D0722850

DISASTERS

Watching the fire that followed the San Francisco earthquake from Russian Hill, April 1906. *(The Bettmann Archive)*

DISASTERS

From the pages of The New York Times

Edited by

Arleen Keylin

and

Gene Brown

ARNO PRESS

New York · 1976

Copyright © 1976 by The New York Times Company.
All rights reserved.

Copyright © 1906, 1908, 1909, 1911, 1912, 1913, 1914,
1915, 1917, 1921, 1923, 1925, 1926, 1927, 1928, 1929,
1930, 1933, 1934, 1935, 1936, 1937, 1938, 1939, 1942,
1943, 1944, 1945, 1946, 1947, 1948, 1949, 1950, 1951,
1952, 1953, 1954, 1955, 1956, 1957, 1958, 1959, 1960,
1961, 1962, 1963, 1964, 1965, 1966, 1967, 1968, 1969,
1970, 1971, 1972, 1973, 1974, 1975
by The New York Times Company. All rights reserved.

Library of Congress Cataloging in Publication Data
Main entry under title:

Disasters: from the pages of the New York times.

      1.   Disasters.   I.   Keylin, Arleen.
II.   Brown, Gene.   III.   New York times.
D24.D55   904   75-43948
ISBN 0-405-06681-3

Editorial Assistant: Sandra Jones

Manufactured in the United States of America

DISASTERS

The New-York Times.

VOL. XXI.......NO. 6257.   NEW-YORK, TUESDAY, OCTOBER 10, 1871.   PRICE FOUR CENTS.

A CITY IN RUINS.

The Terrible Devastation of Chicago.

Three Square Miles in the Heart of the City Burned.

Twelve Thousand Buildings Destroyed---Loss $50,000,000.

Every Public Building, Hotel, Bank and Newspaper Swept.

Appeals to Other Cities and a Noble Response.

Frightful Details of the Disaster from Our Own Reporters.

Special Dispatch to the New-York Times.

[Body text of report largely illegible.]

The Devastation of Chicago—Map of the Burned District as Far as Heard From.

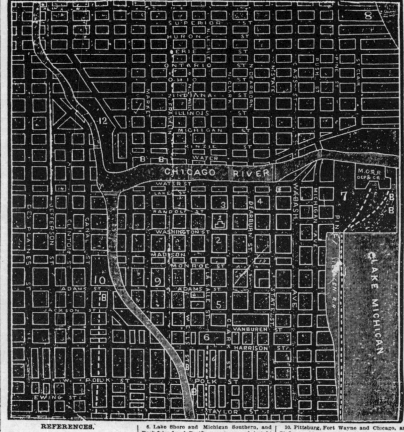

REFERENCES.

1. Court-house.
2. Chamber of Commerce.
3. Sherman House.
4. Tremont House.
5. Pacific Hotel.
6. Lake Shore and Michigan Southern, and Rock Island and Pacific passenger and freight houses.
7. Illinois Central, Michigan Central, and Chicago, Burlington and Quincy freight houses.
8. Chicago Water-works.
9. Chicago City Gas-works.
10. Pittsburg, Fort Wayne and Chicago, and St. Louis, Alton and Chicago Railroad passenger and freight houses.
12. Chicago and North-western Depot grounds.
13. Chicago Tribune office.
14. Chicago Shot-tower.
B. B. B. B. Elevators.

THE VERY LATEST.

Increased Spread of the Fire—The Southern Portion of Chicago Probably Destroyed—Telegraphic Communication with the City Cut Off.

Special Dispatch to the New-York Times.

CHICAGO, Oct. 10—1 A. M.

THE THIEVES CONVICTED

Complete Exposition of the Ring Accounts.

Official Report of the Joint Committee of Investigation.

Nearly $75,000,000 Spent from the Appropriations in Three Years.

The Tax-Payers in Debt One Hundred and Twenty Millions.

Some of the Robbers Pointed Out by Name.

The Schuyler Fraud Traced Home to Tweed.

THE FEELING IN THE CITY.

The Effect Upon Wall-Street—Rapid and Extensive Decline in Western Stocks—A Panic in the Market, Followed by Failures.

Wide World Photos

The Chicago Court House and the downtown area after the fire.

A CITY IN RUINS.

Continued from First Page.

attend to the interests of New-York merchants, and to take charge of all mails coming east.

The Cashier of the German-American Savings Bank announces, in another column, that the Bank will receive and forward all sums, large or small, intended for the relief of the Chicago sufferers.

The Mayor yesterday issued a proclamation setting forth the necessity of sending relief to the sufferers. A meeting of officers and employes of the several Railroad, Express, Steamship and Transportation Companies, in this City, for the purpose of adopting measures of relief is called for 3 P. M. today, at No. 365 Broadway.

Provisions Stored in the Doomed City—Their Value and Amount.

There were a good many exaggerated reports flying about in the vicinity of the Produce Exchange yesterday in regard to the total losses on breadstuffs and other stocks at Chicago. They were variously estimated from $5,000,000 to $40,000,000. The following tables give the amount and value of stocks in store in the ruined metropolis on the 1st of October by which the aggregate loss can very nearly be determined:

Flour, 20,360 barrels, at $7 per barrel; total value, $142,520.

Pork, 16,450 barrels, at $13 per barrel; total value, $213,850.

Prime mess pork, 2,000 barrels, at $11 per barrel; total value, $22,000.

Lard, 8,970 tierces, at $30 a tierce; total value, $270,070.

Bacon, 4,590,000 pounds, at 9½ cents per pound; total value, $43,560.

Wheat, 1,463,418 bushels at $1 20 per bushel; total value, $1,756,101 60. Corn, 868,253 bushels at 46 cents a bushel; total value, $398,396 38. Oats, 749,240 bushels at 30 cents a bushel; total value, $224,772.

Rye, 86,319 bushels at 65½ cents a bushel; total value $56,150 50½. Barley, 686,255 bushels at 58½ cents a bushel; total value, $401,659 13. According to the above list the total value of the stocks in store at Chicago on the 1st inst., was $3,528,809 6[illegible].

THE FEELING IN BROOKLYN.

Action of the Brooklyn Common Council—Intense Feeling of Sympathy in Brooklyn—Real Estate Men Alarmed.

The Brooklyn Board of Aldermen met yesterday, Alderman BERGEN in the Chair, and passed a resolution expressing their deepest sympathy with the authorities and inhabitants of Chicago City, in this hour of great suffering. A committee of five members was appointed to act with the Mayor in calling a public meeting without delay to enable the citizens of Brooklyn to give prompt and practical expression to the sympathy which all so deeply feel. The committee repaired at once to the office of the Mayor, and after a short interview determined to hold a public meeting in the Academy of Music to-morrow. The also sent a telegraphic dispatch to the authorities of Chicago expressing sympathy, and apprising them of the action taken.

The feeling throughout the city yesterday was of the most intense character, and every item of intelligence pertaining to the conflagration was eagerly seized upon and discussed by the populace. The bulletins at the newspaper offices were surrounded by interested crowds, who read and wondered at the dispatches as they arrived one after another from the scene of disaster. A feeling of the most intense sorrow was everywhere manifested for the sufferers.

About 6 o'clock P. M., the news got abroad among business men that many of the City Insurance Companies were absolutely ruined by the fire, and consequently upon that rumor, hosts of real estate men whose property was not within easy access to any of the fire-engines rushed to the head-quarters of Fire Commissioners and besought them that some measures might be taken for the safety of their buildings in case any fire should break out. Many of them acted as though a conflagration was inevitable, and it was only after repeated efforts, that Mr. MASSEY, the Commissioner, succeeded in impressing them with the fact, that all that could be done was already accomplished for the safety of the city. The feeling in the matter, however, is deep, and there is every reason for believing that the meeting, to be held to-morrow, in the Academy, will be one of the largest ever held in Brooklyn.

WASHINGTON.

Feeling at the Capital Over the Chicago Disaster.

Special Dispatch to the New-York Times.

WASHINGTON, Oct. 9.—The terrible calamity at Chicago has completely overshadowed every other subject here today, and has been the sole subject of comment by the crowds who have thronged the telegraph and newspaper offices for the latest intelligence from the doomed city. The President and Secretary of War early in the day anticipated requests that were subsequently received, and directed Gen. SHERIDAN to issue to any extent supplies of tents, blankets and provisions to the houseless and suffering people. The army records of the Department of the North-west, which were deposited at head-quarters in Chicago, are lost with everything else. The destruction of the Post-office and Custom-house occasions considerable uneasiness here, as the Government had in the vaults of the depository there on the last report, a few days since, $1,500,000 in greenbacks and $500,000 in gold. If this money was left in the vault there will probably be no loss whether consumed or not, but if an attempt was made to remove it, then the risk of loss was greatly increased.

AID FROM OTHER CITIES.

Universal Sympathy Expressed and Assistance of Every Kind Freely Offered—Intense Feeling Throughout the Country.

The calamity in Chicago has awakened the deepest sympathy throughout the country, as will be seen by our telegraphic dispatches. The substance we give below:

In Boston a profound sensation was caused among all classes of people, and depressing business of all kinds. Mayor GASTON has telegraphed the Mayor of Chicago expressing sympathy and inquiring in what manner Boston can best extend aid.

A public meeting has been called in Saratoga to-night to raise funds in aid of the sufferers.

The members of the Oswego Board of Trade have contributed $2,000 to the sufferers.

In Philadelphia a special meeting of the Commercial Exchange was held and immediately after the meeting a dispatch was sent to the Mayor of Chicago expressing sympathy and offering material aid in any manner he may indicate. Mayor FOX has issued a call for a meeting at the Mayor's Office, at 12 o'clock, on Wednesday "to take means to meet this appalling emergency."

In Cincinnati the citizens met at the Chamber of Commerce, and Committees on Transportation and Finance were appointed, and subscriptions and cash payments were at once received. The Chamber of Commerce gave $5,000. Many leading firms gave $1,000 each. At 12 o'clock, $25,000 had been subscribed. The Hamilton and Dayton, and Indianapolis and Lafayette Railroad Companies have offered to transport all supplies free of charge. In accordance with this, Mayor DAVIS sent a dispatch to all the cities and towns along the railroad to collect supplies to be taken free. Blankets and clothing will be collected and sent in large quantities, also cooked food. At a meeting of both Boards of the Common Council held at 1 o'clock to-day, it was unanimously resolved to appropriate $100,000 for the relief of Chicago, despite the legal inability to make such appropriation, but pledging themselves individually until legislation to make it legal can be had. A special train was to leave Cincinnati last night, conveying a committee of the citizens and four car-loads of provisions, consisting in part of about 10,000 pounds of cheese, 10,000 pounds of dried beef, 50,000 loaves of bread, 200 barrels of crackers, and 2,000 blankets. The train will run at passenger speed. Donations of provisions continue to be made, and will be promptly forwarded.

The report that three steam-engines were dispatched to Chicago, yesterday, by the Fire Department, proved to be erroneous. Had they been sent they would not have reached there in time for any use.

The Presbytery of New-York, at the regu- Fall meeting, last night, in the Murray Hill Presbyterian Church, took up a collection amounting to nearly $500 for the Chicago sufferers. Further contributions will be received during the remaining sessions of the Presbytery.

The Chicago fire has cast a deep gloom over business circles in Albany, N. Y., many merchants having intimate connection with business firms in the afflicted city and they sympathise deeply with them in their calamity. The Mayor has called a meeting, at the Board of Trade Rooms, on Broadway, today, at 11 A. M., for the purpose of taking measures for the relief of the suffering, and JAMES HENDRICK, President of the Board of Trade, has issued a similar call.

Mayor H. G. EASTMAN, of Poughkeepsie, has called a meeting in Court-house-square, at noon to-morrow, for the purpose of rendering immediate assistance to the Chicago sufferers.

The City Council of Buffalo has authorized the issue of $100,000 of city bonds for the immediate use of the Chicago sufferers, and a Committee of the Council left last night with a car load of provisions for Chicago.

Announcements are coming in from all parts of the West and South-west of liberal subscriptions of money and provisions for the sufferers.

Trains laden with fire-engines and provisions are being sent to Chicago from all points, with promises of more to follow. Wheeling, Columbus, Cleveland, Toledo, Detroit, Indianapolis, Terre Haute, Evansville, Louisville, Memphis and Nashville, as well as larger cities, are contributing liberally.

Mayor BROWN, of St. Louis, received a message from Chicago, asking food for the suffering people of that city. The citizens held, at the Merchants' Exchange, the largest meeting ever held there. Some $70,000 was raised in the space of one hour. At night there would probably be cooked provisions enough ready to load a train. The Merchants' Exchange subscribed $10,000, and many firms and individuals from $500 to $1,000 each.

FORMER DISASTROUS FIRES.

The Conflagrations in London, Constantinople, New-York, Portland and Other Places—Some Account of These Terrible Visitations.

The appalling disaster which has overtaken Chicago recalls like fearful calamities to other cities. Of the great fires of history, those in London in 962 and 1087, in which great portions of the city, including St. Paul's Cathedral, were burned, are still read of with great interest, though the records are but meagre. In A. D. 1212 another great fire devastated the city, beginning on the southward side and communicating to the other, and hemmed in a large crowd of people who were standing on the bridge. Over 3,000 of the unfortunate creatures, in attempting to escape the devouring element by jumping into boats and barges, were drowned. By the fire in London, Sept. 26, A. D. 1666, known as the Great Fire, 400 streets were laid waste, 13,200 houses were burned, eighty-nine churches, which number included old St. Paul's, a second time destroyed, the city gates, Custom-house, Royal Exchange, Lion College, and Guildhall. This terrible fire thus covered with ruins 436 acres, and forced 200,000 people to encamp in the open air in Islington and Highgate fields. London has had many large fires since, but none whose devastations have extended beyond certain districts small in area, except on July 21, 1794, when 600 houses and an East India warehouse filled with saltpetre were burned, £1,000,000 being lost by the conflagration.

The stories of the great fires in New-York City in the last century are interesting. Those who saw these great conflagrations are now slumbering in the grave, but many of their children live to repeat the oft-told story of their childhood. These fires occurred when New-York was occupied by the British troops, the first one breaking out on Aug. 26, 1776, when 493 houses all on the west side of Broadway from Whitehall to Barclay streets were made food for the flames. On Aug. 7, 1778, 300 buildings were destroyed in another conflagration, the buildings being principally located around what was then known as Conger's Wharf on the East River. At both of these fires great difficulty was experienced in obtaining a sufficient supply of water to be of any service. As in Chicago gunpowder was used to blow up the buildings.

On the 16th of December, 1835, New-York was swept by the devouring element, and 648 of the most valuable stores, the Merchants' Exchange, the South Dutch Church and property valued at more than $18,000,000 was lost in the flames. This conflagration took place in the First Ward, east of Broadway, and below Wall-street. On July 19, 1845, another great fire occurred in the City, between Broadway, Exchange-place, Broad and Stone streets, and $5,000,000 were lost.

One of the largest fires in the United States, of late years, was that in Portland, Me., on July 4, 1866. Sixteen hundred buildings were burned, with a loss of $9,000,000,000, upon which there was only an insurance of $3,500,000.

The great fire in Constantinople on the 5th of June, 1870, excited a sensation even at this remote distance. Over 7,000 buildings were burned in this great conflagration, and 1,000 men, women and children lost their lives. About $25,000,000 was the estimated loss.

The New-York Times.

VOL. XXII.——NO. 6720.　　　　NEW-YORK, WEDNESDAY, APRIL 2, 1873.—TRIPLE SHEET.　　　　PRICE FOUR CENTS.

AN AWFUL DISASTER.

Total Wreck of the White Star Steam-Ship Atlantic—Over Seven Hundred Lives Lost.

Special Dispatch to the New-York Times.

HALIFAX, N. S., April 1.—One of the most terrible disasters that has ever occurred on this coast happened at an early hour this morning, when the White Star ocean steam-ship Atlantic went ashore on Mars Head, at Cape Prospect, during a heavy gale. It is understood that over 700 of the unfortunate passengers were lost out of the thousand who were on board.

All of the women and children were drowned.

The news of the awful disaster sent a thrill of horror through the city, and even now excited groups of people stand at street corners discussing the details at hand.

Even at this late hour, the details of the disaster are meagre and unsatisfactory. The first intimation we had of the wreck was a rumor that an ocean steamer had gone ashore down the coast, and that several lives had been lost. So vague was the source from whence the report came, that it was not credited for some time. Subsequently, however, more detailed accounts began to arrive, when it was learned that the ill-fated vessel was the steam-ship Atlantic, of the White Star line, Capt. Williams in command.

It was next ascertained that the Atlantic had attempted to make Halifax harbor on her way from Liverpool to New-York, in consequence of a shortness of coal. A heavy gale prevailed at the time, so that as she neared the coast, in hopes of sighting the light on Sambro Island, the vessel was recklessly carried before the wind and by the strong current that always prevails in that locality, right on to shore, causing her to become a total wreck.

Late this evening further and fresher details were obtained. It appears that there were about fifty cabin passengers on board, together with over 900 steerage passengers, so that, with the crew, the total number of souls on board was over 1,000. During her passage across, the Atlantic encountered very heavy weather, but all was well until yesterday, when it was ascertained that the coal was nearly all gone.

About 12 o'clock last night Capt. Williams and his officers believed that they were making straight for Sambro light, but two hours later the vessel struck.

The scene at that moment was a terrible one. The steamer bumped on the rocks two or three times as the heavy waves lifted her, showing that her doom was sealed. Scarcely had the first shock been felt than the passengers rushed from their berths in cabin and steerage on to the main deck, all being terrified and awe-stricken by the perils that surrounded them.

An attempt was then made to cut away the boats, and one was soon filled with men and women. It was too late, however, for the steamer suddenly careened leeward, falling over on her beam ends, and almost immediately sinking, the boat already spoken of being swamped and going down with her.

So close in to shore was the steamer when she struck, that several of the sailors succeeded in swimming ashore with a line after they found themselves thrown into the sea. Fortunately, the fishermen who live on the coast were on the lookout, and they assisted the third officer and his companions in hauling in a rope by means of the halyards they had so bravely carried ashore. By means of this line some 250 men succeeded in getting safe to land, though, shocking to relate, none of the women or children escaped alive, all going down in the raging sea.

The scene of the wreck, as I have already stated, was on Mars Head, the extreme point of Prospect Cape. According to the official charts the Head is laid down as lying in latitude 44° 30' 10" N., longitude 63° 43' 34" W. It is a rocky, peninsular cape, seventy feet high, and forms the western front of Pennant Bay, the entrance to which is three miles wide and about two miles deep. This little bay is very much incumbered with rocky shoals and irregularly-shaped islands, but it frequently affords shelter to coasting vessels, whose masters are thoroughly acquainted with the passage between them. The land at the head of the bay is moderately high, the highest point, called Hospital Hill, rising fully 250 feet above the level of the sea.

Cape Prospect is sometimes confounded with Mars Head. The cape forms the west side of Bristol Bay, and lies some three or four miles south of Prospect Harbor. The harbor itself, like all of the little bays along this portion of the coast, is incumbered at its entrance by a cluster of small islands. At the back of these lies a considerable inlet called Parker's River.

Prospect Harbor is well known to navigators acquainted with this coast, as a very dangerous port, as it wears at its entrance, right off Mars Head, a very rugged and broken appearance. Whenever rough weather occurs, the reefs, though submerged, are very dangerous, and must have been doubly so in such a heavy gale as that encountered by the Atlantic.

Just off Cape Prospect, or the Head, lies a huge rock, commonly called seventeen feet under water. Its position is due south of the Head, and nearly one-third of a mile from the shore. It is believed that it was this rock that caused the wreck of the Atlantic. The gale probably caused the steamer to beat in shore, and finally drove her heavily on to the Cape at the Head.

The navigation manuals direct masters of vessels to keep outside of this reef, and cautions them not to go between it and the shore. These directions probably proved futile in the gale, and the Atlantic went inside.

LATER.—I have just ascertained that the hull of the wrecked steamer went clear under water when she struck for the fifth and last time. So terrific was the way the vessel struck upon the shore or beach that her bow alone appeared above the surface of the waves. As the majority of the passengers were in their berths or cabins at the time, they were actually drowned between decks, many of them probably being scarcely awake when the waves submerged the ship. We can only imagine the awful scene, for none are here to describe it except, indeed, the third officer, Mr. Brady, who was wholly unable to give any details.

Judging from his statements, the danger was scarcely discovered when all was lost. A few brief moments of terror and dismay, and fully seven hundred men, women, and children found a watery grave. To-morrow I may be able to give you a fuller and more comprehensive account of the disaster, as steamers are being dispatched to the scene from this city.

This coast has long been known as a dangerous one in rough weather, and some notable wrecks have occurred in years past. The most remarkable disaster was the total loss of the French frigate La Tribune, thirty-six guns, which vessel went down on the morning of Nov. 16, 1797, with 300 people on board. On June 20, 1822, the British gun-boat Drake was totally wrecked, when over sixty persons were drowned. On the morning of July 13, 1843, the British troop-ship Albert was wrecked off the coast, having on board the Sixty-fourth Regiment of Foot, a majority of the command being miraculously saved. The last great wreck was that of the United States mail steam-ship Hungarian, which event occurred on the night of Feb. 20, 1860, when 205 lives, all told, were lost.

OTHER ACCOUNTS.

The Earliest Dispatches in Regard to the Disaster.

HALIFAX, N. S., April 1.—The steam-ship Atlantic, of the White Star line, from Liverpool March 20, for New-York, running short of coal, made for Halifax. When about twenty miles from port, off Cape Prospect, at 3 o'clock this morning, she ran ashore on Mars Head. She had on board over 1,000 men, women, and children. Only 250 succeeded in landing. The remainder, including all the women and children, were lost. The Captain and Third Officer were saved; the First Officer was drowned.

On the first receipt of the news of the disaster here, a Cunard and a Government steamer started to the assistance of the Atlantic, but the third officer, who arrived here at 5½ this afternoon, says the vessel and cargo are a total loss.

Private Dispatches.

Mr. J. C. Smith, of the Merchants' Exchange and News-room, kindly furnishes copies of dispatches received by him about the loss of the Atlantic:

FIRST DISPATCH.

HALIFAX, N. S., April 1.—Steamer ashore at Mars Head, near Prospect, thirty miles from here, stated to be the Atlantic, of the White Star Line, from Liverpool, bound for New-York. Steamer and line sent to her assistance. Captain and first officer drowned.

SECOND DISPATCH.

HALIFAX, N. S., April 1.—Government have sent steam-ship Lady Head, and Cunard the Delta, down to the Atlantic. She will be a total wreck. Large number of passengers stated lost.

THIRD DISPATCH.

HALIFAX, N. S., April 1.—Second officer arrived; reports making this port for coal; heavy gale with rain; struck on Mars Head, Cape Prospect, at 3 this morning; had nearly 1,000 passengers; 700 drowned; 250 got ashore, but no women and children saved; Captain saved; first officer supposed lost; ship total wreck; cargo and ship lost; none ashore; may be partially saved.

Another Description of the Calamity—Not a Woman or Child Saved.

HALIFAX, N. S., April 1.—This afternoon a report being current that a steamer had been wrecked on the coast, and several lives lost, was first regarded as a cruel April Fool joke, but this evening the Cunard agents have received news that it was all true, and that only a little of the truth had been told, the fact being that the White Star steamer Atlantic, Capt. Williams, from Liverpool, for New-York, while coming into this port for coal, struck on Mars Rock, near Prospect, twenty-two miles west of Halifax, and became a total wreck. Of about 1,000 souls on board, upward of 500 were drowned. The third officer, Brady, arrived in the city this evening. He says that the Atlantic left Liverpool on the 20th of March, with upward of 900 steerage passengers and about fifty cabin passengers. The steamer experienced boisterous weather during the passage, but all went well until noon on Monday, the 31st of March, when the supply of coal became nearly exhausted. The captain determined to put into Halifax. The captain and third officer were on deck until midnight. The position was then judged to be Sambro Light, bearing north north-west thirty-nine miles. The sea was rough and the night dark. The chief and fourth officers having taken charge, Mr. Brady went below and turned into his berth. The Captain at the same time went to his room to lie down. What occurred between midnight and 2 o'clock, the time of the disaster, Mr. Brady cannot tell, as he was sleeping. He was awakened and thrown out of his bunk by the shock when the steamer struck. She struck heavily, three or four times. Mr. Brady ran up to the deck and found it full of passengers. He found an axe, and with it commenced to clear away the starboard lifeboat. He observed that the Captain and the other officers were engaged in clearing the other boats.

Mr. Brady succeeded in getting his lifeboat out. This was the only boat launched, and it had no sooner touched the water than a crowd made a rush to get into it. Brady had to use force to prevent them crowding in. He put two women and about a dozen men into it, and also got in himself. Just then the steamer fell over and sank. The boat, with its living freight, was carried down with the steamer, and all in it were drowned except Brady.

The hull of the steamer became almost totally submerged, and only the bow and the masts remained above water. The greater part of the passengers were in their rooms below at the time, and were immediately drowned. Indeed, so soon after striking did the steamer sink that many of the passengers who were without doubt sleeping peacefully in blissful ignorance of all that was going on around them, and passed into eternity without a struggle. Of those on deck, numbering several hundreds, many were washed overboard when the ship fell over, and their cries for help, as they struggled in vain for life, were most heartrending. Many, however, had taken refuge in the rigging and on the bow, and were still living, but with the prospect of almost certain death before them, for they knew not where they were, and were in momentary expectation of the ship sinking further and engulfing them all. Even as they were clinging to the rigging, with the sea washing continually their situation was to get into it, and about a dozen succeeded. Just at that moment the steamer fell over on her beam ends and sank. Only one boat had been got out, and that was carried down by the steamer and all in it were lost. Brady scrambled on to the mizen rigging which was above the water, and seeing that he could do nothing there, he then went forward and unrove the halyards, being assisted by Quartermasters Speakman and Owen. Brady then took the halliards and all three swam to the rock, and then a line was handed ashore and a number of the passengers landed by it. A number had got on the rock, but as the tide was rising their position was no better than on the vessel. Just then the fishermen, on the shore came out in boats and rescued those on the rock and a large number from the rigging. Brady remained at the scene until noon to-day, when all who were alive on board had been saved, except the Chief Officer, Mr. Frith, who was in the rigging shouting for help. Brady says he tried to get a crew to go to the rescue of Frith, but the sea was so heavy that nobody would volunteer. Altogether about 250 persons were saved, including Capt. Williams, also the fourth officer, Mr. Brown, the doctor, and several of the engineers and sailors. Not a single woman or child was saved. Most of them, as well as hundreds of the men were drowned in their berths.

The steamer struck about 2 o'clock this morning. The weather at the time was dark, but not thick, and the sea rough. Steamers are going down to Halifax to render what assistance they possibly can. All the people saved from the wreck, with the exception of Brady, are still at Prospect, where the fishermen are giving them all the attention they possibly can.

The Halifax Chronicle's Account.

The following is the *Chronicle's* report of the disaster:

"It is our painful duty this morning to record the most terrible marine disaster that ever occurred on our coast, the loss of a great ocean steam-ship with about 750 lives. Yesterday afternoon a report became current that a steamer had been wrecked somewhere on the coast, and one or two lives lost. The report was regarded as one of the canards put afloat on All Fools' day, and little regard was paid to it. Soon the report became more definite, and we knew that the steamer Atlantic, of the White Star line, was ashore near Prospect, and that several lives had been lost. Even yet the public were inclined to regard the story as a malicious hoax. A little later, however, it became known that the report was well founded, and that but a small part of the true truth had been told. The fact being that the Atlantic had been wrecked on Meagher's Rock, near Prospect, twenty-two miles west of Halifax, and out of about 1,000 souls on board, 750 were lost. Need we say that the terrible announcement created a profound feeling of horror throughout the community.

THE THIRD OFFICER'S STORY.

Having ascertained that one man from the wrecked ship had arrived in town, a reporter went in search of him, and found him in an eating-house in upper Water-street. He proved to be Mr. Brady, third officer of the Atlantic, bruised, worn out, and almost speechless after the terrible events of the morning. He was, as might be expected, in no condition to talk; nevertheless he cheerfully consented to answer the reporter's questions, and gave such information as he could. The Atlantic, Mr. Brady said, left Liverpool on Thursday, March 20, for New-York, touched at Queenstown the next day, to receive the mails and passengers, after which she started on her voyage across the ocean. She had a full cargo of general merchandise and a very large number of passengers. Mr. Brady could not give the precise number, but thought there were more than 800 in the steerage, and about fifty in the cabin. These, with her crew, would probably make the total number not less than 1,000 souls. She was commanded by Capt. James Agnew Williams. Rough weather was experienced, but nothing worthy of note occurred until noon on Monday, the 31st, when the coal being short, Capt. Williams resolved to put into Halifax for a supply. The Captain and Mr. Brady had the night watch up to midnight, when they were relieved by the chief and fourth officers. At that time they judged that Sambro Light then bore north-north-west thirty-nine miles. The sea was rough and the night dark. The chief and fourth officers having taken charge, Mr. Brady went below and turned into his berth. The Captain at the same time went to his room to lie down. What occurred between midnight and 2 o'clock, the time of the disaster, Mr. Brady cannot tell, as he was sleeping. He was awakened and thrown out of his bunk by the shock when the steamer struck. She struck heavily, three or four times. Mr. Brady ran up to the deck and found it full of passengers.

It does not seem possible that any vessel could have stood the shock of striking the ground or coast in the neighborhood of where the Atlantic struck, for it is a mass of flinty rock for scores of miles in each direction. From the terrible loss of life, however awful all on board, it is evident the ship must have gone on to the rocks at a high rate of speed, and boats and rafts were of no avail in the heavy surf and sea which beat in from the broad Atlantic Ocean.

It is probable that the Atlantic did not have over 600 tons of coal on board when she left Queenstown, which, at a consumption of say sixty tons per day, would have lasted her ten days. At this season of the year some aid was expected from easterly winds, and probably she started in the hope of reaching New-York with the 600 tons.

THE CANADIAN FISHERIES.

American Fishermen Warned not to Fish Within the Three-Mile Limit Before July 1, 1873.

WASHINGTON, April 1.—The following circular relative to the fisheries on the coast of the Dominion of Canada, was issued from the Treasury Department to-day:

To Collectors of Customs and Others:

By circulars under date of March 6, 1872, this department notified Collectors of Customs and the public in regard to the restrictions to which American vessels would be subject when employed in fishing on the coasts of the British North American colonies, and that the provisions between the United States and Great Britain, proclaimed July 4, 1871, so far as they relate to the fisheries, would not go into effect until laws required to carry them into operation have been passed by the Imperial Parliament of Great Britain, by the Parliament of Canada, and by the Legislature of Prince Edward Island, on the one hand, and by the Congress of the United States on the other.

The Secretary of State recently assured me that he has been officially informed by Her Britannic Majesty's Minister at Washington, that the Executive Government of the Dominion of Canada, requesting the act of Congress giving effect to the Treaty of Washington as not going into operation till July 1, 1873, has decided that, till that time, American fishermen have no right to fish in the waters within the three-mile limit; that such vessels are liable to seizure for doing so; that we no steps to prevent vessels from fishing within the three-mile limit; that such vessels will have permission to fish so far as that Government can grant it, and that it is not probable that any seizure will be made at the instance of private parties, but that, should such a case occur, the good offices of this Government will be used to advance the release of the vessel and the remission of any penalties incurred.

In view of this communication and liberal act of the Government of the Dominion, you are hereby enjoined to make known to the public under color to the subject, so far as possible, that until the provisions of the Treaty of Washington relating to the fisheries shall go into effect, the liberty of fishing in the waters heretofore to be thrown open to the fishermen of the United States by the operation of those provisions, is permanently only and under its authority of this department, already referred to; and that if American fishermen engaged in fishing within the three-mile limit violate any restrictions which are set forth in the circular of this department, already referred to; and that if American fishermen be seized under date March 6, 1873, they may still be subjected to serious difficulty by private parties, under the provisions of the Dominion of Canada.

(Signed) WILLIAM A. RICHARDSON, Secretary of the Treasury.

New-York Passengers.

NEW-YORK, April 1.—Among the cabin passengers, per the lost steamer Atlantic, are Wm. H. Merritt and wife, of New-York; Miss Merritt, and Miss Scrymser.

History of the Ill-Fated Vessel.

The Atlantic was built by Harland & Wolff, at Belfast, Ireland, in 1870, and launched, we believe, in the month of December of that year. She was 420 feet in length, 40 feet 9 inches breadth of beam, and 23 feet 4 inches depth of hold proper and 31 feet to top of spar deck, and measured 3,600 tons. Custom-house measurement. Her machinery was built by George Forrester & Co., of Liverpool, and consisted of four compound engines, with 41 and 78 inch cylinders, with 60 inches stroke of piston and a nominal horse-power of 600. She had ten main boilers, sufficient to give her a steady pressure of 60 pounds to the square inch, burning, on an average, 80 tons of coal a day, and working her screw up to 60 revolutions per minute. On her trial trip she made 11½ knots per hour. She was fitted with seven water-tight bulk-heads, running from keelson to main deck. She had three iron decks, running fore and aft, to aid in strengthening the long, narrow hull. Her masts, four in number, were of iron and all in one piece, and the yards were also of iron.

In point of equipment the Atlantic was as fine as any of the vessels of the line, and as traced much attention when she first made her appearance in the Mersey. She sailed from Liverpool, on her first voyage early in June, 1871, and arrived at New-York on the morning of Friday, June 23, 1871, having made the run a little short of eleven days, being the second ship of the line, and commanded by Capt. Digby Murray, now relieved from the line. She remained in port until the 1st day of July, 1871, when, at 6:10 P. M., she discharged her pilot off Sandy Hook, homeward bound for the first time, and in eight days and nineteen hours she was off Crookhaven. The voyage was somewhat remarkable for the number of distinguished guests on board, who celebrated the Fourth of July in a manner never known on board of an ocean steamer at sea. The Atlantic has been steadily employed in the trade since she entered it, and until this disaster which has sealed her fate, has never met any serious accident.

This type of vessel has never been considered by American engineers as one likely to stand the slightest rough usage after grounding, and that she should have gone to pieces quickly after striking is no wonder. The enormous length and disproportionate beam renders them an easy prey to the action of waves after they once touch bottom. In this case the seven water-tight bulkheads seem to have proved of no use, as the loss of life shows that there was not enough of the ship left to shelter but a few persons.

The Atlantic sailed from Liverpool on the 20th of March, and probably left Queenstown the next day, and was due here Monday evening, even allowing that she encountered heavy weather. Some anxiety was felt regarding her early yesterday, as she had not arrived up to sundown. Yet there were some who attributed her non-arrival to a broken screw or deranged machinery. Yet none thought that her loss of the news of a terrible disaster to her was to reach the City.

One of the principal causes for the loss of the ship may be set down to the lack of coal to reach this port. It is a well-known fact that the price of coal in England is very high, and that the transatlantic lines buy largely on this side, and endeavor to take over something of a supply to bring them back to this side. It is also true that much of the coal furnished at the present time on the other side is of a very poor quality, and will not make steam as freely as the Welsh coal usually furnished to the first-class steam lines. Another cause for the disaster is that the vessel was considerably out of her true course, either for Halifax or New-York, and the Captain evidently had been running well north to shorten up his longitude. This practice has long been discountenanced by the principal lines, and in some instances the Captains positively forbidden to take the high latitude route which the Atlantic evidently had taken.

FOREIGN NEWS.

Continued Activity of the Spanish Carlists—Narrow Escape of the Cure of Santa Cruz.

BAYONNE, April 1.—The Carlists in Spain are receiving supplies of arms, ammunition, and provisions in various ways, but mostly by the Carlists, who are fortifying them. A body of 400 Carlists, recruited in Navarre, last week, were equipped almost as soon as their organization was formed.

SENOR KLIE, who was the director of the Carlist Committee here, eluded the local authorities, who had orders for his arrest, and crossed into Spain on Saturday last.

It is reported that all the Custom-houses on the frontier except that at Irun have been occupied by the Carlists, who are fortifying them.

MADRID, April 1.—The Cure of Santa Cruznaz surprised yesterday and narrowly escaped capture. Several of his men were taken prisoners.

The insurrection in Barcelona is subsiding. No further outrages have been perpetrated by the populace.

A force of Carlists under the command of the Chieftain Cucala made an attack on Venaros, province of Castellon de la Plano, yesterday. After a short contest, the insurgents were defeated by the Republican troops, and fled in disorder from before the town.

Notwithstanding the efforts of the authorities at Barcelona to preserve the peace in that city, disorder has occurred. The populace, enraged at the burning of Berga and other outrageous acts of the Carlists, attacked several Catholic churches, and seriously damaged the sacred edifices.

Additional reinforcements for the Spanish troops in Cuba were sent to that island by the steamer which sailed from Cadiz, for Havana, yesterday.

PARIS, April 1.—The Spanish Vice-Consul in this city absconded, leaving a deficit in his account to the amount of 70,000 francs, but he has been arrested and sent in custody to Spain.

Characteristic Scene in the French Assembly.

PARIS, April 1.—The Assembly has been debating for two days the Lyons Municipality bill. The discussion to-day closed with a remarkable scene.

M. Le Royer, a Radical, described the committing majority's report which second-panied the bill, as trumpery.

The Marquis de Grammont bitterly retorted, and accused the deputy of intemperance.

President Grevy called the Marquis to order, but the latter refused to retract his language.

The members of the Right, exasperated at the call to order, threatened to quit the chamber.

President Grevy made a dignified speech, in which he intimated that he should resign, and declared the sitting ended.

The tumult broke up amid the intensest excitement.

Deputies of all shades of political opinion waited on M. Grevy to-night, and begged him to overlook the incident; but it is expected that his resignation will be offered to-morrow.

Prince Alexis at Shanghai—The Danish Ministry.

LONDON, April 1.—A dispatch from Shanghai announces the arrival in that city of the Russian Grand Duke Alexis.

COPENHAGEN, April 1.—The Folkething, the Lower House of the Rigsdag, has passed a vote declaring a want of confidence in the Danish Ministry.

THE INDIANS.

Massacre of the Surveying Party on Cinnamon River—The Modocs.

LEAVENWORTH, Kan., April 1.—The surveyors murdered by Indians, were Robert Burt, E. M. Deming, of Arkansas City, J. H. Davies, of Chillicothe, Mo., and an Englishman named Robert Pool.

The Indians were Whirlwind's marauding band of Cheyennes. An expedition has been organized at Arkansas City to go to the relief of surveying parties on the Cinnamon. Much excitement prevails on the frontier.

SAN FRANCISCO, April 1.—It is reported that Gen. Canby is surrounding the Modocs, and will soon oblige them to surrender. Capt. Jack's force is fifty-three.

Suicide of a Well-to-Do Citizen of Wake County, North Carolina.

Special Dispatch to the New-York Times.

RALEIGH, N. C., April 1.—Duncan Glenn, a citizen of Oak Grove Township, Wake County, committed suicide on Friday morning last by hanging himself. Little before daylight Glenn got up and went out of the house, as he usually did every morning. When his wife woke she found that her husband had not returned. She got up and went to look for him, and, on opening the front door, she was horrified to behold her husband suspended from an apple-tree, dead. He had been hanging two hours. It appears that Glenn climbed the tree, tied the rope around his neck, and jumped down. His neck was not broken, and death ensued from strangulation.

The cause of the suicide is unknown. The deceased was a man of property, had money at interest, was not involved financially, or otherwise, lived happily with his wife, and was exceedingly fond of his only child. Glenn never exhibited any signs of insanity, and it is apprehended that he might take his life. The deceased was a good citizen, and generally esteemed by his neighbors. He was forty years old.

War on the Monopolies—The Western Farmers Organizing.

Special Dispatch to the New-York Times.

SPRINGFIELD, Ill., April 1.—The State Central Committee of the Farmers' Organization had a meeting this evening. Mr. Flagg in the chair. The Chairman explained the object of the meeting and of the State organization, which is to meet to-morrow. The object is to organize the producers of the country to resist the extortions of monopolies. The committee organized by appointing T. R. Turner and S. B. Smith as delegates to the National Congress, which will meet in Indianapolis on the fourth Monday of May next. It is anticipated that the convention to-morrow will be largely attended.

Catholic Total Abstinence Union of America.

PHILADELPHIA, Penn., April 1.—The semi-annual meeting of the Board of Government of the Catholic Total Abstinence Union of America embracing officers of the National Union, and Presidents of the various State Unions in the country, was held here to-day. Rev. James McDevitt, of Washington, D. C., occupied the chair. He announced the death of James D. Hawley, of Philadelphia, who filled the position of Sergeant-at-Arms in the National Union. The vacancy occasioned thereby had been filled by the appointment of James M. Kelly, President of the Philadelphia Diocesan Union.

The semi-annual report, which is an elaborate statement of the condition of affairs within the organization, was read, and shows that there are in the country 133 societies of total abstinence, of which 132 are attached to it, there being some 20,000 members, and that there are 200 Catholic total abstinence societies not yet affiliated with the Union.

It was declared to be the sense of the board that, under the constitution, a society which had acquired membership in the General Union on the basis of its status in a subordinate union, and had withdrawn from said subordinate union, can only be admitted again into the General Union on the same terms as societies not connected with subordinate unions.

The following committee was appointed, with a view to connecting the societies of Ireland with those of this country in international union: Rev. J. McDevitt, Washington; J. W. O'Brien, New-Jersey; Dr. J. B. Richmond, New-York; J. M. Kelly, Philadelphia, and John O'Brien, St. John, N. B.

The Executive Committee was instructed to prepare a pledge for societies, to be presented at the next general conference, in New-York, on the 18th of October next.

The board partook of a banquet to-night at the Lapierre House.

A GANG OF FORGERS.

History of Some of the Bank of England Forgers.

Special Dispatch to the New-York Times.

BOSTON, April 1.—Something of the past history of Macdonnell, the Bank of England forger, now under arrest in New-York, is obtained by the Boston *Daily Advertiser*. Macdonnell, under the assumed name of George W. Bradford, operated in a cattle swindle in Portland, Me., several years ago, and while under arrest there was delivered up to late (Detective Coyle, of New-York, who had the papers for him on a swindling operation at Tiffany & Co.'s, the Broadway jewelers, and he was sentenced to Sing Sing for two years. In the Summer of 1868 he and his brother Michael, professing to be commission merchants, attempted to get $5,000 out of the Hide and Leather Bank, of Boston, on a bogus check drawn by a Chicago house, but the bank officers were too smart for them, and they made off to escape arrest. Michael, in October of last year, having in his company a young man named Hills, appeared in Worcester, Mass., and by forging a certified check got $2,300 out of a bank there, and then stole a horse and wagon and went to escape. Michael, taking the name of Hiram Thacker, and Hills, the name of H. B. Conklin. Hills was subsequently arrested in New-Jersey for a forgery perpetrated in connection with Macdonnell on the sturdevant Bank, and got seven years in the State Prison, but was pardoned out last Fall. Since his release he has settled with the Worcester Bank officers for about $1,100. His confederate escaped to California, but he was arrested in Canada, and is now serving time in the State Prison at Wetherfield, to that State. Before he went to prison, and after his sentence, he said that the gang with which he was connected—George, the Bank of England forger, being the inventive head of the organization—had planned a grand quartan system of forgeries in the United States. Deposits in small amounts were to be made in different banks and certified checks obtained thereon, which were to be altered, and by simultaneous action the forges expected to make a haul amounting to the aggregate to hundreds of thousands of dollars. At the forty-five committed this, the certified check was subsequently altered to read $67 and $41, which amounts were raised to correspond with the rest of the cyphers, making the sums drawn $66,700 and $44,100. After Michael had been in prison over a year, George came back and to get him released when the Legislature was in session, but met with no encouragement. Michael then tried to bribe the son of the late warden, Willard, to aid him in securing outside assistance, and gave him a letter to W. W. Bidwell, in New-York, which was never delivered. Thus Bidwell, it now appears, was one of the confederates of George Macdonell in the English robbery. These facts go to show that the gang is an old one, and the New-York detectives in concluding that fact evidently have some motive for it.

The father and mother of George and Michael Macdonell live in Lachine, Canada, and are in good circumstances. Michael Macdonell was in Hartford "for some time before Michael's trial, endeavoring to make a settlement and get him off. The father's name is Michael, and he is reported to be a large holder of real estate in Montreal, where himself and family reside every Winter. Michael's term at the State Prison will expire next Fall, and he will go free now that the Worcester matter has so well settled.

BY MAIL AND TELEGRAPH.

Print cloths, market of Providence, was quiet at 7c. for best 64's.

Augustus Young was run over and killed in a mill near Albany yesterday.

James K. Witbeck, clerk of F. Ruse & Son, Albany, is accused of embezzling $800 and absconding.

A. A. French's house and barn, at Gill, Mass., were burned yesterday; loss $2,500, partially insured.

Mrs. John Goodwin, of Wakefield, Mass., was killed on Monday evening while leaving the train at that place.

About fifty journeymen house-painters in Springfield, Mass., struck yesterday for an advance of wages from $2 50 to $3 per day.

Father L. Lapie, the oldest priest of the Diocese of Ogdensburg, died at Corbeau, N. Y., on Sunday last, aged seventy-four years.

The President has accepted the resignation of Second Lieut. Edward S. Holden, of the Engineer Corps, to take effect March 1.

In the Ohio House of Representatives, yesterday, the bill to abolish capital punishment was defeated, only twenty-one voting for it.

Mrs. Newman and Chas. Ward, arrested last week in Denver, Colorado, for poisoning the woman's husband, were discharged yesterday.

John Callaghan, of Boston and Albany railroad brakeman, was instantly killed by running over a coal car at West Springfield, Mass., yesterday morning.

The proposition to widen Water-street, Boston, on the vicinity of the new Post-office, has been approved by the Board of Aldermen by a vote of 8 to 3.

The Supreme Court in Boston, has ordered execution of the verdict against that city for $10,000 for injuries sustained by Thomas M. Prentiss through a defect in a sidewalk.

Hon. Arthur W. Hunter, Democrat, was elected Mayor of Schenectady, N. Y., by 272 majority, yesterday. Three Republican and two Democratic Aldermen are elected.

The Board of Naval Officers to examine candidates for promotion in the navy, met to-day, at the Naval Observatory, and will re-convene at the Navy Department, in Washington, to-day.

The city debt of Portsmouth, N. H., is $29,000, a reduction of $20,000. The issue and County taxation is increased this year about $10,000. The Portsmouth and Dover Railroad bonds amount to $90,000.

The Secretary of the Treasury yesterday addressed a letter to the House relating to the silver certificate, amounting to $525,000. They are of the denomination of $5,000, and number from 5,750 to 5,881, dating from Jan. 9, 1870, to Aug. 2, 1872.

The eighty-third session of the New-York Conference of the Methodist Episcopal Church will assemble in Hudson, N. Y., to-day, and continue through the week. The members will be entertained by the citizens of all denominations.

The Board of Excise appointed Dr. Henry E. Lindenman Director of the Mint; G. W. Hartell, Melter and Refiner of the Mint at Carson City, Mo. Andrews, superseded, and Wm. H. Doane, Coiner of the Mint at Carson City, John Waite, superseded.

The grand jury of Samuel Wetherell and George W. Connors, proprietors of Charles T. Gardett, deceased, and Martha M. Jones (Administratrix of Samuel Jones, deceased) against the New-Jersey Zinc Company, was begun yesterday in the United States Court at Trenton, N. J. Wm. M. Evarts, George M. Harding, and M. Kelley and others are counsel.

THE GOODRICH INQUEST.

Testimony of Lucetta Armstrong, Alias Meyers—Text of the Mysterious Letter—The Proceedings in Full.

The inquest into the manner of the death of Charles Goodrich was resumed in the court-room of the General Sessions, Brooklyn, yesterday, before Coroner Whitehill. From an early hour in the morning a large concourse of people thronged the court-room and the adjoining corridors, and when the time arrived for the commencement of the proceedings every seat in the room was occupied. A great deal of interest was anticipated from the examination of Lucetta Armstrong, alias Meyers, who has been in custody for some days on suspicion of knowing the circumstances connected with this mysterious murder. She was called immediately on the opening of the inquest, and her testimony, which lasted three hours, was listened to with the utmost attention. Mrs. Armstrong is about thirty-two years of age, and possesses no personal attractions. She had a very wearied expression of features, perhaps the result of her recent imprisonment; her manner was slow and hesitating, and her utterance was somewhat indistinct from the loss of her teeth. Her evident unwillingness to tell everything she knew was so apparent as to induce the Coroner to announce that she should not say anything to criminate herself, as it might subsequently be used against her. Her testimony is herewith reported in full.

THE MYSTERIOUS LETTER.

Coroner Whitehill decided to give the following letter to the Press for publication. It is the one that was mentioned in THE TIMES of the 24th ult., and was the first clue that came into the hands of the police:

BROOKLYN, February, 1873.

Mr. Goodrich:

SIR: I propose to tell the truth. Will you hear it?

For the past eight months I have been living in the second house of the block of new buildings on Degraw-street, the third door from Fifth-avenue. I have lived there unknown to any one except Charles. About one year ago I was married to him secretly, for I trusted, Ee loved him so truly that his word was law to me, and he wished for no one to know of our marriage until some future time on account of property. The reason connected with it he did not fully explain. I was very foolish, but I was alone in New-York, with no friend—only him. I have learned since then that the clergy-man who married me was no minister at all; only a friend of his, Ruben Smith, a doctor, I think, who lives in the City.

In December last—some months ago—our baby was born. Before that and since then Charles has treated me with the utmost cruelty, his cruelty all his own to-ween us. Several days ago, a woman with him came to see to one of the houses after a house he had for her. I was at that time along with which he was connected—George, the Bank of England forger, being the inventive head of the organization—had planned a quartan system of forgeries in the United States. Deposits in small amounts were to be made in different banks and certified checks obtained thereon, which were to be altered, and by simultaneous action the forges expected to make a haul amounting to the aggregate to hundreds of thousands of dollars. The reason I write this and the remembrance under which I write are most painful. I have been trying to work. I have been at work in a store for a week—last Saturday night—I came here to my boarding-house, and was very unexpectedly accosted by a man who had been knocking at the door. He asked me if I wished to see Mr. Goodrich. I told him no, and asked him who he was. He then said he would see himself to the home, and saw all my things gone. Since Christmas of last year—ed in other house that I am in. From all the sight-less that I had lately—the whole writing thus—of me, so. Then words this story, but I'll go to the other house, too, and all my things taken to bribe the son of the late warden, Willard, to aid him in securing outside assistance, and gave him a letter to W. W. Bidwell, in New-York, which was never delivered. Thus Bidwell, it now appears, was one of the confederates of George Macdonell in the English robbery. These facts go to show that the gang is an old one.

It seems that some dreadful nightmare. To-morrow is the Sabbath, and where will I stay? or what will I do? I have no money and no friends. I am afraid of no truck writing thus to you. My life is an eternal with the end of it. I cannot hold my pen; for that reason perhaps it may not be easy for you to decipher or by herself writing. AMY C——.

Saturday evening, Feb. 15.

TESTIMONY OF LUCETTA ARMSTRONG.

Lucetta Armstrong testified, in reply to the Coroner, that she resided in No. 46 Rivington-street—

Q.—Who is the person? A.—Charles Goodrich.

Q.—How long have you known Mr. Goodrich? A.—About two months.

Q.—State about the way with which he became acquainted with him? A.—I can't tell the day, but it is over two months since.

Q.—Since Christmas or before? A.—Since Christmas. I disremember but to the best of my recollection it is about a month.

Q.—Where did you get acquainted with him in New-York or Brooklyn? A.—I saw him first in Brooklyn, but I became acquainted with him in New-York.

Q.—How many times did you see him before you became acquainted with him? A.—Once.

Q.—And I don't well remember that. Had you any correspondence with Mr. Goodrich? A.—No, sir.

Q.—You saw him only once; where was he? A.—No, sir.

Q.—Did you have any conversation with Mr. Goodrich? A.—No, sir.

Q.—Were there any intervals—say of a week that you had not seen him so frequently? A.—No, Sir.

Q.—Did you see him in the course of one day? A.—Sometimes four or five times a week, sometimes not at all.

Q.—You saw him every week, some, or one day, the week you occasioned acquainted with him? A.—Yes.

Q.—Their did you last see Mr. Goodrich? A.—About two weeks ago.

Q.—The Thursday night previous to the murder? A.—I don't remember what day it was.

Q.—Where did you see him last? A.—In Rivington-street.

Q.—Did he call on you? A.—At a corner of Allen.

Q.—You saw him on Thursday night at the corner of Allen and Rivington? A.—Yes, Sir.

Q.—What time in the evening was it? A.—About 7 o'clock, as near as I can tell.

Q.—Was anybody with him when he called? A.—He was alone.

Q.—When was the acquaintance made by whom? A.—Did you meet him after—by appointment? A.—No, sir.

Q.—Did you expect to see him? A.—No, Sir.

Q.—Are you positive it was on the Thursday night before his death that you last saw Mr. Goodrich alive? A.—I am.

Q.—Did you go to his house on any occasion? A.—No, Sir.

Q.—You never were in any of his houses? A.—No, Sir.

Q.—Did you ever know that they were together after the time you have mentioned? A.—No, Sir. They were together three different times, to my knowledge.

Q.—How did you find this out? A.—I saw them, Sir.

Q.—Where did you see them? A.—I saw them in New-York, and in Brooklyn, but I became acquainted with him in New-York.

Q.—When did you first become acquainted with this woman? A.—About a month ago.

Q.—Where did you first meet her? A.—On the street, sir.

Q.—Who introduced you? A.—No one, sir.

Q.—Did you know where she lived? A.—No, Sir.

Q.—What was her name? A.—I don't know.

Q.—How long before Mr. Goodrich commenced she disappeared? A.—I can't tell.

Q.—How did he become acquainted with these parties? A.—Didn't know before.

Q.—Did you introduce her to Mr. Goodrich? A.—No, Sir.

Q.—Did any one else? A.—No, Sir.

Q.—Did you ever hear Mr. Beach speak of a disappear—

The Bettmann Archive

The wreck of the *Atlantic*, April 1, 1873.

The New-York Times.

VOL. XXXVI.....NO. 11,150.   NEW-YORK, FRIDAY, MAY 27, 1887.—WITH SUPPLEMENT.   PRICE TWO CENTS.

POSTSCRIPT.

Friday, May 27, 1887—4:30 A. M.

HORSES DIE BY HUNDREDS

THE BELT LINE STABLES DESTROYED BY FIRE.

NEARLY FIFTEEN HUNDRED ANIMALS PERISH AND THE EQUIPMENT OF THE STREET RAILROAD NEARLY DESTROYED—FRIGHTFUL SCENES OF SUFFERING AND EXCITEMENT.

The greatest fire that has taken place in this city for many years broke out at 1:30 o'clock this morning in the car stables of the Belt Line Horse Railroad, on the west side of Tenth-avenue, between Fifty-third and Fifty-fourth streets. The car stables, with all their contents, were completely destroyed. Over 1,400 horses perished in the flames. One hundred and thirty cars, with a large quantity of harness, feed, and other material, were burned up. Only 40 horses were saved out of the nearly 1,500 in the stables.

The stables occupied the whole front on the west side of Tenth-avenue, and extended down Fifty-third and Fifty-fourth streets half way to Eleventh-avenue. The building was three stories high.

The fire was discovered in the cellar in the extreme western end of the stables and spread so rapidly that it was impossible to enter the building to save the horses.

When the firemen arrived the whole building was in flames, and the heat was so intense that the firemen could not approach close enough to be of any service to save the premises from destruction.

The heat set fire to a row of frame stables and dwellings on the south side of Fifty-third-street, and in a few moments the whole row was blazing. Then the flames leaped across Fifty-fourth-street and set fire to the six-story silk factory of Jacob Dow. A new building, which extends through to Fifty-fifth-street. A row of flats and tenement houses east of the silk factory next took fire, and the flames spread so rapidly that the tenants, rudely awakened from their slumbers, were compelled to fly for their lives.

In some cases the firemen were compelled to tear down the fences in the rear to enable the tenants to escape, as it was impossible for them to leave by the front doors owing to the intense heat.

The five-story brick tenement on the north-west corner of Fifty-third-street and Tenth-avenue, on the ground floor of which Adolph Kruger kept a liquor saloon, was ablaze from cellar to garret in a short time. Next the intense heat set fire to a row of eight two and three story frame buildings on the east side of Tenth-avenue, which were occupied as stores and dwellings.

It did not take many minutes for the flames to sweep through this entire row of buildings from Fifty-third to Fifty-fourth-street, adding to the great heat and blaze.

The first alarm was sent out by the watchman in the stables, and when Acting Chief Colby, of the Ninth Battalion, arrived, he at once sent out a third alarm. This brought eight engines in addition to the three which had responded to the first signal. But in view of the rapid spread of the flames and the great heat this force was practically powerless to stay the progress of the fire. Then followed the "Three-nines" signal, and five companies from all over town were soon hurrying to the scene of the conflagration.

Chief Shay was in command, and those brave fire fighters Chiefs Brannan, Lally, Gicquel, McGill, Reeves, and Fisher were with him doing their utmost to stay the progress of the fire, which assumed alarming proportions and which it was feared would extend beyond the control of the large force of firemen on the scene.

Fortunately the western wall of the stable was an unusually thick wall, built for the purpose of resisting fire, and this stayed the fire from extending beyond the stable to Eleventh-avenue.

It was impossible to pass through either Fifty-third or Fifty-fourth street in a line with the fire, and the firemen made their stand in the rear of the buildings on fire to prevent the flames extending to Fifty-fifth and Fifty-second streets.

The buildings destroyed, besides the car stables and the silk factory, are a row of apartment houses on Fifty-third-street and the frame buildings on Fifty-third-street and on Tenth-avenue.

The entire equipment of the Belt Line Road is destroyed, and the loss of the company will reach nearly $400,000. The other losses cannot be computed, but the value of the other property destroyed will perhaps reach as much more.

When the fire broke out the entire stock of horses owned by the railroad company, sick and well, nearly 1,500 in all, were in their stalls on the second and third floors of the building. The employes of the company who were about the building made desperate efforts to release them so that they might be driven into the street, but the rapid spread of the flames prevented this. The watchmen ran up the runway, and in the few minutes' time that they had, released and drove into the street about 50 of the frightened animals and then they were compelled to abandon the rest. The persons on the north side of Fifty-second-street would have to fly for their lives.

There were 130 cars on the lower floor, the entire equipment of the road. These, with all the harness and an immense amount of hay and feed, were destroyed.

Just beyond these was a little shanty perched on a mass of rocks, which escaped the fire. All of the buildings on the south side of the street opposite the stables were destroyed. These consisted of small wooden buildings occupied by poor families. Policemen Ryan, Grimson, Robb, and Burns went through these buildings, and with difficulty succeeded in getting the frightened people, who were packed. Many of the poor people had cows and horses in little sheds. The majority of the animals were saved. The persons on the north side of the street were Fifty-second-street gave out. The few houses that almost entirely consumed the small buildings on the street above new shot up and threatened to invade Fifty-second-street. Another fire engine was ordered to relieve the one which had given out, and the advance of the flames in that quarter was soon afterward checked.

There was much difficulty in procuring water along Eleventh-avenue. There was said to be only one hydrant there that was available. On the north side of Fifty-fourth-street...

opposite the stables all of the buildings, which were tenement houses of from three to five stories, were destroyed. All of the tenants of these houses were ousted. On the south side of Fifty-fourth-street. The fire did not extend beyond the western walls of stables, but the inhabitants of the buildings for some distance further up the street were burned out. Nearly every family was driven from its home as the fire extended. From Tenth-avenue and burning buildings, stretched a row of house. Almost all the occupants were asleep at the time the flames flashed up, and they scurried out half clad and in dismay. Fifty-second-street was jammed with the refugees guarding much of their household effects as they could snatch away. Some of the people did not get out of their rooms before the fire was swept across the street.

John Roesner lived at 514, and he escaped from a window. He jumped from the second story and badly injured his leg. Mary Geidinger, a young woman, was left alone in the same house when the others fled. She had fallen unconscious, and when some of the men went back they found her drenched and unable to speak. She was carried out insensible.

At the southeast corner of Fifty-third-street and Tenth-avenue, diagonally opposite from the stables, is a three-story brick building. The windows of plate glass in the saloon on the first floor were broken by the heat even when the flames were being blown in the opposite direction. On the top of the building on the southwest corner of Tenth-avenue and Fifty-third-street was wrapped with flames on every side, and after burning for an hour fell with a crash.

CURTIS FILLS THE BREACH.

BRATTON'S SUCCESSOR AS CHIEF OF THE RHODE ISLAND POLICE.

PROVIDENCE, May 26.—Edward F. Curtis was to-day appointed Chief of State Police, vice Charles E. Brayton, resigned. He enters upon his duties to fill the lantern pending the action of the incoming General Assembly, which has power to remove him in favor of another man or abolish the office altogether. The appointment is the mild climax to a long drawn out and somewhat laughable sensation, and if any little surprise was caused by it there was nothing exciting about it.

Chief Brayton's letter of resignation was filed on May 10, to take effect May 20. Some little interest and pleasant expectancy was aroused as to who would take the inevitable office for the brief tenure pending the action of the Legislature. Both Chief Brayton and the Governor declared their desire that the Prohibitionists should put forward their own man to enforce the prohibitory law, and then they could reasonably expect to be pleased with him. To this apparently easy and agreeable task the Prohibitionists applied themselves with partial success, and as an official from the south county was appointed by a secret conference, the ponderous importance of whose position was exaggerated by the universal confidence that they were veiled by the much flattered Prohibitionists.

When the nominee was publicly named it proved to be only a mouse that came out of the mountain after all its labor and pain, and after a few days the Prohibitionists decided they would authorize somebody else. More secret councils were held that only came to an end when it was discovered that nobody who was wanted desired to fool with the office for its last days. One chosen minister, because in part of crooks were in succession produced or suggested in one quarter or another, until the farce seemed ridiculous proportions. Then the solemn councils came to an abrupt end, and the office was put in the market, so to speak, for anybody who was esthetically worthy and would come and take it.

Into the breach walked Edward F. Curtis, with hesitating step. The Governor made out his commission and it was stated his a "speak-quick-yes-or-no" sort of a demand, and Mr. Curtis accepted it, largely to sustain the last traces of dignity of the discomfited party that had been ruthlessly handled into the alluring but uncomfortable predicament. Mr. Curtis is short, rotund, natty in dress, and suave, the opposite of the gigantic ex-Chief of careless attire and general politics. The new Chief is 52 years old, a war veteran, and one who stuck through the whole war, and has an excellent record. He is a Grand Army man, an Odd Fellow, a Methodist, and a Democratic Prohibitionist. He is an all-around good little man, and will be treated fairly and sympathetically by the public until the assembly removes him and the office together, which it is implicitly believed they will do.

CHICAGO BUILDING TROUBLES.

CHICAGO, May 26.—An advertisement will be printed Saturday in all towns having 500 population and upward in Illinois, Indiana, Wisconsin, Michigan, Ohio, and Missouri, offering steady work to 1,000 bricklayers at 45 cents an hour, and protection guaranteed. In this way the master masons of Chicago hope to fill the places of the men they have locked out or who have struck. Ample police protection has been promised, and special safeguards will be provided by the larger contractors. Quite a number of bricklayers applied for work to-day, claiming to be union men, but the contractors are careful about hiring men. Thirty men who applied for work yesterday struck this morning. "It is going to be a long strike," said Contractor William Mayer. "The bricklayers will not give in for weeks. In the meantime the carpenter work will be practically vanished. If the masons should start a full force to-day now morning it would be nearly two months before carpenter work would be fully under way. The non-union carpenters can do all the work there is on hand." Men who seek employment under the master masons are required to read and assent to the platform of principle, which practically puts them outside any union to which a day's work, except Saturday, when all work will be suspended at 12 M. Work to start at 7 A. M. Minimum wages for bricklayers and stonemasons are to be 45 cents per hour. Pay day is to be regularly every two weeks, either Monday or Tuesday.

THE WHEAT MANIPULATORS.

CHICAGO, May 26.—A sudden fright seized the shorts in June wheat to-day, and their efforts to cover ran the price of that future up nearly a cent in five minutes, to 90 cents, the highest price touched by wheat this year. At the latter figure the entire force of clique brokers began selling, and did not cease until the market was beaten down again to its starting point. Close observers of the clique's operations estimated that they sold between 1,000,000 and 1,500,000 bushels. The buying was all done by the shorts, the June future being steadily avoided by fresh traders. In the afternoon the crowd hammered July. Mr. Keene was conspicuous by his offers to sell 1,000,000 bushels at any price. The clique allowed their particular future to slide downward also. The final close was about the lowest point of the day, July 86¼ cents, and June full 2 cents premium. A rumor was in circulation that the deal would culminate in June. This report appeared to grow out of the fact—which is generally admitted—that there have been no indications of important purchases of July or the last minute by the clique, and, moreover, that the process of changing over their lines if begun now would be attended with great difficulty. The more conservative members were disinclined to hazard any opinion as to the length of time manipulation would continue.

BRITISH COLUMBIA AND JAPAN.

OTTAWA, May 26.—Sir George Stephen informed a Cabinet Minister yesterday that the Canadian Pacific Railway steamers would likely be running between British Columbia and Japan within two weeks. The prospects for a good business are very encouraging. It is understood that if the Canadian Pacific railroad Company does not tender directly for the Atlantic mail service under the contract about to be given out several of the Directors are prepared as a private company, will endeavor to secure it. There is a general feeling that the service will have to be considerably faster than at present.

SUNK IN THE MISSISSIPPI.

NEW-ORLEANS, May 26.—The tug Ivy, owned by Walker, Fancher, & McVitie, of Galveston, came here a few days ago with a southern large and started on her return this evening with a caboose laden in tow. In rounding Algiers Point she collided with the British steamer Wydale and sank, carrying down with her the pilot and a son of Capt. Andrews. The damage to the Wydale, if any, has not been ascertained.

AFFAIRS IN FOREIGN LANDS

THE ILLNESS OF THE GERMAN CROWN PRINCE.

GLOOMY FOREBODINGS CAUSED BY DR. MACKENZIE'S REPORT—PRINCE BISMARCK ALSO ILL.

BERLIN, May 26.—The *Reichs-Anzeiger* gives the following account of the course of Crown Prince Frederick William's illness: "In January last his Imperial Highness was seized with an inflammatory affection of the throat, at which the outward indications were a slight cough and intense hoarseness. The symptoms refused to yield under remedies previously applied with success in similar attacks. A course of treatment of several weeks at Ems, though most beneficial to the Crown Prince's general health, failed to remove the local affection. The medical authorities called to consult with the body physician advised that the English specialist, Dr. Mackenzie, be asked to give an opinion. Dr. Mackenzie, after several examinations, found the Prince's condition not so serious as to debar hope that the trouble might be removed with proper treatment in the course of time. The tone of this statement was less assuring than had been expected, and has cast a gloom over official circles. Dr. Mackenzie operated with laryngeal forceps and successfully removed a foreign growth from the Prince's throat, but the Prince remains liable to a relapse from a return of the tumor in a worse form."

Prince Bismarck for several days been suffering from muscular rheumatism. Every sudden movement he makes causes him much pain. His physicians have advised him to take complete rest.

Bishop Kopp will be appointed to the vacant See of Breslau.

The Bundesrath has referred to a committee the proposed Trade Regulation bill for Alsace-Lorraine.

The Franciscans returning to Prussia under the ecclesiastical law are preparing to occupy the old Jesuit monastery at Creusberg, near Bonn.

ENGLAND AND THE IRISH.

MORE CHARGES AGAINST MR. PARNELL—THE STANLEY EXPEDITION.

LONDON, May 26.—The Dublin *Express* (Conservative) accuses Mr. Parnell of cruelty to one of his Avondale tenants named Kennedy. The paper says that although Mr. Kennedy has been a tenant on the Irish leader's estate for nine years, Mr. Parnell has coerced him into exchanging the farm he had occupied and improved for a tract of inferior land. In addition to this Mr. Parnell, the *Express* says, has refused to make the 25 per cent. reduction in rent requested by Mr. Kennedy, and has sued him for a year's rent due only since April.

A despatch from St. Paul de Loanda, dated May 26, gives the details of the arrangements made by Henry M. Stanley prior to the departure of the expedition from Stanley Pool on April 29. In order to provide fuel for the steamers advance corps were sent to various stations along the banks of the Congo. The corps were also instructed to obtain victuals for the Expedition, which were desired to retain the provisions already on board for the land march. The boats were so heavily laden when they left Stanley Pool that it was expected that the journey to Stanley Falls would consume 36 days. All the members of the expedition were well at the time of the last report.

At the Epsom race meeting yesterday a thief stole Sir Charles Russell's watch. Sir Charles pursued the man and recovered his property and then handed him over to the authorities. The thief was arraigned, tried, and convicted and sentenced to three months' imprisonment.

The various British Chambers of Commerce and other associations propose to issue a protest against the import duties on iron and steel imposed by the Canadian Government.

Mr. Gladstone has started for his house at Hawarden to spend the Whitsun holidays.

Ella Russell appeared this evening at Covent Garden Theatre in the opera of "Rigoletto." She achieved a great success.

ASSURANCES OF PEACE.

EMPEROR FRANCIS JOSEPH'S SPEECH CLOSING THE HUNGARIAN DIET.

PESTH, May 26.—The Hungarian Diet was closed to-day. Emperor Francis Joseph, in his speech closing the session, expressed his appreciation of the measures passed by the Diet. He gratefully referred to the patriotic self-abnegation of the Deputies in providing for the safety of the throne and monarchy despite its less favorable condition of the finances. The passage of the landsturm law, he said, had served considerably to increase the defensive strength of the monarchy. The Emperor said further: "While you, equally with us, desire to maintain peace, should this be impossible you have shown that every son of our beloved Hungary is ready to defend with his blood the possessions and interests of the throne, monarchy, and fatherland. While maintaining the present good relations with all the powers the self-sacrificing spirit indicated, coupled with the friendly renewal of the convention with Austria, affords the Government powerful support in their efforts successfully to pursue with increased confidence their policy. This policy, while completely safeguarding the country's vital interests, may, we hope, continue to preserve peace."

THEY WILL MARCH ON BRUSSELS.

BRUSSELS, May 26.—A committee of strikers has written to Premier Beernaert demanding universal suffrage and the abandonment of the Castle bill, and hinting that if he fails to reply before Sunday the strikers will march upon Brussels. A general strike has occurred at Cockerill's works. The glass-workers are obliged to use German coal in consequence of the strike among the miners in the coal districts of Belgium, and the railroads will soon be obliged to do likewise if the strike continues.

The Public Prosecutor has ordered the enforcement of the law against the sale of arms, with the view of checking trade outrages.

An Anarchist rendezvous was surprised by the military in peace, and several men and a quantity of documents were seized.

DE FREYCINET AGAIN DECLINES.

PARIS, May 26.—M. de Freycinet has informed President Grévy that he cannot form a Cabinet.

The Presidents of three Republican groups waited on President Grévy to remove Gen. Boulanger from office.

A hitch has again occurred over the retention of Gen. Boulanger as War Minister. M. de Freycinet, finding that he would be unable to form a Cabinet of all new men, and thus exclude Gen. Boulanger, now insists that the latter must remain at the head of the War Department.

At the meeting of the Chamber of Deputies to-day much discontent was manifested over the delay in the formation of a Cabinet. The Chamber decided, by a vote of 307 to 212, to adjourn until Saturday.

PLOTS TO KILL THE SULTAN.

BUCHAREST, May 26.—A plot to assassinate the Sultan of Turkey was discovered last Thursday. Extraordinary efforts have been made to conceal the discovery from the public. The effect of the plot on the Sultan is visible in the terror he exhibits. He made his usual weekly visit to the mosque hurriedly instead of with the usual slow and pompous parade.

CONSTANTINOPLE, May 26.—It is reported that the Sultan has dismissed a number of officials holding high places in the palace, who were discovered to be engaged in a conspiracy to overthrow him.

CURRENT FOREIGN TOPICS.

VIENNA, May 26.—The Empress of Austria will become patroness of the Home for British Governesses, which is to be founded in honor of the jubilee of Queen Victoria.

ROME, May 26.—At a Papal consistory held yesterday Mgr. Pallotto and Father Hausa were made Cardinals. The Bishops were proconized in France and one in Mexico. The Most Rev. Michael Logue, D. D., Bishop of Raphoe, Ireland, was transferred to the diocese of Armagh, and the Most Rev. F. J. McCormack, Bishop of Achonry, was transferred to Galway. The Pope has proclaimed the new Catholic Bishops of Australasia, making the Bishop of Adelaide, Brisbane, and Wellington archbishops.

SUGAR PRICES ADVANCED.

SAN FRANCISCO, May 26.—The California Sugar Refinery to-day advanced the price of all grades of sugar one-eighth cent, and the American Sugar Refinery met the advance this evening.

O'BRIEN NOW AT MONTREAL

AND ADDRESSES A CROWD FROM A HOTEL.

HIS RECEPTION AT ALBANY BY SPEAKER HUSTED AND HIS ADDRESS TO THE LEGISLATORS.

MONTREAL, May 26.—O'Brien and Kilbride arrived here at 10:45 to-night from Albany and were received at the station by about 200 people. They got into a hack, accompanied by Mr. Cloran, President of the National League, and Mr. Barry, President of the St. Patrick's Society. The crowd was very enthusiastic and insisted on taking out the horses and pulling the hack along the street themselves. The hack driver, mounted on his horse, led off the procession, and the rest followed singing "God Save Ireland" and cheering at times for O'Brien and Parnell. An occasional hearty groan was given for Lord Lansdowne, and on passing Victoria-square there was some hooting at the statue of the Queen. On arriving at St. Lawrence Hall the party proceeded to the parlor and from the open window addressed the crowd below. Mr. Cloran introduced Mr. O'Brien as the apostle of free speech in Canada. He had been attacked time and again by an intolerant and brutal mob and the people of Montreal would have a chance to-morrow night of entering their solemn protest. Mr. O'Brien said he had made several copies of the charges against Lord Lansdowne. Lansdowne might bust for a while in the applause of those who sought their blood in his interest, but there was no better proof of a bad case than that he should to the hilt of people like these, that he should before the world to-day with the brand of guilt on his forehead.

Mr. Kilbride was addressing the crowd when a tumult arose. It appears that two Highlanders named McNeil and McPherson had come to the hall to call as a friend, and McNeil remarked in Gaelic, "That man should not be allowed to speak." The mob made a rush at him, and his comrade, on looking round, saw blood flowing from his mouth. This was too much for his fiery Celtic temper, and he took a hand in. For over a minute the two stalwart Highlanders kept the mob back, and an Englishman coming to their assistance caused a diversion, and all three were pulled into the hotel. There was quite an exciting scene for a few minutes, but the speakers having retired the crowd melted away.

ALBANY, May 26.—Editor O'Brien received a hearty welcome in Albany to-day. Taking a long sleep and a late breakfast at the Delavan House he received John T. McDonough, Dr. John Thompson, John McNally, Thomas Griffin, and Max Kurth, representing the Irish societies of this city, and a few other citizens, and then went to the Capitol just in time to be warmly greeted by the departing legislators. The party reached the Senate Chamber before the adjournment. On the motion of Col. Murphy they were granted the privileges of the floor, and Senators crowded around to shake his hand. After a chat with Attorney-General O'Brien the Irish agitator and his friends crossed over to the Assembly Chamber. The gavel had struck for final adjournment, but Speaker Husted arrested the attention of the members, who were bidding one another good-bye and packing up, amid rounds of applause and loud calls for a speech. Mr. O'Brien, mounting the Speaker's desk, said: "I assure you I cannot find, even if I were stronger, words to thank you for this welcome to myself. I confess I am almost appalled at the kindness I have experienced ever since I set foot on American soil. Since I first saw the Stars and Stripes floating over the sea near Cape Vincent I have had a feeling that there were 60,000,000 friends and freemen around me. I wish I could speak to you in eloquent words as I could desire for this and all the years we have done for Ireland. I know of nothing in all the events of the past few years that has here served the arm of Mr. Gladstone in his great work of reformation and peace than the wonderful volume of American influence and sentiment that has ever been flowing upon him to support and strengthen him. So far as our cause is concerned, thank God, although trouble a few centuries of a struggle that has never been given up by our people and never will be given up. [Applause.] We have got a leader, perhaps the greatest that God ever raised up for the deliverance of a suffering country. We have got the greatest of living Englishmen for our ally—William Ewart Gladstone. [Applause.] We have got the whole sentiment of the civilized world, represented chiefly by the 60,000,000 people in this magnificent country of America; we have pledged to us the whole strength and the whole exercise of the great Liberal Party of England, who have to never yet taken up a reform that they have not succeeded in carrying through. [Applause.] We have only to stand by each other, only to go on quietly and in order until they feel the beats of the Irish people and their leaders never beat higher, more hopeful, than they do to-day, and the hopes of our enemies in Ireland were never lower and their power was never ebbing away faster than it is to-day. I appeal to you a thousand times for having interposed in your proceedings for only a few moments and return you my thanks. Believe me, they come from a heart overflowing with gratitude to you and the whole American Nation for the grand and noble work which you have done for Ireland."

A brief call was next made on Gov. Hill, who welcomed Mr. O'Brien and Mr. Kilbride and exchanged compliments with them. The Governor remarked that the Governor and was a much younger man than he had imagined him to be. O'Brien, who is already fatigued by his exertions and is suffering from his cough this condition in Canada, characterized the parties who made the attacks on him as bloodthirdly and cowardly. "Outside of these gangs of cutthroats and scoundrels," said he, "there is not a man in Canada but who have liberty of action and free speech. The assaults made upon me were no answer to the arraignment I made of Lord Lansdowne. They will have the same effect as assaults and riots of a similar nature had in Ulster in my own country. There the same Orange mob threatened that if we crossed the Boyne that the waters would be red with their threats, with all their threats and mob violence, the Nationalist caucus has steadily advanced until we now have the entire province of Ulster with the exception of two counties, while Derry is as much the skirts of royalty until they hide their heads in shame and disgrace. It is only a few in the Dominion who are thus intolerant. It is not his great mass of the people. They have hoodwinked the American ideas and a very little knowledge of the individual. The effect of the assaults upon us will be a good one, as it will isolate these gangs and rally their powers."

After a drive around town to-day the 1:15 P. M. train for Montreal, where Mr. O'Brien will speak to-morrow night. He hopes to return to Ireland next week, Saturday.

COMMODORE FORBES'S YACHT.

BOSTON, May 26.—The new steel steam yacht just launched from the Atlantic Works in East Boston for Commodore John M. Forbes took her maiden plunge to-day soon after 2 o'clock. As she glided from the cradle she carried about 75 passengers, among them E. Burgess, the yacht's designer. Mr. Forbes has not yet decided what name to give to his new yacht. She is to be used as a family pleasure yacht rather than a racer, although she will probably steam 14 knots an hour. The model is sharp at both ends, and the bow expands to correspond with the general outline as it rises. The stern is rounded above the line of the plankslide sheer and the sides are gracefully rounded amidships. The yacht is 108 feet long on the water line, has 18 feet greatest breadth of beam, and is 10 feet deep. The hull is of steel, and the workmanship on it is excellent. She will go into commission in about a month.

THAT ONE-SIDED BILLIARD MATCH.

WASHINGTON, May 26.—The result of the billiard match to-night was, as it has been for three previous nights, a victory for Mr. Daly. There was no particularly brilliant playing. Mr. Sexton took the lead at the beginning and held it until the sixth inning, when Mr. Daly overtook him and thenceforth was the lead to the end. His run this time was by no means large, and his cut was at a disadvantage. At the conclusion of to-night's playing the score, with everything even, when Mr. Daly's score totals 1,000, Mr. Sexton only 175 points to his credit. The results of the match this year are: Daly 3, Sexton 0. Daily's largest run to-night was 21, 30, and 19; and Sexton's 14, 10, and 21.

AN EIGHTEEN-POUND SALMON.

RONDOUT, May 26.—Albert Munson, of Port Ewen, has caught an 18-pound salmon in the Hudson River near the mouth of Rondout Creek. A despatch from Oceanside states that a 21-pound salmon was caught near there this afternoon. Munson's catch is on exhibition here.

When You Go to the Country use Pearline for washing and cleaning.—Adv.

WRECKS BY WHOLESALE.

THIRTY-ONE FOUND ON THE WEST COAST OF VANCOUVER ISLAND.

SAN FRANCISCO, May 26.—A special from Port Townsend, Washington Territory, says: The United States revenue cutter Oliver Wolcott has returned from a four days' cruise along the west coast of Vancouver Island, where news concerning the ship St. Stephens, which sailed from here on March 29 loaded with 2,200 tons of coal from Seattle for San Francisco. The cutter arrived in Klayuquot Sound last Sunday night. Father McCoy, a Catholic missionary, who recently reported that Indians had found a trunk and other articles belonging to the ship, reside here, and his services were secured. He immediately dispatched several parties of Indians to Cape Cook and other Indian villages in quest of more definite information concerning the wreck.

The party sent to Cape Cook returned on Monday and reported that the St. Stephens had come ashore there during a heavy storm which had prevailed at that point on April 9. The cutter departed for Klayuquot Harbor, a few miles south of Cape Cook, where an Indian villages was found, and personal letters, suits, three boats, the driftwood, pilothouse, compass, ship's stores, and oil paintings belonging to the Captain's daughter, which had washed ashore on April 10, the Indians reported. One white-hull boat, which was carried on the driftwood, was being used by the Indians in having come ashore uninjured. The other two boats appeared to have been crushed by the waves against the sides of the vessel when the crew were endeavoring to leave the ship.

A shoal many 20 miles long, and three miles from the shore, which forms a dangerous reef, exists directly in front of the wreck, which the sea barely covers at ebb tide. It was on this reef that the St. Stephens was wrecked during a heavy southwesterly gale. The theory advanced by Capt. Glover and Bryant is that the vessel was dismasted soon after the dark Barclai Talbot observed her in distress off Cape Beale, and at strong ocean currents exist along the coast the ship was carried a distance of 120 miles to Cape Cook, where she stranded.

Capt. Williams and Capt. Bryant, Hull Inspector, offered a reward of $1,000 to the Indians for information leading to the recovery of the bodies of the crew, and Indians were employed to search the beach for bodies. Nothing more was found except some domestic geese which had come ashore at the time of the wreck. A portion of the hull was seen protruding alongside the reef, indicating that the vessel was carried down after springing a leak on the reef by the immense weight of coal in her hold. Not the slightest trace could be obtained of Capt. Douglass, his family, or crew, numbering altogether about 30. They must have perished while endeavoring to leave the vessel, and the strong current which prevails along the western coast of Vancouver Island has carried their bodies north along the desolate and uninhabited coast.

On Tuesday, when the cutter started on her return voyage, a brig, supposed to be the North Star, was found with head out of the water, and could not be lowered. The word "North" could be dimly be read through a glass. The brig was lumber-laden, from Seattle for San Diego. The hull of the brig frame was found with timbers broken and the house nearly gone. During the passage from Cape Cook to Cape Flattery 31 wrecks were found, and an immense quantity of lumber was strewn along the shore.

At the St. Stephens, Capt. Douglass, was a fine clipper ship of 1,392 tons, built at Bath, Me., by Chapman & Finn in 1877. She was owned by E. P. Flint, and after discharging a cargo from Hong Kong left San Francisco on March 31, under charter to the Oregon Improvement Company, to bring coal from Seattle. The North Star was a brig of 389 tons, built in Boston in 1867. She was owned by J. H. Morehouse and others, and Capt. Traynor was in command.

WABASH TO PAY INTEREST.

JUDGE GRESHAM GRANTS AN ORDER AS EXPECTED.

CHICAGO, May 26.—An order was entered to-day by Judge Gresham in accordance with his decision 10 days ago authorizing Receiver McNulta, of the Wabash, to pay certain interest on the sectional division mortgages of those branches of the system which have earned enough to pay interest. The payments are to be made in accordance with the showings of the books as now kept, and without prejudice to the Chicago Division bondholders to enforce their rights or show that they should not be compelled to pay all the expenses of the Chicago terminals. The Receiver is to pay first the outstanding coupons maturing Feb. 1, 1886, and prior thereto on bonds secured, respectively, by the mortgage of the Lake Erie, Wabash, and St. Louis Railroad Company; by the first mortgage of the Great Western Railroad Company of 1859; by the mortgage of the Decatur and East St. Louis Railroad Company; and by the mortgage of the Illinois and Southern Iowa Railway Company, and also the outstanding coupons maturing on May 1, 1885, and prior thereto on bonds secured by the first mortgage of the Wabash Railway representing coupons belonging to the mortgage bonds above enumerated.

On all the coupons interest shall be allowed from the dates of their maturity to June 1, 1887, at 6 per cent. The Receiver is also ordered to pay six months' interest on the gold certificates issued by the Wabash Road in exchange for unpaid coupons in the above mentioned mortgages. An appeal and supersedeas were allowed to Henry Humphreys and D. A. Lindley and he refused. An order was also entered refusing the application to thumb certain suits brought at springfield to foreclose some of the underlying mortgages. These suits were begun by the Trustees in the mortgages, though other suits were pending for the same purpose, commenced by the bondholders, under order of Judge Gresham.

DAMAGES AGAINST BRADSTREET.

MONTREAL, May 26.—The appeals in the cases of Messrs. S. Carsley & Co. and Mr. E. Carsley against the Bradstreet Mercantile Agency, for heavy damages, were decided this morning by the Court of Appeals. In 1884 a sheet of changes and corrections was sent out by the agency to about 600 of their subscribers, and opposite Mr. Carsley's name were the words "Call at office." This, it was asserted, was intended to convey the information that the agency was aware of something detrimental to the plaintiff's position and standing in business, and was a warning to persons who might feel disposed to deal with him not to do so without calling at the office for such information. When some of the subscribers did call at the office they learned that Mr. Carsley had asked his creditors for an extension of time for the payment of $50,000. The plaintiff urged that this report was false and that he had thereby suffered a loss to the extent of $50,000. In defense the company contended that no detrimental inference could be drawn from the words in the circular, and that they were not guilty of its statement charged. This case was relected to-day, and damages to the amount of $2,000 were granted in each case.

CANADA'S IRON DUTIES.

OTTAWA, May 26.—Sir Charles Tupper, Minister of Finance, spoke to-day to a deputation in regard to the protest of British manufacturers against the new Canadian iron duties. "No further changes," said he, "will be made, despite the representations made to the Colonial Secretary. A similar protest was made in 1879, but the tariff regulation went into effect, but it was only temporary because the English manufacturers soon discovered that the change simply tended to increase Canada's capacity without affecting the imports from Great Britain. The result will prove the same in the present instance. Our trade relations with England will, if anything, be strengthened, while the imports to be given to our rich stores of iron and coal, and we will go a long way toward building up a powerful British nationality in this colony."

ENJOINED FROM BRINGING SUITS.

RICHMOND, Va., May 26.—An injunction was granted by Judge Bond, of the United States Circuit Court, in Chambers, in Baltimore this morning, and filed in the office of the clerk of that court here, restraining unfavorable Attorney from doing anything whatsoever to bring these suits in conformity with the act here brought by the Legislature at the session just closed against persons who tender coupons in payment of taxes. The injunction is granted at the suit of Mr. Cooper, a citizen of England and holder of bonds of the State.

THE DEATH ROLL SWELLING

TERRIBLE RESULTS OF THE OPERA COMIQUE FIRE.

AN ESTIMATE THAT 200 LIVES WERE LOST—MORE THAN 50 BODIES FOUND—MANY DISTRESSING SCENES.

PARIS, May 26.—The bodies of ballet dancers who lost their lives by the burning of the Opéra Comique last night are lying in heaps in the ruins of the theatre. The firemen assert that many bodies are lying in the upper galleries. The number of persons killed greatly exceeds the previous estimated. An excited crowd surrounds the ruins, which are guarded by a military cordon. Many distressing scenes are witnessed.

Forty bodies in a terribly mutilated condition were recovered from the ruins this afternoon. The remains were principally those of ballet girls, choristers, and machinists. Five of the bodies were those of elderly ladies, and one of them was that of a child. The bodies of three men and two women were found in the stage box, where the victims had taken refuge from the flames. It is ascertained that many bodies lie buried in the debris in the upper galleries, whose escape was exceedingly difficult.

Late this afternoon the bodies of 18 ladies, all in full dress, were found lying together at the bottom of the staircase leading from the second story. These ladies and their escorts to the theatre, but no bodies of men were found anywhere near where the women were burned to death.

The walls of the theatre began falling this evening and the search for the bodies had to be temporarily suspended. When the work was resumed to-night several more were exhumed. The official statement says that 50 bodies have already been recovered.

M. Revelliln, a Deputy, speaking in the Chamber of Deputies this afternoon, estimated that at least 200 persons lost their lives in the fire.

To-day 156 missing persons have been inquired for by relatives. They are supposed to have perished in the flames. The bottom of the theatre is flooded with water to the depth of five feet. Sixty bodies have been found floating in the water by the firemen.

The finding of charred bodies continues. The remains are recognizable only by means of trinkets.

The Government propose to close several of the Paris theatres because of their deficiency in exits. The Chamber of Deputies has voted a credit of 200,000f. for the relief of sufferers by the fire.

The library attached to the theatre was entirely destroyed with all its contents, including many valuable scores. Six thousand costumes were burned in the wardrobe. The theatre was insured for 1,000,000f.

Among the audience at the Opéra Comique last night were Gen. Boulanger, Gen. Saussier, Gen. Thibaudin, M. Goblet, M. Berthelot, and the Marquis Ferronnays, Prefect of Police. They all escaped unhurt. An artist named Philippe performed prodigies of valor in saving life. He mounted a ladder three times and saved three persons after they had been abandoned by the firemen.

In the Rue Favart a sudden gust of wind cleared away the dense smoke, when a woman and two men were seen standing in an angle of an uppermost cornice. The woman raised to jump, but the men prevented her. When all were finally rescued the woman was a raving maniac.

A singer had a miraculous escape from a dressing-room in an angle at the top of the building. He says that the wind kept the flames off that part of the building, but a river of molten lead poured from the roof, the course of which he diverted with a board to prevent the weight carrying down the shaky floor.

The officials are endeavoring to underrate the number of bodies found in the building that has alarmed the public.

The Théâtre Château d'Eau announces a performance for the benefit of the sufferers on Monday.

HISTORY OF THE THEATRE.

ACCOUNT OF THE FAMOUS WORKS PRODUCED ON ITS STAGE.

The Opéra Comique has for many years been one of the most famous institutions of Paris. Its importance in the great amusement-life of the great continental metropolis is not readily understood by any one who is unacquainted with the character of the Parisians. Italian opera, pure and simple, has only a spasmodic existence in the heart of France. La Salle Ventadour was the home of Italian music, but it was long ago sold to a banking company, and turned into a substantial business house capable of earning more money even than Patti. Frenchmen are not like Americans; they do not prize imported productions beyond those of native origin. They like the opera as they like their cooking, in French. The most important place of resort for the fashion of Paris is the Grand Opera, and next to that comes, or came, the Opéra Comique.

It may be necessary to remind some readers that comic opera is not always funny; it is simply opera with spoken dialogue in the place of recitative, and is called comic to distinguish it from grand opera. In Paris this class of musical entertainment is indigenous. It does not require the extraordinary attraction of some brilliant name to make it popular with the masses. They like it for its own sake—not for the sake of the performers. Brander Matthews remarks that in his "Theatres of Paris" that the "style in which pieces are put upon the stage was superior to that of the Théâtre National Odéon that it is in our Academy; there was the same polyglot company, with the same reputations in France, the same lack of care and the same taste and attention, the same lack of flourished only in the hotbed of fashion, and but for a sensom's bloomed and to wither.

Many of the operas which we are accustomed to hear in Italian in New-York were originally written in French for the Opéra Comique, and are constantly performed at one theatre or the other.

The Italian opera was, therefore, never on a very firm basis in Paris, and the last attempt to make money out of it were by a publisher, who produced "Aïda," and by Capoul, who produced the Marquis of Ivry's "Les Amants de Vérone," and the Salle Ventadour was transformed from the home of music to the home of gold, and in this case it was a genuine change. The Opéra Comique, on the other hand, has flourished for more than a century, and sought fair to go on flourishing indefinitely. Its home was one of the oldest theatres in Paris. In the early part of the last century companies of strolling players pitched their tents on the suburbs of Paris. This rivalry was not cheerfully received by the royal and privileged companies, and they contrived to have all kinds of heavy and tyrannous weight laid on the companies. At one time the actors were prohibited from speaking or singing. Then the story of the play was told in pantomime, and when words were needed a placard bearing the words was exhibited. The words of necessary songs were arranged and the audience was shown in the same way, and the audience obligingly helped the company out by singing.

The principal strolling troupes joined the theatres known as the Italian Comedy in 1762, and the languages of the house became French. In 1780 all this out of the Italian actors went back to Italy; but the house still continued to make money, and was known as the Italian Comedy. In 1792, when French patriotic feeling was at its height, the name was changed to National Opéra Comique, and took its name from the second republic, the second empire, and third republic, the Orleans branch, the second republic, and third republic, the Opéra Comique has always been popularly associated, but the ominous name of 200,000f. has kept it in a solid when...

The ruins of the Opéra Comique.

to be the most prosperous and popular musical resort in Paris. Not long after its opening it came to be under the management of Favart, husband of the celebrated Mme. Favart, the subject of song and story. It was commonly known among Parisians as the Salle Favart.

During the First Empire an Italian company imported by Napoleon played there; but under the Restoration it returned to its first love, the opera comique. The fire of Wednesday night is not the first in its history, for it was almost wholly burned down in 1838. It had 2,000 seats and was one of the prettiest and best arranged of the older theatres of Paris.

As before said, many of the best known operas in the Italian repertory were originally heard first at the Paris Opéra Comique as comic operas with spoken dialogue. In recent years some American singers have achieved their first success there. It is hardly necessarry to remind music lovers of the receptions accorded Emma Nevada and Marie Van Zandt at this house. They were successful beyond the expectations of their warmest friends. Mlle. Giglio Nordica and Miss Gertrude Griswold also succeeded there. Mlle. Nevada was extremely fortunate in the popularity of her performance of the heroine of Gounod's "Mirella," and Mlle. Van Zandt was accorded high praise for her Lakmé. These ladies have met with less

success in the United States than they had in Paris; but this is easily understood when it is remembered that there they were rated by the standard of comic opera and here by that of grand opera. Moreover, the Opéra Comique has never depended so much upon the particular excellence of a star performer as on the smoothness of its ensemble work. Mme. Galli-Marié, the elder sister of Mme. Irma-Marié, one of the earliest exponents of opera bouffe art in America, and Mlle. Paola Marié created the chief rôles in "Mignon," which was originally produced at this house. They would hardly be received as fitting impersonators of these parts at the Academy or the Metropolitan.

Among the noted singers who appeared at the house were Juillet, Féréol, Vizentini, Leclère, Masset, Audran, Faure, Prilleux, Troy, Nicholas, Achard, Capoul, Mmes. St. Aubin, Duprés, Prevost, Belmont, Jenny Colon, Rossi, Pottier, Miles. Borghèse, Casimir, Anna Thillon, Charton, Louise Lavoye, Ugalde, Decroix, Lefebvre, Miolan Carvalho, Caroline Duprez, and Boulart. From 1807 to 1826 the artists were organized in a society and managed the theatre. In 1826 M. Guilbert de Pixerécourt took the direction of the house. He was succeeded in 1826 by M. Bernard. Other managers have been M. Ducis and M. de St. Georges, Ronsault, Sanger,

Lubbert, Paul Dutreich, Crosnier, Bassett, Perrin, Beaumont, Perrin, Leuven, Du Locle, and Carvalho, in the order named. M. Carvalho was the manager of the theatre up to the date of the fire.

Among the well known works produced at this house are the following: "Richard Cœur de Lion," by Gretry, Oct. 21, 1784; Paisiello's "Barbier de Seville," March 16, 1793; Boïldieu's "Calif de Bagdad," Sept. 16, 1801; Nicolo's "Cendrillon," Feb. 22, 1810; Boïldieu's "Jean de Paris," April 4, 1812; Mozart's "Figaro," Dec. 31, 1818; Auber's "Macon," May 3, 1825; Boïldieu's "La Dame Blanche," Dec. 10, 1825; Auber's "Fra Diavolo," Jan. 8, 1830; Herold's "Zampa," May 3, 1831; Herold's "Pré aux Clercs," Dec. 15, 1832; Adam's "Le Chalet," Sept. 25, 1834; Weber's "Der Freyschütz" under the title of "Robin des Bois," January, 1835; Auber's "Cheval de Bronze," March 23, 1835; Halévy's "L'Éclair," Dec. 30, 1835; Adam's "Postillon de Lonjumeau," Oct. 13, 1836; Auber's "Le Domino Noir," Dec. 2, 1837; Donizetti's "La Fille du Regiment," Feb. 11, 1840; Auber's "Les Diamants de Couronne," March 6, 1841; Halévy's "Les Mousquetaires de la Reine," Feb. 3, 1846; Ambroise Thomas's first opera, "Le Caïd," Jan. 3, 1849; Adam's "Giralda," July 30, 1850;

Semet's "La Petite Fadette," ("Fanchon,") Dec. 28, 1850; Massé's "Galatée," April 14, 1852; Massé's "Les Noces de Jeannette," Feb. 4, 1853; Meyerbeer's "L'Étoile du Nord," which was written for the house, Feb. 16, 1854; Félicien David's "Lalla Roukh," 1862; Ambroise Thomas's "Mignon," 1867; Offenbach's "Fantasio," 1872; Massenet's "Don Cæsar de Bazan," 1872; "Carmen," March 3, 1875; "Piccolino," April 11, 1876; "Les Amoreux de Catherine," May 1, 1876; "Cinq-Mars," April 5, 1877; "Bathyle," May 1, 1877; "La Surprise de l'Amour," Oct. 31, 1877; "Psyche," May 21, 1878; "Lakmé," April 14, 1883; "Manon," Jan. 19, 1884; "Une Nuit de Cléopâtre," April 25, 1885.

"Carmen," "Lakmé," "Manon," and "Une Nuit de Cléopâtre" are among the important works especially written for this theatre. It has not always been devoted simply to operatic productions, for on April 19, 1875, Berlioz's "Requiem" was there made known to the French public for the first time. Paisiello's "Barbier de Seville" was the opera on which that of Rossini was founded, and he also obtained some of his material for "Cendrillon" from Nicolo's opera of the same name.

The New-York Times.

VOL. XXXVII.....NO. 11,399.   NEW-YORK, TUESDAY, MARCH 13, 1888.   PRICE TWO CENTS.

IN A BLIZZARD'S GRASP

THE WORST STORM THE CITY HAS EVER KNOWN.

BUSINESS AND TRAVEL COMPLETELY SUSPENDED.

NEW-YORK HELPLESS IN A TORNADO OF WIND AND SNOW WHICH PARALYZED ALL INDUSTRY, ISOLATED THE CITY FROM THE REST OF THE COUNTRY, CAUSED MANY ACCIDENTS AND GREAT DISCOMFORT, AND EXPOSED IT TO MANY DANGERS.

The storm of wind and rain, which began to sweep over this city and the neighborhood on Sunday evening, gathered force as the night progressed. The temperature began to fall, sleet and snow descended in succession and the wind became boisterous. Before daylight dawned yesterday a remarkable storm, the most annoying and detrimental in its results that the city has ever witnessed, was in full progress. When the people began to stir to go about their daily tasks and vocations they found a blizzard, just like those they have been accustomed to read about as occurring in the far West, had struck the city and its environs and had laid an embargo on the travel and traffic of the greatest city on the continent.

What the presence of a blizzard meant was soon manifest. Before the day had well advanced, every horse car and elevated railroad train in the city had stopped running; the streets were almost impassable to men or horses by reason of the huge masses of drifting snow; the electric wires—telegraph and telephone connecting spot in this city or opening communication with places outside were nearly all broken; hardly a train was sent out from the city or came into it during the entire day; the mails were stopped, and every variety of business dependent on motion or locomotion was stopped.

Thus the city, to a great extent, was at a standstill yesterday, and the prospects are not much better to-day. People vexed at the collapse of all the principal means of intercommunication and transportation became reflective, and the result was a general expression of opinion that an immediate and radical improvement was imperative. So the blizzard may accomplish what months, if not years, of argument and agitation might have failed to do. Probably if it had not been for the blizzard the people of the city might have gone on for an indefinite time enduring the nuisance of electric wires dangling from poles, of slow trains running by horses or by treacherous snows, and showers of sparks from cars drawn by horses and making the streets dangerous with their centre-bearing rails. Now two things are tolerably certain—that a system of a rapid transit which cannot be made inoperative by storms must be straightway devised and as speedily as possible constructed, and that all the electric wires—telegraph, telephone, fire alarms, and illuminating—must be put under ground without any delay.

The elevated roads and the elevated electric wires are not only made useless by a severe storm, but they are made dangerous. The city is able to be put into darkness and the consequent perils. There is also the danger of conflagrations through the failure of the fire alarm wires.

To the great majority of municipal and suburban New-Yorkers the great blizzard was a surprise party of the worst kind. It began soon after midnight, and those who work on newspapers—editors, reporters, compositors, pressmen, as well as the news venders—went home between 2 and 4 o'clock yesterday morning realizing that an unusual tempest had begun. So did the marketmen and milkmen when they turned out for their matutinal labors. The milkmen, in fact, were in many cases unable to get any milk at the stations on account of the non-arrival of the trains; the morning papers all left their homes, the bakers failed to come round with the morning rolls. The tray says that it is the small size of the train were the most; and pealed thousands of New-Yorkers yesterday morning—good, steady, churchgoing heads of families—when they had to get through their breakfasts without their favorite newspaper, their hot buttered rolls, and their fragrant coffee enriched with the boiling milk, began to seriously question whether life was worth living after all, with all these trials and tribulations to undergo.

The other comic journals have made lots of fun over the woes of New-Jerseymen and other suburban residents on account of their morning journeys to the city. Yesterday, on the whole, the Jerseymen, the Staten Islanders, and even Brooklynites as was the ferries had the best of it. It was the New-Yorkers themselves who were in trouble, and they began to realize its extent the moment they left their homes.

An early as 7 o'clock the snow had got a good deal too deep for stout men to travel in with ease, and the rapidity with which it grew worse was simply marvelous. The wind seemed to find in every motion as well as a terrible, direct propelling force. It had a power of slinging the snow into doorways and packing it up close on doors; of sifting it through window frames, of piling it up in high drifts at street corners, of twirling it into hard mounds around railroad stations, such as most New-Yorkers had never seen before. For the first time in their lives they knew what a Western blizzard was.

Not that the wind was at all content with such doings. They were merely its playful tricks. Its spite was shown in driving showers of sleet and icy shot into one's face that stung worse than the wings of the modest hornets. If the hapless pedestrian tried to escape by turning his face away, the first thing he knew an extra cast took him, whirled him around like a teetotum, and, giving him a dose of sleet that blinded him and generally used him up so that he didn't know anything, left him to his fate for once utterly and completely discouraged.

Lots of respectable citizens, who had theretofore rather hugged the flattering delusion to their souls that it took a pretty great man to handle them, came to the conclusion before they had got many rods from their houses, that home was a mighty comfortable place, and that Payne bit the nail on the head when he sang "Home, Sweet Home." Havraz came to that conclusion they turned round, and in a few minutes found that it was true. Their labors of business did not see them thereby stopping. These prudent men had a fine chance to get acquainted with their families. The absence of school kept keep, and Young America, boys and girls, being unable to get out of doors made things as lively and interesting indoors as their great abilities permitted them to do.

Notwithstanding the stay-at-homes outdoor was sufficiently lively. Some thousands of men, women, boys, and girls could not conveniently keep away from their vocations, and most of these tried to get to their destinations by the elevated trains. They didn't do it to any great extent, but as New-Yorkers are apt to do, they got a good deal of fun out of their discomforts. Nobody who participated in any of the itinerant scenes of yesterday can deny that New-Yorkers are the best-natured people in the world. To state it generally, all the transportation lines in the city ceased operations by 9 o'clock in the morning. Most of them were of no use after 7 o'clock. Trains started from Harlem crowded with people—becoming jammed with people as they advanced—who were in a hurry to get to their work. Slowly and more slowly they ran, and at last the doleful information came that they could go no further. Yet there was little or no protest by even among the men. Stories were told, jokes were cracked, and jovial good-fellowship prevailed. Nobody put on any airs. The aristocratic banker and merchant was "halo fellow well met" with the artisan, helpful to the shopgirl, and kind to the inevitable old lady whom even the blizzard couldn't keep at home.

Probably the average time which a citizen occupied yesterday morning in getting from his home anywhere above Twenty-third street to his place of business down town was three hours. About half of the distance was made in the elevated trains and the rest on foot. The walking was the quicker of the two, and perhaps a trifle less dangerous, for one might have the electric wires, dodging falling signs and glass, and incidentally tumbling around in ways which Barnum's most skilled gymnasts could vainly hope to equal, were not altogether consonant with bodily safety. Where the elevated trains were stalled between stations, novel ways of escaping were occasionally devised. For one train, stuck in front of the repair shop of the Fire Department on West Third-street, the shop hands rigged a temporary platform from the windows to which ladders extended, and by that means the passengers were enabled to reach the street.

It is due to the elevated roads to say that they ran longer than the street railroads, and it is due to the street railroads to say that they did better than the cable roads, and that is saying a great deal, for the cable roads did not run at all. There was no effort made to move the cars. The ice and snow frozen over the tracks made it simply impossible for the grips to reach the cables, so there was no ready for use when they can be used. But the horse cars are scattered over the city, standing around promiscuously wherever their drivers and conductors deserted them. There was an abandon, so to speak, in the manner of doing this that was really delicious. Whenever these public servants made up their minds that it was not expedient to continue the performance of their duties any longer, they simply unhitched the horses, mounted them, and rode off. The passengers disembarked at their leisure, and pursued their winding way on foot. The truckmen and even the drivers of express wagons followed the same course. All over town deserted trucks and wagons are to be seen. The fact was the cutting wind and the stinging sleet were unendurable, and bare of these being necessary or of finding a warm spot.

It's an ill wind that blows good to nobody, and even a blizzard threw money into some pockets, particularly those of the cabmen. Those sentry reaped a harvest. Gentlemen who would afford to pay for a little speed—not much, not nearly so much as they expected after Jehu had got them into his power—hired cabs and hacks, and were driven to their offices. The usual fare was $25 from the Hoffman House or any nearer place to the region south of Canal-street. It is a most incredible story, but it was currently reported that in more than one instance Jerseymen refused even these extortionate fares, saying that the lives of their drivers were worth more than money. There is no instance of a cabman himself refusing.

Of course the effect of the storm upon the transaction of business was paralyzing. Yesterday had been selected by several of the great dry goods stores for their "Spring openings." It is needless to say that the "openings" were unavoidably postponed. In fact, most of the stores where many clerks are employed were short-handed, or would have been, if there had been anything to do. Those that employ saleswomen were nearly destitute of help. Therefore all the play little business through lack of operatives. As far as money-making was concerned, about every place in the city might just as well have been shut up yesterday, as open, except the hotels, the restaurants, and the liquor saloons. They were well patronized. The down-town hotels especially were crowded last night. There was not a vacant room in the Astor House, French's, the Metropolitan, or Earle's. Many of the suburban residents who reached the city with courage threw care by means of the ferries made up their minds to "let well enough alone," now that they were here, and to make sure of below in hand for business this morning. They made the hotels lively last evening, and eased the hearts of the landlords to beat with joy. These suburban visitors were mostly Jerseymen and others, who could have reached here by the ferry. Very few persons were brought here by the trains, probably fewer than have ever come to New-York in any day since railroad trains began to run.

While the actual loss of life yesterday was small, the accidents of a more serious nature were numerous, and people overcome, either by the wind and sleet, or by over-exertion, were continually being taken into shops for restoration. Probably all the serious after effects of the storm upon persons will never be known. Hundreds of lives in this city were shortened without any remarkable after effects of injury. It will be not easy to estimate the pecuniary losses on account of the blizzard. The total stoppage of business on the Exchanges means the loss of many thousands of dollars. The cessation of manufactures means the loss of many thousands more. So does the stoppage of transportation by sea and land. How many laboring men will miss their expected day's wages no one can accurately tell. But lots of poor families will have to scrimp and save even a little more closely than usual on that account alone. And the actual damage to property must run into the hundreds of thousands. Empty theatres, deserted and dark streets, howling winds, and general desolation marked New-York after sundown. Most of those whom the unkindness of fate had allowed to reach down town in the morning managed to get home during the afternoon, or to find other quarters for the night. It was well they did; for anything more cheerless than the streets cannot well be conceived. The electric lights were nearly all out, and locomotion was perilous.

In looking back at the events of yesterday the most amazing thing to the residents of this great city must be the ease with which the elements were able to overcome the boasted triumph of civilization, particularly in those respects which philosophers and statesmen have contended permanently marked our civilization and distinguished it from the civilization of the old world—our superior means of intercommunication. Before the fury of the great blizzard they all went down, whether propelled by steam or electricity. The elevated trains became useless; so did the telegraph wires, the telephone wires, the wires for conveying the electric lights, the wires for giving the alarms of fire. And, worse than useless, the last became dangerous.

It is hard to believe in the last quarter of the nineteenth century that for even one day New-York could be so completely isolated from the rest of the world as if Manhattan Island was in the middle of the South Sea.

BUSINESS PARALYZED.

STRANGE SCENES IN WALL-STREET AND ELSEWHERE DOWN TOWN.

There was something almost startling in the sudden paralysis of business down town. The effect of the storm on the big Exchanges, the Government offices, the banks, and the transportation companies was unique and unprecedented.

Lines of communication were almost wholly blocked long before the commercial world is usually astir, and it was extremely difficult for anybody to reach the lower end of the island unless he came by way of the ferryboats or had extraordinary transportation facilities. It was not a matter of doing business, but of getting to the places where business is done. Government officials, bankers, brokers, and clerks living up town, who were determined to do a day's work, offered fabulous sums for cabs, carriages, and wagons to carry them to their destination. Prices ranged from $5 to $40 for anything on runners or wheels that could be propelled against the storm. It was hard on the drivers, but harder on the horses compelled to make the exhaustive trip. Every sort of conveyance was pressed into service, and in about nine cases out of ten the contrast was not carried out, because the locomotive power broke down.

As the street cars had been abandoned at various points along the lines, so the other horse vehicles were left by the wayside, the animals unhitched and driven to the nearest shelter. At one time during the forenoon Broadway below the Post Office contained a funeral-like procession moving toward Wall-street. Carriages and cabs were in Indian file for several blocks, and sandwiched between the black-hooded vehicles with statuesque-looking drivers were Fifth-avenue stages and covered delivery wagons crowded with business men and clerks of every degree.

There was great joy when the tiresome trips were ended and the warm and comfortable offices were reached. Very little attention was given to business matters, as it was generally taken for granted that there would be nothing done. The topic of the hour was the storm, and everybody had a story to tell about his individual experiences after leaving home. It was a great day for rich and poor down town, and as one Wall-street man remarked: "This is an occasion when money won't make the mare go." A solitary cabman in Wall-street shortly after noon was the centre of an excited group of brokers who were bidding for a first choice. The cab cost the lucky bidder $36 to ride up to the Windsor Hotel. During the regular commercial hours down town there is seldom any turmoil enough to confuse and confound a stranger. Yesterday a stranger could have played his way all over historical territory without finding more life than a country churchyard might furnish. It was a great, dreary deserted waste, the whole section below the City Hall, and if New-York had been plague-stricken it is doubtful if the commercial centres would have presented a more cheerless appearance than they did. The holiday or Sunday aspect was missing and in its place were evidences of an evacuation. Telegraph wires were down, signs were broken, too awnings flapped in the wind, and abandoned vehicles, half buried in snowdrifts, were conspicuous objects on the main thoroughfares.

One building was a sight for an artist, and so was St. Paul's, with its highly ornamented with fantastic formations. Huge drifts along the sidewalks almost hid the scattered pedestrians from view, and now and then one was lost to sight who had stepped on a treacherous piece of ice and was precipitated into a snowbank. Those persons who were compelled to foot it adopted the most convenient and comfortable wraps for protection, regardless of style or appearance. The result was that there were many grotesque figures perambulating about the streets during the day. Aristocratic buckled on leggins or tied the lower ends of their pantaloons with cords. Rubber boots and overalls were as common as the plebeian and insignificant rubber overshoes on an ordinary wet day. Messenger boys and laboring men tied up their feet in wrapping paper or packing stuff. A driving trade was done down town in rags with ear lugs, and the unfortunate man without some covering for his ears was a pitiable object. Handkerchiefs were generally utilized for this purpose, especially by the silk and derby hat contingent.

Few of the porters of the big buildings down town made any attempt to keep pace with the storm in clearing away the snow, and as a result there were huge mountainous accumulations along Broadway, Nassau, Wall, William, New, and Broad streets. The ticket-agents along the line of the Sub-Treasury looked as the father of his country might have looked when he crossed the Delaware if he had not worn his cloak and cocked hat.

There were only 30 of the 1,100 members of the Stock Exchange on the floor when the gong sounded at 10 o'clock, and a large majority of the brokers present were residents of Brooklyn. They had a great advantage for once over their New-York associates. The crowd did not increase materially as the storm went on and the floor looked like a deserted ballroom. Only a nominal business was done. The trades were in stocks and represented about 15,000 shares. Out of the 30 or 40 banks which do business for the members of the Stock Exchange only three were supplied with officials. On most days (no deliveries being made Saturday) it was manifestly useless to attempt to continue business, as checks could not be certified, and no deliveries can be made without certified checks; accordingly at noon the board adopted a resolution that no deliveries should be made during the day and further business should be suspended until to-day.

Nothing like this ever happened in Wall-street before, the nearest approach being at the time of the great sleetstorm in 1881, when the telegraph wires of the brokers were all down, and business was delayed but not suspended. The situation on the Produce Exchange, the Cotton Exchange, the Consolidated, and other Exchanges was similar to that on the Stock Exchange. At the Produce Exchange half an hour after the opening the corporal's guard around the wheat pit looked lonely. Only one telegraph wire to Chicago was in working order. The Cotton Exchange was fairly well represented, but no attempt was made to do much business. Out of 23 of the actual members present 18 were from Brooklyn. The oil market slumped off a point, but transactions were light.

The Custom House was run with about half the regular force. Collector Magone reached the office in a cab, soon after the usual hour. The officials of the Sub-Treasury were late in reporting for duty. Owing to the impaired forces in the banks, closing statements were delayed an hour and a quarter. All of the business offices in lower town were not opened at all yesterday, and the ones that were, were not swamped with customers.

WHAT SOME WALL-STREET MEN DID.

Some of the Wall-street men who got down town in the morning were badly disappointed. The accident on the Erie, the phenomenally bad report of the New-York and New-England Railroad's carriages, the declaration of blizzard warfare in the West upon the part of Chief Arthur and his striking locomotive engineers, and a half score of other similarly depressing and distressing financial news nuggets—all these were depended upon by many among the bear contingent for a day that should result in whirling prices rapidly downward. Upon the bull side there were not a few who counted upon yesterday as a turning point for the market's recent downward course; and, for causes that they could recite in a flat a yard long, they were confident that a rising market and better times were right at hand on the Stock Exchange. But, alas! for those that counted so, both bull and bear were saddened in the disappointment of a day that had absolutely not one thing of interest in it so far as a movement in the quotation of stocks was concerned.

Addison Cammack, the great bear leader, staid serenely at home; Thomas W. Pearsall, the bull—"Moses," reposed in bulrushes outside of the Street; Commodore Bateman did not return from Norfolk, where he is spending the month; R. E. Connor did not get beyond the precincts of his American Yacht Club; George Gould tried a journey down town on the elevated road, but he got to his station too late and found that even the son of a hundred millionaire couldn't make the elevated trains run.

Russell sage got down town, but he staid only a little while and got the last train to Forty-second-street, without having accomplished anything for a day's work beyond the opening of his mail.

Charlie Johnea, true to his vow of six months ago, walked every step of the way from his up town to his Wall-street office. He bought a whole hundred shares of stock before the day was done, and then still true to that vow of his, a vow that his will wind up town and down town for one whole year, he trudged through snow and wind and biting cold all the way up to Del-monico's, where last night at 6 o'clock, dining with his friend John O'Brien, he celebrated the smallest day's business ever did in his life.

Mr. S. H. Kneeland and other Wall-street men who live at the Windsor and in Fifth-avenue district round about caught their usual morning train, but before they were half way to the Rector-street station they found themselves at a standstill in midair and had to hire coaches to finish their journey.

Few men in the Wall-street neighborhood found their clerks at their posts when they arrived. The messenger companies had barely 10 per cent. of their boys on hand, and that tenth they were powerless to move.

RAILROADS BLOCKADED.

PEOPLE UNABLE TO GET OUT OF OR INTO THE CITY.

Saturday and Sunday are the two days in the week that travel is heaviest on the New-York Central and Hudson River, New-York and Harlem, and New-York, New-Haven and Hartford Railroads. Between 8,000 and 10,000 passengers go out of town on Saturday and come back on the Monday morning trains. The greater part of this number yesterday had to spend most of their time on the blockaded trains between Dobbs Ferry and this city, and make themselves as comfortable as they could under the circumstances. About 40 trains were blocked on these three lines, and only 2 were able to come in during the earlier part of the day—one on the New-York, New-Haven and Hartford line and the other on the New-York Central. The storm seems to have vented most of its fury right over New-York and in a radius of some 10 miles. It was right in this vicinity that up snowdrifts were the highest, the wind the fiercest, and the snow the most abundant.

Three young gentlemen who had got off a train at the junction at Mott Haven came into the Grand Central Station about 4:30 o'clock in the afternoon. When their train arrived there, they found four trains ahead of them, blocked by the snow. The cars of the trains were crowded with passengers, some of whom were swearing at the delay and their illluck, while others were trying to make themselves as comfortable as possible by sharing songs and crackerjoke jokes. In one thing all the passengers, the impatient and the good-natured, were accord, and that was hunger. Several enterprising people in the neighborhood came around with baskets of sandwiches and sandwiches, and those delicacies were snatched out of their hands at the rate of a quarter of a dollar apiece.

By 5 o'clock in the afternoon the Grand Central station and its vicinity, which is usually so full of activity, presented a most dismal and melancholy appearance. The interior of the station and the yard immediately outside, where the blowing of steam and the clanging of bells is heard day and night, were as silent as a grave. Clouds of snow were driven in like immense drifts, completely stopped up the transparent skylights, and each fell softly on the long lines of trains, covering them with white palls and giving them the appearance of immense coffins of giants laid out and awaiting burial. No sound was audible in the great structure save that of the howling of the wind.

The waiting rooms were crowded with men and women, some who were anxious to get back to their suburban homes, others who were bound for longer distances, East and West, and still others, fathers, mothers, and brothers, anxiously waiting for the arrival of trains bringing near and dear ones. The ticket agents, gate men, and police were all here, but as far as railroad business was concerned there was nothing to do. Several railroad employees were overwhelmed with questions when they could not possibly answer.

The approach to the Grand Central Station was fraught with difficulties. Not a single line of horse cars was in working order, and the fierce wind which swept along Forty-second-street without any break threw down most of the hardiest pedestrians, most of whom had to take shelter in the immediate vicinity of the city, although it blockaded all along as far as Albany. But near the city the snow lay in cuts almost literally choked up with drift. What do we know of what is going on along the line and on the trains?" queried Mr. Toucey. "Why, we know practically nothing. The telegraph wires began giving way in the morning one after another, and by 9 o'clock all telegraphic communication between New-York and Dobbs Ferry was stopped." Mr. Toucey was told that between 30 and 40 telegraph poles were down at Woodlawn, the junction at Mount Vernon.

Reports kept coming in that trains which were buried in 6 and 12 feet of drift just outside the tunnel. The Chicago Express train left Albany at 2 o'clock yesterday morning and reached New-York at 10 o'clock, four hours late, with a small load of passengers who reported the road in a terrible condition, with a fierce wind blowing the four-like snow across the tracks in huge and ever-increasing drifts. Somewhere between Poughkeepsie and Albany the passengers of the Northern express and the St. Louis express were trying to make themselves comfortable. Somewhere between Poughkeepsie and New-York the Peekskill local, the Poughkeepsie local and the local accommodation were lost in the snow drifts. It is doubtful if any train south of Albany will be able to reach the city to-day.

The first train to the city on the Northern Railroad of New-Jersey was brought to a standstill on the west side of Bergen Hill, and the passengers were compelled to wait about two miles to the Erie ferry. Most of them took this by the foxlock and staggered rooms in some of the down-town hotels.

The Rector-Saltiley company of variety performers and burlesque players was billed for New-England town last night. They were gathered in the Grand Central Station and waited and waited for a train. The Japanese wrestler returned that it was catch-as-catch-can in earnest, and doubled himself up in a seat for a snooze. It is safe to say that they did not appear last night.

NO MEANS OF TRAVEL.

ELEVATED ROADS STRUGGLING VAINLY—STREET CAR TRACKS ABANDONED.

Almost every one who works or does business in New-York lives up town or out of town; consequently there are always constant streams of people pouring into the lower or business part of the city from all directions during the early morning hours, just as at night there are similar streams pouring out again. Probably half a million of people patronize the elevated roads, the surface cars, suburban railroads and ferries twice every day in order to get to and from their places of business and their homes. One can easily conceive therefore what the effect must have been upon the minds of half a million of the army of bread-winners when, yesterday morning, they woke up and found, in nearly every case, that the snow-bound elevated railway was forcing into the city, when the elevated trains were blocked in snow, when the surface roads had given up the effort to run, and when the suburban roads were no exception to the general tie-up, and the river was mainly a mass of moving and floating ice. It seemed at first as if the city would really be snowbound for a whole day. A visit to the offices of Superintendent Turner, of the New-York, New-Haven and Hartford, re-

Every Nervous Person Should Use Carter's Little Nerve Pills. 25 cents.—Adv.

vealed that gentleman in the midst of a group of inquirers anxious to know when trains would come in and go out. He was compelled to answer each inquirer with a smiling but unsatisfactory "I don't know." He told a Times reporter that the road was blocked only at the New-York end and that if the tracks from the Harlem River into New-York could be cleared the Boston express of the New-York, New-Haven, and Hartford, via Springfield, arrived about 4½ hours late, at least a dozen regular trains of that road are now stalled just outside the tunnel.

While the Superintendent was explaining about the trains, a man came in and said that 65 Italians were outside anxious to work at shoveling the snow from the tracks. The man was directed by the Superintendent to put them to work and to get as many more men as possible. The New-York Central had an army employed battling with the snow, but their efforts were futile as long as the snow fell and the wind blew, as it did, at 40 miles an hour. The Harlem tunnel presented a most peculiar appearance, looking almost like a big wall which lay inside it, for at the frequent openings the snow sifted in forming bright white patches which were in contrast to the blackness of the tunnel's interior. At the ends of the New-York Central outlining was snowing because all the switches were frozen up and clogged with snow. No sooner would the men clean out the grating of the switches than a gust of wind would bury everything again under a flurry of snow. Finally word was given that no further attempt would be made to clear the tracks until the wind and the snow had ceased. The passengers of both lines were requested, as they were without a rail to take hold of anywhere, to remain at the various stations along the road. The drifts which were being piled up by the fierce wind all day rendered the passage of trains at most points both difficult and dangerous. Passengers as well as freight and stock trains are snowbound in all many points, and the work of clearing off the tracks and starting the trains again cannot successfully be carried on during the continuance of the blizzard.

The train of the Lehigh Valley Railroad, which is due at Jersey City at 7:40 A. M., while running on the Pennsylvania Railroad's tracks near Waverley, N. J., ran into a train of the latter road. The wrecked track was opened about 5 o'clock, when the westbound track was opened from Jersey City, and a relief train of two cars and four engines forced its way through and carried the delayed passengers to the Pennsylvania Railroad, and again inconvenience was caused to those by the block, most of them being unable to reach their homes in Jersey City. The drifts which were being piled up by the fierce wind all day rendered the passage of trains at most points both difficult and dangerous.

The outward-bound Chicago limited vestibuled express train, due at 9:15 A. M., jumped the track at East Newark, and is now drifted in at that place. Many gentlemen doing business in this city reside at points in New-Jersey along the Pennsylvania Railroad, and great inconvenience was caused to those by the block, most of them being unable to reach their homes in Jersey City.

CROSSING THE RIVERS.

THE BROOKLYN BRIDGE IN THE BLASTS—DELAYS ON THE FERRIES.

Nowhere was the storm fiercer than it was on the Brooklyn Bridge Monday morning. The bright—skies—of a snow-storm fairly swept over it and sifted through the great cables and swept the snow in horizontal showers across the driveway and the promenade. It baffled the stalwart policemen and almost tore their coats from their backs. As the night changed into day and the storm grew fiercer it was found best to close the promenade to pedestrians, and the 7 o'clock piers may moving the public was not ventured there.

Just before the order went into effect, however, three or four men made the attempt to cross from Brooklyn to New-York, but one of them, who had reached about the middle of the structure, was whirled around and whirled around when they reached the main body on to the New-York side and the effort to go on was dangerous. A third got as far as the little house at the Brooklyn tower, and there his progress was stopped. Two young men insisted that he must go to New-York and they offered to accompany him. Half way across the railroad tracks on the New-York side the force of the wind was too much for their limbs, and they could go no further. They struggled back to Brooklyn side and abandoned the attempt.

When people began to think about coming across from New-York there was no such thing as a surface road to the city. The Fourth and Sixth Avenue and Broadway lines started out early yesterday but were at once abandoned, and various places along the route. Before 9 o'clock all the surface roads were two feet under the snow on the level and traversed by drifts in some instances seven feet deep. Here and there along the way the deserted street cars, standing in the middle of the road, testified to the futility of horseflesh to make headway against the combined forces of snow-destitution winds and drifting snow. Now and again speculative drivers hitched double teams and attempted to make acceptable conveyances from a batter or two of their stalled cars, but this was temporarily into the business of transporting passengers at twice the rate of a legal fare, and charged from Brooklyn to exorbitant charges, and soon rained with all other surface conveyances before the blizzard's attack. At noon a few straggling hacks could be seen on Broadway, and these were the only wheeled vehicles in motion in the city after that hour.

At-least whatever was being carried to move forced over the Central Railroad of New-Jersey. The management evidently foresaw, when operations began early yesterday, that the storm would be a bad one. The object of keeping the road open for at least communication. A few operations during the day, the trains stalled on the tracks. Jersey City and Elizabeth and Newark. Early in the day, however, it was found that the ferry service was so slow it would be impossible to run the full complement of suburban trains, and they were only started out as the boats came over from New-York. The storm had so increased in violence during the day that any time after 2 o'clock it was impossible to run trains on the time schedule, and from New-York, by 5 o'clock, all down schedules were completely thrown into confusion. The ferry to Jersey City ran at intervals of from one to two hours. From 9 to 12 o'clock boats were run on an hourly schedule.

At Sullivan and Third streets passengers left one of the stalled trains and went to the street by ladders, but one of them, in attempting to walk back to Bleecker-street fell into a snowdrift. Snowplows were attempting everywhere on the stalled surface car lines, but they often did more harm than good. At noon a few straggling hacks could be seen on Broadway, and these were the only wheeled vehicles in motion in the city after that hour.

Policemen of the Ninth and Fifteenth Precincts, and firemen from Engine No. 13 and Truck No. 5, worked busily to rescue passengers from the trains stalled on the Bleecker-street railroad. No. 8 street railroad saturated the ferries. The drifts of snow stopped boats, and several others stalled in places between the wharf and the Elizabeth. The few days, however, it was found that the ferry service was so slow it would be impossible to run the full complement of suburban trains.

Every effort made yesterday by railroad to contend with the storm and to keep some lines open proved to be unavailing.

WIRES DOWN EVERYWHERE.

IN AND OUT OF TOWN COMMUNICATION ALMOST STOPPED.

Destruction almost complete was wrought yesterday on all telegraph and telephone lines both within and without the city. Poles, with their long arms laden with wires and cables, were wrenched and twisted merely by the wind. Snow fixtures, with their tangled masses of wires and broken crosses, lost them in the city, and the crying was caused by the falling of poles and wires in the streets. At many places throughout the city the wires lay tangled on the ground in masses, while the loose ends, lashed by the wind, whirled through the air fiercely.

"The Southern lines are all down," said F. W. Baldwin, the chief of the operating department, "and our wires connecting business we can, taking it subject to delay. The state of things is bad, very bad. In Washington we have suffered as we never did. Fully 100 poles are down there, and between Philadelphia and Baltimore poles are down at intervals of every half mile. On the railroads near entering the city every pole is down. The New-York Central and the New-Haven and New-York are especially bad; the wire along the banks near them. It is between New-York and Boston is almost hopeless. Between averages from half to three-quarters of a mile in a road entering the city by the escaped having some poles up, but at 1:15 this afternoon a solid mass of snow swept out of the sky. Then it was a question whether we could keep communication open at all. Then everything swept away. We can't do anything outside of the city."

The packed passengers on the only train which has been partly cleared and trains, a meeting of the railroad officials held yesterday at which a conclusion was reached that no further effort to get in, and they were assisted by men to reach the Bleecker-street "cuts" made a dangerous "snow-blockade" almost impassable, and they might be closed," at this the passengers from the neighboring blockaded train. As an Irishman in one of the cars—no one but an Irishman could the wires down at intervals of every half mile. On the railroads near entering the city every pole is down.

Special Bargains in new carpet designs of finer makers at $200 cash. Apply to Hardman, Peck & Co., 133 Fifth-ave.

Digging out at Boerum Place, Brooklyn.

The Bettmann Archive

in this wind, but if the storm lets up we will send men out immediately. Two hundred men will cover the out-of-town wires, and 40 men will put the city in shape. Our worst place in the city is the upper part, around One Hundredth-street, while beyond One Hundred and Tenth-street we are completely cut off. Here the wind gets a strong sweep and a power that is irresistible. On the east side there is some delay, but we are reaching every office. Down town the lines are new and in a measure protected by the large buildings. We think they will stand. We have about two-thirds of our full operating force here. At 8 o'clock we had scarcely any one, but they have been dropping in one by one until that number is on hand. The storm is confined to a strip of from 40 to 50 miles inland along the coast, as we hear that at Harrisburg it was clear and cold, and we got the same from other places along the outskirts of the storm line. The Eastern wires were cut off about 11 o'clock yesterday morning."

The same report concerning the condition of the Western Union wires was made last night as during the day. The wires were down everywhere. The cheerful sound of the keys was not heard. Operators gathered in the halls below the operating room and made preparations to bunk for the night. A large portion of the day force was also held in reserve. The girl operators were given the third floor, where over 70 of them bunked together last night. There was one wire working to Buffalo last night and one to Chicago, but the latter was working very poorly, and no business of any account was done over it. At daylight this morning a large force of line men will start out from various cities along the lines and the work of repairing carried on as fast as possible.

The same cry of disaster rather intensified came from the Metropolitan Telegraph and Telephone Company, at 18 Cortlandt-street. "There is but one word for our condition," said General Manager W. H. Eckert, "and that is 'havoc.' If the storm keeps on this way, I don't know where we shall be. The seesawing strain on our guys is fearful, and, if they are unable to hold out, the result will be infinite damage. Things are so bad that it is impossible to know just how much damage has been done. In the lower part of the city the wires are holding well because they are in especially good condition in that quarter. I never saw anything like this storm in New-York before. The entire construction and maintenance force will be on all night, and, if the storm lightens, men will be sent out to make repairs. At present all we are trying to do is to clear away the broken wires in the streets and remove the fallen poles. At the central office only about 80 per cent. of the operating department showed up."

Robert Brown, construction superintendent of the same company, said that in Brooklyn the wires of the New-York and New-Jersey Company were down in all directions. Poles were down in Flushing and Washington avenues. In this city West Eleventh-street had suffered the most, 80 wires being down there, together with two cables which represented about 50 more. In Broadway, between John-street and the Battery, 25 wires were down and at 35 Park-place an entire fixture was completely wrecked; 90 wires were down at Mott Haven.

Mr. Brown, in speaking of the severity of the storm, said: " Our plant was in an excellent condition and capable of withstanding anything ordinary in the way of a storm, but if this storm keeps on I can't say where the mischief will end. I don't think the damage is as great as in the ice-storm of 1884."

The long distance wires of the American Telephone and Telegraph Company were in a similarly deplorable condition. At 11 o'clock yesterday morning its wires to Boston, New-Haven, and Springfield were all cut off, while its southern wires to Philadelphia began to be cut off an hour earlier and continued to drop off, one after another, until at 4 o'clock yesterday afternoon only four out of the 25 were in working condition.

From the windows of the company's office the view stretched over a long vista of intervening roof fixtures and the large wooden frames, with their masses of tangled and broken wires swaying in the wind, was a spectacle forlorn indeed.

The breaking of the telegraph, telephone, and electric light wires, with the danger to vehicles and pedestrians attendant thereon, was added to by the danger of falling poles. At Hudson and Eleventh streets several poles were blown over and almost fell against the houses. They were held up, however, by the mass of wires and the string cables. The same thing was true of the poles in the lower part of the city. The big sticks which line the streets in all directions from the Western Union Building swayed and bent before the blast, but the stoutness of the timber and the weight of the wires kept them from breaking.

About 7 o'clock last evening two wires became crossed at Broadway and Grand-street, just above the sign of William A. Cummings, dealer in neckwear. The contact caused a beautiful display of electricity only equaled by the play of lightning during a tropical storm and was gazed on with admiration by the crowd which had collected until some one shouted "danger." This caused such a wild stampede that several were knocked down, but beyond a roll in the snow no damage was done.

FIRE DEPARTMENT PRECAUTIONS.
WHAT WAS DONE TO OVERCOME THE STORM'S CRIPPLING EFFECTS.

President Purroy of the Fire Department was unable to reach the city from Fordham yesterday, but he was in communication by telegraph with headquarters at Sixty-seventh-street, near Third-avenue. Chief Shay, contrary to his usual custom, spent the forenoon at the old headquarters in Mercer street, near Prince, giving orders for strengthening the force of men and horses and taking every precaution to facilitate action in case of fire. He was in constant communication by telephone with the headquarters and with President Purroy. During the early hours of the day only two alarms of fire were sent in, and both came in correctly. One was a false alarm; the other a small blaze among some rubbish at 403 East Sixteenth-street, and without damage.

The chief operator at headquarters, Mr. Farrell, said that he had never seen such a storm in all his 15 years' experience, though the sleet storm in the earlier part of the seventies did more damage to the telegraph service. So far as his own department was concerned the wires were in working condition, and he did not know of any district where an alarm could not be sent in without delay. Below Fulton-street his reports showed that the fire wires were in good or fair condition. This includes the Wall-street and banking and many wholesale houses, and refers to both box and gong circuits. From Fulton to Houston-street, which includes a very large proportion of the most important dry goods houses, 75 boxes out of a total of 200 were out of condition, but owing to the short distance from one to another, in case of one box failing to respond, little time would be lost in going to the next. Between Houston and Sixty-seventh street, 100 out of 200 boxes were useless, but, like those from Fulton to Houston street, their propinquity to each other would prevent any great delay. Where the greatest confusion existed was from Sixty-seventh-street to the city limit. There are 500 boxes in this district and not more than 100 were in working order; hence, in case of fire, there would be great delay. But this state of affairs, Mr. Farrell said, was offset by the fact that there was less liability of fire there than elsewhere. This was the situation so far as the wires and boxes were concerned.

Mr. Farrell stated that, in a great many cases, the cause was simply the crossing of the telegraph and telephone wires with those of the department, which are always hung with the utmost care, but the strain of snow and ice was so great and continued that many wires had broken. Every effort was making to repair the damage, but the breaks occurred faster than it was possible for the linemen to repair them. The force of linemen and groundmen, or helpers, was largely augmented and every man that could be used to advantage was kept on the go. He did not think much progress could be made, however, until the abatement of the storm, which so materially interfered with locomotion. The districts to be covered were large, some of the circuits being 10 and 12 miles long. If the cars had been running, the damage could have been rapidly repaired. President Purroy, he said, had authorized him by telephone early in the day to spare no expense in making the service as efficient as possible. Seventy-five men were at work, and more will go to work to day.

In many cases, Mr. Farrell said, it would be worth a man's life to attempt to climb one of the high, ice-covered poles, not only on account of the danger from slipping, but also of being blown off by the wind. Another serious drawback was the impossibility of hauling the necessary material from the supply depot to the points of breakage on account of the depth of the snow.

In answer to a query as to the possibility of reaching every fire company in the city, Mr. Farrell said that every company could be reached either by the large band gong, the combination circuit, or, these two modes failing, the telephone. Under the existing state of affairs, so far as concerned the telegraph department, Mr. Farrell thought the damage, unless greatly augmented by a continuance of the storm, could readily be repaired in three days, though one day of clear weather would give them ample opportunity to attain a fairly-efficient basis. "In all my experience," concluded Mr. Farrell, "I have never seen such a snow-storm. In the first years of my present service we had a storm which wrecked the wires to a greater extent than now, but it was comparatively easy to walk around, material could be conveyed wherever desired, and repairs made more easily. So far as the alarm system of the city was concerned it was then worthless, and the city was completely at the mercy of a fire, had one occurred. Now we are comparatively efficient in this department, and little more damage can occur, for the wires which have thus far stood the strain of the blizzard will doubtless weather it through. In fact, the situation is improving, in my opinion. In the operating room the force is complete with one exception, that of an operator who lives in Westchester. I have received orders to keep every man on duty until relieved and have their meals brought in, so in case any of the night operators should fail to come on at 12 o'clock I shall not be short handed. I am on duty myself and expect to remain in the building until all danger is past."

The blizzard caused severe damage throughout the city.

Wide World Photos

At 6 o'clock the following message was transmitted from President Purroy to Chief Shay, who was at the old Fire Department Headquarters on Mercer-street:

"I am snowed in at Fordham. No trains running, and impossible to get to city. Spare no expense in effort to keep department working. If necessary notify Mayor, in my name, so that measures may be taken to keep Broadway and the main streets open."

Chief Shay had already anticipated this measure in a degree, for he was busily engaged all day in going from one to another of the engine houses, doubling up the men, and warning all to be ready at the first call. He experienced no little difficulty in getting sufficient horses, and it was thought that he had done exceedingly well in doubling up the number as rapidly as he did. Every police officer was also specially instructed to be extra vigilant in watching for fires and to lose no time in turning in an alarm. Every precaution that prudence and foresight could suggest was taken to protect the large interests which the Fire Chief had to protect.

Secretary Carl Jussen said that in his opinion the city would be in a worse condition, should a fire occur, than at any time within his experience, on account of the difficulty attending locomotion, which amounted to almost an impossibility with even an empty wagon, not to speak of a heavy engine. Another difficulty would be the hazard attending scaling and climbing, which would amount to almost foolhardiness should it be attempted. Everything that could be done, however, had been done, and extra precautions would be continued till the snow was cleared away and the wires were repaired. Every one about the department spoke and acted in a hopeful and encouraging way, but it could be seen that the time was considered a most critical one.

To overcome the danger from loss of wires and gong service the individual engine companies instituted a sort of patrol service. At intervals a fireman would be sent out to patrol a company's district, and, in addition, the battalion chiefs went about in their wagons.

At Police Headquarters the precinct returns due at 7 A. M. came in straggling, and it was not until 3 P. M. that the last arrived. Many of the policemen who brought them had far to walk. The one who had to bring the record of the Thirty-fifth Precinct walked nearly all the way, as did the messengers from the Thirty-fourth, Thirty-first, Twenty-sixth, and Thirty-third Precincts. Inspector Steers was unable to report for duty, and Inspector Conlin was several hours after his usual time. Inspectors Williams and Byrnes were on time. Superintendent Murray had to hire a coach to get to his office, and he went home in a sleigh. Commissioner French was at Atlantic City, and Commissioners Porter and McClave did not care to brave the weather, but Commissioner Voorhis appeared late in the afternoon. Chief Clerk Kipp was

snowbound in Harlem, and Health Commissioner Bayles was kept away by the weather, as were Col. Emmons Clark and Chief Clerk Golderman. The Central Office perhaps was the most snowbound of the city departmental headquarters. In the rear it was unapproachable, and in Mulberry-street there were drifts from five to six feet and a half high.

Superintendent Murray was anxious when he learned that communication between headquarters and the precincts was almost cut off and the fire alarm service was defective. Messages could be sent only to the Fifth, Tenth, Sixth, Eighth, Ninth, and Nineteenth Precincts, and the sub-station of the Twenty-eighth Precinct at Pier 39 North River in a very unsatisfactory fashion, and occasionally the Eighteenth and Twenty-first Precincts could be "called up." Communication between Firemen's Hall, in East Sixty-seventh-street, and Police Headquarters was stopped. Arrangements were made for inter-precinct communication, and at 11 o'clock, on receipt of a message from Fire Chief Shay that the greatest vigilance was necessary to prevent fires getting headway through failure to transmit alarms, a general alarm was sent out directing all patrolmen, in case of the discovery of a fire, to forthwith go to the nearest engine or truck company's quarters, whether the policeman had sent out an alarm or not, and report the fire, as if no alarm had been sent out. Later in the day Inspector Williams was informed that the electric light companies would not, on account of the many breaks in the wires, light the streets at night, and a general alarm was sent out informing each precinct to this effect.

Messrs. Patterson and Silvey of the Fire Insurance Patrol Committee hired 25 horses from Eahlman & Co., and from the members of the insurance watch organized a mounted fire patrol for the "dry goods" district. This patrol will be kept up at night until the fire department wires are in such a repaired condition that alarms of fire can be sent from the street boxes. On the discovery of a fire on his post the patrol will send in an alarm from the nearest box and immediately ride with all speed to the quarters of the nearest fire company and guide the firemen to the fire.

FIGHTING WIND AND SNOW.
A PEDESTRIAN'S BITTER STRUGGLE UP BROADWAY.

The full effect of the blinding snowstorm and the driving wind could not be appreciated by the fortunate ones who were able to watch the streets through the windows of well-warmed houses and listen to the roar of the gale as it howled down the chimneys. It was only to the

thousands who were forced to brave the power of the blizzard in the open streets that a thorough realization of its discomforts was brought home. The working men and women, boys and girls of a great city like New-York are trained by sad experience to disregard wind and weather, and they thronged out of their homes yesterday morning in as great numbers and with as much eagerness to get to their work on time as they would if the loveliness of a perfect Spring morning had greeted them with cheerful encouragement.

What they did encounter was a snowbank on the stoop, through which they floundered, knee-deep, to a sidewalk covered with snow, in which they sank above the ankles. The wind blew a gale, which sent clouds of snow whirling into their faces, apparently from every quarter of the compass. The cars, surface and elevated, were running, or attempting to run, however, when the average workingman and working woman stepped from their homes, and these once reached formed a haven of refuge from the discomforts of the storm. Later in the morning, when all passenger traffic had been stopped, the unlucky man or woman whom business drove from the house encountered the storm in all its fury, and those who passed through this bitter experience are the only ones who will carry through life a realizing sense of the piercing force of the wind and the blinding effects of the snowstorm.

Among the thousands who were thus forced to bow their heads to the storm and plod their way through the huge drifts of snow which blocked the streets in every direction was a TIMES reporter. It was 10 o'clock when he climbed through the snowbank which formed a barricade before his door and scrambled through the drifts on the sidewalk to the corner where he expected to meet a Sixth-avenue car. He was equipped with a well-constructed umbrella, of approved make and fashion, but one whirl of the wind as he raised it convinced him of the vanity of attempting to utilize it, and for the next two hours he carried it in freezing fingers, heartily wishing it at the bottom of the sea. After shivering for ten minutes on the bleak corner of Varick and Vandam streets, a red-faced policeman informed the reporter that the cars had stopped running, and he started on a run through the drifts, tumbling, floundering, and sprawling, for the Bleecker-street station of the Sixth-avenue elevated road, which he reached, panting and puffing, with a fringe of ice marking his eyebrows, mustache, and whiskers, only to be met by the information that no cars were running. There was but one thing to be done, and that was to battle with the storm and make as rapid progress as possible up town, and to this task, herculean as it proved, the reporter addressed himself.

Broadway, as the leading thoroughfare of the

great city, naturally presented itself to the mind of the pedestrian as the most available route for his progress through the snowstorm, and to this street he pushed his way. It was no easy matter to reach the great artery of the city. Bleecker-street presented a scene such as it never exhibited before. No attempt had been made to clear even a footpath along the sidewalks, and great drifts of snow were piled up on either side of the street, through which men and women were clambering as best they could. The wind, which was blowing a gale, drove through the street from east to west carrying on its wings blinding clouds of snow, which filled the eyes and ears, and piled up little banks of arctic coldness in the pockets of overcoats. Fine particles of the icy snow filtered down the back and sent chilling thrills through the whole system. Men and women bumped against each other, the snow preventing a view of approaching objects at any appreciable distance, and some of the collisions resulted in upsetting both the advancing parties. Good humor was the order of the day, however, and these little accidents were invariably regarded by men and women in the nature of jokes, every disaster being received with peals of laughter and words of banter. From the station at South Fifth-avenue to Broadway is but four short blocks, but the passage occupied as much time as a mile would consume under ordinary circumstances.

Broadway, the pride of the city, might reasonably have been expected to be in better condition than the less important streets. The merchants whose costly palaces line both sides have an interest in keeping the walks partially clear in the severest storm, and many a pedestrian made his way to this great thoroughfare yesterday, hoping, like the reporter, to find a tolerably easy way of pushing forward against wind and storm. Those who were weak enough to cherish this hope were soon undeceived. For once man had been obliged to acknowledge his weakness in the face of the elements. Broadway, as far as the eye could reach, north and south, was one long stretch of white, the only relief to the eye being the hillocks and mountains of snow which the wind had piled up in picturesque bleakness along the sidewalks. Efforts which had been made in the early morning to clear a space in front of the large stores, had been abandoned when it was found that the storm worked faster than the shovels and that the snow piled up faster than it could be taken away. Thousands of feet had toiled up and down the great street since daybreak, and these had left their mark in a little footpath trampled hard along the sides of the buildings. Thousands more were straggling along amid the blinding snow, everybody trying to gain a foothold in this narrow path, pushing, panting, and struggling good-humoredly. The path could accommodate only a single file, and the natural result was that the stronger held the

A horse car stuck in the snow at the Bowery and Cooper Square.

The Bettmann Archive

right of way, while the weaker were forced out into the drifts and floundered along as best they could.

The cars had long since ceased running, and the tracks were hidden by a mantle of snow a foot in thickness. A few cabs and trucks passed slowly along, and the observer found it difficult to decide which to pity most, the poor brutes pulling with all their force to slowly draw the vehicles through the heavy snow, or the drivers, half frozen on their ice-covered perches, who resembled, with their ice-frosted whiskers, and whitened hair, the old pictures of Santa Claus which so delighted the children of a past generation. The telegraph wires were heavily laden with a burden of snow, and sagged and sighed as the wind whistled mournfully through them. The large, strong poles, swayed and surged in the gale which whirled around them. Swinging signs creaked in the wind and threatened to fall on the heads of the passers-by. Avalanches of snow, loosened by the wind and their own weight, came crashing down from awnings and the roofs of the towering buildings. There was danger in that exciting tramp up Broadway in the face of that roaring wind and blinding snow, but nobody seemed to realize it. Every energy was bent to the battle with the storm, and those who braved it had little time to think of danger or of anything but pressing forward to the point at which they aimed.

Opposite the New-York Hotel a single horse car stood on the tracks literally snowed in. Had it been stranded on the prairies of Nebraska it could not have been more perfectly lost. Driver and conductor had abandoned it, taking the horses with them to prevent the poor brutes from freezing by standing in that cruel storm, and the snow had piled and drifted around it until the wheels were hidden, and on the east side a bank had formed nearly up to the windows. Standing there alone and deserted, the car resembled a sort of half-way house in the wilderness of snow which surrounded it, and it was not long before it was utilized by the half-frozen men who spied it on their weary tramp. It was a refuge, a place in which some little warmth could be felt, and into it men piled eagerly for a rest and breathing spell. The Broadway Railroad Company, or, rather, their driver and conductor, by the abandonment of this car, had unwittingly done a service to humanity which will atone for many sins of the corporation. Many a man got the needed rest in this place which gave him strength

to renew the battle with the elements and aided him in his progress up and down town.

New-York has experienced many severe snow and wind storms in the past, but certainly none ever exceeded, if any ever equaled, that of yesterday in the piercing intensity of the force of the storm. The wind at times seemed to make the entire circuit of the compass, and men and women were whirled about by it like so many dolls. The snow was sharp and dry, and as it struck the face impelled by the powerful wind it cut like so many pieces of tiny glass. It clung to whiskers and froze as each successive layer was deposited until the hair on men's faces were transformed into glistening miniature icebergs. When THE TIMES'S reporter, who is decorated with a pair of side whiskers, stepped into the Morton House cafe to thaw out, he pulled from his whiskers masses of ice and frozen snow by the handful, while his hair sent down a torrent of water as the warmth of the room melted its fringe of ice. The frozen snow clung to garments like a covering of wool, and gave to them much the appearance of having just emerged from a meal sack. With all these startling effects of costume and features produced by the storm the procession up Broadway was a picturesque one, which nobody who witnessed it, in spite of the discomforts attending the snow, would wish to have missed.

At Union-square the wind blew the keenest and the storm seemed the fiercest, but the scene was probably the prettiest of any furnished along the entire line of march. Great drifts of snow were piled up in picturesque confusion all through the square, and the paths, which were hidden from sight, were, of course, abandoned. The branches of the trees were bare, the wind preventing the snow from accumulating, and they stood out in grand contrast, with their brownish-black color to the great mantle of white beneath them. The massive bronze statues of Lincoln and Washington and Lafayette stood unmoved amid the raging of the elements, and great banks of snow were piled up against the pedestals, adding to the effect of the bronze. Across the square the wind blew bravely, and it was a brave man who dared to attempt the "short cut" from Fourteenth-street to the square. Most of the pedestrians took the longer course and hugged the buildings on Fourteenth-street to University-place before attempting a crossing. The wind was so strong in the open space bordering the square that it was almost impossible to

stand, and men and women were whisked along without power to govern their movements. At this point a large number of Broadway cars were abandoned early in the morning, and they stood there in a long row until nearly noon, when extra teams were sent from the stables to draw them in. No attempt was made to again move them down town.

That New-York people are remarkably good-natured was never better demonstrated than during the progress of the great storm. The air was so densely filled with the flakes of falling snow, and the wind blew so strongly that the effect was like that of a heavy fog. It was impossible to see a length ahead of one at times, and as heads had to be bent to prevent the snow from filling the eyes pedestrianism was somewhat perilous. The hard-packed paths, where thousands had trodden before, were slippery in places too, and this added another danger to the traveler in the storm. Men and women slipped and tumbled by scores, and arose laughing and joking over each other's mishaps. Men and women were knocked down by innumerable collisions, but in his long walk during which a great number of these casualties were noted, the reporter did not hear one unkind or cross word spoken. ... sentiment seemed to be general that the storm was enough to fight, and men and women had no time to upbraid each other. As a developer of the good nature of the citizens of New-York the great storm was a genuine success.

One of the principal dangers to pedestrians encountered yesterday were the many steps leading to basements, a few of which are to be found on Broadway, and large numbers on the avenues and other principal streets of the city. Down these entrances the snow was carried in huge drifts, in many cases completely covering the top step, and forming a delusive covering for a trap for the foot of man. Many a man unsuspectingly fell into these traps, stepping upon the apparently firm snow only to go through and plunge suddenly down the long flight of basement-steps. Entrances like these from the open sidewalks to basements proved one of the great sources of annoyance and danger, but one who had one made the misstep was on the lookout for these places during the rest of his trip, and no serious results have been reported from accidents of this kind.

FOUR MILES FOUR HOURS FROZEN EAR.

A man who was covered with snow from head to foot, with snow pendants hanging from eyebrows, eyelashes, and beard, ascended to the Fiftieth-street station of the Sixth-avenue elevated road at noon yesterday. The iron gates were closed and the functionary within announced that operations on the road had been completely suspended.

"In the name of goodness, how am I going to get down town?" the traveler asked.

"Walk," was the laconic reply.

The traveler drew his head a little nearer his shoulders to get the more shelter under his upturned overcoat and collar and retraced his steps to the street. He stood for a moment in a doorway on the corner, gazing southward at the waste of snow on earth and in air. He shivered, hugged himself a little closer in the doorway, and reflected as to the possibility of reaching his destination on foot. The case was urgent, and if his physical powers could hold out the importance of his mission would justify the effort. Just as he had made up his mind to start, a cab drawn toilsomely by two despondent-looking horses appeared through the snow mist. "Hi, Cabby!" the traveler shouted, "Are you engaged?"

"No, and I don't want to be," was the answer borne to him through the storm.

"I'll give you $5 to carry me to City Hall!" shouted the traveler.

"Not for $25," said the cabman.

The traveler wanted to argue, but the cabman whipped his horses into a walk and drove away, shouting: "I'm in luck if I get my team to the stable; I don't know but I'm in luck to be alive."

Now the traveler was alone on the street. Not a vehicle or a pedestrian could be seen in any direction. It was then walk or stay and be frozen. With a sigh and look of determination the traveler prepared to meet the blast and turned his face southward. For half a block the wind was on his back and he got along rather comfortably. Quick as a flash of lightning the wind changed to the opposite direction, sending sheets of snow and sleet into his face with venomous energy.

The New-York Times.

VOL. XXXVIII......NO. 11,781.   NEW-YORK, SATURDAY, JUNE 1, 1889.   PRICE TWO CENTS.

DIPLOMAT BLAINE'S IDEAS

THE SAMOA AND THE BEHRING SEA DISPUTES.

THE SECRETARY UNWILLING TO TELL WHAT IS HE IS DRIVING AT—ANXIOUS TO BE ADJUTANT GENERAL.

WASHINGTON, May 31.—There is plenty of room for speculation and excitement about what Mr. Blaine is supposed to be anxious to do in the Samoan matter and in the dispute about the attitude of the Administration on the Behring Sea boundary wrangle, but there is no disposition on the part of the Secretary of State to inform the public of his own country as to what the Government is really driving at in either matter.

There is nothing asserted, or even hinted at in the most guarded way, by any one who can speak at the State Department to justify the assumption that the officers of the United States, in the Revenue Marine or in the Navy Service, have been instructed to use force to assert the jurisdiction of the United States over all of Behring Sea east of a line exactly dividing it between American and Asiatic ground.

ALL TICKERS ORDERED OUT

THE STOCK EXCHANGE WAR ON BUCKET SHOPS.

HEREAFTER QUOTATIONS WILL BE GIVEN MEMBERS ONLY—HOW THE CONSOLIDATED EXCHANGE IS AFFECTED.

Wall-street enjoyed an old-fashioned sensation yesterday. The Governors of the Stock Exchange gave to the brokers a surprise, gave rival exchanges a shock, and created a panic among the pirate bucket shops.

Bucket shops in and out of New York have been established and have thrived through the facilities with which the Stock Exchange's quotations have been obtainable. Bucket shop speculation consists wholly and only of bets made upon the Stock Exchange quotations; and these quotations have been no sort of access to the bucket shop sharper as to the bunker and broker who has paid $25,000 for his membership in the Exchange which makes the quotations.

HUNDREDS OF LIVES LOST

A WATERSPOUT'S DREADFUL WORK IN PENNSYLVANIA.

THE CITY OF JOHNSTOWN SWEPT COMPLETELY AWAY.

A LAKE ON THE NEIGHBORING HILLS BURSTS ITS BARRIERS AND SWEEPS EVERYTHING BEFORE IT—MEN, WOMEN, AND CHILDREN SWALLOWED UP BY THE ANGRY FLOOD—AWFUL SCENES WITNESSED BY SURVIVORS.

PITTSBURG, May 31.—An appalling catastrophe is reported from Johnstown, Cambria County, the meagre details of which indicate that that city of 25,000 inhabitants has been practically wiped out of existence and that hundreds if not thousands of lives have been lost.

A dam at the foot of a mountain lake eight miles long and three miles wide, about nine miles up the valley of the South Fork of the Conemaugh River, broke at 4 o'clock this afternoon, just as it was struck by a waterspout, and the whole tremendous volume of water swept in a resistless avalanche down the mountain side, making its one channel until it reached the South Fork of the Conemaugh, swelling it to the proportions of Niagara's rapids.

THE SITUATION THIS MORNING.

PITTSBURG, June 1.—Additional details of the tempest in Pennsylvania, received at 3 o'clock this morning, are as follows:

Thousands of lives are believed to have been destroyed in the Conemaugh Valley.

ALARM AT WILLIAMSPORT.

CITIZENS POWERLESS TO AVERT A TERRIBLE CALAMITY.

WILLIAMSPORT, Penn., May 31.—Williamsport lumbermen are greatly alarmed over the condition of the river. Since last evening it has been steadily rising.

1,500 LIVES DESTROYED.

PHILADELPHIA, June 1.—A special to THE TIMES from Harrisburg at 2 o'clock this morning says a courier just arrived from Johnstown who saves that at least 1,500 lives were lost by the disaster.

REPORTS FROM ELSEWHERE.

TYRONE, Penn., May 31.—The Juniata River has overflowed its banks at this point and flooded the entire lower portion of the town.

The view on Main Street after the Johnstown Flood.

The Bettmann Archive

and many are drowned out. No trains have arrived on the Lehigh Valley Railroad since noon on account of a bridge west of here being swept away. Advices from points on the Reading Road and branches show great damage. The trains are all late. The damage will aggregate $50,000.

CARLISLE, Penn., May 31.—This afternoon at 2 o'clock a heavy rain and wind storm visited this section. A bolt of lightning, or as some say, a ball of fire, was seen to strike the pavement of the First Presbyterian Church, shattering the pavement and throwing large pieces of bricks some distance. During the flash Miss Mary Kelly of Springfield received injuries and a colored domestic, name unknown, was thrown to the ground and slightly injured. Edward Kramer and a number of others were burned by the flash.

WINCHESTER, Va., May 31.—There has been an incessant downpour of rain for the last thirty hours. At times the winds were very high. Many magnificent wheat fields are laid flat and the wheat is materially injured. All water courses are beyond crossing.

HARRISBURG, Penn., May 31.—A great landslide is reported at Lilly's Station. The water is said to be ten feet deep on the Pennsylvania Railroad tracks.

PHILADELPHIA, Penn., May 31.—A special dispatch to the *Times* from Harrisburg says: At 10 o'clock to-night the rain is descending in torrents, and many occupants of partially-submerged houses residing along Paxton Creek are vacating them. Paxton Creek has expanded into a mighty river, and the rise, unlike customary freshets here, is not due to back water from the Susquehanna River, but to the smaller streams which flow into it. There is danger of the Mount Pleasant School Building, a large structure, situated on the brow of Allison's Hill, being destroyed during the night, a large stone wall sustaining it being gradually washed away by the wildly-rushing waters.

The pressure of the water this afternoon burst the Market-street sewer in the northeastern part of the city at two places, and the street railway tracks have been undermined for long distances. No train has arrived here from the west since 3:30 A. M., and none is expected during the night owing to a wash-out at Lilly's Station, near Johnstown. The trains from the north have been greatly delayed by the high water. The lower portion of Steelton has been transformed into a large lake and many families are getting ready to move out of their residences. Furnaces along the river east of the city will have to be banked on account of the flood. The motor cars running between Harrisburg and Steelton this evening were obliged to push through water reaching the steps of the platform.

RICHMOND, Va., May 31.—The heavy rains of the past twenty-four hours have caused washouts on all the railroads running into this city

except the Richmond and Petersburg. No trains left here to-night on any road except this. People in the lower part of the city are moving their belongings to higher ground. A tremendous freshet in the James River is expected.

LYNCHBURG, Va., May 31.—The James River at this point is 25 feet above ordinary tide, and all communication is cut off on the Richmond and Alleghany Road. On the upper river there have been heavy rains for the past two days, and three inches of rain have fallen since last night up to 12 o'clock to-night. The river is rising rapidly, and much damage has been done in the lower part of the city. The water works are full of water and the city is in darkness.

PIEDMONT, West Va., May 31.—Two hundred families living near the river were forced to leave their houses and flee to the hills. A child of Mrs. Bell's fell from a wagon and was reported drowned but afterward found. Father Meider, while rescuing families from Hendrickson Island, had a narrow escape.

The damage to property in this town is estimated at $10,000. The West Virginia Central and Pittsburg Railway is under water between here and Cumberland, Md. Two bridges have been swept away. Loss in all to that road will be $250,000. No trains are running on the Cumberland and Pennsylvania Road. Two trestles have been washed away. Loss, $20,000. Nine Baltimore and Ohio trains are lodged here and 1,200 emigrants are on the streets. The western end of the road has been impassable since last night and it is hard to say when travel will be resumed. A number of landslides have occurred on the road between here and Grafton. The loss to the Baltimore and Ohio is very heavy, but cannot be estimated at present.

At this hour, 11:30 P. M., the rain has ceased falling and the water is subsiding and no further danger is apprehended.

CUMBERLAND, Md., May 31.—Nearly a hundred families moved out of the lower part of the city to-night in patrol wagons on account of flooded cellars, but no fatalities are as yet reported.

RAILROAD TRAINS STALLED.

PHILADELPHIA, May 31.—Dispatches received up to midnight at the office of the General Manager of the Pennsylvania Railroad indicate that the situation is hourly growing worse. The effects of the storm are now being felt on the middle division of that road, extending between Harrisburg and Altoona. Land slides and wash outs are reported all along the line between these two places.

No trains will be sent out west of Harrisburg until the storm abates and the extent of the damage can be ascertained. A telegram from Pittsburg places the location of the various east-bound trains as follows:

The New-York limited, which was previously spoken of as being safe, is at Wilmore; the At-

lantic Express, which left Pittsburg at 3 o'clock this morning, and the Seashore express, which left Johnstown at an early hour this morning, are both laid up at Portage; the Day Express from Chicago, and the mail train leaving Pittsburg at 5:30 this morning, are at Conemaugh, the foot of the western slope of the Alleghany Mountains.

The Philadelphia express, which started east from Pittsburg at 4:30 A. M., is at Bolivar Junction. The same dispatch says: "We have had no wire east of Conemaugh since noon. We understand that Conemaugh town and Johnstown are entirely washed away and many lives lost. The water is now falling."

The New-York limited, east bound, which is now at Wilmore, had a narrow escape from destruction. The conductor reports that immediately after his train had passed over the bridge which spans the river at South Fork, that structure was swept away by the rush.

FIRE ADDED TO FLOOD.

PHILADELPHIA, May 31.—The tracks west of Johnstown are at some points entirely carried away, and the roadbed is gone. The river for some distance above the bridge is filled with buildings and drift forty feet high, which is on fire and likely to damage the bridge, which is of stone. The fire is beyond control. Johnstown is literally wiped out.

RAIN AND SNOW.

A HEAVY STORM IN INDIANA, ILLINOIS, PENNSYLVANIA, AND VIRGINIA.

DES MOINES, Iowa, May 31.—Frost settled in a great many places in this vicinity last night, especially in the low lands, withering the tenderest vegetation. The corn in fields in river bottoms was ruined, and in some localities the injury extends to the highlands. In Northern Iowa the frost was severe, and the damage to corn is quite general and very serious. The farmers cannot save themselves by replanting without an exceptionally late and favorable season.

Dispatches from all sections of the State speak of the prevalence of frost and the great damage done to the corn, which up this time was in good condition and promised an abundant crop.

CHARLESTON, West Va., May 31.—A heavy rain began falling here at noon yesterday and continued until late last night, which caused a flood in the tributaries of the Kanawha River. The Chesapeake and Ohio Railroad bridge over Cabin Creek was carried away and booms in Elk and Coal Rivers swept away and millions of dollars' worth of timber and lumber and railroad ties swept away. It is feared that a portion of the city will be submerged. The rivers are still rising.

HAGERSTOWN, Md., May 31.—A terrific storm passed over the Potomac River district of

Washington County yesterday afternoon. It seemed to follow the course of the river, leaving destruction in its tracks and blowing down buildings, trees, and fences, and ruining growing crops. Telegraph and telephone wires are down.

WINAMAC, Ind., May 31.—Rain has fallen without ceasing for forty-eight hours, and it changed to a snowstorm yesterday afternoon. There has been nearly twenty-two inches of rainfall, and much damage will be done by floods.

HARRISONBURG, Va., May 31.—There was a great storm in this section last night. The wind blew a perfect hurricane. Wheat was blown down, trees uprooted, houses unroofed, and fences laid low. The damage is great.

WABASH, Ind., May 31.—The heaviest rainfall in years has been prevailing throughout this region for two days. At Benton Harbor, Mich., snow fell to the depth of six inches. Snow is also reported at other places.

GALENA, Ill., May 31.—A heavy white frost visited this section yesterday morning. Corn on low ground was blasted in the sprout, and all kinds of tender fruit killed. The damage is very serious.

MICHIGAN CITY, Ind., May 31.—A northeaster, the fiercest storm known here for years, now prevails. Snow fell here yesterday to the depth of about an inch.

A DAY OF GALES.

The distinctive element of the weather yesterday throughout the East was the wind. All along the coast high winds were reported as early as 8 o'clock in the morning. At that time off Cape Hatteras the wind blew twenty-four miles an hour. Cautionary storm signals were up all along the Atlantic coast.

Here the wind rose from fourteen miles an hour at 8 o'clock to twenty-six miles an hour at noon, and at 3 o'clock in the afternoon it rattled the wind gauge to the tune of thirty-six miles an hour. It blew from the east. The wind was due to the effort of the area of low barometer, central over Toledo yesterday morning, to force its way out through the high-pressure area along the Atlantic coast. All through the States east of the lakes, from North Carolina to Maine, the wind blew from thirty-six to forty miles an hour. The barometer indicated yesterday a fall of only .08 in ten hours.

Cloudy, showery weather accompanied the wind, and rains were general east of the Mississippi. The heaviest rainfall in the morning was at Lynchburg, Va., where two inches fell. Wet weather sprinkled itself very generously all through the Ohio Valley, West Virginia, and Virginia.

The New-York Times.

VOL. XLII....NO. 13,112. NEW-YORK, FRIDAY, SEPTEMBER 1, 1893. PRICE THREE CENTS.

HEARN

22, 24, 26, and 30 West Fourteenth St.

Friday, as Usual, Bargain Day.

DOWN! ....DOWN!! ....DOWN!!!

DOWN THE PRICES GO!

COME EARLY!!
If you can't come early,
Come as early as you can, but Come!!!

AT $2.00 AND $3.00.
Fine Cloth Jackets and Blazers and Cloth and Lace Capes; were $5.00 and $6.00.

AT $4.00 AND $5.00.
Navy, Tan, and Gray Blazers and Jackets, and Embroidered Capes; were $8.50 and $10.50.

AT $6.00 AND $7.00.
Imported Embroidered and Silk-lined Jackets, with and without capes; most colors, were $13.50 and $14.50.

AT $8.00 AND $9.00.
Elegant Novelty Jackets and Capes; were $16.50 and $18.50.

AT $10.00 AND $12.00.
Imported Jackets and Silk and Velvet Capes—richest linings and trimmings; were $22.50 and $24.50.

AT $14.00 AND $16.00.
Finest Imported Jackets and Capes—richest linings; were $28.50 and $34.50.

WASH DRESS FABRICS.
Come early if you can!

(price list)

UPHOLSTERY.
Come early if you can!

(price list)

QUILTS AND COMFORTABLES.
Come early if you can!

(price list)

LINENS AND TOWELS.
Come early if you can!

(price list)

WHITE GOODS.
Come early if you can!

(price list)

NOTIONS AND STAMPED LINENS.
Come early if you can!

(price list)

BOYS' CLOTHING.
Come early if you can!

(price list)

MISSES' DEPARTMENT.

(price list)

CORSET DEPARTMENT.

(price list)

Full list of specialties can be obtained at entrance of our stores........All as advertised........Ushers will give every desired information.

FALSE REPORTS SWORN TO

COMMERCIAL BANK OFFICERS MAY FACE CRIMINAL CHARGES.

MANY STARTLING DISCOVERIES MADE.

Was Insolvent, Superintendent Preston Says, Some Time Before It Closed.

OVERDRAFTS PUT FAR TOO LOW.

An Examination of the Books Yesterday Showed that at the Time of the Last Quarterly Report in June the Total of Overdrafts Was About $11,500—The Report Placed It at $585.62—No Record of Directors' Personal Notes—Objection to Mr. Dykman.

The Directors and officers of the suspended Commercial Bank of Brooklyn may have to face the Grand Jury to answer charges of criminal mismanagement emanating from the depositors of the wrecked institution.

Perjury in swearing to false reports of their condition to the State Department of Banking is one of the charges which may be called upon to defend themselves against in the courts.

Superintendent Charles M. Preston of the State Department of Banking said yesterday to a reporter for THE NEW-YORK TIMES that the last quarterly report of the Commercial Bank to his department, made on the 1st of June, contained an absolutely false declaration as to the amount of overdrafts.

(article continues)

TRAIN AND BRIDGE WENT DOWN

WRECK OF A BOSTON AND ALBANY LIMITED EXPRESS.

FIFTEEN PERSONS KILLED, MANY INJURED.

Four Palace Cars Were Smashed Into Kindling Wood.

HURLED INTO THE WESTFIELD RIVER.

The Bridge Had Been in Use for Nearly Twenty Years and Was Being Strengthened to Meet the Strain of Heavy Engines—When the Train, Running Twenty Miles an Hour, Rolled Upon It the Trusses Collapsed—The Work of Rescuing the Injured and Removing the Bodies of the Dead.

SPRINGFIELD, Mass., Aug. 31.—The Chicago limited express train for Boston broke through a frail iron bridge on the Boston and Albany Railroad one mile and a half east of Chester about 12:30 o'clock to-day, and four Wagner cars were crushed, killing fifteen persons, fatally injuring several others, while at least twenty were badly hurt. The wreck is the worst ever known on the road.

(article continues)

ATTEMPT TO KILL MR. RIDLEY.

A Pistol Shot Fired at the Dry Goods Merchant at Bayport, L. I.

BAYPORT, L. I., Aug. 31.—Arthur J. Ridley of the New-York dry goods firm of Edward Ridley & Sons on a visit here at the Summer residence of Theodore Allen.

(article continues)

MRS. FISKE'S DIAMONDS GONE.

She Loses $4,100 Worth on the Campania and a Letter of Credit for £2,200.

(article continues)

Genesee Wesleyan Seminary.

ROCHESTER, N. Y., Aug. 31.—At a meeting of the Trustees of the Genesee Wesleyan Seminary, held here to-day, the Rev. William H. Rosecrans, A. M.

(article continues)

---

600 VICTIMS

The Number Reported Dead at Port Royal.

THE HORROR MAY GROW

Some Estimate That One Thousand Were Drowned.

FAMINE AFTER FLOOD.

Negroes Are Starving and Desperate.

Tidal Wave Swept Over the Town and Carried Off the Hundreds, Whose Bodies Are Being Fast Recovered—Seven Thousand Negroes Who Had Been Driven to the Place for Shelter Clamor for Food—Small Stock of Provisions on Hand, and When Supplies Are Given Out a Battle Ensues—In One Fight Three Men Were Killed—Not Above Twenty-five of the Drowned Were White Persons and Only Five Were Women, Appalling Scenes About the Streets, Which Are Filled with Women and Children Piteously Appealing for Food and Crying Over the Loss of Some Loved One—The Damage to the Town Estimated at $3,000,000—It Will Take Months to Rebuild the Place—Over Three Hundred Bodies Have So Far Been Recovered and Many It Is Thought Have Been Washed Out to Sea by the Tide.

AUGUSTA, Ga., Aug. 31.—Further and more distressing news of the disastrous work of the hurricane at Port Royal was received to-night.

The number of the dead has been increased from 100 to 600.

(article continues)

INJURED TAKEN TO BOSTON.

Crowds of Friends of Passengers Await Them at the Station.

BOSTON, Aug. 31.—There was weeping on the platform of the Albany station this evening.

(article continues)

14

ings to-night is footed up at $2,000,000. This estimate is considered low rather than exaggerated.

Port Royal is still shut off from telegraphic and railroad communication. The nearest town that can be reached is Coosaw, where boats are taken to carry passengers to the ruined city.

All the rice and cotton crops about there are completely ruined. The stock of provisions in the town has been almost consumed.

The horrors of the devastation can scarcely be imagined and nothing can be extravagantly said of the wreck and ruins.

That part of South Carolina is known as the black district and is almost entirely inhabited by negroes.

Out of the 600 drowned not more than 25 were whites and only five were women. Most of the negroes were adults, though at least 200 helpless children are counted among the dead.

The body of a white woman was recovered this morning, and clasped to her breast was her baby.

A number of bodies are still missing, and many known to have been drowned, and not yet recovered, are supposed to have been carried out to sea by the strong current.

The work of clearing away the débris has not yet been begun. Everybody is assisting in the search for the dead.

It will take at least a year to rebuild Port Royal, to re-establish homes, and to provide work for the laborers who will be indefinitely thrown out of employment.

Most negroes are farm hands, and, as this year's crop is destroyed and plantations still inundated, their labor will not be needed again before Spring.

A telegram just received from your correspondent's associate, who has been at Port Royal all day, says that conservative estimates by some of the most prominent citizens of Port Royal, who are familiar with the surroundings, and thoroughly acquainted with the people, place the aggregate loss of life at 1,000.

Up to this time, 359 dead have been recovered and have been buried.

Citizens are helping in the search for the dead and assisting in digging graves. On nearly every doorknob crape is hung, and men, women, and children are walking the streets crying over the loss of some beloved one, whose body they are searching for.

Telegrams say that on the night of the storm many persons tied themselves to stout trees to save themselves from being blown away.

KEY WEST, Fla., Aug. 31.—The storm signals are flying to-night and another hurricane is expected.

SWEPT THE DRY DOCKS.

Government Improvements Badly Damaged by the Terrific Wind.

COLUMBIA, S. C., Aug. 31.—Several gentlemen from this city, who were in Port Royal or Beaufort during the hurricane, returned to Charleston yesterday on the first train which came into the city over the Charleston and Savannah Railway. They report that the loss of life and the destruction of property at those places and the neighboring sea islands have been fearful.

Among the dead is Dr. Ellis, the newly-appointed quarantine officer for the port.

Paris Island, where the United States dry docks are building, and which stands between the Broad and Beaufort Rivers, was swept by the cyclone. The fatality which has pursued the Government improvements since their inception found its culmination on Sunday night. The injury could not be accurately calculated.

Beaufort, the prettiest island town in the Carolinas, is terribly damaged, notwithstanding the fact that it stands six miles up the river. Many of the residences in the town were ruined, and the wharves are nearly or quite destroyed.

The experience of Capt. Whitely and his wife and family of ten children on Castle Pinckney on the night of the storm was a terrible one. The wind blew the storehouse to pieces and blew away all the ship chandler's stores, and his dwelling was so exposed that it was seen to be dangerous to remain in it. He and his family sought shelter from the fury of the tempest to the leeward of the fort, and with his children he stood out in the storm with occasional waves breaking over the helpless family.

The fury of the winds and waves was so great that some huge masses of iron used for holding buoys and weighing 4,500 pounds were moved from their places and rolled about the beach. Some great anchors weighing from 4,500 to 6,000 pounds were flung about the place like so much timber. The place is a complete ruin, and in spite of it all Capt. Whitely and his brave family are in the castle and are holding the fort.

The missing steamship Seminole, about which so much anxiety was felt, steamed into the harbor yesterday morning.

PASSENGERS OF SAVANNAH.

Party Which Left on Raft Not Returned from Helena Island.

SAVANNAH, Ga., Aug. 31.—The tug that went to Coffin Point, near St. Helena Lighthouse, to bring back the women and children wrecked on the steamer City of Savannah and that was expected to return by 6 P. M., had not arrived here at 10 P. M.

About 6 o'clock this evening the body of a little girl about eight years of age floated down the river. It is reported this evening that twenty-four bodies floated up on the lower end of Hutchinson's Island, near Screven's Ferry. This is not verified.

Dr. Duncan and C. M. Cunningham, thought to have been lost on Wolf Island where they were hunting, and for whom a rescuing party was sent out, are all right. Dr. Duncan came to the city with the rescuing party. Cunningham remained to look after their wrecked boat.

ANXIOUS AT WASHINGTON.

Navy Department Makes an Effort to Get News from Port Royal.

WASHINGTON, Aug. 31.—Now that the Kearsarge and Nantucket have been heard from, the Navy Department people are anxiously awaiting some news from the station at Port Royal, reported to be destroyed by a tidal wave.

There are four officers, some of whom have their families with them, stationed at Port Royal. They are Capt. L. A. Beardslee, commanding; Lieut. Commander W. W. Rhoades, Medical Inspector B. H. Kidder, and Civil Engineer George Mackay.

PRANKS OF THE HURRICANE

ODD SIGHTS ABOUT THE STREETS OF CHARLESTON.

Big Three-Masted Schooner Driven Into a Train Shed and Other Vessels Lodged in the Fronts of Houses—People of the City Not Discouraged—Purse Strings Have Been Loosened and There Is Work in Plenty Clearing Up the Streets and Looking After Repairs.

From a Staff Correspondent of the New-York Times.

CHARLESTON, S. C., Aug. 31.—Already the work of repairing the widespread damage caused by the hurricane is well under way in this city. Only one wire connects Charleston with the outside world, although four days have elapsed since the storm. It leads to Augusta, Ga. Direct communication to the North is yet to be attained.

It is an encouraging sign that the people here show no disposition to sit down and bemoan the losses caused by the big storm. Perhaps the fact that the loss of life was so slight has much to do with this. That only six persons were killed is regarded as little short of miraculous.

Reports of disaster along the coast continue to come in, but owing to the inadequate means of communication it will be several days before the extent of the damage to shipping can be estimated. A dispatch received here this afternoon from Southport, N. C., says that the three-masted schooner Enchantress of New-York, Capt. Frank Rollent, with a cargo of railroad ties, is ashore twenty-five miles south of Cape Fear. Her deck load, boats, cabin, and forecastle have been carried away. The crew was three days without food or water. The mate was washed overboard Sunday night and Capt. Rollent was injured.

The three-masted schooner Jennie Thomas of Savannah, from Savannah to Baltimore with a cargo of lumber, is waterlogged and anchored twenty five miles south of Cape Fear. Her crew is safe.

There are no idlers in this place to-day. Previous to the hurricane there were many unemployed persons owing to the business depression. There is now plenty of work for willing hands. Capital which had been withdrawn from circulation for prudential reasons has come forward now to repair the waste places.

One fact which conduces to philosophy on the part of many who suffered loss is that they held tornado and cyclone insurance. The local agents do not seem desirous of letting the public know the exact amount of this insurance, but it is estimated by business men that the figures will approximate $1,000,000.

Most of the big phosphate companies, the Ferry Company, and the Charleston Bridge Company carried this kind of insurance. It is certain that the insurance companies will have to disburse much money in Charleston immediately, which is gratifying to those who desire to see the city rehabilitated without delay.

Several hundred men are now engaged in cleaning up the streets. The first gang, which set to work Monday, reminded old soldiers of a body of sappers. Armed with axes and hooks, they proceeded slowly along Meeting, King, and other streets, clearing the roadway of fallen trees and other obstructions.

In one locality there was a tangle of huge trees which required hours of labor to remove. Close behind the sappers followed the thirty-six carts of the City Scavenger Department, which carried the débris to the dumping ground.

It is safe to say that in two days more there will be comparatively few reminders of the tempest in the shape of street obstructions.

Sullivan's Island never experienced such a night before. The water rose three feet higher than ever known, and every extra foot meant a proportionate increase in the surge of the waves that dashed across the island. The more exposed houses had been abandoned before dark, and this precaution saved many a life.

The casemates of old Fort Moultrie were crowded with women and children only too thankful to escape the terrors of their wind and wave swept homes.

The appearance of the water front of this city after the storm was one of general devastation. As a general thing nothing remains but rows of piles running out to the channel stringpieces. The destruction of many boats was due to the floating pieces of heavy timber which were dashed about.

The arrival of the Clyde steamer Seminole from Jacksonville yesterday morning relieved many who feared that the six men seen dead on wreckage at sea twenty miles from Savannah were her passengers.

An inland trip through Berkely County, by way of James and John's Island, showed an unbroken sequence of ravaged crops and injured buildings. Cotton, corn, and vegetables have suffered more than 50 per cent. damage. On both banks of the river were stranded small craft, lighters, and pile drivers, some of the boats being a thousand feet from the water and resting in fields recently cultivated.

The death of six colored people was reported in the collapse of houses on the border plantation on John's Island.

Yesterday a cutter, under the command of Lieut. Thompson, carrying Messrs. Earle Sloan and Arthur Simons, proceeded by way of Bass Creek to the front beach of Kiawah Island. Here the beach for miles is strewn with wreckage. Much of it came from the steamer City of Savannah. Cabin doors, saloon chairs, mahogany steps, washstands, mahogany balustrades, as well as cushions, pillows, and hundreds of life preservers, many of them stamped "City of Savannah," were lying about mixed with fragments of the hard-wood finish of the saloon, pieces of lifeboats, and some of the heavy timbering of the superstructure.

The condition of the negroes on Kiawah Island is deplorable. The cyclone destroyed their entire crops and much of their small stock, and with the tide entering their houses swept from them their few personal belongings.

Many were on the beach stripping the canvas from the life preservers to be used for making clothing. One of the cutter's crew reports finding numberless dead seagulls on Kiawah Beach, washed up with the wreckage. This is a strong evidence of the intensity of the storm.

The Italian bark Vincenzo Galatala, which left this port for Hamburg on Aug. 16, was abandoned at sea, off Hatteras, on Aug. 24. Her sails had been blown away, her foretopmast was gone, and she was otherwise disabled when the whaling schooner Hattie E. Smith, Capt. Bourne, which had also suffered damage, came alongside and rescued the crew.

The Galatala had on board 192 casks of turpentine and 3,000 barrels of resin.

Capt. F. V. Abbott, United States Engineer in charge of harbor improvement, does not know whether the cyclone has damaged the Charleston jetties, as his launch has been smashed by a schooner, and he cannot estimate damage before an inspection.

Egan & Friday, contractors for jetty stone work, have lost in material and damage to lighters $20,000, but their machinery is intact and they will continue work next Monday.

One of the greatest losses here was that suffered by the East Shore Terminal Railroad Company, which owns a railroad along the eastern water front of the city and thirteen wharves, which have been damaged $120,000. The stock is owned almost entirely in New-York.

Signal Service Observer Jesunofsky says that a further examination of his anemometer makes the highest velocity of the wind during the storm 128 miles an hour.

Letters from every county in the State give disheartening crop reports. In the low and middle country, where cotton had fully opened, the loss will be enormous, as the plant is flat on the ground, and what little staple can be saved will sell as "sanded cotton." In this section corn is reported in bad condition.

In the upper country the cotton had not entirely opened, and the loss will not be so great. Corn in the river bottoms will be ruined by the freshets which now seem imminent.

News comes to-day that the Combahee rice fields are flooded with salt water, which means destruction to the crops. The Ponpon rice-planters' fields are not as much subject to salt-water overflows, and it is hoped that they have not suffered so severely.

Sea Island cotton has shared the same fate as rice this year. In former years Charleston received 10,000 bags of long cotton. This year she will do well to get 3,000 bales.

The city is still in darkness after nightfall, neither the gas nor electric lights being in working order.

IN THE WRECKED TERRITORY.

Ruining Effect of the Cyclone as It Swept Through the Country.

CHARLESTON, S. C., Aug. 31.—The effects of the hurricane in this vicinity are unprecedented. Men who have been through tropical cyclones, white squalls of the south seas, and Winter gales off Cape Horn say they never before witnessed such storm fury, such destruction, as visited this old town Sunday night.

The city was, to all appearances, in the midst of a howling sea storm. The wind, driving sheets of rain and spray, came tearing along the streets, and the rushing, surging currents swept everything before them. Broken timbers and trees were dashed by the waves against fences and walls, and bolts and bars on shutters and doors soon became useless.

The tidal drains served only to admit salt water, and the parks and gardens were soon raging lakes. Slates, tiles, and chimneypots were flying from the housetops and roofs became as sieves. Literally, the heavens descended and the waters covered the earth.

The result was destruction to household goods from attic to basement. Salt water inundated the streets and squares till sidewalks were from three to ten feet under water. Basements were flooded and cisterns choked with mud or overflowed with salt water.

All this took place at night, and after the electric wires broke down, the gas mains failed. Thus was the city left in darkness.

Along the wharves no man could live by midnight. The water front had taken its way up town. Before nightfall the yachtsmen had battled bravely with the elements to save their boats, but as the piers gave way the débris made all their efforts vain, and one by one the craft were torn to splinters, or luckier ones were swamped.

Fortunately, all the larger yachts, except the Flirt, were off on a cruise, and their friends trusted in the seamanship of their crews to pull them through. They carried barometers, and no particular apprehension was felt, as they were on inland waters and could seek the lee of some friendly shore.

As the storm increased, however, to a hurricane, and the tide rose over five feet above high-water mark, it was realized that no shore existed and that the inland waters had become a part of the raging ocean.

The yachts had all parted or were forced to cut their cables to avoid being overwhelmed by the sea, and they were finally got before the gale, and under bare poles ran into a grove of palmettos and were secured to trees. The launch Diana was first to be hauled off, and her safe arrival in town with the cheering report that all hands were safe and sound gave relief to many.

Then will come the more important work of repairing the damage to business houses and residences. Already mechanics from other cities are making their appearance here.

Progressive business men say the hurricane is apt to prove a blessing. Certain it is that it has loosened the strings of many purses. It has created work in special lines for the masses, and will do more than any legislative act could do in forcing dollars and dimes into circulation.

The absence of excitement impresses the stranger. The people fully understand the magnitude of the disaster, but they have suffered heavily before. They know what is to be done, and they are doing it with a promptness and vim and method that only experience can teach.

The scenes on the streets and the river front are well worth seeing, and the incoming trains are bringing many curious strangers.

"All the News That's Fit to Print."

The New York Times.

THE WEATHER

Generally fair; continued low temperature; north-westerly gales.

COPYRIGHTED, 1898, BY THE NEW YORK TIMES COMPANY.

VOL. XLVII...NO. 15,009.　　　NEW YORK, THURSDAY, FEBRUARY 17, 1898.—TWELVE PAGES.　　　PRICE THREE CENTS.

THE NEWS CONDENSED.

Stock market weak.

Cash yesterday, No. 2 red, $1.05¼; cash corn, No. 2 mixed, 28½c; cash cotton, 6¾c.

FOREIGN—Gen. Pellieux harangued the jury in defense of Count Esterhazy at Zola's trial in Paris with much feeling. M. Labori, Zola's counsel, was not allowed to make a reply. Japan has been asked to allow a postponement of the payment of the war indemnity by China, but it is not thought her finances will permit her to do so. Prince Henry of Prussia has sailed from Ceylon on his way to China. A surgical operation was performed on Sarah Bernhardt in Paris with success. John Dillon moved an amendment to the address in reply to the Queen's speech in the House of Commons, and was supported by A. J. Balfour.—Page 7.

Page 1.

A strike that will bring out 50,000 men on April 1 was threatened at a convention of Pennsylvania miners at Altoona yesterday.

The French Line's steamer Flachat was wrecked on Tenerife and thirty-eight of the crew and forty-nine passengers were lost.

In the town meetings held Tuesday in five counties of the State the Democrats are said to have gained six Supervisors and the Republicans two.

Dr. Dwight Scott Chamberlain, Constable Dunn, and ex-Sheriff Glenn were indicted by the Grand Jury at Lyons, N. Y., yesterday in connection with the "cemetery case."

The Citizens' Union became a permanent local political body last night by the adoption of a detailed plan of permanent organization. The power of the Union rests in a Central Committee of twenty-five members, nineteen of whom are from the Borough of Manhattan and three from the Borough of Brooklyn. This committee may appoint more members and may have sub-committees as it chooses. All partisan ideas are carefully guarded against.—Page 2.

Page 3.

The windstorm caused damage in city and harbor. Vessels were driven ashore and ferry traffic delayed. A man was blown from a roof and may die.

Capt. Frank of the tug Frankie and his engineer were drowned in the bay by the sinking of their boat. The crew and passengers of the ferryboat Carleton saved the two remaining members of the crew.

May wheat in Chicago reached the highest price since 1891, being bid up to 81.05½. Shorts found great difficulty in covering, as there was no wheat offered for sale. Letter brokers were overbidding Armour's agents in the Northwest. Charles Counselman reported great scarcity in European markets.

At yesterday's meeting of the Board of Public Improvements, Commissioner Dalton offered for approval a contract with the Citizens' Water Supply Company of Newtown to furnish water for Long Island City. The contract appeared to be very favorable to the company, and President Bowley of Queens objected. After a long discussion final action was postponed for a week.

Page 4.

The get of the Hermitage and other stud's bring good prices at the Madison Square Garden auction.

At the hearing in the Richardson will contest yesterday it was brought out that the property of "Ben" Richardson, a brother of the "Spite House" builder, disappeared as mysteriously as did Joseph's. "Ben" Richardson, who died eight years ago, was supposed to be worth $6,000,000.

New wheat in Chicago reached the highest price since 1891, being bid up to 81.05½.

The New Jersey Republican Senate bill legalizing the Erie's lease of the New York and Greenwood Lake Railroad.

Members of the Society of Friends in New Jersey have formed plans for the erection of a home for indigent members of that sect, where comforts will be provided at moderate cost. The home is expected to be opened April 1.

C. A. Hart's demand that he be declared elected Supreme Court Justice in the Second Judicial District of Westchester County was yesterday refused by the State Board of Canvassers. He will apply for a writ of mandamus.

Page 5.

At a caucus of Democratic Aldermen yesterday Alderman McCall was chosen leader of the majority in the Board.

A caucus of Republican Senators was held at Albany last night, and it was decided to make the Biennial Session bill a party measure.

Timothy Hogan, a noted mail-box thief, who escaped from Blackwell's Island a year ago, has been arrested near Columbus, Ohio.

The New York Correspondents' Club indulged in a "beefst- k grab," sixty-eight pounds of steak and three kegs of ale being served.

The New York Assembly passed the Senate bill legalizing the Erie's lease of the New York and Greenwood Lake Railroad.

Members of the Society of Friends in New Jersey have formed plans for the erection of a home for the indigent members of that sect.

Page 7.

The funeral of Behrens, the singer, was held in Liederkranz Hall yesterday.

The second act last Tuesday evening dance of the season took place in Sherry's large ballroom last night. Craig W. Wadsworth led the cotillon, dancing with Mrs. Edmund L. Baylies.

Miss Clara Louise Miller was married to William Spencer Frazkard at Christ Church, C. Dundas Drake and Miss Clara Wahle were married at St. Chrysostom's Chapel. Many other weddings of interest took place.

Page 9.

Stock subscription lists of the Woman's Hotel Company were opened yesterday in the Wall Street district.

Page 10.

Col. Wall's body was removed from its grave at Burlington, N. J., and reinterred in Elizabeth. Col. Wall was at one time arrested for treason by order of Secretary Seward, but was quickly released.

Page 12.

The annual meeting of the American Paper and Pulp Association began yesterday at the Waldorf-Astoria.

The School board of the Borough of Manhattan and the Bronx met yesterday and transacted miscellaneous business.

Justice Scott dismissed yesterday the suit of Miss Jessie against former Judge Hilton, on the ground of insufficient evidence.

Cuts in prices of coffee for several Western States were made yesterday by both the American Sugar Refinery and the Arbuckles.

At the sessions of the Newspaper Publishers' Association at the Waldorf-Astoria yesterday many subjects relating to the printing of newspapers were discussed.

The cars of five Brooklyn trolley lines were run across the big bridge yesterday, and

CITIZENS' UNION TO STAY

Its Delegated Committee Adopts Plans for a Permanent Organization in the City.

A CENTRAL BODY NAMED

Partisan Schemes Carefully Guarded Against—Prestige of 1897 to be Maintained—Every Civic Division to be Thoroughly Organized.

The Citizens' Union became last night a permanent political non-partisan organization. This was accomplished by the adoption of the plan for the permanent organization of that body which was drafted by the Special Committee of Seven.

A large and representative meeting of the Committee on Organization was held at the headquarters, 42 East Twenty-third Street, at 8 P. M. It was called to order by James B. Reynolds, and, on motion of Dr. E. R. L. Gould, Joseph Larocque was elected Chairman. Prof. Nicholas Murray Butler presented the report of the Committee of Seven, and moved its adoption. The report is essentially as follows:

The question as to whether or not the Citizens' Union should continue as a permanent organization was not before the committee. That question had been answered in the affirmative by a unanimous and hearty vote of the Committee on Organization. The committee proceeded at once, therefore, to the consideration of the ways in which the Citizens' Union should be best carried into effect.

At this point two divergent policies presented themselves and both were urged upon the committee with vigor and ability. One policy would proceed to build up, at once, a municipal political party on the familiar lines, with enrollments, primaries, conventions, and all the machinery that so delights and employs the professional politician of either party. In support of this policy it was argued that political sentiment could only be gained by thorough organization, that by frankly accepting those devices that have so familiar in our political practice for the purpose of what are known as "getting close to the people" it would be possible to come close to the people.

On the other hand, it was contended that existing party machinery, what-ever may have been its origin and purpose, had become fraudulent and corrupt, and that it was most unwise in forming, frequently, by self-seeking politicians, to advance their own interests and to debauch the voters into believing that they really had some voice in party management and that the party organization in reality was the voters' representative, and that, because of these facts, the Citizens' Union should frankly disavow any intention to create such machinery, and all endorsements, primaries, conventions, and the party machinery of the established form, employing the prestige gained by the fact that 151,540 votes were cast for our candidate for Mayor in 1897.

Against Partisan Organization.

The supporters of this view pointed out that it would be the height of unwisdom for the Citizens' Union to deprive a complete scheme of political organization, for purposes of show of symmetry, that was in advance of local sentiment or that local sentiment could not support; that neighborhood sentiment in favor of the principles and policies of the Union must first be stimulated and allowed to develop naturally, in its own way, about the personalities of its own, voluntarily chosen and to maintain unimpaired the immediate future the opportunities for political action are very few and relatively unimportant, while the opportunities for a campaign of education are constant and obvious; that, therefore a simple form of organization is all that is required at the moment, one that will preserve the continuity and maintain the prestige of the Union now, and that will also inspire and guide the development of neighborhood sentiment in all parts of the city, and provide for the normal formal organization of the supporters of the Union for campaign purposes as soon as local sentiment will fully warrant and support such further organization.

The committee have, in general, adopted the latter of the views just outlined, and their recommendations are made in that spirit and from that point of view. It is of the highest importance that the formation of the committee, to effect these results: (1) To preserve the continuity of the Citizens' Union movement, to represent it before the public, to protect its name and party emblem, and to maintain unimpaired the prestige gained by the fact that 151,540 votes were cast for our candidate for Mayor in 1897; and (2) to allow the utmost freedom to the Citizens' Union sentiment in the several Assembly Districts to develop in its own way, rather than according to some prescribed form; and (3) to enable the formation of a permanent, as broad and representative in its management of all the affairs of the union.

What is Recommended.

The recommendations of the committee fall under three heads, and are as follows:

1. That the Committee of Organization hitherto existing, having served the purpose for which it was called into existence, be dissolved.
2. (2) That the following twenty-five persons—organized on the municipal plan ... [names listed] ... Robert A. Ackley, Charles J. Andrews, Clarence D. Ashley, William M. Bennett, Arthur von Briesen, R. Fulton Cutting, Alfred Frank, Paul Fuller, E. R. L. Gould, Henry E. Howland, Francis Lynde Stetson, Jacob H. Schiff, Edward M. Shepard, R. Ross Appleton, John W. West; Borough of Richmond—William Allaire Shortt; Borough of the Bronx—Fielding H. Marshall—be designated as the Central City Committee of the Citizens' Union, to act in general as the trustees of its interests, with power to fill vacancies in their own number and to add to their number and the final meeting of said committee shall be Feb. 23, 1898, at 8 P. M., at 42 East Twenty-third Street, New York City.
3. That such Central City Committee shall have power: (a) To alter or amend the existing declaration of principles of the Citizens' Union; (b) to represent the Citizens' Union in the formation of clubs in sympathy with the principles and objects of the Citizens' Union, and to keep these principles and objects constantly before the voters of the city; (c) To raise and disburse such funds as may be necessary for the work of the committee, and in particular to secure, if it be possible, an income sufficient for its expenses and subscriptions guaranteed for at least four years; (d) To maintain headquarters and to employ such paid agents as may be necessary; (e) To represent the Citizens' Union at public functions; to promote, with the co-operation of the Mayor, the Municipal Assembly, or elsewhere, in the interest of good government; (f) To aid in the formation of members of the union of political organizations in all the Assembly districts as soon as warranted by the organization in the district; (g) To protect and preserve the right to and enjoyment of the name and party emblem of the Citizens' Union of the City of New York.
4. That such Central City Committee shall have power to leave the San Juan, or rather the basin that would be formed by the Ochoa dam across it, and enter a connecting basin. From the Valley of the San Francisco by a line of embankments 29 miles in hill to the East Divide. Here the river steamer would be abandoned, and the party on foot, took the trail that is being cut out for the Nicaragua Canal Commission. Following this, they scaled the altitude of the principal embankment, crossed the Divide at the site of the great cut, followed the location down the valley of the Desoado, desiring each of the three sites, and at the latter took a hand car over the twelve miles of railroad built by the canal company.

To-morrow they will examine the work that would be required here, and on Friday will leave for Port Limon, Costa Rica, to catch the first steamer to New Orleans.

Some Excitement Follows.

After the adoption of the report some excitement was caused by Thomas Clegg, a member of the Labor Committee during the campaign, who said he did not see the names of any labor men on the Central Committee.

John J. Chapman, President of Good Government Club C, who is not a member of the Committee on Organization, stated that he was opposed to "catering" to the labor element, and that the union might as well put a representative druggist on the committee as a labor man. Chairman Larocque cried in vain to silence him, telling him he was out of order, and while Mr. Chapman was talking to members of the Executive Committee of Good Government Club C, who interrupted him, the "You're no business in here; you are not a member of the Organization Committee." J. W. Sullivan, a member of the Bronx committee, attempted to reply to Mr. Chapman, but pointed at the request of the Chair.

John C. Clark, Secretary of the committee, said, after the meeting, that Mr. Chapman is not only not a member of the Committee on Organization, but that he was not even invited to be present.

The Central Committee will meet and organize at the earliest opportunity and begin a thorough organization in all districts.

KANSAS PACIFIC SOLD.

Government Lien Against the Union Pacific Wiped Out at Topeka, Kan.

TOPEKA, Kan., Feb. 16.—The Government lien on the Union Pacific case was wiped out to-day at the Union Pacific Station in this city.

The Kansas Pacific Road was bought by Alvin W. Krech, representing the Reorganization Committee, for $6,303,000.

There was no competition at the sale. Mr. Krech was the only bidder.

DISCUSSED IN THE SENATE.

Objections to the Sale for Less Than the Government's Full Claim.

WASHINGTON, Feb. 16.—In the Senate to-day there was a discussion of the Kansas Pacific Railroad sale, based on Mr. Turpie's resolution that the sale ought not to be confirmed if the Government received less than the full amount of its claim.

Mr. Hale moved that the resolution be referred to the Pacific Railroad Committee.

Mr. Allen (Pop., Neb.) objected to such reference. He desired the Senate, he said, to take such action as would save the Government the $6,700,000 interest which would be lost if the sale was confirmed.

"How do you propose to prevent the loss?" inquired Mr. Spooner, (Rep., Wis.)

"By redeeming the first mortgage bonds," replied Mr. Allen.

"Then," persisted Mr. Spooner, "you would, by redeeming first mortgage bonds, add about $7,000,000 to the Government's claim, making about $23,000,000 in all?"

"That is precisely what I want," replied Mr. Allen.

"After you did that," asked Mr. Spooner, "how would you hold the road?"

"I would hold it by placing it in the hands of a receiver," said Mr. Allen. "That would be proper and legal."

"Do you think," inquired Mr. Spooner, "that any court in the land would permit you to hold that road and, as you suggest, to operate it, for an indefinite period under a receiver?"

"I think the arrangement to operate the road could easily and legally be made," said Mr. Allen.

In response to inquiries by Mr. Allen, Mr. Spooner replied that if he were disposed to operate the road it would not be as a bad bargain.

In the course of an extended argument in support of the resolution, Mr. Morgan said: "I am sorry to say it, but within the last five or six days the President has been forced to his knees on the subject by the completion of the New York combine—the Fitzgerald combine." Let him take his course, but let him understand that he is responsible to the people of the country."

No action was taken on the Turpie resolution.

INTERCEPTED AT CHICAGO.

Edward Zeller, Who Stole $3,000 from His Father, Arrested.

CHICAGO, Feb. 16.—Edward Zeller, a boy of nineteen, was arrested this evening by a Central police officer as he stepped off a New York train. The boy's father, Lorenz Zeller, a real estate dealer and attorney, at 80 Nassau Street, New York, wired the police early in the day to be on the lookout for his son, who, he said, had stolen $3,000 from him and started for the Klondike. The boy appeared very much chagrined that his trip had been interrupted. He will be taken back home.

50,000 MINERS TO TURN OUT.

Big Strike Threatened on April 1 at a Convention at Altoona, Penn.

ALTOONA, Penn., Feb. 16.—The first official notice of a strike to begin on April 1 in all the States shipping bituminous coal to the Atlantic coast was made this city to-day at a State convention of the United Mine Workers, calling on the miners to provide funds for the strike. The districts affected will be all the coal-mining regions of Pennsylvania, Maryland, the two Virginias, and the Hocking Valley, Ohio. It will bring out at least 50,000 men.

SET FIRE TO HER CLOTHING.

Three Georgia Negroes Attempt to Incinerate a Planter's Daughter.

BAINBRIDGE, Ga., Feb. 16.—Advices have just reached the Sheriff of this county describing the horrible attempt of three unknown negroes to burn to death the sixteen-year-old daughter of James Alday in an obscure district of Decatur on Monday.

It seems that as Miss Alday was going to a spring some distance from her father's residence three negroes sprang from behind a bush, and, seizing her roughly, began to ply her with questions. Upon being informed that she was the daughter of James Alday a prominent planter of that district, two of the men held her while the other two set fire to her clothing. The negroes were dead to her prayers for mercy, and only when they were fully satisfied that her flames could not easily be extinguished did they release her.

Miss Alday broke from the three men and ran screaming to her father's house. Before she had gained her home, however, every stitch of her clothing had been burned from her, and her body was one huge blister. She is now dying.

Nonagenarian for Town Clerk.

MALONE, N. Y., Feb. 16.—Josiah Bailey of Dickinson, ninety-four years of age, has been nominated for town clerk.

THE WEATHER.

The local forecast may be found at the top of this page to the right of the title.

The storm central in New Jersey Tuesday night has moved to the Nova Scotia coast, increasing in intensity and has caused snow or rain in the lake regions, the middle and north Atlantic States. A second storm has moved from Northern Montana to Kansas and has caused light snow in the upper Missouri and upper Mississippi valleys, and violent northwesterly gales in New England, attended by snow showers in the Middle States and lower lake region and west of the Rocky Mountains. It is warmer in the Missouri, the middle and upper Mississippi valleys. Increasing cloudiness and snow or rain may be expected in the Missouri, the middle and upper Mississippi valleys and lake regions, and generally fair weather elsewhere. It will be not quite so cold in the lake regions and southward to the Gulf, and in the north Atlantic States.

The record of temperature for the twenty-four hours ended at midnight, taken from THE NEW YORK TIMES's thermometer and from the thermometer of the Weather Bureau, is as follows:

	Weather Bureau.	TIMES.
	1897.	1898.	1898.
3 A. M.	23	25	22
6 A. M.	22	24	23
9 A. M.	25	30	28
12 M.	30	27	26
3 P. M.	31	23	22
6 P. M.	28	21	20
9 P. M.	23	21	19
12 P. M.	22	20	18

THE TIMES's thermometer is on the street level (that of the Weather Bureau is 314 feet above the street level).

Average temperature yesterday were as follows:

Printing House Square.....32%
Weather Bureau...............23
Corresponding date 1897.....28
Corresponding date last year..25

3 A. M. the humidity was 33 degrees at 12:05 A. M.; the wind was 13 degrees at 11 P. M. The humidity at 8 A. M. was 70, and at 8 P. M., 40.

MUSIC BOXES playing any tune and always in tune. KRELL, 174 Fifth Av., bet. 22d & 23d Sts.—Advt.

THE MAINE DISASTER

Capt. Sigsbee Reports the Number of Dead as 253 and of Survivors as 96.

ONLY THEORY AS TO THE CAUSE OF DISASTER.

All the Information at Hand Tends to Indicate That the Loss Was Due to an Accident.

Most of the Rescued Men Sent to Key West on the Ward Line Steamer Olivette.

Nothing has been learned of the cause of the loss of the battle ship Maine. She is a burned and broken wreck, resting on the bottom of Havana Harbor, and two officers and 251 sailors have perished. There is no evidence to prove or disprove treachery. Naval men tell of many ways in which the disaster could have been caused, but it would be idle to speculate. No facts have been found in the men's sleeping quarters.

It is not yet known how most of the dead men were killed. The supposition is that in most cases the shock of the explosion, which shook Havana itself, so direct death or such injuries that the victims were unable to escape from the quickly following dangers of fire and water.

The meagre accounts gathered from curt official dispatches and press messages indicate that the officers and men who were left alive behaved themselves like American sailors, stuck by their ship and comrades, and were brave, cool, and efficient in the presence of dreadful and sudden disaster.

The Spanish authorities in Havana and Madrid have profusely expressed their regret and sympathy, have tendered kindly offices, and have bestowed them wherever possible. The people of Havana are reported to have done all they could to help the survivors and to show their sorrow for the dead. The newspapers of Madrid reflect in their utterances the course of the Government.

Of the 96 survivors of the Maine, 59 have been sent to Key West, 12 remaining to look after the bodies of the dead, and 25 being so badly that they cannot be removed.

An investigation of the condition of the vessel will be made immediately, and until that has been done nobody can know whether it will be possible to raise and refit her. The inspection is expected to give a clue to the cause of the disaster and to show whether the explosion was within or from without. The officers are reticent. Expressions by some of them indicate their belief that it was an accident to one of the dynamo engines.

Resolutions expressing the sorrow and sympathy of Congress were introduced in the House of Representatives yesterday. Prominent members of both houses expressed suspicions that the Maine was destroyed by foul play, but say they will await evidence.

CABLEGRAM FROM LEE.

Business Suspended, Theatres Closed, and Flags at Half Mast in Havana—Calmness Urged.

WASHINGTON, Feb. 16.—The following cablegram was received by the State Department from Consul General Lee at 9:16 to-night:

Havana, Feb. 16, 1898.

Profound sorrow expressed by Government and municipal authorities, Consuls of foreign nations, organized bodies of all sorts and citizens generally.

Flags at half-mast on Governor General's Palace, on shipping in harbor, and in city. Business suspended, theatres closed.

Dead number about 250.

Officers' quarters being in rear and sea-men's forward, where explosion took place, accounts for greater proportional loss of sailors.

Funeral to-morrow at 3 P. M.

Officers Merritt and Jenkins still missing. Suppose you ask that naval court of inquiry be held to ascertain cause of explosion.

Hope our people will repress excitement and calmly await decision.

LEE.

NOT A SOUND OF WARNING.

The Dead Number 253, and the Explosion Was as Sudden as It Seems Mysterious.

HAVANA, Feb. 16.—It is now known that 251 men and two officers of the United States battleship Maine lost their lives in consequence of the explosion, burning, and sinking of that vessel in this harbor last night. The officers lost are Lieut. Friend W. Jenkins, junior grade, of Pennsylvania, and Assistant Engineer Darwin R. Merritt of Iowa.

The explosion occurred at 9:45. The Maine was anchored 500 yards from the arsenal and 200 yards from the floating dock. The night was intensely dark, the clouds hanging low with the heavy rain that began to fall soon after the catastrophe occurred. The Ward Line steamer City of Washington was swinging from her cables 200 yards away, and the Spanish cruiser Alfonso XII. was also at anchor near by.

Came Without Warning.

The force of the explosion was tremendous. All those on board the Maine agree that the ship was lost. Those in the messroom ran quickly on deck. Lieut. Commander Wainwright struck a match and hurried to the adjoining cabin, which was the Captain's. He found Capt. Sigsbee thrown from his berth, but uninjured. The officers found the following the explosion and immediately began to give orders to the men who appeared for the rescue of the injured and the prevention of further disaster. Capt. Sigsbee's first order was to a seaman to flood the magazine containing

Knew the Ship Was Lost.

The officers say they knew from the great shock that the ship was lost. Those in the messroom ran quickly on deck. Lieut. Commander Wainwright struck a match and hurried to the adjoining cabin, which was the Captain's, to ...

EIGHTY-SEVEN LOST AT SEA.

French Line's Steamer Flachat Wrecked on Tenerife—Fourteen Survivors Reach Santa Cruz.

TENERIFE, Canary Islands, Feb. 16.—The Compagnie Générale Transatlantique Line's steamer Flachat, bound from Marseilles for Colon, was totally wrecked on Anaga Point, this island, at 1 o'clock this morning. Her Captain, second officer, eleven of her crew, and one passenger were saved. Thirty-eight of the crew and forty-nine passengers were lost.

The Flachat struck on Anaga Point during a thick fog. Heavy weather prevailed at the time, and the steamer soon broke in two. The small steamer Suru brought the four survivors to Santa Cruz, and, after landing them, returned to the scene of the disaster to endeavor to render further assistance.

The Flachat was built at Stockton, England, by Pearse & Co., in 1880. She was a twin-screw iron vessel of 1,329 tons net and 2,175 tons gross register. She was 300 feet long, 36 feet beam, and 25.5 feet depth of hold.

SPRING LOCAL ELECTIONS.

Democrats Gain Six Supervisors and the Republicans Two in Five Counties of the State.

ALBANY, Feb. 16.—In the town meetings held yesterday in five counties of the State returns received here indicate that the Democrats have gained six Supervisors and the Republicans two. In Cortland, two; in Schoharie, one; in Chautauqua, one; and in Jefferson, two. The Republicans gain two in Cayuga. This makes twenty-one counties in which Spring local elections have been held, with a net gain for the Democrats of thirty-nine Supervisors and a Republican loss of three.

In next year's Legislature and before an apportionment follows as: In Cortland the Democrats gain one, making two Supervisors and the Republicans two; in the same county where the independent Republicans two, and the regular Republicans seven. The independent Republicans will act with the Democrats, giving them practical control of the county, which was considered rock-ribbed Republican until it elected David W. Van Hoesen, a Democrat in the Assembly last Fall. The town of Cortlandville, which gave Black 1,008 plurality in 1896, elected the fusion local ticket yesterday by 200 plurality. Dissatisfaction with the Platt machine is assigned as the cause of this reversal.

LYONS "CEMETERY CASE."

Dr. Chamberlain, Constable Dunn, and ex-Sheriff Glenn Indicted.

LYONS, N. Y., Feb. 16.—The Wayne County Grand Jury to-day indicted Dr. Dwight Scott Chamberlain on two counts, one for assault and battery and another for attempting to bribe a witness. Indictments were also found against Constable Homer C. Dunn for attempted bribery, and ex-Sheriff William J. Glenn, charged with embracery.

These cases arose from what is known as the "cemetery case." Dr. Chamberlain, who is Secretary of the Lyons Rural Cemetery Association, objected to the burial there of the remains of Mrs. Phoebe Alden, who died last December. The grave was dug several times but was filled up immediately by order of the Secretary. Michael Abert, who reopened the grave, charged the doctor with assaulting him, and the several times he was brought before the Grand Jury about two weeks ago.

A week ago charges were made that Constable Dunn tried to bribe the complainant to keep him from testifying, and that Glenn, Chamberlain, and others attempted to influence some members of the Grand Jury to prevent indictment.

NICARAGUA CANAL SYNDICATE.

Contractors Go Over the Lines of Work and Leave for New Orleans.

GREYTOWN, Nicaragua, Feb. 1.—The syndicate of contractors that has been examining the proposed interoceanic canal route, via Lake Nicaragua, arrived here this afternoon. Here the river steamer Irrawaddy, which they took having examined the Panama work and journeyed the entire length of this route. From Panama the proposed to Corinto, thence by rail to Managua, where they were received by President Zelaya and entertained for several days. From there they came to San Jorge, where the western section of the canal is to leave the lake, and, cutting through a low gap in the hillside, follow the valley of the Rio Grande to the East Divide. That part of the route they made on horseback and greatly enjoyed.

Returning to San Jorge, they crossed the lake to the head of the Rio San Juan, which they descended by river steamer to Ochoa, which is the site of the proposed dam to convert the upper river into an arm of the lake and to maintain the latter at the 110-foot level.

At this point the proposed route leaves the San Juan, or rather the basin that would be formed by the Ochoa dam across it, and

MAINE'S HULL WILL DECIDE

Divers to Find Whether the Force of the Explosion Was from the Exterior or Interior.

SHE WAS AFLOAT FOR AN HOUR

Spontaneous Combustion in Coal Bunkers a Frequent Peril to the Magazines of Warships—Hard to Blow Up the Magazine.

WASHINGTON, Feb. 16.—After a day of intense excitement at the Navy Department and elsewhere, growing out of the destruction of the battleship Maine in Havana Harbor last night, the situation at sundown, after the exchange of a number of cablegrams between Washington and Havana, can be summed up in the words of Secretary Long, who when asked as to what about to depart for the day whether he had reason to suspect that the disaster was the work of an enemy, replied: "I do not, but that I am influenced by the fact that Capt. Sigsbee has not yet reported to the Navy Department on the cause. He is evidently waiting to write a full report. So long as he does not express himself, I certainly can not express himself from the indications, however, that there was an accident—that the magazine exploded. How that came about I do not know. For the present, at least, no other warship will be sent to Havana."

Capt. Schley, who has had experience with such large and complicated machines of war as the New York, did not entertain the idea that the ship had been destroyed by design. He had found that with frequent and very careful inspection fire would sometimes be started in the coal bunkers, and he told of such a fire on board of the New York close to the magazine, and no fear that the best hoboldinested test parttion between the fire and the ammunition before the bunkers and magazine needed. He was not prepared to believe that the Spanish people of Cuba or Spain were supplied with information of the appliances necessary to enable them to make so complete a work of demolition, while the Maine was under guard.

Thinks She Was Blown Up.

An opinion different from this was that of Chief Naval Constructor Hichborne. Looking at the plans of the Maine, and discrediting the report that an explosion in the dynamo chamber, separated from the magazine by the space of an entire deck could have exploded the magazine, he also expressed the opinion that the magazine forward were empty and thus could not have caused fire by spontaneous combustion next to the magazine.

"The Maine," he said, "when fully loaded with coal is down at the head, and it is unsafe to draw upon the forward bunkers first in order to lighten her aft. It is the natural thing for the men to take the coal from the after bunkers near by at the time of the disaster. If they were empty it would be possible to generate gas and provide the material for spontaneous combustion. Now, I do not think the disaster was the result of accident."

There was a very decided aversion, among naval officers, to approve the suggestion that the disaster was accidental, but much because it was deemed in the muster upon an enemy, but because to publish the fact that a battleship was kept by an accident would demoralize the navy more seriously than a fight in which 260 men perished.

Commodore Dickins, Chief of the Navigation Bureau, expressed the opinion to-day that the explosion took from some small ... the disaster naval record of the Maine. He said that this was credited, for the cause had to have a torpedo been fired under the battleship, she would have sunk almost immediately, and the fact that she had not done so was conclusive evidence that the firing of a torpedo was not the cause of the disaster.

Capt. Sigsbee Will Not Talk.

The magazines on the Maine were all closed at 8 o'clock last night, and the keys left hanging in his room. Capt. Sigsbee, yet hanging in his room, Captain Sigsbee, with reference to the explosion, says only this:

"I can not determine the cause; but competent investigators will decide whether the explosion was produced from an interior or exterior cause. I cannot say anything until after such an investigation has been made. I will not and cannot conscientiously anticipate the decision, nor state the reasons for the explosion."

Sending Back the Survivors.

The survivors were sent from here this afternoon on the steamer Olivette of the Ward Line, to Key West, except nine officers, one private, Gunner's Mate Aldrich, and Capt. Sigsbee, who remain to look after the dead, and twenty-five men who are too seriously hurt to be moved. The full list of survivors is as follows:

Officers—Capt. C. D. Sigsbee, Lieutenant Commander R. Wainwright, Lieut. G. F. Holman, Lieut. J. Hood, Lieut. C. W. Jungen, Lieut. Gunior Grade) G. W. Blow, Surgeon L. G. Heneberger, Paymaster C. M. Ray, Chief Engineer L. G. Howell, Lieut. (Junior Grade) J. T. Blandin; Chaplain J. P. Chidwick, Passed Assistant Engineer R. C. Bowers, Lieutenant of Marines A. W. Catlin, Assistant Engineer J. R. Morris, Naval Cadet J. H. Holden, Naval Cadet W. T. Cluverius, Naval Cadet A. Crenshaw, and Naval Cadet Bronson ... [list continues]

Not a Man Flinched.

All accounts agree that the conduct of the officers and surviving men of the Maine was admirable. With a burning and sinking vessel containing thousands of pounds of explosives under their feet, not one of them flinched. A Spanish officer says Capt. Sigsbee was the last man to leave the ship, and stepped into a boat only after he had seen that every living man who could be reached had been taken out.

As well as can be gathered, most of the men lost were killed by the shock of the explosion, which occurred forward, and immediately under their quarters. All the officers are reticent, declining to give definite information in advance of the official report and the statements they will be required to make under oath on the court of inquiry, and were putting out from the shore and the other vessels in the harbor. On the City of Washington an iron truss from the Maine and hurled into the air fell with a crash on the pantry, and other smaller fragments struck in different parts of the vessel.

Spaniards Offered Help.

The Chief of Police Piaglieri of this city went aboard the Maine soon after the explosion and offered his assistance. Capt. Sigsbee was cool and deliberate, and positively declined to express any opinion as to the cause of the disaster.

The Alfonso XII. was in serious danger for a time, and her mooring tackle were slacked so that she could be moved further away from the Maine. This work was done while the wounded were being taken off. The first men to come ashore from the Maine were those of the Machina wharf. Ten arrived there wounded, and were cared for. The Havana Navy Fire Brigade was ordered on duty, and carried stretchers to the wharves for the transportation of the wounded. The Red Cross Society; also sent men to patrol the water front with stretchers to pick up the wounded. The smokestacks of the Maine fell at 11:30 P. M. During all this time the harbor had been a busy and brilliant scene. The water for a long distance round search lights were shining in all directions, assisting the boats at their work of rescue. The Maine finally sank, after another loud explosion, at 2 o'clock, only her superstructure showing above the surface. She went down head first very neatly.

Among those who went out to the Maine from the city were an American friend, Lieut. Commander Wainwright said he thought the explosion was caused by the short-circuit dynamo, but no details of his opinion could be obtained from him. This city is full of rumors and theories regarding the cause of the disaster, but none of them seems to have any authority behind them.

Capt. Gen. Blanco filed his official account of the disaster to Madrid at midnight. Consul General Lee's cable dispatch to the United States Department of State was carried to the palace by Vice Consul Springer at an act of courtesy.

REAR ADMIRAL KIMBERLY'S VIEWS.

Thinks Chemical Action in the Magazine May Have Caused an Explosion.

BOSTON, Feb. 16.—Rear Admiral Kimberly, who commanded the United States squadron at Apia, Samoa, offered the following to the Navy occurred, to-day said he could not imagine how it happened. No hand grenade thrown by a Cuban or Spaniard, as the morning dispatches intimated, could do such damage. A torpedo in the water would have blown up the boat. The accident, he maintained, was evidently not caused by those means. It may have been the result of some chemical action in the magazine, a combustion, perhaps.

"The facts ought to come out later," he declared. "In my judgment, Spain had nothing to do with the affair. Speaking of Spain, I refer to the Government. An enraged Spaniard, or an excited sailor, shall another matter. We know nothing of such incidents. But Spain wants no war with us. She knows too well her position as regards money. The present fully, I know well that there was no sufficient chance of a change in a gun, ball of the explosion of a magazine. It is a grave question of the cause of the affair; but it is my opinion that a spontaneous combustion in the bunker or some cause of some kind took place, and, becoming hot, set off the powder. On the other hand, it would be very difficult to make the magazine of a battleship explode. Every precaution is adopted about ammunition to obviate the chance of its explosion. The records of the Navy Department show that there have been only three or four such cases, and it is not possible the bonds of war. It depends on whether they were empty or contained coal to some degree."

manders to empty the fore bunkers of the ship first, in which case the Maine's bunkers in that quarter were probably empty owing to the length of her stay in Havana harbor.

Spontaneous Fires in Bunkers.

If, however, the bunkers were not entirely empty, they undoubtedly contained within themselves elements of danger that might account for the explosion. The department within recent years has been greatly troubled by complaints of spontaneous combustion of coal in the ships' bunkers which have endangered the lives of the crews and the safety of the ships. The Cincinnati twice at least has been obliged to flood her magazines to prevent their blowing up during fires of this kind, and the cruiser Boston has been in the same condition. In some of these cases shelving in the magazines which separate the powder charges have been charred by the intense heat caused by the burning coal in the adjacent bunkers. Although the bunkers are inspected under the regulations at frequent intervals, so numerous have been these cases of spontaneous combustion that the Navy Department only recently had the special board investigate the subject with the view to applying preventive measures. Unfortunately, this board was prevented from making the thorough investigation necessary because no funds were applicable to the purpose.

Even empty bunkers have exploded. In the case of the Atlanta, some years ago, the bunker exploded with great violence, and the only explanation that could be given was that it probably was caused by the ignition of the vapors arising from the new paint applied to the lining of the bunkers.

The theory advanced by the Spanish authorities that the disaster might have been caused by the explosion of the boiler is accepted at the Navy Department as within the bounds of credibility. The Maine's boiler was separated from the powder magazine at the nearest point by a space of about four feet, usually filled with coal. At least one boiler undoubtedly was kept under almost full steam in order to run the dynamos and move the ship in case of need. The explosion of such a boiler might easily drive through the bulkhead and fire the magazine.

Many Precedents for the Disaster.

Inasmuch as suspicion exists in some quarters that a torpedo was used against the Maine, it may be said that the majority of naval officers believe that the character of the explosion was hardly such as could be attributed to a torpedo. The latter, charged with about 100 pounds of gunpowder or guncotton, it is believed, would have torn a large hole in the bottom or side of the Maine, but was scarcely likely to fire the magazine, which is not near the bottom.

It is said at the Navy Department that there is no lack of precedent for such a disaster as that sustained by the Maine, all of which can be traced to accidental causes. In 1885 the United States man-of-war Missouri, lying at Gibraltar, was totally wrecked by the explosion of her magazine. Another case famous in naval history is that of her Majesty's ship Dolerel, off Puenta Arenas, in the Straits of Magellan, in 1887.

Every confidence is felt at the Department in the commander of the Maine, Capt. Sigsbee, and until it is really established otherwise there is every disposition to charge the accident, if accident it was that destroyed the Maine, to some cause beyond the usual range of human discretion.

The coast survey steamer Bache is now lying at Key West. The Superintendent of the Survey lost no time this morning in inviting Secretary Long to make any use of the vessel in this emergency that he might desire. The invitation was gratefully accepted, and the Bache has been ordered to proceed at once to Havana with wrecking paraphernalia.

While every United States warship is provided with diving outfits, it is probable that the apparatus on the Maine was destroyed in the explosion and sinking of that ship, so it will be necessary to forward another outfit to Havana as early as possible, if an investigation is to be made of the condition of the hull of the ship below water, to determine finally whether the explosion was external or internal. Divers will also be useful in recovering the valuables aboard the Maine, and there is little doubt that her battery of ten-inch and smaller calibre rifle guns can be raised.

A very prominent naval officer who did not wish his name used because of the meagreness of present information as to details, expressed the informal opinion that the accident occurred from spontaneous combustion in the coal bunkers, the heat of which exploded the powder in the supplementary magazines adjoining. Still another prominent officer was very confident that the forward magazine of the Maine could not have exploded. "Had the magazine exploded," said he, "the ship would have been blown to flinders."

BLANCO LAYS IT TO A DYNAMO.

Spanish and Other Diplomats Make Calls to Express the Regrets of Their Governments.

WASHINGTON, Feb. 16.—The news of the Maine disaster was learned at the Spanish Legation with horror, and was the occasion for many expressions of the most profound regret and condolence. Early in the day Señor Du Bosc, the Spanish Chargé d'Affaires, received a message from Capt. Gen. Blanco, which had been filed at Havana at 2 o'clock this morning. It read as follows:

"With profound regret I have to inform you that the American ship Maine, in this harbor, blew up by an undoubtedly chance accident, believed to result from an explosion of the boiler of the dynamo. Immediately following the accident all disposable elements of the capital hastened to the spot to extend every aid possible. These included the force of the Marine Fire Brigade and all the Generals in Havana, among them my chief of staff. There have been deaths and wounded. I have sent an aide de camp to offer every assistance to the North American Consul that he may wish for. I will forward further details as they become available. BLANCO."

Señor Du Bosc expressed the most profound regret at the occurrence. He said: "Of course, I look upon the horror as due in every respect and solely and simply to an accident. That is the clear and unequivocal statement of the authorities at Havana, and all the evidence thus far available goes to sustain it."

Asked if the disaster possibly could have any adverse effect upon the relations between Spain and the United States, he responded with a decided negative and the statement that the affair was wholly an accident.

Señor Du Bosc hastened to the State Department soon after receiving the Blanco cablegram for the purpose of expressing his deep condolence to the authorities and of communicating the Captain General's dispatch to Secretary Sherman and Mr. Day, the Assistant Secretary. To both of them he expressed personally and officially the most profound regret.

The members of the Spanish Legation called at the Navy Department in the afternoon, and left their individual cards as an expression of their personal condolences. Up to 2:30 P. M. the legation had not heard from Madrid. It was stated that the delay doubtless was due to the fact that in a matter of this gravity the Queen Regent herself would send a message of sympathy and regret, and that the message would come later.

The only cablegram from Havana came from Gen. Blanco, and was a request for information from this end.

The Spanish naval attaché, Señor Sobral, who is in New York, sent a telegram to the Secretary of the Navy expressing his profound regret at the news of the loss of so many naval companions.

At all of the foreign establishments there were the deepest interest and solicitude over the affair, and during the day Ambassador Cambon of France, Sir Julian Pauncefote of the British Embassy, and other foreign representatives called on the President or at the State Department to express their regrets.

At all the foreign establishments the occurrence was the one absorbing subject of comment, and the expression was general that, aside from its melancholy feature of death and destruction, it was profoundly unfortunate to the Spanish cause, owing to the natural suspicions which would arise. At the Army and Navy Club and the Metropolitan Club, two centres for the army, navy, and diplomatic circles, the same intense interest was manifested. At these public quarters there was an undercurrent of doubt and questioning as to the coincidence of an accident to this particular vessel at this particular time.

REAR ADMIRAL BROWN'S OPINION.

Says the Explosion Must Have Occurred on the Vessel.

INDIANAPOLIS, Ind., Feb. 16.—Rear Admiral George Brown, who was the highest officer in the navy until his retirement last year, was loath to venture any explanation of the affair, owing to the meagre news received. He said to-day:

"I can offer nothing but vague conjecture as to the probable cause of the destruction of the Maine, although it would seem to me at this time that when an investigation is made it will be found that an explosion occurred on the vessel."

The Admiral was asked if it was possible that a torpedo lying in the harbor could have been accidentally exploded under the ship. He did not think this could have been possible. If a torpedo caused the explosion it must have been sent from shore, for torpedoes are not lying around loose in Havana Harbor, where hundreds of ships are going in and out.

"I am sure no official had anything to do with it, if a torpedo was responsible," he declared; "there could have been no explotion of a torpedo by the dragging of the Maine's anchor or anything of that sort. Nor are there any submerged mines in the harbor. I don't recall any similar affair of this kind in the history of the United States Navy—either in time of peace or in time of war."

NAVAL EXPERTS CONFER.

Effort to Determine the Cause of Disaster—Vessels Sent to Havana.

WASHINGTON, Feb. 16.—Both Secretary Long and Assistant Secretary Roosevelt called a consultation in the forenoon of all the chiefs of the Navy Department and several of the officers of high rank not directly attached, like Commodore Schley, President of the Lighthouse Board, who has a brilliant reputation as a gallant officer and is possessed of great discretion. The purpose of these consultations was to secure the best expert testimony as to the probable cause of the disaster, while at the same time ascertaining to what extent the naval situation has been affected by the loss of the Maine. A good deal of disquiet was exhibited when it was shown that the loss of this fine battleship had done a good deal to destroy the balance of power theoretically between the navies of Spain and the United States. The latter has now left only six serviceable ironclads as against seven in the Spanish fleet.

The beautiful model of the battleship Maine, standing before the door of Secretary Long's office, was surrounded all day by crowds commenting on every feature of the vessel. At intervals telegraph messengers appeared bearing messages from the main telegraph offices. Upon the delivery of each message there would be a rush to the Secretary's room to learn the latest news.

Up to the time Secretary Long went over to the White House, the news was freely and promptly given out as it came. After that five messages were sent direct to him at the White House, and the crowd was obliged to wait for knowledge of their contents until they had been returned to the department.

Commandant Forsyth, at Key West, wired the Navy Department that he had been notified by Capt. Sigsbee of the Maine to inform Admiral Sicard, in command of the North Atlantic squadron, that the Maine had blown up and was destroyed. He requested that a lighthouse tender be sent over to Havana, and added that many were killed and wounded. Commandant Forsyth's message further said that the lighthouse tender Mangrove left Key West at 3 o'clock this morning for Havana, and that the transport steamer Fern would promptly follow her. A second dispatch from Commandant Forsyth said that he had sent the torpedo boat Ericsson, which was at Key West, to Admiral Sicard, who is at the Dry Tortugas, with a message concerning the disaster to the Maine.

BRITISH PRESS OPINIONS.

LONDON, Feb. 17.—The newspapers here express profound sorrow at the disaster to the battleship Maine. The headlines of the afternoon papers yesterday hinted at treachery, either Cuban or Spanish, but the morning papers generally comment very soberly upon the probable cause, which they attribute to accident.

With reference to "certain ominous opinions heard in America," The Times says editorially:

Fortunately for America and for the world, the United States is not governed by persons of this type. So far not only the Governments, but the peoples of America and Spain have acted with good sense, good feeling, and dignity. It is fervently to be hoped the investigation will prove the cause of the disaster an accident, although the conditions which can have led up to such an accident in such circumstances are rather obscure.

The Standard and Daily Telegraph contain similar editorials. The Standard believes the casualty to have been purely accidental, but it suggests that it may be "even feasible to attribute such an outrage to Cuban insurgents, desiring by means, however unscrupulous, to involve Spain in a foreign war."

The Daily News observes:

The disaster reaches the very extremity of horror. The public feeling of the world, shocked by this dire calamity, will do well to imitate the restraint imposed on that of the United States by both the Washington Government and the Captain of the ill-fated ship. For suspicions of foul play there seems to be absolutely no warrant, though naturally they haunt the minds of many Americans. They should be entertained only on absolute compulsion. A spark of misdirected National feeling might cause terrible mischief. The attitude of Spain at this agonizing moment will either efface the memory of the de Lome incident forever or revive it with added circumstances of bitterness and exasperation that cannot be contemplated without a shudder. The calamity sends a pang to every British heart.

The Morning Post, in an editorial of profound sympathy, expresses the hope that certain American Senators who have "allowed themselves to talk rather wildly" will suspend judgment. The paper does not believe in the torpedo theory, and thinks the disaster the result of an accident, but it fears the real cause will never be known.

The Daily Chronicle says: "British sorrow and sympathy are little less vivid than if the casualty had happened to one of our own ships." It thinks the theory that the boilers burst absurd; and, after expressing the opinion that there is "no apparent justification of foul play," it suggests that some new and dangerous explosive, which was on board with a view of experiment should an occasion arise, exploded spontaneously after suffering the process of mechanical decomposition and so fired the magazine. The theory that the officers were overhauling torpedoes at that time of night The Daily Chronicle dismisses as "preposterous."

The Daily Mail remarks:

The suspicion of Spanish treachery exhibited by a section of American opinion looks ill beside the accounts of the splendid gallantry of the suspects in saving drowning Americans; and it indicates an ugly temper toward Spain.

The Globe yesterday afternoon commented as follows:

It is impossible to refrain from the suspicion that the explosion may have been caused by foul means. Although anchored, the Maine would have steam up in one of her boilers for the dynamos and auxiliary machinery. If an infernal machine had been hidden in the coal thrown into the furnaces obviously there would be an explosion of the boiler and, as a result, of a magazine. That this terrible event should have occurred in the harbor of Havana renders a solution of the mystery of international importance.

The last serious disaster of this nature occuring in peace time was in 1881, when H. M. S. Doterel blew up in the Straits of Magellan. The verdict of the court was that it was caused by the formation of coal gas, another suggestion being that a substance called xerotine, a siccative, stowed in the paint room, was responsible. Upon this occasion there were two distinct explosions and 143 out of the crew of 150 perished.

In the following year an explosion on board H. M. S. Triumph killed three men. In this case the disaster was traced to the use of the xerotine siccative.

The St. James's Gazette inclines to the supposition that the disaster was wrought by an explosion in the magazine, "which is beneath the forecastle, and as far as possible from the engine fires," adding:

It remains, however, to be explained how a magazine, carefully guarded, could be fired. As bearing upon this, however, it must be borne in mind that the discipline on American warships, is usually, to English ideas, rather lax. Another possibility which is readily suggested is, that the disaster was produced by an agency outside the vessel, the explosion of a submarine mine or torpedo, caused accidentally or otherwise. This, again, naturally suggests the thought that the outrage was perpetrated by a Spanish conspirator or Cuban insurgents, incensed from whatever motive against the United States.

VIEWS AT THE NAVY YARD

Conflicting Opinions as to the Cause of the Maine Disaster Expressed by Officers.

CONSTRUCTOR BOWLES TALKS

He Thinks that the Explosion Was Probably Caused by Some Force from the Outside of the Warship.

When the news of the destruction of the Maine reached the Brooklyn Navy Yard yesterday morning it caused intense excitement. The opinions of the officers there varied as to the cause of the disaster, and while some contended that it was purely accidental and arose from conditions over which no one had control, others believed the explosion was the result of a plot, and that some one had placed a bomb containing high explosives alongside the vessel. The latter idea, however, was scouted by the majority of the officers, who said that such an act would not be attempted owing to the fact that the Spanish warship Alfonso XII. was anchored near the Maine, and was likely to be in danger from any such disaster to the American ship.

From early morning until the navy yard closed, there was a steady stream of people who visited the office of Rear Admiral Bunce to ascertain the names of the injured and dead. Many of these were the relatives and friends of the officers and men on the Maine. They were disappointed, as no official report had been sent to the yard. They were told to send to the Navy Department at Washington for information. Admiral Bunce is in Washington and will not return for several days. Capt. G. W. Sumner is in charge of the yard in his absence.

One or Two Explosions?

Among the officers who discussed the disaster there was much stress laid on the question whether there was one or two explosions. It is asserted that this was a matter of great importance. All the officers interviewed said positively that the Maine was not destroyed by a submarine mine placed in the harbor for the purpose of defense. It was pointed out that the Spanish authorities would not place a mine where it would hazzard the safety of their own vessels. It was thought by many that the real cause of the disaster would not be known until divers could make a complete examination of the damaged parts of the ship or until she is raised.

Many officers believe that it would have been impossible for the magazines of the Maine to explode, except from some tremendous shock. They base their belief on the situation and construction of the magazines.

"It would be impossible for any explosion to occur in these magazines unless it was caused by shock from a previous explosion," said one of the officers attached to the Ordnance Department, "nor can I imagine any bomb being placed at the side of the vessel sufficiently powerful to cause the damage that has been done If the disaster was caused by a torpedo, the vessel would have gone to the bottom almost immediately. The zone of destruction of a bomb would not be sufficient in itself to cause such great damage as happened; yet the shock of its explosion might have caused the fixed ammunition in the magazines for the smaller guns to explode. This, of course, would happen to the ammunition in the magazine nearest to the bomb. It may be that the boiler used in supplying steam for the electric plant exploded and caused sufficient shock to explode the fixed ammunition.

"The powder used in the large guns is practically free from danger, excepting when it comes in contact with higher explosives, such as fulminate of mercury, used in the electric primers."

Instructor Bowles's Ideas.

Naval Constructor Bowles had a decidedly different opinion. He is one of the best constructors in the navy, and is not only familiar with the make-up of the Maine, but knows every ship in the United States Navy as well as many of those in the foreign navies.

"The only disaster of this kind that I ever heard of on board a warship in recent years," he said, "was due to an explosion of paint. Such a thing would be impossible on the Maine as all explosive materials used in the paint are kept in chests on the deck, and these are kept locked and guarded when not in use. The theory that the Maine was wrecked by an explosion in her magazines seems to me to be nonsense. I have no definite opinion to offer, but I cannot understand how an explosion could have accidently happened. The magazines are opened every day, and the temperature taken. The entrance to them is from the deck under the guns, and when they are not in use they are kept locked, and the keys are in possession of the commanding officer. They are also carefully guarded, and some of the officers are quartered near them.

"It is scarcely possible that guncotton could have caused the disaster. Only a few pounds are kept dry on the vessels. The war heads of the torpedoes are loaded with it, but it is kept wet. These heads are taken out every month and examined. The moisture evaporates slowly, and they are soaked in distilled water at regular intervals.

"All the News That's Fit to Print."

The New York Times.

THE WEATHER. Fair, followed by showers; southerly winds.

COPYRIGHTED, 1898, BY THE NEW YORK TIMES COMPANY.

VOL. XLVII...NO. 15,129. NEW YORK, THURSDAY, JULY 7, 1898.—TWELVE PAGES. PRICE THREE CENTS.

THE NEWS CONDENSED.

Stock market dull and irregular.

Cash wheat, No. 2 red, 92c; cash corn, No. 2 mixed, 38⅝c; cash cotton, 6¼c.

CONGRESS.—The Senate yesterday passed the Hawaiian resolution which Mr. Newlands of Nebraska introduced in the House in June. The House agreed to the Pacific Railroads amendment to the General Deficiency bill, and adopted a number of unimportant resolutions.—Page 7.

FOREIGN—Dr. Cornelius Herz of Panama Canal scandal notoriety in France died at Bournemouth, Eng., where he lived as a refugee from French law. The fourteenth international conference of the Young Men's Christian Association of the World met in Basil, Switzerland, many Americans taking part in the proceedings. President Zelaya of Nicaragua fired an artillery salute in honor of Independence Day. Three persons were killed and six injured by an explosion on board the steamer Manitoba from New York, lying at her pier in London. A London Times dispatch from Montevideo says the ringleaders of the recent revolt have been deported to Buenos Ayres.—Pages 6 and 7.

Page 4.

The United States auxiliary cruiser Yankee arrived in port from Key West, from where she sailed on Sunday. There is no yellow fever on board, as reported.

Cheered by hundreds, the auxiliary cruiser St. Paul sailed for Santiago from the American Line pier with a big cargo and many passengers on board. Among the passengers were Gens. Ames and Henry and their staffs, and the officers and men of the Eighth Ohio Regiment. The St. Paul will be at Santiago this week.

Page 5.

The First New York Red Cross Ambulance Equipment Society issued an address to the public, showing the work already accomplished and setting forth what is intended to be done in the future. Funds are needed.

At the Brighton Beach Racing Association meeting Ornament won the Brighton Handicap in good style, defeating Tillo, George Keene, and Semper Ego. Many horses were withdrawn from the races at the last minute.

Page 7.

At the testimonial war concert in Carnegie Hall, under the auspices of the Soldiers and Sailors' Families' Protective Association, Gen. Stewart L. Woodford presided and Hon. W. Bourke Cockran spoke on "The American Soldier." Gen. Woodford declared that the duty of the hour was to press the war vigorously to a close. The hall was crowded.

Page 9.

The property and franchises of the Suburban Traction Company at Orange, N. J., were sold at auction to the Orange and Passaic Valley Company.

Page 12.

Several millions of the new revenue stamps were sold yesterday in this city. New tax questions were raised and some decided.

Four hundred and forty-six mothers, sick babies, and children were taken on a day's outing in the Floating Hospital of St. John's Guild.

Fire Commissioner Scannell rejected three bids for fire engines, the figures being the same. He said he did not propose to see the city beaten by a combination.

W. F. Doll, who was arrested for riding a bicycle on the Speedway, will make a test case. Lawson N. Fuller and other horsemen object to wheelmen on the thoroughfare.

Arrivals at Hotels and Out-of-Town Buyers.—Page 4.
Marine Intelligence and Foreign Mails.—Page 2.
Business Troubles.—Page 9.
Insurance Notes.—Page 12.
Yesterday's Fires.—Page 5.
Court Calendars.—Page 9.
United Service.—Page 5.
Real Estate.—Page 10.
Legal Notes.—Page 12.
Markets.—Page 8.
Railroads.—Page 9.

SENOR SILVELA HOOTED.

LONDON, July 7.—The Madrid correspondent of The Daily Chronicle says:

"Trouble is brewing. The excitement here is great. I myself saw Señor Silvela hooted a little while ago. He took refuge in the Hotel Roma, from which he drove home in a cab."

SPANISH FOURS DROP.

Declines a Result of the Intention to Continue the War.

LONDON, July 6.—Spanish fours opened at 33⅝ and declined to 33. Yesterday's closing price was 33¼. They closed at 33.

PARIS, July 6.—Spanish fours opened at 32.85 ex interest. Yesterday's closing price was 34.47½. They closed at 32.90.

Business was dull on the Bourse to-day, owing to heavy realizations. Spanish fours were principally weak, due to the announced intention of the Spaniards to continue the war. Copper shares were higher.

MADRID, July 6.—Spanish 4s closed to-day at 56.80. Gold was quoted at 85.

Help for Cuba and Puerto Rico.

LONDON, July 7.—The Madrid correspondent of The Standard says: "Both Government and people seem to face the difficulties with calmness. Anxiety is chiefly felt at the prospect of a more severe blockade of Cuba and Puerto Rico. Fresh attempts will be made to send provisions and war stores by fast steamers."

Rejected Volunteer Kills Himself.

The police of the Alexander Station were notified last night by the Hoboken police that Valentine Wens, thirty years of age, of 639 East One Hundred and Thirty-fourth Street, this city, had shot and killed himself in a saloon in Hoboken. Wens, it is said, was a member of the Seventy-first Regiment, and had been despondent ever since he was rejected on examination to go to the front.

THE WEATHER.

The local forecast may be found at the top of this page to the right of the title.

An area of high pressure, central on the New England Coast, covers the districts east of the Mississippi River. The pressure is generally low in the Rocky Mountain district. The barometer has risen on the Rocky Mountain plateau.

The temperature is higher in the lake regions and lower in the Missouri Valley. Showers and thunderstorms have occurred in the Middle and South Atlantic States, also in the Missouri Valley. Showers are indicated for the South Atlantic and Middle Atlantic States and near the North Atlantic Coasts. Showers will probably occur in the Upper Mississippi Valley.

The temperature will rise slowly in the Atlantic States and New England.

The record of temperature for the twenty-four hours ended at midnight, taken from THE NEW YORK TIMES'S thermometer and from the thermometer of the Weather Bureau, is as follows:

	Weather Bureau. 1897.	1898.	TIMES. 1898.
3 A. M.	70	66	71
6 A. M.	69	66	72
9 A. M.	78	70	76
12 M.	85	71	78
4 P. M.	85	68	76
6 P. M.	81	66	71
9 P. M.	76	65	69
12 P. M.	72	64	68

THE TIMES'S thermometer is 6 feet above the street level; that of the Weather Bureau is 285 feet above the street level.

Average temperatures yesterday were as follows:

Printing House Square	72⅝
Weather Bureau	69
Corresponding date 1897	78
Corresponding date for last 20 years	73

The maximum temperature yesterday was 78 degrees, at 11 A. M.; the minimum was 65 degrees, at 4 A. M. The humidity at 8 A. M. was .54 and at 8 P. M. .63.

CRUISER REINA MERCEDES SUNK

Cervera's Last Ship Destroyed at Entrance of Santiago Harbor.

DRIFTED OUT AT MIDNIGHT

She Was Seen at Once and the Guns of Fleet Riddled Her.

Six-Inch Shell from the Shore Batteries Exploded on Board the Indiana, but No One Was Injured.

Copyright, 1898, by The Associated Press.

HEADQUARTERS OF GENERAL SHAFTER, July 5.—The destruction of the Spanish cruiser Reina Mercedes last night accounts for the last ship of Admiral Cervera's once splendid squadron.

She lies to-day in plain view, her bow resting on the base of the beach under El Morro. Part of the hull is above water, and her masts and two stacks are entirely out of water.

It is not yet known whether she attempted to escape from the harbor, or whether the Spaniards tried to sink her near the hull of the Merrimac and thus block the entrance, to prevent the Americans from getting in.

Her sinking was most dramatic. Just after midnight she was seen drifting slowly out of the narrow entrance by one of the American scouts. In a moment the fleet was ablaze with signals, and, almost instantly, an awful hail of shells was hammering down upon her.

It is not known whether she returned the fire, but the shore batteries opened, and one six-inch shell fell on the Indiana's forward deck, exploding below.

The explosion occurred in the men's sleeping rooms, but all were at quarters and none was hurt.

No other American ship was hit during the engagement, or incident, which lasted only a few minutes.

THE ALFONSO XII. DESTROYED.

Spanish Cruiser Shot to Pieces While Trying to Run the Havana Blockade.

WASHINGTON, July 6.—Secretary Long has received word through Gen. Greely, Chief Signal Officer, that the Alfonso XII. has been destroyed while trying to run the Havana blockade. Gen. Greely had received a cipher message stating briefly that the Spanish ship had been overhauled near Mariel, while trying to get through the blockade, and was a total loss as a result of the fire upon her.

Both the Secretary and Gen. Greely regarded the report as authentic, but there was a desire to get more details, as this has been something of a spectral ship.

The cruiser Alfonso XII. was built at Ferrol in 1887. She was 278 feet 10 inches in length, 42 feet 7 inches beam, with a displacement of 3,090 tons, 4,800 indicated horse power, and could steam 17.5 knots an hour. Her armament consisted of six 2.2-inch Hontoria, two 2.7-inch, six 6-pounder, quick-firing, four 3-pounder, and five Maxim guns.

INCIDENTS OF SUNDAY'S FIGHT.

Terrible Scenes on the Burning Spanish Ships—Our Marines Stopped Atrocities by Cubans.

Special Copyright Cable to The Chicago News.

OFF SANTIAGO, VIA PORT ANTONIO, July 6.—After the destruction of their squadron off Santiago the Spanish sailors who swam from the burning ships were met on the beach by Cubans, who shot or mutilated them. The excited sailors turned toward the advancing boats, terrified and pleading for mercy from the Americans.

Lieut. Commander Wainwright of the Gloucester saw a Cuban shoot at an insensible Spaniard lashed to a floating spar, and fired a blank shell toward the insurgent. Capt. Evans sent his marines ashore to guard against atrocities and to rescue the Spaniards.

What an Officer Saw on the Viscaya.

One of the officers who went to the Viscaya said:

"The American shells had torn holes through her twelve-inch Harveyized stern armor plates. Through them I could see naked men roasting in the shell. Her guns had been left shotted and were exploding from the heat, but we took care and got alongside.

"Her decks and sides were red-hot. Two men, stark naked, were climbing down a davit tackle, and as the ship rolled they would swing against her scorching sides, and out and back again. I took 110 men off the Viscaya, all without clothes. One swam toward me.

"'Are you an officer?' I asked.

"'No,' he answered, 'only a mournful soldier.'"

On the Oquendo and Colon the officers and men took pains to dress as for parade. While their vessel was sinking they put on their best, broke into the stores, and filled their pockets with pies and cakes. Aboard the Colon the men who surrendered were crying "Viva Americanos." Some of the sailors were so drunk that they had to be hoisted in a sling. The Spanish Chaplains, Surgeons, and officers would not assist in caring for their own wounded, but appeared to be taking things contentedly.

Cervera sat on the quarter deck of the Iowa, calm and placid, wearing an American sailor's dirty white hat.

The Spanish officers say it is of no use for Spain to continue the war.

Our Fire Blinded Them.

The third officer of the Maria Teresa, who with his men is on the Harvard, says the Spanish ships were overwhelmed by the intensity of the American fire. "We could not breathe," he said, "and were blinded by the bombardment. We knew from the first we had no chance of escaping."

The Oquendo's Captain put oil on the decks, and then shot himself. The sailors were in such a hurry to surrender that they waved a tablecloth from the forecastle.

The Viscaya hauled down her flag just in time to save the remainder of her crew. The Ericsson was racing swiftly up to her, and was preparing to send out a torpedo when a Quartermaster, looking through the smoke, shouted to Capt. Usher: "Too late, the flag's down!"

SUNKEN SHIPS MAY BE RAISED.

Wrecking Steamers to Try to Save the Cristobal Colon and Others for Our Navy.

HEADQUARTERS OF GEN. SHAFTER, July 5.—Several hours after the Colon went ashore head on she floated off and was beginning to sink. The New York then rammed her several times, using fenders, and pushed her up on the beach without injury to either vessel. It is hoped she will be saved to become part of the United States Navy.

WASHINGTON, July 6.—The Navy Department is already making arrangements to recover as much of the valuable Spanish fleet as can be saved. To-day an agreement was closed with the Merritt & Chapman Wrecking Company to undertake the salvage of as much property as possible from the wrecks. The company's wrecking steamer I. J. Merritt left New York yesterday for Newport News, Va., where she will take on coal and needed supplies, and proceed directly to Santiago. Two large wrecking vessels left Norfolk for Cuba to-day.

Secretary Long is quite hopeful that one or more of the Spanish ships can be saved. Assistant Secretary Allen shares in this belief, and thinks that the Cristobal Colon can be got off the rocks as an entirety, and that the hull, upper works, and guns can be made available. She was the best armored cruiser in the Spanish Navy, and if she can be floated and repaired will make a valuable acquisition to the American Navy. Mr. Allen is hopeful also that the Viscaya and Oquendo can be saved in part. Information has reached the department that the hulls are not badly damaged.

The news which has reached here through the press, however, that a violent tropical cyclone is raging on the south Cuban coast causes the technical officers of the department to fear that the Spanish ships will be entirely destroyed before the wreckers can get to work on them, as their thin hull plates would be quickly torn to pieces on the rocky shore in a pounding surf.

The contract with the Merritt Wrecking Company is by the day, and may be cancelled at any time if the Government finds the salvage is not progressing satisfactorily.

SPANISH PRISONERS MUTINY.

Six Killed and Fifteen Wounded in an Attempt to Overpower the Guards on the Harvard.

HEADQUARTERS OF GEN. SHAFTER, July 5.—About fifty of the 400 Spanish prisoners on the auxiliary cruiser Harvard attempted to escape last night.

In some way a number of them secured guns and made a wild dash for liberty from the steerage, where they were confined.

Their rush was met by the deadly bullet of the guards, and six were killed and fifteen wounded. The firing ended the mutiny.

No American was hurt.

DISPOSAL OF FLEET'S PRISONERS.

Sailors to be Brought to Portsmouth, N. H., and Officers to Boston.

WASHINGTON, July 6.—Sampson has been directed to send his prisoners to the United States. Possibly the Harvard will bring some of them. The St. Louis is filled with the wounded soldiers and cannot be used to convey the Spanish sailors.

The enlisted men and non-commissioned officers among the prisoners will be sent to Portsmouth, N. H., where they will be confined on Seavy's Island, in the harbor. Orders for the immediate preparation of that place for the reception of the prisoners are going forward.

The commissioned officers, from Admiral Cervera himself down to the Ensigns, will be sent to Fort Warren, Boston Harbor, where they will be turned over to the army for safe keeping.

PORTSMOUTH, N. H., July 6.—A. W. Crowninshield, Chief of the Bureau of Navigation, with a corps of assistants, to-day made arrangements for taking care of the Spanish prisoners captured by Admiral Sampson at Santiago de Cuba, who will be brought here. The prisoners will be quartered in eight temporary buildings on Seavy's Island. It is expected that they will arrive on transports within ten days.

The Pope Is Dejected.

LONDON, July 6.—A special dispatch from Rome says the Pope is profoundly dejected at the fresh disaster to Spain.

The dispatch adds that several Cardinals strongly urge his Holiness to make another attempt to arrange peace between Spain and the United States; but the Pontiff declares the failure of his first intervention was so complete that he cannot reinitiate the movement.

Russian Papers Want Peace.

ST. PETERSBURG, July 6.—The Russian newspapers counsel the United States and Spain to "cease this terrible war." They declare that diplomatic intervention has become necessary. The Novosti says:

"In view of her close relations with the United States, Great Britain might, without departing from her neutrality, offer her mediation to President McKinley."

CABINET CRISIS IN SPAIN.

MADRID, July 6, midnight.—The Cabinet was in session to-night, and its resignation may be regarded as threatened.

The sequel probably will be a military Cabinet, under Marshal Martinez Campos.

There also most likely will be a suspension of the constitutional guarantees.

The Ministers on issuing from the council were very reserved. They said the Government had no further news from Santiago, but had only received a dispatch from Gen. Blanco asking for money.

Capt. Aunon denied the report that Admiral Camara would be ordered to return to Spain.

Regarding the statements that Gen. Weyler was organizing a demonstration, Capt. Aunon said: "If this be true, the Captain General of Madrid will attend to the matter."

BLAME FOR BERMEJO.

LONDON, July 7.—The Madrid correspondent of The Daily News says:

"The Ministers fear the effect of the latest disaster upon the garrisons in Havana and San Juan de Puerto Rico. The whole story of Admiral Cervera's squadron, from first to last, is one of unreadiness, indecision, and bungling. Senor Sagasta and Capt. Aunon, Minister of Marine, throw the whole blame upon Admiral Bermejo, former Minister of Marine. Senor Sagasta gave Bermejo a free hand, and he used it to insist on Admiral Cervera leaving the Canaries, to be wafted by a favorable wind across the Atlantic.

"Admiral Cervera went reluctantly, and under protest. When Capt. Aunon entered office things had gone too far to be righted. Coal was scant, and ammunition just sufficient for gun practice, while the gunners were untrained.

"Admiral Bermejo sent the squadron across the Atlantic at Gen. Blanco's suggestion. Señor Sagasta seems to have thought from an early date that Bermejo made a great mistake, and the Government got rid of the Admiral."

WILL SPAIN ASK FOR PEACE?

Reported She Has Appointed Ministers to Make a Proposition to This Country.

LONDON, July 7.—The Madrid correspondent of The Daily Mail says:

"There are persistent rumors here that Duke Almodovar de Rio, Foreign Minister, and Señor Cabano, the Minister of Public Instruction and Public Works, have received full power to propose a suspension of hostilities as a preliminary peace negotiation. The Ministers neither affirm nor deny the rumor.

"Spain, it is alleged, is prepared for peace on the basis of the independence of Cuba and the Philippines, the United States occupying Puerto Rico until the war indemnity is paid.

"Lieut. Gen. Correa, Minister of War, says everything depends upon the course of events at Santiago."

The Madrid correspondent of The Daily Telegraph sends a dispatch to his paper this morning, saying, "I am informed that peace will be demanded to-day."

NO PROPOSITION YET MADE.

WASHINGTON, July 6.—Up to this moment no overtures for peace have come to the Government of the United States from any European nation. The same statement applies to the Pope.

Inquiry at the British, French, German, and other embassies and legations shows that no peace movement is on foot among the great powers of Europe, so far as has been disclosed to the representatives of these powers here. It is the general impression in diplomatic quarters that the annihilation of Admiral Cervera's fleet makes a peace movement opportune, and it is expected that Spain herself will taken the initiative.

When asked how Spain could conduct direct negotiations for peace, one of the best-informed diplomatic representatives said that it might be done through the Pope, as this might excite less irritation than an overture from a power which had a military and naval establishment behind it. There is no intimation, however, that Spain has taken this step, through the Pope or otherwise.

SPANISH PEOPLE ENRAGED.

Great Excitement Prevails Since the Report of Cervera's Fate Was Made Known at Madrid.

MADRID, July 5, via the frontier, July 6.—The enthusiasm aroused by the misleading dispatches of the Spanish Government from Cuba is changed to-day into the wailings of the families of the victims and lamentations over the national disaster. The Ministers are crestfallen and are still concealing the worst.

The utmost extremity of despair, of rage, and recrimination prevails among the population, and the authorities are adopting strong precautions, fearing popular outbursts. Marshal Martinez Campos has been foremost in the endeavors to prevent disturbances.

A Government crisis is imminent and it is regarded as probable that Señor Silvela or Marshal Martinez Campos will succeed Señor Sagasta as Premier and propose peace in order to prevent the Americans from bombarding the peninsula and ruining Spain. The Palace is strongly guarded and the Queen Regent, who is described as being inconsolable, and who did not leave her room yesterday, is receiving the sympathy of the sensible portion of the population; but there is no disguising the fact that grave forebodings are heard as to the future of Spain.

The tone of the general public can be summed up in the remark frequently heard: "God alone knows what will happen."

Señor Silvela, the Conservative leader, declares the present situation is more favorable to peace than to war. But, he adds, the Government alone can judge of what ought to be done under the present circumstances, and he will support the Government in any determination it may reach.

The Republicans say the country is unable to withstand such misfortunes, and that the time has come for a general settlement. The Military Party favors a continuance of the war. Military men say they think Spain could never have expected naval victory, and that so long as she does not meet with disaster ashore she ought not to sue for peace.

The Carlists are anxious for the war to continue.

The Government views are believed to differ. Señor Sagasta, the Premier, says he is awaiting details of recent events from official Spanish sources, adding that he will see the effect which the loss of the Spanish squadron has upon Spain before deciding upon his course. The Spanish Government's decision to continue the war is published, and it is added that the Americans need 600,000 men to continue the operations in Cuba, it being alleged here that the co-operation of the insurgents is practically nothing.

The authorities kept the disaster to Admiral Cervera's squadron a secret as long as possible, and even suppressed the extra editions of the newspapers giving the facts. The official confirmation, therefore, caused a tremendous impression, particularly in naval and military circles, where the Government is accused of ordering Admiral Cervera to make a sortie, despite the known opposition of several naval experts.

The troops are confined to barracks, as disorders are feared, but up to this hour there have been no disturbances in Madrid or in the provinces. Senor Gamazo, Minister of Public Instruction and Public Works, had a long audience with the Queen Regent this afternoon, and subsequently conferred with Duke Almodovar de Rio, the Foreign Minister. These interviews have caused much comment. The Queen Regent has signed a decree promoting Col. Ordonez and Col. Escario to the rank of General.

The Government will transmit to the powers the protest of the Cuban Colonial Chambers against the American invasion of Cuba, which the protest describes as "a brutal attempt to seize territory."

Dining Cars a la Carte,
On the Chicago vestibule limited train, Lehigh Valley R. R., leaving foot of Cortlandt, Desbrosses, and West Twenty-third Sts. daily at 7 P. M.—Adv.

A DAY OF THANKSGIVING

President McKinley Asks the People to Praise God for the Success of Our Arms.

AND OFFER PRAYER FOR PEACE

He Fixes the Next Assembling for Divine Worship for the Observance in All the Churches of the Land.

WASHINGTON, July 6.—President McKinley at 11:40 to-night issued the following proclamation to the American people:

"To the People of the United States of America:

"At this time, when to the yet fresh remembrance of the unprecedented success which attended the operations of the United States fleet in the Bay of Manila on the 1st day of May last, are added the tidings of the no less glorious achievements of the naval and military arms of our beloved country at Santiago de Cuba, it is fitting that we should pause, and, staying the feeling of exultation that too naturally attends great deeds wrought by our countrymen in our country's cause, should reverently bow before the throne of Divine Grace and give devout praise to God, who holdeth the nations in the hollow of His hands and worketh upon them the marvels of His high will, and who has thus far vouchsafed to us the light of His face and led our brave soldiers and seamen to victory.

"I therefore ask the people of the United States upon next assembling for Divine worship in their respective places of meeting, to offer thanksgiving to Almighty God, who, in His inscrutable ways, now leading our hosts upon the waters to unscathed triumph, now guiding them in a strange land through the dread shadows of death to success, even though at a fearful cost, now bearing them without accident or loss to far distant climes, has watched over our cause and brought nearer the success of the right and the attainment of just and honorable peace.

"With the Nation's thanks let there be mingled the Nation's prayers that our gallant sons may be shielded from harm alike on the battlefield and in the clash of fleets, and be spared the scourge of suffering and disease while they are striving to uphold their country's honor; and withal let the Nation's heart be stilled with holy awe at the thought of the noble men who have perished as heroes die, and be filled with compassionate sympathy for all those who suffer bereavement or endure sickness, wounds, and bonds by reason of the awful struggle.

"And, above all, let us pray with earnest fervor that He, the Dispenser of all good, may speedily remove from us the untold afflictions of war and bring to our dear land the blessings of restored peace and to all the domain now ravaged by the cruel strife the priceless boon of security and tranquillity. "WILLIAM McKINLEY.

"Executive Mansion, Washington, July 6, 1898."

HOBSON PROBABLY FREE.

Gen. Shafter Receives a Letter from the Spaniards Agreeing to Exchange Him.

WASHINGTON, July 6.—The War Department posts the following from Gen. Shafter:

Camp Near Santiago, July 5.

Adjutant General, Washington:

I am just in receipt of a letter from Gen. Soul (probably Toral) agreeing to exchange Hobson and men here, to make exchange in the morning. Yesterday he refused my proposition of exchange.

SHAFTER, Major General.

During the morning President McKinley was notified of the assent of the Spanish authorities to an exchange of Lieut. Hobson, the hero of the Merrimac, and his crew. Adjt. Gen. Corbin, soon after receiving the official announcement from Gen. Shafter, which in effect reported a refusal yesterday and an agreement to-day to effect an exchange, communicated the facts to the President. It was most welcome tidings for the President, who has felt keen anxiety over the safety of the Merrimac heroes. He took occasion to express his relief to several of those who conferred with him, stating his profound gratification that Hobson and his men would soon be released and returned to their country in safety.

Copyright, 1898, by The Associated Press.

HEADQUARTERS OF GEN. KENT'S DIVISION, July 5.—Gen. Kent, whose division faces the hospital and barracks of Santiago de Cuba, has been notified by the enemy that Assistant Naval Constructor Hobson and his companions of the Merrimac, are confined in the extreme northern building, over which two white flags are flying.

During the diplomatic conference yesterday Hobson and his fellow-prisoners could be seen through glasses from Gen. Kent's headquarters, looking out of the windows.

BLOW AT "WILDCAT" MINES.

Montana Court Assesses Damages on Holders of Unpaid Stock.

HELENA, Mont., July 6.—The Supreme Court to-day rendered a decision in the Fourth of July mining case. Charles Kelly, injured in 1891, sued and got a judgment for $15,000, but could not recover. The jury found the mine worth $150,000, but capitalized for $7,500,000. The plaintiff contended that the individual shareholders were responsible for the unpaid stock.

In a word the decision of the court is that the individual holders of unpaid stock, in a mining as well as any other company, are liable to the creditors of the company. Stock is held to be unpaid when the property exchanged for it has little value in comparison with the amount of stock issued against it.

The decision will prove a deadly blow to "wild cat" operators in this State, and its influence will be of the most wholesome character. In the promotion of these mining stock schemes it is invariably sought to secure the connection with them of men who may be well known in the community or the State for the influence of their names.

Unless this is done the enterprise does not move along with éclat, nor do shares sell so readily. Under the interpretation by the Court of the Constitution and laws affecting corporations, men of influence, who are at the same time financially responsible, will be slow to become stockholders in corporations that are not of the legitimate kind, having assets somewhere within reach of its capitalization.

Chautauqua Excursion.
$10.00 round trip by Erie Railroad, July 8. Tickets good until August 8th.—Adv.

ST. LOUIS IN A BATTLE.

Reported She Fought the Torpedo Boat Destroyer Terror and Killed Six Men.

CAPE HAITIEN, July 6.—The announcement is made here that a dispatch from San Juan de Puerto Rico, carried to St. Thomas by a carrier pigeon, asserts that to-day the United States auxiliary cruiser St. Louis had an engagement with the Spanish torpedo boat destroyer Terror and killed the engineer and five men.

CAMARA HALTED AGAIN.

Report at Gibraltar that He Has Been Ordered Home with His Squadron.

LONDON, July 7.—The Gibraltar correspondent of The Daily News says:

"Admiral Camara has been ordered to return to Spain immediately to protect the coast, in view of the American threats.

"The Spanish attempts to place batteries in position to seal the Straits of Gibraltar are an illusion, as Ceuta possesses only four modern guns."

SUEZ, July 6.—The Spanish fleet, commanded by Admiral Camara, has arrived here and has been notified by the officials of the Egyptian Government that it must leave this port within twenty-four hours. The Government has also notified Admiral Camara that he will not be allowed to coal here.

ISMAILIA, Egypt, July 6.—The machinery of the Spanish battleship Pelayo is out of order and she has been compelled to stop here since early morning.

Ismailia is a town of Egypt on Lake Timsah, on the Suez and Sweetwater Canals, equi-distant from the Red Sea and the Mediterranean Sea. It was the headquarters of the Suez Canal Company during the construction of the canal and is connected by railroad with Suez and Cairo.

WATSON TO GO AFTER CAMARA.

WASHINGTON, July 6.—Without saying anything about it, the Navy Department is going ahead with the preparation of the Eastern Squadron, which it announced a week ago would be sent to the coast of Spain "immediately." High officials of the department say that no change has been made in the plans for the expedition.

There is ground for the conclusion, however, that its general purpose has been altered so as to make it a case of Admiral Camara's fleet rather than an attack on the coast of Spain.

When the expedition was first decided on the Administration did not believe that Admiral Camara would go through the Suez Canal. Now that it is impossible to say what he will do it is believed Commodore Watson's orders have been changed, so as to send him after the Spanish fleet wherever it may go.

The feeling is strong in naval circles that either Watson or Dewey is destined to catch and destroy this third Spanish fleet as the Asiatic and Cape Verde fleets have been destroyed, leaving Spain with practically no ships upon the seas.

PHILIPPINE REBELS WIN.

They Capture Santa Cruz and Enter Tondo, Their Shots Falling Into Binondo—Gen. Monet Blamed.

MANILA, June 30, via Hongkong, July 6.—The insurgents have captured Santa Cruz, and have entered Tondo, the shots falling into Binondo.

At Malabon they have court-martialed the Mayor for having caused fifteen natives to be executed while the Spaniards were in control there.

There is general indignation at Gen. Monet's desertion of his post on such feeble pretext. One officer proposes to dress him in petticoats or to tar and feather him.

The Spaniards have recaptured Calcocan.

NEXT MANILA EXPEDITION.

WASHINGTON, July 6.—Preparations for the fourth expedition to the Philippines are under way at the War Department. It was scheduled to leave some time between the 6th and the 10th of July, but it is now realized that this is impracticable, unless a much smaller array of transports is started than was at first contemplated. Approximately 12,000 men yet remain at San Francisco awaiting transportation, and a large number of ships will be necessary to take them. The nucleus of a fleet is being gathered, however, and to-day it was stated that the Peru, City of Pueblo and the Titania would in all probability be utilized in the forthcoming expedition.

New York Troops Off for Manila.

The First Regiment, New York Volunteers, will leave this morning for Manila. The companies that are at Forts Hamilton and Wadsworth will leave on boats that will be sent for them at 9 o'clock, and the two companies at Governors Island will be taken away at 10 o'clock. They will be taken on a special train that will leave the Erie Railroad Station at Jersey City at 2:15 o'clock. Col. Barber says the regiment will go right through to San Francisco, and that there will be no stops for ovations.

ADMIRAL DEWEY'S THANKS.

Expresses Appreciation for the Message of the Engineers' Club.

Admiral Dewey has, through his flag officer, expressed his appreciation of the congratulatory telegram sent him by the Engineers' Club of this city, in the following letter which has been received by the Secretary of the club at 374 Fifth Avenue:

Flagship Olympia, May 24, 1898.

Sir: Admiral Dewey wishes me to express to the Engineers' Club of New York his high appreciation of the action of the club in cabling congratulation to himself and to the members of the engineer corps attached to this squadron upon the naval victory of May 1.

The telegram was read on the quarterdeck of all vessels of the squadron with all hands at muster.

Such prompt appreciation of services rendered to the country is a great incentive to continued effort. Very sincerely,

T. M. BRUMBY, Flag Lieutenant.

Maryland Sword for Schley.

CUMBERLAND, July 6.—Gov. Lowndes said to-night that the State of Maryland would at once present her native son, Commodore Winfield Scott Schley, with a suitable sword in recognition of his great achievement in the capture of Cervera and the destruction of his fleet.

Chautauqua Excursion.
$10.00 round trip, via D., L. & W. R. R. July 8. Tickets good until Aug. 8.—Adv.

LA BOURGOGNE SINKS AT SEA

Five Hundred and Sixty-two Persons Lost with Her.

WRECK OFF ISLAND SABLE

French Liner Collides with British Ship Cromartyshire.

IN HEAVY FOG AT DAWN

Out of 725 Passengers and Crew Only 163 Saved.

FIERCE FIGHT FOR LIFE

It Is Charged by Survivors that the Crew Beat Passengers from Lifeboats—Horrible Details of the Disaster.

HALIFAX, July 6.—La Bourgogne, one of the passenger steamships of the Compagnie Générale Transatlantique, was sunk after a collision with the British ship Cromartyshire in a dense fog sixty miles south of Sable Island at 5 o'clock on the morning of July 4.

The British iron ship Cromartyshire was towed in here this morning by the Allan Liner Grecian, with her bow torn away by the collision south of Sable Island with the French steamer, which went down ten minutes later. Of the 725 passengers and crew on board, only 163 were saved.

One woman was saved by her husband.

The Captain and other officers went down with the ship, except the purser and three engineers.

The Cromartyshire laid to and picked up the 163 passengers and seamen who were rescued, transporting them to the Grecian, which came along at that hour.

The log of the Cromartyshire, signed by Capt. Henderson, is as follows:

"On July 4, at 5 A. M., dense fog; position of ship sixty miles south of Sable Island; ship by wind on the port tack, heading about W. N. W., though under reduced canvas going about four or five knots per hour. Our fog horn was being kept going regularly every minute. At that time I heard a steamer's whistle on our weather side or port beam, which seemed to be nearing very fast. We blew horn and were answered by steamer's whistle, when all of a sudden she loomed through the fog on our port bow and crashed into us going at a terrific speed.

"Our foretopmast and maintopgallantmast came down, bringing with it yards and everything attached. I immediately ordered the boats out and went to examine the damage. I found that our bows were completely cut off and the plates twisted into every conceivable shape. The other ship disappeared through the fog. However, our ship was floating on her collision bulkhead, so there seemed no immediate danger of her sinking. We set to work immediately to clear the wreckage, and also to ship our starboard anchor, which was hanging over the starboard bow and in danger of punching holes in the bow. We heard a steamer blowing her whistle on coming back and we answered with our fog horn. The steamer then threw up a rocket and fired a shot. We also threw up some rockets and fired several shots, but we neither saw nor heard anything more of the steamer.

"Shortly after or about 5:30 A. M. the fog lifted somewhat and we saw two boats pulling toward us with the French flag flying. We signalled them to come alongside, and found that the steamer was La Bourgogne, from New York for Havre, and that she had gone down. We ladi to all day, and received on board about 200 survivors from among the passengers and crew, reported to be in all about 600. Several of the passengers were on life rafts without oars, and I called for volunteers from among my crew and the surviving French seamen to bring those rafts alongside of the ship. Some of the passengers and seamen from the sunken steamer assisted us, and we jettisoned some thirty tons of cargo from our forehold in order to lighten the ship. At about 3 P. M. another steamer hove in sight, bound westward. We put up our signal "H. C.," want assistance. Shortly after a steamer bore down toward us. She proved to be the Grecian, bound from Glasgow to New York.

"The Captain of the Grecian agreed to take the passengers on board, and also agreed to tow my ship to Halifax. Owing to the condition of my ship, I accepted the offer, and we proceeded at once to tranship the passengers and get ready our towline. At 6 P. M. we had made a connection and proceeded, in tow of the Grecian, toward Halifax, having put a sail over the broken bow to take part of the strain off the collision bulkhead. There was at that time fourteen feet of water in the forepeak."

Mrs. Henderson's Thrilling Story.

Mrs. Henderson, wife of the Captain, was on board the Cromartyshire with her two children. She tells a thrilling tale of the terrible experience.

The weather was foggy and she had risen from her bunk at an early hour, as was her custom when the weather was thick. Shortly before the vessels came together she detected a steamer's whistle blowing on the port side of the vessel. The Cromartyshire was sounding her fog horn at intervals of one minute. Mrs. Henderson called the attention of her husband to the sounding of the whistle, and a minute later the mate, who was on the watch, also detected the sound. It came nearer and nearer, and Mrs. Henderson stood near the cabin in order to rescue her children should a disaster occur. Suddenly the huge hull of an ocean greyhound loomed up in the mist, going about seventeen knots an hour. Almost immediately there was a fearful crash, and Mrs. Henderson rushed below and found her children awakened by the shock.

She dressed the little ones as quickly as possible and removed them to the deck, unpecting to see her own ship go down any minute. Capt. Henderson had as soon as the collision occurred ordered the boats to be lowered and the damage to be ascertained. As it was found that the Cromartyshire was in no immediate danger the Britisher was put about. The vessel with which they had collided was at that time unknown. A few minutes later her whistle was heard and several rockets were sent up. Capt. Henderson replied in like manner, thinking the steamer was offering assistance, but in a few minutes all was quiet and those on board began to realize the awful results of the collision.

At 5:30 the fog lifted and two boats were seen approaching with only men on board. Later the weather cleared still more, and men were to be seen in every direction clinging to wreckage and floating on life rafts. It was a terrible scene. No pen can picture the appalling sight revealed to the onlookers when the curtain of mist arose. The work of rescue was commenced without a moment's delay, and over 200 persons were picked up and taken on board the ship.

Mrs. Henderson, who had ample opportunity of interviewing those who were rescued, expressed her belief from what she heard that there had been no effort to save the women. There were many foreigners on board who fought for places in the boats. It was fully ten minutes to a quarter of an hour before La Bourgogne went down, and during that time there was ample opportunity offered to rescue at least some of the women and children. As it was only one woman was saved.

Mrs. Lacasse was saved, and she has been on board ever since. She is the wife of A. D. Lacasse, language teacher of Plainfield, N. J.

The crew of the Cromartyshire expressed the belief that there must have been some foul play, considering that only one woman was saved out of 300. Nearly all the first-class passengers were lost, those saved being steerage and sailors. Lacasse and his wife were in the water eight hours, clinging to a raft, before they were picked up by a boat from the Cromartyshire. They lost everything but what they stand in, including money and valuables.

One passenger was going home to France with his two children, his wife having died a month previously. He was saved, but his two babies went down with the ill-fated ship. Mrs. Lacasse says the officers bravely staid by their posts, going down with the ship. The only officer saved was the purser. He went down with the ship, but being a strong swimmer managed to save himself. When the ships struck they were off Cape Sable. The passengers, with the sole exception of Prof. Lacasse, were below decks. Without warning came the terrible shock. Lacasse rushed in haste to his state room, on the saloon deck, got his wife out of bed, and partly dressed. They hastened on deck, to be precipitated into the water on reaching it. They were not long in the water, however, when they found a partly submerged raft, onto which Lacasse lifted his unconscious wife and then clung to it himself. Some of the boats, Lacasse says, capsized and all on board were drowned.

An Awe-Inspiring Scene.

The spasmodic struggles, swishing water, and terrible screams made the situation an awe-inspiring one, never to be forgotten. One man on board La Bourgogne when she sank went out of his mind and jumped to a watery grave. On the morning of the collision, Capt. Henderson was on the poop with his Third Mate, A. C. Stewart. Sailor Haley was on the lookout and First Officer Killman was also on the forecastle deck. The Cromartyshire was making about five knots an hour, with several sails set, and taking in all the time.

Not a sound was heard until the lookout, Haley, saw a large steamer half a ship's length ahead on the port bow. In an instant the Cromartyshire's jibboom was crashing into the Bourgogne's bridge and the sailing vessel crashed into the liner, staving a big hole near her engine room. The Bourgogne scraped the whole length of the Cromartyshire's port side and then she veered off. The Bourgogne blew long mournful whistles for assistance.

Third Mate Stewart of the Cromartyshire says that the Frenchman evidently thought they were another ship, and that they (the Bourgogne) had sunk the colliding vessel.

At the time of the collision Mr. Stewart says the Bourgogne must have been going at the rate of eighteen or nineteen knots per hour through a dense fog, shutting out everything more than twenty yards away. About three hours after the Cromartyshire picked up the survivors the Allan Liner Grecian was sighted and took the Cromartyshire in tow. About 8 o'clock that evening, three miles away, Third Mate Stewart heard the guns and saw three rockets go up, and a blue light, the signal of distress, burning.

The Grecian signaled to the Cromartyshire that she was going to assist the vessel signaling. In a few minutes, however, the light disappeared, and no more guns or rockets were discharged, the vessel certainly having sunk. Prof. La Casse, one of the survivors, is of the opinion that there was a third vessel in the collision, as he saw the Bourgogne sink within ten minutes after the collision.

The second officer of La Bourgogne was the only man of the crew who did anything to help the terrified and helpless passengers. He cut loose all the boats he could, and in fact all the boats that were launched were launched by the brave second officer. He was last seen standing on the deck with his hand on the rigging going resignedly to certain death.

Christopher Brunini, a passenger, was thrown into the water and swam for two hours before he found a boat. He clung to this as his last hope. After some time another man got hold of the same boat, and together they managed to right it. Under the seats they found the dead bodies of four men and three women, who had evidently been drowned by the capsizing of the boat.

Brunini said the crew were cruel in their conduct toward the passengers. He was unable to get in the steamer's boats when he came on deck, being shoved away by the sailors. He saw many of his friends being prevented from getting into the boats by the sailors. He lost everything but what he stood in.

Meholini Secondo, an Italian steerage passenger, is among the saved. When he got on deck he found a raft with five men on it. The raft, however, was tied and chained fast to the deck, and no sailors were near to let it loose. None of the five men had knives. The ship sank rapidly, and they were all precipitated into the water. He was in the water twenty minutes and alone, the others sinking before his eyes. He came across a boat, which he tried to get into. He eventually succeeded, but not before a desperate fight with her crew. He was battered with oars and shoved away with boat hooks. He managed to seize an oar, however, and pulled himself to the boat and climbed in.

Cruelty Charged Against the Crew.

August Pourgi was eager to give an account of his experience. He was in the water about half an hour, and attempted to get into a boat. He was seized when he managed to get half in, and thrown back into the water. Again he tried to enter the boat, but the inhuman savages who manned it were determined to keep him out. He managed at last to get in, and to stay in.

Clinging to the lifeline of a boat not far away he saw his mother, and as if his trials were not enough he was forced to watch a man shove her deep into the ocean with an oar, from which she never rose. He says the man was saved, and was almost sure he can recognize him, though he does not know the man's name.

Fred Miffler, a Swiss, was the most jovial and contented of all the unfortunate passengers. He lost all his money and clothes, with the exception of a pair of pants and a shirt, but he laughed, and now and again cursed the fiendish French sailors with passionate earnestness. He went to bed the night before the collision and slept well. He never heard a sound, but woke in the morning, the same as he would any other morning. He went on deck and saw the splinters. He asked the officer of the watch what was up. The officer replied that it was all right, that the ship would not go down. Miffler, however, got into a lifeboat with some others and remained there until he reached the water, when he thought it was time to leave. None of the sailors ever attempted to let the boat loose. He swam for a long time before he was picked up. He saw an Englishman attempt to get into a boat. But the men in the boat who were sailors of the Bourgogne, hit him over the head with the butt end of an oar. He fell back and sank out of sight.

Charles Liebra, a Frenchman, expressed himself as thoroughly ashamed of his countrymen's conduct. This man is one of the most unfortunate. He had his two motherless boys, five and seven years old, with him. He put them in a boat, but was prevented from entering himself. He could not get in any boat, and went down with the ship. He went down so deep that he thought he was gone, but he came to the surface and at once looked for the boat with his boys. They were nowhere to be seen, and he mourns them as lost. He floated a long time before a boat came along. He tried to get in, but was assailed with oars and boathooks. Mr. Liebra showed your correspondent his arms and body. His arms are black and blue, and his body is terribly bruised from the blows he received. After this boat went off he was in the water eight hours.

Patrick McKeown is an intelligent young Irishman from Wilmington, Del. He is justly indignant at the brutal crew. He is on his way to Paris to turn out leather for a firm there. He was more fortunate than most of his fellow-passengers and got on a raft when the Bourgogne was sinking. He was the only passenger who could have walked through the streets of Halifax without attracting attention.

One of the worst sights he said he ever saw was the murder of an American whom he had become acquainted with on board the steamer. This man, whose name he cannot recall, was from Philadelphia, where he has a wife and family. The Philadelphian was trying to get on a raft not far distant from the one McKeown was on. A French sailor grabbed half an oar and beat him three times over the forehead. The murdered man was on his way to Paris to see a sister. From Paris he intended to go to Ireland to see his father and mother.

Beaten From the Lifeboats.

Charles Duttweilera, a German, could not speak English very well, but by an interpreter he told his story. It is this: He got in a boat which was tied fast to the ship, and stayed in it until he saw it was certain death to remain any longer. He jumped, but was carried down in the whirlpool made by the sinking steamer. He was in the water half an hour, when a boat came within reach, and he attempted to enter it, but the wretches in it shoved him off with boathooks.

His left eye is badly cut by the jabs he received. He saw women shoved away from boats with oars and boathooks when clinging for dear life to the life lines of the rafts and lifeboats. He also says the crew assaulted many passengers. With any implement that came handy, and, if no instrument was to be had, they punched the men and women helpless in the water with their fists.

One of the most important witnesses will be John Burgi, who got into a boat before the ship sank with his aged mother. The sailors in the boat held him and threw his poor old mother into the water to meet a watery grave. The sailors threw him out five times, beat him with oars, and shoved him under the boat. He was in the water nine hours before he was saved by a boat from the Cromartyshire.

Charles Liebra, who lost his two children, also said that he saw five women who were evidently exhausted clinging to the life-line of a boat. The French sailors maliciously, as the women were in no one's way, cut the lines and the women sank, never to rise again.

When accosted, an intelligent looking Frenchman, was asked if he could speak English. He replied "No." Niffler, the Swiss, with a grin then said that this was one of the crew, a waiter. He was questioned further, and it was seen that he spoke English perfectly, but did not wish to give any information. The next person accosted was a young sailor of the Bourgogne. He wrote his name on the back of a scrap of a steerage passenger ticket, Rolleri Gioseppe. He seemed anxious to give information, but the waiter mentioned before said to him in French not to give any. The correspondent said in English, pointing to the waiter: "Never mind him; bad." At this the waiter gave himself away on his "no English" by saying you are bad yourself, and pulled the sailor away, jabbering in French to him.

Gustav Grimaux, a French passenger, heard the shock in his berth, and rushed for the deck. He corroborated the other passengers in their statements about the crew. They did not attempt to cut any boats loose except those which they needed themselves. He saw women shoved away from boats with oars, and not only being shoved away, but shoved deep into the water.

The officers of the Grecian say the passengers and sailors presented a sorry spectacle when they were taken on board from the Cromartyshire. They were dripping wet and had terrible expressions, not having eaten for nearly twenty-four hours. Some are still dazed, and did not know where they were or what they were doing.

The third officer of the Cromartyshire said that one half-drowned wretch whom he pulled in over the side some hours after the collision seized his life belt and asked the steward for his knife. He cut a piece off the life belt and started to eat it, saying it was all he wanted.

AT THE COMPANY'S OFFICES.

Sad Scenes Enacted by the Friends and Relatives of La Bourgogne's Passengers.

Some sad scenes were witnessed yesterday in the offices of the French Line, on Bowling Green. Shortly after 10 o'clock the friends and relatives of those who had sailed on La Bourgogne on Saturday began to arrive, and from that hour until late at night there was a steady stream of men and women passing in and out with anxious faces. None of these lingered very long. There was no hope or comfort to be obtained there.

Until late in the afternoon no information of any kind was given out by the officials of the line. Consternation pervaded the offices when the news that the Bourgogne had been sunk reached there at 8 o'clock. The officials and clerks seemed temporarily stupified, and for a time business was at a standstill. The General Agent of the line, M. Bocande, went to Paris on a business trip about three weeks ago, and Paul Faquet, the Assistant General Agent, is in charge of the offices during his absence.

Within an hour the news of the disaster had spread throughout the shipping district, and many steamship men found their way to Bowling Green. The French Line offices were soon besieged by a crowd of reporters, telegraph messengers, and persons who had been attracted through curiosity. These stormed the clerks and officials for some authentic news, but the latter protested helplessly that they knew nothing officially of the disaster. This was the answer given over and over again.

Those who had relatives and friends on the lost steamer only had two inquiries to make: "How many were saved, and who?" The reply they received was the same as that given to the hundreds of different questions which had been asked by those who came before them: "We know nothing." The officials of the line were plainly confused and staggered by the ever increasing procession of callers. The women were by far the most importunate. They went from one clerk to another, begging that they might be told even the worst, and finally departed unsatisfied.

One of the first callers was Thomas H. Whitney, a banker of Washington, whose wife and child had sailed on the Bourgogne. He was almost distracted with grief and anxiety, and had to be supported by a friend. He could scarcely speak for emotion, and left word that he should be instantly notified when it was learned whether his wife and child were lost.

Some of the Callers.

Later came two young men who had been ushers at a wedding last Thursday, and two days later had thrown rice at the departing bride and groom on the pier, as the Bourgogne bore them away on their wedding journey.

One of the saddest cases that came to light was that of a whole family from Pocantico Hills, Westchester County, which was on the lost vessel. The family consisted of Mr. and Mrs. Frank Fiston, Miss Marie Fiston, and Master Frank Fiston. A big party of friends had seen them off at the dock, and some of these friends were asking about them yesterday and learned that they were dead.

Telegrams were constantly arriving from various cities throughout the country containing inquiries concerning the safety of different passengers on the steamer. These accumulated in a vast heap on the desk of the distracted officials.

Among the callers during the afternoon was the Rev. R. J. Lang, pastor of the German Evangelical Church at Union Hill, N. J. Two weeks ago yesterday he had married Dr. and Mrs. Simon Koppe, who were on the ill-fated vessel on their wedding trip to Paris, where the young physician was to spend two years in study.

Miss Minna Walgemuth, a self-contained little woman, with eyes swimming in tears said that her father had sailed on La Bourgogne for a visit to Switzerland, his native land. She was to have gone with him, but at the last moment had given up the journey. She is a teacher in Grammar School No. 17.

Thus the procession passed throughout the day. There were no violent outbursts of grief and not much noise. Questions were asked and answered in many different tongues, and the general bustle and confusion were continuous, but there was no wild excitement. Only now and then a woman's broken sob varied the low-voiced murmur of the throng.

At 1 o'clock Mr. Faquet announced that he had telegraphed three times to Halifax for the names of the survivors, and had not received any reply.

He said the list of survivors would have to be checked over by by his agents in Halifax before he could get it correctly. No record is kept of the addresses of passengers at the company's office, and the agent was unable to tell how many lived in this city. He said that some of the passengers were booked by out-of-town agents, but he had no information as to where these passengers lived.

THE BOURGOGNE'S CAPTAIN.

Capt. Louis Deloncle, who commanded La Bourgogne, had been in the employ of the Compagnie Générale Transatlantique for about five years. He was formerly Captain of the Normandie, and was considered one of the most efficient and trustworthy officers of the fleet. While on the Normandie he and the Second Captain, Dupont, distinguished themselves by their cool and courageous behavior when the vessel took fire on the high seas, and both officers received gold medals for their gallantry.

Capt. Deloncle came from a distinguished family in France. His brother is an ex-member of the Chamber of Deputies, where he had a seat for seven years, but was defeated in the last election by Count Castellane. The Captain was formerly a "Lieutenant de Vaisseaux," which corresponds to the American rank of navigating officer, in the French Navy. He published a book on marine manoeuvres, which is the standard in French naval schools, and he was teacher of tactics in the School of Gunnery. He was to have commanded one of the new vessels of the company, either the Alsace or La Russie, for the Exposition traffic in 1900. He was forty-four years old, and a wife and four children, who live in Havre, survive him. His eldest son, a boy of seventeen, died two months before he sailed on his fatal trip. He was one of the most popular officers in the service, and was known among his colleagues as "Loup de Mer" (sea wolf) on account of his thorough knowledge of naval affairs.

"All the News
That's Fit to Print."

The New York Times.

THE WEATHER.
Fair and warmer; northerly winds.

COPYRIGHT, 1900, BY THE NEW YORK TIMES COMPANY.

VOL. XLIX...NO. 15,750. — NEW YORK, MONDAY, JULY 2, 1900.—Twelve Pages and Supplement. — ONE CENT In Greater New York; Elsewhere, and Jersey City. TWO CENTS.

TO-DAY, TWELVE PAGES,
WITH FINANCIAL REVIEW AND QUOTATION SUPPLEMENT.

THE NEWS CONDENSED.

FOREIGN.—Reports from Shanghai confirm in the fullest manner the rumors of the assassination of Baron von Ketteler, the German Minister to China. He was slain in Legation Street on June 18, and his body hacked to pieces. The Consul at Shanghai fear that all foreigners in Peking have been killed. Public executions of foreigners are reported to have been begun on June 30. Other dispatches say that the Envoys were alive a week ago, but that their position was desperate, and that they could not hold out more than twenty-four hours. No news has been received about the expedition which started from Tien-Tsin for the capital. Two imperial decrees, upholding the Boxers and calling upon the Viceroys to assist in fighting against the foreigners, have been discovered. Admiral Kempff has sent a list of American casualties in the Peking relief force on June 20. The Deutsche Tageszeitung, in an article charging the German Government for employing diplomacy with the Americans, and advises reprisal as a means to bring the "insolent Americans" to terms. The Archduke Franz Ferdinand of Austria and the Countess Chotek were married in Reichstadt, Bohemia. Archbishop Ireland has been attacked in the French newspapers for his alleged pro-British sentiments. The Kangari relief expedition has been delayed by floods. Gen. Buller is causing the British troops much trouble by his over-petulant tactics. He is endeavoring to make a juncture with the Vet. In Dublin 35,000 children who would not attend the queen's reception to children while she was in Ireland marched through the streets cheering Krüger. Maud Gonne told the boys never to wear the British uniform, as it was "the badge of shame."
—Pages 6 and 7.

The funeral of Admiral Philip will take place to-day.
—Page 12.

ATTACK ARCHBISHOP IRELAND.
Section of French Public Very Hostile to Him Because of His Alleged Pro-British Attitude.

Special Cable to The New York Times.
PARIS, July 1.—It is quite certain that a section of the French public is very hostile to Archbishop Ireland. It is declared that he is an Anglophile, because he has on various occasions referred to Great Britain as the "Home of Liberty."

This is sufficient to condemn the Archbishop completely in the eyes of the "patriotic" pro-army section of the French people, which, though Catholic, is opposed by any principles which tend to extend the domain of individual freedom. These patriots are the Boxers of France, and oppose anything coming from abroad. Americanism, therefore, is to a most serious heresy, and they call Archbishop Ireland the "American Luther."

The campaign principally inaugurated by the articles against Archbishop Ireland and by it meetings that he should be permitted to discourse on the works of the Lafayette Monument on July 4. The Archbishop himself was interviewed to-day, and said that the hostility to him represented a very small section of the French public. He added that any doubt as to his being friendly to France will be set at rest by the oration he will deliver on Wednesday. He intends to stay here several weeks.

CHAOS IN CONVENTION HALL.

KANSAS CITY, July 1.—Eighty laborers were at work in Convention Hall to-day. The regular daily force is three hundred. If the convention were to meet to-morrow its members would find difficulty in getting inside the building. The streets in front and on the side of the structure are filled with rubbish, to remove which a large force will be necessary. The entrances are blocked with material which is to complete the furnishing of the hall.

Mr. Taylor, in charge of the work, says the delay, if any occurs, will be in clearing up. Heretofore no effort has been made to do this, but in order was issued at noon to-day to bar the entrance to the public. Sightseers will not be allowed in the building until Monday night, when a popular concert will be given.

The contractors confidently assert that they expect to turn over the hall to the National Committee Tuesday night. The hall will again be opened to the public on that night, when a drill will be the chief attraction.

All open chairs for spectators are in place except in the southwest corner, where the fixtures are being adjusted to-day.

The work inside the building actually necessary for convention purposes is the placing of 400 chairs for the press, 300 seats on the platform, 1,000 seats for delegates and alternates, and the arranging of one hundred and twenty-six telephones. The wiring for which is finished. The chairs for the platform and press will go in to-morrow, those for the delegates on Tuesday. Camp chairs will be occupied by the workmen in various parts of the convention. The rooms for the committees are yet to be cleared out and furnished.

The decorations are also incomplete barring the entire girders, which are festooned with National colors. All portraits and banners are still packed away, and all work necessary in draping and decorating the platform is embryonic.

HAS FORGOTTEN HIS NAME.
He Loses His Memory in Washington—He May Be a New Yorker.

Special to The New York Times.

WASHINGTON, July 1.—The police of this city have a mysterious case on their hands. It is that of a man who has lost his memory and his name. He is about fifty years old, well dressed, and intelligent. His was found in the Smithsonian grounds last night by two policemen, who, after hearing his story, took him to the station in order that it might be investigated.

The man was unable to tell his name, his occupation, or the place from which he had come. The only incident he could recall was having jumped off a street car in New York City and dodged another which was coming in an opposite direction. He had an impression that he had traveled a great deal and that his friends had called him "doctor." His hat contained the name of a haberdasher in Canton, Ohio, but there were no papers in his possession or other clews to his identity. He remembered having once been interested in some way in the compiling of statistics.

Further than this the man's mind was a blank, but he talked coherently and pressed the police as perfectly sincere. He was detained at the station on a technical charge of insanity, under the name of John Doe.

NO WORD OF THE OREGON.
Naval Officials Can Employ Any Available Means to Save Her.

WASHINGTON, July 1.—Not a word came to the Navy Department to-day regarding the battleship Oregon. The hope is everywhere earnestly expressed that the efforts to float her will be successful, but so that she may be taken to Port Arthur and docked.

The naval officials on the Asiatic station have ample authority to employ whatever means is necessary to save her. Later the grounding will be investigated by Sicsby.

EX-SENATOR HILL CALLED TO LINCOLN
In Conference with Bryan Over Democratic Platform.
AN ANTI-BRYAN MOVEMENT?
Disposition Shown to Rebel Against His Dictation—A Delegate Sent to Notify Him—Croker Will Not Oppose Hill.

Special to The New York Times.

KANSAS CITY, July 1.—Ex-Gov. David B. Hill of New York has gone to Lincoln, Neb., to hold a conference with Mr. Bryan. As he was leaving the breakfast room at the Coates House, shortly after his arrival in Kansas City, he received a telegram from Mr. Bryan, requesting him to come to Lincoln at his earliest convenience.

Before leaving Albany Mr. Hill had received a letter from Mr. Bryan inviting him to Lincoln. On his arrival here he had had a brief talk about the letter with Senator Jones, Chairman Campbell, Executive Chairman Elliot Danforth, and others. When the telegram came from Mr. Bryan, Mr. Hill at once decided to go to Lincoln and started on the first train. He is expected back here late to-morrow afternoon.

Speaking for Mr. Hill and with the approval of Senator Jones, Chairman Campbell said this afternoon:

"Mr. Hill was sent for by Mr. Bryan, and at the urgent request of Senator Jones and Chairman Campbell, of the Democratic National Committee. Left for Lincoln at 10:30 o'clock to-day. He will return to-morrow afternoon. Everything is in statu quo, and will be resumed when Mr. Hill's return. It is up to Bryan and Hill, and all eyes are turned to them. When Mr. Hill does return a programme will be mapped out.

"There will be no meeting of the New York delegation earlier than Tuesday evening. New York has no candidate for the Vice Presidency. A modification of the platform is the main thing, so far as New York is concerned. Whatever is to be done will be done by Bryan and Hill.

"Do you believe that they can arrive at an agreement regarding the platform?

"I certainly do," he replied. "It is an excellent idea for Bryan and Hill to meet. Senator Jones has a heart to heart' talk and Mr. Hill will frankly state his belief of what is best to be done. I am quite satisfied, and Senator Jones agrees with me that Bryan and Hill will certainly reach some kind of an agreement."

"Do you believe Mr. Hill would accept a practically unanimous nomination for the Vice Presidency, regardless of the platform?

"No," he answered decisively, "Mr. Hill will not consent to be a candidate under any circumstances. He will walk out of the convention if an attempt is made to nominate him."

"Theodore Roosevelt also would not accept, but he did."

"That is true," was Mr. Campbell's reply, "but David Bennett Hill is not Theodore Roosevelt."

"Suppose New York should unite in the work, Mr. Hill?"

"It will not," he rejoined. "New York has no candidate for the Vice Presidency."

"How about Sulzer?"

"I repeat," he answered, "that New York has no candidate."

"Will you remain in the National Committee?"

"I will not."

"Who will succeed you?"

"I don't know. Mr. Croker may. Frank K. Mack of Buffalo would accept a position on the committee. By arrangement will probably be chosen at the meeting on Tuesday night. The delegation cannot meet before then, as all the delegates will not be here until that time."

Before he left for Lincoln Mr. Hill was asked about his proposed visit to Bryan. He declined to discuss the matter, but remarked:

"I can say is that after the long trip from New York I am very tired, but I am going to Nebraska because I believe it my duty to do so."

LINCOLN, Neb., July 1.—Ex-Senator David B. Hill is spending the night in Lincoln, coming here from Kansas City, at his solicitation. It is asserted, of William J. Bryan, with whom he was closeted for several hours at the home of the latter. Mr. Hill arrived this evening, and was met by Mr. Bryan and a number of visiting politicians at the Lincoln Hotel, where Mr. Bryan, ex-Senator Hill, Judge Addison Tibbetts, delegate at large from Nebraska; National Committeeman Woodson of Kentucky, and James G. McGuire and Eugene Kreele, district delegates from New York State.

Mr. Bryan and Senator Hill left an hour later for the Bryan home for a conference, which proved to be extended. In the midst of it Mr. Bryan was asked if he or Mr. Hill would make any statement as to the visit of the New Yorker or the subject under discussion.

"So far as I am concerned, I have no statement to make," was the reply. "Senator Hill says he has nothing to say," came a moment later from Mr. Bryan after the question to his visitor.

Earlier in the evening, before leaving the hotel, Mr. Hill excused himself from the newspaper men, insisting he had nothing to say. Senator Hill will return to Kansas City early to-morrow morning.

The feature of the day in Lincoln, aside from the visit of Senator Hill, was the fact that a draft of the Democratic platform said to have the indorsement of Mr. Bryan and meeting the approval of his friends in nearly half the States in the Union has been prepared. It makes the three leading issues of the campaign imperialism, militarism, and trusts, in the order named.

SILVER MEN AGGRESSIVE.
Explicit Declaration. They Say, Is Necessary for Success—Absence of Leadership Apparent.

Special to The New York Times.

KANSAS CITY, July 1.—The talk of the Democrats here justifies the assertion that the conflict here is to be between politicians and idealists, with the prospect favoring the latter. The idea that may dominate the convention is the one held by Mr. Bryan that it is of the utmost importance to require all Democrats to admit that the explicit reaffirmation of the ratio of 16 to 1 is essential to Democratic unity and success. Aside from a little group of politicians whose dissent is more positive than their talk, the Democrats at Kansas City wait upon the news from Lincoln, half a day's journey away. In preference to their own judgment, based upon observation of tendencies and the experience of four years.

A remarkable change is observed in the attitude of some men who were conspicuous in the convention at Chicago four years ago. At that time Senator Jones, ex-Gov. Stone, and other leading men, fighting bitterly the Eastern protest against the adoption of a free-coinage plank, were mustering their forces first to prevent Hill from becoming the temporary Chairman, and then to overwhelm the gold standard Democrats and conservative bimetallists. Now Mr. Jones and ex-Gov. Stone, representing the Democrats who are still theoretically for free silver, but who are sufficiently practical to see that a reiteration of the dogma is dangerous, are doing all that they can do without absolutely abandoning free silver, to bring about an indirect reference to the declarations of four years ago. They are in favor of nominations that will unite rather than further divide the Democracy, and Hill is with them.

A REVOLT AGAINST BRYAN?

Special to The New York Times.

KANSAS CITY, July 1.—A disposition to resist Bryan has developed here and became known late to-night. At the conference which was held late to-day between Senator Jones, ex-Gov. Stone, Richard Croker, and ex-Senator Murphy, and others the frequent reports that Bryan will insist upon dictating every expression of the platform were discussed.

This was regarded by the conference as absurd and unwise, inviting censure of the most intolerable sort. It is asserted that the criticism of Bryan went so far as to amount to a threat that if he persists in his insinuation, the convention will make its own platform and if Bryan will not stand on it another candidate for President will be selected.

The result of the conference was to start an Illinois delegate to Lincoln to see Bryan. The man selected is a school friend of Bryan and is the one of his ardent supporters.

This agent expects to reach Bryan at before Hill leaves him, and will supplement Hill's advice with the warning of the conference.

THE VICE PRESIDENTIAL PROBLEM.

The event of the day here was the departure of ex-Senator Hill for Bryan's home at Lincoln. The last statement from Bryan touching Mr. Hill's candidacy for Vice President was one quoted upon the authority of Mr. Metcalfe, one of Bryan's most intimate and confidential friends, that Bryan would not have Hill as a candidate on the ticket with him. Mr. Hill himself, and Mr. Campbell for him, have both asserted to-day that Hill will not be a candidate, and that the State of New York will not have a candidate. But there are many Democrats who still cling to the notion that Hill will be named, even in spite of himself, and it something like the manner and spirit in which Roosevelt was named in the Republican Convention.

DEMAND OF THE SILVER MEN.

Something of every is added to Chairman Jones's troubles by the persistency with which the ultra-silver men declare that the chief object in calling the convention, next to nominating Bryan, is to make a silver declaration more specific, if possible, than that of 1896. George Fred Williams of Massachusetts is the most conspicuous of the men who rail against a general readoption of the 1896 platform and who insist that the candidate must be a man willing without mental reservation to accept all the doctrines of that platform and to speak and work in order that they may be carried into practice.

"It is not enough to reiterate," said Mr. Williams. "We must go much further than that." And Mr. Bryan's friend, Mr. Metcalfe, says if a specific declaration against trusts, which were denounced in the 1896 platform, is appropriate and desirable, then a new and more specific declaration concerning the policy that was the dominant one in 1896, and that is regarded by the rank and file of the Democratic Party as the one issue that made the Democratic Party differ from the Republican Party.

It is a natural result of the threatened control of the convention by the sanguine idealists that attention is being turned away from political candidates for Vice President. So long as there remains a chance for the nomination of a candidate for political reasons, Hill will continue to be the race, even without his consent. But the delegates from Indiana will not so little surrender without a struggle to a notification from Lincoln that Towne, already named by the Populists, is preferred.

A CASE OF "BRYAN AND BUST."

The arrival of more delegates changes the tone of conversation about candidates and the masterfulness of Mr. Bryan. When Senator Harris and George Fred Williams insist that Mr. Hill cannot be a consistent partner with Mr. Bryan on the ticket, and that Mr. Towne would be, the declarations cause something like a shudder to creep over the perplexing listeners who remember the ingratitude of the Democratic Party in attempting to win support for a Democratic ticket carrying Republican candidates.

The convention may elect Mr. Towne and Mr. Williams's judgment and with free coinage large for New York and Massachusetts to think about. According to a veteran Missouri Democrat, who has participated prominently in many conventions, Bryan will make a reluctant convert to free silver in 1896. "I wother with free silver and so or crazy as to nominate Towne, we might as well write on our banners, 'Bryan and Bust,' for it does not make any difference who the second man is so long as he is to be named without regard for political considerations."

ABSENCE OF LEADERSHIP.

The conviction has flashed over some of the more conservative Democrats here, just as it struck some of the leaders at the Philadelphia convention, that if wise discretion was to have sway it should have been exercised earlier. Mr. Jones is aware of this fact. The absence of leadership, of which so much complaint has been heard all Washington at all Winter, is heard again here. There is a tone of despair and recklessness in some of this allusions to it. Only a policy of letting things go, it is insisted by some of the more conservative men, could have made possible the sanguine hopes entertained by Representative Sulzer that he may be the candidate for Vice President, or the cheerful persistency of James Hamilton Lewis that he shall be considered as a fit soldier companion for Col. Bryan.

It is the lack of leadership that makes it so easy to get the convention to listening every moment for what is said by Bryan at Lincoln and that makes it so hard for delegates to support any platform or to take decisive action, either in making a platform or in choosing a candidate for the Vice Presidency. By the same token the convention is as lacking in enthusiasm for anything except Bryan. There does not appear to be a chance of providing enthusiasm for any of the Vice Presidential candidates except Hill, for whom Towne, the Populist candidate, be chosen, the anticipation that would follow would be perfunctory because from the few enthusiastic devotees.

BRYAN MUST BE PRESENT.

To stir the convention at all it will be absolutely necessary to have Bryan about after his nomination is made to make the speech that is already promised and expected. The tariff has not been mentioned here since the convention crowds began to assemble and talk about the money question. George Fred Williams, disdaining the free-silver question, says only that he wants a Vice Presidential nominee who will with Bryan insist upon dictating every expression of the platform were discussed.

Neither did he show anything but embarrassment when he was reminded of the harmonies and industry with which he labored to prevent the Fifty-second Congress from passing a free-coinage bill, as a measure to the Business interests of the whole country. Mr. Sulzer is the only leader who has had a word to say about reducing the tax burden of the people, and his recommendation goes so further than to take off the war taxes collected on consumption and not on imports.

CALAMITY OF FIRE GROWS IN HORROR
Over 360 Now Estimated To Be Missing.
GREED SACRIFICED LIVES
Captains of Harbor Tugs Rest Under a Grievous Charge.
FIRST BODIES FOUND
Desolation Reigns at the Devastated North German Lloyd Line Piers—Blackened Liners Lie Helpless in the Harbor—The Saale Gives Up Charred Remains — One Body May Be Her Captain's—Bremen and Main Still Burning—Sufferings of the Main's Men—Little Change in Estimates of Property Loss—Mr. Schwab's Statement—Full Insurance.

Dawn yesterday revealed on the Hoboken water front a long stretch of half-burned piles, a tangle of iron work, and heaps of half-consumed merchandise—all that Saturday's fire had left of the American terminal of the North German Lloyd Steamship Company. At the northwest corner of the burned area stood the Campbell stores, from which the fire had eaten most of the contents, and where the firemen of Hoboken and Jersey City at last succeeded in arresting the progress of the conflagration. Smoke still rose from the debris and the streams of water played upon the fire were turned into sprays of steam, giving warning that the heat was still too intense to permit a search to be made for the victims who were trapped upon the piers.

SCARRED AND WRECKED LINERS.

The Kaiser Wilhelm der Grosse, scarred for 200 feet along its starboard side and stripped of many boats, lay at Pier 52, at Jane Street, and soon after dawn was boarded by workmen who had been summoned to prepare the steamship for its sailing to-morrow.

Stranded and partly sunk off Ellis Island lay the liner Saale, still smoking and holding in its fire-eaten, water-filled interior and on its charred and cinder-covered decks the bodies of possibly 128 victims, 127 of the 255 persons in the vessel having been accounted for.

Up the river, beached and still burning, lay the other ill-fated liners, the Bremen and the Main, each stripped of all its upper woodwork and the fire still eating in the interior of the vessels, while the tugs kept on pouring water into them.

ROLL OF THE DEAD GROWING.

According to careful and conservative estimates made late last night the loss of life may reach a total of 361, the estimates being as follows:

Missing from the steamship Saale	128
Missing from the steamship Bremen	74
Missing from the steamship Main	81
Reported missing to date of police	48
Longshoremen, boatmen, and visitors	50
Total	**361**

Less than twoscore bodies have been recovered, and the ruins of the piers, the waters of the harbor, the holds of the three burned and flooded vessels, and the cinder heaps on the decks and in the cabins of the Saale, the Main, and the Bremen have not given up more than an inkling of their secrets.

The bodies of many of those who were drowned in the river, or who, already lifeless, fell from the burning vessels or piers, will never be recovered, and it will never be known how many perished on the burning decks, leaving only their ashes, which cannot be discriminated as human remains.

THE PROPERTY LOSS.

The property loss, according to the most conservative estimates made last night, amounted to $5,615,000, of which the insurance companies, it is estimated, are liable for about $4,075,000, the remaining $1,542,000 falling on the insurance fund maintained by the North German Lloyd Steamship Company.

This total is somewhat less than the estimate on Saturday night, which was $6,175,000, and is far below some of the figures given.

LATE RESCUE OF 22 MEN.

Superintendent Müller of the Bremen piers, starting out late Saturday night in quest of the dead, most unexpectedly rescued twenty-two men. On the tug E. A. Stevens he approached the Bremen and found to his amazement that there were still men living aboard her. This is one of the coal ports the fourth engineer and six of the crew, who had managed to survive the fierceness of the fire in the lower part of the vessel.

Then he visited the Kaiser Wilhelm der Grosse, and seeing Main drifting with the tide he followed in the Stevens to where the still burning liner had gone to the Weehawken flats. Profiting by his experience on the Bremen, he scanned the sides of the vessel closely and descried at one of the coal ports a man who was calling for help. Going to the side of the vessel he rescued this man and fourteen others, all of whom had been in the bottom of the ship, whom roaring above them and working their way ever nearer. The men were at their last stand and would soon have perished.

WARRANTS FOR TUGBOAT CAPTAINS.

The conduct of tugboat Captains who, in the race for salvage, refused to pause to save human lives, caused many bitter comments, and stories of brutality became current. These incidents of the fire. Information was laid before Chief of Police Donovan of Hoboken upon which at least two tugboat Captains will be arrested, warrants having been drawn.

Second Officer Emil Zander of the Saale spoke of the refusal of tugboats to pull his vessel away from the burning pier. Adolph Meyer, a fireman on the Main, who, with five others jumped overboard, hailed a tugboat Captain, who replied:

"How much have you got to give for the job?"

Meyer being too exhausted to reply the tug went on.

SEARCHING FOR THE DEAD.

The work of searching for the dead began early yesterday morning, when the police of Hoboken, Jersey City, and New York, with the harbor police, began the look-out for bodies, finding in all only half a dozen.

The ruins of the piers still defied the approach of the searchers, and it may be a week before they will be able to prosecute the search there.

The New York authorities took possession of the wreck of the Saale and found twelve bodies. Some of them were charred fragments which were picked up among the cinders on the deck. Others were found below by divers.

A portion of a body found on the Saale was supposed to be that of Capt. Mirow, who commanded the vessel, owing to the finding near by of a knife which had a peculiar spring, part of the cover of the log book, and some keys.

No progress was made in the search of the Bremen and the Main, the tugs merely pouring water into the vessels and only a cursory inspection of the wrecked craft being made.

LINE CARES FOR ITS MEN.

In Hoboken the North German-Lloyd Steamship Company, through its agent, Mr. Schwab, supplied clothing to the employes who had suffered from the fire, provided lodgings for its crews, and distributed about $4,000 in cash for the needs of the men and their families. The crowd of applicants, some of them bandaged and many wearing bandages, thronged the company's office in Water Street early in the morning.

Soon the sightseers followed and pressed upon the police lines, and the crowd all day long was so dense that it was difficult to move. Thecrush at the Hoboken Ferry houses was especially great owing to no provision having been made for the rush of sightseers, the boats running on their usual Sunday schedules.

ENDEAVORERS NOT ABOARD.

Some alarm was occasioned by rumors that members of the Christian Endeavor party which was to sail from Boston on the Saale had gotten aboard the vessel here and were to be counted among the missing. There is absolutely no foundation for this. Another rumor circulated with persistence was to the effect that there were over 100 visitors on board the Bremen at the time of the fire. There seems to be no basis for this supposition.

TUGBOAT CAPTAINS ACCUSED.

Information has been furnished Chief of Police Donovan of Hoboken which will cause him to have warrants issued for several Captains of tugboats on a charge of ignoring the applications of people who were thrown into the water during the water-front fire.

At Police Headquarters it was admitted last night that such information had been laid before the Chief which would cause at least two tugboat Captains to be arrested between now and to-morrow night. The charges are that the Captains deliberately allowed human lives to be sacrificed in a frantic race to claim salvage, floundering in the water could not guarantee a sufficient compensation for the trouble of throwing a line and picking them up.

A CHASED COTTON BALES.

Dr. Grahn, the surgeon on the Hamburg-American Line steamer Phoenicia, made the following statement last night: "The third officer of our boat got on board a tug and asked the Captain to aid in rescuing the people who were floating around in the slip just above us. He was specially instructed to succor the Saale." "The Captain of the tug when asked to look after these people replied:

"What is there in it for me?"

"'Help them,' said the third officer, 'and you will be reasonably rewarded.'

"'Not unless I get my price,' replied the Captain of the tug. As a result the third officer of the Phoenicia was taken back to the Hamburg-American Line pier and allowed to go ashore, while the tugboat chased bales of cotton up and down the stream, these bales being worth about $40 each."

"While I personally did not see the incident I got the facts from some of my brother officers. And they are as follows:"

"At the end of Pier 3 of the North German Lloyd Line commonly called the Italian pier, there were twenty-five persons who were compelled to jump into the water."

"LET THE GREENHORNS GO DOWN."

"A tugboat was cruising near the pier did not attempt to help them. Instead, as if I should find the vessel could help, the Captain cried:

"'How much will you pay to be taken on board?'

"Our officer said he heard no response from the drowning people, but he did hear the 'splash of the tug say' Let the greenhorns go down. The names of the tugboats above referred to by Dr. Grahn were furnished last night."

The doctor himself was very reticent, and positively declined to furnish the names himself, but they came from other sources which were perfectly reliable and the Police Department of Hoboken admitted that the detectives are collecting further evidence against the two 'captains.'

THE SECOND OFFICER'S CHARGE.

The story of Second Officer Emil Zander of the Saale is one of many of the experiences with the hard-hearted owners of tugboats. "If the tugs had come to our rescue," said Mr. Zander, "at the time we hailed them there would have been less loss of life on the Saale. I was in my stateroom with Dr. Stabs when the purser called to us, 'Pier 3 is on fire!' I rushed on deck and went to my station aft. The Captain was walking about the streets of Hoboken yesterday showing to whoever would examine it an arm that was a mass of blisters from hand to shoulder, and complaining bitterly of the inhuman treatment accorded him by tugboat Captains after he had jumped from the burning decks of his vessel.

"I was in the fireroom," he said, "when I thought I heard the roar of flames on the deck above. I spoke to some of the other men about it, and six of us started up to see what the matter was. When we reached the deck I saw a mass of flames, and there were men clinging to slip away. They all went down at one, and I was so nearly played out that I had to make for a pier, one end of which was burning.

WRECKS OF GREAT FIRE-SCATHED SHIPS
Sufferings of Men Rescued from the Main's Depths.
THE SAALE'S GHASTLY FREIGHT
Doomed Vessels Still Hold the Dead Trapped in Their Blazing, Furnace-Like Interiors.

Among the most astounding of the stories of the catastrophe at the North German Lloyd Line piers is that of the rescue of fifteen members of the engineer's department of the steamship Main after they had laid for nearly eight hours in an empty coal bunker in the bowels of the blazing ship, the vessel being for all that time in the very vortex of the conflagration. Bone and copper within a few feet of their prison melted and ran like water, and the walls of the bunker itself, except on the one side next the water, were so hot that no one could lay hands on them, yet after the vessel grounded off Shadyside they all tumbled out through an open coal port to the deck of the tugboat Col. E. A. Stevens, burning with thirst, blinded with smoke, and with faces, hands, and bodies blistered by the fierce heat, but not otherwise injured. The rescued men are:

BECKMANN, FRITZ, fireman.
BEHRDER, OSCAR, coal trimmer.
CONRAD, GUSTAV, coal trimmer.
GÜNTHER, ALEX, coal trimmer.
GUNTHER, CHRISTIAN, upper stoker.
HORN, ——, engineer's assistant.
KAHL, OTTO, coal trimmer.
KUBE, MAX, fireman.
MEHL, CARL, fireman.
PETERS, HEINRICH, fourth engineer.
STANGER, ANTON, third engineer.
VON BERGEN, AUGUST, engineer's assistant.
WAGNER, HEINRICH, coal trimmer.
WAGNER, OTTO, engineer's assistant.
WIESNER, JULIUS, fireman.

ONE GOES TO THE HOSPITAL.

Mehl was the only one of the rescued men to go to the hospital. He is lay in a cot at St. Mary's all Saturday night and all day yesterday. He is the oldest of them all, being about forty-five, and while he was subjected to no dangers through which all did not pass he suffered more than all, and for hours the doctors feared that his eyesight was gone forever.

Dr. John McArdle, the house surgeon at St. Mary's, made him the object of his special care, and as soon as he was received injected a solution of atropine between the closed and swollen lids from which tears flowed in unbroken streams. This was to keep the pupils from contracting lest they might never open again. Many times through the night the doctor asked him, in German if he could see and the answer, delivered always in the dull monotone of one suffering was "Nein." Yesterday morning when the man was well up Dr. McArdle repeated his question. The eyelids opened a mere fraction of an inch, and the answer came: "Yes, but faint."

THEIR LAST REFUGE.

Though the vessel had been cooling all day there was one bunker near the mouth of the tunnel into which no coal had been put and they made a dash for it after lying in their first retreat perhaps an hour. It closed with a heavy door which they shut and fastened, believing that the heat less intense. The coal port above their heads was open outside at the ship's side, but was not closed, and so its opening was toward where the Kaiser Wilhelm der Grosse and firemen...

SAW THE BLAZING HULK.

On board the Main was Capt. M. Möller, the Superintendent of the North German Lloyd piers. He and Capt. John E. Gilkinson, who commands the tug, saw the blazing ship approaching, attended by four other tugs and the Hoboken New Yorker. Only one of the little vessels had a line to her, and under her counters were the remains of two coal barges. The ship was glowing from stern to stern with a dull red heat, and flames were rising...

Half Rates Via New York Central to Cincinnati, Account of Baptist Young People's Union of America, will be sold July 10 to 12, inclusive. Call on any New York Central agent.—Adv.

Chicago, St. Louis and all Leading Western Cities are reached readily with comfort and safety by the superb through trains of the Pennsylvania Railroad.—Adv.

Comfort on the Pennsylvania Railroad is a well-known surety. No car speed, and courteous treatment. The dining car service is unrivaled.—Adv.

Avoid noise July 4th; spend day on Long Island Sound. See adv. on the Day Line Str.—Adv. Chapin.

ing to the level of her sides from the barges. Through the upper portholes of the hulk the flames could be seen within, apparently unchecked by any barrier, and fire was rising from some of her forward coal ports, all open and within a few feet of the water line.

The men on the Stevens saw a new peril should the fireship drift against the rescued ships, and the tug was at once turned toward the Main to see if her course could not be checked. She whistled loudly as she bore down upon her, and as she passed on the starboard side Capt. Gilkinson heard screams of men in agony coming from the liner's hulk.

THE BRAVE RESCUE.

He was astonished beyond measure, but could not be mistaken, and running up to the New Yorker told her Captain that there were men aboard, and asked him to drag along her side with his fire-proof vessel, but the firemen paid no heed, he says, and at considerable peril to his own boat he ran slowly alongside the Main, when suddenly from one of the dark coal ports he saw extended an arm waving a lighted engineer's oil torch. The Stevens ran her bow close to the porthole, and her crew crowded forward and tenderly helped the men through to safety.

Some were without any clothing and all had sacrificed the greater part of their clothing. One of them when rescued had but one shoe, and in a semi-delirium he insisted upon going back for the other, and almost fought with the tug's men when they restrained him. But the most of them threw themselves on the tug's deck, and fairly swallowed the fresh, cool air, and then from one and all came the cry, "Wasser, Wasser, ach Himmel, Wasser."

Capt. Gilkinson had just laid in a stock of fresh water. There was a barrel half full of it with a huge cake of ice floating in it, and the men used it nearly all. What they did not drink they poured over their blackened skins, and it seemed to the tug's crew that their flesh soaked it up like sponges. Some of them begged for stimulants, but there were none aboard.

Many lives had been saved by the Stevens during the day, and it was thought that that part of the work was over. She steamed rapidly down to Hoboken, and the men were sent to St. Mary's Hospital, where all but Mehl were found to be in a fit condition to care for themselves.

CAPT. MOLLER'S STORY.

Capt. Moller said last night:

"The Stevens arrived near the Main at about 11 o'clock, soon after she had been beached. My special object was to save as many lives as possible, and though it seemed impossible that any could have lived in the roaring flames that were consuming the whole inner part of the Main, I still hoped that some might be found alive aboard the vessel. It was a forlorn hope, and that there were really men there to be saved appeared half a miracle.

"As I came near the vessel, which was stil sending forth great flames from stem to stern, I heard cries for help and I soon saw the figure of a man at one of the open coal ports. Other boats were around the Main before mine and their crews probably heard the same cries for help and it is strange the men were not taken off sooner than they were. It was dangerous to go too close to the burning ship and maybe fear of injury kept the crews of the tugs away from the men.

ALL TAKEN OUT SAFELY.

"When the Stevens went alongside the upper part of the Main was still all aflame and the tug suffered slightly from the fire. We took aboard the man from the coal port after he had called to his companions to follow and they in turn were taken safely from the bunker where they had found their last resort. With one or possibly two exceptions none of the men was unable to climb up to the port. Only Carl Mehl, who had been half blinded, an older man than the others, had to be half carried up to the openings by some of the last of his companions to leave the empty coal bunker that a little later might have become their grave.

"It is a mystery how those men lived so long. Those who saw the Main burning at her dock surely never thought that beneath that awful fire there were still nearly a score of men who hung on to life. They were rescued just in time; they saw death very near them. The third engineer of the vessel, who was one of the fifteen, said, simply enough, as the tug moved away from the wreck of the Main, 'You got got us just in time; we would have been dead soon.'"

MAIN'S CAPTAIN'S TALE.

Capt. B. Petermann of the Main was about his vessel all day, but was able to do very little in the way of salvage. Capt. Petermann, in telling his story of the fire, said:

"I was sitting in my cabin when I smelled smoke, and ran up on deck. There it seemed as if the ship was walled in with fire. There was a great mountain of flame from the cotton on the pier, and on the other side of us were lighters loaded with cotton which was ablaze. I shouted to the first officer to cut the mooring hawsers, and ran up on the bridge to superintend the work of getting hold of any tug that might be near to give us a tow out.

"When I reached the bridge a blast of hot air knocked me down and stunned me. I got on my feet, but it looked as if I was in the centre of a white-hot furnace. The tide kept us jammed up against the pier, and I saw the vessel would never get out. I scrambled down the side on a rope on to a raft, and was taken away somehow.

"The swiftness of the flames was incredible to me. I can't understand it. It seemed as if the fire just tumbled over on us like a big sea of water, and I don't see how any of my men were able to get up from below. From what I can learn to-day nearly all did get up somehow, and most of those who were lost were drowned."

SAALE YIELDS TWELVE DEAD.

One Body Supposed to be that of Capt. Mirow—Many More Doubtless in the Hold.

The New York authorities took charge of the wreck of the Saale yesterday morning, and for nine hours searched for bodies, finding twelve, including one that is supposed to be that of Capt. Mirow. Of the 252 persons known to have been on board at the time of the fire, 128 remain unaccounted for. It is estimated that at least eighty bodies are still aboard the ill-fated ship. One survivor who was one of the last to be rescued but whose name was not learned, said that in an after compartment from which he escaped there were thirty-seven others besides himself. One body discovered yesterday consisted of fragments of a hip bone.

So fierce were the flames that many bodies must have been consumed without leaving a trace. In one place were found a plain gold ring, a suspender buckle, two keys, and the eighteen-inch blade of a hiltless cutlass, but not the least sign of flesh or bones. As most of the victims had their homes in Germany and as many others had no home excepting on the ship itself it is not expected that even by inquiry the number of missing will ever be definitely determined.

From 8 o'clock in the morning until 5 in the afternoon three divers of the Merritt & Chapman Derrick and Wrecking Company worked in the hold of the Saale. The work of removing the dead, it is now believed, cannot be completed until the hulk has been pumped out and raised.

SAALE'S SAD APPEARANCE.

When the sun rose yesterday morning over the scorched and battered wreck it revealed fully the horror of the night before. The steamship lay in thirty-five feet of water on the Jersey flats, off Ellis Island, where it had been beached the night before. During the night the wreck had settled deeper into the mud, until her upper deck astern was awash with the water at high tide. Her funnels and her masts were burned black. All the woodwork on her decks and upper works was gone. Her deck beams lay exposed, a tangled, twisted mass, and six inches of charred cinders lay strewn ankle deep over the iron plates that had formerly supported her deck, and the paint from her huge hull, once black, hung in sheets.

Capt. Elbert O. Smith of the harbor police at Pier A, who had been on duty until 2 o'clock yesterday morning trying on the specially chartered police boat Mutual to save the Saale's crew, again returned to his post at 6 o'clock. The crew of the Merritt & Chapman Company's derrick Champion had stood by the Saale all night. Roundsman Gilloon and Officer Reardon, who visited the wreck early, reported three bodies found, and those engaged in the work expected to recover shortly from fifty to eighty bodies.

Capt. Smith telephoned to the Morgue to send all available coffins to Pier A. Coroner Bausch soon arrived. Not being sure of their jurisdiction, considering that the wreckage was on the New Jersey side, the Coroner and Capt. Smith offered their services to the New Jersey authorities as a matter of assistance, which Chief Murphy of the Jersey City Police Department accepted. It was also decided to call upon the Department of Charities to send a steamer to take the bodies direct from the Saale to the Morgue.

Mr. Schott, agent of the North German Lloyd Line, and Capt. Moeller, Superintendent of the destroyed docks in Hoboken, landed at Pier A from a visit to the Saale about 1 o'clock. Mr. Schwab announced that from several articles found near one of the bodies, Capt. Moeller believed the body to be that of Capt. Mirow of the Saale.

The body was an unrecognizable mass of charred bones and flesh, evidently the trunk of a man, but from the remains of a pearl-handled penknife with a queer spring which was found next the body, and which the Saale's Captain was known to possess, Capt Moeller was quite sure of the identification. Besides the knife there was found near the body the metal back of a pocket hairbrush, several keys, the partly consumed cover of the ship's log, and a lump of metal, which may have been a gold watch chain melted by the heat of the burning steamship.

The articles were wrapped in a package and marked for identification by Coroner Bausch, who took charge of them.

Mr. Schwab said that the company intended to provide decent burial for all the fire victims and that he had already made arrangements with undertaker Hoffman of Hoboken to look after them.

DEATH LIST INCREASING

Greatest Loss of Life Was on the Steamship Saale.

ESTIMATES NOW REACH 361

This Number Includes Those Missing from the Company's Steamers, and Others Penned In on the Docks.

How many persons perished was the principal query in Hoboken yesterday. The financial loss incurred by the big fire which destroyed the piers of the North German Lloyd Line and wrecked three of its steamers was lost sight of in the eagerness of the people to find out whether or not their friends or relatives were among the victims.

The actual loss of life may not be known for weeks. Conservative estimates now place it at near the 361 mark. The greatest loss seems to have been on the Saale. Purser C. Rablen of that vessel made a careful canvass yesterday of all the men ashore. Later Mr. Schwab prepared this list:

Of the 255 men employed on the Saale, 127 have been accounted for, as follows: Deck department, which includes officers and men who are actually employed as sailors, 27; steward's department, 58, and engineer's department, 42.

Of the 204 men employed on the Bremen, 127 were accounted for, as follows: Deck department, 26; steward's department, 60, and engineer's department, 41.

Of the 137 employed on the Main, 76 were accounted for, as follows: Deck department, 26; steward's department, 19, and engineer's department, 31.

This makes the dead and missing as follows: Saale, 128; Bremen, 77; Main, 61.

In addition to this list of the crews of these vessels, the Hoboken police and Coroner have a list of forty-eight other people who were on the docks or aboard the vessels at the time of the fire who have not yet been accounted for, and the estimates of still others missing are not less than fifty. Unverified rumors place the missing among people who were not actually connected with the steamship line at from 100 to 200.

PATIENT IN HOSPITAL DIES.

Christian Bolghmann, thirty-eight years old, one of the crew of the Main, died at 6:30 yesterday morning in Christ Hospital, Jersey City. He had been badly burned about the face and body, and had inhaled the flame. There was no hope for him from the first, and he was mercifully kept under the influence of opiates to deaden the pain.

SURVIVORS TELL OF NARROW ESCAPES

Stirring Accounts of Rescues at Water Front Fire.

PRIEST ABSOLVES VICTIMS

Frenzied Men Fought Each Other for Places of Safety—Cash Burned in Company Offices.

The chief topic of conversation among visitors to the burned district in Hoboken yesterday as well as among survivors of the tragedy was the hairbreadth escapes and thrilling rescues of the previous day.

Among the many tales of heartbreaking sights is one told by Capt. William H. Cochran of the derrick, Champion.

"Just about as the Saale struck the mud when we tried to beach her, and while the ship was a cauldron of seething flame from stem to stern, the head of a man appeared at a port window in the after compartment. He tried desperately to get out of the window, but it was too small. His room was surrounded by flames and the mystery is the agony lasted so long.

"He called out things in German to us, but we could not understand it. We got as near as we dared and passed a deck hose to him to run water over himself and a bag to wrap up his head in. For an hour and a half the man shouted to us. Then he grew desperate and made a wild attempt to crawl through the window. He got partly through, but could get no further. He was in danger every instant of having his head crushed in by our own boat, and seeing this he tried to get back. Our master diver, Mr. Kelvin, helped him back. We all knew he was doomed, and we had to stand helplessly by and see him.

"I had my wife and little girl aboard at the time. I had invited them for a sail, not dreaming that we would be called out on such a mission before our return.

"For fully an hour after his attempt to get out of the window the man spoke with us. We even handed him coffee. Then, things were getting too hot for him. He called something in German and Captain Muller, who was with us, ordered him to wrap his head in the bag, to soak his clothes with water and to make a break for the deck. We have not seen him since."

"Would you be able to identify him if you saw his body?" some one asked.

"I'd know him if I saw him 500 years from now. My wife says she can't sleep and doesn't know how she ever will again. The moment she closes her eyes she sees that man."

One of the narrowest escapes was that of Superintendent Schmidtem of the Scandinavian-American Line. He was in his office at the extreme northern limits of the burned district, making out his pay roll. The first intimation he had of a fire was when the flames rolled right over the little wooden building. After a hard struggle he succeeded in breaking through the wall of fire and jumped on to a raft which was near the pier. From there he was rescued by a small boat. He had over $3,000 in cash in the office, which was totally destroyed by the fire.

Saturday was also pay day on the North German Lloyd pier, and a large amount of cash was in the office at the end of Pier 3, where the fire started. Of the amount $7,000 in gold was safely removed to the local Post Office.

FATHER BROSNAN ABSOLVES VICTIM

It was Father John Brosnan of the Mission of Our Lady of the Rosary, on State Street, who was seen by hundreds on the deck of a tug administering absolution to many of those who went down with the Saale.

Father Brosnan related the following story of his experience:

"It was about 9 o'clock, while I was walking along the Battery wall, that I saw the floating lighters burning as they came down the river. As I neared the pier of the fireboat New Yorker, I saw tugs bringing in the injured. They were laid on the floor of the firehouse, and many of them were unconscious. I sent at once to the mission and had the holy oils and breads sent over. The Church allows conditional absolution, and I did not stop to ascertain who was of our faith. I administered extreme unction to about thirty before they were carried to the hospitals. Then a fireman provided me with a rubber coat, and I went to the scene aboard the tug Mutual, with Capt. Roberts.

CONSOLATION TO THE DYING.

"We went first to the Saale. By the time we arrived at her side she was slowly sinking. I saw many heads and faces looking out of the portholes. They understood, many of them, and I praise God that He brought me there, for it did seem as though I had brought consolation to some of them. Death they knew was certain. They knew there was no hope of escape. They seemed resigned to die, and spent the last moments in praying with me.

"One man I saw looked out of the second porthole. He was ten feet away from those who could get nearest him. He was a young man apparently twenty-seven years of age. I spoke to him and blessed him, giving him absolution. He understood for he closed his eyes and bowed his head. I will never forget the look on that man's face. It was one of resignation, sublimity, and appeal. Back of him we could see the flames rolling and raging fircely. Perhaps the most horrible suffering next to his was to feel that you were so near him and could not aid him."

Father Brosnan is about thirty-five years of age. He is a native of Killarney, Ireland. He was educated in France and Rome, and has been in this country ten years.

IMPRISONED MEN BECOME FRENZIED

Frank Gatanzaro, one of the survivors who was taken to Bellevue and afterward discharged, was one of the men confined in the hold of the Saale.

"I was working in the hold," he said, "when I heard cries of fire from overhead. With the rest of the men I ran from room to room, but could not get out. I was at one of the portholes when the firemen put their hose through. I lay down in the water, and for a time managed to keep cool, but pretty soon the water got so hot that I could hardly stand it." Gatanzaro could not tell how he was rescued.

Carl Herkelhahn, who is still in Bellevue Hospital, said that when the cry of fire was raised, the men who were with him in the engine room of the Saale were thrown into a state of absolute frenzy. "The stronger ones," he said, "knocked down their weaker fellows and trampled upon them. Some of the latter were evidently suffocated by the smoke, while others sank under the water, which was waist high when I was rescued, and almost scalding hot."

EXPLOSION ON BREMEN.

Herman Lust, who is at St. Vincent's Hospital, said that just before the outbreak of the fire the deck of the Bremen, on which he was working, was crowded with people, there being at least 100 visitors aboard. In describing the scene, he said: "Right after the cry of fire there was a terrific explosion, which seemed to envelop the whole pier and ship with smoke and flames. Then there seemed to be an explosion on the Bremen, and the stern of the vessel gave a great lurch and sank in the water. I and several others were thrown in the water by the sudden movement. I had to dive and swim some distance under water to avoid going under in the struggling mass."

THE PROPERTY LOSSES.

The total property losses sustained in the conflagration aggregate, according to the most conservative revised estimates something in the neighborhood of $5,615,000. This loss is believed to be entirely covered by insurance, either by marine insurance companies, fire insurance companies, or the insurance fund maintained by the North German Lloyd Steamship Company.

From this figure there will be deductions for salvage which are not likely to cut down the losses to any material extent.

The revised estimates of losses are as follows:

Steamship Main of the North German Lloyd service, cost $1,500,000	$1,000,000
Cargo, fittings, and stores	200,000
Steamship Saale of the same service, cost $1,250,000	750,000
Cargo, fittings, and stores	350,000
Steamship Bremen of the same service, cost $1,250,000	800,000
Cargo, fittings, and stores	270,000
Steamship Kaiser Wilhelm der Grosse of the same service	20,000
Pier and property of the North German Lloyd Company on docks	250,000
Freight on the North German Lloyd docks	400,000
Property of the Scandinavian Line on docks	20,000
Property of the Hamburg-American Line on docks	10,000
Loss on twelve barges, fifteen canal-boats, and other craft and their cargoes	150,000
Loss on Campbell's Stores, E, F, G, and H buildings, owned by the Hoboken Land Improvement Company, Stevens estate	50,000
Loss on contents of stores, valued at $1,500,000	1,300,000
Loss on property of the Hoboken Shore Road, terminus, cars, &c.	10,000
Minor losses on floating property	35,000
Total	$5,615,000

"All the News That's Fit to Print."

The New York Times.

THE WEATHER.
Fair; light to fresh winds, mostly easterly.

COPYRIGHT, 1900, BY THE NEW YORK TIMES COMPANY.

VOL. XLIX...NO. 15,811. NEW YORK, TUESDAY, SEPTEMBER 11, 1900.—FOURTEEN PAGES ONE CENT In Greater New York and Jersey City. } Elsewhere, TWO CENTS.

STANCHFIELD IN THE LEAD

All Indications Are that He Will Be Democratic Nominee.

HILL WILL FIGHT FOR COLER

Refuses All Compromises and the Test of the Controller's Strength Will Be Made in the Convention.

Special to The New York Times.

SARATOGA, Sept. 10.—At midnight, with the first session of the Democratic State Convention but ten hours off, the Croker-Murphy-McLaughlin combine has positively agreed on only two of the candidates of the ticket which will be named by the Croker-Murphy-McLaughlin combine. Senator Hill and his friends are in a hopeless minority. They declare, however, that they will carry the banner of Controller Coler into the convention and wave it in the faces of the enemy until they are voted down.

John B. Stanchfield of Elmira is the candidate of the Croker-Murphy-McLaughlin combine for Governor. This declaration was made by Mr. Croker's closest advisers when he dismissed them to-night and retired to his cottage.

Even the Tammany men of undoubted loyalty here can scarcely believe that the convention will nominate Stanchfield, and they ask Mr. Croker and Mr. Murphy why he should be nominated. They get no satisfaction. That the name of Mr. Stanchfield was first taken up by the Croker-Murphy-McLaughlin combine for the purpose of taking away Mr. Hill's fighting ground—Mr. Stanchfield being the protégé and political pupil of Mr. Hill—there can be no doubt. The combine believed that Mr. Hill would have to submit if Stanchfield was put at the head of the ticket.

But Mr. Hill will not submit, and the combine now appears to have determined upon the nomination of Stanchfield simply because they have no other available candidate.

They talk of Judge Earl and they talk of Supreme Court Justice Barrett, but only to add that neither of them would accept the nomination; and so it now stands, Stanchfield for Governor.

The other candidate already agreed upon by the combine is Thomas F. Conway of Plattsburg, Clinton County, for Attorney General. He has been promised the place. At the same time George M. Palmer of Schoharie is advancing claims for the Attorney Generalship which may put him in over Mr. Conway.

Mr. Palmer's friends are even going so far as to urge him as a compromise candidate for Governor, who would be satisfactory to Senator Hill, but Senator Hill says no. If Senator Hill stands throughout as he stands to-night, he will stand for the nomination of Controller Coler until the end. He wants no compromises, will enter no conferences, even if invited to, and seems to be determined—to use a Western phrase—to die with his boots on.

It still looks as though Senator Mackey of Erie would be the candidate of the Croker-Murphy-McLaughlin combine for Lieutenant Governor. Mr. Mackey's friends are shouting that he will have first place or nothing; that he controls 102 votes, and can tie up the convention, but Croker, Murphy, McLaughlin and Company seem to be very well satisfied that Senator Mackey will consider himself very lucky to get the second place on the ticket and pay as the price the delivery of as many votes as he can control to them. They are probably right.

The rest of the slate cannot be predicted to-night with any more accuracy than it was in THE TIMES yesterday morning. The Croker-Murphy-McLaughlin combine are reserving decision in the nominations for minor officers on the ticket so that they will have something to barter with if they find to-morrow that the necessity for dealing confronts them. The situation is very tense.

The men who are bent on the complete humiliation of Hill are silently exulting in their strength. Mr. Hill, in the darkest hour of his political career, is determined and defiant. He has concluded that there is no use accepting crumbs from the hands of the men who would crush him, but that he can gain more by fighting them to the finish even in the face of certain defeat. That is what he says.

In carrying out their programme for the humiliation of Hill the Croker-Murphy-McLaughlin combine played a trump card to-night when they induced Elliot Danforth, supposedly the most loyal of Mr. Hill's supporters, to nominate Senator McCarren, Hill's bitter enemy, for temporary Chairman of the convention. Hill received the news of that action with a sneer, and the statement that it would have no bearing on the fight which he has to make.

It is very hard to compute as to the number of delegates which will be controlled by the Croker-Murphy-McLaughlin combine. It seems safe to say, however, that if they get the majority of the Mackey delegates they will control at least 300 of the 450 delegates.

The Croker-Murphy-McLaughlin leaders learned to-night that the Kings County delegate who would present the name of Controller Coler is Otto Kempner, a former Tammany Hall Assemblyman.

The Kings County politicians spent hours last evening trying to dissuade him from nominating Controller Coler. All efforts were unsuccessful. Mr. Kempner is the author of a book on Richard Croker's life, in which the Tammany leader is exposed as a corrupt politician. Mr. Kempner said last night:

"The book on Mr. Croker's life will be ice water to the speech to be delivered in the convention naming Controller Coler."

Orders were sent to the Tammany Hall orators to prepare for a "debate" on the convention floor. Senator Grady and others will take the Tammany side.

As predicted in THE TIMES yesterday the Albany County delegates, with the exception of Senator Hill, have been driven into the Croker-Murphy-McLaughlin camp by Eugene Wood, whom Mr. Croker recently branded as a "paid lobbyist."

MANOEUVRES OF THE LEADERS.

Hill's Plan to Fight It Out in the State Committee Abandoned—Plans to Name Coler.

Special to The New York Times.

SARATOGA, Sept. 10.—David B. Hill came to town in the dark of the night. His arrival at 1 A. M. was unexpected, and no political lieutenants met him at the hotel or station. Mr. Hill was assigned a suite of rooms in the Grand Union and far away from the cottage headquarters of Richard Croker.

Before 9 o'clock Mr. Hill was holding conferences with the leaders of various country delegations. State Chairman Frank Campbell and Elliot Danforth told him early of the plans of the Croker-Murphy-McLaughlin combine.

The plan to make Senator Patrick H. McCarren temporary Chairman of the convention aroused Mr. Hill's ire. To a friend he said:

"That is a nice way to start a Democratic convention. Mr. McCarren brought in a minority report to the State Legislature in favor of the Sugar Trust."

A Hill plan was at once formed. Political and oratorical batteries were to be unmasked against Senator McCarren and the Croker forces. Senator Hill thought the best method was to make a speech to the State committeemen charging Senator McCarren with being a favorite of the sugar trust, and unfit, therefore, to be called upon to make the opening speech in a convention which would have to adopt resolutions condemning trusts.

Senator McCarren was prepared to reply to the Hill charges. His defense was to be that the trust report written by him was prepared entirely on the evidence which had been brought out at the Lexow trust investigation. He claimed his report was not a defense of the trusts, but a statement that no facts against the trusts had been brought out by Senator Lexow and his colleagues.

HILL'S PROGRAMME CHANGED.

The Hill programme was changed in the afternoon. No reasons were given for the switch in the plan, but all idea of a fight in the State Committee was abandoned.

The Croker-Murphy headquarters was the Mecca of politicians. Richard Croker stood most of the day on the piazza talking to delegates and men who are seeking nominations.

"Sure, all the Hill delegates are jumping hurdles to get to Mr. Croker's cottage," said ex-Sheriff Dunn.

The friends of Senator Mackey from Buffalo and dozens of up-State leaders who for the last twenty years have been taking their orders from Mr. Hill at State Conventions were apparently flocking to the Croker standard. This did not mean that these leaders had forsaken Mr. Hill, but that they were playing shrewd politics and were trying to find out the true state of affairs.

The first startling news of the day was that State Chairman Frank Campbell of Steuben County had lost nearly all of his delegates, and that they had been induced by Tammany men to desert Hill. Mr. Campbell at first denied that he had been deserted by his friends, but late to-night he said:

"The delegates were elected some time before we thought that there would be a fight. Some of my friends may have been induced to desert me."

It was said by the Croker-Murphy leaders that Frank Campbell's would be the only vote in the Steuben County delegation of six which would be cast for Hill in the State Convention.

The inroads into the Monroe County delegation caused Mr. Hill uneasiness. Before noon, however, the sage of Wolfert's Roost had mended the broken fence in this delegation, and said that nine of the twelve delegates would vote with him in the convention.

COLER WILL BE ABSENT.

News which caused a small sensation in the Croker-Murphy camp was the reported arrival in town of Controller Coler.

A cottage had been hired at the United States Hotel, and it was said that Mr. Coler intended to conduct his own campaign and see that his name was presented to the convention. Instead of Controller Coler, Private Secretary Baker arrived with messages. Mr. Coler's decision not to come was said to be based on the advice of Mr. Hill.

The first message was to Assistant District Attorney Littleton of Kings County. He was selected to make the speech nominating Controller Coler. He is from the South, and has the reputation of being an orator of the fire-eating variety who could outdo Senator Grady of Tammany Hall.

"I know nothing about the matter," said Mr. Littleton when asked by a TIMES reporter. "I am not a delegate to the convention, and so far as I know will not be on the floor, as I am only an alternate from my district."

After Secretary Baker and Mr. Littleton had conferred for some time it was said that a decision would be reached whether Kings County would present the name of Controller Coler to-morrow morning.

The plan of Controller Coler's friends was to have Julius Kaufman, a delegate from Coler's home district, in Brooklyn, give way to Mr. Littleton. James Shevlin was confident that the plan would not work and that no one from Kings County would either name or second Coler's nomination.

Augustus Van Wyck, Bridge Commissioner Shea, and Julius Kaufman are the delegates from Mr. Coler's district. The friends of Controller Coler were charging yesterday that Bridge Commissioner Shea, who has for years been Mr. Coler's intimate friend, had decided to cast his lot with the McLaughlin organization.

TAMMANY ON DECK.

The Tammany hosts began to arrive shortly after 2 o'clock. The first section was headed by a brass band and ex-Sheriff Dunn, and there were 300 delegates and their friends.

Then the Keahon cohorts from the Seventh District came up 300 strong. The new district leader headed the procession. On the lapel of each coat was a gorgeous badge with the picture of Patrick H. Keahon. The deposed leader of the district, Bridge Commissioner Boyle, watched the triumph of his enemy from the balcony of the Grand Union Hotel.

From Buffalo there came a crowd of men bearing flags. Desultory cheers were given for Senator William F. Mackey, Erie County's candidate for Governor. The Mackey men were adorned with Mackey buttons, Mackey signs, and Mackey flags.

The Tammany delegations did not cheer, because they had no one to cheer for. At 6 o'clock the State leaders found that some one had been overlooked in the bitter struggle for control between David B. Hill and Richard Croker.

The forgotten one was William J. Bryan. Hardly a Bryan button was to be seen. There was no talk of Mr. Bryan, and there were no Bryan badges waving in the breeze. This oversight was partly repaired by swinging a small banner in front of the Grand Union Hotel with poor paintings of Bryan and Stevenson on it.

MR. HILL'S PLANK SUGGESTIONS.

On the question of platform, the leaders seemed to be just about as much in the air all day as they were on the question of candidates. All sorts of planks were suggested, just as all sorts of slate combinations were made. Senator Grady denies that he is drawing the platform, but the fact remains that he sat up nearly all of last night working on it.

Although Senator Hill did not come here with a platform in his pocket, he did come here with some very well-defined planks in his mind. Expressing some platform ideas to a friend, he said that the only disappointment he would experience through not being permitted to draft the platform would be in the fact that he would not be able to incorporate three planks which had suggested themselves to him. Asked what they were, he replied with a laugh:

"A plank providing for the changing of the ratio every four years, according to the notions of Mr. Croker on the currency question, a strong anti-ice trust plank, and an unequivocal anti-Ramapo plank."

HARMONY IN STATE COMMITTEE

Danforth Springs a Surprise by Nominating McCarren for Temporary Chairman—Hill Absent.

Special to The New York Times.

SARATOGA, Sept. 10.—The meeting of the State Committee, which was called for 8 o'clock, sent the delegates trooping toward the ballroom of the Grand Union Hotel. The general impression seemed to prevail that there was going to be a merry war there between Mr. Croker and Mr. Hill. The news had not been generally disseminated that Mr. Hill had decided that it would be impossible for him to go into the State Committee on a proxy and raise a fighting issue which would result in his certain defeat and accomplish no purpose that he will not be able to accomplish more fully on the convention floor.

The meeting was opened, and the big ballroom was crowded with all sorts of Tammany men. Everybody was talking and smoking, even while the meeting was in progress. The meeting was almost a perfunctory affair, run on lines agreed upon by the bosses during the afternoon. The roll was called, the contests noted, and the routine business transacted.

When it came to the matter of naming a temporary Chairman of the convention—it being well understood that he was to be Patrick H. McCarren—Elliot Danforth, supposed to be Mr. Hill's stanchest adherent, got up and moved the nomination of Mr. McCarren. There was no other candidate, and Senator McCarren was unanimously agreed upon. Why Mr. Danforth, who at the previous meeting of the State Committee had at Hill's bidding presented the name of Mayor McGuire of Syracuse for temporary Chairman, should here move the nomination of Senator McCarren, was something that nobody seemed to understand, except Mr. Croker and other big bosses, and their faces expressed no surprise. Everybody was asking whether even Danforth had been won over by the Croker-Murphy-McLaughlin combination. Mr. Danforth was asked what he meant by making the nomination, and his reply was:

DANFORTH GIVES HIS REASONS.

"Well, somebody had to make it."

"But are you bidding for harmony with the enemy?" was asked.

"Oh, I'm a harmonizer, you know," he said.

"But have you deserted Senator Hill and the standard of Controller Coler?" was asked.

"Oh, no, no," he said. "You'll find me on the convention floor where I have been all along, for Mr. Coler for Governor."

Senator Hill is either one of the best actors in the world or else he was most genuinely surprised and disgusted when he was informed that Mr. Danforth had put in nomination the name of Senator McCarren for temporary Chairman.

"Why didn't he let them make the nomination?" he said, with a show of anger. "Why should he put McCarren in nomination for them? Why did he do it? Oh, I suppose they asked him to. Do I think he did it purely out of good-nature? I don't know. I will have to find out about it."

It was the common talk around the Grand Union Hotel after the meeting that the true reason for Mr. Danforth's action was that both he and State Chairman Campbell had been reached by the Croker-Murphy-McLaughlin combine. This rumor may have done them an injustice, but the fact remains that they were seeking conferences with the leaders of the enemy throughout the day. They even went to Mr. Hill for advice as to what should be done in the event of Mr. Hill's being sent for to confer with the Croker-Murphy-McLaughlin faction, and they seemed a bit perturbed when Mr. Hill replied that that was a contingency which need not be dealt with, as he would not be drawn into any conference under existing conditions.

CROKER AS AN ALTERNATE.

The State Committee adjourned to meet at 6 o'clock to-morrow night, which shows clearly that the Croker-Murphy-McLaughlin forces are not yet in a position to close their dealings and transact the business of the convention. They still hope to bring a pressure to bear upon Mr. Hill's friends which will make them bring Mr. Hill to terms. They do not want a fight on the convention floor.

Richard Croker attended the meeting of the State Committee as a proxy for "Larry" Delmour.

"If you don't mind, I will go to the meeting of the State Committee in your place," said Croker to Delmour.

"I think I can trust you to do the right thing," said Delmour, with mock dignity.

"All right, I won't betray you," said Croker with a laugh.

START FOR THE CONVENTION.

About 1,500 Tammany Men and the Kings County Delegation Leave for Saratoga.

About 1,500 Tammany Hall men started on three special trains yesterday morning for Saratoga to attend the Democratic State Convention. Every Assembly district in the county, with the exception of the Sixth and the Eighth, was represented. The Tammany men in these two districts attended the outing of the Timothy D. Sullivan Association and did not leave for Saratoga until last night.

The first section left the Grand Central Station about 9 o'clock, in chare of State Senator George W. Plunkitt. Among those on this train were John F. Carroll, the deputy leader of Tammany Hall; James J. Martin, Daniel F. McMahon, Police Commissioner John B. Sexton, Thomas F. McAvoy, Matthew F. Donahue, Commissioner of Corrections Francis J. Lantry, George F. Scannell, and State Senator Maurice Featherson.

The second section left the Grand Central Station at 9:20 o'clock, and was in charge of Commissioner James P. Keating. With him were Dock Commissioner Charles F. Murphy, Isaac A. Hopper, President Michael C. Murphy of the Department of Health, Patrick Divver, Coroner Edward T. Fitzpatrick, City Clerk P. J. Scully, Councilman John T. Oakley, City Chamberlain Patrick Keenan, Assemblyman Julius Harburger, Maurice F. Holahan, and John J. Ryan.

The third section, in charge of State Senator Bernard F. Martin, left at 10 o'clock. Among the leaders on this train were Patrick Keahon, who recently defeated Dock Commissioner Boyle for the leadership in the Seventh District; P. J. Ryder, Frank J. Goodwin, who deposed John C. Sheehan from the Ninth District leadership; William Dalton, Peter J. Dooling, Nicholas J. Hayes, President Louis F. Haffen of the Borough of the Bronx, Thomas H. O'Neill, Park Commissioner August Moebus, and Street Cleaning Commissioner Percival E. Nagle.

Care had been take to have the cars well stocked with refreshments, and there was no need for any of the warriors to suffer from hunger or thirst on the trip to the Springs.

The Kings County delegation, in charge of Secretary Patrick H. Keely, left on a special train at 2 o'clock.

COLER TO YOUNG MEN.

Intimates that He Cannot Be Driven Out of Politics.

Controller Coler gave an informal address last night before the Epiphany Club of the Church of the Epiphany, at McDonough Street and Tompkins Avenue, Brooklyn. Mr. Coler's subject was "The Christian and Citizenship." He spoke for a few minutes only, his address being largely devoted to explaining in a general way municipal affairs.

Only once did Mr. Coler make any reference to politics, and that was when he told the young men that they had no right to call themselves American citizens unless they attended the primaries and assisted in the promotion of good citizenship. He said he got into politics in that way, and he intended to remain in because an effort was being made to drive him out.

SERVES WARNING ON CROKER.

Chicago Platform Democracy Against Stanchfield and Machine Men.

James R. Brown, Chairman of the Executive Committee of the Chicago Platform Democracy, declared yesterday that his organization would not support the candidate of the Saratoga Convention for Governor if he should be a man identified with the machine. He added:

"The Chicago Platform Democracy will not support a candidate for Governor whose course in the campaign of 1896 will have to be explained. The Democrats of New York State demand the nomination of a man who is thoroughly honest, one who supported Mr. Bryan four years ago, and one who is not so closely identified with the organization as to be known as a machine man. If the Democrats at Saratoga nominate an objectionable man the Chicago Platform Democracy will place an independent candidate in the field. We have enough votes to spoil any plot the Croker-Murphy combination may hatch."

Mr. Brown added that his organization would not support John B. Stanchfield.

"In the first place," said he, "Mr. Stanchfield is a machine man; then his attitude in 1896 would have to be explained. Besides, he is a corporation lawyer and identified with corporations in other respects."

Mr. Brown said that the Chicago Platform Democracy would support either Con-

Continued on Page 2.

For Nervous Women
Horsford's Acid Phosphate.
Dr. J. B. Alexander, Charlotte, N. C., says: "It is pleasant to the taste, and ranks among the best of nerve tonics for nervous females."—Adv.

MAINE GOES REPUBLICAN

Plurality Over the Democratic Candidates of More than 33,000.

FOUR CONGRESSMEN ELECTED

Prohibitionists Elect Their Candidate for Sheriff in Portland—Congratulations to Mr. Hanna.

PORTLAND, Me., Sept. 10.—The Republican voters elected their State ticket to-day by a plurality over the Democratic candidates of more than 33,000.

The vote was almost as large as four years ago, and the returns up to 11:30 P. M., compared with 1896, showed Republican losses of about 10 per cent., or a Democratic gain of about 18 per cent.

The result must be in a great measure gratifying to both parties. To the Republicans because they polled almost as large a vote as in 1896, and to the Democrats because of the heavy gains over that year.

While thousands of voters who, in 1896, deserted the Democratic ranks, returned to the fold to-day, yet the Republicans were able to make good most of the loss.

The Republican State ticket was elected with all four Congressmen, and a great majority of the Legislature.

There was every incentive for voting. The campaign had been a spirited one, but the vote was not quite as heavy as in 1896, but exceeded that of the 1898 election by many thousands, and the managers of both parties, when the returns from different towns came in, felt that they were fully repaid for their strenuous efforts of the past four weeks.

The Democrats gained considerable satisfaction from the earlier returns, showing, as they did, a gain in four years of from 18 to 20 per cent. This increase over the 1896 vote did not apply to any particular locality, but seemed to be general throughout the State.

The Republicans, however, had rather discounted the falling off in the vote for the Maine ticket from that in 1896, and the managers were not at all surprised at an apparent loss of 12 per cent. which was shown by the returns from the first 150 towns.

Their entire ticket, headed by John F. Hill of Augusta for Governor, was, of course, elected, as were all four of the Congressmen, Allen in the First, (Reed's old district,) Littlefield in the Second, (Dingley's old district,) Burleigh in the Third, and Boutelle in the Fourth.

The campaign throughout the State, except perhaps in Cumberland County, was fought entirely on National issues. In Cumberland County, with Portland as a centre, there was fought one of the most interesting contests in the State.

This was solely on the liquor law, its enforcement or its non-enforcement, the Republican representing the latter and a Prohibition candidate the former issue. The fight was a bitter one.

Returns up to 10 o'clock to-night indicated that the Prohibitionists had landed their candidate for Sheriff, Samuel F. Pearson of this city.

As to the Legislature, there were but few Democratic gains. This body will meet in January and re-elect William P. Frye to the National Senate.

AUGUSTA, Me., Sept. 10.—J. H. Manley, Chairman of the Republican State Committee, sent the following dispatch to Senator Hanna late this evening:

Augusta, Me., Sept. 10, 1900.

Hon. M. A. Hanna, Chairman Republican National Committee, Chicago, Ill.:

Maine stands by the splendid Administration of William McKinley. The voters of the Pine Tree State know when they possess a good thing and are determined to retain it. They believe in an honest currency, in protection, in expansion, and in prosperity.

They have given to-day the largest Republican majority ever given in the history of the State to any party with the single exception of four years ago, when our opponents were completely paralyzed and threw the smallest vote they ever cast in a Presidential year since 1840.

The Republicans, against a determined and united Democracy, have carried to-day every county save one in the State, electing more than 150 out of 181 members of the Legislature, which will return to the United States Senate the Hon. William P. Frye. We have re-elected our delegation to Congress by majorities ranging from 7,000 to 10,000. We have carried the State by 31,000 majority out of a total vote of 115,000.

J. H. MANLEY,
Chairman Republican State Committee.

DEMOCRATIC CHAIRMAN'S VIEWS.

BATH, Me., Sept. 10.—W. E. Hughes, Chairman of the Democratic State Committee, gave out the following to-night:

"The returns received up to this hour indicate a material reduction of the majority of 48,000 given the Republican Governor in 1896. They further show a repudiation of the policy of the present National Administration, and a close analysis of the vote shows that the defections from the Republican Party is confined to no particular locality, but is throughout the State at large. Based upon the meagre returns at hand, the majority of 1896 will be reduced below the predictions of the most conservative Republican managers and is highly satisfactory to the Democratic Party of Maine, which has worked faithfully and well against the largest corruption fund ever used in this State."

PHAETON SHAFT KILLS HORSE.

Special to The New York Times.

HEMPSTEAD, L. I., Sept. 10.—Miss C. Dunlap, the governess in the family of H. Van Rensselaer Kennedy, to-day met with an exciting experience. In company with a coachman, Miss Dunlap was driving a spirited thoroughbred attached to a basket phaeton.

While turning the corner of Greenwich and Front Streets the horse came into collision with a hunter owned by Josiah Newman of New York, which was being ridden by the latter's coachman. The force of the collision was so severe that Miss Dunlap was thrown violently against the wheels of the phaeton, but was not badly hurt. The shaft of the carriage was forced several inches into the flank of Mr. Newman's horse and was broken short off. The injured horse died.

BOUGHT A MADE-OVER HORSE.

Special to The New York Times.

HEMPSTEAD, L. I., Sept. 10.—John Doty of this place, who is known as a shrewd horse dealer, was the victim lately of a sharp trick. Some time ago Mr. Doty came into possession of a fine-looking young horse, but it was averse to all profitable labor. Mr. Doty eventually found a purchaser in John Reidel, a baker, who immediately hitched his new acquisition to the delivery wagon. The price paid was $20.

Mr. Reidel soon discovered the animal's weakness. After much cogitation he decided upon a scheme. Placing the horse in his barn, he commenced a system of nerve-racking stunts, which, after a few weeks, transformed the lazy beast into an animal of much spirit and nervousness. After this he carefully docked the steed's mane and tail, clipped his coat, and, through the hands of an agent, succeeded in unloading his property on the unsuspecting Doty for the sum of $135.

Sun and Matches Start a Fire.

Special to The New York Times.

CHICAGO, Sept. 10.—Matches, carelessly left on a windowsill, were ignited by the heat of the sun yesterday and caused a $500 fire. The fire was in the residence of Ambrose Johnston, 6,350 Chauncey Avenue.

The flames from the exploding matches were communicated to the lace curtains of the window, and thence to the interior of the house.

The New York Central Is First.
"No railroad company in Great Britain has so many miles of railroad protected by the lock and block system as the New York Central."—Extract from address of Mr. John P. O'Donnell, the English expert on block signals, before the American Society of Civil Engineers.—Adv.

NUMBER OF DEAD MAY REACH 10,000

Extent of Texas Disaster Not Realized at First.

MANY SWEPT OUT TO SEA

Victims Along Coast May Outnumber Those in Galveston.

Hundreds of Bodies Already Found Outside of the Wrecked City—Appalling Damage to Property.

DALLAS, Texas, Sept. 10.—From the latest reports which are considered reliable the disaster at Galveston and along the coast has not been exaggerated. The waters of the Gulf and bay met, covering the island to a depth of from six to twelve feet. During this sudden flood a most terrible storm was raging, the wind blowing at about eighty miles an hour.

Many of the dead have been uncovered. Others are still under the débris; others carried out to sea.

It is not possible to give, at this time, a definite report as to the number of deaths. From estimates made by reliable persons who have just come from Galveston it is believed that not less than 1,500, and possibly as many as 5,000 people, were destroyed there.

From Virginia Point north and south along the bay front, at such places as Texas City, Dickinson, Hitchcock, Seabrook, Alvin, and a dozen small intermediate points, the number of dead bodies gathered up by rescue trains and sailing craft had reached at noon to-day more than 700. This is only a small scope of the country devastated.

Hundreds have been swept out to sea and will never be accounted for.

Houston and Texas Central Railroad officials at noon received bulletins from their general officer in Houston that the loss of life will reach 3,000 in Galveston.

The Missouri, Kansas, and Texas relief forces near Galveston and along the coast telegraphed at noon that the loss of life will not be less than 5,000, and may reach 10,000.

THE WRECKING OF GALVESTON.

Story Told in Detail by a Newspaper Man Who Escaped—People Caught Like Rats in Traps.

HOUSTON, Texas, Sept. 10.—Richard Spillane, a well-known Galveston newspaper man, who reached Houston to-day after a terrible experience, gives the following account of the disaster at Galveston:

"One of the most awful tragedies of modern times has visited Galveston. The city is in ruins, and the dead will number probably 1,000. I am just from the city, having been commissioned by the Mayor and Citizens' Committee to get in touch with the outside world and appeal for help. Houston was the nearest point at which working telegraph instruments could be found, the wires as well as nearly all the buildings between here and the Gulf of Mexico being wrecked.

"When I left Galveston shortly before noon yesterday the people were organizing for the prompt burial of the dead, distribution of food, and all necessary work after a period of disaster.

"The wreck of Galveston was brought about by a tempest so terrible that no words can adequately describe its intensity, and by a flood which turned the city into a raging sea. The Weather Bureau records show that the wind attained a velocity of eighty-four miles an hour when the measuring instrument blew away, so it is impossible to tell what was the maximum.

"The storm began at 2 o'clock Saturday morning. Previous to that a great storm had been raging in the Gulf and the tide was very high. The wind at first came from the north, and was in direct opposition to the force from the Gulf. While the storm in the Gulf piled the water up on the beach side of the city the north wind piled the water from the bay on to the bay part of the city.

"About noon it became evident that the city was going to be visited with disaster. Hundreds of residences along the beach front were hurriedly abandoned, the families fleeing to dwellings in higher portions of the city. Every home was opened to the refugees, black or white. The winds were rising constantly, and it rained in torrents. The wind was so fierce that the rain cut like a knife.

"By 3 o'clock the waters of the bay and Gulf met, and by dark the entire city was submerged. The flooding of the electric-light plant and the gas plants left the city in darkness. To go upon the streets was to court death. The wind was then at cyclonic velocity, roofs, cisterns, portions of buildings, telegraph poles, and walls were falling, and the noise of the wind and the crashing of the buildings was terrifying in the extreme. The wind and waters rose steadily from dark until 1:45 o'clock Sunday morning.

"During all this time the people of Galveston were like rats in traps. The highest portion of the city was four to five feet under water, while in the great majority of cases the streets were submerged to a depth or ten feet. To leave a house was to drown. To remain was to court death in the wreckage. Such a night of agony has seldom equaled.

"Without apparent reason the waters suddenly began to subside at 1:45 A. M. Within twenty minutes they had gone down two feet, and before daylight the streets were practically freed of the flood waters. In the meantime the wind had veered to the southeast.

"Very few, if any, buildings escaped injury. There is hardly a habitable, dry house in the city. When the people who had escaped death went out at daylight to view the work of the tempest and the floods they saw the most horrible sights imaginable. In the three blocks from Avenue N to Avenue P, in Tremont Street, I saw eight bodies. Four corpses were in one yard.

"The whole of the business front for three blocks in from the Gulf was stripped of every vestige of habitation, the dwellings, the great bathing establishments, the Olympia, and every structure having been either carried out to sea or its ruins piled in a pyramid far into the town, according to the vagaries of the tempest.

"The first hurried glance over the city showed that the largest structures, supposed to be the most substantially built, suffered the greatest.

"The Orphan Asylum, Twenty-first Street and Avenue M, fell like a house of cards. How many dead children and refugees are in the ruins could not be ascertained.

"Of the sick in St. Mary's Infirmary, together with the attendants, only eight are understood to have been saved.

"The Old Women's Home in Rosenberg Avenue, collapsed, and the Rosenberg schoolhouse is a mass of wreckage. The Ball High School is but an empty shell, crushed and broken. Every church in the city, with possibly one or two exceptions, is in ruins.

"At the forts nearly all the soldiers are reported dead, they having been in temporary quarters which gave them no protection against the tempest or the flood.

"No report has been received from the Catholic Orphan Asylum down the island, but it seems impossible that it could have withstood the hurricane. If it fell, all the inmates were no doubt lost, for there was no aid within a mile.

"The bay front, from end to end, is in ruins. Nothing but piling and the wrecks of great warehouses remain. The elevators lost all their superworks, and their stocks are damaged by water.

"The life-saving station at Fort Point was carried away, the crew being swept across the bay fourteen miles to Texas City.

"I saw Capt. Haines yesterday, and he told me that his wife and one of his crew were drowned.

"The shore at Texas City contains enough wreckage to rebuild a city. Eight persons who were swept across the bay during the storm were picked up there alive. Five corpses were also picked up. There were three fatalities in Texas City.

"In addition to the living and the dead which the storm cast up at Texas City, coffins from one of the cemeteries at Galveston were being fished out of the water there yesterday.

"In the business portion of the city, two large brick buildings, one occupied by Knapp Brothers, and the other by the Cotton Exchange Saloon, collapsed. In the Cotton Exchange Saloon there were about fifteen persons. Most of them escaped.

"Up to the time I left Galveston three dead had been taken from the ruins. They were Stanley G. Spencer, manager of the Elder-Dempster Steamship Company; Richard Lord, traffic manager for George H. McFadden & Brother, and Charles Kelder of the firm of Lammers & Flint.

"How many more corpses there are will not be known until the search is finished.

"The cotton mills, the bagging factory, the gas works, the electric light works, and nearly all the industrial establishments of the city are either wrecked or crippled. The flood left a slime about one inch deep over the whole city, and unless fast progress is made in burying corpses and the carcasses of animals there is danger of pestilence.

EXTRAORDINARY ESCAPES.

"Some of the stories of escapes are miraculous. William Nisbett, a cotton man, was buried in the ruins of the Cotton Exchange Saloon and when dug out in the morning had no further injury than a few bruised fingers.

"Dr. S. O. Young, Secretary of the Cotton Exchange, was knocked senseless when his house collapsed, but was revived by the water and was carried ten blocks by the hurricane.

"A woman who had just given birth to a child was carried from her home to a house a block distant, the men who were carrying her having to hold her high above their heads, as the water was five feet deep when she was moved.

"Many stories were current of houses falling and inmates escaping. Clarence N. Ousley, editor of The Evening Tribune, had his family and the families of two neighbors in his house when the lower half crumbled and the upper part slipped down into the water. Not one in the house was hurt.

"Of the Lavine family, six out of seven are reported dead. Of the Burnett family, only one is known to have been saved. The family of Stanley G. Spencer, who met death in the Cotton Exchange Saloon, are reported to be dead.

"The Mistrot House, in the West End, was turned into a hospital. All of the regular hospitals of the city were unavailable.

"Of the new Southern Pacific works little remains but the piling. Half a million feet of lumber was carried away, and Engineer Feschke says, as far as the company is concerned, it might as well start over again.

"Eight ocean steamers were torn from their moorings and stranded in the bay. The Kendal Castle was carried over the flats to Texas City, and lies in the wreckage of the Inman Pier. The Norwegian steamer Gyller is stranded between Texas City and Virginia Point. An ocean liner was swirled around through the West Bay, crushed through the bay bridges, and is now lying in a few feet of water near the wreckage of the railroad bridges. The steamship Taunton was carried across Pelican Point, and is stranded about ten miles up the East Bay. The Mallory steamer Alamo was torn from her wharf and dashed upon Pelican Flats and against the bow of the British steamer Red Cross, which had previously been hurled there. The stern of the Alamo is stove in and the bow of the Red Cross is crushed.

"Down the channel to the jetties two other ocean steamships lie grounded. Some schooners, barges, and smaller craft are strewn bottom side up along the slips of the piers. The tug Louise of the Houston Direct Navigation Company is a wreck.

HALF THE PEOPLE PAUPERIZED.

"It will take a week to tabulate the dead and missing and to get anything near an approximate idea of the monetary loss. It is safe to assume that one-half of the property of the city is wiped out, and that one-half of the residents have to face absolute poverty.

"At Texas City, three of the residents were drowned. One man stepped into a well by a mischance, and his corpse was found there. Two other men ventured along the bay front during the height of the storm and were killed.

"There are but few buildings at Texas City that do not tell the story of the storm. The hotel is a complete ruin. The office of the Texas City Company was almost entirely destroyed. Nothing remains of the piers except the piling. The wreckage from Galveston litters the shore for miles and is a hundred yards or more wide.

"For ten miles inland from the shore it is a common sight to see small craft, such as steam launches, schooners, and oyster sloops. The lifeboat of the life-saving station was carried half a mile inland, while a vessel that was anchored in Moses Bayou lies high and dry five miles up from Lamarque."

The Galveston News asked to have it announced that all the men of its staff are safe.

THE WORK OF RESCUE.

Awful Scenes Witnessed by a Party Formed as Soon as Movement in the City Was Possible.

GALVESTON, Texas, Sept. 10.—Starting as soon as the water began to recede, the work of rescuing the wounded and dying from the ruins of their homes began.

Screaming women, bruised and bleeding, some of them bearing the lifeless forms of children in their arms; men broken-hearted and sobbing, bewailing the loss of their wives and children; streets filled with floating rubbish, among which there were many bodies of the victims of the storm, constituted part of the scene.

The first loss of life reported was that at Rietter's saloon in the Strand, where three persons lost their lives, and where many others were maimed and imprisoned. The dead were Stanley G. Spencer, Charles Kellner, and Richard Lord. These three were sitting at a table on the first floor, when suddenly the roof caved in, killing all of them instantly. Those in the lower part of the building escaped with their lives in a miraculous manner. The falling roof and flooring were caught on the bar, the people standing near it dodging under the débris. It required several hours of hard work to get them out. The negro waiter who was sent for the doctor was drowned at the corner of the Strand and Twenty-first Street and his body was found a short time after.

The next place visited by the rescuers was the City Hall. Here were congregated fully 700 people, most of whom were more or less injured. One man from Lucas Terrace reported the loss of fifty lives in the building from which he escaped. He himself was severely injured about the head.

In Avenue M several women were imprisoned in a residence by the water and débris. They were rescued by a party headed by Capt. Theriot. Several of them were badly hurt.

Coming back to Tremont Street and going out to Avenue P by climbing over the piles of lumber which had once been residences, the rescuing party observed four bodies in one yard and seven in one room in another place, while as many as sixty bodies were to be seen lying singly and in groups in the space of one block.

The majority of the bodies have not been recovered. They are under the ruined houses, and it will take several days' hard work to get all of them out.

The body of Miss Sarah Summers was found near her home, at the corner of Tremont Street and Avenue F, her hands grasping her diamonds tightly.

INMATES OF HOSPITAL KILLED.

The report from St. Mary's Infirmary shows that only eight persons escaped from the hospital. The number of patients and nurses could not be ascertained, but the number of inmates was seldom under a hundred.

Rosenberg Schoolhouse, which was chosen as a place of refuge by the people of that locality, collapsed. Some of those who had taken refuge there escaped, but many were crushed to death in the ruins.

As Sunday morning dawned the streets were lined with wounded, half-clad people, seeking the aid of physicians for themselves and for friends and relatives who could not move. Police Officer John Bowie was found in a pitiable condition, the toes of both of his feet and two ribs broken, and his head bruised. He reported that his house, with his wife and children, had been swept into the gulf.

The beach resort of Pat O'Keefe, who is known to every visitor to Galveston, was annihilated, not a vestige of the building remaining. Mrs. O'Keefe was drowned.

The great bathing pavilion known as the Pagoda, the big pleasure resort known as the Olympia, and Murdoch's bath house are all swept away into the gulf. There were few bodies on the beach. They had been swept into the gulf or driven up into the rubbish by the waves. Only half a dozen of them were in sight from the point where the workers were.

All the residences which have escaped destruction have been turned into hospitals, as have the leading hotels. There is scarcely one of the houses which are left standing which does not contain one or more of the dead, as well as many injured.

The rain began to pour down in torrents, and the rescuing party went back down Tremont Street toward the city. The rain added greatly to the general distress. Stopping at a small grocery store, the party found it packed with injured, clamoring for food, but the provisions in the store had been ruined. Further down the street a restaurant, which had been submerged by water, was serving out soup

California Excursions.
Daily excursions in Tourist Cars. Personally conducted every Thursday. Chicago, Union Pacific and Northwestern Line. Two fast trains daily from Chicago at 6:30 P. M. and 10:30 P. M. No change of cars. Tickets and information at Chicago and Northwestern Office, 461 Broadway.—Adv.

crackers and cheese to the hungry crowd.

On returning to the Tremont Hotel the death list was found to be swelling rapidly, the accounts coming from every portion of the city. Information from both the extreme eastern and extreme western portions of the city was difficult to obtain, but the reports which were received indicated that those two sections had suffered fully as much as the rest of the city.

Fifteen men, constituting all that remained of a company of regular soldiers stationed at the beach barracks, were marched down Market Street. The loss of life among the soldiers in the barracks, which were destroyed, must have been fully a hundred.

At 11:30 o'clock on Sunday morning the water had receded from the higher portions of the city, but the streets near the bay front still contained from two and one-half to three feet of water.

The Galveston News office, in Mechanic Street, was flooded, and the back end of the building caved in. At the Union Station were scenes similar to those met with in other portions of the city. Baggage Master Harding picked up the lifeless form of a baby girl within a few feet of the station. Its parents could not be located, and are supposed to have been lost. The station building had been selected as a place of refuge by a large number of people. All the windows of the building and a portion of the wall at the top were blown in. The water around the station was probably twelve feet deep.

On the water front the destruction of property was almost as great as on the beach, though the loss of life was not nearly so large. The wharves of the Mallory Company were completely destroyed.

MANY VESSELS STRANDED.

The big steamship Alamo is lying among the ruins of the piers. The wharves of the Galveston Wharf Company are also gone, and the great wharves of the Southern Pacific Company, which have been in course of construction for several months, are damaged to the amount of $60,000.

The Norwegian steamship Gyller, engaged in the Cuban trade, was stranded up the bay beyond where the railroad bridges once stood.

The British steamship Taunton is lying on Pelican Island hard aground. The Mexican, a big British steamer, was driven up the bay and is fast in the mud. Another big ship is lying out near the quarantine station. The Kendal Castle was driven as far up as Texas City, where she is now stranded.

Of the small shipping only a few boats are left. Many of the little schooners were lifted bodily out of the water and flung up on the island. The wrecks of others are scattered along the bay front. The Charlotte M. Allen, the steam ferryboat to Bolivar, is safe. The big dredge used at Texas City was driven inland for half a mile and cannot be saved.

The Pensacola was in port when the storm began, but Capt. Simmons put to sea in the teeth of the storm, and it is feared that the boat and her crew of thirty-six men were lost.

The three grain elevators and the Rey-Merschoffer Mill are wrecks. Their roofs and the top stories are gone, and grain stored therein has probably been ruined by the rain.

The damage to the ships at this time, when the demand for tonnage is so great, is regarded as one of the worst features of the disaster from a business standpoint.

In the business portion of the city the damage cannot be even approximately estimated. The wholesale houses along the Strand had about seven feet of water in their ground floors and window panes and glass protectors of all kinds were demolished. The top of the Moody Bank Building was blown away, and the fixtures of every house in this long business thoroughfare were destroyed.

In Mechanic Street the water was almost as deep as in the Strand. All provisions in the wholesale groceries and goods on the lower floors were saturated and rendered valueless.

The engine house of the Tremont Hotel was caved in by the falling smokestack. The damage to the hotel building will amount to $25,000. The power house of the street railway company was destroyed, and the loss on machinery and building is estimated at $70,000. There are no wires of any sort standing. They are lying in tangled masses across the streets, and will have to be cleared away before horses and vehicles can move about.

WHOLE BATTERY WIPED OUT.

Only 15 Out of 120 Men at Fort San Jacinto Saved—Lieut. Col. C. S. Roberts May Be Dead.

SAN ANTONIO, Texas, Sept. 10.—At Military Headquarters, Department of Texas, the information is that of 120 men stationed at Fort San Jacinto, Galveston, only 15 escaped. Further information is that the Captain in command is among the victims.

Lieut. Col. Cyrus S. Roberts, Adjutant General, Department of Texas, was in Galveston on a tour of inspection. It is not known if he is among the small number at the fort who escaped.

WASHINGTON, Sept. 10.—The War Department to-night received the following dispatch from Gen. McKibbin, in command of the Department of Texas:

San Antonio, Texas, Sept. 10.

Adjutant General, War Department, Washington, D. C.

Start first train to-night. Press reports received here state that all of battery is lost but fifteen men. Both officers lost.

McKIBBIN.

THE CITY STILL ISOLATED.

CHICAGO, Sept. 10.—The following statement of the situation was received to-night from Houston, Texas:

"Up to the present time no full or accurate details of the destructiveness of the storm of Saturday have been received here owing to the prostration of wires, destruction of every bridge, &c. The damage in Houston from wind and water is comparatively light. One life was lost here from falling wires.

"Galveston is yet isolated. The bridges from the mainland to the island are destroyed, and it may take a month to properly repair them. The boats available are few, so that, until a relief party and newspaper men got to the island this morning or afternoon, no one was able to cross since the storm. The Post correspondent at Galveston made his way through the storm yesterday, and it was abating. He reached Houston last night.

"From his hurried view of the disaster yesterday Galveston appears to be one great wreck, and conservative estimates of the dead from drowning run all the way from 400 to 1,500. The water was ten feet deep in parts of the island, and houses were washed away by the hundred. Eight large vessels were wrecked.

"The greatest suffering is for water, as the cisterns were destroyed and the water works wrecked.

"A relief party, with water and provisions and small boats, went from here this morning, but no word has been received from them. Houston is dreading to hear the full details from Galveston, as the story will be one of the saddest for many years, even at its best.

"The party from Galveston yesterday estimate half the property of the city destroyed.

"This is a brief outline of all that we have been able to secure up to this time, after the most strenuous and persistent efforts.

"The need of assistance is urgent, and contributions sent to Gov. Sayers at Austin will be properly and promptly applied.

"R. M. JOHNSTON,
"Editor Houston Post."

A SURVIVOR'S AWFUL STORY.

Only He and His Niece Escaped from House Containing Fifty People, and the Niece Was Drowned Later.

HOUSTON, Texas, Sept. 10.—Among the refugees which the Galveston, Houston and Henderson train picked up at Lamarque, which is about 4½ miles south of Virginia Point, was Patrick Joyce, who resided in the west end of Galveston. Joyce told a harrowing tale of hardships he had suffered to reach the mainland. He said:

"It began raining in Galveston Saturday morning early. About 9 o'clock I left for home. I got there about 11 o'clock, and found about three feet of water in the yard. It began to get worse and worse, the water getting higher and the wind stronger until it was almost as bad as the Gulf itself. Finally the house was taken off its foundation and was entirely demolished. People all around me were scurrying to and fro, endeavoring to find places of safety, and making the air hideous with their cries.

"There were nine families in the house, which was a large two-story frame, and of the fifty people residing there, myself and niece were the only ones who could get away.

"I managed to find a raft of driftwood or wreckage, and got on it, going with the tide, I knew not where. I had not drifted far before I was struck with some wreckage and my niece was knocked out of my arms. I could not save her, and had to see her drown.

"I was carried on and on with the tide, sometimes on the raft and again I was thrown from it by coming in contact with some pieces of timber, parts of houses, logs, cisterns, and other things which were floating around in the Gulf and bay. I drifted and swam all night, not knowing where I was going or in what direction. About 3 o'clock in the morning I began to feel the hard ground, and knew I was on the mainland. I wandered around until I came to a house, and there a person gave me some clothes. I had lost most of mine soon after I started, and only wore a coat. I was in the water about seven hours.

"The Miller residence, where I resided, was about three blocks from the Gulf, and there were fully eight or ten feet of water in this district when I left. Of the other part of the city I know nothing.

"I was in the storm which struck Galveston in 1875, but that one, bad as it was, was nothing in comparison with Saturday's. It will be hard to tell how much damage was done in the city, but it will be something terrible. The Gulf and bay are full of wreckage of every description, and it seems as if every frame house in the town must have blown down, judging from the amount of driftwood that was floating about."

Blames the Harbor Jetties.

Allen Stannard of the New York Custom House, who was for several years Superintendent of the Mallory Line, in Galveston, says he predicted several years ago the calamity that has befallen the City of Galveston. He ascribes the disaster to the effect of the Government jetties upon the harbor. He said yesterday:

"The jetties extend such a long distance across the bay that they prevent the water that comes in from the sea spreading across the bay. When a big storm like this occurs, with the wind in the right direction, it drives the water up between the jetties, and there is no escape for it but to overflow the island and the city."

THE STORM-SWEPT CITY

Galveston's Development as a Port and Railroad Terminus.

MANY SHIPS TOUCHED THERE

Three Railroads Reached the Island Over Trestles—Its Many Banks—Imports and Exports.

As Galveston, Tex., stood on Saturday morning its prospects were of the brightest. Its prosperity and rapid growth as a commercial, financial, and business centre seemed to be assured and those interested in its welfare were confident that great as had been its strides toward equal importance with New Orleans in the last few years, its advance would be still more remarkable in the near future.

The interest taken by Collis P. Huntington in the past had been a factor in its rapidly increasing importance, due to a concentration of business and the speedy completion of some of the most important plans for developing the Southern Pacific system, with the natural result of stimulating the activity of its rivals. Business men predicted with conviction that the bulk of Western-raised produce which goes to Europe and other foreign countries would be exported through Galveston.

The purchase of the city beach property at Denver resurvey and the filling in at Fort San Jacinto by the Government were accepted as guarantees that a military establishment of an important character would be maintained on the island, and there was every reason to believe that the work of deepening the harbor channel to 30 feet by 1,200 feet wide would be promptly started.

Plans to make Galveston an important importing centre had been developed beyond the stage of discussion. All commercial and financial conditions were satisfactory and a profitable and increasing Fall and Winter business was counted on.

As to its wharf and terminal facilities, they were at the time of the disaster almost equal in point of convenience to those of any port in the country. The new pier, B, of the Southern Pacific Company—nine are to be constructed in all—is 1,400 feet long and 650 feet wide. It will have nine acres of sheds and berthroom for seven large ships.

The Galveston Wharf and Terminal Company has from Pier 10 to Pier 36, a lineal wharf frontage of four and a third miles, on which 120 steamships can be accommodated. It owns thirty-three miles of tracks, and its sheds have the capacity of 1,000,000 bales of cotton. A 600,000-bushel grain elevator has just been added to its equipment.

Building operations at Galveston since the Autumn of 1899 had been brisk, and many fine private dwellings and commercial buildings were constructed.

For the development of Galveston Harbor Col. H. M. Robert, Divisional Engineer of the United States Army, presented some important plans before a gathering of representative citizens last May. One was for improvements on existing harbor lines. This contemplates the narrowing of Galveston Channel by enlarging Pelican Island and creating an increased current through Bolivar Roads and the jetties of the Gulf. Another plan is to further increase the enlargement of Pelican Island, and to throw a dike from it to the mainland, and to fill in the water front from Virginia Point to the island, leaving only a narrow water course, where the trestles now pass. The subject will be considered at the next session of Congress.

ITS TRANSPORTATION FACILITIES.

The Port of Galveston gave employment to several thousand laborers and roustabouts and seafaring men for the European, Gulf, coast, and Mexican steamships and sailing craft. At present the Morgan Line is not using the port. The steamship lines active in Galveston's commerce and passenger service are the Mallory Line, for New York and Key West; the North German Lloyd, for Bremen; the Forenede Gulf-Baltic Line, for Aarhuus and Copenhagen; the Rotterdam-American Line, for Rotterdam; the West Indian-Pacific Line, for Liverpool, and the Gulf Ports Steamship Line, for the United Kingdom and the Continent.

There were also the Harrison, Booth, Gulf Ports, Houston, Black Star, and Serra Lines to Liverpool; the Austro-American Line, to Trieste and Vienna; the Texas Line, to Antwerp, Havre, Rotterdam, Hamburg, Bremen, and other European ports; La Flecha Line, to Europe; Castle Line, to Antwerp; Hall Steamship Line, to Antwerp; Manchester Line, to Manchester; Larrinaga Line, to Havre and Bremen; Glynn Line, to Hamburg; Texas-Mexican Line, to Liverpool and Manchester; Anchor Line, to Genoa; Palatine Line, to Hamburg; United States and China-Japan Line of Indra steamers to Japan and China; Munson Line, to Cuba; Watts, Watts & Co., to Copenhagen; T. B. Royden steamers; Benemelis Line, to Cuba; Elder, Dempster & Co.'s steamers to Liverpool and Havre; Magnolia Line, to Bremen, Liverpool, and Havre; Texas Mutual Line, to Europe; Tyzack-Branfoot steamers, to Europe; Head Line, to Belfast; Texas Transport and Terminal Company, to Liverpool, Havre, Bremen, and Hamburg; Galveston and West Indies Line, to Cuba, West Indies, and South America; the Corpus Christi and Galveston Line, to Brownsville and Corpus Christi, and intermediate ports, and the Gulf Transit Company, for Pensacola.

Railroad interests at Galveston were daily increasing in importance through the interest taken in the port by the late Collis P. Huntington, who planned to make it the chief Southern auxiliary to the prosperity of the Southern Pacific system and to spend $3,000,000 to $4,000,000 in improvements and betterments. The system's equities on Galveston Island and its approaches amounted at the time of Saturday's hurricane to more than $1,750,000, including a new pier and wharf yard and another under construction.

Three railroads reached and used the Union Station, at Twenty-fifth Street and Strand, Galveston, owned by the Santa Fé system, by as many trestle bridges from the mainland. These roads were the Gulf, Colorado and Santa Fé Railway of the Atchison, Topeka and Santa Fé system; the Galveston, Houston and Henderson Railroad of the Missouri, Kansas and Texas, and the International and Great Northern Railroad systems, and the Galveston, Houston and Northern Railway of the Southern Pacific Company's system. The trains of the Gulf and Inter-State Railway of Texas left at the foot of Tremont Street by way of the ferry.

The equities of their company at Galveston amounted to about $3,500,000. They did not, as is generally supposed, own the elevators or any part of the docks, water front, or shipping buildings and facilities. These are the property of the Galveston Wharf and Terminal Company, and are worth from $8,000,000 to $10,000,000.

GALVESTON'S CRY FOR HELP.

AUSTIN, Texas, Sept. 10.—Gov. Sayers is in receipt of the following telegram from a prominent Galveston man, who made his way by boat from Galveston to Houston over the submerged country:

"Houston, Texas, Sept. 10.

"Gov. Sayers: I have been deputized by the Mayor and Citizens' Committee of Galveston to inform you that the City of Galveston is in ruins, and certainly many hundreds if not a thousand people are dead.

"Help must be given by the State and Nation, or the suffering will be appalling. Food, clothing, and money will be needed at once.

"The whole south side of the city for three blocks in from the Gulf is swept clear of everything. The whole wharf front is a wreck, and but few houses in the city are habitable. The water supply is cut off and the food stock damaged by salt water. All bridges are washed away and stranded steamers litter the bay.

"When I left this morning the search for bodies had begun. Corpses were everywhere. The tempest blew eighty-five miles an hour, and the Government instruments were carried away. At the same time the waters of the Gulf were over the whole city, having risen twelve feet.

"The water has now subsided, and survivors are left helpless among the wreckage, cut off from the world except by boat."

When asked to-night for an expression as to the flood situation along the Gulf coast, Gov. Sayers said:

"I think it is the most deplorable catastrophe in the history of America, and I feel that every possible aid should be lent the sufferers in their hour of great need. From information received here, I am led to think that hundreds of families have either lost their dear ones or been bereft of their homes, and the case is one that will appeal to every one.

"I have taken active steps to raise relief for every one who can be looked after. I have wired all the Mayors and the county Judges, asking them to secure all funds and provisions possible, and their replies up to to-night are very gratifying. The assistance lent us by the Federal Government in the way of 50,000 rations and 11,000 tents will aid a little in relieving the situation at present.

"The first duty, of course, will be to look after the living, who are thirsting and in hunger, without either water or palatable food to eat, but I think that within a day or so we will have the relief corps working in good order. I will give the matter my personal supervision, and am confident that we will see to it that everybody is looked after. It will require considerable money, however, to do all this. I have located several assistants, and the Adjutant General is near the scene of action and will personally supervise the distribution, while I remain here to answer all inquiries."

DALLAS, Texas, Sept. 10.—The Morning News to-day prints the following appeal:

"There are thousands in South Texas today who are destitute that but a few hours ago were prosperous. There are scores of homes that have been darkened by death that were places of happiness. The News takes this method of announcing that it will receive contributions for the needy and suffering at Galveston and other places visited by the terrible hurricane of last Saturday afternoon and night. The contributions may be either of cash, clothing, or provisions, or of all, for all are needed. In sending them in state whether they are to be applied to the relief of Galveston or of other places. Cash contributions can be sent to The Dallas News. Clothing and provisions should be held subject to order, so that suitable directions may be given."

Two mass meetings were held to-day, and many thousands of dollars were subscribed for the relief of the sufferers.

HOUSTON, Texas, Sept. 10.—The following dispatch was sent from Galveston by boat to the mainland to-day:

"The city is practically without fire protection. The equipment could not get about the city even if there were wires to give alarms. A meeting was held at the Tremont Hotel to consider means of relief for the distressed and homeless people. Medical attention is badly needed as are also disinfectants.

"Relief must come. Human lives are at stake, as actual starvation and death from lack of medical attention faces many hundreds of people.

"The list of dead is growing momentarily, and the first estimate of a thousand deaths is too conservative."

"All the News
That's Fit to Print"

The New York Times

THE WEATHER.

Probably showers and
warmer; winds east.

VOL. LI....NO. 16,331.   NEW YORK, SUNDAY, MAY 11, 1902.—28 Pages, Magazine Supplement and Financial Supplement.   PRICE THREE CENTS.

ERUPTION BEGINS ON ST. VINCENT.

Great Devastation Wrought on the Island.

THIRTY DEATHS REPORTED

The Volcano La Sonfriere Had Been Active Nine Days.

ASHES WERE TWO FEET THICK

Downfall of Dust Very Heavy in Barbados — Loud Reports Resembling Artillery Heard on That Island.

LONDON, May 10.—The following cablegram was received this morning at the Colonial Office from Gov. Sir Frederick Mitchell Hodgson of Barbados:

"The Soufriere volcano on St. Vincent, B. W. I., erupted violently yesterday. Loud reports, resembling artillery fire, were heard at Barbadoes at 3 o'clock in the afternoon. At 5 o'clock there came darkness and thunder, accompanied by a strong downpour of dust, which continued until night. Barbados is covered several inches deep with dust this morning. Have telegraphed Sir Robert B. Llewelyn, Governor of the Windward Islands, offering him all assistance.

"Thirty deaths are reported to have occurred at the Island of St. Vincent, according to a telegram received at the Colonial Office this morning from Governor Llewelyn, forwarded from St. Lucia yesterday evening. The Governor adds:

"'Information incomplete. Eruption continues. I am endeavoring to get back to St. Vincent.'"

Governor Llewelyn of the Windward Islands cables a later message to the Colonial Office from St. Lucia, as follows:

"Leaving at once for St. Vincent. Eruption continues. Break in cable continues. Again urge sending warship."

POINT-A-PITRE, Guadeloupe, May 10.—A message from Caracas at St. Vincent says: "La Soufriere has been in a state of eruption for nine consecutive mornings. On Thursday morning the day broke with heavy thunder and lightning, which soon changed into a continuous, tremendous roar. Vast columns of smoke rose over the mountain, becoming denser and denser, and the scoria-like hail, changing later to fine dust, fell upon all the adjacent estates, destroying a vast amount of property. At Chateau Belair the ashes were two feet deep in the streets.

"In Kingstown they were fully an inch deep, and many large stones fell in the parish of Georgetown. The earth shook violently, and at 4 o'clock in the afternoon a midnight darkness spread over the country. Thirty people are known to have been killed, and the damage to property in the Windward district was very heavy.

"The storm roared about Soufriere all night without cessation, but on the following morning it became intermittent and fainter."

A report from Barbados says that on the 7th the sky was heavily overcast; the heat was excessive, and there was a distant sound of thunder. Later, early in the afternoon, dense darkness set in and a great quantity of vivid dust fell, and continued falling until a late hour. No damage is reported.

WILLEMSTAD, Island of Curacao, May 10.—The Italian steamer Pedemonte, which arrived this morning at La Guayra, reports that while passing near the Island of St. Vincent Thursday night her deck was covered to a depth of two inches with ashes and her passengers were nearly suffocated with the smell of sulphur.

During Thursday all along the coast, especially in the Gulf of Paria, subterranean noises were heard. The Indians were terrorized.

THE ISLAND OF ST. VINCENT.

Scene of a Great Eruption in 1812 and Minor Ones Before That.

Those familiar with the geological and topographical formations of the Windward Islands say that it would not be surprising if both Mont Pelee on Martinique and La Soufriere on St. Vincent, exploded in the same manner. Both of these mountains slope gradually from the coast, both go to about the same height, both have a small lake within their craters, and, curiously enough, each has been known occasionally as "La Soufriere," although the official name of each is different.

The St. Vincent mountain, however, has had a very different history from that of Martinique. Mont Pelee vomited forth volcanic fires in 1851, but soon afterward became inactive, so that both islanders and scientists believed it to be completely extinct. Not so with La Soufriere, of the Morne Garou, of St. Vincent. That mountain was the source of a tremendous eruption in 1812, of another smaller one in 1785, and, according to tradition, of still another in 1718.

The great eruption of 1812 took place on April 27 of that year. There had been disturbances all about the shores of the Caribbean Sea for two years before the great outburst came. On March 26, just a day more than a month before the principal eruption, the coast of Venezuela was vigorously shaken, and the city of Caracas suffered the loss of thousand of its inhabitants.

The seismic convulsion moved to the sea from Caracas, and on the date mentioned reached the little Island of St. Vincent. With a great roar, the gases and fumes, the flames and molten rocks of the earth's interior were thrown into the air, carrying ruin and terror to all the surrounding country. For three days the great volume of smoke that were emitted from the volcano covered the island with darkness. It is said that the noise of the eruption was so great that English soldiers at Barbadoes—sixty miles away—supposed it was the cannonading of a naval battle, and preparations were made to withstand an attack.

Before the eruption of Mont Pelee, little St. Vincent enjoyed the distincting of having produced the most important volcanic disturbance in the history of the Lesser Antilles. The island is only eighteen miles long and eleven miles wide. It lies in the Caribbean Sea, sixty miles west of Barbadoes, and twenty-five miles southwest of St. Lucia. The entire island is of volcanic structure, and La Soufriere rises to a height of 4,048 feet.

This island was discovered by Columbus in 1498. In 1627, when Charles I. granted St. Vincent to the Earl of Carlisle, it was peopled by Caribs; in 1672 the island was given to Lord Willoughby, and in 1722 was granted, along with other islands, to the Duke of Montagu by George I. After hostilities with the French and Caribs, the island passed definitely to Great Britain in 1783. Immigrants were introduced soon afterward, and the plantations of the island were well cultivated.

The "Carib" country is a broad and fertile tract, sloping gently backwards from the sea to the base of the hills of the central mountain range, and it derives its name, obviously, from the aborigines of the country. The valleys are fertile and well watered with fine streams, several of which are spanned with substantial stones and iron bridges. The principal harbor of the colony is Kingstown. The harbor is formed by the projection into the sea of two promontories, the extremities of two spurs thrown out by Mount St. Andrew. The shore is sandy and the sea so smooth, generally, that boats can be beached anywhere along it.

There are about seventy miles of roads running around and through the island, these being for the most part close to the sea coast, and many byways afford very picturesque views of this beautiful island. Communication along the coast is maintained in a very unique manner. The natives propel large six-oared canoes, these plying daily for about twenty miles. It is a favorite custom of visitors to the island to inspect the coast and the peculiar people living along it with these vessels.

Steamers anchor in the bay, and the cargo is transported to and from the shores in lighters called "Moses" boats. These are peculiarly shaped, and are built only in St. Vincent. The town of Kingstown is remarkably well laid out, and is one of the prettiest small ports in the West Indies.

The island of St. Vincent was formerly under the general government of the Windward Islands, Barbadoes being headquarters; but in 1885, Barbadoes was made a separate Government, and Grenada, St. Vincent, Tobago, and St. Lucia were placed under a Governor. The Official Council of St. Vincent is composed of eight members nominated by the British crown.

The population of the island is about 42,000, of whom some 31,000 are negroes. Kingstown has a population of about 5,000. The principal exports are sugar, rum, cacao, spices, and arrowroot. The people trade very largely with the country, the firm of Middleton & Co., 96 Broad Street, this city, having an extensive business in the island. The chief imports are from the United States and England and small hardware.

La Soufriere rises several miles from the shore. Its crater is about three miles in diameter, and there is a lake within it about a quarter of a mile in diameter. The impression the island makes upon travelers passing in steamships was described by Lafcadio Hearn in his book, "Two Years in the West Indies," in these words:

"But over the verge of the sea there is something strange growing visible, looming up like a beautiful yellow cloud. It is an island, so lofty, so luminous, so phantomlike, that it seems a vision of the Island of Seven Cities. It is only the form of St. Vincent, bathed in vapory gold by the sun."

CAUSE OF THE ERUPTIONS.

The Explosion of Steam Subjected to Tremendous Heat in the Bowels of the Earth.

Special to The New York Times.

CAMBRIDGE, Mass., May 10.—Prof. Shaler, Dean of the Lawrence Scientific School and Professor of Geology in Harvard, says of volcanic eruptions:

"Volcanic outbreaks are merely the explosion of steam under high pressure, steam which is bound in rocks buried underneath the surface of the earth and then subjected to such tremendous heat that when the conditions are right its pent-up energy breaks forth and it shatters its stone prison walls into dust. The process by which the water becomes buried in this manner is a long one. Some contend that it leaks down from the surface of the earth through fissures in the outer crust, but this theory is not generally accepted.

"The common belief is that water enters the earth during the crystallization period, and that these rocks through the natural action of rivers and streams become deposited in the bottom of the sea. Here they lie for many ages, becoming buried deeper and deeper under masses of this sediment, which are constantly being washed upon them from above. This process is called the blanketing process.

"Each additional layer of sediment, while not raising the level of the sea bottom, buries the first layers just so much the deeper and adds to their temperature just as does the laying of extra blankets on a bed. When the first layer has reached a depth of a few thousand feet the rocks which contain the water of crystallization are subjected to a terrific heat. This heat generates steam, which is held in a state of frightful tension in its rocky prison.

"Wrinklings in the outer crust in the earth's surface occur, caused by the constant shrinking of the earth itself and by the contraction of the outer surface as it settles on the plastic centres underneath. Fissures are caused by these foldings, and as these fissures reach down into the earth the pressure is removed from the rocks and the compressed steam in them and it explodes with tremendous force."

GUATEMALA'S EARTHQUAKES.

Whole Northwestern Region Said to be in Ruins—Thousands of Dead Still Unburied.

SALT LAKE CITY, Utah, May 10.—In a letter to the Presidency of the Mormon Church, dated April 25, from Paul Henning, Elder and representative of the Church in Guatemala, further details are given of the disastrous earthquakes in that country.

"The whole Northwestern part," says Mr. Henning, "one of the richest in Central America, is in ruins. On the evening of April 18, about 8:20 o'clock, the first shock was felt. This lasted from thirty to forty seconds, and caused the wildest panic. There was no loss of life in Guatemala City, and the property damage was less than at first feared, though walls were cracked all over the city and many old houses were tumbled in ruins. Since then the shocks have continued with more or less violence. The worst damage was done in the City of Quesaltenango, the second largest in the country. Here it is estimated that from five to six thousand people were killed.

"At the time of the first shock a violent storm and rainstorm were raging. The electric lighting plant of the city had been disabled, and when the people, panic-stricken by the rumbling and shaking of the earthquake, rushed from their houses it was only to meet death. Stumbling and falling in the utter darkness, crazed with fright, the people died by thousands under the falling walls, while other thousands were caught like rats, only to die of suffocation or drowning.

"The quaking and rain kept up continually for three days. This made it almost impossible to do effective relief work, and as a consequence now that the hot weather again prevails, the stench from the thousands of bodies in the ruins is unbearable, and fears are entertained of an epidemic. Hundreds of bodies probably never will be recovered."

200 Little Trips

Inaugurating Fresh-to-Tampa, Pullman Trains to Port Tampa and Miami, then short sea voyage. J. J. Farnsworth, F. P. A. Plant System, 200 Broadway.—Adv.

MAP OF THE ISLAND OF ST. VINCENT.

This Tiny Isle is Eighteen Miles Long and Eleven Miles Wide. The Principal Eruption is Reported to be from Morne Garou, Which is Popularly Known as "La Soufriere." Kingstown is the Chief Town of the Island.

SURVIVORS TELL OF ST. PIERRE HORROR

Stream of Lava Burst Forth from Mont Pelee.

PEOPLE IN A WILD PANIC

Pall of Darkness, Broken Only by Flames, Over the Town.

STEAMER RODDAM'S ESCAPE

Captain Describes How It Was Effected — Eruptions Continue in Martinique —The Number of Dead Still Placed at 40,000.

With additional information of the calamity at St. Pierre, Martinique, its horror increases.

A party of survivors who escaped before the final catastrophe and have arrived at Castries, St. Lucia, British West Indies, describe the earlier scenes of the eruption.

Mont Pelee first began to show activity on May 3; on May 4 a downfall of hot ashes hid the mountain from view and covered the city to an inch; on May 5 a stream of lava flowed from Mont Pelee to the sea and 150 persons perished.

Darkness, lit only by flashes of flame from the volcano, wrapped the town in gloom and a panic ensued among the inhabitants, which was heightened by the terrible detonations heard hundreds of miles.

The final catastrophe occurred on the 8th inst.

Capt. Whatier of the Roddam, the only vessel in the harbor to escape, described the scene. A tremendous cloud of smoke and flame seemed to rush with terrific rapidity upon the town and harbor, and a rain of fire fell, destroying the town and every ship in the port except his own.

Reports from St. Pierre are to the effect that the eruptions continue, but are less violent.

The United States Government was quick to act for the relief of the stricken. The Quebec Line steamship Korona, a sister ship of the Roraima, which was lost, has arrived at the Island of Dominica with a number of survivors from the latter vessel. The Korona's Captain reports that the eruption at St. Pierre apparently was from a new crater.

The United States Government was quick to act for the relief of the stricken. The cruiser Cincinnati, which yesterday arrived at San Domingo City, Santo Domingo, has been ordered to proceed to Martinique at once.

The seagoing tug Potomac has left San Juan, Porto Rico, for the ill-fated island. The cruiser Dixie, now in the Brooklyn Navy Yard, has been directed to prepare for sea at once, and will be sent to the scene of the calamity.

Prompt action was taken also by the United States Senate, which passed a bill appropriating $100,000 for the aid of the sufferers. The bill's passage was delayed, however, by objections in the House.

Estimates of the number of dead continue to fix it at about 40,000. But it is now believed that many persons escaped to Morne Rouge, a Summer resort not far from St. Pierre, which, however, is believed to have escaped destruction.

It was learned in this city last night that the French Government has re-established direct cable communication with St. Pierre, but is reserving the use of the wire for Government purposes.

MONT PELEE STILL ACTIVE.

St. Pierre Still in Flames According to Latest Reports—French Warship Carries Food to Refugees.

PARIS, May 10.—The Minister of Marine, M. de Lanessan, has received the following from Fort de France, Island of Martinique, under date of May 10, 4 P. M.:

"Arrived at Fort de France with provisions, passing close to St. Pierre. Fire continues; volcano still emitting ashes with less density. SUCHET."

FORT DE FRANCE, Martinique, May 10.—The earthquakes have ceased, but the volcanic eruptions continue.

Hopes are raised that more of the population of St. Pierre than indicated in the earlier dispatches have been saved.

It is believed that a number of people were rescued from the stricken town by steamers running to Fort de France.

The work of clearing away the débris in the City of St. Pierre will be commenced as soon as it is possible to enter the smoking ruins. Until some semblance of order has been restored and the smoking ruins have been partially cleared away it has been agreed by the municipal and other authorities to burn all corpses found in the streets.

The authorities of Fort de France are sending all procurable necessaries for the sufferers, with medical aid for the injured, the food supplies of St. Pierre being all destroyed.

LONDON, May 10.—Private dispatches received late this afternoon from the West Indies say the eruption at Martinique is decidedly worse.

GRAPHIC STORY OF SURVIVOR.

Captain of the Roddam Tells How St. Pierre Was Overwhelmed—His Vessel's Remarkable Escape.

CASTRIES, St. Lucia, B. W. I., May 10.—Mont Pelee, a volcanic mountain five or six miles north of St. Pierre, the commercial capital of Martinique, the mountain which made a faint show of eruption fifty years ago, on May 3 last began to throw out dense clouds of smoke, accompanied with rumbling noises, lighted the sky over an immense area, causing widespread terror. May 4 hot ashes fell on the whole city quarter of St. Pierre an inch thick and made Mont Pelee invisible.

At noon May 5 a stream of burning lava rushed 4,400 feet down the mountain side, following the dry bed of a torrent, and reaching the sea, five miles from the mountain, in three minutes. In its rush the fiery flood swept from its path plantations, buildings, factories, cattle, and human beings over a breadth of about half a mile.

At the mouth of the Riviere Blanche stood the large Guerin sugar factory, one of the finest in the islands. It is now completely entombed in lava. The tall chimney alone is visible.

One hundred and fifty persons are estimated to have perished here, including the owner's son.

As the lava rushed into the sea the latter receded 300 feet all along the west coast, returning with greater strength. A big wave covered the whole sea front of St. Pierre, but did little damage ashore or afloat.

Terrible detonations, heard hundreds of miles northward, followed at short irregular intervals and continued at night. In the intense darkness the electric lights failed, but the town was lit up by lurid flashes of flame from the mountain. The terror-stricken inhabitants rushed for the hills in their night clothes, screaming, shouting, and wailing—mad with terror.

The Plissono family escaped to St. Lucia in a small steamer.

Thirty-five persons, mostly women and children, arrived here in the forenoon of the 6th and furnished the above details. The men remained at Martinique.

The same afternoon, later, telegraphic communication was interrupted with both the Islands of Martinique and St. Vincent.

During the afternoon of the 8th the British steamer Roddam, which had left St. Lucia at midnight on the 7th for Martinique, crawled slowly into the Castries harbor, unrecognizable, gray with ashes, her rigging dismantled and sails and awnings hanging about torn and charred.

Capt. Whatier reported that, having just cast anchor off St. Pierre at 8 A. M., in fine weather, succeeding an awful thunderstorm during the night, he was talking to the ship's agent, Joseph Plissono, who was in a boat alongside, when he saw a tremendous cloud of smoke and cinders rushing with terrific rapidity over the town and port, completely and in an instant enveloping the former in a sheet of flame and raining fire on board. The agent had just time to climb on board when his boat disappeared.

Several of the crew of the Roddam were quickly scorched to death. By superhuman efforts, having steam up, the cable was slipped and the steamer backed away from the shore, and, nine hours later, managed to reach Castries.

Ten of the Roddam's men were lying dead, contorted and burned out of human semblance, among the black cinders which covered the ship's deck to a depth of six inches. Two more of the crew have since died.

The survivors of the Roddam's crew were loud in their praises of the heroic conduct of their Captain in steering his vessel out of danger with his own hands, though he was badly burned by the rain of fire which kept falling on the ship for miles after she got under way. Beyond burns all over his body the Captain is safe, as is also the ship's agent, though he is badly scorched. Mr. Plissono is believed here to be the sole survivor of the 40,000 inhabitants of St. Pierre. He remained there, for the town and all the shipping in the port have been utterly destroyed.

The West Indian and Panama Telegraph Company's repairing steamer Grappler sank first; then the Quebec liner Roraima, Capt. Muggah of the latter waving his hand in farewell to the Roddam as his vessel sank with a terrific explosion.

The British Royal Mail steamer Esk, which called off Martinique at 10 o'clock last night, reports standing off shore five miles, sounding her whistle, and sending up rockets. She received no answer.

The whole sea front was blazing for miles. The Esk sent a boat ashore, but it could not land on account of the terrific heat, which was accompanied by loud explosions. Not a living soul appeared ashore after the boat had waited for two hours. Fire and ashes fell all over the steamer.

In the afternoon a French coasting steamer arrived here from Fort de France, seeking assistance, as all the country was burned up, the stock was dying, all the plantations were charred, the country people were flocking into the towns, and famine was feared.

The steamer was loaded with food of all sorts and was sent back to Martinique at 7 P. M. The Captain of this vessel reported that some thirty people left St. Pierre by the 6 o'clock boat Thursday morning for Fort de France, and consequently were saved.

All attempts to get to St. Pierre possible showed houses still blazing and streets strewn with charred bodies. It is certain that the whole town was destroyed and the neighboring country for miles was devastated, and it is feared here that few, if any, of the inhabitants escaped.

The volcano of the Island of St. Vincent has burst out in sympathetic eruption. A steamer which returned from there last night reports that the northern third of the island was in flames and cut off from assistance by a continuous stream of burning lava, ashes falling in heavy showers as far as 150 miles away; Kingstown, the capital of St. Vincent, is safe, but people here are very anxious as to the fate of that island.

Dominica and St. Lucia have very active geysers, but they show no departure from normal conditions as yet.

Foodstuffs of all kinds are urgently wanted.

NOTHING LEFT OF ST. PIERRE.

Lloyds' Agent at St. Lucia Fully Confirms the Disaster—England Will Send Help.

LONDON, May 10.—Loyds' agent at St. Lucia, B. W. I., cables that later news fully confirms the disaster at St. Pierre. He says he cannot ascertain the names of the vessels which have been lost, but they include one Italian bark and two steamers, one probably being the Grappler, the cable ship belonging to the West India and Panama Telegraph Company.

Lloyds' agent at St. Thomas, D. W. I., cables that St. Pierre has been totally destroyed by fire and that all the inhabitants perished.

All the vessels in the harbor were lost. These include the Grappler. The steamer Roraima, belonging to the Quebec Steamship Company, took fire in port and was also a total loss.

Cable communication between London and the Island of Martinique is cut off. Communication is still obtainable via the Island of Guadeloupe, (French West Indies,) but the news is congested, owing to the confusion prevailing in the cable

Nearly 350 Hotels and Boarding Houses

in New York and New England in "The Prophet's Chamber," No. 15, of the "Four-Track Series." Sent free on receipt of a 2-cent stamp, by H. N. Daniels, Grand Central Station, New York.—Adv.

The line for California travelers is the New York Central via Chicago, St. Louis, or Cincinnati.—Adv.

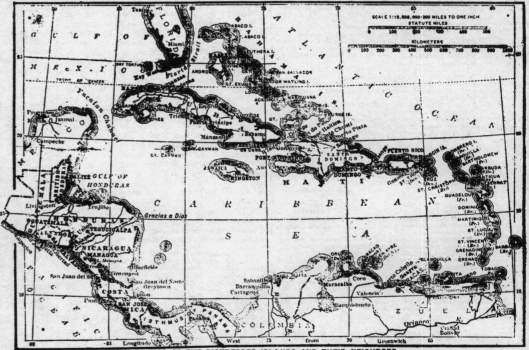
MAP OF THE DISTRESSED ISLANDS AND THEIR NEIGHBORS.
This Diagram Shows the Positions of Martinique and St. Vincent as Related to the Other West Indies and South America.

system and the numerous official messages filed. The receipt of the first direct cable news from Martinique depends on how long the French company will take in repairing the cable to Fort-de-France, (capital of that island,) on which they are now working.

The British Admiralty is communicating with the Commander in Chief of the British naval station, and a war vessel will be directed to go to Martinique.

The French Cable Company received cable dispatches this morning announcing that the eruption at Martinique continues and that ships are afraid to go near the island.

The latest messages indicate that the number of deaths will be about 40,000, several of the smaller islands near Martinique having also suffered. Between 8 in the morning and 8 in the evening of Thursday, May 8, St. Pierre was a mass of fire, and there was also a volcanic eruption at St. Vincent. The Island of St. Thomas is sending help.

It is apparent from the cable dispatches received that the eruption of the volcano on Mont Pelée will not do much damage to the sugar crop, which is chiefly confined to the southern part of the island and the gathering of which is now two-thirds over. However, the wiping out of the moneyed population of the island, centred at St. Pierre, is bound to produce the most serious commercial effect. Not one of the business houses in London has heard a word from or of its agents in Martinique. A partner of the principal English firm dealing with Martinique said to a representative of The Associated Press:

"I suppose all our agents are dead. Not much business is transacted between England and Martinique. Almost everything thence is shipped direct to Bordeaux, which suffers the most. I know Martinique well. The last time I was there, a few years ago, there were only two Englishmen and no Americans resident at St. Pierre, though that town did a good business with America, in the way of foodstuffs. A large proportion of the white population belongs to old French families, who preferred St. Pierre to any other part of the island. We never for a moment dreamed that Mont Pelee would prove dangerous. Fifty years ago some smoke and steam issued from its crevices, but no attention was paid to it. Unless the lava has overrun the whole island, which is not likely, the disaster may not turn out to be as great as it at present seems to be."

A ship which arrived Friday, May 9, at the Island of Dominica, British West Indies, and which was lying off St. Pierre when the eruption commenced, reports that the noise was terrific. A huge cloud of fire appeared over the town and neighborhood, giving the inhabitants no chance to escape.

GUADELOUPE HEARD ERUPTION

Noises Like the Discharge of Heavy Artillery Reached the Island—Story of Roraima's Mate.

POINT-A-PITRE, Guadeloupe, May 10.—The morning of May 5 Guadeloupe learned that the Mont Pelee volcano, in Martinique, had been in a state of eruption since Saturday, May 3, throwing out ashes. The same day violent thunderstorms began here. Tuesday a very heavy storm occurred, and loud detonations were heard. At noon came a rumor that lava was flowing from Mont Pelee and that 300 lives had been lost at St. Pierre. All that day were heard here loud noises, like the discharge of heavy artillery far off. It is now known that these noises were from the Martinique volcano. In the afternoon the cable connections with Martinique disappeared.

A very heavy thunderstorm then broke over Guadeloupe and lasted for a considerable time, and rumors were current that La Soufriere volcano in Guadeloupe was more active. The earth was trembling at Basseterre and volcanic rumblings were heard.

News of the disaster at Martinique reached here by the French war vessel Suchet Friday morning. Nearly every one here has relatives in Martinique, and intense sorrow prevails. All the stores here are closed, and the flags are flying at half mast.

The mountains of Guadeloupe are shrouded in thick clouds, and frequent heavy storms continue. The people are on edge with anxiety, fearing that La Souffriere may become active. A light earthquake shock or a slight increase in the usual smoking of La Souffriere would precipitate a panic here. It is believed, however, that there is no local danger.

The Quebec Line steamship Korona arrived at the Island of Dominica yesterday, bringing a number of survivors from her sister ship, the Roraima. The Captain of the Korona says that the eruption at St. Pierre was apparently from a new crater, and that accompanying the eruption there seemed to be a tidal wave which overwhelmed the shipping.

The first mate of the Roraima thus describes the disaster at St. Pierre:

"Between 6:30 and 7 o'clock in the morning on Thursday without warning there came a sort of whirlwind of steam, boiling mud, and fire, which suddenly swept the city and the roadstead. There were some eighteen vessels anchored in the harbor, including the Roraima, the French sailing ship Tamaya, four larger sailing vessels, and others. All of the vessels immediately canted over and began to burn. The Tamaya was a bark from Nantes, Capt. Maurice, and was on her way to Pointe-a-Pitre. All the boats except the Roraima sank instantly and at the same moment.

"Every house ashore was utterly destroyed and apparently buried under the ashes and burning lava. An officer who was sent ashore penetrated but a short distance into the city. He found only a few walls standing and the streets literally paved with corpses. The Governor of the island, who had arrived only a few hours before the catastrophe, was killed. Both the English and American Consuls, with their families, were reported to have perished. It is certain that no more than 40 out of the above 25,000 could have escaped."

The cruiser Suchet was here yesterday buying provisions for the survivors in the outlying districts. She sailed for Fort de France last night with a large quantity of stores, which were immediately put under military guard.

Negroes are flocking in vast numbers into Fort de France from the surrounding country, demanding food.

A telegram from Fort de France says that hot mud and cinders have been falling all night throughout the island and still continue doing great damage, and that when the final reports are received it will be found that many people have been killed or injured in other parts of Martinique.

THE ENVIRONS OF ST. PIERRE AND MONT PELEE.

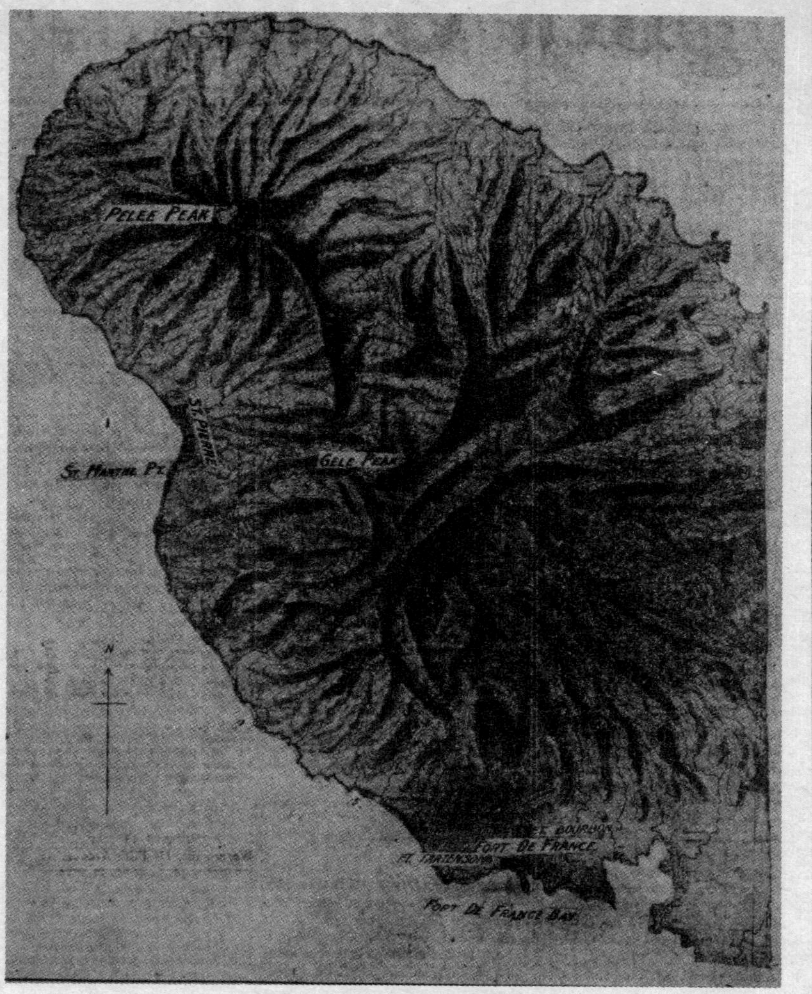

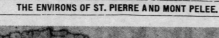

St. Pierre Is About Five Miles from the Crater of Mont Pelee. Morne Rouge Is About Seven Miles from St. Pierre Toward the Opposite Side of the Mountain.

THE PRENTISES MAY BE SAFE.

Wife of the United States Consul at St. Pierre Wrote that Escape Had Been Planned.

Special to The New York Times.

MELROSE, Mass., May 10.—Miss Alice Fry, sister-in-law of Thomas T. Prentis, United States Consul at St. Pierre, thinks that he and his family may have escaped, as a letter she received from Mrs. Prentis this morning indicates that they appreciated their danger when the Mount Pelée volcano first displayed signs of activity, about April 25, which date the letter bears, and had made plans to leave if occasion arose.

Mrs. Prentis writes that the American schooner Anna E. J. Morse was in the Harbor of St. Pierre and that Mr. Prentis planned to sail away on her with his family if things looked threatening. That he was aware of the full gravity of the situation is evident from the fact that he experienced an earthquake while he was Consul at Mauritius in the eighties.

The schooner Anna E. J. Morse, mentioned by Mrs. Prentis in her letter, is a vessel of seventy-three tons, owned by F. W. Clark of Portland, Me. The schooner is engaged principally, it is said, in trade between Philadelphia and the West Indies.

The Prentis family may, however, Miss Fry thinks, have fled to Fort de France. If they arrived there in safety a cablegram is expected at Melrose soon announcing their escape.

The full text of the letter received by Miss Fry is as follows:

"My Dear Sister: This morning the whole population of the city is on the alert, and every eye is directed toward Mont Pelee, an extinct volcano. Everybody is afraid that the volcano has taken into its heart to burst forth and destroy the whole island.

"Fifty years ago Mont Pelée burst forth with terrific force and destroyed everything for a radius of several miles. For several days the mountain has been bursting forth, and immense quantities of lava are flowing down the side of the mountain.

"All the inhabitants are going up to see it. There is not a horse to be had on the island. Those belonging to the natives are kept in readiness to leave at a moment's notice.

"Last Wednesday, which was April 23, I was in my room with little Christine, and we heard three distinct shocks. They were so great that we supposed at first that there was some one at the door, and Christine went and found no one there. The first report was very loud, but the second and third were so great that dishes were thrown from the shelves and the house was completely rocked.

"We can see Mount Pelée from the rear windows in our house, and although it is fully four miles away, we can hear the roar and see the fire and lava issuing from it with terrific force.

"The city is covered with ashes and clouds of smoke have been over our heads for the past five days. The smell of sulphur is so strong that horses on the street stop and snort, and some of them are obliged to give up, drop in their harness, and die from suffocation. Many of the people are obliged to wear wet handkerchiefs over their faces to protect them from the strong fumes of sulphur.

"My husband assures me that there is no immediate danger and when there is the least particle of danger he will leave the place. There is an American schooner, the E. J. Morse, in the harbor, and it will remain here for at least two weeks. If the volcano becomes very bad we shall embark at once and go out to sea. The papers in this city are asking if we are going to experience another earthquake and volcano similar to that which struck here some fifty years ago."

SCIENTISTS SAY THE END IS NOT YET COME

Prof. R. T. Hill Suggests That Further Eruptions May Occur.

Lesser Antilles All of Volcanic Origin, and Present Disturbances May Be Forerunner of a Series

Special to The New York Times.

WASHINGTON, May 10.—It is not improbable that the disaster at Martinique is merely the first of a series of disturbances, either by volcano or by earthquake. Prof. Robert T. Hill of the Geological Survey, who was the geologist of the Agassiz West Indian expedition and is one of the best-posted men in Washington on the subject, said to-day:

"An important item of news in the morning papers, casually mentioned in several places, is that St. Vincent is also exhibiting volcanic phenomena, and it is impossible to say whether this explosion of Mont Pelee is the forerunner or the end of a cycle of disturbances. One thing is certain, that the inhabitants of the West Indies live over smoldering volcanoes which might break out at any moment, although owing to the infrequency of these explosions this is hardly probable except at very long intervals of time."

When asked whether the Martinique explosion will have any results in the United States, Dr. Hill answered:

"It might. Volcanoes and earthquakes are related, and these phenomena often accompany each other, but at other times they may take place independently. The great earthquake of 1812, which destroyed Bogota, and which is supposed to have sunk the swamp lands of Northeastern Arkansas and Southeastern Missouri, was followed in a month by the terrible St. Vincent explosion. In some instances earthquakes precede volcanic explosions. In regions of quiescent volcanism, where outbreaks are not frequent, like Japan, earthquakes are frequently felt.

"The Charleston earthquake several years ago cannot be co-related with any volcanic outbreak. It may have been merely a settlement along the shore line from the loads of sediment. The causes of earthquakes and volcanoes may be classed among the many unsolved problems concealed in the earth's interior, problems which have engrossed the severest thought of scientific men and which are still far from solution."

Speaking of the report that earthquakes were felt in Southeastern Spain Thursday night, Dr. Hill said:

"The present certainly seems to be a marked period of seismic disturbance, with earthquakes and explosions reported from Mexico, Central America, Russia, and Spain. The connection between these phenomena in widely separated portions of the earth, if any, is unknown. The story that earthquakes have cut off the flow of the Beaumont (Texas) oil wells is utterly without foundation.

"There are two classes of volcanic eruptions. There are those which are basic, as they are called, with a great deal of iron in them and less silica, and they usually make the lavas, which flow in a state like molasses and are red hot when they come out. There is another type, of rocks which are called acidic, in which the silica predominates and the metals are less noticeable, and they usually make eruptions of cinders and ashes. These West Indian volcanoes are of the latter type. No doubt in a few days we will be getting the dust from that explosion here.

"That whole group of Caribbee Islands, beginning with Saba, on the north, then St. Eustatius, St. Kitts, Guadeloupe, Dominica, Martinique, St. Lucia, St. Vincent, the Grenadines, and Grenada, are all volcanoes. Although they are entirely built up of the débris of explosions, hardly any of these explosions have taken place since the discovery by Columbus, and the long intervals between them will show how slow these processes are. In Dominica, Guadeloupe, St. Lucia, and St. Vincent there are hot springs, crater lakes, and a few 'soufrieres'—that is, places with escaping steam. But the heat of the waters was so low and these phenomena so inconspicuous that the inhabitants have usually considered themselves out of danger. Only two serious explosions have been known in the history of these islands, and those were in St. Vincent. One was in the eighteenth century and the other in the year 1812, both of which were terrifically disastrous in their effects.

"It is evident, however, that some awful explosions have taken place in prehistoric time. The Grenadines, for instance, 100 little rocky heads barely projecting above the water, are apparently the site of where there was once a great island like Martinique, which had been destroyed by such an explosion.

"The volcanoes of the West Indies are confined entirely to the Caribbee Islands of the Lesser Antilles. St. Thomas, St. Croix, St. Martin, Antigua, and Barbados, although in close proximity to these islands, are of entirely different formation. In the Greater Antilles, Cuba, Jamaica, Haiti, Porto Rico, and their dismembered eastern relatives, the Danish Islands, there has been no volcanic activity in recent geological periods. These islands are composed of sedimentary rocks, with now and then some remnants of very ancient volcanic rocks derived from craters which have long since been obliterated. There have, however, been some terrible earthquakes, notably that which destroyed Port Royal, in Jamaica."

REACH ST. PIERRE BY CABLE.

French Government Reported to Have Re-established Direct Communication with the Stricken Town.

It was learned in this city last night that the French Government has succeeded in establishing direct cable communication with St. Pierre. This was effected by repairs made by the cable ship Pouyer Quertier to the severed cable between Martinique and Paramaribo, Dutch Guiana. Communication was established by way of Lisbon, Madeira, Cape Verde Islands, Pernambuco, (Brazil,) Pinheiros, (Brazil,) Cayenne, (French Guiana,) and Paramaribo. The route from Pinheiros, or Vizen, to Martinique is the system of what is known as the French West India Cable Company, and is dominated by the French Government.

After the Pouyer-Quertier had successfully grappled the cable and made the repair she put operators ashore at St. Pierre, and cable communication with France was established. The French Government, however, seized the cables for its own use, though not to the exclusion of private cablegrams.

It is expected that as soon as the French Government gets some important dispatches through the newspapers of England and France will begin to get something like an accurate account of the calamity at St. Pierre.

The broken cable from Martinique south to St. Lucia, which belongs to the West India and Panama Company, has not yet been repaired, and is not likely to be for some time, as the West India and Panama Company's repair steamer was a victim of the disaster.

It is believed the Pouyer-Quertier has gone to the north of Martinique to repair the break there on the section which runs from Martinique to Puerta Plata, on the Island of Haiti. If this repair is successfully made it will restore direct cable communication between New York City and Martinique, via Haiti.

NEWS RECEIVED OF RESCUED SURVIVORS

Four Hundred and Fifty Have Arrived at Fort-de-France.

Only Fragmentary Reports Have Reached This City, Despite Greatest Efforts of Cable Companies.

The French Cable Company's offices in this city were advised yesterday that their repair steamer Pouyer Quertier had arrived at Fort de France, having rescued 450 persons from St. Pierre. She has returned immediately to the scene of the disaster to search for further survivors.

The Commercial Cable Company sent out the following notice this morning:

> We are advised that a chartered sloop leaves St. Lucia for St. Vincent at noon to-day.

Against vigorous and persistent efforts to secure definite information from Martinique and St. Vincent, only the most fragmentary reports reached this city yesterday. All of those reports indicated, however, that the extent and the awfulness of the tragedy which has been enacted in those islands have not been exaggerated in any reports which have come to hand.

Almost no business was done in the offices of the more prominent West Indian exporting firms of this city. The families of many of them are in Martinique, and all work was suspended until some information telling of the fate of those imprisoned there could be obtained.

The offices of the Quebec Steamship Company, A. Emilius Outerbridge & Co., agents, 39 Broadway, were simply overwhelmed with requests for information. The senior Mr. Outerbridge was kept busy answering the telephone almost all day. Families and friends of the crew and passengers on the ill-fated steamship Roraima were clamoring for every word of news that might be obtained.

Mr. Outerbridge received late Friday night from his agents at Dominica, which is thirty miles north of Martinique, this message:

> We notify you that steamship Roraima has been lost. We do not know whether passengers were aboard or not. Volcanic eruption. Loss terrific. R. H. GORDON & CO.

In response to further requests for details Mr. Outerbridge received this additional message about noon yesterday:

> Dominica, May 9.
> Survivors Roraima on Korona. First Officer Scott and Assistant Purser Thompson in hospital, Fort de France. Morley, second officer; Thompsen, third mate; Moore, Evans, second engineer; Benson, carpenter; Maher, second steward; Leady, quartermaster; stewardess, Mrs. Reed, and three sailors. GORDON.

Mr. Outerbridge said that this probably indicated that the passengers who were on the vessel, as well as the Captain, George Muggah, were lost. The passengers who sailed from this port were Mrs. H. T. Ince and Stanley Ince, mother and son of Dr. J. H. Ince of Buffalo, and a Mrs. Stokes of St. Pierre. There may have been other passengers picked up at the port at which the vessel stopped, but their names are not known here.

Mr. Outerbridge considered it likely that all of the survivors were picked up by the French warship Suchet, and turned over to the Korona, which is a sister ship to the Roraima, and which will arrive in New York in about ten days. It will not be known until the Korona reaches here who the other passengers on the Roraima were.

The Korona is commanded by Capt. Carey.

Capt. Muggah, Captain of the Roraima, was a native of Sydney, Cape Breton, Nova Scotia, and was married. Robert Morley, the second officer, has a mother living in Halifax, Nova Scotia. There was a crew of fifty-two men on board, of whom the following were the officers:

> George Muggah, Captain; E. S. Scott, first officer; Robert Morley, second officer; T. Thompsen, third officer; J. McTear, chief engineer; Evans, second engineer; H. Talmage, third engineer; M. Wensberger, fourth engineer; W. Soucy, chief steward; H. Maher, second steward, and Eugene E. Braun, purser.

Most of these men lived in Nova Scotia, although the remainder of the crew was mainly picked up in West Indian ports.

Several exporting houses in this city had manifested the greatest interest in the welfare of W. P. Lough, a member of the New York Produce Exchange, and related to several families in this city. Mr. Lough was a member of the firm of E. F. Darrell & Co. of the Produce Exchange Building. He had been in the Guianas and was working his way northward from Trinidad. It was supposed that he was on the steamship Roddam, which suffered such trouble, or it was apprehended that he had gone ashore at St. Pierre.

The members of the Darrell firm and also of G. F. Lough & Co. of the Produce Exchange Building made every effort to communicate with Martinique and other points, but without success. Yesterday afternoon, however, this cablegram came from Mr. Lough himself from Dominica:

> Fire has consumed everything on the Boraima. Think it advisable to duplicate orders.

Mr. Darrell of this firm said he could not understand how Mr. Lough reached Dominica, since he was on the Roddam, which had put into St. Lucia. He did not regard it as unlikely that this message was sent by boat to Dominica, and from there forwarded to this city. Mr. Darrell was asked what in his opinion would be the extent of the loss to American firms from the destruction of St. Pierre, and he said:

"It is of course the merest guesswork to name any figures, but it is safe to say that the loss will be very great. The Island of Martinique bought a great many goods from this country, though she sent most of her products to France. She sold a large quantity of sugar and rum here, however. The blow will be a very great one, because the people there have suffered very severely in recent years from the declining prices of sugar and rum.

"There was a time when magnificent estates were maintained in Martinique, and whose owners had mortgaged them three times. Their sugar and rum business was so profitable, however, that they could pay the interest on the mortgages without difficulty, and spend several months every year in Paris. But of late years hard times have come. The people had been accumulating a large amount of sugar anticipating a reduction in this country's sugar duties. Against these accumulations, merchants in this country had loaned money. The death of the merchants themselves, the devastation of the city, and the ruin of the plantations will make it obviously impossible to collect these loans."

Another firm which was greatly concerned about the real condition of things in St. Pierre was the American Trading Company. Henry C. de Medeuil, who manages the French West Indies business of this concern, has a sister and a brother in the city, and he made vigorous efforts to get news from them and from the business houses of St. Pierre in whose welfare he was especially interested.

It being impossible to obtain any information from St. Pierre or Fort de France, cablegrams were sent to France. In response to an inquiry cabled to Bordeaux, this message was received yesterday morning:

> Successive cables announce that several families that took refuge at Morne Rouge are safe. They announce, also, the deaths of the Caminades and Louis Hayot.

The Caminade brothers were members of one of the oldest and most important families in Martinique. Their names were Gaston and Raphael. They owned a large store in St. Pierre, a bakery, several distilleries and sugar plantations. The firm of Middleton & Co., 66 Broad Street, was also very much interested in the fate of these two brothers, and a message was sent to Paris yesterday morning inquiring about them, to which came the brief reply:

"All dead."

Two points in these Paris and Bordeaux messages puzzled the recipients of them. Mr. Medeuil could not understand how refuge could have been obtained for any one in Morne Rouge. That resort is nearer the crater of Mont Pelée than St. Pierre itself. It is true that the village is situated on an elevation, itself somewhat above the slope ascending to the mouth of the volcano, but if the disaster was accompanied by an explosion of the mountain rather than by a huge flow of lava—as is the general understanding—it is difficult to explain how any refuge could have been found at Morne Rouge. The only explanation is that the little resort escaped because it is somewhat toward the other side of the mountain from St. Pierre.

The second point, which was difficult of understanding, was how these reports reached France. The French Cable Company announced early in the morning that cable connection had been obtained with Fort de France by way of the Madeira Islands, Brazil, Guiana, and Trinidad. Messages which were sent over this route cost the sender $2.15 a word, with no special rate for newspapers. It was considered that even if communication could be had with Fort de France, the few survivors would not be likely to have information of specific cases of deaths.

The wife of Henry Tift of Middleton & Co. is a native of St. Pierre and she has numerous relatives there, but so far Mr. Tift has been unable to get any news of them. Charles Testart of 81 New Street, this city, is a son of the United States Vice Consul at St. Pierre, Amedee Testart. Young Mr. Testart also has a sister in that city, Mme. de Messiny. He said yesterday, however, that from reports which had reached the city he feared that the members of his family there had been killed.

A report reached this city late yesterday afternoon, purporting to have come by cable from Port de France, to the effect that General Manager Jelladert of the French Cable Company at St. Pierre had been burned to death.

At the offices of Foulke & Co., 25 Beaver Street, the owners of the barkentine L. W. Norton, which is supposed to have gone down in the harbor of St. Pierre, it was said yesterday that not a word of the ship had been heard. Mr. Foulke said that he was sure that his Captain would report to him at any cost if the vessel was still safe, but that he feared to worst. The ship was chartered by the American Trading Company and had a cargo of about $30,000 value.

Charles R. Leaycraft, head of the firm of Leaycraft & Co., 140 Pearl Street, said that his firm had goods on the Roraima to the value of $540, and that a total of some $800 was due him from merchants in St. Pierre. His firm had not done a large business with Martinique for several years, he said.

Aymer Cater, a traveling representative of Leaycraft & Co., said that he was in St. Pierre in March of this year, and that while he was there the subject of the volcano was never mentioned. He and a friend spent a Saturday and Sunday at a resort right under the mountain, where there were some warm sulphur baths. The idea of fearing danger from the volcano had never occurred to the people there, he said.

Members of the firm of L. W. & P. Armstrong of 106 Wall Street said yesterday that they had heard nothing of their ship, the Talisman. They were still under the belief, however, that the vessel was at Barbados, and that she had escaped the fury of Mont Pelée.

MAP OF THE CITY OF ST. PIERRE.

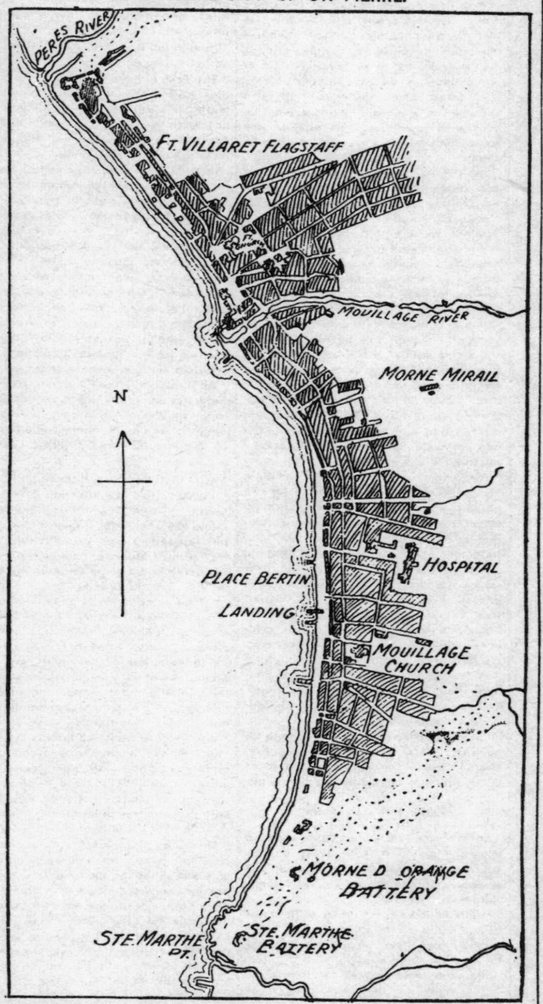

This Diagram Illustrates the Manner in Which the Stricken City Skirts the Shore for a Mile or More. The Land Rises from the Water at a Considerable Slope.

GREAT ANXIETY IN PARIS.

The French Government Sends Relief to Martinique—Fifty Bordeaux Families Bereaved.

PARIS, May 10.—The Minister of Marine has received the following undated dispatch from Pointe a Pitre Island of Guadeloupe, from the commander of the French cruiser Suchet:

"I have obtained the following information of the events of yesterday: About 8 o'clock the volcano threw up a considerable mass of smoke and earth. A whirlwind of fire immediately followed. Instantly the whole town (of St. Pierre) was in flames, and the ships in the harbor were dismasted and burned.

"The shower of rocks lasted a quarter of an hour. I arrived at St. Pierre at 2 o'clock in the afternoon, saving a few persons from the ships. I saw no living creature in St. Pierre, to which it was impossible to penetrate. There were numerous corpses near the quay."

A telegram from the Governor of the Island of Guadeloupe contains news of the Martinique cataclysm received at the Colonial Office. After announcing that the French cruiser Suchet had thirty survivors on board, the Governor of Guadeloupe says:

"Everything tends to the belief that the Governor of the colony, M. L. Mouttet, and Col. Gerbault and their wives perished with the population of St. Pierre. I have ordered the prompt dispatch of provisions from Pointe a Pitre and Basseterre. The Suchet sails for Martinique this evening. All of the people and the supplies of Guadeloupe are at your disposal for relief."

At a meting of the French Cabinet this morning the Minister of Finance, M. Caillaux, was authorized to expend all the money necessary to succor the sufferers by the Martinique disaster. An official of the Colonial Office sailed from Brest for Martinique this morning with 500,000f. ($100,000) in cash.

The Cabinet further decided to order the half-masting of flags over all public buildings for three days, and the Minister of the Colonies, M. Decrais, was instructed to telegraph to the Government of Martinique the condolences of France.

M. Decrais informed the Cabinet meeting that Senator Knight (President of the Legislature of Martinique, who was believed to have lost his life at St. Pierre) had escaped. The wife of Senator Knight has received a cable dispatch from her husband, dated Port-de-Franca, Martinique, at 3 P. M. yesterday, saying: "Well, property safe." The cable dispatch from Senator Knight also said that Morne-Rouge was spared.

An unending procession of inquirers who have friends and relatives on the stricken island is arriving at the Ministry of the Colonies, which has telegraphed to every possible source for information.

A few private telegrams received here renew the hope that some of the inhabitants of St. Pierre escaped. The Bishop of Martinique sent a cable message from Fort de France, forwarded at [illegible] P. M. yesterday, announcing the safety of Pastor King of St. Pierre, who escaped the disaster and sought refuge at Morne Rouge. It is hoped that others fled there.

Cable messages have been received by the southern route. All the northern cables are interrupted.

At least fifty families of Bordeaux are bereaved. Most of the business of St. Pierre was transacted through Bordeaux.

"All the News That's Fit to Print."

The New York Times

THE WEATHER.

Cloudy, warmer; probably snow; fresh west winds.

VOL. LIII...NO. 16,845.　　　NEW YORK, THURSDAY, DECEMBER 31, 1903.—SIXTEEN PAGES.　　　ONE CENT　In Greater New York, Jersey City and Newark. Elsewhere TWO CENTS.

OVER 500 DIE IN CHICAGO THEATRE

Fire Panic in the Iroquois Causes Frightful Loss.

DISASTER AT A MATINEE.

Women and Children Trampled in the Wild Rush.

FIRE STARTED ON THE STAGE

"Mr. Blue Beard" Was Playing and an Electrical Appliance Is Supposed to Have Caused the Fire.

BODIES AT THE MORGUES.

Rolsten	182	Perrigo	19
Jordan	14	Boydston	19
Gavin	79	Hays	21
John Carroll	21	S. E. Cleveland	9
J. W. Hudson	33		
Cook	17	Total	566
Sheldon	47		

RECORD OF THE DISASTER.

The dead........566 Reported miss-
The injured....350 ing .... .250
Identified 196

Special to The New York Times.

CHICAGO, Dec. 31.—Between 550 and 600 lives were lost in ten minutes in a fire and panic in the new Iroquois Theatre between 3:15 and 3:25 yesterday afternoon. The Iroquois Theatre was, the newest, the largest, and, as far as human power could make it, the safest theatre in Chicago.

It is on the north side of Randolph Street, between State Street and Dearborn Street. The stage backs up to Dearborn Street and faces east.

At the morgues are 566 bodies, 100 of which have been identified. More than 500 were injured and more than 200 are missing.

Of the dead a few score were identified last night. Of the unidentified nearly all were so badly burned that recognition was impossible. Only by trinkets and burned scraps of wearing apparel will the bodies of scores be made known to their families.

All night long a horror chained, persistent throng of those whose friends and relatives were numbered among the missing lifted blanket after blanket in the search through the morgues of the city.

Not since the fire of 1871 has Chicago been visited by such a tragedy. It has, over before the city knew that it happened; the news left paralysis behind.

Large Audience Present.

"Mr. Blue Beard" was being performed in the theatre. An audience not only of unusual size, but of unusual composition, was listening to it. It was the matinee audience of the mid-holiday season. Only once in a year could such an audience have gathered; only once in all the twelve months could so many children have been collected within the walls of the theatre. And on this one occasion the sacrifice to flame was demanded.

There were two in the audience, and in the galleries, from which the greatest tribute was demanded, but they were few in proportion to the children. Women died with their arms around their children. There were 2,000 persons or thereabouts in the theatre. Of that number 1,700 had seats.

The rest were massed in the rear of seats on the floor and the first balcony. In the galleries, even the rear seats of the seated gallery, were seated persons who ordinarily would have not been content with anything less than parquet seats. They were mothers, aunts, and elder sisters taking the children for an outing which fitted only to the one afternoon; young fellows from college treating their visiting chums to the theatre; schoolgirls out with their young friends for the same kind of a lark.

Such was the human material provided on one side of the curtain. On the other were 300 members of the extravaganza company. They were dressed in filmy garments trailing with gauze, veils of death once the breath of fire swept over them. Between audience and performers was the curtain line, down which an asbestos fire curtain should have fallen one second after the alarm was given. The curtain never fell.

The fire leaped from the stage as if from a furnace door. The draught from the open stage exits behind drove it upward to the

INDEX TO DEPARTMENTS.

galleries. Over a carpet of the dead it forced its own way through the chimney of the alley doors in the galleries.

The newest theatre in Chicago, the playhouse declared to be fireproof from dressing room to capstone, burned till it was a steel skeleton and its wrecked interior a charnel house. The Coroner to-morrow will begin to learn who, if any one, was to blame; the Building Commissioner will endeavor to learn if the building was overcrowded, and if all the fire ordinances were obeyed.

Asbestos Curtain Did Not Fall.

The only thing plain last night was that the asbestos curtain did not fall. The flyman of the theatre, Charles Johnson, says that for some time past it had been the practice at the theatre to have the curtain high at night so as to permit a good view of the aerial ballet. "They attempted to drop the curtain," he said, " but it would not drop below the height it had been fixed at."

The report made to Manager Will J. Davis was that the curtain caught when a little way down and bulged out under the force of the terrific draught. "Men tried to pull it down," he said. "It would not come." Another report in circulation was that the assistant stage manager, who had immediate charge of the curtain, was not on the stage, but in the audience. He, it was declared, would have touched an electric button, which would have operated the sheet in a second. Without him, according to this rumor, the attempt was made clumsily to run the curtain down by hand.

The fire started while the double octette was singing "Pearly Moonlight," Eddie Foy, off the stage, was making up for his "elephant" specialty.

On the audience's left—the stage right—a line of fire flashed straight up. It was followed by a noise as of an explosion. According to early accounts, however, there was no real explosion, the sound being that of the fuse of the "spot " light.

This light caused the fire. On this all reports of the stage folk agree. As to the manner accounts differ widely. R. M. Cummings, the boy in charge of the light, said last night that it was short circuited. Stage hands, as they fled from the scene, however, were heard to question one another. "Who kicked over the light? " The light belonged to the "Mr. Bluebeard" company.

The beginning of the disaster was slow. The stagehands had been fighting the line of wavering flame along the muslin fly border for some seconds before 'the audience knew anything was the matter. The fly border was tinder to the fire. Made of muslin, it was saturated with paint. The stagehands grasped the long sticks used in their work. "Hit it with the sticks!" was the cry. "Beat it out, beat it out!"

The men struck savagely. A few yards of the border fell upon the stage, and were stamped to charred fragments.

That sight was the first warning the audience had. For a second there was a hush. The players halted in their lines; the musicians ceased to play.

Then the murmur of fear ran through the audience. There were cries from a few, followed by the breaking, rumbling sound of the first step toward the flight of panic.

Eddie Foy's Coolness.

At that moment a strange figure appeared upon the stage. It wore tights, a loose upper garment, and the face was one-half made up. It was Eddie Foy, chief comedian of the company.

Before he reached the centre of the stage he had called out to a stage hand:

"Take my Bryan, there; get hold of there by the stage way!"

The stage hand grabbed the little chap. Foy saw him dart with him to safety as he turned his head.

Freed of parental anxiety, he faced the audience.

"Keep quiet!" he shouted; "quiet! Go out in order."

Between exclamations he bent over toward Herbert Dillea, the orchestra leader. "Start an overture," he commanded; " start anything. For God's sake, play and keep on playing."

The brave words were as bravely answered. Dillea raised his wand and the musicians began to play. Better than any one in the theatre they knew the peril. They could look up and see that the 300 sets of the "Mr. Blue Beard" scenery all were ablaze. Their faces were white, their hands trembled, but they played, and played.

The curtain started to come down. It stopped, it swayed as from a heavy wind, and then it " buckled " near the centre. From that moment no power short of omnipotent could have saved the occupants of the upper gallery.

The coolness of Foy, of Dillea, and of others players, who begged the audience to hold itself in check, however, probably saved many lives on the parquet floor. Panic prevailed, but the maddest of it, save in the doomed gallery, was at the outskirts of the ground floor crowd.

Those in greatest danger through proximity to the stage did not throw their weight against the mass ahead. Not many died on the first floor, proof of the contention that some restraint existed in this section of the audience.

Women were trod under foot near the rear. Most at this point, however, were rescued by the determined rush of the policemen at the entrance and of the doorkeeper and his assistants. The theatre had thirty exits. All were opened before the fire reached full headway, but some had to be forced open.

Only one door at the Randolph Street entrance was opened, the others being locked, according, it appears, to custom, from within and without; these doors were

shattered in the first two minutes after the fire broke out.

Doors Difficult to Open.

The doors of the exits on the alley side, between Randolph and Lake Streets, in one or more instances are declared by those who escaped to have been either frozen or rusted. They opened to assaults, but priceless seconds were lost.

Before this time, Foy had run back across the stage and reached the alley. With him fled the members of the aerial ballet, the last of the performers to get out.

The aerialists owed their lives to the boy in charge of the fly elevator. They were aloft in readiness for their flight above the heads of the audience. The elevator boy run his cage up even with the line of flies, took them in, and brought them safely down.

As Foy and the group reached the outer doorway the stage loft collapsed, and tons of fire poured over the stage. The lights went out in the theatre with this destruction of the switchboard and all stage connections. One column of flame rose and swished along the ceiling of the theatre. Then this awful illumination also was swallowed up. None may paint from personal understanding that which took place in that pit of darkness.

In spite of the terrible form of the destruction, it came swiftly enough to shorten pain. This, at least, was true of those who died in the second balcony, striving to reach the alley exits abreast of them. Six and seven feet deep they were found, not packed in layers, but jumbled and twisted in a struggle with one another.

Opposite the westernmost exit of the balcony was a room in the Northwestern University Building, where painters were working, wiping out the traces of another fire.

They heard the round of the detonation of the fuse and the roar of feet toward the exit across the way. Out on the iron stairway came a man, pushed by a power behind, himself crazy with fear. He would have run down the iron fire-escape, but flame, bursting out of the exit beneath, wrapped itself around the iron ladder.

"A ladder!" shouted one of the painters. "Run it out." It was run out. The man started to cross. The ladder slipped on the frosty window casing. Its burden was precipitated down on the icy ground. The first of the arriving firemen picked up the broken form.

Escape on Planks.

"Wait," cried the painters. "We have planks." Three wide planks were thrust across the alley. The painters dropped to their knees to anchor them. "Come on," they shouted, Hortense Lang, sixteen years old, dragging her sister Irene, eleven years old, was the first to cross.

"I was going to jump," she sobbed, " but I thought of my mother. I just grabbed sister by the hand, and waited for the planks. I don't know how we crossed." The mother, Mrs. L. Lang, 780 Forty-sixth Street, also was in the theatre, on the first floor. She got out safely, and an hour afterward found her children in the Tremont House. The reunited three sat with arms around one another for another hour. Just twelve persons escaped across the plank way. The twelfth was pursued by a pillar of fire, which dashed itself against the wall of the university building. The steel platform was packed with women and children. They died right there.

The bodies of some fell over into the alley. From within the bodies of others fell part way out of the aperture. The helpless watchers peering through the smoke could see the heaps of the dead between the seats and along the outside aisle of the gallery. Firemen crossed the gangway as soon as the tongue of flame drew back and climbed over the ghastly wall to direct the streams of water inward and downward.

They entered too soon. The tongue again and a number of spectators arose to their feet and shouted for order, and did everything in their power to prevent a panic. Then somebody screamed, and everybody apparently lost all control of themselves and ran for the doors. I was knocked down twice by men who seemed to have lost their minds."

The firemen and police retreated stubbornly, but they were driven back. Marshal Campion was in command of the firemen. He saw that the gallery must be for a time abandoned.

The forms of women and children were all about him and his men. No movement was perceptible, but he knew that the living might be buried under the dead. "Is there any living person here?" the Marshal shouted.

The cry echoed through the silent place and no voice answered. Once more he shouted: " If any one here is alive, groan or make some sound; we'll take you out." Not an arm waved in the mounds about him. No moan was heard.

" We will have to fall back," ordered the Marshal. Reluctantly as they defiled over the planks the fire once more billowed to the windows. But this time it claimed no new victim. It needed not to make its work more thorough.

The persons crowded off the fire-escape platform and those who jumped voluntarily by their own death saved persons on the lower floors from injury. Score jumped from the seats in the first balcony to comparative safety on the thick cushion of the bodies of those who preceded them, and who fell from the balcony above.

Other hundreds from the main floor jumped into the same cushion—an easy distance of six feet—without any injury. When the firemen came they spread nets, but the nets were black, and in the gloom they could not be seen.

When the work of removing the bodies to the sidewalk and placing them in the wagons was at its hardest, the lights in the lobby of the theatre and at the entrance were cut out, leaving the firemen to continue in almost total darkness.

Thieves Rob the Dead.

It was a tomb, in which ghouls were plenty. They robbed the pockets of the dead and tore rings from the fingers. In the blackness of the theatre they could

M. Mosquin, Bordeaux, exported thus year 100,000 gallons of Bordeaux and Burgundy Wine to the United States. Taste the Mosquin importation. Ask for price list at M. Mosquin, 426 6th Av., and Mosquin Restaurant, 30 Ann St.—Adv.

Deerfoot Farm Sausages. With increasing knowledge of the danger to health through carelessly prepared food, consumers give more fastidious in their selection. "Deerfoot" means purity, daintiness, cleanliness.—Adv.

A Ready-made Memory. The 1904 Tribune Almanac contains everything you wish to remember. Out to-day. Price 25 cents.—Clark Br'oers.—Adv.

work unobserved, but it was not long before the police had discovered their presence and made war on them.

The police had barred every one from the theatre except newspaper reporters and a few others entitled to enter, but when the blankets were sent from the stores volunteers were called to carry them in.

The thieves seized the opportunity and entered the place of death in the guise of messengers of mercy, but once inside the theatre and hidden by the pall of smoke, they turned into fiends. The first intimation of their presence was when a boyish-looking young man carrying a single blanket crawled bodily over the pile of dead at the fatal angle and pushed past the police.

"The firemen sent me in with the blanket" he shouted. Chief O'Neill caught him by the arm, but the man wriggled loose and pushed toward the interior of the theatre, shouting that the blanket was needed by the firemen.

"Get out!" roared the Chief, who was struggling to dig down through the heap of dead to where the moaning told that some one yet lived. "Men, throw that man out of here; he's a thief." A policeman seized the man and pushed him down stairs.

"Men," he said, " that man was here to rob the dead. You who are not needed here hurry through the theatre and put out everybody not entitled to remain." The police jumped to their work. A fireman crawling on his hands and knees in the smoke saw a figure that he thought at first was that of a victim of the fire.

He drew near it arose and disappeared in the gloom. The fireman found a body on the floor where he had seen the man. After the body of the woman had been carried out it was seen that the fingers were lacerated where rings had been torn away. But the ghouls had little time to ply their work, for the police drove them from the building.

PANIC BALKS ESCAPE

Maddened Audience Unable To Reach the Exits.

Hundreds Were Caught on the Stairways and Vainly Tried to Climb Out Over Bodies.

Special to The New York Times.

CHICAGO, Dec. 30.—When the appalling danger of the fire was flashed abroad, the police came on the heels of the firemen, intent on the work of rescue. Chief O'Neill and Assistant Chief Schuettler ordered all Captains from a dozen stations to bring their men. They rushed to the theatre and led the police up the stairs to the first balcony.

The firemen rushing blindly up the stairs in the dense smoke, had found their path suddenly blocked by a wall of dead bodies ten feet high. They discovered persons in this mass still alive and carried them out to safety. Other firemen crowded over the mass of dead and dragged their hose into the theatre to fight back the flames that seemed to be crawling nearer to turn the fatal landing into a funeral pyre.

The theatre had been constructed but a short time and all its equipment had no means of escape in the rear of the building. The small iron balconies to which the iron ladders were to be attached were up, but the ladders had not yet been constructed. When the panic was at its height a great number of women ran for these fire escapes, only to find as they emerged from this doorway upon the little iron platform that they were thirty to fifty feet from the ground, a fire behind, and no method of escape in front. Those who reached the platform first endeavored to hold their footing and to keep back the crowd that pressed upon them from the rear.

Alarm Turned In.

E. Leavitt, the ticket taker at the theatre, was at the main entrance, and, realizing the gravity of the situation at a glance, he burst open the three doors, and then ran to turn in the fire alarm.

"I heard the cry and saw the mob rushing for the door," said he. " I could not see the fire from where I stood, and I thought that it was not so bad as it really was. When the first of the frenzied audience reached the outside door I tried to calm them, but in less than a minute I saw it was no use, and I burst open the doors.

"Then I ran for the fire alarm box. Coming back, I assisted in the rescue as much as I could, but was overrun with the terrified crowd that pushed and moved each other out of the doorway, and I was caught in the maze of struggling humanity and carried out to the street.

"The first evidence of the fire," he said. " was a thin column of smoke which floated from the stage. This was followed by a sheet of flame which mounted to the ceiling and enveloped the hangings about the front of the stage. The people in the parquette started for the door in an orderly manner.

"The people on the stage, the ushers, and a number of spectators arose to their feet and shouted for order, and did everything in their power to prevent a panic. Then somebody screamed, and everybody apparently lost all control of themselves and ran for the doors. I was knocked down twice by men who seemed to have lost their minds."

Electrician Fights Blaze.

John E. Farrell, the stage electrician, was one of the heroes of the fire. He was the first to discover the blaze when it was a little tongue of flame running up the canvas border of the curtain. He climbed a ladder twenty feet above the stage and sought to extinguish it with his hand. He beat helplessly until his hands were badly burned, and the fire had run up the canvas border into the flies.

Seizing a hand grenade, he dashed it at the fire, and the failing fluid nearly blinded him. With the cry of " Save yourselves!" he fell to the floor, and then running to the rear door of the theatre, he threw it open, calling to the members of the company to rush into the alley.

In the work of assisting the women he was aided by Stage Manager Cummings. As the frightened actors and actresses rushed in a body off the stage, some of them attempted to leap into the orchestra pit. Cummings ran in front of them. " I'll kill the first one that tries to get through the door," he shouted, and the members of the company shrank back.

With the aid of Eddie Foy and Farrell the members of the company were hustled from the rear of the theatre into the alley. Penned below the stage, running about crazed by the panic overhead, were fifty supernumeraries and members of the ballet. They were cut off from the exit by the crowds wedged in the stage stairway. They were saved by James J. Hamilton, a trunk handler attached to the theatre, who led the way to a coal hole in the rear of the building, broke off the cover with his bare flats, and stood guard until all had left the basement.

Search for Friends.

All night and into the early hours of the morning the lower corridor of the City Hall was crowded with men, women, and children, seeking some trace of missing relatives or friends. Husbands were inquiring for wives, parents for children, and children for parents.

James Van Ingen of Kenosha, Wis., who brought his entire family to see the entertainment, reported that all his five children, ranging in age from two to twenty years, were unaccounted for, while the mother was sitting weeping in the Sherman House, beseeching him to get news of them.

A young man living in Englewood came with a list of seven girls who reside in the neighborhood of Yale Avenue and Sixty-third Street. The comrades had made up a theatre party, and not one of them had been heard from since.

Mrs. L. A. Rose, 832 North Clark Street, gave the names of her three children. All had gone to the theatre in company of an aunt, and neither the aunt nor children had been heard from.

ting out through a rear door after assisting the women members of the company to safety. He went into the Sherman House in his stage costume and with his face covered with grease paint in order to secure surgical attendance for some burns which he had sustained.

The workers fell back and the fireman pulled himself over the heap and, helped by the police, gained the other side with a child in his arms, and struggled out to air and safety. Then other firemen from inside the theatre passed out more bodies, handed from one policeman to another, until some on the outside of the heap could take the dead and carry them down stairs.

Another Woman Brought Out Alive.

Suddenly a policeman pulled out a woman. "She's alive, Chief!" he yelled. She was eighteen years old and moaning faintly. Now it was a woman, now a man, and then some little child—dead, unconscious, or wounded. Volunteers assisted the rescuers and helped to reduce the awful pile packed on the fatal landing.

The news of the fire had spread with great rapidity, and in a short time hundreds of men, women, and children were rushing toward the theatre. The building in which the calamity occurred stands midway between State and Dearborn Streets, on the north side of Randolph Street. Although every available policeman within call of the department was immediately hurried to the spot and the men packed in lines at the end of the block, allowing nobody to enter Randolph Street from either Dearborn or State Streets, it was found for a time almost impossible to hold back the frenzied crowd that pressed forward, many of them having friends or relatives in the theatre and anxious to learn something of them.

Break Through Police Lines.

In spite of the efforts of the police, many succeeded in breaking through the lines and did heroic work in rescuing the injured and carrying out the dead. Among these was ex-Alderman William H. Thompson, who, unaided, carried to the street the bodies of eight women. The first newspaper men upon the ground also carried out many of the dead and injured.

The building was so full of smoke when the firemen first arrived that the full extent of the catastrophe was not immediately grasped until a fireman and a newspaper man crawled up the stairs leading to the balcony, holding handkerchiefs over their mouths to avoid suffocation. As they reached the doorway the firemen, whose windows was better trained in such emergencies, seized his companion by the arm, exclaiming, " Good God, man, don't walk on their faces!"

The two men tried vainly to get through the door, which was jammed with dead women piled higher than either of their heads. All the lights in the theatre were necessarily out, and the only illumination came through the cloud of smoke that hung between the interior of the theatre and the street. The two men immediately hurried to the floor below and informed Chief Mussham of the Fire Department that the dead bodies were piled high in the balcony, and prompt assistance must be rendered if any of them were to be saved. The Chief at once called upon all his men in the vicinity to abandon work on the fire and come at once to the rescue.

Job Evans, one of the principals of the Bluebeard company, was in his dressing room on the fourth floor reading the afternoon paper when the alarm of fire was sounded from the stage. He looked out of his dressing room and saw a mass of flames coming from the curtains, coming up into the flies. Leaving everything behind him, he had to dive through that mass of flame down the stairway.

He threw himself down the stairway, got through the flames, and landed three stairways below. He rushed to the stage, and all was in confusion. He helped a number of chorus girls to escape out through the lower basement. Bob's hands and face are burned severely, and he lost all his wardrobe and personal effects.

Chorus Girl's Heroism.

Lola Quinlan, one of Blue Beard's eight dancers, saved the life of one of her companions, Violet Sidney, an eminent peril of her own. The two girls, with five others, were in a dressing room on the flies floor when the alarm was raised. In her haste Miss Sidney caught her foot and sank to the floor with a cry of pain. She had sprained her ankle. Grasping her companion around the waist, Miss Quinlan dragged her down the stairs to the stage and crossed the boards during a rain of fiery brands.

These two were the last to leave the stage. Miss Quinlan's right arm and hand were painfully burned and her face was scorched. Miss Sidney's face was slightly burned. Both were taken to the Continental Hotel.

Herbet Dillon, musical director, at the height of the panic broke through the stage door from the orchestra side, hastily cleared away obstructions with an axe, and assisted in the escape of about eighty chorus girls who occupied ten dressing rooms under the stage.

"My God, man, my daughter is in there; my daughter is in there!" cried a frantic father, who was trying to beat his way past the line of policemen. Behind him and at his side were scores of other men who had jumped from their desks in office buildings as the report that the Iroquois was burning had spread.

"My wife is there!" "My boys are there!" "My family is in there!" These maddened men, with faces convulsive, tear-stained, and twitching with agony, were trying to break through the police, beating them back. "You can't find them!"

Now and then a man got past the struggling line and was found wandering about the lobby of the theatre, cracking the glass of the smashed skylight under his feet, alternately smiling and sobbing, apparently robbed of reason.

"My wife and three daughters were here," said one of these in a whisper to the policeman who led him out. His features were distorted, wet with tears, but he smiled as a man whose mind had been benumbed. "Of course, they got out," said another, as a policeman stopped him at the foot of the stairs to the balcony. " Of course, they got out, officer. Didn't they get out? Nervily everybody got out, didn't they? It's my wife and our little girl. But they got out. Of course they got out!"

The building was so dark and the smoke so thick that it was found impossible to accomplish anything until lights had been secured. Word was at once sent to the Orr and Lockat Hardware Company, two doors east of the theatre, and that firm at once placed its entire stock of lanterns at the service of the department. Over 200 lights were quickly carried into the building and the work of rescue commenced.

Burnett's Extract of Vanilla imparts a superior delicacy of flavor. Try it. Use it.—Adv.

You can't enjoy life if your lungs trouble you. Piso's Cure cures. All druggists.—Adv.

TAKING OUT THE DEAD

Bodies Piled Three and Four Deep in Aisles.

Clothing Torn Completely Off Many Victims and Faces Ground Off by Trampling Heels.

Special to The New York Times.

CHICAGO, Ill., Dec. 30.—As near as can be estimated about two thousand persons were in the theatre. Three hundred of these were on the first floor, the rest being in the two upper balconies and in the hallways back of them. The theatre is modeled after the Opera Comique, in Paris, and from the rear of each balcony there are three doors leading out to passageways toward the front of the theatre. Two of these doorways are at the end of the balcony, and one in the centre.

The audience in its rush for the outer life seems for the greater part to have chosen to flee to the left entrance and to attempt to make its way down the eastern stairway leading into the lobby of the theatre. Outside of the people burned and suffocated by gas it was in these two doorways on the first and second balconies that the greatest loss of life occurred.

When the firemen entered the building the dead were found stretched in a pile reaching from the head of the passageway at least eight feet from the door back to a point about five feet in rear of the door. This mass of dead bodies in the centre of the doorway reached to within two feet of the top of the passageway. All of the corpses at this point were women and children.

The fight for life which must have taken place at these two points is something that is beyond human power to imagine. Only a faint idea of its horror could be derived from the aspect of the bodies as they lay. Women on top of these masses of dead had been overtaken by death as they were crawling on their hands and knees over the bodies of those who had died before.

Others lay with arms stretched out in the direction toward which lay life and safety, holding in their hands fragments of garments not their own. They were evidently torn from the clothing of others whom they had endeavored to pull down and trample under foot as they fought for their own lives. As the police and firemen removed layer after layer of dead in these doorways, the sight became too much even for them, hardened as they are to such scenes, to endure.

The bodies were in such an inextricable mass, and so tightly were they jammed between the sides of the door and the walls, that it was impossible to lift them one by one and carry them out.

The only possible thing to do was to seize a limb or some other portion of the body and pull with main strength. Now and then a shoe would come off, or the skin of the dead would peel away from the face and cheeks, and the sole of the rescuers could be heard even in the hall below where this awful scene was being enacted. A number of the men were compelled to abandon their task and give it over to others whose nerves had not as yet been shaken by the awful experience.

Clothing Torn Off Bodies.

As one by one the bodies were dragged out of the water-soaked, blackened mass of corpses the spectacle became more and more heartrending. There were women whose clothing was torn completely from their bodies above the waist and whose faces were marred beyond all power of identification. Bodies lay in the first and second balconies in great numbers.

In some places they were piled up in the aisles three and four deep, where one had fallen and others tripped over the prostrate forms, and all had died where they lay, evidently suffocated by the gas. Others were bent over backs of seats, where their had been thrown by the rush of people for the doors, and killed with hardly a chance to rise from their seats. One man was found with his back bent nearly double, his spinal column having been fractured as he was thrown backward. A woman was found cut nearly in half by the back of the seat, she having been forced over it face downward.

In the aisles nearest to the doors the scenes were harrowing. Bodies lay in every conceivable attitude; some half naked, agony written on their faces. There were scores of people whose entire faces had been ground off by the heels of those who rushed over them. In one aisle a man was found, the entire upper portion of whose body had been cut into mince meat and carried away by the hundreds of feet that had trampled over it. His head had been torn off.

When the work of removing the dead from the balcony and gallery was begun, few injured were found. The injured had been rescued before the firemen reached the choked exits to the upper floors of the house. Behind the barrier of dead piled in these doorways there were no living persons.

The bodies that were found in masses in the two exits to the balcony and the rear to the gallery in one case completely filled the passageway. In removing these bodies the firemen and police reached above their shoulders to pull down those who had crawled to the tops of the pile in a vain effort to reach the outer stairways.

Until this obstruction of dead bodies had been removed the crowds of people in the street had no idea of the extent of the disaster. They had jumped from the sight of the injured being removed and of the chorus girls being supported along the street. After the injured had been removed to near-by stores and restaurants there was a period of fifteen minutes, in which the crowd waited, half believing that there was nothing worse hidden up the blackened stairway.

It was found necessary, in order to convey the bodies rapidly to the morgue and to the various undertaking establishments, to impress trucks into service, many upon costly blankets furnished by the dry goods stores in the vicinity, and covered with the same material, the dead were hauled away practically like so much cord-wood.

Great Stores Furnish Aid.

The merchants in the vicinity of the theatre rose to the emergency in splendid fashion. Marshall Field & Co., Mandel Brothers, Schlesinger & Meyer, Carson, Pierie, Scott & Co., and other large dry goods stores sent wagonload after wagonload of blankets, rolls of linen, and packages of cotton to be used in binding up the wounds of the injured and to cover the dead. The drug stores furnished their stock to anybody that asked for it in the name of people hurt in the fire. Doctors and trained nurses were on the ground by the score within half an hour after the extent of the calamity was known, and every wounded person who was carried from the building received prompt medical aid. A number of doctors waited at the entrance to the theatre with stethescopes in hand, and as soon as a body which looked as though it might possess life was carried out it was at once examined, and, if dead, placed on the pile lying on the sidewalk. The others were at once placed in ambulances and whirled away to hospitals or to the offices of physicians in the immediate neighborhood.

One large truck ordinarily used for conveying freight to depots was so heavily loaded with dead in front of the theatre that the two large horses attached to it were unable to start, and the police were compelled to assist by tugging at the wheels. When the need for trucks to remove the dead was more pressing, a huge electric delivery wagon, owned by Montgomery, Ward & Co., was hailed by the police.

The automobile headed for the scene, but at State Street encountered so great a press of people that it could not get through. The chauffeur clanged his gong repeatedly, but the crowd refused to part, and the automobile was finally turned away.

Scenes on the Sidewalk.

The side in front of the theatre and Thompson's restaurant was being completely filled with dead bodies, when it was seen that the patrol wagons and ambulances could not remove the bodies which were being borne down the stairways constantly.

They lay outstretched on the sidewalk covered with blankets. Great care in the handling was impossible. As soon as a space on the walk was made by the removal of bodies there were two brought down to fill it.

One of the wagons of the Dixon Transfer Company was so heavily loaded with the dead that the two big horses drawing it were unable to start the truck. Policemen and spectators had to put their shoulders to the wheels.

When once the drays were filled and started there was a struggle to get them through the crowds, so densely were the people packed even without the fire lines, which the police had stretched across Randolph Street at State Street and Dearborn Street.

Policemen with clubs had to precede many of the wagons, and the crowd through which they forced their way was composed mostly of men who had sent wives and children to the theatre, and had reason to believe that one of the drays might carry members of their own family. Eight and ten wagons at a time, half of them trucks and delivery wagons, would be backed up to the curbstone at a time waiting for their load of dead.

Two policemen would grab a blanket at the corners and swing it with its contents up to two others in the wagon. It would be laid beside the others, and so on until a wagon of bodies had been stacked up. Then the police forced a way through the crowd, and another wagon took its place.

Occasionally a body would be identified, and then efforts would be made to remove it directly to the home. Coroner Traeger thus discovered the wife of Patrick P. O'Donnell, President of the O'Donnell & Duer Brewing Company. The body was taken to the residence at 4629 Woodlawn Avenue.

MORGUE OVERFLOWED.

Saloon's Back Room Pressed Into Service—Most Victims Were Women and Children.

Special to The New York Times.

CHICAGO, Dec. 30.—One hundred and thirty-five bodies to-night lay on the floors in the morgue of C. H. Jordan, 16 Madison Street, and in the temporary annex across the alley. The first were brought in ambulances and police patrol wagons. Later, all sorts of conveyances were pressed into service, and for more than two hours there was a procession of two-horse trucks, delivery wagons, and cabs, all filled with ghastly loads.

As carefully as might be, the bodies were carried in and laid on the floors. It was plain from the first that the capacity of the place would be quickly exhausted, and the people who sat drinking and talking about the tables in the back room of the saloon across the alley were quickly driven out, and this also was arranged for use as a temporary morgue.

Two police officers were in charge of each load of the dead, and as soon as the first few bodies were received they set to work searching for possible marks of identification. All jewelry and valuables, as well as letters, cards, and other papers were taken from each body and put in sealed envelopes and properly marked. When this work had been completed all the envelopes were sent to Police Headquarters at the City Hall, and all inquirers after missing friends and relatives were referred to the City Hall.

Many of the bodies last brought in from the theatre were so badly burned and disfigured that identification must be slow, if it is ever possible. Almost all of the faces were badly discolored and the clothing rumpled and wet.

Many of the bodies were distorted so as to show how the unfortunates had struggled vainly for escape. Almost all of them were either women or children, and it was noticeable that the majority had been well dressed. Among them were several old women and lying side by side with them on the floors were little girls and small boys. The men were few. In many cases the flesh of the hands was badly torn as if violent efforts had been made to wrench away some obstruction.

People were strangely slow in coming to the Morgue in search of friends. Many of them had their first suspicion of the catastrophe when members of theatre parties failed to return home at the usual hour. Among the first to arrive at Jordan's Morgue were G. E. McCaughan, counsel for the Rock Island Railroad, and a friend, who came in search of Mr. McCaughan's daughter Helen, who had attended a theatre party in company with a number of other young women. The friend had been in Dearborn Street when the fire broke out, and shortly after had discovered Miss McCaughan's body laid out in Thompson's restaurant. He attached to it a card bearing the name, and, leaving it in charge of a physician, went to the telephone to notify her father. When he returned the body had already been removed, and he and the girl's father searched for hours last night without finding it.

As it grew later the crowd about the doors increased, but almost everybody was turned away. As a matter of fact, it would have been impossible for people to have passed through the long rooms for the purpose of inspecting the bodies, so closely did they lie together. Women came weeping to the doors and beat upon the glass, only to be referred to the City Hall or told to come back in the morning. Later people learned that physicians would be promptly admitted for that purpose.

Two women who pressed by the officer at the door sank half fainting into chairs in the outer office. They were looking for Miss Hazel J. Brown of 94 Thirty-first Street, and Miss Eloise G. Swayze of Fifty-sixth Street and Normal Avenue. They were told to come back in the morning or to send their family physician to make the identification.

"The poor girls had come home from the convent to spend the holiday vacation," sobbed one of the women as she went out.

"Have you found a small, heart-shaped locket set with a blue stone?" would come the call over the 'phone, and the answer would be: "We can tell nothing about that until morning. If you wish to send your physician down, he can inspect the bodies to-night."

DEAD FILL RESTAURANT.

Senator Clark, with a Megaphone, Directs Work of Physicians.

Special to The New York Times.

CHICAGO, Dec. 30.—The scenes in Thompson's restaurant, adjoining the theatre, were ghastly beyond words. Few half hours in battle bring more of horror than the ... hour that turned the place into a charnel house, with its tumbled heaps of corpses, its shrieks of agony of the dying, and the confusion of doctors and nurses working madly over bodies as they strove to bring back the spark of life.

Bodies were everywhere piled along the walls, laid across tables, and flung down here and there. Some were charred beyond recognition, some only scorched, and others black from suffocation. Some were crushed in the rush of the panic.

The continuous tramp of the detachments of police bearing in more bodies, the efforts of the doctors to restore life, and the madness of relatives and friends who poured in through police lines to ransack piles of bodies, made up a scene of horror of which the reader has no conception.

Senator Clark Organizes.

The confusion was already great when Senator Clark leaped upon the coffee buffet and addressed the crowd of rescuers.

"We must have system and order here or we shall never accomplish anything," he shouted. "Let us divide up at once—quick, now, some one give an idea."

"We want a captain," cried one from the groups of physicians who worked at the bodies even while they organized. "I nominate Dr. G. Frank Lydston."

And before Senator Clark could observe parliamentary formality amid the surroundings of increasing ghastliness, the shout went up from the doctors: "Aye, aye—Lydston."

"Dr. Lydston, take command. I'll issue your orders, if you like," answered Senator Clark, who retained his position and began forming a megaphone of a newspaper.

"Doctors," shouted Dr. Lydston, taking instant command and formulating his plans as he proceeded. "Divide up among the tables, three to a table; now form in line and pass along."

TALES OF SURVIVORS

Eddie Foy's Story of How the Fire Started.

Sticking of the Curtain Saved the Actors' Lives—Lights Went Out and Panic Reigned.

Special to The New York Times.

CHICAGO, Dec. 30.—Eddie Foy, the comedian, who had one of the principal parts in "Mr. Bluebeard," and who was the man who ordered the curtain rung down and helped the women on the stage to escape, to-night gave a vivid account of the disaster as he saw it. Said Mr. Foy:

"Just before I came on for the second act I heard a commotion on the stage. I got out and saw that the fly border on the big drop had caught fire from a light or wire. The border was muslin, and the fire crept, crept, crept, while the noise on the stage grew louder, and the people began screaming and running off the stage. My boy was in the entrance, and, as they wouldn't let me go out in front, I grabbed him and gave him to a man, and he rushed him to the outside.

"I went out to the footlights half-dressed, with only my tights on, and called to the people to keep quiet. 'Don't get excited,' I cried. 'Don't stampede; it's all right.' Then I called to the men to drop the curtain, and told the leader of the orchestra to play the overture. He stood up, white as a ghost, and beat his baton, but only a few men played. They had lost their heads, and were too frightened.

"The roar from the fire, the stamp of feet rushing to the outside, and the screams of the women drowned out the music. It was like a penny whistle against the north wind.

"Then I called to the policeman: 'Tell them to go out slowly, to leave the theatre slowly.' By this time the whole border was on fire. Then the narrow strips of the wood cracked with a small explosion, and the whole back of the stage was in flames and smoke. The fire curtain came only half way down. Maybe the man up in the gallery didn't dare to stay. If the asbestos curtain had come down it would have saved the people in the front of the house, I think.

"How did they act in the audience? When I started to talk about 300 people got out in advance, safe, and others were getting out. Then the police came in and tried to stop them. I wasn't there twelve seconds—that's a long time—maybe fifteen. I stayed as long as I could, but I was afraid when the scramble came at the back of the stage that my boy Bryan, only six years old, would be hurt.

"Up in the flies were the German ballet. They were at the top of the theatre, with nothing to bring them down but that elevator. There were about twelve girls. They were all up in there waiting for their turn. It was a case of get out or smother. On the stage they were singing 'Pearly Moonlight.' The sixteen girls tried to finish the song, but the music stopped and the singers screamed and ran off. The first thing I heard was a sudden noise like a small explosion, and some one calling: 'Get a stick; knock it with a pole!' Then I ran out and spoke to the leader and tried to calm the people; but the panic was already on. Something went wrong with the calcium light, and the borders caught fire, or else an electric fuse blew out. I heard both causes given."

Doors Were Fastened Against Egress.

"When I approached the Iroquois Theatre shortly after the outbreak of the fire," said S. I. Shane, President of the Western Wrecking and Lumber Company, "there was an awful crush, and I recognized the necessity of providing more egress for the struggling crowd. I found the doors of the east side of the house securely locked and barred. With the assistance of other men I broke the fastenings and thus relieved the crush from the inside.

"The people coming out of the pitch-dark theatre seemed frantic. Many had become separated from their friends in the wild rush, and after they had reached the vestibule made desperate attempts to get back into the theatre to search for their missing friends and relatives. We did our best to keep the people from returning to the auditorium, calling to them to go to Thompson's and other places next door, where they would probably find the missing ones. Finally the police and firemen arrived and succeeded in restoring order to some extent, pushing the people out of the house as quickly as possible.

"I believe that it was a great mistake of the employes of the house that they did not open all the doors to the auditorium as soon as the fire broke out. A great deal of trouble would have been avoided and perhaps many a life saved by prompt action. The fact that the lights went out in the house when the fire broke out contributed greatly to the terrors of the situation, as it naturally increased the panic and made it difficult for the panic-stricken crowd to find its way out of the house."

A View from the Upper Gallery.

D. W. Dimmick of Apple River, Ill., an old man of seventy, was standing in the upper gallery when the fire broke out.

"I was with a party of four," said Mr. Dimmick. "The second act had begun, when suddenly I saw small pieces of what looked like burning paper dropping down from above at the left of the curtain. At the same time small puffs of smoke seemed to shoot out into the house. On the first floor people began to move about, and a boy in the gallery near me called 'Fire!' but there were plenty of people to stop him.

"'Keep quiet,' I told him, 'if you don't look out you'll start a panic.'

"The musicians came out into the orchestra pit and began to play. Evidently they were trying to still the alarm. Some one of the players, I don't know who, ran out on to the stage and told us there was no danger. All this took but a minute or two. Then, all of a sudden the whole front of the stage and the orchestra pit to the top of the curtain seemed to burst out in one flame. Then it was all off. Everybody seemed to get up and start to get out of the place at once. From all over the house came shrieks and cries of 'Fire!' I and men who were with me started at once, hugging the wall on the outside of the stairway as we went. Almost at once the place seemed to get thick with smoke. I pulled out my handkerchief and held it over my mouth.

"When we got down to the platform where the first balcony opens it seemed to me that people were packed up like cordwood. There were women and children in the lot, but there were some people who, I thought, must be actors, who came running out from somewhere in the interior of the house, and whose wigs and clothes were on fire. We tried to beat out the flames as we went along. We managed to squeeze past the mass of people who were writhing on the floor and practically blocking the entrance.

"As we got by the mass on the floor I turned and caught hold of the arms of a woman who was lying near the bottom, pinned down by the weight on her feet. I managed to pull her out, and I think she got down in safety. One of the men with me also pulled out another woman from the heap. I tried to rescue a man who was also caught by the feet, but, although I braced myself against the stairs, I was unable to get him out.

"When we got down to the ground floor there were six or seven people lying there. I don't know whether they were overcome by the smoke or not, but we ran by them and got out safely. I came in from Apple River to see the sights in Chicago, and I have seen all I can stand."

Victims Packed Like Cordwood.

Dan O'Leary, the professional pedestrian, said: "When I arrived at the theatre the crew of Engine No. 40 were getting a line of hose up stairs into the gallery, making a noble fight of it. On the east side of the first balcony was a mass of bodies piled up like cordwood, men and women together, fifty or seventy-five I should judge.

"Up in the upper gallery, I don't know how many there were, probably fifty or a hundred bodies, anyway. It seems as though they all stampeded, and they must have fought like maniacs to make their escape. As I went up, on the first landing of the galleries lay the bodies of three women and a little girl.

"We went from the bottom to the top of the theatre and down again. I shouted to see if anybody would answer my voice, to see if there were any persons still alive there, but there was no response. All must have been dead."

Could Not Pull Curtain Down.

William " Sellers, the house fireman, who was severely burned in trying to lower the asbestos curtain, spoke of the scene upon the stage and the cause of the fire as follows:

"I was standing in the wings when I heard the explosion, and then immediately afterward a cry of fire from the stage and all over the theatre. Looking up, I saw that the curtain was ablaze, and at once I ran for the fire curtain. We got it half way down when the wind, rushing in from the broken skylights, bellied it out so that it caught, and we could not budge it. With the stage hands I climbed to where it was suspended, and together we tried to push it down. Our efforts were futile, and, seeing that no human power could move that fire curtain and that the stage was a mass of flames, I turned my attention to warning the actors and in trying to save those who were in trouble.

"The women were frantic, and the men not much better. I stood at the stairway leading to the dressing rooms where the chorus people were located, and kept some from going up to get their street clothes. As the others came down I forced them to leave the building. I don't know how they ever got out all those girls and men who came crowding down the stairs—for the stage entrance was blocked by a mass of flames."

The New York Times.

VOL. LIII...NO. 16,989.   NEW YORK, THURSDAY, JUNE 16, 1904.--SIXTEEN PAGES.   ONE CENT In Greater New York. | Jersey City and Newark. | TWO CENTS

1,000 LIVES MAY BE LOST IN BURNING OF THE EXCURSION BOAT GEN. SLOCUM

St. Mark's Church Excursion Ends in Disaster in East River Close to Land and Safety.

693 BODIES FOUND----HUNDREDS MISSING OR INJURED

Flames Following Explosion Drive Scores to Death in the Water.

FIERCE STRUGGLES FOR ROTTEN LIFE PRESERVERS

The Captain, Instead of Making for the Nearest Landing, Runs the Doomed Vessel Ashore on North Brother Island in Deep Water—Many Thrilling Rescues—Few Men on Board to Stem the Panic of Women and Children.

An estimated total of a thousand dead, besides several hundred injured, is the record of the fire disaster which yesterday destroyed the big excursion steamer General Slocum, which was burned to the water's edge before her Captain succeeded in beaching her on North Brother Island. Nearly all the dead and missing are women and children and were members of an excursion party taken out by St. Mark's German Lutheran Church of 323 East Sixth Street.

The estimate that the number of lives lost will be round to reach 1,000 was given by Police Inspector Brooks at an early hour this morning. Fire Chief Croker shared his view, saying that at least 900 persons must have perished.

At 3:30 o'clock this morning the toll Franklin Edson took to the morgue 69 more bodies. Just previously another tug took six, which were burned beyond recognition. Twelve more bodies, also burned, were left at North Brother Island, bringing the total of bodies so far recovered up to 693.

The disaster stands unparalleled among those of its kind. Whole families have been wiped out. In many instances a father is left to grieve alone for wife and children, and there was hardly a home in the parish, whence but a few hours before a laughing happy crowd went on its holiday, that was not in deep mourning last night.

The scenes attendant upon the disaster have seared themselves in the brains of the survivors never to be effaced. Women were roasted to death in sight of their husbands and children, and babes by the score perished in the waters of the East River, into which they had been thrown by frenzied mothers. With death by fire behind them, hundreds leaped to their doom in the river. Out of the awful record there stands forth bright and clear the heroic work of the watermen, the police, nurses, and doctors, who saved hundreds at the risk of their own lives.

It is the opinion of those who witnessed the disaster from the New York shore that Capt. Van Schaick, who commanded the vessel, lost his head. Instead of running the vessel aground on the New York shore near by, he carried her, blazing from stem to stern, to North Brother Island, where she ran on a rocky shore.

Four hundred and ninety-eight bodies were recovered up to midnight. Hundreds of charred remains are still in the hulk of the Slocum, which is now beached at Hunt's Point.

Survivors say the life preservers were worthless and rotted away in the hands of those who attempted to use them.

Coroner O'Gorman said late last night that he had taken more than $200,000 in money, bank books, and jewelry from the bodies of the dead.

Four thousand, frightened thousands had lost relatives thronged the Alexander Avenue station in the Bronx, the Morgue, the piers, and the vicinity of the church all night.

Among the dead is the wife of the pastor, the Rev. George C. F. Haas, and his daughter is missing. It was reported early this morning that the pastor is in a critical condition from shock.

The Captain, two pilots, and some members of the crew are under arrest.

It is believed that the fire started from the explosion of a stove in the galley on the lower deck, where chowder was being cooked.

FATAL TRIP'S JOYOUS BEGINNING.

With Music and Flags A-flutter the Slocum Steamed Up the River.

The annual excursion of St. Mark's Church—Pastor Haas's Church, they call it in the neighborhood—is an event long looked forward to by the communicants

INDEX TO DEPARTMENTS.

and their friends on the east side of the city. Only the tickets calling for passage for adults are taken into consideration while the sale is on, and there were nearly 1,000 of these sold and presented on board the boat before she started. The children are carried free, so that every mother either sent or took her little brood to the outing.

The General Slocum, which had been lately overhauled, started from her pier at East Third Street shortly after 9 o'clock. As she cast off and stood out into the stream her flags were flying, the band was playing a lively air, and her three decks were crowded to their capacity with a happy throng that looked for a pleasant day's outing at Locust Point, on the Sound. The party was to be landed about noon, and the return trip was to be made so that the excursionists would be at home by 11 o'clock.

The excursion was in charge of the social committee of the church, headed by Miss Mary Abendschein of 315 East Eighteenth Street. Miss Abendschein and Pastor Haas, with the other members of the minister's party, were at the dock to welcome the pleasure-seekers. The pastor's wife and daughter, Miss Emma Haas, his sister; Assistant Superintendent Carl Anger, William Slafer, and W. D. Tetamore of Brooklyn.

The Slocum was under command of Capt. William Van Schaick, who has been with the vessel for many years, and with him were two pilots, Edward Van Wart and Edward Weaver. The crew consisted of twenty-three men. Chief Engineer George Conklin was in charge in the engine room. He is believed to have been burned to death at his post.

Accounts differ as to just where the boat was when the fire started. Certain it is that it went through Hell Gate without any evidences of panic being noticed, for the band was playing and persons on shore remarked that the Slocum had a big party on board that was apparently having a good time. With no thought of the coming disaster, no effort was made to keep any of the parties together, and the children ran happily all over the ship, while the mothers gathered on the upper decks and gossiped. They were nearly all German women, who knew each other, and had something in common to talk about.

It was when the boat was about opposite One Hundred and Thirtieth Street in the river that the fire started. Certain it is that it was then that the first warnings were sounded. Some of the survivors say that they saw smoke coming from below before this, but they thought it was from the chowder cooking on the lower deck and paid no attention to it.

Vessel Made Wide Detour.

North Brother Island is about opposite One Hundred and Forty-fifth Street. The vessel was not beached directly at this point, but sailed around the end of the island and ran on the rocky beach several hundred feet further on. The fact is established that Capt. Van Schaick took the Slocum a very long distance before he made any attempt to effect a landing. When the fire was discovered the boat was not more than 300 feet distant from the New York shore, Randall's Island was close at hand, and there were numerous coves and piers on the New York shore at which the boat could have been docked.

The fire started forward. It is believed that it began in the storeroom of the boat on the lower deck. Here a lot of odds and ends of rope, canvas, oily rags, and other truck were stored. In this immediate vicinity, too, was a large stove, on which the people jammed into the water were dropped it and again to the rescue until exhausted. In all, she brought ten persons to safety. Afterward she would take no the fire for the cooking had already been lit.

The dread cry of "Fire!" sounded through the boat about an hour after she left her pier. Almost immediately there was a muffled explosion, and a sheet of flame enveloped the forward part of the boat. It was then that the trouble was first seen from the shore, the boat being opposite One Hundred and Thirty-fifth Street.

Immediately pandemonium broke loose on board. The flames, spreading with incalculable swiftness, forced the passengers to the rear of the boat. Capt. Van Schaick was seen to run from the pilot house after turning the wheel over to Van Wart and

yell to beach the boat on North Brother Island.

The crew made no attempt to get anything like order out of the frightful panic that was in progress. According to some who survive the fire drill was sounded, and they went to their posts. Some say they soon had streams playing on the flames, but even if they had it was like trying to drown out a blazing caldron of oil with a squirt gun. Other say that the pumps would not work, and that the lines of hose were almost immediately abandoned. Some even assert that the hose was torn out of their hands by the frenzied women.

It was only a matter of seconds until the entire forward part of the boat was a mass of flames. The passengers rushed aft, and the boat seemed to be settling by the stern. All this time full speed ahead was maintained, and the flames, fanned fiercely by the wind, ate their way swiftly toward the hapless women and babies that were crowded on all the decks astern.

Fought for Life Preservers.

It was maintained by the survivors that while there seemed to be a good supply of life preservers on board, these were worthless when they came into play. Women tore them from one another and they fell into shreds, and any attempt to use them in some reasonable way was perforce abandoned when the flames were swept closer and closer toward the rear of the boat, driving the frantic passengers before them. With sure death from fire behind, the life crews had they exerted themselves—waited until the flames were upon them, until they felt their flesh blister, before they took the alternative of the river. Babies shrieking with pain, many of them with their clothes on fire, were dropped into the water by scores, and finally the women were forced over the rail and hundreds of them fell into the river.

By this time the boat was opposite North Brother Island and was evidently still under control, for it rounded the point where the dock is located and ran ashore in a little cove, where the jagged rocks jut out into the water. An inspection of the island shows that hardly a worse landing point could have been selected, as the water is deep there and there is no beach. All this time the shrieks of the women and the cries of the children, swelled into a chorus fearful to hear, could be heard on the New York shore, where hundreds of men employed in the various shops and lumber and marble yards had gathered.

Just as the vessel struck the rocks the supports of the hurricane deck gave away, and with a crash the upper works came down. The vessel was then completely enveloped in flames. As the boat struck hundreds jumped or were thrown into the water, and hundreds more were precipitated into the blazing furnace beneath. These remain, a charred, unrecognizable mass, in the hulk of the burned vessel, which is now beached at Hunt's Point, more than a mile from where it first struck.

Meanwhile there were being enacted scenes of bravery that will stand out as among the most heroic in the annals of the country. No men ever braved death more recklessly on the battle field to rescue wounded comrades than did these watermen of the New York river front to save the lives of the women and little ones who were struggling in the waters of the East River or who were still clinging to blazing portions of the wreck. These men saw women and children roasted to death on the burning hulk of the Slocum.

The tug Wade, owned by John I. Wade, who acts as engineer on board and commanded by Capt. Robert Fitzgerald, saved 155 persons. The Wade was lying at the North Brother Island pier when the blazing Slocum hove in sight. She put off and waited to get alongside as soon as the Slocum touched the rocks. As the vessels came together the deck of the Slocum fell in and dozens of women and children, their clothing ablaze, were literally pitched on to the Wade's decks.

The deckhands threw bucket after bucket of water over these, and used every endeavor to make them comfortable after their blazing clothing had been extinguished.

Saw a Policeman Drown.

The crew of the Wade say they saw a policeman drown while engaged in the work of rescue with them. This policeman was one of the first to arrive on the island, and had made eleven rescues. It was while trying to save the twelfth person, a woman, that he was seen to show signs of distress, and before help could reach him he sank. They said the policeman's number was 3,123.

This is the number on the shield of Policeman Thomas Couney of the East Eighty-eighth Street station. He was one of the reserve policemen sent up to One Hundred and Thirty-eighth Street in a patrol wagon when word of the disaster was received.

Capt. Fitzgerald saw a boy climb out on the rail in the rear of the Slocum. His clothing was on fire, and in some unaccountable way he remained upright, a living pillar of flame. Fitzgerald saw him roasted almost to a crisp, when the charred remains tumbled over into the river.

The Wade had kept as close to the burning steamer that her deckhouse caught fire, and when she tried to put off to save herself from destruction it was found that several lines from the larger boat had become entangled in her paddles and she could not get away. Some of the men received had burns while cutting these ropes, and finally, after a bucket brigade had put out the flames on her and the Wade had taken on board a number of nurses and doctors who had meanwhile arrived on the island, she put off to the New York shore.

The city tug Massasoit, which was also moored on North Brother Island, behind the Wade, ran as close as she could to the blazing steamer, but the fierce blaze and the heat made it impossible for her to lie alongside, and her deckhands picked up dozens of women and children who still showed signs of life in the river. Mate Albert Rappaport disrobed, jumped into a small skiff, and picked up a number of children. Capt. Parkinson cut adrift several small boats, into which he saw a number of persons scramble, who were afterward saved. Two of five girls, two boys, and a woman, all of whom were revived when taken to the island.

Flotilla of Rescuing Craft.

From all along the water front on the New York side rowboats and tugs put out to the scene of the blazing wreck, and hundreds of persons who otherwise would have perished were rescued by these intrepid men.

One of the boatmen saw a heap of bodies on the paddle box of the Slocum. A little girl, crying piteously for her mamma, was the only sign of life among the gruesome pile. After repeated attempts the child was taken off. She was unscathed. She said her name was Lizzie Krieger, and that she had seen her mother burned to death. She was taken to the Alexander Avenue Station, where she sat all day in the back room, in sight of the rows of bodies on the floor.

"Mamma is all burned up," was all she could say between her sobs.

While the vessel was racing up stream, enveloped in flames, the watchers on the New York shore all agreed that they were unable to understand why Capt. Van Schaick did not make a landing on the New York side, from which the boat was only a few hundred feet distant.

A watchman who was in the tower of the De La Vergne Refrigerating Company's plant, at the foot of One Hundred and Thirty-eighth Street, was the first to act on what he saw in the river. He noticed the blazing boat several hundred feet away, and, running from his point of vantage which commands a view of the river for miles, turned in an alarm and telephoned to Police Headquarters that a big excursion steamer was ablaze in the river. When he returned, he said, he thought to see the vessel at one of the New York piers, but was astonished to see it rounding the point on North Brother Island. This man in only one of a great number who hold to the same view.

Capt. Van Schaick jumped from the burning vessel to a tug just as the Slocum struck the rocks. He was taken to the Alexander Avenue Station apparently unhurt, although he complained of having strained his back. He and the two pilots as well as several of the crew were then put under arrest and were taken to the hospital as prisoners.

Most of the deckhands were negroes and were apparently unmoved by the terrible sights they witnessed in the police station. All of them had jumped into the water and swum ashore to North Brother Island.

For hours after the disaster the waters around North Brother Island were thick with dead bodies, and these were pulled aboard all kind of craft as quickly as they could be and laid out in the awful rows on the pier. Later they were taken to the Alexander Avenue Station or to the Morgue on various tugs.

Burning Vessel Drifts Away.

The Slocum did not remain at North Brother Island more than ten minutes from the time she struck, but there did not seem to be a living person aboard of her when she drifted off down stream, and finally landed more than a mile away on the beach at Hunt's Point. The fact is that when she reached the water's edge, but when the supports of the decks gave way hundreds of bodies were precipitated into the hold and lay on the lower deck, masses of charred embers. Inspector Brooks last night said that two diving scows had been sent to the wreck and that on these were six skilled divers, including John Rice, who recently rescued the body of Bill Hoar in a New Jersey reservoir.

As soon as word was received of the disaster help was called for from every hospital in the city, and scores of uniformed nurses were soon on their way to the foot of One Hundred and Thirty-eighth Street, whence many were taken over to North Brother Island, while others remained at the docks or in attendance on ambulances to do their part as soon as any survivors were brought ashore.

Every vehicle in the neighborhood was pressed into service as a dead wagon, and in a short time wagons laden with bodies were on their way in a steady stream to the Alexander Avenue Station. There Coroner Berry of the Bronx was in attendance, and he later had a conference with Assistant District Attorney Garvan, who had been sent to take preliminary charge of the case. Mr. Garvan arrived went to North

Brother Island with ex-Fire Marshal Freel to make an investigation.

Coroner O'Gorman, who went to the island, said that he had taken from the bodies so far recovered upward of $200,000 in money, bank books, jewelry, and various kinds of valuables.

Scenes that beggar description were enacted around the Alexander Avenue Station, the Morgue, and in the vicinity of St. Mark's Church. Strong men nearly went mad when they told of having lost whole families. One said his wife and six children had gone on the excursion, and he had received not a trace of any of them.

Mrs. Albertina Lembeck of 427 East Ninth Street, one of Pastor Haas's parishioners, her head and neck swathed in oil bandages, ran shrieking about the corridors of the Lincoln Hospital, bemoaning the fate of her five children. There were Herman, fourteen; Dora, eleven; Ernestine, nine; Henry, seven, and Albert, four. She told how she had thrown Ernestine and Albert overboard when her clothing caught fire. The other children became separated from her in the panic, and she never saw a hundred bodies.

One little man, six years old, was brought into Lincoln Hospital hugging a toy hobby horse in his arms. There was not a scratch on him. He had jumped overboard with the toy in his arms and when picked up was still hugging his treasured possession.

Yacht Club Victims to Their Fate.

In marked contrast to the heroic actions of the river men is the story, vouched for by an engineer working on North Brother Island and by several watchers from the New York shore, that a yacht, flying the pennant of the New York Yacht Club, followed the ill-fated vessel up the river from the time she caught fire, and when she saw her go on the rocks put about and steamed away. All reports agree that the yacht made no effort whatever to pick up any of the women or children who had jumped overboard near her or to render any assistance at North Brother Island.

From the stories of a number of survivors it appears that the fire may have been started from the oil stove in the galley on the lower deck, on which the chowder was to have been cooked. This was one of the first theories advanced, and Pastor Haas also inclines to it. There are those among the survivors who say that while they were standing near this place they saw a puff of flame from the stove, heard a muffled explosion, and then saw a greater burst of flame that soon ran through the ship.

It is worthy of note that hardly a survivor or a dead body picked up was found to have a life preserver. It is asserted by several survivors that they tried on a number of these appliances, and that the shoulder straps were rotten, making the so-called preservers useless.

Capt. Van Schaick told four different stories to a Times reporter in the Alexander Avenue Station. He said that he had tried to put into the New York shore, but had been warned off. This is denied by at least a score of persons who watched the progress of the burning vessel up the river. He said that it was not over four minutes from the time he first heard there was fire on board until he had run the vessel on the rocks. It was pointed out that this was manifestly impossible, and then he said that it might have been longer, but it did not seem longer to him. He said that—a fire-drill had been answered and the hose was working, and a moment later contradicted this by the statement that the hose had been torn from the hands of the men while they were endeavoring to bring them into play.

Finally he refused to make any further statement and was taken to the hospital.

One of the mournful incidents of the disaster was that every dead woman brought into the Alexander Avenue station wore on the third finger of her left hand a heavy gold wedding ring.

"Wives, all of them," said Coroner Berry, "and mothers, too, I don't doubt. It is the most awful sight I have ever seen."

ONE THOUSAND DEAD.

Inspector Brooks's Estimate of the Loss—Finding Bodies Fast.

At 1 o'clock this morning Inspector Brooks said the total number of bodies recovered was 498. At 2:30 o'clock it was 606. He estimated the final loss at 1,000. In the night the Merritt Wrecking Company was hard at work on top of and around the wreck of the General Slocum, tearing away decking and sending divers down after the bodies. Besides these workers, policemen dropped floodlights from launches and pulled up the and three bodies at a time.

Shortly after midnight twelve bodies were taken out of the hold. One woman was found tightly clasping her baby around the neck. Another had her arm around a seven-year-old boy. Many of the women and children were locked in one another's arms so that they could hardly be pulled apart. There were three divers at work constantly.

According to Inspector Brooks, the decking had dropped into the hold, forming a V-shaped, immovable mass. With the fall it had pushed dozens of persons below and pinned them, to be burned or smothered to death.

ISLANDERS SAVED SCORES.

Doctors and Nurses Dashed into the Water and Dragged Victims Ashore.

When the Gen. Slocum neared the landing at North Brother Island, in an effort to run ashore, she ran into a bank that drops at an angle of about forty-five degrees into deep water. The doctors, nurses, and employees from the Isolation Hospital ran to the water's edge, where, without thought of their own danger, they proved themselves possessed of the greatest courage.

Using everything at hand in their efforts at rescue, two ladders, several footbaths, a hose, and themselves as a human chain, they succeeded in bringing many people ashore, scores of them in immediate need of medical attention, so that the force of rescuers was depleted of those who had to work over the unconscious there and then in order to keep them alive.

Nellie O'Donnell, assistant matron, was first in the water. She had often remarked to the other attendants that she wished she knew how to swim, as she believed everybody ought to know how to keep afloat in case of accident, but she had never had the necessary courage. When she saw the people jumping into the water and many drowning before her eyes, she forgot all about the necessary courage and plunged in to save whom she could. To her subsequent amazement, though she thought nothing of it at the time, when she got into the deep water she found that she could swim.

Miss O'Donnell is strong, and when she

realised that she was really swimming she grabbed a small boy by his collar and towed him ashore. Then she went back again and again to the rescue until exhausted. In all, she brought ten persons to safety. Afterward she would take no credit, saying that it was all a miracle. As to her new found art of swimming, it would be of no value to her, as after what she had seen and heard, she would never again dare to venture into water over her depth.

Rescuers Formed Human Chain.

James F. Gaffney, the engineer on the island, attracted by the blowing of whistles and seeing the burning boat coming ashore summoned the fire-fighting force and plunged into the water with the hose, which had been quickly attached. Seeing that the stream he had would be of no use, he dropped it and again to a woman struggling in the water. Coming back with her, he picked up a boat.

He and the five men under him formed a human chain, Gaffney the outermost. He caught in all twenty persons, who were passed back to safety. In addition, these men recovered something more than half a hundred bodies.

Dr. McLaughlin, in charge of the tuberculosis patients on the high island to the float, and jumping into a small rowboat, rowed around the point, where he rescued six people. Landing with them he was about to put out again when he saw that a small boy of the party he had rescued needed his attention. By the time he had brought the little fellow around there was no further chance at rescue. The ill-fated Slocum had drifted away, and there was much for him to do with the other doctors in restoring those who had been brought ashore nearly drowned.

George W. Johnston of the Riverside Hospital, mate of the Franklin Edson, whose day it was to be off, had gone to the island to see a friend of his, James Owen, a bricklayer. The two men went close to the fine steamer, running in close to her stern. They shouted to the terrified people there to jump, and when they seemed afraid Johnston, who is a strong swimmer, to encourage them to plunge overboard, jumped into the river.

This gave courage to the passengers, and they commenced jumping three and four at a time. The boat was soon filled to the danger point, so Owen rowed ashore, saving twenty-five people. By the time he was able to row back again out by Owen and climbed in the boat with his charges, as he was nearly exhausted. When they rowed back again there was none to save. Johnston, in describing the vain rescue, says:

Oars Struck Bodies of Dead.

"It was simply awful. The boat was drifting away, and we were impeded by the dead, our oars striking them every now and then, and then, too, we would run into them. The worst was the sight of the stern of the boat, where there was a small boy burning and in some way caught so that he could not free himself. He was dead, but close to him was a little fellow with long golden hair. This was on fire, and he was doing his best to beat it out. The heat was blistering, but we tried to get to him.

"We were still some distance off when he fell back into the flames. This was almost gone with what I had seen and the struggle in the water. Poor Owen was crying like a baby and the two kids in the bottom of the boat were shivering and pleading for their mothers. We couldn't be of any more use, and it did not then seem worth while to try and pick up the dead, so we rowed back through them to the shore.

"There is one thing I want to say, and that is that with the exception of the patients there wasn't a person on the island who did not do his duty. When Nellie O'Donnell was finding out that she could swim and bring them like a man, five of the other nurses joined hands, and in this way, one of them lying down in the shallow water so that the rope would be longer, they pulled in a lot. Drs. Watson, Weisman, Lord, Cannon, and Halderson, by keeping out of the water and reviving those brought ashore, were just as much heroes as anybody else. Without their aid many of those brought ashore might just as well have been left in the water. And there is another thing. They, too, would have gone out in a boat like Dr. McLaughlin, but they were in the wards, and by the time they got out and down to the water front there was work there for them to do."

Mary McCann, one of the measles patients, convalescent enough to be employed about the ward, was near the beach when the burning vessel came ashore. She waded in until only her head was out of water and dragged several half-drowned people ashore. Miss McCann was the last woman pulled out with twenty rescues.

She collapsed as she dragged in the last one and was carried back to her ward, where everything is being done for her. The doctors cannot tell how serious her exertions in the cold water may prove, especially as she had not fully recovered her strength after her illness.

POLICE RESCUED MANY.

Their Prompt Response to Summons Saved Scores of Lives.

The police arrangements to handle the great crowds that congregated on the Manhattan shore yesterday, attracted by news of the disaster, could not have been improved upon. As soon as Police Headquarters received information of the disaster Chief Inspector Cortright designated Inspector Brooks to proceed to the scene and assume command of the police.

The reserves from all the neighboring precincts were called out, the number on duty being about five hundred men. Inspector Albertson was among the first of the police officers to reach the scene. With Capt. Geohegan of the Alexander Avenue Station and a squad of men, he boarded the fireboat Zophar Mills and steamed quickly out to the burning vessel.

As they neared the Slocum they found a veritable sea of bodies, and Patrolmen David Goss, Daniel Sullivan, and George Young jumped into the water and assume command of the boats. These three men saved fifteen women, all of whom were cared for on the Zophar Mills, and stuck to their heroic work until it was known beyond a doubt that no more living remained among the scores of bodies that filled the water.

Another patrolman who did great work was John Q. Schwing, also of the Alexander Avenue Station. Schwing went out to a boat alone. He saved five people—Annie Klipp of 1,834 Lexington Avenue, Barbara Becker of 1,157 Third Avenue, Barbara Duhofer of 121 Avenue A, and Andrew Sommer of 17 East Sixth Street.

GRIEF-CRAZED CROWDS VIEW LINES OF DEAD

Scores Prevented from Throwing Themselves Into River.

BOAT LOADS OF BODIES

Immense Crowds Weeping and Struggling Seek to Identify Them.

MANY PATHETIC INCIDENTS

Measures Taken by Officials to Safeguard Interest of Relatives—Over $200,000 in Valuables Found on the Victims.

Scenes terrible, heart-breaking, indeed, able were witnessed yesterday at the hospitals, police stations, and the East River piers, where the injured and dead of the General Slocum catastrophe were taken.

Fully 10,000 men, women, and children seeking relatives and friends among the dead swarmed into East Twenty-sixth Street last night after 6 o'clock, completely choking that thoroughfare from First Avenue to the water front, where New York's principal Morgue is located. It was a mad, excited crowd, frenzied with grief to a point that meant self-destruction if unrestrained. Men and women wept and cried aloud as they fought and elbowed their way toward the big pier at the foot of the street, where hundreds of charred and mangled corpses rested in rows of rude pine boxes.

The police reserves of several precincts, who had been hastily summoned, and all they could do to prevent the crowd from plunging madly into the river. Those in the crowd who had been told of the identification of relatives among the dead completely lost control of themselves. They forced their way to the stringpiece at the side of the pier, and would have leaped into the river had not they been prevented forcibly from so doing by the police.

The constant clanging of the ambulance gongs told of men and women come fainting, some temporarily insane from grief, who needed medical attendance, and who were dragged through the hospital gates of Bellevue, where they got relief. Finally, with great difficulty, at 7 o'clock, the police succeeded in establishing a line of waiting persons by the aid of ropes, and from that time on the work of identification proceeded with a semblance of order.

The facilities of the Morgue, which is said to be the best in the United States, were wholly insufficient to accommodate the number of bodies brought in by the steamers which conveyed them from North Brother Island and other places in the vicinity of the disaster. For this reason the bodies were laid along the big pier of the Department of Charities, which Commissioner James H. Tully turned over for the purpose, all business of his department now that of attending to the results of the disaster being suspended. Only those bodies which were badly burned or charred beyond recognition were taken to the Morgue proper.

First Boatload of Bodies.

The first boatload of dead reached the Morgue shortly before 4 o'clock. This was the Fidelity, the Potter's Field boat, and it brought thirty bodies, all of persons who died from flames. The bodies being beyond recognition except from the jewelry and the few pieces of clothing which still clung to them. An hour later the Massasoit of the Department of Correction docked at the Charities Department pier, bringing in more than eighty bodies, most of which had been taken from the water in the vicinity of the disaster.

All of the bodies brought to the Morgue and to the pier were wrapped in blankets secured from some of the various hospitals which sent aid, or else covered with tarpaulins or other coverings which were to be found on the steamers.

Before the boats reached the docks hundreds of rude pine coffins had been secured, the sizes ranging from those for babies in arms to adults, and each body was placed in one of these coffins before being removed to the Morgue or to the pier. On the pier the bodies were placed in long double rows, so that the line of persons seeking to identify those missing might pass up one side and down the other and thus see each body laid out.

At one time last night more than two hundred bodies were lying side by side on this pier. Each body had been tagged with a number, to aid in the work of identification, and by 7 o'clock, when the waiting crowd was admitted, Coroner Scholer, Goldenhaus, Jackson, and Brown of Manhattan, and Coroner O'Gorman of the Bronx, with their clerks and assistants, were in readiness to expedite the work of removing bodies as soon as identification had been established.

In a steady line, two abreast, the waiting crowd then was admitted to the pier, passing out toward the river on one side of a row of bodies and coming back toward the land on the other side of another row. The boxes in which the bodies were placed were emergency affairs, the bodies themselves without robing in as best the men could arrange them in the space of time they had to make the arrangements, and it was hard work in many cases for the relatives and friends to pick out the missing ones.

Police were stationed every few feet, and theirs was the trying task of restraining husbands and fathers from throwing themselves in a frenzy on the bodies of wives and children as they finally found them in the mute and gruesome line that moved in the glare of the searchlights. Every few minutes a man or a woman would either shriek in agony and try to throw himself or herself on a prostrate form, or else would collapse entirely and have to be carried in a fainting condition to the outer air, to be revived by the hospital

For Nervous Women.
Horsford's Acid Phosphate quiets and strengthens the nerves, relieves nausea and sick headache, and induces refreshing sleep.—Adv.

Easy to Remember
"Every Other Hour, on the Even Hour." Royal Blue Trains of the Baltimore and Ohio Railroad leave New York at 8, 10, 12, 2, 4, 6, and 7 o'clock, during the day, for Baltimore and Washington. Ticket Offices, 434 and 1,300 Broadway and 4 Astor House, 343 Fulton Street, Brooklyn.—Adv.

Burnett's Extract of Vanilla
Is the best, perfectly pure, highly concentrated.—Adv.

Ever used up? Brain overworked? Spencer's glasses, 12 Maiden Lane.—Adv.

physicians before they could appear before the Coroner to give the number of the body identified and secure a permit for its removal.

Death Certificates Held Ready.

All of the Coroners and their clerks had death certificates in readiness for filling out, and as soon as a body would be identified, the identifier and an officer would go before a Coroner to secure a permit, and then would have an undertaker take the body away.

All during the night there was a line of undertakers' wagons in East Twenty-sixth Street extending all the way from the pier to First Avenue, and at times turning well into the avenue. Among the persons seeking to identify dead were many children, some not more than four or five years old, who had been brought by friends, in whose care they had been left, to identify mothers and brothers and sisters. In many cases mistakes in identification were made at first, but every precaution was taken to prevent this and also the false identification of any body for the purpose of dishonestly taking possession of property belonging to any of the dead. Where missing friends and relatives were not found in the line of dead on the pier, most of the bodies there being those of victims who died by drowning, the persons seeking friends went through the Morgue proper to look at the burned bodies and the clothing that remained.

It was nearly 11 o'clock in the morning when Charities Commissioner Tully received word of the disaster at his office on the East Twenty-sixth Street pier. He immediately suspended all business of the office and detailed his entire staff to various points to handle the work of the accident. All of the boats of the department were pressed into service.

The Commissioner personally took charge of affairs at the Morgue and on the pier, aided by Deputy Commissioner R. J. Dougherty and Superintendent George W. Meeks of the Outdoor Poor. William J. Lee, Assistant Secretary to the department, was assigned to look after the property of all the dead brought in, and he worked in conjunction with John Fane, the keeper of the Morgue, and Jefferson Morrell, the police officer detailed to the pier. Clerks at once were put to work numbering tags for the bodies and corresponding envelopes to hold the jewelry and like property of the dead.

Preparations also at once were begun at the Morgue to handle the bodies which later were brought in. As the refrigerating plant and Morgue accommodations were wholly insufficient for the emergency, load after load of ice was ordered and taken to the pier during the afternoon preparatory to the establishment of the temporary morgue on the pier.

By noon the crowd began to gather around the Morgue and a detail of police was sent for from the East Thirty-fifth Street Station. Police lines were established and all persons were kept outside the lines until the bodies should arrive and be prepared for the work of identification. All during the afternoon the gathering crowd grew larger and larger, many of the survivors of the disaster coming to get what word they could of the other members of their parties.

Doctors Rush to Aid Victims.

When the word first reached Bellevue Hospital Dr. J. C. Ayre, the visiting surgeon, went to Acting Superintendent Ricard and arranged to go to the scene of the disaster. Taking his instruments and two physicians, he jumped into a big forty-horse-power automobile and raced up First Avenue to One Hundred and Thirty-eighth Street, followed as fast as possible by two ambulances and six more physicians. All worked during the rest of the day, giving all possible aid.

In the crowd that gathered during the afternoon about the Morgue there were many pitiful scenes. When Commissioner Tully got word that the Fidelity and the Massasoit were on their way with their sad cargoes, many reported to the officials the names of the missing they sought. One of the first to do this was Mangus Hartwig, a tailor of 13 West Twenty-ninth Street, and living at 342 East Twenty-first Street. His wife and six children were on the ill-fated boat and he had heard nothing from any of them after the disaster. It was only by the greatest effort that the man could stand the strain of waiting in suspense for word which he felt would be the worst. The wife, Louisa, was forty-five years old, and the children ranged from Minnie, aged twenty-four, and a singer in the choir of St. Mark's, down to little Elsie, aged six. The other children were Frances, a teacher in the Sunday school and aged seventeen; Harry, aged fifteen; Nellie, thirteen, and Clara, eleven.

Henry Gordes, a clerk, living at 417 East Sixteenth Street, and one of the survivors, came around looking for his mother, a brother, a sister, and two friends. Cordes, who is seventeen years old, started on the excursion with his brother Charles, aged eighteen, a brother Frederick, aged fourteen, his mother, Mrs. Maida Cordes, aged fifty-five, a sister Etta, aged twenty-three, and Mrs. Mary Rosenberger, all of the same address. With them was Mrs. Mary Wolff of 420 East Sixteenth Street. Henry and Charles were on the upper deck when the fire started, the rest of the party being on the main deck.

"The fire seemed to get right on us all at once," he declared. "The crew did everything in their power to quiet the crowd and to play the hose on the fire, but they could not accomplish anything. The fire came up from the lower part of the boat, and spread everywhere in an incredibly short time. There were few men aboard, most of the crowd being women and children. Charlie and I were separated from the rest of the party, and I don't know what happened to them. Charlie and I both jumped into the river, he landing on a tug all right, while I went into the river. Men in a rowboat pulled me in and took me with others to North Brother Island, where I got some dry clothes and then rushed home, but heard from no one, and so came over here."

William Beck, a clerk in the Columbus Distilling Company's office at 23 Pearl Street, and living at 313 East Ninth Street, came to the Morgue in the afternoon looking for his mother, Mrs. Christina Beck, aged fifty-seven; a sister, Mrs. Charles Horway, aged twenty-seven, and Mrs. Horway's two children, Adele, aged six, and Carl, aged two, all of whom lived with him. Late at night Beck found his mother's body among those lined out on the pier.

TALES OF HORROR TOLD BY SURVIVORS

Eye-Witness Stories of Swift and Awful Panic.

FAMILY PARTIES WIPED OUT

Mrny Brave Deeds on Board the Doomed Steamboat Amid Scenes of Wild Panic.

Stories told by the survivors of the burning of the General Slocum give a disjointed but vivid picture of the terrible swiftness with which death swept the vessel, of the panic which raged over her decks, and of the sudden tragedy which took hundreds of the helpless. Many of those who were rescued have no very clear idea of how they escaped. A man dragged them into a boat or a swimmer brought them ashore. Further details very few of them can give. Two things they all agree upon: the tragedy fell with awful swiftness, and the panic aboard the steamer instantaneously swept away every semblance of calmness.

The Rev. Julius G. Schulz of Erie was a passenger on the General Slocum, and witnessed the frightful scenes that followed the burning of that craft. Mr. Schulz is of the opinion that Capt. Van Schaick used bad judgment in running the Slocum up stream instead of beaching her on the sunken meadows.

"It is absolutely impossible," said Mr. Schulz, "to describe the horrible scene on the Slocum. The flames spread so rapidly and it seemed only a second before the whole craft was ablaze from end to end. Women and children jumped in the wildest manner to their death, while the efforts of mothers to save their little ones was the most heartrending spectacle I have ever witnessed.

"Poor Mr. Haas did his best to save his wife, but in the excitement somebody pushed in between the two and Mrs. Haas was lost. I myself was among fifty others that were saved by a boat, the name of which I do not know.

"Yes, I am confident that something was radically wrong in the management of the Slocum. Why the Captain did not attempt to make the Manhattan shore or to beach the ship in the meadows is past my comprehension. Had he beached her hundreds of women and little children would certainly have been saved. Of that I am certain.

Miss Marie Kreuger of 451 West End Avenue, who suffered from burns, and was taken to Harlem Hospital, said: "I was on the upper deck when I was startled by a cry of 'Fire!' Then the men came along and told the women to be quiet. The advice fell on deaf ears, however, for every one became panic stricken the minute the alarm was given.

"I myself slid down a pole to the water and managed to get hold of a rope that was hanging alongside the boat. I had to relinquish this, however, in short order, for the flames began to shoot out of the portholes right above me. Alongside of me was a little boy, and he was holding on to a life-preserver. Near us was a coal barge, and a deckhand on that threw us a rope and pulled us on board the barge. I had a sister and a cousin on the Slocum, and I do not know whether they were saved or not."

Freda Gardner, eight years old, of 420 Willis Avenue, was rescued after being in the water fifteen minutes. She was picked up by a man in a row boat. She says that the first thing she knew of any trouble was when everybody started shouting and running to the stern of the boat. She was knocked down, but managed to get to her feet again.

A big man stopped and put a life-preserver about her. He was praying all the time, and hurried on to help another child. She fell again, and, as she was getting up, somebody, she thinks it was a woman, tore off the life-preserver. The smoke was stifling, and it was terribly hot. She managed at last to get to the outer rail, but was afraid to jump.

"A man picked me up and threw me into the water," she said. "I saw him a second later swimming toward me, and it gave me courage. Then he disappeared. A plank came floating by, and I grasped it. It easily supported me. Somebody caught hold of my foot, but let go. All the time I was trying to pray, but could not, because I had gone on the excursion without the knowledge of my mother.

"A man grabbed the plank and was pulling himself up on it, when a woman threw her arms about his neck, and the two slipped back into the water. I managed to say a prayer then and felt better, and I then resolved never again to disobey my mother. I started to pray again, when a man in a rowboat reached out and pulled me in. He took me to the foot of One Hundred and Thirty-eighth Street."

There Freda found a great many other little boys and girls, whom several ladies were undressing, rubbing, and wrapping in blankets. There wet clothing was spread out to dry. Freda, when it was seen that she was in need of medical attention, was taken home in a buggy. There was the greatest surprise on the part of the mother when her little daughter, wrapped in a great blanket, was carried into the house with her clothing, still wet, in her arms. There was no scolding for the truant girl. As the man who had brought her home departed he saw the mother and her little girl, who was still wrapped in a blanket, kneeling by the sofa thanking God for His Mercy.

EAST SIDE'S HEART TORN BY THE HORROR

Scenes in and Around St. Mark's Church.

SEARCH FOR RELATIVES

Stories Told by Anxious Seachers—Moaning of the Bereaved in Every Street and Alley.

It is an extraordinary tragedy that changes the entire aspect of New York's swarming east side, that makes its echo heard on every street corner, that fills the streets with lamentations, and makes the tens of thousands almost forget their business, their pleasures, and even their individual troubles. Such a tragedy was the burning of the steamboat General Slocum. Not a block but mourned from East Fourteenth to Houston Street, and few that did not feel the shock directly or indirectly throughout the lower part of the city.

From the time when the first news of the disaster reached the neighborhood of the Evangelical Lutheran German Church until the early hours of this morning, every street and alley resounded with the weeping of the grief-stricken fathers and mothers and brothers and sisters of the victims. On every tenement stoop groups of excited men and women talked of nothing but the great disaster. In front of the church thousands gathered to read the hastily prepared bulletins posted there. Hundreds of carriages and wagons passed to and fro throughout the afternoon and evening, each bringing home some injured survivor of the steamboat or restoring to their waiting relatives those who had been fortunate enough to escape unscathed.

A little before noon a woman alighted from a Second Avenue car at Sixth Street, the tears streaming down her face, and her hand clinching an afternoon newspaper in which was the first news of the disaster. She rushed to the church, half a block away, and, upon finding the doors closed, fell weeping and hysterical to the sidewalk.

It was the first tidings Sixth Street had received of the accident. The woman was the first of the hundreds who had lost kin or friends on the excursion boat. Ten minutes after her arrival the whole vicinity was aroused. Newsboys with extra editions thronged the sidewalks. In front of the church a crowd had collected. Another excited crowd had gathered into Seventh Street, and was vainly seeking information at 64, the home of the Rev. G. C. F. Haas, pastor of the church.

Pastor's Son's Suffering.

Inside the minister's house his nineteen-year-old son, the only member of the family who had not gone on the excursion, was hearing over the telephone that his parents, two aunts, and a sister were supposed to have perished in the flames. Hours passed before he heard of his father's safety.

While the streets roundabout grew more excited and scattered survivors began to find their way down town from hospitals or police stations or piers, the minister's house became a general bureau of information, and a score of the family's friends went in to give their aid.

From these church members and from the church records in the house, it was learned that the annual excursion of the Sunday school had been a custom of the last seventeen years. The record attendance on the excursion for the past was about 1,500, but none of the members yesterday knew exactly how many tickets had been sold for this one.

"I estimate that there were between 1,200 and 1,500 on the General Slocum," said the minister's son.

The picnic was organized by the Social Committee of the Sunday school teachers, most of whom are young unmarried women. Miss Mary Abendschein of 325 East Eighteenth Street was Chairman of the committee this year. The tickets—costing 50 cents for adults and 25 cents for children—were distributed among the scholars to be sold. While most of them undoubtedly went to German Lutherans, not a few were held by others. Among the excursionists was a scattering of Jews, Italians, and others.

Although lunch-counter privileges were sold for the steamboat, most of the provisions, such as sandwiches, ice cream, and the like, were contributed by church members, and, according to the annual custom, many who bought tickets never intended to go on the trip, but merely paid to help along the outing. Locust Grove, on the Sound, had been the picnic grounds of the Sunday school ever since the church members could remember, and the start always had been made from the same pier—at the foot of East Third Street.

Students Came from All Over.

The students, like the teachers, came from varied districts, though most of them were of the east side. There were some from as far away as Hoboken and Flatbush. The church for fifty-seven years has been growing steadily, and its membership has spread more than ever in the twenty-seven years of Mr. Haas's pastorate. It was estimated that practically all of the 500 students were on the excursion. Added to these were the scores of infants in arms, mothers, invited friends, and a few fathers and other male relations.

"The proportion of men was very small," said the Rev. John A. W. Haas, brother of the minister of the church and formerly pastor of St. Paul's Lutheran Church in this city. "Among the children were many so small that their mothers took them aboard the boat in baby carriages. In the party that left this house, besides my brother, were Mrs. Haas, her sister, Mrs. W. B. Tetamore of 1,471 Bushwick Avenue, Brooklyn; Gertrude Haas, my brother's thirteen-year-old daughter; Miss Emma Haas, my sister, and Mrs. Hansen, Mrs. Haas's mother."

The crush of anxious relatives became so great around the pastor's house that it was decided shortly after noon to establish a temporary bureau of information in the church in Sixth Street. Long tables were placed just inside the entrance, and conspicuous bulletins were posted outside, announcing that survivors should report their safety inside, and that relatives should come in to inquire about those who were missing.

Within a few minutes the street was packed from Second Avenue to First Avenue. A score of policemen, detailed to keep order, were busy all day and night maintaining the line of those who wanted to enter. As news came from the scene of the wreck it was posted outside. Before nightfall the reporters and church members sitting at the inquiry tables had catalogued hundreds of names, sent out as many alarms to the police, and listened to the weeping stories of scores of those who had lost their relatives or in some cases their whole families.

Probably the most heartrending tale of the day was that of Mrs. William Klein, mother and grandmother, who narrated between her tears the loss of nine members of her family and a score of friends. One little girl, her youngest, had been the only one to return home out of her immediate circle, although she had heard of the rescue of her daughter-in-law, Mrs. Annia Klein of 331 East Sixteenth Street.

Attempt at Suicide.

At First Avenue and Sixth Street another man who had lost his entire family was about to stab himself with a butcher's knife when two of his friends seized his arm and took the knife away from him. They led him to his home, saying they would watch him for the remainder of the night.

"All the News That's Fit to Print."

The New York Times.

THE WEATHER.
Fair to-day and to-morrow; rising southerly winds.

VOL. LV...NO. 17,617. NEW YORK, THURSDAY, APRIL 19, 1906.—TWENTY TWO PAGES. ONE CENT In Greater New York, Jersey City and Newark. | Elsewhere, TWO CENTS.

OVER 500 DEAD, $200,000,000 LOST IN SAN FRANCISCO EARTHQUAKE

Nearly Half the City Is in Ruins and 50,000 Are Homeless.

WATER SUPPLY FAILS AND DYNAMITE IS USED IN VAIN

Great Buildings Consumed Before Helpless Firemen—Federal Troops and Militia Guard the City, With Orders to Shoot Down Thieves—Citizens Roused in Early Morning by Great Convulsion and Hundreds Caught by Falling Walls.

SAN FRANCISCO, April 18.—Earthquake and fire to-day have put nearly half of San Francisco in ruins. About 500 persons have been killed, a thousand injured, and the property loss will exceed $200,000,000.

Fifty thousand people are homeless and destitute, and all day long streams of people have been fleeing from the stricken districts to places of safety.

It was 5:13 this morning when a terrific earthquake shock shook the whole city and surrounding country. One shock apparently lasted two minutes, and there was almost immediate collapse of flimsy structures all over the city.

The water supply was cut off, and when fires started in various sections there was nothing to do but let the buildings burn. Telegraph and telephone communication was cut off for a time.

The Western Union was put completely out of business and the Postal Company was the only one that managed to get a wire out of the city. About 10 o'clock even the Postal was forced to suspend.

Electric power was stopped and street cars did not run, railroads and ferry-boats also ceased operations. The various fires raged all day and the fire department has been powerless to do anything except dynamite buildings threatened. All day long explosions have shaken the city and added to the terror of the inhabitants.

Following the first shock there was another within five minutes, but not nearly so severe. Three hours later there was another slight quake.

First Warning at 5:13 A. M.

Most of the people of San Francisco were asleep at 5:13 o'clock this morning when the terrible earthquake came without warning.

The motion of the disturbance apparently was from east to west. At first the upheaval of the earth was gradual, but in a few seconds it increased in intensity. Chimneys began to fall and buildings to crack, tottering on their foundations.

The people became panic-stricken, and rushed into the streets, most of them in their night attire. They were met by showers of falling bricks, cornices, and walls of buildings.

Many were crushed to death, while others were badly mangled. Those who remained indoors generally escaped with their lives, though scores were hit by detached plaster, pictures, and articles thrown to the floor by the shock. It is believed that more or less loss was sustained by nearly every family in the city.

Steel Frame Buildings Stand.

The tall, steel-frame structures stood the strain better than brick buildings, few of them being badly damaged. The big eleven-story Monadnock office building, in course of construction, adjoining the Palace Hotel, was an exception, however, its rear wall collapsing and many cracks being made across its front.

Some of the docks and freight sheds along the water front slid into the bay. Deep fissures opened in the filled-in ground near the shore, and the Union Ferry Station was badly injured. Its high tower still stands, but will have to be torn down.

A portion of the new City Hall, which cost more than $7,000,000, collapsed, the roof sliding into the courtyard, and the smaller towers tumbling down. The great dome was moved, but did not fall.

The new Post Office, one of the finest in the United States, was badly shattered.

The Valencia Hotel, a four-story wooden building, sank into the basement, a pile of splintered timbers, under which were pinned many dead and dying occupants of the house. The basement was full of water, and some of the helpless victims were drowned.

Fires Start in Many Places.

Scarcely had the earth ceased to shake when fires started simultaneously in many places. The Fire Department promptly responded to the first calls for aid, but it was found that the water mains had been rendered useless by the underground movement.

Fanned by a light breeze, the flames quickly spread, and soon many blocks were seen to be doomed. Then dynamite was resorted to, and the sound of frequent explosions added to the terror of the people. These efforts to stay the progress of the fire, however, proved futile.

The south side of Market Street, from Ninth Street to the bay, was soon ablaze, the fire covering a belt two blocks wide. On this, the main thoroughfare, were many of the finest edifices in the city, including the Grant, Parrott, Flood, Call, Examiner, and Monadnock Buildings, and the Palace and Grand Hotels.

At the same time commercial establishments and banks north of Market Street were burning. The burning district in this section of the city extended from Sansome Street to the water front, and from Market Street to Broadway.

Fires also started in the Mission, and the entire city seemed to be in flames.

Long Detours Around Fires.

The flames, fanned by the rising breeze, swept down the main streets until within a few hundred feet of the ferry station, the high tower of which stood at a dangerous angle.

The big wholesale grocery establishment of Weelman, Peck & Co. was on fire from cellar to roof, and the heat was so oppressive that passengers from the ferry boats were obliged to keep close to the water's edge, in order to get past the burning structure.

It was impossible to reach the centre of the city from the bay without skirting the shore for a long distance so as to get entirely around the burning district.

About 8 o'clock the Southern Pacific officials refused to allow any more passengers from trans-bay points to land, and sent back those already on the boats. The ferry and train service of the Key Route was entirely abandoned owing to damage done to the power house by the earthquake at Emeryville.

Lack of Dynamite Felt.

There was little dynamite available in the city. The Southern Pacific soon brought some in. At 9 o'clock Mayor Schmitz sent a tug to Pinola for several cases of explosives. He sent also a telegram to Mayor Mott of Oakland. At 10:30 he received this reply to his Oakland message:

"Three engines and hose companies leave here immediately. Will forward dynamite as soon as obtainable."

The town of San Rafael, despite its own needs, sent fire fighting apparatus here.

Mayor Schmitz gave orders to use dynamite wherever necessary, and the firemen and United States soldiers, who assisted them, blew down building after building. Their efforts, however, were useless, so far as checking the headway of the flames was concerned.

The shortage of water was due to the breaking of the mains of the Spring Valley Water Company at San Mateo. The water needed so badly in the city ran in a flood over San Mateo.

Burning of the Opera House.

The fire swept down the streets so rapidly that it was practically impossible to save anything in its way. It reached the Grand Opera House on Mission Street, and in a moment had burned through the roof. The Metropolitan Opera Company from New York had just opened its season there, and all the expensive scenery and costumes were soon reduced to ashes.

From the opera house the fire leaped from building to building, leveling them almost to the ground in quick succession.

The Call editorial and mechanical departments, in the handsome building at Third and Market Streets, were totally destroyed in a few minutes, and the flames leaped across Stevenson Street toward the fine fifteen-story stone and iron building of Claus Spreckels, which, with its lofty dome, was the most notable structure in San Francisco. Two small wooden buildings furnished fuel to ignite the splendid pile.

Thousands of people watched the hungry tongues of flames licking the stone walls. At first no impression was made, but suddenly there was a cracking of glass and an entrance was effected. The inner furnishings of the fourth floor were the first to go. Then, as if by magic, smoke issued from the top of the dome.

This was followed by a most spectacular illumination. The round windows of the dome shone like so many full moons; they burst and gave vent to long, waving streamers of flames. The crowd watched the spectacle with bated breath. One woman wrung her hands and burst into a torrent of tears.

"It is so terrible," she said.

The tall and slender structure which had withstood the forces of the earth appeared doomed to fall a prey to fire. After a while, however, the light grew less intense, and the flames, finding nothing to consume, gradually went out, leaving the building standing, but completely gutted.

At California and Sansome Streets stood the Mutual Life Building, a modern structure of architectural beauty, to which the flames were soon communicated. An attempt was made to save it, but the fire was irrepressible. The flames gained, and in a few moments the big building was beyond hope. The Anglo California Bank was swept by the flames and came down in a rush.

Time and again attempts were made with dynamite to clear a space which should prevent the flames from spreading to other buildings, but freely as the explosive was used the fire crept and climbed from one structure to another.

An unusually loud report showed that a gas house at Eighteenth and Market Streets had blown up. The fire caused by the explosion quickly communicated in various directions. As the gas house exploded a feeling of despair overcame the men who were performing the rescue work.

Scare at Palace Hotel.

The Palace Hotel, the rear of which was constantly threatened, was the scene of much excitement, the guests leaving in haste, many with only the clothing they wore. Finding that the hotel was surrounded on all sides by streets, and was likely to remain immune, many returned and made arrangements for the removal of their belongings, though little could be taken away owing to the utter absence of transportation facilities.

The Parrott Building, in which was located the chambers of the State Supreme Court, the lower floors being devoted to an immense department store, was ruined, though its massive walls were not all destroyed.

A little further down Market Street, the Academy of Sciences and the Jennie Flood Building and the History Building kindled and burned like so much tinder. Sparks carried across the wide street, ignited the Phelan Building, and the army headquarters of California, Gen. Funston commanding, were burned.

Still nearing the bay, the waters of which did the firemen good service along the docks, the fire took the Rialto Building, a handsome skyscraper, and converted scores of solid business blocks into smoldering piles of bricks.

Thousands Watch the Flames.

Banks and commercial houses, supposed to be fireproof, though not of modern build, burned quickly, and the roar of the flames could be heard even on the hills, which were out of the danger zone. Here many thousands of people congregated and viewed the awful scene.

Great sheets of flame rose high in the heavens, or rushed down some narrow street, joining midway between the sidewalks, making a horizontal chimney of the former passageway.

The dense smoke that arose from the entire business district spread out like an immense funnel and could have been seen miles out at sea. Occasionally as some drug house or place stored with chemicals was reached, most fantastic effects were produced by the centred flames and smoke which rolled out against the darker background.

One of the first orders issued by Chief of Police Dinan this morning was for the closing of every saloon in the city. This step is taken to prevent drink-crazed men from rioting in the streets.

Mayor Schmitz sent out word to the bakeries and milk stations throughout the city that their food supplies must be harbored for the homeless. Provisions were made to place tents in every park in the city, and those who have lost all will be given food and shelter.

Early in the morning the prisoners confined in the city prison on the fifth floor of the Hall of Justice were transferred in irons to the basement of the structure. Later they were removed to the Broadway Jail, and if necessity arises they will be taken to a branch county jail on the Mission Road.

The Mayor also established a base of rescue, and soon had forces out where they could accomplish most. Many men were sent down to the lodging house district near Market Street. There it was found that many frame buildings, packed with people, had collapsed, burying their occupants in the ruins.

The rescuers jumped into the wrecks and pulled out the dead, the dying, and the injured. Practically every physician in the city immediately volunteered his assistance, and soon there was a well-equipped medical corps organized which began ministering to the injured.

For hours bodies were taken out in the lodging house district, and hundreds of men volunteered to go into the ruins to get more.

The pretentious City Hall, bounded by Larkin and McAllister Streets and City Hall Avenue, was badly shattered by the earthquake, and the ruins later were burned. It took twenty years to build the City Hall, the pride of the coast. When the first shock was felt the building rocked and swayed until it cracked. Part of the interior fell and the ruins caught fire. An alarm was turned in and the firemen responded. Chief Sullivan, awakened by the shock at his quarters in a firehouse, hastened to put on his clothes. As he reached for them the tower of the California Hotel dropped upon his building and crushing through the roof killed him.

The firemen arrived at the City Hall, but were helpless. They hitched their hose to the fire plugs, but there was no water supply.

Every possible precaution has been taken to guard property. Immediately after the destructive shocks the police turned out on guard, and the Governor and Gen. Funston, commanding the Pacific Division of the United States Army, were asked to send troops.

A thousand men from the Presidio, sent by Gen. Funston, arrived downtown at 9 o'clock to patrol the streets. The Thirteenth Infantry, 1,000 strong, arrived from Angel Island a little later and went on patrol duty at once.

The soldiers were ordered to shoot down vandals caught robbing the dead and to guard with their lives the millions of dollars' worth of property placed in the streets to escape the flames.

The First California Artillery, 200 strong, two companies, was detailed to patrol duty on Ellis Street. Two more companies patrolled Broadway in the Italian section. The Ellis Street contingent of guardsmen were under the command of Capt. G. A. Grattan. Capt. William A. Miller commanded the forces on Broadway.

The city is under martial law, and all the downtown streets are patroled by cavalry and infantry. Details of troops are also guarding the banks.

Early this morning Mayor Schmitz, who established his office at Police Headquarters, named the following citizens as a Committee of Safety:

James D. Phelan,	Paul Cowles,
Herbert Law,	M. H. De Young,
Thomas Magee,	Claus Spreckles,
Charles Fee,	Rudolph Spreckles,
W. P. Herrin,	C. W. Fay,
Thornwell Mullalley,	John McNaught,
Garret W. Enerney,	Dent Robert,
W. H. Leahy,	Thomas Garrett,
J. Downey Harvey,	Frank Shea,
Jeremiah Dinan,	James Shea,
John J. Mahoney,	Robert Pisis,
Henry T. Scott,	T. P. Woodward,
I. W. Hellman,	Howard Holmes,
George A. Knight,	George Dillman,
I. Steinhart,	J. B. Rogers,
S. G. Murphy,	David Rich,
Homer King,	H. T. Cresswell,
Frank Anderson,	J. A. Howell,
W. J. Bartnett,	Frank Maestretti,
John Martin,	Clem Tobin,
Allan Pollock,	George Toumey,
Mark Gerstle,	E. D. Pond,
H. V. Ramsdell,	George A. Newhall,
W. G. Harrison,	William Watson.
R. A. Crothers,	

THE BUILDINGS DESTROYED.

A Partial List of the Structures Torn Down or Injured.

SAN FRANCISCO, April 18.—The following is an incomplete list of the buildings destroyed or injured:

Call Building, entirely destroyed.

Claus Spreckels Building, burned out.

Hearst Building, collapsed.

New Chronicle Building, hardly damaged.

The White House, walls badly cracked; all plate glass windows gone; every piece of stock in building removed before 9:30 A. M.

Winchester Hotel, Third Street, totally destroyed by earthquake shock.

Grand Opera House, entirely destroyed.

Claus Spreckels house and stables, Van Ness Avenue, badly damaged and will have to be largely rebuilt.

St. Luke's Episcopal Church, Van Ness Avenue, will have to be pulled down.

Mechanics' Library Building, Post Street, cornices fell to street; building slightly injured.

Crocker Building, Market and Post Streets, slightly damaged, principally around light shaft.

Lick House, walls and roof largely caved in.

Upham Building, Pine and Battery Streets, totally destroyed; loss, $550,000.

Fire house adjoining California Hotel in Bush Street; Chief Sullivan and wife, sleeping in engine house, severely bruised by bricks crashing through roof from hotel.

California Hotel, Bush Street, upper walls collapsed and upper floors wrecked.

The building in course of construction to be occupied by the Hamman baths will have to be rebuilt. It is in Post Street near the Olympic Club. The walls are badly warped and twisted and the roof has fallen in.

San Francisco Gas and Electric Company's Post Street plant, only slightly injured.

St. Francis Hotel, exterior slightly cracked and seamed, but not seriously injured.

Pacific Union Club, Post and Stockton Streets, front injured and fissures in rear wall.

St. Dominic's Church in Pierce Street, total loss. The interior of the church is wrecked and there are fissures in the walls. The structure will have to be pulled down. The parochial house in the same block is nearly a wreck. It is estimated that the loss to the parish is $300,000.

The ornamental top on St. Dunstan's, the apartment house at Sutter Street and Van Ness Avenue, fell into the street.

The Concordia Club building in Van Ness Avenue has several fissures in the side, and rebuilding will be necessary.

The Hotel Grinado, badly damaged; stone coping about roof fell.

EARTHQUAKE'S AUTOGRAPH AS IT WROTE IT 3,000 MILES AWAY.

Tracing Made by the Seismograph Needle in the Office of State Geologist John M. Clarke, State Museum, Albany, Showing How the Earthquake Traveled Across Continent in 19 Minutes.

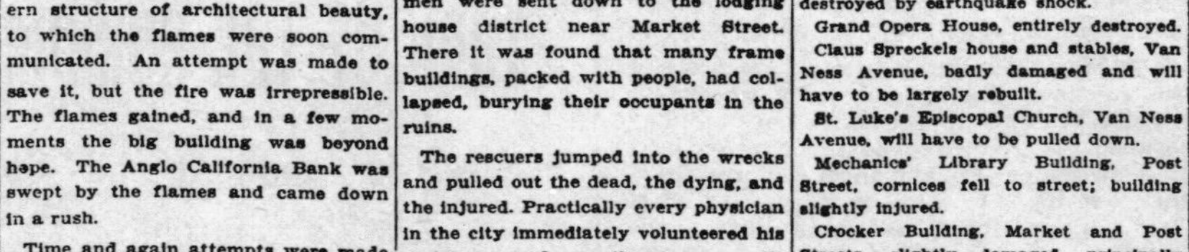

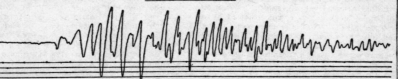

The drawing represents the vibration of the north and south pendulum of the seismograph during the time of the most intense activity, beginning in San Francisco at 5:13 A. M., in Albany at 8:32. In Albany the violent agitation ended at 8:43 A. M. The straight lines at the side of the wavy line indicate the normal condition of the record as the recording drum revolves, and this serves to show the contrast between the ordinary progress of the record and that during a disturbance. The spaces between the dots indicate lapses of one minute each.

The same violent disturbance was noticeable on the seismograph at Washington between 8:32 and 8:35 A. M., thus verifying the time of transit across the continent—19 minutes.

The Fastest Long Distance Train in the world is Twentieth Century Limited, the 18-hour train between New York and Chicago by "New York Central Lines."—Adv.

Absolute purity and old age make Dewar's Scotch welcomed everywhere.—Adv.

For trains to Detroit, Chicago, and St. Louis by West Shore Railroad. Ask a West Shore ticket agent for particulars.—Adv.

After all, Usher's the Scotch that made the highball famous.—Adv.

ALL SAN FRANCISCO MAY BURN; CLIFF HOUSE RESORT IN SEA

Flames Carried From the Business Quarter to Residences

PALACE HOTEL AND MINT GO; BIG BUILDINGS BLOWN UP.

Other Shocks Felt During the Afternoon—Insane Asylum Is Wrecked and Hundreds of Former Inmates Are Roaming About the Country—Reports of Heavy Loss of Life at San Jose.

SAN FRANCISCO, Thursday, April 19.—12:15 A. M. (3:15 A. M. New York Time.)—At midnight the fire still roars. Fleeing inhabitants can see from miles around the pillars of fire towering skyward. The crash of falling ruins and the muffled reports of the exploding dynamite reach the ear at regular intervals.

A disaster that staggers comprehension and in point of terror and damage is unprecedented on the coast has not yet reached its culmination.

The Merchants' Exchange Building, one of the handsomest and most substantial edifices in the city, is in flames, as is also the Crocker-Woolworth Building.

The former building is a fourteen-story structure, seven floors of which are occupied by the Southern Pacific Railway Company as offices. The Crocker-Woolworth Building is a twelve-story terra cotta and granite structure and stood directly opposite the Palace Hotel.

The immense D. O. Mills Building is surrounded by fire and probably will burn. The Lick House, the Occidental Hotel, and the Russ House in this immediate vicinity are in immediate danger.

The exact loss of life never will be known. Hundreds have been incinerated. To-night the city resembles one vast shambles with the red glare of the fire throwing shadows across the worn and panic-stricken faces of the homeless.

At the morgue in the Hall of Justice fifty bodies lie. Before the eyes of an Associated Press reporter three thieves were shot dead.

The Japanese quarter has been burned and the people fled in terror, packing on their backs what household effects they could tie together.

At 9 o'clock to-night an Associated Press man who went to a high hill overlooking the city noted that the sky on the east and south sides was illuminated for a distance of four or five miles. The illumination on the southern side was in a duller glow, showing that the flames were not consuming property of such great proportions as was the case on the east side.

In the business district toward the water front the flames were either checked or blocked at about Washington Street, and at the corner of Kearny Street the Hall of Justice could be noted standing, but it was impossible to determine what damage had been done to the interior. From the Hall of Justice to the south the fire cut its way through some of the choicest buildings in the city, the Pacific Mutual and the Italian-American Bank Building being reduced to ashes.

Down Kearny Street on both sides at 10 o'clock the conflagration was still raging with fury, but the direction of the wind prevented its advance up the hills to the west toward the residence quarter.

To the west of Kearny, up to Dupont, most of the buildings were burned as far south as California Street. All around the new fourteen-story Merchants' Exchange Building the fire burned fiercely, licking the sides of the steel giant, but it resisted the influence of the heat.

Then came the destruction of the Western Union Building, at the corner of Pick and Montgomery Streets. In this building were the offices of the Associated Press. Earlier in the day the occupants had been ordered out by the authorities on account of danger, and The Associated Press established a temporary station in The Bulletin editorial rooms. Then the latter place was closed, and this dispatch is written on a doorstep near Chinatown, the illumination of the burning buildings furnishing light for the writer.

It appeared that the great Mills Building would block some of the southward sweep of the blaze, as it had already checked an advance northward earlier in the night. If this proves true the limits of the fire will be determined, but predictions on this point are as unreliable as the strong wind, which every five minutes is changing from one direction to another.

The city to-night in face of its appalling disaster, is fairly quiet and orderly. Liquor cannot be had anywhere and the formidable presence of Federal troops, militia and naval reserves has had its effect on the element that might be disposed to be disorderly.

The Mayor's proclamation authorizing the shooting of looters on sight has been scattered broadcast in circulars and few reports of thieving are received.

It is impossible to give anything like an accurate statement concerning the killed. Unquestionably many people were either killed outright, imprisoned or rendered unconscious in collapsed buildings which were afterward burned.

At 10 o'clock the Occidental Hotel began burning and the great Crocker Building containing the Crocker-Woolworth National Bank was ablaze.

On Geary Street the Albert Pike Memorial Temple of the California bodies of the Scottish Rites Masons, containing scenery that cost $20,000 and costumes valued at $15,000, collapsed. The new Jewish synagogue adjoining was cracked to its foundations.

While five dying men were taken from a collapsed building at Second and Jessie Streets Fathers Hogan, Rogers, and Huber of St. Patrick's Church granted them the last rites of the Catholic Church. This ceremony was performed while a mass of coping overhead threatened to crush the priests to death. Three of the men died.

A shoemaker, Joseph Lindsay, was four hours in a demolished building and when dug out it was found that he had not been hurt.

The entire Larkin Street frontage of the City Hall for a distance of several hundred feet was thrown out into the street, and that thoroughfare for two blocks is piled high with boulders of mortared brick and twisted iron.

Latest reports from Leland Stanford University at Palo Alto indicate that the magnificent stone buildings of that institution have suffered severe damage. Many of the buildings were ruined by cracks that split them from cornice to foundation.

The University of California at Berkeley, across the bay, escaped serious injury. The buildings are intact. Only a few structures collapsed in Berkeley, the shock being slight there.

Artillerymen from the Presidio with their supply wagons and the army commissary wagons are aiding in getting the fleeing inhabitants and their baggage out of the threatened quarters.

270 Dead in an Asylum.

The insane asylum at Agnews is a total wreck, 270 of the inmates being killed. It is reported that the attachés of the institution who were about at the time of the earthquake were saved. The ruins took fire shortly after the collapse. One hundred and twenty bodies have been removed.

There were about 700 persons in the building. Hundreds of the inmates who escaped death are roaming about the country in a state of panic.

Half San Francisco Gone.

OAKLAND, Cal., April 18, 10 P. M.—It looks now as if the entire City of San Francisco would be burned.

At 10 o'clock to-night the fi

San Francisco's City Hall was almost completely destroyed.

The Bettmann Archive

was unabated, and thousands of people are fleeing to the hills and clamoring for places on the ferryboats to cross the bay.

Correspondents are trying to get matter to Oakland by boat, but they are very uncertain. The Government is furnishing tugs, but the confusion is so great that they cannot be relied upon. It will be impossible to send full details for several days.

From the Cliff House comes word that the greatest pleasure resort and show place of the city, which stood upon a foundation of solid rock has been swept into the sea. Not a thing stands to tell where the monster stone building once stood. It has been leveled to the foundation and only the rock lining the sea coast remains intact.

At this hour the fire is increasing in violence. It is spreading in all directions in both the business and residence quarters.

Practically the entire district south of Market Street, from the water front to the Mission, has been swept clean by the flames.

At 5 o'clock to-night, in the northern part of the downtown business section, the fire swept around the Hall of Justice and communicated to China-

town, thence proceeding westward into the heart of that colony. It then began rapidly eating its way southward on both sides of Kearny Street, and at 7 P. M. was within a block of the California Hotel.

This point was near the plant of The Evening Bulletin, in which the three morning papers had agreed to join to issue a four-sheet paper to-morrow morning. The plan was abandoned, as The Bulletin lay directly in the path of the flames.

One of the big losses of the day was the destruction of St. Ignatius Church and College, at Van Ness Avenue and Hayes Street. This was the greatest Jesuitical institution in the world, and was built at a cost of $2,000,000.

At 7 o'clock the fire had swept from the south side of the town across Market Street into the western addition, and was burning houses at Golden Gate Avenue and Octavia Street. This result was reached after almost the entire southern district, from Ninth Street to the eastern water front, had been converted into a blackened waste. In this quarter were hundreds of factories, wholesale houses and many business firms, in addition to thousands of homes.

On the north side, the fire to-night was not making such rapid headway as in the western addition, where there is a limited water supply available. The firemen were making desperate efforts to stop the flames.

Temporary headquarters were established in tents in Portsmouth Square this evening for Mayor Schmitz, Chief of Police Dinnan, and Gen. Funston, but this site became too dangerous about 6 o'clock and was abandoned. Later the flames swept the square.

Wide fissures have been made in the streets, street railways have been twisted out of line, sewers and water pipes have burst, and it is feared there will be an epidemic of disease.

Water Sold by the Glass.

Provisions are sold at fancy prices, and even water is vended by the glass.

As the flames spread into the residence districts people left their homes and fled to the parks and squares. A series of rather severe earth shocks at 7 o'clock further increased the terror, and many left homes that were not in danger.

A Finance Committee, with James D. Phelan at the head, has been appointed, and Mayor Schmitz has been instructed

to issue drafts for all funds needed on this committee. A general meeting of the Citizens' Committee has been called for to-morrow morning.

A message from President Roosevelt was received this morning, and it had a cheering effect. George Gould also telegraphed, offering assistance.

Throughout the city, wherever there is a public square, a scene of desolation is presented. Tents have been pitched by fortunate possessors of canvas, but most of the homeless people are huddled in frightened groups about the household belongings they managed to save from the general ruin.

From Golden Gate Park comes news of the destruction of the immense building covering a portion of the children's playground. The walls are shattered beyond repair. The roof has fallen in, and the destruction is complete. The pillars of the new stone gates at the park entrances are twisted and torn from their foundations. Some of them, weighing nearly four tons, were shifted as though they were constructed of cork.

Nearly every noted landmark that has made San Francisco famous has been laid in ruins or burned to the ground. Never has the fate of a city

Market Street, one of San Francisco's busiest thoroughfares, was devastated by the earthquake.

The Bettmann Archive

been more disastrous.

In Union Square Park, where a number of homeless now have temporary shelter, the mighty Dewey Monument has been shifted from its base. It now stands leaning at an angle of 10 degrees. There is danger of the immense stone structure falling.

No afternoon papers were issued, and it is doubtful if the morning papers will appear.

The papers in San Francisco estimate the dead at from 500 to 700, and 20,000 homeless.

The Palace Hotel is destroyed. The Postal and Western Union buildings and the magnificent new Union Trust Company Building, eleven stories high, have been dynamited.

It is reported that the Mint in San Francisco is ablaze, and from the outside indications it will be impossible to save it. The fire surrounds it on every hand.

A Western Union operator has just been along Montgomery Street to the section formerly occupied by the Western Union Building. He says that this whole section is aflame and is surrounded by United States troops. The block bounded by Montgomery, Bush, Pine and Sansome Streets is doomed. Fifteen or twenty blocks along the water front are now a mass of flames.

All efforts to prevent the fire from reaching the Palace and Grand Hotels were unsuccessful, and both were completely destroyed, together with all their contents.

Commissioner E. Myron Wolf has announced that the eighty-odd fire insurance companies interested had decided to pay dollar for dollar to every one insured with them. The companies will not discriminate between fire and earthquake, and every one insured will be paid to the extent of the loss. But two of the companies affected are Pacific Coast concerns, the others having principal offices in the East or in Europe, and all will stand the loss without danger of failure.

Another sharp shock of earthquake was felt on this side of the bay after 6 o'clock this evening. It was of short duration, lasting about five seconds.

The city is under martial law and precautions have been taken to prevent disorder and looting to-night. Four thieves were shot by soldiers to-day for looting. The soldiers have orders to shoot without warning any person acting in a suspicious manner.

The greatest destruction was wrought in that part of the city which was reclaimed from San Francisco Bay. Much of the devastated district was at one time low, marshy ground, covered by water at high tide. As the city grew it became necessary to fill in many acres of this low ground in order to reach deep water.

The Merchants' Exchange Building, a fourteen-story steel structure, was situated on the edge of this reclaimed ground. It had just been completed and the executive offices of the South-

ern Pacific Company occupied the greater part of the building.

The damage by the earthquake to the residence portion of the city, the finest part of which is on Nob Hill and Pacific Heights, seems to have been slight. On Nob Hill are the residences of many of the men who in the early seventies became wealthy through mining investments or the construction of the Central Pacific Railroad. They include the Stanfords, Huntingtons, Hopkinses, Crockers, Floods, and others.

The magnificent Fairmount Hotel, not yet completed, stands on the brink of Nob Hill, overlooking the bay. The hotel was not seriously damaged. The construction of the hotel was started by Mrs. Hermann Oelrichs of New York as a monument to her father, United States Senator Fair, but she recently sold it for $3,000,000. To the westward of Nob Hill, on Pacific Heights, are fine new residences, but little injury was done to any of them.

The Palace Hotel was a seven-story building, about 300 feet square. It was built thirty years ago by the late Senator Sharon, whose estate was in the courts for many years. At the time it was erected the Palace Hotel was the best-equipped hotel in the West.

The Post Office is a fine graystone structure, and has been completed less than two years. It covers half a block on Mission Street, between Sixth and Seventh Streets. The ground on which the building stands was of a swampy character, and some difficulty was experienced in obtaining a solid foundation.

The City Hall was a mile and a half from the water front. It was an imposing structure, with a dome 150 feet high. The building covered about three acres, and cost more than $7,000,000.

Best Theatres All Burned.

All of San Francisco's best playhouses, including the Majestic, Columbia, Orpheum, and Grand Opera House, are a mass of ruins. The earthquake demolished them for all practical purposes, and the fire completed the work of demolition.

The scene at the Mechanics' Pavilion in the early hours of the morning and up to noon, when all the injured and dead were removed because of the threatened destruction of the building by fire, was one of indescribable sadness. Sisters, brothers, wives, and sweethearts searched eagerly for some missing dear ones. Thousands of persons hurriedly went through the building inspecting the cots on which the sufferers lay in the hope that they would locate some loved one that was missing.

The dead were placed in one portion of the building, the remainder was devoted to hospital purposes. After the fire forced the nurses and physicians to desert the building, the eager crowds followed them to the Presidio and the Children's Hospital, where they renewed their search for missing relatives.

Up to a late hour this afternoon more

Refugees having their dinner on Franklin Street.

The Bettmann Archive

than 750 persons who were seriously injured by the earthquake and the fire had been treated at the various hospitals throughout the city.

The front of the Bailey & La Costa Building on Clay Street, near Montgomery, fell in and three men and seven horses were killed.

Capt. Gleason of the Police Department was severely injured at noon by falling tiling.

The stereotypers and the pressmen of The Examiner and The Call, as soon as the shock was felt, rushed out of their buildings and found that the coffee house at Stevenson and Third Streets had collapsed. They immediately set to work with axes and other implements to rescue those inside.

The sheds over the Southern Pacific long wharf on San Francisco Bay completely collapsed. Many of the bunkers fell into the bay, carrying with them thousands of tons of coal. The long wharf was one of the most important shipping points about the bay, and freight traffic will be interrupted considerably.

At Eighteenth and Valencia Streets to-night there is a crevice six feet wide in the pavement, and the entire sidewalks are torn up. The street car tracks at this point are twisted into fantastic shapes.

When the time arrived for the banks to open this morning there was a rush by many depositors to withdraw their accounts. The banks, however, kept their doors shut, and would give money to none of the depositors.

The Board of Supervisors has been called together and will decide on the proper measures which should be immediately adopted to afford first aid to persons who have been driven from their homes.

A. W. Hussey came to the station at the Hall of Justice shortly before 10 o'clock this morning and told how, at the direction of a policeman whom he did not know, whose star number he gave as 615, he had cut the arteries in the wrists of a man pinioned under

timbers at the St. Katherine Hotel.

According to the statement made by Hussey, the man was begging to be killed and the policeman shot at him, but his aim was defective and the bullet went wide of the mark. The officer then handed Hussey a knife, with instructions to cut the veins in the suffering man's wrists, and Hussey obeyed orders to the letter.

Chief of Police Dinan directed that Hussey be locked up. There has been no opportunity to investigate his story, but the police believe that the awful calamity rendered him insane and that the incident reported to them has no existence excepting in the imagination of the man who made the report.

Sixteen-year-old Otto Settner of 3234 Pierce Street rushed into the room of his father when the big shock came and shouted: "Oh, papa, I am dying!" The child fell dead in his father's arms.

Measures have already been taken for the care of the destitute. They will be fed and protected in Golden Gate Park and the public squares.

The Southern Pacific Railroad is carrying out of town all those who want to leave. No one is allowed to enter, and those who have left will not be able to get back for several days at least.

It is reported that while a building was being blown up with dynamite a premature explosion killed fifteen men.

The Terminal Hotel, at the water front and Market Street, fell to-day and buried twenty persons under the debris. They were incinerated and there is no possibility of learning their identity.

The Court House at Redwood City and other buildings collapsed. Menlo Park, Burlingame, and other fashionable suburban towns suffered. Santa Rosa, to the north; Napa, Vallejo, and all towns around the bay were damaged. These reports, alarming as they were, created little interest in San Francisco, where the people were in a frantic state.

To-day's experience has been a testimonial to the modern steel building.

A score of these structures were in course of construction, and not one suffered from the earthquake shock. The completed modern buildings were also immune to harm from the seismic movements. The buildings that collapsed were all flimsy wooden and old brick structures.

The damage by earthquake does not begin to compare with the loss by fire. The heart of the business quarter of San Francisco has been destroyed by fire. Fire has done the great damage. An area of thickly covered ground of eight square miles has been burned over, and there is no telling when the fire will be under control.

The principal damage done in Oakland was caused by falling chimneys.

WASHINGTON, April 18.—The War Department has received the following message from the Western Union at San Francisco:

"Although water has been secured to the firemen in many sections, the fire is by no means under control. It is raging around Pine and Montgomery Streets, and the Western Union Building has been abandoned to its fate. At the Oakland ferry house, where the company has established an office, it is difficult to obtain information concerning current events."

LOS ANGELES, Cal., April 18.—Many rumors are in circulation that additional shocks occurred at San Francisco during the day. All wire communication with San Francisco was lost early to-day. The Postal Telegraph Company had two wires working to Oakland, across the bay from San Francisco.

A special train of four cars with about seventy-five doctors and nurses on board left Los Angeles for San Francisco over the Southern Pacific Railroad this evening. The train is due in San Francisco to-morrow forenoon.

An equal number of doctors and nurses who tendered their services was

turned away on account of lack of accommodation on the train. Another special will leave to-night with more nurses, doctors, and policemen.

CHICAGO, April 18.—Henry Forsland, racing correspondent at San Francisco, wired his paper from Oakland this afternoon:

"All means of transit from San Francisco to Oakland closed. No one is allowed to enter the city from outside points, martial law having been declared. A number of racing folk said to have perished in the St. Nicholas Hotel."

FUNSTON ASKS AID.

Sends to Washington for Tents and Rations for 20,000 People.

WASHINGTON, Thursday, April 19.—The Secretary of War early this morning received the following second dispatch from Gen. Funston:

"OAKLAND PIER, Cal., April 18, via Union Pacific special wire via New York.—We are doing all possible to aid residents of San Francisco in the present terrible calamity. Many are homeless, and I shall do everything in my power to render assistance, and trust to War Department to authorize any action I may have to take. Army casualties will be reported later. All important papers saved. We need tents and rations for 20,000 people.
"FUNSTON."

A dispatch received early this morning from Army Department Commissary Trauthoff, is as follows:

"Oakland Pier, Cal. April 18, via Union Pacific Railroad special wire, via New York.—Depot destroyed by fire. Everything lost. Local troops supplied. Will wire in reference to Manila shipments.
"TRAUTHOFF."

From Benica, Arsenal, Cal., comes the following addressed to the Chief of Ordnance:

"Damage by earthquake chiefly to chimneys and ceilings. Probably not over $1,500. Report will follow. No one injured here. BENET, Commanding."

This dispatch was sent to General Funston by Commissary General Sharpe:

"The Secretary of War has directed the Commissary at Vancouver Barracks to forward to the Depot Commissary at San Francisco 200,000 rations. Is the railroad open to Portland?"

"All the News That's Fit to Print."

The New York Times.

THE WEATHER.
Fair to-day; rain, warmer Friday; north winds, becoming variable.

VOL. LVII...NO. 18,303. * * * NEW YORK, THURSDAY, MARCH 5, 1908.—FOURTEEN PAGES. ONE CENT In Greater New York, Jersey City and Newark. { Elsewhere, TWO CENTS.

OMAHA CROWDS MEET AUTO RACE LEADER

Cannons Boom and Whistles Shriek When Thomas Car Enters City.

ZUST CUTS DOWN LEAD

De Dion Still at Cedar Rapids, Iowa—Protos Reaches Chicago and Motobloc Remains There All Day.

22D DAY OF THE RACE.

Car.	Arrived.	Time. A. M.	Distance.
Thomas	Omaha, Neb.	11:45	1536
		P. M.	
Zust	Vail, Ia.	6:45	1458
*De Dion	Cedar Rpds, Ia.	....	1262
*Motobloc	Chicago	....	1043
Protos	Chicago	7:10	1043

*Spent day there.

FORECAST FOR RACING WEATHER TO-DAY—Rain, followed by falling temperature and snow.

Special to The New York Times.

OMAHA, Neb., March 4.—The Thomas car in the New York to Paris race arrived at Omaha at 11:45 this morning and will leave for Cheyenne early Thursday morning.

The trip from Logan, Iowa, where we stayed last night, to Council Bluffs was devoid of incident until we reached the outskirts of Omaha, where we met with the grandest reception given us yet. The car has been equal to Iowa mud and has stood up wonderfully. Never before have I piloted any car through such fields of mud, through such horrible road conditions as have been found in the last 200 miles.

We have plowed a trail in the road where enterprising Western farmers can plant their grain and reap a harvest at our expense. To-day American flags greeted us all along the road. No matter how humble the farmhouse, an American flag was displayed, evidencing the patriotism of the West.

Words are inadequate to describe our reception in Omaha. The moment we reached Missouri Valley, twenty-four miles east of Omaha, the fact was announced by the screeching of a large siren whistle at the Union Pacific shops. Incidentally, permission must be obtained from the city fathers before the whistle can be blown. The siren was heard all over Omaha hearalding our approach.

When we reached the bridge between Council Bluffs and Omaha eight cannon were fired, and every whistle in the city was let loose. When the people of Omaha do anything, they do it thoroughly.

They tell me that such mammoth crowds, through which we were actually compelled to fight our way for a mile, were never before seen in Omaha. Policemen and officers on horseback in front of us were responsible for our final successful effort to reach our garage. Flowers and flags thrown at us during our passage through this vast concourse of people mingled in gay confusion with Iowa mud.

This is the grandest reception we have had, not excepting New York City. The interest taken in this race is amazing to me. I have never seen such enthusiasm. I hope the same courtesy will be extended the foreigners when they arrive, and I am sure it will. H. E. Frederickson, the Omaha agent for the Thomas cars, met us twelve miles east of Omaha, and will probably pilot us through to Cheyenne. We start in the morning, after the gumbo (Iowa mud) has been knocked off the car and fresh tires put on. My trip ends at Cheyenne, which I regret, as I have long fostered a great regard for my car, which has stood the strain so well, and carried us thus far in safety. I hate to leave "old baby" and turn her over to strange hands, although my rugged companion, George Schuster, assures me that he will see she is not mistreated.

Well, I want to get back to the subject of Omaha. I have been here only a few hours, and for the first time since leaving New York I feel at home. The people of Omaha have a way of taking you into their "bosom" that at once appeals to you as sincere. The managers of the Hotel Schlitz, Messrs. Philbin and Murphy, extended the courtesy of their house tous, and treated us to the finest noonday repast it has been my fortune to partake of since leaving Chicago.

The Secretaries of the Omaha Club and the Omaha Automobile Club, Lee Moshan, and other officials, are preparing a banquet for this evening at the Hotel Rome, and I anticipate a great time. Omaha has declared a holiday for this afternoon, and festivities are under way. Immense crowds are forever following us, and when we seek a secluded nook for a moment's respite, they still follow.

Capt. Hans Hansen joined us to-day at Omaha and enjoyed his first ride in the American car. The local papers express great interest in this fact. I was glad to see the Captain, who proudly produced a silk American flag and waved it as his credentials. Remember we are off again to-morrow morning and will keep the lead.

Col. William F. Cody, "Buffalo Bill," was on the Reception Committee, which accounts in a large measure for our good time. The Colonel is about to buy a drink for the crowd, and I must end this story.

MONTAGUE ROBERTS.

ZUST COVERS 89 MILES.

Reaches Vail, Iowa, After Difficult Day of Drizzling Rain.

Special to The New York Times.

VAIL, Iowa, March 4.—The Zust (Italian car, second in the New York to Paris race, arrived here at 6:45 o'clock to-night, covering only eighty-nine miles to-day.

A breakdown outside of Jefferson at 11 o'clock spoiled the chances of the Italian car making a better record, though because of the delay of the Thomas car at Omaha the Italians actually reduced the American's lead from 132 to 78 miles. The trouble encountered was a repetition of the steering gear difficulty which has retarded the car ever since its breakdown in Rochester, N. Y.

After two hours' work repairs were effected and the car proceeded.

The record of eighty-nine miles under

Continued on Page 8.

WINANS ANGRY WITH SON.

Announces His Disapproval of the Young Man's Marriage.

Special to The New York Times.

BALTIMORE, March 4.—Gen. F. C. Latrobe, personal counsel for Ross Winans, to-night announced that Mr. Winans authorized him to say that his son, Thomas Winans, had married without his consent and was now living in Paris on an allowance paid by his father. It is said the father is greatly displeased with his son, and that the young man will not inherit the Winans millions.

When Mr. Winans several months ago started for America with the bodies of his wife and another son he expected that his son Thomas would cross the ocean with him. The steamer on which they were to sail was scheduled to leave Liverpool early in the morning, and Mr. Winans and his son went on board the night before. When Mr. Winans awoke the next morning with the steamship well down the Irish Channel he found that his son had slipped off the night before.

The son went straight from Liverpool to Paris and married a Spanish actress, in spite of the most strenuous objections on the part of his father. Mr. Winans's anger was so great when he learned his son had contracted what he believed to be a mesalliance that he is alleged to have decided to leave the bulk of his millions to others than the son, who would have received them in ordinary circumstances.

NAVAL SECRETS REVEALED.

Duma Hears That Russian Processes Were Disclosed to English Firm.

ST. PETERSBURG, March 4.—An interpellation was introduced in the Duma today demanding explanations from Admiral Dikoff, Minister of Marine, of the charges current in navy circles that Russian naval secrets had been communicated to Vickers's Sons & Maxim, the English shipbuilders, in connection with the construction of the new Russian cruiser Rurik by this firm. These secrets were thereby rendered available to other nations.

It is alleged that the armor, guns, and shells manufactured by Vickers's Sons & Maxim were unsatisfactory, and that the Ministry of Marine, instead of replacing this material direct from Russian factories ordered supervising experts to instruct Vickers's Sons & Maxim to prepare the armor according to a secret process worked out at the Kolpine factory, and furnished plans of Russian eight and ten inch guns to the English firm when the English shell failed to meet the high-velocity requirements insisted upon by Russia. It also is charged that the Ministry communicated the Russian method of attaching rifling bands to armor-piercing guns, which was one of the cherished secrets of the Odoukhoff arms factory.

NOTES SIGNED U. S. GRANT, JR.,

Are Fraudulent and Void, Wall Street Hears—Three U. S. Grants.

This warning, to which the name of the man concerned gave interest, was sent out by a Wall Street news agency yesterday:

U. S. Grant, Jr., has given notice that there are no notes or personal obligations bearing his signature upon the market for sale or discount, and he warns all persons that if such are offered they are fraudulent and void.

Ulysses S. Grant, son of the late President, usually known as U. S. Grant, Jr., lives in San Diego, Cal., most of the year. U. S. Grant, nephew of the late President, who is not junior, has a post in the United States Sub-Treasury. He said yesterday that he did not know whence the warning came or why it was issued. It did not come from him.

Gen. Fred D. Grant, commander of the Department of the East, stationed at Governors Island, has a son, Ulysses S. Grant, third, who is a graduate of West Point, and is stationed at Boston. Gen. Grant said that the warning, he was sure, had not been sent out by his son, and he did not think his brother had sent it out, either.

OFFICERS CRITICISE HALE.

Action in Cutting Short Commander Sims's Testimony Raises Row.

Special to The New York Times.

WASHINGTON, March 4.—The action of Senator Hale and other Senators in cutting short the statement with which Commander Sims sought to open his testimony in the naval investigation yesterday has resulted in a storm of criticism among naval officers.

Commander Sims gave out a statement to-day covering his preliminary remarks before the Senate Committee. He prefaced it by saying that his remark about the poor gunnery in the Spanish war was not intended to be a reflection on the personnel, which he declared "is the best in the world."

The shooting in the war was bad "simply because the system in vogue then did not develop the ability of the gunners or of the material. Our men are the superiors of any others in the world, and since the present system of gunnery training was established they have shown that they can beat any other navy in the world."

The narration of his criticisms, he said, would "involve relating some unpleasant incidents, including apparent resistence to criticisms, and to the remedying of serious defects, the disappearance of official reports, and the practical secretion of official documents."

"You can't handle powder, and handle it fast, without having accidents. And you have got to handle it fast—you must reach your gun before the other fellow gets to his. You must hit the other fellow quick, and as many times as you can before he gets at you."

These expressions are taken from the testimony of Rear Admiral William S. Cowles, chief of the Bureau of Equipment of the Navy Department, before the Senate Committee on Naval Affairs to-day in the investigation of criticisms of battleship construction.

Admiral Cowles said that the American ships were the equal of any afloat, and indorsed in positive terms the open turret and direct ammunition hoist with the improvements made since the Missouri and Georgia accidents.

Rockefeller Estate Liens Satisfied.

Two of the four mechanics' liens filed against the John D Rockefeller estate at Pocantico Hills recently were satisfied yesterday in the County Clerk's office in White Plains. These liens were filed by Harry A. Leoder and Thomas Conroy of the firm of Leoder & Conroy because of a dispute as to payments by contractors for the building of a laundry.

PALM BEACH—ST. AUGUSTINE—MIAMI Seaboard Florida Limited—daily—all Pullmans. Shortest Florida Route. Office, 1,183 B'way.—Adv.

EXTORTION CHARGE AGAINST VIDAVER

Attorney General's Special Deputy Arrested After He Accepts $500 in Marked Bills.

MONEY FROM MONTGOMERY

Former President of Hamilton Bank Accuses Him of Threatening to Close Proposed New Bank.

Nathan Vidaver, Special Deputy Attorney General for the State and candidate in turn for the Supreme Court and Court of General Sessions on the Hearst Independence League ticket, was arrested yesterday at the Astor House with $500 in marked bills in his possession.

The District Attorney's office asserts that this money was obtained from William R. Montgomery, formerly President of the Hamilton Bank, as the result of attempted extortion, the money having been accepted by Vidaver ostensibly as a "fee" to muzzle the newspapers and keep Attorney General Jackson's office from interfering with a plan Montgomery had on foot for the opening of a new bank in Seventh Avenue.

For several months Vidaver has been active in the work of the Attorney General's department. It was he who conducted the Grand Jury investigation of the Kissena Park scandal in Queens Borough. It was he also who prosecuted the charge of neglect of duty made against William Leary, State Superintendent of Elections, by Max Ihmsen, candidate for Sheriff in the last municipal campaign. At the present time Vidaver represents the Attorney General in the Metropolitan Street Railway investigation.

Vidaver denies the charge upon which he was arrested, but admits that he received the marked money. He explained that it was accepted merely as a "retainer for his services as associate counsel for Montgomery."

Trap Laid for Him.

His arrest was the result of a cleverly executed plan arranged by District Attorney Jerome, to whom Montgomery had gone with a report of his negotiations with the Special Deputy. The report made by the ex-bank President appears to implicate another lawyer in the transactions leading up to the passing of the marked money and Vidaver's arrest.

Vidaver was arraigned before Magistrate Herrman in the Tombs Court and released on cash bail, pending an investigation of the charges against him. The evidence will be placed before the Grand Jury to-day.

On the authority of an official connected with the District Attorney's office the evidence will show that the money was obtained from Montgomery under threats of serious injury to his business plans. This evidence will be given by policemen who overheard conversations between the principals in the case, supplementing the written evidence of a stenographer who, while hidden in a clothes closet in Montgomery's home early yesterday morning, took down in shorthand a conversation between Lawyer Moses H. Grossman and Montgomery.

According to the District Attorney Grossman acted as the go-between during most of the dealings between Vidaver and the former President of the Hamilton Bank. He is accused of arranging the meeting yesterday afternoon between Vidaver and Montgomery at the Astor House, although he was not present when the $500 was paid over to Vidaver.

This $500 in marked bills was not the first money Vidaver had received from Montgomery, according to evidence which is in the hands of the District Attorney. There was a check for a like sum which Vidaver received last year.

When He First Met Montgomery.

According to the information received by Mr. Jerome, the dealings between Vidaver and the banker began last November, a few weeks after the Hamilton Bank was closed by order of the Superintendent of Banks, and Montgomery, who had succeeded E. R. Thomas to the Presidency of the suspended institution, was making vigorous efforts to get the depositors' consent to a plan for resumption.

The newspapers were commenting unfavorably on the bank on reports of its affairs that emanated from the office of the Attorney General, which at that time was making an investigation in conjunction with the State Banking Department.

There was a meeting between Montgomery and Vidaver, who at that time was not connected with the Attorney General's office, but was associated with Clarence J. Shearn as counsel for the Independence League and stood close to Attorney General Jackson. What transpired at that interview will be told to the Grand Jury today by Montgomery himself.

The version that has come to the District Attorney's office is that Vidaver offered to muzzle the newspapers by shutting off the information concerning the Hamilton Bank affairs which was cropping out of the Attorney General's office.

Montgomery wanted to know what such a service would cost, so the story goes, and was told that it would be $1,500. Moses H. Grossman was thereupon seen by Montgomery, and a little later Vidaver received a check for $500, signed with Grossman's name. On this check, it is said, there appeared an indorsement indicating for what the money was paid. Grossman said yesterday that he had never received that $500 from Montgomery, and that it came out of his own pocket.

An official connected with Mr. Jerome's office asserts that no more Hamilton Bank news came out of the Attorney General's office for a while after the receipt of that check. Frank White was receiver for the Hamilton Bank some weeks past. Then came the dissolution of the receivership by a court order and the indictment of Montgomery on the charge of overdrawing his account. This indictment still hangs over his head.

Plan for a New Bank.

Relieved of all connection with the Hamilton Bank Montgomery some time ago began to lay plans for another bank to be opened in Seventh Avenue. He consulted Grossman, who advised him to see Vidaver. There were several meetings between Vidaver and Montgomery. According to the District Attorney a threat was made finally that unless Montgomery paid a certain sum of money the Attorney General's office would close up any such bank.

Montgomery says he was told also that if $500 was paid over to Vidaver the Attorney General's office would not be averse to the District Attorney dropping the pending prosecution of the overdraft charge.

That was several days ago. Montgomery communicated with Mr. Jerome, and made a full statement of the case. The Dis-

Continued on Page 3.

BLAIR ESTATE FIGHT ENDS.

Five Grandchildren Get $500,000 Each; Son $47,500,000.

After being eight years in the courts of New Jersey, the John I. Blair $50,000,000 estate was straightened out before Vice Chancellor Emery in Newark yesterday, when the executor was discharged and the steps he had taken in settling the difficulties approved.

The five grandchildren of the testator were paid $500,000 each in cash and securities. These heirs are Isabella Scribner, Charles Scribner, Arthur H. Scribner, Clarence Blair Mitchell, and Emma Scribner Larned. They said they were satisfied with the terms. The bulk of the estate goes to the executor, De Witt C. Blair, a son.

John I. Blair of Blairstown, N. J., died in December, 1899. Five trusts were named in his will for his five grandchildren. It was found, however, that many of the stocks specified in the trusts had been sold. The grandchildren brought suit to compel the executor to replace these shares with others not specified, to make the bequests the same amount as that named in the will.

MAILS WAIT ON SOCIETY.

Great Neck Can't Get Rural Delivery Without Rich Residents' Consent.

Special to The New York Times.

GREAT NECK, L. I., March 4.—On the approval of Meadow Brook colonists and other wealthy property owners of the section alluded to as the "Newport of Long Island," depends the fate of the newly proposed rural free delivery route for Great Neck. The proposed route is skirted by the estate of some of the wealthiest residents of Long Island, and as they own automobiles and can readily collect their own mail at the village Post Office, Postmaster Hicks says their sanction to the rural route is necessary before the less fortunate residents who live in remote sections can have free delivery.

Among the prominent residents whose approval is asked for are William R. and J. P. Grace, Henry P. Booth, Charles Gignoux, Hazen L. Hoyt, Silas McBee, Cord Meyer, Mrs. H. S. Kerr, Roswell Eldredge, Clarkson Cowl, August Jannsen, William Astor Chanler, Leo Kohn, Mrs. E. M. Scott, A. H. Alker, J. F. O'Rourke, Daniel Winant, Paulding Farnham, and C. B. Wilson.

AUDUBON YACHT CLUB BURNS.

Young Women Help Save Property at Spectacular River Front Fire.

A spectacular fire, caused, it is believed, by sparks from a New York Central locomotive, destroyed last night the premises of the Audubon Yacht Club, John Dalton's Launch Club, and the Fort Washington Canoe Club, all of which were along the river front at 168th Street and the Hudson River. Fifteen launches and twenty canoes stored in or near the clubs were also burned. The damage was estimated at about $15,000.

Miss Gladys Springer, daughter of John H. Springer of the Grand Opera House, Twenty-third Street, was the first to notice the fire, which started in Dalton's. She telephoned to Fire Hall, and then, in company with Miss Clara Anway, Miss G. Sturges, and several others, including Capt. Payne Kretzner, Commodore of the Knickerbocker Canoe Club, formed a bucket brigade and did great work in saving several of the launches and canoes, pending the arrival of the Fire Department.

"TIN CANS" IN THE SUBWAY.

New Cars So Named by Guards—The Side-Door Problem.

The order requiring the Interborough Rapid Transit Company to show cause why all the Subway cars should not have side doors came up for hearing before Public Service Commissioner Eustis yesterday, but was postponed until April 8, owing to the inability of Bion J. Arnold, the commission's expert, to be present.

Alfred A. Gardner, counsel for the company, said the company would not consent to have side doors in all the new cars, providing the commission would drop that part of the order requiring the changing of the cars at present in use.

The first installment of the recent purchase of new steel cars for the Subway has been received and put in operation on the Subway expresses. The cars have doors nearly twice as wide as the doors of the older type of car, and the platforms are correspondingly larger. It is said the new cars cost about $5,000 less each than did the first steel Subway cars. The ceiling instead of being aluminium is steel. The cars rattle a good deal, and some of the train guards have dubbed them "tin cans."

HAD A SECRET WEDDING.

George Quintard, Jr., and Miss Maie Woods Were Married in November.

Special to The New York Times.

WHITE PLAINS, March 4.—Following an automobile ride to Mount Vernon Miss Maie Woods, famous since the Brewsters wreck on the New York Central, and George W. Quintard, Jr., grandson of the wealthy iron manufacturer, were married on Nov. 16, 1907, in Mount Vernon. The facts concerning the wedding did not get out until to-day.

The bride displayed great courage when the Brewster Express was wrecked on Feb. 18, 1907. She was on her way to her home in White Plains, and though badly injured she aided women passengers to escape from the car, which overturned, by dragging them through windows.

CUBAN IMPORTS FALL OFF.

Customs Receipts for February Amounted to Only $1,604,730.

HAVANA, March 4.—The customs receipts at Havana for February amounted to only $1,604,730. In January the receipts were $2,225,042, and in December $2,221,000.

The February receipts were less than those of any month since the evacuation of Cuba by the Spanish, excepting the month of September, 1906.

The country merchants complain they have been compelled to curtail their orders owing to the refusal of the Havana bankers to extend their credits. There is a disposition here to attribute the situation to a lack of confidence in the American declaration that a republic will be re-established next February.

POLAND WATER. Leads all in Reputation, Purity, and Medicinal Properties. Hiram Ricker & Sons, Proprietors, New York Depot and Office, 1,180 Broadway. B. S. Robinson, Manager.—Adv.

BLACK ATTACKS THE RACING BILLS

Says if Gambling at Race Tracks Is to Go, Bets of Candy Are Punishable.

REGULATION, SAYS POTTER

Compromise Proposition Offered by The Jockey Club Would Favor Credit Betting.

Special to The New York Times.

ALBANY, March 4.—Ex-Gov. Frank S. Black appeared this afternoon at the joint hearing before the Codes Committees of both houses against the Agnew-Hart bills, recommended by Gov. Hughes and framed with a view to check betting on races.

He argued that if the Legislature desired to abolish gambling at the race tracks, it must also make it a prison offense for a young girl to bet a box of candy on the result of a college boat race. When he was through speaking, Louis Marshall of the law firm of Untermyer, Marshall & Guggenheim said:

"I withdraw my request for time to answer Mr. Black. He has answered himself. All I want Gov. Black to do is to read his own speech from the transcript of the stenographers' notes, and if he does not blush with shame over his performance I will blush for him."

The arguments of the friends of the proposed reforms were sandwiched between the speeches of the attorneys of the racing interests and ex-Gov. Black, who ostensibly appeared as the representative of the agricultural societies, with no opportunity for rebuttal. This was a departure from the usual proceedings at hearings before the legislative committees, where the opponents of a bill are heard first and then the proponents.

Belmont's Compromise Plan.

A letter from August Belmont, President of The Jockey Club, proposed a compromise plan for the further restriction of race-track betting. This plan, urged by the stewards of The Jockey Club after a consultation with Police Commissioner Bingham and several Justices of the Supreme Court, contemplates the prohibition by statutory enactment of the passing of money in betting at the tracks. This would have for its result the inauguration of credit betting, something akin to the system now in vogue at the English tracks.

Bishop Pootter for Regulation.

Something of a sensation was caused by the reading of a letter from Bishop Potter of New York, in which he said it is his conviction that not abolition, but regulation would provide the best means of meeting the betting evil. A similar letter from the Rev. Dr. Thomas R. Slicer of New York had already been read.

To-day's hearing was held with a view of giving the agricultural societies who have been represented as opposed to any change in the law a chance to be heard. Only thirty out of sixty-one county fair associations in the State were represented.

Louis Marshall, who made the principal speech in favor of the bill, was a member of the Constitutional Convention of 1894, which proposed the omnibus prohibition against gambling. He declared that the Percy-Gray law evaded the Constitution and fell short of meeting the intentions of those that revised it.

"The ordinary citizen, who on one day visits a race track and observes the operation of the pool seller in an inclosure specially provided, known as the betting ring, from a hundred different stands, at which attractive odds are offered, and who finds that these operations have apparently the sanction of law, is unable to understand why he cannot, on the succeeding day, visit a poolroom and bet on the same horses without contributing to the commission of a State prison offense.

Ex-Gov. Black's Speech.

After several speakers had been heard in favor of the bill ex-Gov. Black got the floor.

"This is not a moral question," he said. "It is a purely practical question. There is not a profession in the world, the members of which would not divide upon the question of whether gambling is right or wrong.

"You should not be guided, whether you come from Chemung, Buffalo, or Brooklyn, by the sentiment in your districts which may foil you in your desire to come back to the Legislature if you should run counter to it. Should you let yourselves be guided by any local breezes like that, then you are not fit to be here at all."

Mr. Black declared that the Constitution was against all forms of gambling and said the legislators would not do their full duty if they singled out one special form of gambling to make it a crime. He declared that if it was wrong for a man to bet money at the track it was equally wrong for a woman to bet a pair of gloves or a box of candy on a boat race or anything involving an element of chance.

"Never unless it be written in the statute book can betting be regarded as a crime. It is a question of personal liberty. It is a question of right. You can't stop betting."

When ex-Gov. Black read the letters from Bishop Potter and Dr. Slicer he supplemented the reading with the remark that that would about even things up between both sides as far as the support of the Church was concerned. He said he had only heard one minister of the Gospel—the Rev. Dr. Walter Laidlaw of the American Federation of Churches—speak in favor of the bills. At that point clergymen bobbed up in every part of the Assembly chamber. There were more than a score of them, and they all declared they were in favor of the reforms.

Assemblyman Hart of Utica, who introduced the bills in the lower house, read a telegram from Gov. Folk of Missouri, telling the story of the abolition of race-track gambling there.

MORE FINE HORSES NOW.

Gov. Folk Says Anti-Gambling Laws Do Not Stop Their Raising.

JEFFERSON CITY, Mo., March 4.—Anti-gambling laws do not interfere with the breeding of fine horses in Missouri, according to a statement made to-night by Gov. Folk. Gov. Folk said:

"From the best reports obtainable I say there have been more fine horses raised in Missouri during the past three years when there has been no race-track gambling than when gambling on race tracks was licensed."

TOUR TO SEE WASHINGTON. Only $12.00 or $14.50 covers necessary expenses for three days. Leaves Thursday, March 12, via Pennsylvania Railroad.—Adv.

WHIP BARRED FROM SCHOOLS.

Board of Education Rejects Corporal Punishment by a Vote of 21 to 17.

By a vote of twenty-one to seventeen the members of the Board of Education last night defeated the proposal to introduce corporal punishment in the public schools of this city.

The special committee appointed to consider the subject, composed of Nathan S. Jones, Dr. Dennis J. McDonald, and George A. Vanderhoff, said that 470 letters had been received from all parts of the country, 270 favoring the reintroduction of corporal punishment.

Supt. Maxwell was among those who approved the plan.

FOUND NEW SATELLITE.

Observer at Greenwich, England, Saw It on Eight Different Nights.

CAMBRIDGE, Mass., March 4.—The discovery of a new planet or satellite is announced in a cablegram received from the observatory at Kiel, Germany, by the astronomers at the Harvard Observatory at Cambridge.

According to the cablegram, the new body was observed on eight different nights by Observer Melotte at Greenwich, England, and is visible in a large telescope. Its position on Jan. 27 was given as follows: .5306, Greenwich mean time, it was in right ascension 8 hours 46 minutes 7.2 seconds, declination plus 18 degrees 3 minutes 84 seconds.

The Harvard astronomers are inclined to the belief that the object is a satellite.

$16,000 FOR A JARDINIERE.

One of the Famous Dickens Porcelains Sold at Christie's.

LONDON, March 4.—The sale at auction at Christie's of the famous Dickens collection of porcelains, which includes fine Dresden and Sevres examples, attracted a host of foreign dealers to-day.

Despite the financial depression, good prices were realized, 104 lots bringing $100,000.

The highest prices were $16,000 for a Sevres jardiniere 8½ inches high, painted by Morin and Scioux, and $16,800 for a set of three Sevres vases and covers painted by Morin and gilded by Vincent.

BROKAWS SOON TO GO SOUTH.

Parents of Ill Wife Hear That She Will Accompany Her Husband.

Special to The New York Times.

HIGH POINT, N. C., March 4.—It is understood that the Blairs, parents of Mrs. William Gould Brokaw, who are now at Fairview Lodge, have been advised that Mr. Brokaw has decided to wait several days longer in New York before returning South in order that Mrs. Brokaw, who is still in a hospital, may accompany him. William Gould, uncle of Mr. Brokaw, has telegraphed from New York, denying the report that Mr. Brokaw had deeded the Fairview estate to him.

The parents of Mrs. Brokaw say that rumors of a separation are unfounded.

SIXTEEN MINERS ENTOMBED.

English Colliers Cut Off by Fire—Feared They Must Perish.

BIRMINGHAM, England, March 4.—A fire broke out this evening in the Hamstead colliery, near here.

Sixteen miners are entombed and rescuing parties have not been able to reach them. It is feared that they have perished.

BOTH FIGHTERS MAY DIE.

Rival Grocers in a Desperate Battle Following a Trade Dispute.

Special to The New York Times.

PASSAIC, N. J., March 4.—Samuel Zuritsky and Louis Alper fought each other so desperately in a lonely section of Garfield yesterday afternoon that they had to be carried home, and both may die from their injuries.

The men are grocers, Zuritsky having purchased his store from Alpers on condition that Alpers should not resume business within ten blocks. Alper's wife started a new grocery store a block away from the old stand, and her husband and Zuritsky fought yesterday in consequence. Alper was kicked in the face and stomach, but fought until he knocked his assailant down. In falling Zuritsky sustained a fracture of the skull, and this ended the fight.

NO THREATS TO CHINA.

But Japan Expects Release of Vessel, an Apology, and Damages.

TOKIO, March 4.—Officers of the Foreign Office to-day made this statement:

"Japan has issued no ultimatum and has made no threats to China in connection with the steamer Tatsu's illegal seizure. We are depending on the good sense of the Chinese Government to release the vessel, express regrets, and pay damages."

LONDON, March 5.—A special dispatch to The Morning Post from Shanghai says that the relations between China and Japan are seriously strained owing to the seizure by China of the Japanese steamer Tatsu Maru off Macao. The dispatch further says that Japan declares that it will regard the refusal to release the steamer as a casus belli.

BETRAYED BY A COCK CROW.

Prisoners Said Valises Held Clothing, but Rooster Wouldn't Keep Still.

Sergt. Treanor of the East 126th Street Police Station congratulated himself last night on having broken up a cockfighting main which he believes was to have been "pulled off" somewhere in Harlem. The Sergeant stopped three men whom he saw carrying valises in 126th Street, near Madison Avenue, and when one of the men dropped his valise and ran Treanor grabbed the other two.

Both asserted that they had only clothing in their grips, but just then Treanor heard a muffled crowing. He took the men to the station house, where the valises were found to contain six fighting cocks, two birds in a valise, all clipped and ready for the fray.

The men said they were Harry Hudson, 25 years old, of Englewood, N. J., and Albert Keitz, 30, of the same town. Keitz had $100 in his pocket. They were locked up as suspicious persons.

Artist De Severius Sued for Divorce.

Through her attorney, Mrs. Lillian Georgiana de Severius, the wife of Alhanis de Severius, an artist, yesterday applied to Supreme Court Justice Crane, in Brooklyn, for alimony and counsel fee in a suit for divorce brought against her husband. Justice Crane reserved decision. Mrs. de Severius names a Brooklyn woman in her suit. All the allegations are denied by the artist.

NEW YORK TO PACIFIC COAST $55. Lehigh Valley, 355, 1,460 B'way.—Adv.

165 CHILDREN PERISH IN FIRE

Penned In by Flames and Jammed Against Locked Door in Collinwood (Ohio) School.

MANY TRAMPLED TO DEATH

Broke from Fire Line as Flames Swept Up Stairway and a Panic Followed.

INCENDIARISM IS SUSPECTED

No Wires to Ignite the Woodwork Where the Flames Started in the Basement.

TWO TEACHERS ARE VICTIMS

Parents Fight with Firemen in Desperate but Vain Effort to Rescue the Little Ones.

Special to The New York Times.

CLEVELAND, Ohio, March 4.—In a fire that may have been incendiary between 160 and 170 children lost their lives this morning when Lake View School, in the suburb of Collinwood, burned.

Penned in narrow hallways and jammed up against doors that only opened inward, the pupils were killed by fire and smoke and crushed under the grinding heels of their panic-stricken playmates. All of the victims were between the ages of 6 and 14 years. There were about 310 children in the school.

Two teachers, in vain efforts to save the little ones, perished. To-night 165 bodies are in the morgue at Collinwood, of which more than 100 have been identified and 57 are still unidentified. Thirteen children are still unaccounted for, and all the hospitals and houses for two miles around contained children, some mortally and many less seriously injured.

Fire's Origin a Mystery.

What caused the fire is a mystery. There are hints that it was incendiary. There were no wires to cross and ignite the woodwork. There was no rubbish where the flames began, to ignite from spontaneous combustion. All that now seems to be known is that three little girls coming from the basement saw smoke. Before the janitor sounded the fire alarm a mass of flames was sweeping up the stairway from the basement. Before the children from the upper floors could reach the ground egress was cut off and they perished. It was all over almost before the frantic mothers who gathered realized that their children were lost.

With the call for fire engines calls for ambulances were sent in. Every ambulance from the eastern end of Cleveland was pressed into service. Wagons were used to carry off the dead.

Rescuers were present by the hundreds, but they could not save the life of one child, so dense was the jam at the foot of the stairways.

The Lake View School was a three-story structure. Under the stairway in the front of the building was the furnace. Owing to the mild weather there was less fire than usual, and it is certain that the fire did not start there. On the first floor four rooms were in use when the fire started, and the children of this floor escaped with few exceptions. They believed the ringing of the fire gong was the usual fire drill signal and marched out in order. The pupils on the second and third floors became panic-stricken and rushed to death.

Rear Door Was Locked.

The number of pupils was more than normally large, and the smaller children had been placed in the upper part of the building. There was only one fire escape, and that was in the rear of the building. There were two stairways, one leading to a door in front and the other to a door in the rear. Both of these doors opened inward, and it is said that the rear door was locked as well.

When the flames were discovered the teachers, who throughout seem to have acted with courage and self-possession, and to have struggled heroically for the safety of their pupils, marshaled the little ones into columns for the "fire drill," which they had often practiced.

Unfortunately the line of march in this exercise had always led to the front door, and the children had not been trained to seek any other exit. The fire to-day came from directly under this part of the building.

When the children reached the foot of the stairs they found the flames close upon them, and so swift a rush was made for the door that in an instant a tightly packed mass of children was piled up against it. From that second none of those who were upon any portion of the first flight of stairs had a chance for their lives. The children at the foot of the stairs attempted to fight their way back to the floor above, while those who were coming down shoved them mercilessly back into the flames below.

In an instant there was a frightful panic, with 200 of the pupils fighting for their lives. Most of those who were killed died here. The greater part of these who escaped managed to turn back and reach the fire escape and the windows in the rear.

What happened at the foot of that first flight of stairs will never be known, for all of those who were caught in the full fury of the panic were killed. After the flames had died away, however, a huge heap of little bodies, burned by the fire and trampled into things of horror, told the tale.

As soon as the alarm was given Mrs. Kelley ran from her home, which is not far from the schoolhouse, to the burning building. The front portion of the structure was a mass of flames, and, frenzied by the screams of the fighting and dying children which reached her from the death trap at the foot of the first flight of stairs and behind that closed door, Mrs. Kelley ran to the rear, hoping to effect an entrance there and save her children.

She was joined by a man whose name is not known, and the two of them tugged and pulled frantically at the door. They were unable to move it in the slightest, and there was nothing at hand by which they could hope to break it down. In utter despair of saving any of the children, they turned their attention to the windows, and by smashing some of these they managed to save a few of the pupils.

"They could have saved many more," said Mr. Kelley to-night, "if the door had not been locked. Nobody knows how many of the children might have made their way out before my wife reached there if the door had not been locked. If half a dozen men had been there when my wife and her companion arrived at the schoolhouse, perhaps they might have broken down the door, but the two could do nothing, and the flames spread so rapidly that it was all over in a few minutes."

Parents Fight with Firemen.

The suburb of Collingwood contains about 8,000 people, and within a half hour after the outbreak of the fire nearly every one of them was gathered around the blazing ruins of the school house, hundreds of parents fighting frantically with the police and firemen who were busily engaged in saving the lives of the children caught in the burning building and doing their best to extinguish the fire.

The police were utterly unable through lack of numbers to keep away the crowd that pressed upon them, and the situation soon became so serious that a number of the more cool-headed men in the throng took it upon themselves to aid in fighting back the crowd, while others worked to help the firemen and the police.

Among the latter were Wallace Upton, who reached the building shortly after the front door had caved in, and disclosed to the horror-stricken crowd the awful scenes that had occurred there. Just in front of Upton's eyes was his own ten-year-old daughter, helpless in the crush, badly burned, and trampled upon, but still alive. The fire was close upon her, and if she could not be saved at once she could not be saved at all.

Upton sprang to help her, and with all his strength sought to tear her from the weight that was pressing her down and from the flames which were creeping close. Although he worked with a desperation of despair, his strength was unequal to the task. He fought on until his clothing was partly burned from him and the skin of his face and hands was scorched black. Other men attempted to induce him to move, but he refused until he saw that his girl was dead, and that he could not save her life by sacrificing his own. He then withdrew from the schoolhouse, and, although so seriously injured that he may die, lingered about the place for several hours, refusing to go to a hospital or to seek medical attention.

Flames Spread with Rapidity.

The flames spread with such terrific rapidity that within thirty minutes from the time the fire was discovered the schoolhouse was nothing but a few blackened walls, surrounding a cellar filled with corpses and débris.

The firemen dashed into the blazing wreckage and with their bare hands worked in the most frantic manner with the hope of saving a few more lives. They were unsuccessful, for none was taken alive from the ruins after the floors collapsed.

The greater majority of the little bodies that were taken from the ruins were burned beyond all possible recognition. And it is no small part of the sorrow which is bearing down the people of Collinwood that positive identification of many of the children will never be made.

Piled Against Locked Door.

One of the scenes of horror that attended the fire occurred at the rear doorway of the building before the firemen arrived. This door, like the one in front, opened inward and it was locked. The children were piled up high against it, and when it finally was broken down by their weight and by the fire that had partly burned and weakened it the women who had gathered outside saw before them a mass of white faces and struggling bodies. The flames swept over the aisle, while the women stood helpless, unable to lend a hand to aid the children. Many of the women were unable to withstand the sight and dropped fainting to the ground.

The Fire Department was late in reaching the building, and when it came the apparatus was inadequate and the men were volunteers, there being no paid Fire Department in the suburb. The water pressure was not sufficiently strong to send a stream to the second-story windows. Moreover, the firemen had no ladder that would reach to the third floor. The volunteers did what they could, but within a few moments after their arrival the task was one for ambulances alone.

After the bodies had been taken to the extemporized morgue in the Lake Shore shops, they were laid in rows of ten. The first identification was that of Nels Thompson, a boy, who was identified by his mother, who knew his suspender buckle.

Henry Schultz, 9 years of age, was known only by a fragment of his sweater. The third identification was that of Irene Davis, 15 years of age, whose little sister pointed out a fragment of her skirt.

Among those who sought vainly through the Morgue for their children was Mrs. John Phillis of Poplar Street, whose fifteen-year-old daughter is among the dead. Her attention was called to the fire by her four-year-old son, who called her to come to the window "and see the children playing on the fire-escape." Mrs. Phillis ran to the schoolhouse and found her daughter among those penned in around the front door. She took hold of her hands, but could not pull her out.

"I reached in and stroked her head," said Mrs. Phillis, "trying to keep the fire from burning her hair. I stayed there and pulled at her, and tried to keep the fire away from her till a heavy piece of glass fell on me, cutting my hand nearly off. Then I fell back, and my girl died before my face."

Dan Clark, 8 years old, was identified by a little pink bordered handkerchief in which he had wrapped a new bright green marble. The body of Russell Newberry, 9 years old, was made known by a fragment of a watch chain.

At 10 o'clock to-night it was said that sixty bodies had been identified.

Deputy Coroner Harry McNeil, who was to-night in charge of the Morgue in the Lake Shore depot, declared that the faces of nearly all the bodies were so badly burned that it would be impossible to identify many of them. Mr. McNeil said:

"I have many portions of bodies and dozens of hands and feet which have been torn off and burned away, but which cannot possibly be identified. Two of the bodies are of women."

At the office of the firm of architects who designed the building the plan exhibited to-night showed that the doors were originally designed by them to open outward.

The statement that the back door of the building was locked was made by Walter C. Kelley, the editor of the sporting department of The Cleveland Leader, two of whose children were killed.

Janitor Herter could remember little of what happened after the fire started.

"I was sweeping in the basement," he said, "when I looked up and saw a wisp of smoke curling out from beneath the front stairway. I ran to the fire alarm and pulled the gong that sounded throughout the building. Then I ran first to the front and then to the rear doors. I can't remember what happened next, except that I saw the flames shooting all about, and the little children running down through them screaming. Some fell at the rear entrance, and others stumbled over them. I saw my little Helen among them. I tried to pull her out, but the flames drove me back. I had to leave my little child to die."

Herter was badly burned about the head.

County Coroner Burke immediately after the fire said: "The construction of the school house was an outrage. The hallways were narrow and there was practically only one mode of exit. The children were caught like rats in a trap."

Youth Dies Rescuing Children.

Hugh McIlrath, who was killed in the fire, was the son of Charles G. McIlrath, Chief of the Collinwood Police. He lost his life in an effort to save a number of smaller children. When Chief McIlrath reached the burning building he saw his son leading a crowd of younger children down the fire escape. From the bottom of the escape to ground was a long leap, and the children refused to take it in spite of young McIlrath's efforts. Some of them turned back into the building and McIlrath hastened after them to induce them to come out again, but was caught by the flames before he could do so.

Glenn Sanderson, a boy 12 years of age, met his death in plain view of a large crowd which was utterly unable to help him. He was on the third floor in the school auditorium in which were a number of pieces of scenery, the floor beneath him was on fire, and young Sanderson swung from one piece of scenery to another trying to reach the fire escape. He managed to cross the stage about half way when he missed his grasp and fell into the fire.

George Getzien, Superintendent of the local telephone company, was in his buggy not more than 200 feet distant from the school when he saw the fire shoot out from the front of the building. In relating his experience he said:

"I went to the rear door and tried to force an entrance. Aided by Policeman Charles Wall, we managed to get in, but both of us were driven out by the fire. There were no children near the door at that time, as I remember it. We ran around to the front door, but could not force it open. My opinion is that it opened inward. The fire was so hot that within fifteen minutes after I saw the flames I could not remain near the building."

Henry Ellis, a real estate dealer, was one of the first to reach the building. With him was L. E. Cross, Superintendent of the Lake Shore & Michigan Southern roundhouse. Together they attempted to rescue some of the children jammed at the rear door, and Ellis remained at the work until his hands and face were badly burned.

"When I reached the school," he said, "the front door was closed and below I could see the flames coming through the floor. We knew we could save none of the children there, and Cross and I went to the rear. The door had been broken open and the children lay five or six deep, the fire had already reached them, and I could see the flames catch first one and then another. I saw one girl who could not have been more than 10 or 11 years old protect her little brother, who was not more than 6.

Fire Caught Them in a Minute.

"He cried for help and clung to her hand. She encouraged him and covered his head with a shawl she was wearing, to keep the flames away. The fire caught them in a minute and both were killed. Cross and I thought that the work of getting the children out would be easy, but when we attempted to release the first one we found it was almost impossible to move them at all.

"We succeeded in saving a few who were near the top, but that was all we could do. The fire swept through the hall, springing from one child to another, catching their hair and the dresses of the girls. Their cries were dreadful to hear."

Deputy State Fire Marshal Nathan Feigenbaum made an inspection of the ruins after the fire and to-night declared positively that the doors of the schoolhouse opened toward the inside, and that the rear door was locked when the children reached it. He declared that his investigation had so far failed to establish the cause of the fire.

TOOK PUPILS ON FIRE ESCAPE.

Miss Bodey Saved Almost Fifty of Her Class.

Special to The New York Times.

CLEVELAND, Ohio, March 4.—Miss Laura Bodey, teacher of the fifth grade on the third floor, said:

"When the gong sounded I thought at once of the fire drill. I didn't think at first it was a real fire. But I formed my pupils just as we have often done in practice. We had no more than formed in line when smoke began creeping into the room. Our practice taught the children to go down the fire escape, but when the smoke began coming in some of the pupils cried to the others to go down the rear stairs.

"Seven or eight broke from the line and started for the stairs. The rest I managed to keep under control. I got them on the fire escape and to the ground in safety. The poor children who rushed down the back stairs must have perished, for I know they never came back to the room again. I was the last to leave and watched for them to return until the heat and the flames drove me down the fire escape. I had about fifty pupils in my room, and all escaped but the few who left the line and rushed for the stairs."

Besides the children who were killed inside the building, three little girls, Mary Ridgeway, Anna Roth, and Gertrude Davis, were instantly killed by leaping from the attic to the ground.

Miss Ethel Rose, a teacher on the first floor of the building, whose pupils were the younest in the school, managed to get all but three of her charges out of the building in safety. Two of the smaller ones she carried in her arms.

Miss Anna Moran, the Principal of the school, and two of the teachers, Miss Gollmar and Miss Rowley, escaped by one of the windows in the rear. They remained with the panic-stricken children until they could do no more for them, and then sought their own safety.

Little Girl Saves Her Brother.

One of the heroines of the catastrophe was little Marie Witman of 5,217 Lake Street. She ran through the smoke-filled halls and grasped her little brother, whom she managed to drag from the room and take out through a window, both of them being nearly strangled with smoke.

Miss Gollmar said:

"It was awful. I can see the wee things in my room holding out their tiny arms and crying to me to help them. Their voices are ringing in my ears yet, and I shall never forget them. When the alarm gong rang I started the pupils marching from the building. When we started down the front stairs we were met by a solid wall of flame, and clouds of dense smoke. We retreated, and when we turned the children became panic-stricken and I could not do anything with them. They became jammed in the narrow stairway, and I knew that the only thing for me to do was to get around to the rear door if possible and help those who were near the entrance.

"When I got there, after climbing out of a window, I found the children so crowded in the narrow passageway that I could not pull even one of them out. Those behind pushed forward, and as I stood there the little ones piled up on one another. Those who could stretched out their arms to me and cried for me to help them. I tried with all my might to pull them out, and stayed there until the flames drove me away."

Teacher Narrowly Escapes Death.

Another teacher, Miss Pearl Lynn, narrowly escaped death. She was carried toward the rear entrance by the rush of the panic-stricken pupils and fell at the bottom of the stairs with numbers of the children on top of her. She lay there unable to rise because of the weight of the bodies upon her. She was dragged from the mass of dead children just in time to save her own life.

TWO TEACHERS PERISH.

Belief That Miss Fiske Died Hurrying Pupils to Fire Escape.

Special to The New York Times.

CLEVELAND, Ohio, March 4.—Of the nine teachers in the burned Lake View School, all escaped with their lives but two. Those who met death in the flames were Miss Katherine Weiler, 2,217 East Eighty-first Street, and Miss Grace Fiske, Orville Avenue, Cleveland.

Miss Fiske was a teacher of the first grade class, on the first floor. She was carried from the building still breathing and hurried to Glenville Hospital, where she died shortly before noon. Miss Weiler taught a class on the second floor. She perished with many of her pupils. Her body was recovered at 1 o'clock.

How Miss Fiske died will probably never be known. One of her pupils who escaped down the fire escape said he remembered seeing her trying to gather the children together as the flames burst through the doors leading to the hallway. Her room was the first to be reached by the fire coming from the basement, and there was scarcely an instant's warning of their impending fate. It is supposed Miss Fiske died in attempting to hurry her pupils to the fire escape. The flames must have caught her before she could reach the windows.

Miss Weiler was the daughter of the Rev. Gustave Weiler of 167 Fortieth Street, Pittsburg, Penn., pastor of the Second German Methodist Episcopal Church. She was 27 years old. The family formerly lived at Wheeling, West Va.

When 18 years old Miss Weiler began teaching at North Baltimore, Ohio, going from there to Berea and then to Collinwood. She has been in the schools here for two years. Miss Weiler was President of the Cuyahoga County Primary Teachers' Association.

The New York Times.

THE WEATHER.

Snow or rain, warmer, to-day; cold wave, possibly snow, Thursday.

VOL. LVIII...NO. 18,603.   NEW YORK, WEDNESDAY, DECEMBER 30, 1908.—EIGHTEEN PAGES.   ONE CENT   In Greater New York, Jersey City, and Newark.   Elsewhere TWO CENTS.

ENGINEERS CHOSEN FOR CANAL INQUIRY

Davis, Freeman, Hazen, Randolph, Schuyler, and Stearns Will Accompany Taft.

TWO FAVORED LOCK PLAN

President Wants an Unbiased Report on Which to Act Before He Leaves Office.

Special to The New York Times.

WASHINGTON, Dec. 29.—Formal announcement was made at the White House to-day of the composition of the new Board of Consulting Engineers who are to make an examination of the Panama canal for the special purpose of reporting to President Roosevelt their opinion as to the proposed Gatun Dam and the comparative advisability of the board, all civilians, and all but one outside the Government service. They are:

ARTHUR P. DAVIS, chief engineer of the Reclamation Service.

JOHN R. FREEMAN, Providence, R. I.

ALLEN HAZEN, New York.

ISHAM RANDOLPH, Chicago.

JAMES DIX SCHUYLER, Los Angeles, Cal.

FREDERIC P. STEARNS, Boston.

Of the six Messrs. Randolph and Stearns were members of the consulting board, consisting of American and foreign engineers, which reported on the type of canal in February, 1906. The majority of eight said a lock canal was not feasible. Messrs. Randolph and Stearns were included in the minority of five who favored a lock canal. President Roosevelt and Congress upheld the minority, and the canal is being built according to the plans they outlined.

All six of these men were chosen by the President upon the recommendation of Alfred Noble, who was the first man asked to undertake this commission. Mr. Noble, who also was of the lock canal minority in 1906, would have been Chairman of the board if he could have accepted the appointment, but he was compelled by his private engagements to decline. It is expected that the board will sail for Panama with Mr. Taft the latter part of next month, but it may be that they will go down in the Isthmus about the time that he arrives.

The purpose of the President in sending this new board to the Isthmus is simply to secure a last disinterested judgment of the work he has directed before he goes out of office. He has chosen the most competent experts he could find and is prepared to abide by their opinion. There has been a great deal of talk, very little of it, it is true, reaching higher than mere gossip, to the effect that the adoption of the lock level for the canal was a stupendous blunder. Every accident that has happened, serious or insignificant, has led to further assertions that the lock level was wrong, and there has been a steady fire of accusations and argument from certain men who based either have shown honestly in favor of the sea-level plan or were disgruntled for one reason or another.

[Column text continues...]

GIRLS AVERT OPERA SCARE.

Alcohol Lamp Explodes Behind Metropolitan Boxes, and Set One Afire.

The presence of mind of three young girls, it was learned yesterday, averted what might have been serious consequences of a small fire at the Metropolitan Opera House on Saturday afternoon.

The accident was kept quiet then, but the facts leaked out yesterday.

The Directors of the Opera House have established a refreshment place in the large room back of the grand tier boxes. This stand is in charge of three young girls—Miss May Mae, Miss Anna Brummer, and Miss Bessie Harris—whose duty it is to serve the patrons of the house between the acts.

On Saturday afternoon the double bill of "Le Villi" and "Pagliacci" drew an immense audience to the house, and the crowd at the refreshment stand between the acts became so large that the girls were compelled to move a small alcohol lamp used for heating coffee from the stand to a table near by.

After the curtain had risen on the first act of "Pagliacci," when the crowd had returned to the auditorium, Miss Brummer went to the table to carry the lamp back to the stand. As she reached the table she noticed that the lamp was burning queerly. She called to Miss Mae, who hurried to the table and picked up the lamp. As she did so the alcohol exploded, setting fire to Miss Mae's skirt and sending a shower of sparks all over the room.

Miss Mae, stifling a scream, dropped the lamp and attempted to beat out the flames with her hands. This she was unable to do. Miss Brummer, seeing her companion afire, snatched the cloth from the table and told her to lie on the floor. Miss Mae did so and Miss Brummer wrapped the cloth about her, and, rolling her around vigorously, succeeded in extinguishing the fire.

In spite of the fact that the hands of both girls were severely burned, and Miss Mae's skirt was in ruins, they, with the assistance of Miss Harris, began to stamp out the sparks which were threatening to set fire to the heavy window curtains. Then, when all further danger had vanished, Miss Mae went home to get a new skirt. Miss Brummer and Miss Harris returned to the stand to serve the throng that had happened.

Had the room caught fire the consequence might have been serious, as boxes, orchestra, and galleries were crowded with an audience consisting mostly of women and children, and the room is directly behind the main stairway. Even had the girls lost their heads and screamed the result might have been different.

BURIED IN THE CELLAR.

Missing Woman's Body Dug Up—Husband Accused of Murder.

The body of Mrs. Matilda Breitag, 40 years old, whom her husband had reported to the police as missing three weeks ago, was dug up by the police in the cellar of their home at 221 Fifty-third Street, Brooklyn, last night. She had been choked to death.

The house is a two-story affair in South Brooklyn. The whole house is occupied by the Breitag family, consisting of Charles Breitag, a foreman employed at Bush's stores, his wife, and his stepdaughter, Aloina, who is 16 years old.

The neighbors have been commenting recently that they had not seen Mrs. Breitag since Sunday, Dec. 6. They talked to Breitag about it, and he said she had gone away somewhere, he did not know where.

Later Breitag reported to the police of the Fourth Avenue Station that his wife had disappeared. A general alarm was sent out for her.

Last Saturday Breitag bought some cement and refloored his cellar. Meantime the suspicions of the neighbors had been growing. Yesterday some of them communicated these to the police.

Last night detectives went to the house to investigate. When they started to the cellar Breitag seemed to be uneasy. When they proposed to dig up the floor Breitag objected. When they insisted he confessed that his dead wife lay under there. He had choked her to death, he said.

The police dug down two feet under the concrete and exposed one of the woman's feet. Then they called for the Coroner and arrested Breitag.

Pending further inquiry, the police detained Breitag's stepdaughter at the station. The murder is supposed to have been due to the wife's jealousy of this girl.

RICH BOOK BUYERS CALLED.

Purchasers of "De Luxe" Editions to Testify in Chicago Case.

Special to The New York Times.

CHICAGO, Dec. 29.—Several wealthy people have been subpoenaed to appear as witnesses against W. N. Cooper and Samuel Warfield, who are accused of defrauding Mrs. James A. Patten to the extent of $22,000 on "De Luxe" books.

Alexander Sellers, a retired manufacturer of Philadelphia, and Ferdinand A. W. Kieckhefer, a Milwaukee business man, appeared in court to-day prepared to tell of their deals with the bookmen, but were not called as witnesses. It is likely that they will be asked to testify to-morrow.

Among the other lovers of "De Luxe" editions and "art publications" who may be called to tell of the methods of the accused men are Mrs. Hoxie, Chicago; Mrs. Mary J. Mermod, St. Louis; Mrs. I. L. Ellwood, De Kalb, Ill.; Mrs. A. L. Root, Alton, Ill.; Mrs. W. J. Conselman, Pekin, Ill.; Mrs. Warren Lamson, Chicago; Mrs. Ludy A. Roe, Evanston; Mrs. A. L. Fort, Lacon, Ill., and Mrs. W. F. Wolfner, Chicago.

All of these women are scheduled as among the purchasers of the high-priced literature, the amounts they paid ranging from $10,000 up to $44,000. Mrs. Mermod is declared to have paid the highest price.

Latest Shipping News.

The steamship Teutonic was reported by Marconi wireless 300 miles west of the Lizard at 5 P. M. off Plymouth 5 P. M. Arrived—SS. Massachusetts, London, Dec. 17.

AMERICA DECLINES A CHINESE ALLIANCE

Ambassador Tang Fails to Commit United States to His Government's Plan.

EASTERN WAR NOT WANTED

Assurances Given, However, of American Sympathy with the Development of the Empire.

Special to The New York Times.

WASHINGTON, Dec. 29.—It was learned to-day that the real diplomatic mission of Dr. Tang Shao Yi, the special Ambassador of the Chinese Government, is practically a failure. He is aiming at something which would have practically the effect of an alliance between China and this country. An alliance in form, he knew, of course, when he came here, was impossible. But an alliance in effect, he hoped to obtain by diplomatic means. He will get nothing from this Government that can by any construction be made to serve the purpose of an alliance.

Dr. Tang came to the United States with two missions, one apparent and one real. The apparent one was to convey to this Government in the most formal and ceremonious fashion possible the thanks of the Chinese Empire for the remission of about $14,000,000 of the unpaid indemnity growing out of the Boxer outbreak of 1900. He brought with him an elaborate retinue, took a house here, and prepared for a season of social festivities, all of which should obscure his diplomatic activity.

That part of his mission having to do with the communication of China's thanks was duly carried out. The social activities were delayed by the death of the Emperor and Dowager Empress. But the diplomatic activities have been carried on with unremitting energy for some time. Despite the caution of Ambassador Tang, it has been noted, especially in diplomatic circles, that he was frequently in consultation with Secretary Root at the State Department.

It is learned from a well-informed administration source, however, that there is no disposition on the part of this Government to accede to the wishes of Dr. Tang. There is no question that this Government is in sympathy with the Chinese Government, but Dr. Tang has been informed plainly that any form of alliance is out of the question.

Dr. Tang has given this Government to understand that he appreciated that fact. He wanted from China, but his superiors in Peking were inclined to believe that some kind of an arrangement might be brought about which would give assurance to China of more than the merely moral support of the United States.

The repeated declarations of this Government concerning the preservation of the territorial integrity, the independence, and the administrative entity of China had led some of the Chinese authorities to hope, if not to believe, that the United States would take a more positive stand in the matter than had been done heretofore.

Dr. Tang's appreciation of the difficulty of the diplomatic task which was laid upon him has not diminished his activity in the effort to make some progress with it, and he is continuing his visits to Secretary Root. He has been assured that this Government will unfailingly use its good offices with other Governments in behalf of China wherever possible, and will do all it can to further the diplomatic efforts of the Chinese. But at the same time he has been told bluntly that the United States will not do anything which might involve them in a war upon the Asiatic mainland. It has been confirmed that China would not make any support any administration in a war aiming out of the question whether Chinese or Japanese, for instance, should control Manchuria.

Both President Roosevelt and President-elect Taft are much interested in the Far Eastern question. Both are firm believers in the great destiny of the Chinese Empire, and are anxious to do all they can to further a rapidly progressing Chinese development. Neither has the least concern about the so-called "yellow peril." Neither gives any credit to the idea of the military menace to the rest of the world of an awakened and militant China.

The President believes that China in her present enfeebled and helpless condition is a far greater menace to the peace of the rest of the world than she would be with her army reorganized and on such a basis of preparedness as would enable her surely to protect herself from foreign aggression. Both the President and Mr. Taft are concerned to see the Chinese complete the army reorganization which they have begun, and carry on the general development which has been so well undertaken.

In discussing the matter with an Administration official this evening it was suggested that possibly there might be an exchange of notes between China and the United States, following the Japanese policy, in which each would cover some of the points of Dr. Tang's mission without giving more than moral force to the statement. But it was said by the official that even that much was out of the question, owing chiefly to the fact that China has nothing to give this country in return for such an expression on its part.

From all this it is apparent that the results of Dr. Tang's mission will be confined practically to the very successful expression of the thanks of his Government for the remission of the unpaid Boxer indemnity, and that he will not get much beyond that.

DWIGHT T. GRISWOLD DEAD.

Yale Oarsman Who Collapsed in Harvard Race Never Regained Health.

NEW HAVEN, Conn., Dec. 29.—According to a message received here to-day, Dwight T. Griswold, who stroked the Yale 'Varsity eight-oared crew in New London last June, died to-day in San Francisco. Mr. Griswold's home was in Erie, Penn. No particulars are known.

Dwight T. Griswold was 24 years of age. He rowed in the freshman crew in his first year, although then considered not fit physically. He went out for the 'varsity crew two years later, but did not make it. He tried again his Sophomore year, and as Yale was short of material for the stroke position Griswold was put in. Griswold stood 6 feet 1 in his stockings and weighed 159 pounds. He was always inclined to be nervous, and for this reason there was some discussion as to his fitness when it was discovered that he would row in the big race.

He trained hard for the contest, but after rowing one-half of the course in the contest he collapsed completely. This proved too great a handicap for the rest of the crew and the race was lost. Three days later Griswold was graduated from the university and left for the coast to improve his health.

TAFT TO OPEN FLOWER FEAST.

To Press a Button to Start Portland's Annual Festival.

PORTLAND, Ore., Dec. 29.—In a letter to the Rose Festival Association of this city President-elect Taft consents to inaugurate Portland's annual feast of flowers on June 7 by pressing an electric button at the White House in Washington. This is said to be the first function the newly elected Chief Executive has consented to lend his official stamp of approval to.

NEW YEAR IN TIMES SQUARE.

Times Tower Illumination Will Announce the Arrival of 1909.

As in former years, Times Square is likely to be the chief centre of the New Year's celebration in this city. The restaurants are already booked to the fullest capacity.

For one night, at any rate, there will be no sign of financial depression, and the resources of the kitchens and cellars will be ransacked to meet the demands of the feast. Not a customer will be permitted to enter the restaurants unless he can show proof that he has already engaged a table.

The Times itself will announce the arrival of the new year to all within sight of its tower, which is practically the whole city. All evening the building will be illuminated. Every window will be ablaze with light, and from the summit of the building a searchlight of 2,000,000 candle power, the largest in the world, will play. With the possible exception of the Sandy Hook light, will play.

At midnight precisely, by official time, the ball will drop. It will herald the coming in of the new year to the thousands waiting in Times Square. As it touches the base of the mast it will establish a connection which will cause the illuminated figures six feet high on all four sides of the cupola, will shine forth—1909.

It will be the announcement of the passing of 1908, and will give notice to the throngs in the cafes near by to drink to the coming year.

$10,000 FOR WIFE'S LOSS.

Actor McCullough Wins Alienation Suit Against Dr. Henninger.

Special to The New York Times.

CHICAGO, Dec. 29.—Walter O'Mellah, known on the stage as Walter McCullough, recovered a judgment for $10,000 to-day against Dr. Joseph Henninger for alienation of the affections of his former wife. The suit has been noted, especially in diplomatic circles, that he was frequently in consultation with theatregoers as Mabel Montgomery.

The suit recalls the marital difficulties of the O'Mellahs and of Dr. Henninger and his wife in 1906. One of the many incidents in the tangle was the horsewhipping of Mabel Montgomery by Mrs. Henninger. Following this Mrs. Henninger was placed in the insane asylum at Elgin, but soon afterward she was released through the aid of friends, and she charged that Dr. Henninger had caused her to be placed in the institution so she could not interfere with him and the actress.

Jankowski grappled with the runner. They struggled a moment. The burglar slipped through his hands and ran on, followed by Jankowski, with the two policemen close behind. They kept firing their pistols, hoping to frighten the burglar, but he paid no attention to them. The burglar was getting into the dark when he was overhauled by Jankowski. After a brief struggle the burglar whipped out a pistol and shot his captor through the heart. The one bullet killed him.

A divorce suit followed and Mrs. Henninger got a decree.

LEEDS ESTATE $14,064,455.

Widow Gets the Bulk of the Property Under the Will.

Special to The New York Times.

MINEOLA, N. Y., Dec. 29.—Eugene Kirwin, Nassau County Tax Appraiser, filed numerous appraisals of the estates of prominent persons to-day in the Surrogate's office here. Among the most prominent was that on the estate of William B. Leeds, who died in Paris last June 23.

The estate is valued at $14,064,455. In payment of debts and expenses of administration, the sum of $5,854,215 is deducted, the balance being $8,210,250.

To his wife, Marie Stuart Leeds, Mr. Leeds left $5,482,233, the house at 987 Fifth Avenue, valued at $235,050, and the building at 114 West Fourteenth Street, valued at $190,000; wearing apparel, bric-a-brac, automobiles, stable, box at the Metropolitan Opera, amounting to $55,258.

The Newport house and furnishings, which are given as not taxable, are valued at $240,065. The tapestries in the town house are valued at $5,000, while paintings are valued at $30,000. Other household furnishings are given as follows: linings room silver, $2,250; dining room tapestries, $500; painting by Watteau, $3,500; painting by Sir Thomas Lawrence, $2,500. The yacht Nora, which is also bequeathed to Mrs. Leeds, is valued at $150,000.

William B. Leeds, Jr., the eldest son, benefits from the will to the extent of $1,611,130; Raleigh Gaar Leeds of Richmond, Ind., receives $10,000; James N. Elder, Mr. Leeds's secretary, gets $25,000 outright. Mr. Leeds's servants are given bequests.

FEW GUNS FOR AN ARMY.

Not Enough Rifles to Equip a Force of 500,000 Men in This Country.

Special to The New York Times.

WASHINGTON, Dec. 29.—With 9,000,000 men in the United States able to bear arms, there are not enough rifles to equip an army of much more than 500,000, and two-thirds of these rifles are practically obsolete. In addition, the army establishment has not enough field artillery of the modern type to equip an army of 250,000 properly.

Brig. Gen. William Crozier, Chief of the Bureau of Ordnance, not only acknowledges this fact, but adds that it will require several years to remedy the lack. He blames the conditions on the failure of Congress to appropriate funds sufficient in the past to meet the demands.

The disclosures of deficiencies in the army came as the result of a quiet investigation undertaken by the Inspector General's office. This Inspector recently said that if it were necessary to gather an army of 2,000,000 the majority would be armed with shotguns and scythes.

The result of the investigation sustained the President's declaration. It disclosed that there are not enough of the new Springfield rifles to arm more than 350,000. There are enough of the now obsolete Krag-Jorgenson and old Springfield rifles to equip 350,000 men, and these are pretty well distributed among the militia of the several States.

S. P. C. A. SHED WRECKED.

Gas Tank Blew Up in Asphyxiating Dogs—Dozen Killed, Helper Hurt.

A gas tank exploding in the shelter shed of the Society for the Prevention of Cruelty to Animals, at 448 East 102d Street, yesterday afternoon, partly wrecked the shed, killed a dozen dogs, and severely injured Hugh Dunlevy, who was in charge.

The tank is used by the society agents to kill the stray dogs which have not been called for. Dunlevy had put a dozen in the tank and had turned on the gas when there was a deafening explosion which knocked Dunlevy off his feet. Nearly all of the windows in the building were broken. The east wall was shattered and a partition was knocked into kindling wood. Dunlevy was burned about the head, arms, and hands and cut by flying glass. He was taken to the Harlem Hospital by Dr. Moeckel. He could not tell what caused the explosion.

SHOT IN THE HEART BY FLEEING BURGLAR

Pursuer Killed at Lakewood After Second-Story Thief Attempts to Rob a Hotel.

BELLBOY GIVES THE ALARM

Police Overhaul the Desperado a Moment After He Shoots Down His Pursuer.

Special to The New York Times.

LAKEWOOD, N. J., Dec. 29.—While practically all of the Winter colony here was attending amateur theatrical performances in the theatre of the Hotel Manhattan to-night at 10 o'clock, a burglar got a ladder and set it up against one side of the hotel. He was seen and an alarm given. A posse started in pursuit. Frank Jankowski, one of his pursuers, was shot and killed. The burglar was then arrested. He refused to say a word about himself.

There were two one-act plays at the Manhattan. One of them, "A Happy Medium," written by Miss Bettie Hammond, a sister of John Hays Hammond, was on the stage at 10 o'clock. Nearly everybody in town who could get out was there, and all the patrons of the hotel were in the auditorium, far removed from the side picked out by the burglar.

One of the bellboys happened to go out into the yard and saw the burglar fumbling at a second-story window. He shouted for help and Policeman George Matthews, who happened to be within a block, ran up to the hotel, firing his pistol in the air to call to his assistance his brother protector of Lakewood, Walter Curtis.

Curtis soon joined Matthews and the two gave chase to the burglar. Meanwhile no one in the theatre knew what was going on. The burglar ran through Sixth, Fifth, Fourth, and Third Streets. At Lexington Avenue and Second Street stands the Bartlett Inn, and out of that was coming at the time Frank Jankowski, the bartender, on his way home.

By this time Matthews and Curtis had come up. They arrested the runner and locked him up, charged with attempted burglary and homicide.

MRS. LONGWORTH'S ESCAPE.

Almost Run Down in Washington Street—Policeman Saves Her.

WASHINGTON, Dec. 29.—Mrs. Alice Roosevelt Longworth had a narrow escape from death or serious injury to-day beneath the feet of a pair of spirited horses, and only for the prompt action of Police Sergeant John Catts might have been trampled upon.

Mrs. Longworth was hurrying to attend the afternoon concert of the Philadelphia Symphony Orchestra, at which she was the guest of Mrs. Lawrence Townsend. She drove her electric runabout to the house across the street from the theatre, and, bringing it to a stop, alighted and hurried through the crush of vehicles.

Just as she reached the middle of the street a brougham, drawn by a pair of spirited horses, swept down upon her. Seeing her peril, Sergt. Catts sprang from the curb and, seizing the horses by their bits, threw them almost on their haunches. He escaped injury. Mrs. Longworth looked frightened as she hurried into the theatre.

A moment later Representative Longworth, who had been held up some distance from her, came up and being told of his wife's narrow escape returned to the street and shook hands warmly with the policeman.

MINE EXPLOSION ENTOMBS 36

Fourteen Others Rescued at Lick Branch, Va.—Four Dead.

ROANOKE, Va., Dec. 29.—Meagre reports of a coal mine disaster at Lick Branch, Va., reached here to-night. A message received at 10 o'clock at the general offices of the Norfolk & Western Railway in this city says that fourteen men have been taken out of the mine and that four of this number are dead.

It is now practically settled that fifty miners were at work in the mine when the explosion occurred and that there yet remain thirty-six in the death pit. The rescue work is very slow. The damage to the mine is reported to be great.

The cause of the explosion has not yet been determined, and as the rescuers have not yet reached the seat of the trouble, Lick Branch is a coal town on the Pocahontas Division of the Norfolk & Western Railway.

STORY SUITS ARE SETTLED.

Widow of the Suicide Agrees to Accept $200,000 as Her Share.

Special to The New York Times.

WHITE PLAINS, N. Y., Dec. 29.—According to an agreement signed by William B. Coster, executor of the will of Marion Story, who committed suicide at his home, Brook Farm, near Port Chester, against Elizabeth S. Grey, in connection with the will, has been settled by agreement with Mrs. Story.

Mr. Story left a large mansion at Rye, surrounded by hundreds of acres, all valued at $250,000. The widow agrees that all litigation is stopped and the probate of the will continued, she will accept $200,000 as her share of the estate. Justice Keogh has signed an order, accordingly, allowing the withdrawal of the suits.

WITHDRAWS ITS AMBULANCES

Roosevelt Hospital's Reply to Criticism of Transferring Patients.

At a meeting of the Board of Governors of Roosevelt Hospital, held yesterday, it was decided to discontinue the ambulance service of the hospital after March 1, 1909. It is believed this action of the board was caused by the criticism of the hospital authorities in connection with the transferring of patients to Bellevue Hospital.

The territory covered by Roosevelt Hospital is a large and important one on the west side of the city. The action taken by the Board of Governors follows swiftly on the recommendation of a Coroner's jury two weeks ago that the facts attending the death of a young woman who died in a Roosevelt Hospital ambulance while she was being transferred to Bellevue, be brought to the attention of the District Attorney, and, if necessary, the Grand Jury.

The young woman, May Davis, died in the ambulance on the way to Bellevue. She had been a patient in Roosevelt Hospital, and her condition was at all times critical. The ambulance surgeon, Dr. Ward, who was in charge of the ambulance at the patient, testified at the inquest that the woman was "only a charity patient." Following this verdict the Coroner's jury brought in a verdict censuring the hospital authorities.

Post Office Safe Dynamited.

HEWLETT, L. I., Dec. 29.—An attempt was made early to-day to rob the Post Office at this place. The burglars effected an entrance to the building by cutting out a panel in the rear door. Inside, the burglars bored a hole just above the combination, and after filling it with dynamite touched off a fuse, with a match, and blew the safe open. The explosion made by the charge was loud, and it frightened the burglars so that they fled without waiting to take any of the contents of the wrecked safe. In the safe was more than $2,000 in money, and $200 worth of stamps.

C. F. KING GUILTY.

Boston Jury Convicts Promoter on 27 Counts in $25,000 Larceny Case.

BOSTON, Dec. 29.—Guilty on twenty-seven counts was the verdict returned by a jury in the Suffolk County Superior Court at midnight against Cardenio F. King, formerly well-known as a financial agent and promoter in this city and New York.

King has been on trial for two weeks for the alleged larceny of $25,000 from patrons.

YAQUIS MAKE PEACE.

Indians Sign Treaty with Mexican Authorities—Hold a Love Feast.

NOGALES, Arizona, Dec. 29.—The long war with Yaqui Indians in Mexico, in which scores have been killed at different times, including many Americans, has been terminated in a treaty of peace agreed upon by three Indian chiefs and 168 of their followers and the Governor of the State of Sonora, Mexico.

The scene enacted at the treaty agreement was a remarkable one, concluding with the Mexican soldiers embracing the Yaquis and participating in a joint celebration lasting all night.

DEPUTY SHERIFF DROWNED.

W. C. Forest of the Watershed Police Loses His Life While Skating.

WHITE PLAINS, N. Y., Dec. 29.—Deputy Sheriff William C. Forest of Tuckahoe, who was attached to the New York watershed police, was drowned this afternoon while skating on the Cornell reservoir near Purdy's Station, Westchester County.

The Deputy Sheriff was alone on the lake. James Brearton and Howard Holbrook, who were skating home from school, heard his cries and tried to save him, but they were too late. The body, which was under the ice, was recovered. Forest was advised not to go on the reservoir, as the ice was too thin. He leaves a wife and family at Tuckahoe.

TAUGHT IN CHURCH 71 YEARS.

Some of Mrs. Van Tassel's First Pupils Now Grandmothers—Purse Given Her.

Mrs. J. W. Van Tassel, who has lived all her ninety years in Tompkinsville, S. I., where she was born, and who for seventy-one years has taught the infant class in the Sunday school of the Brighton Heights Reformed Church, Tompkinsville, and is still teaching it, received a purse of $125 last night at a Christmas celebration in the church.

Ex-Superintendent A. L. Schwab of the Sunday school in his speech noted that Mrs. Van Tassel had taught Tompkinsville infants in her class who were now grandmothers in the neighborhood. Mr. Schwab presented the purse to Mrs. Van Tassel, who rose and bowed her thanks. The Rev. J. C. Lenington, pastor of the church, also spoke.

MAY VOTE ON SUNDAY LIQUOR

Atlantic City Will Settle the Question at the Polls if Bill Passes.

Special to The New York Times.

TRENTON, Dec. 29.—Assemblyman Martin E. Kelfer of Atlantic County was at the State House to-day, and in discussing the Atlantic City excise question said that either he or Senator Wilson would introduce a bill in the coming Legislature permitting Atlantic City to vote on the question of the hotels selling liquor on Sundays.

He said that he knew that the people of Atlantic City, especially those who catered to the important transient public, favored this, and he held that almost everybody there was in favor of giving the widest liberty to the resort compatible with peace and order.

DEAD IN QUAKE MAY BE 100,000

Reports Slowly Reaching Rome Show Disaster to be Greater Than Was Thought.

WHOLE TOWNS WIPED OUT

Entire Population of Reggio, Numbering 45,000, Believed to Have Perished.

MESSINA'S TERRIBLE LOSS

Dead May Reach 50,000—American Consul Cheney and Wife Probably Dead.

RUIN BY THE TIDAL WAVE

Vandals Plundering in the Ruins of the Wrecked Cities—Troops Sent for Police Duty.

REFUGEES TELL OF HORRORS

British Vice Consul at Messina Loses His Wife—King and Queen Start for Scene to Give Aid.

ROME, Dec. 29.—One hundred thousand dead; Messina, in Sicily, and Reggio and a score of other towns in Southern Italy overwhelmed, and the entire Calabrian region laid waste—this is the earthquake's record so far as it is at present known from the reports that are coming into Rome slowly, on account of the almost complete destruction of lines of communication to the stricken places.

The death list in Messina ranges from 12,000 to 50,000; that of Reggio, which with its adjacent villages, numbered 45,000 people, includes almost the entire population. At Palmi, 1,000 are reported dead, at Cassano 1,000, at Cosenza 500, and half of the population of Bagnara, about 4,000.

The Monteleone region has been devastated, and Riposto, Seminara, San Giovanni, Scilla, Lazzaro, and Cannitello, and all other communes and villages bordering on the Straits are in ruins.

The first official news concerning Reggio reached the home office this evening from Grace Marina, from which point an army officer who escaped from that place telegraphed that the town had been entirely destroyed, and that the dead were numberless. Five distinct earthquake shocks, all terrible in their effects, had been felt.

Several hundred soldiers were killed at Catanzaro, and many policemen were killed and wounded. Thousands of charred bodies have been seen floating in the straits. At Palmi 300 corpses have been discovered, and many hundreds more are still beneath the wreckage of the town. Every house in Bagnara was leveled. All the railway stations between Messina and Rometta were destroyed. Every little village has its quota of dead.

Latest reports received here state that 4,000 soldiers in the various barracks at Messina were buried under the ruins.

The Rock of Charybdis now blocks the entrance to the Strait of Messina. The tidal wave wrecked the lighthouses in the strait, including Faro Beacon, and they crashed into the sea.

English and Germans Buried.

The Minister of Marine received a wireless dispatch this afternoon estimating the dead at Messina at 50,000. It added that the bodies of seventy English travelers and thirty Germans are buried beneath the ruins of the Hotels Trinacria, Victoria, and Bellevue at Messina.

The King and Queen of Italy are now on their way to Messina, having sailed to-night from Naples aboard the battleship Vittorio Emmanuele.

The Pope has shown the greatest distress at the calamity, and he himself was the first to contribute, giving a sum amounting to $200,000 to the relief of the afflicted.

It is feared that many foreigners have been killed, as a number of the hotels at Messina, and doubtless at other places, were crowded with tourists.

Little is known of the fate of the diplomatic representatives of the foreign powers stationed at these posts, although the Italian Government is using every effort to relieve the anxiety felt on their account.

Italy Stunned with Grief.

Stunned at the magnitude of the calamity which has overtaken their fellow-countrymen, all Italy mourns to-night for the stricken Province of Calabria and the Island of Sicily. Accustomed for centuries to earthquakes, Italy stands in dread, but none was prepared for the disaster which in the fraction of a minute yesterday devastated these cities and caused the death of thousands.

The streets in Rome are jammed with...

people who snatch the special editions from the newsboys. The people are plunged in grief, and lamentations are heard on all sides. Here and there one asks another. "When will end this awful repetition of devastation and death in our country?"

Relief funds have already been started, and a hundred ships and trains are on their way carrying supplies and reinforcements to the south. Rome, Milan, Florence, Naples, and other cities are sending physicians, police, and firemen. To-day all the Ambassadors and Ministers expressed sympathy with M. Tittoni, Minister of Foreign Affairs, whose emotion was profound. The Bourses and theatres have been closed throughout Italy, and dispatches of sympathy continue to pour in from all quarters of the globe.

The hands of all the nations have been extended to Italy in her affliction. From rulers have come messages of condolence and from the peoples spontaneous promise of that aid which brings the world closer together in times of great calamity.

Foreign Sailors Aid Rescue Work.

Already British and Russian squadrons have arrived at Messina. French warships are on the way. Sailors and marines have been disembarked, and they have performed courageous acts in rescuing the injured and wounded. A large number of survivors have been transferred to the warships, which are transformed into great floating hospitals.

It is imperative that the dead be removed from the ruins, in order to avoid a pestilence. Steamers with doctors, druggists, firemen, and workmen have arrived at Messina from Catania and other places.

Urgent messages have been sent from Rome to Messina, but these remain unanswered, and fears are entertained that Fort Spuria, near Messina, has been destroyed, as the wireless station installed there, one of the most powerful in Italy, is evidently not working.

The catastrophe has excited the superstitions of the entire populace, who are running about the country calling upon all the saints and imploring the mercy of Heaven. Their superstition has been increased by the rumor that in the general destruction of Messina the statue of St. Rose remained uninjured.

Harrowing Scenes at Messina.

The work of rescue at Messina, according to the meagre details received here to-night, presented harrowing scenes. Hundreds of people were pinned under walls and rafters, alive but terribly injured, for thirty hours. One of the rescuers found under the ruins of a house five children alive, but unable to speak, clinging around the corpse of their mother.

In some cases heroic rescuers met death in the falling débris. In one house twenty persons were suspended on the fifth floor and unable to reach the street. The floors had been torn away. They were rescued with a rope by a sailor.

Vandalism of the worst kind has broken out, and the Government has adopted the most energetic and severe measures for its repression. Robbers and looters are shot on sight. Six criminals were killed while attempting to loot the Bank of Sicily, where cash amounting to half a million dollars lay in plain view.

The prison at Messina collapsed. Some of the prisoners were killed, but the survivors made their escape and joined the hooligans who were sacking the city. Such confusion reigned that the robbers met with no resistance. The local Chief of Police lies dead in the rooms of his office.

The barracks at Messina were demolished. The commander of the troops was killed outright, and there are many victims among the enlisted men.

Vandals Rob Buildings and Bodies.

The robbers pillaged the ruins of shattered buildings, and even stole clothing and valuables from the corpses of the victims. They were not deterred by the flames that broke out in several sections of the city, but took advantage of the light for their vandalism. The night in Messina was one of horror indescribable—fire, robbery, dead and dying on every side, the city in the utmost confusion, and the people panic-stricken and under a spell of terror.

The Government is sending troops with the utmost dispatch by land and by sea to the scene of the disaster. Four thousand men from the garrison at Rome already are on their way. Various steamship companies have placed vessels at the disposition of the Government, and the existing system of wireless communication is being increased. Wireless messages will be transmitted by warships from the Straits.

Troops began to pour into Messina last night, and this morning a number of steamers arrived from the Peninsula with soldiers on board. Patrols were at once organized, and efforts made to bring some order into the situation. Bands of citizens were formed and helped heroically in the work of rescue. Many courageous acts were performed by soldiers and citizens alike, and in some cases the rescuers themselves lost their lives in trying to help others.

Toward morning several of the worst fires had been extinguished, the looting was under partial control, and comparative order had been established. Everything possible is being done to succor the wounded, but the relief measures are still utterly inadequate, owing to the immensity of the disaster.

Wireless telegraphy has been of the greatest assistance in getting in reports from the devastated regions, and in helping the authorities to realize the extent of the disaster, and to send help to the places where it was most urgently needed.

A flying squadron of the Italian Navy, composed of the three best battleships, had left for a cruise on the Atlantic before the first news of the disaster came to hand. Through the medium of wireless telegraphy it was possible to reach these vessels and order them to proceed at full speed for Messina.

Strait Altered Beyond Recognition.

The Strait of Messina was shaken and twisted by the earth's tremblings, for mariners report the channel altered beyond recognition. The ports and villages on both the Continental and Sicilian sides were wrecked or inundated, and all lighthouses along the coasts were swallowed up. Navigation now is dangerous and in some places impossible.

Starving, bleeding from injuries, and almost insane from their terrifying experiences, Messina's survivors are fleeing in all directions. The spectacle presented by the ruined seaboard is described as terrifying. Tumbling buildings killed and mutilated, while hundreds of the injured, imprisoned in the wreckage, were abandoned to their fate by the fleeing populace. One of those who escaped said:

"The earth seemed suddenly to drop and then to turn violently on its axis. The whole population, precipitated from the houses rent in twain, were spun around like tops as they ran through the streets. Many fell crushed to death, and others, bewildered, took refuge for breath beside the tottering walls, where they soon met the fate of their companions."

How the Tidal Wave Came.

At the time of the earthquake the torpedo boat Sappho was lying in the harbor at Messina, and one of the officers has told of the occurrences as follows:

"At 5:30 o'clock in the morning the sea suddenly became terribly agitated, seeming literally to pick up our boat and shake it. Other craft near by were similarly treated, and the ships looked like bits of cork bobbing about in a tempest. Almost immediately a tidal wave of huge proportions swept across the strait, carrying everything before it. Scores of ships were damaged, and the Hungarian mailboat Andrassy parted her anchors, and went crashing into other vessels. Messina Bay was wiped out, and the sea was soon covered with wreckage, which was carried off by the receding waters."

Further stories told by the officers of the Sappho show the tremendous force of the great wave that swept completely over the city, from which a dense cloud of dust arose as the buildings fell, while the air was rent by cries for help.

Only at sunrise was it possible to get even a faint idea of what had happened. Almost the entire city was reduced to ruins in the twinkling of an eye, and in the midst of these still stand the gigantic and sinister walls of the great Hotel Trinacria, where a hundred foreign guests met their death; the municipal palace, and a line of what were once splendid edifices along the sea front.

From a dozen sections tongues of flame were seen shooting out of the ruins, and shortly half the town was enveloped in flames, the smoke from which was carried in great masses far over the bay.

MOUNT ETNA, SEEN FROM ST. NICOLAI.

Sailors from the Sappho, under the command of the head engineer, succeeded, after a mighty struggle against the waves, in reaching the land, and they were among the first to penetrate into the town and begin the work of rescue. At every step they came upon the dead and dying, and they joined the others in trying to save those caught in the ruins.

The escaped prisoners from the jails were soon at work sacking the empty houses, paying particular attention to the Bank of Sicily, the military college, and other public buildings.

Officers and men from Italian and British steamers went ashore as soon as possible. The Britishers saved a family of five who were imprisoned in a burning house. Many prisoners from the jails made their escape and looted right and left. Hundreds engaged in the work of robbing the banks and business houses. In the opinion of the officers of the Sappho, half the population of Messina perished.

It is reported that the Prefect of Reggio was killed. The Prefect is the head of the province, the post corresponding to that of Governor of a State in America.

Refugees from Reggio who reached Catanzaro this afternoon said that they could see huge columns of smoke arising from the ruins of Messina. They affirmed that Reggio, Cannitello, and Lazzaro were destroyed. A tidal wave demolished the railroad between Lazzaro and Reggio, and a small army of men are working desperately to re-establish communication with the latter place, for which a train with troops and telegraphers has started.

STORIES OF SURVIVORS.

Refugees from Messina Describe the Terrifying Spectacle of Ruin.

CATANIA, Dec. 29.—Tales of terror and suffering are told by the Messina refugees who have reached here. The majority of these are being treated in the hospitals, while the others have secured shelter in private homes. A woman who escaped unhurt told of her experiences.

"We were all sleeping in my house," she said, "when we were awakened by an awful trembling, which threw us out of our beds. I cried out that it was an earthquake, and called to the others to save themselves, while I quickly pushed a few clothes into a valise. The shocks continued, seeming to grow stronger. The walls cracked and my bureau split in two and then crashed to the floor, nearly crushing me. My hands trembled so that I could scarcely open the doors.

"To increase the terror a rainstorm, accompanied by hail, swept through the broken windows. Finally, with my brother and sister, I succeeded in gaining the street, but soon lost them in the mad race of terror-stricken people who surged onward, uttering cries of pain and distress. During this terrible flight chimneys and tiles showered down upon us continuously. Death ambushed us at every step.

"Instinctively I rushed toward the water front, but there found the grand promenade transformed into a muddy, miry lake, in which I slipped and often fell. I learned afterward that I was rescued senseless by a soldier and carried to a train."

Refugees Stupefied with Terror.

Refugees are pouring into Catania by trains, steamers, and automobiles. They are half naked and stupified with terror. Some of them appear almost insane from the horrors through which they have gone. In the beginning they could only babble "Messina has been devastated; the city has been annihilated." Little by little some idea of the indescribable horror at Messina was obtained from these unfortunates.

They declare that thousands of demented survivors are still wandering about among the ruins of the city. A wounded soldier said:

"The spectacle was terrifying beyond words. Dante's 'Inferno' gives but a faint idea of what happened yesterday morning at Messina. The first shock came before the sun had risen. It shook the city to its very foundations. Immediately the houses began to crumble. Those of us who were not killed at once made our way over undulating floors to the street. Beams were crashing down through the rooms. The stairs were equally unsafe.

"I found the streets blocked by fallen houses. Balconies, chimneys, bell towers, entire walls had been thrown down. From every side arose the screams and moans of the wounded. The people were half mad with excitement and fear. Most of them had rushed out in their night clothes. In a little while we were all shivering under a torrential downpour of rain. Everywhere there were dead bodies, nude, disfigured, and mutilated. In the ruins I could see arms and legs moving helplessly. From every quarter came piteous appeals for aid.

Swept Away by Tidal Wave.

"The portion of the town near the water was inundated by the tidal wave. The water reached to the shoulders of the fugitives and swept them away.

"The City Hall, the cathedral, and the barracks crumbled, and churches, other public buildings, and dwellings without number were literally razed to the ground. There were 200 customs agents at the barracks; only forty-one of them were saved. At the railroad station only eight out of 280 employes have been accounted for.

"Many of those who succeeded in escaping with their lives are incapable of relating their experiences coherently. I questioned all who were in a condition to talk. Most of them told the same story. They said the first thing they knew they were thrown out of bed, and amid crashing ceilings and falling furniture managed to make their way to the street. Then, in the blackness of night and amid pouring rain that added to their horror and distress, they rushed blindly away amid the crash of tumbling buildings and the shrieks and groans of those buried in the ruins. Many were struck down while trying to escape by falling balconies and masonry, and still many others lost their reason and to-day are wandering aimlessly in the open fields outside the city or up and down the ruined streets they knew so well. The looters and robbers were shot dead by the rifles of the soldiers."

"All the News That's Fit to Print."

The New York Times.

VOL. LIX...NO. 18,922.   • • •   NEW YORK, SUNDAY, NOVEMBER 14, 1909.—66 PAGES, In Seven Parts, Including Picture Section.   PRICE FIVE CENTS.

THE WEATHER.

Fair to-day; increasingly cloudy Monday; moderate east winds.

COLD TOWARD SUGAR FRAUDS

Investigator's Own Story of the Persistent Attempts to Block His Work.

ORDERED TO DISTANT CITIES

Replaced by Another, His Diary Stolen, Home Shadowed, and Efforts Made to Bribe Him.

BUT ROOSEVELT BACKED HIM

On the Strength of That He Disobeyed Treasury Orders—Stimson Once Had Him Put Back at Work.

The charge that the Treasury Department at Washington, under the Administration of President Roosevelt, displayed apparent indifference to the efforts to procure evidence of Sugar Trust frauds in this city was made yesterday by Richard Parr, Chief of the weighers' division of the Custom House. For three years Parr has devoted his time to getting evidence that the Sugar Trust has been cheating the Government in the weighing of sugar at its Williamsburg pier, in this way evading the payment of full duty on many importations.

In making his charge of lack of interest in the work of the Custom House officials to uncover the frauds, Mr. Parr made it clear, however, that in all his efforts he had the full support of President Roosevelt. The President personally expressed to him at one time, he said, his desire that he should not waver in his activities, and that all the evidence he obtained should be used in an effort to punish those in the trust employee who were guilty of the frauds perpetrated on the Government.

President Roosevelt even went so far, says Parr, as to express the hope that if Parr's investigation showed that any of the men "higher up" in the Sugar Trust were guilty of having connived at the frauds he would not hesitate to lay the evidence concerning it before the United States District Attorney.

The Investigator's Troubles.

In pursuing his investigation as a Special Agent of the Treasury Department, Parr declared, he encountered obstacles from the outset. He was shadowed by detectives and offered bribes to leave the country. Once, when he was about to testify before United States Commissioner Shields in connection with discoveries he made at the Williamsburg pier of the tampering with scales on which the sugar was weighed, the Treasury Department ordered him out of town. He was cheating him of an indication that there was a desire to get him away before he could give the evidence he had been so long in getting.

The particular Treasury official whom Parr described as seemingly disposed to discourage his sugar fraud energies by ordering him to distant cities at inconvenient times was James Burton Reynolds, who at that time was an Assistant Secretary of the Treasury, and is now a member of the Tariff Board. George B. Cortelyou was then Secretary of the Treasury.

Parr did go away, but not before he had appeared before the United States Commissioner and made his revelations. As that appearance before the Commissioner Parr told of the theft from his desk at the Custom House of a diary in which he had jotted down various bits of evidence against the Sugar Trust that he had some across. This was taken at night, the desk having been broken open. Parr suspected a former Secret Service man who had been transferred to special work in the Custom House.

Leeb Procured Suspect's Discharge.

On communicating his suspicions against this former Secret Service man to William Loeb, then Secretary to President Roosevelt, so Parr said, an order was quickly sent to the Treasury Department to have the suspect discharged. As soon as the man had lost his place he was employed by the Sugar Trust.

An echo of the theft of the diary from Parr's desk came last week, when it was learned yesterday that the former Secret Service man was summoned before the Federal Grand Jury here. It was learned at the Federal Building that he had been asked questions with reference to the sugar frauds, and it was surmised that he had been offered immunity from prosecution on the theft charge if he would aid in the prosecutions now under way.

For three days the Sugar Trust employee went before the Grand Jury. District Attorney Wise, when asked if it was the purpose of his office to use him in the effort to connect the men "higher up," he would not commit himself. Mr. Wise was not inclined to discuss the man's value to the prosecution from any point of view.

There was a keen impression in the Federal Building that Mr. Wise had no intention, in bringing the former Secret Service man into the investigation at this time, of pushing the charge of theft against him, for the actual evidence of his perpetration of that crime is declared to be only vague. This forced the conclusion that it has shown an inclination to give information to the District Attorney, or at least that an attempt is under way to compel him to reveal what he knows.

Evidence Leading Higher Ready.

In connection with the effort to fasten guilt upon the higher officials of the Sugar Trust, it became known yesterday from an authentic source, that the Dis-

Continued on Page 3.

TRAIN TO FLORIDA, AUGUSTA. "PALMETTO LIMITED," 3:23 P.M. W 23d St., Penna. Ferry. Also 3:25 P.M. 9:25 P.M. Best service to Florida and South. Atlantic Coast Line.—Adv.

MRS. HENRY S. KIP SUES.

Wall Street Broker's Wife Asks Divorce in Reno, Charging Desertion.

Special to The New York Times.

RENO, Nev., Nov. 13.—Mrs. Fannie Kip, who has been in this city since last January, filed suit for divorce to-day against Henry Kip, a stock broker at 7 Wall Street, New York. Mrs. Kip alleges in the complaint that they were married in New York on Oct. 23, 1902, and that they lived together until Nov. 12, 1908, when her husband deserted her at the Osborne Apartment, at Fifty-seventh Street and Seventh Avenue, New York. She says there is one child, William Bergh Kip, 4 years old, who is with his father. She does not ask for the custody of the child, although she said when she first came here that she intended to win it.

In her complaint Mrs. Kip alleges non-support and desertion, and says that for several years her husband wilfully refused to contribute to her support, although he was abundantly able to do so. She asks that her maiden name, Frances Coster Jones, be restored to her. She says that there is no community property.

Shortly after her arrival in Reno Mrs. Kip went to San Francisco. While there she said she went to Reno for her health, and that she intended to study music to take up the career of an opera singer.

The Kips have been prominent in society circles of New York and Newport for many years. Entertainments which they gave at their home in West Fifty-seventh Street in this city attracted a great deal of attention. Mrs. Kip has a soprano voice, and she often told her friends that nothing would please her more than to be an opera singer. With this in view she went abroad in 1907, where she took up study under the direction of Jean de Reszke.

Mrs. Kip returned to this country in December, 1908. She said that Mr. Kip had decided that she could pursue her musical studies in the city as well as abroad. About two weeks after the couple separated Mrs. Kip took apartments at the Hotel Savoy, while her husband went to live at the University Club.

Mrs. Kip is the daughter of Mr. and Mrs. Alfred Renshaw Jones. Mr. Kip is a son of the late Major William Bergh Kip of Rhinebeck. He is a graduate of Yale, class of '96.

In 1904 Mr. and Mrs. Kip gave a baby party which attracted a great deal of attention. All the guests were clad in bibs and aprons. Mrs. Kip wore a white muslin frock, such as children wear, and her husband appeared on the scene in a Buster Brown outfit.

Mr. Kip is associated with the brokerage firm of Herrick, Hicks & Colby.

BRANDENBURG CONVICTED.

Fined $500 in St. Louis for Kidnapping His Stepson.

Special to The New York Times.

ST. LOUIS, Mo., Nov. 13.—Broughton Brandenburg was found guilty to-day of enticing James Shepard Cabanne, Jr., his stepson, from the home of the boy's grandmother, to San Francisco, and the minimum punishment of $500 was assessed. Brandenburg declared he would ask for a new trial.

Mrs. Brandenburg says that at the next trial there will be developments. "We have lots to tell," she said, "and we will tell it all."

"We will appeal at once," Brandenburg's written statement says, "and fight this case through to the limit. If the whole evidence that really pertains had been presented so intelligent a jury would have drawn a different conclusion.

"Under the charge to the jury and the butchered testimony there was little else that they could do, and their true attitude is shown by the small amount of the very least fine that the law allows."

A bondsman was at hand to release Brandenburg on a $500 bond, pending the result of the motion for a new trial and appeal.

It was revealed in the courtroom that Mrs. Brandenburg, who has avoided Mr. Cabanne, her former husband, all during the trial, went to the Cabanne home on Monday to see her son.

WON THE GIRL SLEUTH'S HAND

Dentist She Was Shadowing Found a Way to Clear His Title.

Belle Conro of 802 East 160th Street, the woman detective employed by the New York State Dental Society to apprehend dentists who practice the profession illegally, was married yesterday to Dr. Joseph J. Gulishan, a dentist she tried to catch.

Some time ago Miss Conro dropped into Dr. Gulishan's office in the Bronx, and asked him to examine her teeth. Her teeth, by the way, are in excellent condition, and always have been, but she had them examined a score of times every week, for that is the way she goes about her detective work. Dr. Gulishan made an examination and declared the well-shaped ivories faultless.

Miss Conro was satisfied during her stay in the dentist's office that there was nothing wrong with his certificate. Their acquaintance was renewed a short time later, and it developed from friendship to love, although he looked in perfect condition. He and Yancey did most of the time plunging during the game, and as the accident happened five minutes before the close of the final period I am inclined to think that it was somewhat tired, which caused him to stumble.

They were married at St. Anselm's Roman Catholic Church, 153th Street and Clinton Avenue, by the pastor of the church, the Rev. Father Bernard. Mr. Carrie McCauley, probation officer in the Harlem Court, was the bridesmaid, and Dr. William J. Hogan of Carrington, Conn., a classmate at Yale with Dr. Gulishan, the best man. Several City Magistrates and attaches of the Harlem Court were specially invited guests.

DRY SUNDAY FOR WILMINGTON

Liquor Selling by Clubs to be Stopped and Stores Closed.

Special to The New York Times.

WILMINGTON, Del., Nov. 13.—As an outcome of complaints made by confectionery dealers against Greek candy merchants a Sunday-closing crusade will be undertaken to-morrow by the Law and Order Society. The movement will be general, and will include everything, almost, except restaurants and drug stores. Detectives have been employed to get evidence, and a large number of prosecutions may result.

The plan is the most sweeping of the kind ever inaugurated in Delaware. The running of trolley cars and the sale of newspapers will not be disturbed. Secretary Wescotts of the Law and Order organization declared to-night that private clubs where liquor is sold to members on Sundays will be prosecuted.

The handsome WYOMING APARTMENT HOUSE, 55th St. & 7th Av., has a CASEMENT ROOF. Estb. 1867. 166 5th Av. (21st St.).—Adv.

HURT AT FOOTBALL, PLAYER MAY DIE

Virginia Athlete Injured in Mass Play, Which Has Caused Many Other Accidents.

HAS CONCUSSION OF BRAIN

Quarter Back on Ohio Team Also is Suffering from Similar Hurt—Agitation Against Game Begun.

Special to The New York Times.

WASHINGTON, Nov. 13.—After playing the star game for years, Archie Christian, Jr., of Roanoke, Va., left half back on the University of Virginia eleven, was seriously, it is feared fatally, injured in a game of football here this afternoon with Georgetown University. Christian was carrying the ball for his victorious team, two of his men running with him, when he was thrown to the earth and buried beneath a pile of kicking players. When doctors made an examination he was found to have suffered concussion of the brain. He was operated on, and late to-night it is a question whether he can recover.

Christian did not recover consciousness after the operation. The surgeons removed three blood clots from the brain. Christian's respiration improved, and the surgeons said there was about an even chance for his recovery.

The accident occurred five minutes before the end of the game, which was played out without him, and ended, largely through his efforts, in Virginia's victory by a score of 21 to 0. Christian's mother had been on the field, but in order to catch a train home she had left and was at the Union Station when she was summoned to her son's bedside in the hospital. She arrived before the operation was commenced.

How the Accident Occurred.

Shortly before the end of the game, Virginia made a number of continuous line plunges, and worked the ball into Georgetown's territory. At last the Virginia quarter back called the signal for Christian to carry the ball on a mass play just outside of Georgetown's right tackle. The quarter back and Bowen formed the interference, and Stanton and Capt. Yancey were on either side of Christian, dragging him over Georgetown's line.

Georgetown's secondary defense was playing five yards behind the line, and when Christian had been dragged over the first defense the backfield players made a rush for the Virginia half back. Just as the Georgetown secondary defense reached a point two yards from where the line had failed to hold the onslaught of the Virginians, Christian stumbled and fell to the ground.

Stanton and Yancey stopped to break the combination of Georgetown players, who were making a desperate effort to reach the struggling half back. Just as Christian was getting on his feet three Georgetown players hit him at one time, knocking him to the ground again. When he fell he landed on his back, both feet staying in the air. It seemed as if none of the members of the Virginia or Georgetown teams realized that Christian was on the ground, and twenty players piled on the youth. The referee's whistle blew, telling the players that the down had been made. They scrambled to their feet, but Christian remained on the ground, his right leg in the air. The Virginia substitutes, "Pop" Lannigan, the trainer, and many spectators, rushed on the field. Lannigan carried Christian to the side line, where he was wrapped in a blanket.

Is Taken to Hospital.

Dr. William B. Carr, who was in the Virginia stands, went to the side lines and worked over the injured half back. It was soon seen that his condition was serious, and he was taken to Georgetown University Hospital.

Christian was unconscious when taken into the institution, and was immediately carried to the operating room. It was then that his mother entered the room. Mr. Christian bore up well under the strain. She was constantly at the side of her boy, and could hardly be prevailed upon to leave him while the delicate operation was being performed.

Quarter Back Gooch, who with Bowen formed the interference in the play which resulted in Christian's injury, said that Christian had made the play many times during the game.

"Early in the first half," said Gooch, "I broke through Georgetown's right tackle without any of the interference and carried the ball ten yards. He must have been very weak, although he looked in perfect condition. He and Yancey did most of the time plunging during the game, and as the accident happened five minutes before the close of the final period I am inclined to think that it was somewhat tired, which caused him to stumble."

The accident, it is expected, will result in a cancellation of all the games that remain to be played on the schedules of both universities. In addition, a movement is afoot to-night among the parents of students in the High Schools of the District of Columbia to have football proscribed in the schools, if not barred entirely from the capital.

The death of Cadet Byrne of West Point and the nearly fatal injuries of Midshipman Wilson in the game at the Naval Academy are put forward as reasons why the game should be abolished at least as now played.

CLEVELAND, Nov. 13.—Raymond Austin, quarter back of the Ohio Wesleyan University football team, is in a hospital here to-night suffering from concussion of the brain as the result of injuries received in the game between his team and Case School of Science of Cleveland to-day. After being hurt Austin remained on the side lines until the close of the game, but later was taken to the hospital. Early this evening he was reported to be improving rapidly.

GRAND RAPIDS, Ohio, Nov. 13.—Roy Vogel, a schoolboy injured two weeks ago in a football game, died last night. A blood vessel in his head was ruptured and he was unconscious for thirteen days.

MAILLARD'S VANILLA CHOCOLATE. Choicest of all confections made, and as a drink is unequalled for dainty luncheons, &c.

TO-DAY'S ISSUE OF The New York Times CONSISTS OF SEVEN PARTS

I. Pictorial Section.
II. News Section.
III. Cable News Section.
IV. Sporting News Section.
V. Magazine Section.
VI. Fashion Section.
VII. Real Estate Section.

GAGE, AT 73, WILL TAKE A THIRD WIFE

Ex-Secretary of the Treasury to Wed a San Diego Widow on Thanksgiving Day.

A CONVERT TO THEOSOPHY

They Will Live in a Cottage Which Gage Has Had Erected at Mrs. Tingley's Colony.

Special to The New York Times.

SAN DIEGO, Cal., Nov. 13.—The mystery of the $25,000 home that Lyman J. Gage, ex-Secretary of the Treasury, is building at Point Loma, the home of Mrs. Katherine Tingley's Theosophical Society, was solved to-day when it became known that he was to be married on Thanksgiving Day to Mrs. F. Ada Ballou.

Mr. Gage has had men at work for some months on his cottage, and gossips have guessed that he would take a bride, because it is most unusual for members of Mme. Tingley's colony to build elaborate residences in the Theosophical preserve for their own use. The suspicion of the gossips was confirmed to-day when Mrs. Ballou admitted that she was to become Mrs. Gage on Thanksgiving.

Mrs. Ballou was interviewed to-day at her apartments at Coronado, where she has taught music.

"Is it true that you and Mr. Gage are to be married?" she was asked.

"Yes, we are to be married on Thanksgiving Day," she replied. "But I do not think that Mr. Gage wanted it to be known before the ceremony. Have you seen our home at Point Loma? Isn't it splendid? We shall take no honeymoon trip, but shall just settle down at our new home as soon as we are married. Mr. Gage has made a life unhesitatingly in a futile effort to save his comrades. Standing at the bottom of the shaft he carried the bodies of five men into the cage, the only way of escape. As the last was carried in he fell across the body.

He was dead, as were all his companions, when the cage was lifted to the top.

No Hope, Survivors Say.

A few survivors were surrounded by groups of the women, and the answers of these men to inquiries only added to the terror of the women. Almost to a man the survivors declared that there was no hope for those still in the mine. Almost 200 of the men imprisoned, they declared, were in the third vein, the only entrance to which was from the second vein, almost 500 feet from the main shaft of the pit.

When the extent of the fire was realized the officials saw that ordinary measures were ineffectual. The fire had burned away the timbers of the shaft and the flames also reached the escape shaft. A few minutes later the fan which supplied air to the shaft collapsed and tumbled through the opening. The flames then swept on to the mouth of the pit, where they were carried to the surface, forcing back all those who remained near. The officials knew that the fire must be eating its way back in to the shaft, and then the measure of sealing the mouth of the pit was adopted.

Before this water had been poured down the escape shaft, but with no better effect than to flood the floor and render hopeless any effort of those inside to escape.

That those of the men who were able had retreated to the furthermost ends of the veins was the statement of the miners on the surface. There they might huddle together, gasping what little oxygen remained in the sealed and burning mine in the hope that the rescuers might reach them before it was exhausted. The most hopeful of those seeking to aid the prisoners could that more than a few were alive, and that even these at a few score will be found alive when that aid comes.

Carelessness Cause of Fire.

The only men to escape were those near the main shaft when the fire started. They declared that a careless miner had thrown a torch on a bundle of hay used to feed the mules stationed in the mine. No attention was given the smouldering hay for a few minutes. Then two miners threw the burning mass on a cart and started toward the main shaft, about 150 feet away.

Before it was reached an explosion occurred, and in a few moments the entrance to the vein from the shaft was filled with smoke and flames.

Those nearest the cages hurried to them.

Continued on Page 2.

DEWEY'S WINE HOUSE & RESTAURANT. Only half block east of Fulton St. Sub-Station. H. T. Dewey & Sons Co., 136 Fulton St., New York.—Adv.

---

400 CAUGHT IN MINE; ALL BELIEVED DEAD

Imprisoned by Fire, Following Explosion, There is Little Hope for Escape of Any.

12 BODIES ARE RECOVERED

Six Men Descend in Burning Shaft at Cherry, Ill., and Lose Lives in Vain Attempt at Rescue.

CHERRY, Ill., Nov. 13.—About 400 men were entombed in the mine of the St. Paul Coal Company here to-day by an explosion, which was followed by fire. Mine officials believe that all of the 400 men are dead.

Twelve bodies have been taken out. Six of these were bodies of heroes not employed in the mine, who gave their lives in a futile effort to save the entombed workers.

Mine Superintendent James Steele declared, five hours after the explosion, that it was almost impossible that any of the miners still imprisoned could escape death.

The mine had a day shift of 484 men. Of these, fifty left the mine at noon. Twenty-five or more escaped after the fire started. The others are believed to be dead.

The entrance to the mine has been sealed up in the hope of checking the flames. The building above the pit entrance has fallen, and is burning in the little town of Cherry. Despite the frantic efforts of the officials and the scores of volunteer assistants in the little town of Cherry, it seemed assured at 9 o'clock that only bodies of the dead would be taken from the mine.

Resume Rescue Work To-day.

Until to-morrow morning, when the covering will be removed and rescuers endeavor to penetrate the smoke and gas choked shaft and veins, the fate of the inmates cannot be learned definitely.

The fire causing the explosion, which may prove one of the greatest tragedies in the list of mine horrors, had an origin almost trivial. A pile of hay, allowed to smolder too long, finally ignited the timbers of the mine, and before the workers realised their danger the mine was filled with smoke, gases, and flames, and all exit was impossible.

Kerosene such as is rarely exhibited was shown by officials of the company as one of the causes of the fire. These men, who were outside the mine when the fire originated, contributed six to the list of twelve known dead.

Alexander Nerberg, a pit man, gave his life unhesitatingly in a futile effort to save his comrades. Standing at the bottom of the shaft he carried the bodies of five men into the cage, the only way of escape. As the last was carried in he fell across the body.

He was dead, as were all his companions, when the cage was lifted to the top.

Those who had gone into the pit with him were John Bundy, the mine Superintendent; John Flood, Isaac Lewis, a merchant of Cherry, Dominic Fonenti, and a miner named Rubinski. Dr. W. Howe, a physician of the city, who had sought to go with the men when they descended in the cage, was thrust out by Bundy, who exclaimed: "They will need you at the top if we get any one out. You must not risk your life down here."

The physician vainly sought to resuscitate the men when they were carried to him a few minutes later. He said they had died of suffocation.

At the entrance of the shaft a scene was enacted such as is seen only at a disaster of this kind. Hundreds of screaming women, weeping children, and frantic, helpless men crowded about the place.

THANKSGIVING FORGOTTEN.

Taft, However, Is Likely to Issue the Proclamation on Monday.

WASHINGTON, Nov. 13.—In the hurry of his long trip across the continent, President Taft has forgotten that Thanksgiving Day is at hand. No proclamation of the holiday has been issued, and inquiries lately have been coming in.

There is no law compelling the issuance of a proclamation, but the custom has been invariable for many years. The proclamation comes out through the State Department, and when the question of its non-appearance was raised there to-day it was met by an uneasy grin. It was explained as an oversight, and the intimation was that the proclamation might be forthcoming on Monday.

It was emphatically denied that the President's gastronomic powers had been so tested on the long trip over the country that he had decided against a feast day so soon after his returning.

NOTHING WRONG—ROOSEVELT

Word Received from Him at Mombasa—High Climb by Loring.

MOMBASA, British East Africa, Nov. 13.—News of the American hunting expedition was received here by direct from Col. Theodore Roosevelt. The message states that there is nothing whatever wrong with the party.

NAIROBI, British East Africa, Nov. 13.—Major Mearns and J. Alden Loring, the naturalist, have arrived here with splendid collections of photographs, birds and mammals. Both men are in excellent health.

In his climb of Mount Kenia Loring reached an altitude of 16,500 feet. He will go to Lucania Hill Monday. Major Mearns will remain here to pack the specimens for shipment to America.

PEARY TO BE A CAPTAIN.

Promotion in the Navy to Come Through the Regular Channel.

WASHINGTON, Nov. 13.—Commander Peary, the arctic explorer, will be promoted to the rank of Captain Oct. 30, 1910, according to Assistant Secretary Winthrop of the Navy Department.

On that date Capt. U. H. G. White will be retired on account of age. Peary is the only civil engineer in the navy with the rank of Commander, and his promotion to a Captaincy will come as a natural advancement.

TO EXAMINE COOK'S RECORDS.

Prof. Ellis Stromgren Chosen as Head of Danish Committee.

COPENHAGEN, Nov. 13.—Dr. Torp, rector of the University of Copenhagen, has selected Prof. Ellis Stromgren, Director of the Astronomical Observatory, as head of the committee to examine Dr. Frederick A. Cook's records.

These are expected here about Dec. 7, coming on the Scandinavian-American steamer United States.

NOBEL PRIZE FOR EDISON.

His Name the Only One Mentioned in Chemistry Award.

STOCKHOLM, Nov. 13.—Rumors of the probable Nobel prize winners this year are uncertain.

Up to the present only Thomas A. Edison has been mentioned in connection with the physics and chemistry prize.

LORD ESTATE SETTLED.

Personal Property and Realty Valued at More Than $6,000,000.

Special to The New York Times.

MINEOLA, L. I., Nov. 13.—Surrogate Edgar Jackson placed his signature to-day on the judicial settlement of the Franklin B. Lord estate. Mr. Lord died some time ago, leaving his fortune to his wife and several relatives. She survived him only a short time.

The executors of the estate are Lucius H. Beers, Henry De Forest Baldwin, and Franklin Lord. The personal estate was appraised at $1,111,397, and the real, which cannot be exactly estimated, at more than $5,000,000.

AUTO RUNS OVER A BOY.

Doctors at St. Vincent's Hospital Unable to Revive Him.

Daniel De Grosse, 14 years of age, of 142 Baxter Street, Richmond Borough, was run down and fatally injured last night near his home by an automobile driven by Bert Tarlan of Matawan, N. J. The little fellow was crossing the street. Two of the wheels passed over aim. He was hurried to St. Vincent's Hospital, but the doctors there have been unable to revive him despite all their efforts.

Tarlan was arrested and locked up at the West Brighton Police Station. The car is owned by Peter Devlin of Matawan.

POLICE MATRON ARRESTED.

Store Detective Says She Was Caught in Act of Shoplifting.

Mary Merrill, matron of the East Thirty-fifth Street Police Station, was arrested in a Broadway department store yesterday and taken to the West Thirty-seventh Street Station. When the prisoner was hailed out the police would not say who had given a $1,000 bond for her release.

Tillie Drew, a store detective, says she saw the woman pick up half a dozen women's collars which she concealed in her handbag.

Mrs. Merrill wore the little police matron's badge when arrested. The badge was taken from her. She is a widow, and lives at 213 East Twenty-first Street, 1892. The half dozen collars she is alleged to have stolen were valued at $2.72.

TO REVIVE A RAILROAD.

Jersey Central Branch to Have Daily Instead of Twice-a-Week Trains.

GERMAN VALLEY, N. J., Nov. 13.—A railroad practically dead for ten years will be resurrected. Because of the efforts of the citizens along the line, the Central Railroad of New Jersey will place the Chester Branch, a railroad six miles in length, connecting this town and Chester, on the railroad map again. Heretofore the company ran two scheduled trains weekly over the road to maintain its charter. Preparations are being made by the company to repair the roadbed and bridges, and a daily service will be established.

817—Broadway—817. The office of the Manhattan line for all Southern resorts. Call or telephone 3395 Spring for tickets and reservations.—Adv.

JURY ACQUITS MME. STEINHEIL

Woman Faints as Crowd in Paris Courtroom Cheers the Verdict.

STARTED FOR CONVICTION

Then Jurors Shifted and Decided She Did Not Kill Husband or Stepmother.

WAS BITTERLY ASSAILED

Woman's Career Exposed and French Officials Were Involved—Notable Case Has a Dramatic Ending.

Special Cable to The New York Times.

PARIS, Nov. 14.—Mme. Steinheil, who was on trial for the murder of her husband, Adolphe Steinheil, an artist, and her stepmother, Mme. Japy, was acquitted fifty-five minutes after midnight. Amid wild cheering in the court and tremendous excitement outside, Mme. Steinheil heard the verdict with a smile, and then fainted dead away.

The jury sent for the Judge three times during their deliberations, which lasted three hours. How they stood on the main question was not accurately reported to the assembled journalists at intervals. The majority was for conviction nearly until the end. Then a small majority voted for acquittal.

Cheers Greet Mme. Steinheil.

By the time the final decision was reached everybody in the courtroom fully expected conviction. When Mme. Steinheil was brought in to hear the verdict, she evidently felt certain her cause was lost, but she was arrested by a tumult of cheers which at once conveyed to her the truth. A smile spread over her worn-like features, which in that moment were wondrously beautiful. Then, without an instant's warning, she fell back in a dead faint, to be carried out by the guards.

An immense crowd throughed the neighborhood of the Palace of Justice and gave vent to a noisy excitement, which spread throughout the city as fast as the news of the verdict could travel.

The argument of Mme. Steinheil's defender had not been concluded until 10 o'clock, and there had been an exceedingly painful scene when the Judge read to the jury the questions they must answer. As he began to read the first question, which accused Mme. Steinheil of having murdered her husband, the woman was livid. With emotion and every syllable was heard by the audience in deathlike stillness. When at last he reached the word assassin, Mme. Steinheil's head went down upon the rail in front of her with a loud bang. Two municipal guards sprang forward, lifted her in their arms, and carried her out motionless. She did not return to the court until the verdict had been brought in.

Most Brilliant Audience of Trial.

The last day of the proceedings attracted the most brilliant audience in the whole course of the trial. President de Valles must have winked at violations of the stern rule against the admission of women as spectators, for Mme. Regnas was present and some other actresses as well. Some of the poor creatures who had kept the all-night vigil at the entrance of the court sold their places, which stand-ing room only, for 100 francs each.

When the court convened it was discovered that the foreman of the jury was absent, and this not only caused a long delay, but was regarded as an omen of a miscarriage of justice. The absentee sent a telegram, pleading "physical and moral fitness," and was excused, and not until a dozen had been sent to verify his condition, a supplementary juror, who had been in attendance all the time, being put in his place. The "moral fitness" of the absentee was said to be due to the agonizing doubt which the Advocate General had produced in his mind as to the guilt or innocence of the accused.

Mariette Wolf Makes Scene.

Mariette Wolf made a scene by declaring from her way to the bar and demanding of the court a retraction of the imputation of complicity which was cast upon her and her son Alexandre in Advocate General Trouard-Riolle's address to the jury Friday. The demand was granted.

Maître Aubin then for several hours set himself to rehabilitate Mme. Steinheil. The woman sobbed in her seat most of the time her advocate was speaking, and looked even paler than she did the day before. Some of the gossips, to be sure, declared that this additional pallor was due to a thicker application of face powder.

Maître Aubin dwelt with almost unctuous emphasis upon his client's relations with the late President Felix Faure from 1893 to 1899, pointing out the opportunity they afforded for mercenary profit. Yet, said he, in 1899 there was a grave deficit in the Steinheil exchequer. One of Maître Aubin's arguments was that the accused could

400 CAUGHT IN MINE; ALL BELIEVED DEAD

Continued from Page 1.

and were hoisted to the surface. After about four trips the cages ceased moving, and no more miners came from the shaft. What disaster occurred in the mines following the escape of the men near the shaft is unknown.

After waiting a few minutes at the head of the shaft, Mine Superintendent Bundy leaped into the cage, calling Nerberg and two miners. The miners were afraid, and from the small group of residents who had gathered near the entrance volunteers came who were eager to assist Bundy in the work of rescue.

Flood, Lewis, Fonenti, and Rubinski entered the cage and descended. The next trip of the cage, operated from below, carried up the bodies of six miners. Then a few minutes elapsed, which seemed an hour to those waiting at the top. Then the cage again ascended, this time bearing the unconscious bodies of three of the rescuing party. Again it was lowered, and the bodies of the last three of the six, including Nerberg, were brought up.

Thinks All Died Quickly.

City Attorney Hallorick of Spring Valley, who was at the scene, expressed the belief that not one of the miners would be taken out alive. He is familiar with the construction of the mine and believes that the fire caused the death of all the men before the opening had been sealed.

About the little town of Cherry wild scenes followed. Stores and residences were vacant, and almost the entire population of 5,000 gathered about the mine. From all directions teams and pedestrians hurried into the city from districts which had been notified by telephone.

Every physician in the city and many from nearby towns were caring for hysterical relatives of those imprisoned in the mine. The town officials had hastily improvised hospitals and provided nurses and physicians for those who might be taken from the mine, but the physicians were needless.

Chief. Supt. W. W. Taylor of the mine was not in the city when the accident occurred.

The Cherry mine is seven miles north of Spring Valley on a branch of the Chicago, Milwaukee & St. Paul Railway. The mine is owned by the St. Paul Coal Company. Nearly all the miners employed there were Austrians and Italians. Cherry has a mining population of 3,000.

As soon as the news of the disaster spread abroad great crowds from the neighboring towns collected at the mouth of the mine

State Mine Inspector James Taylor (on the left) and Henry Smith, a volunteer, preparing to enter the mine

Women and children, whose husbands and fathers were imprisoned in the mine, waited in vain at the mouth of the pit for any reassuring news

Lowering into the airshaft mine experts, equipped with oxygen helmets and electric lanterns, in an endeavor to rescue some of the workers

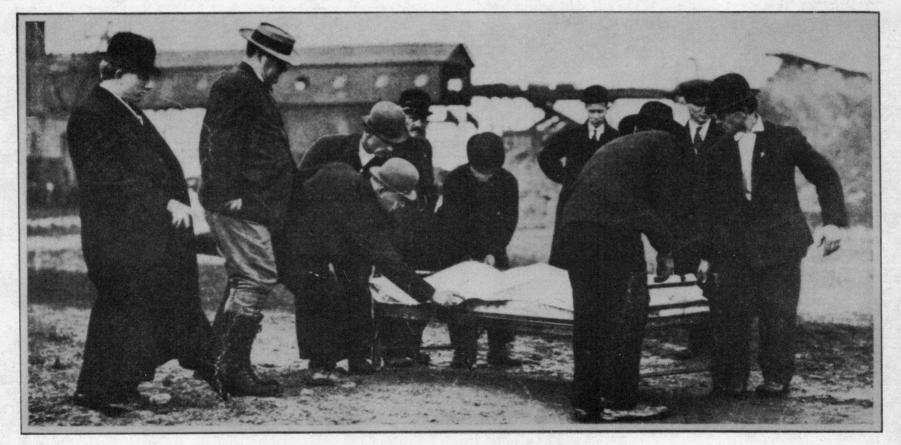

Removing the remains of one of the twelve rescuers, all of whom were literally roasted alive while riding in the cage as it passed through the flames in the shaft

THE MINE DISASTER IN ILLINOIS

"All the News That's Fit to Print."

The New York Times.

THE WEATHER.

Fair, warmer Sunday; rain probably Monday; moderate south winds.

For full weather report see Page 10, Part 3.

VOL. LX...NO. 19,419. * * NEW YORK, SUNDAY, MARCH 26, 1911.—90 PAGES, In Eight Parts, Including Picture Section and Review of Books. PRICE FIVE CENTS.

LIMANTOUR, VICTOR, PROMISES REFORMS

He Remains in Mexican Cabinet and de la Barra Will Displace Creel.

FORCE WILL MEET FORCE

Minister, However, Appeals to Mexicans and Nations to Believe in the Government's Good Faith.

FROM VICE PRESIDENT CORRAL.

Mexico City, March 25.

To the Editor of The New York Times:

The resignation of Gen. Diaz's Cabinet has been well received, because its object is to make it easier for the President to introduce reforms in public administration which it is thought will contribute to reestablish peace.

RAMON CORRAL.

FROM MINISTER OF WAR COSIO.

Mexico City, March 25.

To the Editor of The New York Times:

I am not in a position to answer your question since it is for the public to discuss the effects of the resignation.

G. COSIO.

Señor Limantour seems to have gained full sway in the Mexican Government. He is to remain as Minister of Finance. Ambassador de la Barra, with whom he had long consultations in New York, has been summoned from Washington to be Minister of Foreign Affairs in place of Enrique Creel, Limantour's rival. Four other new names are on the Cabinet slate.

Señor Limantour in an interview appeals to all Mexicans to rally to the Government. He promises needed reforms, but declares force will be met with force.

The Maderos, who were in New York, have gone to Texas to be nearer to Francisco I. Madero, the rebel leader.

Insurrectos have appeared at new and widely scattered places. Successful operations are reported in Coahuila and Neuvo Leon in the North and Guerrero and Oaxaca in the South.

APPEAL BY LIMANTOUR.

Assures Mexicans of Reform and Appeals for Their Support.

Special to The New York Times.

MEXICO CITY, March 25.—Señor José Yves Limantour, whose return to this city has been followed by the upsetting of the Diaz cabinet, and who is expected to be a figure of great importance in the new Ministry, in an interview with the correspondent of THE NEW YORK TIMES this afternoon outlined the policy which he believes will be followed by the Government. Señor Limantour, whose resignation went in with those of his colleagues, spoke as an individual.

"I hope and earnestly trust," he said, "that the present difficulties will soon be solved in the best interests of the country and to the satisfaction of all reasonable and patriotic citizens; and I feel that I can say that the administration of Gen. Diaz is prepared to take such measures and implant such reforms as will satisfy the best public opinion of the country; and that, while meeting force with force, it will leave nothing undone in the present circumstances to unite all good Mexicans.

"A united Mexico is our watchword. I ask all patriotic and progressive Mexicans to be patient, and while the Government is working at the problem before it that they practically display the love of the fatherland, which has been and must be the basic principle of Mexico's proud position in the world. The putting aside of all personal resentments is imperatively demanded and a common cause to overcome a national difficulty is a necessity.

"If the citizens and friends of Mexico will continue to prove their devotion to the glorious past and the promising future of this nation in a brief time all complexities can readily be overcome. The Mexican people and the Governments friendly to us must believe—and I say this in all solemnity of verity—that the Government is determined to properly and progressively satisfy all legitimate demands for reformative measures, and that it is doing this in its line of duty as a representative Government, honestly, sincerely, and fearlessly."

The resignation of the Cabinet yesterday is taken as an indication that Señor Limantour's policies are prevailing with President Diaz. Señor Limantour's recognized value in his present office and his unfamiliarity with diplomatic duties is advanced as a strong argument against a change in his office, and he will remain as Finance Minister.

While high officials will not admit that Gen. Bernardo Reyes has been recalled from Europe, it can be stated, with practical certainty that the summons has gone to him. To Gen. Reyes, who has long been called the "idol of the Mexican Army," may be intrusted the task of handling the rebellion, as Minister of War and Marine. He will succeed the aged Gen. Cosio, who has been severely criticised for the campaign so far conducted. Gen. Reyes, who has long been abroad on a mission to study the military methods of Europe, was last heard from in Rome, whence he had gone from Paris.

Six Chosen For Ministry.

MEXICO CITY, March 25.—Although no official announcement has been made, it is known that five of the new members of President Diaz's Cabinet have been chosen and it is almost certain that José Yves Limantour will remain as Minister of Finance. Other selections besides that of Señor de la Barra as Minister of Foreign Relations, are:

DEMETRIO SODI, Judge of the Supreme Court, Minister of Justice, succeeding Justino Fernandez.

NORBERTO DOMINGUEZ, Postmaster General, Department of Communications, succeeding Leandro Fernandez.

MANUEL MARROQUIN, well-known civil engineer, Department of Fomento, succeeding Olegario Molina.

JORGE VERA ESTANOL, attorney, Minister of Education, succeeding Justo Sierra.

So far as official announcement of the

Continued on Page 9.

TO-DAY'S SUNDAY TIMES

CONSISTS OF

WIRELESS NEWS BY KITES.

Got Calls 4,000 and 6,000 Miles Away, Say San Francisco Men.

SAN FRANCISCO, March 25.—Notable achievements in wireless telegraphy are reported by a party that conducted experiments in receiving messages with the aid of high-flying kites on a beach near the Golden Gate last night.

The experimenters say they have distinctly heard calls from San Juan, Porto Rico, Washington, D. C.; Key West, Fla.; Brooklyn Navy Yard, Colon, Guantanamo, Cuba, and the station at Otichishi, Japan, which is 4,900 miles distant. They also detected an indistinct Marconi spark, which they believe was sent from Cornwall, England, a distance of 6,500 miles.

The receiving aerials were strung between two pairs of 16-foot kites, which rose to a height estimated at 1,500 feet.

To-day reports of the experiments are being prepared for transmission to the War Department, together with suggestions for the use of such an appliance for the detection of distant activities of enemies.

SENDS WIRELESS 2,500 MILES.

The White Star Liner Megantic Forwards a Message to England.

HALIFAX, N. S., March 25.—What is said to be an entirely new feat in direct wireless communication, the sending of a message over the Atlantic a distance of 2,500 miles from a ship at sea to England, was reported by the White Star Dominion liner Megantic, which arrived today from Liverpool.

While off the coast last night Purser Pomeroy of the Megantic sent a wireless dispatch to Liverpool via Poldhu, Cornwall. The message was received and to-day when the ship docked, a reply by cable was handed to the purser.

Hitherto messages from ships in this part of the Atlantic have gone by way of Cape Race or Glace Bay and a range of 600 miles has been considered as practically the limit.

RAILROAD STRIKE IS OFF.

Queen & Crescent Firemen Return to Work, Both Sides Yielding Points.

Special to The New York Times.

CINCINNATI, Ohio, March 25.—The strike of firemen on the Queen and Crescent road, which caused considerable loss of freight and passenger service, was called off late to-night following a conference of the road's officials and representatives of the Firemen's Union. Both parties found it necessary to concede points of difference.

The company retains the right to employ such firemen as are now in service between Oakdale and Chattanooga, and to give them one-half the passenger and preferred freight runs.

It is understood that the strike, which has lasted sixteen days, has cost the company at least $250,000, besides the cost of operating trains with new firemen.

It is significant that the agreement is not signed by Vice President Powell of the road, who took the matter out of the hands of General Manager Baker. It is signed by Baker for the road and Vice President H. O. Teat, Chairman J. L. Payne, Vice Chairman G. A. Odenwald, and Secretary-Treasurer J. L. Fetterman of the Firemen's Union.

Smith Premier Typewriters in Servia.
After testing fifteen various makes the Belgrade Government has placed an order for one hundred Model 10 Smith Premiers.—Adv.

TALK OF CHARGES AGAINST THE MAYOR

Civic Organizations Taking Up Magistrate Corrigan's Attack—Want Police Control Shifted.

MAY GO TO THE GOVERNOR

Former District Attorney Philbin Says the Force Is Demoralized and Gaynor Doesn't Understand It.

An attempt was made yesterday to start an official investigation of police conditions in this city. Various civic organizations communicated with Magistrate Joseph E. Corrigan, who in a letter to the newspapers described the situation as intolerable and put the blame directly upon Mayor Gaynor.

It is the intention of the organizations to find out if things are as bad as has been set forth by Magistrate Corrigan and to have the responsibility placed somewhere.

Magistrate Corrigan has been asked to submit all the information and data relating to the subject he has on hand or can get, and he will comply with the request. This is as far as the Magistrate will go, he said, as he considers that he has done his duty in drawing the attention of the public to the abuses.

"I have nothing to add to what I stated in my letter," said Magistrate Corrigan yesterday, "but I am ready to stand by everything I wrote. My deductions are more than borne out by the letters which I receive by every mail. Most of these are from responsible people and contain specific instances of how the police of New York City are demoralized. These letters I am willing, with the consent of the owners, to turn over to any investigating committee, with any other information which I possess. I hope a full investigation will be made, either by the Grand Jury or some civic body."

Magistrate Butts Takes Notice, Too.

It was reported that the civic organizations will endeavor to have police control taken entirely out of the hands of the Mayor. It was said that they will even go so far as to bring charges before the Governor against the Mayor if he does not remedy defects of his own accord.

City Magistrate Butts substantiated in a measure yesterday the charges of Magistrate Corrigan. On Thursday Magistrate Butts praised Magistrate Corrigan's sincerity and courage, and he was not invited to the meeting of Magistrates on Thursday evening at which thirteen Magistrates disclaimed sympathy with Magistrate Corrigan's attack.

Magistrate Butts's position was defined when two policemen from the West 126th Street Station offered newspaper clippings in the Harlem Court describing proceedings at the Polo Athletic Club as a basis for warrants for the boxers. They said they had been unable to get into the club.

"It is a barefaced confession of the general inefficiency of the Police Department for you to offer me such evidence," said Magistrate Butts. "It reflects small credit on the police affairs of the city. How absurd it is for you men to come here and ask for a warrant or even a summons, when you make no straight charge based upon any real evidence that a crime has been committed.

"Now, understand me: I do not blame you two men or your Lieutenant or your Captain, but it certainly shows inexperience, if not stupidity, in the police administration of the City of New York. The court is powerless to put in motion its processes on such 'evidence' as this. The application for a warrant is denied."

Among those who openly backed up Magistrate Corrigan's charges yesterday were former District Attorney Eugene A. Philbin, who helped to break up the old police "system," convicting a number of Captains for neglect of duty and forcing others to retire from the department.

Force Demoralized, Says Philbin.

"I consider the police force of New York the finest body of men in the world for its size," said Mr. Philbin. "For the most part it is made up of splendid fellows, but they are now working purely under the stimulus of their own innate virtue. The force as a force is demoralized; never in my time has it been in such a state, and I believe that whether his statement was judicious and well timed or not, Magistrate Corrigan was entirely correct in his description of the conditions.

"Men are afraid of their commanding officers, not in the old sense of knowing that they must obey them, but in the sense of having no confidence in them. They are afraid to make an arrest, almost to call their souls their own. Of course, such a condition is intolerable.

"A Captain in the old days was held strictly accountable for what happened in his precinct, and although an honest patrolman, with a grievance or a wrong to report, did not have a chance in the world if he went to Headquarters with it, the discipline was splendid and New York was protected. I did my best to destroy that old system while I was in the District Attorney's office, thinking that thereby I could do a permanent good to the city. It seems, however, that I really did an injury, as so far nothing has been found as a substitute for what was called the police 'business.'

Criticisms of the Mayor.

"I do not believe that Mayor Gaynor is fully informed on police matters, or so thoroughly conversant with them as those who have studied them for years. In my opinion the only solution is to appoint a Police Commissioner for a long tenure of office, say fourteen years, so that he may be free from all influence.

"I am convinced that all the Magistrates who signed the statement condemning the action of Magistrate Corrigan, though they believed it impolitic and, perhaps, tending further to upset the discipline and efficiency of the force, really agreed with him."

James Forbes, Secretary and Director of the National Association for the Prevention of Mendicancy and Charitable Imposture, who is well acquainted with police conditions in New York, also supports Magistrate Corrigan.

"There is no question about it," he said, "the whole police force of the city is utterly demoralized. The police realize that the Mayor dislikes the police, mistrusts them, takes every opportunity to side against them.

"Now, the police force is a peculiar body, with a psychology all its own. They are very closely bound together, so that the slightest influence spreads at once through the entire force, and the Mayor's constraint, which has been carried to the extent of persecution, has simply wiped out their spirit."

Letters to Corrigan.

Letters from all kinds of people praising him for the stand he has taken in regard to the police continue to pour in on Magistrate Corrigan. The following is from a prominent lawyer:

"I congratulate you on having at last brought the public to a realization of present conditions. Whatever the other

Continued on Page 8.

LAKEWOOD Healthful Open Air Life.
Ideal Motor Run—Polo Carnival—Golf.
LAUREL HOUSE, LAUREL-IN-THE-PINES.
—Adv.

141 MEN AND GIRLS DIE IN WAIST FACTORY FIRE; TRAPPED HIGH UP IN WASHINGTON PLACE BUILDING; STREET STREWN WITH BODIES; PILES OF DEAD INSIDE

The Flames Spread with Deadly Rapidity Through Flimsy Material Used in the Factory.

600 GIRLS ARE HEMMED IN

When Elevators Stop Many Jump to Certain Death and Others Perish in Fire-Filled Lofts.

STUDENTS RESCUE SOME

Help Them to Roof of New York University Building, Keeping the Panic-Stricken in Check.

ONE MAN TAKEN OUT ALIVE

Plunged to Bottom of Elevator Shaft and Lived There Amid Flames for Four Hours.

ONLY ONE FIRE ESCAPF

Coroner Declares Fuilding Laws Were Not Enforced—Building Modern—Classed Fireproof.

JUST READY TO GO HOME

Victims Would Have Ended Day's Work in a Few Minutes—Pay Envelopes Identify Many.

MOB STORMS THE MORGUE

Seeking to Learn Fate of Relatives Employed by the Triangle Waist Company.

The Burning Building at 23 Washington Place.

Three stories of a ten-floor building at the corner of Greene Street and Washington Place were burned yesterday, and while the fire was going on 141 young men and women—at least 125 of them mere girls—were burned to death or killed by jumping to the pavement below.

The building was fireproof. It shows now hardly any signs of the disaster that overtook it. The walls are as good as ever; so are the floors; nothing is the worse for the fire except the furniture and 141 of the 600 men and girls that were employed in its upper three stories.

Most of the victims were suffocated or burned to death within the building, but some who fought their way to the windows and leaped met death as surely, but perhaps more quickly, on the pavements below.

All Over in Half an Hour.

Nothing like it has been seen in New York since the burning of the General Slocum. The fire was practically all over in half an hour. It was confined to three floors—the eighth, ninth, and tenth of the building. But it was the most murderous fire that New York has seen in many years.

The victims who are now lying at the Morgue waiting for some one to identify them by a tooth or the remains of a burned shoe were mostly girls of from 16 to 23 years of age. They were employed at making shirtwaists by the Triangle Waist Company, the principal owners of which are Isaac Harris and Max Blanck. Most of them could barely speak English. Many of them came from Brooklyn. Almost all were the main support of their hard-working families.

There is just one fire escape in the building. That one is an interior fire escape. In Greene Street, where the terrified unfortunates crowded before they began to make their mad leaps to death, the whole big front of the building is guiltless of one. Nor is there a fire escape in the back.

The building was fireproof and the owners had put their trust in that. In fact, after the flames had done their worst last night, the building hardly showed a sign. Only the stock within it and the girl employes were burned.

A heap of corpses lay on the sidewalk for more than an hour. The firemen were too busy dealing with the fire to pay any attention to people whom they supposed beyond their aid. When the excitement had subsided to such an extent that some of the firemen and policemen could pay attention to this mass of the supposedly dead they found, about half way down in the pack, a girl who was still breathing. She died two minutes after she was found.

The Triangle Waist Company was the only sufferer by the disaster. There are other concerns in the building, but it was Saturday and the other companies had let their people go home. Messrs. Harris and Blanck, however, were busy and their girls—and some men—stayed.

Leaped Out of the Flames.

At 4:40 o'clock, nearly five hours after the employes in the rest of the building had gone home, the fire broke out. The one little fire escape in the interior was never resorted to by any of the doomed victims. Some of them escaped by running down the stairs, but in a moment or two this avenue was cut off by flame. The girls rushed to the windows and looked down at Greene Street, 100 feet below them. Then one poor, little creature jumped. There was a plate glass protection over part of the sidewalk, but she crashed through it, wrecking it and breaking her body into a thousand pieces.

Then they all began to drop. The crowd yelled "Don't jump!" but it was jump or be burned—the proof of which is found in the fact that fifty burned bodies were taken from the ninth floor alone.

They jumped, they crashed through broken glass, they crushed themselves to death on the sidewalk. Of those who stayed behind it is better to say nothing—except what a veteran policeman said as he gazed at a headless and charred trunk on the Greene Street sidewalk hours after the worst cases had been taken out:

"I saw the Slocum disaster, but it was nothing to this."

"Is it a man or a woman?" asked the reporter.

"It's human, that's all you can tell," answered the policeman.

It was just a mass of ashes, with blood congealed on what had probably been the neck.

Messrs. Harris and Blanck were in the building, but they escaped. They carried with them Mr. Blanck's children and a governess, and they fled over the roofs. Their employes did not know the way, because they had been in the habit of using the two freight elevators, and one of these elevators was not in service when the fire broke out.

Found Alive After the Fire.

The first living victim, Hyman Meshel of 322 East Fifteenth Street, was taken from the ruins four hours after the fire was discovered. He was found paralyzed with fear and whimpering like a wounded animal in the basement, immersed in water to his neck, crouched on the top of a cable drum, and with his head just below the floor of the elevator.

Meantime the remains of the dead it is hardly possible to call them bodies, because that word suggests something human, and there was nothing human about most of these—were being taken in a steady stream to the Morgue for identification. First Avenue was lined with the usual curious east side crowd. Twenty-sixth Street was impassable. But in the Morgue they received the charred remnants with no more emotion than they ever display over anything.

Back in Greene Street there was another crowd. At midnight it had not decreased in the least. The police were holding it back to the fire lines, and discussing the tragedy in a tone which those seasoned witnesses of death seldom use.

"It's the worse thing I ever saw," said one old policeman.

Chief Croker said it was an outrage. He spoke bitterly of the way in which the Manufacturers' Association had called a meeting in Wall Street to take measures against his proposal for enforcing better methods of protection for employes in cases of fire.

No Chance to Save Victims.

Four alarms were rung in fifteen minutes. The first five girls who jumped did so before the first engine could respond. That fact may not convey much of a picture to the mind of an unimaginative man, but anybody who has ever seen a fire can get from it some idea of the terrific rapidity with which the flames spread.

It may convey some idea, too, to say that thirty bodies clogged the elevator shafts. These dead were all girls. They had made their rush their blindly when they discovered that there was no chance to get out by the fire escape. Then they found that the elevator was as hopeless as anything else, and they fell there in their tracks and died.

The Triangle Waist Company employed about 600 women and less than 100 men. One of the saddest features of the thing is the fact that they had almost finished for the day. In five minutes more, if the fire had started then, probably not a life would have been lost.

Last night District Attorney Whitman started an investigation—not of this disaster alone but of the whole condition which makes it possible for a firetrap of such a kind to exist. Mr. Whitman's intention is to find out if the present laws cover such cases, and if they do not to frame laws that will.

GIRLS JUMP TO SURE DEATH.

Fire Nets Prove Useless—Firemen Helpless to Save Life.

The fire, which was first discovered at 4:40 o'clock on the eighth floor of the ten-story building at the corner of Washington Place and Greene Street, leaped through the three upper stories occupied by the Triangle Waist Company with a sudden rush that left the Fire Department helpless.

How the fire started no one knows. On the three upper floors of the building were 600 employes of the waist company, 500 of whom were girls. The victims were mostly Italians, Russians, Hungarians, and Germans were girls and men who had been employed by the firm of Harris & Blanck, owners of the Triangle Waist Company, after the strike in which the Jewish girls, formerly employed, had become unionized and had demanded better working conditions. The building had experienced four recent fires and had been reported by the Fire Department to the Building Department as unsafe, on account of the insufficiency of its exits.

The building itself was of the most modern construction and classed as fireproof. What burned so quickly and disastrously for the victims were shirtwaists, hanging on lines above tiers of workers, sewing machines placed so closely together that there was hardly aisle room for the girls between them, and shirtwaist trimmings and cuttings which littered the floors above the eighth and ninth stories.

Girls had begun leaping from the eighth story windows before the firemen arrived. The firemen had trouble bringing their apparatus into position because of the bodies which strewed the pavement and sidewalks. While more bodies crashed down among them, they worked with desperation to run their ladders into position and to spread firenets.

One fireman, running ahead of a hose wagon, which halted to avoid running over a body, spread a firenet, and two more seized hold of it. A girl's body, coming end over end, struck on the side of it, and there was hope for an instant that she would be the first one of the score who had already jumped to be saved.

Thousands of people, who had crushed in from Broadway and Washington Square and were screaming with horror at what they saw, watched closely the work with the firenet. Three other girls, who had leaped for it a moment after the first one, struck it on top of her, and all four rolled out and lay still upon the pavement.

Five girls who stood together at a window close to the Greene Street corner held their places while a fire ladder was worked toward them, but which stopped at its full length two stories lower down. They leaped together, clinging to each other, with fire streaming back from their hair and dresses. They struck a glass sidewalk cover and crashed through it to the basement. There was no time to aid them. With water pouring in upon them from a dozen hose nozzles the bodies lay for two hours where they struck, as did the many others who leaped to their deaths.

One girl, who waved a handkerchief at the crowd, leaped from a window adjoining the New York University Building on the westward. Her dress caught on a wire, and the crowd watched her hang there till her dress burned free and she came toppling down.

Many jumped whom the firemen believe they could have saved. A girl who saw the glass roof of a sidewalk cover at the first-story level of the New York University Building leaped for it, and her body crashed through to the sidewalk.

On Greene Street, running along the eastern face of the building, more people leaped to the pavement than on Washington Place to the south. Fire nets proved just as useless to catch them and the ladders to reach them. None waited for the firemen to attempt to reach them with the scaling ladders.

All Would Soon Have Been Out.

Strewn about as the firemen worked, the bodies indicated clearly the preponderance of women workers. Here and there was a man, but almost always they were women. One wore furs and a muff, and had a purse hanging from her arm. Nearly all were dressed for the street. The fire had flashed through their workroom just as they were expecting the signal to leave the building. In ten minutes more all would have been out, as many had stopped work in advance of the signal and had started to put on their wraps.

What happened inside there were few who could tell with any definiteness. All that those who escaped seemed to remember was that there was a flash of flames, leaping first among the girls in the southeast corner of the eighth floor, and then suddenly over the entire room, spreading through the linens and cottons with which the girls were working. The girls on the ninth floor caught sight of the flames through the windows, up the stairway, and up the elevator shaft.

On the tenth floor they got them a moment later, but most of those on that floor escaped by rushing to the roof and then on to the roof of the New York University Building, with the assistance of 100 university students who had been dismissed from a tenth story classroom.

There were in the building, according to the estimates of Fire Chief Croker, about 600 girls and 100 men. The bodies of those

DEWEY'S PURE GRAPE JUICE
Purifies the blood, is very nourishing.
H. T. DEWEY & SONS CO., 138 Fulton St., N. Y.
—Adv.

ASHEVILLE "THE LAND OF THE SKY."
Marvelously blue sky—Clear Streams Sparkling cascades—Elegant hotels. Reached by Southern Ry. From New York a few hours. N. Y. Office, 264 Fifth Ave., cor. 29th St.—Adv.

killed and burned to death were found principally on the ninth floor, where over 50 perished in front of a closed doorway, which they had jammed shut; in the two elevator shafts 30 or more were piled up in the bottom after the elevator had ceased running; at the bottom of a single iron fire escape in an air shaft in the building's rear and on the fire-proof stairways between the eighth and ten stories, up which the fire from the burning sewing machines on the eighth floor went with a rush of air toward the roof.

When the Fire Was Discovered.

Samuel Bernstein, the waist factory's foreman, and Max Rothberg, his first assistant, were standing together on the eighth floor when the screams of girls attracted their attention to the southeast corner of the large room. They rang for the elevators, of which two were in the south side of the building, and Rothberg telephoned to the Fire Department and Police Departments. Two hundred girls were working on that floor, most of them still at their machines in the narrow aisles that gave them hardly room to move about. Dynamos, used to operate the sewing machines were in the corner from which the fire was spreading.

The two men attacked it with buckets of water, feeling confident at first they would be able to put it out. In the meantime the girls, screaming loudly and in a panic, rushed for the elevator shaft and the staircase, where they encountered a closed door.

Dora Miller of 10 Cannon Street got the door part way open, but it was jammed shut again by the press of people behind her. She struck a glass panel in it with her fists until she had made a hole large enough to climb through, and she escaped. Twenty others followed her before the flames reached them, and the rest of those caught on the floor were only discernable as a mass of charred bones when the firemen at last worked their way up the staircase.

Bernstein and Rothberg escaped by way of the elevator on its last trip to the floor.

Factory Owners Escape.

The two partners, Harris and Blanck, were both in the building, Harris being on the ninth floor and Blanck on the eighth. With Blanck, according to a statement of Joseph Zito, an elevator man, were his two daughters and a governess. He was telephoning for a taxicab to take them home when the alarm was sounded.

Blanck told Zito, the latter declares, to keep his elevator running and take out the women first.

The two passenger elevators, in charge of Zito and another operator named J. Gaspar, made several trips, but never went above the eighth floor, as they found more than enough people surrounding the entrance on that floor each time they reached it.

One of the men—which one was not made clear in the various versions of the affair offered—deserted his elevator and ran away, crying "Fire" as he ran.

Max Steinberg, a New York University law student, saw him running through Washington Place, and at the same time saw a girl leap from an eighth story window. He pulled a fire alarm box in Washington Square East and then ran to the building, where he entered the deserted elevator and ran it for four more trips before the heating of the cables put it out of commission.

Trapped on the Ninth Floor.

On the ninth story, which like the eighth was filled with sewing machines and was used for cutting and sewing shirtwaists, the girls fared worse than those on the floor below. They crowded about the elevator shaft, but no cars responded to their frantic ringing of the bell. Time after time they saw the cars approach, only to be filled at the eighth and go down again.

Girls who rushed to the staircase were met with flames which bore them down before they could retreat. Those who reached the windows and waited there for firemen saw the ladders swing in against the building two stories below them.

The one little iron fire escape, leading from a rear window, was pitiably inadequate, and it was from this floor that most of those came who fell like paper dolls, end over end, to the pavement.

There were about 20 men on the ninth floor. Calmer than the girls, they lined the southerly tier of windows first and tried to force the girls back to prevent them from jumping. Several girls they dragged back, after they had reached the window sills, and some they induced to lift themselves in again after they had climbed outside and were clinging only with their hands.

Zito, the elevator man, said that on his last trip down he could hear the thud of bodies striking the roof of his car as women jumped from the ninth floor after giving up hope that he would reach them. He heard the rattle of silver from their pay envelopes as it came through the iron grating into the car.

The loss on this floor was not known to the firemen and police until nearly 7 o'clock, when Deputy Fire Chief Binns reached it on the concrete stairway, which remained perfectly solid and unharmed. Binns found the bodies of fifty or more women, those who had not been burned beyond recognition seeming to be mere girls. They were lying in heaps upon the floor, as if they had huddled together near the stairway and the elevator shaft, and had been overtaken there by the flames. Money from the pay envelopes was strewn about close to them.

The tenth floor was the only one on which men were employed in any numbers. On this floor was the packing room, where the finished shirtwaists were prepared for shipment, and the showroom, where customers were made welcome.

East Side of Building---40 Bodies on Sidewalk.

One Hour After This Picture Was Taken Two of the Victims Were Discovered to be Alive.

Students Save Some Lives.

The men and women on this floor rushed for the roof. The smoke issuing from the windows was seen by Prof. F. Somner, who was teaching twenty-five young men the principles of the New Jersey Code on the tenth floor of the law school.

Prof. Somner ordered his students to rush to the roof and lower ladders to the roof of the factory building. The New York University building is one story higher than the waist factory building. One ladder was procured and a student named Kremmer descended on it to the roof of the building on fire. Another student, at the top of the ladder, grasped the women as they climbed toward the top, while Kremmer kept them from blocking the bottom rungs.

Men, panic-stricken, fought with the women to get to the ladder, but Kremmer shoved them away and let the women out of the danger zone first. Over 100 women and 20 men escaped this way. Another hundred reached a building north of the burning one, whose roof was only five feet higher and could be reached without a ladder.

How many reached the streets through the stairways nobody knew, as they were foreigners who spoke little English and fled for their homes in the lower east side as soon as they gained the sidewalk.

The task of the police and firemen outside the building was hardly started before the fire had caused its full damage in loss of life. The three burned stories, after it was all over and Fire Department searchlights played upon them, were seen to be wholly intact except for their wooden window trim and wooden floor coverings. Red tiling flashed the searchlight glow back to the street below from all the ceilings, and steel and concrete layers made the floors as firm to the tread of the firemen as if they had been newly built.

Police and Firemen Arrive.

The call to the police reached Headquarters over the telephone in a brief message that said girls were jumping from the Triangle Waist Company windows. The police were familiar with the place, as it had played a centre rôle in the opening phases of the shirtwaist strike.

Headquarters, from First Deputy Commissioner Driscoll and Chief Inspector Schmittberger to the last clerk and doorman, emptied itself, at Driscoll's orders, into the fire zone. Inspector Daly and twelve Captains reported to Schmittberger a few moments after he arrived.

Capt. Dominick Henry of the Mercer Street Station had preceded Driscoll and Schmittberger, and was attempting to establish fire lines when they arrived. Twenty-five patrol wagons from all the downtown precincts and 150 men came into the fire zone. They made one line on Washington Square East, forcing the people to the west side of the street, another line at Broadway, and cross-street lines at Waverly Place and on Fourth Street.

The second, third and fourth fire alarms were turned in before any apparatus had appeared, on the receipt of information at Fire Headquarters that there were twenty or more dead on the sidewalks. Chief Croker arrived in time to see his men spreading hopelessly their small and one or two large life nets, and saw many jump to their deaths.

Ambulances from Bellevue and New York and St. Vincent's Hospital—twenty or more in number—lined the street in Washington Square East and in Washington Place.

Ten surgeons from Bellevue, under Drs. Byrne, Read, and Kempf, threaded their way among the firemen gathering up the dead. They worked at this task from 6 o'clock until 7, and then policemen came to their assistance. The bodies found on Greene Street were taken to the east sidewalk, while those in Washington Place were laid in lines on both sidewalks.

Tarpaulins, laid over them, protected them somewhat from the deluge of water which, pouring from the high-pressure towers like a miniature niagara, flowed down the side of the building and into foot-deep flood along the pavement.

The surgeons could offer little aid except to cover over the bodies of the dead. Here and there from near-by stores reports came of injured, and a few ambulances drove away with these to the hospitals. Mostly all there was to do was to determine that life was extinct in the bodies on the pavement, and cover them over.

Deputy Police Commissioner Driscoll sent in an order at 6:30 o'clock for seventy-five coffins, and later another order for seventy-five more. It was not known to the firemen and policemen at first that the death roll would reach anything like its final proportions.

How Many Died.

A thirteen-year-old girl hung for three minutes by her finger tips to the sill of a tenth floor window. A tongue of flame licked at her fingers, and she dropped to death.

A girl threw her pocketbook, then her hat, then her furs from a tenth-floor window. A moment later her body came whirling after them to death.

At a ninth-floor window a man and a woman appeared. The man embraced the woman and kissed her. Then he hurled her to the street and jumped. Both were killed. Five girls smashed a pane of glass, dropped in a struggling tangle, and were crushed into a shapeless mass.

A girl on the eighth floor leaped for a fireman's ladder, which reached only to the sixth floor. She missed, struck the edge of a life net, and was picked up with her back broken. From one window a girl of about 13 years, a woman, a man, and two women with their arms about one another threw themselves to the ground in rapid succession. The little girl was whirled to the New York Hospital in an automobile. She screamed as the driver and a policeman lifted her into the hallway. A surgeon came out, took one look at her face and touched his hand to her wrist.

"She is dead," he said.

One girl jumped into a horse blanket held by firemen and policemen. The blanket ripped like cheesecloth, and her body was mangled almost beyond recognition.

Another dropped into a tarpaulin held by three men. Her weight tore it from their grasp and she struck the street, breaking almost every bone in her body.

Almost at the same moment a man somersaulted down upon the shoulder of a policeman holding the tarpaulin. He glanced off, struck the sidewalk, and was picked up dead.

Chief Croker thought at first it would not go over twenty-five. Then he placed the number at sixty-five—the total on the streets and reported from the inside. At 7 o'clock, over two hours after the firemen had come, the dead on the ninth floor were found, and those in the elevator shaft, each find sending the total up beyond the largest estimates previously made.

In getting out the bodies, the task proved so formidable that it was late in the night before it was reasonably complete.

Taking the Bodies Away.

Coroner's Physician O'Hanlon, with Coroners Holtzhauser and Lehane, arrived at 6:45 o'clock along with District Attorney Whitman and several of his assistants. O'Hanlon explained that he had cared for the dead from the Slocum disaster on the recreation pier, and it would be better to handle these in the same manner, as the Morgue would prove hopeless to the task of accommodating them.

Scenes Attending the Disaster in Washington Place.

Entering New York University Building, Looking for Bodies of the Dead.

Water Tower and Ladder Opposite Building in Washington Place.

PHOTOS. COPYRIGHT BY AMERICAN PRESS ASS'N

Firemen Carrying the Body of a Woman Who Jumped from the Ninth Floor.

He said he had still some of the tags such as were used in the Slocum disaster, and he proposed that each body be tagged exactly where it lay, and that records be made by number. He was told by Coroner Holtzhauser to proceed in this manner, and did so with the assistance of 100 or more policemen.

As fast as bodies had been looked over for identifications and tags fastened to them, coffins were brought from a supply depot established in East Washington Place. In these rude wooden boxes, coverless, the bodies were placed in patrol wagons and driven away.

At 7:45 o'clock the searchlights from four Fire Department engines were playing in the upper windows, and a glow came out of them from torches carried within by firemen. Suddenly a black shadow swung out of the ninth-story window, and the creaking of pulleys and a rope and tackle began, as the black mass descended speedily toward the ground. Firemen in windows on the lower floor guided the ropes. It was the beginning of the work of bringing out the bodies from the floor where the death roll was the largest.

The pulley system worked for an hour, each body being lowered after it had been wrapped in black cloth and tied securely until it resembled just such packages as go up and down daily in the business district, rope-and-pulley fashion.

Coroner's Statement.

The scene was more than Coroner Holtzhauser could stand. Sobbing like a child, the Coroner, who was first to open the fireplace where Ruth Wheeler's body was incinerated in the Wolter flat, said that that scene was easy to stand compared with this.

"And only one miserable little fire escape!" he said. "I shall proceed against the Building Department along with the others. They are as guilty as any. They haven't been insistent enough, and these poor girls who were carried up in the elevator to work in the morning—now they come down on the end of a rope."

That investigations from many centres would be started was early made apparent. Building Department officials who arrived at 7:20 o'clock, said they would begin one this morning. Fire Marshal Beers said he would begin another. The District Attorney made a list of witnesses that he will question.

Chief Croker's View.

Fire Chief Croker, after the fire had flickered down to a few embers still glowing here and there, spoke vigorously against the men who have opposed his plans for better fire protection. "Look around everywhere," he said, "nowhere will you find fire escapes. They say they don't look sightly. I have tried to force their installation, and only last Friday a

manufacturers' association met in Wall Street to oppose my plan and to oppose the sprinkler system, as well as the additional escapes."

"This is just the calamity I have been predicting," said Chief Croker. "There were no outside escapes on this building. I have been advocating and agitating that more fire escapes be put on factory buildings similar to this. The large loss of life is due to this neglect."

He said that there was only one fire escape from the building. An old-time perpendicular affair, he said, leading to the courtyard in the centre of the block of buildings, which would only allow of one person's escape at a time. When he examined this escape, he said, he found on the upper floors that it had become very loose, and it was a dangerous matter to escape by that route.

"A repetition of this disaster is likely to happen at any time in similar buildings," he said. He advocated balcony fire escapes with a wide iron staircase.

The staircases in the building, the Chief said, were of the ordinary three feet six inches wide type, but he believed that if escape had been sought by that route, the death list would not have been so appalling.

There were rumors that the fire started by a gasoline explosion, but the survivors said that they had heard no explosion.

Fire Commissioner R. Waldo being out of town yesterday, the fire was in charge of Deputy Commissioner Arthur J. O'Keefe, in charge of Brooklyn and Queens, who is taking the Commissioner' place.

He and Coroner Holtzhauser had a dispute concerning the cause of the fire at 11:20 o'clock. Holtzhauser remarked that there was terrible responsibility for the Fire Department to meet.

"And for some other departments, too," O'Keefe replied. "Commissioner Waldo to my certain knowledge had reported this place to the Building Department within the past three months as a building unsafe for use as a factory, since there were insufficient means of egress by stairways, and there were not sufficient fire escape facilities.

"Oh, that makes a difference, then," Holtzhauser concluded.

Winfield R. Sheehan, Commissioner Waldo's secretary, joined the group at that juncture. He said that he personally had mailed the protest to the Building Department and knew of Commissioner Waldo's anxiety because of the unsafe condition of the building and his inability to force the making of changes.

Alfred Ludwig of the Department of Buildings was acting in the capacity of Superintendent during the absence of Supt. Rudolph P. Miller, who was out of town last night.

SCENES AT THE MORGUE.

Men and Women Gather in a Frantic Throng in Quest of Loved Ones.

A few minutes after the first load of fire victims was received at the Bellevue Hospital Morgue the streets were filled with a clamoring throng, which struggled with the reserves stationed about the building in an effort to gain entrance to view the bodies of the dead in the hope of identifying loved ones.

The frantic mob was reinforced as the hospital wagon brought more of the dead to the institution. The sobbing and shrieking mothers and wives, and frantic fathers and husbands of those who had not been accounted for struggled with the police and tried to stop the wagon that was bearing the dead on its trips to the Morgue. Mothers and wives ran frantically through the street in front of the hospital, pulling their hair from their heads and calling the names of their dear ones.

A few of the surging mob who viewed the situation in a calmer manner attempted to calm the excited ones, but in vain. The police were abused because they would not allow the surging mob in the Morgue, and in many instances they were threatened and had to resort to the use of their nightsticks to keep the struggling mass from breaking in.

Two members of the throng who succeeded in gaining entrance to the Morgue were Mrs. Josephine Pannel of 49 Stanton Street and her son-in-law, who came in search of her daughter, Mrs. Jane Bucalo, 18 years old. She was last seen struggling to get into the elevator on the eighth floor of the building. Mrs. Pannel walked up and down the aisle that was formed between the rows of the unidentified dead and looked in vain for her daughter.

She was filled with hope, however, when an attendant announced that the wagon had just arrived with another load of the fire victims. The newly arriving dead were brought into the Morgue and stretched out, and Mrs. Pannel and her son-in-law ran frantically up and down the lines trying to find the one they sought. When the mother found that her search was in vain, she ran shrieking to her son-in-law and began tearing out her hair. Bucalo stood as a man in a trance, gazing at the rows of blackened bodies. Suddenly he reeled and fell to the floor. He was assisted to his feet by the attendants.

Presently Mrs. Pannel became calmer, and, seeing that there was no body among the dead that would answer the description of her daughter, she grew more composed, and thought it was probable that her daughter had escaped from the burning building alive.

At the door of the Morgue Mrs. Pannel met a reporter, and told him of her miraculous escape from the burning building, and the cause of her frantic search for the body of her daughter. According to her story, she was in the reading room of the factory when the fire was discovered. She, with others, ran to the elevator shaft, and when the car reached the eighth floor they fought to get into it. She said that she seized her daughter by the skirt before leaving the cutting room, and as she was being carried into the elevator by the frantic mob that was surging behind her her hold on her daughter's dress was torn away, and she remembers seeing the terrorized face of her daughter as the car was started downward. She called to her daughter, and thought that she saw her reel and fall to the floor as the car shot downward.

Mrs. Pannel described graphically the surging throng that clamored in the hall of the eighth floor and the struggle of the employes to gain entrance to the elevator car. She told of the rush of the occupants of the car when the elevator reached the ground floor on its last trip. She said she had a dim recollection of persons being trampled under foot by the excited mob as they dashed from the car to the entrance of the building, and that she believed many who were trampled upon perished in the bottom of the elevator car.

She also said that when the car left the eighth floor, some of the employes made a vain attempt to leap on the top of the car and that a few, being pushed forward by the struggling mass behind them, fell down the shaft through the open doorway of the shaft on the eighth floor and were dashed to death upon the roof of the car.

Police Work Desperately.

A hundred policemen, most of them ashen and with trembling lips, worked at the heart-rending task of keeping back, without undue roughness, the maddened thousands.

"For God's sake," one cried to a reporter, who was wedging his way out of the mob, "get me a drink!"

The poor bluecoat needed it.

Every few minutes a patrol wagon or a hastily improvised morgue wagon that had done duty as an auto truck earlier in the day appeared at the head of the mob at First Avenue and Twenty-sixth Street, and the reserves of six precincts had to force open a narrow path through the crowd for it. As soon as the path was opened in front, however, the crowd surged in behind it. At the sight of the bodies the crowd broke into fresh weeping and screaming, each seeming to see in the charred and often unrecognizable remains a loved one.

Twelve patrol wagons from as many stations, besides dozens of hastily impressed dispensary wagons of the Police

Police Numbering the Bodies in the Street.

POLICE TRYING TO IDENTIFY VICTIMS

Department and the Department of Public Charities and a few auto trucks were used in transporting the dead from the fire to the Morgue. The Morgue itself became too crowded, early in the evening, for further storage of bodies, and the Charities Department decided to throw open the long public dock adjoining it. Here, as night settled over the city, the bodies were taken from the wagons and laid out, side by side, in double rows along either side of the long docks.

Besides the thirty attendants regularly at the pier, twenty derelicts who had applied at the Municipal Lodging House in East Twenty-sixth Street for a night's rest, were pressed into service for the ghastly work.

Considerable confusion was caused on the pier in numbering the dead. The police of the various precincts had received from the Charities Department small, colored tags bearing numbers to tag the different boxes as soon as the bodies were laid in them. There turned out to be three separate systems of numbers, and the enumeration had to be done all over again.

At 11:30 o'clock, with the mob still storming more and more outside, the police had counted in the Morgue and on the pier 136 bodies—thirteen men and 123 women. Fifty-six of these were burned beyond all but human semblance and may never be identified. The thousands of clamorers outside could not have identified them, even if the police had let them swarm in on the pier.

As the maddened throng swarmed around the ghastly laden patrol wagons and improvised hearses their misery wrung even the hardened habitual handlers of the dead in the Morgue, making them frequently turn away from their work. There were hundreds scantily clad and shivering, despite their raving, in the cold night air. Many of them had no money. Their week's funds were in the pay envelopes, found in dozens, on the scorched and irrecognizable bodies on the pier. One woman, her head charred to a mere twisted blurr of black, carried in her stocking $600 in tightly crumpled bills. Dozens of the girls whose bodies were laid out on the pier were found to have carried their scant savings in this way.

Clung Together in Death.

Two girls, charred beyond all hope of identification, and found in the smoking ruins with their arms clasped around each other's necks, were conveyed to the pier, still together, and placed in one box.

Horrible cries had burst from the misery stricken mob outside when these two were carried through the narrow ane in the street, and a few of the clamorous throng had forced their way to the wagon and lifted the dark tarpaulin. Everywhere burst anguished cries for sister, mother, and wife, a dozen pet names in Italian and Yiddish rising in shrill agony above the deeper moan of the throng.

Now and then a reporter, the way cleared before him by a broad, white-faced policeman, forced his way to the nearest telephone, to send to his office a report of what was happening there. Each time a hundred faces were turned up to him imploringly, and a hundred anguished voices begged of him tidings of those within. Had he seen a little girl with black hair and dark-brown cheeks? Had he seen a tall, thin man, with stooped shoulders? Could he describe any one of the many he had seen in there? The poor wretches were hunting for a " story," too.

STORIES OF SURVIVORS.

And Witnesses and Rescuers Outside Tell What They Saw.

The rapidity of the flames is shown in the experience of Max Rother, a tailor in the employ of the Triangle Waist Company, who was on the eighth floor of the building when the fire started. Rother was on the Washington Place side when he heard the cry of alarm coming from the Greene Street side of the loft. Hanging over the heads of the operators at the machines in the room was a line of clothes ablaze. With the manager of the firm, Max Burnstein, he tried to put the fire out with pails of water. While at this work the rope on which the clothes were hung burned in half and the burning clothes fell over their heads.

Soon the room was in flames. Rother ran for the stairs on the Greene Street side of the building and escaped. He does not know what became of Burnstein, the manager.

Cecilia Walker, 20 years old, who lives at 29 Stanton Street, slid down the cable at the Washington Place elevator and escaped with burned hands and body bruises. She was on the eighth floor of the building when the fire started. Running over to the elevator shaft she rang for the car, but it did not come. As she passed the sixth floor sliding on the cable she became unconscious, she said, and does not know what happened until she reached St. Vincent's Hospital, where she is now.

"A girl and I," she told the doctors at the hospital, "were on the eighth floor, and when I ran for the elevator shaft my girl friend started for the window on the Washington Street side. I looked around to call her but she had gone."

Jump Before Firemen Arrive.

According to several eye witnesses, the flames were pouring from the windows and the girls jumping to the sidewalk for several minutes before the first fire truck with ladders arrived. Benjamin Levy of 995 Freeman Street, the Bronx, one of the first men to arrive at the burning building, says that it was all of ten minutes after the fire started before the first engine arrived. Mr. Levy is the junior member of the firm of I. Levy & Son, wholesale clothing manufacturers, just around the corner, at 3 and 5 Waverley Place.

"I was upstairs in our work-room," said he, "when one of the employes who happened to be looking out of the window cried that there was a fire around the corner. I rushed downstairs, and when I reached the sidewalk the girls were already jumping from the windows. None of them moved after they struck the sidewalk. Several men ran up with a net which they got somewhere, and I seized one side of it to help them hold it.

"It was about ten feet square and we managed to catch about fifteen girls. I don't believe we saved over one or two, however. The fall was so great that they bounced to the sidewalk after striking the net. Bodies were falling all around us, and two or three of the men with me were knocked down. The girls just leaped wildly out of the windows and turned over and over before reaching the sidewalk.

"I only saw one man jump. All the rest were girls. They stood on the window sills, tearing their hair out in handfuls, and then they jumped.

"One girl held back after all the rest and clung to the window casing until the flames from the windows below crept up to her and set her clothing on fire. Then she jumped far over the net and was killed instantly, like all the rest."

One of the policemen who were checking up the bodies as they were being shipped to the Morgue told of one heap in which a girl was found still alive when the others were taken off her. She died before an ambulance doctor could reach her.

Elevator Made One Trip.

Samuel Levine, a machine operator on the ninth floor, who lives at 1,982 Atlantic Avenue, Brooklyn, told this story when he had recovered from his injuries at the New York Hospital: "I was at work when I heard the shout of ' Fire.' The girls on the floor dropped everything and rushed wildly around, some in the direction of windows and others toward the elevator door. I saw the elevator go down past our floor once. It was crowded to the limit and no one could have got on. It did not stop. Not another trip was made.

"There were flames all around in no time. Three girls, I think from the floor below, came rushing past me. Their clothes were on fire. I grabbed the fire pails and tried to pour the water on them, but they did not stop. They ran screaming toward the windows. I knew there was no hope there, so I stayed where I was, hoping that the elevator would come up again.

"I finally smashed open the doors to the elevator. I guess I must have done it with my hands. I reached out and grabbed the cables, wrapped my legs around them, and started to slide down. I can remember getting to the sixth floor. While on my way down, as slow as I could let myself drop, the bodies of six girls went falling past me. One of them struck me and I fell to the top of the elevator. I fell on the dead body of a girl. My back hit the beam that runs across the top of the car.

"Finally I heard the firemen cutting their way into the elevator shaft, and they came and let us out. I think others were taken out alive with me."

M. Samilson of the firm of Samilson & Co., on the second floor of the building, was standing at one of the windows of his office just after the fire was discovered. In the next few minutes, he said, he saw several bodies shoot past the window from above, most of them girls. When the firemen reached him, at nearly 6 o'clock, he was still standing there, horrified. He says he could not tear himself away.

Few of the girls that fell from the windows on the ninth floor, it was learned, jumped of their own accord. They were pushed forward by the panic-stricken crowd in the room behind them.

"All the News That's Fit to Print."

The New York Times.

THE WEATHER.

Unsettled Tuesday; Wednesday, fair, cooler; moderate southerly winds, becoming variable.
For full weather report see Page 23.

VOL. LXI...NO. 19,806.   NEW YORK, TUESDAY, APRIL 16, 1912.—TWENTY-FOUR PAGES.   ONE CENT   In Greater New York, | Elsewhere, Jersey City, and Newark. | TWO CENTS

TITANIC SINKS FOUR HOURS AFTER HITTING ICEBERG; 866 RESCUED BY CARPATHIA, PROBABLY 1250 PERISH; ISMAY SAFE, MRS. ASTOR MAYBE, NOTED NAMES MISSING

Col. Astor and Bride, Isidor Straus and Wife, and Maj. Butt Aboard.

"RULE OF SEA" FOLLOWED

Women and Children Put Over in Lifeboats and Are Supposed to be Safe on Carpathia.

PICKED UP AFTER 8 HOURS

Vincent Astor Calls at White Star Office for News of His Father and Leaves Weeping.

FRANKLIN HOPEFUL ALL DAY

Manager of the Line Insisted Titanic Was Unsinkable Even After She Had Gone Down.

HEAD OF THE LINE ABOARD

J..Bruce Ismay Making First Trip on Gigantic Ship That Was to Surpass All Others.

The admission that the Titanic, the biggest steamship in the world, had been sunk by an iceberg and had gone to the bottom of the Atlantic, probably carrying more than 1,400 of her passengers and crew with her, was made at the White Star Line offices, 9 Broadway, at 8:20 o'clock last night. Then P. A. S. Franklin, Vice President and General Manager of the International Mercantile Marine, conceded that probably only those passengers who were picked up by the Cunarder Carpathia had been saved. Advices received early this morning tended to increase the number of survivors by 200.

The admission followed a day in which the White Star Line officials had been optimistic in the extreme. At no time was the admission made that every one aboard the huge steamer was not safe. The ship itself, it was confidently asserted, was unsinkable, and inquirers were informed that she would reach port, under her own steam probably, but surely with the help of the Allan liner Virginian, which was reported to be towing her.

As the day passed, however, with no new authentic reports from the Titanic or any of the ships which were known to have responded to her wireless call for help, it became apparent that authentic news of the disaster probably could only come from the Titanic's sister ship, the Olympic. The wireless range of the Olympic is 500 miles. That of the Carpathia, the Parisian, and the Virginian is much less, and as they neared the position of the Titanic they drew farther and farther out of shore range. From the Titanic's position at the time of the disaster it is doubtful if any of the ships except the Olympic could establish communication with shore.

Titanic Sank at 2:20 A. M. Monday.

In the White Star offices the hope was held out all day that the Parisian and the Virginian had taken off some of the Titanic's passengers, and efforts were made to get into communication with these liners. Until such communication was established the White Star officials refused to recognize the possibility that there were none of the Titanic's passengers aboard them.

But by nightfall came the message from Capt. Haddock of the Olympic to Cape Race, Newfoundland, telling of the foundering of the Titanic and of the rescue of 655 of her passengers by the Cunarder Carpathia, which, the wireless message said, reached the position of the Titanic at daybreak. All they found there, however, was lifeboats and wreckage. The biggest ship in the world had sunk at 2:20 o'clock yesterday morning.

Mr. Franklin admitted late last night that the Parisian and the Virginian, though they were among the first to answer the Titanic's calls for help, could not have reached the scene before 10 o'clock yesterday morning, seven and a half hours after the big Titanic buried her nose beneath the waves and pitched downward out of sight. The Carpathia, so the wireless dispatch from Capt. Haddock to Cape Race announced, reached the scene of the Titanic's foundering at daybreak, several

The Lost Titanic Being Towed Out of Belfast Harbor.

CAPT. E. J. SMITH,
Commander of the Titanic.

hours before the expected arrival of the Virginian and the Parisian.

THE PROBABLE LOSS.
Number Aboard.

First cabin	325
Second cabin	285
Steerage	710
Crew (estimated)	900
Total	**2,120**
Saved.	
By the Carpathia	866
Probably drowned	1,254

1,465 Lives Lost First Report.

It is unbelievable, so White Star Line officials were compelled to concede finally, that the Carpathia should have failed to pick up every lifeboat which still floated on the waves. If they failed to pick up more than 655 passengers, it was because the others of the ship's complement had gone with her to the bottom.

But it was not until nearly nightfall that the extent of the disaster was realized. Before that the reassuring nature of the bulletins issued by the White Star line was sufficient to quiet the fears of those who had relatives or friends aboard the unfortunate ship and to prevent widespread belief in a serious disaster.

Capt. Haddock's message from the Olympic, which is printed in another column of THE TIMES, strongly indicated that none but the 655 taken from life boats by the Carpathia had been saved. This message was re-

layed immediately to the White Star offices, but Mr. Franklin positively declined to make the text of the message public. He offered still the hope that passengers were aboard the Parisian and the Virginian, and even when the admission was wrung from him that there seemed little hope of the saving of any others than the 655 aboard the Carpathia, he clung to the hope that in some unexplained way there were other passengers aboard the two Allan liners.

First Reported Titanic in Tow.

Throughout the day there had been reassurances that the Titanic was being towed to port by the Virginian,

and when Capt. Haddock's message proved this to be untrue only the admission was made at the White Star offices that the Titanic had sunk. Mr. Franklin said that Capt. Haddock's message was brief and "neglected" to say that all the crew had been saved." But the inference was not that all the passengers had been saved. Rather it was that many of them had died, and presently Mr. Franklin admitted the fear that there had been a terrible loss of life on the Titanic.

This version of Capt. Haddock's wireless had been given at the White Star offices:

Capt. Haddock of the Olympic sends a wireless message to the White Star offices here that the steamer Titanic sank at 2:20 A. M., after all the passengers and crew had been lowered to life boats and transferred to the Virginian. The steamship Carpathia, with

several hundred passengers of the Titanic, is now en route to New York. At 9 o'clock, however, he modified this statement, declaring:

As far as we know the situation, there have been rumors from Halifax that three steamers were at the scene of the Titanic's sinking, namely, the Virginian, the Parisian, and the Carpathia. We have heard from Capt. Haddock of the Olympic, who says that the Titanic sank at 2:20 o'clock this morning. Haddock also informs us that the Carpathia has 675 survivors on board. It is very difficult to say whether the Virginian and the Parisian have any survivors on board until we can get a report from those vessels.

We are hopeful that the rumors which have reached us by telegraph from Halifax that there are passengers aboard the Virginian and the Parisian will prove to be true, and that these vessels will turn up with some of the passengers. It is the loss of life that makes this thing so awful. We can replace the money loss, but not the lives of those who went down.

Another version of the message from the Olympic was current last night and included the sentence: "Loss likely total 1,800 souls." This sentence was not in the message received by THE TIMES from Cape Race nor in that sent to the White Star line offices.

Fears Serious Loss of Life.

We have asked for that report from Capt. Haddock, and we are expecting a reply at any time. The Carpathia

Biggest Liner Plunges to the Bottom at 2:20 A. M.

RESCUERS THERE TOO LATE

Except to Pick Up the Few Hundreds Who Took to the Lifeboats.

WOMEN AND CHILDREN FIRST

Cunarder Carpathia Rushing to New York with the Survivors.

SEA SEARCH FOR OTHERS

The California Stands By on Chance of Picking Up Other Boats or Rafts.

OLYMPIC SENDS THE NEWS

Only Ship to Flash Wireless Messages to Shore After the Disaster.

LATER REPORT SAVES 866.

BOSTON, April 15.—A wireless message picked up late to-night, relayed from the Olympic, says that the Carpathia is on her way to New York with 866 passengers from the steamer Titanic aboard. They are mostly women and children, the message said, and it concluded: "Grave fears are felt for the safety of the balance of the passengers and crew."

Special to The New York Times.

CAPE RACE, N. F., April 15.—The White Star liner Olympic reports by wireless this evening that the Cunarder Carpathia reached, at daybreak this morning, the position from which wireless calls for help were sent out last night by the Titanic after her collision with an iceberg. The Carpathia found only the lifeboats and the wreckage of what had been the biggest steamship afloat.

The Titanic had foundered at about 2:20 A. M., in latitude 41:16 north and longitude 50:14 west. This is about 30 minutes of latitude, or about 34 miles, due south of the position at which she struck the iceberg. All her boats are accounted for and about 655 souls have been saved of the crew and passengers, most of the latter presumably women and children.

There were about 2,100 persons aboard the Titanic.

The Leyland liner California is remaining and searching the position of the disaster, while the Carpathia is returning to New York with the survivors.

It can be positively stated that up to 11 o'clock to-night nothing whatever had been received at or heard by the Marconi station here to the effect that the Parisian, Virginian or any other ships had picked up any survivors other than those picked up by the Carpathia.

First News of the Disaster.

The first news of the disaster to the Titanic was received by the Marconi wireless station here at 10:25 o'clock last night [as told in yesterday's New York Times.] The Titanic was first heard giving the distress signal "C. Q. D.," which was answered by a number of ships, including the Carpathia.

PARTIAL LIST OF THE SAVED.

Includes Bruce Ismay, Mrs. Widener, Mrs. H. B. Harris, and an Incomplete name, suggesting Mrs. Astor's.

Special to The New York Times.

CAPE RACE, N. F., Tuesday, April 16.—Following is a partial list of survivors among the first-class passengers of the Titanic, received by the Marconi wireless station this morning from the Carpathia, via the steamship Olympic.

Mrs. JACOB P.—— and maid.	Mr. C. ROLMANE.	Mrs. WILLIAM BUCKNELL.
Mr. HARRY ANDERSON.	Mrs. SUSAN P. ROGERSON. (Probably Ryerson).	Mrs. O. H. BARKWORTH.
Mrs. ED. W. APPLETON.	Miss EMILY B. ROGERSON.	Mrs. H. B. STEFFASON.
Mrs. ROSE ABBOTT.	Mrs. ARTHUR ROGERSON.	Mrs. ELSIE BOWERMAN.
Miss G. M. BURNS.	Master ALLISON and nurse.	
Miss D. D. CASSEBERE.	Miss K. T. ANDREWS.	The Marconi station reports that it missed the word after "Mrs. Jacob P." In a list received by the Associated Press this morning this name appeared well down, but in THE TIMES list it is first, suggesting that the name of Mrs. John Jacob Astor is intended. This supposition is strengthened by the fact that, except for Mrs. H. J. Allison, Mrs. Astor is the only lady in the "A" column of the ship's passenger list attended by a maid.
Mrs. WM. M. CLARKE.	Miss NINETTE PANHART.	
Mrs. B. CHIBNACE.	Miss E. W. ALLEN.	
Miss E. G. CROSSBIE.	Mr. and Mrs. D. BISHOP.	
Miss H. ROSEBIE.	Mr. H. BLANK.	
Miss JEAN HIPACK.	Miss A. BASSINA.	
Mrs. HY. B. HARRIS.	Mrs. JAMES BAXTER.	
Mrs. ALEX. HALVERSON.	Mr. GEORGE A. BAYTON.	
Miss MARGARET BAYS.	Miss C BONNELL.	
Mr. BRUCE ISMAY.	Mrs. J. M. BROWN.	**NAMES PICKED UP AT BOSTON.**
Mr. and Mrs. ED. KIMBERLEY.	Miss G. C. BOWEN.	BOSTON, April 15.—Among the names of survivors from the steamer Carpathia here to-night were the following:
Mr. F. A. KENNYMAN.	Mr. and Mrs. R. L. BECKWITH.	
Miss EMILE KENCHEN.	Miss RUTH TAUSSIG.	Mr. and Mrs. L. HENRY.
Miss G. F. LONGLEY.	Miss ELLA THOR.	Mrs. W. A. HOOPER.
Mrs. A. F. LEADER.	Mr. and Mrs. E. Z. TAYLOR.	Mr. MILE.
Miss BERTHA LAVORY.	GILBERT M. TUCKER.	Mr. J. FLYNN.
Mrs. ERNEST LIVES.	Mr. J. B. THAYER.	Miss ALICE FORTUNE.
Miss MARY CLINES.	Mr. JOHN B. ROGERSON.	Mrs. ROBERT DOUGLAS.
Mrs. SINGRID LINDSTROM.	Mrs. M. ROTHSCHILD.	Miss HILDA SLAYTER.
Mr. GUSTAVE J. LESNEUR.	Miss MADELEINE NEWELL.	Mrs. P. SMITH.
Miss GIORGETTA A. MADILL.	Mrs. MARJORIE NEWELL.	Mrs. BRAHAM.
Mme. MELICARD.	HELEN W. NEWSOM.	Miss LUCILLE CARTER.
Mrs. TUCKER and maid.	Mr. FIENNAD OMOND.	Mr. WILLIAM CARTER.
Mrs. J. B. THAYER.	Mr. E. C. OSTBY.	Miss CUMMINGS.
Mr. J. B. THAYER, Jr.	Miss HELEN R. OSTBY.	Miss FLORENCE MARE.
Mr. HENRY WOOLNER.	Mrs. MAMAM J. RENAGO.	Miss ALICE PHILLIPS.
Miss ANNA WARD.	Mlle. OLIVIA.	Mrs. PAULA MUNGE.
Mr. RICHARD M. WILLIAMS.	Mrs. D. W. MERVIN.	Mrs. JANE
Mrs. F. M. WARNER.	Mr. PHILIP EMOCK.	Miss PHYLLIS O.——
Miss HELEN A. WILSON.	Mr. JAMES GOOGHT.	HOWARD B. CASE.
Miss WILLARD.	Miss RUBERTA MAIMY.	Miss MINEHAN.
Miss MARY WICKS.	Mr. PIERRE MARECHAL.	Miss BERTHA
Mr. GEO. D. WIDENER and maid.	Mrs. W. M. MINEHAN.	
Mrs. J. STEWART WHITE.	Miss APPIE RANELT.	
Miss MARIE YOUNG.	Major ARTUR PEUCHEN.	
Mrs. THOMAS POTTER, Jr.	Mrs. KARL H. BEHR.	
Mrs. EDNA S. ROBERTS.	Miss DESSETTE.	
Countess of ROTHES.		

is proceeding to New York direct. We very much fear that there has been serious loss of life, but it is impossible for us to say definitely concerning this sad part of the situation until we are able to reassure ourselves whether or not any of the Titanic's passengers are aboard the Allan liners.

Continued on Page 2.

POLAND WATER promotes Health. Avoid contagion by drinking purest water in world. Off. 1,180 B'way. Tel. Med. Sq. 4715.—Adv.

CRETA CREME HAND SOAP. Instantly removes stains. Large 10c.—Adv.

GREAT BEAR SPRING WATER. 80c. per case of 6 glass-stoppered bottles.—Adv.

the Baltic and the Olympic. The Titanic said she had struck an iceberg and was in immediate need of assistance, giving her position as latitude 41:46 north and longitude 50:14 west.

At 10:55 o'clock the Titanic reported she was sinking by the head, and at 11:25 o'clock the station here established communication with the Allan liner Virginian, from Halifax for Liverpool, and notified her of the Titanic's urgent need of assistance and gave her the Titanic's position.

The Virginian advised the Marconi station almost immediately that she was proceeding toward the scene of the disaster.

At 11:36 o'clock the Titanic informed the Olympic that they were putting the women off in boats and instructed the Olympic to have her boats ready to transfer the passengers.

The Titanic, during all this time, continued to give distress signals and to announce her position.

The wireless operator seemed absolutely cool and clear-headed, his sending throughout being steady and perfectly formed, and the judgment used by him was of the best.

The last signals heard from the Titanic were received at 12:27 A. M., when the Virginian reported having heard a few blurred signals which ended abruptly.

The Virginian Still Searching.

ST. JOHNS, N. F., April 15.—The steamer Virginian will proceed from the scene of the wreck after daylight to-morrow morning, bringing such survivors of the steamship Titanic "as she may be able to rescue," according to wireless advices received here late to-night.

These advices did not clear up the uncertain point as to whether or not the Virginian had on board any of the passengers or crew of the Titanic. The message was taken as indicating in the words "which she may rescue" that there were no survivors aboard at the time.

The only information received here to-night regarding the Titanic disaster was that the Carpathia had 675 persons aboard, including passengers and some of the crew, and was proceeding to New York with them.

The steamers Parisian and Virginian were reported searching for others of the Titanic's people. The Virginian was to give up her search after daylight and proceed here on her way to Liverpool. Being a mail boat, she is forced to make the utmost haste to her destination.

Other Ships Probably Too Late.

MONTREAL, April 15.—The two Allan Line steamships Vir-

ginian and Parisian, which were reported as having steamed toward the scene of the Titanic disaster, had not reported to the company here up to 10 o'clock to-night any definite news of what they had done.

The report that the Virginian had sent a wireless to the effect that she had rescued a number of passengers and then had re-transferred them to the Carpathia was not confirmed.

George Hannah, General Passenger Agent of the line, is of the opinion that the Virginian arrived on the scene too late to be of any assistance, and, being a mail boat, she proceeded on her voyage. She may not be in touch with the world until she nears the Irish coast.

Mr. Hannah thinks that the Parisian may have arrived in time to be of assistance to the Titanic. If she did not, he thinks she would probably have spent some time cruising around in search of persons clinging to wreckage, and it is possible that some were saved in this way.

Sir Montague Allan, head of the Allan Line stated to The New York Times's representative to-night:

"We have heard no word from the Virginian, and have received no official message as to the whereabouts of the passengers. We have received, however, a Marconigram dispatched to New York stating that the Carpathia had arrived on the spot where the Titanic had been, that all the Titanic's boats had been accounted for, and that 655 of the passengers had been saved, but that the rest had gone down with the Titanic. This is not official

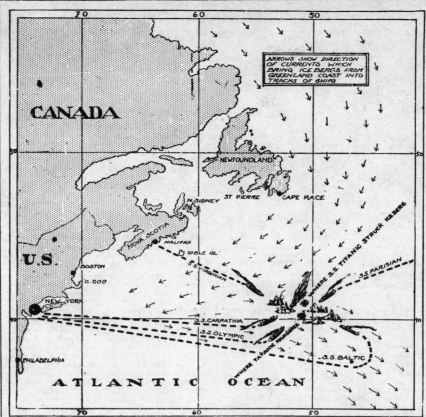

Where the Titanic Hit the Iceberg, and Where She Foundered, and How Other Liners Answered the Wireless Calls for Help.

and we have no official news yet. I shall be very glad to make public the text of any official news we receive."

LINER'S GRAVE TWO MILES DEEP

Location of Titanic's Deathbed Placed by Canadian Marine Official.

HALIFAX, April 15.—The deathbed of the ten-million-dollar steamer Titanic, and of probably many who must have been dragged down with her, is two miles, at least, below the surface of the sea.

The calculation was made by an official of the Government Marine Department, who finds that depth on the chart at a point about 500 miles from Halifax and about 70 miles south of the Grand Banks, where he believes the Titanic went down.

This location is midway between Sable Island and Cape Race, and in line with those dangerous sands, which, however, might have proved a place of safety had there been time to run the Titanic there and beach her.

The Canadian warship Niobe, which has one of the most powerful wireless equipments of any vessel in this vicinity, was unable to get in tune with any of the ships in the vicinity of the Titanic disaster, and the Government station at Camperdown heard only fragmentary relays of messages.

Lloyds agent here had not received late to-night any official notification of the loss of the Titanic.

EXCITED CROWDS AT WHITE STAR OFFICE

Continued from Page 1.

Mr. Franklin said it was an error, and that the loss would certainly not reach that figure if the Carpathia had saved the number reported. THE TIMES dispatch reported that number as 655.

It may be relied upon that everything that reached Cape Race concerning the loss of the Titanic is contained in THE TIMES dispatch from that point.

Mr. Franklin admitted at 10 o'clock last night that he had not been able to get into communication with the Parisian or the Virginian. He admitted then for the first time that Capt. Haddock's message had held out little hope that the passengers had been taken aboard these steamers.

"What Capt. Haddock did say," conceded Mr. Franklin, sadly, "was discouraging to such a belief."

Vincent Astor Weeps in Office.

So reassuring was the tenor of the first reports of the accident and so late was it before the truth concerning the

disaster became known, that up to 11 o'clock last night there were few visitors at the White Star offices, though the telephones there were constantly in use answering inquiries of anxious friends and relatives of the Titanic's passengers.

Several frightened women, crying with anxiety, were among the first visitors, and presently Vincent Astor, son of Col. John Jacob Astor, arrived at the offices. He and A. J. Biddle, who accompanied him, were closeted with Mr. Franklin for some time, and when they left young Mr. Astor was crying. He refused to answer questions as to what he had heard about his father.

Vincent Astor reappeared in the offices of the steamship company shortly after 1 o'clock to-day. When told no list of the survivors had been received he buried his face in his hands and sobbed.

Sylvester Byrnes, private secretary to Isidor Straus, was another visitor at the offices. He said Jesse Straus, a son, was on the Hamburg-American liner Amerika and probably at that moment was passing the spot where the vessel carrying his father had sunk. Another son, Herbert, said Mr. Byrnes was on his way to Halifax, where, it had been at first reported, the passengers of the Titanic would be landed. He will not learn until this morning that the Titanic is at the bottom of the sea.

Shortly before midnight last night a brother of Frederick M. Hoyt, Commander of the Larchmont Yacht Club, who, with his wife, was a passenger on the Titanic, made inquiry at the offices of the steamship company, as did Leo Greenfield of 1,239 Madison Avenue, whose wife and son were in the ill-fated steamer.

A young man and woman, who declined to make known their identity, entered the offices of the company just before midnight.

"Is it true that the Titanic has sunk —are the stories in the evening papers true?" the young man inquired of a clerk.

He was told that the steamship had gone to the bottom.

"My God!" he exclaimed; "we are ruined. They are all lost."

The young woman became hysterical.

A Mr. Mardhoff also called to inquire whether Arthur Ryerson and the latter's family were safe. Mr. Ryerson, his wife, two daughters, and a son were coming back from England to attend the funeral of another daughter in Philadelphia, Mr. Mardhoff said.

J. B. Fourman called to ask for news of his brother.

Notables on the Steamer's List.

Notable passengers on the Titanic, whose faith was in doubt in the lack of definite advices as to the identity of the survivors, were Mr. and Mrs. John Jacob Astor, Major Archibald Butt, Aid to President Taft; Charles M. Hays, President of the Grand Trunk Pacific of Canada, his wife and daughter; W. T. Stead, Benjamin Guggenheim, F. D. Millet, the artist, and J. G. Widener of Philadelphia; Mr. and Mrs. Isidor Straus, Mr. J. B. Thayer, Vice President of the Pennsylvania Railroad, J. Bruce Ismay, President of the International Mercantile Marine, Henry B. Harris, the theatrical manager, and Mrs. Harris, and Col. Washington Roebling, builder of the Brooklyn Bridge.

A ray of hope appeared shortly before 11 o'clock last night in a message to New York from the operator of the Marconi wireless station at Sable Island, near the scene of the disaster. Answering an inquiry regarding the delivery of wireless messages to the passengers of the Titanic, the operator reported that it was difficult to deliver them, "as the passengers are believed to be dispersed among several vessels."

Even this faint indication that other vessels than the Carpathia had picked up survivors of the Titanic was eagerly seized upon by thousands of relatives and friends of those who had set sail on her.

Solomon Guggenheim, Robert and Mrs. Robert G. Guggenheim with Miss Nettie Gerstle and Louis Rothschild, heard of the sinking of the Titanic as they left a Broadway theatre last night. Benjamin Guggenheim was a passenger on the Titanic, and his relatives had believed him safe. They hurried to the White Star offices, but could get no information beyond the statement that 675 persons were on the Carpathia.

Among those who made inquiry in the offices of the company last night was Miss Wheelock of 317 Riverside Drive, who requested information relative to the safety of her brother-in-law and sister, Dr. and Mrs. D. W. Marvin, who, she said, were returning in the Titanic on a honeymoon trip.

Shortly after 11 o'clock last night Mr. Franklin said he had received a dispatch stating that the Carpathia rescued survivors from a small fleet of lifeboats of Canada, his wife and daughter more than eight hours after the Titanic is reported to have sunk. In his opinion, the Carpathia is hastening with all possible speed to New York City, in order that the persons

Side View of the Lost White Star Liner Titanic, the Largest Steamship Ever Launched.

Length over all, 882 feet 6 inches. Breadth over all, 92 feet 6 inches. Breadth over boat deck, 94 feet. Height of funnels above boat deck, 81 feet 6 inches. Distance from top of funnel to keel, 175 feet. Number of steel decks, 11. Passengers accommodated, 2,500. Crew, 860. Tonnage, registered, 45,000. Number of Watertight bulkheads, 15. Tonnage, displacement, 66,000. Approximate cost, $7,500,000. Height from bottom of keel to top of captain's house, 105 feet 7 inches. Height of funnels above casing, 72 feet.

taken from the lifeboats, who were suffering from exposure, might obtain medical attention with the least possible delay. In the cabins were 230 women and children, but it is not known how many there were among the 710 third-class passengers. In the first cabin there were 128 women and 15 children, and in the second cabin 79 women and 8 children.

The rush to the White Star's offices will come to-day. Then the public will know of the disaster to the Titanic, and White Star officials prepared last night to receive the throngs they expect to-day.

Not until Thursday night, however, and possibly not until Friday morning, can first hand knowledge of the wreck be obtained, for it is not until then, Mr. Franklin said last night, that he expected the Carpathia to reach this port. Already he has wired to Capt. Haddock and has tried to reach the Carpathia to obtain a list of those who were rescued. This will probably be obtained by wireless before the Carpathia reaches port. What names may appear upon it none can tell except that Mr. Franklin and steamship men in general realize that of all the 655 there probably will be the name of only a man or two.

The "rule of the sea," that law by which the women and children are always first taken from a sinking ship, is frequently written of in romances of the sea. There is no such rule that seafaring men recognize, but there needs no rule to cause men to stand aside in time of danger, said Mr. Franklin last night.

"It is a matter of courtesy extended by the stronger to the weaker, on land as well as on sea," he added, "and we know, therefore, that mostly women and children—perhaps only women and children—are passengers aboard the Carpathia. Capt. Smith, I am sure, went down with his ship. Capt. Haddock said no word of him, but I know Capt. Smith. He is that kind of a man."

So far no details have been received as to how such passengers as were rescued were taken from the doomed steamer. All these must wait until the Carpathia reaches here or until she gets within wireless range.

Capt. Haddock's wireless telling of the sinking of the ship and the records of the Cape Race wireless station which received the Titanic's first call for help afford some idea of what must have happened aboard the now sunken vessel.

The Titanic struck at 10:25 o'clock Sunday night in latitude 41.16 north and longitude 50.14 west. The huge iceberg with which she collided stove in her bow plates, and just half an hour later the big ship flashed out over the sea the news that she was sinking by the head. From then until 12:27 o'clock yesterday morning the Titanic's wireless flashed news of her condition and appeals for immediate help out over the water. Then the last crash of the instrument died out in an indistinguishable blur.

Did the Titanic sink then? It is just possible she did, for until that instant the sending of the operator aboard the big steamer had been clean cut and deliberate. His touch was as sure and steady as though his ship was in no danger, and his brother operators at Cape Race are certain that while the ship rode the waves and his instruments were intact the Titanic's operator would have kept up his messages to the world.

If the vessel disappeared from sight then, however, such of her lifeboats as had put off from the ship must have been at a safe distance to escape the suction of the huge steamer as she passed out of sight. It was at exactly 11:36 o'clock that the Titanic's wireless notified the Olympic, then speeding to her rescue that the women and children were being put off in boats. With the work started at this time there remained time for the life boats to be propelled far from the sinking vessel in the fifty-one minutes that intervened.

There is the chance, however, that the smaller boats could not live in the ice field into which the Titanic had run, or keeping afloat there, could not be driven through a sea as thick as molasses to a safe distance from the Titanic. Some of them may have been drawn down with the mother ship. The bigger vessel's extraordinary powers of suction were exemplified when she left her Southampton pier and jerked the steamer New York from her moorings. But for the occupants of such lifeboats as lived the scene must have been almost as terrible as for those whose lot it was to stay aboard the doomed vessel.

It was night, and the darkness must have redoubled the terrors of embarking in lifeboats in a sea of ice. From the Titanic it is probable that rockets were sent up and Coston lights burned to cast their wierd light over the scene, and as boat after boat, loaded to its capacity with women and children, was pushed off from the side, the attempts at cheers which must have gone up from those left behind only can be imagined until the survivors reach here to tell of it.

Wives and sisters must have sat in the small boats, slowly drawing away from the wounded leviathan, from whose decks husbands and brothers waved farewells. At the gangways there must have been partings like those in a death-chamber, for the fate of those who remained aboard must have been known. With the Titanic in such shape that it was necessary to send off the women and children within an hour of the time the steamer struck, there could have been none aboard so optimistic that he could see hope of relief.

Capt. Smith and his officers must have known that their vessel, the biggest one afloat, was gasping and straining in her last effort to keep her bow above water. They must have felt in the shiverings and trembling of the big vesel that the end was a matter of minutes only, and yet knowing this, Capt. Haddock's dispatch says simply that the women and children were put off. There is no rule of the sea, but the courtesy of the sea must have been observed by cabin passenger and steerage traveler alike.

What provision had been made to meet such a catastrophe aboard the Titanic is not known here. Mr. Franklin admitted that he did not even know the number of lifeboats the big steamer carried, except that they were in such number as were required by the British law.

Satistics of the Titanic's life-saving equipment were not available at the office of the Local Steamboat Inspecting Service, for the vessel had not yet entered this port, the cruise which had ended beneath an ice covered sea off Newfoundland being the Titanic's maiden voyage for this port. The statistics for the Olympic, the Titanic's sister ship, were available, however, and it is probable that there was very little difference in the equipment provided for the Titanic and that of the Olympic, for the vessels are almost identical in size and capacity.

These are the figures for the Olympic. She carries sixteen lifeboats and four collapsible boats, or rafts. These are calculated to carry at least 1,180 people. The requirements do not make it obligatory for a vessel to carry accommodations sufficient for its complete passenger and crew list. It would be an impossibility to do so, it was pointed out yesterday, for it would be impossible to carry such a number of lifeboats and the rafts in positions where they could be quickly lowered into the water.

The life preserver requirement demands a sufficient number to accommodate passengers and crew, even when the vessel is filled to capacity. The Olympic carries 3,455 life preservers and 48 life buoys. This fulfills the requirements of the British Board of Trade, and the United States Inspection Service simply sees that each vessel meets the requirements of its own Government.

But the life preservers and buoys which the Titanic carried can have been of little service in the emergency which the big ship encountered. Between the time she collided with the iceberg and the probable time that the big vessel sank there were just two hours and two minutes to transfer all of her passengers and crew, 2,120 persons all told, into the lifeboats. The sixteen lifeboats and four collapsible rafts were calculated to accommodate 1,171 persons, more than one-half of those who awaited rescue aboard the Titanic. There was time for every one to leave the ship, but the means of taking them off were lacking.

Had it been possible for the Carpathia, the Parisian, the Virginian, or the big Olympic to reach her in time, the Titanic might have relayed her passengers to any of these boats in the two hours and two minutes of life which remained to her after the collision.

But it was not until daybreak that the Carpathia arrived on the scene, and she was the first by probably five hours to get there. Just what the Carpathia found will not be known in detail until she gets within wireless range or reaches this port. It can be imagined readily, however, that what her crew and passengers saw when they drew close to the scene of the collision, was several small boats in a sea of ice, jammed to overflowing with women and children, and with only men enough aboard to handle the craft. About them floated bits of wreckage from the giant Titanic, and besides this only ice.

It would not have been until they were almost upon the small boats that the Carpathia's crew could have seen them, but those in the lifeboats must have strained their eyes, peering through the lifting gloom for a glimpse of smoke which should tell them that rescue was at hand. It was about daybreak when the Carpathia sighted the survivors.

With the last of her life the big ship screamed out her location that all might hear and hasten to the spot. Steamers from every point of the compass had heard and had heeded her wireless calls. Those in the small boats could not but know that from all sides help was coming as fast as power could be generated to drive the engines.

For hours in the darkness the small boats must have drifted about, their helmsmen bringing them back over the scene of the disaster as fast as they fell away, and as the first dim rays of daylight began to break up the black covering of night, there must have been eyes in every boat sweeping the sea in all directions for a glimpse of the ship that was to save them.

What caused the big steamer to sink may never be known. Probably those who could tell with authority carried the secret of the vessel's sinking to the bottom with them. She struck the iceberg bow on. So much is known from the first wireless which the Titanic sent out, and from this very fact it was concluded at first that the big steamer was in no danger.

Mr. Franklin called her unsinkable, and last night when he knew at last that the pride of his line was beneath the ocean he could not seem to comprehend that the steamer had sunk.

Nor can any one else ashore say now what sent the big vessel to the bottom. It may have been that the shock deranged the mechanism by which her water-tight compartments are closed. Another conjecture advanced last night was that there was a spur of the iceberg under water on to which the Titanic ran when she collided with the visible part of the berg, and that this spur opened holes in plates further back along the keel. Either or both of these things may have happened.

NOTED MEN ON THE LOST TITANIC

Col. Jacob Astor, with His Wife; Isidor Straus and Wife, and Benj. Guggenheim Aboard.

BRUCE ISMAY, LINE DIRECTOR

C. M. Hayes of Grand Trunk and J. B. Thayer of Penn. Lines Also Passengers.

MAJOR BUTT ON THE LIST

Clarence Moore, George D. Widener, H. B. Harris, W. D. Stead, and Frank D. Millet Among the Others.

Following are sketches of a few of the well-known persons among the 1,300 passengers on the lost Titanic. The fate of most of them at this time is, of course, not known. Col. John Jacob Astor and Mrs. Astor, Isidor Straus and Mrs. Straus, J. Bruce Ismay, Managing Director of the White Star Line; Benjamin Guggenheim, and Frank D. Millet, the artist, are perhaps the most widely known of the passengers.

Others are Charles M. Hays, President of the Grand Trunk Railway; Henry B. Harris, the theatrical manager; James B. Thayer, Vice President of the Pennsylvania Railroad; William T. Stead, Jacques Futrelle, the author; George D. Widener of Philadelphia, Clarence Moore of Washington, and Major Archibald Butt, President Taft's aid.

COL. JOHN JACOB ASTOR.

Wealthy Society Man and an Author and Inventor as Well.

Col. John Jacob Astor, the American head of the Astor family, has held a prominent place in the life of this city for many years. Not alone has he been a conspicuous club member and leader of society, but he has engaged in vast business activities that gave him a place of rank apart from his immense fortune and social attainments.

Col. Astor put up and owned more hotels and skyscrapers than any other New Yorker. At one time he was a Director in twenty or more large corporations, including railways. His fortune has been estimated at from $100,000,000 to $200,000,000.

Col. Astor was born at the old Astor estate at Ferncliff, Rhinebeck-on-the-Hudson, July 13, 1864. He was the son of William Astor, a grandson of William B. Astor, and great-grandson of the original John Jacob Astor, founder of the house in America.

John Jacob Astor spent his early schooldays at St. Paul's, Concord, N. H. Thereafter he went to Harvard, where he was graduated in 1888. After exten-

Some of the Notable Passengers Who Were on Board the Titanic.

Henry B. Harris · Major Butt · © Harris & Ewing – Col. W. Roebling · J. M. C. Smith · Isidor Straus · J. B. Thayer · F. D. Millet · Mrs. G. D. Widener

Mrs. J. J. Astor · Mrs. and Mr. B. Guggenheim · J. J. Astor © Underwood & Underwood.

FOUR NEW YORKERS ON THE SUNKEN LINER.

sive travels through Europe and the West Indies, he returned to this city to devote himself to the management of the great estates which had been left to him by his father. Unlike his cousin, William Waldorf Astor, who became a British subject, Col. Astor declared repeatedly that he was proud to be an American.

Three years after leaving Harvard he was married, in 1891, to Miss Ava L. Willing of Philadelphia. They had two children—William Vincent Astor, who is now 20, and Alice, 10 years old. Soon after his marriage Col. Astor began building large hotels, among them the old Waldorf, later joined to the Astoria; the St. Regis, Knickerbocker, and the Astor. He also owned the Astor House.

Col. Astor got his title by appointment on Gov. Morton's staff, and afterward served in the Spanish-American War. Long before that time, however, he developed a bent for invention in the laboratory of his Fifth Avenue house, working out, among other inventions, a pneumatic device for renovating macadam roads, for which he was awarded first prize at the Chicago Exposition. He wrote several books also, among others "A Journey in Other Worlds," a curiously imaginative work, dealing with supposed life on Saturn and Jupiter.

In October last Col. Astor's estate was assessed for \$107,000,000 on 700 separate city parcels, the complete list of which was published for the first time in THE NEW YORK TIMES. This did not include all that the first John Jacob Astor had, huge slices having gone to the Chanlers, Jays, and others.

JOSEPH BRUCE ISMAY.

Chairman and Managing Director of the White Star Line.

Joseph Bruce Ismay has been considered one of the most prominent ship owners in the world. As chairman and managing director of the White Star line he took passage on the Titantic on her maiden voyage.

He was born in Liverpool on Dec. 12, 1862, and was the son of the late Thomas Henry Ismay, of Dawpool, Cheshire, England. In 1888, he married Julia Florence Schieffelin, daughter of George R. Schieffelin, of this city. They have two sons and two daughters.

Mr. Ismay was educated at Elstree and Harrow. His residence is at 15 Hill Street, Sandheys, Mossley Hill, Liverpool. He has been a member of the Reform Club of that city, and a prominent clubman in London.

STRAUS A FAMOUS MERCHANT.

Member Both of R. H. Macy & Co. and Abraham & Straus.

Isidor Straus, who, with Mrs. Straus, was aboard the Titanic, was born in Rhenish Bavaria on Feb. 6, 1845. His father's family came to this country in 1852 and settled at Talbotton, Ga. Isidor obtained a common school education, which he supplemented with a classical course at Collinsworth Institute. It was his ambition to enter West Point Military Academy, and probably he would have done so had not the war broken out just at the time that he had prepared himself for that institution. He was then 16 years old, and, with the war fever in the air, he volunteered for the Confederate Army. He assisted in the organization of a company of which his comrades had chosen him Lieutenant.

When he offered himself, however, he was informed that the Confederacy did not have the guns sufficient to arm its men, and wanted no boys, and the only thing left for him to do was to enter his father's store and take the place of a clerk who had joined the Southern Army. Here he remained for two years, when an opportunity came to him to go to England and remain in the employ of a company there until the close of the war. His father had in the meanwhile moved to Columbus, Ga., and was seriously thinking of moving to Philadelphia to start anew in business. His son favored New York instead, and, his advice prevailing, the family came to New York and the firm of L. Straus & Son was organized and began dealing in earthenware. The success of this venture led the firm to branch out into porcelains and chinaware, and as the other sons of Lazarus Straus reached the age at which they could enter business the firm name was changed. From that time the firm of L. Straus & Sons grew in reputation until it was known not only in this country, but throughout the world.

CLARENCE MOORE.

Washington Banker One of the Best-Known Sportsmen in America.

Special to The New York Times.

WASHINGTON, April 15.—Clarence Moore of 1,748 Massachusetts Avenue, a passenger on the Titanic, is one of the best-known sportsmen in America. He is Master of Hounds of the Chevy Chase Hunt, and on his visit to England from which he is returning he is said to have purchased twenty-five brace of hounds from the best packs in the north of England. His present wife is Miss Mabelle Swift, daughter of the late E. C. Swift of Chicago. She said to-day that her husband's trip abroad had been for pleasure.

Mr. Moore is a member of the New York Yacht Club and the Travelers' Club of Paris, besides the Metropolitan, the Chevy Chase, and the Alibi Clubs of Washington. Socially he is one of the best-known men in Washington.

He was born in Clarksburg, West Va., in 1865, and when he finished his education in Dufferin College in Ontario he interested himself in the development of mineral wealth of that State as did the late Senator Stephen B. Elkins and Henry Gassaway Davis. Since 1890 Mr. Moore has lived in Washington, having business connections with the banking and brokerage firm of Hibbs & Co.

Mr. Moore's first wife was Alice McLaughlin, daughter of Franklin McLaughlin of Philadelphia. She died in 1897, leaving two children, Frances Sarah Preston and Samuel Preston Moore. He married Miss Mabelle Swift on June 20, 1900. By his second marriage he has two children, Jasper and Clarence, Jr.

FRANK D. MILLET'S CAREER.

Noted Artist Famed as War Correspondent and Traveler.

Frank D. Millet, a noted artist and correspondent, was born at Mattapoisett, Mass., in 1846. His adventurous temperament led him to enlist as a drummer boy at the beginning of the Civil War. He was soon promoted to the position of assistant in the surgeons' corps, which he held for a year, seeing a great deal of active service.

When the war was over, he returned to Massachusetts and entered Harvard. On graduation he went into journalism, joining the staff of the Boston Advertiser. Later he was City Editor of the Boston Courier and head of the Boston Saturday Evening Gazette.

In 1871 he took up the study of art at the Royal Academy in Antwerp, where he won a much-coveted prize in his first year. His success obtained for him the position of secretary to Charles Francis Adams when the latter was appointed commissioner to the Vienna Exposition of 1873. Though only 27, Millet managed there to keep up his art studies, do his duties as secretary and report the exposition for two New York newspapers.

In 1876 he returned to his native country and got to work harder than ever. Not only did he report the Centennial Exposition at Philadelphia for the Boston Advertiser, but he found time to assist John La Farge in decorating Trinity Church, Boston's most famous place of worship.

In 1877 he became war correspondent for the New York Herald in the Russo-Turkish War and acquitted himself so brilliantly that his work attracted the attention of the editors of the London Daily Mail, who appointed him their correspondent to succeed the celebrated Archibald Forbes. Millet was by the side of the Russian General Skobeleff in a good part of the liveliest fighting in the war and wrote thrilling descriptions of the big events of the campaign. He also drew graphic sketches, and emerged from the war with no less than six decorations for bravery under fire.

After that he went to Paris and devoted himself for a while to serious art study. He was chosen a member of the Fine Arts Jury of the Paris Exposition in 1878. Returning to Boston, he married and settled down for a while, but in 1881 he was again on the move, making sketches for the Harpers in Europe. Soon after he settled down in Worcestershire, England, where his home has been ever since.

HENRY B. HARRIS.

Well-Known Theatrical Manager Who Has Won Many Successes.

Henry B. Harris, who leaped into prominence in the New York theatrical field only about half a dozen years ago as manager and producer, was, nevertheless, a veteran of many years' standing before metropolitan fame came to him, and is a member of an old theatrical family.

He was born in St. Louis Dec. 1, 1866. His father, William Harris, a theatrical manager of note, is now associated with the firm of Klaw & Erlanger. The son received his education at the public schools in that city and later in Boston, to which city his parents moved while he was yet a boy. It was in the Massachusetts capital that Harris got his first training as a theatrical man, becoming connected with the famous old Howard Athenaeum there. He remained identified with that house for several years, leaving it to become a partner in the firm of Rich & Harris, for many years active in the theatrical history of Boston. It was during his association with this firm that he laid the foundations of his future success by a number of highly successful ventures. Among the stars whom he managed in a number of successful plays at this time were May Irwin, Pete Dailey, and Mrs. Langtry.

MAJOR ARCHIBALD BUTT.

President's Aid Had Gone on a Special Mission to the Pope.

Special to The New York Times.

WASHINGTON, April 15.—Major Archibald Willingham Butt, President Taft's Military Aid, was returning on the Titanic after a visit to Rome, where he went to see the Pope and King Victor Emmanuel. He undoubtedly went there as a personal messenger from the President. He is supposed to have been bearing home to President Taft an important message from the Pope.

Major Butt has been one of the most popular officers in the army. He was born in Georgia forty-one years ago. For several years before the Spanish war he was a newspaper correspondent in Washington, representing at one time The Louisville Post, The Atlanta Constitution, The Nashville Banner, The Augusta Chronicle, and The Savannah News. From his first arrival in Washington he has been popular in society.

He accepted the position of First Secretary of the United States Legation at the City of Mexico when former Senator Matt W. Ransom of North Carolina was Minister, and remained there until the death of Ransom, when he returned to newspaper work in Washington. One of his diversions during his years of work as a newspaper writer was to write for magazines, and he produced several novels based on his life in Mexico and the South that rose to a more than ordinary level of finish and interest.

His entry in the army was due to the late Major Gen. H. C. Corbin, who was Adjutant General during the Spanish War and the years following, and who selected Butt as one of twenty young officers to go into the fifteen new volunteer regiments to go to the Philippines.

PHILADELPHIANS ON BOARD.

All Prominent Socially—Mr. and Mrs. George D. Widener Among Them.

Special to The New York Times.

PHILADELPHIA, Penn., April 15.—Relatives of passengers on board the Titanic who live in this city were frantic tonight over the lack of news from their friends, and the alarm grew as it became known that there was probably large loss of life on the steamship.

Mr. and Mrs. Arthur L. Ryerson, with their two daughters and son, were on the liner bound to this city to attend the funeral of their son, Arthur Larned Ryerson, Jr. He was killed in an automobile accident at Bryn Mawr a few days ago with J. Louis Hoffman of Radnor. The home of the family is at Haverford.

On the Titanic were George D. Widener of Lynnewood Hall, Elkins Park; his wife, who was Miss Eleanor Elkins, and their son, Harry Elkins Widener. The Wideners went abroad a short time ago to purchase a trousseau for Miss Eleanor Widener, their daughter, and were presumably bringing the trousseau with them. Miss Widener remained in this city. Her engagement to Fitz Eugene Dixon, son of T. Henry Dixon of Chestnut Hill, was announced recently. Joseph E. Widener, brother of George D. Widener, who is one of the leading financiers of the country, said that the family was making every effort to obtain news.

Mr. and Mrs. John B. Thayer and their son, John B. Thayer, Jr., of Haverford, were on the liner. Mr. Thayer is Second Vice President of the Pennsylvania Railroad. Mrs. Thayer was Miss Marian L. Morris. Their son was a famous University of Pennsylvania football player. Efforts were made from time to time all day by relatives and Pennsylvania Railroad officials to reach them by wireless.

C. Duane Williams and his son, Richard Morris Williams, Jr., of Geneva, Switzerland, were on their way to visit Richard Norris Williams of Chestnut Hill. Mr. Williams said last night that his brother has lived in Geneva many years. He recently received a letter from him saying that he was coming to this country on the Titanic.

William C. Dulles of 319 South Twelfth Street, who has a country residence at Goshen, N. Y., was a passenger. He is a son of Mrs. Andrew Chevis Dulles. Keatly C. Dulles, a broker, of this city, is a cousin.

"All the News That's Fit to Print."

The New York Times.

THE WEATHER.
Rain to-day, colder to-night; fair, colder Friday; high, shifting winds.
For full weather report see Page 16.

VOL. LXII...NO. 20,151. NEW YORK, THURSDAY, MARCH 27, 1913.—TWENTY-TWO PAGES. ONE CENT In Greater New York, Jersey City and Newark. | Elsewhere, TWO CENTS.

FLOOD COSTS 3,000 LIVES IN TWO STATES; $100,000,000 WORTH OF PROPERTY WIPED OUT; FIRES ADD TO HORROR IN STRICKEN DAYTON

ADRIANOPLE WON BY THE ALLIES

Fortress Is Stormed and Captured After a Terrible Battle Lasting Three Days.

TURKS SET FIRE TO CITY

Blow Up Barracks and Magazines—Flames Devastating Many Quarters.

SHUKRI PASHA SURRENDERS

Hands Sword to Savoff—Mines Destroy a Bulgar and a Servian Regiment.

TCHATALJA ALSO CAPTURED

Town Taken by Bulgarians After Fierce Two-Day Battle — Europe Thinks Latest Carnage Unjustified.

MUSTAPHA PASHA, March 26.—The fortress of Adrianople was taken by storm by the Bulgarians this morning after fighting of the most terrible character that had continued since Monday.

Flames are devastating the city at many points.

After the outlying fortifications had been captured the Turkish troops set fire to all their depots and stores as well as to the arsenal and the artillery park. They also blew up the barracks and a number of powder magazines.

Most of the population fled.

SOFIA, March 26.—Shukri Pasha, the Turkish commander in chief of Adrianople, surrendered to Gen. Savoff this afternoon. Bulgarian cavalry had previously entered the city.

An official account of the operations in the capture of Adrianople says:

"The commander of the second army received orders on March 23 to attack and carry the outlying positions of the Turks in the eastern section. The following day at 2 o'clock fire was opened in all sections by the field batteries, the Turks replying with siege guns. The duel lasted until 8 o'clock in the evening.

"Toward 3:30 o'clock the next morning the Bulgarian infantry advanced on the Kumdere, which they crossed at 4:15. At the same time the siege guns opened on the Turkish positions. The enemy replied with a violent infantry and artillery fire on the advancing columns, which, however, pushed forward, and at daybreak, at the point of the bayonet, carried the outlying positions. Twelve guns and 300 men were captured.

"Simultaneously the troops in the southern section captured Pamukryrty, and carried on an offensive action against Ouktabir and Dudjaror, while the Servian infantry occupied the hill to the northwest of Kadikeui and another Servian division captured Ekmktchikeui. The Danube Servian division attacked Papastepe.

"The siege artillery tried all day to master the Turkish guns and destroy the forts. Under cover of this the troops of the Eastern division continued to advance, and at 10 o'clock reached within 800 yards of a fort where 1,000 men and twenty-one guns were captured. These guns were at once brought into action against the enemy, and other forts were taken.

"In the course of the night the infantry destroyed a series of artificial obstacles, and at daybreak carried at the point of the bayonet the whole line of forts. The Turks began to destroy their stores, barracks, hospitals, and other buildings, and the city is on fire at several points."

Inhabitants Panic-Stricken.

At an early hour this morning fires were raging in various sections of the city. The maddened population, whose nerves had been shattered by the almost incessant bombardment for a period of over five months, were fleeing about the streets from one point to another, not knowing where to find shelter. Some of them rushed along the line of forts, daring the heavy infantry and artillery fire that was in progress.

The great artillery arsenal in the city was burning, and the barracks lying between the hospital and the northern forts were also in flames.

The entire line of fortresses defending the eastern side of the city was captured by the Bulgarians after a most spectacular assault at the point of the bayonet by long lines of infantry, which were strengthened rapidly by the second or reserve line.

In the advance on Adrianople herds of cattle were driven forward in order that the danger of mined trenches might be avoided. Soldiers clad in cuirasses and provided with shields cut and divided the wire entanglements surrounding the forts and bastioned walls, which were carried at the point of the bayonet.

The Mir says that the Servians in the northern and western sections fought valiantly, "although it was not their lot to capture the forts."

Fierce Battle at Tchatalja.

LONDON, Thursday, March 27.—Adrianople has fallen, after one of the most stubborn defenses in the history of warfare, and the Town of Tchatalja, according to a telegram received by the Bulgarian Legation in London last night, has suffered a like fate, falling into the hands of the Bulgarians after two days' desperate fighting. The Allies made just as determined an attack on the Tchatalja lines as they did on Adrianople.

Shukri Pasha, the defender of Adrianople, who held the town for 153 days against great odds, which included, be-

Continued on Page 7.

USHER'S GREEN STRIPE SCOTCH Is a Whisky of Matchless Merit.—Adv.

WE MAY GET SNOW TO-DAY.

Forecaster Scarr Predicts Passing of the Storm and Colder Weather.

Forecaster Scarr said last night that the unusual weather in and around New York in the last few days had been caused by the heavy rainfall which extended from the great lakes south to New Orleans and which centred last night over Cincinnati.

"We are getting a share of the rainstorm to-night," said the forecaster, "and for the twenty-four hours ending at 10 P. M. the rainfall in New York has been 1.24 inches. The temperature has been very varied during the storm. To-night it is at freezing point in Buffalo and 50 degrees in this city. The rain will continue until the centre of the storm has passed New York, to-morrow, when it will probably turn to snow, as it has done in Illinois and Iowa, and the temperature will be much colder."

When asked if New York was likely to be visited by a windstorm, Mr. Scarr said that he did not think so. The greatest velocity of the wind was forty-eight miles an hour at 11 o'clock yesterday morning. It might increase to that figure again to-day, but was not likely to blow harder than forty-five miles an hour.

With regard to the dark cloud that hovered over the city yesterday forenoon and caused some nervous people to get the idea a tornado was coming, the forecaster said that was ridiculous because New York was out of the tornado belt. That was only a squall, during which the wind rose to forty-five miles an hour and then died down again. The topographical conditions of New York prevent the city being subjected to tornadoes, he said.

POPE CELEBRATES MASS.

But His First Collective Audience Is Postponed Till April 4.

ROME, March 26.—Pope Pius celebrated mass early this morning, when he administered the communion to the servants of the household.

The physicians in attendance visited and examined the Pontiff both before and after the mass, and expressed their satisfaction with his condition. They, however, advised him to maintain caution and again to postpone his collective audience.

It was then decided that on April 3 the Pope would receive some of the Bishops, and on April 4 give his first collective audience since he was taken ill.

CUBAN PROBLEMS DELAYED.

Congress Closes Without Acting on Amnesty Bill or Solo Case.

HAVANA, March 26.—The session of Congress terminated this evening. The new Congress will convene on April 7.

The Senate passed the bill consenting to the submission to arbitration of the claims of Great Britain, France, and Germany for damages in the revolution of 1895-98, but in amended form, necessitating its resubmission to the House of Representatives.

No effort was made to obtain the permission of the House for the prosecution of Representative Solo, the author of the libelous attacks in the newspaper Cuba on American Minister Beaupré and Secretary of Legation Gibson.

The Amnesty bill was also left over for the new Congress.

SENATE PASSES HOME RULE.

Cullen Bill to be Sent to Assembly for Concurrence.

ALBANY, March 26.—Without opposition, the Senate passed to-day the Cullen bill designed to provide home rule for cities throughout the State. This measure carries amendments not included in the Levy home rule bill, which has passed the Assembly, and will be sent to that body for concurrence.

The Senate Insurance Committee's compromise workmen's compensation bill was reported favorably to-night.

The Wagner bill, designed to regulate labor in tenement houses, passed the Senate.

BLIZZARD IN SOUTHWEST.

Oklahoma and Northwest Texas in Clutch of a Snowstorm.

OKLAHOMA CITY, March 26.—A storm of the blizzard type has been raging in Oklahoma since midnight. Snow has fallen to a depth of three inches and is still falling. Street car service is blocked and train service is slow.

DALLAS, March 26.—An unusually heavy snowstorm swept Northwest Texas to-day, moving rapidly eastward. The storm visited sections where fields and gardens already are green. No serious damage resulted, the temperature barely touching the freezing point

LOST SAVING GRANDCHILDREN

Paralytic Man Got Two Out and Died Himself in Burning House.

When Michael Wehr's cottage at Town Dock Road and Hutchinson River, the Bronx, was burned last evening, Mr. Wehr, a retired business man of 67, partly disabled from paralysis, succeeded in rescuing his two grandchildren, who were asleep on the second floor, but he himself was penned in by the flames and suffocated before any one could get him out. The house was completely destroyed.

The children were the son and daughter of his daughter, Mrs. Samuel McCoy. Mr. and Mrs. Wehr and Mrs. McCoy were sitting in the living room downstairs when the fire was discovered. Mr. Wehr sent them to safety, and went upstairs for the children. He carried little Mamie downstairs and out to the porch. Then he made his way back through the smoke, and lifted his grandson, Samuel, in his arms, but before he could descend the stairs gave way with the onrush of the flames, and he stumbled to a window overlooking the garden. There young Christian Bloz, a neighbor, boosted another neighbor, Jack Matthews, until the latter was able to reach his arms to the little boy and jump with him to the ground. But the sweep of the flames drove Wehr from the window, and when they finally reached him he was dead.

The house stood at a part of the Bronx so remote and with thoroughfares so unlike the pavements further downtown, that the fire engines from the station at 229th Street and White Plains Road could not make their way through the mud, and had to reach the Town Dock Road by way of Mount Vernon. They came too late.

Latest Shipping News.

BY MARCONI WIRELESS—SS Celtic, (White Star Line,) from Liverpool to New York, was reported 1,184 miles east of Sandy Hook at 6:15 P. M.; due 30th, 8 A. M.

25 HOURS TO FRENCH LICK SPRINGS. "St. Louis Limited" via Baltimore & Ohio. Leave New York daily 10 A. M., arrive Springs 1:10 P. M. Through Sleepers to Mitchell, Ind. Parlor Cars beyond. Double daily service returning. Ticket Offices, 379 & 1,490 B'way, 7 Cortlandt St., and 4 Court St., Brooklyn.—Adv.

TOLL TAKEN BY THE FLOOD.

Lives	3,000
Property	$100,000,000

ESTIMATE OF THE DEAD.

OHIO.		INDIANA.	
Dayton	2,000	Peru	60
Piqua	540	Brookville	40
Columbus	100	Newcastle	3
Delaware	50	Lafayette	2
Middletown	100	Fort Wayne	6
Sidney	50	Indianapolis	50
Hamilton	12	Noblesville	2
Tippecanoe	3	Scattering	25
Tiffin	50	Total	188
Fremont	11		
Scattering	200		
Total	3,116		

Total in both States 3,304

NATION'S FORCES AID ON A HUGE SCALE

Wilson Puts Entire Government Machinery in Motion to Succor Flood Victims.

ARMY RATIONS FILL TRAINS

War Department Never Such a Hive of Industry in Time of Peace—National Appeal by Wilson.

Special to The New York Times.

WASHINGTON, March 26.—When President Wilson read the newspapers this morning and learned of the terrible loss of life and devastation caused by the floods in Ohio he hurried over to his office in the Executive Building and immediately set about finding ways and means of furnishing Federal aid to the stricken people of that State.

One of the first steps he took was to issue the following appeal to the Nation:

The terrible floods in Ohio and Indiana have assumed the proportions of a National calamity. The loss of life and the infinite suffering involved prompt me to issue an earnest appeal to all who are able, in however small a way, to assist the labors of the American Red Cross to send contributions at once to the Red Cross at Washington or to the local treasurers of the society. We should make this a common cause. The needs of those upon whom this sudden and overwhelming disaster has come should quicken every one capable of sympathy and compassion to give immediate aid to those who are laboring to rescue and relieve.

WOODROW WILSON.

The President also sent the following telegram to both Gov. Ralston at Indianapolis and Gov. Cox at Columbus, Ohio:

"I deeply sympathize with the people of your State in the terrible disaster that has come upon them. Can the Federal Government assist in any way?"

250,000 People Unsheltered.

The following telegram then came from Gov. Cox at Columbus, Ohio, to President Wilson:

"We have asked the Secretary of War this morning for tents, supplies, rations, and physicians. In the name of humanity see that this is granted at the earliest possible moment. The situation in this State is very critical. We believe that 250,000 people were unsheltered last night, and the indications are that before night the Muskingum Valley will suffer the fate of the Miami and Scioto Valleys."

The President telegraphed to Gov. Cox as follows:

"Have directed the Secretary of War immediately to comply with your request and to use every agency of his department to meet the needs of the situation."

Gov. Cox's appeal was for 50,000 tents and 100,000 rations.

Secretary of War Garrison was summoned and was with the President a good part of the day discussing the situation and giving directions to subordinate officers of the War Department for carrying out the measures of relief decided upon.

One of the first things that the President learned was that there was no authorization of law for sending Federal supplies to the distressed districts in the West. But he learned also that in cases of emergency his predecessors had directed the War Department to ship tents, rations, and medical stores to places where they were sorely needed, and that Congress had always subsequently authorized the expenditures made in these directions. President Wilson decided to follow the practice, law or no law, and in consequence the offices of the Quartermaster General and the Surgeon General of the Army were hives of industry within a brief time after the President and the Secretary of War got into action. Officers were ordered to the stricken districts, and telegrams for the shipment of tents, food, and medicines were transmitted to the proper offices at the nearest available points.

Press dispatches and information received from official sources brought home to the President that the emergency called for all the help that it was possible for the National Government and the people of the country to extend. His appeal for funds followed a call of Miss Mabel Boardman, Chairman of the Relief Board of the Red Cross, at the White House.

Wants Relief Steps Sanctioned.

In the course of the day President Wilson had a telephone conversation with Representative Oscar W. Underwood of Alabama, majority leader in the House of Representatives, in which he urged Mr. Underwood to propose legislation as soon as Congress meets in extra session sanctioning the use of War Department funds and supplies for the stricken people in the West and providing for recompensing the War Department for these expenditures. Mr. Underwood said he would give the matter his personal attention, and indicated there would be no difficulty in having the proposed legislation enacted. The President sent telgrams also to Senator Thomas S. Martin, Chairman of the Senate Committee on Appropriations, at Charlottesville, Va., and Representative John J. Fitzgerald, Chairman of the House Committee on Appropriations, at Brooklyn, telling them of his directions to the War Department, and asking them to see that money was appropriated when Congress assembled to enable the War Department to purchase supplies to replace those sent to the West.

Orders were issued by direction of Secretary Garrison to provide for the entire flood region of Indiana and Ohio the same service that was maintained last year in the Mississippi River floods. Major James E. Normoyle, Depot Quartermaster at Washington, and Major James A. Logan, Quartermaster, now on duty at the War College, were ordered to proceed to Columbus and organize an adequate system for the housing and feeding of the many thousands of homeless people. A sufficient number of officers from the Quartermaster Corps and the Engineer Corps will be assigned to duty under Major Normoyle to provide for depots for the care of the suffering in all the smaller towns in the Miami Valley.

Major Powell C. Fauntleroy of the Surgeon General's Office in Washington was ordered to proceed to Columbus and take charge of the organization of hospital facilities throughout the flood section. Major Gen. Carter at Chicago was directed to order eight medical officers from posts within convenient reach of Columbus to proceed there to be in readiness for duty in the field. The St. Louis depot of the Medical Department of the army was ordered to send at once by the first available train fifty hospital corps stewards and a complete store of supplies and medicines for a field hospital.

Gov. Cox, in addition to asking the Secretary of War for rations, tentage, and cots, requested 500 boxes of reserve dressing, 10,000 vaccine points, and 5,000 anti-typhoid vaccine ampules. All these supplies were started on the way to Columbus by express in sufficient quantity to meet present requirements.

Orders Troops to Be Ready.

The Secretary of War also took another step to provide for a possible demand for more help, and issued orders to all troops stationed in Western New York and in the Central Department in the States of Ohio, Michigan, Indiana, Illinois, and Missouri to be in readiness to entrain for the flood district at an hour's notice to render aid to the sufferers. Several thousand blankets were ordered shipped to Columbus, and a large number of stoves, both for camp kitchens and for warming hospital tents, were also ordered from St. Louis. Gov. Cox in his telegrams to the department said that thousands of people would probably have to live in army tents for a month or more.

In the opinion of the United States Weather Bureau, the flood situation in the West will grow worse instead of better, and additional flood warnings were issued to-day. Prof. Alfred F. Henry, who is in charge of the Bureau's River and Flood Division, said that the situation in the Mississippi and Ohio Valleys was grave, and there were indications of more rains in both valleys.

Prof. Henry's reports show that the Ohio River at Pittsburgh is nearing the flood stage, and it is believed that the water will have risen 26 feet, or 4 feet above the flood-mark, by to-morrow morning. At Cairo, Ill., where the Ohio River joins the Mississippi, the Ohio was 1½ feet below the flood stage to-day and was rising rapidly. South of Memphis the Mississippi is up to the flood limit, but Prof. Henry was unable to tell how serious conditions would be. There is grave danger of an overflow of the Ohio from Evansville to the mouth of the river. The conditions at Pittsburgh, he said, were the keynote to the situation, and it could not be determined what the result would be in the lower Ohio until these conditions had developed thoroughly.

The most encouraging thing, said Prof. Henry, was that the water at Dayton would go lower instead of higher. He attributed much of the damage done at Dayton to the fact that the banks of the river were low there, and not much of a rise was necessary to cause a flood.

Whole Federal Machinery Moving.

The entire machinery of the Government was put into operation for the relief of the stricken districts. The measures undertaken have never been equaled in time of peace. Within ten minutes after Gov. Cox's appeal was received by President Wilson the War and Treasury Departments and other Governmental agencies were rushing preparations for relief on an unprecedented scale.

The War Department received word late this afternoon that 300,000 rations would be shipped from Chicago this evening and 700,000 had been prepared, ready for shipment as soon as possible. In the emergency an arbitrary ration was arranged for

Continued on Page 5.

RUTLAND RAILROAD TO MONTREAL. Sleepers leave Grand Central daily 7:46 P. M. Particulars 1,216 B'way. 'Phone 6810 Madison.—Adv.

Gov. Cox Asks Nation's Aid in Meeting the Great Disaster.

FEW BODIES RECOVERED

Many Swept Away and Others in Houses Isolated by the Torrents.

FLAMES IN BUSINESS CENTRE

Beckel House Probably Destroyed—Fate of 250 Refugees There Is in Doubt.

65,000 PERSONS MAROONED

Piteous Appeals for Drinking Water and Food Made to Passing Boatman.

LIFE SAVERS ON THE WAY

Food Supplies Being Rushed from Cities—New York Relief Train Starts.

INDIANA SUFFERS LESS

Hopes to Care for Its Own Victims—Wilson Puts Federal Forces at Work to Aid Ohio.

DAYTON, Ohio, March 26.—Flames that destroyed eight buildings in Dayton's submerged business section early to-night cast a red glow over the flood-stricken city, adding to the alarm of thousands of refugees and marooned persons and causing those in safety to fear that some of the flood's prisoners in homes and office buildings might fall victims to this new danger.

Soon after the fire started notices were posted at the headquarters of the Emergency Committee that the city was under martial law, several companies of soldiers having arrived from neighboring Ohio cities.

The soldiers are being employed to patrol edges of the burned district and prevent further looting of homes which have been freed from the flood's grasp.

At 1:15 o'clock this (Thursday) morning State guardsmen shot and killed a man attempting to loot the homes of flood victims in Fifth Street.

The fire, which seemed to threaten the business section, was confined at first to the block bounded by Second and Third Streets and Jefferson and St. Clair Streets. In the block are the Fourth National Bank, Lattiman Drug Company, Evans Wholesale Drug Company, and several commission houses. It was impossible to get within two miles of the fire, and from that distance it looked as if explosions, probably of drugs, made the fire seem larger than it was.

At 9 o'clock the fire seemed to be dying out, but at 11:30 o'clock the flames started up again and obtained new headway.

It is impossible to tell accurately what buildings are burning, as the rushing torrents of water down the principal streets prevent any approach to the scene.

Reports are persistent that the Beckel Hotel has been burned. It is said that 250 persons took refuge there, but their fate is not known.

Scores of watchers on the National Cash Register building, nearly two miles from the scene, agreed in believing that the hotel had been destroyed, probably after 10 o'clock.

To-night's outbreak of flames followed several sporadic fires, which were believed to have been caused by natural gas, which is supplied to the city from the Indiana gas region.

One fire that broke out in the submerged centre of the city late this afternoon burned to the water's edge buildings between St. Clair and Jefferson Streets on the north side of East Main Street and threatened the business section.

One fire was started by an oil tank containing hundreds of gallons, which bumped into a submerged building near Fourth and Jefferson Streets.

The Dayton fire department worked from boats and dynamited the upper stories of several buildings in successful efforts to halt the flames.

Rescue squads worked frantically all day to-day, but up to a late hour to-night it was impossible to make any accurate estimate of the number who lost their lives in the flood. Conserva-

Distinguished scientists recommend the use of malt. In MALT BREAKFAST FOOD it is in its simplest and most useful form.—Adv.

"OUR GREATEST TRAGEDY," SAYS GOV. COX

He Estimates the Loss in Dayton at 1,000 Lives, in Telegram to The Times.

By Telegraph to the Editor of The New York Times.

COLUMBUS, Ohio, March 26.—The exact extent of the appalling flood in Ohio is still unknown. Every hour impresses us with the uncertainty of the situation. The waters have assumed such unknown heights in many parts of the State that it will be hardly less than a miracle if villages and towns are not wiped out of existence in the southern and southeastern parts of Ohio. The storm is moving south of east.

Please give great publicity to our appeal for help. My judgment is that there has never been such a tragedy in the history of our Republic.

Columbus was the centre of all activities to-day in behalf of the stricken cities. Every hour has apparently been filled with an accumulation of dramatic circumstances.

Piteous appeals have been made by men who were surrounded by water and confronted by the approaching conflagration in the City of Dayton. Every human energy has been exerted to give relief, and yet the measure of assistance has been comparatively small. It is the belief, however, that by daylight to-morrow those imprisoned in the business section of Dayton can be relieved.

The day began by a storm signal from the Weather Bureau, advising that there would be a dangerous rise in the waters of the Muskingum River.

All towns along its course, including Zanesville and Marietta, were advised. Before noon the situation assumed a critical aspect at Zanesville, and the historic "Y" bridge was blown up with dynamite. The loss of life in Zanesville is uncertain, because all telephone communication ceased at noon.

Marietta lies further south on the Ohio River. It cannot be reached, but it is safe to assume that the same devastating results at Zanesville were carried on to Marietta.

A flood situation developed in the Maumee and Sandusky Valleys, in Northwestern Ohio, but the damage to life and property was nothing compared to that in the south.

The one great tragedy remains—the Dayton situation. In many respects it is absolutely without parallel in the history of the Republic.

The early morning reports were that the water was receding, and that the loss of life would not be more than one hundred. It soon developed, however, that this city, which is built on several hills and in the valleys of four streams, is unable to send to the outside world any accurate idea of the real loss that has been sustained.

North Dayton reported in itself a loss of 100 lives. Later precisely the same situation was reported from Riverdale. West Dayton is almost completely under water, and the houses in Edgemont, a residential section, are so deep in the flood that great destruction to life and property has certainly ensued there.

On the high lands of South Park and East Dayton pockets had been developed and people were drowned on apparent elevations where it would seem naturally impossible.

The water at Fifth and Brown Streets, which is twenty-five or thirty feet above the elevation in the business section, is reported to be ten feet in depth.

At this time a river, wild and turbulent, four miles wide, is sweeping through the business section of Dayton, to say nothing of the overflow in the residential sections.

Telephone communication was established before the day was over with four points in the city. Bell, the intrepid telephone operator, reported first that he had sent scouts into the different parts of the city by boat.

His belief at daylight was that the loss of life had been overestimated, but by 10 o'clock it was known that easily 500 persons had been drowned. This evening we cannot resist the belief that the loss will not be less than 1,000.

Little by little the facts are becoming known. The Miami River enters Dayton directly north and south, separating North Dayton from Riverdale. It then makes a complete turn west and runs about three-fourths of a mile before it turns directly at right angles to the south. These bends have been the undoing of the city and caused the breaks in the levee.

Not until to-day was it apparent that between 10,000 and 12,000 people are penned up in the business houses, skyscrapers, hotels, and the Young Men's Christian Association, making it apparent that the flood came so rapidly that the business community was unable to reach the hills of the city.

The City Hall is patrolled by a number of policemen inside, and it is so situated as to enable the officers to make more or less accurate estimates of the number of people in the business section.

Fire broke out in the square bounded by St. Clair, Jefferson, Second and Third Streets soon after noon. The blaze was noticed first in a drug store. It swept north and destroyed the St. Paul Evangelical Church, fronting on Library Park. The flames then shot to the south through the wholesale district, consuming two large wholesale liquor houses and threatening the Fourth National Bank Building.

The fire is still burning to-night. We were advised by telephone to-night that people could be seen on the roofs of the buildings in the imperiled square, and that they were jumping from one structure to another, keeping safely out of the way of the flames. The water at this time had receded to about five feet in that part of the city.

The appeal came in very dramatic words over the telephone to the State House that unless boats were sent at once from some part of the stricken district the loss of life would be tremendous.

This evening it developed that the rescue from this square was complete, and that no sacrifice in human life ensued.

The Beckel Hotel, immediately across the street, was on fire at noon, but the flames were put out. Howard, from the Home Telephone Building, reported that the roof of the Beckel House was black with people, standing guard over their safety point.

South of the stricken square is another wholesale section, and it developed that about thirty-five women and children were in several of the buildings.

About 3 o'clock the flames leaped across Third Street and attacked the square bounded by Third, Fourth, Jefferson, and St. Clair Streets. Lowe Brothers' paint store was destroyed, and another tremendous sacrifice in human life was imminent.

Fifteen men in the Home Telephone Building succeeded, however, in rescuing the women and children by the aid of a block and tackle, getting them into the Beaver Power Building, a fireproof structure, where they are to-night.

Instructions have been given from Columbus to the militia in the southern part of Dayton to give vigilant eye to the fire district, and if the flames start in the direction of the Home Telephone Building and the Beaver Power Building to risk passage through the turbulent river, which is now running through the city, with boats.

To-morrow morning at daylight fifty boats will go into the business district from South Park. The naval militia, with 100 boats, leave Toledo at midnight.

The Federal life-saving crew, with equipment, will arrive at Dayton from Cleveland by way of Toledo at daylight. So, unless the developments during the night are unseemly, the whole situation ought to be measurably well in hand to-morrow forenoon.

We are disquieted, however, to-night by the report from the Lewistown Reservoir that the wind has changed to the north and the water is beating against the banks on the south shore, which has been standing the pressure and impulse of the waves for ten days.

If the reservoir should give way, then the wildest imagination could probably not bring an accurate impression of what will happen in Dayton.

JAMES M. COX, Governor.

tive estimates put the number at 500 and 800, while others figured that it was likely to reach 2,000.

George F. Burba, representing Gov. Cox, and J. H. Patterson, head of the relief work here, thought at noon that the loss of life from the flood would be between 500 and 1,000 persons. Both said, however, that the estimates were based solely on conjectures and rumors, and that the death list might be much greater or much less.

At 6 o'clock this evening J. H. Miller, Secretary of the Board of Health, estimated that the death list would reach 800.

It was reported that the National Cash Register Company had ordered 800 coffins for immediate delivery.

The known dead are:

ANTON SAETELL, grocer, Vine and Main Streets, killed in an explosion.
Mrs. ANTON SAETELL, drowned.
Unknown woman found near by, hanging on wire.
Mrs. A. B. BISH, aged 65.
Miss FLORENCE BISH, aged 27.
Miss VIOLA BISH.
Mrs JOHN BISH.
Mrs. LUCY ABEL, aged 50, died after being rescued near Miami Hospital.

The entire Bish family excepting John, son of one of the drowned women and husband of another, perished in the flood.

Reports that Fire Chief Ramby lost his life while attempting to reach a floating house have not been confirmed.

The arrival of motor boats late to-night gave hope that by to-morrow the northern section of the city, now cut off by the Big Miami's waste of waters, may be penetrated, and then may be learned the fate of hundreds who were imprisoned by the torrent sent down from the broken reservoir.

It was impossible to ascertain, even approximately, the number of persons who might have been marooned in this section and died after being trapped by flood and fire. Nevertheless, rescue work went steadily on, and about 3,000 persons were housed in places of refuge to-night, most of them in buildings of the National Cash Register Company.

Late this afternoon several refugees brought in from Simpson Street told stories that gave an insight into conditions in East Dayton, hitherto unreached. They said they knew of no loss of life in that section, because many had taken warning and fled.

Sixty-five persons were marooned in the Central Police Station.

Nothing had been heard up to to-night from Mayor Phillips of Dayton or from Adjt. Gen. Woods, marooned, it was believed, in North Dayton.

At least 65,000 persons are imprisoned in homes and business buildings. It is feared that their two days' imprisonment, with accompanying hunger and fright, have caused tremendous sufferings. The flood came with such suddenness that food supplies in homes were whisked away by the torrent that reached to second floors in almost the flash of an eye. Skiffs skirted the edge of the flooded district, attempting to take food to those whom it was impossible to carry off, but the fierce current greatly retarded this work.

Two oarsmen, Fred Patterson and Nelson Talbott, who braved the current that swirled through the business section of the city to-day, reported that the water at the Algonquin Hotel, at the southwest corner of Third and Ludlow Streets, was 15 feet deep.

From windows in the hotels and business buildings hundreds of marooned begged piteously for food. The oarsmen think many persons must have perished in the waters' sudden rush through the streets.

Houses Drift Down Main Street.

At the intersection of Main and Third Streets, the city's principal corner, they said they saw houses and many small structures drift swiftly down between imposing office buildings that formed banks for the muddy torrents.

"By careful steering and strong rowing we penetrated to almost the centre of the city," said Mr. Patterson. "Our route was Warren Street to Jefferson, up Jefferson to Main, thence to Third Street, to Ludlow, to Second. Everywhere people yelled to us to rescue them, but it was impossible, for we were barely able to keep afloat.

"Large amounts of money were offered us to take persons from perilous positions. The windows of the Algonquin Hotel seemed filled with faces, and the same conditions prevailed at most of the buildings we passed. We did not see any bodies, but the loss of life must have been great."

Oarsmen who worked into the outskirts of the business section to-night reported that 250 persons were marooned in the Arcade Building and 200 in the Young Men's Christian Association Building. They were begging for water, while children in all the houses were crying for milk.

Volunteers were called for to-night to man boats that will brave the dangerous currents to-morrow in an attempt to get food to the suffering.

"Our greatest need is a dozen more motor boats and men to run them," was a sentence in an appeal sent out by J. H. Patterson, President of the National Cash Register Company, who is chairman of the Relief Committee. This gives an insight into the flood situation. Skiffs and rowboats cannot live in the torrents rushing through the city's principal streets.

Floods Hold Up Food Trains.

A shortage of provisions was threatened this afternoon, when it was reported that many relief trains, bound to Dayton from neighboring cities, had been stopped by high water. Every grocer in the city had been "sold out" before noon.

Late to-night, however, the first trainload of provisions from Cincinnati, together with a detail of policemen to help in the rescue work, reached here after being twelve hours on the road. This, with two cars from Springfield, relieved the immediate suffering. Word was received that a carload of supplies was on the way from Detroit.

The list of six known dead was added to this afternoon by the death of a refugee. It was reported late to-night that a number of dead had been found in houses at Fifth and Eagle Streets, but when rescuers worked their way into the partly submerged buildings they found some flood prisoners, who were weak from fright and hunger.

It is feared that the loss of life on the north side of the Great Miami River will be large. The water stood 7 feet deep in a large section of the city, lying across that river, when the rush from the break in the Laramie levee came. . There has been no communication with that part of the city since early Tuesday. Opinions differ as to whether persons, living there, knew the levee had let go before the water overwhelmed their homes.

A report that the dam above Dayton threatened to break added to the city's terror to-night. If the dam breaks it will pour in a flood that will hold up rescue work for days.

Vandals Have Been Looting.

A gang of roughs went through the southern part of the city to-night in-

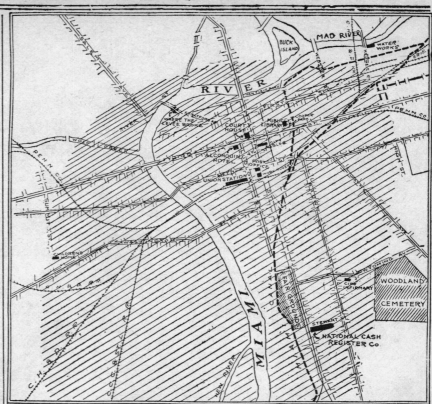

The Flooded Area of Dayton.

Water Covered the Lightly Shaded Portion to Depths as Great as Eighteen Feet. This Area, Which Is the Heart of the City, Is Two and One-Half Miles Wide and Three Miles Long.

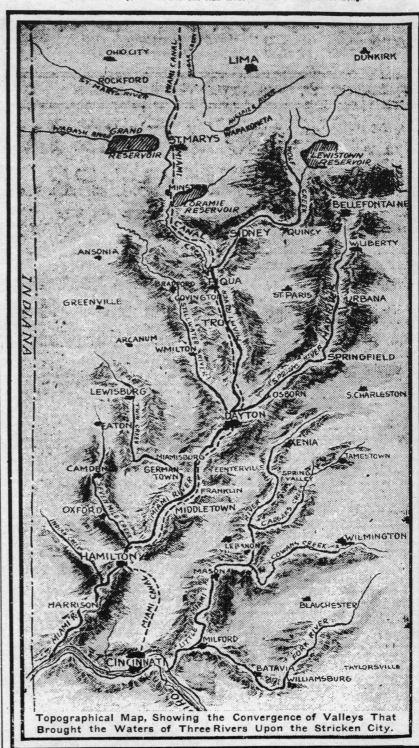

Topographical Map, Showing the Convergence of Valleys That Brought the Waters of Three Rivers Upon the Stricken City.

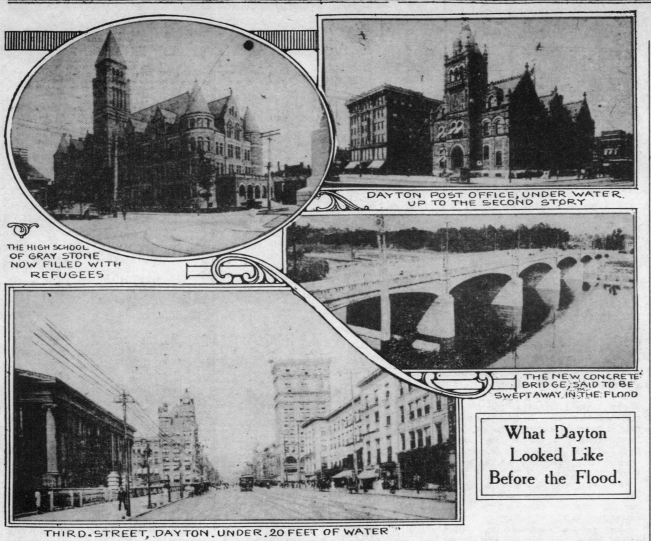

THE HIGH SCHOOL OF GRAY STONE NOW FILLED WITH REFUGEES

DAYTON POST OFFICE, UNDER WATER. UP TO THE SECOND STORY

THE NEW CONCRETE BRIDGE, SAID TO BE SWEPT AWAY IN THE FLOOD

THIRD STREET, DAYTON. UNDER 20 FEET OF WATER

What Dayton Looked Like Before the Flood.

structing people to extinguish all lights for fear of a gas explosion and then began raiding. University students from Cincinnati and the traffic officers dispersed them.

Numerous stories of looting have been told. In most cases the vandals had entered houses and had been searching for valuables. Repeated revolver shots last night gave rise to the reports that desperate householders had shot themselves rather than drown. When some of the shots were traced to-day, however, they proved to have been fired in an effort to attract rescuers.

Dayton was practically cut off from wire communication until late this afternoon. Then two wires into Cincinnati were obtained, and operators plunged into great piles of telegrams from Dayton citizens almost frantic in their desire to assure friends outside of their safety. Operators at opposite ends of the wires reported that thousands of telegrams were piled up at relay offices. These were from people anxious over the fate of Dayton kinsmen.

Railroad trains have been unable to enter, and the nearest telephone or telegraph station in operation during most of the day was from Lebanon, eighteen miles away, where a single wire allowed the news to be sent out.

Excepting a railroad bridge or two, all such structures leading into the city have been washed away.

Waters Slowly Receding.

The crest of the flood was passed at midnight last night and the waters began to recede slowly thereafter.

The rain, which had persisted for forty-eight hours, stopped at daylight, and by 10:30 o'clock this morning the depth of water had been lessened by about two feet. Rain again began to fall at noon.

The low temperature, ranging about 35 degrees at daylight, added to the dismal situation. This condition was welcomed, however, because a hard freeze would aid materially in holding back the innumerable tributaries of the flooded streams and assist the earth in retaining the moisture that has been soaked into it steadily for the last five days.

In front of the Central Union Telephone office the water was still running so swiftly this morning that horses could not go through it without swimming. The telephone employes in that building fished chairs, dry goods boxes, and other floating property from the flood.

Débris has been swept down the main business street with such force that every plate glass window has been smashed by floating logs and boxes.

Only one building of any size had collapsed, so far as the watchers in the telephone office could learn. This structure, an old one, was a three-story affair near Ludlow Street, occupied by a harness manufacturing concern.

The rumor circulated last night that St. Elizabeth's Hospital, with 600 patients, had been swept away, proved to be untrue. Although it has been impossible to reach the hospital, field glasses show the building is still standing. The water is not thought to be much above the first floor of the building, and it is believed the patients have not suffered.

Waters Cover Fifteen Square Miles.

The inundated district in the city is estimated to-day as covering an area of more than fifteen square miles, most of which is under from six to eighteen feet of water.

The water extends from River Street on the north, Summit Street on the west, and High Street on the east down past the southern borders of the city. This covers the main part of the town and the most thickly populated section. All stores and factories in the main part of the town are flooded to a depth of eight to ten feet.

It is thought most of the fatalities occurred on the west and north sides of the river, where the water rushed in suddenly with the breaking of the levee. Here the residents were almost entirely foreign-born, and they refused to obey the warning to leave on the night before the levee broke.

Except in a few instances, where houses were notably unstable, there was less loss of life in Riverdale or the south and east sections, where residents had warning.

The early breaking of the levee had the effect of keeping down the loss of life in the commercial section. By 8 o'clock yesterday morning the business streets were impassable because of the flood, and many employes in the stores and offices were prevented from reaching their places of employment.

Many were driven to the outskirts of the city far from their homes, however, and were unable to communicate with friends who feared they were lost.

Probably more than 70,000 persons were unable to reach their homes or were held in their water-locked houses and unable to reach land.

Systematizing the Rescue Work.

Rescue work, which yesterday was being done in disconnected fashion, was undertaken with something like system to-day.

Many boat loads of women and children were taken out of houses in the flood zone. The powerful current on each cross street, however, made it impossible for those managing the boats to pass a street crossing without the aid of tow ropes. Automobiles meet the boats and the refugees are taken at once to hospitals.

Expert oarsmen, who braved the tide in the business section of the submerged city this afternoon, came back nerve-wracked to tell narratives of pitiable appeals made to them by hundreds marooned in upper floors of tall buildings about whose lower stories swirled a flood that threatened the structures' foundations. The dark colors in the narrative were lightened here and there by stories of bravery shown by many of the prisoners of the flood.

A woman with three children marooned in the upper floor of her home on the edge of the business district called to the oarsmen:

"Oh, I know you can't take me off," she cried, "but for the love of humanity, please take this loaf of bread and jug of molasses to Sarah Pruyn, down the street. I know she's starving."

Twice the boatmen attempted to take the food, but waves that eddied about the submerged house hurled them back.

Further on, in the high grade residence district, large amounts were offered them for rescue.

Their narrative inspired an effort late this afternoon to launch a boat for navigation on the river, but up to a late hour the craft had been unable to pass beyond areas already reached on the fringe of the flooded district.

Human Clearing Houses Started.

Missing members of families were restored to their loved ones through human clearing houses, established at several points on the fringe of the flood district. Great ledgers filled with names, presided over by volunteer bank clerks, were at the disposal of persons seeking missing kinsmen. If these had registered in the clearing house, their addresses were quickly given to the inquirers.

Up to 7 o'clock this evening 3,000 of the homeless had been housed in different places of refuge, most of them being cared for at the plant of the National Cash Register Company.

Scores of the flood victims were being carried from their places of imprisonment late this evening, and leaders of the rescuing parties were arranging for relays of torch bearers to light the work during the night.

All the cash register buildings available have been filled with cots and means for providing food for the sufferers.

The crop of flood babies was increased to-day by two, making five little ones to be born in the hospital rooms of the factory within twenty-four hours.

Hundreds of homeless persons are being cared for by citizens whose homes were above the water level.

A plan by the Relief Committee to make a systematic effort to penetrate the downtown district to-day failed through the non-arrival of several motor boats which had been ordered. These are expected to-morrow.

Appeal of Relief Committee.

Local relief committees to-day issued the following statement:

"An awful catastrophe has overtaken Dayton. The levees have broken. The centres of Dayton and the residence districts from the Fair Grounds Hill to the high ground north of the city are under water.

"Some of our buildings are used as shelter for the homeless and sick of the south side.

"Bring potatoes, rice, beans, vegetables, meat, and bread, and any other edibles that will sustain life.

"We have cooking arrangements for several thousand. We are sending trucks to near-by towns, but ask that you haul to us, as far as possible."

Red Cross officials also sent out urgent requests for aid.

The immediate pressing need of Dayton to-day was food and medical supplies. The great demand for food exhausted the emergency supplies in the outskirts of the city, and survivors are now depending entirely on what may be brought in.

Those who are flood-bound in offices and stores will suffer from hunger and thirst unless the flood soon subsides, but they are in no danger from the water.

All roads that are passable are being used by parties of relief. From north, south, east, or west persons bent on rescue work wended their way to Dayton to-day. All day and all night strings of automobiles were going back and forth.

Farmers in the surrounding country have offered their teams to haul toward Dayton any supplies that can be gotten together.

Peace officers of Dayton who are able to get about at all are swearing in all available men as Deputies, commandeering provisions and charging the expense to the State. The available supplies are so slender, however, that 1,000 persons on the north side of the river are destitute.

Efforts to learn the conditions of the 2,500 inmates of Old Soldiers' Home on the west s de brought a report that the institution was in no danger because of its high location.

According to report, a boat which was engaged in rescue work capsized and all the crew but Robert Patterson, son of John P. Patterson of the National Cash Register Company, were drowned.

ALL OHIO IN GRASP OF BOILING FLOODS

Over 100 Persons Lose Their Lives in Columbus—Whole West Side Under Water.

PANIC OVER WILD RUMOR

Delaware Suffers Severely—Great Distress in Youngstown—Many Bridges Go Out.

COLUMBUS, Ohio, March 26.—Ohio is experiencing the worst flood in its history. The property damage is enormous. Darkness to-night brought no relief to the scores of cities and towns of the State that are inundated and cut off from the outside world. Thousands of persons are marooned by the swollen waters. Although the floods in some places are reported to be receding slowly, there is no immediate relief in sight. Rain continues to descend, at times in a drizzle and more frequently in torrents.

The reports received from flooded cities to-day were so appalling that in many cases they were disputed, and in some instances totally disregarded. Later reports from these same districts, however, many times confirmed what seemed to be wild rumors. The various news agencies of the State are working under great difficulties in obtaining accurate reports because of crippled wire service. This city itself suffered severely from the flood.

As a result of the flood in the Scioto and Olentangy Rivers, it is estimated that from 100 to 150 persons lost their lives. The west side of the city is flooded. Many persons say that they saw scores of bodies float downstream. Many persons were carried away in their houses. Among those reported dead are William A. Sexton, probation officer; Edwin D. Daniel, Albert Gore, Mr. and Mrs. E. M. Hayes, Mrs. George Cook and baby, Mrs. L. H. Mack and three children, and Mr. and Mrs. George Eckert and seven children.

The isolation of the western part of the city again became real when the last remaining bridge gave way before the torrent this afternoon. A report became current late to-day that the storage dam several miles north of the city had broken and was sending its waters to augment the Scioto River flood. At once there was a wild panic in all parts of the city. Policemen, soldiers, and citizens in automobiles with tooting horns warned every one to seek safety in the highlands and on the east side. Many, stunned by the supposed impending disaster, collapsed from fear or gave way to hysteria.

It was more than an hour before the report was officially denied. Responsibility for its origin has not been fixed. Policemen say that the report was given to them by persons connected with the militia.

City officials said to-night that the storage dam was holding fast against the millions of gallons of water that were being poured against it, and they expressed confidence that it would continue to do so.

The flood is the greatest ever known in Columbus. Business activities are practically paralyzed. The water works shut down last night and will not be in condition to furnish water for a week, as two large mains have been washed out by the flood, which took away every bridge in the city. The city was in darkness last night, as the municipal electric light plant was flooded. Gas pressure is low.

The flood in the Scioto and Olentangy Rivers came so suddenly yesterday that workers who had crossed them early in the day were unable to return to their homes in the west side when the torrents tore loose the bridges connecting both sides of the city. All available State offices were thrown open to refugees and thousands of dollars have been raised to care for them.

According to a wireless report received at the Ohio State University late this afternoon from Mount Vernon, that town was hit hard by the flood, and probably one hundred lost their lives. This report could not be verified to-night.

Communication with Zanesville was cut off early to-night, when the telegraph company's office was flooded. The operator's last words were that the town was under water, that a building near the telegraph office had fallen, and that he would have to get out.

All points below Zanesville, extending east to the Ohio River, were cut off from the outside world to-night. The last available information received here from these places was that they were partially or wholly submerged. Marietta and McConnellsville at that time were reported to be under several feet of water. The Muskingum River was reported to be more than ten feet higher than ever before. Chillicothe, Circleville, Portsmouth, Ironton, and all points in the Miami Valley south were cut off from communication with this city late to-night. All are either partly or almost wholly under water. At Chillicothe the telephone and telegraph offices were flooded early to-day.

Reports received here from Akron late to-day were that at least 500 families are homeless, and that there undoubtedly would be fatalities. Massillon, New Philadelphia, Marion, and Lima also, it was reported here, were partly inundated and were wholly cut off from communication.

PIQUA SAID TO BE ON FIRE.

Midnight Report Told of the Peril of Ohio Town.

PHONETON, Ohio, March 26.—A report received here at midnight said that the town of Piqua was on fire. There was no positive confirmation of this report.

ZANESVILLE IS CUT OFF.

Two Bridges Go Down and Many Persons Are Marooned.

ZANESVILLE, Ohio, March 26.—(By Telephone to Pittsburgh.)—Six persons are believed to have drowned in the Muskingum River here this morning, when the mill of the Zanesville Woolen Company, whose foundations had been weakened by the high water, washed down against the Sixth Street bridge. The bridge collapsed, and the mass of debris was carried away by the current. The Baltimore & Ohio Railroad bridge went out later in the day, completely severing communication between the east and west sides of the city. On the west side are scores of persons marooned in their homes. It is thought that the loss of life there will be heavy, as it is impossible to reach them. Many of them were warned by the police at daybreak, but they refused to leave their houses.

The city is entirely cut off from the outside world except by one telephone line. The rising waters of the Muskingum and Licking Rivers have flooded the electric light plant, and notice was given by the gas company at noon that the suply would be shut off this afternoon.

Before the wires went down the news came from Coshocton, Ohio, thirty miles north of here, that the Tuscarawas and Walhonding Rivers had overflowed their banks, and were raging torrents. Thousands of acres of the richest farm lands in Ohio were under water, and the loss of live stock was heavy.

A railroad bridge on the Columbus division of the Panhandle Railroad went out during the night, and scores of highway bridges were washed away. All streams throughout this section are raging torrents, and the loss will be very heavy. There are no trains or trolley cars running into Zanesville.

The Muskingum River is ten feet above normal, and is rising at the rate of five inches an hour.

Towns in Ohio and Indiana Suffering from the Flood.

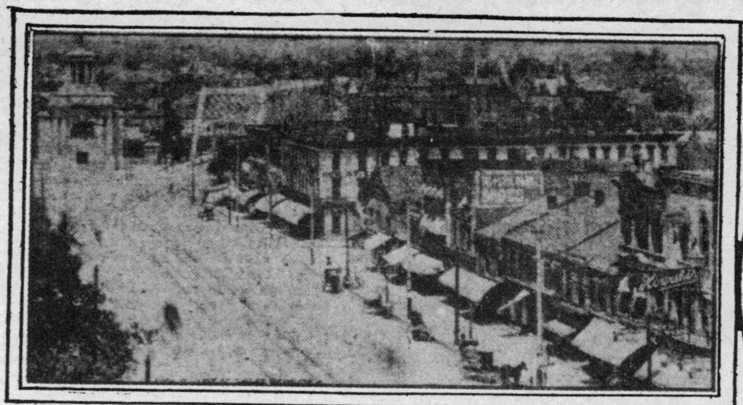

A VIEW OF HAMILTON O. WHERE MANY LIVES ARE LOST

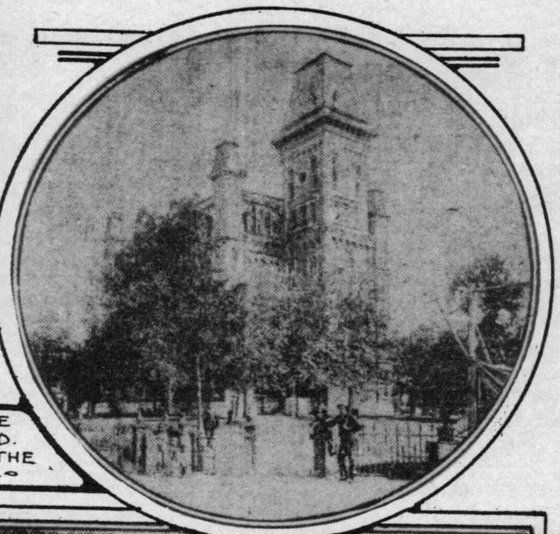

COURT HOUSE AT PERU, IND. CAUGHT IN THE FLOOD

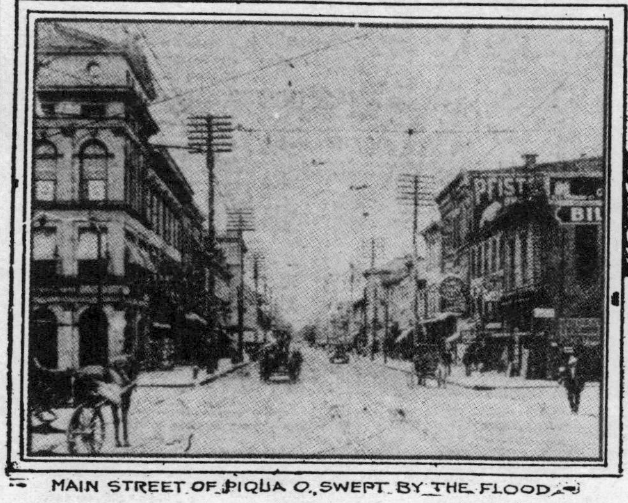

MAIN STREET OF PIQUA O., SWEPT BY THE FLOOD

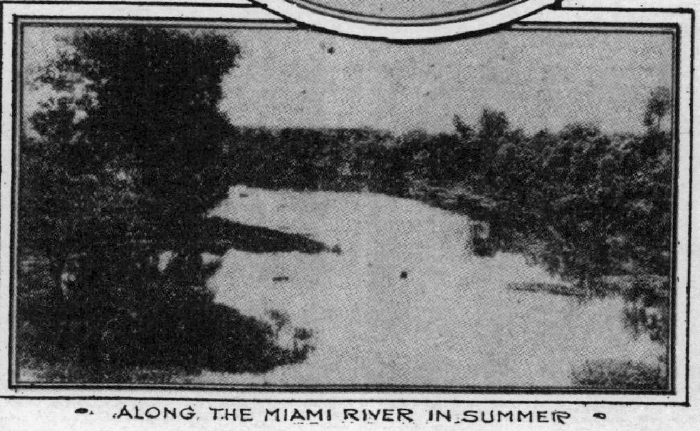

ALONG THE MIAMI RIVER IN SUMMER

INDIANA DEATH TOTAL NOW PLACED AT 200

Reports from Remote Localities May Swell Number of Fatalities in State.

PERU HAS 7,500 HOMELESS

Refugees in Stricken Town Packed in Court House, Where Six Die of Suffocation.

INDIANAPOLIS, Ind., March 26.—Night fell upon flood-swept Indiana with little comfort for its many thousands of sufferers. The most conservative reports put the loss of life in the State at 200, while persistent statements from various points indicate that more than that number may have perished. No one has attempted to even guess at the property damage. The total number of fatalities in this city is roughly estimated at 50.

Communication established with Connersville brought definite information that at least 40 persons perished at Brookville, Franklin County, during Monday night in the flood caused by the overflowing of White Water River. Dispatches from the same region bring the news that the smaller towns of Metmora, Cedar Grove, and Trenton have been swept away.

Late afternoon advices from Peru, sent by telephone through South Bend, say that 12 bodies were recovered from a single house there, and insist that the largest death figures for that city are not exaggerated. Peru probably suffered more than any other town in the flood districts of Indiana., but Fort Wayne, Logansport, Lafayette, and Terre Haute have experienced loss of life and great property damage.

Indianapolis suffered heavily through loss of life in the great flood expanses along White River, and inestimable property loss in the most substantial residence districts. Water fell rapidly in the latter district during the day, but there was no abatement of the waters in West Indianapolis.

There are three distinct flood districts in the State, each only a few miles wide, but sweeping across the entire width of Indiana. In the north all the towns and cities along the Wabash and its larger tributaries are affected; White River sweeps through Central Indiana, with In-

HALF OF PERU HOMELESS.

Thousands Marooned in Flooded District and Hundreds Injured.

PERU, Ind., March 26.—Most of the 15,000 residents of Peru are huddled to-night in the upper stories of the business blocks near the Court House, which is the centre of the relief work. All day they watched the muddy waters rush through the streets, hoping for the flood to subside so they might search the houses near the river, where they believe the bodies of at least fifty flood victims will be found.

City officials and members of the Citizens' Committee assert that the death list will not be less than fifty. One man who came from the West Peru district to-day said he saw twelve bodies floating in one house. The only person who visited Canal Street, where the greatest loss of life is believed to have occurred, has not returned.

It is impossible to establish the exact number of dead, because many bodies are hidden in houses still wholly submerged. Fully 7,500 persons are homeless. Two hundred and twenty-five injured or sick persons have been rescued and removed to a temporary hospital at Plymouth, Ind. The property loss is estimated at $2,500,000.

Only two of the dead have been identified. They are Mrs. Rose Whittle and Mrs. Elsie Smith, tenants of what was known as Walnut Row, composed to twelve frame cottages, where twelve families were drowned.

The Winter quarters of a big circus and menagerie were destroyed, about 500 animals being drowned. These include lions, tigers, bears, camels, elephants, ponies, monkeys, and a rare collection of birds.

The citizens have organized a Vigilance Committee, with orders to shoot any person caught looting houses.

Several thousand persons are marooned in the Court House, hospital, factory buildings, and other structures, because the various relief parties sent from South Bend and other cities had not sufficient boats to carry them to the nearest dry land three miles away. A heavy snow is falling and suffering is intense because of the lack of heating facilities. The town is in darkness except for a scant supply of lanterns.

The town is without electric light power, and has no drinking water supply. The only means of communicating to the outside world is over a feeble telephone line. Much food, clothing, and blankets already have arrived, but more help is needed.

The difficulty of giving anything like a list of the dead and injured is explained by the fact that the rescue parties devoted the entire day to carrying away the survivors who had climbed to perilous positions on icy roofs. Ten men who had remained for two days on top of the tank at the water works became panic-stricken at the sight of the first rescue boat. Most of these men fell into the water in attempting to jump into the boat and several of them were carried away.

It is impossible to tell how soon, if ever, the names of all the dead will be listed or the number known.

"All the News That's Fit to Print."

The New York Times.

THE WEATHER.
Snow or rain, warmer, to-day; cold wave, possibly snow, Thursday.

VOL. LXIII...NO. 20,580. .... NEW YORK, SATURDAY, MAY 30, 1914.—TWENTY PAGES. ONE CENT In Greater New York, Jersey City and Newark. { Elsewhere TWO CENTS.

LINER SINKS IN 14 MINUTES WITH 954 LIVES; EMPRESS OF IRELAND LOST IN ST. LAWRENCE; WIRELESS BRINGS PROMPT AID; 433 ARE SAVED

KARLUK IS SUNK IN ARCTIC ICE; CREW ARE SAVED

Capt. Bartlett, Picked Up on Siberian Coast, Brings Loss of Stefansson Ship.

TRUDGED 500 MILES FOR AID

Leaving Men on Wrangel Island, Peary's Old Commander Starts Across Floes.

VESSEL WENT DOWN JAN. 16

Caught in the Ice, She Had Drifted Nearly Four Months at Mercy of Currents.

LOST 60 MILES FROM SHORE

Relief That Expedition's Members Reached Land by Sledge Journey.

BARTLETT AT ST. MICHAEL

Steamer Which Rescued Him Will Go North Later for Others of the Expedition.

NOME, Alaska, May 29.—The 330-ton wooden Whaler Karluk, flagship of the Canadian Government's Arctic exploring expedition, under command of Vilhjalmar Stefansson, was crushed in the ice and sunk on Jan. 16, near Herald Island, northeast of Siberia.

The entire white crew, excepting Capt. Robert A. Bartlett, is now on Wrangel Island, with a plentiful supply of food and wood. Capt. Bartlett made his way across the ice to North Cape, Siberia, and then proceeded over land to Whaler Bay, Siberia. There he was taken on board the whaler Herman, which carried him to St. Michael, where he now is and from which point information of the Karluk's fate came by cable.

It is assumed by Arctic authorities that when the ice closed on the Karluk last January, the 24 men on board got their supplies out on the ice and along with the dog teams were able to reach land well equipped for the remainder of the Winter. It is assumed, also, that as soon as the days became of sufficient length to permit of travel, Bartlett, accompanied by the five Eskimos on board, set out for Bering Sea.

The frozen sea was quite safe for travel. Probably he drove his dogs over Siberia from North Cape to Whaler Bay on the Bering Sea shore of Siberia, where he met the whaler Herman, which sailed from San Francisco about March 25.

The Herman took him to St. Michael, where there is a cable station.

The mouth of the Yukon and the roadstead at Nome are free of ice already, an unusually early melting. It is said that the Herman will go to the relief of the Karluk's crew as soon as she can get through Bering Straits into the Arctic.

Stefansson is at the mouth of Mackenzie River, having left the Karluk on Sept. 10 to hunt caribou ashore. When he returned to the point where he had come ashore, he found that the Karluk had been blown away by a storm. It will not be possible to send dog teams to Wrangel Island now, for the ice is rotting.

Wrangel Island contains food animals, and is especially noted for its polar bears, a hunting and picture expedition few years ago having counted twenty-two in a single day. It is 250 miles in a straight line from North Cape. Whaler Bay is 225 miles southeast of North Cape.

Herald Island is a small, rocky island, named for the British warship Herald, whose Captain discovered it.

HAD DRIFTED FOR MONTHS.

Whereabouts of Explorer's Flagship Was Long an Arctic Mystery.

The whereabouts of the Karluk had been a mystery for months—since the last Fall when, after Stefansson had gone ashore on a land exploring trip, she was caught in the ice and drifted away. There has been much speculation over her fate.

Herbert L. Bridgman of Brooklyn, the firm friend and supporter of Rear Admiral Peary, received yesterday this dispatch from Hugh J. Lee, Deputy United States Marshal at St. Michael, Alaska:

Bridgman, Standard Union, Brooklyn.
Karluk crushed ice January, sixty miles off Herald Island. Bartlett arrived here last evening. Whaler Herman, from Siberia, assistance for crew Wrangel Island.
LEE.

In the message to Mr. Bridgman not a word is said of how Capt. Bartlett reached Alaska, but from advices received from San Francisco and Nome it appears that Bartlett, after establishing his men safely ashore, set out on a long tramp across the ice to reach a point where he could get into touch with civilization and summon help for his imprisoned party.

It is estimated that Capt. Bartlett trudged 500 miles over the ice on his journey to get aid for his crew.

His long journey to get aid for his

Continued on Page 7.

$90,000 FINE FOR BAVARIA.

Imposed by American Authorities for Illegal Landing of Arms.

VERA CRUZ, May 29.—Capt. Stickney, Collector of the Port, has imposed a fine of 180,000 pesos ($90,000) upon the Hamburg-American steamer Bavaria for having entered the port without a manifest and for having landed a cargo of ammunition at Puerto Mexico which was consigned to Vera Cruz.

The imposition of the fine is an effort to enforce the Mexican navigation laws, and the ship master has sent a cablegram to the Hamburg-American office in Germany for instructions. Clearance of the liner is refused until some arrangement has been reached.

It is understood that similar procedure will be taken against the Ypiranga if she returns here, as it was previously announced she would do. In such an event the Ypiranga's fine would be many times greater than the Bavaria's, because of her larger cargo.

EARTHQUAKE IN ALASKA.

Severe Shock at Fairbanks Accompanied by Rumbling.

FAIRBANKS, Alaska, May 29.—The severest earthquake shock since that of July, 1912, when the Katima volcano broke its bonds, was felt here at 6:05 o'clock this morning. It was accompanied by rumblings of the earth.

The shock was the fifth in 48 hours.

JUDGE HORNBLOWER WORSE

Suffers a Relapse at His Home in Litchfield, Conn.

Judge William B. Hornblower, of the State Court of Appeals, who has been ill with heart trouble since the middle of last April, was reported last night to have suffered a relapse.

For some time it was thought that Judge Hornblower was recuperating, but partial paralysis has made his condition serious. He was moved from his home at 512 Fifth Avenue to his country place at Litchfield, Conn., recently.

MUST RESTORE $1,096,000.

Order Served on Directors of "Plundered" San Francisco Railroad.

SAN FRANCISCO, May 29.—The California Railroad Commission issued an order today that the Directors of the United Railroads of San Francisco restore to the company's funds $1,096,000 which the commission charges Patrick Calhoun, former President of the United Railroads, diverted to his personal use.

The order fixes July 17 as the date on which the Directors shall appear before the commission with proof that the missing money has been restored, or present an adequate plan for the restoration of the fund. At the same time, a sweeping investigation of the company's finances will be begun.

In a recent opinion the Railroad Commission charged that the United Railroads had been "plundered" of $1,096,000 by Calhoun, and that he used the sum in a private land deal.

FIGHTS OWN RE-ELECTION.

Bartholdt Opens Headquarters to Resist His Constituents.

Special to The New York Times.

ST. LOUIS, May 29.—The unique situation of a man maintaining headquarters in a campaign against his own re-election is presented by Representative Richard Bartholdt of St. Louis, who is fighting against being forced into the race for Congress from the Tenth Missouri District. He has employed extra typists to warn his friends that he will not accept a renomination in the district, which is strongly Republican and which he has carried for years by big majorities.

Last December Mr. Bartholdt informed his constituents in a formal statement that he did not wish again to be a candidate. A deluge of telegrams and letters of protest was the result. It soon became necessary to employ extra stenographers to take care of his mail on the subject. Mr. Bartholdt issued another formal statement, and still the constituents wrote. Now he has established campaign headquarters to prevent the election being forced upon him.

COMMUTES IN YACHT.

Col. Hayden Starts Frequent Trips Between Newport and New York.

Special to The New York Times.

BOSTON, May 29.—The last word in comfortable commuting that will afford great pleasure to an enthusiastic yachtsman is planned by Col. Charles Hayden of Hayden, Stone & Co. for the Summer. He will make frequent trips between New York and Newport in the steam yacht Sovereign, which he leased recently from the estate of M. C. D. Borden.

The Colonel is a member of the New York and Eastern Yacht Clubs.

Special to The New York Times.

NEWPORT, R. I., May 29.—All records for speed in yachts between New York and Newport were broken today by the steam yacht Sovereign, chartered by Col. Charles Hayden of Boston and New York, which left the East River station of the New York Yacht Club at 1.08 this afternoon and moored to the yacht club station here at 7:07 tonight, covering the distance in six hours and three minutes, and without pushing to full capacity.

The Sovereign is 150 feet long, burns oil fuel, has three Curtis turbines and three propellers. She has a record of forty miles an hour.

SIX FALL TO DEATH IN MINE.

Cage in Which They Were Being Hoisted Turns Turtle—Two Hurt.

TAMAQUA, Penn., May 29.—Six miners were killed and two badly injured at the Mary D. colliery late today, when the cage in which they were riding to the surface turned turtle after it had gone forty feet into the air past the landing where the men were supposed to disembark. The dead were all foreign-born workers.

One of the victims jumped while the cage was twenty feet in the air. He landed on a beam, and his skull was crushed. The other five men plunged 700 feet into a sump at the bottom of the shaft and were so badly crushed that it was not until a late hour tonight that it was possible to identify the bodies.

Andrew Durkin saved his life by grasping a chain. A foreigner, whose name has not been ascertained, caught on a projection and escaped with a broken leg.

The colliery is operated by Wentz & Co. of Philadelphia, and employs 500 men. No official statement as to the cause of the accident was given out, and it is not known whether it was due to negligence or some mechanical defect.

THE ALLTOGETHER POUCH
Holds pipe and tobacco. At the Schulte Stores.
—Adv.

ENVOYS RECEIVE CARRANZA AGENT, BUT WON'T DELAY

Permit Urquidi to Present First Chief's Request to Enter the Conference.

URGED BY WASHINGTON

Mexicans Are Opposed to Admitting Rebels Unless with Full Powers.

BUT BRYAN FAVORS IT

Administration Thinks Rebel Participation Will Increase Chances of Lasting Peace.

CARRANZA IS UNYIELDING

Urquidi Says He Holds That Conference Should Not Deal with Internal Affairs.

HUERTA SEEMS OBDURATE

Minister Alcocer Says That He Won't Yield the Presidency to a Constitutionalist.

Special to The New York Times.

NIAGARA FALLS, Ont., May 29.—At the earnest request of Justice Lamar and Mr. Lehmann, the American delegates to the peace conference, the three A B C mediators this evening agreed to receive a communication from Gen. Carranza, First Chief of the Constitutionalists, asking that his faction be permitted to participate in the conference. The mediators took the matter under advisement and later let it be understood that if a Carranza delegate were admitted to the conference it would be on condition that he should not offer suggestions that would make for delay in the settlement.

The only official statement made regarding the visit of the Carranza agent was the following bulletin, issued tonight:

> The mediators have received a communication from the representative of Gen. Carranza in Washington, the tenor of which differs entirely from the version contained in a news dispatch this morning from Durango, and does not disturb the course of the negotiations.

Gen. Carranza's communication was presented by Juan Francisco Urquidi, brother of Manuel Urquidi, who was sub-Secretary of Communications under the late President Madero. It had been telegraphed by Gen. Carranza from Durango to Washington, and was brought to the Falls by Señor Urquidi, who arrived here this morning.

Envoys' Course in Doubt.

What action will be taken by the mediators has not been determined formally. They are known to be indisposed to permit Constitutionalist participation in their deliberations at this late day, and would have given no consideration to Gen. Carranza's requests if the American delegates had not asked them to do so. Before any answer is given to Señor Urquidi, the Mexican peace delegates, Señores Rabasa, Elguero, and Rodriguez, will ask Gen. Huerta for instructions as to what their course should be if the mediators should give favorable consideration to the rebel application.

The Mexican delegates are opposed to such action, and it seems to be settled in advance that neither they nor their Government will agree that a Constitutionalist delegate be admitted to the conferences unless he has full authority to arrange a plan for the adjustment of Mexico's troubles.

No reference was made in Gen. Carranza's telegraphic note as to the character of the credentials that would be given to his delegate if he were admitted to the peace parleys. A simple request for the participation of a representative of Gen. Carranza is understood to have been all that the note contained. No credentials or explanatory statement accompanied it.

It is understood that the note followed in only a very vague way the lines of the following message, published from Durango today, as a reported dispatch through the junta at Washington to the A B C envoys:

> Six days ago conferences began to treat the international conflict between the United States and Mexico occasioned by the arrest of several American sailors by soldiers of Huerta at Tampico. To solve this conflict you offered to the Government of the United States, to Huerta, and to me your good offices, inviting me to appoint delegates who would represent the general headquarters of the Constitutionalist army, which is under my orders.
>
> I answered you that in principle I would accept your good offices and later in a separate message I asked the points which would be dealt with in the peace conference. Awaiting an answer to that dispatch I have not named delegates.
>
> I am surprised that you have continued to treat for a solution of the conflict between the United States and Mexico without representations from the Constitutionalist Army, which

Continued on Page 5.

Small Coal Steamer Hits Liner in a Dense Fog.

VESSEL'S SIDE TORN OUT

Ship Lists So Suddenly That Many of Her Lifeboats Are Rendered Useless.

EXPLOSION FOLLOWS CRASH

Laurence Irving, Sir H. Seton-Karr, and Many Salvationists Among the Missing.

CAPT. KENDALL'S BRAVERY

Urges Coal Ship to Stand By to Close Hole in His Vessel's Side.

AID COMES IN 20 MINUTES

Government Vessels Pick Up Chilled and Dying Victims—Search for Dead Throughout the Day.

RIMOUSKI, Quebec, May 29.—Of a total of 1,387 persons on board the Canadian Pacific liner Empress of Ireland when she sailed yesterday from Quebec for Liverpool 954 were lost when the liner was rammed by the Danish collier Storstad and sank off Father Point, in the St. Lawrence River, before daylight today. Only 433 are known to have been saved.

Of the 87 cabin passengers, the late figures show 29 to have been saved. Of the 153 in the second cabin 29 were rescued; of the 715 third class passengers there are 101 survivors, while 237 of the crew of 432 were brought ashore.

These figures account for the 396 survivors landed here and taken by train to Quebec, where they arrived tonight. Thirty-seven rescued persons remained, completing the total of 433 known survivors.

Among the notable passengers lost were Laurence Irving, the actor, son of Sir Henry Irving; his wife, Mabel Hackney, and Sir Henry Seton-Karr. The Empress of Ireland also had on board a large number of Salvation Army delegates to a London conference.

The Empress of Ireland, in command of Capt. H. G. Kendall, R. N. R., left Montreal on Wednesday afternoon, stopped at Quebec, and proceeded from that port on her voyage to Liverpool at 4:20 o'clock yesterday afternoon.

Quick Work of Wireless.

So deep was the gash in the stricken liner's side inflicted by the sharp prow of the heavy laden collier, and so fast the inrush of the water, that although the first rescue steamer catching the wireless S O S call and hastening out from Father Point reached the scene within twenty minutes after the collision, the liner already had gone down.

The wireless could hardly have worked to better effect or the response been more prompt. Yet, within sight of shore, in landlocked waters, with help close at hand, nearly 1,000 persons lost their lives by drowning when fog obscured the vision of the river navigators and two vessels, one virtually at a standstill as a measure of precaution, and the other, from all accounts, moving at not more than moderate speed, crashed together in a fatal impact.

Investigation of the cause of the disaster is to be started promptly.

The story of the Storstad, which, after picking up a few of the survivors and landing them here, resumed her way up the river, will not be told until tomorrow when she reaches Quebec, whence she was bound from Sydney with a cargo of coal. From the evidence of officers on the Empress of Ireland, however, the liner had come to a dead halt in the fog and was blowing her whistle as a warning of her presence.

The fate of the smartly equipped and speedy liner, queen of her fleet, seems to have been hastened by the unfortunate and probably unintentional withdrawal of the Storstad's bow from the gash she had inflicted in the passenger vessel's side. As the waters rushed in the liner quickly inclined sideways at a sharp angle, the sea found the boilers, and an explosion followed that ripped apart still further the vessel's sides and sealed her doom.

Passengers who had crowded the upper works, hoping for rescue, were blown into the river. Others, who had escaped death or injury in the splintering of wood and smashing of steel in the collision, met their fate below decks.

Looming up through the river mists, as the Empress of Ireland was lying

Continued on Page 2.

DEATH TOLL OF THE EMPRESS OF IRELAND

954 Lost of the 1,387 Persons Aboard—196 Passengers and 237 of the Crew Saved.

THE DEAD.		THE SAVED.	
Passengers	778	Passengers	196
Crew	176	Crew	237
Total	954	Total	433

Total number aboard, 1,387.

A complete list of the passengers and crew of the sunken ship is not at present available. The complete first and second cabin passenger list is printed on Page 4 of THE TIMES. The names of the survivors, as far as obtained, appear below. This list is far from complete, and until it is it will not be possible to determine from the passenger list exactly who were lost.

THE SURVIVORS.

First Cabin.

AITKINSON, JOHN.
BURT, C. R.
DUNCAN, J. FERGUS, member of firm of Kimber, Bull & Duncan, solicitors, London.
EASTERNS, Miss.
FENTON, WALTER, Manchester, England.
GALLAGHER, ———.
GOSSELIN, L. A., Montreal.
HENDERSON, G. W. S., Montreal.
KOHL, Miss GRACE, Montreal.
LEE, Miss ALICE, Nassau, N. P.
O'HARA, H. R., Toronto.
O'HARA, Miss HELEN, Toronto.
PATON, Mrs. W. E., Sherbrooke, sister of Frederic Grundy, European manager of The New York Sun.

Second Cabin.

BLACK, J. W., Ottawa.
BLACK, Mrs. J. W., Ottawa.
BUNTHORNE, ALEXANDER.
COURT, Miss E., Liverpool.
DANDY, J. F., Person, Manitoba.
DAVIES, WILLIAM, Toronto.
DAVIES, Mrs. WILLIAM, Toronto.
ERZINGER, J., Winnipeg.
HUNT, Miss E. DE V.
JOHNSTON, GEORGE, San Francisco.
LANGSLEY, J. W., Vancouver.
LANGSLEY, Miss M. E., Vancouver.
LAW, E., Calgary.
LAW, Mrs. E., Calgary.
LAW, Master, Calgary.
LENNON, J., Winnipeg.
LISTON, Miss A., London.
McALPINE, A., Montreal.
MATTIER, A., Indianapolis.
MOIR, Mrs. CHARLES, Toronto.
MORGAN, J., Winnipeg.
PETERSON, H., Winnipeg.
PETERSON, Mrs. H., Winnipeg.
SIMONDS, Mrs. Reynold, London.
WIENICH, B., Montreal.

Salvation Army Members.

ATWELL, Major, Toronto.
ATWELL, Mrs., Toronto.
BALES, ALICE, (address not given.)
BROOKS, FRANK, Toronto.
DELAMONT, ———, (one of two brothers,) Moosejaw, Sask.
DELAMONT, ———, (one of two brothers,) Moosejaw, Sask.
FOORD, ERNEST, Toronto.
GREEN, ERNEST, Toronto.
GREENAWAY, THOMAS, Toronto.
GREENAWAY, Mrs. THOMAS, Toronto.
GREENAWAY, HERBERT, Toronto.
HANNAGAN, GRACE, 8 years old, Toronto.
JOHNSTON, JAMES, Toronto.
KEITH, Lieut. ALFRED, Toronto.
McAMMOND, Staff Capt. D., Winnipeg.
McINTYRE, KENNETH, Toronto.
MEASURES, WILLIAM.
MORRIS, Major FRANK, Divisional Commander of London Department, London Division, Lindsay, Ont.
SPOONER, Capt. RUFUS, Toronto.
TURTIN, Major RICHARD, Manager Trade Department, Toronto.
WILSON, Capt. GEORGE, Toronto.

Men of Crew.

BOMFORD, EDWARD, second Marconi operator.
BORAH, T., Quartermaster.
DUCKWORTH, M. D., electrician.
ELLIOTT, A., baker.
FERGUSON, RONALD, first Marconi operator.
GAADE, A. W., chief steward.
GRANT, Dr. J. F., surgeon.
HAYES, ERNEST, first assistant purser.
HELM, S. F., bugler.
JOHNSTON, Dr., Chief Medical Officer.
KENDALL, H. G., Captain.
PERKINSON, R. H., steward.
ROWEN, ———, steward.
RUDLEY, A., boatswain's mate.
SAMPSON, ———, first engineer.
SPENCER, C. S., bellboy.
SPRAGUE, T., Quartermaster.
STARR, ———, baker.
SWANN, ———, engineer.
VELL, J., bellboy.
WHITE, ———, steward.
WILLIAMS, J., steward.
———, ———, second assistant purser.
———, ———, second engineer.

Men of Crew or Steerage Passengers.

None of these names appears on the first cabin or second cabin list.

BLYTHE, Miss.
BOYLE, R.
BANTALA, ——.
BROWN, WILLIAM.
BYRNE, JOHN.
BACKFORD, Miss.
BRENNAN, R.
BURROUS, W. T.
CANEPA, W.
CAPPLIN, GEORGE.
COLBAEBA, A.
CLANDON, ——.
CLARKE, CHARLES.
CLARKSON, H.
DONOVAN, G.
DORTS, JOHN.
DAVIES, JOHN.
DAVIES, PETER.
DARCY, P.
DOOLIX, ——.
ELGEVISH, A.
EVANSON, ARTHUR.
ELLIS, ALEC.
FAVORSTONE, Mrs.
FLAIR, ROY.
FRONT, ——.
FITZPATRICK, JOHN.
FENEDAY, ARTHUR.
FUGENT, WILLIAM.
FOSTER, E.
FERGUSON, A. C.
GRAY, ARTHUR.
GRAY, E. C.
GRIVERI, ALEC.
GARD, J.
GRATWICK, ——.
HARBANAN, RENNE.
HOHN, S. F.
HUGHES, W. H.
HONRALAIN, W.
HAMPTER, W.
HANON, T.
HELLER, W.
HOLT, R., (steward).
HOUGHES, HUGH.
HARBANE, ——.
HARRON, ——.
JOHNSTONE, J.
KORONIC, MICHAEL.
KING, ——.
LEDDELL, R.
LYON, CHENA.
LAWLER, PHILLIP, Brantford, Ont.
LOMMI, WALTER.
LASKIO, K.
MERE, ——.
METCALFE, G. J.
McCONE, J.
McDONALD, C. P.
McWILLIAMS, R.
McDOUGALL, D.
McCREADY, THOMAS.
MALTE, ——.
MORELAND, ——.
MURPHY, O. S.
NISITO, F.
NOSEAL, ——.
NOVEK, ——.
OWEN, W. S.
POTVERT, ——.
PROBSI, ——.
QUINN, WILLIAM.
REGINALD, A.
RIOULENTE, FEDOR.
ROBERTS, W.
ROMANUS, JOHN.
RYAN, JOHN.
SAMUELSON, C.
SAPETE, ——.
SALIO, J.
SAVEIN, ——.
SCOTT, ——.
SELINSKI, W.
SHANNON, EDWARD.
SIMS, JUBAINER.
SIMS, JOHN.
SIMON, J. R.
SMITH, C. H.
SMITH, H. H.
SMITH, J.
SUZZERA, ADAM.
SPEDDON, ——.
TALBACHA, ALEX.
THORNE, ——.
TIDDELL, ——.
TOCK, ——.
WALINSKI, ——.
WEISS, ALEX.
WEYKE, ——.
WHITE, J. B.
WILLIAMS, A.
WILLIAMS, O.
ZUH, H.

The Chief Officer and the Purser are among the missing.

Wireless Operator Tells of Rescues and Search for Dead; Praise for Capt. Kendall, Whose Ship Sank Under His Feet

By the Wireless Operator at Father Point.

Special to The New York Times.

FATHER POINT, Quebec, May 29.—All day long the search has continued at the scene of the collision which sank the Empress of Ireland. The Government steamers Lady Evelyn and Eureka at nightfall had found five men and one woman. Four of the men were living, but unconscious. Two hundred and fifty bodies had been recovered. The list of saved totals 400.

Capt. Kendall was injured, and, from all accounts, he behaved like a true British sailor while his ship stood under his feet. While the Storstad's stem was stuck in the side of his ship Capt. Kendall is said to have urged the collier's Captain to keep going ahead so that his stem would plug the hole in the Empress's starboard side. But the Storstad dropped back and the Empress filled and foundered.

Capt. Kendall stood on his bridge as the ship went down. He was picked up by one of his boats and went on with the work of rescue until the lifeboat he was in was loaded to the gunwales.

The Canadian Pacific Railroad sent a special train down and took several carloads of the rescued to Quebec. The company is doing everything that money can do to relieve the sufferings of the survivors. A medical staff also has been sent down.

Very few of the bodies have been identified. The Coroner's inquest takes place tomorrow.

The prompt Marconi service doubtless saved many lives, as one of the rescue steamers, the Eureka, was on the spot about twenty minutes after the disaster, and the Lady Evelyn was close on her heels. The prompt arrival of these vessels enabled the lifeboats to be overfilled without danger.

The scene at the Rimouski wharf, where the bodies lie, is a heartrending one. The Empress had eighty-seven saloon, 256 second cabin, 710 steerage, and a crew of 425. It appears from the evidence of officers that the Empress was dead stopped in the fog and blowing her whistle. The search will continue for more bodies.

J. McWILLIAMS.

Throng Bare Heads As the Survivors Arrive at Quebec.

ESCAPES BY PORTHOLE

Dr. Grant Pulled Out to Liner's Horizontal Side, Upon Which 100 Persons Stand.

TWO LITTLE GIRLS SAVED

One Goes Overboard with Father, Who Is Lost, While She Swims to Safety.

REUNITED WITH HIS BRIDE

Salvation Army Man Finds Wife, After Sinking, Has Awakened Afloat on Chair.

PATHETIC SCENE ON TRAIN

Ill Clad Passengers, Who Lost Clothes, Harrowed by Grief and Suffering from Injuries.

Special to The New York Times.

QUEBEC, May 29.—A special train tonight brought here 396 survivors of the wrecked steamship Empress of Ireland, and 37 were still at Rimouski. These 433 probably were all the saved, leaving a total death list of 934.

Almost all the survivors told the same story of the disaster. The Empress was running slowly when struck by the Storstad, between 1 and 2 A. M. The collier rammed her amidships with terrific force, smashing bulkheads and tearing out a good part of the interior.

Then the collier backed off and the Empress immediately began to roll over and sink. There was no lowering of boats at all. They simply broke away and floated off. Most of the passengers were drowned in their cabins. Those who escaped leaped, for the most part, from the starboard side of the ship when the deck was almost perpendicular.

Those that slid off the deck on the low side as it was becoming submerged, either were crushed to death by the fall of deck structures or boat tackle, or were carried down by the suction as the ship careened and sank.

During all this time the screeching of women and children was described as fearful. Many of the saved owed their lives to the fact that they could swim, though some were kept afloat by life belts. Not many outside of men of the crew had time to adjust these. Some fifteen or twenty who were picked up alive died.

Capt. Kendall fell from the bridge to the deck and fractured his shoulder. He suffered other injuries also. An unconfirmed rumor said he had died.

Out of thirteen stewardesses on board only two were saved. Mrs. Paton of Sherbrooke, P. Q., a sister of the Messrs. Grundy, who are respectively the London and Paris correspondents of The New York Sun, was one of the women saved.

The scene on the train was most pathetic. Many of the survivors were bruised and ill, others were bowed in grief over the loss of a relative, while all showed the strain which they had suffered. There was no distinction of class or station among those who had fought so hard and helped one another when the liner sank. Most of them were clothed in attire which was furnished at the Rimouski stores.

Stories of a panic in the dark as the ship listed and her lights went out, of the futile effort of the crew to lower the boats, which was made impossible by the list of the ship, and of desperate struggles in the water after the ship went down, were told by the survivors.

Special praise was given to the heroic work of Dr. James F. Grant of Victoria, B. C., who was ship's surgeon on the Empress of Ireland. It was thought that by his coolness and his authority over the survivors he managed to save many who after their rescue would have perished had they not received prompt medical assistance.

There was also repeated mention of the open-hearted hospitality shown by the French-Canadian people at Rimouski, who deprived themselves of

Where the Empress of Ireland Sank with 900 Lives.

The Steamer Empress of Ireland.

the comforts of their homes that they might help the shipwrecked passengers.

Dr. J. V. Grant's Bravery.

Every such disaster as that which befell the Empress of Ireland seems to bring out one or more men of supreme coolness, resource, and courage.

The survivors united in praising Dr. James F. Grant, the ship's physician. They praised the manner in which he calmed the terror-stricken, kept hope alive in the breasts of those whose loved ones were in peril, and gave medical aid to the injured. The doctor was pulled from a port hole by those who stood on the side of the ship after she had canted over. He slid into the water as the great hull dropped from under him, and swam toward the Storstad.

Dr. Grant was picked up by one of the boats of the collier, and on his return to the scene of the wreck he aided in the rescue work. Then he boarded the Storstad, and out of the confusion that made the grimy collier a place of horror, brought a semblance of order. Women died as they reached the deck and he took charge of the bodies, directing where they should be laid. Down in the engine room men were shrieking in terror, and women were trying to warm their chilled bodies and dry their clothing. The physician took charge of these sufferers and gave them every possible aid.

Dr. Grant told the following story of the collision:

"We left Quebec on May 27 at 4:30 P. M. and had an uneventful trip during the evening. During the early morning a fog dropped around us and we proceeded slowly. At 1:30 A. M. we put the pilot off at Father Point. At 1:52 the collier Storstad rammed the Empress of Ireland. The vessel's lights had been sighted by the watch, who reported to Capt. Kendall, who was on the bridge.

Capt. Kendall's Signal.

"The captain signaled with three blasts of the whistle, 'I am continuing my course.' The collier answered but what the reply was I have not learned. Capt. Kendall sounded the whistle twice, saying, 'I am stopping.'

"The light of the collier could be seen approaching. The captain of the Empress signaled to reverse and steam full astern. But the big liner could not avoid the small ship. She was rammed amidships in the engine room on the starboard side. The plates were ripped open to an enormous length. Then the collier backed off about a mile.

"In a few moments the Empress began to list to one side. She made an attempt to right herself, and then canted still further to starboard. As the water forced its way in through the gaping break in her side she lurched further and was doomed.

"An attempt was made to lower the boats on the starboard side. The first one was thrown clear and the sailors in it were thrown out. That boat was overturned. Then some of the port boats were flung across the deck by her list and several persons were killed.

"They were crushed to death against the rail. I believe that the chief officer, Mr. Steede, lost his life when these boats catapulted their way through the crowd.

"There was no disorder among the crew. The Captain and other officers remained on the bridge until the vessel sank. It was just seventeen minutes from the time she was rammed until she sank below the surface. Comparatively only a few were able to obtain life belts, and practically all were forced out in their night clothes into the water.

Hundreds Clung to Ship.

"Several hundred clung to the ship until she sank, holding to the rail until the vessel canted over so far that it was necessary to climb the rail and stand on the plates of the side. Then as she keeled over further they slid down and into the water as though they were walking down a sandy beach into the water to bath.

"There were several hundred souls swimming around in the water, screaming for help, shrieking as they felt themselves being carried under, and uttered strange, weird moans of terror undisguised.

"The lifeboats of the Storstad were launched, and came rapidly to the rescue. Not one went back that was not well loaded. About five of the Empress's boats also got away. The entire catastrophe was so sudden that scores never left their bunks.

"The passengers had been on the ship only a day, and were not yet familiar with their surroundings. In the confusion and the semi-panic, many could not find their way to the decks, and only a few knew how to reach the boat deck. This was largely responsible for the terrible toll of death.

"The survivors were taken on board the Storstad and the Lady Evelyn which was summoned by wireless. There everything possible was done for them. In at least five cases, however, the shock and exposure were too severe.

"Four women perished after they reached the Storstad. In each case I was called, and the unfortunates died before anything could be done. The last spark of energy had been exhausted. One other woman died just as she was being taken ashore."

All this time the doctor had said nothing regarding his own experiences. He was asked to relate his own story.

Escape of Dr. Grant.

"I knew nothing of what was occurring," he said, "until I was rolled out of my berth by the listing of the boat. At once I knew that there was something wrong, and I tried to turn on the lights. But the power was off. The dynamos had been stopped by the inrush of water a few moments after the collision. I could not find the door. I heard screams of terror and the sound of rushing water. I did not know what was wrong, nor was there anything to guide me as to the danger.

"I managed to get out of my stateroom, but I was unable to walk up the alleyway because of the tilt of the boat. I tried to crawl, but could not.

"So I scrambled along the wall and grasped a porthole. I got my head out, and what was my astonishment to find the side crowded with people, standing there as though it was the deck. I called, and some one reached down. I was trying to get my shoulders through the opening. This man pulled me out, and I, too, stood there with them for a moment. There were fully 100 people around me. There was no time to question. I had no time to think. The ship sank from under, and we were all struggling in the water.

"The fog had been all around us. Just as soon as the boat sank this mist, as though it had accomplished its purpose, rolled up like a curtain, and low in the water I could see, about a mile away, the lights of the collier that I afterward learned had struck us. I swam to it and was picked up by a lifeboat which had just been launched. In it I returned to the spot where the ship had gone down and helped to pick up those who were struggling in the water."

Two little girls, one 8, the other 10, went over the side of the Empress of Ireland and reached safety. The younger fell off the boat, the other dived into the black waters in her father's arms. The father perished there. The younger girl, now an orphan, is not aware that her father and mother did not have the luck to find a piece of wood to which to cling.

"They'll be on the next boat. You wait and see," said she, gaily. She was Gracie Hannagan, 8 years old, daughter of Bandmaster Hannagan of the Salvation Army at Toronto.

The other child was Helen O'Hara, daughter of Mr. and Mrs. H. R. O'Hara, also of Toronto. Mr. O'Hara was a prominent stock broker of that city. She, too, was discovered in the special train, in the private car of Mr. G. G. Grundy, which had been turned into a hospital. Here the sick were being cared for. Near her mother, trying in her childish way to comfort her, was Helen. In an artless manner she told how she had been rescued.

Child Swam to Safety.

"When I woke, the boat was leaning over and every one was hurrying," said she. "I only had time to get my combinations on, and a coat when papa picked me up in his arms and we went up on deck. I don't know what became of mamma then. Papa waited until the boat nearly fell over and then he jumped. I fell out of his arms and into the water. It was awfully cold.

"Then I saw a piece of wood and I swam over and clung to it. I lost it after a while and then I had to swim to where there was a lot more. After a while I saw a boat, so I swam over to it and held on to a man who had hold of the boat, and then they took us in. I was very glad that I have taken swimming lessons at Havergal, where I go to school.

"Everything was all mixed up and when they took us on the ship I asked if we were on a boat. And I did not find Mamma until I got to shore."

Few of these who came alive from the maelstrom of death off Rimouski had so stirring experiences as befell Mr. and Mrs. Thomas Greenaway of the Salvation Army band. It was their honeymoon trip. They had been married in Toronto but a week ago. In the disaster each gave the other up for lost. They floated a short distance apart. He tried to die because he felt that life without his bride would be too sad. In the brightness of the sunshine that flooded the little town of Rimouski they found each other again.

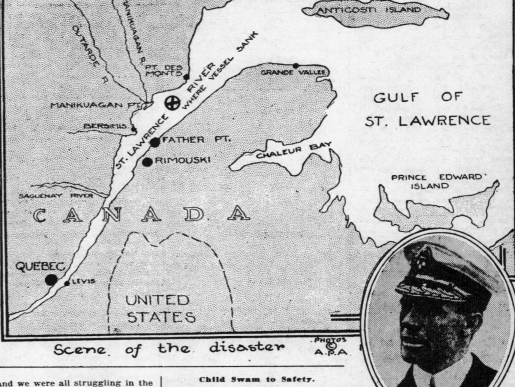

Scene of the disaster.

Capt. Kendall.

"We were notified to go on deck after the crash," said Mrs. Greenaway, "and, without feeling very nervous, we threw on a wrap or so and left our cabin. In the confusion I lost my husband. I do not know how it happened.

"But I found some friends, and one of them put a lifebelt on me. All this time I was looking for Mr. Greenaway, but he was no where to be seen. The boat tilted further, and we were all holding to the rail for dear life. It kept going over, and we were forced to climb the rail and stand on the side.

"The boat was nearly under by now. I felt that all was over and I began to pray. As I stood there asking for Divine help I felt the water swiftly mounting. The suction drew me down, deep down in the swirling black water. I could not seem to realize that death was very near, even though I had given up all hope. And then I seemed stunned. That was the explosion. My ankle was cut and I was burned and bruised about the body.

Woman's Remarkable Escape.

"When I regained consciousness, it must have been but a moment or so later, I found myself lying across a deck chair in the water. I have no idea how I got there. I think that the explosion must have blown me out of the water. Then I made myself secure and waited. Soon a raft with two men on it floated near me. A huge, big man and another were on it.

"The big man held out a paddle to me and asked, 'Are you alive?' I guess I moaned, because the cut in my ankle and my burns were hurting me. I caught hold of the stick, and he pulled me up on the raft. Then he said, 'Don't be afraid, little girl. My wife's gone.' I answered, 'I've lost my husband.'

"After a while I said that I was cold. He opened his coat and vest and drew me over close and buttoned them around me. That kept me warm and I think it saved my life. I don't remember anything more until I found myself on board the collier."

Mr. Greenaway told of the separation and his subsequent adventures.

He went back to get some wraps for his wife, and also to close the window to prevent the water from washing in and spoiling their clothes. None of the passengers, it seemed, realized the danger. They all evidently thought until the last that everything would be all right.

"When I reached the deck," said he, "I could not find my wife. Several members of the party had seen her, but where she was they did not know. As the boat went over I climbed over the rail to the side with the others. I looked around for her, but she was not in sight. I decided that she must be gone."

All this time Mrs. Greenaway stood but a few feet away in the darkness.

"Then I decided to go down with the ship," her husband continued. "I grasped the rail firmly, and down we went. Then came the explosion that loosened my grip, and I came to the surface.

"The first thing I saw was the leg of a table. I am not a swimmer, but I managed to reach it, and there I clung until the pilot boat picked me up. I was taken ashore, and received splendid treatment in a hospitable home. And then this morning I went out to see if my wife could have been saved. I found her at the hotel. We wept together for pure joy."

The nine survivors of the Salvation Army band were, indeed, a sorrowful lot. Ernest Green, one of the band, lost his father, Adjt. Harry Green; also his mother and his sister, Jessie. He was now the only remaining member of the family. William Measures, another member of the band, living at 72 Withraw Avenue, Toronto, went to his home alone, while both Major Findlay and his wife were drowned. Besides the Greenaways, the saved Salvationists comprised the bridegroom's brother, Herbert Greenaway; A. L. F. Keith, Kenneth McIntyre, an American from New York; Frank Brooks, Capt. Spooner, and Capt. Wilson.

One of the most self-possessed passengers among the rescued was Mrs. W. E. Paton of Sherbrooke. Mrs. Paton was rescued in a lifeboat and did not get the least bit wet. Owing to her remarkable courage she was able to give much valuable assistance to the sufferers.

The crew of the Empress said a majority of those saved had to swim. All that was possible was done to lower boats, but the list of the ship made it impossible to lower more than five boats, they said.

Women Hurled Against Cabin.

M. J. Fergus Duncan, an advocate of London, England, who has been in Canada on business, told how the first boat lowered upset and those who had crowded into it were plunged headlong into the water.

"My berth was on the starboard side," said Mr. Duncan. "I heard the whistles and foghorns as well as the reversing of the engines. Then came the crash. I went out on deck, which was empty, and looking over the side I saw the collier moving away. A boat was lowered from the bridge, but one of the davits worked more quickly than the other, and the living cargo was shot clean into the water. I hurried back to my cabin, and then as the boat took another list I did not wait longer, but went out again.

"Frightened passengers were asking what the trouble was and began donning lifebelts. As the ship tilted I could not stand upon the deck any longer, and had to climb up on to the railing. It was awful to see those poor women who had not strength to keep their hold on the railing, as they were hurled back against the cabin. What became of them I do not know.

"As the ship settled for the final plunge I slid down the plates of her side into the sea. As I reached the water the steam came bursting out of the side of the ship, causing a great commotion. When the last plunge came I was sucked under, and, coming to the surface, I saw no boat around, so I struck out for the other ship. One of the liner's lifeboats came by, so I clung to the ropes and eventually got into the small vessel, exhausted and nearly frozen. We were taken on board the Storstad and placed in the engine room.

"Some of the survivors were raving mad from the shock and hardships. Dr. Grant, the ship's surgeon, was very calm, and by the attention he gave the survivors he surely saved many lives. There were no officers there, and he simply stood out and controlled the situation.

"The passengers lost nearly everything. The women were extremely brave and they showed much courage. Helen O'Hara of Toronto, a child of 10, whose father was drowned while trying to save her, told a pathetic story.

"My papa awakened mamma and brought me up on deck. When the ship began to sink he took me under one arm and jumped into the water with me. He then began to swim with me and placed me on a piece of wood. I did not see my papa after that. I swam with the piece of wood and soon I came to a boat and was taken in."

"Where did you learn to swim?" asked one of the group, listening to the child's story.

"I took lessons at Haverhill College," she said.

Few women were saved from the river. The lists so far show twenty-two rescued. Assistant Purser Hayes said Capt. Kendall bade him goodbye on the bridge, as the water was lapping their feet.

The Captain had a life preserver, but handed it over to a passenger. Hayes and the Captain jumped together, and Hayes was picked up by a lifeboat. Thirty minutes later the ship had foundered and Capt. Kendall was discovered clinging to a piece of wreckage. He was taken into No. 3 boat and immediately took active command and saved seventy-three lives in that boat alone.

Two Victims of the Steamship Disaster.

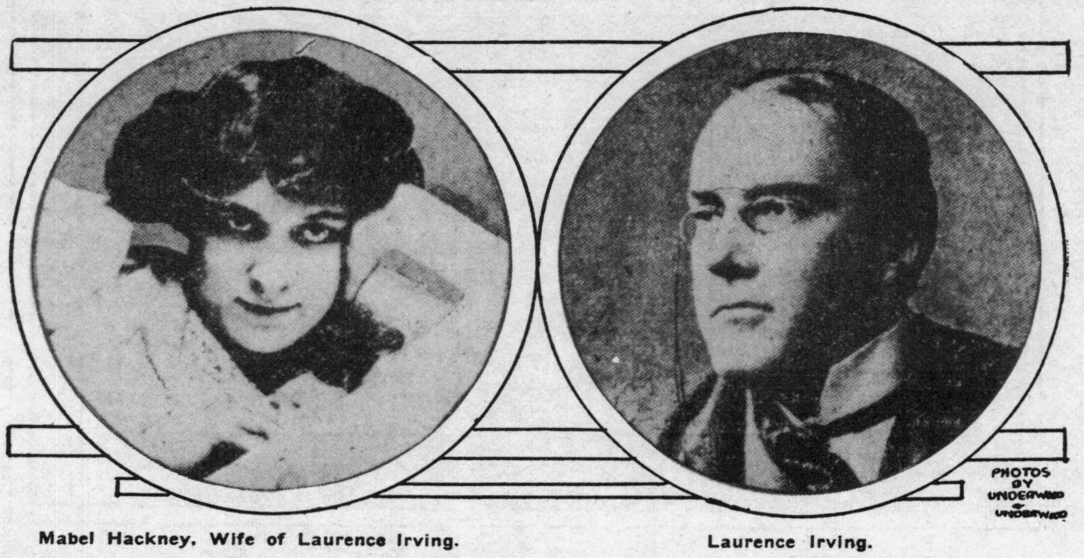
PHOTOS BY UNDERWOOD & UNDERWOOD

Mabel Hackney, Wife of Laurence Irving. Laurence Irving.

By The Associated Press.

Ambulances in Readiness.

QUEBEC, May 29.—A full equipment of ambulances supplied by the City of Quebec, the town of Levis, on the opposite side of the river, and the Army Medical Corps, was awaiting at Levis when the survivors' special train arrived, and the passengers were immediately disembarked and removed to the ferryboat Polaris, which had been waiting at a wharf especially chosen to facilitate the transfer to Quebec.

It was a pitiful sight when the Polaris docked on the Quebec side at 8:30 o'clock and the 396 men and women trooped, faltering, down the gangway. The faces of all plainly registered the frightful experience they had gone through. Very few of the survivors possessed a complete outfit of clothes. The majority wore only shirts, trousers, and boots.

Crowd with Heads Bared.

Heads were bared as the injured were brought ashore, supported by friends and by officials of the company. The second and third class passengers and the crew were immediately made comfortable on the Allan liner Alsatian, which was lying in an adjoining berth at the breakwater. The injured first-class passengers were transferred in automobiles and other vehicles to the Château Frontenac. A staff of physicians and nurses took charge of the injured.

Among the survivors of the first cabin there were eight women and one child, and, strangely, among the twenty-nine rescued from the second cabin there were also eight women and one child. Of the 101 persons saved from the steerage four were women.

Among the passengers left in Rimouski were a number who were so ill or so badly injured that they had to be taken to a hospital.

Survivors gave special praise to the heroic work of Dr. James F. Grant of Victoria, B. C., ship's surgeon on the Empress of Ireland. To his coolness was credited the saving of many persons taken out of the water who probably would have perished had they not received prompt medical attention.

A story to the effect that there was a tremendous explosion on board the Empress of Ireland after she was hit by the Storstad was told by Philip Lawler, a steerage passenger from Brantford, Ont. Lawler was on his way to England with his wife and his son, Herbert, 15 years old.

When the collision occurred the Empress of Ireland listed under the severe shock and water rushed into the steerage quarters. A few seconds later an explosion shook the vessel. Lawler said this probably was when the water reached the boilers.

Shot Into Water by Blast.

"People were simply shot out of the ship into the river by the explosion," Lawler continued. "I was pushed overboard with my wife and boy. The boy could swim, and so I tried to take care of my wife, but somehow she slipped from my grasp and sank."

Dr. Johnston, chief medical officer on the Empress of Ireland, said that had not the Storstad backed out so soon a larger number of persons would have been saved. He asserted that when the collier pulled herself free the sea surged into the hole she had torn in the side of the Empress of Ireland, and the liner quickly sank.

Hayes, chief Marconi operator of the Empress of Ireland, told of the sinking of the vessel.

"As soon as I felt the shock of the collision," he said, "I was ordered to sound the danger signal, and the flash of my S O S was immediately picked up by the operator at Father Point and was answered back. But I could not talk with him, for five minutes after the impact my dynamos failed, and seventeen minutes after the collision out boat went down."

Woman's Plucky Struggle.

To leap pluckily from the deck of the sinking liner and swim around for nearly an hour in the river and then to drop dead from exhaustion on the deck of the pilot boat Eureka was the fate of an unidentified woman. She had on little clothing.

The noise of the water rushing into his cabin awakened W. E. Davis of Toronto and his wife. They fled upon deck but in the rush of passengers were separated. Mr. Davis was saved but it was feared his wife was drowned.

Only two children were known to have been saved from the wreck. A wonderful rescue was one of these—little Gracie Hanagan, 8-year-old daughter of the leader of the Salvation Army band. Her father and mother both were drowned. Gracie was not told of their loss, and believed tonight they would come to Quebec on the next boat.

When asked how she was saved, Gracie said: "Oh, I saved myself."

The child, her hair hanging in braids down her back, was entirely unconcerned, apparently not realizing what she had been through. No lifeboat was near when she was thrown from the Empress of Ireland, and she sank at once, but rose to the surface in a moment, saw a piece of floating wood near her and seized it. Later she was pulled into a lifeboat. She was numbed by the chilly air and cold water, but was revived and soon was entirely restored.

Sank with Wife Thrice.

Major Atwell of Toronto and his wife were among the saved.

"I got a lifebelt for my wife," said Major Atwell, "and we both jumped into the water together when we saw that the vessel was doomed to go down. We both sank three times, being carried under by the suction of the foundering vessel. When we came up the third time I saw a lifeboat near and I swam to it, pulling my wife after me. Then those in the boat pulled us in and we were saved.

"The impact was just sufficient to waken us. It sounded as if our boat had struck a rock. It was very slight, and I was surprised when I afterward came to realize the awful consequences of the crash. When we got on the deck there were very few persons to be seen. In fact, the people on the deck were so few that they were hardly noticeable.

"The reason for this is that when the boat had listed to one side the stairs from the sleeping apartments up to the boat decks were very difficult, almost impossible to mount. I did not see the hole in the side of the ship as I rushed for the stairs, but I did see the water pouring in in such volume that it threatened to drown us before we could mount them."

Awakened by Crash.

K. A. McIntyre was in the second cabin with most of the other Salvation Army passengers. He told a vivid story of his own experiences and of what he saw as he swam to safety.

"Virtually every leading officer of the Salvation Army in Canada," he said, "is gone. Commissioner Rees and his wife and children went down, and only three of this family survive. And out of our Salvation party of 150 on board probably fewer than twenty were rescued.

"I was on the upper deck and therefore had a betterchance to get to safety than those in the lower ones. The water came in through the port holes of the lower decks before the passengers there realized their danger, or that there was danger at all.

"I was aroused from my sleep by the impact and awakened the others in my cabin. I could plainly hear the rush of water, and I felt sure that something serious had happened. I also heard the machinery of the boat running. It did not stop immediately after the crash but continued until the explosion occurred.

Gave Life Belt to Woman.

"I grabbed a life preserver and went out on the deck. On deck there were no life belts, and people were standing about apparently unable to determine what to do. I gave my belt to Mrs. Ford, one of our party. I tied the belt on her myself.

"My three comrades went to the bottom. I swam in the direction of the vessel that ran us down, and was pulled into a lifeboat of the collier. I saw the collier not far from where the Empress foundered. She was all lighted up.

"When I was taken on board I saw many men rescued practically unclothed. I was almost naked myself, and the rest of those on board were shivering and in a bad state from the icy water of the river and the chilly morning air. Soon we were attended to by those on board the collier and made warm and comfortable.

"As I swam through the icy waters I heard the dull explosion caused by the water reaching the engines. It was followed by a burst of steam that spread to all parts of the vessel. There came a quick listing of the liner, and she turned over. It looked to me as if she turned turtle.

"I do not think there were many first-class passengers saved. I saw only one of the first-class boats lowered.

Behavior of Crew Commended.

"The weather was virtually calm and there was plenty of light on the water when I went on deck. I saw no fog. I thought at first we had hit a rock. Some officers of the vessel said that the ship would not go any further, for bottom had been struck.

"The behavior of the crew was, on the whole, good, though it must be said that the men hardly had time to collect themselves or to effect rescues in any systematic way. The boat was really sunk before the crew or anybody else realized it or could do anything.

"Those of the crew who got to the deck tried to launch a boat on the upturned side of the vessel, but this was impossible, because the list was such that the boat could not be put into the water and it landed on the side of the vessel.

"The decks were almost perpendicular, so that to escape many passengers had to slide down from the higher side to the lower or water side."

THE EMPRESS A FINE SHIP.

One of the Most Palatial Vessels in North Atlantic Service.

The Empress of Ireland was one of the finest steamers engaged in the North Atlantic trade, as the Canadian service is termed. She was 570 feet long, 65 feet 6 inches beam, 14,500 gross tonnage and 18,000 horse power. She had accommodations for 350 first, 350 second, and 1,000 third class passengers. She was valued at $2,000,000.

The vessel was equipped with the latest appliances for safety at sea, including longitudinal and transverse water tight steel bulkheads, submarine signalling and wireless apparatus. Her cabins were well furnished and spacious.

The steamer Storstad, Capt. Andersen, is a vessel of 3,561 tons register, built for the coal trade, and is capable of carrying 7,000 tons dead weight. She has been engaged for some time carrying coal between Sydney, Quebec, and Montreal. She had a crew of about forty-eight men.

Father Point, near which the wreck of the Empress of Ireland occurred, is a small village on the south bank of the St. Lawrence River about 200 miles down the river from Quebec. At this point the river is thirty miles wide.

Father Point is a station on the Intercolonial Railroad and receives mail by a cutter running from the town to the Canadian Pacific liners, and is also a pilot station. The pilots are all French-Canadians, who form a very close corporation, and in the Winter, when the St. Lawrence is frozen, they spend their time on their farms in the section around Father Point and Rimouski.

In the early Summer the St. Lawrence often is visited by dense fogs which sometimes hold up the liners for 24 to 48 hours as the course up to Quebec is a zigzag one and very dangerous to navigation.

Wireless Station That Brought Help and a Rescue Ship.

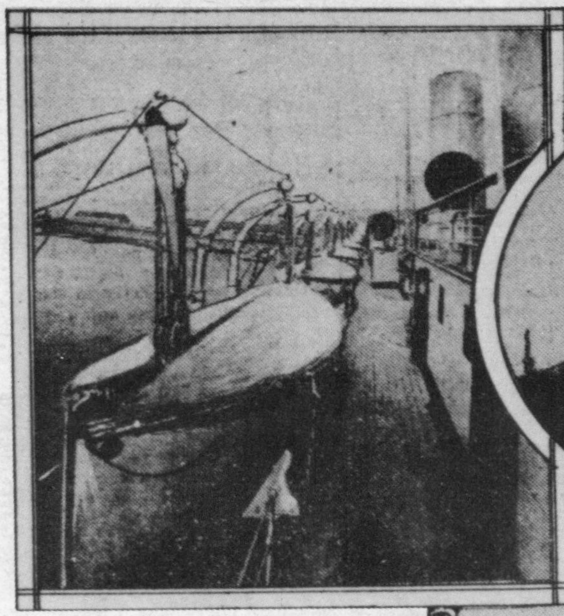
Lifeboats on the steamer Empress of Ireland.

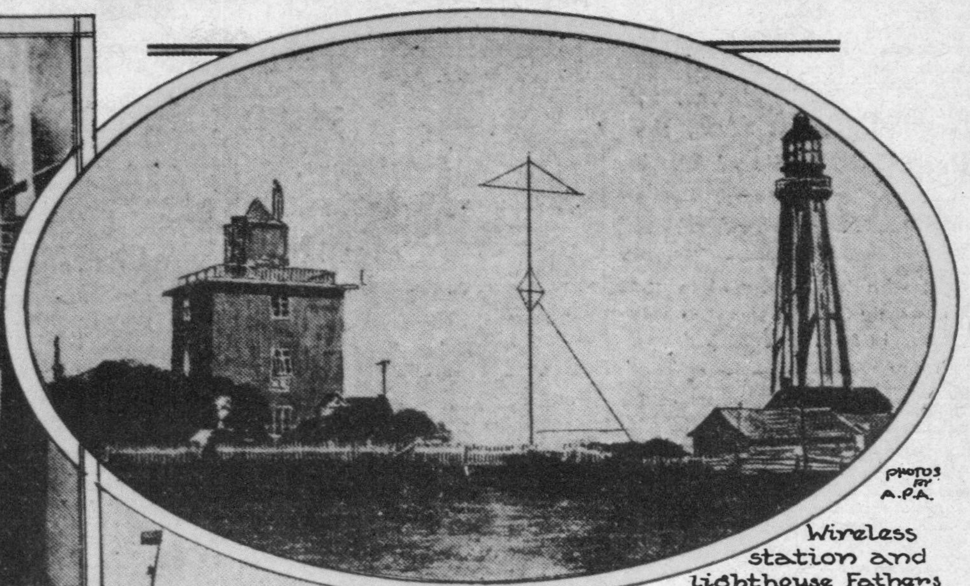

Wireless station and lighthouse Fathers Point.

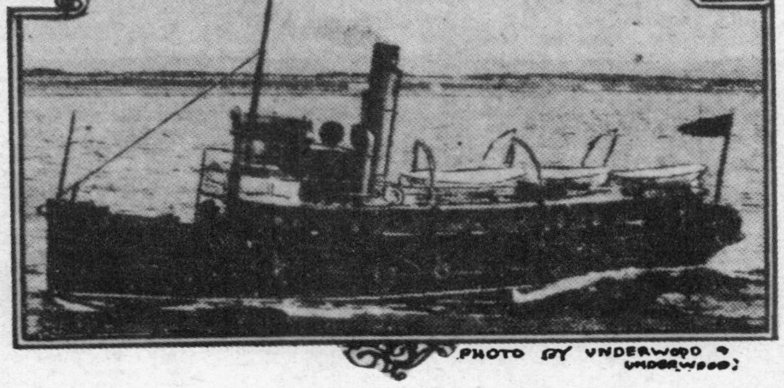

Canadian Revenue Cutter Eureka.

LINER IN COLLISION SINKS, 934 LOST

Continued from Page 1.

to, waiting for the fog to lift, or day to break, the Danish collier Storstad crashed bow-on into the side of the big Canadian liner, striking her about midway of her length and tearing her side open to the stern.

According to some of the officers, when the lights of the Storstad were sighted it was reported to Capt. Kendall on the bridge, and he at once signaled with three blasts of the whistle, "I am continuing my course."

As the collier approached Capt. Kendall signaled full steam astern, but the Storstad came on, ramming the Empress amidships on the starboard side. Instantly the Empress began to list.

The crash occurred not far from the shore off Father Point, 150 miles from Quebec, and ten miles from this point on the St. Lawrence. In reality, therefore, the disaster was not one of the ocean, but of the river. Unlike the Titanic's victims, the Empress of Ireland's lost their lives within sight of shore—in land-locked waters.

As soon as the ship's officers recovered from the shock of the collision and it was seen that the vessel had received a vital blow, a wireless S O S call was sent out. The distress signal was picked up by the Government mail tender Lady Evelyn here, and the Government pilot boat Eureka at Father Point, and immediately both set out to the rescue. So deep was the hurt of the Empress, however, and so fast the inrush of waters that long before either of the rescue boats could reach the scene she had gone down.

Died in Ice-Chilled Waters.

Only floating wreckage and a few lifeboats and rafts from the steamer, buoying up fewer than a third of those who had set sail on her, were to be found. The others had gone to the bottom with the vessel, had been crushed to death in the collision, or had been forced, from exhaustion and exposure in the ice-chilled waters, to loose their hold on bits of wreckage that had supported them and had drowned.

Only a few persons were picked up by the Storstad, which was badly crippled by the collision, and these were brought here by the collier, together with those saved by the Eureka and the Lady Evelyn. Twenty-two of the rescued died from injuries or exposure. The others, most of whom had jumped into the boats or plunged into the water from the sinking ship, were scantily clad. They were freely provided with such clothing as the town could supply, and later those who were able to travel were placed on board a train and started for Quebec, where they arrived tonight.

All reports agreed that in the brief space of time—not more than fourteen minutes—between the shock of the collision and the sinking of the vessel there was little chance for systematic marshaling of the passengers. Indeed, everything indicates that hundreds of those on board the steamer probably never reached the decks. Very few women were among the saved—not more than a dozen—the lists make it appear.

Awakened by Frenzied Cries.

"It all happened so quickly that we did not really know what was going on, and nobody had time to cry 'Women first!'" one of the passengers told Capt. Bellinger of the Eureka. "The stewards did not have time to rouse the people from their berths," the survivor said. "Those who heard the frenzied calls of the officers for the passengers to hurry on deck lost no time in obeying them, rushing up from their cabins in scanty attire. They piled into the boats, which were rapidly lowered, and were rowed away. Many who waited to dress were drowned."

In the interval during which the Empress of Ireland was rapidly filling, and while frightened throngs were hurrying to escape before she sank, there was an explosion which shook the ship and added horror to the situation. According to one of the rescued, the explosion, probably caused by the water reaching the boilers, bulged the liner's side and hurled many persons from her decks and plunged them into the water.

The ship's heavy list as the water poured into her made the work of launching boats increasingly difficult from moment to moment, and when she finally took her plunge to the bottom scores still left on her decks were carried down in the vortex. Only a few were able to clear her sides and find support on pieces of wreckage.

From all accounts Capt. Kendall bore himself like a true sailor so long as his ship stood under him. Capt. Kendall retained such command of the situation, that while the Storstad's stem still hung in the gash it had made in the Empress's side, he begged the master of the collier to keep his propellers going so that the hole might remain plugged. The Storstad, however, dropped back and the Empress filled and foundered.

The Storstad is on her way to Quebec tonight, badly damaged, but under her own power.

Capt. Kendall stood on his bridge as the ship went down. One of the boats from the liner picked him up, and he directed its work of saving others until the craft was loaded to the gunwales. The Captain was injured in the crash and suffered from exposure, but his hurts are not dangerous and his speedy recovery is expected.

When day broke this morning the rescue boats had not yet returned from the scene of the wreck. People standing on shore at Father Point scanned the horizon with telescopes, saw the rescue steamers picking up boats in the river, and prepared to give help to the survivors.

When the rescue ships docked here the station platform was converted into a hospital and the townspeople, bringing food and clothing, united in a common effort to aid the sufferers. Twelve bodies, with faces covered, lay side by side on the wharf.

The residents of Rimouski, numbering only 800, came silently to the pier where the dead and exhausted were being landed, and, under the direction of the Mayor, H. R. Fiset, gave aid wherever possible. Every doctor in the town was on the pier, and many of the injured were taken to private homes. From cedar chests and closets the townsfolk brought garments of all descriptions for those who had lost their belongings. Two headquarters were established—at the wharf and at the station of the Inter-Colonial Railway. At the station those injured and not removed to homes were cared for.

The rescue boats Eureka and Lady Evelyn found, on reaching the point where the Empress sank, a scene not unsimilar to that which greeted the liners which rushed to the Titanic's aid. The ship had vanished, and the surface of the water, fortunately calm, was dotted with lifeboats and smeared with floating debris.

Many Injured in Lifeboats.

In the lifeboats were huddled the survivors, dazed and moaning, some of them dying of injuries sustained in the rush of leaving the sinking vessel. Few could give anything but incoherent, almost hysterical, accounts of what had happened. J. L. Black and Mrs. Black of Ottawa said they had jumped into the river together. They had been roused by the shock of the collision, and, unable to get into a lifeboat, had rushed to the ship's side and jumped overboard. They were picked up by a boat from the Lady Evelyn.

Both the first and second Marconi operators of the Empress were saved. Edward Bomford, the second operator, was coming on duty when the vessel was hit. He caught the Father Point Marconi station and called for help. Bomford was saved by falling into a lifeboat. The other operator, Ronald Furgusson, had to swim for the boat. Both operators came back to Rimouski on board the Eureka.

Passengers were loud in their praise of the Captain and the pilot of the Lady Evelyn and Capt. Belanger of the Eureka and their crews. All of them displayed the greatest bravery, it was said.

All of the authorities of Rimouski and Father Point joined in caring for the survivors. They were sorely in need of help, as most of them had on little clothing, and the temperature was almost down to the freezing point. When they had been cared for and sent on their way to Quebec the work of recovering the bodies was undertaken.

The rescue steamers themselves had brought in nearly fifty of these and tonight, after they had continued their search the entire day, a total of about 300 bodies had been recovered. One woman and four men still living, but unconscious, were picked up during the day by the steamers. Few of the bodies had been identified tonight.

The wireless is credited with having saved many lives from the sinking liner. Responding promptly to the S O S call, the Eureka was on the spot approximately twenty minutes after the disaster, and the Lady Evelyn but little later.

About 300 bodies of dead from the Empress of Ireland lie tonight in the sheds at the wharf here. Some of the bodies have been identified and claimed, the others will be kept here until friends or relatives give orders for their disposal. Among the bodies on the wharf is that of a woman whose arms are clasped tightly about her child.

It was noticeable that on board the train that took the survivors from Rimouski to Quebec the greater number of those who had been saved from the sea were men.

Capt. Kendall was downcast over the disaster when he was brought ashore here.

"I wish I had gone to the bottom with her," he said.

TELLS OF PRECAUTIONS.

Manager of Line Says Drills Showed Efficiency of Crew.

Special Cable to THE NEW YORK TIMES.

LONDON, Saturday, May 30.—Mr. Kensey, Managing Chief of Ocean Services of the Canadian Pacific Railway and Allan Lines, said today:

"I was in Liverpool at the Board of Trade inspection of the Empress of Ireland on May 15 when all the boats were very smartly swung out in less than a minute. They had a bulkhead drill, when every single bulkhead door in the ship was closed. Then there was a fire drill. The men also drilled at sea during the voyage. There was a bulkhead door drill every day.

"In addition to these precautions, we recently appointed Capt. Staunton, R. N. R., from the Orient Line, one of our Marine Superintendents, with special duties of inspecting the boats and life-saving apparatus for the whole service. He was required constantly to travel to and fro. He is now in Montreal, putting three ships through their drill, seeing to the lowering of boats, putting crews in shape, and trying to make every one of the crew into an efficient boat hand."

The letter of instructions sent to Capt. Kendall by the manager of ocean service on behalf of the Canadian Pacific Railway when he took over the command of the Empress of Ireland contained the following passages:

"I desire particularly to call your attention to the importance of your command, to the value of the ship and to emphasize to you the instructions of the company relative to the care of your vessel and the lives of your passengers.

"It is to be distinctly understood that safe navigation of the ship is to be in all instances your first consideration. You must run no risk which by any possibility might result in accident. You must always bear in mind that the safety of the lives and property intrusted to your care is the ruling principle by which you must be governed in the navigation of your ship, and that no saving of time on voyage is to be purchased at the risk of accident.

"I cannot sufficiently emphasize my desire that these instructions shall be carried out to the letter. It is expected that all officers of your ship will bear this in mind and will be specially cautioned by you."

"All the News That's Fit to Print."

The New York Times.

THE WEATHER
Fair today and Friday; moderate temperature; moderate east and southeast winds.
For full weather report see Page 21

VOL. LXIII...NO. 20,607. ... NEW YORK, FRIDAY, JUNE 26, 1914.—TWENTY-TWO PAGES. ONE CENT In Greater New York, Jersey City and Newark. | Elsewhere, TWO CENTS.

WILSON PREDICTS A GIGANTIC BOOM

Sure to Follow Passage of His Anti-Trust Bills, the President Tells Editors.

SEES SIGNS OF REVIVAL

His Programme, "A New Constitution of Freedom for Business," to Quiet All Fears.

WILL NOT BE THWARTED

With Clenched Fist He Declares He Will Permit No Postponement of Pending Legislation.

Special to The New York Times.

WASHINGTON, June 25.—Addressing a delegation of visiting Virginia editors, President Wilson today declared that the United States was on the eve of the greatest business boom in its history. Signs of revival already were discernible, he said.

The boom, said Mr. Wilson, would come as a result of the "new constitution of freedom for business" incorporated in his pending anti-trust legislation, which, he declared, would not be postponed—and his jaws snapped in his earnestness as he made the assertion—but would be pressed to successful enactment, and, he added, that would not take long.

The President made his remarks shortly after he had heard of the H. B. Claflin Company failure in New York, although no official ventured to say that he had that in mind while speaking. That he was tremendously in earnest was evident. His eyes flashed and at times he clenched and raised his fist for emphasis.

The address was delivered in the East Room. While the President spoke to a small group, it was implied that his assurances were meant for the country. A military aid, in full-dress uniform, stood beside the President, and there was every indication that the speech was meant to be one of the most important of the Administration.

For ten years, the President said, business had been uneasy because of attacks on it. He contended that his Administration was the first in years that had been the real friend of business, and he added that his Administration was going to prove its friendship by clearing away all anxiety among business men over what was to come.

In declaring that signs of business revival already were to be seen throughout the country, Mr. Wilson seemed to feel sure of his ground. He declared that, through Governmental agencies and extensive correspondence, he was better able to judge conditions than any one else in the country. He compared the condition of business in recent years to a man about to undergo an operation who feared that it would be a capital one. He added that it had become apparent that only minor operations were necessary, and that it would be dangerous to postpone them.

Nothing would be more unfair to business, the President declared, than to keep it guessing. During the pendency of the Tariff and Currency bills, he said, business shivered, but there were no serious effects. He declared that there was no reason to think that the result would be more serious after the anti-trust bills were passed.

Mr. Wilson's speech follows in full:

Best Able to Judge Conditions.

I think it is appropriate in receiving you to say just a word or two in assistance of your judgment about the existing conditions. You are largely responsible for the state of public opinion. You furnish the public with information and in your editorials you furnish it with the interpretation of that information.

We are in the presence of a business situation which is variously interpreted. Here in Washington, through the Bureau of Commerce and other instrumentalities that are at our disposal and through a correspondence which comes to us from all parts of the nation, we are perhaps in a position to judge of the actual conditions of business better than those can judge who are at any other single point in the country; and I want to say to you that as a matter of fact the signs of a very strong business revival are becoming more and more evident from day to day.

I want to suggest this to you: Business has been in a feverish and apprehensive condition in this country for more than ten years. I will not stop to point out the time at which it began to be apprehensive, but during more than ten years business has been the object of sharp criticism in the United States, a criticism growing in volume and growing in particularity; and, as a natural consequence, as the volume of criticism has increased business has grown more and more anxious.

Business men have acted as some men do who fear they will have to undergo an operation and who are not sure that when they get on the table the operation will not be a capital operation. As a matter of fact, as the diagnosis has progressed, it has become more and more evident that no capital operation was necessary—that at the most a minor operation was necessary to remove admitted distempers and evils.

The treatment is to be constitutional, rather than surgical, affecting habits of life and action which have been hurtful. For on all hands it is admitted that there are processes of business, or have been processes of business, in this country which ought to be corrected; but the correction has been postponed, and in proportion to the postponement the fever has increased—the fever of apprehension.

There is nothing more fatal to business than to be kept guessing from month to month and from year to year whether something serious is going to happen to it or not, and what in particular is going to happen to it, if anything does. It is impossible to forecast the prospects of any line of business unless you know what the year is go-

Continued on Page 2.

BENTON'S SLAYER KILLED.

Col. Fierro Fell at the Taking of Zacatecas, Shot by His Men.

Special to The New York Times.

EL PASO, Texas, June 25.—Col. Rodolfo F. Fierro, "the Butcher," as he is known throughout Northern Mexico, died at the taking of Zacatecas, a victim of the hatred of his own men. His death will probably mean that no one will ever be brought to justice for the killing of William S. Benton, the British rancher, for even Constitutionalists tacitly admit that Fierro was the man who killed the Englishman.

That Fierro met death at Zacatecas was the information contained in a telegram received here by A. Benavides from his brother, the commander of the famous Zaragoza brigade.

Confirmation of the report of the death of Gen. Trinidad Rodriguez and the serious wounding of Gen. Monclovio Herrera was also contained in the message.

JABS "WHITE HOUSE PETS."

Looking After Fences, Says Humphrey, While Congress Patriots Sizzle.

WASHINGTON, June 25.—Declaring that "if enough of us would go away so that it would be impossible for the rest of us to transact any business it would be a blessing upon this harassed country," Representative William E. Humphrey, Republican, of Washington, today charged in the House that it was "the little leaders by Executive order" who were keeping Congress from adjourning.

"We're being kept here by Executive order," said Mr. Humphrey. "Looking on the Democratic side, I note the absence of the gentleman from Texas, Mr. Henry. Why is he not here attending to business? He is one of the White House favorites. I also note the absence of the distinguished gentleman from Georgia, Mr. Hardwick. His interests at home have become greater than those of the country. He is another White House favorite. Why is he not here attending to business? I see also that the gentleman from Pennsylvania is absent. He so seldom comes on the floor that the new members are not familiar with his distinguished appearance. He is another White House favorite.

"Why are not those pets of the teacher here attending to business? I note that the distinguished gentleman from Alabama, Mr. Underwood, and the distinguished gentleman from New York, Mr. Fitzgerald, and the great Speaker of this House are staying here attending to business, but these little leaders, by Executive order, who are out preaching that we must stay in session so the country may be saved—where are they?

"What has become of the leaders by White House dictation? They are out preaching the doctrine of repudiation. They are telling the people what a grand thing it is to be under the British flag and the transcontinental railroads. They are telling the rest of us to stay here this Summer, while they are looking after the fences.

"I hope this statement will be taken to the White House, showing where these special favorites are and what they are doing, and showing how the men whose judgment the President does not value and whose influence he will not take are blessing the country by staying here and attending to business, while his favorites are running around trying to be re-elected."

BRASSEY ARRESTED AS SPY.

Kiel Harbor Policeman Takes Naval Expert Into Custody.

Special Cable to THE NEW YORK TIMES.

KIEL, Friday, June 26.—A most extraordinary incident occurred to mar the even tenor of the Anglo-German naval love feast in the harbor here yesterday.

Lord Brassey, who arrived here Wednesday in his famous steam yacht Sunbeam, was arrested by the harbor police late yesterday afternoon on suspicion of espionage. Lord Brassey had left the Sunbeam in a dinghy to go around the harbor. As he was passing near the imperial dockyard he was suddenly accosted from the shore by a policeman, who informed him that he was under arrest.

Other details at this late hour are unavailable, except that it took Lord Brassey an hour and a quarter to establish his identity and obtain his release.

The huge floating dock in the imperial dockyard, near which Lord Brassey was arrested, has for several years, since the outbreak of the spy mania in Germany, been adorned by a legend, in letters two feet high and extending the full length of the dock, warning trespassers that they will be punished to the full extent of the espionage law.

KIEL, June 25.—The German Emperor today visited the British flagship of the Second Battle Squadron, King George V., on which his flag as Admiral of the fleet was hoisted. Vice Admiral Sir George Warrender, commanding the squadron, who was outranked by the Emperor in the latter's capacity as a British Admiral, transferred his own flag to the Centurion.

The Emperor remained an hour on board the flagship, during which time he was nominally in supreme command of the British fleet. On leaving he was saluted with an Admiral's twenty-one guns, instead of a ruler's twenty-three.

Lord Brassey is known the world over as the founder and first editor of The Naval Annual. He has been a Civil Lord of the British Admiralty, has served on various royal commissions dealing with the problems of navigation, and is Lord Warden of the Cinque Ports.

PAY $50,000 LABOR PENALTY

Record Collection Under Alien Contract Law from Boston Concern.

WASHINGTON, June 25.—An agreement, announced today, between attorneys for the Department of Labor and the Dwight Manufacturing Company of Boston, provides for payment by the company of $50,000, the largest single penalty ever collected for violation of the alien contract labor law.

The company was charged with importing a number of laborers, mainly Greeks, to work in its cotton mills in Chicopee, Mass., and Alabama. The case had been pending since 1910, and when it was ready to be brought to trial the company offered to settle for $50,000, and the Government accepted.

HAAN'S (DOWNTOWN) RESTAURANT, Park Row Building. Coolest, pleasantest, best. Superior food. Moderate prices.—Adv.

PAN-AMERICANISM NOW A REALITY

Mediators Think Their Purpose Achieved, Even if Mexicans Don't Confer.

BUT PARLEYS ARE EXPECTED

Calderon and Colleagues Are Looked For at the Falls by Tonight—A Day of Waiting.

4,500 DEAD IN ZACATECAS

Villa's Victory Cost Him 500 Men and the Federals 4,000, He Reports.

Huerta Says Mediators' Object Is Accomplished In Protocol.

Special Cable to THE NEW YORK TIMES.

MEXICO CITY, June 25.—THE NEW YORK TIMES cablegram telling of the signing of the peace protocols at Niagara on Wednesday night was shown to President Huerta today, and he said:

"The motive of the conferences at Niagara Falls has been the satisfactory adjustment of the international difference between Mexico and the United States. The country's internal questions never have been, are not, and will not be the subject matter of discussion in the conferences to which I refer, because they appertain exclusively to the republic."

Special to The New York Times.

NIAGARA FALLS, Ontario, June 25.—The South American mediators are congratulating themselves upon the accomplishment of the object for which they tendered their good offices to the American and Huerta Governments nine weeks ago.

Even if the Carranza delegates who have been appointed should not confer with the Huerta plenipotentiaries, or if conferences between them should be futile, the success of the mediation movement has been assured, they hold, through the prevention of further hostilities involving the American Government. Although they are not making any declaration on the subject, the mediators believe that what has been accomplished through their efforts has established the advisability of concerted action by American nations in all matters of dispute affecting two or more of the republics on this hemisphere. This is equivalent to saying that Pan-Americanism has become a reality, after many years of more or less academic discussion.

The mediators are greatly encouraged over the prospects of peace in Mexico afforded by the arrangement for Constitutionalist parleys with Gen. Huerta's delegates and pleased with the terms of the protocols agreed to last night by the American and Mexican Commissioners. They are convinced that the protocolized articles dealing with the Tampico indignity and the capture of Vera Cruz by the American armed forces have removed the danger of war between Mexico and the United States. With the international difficulties settled by last night's amicable arrangements, they believe the way has been paved to an adjustment of Mexican internal troubles.

Positive statements attributed to Constitutionalist leaders that representatives of Gen. Carranza would not participate in the proposed conferences with the delegates of Gen. Huerta at Niagara Falls have not discouraged those concerned in the mediation movement. Assurances have been given from the proper authority that the Carranza delegates will come here to negotiate a settlement of Mexico's internal troubles, and they are expected to arrive before the week is out.

It is the understanding here, based upon advices from Washington, that the time of the arrival of the Carranza delegates will depend upon the arrangements of Señor Calderon, Gen. Carranza's chief representative, who is expected to reach Washington tonight. It would not surprise anybody in the mediation circle if Señor Calderon and his colleagues arrived in Niagara Falls tomorrow. In fact, it is the expectation that they will be here before tomorrow night.

From now on the mediation conference will resolve itself into a series of meetings between the delegates of Gen. Huerta and those of Gen. Carranza, provided the latter come to this place in accordance with the arrangements made after the White House conference last Friday between President Wilson, Secretary Bryan, and Minister Naon, the representative of the board of mediation.

Señor da Gama, the Ambassador of Brazil and the senior member of the board, left Niagara Falls tonight to join Señora da Gama at Long Branch, and there is no certainty as to when he will return. Dr. Naon and Señor Suarez Mujica, the other mediators, will remain here, although Señor Suarez Mujica plans to make a short visit to Washington to see his family. If the Huerta and Carranza delegates reach an amicable agreement on a mode of settlement of Mexico's internal problems, the mediation conference may be concluded in Washington. Constructively, however, the mediation negotiations are still being conducted at Niagara Falls.

What course the American delegates, Justice Lamar and Mr. Lehmann, will follow while conferences are in progress between the representatives of the Mexican factions has not been determined. They cannot adopt any method of procedure until after the Carranza agents reach here. The American delegates do not expect to have any part in the new series of conferences, but they are inclined to remain here, marking time, as it were, in the idea that they may be of assistance in the conclusion of any

Continued on Page 5

GREEN STRIPE SCOTCH Ask for the Non-refillable bottle with the Green Stripe. ANDREW USHER & CO., Edinburgh.—Adv.

"Clover Time"—a Charming Picture in Rotogravure

A chubby figure flung out under a tree in waving grasses and pink clovers—this is the subject that the artist, C. Bergen, has painted, and which will be reproduced by The Times's new process of printing, rotogravure,

IN NEXT SUNDAY'S TIMES.

ROOSEVELT'S BAN ON WHITMAN FUSION

Says He's Barnes's Man and the Progressives Will Go It Alone.

MORE TALK OF "DRAFTING"

District Attorney Says He Will Never Be Subservient to Either Barnes or Roosevelt.

Special to The New York Times.

OYSTER BAY, N. Y., June 25.—After a conference of Progressive leaders at Sagamore Hill today it was announced that District Attorney Whitman will under no circumstances receive the indorsement of the Progressives in the event of his nomination by the Republicans. The Progressive Party will go it alone.

Col. Roosevelt made his position known in a vigorous statement in which he characterized Mr. Whitman as a Barnes candidate and a man who, if elected, would be subservient to the Republican State Chairman. The Colonel is satisfied that Mr. Whitman will be the nominee of the Republicans. He is satisfied also that Mr. Whitman will not subscribe to the principles of the Progressive Party.

The Colonel said he himself would support the ticket the Progressives place in the field. Whether he would accept if the Progressives nominated him for Governor at the primaries the Colonel did not say. He refused to comment upon that phase of the situation. Several of the Progressive leaders, however, said they thought there was little hope of inducing the Colonel to run.

Says Whitman Is Barnes's Man.

Here is what Col. Roosevelt had to say:

"It is evident to me that the decent citizens of this State demand that the State fight this Fall shall take the shape of a clean-cut movement against both old party organizations, controlled as one of them is by Mr. Barnes and the other by Mr. Murphy.

"I am struck by the statement in The Tribune today that the Whitman candidacy is being engineered by Mr. Barnes and his personal lieutenants in Albany County. I have similar information from other sections of the State.

"It is evidently the intention of the Barnes machine to run either Mr. Whitman or some other man on whose real subserviency they can count—in short, to have a rubber stamp ticket from top to bottom, a ticket of which the personnel would be wholly unimportant because the directive force behind would be Mr. Barnes. In my judgment neither the Progressives nor the Independent citizens will accept either Mr. Whitman or any one else who has failed already to show as a matter of principle and not as a matter of expediency by clean-cut statements in the open that he is as unalterably opposed to the Barnes machine as to the Murphy machine.

"I shall of course fight for the Progressive Party in this State just as I shall fight for the Progressive Party in the nation and when the Progressive Party has nominated its State ticket, as I am sure it will, on a basis of frank and utter antagonism to the boss-controlled organizations of both the old parties, alike to the Barnes organization and the Murphy organization, I shall do all I can to aid in the election of that ticket and as far as my voice will permit, I will speak in every section of this State from one end to the other in support of the cause to which I think I have a right to expect all good citizens in the State to subscribe."

Big Moose at Conference.

All the details of what took place at the conference at which Col. Roosevelt decided definitely to toss Mr. Whitman into the discard as far as the Progressive Party was concerned, and come out against any form of amalgamation with the Republican Party in the State were not made known. Enough was learned, however, to indicate strongly that Col. Roosevelt did not put aside the thought of joining forces with the independent Republicans without a measure of regret.

He was told, it is understood, that there was no hope of a successful outcome of the plan once hinted at, of forcing the Republicans to nominate a man who would denounce William Barnes and be acceptable to the Progressives. Mr. Whitman, he was told, seemed certain of obtaining the Republican nomination, and Whitman, he also learned from the scouts, had no intention of coming out openly for several of the more radical innovations in State government on which the Progressive Party has built its house, such as the recall, referendum, and initiative.

Those who attended the conference included George W. Perkins, Chairman of the Executive Committee of the National Committee; State Chairman Theodore Douglas Robinson, County Chairman Francis W. Bird, Horace S. Wilkinson of Syracuse, who has been canvassing the situation to prove to the Colonel that he would sweep the State if nominated for Governor; ex-State Chairman William H. Hotchkiss, Judge William L. Ransom, Henry L. Stoddard, Chauncey J. Hamlen of Buffalo, William H. Childs, ex-Senator Frederick M. Davenport, Walter F. Brown, State Chairman of the Progressive Party in Ohio, and John M. Parker, State Chairman in Louisiana.

Bird Reads Duell Out of Party.

When the conference broke up, about 7 o'clock tonight, Mr. Robinson announced, with a smile on his face, that

Continued on Page 3.

Chas. E. Matthews, the Desk Man, now 81 E. 28th St.; also Commercial Stationery.—Adv.

OCEAN FLIER NEEDS MORE LIFTING POWER

America, with Larger Hydroplanes, to be Tested with 1,000 Pounds More Weight Today.

FLIGHT MAY BE DELAYED

Porte Quoted as Saying He Will Not Attempt Trip Unless Improvements Are Made.

Special to The New York Times.

HAMMONDSPORT, N. Y., June 25.—The critical test of the America, Rodman Wanamaker's transatlantic flyer, will take place tomorrow when the lifting power of the airboat will be tried out with a load of more than 1,000 pounds of concrete.

On its trial flights so far the total weight of the America and its crew was about 3,300 pounds. This is about 1,700 pounds less than its total weight will be when it is loaded with 300 gallons of gasoline for its transatlantic flight.

No attempt to fly the America with much weight has been made as yet, because the hydroplane boards which enable the airboat to climb out of the water, have not worked as well as was expected. The original hydroplane boards, which are like fins fitted to the keel of the boat, were ten by eighteen inches.

A new pair of hydroplane boards, or elevators, have been built at the Curtiss factory. They are 10 by 24 inches and increase the lifting power considerably. A crew of six men worked all night at the Aviation Field fitting up the new boards, and they will be ready for the America's flight tomorrow evening. Mr. Curtiss is confident that the new boards will meet the difficulty that was feared when the airboat should attempt to fly with a heavy load.

The original hydroplane boards each had a surface of 180 square inches. Mr. Curtiss calculated that when the America was making forty-five miles an hour each square inch would have a lifting power of thirty pounds, so that the two boards should be capable of lifting 10,800 pounds, more than twice the weight of the America on its proposed ocean flight.

Nevertheless, it was found that the boards would have to be enlarged in order to allow the America to jump into the air without first racing through the water for any distance. This is important, especially since the America may have to alight and rise from the ocean. The difficulty of climbing into the air would be increased considerably in rough water.

May Soon Be Ready.

In case the new hydroplane boards prove successful, Mr. Curtiss said today that only two or three more trial flights would be necessary to demonstrate the America's fitness for the transatlantic attempt.

On the other hand, if the new boards are not considered perfect, structural changes may have to be made in the America. This would involve much delay. If the America does not make a perfect ascent from the water when she flies tomorrow with the new boards and extra weight, it is probable that Lieut. Porte will decided to postpone his start from Newfoundland until about Aug. 5, when he will be aided by a full moon.

Lieut. Porte was anxious to make the flight with the full moon in July, but the America could not be completed in time to make that possible. He was still in favor of flying in July, without the benefit of the moon, however, for the reason that weather conditions between the Azores and Spain are better in July. Cyclonic storms occur frequently in August.

Mr. Curtiss said today that the flight could not very well be undertaken until after July 20. It was decided today that the America should not be shipped until July 11. She should arrive at St. John's, Newfoundland, on July 16 or 17. Three days will be required to set up the craft. Trial flights will have to be made.

After that the flight will take place as soon as weather conditions are sufficiently favorable. Special reports on weather conditions in the Atlantic will be cabled to Lieut. Porte from the Weather Bureau at Washington. If weather conditions delay the flight for many days it is believed that Lieut. Porte would wait for the full moon on Aug. 5 and fly then, taking the risk of encountering storms.

It was intended until to-day to ship the America on July 3, when Lieut. Porte expected to sail for Newfoundland. The postponement was made, however, in order to insure sufficient time for the trial flights.

The America made a short flight at 7:20 o'clock this evening in order to try out the propellers under a different method of operation. Heretofore, the propellers have turned "inboard," the two blades driving so that the currents of air from each converged. It was found that the powerful air currents forced down the trial planes, giving the America her tendency to rise.

Today the twin propellers were reversed, so that they drove their currents "outboard," or away from each other. This relieved the pressure of air on the tail planes and counteracted the tendency to soar. On landing Lieut. Porte said the new trial had been "very pleasing." During the trial the America reduced speed to forty-five miles an hour and rode with her keel drawing two inches of water. The reduced speed enabled Mr. Curtiss to keep alongside the flyer in a powerboat and observe the effect of the new propeller arrangement. He said the America had behaved beautifully with her propellers driving outboard and that they would remain that way.

Can Carry Ton of Gasoline.

The contract with Rodman Wanamaker calls for acceptance of the America when she demonstrates her ability to fly with gasoline to carry her for twenty hours and a 20 per cent. margin over that. This totals about 230 gallons, according to bench tests, or a weight of a

Continued on Page 4.

Drink Dewey's Haut Sauterne and you will work, sleep, and feel better. 138 Fulton St.—81 Nassau St., New York.—Adv.

SALEM SWEPT BY $10,000,000 FIRE

More Than Three Square Miles of Ancient Seaport Are Burned Over.

THOUSANDS ARE HOMELESS

Great Factory District Is in Ashes, but No Loss of Life.

OLD WITCHES' HOUSE GONE

Fine Colonial Homes and Many Public Buildings Also Destroyed.

Special to The New York Times.

SALEM, Mass., June 25.—The old City of Salem fought a fire today which for hours threatened the city's destruction. It swept over more than three square miles of territory. The property loss at 10:30 o'clock tonight was estimated to be from $10,000,000 to $15,000,000. The fire at that hour was said to be under control.

It was estimated late tonight that 10,000 persons were homeless. The city has 45,000 inhabitants. In all at least 1,000 buildings were destroyed. Inadequate water pressure was the cause of the disaster.

It is believed that all of the famous historic and literary landmarks except the Witches' House escaped destruction. These included the Peabody Museum, Essex Institute, Old Custom House, where Nathaniel Hawthorne did much of his literary work, and "The House of Seven Gables" made famous by the novelist.

Thousands of the homeless were encamped on Salem Common tonight, with such household goods as they could save piled around them. Long lines of refugees, most of them on foot, and others in wagons, carriages, and automobiles, crowded the road leading to Beverly, where hundreds spent the night in the parks.

The fire spread with such rapidity that early in the evening buildings were blown up with dynamite to stay its progress. It was several hours later, however, before it was in check.

The Boston & Maine Railroad station was threatened by the fire about 9 o'clock. The authorities at that hour, thoroughly alarmed, feared that there was no hope for the city, but with more reinforcements of firemen from other towns the fight was kept up and the flames were diverted from the station. When the station was saved as a matter of fact the fire was got under control.

The fire started in the leather factory of W. J. Korn & Co., in the Blubber Hollow district. There were many leather shops built of wood in this neighborhood. In the shadow of the famous Gallows Hill, where witches were once hanged, half a dozen factories were aflame in a few minutes, and employes were running for their lives.

There was a report early in the evening that twenty girls lost their lives in the Korn factory, but later reports were that only one person was injured.

Old Witches' House Goes Early.

It was hoped early in the evening that all of the relics of Salem's famous days at the leading seaport of the country would be saved. They were housed, far down Essex Street, in the Essex Institute and the Peabody Museum.

The old Witches' House, however, one of the historic landmarks of the city, where dwelt in Colonial days women who met death on Gallows Hill, was one of the first buildings to be consumed.

The electric light station burned early in the evening and the city was without electric power.

It was 2 o'clock in the afternoon when, from an unexplained explosion, the fire started in the factory of W. J. Korn & Co., at Proctor and Boston Streets, in the western part of the city.

Fanned by a brisk northwest wind, the flames swept rapidly through this district, destroying factory buildings there and scores of dwellings and small stores. There was a panic among the employes in the Korn factory, but only one person was seriously hurt in leaving the building. All the storehouses and other buildings along both sides of Boston Street from Putnam Street to Essex Street, and thence up Essex Street to Jackson Street, were burned early in the day.

The Korn factory is distant a mile from the centre of the city, but so rapidly did the flames advance that the flames at 7 o'clock were consuming houses on Endicott Street, at the end of the Boston & Maine Railroad station platform, only a block or two from Town House Square, the centre of the business district.

In the meantime dwelling houses were burning in the French district at South Salem, a mile away from where the fire began. The wind had carried embers there from the original blaze, and this district was well burned over before the flames reached the central business district.

Resort to Dynamite.

The city authorities early in the afternoon saw that they could not control the fire and they sent frantic calls to Boston and all the smaller cities hereabout for help. Firemen from these cities responded quickly. In a desperate effort to stop the progress of the fire six structures on Boston and Endicott Streets were blown up with dynamite early in the evening. The Lincoln Primary School at Federal and Fowler Streets was destroyed in this manner.

At the start the water pressure was low and when the fight had become desperate a great water main near the Beverly Bridge broke, and the firemen practically were helpless.

In response to the calls for assistance apparatus ranging from the most antiquated tubs from towns and villages to the new high pressure automobile engine of the Manchester, N. H., Fire Department, responded. The Manchester engine undertook to pump water from the ocean. Boston, Lynn, and

Continued on Page 4.

PRINCE DODGES MILITANTS.

Dives Into Lake at Camp When He Sees Two Women Approaching.

Special Cable to THE NEW YORK TIMES.

LONDON, June 25.—The Prince of Wales is taking no chances with the suffragettes. During a bathing parade at a lake at Kochett, near Aldershot, today the Prince, who is in camp there with the Oxford University officers' training corps, of which he is Lance Corporal, was standing on the bank when he saw two women coming toward him.

Shouting to a comrade near him, he jumped into the water and quickly put some distance between himself and the bank. The Prince joined in the merriment caused by the incident.

$20,000 SUIT OF CLOTHES

Made for King Otto of Bavaria and Has 8,000 Real Pearls.

What was described as the most valuable suit of clothes made in the last 100 years was sent from the Red Star Line pier yesterday to the Public Stores to be appraised for duty. It is studded with gold, silver, and pearls, and was made to order for the late King Otto of Bavaria.

The suit was brought to New York on the Zeeland by Miss Anita Koeck, who has the necessary affidavits to prove its genuineness. The attestation made before the United States Consul in Stuttgart, Germany, places the value of the coat, waistcoat, and trousers, with an elaborate hat, at $20,000. There are 8,000 real pearls embroidered on the coat and waistcoat. The $20,000 suit will be exhibited in the windows of a Fifth Avenue jeweler.

WILKINSON IN GLOOM.

Promoter Says His Enemies Have Killed a Great Enterprise.

Special to The New York Times.

PHILADELPHIA, June 25.—With an announcement today from James T. Cortelyou, Chief Postal Inspector here, that Frank W. Smith and J. V. Holtby, two of his men, would be sent to Spring City, Tenn., to investigate the Central Tennessee Development Company, came a statement from "Col." George Wilkinson, President of the company, in which he said he was not quite certain whether he would attempt to complete his plan to transform Spring City into a metropolis.

Wilkinson and Mahlon Van Boeskirk, a patent attorney who drew up the company's charter, are under $2,500 bail each for a further hearing on July 8 in connection with the project. They are accused of using the mails for fraudulent purposes.

"The company's future is now merely conjecture," Wilkinson said today. "All of this is a great mistake. I'm as honest as the day is long. My enemies may have killed a great proposition for all concerned."

Chief Cortelyou said the company's scheme was one of the most amazing he ever heard of, and that he would have some of the investors brought here to give full details of the "town booming" proposition at the next hearing.

WESTINGHOUSE STRIKE VOTE

Only 500 of the Men Cast Ballots on Company's Invitation.

Special to The New York Times.

PITTSBURGH, June 25.—H. P. Herr, Vice President of the Westinghouse Company, today sent a letter to C. L. Bradley, Financial Secretary of the Allegheny Congenial Industrial Union, outlining a plan which he hoped might end the Westinghouse strike. It was proposed to conduct a secret ballot this afternoon on the subject, "Shall we return to work or shall we continue on strike?" the voters to be the Westinghouse employes.

The men were asked to put in their votes at the company's pay window. There tellers under oath were to count the votes and announce the result. Secretary Bradley was invited to be one of the judges.

The communication brought no reply from the strikers, but between 1 and 3 P. M. about 500 strikers drew their pay. Only about one-fourth of them voted. The result of the vote has not yet been announced.

Bridget Kenny, the real leader of the strikers, said today that the situation was slowly working toward success for the workmen.

"We could call out the men at Trafford City in the Westinghouse Foundries Company's plant tomorrow if we wished to do so, but it would only be an additional burden on the union," she said. "We are biding our time and will win."

DEFENDS T. D. JONES.

No Better Man Possible for Reserve Board, Says E. D. Hulbert, Banker.

Special to The New York Times.

CHICAGO, June 25.—E. D. Hulbert, Vice President of the Merchants' Loan and Trust Company, a Marshall Field institution, made a vigorous defense today of the appointment of Thomas D. Jones of Chicago to membership on the Federal Reserve Board and criticised very sharply the fight that was being made on him. Mr. Hulbert, who has long been a close personal friend of President Wilson, said:

"It is one of the idiosyncrasies of politics that the one who, above all others whom the President has appointed on the board, should be free from any possible objectionable qualities is the one against whom the fight is being directed. I regard the attacks which are being made on Mr. Jones as entirely unjust, unwarranted, and the result of some sort of disorder which I cannot understand in the physical make-up of man. No cleaner, stronger, abler, better man could have been selected than Mr. Jones. I do not doubt that Mr. Jones will be confirmed, in spite of the attacks on him."

GRONNA AND HANNA WIN.

Renominated in North Dakota—Other Results of State Primary.

GRAND FORKS, N. D., June 25.—United States Senator A. J. Gronna and Gov. L. B. Hanna were renominated on the Republican ticket by safe pluralities, according to incomplete returns today from yesterday's Statewide primary election. F. O. Hellstrom probably received the Democratic Gubernatorial nomination, while the contest between W. L. Purcell and G. P. Jones for the Democratic Senatorial nomination is close.

Congressman G. M. Young was renominated in the Second District by a safe majority. In the Third District, where Congressman P. D. Norton sought renomination, the result was in doubt.

Best Electric Wiring—Home, Office, Factory. DENNIS G. BRUSSEL, [illegible] West 38th Street.—Adv.

RECEIVERS TAKE H. B. CLAFLIN CO., ALLIES SOUND

Big Dry Goods Firm Itself Has $44,000,000 Assets Against Its $34,000,000 Liabilities.

HOLDING COMPANIES SOLID

Neither Associated Merchants Nor the United Dry Goods Companies Involved.

BANKS HAD OFFERED AID

John Claflin Refused It and Put Under Way the Present Move for Reorganization.

NOTES HELD BY 5,000 BANKS

Situation Due to Changed Trade Conditions and Too Rapid Growth for Company's Money Supply.

The H. B. Claflin Company, the great wholesale dry goods concern, which is also a holding company for retail stores in various parts of the country outside of New York City, was put in the hands of receivers yesterday as the result of its inability to meet maturing notes of its subsidiaries bearing its indorsement.

The amount of these notes outstanding was officially estimated yesterday at $34,000,000. It will be several days before the receivers are able to determine the amount of the assets, but they were estimated on the basis of statements made to bankers in the last few days by John Claflin, President of the company, at $44,000,000.

The same receivers—J. B. Martindale, President of the Chemical National Bank, and Frederic A. Juilliard of A. D. Juilliard & Co.—were put in charge of the Defender Manufacturing Company of 214 Avenue C, makers of underwear. A number of the twenty-seven stores controlled by the H. B. Claflin Company also went into receiverships for their own protection in this crisis. Among these were the H. Batterman Company and the Bedford Company, both in Brooklyn; the Jones Store Company of Kansas City, and the Fair Company of Montgomery, Ala.

Bankruptcy Petitions Filed.

Immediately after the naming of receivers for the New York and Brooklyn companies, which was done upon the application of associates of Mr. Claflin, petitions in involuntary bankruptcy were also filed against the H. B. Claflin Company and the Defender Manufacturing Company by Gregg & McGovern of [illegible] Broadway, representing individual creditors. Hearings on these petitions were set for July 2.

Yesterday's events marked the fourth financial crisis of the H. B. Claflin Company since it was first established in this city, in 1843, with the firm name of Bulkley & Claflin. It was tided over financial difficulties during the civil war, when Southern debtors refused to meet their Northern obligations; again in the panic of 1873, and again in the panic of 1907, when, it is understood, J. P. Morgan & Co. came to the rescue.

The large dry goods stores in this city affiliated with the Claflin interests are not controlled by the H. B. Claflin Company and are not concerned in the proceedings. James S. Alexander, President of the National Bank of Commerce and Chairman of a committee formed among the banks holding paper indorsed by the Claflin Company, emphasized this fact yesterday and declared that they were in no wise affected. They are controlled by the Associated Merchants Company or the United Dry Goods Companies. Mr. Claflin was President of both of these corporations, but resigned yesterday afternoon to devote his attention to the affairs of the H. B. Claflin Company, and his place was taken by Cornelius N. Bliss, Jr.

Twenty-seven Stores Affected.

The stores controlled by Mr. Claflin or the H. B. Claflin Company are:

BEDFORD COMPANY, Brooklyn, N. Y.
J. BACON & SONS, Louisville, Ky.
CASTNER-KNOTT DRY GOODS COMPANY, Nashville, Tenn.
M. J. CONNOLLY COMPANY, Butte, Mont.
THE FAIR, Cincinnati, Ohio.
JOSLIN DRY GOODS COMPANY, Denver, Col.
KLINE BROTHERS, Altoona, Penn.
LORD & GAGE, Reading, Penn.
LION DRY GOODS COMPANY, Toledo, Ohio.
GEORGE W. McALPIN COMPANY, Cincinnati, Ohio.
McCREERY & CO., Pittsburgh, Penn.
MONTGOMERY FAIR, Montgomery, Ala.
PEOPLE'S STORE COMPANY, Tacoma, Wash.
ROOT DRY GOODS COMPANY, Terre Haute, Ind.
SPRING DRY GOODS COMPANY, Grand Rapids, Mich.
WHITEHOUSE COMPANY, Spokane, Wash.
J. B. WHITE & CO., Augusta, Ga.
H. BATTERMAN COMPANY, Brooklyn, N. Y.
WATT, RETTEW & CLAY, Norfolk, Va.
THOMAS C. WATKINS, LIMITED, Hamilton, Canada.
HENNESSY COMPANY, Butte, Mon.
COPPER CITY COMMERCIAL COMPANY, Anaconda, Mon.
McDOUGALL & SOUTHWICK, Seattle, Wash.
JONES STORE COMPANY, Kansas City, Mo.
LAZARUS BROTHERS, Wilkes-Barre, Penn.
THE HIGBEE COMPANY, Cleveland, Ohio.
MacCULLUM & CLOUTIER, Anaconda, Mont.

These Are Not Concerned.

The Associated Merchants' Company owns half the stock of the Claflin Company and also, outside of the Claflin Company, controls these stores:

McCREERY & CO., New York.
STEWART & CO., Baltimore, Md.
O'NEILL, ADAMS & CO., New York.
J. N. ADAM & CO., Buffalo.
C. G. GUNTHER, New York.

The United Dry Goods Companies own a majority interest in the Associated

The great fire at Salem, Massachusetts.

United Press International

SALEM SWEPT BY $10,000,000 FIRE

Continued from Page 1.

other cities sent policemen as well as fire apparatus. The combined efforts of the greatest aggregation of fire fighting apparatus that has been seen here seemed futile. It was then that resort was had to dynamite. But this did not seem to be of much avail as the fickle wind, which shifted four times, carried destruction in a new direction.

West Side Devastated.

The first spread of the fire was on the west side of the city at the foot of Gallows Hill. A territory about two miles long and more than half a mile wide, extending from Proctor and Boston Streets on the north to Jefferson Avenue on the south, early was devastated. In this district are Proctor, Pope, Broad, Hawthorne, Winthrop, Mount Vernon, Endicott, and Peabody Streets, where practically all structures were destroyed.

In the meantime the falling embers had started fires in South Salem and the more exclusive residential part of the city. All the available fire-fighting apparatus was in the Gallows Hill district and South Salem was without protection. One building after another burst into flames.

For several hours the fire in this district was confined to a small oval, extending from Porter Street on the north to Hancock Street on the south and from the canal to Lafayette Street. As evening approached the flames spread in all directions, destroying hundreds of residences in the district, including many handsome homes on Lafayette Street, the most fashionable thoroughfare in Salem.

Orphan Asylum Destroyed.

The City Orphan Asylum, on Lafayette Street, sheltering 150 persons, early was destroyed. All the children were taken by the nuns to a place of safety.

The Salem Hospital next was attacked. The patients were removed to safety on stretchers. In the excitement a daughter was born to Mrs. Rossetti, an inmate.

Up Lafayette Street the fire swept, making a clean path from the State Normal School north to Cedar and Everett Streets. From this point the front of the fire moved like a huge sickle across Salem and Park Streets to the water front.

There was no apparatus here to check the flames, which licked up scores of tenements and high wooden apartment houses.

St. Joseph's Church, a huge new brick structure with lofty twin towers, and the adjoining school and convent buildings recently erected at a cost of $250,000 made ready fuel.

Late in the evening a fourth fire was kindled by brands in the plant of the Salem Oil Company, in Mason Street, northwest of the Essex County Court House. A terrific explosion occurred when the oil tanks blew up, and showers of sparks fell threateningly on that part of the town that before had not been in imminent danger. This fire, however, was checked after it had destroyed the oil company's plant and thirteen houses.

The fire made intense heat, and more than fifty firemen were overcome. Many persons also received injuries which called for medical attention. Twelve employes who leaped from the third floor windows of the Korn factory were taken to a hospital for treatment.

The new high school, police station and City Hall were thrown open to care for the homeless. Automobiles and wagons carried their personal belongings to safety.

Panic in the Streets.

While the fire was at its height there was a semi-panic in the business and residential districts. Women ran about the streets calling for help. Some carried bedding and other household furniture in their arms. Many women collapsed on their doorsteps and in the street from excitement. Others tried to put out fires on roofs with brooms and pails of water. More than 100 automobiles were drawn up at the edge of the fire zone, taking household articles away. Even the moth-spraying machine of the city was used in an effort to put out some of the smaller fires.

Charles Lee, an employe of the Korn factory, jumped from a third-story window and broke both legs. The explosion in this factory which caused the fire has not been explained. All traffic between Peabody and Salem was stopped, and many telephone lines were put out of commission. Numerous roof and grass fires caught from flying sparks. Thousands of men and women were employed in the burned factories, but most of them were able to get out without being hurt, although many girls fainted from excitement.

Company H of the Eighth Regiment and the Second Corps Cadets, both Salem organizations, were called out. The police asked for help in handling the thousands of persons who flocked from other places.

Cemetery Place of Refuge.

The Broad Street cemetery, in the heart of the fire district, was used to store household furnishings which were saved. Militiamen patrolled the cemetery to guard against looting. The city authorities had tents pitched in the cemetery so that homeless persons could sleep there through the night. Men, women and children, in a panic, were racing through the street just before nightfall seeking safety.

Many families were separated in the confusion. Little children who had lost their fathers and mothers, and many of them their homes, ran about crying.

Report That Four Were Trapped.

There was an early unconfirmed report that four persons, trapped in a boarding house at Orne Square, were burned to death. The authorities had no verification of this late tonight.

The 100 children in the orphan asylum and twenty aged women who were cared for there had a narrow escape. They were hemmed in on three sides by the fire. The only avenue of escape was by water, and they were removed in boats. They were taken out by the Sisters of Charity, aided by Father J. J. Cronin. Sisters knelt in prayer in the yard while the rescue was in progress.

Gov. Walsh, informed of Salem's peril, hurried here from Boston early in the evening. Before he left Boston he directed Adjt. Gen. Cole to send 500 cots and blankets here. The armory was used to shelter more than 500 people tonight.

Some Burned Buildings.

The buildings burned included the plants of a score of manufacturing companies, among them the big plant of the Naumkeag Cotton Mills, the American Hide and Leather Company tannery on Goodhue Street; the Ryan & White Shoe Factory, Boston Street; the Matthew Robinson Tannery in Goodhue Street, and the factories of the Carr Leather Company, the Marrs Leather Company, the Dane Machine Company, the A. T. Way Leather Company, the O'Keefe Leather Company, and the Brennan Leather Company.

Twenty dwellings on Boston Street were consumed, twenty on May Street, fifteen on Essex Street, three on Warren Street, twelve on Phelps Street, fifteen on Vale Street, fifteen on Green Street, twenty two-family houses on Orne Square, and one house on Winthrop Street.

Colonial Homes Destroyed.

The fire destroyed many of the handsome Colonial homes on Chestnut Street. These have been described as the finest types of that style of architecture in the country. The Public Library also was destroyed. It was a queer, sickle-like jump that the flames took. Starting in Blubber Hollow, they worked in a curve to the waterfront when sparks leaped over a gap of a mile and one-half. While all the energies of the firemen were in the leather district sparks kindled the new French Church, on La Fayette Street. It was soon aflame. Many three-story houses occupied by French people next caught fire.

The French Church was a sort of dividing line between the residence district of the wealthy on La Fayette Street, which is a motor highway between Lynn and Salem, was swept by the fire from the State Normal School to Cedar and Everett Streets.

The fire that wiped out the homes of the French-speaking population also destroyed the magnet that made them live in the congested district of South Salem—the Old Naumkeag Cotton Mills, employing 5,000 hands.

FAMOUS AS CITY OF WITCHES.

Twenty Persons Were Put to Death to Stamp Out Black Art.

Salem is famous in early Colonial history for its witches. The delusion which led to the execution of twenty persons and the torture of fifty originated through the hysteria of the children of the Rev. Samuel Parris. In the Winter of 1691-2 his daughter Elizabeth, aged 9; his niece, Abigail Williams, aged 11, and several friends used to meet to practice tricks. A half-negro slave, Tituba, began to teach them what she called the "black art," and soon they were barking like dogs or screaming at some object that they said they could see although invisible to every one else.

Witchcraft was a very real thing to the people of the seventeenth century, and Cotton Mather and his teachings encouraged the belief in it. Some one had to be blamed for the folly of the girls, and Parris beat Tituba until she admitted that she had bewitched the children.

John Indian, her husband, through fear, accused others, and the young people of Salem, notably Ann Putnam, spread the stories. At length a regular reign of terror prevailed in the village. Any one who had a grudge against another could accuse him, and, strangely enough, some of those thus calumniated admitted that they really were obsessed. A special court was formed to try those who had sold themselves to the devil, and it was unsafe to express doubt of any one's guilt.

Parris got the Rev. George Burroughs, pastor of Salem, hanged as friend of the witches, and one colonist, Giles Corey, a man of 80, in connection with the craze achieved the distinction to be the only man ever slain in America by the old punishment of peine forte et dure. Accused by Ann Putnam, he was determined to do all he could to save his property for his family. If he was brought to trial and convicted it would be confiscated, and the one way he could avoid this was to refuse to plead. So he stood mute as the charge was read to him, and, acording to custom, his obduracy was punished by the peine forte et dure. Iron weights were piled upon him, but not quite enough to crush him. Then he was left to linger in agony and fed with only enough bread and water to keep him alive.

"All the News That's Fit to Print."

The New York Times.

THE WEATHER
Fair today and Sunday; fresh to strong southwest to west winds.
☞ For full weather report see Page 21.

VOL. LXIV...NO. 20,923.   NEW YORK, SATURDAY, MAY 8, 1915.—TWENTY-FOUR PAGES.   ONE CENT In Greater New York, Jersey City and Newark. | Elsewhere TWO CENTS.

LUSITANIA SUNK BY A SUBMARINE, PROBABLY 1,000 DEAD;
TWICE TORPEDOED OFF IRISH COAST; SINKS IN 15 MINUTES;
AMERICANS ABOARD INCLUDED VANDERBILT AND FROHMAN;
WASHINGTON BELIEVES THAT A GRAVE CRISIS IS AT HAND

SHOCKS THE PRESIDENT

Washington Deeply Stirred by Disaster and Fears a Crisis.

BULLETINS AT WHITE HOUSE

Wilson Reads Them Closely, but Is Silent on the Nation's Course.

RUMOR OF CONGRESS CALL

Loss of Lusitania Recalls Firm Tone of Our First Warning to Germany.

CAPITAL FULL OF RUMORS

Reports That Liner Was to Be Sunk Were Heard Before Actual News Came.

Special to The New York Times.

WASHINGTON, May 7.—Never since that April day, three years ago, when word came that the Titanic had gone down, has Washington been so stirred as it is tonight over the sinking of the Lusitania. The early reports told that there had been no loss of life, but the relief that these advices caused gave way to the greatest concern late this evening when it became known that there had been many deaths. Although the higher officials are profoundly reticent, officials realize that this tragedy, probably involving the loss of American citizens, is likely to bring about a crisis in the international relations of the United States.

It is pointed out that the sinking of the Lusitania is the outcome of a series of incidents that have been the cause of concern to this Government in its endeavor to maintain a strictly neutral position in the great European war.

It is impossible to say tonight what effect the loss of American lives on the Lusitania will have on the Government. Judged from the little that can be learned it is a safe prediction that President Wilson will endeavor to ascertain all the facts, including evidence as to whether a German submarine was responsible for the sinking of the vessel, before proceeding to determine the course to be pursued. The news that many lives had been sacrificed, probably as many as a thousand, was given to him at the White House about 1 o'clock this evening, but no word came from him as to what effect this intelligence had on him.

The State Department tonight sent instructions to the American Embassy in London to send the names of any Americans who might have been killed or injured in the disaster. A bulletin from THE TIMES, saying probably 1,000 lives had been lost, was sent to the White House as soon as received and laid before President Wilson. The news that two torpedoes had been fired into the Lusitania by a submarine and that the Lusitania sank fifteen minutes afterward was also sent to the White House, but it reached there after the President had gone to bed. The President retired about 11 o'clock.

Rumors of Congress Session.

There were reports this evening that Congress would be called in extra session, but these were not justified and the most that can be said is that while the Government is greatly concerned over the situation, it has shown no inclination toward excitement or taking hasty action.

This afternoon and early this evening officials were relieved over the reports that no lives had been lost. But in spite of the calmness in the upper official circle during this period, there was little effort elsewhere to conceal the view that even if no Americans went down with the liner this Government might find itself face to face with a grave situation.

The statement from London that the Lusitania was torpedoed without warning was regarded as showing the decency of the situation, for this Government, in the warning it delivered to Germany concerning the proposed submarine warfare on merchant ships, laid down the principle that the obligation to visit and search a merchant ship before sinking or taking her

Continued on Page 2.

BOSCA BRUT—Dry. Exquisite Flavor. Favored by those who like dry champagne.—*Advt.*

Continued on Page 2.

Roosevelt Calls It An Act of Piracy.

Special to The New York Times.

SYRACUSE, N. Y., May 7.—Colonel Roosevelt tonight characterized the sinking of the Lusitania as "an act of piracy."

"I do not know enough of the facts," said the Colonel, "to make any further comment or to say what would be proper for this Government to do in the circumstances.

"I can only repeat what I said the other day when the Gulflight was attacked. I then called attention to the fact that months before the German war zone was established, and deeds such as the sinking of the Lusitania were threatened, that if such deeds were perpetrated they would represent nothing but mere piracy."

captive was imposed on the German Government.

But it is too soon to say, or even to attempt to predict, what course the United States Government will adopt. It is clear that the first move of the Government will be to ascertain all the facts obtainable and that the inquiry will be pursued, as far as possible, by officers of the United States. Until such an investigation has been completed and President Wilson and his advisers have determined what attitude the facts warrant the Government in adopting, no formal diplomatic action may be expected. For the present the higher officials refrain from committing themselves with a refusal to answer questions as to the position likely to be taken and with expressions of the hope that the early reports that no lives were lost in the Lusitania are true. That was Secretary Bryan's way of treating the matter before the alarming bulletins began to arrive.

What impresses Washington most tonight is that the loss of American lives was apparently the result of the action taken in the face of the warning given to Germany that such an outcome of a German attack might bring about a rupture in the friendly relations between the two countries. The language employed in that warning note was regarded as too drastic by some public men here, but the defense of its use was that it would be better to be outspoken before any critical incident than to wait until it occurred, when public feeling in this country might be aroused to the highest pitch and demands made for redress against Germany.

While there was interest here in the last voyage of the Lusitania on account of the risk she ran, it was not an intense interest. The feeling among officials and others appeared to be that the Germans would not go to the extreme of sinking a passenger vessel with women and children and many American citizens aboard. Even the advertisement inserted in American newspapers last Saturday by the German Embassy, warning Americans not to take passage for Europe in the ships of Germany's enemies, did not cause any alarm here with particular reference to the Lusitania, although it produced a feeling of irritation.

President Wilson Shocked.

President Wilson had just finished luncheon and was preparing to go golfing when the first news of the Lusitania disaster reached the White House. It came in the form of a newspaper bulletin and was received by Rudolph Forster, the executive clerk to the President. Mr. Forster, who was in the executive offices, wrote a note to the President telling him of the report. It was said afterward that the President was greatly shocked and perturbed, but that he expressed thankfulness that no lives had been lost, as the bulletin had it.

The President canceled his golfing and decided to remain at the White House. A little later, when further bulletins were received in the news that lives had been lost, the President went motoring. Tonight he received press bulletins concerning the Lusitania in his study in the White House. These were sent to him from the telegraph room of the executive offices. It was said that he had no visitors during the evening. A report saying that probably 1,000 lives were lost in the disaster was sent to him shortly before 10 o'clock.

Secretary Bryan was at luncheon at

Cunard Office Here Beseiged for News; Fate of 1,918 on Lusitania Long in Doubt

Official news of the sinking of the Lusitania yesterday reached New York in fragmentary reports, and several hours elapsed between the first unverified rumor of the disaster and the cable messages that told at night of the saving of some of the passengers and gave meagre details of the most sensational incident of its kind in the war.

The early bulletins that reached the local offices of the Cunard Line, 21 State Street, at 11:41 o'clock yesterday morning, but was not made public until late in the afternoon. The message, which was sent from the head office in Liverpool, read:

The Lusitania, we regret to state here in an unconfirmed report states to have been torpedoed by a submarine at 2 P. M. Friday, ten miles from Kinsale, and sunk at 2:30. There is no news as to the safety of passengers or crew.

Following this dispatch there was a message which had been picked up by the wireless station at Land's End, evidently a distress call from the liner, which said:

Come at once. Big list. Position ten miles west Kinsale.

A third dispatch from Queenstown stated:

All available craft in harbor dispatched to assist. Weather here beautifully fine. Wind northwest, light.

By 3 o'clock in the afternoon the news of the sinking of the Lusitania had been spread in the city and the Cunard offices were besieged by relatives and friends of the passengers on board. Owing to the alterations in and addition of the Lusitania's departure from Saturday, it took some time to get the correct figures, which were finally given out at 290 first, 601 second, and 367 third class passengers. Of the cabin passengers thirty-six had been transferred from the Cameronia on Saturday morning. This delayed the Lusitania's departure from 10 o'clock to 12:28.

1,918 Persons on Board.

The officers and crew numbered 665, instead of the usual complement of 850, on account of fewer men being carried in the engineers' and steward's departments. Thus there were in all 1,918 persons on board.

To all inquiries that they would give out the messages as fast as they were received and had no intention of keeping back the news from the public. Several bulletins were received from the Liverpool office, but few of them contained any definite news as to who had been saved or to make... more accurate we are going through hostile sailing houses, &c. tonight, and it may be necessary to slide in... in the meantime injured and dead are taking up our attention (late) here.

CUNARD, Liverpool.

Reports 450 Rescued.

The following was given out at the Cunard offices at 10:30 o'clock at night:

Liverpool, May 7, 9:45 P. M.
Queenstown wires that the tug Stormcock landed 150, including passengers and crew. It is reported that the trawlers Bock and Daniel Lucas have taken 200 on board, the tug Flying Fish has 100, and three torpedo boats brought in 15 living and 4 dead. We are putting the survivors for

Continued on Page 3.

sengers and crew had been saved in small boats and rafts. This information was given out to the people waiting in the Cunard office, and many of them went home. It was estimated that fully 200 inquiries were received by telephone and telegraph in the afternoon from relatives and friends of passengers on board. Long-distance calls were received from St. Louis, Atlanta, Montreal, and Toronto.

The next bulletin made public at the Cunard office was the following:

Liverpool, May 7.
1:51 P. M. (New York Time.)
Following received by Admiralty. Old Head Kinsale. Several boats, apparently survivors, southeastern miles. Greek steamer proceeding to assist.

The next bulletin was:

2:25 P. M. (New York Time.)
Queenstown wires Old Head: Large steamer just arrived in vicinity, apparently rendering assistance. Tugs, patrols, &c., now in the spot, taking boats in tow. Steamer assists with two Lusitania boats bearing probably for Kinsale. We have wired Kinsale agents to render every assistance to advise us if any boats are towed in there.

This was followed by:

3:08 P. M. (New York Time.)
Cork newspaper reports that 200 passengers landed at Queenstown. Old Head wire begins: Cancel last message. Stormcock taking passengers and boats from motor fishing boat, proceeding Queenstown.

First News of Loss of Life.

The first word of the sinking of the Lusitania received here reached the local offices of the Cunard Line, 21 State Street, at 11:41 o'clock yesterday morning, but was not made public until late in the afternoon. The message, which was sent from the head office in Liverpool, read:

8:28 P. M. (New York Time.)
Admiralty have just received from Queenstown saying between 500 and 600 landed at Queenstown, including many injured cases, some of them from the Old Head landed at Kinsale.

CUNARD, Liverpool.

At the same time that the Cunard Line gave the following cablegram from its Liverpool office in reply to a private inquiry:

Brethrenn and family are safe.

The message evidently referred to Mrs. Cyril E. Bretherton of Los Angeles and two children, who were in the second cabin. Mr. Bretherton came here from Los Angeles with his wife and children for a visit to relatives in England. He remained in New York for a long time before sailing.

A report that Charles Vanderbilt had received a cablegram that his brother, Alfred G. Vanderbilt, who was a passenger on the Lusitania, was denied by Mr. Vanderbilt when he was called by telephone at his home at West Orange, N. J., waited. Robert S. Franks, Vice President of the Carnegie Corporation of New York, who lives at West Orange, N. J., waited all afternoon to get news of his niece, Miss P. Hutchinson.

Toward evening the crowd diminished in the office, as it was believed that no more news would be received until noon.

The Cunard Company gave out the following statement late in the afternoon:

The Cunard Company's whole concern is with regard to the possible loss of life of passengers and crew. The material loss is covered by insurance. Accurate details to meagre reports so far received the Lusitania was torpedoed without warning, and sank within a very short space of time. A large number of ships are known to be in distress, and the weather is reported to be fine and through hostile waters we are unable to obtain further details and all information will be published without delay.

The Cunard office gave out the following bulletin shortly before 10 o'clock:

LIVERPOOL, May 7, 9:25 P. M., (New York Time.)—Queenstown wires that First Officer Jones states about 500 to 600 lives saved. This includes passengers and crew.

The statement contained no definite news as to who were saved.

Scene in the Strand.

There was a remarkable scene in the Strand when the news first became known. A newsboy shouting out the contents of a bill of an evening paper "Lusitania torpedoed and sunk, official," was stopped outside the Hotel Cecil by a police constable, who refused to believe the news. He intimated that he would be arrested if it were shown he was crying out false news. The boy promptly showed the policeman the official news of the disaster, and

---

THE LOST CUNARD STEAMSHIP LUSITANIA

Loss of the Lusitania Fills London With Horror and Utter Amazement

Special Cable to THE NEW YORK TIMES.

LONDON, Saturday, May 8.—Stupefaction is the word which best describes the first impression created by the news of the sinking of the Lusitania. People seemed unable to realize that at this stage of the world's progress such a deed could be committed as an act of war.

"I have no words for it," said Lord Rosebery, and everywhere one found the same sentiment repeated.

It was some hours between the time the first reports of the disaster were received at the Admiralty and the time the news was made public by a communiqué from the Press Bureau. During this interval the news spread quickly through official, Parliamentary, shipping, and newspaper circles.

At the Cunard offices in the later hours of the evening men rushed in asking, "Is it true?" When and how they heard the news was a mystery. Shipping offices could give little or no information until the official statement was issued that the Lusitania was sunk by a submarine at 2:33 P. M., eight miles south of West Kinsale.

Shortly after 7 P. M. a dispatch reached THE NEW YORK TIMES correspondent from Liverpool that it was stated that many passengers were unofficially reported saved. But at that hour this information was without foundation. The chief reports here were to the effect that only 500 out of 1,900 souls on the mammoth liner had been saved. Seeing that the vessel had sunk so quickly, it was argued that the loss of life must have been great, that the torpedo must have created such havoc that an immediate heavy list would follow, and in that event the boats were already hanging out on their davits the difficulty of manning and filling even half of them in the time available would have been so great that the possibility of saving a majority of the people aboard was minimized.

When first moments of dull horror passed speculation began. One of the first theories advanced was that to have caught the Lusitania the German submarine could not have given the speedy liner any warning. Previously reported activities of German submarines in the waters to the southwest of Ireland encouraged the belief that several vessels of the underwater fleet must have been on the lookout for the Cunarder so as to demonstrate to the world that German warnings were not empty threats. It was suggested that as the incoming transatlantic liners usually followed a certain distinct track, running close to the southern shore of Ireland it was an easy matter for two or more submarines to lie in wait for the Lusitania, and once she was observed to let torpedoes go at her last length presenting a huge target.

Early in the afternoon it was not known at the Cunard offices where the Lusitania had met destruction. It was suggested that the company was anxious where she was steaming to Liverpool by the north or south of Ireland and that her chance of course was probably directed by Admiralty orders received by her captain. That she was being convoyed was generally assumed, and as an addendum to the assumption it was believed that Germany would invoke the fact of convoy as a reason wherefore no warning could be given.

aster in the "stop-press column" and he was allowed to proceed. The incident attracted a huge crowd and in a few minutes the bill had sold all his papers.

The official news was first published at 7:45 P. M. and created a profound impression on the public, and especially in the west end hotels where the guests gathered round the newspaper men.

Among Americans, mostly business men are at present staying at the Hotel Cecil, Savoy, and other big hotels in Northumberland Avenue and those who had expected relatives and friends to arrive in London today hurried in taxicabs to make inquiries at the Cunard offices. Americans in evening dress rose hurriedly from the dinner table when they heard the news and drove off to the shipping office in Cockspur Street. Americans did not attempt to hide their anger. A group outside the Carlton Hotel balls's a newsboy and on glancing at the official statement became infuriated, shouted and shook their fists in disgust.

Vain Inquiry At Ship Office.

Describing the scene inside the London Cunard office, says The Chronicle: "One or two middle-aged ladies sat about quietly reading newspapers splendidly hoping against hope. Early in the long vigil the overstrung nerves of one young girl gave way and she shrieked in hysterics she had a brother and sister on the vessel, but all she could be told was that the boat had gone down and that it was hoped that the passengers were safe.

"Only three days ago I received a letter from Mr. Frohman, written in New York April 21," said Mr. Harrison. "In it Mr. Frohman, who spoke of his intention to make a trip to see me and other theatrical managers on business, wrote: 'I hope to see you soon.' From the letter I took it he was sailing within a few days."

"All I can say is that the theatrical profession loses a clever man and a very kind friend. Mr. Frohman had a tremendous influence in the theatrical field and his energies were directed the right way. The sinking of the Lusitania is a terrible act and Germany ought to be held by America to the fullest accountability."

Admiralty Puts Embargo On News Dispatches

LONDON, May 8.—It is stated that the British Admiralty is not withholding any verified facts regarding the Lusitania, but declines to pass dispatches based merely on rumor.

It is expected that the Admiralty will issue a statement as soon as authenticated facts are available.

DEATH OF FROHMAN IS FEARED IN LONDON

"What Is America Going to Do About It?" Asks British Colleague of Manager.

Special Cable to THE NEW YORK TIMES.

LONDON, May 7.—The theatrical world of London is stunned over the reported fate of Charles Frohman. Mr. Frohman is a familiar figure in the theatrical life of London, and theatre managers and players alike regarded him highly. Speaking tonight, Frederick Harrison, lessee of the Haymarket Theatre, after expressing his intense shock over the report of Mr. Frohman's drowning, asked abruptly:

"What is America going to do about the torpedoing of the Lusitania? What is Washington to say about the drowning of American citizens? Is America going to take it lying down?"

Mr. Harrison spoke of Mr. Frohman as one of his most intimate friends and a man whose loss the entire theatrical world, here and abroad, would feel keenly.

AMERICANS IN LONDON ARE DEEPLY STIRRED

A. J. Drexel Denounces Sinking of the Lusitania — Pinchot Refrains from Commenting.

Special Cable to THE NEW YORK TIMES.

LONDON, May 7.—A. J. Drexel, at his home in Grosvenor Square, denounced the sinking of the Lusitania to THE NEW YORK TIMES correspondent. "The most infernal outrage that has happened during the war," Mr. Drexel said on the Lusitania on March 13, when Captain Dow was in command. He came back on the American liner New York with Harry Lehr because of Mr. Lehr's fear of sailing on a steamer flying other than the American flag.

"I don't care how the American Government," said Mr. Drexel, "can anything but go into the war itself. If the lives of its citizens are to be snuffed out this way by the Germans America must act sternly. If Americans are to feel that the protection of their country means anything. Can it be that America will supinely allow the Germans to murder her citizens? For my part, I expect the Government at Washington to take drastic measures now with Germany. If it means war to protect our citizens, then war it is. I can't begin to express my feelings of dismay and horror over this abominable thing. How do we know the Germans will not torpedo a ship flying the American flag? Where is this terrible work of the Germans to end? What is to be done with the Kaiser, who has the blood of innocent American men and women on his hands? America to close no doubt in condemning this worst crime of the war, but I don't want to see any uncertainty sounding from America. I feel certain the Government is going to act quickly and sternly."

"Her protest must be in thunderous tones, made of bronze, that strike to the depths of the Berlin conscience."

Gifford Pinchot, who says he still holds an official commission from the American Government in the war relief work, expressed himself concerning the sinking of the Lusitania at his home of his brother-in-law, Sir Alan Johnstone, where he has been staying since the German escorted him out of Belgium, would not speak of the Lusitania case "because of his connection with the Government.

"I wish I were able to speak, but I must remain silent," he said as tears came to his eyes. Mr. Pinchot had arranged to return to New York on the Lusitania a week or two tomorrow, having got a cabl from Washington several days ago that it was inadvisable for him to try to carry out his work in France just now. When he heard of the torpedoing of the Lusitania he got into touch with the American Line to make reservation on the St. Paul tomorrow for himself and wife. When he talked with THE TIMES correspondent he had not been able to get the accommodations he wanted, and said he might have to postpone going.

"But I'll go back to New York on a steamer flying the American flag," he said.

Lord Rosebery said regarding the torpedoing of the liner: "The thing is beyond all expression."

Insist on ANGOSTURA BITTERS in your Martini; splendid tonic; delicious flavor.—*Advt.*

SOME DEAD TAKEN ASHORE

Several Hundred Survivors at Queenstown and Kinsale

STEWARD TELLS OF DISASTER

One Torpedo Crashes Into the Doomed Liner's Bow, Another Into the Engine Room

BOATS PROMPTLY LOWERED

But Ship Goes Down So Quickly Many Must Have Gone with Her —No Officers Reported Saved.

ATTACKED IN BROAD DAY

Passengers at Luncheon—Warning Had Been Given Before the Ship Left New York.

LONDON, Saturday, May 8.—The Cunard liner Lusitania, which sailed out of New York last Saturday with 1,918 souls aboard, lies at the bottom of the ocean off the Irish coast.

She was sunk by a German submarine, which sent two torpedoes crashing into her side, while the passengers, seemingly confident that the great, swift vessel could elude the German underwater craft, were having luncheon.

How many of the Lusitania's passengers and crew were rescued cannot be told as present. Official statements from the British Admiralty up to midnight accounted for not more than 500 or 600, and unofficial reports tell of several hundreds landed at Queenstown, Kinsale and other points.

Up to midnight 520 passengers from the Lusitania had been landed at Queenstown from boats. Ten or eleven boatloads have come ashore and others are expected.

A press dispatch says seven torpedoes were discharged from the German craft and one of them struck the Lusitania amidships.

Probably at least 1,000 persons, including many Americans, have lost their lives.

Sank in Fifteen Minutes.

The stricken vessel went down in less than half an hour, according to all reports. The most definite statement puts fifteen minutes as the time that passed between the fatal blow and the disappearance of the Lusitania beneath the waves.

There were 1,253 passengers from New York on board the steamship, including 290 who were transferred to her from the steamer Cameronia. The crew numbered 665.

No names of the rescued are yet available.

Story of the Attack.

The tug, Stormcock, has returned to Queenstown, bringing about 150 survivors of the Lusitania, principally cabin passengers, among whom were many women, several of the crew and one steward. Describing the experience of the Lusitania, the steward said:

"The passengers were at lunch when a submarine came up and fired two torpedoes, which struck the Lusitania on

---

BERESFORD BLAMES A LACK OF CRUISERS

Great Britain Needs More to Protect Her Trade Routes, Says Naval Critic.

Special Cable to THE NEW YORK TIMES.

LONDON, Saturday, May 8.—Lord Charles Beresford, asked for an expression of opinion on the sinking of the Lusitania, said he thought it was due to a shortage of cruisers to protect the trade routes.

This had been his opinion for years, he said.

PRESIDENT WILSON SHOCKED AND WASHINGTON FEARS THE DISASTER MAY CAUSE A CRISIS

Longitudnal Section of the Lusitania, Showing Her Construction and Where She Was Hit

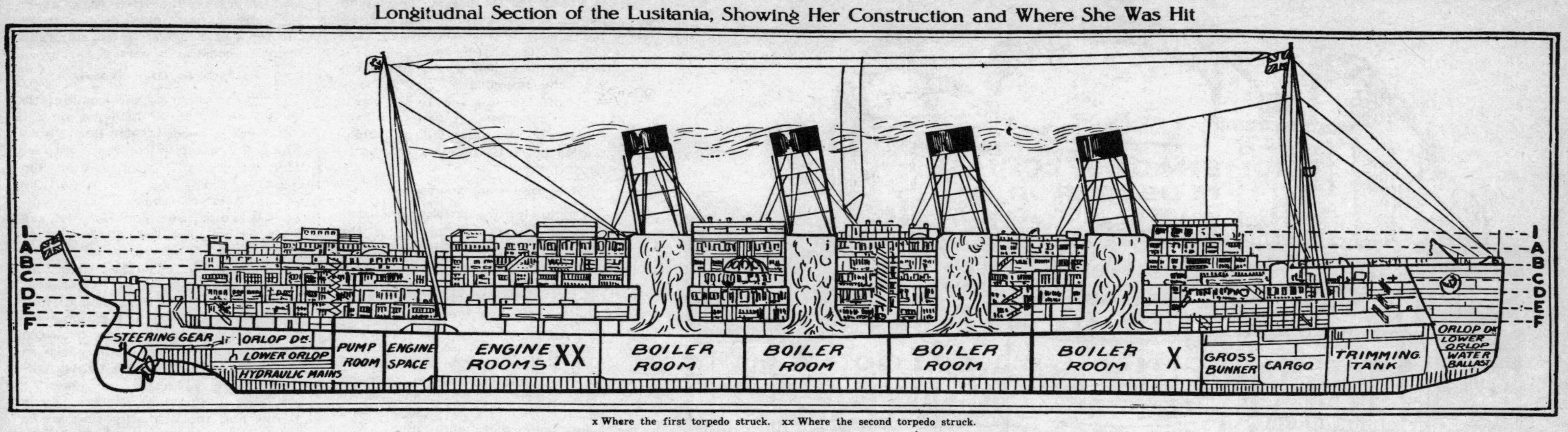

x Where the first torpedo struck. xx Where the second torpedo struck.

NO. 1—Navigating Bridge, Officers' Rooms, Roofs of Public Rooms, Marconi House and Docking Bridge.
A, OR BOAT DECK—Captain's Rooms, First Class Library, Grand Entrance, Passenger Elevators, First Class Lounge, Music Room, Smoking Room and Veranda Café, Second Cabin Promenade and Lounge.
B, OR PROMENADE DECK—Forecastle Head, Head Front of Promenade Deck, Observation Corridor, First Class Staterooms, Regal Suites, En Suite Rooms, Grand Entrance and Passenger Elevators, First Class Staterooms, Dome of Dining Saloons, Second Cabin Promenade, Drawing Room, and Second Cabin Smoking Room.
C, OR UPPER DECK—Forward Capstan and Windlass Machinery, Third Class Smoking Room and Ladies' Room, Third Class Covered Promenade, Third Class Main Entrance, First Class Children's Dining Saloon and Nursery, Grand Entrance and Passenger Elevators, First Class Grand Dining Saloon, Engineers' Quarters, Second Cabin Main Entrance, Second Cabin Staterooms and Promenade.
D, OR SALOON DECK—Stewards' Quarters, Third Class Main Dining Saloon, First Class Staterooms, Grand Entrance and Passenger Elevators, First Class Grand Dining Saloon, Galleys and Pantries, Second Cabin Dining Saloon, Second Cabin Staterooms, Stewards' and Cooks' Quarters.
E, OR MAIN DECK—Seamen's Quarters, Third Class Cabins, Grand Entrance and Passenger Elevators, First Class Staterooms, Firemen's Quarters, Second Cabin Staterooms, Stewards' Quarters.
F, OR LOWER DECK—First Class Baggage Rooms, Third Class Cabins, Coal, Stores, Wine Rooms, Firemen's Quarters, Mail Room, Mail Sorting Room, and Stewards' Quarters.
BELOW DECK F—Boilers, Engine Room, Pump Room, Tanks, and Shaft Tunnels.

the starboard side, one forward and another in the engine room. They caused terrific explosions.

"Captain Turner immediately ordered the boats out. The ship began to list badly immediately.

"Ten boats were put into the water, and between 400 and 500 passengers entered them. The boat in which I was, approached the land with three other boats, and we were picked up shortly after 4 o'clock by the Storm Cock.

"I fear that few of the officers were saved. They acted bravely.

"There was only fifteen minutes from the time the ship was struck until she foundered, going down bow foremost. It was a dreadful sight."

At the time this dispatch was sent from Queenstown two other vessels were approaching the port with survivors.

The Cunard Line received a message saying that a motor boat, towing two boats containing fifty passengers, and two tugs with passengers, was passing Kinsale. A majority of the rescue boats are proceeding to Queenstown.

An Admiralty report states that between 500 and 600 survivors from the Lusitania have now been landed, many of them being hospital cases. Several of them have died. Some also have been landed at Kinsale, but the number has not yet been received.

Hit 10 Miles Off Kinsale Head.

This greatest sea tragedy of the war, because of the terrible loss of lives of non-combatants and citizens of neutral nations, took place about ten miles off the Old Head of Kinsale about 2 o'clock in the afternoon.

A dispatch to the Exchange Telegraph from Liverpool quotes the Cunard Company as stating that "the Lusitania was sunk without warning."

According to a Queenstown dispatch the Lusitania was seen from the signal station at Kinsale to be in difficulties at 2:12 P. M. and at 2:33 she had completely disappeared.

This indicated, the dispatch added, that the liner was afloat twenty-one minutes after what evidently was the beginning of her trouble.

Official announcement was also made here last night by the Cunard Line that the Lusitania remained afloat at least twenty minutes after being torpedoed, and that "twenty boats were on the spot at the time." Sixteen more boats, officials of the line said, had been dispatched to the scene for rescue work.

As soon as the Lusitania's wireless call for assistance was received at Queenstown at 2:15 o'clock, Admiral Coke, in command of the naval station, dispatched to the scene all assistance available.

The tugs Warrior, Stormcock, and Julia, together with five trawlers and the local life boat in tow of a tug, were hurried out to sea. It was thought it would take most of them about two hours to reach the spot where the Lusitania was reported to be sinking.

One dispatch received here said the liner was eight miles off the Irish coast when she finally went down.

London Torn With Anxiety.

All the afternoon, following the first startling message from Ireland and the fragmentary bulletins, indicating a possibility of heavy loss of life, London waited with intense anxiety for further news.

This anxiety grew steadily through the evening as hour after hour passed without any definite statement from an authoritative source as to the extent of the disaster.

The Cunard offices, which will remain open throughout the night, were besieged by a great crowd, largely composed of women, many of them weeping bitterly as the hours passed and no definite news came of those aboard the Lusitania.

Accommodation was provided inside the offices for those who had relatives or friends on the steamer, while hundreds waited outside, eagerly reading the scanty bulletins which told of rescue boats arriving at Kinsale and Queenstown, but gave no names of the saved, and consequently did not allay the anxiety.

Flickering Gleam of Hope.

There was a gleam of hope in the general gloom soon after 8 o'clock, when this announcement was made unofficially:

The Cunard Company has definitely ascertained that the lives of the passengers and the crew of the Lusitania have been saved.

This was speedily proved untrue, however, but the more optimistic still refused to credit the early reports of the swift sinking of the big liner. It was believed that her watertight bulkheads would tend to keep her afloat, and if she floated a reasonable length of time before going down, it was possible that rescuing ships got to her side in time to save all on board.

Owing to the fact that all the news of the Lusitania came through the Admiralty, and that only fragments filtered through at intervals, the crowds got increasingly more impatient, though the Cunard officials posted quickly all bulletins received.

Late in the evening the Admiralty felt compelled to give out notice that it was not holding back any known facts, but did not feel justified in giving out rumors.

Americans Besiege Embassy.

The American Embassy and Consulate and the American newspaper offices were flooded with telephonic inquiries from Americans as to the fate of the passengers on the Lusitania, but there was no definite news there until after midnight, and the only hope that could be held out was that some boats had landed survivors and others had been seen making for the shore. The Embassy decided to remain open all night, so that any news that was received could be made public.

Up to 1 o'clock no news tending to allay the public anxiety had been received in the city. Then dispatches, issued by the Admiralty, indicated that among the survivors landed at Queenstown were some injured, presumably by the explosion.

A later dispatch from the same source increased the apprehensions in this direction. Those wounded are being sent to the naval and military hospitals.

A press dispatch from Queenstown reported that 400 pasesngers and crew had been landed at Kinsale. This stated that none of the first-class passengers had been saved, but this is proved not true by private dispatches.

An Admiralty statement states, however, that the survivors from the Lusitania landed at Kinsale numbered about eleven.

A private telegram from Clonakiety to Dublin says that several hundred passengers had landed that from the Lusitania.

FEARED FOR LINER'S SAFETY.

Washington Heard Alarming Rumors Before the News Came.

WASHINGTON, May 7.—Information gathered among officials of the Government and in diplomatic quarters confirms the belief that plans for the destruction of the Lusitania were made several weeks ago. First, the German Embassy was instructed to advertise in the leading newspapers of the United States warning passengers against traveling on ships belonging to enemies of Germany. Anonymous warnings then were said to have been sent to individuals who proposed sailing on the Lusitania. Most significant of all were letters received here from officials in Germany by individuals saying that the Lusitania surely would be destroyed.

From the day the ship sail from New York officials here have received inquiries from many sources almost daily as to the safety of the vessel. One official was told with mpch positiveness today that this was the day selected for the destruction of the vessel.

The naval radio station at Arlington has been on the alert for news, and from time to time has been reported as having picked up messages saying the vessel was sunk. Inquiry at the Navy Department each time failed to confirm the reports, and they were not circulated because it was feared they would sprad unnecessary alarm.

At the German Embassy, while no comment was made as to whether it was known that the vessel was to be destroyed, it was said the Embassy knew the Lusitania carried arms and ammunition and, being advised of the resolution of the German Admiralty to attack ships that carried, officials had believed she would be attacked. At the embassy and among diplomats friendly to Germany there was a general satisfaction amounting almost to relief when the first reports came that no lives were lost, for it was urged that the purpose the German submarine campaign was only to destroy British commerce and ships, but no lives. There was a disposition on the part of the Germans to inquire also wether the Lusitania carried any guns on her decks, which might place her in the class of a warship and make unnecessary, according to the rules of international law, the giving of warning.

BULLETINS STIR UP WAR SYMPATHIZERS

Arguments and Fights Follow Sinking of the Lusitania —One Arrest.

The first reports of the sinking of the Lusitania, by a German submarine posted on the bulletin boards around the city caused great crowds to gather and stirred heated arguments and a number of personal encounters. The police stationed at these places had their hands full keeping the peace.

When Paul Zeider of 416 West 126th Street passed Times Square at 6:30 o'clock last evening he saw on the bulletin board the news that the Germans had sunk the Lusitania. He shouted: "Hurragh for the Germans!" and threw his hat in the air. There was an angry outcry, and a dozen men rushed for him. When Traffic Policeman MacDonald, stationed at Broadway and Forty-third Street, had shoved his way into the centre of the small riot, he had to call Patrolman Foley to help rescue Zeider. The German sympathizer failed to appreciate this service, and began struggling with the policemen. He was then taken to the West Forty-seventh Street Police Station and locked up on a charge of disorderly conduct.

In front of THE TIMES bulletin board, in Herald Square, in Park Row, and, in fact, everywhere people congregated to talk about the sinking of the Lusitania, there were angry arguments.

WILSON SHOCKED AT TORPEDO BLOW

Continued from Page 1.

the Shoreham Hotel when the first bulletin was received here. With him were Secretary Garrison, Secretary Daniels, Secretary Lane, Secretary Wilson, and Mr. Tumulty, the Secretary to the President. As the party finished luncheon and was leaving the dining room a newspaper man handed Mr. Bryan the bulletin telling of the sinking of the big Cunarder.

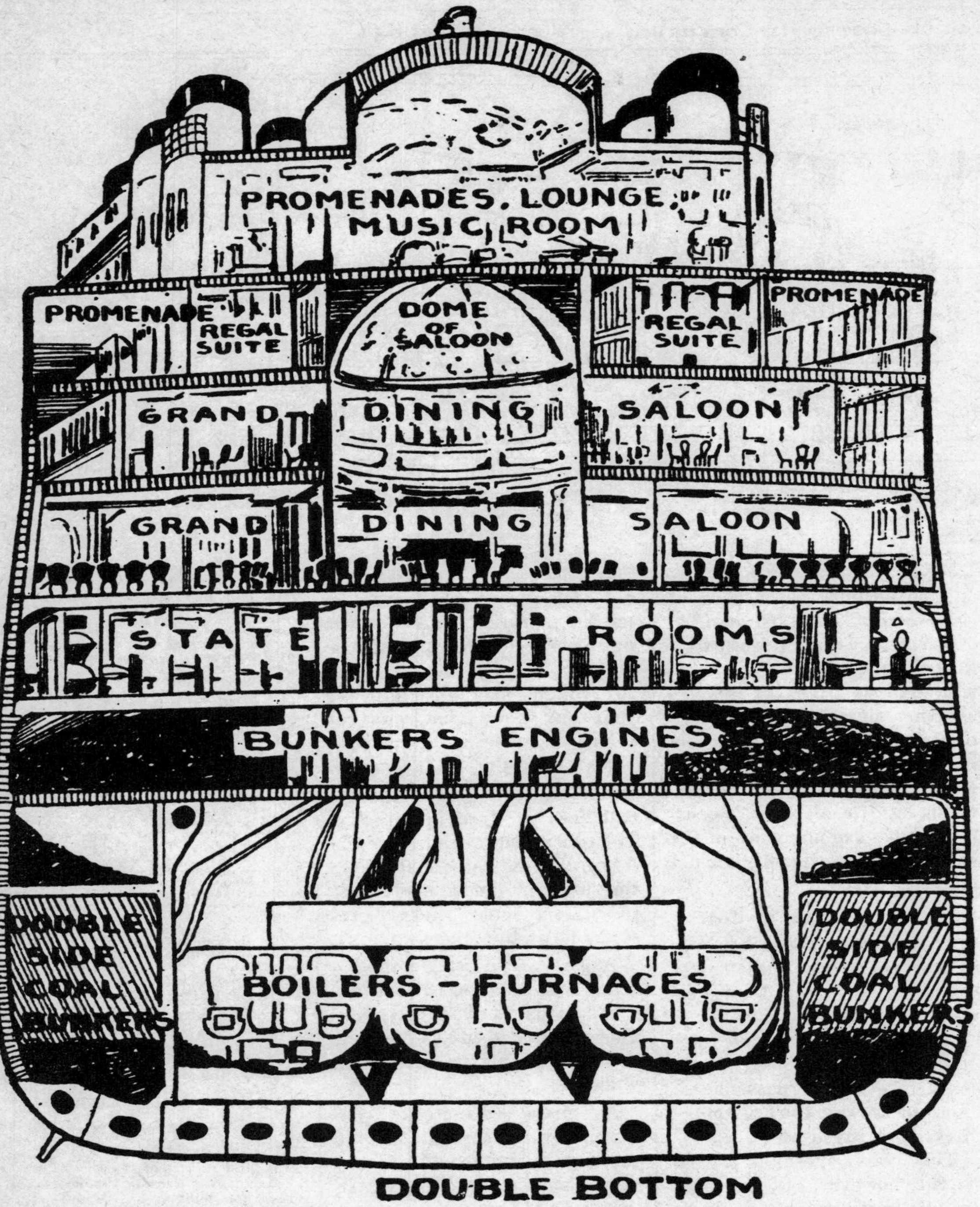
PROMENADES, LOUNGE
MUSIC ROOM
PROMENADE
REGAL SUITE
DOME OF SALOON
REGAL SUITE
PROMENADE
GRAND DINING SALOON
GRAND DINING SALOON
STATE ROOMS
BUNKERS ENGINES
DOUBLE SIDE COAL BUNKERS
BOILERS - FURNACES
DOUBLE SIDE COAL BUNKERS
DOUBLE BOTTOM

Cross Section of the Lusitania.

Bryan Hurries to Office.

It was read eagerly by all the Cabinet officers and Mr. Tumulty. Secretary Bryan nurried to the State Department and asked if any official news of the disaster had been received. Nothing had come, however. It was an hour later before the official news reached the Department.

This was in the form of a cable message from Walter H. Page, the American Ambassador in London, received at 3:05 P. M., and was as follows:

"The Lusitania was torpedoed off the Irish Coatst, and sunk in half an hour. No news yet of passengers."

This message was repeated to the White House over the Government telegraph wire.

No other official information came until after 9 o'clock tonight, when the State Department received this message from Consul Frost at Queenstown, Ireland:

"Lusitania sunk at 2:30. Probably many survivors. Rescue work progressing."

Secretary Bryan declined to comment on the Lusitania disaster when he was questioned by newspaper men. He expressed satisfaction over the reports that no lives had been lost, but he declined to go beyond that. His reticence was typical of the attitude displayed throughout official circles, where there was an evident appreciation of the seriousness of the situation.

May Group Protests.

In the absence of any authoritative statement of the Government's position, opinion here is inclined toward the view tha the United States will group the Lusitania case with those of the American tank steamer Gulflight and the British passenger steamer Falaba. In the sinking of the Falaba by a German submarine Leon C. Thrasher, an American citizen, lost his life. Two members of the crew of the Gulflight jumped overboard and were drowned when the vessel was torpedoed, and the Gulflight's Captain died of heart failure sixteen hours afterward.

No representations have ever been made by the United States to Germany on the subject of Thrasher's death. An investigation is now being made by American officers in England and Germany in an effort to get at all the facts connected with the Gulflight affair, with the primary purpose of determining whether a German submarine was responsible for the attack on the vessel. It was suggested here this evening that when the Government came to make representations to Germany concerning the death of Thrasher it probably would include in its note references to the explosion against the bow of the Gulflight, provided evidence was obtained to show beyond a reasonable doubt that the injured had been done by a German torpedo, and to the sinking of the Lusitania, granted also that there was evidence of a German attack.

In grouping these three incidents the Government, it was said, would be in a position to maintain the contention that Germany had disregarded the warning of the United States concerning attacks by German submarines on American merchant vessels and on foreign vessels carrying American citizens.

In that warning, which was addressed to Germany in the form of a diplomatic note pertaining to the German war zone order, with its consequent submarine warfare against merchant vessels, this Government said that if a German war vessel should destroy on the high seas an American vessel or the lives of American citizens, "it would be difficult for the Goernment of the United States to view the act in any other light than as an indefensible violation of neutral rights which it would be hard, indeed, to reconcile with the friendly relations now so happily subsisting between the two Governments."

The War Zone Order.

To obtain an idea of the bases of the position that may be assumed by the United States Government, it is necessary to keep in mind the several diplomatic notes and certain occurrences that have to do with the German war zone order, which provided for hostile operations by German submarines against merchant ships of Germany's enemies. The points of these bases may be set forth as follows:

1. The German Government issued a decree providing that food supplies of the civilian population of the empire should be taken over and distributed by the Government.

2. Great Britain construed this action as meaning that all food supplies in Germany, or shipped to Germany for the use of the civilian population, were to be taken over by the German Government for the use of its armed forces. Great Britain then took action indicating that she intended to prevent any foodstuffs from going to Germany. Up to that time she had permitted foodstuffs for the civilian population to go to Germany if carried in neutral vessels.

Our Flag Protest.

3. Following the action of the British Government in detaining the Wilhelmina, an American ship loaded with food suplies from the United States for the civilian population of Germany, the German Government issued its war zone order, providing that a submarine warfare should be waged against British, French, and Russian ships within a prescribed area of water adjacent to the coast of the British Isles, and warned neutral nations that they should keep their merchant ships away from the war zone, on account of the danger that they might be mistaken for ships of the enemy and made to suffer the consequences.

4. The Lusitania, the vessel sunk today, flew the American flag on a voyage from New York to England, and Germany took advantage of this incident to justify the war zone order. The use of the flag was the subject of a protest by the United States to Great Britain.

5. The United States Government protested against the war zone order as far as it might apply to American ships, and insisted that the well-defined right of visit and search to determine the nationality, destination, and cargo of a merchant vessel should be exercised by Germany in order to prevent the possible sinking of an American vessel by a German submarine or other warship. At the same time, this Government warned Germany that friendly relations between Germany and the United States might be severed if a German warship should destroy an American vessel or cause the loss of American lives through sinking a vessel of other nationality with Americans on board.

6. The war zone order caused the British Government to issue the Order in Council providing for stopping all supplies to Germany, even if carried in neutral bottoms and intended for civilians.

7. The British passenger ship Falaba, bound for Africa, was torpedoed by a German submarine and Leon C. Thrasher, an American citizen, was drowned.

8. The American ship Gulflight was sunk off the Scilly Isles, supposedly by a torpedo fired by a German submarine, and two members of the crew were drowned. All others on the Gulflight were saved except the Captain, who died from heart failure.

Modus Vivendi Failed.

After the issuance of the German war zone order, and the promulgation of the British Order in Council, which carried into effect the practice of the British Government in nolding up neutral vessels with cargoes of foodstuffs for Germany the United States Government endeavored to effect an arrangement in the form of a modus vivendi by which American foodstuffs were to be permitted to go to Germany under a guarantee from the United States that they would be distributed only to non-combatant civilians. These negotiations failed.

Examination of the official British Admiralty chart of the south coast of Ireland in the Navy Department late this afternoon in connection with the various bulletins from London, Liverpool, and Queenstown threw considerable light on the difficulties that would be encountered in rescuing the 1,900 persons constituting the passengers and crew of the Lusitania. According to the only message that appears to have come from the Lusitania in the form of distress calls received by the Land's End wireless station the position of the Lusitania was given as ten miles south of Kinsale. Interpreted in the light of subsequent messages, this message from the Lusitania was accepted as meaning that her position was about ten miles south of Old Head of Kinsale, a rocky promontory on the Irish coast about six and one-half miles due south of the town of Kinsale, which stands in from the coast on a narrow harbor.

Struck in Deep Water.

The point given by the Lusitania is located in water 49 fathoms, or 294 feet, deep. The 40-fathom line, within which the water is less than 240 feet deep, is nearly 4½ miles from the coast at Old Head of Kinsale, the nearest point of land to the accident. The 30-fathom line, behind which the water is not over 180 feet deep, runs 1 2-3 miles from the coast at Old Head of Kinsale. The 20-fathom line, behind which the water is not over 120 feet deep, is a mile from Old Head of Kinsale, and the 10-fathom (60 feet depth) is a half a mile from Old Head. These measurements based on official soundings by the British Admiralty are sufficient to show the precipitous shelving of the ocean depths and the difficulty that would be encountered in trying to beach the Lusitania.

If the Lusitania was struck ten miles from Old Head of Kinsale, as indicated by the Lusitania's message, it would have been necessary for the giant Cunarder to travel not less than 8¼ miles in order to reach water in which there would be a depth of 20 fathoms, or 120 feet, and this water would be too deep for beaching. The nearest point at which the Lusitania could reach water of not more than ten fathoms, 60 feet depth, would be 9½ miles from the point of torpedo attack, and within a half mile of Old Head of Kinsale. It is not thought that the Lusitania could have been beached at all off Old Head of Kinsale, the shores of which are of rock and almost vertical. To beach the Lusitania its Captain would have been compelled to steer into Courtmacsherry Bay, a large arm of the ocean, west of Old Head of Kinsale, and bounded on the west by a promontory known as Seven Heads. To be beached in Courtmacsherry Bay the Lusitania would have been forced to travel not less than twelve miles after being struck.

Twenty-eight Miles from Queenstown.

The air-line distance by water from Queenstown to the place where the Lusitania was struck is shown by the British Admiralty chart to be twenty-eight miles from Queenstown. This means that vessels sent in the rescue fleet from Queenstown had to travel about sixty miles in making the round trip, and this could not be done in less than about six hours.

The three nearest points of the Irish coast to the point where the Lusitania was torpedoed were the promontories of Old Head of Kinsale, Seven Heads, and Galley Head. Old Head of Kinsale is fifteen miles southwest of Roche Point, the entrance to Cork Harbor, which leads to Queenstown and Cork. Seven Heads is seven miles west-southwest of Old Head of Kinsale and ten miles northwest of the point where the Lusitania was torpedoed.

Galley Head is ten miles west southwest of Seven Heads, and seventeen miles west-northwest of the point where the Lusitania was struck. Some of the wireless messages received at Liverpool came from the Admiralty wireless station at Galley Head, which is on the Galley Head promontory, just mentioned. One of the cable messages received by the Cunard Company in New York this afternoon from Liverpool stated that a Cork newspaper reported that 300 passengers had landed at Clonakilty.

This probably means that these passengers landed at Clonakilty Bay, which is situated between Galley Head and Seven Heads and fifteen miles from the point where the tragedy occurred. The town of Clonakilty is two miles inland from the head of this bay. There are two landing coves in Clonakilty Bay. These are Dunnycove Bay, on the west side of Clonakilty Bay, three and one-half miles south of the town of Clonakilty, and Barry Cove, on the east side of Clonakilty Bay, five miles southeast of the town of Clonakilty.

No Railroad There.

No railroad touches the shore of Clonakilty Bay. Any passengers landing on that bay would have to travel over rocky roads to Clonakilty, the end of the Clonakilty branch of the Cork and Bandon Railway. Once at Clonakilty these passengers, in order to reach Queenstown, woud travel over this branch railway to Clonakilty Junction, a distance of eight miles, then go eastward through Bandon to Cork, about twenty-two miles, and thence by rail about ten miles to Queenstown.

One of the Cunard Line's messages from Liverpool said the Admiralty wireless station at Galley Head reported having sighted several boats apparently containing survivors nine miles southeast and that a Greek steamer was proceeding to assist. Nine miles southeast of Galley Head would mean that these boats had gone considerably off their course, and would mean that their boats had drifted a little south of west about ten miles from the place where the Lusitania was struck.

The nearest point of approach to shore for persons in boats making away from the place where the Lusitania was struck would be Courtmacsherry Bay, ten miles distant from the point of attack, and five miles nearer than Clonakilty Bay. Courtmacsherry Bay is between the promontories of Seven Heads and Old Head of Kinsale, and there are many places on its shore where passengers in small boats might safely land. Arms of Courtmacsherry Bay are Seven Heads Bay, Boat Harbor, Garylucas, Ringalurisky Point, and West Holeopen Bay. Those who may have succeeded in landing on the west side of this bay would take the Owenkeagh Railroad from the town of Courtmacsherry to Ballinascarty, on the Clonakilty Branch Railway, and then go through Bandon to Cork. Those landing on the east side of this bay would have to travel by highway to the town of Kinsale, whence they could proceed by the Kinsale Branch of the Cord and Bandon Railway to Cork and Queenstown.

A high Government official, who is an expert in nautical and maritime matters, ventured the suggestion tonight that perhaps only half of the lifeboats of the Lusitania could have been used in the circumstances of the loss of the vessel as reported.

"The press and official dispatches agree that the Lusitania sank in half an hour," he said. "To have sunk so rapidly the Lusitania probably listed quickly and heavily. Otherwise the vessel, constructed as she was, would have gone down very slowly if she had settled straightaway without any heavy list. If complete developments show that the vessel listed rapidly it will probably be found that the lifeboats on one side were not used, or only part of them used. If the vessel listed to the starboard very quickly it would have been difficult to use the lifeboats on the port side because these boats would not reach the water. They would strike the side of the vessel and turn over. The lifeboats on the starboard side could have been, of course, used while the vessel was listing to starboard. The Lusitania was heavily bulkheaded. There were coal bunkers built along both sides to protect the machinery against shell attack.

But this coal would not give protection against torpedo attack. A torpedo tearing a great hole in the side of a vessel would let in the water, but if the hole were near the bunkers the coal would impede the inflow of the water somewhat. If the Lusitania settled straightaway without listing, I think it would have been possible to get off the 1,900 persons in half an hour, but it would be quick work and depend altogether on conditions met at the time. With the vessel listing, if only half of the lifeboats were used, that would account for heavy loss of life."

171 ABOARD WERE AMERICANS.

Nationalities of First and Second Cabin Passengers Announced.

The first and second class passengers on the Lusitania, according to the Cunard office here, are divided into the following nationailties: British, 700; American, 171; Dutch, 5; Russian, 3; Greek, 3; Swedish 1; Mexican, 1; Swiss, 1; Italian, 1.

A table was prepared showing the nationality of the third-class passengers, bupt it was made on the assumption that the third-class paseengers of the Cameronia had been tionalities who, it was learned later, had not gone aboard the Lusitania. All of those who left on the Lusitania were provided with passports from their Consular representatives, which had been approved by the British Consulate here.

LOST SHIP WAS LONG QUEEN OF THE SEAS

Cut Six Hours from Record on Maiden Voyage and Twice Reduced Her Own Time.

BUILT TO BEAT GERMANS

Depended on Speed Against Submarines, but Used U. S. Flag Once When in Danger.

The sinking of the Lusitania came just seven years, seven months and twenty-three days after she was hailed Queen of the Seas upon her arrival off Sandy Hook on her maiden trip, six hours ahead of the fastest record made up to that time.

It was her great speed that was relied upon to save her from submarine attack, although in February last, on her way from Queenstown to Liverpool, fear of such attack caused her to raise the American flag, an act that roused astonishment on both sides of the ocean and resulted in a statement by the British Foreign Office justifying the use of a neutral flag under such circumstances.

Her first run to sea, when she was completed in the Summer of 1907 by the shipbuilding firm of John C. Brown & Co., at Clydebank, as England's challenge to the supremacy of the German transatlantic liners, carried her over the spot where she was torpedoed.

It was a 900-mile spin around Ireland, and the speed the Lusitania showed made all England joyful, because she promised to do what she had been built to do—to bring back to England the transatlantic record which the Germans had wrested and held for the ten years preceding.

The first four-propellered turbine steamship, which it was the delight of the English to describe as "a floating first-class hotel," the Lusitania was welcomed to New York on her first arrival by more steam whistles than had ever before disturbed the air above the lower bay.

The late J. P. Morgan went out to greet the liner on his yacht, the Corsair, while the crack steamship of the French Line, La Provence, preceded the Lusitania up the bay, by way of showing how great an advance "Big Lucy" was over the best ships of the older days.

Breaks Her Own Speed Record.

The Lusitania gained fame each year and twice managed to break her own records—once in 1908 and again in 1909. She brought to this country the first two-cent mail from England, and she was the first steamship from which a wireless message went out to the world that a dream of shipbuilders had been realized in a ship that could average for a whole day's run more than 25 knots. This great run was made on Wednesday, May 25, 1908, and the twenty-four hours average was 26 1-3 knots.

In the ship's early days a favorite devise for illustrating her size was to print pictures showing the Park Row building, the Flatiron building, and the St. Paul building piled end on end. The Lusitania, sketched alongside the three, was just short of equalling their combined height. Another favored way of describing her size was to contrast her to the leviathan which preceded her—the Great Eastern. Her length of 790 feet was a gain of ninety-eight feet over the Great Eastern, her beam of eighty-eight feet, an increase of eight feet and her displacement of 45,000 tons, an increase over the Great Eastern of 22,300 tons. Her four screws gave an increase of 13 knots over the Great Eastern's speed of 13.

The Lusitania came sixty-seven years after the Britannia, the first Cunard steamship to cross the ocean, had attested Great Britain's supremacy in trade with the United States. At her launching 10,000 British throats sang "Rule Britannia" until they were hoarse.

From Friday, Sept. 13, 1907, the day of the Lusitania's first great triumph when she took from the North German Lloyd line the sea's speed laurels, men of the salt water on both sides of the Atlantic began to express forebodings about her. There was always present in the literature that grew up around her name, the undertone of foreboding because of the way "Friday the Thirteenth" came to be associated with her career afloat.

A Ship of Colossal Dimensions.

It was said that a third of the Lusitania's possible cabin room was sacrificed to spaciousness. Even with this sacrifice there was room for 500 first-class passengers, 550 second, 1,200 third, and a crew of 910 men, 3,160 souls in all. The cost of the Lusitania was never made public, although it was roughly estimated at $6,250,000 at the time of her launching. When she was fitted and ready for sea she was supposed to represent $10,000,000 invested.

The Lusitania's builders worked definitely, with Admiralty reports before them, based on experiments with the warship Monmouth, to get an increase of one and one-half knots over the speed of the North German Lloyd's champion of the transatlantic race course, the Kaiser Wilhelm II. To obtain this result the Cunard people installed additional furnaces and boilers to provide 52,000 square feet more heating surface than that of the crack liner of the Germans.

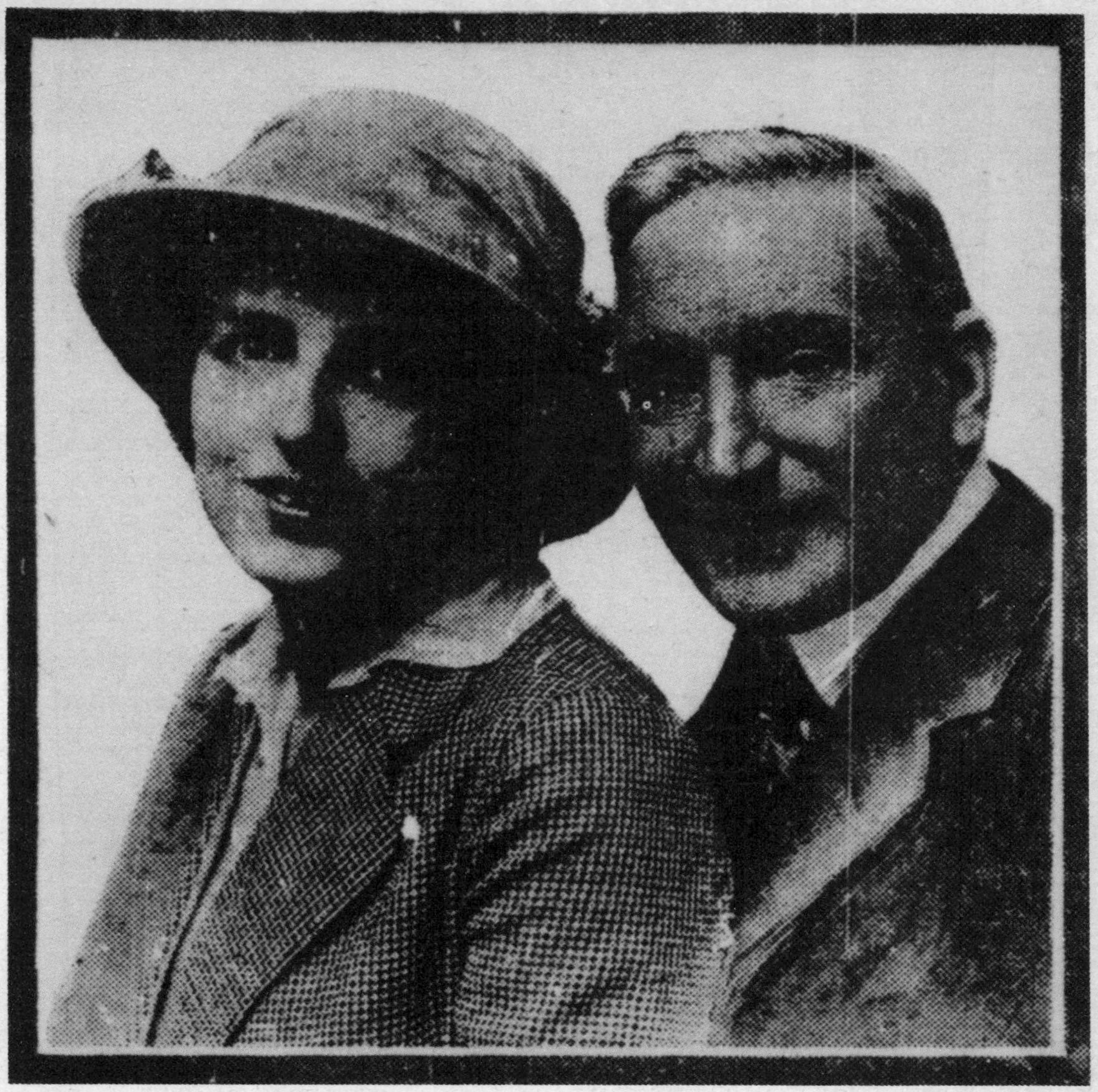

Capt. Turner of the Lusitania and His Niece, Miss Desmore.

The double-bottom system was adhered to in the Lusitania, and doors connecting the various water-tight compartments, of which 170 were provided, were planned to be closed automatically from the bridge in a few seconds.

In the ship's hull 26,000 steel plates, many of which weighed five tons each, were used, while 4,000,000 rivets, weighing 500 tons, held them in place. There were eight decks, and everything about her was of colossal dimensions. Her rudder weight 65 tons, and the three anchors weighed 10 tons each. The main frames and beams, if put end to end, would extend thirty miles. There were 1,200 sidelights and windows, 5,000 incandescent lights, and 200 miles of electric wiring.

Dips Her Pennant to Mauretania.

The various records of the Lusitania became the wonder of the maritime world, but finally her glory as queen of the seas was taken by the Mauretania, her sister ship, which is now in the service of the British Navy. The trip which attracted the eyes of all the world to the Lusitania was made westward in 5 days and 54 minutes. The record that added even more to her fame was 4 days, 11 hours and 42 minutes, but the Mauretania made a trip in 4 days, 10 hours and 41 minutes—a record which still stands.

One of the eventful days in the Lusitania's career was Sept. 16, 1911, when she appeared bedecked in bunting from stem to stern, before thousands of spectators who lined the Battery, completing her third trip across the Atlantic in less than three weeks.

Inasmuch as she was the greatest prize the Germans could hope to win, the trips of the Lusitania since the war began have been watched with much concern. British shipping men insisted that it was safe for her on the ocean because the British fleet was keeping the German fleet in check, and had cleared the ocean lanes of hostile ships. They felt that her speed would carry her through, even if a submarine should try to sink her. Three days after war was declared the Lusitania left New York on one of her regular trips to Liverpool. She slipped out of the harbor in darkness, and it was reported while she was at sea that German warships had captured her and, subsequently, that she was fleeing to some American port.

On Dec. 24 last the Cunard Line paid $50,000 in premiums to insure the Lusitania for a voyage from Liverpool to New York and return, the policy being for $10,000,000. It was the largest sum ever paid for a marine policy.

On her first trips after the war began the Lusitania sailed with her smoke stacks painted plain black, so that she would not be so easily distinguished, but last November she came out again in the Cunard colors, which was taken as a sign of returning confidence, due to the freeing of the seas of German warships.

On Feb. 20 of this year the Lusitania arrived under merchantman's colors, discarding for the first time the blue flag of the Royal Naval Reserve which she was entitled to fly.

INQUIRERS BESIEGE CUNARD OFFICE HERE

Continued from Page 1.

different hotels and boarding houses, but cannot give a list of the survivors, as the passengers are in such a state that their immediate wants must first be considered.
CUNARD, Liverpool.

Denial by Mr. Stone.

The first inquirers were assured by clerks at the Cunard office that there had been no loss of life for the reason that Charles P. Sumner, General Manager of the Cunard Line in Aerica, had received word from Melville E. Stone, General Manager of The Associated Press, that the Lusitania had been beached, and that all on board had been saved. This, according to employes in the Cunard offices, had been corroborated by Lloyds. Later in the afternoon Mr. Stone sent out a denial of this story from The Associated Press offices.

Inquiries were made from the Cuban Consulate for Julian de Ayala, Consul General for Cuba at Liverpool, who sailed on the Lusitania, and from a representative from the headquarters of the Carranzistas in this city. There were inquiries for Frederic G. Padilla, Consul General for Mexico at Liverpool, who also was on the Lusitania.

Many inquiries came in the afternoon for the safety of Charles Frohman. One of the first long-distance calls was an inquiry about Lady Allan and her two daughters. Reassuring replies were made to all these messages. Because of the optimistic reports in the day, there were only a few inquiries in the evening, most of them by telephone'

More Rescues Reported.

At 10:42 o'clock at night the Cunard office received the following from Liverpool:

Mrs. J. T. Smith and George Kessler are safe.

At 10:45 the following cablegram was received from the Liverpool office:

General Lassetter's wift and son are safe.

The Cunard office was closed at 11 o'clock at night.

LINER UNPROTECTED, CAPTAIN COMPLAINED

"Admiralty Never Trouble to Send Out to Meet Lusitania," Turner Said.

WARNED OF MINES BEFORE

Officer Now Here Asserts the Only Vulnerable Spot Was Right Under Engine Room.

In spite of the warnings that had been received from time to time that the Germans would make an attempt to blow up the Lusitania, Captain William T. Turner expressed no fear for the safety of his ship when he sailed from New York last Saturday.

"I wonder what the Germans will do next?" was his only comment when he read the advertisement in THE NEW YORK TIMES sent out by the German Embassy warning Americans that they sailed at "their own risk" on British ships, which were liable to destruction in the war zone.

When Captain Turner was questioned by a TIMES reporter regarding the ship being met off the Irish coast by British torpedo destroyers, he replied:

"The Admiralty never trouble to send out to meet the Lusitania. They only look after the ships that are bringing the big guns over, like the Orduna and the Transylvania, last voyage. On the eastward trip I never saw a warship until we reached Liverpool. The ship is steaming under three sections of boilers, and will average about twenty-two knots if the weather is fine, which ought to bring her into Liverpool about Friday evening."

One of the Cunard officers now in port, who was on the Lusitania on her last voyage, yesterday confirmed Captain Turner's statement that the liner had not sighted a single warship before arriving at Liverpool.

"All the News That's Fit to Print."

The New York Times.

THE WEATHER

Generally fair Sunday and Monday; light, east winds.

For full weather report see Page 62.

VOL. LXIV...NO. 21,001.   NEW YORK, SUNDAY, JULY 25, 1915.—90 PAGES, In Seven Parts, Including Picture and Rotogravure Sections and Review of Books.   PRICE FIVE CENTS

BERLIN HOLDS UP NOTE'S FULL TEXT; CURBS COMMENT

Newspapers Get Only a Scant Summary and Publish It Inconspicuously.

DENY THAT IT IS FINAL

Lokalanzeiger, Reflecting Official View, Thinks It Leaves Way for Further Parley.

SOME STRONG EDITORIALS

American Attitude Is Neither Friendly Nor Neutral in Spirit, Says Tageszeitung.

DELAY EXPECTED HERE

Washington Thinks Germany Will Withhold Reply in Deference to Sentiment at Home.

From a Staff Correspondent.

Special Cable to The New York Times.

BERLIN, July 24, (via London.)—The full text of the American note has not been printed here, and apparently the word has gone out to be cautious in commenting on it. As a result the afternoon papers do not refer to the note in their headlines and publish only very short summaries of its contents.

The Lokalanzeiger says: "The note fully comes up to the expectations which we have repeatedly expressed. It affords ground on which further negotiations with Washington can be conducted. Throughout it is correct in tone and is couched in the usual forms of politeness customary between States, yet at the same time it is outspoken."

After summarizing the Lokalanzeiger, with all the earmarks of higher inspiration, significantly concludes: "The questions raised in the American answer must naturally be exhaustively looked into by the various German authorities concerned. Therefore, at present there is nothing to say as to the nature of the answer. The report emanating from English sources that the American answer is meant to be final is absolutely without foundation. In any event, after the previous negotiations, we may have every confidence that Germany will continue to use the valuable war weapon of the submarine in future in such a way as may seem useful for us and the least harmful for neutrals. We had and have, of course, no interest in arousing neutrals against us. On the contrary, it can only be our purpose to avoid everything that would be likely unnecessarily to imperil the rights of neutral States."

The Berliner Tageblatt does not publish a line of comment and devotes a single paragraph to "the contents" of the American note.

The Vossische Zeitung also devotes one paragraph to the contents, while it modestly runs under a Washington cable telling that President Wilson and Secretary Lansing are planning a new note to England under the headline, "American Protest Note to England."

Says We Stick to England.

The Kreuz-Zeitung says:
"The contents of the note proves anew that the American Government stands closer to England than they care to admit. The note indicates not the slightest effort to do justice to the German standpoint, but clings obstinately to the alleged right of American citizens to travel on belligerent ships, although being endangered, even when those ships are freighted with bombs and shells. America wants to give a free pass to contraband for England by means of its citizens. That is not neutrality, but most decided partisanship. If America had the least bit of good will the demands of the note would have been limited to safe passage for such ships as carried no contraband.

"In saying that the undertakings of warring countries must be subordinated to 'the rights of neutrals' the note goes counter to the most elementary principles of international law. Everywhere in land and sea warfare, no consideration can be given to neutrals. The rule is, 'he who goes into danger does so at his own risk.' America could with equal right contend that American citizens have a right to live unendangered in Paris or Dunkirk, and say, 'if you bombard these cities, we will consider it as an intentionally unfriendly act.' We do not know what the German Government considers answering, but we have confidence that it will not abandon the submarine war. We have shown that we are prepared to make every possible concession to the neutrals, but the compromise must

Continued on Page 4.

ROOSEVELT AND BRYAN REFUSE TO COMMENT

Former Says He Hopes America Will Act on the Sentiments He Expressed at Syracuse.

Special Cable to The New York Times.

SAN FRANCISCO, July 24.—After studying the latest note to Germany, Colonel Roosevelt declined to discuss it in detail or to express an opinion concerning it.

"I have only this to say," said Colonel Roosevelt. "If you will refer to my statements at Syracuse after the sinking of the Lusitania, you will find the sentiments I held then and hold at this time. I can only add that I hope Uncle Sam will act on them."

In the statement received to-day, Colonel Roosevelt declared, in brief, that the sinking of the Lusitania was piracy and wanton slaughter of innocent men, women, and children.

In speeches made here to-day ex-President did not refer to the latest note to Germany.

Ex-Secretary Bryan is now en route from Los Angeles to San Francisco, and will not arrive here until late this evening. Before departing from the south, and after a hurried perusal of the note, he said:

"This is interesting, but, of course, until I have read the note through and analyzed it carefully I cannot discuss it. It would be impossible for me to give any opinion on the note until I have gone over it with the greatest care."

BRITISH PLEDGE TO FIGHT IT OUT

Anniversary Meetings Throughout the Empire Will Take a Vow to Continue on to Victory.

LONDON, July 24.—The anniversary of Great Britain's declaration of war on Germany, Aug. 4, will be marked throughout the empire by reaffirmation of the determination of the British peoples to continue the struggle unwaveringly.

The pledge will be embodied in the following resolution, approved by Premier Asquith:

"That on this anniversary of the declaration of a righteous war this meeting of citizens of ——— records its inflexible determination to continue to a victorious end the struggle for the maintenance of those ideals of liberty and justice which are the common and sacred cause of the Allies."

Meetings have been arranged throughout the empire, at which the resolution will be put. Members of the Cabinet and of Parliament and other public officials are co-operating in the arrangements, and the dominions and colonies are all joining in the movement.

TWO MORE VESSELS TORPEDOED AND SUNK

Russian Ship Rubonia and a Trawler—Crews Landed on Orkneys.

LONDON, July 24.—The Russian ship Rubonia has been torpedoed and sunk by a submarine. Her crew of thirty were landed on the Orkney Islands.

The trawler Star of Peace also was torpedoed and sunk off the Orkneys. The crew were landed at Stromness.

No Russian ship Rubonia is on the marine lists. The Russian steamer Rubonia is listed. Her length is given at 250 feet, with beam of 45 feet and of 25 feet, and tonnage of 3,424 gross. She was built at Newcastle in 1906.

SERBIAN ARMY BETTER EQUIPPED THAN EVER

But Is Still Inactive—Typhus Stamped Out, Foreign Doctors to Go Elsewhere.

Special Cable to The New York Times.

LONDON, July 24.—The Daily Chronicle's Nish correspondent writes:

"Serbia has now completely recovered. Since April I lost her little army, in fine fettle and perhaps better equipped than ever before, has been massed round her frontiers ready to take up arms if called upon at any given moment and from any given point. Yet so far, except for skirmishes in Albania, she has struck no blow, nor has any big blow been dealt her.

"The inactivity along the Serbian soldiers has meant almost equal inactivity among many hundreds of doctors and the British and American units which have been scattered so freely up and down the country. Since typhus has practically been wiped out of the country many hospital workers have been heard on all sides lately bemoaning the fact that they have little or nothing to do. Accordingly, Sir Ralph Paget, the British Red Cross Commissioner in Serbia, has at last given permission for all hospital units employed units to apply for disbandment should they wish, provided there is no resumption of hostilities by July 21.

"On the expiration of the time limit, it now seems probable, large detachments of doctors, nurses, and orderlies will be set free to take up work in other war areas where their services are most urgently needed."

FIND LINDON BATES'S BODY.

Identification of Lusitania Victim from Documents and Linen.

QUEENSTOWN, July 24.—A body washed ashore at Kilcolgan Galway, on the Irish coast, has been identified from documents found in the coat pocket and from the name on the linen as that of Lindon W. Bates, Jr., one of the American victims of the sinking of the Lusitania by a German submarine.

A body recently washed ashore in County Limerick, was at first believed to be that of Lindon W. Bates, Jr., son of Lindon W. Bates, Vice Chairman of the Commission for Relief in Belgium, but the identification was afterward doubted, and messages received by the family in this country stated that the body had been buried as that of another Lusitania victim.

The effects found on the body were sent to London for closer examination.

GERMANS TIGHTEN GRIP ON WARSAW FROM THE NORTH

Strong Forces Cross the Narew After Storming Two of the Fortresses.

DIRECT DRIVE IS HALTED

Russians Also Hold Lines on Lublin-Chelm Railroad—Driven Across Vistula at Ivangorod.

OPEN BATTLE IN COURLAND

Berlin Reports Crushing Defeat of the Russian Army, Which Was Caught in Retreat.

ITALIANS PRESS CAMPAIGN

Cadorna Is Directing the Attack on Gorizia Under the Eye of the King.

LONDON, July 24.—The Austro-German Armies seem unable to force the Russians from the important positions to the immediate west of Warsaw, and from the line along the Lublin-Chelm Railway, but the German victories in Northern Poland and north of the Polish capital have tightened their grip on the city, and military critics say that the abandonment of Warsaw by the Russians again becomes more probable.

After weeks of battling the German forces for the first time have crossed the Narew River north of Warsaw, and now have a considerable weight of men on the east bank of that river between the Fortresses of Rozan and Pultusk, which a Berlin official statement describes as having been "stormed irresistibly." The communication, however, does not state whether the fortresses capitulated.

The fight in Southern Courland, according to German claims, has resulted in something akin to a crushing victory such as was familiar in the earlier years, General von Bülow's forces having cut off the Russian retreat and delivered a body blow. It is stated that the Germans cut up the retiring troops badly, dispersing those which were not killed, wounded, or captured.

That the Russians are holding the immediate Warsaw front is plainly evidenced by a German official statement which refers to only minor operations in this area and tells of a comparatively insignificant number of prisoners taken. Military critics say this indicates that there have been no serious attacks on either side, which probably means that the Germans are dug in, waiting reinforcements for a more favorable circumstances, while the Russians, from their strongholds, are risking nothing in counter-attacks.

The report of the investment of Ivangorod is now patently erroneous, as the German speak of attacks west of the city and, though claiming that they buried the Russians across the Vistula to the northwest of the city, do not contend that their forces obtained a foothold on the eastern bank.

Reuter's Amsterdam correspondent sends the following received from Berlin:

"The war correspondent of the Lokal Anzeiger on the eastern front telegraphs the warning that while 'the Russians are being continually pressed back along the entire front, it cannot be concealed that only now we succeeded in breaking down the strong hostile armies. The battle for the Russian central positions may be of an extremely varying character,' continues the Anzeiger's correspondent. 'The Teutonic allies are aware of that, but the battle may also be propelled toward the falling side of the east-side of actions and sisters to keep from falling. The whole cargo was impelled toward the falling side of the lower port holes.

None of the passengers had put off. Orders had been given to cast off, notwithstanding that for a considerable time the boat had been gradually listing. When the order to cast off was given it was too late. Before it could be carried out the boat had turned on her side, the hawsers, still attached to the ship, tearing the piling from the pier. The hawsers are still attached to the semi-sunken steamer, the Federal and local authorities having given strict orders that they are not to be disturbed, pending investigation.

Screams from passengers attracted the attention of fellow-excursionists on the pier awaiting the next steamer. Wharf-men and picnickers soon lined the edge of the embankment, reaching out helplessly toward the wavering steamer.

For nearly five minutes the ship listed before it finally dived under. Then there was a plunge, with a sigh of air escaping from the hold, mingled with crying of children and shrieks of women, and the ship was on the bottom of the river.

All Over in Six Minutes.

Hundreds on the upper deck were thrown into the water, and a few escaped. Most of the other passengers, caught below in the cabins or on the lower decks, perished without a chance for life. They were swallowed up in the sight of other thousands crowding the Clark Street Bridge, the wharves, and adjoining streets on their way to the south.

It was all a matter of only a few minutes. Many witnesses say it was all over in six minutes.

The surface of the river was thick

Continued on Page 6.

1,800 DROWN AS EXCURSION STEAMER CAPSIZES, LOADED TO CAPACITY, IN THE CHICAGO RIVER; TOPHEAVY, SHE WAS STARTED WHILE MOORED

SINKS IN BARELY SIX MINUTES

Great Majority of Victims Women and Children, Bound for Picnic.

HUNDREDS TRAPPED BELOW

Throngs Dumped from Upper Decks Into the River to Struggle and Die.

CHICAGO PUTS ON MOURNING

Rows of Bodies, Awaiting Identification, Fill Armory—Heroes Not Lacking.

Special to The New York Times.

CHICAGO, July 24.—Approximately 1,800 persons, most of them women, children and babies, lost their lives in the murky little stream called by courtesy the Chicago River, this morning, when the excursion steamer Eastland turned over at her pier between Lasalle and Clark Streets.

There were 2,500 passengers on the Eastland and a crew of 72, commanded by Captain Henry Pedersen, according to a statement issued this evening by W. J. Greenbaum, general manager of the Indiana Transportation Company, after he had checked up the returns of the ticket takers.

At midnight 880 bodies had been taken to morgues and the work of taking out the bodies was still proceeding.

Besides these, 762 persons are known to have been rescued, and careful checking has shown 921 missing. It is feared that practically all the missing are drowned. This would make the death list about 1,800.

Trying to Fix the Blame.

The task of establishing the cause and of fixing responsibility has begun. A special Federal Grand Jury, called by Judge Landis, will begin an investigation at once. State's Attorney McClay Hoyne opened an inquiry within two hours after the tragedy.

Aboard the Eastland at the hour set for sailing, 7:40 A. M., were approximately 2,500 excursionists. Some say there was danger of overloading the steamer. It is known that United States Custom House officials boarded the boat a short time before she went down and caused between 400 and 500 persons to be removed on finding that the steamer was carrying many more passengers than allowed by law.

The excursionists were a part of five boats chartered for the excursion. About 7,000 tickets had been distributed and a fleet of five steamers had been chartered to take the picnickers across the lake to Michigan City, Ind., where there was to be a big parade and great festivities. The Eastland was the first of the fleet scheduled to depart for Michigan City, and a great throng clamored for admittance.

Cables News Were Cut Off.

Business and social life have been at a standstill all day. The city is overwhelmed by the great disaster. Flags are at half staff on all buildings; there are crowds in the vicinity of the Chicago River which the police find difficult to hold in check, the downtown streets are congested with hearses and auto trucks carrying away the dead, and at the morgues there are lines of people stretching for blocks awaiting admission to identify and recover lost friends or relatives. In the horrors of the day strong men have wept like children, and some have become hysterical. Chicago never before suffered such a tragedy, and is overwhelmed with grief.

All day long and tonight great crowds thronged the river's edge and choked the streets leading to it. On the side of the boat which protruded several feet above the water groups of men gathered around holes burned with gas flames through the steel hull and with ropes dragging up the bodies as fast as the divers could get them. Many are still in the boat, while the river still holds bodies, and it will be days before the exact number of dead is established.

Tonight electric wires have been stretched along the upper side of Eastland to enable the firemen, the divers, and the lifesavers to continue their work through the night.

Policemen drafted from practically every station in the city had a hard fight all day to hold back the hundreds of thousands of persons who pressed toward the Clark Street bridge, intent on seeing the overturned boat and the work of recovering the bodies. The bridge approaches from either side to the south to Austin Avenue on the north were held by a dozen police lines. No strict and Chief Schuettler's orders that even officials and newspaper men had difficulty getting through the lines.

Too Late for Respirators.

Inside the innermost of the police lines and on the deck around us and at her I'd rather be off her this minute. Finally they were all aboard about 7:30 o'clock, maybe a few minutes later. We got orders to cast off the stern lines and were working at that when she began slowly to list again.

"My mate and me heard them hollering on the deck around us and at her I'd rather be off her this minute. Finally they were all aboard about

Continued on Page 2.

SCENES DRIVE DIVER MAD

Unable to Withstand the Shocking Experiences in Hold Among Dead.

STORIES OF THE RESCUED

Deckhand Pictures Victims Dropping by Hundreds Into the River.

BOAT'S STAIRWAYS JAMMED

Panic's Growth as Vessel's List Increased—Swimmers Dragged Under.

Special to The New York Times.

CHICAGO, July 24.—A city diver engaged in the work of taking bodies from the Eastland became violently insane tonight, after several visits to the hold of the vessel, because of the scenes he witnessed there. He discarded his suit, and, raving, started to run across the hull of the boat. He was overcome and placed in a patrol wagon and driven away.

Two women, their clothes in shreds, their fingers torn and bleeding from clawing at the iron hull of the overturned steamer, were taken alive this afternoon from the interior of the Eastland.

They had been imprisoned in a stateroom when the boat turned over. The imprisoned air held back the first rush of water, which, however, seeped in gradually. The two women heard the shrieks of the drowning, but the door of their stateroom was jammed fast, and the port hole was too small for them to crawl through.

Gradually the air leaked out and the water seeped in. First it swirled about their feet and soon rose to their knees. Then it rose to their waists as they struggled in vain for freedom.

Then they became aware that their cries were heard by the rescuers. They heard the blows of sledge hammers above their heads for a time, but these ceased as the rescuers realized that they could make no impression on the steel hull. Then they gave up hope. All the time the water rose higher.

In the meantime the rescuers got acetylene torches, and the blue flame began to eat through the steel plates. Soon a hole was pierced, but this released the air in the hull and the water came in with a rush. Just as the water reached the heads of the victims the iron plate fell in and the rescuers seized the choking and gasping women by the hair and dragged them out. They were carried to Reid, Murdoch & Co.'s plant. Their ultimate recovery is in doubt. A man who had had an experience almost as thrilling was saved from the boiler room of the vessel, where his life had been preserved by a similar air pocket.

For nine hours, or from the time the disaster occurred until about 2 o'clock this afternoon, a boy of 10 years was penned in a section of the hold of the Eastland. Finally, when a hole had been burned through the steel plates, rescuers found him clinging to a stanchion just above the water. He was helped out by firemen. He was too weak to talk for a few moments. When he recovered his strength, however, he got up from the side of the boat and ran to the dock apparently driven frantic for the time being by his terrible experience. His name was not learned in the crowd ashore. His name was not learned.

SAW HUNDREDS FALL TO DEATH IN RIVER

Deck Hand Tells of the Panic—Stairways Jammed—Swimmers Dragged Under.

Special to The New York Times.

CHICAGO, July 24.—Survivors of the Eastland disaster told thrilling stories of their experiences. One survivor owes his life to the fact that his coat caught on a nail and he was held above water. One woman managed for a time to hold her little daughter and son as well as herself above water, but, with her arm benumbed, she finally had to let the daughter go.

Harry Miller, a deckhand of the Eastland, gave a vivid picture of the disaster. His story follows:

"The Eastland began to list about 7:30 o'clock, while crowds were still pouring on her. She listed then, so much the gangplank lifted two or three feet at the ship's side. They stopped the crowd coming on and got all on board over to the shore side of the ship. That righted her. Then they let the rest of the crowd come aboard.

"I didn't like the way she acted and I said to my mate 'I'm scared off her.

Continued on Page 2.

Previous Ship Disasters Show No Such Record of Lives Lost

	Lives Lost.
Titanic, April 14, 1912, off Newfoundland Banks	1,500
*Lusitania, May 7, 1915, Atlantic Ocean	1,100
Empress of Ireland, May 29, 1914, St. Lawrence River	1,024
General Slocum, June 15, 1904, East River, N. Y.	959
*Bourgogne, July 4, 1898, off Newfoundland Banks	571
Princess Alice, Sept. 3, 1878, in Thames near Woolwich	600
Utopia, March 17, 1891, off Gibraltar	574
Norge, June 25, 1904, off Rockall Reefs	600
Mainz, March 12, 1906, off coast of Japan	380
Ship Kapunda, March 20, 1887, off coast of Brazil	300
Lady Elgin, Sept. 8, 1860, Lake Michigan	287
Excursion steamer, April 24, 1909, at Montevideo	200
Nile River steamer, April 8, 1912	200
Larchmont, Feb. 12, 1907, Long Island Sound	183
Volturno, Oct. 11, 1913, Atlantic Ocean	125
State of Florida, April 18, 1884, off Canadian coast	128
Libau, June 7, 1908, off Marseilles coast	100

Eastland's Death List 1,810, Latest Official Figures Show

Special to The New York Times.

CHICAGO, Sunday, July 26.—The latest figures obtainable on the casualties in the Eastland disaster would indicate a loss of 1,810 lives, assuming that the figures given by the United States Custom House Inspectors of the number of passengers on the boat is accurate.

At midnight 889 bodies had been recovered and tagged, of which 103 have been identified. Rescued persons to the number of 762 at the same hour had been tabulated.

On the basis of 2,500 passengers and 72 crew there were 2,572 aboard. Of these 762 have been accounted for as rescued and 889 bodies have been recovered. Total of 1,651, leaving 921 persons missing and unaccounted for.

The following table gives the official figures:

Passengers on Eastland	2,500
Crew on Eastland	72
Total	2,572
Number of dead recovered	889
Number of persons rescued	762
Total	1,651
Missing and unaccounted for	921
Total dead and missing	1,810

THIRTY PUT UNDER ARREST

City, State and Federal Authorities Begin Investigations.

VESSEL ALWAYS UNSTABLE

Overloading and Unseaworthiness Alleged as Causes of the Disaster.

CALLS FEDERAL GRAND JURY

Contradictory Stories Told of Tug's Part in Dragging the Eastland Over.

Special to The New York Times.

CHICAGO, July 24.—The most important move toward the investigation of the Eastland disaster and the punishment of those who may be found responsible for it was the arrest tonight of the St. Joseph-Chicago Steamship Company, owners of the steamer. Captain Pederson and twenty-nine members of the Eastland's crew had already been put under arrest, and Coroner Hoffman had ordered the arrest of every official of the Indiana Transportation Company, which had leased the boat for today's excursion.

The State's Attorney late in the day issued an order to let no one get away until responsibility for the tragedy had been fixed.

He had Capt. H. Pedersen, Chief Engineer C. Erickson and other officers of the boat, together with thirty of the crew, at his offices at the Criminal Court Building. There they were examined by Coroner Hoffman carefully going over every official of the Indiana Transportation Company, which had leased the boat for today's excursion.

Many theories are advanced as to the cause of the disaster. The real cause may not be known until expert testimony is presented to the Federal Grand Jury next week. Among the causes assigned are these:

1. Overcrowding—Thirty-two hundred tickets are said to have been sold for the Eastland, although Government inspectors say that only 2,500 persons went aboard—the number allowed by law.

2. Uneven ballast—The starboard side water ballast tanks are said to have been full and the port side tanks empty. Members of the crew say the ballast pumps were started only after the boat began to list. The rush of passengers to one side, they say, caused the boat to list badly. It was a report which some received aboard so as to lighten the steamer.

3. Probable unseaworthiness—It is declared that the Eastland was condemned on Lake Erie as unsafe and was altered before being brought to Chicago last year; her top deck being added, it is said. The Eastland suffered several mishaps on Lake Erie, but without loss of life.

Federal Grand Jury to Act.

Federal Judge K. M. Landis has ordered a Federal Grand Jury investigation of the catastrophe. Twelve Deputy United States Marshals were sent out with subpoenas for a panel of sixty men. The new Grand Jury is ordered to convene on Thursday afternoon.

This is the first time in Chicago that a special Federal Grand Jury has been ordered to investigate a disaster. It was explained that it was because a vessel plying the navigable waters of the United States had sunk at her pier, and it lies within the province of the Federal Government to ascertain whom the blame lies.

While no official would discuss the culpability of any person connected with the steamboat company or the Federal inspectors' office, it was declared that the vessel may have been passed as safe, while in fact it was not really so.

Edward Willard, members of the crew are in custody at the Cook County authorities pending an investigation by State's Attorney Hoyne.

W. K. Greenbaum, manager of the Indiana Transportation Company, made the following statement late in the day:

"The Indiana Transportation Company expresses its deepest sorrow and sympathy for the bereaved in the Eastland disaster. The Eastland was not overloaded. There were 2,408 tickets taken up at the Eastland gangway by the Eastland collectors under Federal supervision. The Government capacity mark is set at 2,500.

At this time the Indiana Transportation Company is unable to place an opinion on the cause of the accident because the Eastland was hired for the day and the Captain and crew were not employes of the Indiana Transportation Company.

"We are doing everything in our power and will continue to do so both in the work of rescue and in aiding all investigations both by legal authorities and by the press.

"To both we have thrown open every facility for information every aid in our power."

Alleged Misuse of Ballast.

Steamboat Inspector William Nicholas, giving a testimony report that water ballast was pumped from the hold of the Eastland as the passengers boarded, so that the boat would raise and discharge

(continued)

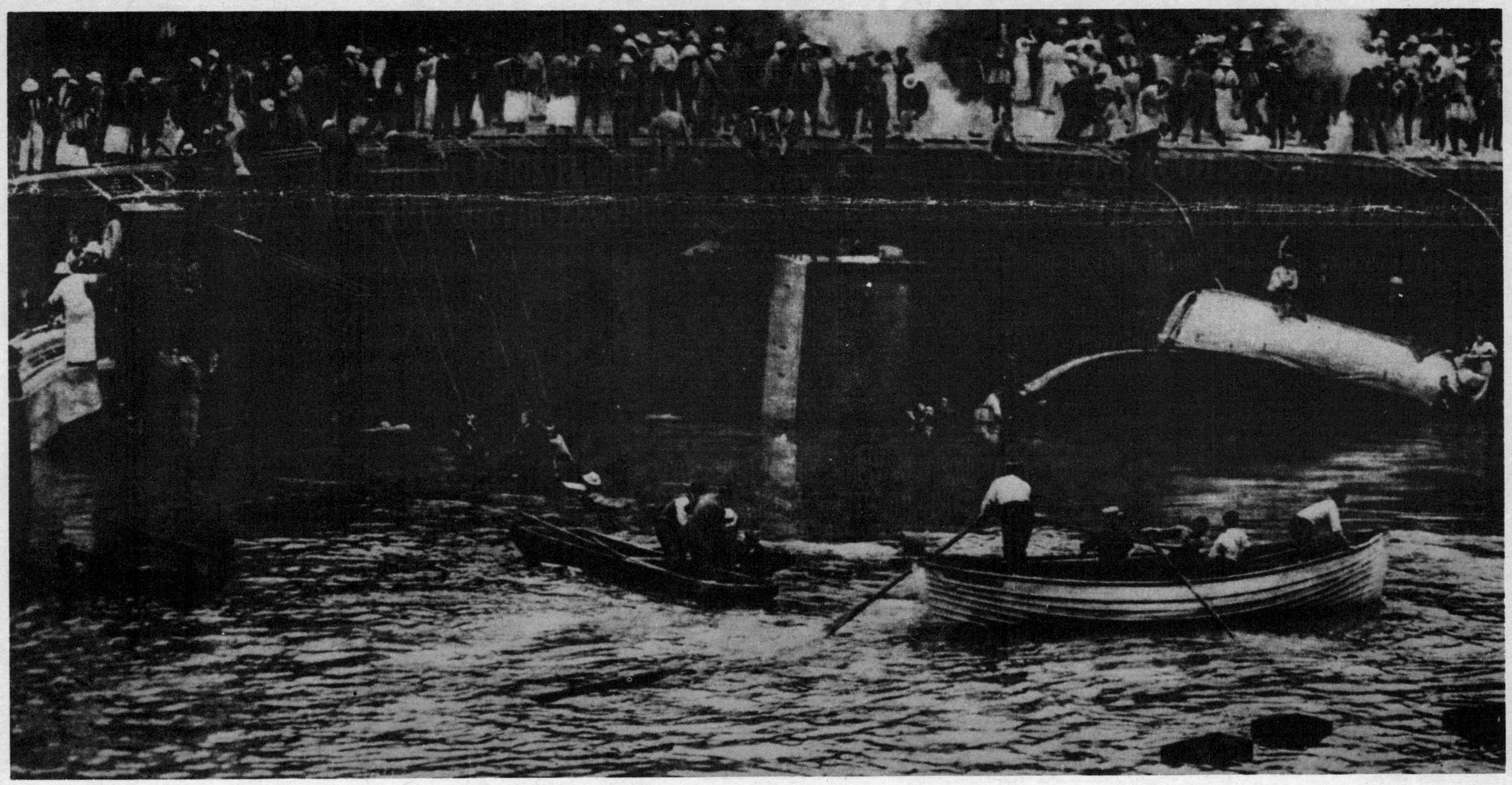

Efforts to rescue the *Eastland's* passengers.

lowing is that the steamer had stuck in the mud and had failed to free herself when the engines were started, causing the outer side of the steamer to list. The weight of the large crowd aboard augmented this to such an extent that the boat could not right itself but caused the hawsers to pull out the piles and the boat continued to list until it overturned.

William Flanagan, one of the Eastland crew, who was in charge of the lines which were to be passed to the tugs to haul the vessel out into the lake, was taken by the police to the office of Assistant States Attorney Case, where he was questioned with regard to the part played by the tug in bringing about the disaster.

"I was standing on deck, ready to pass the lines to the tug," he declared. "I didn't see the Captain, but from the lookout I received the signal to pass the lines over. I did so, and no sooner had the lines been made fast than the tug started away. The ship was listed, anyway, and it began to turn."

"Were the cables that fastened it to the pier still attached?" Flanagan was asked.

"Yes."

"What effect did this have on the turning?"

"None whatever, I believe," was the reply. "The natural effect of this would be to check the roll, but the lines were too weak. The ship was so heavily loaded that the lines parted and it turned over."

"Is it usual for the tugs to start up before the lines to shore are cast off?"

"No, it is not."

"Who was in charge of having the shore lines cast off?"

"The Captain."

"Suppose the Captain, seeing that the tug had started, would have immediately given the order to cast off the shore lines, what effect would that have had?"

"I don't know. It is impossible to say. I don't think it would have had any effect, because the lines parted anyway when they received the full weight of the ship."

Denies Tug Had Started.

Arthur McDonald, engineer of the tug Kenosha, which had received the lines from the Eastland, contradicted Flanagan's statement when questioned in the State Attorney's office.

"I was in the engine room at the time," he said. "It is true that the lines had been passed across, but the tug had not started, nor had I even received orders to start my engines. It is pretty obvious that if the engines were not even turning the tug could not have been pulling the steamer, isn't it?"

McDonald further said that the dangerous list of the steamer was noticed by the crew of the Kenosha and commented on before the boat turned over. "For fifteen minutes before it actually rolled we noticed the list was growing worse and worse all the time. Everybody was onto it, and all of our crew were saying that it wouldn't take much to send the craft over on its side."

Coroner Hoffman began the inquest late today. He had a number of photographs of the boat taken, and then ordered it pumped out and raised. Chief of Police Healy, who inspected the hull late in the afternoon, expressed the opinion that there were still 300 bodies in the boat which cannot be recovered until the boat is raised.

Coroner Hoffman impanelled the following jury:

Dr. William A. Evans, former Commissioner of Health.
William F. Bodem, Vice-President of Reid, Murdoch & Co.
Henry A. Allen, mechanical engineer in charge of the Department of Public Works.
J. S. Keogh, General Manager of W. F. McLaughlin & Co.
Eugene Beifield, Manager Hotel Sherman.
Harry Moir, proprietor Hotel Morrison.

Dr. Evans was chosen foreman and then the jury spent several hours viewing the bodies of the victims and adjourned subject to call.

That a sudden rush of persons on the deck of the Eastland to the port side to look at a speeding launch caused the catastrophe was the assertion of Jack Elbert, gauge tender of the steamer. He said he and J. M. Erickson, chief engineer, escaped drowning by wading through water in the hatch and crawling out of a porthole into the river.

Ordered to "Steady Her Up."

"The steamer Eastland was kept stable by means of a water-ballast system," said Elbert. "Water is pumped into the chambers in the ship until she becomes steady. This was done before even freight is taken on board. The first thing I noticed this morning was that the Eastland began to lean to starboard. Erickson, the chief engineer, was in charge of the pumps used to pump the water into the chambers. He said 'Boys, steady her up a little,' and then we pumped water into the other side until she was up even and all right. We had just evened her up when a launch came down the river and past the Eastland and the crowd on the Eastland rushed over to portside to look at it. The weight all on one side apparently proved too much and the Eastland began to list badly.

"We worked frantically at the pumps to try to bring her back, but she was too far gone."

Eyewitnesses informed the police that there was a man in the launch with a moving-picture camera and that this attracted the attention of passengers on the Eastland, who rushed to one side of the boat.

Captain Harry Peterson, 57 years old, of Benton Harbor, Mich., who was in command of the boat, said:

"I was on the bridge, and was about ready to pull out, when I noticed the boat begin to list. I shouted orders to open the gangways nearest the dock and give the people a chance to get out. The boat continued to roll, and shortly afterward the hausers broke and the steamer turned over on its side and was drifting toward the middle of the river. When she went over I jumped and held on to the upper side. It all happened in two minutes. The cause is a mystery to me. I have sailed the lakes for twenty-five years, and previous to that sailed on salt water twelve years, and this is the first serious accident I ever had. I do not know how it happened."

REDFIELD ORDERS INQUIRY.

Eastland's Owners Only Lake Shippers to Complain of New Law.

Special to The New York Times.

SYRACUSE, N. Y., July 24.—Secretary William C. Redfield of the Department of Commerce has taken steps to insure a searching inquiry regarding the Eastland disaster. Immediately on receipt of news of the accident he wired Deputy Supervising Inspector General Hoover of the Steamboat Inspection Service to leave Washington at once for Chicago. Later he sent the following dispatch to be handed to Mr. Hoover on arrival in Chicago:

> Leave nothing undone to determine cause of sad disaster to steamer Eastland, and to fix responsibility for same. Inquire strictly and fearlessly whether any official neglect or incompetence. None is now assumed, but none can be pardoned. You will be given on call any needed assistance from Washington. Go to the bottom of the matter.
>
> (Signed) REDFIELD, Secretary.

Hoover was designated to take general charge of the investigation because the Supervising Inspector General is at the San Francisco Exposition.

Deputy Secretary Sweet of the Commerce Department will arrive in Syracuse tomorrow morning to confer regarding the disaster with Secretary Redfield, who is the guest of his daughter, Mrs. Charles K. Drury. He also will bring here official files containing data regarding the Eastland and correspondence pertinent to the subject.

An interesting incident in connection with the Eastland, Secretary Redfield said, was that it was owned by the only shipping company on the Great Lakes, which had made many objections to the Seaman's act, effective next November. Some time ago an official of the company wrote to the department that the Seaman's act would require it to cut down the number of passengers carried. This was true, Mr. Redfield said, unless additional life-saving equipment was installed. The Eastland was licensed to carry 2,500 passengers and a crew of 70. The law now requires a life preserver for each person on the boat and floats and rafts for 30 per cent. The new act will require life boats for 50 per cent.

In another letter received ten days ago the same official wrote Secretary Redfield that the company could not install any more life-saving equipment on account of lack of room. Under the Seamen's act, when it becomes effective, with the safety equipment as heretofore, Mr. Redfield said the Eastland could only carry 1,552 passengers. He wrote the official immediately saying that, as the Eastland, which is a Summer excursion boat running across Lake Michigan, was frequently over twenty miles from land and distant from other vessels, he thought the requirement of the Seamen's act was in the interest of public safety.

1,800 DROWN AS STEAMER CAPSIZES

Continued on Page 2.

came forth stiff and cold, the lung motors were gradually retired from use. The physicians contented themselves with administering injections of strychnine. In the rare cases in which the powerful stimulant seemed to awaken a spark of life the respirators were called into service again.

Coroner's Physician Joseph Springer examined most of the bodies as they were brought ashore. By pinching the throat of each victim with his fingers the physician determined how he had met death—whether by drowning or suffocation. Dr. Springer said the majority had been suffocated.

As evening approached the stream of bodies through the two great holes cut in the vessel's side continued at the rate of one every three minutes. Coroner Hoffman swore in an inquest jury in the Reid-Murdock warehouse, where 600 bodies lay.

Although the Eastland was known over the lakes for its lack of stability, neither officers nor crew told the passengers of their danger until it was too late. On that the stories of the survivors, however incoherent, agree.

Question of Responsibility.

There are two big questions which the various investigating bodies will seek to have answered:

1. Was it because of a defect in its water ballast system that the Eastland capsized?

2. Were more passengers permitted aboard than its official carrying capacity of 2,500?

Already there have been several answers to these questions. R. H. McCrary, Navigation Inspector, says he turned away all prospective passengers after his automatic counter registered 2,500.

Contradicting McCrary's assertion is the estimate of two officials in charge of the outing that 3,700 persons, of whom the women outnumbered the men four to one, had crowded on board the Eastland.

Among the first to appear before State's Attorney Hoyne was W. K. Greenbaum, General Manager of the Indiana Transportation Company, which had chartered the Eastland for the day from the St Joseph-Chicago Steamship Company. He said that as soon as the listing began he started the work of rescue.

"About 7:20," he testified, "I was standing at the docks watching the Theodore Roosevelt loading, when shouts warned us that something was wrong on the Eastland. Rushing up to the street level, I saw she was listing to port. Returning to the Roosevelt, I ordered the Captain to blow the emergency whistle, lower the lifeboats, and send the crew among the passengers, begging them to throw life preservers and life rafts overboard to drift down the river into the next block, where the Eastland was turning over.

"This assistance from the Roosevelt saved many people. One boat returned with thirty-five. I did not see the Eastland go over because I was occupied with rescue work on the Roosevelt. I am informed that Government Inspectors were present, and that when the Eastland had been loaded to capacity, further admission was denied."

Cause of the Listing.

Two general theories for the listing are advanced, in addition to the alleged overcrowding.

The first is that the water ballast was let out of the hull to enable the boat to navigate the river in the turning basin above the La Salle Street tunnel. This made it top-heavy, and when the listing began there was no counter-weight to prevent its capsizing.

The other theory is that the lines were not cast off before the tug began pulling the vessel toward the river, which destroyed the equilibrium.

This second theory is advanced by William Flannigan, a lineman on the boat, who says the tug was pulling at the Eastland, although its lines had not been cast off. This is denied by Arthur McDonald, engineer of the tug, who says that when the Eastland turned over the towline had not been attached.

The police officer on duty at the dock says when the listing began the strain on the moorings was so great that the post over which the bowline was thrown began to break. He at once sent in an emergency call. Some of the witnesses say the listing was first noticed fifteen minutes before the capsize and before the gangplank was taken in.

The theory of insufficient ballast is founded on reports from members of the crew, who say that to get up the river part of the ballast was removed, to avoid danger of scraping the roof of the La Salle Street tunnel.

The boat has always been deemed unsafe by lake Captains. The shape of the hull is such that marine experts regarded the boat with suspicion. It careened once before in Cleveland Harbor, and when in the South Haven excursion trade it often listed as it left the river at South Haven, with crowds flocking to the rail on one side. After she was built the top deck was taken off, because of her tendency to list under any overbalancing weight.

The Eastland's gauge tender came forward late in the afternoon with the St. Joseph-Chicago Steamship Company's version of the capsizing.

A sudden rush of passengers of the port side of the excursion boat to view a passing launch carried the Eastland over, he said. But in their stories the survivors say there was no such rush, that the crowd, great though it was, seemed evenly distributed over the vessel.

No Lack of Heroism.

Instances of heroism were almost as numerous as the number of persons on the scene. Boats as soon as full took rescued passengers to the wharf or to the steamer Theodore Roosevelt, which was tied up opposite the Eastland. One man was seen to cling to a pile in the side of the wharf while two women and three children walked upon his body as on a ladder to safety. He fell exhausted into the river as the last one of the five reached the pier.

In an hour the water was cleared of excursionists. Those who had not been taken to land had sunk or were swirling down the river toward the drainage canal locks at Lockport, Ill., many miles away. The locks were raised to stop the current and arrangement were made to take bodies from the river along its course through the southwest part of Chicago.

Shortly after the water was cleared, city firemen, ship engineers and helpers were on the exposed side of the Eastland's hull cutting through its steel plates with gas flames, divers were hurried into under-water suits and a tug was moored as a bridge between the pier and the capsized ship.

As the divers gained entrance to the hull the scene of distress moved for the time being from the river to the extemporized morgues. Warehouses of wholesale companies along the river were thrown open and bodies were placed in rows on the floors. Scores of persons rescued from the water were injured, and these were taken to the Iroquois Hospital.

"All the News That's Fit to Print."

The New York Times.

THE WEATHER
Fair, fresh northeast winds today; tomorrow fair, continued cold.
For full weather report see Page 21.

VOL. LXVII...NO. 21,867. ... NEW YORK, FRIDAY, DECEMBER 7, 1917.—TWENTY-TWO PAGES. ONE CENT In Greater New York. | TWO CENTS Within Commuting Distance. | THREE CENTS Elsewhere.

MUNITION SHIP BLOWS UP IN HALIFAX HARBOR, MAY BE 2,000 DEAD; COLLISION WITH BELGIAN RELIEF VESSEL CAUSES THE DISASTER; TWO SQUARE MILES OF CITY WRECKED; MANY BURIED IN RUINS

WAR ON AUSTRIA; NOT ON TURKEY OR BULGARIA

Hope of Separate Peace Dissipates Congress Sentiment for a Sweeping Declaration.

TIP BY STATE DEPARTMENT

Given to Senate Committee and Alluded To in Debate in the House.

BOTH BODIES ACT TODAY

Will Pass Resolution Against Austria with Little Debate—House Committee Report.

Special to The New York Times.

WASHINGTON, Dec. 6.—Congress tomorrow, it is expected, will formally declare that a state of war exists between Austria-Hungary and the United States. Steps preliminary to such action were taken by both branches of Congress today. A favorable report on the war resolution was made so that it be considered and disposed of tomorrow. Acceptance by the Senate tomorrow of a similar resolution, is reported today by the Foreign Relations Committee, is expected.

Unless unexpected opposition develops, Congress will observe the President's wishes and confine the declaration of war to Austria-Hungary. Conclusion of the new war legislation is expected by Saturday.

Sentiment in the Senate committee in favor of declaring war against Turkey and Bulgaria, as well as Austria-Hungary, was dissipated by the receipt of information from the State Department that strong hopes were entertained of a separate peace with Turkey and Bulgaria. Other reasons against expanding the war declaration were also given by the State Department, but these were not made public.

The scene in the House today when Representative Flood, Chairman of the Foreign Affairs Committee, reported the war resolution indicating Austria-Hungary for fomenting labor troubles in the country and for other offenses, was one of enthusiasm. That there was an inclination to include Bulgaria and Turkey in the war resolution was emphasized in a stirring plea made by Representative Charles Miller of Minnesota. This sentiment was cooled considerably, however, when Representative Flood said in reply that there was excellent reason for excluding these nations at the time, at the same time intimating that if conditions developed contrary to the expectations of the President war would be declared promptly against the remaining allies of Germany.

Refuse to Cut Debate Short.

After listening to the indictment of Austria-Hungary by Representative Flood, the House unanimously consented to take up the resolution tomorrow and act upon it before night. Mr. Flood failed to obtain an agreement to limit the debate to one hour on each side, and it is expected that a longer time will be given to consideration of the resolution.

Another reason advanced for waiting was that there were American citizens in Turkish territory who must be got out before war was declared. When Mr. Flood said the President would ask for a declaration of war against Turkey and Bulgaria when he deemed it expedient there was a demonstration of cordial approval, and the opposition to the resolution apparently disappeared.

Report on House Committee.

The report presented to the House enumerated the reasons why war should be declared against Austria-Hungary and reviewed the conduct of Ambassador Dumba in meddling with domestic affairs. The report follows:

"The Committee on Foreign Affairs, to which was referred the joint resolution (H. J. Res. 169) declaring that a state of war exists between the Imperial and Royal Austro-Hungarian Government and the Government and the people of the United States and making provision to prosecute the same, having had the same under consideration, reports in

Continued on Page 2.

Denies Franco-British Deal To Act Against Vatican

LONDON, Dec. 6.—In the House of Commons today Lord Robert Cecil, Minister of Blockade, denied that England and France had entered into any treaty or understanding to support Italy against the Holy See if it should first attempted to take steps towards peace.

Asked why he reasoned reply to the Pope's note was made by England, France, or Italy, he said:

"The British, French, and Italian Governments considered no reply necessary beyond that returned by President Wilson."

TEUTONS CAPTURE 11,000 ITALIANS AND SIXTY GUNS

Advance Their Lines in New Great Drive on Mountain Barrier.

ALPINE TROOPS CUT OFF

Rome Admits Retirement to New Positions on the Asiago Plateau.

DESPERATE ALL-DAY BATTLE

Foe's Attempt to Break Through Front in Upper Brenta Valley a Costly Failure.

BERLIN, Dec. 6. (via London.)—Eleven thousand Italians have been captured by the Austro-Germans in their new offensive on the mountainous front of Northern Italy, it is officially announced today by the German War Office.

Strong Italian positions in the Meletta region of the northern front were taken and held by the Teutonic forces, who also captured more than sixty guns, the statement says.

ROME, Dec. 6.—After fighting all day, the Italians withdrew from the slopes south of Monte Castelgomberto to the Frenzela Spur, on the northern front, the War Office announces, adding that on Monte Fior and Monte Castelgomberto some Alpini detached their defense to the bitter end to retirement. The text of the statement reads:

"British Headquarters beginning at dawn yesterday the battle was renewed with violence. The enemy, profiting by the advantages gained the previous day between Monte Tondarcar and Monte Badanecche, brought the action up to its fullest extent in order to carry from the rear the formidable bastion of Monte Castelgomberto-Meletta di Gallio, which effort he had to give up and attack frontally. The fighting continued fiercely the whole day from the slopes south of Monte Castelgomberto to the Foza Spur. The ponderous effort of the enemy, carried out with crushing numerical preponderance, met with stubborn resistance and numerous counterattacks by our troops which were defending the Meletta strong point, ground being yielded foot by foot. Only when the rear line defense was being garrisoned by our men was the order given to withdraw to that line.

On Monte Fior and Monte Castelgomberto some Alpini troops which had remained isolated to retire the eventuality of an uncertain retirement a glorious sacrifice and an heroic defense to the bitter end.

A powerful enemy attempt to carry our line of defense in the Upper Brenta Valley was repulsed with heavy losses.

Masses Fight Hand to Hand.

ITALIAN ARMY HEADQUARTERS IN NORTHERN ITALY, Wednesday, Dec. 5.—(Associated Press.)—The furious enemy attack on the Asiago Plateau has been repulsed with heavy losses, except at the northeastern sector, around Monte Tendarcar, where after a desperate struggle which lasted until this morning the enemy succeeded in occupying some of the advanced Italian lines, which were retired to more secure positions.

The fighting has been extremely heavy, with masses of infantry engaged in hand-to-hand combat. The first attack on the Italian left was not repulsed by the 2d Corps, with large enemy casualties. Many prisoners were taken. The main attack on the Italian right was contested thirty-six hours by our corps, which inflicted heavy losses before yielding ground.

The attacks reached the maximum of intensity toward 4 o'clock yesterday afternoon. They came from two directions, the first on the left of the Italian line around Meletta Heights, and from on the right, around Monte Tondarcar. The first assault on the left was met by strong artillery fire, which mowed down the advancing infantry with heavy losses and the capture of a number of groups of prisoners. Toward 5 o'clock the infantry rushes were definitely repulsed, and the enemy's action on the left became a sullen bombardment with heavy and middle calibre guns.

At the same time the main action shifted to the Italian right, with an intense shelling, which lasted for five hours. This was followed by the loosing of gas and by infantry attacks in force near Monte Tondarcar. Here the fighting was sanguinary—both in attack and counterattack.

The Italian First Army, which is meeting the brunt of the attack, is giving splendid evidence of its offensive and defensive qualities. The spirit of the men is high, and the German commanding the First Army has gone ahead with

Continued on Page 2.

Emperor Again Expresses Longing for Peace; Czernin Outlines Austria-Hungary's Terms

AMSTERDAM, Dec. 6.—At the reception of the Austrian delegations, says a Vienna dispatch, the Emperor remarked to the Presidents of the Parliaments:

"It will be the finest day of my life when I can conclude peace."

Another dispatch from Vienna says that in the course of a long review of the war situation to the Foreign Affairs Committee of the Hungarian delegation Tuesday, Count Czernin, the Austro-Hungarian Foreign Minister, said:

"We can await the dawn of peace in a confident spirit. The only Government which took up our idea was the Provisional Government of Russia. Our aim is to conclude a peace by which the freedom, independence, and territorial integrity of Austria-Hungary shall be maintained inviolate.

"We are striving for no territorial extension by force, and no economic oppression. We only demand effective guarantees for free and unhampered future development. Agreements on a gradual simultaneous and mutual reduction of armaments and the freedom of the seas, with a simultaneous introduction of obligatory arbitration provided with corresponding guarantees, might offer us such guarantees that we thus would be prepared to conclude a peace with our enemies, a general, just, and honorable peace safeguarding the territorial integrity of the monarchy and its future for free development to political and economic domain.

"I must declare, however, that it is impossible for me to bind myself for all future time as regards our unselfish war aims, as against the openly admitted annexation desires of those enemies who would insist on a continuation of the war.

"I cherish the hope that we may attain peace by way of an understanding. Otherwise, I am convinced we shall obtain it by force."

BRITISH GIVE UP BOURLON SALIENT

Byng Withdraws at Night to Stronger Front—Retains Part of Hindenburg Line.

GERMANS OCCUPY VILLAGES

Berlin Announces a 2½-Mile Gain, 9,000 Prisoners and 148 Guns Taken Recently.

BRITISH HEADQUARTERS IN FRANCE, Dec. 6.—The British have withdrawn from the salient about Bourlon Wood to a prepared line which should make their position much stronger and more desirable in many ways. The retirement was carried out successfully mainly between the hours of midnight and 4 o'clock Wednesday morning and under cover of darkness. Not until many hours later did the enemy discover he was facing evacuated territory.

The Germans today had swarmed over much of the vacated zone and were digging themselves in about the advanced line, but as late as 1:30 o'clock yesterday afternoon they were still shelling Bourlon Wood, and between noon and 1 o'clock they launched a heavy attack against the empty trenches near Moeuvres, showing that they were uncertain of the situation even then.

The successful manner of the withdrawal places it in the category of a remarkable military achievement, for had the Germans become aware that it was impending grave losses might have resulted to the retiring troops. The question of abandoning the salient must have been under careful consideration some time over.

Wednesday's retirement cannot be designated as a retreat for there is no reason to believe that the British could not have maintained themselves here. However, the position was not desirable and it would have cost the lives of too many men to have held on to the sharp salient, which could be swept by enemy gunfire from several directions.

The ground, as abandoned, was cleared thoroughly, and not a gun or any other material appeared to have been left behind. Moreover, the vacated positions were rendered temporarily untenable, so that the enemy would be forced to construct new defenses and dugouts. The British prepared the new line while they still held Bourlon Wood.

How the Troops Retired.

About midnight Tuesday the British silently began to pull back from the northern edge of Bourlon Wood. The British rifles and machine guns continued to spit fire along the line and the artillery maintained its customary hammering of German positions.

By 3 o'clock in the morning the main British body had passed into the new positions, and Bourlon Wood was virtually stripped of soldiers, with the exception of a few rearguards. A little later even the rearguards had followed and the great forest was left silent, save for the bursting of shells.

Germans Charged Vacated Post.

The British troops from their distant positions watched the maneuvres of the German with delight. These culminated in a fine charge in mass formation against the former British line. As the Germans reached the trenches they paused in evident surprise, and a halt was called for a consideration of the situation.

About 2 o'clock in the afternoon the Germans were seen coming over the ridge on both sides of Bourlon Wood in large numbers and proceeding toward the Bapaume-Cambrai Road. A considerable force of them was caught in the artillery fire to the west of the wood and suffered heavy casualties.

Throughout Wednesday forenoon the

Continued on Page 2.

ANTI-PEACE MOVE IN RUSSIA GAINS

Ukraine Opposed to Truce—Caucasus Army Asks Britain for Financial Aid.

KERENSKY HEARD FROM

Is Candidate for Assembly—Bolsheviki and Germans Make 10-Day Armistice.

LONDON, Dec. 6.—While the Bolsheviki are officially to the Berlin War Office, powerful and growing opposition to the peace overtures is shaping itself in Russia, as appears from advices from various sources.

The Ukrainian Official Bureau, according to a dispatch by way of Geneva, has made the following announcement:

"Neither the Ukrainian Parliament nor the Government has opened negotiations for a separate peace with the Central Powers, despite German affirmations to the contrary."

A dispatch to the Central News from Copenhagen says:

"The Russian Legation in the Danish capital has published a telegram received from the Russian Legation in Teheran, Persia, saying the Administration and the army command in the Caucasus are opposed to the Bolsheviki and that a special delegation has arrived in Teheran to negotiate with the Russian and British Legations concerning the continuation of the war. The dispatch adds that the Caucasians will not stop fighting against the Turks, but that they will need financial support."

Kerensky Denounces Bolsheviki.

Petrograd advices announce that the Social Revolutionary newspaper Dielo aroda (the People's Work) publishes a letter from Kerensky, the former Premier, in which the following passages occur:

"Do you not see that happiness is being made use of and that you are being deceived? You were promised peace with the Germans within three days. Where is it? Where is the liberty which was promised you?

"It is dishonorable, infamous! Fools! It is I, Kerensky, who tell you this. For eight months I safeguarded the liberty of the people and the future happiness of the masses of workers. Now they realize that when I was in power they had—and democracy really existed."

The Helsingfors Huvudstadsbladet reports that Kerensky is in a place of complete safety. The newspaper says he is engaged in preparations for the Constituent Assembly, and already has been placed on the list of candidates at many places throughout the empire.

It is stated that M. Prokopovitch, former Minister of Supplies, after signing the recent proclamation in the name of the Kerensky Government, insisting on the calling of the Constituent Assembly, escaped arrest and joined General Kaledines, Hetman of the Don Cossacks, in the south. There also arrived in Kaledines's headquarters four other former Ministers of the Provisional Government. Under former procedure the five Ministers constitute a quorum. It is reported that General Kaledines has come to an agreement with the Ukraine Government not to invade Ukraine territory.

The last message sent to the troops by General Dukhonin, the Commander in Chief of the Russian forces, before the Bolsheviki forces captured his headquarters at Mohilev and Bolsheviki troops killed him, solemnly warned them against breaking a treaty with the Entente Allies and alienating the defenders of the Russian democratic regime. The message declared that the Russian would become slaves if they signed a separate peace, while cunning and lies prevented the exercise of justice and freedom of conscience. Germany, he added, would never tolerate the free and democratic Russian people by her side.

The foreign military advisers have left Army Headquarters for Kiev.

The newspaper Svobodnaya Ryetch of Petrograd, according to a Petrograd dispatch, reports that the Entente diplomatic representatives in Russia have

Continued on Page 2.

WILSON TAKES UP RAILROAD CRISIS

Cabinet Likely to Decide Today on Sixty-Day Test of Unit Operation or Control.

ASK BILLION DOLLAR LOAN

Newlands Confers with Executives and Declares Financial Aid Is Imperative.

Special to The New York Times.

WASHINGTON, Dec. 6.—The whole railroad situation, with particular reference to Government control for war purposes, will be discussed at the regular meeting of the Cabinet tomorrow, when it is expected consideration will be given to a suggestion advanced today within the Cabinet circle that the Eastern railroads be permitted to continue their present operations as a unit for sixty days under the direction of the Railroads' War Board. At the end of the two months' period it would be more apparent whether railroad or Government operation was desirable.

This seems to be the immediate step the Government will take in the greatest of the domestic war problems. The situation, recognized as very serious, was brought to a focus by a report submitted to Congress yesterday by the Interstate Commerce Commission, suggesting the suspension of restrictive laws on railroad pooling; or as an alternative to have the President operate them as a military necessity.

The solution, which has been the subject of Government and railroad thought for many months, has not yet been found and those involved are greatly troubled in their efforts to outline a plan that will make for the success of the nation in the war and at the same time avoid injustice to those whose material interests are concerned and industry generally.

President Wilson held a long conference with Chairman Hall of the Interstate Commerce Commission, discussing with him the recommendations of the commission and the present financial needs of the carriers. The President learned the exact situation and was informed of the relief that would be afforded to the railroads should the commission award them a 15 per cent. increase in freight rates. It is supposed that the brotherhoods for increased wages was also brought before the President an another difficulty the roads now face.

Roads Need a Billion Dollars.

This was a day of conferences. Senator Newlands, Chairman of the Joint Congressional Committee on Railroads, saw the Railroads' War Board, and went over the situation with the members with the purpose of offering legislative aid if possible. After the conference he announced that the Government must loan or guarantee loans of $1,000,000,000 to the railroads almost immediately. This loan is necessary in addition to the relief expected from the 15 per cent. increase on freight rates.

The billion dollars is needed, Senator Newlands explained, to place the railroads in a condition to meet the abnormal demands being made upon transportation by reason of the war. It must be used in the purchase of additional equipment, in the creation of additional terminal facilities, and in the construction of new trackage, particularly on the Eastern trunk lines leading to the seaboard, he said. Congress must decide whether to appropriate the money for a plan to the railroads or whether to enact legislation pledging the Government as security for any money which the railroads may be able to borrow in the market up to a billion dollars.

The railroad executives left the conference with an understanding that they would submit to Senator Newlands a detailed estimate of their additional financial needs either on Saturday or Monday. Senator Newlands intends to lay this estimate before President Wilson on Monday afternoon, when he has an appointment at the White House.

Those who attended the conference were Samuel Rea, President of the Pennsylvania Railroad; Fairfax Harrison, President of the Southern Railroad; Julius Kruttschnitt of the Southern Pacific Railroad, and Hale Holden of the—

Continued on Page 3.

Halifax Thought of German Shelling as Shock Came.

CITY CUT OFF FOR HOURS

Count of Dead Is Slow Amid Burning Ruins of Wrecked District.

EXPLOSION HEARD 61 MILES

Came 17 Minutes After the Collision, When Flames Reached Munitions Cargo.

MANY VICTIMS ON SHIPS

Harbor Crowded with Boats on War Duty—American Bluejackets Aid in Rescue Work.

Special to The New York Times.

HALIFAX, N. S., Dec. 6.—One thousand tons of munitions on board the French Line steamship Mont Blanc exploded in the harbor at 9 o'clock this morning as the result of a collision with the Belgian Relief steamship Imo, killed 800 to 2,000 persons, injured 3,000 or more others, many of them probably fatally, and laid waste a wide area of this city, causing millions of dollars damage.

Practically all the northerly part of Halifax, known as Richmond, was shattered by the terrific concussion or wiped out by the fires that started at once. The more modern part, between North Street and Pleasant Point, was shaken as by an earthquake, but the more solid buildings resisted serious damage to a large extent.

The monstrous energy suddenly released by the blast swept irresistibly over the country about Halifax, did vast damage in Dartmouth, across the bay; broke windows sixty-one miles off, and by the force of its concussion killed a telegrapher at his desk four miles from the bay.

The munition ship, bound in from New York, had almost passed through the narrows leading down the outer harbor into Bedford Basin to the northwest, when the collision occurred. The Imo, westward bound, was just putting to sea.

The weather was clear and the two ships had room in which to pass. Because of a misunderstanding of signals, however, they headed for each other. Their efforts to avoid each other were unsuccessful and the Mont Blanc was pierced on the port side. A few minutes later flames burst from the wreckage.

People Vainly to Check Blazes.

The pilot of the Belgian relief ship, who is a survivor, says the Mont Blanc carried benzine tanks forward and that soon after the collision the burning oil spread fiercely over the port of the ship.

Witnesses of the disaster who escaped reported that the crew of the Mont Blanc began to leave desperately to check the flames, knowing that their own lives, at least, were at stake. Men on the waterfront and on ships in the harbor within sight of the Mont Blanc saw the crew driven back step by step by the flames until finally they abandoned hope and fled for the boats. They rowed as hard as they could toward the shore, while the Mont Blanc drifted.

Seventeen minutes after the collision the munitions ship blew up. The harbor at this point is less than half a mile wide. On the south shore is the Richmond section of Halifax. On the north shore is the town of Dartmouth. On each side the land slopes rather sharply upward from the waterfront, so as to form a trough, confining the explosion in some degree and increasing its destructiveness.

The main waterfront works, piers for loading ships, and warehouses of supplies and munitions, are located between the ocean and a point some distance to the southward of the scene of the explosion, so that they escaped the full effect of the blast. They were damaged badly, but reports late last night indicated that the explosion had not crippled the principal waterfront developments used by the Government in loading transports and munitions ships. The finest buildings and best residences of the town are on slopes of the hills lying back of the principal waterfront works, and thus at a distance from the explosion. This section, which includes the public buildings and the finest residences near the Citadel which looks over the city, escaped the withering blast of flames. The shock, however, rocked it tremendously and shattered windows everywhere.

Richmond a Whole Waste Section.

The great loss of life was in the Richmond district. This is built up for the most part of small wooden dwellings

Confusion of Signals Caused Collision; Benzine Started Fire That Reached Munitions

HALIFAX, Dec. 6.—Pilot Frank Mackie of the munitions steamer Mont Blanc declared tonight that the collision today resulted from a confusion of whistles sounded by the Imo. He believes the fire which caused the explosion was due to the fact that the munitions ship carried a deck load of benzine.

An official of the Norton & Lilly Company said last night that the relief ship which collided with the Mont Blanc was the Norwegian freighter Imo of Christiania, which left New York about eight days ago with a cargo of 8,000 tons of grain for Rotterdam, and was scheduled to call at Halifax for examination. She was built in Belfast at Harland & Wolff in 1881 as the White Star liner Runic, and was sold a few years ago to the South Pacific Whaling Company of Christiania.

The Imo carried a crew of sixty men and was commanded, according to the shipping records, by Captain From. She was a four-masted iron vessel of 5,043 gross tonnage, 430 feet long, 45 feet 2 inches beam, and 30 feet 3 inches depth of hold.

The Mont Blanc was a French Line boat under charter to the British Admiralty and left here with 1,000 tons of munitions.

Point of Collision and Devastated Area.

The star in the Narrows in the above map shows where the two ships came together and the Mont Blanc blew up. The shaded part of the city was devastated.

railway station as far north as Africville to Bedford Basin, the district also known as Richmond. From the water the devastated district extended back to a point running parallel with Gottingen Street. Nothing has been left standing in this section of the buildings which were not damaged and crushed in a twinkling when the buildings sprung down on them like traps. The terrific heat of the blast from consuming gases of the munitions swept an area strewn with thousands of tons of kindling wood.

When those who had escaped crushing in the wreckage could recover themselves they found fire racing through splintered woodwork in several spots in the Richmond section. Nothing could save great tracts from being burned over, and tonight it appeared that nearly half of the area of the city was in ruins.

The dead will probably never be more than approximately known because of the many families of whom no trace except burned bones is left.

TWO SQUARE MILES IN RUINS.

City Laid Waste by Shock, and Then by Flames.

HALIFAX, Dec. 6.—Eight hundred to 2,000 persons were killed and two square miles of this city were laid in ruins today, following the blowing up of the French munitions ship Mont Blanc in the harbor after a collision with the Belgian relief steamship Imo at 9 o'clock this morning.

Late tonight five cartloads of dead were brought to the Morgue, and the Chief of Police estimated that the dead would reach 2,000. Other officials thought the total would exceed that number.

Thousands of persons were injured in the square of business buildings, due to the shock of the explosion, or in the fires that started almost immediately in the devastated area and were not brought under control until after nine hours' hard fighting. Many of these injured are likely to die.

Tonight, as the dazed city is recovering from the terrible disaster, dead bodies lie in scores in the streets and in overthrown buildings or buried beneath the débris of fallen walls. Rescue parties are busily at work.

The hospitals are filled to overflowing with victims, and many private houses are crowded. Temporary hospitals and morgues have been opened in schoolhouses in the western section of the city. Systematic efforts are being made tonight to identify the dead, but great difficulty is encountered, as so many who were killed suffered injuries that made recognition impossible.

Soldiers and Sailors Patrol City.

All business has been suspended, while armed guards of soldiers and sailors are patrolling the city and are searching among the ruins for, the dead and injured. The Canadians are being assisted in this work by bluejackets from an American warship in the harbor. Not a street car is moving, and most of Halifax is in darkness tonight.

Virtually all the north end of the city is laid waste, and the property loss will run far into the millions. Part of the town of Dartmouth, across the harbor from Halifax, also is in ruins. Nearly all the buildings in the dockyard are wrecked.

The scene of destruction in the harbor is indescribable.

Houses Blown to Atoms.

In the west and northwest sections the damage was more extensive, and there the walls of many houses were blown to atoms.

It was in Richmond, opposite scene of the explosion, however, that the havoc was greatest. Here whole blocks of dwellings, most of frame construction, were leveled. Here one street was laid in ruins, and structures which were left standing by the explosion were destroyed by fire which broke out simultaneously in a score of places, and which it was impossible to check until they had burned themselves out.

Many of the fires were caused by overturned stoves, and these generally in wooden frame houses that lent themselves readily to the flames.

It is believed that scores of persons who lost their lives were burned to death or asphyxiated. Many injured in homes of their homes perished in the flames from which they were helpless to escape. The fire in the district were extinguished tonight.

rink, military gymnasium, sugar refinery, and elevator.

Among other structures wrecked was St. Joseph's Church, and the school building adjoining. An immense cotton factory in the Richmond district also was demolished.

The concussion shattered the big gas tanks of the city. All power plants are out of commission and newspaper offices have been so badly wrecked that publication is impossible.

Only a pile of smoldering ruins marks the spot where the great building of the American Sugar Refining Company stood.

The drydock and the buildings which surrounded it were all destroyed. A Richmond school, which housed hundreds of children, was demolished, and it is reported that only three children escaped.

It was reported tonight that all the guests in the hotels of the city were safe. Some of them were cut by flying glass, but none was seriously injured.

Two members of the crew of the Canadian cruiser Niobe, which lay at her dock, were killed by the explosion and several were injured.

Feared Fleet or Air Raid.

Five minutes after the explosion the streets in all parts of Halifax were filled with frenzied, panic-stricken throngs striving to reach the outskirts in an effort to escape what they believed was a raid by a German fleet. Hundreds of the fugitives had been cut by the showers of glass from windows shattered by the concussion.

The fear of an air raid possessed the minds of many when the explosion on the Mont Blanc shook the town. There were three distinct shocks. First came a comparatively light rumble like a seismic disturbance. A moment later a terrific blast made even the citadel quake. Then a crash of glass throughout a wide area completed the confusion.

Thousands, rushing into the open, saw a thick cloud of gray smoke hanging over the north end of the city. This strengthened their conviction of an attack from the air.

It was feared that other explosions would follow, and as far as possible the frightened ones were herded in the southern part of the city. Great crowds gathered in open lots and remained [illegible] for hours until they believed that all danger was passed.

In the Richmond section injured men and women crawled out of the wreckage of their homes and lay in the streets until they were removed in ambulances and automobiles to hospitals. Those less seriously hurt aided those more gravely injured.

In the streets, piled high with débris, were found the shattered bodies of many women and children. Several children were crushed to death when they were hurled against telegraph poles by the force of the explosion.

In scores of cases occupants of houses who had escaped without injury or were only slightly hurt were baffled by the flames in their search for members of their families and were forced to stand by impotent, while what once had been their homes became funeral pyres for their loved ones.

A Government employe, A. B. Macdonald, who made all speed to reach his home after the explosion, found that his wife and four children had perished. His two-year-old daughter had been killed while playing in the yard of her home.

Among those killed were the Chief of the Fire Department and his deputy, who were hurled to death when a fire engine exploded.

Scores of children in the public schools in the North End lost their lives. Many others suffered broken limbs and were rescued with difficulty from the ruined buildings. The teachers who escaped injury worked heroically to save the lives of the children under their charge.

Lebaron Coleman, manager of the Canadian Express Company, was killed when the roof of the company's building collapsed.

Quick Organization of Rescue.

In less than half an hour after the disaster 5,000 persons had gathered on the Common and thousands of others had sought refuge in fields outside the city. Hundreds were reported missing by their relatives, and it was not known whether they were alive or dead.

The work of rescue and relief was promptly organized. The Academy of Music and many other public buildings were thrown open to house the homeless. Five hundred tents were erected on the Common and will be occupied by the troops, who surrendered their barracks to the women and children.

Every nook and cranny in all available public and private buildings was made ready within an hour to receive the wounded. A steady stream of ambulances and automobiles arrived at hospitals, which soon were filled to capacity with the injured.

Doctors, nurses, and volunteers toiled ceaselessly in the work of succor. Their ranks were swelled by others who arrived in constantly increasing numbers from nearby towns.

Those who were only slightly injured were sent to their own homes or to those of friends after their wounds had been treated. There were hundreds of cases of serious injury, however, and it is expected the death list will be greatly increased by those who succumb to their wounds. Before nightfall twenty-five of the injured had died.

Automobiles are scurrying about all sections of the city tonight carrying blanket-clad burdens.

A committee of citizens already has been formed and assistance is asked from all outside points. The supplies most needed are glass, tar paper, beaver board, putty, bedding, and blankets. The Mayors of all towns in the province have been asked to rush supplies to Halifax.

Fear of food shortage is entertained by some, though encouragement is found in the word that train loads of provisions are already on the way here from several points. The immediate feeding of homeless ones amid the confusion remains, however, a serious problem. Everything possible is being done to systematize the distribution of food as well as of clothing and bedding.

There was much suffering among the homeless tonight. The temperature, while not low for this district, held below freezing.

All Wires Thrown Down.

The force of the explosion was felt at Truro, sixty-one miles away, where windows were shattered. All telegraph and telephone wires were torn down, and for several hours Halifax was completely isolated from the outside world.

This afternoon a telegraph line was worked for a short time into Halifax, establishing the first communication with the city since the brief period that followed the explosion.

A second outlet for news of the disaster was established after several hours of emergency labor late today. Following the restoration of one telegraph wire, the cable line to the New England coast was repaired.

Charles Prest, gasoline engineer on the steamer Wasper B, which had been in drydock, had a narrow escape from death.

"We had 80 gallons of gasoline in our tanks when a shell from the munitions ship struck us," he said. "We had just left the drydock to go to Bedford Basin to get some plates and were opposite the Lorne Club when we saw the [illegible] coming down from the basin and the Mont Blanc going up.

"I heard the Belgian steamer's whistle blowing, and then I saw that the munitions ship was on fire on the starboard side. We tried to turn back to warn the officials at the drydock, but before we reached there a shell struck us. I believe I was the only one of the [illegible] on board the Wasper B to escape. [illegible] was blown up. My son, who worked with the drydock, was killed."

[illegible] Mackenzie Bell, who spent two [illegible] on the [illegible] line in Flanders, [illegible] tonight [illegible] he never had seen anything on the battle front to equal the scenes of destruction that he witnessed in Halifax today.

View of Halifax Harbor, Where Explosion Occurred.

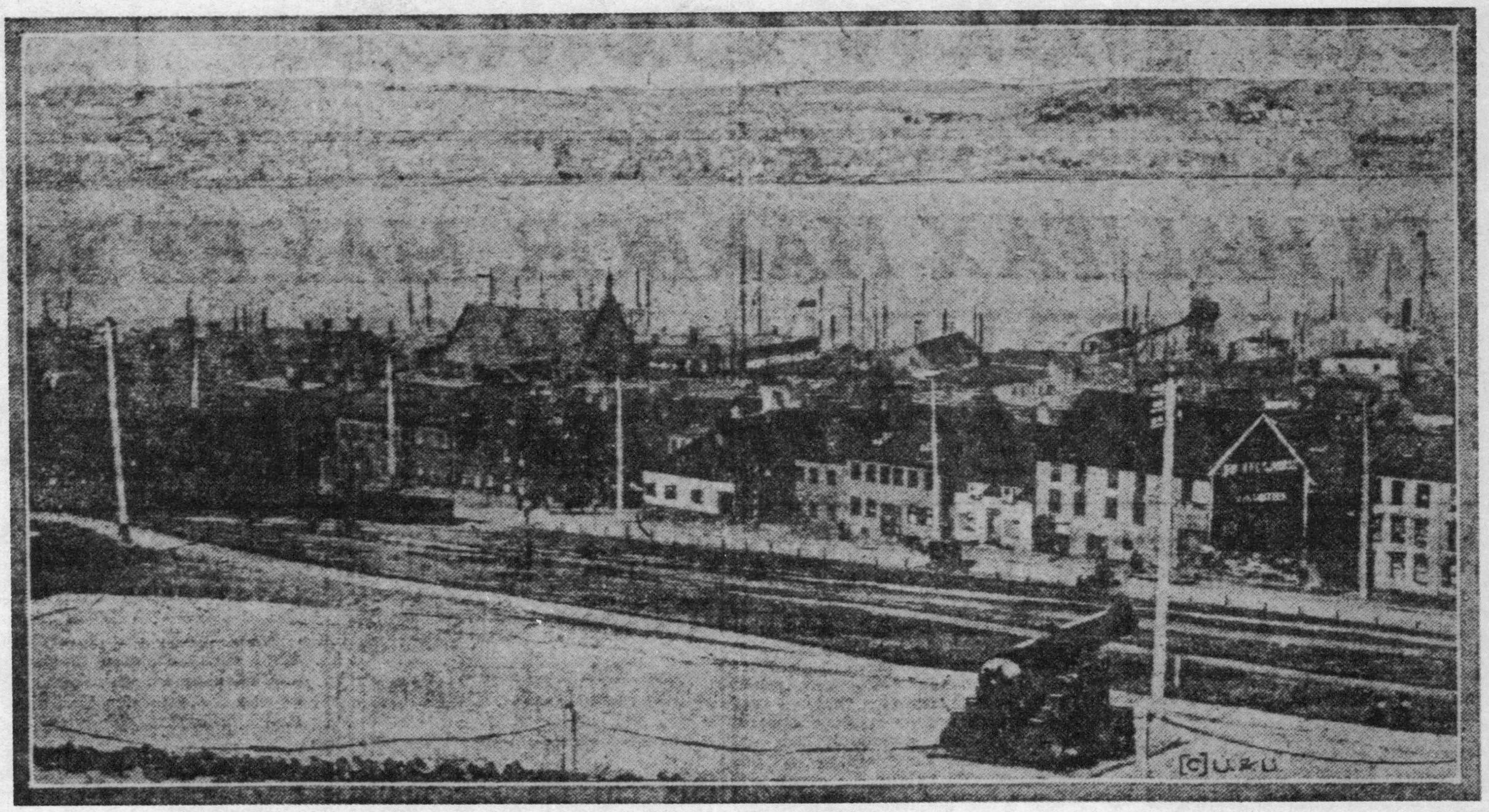

SHOCK CAUSED A TIDAL WAVE.

And Dock Workers by Hundreds Were Engulfed.

TRURO, N. S., Dec. 6.—Survivors reaching here from Halifax tonight reported that the explosion caused a great tidal wave in The Narrows, which resulted in the deaths of hundreds of workers in the busy dock district.

George Graham, manager of the Dominion Atlantic Railway, who was on the train, was one of the first to reach the devastated area. He reported that in walking from the waterfront to the Richmond district, he counted twenty-five dead railway men.

Another man from Halifax said that every building on both sides of Barrington Street, between the Queens Hotel and Richmond station was wrecked.

I. M. Soy, General Officer of the Maple Leaf Lumber Company, told a graphic story of his experiences.

He was sitting in the Queen's Hotel, on the southernmost edge of the ravaged district, when he was thrown out of his chair by a terrific explosion. He rushed into the street with hundreds of others.

The hotel guests, he said, were surprisingly cool.

"It is an air raid," was the general version. The possibilities of a raid by Zeppelins had been frequently talked about and all had prepared themselves for eventualities.

Going to the North Street station, he found that the immense glass roof had been carried away. Many were killed at that point. He thought the number might reach twenty-five, but said it was impossible to give an accurate estimate. In the portion of the district he was able to penetrate he thought the dead numbered at least 500.

Among the dead in the city are Edward Condon, Chief of the Fire Department; William Brunt, Deputy Fire Chief; Captain Peter S. Broderick of the Fire Department; the wife and son of the Rev. W. J. Sweatman of the Kaye Street Methodist Church, and Dr. Murdock Chisholm.

Within a few hours all the Halifax hospitals were overcrowded. The relief trains from this city, Sydney, Amherst, Monoton, and other cities are returning with such of the injured as can be moved.

HEARD 61 MILES AWAY.

Nova Scotia Cities Rush Help to Halifax.

AMHERST, N. S., Dec. 6.—The explosion at Halifax was so terrific that it destroyed the installation in telegraph and telephone offices for thirty miles around the city, while it was heard at Truro, sixty-one miles away.

Messages asking for fire engines and fire fighting apparatus, doctors and nurses, hospital supplies, &c., were received from Halifax by many localities in Nova Scotia. Special trains were made up, with everything required that could be obtained.

At Truro, Windsor, and Amherst the City Councils met in the morning and decided to take immediate steps to render aid to the afflicted people at Halifax.

It is understood that large quantities of food were destroyed and that the citizens of Halifax may soon be in danger of starving. It was decided to rush carloads of food to the city.

Special trains from Moncton and St. John passed through Amherst tonight, carrying doctors, nurses, and druggists to Truro, where injured from Halifax are being brought.

WAR MADE HALIFAX BUSY PORT OF CALL

Harbor Was Constantly Studded with Troop-Laden Transports and Munition Freighters.

GREAT RAILWAY TERMINUS

Millions Invested There Since 1914 in Piers, Warehouses, and Shipyards—Used as Base by Navy.

Halifax is built on the eastern slope of a peninsula in Halifax harbor. The harbor consists of a neck of water a mile wide and six miles long, which ends in Bedford Basin, a large sheet of water open all the year and affording a safe anchorage for vessels of any size.

Hills on either side of the narrow harbor form a trough calculated to increase greatly the violence of any large explosion in the waters of the harbor. Since the war Halifax has grown from a comparatively small port of provincial importance to one of the greatest gates of ocean traffic in North America, and its waters have been constantly studded with transports and freighters carrying munitions and supplies. Most of the Canadian troops now in Europe, supposed to number about 400,000, sailed from Halifax harbor.

In 1911 Halifax had a population of 47,000, according to the census of that year, but this is believed to have more than doubled, with the enormous growth of the military and naval importance of the city. It is the nearest North American port of consequence to Europe, and this, combined with the fact that it possessed a magnificent natural harbor and was the terminus of the great Canadian railroad systems, produced its great importance since the Summer of 1914. It is the eastern terminus of the Canadian Pacific Railroad, the Canadian Government railroads, and local lines.

Places in Devastated Area.

Steamship lines operate between the port and points in Newfoundland, Great Britain, the United States, and the West Indies. The greatest developments, which have taken place since 1914, have been the building of piers, warehouses, shipyards, and railway facilities to handle the vast streams of munitions and troops bound for Europe. These structures were naturally the most exposed to destruction from an explosion on the water.

The most important part of the waterfront lay in the area of damage from the explosion, dispatches indicate. In addition, there were many churches and schools, the main railway station, some of the Government dockyards, Wellington Barracks, the Admiralty House, (the official residence of the Admiral in command of the North American British Squadron,) the Military Hospital, Garrison Chapel, the Post Office, the Provincial Parliament Building, the City Hall, and Ordnance Department, most of the large stores, all of the telegraph and cable buildings, and a few hotels. One of the institutions in the area is the Deaf and Dumb Asylum and the Home for Aged Women. A large cotton mill and a sugar refinery were among the chief manufacturing plants.

Most of the devastated section was the old part of Halifax, in which are many buildings erected by the original settlers. The section is thickly populated. The lay of the streets and the character of the buildings were such as to increase the danger from a conflagration. Many of the buildings were frail wooden structures, crowded together, and the blocks were separated only by narrow streets. Hollis Street, the principal business thoroughfare, had many substantial buildings and many of the residence streets were lined with fine homes.

Within the area damaged, as indicated in dispatches, is Citadel Hill, the eminence which dominates the entire city. This is 255 feet above the sea. It was frequented by tourists because of the magnificent view which it commands of the town and harbor. This has been a military strong point since the French and Indian war and was heavily fortified in 1778. Near the head of the hill stands the Halifax County Academy, a large and handsome building in red brick. Near it are extensive barracks, which were occupied before the war by the Royal Engineers and Artillery.

RAILWAYS SUFFER HEAVILY.

Scattered Reports to Outside Points Tell of Damage.

TORONTO, Ontario, Dec. 6.—A message received by J. D. Reid, Canadian Minister of Railways, from Assistant Chief Engineer Duff of the Intercolonial Railway at Halifax, said that every building north of the Queen's Hotel was wrecked.

"The North Street Station is in ruins," the message said, "as well as our plant at Willow Park, and there is just one mass of wreckage and dead bodies in the north end of the city. Special trains from Sydney with doctors, nurses, and hospital supplies are on their way. I am also arranging for food supplies and to send coaches to Halifax to take people away."

AMHERST, N. S., Dec. 6.—The Canadian Government depot, used by the Canadian Pacific Railway, is described as having entirely collapsed.

Freight cars were blown off railway tracks along a stretch of nearly two miles. Storage sheds along the waterfront for a mile and a half were leveled.

Pieces of iron and shrapnel have been found three miles from the Halifax waterfront.

"All the News That's Fit to Print."

The New York Times.

THE WEATHER
Fair today and Friday; moderate temperature; moderate east and southeast winds.
For full weather report see Page 21.

VOL. LXX....No. 23,224. NEW YORK, THURSDAY, AUGUST 25, 1921. TWO CENTS In Greater New York | THREE CENTS Within 200 Miles | FOUR CENTS Elsewhere

16 AMERICANS, 27 BRITISH, DIE IN ZR-2 WRECK; ONLY 5 ARE SAVED; EXPLOSION RENDS AIRSHIP; SHE FALLS BLAZING INTO THE RIVER HUMBER

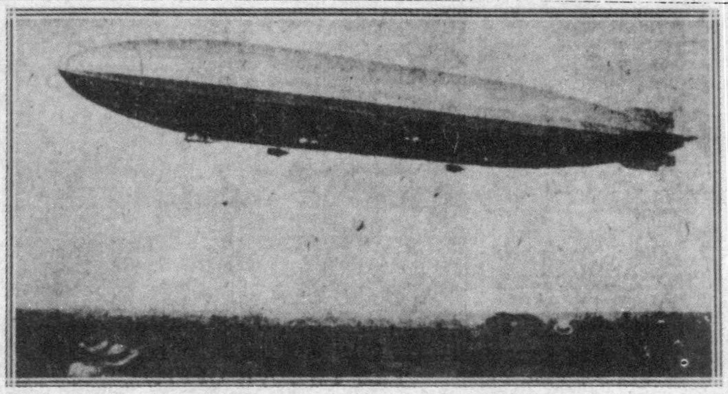

THE ILL-FATED ZR-2 IN FLIGHT.

DOCTORED RECORDS IN GRAFT CASE BARE MYSTERIOUS $3,500

Chemicals Restore Erased Entries in Books of Butcher Who Got Market Permit.

$500 FOR THE McMANUS

Permit Issued by O'Malley When Adolph Kahn Visited Him After Drawing $3,000.

SWANN TO AID COMMITTEE

Promises Prosecutions and Protection of Witnesses Whose Permits Are Revoked.

Adolf Kahn, a wholesale butcher in West Washington Market, admitted before the Meyer committee yesterday that he had cashed a check for $3,000 on the morning of April 11, 1921, had visited Edwin J. O'Malley, Commissioner of Public Markets, at the Municipal Building immediately thereafter, and had walked out of his office with a valuable permit for trading in West Washington Market.

Mr. Kahn on the same day made out a check for $500 in favor of Thomas J. (The) McManus, the Tammany politician and leader of the Fifth Assembly District. Mr. Kahn said, however, that he "thought better" of this and did not issue the check with the name of McManus on it. Instead, he made out a check for $500 payable to bearer and it was duly cashed by the bearer.

Just what the $3,000 cash and the $500 check were used for was the subject of a good deal of contradiction. Facts tending to explain the transaction were drawn from reluctant witnesses, from erased and rewritten checks and from pages of Mr. Kahn's books the writing on which had been obliterated with chemicals.

Drew Check to "Surprise" McManus.

Mr. Kahn issued a statement to the press explaining that he had originally drawn the check for McManus in order to "surprise" him. Then he changed his mind and gave Mr. McManus not a single cent. He said he cashed the check himself on the same day, April 11, and bet the money even that Jack Dempsey would defeat Georges Carpentier. He testified that the $3,000 in cash which he drew a few minutes before calling on Commissioner O'Malley had been turned over at the bank as a loan to his brother-in-law.

An erased entry in Mr. Kahn's books, later restored with chemicals by the Meyer committee, showed that he had originally credited the $3,500 to his investment in the West Washington Market property, which he acquired by permit from Commissioner O'Malley. The whole page recording his expenses in connection with this transaction had been washed with ink-bleaching chemicals. A new investment account had been written up on another page. This account did not contain any reference to the $3,000 in cash or the $500 bearer check. But on another page the $3,500 was succinctly recorded as "withdrawn from capital."

Nearly the whole day was consumed with an intensely interesting development of the mysterious Kahn-O'Malley-McManus transaction; of the manner in which Kahn originally heard that an applicant for a market permit should see McManus; of his quick migration from the bank to Commissioner O'Malley's office; of the number of telephone calls sent out by Kahn on the Saturday he received his subpoena to appear before a Meyer sub-committee; of his consultations and attempted consultations with legal and political advisers, relatives, friends, employes and an expert accountant; of his orders and countermanded orders to his employes; of a gathering on Sunday at his office where his books were kept, and of his appearance on Monday before the Meyer committee with books erased, chemically treated and revised.

To Trail That $3,000 Today.

Today's session will be devoted to an investigation of the real destination of the $3,000. The facts already developed are regarded by counsel for the committee as pretty conclusive as to the recipient of the $500 check to bearer.

"Who got the $3,000 in cash?" To this question the committee will attempt to find an answer today. More definite evidence than is usually obtainable in bribery transaction is said to be forthcoming tomorrow, involving a member of Mayor Hylan's official family.

The committee took prompt action to protect the witnesses—Christian Haslob and Stephen Woolsey—whose permits to do business in Washington Market were revoked by Commissioner O'Malley after they had testified to the payment of bribes demanded of them as the price of permission to do business under Commissioner O'Malley.

The committee engaged Cyrus R. Miller, a lawyer of 261 Broadway, to fight any overt steps taken by Commissioner O'Malley against these men. O'Malley caused them to be notified that their permits would be revoked, but he took no steps to dispossess them. An application for an injunction will be made, according to Leonard A. Wallstein of counsel for the committee, as the first step to prevent dispossession.

Swann to Support Committee.

District Attorney Edward Swann assured the committee that he would give them full support, both in prosecuting crime brought to light by the committee and in crushing attempts to interfere with the committee's work.

"I deem it to be of greater importance," said Mr. Swann, in a letter to the committee, "to drive from the public service any public official who has been guilty of exacting tribute from a citizen, or receiving compensation for the

Continued on Page Three.

BELL-ANS IS A WONDERFULLY FINE THING FOR INDIGESTION.—Advt.

Save Girl as Plane Plunges Into Ocean

Special to The New York Times.

PHILADELPHIA, Aug. 24.—Perched precariously on the fabric-covered tail of a fallen airplane, a Stone Harbor (N. J.) girl calmly awaited rescue in the ocean off Sea Isle City last night while life guards and coast guards fought their way to her through a heavy surf.

With her were Captain Frank Little of Philadelphia and Walter Krouse, son of Mayor Clarence A. Krouse of Stone Harbor, owners and pilots of the plane, and both former members of the Royal Flying Corps. It was their first accident in more than 1,500 hours in the air.

The aviators, with their passenger, whose name they refused to disclose, had flown from Stone Harbor to Atlantic City and were returning by moonlight. Flying low off a pier at Sea Isle City, the plane, for an unknown reason, fell into the sea. It was a land machine, equipped with wheels instead of the pontoons of a seaplane, and its forward end, weighted by the motor, sank into the water. The fabric of the wings and lighter tail held it afloat, with the tail, elevators and rudder pointing upward.

The men helped the girl from the cockpit to the tail, and the three clung there until they were rescued by the guards.

TECHNICALITY HOLDS UP GERMAN TREATY

Signing Postponed Till Dresel Can Get a Ruling From Washington.

AUSTRIAN TREATY SIGNED

Terms Not Disclosed—Text of That With Germany to Be Published When It Is Signed.

BERLIN, Aug. 24 (Associated Press.)—The Peace Treaty between the United States and Germany was not signed today, as had been intended.

The delay in signing resulted from an unexpected technical point raised in connection with the formalities as arranged by Ellis Loring Dresel, the United States Commissioner, and Dr. Friedrich Rosen, the German Foreign Minister, yesterday.

The ceremony of signing was to have taken place at noon today at the Foreign Office, but it was postponed at the request of Mr. Dresel, who asked the privilege of querying the Washington Government on the mooted point.

At the headquarters of both the American Commission and the German Foreign Office it was said that the technicality which involved the delay did not affect the contents or character of the treaty, as both Governments had reached a full accord on the official text some days ago. German editors had been summoned to the Foreign Office for a discussion of the treaty this afternoon, but the conference was postponed pending the receipt by Commissioner Dresel of a reply from Washington.

Although the point which was referred to Washington is said to be of minor technical importance, Commissioner Dresel preferred to obtain a ruling on it from the American State Department. If this reply is received early Thursday it is probable that duly executed copies of the treaty will be exchanged that day.

The signing in Vienna today of the peace treaty between Austri and the United States was said to be a mere coincidence with the date on which the German peace treaty was to be signed, as it was declared that neither German nor American officials here had been informed of the signing of the Austrian treaty.

Simple Ceremony in Vienna.

VIENNA, Aug. 24 (Associated Press.)—The treaty of peace between the United States and Austria was signed here this afternoon, Arthur Hugh Frazier, American Commissioner in Vienna, acting for the Washington Government.

Such expedition and secrecy attended the preliminary negotiations and today's simple ceremony that the late newspapers today furnished the first news that the United States and Austria were no longer even technically enemies.

The terms of the treaty are being withheld for the present. It is understood that the Government does not desire public discussion of the treaty pending its ratification by the Foreign Affairs Committee of the Parliament. The committee will meet Saturday to prepare the resolution of ratification of the treaty for consideration by Parliament when it reassembles.

The ceremony of signing was devoid of formality. Mr. Frazier, accompanied by Secretary Shocraft, arrived at the Foreign Office at 12:57 o'clock this afternoon. They went immediately to the Chancellor's office, where they were received by Chancellor Schober and a few other officials. The document was in readiness and was signed at once.

A brief and informal exchange of congratulations followed, Commissioner Frazier expressing the hope that the signing would have a great moral as well as material effect upon Austria. Chancellor Schober, with ill-concealed emotion, voiced his deep gratification at the restoration of friendly relations with the United States.

Treaty Before Senate Committee.

Special to The New York Times.

WASHINGTON, Aug. 24.—President Harding in a conference at the White House this morning took Senator Lodge and other Republican members of the Senate Foreign Relations Committee into the confidence of the Administration respecting the terms and character

Continued on Page Six.

When you think of writing, think of WHITING.—Advt.

LEVIATHAN SINGED, ARMY PIERS BURNED, SOLDIER DEAD SAVED

New York and Jersey Firemen Battle With Flames Lighting Hudson a Mile.

TWO HOBOKEN PIERS GONE

400 Caskets Containing Bodies of Veterans Rescued by Volunteer Corps.

WIND SHIFT SAVED SHIP

Bridge Slightly Charred, Lifeboats Damaged—Fireboat's Water Barrage Helped.

A fire which for a time yesterday evening threatened to destroy all the army piers in Hoboken, the huge liner Leviathan, and to jump River Street and invade the city itself, gave the Hoboken Fire Department, with aid from Jersey City and New York, the hardest tussle they have had since the great pier fire of twenty-one years ago. Pier 5 was destroyed, Pier 6 partly wrecked, the Leviathan was scorched, and the army headquarters building and barracks were burned.

The bodies of 1,500 soldier dead on Pier 4 were in danger for a time, but a shift in the wind saved both the Leviathan and the pier with its precious burden from destruction. More than 400 caskets in two large rooms in a connecting warehouse between Piers 4 and 5 were removed by army officers and soldiers with the aid of a hundred civilians recruited from among an eager crowd on the street. They worked in blinding and chocking smoke for an hour.

Ammunition Blown Up.

The fire was a brilliant spectacle, lighting up the shore front for a mile as pillars of flame roared up from the combustible material in the barracks and warehouses filled with army stores. In the barracks were many cases of small arms ammunition, some of which were carried to safety. What was left went off in staccato barks like a machine gun, and spectators backed up as crackling explosions reached them. No one was injured by the bullets, which were confined by brick walls.

So fiercely did the fire burn that to the watching thousands along New York's shore front and the huge throngs which packed the streets near the Lackawanna ferry entrance it seemed that the entire city was menaced. Marine Inspector Hallock from the police boat John F. Hylan sent back wireless bulletins of the fire to New York headquarters, and at one time warned that all available water apparatus be sent, becuse he feared that the fire would spread to buildings in the city.

Men who watched the fire with gloomy foreboding in its early stages recalled that it was just about in this spot that the great fire which destroyed the North German Lloyd piers years ago started. The steamships Main, Saale and Bremen were burned then with considerable loss of life. The two piers which burned yesterday were the two wooden piers left after that great conflagration.

Just how the fire started last night the firemen were unable to learn. Both piers have been empty for some time, the Leviathan being tied to Pier 4 in the slip between 4 and 5. The fire started on Pier 5, at the end of which a scow was tied. It began slowly, but the dry timbers of which the pier was built were eaten into with increasing rapidity, until in a few minutes the entire breadth of the pier was in flames.

Three Fireboats Sent From New York.

Chief John Gilday knew he had the fight of his life on his hands as soon as he arrived. Every bit of apparatus in the city was called, and a call for help was sent to Jersey City and New York. Three fireboats, the New Yorker, the Strong and the Duane, were sent from this city, and Jersey City sent two companies of land apparatus. By the time they arrived the pier was a furnace, shooting great clouds of sparks in the air. Pier 6 soon caught and added to the heat, which cracked windows in buildings near by.

When the Duane arrived she nosed into the narrow space between the Leviathan and Pier 5, a place of whirling smoke and blistering heat, all her port and starboard nozzles shooting high pressure streams. She created a water barrage, which, with the aid of a shift in the wind, saved the Leviathan. Up and down the slip she moved, spraying the sides of the Leviathan, where paint was curling and peeling off, and shooting into the flames on Pier 6 that made a heat almost unendurable.

William F. Gibbs, chief constructor for the International Mercantile Marine, who has been in charge of the maintenance of the Leviathan for the last eighteen months, discovered the fire as he was leaving his office at 11 Broadway, New York. He found when he reached the ship that the crew of engineers, mechanics and others aboard the vessel already were fighting the blaze, with the aid of Companies 1 and 4 of the Hoboken Fire Department. All the lifeboats on the side next to the fire were aflame and the heat had broken the port lights.

Auxiliary machinery aboard the vessel had been kept in running condition for a year and a half and sufficient steam to operate the auxiliary engines and pumps had been kept up in the face of some criticism because of the expense. Mr. Gibbs felt that the saving of the vessel was due to insistence upon these precautions. The bridge was slightly charred and some of the lifeboats destroyed, but aside from some paint that was the only loss on board.

The Strong moved about off the end of Pier 5 with her pumps throwing tons of water into the blaze, while the New

Continued on Page Four.

THINK FRAME BUCKLED

Naval Aviation Experts Ascribe Accident to Structural Weakness.

DEAD HAILED AS MARTYRS

Secretary Denby Sends Message of Condolence to British Air Ministry.

SHIP NOT YET TAKEN OVER

But Navy Department Estimates Payments of $1,500,000 Had Been Made on ZR-2.

Special to The New York Times.

WASHINGTON, Aug. 24.—No information whatever reached the Navy Department tonight from London, Hull or Howden, giving an official account of the manner in which the great British built dirigible ZR-2—the largest in the world—which was scheduled to make its first flight across the Atlantic early in September under command of American naval officers and manned by an American naval crew, met its fate.

The meagre information received merely dealt with the loss of the American naval officers and men on board, and beyond stating that the dirigible had been lost as the result of a terrific explosion did not attempt to give the cause.

But the more American aviation officers think of the accident, in the light of previous reports the more they are convinced that the accident resulted from another buckling of the frame of the big dirigible and that the terrific explosion described in press and official dispatches followed instead of preceding such a buckling.

It can be stated that even before the tests were begun yesterday, American officers were much concerned over the structural qualities of the ZR-2, and American officers abroad were, for that reason, observing the tests most closely. The vessel had to be absolutely airworthy before the Navy Department would undertake the voyage, originally set to begin tomorrow, but which, on account of delay in the trials, had been postponed until later.

Information regarding the accident reached the Navy Department piecemeal. Until soon after 9 o'clock tonight the department did not know officially how many American officers and men were on board during the flight. Forty-four officers and men were in England ready to make the transatlantic voyage whenever the tests were completed and the rigid airship declared safe and airworthy. But only seventeen of these appear to have been among those that made the test flight which began yesterday, and was in progress when the accident occurred near Hull.

Call Dead Martyrs to Aviation.

Press dispatches had stated that six officers and eleven men were in the accident, and that the only survivor, Quartermaster Norman O. Walker, had subsequently died, and official dispatches, while not confirming the death of Walker, indicated that none of the others had been saved.

On receiving the names of the six officers and eleven men the department announced the names of the next of kin of these newest martyrs to the cause of aviation development. That they were martyrs is the conviction of aviation officers, both of the army and navy, who, while not permitting themselves tonight to be quoted for publication, asserted their belief that it would be unfortunate if the accident to the ZR-2 should operate to delay the subsequent acquisition of other large rigid dirigibles for the use of the American Navy.

It is the opinion of aviation experts, familiar with the reports received relative to the previous trials of the ZR-2, that it will be found that she was not structurally strong enough to stand the stress of weight she was designed to carry, and that the fault was primarily one of design.

Admiral Moffett, head of the Naval Air Service, would not comment on the probable cause of the accident tonight. He deeply regretted that so many good aviation officers and men should have lost their lives, but also thought it would be unfortunate if the accident should interfere with the development of rigid dirigibles for the United States.

"We will carry on and build and operate," Admiral Moffett said, "as many big, rigid dirigibles as are necessary, so that these brave men shall not have given their lives in vain."

Those who believe the accident was caused by a buckling of girders think this buckling severed pipes, &c., and allowed hydrogen gas to escape, and that this when ignited would have been sufficient to have wrecked the airship. This belief is strengthened by the report which the Navy Department recently received on the buckling of the ZR-2 in the third test flight which was held in July and as a result of which the airship had to be strengthened before the fourth flight, which resulted so disastrously today, could be undertaken.

The official report to the Navy Department on the third test flight stated that while the dirigible was proceeding at a gait of fifty miles an hour on four

Continued on Page Two.

AMERICANS SHOWED NO FEAR OVER TRIP

None of Them Had Any Thought of Serious Trouble in ZR-2'S Trial Flights.

ESTERLY "NOT WORRIED"

Others "Teased" Him About Precaution for Sea Voyage—Wife Sees Maxfield Leave.

HOWDEN, England, Aug. 24. (Associated Press.)—Conversations among the American officers just before they boarded the ZR-2 here yesterday morning for the flight which had such disastrous results indicated that not one of them had the slightest idea that an accident was likely to be met in the course of the air voyage.

"Are any of you ever troubled with thoughts of being wrecked?" the correspondent of The Associated Press asked Lieutenant Marcus H. Esterly, radio officer of Washington, just before he embarked.

"We are not worried," replied Esterly, "but, all the same, we have gone ahead and made all preparations against every emergency. The others tease me as being too fearful of accident. But all the same, I have figured that it was best to get ready for anything that might happen, and then, if the worst comes, we ought to have at least a fighting chance."

The officer told how he had rigged up an emergency radio set to be carried up 250 feet by means of a balloon, so that if the ZR-2 were disabled in mid-Atlantic, help could be summoned.

Lieutenant Esterly indicated that the possibility of serious trouble occurring in the trial flights had not been thought of by the Americans.

Before the fateful flight started, the correspondent found Brig. Gen. F. M. Maitland, British Air Marshal, strolling under the mammoth air craft in its hangar while she was being made what was termed "air light," meaning the discharge of sufficient ballast to make the weight of the great gas bag nil.

"Now she is as light as a feather," remarked General Maitland as this stage of the preparations was concluded. With evident pride he enumerated the points of excellence in the craft, which, he remarked, "is the greatest improvement on balloons, with which I started experiments in aeronautics thirty years ago."

"She is beautiful," declared General Maitland as the enormous hulk was cleared from the hangar by her party of 300 attendants.

He waited until the six motors had been tested and the ship's signal bells tried out by Lieutenant Wann, the British commander of the aircraft. Satisfied that all was well, the General, with a cheery good-bye and "I will see you in Pulham," climbed up the ladder and disappeared in the great silvery shell.

A moment later Commander Louis H. Maxfield, U. S. N., was boosted up into the control car alongside Lieutenant Wann. Then the civilian observers boarded the ship, and the aircraft was off on her journey.

MAXFIELD'S WIFE AT HOWDEN.

She and Daughter Saw Him Leave—Pulham Expected Airship.

Copyright, 1921, by The New York Times Company.

Special Cable to THE NEW YORK TIMES.

PULHAM, England, Aug. 24.—Among those who saw the ZR-2 leave Howden were the wife and daughter of Commander Maxfield, who was on board and was to have taken charge of the airship on its voyage to America.

There was a parachute for each man on board and a special one for the kitten mascot which was to be taken across to the United States in the airship. It was so arranged that it could be fixed to one of the parachutes for the men's use.

PULHAM, England, Aug. 24.—Everything had been in readiness here for the expected arrival of the ZR-2 when word came by radio from her commander that he had decided to return to Howden, as he was making speed tests, for which kite balloons are essential in estimating distances. It was known that no such balloons were at the Pulham station, and that some had been run up 2,500 feet at Howden.

Notwithstanding this seemingly plausible explanation of the ship commander's reason for not berthing at Pulham, officers here expressed some surprise.

Apparently the airship was driven from her course by a terrific electrical and rain storm early this morning.

List of American Victims Of the Airship Disaster

Special to The New York Times.

WASHINGTON, D. C., Aug. 24.—The Navy Department announced tonight that official word had been received that six officers and eleven of the men of the non-commissioned personnel of the navy were on board the ZR-2 when the disaster took place. According to the department's information the bodies of two officers had been recovered, and one enlisted man had died in a hospital after being rescued. Later reports say he is still alive. He is Norman O. Walker of Commerce, Texas. The others are reported as missing.

The department gave out this list of officers figuring in the accident, with names of next of kin:

OFFICERS.

Commander Louis H. Maxfield, brother, A. C. Maxfield, 627 Goodrich Avenue, St. Paul, Minn.

Lieut. Commander Valentine N. Bieg, mother, Mrs. F. G. Bieg, 120 South Fairfax Street, Alexandria, Va.; wife, care of Mrs. Ronald Barlow, Haverford, Pa.

Lieut. Commander Emery Coil; wife was with him in England.

Lieutenant Charles G. Little, father, Henry B. Little, 227 High Street, Newburyport, Mass; body recovered.

Lieutenant Marcus H. Esterly, wife, M. E. Esterly, 242 Auburndale Avenue, Youngstown, Ohio; body recovered.

Lieutenant Henry W. Hoyt, mother, Mrs. R. D. Hoyt, Clearwater, Fla.

NON-COMMISSIONED.

Charles I. Aller, father, H. L. Aller, 1,200 Thirteenth Street, Denver, Col.

Maurice Lay, wife, Mabel R., 400 Eugene Street, Greensboro, N. C.

A. S. Pettitt, wife, Margaret H., 326 East Thirty-fifth Street, New York.

Robert M. Coons, mother, Kate, 812 Allen Street, Owensboro, Ky.

Lloyd E. Crowel, wife, Minnie 26 Savage Street, Charleston, S. C.

J. T. Hancock, father, John, 17 Godwin Road, London, England.

William Julius, mother, Frieda J., 356 Seventy-seventh Street, Los Angeles, Cal.

Albert L. Loftin, father, James Benjamin, 710 Shattuck St., Lake Charles, La.

William J. Steele, wife, Lena C., Bainbridge, Ind.

George Welch, sister, Elizabeth Kimmerman, 159 Valley Road, Montclair, N. J.

LAST MESSAGES THE AIRSHIP SENT

The Final, Timed 5 P. M., Notified Air Ministry She Would Land at Howden at 6:30.

Copyright, 1921, by The New York Times Company.

Special Cable to THE NEW YORK TIMES.

LONDON, Aug. 24.—An official statement from the Air Ministry says that the ZR-2 left the Howden base at 7:10 A. M. yesterday for her fourth trial, under command of Flight Lieutenant A. S. Wann. She reported her position at various times throughout the day and proceeded to carry out different tests which had been arranged beforehand. At 8 o'clock last night she signaled the following message:

"Will remain out tonight to complete necessary trials. Several have already been successfully accomplished. Will land tomorrow."

The cruise, therefore, continued during the night, and at 7 o'clock this morning the airship reported that she was flying in the neighborhood of Howden, from which she had started. She continued flying over the area between Howden and Pulham during the day, and at 1:15 o'clock signaled:

"Will not land at Pulham until cloud height increases. Trial proceeding satisfactorily."

Later she requested Howden to fly a kite balloon at 3,000 feet and to give the probable winds at that height, as she was going to carry out full speed trials, which were expected to take about an hour. This message was sent at 3:50, and was followed by a further one timed 4:30, saying: "Carrying out full speed trials."

Half an hour later a message was sent both to the Air Ministry and Pulham, saying: "Landing at Howden 6:30." Earlier in the day she had requested both Pulham and Howden to keep landing parties standing by, as the captain of the airship wished to be in a position to land at the station which he considered most favorable from a meteorological point of view.

The last wireless transmission from

Continued on Page Two.

SURVIVOR THINKS ZR-2 GIRDER BROKE

Bateman Says That After Several Shocks the Airship's Petrol Tank Exploded.

HIS PARACHUTE ENTANGLED

American Officers in London Believe That Escaping Gas Became Ignited.

LONDON, Aug. 24 (Associated Press).—Harry Bateman of Halifax, one of the physical laboratory assistants on the ZR-2, talking to the correspondent of The Daily Mail at Hull after today's disaster, said:

"I was seated in the tail of the ZR-2. She first flew over the North Sea and toward Pulham. She was in perfect flying condition until 5:30 o'clock this evening, at which time the controls on the ship were being tested while the vessel was proceeding at high speed.

"I assume that a girder broke amidships. After a few short shocks the ship began to fall and the petrol tank exploded. I saw smoke afterward up forward about the ship, which began to fall, nose downward, toward the Humber.

"Immediately after the explosion I was thrown into the cockpit at the tail of the ship. I then attached myself to a parachute and jumped overboard. The rope of the parachute, however, had caught in some wires, and I was unable to extricate myself. Shortly afterward, with two other persons, I was picked up from the water by a barge and taken to the police station."

Ernest Davies, one of the British members of the crew of the ZR-2 who was saved, said in an interview with The London Times at Hull:

"We had a terrible time. It was all over in a moment. The petrol tanks exploded and volumes of smoke and fire issued from the ship.

"Some of the men jumped, but I stuck to the ship and went down with the stern section, which struck a sand bank, from which I was rescued. Some of the poor fellows had no chance whatever, especially those in the control car."

Lieutenant Newton H. White, Aviation Attaché of the American Embassy, and Lieut. Commander Richard E. Byrd of the American Air Service, who was to assist in the navigation of the ZR-2 to the United States, went to Hull tonight to take charge of the bodies of the American officers and men killed in the disaster.

American naval officers here express the opinion that the wreck of the ZR-2 was due to hydrogen escaping from one of the ship's gas bags being ignited by the exhaust from one of her six motors. What they say they are unable to understand, however, is how it was possible that a gas leak sufficient to make an explosion possible could have occurred without it having been detected through the pressure gauge fitted to each gas bag.

One of the points in the construction of the airship which her builders repeatedly pointed out to visitors at Bedford, where the ZR-2 was built, was the way in which her six motor gondolas were slung several feet from the outer shell of the craft. This, the builders declared, would greatly safeguard the ship from the danger of leaking gas coming in contact with the backfire flame from a motor.

Air Commodore Maitland, who was lost with the ZR-2, was one of the foremost of the British air pioneers, and his loss will be deeply felt. Many rumors have been afloat for the last few days concerning the stability of the airship, and Commander Maitland was quoted, whether rightly or wrongly is not known, as saying that the future of lighter-than-air travel largely depended upon the results this airship showed.

Lieutenant Wann, commander of the ZR-2, was brought ashore at Hull about an hour after the disaster to the airship, says a dispatch to The London Times from Hull. He was badly cut about the head and bleeding profusely, but was conscious. At a late hour he was reported as doing well at the hospital.

BIG DIRIGIBLE COLLAPSES

Envelope Breaks Into Two Parts After Several Explosions.

PARACHUTES SAVE THREE

Commander Wann Is Thought to Have Steered Over River to Protect City.

PANIC FROM CONCUSSION

Structural Weakness Is Said to Have Been Found in Tests of Airship.

One American Is Alive; N. O. Walker, a Rigger, Escapes

HULL, Eng. Thursday, Aug. 25 (Associated Press).—Norban O. Walker, a rigger, was the only American to escape when the ZR-2 was destroyed here last evening. It was reported early in the night that he had died in a hospital, but inquiry has established the fact that he is still alive. His home is in Commerce, Texas.

Copyright, 1921, by The New York Times Company.

Special Cable to THE NEW YORK TIMES.

HULL, England, Aug. 24.—Forty-four of the forty-nine officers and men on board the dirigible ZR-2, which was about to the transferred to the United States Navy, were killed when the great airship was wrecked over this city about 6:30 o'clock this afternoon. All but one of the seventeen Americans on the airship perished.

The disaster occurred when the ZR-2 was about to conclude a long trial flight. It was suddenly noticed to crumple in the middle, burst into flames and drop. A terrific explosion followed and the airship fell into the water.

Thousands of people rushed to the pier, and a large part of the airship's envelope could be seen floating half way across the River Humber and in a direct line between Hull and New Holland. This represented only a portion of the ship, and large part of it having sunk. Burning débris was floating.

Vessels rushed to the scene and a few men were picked up alive. The commander, Flight Lieutenant Wann, was saved, but was severely injured.

Eye witnesses state that as they were watching the progress of the ZR-2 in midair it was seen to break suddenly in the centre and drop. Two terrifying explosions followed immediately. One witness of the tragedy states that it was just over the centre of the pier and had been noticed to be dipping for some time. Suddenly the nose end seemed to break away from the body and the airship broke in two. Two parachutes were seen to fall.

Explosions Shake City of Hull.

Before the airship touched the water one of the halves was scattered in an explosion, and a few seconds afterward there was a second roar. The explosions were like the bursting of two huge rockets. When the wreckage touched the water of the Humber a huge column of flame and smoke was all that could be seen.

As a result of the explosion a great amount of damage was done to windows in the central part of Hull, also in the streets adjacent to the pier.

At a late hour tonight twelve bodies had been recovered. Those of Lieutenant Montague and Lieutenant Esterly have been identified. But the others are so badly disfigured by burns that identification is almost impossible. The Hull police authorities say there is very little chance of any further survivors. The work of recovering the floating bodies is difficult owing to the darkness.

The bodies of the Americans, it is stated, will be embalmed and sent to America.

According to one eyewitness of the disaster three men were seen clinging to one parachute. Another parachute was seen to fall into a patch of blazing petrol floating on the river which had come from the wrecked airship.

The dead and injured were brought in tugs to the Corporation pier and there were scenes of great excitement. The first man landed was unconscious and he had received terrible wounds on the face, while the second, a young man, was able to walk to an ambulance, the crowd around the pier cheering loudly when they saw that there was a man alive.

The Humber was at low water at the time of the disaster, and the airship's stern, when it fell, landed in the middle shoal. As a consequence boats cannot get close to it. It is supposed that before the final crash the commander, realizing that a disaster was impending, made the utmost speed to get clear of Hull and over the Humber.

Airship Broke Into Two Parts.

I have interviewed several people who were at the scene of the disaster. One was Mr. Martin, a pier master, who is an old navy man. He said:

"I had been watching her for some time. She turned in from the northwest and was heading for the southwest. She was not very high, and her engines were working at great speed. As she mine closer the envelope appeared to wrinkle in the centre. There was no flame, but the scene appeared to be surrounded by a slight fog. Possibly it was her own escaping gas.

"All this time she was coming lower. She cleared the land and had got some little distance across the river toward New Holland, on the Lincolnshire side, when the crumpling of the envelope became worse, and suddenly she broke clean in two.

"Up to that time I had seen no flames, but all at once there was a terrific explosion and the falling envelope burst into flames. In a few seconds it touched the water and then the second explosion occurred.

"Before the disaster I had noticed that the engines were working at terrific speed and it is a mercy that the airship got over the river before any explosion took place. If it had occurred over the crowded town I shudder to think what would have followed. I am an old naval man and I know what big guns can do, but I don't think they could have caused a more terrible disaster than those awful explosions would have done."

Sergeant Bushby, of the American air force who witnessed the disaster from the river front, said:

"I consider that there was some fire amidships. She collapsed in the centre, her stern coming down first. She was just turning when the disaster took place and the wrecked envelope and gondolas came speeding down to land. It is God's mercy that the disaster did not occur over the town."

Pilot William Henry Smith, who was one of the first to get to the sinking airship, said:

"The airship at the time of the disaster was about 1,000 feet high. I saw men, beds and blankets dropping from her, but whatever dropped fell into another portion of the wreck, which when it reached the river was a mass of flames."

Pilot Osborne was the first man alongside the wreck. He said:

"Five men have been saved. We cut different sections of the envelope with jackknives to get them out. We were unable to extricate any of the dead bodies. We saw the body of a young man in American uniform among the wreckage and tried to get hold of it with a boathook, but just as we were succeeding a swell of the tide washed us away. Another body, also in American uniform, could be seen, but we were unable to reach it.

One of the eyewitnesses said:

"The airship had been sailing around and over Hull for some time during the afternoon, during which there was a slight wind from the northeast. About twenty minutes to 6 o'clock I saw her coming down easily before the wind, approaching from the town and the Hive. Humber. The streets were crowded in all parts of the city. I was about a quarter of a mile from the Humber.

"Suddenly I heard the loudest explosion I have ever known, its concussion shook the whole town and the airship immediately began to fail. I had advanced not more than a dozen steps when there was a second explosion, if possible, of greater violence, accompanied by a crashing of glass.

"There was something approaching panic for a moment, but as soon as it was realized what had happened, every feeling of personal alarm was smothered in fears and sympathy for the gallant men who were in the airship. A huge cloud of smoke was seen to be rising from the direction of the harbor, and instantly a great crowd commenced to run toward the pier.

"When I reached it, the first thing I saw was a portion of one end of the airship resting in the river. It was dead low water. The river was perfectly calm and many steamers were gently swinging at their anchors. A brilliant sun was shining over the whole scene. Close to the wrecked envelope I could see floating small pieces of flaming material which had fallen. Tugboats were making their way toward the remnants of the envelope, but were not able to approach close to it, the envelope having fallen on a shoal of mud which was nearly exposed at low water.

"Being unable to get close to it, they launched their boats and began a search of the vicinity. In a little time other tugboats were launched and dashed away in the hope of being able to render assistance. One of the tugboats returned with a man whose clothes were wet and who had a wet handkerchief covering his face. One could see by the slight movement of his mouth that some remnant of life remained. He was immediately placed in a motor ambulance and taken to the infirmary, where I also found Captain Wann, master of the airship. He was suffering not only from injuries to the body but also as a result of his immersion.

"Immediately after this several bodies were landed and other boats brought in those they had rescued for examination. The melancholy business of these landings continued for some time. Immediately on reaching the pier medical men who were in attendance examined those brought in and any who were alive were hurried off to the infirmary, while those who were beyond assistance were taken to the city mortuary."

Two of the bodies were those of Captain Rupert Samuel Montague of the Royal Air Force and Flight Lieutenant Marcus H. Esterly, 30 years of age, belonging to the United States Navy. Both were badly burned as if by petrol and had suffered terrible injuries. Esterly was wearing a portion of his belt. A relative of Esterly was in town at the time and has arranged for the body to be embalmed.

The district naval intelligence officer at Hull gave the following description of what he saw:

"The airship was just off Corporation Pier when the thing happened, and it could be seen that several men jumped into the sea.

"The back of the gondola could not be seen. It was probably blown to atoms.

"Terrible scenes were witnessed when the sky had cleared and everything could be observed. The great majority of the crew were blown to pieces and for hours afterward parts of their bodies could be seen floating in the river. Shrieks could be heard, but amid the general confusion and sound of windows falling out it was hard to tell whence they were coming.

"The engines fell into the river some distance from the pieces of the gondola's Within five minutes of the first explosion all that was left of the great airship were tangled pieces of envelope and wood and wires floating in the oil-stained water."

Steered Craft to the River.

Another eyewitness said:

"While we were still watching the airship as her long, graceful shape came out of the light Summer cloud that had half hidden her for a few seconds, she kinked and buckled and then broke into two pieces. At the same moment flames shot from her sides with puffs of smoke that floated in the calm air. The forepart seemed to rise, while the other half began slowly to descend.

"Then as a loud explosion burst over the city, while women screamed and one heard the tinkle of breaking windows, the whole mass fell headlong into the river. Many of the spectators were in panic, for it seemed certain that some at least of the blazing wreckage would fall into the busy streets and people began to run in all directions for shelter.

"So far as one could judge, the navigating officer had had a few seconds warning of the coming crash and with a supreme effort that navigated his craft at speed to get clear of the city and over the Humber. This last thought for others by a man facing death achieved its purpose, and what might have been a yet more terrible disaster was averted."

As parachutes broke from the doomed airship crowds watched them with breathless anxiety. When the two portions of the airship fell, a heavy mass, apparently an engine and one of the gondolas or cars for the crew, detached itself and pitched down with terrific speed.

I have heard since that the shock of the explosions was also felt in Grimsby, fifteen miles away, across the mouth of the river, where windows shook and rattled.

Three survivors were brought to the pier at 7:30 o'clock and taken to the infirmary. All of them were terribly burned and two of them it is feared are beyond recovery.

It is believed that at the time of the disaster rudder tests were being carried out. One of the survivors states that he was at the tail end of the ship taking photographic records of experiments with the rudder when the airship took a sharp turn over the centre of Hull toward the Humber. Another survivor is understood to have said that one of the main girders of the airship failed to take the strain when this sudden manoeuvre was made.

In this connection I may recall that during the earlier trials certain weaknesses were discovered which led to some modification in the structure. These included alterations of some of the more features of the framework and a renewal of some of the latter.

A late tour of the city and the waterside shows that windows were broken by the force of the explosion within a radius of at least a mile of the place where the blazing wreckage fell. Several people in the streets were thrown down by the concussion, and a number were treated at the infirmary for injuries caused by falling glass. They said that the broken glass lying about the streets and the shattered windows recall the scenes which followed the Zeppelin raids.

Officers Who Were Aboard.

Besides the commander of the airship, Flight Lieutenant A. H. Wann, there were six other British flying officers aboard, in addition to Air Commodore E. M. Maitland, who was in command of the airship base at Howden and who made the double Atlantic trip in the R-34. There were also three representatives of the British National Physical Laboratory and two representatives of the British Royal Airship Works. Of the other ranks aboard there were nineteen British.

Of the seventeen Americans aboard there were six officers and eleven of other naval ranks. The officers were Commander Maxfield, Lieut. Commanders Bieg and Coil and Lieutenants Hoyt, Little and Esterly.

Flight Lieutenant Pritchard of the English crew made the trip with the R-34 to America and descended by parachute to the landing field at Mineola. C. J. R. Campbell, Superintendent of the Royal Airship Works at Cardington, was also aboard. He was the chief designer in charge of the construction of the ZR-2.

The Hull authorities intend to save the wreck for examination if possible. Preparations are being made for a diver to enter the submerged gondolas tomorrow morning and to drag the river for bodies.

A mascot carried aboard the airship perished in the disaster. It was a black cat named "Snowball" and was a great pet with the American crew.

The ZR-2 set out on her last trip from Howden, 21 miles west of Hull, in Yorkshire, Tuesday morning. It had been expected that she would land at Pulham, in Norfolk, where the British Air Ministry has a station, that evening, but a mist crept up and the officer commanding decided to remain in the air all night. Early today she had been reported cruising off the Norfolk coast, and this afternoon she put in an appearance over Hull, sailing over the town for some time before the disaster occurred.

Why after being off the Norfolk coast in the neighborhood of Pulham, where she was to have ended her trial trip, she had turned back north and steered to Hull is one of the mysteries connected with the disaster. According to a statement issued by the British Air Ministry tonight the cause of the accident is unknown.

Frame Is Said To Have Buckled.

HULL, England, Aug. 24 (Associated Press).—One theory of the cause of the disaster to the ZR-2 is that while the airship's rudders were being tested the giant craft took a sharp turn, which caused her framework to buckle, and that the explosion of a gasoline tank completed the tragedy of the air. The actual cause, however, never may be known.

A rumor has been afloat for some days that the ZR-2 was structurally weak, but this was stoutly denied by all in authority.

Tens of thousands of spectators saw several men climb outside the balloon and drop from the falling mass, which was enveloped in smoke, and others jumped into the Humber as the crippled craft came over the water. As the dirigible struck the wreckage above the water was burning, and there was slight chance for any of the men caught inside to escape.

Tugs immediately put out into the stream and brought ashore the five survivors, who were taken in ambulances to hospitals. Among those found alive was the American Quartermaster, N. O. Walker, who died soon after reaching the hospital from burns. Lieutenant Little also was rescued from the débris alive, but succumbed to his injuries on reaching the infirmary.

Maxfield's Name Found in Coat.

A rescue tug pulled another American out of the water. He was dead. Inside of his coat was the name "Commander Maxfield." Early reports were to the effect that Lieutenant Esterly had been saved. Later this proved to be without foundation.

One member of a rescuing party said that when they got alongside the burning airship the pilot of the tug asked for volunteers to board one part that still was almost intact. Jumping upon the wreckage the rescuers ripped open the débris and pulled away by means of ropes. The task was a hazardous one, because one of the balloonettes was still filled with gas and another explosion was feared.

Among the wreckage an American naval man was to be seen hanging by his coat to a girder in the frame of the airship. It was believed that he was dead, owing to the position of the body, which was not recovered. Another rescuer said that one man was hanging to the tail of the ship, apparently uninjured, while another was found floating in the water. Both of them were saved.

While the rescuers were at work the balloon began to turn over and the party had to return to the tug.

When first seen from Hull the ZR-2 was approaching the city, coming from a southeasterly direction over the Humber. While sailing on an even keel above the city, according to some eyewitnesses, a huge cloud of dense smoke burst from the tail of the aircraft. It was thought that the ZR-2 was sending out a smoke screen as an exhibition, but, to the horror of thousands of spectators, it was seen that she had broken in two and was taking a tremendous nose dive, which apparently would bring her down into the thronged streets.

Concussion Area a Mile Square.

Then there came a loud explosion and a great crash, followed by another explosion, which was accompanied by the breaking of glass in windows on land, the whole being reminiscent of war times, when German airships bombed Hull and explosions shook the whole town. Today's concussion was so great that it wrecked windows over an area of about a mile square.

Some spectators say that the airship began to buckle before any flame or explosion was seen or heard. The broken halves of the ZR-2 reached the water nearly a mile apart.

THE TWELVE OFFICERS OF THE ZR-2. SIX OF THEM WERE LOST.

The officers, reading from left to right, are:

Top Row—Lieutenant M. H. Esterly (lost), not identified; Dr. Taylor; Lieutenant T. B. Null, not identified; Lieutenant J. B. Anderson.

Bottom Row—Lieutenant H. W. Hoyt (lost), Lieut. Commander E. Coil (lost); Commander L. T. Maxfield (lost); Lieut. Commander V. N. Bieg (lost); Lieutenant R. Y. Pennoyer, not identified.

The New York Times.

THE WEATHER.
Clearing; fair Friday; no temperature change; southwest winds.
Temperature—Max., 71; Min. 40.
For weather report see next to last page.

VOL. LXXI....No. 23,252.   •••   NEW YORK, THURSDAY, SEPTEMBER 22, 1921.   TWO CENTS In Greater New York | THREE CENTS Within 200 Miles | FOUR CENTS Elsewhere

---

CONGRESS RESUMES AS PRESIDENT SENDS TREATIES TO SENATE

Foreign Relations Committee Will Consider Conventions Today and Hasten Its Report.

DEBATE WILL BE PUBLIC

Borah Expected to Lead in Effort to Defeat the German-American Compact.

TAX BILL GOES TO SENATE

Finance Committee Makes Change in Provisions Covering Capital Net Gain Levies.

Special to The New York Times.

WASHINGTON, Sept. 21.—Congress resumed work today after a month's recess, the Senate being faced with a difficult calendar, including consideration of the treaties with Germany, Austria and Hungary, the Tax and Tariff bills and the Anti-Beer bill, as well as the Panama Canal tolls resolution. The House had already passed the taxation and tariff bills, and it arranged today to transact practically no business before Oct. 1, meeting only every three days up to that date.

While the Tax bill is admitted the most important Administration measure before the Senate, it was announced today by Senate leaders that every effort would be made to force the ratification of the treaties as soon as possible, so that they would be out of the way by the time the conference on the limitation of armaments meets on Nov. 11. If necessary, night session will be held at which the treaties will be discussed, the days being devoted to consideration of the Tax bill.

The treaties reached the Senate accompanied by a formal note of transmittal from President Harding. They were referred at once to the Foreign Relations Committee which will meet tomorrow morning and hurry their consideration, as it is understood that all the Democratic members of the committee will vote for the treaties and, therefore, Senator Lodge Chairman of the committee has decided to dispense with hearings and the appearance of witnesses, it was said today. The Senator conferred at the White House today with President Harding on the treaty situation.

Borah to Oppose Treaty.

It does not follow that even if the treaties have easy going in the Foreign Relations Committee they will be smooth when they reach the Senate floor. Senator Borah, of the irreconcilable group, will oppose the German-American treaty on the principle that it involves this country in European affairs and binds the United States to what he calls "some of the most objectionable" features of the Versailles compact.

Senator Lodge announced today that the treaties would be considered in open instead of executive session, something which Senator Borah and others have insisted upon for months.

Whether this same publicity will be approved by the Senate for the disarmament conference is not at all sure. It is not believed that the Senate will pass a resolution introduced by Senator Harrison demanding that all sessions of the disarmament conference be open to the press.

The Senate is now in session only a short time today, finishing its work with an executive session, at which several nominations sent in by President Harding were confirmed.

The pending unfinished "business" before the Senate is the Panama Canal tolls matter, but as an agreement has been reached to vote on this on Oct. 18 it will be displaced by the tax bill.

Senator Lodge was not at all pleased with the attendance of Senators today. Only 54 were present, 36 Republicans and 15 Democrats failing to answer to their names when the roll was called. The attendance in the House was so small that only the most formalities were had. When the roll was called 57 members replied to their names and the House was organized, committees, in ses sion, then recessed until tomorrow.

SPEED ASKED ON TAX BILL.

Finance Committee Changes Provision Covering Capital Net Gain.

WASHINGTON, Sept. 21.—The amended House Tax Revision bill was presented formally to the Senate today by Chairman Penrose of the Finance Committee, who gave notice that he would submit the majority report tomorrow and urge at that time that the measure be considered as soon as other business of the Senate would permit. The bill is designed to raise approximately $3,250,-000,000 in revenue this fiscal year.

An important change in the House bill not heretofore made public deals with taxes on capital net gain. The Senate committee measure provides that if any taxpayer derives a capital net gain in any taxable year "such capital net gain shall be stated separately from the ordinary net income in the taxpayer's return, and only 40 per centum of such capital net gain shall be taken into account in determining the amount of the net income on which taxes are imposed by Sections 210, 211 and 230 of this title (the normal income, surtax and corporation tax sections). In any such case the tax shall be collected and paid upon the sum of the amount derived from the ordinary net income in the taxpayer's return at the per centum of the amount of the capital net gain.

The House bill provided that in the case of any taxpayer, other than a corporation, whose ordinary net income and

Continued on Page Four.

The full text of the revised tax bill, now before the Senate, is printed in full this morning, in The Journal of Commerce.—Advt.

German Commission Backs Plan For Indemnity Credit Funds

BERLIN, Sept. 21 (Associated Press).—The German Reparations Commission, which is dealing with the problem of raising funds for future German indemnity payments, approved at yesterday's meeting a plan elaborated by one of its experts, Dr. Machenburg, looking to the creation of a collective credit organization embracing all industries, banks and realty owners, on the principle of limited liability.

The plans contemplate the mortgaging to the State by each member of a fixed proportion of his holdings in return for which certain abatements of taxation would be granted.

MURPHY EXPECTS 70 OF 72 VOTES TO KEEP HIM AS LEADER

Minimizes Hines's Revolt, Through Statement Made by Tammany Secretary.

WOULD IGNORE INSURGENT

Decides Not to Protest Against Seating Him in Committee Tonight.

RECOUNT TO BEGIN TODAY

Hines Deposits $2,500 With Election Board to Cover Expenses of Examination of Ballots.

When the seventy-two district leaders who comprise the Executive Committee of Tammany Hall meet tonight to organize for the ensuing year of them will vote for the re-tention of Charles F. Murphy as leader of the Tammany organization. The two insurgent leaders, of course, will be James J. Hines and Mrs. Ernestine F. Stewart, his co-leader in the Eleventh Assembly District.

This announcement was made yesterday by Thomas F. Smith, Secretary of Tammany Hall, and is regarded as the first recognition that Mr. Hines revolt. In his statement Mr. Smith sought to show that the vote which Hines received on Primary Day, when he carried eight Assembly districts in his contest for the nomination for Borough President of Manhattan, against Julius Miller, the regular Tammany candidate, did not indicate that the revolt against Murphy's leadership extended beyond Mr. Hines's own district. Mr. Smith also sought to show that other Tammany leaders who have fought Murphy's control in the past have made a better showing than did Hines.

Mr. Murphy reached the conclusion yesterday to make no protest against the seating of Mr. Hines and Mrs. Stewart at tonight's meeting. There will be no fight in the Executive Committee against them, but both will be ignored by Murphy and the other leaders. That will be the procedure, at any rate, unless Mr. Hines decides to make an attack on Murphy. In that event, Tammany leaders said, there was no telling what would happen, as Murphy's friends who will be in the vast majority in the committee, will rally around their leader.

"If Jimmie Hines starts any fireworks," said one Tammany leader, "he will get all the trouble he is looking for. That little affair on primary night in which his campaign manager was beaten up will be a Sunday school affair in comparison to what will happen if Hines attempts to get unruly."

500 Hines Defenders.

Hines will have a force of 500 ablebodied men and women on hand to take his part, this being the number of the County Committeemen elected from his district, but the number will be lost in the 8,000 or more County Committeemen from the other districts. The members of the County Committee are scheduled to meet for reorganization in the big assembly room of the hall at 8 o'clock, an hour after the Executive Committee meets downstairs. Of course, not all 8,000 are expected to be on hand, but indications are that most of them will show up just to show Murphy that they are with him in his fight against the Hines clan. The assembly room will not accommodate more than 3,500. Anticipating disorder, a large force of policemen will be detailed to the hall.

"When the Executive Committee meets tomorrow night," said Secretary Smith, "of the seventy-two district leaders who were elected at their district clubhouses on Tuesday night, seventy will be solidly behind the leadership of Charles F. Murphy. Only two, Hines and Mrs. Stewart, his co-leader, will oppose him. Of the eight Assembly districts which Hines carried in the primaries, seven of them have re-elected pro-Murphy leaders.

"A careful analysis of the Hines vote in the primaries shows that the support for Mr. Hines is not abnormal and did not in any way reflect an opposition to Mr. Murphy's leadership. Mr. Hines received 20,167 votes out of a total enrolment of 180,153. John J. Hopper, an independent candidate for the nomination for the office of Register, running in the Democratic primaries without any organization and without any publicity, polled 13,423 votes. Mr. Hines's own Assembly District, the Eleventh, gave him 3,000 votes. Excluding these votes from his own district, his total in New York County was little more than the vote cast for Mr. Hopper.

"In 1917, with only one voting Thomas E. Rush, candidate for the Supreme Court on an anti-Murphy issue, polled 17,448 votes out of an enrolment of 133,438. Thus the vote cast for Mr. Hines in 1921, which seems to be regarded by Republican newspapers as a protest against Mr. Murphy's leadership, was considerably less, in percentage, than that cast for Rush.

"As an evidence of the vote which can be polled by any disgruntled candidate running against the organization's choice of any party, we have the 19,750 votes cast in the recent Republican primaries for Frank Hendrick for Judge of General Sessions. Mr. Hendrick had no organization and little, if any, publicity."

Mr. Murphy's leadership of Tammany Hall rests absolutely with the members of the Executive Committee. Any time the Executive Committee desire to oust Mr. Murphy from his leadership, it is wholly within its power to do so. When the Executive Committee meets tomorrow night Mr. Murphy will have absolutely behind him seventy of the seventy-two district leaders.

Mr. Hines deposited yesterday with

Continued on Page Two.

When you think of writing, think of WHITING.—Advt.

Mayor Assails Press in Proclamation; Defends Police Handling of Unemployed

Mayor Hylan issued a proclamation to "business men" yesterday in which he said that the "hate-crazed newspaper publishers" were advertising the city as a "paradise for criminals" and "doing everything they can to wreck the town commercially." The proclamation read as follows:

City of New York, Office of the Mayor.

Proclamation.

To the Business Men, Merchants and Shop Keepers of New York City:

You support the newspapers of the city and you have the right to expect them to be loyal to your interests, but some of them, in their mad fury to do "anything to beat Hylan" are not giving you a square deal. In fact they are doing everything they can to wreck the town commercially and it is time you realized it.

The other night the police broke up a near-riot in Bryant Park that would have made the world think that New York was as lawless as an old-time mining camp—if it had been allowed to spread. Certain newspapers, instead of commending the police for their determined and courageous work, are now trying to create the impression that the police were cruel and brutal to a lot of inoffensive citizens. New York, like all other big cities, is at the present time facing an unprecedented situation, due to the vast army of unfortunates who are unable to secure employment. It also has its share of criminals, but our conditions are made worse by the influx of out-of-town rascals, who are persistently told by certain New York newspapers that New York is a good mine for thieves and that the New York police are incompetent and crooked. It is no wonder that the crooks of the whole want to come here when the political propaganda of disloyal newspaper

publishers assures them that this is a safe and profitable place for them to prey upon the public.

Mr. Business Man, Mr. Merchant, Mr. Shopkeeper, when these hate-crazed newspaper publishers besmear New York and advertise it to the world as a paradise for criminals, they are asking you to pay the price of their political spite. The same "crimewave" propaganda that practically invites the crook to come to New York operates at the same time to frighten away the visitors, shoppers, tourists and business men from other parts of the country.

Think this over, place the blame where it belongs—and act accordingly. In witness whereof, I have hereunto set my hand and affixed the seal of my office this twenty-first day of September, one thousand nine hundred and twenty-one.

JOHN F. HYLAN.

By the Mayor: JOHN F. SINNOTT,
Secretary to the Mayor.

The Mayor sent a copy of his proclamation to each of the newspapers with a note urging its publication. The note addressed to THE TIMES follows:

New York, Sept. 21.

To the Publisher of THE TIMES:

Dear Sir: As Mayor of New York I ask you to give a prominent place in your columns to the enclosed proclamation which I have this day promulgated.

No newspaper publisher who does not feel accused by the terms of this proclamation will refuse to print in full nor will he "edit" it or prefade it in any way.

I rely on your public spirit to print this proclamation in full.

Respectfully,
JOHN F. HYLAN, Mayor.

MACHINE OPPOSES ANDREWS FOR JUDGE

Members of Old Guard, Gathering in Syracuse, Push Justice Cochrane.

CONTEST SEEMS CLOSE

New York Delegates May Hold Balance of Power in Keen Struggle.

Special to The New York Times.

SYRACUSE, N. Y., Sept. 21.—In full battle array the Old Guard in the Republican organization is here, prepared to make a fight in the State convention which will open tomorrow against the nomination of Associate Judge William S. Andrews of the Court of Appeals for the place in that tribunal which became vacant when Judge Emory A. Chase of Greene died suddenly on June 25. Judge Andrews, one of the leading jurists in the State, is now sitting with the Court of Appeals under designation from Governor Whitman.

The Old Guard's candidate for the nomination is Supreme Court Justice Aaron V. S. Cochrane of Columbia County. Justice Cochrane, who has been on the bench sixteen years, is at present a member of the Appellate Division in the Third Department.

It looks as if Judge Andrews and Justice Cochrane would be the only candidates on the early ballots with the contest between them developing into a sharp one. A deadlock and a compromise candidate are not thought out of the question, in which event it is likely that the name of Supreme Court Justice Russell Benedict of Kings may go before the convention. Delegates from Kings County say that Justice Andrews is definitely eliminated from the fight.

That so far the backing of Judge Andrews appears to be confined to a group of militant and influential Republicans from this city, which is his home. Apparently the two candidates will enter convention with almost equal strength. Under the circumstances the delegates from New York City, who have come prepared to play an inconspicuous part in the convention, being outnumbered more than three to one by representatives of up-State localities, may find themselves in a position where they will hold the balance of power and decide the contest.

The time-worn argument, that Judge Andrews, coming from Syracuse, which has furnished two Judges in the Court of Appeals as well as the Governor and the Chairman of the Republican State Committee to boot, is "geographically" ineligible for the nomination, even if his recent decision invalidating the $45,000,000 bond issue voted by the Legislature to provide bonus payments to veterans had made his nomination politically unwise, is being dinned into the ears of delegates by the supporters of Justice Cochrane's candidacy, but there is more to the opposition than appears on the surface.

The devotion to William Barnes of some of the Old Guard leaders, who are fighting Judge Andrews, is a factor in their opposition to him, possibly more weighty than the reasons that are being advanced by them in attempting to make converts for Justice Cochrane.

They have not forgotten that Justice Andrews presided in the Roosevelt-Barnes criminal libel trial in which Colonel Roosevelt was acquitted of blame, though he had called William Barnes a "boss." Some of the rulings of Justice Andrews at that time were objected to by friends of Mr. Barnes, who attributed to them the verdict of "not guilty" brought in by the jury.

Local politics in the counties included within the Third Judicial District also are an important factor in the fight made upon Judge Andrews. The nomination of Justice Cochrane would create a vacancy on the Supreme Court bench in this district, making three in all and supplying every need for the satisfaction of lawyers in the district who harbor aspirations. Already there are two candidates in the field for nomination to the Supreme Court, both powerful enough to require consideration from the leaders. One is Conservation Commissioner Staley of Albany, who, when

Continued on Page Two.

POLICE PROMISE AID TO FEED CITY'S IDLE

Change Tactics and Invite Club Members to Distribute Alms When They Like.

GUARD GRANTED LEDOUX

He Will Give Out Rolls Today in Park Where He Was Barred—Hylan Calls Relief Meeting.

The police yesterday did everything possible with one exception, to co-operate with men and women who are attempting to alleviate the condition of the unemployed, and showed a complete reversal of the temper with which they greeted Urbain Ledoux when he tried to repeat in this city his experiment of auctioning jobless men. Ledoux said yesterday that he doesn't need to hold the auction now, because his purpose of attracting publicity had been accomplished.

The Mayor also wrote two letters on unemployment, one to Bird S. Coler, Commissioner of Public Welfare, in which he commended the Commissioner for the work already done to alleviate distress through the Industrial Aid Bureau. He called attention to a gathering of business men in the City Hall today at 2:30 o'clock to discuss measures to relieve unemployment.

Dennis O'Sullivan, an attorney, Chairman of the Bronx Unemployment Committee, also received a letter thanking Mr. O'Sullivan for suggesting that the city take action to obtain the use of the armories to house shelterless men," and said the city would be glad to act on any practical suggestion to relieve conditions which Mr. O'Sullivan might make.

Police Invite Food Distribution.

Members of the Sunset Club, who were told by a policeman to leave Bryant Park when they tried to give food to the men there, and who were knocked down by the policeman, were called up several times yesterday by police officials. They were invited by Inspector Boettler to meet this morning and make charges against the policeman, and promised protection when they wished to distribute food again.

Urbain Ledoux, who was prevented from giving away food in Cooper Square and Bryant Park on Monday, will be allowed, at 2:30 o'clock this afternoon, to give out rolls in the square at the same spot this morning under police protection. Two detectives escorted him in his patrol of the Bowery yesterday.

The only disagreeable experience was taken up by Commissioner Enright yesterday today came when Mrs. Harriet MacDonald of 37 West Ninety-fifth Street, a member of the Sunset Club, called the Chief Inspector's office at Police Headquarters and asked for an appointment with Commissioner Enright to lay her complaint before him. Some one in the office who answered the telephone spoke to her so sharply that she asked him to repeat his words so that she could have a stenographer write them down.

"You are the kind of woman who make trouble," she was told. "If you are like the I. W. W. agitators of three years ago, and if you keep on opposing the police instead of co-operating with them, you will have riots and men marching up Fifth Avenue as they did then. If you want to feed people, feed them in your own homes."

When Mrs. MacDonald protested that she was not used to being addressed in this way and wanted the official's words recorded by her stenographer, he became apologetic and said if he was not trying to compare her methods to those of the I. W. W. He finally referred her to Inspector Boettler.

Police officials have been calling me up all day from everywhere," she said yesterday, "to talk to me more nicely and of what will happen when I go to the West Sixty-eighth street station tomorrow to see the Inspector. He was so courteous, however, that he somewhat allayed my fears. I never expected to get into a mess of this kind when I started out to feed a few hungry men."

Algernon Lee, who was floor leader for the Socialists in the Board of Aldermen last year, sent a letter to Mayor Hylan yesterday protesting the rough methods of the police in breaking up a gathering of which Ledoux was the centre on Monday.

"The treatment of unemployed workingmen by the police Monday and yesterday is nothing less than infamous," he said. "You are the Chief Executive of this city, vested with ample power to

Continued on Page Three.

MEYER TRAIL LINKS POLICE WITH COSTLY PRIVATE DETECTIVES

Favoritism, Forcing Business Firms to Pay Large Sums for Protection, Charged.

ENRIGHT EXPLAINS OIL DEAL

Denies It Was "Fictitious"— Asked if He Had Other Deals Says "No, but I Have Hopes."

SEEKS $4,825,741 INCREASE

Reads Many Records to Show Leniency by Arthur Woods Toward Police Offenses.

Investigation of the alleged relation of officials of the Police Department with certain private detective agencies, which has resulted in business firms paying large amounts for protection of business, was begun yesterday by the Meyer legislative investigating committee at its public hearing in the Aldermanic Chamber in City Hall.

Anthony P. Vachris, formerly a Police Lieutenant and now head of a detective agency bearing his name, testified that he had lost the job of policing Piers 56 and 97 in the Hudson River, leased by the Navigazione Generale Italiana, because he did not have a pull with the police. He said his watchmen had been beaten up on their way home from the piers, and that he had been unable to get them appointed special policemen or to get police protection for the company at the request of Vachris without effect, were appointed special policemen after Cross came in.

Enright Tells of $12,000 Profit.

Richard E. Enright, Police Commissioner, who occupied the witness stand at the forenoon session, brought up the $12,083.29 profits he had received from Allan A. Ryan, Special Deputy Police Commissioner, on an oil stock deal and complained that he had been unfairly treated because former Senator Elon R. Brown, counsel of the committee, had applied the adjective "fictitious" to the transaction, and had dropped his questioning on this matter just before adjournment the preceding day without giving the witness an opportunity to explain.

Mr. Enright said Mr. Ryan had spoken to him about an investment and that he had told him he would put up whatever was needed.

"Had there been any loss in this thing," Commissioner Enright said, "I would have been obliged to take care of it."

"I found that it had practically been junked in the lot were included 24 wheel chairs that had cost us about $85 each. There were 18 or more Morris chairs for which we had paid about $60. I cannot give the exact amounts, but we are checking the figures up now for reference. There also were a great many bedsteads and other hospital furniture of all sorts of enamel ware, including bowls, pitchers and jars, that had formed part of the equipment of our private rooms. These are cost but between $20 and $30, and also the valuable pieces of furniture and bric-a-brac that had been discarded. A set of $11 and John A. Blanco, formerly night superintendent, to see what had happened to the Polyclinic.

Material Junked, Says Dr. Wyeth.

Plan to Fight Unemployment To Be Ready Within a Month

WASHINGTON, Sept. 21.—Recommendations for a practical policy to combat unemployment throughout the country are expected to be ready for consideration by the Administration within a month, officials said today. The National Conference on Unemployment, which will convene here on Monday, officials asserted, will attempt to solve as rapidly as possible the problem of the immediate needs of the workers. Special committees, it was asserted, might continue the investigation of various phases of the unemployment situation for some time, but the main conference, it was expected, would complete its labors in three or four weeks.

CHARGES ATTEMPT TO RUIN POLYCLINIC

Dr. John A. Wyeth Declares Government Is Trying to Buy It in Hospital It Now Controls.

CITES LOSS OF EQUIPMENT

Gotham Bank, Restaurateurs and Columbus Circle Association Join Drive.

An attempt to force the Polyclinic Hospital of New York into bankruptcy so that its property in West Fiftieth Street, near Eighth Avenue, might be acquired for the Government at the latter's own price was charged yesterday against officials of the Government, not named, by Dr. John A. Wyeth, founder and Trustee of Polyclinic Hospital, when he asked the support of the Society of Restaurateurs in the campaign for return of the hospital to its rightful owners. Dr. Wyeth, in the presence of Henry States, counsel and Trustee of Polyclinic Hospital, made the accusation at the course of a conference with Paul Henkel of Keen's Chop House, who is a Director of the Society of Restaurateurs. Dr. Wyeth further accused the Government representatives of having failed to take the proper care of the property while under control of the War Department and the Public Health Service, and asserted that it would cost at least $150,000 to recondition the hospital.

One of the evident injustices inflicted upon Polyclinic Hospital since the Government took control of the institution, according to Dr. Wyeth, was the removal last December of 982 pieces of material and furniture from the Fox Hills Hospital, Staten Island, where this equipment was placed unprotected from weather in a vacant lot and left to the rain.

"We have the most uncontrovertible evidence that they took this equipment from the hospital without communicating with me or with any other member of the Board of Trustees," complained Dr. Wyeth to Director Henkel of the Society of Restaurateurs. They dumped it in an open lot at Fox Hills ground.

"The first we knew that this valuable furniture and material had been disposed of in such manner was last June, when we received a request from the Public Health Service to send a representative to Fox Hills in order to check up an inventory of the articles. When the nature of this request was made known to me I hastened with my wife, who was then Dietitian at Polyclinic, M. T. Cooper, former druggist and purchasing agent for the hospital, and John A. Blanco, formerly night superintendent, to see what had happened to the Polyclinic.

"I found that it had practically been

Continued on Page Three.

1,000 TO 1,500 PERISH AS BLAST WRECKS GERMAN DYE PLANT

Two Thousand Others Injured and Town of Oppau Almost Destroyed.

FIRE FOLLOWS EXPLOSIONS

Badische Company Officials Believe Gas Generator Burst in Room Where 800 Worked.

SHOCK FELT FOR 50 MILES

Left Hole In Ground 130 Yards Wide and 45 Deep—Factory Made First Poison Gas.

Copyright, 1921, by The New York Times Company.
Special Cable to THE NEW YORK TIMES.

BERLIN, Sept. 21.—The greatest explosion catastrophe in German industrial history described here at 7:30 o'clock this morning the synthetic nitrate plant of the famous Badische Anilin concern in Oppau was destroyed with hundreds of casualties.

The village was laid waste and all its foundations high into the air, and it fell back a rubbish heap, surmounted by an impenetrable fog of chemical fumes. All workers in and about the plant are believed to have been killed.

Three trains just pulling in loaded with workers for the new shift were caught and hundreds were buried in the ruins.

Further explosions are feared. So far as could be learned, the explosion was not directly connected with the manufacturing process of synthetic nitrates, but was caused by an explosion of a gas compressor in a subsidiary building of the nitrate plant.

Wives and children of workmen were trying to break through the strong cordon drawn at a wide radius around the scene of disaster. Firemen and police, with gas masks, were trying to keep through the chemical barrier which was frustrating rescue work.

All Hospitals Filled.

Many children bound for school were killed or injured.

All available transportation rushed to the catastrophe from the surrounding countryside and the nearest cities. The French garrison at Ludwigshafen reported that it was holding itself in preparedness as a result of the explosion.

Its horses were transported across the Rhine from Mannheim.

The Oppau plant manufactured nitrates, employing nitrogen extracted from the air by a famous process discovered by Fritz Chandler Haber, who won a Nobel prize for his achievement. The plant was built on a small scale at first and saved Germany from a military collapse in the Spring of 1915 by supplying artificial nitrates when the British blockade cut off the Chile saltpeter supply.

The present Reconstruction Minister, Dr. Rathenau, has laid stress on the raw materials section of the Prussian War Ministry, in the Fall of 1914 recognized the imminent danger of an ammunition shortage from the lack of Chile saltpeter, and, stimulated by Rathenau's genius, scientists enormously increased the output of synthetic nitrogen by mammoth proportions with an output of 100,000 tons of synthetic nitrate annually, or one-third of Germany's total requirements.

The following catastrophe seriously offered to the Government for each purpose with the understanding that the hospital would be returned to its rightful owners as soon as possible.

Whereas, The Society of Restaurateurs approves of the effort of its fellow members, and considers the matter of sufficient importance to warrant action by the organization as a whole, be it

Resolved, That the Trustees of the Polyclinic Hospital have offered to effect a return of their property to them as an act of justice to the community and as an aid to the medical institutions of the city.

It is interesting to observe that Berlin has so far returned to normalcy that the public has forgotten war casualties and was more concerned over the Berlin reports of 1,000 dead. The large number of casualties was freely discussed in public places.

Explosion on Shifts Change.

MAYENCE, Germany, Sept. 21 (Associated Press).—A great explosion occurred at the chemical products plant of the Badische Anilinfabrik Company at Oppau, on the Rhine, wrecked the factory and buildings and spread death and destruction in every hand.

The number of killed is variously estimated from 1,000 and 1,500, and the injured close to 2,000. One report says that 3,000 men were on duty at the moment of the explosion and it is believed that about half of them were killed.

Two explosions occurred at about 7:30 o'clock this morning during a change of working shifts. The shock was felt and damage was done within a radius of fifty miles.

The entire factory building was blown to its foundations high into the air and it fell back a rubbish heap, surmounted by an impenetrable fog of chemical fumes.

Oppau is a scene of utter desolation.

Continued on Page Two.

more than a third of the houses having been completely destroyed. The roofs of the others were swept off as if by a whirlwind. Here also many were killed or injured.

The explosion is attributed by some to excess pressure in two adjoining gasometers, the whole of that part of the works being demolished. Where the gasometers stood is now a funnel-shaped hole 130 yards wide and 45 yards deep, and twisted girders and debris lie scattered about. For several hundred yards not a wall is left standing.

Directors of the company are quoted as saying that the explosion occurred in a storehouse containing 4,000 tons of nitrous sulphates, which had previously been examined and were believed to be free from danger of explosion.

All the workmen's dwellings in the vicinity were razed to the ground. At Mannheim, on the opposite side of the river, thirty-five persons were seriously injured and 200 or more slightly injured. Ludwigshafen reports say that three workmen's trains were buried under the wreckage and that many children on their way to school in that town were injured.

At the little cemetery on the outskirts of Oppau, there are already more than 200 bodies laid out on the grass. Numerous tombstones were lifted and hurled in various directions by the force of the explosion. There was not a door or window left intact for a radius of three miles.

French medical units are aiding in the rescue work. Assistance also has been rushed from all the neighboring towns, and all public and private motor cars and vehicles were requisitioned. The roads leading to Oppau were soon crowded with persons making their way to the scene of the disaster.

A regiment of Colonial Infantry and the first Madagascar regiment from Ludwigshafen immediately proceeded to Oppau to preserve order and aid in the work of rescue. Describing the disaster, a captain of the First French Colonial Infantry, who was an eyewitness, said:

"I was riding close to the factory at 7:30 o'clock in the morning, when suddenly I heard a dull rumbling. The earth seemed to quiver and an immense column of flame and smoke shot up a few hundred yards from me, followed immediately by an explosion and a rush of air which hurled me and my horse to the earth.

"When I picked myself up, an immense cloud of dust and smoke hid that part of the factory near the gasometers. All sorts of objects, beams, blocks, stones and bricks rained upon the road.

"Hearing cries behind me, I turned and saw that the village of Oppau was destroyed as by an earthquake. Shortly after, the main buildings of the plant burst into flames and the air was filled with the fumes of ammonia. Twenty minutes after the first explosion, there was another, but less violent.

"The alarm was quickly given and in less than half an hour after the first explosion help arrived. Unfortunately, as further explosions were feared, the rescue parties were not able to get to work properly before 9 o'clock."

A late statement issued by the management of the Oppau factory says that the explosion occurred in a reservoir containing 200 tons of ammonium sulphate. It adds that all necessary precautions had been taken during the process of manufacture and storing the product, so that an explosion appeared impossible. An inquiry has been opened.

The first explosion occurred when the shifts were being changed at 7:45 o'clock this morning in a laboratory where 800 men were working. All of these are reported to have been killed. This explosion was followed by a rapid succession of others, which rendered assistance to the first victims impossible.

The concussions were so terrific that they were felt in this city, about thirty-five miles from the scene, while at Mannheim, thirteen miles away, every window was shattered. The shock was felt as far as Frankfort, more than forty miles away, and many windows were broken there.

The whole district was enveloped in thick smoke, which, with the cutting of telegraph and telephone communication with neighboring towns, hampered the efforts at assistance. All the available fire brigades were rushed to the spot, but the work of rescue was found by the relief parties to be exceedingly difficult.

One report of the disaster says the first explosion occurred in Laboratory 53 of the old plant of the Badische Company in Oppau. The laboratory was raised bodily by the air pressure from the shock and then collapsed.

All of French Guard Killed.

LONDON, Sept. 21.—A dispatch to The London Times from Mayence says that all the members of a party of French soldiers on guard duty at the Oppau works were killed and that several French soldiers on a French transport unloading in Mannheim Harbor were injured.

The dispatch adds that the old palace in Mannheim was badly damaged and that the National Theatre was rendered unsafe and performances in it were forbidden.

BERLIN, Sept. 21.—The Ludwigshafen correspondent of the Allgemeine Zeitung says that the disaster at Oppau was caused by the explosion of a nitrogen tank, after which four other tanks exploded.

In the building at the time were 800 workers and it is feared that all of them perished. Pieces of machinery weighing half a ton were hurled into Ludwigshafen.

The correspondent says he learns that a new process of manufacture was being tested in the laboratory.

An aerial view showing the enormous crater-lake formed by the explosion which devastated the chemical works at Oppau, Germany.

United Press International

MADE FIRST POISON GAS.

Badische Works Target in Air Raids —British Knew Its Importance.

LONDON, Sept. 22.—"The name of the Badische works has an evil sound in allied ears," says The Daily Mail, "for there the first poison gas used in the war was produced, and throughout the war chlorine, phosgene and lachrymatory gases were manufactured for the German Army.

"The works did more than any other German industrial concern to prolong the war by remarkable achievements in supplying high explosives. They were severely damaged in the course of twenty-nine air raids which the French and British made on Mannheim, one of the chief objectives of the allied bombing squadrons.

"The Badische works are recognized as the largest dye and high explosive concern in the world. More than 10,000 persons were employed there before the war, and recently between 15,000 and 18,000. The concern has wide ramifications in the German copper, coal and sugar industries."

PLANT COVERED 20 ACRES.

Agent Here Expects Reports Today —Other Disastrous Explosions.

Adolph Kuttroff of Kuttroff, Pickhardt & Co., 128 Duane Street, American representatives of the Badische Anilin-fabrik, said last night that the nitrate plant of the German dye works covered twenty acres and employed approximately 8,000.

He said that there were several plants, one of which was devoted exclusively to the production of dyes. This plant is near Ludwigshafen and employs about 8,500 men.

"As soon as I read accounts in the newspapers," said Mr. Kuttroff, "I asked that information be cabled as soon as possible. I expect to have some information tomorrow.

"I should judge from cabled reports that the explosion occurred in the nitrate buildings, which are two to three miles from the soda works. The ammonia plants are not so far away."

Property loss estimated at more than $11,000,000 was caused by an explosion of munitions on Black Tom Island, in New York Harbor, early on the morning of July 30, 1916. The concussion shook Manhattan Island so severely that windows were broken and cornices jarred loose from buildings. In January, 1917, followed the explosion of the munitions plant of the Canadian Car and Foundry Company, at Kingsland, N. J., with a loss of $1,500,000.

When the shell-loading plant of T. A. Gillespie & Co. at Morgan, near Perth Amboy, N. J., was demolished by an explosion in October, 1918, 94 lives were lost. In May of the same year 100 men were killed and 300 injured in an explosion that destroyed the Oakdale plant of the Aetna Chemical Company at Pittsburgh.

About 1,266 were killed in the explosion of the munitions ship Mont Blanc in the harbor of Halifax in December, 1917.

"All the News That's Fit to Print."

The New York Times.

THE WEATHER
Partly cloudy today; Monday unsettled; probably showers.
Temperature yesterday—Max. 82.7 min. 65.
For full weather report see Page 23.

VOL. LXXII....No. 23,962.   ....   NEW YORK, SUNDAY, SEPTEMBER 2, 1923.   Including Rotogravure Section in two parts—Book and Magazine Sections.   FIVE CENTS In Manhattan, Bronx and Brooklyn | TEN CENTS

GREAT EARTHQUAKE AND FIRE RAVAGE TOKIO AND YOKOHAMA; MANY PERISH, BUILDINGS COLLAPSE; SURVIVORS FLEE IN PANIC; ITALY SEIZES TWO MORE ISLANDS; LEAGUE TAKES UP THE CASE

COAL STRIKE FORCES 100 PER CENT. TIE-UP; RECESS IN PARLEYS

All of 158,000 Miners, Except Maintenance Men, Drop Tools and Quit.

DISPUTANTS CONFER AGAIN

Meet With Pinchot for Half an Hour and Then Adjourn Until Wednesday.

GOVERNOR MORE HOPEFUL

Expects Rest to Help His Cause, and Meanwhile Asks Expression of Public Opinion.

Special to The New York Times.

HARRISBURG, Pa., Sept. 1.—There is a total suspension of work today in the anthracite coal fields. Reports received here by anthracite operators and miners indicated that all but 4,000 of the 158,000 hard coal miners had walked out. Those who remained to work are the maintenance men whose duty it is to keep the mines free of water and gas and to prevent cave-ins.

Representatives of the operators and the miners met Governor Pinchot for half an hour today and decided to reconvene on Wednesday at 2 P. M. The Governor expressed himself as very much encouraged by the willingness of both sides to meet him again and issued a statement declaring that as the disputants would spend the recess getting over the situation, each from its own point of view, "this seems to me like a good time for the people to consider their own interests also, and to make their will known through the fullest public discussion."

After pointing out the hardships caused to the public by a coal strike the Governor said he welcomed the breathing space for the hard-pressed leaders on both sides and urged them to use it "in acquiring a realizing sense of the public point of view."

"This is not a private quarrel," he added. "Neither miners nor operators have any right to disregard or overlook the public suffering which would follow a prolonged strike. The patience of the people is very near its end. We have seen it pushed beyond endurance before and we have seen the results."

Neither the Governor nor the disputants would make any definite statement as to the proceedings in the conference today. It is understood that both sides remained firm in their attitude as expressed by their formal replies yesterday. None of the leaders would hazard a guess as to how long the suspension which began last midnight would last.

Undercurrent of Hopefulness.

The check-off of union dues, arbitration and a wage increase still bar the way to peace in the anthracite dispute. Despite the pessimistic attitude of the leaders on both sides—a "professional pessimism" it was called—the first breath of optimism that has entered into the situation for weeks was noted today. There was no general hilarity around the miners and operators' headquarters at the Penn Harris Hotel but there was an indefinable undercurrent of hopefulness that had not previously existed. The official attitude of both sides and operators was "no progress," but next Wednesday's conference is the ray of hope on which both sides cling.

The following basis for a possible agreement was indicated today. Elimination of the check-off demand by the miners if the operators drop their demand that all future wage disputes shall be arbitrated; the 10 per cent. wage increase to stand for contract miners and some adjustment that would give the day men a larger actual increase to be made, and a two-year agreement.

Those who have been following the negotiations would not be surprised to see a new contract drawn up with the foregoing features comprising its main essentials. In that demand for the check-off, the miners encounter the refusal of the operators. The latter are willing to grant the 10 per cent. wage increase suggested by Governor Pinchot if arbitration is agreed to as a permanent method of arranging contracts. There is a feeling prevalent here that if the miners drop their demand for the check-off the operators will forego their desire for arbitration. The miners want it to last one year. A compromise of two years is possible. The miners are vigorous in their insistence that the day men, 90,000 of whom earn between $4.20 and $5.00 a day, shall receive more than a 10 per cent. increase. This point may be settled by granting the day men an actual dollar and cents increase to equal the per cent. granted to the contract workers.

This does not mean that miners and operators will necessarily return to Governor Pinchot on Wednesday and immediately agree on a contract. Protracted negotiations are likely. But the Governor is hopeful of a successful termination of the negotiations and so are those close to him.

The miners and operators met the Governor at 9:25 o'clock this morning and adjourned with him for half an hour, after which they left town, scattering to their various homes and headquarters.

Continued on Page Six.

Policeman Slain as He Orders Four to Move; Eyewitness Gives Names of Two Assailants

The list of policemen murdered in the performance of their duty was increased last night when Patrolman John E. Egan of the Westchester Station was shot three times and killed at the northwest corner of Benson and Tremont Avenues, the Bronx.

With the murders of Patrolman Reynolds and Romanelis still unsolved and apparently no clue to the identity of the man who killed them at Sixty-fourth Street and Second Avenue several months ago, the police were spurred into new activity last night by the news of Patrolman Egan's murder.

Arrests of the men implicated in the Egan murder are expected momentarily by the police. They say they have the names of two, one of whom did the killing.

Through the aid of a young woman who was passing when the policeman was murdered, detectives of the Sixth Inspection District, working under Acting Captain Henry Bruckman, learned what occurred.

Egan was doing special duty in plain clothes, an assignment that carries a roving commission to patrol anywhere within the precinct on the watch for vice, gambling or disorderly persons. The patrolman was on the southeast corner of Benson and Tremont Avenues shortly after 10 o'clock when he saw four men standing on the northwest corner.

As he noticed them they started scuffling among themselves, but whether or not any earnest could not be learned.

He walked over to them and ordered them to leave. As he did so, one of the men, whose name was given to the police, struck the patrolman a blow in the face with his flat. As the four men sprang at him Egan threw off his coat and fought back. He shouted to the men that they were under arrest and drew his pistol. One of the four men, whose name also was given to detectives by the young woman, snatched the revolver away from him and fired.

As the patrolman turned toward him the man fired again and fired again. Egan, falling, had turned slightly away from the man and the third bullet, the one with which he believed to have killed him, struck him in the left side of the back.

As the patrolman fell the four men turned and ran, the man with the patrolman's pistol still holding the weapon. In the excitement that followed no one noticed which way they went. It is believed they ran a short distance and then hired a taxicab.

Patrolman Egan had been a policeman for a little more than a year. About three months ago he received commendation for a spectacular bit of police work when while riding a Police Department horse he chased a runaway horse for almost five miles through Bronx streets and was injured while bringing the runaway to a halt. He was 24 years old and lived at 1222 Boynton Avenue, the Bronx, with his wife and two children.

PHYSICIANS DENY HYLAN HAS CANCER

Dr. John J. McGrath, President of Bellevue Hospital, Visits the Mayor.

PATIENT NEEDS A REST

Resting Comfortably, but Must Remain in Bed a Week or Ten Days.

Special to The New York Times.

SARATOGA SPRINGS, N. Y., Sept. 1.—Dr. John J. McGrath, President of Bellevue and Allied Hospitals, who returned on Friday from Europe, where he studied the advances recently made by German physicians in the treatment of cancer, arrived here today to examine Mayor John F. Hylan of New York City.

Dr. McGrath, after an examination this afternoon, denied that the latter was suffering from cancer. In answer to a specific question as to whether the Mayor had cancer, Dr. McGrath said:

"There is no indication of any such condition."

Dr. McGrath also said that the laboratory tests that had been made did not indicate any condition of that character. He said he made a thorough examination of Mayor Hylan and would make another examination tomorrow.

"The condition of the throat has improved and the Mayor's general condition is satisfactory," he added. "The fever is decreasing and the pulse is not rapid and is of good quality. Altogether Mayor Hylan's condition is quite satisfactory."

Finds No Serious Ailment.

The arrival of Dr. McGrath revived reports that Mayor Hylan was suffering from some affliction, promoted merely an inflammation by the attending physicians, was worrying the members of his family. Rumors that the Mayor's throat trouble indicated the possibility of a serious ailment have been denied by Dr. George P. Comstock, the Saratoga physician who has been attending Mayor Hylan since the beginning of his illness, and by Dr. Harmon Smith, the throat specialist, who was called to examine the Mayor on Tuesday.

Both Dr. Comstock and Dr. Smith insisted on Friday that the condition of the Mayor was greatly improved, commenting upon the persistent reports that the Mayor was suffering from an incurable throat infection. Dr. Smith then said:

"Absolutely nothing to it. Mayor Hylan has no disease of an incurable nature."

Dr. Comstock also denied tonight that there was any suspicion that Mayor Hylan was suffering with cancer. "It is absolutely out of it. The Mayor is suffering from influenza which has caused a throat inflammation."

Dr. Comstock said that Dr. McGrath arrived in Saratoga at 4:30 this evening and that he left word for him to examine Mayor Hylan without waiting for him. He could be understood that Dr. McGrath examined the Mayor generally, and in the course of this examination made an examination of his throat. He said he talked with Dr. McGrath later and that Dr. McGrath said there was nothing of cancer in the Mayor's throat infection.

Despite the arrival of Dr. McGrath,

Continued on Page Seventeen.

ALIENS ON FOUR SHIPS TOO SOON TO ENTER

Most of 1,896 Who Arrived Before Instead of After Midnight Must Go Back.

CAPTAINS DISPUTE TIME

Say Chronometers Showed Midnight Before Arrival—Estonia Reported 15 Seconds Early.

Because the immigration authorities say that four steamships reached Quarantine on Friday before midnight, the 1,896 immigrants on board will be counted in the virtually exhausted August quota, which means that nearly all of them will have to return to their native land.

Commissioner of Immigration Henry H. Curran telephoned from Ellis Island to Commissioner General of Immigration Husband at the Department of Labor yesterday in Washington and asked him if he intended to enforce the quota law on the four steamships, which arrived a few minutes before Sept. 1. The Commissioner General said yesterday that it was deplorable that these immigrants had to be refused to their native countries, but he admitted that he could not set aside the ruling of the Commissioner General. He pointed out that the immigrants will have to suffer because of the eagerness on the part of the steamship owners to race their ships into Quarantine in order to land the passengers before the quota is exhausted.

Seven Ships Jammed in Channel.

The Commissioner again saluted to the danger of having a number of steamships in such a narrow channel jockeying for a place of vantage to start in the race for Quarantine at midnight. In the case of one ship, the Greek liner Byron, the captain had to go full speed astern to avoid ramming a vessel ahead of him. After shifting his helm he had to go full speed ahead to prevent another vessel hitting his ship on the starboard quarter. At 11:45 P. M. Friday seven ships were in the race for Quarantine. They were the Estonia of the Baltic-American Line at 11:59.45, fifteen seconds before midnight.

The four steamships within the official observers eyes crossed the imaginary line between Fort Wadsworth and Fort Hamilton before midnight on Friday were the Esperanza of the Ward Line, 11:55 P. M.; the Braga of the Fabre Line, 11:56; the Gryck steamship Byron, 11:57, and the Estonia of the Baltic-American Line at 11:59.45, fifteen seconds before midnight.

The Esperanza from Cuba and Mexico brought 40 Spaniards, 3 Greeks and 46 Portuguese who are above the August quota and will have to go back by the Commissioner General's ruling. One of the Greeks was here before the July quota and arrived too late. His wife gave birth to a son on the immigration barge that was conveying her to Ellis Island from the ship, and the family went back to Cuba. The Fabre liner Braga from Naples brought 7 Africans, 62 Albanians, 1 Egyptian, 21 Greeks, 16 Italians and 1 Palestinian. The Ponsler's quota from Albanians is only fifty-eight, so those a surplus of forty even if the Braga had reached Quarantine after midnight. The Greek liner Byron from Patras and other ports in the Levant had 464 Greeks, 219 Turks, 25 Albanians, 9

Continued on Page Three.

MORE GREEK ISLANDS SEIZED

Italian Forces Occupy Paxos and Antipaxos, Strategic Points.

GREEK STEAMER FIRED ON

Channel Is Under Blockade, Italian Submarine Commander Tells Merchantman.

NO MORE SEIZURES LIKELY

But Rome Orders Other Naval Units to Lower Adriatic Ready for Action.

ROME, Sept. 1 (Associated Press).—The small islands of Paxos and Antipaxos, part of the Ionian group, in the vicinity of Corfu, have been occupied by the Italians.

The Government here has officially announced that the occupation of Corfu probably will be the limit of Italian advances for the enforcement of sanctions and that consequently there probably will be a short breathing spell.

A message received by way of Corfu says the Greek ships at Phaleron have been moved to Salamis.

Italian naval units which had been stationed at Spezia and Venice, however, now are steaming for Southern Adriatic waters in full war status, and eight transports are held in readiness in case there are further eventualities.

Official announcement was made this afternoon that there was no truth in the reports circulated in foreign countries that Italian forces had occupied either the island of Samos or of Crete.

A dispatch from Brindisi states that the Greek steamship Attmonitos, which had been held up there, was allowed to proceed toward Corfu, but was required to fly the Italian flag at its mainmast. Three Greek journalists expelled from Italy were on board the vessel.

Say Bombardment Was Necessary.

The Greek authorities at Corfu were blamed by the Italian Government in a semi-official statement for the necessity of the firing at Corfu yesterday.

The statement said that the Italian Admiral did not fire until he had given the Greek authorities time in which to effect the evacuation of refugees and other civilians from the old fortress. This statement estimated the number of wounded at ten.

"It was necessary," said the statement, "to fire with small-calibre guns against the fortress at Corfu, following the refusal of the Greek authorities to hoist a white flag after they had been requested by the Italian authorities to do so, according to the customs of International law, as yet and persons within the fortress were wounded."

Reports Calm in Corfu.

The occupation was effected with the greatest military discipline and perfect calm, according to reports reaching Rome. All the Italian units maintained strict order and took their positions with marked regularity.

The Italian naval squadron arrived off Corfu yesterday morning and the various units took their positions around the island so as to prevent any departure.

Admiral Solari, commanding the Italian troops at Corfu, has addressed a proclamation to the people of the island, outlining the causes and nature of the occupation, which he says is of a temporary and peaceful character. It will continue, he says, until the island. At the question in issue the settlement of the question which called forth the conflict between Italy and Greece.

The proclamation is along the lines of Premier Mussolini's statement of Italy's representative abroad. In this speech the Premier, declaring that the Greek Government had replied to "unjust demands of Italy" in terms substantially equivalent to a complete rejection, asserted that by the occupation of Corfu Italy had no intention of committing an act of war and was only seeking "to safeguard her prestige and manifest her unshakable determination to obtain the reparation due her in conformity with custom and international law." The occupation, he said, was a temporary measure.

Italy Halls Mussolini's Action.

Premier Mussolini's decision that the Greek reply to Italy's demands could not be accepted has been received everywhere with the greatest enthusiasm. Many supporters of the Government's course point out that the Allies always insisted on ample indemnity when a French or British subject was killed in Germany, and that Italy has now felt by asking the sum she thinks the situation warrants.

Signor Mussolini continues to receive innumerable telegrams from civil and patriotic organizations of all classes expressing indignation at the massacre of the Italian mission and expressing confidence in his Government and in the steps he can take to preserve the dignity and prestige of the nation. Various officials assert as amount he is a plebiscite which records the chief of the Government unlimited confidence.

In some quarters it is urged that Greece should make a quick settlement to avoid an increase in the amount of Italian reparations which would be caused if armed occupation were necessary.

What is regarded here as the hostile

Continued on Page Three.

AREA OF EARTHQUAKE DAMAGE IN JAPAN.

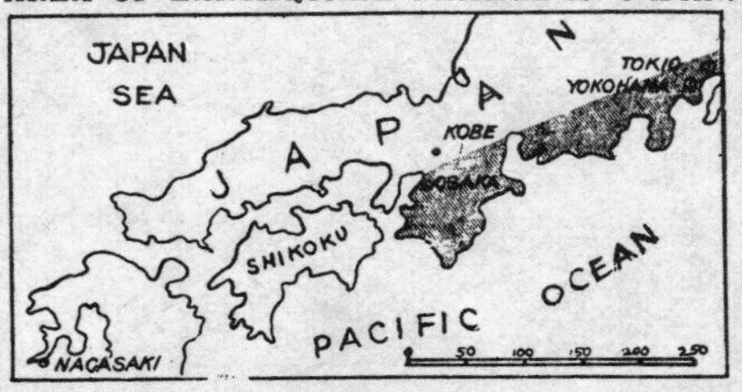

Coolidge Cables Sympathy to Emperor of Japan; Navy Orders Vessels to Yokohama for Relief

WASHINGTON, Sept. 1.—President Coolidge tonight addressed to Emperor Yoshihito of Japan a message of sympathy on the part of himself and the American people for the sufferers from the earthquake in Japan.

The President's message read:

At the moment when the news of the great disaster which has befallen the people of Japan is being received, I am moved to offer you in my own name and that of the American people the most heartfelt sympathy, and to express to your Majesty my sincere desire to be of any possible assistance in alleviating the terrible suffering of your people.

Orders were given tonight to the American Asiatic squadron to rush ships to Yokohama to assist in relief measures.

Admiral Anderson, commanding the fleet, was instructed to use all possible speed in dispatching the vessels and their commanders to render every aid possible.

The Asiatic fleet is now near Port Arthur, and Admiral Eberle, Chief of Naval Operations, said it was probable that Admiral Anderson had already dispatched a squadron of destroyers to Yokohama, where an American naval hospital is located. He added, however, that in order to assure the presence of American relief ships there, specific orders were dispatched.

LEAGUE OF NATIONS CALLS FOR TRUCE

Council Enters Greco-Italian Controversy on Athens' Appeal—Hears Spokesmen.

ITALY SEEKS MORE TIME

Salandra Questions Right of Geneva to Act and Gains Delay Till Tuesday.

GENEVA, Sept. 1 (Associated Press).—The Council of the League of Nations today decided to take up the Greco-Italian controversy immediately and expressed the hope that meanwhile the two countries would commit no acts of such a nature as to aggravate the situation.

The communication from Greece submitting the crisis to the League was received today at the League headquarters, thus automatically bringing the conflict before the Council.

Antonio Salandra, the Italian representative, announced that he had received no instructions from his Government and asked that the session be adjourned until he could hear from Rome. In the meantime, he said, he wanted to inquire whether the Council was competent to take up the question in view of the fact that it already was before the Council of Ambassadors in Paris.

Nicholas Politis, the Greek spokesman, was heard immediately after the session under the Presidency of Viscount Ishii, of Japan. Greece's former Foreign Minister made a good impression, and the opinion in League circles tonight is that the grave question comes before the Council in shape favorable for settlement.

Acts Under Articles 12 and 15.

M. Politis, in explaining the Greek demand for intervention by the League, said that his Government had invoked only Articles 12 and 13 of the covenant, although it might also have invoked Article 10, which provides for a blockade, upon the certainty that the covenant his Government, he declared, omitted this article because it desired to approach the question in the most amicable spirit possible. It announced that Greece would accept whatever decision the Council might make for a settlement. Lord Robert Cecil, of the British delegation, declared there was no doubt of the competence of the Council to deal with the conflict, nor of its duty to do so.

Hjalmar Branting, the Swedish representative, agreed with Lord Robert and said that the whole world was looking to the League for action. Then Signor Salandra said that he wanted simply to reserve the right to speak again on the question of the competence of the League after he had heard from his Government.

The Council adopted unanimously a resolution to the effect that, while it agreed to a short adjournment so that an examination of the question might be made, it hoped that the two countries would refrain in the meantime from any act of a nature to aggravate the situation.

As he came out of the meeting, Signor Salandra, said that he hoped to have word from his Government by Tuesday.

"It is ridiculous," asserted Signor

Continued on Page Two.

FEAR FOR AMERICANS IN EARTHQUAKE ZONE

Many Trading in Tokio Live in Yokohama, Occupying the Higher Sections of Town.

RED CROSS OFFERS ITS AID

American Naval Hospital in Yokohama May Help If It Survives.

WASHINGTON, Sept. 1.—Reports of a severe earthquake and fire in Yokohama, Japan, caused unusual anxiety here today because of the large number of Americans who make their home in that city.

It is estimated that more than 1,000 citizens of the United States who have business connections in Tokio live in the section reported affected by the earthquake. More than half of all the Americans in that part of Japan are said to have chosen Yokohama as their place of residence. It is only a half hour's ride from the capital.

The American Red Cross, through John Barton Payne, its Chairman, offered to the Japanese Embassy the aid of the organization in rescue work made necessary by the earthquake in Japan. The sympathy of the Red Cross was extended.

The offer of assistance was cabled to Tokio by the Embassy. In the event Red Cross officials said the aid probably would be in the form of financial advances to the Japanese Red Cross, that organization being described as highly efficient and well able to take care of the situation. It was recalled by these officials that at the time of the San Francisco fire the Japanese Red Cross was among the first organizations to offer aid.

Continued on Page Two.

FIRES RAGE IN WHOLE TOKIO DISTRICT

All Yokohama Burning and Neighboring Towns Are Involved as Water Systems Are Wrecked—Business Suspended.

TREMENDOUS LOSS OF LIFE AND PROPERTY INDICATED

700 Are Killed in the Asakusa Tower—People Flee to Ships—Earthquake Centres in the Extinct Volcano of Fuji—Cables Interrupted.

SAN FRANCISCO, Sept. 1 (Associated Press).—Tokio is afire, many buildings of the city have collapsed, the water system is destroyed, the loss of life is heavy, all traffic has been suspended and the flames are spreading to surrounding towns, following a terrific earthquake, according to a message received here tonight by the Radio Corporation of America from the superintendent of the company's station at Tomioka.

[Other messages report that the whole city of Yokohama is burning and that great loss of life and property has been caused.]

The Radio Corporation's superintendent said he obtained his information from a morning paper at Sendai, a large seacoast town about 200 miles north of Tokio. Tomioka is about 144 miles north of Tokio.

Casualties Very Heavy.

The message said:

"Severe earthquake Tokio and vicinity at noon yesterday. Railway stations near Tokio collapsed and no means to reach Tokio. Heavy damage in Tokio. Water system destroyed and many big buildings collapsed, with outbreak of fire in various places.

"Flames spreading toward Asakusa, Kanda, Hongo, Fukagawa and Shitaya. Heavy casualties reported. Rumor afloat that all traffic suspended throughout Tokio. Refugees running in all directions.

"Principal buildings burned down are Matuzakaya Department Store at Ueno; twelve-story tower at Asakusa; Manseibaishi railway station at Kaije; the building occupied by the Peers' Club, and the Tokio arsenal.

"Many disastrous accidents have been reported, a number of trains running to Tokio having been wrecked during the quake. It is also reported that a severe tidal wave struck the coast at Shizuoka. No damage western side of Shizuoka."

[This message was probably filed in Japan after midnight, which would make the "yesterday" mean Saturday.]

700 Killed When Tower Falls.

At 8:20 o'clock tonight the Radio Corporation received a message from its station at Tomioka which said that 700 persons were killed when the twelve-story tower at Asakusa fell.

Many boats sank in a tidal wave in the Bay of Suruga. Most of the houses at Numazu collapsed, the message said.

In Tokio the Imperial Railway station was swept by fire and the Imperial Theatre collapsed. The railway station at Ueno burned.

It is rumored that the Imperial Palace is in danger.

The reports from Suruga and Namuza indicate that the earthquake was widespread. Suruga is 62 miles southwest of Tokio; Numazu is 84 miles from Tokio in the same direction. Ueno is about 30 miles west of Tokio. Numazu is a resort and the location of an Imperial villa. The population is 13,000.

The Asakusa Tower which collapsed is 220 feet high. It stood in Asakusa Park, near the "Floral Hall," an establishment devoted to entertainment features. The tower's top commanded an extensive view of the streets surrounding the park.

Prince Regent Hirohito and his household are safe, according to a message received by the Radio Corporation from its station at Tomioka.

Tokio Refugee Tells of Disaster.

The Radio Corporation of America tonight also received from its station at Tomioka a first-hand story of the earthquake and fire in Tokio from a refugee. The refugee said that at the first shock fires broke out at various places in the city.

The flames originated in the Mitsukoshi Department Store and spread to the Metropolitan Police Board's building and the Imperial Theatre. These were burned to the ground, as were many other large buildings.

The city, the refugee said, is still in flames and the fire is spreading from Senju [the northern tip of the city] to Shinagawa [the extreme southern point]. The flames can be seen seven miles away from Tokio.

All railway bridges are destroyed and in many places there is no traffic at all.

The refugee said the number of dead and injured was incalculable.

All Yokohama Ablaze.

A message received earlier in the day by Radio Corporation said the entire city of Yokohama was afire and numerous casualties had occurred as a result of a conflagration which broke out after the severe earthquake shock.

The message, from the Japanese radio station at Iwaki, follows:

"Conflagration subsequent to severe earthquake at Yokohama at noon today (Saturday). Practically whole city ablaze. Numerous casualties."

The Radio Corporation announced here at 9:20 A. M. that all connection with Japan had been lost. Word from Japan received shortly before that hour said that apparently all land lines in the northeastern section of Japan were down.

The Postal Telegraph Company said it was making an effort to reach Tokio by way of Manila and Shanghai.

At 10 A. M., the cable department of the Postal Telegraph Company said cable connections between Guam and Tokio had been interrupted.

Meagre reports received here indicate the earthquake in Japan has been most severe on the eastern coast of Hondo, the principal island of the Japanese archipelago. The range of the damage apparently is at least 300 miles, running from Osaka and Kobe in the south to Sendai in the north.

Native Houses Firetraps.

The locality of the present quake is the most thickly settled section of Japan.

Residents of San Francisco who have been in the Orient said that an earthquake now, if violent, would have more consequences than a similar quake would have had a few years ago, for the reason that there are so many foreign buildings whose collapse would endanger life.

The danger among native houses would be greatest from fire, it was said, because of the lightness of their construction and their inflammability.

Communication with Japan, interrupted by the earthquake at noon, Tokio time, today, was still virtually at a standstill twenty-six hours later. The only means of obtaining news from Japan since the shocks has been through the Tomioka station of the Radio Corporation, located in an isolated position 144 miles from Tokio.

Two big passenger liners plying between San Francisco and Far East points are believed to be in the harbor of Yokohama today. They are the President Pierce, operated by the Pacific Mail Steamship Company, and the Korea Maru, operated by the Toyo Kisen Kaisha.

Both vessels are bound for San Francisco. The Korea is due here on Sept. 18 and the President Pierce on Sept. 20.

People Flee to Boats.

NAGASAKI, Japan, Sept. 1.—A naval wireless message received at Saseho from Funanash says that there have been repeated earthquakes, accompanied by a severe rainstorm, in Tokio today.

Another message reports that fire has broken out in Yokohama and that the inhabitants are seeking refuge in the ships in the harbor.

Nearly All of Tokio Ablaze.

OSAKA, Japan, Sunday, Sept. 2 (Associated Press).—With the exception of the Shiba Road, the whole of Tokio is burning.

Part of the Imperial Palace at Tokio is reported to be ablaze.

An earthquake shock lasting over six minutes was felt here at noon today. It was accompanied by an "up and down movement." The shock stopped all clocks here.

Telephonic and telegraphic communication with Tokio has been interrupted. It is feared that the shock has had a serious effect in Tokio and that great damage has been done there, in Yokohama and Yokusuka.

According to information reaching the railway station all railway lines entering Tokio have been dislocated within a radius of 100 miles of the city.

The Tokaido railway line has been seriously damaged in several places.

Reports indicate that the earth shocks have been most violent in the districts surrounding Mount Fuji, which is a dormant volcano. Mount Fuji is about sixty miles southwest of Tokio.

According to the observatory at Osaka, the seismic tremor probably centred in the Zu Peninsula.

The seismograph reported tremors lasting nearly an hour and a half. Slight vibrations were felt again at 2:25 today.

Destructive Tremors Frequent.

Japan has about 1,500 earthquakes a year, or an average of four shocks a day, most of which are not violent. In Tokio a shock is felt on an average of once a week.

More or less destructive earthquakes occur in Japan on an average of once in every two years and a half. The greatest earthquake of the 230

A BIRDSEYE VIEW OF CROWDED TOKIO
© Newman Traveltalks & Brown & Dawson.

serious ones that have occurred since the fifth century was in 1707. It shook the entire southwestern portion of Japan over an extent of about 500 miles. It originated beneath the ocean and was followed by huge tidal waves.

On Dec. 23 and Dec. 24, 1854, there were two violent tremors, after which tidal waves crossed the Pacific Ocean in twelve hours and forty minutes, leaving traces on the tide gauge diagrams at San Francisco and San Diego.

Some of the most violent earthquakes in Japan were as follows:

684 A. D.—An area of about three square miles in Tosa was submerged.
869 A. D.—Earthquakes with tidal waves visited Mutsu; thousands killed.
1361—Severe earthquakes around Koyti.
1498—Quake at Tokaido killed 20,000; Hamana Lagoon was formed.
1596—Bungo, Kyushu, visited by a quake; 700 killed; Kyoti shaken.
1792—At Hizen. 15,000 killed.
1844—At Shinano, 12,000 killed.
1866—In Shanriku districts, 27,000 killed.

There are many large modern buildings in Yokohama. Among them are the Pacific Mail offices, the Toyo Kisen Kaisha offices, the American Express Building, Cook's (tourist) Building, Arthur & Bond, department store; banks, hotels and hospitals.

FEAR FOR AMERICANS IN EARTHQUAKE ZONE

Continued from Page 1, Column 6.

Madison Avenue, born and brought up in the Japanese city. There are about 1,000 British there and several hundred Frenchmen.

Basing his opinion merely on the somewhat meagre details that were available last night, Mr. Austin said he thought most of the foreigners and the richer Japanese probably would escape the disaster, as during this period of the year those who can afford it live at Karuizawa, a Summer resort, located about fifty miles up in the hills from Yokohama.

The American and British homes are located on a bluff, one or two of which put the city itself in a sort of valley between. Due to this, if sparks have not been carried to the higher part of the city, Mr. Austin was inclined to think the better residential section may have escaped. His own home is located on the bluff, as is the home of the late F. W. Horne, an American business leader of Yokohama. The Horne home is called "Temple Court," because it was fashioned after a famous Japanese temple. It is now owned by the principal shareholder of the chief Japanese steamship line, the Nippon Yusen Kaisha, and passengers on the line's vessels are frequently entertained there.

Fire Apparatus Inadequate.

Mr. Austin reported that Yokohama's fire-fighting apparatus is of the slenderest. He said it was only within the last few years that some pieces of modern fire-fighting equipment were added to the antiquated methods of the department there. The old hose employed furnished a stream something like a garden hose, and it was well nigh useless in fighting a fire of any dimensions. Although the homes of the foreigners and the richer natives are constructed

on more substantial lines, the native homes and even business structures are of flimsy construction and would quickly take fire. In connection with the inadequate fire protection, Mr. Austin pointed out that the earthquake that preceded the blaze undoubtedly had broken the mains, so that water would not be available for fighting the spread of the flames.

Most of the native houses, said Mr. Austin, were constructed with foundation posts set into grooved stones, so that when an earthquake occurred—a matter of frequent happening—the buildings would sway rather than fall. Mr. Austin and his wife reported having passed through many quakes of slight power, and told how the chief danger came from toppling chimneys. The residents of Yokohoma are warned to remain indoors during an earthquake, and when the warning is sounded the folks indoors, said Mr. Austin, usually posted themselves in doorways.

This, as his wife explained, was to get the benefit of the stouter supports of the doorways. Mrs. Austin said that occasionally the tumbling tiles of a

chimney would crash through the roof and down through the slight floors, but the frame of the doors would halt the flight of a chimney admirably.

Due to the frequency of earth tremors, said Mr. Austin, insurance against fire from earthquake was almost unobtainable.

Many American Firms There.

Among the American corporations owning buildings and plants in Yokohoma are the Standard Oil Company, the International Banking Corporation, which has a large structure there; F. W. Horne & Co., and the Sale-Frazer Company, importers and exporters, with a local office at 30 Church Street. The larger hotels are the Grand Hotel and the Oriental Palace which, presumably, suffered as they were located in the lower part of the city.

The city is the chief seaport of Japan, serving as an outlet for the sea for Tokio, which is located about eighteen miles northward. Yokohoma is on the west shore of the island of Hondo and, roughly, may be divided into three parts; Kwan-Nai, Kwan-Gwai and Minami-Yamati.

Kwan-Nai, facing the harbor, is the location of the business houses, the Prefecture, Post Office, hotels and the official buildings of the municipality. It is a medley of Japanese and Occidental architecture. The western part of the city is known as Kwan-Gwai, and is the native part, typically Japanese, with shrines, native theatres, homes and business shops.

Minami-Yamati, the third quarter of the city, is the home of the foreign residents, and is on the bluff overlooking the city proper. Another bluff, not quite so high, is located to the northwest of the city, and is called Nogeyama. There are the homes of the more wealthy of the Japanese, each house surrounded, as are the homes of the foreigners, by large gardens. These homes are, for the most part, of frame construction, however.

TROLLEYS IN AN ANCIENT SETTING—TOKIO
© Underwood & Underwood.

"All the News That's Fit to Print."

The New York Times.

VOL. LXXIV....No. 24,526. NEW YORK, THURSDAY, MARCH 19, 1925. TWO CENTS In Greater New York | THREE CENTS Within 200 Miles | FOUR CENTS Elsewhere in the U. S.

THE WEATHER

Rain today, colder tonight; tomorrow fair; strong westerly winds.
Temperature yesterday—Max., 56; min., 40.
For weather report see Page 42.

BREAKERS AND PALM BEACH HOTEL BURN; $2,500,000 BLAZE IN FLORIDA RESORT; GUESTS LOSE PROPERTY, TROOPS CONTROL

PANIC AS FLAMES START

Guests Rush Back to Breakers to Save Their Luggage.

LITTLE PROPERTY SAVED

Some Thrown From Windows, but Rush of Flames Makes the Loss Heavy.

10,000 WATCH FROM BEACH

Embers Fire Second Hotel—Royal Poinciana and Bradley Club Are Saved.

Special to The New York Times.

PALM BEACH, Fla., March 18.—Fire late this afternoon destroyed the famous Breakers Hotel, said to be the largest wooden structure in the world, wiped out the smaller Palm Beach Hotel and destroyed several other smaller buildings.

For a short time tonight it looked as if the Royal Poinciana Hotel and the noted Bradley Club might also be wiped out, but these were saved by the hard work of the firemen.

By nightfall all that remained to mark the site of the two burned hotels was seething masses of embers and a few blackened smokestacks.

There were reports of loss of life, particularly of an elderly couple said to be missing, but the reports were not confirmed.

Damage through the loss of the hotel and private property at the Breakers is estimated at $1,500,000. At the Palm Beach Hotel the damage is estimated at about $750,000.

According to the Palm Beach Fire Chief the blaze at the Breakers was started by an electrical appliance used by a guest there.

Tonight nearly 300 of the 500 guests at the Breakers, left without even so much as a change of clothing, are rummaging among piles of luggage rescued at the last moment in an effort to discover their own baggage.

Thousands of dollars' worth of valuable dresses, cash and jewelry were stolen from the hotel rooms, to which almost any one was permitted access through the absence of police fire lines.

It was said tonight that much of the jewelry owned by wealthy guests of the Breakers was in the concrete vault of the hotel and would be safe. Mrs. Jesse L. Livermore, wife of a New York broker, is reported to have had nearly a million dollars' worth of jewelry in the vault.

Many of the society people residing here have risen to the occasion by throwing open their homes to persons who could not obtain accommodation at the Royal Poinciana or Royal Danell Hotels, and in some cases they have even come forward with clothing and money.

Fire Started on Top Floor.

There were few persons in The Breakers when the fire started. William E. Hayes, the room clerk on duty, was alone in the office about 4 o'clock in the afternoon. He had just replied to a question from Mrs. Edward F. Hutton and Miss Billie Burke, who were seeking friends in the hotel, when a woman called him aside and whispered that she had smelled smoke on the top floor.

Without a word Hayes hurried up stairs in the southern wing, which was the direction from which the smoke was reported to have come, but he could find nothing. Seeing a light in the room of Mrs. William Hale Thompson, wife of a former Mayor of Chicago, who had been ill in bed several days, Hayes knocked at the door. There was no response. Mrs. Thompson had gone out for a walk.

But the smell of smoke coming from the room was strong and Hayes burst open the door. He found the inside of the room already ablaze, and hurrying downstairs notified the manager of the hotel, John Greene, and turned in a fire alarm. Then with a list of all the persons in the hotel known to be ill in bed, Hayes commandeered a squad of bell boys, went to the rooms occupied by sick people and removed them to a place of safety.

Among these were Mrs. M. J. Murphy of Detroit, Douglass Mabee of Saratoga, Mrs. W. H. Cowen of New York and a child of Mrs. E. E. Work of Cincinnati.

All this was done so quietly and with such dispatch that few people in the hotel knew that the place was afire until the sick had been removed. Then two women who had been sitting on the veranda sipping orangeade and playing mah jong saw smoke coming from the south wing and rushed into the lobby to give the alarm.

Meanwhile scores of persons on the beach had seen the smoke and hurried over. A fire brigade was recruited from bellboys, guests of the hotel, life guards and bathers, many of whom still were in bathing suits.

By this time the top floor, where the fire had started, was filled with smoke. The first thing the volunteer fire fighters did was to throw open all windows to let the smoke out. This created a draft and the fire, with a good thirty-mile wind right from the ocean, did the rest.

Fire extinguishers were turned upon

Continued on Page Three.

FLORIDA AND CAROLINAS Leave N. Y.: Seaboard Florida Limited, 3:20 P. M.; Orange Blossom Special, 12:45 A. M.; Floridian, 9:05 A. M.; Carolina-Florida Special, 3:10 P. M. Seaboard, 142 West [illegible] Street. Tel. [illegible]—Advt.

Military Are Put On Guard in Palm Beach; At Least Two Lives Reported Lost in Fire

PALM BEACH, Fla., March 18 (Associated Press).—Martial law was put into effect tonight by Governor Martin at the request of local authorities after police in West Palm Beach had captured two motor trucks and several automobiles loaded with valuables stolen from the ruins, arresting eight negroes and one white man.

State troops were at once placed on guard at all bridges between the resort and West Palm Beach. Before midnight the militiamen and police had rounded up more than a score of alleged looters in Palm Beach and West Palm Beach.

Most of the prisoners were negroes. They had jewels, money and clothing valued at many thousands of dollars belonging to those who had been driven from the hotels. Trunks, furniture and other articles valued at $50,000 were assembled under guards in a vacant space adjacent to the Palm Beach Hotel site.

An elderly man and woman, whose identity had not been learned, were burned to death in the Breakers Hotel in the fire that destroyed the two hotels.

Some of the local authorities expressed fear that the rapidly spreading flames had taken other toll of life.

SINCLAIR DEFENSE ASSAILS POLITICIANS

Littleton, in Opening, Refers to 'Senate Jungle Hunt' and 'Burning Plains' of Campaign.

LEASE CALLED NECESSARY

Court Hears Admiral Robison's Deposition, Which Is Relied Upon to Disprove Fraud.

Special to The New York Times.

CHEYENNE, Wyo., March 18.—Opening the defense side of the Teapot Dome case, Martin W. Littleton of New York, of counsel for Harry F. Sinclair and the Mammoth Oil Company, declared today that Mr. Sinclair was delighted that he had at last reached the sanctuary of the courts, after being "hunted through the fetid jungles of Senatorial scandals and chased across the plains of Presidential politics." He did not once refer to the Continental Trading Company phase of the case.

While Mr. Littleton was making the opening plea for Mr. Sinclair, Albert B. Fall, former Secretary of the Interior, who was subpoenaed by the Government but not called to the stand, was packing his grip for the return trip to Three Rivers, N. M.

Just before he departed Mr. Fall broke a silence of more than a year to make a reference to what he described as "wild charges and cheap attempts to make reputations by defamatory oratory." But he had nothing to say about the oil reserve leases or the part he had in making them. At the proper time, he intimated, he will break his long silence.

Fall Repeats That He Is Gratified.

"I have made no statement concerning the pending case for the cancellation of the Mammoth oil lease, nor about any other case, criminal or civil, concerning oil matters, since the cases were filed or indictments found," he said, "except, practically one year since, to the effect that I was gratified to know that the cases were finally in court, where rights of parties and witnesses, both for the Government and the private parties, could and would be respected and protected without regard to wild charges or cheap attempts to make reputations by defamatory oratory.

"All these cases are yet pending either here, in California or in Washington. Up to the present time the feeling of gratification that the cases were in the courts has in no sense been lessened.

"I have made no statement since being subpoenaed as a witness in this case now on trial as to what I might testify to when called upon the stand, nor that I should decline to testify. I have been notified that I would not be called as a witness and that I could return to my home. I shall return, maintaining until what I consider to be the proper time that silence which I have adhered to up to the present."

Opening for the defense, Mr. Littleton said that the Sinclair side of the Teapot controversy are gratified to find themselves at least in the "clear atmosphere of a court of justice." He asserted that in the making of the Teapot lease the controlling questions were "national defense and necessity."

"The only evidence before the Court that sends anything directly or indirectly from Mr. Sinclair or the Mammoth Oil Company into the hands of Mr. Fall," said Mr. Littleton, "is the $25,000 loan of June 1923."

The defense, he declared, would prove that this was a bona fide loan made long after Mr. Fall resigned from the Harding Cabinet and at a time when he had been retained by Mr. Sinclair to aid him in certain European negotiations. This loan, which he said was made in Liberty bonds, was not related in any way to any other bond transaction which the Government has alleged figures in the case.

After tracing the history of public land legislation up to the enactment of the general leasing law of 1920, Mr Littleton took up the executive order of May 31, 1921, which order, signed by President Harding, authorized the Secretary of the Navy to give over the management of the naval oil reserves to the Department of the Interior.

He declared there was not a scintilla

Continued on Page Five.

Popular price Matinee Today. Leon Errol Ziegfeld Greatest Louis the 14th. Ziegfeld Cosmopolitan Theatre.—Advt.

Matchless golf, baths and W. S. S. Water —nothing in Europe is better than The Greenbrier at White Sulphur.—Advt.

SHEPHERD IS JAILED ON MURDER CHARGE

Habeas Writ Is Dismissed and His Counsel Vainly Offers Bail Up to $500,000.

FAIMAN ONLY IN CUSTODY

Head of Medical School and Heir of McClintock Are Identified as Guests at Hotel Grill.

Special to The New York Times.

CHICAGO, March 18.—William Darling Shepherd, formally charged with the murder of young William McClintock for the purpose of inheriting the lad's $1,000,000 estate, occupied a cell in the County Jail tonight, but not until his attorneys had waged a bitter fight to spare him this humiliation.

Dr. C. C. Faiman, the bacteriologist who confessed he plotted with Shepherd to administer typhoid bacilli to young McClintock, and expected Shepherd would pay him $100,000 according to an alleged agreement for his share in the murder, was not served tonight with the capias issued upon the return of the indictment in which Dr. Faiman is jointly accused with Shephard. Instead, he will continue in the custody of the State's Attorney.

Shepherd was not required to plead to the indictment today. William Stewart of his counsel, however, announced that "our plea is, has been and will be not guilty."

Shepherd was led into the jail late in the day, ordered into a change of clothing, given a bath and put through the rest of the new prisoner's routine. Captain Wesley Westbrook, Warden of the jail, said Shepherd would be treated the same as any other prisoner.

Shepherd was formally placed under arrest in the courtroom of Chief Justice Hopkins, before whom the indictment was returned. The pending writ of habeas corpus sought for Shepherd's release was dismissed.

Shepherd's scheduled arraignment was delayed by sudden and decisive activity on the part of his attorneys, William Stewart and W. W. O'Brien. He was brought into the Court Building at 2 o'clock to appear before Chief Justice Hopkins in the hearing on the writ of habeas corpus obtained when he was first taken into custody by the State's Attorney.

Earlier in the day the forty-three-page indictment of twenty-two counts, charging him with the murder of his ward and benefactor, McClintock, had been returned by the Grand Jury and in the ordinary course of events the automatic collapse of the writ hearing would have been followed by Shepherd's arraignment on the murder charge.

The entire interest of the spectators was focused on Shepherd, although there had been some speculation as to how Dr. C. C. Faiman, his accuser and co-

Continued on Page Eight.

HOTEL BREVOORT—FRENCH RESTAURANT should not be confused with sale of "Brevoort Home." Hotel Brevoort not sold. Advt.

John McCormack Receives Art Treasures By the Will of a Riviera Admirer

Copyright, 1925, by The New York Times Company.
By Wireless to THE NEW YORK TIMES.

NICE, March 18.—An aged British resident of Mentone, Henry Osborne O'Hagen, whose musicals have formed a feature of the fashionable Riviera season among Anglo-American visitors and were staged regardless of expense, has made a will leaving the majority of his wonderful art treasures to John McCormack, the singer.

O'Hagen has been a devoted admirer of McCormack for many years. The art collection is said to be very valuable, one estimate valuing a single item at $500,000.

When the above dispatch was communicated to John McCormack at Muncie, Ind., by telephone last night Mr. McCormack expressed both surprise and doubt. He said that Mr. O'Hagen had been his friend since 1920, that he had sung at the O'Hagen villa and had been royally entertained by its master on the occasion of visits to Monte Carlo, but that he never had received any intimation that Mr. O'Hagen meant to remember him in his will.

Describing Mr. O'Hagen as an aged gentleman who is retired and whose business history he did not know, Mr. McCormack added that he never had heard that his friend was the possessor of any notable art collection, although he had seen in the villa one very fine piece of sculpture. Mr. McCormack did not know whether Mr. O'Hagen was wealthy, but was quite sure he was "not poor."

DAWES WILL CARRY SENATE RULE FIGHT BEFORE THE PEOPLE

Vice President Hopes to Arouse the Country to Need of Reform in Procedure.

WILL MAKE SIX SPEECHES

First Onslaught Will Be Before The Associated Press in This City in April.

Special to The New York Times.

WASHINGTON, March 18.—Vice President Dawes will carry to the country this Summer his issue against the Senate in favor of an amendment of the rules to enable it to expedite the transaction of public business.

No formal announcement of the plans of the Vice President in this respect has been issued. They are still formulative so far as detail is concerned.

The Vice President's decision was reached after conferences with certain of his friends, among them certain Senators who have assured him they intend to support resolutions to be brought forward in the Senate contemplating adoption of a closure rule and other rule changes intended to prevent undue delay in the consideration of legislative business.

The plan of the Vice President is to deliver about six speeches in which he will deal with the subject of Senate rules reform at considerable length. He will elaborate his position in detail and try to convince the country of the necessity for such reforms.

Mr. Dawes has several invitations to speak. He has not selected any of the places where he will discuss the rules issue except that the first address will be delivered before the annual meeting of The Associated Press in New York City on April 21. This speech will be given wide publicity, as present plans contemplate broadcasting it.

Although he has not chosen the places for his other speeches Mr. Dawes desires to deliver one in Indiana and another possibly in Ohio. The others probably will be heard in the region west of the Mississippi River.

The Vice President does not regard the rules issue as partisan. For that reason it is not his intention to make his "issue" speeches before partisan political gatherings, but before non-partisan meetings. He will emphasize his conviction that some form of closure rule should be adopted by the Senate. It is not understood to be his purpose to indicate in detail the changes which should be made, as he feels that this should be left to the judgment and wisdom of the Senate.

Mr. Dawes has received nearly a thousand telegrams and letters endorsing the stand he took in his inaugural address. These communications have come from all parts of the country, and while several have come from prominent men of affairs, he has received many from the "general run" of citizens.

The Vice President will leave Washington next Saturday for his home in Evanston. He will remain there until he starts for Boston, where he will deliver a speech April 19, the 150th anniversary of the Battle of Lexington. This speech will be historical and will be delivered in the Old North Church, where the lantern was hung during Paul Revere's ride. Mr. Dawes's great-great-grandfather, William Dawes Jr., was with Revere on that ride.

From Boston General Dawes will go to New York for the Associated Press luncheon and will return to Washington to attend the Gridiron Club dinner April 23. A few days later he will go to Evanston, and by that time he expects to have decided where he will deliver the remainder of his speeches dealing with the rules issue.

12,000 Are Made Homeless by Tokio Fire Which Burns 2,600 Buildings in the City

By WILFRID FLEISHER.

Copyright, 1925, by The New York Times Company.
By Wireless to THE NEW YORK TIMES.

TOKIO, March 18.—A great fire started in the suburbs of Tokio early this afternoon and later spread within the city limits. More than 2,600 houses had been destroyed by a late hour tonight, making fully 12,000 persons homeless in the overcrowded slum districts.

The fire originated in Nippori suburb, situated beyond the Uyeno station on the northern limit of the city, at 3 P. M. Fanned by a strong wind which was blowing toward the city, it spread with such rapidity that 600 houses were engulfed within two hours.

Although all the available fire apparatus in Tokio was rushed to the scene, the firemen were powerless to check the blaze, due to the insufficient water supply.

A second fire started at Ikegukuro, another northern suburb and destroyed sixty houses. A third fire occurred simultaneously at Oimachi, also a suburb, where fifty houses were burned.

The greatest confusion prevailed among the inhabitants of the surrounding districts, who rushed in all directions with their belongings to take them from the path of the advancing flames.

The number of casualties is unknown, but it is thought that some perished in the flames.

The sections where the fire raged were poor districts which were greatly overcrowded, and there is great distress among the refugees tonight.

Several famous Buddhist temples were destroyed in the Yanaka district, which is noted for its temples. The same districts were wiped out during the fire which followed the great earthquake and had been rebuilt mostly with wooden shacks. The glow of the fire was visible in the sky all over Tokio tonight.

Kellogg Cables Offer of Help.

WASHINGTON, March 18.—Secretary Kellogg cabled instructions late today to Ambassador Bancroft, at Tokio, directing that inquiry be made at once to ascertain if American assistance was needed in caring for those injured or made homeless by the fire there.

Let Davey Tree Surgeons examine your trees without cost. Phone Murray Hill 1517.—Adv.

LINCOLN MOTOR CARS. [illegible], 317 W. 57. Open [illegible]—Advt.

REPUBLICANS READY TO VOTE FOR TAX CUT; MAKE FINAL STAND

Will Lower Appropriations to Allow Reduction if Governor Slashes Them.

HE ACCEPTS CHALLENGE

Opponents Send List for Him to Pare Containing $15,000,000 Over Previous Estimates.

Special to The New York Times.

ALBANY, March 18.—With every realization that their fight is as good as lost, the Republican leaders in the Legislature tonight are making their final stand against Governor Smith's proposal for a 25 per cent. reduction in the personal income tax.

They threw up a barricade of figures this afternoon when they delivered into the Governor's hands a statement in which is embodied a list of appropriations, already pending, which they insist that he must dispose of before they can discuss tax reduction of any kind with him.

It was this statement, prepared at conferences held by the Republican leaders during the night hours and completed this afternoon, to which reference was made last night by Speaker McGinnies of the Assembly, as one which might pave the way for an agreement with the Executive with regard to tax reduction.

It included a list of appropriations aggregating $15,930,702 which his opponents insist the Governor had not included in his estimates of the State's needs when he made his public declaration by radio, backed by figures, to show that the 25 per cent. reduction would be feasible and that $4,000,000 would be left at the end of the fiscal year as a surplus after $8,500,000 had been slashed from the income tax.

Governor Accepts Challenge.

The statement was placed in the hands of Governor Smith early this evening by Senator Hewitt and Assemblyman Hutchinson, Chairmen of the Senate Finance and Assembly Ways and Means Committees, who acted as emissaries for their Republican colleagues. The statement had first been formally accepted by the majority Senators and Assemblymen at separate conferences held during the day.

The Governor, after receiving it, said he had no immediate comment to make, but that, after studying it, he would frame an answer which he hoped would be satisfactory to the Republicans. It may be stated that he is quite willing to accept this new challenge and confident that the plan he is working out will result in income tax reduction or at least show to the satisfaction of all the people that such a reduction can be made.

The Governor's proposal is winning more and more support among individual law makers of the opposition party. Today the entire Republican delegation from Westchester County, composed of five Assemblymen and two Senators, all Republicans, made it known that they will vote in support of reducing the income tax if the opportunity is given to them.

Word was said to have come from William L. Ward, the veteran Republican leader of Westchester, that the sensible thing to do was trail along with the Governor in the situation which has grown out of the stubborn opposition of a few Republican leaders in the Senate to his proposal.

Included in the figures submitted in the Republican statement is $9,000,000 for State aid to the rural schools, which admittedly cannot be used before May of next year.

Want Responsibility on Smith.

The Republican leaders made it clear that they wanted the Governor to veto the bill making this provision, thus assuming full responsibility for the appropriation being deferred until the next Legislature meets.

Governor Smith said this afternoon before the statement had been received by him that he was willing to do this and that it would take him just about three minutes to send it back to the Legislature with a veto message attached.

"Let the Governor assume the responsibility for making the cuts and we will do the rest," summarizes the attitude of the Republican leaders at this particular stage of the fight. They fully realize that the Governor has the popular side of the argument and that to turn down his demand will mean a loss of votes to them in the Assembly elections this Fall.

According to one of the Republican leaders the statement was sent to the Executive Chamber largely to put on record the stand they have taken to which they will be in a position to point

Continued on Page Six.

PINEHURST, N. C. 16 hours from New York. Many sport tournaments. Rest [illegible]—Advt.

950 KILLED, 2,700 INJURED BY TORNADO IN ILLINOIS, INDIANA AND MISSOURI; SEVERAL TOWNS WIPED OUT; FIRES RAGING

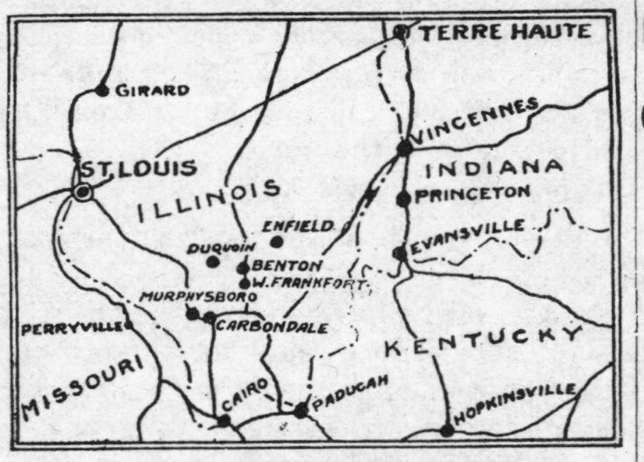

THE AREA SWEPT BY THE TORNADO.

CONFUSION REIGNS IN ZONE

Communications Are Cut, Water Mains Burst and Towns in Darkness.

HOSPITALS ARE CROWDED

Hundreds Are Buried in Debris and Check of Total Casualties Is Impossible.

1,000 IN WEST FRANKFORT

Parrish Has 497, Murphysboro 250, De Soto 150, Carmi 150, Princeton 100 and Gorham 87.

By The Associated Press.

CHICAGO, Ill., March 18.—A tornado tore through Southern Illinois today after lashing Eastern Missouri, and then caused considerable damage in Indiana before it died out to the northeast after collecting a reported toll of 3,631 persons dead or injured on the basis of estimates available tonight from the storm-swept regions, where communication was largely destroyed.

While darkness and prostrated wires made the collection of data difficult, estimates which came in through various sources with ever-increasing totals placed the total dead at 957 and the injured at 2,674 before midnight.

The latest list of casualties, with the towns listed in the order in which the storm struck them, is as follows:

Town.	Dead.	Injured.
Annapolis, Mo.	2	50
Biehle, Mo.	10	20
Altonburg, Mo.	1	10
Cape Girardeau, Mo.	12	50
Gorrin, Ill.	..	50
Murphysboro, Ill.	100	300
Gorham, Ill.	7	80
De Soto, Ill.	100	300
Bush, Ill.	5	60
Hurst, Ill.	6	40
West Frankfort, Ill.	350	650
Denton, Ill.	..	50
Logan, Ill.	2	30
Parrish, Ill.	75	422
Thompsonville, Ill.	8	40
McLeansboro, Ill.	17	80
Carmi, Ill.	2	25
Crossville, Ill.	1	10
Griffin, Ind.	75	75
Owensville, Ind.	75	100
Princeton, Ind.	100	200
Poseyville, Ind.	5	20
Elizabeth, Ind.	..	12
Totals	957	2,674

West Frankfort, Ill., a mining town, on the face of tonight's reports suffered the greatest loss of life, estimates of the dead and injured running as high as 1,000.

Murphysboro, thirty miles southwest of West Frankfort, with a population of 11,000, suffered severely, with a casualty list reported as high as 250. Great havoc was wrought to buildings in this city and fire broke out in the débris.

On reports of this situation an effort was made by Governor Len Small to send troops to Murphysboro, while relief trains and Red Cross workers prepared to depart from Chicago and St. Louis for the storm area.

Among the other towns and cities to report damage and loss of life were De Soto, Ill., with 150 casualties reported; Parrish, Ill., with all but three of a population of 500 reported either killed or injured; Princeton, Ind., with an estimate of 100 casualties; Griffin, Ind., with twenty; Gorham, Ill., with eighty-seven; Carmi, Ill., with 150, and Crossville, Bush, and Hurst, Ill., reporting serious damage and numerous casualties.

Frantic People Hunt for Friends.

Darkness descended over the desolated area shortly after the wind had twisted its way to the northeast, and the streets of the demolished towns were filled with frantic inhabitants clambering over the piles of wreckage seeking missing friends and relatives. From the recesses of the jumbled timbers came the cries of injured persons who were pinned beneath the wreckage, while the bodies of the dead could be seen far down in the débris, whence it was impossible to extricate them.

The twisting wind apparently assumed its dangerous proportions in Eastern Missouri soon after 1 o'clock this afternoon. It wiped out most of Annapolis, Mo., and then tore its way across the Mississippi River into Illinois, apparently lifting its devastating force and spreading out like a river delta until the various twisters descended some twenty-five miles east of the Mississippi.

It was around 3 o'clock when the tornado again touched earth with its mighty swish, swinging through Murphysboro and De Soto and laying those places waste in the twinkling of an eye. The wind rushed on close to earth for fifteen or twenty miles, and then apparently lifted until it came to Carmi, Ill., near the Indiana line. After taking its toll in that region the storm again rose, only to descend once more twenty miles from the State line at Princeton, Ind.

From the region of Princeton the tornado apparently died out as it went on toward Indianapolis.

In all the ruined towns and cities all the inhabitants who escaped serious injury or death turned out at once to rescue the injured, recover the dead and fight any fires that might result from the wrecking of buildings.

The churches and schoolhouses were turned into hospitals and morgues, and despite the difficulties faced by the rescuers, hundreds of persons were gathered into these places of refuge before darkness settled over the scene.

Where [illegible]

DRY HOPES KILLED BY SENATOR WHITLEY

Monroe Republican Continues Opposition to Wales-Jenks Enforcement Bill.

IT IS FAVORABLY REPORTED

But With Four Senators Opposed Supporters Cannot Gain the Necessary Majority.

Special to The New York Times.

ALBANY, March 18.—The Wales-Jenks Prohibition Enforcement bill, which has passed the Assembly, was reported out today by the Senate Codes Committee, the vote standing 6 to 5. Two Republican members, Senators Whitley of Monroe and Lipowicz of Erie, were recorded in the negative.

Developments in the Senate today point conclusively to the defeat of the measure, despite the tremendous effort that has been made by Chairman Morris of the Republican State Committee, Lieut. Gov. Lowman and other "dry" Republican leaders in the supper house to whip a sufficient number of votes in line for the bill. The failure of United States Senator Wadsworth to lend his influence to that purpose is held responsible by the Anti-Saloon League for failure of the drive.

The bill had its first setback the moment it was reported. Senator Knight urged that it be advanced to third reading. At once Senator Courtlandt Nicoll of New York County was out of his seat protesting. The one objection necessary to send the bill into Committee of the Whole and thus retard its progress was interposed by him at a time when a dozen Democrats were prepared to perform the same service.

Chairman Morris spent hours yesterday trying to win over the one Republican vote lacking to give the necessary majority of twenty-six to see the bill through. He admitted failure.

One of the four "wet" Republican Senators, James L. Whitley of Monroe, who had been singled out as the one most likely to yield to persuasion, settled for good and all today where he stands. He filed a brief with the Codes Committee in which he set forth beyond equivocation his opposition to the measure and his determination to oppose it at every stage. The other "wet" insurgents are Senators Nicoll, Karle of Queens and Lipowicz. Senator Whitley said in his brief:

"In order that my attitude on this proposed legislation may be understood I desire to express my views on the two bills before us. I have no apologies to make to the Anti-Saloon League and others advocating these measures. I believe if the time consumed in consideration of these bills were used in considering more important legislation we would be performing our duty to the people of the State. There never has been any doubt as to my attitude on this legislation. In 1923 it was my privilege to vote for the repeal of a similar law. This fact was known to the voters in my district. I was not nominated and elected to the office of Senator by sham or misrepresentation.

"The Volstead act is now the law of this State; every city, town and village is subject to all of its provisions. The enactment of this proposed legislation will give us more law but no more enforcement. It may be asked, if it is now the law, what harm can come if the State re-enacts it?

"We had a similar law on our statute books in 1921 and before the signature of the Governor who signed it was dry the Anti-Saloon League began to pass the hat for funds to secure the passage of legislation authorizing cities, towns and villages to enact similar legislation for the subdivisions of the State.

"You can prevent a man from stealing by tying his hands behind, but you cannot make him honest; neither can you secure enforcement of prohibition by passage of laws. The enactment of this law will go further in increasing the most scandalous corruption and scandalous contempt for law than we are witnessing under the Volstead law. It will only multiply the number of spies, pretenders, extortionists, blackmailers and hypocrites.

"Why should I, for the support and applause of the Anti-Saloon League, concur in its enactment? There are people whose moral code for public regulation is concerned solely with the enactment of this law, and they have no time for any other law. Their standard of personal respectability and honesty in public service is prohibition. Their only requirement as to qualification of a legislator is that he vote dry and thus close further examination of his record. There are many sincere advocates of State enforcement, but I know of many, in and out of the Legislature, whom, when I hear them cry out for enforcement, I feel inclined to tap on the hip."

When you think of Writing Think of Whiting.—Advt.

TAXI RULE BY POLICE VIRTUALLY ASSURED

Aldermen's Committee on Laws Votes for It After Spirited Public Hearing.

CORRUPTION IS INSINUATED

Foe of Yellow Company Declares $175,000 in Stock Went "a Certain Way."

Mayor Hylan's bill, transferring the licensing of taxicabs and their drivers from the Bureau of Licenses to the Police Department, was advanced a long step toward adoption last night, when the Committee on Local Laws of the Aldermanic branch of the Municipal Assembly voted to report it favorably out of committee for action by the board.

The measure already has passed the Board of Estimate branch of the Municipal Assembly. It virtually is assured of a large majority in the Aldermanic branch and will become effective as soon as the Mayor signs it.

The Aldermanic committee acted affirmatively in executive session last night after a public hearing which crowded the Aldermanic Chamber and lasted more than four hours. Scores of spirited speeches were delivered for and against the measure in the hearing.

As in earlier hearings, officers and drivers of the city's "independent" taxicabs voiced opposition to the proposed transfer. Again the police were accused of favoring the Yellow Taxicab vehicles and their drivers.

Members of civic associations, including the Merchants' Association and the Fifth Avenue Association, filed briefs or delivered addresses warmly approving the transfer, which would involve 17,500 taxicabs and more than 30,000 operators.

John Ullman, Secretary of the Empire State Taxicab Chamber of Commerce and editor of a taxicab trade publication, created a sensation at the afternoon hearing. He had been saying that the Yellow Taxicab Company had established its supremacy in Chicago by placing blocks of stock where they might do the company good. He turned to the New York situation, and, while careful to name neither individual nor corporation, declared that he had been informed on what he believed reliable authority that "$175,000 worth of taxicab stock went a certain way."

Speaker Is Challenged.

Immediately Alderman George U. Harvey, Republican, of Queens, amid an audible murmur in the chamber, challenged the speaker to specify what he meant by his insinuation. As Chairman of the committee, he said:

"If you can produce any concrete evidence of the charge you have just made I pledge you my word that this committee will sift it to the bottom, no matter whither it may lead."

Mr. Ullman replied calmly, "I am not a man who is in the habit of going off half-cocked. I have no proof at present, nor could I swear that anything of the kind I have intimated has taken place. I believe the story to be true. But the man who told it to me advised me that if I ever tried to make it public he would deny ever having spoken to me on the subject. Although I have no proof to offer now, I assure you, gentlemen, that I am going out to try to get it, and if I succeed, I will bring it to you."

Ullman declared that the taxicab industry in New York City produces $100,000,000 revenue a year and that the daily income of the 17,500 taxicabs operating here amounts to $350,000. Of the city's 17,500 cabs, he said, the Yellow Taxicab Company operates 1,400. He declared the Mayor's bill was intended to intrench the Yellow Taxicab Company in the position of a monopoly and exterminate competition. He warned that if the proposal went through, New York was likely to see a "bloody taxicab war" like the violence in Chicago during a dispute over taxicab monopoly there.

"If you give the police entire supervision over taxicabs," he declared, "you will make the streets of this city a private right of way for a monopoly. The hotels of this city are fostering the Yel-

Continued on Page Two.

The Nassau Hotel, Long Beach, L. I., opens Decoration Day; same management.—Advt.

Always drink POLAND WATER. Sold on all Ocean Liners.—Advt.

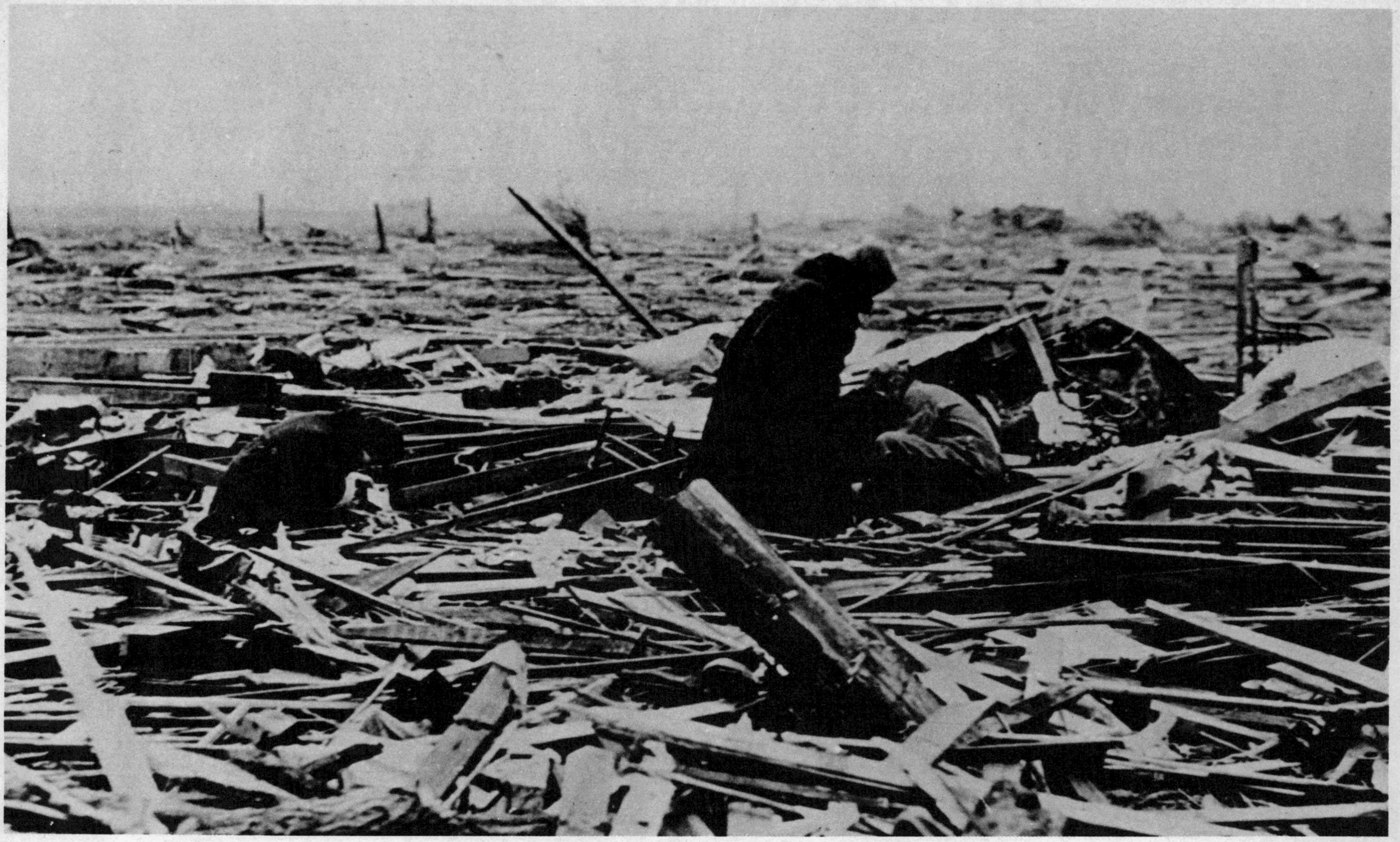

In Griffin, Indiana, survivors search debris for their belongings.

The Bettmann Archive

so arranged that the rescue work might continue during the night.

In other towns bonfires were lighted and automobiles and hand searchlights were brought into use to aid the workers. Such railroads as could operated special trains to convey many of the injured to near-by towns where hospital facilities were available.

By nightfall all the hospitals in Carbondale were filled to overflowing with those who were hurt at Murphysboro.

Many of the rescuers at Murphysboro and De Soto had to be detached as night fell to combat flames that broke out in the ruins. As most of the towns hit by the storm were small, pleas for relief were sent out intermittently whenever a wire could be found to carry a message or an automobile could make its way from the devastated regions to other towns that had escaped the fury of the storm.

Churches and schools were razed at various places and 200 persons, mostly children, were killed or injured when the elements ripped open the Joiner School at Murphysboro.

Express Trains Delayed.

Despite the wide sweep of the storm after crossing the Mississippi River several of the best trains running between the Southern resorts and Chicago escaped its fury, so far as reports showed tonight, but the scores of passengers were delayed somewhat in reaching their destination, as the trains had to feel their way through the storm region for fear that obstructions might have been thrown across the tracks or bridges torn down.

At 7 o'clock tonight The Chicago Herald and Examiner organized the first relief train, which left at 10 o'clock for the stricken area with 200 doctors, nurses and assistants aboard. Four Pullman cars, two baggage cars of medical supplies and a car of tents sufficient to establish a tented city comprised the special.

The train was in charge of Dr. Thomas A. Carter, who, upon his arrival in the stricken area, will place his command at the disposal of the authorities.

Later in the evening The Chicago Tribune, at the request of Mayor Dever, started a financial relief fund. The newspaper gave $1,000 and added subscriptions were reported.

Murphysboro Virtually Destroyed.

CENTRALIA, Ill., March 18 (Associated Press).—Striking with unprecedented fury, a severe tornado late this afternoon virtually destroyed the town of Murphysboro, practically obliterated Parrish and severely damaged De Soto, Duquoin, West Frankfort, Thompsonville, Logan and scores of other towns in Southern Illinois, causing an unestimated number of casualties, according to reports reaching here.

Only three persons out of a total population of about 500 are said to have escaped injury in the storm which struck Parrish. West Frankfort reported more than 250 dead; Murphysboro in excess of 100 dead and injured, while other towns reported that their casualties ranged from a few to several scores.

So terrific was the storm at Parrish and West Frankfort, eye-witnesses said, that in some cases bodies were blown about a mile and a half out of town.

At De Soto, the heaviest toll of death was taken at the De Soto public school. One hundred and twenty-five students and teachers were in the building at the time and only three are known to have escaped, the reports said. Eighty-eight bodies were recovered from the ruins, it was said.

A southbound passenger train on the Illinois Central that left here at 3 P. M. with three empty refrigerator cars stopped at De Soto and filled the cars with bodies, Conductor Redus reported late tonight. There was no building more than ten feet high left standing in the town, he said.

Only one building was reported standing in Hurst, a town of 1,200 population. Fire which followed the storm was said virtually to have destroyed De Soto.

The storm struck without warning, increasing in intensity as it progressed.

Starting at Tamaroa, where slight damage was done, the tornado struck Dubois, doing considerable damage. It then skirted Hallidaysboro, again dropping on De Soto, where a two-story brick schoolhouse was demolished, killing several children and injurying many.

West Frankfort, in Franklin County, was the next town reported to have been struck, being partially demolished, with a consequent heavy loss of life and property.

Reports next were received from Murphysboro. Dropping with all its fury, the storm virtually devastated this little mining town, demolishing buildings and killing and injuring almost all within its path.

In some instances the suffering from the storm was intensified by fire which broke out.

Meanwhile, reports began to be received from Logan, Thompsonville, Parrish and other intermediate towns, each detailing damage more widespread than the other, culminating in the advices from Parrish which said that only one house was left standing after the storm had passed.

The Orient mine, said to be the second largest coal mine in the world, was completely destroyed, the advices said.

A special train carrying doctors and nurses is being rushed from here by the Illinois Central Railroad to West Frankfort.

Report 200 Dead in Indiana.

EVANSVILLE, Ind., March 18.—At least 200 persons are believed to be dead as the result of a tornado that struck Southern Indiana, razing the towns of Princeton, Griffin, Owensville and Poseyville this afternoon, according to conservative estimates available up to late tonight.

The death toll is figured thus:

Princeton, 75 to 100 dead; hundreds injured.

Griffin, 60 to 75 dead, 200 injured.

Owensville, 25 dead; scores injured.

Poseyville, five dead; thirty injured.

Princeton is under martial law, declared by Captain N. E. Hart, commander of Battery D, Nineteenth Field Artillery, stationed there.

Griffin, a town of 400 people, is a total ruin. Projecting above the débris are parts of four buildings, all that remain standing out of more than 200. Fire swept the town and brought death to many injured who could not help themselves. Nine bodies have been recovered.

In Owensville the public library has been converted into a temporary hospital. Twelve bodies have been recovered and identified.

Late tonight Miss Grace Wright, Red Cross agent, had organized a special train carrying several scores of volunteer workers to Griffin, where the scenes were said to be beyond description.

Open cisterns claimed some of the rescue workers as they searched through the ruins after dark. The only way to locate the injured was by estimating their cries. Persons who were stunned are believed to have been caught by the flames that quickly followed the disaster.

LOUISVILLE, Ky., March 18.—An undetermined number of persons were hurt when a tornado struck Elizabeth, Ind., fifteen miles southwest of New Albany, early tonight, reports received in New Albany said. Due to the confusion, definite information was not available.

SPRINGFIELD, Ky., March 18.—Two negroes were killed and twenty-five others injured, some seriously, at Jimtown, a negro settlement near here, early tonight when a severe windstorm practically destroyed the negro quarters.

INDIANAPOLIS, Ind., March 18.—Griffin, Ind., a town of 400 inhabitants, twelve miles northwest of Poseyville, is "burning up" following the tornado, according to a telephonic report from Evansville. All communication with Griffin has been severed.

Carbondale Asks for Help.

CAIRO, Ill., March 18.—Mayor Hill of Carbondale, Ill., in a telephone call to W. N. Wood, Mayor of Cairo, early tonight appealed for assistance in "every form" for the storm-swept section about Carbondale. He urged especially that relief workers be rushed to the scene.

Mr. Hill did not attempt to estimate the number of dead or injured. Company K, 157th Infantry, Illinois National Guard, stationed here, was immediately mobilized and held at its armory for orders. Fire, it was reported, had destroyed the entire western portion of the town.

The armory and hospitals at Carbondale have been filled to capacity with the bodies of persons killed, and relief workers have found it necessary to send other bodies to Duquoin.

A fire is now raging in Murphysboro and threatening to destroy the entire town, according to reports received here.

Mayor Decker of Grand Tower, Ill., in another telegram to Mayor Wood said:

"City of Gorham destroyed by tornado, town burning up. Impossible to estimate number of dead and injured. All people are homeless. What is needed immediately is a Red Cross unit, doctors and nurses and 500 tents for the homeless. The roads are nearly impassable."

Report City in Flames.

ST. LOUIS, March 18.—Passengers arriving in St. Louis at 8:45 o'clock tonight on a Mobile & Ohio train, which passed through Murphysboro, Ill., two hours previously, reported that the city is "completely in flames." Water mains have burst, they said, and there are no lights. As the train stopped to take on fifty refugees, citizens by the hundreds were seen running frantically through the streets, some clad only in blankets. Estimates of the dead in Murphysboro ranged from 100 to 180.

Chester, Gorham and Duquoin were reported hard hit.

A man named Stewart was killed, scores of persons were injured and all but three buildings were destroyed at Annapolis, Mo., a village of about 200 people, at 1:20 o'clock this afternoon, according to reports brought to Ironton, Mo., late today by C. E. Pyrtle, a Kansas City traveling man.

Many of the injured, Pyrtle said, received broken arms and legs from flying missiles. One sick woman, he said, was removed from her home just before it burst into flames.

CAPE GIRARDEAU, Mo., March 18.—One man was killed when his home at Allenburg, Mo., thirty miles north of here, was wrecked in the storm late today and ten children were injured in the collapse of an Allenburg parochial school, according to advices received here tonight.

EAST ST. LOUIS, Ill., March 18.—An Illinois Central train left here late this evening with seventeen physicians aboard, bound for the storm-stricken area. It was announced at the relay station that another special train was being held in readiness to take additional physicians and medical and food supplies to the storm sufferers.

TELLS OF SCENES AT DE SOTO.

Visitor Finds It a Town of Ruins, With Dead Bodies in Streets.

Special to The New York Times.

CENTRALIA, Ill., March 18.—Max Burton, telegraph operator for the Illinois Central at Tamaroa, interviewed last tonight after a visit to De Soto, declared the town was a mass of bodies, maimed residents, débris and burning buildings.

"It seems to me there was not an entire house in the town," said Burton. "People were going out on the hard road, north and south, with a few belongings clutched in their arms, more for protection against the storm than anything else, so far as I could see.

"I went directly to the school house, after running and walking two and a half miles, and the first thing I saw were the bodies of about twenty little children laid out on mattresses and blankets. There was no one there to claim them, so I thought the people I had seen on the hard road were their parents, but I learned later that the children's parents had been killed or wounded and those who were not dead were being hurried by automobile, special relief train and ambulances to the hospitals at Carbondale and Duquoin.

"The Principal of the school was on hand and he was trying to identify the bodies of the pupils and was also worrying over the whereabouts and safety of two girl teachers who were unaccounted for. The Principal was bloody from his injuries and staggered in his walk. He had barely escaped with his life.

"About twenty-five bodies of school children were piled up just outside the playgrounds and they were still seeking for others in the ruins. While I stood there they took some of the bodies away and brought others out of the building, which by then was a mass of smoulder-ering ruins, fire having destroyed what the cyclone did not.

"The hallway of the house had caved in and what few rescuers were on hand were trying to uncover other bodies of pupils and locate the two missing teachers.

"I walked out beyond the school grounds and near the city limits I saw the bodies of two babies, apparently about six or eight months old. They were dead and their baby clothes had been torn from them.

"Every tree that was left standing and every fence had garments, bed clothes and household goods blown against the west side of them. It looked to me as if the tornado began in the west and traveled eastward. I saw furniture, automobile tops and clothing scattered everywhere and saw many people fleeing from the town with hardly any garments.

"The business section was practically destroyed by fire and wind and nearly every home was flat.

"I saw about forty automobiles piled up in one big heap and thought this was a garage that had been struck.

"Then I saw another car just outside of town that looked like the people were trying to get away, but had failed. The car had blown from the road over to the railroad right of way and was wrecked, but I could find no bodies.

"I offered what help I could and they told me the bodies were first taken south to Carbondale, but that the hospital there was filled and they were taking the injured to the Duquoin Hospital, north of De Soto.

"I met two girls on the hard road on my way back to Tamaro. Their faces were bleeding and their clothes were torn. One of them said, 'How did you get out?' and the other answered, 'I climbed out the window,' and asked, 'How did you get out?' The first said, 'I don't know.' They were wandering up the road and seemed not to know where they were going."

"All the News That's Fit to Print."

The New York Times.

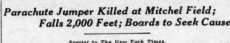

THE WEATHER
Fair, warmer today; showers tonight or tomorrow and cooler.
Temperature Yesterday—Max. 73; Min. 62.
For weather report see Page 54.

VOL. LXXVI....No. 25,078. NEW YORK, WEDNESDAY, SEPTEMBER 22, 1926. TWO CENTS in Greater New York | THREE CENTS Within 200 Miles | FOUR CENTS Elsewhere in the U. S.

400 KILLED IN FLORIDA, 150 MISSING; PENSACOLA DAMAGED, NO LOSS OF LIFE; CITIES MOVE TO AVERT AN EPIDEMIC

FONCK PLANE BURNS, 2 DIE AT START OF PARIS FLIGHT; ACE AND CURTIN ESCAPE

WRECK BURSTS INTO FLAMES

Machine a Crumpled Ruin Three Minutes After It Takes Off.

OVERLOADING IS BLAMED

French Flier Unable to Lift Giant Into Air—Wheel Breaks, Craft Dives Into Ditch.

MEN PERISH IN DEBRIS

Mechanic Islamoff and Radio Operator Clavier, Probably Stunned, Unable to Escape.

Three minutes after the giant Sikorsky airplane, which was to have started from Roosevelt Field yesterday morning for Paris, trembled and moved forward over the ground in the cold gray light of dawn, it was a tangled and twisted heap of burning wreckage at the bottom of a gully at the other end of the field. Two of the crew were caught in the flames that roared fifty feet into the air and were burned to death.

Captain René Fonck, the French ace who was at the controls, and Lieutenant Lawrence W. Curtin, U. S. N., his navigator, who was seated beside him, crawled to safety from the cockpit a moment before the flames would have made their escape impossible. They stood, dazed and heart-broken, a moment, looking back at the funeral pyre of their comrades, Jacob Islamoff, the mechanic, and Charles Clavier, radio operator, and then were led away by friends. The pilots were only slightly scratched.

There was no possibility of saving the other two, who apparently had been knocked unconscious in the terrific crash with which the plane "cartwheeled" around on its right wing when the landing gear gave way, for no sound came from the plane as the first huge puff of flame enveloped it. Inside there had been a quantity of oil cans and baggage and the men must have been hurled under this mass and burned before they knew what had happened.

Crash Laid to Overloading.

The accident was attributed to overloading and the inability of Captain Fonck to stop the machine in time to prevent its dropping over a steep declivity of about twenty feet at the end of the runway. He had hoped that sufficient flying speed would be attained by the time he reached this spot to permit him to float into the air, but the plane merely dropped, smashing the big right wheel as if it were a toy, and then twisting around into a collapsed and broken mass, from which the flames sprang as if from a miniature oil tank. There were 2,380 gallons of gasoline in her huge tanks, and the flames billowed up for nearly an hour; black, thick smoke, around a belching red centre.

Captain Fonck said he lost control of the plane soon after he started when the auxiliary landing gear began to break away and tore off the lower part of the left rudder. He could not steer the huge machine, and it did not pick up flying speed, never going faster than sixty-five miles an hour. The tail dragged all the way. In this he was corroborated by Lieutenant Curtin, who told of trying to help Fonck use the right rudder when the French ace motioned to him that he was unable to curb the left swing of the machine. At the end, when it was seen that a crash was inevitable, Captain Fonck tried to make a landing as the plane pitched over the bank, and might have done so if the landing gear had not given way under the terrific strain.

Both Ready for Another Trial.

Both pilots said that there was nothing they could have done to avert the crash. Half an hour afterward both expressed themselves as willing to make another attempt in another machine built by Igor Sikorsky. They said the end was inevitable, one of those accidents for which all fliers are at all times prepared. Their own escape, while their fellows died, they regarded as miraculous, having believed that the most dangerous place was in the cockpit of the machine.

Captain Fonck and Lieutenant Curtin told their stories to District Attorney Elvin N. Edwards at the Nassau County Court House, a few hours after the disaster, and Mr. Edwards said he was convinced that the accident was unavoidable and that everything possible had been done to make the start as safe as any such undertaking can be.

Things began to go wrong as soon as the big plane was taxied from the hangar to the end of the runway in pitch darkness, purple flames spitting from her exhaust pipes. On the way the tail skid slipped off the "dolly" as the wheels are called which held it up to prevent unnecessary bumping, and the lower end of the centre rudder

Continued on Page Three.

6 BELL-ANS BEFORE BREAKFAST is Marvelously Beneficial. Try it.—Advt.

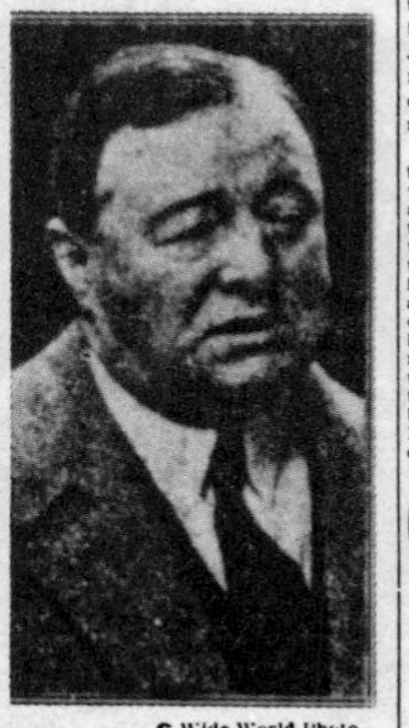

© Wide World Photo.
JOSEPH A. GUIDER,
Borough President of Brooklyn, Who Died Early This Morning.

JOS. A. GUIDER DIES AFTER AN OPERATION

Brooklyn Borough President, Stricken Monday, Succumbs to Peritonitis.

HE WAS 56 YEARS OF AGE

Served Five Terms in Assembly and Had Been Commissioner of Public Works.

Borough President Joseph A. Guider of Brooklyn died at 1:30 o'clock this morning at the Skene Sanitarium, 759 President Street, Brooklyn, to which he had been taken on Monday night for an operation to remove his appendix. It was found that the appendix was ruptured and peritonitis had set in, while a weak heart and low pressure also combined to cause the Borough President to lose his fight for life.

Throughout yesterday Mr. Guider's condition became steadily worse. Dr. George F. Herrity, a personal friend of Mr. Guider and his physician for ten years, called in Dr. Edward Cornwall, a physician of 1,218 Pacific Street, Brooklyn, and later they were joined by Dr. Marcus Searle. A priest was summoned to the patient's bedside and administered the last rites of the church.

At 8 o'clock last night Mr. Guider's condition became critical and from then on the physicians in attendance knew they were waging a losing fight with death. For an hour before he died Mr. Guider was kept alive only through the administering of oxygen. During the day digitalis, strychnine and strophantin were given to him in an effort to quicken the heart action.

Relatives at the Bedside.

Grouped about his bedside when Mr. Guider died were a niece, Sister Francis Joseph, from Whitestone, L. I.; a sister of Mr. Guider's, Catherine Lubbe of 782 Franklin Avenue, Brooklyn; another niece, Marie Guider, who is staying with Mrs. Lubbe, and a nephew, Cornelius Guider, who had come from Seton Hall in South Orange, N. J., when he heard of his uncle's illness. They had been at the hospital throughout the day.

Below in a reception room were a number of the political leaders of Brooklyn, who were long time friends of Mr. Guider's. Prominent among these was John H. McCooey, Kings County Democratic leader. Mr. McCooey was present at the hospital on Monday night when Mr. Guider underwent the operation and had scarcely left the hospital since.

Others in this group were John J. Curtin, who was Mayor Walker's campaign manager in Brooklyn last year; Fire Commissioner John Dorman, Supreme Court Justice Edward Riegelman, who preceded Mr. Guider as Borough President, and Assistant District Attorney Joseph Gallagher. There had been scores of callers earlier in the day, including Commissioner of Public Works James J. Byrne and many other political leaders and friends.

Mr. Guider was a widower and had lived alone.

For several months the Borough President has been far from well, but continued to work, despite cautions from his friends. Two weeks ago, while at Atlantic City with his friend Cyrus B. Gale, who was in the Legislature with him thirty years ago, Mr. Guider collapsed. He was advised to take a vacation, and went to Hot Springs, Va., but insisted upon returning to vote in the primaries last week.

Successful As a Builder.

Joseph A. Guider, Borough President of Brooklyn, was born in the old Ninth

Continued on Page Sixteen.

Parachute Jumper Killed at Mitchel Field; Falls 2,000 Feet; Boards to Seek Cause

Special to The New York Times.

MITCHEL FIELD, L. I., Sept. 21.—When his parachute failed to open after he had made a practice jump from an airplane flying at an altitude of 2,000 feet, Charles C. Turner, a Private, First Class, and a member of the Eighth Photographic Section of the army, was killed here this morning. Turner, with First Lieutenant Joseph A. Wilson as pilot, took off from the flying field soon after 11 o'clock. After reaching 2,000 feet Turner prepared for his descent.

His jump was delayed but he cleared the plane safely. Then something went wrong and his body landed on a grass plot between the barracks of the Fifth Observation Squadron and the mess hall. Major I. B. March, the post surgeon, lost no time in reaching Turner, whose hand was wrapped around the ring of the emergency chute. Officials at the post are at a loss to determine why Turner did not release the main parachute. Army regulations require the jumpers to carry two parachutes, the main one on the back and the emergency on the chest. Each is controlled by a large ring easily accessible to the jumper.

The ring of the emergency parachute had been pulled and the apparatus was partly opened when Turner's body was picked up. Apparently no effort had been made to release the main parachute.

Lieutenant Wilson is the post parachute officer. He declared that Turner, for some undetermined reason, had failed to release the main parachute and pulled the ring controlling the emergency parachute when too near the ground and too late to save himself.

A board of officers has been appointed to determine the cause of the accident. On the board are Major March, First Lieutenant Wilson and First Lieutenant Roland Birnn. Another board has been appointed by Lieut. Colonel B. D. Foulois, commandant of the flying field, to investigate the condition of both parachutes, to determine if they were defective. On this board are Captain Vernon L. Burge, Lieutenant Wilson and Lieutenant Birnn.

The findings of both boards will be forwarded to Washington.

Turner's home was in Auburn, N. Y. He was serving his second enlistment.

GOV. SMITH MOVES FOR PARTY PEACE; MAY REVISE SLATE

He Tells Shuler, Who Promises Fight for Controller, That Ticket Is Only Tentative.

SHERMAN FRIENDS ACTIVE

Protest to Olvany That He Was Dropped for Attorney General Because of Religion.

There were indications yesterday that the Democratic slate tentatively agreed upon at a conference last week at the Executive Mansion at Albany will be revised. Governor Smith has been compelled to take a hand, and yesterday he communicated with at least one of the aggrieved aspirants for a place on the ticket who has threatened to take his fight to the State convention.

Major George Kent Shuler, who asserts he has the support of thirty-four up-State Democratic county organizations for the nomination for Controller and who found last week that it had been decided at the Albany conference to place Morris Tremaine, a wealthy Buffalo man, on the ticket as a candidate for that office, was summoned by Governor Smith for a conference after the Governor had read of the threatened insurgency by Major Shuler and Carl Sherman, former Attorney General, who wants his old office back. At last week's conference he had been passed over in the interest of Benjamin Stoltz of Syracuse, who was said to have the backing of William H. Kelley, Democratic leader of Onondaga, for this nomination.

Major Shuler, it was learned last night, told the Governor bluntly that if the slate made at the Albany conference was intended to stand he would take his fight to the convention and would keep on fighting until nominations had been made. Major Shuler is the fighting kind of Democrat, both in and out of politics. He saw service with the United States Marine Corps before he was drafted in 1922 as a candidate for State Treasurer on the Democratic ticket.

Slate Tentative, Smith Says.

The Governor told Major Shuler what he has told others—that no decisions were reached at the Albany conference, that everything done there was tentative and that nothing definite could be done until the Democratic leaders gathered at Syracuse for the convention, which will open on Monday. Last night the Governor had a talk with the sponsor for Stoltz, Mr. Kelley.

Major Shuler said last night that his attitude had not changed, that he was still a candidate and would continue to be. In one respect his plans have undergone a change since he talked with the Governor. Where it had been announced by friends of the Major that he had pooled issues with Mr. Sherman and that they would win or lose together, it was said last night that the alliance was off.

Major Shuler has the active backing of Franklin D. Roosevelt, who, during a long talk with Governor Smith on Monday evening over other matters, told the Governor he would like to see Major Shuler nominated for State Controller. It was after this talk and the reports of coming trouble which appeared in the newspapers that Mr. Shuler was sent for and came to the Biltmore. The Governor reminded Major Shuler that he had been defeated for State Treasurer two years ago. Major Shuler told the Governor that 1924 being a Presidential year, when all the other Democratic candidates for State officers except the Governor himself, went down to defeat, it could not be held against him. He reminded the Governor of the defeat the latter had suffered at the hands of Nathan L. Miller in 1920, another Presidential year. The Governor laughed at the reminder.

Sherman's Friends Active.

Friends of ex-Attorney General Carl Sherman were very active yesterday. A large delegation went to Tammany Hall, by appointment they said, to plead with Tammany Leader George W. Olvany in behalf of Mr. Sherman's candidacy. Mr. Olvany, however, was not there. They went away disappointed, leaving behind a statement in which they called attention to reports in circulation several months ago, when Mr. Sherman aspired to the nomination for United States Senator, to show that he was being discriminated against because he is a Jew.

The delegation was made up of men

Continued on Page Twelve.

Glorious days at Hotel Briarcliff Lodge, America's Foremost Resort, Briarcliff Manor, N. Y., for Rest, Health and Sports.—Advt.

NEW WRIT SOUGHT TO STOP BIG BOUT; PURSE IS ATTACHED

Hearing Set for Today on Move by Clements, Who Got the Indiana Injunction.

DEMPSEY MONEY TIED UP

Another Court Action Garnishees Rickard—$600,000 Bond Posted by Promoter.

PHILADELPHIA, Sept. 21 (AP).—The heaviest legal barrage to which the Dempsey-Tunney battle has yet been subjected was laid down today.

Firing from the legal bulwarks resulted in no less than six court shots being directed at Dempsey, as well as Promoter Tex Rickard and Billy Gibson, Tunney's manager, by the two outstanding foes of the champion—Jack Kearns, the champion's former manager, and B. C. Clements, Chicago promoter, who is fighting to sustain the validity of a contract to match Dempsey and Harry Wills.

Application for an injunction to stop the fight, made by Clements, was the outstanding development in the court manoeuvres and loomed as the only possible obstacle to the bout being held as scheduled on Thurdsay night in the Sesquicentennial Stadium.

Hearing at 1:30 P. M. Today.

This will not be decided, however, until tomorrow at a hearing in Common Pleas Court at 1:30 P. M. Clements based his application on the grounds which resulted in an Indiana court granting an injunction, which was not recognized here. The Chicago promoter claims that Dempsey, in signing with Rickard to meet Tunney, violated a prior agreement to meet Wills in Chicago, but the champion's answer had been that Clements did not live up to his own contract terms.

Clements simultaneously filed four actions, claiming damages individually and collectively against Dempsey, Rickard and Gibson, while Kearns, in addition to moves already made in New York and Atlantic City, obtained a writ of attachment here against Dempsey's share of the purse. Rickard was named as garnishee in the writ and bail was fixed at $600,000, representing twice the amount of Kearns's claim. This was covered by surety bonds arranged by Rickard.

Dempsey's Share $450,000.

Dempsey's share of the purse, it was revealed by Frank Wiener, Chairman of the Pennsylvania Boxing Commission, is $450,000, while Tunney's is put at $200,000. No percentages are involved, according to Wiener, who quoted from a copy of the contracts with the fighters given him by Rickard.

Kearns's writ, which is expected to mean tying up of the gate receipts, was obtained after withdrawal of an attempt to stop Rickard from paying either of the fighters before the bout, in violation of the Pennsylvania boxing law. Rickard himself took the stand to deny that he had paid money either to Dempsey or Tunney out of the receipts for the fight, although the promoter admitted he had made personal loans to both.

Rickard, after spending most of the morning in court, expressed confidence that none of the pending legal moves would block the fight, and devoted the rest of the day to inspectin the construction work at the stadium.

Dempsey Assails Kearns.

ATLANTIC CITY, N. J., Sept. 21 (AP).—Charging that Jack Kearns, his former manager, is an ex-convict and had defrauded him out of $500,000, Jack Dempsey today filed an answer to the suit which has thrown him into temporary receivership. The case was continued for two weeks on the plea of Richard J. Mackey of Jersey City, Dempsey's attorney, because he said he had had no time in which to prepare a defense.

Dempsey did not appear in court, disappointing many spectators who jammed the chambers of Vice Chancellor Robert H. Ingersoll. He filed his answer through his counsel, who appeared with Gene Normile, his business manager.

Dempsey's affidavit was sensational in its charges against his former manager. He swore that:

He had learned that Kearns was an ex-convict, having served time in the

Continued on Page Twenty-one.

GULF LOSSES IN MILLIONS

Railroads and Vessels Are Heavy Sufferers at Pensacola.

CITY CUT OFF 24 HOURS

Restoration of Communication Relieves Fear of Serious Loss of Life.

WHARF FRONT DEMOLISHED

Barometer There Lowest in 50 Years—Cotton and Pecan Crops Badly Damaged.

PENSACOLA, Fla., Sept. 21 (By Wireless to New Orleans) (AP).—Damage from the hurricane here was confined to ships aground, roofs torn from buildings and bridges washed away, it was shown today by a survey of Pensacola and vicinity.

There was no loss of life here and reports from surrounding territory tell of only three children drowned in Baldwin County, Ala.

Several fishing schooners broke away from their moorings and went adrift and two foreign vessels stuck their noses in the mud.

Pensacola citizens are preparing to raise funds for cities that suffered damage in Florida and Alabama. Lack of communication with South Florida prevents immediate aid being offered.

During the hurricane the wind velocity at times reached 120 miles an hour.

Santa Rosa Island, a natural breakwater, prevented damage to a great extent from the storm here.

[The above dispatch is the first to come out of Pensacola except for the telephone report from The Pensacola Journal to The Mobile Register. This dispatch was sent to The Associated Press by its Pensacola correspondent over naval radio to New Orleans.]

Force of Storm Now Spent.

NEW ORLEANS, Sept. 21 (AP).—Property losses and crop damage estimated at millions of dollars resulted along the Gulf Coast from the tropical hurricane which veered northwestward from Southern Florida and careened across the western top of that State and lower Alabama before spending its full force late tonight in Southern Mississippi.

The first word from Pensacola, which had been cut off from communication for twenty-four hours after the hurricane, came when a telephone line to Mobile was repaired today and a brief message ended fears that lives had been lost. The destruction of the railroad station and other property north of the city was disclosed, and it was estimated that it would be two days before trains could get through.

The bridge connecting the Naval Station with Pensacola proper was greatly damaged by the storm, rendering it impassable and hindering communication with the city proper.

Mobile Buildings, Unroofed.

Mobile, the largest of the Gulf cities visited by the hurricane, suffered property damage, but dispatches said there had been no loss of life and no reports of persons seriously injured. Property losses consisted chiefly of unroofed structures and consequent water damage to stocks of goods in business houses an dto residences.

Mobile was in the grip of the storm from 5 o'clock Monday morning until midnight Monday, with the greatest wind velocity at ninety-four miles an hour. The barometer reading was the lowest in the fifty years of the Weather Bureau station there. Trees and telephone poles were blown down, making streets impassable and throwing some 3,000 telephones in the city out of order. Communication with the outside world also was cut off until this afternoon, when dispatches were sent through direct disclosing the extent of the damage.

Lives Reported Lost in Alabama.

Surveys are now under way to determine the extent of the damage to small villages along Mobile Bay and in the interior. There were unconfirmed reports of some loss of life at Jackson and Bay Minnette, Ala.

Pascagoula, Miss., suffered heavy damage, but there was no loss of life. Charles Farrar, special agent of the Louisville & Nashville Railroad, reported. Property losses, he said, in Jackson County, Miss., would run into the hundreds of thousands of dollars, principally to the pecan crop.

The cotton crop in Southern Alabama was said to have sustained considerable damage, but outside of Mobile there were no reports of damage to shipping or the fishing fleets, which base on the numerous bayous

Continued on Page Two.

POPULAR MATINEE TODAY.
Greatest Show Ziegfeld ever producted.
Ziegfeld Revue, Globe Thea.—Advt.

Bahamas Are Hard Hit by Hurricane; Thousands of People Homeless on 3 Islands

GRAND TURK, Turk's Island, Bahama, Sept. 21 (AP).—Four thousand persons are homeless and great property damage has been caused on Turk's and Caicos Islands as a result of the recent hurricane which swept from the West Indies across the State of Florida.

MIAMI, Fla., Sept. 21 (AP).—Reports reaching here today indicated that the Island of Bimini, 135 miles from Nassau, in the Bahamas, was devastated by the tropical hurricane of last week which ravished the east coast of Florida. Nassau was not hard hit but felt the effects of the hurricanes, the report said.

The reports that Bimini suffered severely were confirmed by crew members of tugboats which arrived here today from that vicinity. They did not attempt to land or check for dead or injured.

Efforts have been made repeatedly to gain information by radio as to the effect of the storm in the Bahamas. Nassau was heard but not clearly. It was learned then, however, that only property damage had resulted there from high winds and waves.

SIX SHIPS ARRIVE FROM STORM AREA

Trinidad Liner Was Helpless in Heavy Seas for Two Days When Steering Gear Broke.

MOREAS LOST LIFEBOATS

Operator of Siboney Describes Relaying First Message of Disaster at Miami.

Six more storm-battered ships arrived in New York yesterday from the hurricane area. The officers of one, the 4,000-ton Matura of the Trinidad Line, which docked at the foot of Amity Street, Brooklyn, reported that she had wallowed helplessly in the trough of enormous seas for nearly twelve hours when both steam and hand steering apparatus were disabled. Officers of the others described winds of unusual violence and heavy weather both off the coast of Florida and in the North Atlantic.

According to Captain John Kirkby of the Matura, that vessel, which carried twenty-eight passengers and a cargo of asbestos, owed her safety to the accident to her steering gear. He said that but for the delay it caused she would have found herself in the vortex of the hurricane and expressed the opinion that she might have foundered.

Lost Wireless for Two Days.

"The Matura left Dominica on Sept. 13 and was north of Saba, which is ninety miles north-northwest of St. Thomas, when we received the first warning at 2 A. M. on the 14th," he said. "At 4 A. M. the hurricane broke. The steam steering gear was disabled at 7 A. M. when we were trying to bring the ship around, and shortly afterward the hand gear went out of commission. The electric lighting plant also stopped working at this time and a little later the wireless aerial was blown down. William Moore and Reginald Harrington, who went on deck to try to rig up a new one, were nearly washed overboard, and the ship did not have her radio again for two days."

According to Captain Kirkby it was not until late afternoon that jury steering apparatus was in operation. During the interval the ship was at the mercy of the storm. A starboard lifeboat was carried away, the saloon and wireless room were flooded, a number of stanchions were twisted loose and several portholes smashed in. While in the saloon attempting to reassure the passengers, Helen Kirkby, the captain's daughter, was thrown violently to the deck, but escaped with bruises.

Captain Kirkby said that the waves following the storm were even higher than those in the midst of it. He said that, according to his calculations, the vortex of the storm hit Sombrero Island when he was off Barbados, a little to the southeast.

Moreas Battled Storm 38 Hours.

The Moreas of the Greek Line, formerly the Anchor liner Columbia, arrived two days late on her first trip from Piraeus. According to Captain William Koutsoukos, commander of the vessel, she struck a side swirl of the storm on Sept. 17 off the coast of Newfoundland. For thirty-eight hours she battled terrific seas and hurricane winds, keeping full steam ahead. When at the end of this time he was able to take a sextant observation of the sun for his position he found that he had been blown thirty miles backward.

At the height of the storm the wireless antennae were blown down, but they were soon in place again. Three of the lifeboats were smashed in by waves described as thirty to fifty feet in height. One of the vessel's 194 passengers, Miss Kenella Jarvis of Athens, had her head cut open when she was thrown to the deck by a big wave.

Siboney Gave First Miami News.

The Ward liner Siboney, which sent north the first message of the disaster at Miami, docked yesterday. She passed eleven miles off Miami late Saturday night. The first intimation her officers had that there had been a disaster there was when the chief officer failed to see the familiar blaze of light ashore.

Her wireless operator, Raymond D. Hutchens of Chicago, told of receiving

Continued on Page Two.

SURVIVORS PICTURE HURRICANE HORRORS

Aviator Tells of Scores of Persons and Cars Blown to Sea From Causeway.

HOTEL LIKE A SHIP AT SEA

Jersey City Lawyer Says Scene in Miami Was Worse Than Shell Fire in France.

Special to The New York Times.

TAMPA, Fla., Sept. 21.—R. T. Freng, pilot for the Florida Airways Corporation, reached Tampa last night after spending Friday and Saturday in Miami, bringing a first-hand account of the storm's destruction.

The most terrific loss of life, according to Freng, was on Miami Beach and on the Causeway leading from Miami to the beach across Biscayne Bay. Hundreds were in bathing early Saturday morning when the hurricane descended, he said. There were hundreds in motors and on foot crossing the Causeway from the beach to Miami who already had had their morning plunge. Many of these were washed out to sea. It may be weeks before the exact number of dead is known.

When the storm started Friday night Freng left Hialeah, where he was staying, and went out to the airport to care for his plane. At midnight the wind was blowing sixty-five miles an hour. Terror-stricken women and children deserted their homes in Hialeah and ran aimlessly about the streets. Some took to open spaces, many got in their automobiles to ride around blocks in frantic attempts to find shelter.

Many Escaped in Cars.

Curiously, Freng says, many of those who fled to their cars escaped injury, while many of those who remained in their homes were trapped by the wind and killed or injured. At 1:30 A. M. the wind had reached a velocity of 90 to 100 miles an hour. This it maintained until 3:30 A. M., when it died out, and spent four hours and a half switching around to the south. During the hours of dawn emergency hospitals were brought into use, hotels, restaurants, even the police station, provided shelter or became improvised morgues for the dead which had been struck down by this early blow.

At dawn many persons made their way to the beach to take advantage of the high waves. Here they romped and frolicked for a couple of hours. Five or six hundred, somewhat frightened by the midnight storm, played along the beach. Toward 8 o'clock about 100 of them were on their way back to Miami. Scarcely had they got well on their way across the long causeway when the hurricane in its second and worst phase struck them. A gate tender on the Miami end of the causeway told Freng a mountainous wall of water suddenly rose from Biscayne Bay as the wind developed and crashed across the bridge. The bathers were tossed off like leaves. Those who still were in bathing were also carried away.

A huge apartment building on Miami Beach, housing, it is estimated, at least 100 persons, collapsed.

On his way to Miami, Freng says the wind was blowing 120 miles an hour. He took shelter in a gutter alongside the road, lying there from 9 o'clock A. M. until 12:30 P. M. At the outset of the second storm he and two comrades tried to save the life of a woman who but a minute before had given premature birth to a child. As they were carrying the woman and the child out of the wreckage of her home, a telephone pole in front of the door was wrenched loose and thrown against her husband, killing him.

Broken Bones Are Common.

Broken backs and limbs were the most common injuries in the emergency hospitals following the storm, Freng says. Full size trees, branches of all sizes, lumber, pipe, tiles, débris of all kinds. Even small autos, were flying through the air during the hard blow. Children, separated from their parents, shrieked and ran or were blown helplessly about, scores of them

Continued on Page Eight.

MIAMI DEAD PUT AT 250

Figures Rise as Bodies of Victims Washed Out to Sea Are Found.

5,000 HURT, 50,000 IN NEED

Medicine, Food and Clothing Are Being Hurried to Scene to Meet Great Emergency.

DESOLATION IS APPALLING

Despite Efforts of Residents to Restore Semblance of Order the Picture Has Changed Little.

By WARREN IRVIN
Staff Correspondent of The New York Times.

MIAMI, Fla., Sept. 21.—With almost every relief agency in Florida cooperating in rushing aid to the storm swept area in and about this city, local and State health authorities began today to prepare against a possible epidemic of typhoid, which now is considered as the greatest menace.

Meanwhile the task of counting the dead and hunting the missing continues. At a late hour tonight the known dead was still below 400, but there were 150 persons unaccounted for.

To meet the chance of epidemic, vaccine serum, sent from Jacksonville, was distributed in Miami, but because of the small quantity available, many towns nearby are still without it. Already two cases of typhoid have been reported at Fort Lauderdale and eleven are said to have been discovered in Hialeah.

While health authorities insist that there are no more cases of this disease in the storm area at present than are usually there, rigid precautions are being taken. All towns in the affected area have posted bulletins warning citizens against drinking water at Miami and Fort Lauderdale, and Dr. W. A. Claxton, City Health Officer of Miami, announced today that he had advised the chlorination of water there.

Rigid daily insections are being carried on at all tourist camps in the affected area and sanitary inspectors have been instructed to pour oil on all puddles in the vicinity of these camps.

The greatest danger, health officials say, lies outside the City of Miami in towns which have no city sewage disposal systems. In nearly all septic tanks are used and thousands of these tanks were broken during the storm or overflowed because of the saturated condition of the soil. Health officers say this condition threatens to result in soil pollution and unless proper safeguards are taken in general, spread of typhoid is almost certain.

Repair of Damage Begun.

The work of repairing the damage done by the storm is being carried on everywhere. Fort Lauderdale, Hollywood, Dania and Hialeah appear to have suffered worst. Miami already has cleared away much of its wreckage, although the absence of electric signs on the principal streets and the empty windows of all the large skyscrapers still attest the fury of the hurricane.

Several Places Lightly Touched.

The storm did little damage in the Palm Beaches. In Palm Beach proper a few small shacks were overturned and one or two residences lost small sections of roof. The roof of White Hall was slightly damaged and the New Breakers, which is being rushed to completion, was damaged slightly.

All of the streets were filled with water to a depth of about three feet, and a number of small craft in Lake Worth were either sunk outright or landed high and dry on Lake Shore Drive in West Palm Beach. There, too, the damage was slight and principally from water.

Lake Worth, Boynton, Del Ray and Boca Raton also reported but little damage. Golf courses of the Gulf Stream and other clubs were

flooded and roofs were ripped from several small frame shacks and the Ocean Boulevard was rendered impassable from Boca Raton to the inlet north of Palm Beach.

But the only casualties were a few persons who were slightly bruised by flying debris.

As one moves southward from Del Ray, however, the work of the storm becomes more and more evident. The gaunt trunks of giant Australian pines which line the road in many places are completely stripped of their bark. Telegraph and telephone poles are down on all sides and wires litter the highway.

At Deerfield the freight station of the Florida East Coast Railroad was completely demolished, two garages were hurled down upon the automobiles stored within and many houses shorn of their roofs. At Pompano the Ford motor station and a hardware store were toppled in.

The Floranada Club, the once brilliant dream of a fashionable Anglo-American society Winter resort, has been transformed into a swamp, above which the long rows of street lamps, all bent double, appear to bow mockingly.

Fort Lauderdale Trail of Ruin.

Just north of Fort Lauderdale one strikes the real storm area. Here giant pines have been torn up bodily by the roots, carrying with them great clods of earth and leaving great voids in the soil like huge shell craters.

Clusters of small frame bungalows which line the road thereabouts have been tossed about by the wind and lie in all postures. Some stand upside down, others lie crazily on their sides and still others, shaken on their foundations, lean all awry.

Fort Lauderdale, where the hurricane raged at a velocity of 125 miles an hour, has scarcely a house left intact. The main street of the town is lined with buildings from which the upper stories are missing. Automobiles hang threateningly from the upper floors of storehouses or garages, the walls of which are gone.

Although the populace of the town has worked day and night since the storm abated to repair the damage, they have scarcely begun the work of clearing away the wreckage. Up to tonight twelve dead bodies had been removed from the ruins and fifty persons seriously injured were in the hospitals. But it was impossible to say how many more bodies lie beneath the wreckage.

The proximity of the Gulf Stream, which is three miles off Las Olas Beach and six miles east of Fort Lauderdale proper, is generally credited with breaking the force of the waves and saving the town.

Water Swept Eight Miles Inland.

As it was, however, the water washed inland for nearly eight miles, carrying with it barges, houseboats and small motor craft.

A Coast Guard seaplane was dashed against a bridge and demolished. The houseboat Moccasin, which draws eight feet of water, was carried clear across New River Sound, a shallow inland waterway not more than four feet deep, and the launch Elizabeth V. of New Brunswick was perched in the middle of a highway this morning, nearly a mile from the nearest waterway, and two miles from the beach.

Governor John W. Martin of Florida visited all towns in the stricken area today, and following his visit efforts to organize relief work, which had been somewhat handicapped by local rivalries, appeared to be making better headway.

Refugees were being transported to towns further north, where they were taken in and cared for in private homes. Before leaving all were compelled to register, so that the city authorities might be able to aid friends and relatives in finding them.

Objection to Martial Law.

Up to the time of the Governor's arrival the city had considered itself under martial law, a measure proclaimed as necessary by Mayor John W. Tibbaugh.

Troops of the Florida National Guard were in full command of the town and many posters, prominently displayed along the main street, gave notice to the public that they would be compelled to bathe at the beach once a day. This order was signed by the local National Guard officer in charge.

The Broward County authorities were very much incensed over the high-handed methods of the guardsmen, so that when Governor Martin arrived they immediately went to him with their complaints. He assured them he had at no time proclaimed martial law and had ordered out the National Guard merely to supplement and aid the local police.

Thus assured, Sheriff Paul C. Bryan went to the City Hall, which the guardsmen had made their headquarters, and took charge of things.

Sanitary Corps Organized.

Physicians of the city organized a special corps to carry on sanitary work. Hand bills were distributed to the public warning them not to drink any water without first boiling it.

Chloride of lime was distributed free of charge at the City Hall and all persons were advised to chlorinate their drinking water.

Medical supplies in large quantities were arriving with each train coming in from the North. **One hundred and fifty nurses arrived in the morning from Palm Beach.**

Dr. D. L. Campbell, former City Health Officer, said this afternoon that there was no immediate danger of an epidemic at Fort Lauderdale.

He said the authorities were preparing a campaign to inoculate all persons there against typhoid. They would begin work as soon as the necessary serum arrived. He expected the first shipment tomorrow morning.

Although fifteen persons had previously been listed as dead in Fort Lauderdale, it was discovered that four unidentified dead were being carried by mistake on the list of casualties.

It was thought the real number of dead was eleven. Later in the day, however, the body of an unidentified negro was discovered among the debris of his small cabin. He had been pinned down by a rafter and drowned.

Lighting System Disrupted.

Commander C. G. Porcher, in charge of the Coast Guard base there, said the barometer dropped to 28.40 during the storm, the lowest he had ever seen recorded.

Soon after the storm subsided the old city water tower, which had been stripped of its cover by the storm but which had not been overturned, was pressed into service and has been doing duty ever since. The city thereby was able to avert water shortage.

But the lighting system has not been repaired and all telegraph and telephone wires are still down.

The plant of The Fort Lauderdale News was badly damaged and the paper has been getting out a handbill every day, giving merely the high spots of the news.

Although there was some looting in Fort Lauderdale after the storm subsided, most of it is said to have been done by persons without clothing who sought to find something to wear.

One shopkeeper, who was knocked down and pinned beneath a beam, told how two men had entered his store as he lay there crying for aid and emptied his cash register of its contents.

Hospital authorities say that several babies were born during the height of the storm.

Efforts to communicate with a band of fifty Seminole Indians under Chief Tony Tommy, who were last heard from at Davie, five miles west of Fort Lauderdale, have not been successful so far, and some fear is felt for their safety.

Throngs Watch Death Lists.

Dania and Hollywood also suffered heavily in the storm. Thirty-six bodies had been recovered tonight from ruined stores and homes in these towns, and it is impossible to say how many others have been killed.

All day long crowds of persons looking for missing relatives or friends stood outside The News Building in Hollywood watching the lists of dead and injured.

An enterprising promotion manager, determined not to miss such an opoprtunity for publicity, posted alongside the death list a large placard which read:

"Hollywood is rebuilding bigger and better than ever. More than a million has already been paid out in tornado insurance."

It was explained that this money was paid out by private insurance companies through an insurance division of the corporation organized when its development began four years ago.

Another placard on the bulletin board announced that free transportation would be furnished by the Hollywood Company to all destitute and homeless people there to any part of the United States on special trains which will be sent out daily.

Ten Killed in Dania Church.

The main street of Dania resembles a scene in a shell-torn village in France during the war. The Methodist Church was completely destroyed and ten persons who sought shelter inside it were killed. The steeple toppled into the street and still lies there.

Every house in the town is damaged to some extent.

The situation in Hollywood is the same, although, whereas in Dania the wind was responsible for nearly all the damage, much of the damage in Hollywood was caused by water. The Hollywood Hotel was damaged to the extent of $500,000, it was said, and damage elsewhere in Hollywood is estimated at nearly $400,000.

Residents of Hollywood say that in addition to the hurricane they experienced a tidal wave there. It started, they said, at a height of five feet at the beach and when it reached the west side of the town had dwindled to three feet. Then it

The town of Hallandale also was badly damaged. Despite reports to the contrary, the damage at Miami Beach does not compare with that in Fort Lauderdale and other sections. Although many homes in Miami Beach were stripped of small sections of their roofs and had all their windows shattered, very few collapsed.

The same applies to the business district of Miami, where only a few buildings caved in, and these were badly put together. Miami's streets are now practically cleared of debris, although in Miami Beach the streets still are partially blocked by fallen cocoanuts, palms and other trees.

In the outlying sections of Miami, where the houses were all of the frame-bungalow type, however, conditions are identical with those at Dania and Hollywood. Household furnishings are scattered in all directions, and of many bungalows only heaps of splintered timbers remain.

Of all the buiuding sections of Miami, Hialeah probably suffered most. It is impossible to tell how many persons were killed there. The relief workers openly acknowledge that they do not know, but their guesses range from twenty to forty dead and from 200 to 400 injured.

The Hialeah Race Track lost large portions of the roof from the grand stand and several of the stables were blown down. The arena of the Jai Alai games lost its roof and much of the walls. Both of the dog racing tracks were partially demolished, and in Hialeah proper seventy families were rendered homeless.

Federal Health Survey Coming.

Dr. C. F. Roche, Health Officer of Miami Beach, said that the same precautions against the possibility of a typhoid epidemic were being taken there and elsewhere.

Governor Martin announced tonight that he had received word that Surgeon General Hugh S. Cummins is sending Government experts by airplane to Miami to make an immediate survey of health conditions in the storm zone.

When Governor Martin asked Acting Mayor James H. Gilman of Miami what the city needed, Mr. Gilman replied, "Money with which to rebuild." He said that further shipments of food were unnecessary, as there is no food shortage and the city has ample food with which to provide for everyone.

It will probably be many days before an accurate check-up can be made of the persons killed and injured in the storm.

Miami's death list at present contains ninety-two names, including persons killed in Hialeah, Allapattah and Coral Gables.

With the eleven persons killed at Fort Lauderdale and the sixteen at Dania and Hollywood this brings the present number of known dead to 138.

It is impossible to get an accurate list of the injured, since hundreds of them are being rushed to towns north of the storm area.

In the Town of Moorehaven, at the southwest corner of Lake Okeechobee, 160 persons were killed and many other towns in that vicinity were entirely wiped out. There are also scores of tiny settlements in the Everglades which are completely out of touch with civilization and from which nothing may ever be heard.

Insurance Payments Soon.

Insurance agency officials in Miami estimated yesterday that from $20,000,000 to $50,000,000 in insurance was carried by victims of the storm in the Miami district. They said that the work of paying claims would begin within a few days and would be carried on as expeditiously and with as little red tape as possible.

All dead removed from ruins in the storm area are being sent home for burial or buried immediately here. Where burial is made here, officials explained, relatives will receive permits to disinter bodies whenever they desire, should they care to have them buried elsewhere.

A force of 5,000 men has been engaged to clear the debris from the streets of Hollywood.

J. W. Young, developer of Hollywood, returned from New York yesterday and immediately took personal charge of the relief workk.

Known Dead Grow Slowly in Number.

MIAMI, Fla., Sept. 21 (AP).—At least 400 persons dead, 150 or more missing, 5,000 injured and 50,000 homeless—this was the known sum tonight of human life and suffering in cities and towns along Florida's southeastern coast in the tropical hurricane.

At Miami the death total increased as Biscayne Bay gave up more of its dead. Authorities said the list probably would reach 250, although it was approximately 200 tonight. Hospitals and Red Cross stations here treated more than 3,000 injured during the day, many of them only slightly hurt.

At Hollywood the list of known dead was thirty-two, with possibly eight other bodies to be brought in and with seventy persons listed as missing.

Fort Lauderdale's death list remained at eleven during the day, but the list of seriously injured increased to 300. There are 500 others less seriously hurt in the Fort Lauderdale, Floranada and Progresso neighborhood. The Red Cross relief stations were crowded with injured and refugees.

Reports from other localities indicate little change in the death list with the exception of Dania and Davie, both of which reported several additional bodies found.

Actual damage to homes and business buildings was estimated at nearly $50,000,000, but many held that the value of the millions of palms and pines which were uprooted or cut to the ground would double the damage estimate. Paved roads, sidewalks, development gateways and clubhouses also had to be added, as well as the loss to business firms by the cessation of work, due either to storm damage or lack of power or water.

Reports from farm and citrus growing areas show a steadily mounting estimate of damage to crops. In the Homestead section of the Redlands district in the southern section of Dade County, $2,000,000 is believed to have been the toll in damage to the orange, grapefruit and avocado crops, while Fort Myers, on the west coast, reported an estimated loss of more than $1,000,000 to the crops from high winds.

In the devastated area where the waters have receded millions of fish were left to die. **Countless thousands of crabs and fiddlers swarm over the land in search of the watering places from which they were swept last week.**

Specific appeals for assistance reached the Red Cross unit from different points. West Palm Beach reported imperative need for cots, bedding and clothing. A carload of foodstuffs was forwarded to Sebring, where 1,000 refugees from Moore Haven, casualty centre of the interior, were quartered.

Another carload of cots, lanterns, candles and clothing, especially for children, was assembled for Fort Lauderdale and Hollywood. For the same two communities a special effort was made to obtain two cars of chloride of lime from Atlanta.

Money for rehabilitation operations is becoming a greater need than food and other supplies, the Jacksonville Red Cross Chapter announced. In response to an appeal from Sebring for funds to aid in the care of the Moore Haven refugees, $3,000 was forwarded by the Citizens' Committee of Jacksonville.

An airplane shipment of tetanus antitoxin, one of the pressing needs of the devastated region, left Jacksonville this afternoon for Miami after a delay of twenty-hour hours, due to the breaking of a propeller when the plane landed upon its arrival from Richmond yesterday. A new propeller was obtained by Lieutenant Bissell, the pilot.

Miami was recovering encouragingly today while the relief trains brought tons of food and clothing.

"All the News That's Fit to Print."

The New York Times.

THE WEATHER
Today cloudy, showers in afternoon or night; tomorrow cloudy, cooler.
Temperature Yesterday—Max. 76; Min. 61.
For weather report see Page 50.

VOL. LXXVII....No. 25,451. *** NEW YORK, FRIDAY, SEPTEMBER 30, 1927. TWO CENTS In Greater New York | THREE CENTS Within 200 Miles | FOUR CENTS Elsewhere in the U. S.

5-MINUTE TORNADO KILLS 69 IN ST. LOUIS; 600 ARE INJURED, DAMAGE IS $75,000,000; WEALTHY WEST SIDE SUFFERS HEAVILY

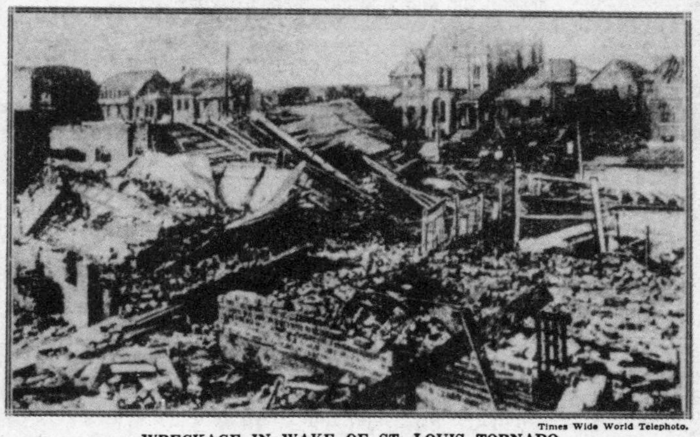

Times Wide World Telephoto.

WRECKAGE IN WAKE OF ST. LOUIS TORNADO.
The Ruins of a Garage and Bakery at Sarah Street and McPherson Avenue, From Which a Girl Was Removed Uninjured After She Had Been Covered by Debris.

5,000 HOUSES DESTROYED

Falling Walls Trap Many and Fires Start in the Ruins.

SIX SQUARE MILES SWEPT

Troops Mobilized and Police Are Told to Shoot Looters on Sight.

SCHOOL CHILDREN ESCAPE

March Out When Part of Building Collapses—Rain Adds to Terror and Confusion.

Special to The New York Times.

ST. LOUIS, Mo., Sept. 29.—A tornado and rainstorm, sweeping over St. Louis and vicinity this afternoon with unprecedented fury, blasted an area of six square miles through the residential and outlying business sections of the city and took a toll of sixty-nine lives and did property damage that may exceed $$75,000,000.

With rescuers working through the night it is probable that the death list may reach 100 and that the list of injured, which now stands at 600, may reach 1,000 to 1,500. More than 5,000 houses were destroyed.

The storm struck with sudden fury at 1 o'clock this afternoon, lasting in its full force only five minutes. Its first intensity was noticed at Manchester and Taylor Avenues. Then with ever-increasing intensity it swept north in a widened area to Prairie Avenue, west to Kings Highway and east to Glasgow Avenue. This area measured approximately six square miles and embraces both residences and business blocks, but the downtown business section escaped unharmed.

It was the beautiful West End which bore a large part of the tornado's wrath, a section of beautiful boulevards and homes, where many wealthy residents live.

The violent wind, which, according to the Weather Bureau, reached a velocity of ninety miles an hour, was accompanied by a terrific rainstorm, which added to the desolation.

Buildings Wrecked Like Toys.

Trees were uprooted, houses and factories were overturned like so many toys, telephone poles were snapped off at the ground and electric light wires were scrambled on the ground.

Hundreds of persons were moved to the hospitals after being dragged from the wreckage.

Wire communication was paralyzed and fires dotted the wrecked residential area. Some of St. Louis's finest homes and streets were in ruins, and business places and factories, supposed to be storm proof, were a mass of wreckage.

Thousands of rescuers were digging in the ruins, extricating the dead and injured. It was estimated that 5,000 residences were leveled to the ground.

Except for a hard blow and heavy rain, most of the downtown section was spared, as were the Cabanne district of the West End, sections to the north of it, and the South Side, which was the centre of damage in the tornado of 1896.

In the sections hit by the storm pedestrians were swept from their feet by wind, roofs were lifted wholly or in part, automobiles were blown about and their tops damaged, trees were blown down or stripped of limbs, and the wrecking of poles, wires and windows was general. Telephone and telegraph lines were disabled.

Silence Precedes Storm's Fury.

For an hour before the storm struck with lightning like swiftness, a desultory thundershower had played about the Western horizon. There were jagged flashes of lightning, almost incessant, the continuous low rumble of thunder, interspersed with an ominous crackling, and a gathering darkness.

A tense silence, which made people's ears ring, and a sense of oppression heralded the coming of the tornado. There was a dull drumming sound as of innumerable wings being flapped high in the air, and the swirl of black dust about the sky. Then a spiral of loosely woven clouds headed downward, an inky blackness in its wake, and the twister began its devastation.

Everywhere the sound of crashing glass could be heard. The air was filled with huge missiles, which tore off chimneys and cornices and the corners of sturdy blocks. Great sections of roofs from buildings where the tornado first struck were tossed about like straws.

Bricks, tiles from roofs, tops of automobiles, great chunks of glass, huge limbs of trees, signs and movable objects of every conceivable size and variety were blown along, the larger missiles bowling over anything in their paths, and through it all a grayish-black dust swirled, pouring in streams through shattered win-

---

SMITH FORESTALLS REPUBLICAN ATTACK IN CONVENTION TALK

Replies in Advance to What He Expects Roosevelt to Say in Speech Today.

HE IS SILENT ON 1928

And No Other Speaker at Democratic Gathering at Albany Mentions Governor's Boom.

STATE ISSUES OUTLINED

Smith Opposes Four-Year Term, but Asks Approval of Other Amendments—Wet Move Fails.

From a Staff Correspondent of The New York Times.

ALBANY, N. Y., Sept. 29.—Refraining from the slightest mention of his aspiration for the Presidential nomination, Governor Alfred E. Smith launched his campaign to defeat the proposed constitutional amendment to lengthen the term of the Governor to four years, with the election in Presidential years, in a speech at the Democratic State Convention here today.

The Governor, anticipating an attack upon him and his Administration for alleged extravagance at the Republican State Convention at Rochester tomorrow, replied in advance to what he said he expected would be the arguments advanced by Colonel Theodore Roosevelt, who is to be the Chairman of that convention, and served notice on "the young Colonel," as he called him, that he would require him or any other Republican to sustain such charges in an appeal to the voters of the State.

An opportunity for a demonstration such as usually greets Governor Smith in his appearances before a State convention of his own party was lacking, as there was an obvious effort to prevent anything which might have been interpreted as the launching of his Presidential boom.

Presidential Boom Under Cover.

The willingness of the delegates to acclaim the Governor as the next Democratic candidate for President was apparent, and there was little talk of anything else in the corridors of Harmanus Bleecker Hall, where the convention was held, and in the lobby of the Hotel Ten Eyck, where the delegates gathered before and after the convention.

Only once in the convention was there a statement which the delegates took to refer to the Governor's Presidential candidacy, and that was when Warnick J. Kernan of Utica, the Chairman, in introducing Governor Smith said:

"New York has had many great Democrats. It had Samuel J. Tilden, the nominee of his party for President. It was from the ranks of the Democratic Party in this State that Grover Cleveland was drafted for the Presidency. New York has had many great Democrats, but none greater than our great Governor, Alfred E. Smith."

Long and sustained cheering greeted this introduction, but the Governor checked the demonstration and went on with his speech without referring in any way to the campaign being made to obtain for him the Democratic Presidential nomination.

This was about the only time the delegates and spectators had a chance to cheer. They came here from all parts of the State to cheer for "Smith for President," but were told to put on the "soft pedal" after they reached here.

Name Judge O'Brien Unanimously.

The convention disposed of its necessary business very quickly, and named Judge John F. O'Brien as the party nominee for Associate Judge of the Court of Appeals by acclamation.

Former Representative John B. Johnston of Brooklyn placed Judge O'Brien in nomination. The nomination was seconded by Representative John J. O'Connor of Manhattan and Miss Harriet May Mills of Syracuse.

Cornelius F. Byrne of Troy offered the resolution to empower the State Committee to appoint the delegates-at-large and the alternates-at-large to the Democratic National Convention, thus avoiding the necessity of a Spring convention for the election of these delegates next year. Under Mr. Byrne's resolution there will be eight delegates-at-large, each with a one-half vote, and the same number of alternates. There will be two delegates from each Congressional district to be elected at the Spring primary election.

Mr. Byrne's resolution was according to schedule and its adoption is intended to prevent possible embarrassment to the Governor, perhaps a clash on the prohibition issue which might be caused by holding a Spring convention.

Such a clash was avoided today by the simple expedient of preventing Assemblyman Louis A. Cuvillier, head of the National Constitutional Liberty League of America, who had announced his intention of offering a resolution for the repeal or modification of the Eighteenth Amendment, getting a proxy to sit as a delegate in the convention.

Mr. Cuvillier had expected a proxy from an Erie County delegate, but was told later by this delegate that he could not give it to him. Immedi-

Continued on Page Sixteen.

Bonds Stolen From Garfield Bank Here Used in Pennsylvania Election Campaign

Special to The New York Times.

WILKES-BARRE, Pa., Sept. 29.—Four men were taken into custody here today in connection with the theft of $79,000 worth of Bridgeport (Conn.) municipal bonds which were stolen some time ago from the desk of R. W. Poor, general manager of the Garfield National Bank of New York City.

B. H. McKeehan of Wyoming, Pa., an insurance and real estate man, was arrested on a bench warrant signed by Judges Jones, McLean and Fuller, and is charged with conspiracy, larceny and receiving stolen goods. He was committed to the county prison in default of $20,000 bail.

John J. Walsh, merchant, of Plains Township, Pa.;; Squire D. F. Mulligan of Wilkes-Barre Township and A. M. Bernstein, a merchant of Wilkes-Barre, are each held under $5,000 bail as material witnesses.

The bonds were distributed among banks in Wilkes-Barre, Plymouth and Scranton, being put up as security for 80 per cent. of their value for loans. Part of the money taken from the local banks, it is charged, was dumped into a pool to back the candidacy of Dr. Frank D. Thomas, who sought the Republican nomination for Sheriff in Luzerne County.

McKeehan, Walsh and Mulligan were campaign managers of Dr. Thomas, and, despite their use of thousands of dollars, Thomas ran a poor fourth in the contest.

McKeehan, according to testimony offered today, met on the street a stranger, who made himself acquainted on the strength of fraternal society relationship and said his name was Harris.

The man suggested that McKeehan could get money for the Thomas campaign by obtaining bank loans on Bridgeport municipal bonds in his possession.

Walsh, Mulligan and Bernstein then came into the picture and they each helped in getting loans from $3,500 up.

Captain William Clarke of the State Police testified that McKeehan turned over some of the bonds for the campaign. The proceeds of the rest, he said, went to "Harris" after McKeehan had received 20 per cent. for himself.

It is said by county detectives that more than $100,000 in stolen bonds were floated among the banks in Wyoming Valley and that most of this was dumped into the Thomas campaign.

Dr. Thomas said tonight that he knew nothing whatever about the bonds and that no money for his campaign was handed him.

STATE REPUBLICANS PLAN WAR ON SMITH

The Convention at Rochester Awaits Roosevelt's Keynote Broadside Today.

ARE TOLD COOLIDGE IS OUT

Washington Officeholders Bear Definite Word Another Must Be Sought.

From a Staff Correspondent of The New York Times.

ROCHESTER, N. Y., Sept. 29.—Federal officeholders who are here in force for the Republican State Convention, which will meet here tomorrow, have brought word to the party leaders in this State that President Coolidge in his "Do not choose" statement definitely took himself out as a prospective candidate for the Presidential nomination next year and furthermore that any effort to "draft" Mr. Coolidge, except in the face of some grave emergency, which is not likely to arise, is bound to come to naught because of a fixed determination on the part of the President not to remain in his present office beyond March 4, 1929.

The Federal officeholders were earlier on the ground than most of the party leaders, but tonight, with the Republican clans gathering for tomorrow's event, it is evident that the last lingering hope with regard to the possible availability of Mr. Coolidge as a standard bearer in next year's national fight has been snatched from those who harbored it. From now on, it is predicted, Republicans in this State will begin to cast about for some other man and a new allegiance.

Little Talk About Hughes.

Oddly enough, little talk is heard about Charles E. Hughes in that connection, even though it is likely that unless some word from him should render such a course impossible the delegation from this State to the Republican National Convention next year may be pledged to him as the "favorite son" of the Empire State. The "Federal crowd" was talking Hoover so persistently that they made a decided impression among delegates here for the State Convention.

"Hughes would be strong in this State and probably in the East generally, but it would be an up-hill fight in the West with Hughes heading the ticket," was the explanation volunteered by a prominent Republican leader occupying a high official position in Washington. "Hoover will carry this State against Smith, although perhaps, by a somewhat smaller plurality."

With Hoover talk predominating and a notion pretty generally prevailing, owing undoubtedly to the source from which it sprung, that it may have been "inspired," there has been some talk about Frank O. Lowden, former Governor of Illinois, whose supporters are preparing to make a drive for delegates from this State. Oddly enough, the Lowden talk appeared to emanate from a group of Republican women who will sit as delegates at tomorrow's convention and was first heard following the arrival of Miss Sarah Schuyler Butler, Vice Chairman of the Republican State Committee in charge of the women's division.

Program Puzzles Delegates.

But for the fact that tomorrow's State convention was designed by the Republicans primarily as a curtain raiser for 1928 and that the national contest next year will project its broad shadow over the proceedings, the event would be almost barren of interest for party men. As it is, bewildered delegates contemplating the program proposed by Chairman George K. Morris of the Republican State Committee are asking what it is all about.

This program contemplates the nomination by a Republican State convention of Associate Judge John F. O'Brien for the Court of Appeals bench, a Democrat and an appointee of Governor Smith, for the position he will continue filling until the end

Continued on Page Sixteen.

CALLES, ON 'PHONE, GREETS COOLIDGE

At Opening of New Service Both Presidents Predict It Will Improve Relations.

NEEDLESS DISPUTE DECRIED

Calles Hopes for New Era That Will End Clashes—Ceremonies in Two Capitals.

Special to The New York Times.

WASHINGTON, Sept. 29.—Telephone service between Mexico and the United States was formally started late today by President Coolidge and President Calles of Mexico and officers of their respective Governments.

Over a line 3,357 miles long stretching through New York, Chicago, St. Louis, San Antonio, Laredo, Saltillo and other Mexican cities, the Chief Executives addressed each other in direct conversation, making the occasion an opportunity for expressions of international good-will and mutual esteem.

The ceremonies here were conducted in the Hall of the Americas of the Pan American Union in the presence of a distinguished gathering which included members of the Cabinet, ranking officers of the army and navy and members of the Latin-American diplomatic corps.

Those in Mexico City were conducted at the National Palace.

President Coolidge referred to the new long-distance telephone link between the two countries as new facilities that "will promote a better understanding between the peoples of our countries."

Calles Hopes for "New Era."

President Calles, in response, declared "this event will undoubtedly improve international relations between Mexico and the United States of America."

He wished, he said, to renew his "ardent hopes" for the beginning of a new era for the two Governments, "an era of good-will and mutual understanding which cannot fail to put an end to all those needless misunderstandings that so frequently exist with prejudice to the moral development of nations."

Neither President could understand the other when he was speaking, but Mr. Coolidge's address was translated into Spanish for the Mexican Executive and the process was reversed for the American President.

The Presidents were followed in the telephonic conversations by Wilbur J. Carr, acting Secretary of State, and Genaro Estrada, acting Secretary of Foreign Affairs of Mexico; Manuel C. Tellez, Mexican Ambassador here, and H. F. Arthur Schoenfeld, American Chargé d'Affaires in Mexico City.

Each guest here has a set of head phones and was able to listen in to all the conversations.

Dr. L. S. Rowe, Director General of the Pan American Union, presided. Walter S. Gifford, President of the American Telephone and Telegraph Company, in an address explained the achievement by which the two countries had been telephonically united. Mr. Gifford announced that service between the two countries would be open to the public after 8 o'clock tomorrow morning.

Following this, the United States Army Band from the patio of the Pan American Building played the national anthem of Mexico, and the band of the Federal District in Mex-

Continued on Page Four.

ATTORNEY INDICTED FOR SHIELDING BEACH IN MURDER MYSTERY

Charged With Hiding a Witness and Spiriting Away a Man Wanted for a Crime.

WILL SURRENDER TODAY

Hedges Declares He Has No Idea Now of His Fugitive Client's Whereabouts.

BOY SAYS HE SAW SLAYING

Will Be Questioned Today—Cross Is Burned on Lawn of Lilliendahl Home.

Special to The New York Times.

HAMMONTON, N. J., Sept. 29.—Edison Hedges, attorney for Willis Beach, fugitive, under a charge of being an accessory in the Lilliendahl murder case, was indicted on two counts today by the Atlantic County Grand Jury at Mays Landing. The lawyer was charged with spiriting away a material witness in the first count, and in the second with spiriting away a man wanted for a crime.

The indictment was handed to Common Pleas Judge William H. Smathers, whose clerk, William A. Blair, issued bench warrants. The warrants were withheld, however, and Hedges is to surrender at 9 A. M. tomorrow to County Prosecutor Louis Repetto in Atlantic City. Mr. Hedges had no comment to make on the action of the Grand Jury.

The indictment was based on the attorney's advice to Beach to leave the jurisdiction. Beach is still missing and although Mr. Hedges had maintained that he knew where he was and could produce him for the courts, the lawyer admitted today that he had no idea where his client was now. Neither had the police.

Crime Act Violation Charged.

The charge against Mr. Hedges is a violation of Section B-35 of the New Jersey Crimes act. It is a misdemeanor carrying alternative maximum penalties of three years in jail or $1,000 fine. It was said that most of his colleagues of the criminal bar in Atlantic County indicated today that they supported Mr. Hedges's interpretation of his duty to a client.

County Detective Nat Kashel of Atlantic County went to Hoboken tonight to get a youth who said he was Alfred Longben, 18 years old, of Buffalo Avenue, Egg Harbor. The Prosecutor's office was notified by the Hoboken police that Longben had said he was an eyewitness to the Lilliendahl murder, and had said the killing was done by a negro.

Longben was held here for questioning tomorrow.

The Grand Jury convened at 1 P. M. and S. Cameron Hinkle, Assistant Prosecutor, presented the evidence. The first witnesses called were State Trooper N. Robert Woodward, Chief County Detective Frank I. Harrold and County Detective Richard Black. Several newspaper men testified next. They were called to tell of an interview with Mr. Hedges in which they said the lawyer admitted advising Beach to leave the State. The reporters and their newspapers were: Miss Irene Kuhn, The Daily Mirror, New York; George Dixon, Philadelphia Inquirer; Ralph Cropper, Philadelphia Evening Public Ledger; John J. Fitzgerald, Camden Courier; Raymond Baker, Philadelphia Record, and Robert Conway, The New York American.

No Other Warrants Planned.

"All that I can truthfully say," said Mr. Hinkle, "is that the investigation is progressing as rapidly as we can hope for. The mystery is nearing a complete solution. In order that we may be absolutely certain, or as nearly certain as possible, we are taking every precaution that no one need be accused who is innocent and that no one who is guilty will be overlooked."

"We are of the opinion that the shots were fired by one person, but I cannot at this time disclose what person or persons may have been otherwise connected with the murder. We are not issuing any other warrants just now.

"This Hedges phase of the investigation will disclose whether a lawyer can obstruct justice and stifle an inquiry of this sort. It will show whether one lawyer is bigger than the whole State of New Jersey. The claim that third-degree methods were used on Beach is entirely untrue. Beach was treated with a great deal of courtesy and consideration."

Despite Mr. Hinkle's optimistic

Continued on Page Thirteen.

French Reds Mutiny in Toulon Naval Prison; Free 100 Before Sailors Quell Protest Riot

Copyright, 1927, by The New York Times Company.
Special Cable to THE NEW YORK TIMES.

PARIS, Sept. 29.—Twelve Communist inmates of the Naval Prison at Toulon attempted a mutiny yesterday afternoon as a protest against the sentences imposed on André Marty and other Communist leaders in Paris a few days ago.

Shouting, "Down with the army! Long live Marty!" and armed with picks and other tools, which had been introduced into their cells in a manner not yet accounted for, they succeeded in liberating nearly 100 other prisoners and smashing everything in sight.

The prison guards were unable to cope with them, and the naval authorities were notified. They sent a detachment of naval gendarmes and armed sailors, who soon succeeded in rounding up the mutineers. The latter were placed in camions and rushed to the prison annex at Malbousquet, where they could be better guarded.

However, before this happened, the Communist centres in the vicinity must have received word of trouble. At 5:30 o'clock, 200 workers from the arsenal assembled at the entrance of the prison. They began singing the "Internationale" in evident sympathy with the mutineers, and were only dispersed on the arrival of a detachment of police.

N. Y. CENTRAL TRACKS LAID ON CITY'S LAND

Mayor Orders Inquiry When He Hears That New Lines Are Put Down in Riverside Park.

STATE BOARD APPROVED

Transit Engineer Sees Walker Uninformed on Plan for Grade-Crossing Elimination.

Mayor Walker, while presiding yesterday over the meeting of the Board of Estimate, expressed surprise when he was informed that the New York Central Railroad Company, with the ostensible sanction of the Public Service Commission, has been laying lines of from four to eight additional tracks on city property west of its right-of-way between 145th and 153d Streets, in the Riverside Park area.

The Mayor consulted Arthur S. Tuttle, Chief Engineer of the Board of Estimate, and ordered that a special report upon the situation be made as early as possible.

Doubts Board's Power.

"I am inclined to doubt the right of the Public Service Commission," said the Mayor, "to permit the use of city property by a railroad without regular judicial proceedings. That, however, is a moot question. We cannot act too hastily, remembering that to a great extent we depend upon the railroads for our food and merchandise. But, of course, that fact alone would not entitle a railroad to take city property."

"Our waterfront is very precious to us and we don't want to lose it," declared Mrs. John Jerome Rooney, President of the West 145th Street Taxpayers' Association. She, with Mrs. John Clapperton Kerr, representing the Women's League for the Protection of Riverside Park, had appeared in the meeting and had informed the Mayor of the new tracks laid by the railroad.

Chief Engineer Tuttle said the Public Service Commission had permitted the laying of the rails and spoke of the work having been done under an "adjustment," presumably in the course of negotiations with the railroad looking to the development of the west side improvement.

Fears Use by Railroad.

Mrs. Rooney protested that, from past experience, she thought it would be difficult to persuade the railroad to relinquish anything after having once acquired it.

"I want to assure you," said the Mayor, "that no title will be given to the railroad."

Mrs. Kerr said after the meeting: "The property which the railroad has taken is sorely needed for playgrounds and other recreational purposes. The city must get back that property or the people will want to know why not. There has been enough invasion of our incomparable Riverside Drive waterfront. It should stop right now."

Colonel Lancaster's Views.

The opinion that Mayor Walker was not entirely conversant with all the plans under which the Transit Commission some time ago arranged for elimination of New York Central grade crossings along the Hudson and under which the present track laying presumably is being done, was expressed last night by Colonel William C. Lancaster, chief engineer of the Transit Commission and Chairman of the Board of Engineers which formulated the plans.

"When the New York Central Railroad was ordered to eliminate grade crossings between 125th Street and 138th Street along the Hudson River, a set of plans was drawn up by a board of engineers representing the State, the city and the railroad," Colonel Lancaster said. "The work was a part of the general scheme for west side improvement, which

Continued on Page Three.

Man Is Sentenced for Life For Possessing Pint of Gin

Special to The New York Times.

LANSING, Mich., Sept. 29.—Fred Palm, aged 29, of Lansing, will start serving a life sentence in State prison tomorrow for possession of one pint of gin. He was sentenced this afternoon by Judge Leland Carr in Ingham County Circuit Court after he had been convicted of illegal possession of liquor.

He is the first liquor law violator in Michigan to be arraigned and sentenced under Michigan's Baumes law, making life imprisonment mandatory following conviction of four felonies.

Palm's crimes with one exception have all been violations of the prohibition law. He was sent to Leavenworth in 1920 for raising currency.

GOVERNMENT CURBED ON ALCOHOL POLICY

Manufacturers Need Not Prove to Whom They Sell Finished Product, Court Rules.

FAR-REACHING EFFECT SEEN

Dry Men Had Employed That Method to Trace Ultimate User—'Tyranny' Viewed as Ended.

Federal Judge Joseph C. Hutcheson Jr. of the United States Court of Texas, sitting in New York by designation, handed down a decision yesterday in which he held that the action of Prohibition Administrator Maurice Campbell, in seeking to impose terms as a condition for further withdrawals of denatured alcohol by a perfume manufacturer, had been "merely personal and arbitrary and without support in regulation or law."

Judge Hutcheson ruled also that manufacturers who hold permits for the withdrawal of denatured alcohol do not have to prove to the Administrator's satisfaction that they sell their finished products to recognized dealers in the trade only, but need show only actual confirmations of their sales. The decision is considered far-reaching and of great importance to manufacturers.

It has been the contention of the Government that it had the right to require a manufacturer of a product requiring denatured alcohol to tell to whom he sold his finished product and then to make that purchaser tell who his customers were.

The case in which the decision was rendered was that of Nicke Weste, a perfume manufacturer, against Mr. Campbell, Prohibition Commissioner James Doran and Secretary of the Treasury Mellon. The Government was represented by Assistant United States Attorney U. S. Grant. Lewis Landes, who appeared for the plaintiff, said of the decision:

"Judge Hutcheson's opinion, it will be noted, puts a stop to the indiscriminate tyranny of the Administrator in refusing to grant that which is a right to the applicants for permits, and prohibits the prohibition authorities from trying to regulate and control the activities of businessmen."

Judge Hutcheson's decision follows in part:

"Plaintiff asserts that his permit is, in effect, canceled in that by an order issued by the Prohibition Administrator on April 8 he was not permitted to withdraw any denatured alcohol until he should submit to the Prohibition Administrator orders for merchandise from persons having a recognized standing in the perfumery industry and who stood ready to satisfy the Administrator as to the dis-

Continued on Page Eleven.

LAWYER ACCUSED AS FOOD GRAFTER

Pecora to Present Evidence to Grand Jury Involving Bar Member in Scandal.

NEW DISCLOSURES HINTED

Unidentified Man Said to Be in Position to Name Others—Tompkins Ends Inquiry.

Assistant District Attorney Ferdinand Pecora concluded the presentation of evidence in the John Doe milk and poultry graft inquiry yesterday before Supreme Court Justice Arthur S. Tompkins at the County Court House. Justice Tompkins said he would hold himself in readiness for further sessions should occasion demand. Mr. Pecora will prepare a digest of the testimony, which involves some twenty former Health Department employes in about seventy-five distinct alleged crimes. After Justice Tompkins has studied it he will forward his findings to District Attorney Banton, indicating what cases he believes warrant presentation to the Grand Jury.

Mr. Pecora told the Court that in addition to the cases developed at the public hearings he would present directly to the Grand Jury evidence involving three persons already convicted in connection with Health Department grafting and "also another case where the allegations affect a member of the bar."

The three convicted persons are believed to be Thomas J. Clougher, once Secretary to former Health Commissioner Monaghan; Frederick W. Kautzmann, a former inspector, and William H. Kehoe, once Assistant Corporation Counsel assigned to duty at the Health Department. Clougher and Kautzmann are in Sing Sing and Kehoe's appeal from his conviction is pending before the Court of Appeals.

No Intimation of His Identity.

No intimation was given yesterday as to the identity of the lawyer said to be involved. He has been referred to as the "attorney general of the slaughter house grafters," in much the same way that Kehoe was termed "attorney general of the milk graft ring."

It is understood that the unnamed attorney is regarded as being in a position to make sensational disclosures concerning poultry slaughter house graft, in which it is alleged a regular scale of prices obtained for the granting of permits, ranging from $5,000 in Manhattan to $2,500 and less in other boroughs. Should the indictment and conviction of the unidentified lawyer follow it is hoped that further evidence of the "greatest importance" will become available involving persons thus far unnamed, it was said yesterday.

Justice Tompkins will open the October term of the Supreme Court in Orange County at Goshen next Monday and it is thought likely that District Attorney Banton will receive Justice Tompkins's findings some time next week. Following the adjournment of court at Goshen Justice Tompkins will hold another John Doe investigation in Brooklyn at the request of District Attorney Charles J. Dodd of Kings County. The evidence collected by former Supreme Court Justice Charles H. Kelby during his investigation of more than a year will be the basis of the inquiry, as it was of the hearings in New York County.

Two witnesses yesterday, Samuel Sahn, a live poultry wholesaler at 614 Flushing Avenue, Brooklyn, and David Danziger, in the poultry business at 730 Park Avenue, Brooklyn, suffered lapses of memory at the morning session. After consultation with Hyman Bushel, their counsel,

Continued on Page Nine.

An apartment building in St. Louis which was struck by the tornado.

United Press International

dows and sticking fast to everything it touched.

Sheets of flame, their origin a mystery to the beholder, swept past in uncanny fashion. Great gobs of blazing material which shed showers of brilliant sparks in the murk of night, which enveloped everything, were flung along, leaving a trail of fireworks as they suddenly disintegrated against some more substantial object. Awnings, articles of clothing, flag poles, lawn swings, pots, which a moment before had housed the brightly blooming shrubs of Autumn, pieces of fence, doors from garages and small outbuildings followed each other in a bewildering succession.

Calls to the City Hospital, begining immediately after the five-minute period of the storm's greatest intensity, caused ambulances to be sent in all directions, and the hospital soon after began to receive the injured.

Troops Are Mobilized.

All of the 1,500 members of the Police Department, regardless of their regular hours of duty, were called out to take part in rescue and relief work. Two members of the Police Department were reported among the dead. The Red Cross began mobilizing its relief forces.

"Shoot to kill" was the order issued by Chief of Police Gerk to all police stations. "Make a Coroner's case out of every one you catch looting in any form whatever."

Rescuers Work Frantically.

A picture of the storm area tonight was one of a wilderness of crumpled houses, fallen trees, wrecked factories, streets strewn with débris so dense traffic was unable to move through it; policemen shouting hoarse words of warning against the danger of live wires and collapsing walls; weeping women running frantically without direction, seeking children whom they believed buried in the ruins; men digging in vast heaps of brick and stones in desperate effort to reach persons buried below; ambulance bells clanging as cars swept by on missions of rescue; the shrill sirens of the fire fighters, and, over all, the pall of another approaching storm.

Hospital Patients Carried Out.

With the entire police force mobilized for action, the storm area was quickly blocked against the curious, but behind the cordon were a thousand or more men organized into makeshift units of relief. Men in overalls and men in smart business suits lent a hand at carrying the injured to the hospitals or to their homes. Boy Scouts became traffic officers and flappers drove their motor cars converted into ambulances.

At the Mullanphy Hospital there were pathetic scenes as the patients were carried out to places of greater security. In the basement hall of the building a white-capped Sister of Mercy stopped long enough to exclaim that "it was a miracle that all were not killed."

There were sixty-three patients in the hospital at the time the storm broke, the wind sidewiped the building, ripped the entire west wing to shreds, and sent the roof and upper floor crashing to the ground. This fourth floor is the quarters used by the nurses, and none was in that section at the time, but below were a score and more of expectant mothers or mothers with babes in arms—the maternity section.

Child Disappears in Air.

At the corner of McPherson Avenue and Sarah Street Carl Henry, manager of a filling station, sat in the doorway as the storm approached.

"When the wind hit," he said, "I could hear it, zooming, like a distant airplane engine. I jumped back into the station, but before I could close the door I was thrown by the wind over against that wall.

"You see over there that ruin? That is Hyman Appel's bake shop. I could see it from the window. I saw the wind hit it, and the walls were forced apart, like some great force from inside. And then the wind blew a little girl right through those walls. The building fell then, and one man was in it. The storm had passed. I rushed over and helped them dig Frank Cape out."

Across the Mississippi River from St. Louis, the suburbs of Venice, Madison and Granite City, Ill., were in the path of the storm. The dead there were said to number five, with twenty injured, of whom three were workers who were burned when the storm upset a crucible of molten steel. These three are not expected to live. The damage in the suburbs will run into hundreds of thousands of dollars.

Plants Collapse, Killing Many.

Three men were killed at the Hydraulic Press Brick Company plant, 5,100 Manchester Avenue, when part of the building collapsed. Three perished at the Polar Wave Ice plant, Union and Newstead Avenues, by the falling of a wall, and three other men lost their lives at the Blackmer & Post Pipe Company, 2,801 Hereford Street. The bodies were taken to the morgue.

A man having in his pockets letters addressed to William Owsley, 4,440 Easton Avenue, was found unconscious in an automobile on Kings Highway, just south of Oakland Avenue, near the southeast corner of Forest Park. A heavy piece of lumber had been blown into the automobile, striking the man's head. He died in an ambulance on the way to the City Hospital.

One man was killed and six injured when the wind blew down a telegraph pole that crashed through the roof of the Federal Motor Car Company, 4,060 West Pine Boulevard. The man's body was taken to the city morgue and the injured to the City Hospital.

In the collapse of a building at 3,700 Easton Avenue two men were reported killed.

"All the News That's Fit to Print."

The New York Times.

THE WEATHER
Colder today, with rain this morning; tomorrow, fair and colder.
Temperature yesterday—Max., 51; min., 40.
For weather report see Page 5?.

VOL. LXXVII....No. 25,617. **** NEW YORK, WEDNESDAY, MARCH 14, 1928. TWO CENTS in Greater New York | THREE CENTS Within 200 Miles | FOUR CENTS Elsewhere in the U. S.

HINCHLIFFE TAKES OFF FOR AMERICA WITH DAUGHTER OF LORD INCHCAPE; PASSES IRELAND AND HEADS OUT TO SEA

BOUND FOR MITCHEL FIELD

British Flier Told Wife That Was His Goal—East Wind Favors His Flight.

MYSTERY IN SUDDEN START

"Starting Out to Fly Atlantic," He Says in Message as He Leaves Cranwell Airdrome.

COMPANION KEPT SECRET

Girl's Identity Is Hidden Till After Departure—She Helped Prepare Their 'Iron Rations.'

Newfoundland Deep in Snow; Plane Could Land, but Not Rise

Copyright, 1928, by The New York Times Co.
Special Cable to THE NEW YORK TIMES.

ST. JOHN'S, N. F., March 13.—Weather conditions here are favorable for the landing of Captain Walter Hinchliffe's plane if he succeeds in passing the ice floe region off the coast.

It is improbable that he would be able to leave again, however, even if he lands anywhere in this country because of the deep snow.

Harbor Grace airport is thickly covered with snow and every other level spot near by is also obstructed by a dense white covering.

Copyright, 1928, by The New York Times Company
By Wireless to THE NEW YORK TIMES.

LONDON, March 13.—Captain Walter Hinchliffe, with a companion at first reported to be "Captain Gordon Sinclair," later proving to be Miss Elsie Mackay, the daughter of Lord Inchcape, quietly took to the air at 8:35 o'clock this morning from the Cranwell Airdrome in Lincolnshire with the intention of flying over the Atlantic from east to west, a feat never yet accomplished in an airplane.

It did not come out with any definiteness until late tonight that Captain Hinchliffe's mysterious passenger was Miss Mackay. It would seem that "Gordon Sinclair," who was said to be a reserve army officer, exists in name only. From all the information received from various sources there is apparently no doubt that the daughter of Lord Inchcape is actually accompanying Captain Hinchliffe's on his transatlantic flight.

The meteorological office report on Atlantic weather conditions indicates that they are favorable as far as mid-ocean but that Hinchliffe is likely to strike squally weather and adverse winds as he approaches Newfoundland. The report reads:

"From midocean westward to Newfoundland, wind changing to a northwesterly direction with squally showers, snow and sleet. Visibility good, apart from showers."

Leaves Ireland With Wind.

No definite news of his progress has yet been received, but an airplane thought to be his was reported at 11:30 A. M. over Kilmeadan, County Waterford, Ireland, at 12:30 P. M., ten miles from Cork, and at 1:30 P. M. over Mizenhead, County Cork, about 465 miles from Cranwell.

A later message states that a plane going very fast was sighted on the south Irish coast going in a westward direction and believed to be Captain Hinchliffe's, but, owing to a heavy snowfall and low visibility the markings of the plane were not seen clearly.

With a strong easterly wind blowing off the Irish Coast it is thought that Captain Hinchliffe, if it was his machine, had decided to go straight on and take advantage of the favorable weather.

Plane Kicks Up Snow in Wake.

Captain Hinchliffe revealed to no-one at the Cranwell Airdrome where he intended to land. Officials had the impression that Baldonnel was his destination.

He gave instructions last night to be called early today. Only the night porter at the hotel saw the flier and his companion leave for the airdrome soon after dawn.

They arrived at the airdrome about 8 o'clock and immediately gave orders to wheel the Adventure from its hangar. After the engine was tested for some time to its fullest capacity, Captain Hinchliffe and the person later identified as Miss Mackay took their seats in the cockpit.

With a roar the machine taxied across the snow-covered ground to the far side of the airdrome before it took to the air gracefully, almost disappearing in the mist. In a minute it had returned, dipping slightly as if to bid farewell to the little group of airdrome officials and civilians on the spot, and, then, flying

Continued on Page Four.

MARILYN MILLER in "Rosalie" with Jack Donahue. Matinee Today, New Amsterdam Theatre, West 42d St.—Advt.

OFF ON A GREAT AERIAL ADVENTURE.

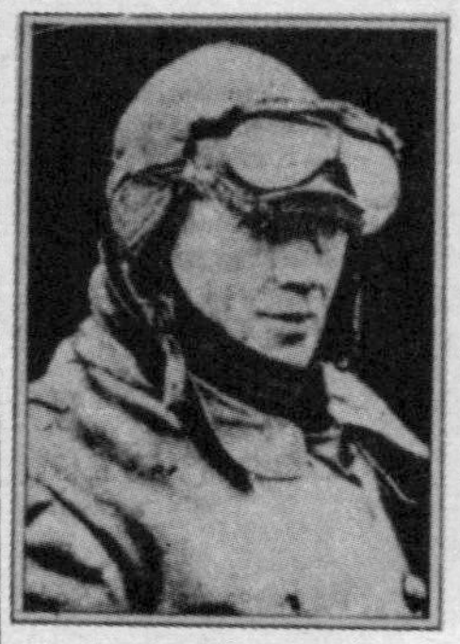

CAPT. WALTER HINCHLIFFE.
Famous British Flier, Who Is Trying the Westward Atlantic Flight.

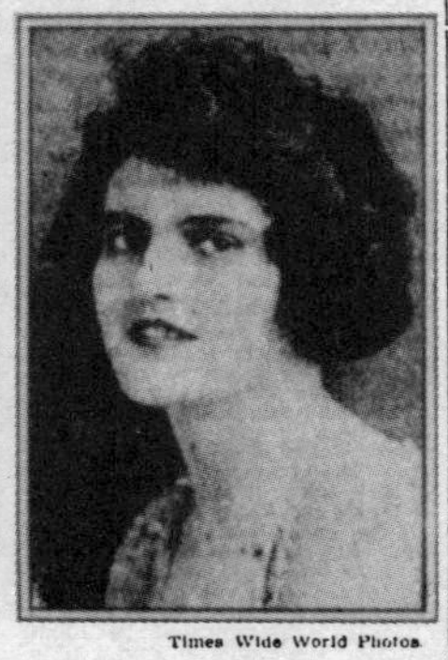

Times Wide World Photos.
THE HON. ELSIE MACKAY,
Daughter of Lord Inchcape, Who Is Hinchliffe's Passenger.

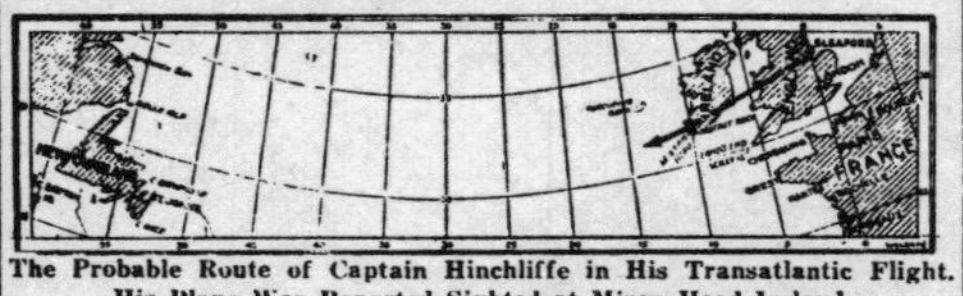

The Probable Route of Captain Hinchliffe in His Transatlantic Flight. His Plane Was Reported Sighted at Mizen Head Ireland.

HORTHY FOES JEER KOSSUTH DELEGATION

Police Quell Two Riots After Arrival on the Olympic to Unveil Statue.

FIRE SHOTS INTO THE AIR

Night Sticks Freely Used to Disperse Angry Mob Demanding Freeing of Prisoners.

The arrival on the Olympic last night of a delegation of 480 Hungarians to participate in the unveiling of a statue to Louis Kossuth at Riverside Drive and 113th Street tomorrow precipitated two riots last night, in one of which shots were fired into the air and night sticks used freely by the police on a mob of some 500 agitators against the Horthy Government, who also demanded the release from prison of Baron Ludwig Hatvany, a Liberal Hungarian editor.

The first disturbance occurred in Eleventh Avenue between Seventeenth and Nineteenth Strets soon after the Olympic had been warped into Pier 59. Before that time, although some officers and members of the Anti-Horthy League had been loitering in the vicinity, there had been no indication of an organized agitation against the visiting delegation of Hungarians. Suddenly, however, crowds began to pour into Eleventh Avenue.

Police Act Promptly.

Members of Traffic A, mounted policemen, reserves of the entire Third Inspection District and a detachment from the Bomb and Industrial Squads acted promptly. Mounted and afoot they charged the throng, which retreated without appreciable resistance. Believing they had the disturbance in hand the police returned to their stations along Eleventh Avenue.

There they discovered that the mob was returning, this time carrying placards denouncing the Horthy régime and others reading, "Free the Thousands of Hungarian Prisoners." "Will Walker Shake Hands With Hejjas, the Mass-Murderer?" and other "slogans" of the agitators. The police charged again, but this time the placard bearers resisted. There was the swish and thud of night-sticks, cries of anger and of pain, and then a loud explosion led to the general belief that a bomb had been exploded.

Flashlight Powder Causes Scare.

Investigation disclosed that Rudolph Arnold, a photographer for The Evening Graphic, had been severely burned by an explosion of his flashlight powder. He was taken to St. Vincent's Hospital in a taxicab. There it was said he probably would lose two fingers of his right hand. He was also severely burned about the face.

Seeing the retreating crowd and hearing the explosion, policemen of the New York Central Railroad in the yards south of Eighteenth Street fired several shots into the air to drive them back. Police Captain Edward McDonough later admitted that some of his men had fired their pistols, but said he understood the members of the mob had fired first.

The mob gave battle to the police for about ten minutes before Eleventh Avenue was again cleared. Meanwhile, fearing some trouble, members of the Hungarian delega-

Continued on Page Fourteen.

Enjoy the beauties of Briarcliff Lodge, Briarcliff Manor, N. Y. Winter rates now. Tel. Briarcliff 1640.—Advt.

NICARAGUAN HOUSE REJECTS OUR HELP

McCoy Bill for Supervision of Elections Is Defeated by 23 Votes to 17.

WILD CHEERS GREET RESULT

Congressional Palace Guarded During Debate by Guards With Fixed Bayonets.

By HAROLD N. DENNY.
Copyright, 1928, by The New York Times Company
By Tropical Radio.

MANAGUA, Nicaragua, March 13.—The Nicaraguan House of Deputies at 6 o'clock this evening voted down American supervision of the elections, bringing to an end the tensest day in Nicaraguan politics since the stormy times of Chamorro's de facto Presidency more than a year ago.

The vote was 17 in favor of the McCoy bill and 23 against its passage. The vote was almost completely along factional lines, with the Chamorro bloc solidly against the measure with the exception of one defection. The Liberals, as well as the Moderate Conservatives, voted solidly for it.

This flat rebuff of American policy was delivered in the Congressional Palace lined by Guardia Nacional troops with bayonets fixed to guard against demonstrations usual when hard-fought matters are at stake. The debate raged within the small chamber where two months ago Lindbergh received the Nicaraguan Medal of Honor, and American policy was denounced in the glaring light which beat in at the same window from which Lindbergh received the ovation of the crowd as America's "eagle without wings."

Anti-Americanism Not Dominant.

Anti-American feeling welled up occasionally and then violently, but it was not the dominant note and

Continued on Page Three.

MELLON AND BUTLER DEFEND OIL SILENCE; HAYS UNDER HOT FIRE

Secretary and Chairman Say Their Refusal of Bonds Justified Reticence.

'IRRELEVANCY,' HAYS'S PLEA

Ex-Chairman Testifies 'Dummy' Gift Deals Have No Bearing on Oil Cases.

WALSH ABSOLVES MELLON

Calls His Course Creditable—$249,000 Osler Deposit Linked to Republican Fund.

Special to The New York Times.

WASHINGTON, March 13.—The Senate oil investigating committee turned a heavy fire of questioning today upon Andrew W. Mellon, Secretary of the Treasury; William M. Butler, Chairman of the Republican National Committee, and Will H. Hays, former National Republican Chairman, in an effort to have the three party leaders explain their silence of more than four years regarding Mr. Hays's efforts to conceal $260,000 in Liberty bonds given by H. F. Sinclair to help wipe out the 1920 Republican campaign deficit.

Secretary Mellon and Chairman Butler gave as their reason for not volunteering the information long sought by the Senate Committee that they had turned down Mr. Hays's proposal to make "dummy" contributions and thus felt that their knowledge of the facts would not be of public importance.

Mr. Hays in his turn took the position that the whole question of the bond transactions was irrelevant to the oil lease inquiry and for that reason he had not deemed it incumbent upon him to disclose the details to the Senators.

It was a notable day among many notable ones in the Walsh committee's long trail. First Secretary Mellon took the witness chair and for one hour and forty minutes stood the ordeal of a searching examination by Senator Walsh and his colleagues. Secretary Mellon was a willing witness and he managed to keep on good terms with Mr. Walsh, and when it was all over the Montanan gave it as his opinion that Mr. Mellon's part in the Republican deficit business had been a creditable one.

Butler Springs Surprise.

Then came Mr. Butler, who began by saying that he knew nothing about the Continental Trading Company phase of the oil investigation.

In the end, however, he surprised the committee when he volunteered the information that Mr Hays had proffered to him $25,000 of the Sinclair bonds, to be held as security for a "fake" contribution of the same amount to be entered on the public records as a gift from Mr. Butler.

"I could not make a contribution by using somebody else's money and I didn't," said Mr. Butler.

When Mr. Butler, a former Senator from Massachusetts, slowly marched back to his seat in the audience, Mr. Hays, the 1920 National Republican Committee Chairman, stepped briskly forward. His face was pale and there was no question but that he appreciated the gravity of the occasion so far as he was concerned.

The steely eyes of Walsh, it seemed, almost bored through the slender little man from Indiana, now the motion picture "czar." It proved a rough battle and without gloves. Walsh bluntly accused Hays of giving misleading testimony in March, 1924, when he swore that the sum total of Sinclair gifts for the deficit as well as the campaigns of 1916 and 1918 had amounted to not more than $75,000.

At times Senator Walsh was on his feet bending far over the table, looking Mr. Hays straight in the eyes, and demanding a "yes" or "no" to this or that question. Walsh sought to show that Hays had adopted a

Continued on Page Sixteen.

Two-Ton Whale Seized in Gowanus Canal; Puts Up Terrific Fight; Museum Will Get It

The waters of the Gowanus Canal and the Erie Basin off Brooklyn echoed for three hours yesterday morning to the din of what is believed to be the first whale hunt in the history of New York Harbor.

So titanic was the struggle and so many versions of it were spread that the hunt has already become a legend in Brooklyn, although the whale was tied last night at the foot of Clinton Street in the Clinton Basin.

It is a baby whale, not more than 2 years old, but in size it is no minnow. According to Dr. George G. Goodwin of the American Museum of Natural History, the mammal is a sperm whale, eighteen feet long, and weighs more than 4,000 pounds. How it came to New York Harbor is a mystery to the scientist, for the whale's habitat is far at sea.

Four jobless ironworkers caught the whale and earned a reward of $50 from Dr. Goodwin, who said that the museum would exhibit the skeleton in the new Oceanic Hall of the institution. Winches towed the monster out of the water last night and today it will be taken in a truck to the museum.

The story of the capture of the whale is shrouded in myths. According to the most plausible version, John McGibney, an unemployed ironworker, saw the whale spouting off the foot of Court Street. With three other men, Harry Dolan, Henry Steele and William Lynch, McGibney borrowed a motor boat belonging to a barge captain and approached the whale. When they came closer they saw it was bleeding from a large wound near its fin and that it was feebly lashing the water with a bruised tail. When it spouted the vapor was mixed with blood.

Making a lasso of a steel cable with which they had provided themselves, the men slipped a noose over the whale's tail and started back for shore. They towed it a block to Clinton Street, while Dolan used the boathook with a professional whaler's flourish. Another noose was slipped over the whale's head and, enlisting the help of a dozen men, the captors prepared to haul it ashore.

The men were tugging at the cable when the whale suddenly began thrashing so savagely with its tail that they were forced to drop the line. For fifteen minutes the monster churned the waters of the basin in its death throes. Seagoing tugboats near by were rocked by the commotion. Then the whale became still.

274 PERISH, 700 MISSING, IN TORRENT LOOSED BY BURSTING CALIFORNIA DAM; FLOOD ENGULFS VICTIMS AS THEY SLEEP

THE RUINS OF THE BROKEN ST. FRANCIS DAM.

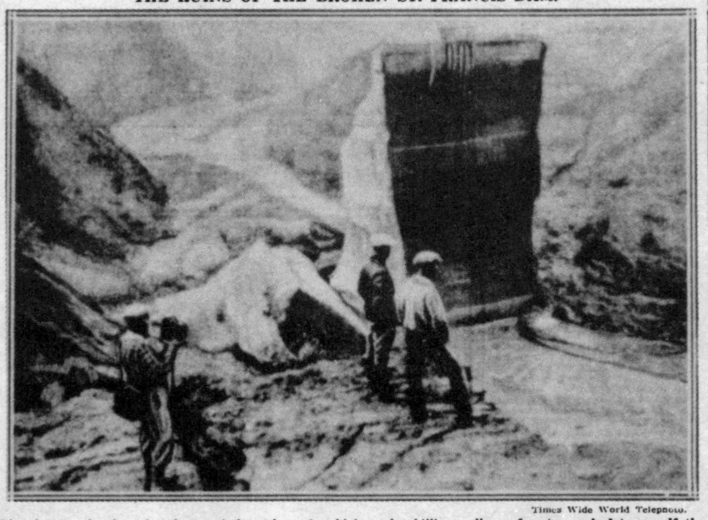

Times Wide World Telephoto.
This picture, showing the shattered dam through which twelve billion gallons of water rushed to engulf the Santa Clara Valley in California, was taken yesterday morning and reached The Times Annex yesterday afternoon. Coming over the American Telephone and Telegraph Company's wires, it was transmitted in seven minutes.

WATER WALL 78 FEET HIGH

Homes, Ranches and Roads Are Swept Away in 20-Mile Canyon.

PACK TRAINS HUNT BODIES

Many Are Buried in Silt Left by Loosing of Huge Reservoir North of Los Angeles.

TOWNS ESTABLISH MORGUES

Red Cross Units and 1,500 Officers Carry On Relief—Troops Are Mobilized.

Special to The New York Times.

LOS ANGELES, March 13.—Collapse of the great St. Francis Dam of the Los Angeles water supply early this morning poured a sudden flood into the San Francisquito Canyon, from which the known death-toll tonight stood at 274 persons.

The valley of the Santa Clara River was laid waste. With 700 residents of the section missing, search for the bodies of additional victims went on tonight.

At temporary morgues at Newhall, Piru and Fillmore were the bodies of 167. Other bodies were in morgues at Santa Paula, Ventura and Moorpark.

Of the dead recovered in the stricken area forty miles north of here, only fifty-two had been identified.

Wall of Water Hits Valley.

At 1 o'clock this morning the great dam gave way and in an instant 38,000 acre feet, totaling 12,000,000,000 gallons, of stored water was rushing on its mad race to the sea. The dry bed of the Santa Clara River provided the initial outlet, but in a short time the bank broke and a strip of country sixty miles wide in some places was at the mercy of the flood.

What little warning there was of the wall of water that swept the floor of the valley was insufficient to give any of the inhabitants of the upper part of the canyon time to flee its fury.

Caught in the swirl of the raging flood, the hundreds of ranch houses that once dotted the canyon were crushed like egg shells and their inhabitants in most instances swept to their doom.

Mute evidence that the first roar of the oncoming waters told many of those trapped that the dam had broken was seen by relief workers in the fact that many of the bodies recovered were partly clad. The majority, however, were in night clothes, or with even these torn off by the force of the waters.

Just at the break of dawn, two deputy sheriffs of the relief squads came over a hill from an islet in the receding flood waters carrying a small child, about three years of age. Over her nightgown a worn and tattered coat and one shoe with the strings untied told of the frantic effort some member of her family had made to gain safe ground.

Markers Are Put at Bodies.

Two hours after sunrise, when the rescue work had become well organized with more than 2,000 volunteers aiding Deputy Sheriffs and police, little sticks with white handkerchiefs or a piece of rag waving from their tops began to tell the story of the flood's toll.

Each stick was a marker that another victim of the tragedy had been found.

At the entrance to the canyon road, where it abruptly halted at the edge of a twenty-foot wall sheered off by the flood, stood three ambulances and as many police cars from the Los Angeles Department.

On the Carey trading post road, also at the edge of the canyon, another train of ambulances was posted.

All these were waiting for the volunteer workers to complete the difficult task of carrying the bodies from out of the silt and mudwash to dry land, where they were transferred to the ambulances and carried to the temporary morgue at Newhall.

More than a score of pack horses from the Baker ranch were taken down into the canyon and as rapidly as possible the bodies of the victims were transported to dry land.

At every road leading down to the edge of the chasm a similar scene was enacted.

Towns and Villages Damaged.

Towns and villages have been devastated, ranch homes destroyed and farm land laid waste. Warnings were sent out by telephone, but in few places near the dam were inhabitants able to escape the great tide as it swept toward the ocean seventy-five miles away.

The city of Los Angeles and the San Fernando Valley were protected from the flood water by a low range of mountains between here and the dam. The nearest the flood reached this city was at Saugus, thirty-five miles to the north, where some property was destroyed.

When the first officers arrived at the scene of the flood soon after 1 o'clock in the morning the torrent was still at its peak, and it did not begin to recede until nearly 3 o'clock.

It was soon after that the bodies of the first two victims of the flood were recovered when they were

RADIO SHARES SOAR IN FACE OF INQUIRY

Up Another 7½ Points, With Sales of 332,600 Setting Exchange Record of 3,947,530.

BIG PROFIT FOR MEEHAN

Man Who Engineered Coup That Astounded Wall Street Once Sold Theatre Tickets.

With a technical corner perilously near in Radio Corporation common, the New York Stock Exchange announced yesterday morning, after there had been an overnight gain of 21½ points in market value, that an investigation was under way to determine the stock's status.

The immediate effect of the announcement was a perpendicular decline of 20 points that jarred the whole market. It failed, however, to put a curb on speculative enthusiasm and within a few minutes Radio had resumed its upward march, carrying in its train a large number of other stocks. There followed another runaway market that lasted until near the close and that wrote up a new record for volume of trading. Final prices were irregular, with a weak and nervous tone.

The turnover on the Stock Exchange totaled 3,947,530 shares, or 71,620 shares greater than the previous record of 3,875,910 shares established on the day before. Yesterday's market saw the seventh 3,000,000-share turnover of the year. The business was so close to 4,000,000 shares that the majority of the stock market community left for home in the afternoon with the impression that this figure had been exceeded. It was several hours after the close of the market before overworked statisticians were able to compute the total.

Leading Stocks Are Erratic.

Radio swung up and down with such violence after the announcement that the Stock Exchange was making an investigation that it looked for a time as if the whole speculative structure would topple over. The fear of such a development was not entirely dispelled at any time during the day and a feeling of apprehension was reflected in the nervous, erratic movements of leading stocks.

Price movements in nearly all departments of the market were highly irregular. Even such stalwarts as United States Steel, General Electric and New York Central wabbled about as if in doubt as to which way they should move. Radio was an uncertain factor all day. Although recovering a good part of the early break, it drove about like a sapling in a storm, always shaky and unstable.

Harassed short traders who were heartened by the nose-dive which followed the Exchange's announcement soon had their hopes dashed. At the day's lowest price, 140, Radio was still selling 1½ points above the close of the day before. Few of the shorts took advantage of the early break, but, true to their nature, hung on and hoped for a wide-open crack that would get back for them a larger part of the huge paper losses which they had seen marked up in the 40¼-point net rise of Monday, Saturday and Friday. When the decline halted, they refused to be convinced that the downturn had been arrested. Brokers reported that a large number of traders continued to take on short contracts as the day wore on.

The opening was a tense moment for the Radio shorts. No one outside of the Business Conduct Com-

Continued on Page Thirteen.

Tammany Hall Will Move Temporarily to 2 Park Av.

Tammany Hall will be located temporarily on the eighteenth floor of 2 Park Avenue, a new building on the site of the old Park Avenue Hotel, pending the completion of the new Wigwam at East Seventeenth Street and Union Square, George W. Olvany, leader of Tammany, announced yesterday. The removal from the present Fourteenth Street building will be started immediately after July 4, when the customary Independence Day exercises will be in the nature of a farewell.

There will be approximately the same floor space available in the Park Avenue quarters as in the present building. There will be an executive committee room, an assembly room, a room for the Speakers' Bureau and an office for Judge Olvany.

The present Tammany Hall was sold recently through Joseph P. Day and resold to the Consolidated Gas Company. It is expected that the new Tammany Hall will be completed by or soon after Jan. 1.

HOOVER, SMITH WIN IN NEW HAMPSHIRE

Returns From Majority of 294 Towns Put Them Far Ahead in Presidential Primary.

By The Associated Press.

CONCORD, N. H., March 13.—New Hampshire Republicans and Democrats expressed preference, respectively, for Secretary of Commerce Hoover and Governor Smith of New York in today's Presidential primaries.

At midnight, with returns from 187 towns and wards in the Republican primary and 175 in the Democratic, out of 294 in the State, party leaders admitted that solid Hoover and Smith delegations at large would go from New Hampshire to the Kansas City and Houston conventions.

In the Republican race the single candidate pledged to President Coolidge was trailing a field of fourteen contesting for seven places on the delegation-at-large.

On the Republican side, in the face of these returns, the "Big Four" of the party in the State—Governor Spaulding, Senator Moses, former Governor Winant and Thomas C. Cheney—were heading the list in that order.

New Hampshire Republicans have pointed the way for members of their party in other States, Senator Moses said tonight.

"New Hampshire Republicans have taken the President at his word and have paid their tribute to his sincerity by declining to embarass him in their choice of delegates," the Senator said.

In the Democratic race seven candidates pledged to Governor Smith were at the head of the list, while Robert Jackson of Concord, Chairman of the Democratic State Committee and favorable to Governor Smith, was in the upper eight.

Considerable interest was injected into the election today when circulars signed by the Rev. E. L. Converse, State Superintendent of the Anti-Saloon League, were distributed. These read:

"Al Smith has been a constant supporter of the saloon. He was the leader in repealing the New York Enforcement code. Tammany was a thorn in the flesh of President Wilson. Al Smith is a thorn in the flesh of the better element of the Democratic Party."

LINES IN EAST DRAFT RAIL CONSOLIDATION

Pennsylvania, Baltimore & Ohio, New York Central and Nickel Plate Reported in Plan.

LOREE'S DECISION AWAITED

Executives Expect Him to Drop Trunk Line Idea and Accept the Van Sweringen Chairmanship.

By J. F. ESSARY,
Washington Correspondent of The Baltimore Sun.
Copyright, 1928, by The Baltimore Sun.

PHILADELPHIA, March 13.—After more than three years of negotiation, interrupted from time to time by deadlocks, executives of the Eastern Railways have found the basis of a compromise upon a four-party scheme of consolidation of their territory and will consider it at what may be a conclusive conference to be held in New York on Friday of this week.

These facts became known upon indisputable authority today and at the same time it became known that the major demands of the Pennsylvania Railroad in the allocation of the smaller lines have been met, that this company is now ready to join in extinguishing the proposed Loree fifth trunk line and is ready to approve the compromise.

Loree a Vital Factor in Plan.

The success of this new deal in the Eastern transportation territory, so far as the railroads are concerned, depends only on an abandonment by L. F. Loree, President of the Delaware & Hudson, of his project for a fifth trunk line from New York westward.

Also a good deal depends on the final decision of the Interstate Commerce Commission in the Chesapeake & Ohio-Erie-Pere Marquette merger now pending—so much, in fact, that the interests which now are moving toward a final plan of Eastern mergers may hol dtheir program in abeyance until the commission has laid down a rule in the C. & O. case.

The executives of the Pennsylvania, Baltimore & Ohio, New York Central and the Nickel Plate, upon whose present properties the new systems would be built, are convinced that Mr. Loree is now willing, in the interest of peace and progress, to forego his scheme and to assist in developing a four-party plan which may be acceptable to the Government.

Reasons to Expect Loree's Aid.

Mr. Loree will be pursuaded to do this, his associates declare, first because of the manifest distrust on the part of the Interstate Commerce Commission of the Delaware and Hudson-Lehigh Valley-Wabash combination; next, because of the powerful pressure upon him by the financiers; again because he is offered an important part by the Van Sweringens in the great merger enterprise, and lastly, because of the withdrawal of support of his project by his one ally, the Pennsylvania Railroad.

Without this support of the Pennsylvania Mr. Loree would have had no part in the Eastern railroad consolidation scheme, except the small part given him through his Presidency of the Delaware & Hudson.

But with the Pennsylvania backing him, he was able to acquire control of the Lehigh Valley, and the Wabash, to play for control of the Buffalo, Rochester & Pittsburgh, to negotiate for trackage rights over more than 200 miles of Pennsylvania line and to block all proposed com-

Continued on Page Eleven.

hurled against the bank of the highway near Castaic. They were partially identified at that time as the sons of J. H. Barnett, a rancher located in the canyon two miles above that point.

By 5 A. M. more than 600 deputy sheriffs, police officers and State motor vehicle officers had arrived on the scene, and Sheriff Traeger and his chief deputies, Eugene Biscaliuz and William Bright, began the organization that was to carry on the work of rescue and maintenance of order.

Temporary Morgue Established.

Five ambulances had arrived at Saugus by 5 o'clock, and a few minutes later the temporary morgue at Newhall was established. Red Cross units were operating by daylight and the Newhall emergency hospital became the headquarters for scores of physicians rushed to the scene.

Damage to the valley as a whole had been variously estimated at from $15,000,000 to $30,000,000, but an accurate figure will not be available for several weeks, according to city officials.

At least 400 houses in the upper portion of the valley, between Piru and the dam, a distance of sixteen miles, have been swept away, not a sign of their foundation remaining.

At Santa Paula, 300 houses in the southern section of the town were wrecked and swept into a tangled mass of débris as the raging waters whirled through there down the Santa Clara River bed. The death total at Santa Paula was more than thirty.

Thirty or forty houses had been carried away in Fillmore and at Piru fifteen were destroyed.

As the waters swept down the river they carried away the State highway bridge at Castaic and the steel bridge of the Southern Pacific branch from Saugus to Montalvo.

Back at Daylight to Search.

It was a hardy lot of people who settled in and farmed the San Francisquito Canyon, and the stoicism developed in their fight to till the desert country of the Saugus district stood them in good stead.

"Well, Uncle Jeff's gone too," declared Constable Jim Biddleton, lifetime friend of Jefferson Hunick, who was whirled to his death before the eyes of his nephew, Charles, when their farm, one mile and a half above the Carey post, was swept over by the 78-foot wall of water at that point. The nephew returned to the scene at daylight and took up the work of searching for "Uncle Jeff."

At the little town of Castaic, where a camp of the Southern California Edison Company was established, 130 men were reported missing. From Saugus, officers report seeing twenty bodies.

The dam was part of the great Owens aqueduct system which supplies the City of Los Angeles and the San Fernando Valley with water for irrigation and domestic purposes.

The St. Francis Dam, as the structure is called, is located in the highlands. Leading from it about 75 miles to the ocean is the bed of Santa Clara River, a sluggish stream with little water in it except at flood times. It was through this channel to sea that the water rushed toward an outlet and left a path of death and desolation in its wake.

Power plant No. 2 of the Los Angeles water system, located eight miles below the dam, was completely destroyed as the flood tide swept over it.

Investigations to Be Made.

State and local officials are at a loss to find a reason for the sudden collapse, and searching investigations are to be launched at once, Edward Hyatt Jr., State Engineer, said this morning.

"According to our reports, the dam was in perfect condition and had been inspected regularly under State supervision. It does not seem likely that it could have been dynamited, as a tremendous quantity of explosives would have been necessary. We expect to go to the bottom of the affair."

All the bridges through the Santa Clara basin have been swept away, including an important railway bridge between Ventura and Oxnard. It will be twenty-four hours or more before rail connections are established between Los Angeles and the north by way of the coast route.

All Red Cross chapters in this section are prepared to move to the scene of disaster. According to D. C. Waters, head of the Los Angeles chapter, the elaborate equipment used at the Santa Barbara earthquake is available for immediate service.

The 160th Regiment, California National Guard, is mobilized and will go to the stricken section for guard and other duty. An army of deputy sheriffs from Los Angeles County has been on duty since a few minutes after the first alarm.

Search Halts for the Night.

NEWHALL, Cal., March 13 (AP).—Searchers for the dead tonight halted their efforts in the slime of San Francisquito Canyon, the peaceful valley that was turned into a graveyard today when the St. Francis Dam broke and engulfed it.

In announcing abandonment of a plan to continue the search throughout the night with the aid of powerful arc lights, under Sheriff Eugene Biscailuye said:

"We have abandoned the proposed night search after a conference between officials in charge. Many of the bodies are unquestionably buried deep and could not be found in daylight and it would be useless to search for them all night.

"Instead, every available Deputy Sheriff, including those who worked today and all others who can be pressed into service, will renew the search early tomorrow morning."

Howard Durley, Under Sheriff of Ventura County, estimated the bodies to be recovered in Ventura County alone would aggregate 200.

Over the whole of the canyon a deep layer of yellowish silt was deposited and beneath this, rescue officers believed, undetermined scores of dead may be buried.

Fifteen hundred Los Angeles peace officers, ranchers and other dwellers in the rolling hill country north of Saugus carried on the rescue work during the day.

The valley presented a scene of utter desolation. Rescuers plodded through mire knee deep in search of the dead. Temporary morgues, hospitals and rescue stations were set up early at Saugus, Newhall, Oxnard, Fillmore, Piru, Moorpark and other inland towns along the route of the flood.

Destruction Viewed From Plane.

An Associated Press correspondent flew over the devastated area and found only the central section of the dam standing. The east and west wings had crashed outward under the force of the tons of water released from the reservoir stretching back five miles.

A few ranch houses had escaped and from the air it appeared as if the wall of water had missed them only by inches.

In one eddy of the stream floated the floors of what had been two houses, the superstructures of both having been carried away.

The rails of the Southern Pacific Railway's branch running up the valley added their bit to the picture of destruction. For a distance of half a mile the metals looked like two badly twisted strings of spaghetti, the sleepers hanging from them at all angles.

A deep gully, half a mile wide, in the mire of whose bed could be seen the bodies of animals, wreckage of every description, and here and there a rescue group seeking more bodies of the human victims, replaced what yesterday had been green fields, orchards and homes. Vultures circled overhead.

Viewed from aloft the power house of reinforced concrete located below the 185-foot dam and filled with tons of machinery, showed nothing left but two turbine engines. Near the power station, where previously had nestled almost a score of workmen's cottages, the ground seemed to have been swept clean as with a gigantic broom.

Mountain sides that slid past below the plane showed the scars of the terrible night. Swift, high waters had whipped every bit of vegetation from their slopes, leaving sharp rocks protruding.

In the upper reaches of the canyon, boulders could be seen still bounding down the hillsides into the diminishing stream, while here and there landslides skidded down to the canyon floor.

River Bed Is Raised by Silt.

Another correspondent on foot cut across the deluged low country from Saticoy to Piru. From Piru to Fillmore he traveled by foot a district that resembled a flooded delta.

Fears had been expressed outside the stricken area for the safety of both Piru and Fillmore, but both were found to have suffered only little apparent damage.

The country between, however, and back to Saticoy was a succession of running rivers and rivulets, interspersed with mud holes. So much silt had been carried down the valley by the tremendous force of the released torrent that the Santa Clara River bed in in some places had been raised thirty feet above its former level.

The undertaking parlors were filled with bodies. At Filmore, Santa Paula, and Moorpark, more than ninety bodies of flood victims have been brought in. Nurses were rushed from Santa Paula to Filmore where there was not a single one available.

The Santa Paula school house was converted into a Red Cross station where food and clothing were supplied to refugees and about one hundred cases of minor injuries treated. Most of the injured were members of parties engaged in recovering bodies who had stepped on nails and jagged rocks.

Rescue camps presented pitiful figures of those who came through with life only, many with loved ones left dead in the gutted valley.

They told stories of how houses and cabins were tossed about like corks on the crest of the tremendous wave, dashed against trees, poles or anything that stood in the way.

CALIFORNIA DAM WHICH BURST AND ITS LOCATION.

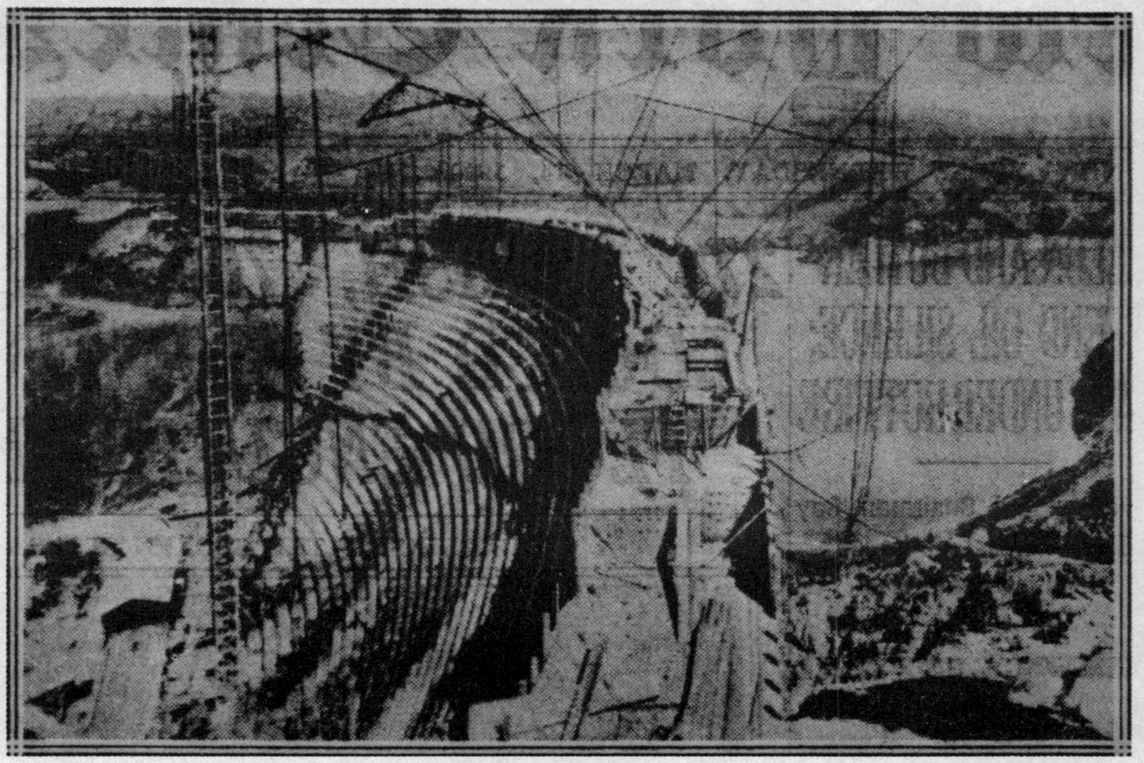

Associated Press Photo.

The Huge St. Francis Dam in San Francisquito Canyon, California, Which Gave Way Yesterday and Flooded the Santa Clara Valley, With Huge Loss of Life and Enormous Property Damage. This Photo Was Made When the Dam Was Under Construction.

Tells of Baby Being Torn Away.

Mrs. Ann Holzcloth, in the emergency hospital here, related how a freakish eddy in the current of the flood, which washed her home away, had thrown her to safety and at the same time whirled her baby from her arms to its death. An older child of hers was also washed away by the flood.

"The baby was sleeping with me," she sobbed. "I clutched him tight as we were swept out on the water in the dark.

"I managed to grab hold of some sort of timber from the wreckage of the house. With my other arm, I held the baby out of the water the best I could. I know that he was alive when we hit a whirlpool that took him away from me.

"The whirl of the eddy wrenched him from me and threw me in the other direction. I landed on dry land. Why did I have to live?"

The Harry Carey ranch near here, where the film actor-owner has staged many rodeos, was a picture of ruin. Everything had been covered by the rush of water except the owner's cottage.

On a hillock there stood the pitiful figure of a woman, huddled in a vivid red sweater, wringing her hands. She told the correspondent she was Mrs. Russell Hallen. Her little daughter had lived with her grandmother up San Francisquito Canyon.

She pointed to the place where the grandmother's home had stood, beside a cottonwood tree. It was nothing but a tablelike surface of yellow sand and the cottonwood tree had been stripped even of its bark by the wild waters.

A grotesque figure in a long fur coat waded up and down the dwindling stream which followed in the wake of the 75-foot-high torrent. It was Kimmy Errachow, a rancher, half crazed by the disaster, searching for the bodies of his wife and baby.

Gives His Life to Warn Men.

Out of the disaster rose a hero, who paid with his life for his courage. He was E. Locke, watchman at the Southern California Edison Company's power switching station at a camp in the canyon.

Suvivors from the camp told of Locke running from cabin to cabin, from tent to tent, warning the workers to flee. Scores of these were able to save themselves, but Locke died.

The payroll at this camp, company officials stated, carried 170 names. Of these men, sixty had been definitely accounted for and six bodies had been recovered. Among them was that of Locke.

C. H. Hunick, 80 years old, related in the emergency hospital how he was rescued by one of his sons from the swirling waters of the flood just as he had given up all hope of being saved.

"Our ranch house," he said, "was located a mile and a half below the dam. When the water hit it, the house crumpled as though it were built of cards. I could not see a thing in the darkness, but found myself clinging to what turned out to be a part of the roof of our home.

"Down, down with the current we went. I held on desperately. I kept saying to myself every second was my last. I knew that I could not last long. I am old and my strength was going fast, but I hung on.

"Then—I must have floated for miles—somebody grabbed my arm in the darkness.

"'Is it you Dad?' I knew that it was one of my sons. He got me over to the plank he was on. I don't remember much after that. I wonder if they saved the other two boys?"

The attendants did not tell the old man that the bodies of the two sons for whom he inquired lay in the temporary morgue near-by.

Electric Flash Gives Warning.

The first report from the scene of disaster early this morning said that an earthquake had wrecked the dam, but no temblors were reported elsewhere. Later, an inspection of the wrecked structure indicated that seepage through the hill to which the west wing of the dam was anchored had allowed it to bulge and crash; then the east wing followed, and only the central portion remained, while the great cataract poured through the breach to blot out life in San Francisquito Canyon.

The dam itself had sent out one warning of disaster as its crumbling walls loosed the flood on the canyon. Dr. C. O. Ashley, proprietor of a sanitarium at Saugus, reported that soon after midnight he saw two tremendous flashes, evidently from the breaking of a power line. Scenting trouble, he ordered his assistants to stand by to render aid.

The break, which occurred about 1 A. M., unleashed the flood at high speed and in three hours it was more than twenty miles down the valley.

Red Cross workers were early on the scene, but their first efforts to save lives were regarded by the Sheriff's officers as useless. William Bright, in charge of the Sheriff's rescue squad, declared there would be little use for such work, as he felt virtually all the inhabitants of the canyon had perished.

Bright recruited between 500 and 600 men and deputized them to preserve order and search for bodies in the stricken area.

Pack Trains Go Into Area.

Pack trains were organized late in the day to enter the flooded area and take out the bodies. The silt and mud washed onto the roads made any other type of transportation impossible.

The Los Angeles City Council ordered its Water and Power Committee to start an investigation into the cause of the disaster. The Board of Water and Power Commissioners voted $25,000 for relief work.

Fred T. Beatty, member of the Board of Supervisors of Los Angeles County, inspecting the site of the collapsed dam, picked up a piece of concrete and declared that he had crumbled it between his fingers. Mr. Beatty said:

"Yes, it came from the dam, but judgment must not be passed until a competent board of engineers has conducted a searching investigation and has reported to Governor Young."

Leaks in Dam Caused Fears.

Mrs. A. M. Rumsey, postmistress at Saugus, a near-by town, declared tonight that for ten days ranchers living in the shadow of the St. Francis Dam had "talked of nothing else" but reported leaks in the structure and the possibility of the disaster that wrecked their homes and wiped out their families today.

Supporting Mrs. Rumsey's statement of rumored leaks in the dam, were reports obtained by investigating officers from motorists who had driven through the canyon late yesterday.

One auto driver, according to the investigators, stated that, while driving up the canyon road with his wife and family, he saw an unusual quantity of muddy water coursing through the ordinarily dry steam bed.

The autoist, said the officers, drove up to the dam, expecting to see the water coming over the spillway, but found none flowing. Driving closer, he said he noticed that the water behind the buttress was within three feet of the top and that the spillway gates apparently were closed, although there was a good stream running down the canyon.

Further along the road, the autoist reported, he found a gang of workmen drilling holes apparently in preparation for dynamite blasts to blow off the shoulder of a hill not more than 200 feet from the dam.

"And it was then," the officers reported the autoist as saying, "I remarked to my wife that it looked like a pretty heavy charge to set off so close to the dam. We were in the hills until nearly 7 o'clock in the evening, and I am certain the blast was not set off until that hour, for undoubtedly we would have heard it."

"All the News That's Fit to Print."

The New York Times.

THE WEATHER
Rain, gales today; tomorrow clearing, continued cool.
Temperature Yesterday—Max., [illegible]; Min., [illegible].
U. S. Weather Forecast—For details see Page 58

Copyright, 1928, by The New York Times Company.

VOL. LXXVIII....No. 25,806. NEW YORK, WEDNESDAY, SEPTEMBER 19, 1928. TWO CENTS In Greater New York | THREE CENTS Within 200 Miles | FOUR CENTS Elsewhere in the U. S.

200 TO 400 KILLED IN FLORIDA HURRICANE; STORM, WEAKER, SWEEPS INTO CAROLINAS; FOOD RIOTS IN PORTO RICO; RELIEF RUSHED

PALM BEACH WANTS TROOPS

Council Acts on Looting—National Guard Called Into Service.

LOSS THERE IS $25,000,000

Many Big Homes in Ruins—Number of Drowned in the Lake Regions Mounts.

STORM BATTERS GEORGIA

Heavy Rains Damage Coast as Gale Drives Through Carolinas Toward Newport News.

Special to The New York Times.

PALM BEACH (By Radio, via Middletown, Ohio), Sept. 18.—The death toll in the hurricane is now mounting rapidly and, it seems, will be more than 200. Some estimates put the total as high as 400. This is based on the latest figures released by the Red Cross and on news arriving from the Everglades section that was ravaged by destructive winds throughout yesterday and then inundated by the waters of Lake Okeechobee when the protective dike gave away, flooding miles of the section. Several hundred injured so far have been counted. The situation resembles that of Miami in 1926.

The local chapter of the Red Cross through its Chairman, Howard Selby, gave out as an unofficial estimate of property damage the figures of $10,000,000 for Palm Beach and West Palm Beach and another $10,000,000 for the rest of Palm Beach County. Elmer Schultz, Fire Chief of Palm Beach, stated that the property damage for the twin cities would be more than $25,000,000.

A returning ambulance tonight brought many from Belle Glade tonight, who stated that many dead were left floating in the water in that region.

Harold Ferguson of the Ferguson Undertaking Company of West Palm Beach stated that he had a list of ten dead and that he estimated the white dead at forty and the colored at sixty. These seem to be conservative figures.

It was a grim tale of horrifying and harrowing experiences that these Glades settlers related.

The brunt of the storm had hardly hit them when the dike gave way, allowing tons of water to flood the lands. The waves broke windows, tore away foundations and leveled homes. Only the Glades Hotel was left standing, according to R. G. Reest, one of the rescued.

Waded Six Miles Through Water.

These people who had witnessed death and destruction had to walk six miles through water over their waists, shunting floating débris, before reaching the ambulances to bring them to safety.

Thomas H. Benton and James Maxwell of Pahokee, eighteen miles northwest of Belle Glade, made urgent appeals for aid. They said that the full force of the storm struck Pahokee about 9 o'clock Sunday night with nerve-wracking fury, and that refuge in a newly completed school saved more than 200 lives.

A Mr. Reest, relating his experiences at Belle Glade, stated that reports that they had received told of the destruction of South Bay, another lake village. No estimate was made of the loss of life there.

The Town Council of Palm Beach asked for military control this evening, and radio operators in Lima, Ohio, and Asheville, N. C., are working to get their messages to the capital.

Passes Required at Night.

Meanwhile in West Palm Beach the local unit of the National Guard was pressed into service Monday morning at the order of James McIntosh. A few attempts at looting have been reported. The police are keeping persons off the street at night and passes from police chiefs are required for those in the city.

It is expected that lights will be off for a week. Hundreds of linemen are being rushed South to repair damages.

George W. Carl, General Chairman of the Relief Committee, has issued an appeal for volunteer workers.

Radio Operators Ralph Hollis and Forest Dana have been on constant service here with emergency transmitters since the start of the storm Sunday afternoon. They have been working with Florida stations in the early evening, but a storm was reported there and connections were made with Ohio and North Carolina.

This hurricane is appearing more and more to be the worst that ever struck the State. All public and semi-public buildings within Palm

Continued on Page Fourteen.

Gale Expected to Hit New York Today; Related to Hurricane, but Not Part of It

High winds of gale intensity, accompanied by rain, are expected to strike New York before daybreak today, according to indications from the Weather Bureau last night. At the same time an earlier prediction of a northeast storm was amplified by a warning of a full gale on the Atlantic Coast from the Virginia Capes to Atlantic City.

The storm here, according to information obtained from James H. Scarr, chief of the New York office of the Weather Bureau, yesterday afternoon, would be related to the hurricane, but not part of it.

As to the hurricane itself, Mr. Scarr said: "There is only one chance in a thousand that the hurricane will hit here. We will get some rain, and we probably will get some winds of gale force."

It was explained at the Weather Bureau office here that there was a high barometer reading to the northwest of New York, and that there also were strong northeast winds south of New York, between us and the low pressure area' which has been a factor in the hurricane.

The big question, in the view of Mr. Scarr, was whether the hurricane would take a course off the coast or follow along it.

The indications yesterday were that the hurricane would leave the vicinity of Cape Hatteras and move out to sea.

Special to The New York Times.

ASBURY PARK, Sept. 18. A wind of galelike proportions began blowing along the North Jersey shore shortly after 7 o'clock tonight. During the day storm warnings had been heeded and along the beach front section loose objects had been battened down in preparation for a blow.

TROOPS PATROLLING PORTO RICO TOWNS

Nine National Guard Companies Called for Duty to Halt Looting of Stores.

SURVEY OF NEEDS STARTED

H. M. Baker and Red Cross Aides Take Charge—Jamaica Reports Heavy Damage.

Wireless to The New York Times.

SAN JUAN, Sept. 18.—The Porto Rico National Guard, comprising about 2,000 men, was called out by Governor Horace M. Towner to patrol twenty-three towns of the island today, as reports of food riots and looting of stores were received. Twenty-five volunteer reserve officers were detailed to go to every island town carrying the first relief in money and supplies and assurances that additional aid was at hand. They also were instructed to make an estimate of requirements.

The overwhelming enormity of Porto Rico's total loss, of about 1,000 lives and $100,000,000 in property damage, began to be obscured to a certain extent by more individual aspects of the catastrophe. Relief and reconstruction were visualized as personal problems.

After the arrival of Henry N. Baker, Red Cross disaster relief director, and his assistants, Mayors of a number of towns reported that stores were being raided by the desperate citizens in search of food. They said they did not dare to return to their home towns without supplies or money.

Distribution Is Problem.

With foodstuffs and other stores being unloaded by the transport St. Mihiel and with other ships due before the week-end, the chief problem is not so much in having enough food and clothing, but in their distribution to points where they are most needed. This problem, it is expected, will be definitely tackled tomorrow with the help of Mr. Baker and his assistants.

Conditions as they exist in the country were told by Elmer Ellsworth, son of J. H. Ellsworth of the American Telephone and Telegraph Company of New York, who lives at Cidra, near the centre of the island.

"As I stand in my home on the hilltop and look out over the hills and valleys, I do not see Porto Rico, but a landscape that reminds me of the barren lands of Arizona or New Mexico. The country is blasted. Land under cultivation before the storm is now as hard as concrete. There is no human life apparent, but at night here and there fires may be seen, and where those fires are homes had been and homes are being restarted."

Stores Being Exhausted.

Where the country stores had any supplies left, Mr. Ellsworth said, they were rapidly disappearing, with sugar, coffee and other products of the country generally exhausted. Work and food are the only salvation, he said.

Much of San Juan in the business section tonight is lighted with candles. Power is used during the day for the essential industries. Newspapers are again being published and news of plans for relief are being circulated

In the residential districts the formerly well-lighted streets seem like country roads except for lights from automobiles. The Hotel Condado Vanderbilt is lighted by candles spaced along the corridor floors and the servants carry barnyard lanterns.

Baker Organizing Relief.

SAN JUAN, Porto Rico, Sept. 18 (AP).—Nine companies of the Porto Rican National Guard were called out this afternoon for police and other duties in twenty-three towns of the island by Governor Horace M. Towner.

Henry M. Baker, National Director of Disaster Relief for the Red Cross,

Continued on Page Fourteen.

'WINDMILL' PLANE FLIES THE CHANNEL

De la Cierva, in Autogiro, Crosses From London to Paris in Four Hops.

DESCENT ALMOST VERTICAL

Experts Acclaim 'Foolproof' Machine as Sensational Advance in Science of Aviation.

Special Cable to The New York Times.

PARIS, Sept. 18. The curious looking airplane which has been described as a "foolproof flying machine" today spanned the English Channel in a successful London-Paris flight made in four hops. It was invented by a former member of the Spanish Parliament, Señor Juan de la Cierva, who calls his plane, which is a development on the helicopter principle, the "autogiro."

Without reservation European aeronautical experts acclaim the new plane as a sensational advance in the progress of the science of aviation. It embodies a radical departure in aircraft construction. Its two ridiculously small wings, unsupported by struts, closely resemble garden spades, even to the handle-like rods by which they are attached to each side of the fuselage.

The most striking feature, however, is the "windmill" arrangement surmounting the fuselage. This consists of four lengthy propeller-like blades which rotate on an almost vertical mast. The motive power comes from a conventional propeller on the nose of the plane, though it is somewhat smaller than the type used on an ordinary plane.

Air Bumps Less Severe.

The "autogiro" left Croydon Airdrome at 10:05 A. M. today. After a brief stop at the Lympne field on the English side of the Channel it proceeded as far as St. Inglevert, where it landed at 11:06 A. M. Leaving St. Inglevert at 12:53 P. M., the machine next landed at Abbeville and from there continued to Le Bourget, completing the flight at 4:20 this afternoon.

The inventor himself piloted the autogiro, taking as a passenger M. Baschet, director of the Paris weekly review, L'Illustration. An Air Union commercial plane accompanied the autogiro to give aid in case of emergency. This precaution was taken because the new machine is not equipped with radio.

The passenger reported that he felt air bumps but that they did not seem to be as abrupt as in an ordinary plane. With a wind blowing at ten miles an hour behind it, the autogiro easily attained a speed of

Continued on Page Nine.

Archer M. Huntington Donates $100,000 For Development of American Sculpture

The greatest gesture ever made by an American philanthropist toward the development of national sculpture, in the opinion of sculptors here yesterday, is an unsolicited gift of $100,000 just made by Archer M. Huntington to the National Sculpture Society for the arrangement of the largest exhibition of sculpture ever held in this country.

The National Sculpture Society is already making plans for the exhibition, which is to be opened in the California Palace of the Legion of Honor in San Francisco, on next April 1. Notice is about to be broadcast to American sculptors all over the world to submit photographs of any work they may wish to have judged for inclusion in the exposition.

Any piece executed in this country, provided that it has not already been shown in California, will be eligible, as will also any work done by an American abroad. A jury of fifteen members has been selected by the society to select the works for showing in the sixteen indoor galleries and on the grounds of the San Francisca art museum. The exhibition is intended to represent American sculpture in its widest sense and no piece is to be rejected either because of academic or modernistic tendencies.

The gift will permit the works selected for exhibition to be packed, shipped to San Francisco, and returned to the sculptor without cost to him. A second gift of $20,000 has been provided by citizens of California for the purchase of selected pieces of sculpture for the permanent collection of the San Francisco museum. It is estimated that about 1,500 works of art will be included in the exhibition, which will require two months for assembling and arrangement.

In 1923 Mr. Huntington sponsored a similar but smaller exhibition of American sculpture at the Hispanic Society Museum here, of which he is founder and President. In the same year he married Anna Vaughn Hyatt, famous American sculptress. He is an adopted son of the late Collis P. Huntington, whose nephew, the late Henry E. Huntington, assembled and willed to the public one of the greatest libraries and art collections in the world.

POWERFUL CHINESE PLOTTING TO UPSET NANKING IN OCTOBER

Disaffected Leaders Have Spent 30,000,000 Mexican Dollars and Enlisted 200,000 Men.

NATIONALISTS JOIN THEM

Plan to Abolish Rule by Committees and Follow American Governmental Scheme.

By HALLETT ABEND.

Wireless to The New York Times.

DAIREN, Manchuria, Sept. 18.—Before the Nationalist régime at Nanking has had time to bring order out of chaos in supposedly unified China, a gigantic conspiracy has taken form to overthrow the present heads of the Government, abolish the committee form of rule, move the capital back to Peking and revert to an imitation of the American system, with a President and two legislative branches.

Wu Pei-fu has been agreed upon as the man to become President, but he would be a dummy figure. The real governors of China would be the ultra-conservative leaders of the Kuangsi faction of Shansi, powerful survivors of the Chihli-Shantung clique, and Manchurian conservatives. The still powerful Anfu Party leaders are assisting with money and advice and suggest Tuan Chi-jui for Vice President, with more power than Wu Pei-fu. Even Li Chai-sum, head of the Canton anti-Communist régime, is understood to have given a promise of cooperation.

While the Nationalist label will be used by the new coalition and while its foreign policies and treaty attitude will be strongly Nationalist, the scheme really marks a reversion to conservatism in internal affairs. A great degree of local and provincial autonomy will be insisted upon and the hopes of the originators of the conspiracy seem to be for a revival of the system of semi-independent satrapies with a "central government" assured of full backing in foreign affairs and the necessary modicum of financial support.

Advance Officers in Disguise.

Already 300 well-trained military officers and men, formerly commanders of the Mukden or Chihli-Shantung armies, have made their way, disguised as coolies and peddlers, up the Yangtse River into Szechuan Province, where Wu Pei-fu now is supposedly a refugee but in reality is actively working with Yang-sen, buying the adhesion of mercenary forces and persuading leaders of the Szechuan factions into support of the plan.

Within the last two months more than 30,000,000 Mexican dollars have been sent into Szechuan to finance

Continued on Page Twenty.

Ford Interests Buy Philadelphia Airport Site For Eastern Terminal to Cost $1,000,000

Special to The New York Times.

PHILADELPHIA, Pa., Sept. 18.—Backed by Henry Ford and a group of Philadelphia and Detroit bankers, an airport representing an investment of $1,000,000 to $1,500,000 is to be established on a 140-acre tract in South Philadelphia to serve as the Eastern terminus for the proposed cross-country air line of the Ford Motor Company's aeronautic division. The Philadelphia Air Terminal, Inc., is the name taken by the financial backers.

The site, which is only three and two-tenths miles from City Hall, will give to Philadelphia, it is stated, an air field nearer the heart of the city than any other municipality in the world. The field when completed, with six runways 2,300 to 2,500 feet long will be drained to provide safe landing under all conditions.

According to Stuart A. Howard, spokesman for the Detroit interests, there is a possibility that the recently formed Aviation Company of America, scheduled to establish an air line starting at Montreal and flying over the Pan-American route of Colonel Charles A. Lindbergh, will make the local airport its principal stopping place on the Eastern seaboard.

The proximity of the Pennsylvania Railroad tracks, a few hundred yards from the proposed site, eventually may lead to the use of the airport as a link in the Pullman-to-airplane service inaugurated by the Pennsylvania, it was said.

Work on the site, it was announced, will begin Oct. 1 and will be completed early next May.

"Immediately upon the completion the Stout Air Service, Inc., which is the airplane division of the Ford Motor Company, will inaugurate a regular passenger and freight service between this city, Chicago, Detroit, Cleveland, Buffalo and Pittsburgh," the announcement of the Philadelphia Air Terminal, Inc., said.

It also was learned from officials of the company that the Sky View Lines, using Ford-Stout tri-motored craft, will operate a short-flight and sightseeing service. Similar trips are now being conducted by this company over Detroit, other mid-Western cities and Niagara Falls.

The airport tract lies between Fifth and Swanson Streets and Packer and Pattison Avenues.

PATTEN WINS EASILY, ROUTING TAMMANY; MRS. PRATT WINNER

Queens Borough Head Crushes Hallinan, Whom Olvany Aided—8,500 Indicated Plurality.

CARRIES TICKET WITH HIM

Phelps Beaten for Congress by About 1,900—Dempsey Victor in Up-State Primary.

In one of the most bitterly fought primary contests in the history of the city, Borough President Bernard M. Patten of Queens, candidate of the regular Democratic, or Connolly organization, won yesterday the Democratic nomination for the office he holds in the primary election, and administered a crushing defeat to Tammany and its leader, George W. Olvany.

Mr. Patten, who had to bear the burden of the Queens sewer scandals in his campaign, won by a large margin over James T. Hallinan, candidate of the Democratic Organization for Clean Government, who was backed by Judge Olvany and Tammany. United States Commissioner Garrett W. Cotter and former Assistant District Attorney William J. Morris Jr., the two other contestants in the four-cornered race, each received an insignificant vote.

Plurality of 8,500 Indicated.

Semi-official returns from 400 out of the 500 election districts in the borough gave Patten 31,210, Hallinan 24,395, Morris 1,341 and Cotter 1,234. This actual plurality of 6,805 for Patten in four-fifths of the election districts indicated a plurality of more than 8,500 for him in the entire borough.

Mrs. Pratt Beats Phelps.

In the other outstanding contest in New York City, that for the Republican nomination for Representative in the Seventeenth Congressional District, Mrs. Ruth B. Pratt, member of the Board of Aldermen, won from Assemblyman Phelps Phelps by an estimated plurality of 1,893. Complete returns gave Mrs. Pratt 4,507 and Phelps 2,814.

According to unofficial returns collected by Mrs. Pratt's campaign headquarters, she carried her own Assembly district, the Fifteenth or "silk stocking" district, by nearly 1,800, the Seventh Assembly District by about 250 and the small parts of the Fifth and Ninth Assembly districts in the Congressional district by smaller margins. It was admitted at Mrs. Pratt's headquarters that Mr. Phelps had carried his own Assembly District, the Tenth, by about 200.

Mrs. Pratt, who is the widow of John T. Pratt, Standard Oil capitalist, is co-leader of the Fifteenth Assembly District. She first became active in Republican politics when she supported Herbert Hoover for the Republican nomination for President in 1920 and was a strong supporter of the Republican Presidential nominee in the pre-convention campaign this year. She later became co-leader of the Fifteenth Assembly District and is serving her second term as a member of the Board of Aldermen, where she has been a frequent and caustic critic of Tammany and the Walker Administration. Posessing wealth and social position, Mrs. Pratt is very popular among all classes of her acquaintances.

Representative S. Wallace Dempsey of Lockport, Niagara County, Chairman of the House Committee on Rivers and Harbors, won renomination in the Fortieth Congressional District after a bitter fight against Henry W. Hutt of Buffalo. Despite the loss of the Erie County part of the district by 171 and the opposition of Fred A. Bradley, Erie County Republican Chairman, Mr. Dempsey rolled up a majority of more than 2,000 in Niagara County to give him victory. Other up-State Republican

Continued on Page Four.

SMITH AT OMAHA ADVOCATES PRINCIPLE OF M'NARY-HAUGEN BILL; SILENT ON FEE; ANSWERS POINTED QUESTIONS ON LIQUOR

PROHIBITION NOT MAIN ISSUE

Admits All He Can Do Is to Advise Congress on the Subject.

AND TELL PEOPLE ABOUT IT

Is Sure Drys Can Stay in Party—Explains Stand on State Control of Liquor.

TARIFF QUESTION 'TRICKY'

But He Replies—Expresses Hope That Same Questions Will Be Put to Hoover.

From a Staff Correspondent of The New York Times.

OMAHA, Neb., Sept. 18.—After he had concluded tonight his address here in which he dealt exhaustively with the question of farm relief, Governor Smith proceeded to answer eight questions directed to him in an advertisement in an Omaha newspaper, and provided thereby one of the most interesting features of the evening.

The questions were addressed to the Governor by ten Nebraska citizens. Picking up a copy of the paper, he said:

"When I arrived in Omaha today my attention was called to some of the newspapers published here, with a large number of questions. Some interesting citizens of Omaha desired to ask me some questions. And they are so kind about it, starting with 'Dear Governor' [laughter], I thought I would rather accommodate them a little bit. [Applause.]

"But entirely aside from my desire to be neighborly and kind to them on my visit to Omaha, I said in the beginning of this speech tonight that I believe in talking out frankly and plainly and openly. So that if this was intended as any embarrassment to me, it doesn't hit that way. [Laughter and applause.]

Answers on Farm Legislation.

"Question No. 1: 'What specific Federal legislation do you propose for farm relief?'

"If these gentlemen had read my speech of acceptance there would be no occasion for that question. I made that clear in Omaha tonight, that the legislation working out the principle of lifting the surplus is to be handed to a commission to be worked out during the Winter. That is No. 1.

"No. 2: 'Do you believe the country will be more prosperous with liquor or without? Why?' [Laughter].

"Well, I assume that this is an intelligent group of men that have an understanding of what is going on around the country. Nobody, no living person, no matter how wise, no matter how well informed, no matter how far-seeing, could make any answer to that question, because there has never been liquor out of this country.

Denies Liquor Is Chief Issue.

"No. 3: 'Do you believe that liquor is the great issue in this campaign?'

"I certainly do not.

"No. 4: 'How can you square your support of Democratic candidates for Congress pledged against liquor with what you say you will do for liquor?'

"Why, I don't know what idea these men must have of the debates, the platform and the speeches of acceptance. If they paid the slightest attention to any one, they could not ask that kind of a question, because there is nothing that the President can do about liquor. All he can do is recommend to Congress, and he can assume the leadership of the American people in an effort to show them that his recommendation is right. That is what I propose to do. And let the American people make the decision, as they will have to do.

"How can I support a Democratic candidate for Congress?

"That question came up in the national convention. And the national convention deliberately, through the report of the Committee on Credentials, left every Democrat in the United States free to express his own individual opinion of what he thought on that subject.

"Now, you have an admirable, scholarly gentleman running for United States Senator here, Mr. Metcalfe. I understand that Nebraska is dry, but I would never ask Mr. Metcalfe to turn his back on the people of his State until such time as he can come out here and convince them that they are not tackling the problem the right way.

Defines Views on States' Rights.

"No. 5—'How will your proposal for the sale of liquor in a few States meet your issue of personal liberty in the other States?'

"The prevention of the sale of

Continued on Page Three.

Montana Women Registered In Their Kitchens to Aid Hoover

Special to The New York Times.

WASHINGTON, Sept. 18.—A new plan of campaign has been adopted by Republican women workers in Montana—the registration of women in their own kitchens by deputy notaries—Mrs. George H. Berry, Republican National Committeewoman from that State, revealed while here today. She said it meant that virtually the full female Republican vote in the State will be polled this year.

"As the great majority of women in our State, once registered, will vote for Hoover, we consider this one of the most important activities we are undertaking," Mrs. Berry said. "Our great need is for farm relief. Mr. Hoover's promise of attention to that all-important question has won him the support of our women.

"Seven Indian reservations in Montana are providing campaign work for Republican women," Mrs. Berry added. "Workers there are basing their pleas largely on the Indian ancestry of Senator Curtis. They are conducting classes to instruct the Indian women how to register and how to vote for the Hoover-Curtis ticket."

HOOVER MAKES PLEA FOR UNITY IN JERSEY

At Newark Luncheon of Leaders He Calls State a Critical One and Asks Harmony.

AGAIN BANS PERSONALITIES

He Completes Auto Tour, Gets Assurances of Victory and Returns to Washington.

Terming New Jersey a critical State to the success of the Republican Party, Herbert Hoover pleaded for a unified party in this year's Presidential campaign, in an address at a luncheon in Newark yesterday.

The Republican candidate made his request for united support before active political leaders and workers who were guests of Senator Walter E. Edge. His remarks were regarded as significant because many in the gathering were only recently at cross purposes in a bitter primary campaign. The fact was also pointed to that he was bidding for solid support in a State where several prominent Republican wets have bolted to the Democrats.

Mr. Hoover added to his urging of Republican regularity a statement banning personalities from the campaign where so-called "whispering" has been so often mentioned. He concluded his speech with a laudation of the record of President Coolidge, which brought cheers from several hundred men and women who crowded the Newark Elks Club for the luncheon.

The candidate's speech on Monday night at the Newark Armory, in which he appealed to labor, warned against a tariff cut and told the workers that they owed their welfare to Republican policies, brought much praise from Eastern leaders during the day. Senator George H. Moses, the Republican "coordinator," Representative John Q. Tilson, head of the Eastern Speakers' Bureau, and William H. Hill, New York Hoover-Curtis campaign executive, were among those to acclaim the address on the problems of labor. John L. Lewis, President of the United Mine Workers, according to an Associated Press dispatch from Springfield, Ill., also commented favorably.

Goes Back to Washington.

Last night Mr. Hoover reached Washington on a special train after having completed a wide automobile tour of the State. Mr. Hoover carried with him, despite his own statement of the critical situation there, the assurances of Senator Edge and other leaders that New Jersey would give him a decisive plurality in November. They also assured him that the request he made in his address, that he receive the support of another Republican New Jersey Senator through the election of Hamilton F. Kean, would be fulfilled by the party organization working in harmony.

Mr. Hoover's tour, during the second day of his visit to New Jersey, took him from one end of the State to the other and it brought him into the obviously hostile territory in Hudson County—just across the river from New York—where Frank L. Hague, Democratic leader, holds sway. In contrast to the large throngs which he encountered on Monday on his motor tour into Essex County, he found an apathy in Hudson County and other parts of the State where small and quiet groups gathered on the sidewalks.

In Passaic, Paterson, Trenton and several other communities big crowds

Continued on Page Two.

ATTACKS HOOVER POSITION

Governor Declares Rival Had Direct Part in His Party's Delay.

TARIFF ALONE WON'T DO

Crowded Auditorium Hears Him Make His First Campaign Address to West.

GREAT RECEPTION IN CITY

45,000 Line Streets as Governor Arrives—Packing Workers Call Him 'Al.'

From a Staff Correspondent of The New York Times.

OMAHA, Neb., Sept. 18.—Governor Smith invaded the Corn Belt today with what he called a message of "immediate and adequate farm relief."

Warmly received by great throngs on his arrival here this morning, he spoke tonight in a crowded auditorium, pledging support to the purpose and principle of the McNary-Haugen bill. It was the first time that he had mentioned that measure by name in a formal address.

The Governor did not mention the equalization fee by which the sponsors of the bill in Congress sought a method of assessing the cost of bringing the desired aid to agriculture, but he made clear his intention not to urge it and his feeling that it was not satisfactory when he said:

"I do not limit myself to the exact mechanics and method embodied in that bill."

In general the speech he delivered followed the outline and sometimes the wording of the speech he had prepared. To make sure that there would be no mistake, he read his reference to the McNary-Haugen bill and his concluding paragraphs on farm aid.

Gives Pledge on Surplus Control.

After a detailed criticism of the record of the Republican Administration on farm relief, in which he attributed to the Republican Presidential candidate, Herbert Hoover, a direct responsibility for "seven and a half years of promise and no performance," the Democratic nominee said he based his solution of the agrarian problem on the control of the exportable surplus in the major cash crops, and the fixing of the cost upon the commodity benefited.

On that method of aid, which, he said, the McNary-Haugen bill expressed, the Governor definitely drew the issue with the Republican candidate.

"For that principle I squarely stand," the Governor asserted. "Mr. Hoover stands squarely opposed to this principle, by which the farmer could get the benefit of the tariff. Here is a clean-cut issue, which the farmers and voters of this country must decide."

As the Governor slowly read the paragraph containing his indorsement of the McNary-Haugen relief principle, the 7,000 people who jammed the floor, balcony and aisles of the flag-decked building rose to their feet, shouting, tossing their hats and waving their arms.

It was the culmination of an hour of demonstrations while the crowd took noisy joy in the extemporized sallies of the Governor on the Republican attitude on farm relief, cheered his satirical references to utterances of President Coolidge and Herbert Hoover, and applauded his humorous remarks on incidents in his own life.

Several thousand more, listening at amplifiers outside the auditorium, added their distant cheers at times.

Refers to Senator Norris.

There was more than a hint in the Governor's speech tonight that he was bidding for support from Senator George W. Norris, insurgent Republican of Nebraska, who has failed to endorse Hoover and who, according to rumor here, will meet the Democratic candidate before he returns to the East.

Twice the Governor quoted him as "an authority on farm conditions." Once he referred to the other's characterization of the farm plank in the Republican platform as "a direct slap" at the farmers of the country. Again he quoted the Senator's criticism of President Coolidge for standing against the relief measures offered by Congress and making "no constructive suggestions."

The Governor also referred to the threat of Governor Adam McMullen of Nebraska to lead an army of farmers to the Republican convention and to Frank O. Lowden's declaration that the failure of the Republican convention to "rescue agriculture" demanded the withdrawal of his name as a Republican Presidential candidate.

Most of the Governor's speech was an arraignment of the Republican attitude toward agricultural needs.

"I charge that they violated their platform promises, that they de-

Continued on Page Three.

POPULAR MAT. TODAY—New Amsterdam Thea., Marilyn Miller in "Rosalie," with Jack Donahue. Ziegfeld Prod.—Advt.

These are glorious days at Hotel Briarcliff Lodge, Westchester Co., for a luncheon, a day, or longer. Tel. Briarcliff 1640.—Advt.

Perfect Golf Weather "in the Land of the Sky." Five beautiful courses. Excellent accommodations. Variety of sports and entertainment. Grove Park Inn, Asheville, N. C.—Advt.

LOW RATES TO THE NORTH! [illegible] trip to Albany or Troy—Less than half fare via the NIGHT LINE [illegible] only [illegible] now. Call WAlker 5210.—Advt.

MAT. TODAY, "CROSS MY HEART." Tuneful and gay musical comedy. Knickerbocker Thea., B'way & 38th St.—Advt.

FLORIDA DEAD, 200; LOSS IN MILLIONS

Continued from Page 1, Column 1.

Beach are strewn with storm débris on every hand.

Royal Poinciana Badly Hit.

The damage to the Florida East Coast Hotel Company is estimated at more than $1,500,000. This figure comprises damage done to the historic Royal Poinciana, which is judged to be almost a loss by one of the officials, and the damage to The Breakers, still majestic in its position surveying the ocean, but now without a roof on either its north or south wing; the roof on the northeastern wing is also partially off. Water damage, according to this same official, will undoubtedly be great.

Practically all the botanical garden in the grounds of the Royal Poinciana is destroyed. Hundreds of rare plants and trees, imported from many lands, have been whipped to pieces by the hurricane and gales and rain that have been incessantly pounding here.

The golf club at the Poinciana course has twisted and its roof slopes to meet the floor on the north. Water from several inches to several feet inundated the golf course. The bunkers are hardly visible.

Property damage is greatly increased by the loss of the Ocean Boulevard in many places. The ocean last night flooded the front lawn of the J. Leonard Replogle home and took foliage and trees with its receding waves.

Elmirosal, the palatial estate of Mr. and Mrs. Edward T. Stotesbury on the North Ocean Boulevard, represents a scene of destruction. Noted for its trees, the place looks like a forest at the front during the war.

Rodman Wanamaker Home Ruined.

The Frazier home just south of the Breakers Hotel reported that it would take $60,000 to replace only two paintings that were ruined.

The Rodman Wanamaker home on the North Ocean Boulevard, which cost more than $240,000, was a complete wreck.

Leland Hatch of Hatches, Inc., reports that about 50 per cent. of the stock of the store was damaged by the incessant rain.

The winds were unmerciful in Palm Beach. No street is without its loss.

The Alba, a large lakefront hotel, appears water-damaged. The Whitehall has suffered greatly from the water. The New Palm Beach and the Royal Daneli Hotels also suffered slight damage.

With high tide last night the ocean came over the boulevard, raking the beach clean of every bathing paraphernalia on it. Débris was carried several hundred yards from the beach.

All the yachts, although they had been taken to apparently safe retreats, have been damaged. Seven in the Palm Beach Canal are partly on the mainland, blown there by the southeast winds after the lull. The same is true of boats in the Everglades Basin.

The western approaches to the Royal Park Bridge and the Southern Boulevard Bridge were washed away. Only the Florida East Coast Bridge is open to a thin stream of traffic, and its railing has been blown down.

Streets Are Being Cleared.

The streets of West Palm Beach are slowly being cleared of wreckage. Train and extra crews are gathering the tar paper confetti tossed about by the antics of the wind. Practically all the glass fronts along Clematis Avenue are out, with many of the building fronts damaged.

Practically all businesses have suffered. The loss in foodstuffs has been great. Emergency food supplies are being prepared for distribution by the Red Cross.

The Flamingo district in the southern part of the city suffered greatly. First Street, West Palm Beach's auto row, is a mass of débris. Not a front is standing on the north side of the block between Olive and Poinsetti Streets. Most of the construction was with concrete.

School bells that were intended to ring today were mournfully quiet. Local schools were damaged by water. Others in the country were partially destroyed or demolished. A score or more persons seeking shelter in the Boynton School were injured, none seriously, when the recently completed building blew down.

Delray Beach reports a large property loss. Almost every business building in the town is demolished. Mrs. L. B. White was killed there and her grandchild injured when their home toppled.

In Boca Raton seventeen cars of a freight train returning empty that had been sidetracked for the storm were blown over. No loss of life was reported.

Deerfield had its main buildings strewn over the street.

Barometric Record Claimed.

At Pompano newly opened structures were flattened.

Fort Lauderdale suffered damage but not nearly so much as cities to the North. It will probably amount to more than $25,000.

People are beginning to feel the want of water which has been off for twenty-four hours now. No one knows when electric power will return. The high tension line is down south of Fort Lauderdale. Poles dot the roadbeds south with wire stringing over all.

Lumber warehouses are jutting timber to the four winds.

It is calculated by barometric readings that Palm Beach was in the storm centre. The local glass dropped from 29.12 to 28.12 in two hours between 3:20 P. M. and 5:40 P. M.

Then, from 5:40 P. M. to 6:20 P. M., the barometer dropped from 28.12 to 27.57. That is said to be the lowest barometric reading ever known in the United States.

The storm started here soon after noon Sunday after a hard gale that morning and increased in fury until the wind reached a peak of about 120 miles an hour. Then came a lull for more than an hour, and then the wind started from the southeast, slowly shifting to the southwest, from which direction it proved the most destructive. Its velocity then was 150 miles. All line poles down are pointing eastward. Yachts wrecked about Palm Beach and West Palm Beach were blown toward the northwest.

On the Palm Beach at the Everglades Basin the "Marchoness" property of D. H. Conkling was a total loss.

Reports coming in now indicate that there was much damage as far north as Olympia or Hobe Sound, another Winter rendezvous of the wealthy.

Amateur wireless is depended on for transmission of messages out of this area.

Known Dead Reach 250.

JACKSONVILLE, Fla., Sept. 18 (Æ).—The appalling extent of hurricane disaster assumed an ever widening scope late tonight as reports from the stricken areas counted the known dead in Florida at more than 250 and estimated damage to property high in the millions.

With many persons reported missing, expectations were that the total death list would be much greater. Red Cross officials estimated that it would reach 400 in Palm Beach County, one of the hardest-hit regions, alone.

The same source placed the damage at approximately $25,000,000, while other estimates reported by Senator Robinson increased this figure to between $75,000,000 and $100,000,000.

Relief expeditions penetrated the territory from Miami and wired back for more aid for those made homeless and helpless by the storm.

One hundred National Guardsmen were ordered to the Palm Beaches for duty and two batteries of artillerymen were dispatched to Lake Okeechobee.

Refugees in need of food, clothing and medical supplies, wrecks of homes and other structures faced Red Cross and other workers who bent every effort to succor the injured and needy.

Of the dead, eleven are identified and 138 unidentified. Seventy-six of the unidentified dead are negroes, two at Jupiter, four at Delray Beach, fifty at Tahokee and twenty at South Bay. In addition there were reported ten unidentified whites among the dead at Tahokee, twenty at Belle Glade, fifteen in the Okeechobee City area and seventeen in the Palm Beaches area.

Reports Looting in Palm Beach.

A message received by the Governor through Asheville, N. C., and signed by the Palm Beach Town Council advised that the situation was "serious" and that "nearly all houses had been damaged and are open." The police force, the message said, was insufficient to cope with the situation.

Another message received by the Governor and signed Clark J. Lawrence, President of the State Reserve Officers Association of Palm Beach, said the situation there was serious.

"Expensive homes wide open and being looted. Recommend martial law for Palm Beach only. Advise sending at once companies for guard duties." the message said.

View of West Palm Beach showing damage wrought by worst tropical storm ever to hit this country.

Wide World Photos

PROGRESS OF THE STORM NORTH FROM FLORIDA.
Though Weaker, It Still Sweeps On, Passing Through Georgia and South Carolina, and Now Nears Cape Hatteras.

"All the News That's Fit to Print."

The New York Times.

THE WEATHER
Cloudy today, followed by showers; tomorrow fair and cooler.
Temperature yesterday—Max. 81, min. 58.

Copyright, 1929, by The New York Times Company.

VOL. LXXVIII....No. 26,045. ++++   NEW YORK, THURSDAY, MAY 16, 1929.   TWO CENTS In Greater THREE CENTS | FOUR CENTS Elsewhere

ZEPPELIN STARTS TRIP TO LAKEHURST BY SOUTHERN ROUTE

Bad Weather Forces Eckener to Select Longer Course —Due Here Sunday.

NEW YORK WOMAN ABOARD

Mrs. Mary Pierce, Despite the Pleas of Husband and Mother, Embarks on Trip.

SHIP TO FLY VIA BERMUDA

She Will Send Radio Reports of Progress—Lakehurst Rehearses to Receive Her.

By WYTHE WILLIAMS
Special Cable to THE NEW YORK TIMES.

FRIEDRICHSHAFEN, Germany, Thursday, May 16.—The dirigible Graf Zeppelin took off from here on her second voyage to America at 8:57 this morning (12:57 A. M., New York Daylight Saving Time).

The airship had fine weather conditions for her departure, but Dr. Hugo Eckener, her commander, said that bad reports would force him to take a more southern course, and increase the route by 700 kilometers (about 435 miles). He did not expect to arrive at Lakehurst before Sunday morning.

At 5:45 the Zeppelin was taken out of the hangar, her newly painted body shining in the morning sunlight. Enthusiastic "Hochs!" went up amid resounding farewells to the crew of forty-two and eighteen passengers. Handkerchiefs were waved from ship and ground while the shriek of sirens rose above the noise of the motors.

At 6:05 the airship was crossing Lake Constance and she soon disappeared in the mist to the west.

Captain Eckener expects to reach the Atlantic at noon on account of the favorable wind and he is determined to establish a speed record if he can.

Three more stowaways were found this morning in the hangar. Mrs. Mary Pierce of New York decided to make the trip and posed for photographers. She is the only woman passenger aboard.

By dusk last evening suitcases and baggage had been stowed in the cabins, the gorilla Susie, who passed the day in the company of the ship's officers, had gone aboard again and some of the passengers had gone for a few hours' sleep. Others made merry in the hotel's dining room all night until automobiles arrived to take them to the Zeppelin field at dawn.

Weather Becomes Colder.

The sudden change from Summer to near-Winter weather, which has forced every one into heavy wraps, would, Dr. Eckener admitted, force him to take the southern instead of the short course he had planned had he been able to start on time. But he compared the weather with the "political" situation which prevented an earlier take-off. Although the rain still came on in quick gusts during the evening and gray clouds still banked on the horizon, nevertheless the thunder was receding in what he declared to be the same manner as the French Government modified the terms under which the airship might fly above French territory.

However, the flight commander was still annoyed over what he believed to have been deliberate obstruction in the way of what otherwise might have been a record trip.

"But France evidently forgot that the Zeppelin on this occasion was bound for the United States," he said, "and not for some little nation, and that the American public would fail to appreciate such tactics."

Dr. Eckener then thanked the American correspondents for their dispatches which, he believes, caused the French authorities to see the situation in a new light.

Explanations arrived all during the day as to just when and how the French got the German request for a permit and the speed with which they replied. One report was that the request had been made only on Monday. This the Zeppelin authorities stoutly denied.

Details of First Permit.

Meanwhile they produced the French permit order, which, according to the telegraph stamp, was filed at 8:50 last night and received here at 8:30, well after the news cabled to America had time to be recabled to Paris. This permit insisted that the Zeppelin cross French frontiers only between the hours of 7 and 9 A. M., that the War, Navy and Air Ministers be notified, that the ship could not fly above the La Creusot Arms Works and, furthermore, that no mail, either official or picture postcards from passengers, be dropped overboard while the airship soared above France.

Asked why there were these restrictions, Dr. Eckener replied sarcastically that he did not know "unless the French Air Squadron wished to meet us and give us an escort." He added that he would willingly go "as possible," and would not go that way if northern weather conditions were favorable.

He then explained those identical conditions now prevail over the Atlantic as at the time of his first transatlantic flight, so that he counted on the voyage lasting about eighty hours instead of sixty-five as planned. He expected then to leave Europe south of Cape Finisterre and, flying by way of Bermuda, to strike the American coast at the Virginia

Continued on Page Three.

Straw Hat Season Opens With Thermometer at 80

Storm clouds loitered on the horizon yesterday, but their threatening aspect failed to delay the opening of the straw hat season. With the thermometer hovering around 80 degrees, loyal observers of the seasonal styles donned their skimmers or panamas and braved the possibility of thunder showers. The day was the warmest thus far this month. The mercury climbed from 58 degrees at 2 A. M. to 81 degrees at 6 P. M. Then it made a slight descent.

Yesterday's maximum of 81 was two degrees higher than last Sunday's maximum, and 22 degrees higher than the maximum for May 15 last year, but it was not a record temperature. Weather Bureau records show that the maximum for May 15, 1900, was 89 degrees. The lowest ever recorded on that date was 43 degrees in 1880.

The forecast for today is cloudiness followed by showers in the late afternoon.

D. F. DAVIS HAS OFFER OF PHILIPPINES POST

Former War Secretary Confers With Family at St. Louis on Accepting It.

FRIENDS SAY HE WILL DO SO

Taking of Appointment as Governor-General Declared Dependent on Wife's Health.

Special to THE NEW YORK TIMES.

ST. LOUIS, May 15.—With the announcement at Washington today that President Hoover had offered the Governor Generalship of the Philippines to former Secretary of War Dwight F. Davis, Mr. Davis returned to his home here for a series of conferences with friends and relatives, conferences which, his friends say, will probably lead to his acceptance of the post.

The announcement as to the offer of the Governor Generalship, in succession to Henry L. Stimson, who left Manila to become Mr. Hoover's Secretary of State, was accompanied by a White House statement to the effect that the names of other men would not be considered for the position until Mr. Davis had decided upon his course.

The former Secretary of War arrived from the capital and for the greater part of the day closeted himself with his brother, John T. Davis, at the latter's office. The former Secretary declined to discuss the proffer of the appointment, saying only that he conferred with the President several days ago.

Had Desired European Post.

The offer of the insular post was said to have been a considerable surprise to Mr. Davis, as it was to Republican leaders here. Friends said that Mr. Davis had at first been desirous of obtaining a diplomatic post in Europe under the Hoover Administration.

A principal factor in Mr. Davis's hesitation as to accepting appointment to Manila, it was declared, was the consideration of Mrs. Davis's health. It is believed he is becoming convinced that the climate of the islands would be no obstacle to her accompanying him there.

The fact that Mr. Davis announced he will remain here for perhaps a week has led to the belief that he will think the matter over for several days before coming to a decision.

At any rate, friends here are certain his nomination, if as has been reported, and point to the fact that the upper house will be in session from time, when it will give him opportunity to consider the appointment thoroughly its revenues during the members of his family.

Clements Expects Him to Accept.

About a week ago, Dr. E. B. Clements, Republican National Committeeman for Missouri, was in Washington, and at that time he mention was made of offering Mr. Davis the Philippine Governorship. Mr. Clements said today. It was only today that he heard of the news, he said.

Dr. Clements was enthusiastic about the offer and expressed the hope that, Mrs. Davis's health permitting, the former Secretary would accept.

"The position should present a great opportunity for Mr. Davis and should prove a stepping stone to higher office, as it has for others," said Dr. Clements.

"Mr. Davis, through his experience as Assistant Secretary of War and later as Secretary under President Coolidge, has been in direct contact with Philippine affairs, as the islands are administered under the Secretary of War, and he should be eminently fitted for the post."

Surprise in Washington.

Special to THE NEW YORK TIMES.

WASHINGTON, May 15.—The offer of the Governor Generalship of the Philippines to Dwight F. Davis was a surprise here, as it had been generally understood that Mr. Davis was under consideration for a high diplomatic post.

Only a few days ago Representative Edgar R. Kiess of Pennsylvania, who was chairman in the last Congress of the House Committee on Insular Affairs, urged the President to appoint Eugene A. Gilmore, the present Vice Governor.

President Hoover's announcement today disposed of months of speculation and discussion.

HOUSE WILL REBUKE SENATE FOR ACTION ON DEBENTURES PLAN

Likely to Make Retort on Constitutional Rights Mild to Avoid Deadlock.

CALLED A REVENUE SCHEME

Republican Steering Committee Will Decide on Exact Tone of the Declaration Today.

AGAINST KILLING FARM AID

But Leaders Favor Conference on Bill Only After Insisting on Rights.

By RICHARD V. OULAHAN.
Special to THE NEW YORK TIMES.

WASHINGTON, May 15.—The House of Representatives will administer a rebuke to the Senate for incorporating the export debenture plan in the farm relief bill.

A heavy majority of the House membership is convinced that the Senate infringed on the constitutional rights of the House in originating what the latter holds to be a provision affecting the revenues. The Constitution provides that all measures for raising revenue shall originate in the House.

Whether the rebuke will be mild or a slap in the Senate's face will be determined tomorrow at a meeting of the Republican steering committee of the House. Everything indicates that it will be a mild rebuke. Speaker Longworth and Chairman Snell of the Committee on Rules are understood to have become convinced that the wiser course to follow is to agree to a conference between the Senate and the House on the farm bill, but at the same time tell the Senate plainly that it violated the Constitution.

Would Expedite Legislation.

The communication to the Senate according to present plans, will set forth that because of the importance of the agricultural legislation and to expedite its enactment the House will agree to the Senate's request for a conference, but wishes it understood that this action is not to be regarded as a precedent in connection with other measures from the Senate which infringe on the exclusive right of the House to originate legislation affecting the revenues.

Many Democratic Representatives are fully in accord with the procedure to rebuke the Senate. Some of them would go to the extreme of slapping the Senate in the face by refusing to receive the farm bill. Others prefer the milder method of agreeing to a conference, while telling the Senate that it has assumed rights which it did not possess.

There is a marked division in the Democratic ranks in the House over the debenture plan. Representative Garner of Texas, the party's floor leader, is for it. Representative Aswell of Louisiana, who will be senior Democratic member of the House committee which will confer with the Senate, is opposed.

Unlike Democrats in Senate.

The situation among the House Democrats thus is different from that prevailing in the Senate. Although a conference of Democratic Senators several weeks ago had shown that the general opinion was one of opposition to making the debenture proposal a party matter, their leaders lined up enough reluctant Democrats to cause the adoption of the debentures amendment with the cooperation of insurgent Republicans.

The former were appealed to on the score that it was desirable to have as many Democratic votes as possible for the plan. Four of those opposed to the debenture scheme refused to be brought over on that plea, but others sacrificed their principles for the sake of party loyalty, and the provision was adopted by the Senate.

The willingness of Republican and Democratic Representatives to let the Senate's bill go to a joint conference committee of the two houses is due primarily to the desire to save farm legislation. They perceive that there may be an entire failure of farm relief if the House refuses to receive the Senate measure.

Would Prefer Tariff Bill Action.

Some of the Republicans express the opinion that the Senate's Democratic leadership is anxious to have the legislation fail, so they may be able to go to the country in next year's Congressional elections with the contention that President Hoover has not carried out his pledges to the farmers.

Members of the Republican farm group in the House said today that if the House refused to confer with the Senate because of the difference over the debenture amendment, there will be "chaos." They would prefer, they said, that the plea should ultimately be shifted to the pending tariff bill.

In that they expressed a thought that is much in the minds of many Senators and Representatives, the feeling among whom is that the handling of farm relief through the tariff bill would expedite the revenue-raising measure. The utmost care is to be taken in the handling of farm relief. Only small

Continued on Page Two.

POISON GAS KILLS 100 IN CLEVELAND CLINIC; EXPLOSIONS SPREAD FUMES, FIRE FOLLOWING; PATIENTS, NURSES, DOCTORS DIE IN FLIGHT

CLEVELAND CLINIC WHERE SCORES DIED FROM GASES AFTER EXPLOSION OF X-RAY FILMS.
Times Wide World Telephoto.

FALL AS ON BATTLEFIELD

Victims of Deadly Fumes Stricken as They Wait or Are Being Treated.

MORE THAN 100 INJURED

Firemen Use Pulmotors on Roof While Holding the Blaze at Bay.

FIRE STARTS IN X-RAY ROOM

Dr. John Phillips One of Victims —Dr. Crile, Fellow Founder, Gives Blood in Vain.

Special to THE NEW YORK TIMES.

CLEVELAND, May 15.—Yellow gas fumes, emanating from the X-ray room in the basement of the Cleveland Clinic and following a deafening explosion ended today the lives of 100 patients, doctors, nurses, hospital aides and rescuers in the greatest tragedy in the history of this city.

More than 100 were injured and 38 of them are in hospitals, several near death. One of those who succumbed tonight was Dr. John Phillips, one of the "founders" of the clinic.

Other prominent persons who lost their lives in the disaster were J. Barker Smith, secretary-manager of the Cleveland Athletic Club and former potentate of Al Koran Shrine; Dr. Max Bartholomew and Dr. C. L. Locke of the clinic staff and Mrs. Charles W. Stage, wife of the general counsel for the Van Sweringen interests, who was in Washington.

Die as They Try to Escape.

Gasping for breath, waging a frantic battle to reach fresh air, men and women, trapped in the building, dropped in the halls to expire, unable to escape the deadly fumes. The explosion blasted the gas upward through ventilator shafts, up stairways and through halls.

A fire which blazed up immediately swept up the rear stairway, feeding on the woodwork. It caused walls to bulge and windows to burst. About 300 people were in the clinic at the time of the explosion. Many were in bed. Others were on operating tables.

Not since the tragic Collingwood School fire of 1908 has Cleveland been visited by such a tragedy, and never in the history of medical science anywhere in the world has such a strange disaster demolished an institution of mercy.

Never in the annals of hospitals has such destruction of valuable records, equipment, statistics, test specimens and delicate instruments and observations been coupled with such loss of life.

The instrumentalities of advanced science turned against their users, for the greatest cause of death was the gas produced by the burning and explosion of the cellulose and sensitized X-ray and photographic films.

The drama could not have been more gripping if a bomb had suddenly hurtled from an airplane during wartime, releasing death-dealing gas upon a peaceful community.

Doctors and nurses were bustling about, taking care of patients, when a deafening detonation shook the building. Immediately there was a stampede, men and women scrambling for doors, windows and elevators.

Police and firemen made an effort to enter the blazing building, but were driven back by the fumes. Ex-mero Stabb, a policeman directing traffic on the corner, rushed into the structure and started to carry out a woman. He staggered, fell, regained his feet, and then dropped again. Fellow-officers found him dead fifteen minutes later.

Find Fire of Dead and Living.

Firemen under Battalion Chief Michael Graham, turned back by wall of gas at every entrance, finally reached the top of the building by a motor-controlled ladder. Two of the firemen, Howard McAllister and Peter Rogers, hacked their way through the skylight, fastened ropes under their arms and were lowered into the building. They had to swing themselves until they had gathered sufficient force to drop inside the mezzanine rail that circles the fourth floor.

They found bodies packed deep in the space between the elevator and the stairway. A trap door on the roof was cracked open and fifteen victims were lifted up to the roof.

Several who were crushed in the bottom of the elevator were dead, but the number were still living when pulled out into the open and carried out to the roof and later gathered unconscious forms had been lifted.

Chief Graham was three lowermost into the building. He found the

Continued on Page Two.

STRICT RULES GUARD HOSPITAL FILM HERE

Fire Underwriters Impose Stringent Regulations, but Find Enforcement Hard.

URGE SAFETY NEGATIVES

Now Used by City Institutions and Many Private Ones, Says Fire Bureau.

While fire underwriters here last night urged legislation compelling the replacement of nitrocellulose X-ray films such as are believed to have caused the Cleveland Clinic Hospital fire yesterday, with safety (acetate cellulose) films for all X-ray work, New York Fire Department officials insisted upon the extreme unlikelihood of such an occurrence in this city.

The plea for greater safeguards was made by spokesmen for the National Board of Fire Underwriters, 85 John Street, as necessary to prevent fire and loss of life in the future.

Both medical men and Fire Department officials here, basing their judgment on reports of the origin of the Cleveland fire, expressed the belief that the explosions were caused by the ignition of inflammable nitro-cellulose film, perhaps in combination with various substances used in the emulsion on the film. They were of the opinion that the flames had released the fumes in the emulsion in the form of a vapor similar to that used in war gas.

Regulations are Stringent.

But stringent regulations governing the storing of such films are in force here. Peter S. Spence, Chief of the Bureau of Fire Prevention declared yesterday. He also asserted that much of the film used in the X-ray laboratories of New York hospitals is of a non-inflammable variety invented by the Eastman Kodak Company at the solicitation of the New York Fire Department.

"When inflammable film is used," added Mr. Spence. "Some years ago the Eastman company, at our request, developed an acetate film to take the place of the ordinary nitrocellulose film. The acetate film is rated as non-inflammable. It burns about as paper does, and has none of the explosive qualities of nitrocellulose.

"The city hospitals and most of the private ones use this new type of film. Two years ago the superintendents of the hospitals met with officials of the Fire Department and received thorough instruction on the fire hazards of X-ray film. They have cooperated thoroughly with us.

"I do not think that anything like the fire in Cleveland could occur in New York," said Dr. George Palmer Ratner, director of the X-ray laboratories of New York, 500 Fifth Avenue. "The utmost care is taken in the handling of film. Only small

Continued on Page Two.

kSEAPLANES for charter to the boat races. Coastal Airways, Inc.; Bryant 9450.—Advt.

List of the Identified Victims

Special to THE NEW YORK TIMES.

CLEVELAND, May 15.—Following is the list of identified dead and injured of the Cleveland clinic disaster:

THE DEAD.

ANDISON, Dr. HARRY, Cleveland Heights, member of clinic staff.
AIT, Miss CHARLOTTE E., a patient.

BAKER, PHILIP, B., Cleveland, a salesman.
BARTHOLOMEW, Dr. MAX, Cleveland, of clinic Hospital staff.
BERNASE, EVELYN, a high school student, Cleveland.
BISSELL, R. E., 38, Cleveland, an engineer.
BORELLO, Dr. HAL, Cleveland.
BRENNAN, Dr. RAY A., Lakewood, Ohio.
BROWNLOW, WILLIAM A., Cleveland.

CAISE, MAE V., address unknown.
CASINO, ROMEY, Cleveland.
CASINO, ROSA, Cleveland.
COSTLEY, Miss MINNIE E., Cleveland.

DANFORTH, W. H., address not known.
DANIELS, JOHN, address unknown.
DORROW, FANNY, Cleveland.
DORBELLO, Dr., address unknown.

EPSTEIN, Mrs., wife of Dr. Epstein, Detroit.

FAY, Miss ZANNA, X-ray nurse at clinic.
FELIX, HUGO, Akron, Ohio.
FISHER, Miss ——, nurse, Cleveland.
FLEMING, ALVIN, Cleveland.
FLEMING, V. M., address unknown.
FLIT, LILLIAN, address unknown.
FOWLER, GEORGIANA, clerk, St. Petersburg, Fla.
FUELST, HERMINE, Cleveland.
FULTON, R. B., Lakewood, Ohio.

GIBSON, Miss GLADYS, Cleveland, telephone operator at clinic.
GLERTO, Miss ——, address unknown.

HAAS, SAMUEL, address unknown.
HELWIG, Mrs. CARL, Cleveland.
HOLTENBACH, LENA, Cleveland.
HUNTSRI, Dr. E. S. A., Cleveland, of the clinic staff.

KORINISHSKI, Mrs. SAMUEL, Akron, Ohio.

LEUSIA, JULIA, address unknown.
LOCKE, Dr. C. E., Cleveland.
LONG, C. L., Barberton, Ohio.
LONG, FRED, Parsons, W. Va.

MADDLER, Mrs. HOPE, address unknown.
MARKELL, Mrs. MARY E., Madison, Ohio.
MARKELL, CLIFFORD, Madison, Ohio.
MATZ, Miss SUE, nurse at clinic.
McKENNA, MARGARET, East Cleveland.
MOELLER, Miss ELLA, Cleveland, clinic stenographer.
MOORE, CHARLES, East Cleveland.

MORGAN, EDITH, Cleveland, an employe at the Clinic.
MULLEN, Mrs. FLORENCE E., Cleveland.

O'CONNELL, HELEN, Elyria, Ohio.
O'KEEFE, Mrs., Rome, Ga.

PARDON, EVELYN, Akron, Ohio.
PERKINS, RITA F., Cleveland.
PHILLIPS, Dr. JOHN, Cleveland.
PORTER, Miss, address unknown.

QUAYLE, Miss ALICE, Hotel Alcazar, Cleveland.

RALSTEIN, JOHN, address unknown.
RAASK, MARY, East Cleveland.
HANAUKA, MARGARET, died at Mount Sinai Hospital.
REESE, JAMES, address unknown.
RENZ, HELEN, Cleveland.
RICHARDS, MAY, Ashtabula, Ohio.
ROBERTS, Miss DAHNA, Cleveland.
ROBERTS, GRACE, Sharon, Pa.
ROCKMORE, PAUL, employe in clinic photo room.
ROGERS, W. T., Cleveland, chief accountant of the White Motor Company.
ROTHSCHILD, Mr. MATTIE, Cleveland.
ROQUEMORE, PAUL, Dallas, Texas, X-ray clerk.

SCHMIDT, C. E., Lakewood, Ohio.
SCHRAFFT, GEORGE, address unknown.
SERTELLA, FRANCIS, address unknown.
SEWALL, CHARLES, Cleveland.
SEYMORE, T. W., Akron, Ohio.
SHAFFER, MARY, East Cleveland.
SHERMAN, Mrs. AGUSTO, address unknown.
SMITH, J. BARKER, secretary-manager of the Cleveland Athletic Club.
SOGAL, FRANCIS, address unknown.
SPELLMAN, W. J., Forest, Ohio, died in Huron Road Hospital.
STAHL, ERNEST, Cleveland, emergency police squad.
STAGE, Mrs. Charles W., Cleveland, wife of an attorney.
STARK, Miss ANNA, Youngstown, Ohio, wife of J. T. Stark.
STRAPP, GEORGE, Cleveland, a fireman.
STRENBERG, HARRY, Denver, Col.
STERLING, HARRY, Denver, Col.

TIGHT, ADAM, Sandusky, Ohio, salesman.

WALD, CHARLES, Cleveland.
WARD, JOHN, Cleveland.
WILDY, RUTH, Boulder, Col.
WORDEN, Mrs. MAY, Cleveland.

YOUNG, MABEL, Cleveland.

THE INJURED.

ADAMS, WALLER, badly burned, in Cleveland Hospital.
ALEXANDER, C. H.
ANDERSON, Dr. J. R., suffering from gas.
ASADORAIN, Miss.
BELCHER, Dr. GEORGE, Cleveland.
BICKSON, Dr.
BISHOP, Mrs. CORY, 30, St. Joseph, Mo.
BOWEN, Miss, a nurse.
BUEDEMANN, Dr.
BUELL, Miss.
CARBOLL, Dr.
CHIPEANI, THOMAS.
CREADY, Miss.
CRITCHEN, ENID.
DAVIES, Dr.
DECKER, an interne.
DINSMORE, Dr. ROBERT S., surgeon at clinic, fractured leg.
DUNCAN, Dr. WALLACE, injured in fire, is suffering from gas.
EBLING, Dr.
FARRELL, Dr.
FIELOFF, Miss.
GLEASON, Miss.
GRAULWIN, M. R., Cleveland.
GRAY, Dr.
GRIFFITH, Miss.
GRUNDEM, Miss.
HARTBOCK, Dr.
HARRISON, Dr.
HEINESS, Miss RUTH.
HOLLAND, Dr.
HORWITZ, JEANETTE, Cleveland.
HUGHES, HARRY, patrolman, overcome by gas.

HYDE, Miss DOROTHY.
JALINEK, J., an orderly.
JOHNSON, MARGARET.
JONES, Dr.
LANGTON, Mrs. WILLIAM.
McCULLOUGH, Dr. Percy, Vancouver, suffering from gas.
McDONALD, Dr. R. H., suffering from gas.
MAZNEY, Miss ANNA.
MERWIN, Miss.
MORTON, Mrs. HENRY.
MUTCH, Miss.
NETHERTON, Dr.
PEART, Dr. WILSON J., Cleveland, head of clinic dental department and one of its founders; badly gassed.
PERHIM, Miss EMILY, Shaker Heights, Ohio.
RICHARDS, Mrs. ART.
RICKSECKER, Dr.
ROGERS, PATRICK, Cleveland, a fireman, slightly injured.
RUSS, Miss.
SHEARER, Mrs. EDWARD L., Cleveland.
SHEARER, Dr. EDWARD L., Cleveland.
SWAFFORD, Dr. JOHN H.
SWANDT, Miss.
THOMPSON, Dr.
TROCK, ROBERT, an orderly.
WALTER, RUTH.
WINTERS, Miss.
YAWBERG, MURIEL, Cleveland.

When you think of Writing Think of Whiting.—Advt.

EXPERTS DIVIDED ON NATURE OF GAS

Bromine Fumes Blamed by Some—Others Think It Nitric Gas.

CAUSED MOST OF DEATHS

Burning X-Ray Films Would Throw Off Three Compounds, Experts Say.

By The Associated Press.

CLEVELAND, May 15.—Investigation tonight of the explosion and fire at Cleveland Clinic Hospital today, which claimed nearly 100 lives, established that many of the deaths were caused by a deadly gas, but its identity was argued over.

Pharmacists said that it was a bromine gas, but doctors said that it probably was a form of nitric gas.

It is probable, however, that it was a mixture of gases coming from many forms of chemicals in the building which were liberated when containers were broken by explosion of celluloid X-ray films. In addition, the burning films gave off a gas said to be bromine.

Whatever the gas was, it was powerfully penetrating and most deadly. Many patients were killed in seemingly less than a minute. Others in remote parts of the building died later.

According to general opinion the poisonous gases were due to the burning of X-ray film in large quantities. The photographic film, which has much the same composition as guncotton, in addition to exploding also threw off three kinds of compounds as the result of combustion. These were camphor and carbon monoxide and the gases nitric oxide or other nitrogen compounds.

Inhalation of the carbon monoxide resulted in death similar to the breathing of exhaust gas from an automobile in a closed garage. Camphor vapor settled on the walls of the clinic as a brown, tarry substance.

The presence of nitric oxide, some experts said, accounted for a brown vapor which was at first mistaken for bromine gas. There was not enough of bromine or chlorine compounds in the X-ray film, it is asserted, to account for the large amount of what was thought to be bromine gas in the wrecked building.

Had Effect of War Gas.

Dr. William E. Lower, one of the founders of the clinic, said late tonight:

"The deaths were apparently due to gas poisoning. Persons in the building collapsed and were dead less than a minute after the gas was inhaled.

"I do not know what gas it was, but from the behavior of its victims it was similar to phosgene gas such as was used in the World War.

"I have talked to one of the doctors who was in the building, and he told me he was seated in the reception

Continued on Page Two.

crushed bodies of about ten people who had been trampled to death in the mad stampede to reach the elevator.

"As soon as the smoke had cleared a little and we could see our way around. I noticed a man sitting in a chair in the lobby on the second floor," Chief Graham said. "He looked as though he had just started to take a short nap when the fumes began rolling through the building and caught him.

"I also found one of the nurses seated in her chair in one of the second story offices. She seemed to be still alive, but we worked over her for an hour without bringing her back to consciousness."

When it became apparent that the smoke-filled lower corridors would block the passages by which policemen and firemen could enter with stretchers, Chief Graham ordered pulmotors brought into the building, and while firemen with hose stood alongside beating back the flames, others applied the respirators and restored several victims so that they could walk to the ladders.

Shortly after the policemen and firemen entered the building the large lawn in front of the clinic was filled with the dead and dying. The city's hospital and ambulance facilities were tested to the utmost, and the metropolis of 1,250,000 people became as a small town choked with stricken people inquiring dazedly for their relatives.

Police and ambulance sirens screamed as the automobiles sped through crowds which lined the streets near the wrecked clinic. Taxicabs were summoned and used to transport the dead and injured to hospitals and morgues.

An hour and a half earlier everything was quiet and peaceful in the clinic, made nationally famous by Dr. George W. Crile, surgeon and technician, and his brother specialists. One moment a hundred or more patients, suffering from chronic and complicated diseases, were undergoing examination on medical tables. The next instant death belched from the X-ray room in the basement.

The building rocked, glass burst from the windows, the skylight fell in, plaster collapsed and the clinic became a charnel house.

Most of the victims were trapped without a chance and asphyxiated by the thick yellow fumes, believed to be principally nitric oxide, accompanied by bromine and chlorine gases. Struggling to reach stairways and windows, they choked and died where they fell or on tables, or in chairs in the outer offices.

Crushed Beneath Debris.

Others, some of them unclothed or partly disrobed, were crushed beneath falling debris, heavy diagnostic apparatus or operating tables. Physicians, chemists and nurses fell with instruments, test tubes and charts in their hands.

Death halted them as they gave relief from pain. As the yellow colored smoke rolled out the doors and windows of the clinic the screams and yells of the trapped patients could be heard for blocks.

A fireman donned a gas mask and groped his way in. In a minute he staggered out.

"Can't make it, it's killing," he moaned as he fell into the arms of the Chief.

Screaming figures on the roof were dimly seen through the rolling orange hued fog, inarticulate wails came from the blackened windows on the upper floor, automobile horns tooted and spectators in quivering groups gasped.

"Up the ladders, up the ladders! Get them from the top," yelled Chief Graham.

Louis Hildebrand, a fireman, climbed the ladder to the roof.

"Down the airway, quick, they're trampling them to death down there," Graham shouted.

Hildebrand rushed to the skylight and looked down.

"I never hope to have to look at anything so horrifying again," he said. "Lord help me, as far down the stairway as you could see were bodies, bodies, bodies. Twisted arms and legs, screaming men and women. Bodies and screams."

The patients, thirty or more of them, were jammed so closely together during their frenzied flight to the roof that they couldn't move, the firemen said.

Some of them, caught without clothes, were protected only by sheets wrapped around them as the explosion sent glass hurtling from the skylight to the second floor foyer.

"It took three firemen to force a way down that stairway and to lift the top one to men on the roof," Chief Graham related. "For five minutes we were lifting those bodies to the skylight before we could get to the third floor, where the screaming was the worst."

When the firemen could get down to the third floor, clambering over piles of bloody clothing, scraps of plaster and débris they found a panic-stricken group of patients trying to get down to the first floor.

When they once got into the building the firemen brought victims out so fast that workers on the street and front lawn could hardly treat them fast enough. Some of the patients protested that they were all right.

"Don't have to do a thing for me," one man said as firemen sought to pump fresh air into his lungs. "The gas didn't bother me. Get the others who are dying."

Five minutes later he collapsed. Firemen lifted him into an ambulance and started him for a hospital. He was dead before he reached there.

Apparently Unharmed But Die.

Paul Roquemora of East Dallas, Texas, an X-ray salesman in the clinic at the time of the explosion, was able to get out unassisted. He turned at once to helping firemen.

"Better go to a hospital," one of the rescue squads warned. "You don't know what that gas can do."

He worked for a little while longer and then went to a hospital where he presented himself, with a laugh, for treatment. Ten minutes later he was dead.

The largest number killed at any one place were those caught on the stairway and in front of the elevator on the third floor, in the opinion of the four firemen who carried out all the patients on that floor.

Not more than one or two of those who rushed toward the elevator came out of the building alive, Fire Lieutenant T. W. Reese, who led the rescue work on that floor, said tonight.

"When we smashed in a window at the west side of the building we could see through the smoke one huge pile of people," said Reese. "They had evidently rushed toward the elevator, for most of them had fallen toward the doors of the shaft."

While one fireman virtually bored a hole through the smoke with a high pressure hose, three others pulled bodies from the pile and carried them to the window where other fire fighters waited to take them to the ground.

"We had a line of persons strung from the hallways to the stairs, where they were trapped, clear to the window," Lieutenant Reese said. "It looked like a hopeless job to begin with, everybody seemed so entangled in the pile. Not a one of those we dragged out appeared to be living."

The firemen found in that crush only one they thought was still living. She was a nurse. They carried her to an office at the east side of the building, closed the door to shut out the smoke, broke a window to admit air and began applying artificial respiration, but as they did so she expired.

Not for four or five hours was it possible to even begin to identify the dead. The bodies, lying in row after row in hospitals and morgues were too numerous. The list grew hourly as seemingly healthy patients who had escaped from the death trap reeled and died from gas in their lungs.

Through it all, with his fellow specialists either injured or killed, his young doctors and aides lying dead or lying around him, Dr. Crile, mainspring of the clinic, moved like the former World War surgeon that he is. Refusing to lose his head, the world famous physician who had perfected goiter operation technique, who had become one of the renowned figures that emerged from the base hospitals of the war, called for ambulances, ordered emergency telephones installed, directed policemen and firemen how to help and then visited hospitals where victims were taken.

Crile Gives Blood for Friend.

He visited all of the hospitals, taking a census of the friends and patients who were swept away by the tragedy. Late in the afternoon he went to the Wade Park Manor and there underwent a blood transfusion in a vain attempt to save the life of his friend and protégé, Dr. John Phillips. Dr. Phillips is the man who rushed with oxygen tanks to the Gates Mill home of Myron T. Herrick last Fall, when Mr. Herrick was suddenly stricken with a bronchial attack and nearly died for lack of oxygen.

The dead and injured were taken to every hospital within easy reach of the Clinic. Mount Sinai received forty-five of the dead. Huron Road fifteen, and others from five to ten.

As evening drew on, the throngs which had crowded the sidewalks around the Clinic moved downtown to the county morgue, which was housing the greatest number of dead at any one time in its history. There were not enough slabs to accommodate the victims, so they were stretched out in long rows upon the floor in room after room.

Gradually, one by one, they were identified. Frantic mothers and fathers, sisters and brothers, from all over Northern Ohio, called by telephone to newspaper offices and post-office stations and described their loved ones who were in the clinic at the time of the explosion.

Prominent people as well as ordinary workingmen, doctors as well as patients, nurses and record clerks were among the victims.

The bodies of all the victims were yellow tinged as were the walls of the rooms. The interior of the building looked as though it had been swept by a tornado.

Oxygen Running Short.

CLEVELAND, Ohio, May 15 (AP).—In the hospitals authorities were tonight administering respiration to victims of the clinic disaster. Sufferers were dying at short intervals and physicians sent out appeals for additional oxygen in the fear that the supply in the city might prove insufficient. Oxygen is declared the only effective means of overcoming the gas burns.

Nearly all of the deaths were attributed to the deadly gas which filtered through the four-story brick building slowly at first and then, augmented by a second and greater explosion than the first, rushed up from the basement and cut off escape down the stairways and elevators.

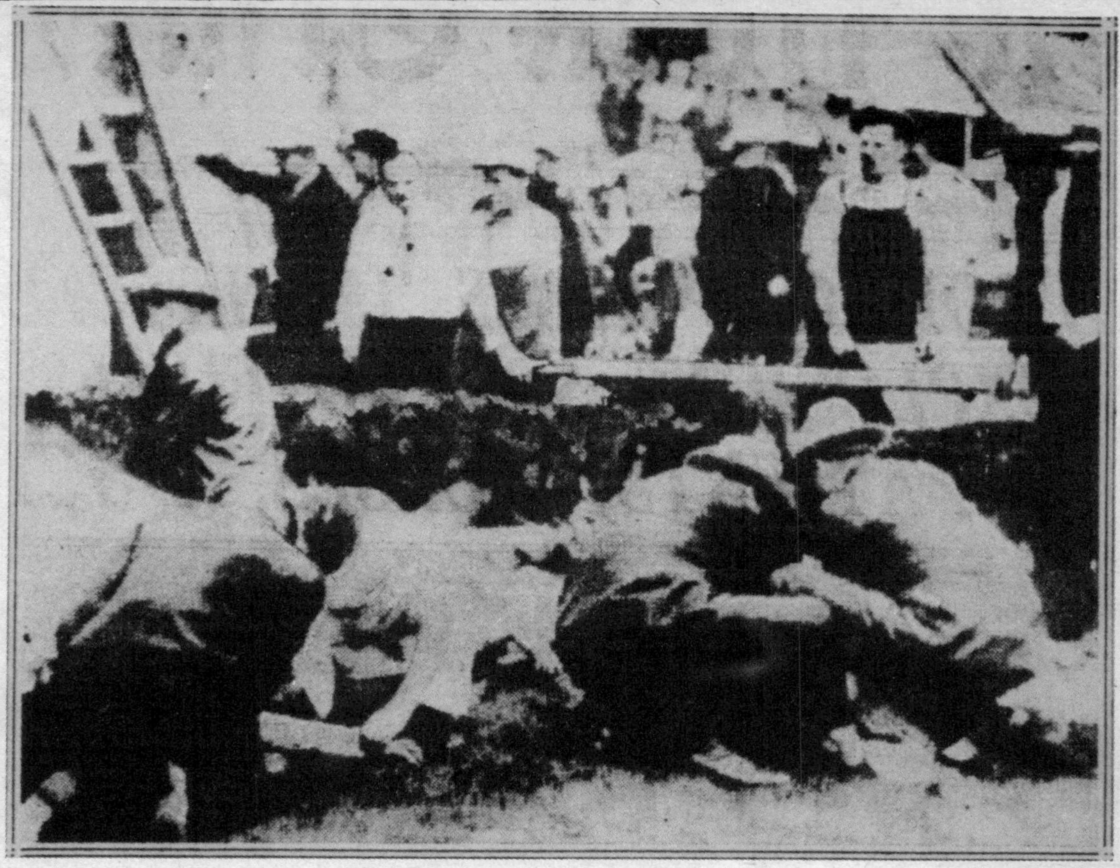

Associated Press Telephoto.

TREATING VICTIMS OF THE CLEVELAND CLINIC DISASTER.

Doctors Working Over Persons Stricken by Deadly Gases Following Explosion of X-Ray Films and Chemicals in the Clinic's Laboratories.

Policeman Dies After Taking 21 Out of Gas-Filled Clinic

CLEVELAND, May 15 (AP).—Policeman Ernest Stabb, 30, of No. 1 Emergency Wagon, sacrificed his life to achieve the removal of twenty-one persons from the blazing gas-filled Cleveland Clinic.

Stabb arrived while the fumes still clogged the entrance and time after time pushed his way into the darkened halls.

Some of those he removed were alive tonight, some died as he carried them to the open air.

Stabb worked away as the fatal gas slowly destroyed his lungs. He collapsed after carrying out his twenty-first burden. He followed those he rescued to an emergency cot at Mount Sinai Hospital and died a few hours later.

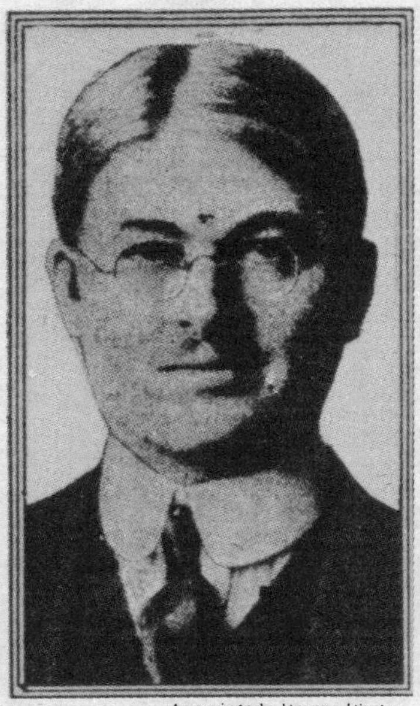

Associated Press Photo.

DR. GEORGE W. CRILE,

Famous Physician and Head of the Clinic, Who Escaped the Gases and Led the Rescue Work.

Fire Carried Fumes.

Survivors said the faces of those asphyxiated turned a sickly yellowish brown color within two minutes after they had inhaled the gas. The fumes were given off by fire of undetermined origin which destroyed X-ray films in the basement. Some pharmacists said it was bromine gas, while Dr. W. E. Lower, one of the founders of the Clinic, said it resembled the deadly phosgene gas employed in the World War.

The first explosion came wh X-ray films stored in the basement caught fire, releasing deadly fumes which penetrated to the waiting room on the floors above.

The hollow centre of the building soon filled with gases. The intense heat below sent the fumes swirling upward. Before any one had opportunity to escape a second blast blew out the skylight and filled every corner of the building with an atmosphere of death.

Those in the Clinic had no way of escape but the windows, and few were able to reach them. Even these were enveloped in the fumes and collapsed. The two street entrances were choked, and the stairways leading to the roof were heavy with the poisoned air. Every piece of fire apparatus available was centred at the Clinic and every vehicle possible was commandeered to remove the bodies. An hour and a half later all had been taken to near-by hospitals.

An army of volunteers, taking orders from police officials and executing them with amazing coordination, performed heroic rescue work. Men from all walks of life, men in gray and blue business suits, overalls, taxi uniforms, even rags, stood at the beck of policemen and helped in taking the injured and dead from the clinic building while it still was filed with death-dealing gases.

Inspector George J. Matowitz, who rushed from Central Police Station with flying squads, found huge billows of smoke and gas enveloping the structure, and with other police officials he commandeered all vehicles in sight as ambulances and then pressed every available man in the vicinity into duty as fast as he volunteered.

While delivery trucks, drays, transfer wagons and private automobiles stood ready to take away the dead and injured, butchers, grocers, dentists, sailors, brokers, taxi drivers and clerks, working in small groups under uniformed men, waded through water left by the fire hose and tore away obstructions as they helped carry on the first rescue work.

Back of the clinic the fence was lined with volunteers, grim-faced men waiting their call. At a word from a fireman or policeman they plunged in and performed the duty assigned them.

The rescuers found evidences of the suddenness with which disaster came to those inside the building on every hand. Hats and shoes were scattered about.

Pedestrians Near-by Overcome.

The suction after the explosion shattered glass doors reinforced with steel. Compression in the hollow centre of the building packed air into the halls and staircases, and when this force was released by the blast the air rushed back into the centre of the building, smashing the doors with the force of battering rams.

The heavy fumes hung about the building and for two hours after the blast rescuers were unable to remain inside for long intervals. The first explosion came at a few seconds past 11:30 A. M. A clock on the third floor balcony stopped at that time. The fumes were so strong as to act almost instantly. Pedestrians outside the building toppled to the ground and lay unconscious until dragged to safety when the gas lifted.

Some at unbroken windows pounded weakly against the glass and then dropped from sight as the gas choked them.

"All the News That's Fit to Print."

The New York Times.

Copyright, 1930, by The New York Times Company.

THE WEATHER
Rain early today, cooler tonight; tomorrow fair.
Temperatures yesterday—Max. 52, min. 42.
U. S. Weather Forecast—For details see Page 33.

VOL. LXXIX....No. 26,386. NEW YORK, TUESDAY, APRIL 22, 1930. TWO CENTS In Greater New York | THREE CENTS Within 200 Miles | FOUR CENTS Elsewhere Except 7th and 8th Postal Zones

FIVE POWERS SIGN NAVAL TREATY TODAY; EUROPEAN NATIONS TO CONTINUE TALKS; STIMSON CALLS PACT STEP TO BANISH WAR

STIMSON WILL SIGN FIRST

Heads of Delegations to Deliver Addresses at Final Session.

PACT IS DIVIDED IN 5 PARTS

Limitation Provisions Apply Only to America, Britain and Japan.

ALL AGREE TO REMAINDER

France and Italy Included in Capital Ship Holiday and Submarine Humanization.

By EDWIN L. JAMES.
Special Cable to THE NEW YORK TIMES.

LONDON, April 21.—The London naval treaty will be signed at a plenary session at St. James's Palace tomorrow morning. The ceremony will begin at 10:30 A. M. (4:30 A. M. New York Time), and there will be addresses by the heads of the five delegations, as well as by representatives of the British Dominions. These speeches, with the translations, will require about two and a half hours for delivery, so the actual signing will not occur before 1 P. M. at the earliest.

Secretary Stimson will be the first to set his name to the document. He will be followed by Ambassador Dawes, Secretary Adams, Senator Robinson, Senator Reed, Ambassador Gibson and Ambassador Morrow. Foreign Minister Briand and his colleagues of France, the next nation in alphabetical order, will come after them.

The representatives of the British Empire will follow, headed by Prime Minister MacDonald. Foreign Minister Grandi, who is ill in Rome, will not be present and Admiral Sirianni will lead the Italians, the next to sign, and the Japanese, headed by Reijiro Wakatsuki, will be last.

European Talks to Go On.

In addition to the treaty, the delegates will adopt a resolution providing for the continuance of negotiations by Britain, France and Italy, and also a letter which Prime Minister MacDonald, as president of the conference, will send to the Secretary General of the League of Nations, notifying him of the London treaty.

At 2 o'clock tomorrow morning copies of the treaty will be distributed at St. James's by the secretariat of the conference to be released for publication after the actual signing, which will be about 7 A. M., New York Time.

The treaty fills thirty-four printed pages, printed in parallel columns of English and French. It runs about 10,000 words, two-thirds of which is the treaty proper and the rest annexes. It contains nothing surprising. All its provisions have been published in these dispatches. It contains a preamble and twenty-six articles, divided into five parts.

In form it is a five-power treaty among America, Britain, Japan, France and Italy. Its naval limitation provisions apply only to the United States, Great Britain and Japan. The parts which are binding also on France and Italy include the capital ship holiday and submarine humanization.

The preamble, which is short and simple, contains reference neither to the Kellogg pact nor the League of Nations, since America opposed mentioning the League and the other powers would not name the anti-war pact without giving credit also to the League. It says the nations desire to prevent danger and to reduce the burdens of competitive armament and desire to carry forward the work begun by the Washington naval conference and to facilitate the progressive realization of general limitation and reduction of armaments.

Provisions Outlined.

Part I contains the first five articles. Article 1 provides for a capital ship holiday until 1936, permitting France and Italy to build the battleships they had a right under the Washington treaty to lay down in 1927 and 1929.

Article 2 lays down how England, America and Japan shall bring down their number of battleships in 1931 to fifteen, fifteen and nine, respectively. The United States is to scrap the Florida, the Utah and the Arkansas or the Wyoming; England is to scrap Benbow, the Iron Duke, the Marlborough, the Emperor of India and the Tiger; Japan is to scrap the Hiyei. Of these ships the United States may retain for training purposes the Arkansas or

Continued on Page Two.

"Three Little Girls," sensational musical hit. Shubert Thea. Mats. Wed. & Sat.—Advt.

Says France Plans to Build 27,000-Ton Cruiser at Once

Special Cable to THE NEW YORK TIMES.

LONDON, April 21.—On the eve of the signing of the naval treaty it is reported here that France intends to proceed immediately with the construction of a cruiser of about 27,000 tons displacement, carrying twelve eight-inch guns.

This vessel, according to The Daily Telegraph, will be incomparably superior in every respect to the Ersatz Preussen, Germany's "pocket battleship," and practically equal in fighting power to any battle-cruiser now afloat with the single exception of the British battle-cruiser Hood.

The French decision to build the vessel is said to result from the recent action of the German Reichsrat in restoring the naval estimates vote for a second vessel of the Ersatz Preussen type. The cost of the proposed French ship is estimated at $20,000,000, and it will take three years to complete.

FIGHT ON M'DONALD VOTED BY LEFT WING

Independent Laborites Call for Ousting of Government as Reactionary.

FOR SOCIALIZING INDUSTRY

Birmingham Conference Plans Separate Party Action for Radical Changes.

By CHARLES A. SELDEN.
Special Cable to THE NEW YORK TIMES.

BIRMINGHAM, April 21.—When Parliament reconvenes next week the thirty members of the House of Commons who were elected a year ago as candidates of the Independent Labor party will come back as avowed opponents of the MacDonald Government. That situation was clinched at the sessions today of the Independents' conference in this city.

While these thirty men and women under the leadership of James Maxton have already voted of their own volition against the Parliamentary Labor party on various government measures before the Commons, they now have their party's endorsement of their action and, moreover, definite instructions to continue.

This means that Prime Minister MacDonald's assured strength within the Labor party in the House of Commons is cut from 289 to 259 in the total Parliament membership of 615. But this loss no doubt will be more than made up by the support of practically all of the fifty-nine Liberal members. That Premier MacDonald and the members of his Cabinet do not fear a disastrous result is indicated by the fact they have defied the Independents to do their worst.

The Birmingham conference further undertook to undermine the Parliamentary Labor party not only in the Commons but generally with the electorate and to work for new leadership of the party, reorganized on a basis of much more extreme socialism than the present government contemplates.

Resolutions were adopted holding the MacDonald Government responsible for the present disturbances in India and demanding complete independence both for that country and Egypt. The Independents declared that complete solidarity existed between them and the Indians.

J. H. Thomas, Lord Privy Seal in the MacDonald Government, was accused of doing more for the capitalists in the last ten months than the Conservatives had been able to do in five years. In that connection a resolution was adopted demanding a complete reorganization of industry through the socialization of land, banking, the export and import trade, transportation and all other key industries.

Complete Break Is Expected.

BIRMINGHAM, April 21 (AP).—There were storms of protest at the conference of the Independent Labor party here when the right of "Left-Wingers" in Parliament to vote against the Labor government was again upheld. There was much criticism of the government, particularly in regard to its unemployment policy, but a motion of censure was defeated.

From several delegates came suggestions that the outcome would be a left-wing party distinct from the Parliamentary Labor party. One delegate, indeed, urged the independents to prepare by getting into contact with workers in shop and factory.

One motion before the conference urged the I. L. P. group in Parlia-

Continued on Page Two.

VILLEPIGUE'S NOW OPEN. Shore Dinners and A la Carte. Phone Sheepshead Bay 1000.—Advt.

SECRETARY TALKS ON RADIO

He Tells Publishers Here Kellogg Pact Helped Build Confidence.

URGES US TO LEAD IN PEACE

Naval Limitation, He Says, Is Best Approach—Sees Gain for Methods of Diplomacy.

HOOVER GREETS MEETING

Asserts The Associated Press Aided in Accord 'Fruitful of So Many Blessings.'

Speaking over the radio from London yesterday, Secretary of State Henry L. Stimson told nearly 1,000 members of The Associated Press, at the annual luncheon in the Hotel Commodore that the fruits of the naval parley would be potent in outlawing war. He said that the success of the conference was the outcome of greater confidence among the nations which had been inspired by the Kellogg-Briand compact.

"The past fourteen weeks," said Colonel Stimson, "have given me more confidence in my belief that the peaceful methods of diplomacy can eventually take the place of war than anything I have witnessed since the last war drew to a close."

Before the secretary spoke, Frank B. Noyes, publisher of The Washington Star and president of the news agency, read a message from President Hoover, praising The Associated Press for the reliability and impartiality of its news. After Colonel Stimson's address, Kent Cooper, marking his fifth year as general manager of The Associated Press, discussed the changes he had made and told of his aspirations for the future. He paid tribute to the late Melville E. Stone, his predecessor.

Stimson Is Heard Clearly.

The voice of the Secretary of State came through clearly during the fifteen-minute period of his speech, spanning 3,000 miles of ocean with virtually no static. Colonel Stimson had promised months ago to attend the luncheon and deliver his address in person. This being impossible, he stood before the microphone at London's dinner hour and was heard as distinctly as if he had been standing in the Commodore ballroom. The transmission, handled in England by the British Broadcasting Company and here by the National Broadcasting network, was the first fully successful bringing by radio of a speaker's voice from one side of the Atlantic to an assemblage he was addressing on the other side.

Declaring that limitation and reduction of naval armaments was the surest way in which to make realities of the pledges of the Kellogg-Briand compact signatories, Colonel Stimson said that the United States should lead the way. The position of this nation, strategically, made this mandatory. He added that this country should "refrain from criticizing others less fortunately placed."

"The message which I should like to make clear to you all today is that the success of the London naval conference is necessarily related to the success of the Kellogg-Briand pact," he said. "The good resolutions of that pact cannot stand alone. They must be followed by national effort, prompt, constant, unremitting effort to make them good, and no line of effort offers a better earnest of its success than the line of naval armament. In selecting that line President Hoover laid his finger upon the best method of insuring that our solemn promise of two years ago should be fulfilled."

Sees Two Naval Problems.

The naval conference's work, as viewed by the head of the American delegation, dealt with two distinct naval problems. The first was that of the relations between the navies of the United States, Great Britain and Japan. The second concerned the navy strength to be maintained between Great Britain, France and Italy.

The first problem has been solved, he said, "and this is a great achievement in itself." The second problem was more complex and any discussion of naval quotas, he said, involved the political questions controlling the relations of Italy, France and Great Britain. The United States at the conference had not gone into the political phases, but the delegates, as observers on the sidelines at the meetings to discuss the Italian, French and British ratios, had seen many issues clarified.

"This came not only by clarifying the results of their discussion," said

Continued on Page Twenty-two.

"WHEN YOU THINK of Writing, Think of Whiting."—Advt.

WALKER VETOES BILL RAISING TAXI FARE; ORDERS NEW STUDY

Expresses Belief City Has No Right to Deprive Public of Benefits of Competition.

SPLIT WITH WHALEN SEEN

But Mayor Shows "Sympathy" With Commissioner's Argument for Better Service.

NAMES WALSH BOARD HEAD

Lawyer and Four Others to Make a Thorough Survey of Taxicab Industry.

Mayor Walker vetoed last night the taxicab rate ordinance passed by the Board of Aldermen on April 8 fixing a minimum fare of 15 cents for an initial quarter-mile and 5 cents for each additional quarter mile and increasing the waiting time charge from $1.50 to $2.40 an hour. His veto message, signed at 7:15 P. M., announced also his appointment of a five-man commission, headed by Frank P. Walsh, former co-chairman of the War Labor Board, to make a survey of the taxicab situation and report to him its findings and recommendations.

Besides Mr. Walsh, the commission will comprise Daniel L. Reardon, executive vice president of the United States Trucking Corporation; an engineer to be suggested by Day & Zimmermann, Inc., who recently completed a comprehensive traffic survey of the city; a member to be named by the Merchants Association, and one to be named by the State Chamber of Commerce.

Believes Measure Unconstitutional.

Mayor Walker's veto was based mainly upon his conviction that the City Government had no power to deprive the public of the benefit of any lower taxicab fare to be obtained from a competitive system. Although the message did not specifically declare his belief that the ordinance was unconstitutional, it is known that he has held that view since the measure was first introduced in the Board of Aldermen by Dennis J. Mahon, majority leader.

Mayor Walker's formal veto will be placed before the Board of Aldermen at its meeting today. Although the board has the power to override it by a two-thirds vote, it is a foregone conclusion that no such action will be taken. It is also unlikely, in view of the appointment of a survey commission, that Alderman Murray Stand will introduce his proposed bill to establish a "standard" or fixed taxicab fare.

The veto decision followed a three-hour conference at which Mayor Walker discussed the ordinance with Mr. Walsh, Alderman Mahon, Public Works Commissioner Joseph Johnson and Bill Drafting Commissioner Cahill. The veto message was signed after Mayor Walker had studied and considered an eight-page memorandum urging its approval submitted last week by Police Commissioner Whalen.

Mayor Walker's veto message characterized the taxicab industry as one without system or standardization and described the ordinance as an "earnest effort to improve these conditions," made at the request of the Police Department and citizens. Expressing sympathy with Mr. Whalen's argument that the ordinance would cut down taxicab accidents, improve service, relieve traffic

Continued on Page Twelve.

Reds Get Police Permit for May Day Parade, But Must Wait Till Veterans Leave Union Sq.

The Communists will parade under police escort on May Day and will meet in Union Square as the result of an agreement made by them yesterday with Police Commissioner Whalen. The commissioner granted a permit for the meeting and parade on condition that the march be diverted away from the congested centre of the east side and that the meeting be held from 3 to 4:45 P. M.

To avoid a clash between Communists and the Veterans of Foreign Wars, who received a permit yesterday to hold their meeting from noon to 2 P. M., Commissioner Whalen fixed 3 o'clock as the starting hour for the Communists' demonstration.

Announcement that a permit would be granted today to the Communists was made last night by Commissioner Whalen after a talk at Police Headquarters with Herbert Benjamin, head of the United May Day Conference. Benjamin agreed to have the Communist parade from Rutgers Square to Union Square traverse the route prescribed by Mr. Whalen, from Rutgers Square east to Pitt Street, to Avenue C, to Seventeenth Street and to Union Square. The Police Commissioner said that if the Communists pursued a peaceful policy in the future they would be accorded every possible courtesy and consideration by the Police Department.

Benjamin went to Police Headquarters late yesterday afternoon when he learned that Commissioner Whalen wished to talk with him concerning the application for a permit made to the police. The application, said by Mr. Whalen to be the first time that the Communists have asked permission of the police to parade, declared that "the working class will not give up its right to demonstrate for its demands and for international solidarity in the struggle against capitalism in Union Square on May 1."

"The right of the workers to Union Square has been established," the letter continued. "We intend to maintain that right."

Earlier in the day Commissioner Whalen granted a permit to Henry B. Fairbanks, retired colonel, for a parade and meeting of the Veterans of Foreign Wars, in which, it was said, about 10,000 soldiers will participate.

The veterans will assemble at 9:30 at Fifth Avenue and Twenty-fourth Street and will parade to Union Square. The police arrangements in the Square will be similar to those in effect on March 6. Mr. Whalen will direct his command from the garden house at the north end of the square.

HOTEL VICTORIA, 7th Ave. & 51st St. Radio in Every Room, $3 to $4.—Advt.

CRESCENT LIMITED, De Luxe All-Pullman train New York-New Orleans, leaves Penna. Station 8:40 P. M. daily. Reservations, Tickets, Southern Railway, 152 W. 42nd St. Phone Wisconsin 2205.—Advt.

335 CONVICTS DIE IN OHIO PRISON FIRE; TROOPS SUBDUE 2,000 FREE IN THE YARD; THREE OTHER FIRES SET IN ESCAPE PLOT

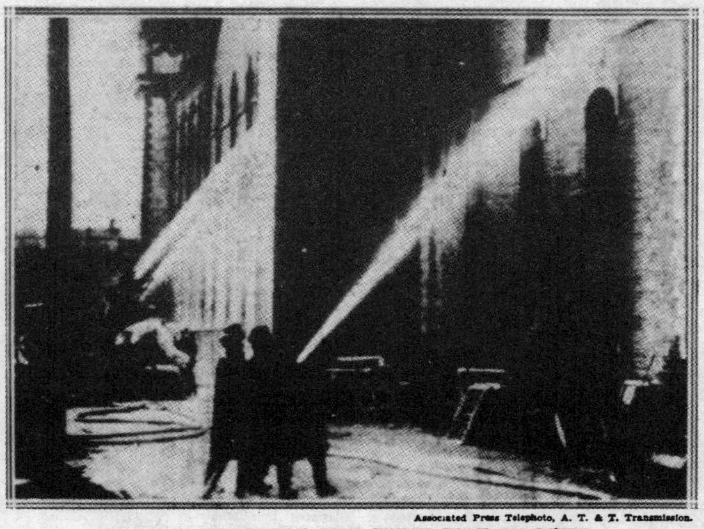

Associated Press Telephoto, A. T. & T. Transmission.

FIGHTING THE PRISON FIRE WHICH TOOK 300 LIVES.

This photograph was made last night at the Ohio State Penitentiary while the first of the series of fires there was raging. It was taken by airplane to Cleveland and transmitted from that city to New York by wire.

INMATES TRAPPED IN CELLS

Burned and Suffocated While Rescuers Try in Vain to Reach Them.

YARD LIKE A BATTLEFIELD

Dead and Dying Cover Ground as White-Robed Doctors Try to Save Them.

4,300 IN CROWDED PRISON

Prisoners and Guards Show Heroism—Regulars and Militia Called to Prevent Outbreak.

311 Bodies in Prison Yard; 24 Others Lying in Basement

By The Associated Press.

COLUMBUS, Ohio, Tuesday, April 22.—A count of the dead in the Ohio penitentiary fire disaster, completed early today, indicated that the fatality list would run well above 300.

Hospital attaches said that 311 were counted in the prison yard and twenty-four dead were in the hospital basement. Of the 150 injured, they feared that many would succumb.

No effort was being made by prison heads to get an official death count until all the bodies had been removed to the temporary morgue.

Special to The New York Times.

COLUMBUS, Ohio, April 21.—The Ohio State Penitentiary, housing 4,300 prisoners in accommodations designed for 1,500, was transformed into a human pyre tonight when fire swept through four cell blocks and wiped out the lives of more than 300 men in the brief space of about an hour.

Late tonight it was feared that the death toll would mount to more serious proportions, with more than 100 other victims suffering from the effects of smoke.

Just before midnight regular army soldiers and militiamen had got under control the 2,000 prisoners who were loose and threatening violence in the prison yards.

Originating at about 6 P. M. as a seemingly trifling blaze and developing with rapidity into a major disaster, the fire was believed to be the work of incendiary inmates, who hoped in the ensuing excitement to make a successful dash for liberty.

Just before midnight, after hours of destruction and disorder, floodlights in the prison yard revealed the grisly results of the incendiaries' handiwork.

Hundreds of Bodies on Grass.

Several hundred bodies lay about on the damp grass. Nurses and doctors were administering first aid to those suffering from smoke. Towering over the dead and suffering were the fire-swept cell blocks. And as a background to the night's grim festival of death and destruction uniformed soldiers of the regular army, Ohio National Guardsmen, all available city police and prison guards were patrolling in and around the prison, victors in a struggle to restore order among the thousands of helpless, milling convicts.

As Warden Preston E. Thomas began a conference late tonight with State officials it was agreed, in practically all official quarters, that the first fire, as well as others that followed, had been the work of prisoners.

The first fire alarm was sounded at 5:50 P. M., when all the prisoners had been locked in their cells for the night. The fire was discovered in the northwest section of the prison, in the roof of G and H cell blocks, which are under reconstruction. Speedily it ate its way along the roof southward to the southwestern corner and then took an eastward course, threatening the administration section of the exposed southern wing.

New Fires Are Started.

About 8 o'clock the fire fighters considered that they had the original blaze under control. By that time the list of known dead had mounted to more than 250. Then, about half an hour later, new fires broke out, this time in the cotton and woolen mills, about 900 feet away from the scene of the first blaze, which had been set alight by oil-soaked cloth. The Catholic chapel was also set on fire.

Tense scenes were enacted in the cell blocks and in the prison yard

Continued on Page Three.

RED LEADERS JAILED 6 MONTHS TO 3 YEARS

Foster and Three Aides Get Maximum Terms After Denouncing Judges as Prejudiced.

REBUKED FOR OUTBURST

Insist on Their Right to Speak Before Sentence—Fifth Red Rioter Gets 30-Day Term.

After delivering court room orations of vilification, four of the five Communist leaders convicted of unlawful assembly for the riot in Union Square March 6 received indeterminate penitentiary sentences yesterday in the court of Special Sessions. The fifth, who held his tongue, escaped with a thirty-day sentence to the workhouse.

William Z. Foster, Robert Minor and Israel Amter, national leaders of the revolutionary party, and Harry Raymond, who joined the others in criticising their conviction as an "outrageous example of capitalist justice," received maximum sentences from Justices Max Salomon, James J. McInerney and Daniel F. Murphy. Joseph Leston, who alone waived his right to address the court before sentence was imposed, was called "an instrument" in the hands of the "prime instigators and leaders" of the riot and got the lighter punishment. Leston appeared on the court record as Joseph Lester.

Indictments charging each of the five prisoners with felonious assault still are pending. April 30 has been set for a hearing. If convicted of this charge the Communist agitators

Continued on Page Twenty.

'Star-Spangled Banner' Bill, Thrice Beaten, Passed in House

Special to The New York Times.

WASHINGTON, April 21.—The House voted today to adopt the "Star-Spangled Banner" as the national anthem, after turning down Representative Linthicum's bill three times at the present session.

Representative Collins of Mississippi, who has objected every time the bill was brought up, opposed it today, but Representative Snell of New York, acting speaker, refused to entertain the objection.

The bill now goes to the Senate.

COMMITTEE, 10 TO 6, REJECTS PARKER

Vote for Adverse Report on Nomination Follows Refusal, 10 to 4, to Call Judge.

SWIFT AND UNEXPECTED

Action on High Court Nominee Taken Without Debate—Hoover Firm in Face of Senate Fight.

Special to The New York Times.

WASHINGTON, April 21.—The Senate Judiciary Committee voted 10 to 6 today to report adversely on the nomination of Judge John J. Parker of North Carolina to be associate justice of the United States Supreme Court.

Previously, by a vote of 10 to 4, the committee had rejected Senator Overman's motion to invite Judge Parker to explain his labor decision and alleged utterances regarding Negroes. This motion occasioned long debate, and, when it ended, Chairman Norris perfunctorily asked the committee whether the nomination should be reported favorably or adversely.

Without debate the vote was taken for an adverse report. The action was unexpected, the fight of many weeks, backed by organized labor and Negro associations, taking a sudden turn that surprised even the opposition Senators.

The opposition declared tonight that the decision of the committee would strengthen its fight on the Senate floor and that Judge Parker would finally be rejected.

Hoover Stands by Nominee.

It is generally understood, however, that President Hoover will not withdraw Judge Parker's nomination and that he feels that the Senate has no justifiable grounds for rejecting him.

There is some talk that Judge Parker may request that his nomination be withdrawn, but unless he does so the President will not act.

The White House will do nothing to influence the long fight expected on the floor. Friends of Judge Parker probably will move to recommit the adverse report to the committee when the Senate receives it and takes it up in open executive session this week.

If the nomination should recommitted and action in the Senate post-

Continued on Page Twenty-three.

WHEN BUYING BITTERS, DEMAND Abbott's Flavors Beverages.—Advt.

WHALEN DUE TO QUIT AT DINNER ON MAY 6

Walker Is Said to Have Told Police Head He Need Not Continue Salary Sacrifice.

CONSIDERING A SUCCESSOR

Inspector O'Brien and Patterson Suggested—Commissioner to Return to Store Post.

Grover A. Whalen is expected to announce his resignation as Police Commissioner at the dinner to be given for him on May 6 by a committee of prominent citizens, it was learned yesterday on excellent authority. The resignation, it was said, will take effect the following day and Mr. Whalen will return to the place as general manager of Wanamaker's which he left on leave of absence to become the head of the Police Department.

Information to this effect is believed to have been conveyed to Mayor Walker, who will be one of the principal speakers at the dinner. The Mayor is said to have informed Mr. Whalen some time ago that he was prepared to name his successor and that Mr. Whalen need not continue to make a financial sacrifice by remaining in office any longer than he desired.

The Mayor, however, did not indicate to Mr. Whalen whom he had in mind for his successor and it is probable that he has not decided on a selection. The latest speculation favored the appointment of Richard C. Patterson Jr., Commissioner of Correction, unless the Mayor decided to take a man from the uniformed force, possibly Chief Inspector John O'Brien. Mr. Patterson has made an excellent record as Commissioner of Correction, and his appointment or that of Chief Inspector O'Brien would be accepted as being made without regard to partisan politics.

No Move for Higher Salary.

Members of the Whalen dinner have informed Mayor Walker that the published report that the dinner would be made the occasion of an attempt to get the salary of the Police Commissioner raised from $10,000 to $25,000 or $35,000 a year for the purpose of getting Mr. Whalen to remain were without foundation. It was learned that this project, which originated with Stewart Browne, president of the United Real Estate Owners' Association, one of the organizations participating in the dinner, never received any substantial support.

Mr. Browne approached Mayor Walker on the matter, it was said, but received no encouragement. He then suggested it to sponsors of the dinner, who declined to have anything to do with such an attempt. It also was learned that Mr. Whalen's decision to resign as Police Commissioner was final, and, so far as could be learned, no further attempt has been made to push the salary increase project with a view to retaining Mr. Whalen as commissioner, although there has been a general agreement among those

Continued on Page Four.

"THE TAMIAMI" Fast New Train to Florida. From Penn. Sta. daily 8:10 a. m. Atlantic Coast Line, 8 W. 40th St. Tel. Lac. 7080.—Advt.

FOUND CONDITIONS BAD AT OHIO PRISON

Investigation in 1928 Told of Overcrowding of Plant and Convicts' Idleness.

O. HENRY ONCE HELD THERE

Famous Author Collected Material for Some of His Stories While in the Penitentiary.

The Ohio State Penitentiary, which was established in 1815 and was moved to its present site in 1830, was condemned as one of the worst in the country, due to conditions of overcrowding, in a report in The Handbook of American Prisons and Reformatories of 1929. The penitentiary is now entirely surrounded by the city of Columbus.

The report, compiled by the National Society of Penal Information, says:

"The ancient plant at the State Penitentiary in Columbus, one of the largest prisons in the country, suffers from overcrowding worse than that in any other large prison. The need of another institution in the Ohio penal system has been apparent for many years. * * *

"Not only can Columbus not care for an increased population, but it is already too large a prison to be operated on any other lines than those of a blanket treatment. The present situation should not be tolerated."

"Ohio, like many other States," the report continues, "has allowed its prison population to get far ahead of its building program, and socially minded citizens should demand legislative and Executive action without delay. When overcrowding is coupled with the amount of unemployment found here, the state of affairs becomes increasingly critical."

The report criticizes the low salaries of attendants. It refers to a scandal caused by an escape by bribing a guard, and adds:

"A second occurrence which received widespread publicity was the fire which destroyed a wooden building used as a dormitory for prisoners at the brick plant. The shocking loss of life which took place, when prisoners were unable to free themselves from the burning building, called attention to a condition which is paralleled in many other States where prisoners, especially on the farms, in road camps and on other outlying details, are quartered in buildings that are firetraps, with inadequate provision for their immediate release in case of fire."

The report concludes:

"It would require a thorough survey of this prison, made with entire freedom from restriction, to determine to what extent Ohio is reaping the fruits that may reasonably be expected from conditions of grave overcrowding and idleness, and restricted space in an institution which has not grown away from the old ideas of penology to the degree that institutions have in many other States."

William Sydney Porter—O. Henry to most persons—served three years and three months of a five-year sentence for embezzlement at the Ohio State Prison at Columbus and during his term there collected the material for some of his most famous stories.

Professor C. Alphonso Smith of the University of Virginia in a biography of O. Henry says that it was through his prison experiences that he made the step from journalism to literature.

O. Henry entered the prison in April, 1898, and was released in July, 1901.

Built to House Only 1,500.

COLUMBUS, Ohio, April 21 (AP).—Ohio Penitentiary was built in 1890 and was designed to house only 1,500 men. A roll-call this morning showed the total enrolment today was 4,300.

The prison covers about five acres, within a stone's throw of downtown Columbus. Within the walls are a score of buildings, including eight cell blocks, a hospital, mills, a chapel, dining halls and other structures.

Preston E. Thomas has been warden for about fifteen years. He is noted as an expert. Under his rule there have been no major riots, but there have been many deliveries and escapes, including one when thirteen convicts of Company K, the "bad gang," got loose.

STATE NEGLECT CHARGED.

Ohio State Journal Editorial Denounces Prison Fire Hazard.

Special to The New York Times.

COLUMBUS, Ohio, April 21.—In an editorial The Ohio State Journal tomorrow morning will say:

"Ohio has supplied one of the most frightful disasters in the history of American prisons.

"More than 300 human beings, locked in steel cells at the Ohio Penitentiary, were burned to death. * * *

"They were prisoners doing time for violation of the law, but they were human beings, each with a soul, each with a love of life, each entitled to fair play from the great State that imprisoned them. * * *

"It is a bitter and terrible reproach that in any great State a prison should be fireswept. These buildings should be fireproof; there should be adequate fire-fighting equipment. These safeguards should have been increased as the population was becoming congested during recent years.

"Men in Columbus have pleaded many times with the Legislature for betterment of prison plants and conditions, but their pleas fell on deaf ears. The tax spenders and professional politicians always had other uses for the taxpayers' money and the pleas to protect the lives of prisoners and the good name of the State were thrust aside."

PRISON IN WHICH HUNDREDS BURNED TO DEATH

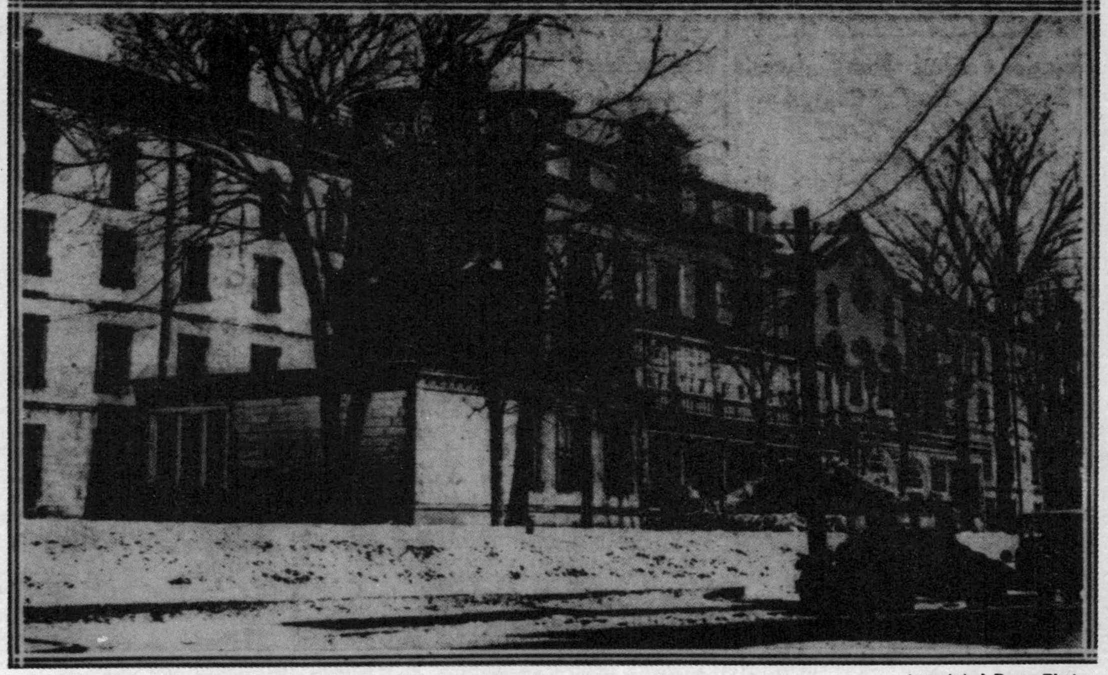

Associated Press Photo.

Front View of the State Penitentiary at Columbus, Ohio, Where Flames Swept Dormitories and Part of the Main Cell Blocks.

335 CONVICTS DIE IN OHIO PRISON FIRE

Continued from Page 1, Column 8.

before a semblance of order was finally restored by the soldiers and guards, scenes of suffering, swift tragedy, human endurance and heroism. Some of the locked-in convicts were burned to a crisp. Smoke suffocated many.

If the words of some prisoners could be taken the lives of many of the victims could have been saved if their cells had been unlocked when the fire started and when there was still time.

In one case, the survivors said, a guard had told the convicts that he had no authority to release them from their cells, explaining that he had to wait for the command from his superiors. However, as the flames gained headway the prisoners in the cells that were threatened were released.

The most tragic scenes took place in the fifth and sixth upper tiers from the middle of the western sections of G and H blocks southward and along the section of the prison with the southern exposure.

Here, amid the cries of the dying, deeds of heroism were enacted. One guard, a man named Baldwin, worked with feverish haste, exposing himself to the fate of the others, to release the helpless convicts.

In some instances keys to the cells could not be found quickly and men perished as the flames shot along the roof, burning them and sending flaming débris showering down their bodies. Streams of water, shot from the fire hoses in the yard below, seemed utterly inadequate to give relief.

Start of the Disaster.

The catastrophe began with a sudden burst of fire and a dense cloud of smoke. The flames first shot out of the cell block where a new structure inside the prison walls was under construction, and inside forty minutes had reached the southwest corner. Aided by a brisk wind they reared a furnace in and around the cell blocks.

In a short time utter disorder reigned. Prison guards, National Guardsmen, regular army troops and reserve guards fought heroically to rescue the trapped men and maintain order.

Above the cracking of the flames and the shrieks of the prison siren could be heard the screams of the panic-stricken prisoners, some held fast in locked cells, others being burned alive.

At the first outbreak all telephones in the institution were rendered useless, a circumstance which strengthened the suspicion that the fire was an attempt at a wholesale prison break. News of what was happening ran through the city like magic and crowds began to gather outside the prison walls even before the arrival of the two Fire Department units.

As the fire gained headway, hurried calls for aid brought more fire apparatus, an extra force of reserve guards, National Guard units and regular army infantrymen. More appeals brought upward of 100 nurses from all of the city hospitals, but Warden Thomas at first refused to admit them because of the danger inside the walls.

Radio appeals also brought doctors and nurses from as far away as 300 miles, but long before their arrival there were so many at work that they could not be used.

Scores of doctors and nurses worked at top speed as inert body after body was placed before them. Around the fire engines milled excited prisoners, many adding to the confusion even in their attempts to rescue their fellows, and the troops had trouble in controlling them. Firemen later reported to the prison Warden that some convicts had tried to cut the fire hose and set fire to the firemen's gasoline wagon.

Steadily the prison yard was being strewed with the dead or dying and those less seriously stricken, while the growing crowd of prisoners in the yard became more and more unmanageable. With the doctors and nurses, many wearing their white hospital uniforms, the yard resembled a besieged fortress.

From first to last, all precautions were taken to avert a wholesale dash for liberty. Police and National Guardsmen were posted on the walls of the prison, augmenting the regular prison guards, with orders to keep their machine guns ready for instant action.

The first indication that the original fire was of incendiary origin came from State Fire Marshal Ray Gill. He expressed the belief that it was set in several places simultaneously in the I and K cell blocks. He asserted that the later fires in the cotton mill also were incendiary.

A number of investigations are expected to start tomorrow, with Governor Myers Y. Cooper directing one of them.

John J. Chester, Prosecuting Attorney of Franklin County, gathered data for his investigation at first hand tonight. He was inside the prison grounds while the bodies of the victims were still being carried away. The State Fire Marshal's Department is to conduct an inquiry also.

Governor Cooper was notified of the fire at White Sulphur Springs, Va., where he had been enjoying a rest from his official duties. He started for home at once, and is expected here at 7:30 A. M. tomorrow.

The most difficult problems facing the investigators are to discover the cause of the fires and decide the truth of the reported delay in the release of the prisoners from their cells.

William Wade, Warren, a big Negro prisoner, broke down a cell door with a sledge hammer and released twenty-five men. He was driven away by the heat. He was confined in another part of the prison and was released at the second alarm. Like others, he was bitter in his denunciation of the officials. "They could have saved these men," he said. "They let human beings burn to death."

George Johnson, a Cleveland Negro, said he seized the keys from the hand of a guard, went to the higher cell tiers and released many prisoners. Leo Matlock of Columbus, who is serving a life sentence for murder, got possession of keys and released prisoners.

"Prisoners worked in the flames, smothered and suffocated," said one convict. "Nearly all the prisoners behaved themselves. There was not an attempt to escape. Women were in the yard working. No one was insulted."

One story was simply told. It was a note written by a prisoner before he died of suffocation. It read: "Gus Socka. Notify John Dee, 93 Armory Avenue, Cincinnati."

Charles Greene, a Cleveland prisoner, said he helped carry out forty-two dead men, fighting his way through hot steel corridors and blinding smoke.

Roy Tyler, a Cleveland convict, who was due for liberty under a recent Supreme Court decision for "good time," was a victim.

Liston G. Schooley, a former Cleveland Councilman, who is serving a sentence in connection with land fraud cases, is credited with sounding the first alarm.

Says 100 Could Have Been Saved.

Glenn Pierce, one of the prisoners, declared that the lives of 100 men would have been saved had the guards consented to open the cells and release the men inside. Pierce was one of the first to be released and he with others immediately began to batter down doors still locked with an iron bar. Virtually every man on 5H, he said, knew that death was inevitable because all efforts of the rescue party could not take them beyond the 3-H range.

Convicts asserted a guard in the new cell block ran to the office of the penitentiary when the fire was discovered, after refusing to unlock the cells. Another guard raced to the office, they said, obtained the keys to the upper two tiers and turned them over to a convict with instructions to unlock the cells.

When the order for a general unlocking of cells was given the upper tiers had become red hot and many of their occupants had perished.

The old cell blocks were of six ranges, seventeen cells to a range, with four men in each cell. The fifth and sixth ranges at the top suffered most heavily. There more than 200 men died.

Men in the fifth and sixth tiers of the west cell blocks begged to be shot as they watched the flames approaching them.

Even after men had reached the lower floor during the first part of the blaze there was reluctance to allow them to get to the yard, it is said.

Holward Jones, who had been released after a twelve-year term and was resentenced for theft, proved himself a hero. He seized a sledge hammer and single handed released 136 convicts by hammering the locks off their cell doors.

Lying on a blanket gasping for his breath was another convict who had saved twelve lives.

Warden's Daughter Directs Fight From Office, Calling Help for Him as He Battles Amid Flames

By The Associated Press.

COLUMBUS, Ohio, April 21.—With Warden Thomas inside the prison walls during tonight's death-dealing fire in the Ohio Penitentiary, the situation in the prison outer office was handled by Miss Amanda Thomas, his daughter.

This young woman ordered guards to their posts, issued machine guns and ammunition, called doctors and nurses, summoned troops and performed many other duties.

She was calm and collected until the fire threatened her home in the penitentiary main building. Then she turned her attention to the house, ordering her valuables removed.

Big Jim Morton, a notorious Cleveland bank robber, was a hero of the fire. Big Jim, loose in the yard when the fire started, rescued a score of men from K cell block.

He continued working at top speed until he was overcome by smoke. He was unconscious for a time, but was revived and suffered little ill effects.

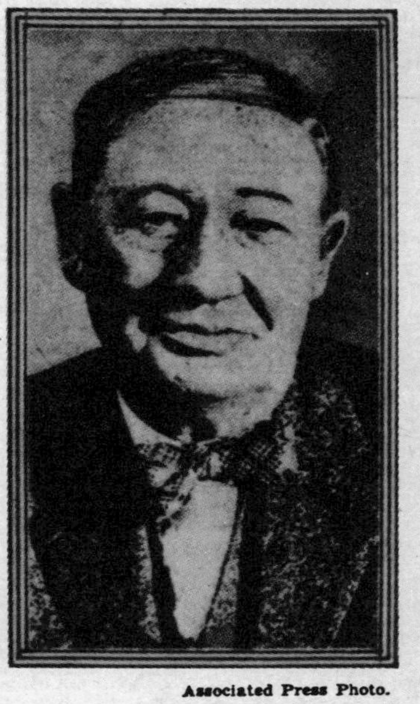

Associated Press Photo.

Preston E. Thomas, Warden of the Fire-Swept Prison.

"All the News That's Fit to Print."

The New York Times.

Copyright, 1930, by The New York Times Company.

THE WEATHER
Generally fair today and tomorrow; little change in temperature.
Temperatures yesterday—Max. 84, min. 68.
U. S. Weather Forecast—For details see Page 37.

VOL. LXXIX....No. 26,479. **** NEW YORK, THURSDAY, JULY 24, 1930. TWO CENTS in Greater New York | THREE CENTS Within 200 Miles | FOUR CENTS Elsewhere Except 7th and 8th Postal Zones

679 KILLED IN ITALIAN EARTHQUAKE; INJURED PUT AT 1,500; RELIEF RUSHED; NAPLES IN TERROR AS HOUSES CRUMBLE

10,000 PERSONS HOMELESS

Shocks Came While the People Slept, Adding to the Panic.

DEATH LIST IS MOUNTING

Villanova Is Virtually Wiped Out in Disaster—Quakes Centre in Melfi in Apennines.

PREMIER AND POPE GIVE AID

Relief Hampered by Collapsing of Train Tunnels and Roads—Americans in Area Are Safe.

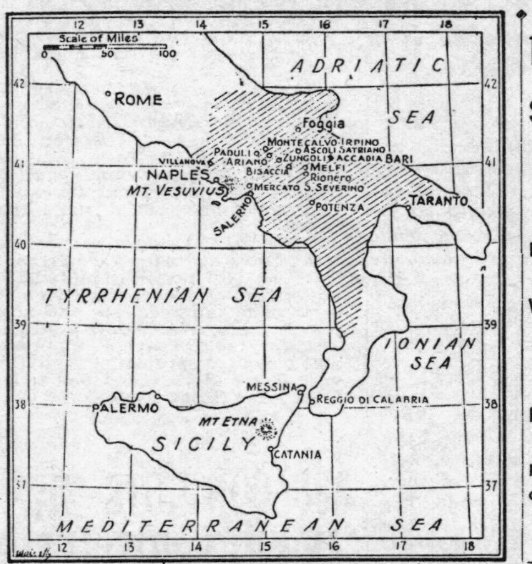

AREA IN ITALY STRICKEN BY QUAKE.

By The Associated Press.

ROME, July 23.—Official reports from provincial prefects to the government tonight accounted for 679 dead in today's earthquake disaster. The reports included Accadia 70 and Anzaho 30, among other newly reported towns. The injured counted were 1,500.

By ARNALDO CORTESI.

Wireless to THE NEW YORK TIMES.

ROME, July 23.—More than 500 persons are known to have been killed and many hundreds injured in the earthquake which early this morning rocked the region between Naples and Bari, causing great damage as far north as Foggia and Benevento and as far south as Potenza.

The centre of the disturbance was at Melfi, in the middle of the Apennine Mountains, almost exactly half-way between Naples and Bari. In this town alone more than 100 persons were killed and thousands rendered homeless when scores of houses collapsed.

Fifty more dead were reported in neighboring villages, but the complete figures on the disaster are not yet available, as news has not been received from many scattered villages.

The first news of the earthquake was received from Naples. Then dispatches began pouring into Rome from the prefects of almost all the southern provinces, asking urgently for relief and telling of extensive damage and loss of life.

Rail Damage Hampers Relief.

As soon as the gravity of the disaster was realized in Rome, relief work was organized with the greatest dispatch. Within an hour of the first news, relief trains were on their way from Foggia to Melfi, bearing medical stores, food and blankets. The trains, however, were unable to reach Melfi because the railroad tracks had been severely damaged by the earthquake. So the relief provisions were transported the rest of the way on motor trucks, reaching Melfi in the morning.

Premier Mussolini, immediately on hearing of the disaster, summoned Senator Cremonesi, President of the Italian Red Cross, and sent him and the Under-Secretary of Public Works to the stricken zone with a special relief train. They will be in charge of all the relief work.

At the same time all available troops in the damaged and adjacent areas were mobilized and sent wherever their services were most needed. Regional Fascist militiamen also were mobilized and sent to the scene of the disaster.

The Vatican also decided to aid in the relief work. Beginning at about noon, telegrams began to pour into the Vatican from Bishops in all the stricken zones, telling of the terrible damage done by the earthquake and urging immediate help for the people, who in many cases have lost not only their homes but all their possessions. The Pope, who was deeply moved by the disaster, immediately telegraphed words of condolence and encouragement to the Bishop of Melfi and at the same time gave instructions that he be informed immediately of any new developments.

The Pontiff began immediately to make arrangements for dispatching relief to the damaged region.

Naples Panic Stricken.

The earthquake came soon after 1 o'clock this morning, when almost every one was asleep. The people were awakened first by loud subterranean rumblings. Residents of Naples thought these were a prelude to an eruption of Vesuvius.

The rumblings, however, were followed by the creaking of the walls of houses, with furniture moving about on the floor. Many sleepers awakened to find themselves thrown out of their beds.

No sooner had the populace of Naples realized what happened than

---

AMTORG THREATENS RED TRADE BOYCOTT UNLESS ATTACKS END

Bogdanov, Alleging Unjustified Accusations, Gives a Veiled Warning at Inquiry.

REPRESENTATIVES SEE SOON

Nelson Says Commerce With Soviet Undermines Economic Order and Is Suicidal.

RUSSIAN AGENCY DEFENDED

Chief Asserts It Has Not Had 'Shadow on Record' in Six Years—Puts Our Exports at $100,000,000 a Year.

With the documents made public by former Police Commissioner Whalen charging that the Amtorg Trading Corporation, the Soviet commercial agency in the United States, was a channel of subversive Communist propaganda again the centre of attention before the Congressional committee investigating Communist activities, yesterday's session of the committee developed a line of inquiry affecting the whole question of Russo-American trade relations.

Peter A. Bogdanov, chairman of the Amtorg, in a long statement read into the record, made the veiled threat of withdrawing all Russian trade from this country unless there were a halt to what he denounced as unfair and unjustified attacks on the Amtorg and Soviet Russia. Members of the committee suggested that such withdrawal might be a boon to American interests and threatened again to have Mr. Bogdanov driven out of the United States as a Communist who should never have been permitted to come here.

Questions Wisdom of Trade.

The larger question of the wisdom and desirability from the American point of view of helping in the economic rehabilitation of Russia under the Soviet régime was raised by Representative John E. Nelson of Maine. In a lengthy interrogation of Mr. Bogdanov Mr. Nelson asserted that by dealing with Soviet Russia American industrialists were merely helping communism to undermine the existing economic order in this and other countries. He charged that Soviet Russia was preparing to dump hundreds of millions of bushels of wheat, large quantities of coal and lumber, as well as other products, at cheap prices upon the American market, to the detriment of this country.

It is suicidal for the United States, Mr. Nelson suggested, to supply Soviet Russia with credits, machinery, equipment and technical talent to enable the Soviet Government, with the aid of a highly centralized state industrial apparatus and cheap labor, to compete with America economically.

Mr. Bogdanov took issue with this view, arguing that there were mutual advantages to the United States and Russia in promoting their trade relations. Despite his earlier veiled threat to withdraw all trade from the United States, he urged that the two countries enter into a commercial treaty which would promote Russo-American commerce on a higher scale than has been possible hitherto.

Documents Again Challenged.

Although several hours were devoted by the committee to questions dealing with the Whalen documents, the interrogation failed to cast any further light on these papers, but produced additional denials of their authenticity by Mr. Bogdanov and a repetition of his former challenge to Mr. Whalen to prove that the documents are genuine. On his own part and through Louis Connick, counsel for the Amtorg, Mr Bogdanov protested against what he and Mr. Connick characterized as an effort by the committee to relieve Mr. Whalen of the burden of proof and place this burden upon the Amtorg.

"It is not the Amtorg which should be called upon to disprove the authenticity of these documents," Mr. Connick said. "Mr. Whalen, who made the charges, should be made to produce the evidence."

Mr. Bogdanov offered to present to the committee a detailed memorandum prepared by attorneys for the Amtorg containing an analysis of the Whalen documents and showing where, in the opinion of the attorneys, the documents are false and erroneous. The committee did not make it clear whether it would receive the memorandum, but it was assumed that the memorandum would be read before the hearings are concluded.

In connection with this, Mr. Fish revealed that the committee had not yet visited Police Headquarters, where, in accordance with its understanding with Mr. Whalen, it is to

Continued on Page Twelve.

IT'S COOL AND COMFORTABLE. Hotel Nassau, on ocean, Long Beach, Long Island. Bathing from your room. Dining on beach. Day, week or season. Phone Long Beach 100.—Advt.

Cruiser Hindenburg Is Floated After 11 Years at Sea Bottom

Wireless to THE NEW YORK TIMES.

LONDON, July 23.—More than eleven years after the proud German fleet was scuttled in Scapa Flow the 28,000-ton battle cruiser Hindenburg has been successfully raised and floated with her deck clear of water.

It is the greatest salvage feat of the kind ever accomplished and there was a note of jubilation in the news received in London today from E. F. Cox of the salvaging company of Cox & Banks, who, since 1926, has been in personal charge of the operation.

Twice before the Hindenburg was brought to the surface, but owing to a dangerous list was allowed to sink again. It is now hoped to move the Hindenburg to Mill Bay, in the Orkneys, where she will be prepared for a journey to the south for breaking up.

This is the fifth vessel to be salvaged from the sunken fleet. Previously the Moltke, Seydlitz, Kaiser and Bremse were raised, and Mr. Cox now hopes to salvage the Prince Regent, Luitpold and Von der Tann.

VAST REALTY PASSES TO LAST OF WENDELS

Sixth Sister Gets $100,000,000 Holdings, Assembled Over Two Centuries, as Fifth Dies.

ALL LIVED IN SECLUSION

Kept in 5th Av. 'Mystery House' by Brother Who Held Marriage Would Disperse Property.

Mrs. Rebecca Wendel Swope died last Sunday in the Summer home of the Wendels at Quogue, L. I., at the age of 87, leaving to the last of the six Wendel sisters, Ella, who is 80, an unbroken real estate accumulation of two centuries. It has grown in value to more than $100,000,000 since the first John Wendel left the fur business at the same time as the first John Jacob Astor and laid upon his descendants the duty of never buying anything but choice New York real estate and never thereafter letting it go.

Mrs. Swope was the only one of the six sisters to escape from this duty as construed by their only brother, John Gottlieb Wendel, who opposed marriage for his sisters on the ground that it would disperse the accumulated property and put it under other names than Wendel. To prevent this he kept them in the four-story brick and brownstone house which has stood on the corner of Fifth Avenue and Thirty-ninth Street since 1856, and stands there now just as it was built, lighted inside only by gas, without telephone, dumbwaiter, radio or phonograph, and shuttered outside with a dusty look that has caused it to be pointed out from sightseeing buses as the "House of Mystery."

Inside lived six sisters who were taught that they must not marry or waste or dissipate their stewardship and that publicity was demeaning. They continued, until they died, to wear the round sailor hats that were popular in their 'teens in the '60s and '70s, and to make their own clothes without the aid of a sewing machine, always in black, with full skirts cut for hoops. They wore them until shabby. Their brother seldom entertained.

Even Rebecca Wendel did not decide to oppose her brother until late in life; then, despite his violent opposition, she married Professor Luther A. Swope, a friend of the vicar of Trinity and also the son of an old New York family. Thereafter John Wendel discouraged his sisters from going to church.

The only other rebellion took place

Continued on Page Four.

FAVORITISM CHARGE BRINGS TAX BUREAU INTO HIGGINS INQUIRY

Mayor Consents to Subpoena for Republican Leader Who Accused Commissioners.

THOMAS PRESSES ATTACK

Says Harvey's Reply Virtually Admitted Irregularities in Paving—Klein Scouts Letter.

WNYC OPEN TO HARBORD

Mayor Offers Use of City Radio for Republican Reply—Socialist Leader Wants Privilege Also.

The inquiry begun on Monday by James A. Higgins, Commissioner of Accounts, into the Dock Department and the Board of Standards and Appeals by order of Mayor Walker widened last night to include the Department of Taxes and Assessments when the Mayor declared he could see no reason why Commissioner Higgins should not call Irwin Kurtz, Republican leader, to substantiate his charges of irregularity in that department.

Mr. Kurtz declared a few days ago that the Department of Taxes and Assessments showed favoritism toward certain individuals in the fixing of taxes and assessments. His charges were met by George Henry Payne, Republican member of the department, with a demand upon Commissioner Higgins to make Mr. Kurtz substantiate his allegations. Mr. Kurtz questioned Mr. Higgins's right to call him as a witness on the ground that he was not in city employ and announced that he would refuse to answer a subpoena, in order to test the commissioner's powers.

Defends Wide Right of Subpoena.

Commissioner Higgins asserted his right to call any one he chose, citing a decision of the Court of Appeals upholding Section 119 of the City Charter. The section invests the Commissioner of Accounts "with full power to compel the attendance of, to administer oaths to and to examine such persons as he may deem necessary as witnesses for the purpose of ascertaining facts in connection with the examination."

The Commissioner of Accounts denied allegations that his investigation would be "hamstrung" if he warned witnesses that they need not make incriminating answers. He said it was necessary to inform witnesses of their constitutional rights and added that warning witnesses in the street cleaning inquiry two years ago had not impeded his investigation. He said his failure to warn these witnesses would have made their testimony inadmissible in court and recalled that sixteen indictments and thirteen convictions had been obtained in that inquiry.

"Anything any witness says to me can be used against him," Mr. Higgins declared. "At some of the street cleaning trials in Kings County Court some of the defense attorneys and some of the judges—I think Vause and Taylor—demanded to know if witnesses before me had been advised of their constitutional rights and told that they could refuse to answer on the ground that the answers might tend to incriminate or degrade them. I have done just that in every case since I have been Commissioner of Accounts. Frank Gannon, Brooklyn Street Cleaning Superintendent, refused on that ground and was haled into Special Sessions on my sworn complaint and tried, but was acquitted on a technicality."

"There is nothing much to report

Continued on Page Six.

Two More Die in Day of Moderate Heat Here; 84 Degrees High Mark; No Further Rise Today

Some captious critics might have said that yesterday afternoon was hot, but most persons, with the unpleasant memory of the record-breaking temperatures of the past few days, agreed with the Weather Bureau that it was comfortably warm and were thankful.

The official thermometer did not reach 80 until afternoon and it never went above 84 degrees. Today will be about the same, the official observers said.

Even with the fall in temperature however, two deaths and one prostration were reported in New York City and New Jersey. In the latter State it was estimated that the storm which broke the heat wave caused damage in excess of $100,300.

The Dead.

BLESSEDELL, CECIL, 34, succumbed to a heart attack following heat prostration at his home, 75 West Forty-eighth Street, Bayonne, N. J.

ECKHOFF, DORA, 51, 405 West Forty-fourth Street, Manhattan, removed from her home to Bellevue Hospital Monday suffering from heat prostration and died there yesterday.

Prostrated.

NACENA, SADEGH, 26, 600 West 134th Street, overcome by the heat at home and removed to Knickerbocker Hospital.

In the forenoon the temperature ranged from 70 to 75 degrees. Between 11 A. M. and 1 P. M. it jumped from 75 to 80 degrees and remained there until 3:50 o'clock when it reached 84. Fresh breezes and low humidity prevented serious discomfort.

New Brunswick, N. J., which was swept by a cyclonic wind and rain storm Tuesday evening, reported that about 100 homes had suffered minor damage. Seven per cent of the city's telephones, about 1,000, were put out of commission and street lights in many sections were extinguished by broken wires. The damage in New Brunswick was estimated at $125,000.

Trenton also reported considerable damage by wind and Esau Lindquist, a laborer on the new Burlington-Bristol Bridge was blown off the structure into the Delaware River, where he drowned, bringing the deaths in the storm to two. Mrs. Marianna Vennisac was crushed to death when her home in New Brunswick was blown down upon her.

Two deaths in the storm were reported in Philadelphia where lower temperatures were recorded yesterday. Virginia and the Carolinas still reported exceptionally high temperatures but Georgia and Florida found the weather "normal." Other Southern States were shielded from the sun by clouds. The Associated Press reported from Ithaca that the United States Agricultural Bureau at Cornell University had found that the hot dry weather of the past week had been beneficial to the harvesting of the hay crop.

Store Under Mulrooney Home Held Up While He Is Asleep

Two hold-up men took a wrist watch and $190 in cash last night from the drug store of Herman Juster, on the ground floor of 760 Mott Avenue, the Bronx. Police Commissioner Mulrooney lives in the house, on the fifth floor. He was asleep at the time, and later reporters found he had left orders with the superintendent that he was not to be disturbed.

Jack Gilbert, pharmacist; Morris Goodman and William Capeher, soda clerks, and Benjamin Fredericksen, superintendent of the building, were in the store when the hold-up men entered. Displaying pistols, the intruders ordered the men into a rear room and locked them in. They took Gilbert's wrist watch and the money in the cash register.

The clerks hoisted Fredericken to the window of the room in the meantime and he put his head out, shouting until he had awakened the tenants. Before he could crawl through the window and come around to the front of the store the hold-up men had left in a taxicab, which had been waiting.

BORAH MAPS DRIVE AS FARM BOARD FOE

He Will Begin Campaign in the Northwest on Completing Treatment Ordered by Physician.

BACKED DEBENTURE PLAN

Shouse Retorts to Legge's 'Political Bunk' Charge by Calling It Political, Too.

Special to The New York Times.

WASHINGTON, July 23. Senator Borah, mapping plans for the Fall election campaign, plans to raise his voice in the West in opposition to the administration farm relief measures, including the work of the Federal Farm Board.

Revelation today of the Senator's intention recalled the events of the session of Congress just closed, in which he saw the export debenture feature eliminated from the tariff act over the protests of the insurgent group with which he was allied, while his endeavors to have the tariff revision confined to those items affecting the farmer were unsuccessful. His campaign will be delayed, however, until he has undergone treatment prescribed by his physician, which may last until the latter part of September.

Senator Borah's appearance on the campaign platforms of the Northwest, where he has been asked particularly to speak and where he indicated he would accept engagements, will differ from two years ago, when he was one of the chief supporters of the Hoover candidacy.

Unlike the addresses of 1928, the Senator this Fall will express the Republican opposition's view of the conflict between the administration and the insurgent bloc in the Senate over the tariff and agricultural measures.

Shouse Replies to Legge.

Saying that the National Democratic Committee "did not write the quotations of the present prices of wheat, corn and cotton," Jouett Shouse, Chairman of the Democratic National Executive Committee, issued a statement today taking to task Alexander Legge, chairman of the Federal Farm Board, for terming attacks on the farm relief program "political bunk."

Accusing Mr. Legge of adapting the devices of politics to his own uses while disclaiming any interest in politics, Mr. Shouse charged the board with "dabbling in the wheat market, with the result that no inconsiderable portion of its investment went to fatten the gains of the Chicago grain speculators, who knew more about rigging the market than Mr. Legge and his conferees."

Mr. Shouse was referring to the purchase of 69,000,000 bushels of the 1929 wheat crop by the Stabilization Corporation, organized by the Farm Board. The wheat will be withheld from the market until conditions improve. Mr. Legge indicated recently, after beginning his campaign for a reduction of wheat acreage and regulation of production within the limits of domestic demand, that the board intended to buy no more wheat as a price-stabilization move.

The statement issued by Mr. Shouse read in part:

"Chairman Legge of the Farm Board, protesting that he is not in politics, has neatly adopted the politician's alibi in reply to criticisms.

"When the Democrats and Progressive Republicans in the Senate were tilting against the exorbitancies of the Grundy tariff bill, its supporters gravely asserted that these protests were mere political propaganda.

"When the Senate was engaged in refusing confirmation as a member of the Supreme Court for Judge Parker of North Carolina, those who advocated confirmation of the Presidential nominee announced that the opposition was pure politics.

"The President himself in his letter, about 'hair shirts' gave the same explanation of criticism of his policies.

"It did not take Chairman Legge long to learn the patter of the officials whose work is unsatisfactory to the public.

"The Democratic National Committee and the orators mentioned by

Continued on Page Four.

KILLING OF BUCKLEY AROUSES DETROIT; HINT OF RACKETEER

Radio Announcer, Shot in Hotel, Accused by Bootlegger of Extortion, Police Say.

HAD FOUGHT MAYOR BOWLES

Many Foes Had Been Made by His Attacks on City Conditions, Say Friends

USE OF TROOPS THREATENED

Governor Green Demands Clean-Up After Eleventh Gang Killing in City in 19 Days.

Special to The New York Times.

DETROIT, July 23.—Every law enforcement agency of the State as well as of Detroit was working tonight toward a solution of the murder of Gerald E. "Jerry" Buckley, radio announcer for station WMBC, who was shot to death early this morning by three gangsters as he sat reading a newspaper in the lobby of the La Salle Hotel.

In addition to the city investigation, begun at once by Police Commisioner Thomas C. Wilcox, the State police were ordered by Governor Green to investigate the murder independently. The governor, who flew to Detroit early in the day from Holland, Mich., said that if necessary he would call out the militia to put an end to further lawlessness in Detroit.

The murder of Buckley was the eleventh committed by gangsters in the Michigan metropolis in nineteen days. Although city police are said to have in their possession a sworn statement to the effect that Buckley extorted $4,000 from a racketeer, Paul Buckley, a brother of the slain man and a former assistant prosecutor in Wayne County, insists that Jerry Buckley was murdered because of his activities in the campaign to recall Mayor Charles Bowles.

The affidavit in the hands of the police, Commissioner Wilcox said, was made by a confessed bootlegger.

Told of Threatening Letters.

W. Wright Gedge, secretary of the Michigan Broadcasting Company, which operates Station WMBC, says that Buckley told him he had received several threatening letters after speaking over the radio on behalf of the recall and had expressed the opinion that gangsters were out to get him.

A few hours before he was killed Buckley, in his last talk over the radio, had announced the success of the election which called Mayor Bowles from office by a majority of more than 30,000 votes. Of the 210,770 votes cast, 120,863 were for recall and 89,907 against.

As a result a new city election will have to be held within thirty days, although Mayor Bowles automatically becomes a candidate for re-election and, in any event, will remain in office until a successor is chosen.

The spot where Buckley was murdered was less than fifty yards from the entrance in front of which George Collins and William Cannon, Chicago gangsters, were shot to death three weeks ago. Buckley witnessed that shooting from a window of the hotel.

Station WMBC is located in the hotel. After making the final announcements last night Buckley went downstairs to the lobby with Miss Evelyn O'Hara, his secretary. He left her at the front door and, going back into the lobby, sat down in a big armchair. Jack Klein, a motion picture operator, was sitting in a chair close by.

Hit by Eleven Bullets.

According to Klein, who was held by police as a material witness, at about 1:50 A. M., while Buckley was glancing through a copy of an election extra, three men walked across the lobby and, standing around Buck-

Continued on Page Five.

GLENN CURTISS DIES, PIONEER IN AVIATION

End Comes Suddenly in Buffalo Hospital During Convalescence From an Operation.

MOURNED BY AIR LEADERS

His Inventive Genius and Skill in Flying Lauded as Contributing to World Progress.

Special to The New York Times.

BUFFALO, N. Y., July 23.—Death came suddenly to Glenn H. Curtiss, aviation pioneer, in the General Hospital here this morning. On July 11 Mr. Curtiss was operated on for appendicitis. His condition since then had been reported daily by surgeons as excellent. Early today he lapsed into a coma and before relatives could reach his bedside he died. Hospital officials gave the cause of death as pulmonary embolus, a blood clot in an artery near the heart.

A patent suit against Mr. Curtiss, brought by the Herring-Curtiss Company in Federal court at Rochester before Judge William S. Andrews, involving about $1,000,000 in royalties and corporation funds, came to an abrupt end two weeks ago when Mr. Curtiss was unable to appear as a witness.

He had suffered several appendicitis attacks earlier and on the eve of his court appearance he was stricken with an acute attack. Dr. Thew Wright of Buffalo, a close personal friend as well as family physician, was called to the Curtiss home on Lake Keuka, Hammondsport, and upon his orders Mr. Curtiss was rushed to the hospital here. The operation took place the following day.

Hundreds of Western New York citizens mourn the death of Mr. Curtiss. After his early flying experiments and manufacturing in Hammondsport, Mr. Curtiss moved most of his factory to Buffalo, and opened another plant on Long Island. Several plants in Buffalo built hundreds of machines for war use and Mr. Curtiss became an intimate figure in the city's life during that period.

Late today the body of Mr. Curtiss was taken to his late home in Hammondsport, where funeral services

Continued on Page Twenty-one.

NAVAL TREATY BILL ADVANCED IN BRITAIN

Enabling Act Is Accepted by Commons Without a Vote at Second Reading.

RATIFICATION IS ASSURED

Chief Objector in Brief Debate Is Baldwin, Who Says Step Is Premature.

Special Cable to THE NEW YORK TIMES.

LONDON, July 23.—Without a vote being taken, the House of Commons agreed tonight to the second reading of the London naval treaty bill. This step is designed to enable effect to be given to the four-power treaty signed here in April and to repeal Section IV of the Treaties of Washington act of 1922.

At the outset the speaker ruled against any discussion of the actual terms of the treaty. The perfunctory debate was marked by two protests: Commander A. R. Southby, Conservative, said it would have been "wiser, better and more courteous to the Dominions if the bill had been delayed until after the forthcoming Imperial Conference," while Lieut. Commander J. M. Kenworthy, on behalf of the pacifist section of the Labor party, regretted that Clause 2 of the new bill abrogated that part of the Washington Treaty of 1922 providing for the trial and punisment of persons violating the rules of war.

Baldwin Calls Bill Premature.

Arguing that it was premature to offer the bill now, former Prime Minister Stanley Baldwin asked whether the government had assurance from the dominions, including the Irish Free State, that they would give effect to such legislation as might be necessary under Section 1 of the bill limiting shipbuilding.

"Under the original act of 1922," he said, "the dominions were especially excluded. It is essential that if we tie our hands with regard to shipbulding here, equal legislation should be applied in all the dominions, including the Irish Free State. If we do not get a satisfactory reply from the government on this point we will feel bound to press the matter in future stages of the bill."

Albert V. Alexander, First Lord of the Admiralty, said on behalf of the government, that all the dominions represented at the London conference had indicated their intention of fully ratifying the naval treaty and the government had no doubt that the dominions would pass such legislation as would be necessary to carry out their obligations under that decision.

Says Doubts Can Be Settled.

"If there is any doubt on that point," he added, "it can be settled at the imperial conference. But that is no reason why the passing of this bill should be delayed. If the country is to ratify a treaty which will in any way limit the action of its nationals it is important that the treaty should be implemented immediately. It is declared that our nationals should not build ships for other powers which we have undertaken not to build for ourselves."

The limitation of aircraft carriers, Mr. Alexander then explained, was intended to prevent the building of

Continued on Page Two.

"WHEN YOU THINK of Writing, Think of Whiting."—Advt.

Coast Guardsmen Wound Two in Seizing Boat Off Woods Hole, but Find No Liquor Aboard

Special to The New York Times.

WOODS HOLE, Mass., July 23.—Charges that Coast Guardsmen fired today without warning upon the speedboat Marge, raking her decks with machine gun bullets which slightly wounded two New Bedford men, were made by Captain Charles Kingsley of New Bedford, skipper of the craft, which is owned by Howard Jackman of Lynn.

Commander Frederick A. Nichols of Coast Guard Base 18 here said that the patrol boat 2,378 signaled with a searchlight and made every effort to halt the Marge before firing. He expressed regret that the men were wounded.

Although no liquor was found on board, Commander Nichols said that the Marge was known to Coast Guardsmen as a rum-runner.

Frederick Stone and Daniel Conway were wounded in the legs by the gun fire. The Marge had just come through the Cape Cod Canal and was running with all lights on, according to their story.

"It might well have been another Black Duck case," Stone said, "there was no warning, except a flash of the searchlight. We had no rum aboard, nor had we had any."

The Coast Guard called for a physician and the injured men were treated at the base here.

Captain Kingsley said that he would take legal action against the officers of the patrol boat.

Boatswain's Mate A. H. Calder, skipper of the 2378, said that two speed boats were sighted running without lights, one being the Marge. The other, her decks piled with cases of liquor, threw out a smoke screen and escaped, he said, adding that when he fired a warning shot across the bow of the Marge it was disregarded.

WHEN BUYING BITTERS, DEMAND Abbott's Flavors Beverages.—Advt.

they fled into the streets in a panic. They fled in their sleeping clothes and the streets were soon filled with frenzied crowds rushing blindly this way and that. The scene was rendered hideous by electric trolley wires which had been broken by the quake and had fallen to the ground and were emitting sparks, while masonry was crashing on sidewalks. Then the city was plunged into darkness, increasing the panic and confusion.

The night was rent by shouts of mothers and fathers for their children, by the groans of the injured, the roar of falling houses, the shrieks of the sirens of ambulances and firemen rushing to make rescues in the most severely damaged quarters of the city.

Blindly fleeing in darkness and under the hail of falling masonry, the crowds eventually made their way to open squares or to the seashore, where they could rest in comparative safety. They remained there all night, standing huddled together, because all available open space was so crowded that there was no room to sit or lie down.

Dawn restored some measure of confidence and some of them were prevailed upon to re-enter their homes. Others, however, stubbornly refused and camped out in the open. Some of the residents used motorcars to flee from the city.

Duchess Aids in Relief.

Immediately after the earthquake occurred a meeting was held in the office of the High Commissioner of Naples and arrangements were made to face the sudden crisis. One of the first volunteer helpers to arrive was the Duchess of Aosta, who drove from the royal palace to place her services at the disposal of the city of Naples.

Having had long training as a nurse at the front during the war, she spent the whole night going from one danger point to another caring for the injured and encouraging the panic-stricken populace. The relief workers soon were joined by the bolder spirits of the populace, who, after momentary panic, threw themselves into the task of helping. They helped to disengage hundreds of persons pinned under wreckage and assisted firemen in extinguishing many fires caused by gas escaping from broken mains and set aflame by electric sparks.

Escaping gas proved a great danger to some persons pinned under masonry and several died of asphyxiation.

Terrifying as the scenes are at Naples, they are even more terrible in the smaller centres, especially those like Melfi. Here the number of houses which collapsed or were rendered uninhabitable was extremely high, and a considerable portion of the population was left homeless and completely destitute.

Especially in the small villages the absolute lack of proper organization for facing the disaster left the inhabitants helpless. Luckily a relief organization which was set in motion outside the stricken zone worked with great efficiency and help arrived in the early hours of the morning. There still, however, is a crying need for tents and huts to house the homeless.

Many Children in Asylum Killed.

Excruciating scenes occurred at Foggia, where many children in an infant asylum were killed or wounded. The body of one woman was found there with three dead children under her outstretched arms. Her position indicated she had attempted to shield them with her body from the falling masonry.

Other acts of heroism were noted from almost all the places in the 'quake zones. Troops and Fascist militia have been commended for their devotion to duty and the zeal with which they threw themselves into the rescue work.

The actual earth tremors lasted less than a minute, so that the inhabitants had little time to flee from their houses before they collapsed. In view of this fact, the number of victims may be considered extremely low. Reports from the stricken provinces, however, are coming in rapidly, so it is hoped a complete picture of the disaster may be had soon.

In the region around Melfi the panic was increased by the fact that the earthquake was followed later in the morning by three other shocks. They did no particular damage, but confirmed the inhabitants in the opinion that it was unsafe to re-enter their houses. The whole populace, in fact, is still camping in the fields.

Wide World Photos

View of the remains of a house in Naples, Italy, after the earthquake.

The damage is some regions is so extensive that it cannot be taken care of by the ordinary means at the disposal of the municipalities and provinces. It is expected, therefore, that the government will appropriate funds for rebuilding the wrecked houses and repairing those still standing.

NAPLES OFFICIALS GET DEATH TOTAL OF 700

Many Persons in That City Afraid to Go to Bed—Countryside Shows Great Desolation.

NAPLES, July 23 (AP).—A darkened band, twenty to forty miles wide, tonight reached across the boot of Italy about at the "ankle." This city was the northwestern corner of the zone. Across this belt an hour after midnight today a terrific undulating earthquake dealt death to hundreds of sleeping persons, burying them in the ruins of scores of cities and hamlets and effectively blotting out all of the electric power in that territory.

It was related here tonight that more than 700 persons had been killed without a chance to try to save themselves and that more than 1,500 were treated for serious injuries during the day, figures which Naples officials said had been compiled with the greatest difficulty owing to the isolated positions of many villages and the reluctance of local authorities to reveal the truth.

Melfi Scene of Desolation.

Melfi, picturesque mountain city, perched perilously upon the crater of the extinct Monte Vulture, was an area of ghastly debris Even the ancient cathedral the history of which goes back to the ninth century was wrecked.

The almost inaccessible nature of some of the areas devastated made difficult the work of succor and the enumeration of casualties. Most of the towns hit the hardest are off the beaten paths, with poor transportation and almost inaccessible altitude.

Several supply trains have been sent to points on the railroads in the interior from Naples and hundreds of relief workers tonight were penetrating the recesses of the agricultural area offering relief to the terror-stricken victims.

The quake has stunned all Italy. It was the worst since Messina was all but obliterated in 1908 The first shock came an hour after midnight, and its own awful nature was aggravated by a tremendous electrical storm over virtually the whole affected area.

The area extended from the Tyrrhenian Sea to the Adriatic, the coast settlements suffered less in proportion than the mountain populations. Naples experienced several hours of panic, when many persons ran from their homes and there were scores of casualties. Among this city's victims was the Countess' de Rossi Vargas. Never in all Neapolitan history had this classic city experienced such stark fright. A frenzied populace raced through the streets, apparently heading nowhere.

Tonight the work of rescue proceeded as rapidly as the means available would permit. Wrecked bridges, snapped communication wires and many other obstacles had been tossed in the path of the relief workers by the upheaval of nature. Motor cars made little progress over unaccustomed routes. The highways of the area are notoriously undeveloped, and rail lines passed through many gorges, into which the quake had tumbled avalanches.

Last night one could look out on a happy countryside embracing this classic city. The fragrance of ripening vineyards was in the air. In the streets the populace strolled carelessly. Tonight the countryside had been churned in forty-five seconds into a veritable no-man's land by the most disastrous earthquake this light-hearted country has experienced in a generation.

Instead of proceeding peacefully to their homes tonight, the people of the city slept in cleared spaces in the public squares, panic still gripping them. Their single emotion since the stunning happenings of the last twenty-four hours seemed to be fear that they might be caught like rats in a trap by another earth shock.

Bedding Taken to Parks.

The people brought their bedding into the parks. Practically every one believed there would be a repetition of the crushing blow. The squares of the Plebiscito, Carmine and the Villa Communale and the wide plaza before the railway station were thronged by thousands who were almost afraid to go to sleep but were too weary to stay awake.

Ordinarily one may stand in the plaza and gaze at myriads of twinkling hamlets in the distant hills. Tonight no single light gleamed there. Lighted by lanterns, flares and torches, the citizens of many towns among the hills and miniature cities high up among the Apennines either slept exhausted from their day's rescue exertions or delved among the litter that had been their homes, stores and public buildings yesterday.

Firemen, soldiers and Fascisti searched tirelessly for victims. These little mountain towns were the hardest hit by the quake. Coastal cities suffered the least. The churches here and in all surrounding towns were open tonight and in them went on the work of relief, while thousands prayed for the victims and besought deliverance from another quake.

Across the Bay of Naples Vesuvius glowed dully tonight and was watched with dread by Neapolitans and all who dwell on the bow of the bay. Belief that the earthquake would almost immediately be followed by a tremendous eruption of the terrible old volcano prevailed throughout the day. When no eruption occurred every one breathed more freely.

There was widespread comment today on what citizens declared to have been a miracle—the fact that practically all of the city's church bells pealed forth at the moment of the first quake as if to warn the inhabitants to flee for their lives.

This was explained, naturally, by the fact that the undulating earth tremors set the bell towers to oscillating.

Town and church clocks throughout all the province were running again this evening. The quake had stopped them as if automatically at the moment of the shock, 1:10 A. M., thus giving the clearest evidence of the time of appearance of the subterranean upheaval.

This afternoon a trip through some of the towns among the mountains revealed the desolation and tragedy difficult to describe. Whole suburbs and whole families went down in the ruins. Old houses built of stone, with little mortar, crumbled like castles of cards.

Relatives in Pathetic Search.

As the hot South Italian sun beat down upon them the rescuers extricated body after body from the ruins. At Villanova and Melfi there seemed no place left to put the dead. The provincial headquarters were filled with bodies.

Here and there in pathetic groups relatives of the missing persons gathered, hoping that by the miracle for which they prayed to their patron saints their loved ones remained alive in the tangled débris of timbers and masonry.

This morning only a score were known to be dead. At noon the figure rose to 100. This afternoon they said several hundred had perished. Tonight, with more than 500 accounted for, bodies still were being drawn from the wreckage.

At Potenza, a hospital centre, the injured poured in by hundreds throughout the day. This was a scene duplicated at Avellino and Ariano.

All day long crash after crash echoed through the still Apennine Valleys as house after house, weakened by the quake, was pulled to the ground by firemen or soldiers to prevent its falling upon passers-by.

Fear, uncertainty and foreboding tonight were all that many thousands of dwellers from Naples to Brindisi had left as their portion of the convulsion.

Section 1

"All the News That's Fit to Print."

The New York Times.

THE WEATHER
Fair and cool today; tomorrow cloudy; little change in temperature
Temperatures yesterday—Max. 61, min. 46.
U. S. Weather Forecast—Page 12, Section 11.

Section 1

Copyright, 1930, by The New York Times Company.

VOL. LXXX....No. 26,552. **** + NEW YORK, SUNDAY, OCTOBER 5, 1930. Including Rotogravure Picture Section in three parts—Magazine and Book Sections in Rotogravure. FIVE CENTS In Manhattan, Bronx and Brooklyn | Elsewhere TEN CENTS Except in 7th and 8th Postal Zones

BRITISH AIRSHIP R-101 IS DESTROYED IN CRASH AND EXPLOSION IN FRANCE; 46 ABOARD PERISH, 7 BADLY INJURED

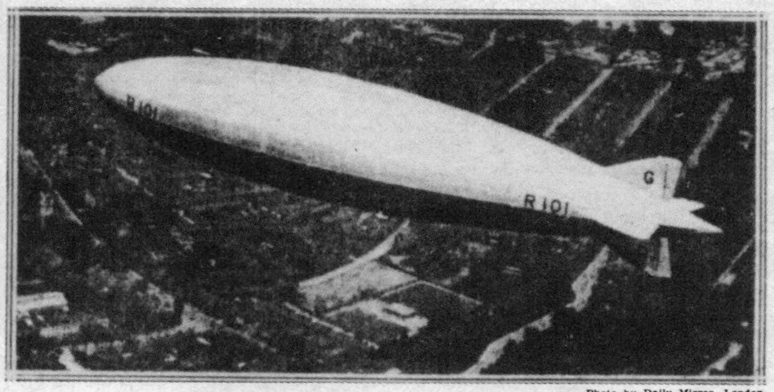

Photo by Daily Mirror, London.

THE R-101, DESTROYED IN FATAL EXPLOSION.
A Photograph of the Great British Dirigible, the Biggest in the World, on One of Its Test Flights in England Before the Start of the Flight to India.

REVOLUTION SWEEPS BRAZIL; SPREADS QUICKLY ON SIGNAL FROM STATES IN THE SOUTH

RIO GRANDE IN REBEL HANDS

Flare-Up There Brings In Others as Far North as the Amazon.

AIM TO BAR NEW PRESIDENT

And "Wipe Out the Clique That Has Dominated Brazil for the Past Forty Years."

CAPITAL ACTS TO STEM TIDE

Chamber of Deputies Votes State of Siege, but the Federal Forces Are Weak.

Special Cable to THE NEW YORK TIMES.

SAO PAULO, Oct. 4.—Revolution has broken out in the States of Rio Grande do Sul, Parana, Minas Geraes and Rio de Janeiro but on account of the strict censorship the details and extent of the uprising are unknown.

Fighting is reported to have taken place yesterday at Porto Alegre, Sao Paulo and in the State of Parana. Despite denial by the government, the newspapers here and elsewhere state that the President and the former President of Minas Geraes have been arrested, while fighting is reported to have taken place in a number of cities in that State.

Railway traffic between Minas Geraes and Rio de Janeiro has been suspended. The telegraph service within the country is paralyzed. All plain-language messages pertaining to the revolution are not being accepted by the cable company, and at noon today the Western Telegraph Company, Ltd., refused to accept even code messages.

Rebellion Starts in South.

Special Cable to THE NEW YORK TIMES.

MONTEVIDEO, Oct. 4.—The threatened revolt to prevent the inauguration of Dr. Julio Prestes as President of Brazil has begun in the State of Rio Grande do Sul, and dispatches reaching here late this afternoon announce the triumph of the revolutionary movement throughout that State, rebels being in possession of all the important cities, including Porto Alegre, the State capital.

The outbreak in Rio Grande had been agreed upon as a signal for a simultaneous uprising in Minas Geraes, Parahyba and other States, and a brief telegram from Rio de Janeiro this afternoon said that it was reported there that a movement had started in the State of Minas Geraes.

Field Marshal Diaz Lopez, who has been directing the revolutionary plans in the Uruguayana District from the Argentine city of Paso de Los Libres, states this afternoon that five States have joined the revolutionary movement, but this is as yet unconfirmed.

Revolt Carefully Planned.

The revolt in Rio Grande do Sul, which had been carefully planned for several months, broke out Friday simultaneously in all the important cities of the State. The entire general staff of Federal troops stationed within the State were taken prisoner at Porto Alegre when they refused to join the movement.

Later dispatches from the State of Rio Grande do Sul say that General Pereyra da Souza has assumed the provisional government of the State.

Rio de Janeiro reports that Federal troops are patrolling the city, and three Opposition newspapers have been closed by the Federal authorities.

Federal troops in thirteen localities of Rio Grande do Sul are reported to have gone over to the revolutionists, as have those at three cities in the State of Minas Geraes, including Ouro Preto and two cities in the State of Parana.

Among the prisoners taken by the revolutionists at Porto Alegre is General Gildo de Almeida, commander-in-chief of the Federal troops in Rio Grande do Sul.

The Fifth Calvary Regiment and a battery of artillery at Uruguayana, with all but a few officers, went over without resistance. At Sant'Ana do Livramento all the officers of the Seventh Infantry Regiment and a battery of the Fifth Artillery Federal troops were captured in their hotel, after which 8,000 well-trained, well-equipped State troops and police sur-

Continued on Page Three.

Royal Meissen authentic Dresden dinnerware, open stock, available. Slobodkin, 20 W. 23d.—Advt.

Houston Asks Writ to Block Atlanta's Census Claims

Special to The New York Times.

WASHINGTON, Oct. 4.—The city of Houston and its Chamber of Commerce petitioned the District of Columbia Supreme Court today for leave to intervene in the suit filed by the city of Atlanta and business firms to compel W. M. Steuart, Director of the Census, to publish Atlanta's population as 360,692 instead of 270,367.

The city of Houston declares that it will suffer great injury if the Census Director grants Atlanta's request and that it will be reduced from the second city in the South to the third and from the twenty-seventh city in the United States to the twenty-eighth. Houston's population is 289,570, according to the 1930 census.

CUBAN POLICE BARE ASSASSINATION PLOT

Arrest Ringleader With Arms and Dynamite in Alleged Plan to Kill High Officials.

MARTIAL LAW AVAILABLE

President Signs the Act Which Suspends Guarantees, but Won't Use Power Now.

By The Associated Press.

HAVANA, Oct. 4.—National police tonight announced the discovery of a plot against the lives of a number of high government officials and placed under arrest Justo Martin of Mariano, said to be a habitual criminal, as the chief conspirator.

A large quantity of dynamite, several machine guns and a number of small arms, with much ammunition, were said to have been found at Martin's home when police raided it.

Martin was reported to have confessed planning to use the dynamite to destroy the Regla aqueduct and to have been the leader of a group of Communists planning the assassination of several members of President Machado's Cabinet.

The final step in legislation authorizing President Machado to suspend constitutional guarantees in the Cuban Republic was taken tonight.

Publication in the Official Gazette of the act of Congress ratified last night following an all-night session automatically made the bill a law, but it is understood that the President has decided against putting into effect immediately the new weapon at his command.

On Fishing Trip.

President Machado was reported as intending to spend the week-end at Mariel, where he went fishing early today. The decree was taken to him shortly before noon and he signed it, but he made no indication relative to the time when he would give the signal putting it into force.

The measure stipulates that President Machado may create a virtual state of military law in Havana and its suburbs, extending the condition to the whole republic at his discretion, for a period of twenty days preceding the elections on Nov. 1.

The decree, drafted by the President when a number of outbreaks in various parts of the island indicated that Cuba might be following in the revolutionary footsteps of other Latin-American republics, gives him full power to use any measures he may consider necessary in case of emergency.

The Nationalists, other than issuing a manifesto signed by Colonel Carlos Mendieta, setting forth that the suspension of constitutional rights "had been in effect for a long time previous to its legal sanction by Congress," were silent today following Congress's favorable attitude toward the decree.

The following are the constitutional guarantees subject to suspension at the discretion of the President:

"Article 15—No one shall be arrested except in cases and under forms prescribed by the law.

"Article 16—Those arrested shall obtain their liberty or be entitled to a hearing within twenty-four hours.

"Article 17—If there is no proof of guilt of the arrested parties they shall receive their liberty within seventy-two hours.

"Article 19—No one shall be indicted or sentenced except by a competent tribunal.

"Article 22—Secrets of correspondence are inviolable.

"Article 23—A man's home is in-

Continued on Page Sixteen.

The Weekly Kansas City Star has the largest circulation of all farm papers circulating in Missouri and Kansas and the largest weekly rural route circulation in America.—Advt.

Cardinals Take Third Game of Series, 5-0; Yale, Harvard, Princeton Win at Football

World's Series—The Cardinals defeated the Athletics, 5 to 0, in the third game of the world's series in St. Louis yesterday before 38,000 persons. It was the first victory for the Cardinals in the series. The fourth game will be played in St. Louis today.

Football—Albie Booth scored two touchdowns and led a strong forward-pass offense as Yale triumphed over Maryland, 40 to 13, at the Yale Bowl. Harvard launched its football campaign with a 35-to-0 victory over Vermont. Princeton defeated Amherst, 23 to 0; Columbia beat Union, 25-0; N. Y. U. upset West Virginia Wesleyan, 41-6, and Fordham blanked Buffalo, 71-0. Notre Dame conquered Southern Methodist, 20-14.

Racing—Harry Payne Whitney's Equipoise, 1-to-5 favorite, was beaten by a length by Twenty Grand, 7-to-1 shot, in the Junior Champion Stakes at Aqueduct. Land Boy beat Falmouth by 250 lengths in the steeplechase feature at Bowman Park, gaining permanent possession of the $5,000 Gold Cup for A. F. Goodwin of Boston.

Complete Details in Sports Section.

GOVERNOR EXPECTED TO REFUSE TO WIDEN JOB-BUYING INQUIRY

He Is Said to Have Accepted View That Law Limits Ward to the Ewald Case.

REPLY TO GRAND JURY SENT

Special Body Moves to Invoke Election Act to Investigate Other Judges Here.

Governor Roosevelt, it was understood last night, has decided to refuse the Ewald grand jury's request that he remove the limitations he imposed upon Attorney General Hamilton Ward. He is reported to have based his decision upon the advice of noted counsel, who advised him he lacked the power to accede to the proposal.

Anticipating a denial of their request, Hiram C. Todd, the special prosecutor appointed by Mr. Ward, and the members of the grand jury were preparing to continue their inquiry into general charges of office-buying in New York County under the elective franchise law without further authorization from the Governor.

Such other suspected crimes as do not come within the terms of the election laws and are not related closely enough to the Ewald-Healy case to be acted upon by the special investigating body, it was understood, will be referred to District Attorney Crain and the regular grand jury of New York County, which is being held over for that purpose.

Grand Jury Awaits Letter.

Meanwhile the scheduled attempt of I. Nicholas Gordon, attorney for former Magistrate George F. Ewald, Mrs. Bertha E. Ewald and Peter Eckert, her father, to terminate the activities of the special grand jury suffered an enforced delay until tomorrow, when a letter containing the Governor's answer to the grand jury's plea will be made public.

Samuel Untermyer and the group of lawyers assisting him in advising John F. Curry, leader of Tammany Hall, on the maze of legal technicalities that have cropped up in connection with the judicial inquiries, hastened to dissociate themselves from Mr. Gordon's move. At the same time other attorneys cast serious doubt upon the efficacy of Mr. Gordon's plan "to confine this inquiry to legitimate channels."

Mr. Untermyer's statement said:

> There is no basis for the varying stories in the newspapers, either as to the organization, formal, informal or otherwise, of a legal or other staff of defense, or of advice to either Mr. Curry or the district leaders or any of them, nor as to the connection of any of the men named, with any application to the court to limit the activities of the Ewald grand jury by injunction or otherwise.
>
> No such topic was discussed or even mentioned and we know nothing of it. The first advice as to such proposed action was gathered from this morning's newspapers.

Terence McManus, attorney for Mayor Walker, and another member of the alleged legal board of strategy which Tammany Hall was said to have created, insisted there "is scarcely a scintilla of truth in the story." Mr. Gordon, insisting that he acted independently on behalf of Mr. Eckert, who, he said, had suffered from continued prying into his private affairs, admitted that his move, if successful, would operate to the advantage of any witness.

With the Governor's reply to the grand jury already formulated and drafted and on the way to Robert Morris, the foreman of the body, which reconvenes tomorrow, its contents caused much speculation. Persons who discussed the situation with Governor Roosevelt in the past few days reported him as "hostile" to the

Continued on Page Twenty.

With their flavor and individual rich red radiant color no fruit sauce awakens a sluggish appetite more delightfully than fresh Ten Minute Cranberry Sauce made from fresh Eatmor Cranberries.—Advt.

ECONOMY PROGRAM OF NAVY COMPLETED; PERSONNEL TO BE CUT

General Reorganization Is Included in Steps Recommended by Admiral Pratt.

SUBMARINES TO BE REDUCED

Prediction Is Made That Some of the Destroyers Also Will Be Retired.

Special to The New York Times.

WASHINGTON, Oct. 4.—Plans for a general reorganization of the United States fleet and of naval shore establishments have been practically completed. They are designed to meet President Hoover's demands for economy, bring the navy closer to the strength provided for it under the London naval treaty and carry out ideas of Admiral W. V. Pratt, chief of naval operations, for increased efficiency.

Orders received at Pearl Harbor yesterday to send two division of R-type submarines to Atlantic ports in December are steps in this reorganization. While there is every reason to believe that the submarines withdrawn will be replaced in whole or in part by newer-type submersibles, there are ample grounds for believing that a number of the older submarines will be decommissioned shortly.

It is understood that as a purely economic measure orders have been issued to dismiss several hundred men at navy yards and stations along the Atlantic and Gulf coasts. How many employes and what yards are affected is not divulged, although it is indicated that the New York navy yard is not affected.

Yards to Be Retained.

The belief has long existed in naval circles that several of the yards are not needed, but have been retained because of political pressure from the districts in which they are located. For this reason it is not expected that any of the yards will be closed, although it is understood that such a recommendation has been placed before Secretary Adams.

Not only have cuts been made in civilian staffs but recruiting has been slowed up and an order is expected soon to stop recruiting temporarily so as to reduce the enlisted strength of 84,500 by from 2,500 to 5,000. The Marine Corps' 18,000 men may be reduced by 500.

The prediction is made that a number of destroyers may be laid up, and Admiral Pratt is working on his operating schedule for the 1931 fiscal year along lines that may result in some cuts in the control and fleet base forces. Should these reductions be made the need for one Rear Admiral would be eliminated.

The recent decommissioning of three battleships of the scouting fleet to bring battleship strength to the fifteen specified in the London treaty will release 2,100 men for distribution among other units of the fleet, while the laying up of submarines and destroyers would provide still more. Hence the loss of a few thousand men in the enlisted strength would not be seriously felt and sufficient men would be available to man the new 10,000-ton cruisers. Three more of these vessels are to be commissioned early in 1931, requiring a personnel of 1,500.

The understanding is that no disturbance of the balance of strength between the forces in the Pacific and the Atlantic is contemplated. Several of the steps in prospect are believed to embody recommendations made by Admiral Pratt in his last annual report as Commander-in-Chief of the United States Fleet. This report, which has never been made public, was submitted after Admiral Pratt had returned from the London conference, and is said to embody conclusions, resulting from commanding the fleet and participating in the London conference, aimed at providing the best fleet possible under the treaty while effecting economies.

Present indications are that while

Continued on Page Twenty-four.

PRESENT LIQUOR FLOW 40% OF THAT IN 1914

Woodcock, Dry Chief, Puts the Possible Production in 1930 at 876,320,718 Gallons.

SEVEN FOR EACH PERSON

The Commissioner Estimates That Consumption of Illegal Spirits Is Decreasing.

Special to The New York Times.

WASHINGTON, Oct. 4.—The possible production of illicit liquor of all classes in the United States for the fiscal year ending June 30, 1930, was placed at 876,320,718 gallons, or approximately seven gallons to each person in the United States, by the Bureau of Prohibition in the first of its reports on consumption and sources, made public today by the prohibition director, Colonel Amos W. W. Woodcock.

The figures given in the bureau's survey were somewhat under those issued earlier this week for 1929 by the Association Against the Prohibition Amendment. Mr. Woodcock emphasized that he had used the words "possible production" in the absence of a basis for actual figures. Contrary to the anti-dry body, his conclusion was that "consumption of alcoholic liquor in the United States is growing less from year to year." Statements to the contrary were characterized as "unwarranted."

The bureau's report made a comparison of the estimated "possible production" of the last fiscal year with that of 1914, the last year of normal full production of legal liquor, when actual figures showed a legitimate withdrawal of 2,256,272,765 gallons and added the calculation that the apparent present consumption was only about 40 per cent of that year.

Mr. Woodcock's report emphasized over and over again that it was not intended as an argument for or against any one's figures, but represented "a scholarly and unbiased effort to find the truth." It maintained that "it is not scientifically possible to ascertain the exact amount of alcoholic beverage consumed," but added that a "fairly close" guess could be made by surveying the production of the commodities from which liquor is made, discounting the amounts of these commodities known to have been used in legitimate manufacture.

In a survey made on that basis, taking into consideration figures obtained from the Departments of Commerce and Agriculture and the Census Bureau, coupled with a special survey made by investigators of the Department of Justice and the Treasury, the following amounts were listed as the Prohibition Bureau's figures on bootleg liquor production in the fiscal year ended June 30, 1930:

	Gallons.
SPIRITS.	
Distilled spirits from corn sugar	45,900,000
Distilled spirits from cane or beet sugar	10,000,000
Distilled spirits from grains	4,000,000
Diverted industrial alcohol	9,929,218
Smuggled spirits	3,557,500
Total spirits	73,386,718
WINE.	
Wine made from grapes & raisins	118,320,300
Smuggled wine	155,900
Total wine	118,476,200
BEVERAGE LIQUOR.	
Malt liquor (home brew)	683,032,000
Malt liquor smuggled	1,144,800
Total malt liquors	684,476,800
ALL BEVERAGE LIQUOR.	
Spirits	73,386,718
Wine	118,476,200
Beer	684,447,800
Total possible production	876,320,718

The report made an immediate comparison with the liquor records of

Continued on Page Six.

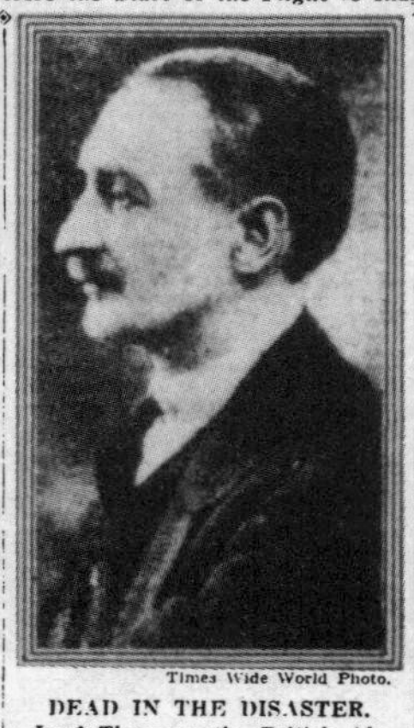

Times Wide World Photo.

DEAD IN THE DISASTER.
Lord Thomson, the British Air Minister.

R-101 HAD A CAREER OF LESS THAN YEAR

Launched in England on Oct. 12, 1929, Craft Was Largest Airship in the World.

The R-101, sister ship of the R-100, which recently made a successful round trip from England to Canada, was launched at Cardington, England, on Oct. 12, 1929, and was the world's biggest airship. Although originally she had sleeping accommodations for 100 persons, these were reduced recently to fifty-two, as part of an extensive program of alterations designed to give the airship greater lifting power. Her lifting power after the alterations was estimated at 172 tons, compared with 156 tons for the R-100.

These alterations, which were made during a six months' period, increased the ship's length by 35 feet and her hydrogen gas capacity by 500,000 cubic feet, to a total of 5,500,000 cubic feet. In order to make the alterations the ship was cut in two and new central bays installed between the separated halves. The change made practically no difference in the streamline shape of the craft, except to give emphasis to her speedy lines.

The cost of the airship R-100 was upwards of $2,500,000 and the R-101 cost considerably more.

Visitors who looked over the airship when the work was completed described her as a marvel of luxury. The gangway was in the nose and led down along an enclosed corridor, slightly larger than that of a Continental train, along the longitudinal girders to the two passenger decks.

Last Word in Airship Luxury.

The airship's two-berth staterooms compared favorably with those of many ocean liners, while the spacious lounge that extended across her entire breadth was held to be the last word in airship luxury. Wide windows on either side gave passengers an excellent view of the terrain below, while there was also a broad promenade equipped with deck chairs.

The spacious dining room was lit by large celluloid windows in the ship's sides. Beneath it was the electric kitchen, equipped with electric cookers and aluminum stoves. All the water containers and pipes were of the same material.

The smoking room, an interior compartment fed by forced air circulation and isolated from the gen-

Continued on Page Two.

Cavalier Hotel, Virginia Beach, Va., Two 18-hole Golf Courses, 12 hrs. from N. Y.—Advt.

ELEVEN NOTABLES ON THE TRAGIC TRIP

Lord Thomson, Air Minister of Labor Government, Among 53 on Board.

SIR SEFTON BRANCKER ALSO

Wing Commander Colmore and Major Scott, Captain of R-34, Were Passengers.

By The Associated Press.

LONDON, Sunday, Oct. 5.—Lord Thomson, Air Minister of the Labor Government, and fifty-two other persons were aboard Britain's giant air liner, the R-101, destroyed in an explosion near Beauvais, France, this morning.

Sir William Sefton Brancker, Director of Civil Aviation; Wing Commander R. B. B. Colmore, Director of Airship Development, and Major G. H. Scott, famous airman and commander of the historic R-34, were among the eleven passengers. The officers and crew totaled forty-two.

The airship was commanded by Flight Lieutenant H. C. Irwin. The navigator was Squadron Leader E. L. Johnston, and the first officer Lieut. Commander N. G. Atherstone.

Many Had Notable Careers.

Christopher Birdwood Thomson, P. C., C. B. E., D. S. O., was created first Baron of Cardington in 1924. He twice held the post of Secretary of State for Air in Great Britain and had a brilliant record as a soldier and statesman. He was a subaltern in the Boer War and a Brigadier General in the World War.

Born April 13, 1875, the son of Major Gen. David Thomson and Emily Birdwood Thomson, he was educated at Cheltenham College and the Royal Military Academy at Woolwich. He was commissioned first in 1894 and served in the Mashonaland campaign and the Boer War. His services in the latter war won him the rank of brevet Major.

From 1902 to 1905 he was an instructor of the Military Engineering School at Chatham and subsequently at the Staff College and in the War Office. After the World War he was Military Attaché and chief of the Military Commission to Rumania. He was also a member of the British Supreme War Council at Versailles. He retired from the army with the rank of Brigadier General in 1919.

Why Thomas Was Laborite.

The following year he became active in the Labor party in England. Explaining his attachment to the Labor cause, he once said:

"I joined the Labor party because I attended the Versailles Conference and saw face to face the utter incapacity, folly and dishonesty of the politicians assembled there to dispose of the destinies of the world. I had been in the army twenty-six years, but I had never seen anything like the thickheadedness of the Versailles statesmen.

"I came away with the conviction that that sort of thing must not happen again. I resolved that I would devote my life to the prevention of war. This, not in spite of my being a soldier, but because I was a soldier."

In 1924, during the first brief stay of Ramsay MacDonald's Labor party in power, Lord Thomson served in his Cabinet as Secretary of State for Air. When the Labor party again came into power in 1929 he was again appointed to that post and had served in that capacity since.

He had written many of the lead-

Continued on Page Two.

WHEN Buying Bitters, demand Abbott's. Flavors beverages.—Advt.

CRASHES IN VIOLENT WIND

Air Minister Is Killed by Flames—Survivors in Beauvais Hospital.

SOME LEAPED DURING FALL

Smoking Permitted for First Time on Such Craft, Causing Debate on Part in Tragedy.

DIRIGIBLE ON WAY TO INDIA

Major Scott Revealed at Start From Cardington Project for Australian Service.

R-101 Crashed on Top of Hill, Survivor Phones to London

By The Associated Press.

LONDON, Sunday, Oct. 5.—H. J. Leech of the engineering staff of the R-101, survivor of the disaster that overtook the giant dirigible near Beauvais, France, this morning, telephoned to London an account of the crash.

"We crashed on top of a hill," he said. "There was no warning. As the airship lurched to the earth it burst into flames and, then crashed."

Two other survivors of the disaster were J. H. Binks and V. Savory. Both were members of the engineering staff.

By The Associated Press.

BEAUVAIS, France, Sunday, Oct. 5.—Britain's giant dirigible R-101, the largest lighter-than-air craft in the world, was completely destroyed this morning about seven hours after leaving her base at Cardington, England, on a flight to India.

The airship burst into flames in a field five miles south of here.

Lord Thomson, Air Minister of the British Labor Government, a passenger, was burned to death with forty-five men of the airship's complement of fifty-three officers, crew and passengers.

Survivors Badly Burned.

Only seven persons were saved. All of these were badly burned and otherwise injured. They were rushed to the Beauvais Hospital after receiving first aid.

The disaster occurred at 2:30 A. M. (9:30 P. M. Saturday, New York time) as a gale was blowing in from the Channel.

The big airship, cruising at an altitude of 400 feet on her way south to Bordeaux, crashed into a farmer's field near the village of Alonne.

By the time neighboring farmers, roused by the sound, had reached the field, the pride of Britain's dirigibles was a mass of fiercely burning flames.

The authorities at Beauvais Prefecture were notified by telephone, and rushed with the police to the field. They were too late to save more than seven of all the brave and distinguished men who set out cheerfully for the East yesterday afternoon.

French Explain Disaster.

French Air Ministry officials ascribed the disaster to high wind. They said the R-101 hurtled downward into the field, burst into flames and exploded.

A communiqué from the French Air Ministry states:

> The Air Ministry was constantly in touch with the dirigible, which sent out messages every ten minutes.
>
> At 1:50 A. M. (8:50 P. M. Saturday, New York Time) the dirigible gave its position as a mile and a quarter north of Beauvais. After this no message was received direct from the ship.
>
> Later it was learned that the dirigible, probably in trouble through bad weather, came down to a low altitude. Shortly afterward, doubtless as the result of a violent cross current wind, the dirigible crashed to the ground in a woodland a few miles south of Beauvais.
>
> It caught fire and exploded. Several victims, gravely injured, were removed from the débris and transported to the hospital at Beauvais. Laurent Eynac, Minister of Air, left immediately for the scene of the disaster.

The Air Ministry's announcement said that the crew of the R-101 was composed of five officers and forty-three men and that she carried nineteen passengers.

Since early evening the wind had been rising over the French channel coast, heralding a storm out in the Atlantic. It struck heavily soon after midnight.

At first the fact that smoking was permitted on board was considered as a possible cause of the explosion.

In addition to Lord Thomson, many of Britain's foremost aircraft authorities were aboard the R-101. They included Sir Sefton Brancker, Director of Civil Aviation; Major G. H. Scott, commander of the R-34, and Wing Commander R. B. B. Colmore, Director of Airship Development.

The police mobilized all the available farmhands of the region, as well as many citizens of Beauvais for rescue work and to search for bodies.

They learned that about a dozen bodies were strewn through the wooded land where the airship crashed. It is believed that some persons leaped from the gondola at a low altitude when she was coming down.

About a hundred men hunted around the spot, but darkness hampered their work.

All Beauvais was speculating whether pipe and cigarette smoking aboard the airship had played any part in the disaster. For the moment it was impossible to say.

It was exactly 2 o'clock in the morning when the inhabitants of Beauvais, a city renowned for its cathedral and frequently visited by Americans, were awakened by the roar of gigantic motors. Many people looked up through their windows and saw the dirigible at a low altitude. Despite the rain and slight fog, the ship's red and green lights were distinctly seen. The craft seemed to be in difficulty.

A few seconds later there was a terrific explosion. Streaks of light illuminated the sky. Many hastily donned their clothes and rushed in the direction of the dirigible, which was already a mass of flames outside the city on the road to the city of Pontoise. They could not approach the R-101 because of the unbearable heat.

Last Report to London at 1 A. M.

By The Associated Press.

LONDON, Sunday, Oct. 5.—The last report the Air Ministry received from the R-101 was at 1 A. M. (8 P. M., New York Time). At that time the airship was over Abbeville, France, and reported all was well. Abbeville is about fifty miles north of Beauvais.

The airship, largest lighter-than-air craft in the world, left Cardington, England, at 7:37 P. M. British standard time (2:37 P. M. Saturday, New York time).

She was bound on a trial run to India and back, her first port of call being Ismailia, Egypt. She was due there Monday.

The R-101 is a sister ship of the R-100, which made the transatlantic flight to Canada last Spring. Recent alterations had made her larger than the R-100.

Her flight today was in the nature of a test to determine the feasibility of inaugurating regular airship service from Great Britain to India.

Early in the evening she passed over London almost hidden by low-hanging clouds. The great gas bag was invisible, but observers saw the red, white and green lights at her prow and her stern.

Before her launching at Cardington in October, 1929, the big airship had been called "obsolete and a failure." Commander Dennistoun Burney, airship designer, predicted that she would be of little commercial value. Alterations were subsequently made and she was refitted for the voyage to India last August.

Smoking Permitted on Airship.

Special Cable to THE NEW YORK TIMES.

CARDINGTON, England, Oct. 4.—The world's largest airship, the R-101, floated away from her mooring mast here tonight on a voyage to India.

Carrying Lord Thomson, Air Minister, and fifty-two others, she soared off into the darkening evening sky bound for Karachi, India, with one landing at Ismailia, Egypt, 2,500 miles from London.

No airship has ever attempted to cross the hot desert country east of Suez and only two have ever ventured into the tropics before, the German Zeppelin, which flew from Bulgaria to East Africa during the war and the Graf Zeppelin on its flight across Africa and the South Atlantic to Brazil.

There was no sign at Cardington tonight that anything epoch-making was being attempted. A crowd of 300 waited around the mooring mast for the giant ship to rise. At 7:37 P. M. there were a few sharp words of command, her nose slipped free of the mooring mast, and while the crowd waved farewells the R-101 backed off and rose into the air.

For the first fifty miles her commander, Flight Lieutenant H. C. Irwin, pointed her nose due south over Hertfordshire and London. Soon after starting the flight he decided to fly between Rouen and Paris and thence south to Bordeaux.

Instead of carrying gasoline fuel the R-101 had twenty-five tons of heavy oil fuel for her five Diesel engines. Thus, although oil engines are heavier than gasoline engines, the R-101 was the first airship in the world on which smoking is possible.

"We are greatly relieved that we can smoke on board, said Major G. H. Scott, commander of the historic R-34, before starting on his latest airship adventure today, "for the trip to Canada on the R-100 it was forbidden and we all longed for a cigarette."

Major Scott revealed that the R-101's flight was intended to blaze an airship trail to Australia and that it will decide whether the Arabian route or the Atlantic-Pacific route via Canada and the Fiji Islands is more practicable.

The airship has the most comprehensive system of weather reporting ever employed on an airship voyage. A chain of five Royal Air Force stations will supply reports at six-hour intervals.

Thomson Confident at Start.

Just before boarding the airship Lord Thomson said he was completely confident of the trip's success.

"I have promised the Prime Minister I shall be back in London by Oct. 20," he said.

The present plan is to keep the R-101 at her Karachi masthead four days and then return to England without further flights over India.

Other notable passengers include Air Vice Marshal Sir Sefton Brancker, Director of Civil Aviation, and Lieut. Col. V. O. Richmond, designer of the airship.

An assistant coxswain in the crew is W. A. Potter, who has been working with airships since 1915 and is one of the five survivors of the R-38 disaster ten years ago.

The departure tonight was delayed more than fifteen minutes by failure of the starboard forward motor. The starting mechanism refused to function but the four other engines whirred into action perfectly. Darkness made it necessary to turn on the huge floodlight which shone on the silvery envelope until the balky engine could be started.

Special Cable to THE NEW YORK TIMES.

LONDON, Oct. 4.—With lights twinkling faintly beneath her the R-101 sailed over London in a drizzling rain about 9 o'clock. She was only dimly discernible in the haze and vanished to the southward in the darkness.

R-101 Moored to Her Mast in Cardington, After a Recent Test Flight.

International Newsreel Photo.

Control Room of the R-101. Lieut. Commander Atherstone Is Seen Taking a Compass Bearing.

Times Wide World Photo.

ELEVEN NOTABLES ON THE TRAGIC TRIP

Continued from Page One.

Continued from Page One.

ing aeronautical books on military subjects and numerous magazine articles. Among the books were "Old Europe's Suicide," "Victors and Vanquished," "Samaranda" and "Air Facts and Problems."

Lord Thomson, a pronounced exponent of lighter-than-air operations over long-distance routes on sea and land, said in one of his most recent volumes:

"Airship routes will be mainly over sea routes. Over land the airship is much slower than the airplane and not much faster than the express train, while over the sea it will travel twice as fast as the fastest steamer. * * * Owing to the fact that the surface of the sea, even in the tropics, maintains a fairly even temperature, atmospheric disturbances are less disruptive to airships there than those encountered over land in the tropical or semi-tropical climates. Vertical gusts are generated over sun-baked plains which may attain a velocity of 1,000 feet per minute. It was a gust of this description which caught the ill-fated Shenandoah.

"Another disaster like that which befell the Shenandoah would delay development for many years."

Major Scott, who stated shortly before the airship left Cardington that "we are greatly relieved that we can smoke on board," was for a number of years Assistant Director of Flying for the British Government. He was captain of the R-9, the first British rigid airship to fly, in 1912.

In 1919 he commanded the R-34 in its historic flight from Scotland to the United States. More recently he was aboard the R-100 in its flight from England to Canada in July. It was he who invented and planned the St. Hubert mooring tower and base at Montreal, at which the R-100 was landed.

In 1926 Major Scott was aboard the dirigible Norge, in which the Amundsen-Ellsworth-Nobile expedition flew over the North Pole, during its test flight from Rome over the Mediterranean and Southern France. In an advisory capacity as one of Britain's leading air pilots, he took great interest in the flight.

While in Toronto, after the flight of the R-100 to Canada, he predicted that there would be a daily dirigible service between England and Canada in ten years.

Brancker's Career.

Air Vice-Marshal Sir William Sefton Brancker, K. C. B., was born

The Course of the R-101 on Her Last Trip.

in 1877, a son of the late Colonel W. G. Brancker, Royal Artillery, and began his military career during the South African War, serving with the artillery. He held various commands in the British Air Service, including that of Director of Air Organizations and Deputy Director General of Military Aeronautics, the latter post from 1914 until 1917. He was appointed Controller-General of equipment in 1918, and was Master-General of Personnel, Air Council, in 1918 and 1919.

In 1922 Sir William was appointed Director of Civil Aviation in the Air Ministry. He was the British representative on the International Commission of Air Navigation and was a past president of the Royal Aeronautical Society and of the Institute of Transport.

He wrote extensively on matters concerning aviation and recently declared that the world was at present on the threshold of vast developments in aerial commerce. He had always been an enthusiastic supporter of lighter-than-air craft.

Lieutenant H. C. Irwin, who acted as commander on the flight yesterday, had for many years been connected with flying, both in the army air service and more recently in the commercial field. On the first flight of the R-100, on Oct. 15, 1929, when the craft was taken from Cardington, England, on a test flight over London, Lieutenant Irwin took a prominent part as Flight Lieutenant. He did not make the trip from England to Canada last Summer.

Designer Aboard.

Lieut. Col. V. C. Richmond was aboard the ship in his usual capacity of observer and adviser. The designer of the dirigible, he took a keen interest in its test flights.

"All the News That's Fit to Print."

The New York Times

LATE CITY EDITION
WEATHER—Fair today; tomorrow rain; temperature unchanged.
Temperatures Yesterday—Max., 46; Min., 40.

Copyright, 1933, by The New York Times Company.

VOL. LXXXII....No. 27,465. Entered as Second-Class Matter, Postoffice, New York, N. Y. NEW YORK, WEDNESDAY, APRIL 5, 1933. P TWO CENTS In New York City. | THREE CENTS Within 200 Miles | FOUR CENTS Elsewhere Except in 7th and 8th Postal Zones

73 LOST IN AKRON CRASH, 3 SURVIVORS HERE; SHIP DRIVEN DOWN IN STORM, CAUSE IS UNKNOWN; RESCUE BLIMP FALLS, 2 KILLED, 5 ARE SAVED

FORCES FOR REPEAL WINNING WISCONSIN, WITH VOTING HEAVY

Wet Sweep of All 15 Delegates at Large Rolling Up in Sequel to Michigan Poll.

LEADING 4 TO 1 IN RETURNS

Margin 2 to 1 in Rural Area, Disappointing Drys, and 10 to 1 in Milwaukee.

DECISIVE VOTE DEMANDED

Electorate Warned in Wet Appeal of Example to Nation—93 of 100 Michigan Delegates for Repeal.

By The Associated Press.

MILWAUKEE, Wis., Wednesday, April 5.—Following Monday's example of Michigan, sentiment for repeal of the Eighteenth Amendment was sweeping Wisconsin as returns were being tabulated early today showing a rejection of prohibition in yesterday's referendum by a margin of about four to one.

Returns from 1,174 of the 2,899 precincts in the State gave: 237,108 for repeal, 58,593 against it.

In heavy voting town and country alike turned in thumping wet majorities. First returns were from rural districts, where drys had held some hope of showing strength. But even they favored repeal by a two-to-one majority.

Then the cities of the eastern part of the State, where polls closed late, began piling up the wet lead.

Milwaukee, where the breweries are humming to produce the beer which will become legal Friday went wet by a margin of more than ten to one.

In thirty-seven precincts in Milwaukee the vote was: for repeal 30,037, against it 866.

In Racine, Sheboygan and Kenosha it was the same story.

Vote Asked as Guide to Nation.

Wisconsin voters selected fifteen of thirty candidates for delegate to the constitutional convention. The fifteen drys and fifteen wets were listed separately. None of the candidates made personal campaigns and all were definitely committed as to how they would vote in the convention. The constitutional convention accordingly will merely be a formality to carry out the mandate of the voters.

On the basis of the present trend wet leaders were predicting that every one of the fifteen delegates to a constitutional amendment convention to be held at Madison April 25 would be committed to vote for repeal. A bare majority is required to cast the State's vote one way or the other.

Dr. J. J. Seelman, Milwaukee chairman of the State branch of the Association Against the Prohibition Amendment, said that the result was about what was expected. He expressed belief that a decisive Wisconsin vote for repeal would have a "stimulating effect" in other States which soon are to pass on the proposal.

In an appeal to the electorate to cast a "decisive vote," Dr. Seelman had said:

"The eyes of the nation are on Wisconsin. A close vote will have a bad psychological effect in States where wet and dry sentiment is almost balanced."

Referring to the vote of 350,337 to 196,402 by which the State repealed its own prohibition law four years ago, Dr. Seelman urged that today's mandate be made "the most decisive yet extended by the people of Wisconsin."

In his plea for a large turnout of voters to exercise their franchise on the prohibition question Dr. Seelman had the support of Governor Schmedeman and the State's members in the United States Senate, Robert M. La Follette Jr. and F. Ryan Duffy.

The Rev. Warren Jones of Madison, State superintendent of the Anti-Saloon League, conceded a wet victory.

A State Supreme Court Justice and State Superintendent of Instruction, in addition to municipal officers, judges and school board members, are also being elected.

Speedy tabulation of the votes was expected because of a new State law which requires the filing of election results immediately after the polls close. Closings were set at 8 P. M., Central Time, in the cities and 6 P. M. in rural areas.

93 of 100 Michigan Delegates Wet.

Special to THE NEW YORK TIMES.

DETROIT, April 4.—In the first State referendum on repeal of the Eighteenth Amendment the voters

Continued on Page Two.

Mary Elizabeth's—Dine and Play Games—Dinner-a-Dollar. 5th Ave. at 38th St.—Advt.

Chamberlain Refuses Reply To Debt Question in Commons

Wireless to THE NEW YORK TIMES.

LONDON, April 4. — Neville Chamberlain, Chancellor of the Exchequer, was asked in the House of Commons today whether he would tell the United States that future war debt payments, if any, would take the form of short-term credits without interest to be placed by this country at the disposal of the United States to be used for the purchase of British goods and services. He replied it was undesirable to say anything about the debts pending future discussions.

In reply to another question Mr. Chamberlain said the amount already paid the United States, including last December's instalment, was £355,200,000, which was £162,800,000 more than Britain had received from reparations and war debt payments by the Allies. [The pound is currently worth $3.42½.]

GERMANY WILL KEEP GRIP ON FOREIGNERS

Permits to Leave to Be Denied to Persons Suspected of "Untruthful" Designs.

BOYCOTT FORMALLY ENDED

Our Embassy Protests Charge Berlin Consulate Is an "Atrocity Lie Factory."

By FREDERICK T. BIRCHALL.

Wireless to THE NEW YORK TIMES.

BERLIN, April 4.—All foreigners, including Americans, who find themselves in Germany will henceforth be unable to leave it without a police permit.

The optimistic declaration of the United States Consulate when the visa regulations were formally decreed yesterday, that it had had official assurances that the decree would not be applied to foreigners, was withdrawn today in the light of fuller information.

Any doubt that the regulations covered "all persons" was dissipated by an announcement of supplementary instructions by Captain Hermann Wilhelm Goering, Minister Without Portfolio and Prussian Interior Minister. The instructions are as follows:

1. That permission can be refused if action justifies the supposition that the person leaving Germany intends to act abroad in a manner hostile to the Reich or against a German State, or that he intends to insult or hold up to scorn abroad the President of the Reich or members of the government of a German State, as well as other organs, institutions or authorities of the Reich or of a German State.

2. That permission can be refused if there is danger that the person leaving Germany will spread untruthful news abroad that might damage the vital interests of the Reich or of a State.

Boycott Formally Called Off.

Formal announcement of the calling off of the anti-Jewish boycott was officially made today in these terms:

With satisfaction the Government of the Reich has taken note of the fact that the defensive boycott against anti-German agitation has not failed to produce its effect on other countries. Aside from small remnants of atrocity agitation against Germany, the agitation has been completely abandoned.

The Government of the Reich therefore takes the stand that there is no purpose in further opposing these remnants by means of the boycott, especially since it is agitation that has its origin among the Communists. The German defensive boycott will not be resumed tomorrow because it has become superfluous.

The Government of the Reich emphasizes, however, that the defensive organization of the National Socialist party is being maintained intact so that it can resume the defensive battle in case the agitation should revive.

Any addition to the simple terms of this outgiving, including the assumption about the Communists, would be to superimpose gilding upon pure gold. It should, however, be recorded that while the boycott is being called off at the front door other measures meanwhile are in preparation in the rear of the house.

May Form Committee on Race.

From the Munich headquarters of the Central Defense Committee Against Jewish Atrocity and Boycott Agitation, the Nazi organization that engineered and managed Saturday's boycott, Dr. Julius Streicher, the Reichstag Deputy who is its chairman, announced that despite the cessation of the movement "the responsible authorities will continue to enlighten the

Continued on Page Ten.

CURB INVESTIGATION CALLED BY BENNETT TO BE BEGUN TODAY

Exchange Head Is Summoned for Questioning on Listing Practices.

UNLISTED TRADING SCORED

Attorney General Plans to End This as "Presenting Opportunity for Serious Abuses."

INVESTORS HELD MISLED

Many Buy Stock Not Knowing That It Has Not Been Scrutinized by Exchange, It Is Said.

An investigation into the listing practices of the New York Curb Exchange was ordered yesterday by State Attorney General John J. Bennett Jr. He announced that Howard C. Sykes, president of the Curb Exchange, would appear at 11 o'clock this morning at the State Bureau of Securities offices, 80 Centre Street, for examination. Mr. Sykes will be followed by other officers of the Exchange.

Mr. Bennett issued the following statement:

"Attorney General John J. Bennett Jr. today announced that, following the receipt of several complaints during the past few days, an investigation will be immediately instituted into the listing practices of the New York Curb Exchange.

"Howard C. Sykes, president of the New York Curb Exchange, has been called for examination on Wednesday morning. The investigation will be conducted by Assistant Attorney General John F. X. McGohey, in charge of the Bureau of Securities, and Assistant Attorney General Ambrose V. McCall.

"Pending the investigation Mr. Bennett refused to make any extended comment. However, he did state:

"'As a result of a preliminary survey made of the listing practices on the New York Curb Exchange it appears that listed and unlisted securities are traded in without discrimination.

"'There is a widespread belief among the investing public that all securities traded on the Curb Exchange conform to the standards for listed securities established by that Exchange. The practice of admitting stocks and bonds to unlisted trading privileges presents an opportunity for serious abuses and my investigation will have for its object the elimination of this so-called unlisted trading.'"

Most of Securities Not Listed.

One of the State officials said that a large part of the investing public did not know that the majority of the securities dealt with on the Curb Exchange had not been formally listed and consequently the many rules of the Exchange did not apply in any way to the corporations which had issued such securities. It was pointed out that in trading unlisted securities it was possible to trade in the securities of a corporation that did not want its stock traded in the market.

It was also stated that many investors did not want to purchase stock that was not listed on the Exchange, and often bought under misapprehension unlisted securities in the belief they had been sub-

Continued on Page Four.

Three Survivors of Disaster Suffered No Serious Harm

The condition of the three survivors of the wreck of the Akron was described at the Brooklyn Naval Hospital yesterday afternoon as generally good. None of the men was suffering from anything more serious than exposure, fatigue and shock.

As given by Captain Robert E. Stoops, Medical Corps, executive officer of the hospital, the condition of the men follows:

Lieut. Commander Herbert V. Wiley—No bodily injuries. In good condition except for evidences of fatigue.

Richard Edward Deal, boatswain's mate, second class—A few minor abrasions about legs and arms, and general effects of fatigue and shock.

Moody Eugene Erwin, aviation metalsmith, second class—Very good condition. Only a small abrasion on left wrist and general effects of fatigue and shock.

The body of Robert W. Copeland, chief radioman, who died aboard the German tanker Phoebus, apparently of exposure, was taken to the hospital morgue.

CONGRESS SPEEDS INQUIRY INTO WRECK

Future Aircraft Policy Will Depend on Investigations Put Under Way Today.

NAVY STAND UNCERTAIN

Too Early to Decide, Swanson Says—McClintic Predicts No More Will Be Built.

Special to THE NEW YORK TIMES.

WASHINGTON, April 4. — The House Committee on Naval Affairs will meet tomorrow and order a complete investigation of the loss of the Akron. Representative Vinson of Georgia, chairman of the committee, was in frequent communication with the Navy Department during the day.

Senator King announced that he would introduce a resolution tomorrow for a Senate investigation to determine the advisability of further expenditures for such craft. Senator Trammell, chairman of the Senate Naval Committee, was not ready, however, to say that the disaster marked the end of dirigible construction by the government.

Representative Vinson indicated that until all the facts are known the House Committee would make no statements regarding its future policy on lighter-than-air craft. This is also the position of Representative Britten of Illinois, the ranking Republican member of the committee.

End of Such Craft Predicted.

Many members in Congress and other officials of the government foresaw the end of dirigible construction for the national defense services as a result of the disaster, but others, including Secretary

Continued on Page Fifteen.

Opera Fund Near Goal With $270,000 Raised; 'Salome,' Long Barred, Planned for Next Year

With $270,000 of the $300,000 needed to insure continuance of the Metropolitan Opera next year already pledged, plans for a fourteen-week season to open Dec. 25 or 26 are now being formulated, it was learned last night. The signing of contracts and definite decisions on répertoire will not be made until the entire sum has been raised, however.

Hopes that most or all of the necessary balance of $30,000 will be realized through the Opera Ball scheduled for the night of April 23 are held by its sponsors. The fund-raising committee, headed by Lucrezia Bori, is attempting to raise as much as possible over $300,000 as a safeguard in the event that some of the pledges which have been given are not fulfilled, it is understood.

At least three important novelties will mark the coming season, according to present plans. They are the American opera "Merry Mount," with book by Richard L. Stokes and music by Howard Hanson; Donizetti's "Linda di Chamounix," which is intended to provide another vehicle for Lily Pons, and Richard Strauss's "Salomé."

The last named is not strictly a novelty, as it had a single performance at the Metropolitan in January, 1906, under the management of Heinrich Conried. It created a great furor and after the performance the directors of the Metropolitan Opera and Real Estate Company issued a statement terming it "objectionable and detrimental." In 1910 Oscar Hammerstein presented it with Mary Garden in the title rôle, but it has not been seen in New York since then.

"Merry Mount," which will be the fifteenth American production under the Metropolitan's present management, was announced for last season but postponed. It will be produced in concert form at the Ann Arbor Festival next month. The Metropolitan production will probably have Lawrence Tibbett in the leading rôle.

Donizetti's "Linda di Chamounix" has never been presented at the Metropolitan, but it was seen at the Astor Place Opera House in 1848, and again at the old Academy of Music in 1883-84 with Adelina Patti in the title rôle.

WIND WRECKS THE J-3

Crowds on Shore See New York Police Plane in Daring Rescue.

BLIMP PLUNGED INTO SEA

Blown Back Over Water at Beach Haven After Nearly Reaching Land Safely.

TINY PLANE FIGHTS SURF

Unable to Reach Two of Crew—One Rescuer Injured by the Propeller.

Special to THE NEW YORK TIMES.

BEACH HAVEN, N. J., April 4.—Fighting landward in the teeth of a forty-five-mile off-shore wind after a dangerous but fruitless search at sea for survivors of the wrecked dirigible Akron, the navy non-rigid blimp J-3 plunged into the ocean here at 1:45 P. M. today, 300 feet off Long Beach bar. Hundreds saw her dive.

Five of the crew were pulled from the waves by two policemen who landed beside the wreck in a tiny Savoia-Marchetti seaplane owned by the New York Police Department. Clinging to the deck of the plane, they were taxied through the surf, with the spray cutting their faces and blinding them, but all reached shore safely.

Two of the blimp's crew were lost. Pasquale Bettio, aviation machinist mate, first class, of Lakehurst, N. J., was dead when a Coast Guard cutter found his body floating near the submerged blimp an hour or so after the plunge.

Lieut. Commander David E. Cummins, who lived in Prescott, Ark., was picked up about the same time by the Coast Guard seaplane Sirius, piloted by Lieut. Commander E. F. Stone. He died in the plane on the way to Atlantic City Hospital.

Those Rescued From the J-3.

The five who were rescued are:

Lieutenant JOHN H. THORNTON, who commanded the J-3. His home is Greensboro, N. C.

Lieutenant (Junior Grade) WILLIAM A. COCKELL of Oswego, N. Y.

C... Radioman H. E. MANLEY, Brattleboro, Vt.

Aviation Machinist Mate (first class) A. A. SPRAGUE, Henderson, N. Y.

Aviation Machinist Mate (first class) W. H. MYERS, Bridgeport, Conn.

Otto A. Kafka, pilot of the police plane, and Acting Sergeant John W. Forsythe, who flew with him as observer, were hailed as heroes tonight when they landed at the police plane base at Floyd Bennett Field, Brooklyn. Their rescue of the blimp crew was breath-takingly sensational, according to witnesses.

The J-3 left the naval air station at Lakehurst this morning at 10:45 o'clock. Lieutenant Commander Cummins was aboard, though he had just returned to the field after a two-hour search in his own plane for some sign of the unfortunate Akron.

The skies over the field were thick and gray and rain was falling when the blimp left the ground. Lieut. Commander Kenworthy, in charge at Lakehurst, had received reports that survivors of the Akron had been seen clinging to débris in the ocean off Barnegat.

Ceiling of Only 200 Feet.

"There is a ceiling of only 200 feet," he told the Navy Department by telephone. "The planes cannot go out at Atlantic City. Just at the moment the weather is a little more favorable, although the wind is due to increase in about two hours. If necessary the crew can pull the rip cord. The loss of the blimp would not be much."

Soon afterward the blimp was on its way, with enough fuel aboard to feed its two motors for thirteen hours. The crew had orders to fly low, go out over the ocean about thirty miles and search as long as possible for Akron victims and to "crash" the blimp if necessary to save the lives of its crew.

Lieut. Commander Kenworthy got Philadelphia Navy Yard and asked that a stand-by ground crew be detailed at once to Cape May, at the southern tip of New Jersey, to help the J-3 to a landing if she should be forced that far south. He in-

Continued on Page Fifteen.

FINE PHOTOGRAPHS $1.50 Each, Mounted Size 6"x10", Sarony, 265 Fifth Ave.—Advt.

Roosevelt Grieves at Loss to the Nation; Says We 'Can Ill Afford to Lose Such Men'

Special to THE NEW YORK TIMES.

WASHINGTON, April 4.—Grief and bewilderment greeted the news here today of the loss of the Akron. Officers at the Navy Department, many of whom had personal friends among the crew and passengers of the wrecked airship, suspended routine work in an unofficial mourning period. President Roosevelt, Cabinet officials and members of Congress discussed the disaster, and the public talked of little else all day.

The centre of most intense grief in the Navy Department probably was the office of the Chief of the Bureau of Aeronautics. Rear Admiral William A. Moffett had occupied that post uninterruptedly since its creation in 1921, and many members of the personnel of the office have served with him for years.

President Roosevelt issued the following statement early in the day:

> The loss of the Akron with its crew of gallant officers and men is a national disaster. I grieve with the nation and especially with the wives and families of the men who were lost.
>
> Ships can be replaced, but the nation can ill afford to lose such men as Rear Admiral William A. Moffett and his shipmates who died with him, upholding to the end the finest traditions of the United States Navy.

Wiley Hails Heroism of Men As the Akron Plunged Into Sea

No Noise or Confusion After Order "Stand by for Crash!"—Survivor Says Ship Fell 1,600 Feet Amid Lightning Flashes—Tells of Struggle as Rudder Wires Snapped.

Lieut. Commander Herbert V. Wiley of the United States Navy, the only officer who survived the wreck of the Akron, stood half-way down a flight of stairs in the Brooklyn Naval Hospital yesterday afternoon and in calm, clear phrases told of the last hours of the world's greatest airship.

Caught in the centre of a turbulent storm, with lightning flashing all about her, the Akron was forced down into the sea after the rudder control wires had snapped, he said. The great mass of duralumin, with its fragile skin of rubberized fabric, was quickly ground up by the choppy rollers into jumbled wreckage.

Commander Wiley declined to venture any opinion as to the cause of the accident, but added that he did not believe the ship had been struck by lightning. The discipline of the crew, he said, was excellent, the engine cars answered all orders up to the last and the Akron plunged into the sea with the officers and men in the control car standing calmly by their posts, awaiting orders.

He added that there had been no explosion nor fire aboard the Akron.

Later in the day, speaking over a nation-wide radio network, he repeated the story of the disaster.

There was nothing of boastfulness about the way Commander Wiley told his story, nor was there apology. He was clad only in a bathrobe, hospital pajamas and slippers, and there were deep circles under his dark eyes. He stood erect; he spoke firmly.

Permits No Questions.

"I am going to just about conduct this interview myself," he announced to the throng of newspaper men, in prefacing his description of the disaster. "I am not going to answer any questions as to opinions or technical observations."

He paused a moment, glanced down at a few papers he held in his hand, and rubbed his cheek with a pencil.

"We left Lakehurst last night at 7:30 on a regularly scheduled flight," he said. "One object of the flight was to calibrate some radio stations in New England. Since this calibration could not begin until daylight, and it was foggy over the sea, we decided"——

He paused a moment, smiled faintly and corrected himself.

"——or, rather, it was decided to cruise inland where the ground could be seen, and we were over Philadelphia about 8:10 and headed south, following the Delaware River. It was expected it would be foggy south of New Jersey and that the fog at sea would clear in the morning. About 8:45 last night, when twenty or thirty miles south of Philadelphia, lightning was seen ahead, and in a few minutes we had a report of a thunderstorm over Washington. We headed east and northeast."

After a quick look at the papers in his hand he went on: "We headed east and northeast toward the ocean, flying at about 1,600 feet altitude. The ground was obscured by fog, but we knew our position quite accurately and occasionally we would glimpse a light or group of lights indicating a town which checked with our course. The ship was in good flying condition, slightly heavy.

"The lightning to the south became quite extensive and also appeared to the west. About 10 P. M., just after we had left the Jersey coast—that is, we were over the water—the storm became general all around us."

Commander Wiley paused, then continued deliberately:

"I do not think the ship was struck by lightning, as there was no indication of it at any time, although there was plenty of lightning all around us.

Watched Lights on Shore.

"We continued to the eastward for about one hour and then reversed the course. When we reached the land again we saw a group of lights and identified the shore line. This was about midnight and the course was changed to the southeast. About thirty minutes later the ship began to descend rapidly from about 1,600 feet and I dropped emergency ballast forward, and the fall was stopped at about 800 feet. We rose rapidly and leveled off at 1,600 feet again. While we were falling the engines were speeded up to full speed and when we regained altitude changed to standard speed again.

"About three minutes later the air became exceedingly turbulent and the ship was tossed about violently. I knew we were near the centre of the storm, because the air is most disturbed near the centre, and called all hands for landing stations; that is, I gave the signal for all hands to landing stations to have them available and not in their bunks.

"The ship took a sharp lurch and the rudder control wires to the upper rudder carried away."

"They did what?" a voice interrupted.

"They carried away; they broke." Commander Wiley explained patiently. "I unclutched the upper rudder and tried to steer with the lower rudder. I was on the right side, that is, the starboard side, of the control tower and superintended the rudder, and the Captain was on the left side and superintended the elevators; that is what is used to send the ship up and down."

Again he paused, his eyes looking out into the crowd of upturned faces before him.

Stationed in Control Car.

As executive officer, second in command of the Akron, Lieut. Commander Wiley's station was in the control car on the starboard side near an open window. The station of the commanding officer, Commander F. C. McCord, was on the other side of the car near another open window.

"I had the steersman steer with the lower rudder," he continued. "However, within less than a minute afterward I heard a popping noise and the lower rudder control rope was also broken.

"The elevator man repeated several times that the ship was falling and I heard him report '800 feet.' By this time the bow of the ship was inclined up about twenty degrees, but the ship was falling quite rapidly.

"In the fog nothing could be seen. I asked the altitude and the answer was '300 feet.' I gave the order—'Stand by to Crash,' and that sig-

Continued on Page Fourteen.

HUNT FOR SURVIVORS VAIN

Planes and Naval Ships Balked by Weather—Hope Abandoned.

LIGHTNING CAUSE DOUBTED

Airship, Caught in Centre of Storm, Was Smashed as It Struck Ocean.

ADMIRAL MOFFETT LOST

President Orders Navy to Give the Fullest Information to the Public.

Seventy-three officers and men, including Rear Admiral William A. Moffett, chief of the navy's Bureau of Aeronautics, were lost in the wreck of the navy dirigible Akron during a storm early yesterday in the Atlantic Ocean off the New Jersey coast—the worst airship disaster in history.

There are only three survivors. Four of the seventy-six aboard the Akron were rescued, but one died later of exposure. The body of another was found at sea. Seventy-one were still missing last night.

Two more lives were lost yesterday afternoon when the navy blimp J-3, taking part in the search for wreckage and survivors of the Akron, fell into the ocean off Beach Haven, N. J. Five of the J-3's crew of seven were rescued.

Only a few scattered pieces of the Akron's wreckage were found. It was believed that the greater part had sunk or had been carried miles away by wind and tide. Navy and Coast Guard ships and airplanes, which searched the Jersey coastal waters all yesterday, will continue the hunt today.

The steamship George Washington notified the Navy Department at Washington by radio last night that it had passed an inflated fabric like the outside cover of an airship, with some wreckage around it, at 5:45 o'clock yesterday afternoon, at approximately latitude 39.31 longitude 74.12. This is some miles from the scene of the disaster and further down the Jersey coast. The cruiser Portland was ordered to the scene.

Federal Inquiries Speeded.

The cause of the disaster will be investigated by the Committee on Naval Affairs of the House of Representatives at Washington, which announced last night that it would meet today to order a complete and thorough inquiry. The Navy Department also announced that it would begin an official inquiry without delay.

Henry Latrobe Roosevelt, Assistant Secretary of the Navy, whom President Roosevelt sent to the Naval Air Station at Lakehurst, N. J., promised yesterday that "a complete investigation" would be made to determine the cause of the crash. He added that President Roosevelt wished the people to have the fullest information as quickly as it could be obtained.

Such was the fury of the storm at the time of the accident that little hope is held out that any one who was not picked up immediately is still alive. As is always the case when men are lost at sea, the wives and families of the missing ones are hoping against hope that they may still be found.

The three who were rescued were Lieut. Commander Herbert V. Wiley, executive officer and second in command, of Lakewood, N. J.; Moody E. Erwin, metalsmith, of Memphis, Tenn., and Richard E. Deal, boatswain's mate, of Lakehurst, N. J.

The man who died after being rescued was Robert W. Copeland, chief radio operator, of Lakehurst, N. J.

The body of Lieut. Commander Harold E. MacLellan of Westerly, R. I., was found near the scene of the wreck about noon yesterday.

Those who lost their lives in the accident to the J-3 were Lieut. Commander David E. Cummins of Prescott, Ark., and Pasquale Bettio, chief machinist's mate.

Crashed During Heavy Storm.

The Akron crashed about 12:30 A. M. yesterday, twenty miles off Barnegat Light. This is at Barnegat City, midway down the New Jersey

Continued on Page Fourteen.

WILEY DESCRIBES FIGHT TO SAVE SHIP

Continued from Page One.

nal was rung up to the engine cars. Almost immediately we hit the water.

"We had, as I remember, a list to starboard; that is, to my side of the car, and the water rushed in my window and carried me out the other window. I tried to swim as rapidly as I could to get from under the ship and finally came to the surface.

"I could see the ship drifting away from me when the lightning flashed. The bow was pointed up in the air and the whole structure was a general wreck. I saw two lights on what I thought was the stern and, looking to one side of them, I saw the lights of a ship. I also thought I could see the glare of Barnegat Lighthouse.

Clung to a Board in Sea.

"I swam toward the ship and after about ten minutes I found a board about three feet square, which I clung to the rest of the way. I saw some men in the water, but none very close that I thought I could help. When I was within fifty yards of a man I did not have my board. When I got about 400 yards off the ship the wind changed and the waves began hitting me in the face, instead of being behind me.

"The captain put his ship broadside into the sea and floated down toward me. I think he must have already heard the cries of men in the water. I swam easily to the steamer and they threw a lifebuoy to me and hauled me aboard. They had boats out and picked up three men with their boats, but I did not see the boats until I was aboard.

"As soon as I had recovered my strength a little—in about an hour —I sent a message giving the names of the people on board."

Commander Wiley praised his rescuer.

"The German captain was an excellent seaman and did everything he could to save life," he said.

"That's my story."

Commander Wiley was asked if the water was cold.

"Yes, sir," he replied emphatically, smiling.

Moffett Asleep During Evening.

"Where was Admiral Moffett at the time of the crash?" he was asked.

"Admiral Moffett was asleep until midnight and then he came down to the control cabin. For five minutes previous to the disaster I did not notice him in the cabin."

Last night in his broadcast account Commander Wiley amplified this:

"About thirty minutes after we left the coast—that is, about 12:30— Admiral Moffett came into the control car and spoke to me about the severity of the storm and compared it with one which we had encountered when he was on board a year ago January in Alabama."

Commander Wiley was asked how many officers were in the control car at the time of the crash.

"Lieutenant Redfield," he began. "No, he had just been relieved at 12 o'clock by Lieutenant Clendenning. Lieutenant Calnan appeared soon after I dropped ballast the first time and took his station at the ballast board. Two enlisted men were at the two control wheels. There may have been other officers out of my sight in the control car."

"There was no noise or confusion of any kind in the control car," he said in answer to another question. "All orders were given and carried out efficiently. There was no conversation after I said, 'Stand by for a crash.'"

Again an answer to a question Commander Wiley estimated that it was about three minutes from the time of the first drop of the Akron until he gave the "stand by" order.

Crash Came Quickly.

"From 'Stand by to crash' to the actual crash was only about thirty seconds," he added. He said that he did not believe many, if any, of the crew were in their bunks at the time of the accident; he believed they had had time to get to their landing stations after the first alarm.

"Did you see Captain McCord after the crash?"

"The water just swept me out of his window. I don't know what happened to him. I never saw him after the crash."

The engines functioned until the

last minute, he said, and all signals from the control car were answered until the crash.

He said he never saw the wreckage of his ship again after he was hauled aboard the Phoebus; even before that owing to the foggy weather and the steady rain the shattered ship had drifted out of his sight.

"The Phoebus searched from 12:30, the approximate time of the wreck, until after daylight," he said, "and did all she could."

Finally, closing the interview, Commander Wiley, though declining to give any opinion as to the cause of the disaster, reiterated that he did not believe the ship had been struck by lightning, although he conceded that it was possible that this might have happened without his knowledge.

"I think we'd have known it if we had been," he said, "but we might not have known it, because we're not afraid of it."

Gives General Observations.

In his radio address Commander Wiley prefaced his description by saying that "very reluctantly I consent to speak so soon after the loss of so many shipmates of long association, but because of the widespread interest in this disaster to our navy, I wish to give you a general report of my observations."

"The Akron flew about 425 hours the first three months of this year in all kinds of weather," he continued. "The start of yesterday's flight was routine, except that we had on board that distinguished naval officer, Admiral Moffett, our beloved Chief of the Bureau of Aeronautics of the Navy."

"Daylight was about 6 o'clock and about 7 o'clock the Coast Guard destroyer Tucker arrived. Shortly after, two Coast Guard cutters arrived and the navy cruiser Portland came into sight. I was transferred to the Tucker with the two enlisted men and the body of one man who died aboard the tanker, and arrived in New York about noon.

"In spite of this accident," Commander Wiley concluded, "I have every confidence in airships and hope that our people will still continue to see the value of them, both commercially and for naval uses, and that they will be allowed to continue as a part of our national progress."

The others brought on the Tucker with Commander Wiley were Richard Deal and Moody Erwin. Erwin, exhausted, was carried off in a stretcher and put in a waiting ambulance. Deal, with a blanket around his shoulder, leaned on the arm of a Coast Guardsman, and Commander Wiley came last. He was in borrowed trousers, too short for him, and a shrunken khaki flying blouse which had been dried over the destroyer's boilers. A pair of too-large shoes, unlaced, completed his attire.

"I'm feeling fine," he said to reporters as he climbed in the ambulance and went off with his men to the Brooklyn Naval Hospital, where he and the other two survivors will be kept for observation today.

Associated Press Photo.
The Navy Blimp J-3 Sinking in the Sea After Its Crash in Searching for Akron Survivors.

Times Wide World Photo.
Survivors being landed at Brooklyn Navy Yard. Boatswain's Mate R. E. Deal is being carried on a stretcher. At the right is M. E. Erwin of the crew (with the blanket), and at his right, in light coat, is Lieut. Commander Herbert V. Wiley.

Wide World Photos
Section of wreckage, girders and silk fabric, of the *USS Akron* being hauled from the ocean depths.

NRA U.S. WE DO OUR PART

"All the News That's Fit to Print."

The New York Times.

LATE CITY EDITION
WEATHER—Clearing today; tomorrow generally fair.
Temperatures yesterday—Max., 72; Min., 64.
Detailed Weather Report, Page 10, Sec. 3.

Section 1

Copyright, 1934, by The New York Times Company.

VOL. LXXXIII....No. 27,987. | Entered as Second-Class Matter. Postoffice, New York, N. Y. | NEW YORK, SUNDAY, SEPTEMBER 9, 1934. | Magazine and Book Sections, Including Rotogravure Picture, | F + | TEN CENTS | TWELVE CENTS Beyond 200 Miles. Except in 7th and 8th Postal Zones.

MORRO CASTLE BURNS OFF ASBURY PARK; 200 TO 250 ARE LISTED AS DEAD OR MISSING

GORMAN PROPOSES STRIKE ARBITRATION IF ALL MILLS CLOSE

Union Leader Would 'Avoid Murders' While President's Board Settles Issue.

BUT WIDENS WALKOUT

Calls Out 50,000 More Workers as Employers Plan Mill Openings Tomorrow.

HOSIERY STRIKE ORDERED

Labor Chiefs Direct 85,000 to Quit Wednesday—Green Confers on Textile Peace Plan.

By LOUIS STARK.

Special to THE NEW YORK TIMES.

WASHINGTON, Sept. 8.—Francis J. Gorman, chairman of the textile strike committee, proposed tonight that President Roosevelt's textile board arbitrate the issue in the textile strike which began Sept. 1.

In a radio broadcast over the Columbia System, Mr. Gorman suggested that arbitration begin on Monday, that both sides agree to accept the findings of the textile board and that pending arbitration the mills be closed "so that further murder of our fellow workers may be avoided."

An additional 50,000 textile workers in miscellaneous lines will be called out on Monday, said Mr. Gorman. These operatives are in the plants making upholstery and drapery, carpets and rugs, pile fabric, plush and velvets. The strike extension is made in face of the reported plan of employers to open next week mills closed by the general textile walkout.

While Mr. Gorman was still speaking over the radio, the National Executive Board of the American Federation of Hosiery Workers at an emergency session issued an order calling a strike at midnight Wednesday in all hosiery mills where no contractual relations exist between employers and employes. The order covered both seamless and full-fashioned sections of the industry and applied to about 85,000 workers in twelve States, union spokesmen said.

Strike Threat in Dye Industry.

Mr. Gorman announced that unless employers in the dye industry met demands of the union employes in that industry would be called out some time next week.

Governor J. G. Winant, chairman of the textile board, declined tonight to comment on Mr. Gorman's arbitration proposal. He would not say whether the board would take the initiative and seek the view of the employers on the arbitration request or await instead the unsolicited action of the manufacturers.

Under the President's executive order the Winant Board is authorized "upon the request of the parties to a labor dispute, [to] act as a board of voluntary arbitration or select a person or agency for voluntary arbitration."

The textile board's next appointment with George A. Sloan, president of the Cotton Textile Institute, is scheduled for Tuesday.

Green Discusses Arbitration.

Arbitration as a way out was also discussed before the board this afternoon by William Green, president of the American Federation of Labor. On leaving the board's offices Mr. Green said that he had brought up the subject of arbitration as a possible way to end the controversy peaceably, but that no concrete or definite line of procedure had been outlined.

No comment was obtainable here as to the view of the manufacturers on the union arbitration proposal.

In making his announcement Mr. Gorman stressed the need for a peaceful atmosphere before the controversial issues could be settled. He declared that the employers have stated that they would open the mills on Monday, asserted that "they have hired guards, and in some places misled members of the American Legion are reported to be working with these private armies of so-called guards."

In a telegram to Edward A. Hayes, commander of the American Legion, Indianapolis Mr. Gorman said that Mr. Sloan had announced the closed mills would resume operation on Monday. He declared that "great bands of strike-breakers have been deputized and armed and American Le-

Continued on Page Two.

Sailor Missing 12 Years 'Found' on Morro Castle

By The Associated Press.

ST. LOUIS, Sept. 8.—A St. Louisan, given up for dead by his family more than a decade ago, came back into the world for them today as a result of the Morro Castle disaster.

A crew member of the stricken vessel, carried on the roster as Roger Klinger, was identified by his brother today as Gustav Lehmann, who left his home here twelve years ago.

The brother, Edward H. Lehmann, said his missing relative had assumed "Klinger," the name of another branch of the family, to avoid rejection by navigation companies. He was turned down as Gustav Lehmann for failure to pass a physical examination the brother said.

"The last time we saw Gustav," Edward said, "was twelve years ago. He went to Detroit after that and that was the last city from which we ever received a letter from him."

5 LOST IN STORM WHEN BOATS UPSET

3 Missing, 5 Washed Ashore Off Jersey—Two on Tug Drowned in Bay.

4.8 INCHES OF RAIN HERE

Floods Disrupt Land Travel—Ships Torn From Moorings by Wind in Hudson.

A wind and rainstorm lashed the New Jersey and Long Island coasts last night, disrupting land and water transportation and capsizing two boats, causing a loss of five lives.

Two seamen were drowned and three others rescued after they had been in the water two hours when a tugboat of the Tracy Towing Company overturned in New York Bay off the foot of Sixty-fifth Street, Brooklyn. The tug, the William Tracy, was steaming from Brooklyn to New Jersey when she overturned without warning in a sudden gust of wind and plunged the five men into the water.

The drowned were Robert Whittaker, fireman, and Benjamin Elder, deckhand, both of Brooklyn. Those rescued, all of Brooklyn, were Captain William McNally, John Duffy and David Davidson. They were landed in Jersey City and taken to the Jersey City Medical Centre, where they were reported to be in serious condition.

The thirty-five-foot schooner Neshaminy, with a party of eight men aboard, was capsized two and one-half miles off Brigantine Beach, N. J. Five of the men succeeded, with the aid of life-preservers, in reaching shore. Coast Guardsmen searched for the three others without success.

Boat Is Washed Ashore.

The missing men are Captain Robert McCleary, 35, Harry Clayton, 45, and Edward Clayton, 30, his brother, all of Philadelphia. Coast Guard boats put out to search for them after the five survivors had been washed ashore. At 8:30 P. M. the Neshaminy, the boat in which the party of eight had been fishing, was washed up at Brigantine.

Those rescued are James Sharp, 35, of Langhorne, Pa.; George Oldham, 30, of Newportville, Pa., and Earl Widdop, 35, Claude Pieminck, 32, and Charles Wensel, 28, of Philadelphia. Wensel and Oldham were in a serious condition at Atlantic City Hospital.

They said that, although their boat was seaworthy and in good condition, it was no match for the gale that blew out of the northeast. Sharp, Harry Clayton and Oldham were in the pilot house when a big wave came along and turned the craft over. They had to break through glass windows to get free.

Craft Break Loose in Hudson.

Shipping in the Hudson River had a bad time at the height of the storm. The U. S. S. Oklahoma, anchored in midstream off Seventy-ninth Street, was forced to pull her hook and manoeuvre about to escape being hit by a lighter with a derrick aboard, which had broken moorings on the Jersey side.

From the Oklahoma signals telling what was going on were flashed to the shore patrol, in command of Ensign Albert G. Pelling. He notified the Police Department, and marine division boats, as well as

Continued on Page Thirty-five.

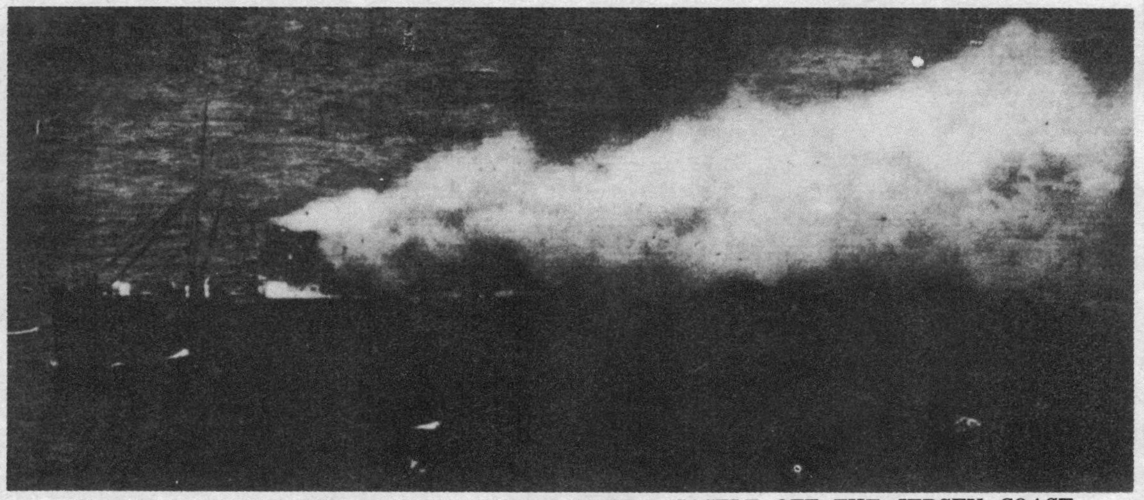

AN AIR VIEW OF THE BURNING LINER MORRO CASTLE OFF THE JERSEY COAST.

Rescue Liners Pick Up 157; Craft Near By Speed to SOS

Four Large Vessels Put Out Lifeboats to Circle Water With Coast Guard—Many of the Saved Are Injured.

From north, east and south passenger and freight ships altered their courses yesterday to go at full speed to the fire-illumined point off Shark River Inlet, above Sea Girt, N. J., where the Ward liner Morro Castle with 318 passengers and a crew of 244 was burning.

Off Ambrose Light the Monarch of Bermuda and the City of Savannah turned around and sped southward through the dark about twenty miles to the distressed ship. From the east, seven miles, came the freighter Andrea S. Luckenbach. From the south, further away than the others, the President Cleveland sped through the night.

The S O S from the Morro Castle was received by the Monarch and the Savannah line vessel at about the same time, 4:30 A. M. daylight time. The Luckenbach ship had been attracted by the sight of the flames and radio confirmation that the Morro Castle needed help came from a land station.

Rescues Began in the Dark.

The sea was turning the color of gun metal in a murky dawn when the Monarch and the Savannah arrived to find that the Luckenbach was already on the scene, as well as several Coast Guard craft.

They came upon a scene of confusion and horror. The liner was blazing from B deck upward. On the surface of the water were passengers and members of the crew who had jumped.

The water was being combed by the Coast Guard craft and two lifeboats from the Luckenbach. Four of the lifeboats from the Morro Castle had been successfully lowered, six on the port side having been made inaccessible by the flames.

The rescuing ships stood by until they could no longer be of service, and then steamed for New York, carrying in all, 157 survivors including at least forty members of the Morro Castle's crew, and one woman who was dead when taken from the water.

The work of rescue began at about 6 A. M., daylight saving time, when the Morro Castle had been burning at least two hours. By 10 o'clock there were apparently no more living persons to be taken from the water.

The Monarch of Bermuda had gathered seventy-one survivors and the body. The City of Savannah—both of these ships pushed to within 100 feet of the flaming liner—had sixty-five and the Luckenbach twenty-one. The President Cleveland, from a point about half a mile away, lowered two boats, but these returned without having lifted any person from the water.

Captain A. R. Francis of the Monarch stood by for two and half hours in a choppy, wind-beaten sea while four power-driven lifeboats he had lowered circled the immediate waters. In this way those aboard listed to safety persons, old and young, exhausted, hysterical and unconscious.

At times his ship swept within sixty feet of the burning ship, and then, learning that he had nineteen persons aboard with injuries, twelve of them in a critical condition, Captain Francis headed for New York so the injured could receive adequate hospital attention as quickly as possible.

Leaves Burning Ship at Anchor.

He left the Morro Castle anchored with her bow to the wind, the flames being thus swept to stern.

A few valiant seamen, 14 to 20, of them, on the fire-free forecastle determined not to leave their ship.

Captain Francis said his ship was off Ambrose Light when, at 5:30 A. M., daylight saving time, he received an S.O.S. from the Morro Castle. He turned his ship about and made all speed (20 knots) toward the spot off Sea Girt, N. J., about twenty miles away, where the Morro Castle reported she had anchored.

It was not yet daylight, the weather was squally with a heavy sea, as the Monarch headed south. The Andrea S. Luckenbach, freighter, of the Luckenbach lines, was at least a half-hour nearer the Morro Castle than was the Monarch.

"I messaged the Luckenbach," Captain Francis said, "and the message came back that she could be there in a half-hour. I needed an hour. I messaged again—'Do you want assistance?' and the word came back, 'Yes.'

"We reached the Morro Castle at about 7:30 A. M. It was turning daylight. From four or five miles away we could see the great red glare of light on the gray sea. We came within 100 yards of the Morro Castle and lowered four boats. One, under the command of Staff Captain Leslie Banyard, picked up thirty-one persons. We took them mainly out of the water and off the poop deck."

Acts of Heroism Related.

Passengers on the Monarch of Bermuda, disturbed by the bustle, were awake and about. They could feel the heat of the burning ship, see the flames climbing from A and B decks upward, shooting fifty to sixty feet in the air.

Passengers and members of the crew dotted the water or hung over the sides on ropes afraid to let go. Some still were jumping from B and C decks. One passenger saw a stewardess with a child on her back jump into the water and swim toward one of the rescue boats. Captain Francis, who stayed on his bridge, saw a seaman, with 4-year-old Robert Lione of Long Island City, enact a similar scene of heroism. The boy was lifted into one of the Monarch's boats.

On the waters around the flaming ship by that time were boats from the Luckenbach, the City of Savannah, Coast Guard boats, from the Jersey shore and from Staten Island. Two boats put out from the President Cleveland of the Dollar Line anchored half a mile away.

Aboard the Monarch two primary concerns were manifest. One was to get as adequate as possible medical attention for the injured, most of whom were suffering from surgical shock, smoke-injured eyes, and exhaustion, and the other was to

Continued on Page Twenty-eight.

List of Victims in Sea Disaster and Survivors

Passengers and members of the crew reported accounted for, injured or missing, together with a list of the identified dead in the burning of the Ward liner Morro Castle, on the basis of the latest available information, were as follows:

SURVIVORS.

Passengers.

ADAMS, JANE, Point Pleasant, N. J.; injured, shock and submersion.
AGUIAR, VAL, Las Vegas, Venezuela.
ARNETH, PAUL, Brooklyn.
ASCHOFF, THORP H., 150-15 Stoneford Avenue, Flushing, Queens.
ATICELLO, MARCO, Brooklyn.
ASCHOFF, Mrs. T. H., same address.
BARSTEAD, LLOYD C., 1,891 Harrison Avenue, Bronx.
BARSTEAD, Mrs., same address.
BECK, Miss EMILY C., Philadelphia.
BEACH, AGNES, 205 East Seventy-eighth Street.
BEHR, Miss C.
BEHR, Miss E.
BERGENSTEIN, Miss DOROTHY.
BIREN, ROSE, Philadelphia.
BLANCO, BOB, Havana.
BLONDEAU, Mr. JULES, Philadelphia; shock and submersion.
BLONDEAU, Mrs. JULES, Philadelphia; shock and submersion.
BODNER, S., 85 Summit Road, Elizabeth, N. J.
BODNER, Mrs. S., same address.
BORMAN, H., 352 Roosevelt Avenue, Freeport, L. I.
BRADY, Mrs. E. J., Overbrook, Pa.
BRADBURY, Miss MARTHA, Pennsylvania.
BREGSTEIN, Dr. J. JOSEPH, 7,825 Fourth Avenue, Brooklyn.
BREGSTEIN, MERVIN G., same address.
BRINKMAN, HARRY, Brooklyn.
BRINKMAN, Mrs.
BRODIE, Miss H.
BROWN, Miss FLORENCE.
BROWN, Miss IDA, Philadelphia.
BUDLONG, Miss MARJORIE, Hillside, N. J.
BUQUETS, OFELIA
BUQUETS, Mrs.
BUQUETS, FRANCOIS
BURRELL, Dr. J. H., Buffalo.
BURRELL, Mrs. J. H.
BUTE, JAMES, Brooklyn.
BYRNE, W. E., 330 West Ninety-fifth Street; burns.
CALEYA, JUAN, Cuba.
CANNAVAN, Miss K., 20 Butler Place, Brooklyn.
CANNON, THOMAS.
CARPENTER, Miss MADGE, 41-08 171st Street, Flushing, Queens.
CASEY, CAROLINE, Philadelphia.
CHRESLER, Miss L., Brooklyn.
CLARKE, WILLIAM F., 156-14 Channel Street, Howard Beach, L. I.; injured.
COCHRANE, Dr. CHARLES, Brooklyn.
COCHRANE, Miss C. M.
COHEN, A., Hartford, Conn.
COHEN, Mrs. A., Hartford, Conn.
COHN, Miss GERTRUDE.
COLL, Mrs. J. P.
CONROY, Miss ANNE.
CONWAY, Miss ANNE, Brooklyn.
COTTER, Miss M. V.
CULLEN, Miss UNA
DAVIS, Mrs. MINNIE, 200 Pine Street, Brooklyn, burns on both legs.
DAVIDSON, Miss LILLIAN, 33 Athens Street, Clifton, N. J.
DAVIDSON, SIDNEY.
DAVIDSON, Mrs. SIDNEY.
DESVERNINE, MADELINE.

Continued on Page Twenty-six.

Survivors Tell of Leaping Into Sea to Escape Flames

Many Sang and Prayed on Decks—Reluctant Women Pushed Overboard or Into Boats—Ship's Plates Red Hot.

Survivors of the Morro Castle, telling of their experiences on the fire-swept liner yesterday, painted in broad strokes a story of heroism and of panic.

Some of them told of jumping from the flame-swept decks of the Morro Castle and swimming for six or seven hours before coming ashore or being picked up off the Jersey coast. Others, brought to New York on the rescue vessels, told of being picked up from the water.

Many told of being forced to jump into the sea many feet below from the crowded decks when the approaching flames left them no other course. Members of the crew described a gallant attempt to subdue the fire—a fight doomed from the start because of low water pressure.

Others told of how frightened passengers crowded aft in the vessel and were cut off from the bulk of the crew by the flames which were sweeping the midsection. They told of women weeping and praying, and of men and more courageous women banding together and singing such songs as "Hail, Hail, the Gang's All Here" in an attempt to bolster the courage of the rest.

Chief Officer Takes Charge.

The outstanding hero to the crew was W. F. Warms, the chief officer who became the acting captain of the Morro Castle. They told of his standing on the liner's bridge as it was aflame, shouting orders to his men, thinking only of saving his passengers and crew. All the passengers told of the few members of the crew who apepared among them. The crew members explained that this was due to the fact that they were cut off from the aft section of the vessel by the flames amidship.

A small group of seamen and stewards, however, aided greatly in adjusting life belts for passengers and forcing them to jump into the sea, where they stood at least some chance for their lives.

Rescued stewards laid part of the death toll to the modesty of women passengers who waited in their cabins to dress—waited too long—and found themselves cut off by the flames.

The rough weather, too, was blamed by some of the crew for the heavy loss of life. At least a third of the passengers were seasick at the time the fire began, they said. Many of these, survivors believed, were likewise trapped in their cabins.

The virtual cutting in two of the ship by the fire made it impossible to lower many of the lifeboats. All those on the port side were burned. There were ample life belts, however.

The survivors told their stories in hospitals and impromptu shelters along the Jersey coast, where they were housed after they were brought ashore. Others described their experiences when they arrived in New York on the rescue ships.

At least five couples jumped from the rails together to swim to shore and safety. Two of them made their way to the Jersey coast. Another couple were picked up by rescue boats. In two other instances, however, the wives were saved after they had seen their husbands drown.

At least a score of these safe in New Jersey told of swimming ashore, or nearly ashore, from the burning liner. Some, including several women, were in the water for as long as seven hours. Several were picked up by Coast Guard boats less than 100 yards from the beach at Sea Girt.

The outstanding swimming feat was that of Antonio Mato, 20, a Cuban mess boy. He swam from ship to shore without a life belt and was rescued from the surf off Sea Girt just as he collapsed. However, several of the passengers, aided by life belts, made their way through the ocean from the burning ship to the Jersey coast.

When the rescue ships arrived here late yesterday afternoon the piers were thronged with anxious relatives and friends. There were joyous, sometimes tearful, reunions.

A few of the passengers and most of the members of the crew who had landed in Jersey were brought to the city during the afternoon by train, the passengers going to the Hotel New Yorker and the crew to the Seamen's Church Institute or to their homes.

Doctor Awakened by Smoke.

Dr. Charles Cochrane of Brooklyn, one of the passengers, told a vivid story of his experience after he had been brought ashore at Long Branch, N. J.

Dr. Cochrane is a well-known Brooklyn surgeon. He is a fellow of the American College of Surgeons and of the American Medical Association. He is chief of the urological staff of Kings County Hospital and is a consulting surgeon at the Carson C. Peck Memorial Hospital.

"I was awakened from a sound sleep, at just what time I don't know, by clouds of suffocating smoke filling my cabin," said Dr. Cochrane. At almost the same time some one banged and hammered at my cabin door and shouted something unintelligible.

"Confused by my sudden awakening, and choking and unable to see because of the dense smoke in the cabin, I tried vainly to find the door. Just in time my groping hands came in contact with a port hole. I crawled through it and dropped to the deck outside.

"There was no apparent panic. The crew was making frantic efforts to launch the boats. All the time the flames were creeping nearer.

"Suddenly some one gave me a violent push and I half fell and half staggered into the lifeboat. There was trouble in launching it and it seemed almost a half hour before we were in the water and pulling away from the Morro Castle. The front of the ship was a pillar of flame by this time.

"A strong gale was whipping up

Continued on Page Twenty-seven.

MANY BURNED IN CABINS

Flames Cut Off Escape of Tourists Returning From Cruise to Cuba.

STORM HAMPERS RESCUERS

Darkness and Pounding Seas Add to Death Toll—Captain Had Died Shortly Before.

SWEEPING INQUIRIES SET

Speed of Conflagration and Cause a Mystery—Crew Is Praised and Scored.

A page of photographs of the Morro Castle disaster, Page 24.

By RUSSELL B. PORTER.

In one of the worst marine disasters on record, the liner Morro Castle was swept by fire of unknown origin early yesterday morning off the New Jersey coast, with heavy loss of life.

The scene of the tragedy was not far from where the dirigible Akron was wrecked during a storm off Barnegat Lighthouse last year.

By a strange coincidence, Captain Robert Willmott, master of the Morro Castle, died of a heart attack following acute indigestion about 8:45 o'clock Friday night, nearly eight hours before the SOS went out at 4:23 A. M., New York daylight time. When the fire started, the liner was under the command of Chief Officer William F. Warms, who remained aboard the burning ship until taken off by a Coast Guard cutter late yesterday afternoon.

The exact number of dead and missing was not finally determined last night, but it was believed to be between 200 and 250.

Reports to the offices of the Ward Line, operators of the Morro Castle, were that 161 passengers and 147 of the crew, or a total of 308 persons, were known to have been saved. According to the line, the ship had carried a total of 562 persons, including 318 passengers and a crew of 244. This would indicate a death list of 254, but it was emphasized that other survivors may not yet have been reported.

Later information indicated that the survivors numbered at least 325, for, in addition to the 268 survivors here or bound here, there were thirty-six in the Fitkins Memorial Hospital at Asbury Park and twenty-one in the Point Pleasant (N. J.) Hospital last night. This would cut the possible dead to 237.

171 Bodies Are Recovered.

The New Jersey National Guard, which was assembling at Camp Moore, Sea Girt, all the bodies washed ashore at fifteen or more coast communities, estimated that reports from these places indicated that a total of 171 bodies had been recovered.

At midnight last night fifty-eight bodies of unidentified dead had been taken to Camp Moore from various New Jersey communities. Thirty-three were men, twenty-two women and three children. Other bodies were to be taken there during the night.

Confusion existed over the number of survivors and dead partly because of the many places to which survivors and bodies were taken at first and partly because the steamship line did not have an accurate list of the crew. The figure finally announced for the crew may be revised.

Two hundred and fifty-four survivors were brought to New York and Jersey City during the afternoon and night. These included seventy-one persons rescued by the Monarch of Bermuda, sixty-five by the City of Savannah, twenty-one by the Andrea S. Luckenbach and ninety-seven brought here by train from Jersey coast points where they had gone ashore. Fourteen more were on their way here aboard a Coast Guard vessel.

Of the 268 here or on their way here last night, 140 were members of the crew and 128 were passengers.

Nine bodies were brought to New York, and were taken to the Morgue at Bellevue Hospital. Five were men and four were women.

Continued on Page Twenty-five.

Throngs at Piers Wait Anxiously for Arrival of Rescue Ships With Survivors

CROWDS AT PIERS AWAIT RELATIVES

Many Search in Vain as First Survivors Are Landed by Two Rescue Ships.

SOME JOYFUL REUNIONS

Others Cling to Slender Hope When Those They Seek Are Not Among the Saved.

At three of the city's piers yesterday, relatives and friends of those aboard the Morro Castle underwent the agony of waiting for news that was long in coming. In many instances, when it did come it only substituted sorrow for uncertainty.

At the Ward Line pier on the East River at the foot of Wall Street, about 200 persons spent virtually the entire day. That was the pier from which the Morro Castle sailed and to which it was to have returned. Those who waited despondently witnessed a gay sailing party. The Iroquois put out on a cruise as a substitute ship pressed into service at the last minute to fill the Morro Castle's schedule.

There was a wedding party aboard the Iroquois. Mr. and Mrs. R. Suriano of 7,403 Seventeenth Avenue, Brooklyn, were showered with rice as they went up the gangplank. Wedding guests called spirited farewells to them. The departure of the Surianos gave those who awaited news of the Morro Castle something to watch.

Other groups took up their vigil at the pier at the foot of Thirty-third Street in Brooklyn, where the Andrea F. Luckenbach, one of the rescue ships, brought in twenty-two survivors, and at the City of Savannah's dock, at the foot of Tenth Street, North River. The Savannah brought in sixty-five survivors.

There were brief happy reunions as the two vessels docked, but officials quickly took charge and speeded the rescued men and women to hospitals.

At both the piers used by the rescue ships, lists of those reported to be aboard were given out long before the vessels arrived. But these lists were hurriedly made; they contained numerous errors, and those who waited could not be certain until they saw their relatives with their own eyes.

Awaited Ones Do Not Arrive.

Before noon the Luckenbach offices received from the master of their ship a message saying: "Arrive 11:30. Have ambulance. Twenty-two survivors from Morro Castle."

When the freighter docked, sixteen ambulances, from Coney Island, Norwegian and Kings County Hospitals, from the Department of Hospitals and the Holmes Ambulance Service, were on hand. All of them were used to speed the removal of the survivors.

William and Margaret Sigmund of Bardonia, N. Y., were on hand early, hoping that their mother, Mrs. Clara Sigmund, would be aboard. They did not find her, and they started out to search elsewhere.

E. O. Eriksen of 41-12 171st Street, Flushing, Queens, looked for his niece, Miss Jennie Eriksen, and their neighbor, Miss Madge Carpenter of 41-08 Seventy-first Street. He too, was unsuccessful, but he refused to lose hope and continued his search.

Before the Luckenbach came in, those who hoped their relatives would be aboard huddled together in a corner of the big pier, trying to keep one another's courage up. Occasionally some one would detach himself from the group and go outside in the rain to ease his nerves with a cigarette. Smoking is forbidden on the piers.

Some Have Joyful Reunions.

One of the most pathetic cases concerned the Jacobys. Henry Jacoby of 61 Ridgewood Avenue, Brooklyn, and his son, Henry Jr., were on hand, hoping they might greet Mrs. Josephine Jacoby, wife and mother. They had received a message that a woman named Jacoby was aboard. But the woman turned out to be Miss Ella Jacoby, who was employed on the Morro Castle.

James G. Featherstone of 59 Pineapple Street, Brooklyn, was overcome with joy when he saw, before the arrival of the Luckenbach, that his sister, Mrs. James Sheridan, was among those aboard.

"She went on a pleasure cruise," he said, "and see how it ended!"

Mrs. Sheridan's son, Arthur, was with her on the cruise, but Mr. Featherstone had no information as to what had happened to the boy.

When the rescue ship came in the police took immediate charge. Stretchers were hurried aboard. They were necessary for about fifteen of the survivors, who were heavily bundled in blankets, only their faces showing as they were carried down the gangplank to the waiting ambulances.

As each survivor appeared the police called out a name for the benefit of those who were waiting. Occasionally some one exclaimed "Thank God!" and rushed forward. But no lengthy reunions were allowed; there was too much work to be done.

Mother Finds Son, 17, Safe.

Some of those who waited for news at the Ward Line offices had gone there with no knowledge that the Morro Castle had met with disaster. One of these was Mrs. Jean Tripp of Dorcester, Mass., mother of William Tripp, 17 years old, a student at Massachusetts Institute of Technology. None of the rescue ships came in at the Ward pier, but as soon as young Tripp reached shore he hurried here, for he knew his mother would be waiting. Happily, she took him in her arms.

Many of those who were rescued made for the Ward Line offices for the same reason that impelled young Tripp. Some of them still were clad in the clothing that was furnished by their rescuers. Pajamas peeped out from under women's coats and girls were clad in sailors' dungarees.

Herbert and Arthur Davis, brothers, of 200 Pine Street, Brooklyn, arrived at the Ward Line offices shortly after officials had given out a partial list of those rescued. On the list they saw the name of Mrs. Minnie Davis.

"Mother! Mother!" said Herbert. He walked away weeping.

There was a particularly happy reunion among Roger V. Toole of 276 Lefferts Avenue, Brooklyn, his brother Dan, an assistant purser on the liner Orizaba, and their grandfather, who is superintendent of police at the Ward pier.

Roger was aboard the Morro Castle. Within a few days Dan Toole is to be married, and Roger had promised to be his best man. The wedding will go on as scheduled.

When the Iroquois sailed on her cruise, officials of the line announced that about fifty of the 300 reservations had been canceled as a result of the Morro Castle disaster. They thought, in the circumstances, that the number was not surprisingly large.

Elderly Couples Are Saved.

About fifty persons congregated at Pier 46, North River, to await the arrival of the City of Savannah. Among those who came down the gangplank when the ship docked were several elderly couples. They appeared dazed by the experience they had been through, but they pluckily came back to land on their own legs.

The police protected the survivors from every one except relatives and friends. Most of them were placed immediately into ambulances from the Marine, Gouverneur, St. Vincent's, Broad Street and Beekman Hospitals.

The rescued passengers wore all sorts of fantastic clothing. Members of the crew of the City of Savannah said some of them had been nude, aside from their lifebelts, when they were picked up. As they came ashore they were wrapped in blankets and attired in sailor garb. Only about six in this group of survivors needed stretchers to get to the ambulances. Eyes were swollen and faces still were white and drawn.

G. M. Phelps Jr. of 155 East Seventy-ninth Street and Nathan Feinberg of 12 West Seventy-second Street were among those on the Savannah. Mr. Phelps said he understood his father was missing.

Consul's Wife Cancels Concert.

Because of grief over the death of a number of her countrymen in the Morro Castle catastrophe, Señora Natalia Arostegui de Suarez, wife of the Cuban Consul General, canceled an engagement to sing yesterday afternoon at the Brooklyn Museum. She was to have repeated a program she gave Wednesday, when she made her American début as a soprano soloist with the New York Civic orchestra at the American Museum of Natural History.

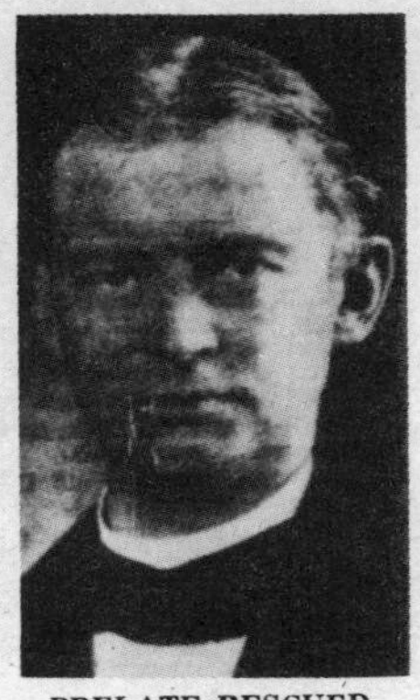

PRELATE RESCUED.
The Right Rev. Hiram R. Hulse, Bishop of Cuba.

BISHOP AND HIS WIFE, LOST IN SEA, REUNITED

Separated in Escape From Morro Castle, They Meet Again on Board Rescue Ship.

A dramatic escape from the burning Morro Castle and the reunion on the rescue ship Monarch of Bermuda of a couple lost at sea were disclosed yesterday on the arrival of the Right Rev. Hiram R. Hulse, Episcopal Missionary Bishop of Cuba, and Mrs. Hulse at Pier 95. They were taken to St. Luke's Hospital, too ill to recount their experiences in detail, but were expected to recover in a few days from exposure and submersion.

After the warning that the ship was on fire had been sounded, the Bishop became separated from his wife when they were called on deck to leave the ship in lifeboats. Unable to find her husband and with flames spurting out behind her, Mrs. Hulse grasped a rope that had been tied to the deck of the ship and slipped over the side.

Clutching the rope that left her dangling over the side of the ship, she slid toward the water. Before she reached it, however, she lost her hold of the rope and fell into the sea unconscious.

Mrs. Hulse said she had no further recollection until she regained consciousness several hours later on the Monarch of Bermuda. Unaware of the fate of her husband, she sent a radio to her daughters, the Misses Emma A. and Frances Hulse at 501 West 111th Street, New York, informing them of her safety.

A check-up of survivors on the rescue ship showed that the Bishop also had been rescued, but he, too, was unable to recall the details. Both apparently had been picked up from the sea by members of the crew of the Monarch of Bermuda and taken on board in rescue lifeboats.

Upon learning that the Bishop and his wife were on the rescue ship, D. W. MacCormack, banker and publicist of 439 East Fifty-first Street, arranged for an ambulance from St. Luke's Hospital to meet them. Bishop Hulse was coming from Cuba to attend the triennial general convention of the Episcopal Church in Atlantic City next month.

TRAGEDY WATCHED BY SHORE THRONGS

Helpless Straining of Eyes Through Storm Gives Way to Eager Aiding of Rescued.

RAIN VEILS EARLY FLAMES

Only With Daylight Do Jersey Crowds Get Inkling of Extent of Ship Disaster.

Spreading flame that stained the black sky and the rain-lashed sea eight miles off Belmar, N. J., at 4 o'clock yesterday morning caught the sharp eyes of Coast Guard beach patrols and lookouts in beach watchtowers and gave the first signal of the Morro Castle disaster along the Jersey Coast.

As the flame burned higher and higher—shut out altogether at times by fierce rain squalls—the Coast Guardsmen in dripping oil skins, fishermen and owners of pleasure craft assembled along the New Jersey shore or prepared to take to the heavy, pounding sea. Women joined them to offer what little aid they could.

The boardwalks at the various beach resorts became crowded as visitors jammed the rails, straining their eyes through the rain and the mist for a glimpse of the burning liner. In many cases, however, it was hours before the watchers knew what ship was burning and had an inkling of the extent of the disaster.

Tragedy Veiled by Rain.

Dawn broke gray and muddy and obscured by the squalls. The Morro Castle stood about six miles off shore, a dark hulk with great clouds of white smoke belching upward from her. The veil of rain prevented shore watchers from seeing the men and women leaping into the sea, the launching of the lifeboats.

As day broke Coast Guard boats, pitched and tossed by whitecaps, made tortuous progress toward the burning ship. They swarmed up from Cape May, Shark River, Beach Haven, from Barnegat, Sandy Hook, Spermacetti Cove, Monmouth Beach and out of Spring Lake, Manasquan, Deal and Long Branch.

Few of the Coast Guard "pullboats"—dories manned by four oarsmen—were able to get through the crashing and towering surf that rolled in on the beaches, but the men who had the advantage of the comparative calm in Manasquan Inlet got through.

See Rescue Ships Arrive.

In the meantime patrol boats and picket boats were ploughing through a smother of spray and staggering walls of dirty green water toward the stricken Morro Castle, and large craft—the Monarch of Bermuda and the City of Savannah—were looming vast and gray out of the morning mist toward the same objective.

The drenched watchers at last made out the shapes of some of the Morro Castle's lifeboats, tossing and riding crazily on plunging waves. Manoeuvring toward them were two Coast Guard boats out of Shark River and two other craft from Manasquan station. The regular off-shore patrols were edging in.

It was about 6 o'clock when the first of the burning liner's lifeboats neared the beach at Spring Lake. Hundreds of men and women lining the shore—many wringing their hands in sheer nervousness and excitement—watched the perilous approach. Now they saw the boat—now they did not. Great combers had the lifeboat, then tossed it back into view.

It was Lifeboat 10 from the Morro Castle. It carried seven of the crew and three women passengers. As it drew closer, bucking a nasty squall, the shore crowds saw that it had a small sail. This was hauled down as the beach came in sight.

Lifeboat Reaches Pier.

The stalwarts at the oars manoeuvred the lifeboat expertly alongside the South Side Recreation Pier and eager hands reached down to help the occupants onto firm planking. The metal plates of the lifeboat, it developed on close inspection, were dented and the combings were ripped and battered, as if the craft had brushed the hull of the Morro Castle in getting away.

Sheer exhaustion was written in the faces of the survivors. Their bodies sagged and their hair and clothing were plastered down by the beating rain. Blankets were thrown around their shoulders and they were hurried to the first aid headquarters, to the police station and to the fire house, where bubbling hot coffee, prepared by the women volunteers, was ready for them. They gulped it down eagerly.

After the coffee the stories of the fire and the escapes from the ship began to unfold.

One by one, the other lifeboats from the Morro Castle came pitching shoreward under the fierce southward drive of the tide and the wind. Most of them were all but empty save for the crews at the oars. Lifeboats 5, 3 and 9 arrived and about ninety members of the crew and about ten or twelve passengers were ashore. As fast as the boats shot them in to shore the survivors were lifted out, rushed to the relief stations, rubbed, shaken, supplied with scalding black coffee or whisky, and given a chance to get their breath. Most of them seemed in fairly good shape, except for exhaustion.

Ambulances Race to Shore.

By this time the nurses, doctors and volunteer stretcher bearers had been organized. Twenty ambulances from coast towns and villages and from inland communties within a radius of fifty to sixty miles were carrying the injured to the hospitals. Captain C. W. Brahn of Spring Lake directed the work. Dr. Louis F. Albright was in charge of the medical force.

Mounds of dry clothing, boots, shoes and other articles of dress appeared as if by miracle and were distributed to the survivors. Many of the men were led to army cots or to stretchers laid out on the floors. They gasped for air or quivered as tense muscles let down.

These scenes were being duplicated all along the Jersey shore, at Point Pleasant, at Brielle, at a dozen other places. As the daylight grew stronger, the thousands on the rocks and on the beaches could make out in the water the figures of men and women who had flung themselves from the decks of the Morro Castle. They fought their way toward shore. Some had life jackets, some did not. Here and there the dead tossed on the hissing combers.

The Diana of the Manasquan fishing fleet brought in the body of a girl that was found drifting shoreward. The body was nude. She had probably cast off what clothing she wore in her effort to swim to safety. Mr. and Mrs. Abraham Cohen of Hartford, Conn., swam the distance from the Morro Castle to Sea Girt, with one life preserver between them, then collapsed and were rushed to the hospital.

Legion Delegates Help.

Summer residents in shore cottages picked up many exhausted swimmers and many of the dead. Along the boardwalks and along the sands the crowds kept shifting to a new point every time a boat, a swimmer or a body was sighted. The ambulances caught up the patients as fast as they could and went whirling down the main roads toward the hospitals.

Members of the American Legion who were in convention at Belmar delegated fifty of their men to act as traffic officers to clear the roads for the ambulances and to help the State Troopers guide the frantic relatives of Morro Castle passengers who had begun to stream into the shore resort area by motor car from New York City and vicinity. Other Legionaires acted as stretcher bearers.

A lifeboat that had put off from the City of Savannah in the pounding sea was unable to get back to its ship. It rode into Manasquan Inlet and a safe haven. It was commanded by John Babbinger and R. C. Davis of the Savannah and had on board several members of the crew of the Morro Castle.

Meanwhile, pleasure boats and Coast Guard rescue craft were throwing lines to oared rescue units and were towing them in under motor power.

Through into the night thousands patrolled the sands and rocky points along the New Jersey shore watching for bodies and for any possible survivors who might still be fighting shoreward. At many points beach fires were lighted and searchers paraded in the rain hoping their beacons might lead any swimmers to safety.

Morgue Set Up at Camp.

The old canteen and mess hall at Camp Moore, Sea Girt, was converted into a temporary morgue for the unidentified dead. Bodies were taken from private morgues along the coast and brought in ambulances and trucks manned by nurses to the wooden army building. The procedure was primarily to facilitate identification.

By late last night the vehicles had brought the bodies of eighteen women, thirteen men and two children. Friends and relatives gathered. The first identification was that of Charles Bader, 22 Oakmere Drive, Baldwin, L. I. It was made by Theodore C. Wenzl, 175 Orange Avenue, Irvington, N. J. Mr. Bader was his prospective father-in-law, Mr. Wenzl said.

Officers of the National Guard were on duty. Brigadier General Winfield Price canvassed undertaking establishments and estimated that the total of bodies recovered was 171. Major Gen. John J. Toffee, in command of the State militia, who had sped from the war game, opened the facilities of Camp Moore for relief workers and for the survivors. Twenty-four permanent buildings were available and preparations were made to transfer survivors from private homes.

Fishing Boat Picks Up 67.

By The Associated Press.

BRIELLE, N. J., Sept. 8.—A picture of the horror as survivors of the burning Morro Castle floundered in the water screaming for help was given by members of the crew of the fishing boat Paramount, which rescued 67 persons.

"It was the most horrible sight I ever saw," said John Bogan, owner of the little craft which for four hours ploughed through the stormy water taking survivors aboard. "The water semed to be full of dead people."

The skipper of another rescue craft, the Diana, which brought in 12 bodies, said sharks added to the terror of the disaster. He said he counted three sharks in the area where survivors were struggling.

Jeff Bogan, 21-year-old captain of the Paramount, said he saw the blaze on the Morro Castle as his craft started out on its daily fishing trip. He turned back to Brielle, notified the Coast Guard, and then made for the burning liner.

Rescued Piled in Heaps.

The Paramount kept blowing its horn to call out other boats because the crew feared it would not be big enough to hold all the survivors.

"We didn't stop until we heard no more screaming," said John Bogan Jr. By that time we had 67 on board, many more than the boat could hold normally. The people we picked were so exhausted they just lay in heaps on the deck like dead people."

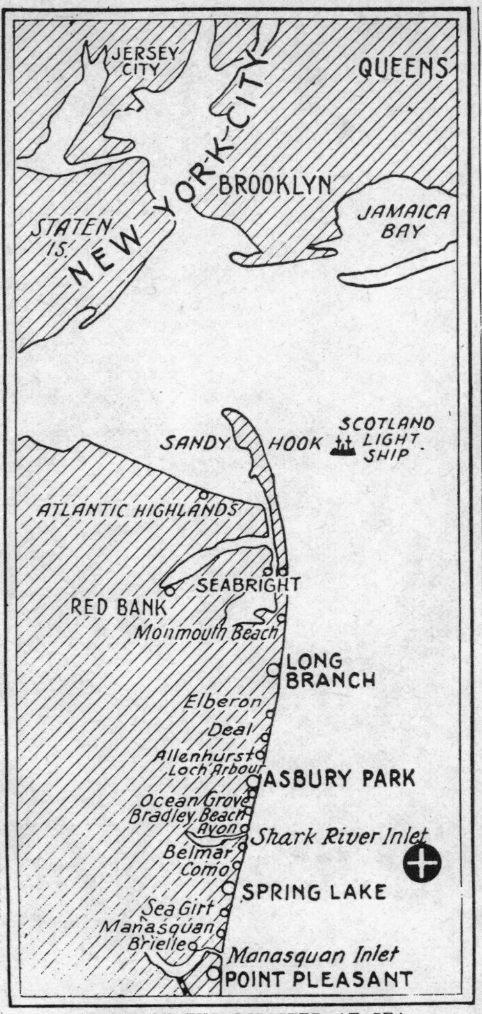

SCENE OF THE DISASTER AT SEA.
The Cross at Point Off Shark River Inlet Indicates Where the Morro Castle Burned.

2 Canceled Trip on Liner The Day of Her Sailing

By The Associated Press.

NEW CANAAN, Conn., Sept. 8.—John H. Andrews Sr. and his son, John J., the latter a New York insurance broker, who make their home here, missed being passengers on the Morro Castle only through the insistence of a moving agent.

The father and son, steamship agents here disclosed today, had booked passage on the liner and were ready to leave for New York Sept. 1, the ship's sailing day, when they were reminded by the moving company they had contracted to move that day.

The two immediately canceled their booking.

Young Andrews was on the maiden voyage on the ship when it was launched and since then had made nineteen round trips on the vessel.

SONS SAVED, LOSES WIFE.

Cincinnati Man to Learn Today of Rescue of His Boys.

SPRING LAKE, N. J., Sept. 9 (AP).—Mrs. R. A. Holden of Cincinnati is dead, a victim of the Morro Castle sea tragedy, but her husband and her sons sleep in separated places tonight, unknowing of her fate. Mr. Holden, exhausted, is in the Monmouth Hotel. The sons, 15 and 10 years old, are in a private home.

W. J. Lippincott, a cousin, located Mr. Holden and then the boys. Tomorrow, when they awaken, he intends to bring them together. He also identified the body of Mrs. Holden.

ALL RADIO STAFF OF SHIP RESCUED

Chief Operator Wirelesses That He Is Aboard Cutter —One Aide With Him.

OTHER IN MARINE HOSPITAL

All Three Declared to Have Stuck to Posts Until Fire Drove Them Away.

George W. Rogers, 37-year-old chief radio operator of the Morro Castle, last night radioed his chief, John B. Duffy, general superintendent of the Radio Marine Corporation, that he was safe on board the Coast Guard Cutter Tampa.

Mr. Duffy said that the message merely contained assurances of the well-being of the sender, containing none of the details of the disaster. The radio official said that he telephoned the message to Mrs. Rogers who was hopefully waiting for news in her home at 601 Avenue E, Bayonne, N. J.

From a source that preferred to remain anonymous, however, some of the details of the functioning of the ship's radio staff during the fire were learned.

Rogers was not on watch at the time. As soon as he was notified of the fire by one of his two assistants, he rushed to the room and took charge, personally sending the rescue messages at the direction of superiors. He remained there with his two assistants, George Alegna and Clarence Maki, until flames drove them away.

The first rescue appeal, as near as can be determined, was radioed at 3:28 A. M., standard time. A report that Rogers had encountered atmospheric disturbances was explained by a radio official, who said disturbances are common at this time of the year.

With Rogers's safety assured, the whole radio staff of the Morro Castle is accounted for. Alegna, the first assistant, is with his chief on board the Tampa, and Maki is in Marine Hospital, Ellis Island, suffering from exhaustion and submersion.

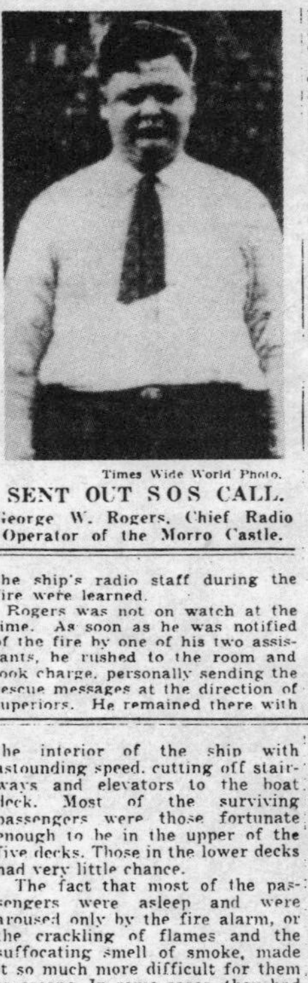

Times Wide World Photo.
SENT OUT SOS CALL.
George W. Rogers, Chief Radio Operator of the Morro Castle.

SAW LIFEBOATS SMASHED.

Photographer Tells of Wreck After Own Plane Is Grounded.

Special to THE NEW YORK TIMES.

LONG BRANCH, N. J., Sept. 8.—A balky engine forced an amphibian plane carrying a newspaper photographer to the scene of the Morro Castle disaster to land here on the golf course of the Long Branch Country Club. The passenger and the crew of two were unhurt.

The pilot, William Cleveland, told of seeing in a previous visit to the scene attempts to rescue the passengers of the Morro Castle. He said that as he circled the ship two lifeboats filled with survivors were dashed against the side of the burning hulk and the occupants of both thrown into the sea.

THE MORRO CASTLE BURNS OFF ASBURY

By RUSSELL B. PORTER.
Continued From Page One.

Of these, five men and three women were picked up by a Coast Guard cutter off Sea Girt, N. J. All wore life preservers. One woman was tentatively identified as Mrs. William Price, wife of a policeman. The body of another woman was brought here by the liner Monarch of Bermuda.

Bodies definitely known to have been recovered, besides the nine in New York, included forty-two at Manasquan Morgue, fifteen at the Coast Guard station in Manasquan and thirty-one at the Point Pleasant First Aid Association.

Agonized crowds of relatives and friends of Morro Castle passengers gathered yesterday at the Ward Line pier at the foot of Wall Street in the East River, where the liner was to have docked. Others rushed to the piers where the rescue ships landed and to the Jersey shore communities where survivors were landed and where bodies were washed ashore.

The burning hulk of the Morro Castle was towed by the Coast Guard cutter Tampa and two tugs toward Sandy Hook late yesterday, but broke away because of the heavy seas, and was beached at the foot of Sixth Avenue, Asbury Park, at 7:35 o'clock last night.

The Morro Castle was still burning, and fears were felt that, because of the heavy storm, she might be swept against the new Asbury Park convention hall on a pier extending out over the ocean. She struck the beach broadside with her bow pointed north.

Last night the wind shifted from northeast to northwest, thereby lessening the danger that sparks from the burning ship might set fire to the Convention Hall or other resort buildings. The ship was beached about 150 feet offshore. Fire was plainly visible through the portholes, and smoke was still pouring out of the vessel.

Late last night the liner was listing gradually to starboard as the tide went out. Coast Guard officers at Asbury Park predicted she might keel over on her side at low tide. Three port side lifeboats, two appearing to have been slightly lowered, hung from their davits. A crowd of 10,000 persons had gathered on the boardwalk to watch the stricken ship.

It was learned that the Coast Guard cutter Tampa was slightly damaged when the hawser by which she was towing the Morro Castle parted shortly before the liner beached. The Tampa's propeller was fouled, and she was being towed slowly to New York late last night by the Sebago, another Coast Guard cutter.

Was Near End of Cruise.

The disaster occurred just a few hours before the Morro Castle was to have docked at New York at the end of a seven-day Labor Day holiday cruise to Havana. The scene of the tragedy was about twenty miles south of Scotland Light, past which ships turn into Ambrose Channel and the safety of New York Harbor, and only about eight miles off the New Jersey coast, near Asbury Park and Shark River Inlet.

The stricken liner sent her SOS at 4:23 A. M., New York daylight saving time, less than four hours before she was scheduled to dock. In that message, the radio operator reported that the flames were under the radio room. "Can't hold out much longer," he flashed." No further word was heard from him.

The horror of the fire was increased by the storm that was raging. Wearing nightclothes or nondescript outergarments thrown on when they were awakened, those passengers who were able to reach the lifeboats, or dive into the sea, then had to contend with a strong northeast gale, heavy seas, and driving rain.

Several ships at sea, together with Coast Guard vessels from New York and New Jersey and fishing boats, set out to the rescue immediately on receipt of the SOS. It was after 6 o'clock before the rescue ships arrived in any force, and meanwhile scenes of terror and tragedy had taken place aboard the burning liner, and in the sea about her.

Passengers were trapped in their cabins, and members of the crew below deck fought each other to climb to safety. The flames swept the interior of the ship with astounding speed, cutting off stairways and elevators to the boat deck. Most of the surviving passengers were those fortunate enough to be in the upper of the five decks. Those in the lower decks had very little chance.

The fact that most of the passengers were asleep and were aroused only by the fire alarm, or the crackling of flames and the suffocating smell of smoke, made it so much more difficult for them to escape. In some cases, they had to die in their cabins, helpless to force their way through the burning passageways. In others, they broke their stateroom windows and crawled out on deck.

Even there, many found themselves still trapped by the flames. Some could not reach the lifeboats, which were already afire along one side of the ship. Others could not get to that side of the ship where the lifeboats were free of the fire.

Men, women and children, unable to reach the lifeboats, jumped into the water, some with, others without life preservers.

There were conflicting reports as to the behavior of the crew. Some passengers could not speak too highly of the courage and efficiency of the members of the crew with whom they had come in contact. They told many tales of heroism by both crew and passengers.

On the other hand, others made serious criticism of the conduct of the crew, charging that members crowded into the lifeboats and left passengers to burn to death or jump into the dangerous sea.

It was pointed out by some passengers that there was a disproportionate number of the crew saved in relation to the passengers rescued in the lifeboats which made their way to New Jersey points. Many passengers were picked up from the sea by the rescue ships or swam or drifted ashore in their lifebelts, while many of the crew reached safety in the lifeboats.

Searching Inquiry Ordered.

Secretary of Commerce Roper from Washington ordered a thorough investigation, which is expected to cover the question of how the crew behaved and their training for such an emergency. How the fire started, why it gained such headway before it was discovered and why the supposedly up-to-date fire-fighting equipment of the Morro Castle, which was built in 1930 and was regarded as one of the most modern and safest vessels afloat, was not sufficient to put out the blaze, will also be investigated.

Rumors of possible sabotage resulting from labor troubles, or a radical plot, will be investigated, although officials of the Ward Line, which operates the Morro Castle, scouted them. The rumors originated in Havana, but gained some support when an assistant engineer of the ship, who was rescued, said that the fire seemed to start in half a dozen places at once, and hinted at incendiarism.

Most of the passengers and members of the crew who survived said that the fire started in the smoking lounge or in the library. No one spoke of an explosion. Some suggested that there were some gay parties in the smoking room on the last night before the liner was due in New York, and that the cause of the fire might have been a cigarette tossed carelessly in or near inflammable material.

New mystery was added to the question how the fire started and got such headway before being discovered, by a statement last night from W. M. Tripp, an 18-year-old M. I. T. student of Dorchester, Mass., an engineer cadet aboard the Morro Castle.

Tripp, who logged the orders from the bridge in the engine room Friday night, said the bridge gave the stand-by signal at 4 o'clock, daylight saving time, and a few minutes later asked if there was a fire in the engine room. This would indicate that the bridge had just been informed there was a fire and had not located it.

According to Tripp, the next order was one at 4:10½ for full speed ahead on the starboard engine, presumably to turn the ship toward shore. About 4:30 there was an order to stop the engines, but then the lights had gone out, and he could not log accurately.

Early reports, made by some of the first members of the crew to come ashore, that the ship had been struck by lightning during the storm, were not substantiated by later accounts given by members of the crew.

The immediate investigation will be in charge of D. N. Hoover, Assistant Chief of the Bureau of Navigation and Steamboat Inspection of the Department of Commerce. Mr. Hoover was ordered here yesterday by Secretary of Commerce Roper.

Martin J. Conboy, United States Attorney for the Southern District of New York, also began an investigation as to the responsibility for the disaster, and the New York and Havana police announced investigations.

Henry E. Cabaud, executive vice president of the Ward Line, asserted that the Morro Castle was equipped with every safety device, but that he could not comment on the way in which the fire apparatus functioned until after the inquiry. Inspectors of the Steamboat Inspection Service, who checked the ship as late as Aug. 4, expressed surprise that she should have burned as she did. They said they had regarded her as one of the best equipped ships at sea for contending with fire.

Members of the crew who were questioned about the criticism of their conduct by some passengers indignantly denied the charges. They said that they did everything that was humanly possible for the passengers, but that most of them, like the passengers, were caught unawares by the rapidity with which the flames spread, and were unable to reach passengers trapped in their staterooms or on the lower decks. It was only when every hope for the trapped passengers was seen to have vanished, the crew said, that they themselves got into the lifeboats.

Members of the crew said that those of their companions who were not cut off from the passengers by the flames, had done valiant service. They declared that a small crop of seamen and stewards, who were able to reach the trapped passengers on deck, helped them put on their life preservers and forced some of them to jump overboard before the flames reached them, so that they would have at least a chance to be picked up.

Fourteen of the crew, including Chief Officer Warms, remained aboard the Morro Castle after all others able to do so had abandoned ship. The fourteen were taken off the still smouldering liner late yesterday afternoon by the Coast Guard cutter Tampa and the Pilot Boat Sandy Hook.

Passengers and crew united in praising the heroism of Chief Officer Warms and the other crew members who stayed with the ship long after the others had left. They had to huddle up in a small section of the fore part of the vessel to escape the flames which swept the ship fore and aft, and which generated such terrific heat all through the craft that the plates they stood on burned the soles of their feet.

Work of Rescuers Praised.

Praise was heaped upon the officers and crew of the steamships which went to the rescue, especially the Monarch of Bermuda, which was one of the first to reach the scene, and which rescued more than any other ship. The City of Savannah and the Andrea H. Luckenback also did valiant work. The President Cleveland went to the scene, but found no remaining persons to be rescued either from the burning ship or from the surrounding waters.

Coast Guard cutters from New York, Coast Guard lifeboats from all along the New Jersey coast, fishing boats from various shore communities, and National Guard aviators who flew over the burning ship to help direct the recuers, all came in for honors.

Survivors and others who observed the rescue work asserted that the rescuers, both seafaring men and fliers, deserved special commendation because of the adverse and dangerous weather conditions under which they worked.

Even in small fishing boats and lifeboats men risked their lives in the thick northeaster, with its huge running seas and beating rain, without regard for their own safety. Along the shore, as swimmers and persons floating on life belts came in, lifeguards and others rushed out into the treacherous surf to help the survivors struggle to the beach.

Some members of the crew, however, criticized the rescue ships, saying that they stayed offshore of the burning liner, whereas if they had manoeuvred between her and the shore, they could have picked up more of those in the water.

Officers of the rescue ships said that the Morro Castle was ablaze from bow to stern when they came on the scene, that they manoeuvred as close to her as they could, and that they sent out lifeboats which circled her several times before giving up the hunt for further survivors in the water.

It was said that the strong northeast gale and the current had caused many of the people in the water to drift far out of sight before the rescue ships appeared on the scene.

The fog which settled over the coast line after day broke made the rescue work all the more dangerous, especially for the fliers, but no one shirked it.

THE STORY OF THE MORRO CASTLE DISASTER TOLD IN PICTURES

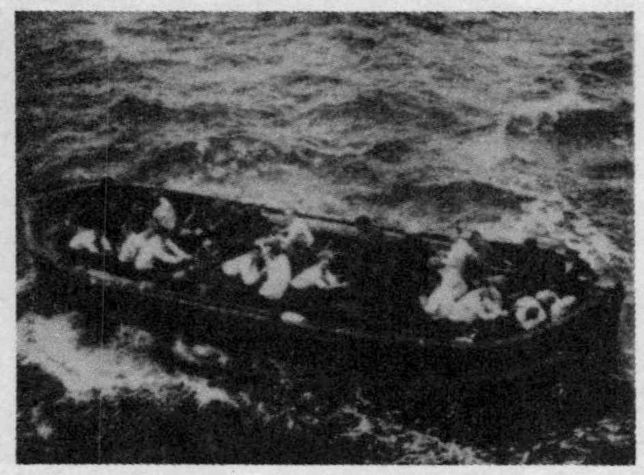

Associated Press Photo.
Lifeboat of Survivors Approaching the Monarch of Bermuda.

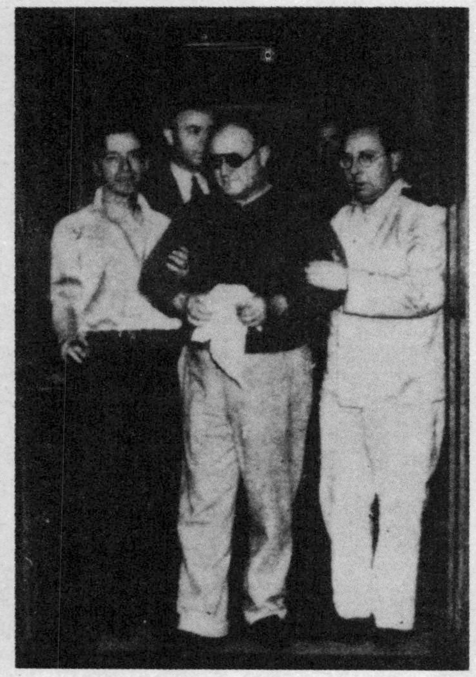

Henry Speirman, Chief Steward of the Morro Castle, Landing Here Assisted by Members of the Crew of the Monarch of Bermuda.

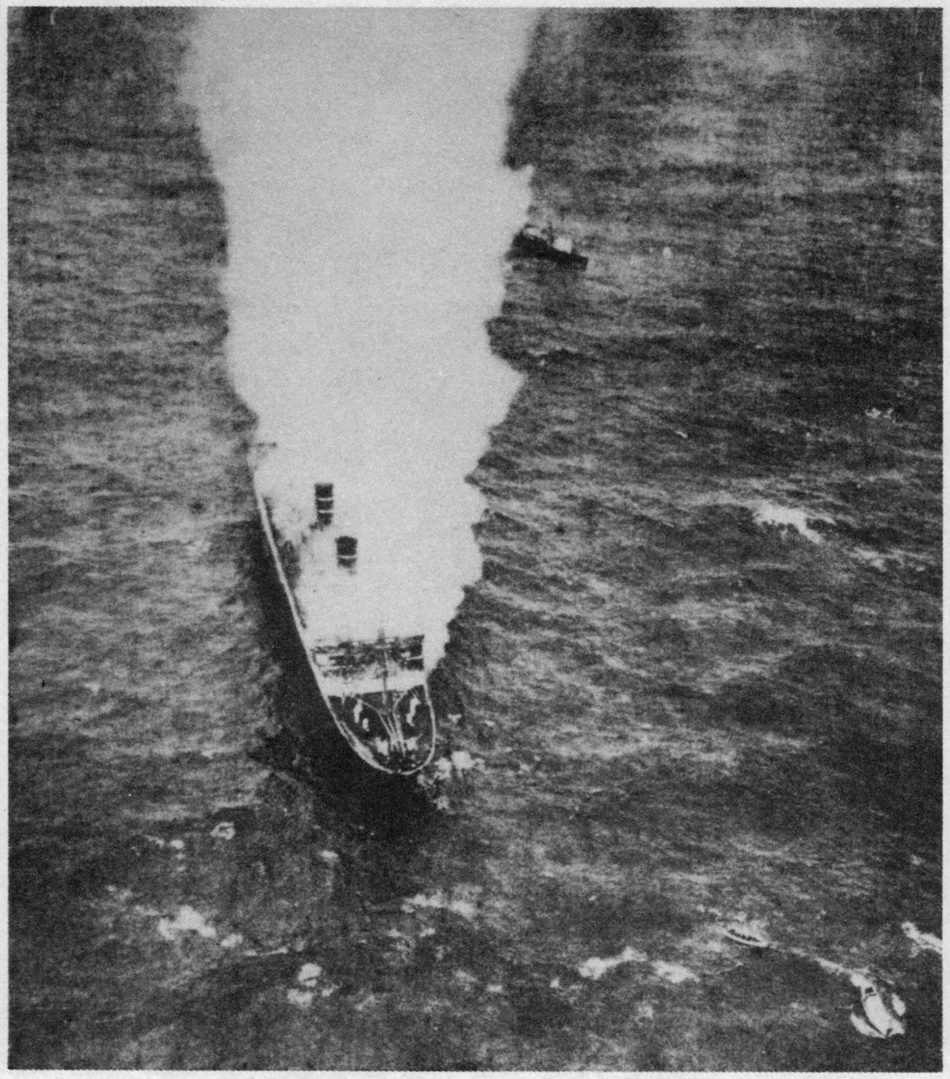

The Morro Castle Afire Surrounded by Lifeboats in Which Passengers and Members of the Crew Are Pulling Away Toward the Rescue Ships.

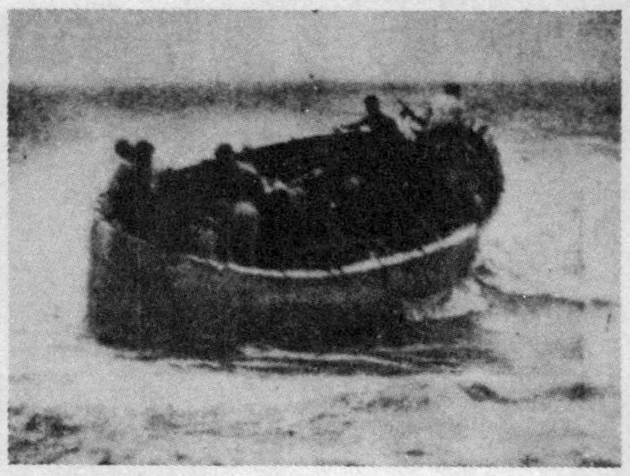

Some of the Passengers Being Hauled to Shore at Spring Lake.

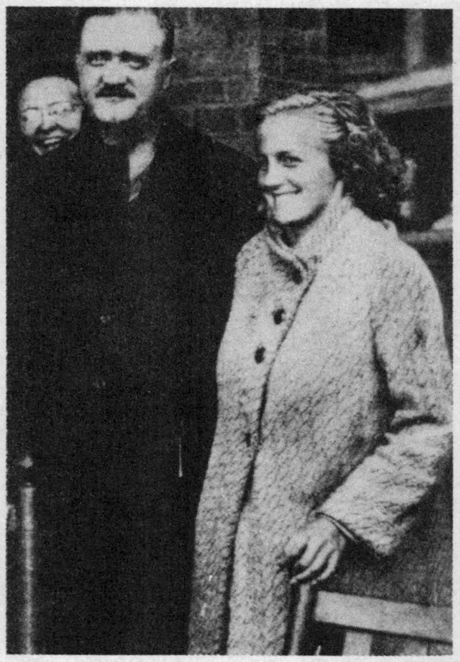

Times Wide World Photo.
Dr. Charles S. Cochrane of Brooklyn and His Niece at the Emergenc Headquarters in Spring Lake After Drifting Ashore in a Lifeboat.

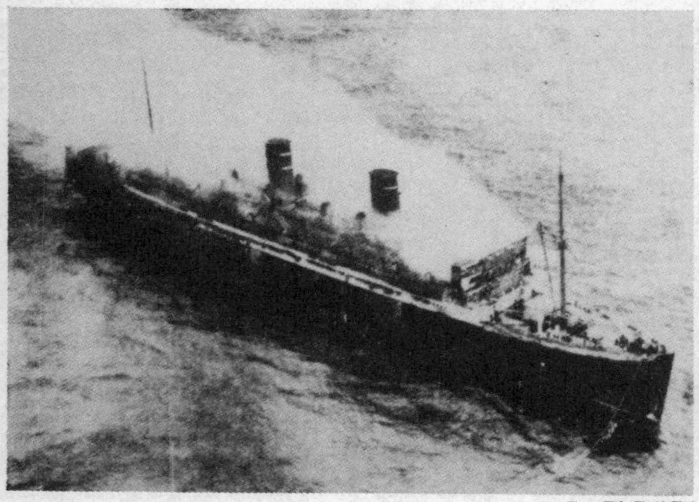

Times Wide World Photo.
A View of the Helpless Steamer Morro Castle, Still Afire Yesterday Afternoon With Some of Her Crew Still Aboard.

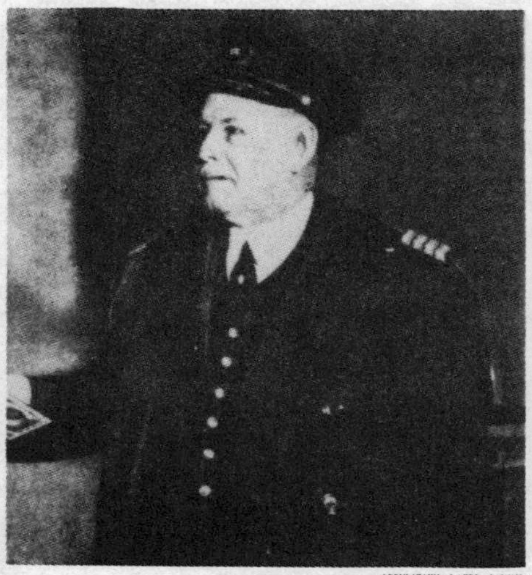

Associated Press Photo.
Captain R. R. Willmott, Master of the Ill-Fated Vessel, Who Died of Heart Disease Aboard His Ship Before the Disaster.

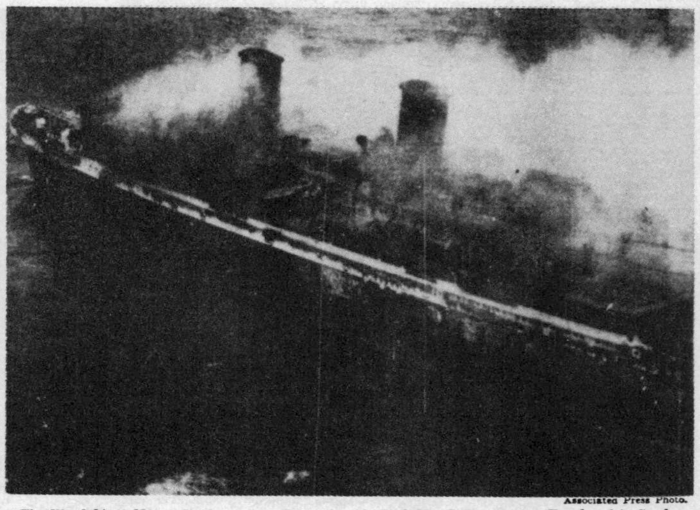

Associated Press Photo.
The Ward Liner Morro Castle as Seen From the Air With Her Superstructure Enveloped in Smoke.

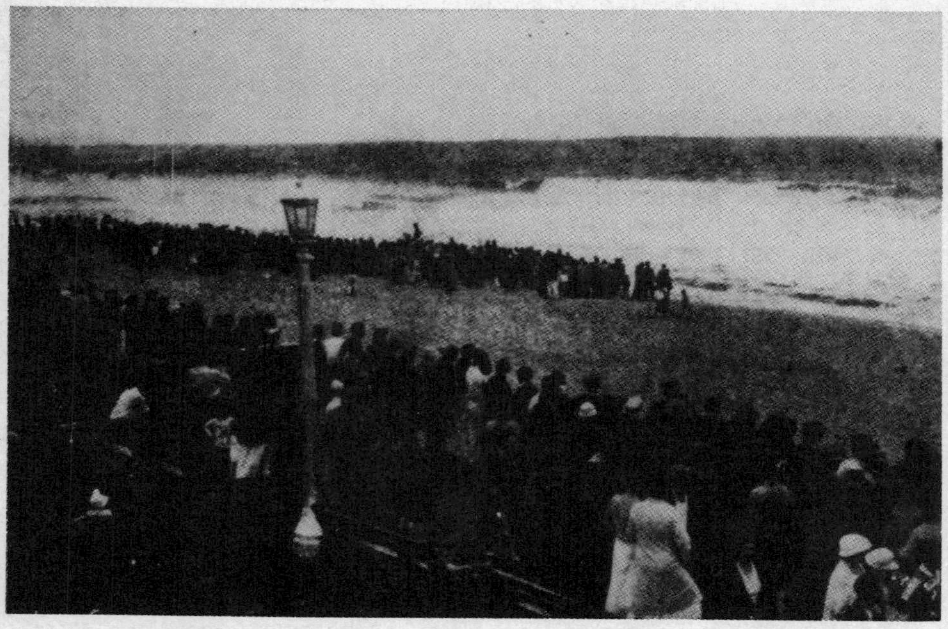

Associated Press Photo.
The Crowd on the Shore at Spring Lake, N. J., Awaiting the Arrival of Survivors of the Morro Castle in Lifeboats.

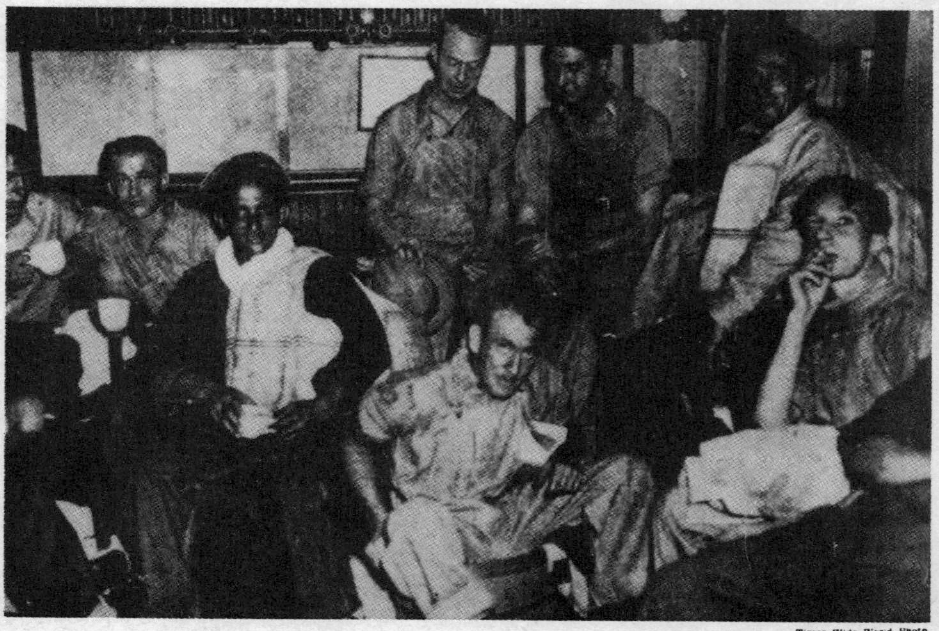

Times Wide World Photo.
Members of the Crew of the Morro Castle, Still Showing Signs of Their Harrowing Experience, After Being Landed at Spring Lake.

Survivors Describe. Frantic Efforts of Passengers to Flee the Burning Vessel

TWO WIVES SEE HUSBANDS DROWN

Men, Exhausted, Unable to Go On After Swimming for Hours With Their Companions.

5 COUPLES LEAP TOGETHER

Bride and Groom Separated, but Both Are Rescued—Others Reach Safety.

At least five married couples, and probably more, jumped hand in hand from the decks of the burning Morro Castle and started to swim to shore.

Two couples, both young, were successful and reached the Jersey coast in safety. In another case both husband and wife were picked up by rescue craft, although for several hours each thought the other dead.

In the case of the other two couples, both middle aged and both from Philadelphia, the wife was saved after seeing her husband drown.

The two young couples who swam to safety were Mr. and Mrs. Abraham Cohen of 18 Townley Street, Hartford, Conn., and Mr. and Mrs. Jules Blondeau of 2,414 Locust Street, Philadelphia.

Both couples were in the water for more than six hours.

The escape from death of the Cohens was especially dramatic. They had only one lifebelt between them and Mrs. Cohen could not swim more than a few strokes. They were in the water six hours and were on the verge of collapse when rescued off Sea Girt. Friends of Cohen in Hartford attributed his and his wife's safety to Cohen's excellent physical condition. He was on the Dartmouth football squad of 1924 and 1925. The Cohens were on their honeymoon.

Picked Up by Coast Guard.

Mr. Blondeau and his wife swam ashore and were picked up at Sea Girt at 11 A. M. They were exhausted but in good condition when a Coast Guard boat picked them out of the surf.

They told their story lying on cots in the American Legion Hall in Point Pleasant, which had been fitted up as an emergency hospital. They said they were awakened by persons running along the C deck corridor. Mr. Blondeau looked out, and saw passengers wearing life belts.

"We put coats on over our night clothes," said Mr. Blondeau, "put on our life belts and went to the stairway to B deck above. There were flames in the corridor but we squeezed by in safety. All the passengers were aft on B deck. The women were crying, some of them, others were praying and a few were singing.

One of the rescues was made by Lloyd Barnstead, a New York City accountant, who swam six miles to shore with his wife, Grace, 28, and Mrs. Pearl Panimo of Bangor, Pa. According to Barnstead, some of the passengers were badly frightened.

He, his wife and Mrs. Panimo jumped from the liner into the sea. There was no use trying for the lifeboats, he explained, since five of them were already on fire. For the last half of the six-mile swim Barnstead assisted the two women, who were exhausted. All three had donned life preservers before leaping into the sea.

"The ship was going very fast toward the shore. This and a strong wind blew the smoke and the flames aft. It got so hot we all went down again to C deck. Some of us got together and sang, 'Hail, Hail the Gang's All Here' to try and cheer up the rest.

"There were only two officers on the deck with us, the cruise director and his assistant. They were calm and were walking around without life belts reassuring the passengers. They told us not to worry.

"Finally it got so hot my wife and I were forced to jump into the ocean. The waves were eight to ten feet high. I saw a life ring, swam to it and then towed it back to where my wife was floating. We swam away from the ship. We were afraid it would explode and sink and that we would be carried down by the suction."

The couple were carried along by the current and were picked up off Sea Girt, as were many others. Neither of the Blondiaus is a good swimmer. Both were worried over three other members of their party, George Watrimez and Dr. and Mrs. James P. Coll,, all of Philadelphia.

Dies Saving His Wife.

Mrs. Freda McArthur, 38, of 2,019 Bleigh Street, Philadelphia, leaped into the sea hand in hand with her husband, Alexander, 42, only to have him die of exhaustion before rescuers arrived. He had tired himself out trying to keep his wife above water. Mrs. McArthur told her story in Spring Lake.

"I am a light sleeper," she said, "and some time during the night—it might have been between 3:30 and 4 o'clock—I awoke and noticed sparks outside the porthole of our stateroom.

"I watched for a minute and then got up and put my head out the porthole. Smoke was curling down from the deck above and it nearly suffocated me. I awakened my husband and just then we heard a cry from some place in the corridor telling every one to put on a life-preserver. Then there were other noises. People were running around and there was a lot of excitement.

"We both were completely bewildered, but we knew something dreadful had happened. We dressed quickly, put on life-preservers and went up on deck. Every one was running to and fro and didn't seem to know what they were doing.

"We went down to the lower deck and saw there was the same confusion there. Every one was jumping into the water and my husband and I took hold of each other's hands and leaped. My husband is an excellent swimmer, but I can scarcely tread water. We kept hold of each other in the water and my husband helped me keep my head above the waves several hours. Finally he became exhausted.

"When the Coast Guardsmen threw me a rope I managed to get hold of it with one hand and to keep hold of my husband's life belt with the other. They shouted to me to let my husband go because they could not take dead persons on the boat. I wouldn't do it at first, but finally I released my hold and then they lifted me on board. That was the last I saw of him."

Physicist Is Victim.

A similar story was told by Mrs. Adele Brady, 48, of 70-48 Greenhill Road, Overbrook, Pa. Her husband, Edward J. Brady, chief physicist of the United Gas Improvement Company, was drowned after swimming by her side for seven hours. Their daughter, Nancy Ann, 17, was rescued.

"We were awakened by the alarm bell," Mrs. Brady explained as she told her story in the Point Pleasant Hospital. "Nancy rushed up on deck first and we didn't see her again. My husband and I put on life belts and then we jumped into the water together, holding on to each other.

"My husband had been ill and it was for his sake that we took the Havana cruise, but he insisted on trying to help me. Some time after daybreak, I don't know how many hours, my husband's strength became exhausted. He said to me: 'I don't think I can make it, but I don't mind. I am very tired.'

"I tried to encourage him. I told him a boat would be along to rescue us any minute. He reached into his pocket and took out his wallet with his money in it. He handed it to me, telling me to put it in my pocketbook.

"Then later, it must have been about 10:30, his last bit of strength left him. I was holding on to him, but he gathered together his last ounce of strength and pushed me off. 'Save yourself,' he said. Then I saw a ship approaching me, and I was taken on board."

Brady's body was later recovered and brought to shore.

Benjamin Hirsch, owner of a Philadelphia haberdashery chain, was one of those rescued by the Monarch of Bermuda. His leg was broken. Hirsch and his wife, Katherine, were on their honeymoon. They jumped over the rail into the sea together.

"I don't know what happened," he muttered. "I only remember I found myself in the water. That's all."

"And your wife?" he was asked.

"Dead," was his reply.

However, it developed later that the wife had been picked up by another rescue boat and brought to this city. She was taken to St. Vincent's Hospital suffering from exhaustion. Both she and her husband were told of the other's safety.

RED CROSS MOBILIZES ITS RELIEF SERVICE

New York Chapter Gives Aid to Survivors of Liner Who Are Landed Here.

The New York Chapter of the Red Cross mobilized its Disaster Relief Service yesterday to care for survivors of the Morro Castle, arriving at this city in rescue ships.

Shortly after receiving word that many of the survivors would be brought to this city, Douglas Gibbons, director of the chapter's service, ordered an ambulance laden with first-aid equipment, clothing and blankets to Pier 46, North River, at the foot of West Tenth Street, where many of the survivors were landed.

Six nurses, a doctor and two aides from headquarters of the chapter at 315 Lexington Avenue went to the pier with the ambulance to attend the rescued men and women. The Red Cross workers gave emergency treatments to those suffering from burns, exposure and submersion, supplied clothing to those who had been forced to leave the ship before they were dressed fully and sent the injured to hospitals in the chapter's ambulance.

Mr. Gibbons said that arrangements had been made with chapters of the Red Cross in Brooklyn and cities in New Jersey to provide medical treatment, ambulance service and clothing to survivors landed at piers in Brooklyn and New Jersey.

Members of the New York chapter were on duty all night gathering information to assist relatives and survivors to get into touch and to render other relief, including the finding of places to stay for survivors who were without relatives or other means of assistance in this city.

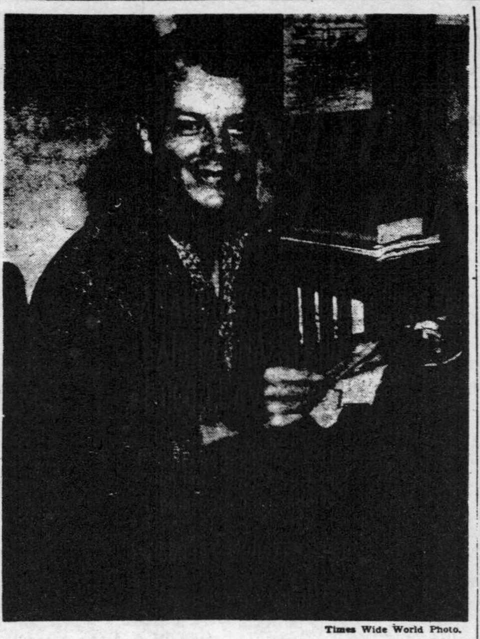

Times Wide World Photo.

CLUNG TO BURNING LINER FOR SIX HOURS.

Gouverneur Morris Phelps Jr., who was picked up by a lifeboat from the steamer Luckenbach, recovering from his experience at the home of his parents here last night.

Puppy, Ship's Mascot, Saved.

SPRING LAKE, N. J., Sept. 8 (AP).—A mongrel puppy, mascot of the crew of the Morro Castle, jumped to the beach as one of the first lifeboats made the sand today.

PARENTS AND SON PART AMID FLAMES

Dr. G. M. Phelps and Wife Leap Into Sea and Swim Ashore—Young Man Waits 6 Hours.

CLINGS TO ROPE AT STERN

After Seeing Several Lifeboats Pass While Men and Women Drown, He Is Finally Saved.

Gouverneur Morris Phelps Jr., 25 years old, Harvard '31, sat in his father's study at 155 East Seventy-ninth Street last night, still clad in oil-room dungarees. He told how, with his body in the water, he clung to a rope hanging from the burning Morro Castle for almost six hours, while fellow-passengers were dying, before he was taken aboard a lifeboat from the freighter Andrew W. Luckenbach.

Dr. Gouverneur Morris Phelps, a prominent surgeon, and his wife, Mrs. Katharine Brower Phelps, formerly of Babylon, L. I., plunged into the sea a full half hour before their son did, and managed to reach the New Jersey shore near Manasquan. Many hours passed before they got word from Manhattan that the young man was alive and back home.

"I woke up about—this is guesswork, of course—3 o'clock, in my stateroom, 221 on C Deck, coughing and choking. The room was filled with smoke. Thought I'd dropped a cigarette before I fell asleep and started the fire myself. I opened the stateroom door, looked down the hall and saw it all aglow with a bright orange flame and dense with smoke.

"I pulled my head in, shook my room-mate, Ed Kendall, and told him the ship was afire. Then I stuck my head through the porthole and my blood ran cold. I could see a perfect inferno of flame along the full length of the ship, great sheets of it leaping high above the lifeboat level.

Played Hose on Flames.

"We ran into the corridor and tore a line of hose from the wall. We got it started with tremendous pressure and turned on the stairway, sort of trying to blow our way out. We yelled "Fire!" and tried to rouse the other people. We banged on stateroom doors. Then we realized the hose was no help. The flames got worse and the smoke rolled down on us—black, bitter smoke, and we had to run for it.

"I ran around to the other corridor, to stateroom 209, where my father and mother were asleep. I pounded on their door and called their names and finally they came, sleepy-eyed and wondering what all the noise was for. They were calm—took hold at once. After an instant's pause they turned back into the cabin, got their lifebelts and their money and came out again. Then we three fled through the smoke toward the after deck, pounding on doors and trying to hammer other sleepers into wakefulness.

"Father, mother and I got to the stern rail on C deck. The others came crowding up, too, and the smoke poured down upon us with ever-increasing volume. Many of the passengers were terrified. Then the lights went out and matters became worse. Darkness brought real panic. Around us we could hear men and women praying."

Many Scream in Pain.

Terror increased, Mr. Phelps declared. Men came by, dragging burned friends or wives whose screeches of pain chilled the hearts of all who heard them. The burned and the injured kept calling for doctors.

"Father stood by the rail and stared intently toward shore, where we could see land lights," he continued. "He would have helped those injured, but how could he in the dark, without instruments or anything else? He was powerless to help. Suddenly he turned to mother and said:

"'Katharine, that light over yonder must be Scotland Light and that one over there must be Ambrose. That means that the beach over there must be less than seven miles away. I know this part of the coast.' [Young Mr. Phelps explained that his father had fished and cruised along the New Jersey shore for years.]

"'The wind is blowing directly toward shore. I think, dear, our only chance is to go over the great rush and try to make the beach, on our own. Will you come?' Mother smiled through her tears and nodded. That's all. She couldn't speak. Then father turned to me and said: 'Govvie, I have all I can do to take care of Katherine. You're a man now. You can take care of yourself. Don't wait too long. Promise me you'll go over before that partition burns through. Good luck, boy.' The wind was high. He talked into my ear.

"There was no shaking of hands. The fire threatened to break through the second-class dining salon partition at any moment. Dr. Phelps lifted his wife over the rail and let her drop into the water. The stern lifted under the heave of a strong wave and then he went over after her. I thought I heard the splash when he hit. He's six feet, you know, and weighs about 200.

Officer Calms Crowd.

Mr. Phelps recalled that he saw an officer trying to calm the crowds at the aft rail. "I could hear him shouting, but I couldn't make out the words," he said.

As other passengers followed the example of Dr. and Mrs. Phelps and plunged into the sea, young Mr. Phelps suddenly realized that in his anxiety to warn his parents he had forgotten to take his life-jacket.

"The flames, whipped by the wind, threw a bright glare on the water," he said, "and I could see bodies floating around the stern and people trying to swim. It wasn't until then that the awful horror of the situation struck me. I thought of my father and mother out in that blackness and wondered if they were clinging to each other."

Some one had lowered the warping cables from the deck into the water. A number of the passengers slid down rather than take a chance on jumping, and Mr. Phelps did the same. A man named Chalfonte, a boat acquaintance with whom he had played bridge earlier in the evening, came up wearing a lifebelt and suggested they go over together and that Mr. Phelps cling to him. Mr. Phelps shook his head.

"He implored me to go with him and use his belt, but I couldn't do that. A half hour or more had passed after my parents went over before I slid down the mooring rope. When I got into the water I could see another rope dangling about 20 feet away. I made for that. A wave lifted me and threw me within arm's reach of it. That was sheer luck."

Then began the six-hour wait for rescue, pounded by the waves, pelted by falling bits of hot metal, wood and splashes of paint.

"I had seen a lifeboat, apparently manned by some of the ship's crew, pass through the water where men and women were yelling and screaming and imploring to be taken in," said Mr. Phelps. "There seemed to be only about eight or nine men in that boat. They didn't stop to pick any one up. It was one of the boats that got away early.

"Later I saw a second lifeboat go through those struggling people, making no effort to help or take any one on board. Some of the men in the boat seemed to be having difficulty with the oars and some of them seemed to be just clinging to the seats. People in the water tried to clutch at the gunwales, but they all seemed to miss and the boat drifted on."

Several women, some of whom Mr. Phelps recognized, struggled toward a cluster of dangling ropes close to 'midships, but he was too far gone to help them. They held on only for brief periods before the waves tore them away into the dark.

"I had to watch those women drop off one by one and float off and hear their desperate and familiar voices pleading," he said. "I'd met them and danced with them."

Waves Lift Ship's Stern.

After daybreak a huge wave lifted the stern of the Morro Castle and hauled Phelps clear of the water. He dropped and sank. As the stern smacked down again and he came to the surface a man named Burne, whom Mr. Phelps had helped to get to another rope, caught his wrist and helped him regain his rope. A few minutes later he had to perform a similar service for Byrne.

A lifeboat appeared around the opposite side of the stern, but it was already full and left them. About that time, Mr. Phelps recalled, the fire burst through the salon partition. He could hear the roar—and a veritable "rain of people, a hundred or more" came leaping over the side to escape the suddenly released flame; they hit one another in the descent; many sank out of sight immediately.

Another half-hour passed before the Luckenbach lifeboat pulled up. Some one reached down and hauled Mr. Phelps aboard by the slack of his pajamas. He fell in a faint in the bottom of the boat.

Hot coffee, a suit of dry dungarees and medical attention restored him. When the Luckenbach docked at her Brooklyn pier he left the ship with a police chaplain who drove him home. He learned then of his parents' safe landing and told his mother over the telephone about his rescue. His parents spent the night at the home of a Dr. Ramsdell in Point Pleasant.

INSTITUTE CARES FOR 90.

Many Injured Among the Vessel's Seamen Arriving Here.

About 90 survivors of the crew of the Morro Castle were brought to the Seamen's Church Institute here, 25 South Street, late yesterday afternoon. Thirty-four remained there, the others going to their homes or to the homes of friends and relatives in the metropolitan area. Many of them were suffering from burns and other injuries received in the disaster.

All but five of those brought to the institute came on a special train from Spring Lake which arrived in Jersey City about 5:15 P. M. They were ferried across the river to Cortlandt Street and then taken to the institute in taxicabs. The other five were brought to New York earlier in the day by the Monarch of Bermuda.

The men were rescued in a variety of ways, some in lifeboats, others by rescue craft. They were assembled at the Spring Lake Police Station for transportation to New York.

Officials at the institute assigned the entire ninth floor for the use of those remaining there. Each man received an individual room, hot food, extra clothes and cigarette money.

Memorial services for the members of the Morro Castle's crew, who died in the disaster, will be held next Sunday at 8 P. M. in the chapel of the Seamen's Church Institute, 25 South Street, it was announced last night at the institute.

SURVIVORS TELL OF LEAPS INTO SEA

Continued from Page One.

the sea. It seems miraculous that the boat lived through it and brought us ashore. When we left the ship her plates were red hot."

Antonio Georgia, an oiler on the ship, who came ashore at Spring Lake, described the panic in the hold of the ship.

"I was lying down in the petty officers' room, having come off duty at midnight," he said. "I was suddenly awakened by screams for help and found the room filled with smoke. I opened the door. Flames were everywhere. The hold was a bedlam of fighting men. Three times I started up the stairs and three times my legs were grabbed and I was dragged down as men fought like beasts to get up the narrow ladder stairway.

"The flames were thickest on the port side, it seemed. It was there that most of the women were gathered. I saw many women burned to death, but could not get near them because of the terrific heat from the fire. I finally reached the deck and crawled into one of the lifeboats. The boat quickly filled with people. We were horrow-stricken when we found the lifeboat would not swing over the side. Its tackle was jammed. Finally the electrician freed the boat, but many of the people had jumped out and leaped into the sea.

"We got the boat into the water, but couldn't row because of the high seas. Luckily the wind came up and blew us to shore. The waves half swamped us and we had to bail constantly. One huge wave swept the chief engineer out of the boat, but the next swept him back in again. His arm was broken."

Georgia's hands were lacerated and blistered from the hours of steady bailing. The boat drifted about three hours before coming ashore at Spring Lake.

Work of Crew Praised.

The behavior of the crew was praised by Leroy Kelsey, a seaman, who was in charge of the first lifeboat to land at Spring Lake.

"We had a bad time and once almost overturned," he said. "The crew and every one else did all they could to save the passengers. I understand the wireless operator was burned to death in his shack."

The fire, Kelsey said, seemed to centre in the main saloon between A and B decks.

"We had to get off or burn," he said. "The passengers all ran aft because the flames were amidships. That is where most of the lives were lost. I was sleeping in the forecastle when I heard the general alarm. It was the bell, not the ship's whistle. We ran out on deck and I shoved three women into the lifeboat. Their courage was splendid in spite of the fact that they were deathly seasick."

The first assistant engineer, Anthony Bujia, would not discuss the catastrophe other than to say that the fire seemed to have started in a half dozen places at once and to hazard the suspicion that it might have been "set." He would not explain his suspicion of incendiarism.

Joseph O'Connor, 50, the ship's night watchman, who discovered the fire, said he had turned in the alarm at 2:50 A. M. He smelled smoke on B deck and looked into the recreation room amidships to find it a roaring furnace. The library and lounge adjoining were also in flames, he said. He joined the fire-fighting brigade and then, when all hope of putting out the fire was abandoned, took to a lifeboat.

He explained the heavy loss of life among the passengers by the fact that at least a third of them had been seasick and that the fire spread quickly through the corridors, cutting off this means of escape from cabins. Many passengers were trapped in their berths, he believed.

Nine passengers and Robert J. Smith, the cruise director, arrived at Pennsylvania Station at 4:14 P. M. in the rear half of a special six-car train from Spring Lake. The first three cars of the train, bearing eighty-six members of the crew, was routed to Jersey City at Manhattan Transfer.

The stories told by the surviving passengers varied widely, but each stressed the general confusion at the start, when no one seemed aware of what had happened.

Miss Renée Mendez Capote, 32, of Havana, said to be a daughter of a high Cuban official, who was making her eighth trip to New York, said:

"I was in my stateroom on A deck, No. 15—and I just woke up, I don't know why. There was a strange noise outside the door. I opened it to see what was going on, but I shut it again because the smoke and flame rushed in.

"Then I tried to open the window, but I couldn't, so I opened the door again. But the smoke and flames were worse, so I shut it again and tried the other window—there were two in my cabin, a de luxe stateroom. I managed to open it and climb out to the deck where the lifeboats were. One of the men of the crews was very nice and very brave, and he put me in a crew lifeboat. I was the only woman in the crew lifeboat."

When the boat was picked up hours later, Miss Capote received a loose-fitting white garment like a nurse's to replace her soaked and torn sleeping outfit. She said she lost considerable cash and jewelry.

Paul Arneth, a butcher, of 5,844 Catalpa Avenue, Brooklyn, told his story as follows:

"I ran to the deck and found the fire raging all around me. I gave a hand with the hose, but was cut off by fire at the front part of the boat. Finally, myself and three others got into a lifeboat. It was awfully hot, but we managed to launch it, and were picked up two hours later. I had on a pair of trousers and a dressing gown, I lost everything else. Yes, you could call it a sort of alleged vacation."

Miss Una Cullen, 21 years old, a stenographer of 68 Chauncey Street, Astoria, L. I., said:

"I was alone with Mary Maloney and two friends having cocktails in the lounge. It was about 4 A. M. I don't know what happened. I first saw smoke, but didn't think it was much because the stewards said not to worry, it would be put out easy. So we went to see what was going on and suddenly the fire just jumped at us. I ran down and woke my roommate, Helen Williams, and got a coat and a life preserver.

"I was all for jumping overboard right away, but they told me to wait. Then I tried to go down a rope ladder, but my high heels caught in the second step and I fell in the water. I was in the water seven hours, I think."

Miss Cullen said she had been wearing a trailing velvet evening gown. On the train, huddled in a gray blanket, she wore a blue-green and white house dress and old black shoes. Her black hair was wet and tousled. A jeweled crucifix hung at her throat. She was met at the station by her parents, Mr. and Mrs. Thomas Cullen, and other members of the family.

Miss Sydney Folkman, 230 Riverside Drive, said:

"I was in my room on B deck with Miss Gertrude Cohn of 600 West 168th Street, my roommate. I was sleeping. I was awakened by the smell of smoke, and nearly choked. I woke my roommate and we pulled on some clothes and went up on deck. Women were screaming all around, but some were praying. I heard one woman say, 'I have three children at home, what'll they do?'

"Every one seemed panic-stricken and the crew did nothing as far as I could see to help the passengers out. The passengers had to do everything for themselves. A great cloud of smoke and flame drove all of us to the rear of the boat. People began to jump overboard, so I jumped too.

"When I came to the surface—held up by my life preserver—I found a member of the crew, I think he was a steward, floating near me. Miss Cohn was near me too. We saw a floating log in the gray light and made for it. Five of us, including the crew man, clung to it for eight hours at least. The steward told us to be calm, we were bound to be picked up sooner or later. Finally a Coast Guard cutter did pick us up."

Others on the train were Charles Hoffman of 6,926 Cooper Avenue, Glendale, L. I., and his son, Charles Jr. Both were severely injured, the father's eyes being swathed with bandages. They lay on impromptu stretchers on the train, but were transferred to wheel-chairs at the station and taken to the Hotel New Yorker, where an emergency hospital had been set up.

The relief train, which left New York early in the morning, left Spring Lake at 1:29 P. M., standard time. The survivors were in the care of five nurses from the Monmouth County volunteer Red Cross unit, five State troopers and Julius Sachs, Pennsylvania transport agent. A considerable crowd was at the station to meet the train. Uniformed immigration officials boarded it immediately and after briefly conferring with the passengers allowed them to leave the coaches.

John Holden, 12, of Cincinnati, told his story at Spring Lake, sitting bundled in blankets waiting for dry clothes. Next to him was his 16-year-old brother, Rubin. The two boys talked of their anticipated reunion with their parents, also passengers. The parents are not listed among the saved.

"Mother kissed us all on deck," said John, "before she, my father, my brother and myself leaped into the ocean. We had on life preservers and she told us that if we got separated to meet her and dad at the Roosevelt [the Hotel Roosevelt here].

"Rubin and I kept together in the water. We hailed six lifeboats but they didn't hear us. We saw another one coming and swam right in front of it, so they either had to pick us up or run us down. They pulled us into the boat."

Members of the crew spoke freely soon after they were rescued, but were silent later on when their officers told them not to talk. Ernest Abbott, junior engineer, told of seeing the first mate—the acting captain—on the bridge shouting orders.

"The bridge was burning furiously and I could hardly see the mate because of the flames," he said.

"False modesty" on the part of women cost many lives in the opinion of John Smith, a steward. Quite a few were caught in their cabins by the flames because they waited to don clothing, he said. Smith added that the water pressure on the ship's fire fighting system failed.

Joseph Markov of Flushing, another steward, told of fighting the fire until forced to take to the lifeboats.

"All the sailors were asleep when they were aroused by the ship's bells and fire siren," he said. "Passengers must have been asleep, for three women were all that I saw after fighting the blaze on the forward B deck for at least an hour.

"I ran to the lifeboats on the promenade deck and after breaking down a door managed to release two screws which held the boat in position. I saw three women and called them to come up. By that time lifeboats 8 and 12 were on fire and we were between the flames, trying desperately to get the lifeboat down.

"We had trouble releasing the forward hook after the boat almost reached the ocean, which was pounding against the side of the ship. Nearly all of us narrowly escaped being thrown overboard before we were able to release the hook while the lifeboat hung at an angle of forty five degrees.

"Showered with hot broken glass from the upper decks, we drifted in the surf. We saw nothing in the water but the red glare of the flames. The smoke was streaming from the port side of the boat. As we managed to row the lifeboat around the ship we could see that the decks were filled with passengers screaming, crying and waving frantically. We rowed for an hour with what few oars were available. We had lost some overboard while we were trying to lower it.

"Finally, after rowing until we were all in, we found a piece of canvas and hoisted it as a sail with a jury rig. The wind blew us toward the shore. Just then the lifeboat began to fill with water. We found the drain plug in the bottom was out. I took off my shirt and stuffed it in the hole and stopped the leak. We thought the Morro Castle would blow up any minute. It was a terrible sight and a terrible night.

"We did not see any other ship and we didn't know what had happened to those on board. I lost everything I had except a belt and that isn't mine."

Survivors who arrived in port late yesterday afternoon on the rescue ships had their stories to tell of the fire. Many of them would not tell of their experiences, however. Relatives of passengers thronged the pier and there were many joyous reunions as well as much weeping, mostly for joy.

David Schneider, textile exporter of 1,214 Broadway, who also arrived on the Monarch of Bermuda kept muttering: "They were jumping over like fleas. You never saw such praying in all your life," he added.

Five members of the Morro Castle's crew, picked up by the same liner, were taken from the pier to the Seamen's Church Institute. All of them were near collapse. One of the five, Albert Sorel, 30, of Fall River, Mass., a seaman, told a graphic story of the fire.

"I went up forward and ran to A deck," he said. "I pulled out the hose, but the fire had too big a start. We went aft around No. 1 lifeboat. Then we couldn't get back forward again or even amidships because of the fire and smoke.

"The anchor was dropped and the ship pointed into the wind. The fire and smoke poured aft. We managed to hold back the flames from the passengers with the hose until daylight, but then it got the best of us.

"On B deck the smoke was so bad the passengers couldn't stand it and I saw dozens of them jump overboard. On C deck the women passengers were panicky and refused to go overboard when they were told to do so by members of the crew, who were adjusting life belts to them and dropping them into the ocean. But we made them go overside."

Katherine Liebler, 27, of 38 Huron Road, Bellerose, L. I., was one of the few survivors landing on the Andrea Luckenbach in Brooklyn, who was able to talk about her experience.

"I was in bed and I heard some noise as though a party was going on outside my room," said Miss Liebler. "When I got the sleep out of my eyes I realized it was one of the stewards calling into the room. I still couldn't understand what was going on, but I woke my girl friend, Mildred Weiser. Poor Mildred, I don't know where she is now.

"We went out on deck. It was then about 4:30. We smelled smoke and knew the ship was on fire, but we did not get excited. Everybody seemed very quiet. There was some screaming, but not nearly as much as you'd think there would be at a time like that. It kept getting hotter and hotter all the time and we were all waiting until the last minute before leaving the ship. The water looked so cold and black.

"Every one around me had on life-preservers. They were given to us before we left our cabins. Finally it got so hot we could stand it no longer. I guess it was about 6:15 when I went down the rope and hit that icy water. I was in the water for about half an hour before I was picked up by one of the life boats from the Luckenbach. It was a frightful experience, but I did my best to stay calm.

"I saw no panic on board and I think the men passengers and the members of the crew did everything they could do for people in distress. Everybody seemed to be trying to pacify one another."

Miss Liebler, dressed in blue polka dot pajamas, a gray sweater and a blue raincoat, said she did not know where the latter two garments had come from.

"Somebody slipped them on me, I guess, when I was taken out of the water," she said.

Miss Liebler was taken to the Hotel Pennsylvania. She said she expected to leave for her home as soon as she could get some clothes. She sailed a week ago yesterday for a pleasure trip, she said, having worked all year as a secretary in a law office.

Wandered Through Corridors.

Miss Lillian Wallace, 23 years old, of 9 Vernon Avenue, Hartford, Conn., was removed to the Coney Island Hospital, Brooklyn, after the arrival of the Luckenbach. She was burned about the head and body.

Miss Wallace told of wandering through the corridors of the Morro Castle and jumping through a mass of flames to reach the deck. She said she waited on deck for more than two hours with a lifebelt strapped around her.

"When it got too hot, I jumped," said Miss Wallace. "I saw a lot of people floating around. Some were probably dead. I tried to do something to help, but I needed help myself. I don't know who picked me up, but here I am."

Mrs. Mary Lione of Long Island City was among the injured on the Monarch of Bermuda. Her son, Robert, 4, was also aboard. Her husband, Anthony, and another son, Raymond, 8, were among the missing.

Robert could not tell the story of his rescue. He was bewildered by the attention being showered on him. An unnamed but heroic seaman had saved his life, other persons aboard the rescue boat said, by taking Robert on his back and jumping from the flaming ship, managing to stay afloat until he delivered his human cargo to the lifeboat. He also was rescued.

E. Rhinehart of Philadelphia told of his experience.

"I was awakened by noise and smoke and when I opened the door of my cabin on B deck I was met with a burst of flame. I shut the door and climbed out of the cabin window, a few feet away, onto a portion of the deck which was not burning. I stood there with fire crawling toward me from both directions on the deck, not knowing what to do. Finally, I followed the course of the others—I jumped. I was unconscious when they pulled me out of the water.

Mrs. Molly Weinberger, 25, of 4,356 York Road, Philadelphia, who is in a Spring Lake hospital, was overjoyed last night when she was told that her husband, Dr. M. E. Weinberger, whom she had feared was dead, was safe in St. Vincent's Hospital here suffering from a broken arm. She had not seen him since he had put a life belt about her and tossed her over the side of the burning liner.

No Confusion, Says Waiter.

Carl Wright, 32, headwaiter on the liner, told his story of the fire on board the train which brought the crew survivors to New York.

"There was very little confusion," said Wright. "The fire was mostly forward, but the smoke was suffocating and when I left C deck aft over the side only a few of the crew were left on deck. Several passengers were hurt by jumping on top of each other. The little girl I tried to save was badly burned on the hands and face."

According to members of the crew, the ship's steering apparatus, including the emergency gear, failed soon after the fire started, making the vessel unmanageable. Several passengers were drowned or injured because their lifebelts were improperly adjusted and came off when they leaped into the sea, members of the crew said.

Among the survivors rescued by the City of Savannah, which docked at Pier 46 at 3:45 yesterday afternoon, were Dr. and Mrs. Harry J. Brinkman of Bellerose, Queens. Many of the survivors were dressed in makeshift clothes borrowed from members of the Savannah's crew, some of the rescued passengers being clad only in night clothes and blankets.

Miss Margaret Cotter, 22, of 68 Court Street, Springfield, Mass., said she owed her life to her ability to swim. She said:

"The flames and smoke were so bad I was afraid of being suffocated and I put on a life preserver and jumped overboard. I swam for five hours and at last saw a lifeboat from the City of Savannah. I reached the boat and was helped in.

"While in the water I passed near several bodies and saw several people who could not swim drown in front of me before I could move toward them."

Nathan Feinberg of 12 West Seventy-ninth Street, another survivor, said the crew of the City of Savannah did fine work in the rescue.

"I was in the water seven hours," he said. "I'd rather not say anything about the crew of the Morro Castle. I was awakened before dawn by a passenger—and did not see any officer or sailor even to ask what had happened. I was picked up at 7:30."

Seymour Saffir of 1,687 Carroll Street, Brooklyn, spent seven hours in the water before being rescued by a lifeboat from the Savannah. He is the son of Abraham Saffir, Republican leader of the Eighteenth Assembly District in Brooklyn. Seymour, a student at Pennsylvania State College, had spent the Summer as a bellboy on the Morro Castle. Another youthful survivor was José Hidalgo y Garcia, Brooklyn High School student, who also swam around for seven hours before being picked up.

Mr. and Mrs. Thorpe Aschoff of 150-15 Sanford Avenue, Flushing, were on their wedding trip, having been married on Sept. 1. Both leaped into the sea shortly after the outbreak of the fire. Aschoff, a strong swimmer, gave away his life preserver first. They were in the water about five hours, the husband helping his wife to remain afloat. Picked up by a lifeboat from the City of Savannah, they landed safely and were taken to the home of the bride's mother, Mrs. Charles C. Lawrence, 41-52 150th Street, Flushing.

Two young women from Shrewsbury, Mass., Ethel and Jean Knight, performed deeds of heroism. The two sisters, both in their twenties, leaped from the burning ship and started to swim to shore. En route they found Benito Rueda, 7, and his younger brother battling the waves. Each young woman took a child in tow and struggled through the waves to the shore. When they reached land, worn and exhausted, Benito was taken to the Fitkin Hospital at Asbury Park. The other child was dead.

W. M. Tripp, an 18-year-old student of 14 Sayward Street, Dorchester, Mass., who was an engineer cadet on the Morro Castle, gave a graphic description of the scene in the engine room, where he was on duty when the fire started.

"At 3 in the morning the bridge signaled us to stand by," he said. "A few minutes later they telephoned, ordering us to search the engine room for signs of fire. At 3:10, full speed ahead on the starboard engine was ordered, in order to swing her head toward the coast, I suppose.

"Shortly after that the lights went out and we could see the wind driving the fire along the ship. At about 3:30 came the order to stop the engines. This was a difficult task, as we had to grope our way through the smoke and darkness to reach the valves and controls so we could stop the screw and shut off the boilers to prevent danger of the ship blowing up. Then we crawled aft through the shaft and out on the upper deck."

Pietro Yaines, a steward, said he had been awakened by the alarm and ran on deck and then jumped overboard. "I swam for a while and was then picked up by a lifeboat. Many people around me were drowned because the boat was still under way and they were sucked in."

Colin Houston of 62 Chestnut Avenue, Ridgefield Park, N. J., a fireman on the Morro Castle, told this story:

"I was asleep in the E deck quarters when at 2:30 a wiper shook me and told me the boat was afire. When we reached forward deck five minutes later, going through smoke which became denser all the time, we found the midships in flames. We were ordered to man the hose but the flames were so hot there was little we could do. We were forced away. Then the wind changed to port, the flames licking under the lifeboats.

"We were sent along to try to get the passengers to the boats. They were trapped in their staterooms. We could not go through the passageways because of the flames, so we broke the windows of the staterooms, pulling some of the people through.

"We were driven to the lifeboats. An officer pushed me into the boat and later we landed at the beach here [Spring Lake]. We tried to pick up the passengers in the water, but it was dark and the waves carried them away."

According to Doris Watcher of Roselle Park, N. J., the fire was first discovered by passengers at 2:30, when a group of young people passed the lounge. She was one of the group.

"We saw the fire in the lounge at about 3 o'clock," she said. "We went to arouse the passengers, but members of the crew throwing buckets of water on the blaze stopped us. However, we did get away and started to awake the passengers—I went first and called father and mother."

NRA U.S. WE DO OUR PART

"All the News That's Fit to Print."

The New York Times.

LATE CITY EDITION
WEATHER—Fair today, no change in temperature; tomorrow showers.
Temperatures Yesterday—Max., 76; Min., 60

Copyright, 1935, by The New York Times Company.

VOL. LXXXIV....No. 28,252. Entered as Second-Class Matter. Postoffice, New York, N. Y. NEW YORK, SATURDAY, JUNE 1, 1935. PP TWO CENTS In New York City. | THREE CENTS Within 200 Miles | FOUR CENTS Elsewhere Except in 7th and 8th Postal Zones.

20,000 DIE IN INDIAN QUAKE; WIDE AREA IS DEVASTATED; 43 BRITISH AIRMEN VICTIMS

BALUCHISTAN IS STRICKEN

Quetta, the Capital, Is Shattered, With 100 Europeans Killed.

AIR FORCE HANGARS CRASH

Military Authorities Act to Prevent Looting by Wild Tribesmen Along Border.

AFGHAN TOWN IS IN RUINS

Kandahar Razed by Tremors—Shocks in Early Morning Cause Scenes of Terror.

Wireless to THE NEW YORK TIMES.

KARACHI, India, Saturday, June 1.—An extensive area along the valley of Baluchistan, in which the town of Quetta, the capital of Baluchistan and an important military and railway centre with 60,000 inhabitants, is located, was devastated early yesterday morning by one of the worst earthquakes in Indian history.

The shattering of communications made the huge loss of life difficult to estimate, but some radio messages from Quetta now put the death roll in that city alone at between 15,000 and 20,000. The total of European casualties in the town is now placed at 100 dead, including forty-three members of the British Royal Air Force, and 200 injured.

The number of casualties in the surrounding district has not been ascertained, but the stricken area is now known to extend southward from Quetta for more than 100 miles.

[Kandahar, the second largest city in Afghanistan, which is 125 miles northwest of Quetta, was reported in ruins with an unknown number of casualties, according to an Associated Press dispatch. It has a population of 60,000.]

Act to Prevent Looting.

Effective steps have already been taken by the military authorities to prevent looting by wild frontier tribesmen, which is one of the menaces stalking hand in hand with fire, pestilence and famine throughout a large part of the devastated district.

The first shock was felt in Quetta at 3:04 A. M. [about 7:04 P. M. Thursday, New York daylight-saving time], and others varying in intensity and lasting thirty to sixty seconds quickly followed. Crying "Ram, Ram!" the popular invocation to the Hindu god Rama, the terrified native populace rushed from their tottering houses into the open and the parks.

The town was crowded with British officials, students and members of the trading community spending the customary vacation in the hills during the hot weather.

Apparently the casualties were heaviest in the more solidly constructed buildings and barracks such as those in which the Royal Air Force was housed. Hangars collapsed, burying scores of costly aircraft beneath tons of tangled steel and masonry. Fragmentary radio messages reaching here from portable sets of the Air Force units gave first indications of the disaster.

Upheaval Like Tidal Wave.

According to one message, destruction came like a "tidal wave" in a land upheaval that swept in a few moments from Mastung along the low level of the valley of Datibdaulta, or the Plain of No Riches, to Quetta. Four-fifths of the buildings in both towns are reported destroyed.

Strangely enough, few casualties appear to have befallen the large numbers of British and Indian troops encamped in open cantonments on the outskirts of Quetta. Nevertheless, all civil and military railways have been demolished over the entire area and the flying fields were so damaged that rescuing airmen were warned by radio not to attempt a landing anywhere in the Quetta region.

Kalat, another town in the affected area, was also severely damaged, four persons out of five, according to dispatches here, being either killed or injured.

Fortunately Quetta, which is the jumping-off ground for military operations along the northwest

Continued on Page Three.

SMITH BROTHERS RESTAURANT, Poughkeepsie, N. Y. Open Sundays.—Advt.

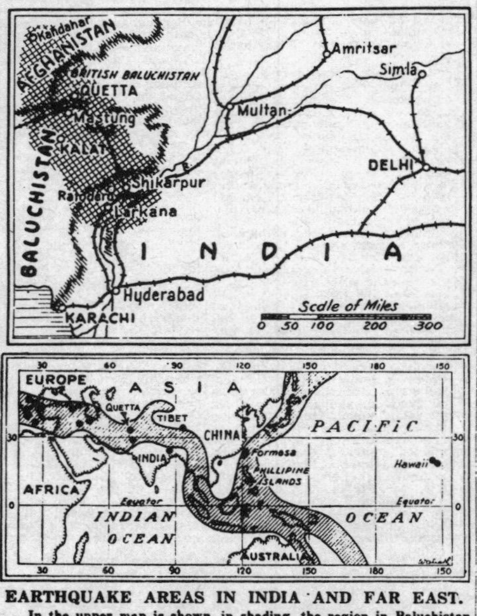

EARTHQUAKE AREAS IN INDIA AND FAR EAST.

In the upper map is shown, in shading, the region in Baluchistan and Afghanistan which was devastated by yesterday's shock. In the lower map the shading shows the great earthquake zones extending from Europe through Asia and Western Pacific islands. The dots show where severe quakes have occurred this year.

22 DEAD, 20 MISSING IN WESTERN FLOODS

Torrents Spread Destruction in Sections of Colorado, Wyoming and Nebraska.

TWO TOWNS 'WIPED OUT'

Houses and Bridges Are Swept Away—Trains Marooned, Vast Areas Inundated.

By The Associated Press.

DENVER, May 31.—Boiling waters of a tri-State flood, born of Spring rains on the eastern slope of the Rockies, raged eastward toward the already rising Missouri tonight, leaving twenty-two dead, more than a score missing, reports of other deaths and property damage in the millions.

The extent of the toll in Northern Colorado, Southwestern Wyoming and Southwestern Nebraska was pieced together slowly over crippled communication lines as heavy precipitation carried the flood menace to parts of other States in the mid-continent.

By a quirk of the weather, dust blew again in Southeastern Colorado's drought area. Searchers combed flood débris for bodies of three missing persons amid a dust storm at Seibert.

Floodwater sprawled over the banks of the South Platte River at Fort Morgan, Col., and Beaver Creek poured a three-foot deluge through the town's main street. About thirty miles of lowlands were reported inundated.

Wires Snapped in Nebraska.

McCook, Neb., was a danger point isolated by the snapping of wires after fragmentary reports of the death of six men in the collapse of a bridge, efforts to rescue fourteen workmen marooned atop a light plant and the wiping out of the villages of Parks and Max.

Four were listed as dead at Colorado Springs, three at Kiowa, three at Elbert, three at Seibert and two at Bennett, all in Colorado, and seven in Wyoming.

Other high water caused property damage and drove scattered families from lowland homes in Kansas, Oklahoma, Missouri and Texas.

Hundreds of farm families along Missouri River bottoms between Kansas City and St. Louis were moving to higher ground tonight as heavy rains brought the "Big Muddy" above flood stage.

At Boonville, Mo., the swirling river was three feet over flood stage and a further rise of two or three feet during the night was predicted.

The floods which ravaged the region of Colorado Springs and the district immediately northeast had subsided tonight.

Colorado Springs decide to ask

Continued on Page Nine.

DROUGHT FELT HERE IN RISING MEAT COST

Greater Advances Predicted Unless Consumers Turn to Fish and Vegetables.

PORK ROSE 48% IN YEAR

AAA Plan Held Responsible in Part—Beef Next With Price Gain of 30%.

By RUSSELL B. PORTER.

With meat prices rising almost to pre-depression levels, angry housewives picketing storage plants and retail stores, and with thousands of butcher shops closed, New York City is beginning to feel at first hand the effects of the great drought of 1934.

It may suffer even more in future months, for predictions in Federal Government circles, based upon the state of supply, are that beef and pork prices will continue to rise unless the present complaints are followed by a considerable reduction in demand. If city workers' incomes are reduced by the abolition of the NRA, it is pointed out, the situation may become even more acute.

The long dry spell, the scorching sun, the hot winds and the terrible dust storms of the worst drought the United States has known in many years laid waste large areas of the Middle West, the nation's food basket. Feed crops were destroyed in many States. Millions of head of cattle were slaughtered to keep them from starving. For lack of feed, millions of hogs which normally would have been grown could not be raised.

On Top of AAA Program.

This came on top of the 1933 "slaughter of little pigs" in the AAA corn and hog reduction program. The purpose of that, as in the whole agricultural curtailment plan, was to reduce farm surpluses and restore farm income and purchasing power. As the AAA increased farm income, the natural rise in food prices was to have been overcome by the NRA increase in the income of the city masses.

Now, with the drastic increases in meat prices from the unforeseen drought and with the uncertainties attending the end of NRA, another stage seems to be developing in the historical cost-of-living cycle of city versus country.

Complaints of housewives, increasing throughout the past Winter, have reached a climax. The dissatisfaction has been organized into a consumers' boycott, and a strike committee has been formed to picket retail shops and wholesale storage plants. Communists and other left-wing groups have seized upon the situation as a focus for agitation. The strike committee demanded that the city, with one-

Continued on Page Eight.

BRITISH SET PARITY IN AIR AS CONDITION OF PACT WITH REICH

Eden Says Nation Won't Rest Its Fate on Agreement for Help From Others.

BUILDING WILL BE PUSHED

Laborite Plea for a Halt in Aviation Program Rejected by the Government.

By CHARLES A. SELDEN.
Wireless to THE NEW YORK TIMES.

LONDON, May 31.—Great Britain will insist upon parity in any air agreement with Germany, Anthony Eden, Lord Privy Seal, told the House of Commons today.

"The yardstick for the collective security of the four great powers concerned [Britain, France, Italy and Germany] is parity," Mr. Eden said. "This country cannot have a lower air level than the other powers on the assumption that they would take care of us if we got into trouble."

The debate today in the Commons on the proposed Western air pact as part of the Locarno treaty was noticeably cramped by the collapse of the French government. Sir John Simon, Foreign Secretary, told the House he had received from Chancellor Hitler a draft of such a convention as Germany would be willing to sign but gave none of its details.

Reports French Assurance.

He seemed influenced by a desire not to rush matters or reveal too much while France was too preoccupied with her domestic political crisis to give full attention to the international situation. He said he had communicated with Pierre Laval, French Foreign Minister, just before the debate and had his authority for stating that the air negotiations would receive the careful consideration of all Locarno signatories.

Sir John, however, gave no intimation that it was feared in London that the French, despite willingness to consider a Western air pact, would not sign such a document unless it was taken in connection with other items of the Anglo-French agreement of Feb. 3.

There is real anxiety lest Herr Hitler's proposal of the last week, which Stanley Baldwin, Lord President of the Council, and the British Government and Parliament generally welcomed with such enthusiasm, may fall through because of eventual French refusal to act upon it separately.

This new doubt on the part of the British probably was the cause of Sir John's insistence today in going on with the full program for trebling the air force of this country without awaiting further negotiations. A week ago there was an official intimation that Britain might not be obliged to carry out this plan in its entirety because of the new hope of limitation inherent in the Hitler proposal.

The only party leader urging delay in the construction today was Sir Stafford Cripps, speaking for the Labor Opposition, who asked the government to reserve the expansion program as a bargaining factor until October and then pro-

Continued on Page Nine.

CABINET IS FORMED IN PARIS ON PLEDGE OF FULL AUTHORITY

Fernand Bouisson, Supported by Radicals and Other Parties, Faces Deputies Tuesday.

LAVAL IS IN FOREIGN POST

Bank of France Meets All Gold Demands—Bourse Remains Open and Shows Strength.

By P. J. PHILIP.
Wireless to THE NEW YORK TIMES.

PARIS, May 31.—For the ninth time since the present Chamber of Deputies was elected just three years ago a new government has been formed tonight. It is much the same kind of government as most of its predecessors, but has a new titular head in Fernand Bouisson, who for years past has been elected and re-elected President of the Chamber of Deputies.

M. Bouisson is a former Socialist, but as President of the Chamber become known as a non-party man, and with that as his main qualification was asked last night by President Albert Lebrun to try to form a Cabinet to succeed that of Pierre-Etienne Flandin.

His first stipulation was that he should have the full powers that M. Flandin asked for and which the Chamber rejected. After long negotiations the Radical Socialist party agreed with only twelve dissenting votes, and on that basis a Cabinet has been formed. It will go before the Chamber Tuesday morning and ask to have its full powers ratified, and so it is likely to have a chance to live at least until it must give a report on how these powers have been exercised.

Members of the Cabinet.

The composition of the new Cabinet is as follows:

Premier and Minister of the Interior—FERNAND BOUISSON.
Ministers of State—JOSEPH CAILLAUX, LOUIS MARIN, EDOUARD HERRIOT, Marshal PHILIPPE PETAIN.
Foreign Affairs—PIERRE LAVAL.
Finance—MAURICE PALMADE.
Commerce—LAURENT EYNAC.
War—General LOUIS FELIX MAURIN.
Navy—FRANCOIS PIETRI.
Air—General VICTOR DENAIN.
Justice—GEORGES PERNOT.
Labor—LOUIS FROSSARD.
Pensions—CAMILLE PERFETTI.
Colonies—LOUIS ROLLIN.
Communications—GEORGES MANDEL.
Public Works—JOSEPH PAGANON.
Merchant Marine—WILLIAM BERTRAND.
Agriculture—HENRY ROY.
Education—MARIO ROUSTAN.
Health—ERNEST LAFONT.
Under-Secretary to Premier—PIERRE CATHALA.

The whole interest in today's negotiations centred on whether the Radical Socialists would agree to enter the Cabinet and would give it full powers, which a large number of its members last night refused to give M. Flandin.

There were numerous long discussions. It was at first announced that the Radical Socialists had agreed on M. Bouisson's choice of personalities, but that points of principle remained to be cleared up. When these points of principle were agreed to, or swallowed, M. Bouisson had not disclosed any more than had M. Flandin on the use he would make of the powers he was asking for beyond a general statement that he would use them to protect the franc, develop

Continued on Page Two.

Normandie Breaks Speed Mark for Liners; Expected to Set Even Better Record Today

By NEIL MacNEIL.
Wireless to THE NEW YORK TIMES.

ON BOARD THE LINER NORMANDIE, May 31.—The world's greatest liner broke the speed record for commercial ships in its run from noon yesterday until noon today, despite a twenty-five-mile head wind and adverse currents.

The Normandie traveled 744 nautical miles, beating the mark of the Rex of the Italian Line by eight miles and averaging 29.76 knots for twenty-five hours. After doing a little better than 29 knots throughout yesterday, she speeded up during the night, averaging 30.2 knots from 4 P. M. until 5 A. M.

Today, there has been a freshening head wind to thirty-five miles an hour and an adverse current of 0.4 knot, but officials expect a still better mark by noon tomorrow. Commandant-Adjutant Thoreux frankly admitted to the press today that he expected to have eclipsed all records on arriving in New York, explaining that he would increase his speed after crossing the Gulf Stream when the currents would be favorable.

A visit to the engine room revealed that the ship was operating at 128,000 horsepower while it is capable of an output of more than 160,000, confirming the assertions of officials that the ship is running at a commercial speed.

Asked about the reserve power, M. Thoreux replied:

"There is plenty."

The ship is following the southern course to avoid icebergs. The officials refuse to give the mileage, asserting that several Paris papers have contests on the figure, but the data posted in the purser's bulletin tell the story. For to noon Thursday it gave 228 miles, 744 from noon Thursday until noon today, and an added 2,220 more to go, totaling 3,192.

This ship's officers expect to calculate the time for the record from Bishop's Rock, which was passed at 11:48:24 Thursday morning, instead of from St. Catherine's Light.

Mme. Albert Lebrun, wife of the French President, formally opened the grill and cafe today. Tonight it was the scene of gay parties.

Mme. Albert Lebrun will be the guest of honor Monday night at a dinner at the Waldorf-Astoria that has been arranged by Mayor La Guardia's reception committee.

She will leave Tuesday for Washington to be received by Mrs. Roosevelt, wife of the President, and will be entertained at dinner Tuesday evening at the White House. On Wednesday evening an official dinner will be held aboard the Normandie, after which Mme. Lebrun will return to the Waldorf-Astoria to attend a fashion show featuring French mannequins who are also passengers on the Normandie.

PRESIDENT SAYS END OF NRA PUTS CONTROL UP TO PEOPLE; WILL ACT TO HALT DEFLATION

Stocks Break on President's Views; Commodity Prices Fall Sharply

Cotton Drops $4.15 a Bale From High of Day and Sugar Takes Widest Plunge in 11 Years as Wall Street Reacts Swiftly to Statement—Shares Lose Up to 2½ Points.

Stocks and commodities declined sharply yesterday following the publication by news tickers of President Roosevelt's reaction to the Supreme Court's NRA decision. It was the third consecutive downward movement in the financial markets since the court ruled NRA unconstitutional last Monday.

Wall Street interpreted the President's remarks as indicating that no attempt would be made at this session of Congress to revive NRA.

The financial community attached great importance to the President's statement that the court's decision imperiled crop-adjustment plans, and that if these plans were abandoned this country might see cotton at 5 cents a pound and wheat at 36 cents a bushel. At present the government is lending to farmers 12 cents a pound on cotton, and wheat is quoted at 82⅝ cents a bushel in Chicago.

Cotton showed acute weakness as traders digested the President's views, which began to appear on the news tickers a little after 2 P. M. On the Cotton Exchange futures market, prices declined as much as 83 points, or $4.15 a bale from the highs for the day, and the closing quotations were from 61 to 67 points lower.

The Chicago wheat market did not have an opportunity to appraise all of the President's remarks before it closed at 2:15 P. M. Wheat futures declined about ¾ of a cent a bushel.

Sugar futures sustained the widest break in eleven years on the New York Coffee and Sugar Exchange, closing around 25 points, or a quarter of a cent a pound lower, the largest decline permitted by the rules of the Exchange; raw silk futures dropped 3 to 4 cents a pound, and raw hide futures, 3 to 13 points.

The turnover on the Coffee and Sugar Exchange was 89,950 tons, the largest for any session since July, 1933. Sugar, it was pointed out, was in a particularly advantageous position under the Jones-Costigan Act, which called for processing taxes and the fixing of market quotas by the AAA.

Beginning 1935 at 2.02 cents a pound, the December sugar contract advanced to a high of 2.71 last Monday. Yesterday it was quoted at 2.30 cents a pound, having lost nearly 58 per cent of the year's gain.

On the New York Stock Ex-

Continued on Page Six.

CURB ON NATIONAL RULE

Roosevelt Holds Court Stripped Washington of Commerce Power.

BACK TO 1789, HE ASSERTS

Doubts Raised as to Validity of AAA and of the Securities and Exchange Act—FACA Dead.

PRIOR DECISIONS CITED

Analyzing Ruling for Newspaper Men, He Implies Need to Change Constitution.

By CHARLES W. HURD.
Special to THE NEW YORK TIMES.

WASHINGTON, May 31.—The right of the government to regulate nation-wide economic and social conditions in the United States was made the paramount political issue by President Roosevelt today.

He thrust forward the problem which is expected to be fought on the field of the 1936 elections when, at a White House press conference, he said that the implications of the Supreme Court's NRA decision deprived the government of all control over economic and social conditions, by interpretation of the interstate commerce clause of the Constitution in the light of the "horse-and-buggy" days of 1789, when it was written.

In a press conference which lasted for an hour and twenty-five minutes, talking to newspaper men in an unbroken thread, the President termed the Schechter decision the most important rendered by the Supreme Court since that in the Dred Scott case in 1857.

He said that by implication the decision raised grave doubts as to the constitutionality of the Agricultural Adjustment Act, the "truth in securities act" and the Securities and Exchange Act, as well as of all pending social legislation.

Commerce Clause Sole Weapon.

Mr. Roosevelt termed serious the court's expressed view on the delegation of Congressional powers to the Executive, but said the greatest question revolved around its interpretation of governmental powers over interstate commerce. Those powers, he emphasized, constituted the only weapon in the government's hands to fight conditions not even dreamed about 150 years ago.

Turning again and again to the implications of the decision, which quoted a previous decision designating building construction, manufacturing, mining and the growing of crops as local occupations, Mr. Roosevelt drew the deduction that not only business recovery efforts, but social security, including unemployment insurance and pending labor legislation, had been jeopardized.

He declined today to submit a formula, although his listeners drew the plain inference that the President felt that if the Constitution made his Federal program for regulating economic conditions impossible, the Constitution must be changed.

The President made no commitments, but promised an announcement of immediate plans within four or five days. In the meantime, he said, his sole desire was that the press and radio should make clear to the public the implications of the decision invalidating the NRA.

Many Suggestions Impossible.

His desire for such clarification was prompted, the President said, by the obviously uninformed condition of the public mind as shown by thousands of telegrams received at the White House pleading for immediate action and coupling the pleas with suggestions impossible of accomplishment in the face of the Supreme Court's decision.

The press conference was the first of its kind in White House history where a President, speaking informally to newspaper men who would write their stories only from such penciled notes as they could make, outlined without reference to a manuscript an issue which appeared to him as second in importance only to war.

He spoke usually with a smile, but this did not mask the serious trend of his thought or the apparent irritation he felt over a governmental system which requires the

Continued on Page Six.

MANY IN CONGRESS OPPOSE ROOSEVELT

Republicans in Senate Reject and Democrats Split on Constitution Change.

MOST ARE NON-COMMITTAL

Robinson Insists President Is for States' Rights, Replying to Liberty League Attack.

Special to THE NEW YORK TIMES.

WASHINGTON, May 31.—The immediate reaction in Congress to President Roosevelt's statement of the issue created by the Supreme Court's decision against the NRA indicated that the legislative branch might not be ready for so great an expansion of Federal powers as he seemed to suggest.

The American Liberty League, representing certain business groups, took issue with the President's remarks. Jouett Shouse, president of the league, said that Mr. Roosevelt planned "to assume unwarranted power" and accepted for his organization what he termed a challenge to make the idea of Federal expansion an issue before the people.

The only really condemnatory comment in Congress came from partisan sources, but it was clear from the utterances of faithful Democrats that they either did not understand the full purport of the President's statement or did not relish its content. Their comment was indefinite and noncommittal.

Robinson Explains Talk.

Practically all of the Congressional reaction came from the Senate. The House adjourned early until Monday and several of its leaders had gone to North Carolina on a fishing expedition, unaware that a development of historical significance was about to take place in Washington.

The epitome of the reaction of New Deal Senators was voiced by Senator Robinson, the Democratic leader, who sat with the President as he expounded his views. Mr. Robinson said:

"The President gave emphasis to the difficulties that are to be anticipated from the decision and made clear the importance of the issues associated with questions pertaining to powers of Congress to deal with economic and social problems that are of national importance."

This evening, in a second statement, issued through the publicity bureau of the Democratic National Committee, Senator Robinson declared that the President had not "renounced" the Democratic theory of States' rights, as charged by Mr. Shouse.

In this statement Mr. Robinson said:

"The President has not renounced the Democratic theory of States'

Continued on Page Seven.

TWO NRA PLANS PUT BEFORE LEADERS

Officials Begin Study of the Detailed Proposals to Salvage Principles.

ONE SETS UP NEW AGENCY

Grimes Proposes Federal Incorporation—Kennedy Asks Revised Labor Pact.

Special to THE NEW YORK TIMES.

WASHINGTON, May 31.—Fortified by a veritable avalanche of telegrams and letters from all parts of the country begging him to "do something," President Roosevelt decided today to send Congress in a few days a bill designed to stem the tide of deflation that has been rising with increasing momentum in the nation's industrial centres since last Monday when the Supreme Court "threw out the baby with the bath" in the Schechter case decision.

Those of the President's advisers, led by General Johnson, who urged him to assert his leadership and "get tough," won the battle for immediate action.

Resolutions sent to the White House by trade associations, calling on members to abide voluntarily by wage, hour and child labor provisions of the now defunct codes, failed to overcome the impression created by widespread reports of strikes engendered by wage cuts and lengthening of hours, on the heels of the court ruling.

Leaders Study Two Proposals.

Scores of plans and measures of all sorts have been pouring in on administration officials, while the NIRB wrestled today with its own program of legislative suggestions.

General Johnson, who again called at the White House, made recommendations for legislation.

Important administration circles are considering proposals by two government officials, one for a temporary arrangement to replace the NRA and one based on long-range policy.

One of these plans was explained to Senator Harrison of the Finance Committee and an outline of both plans went to Solicitor General Reed.

The temporary plan was offered by John Drummond Kennedy of New York assistant NRA administrator in charge of food codes, and the permanent proposal was advanced by Charles P. Grimes of the NRA legal division, formerly associated with the New York law firm of Cravath, de Gersdorff, Swaine & Wood.

The Kennedy or temporary plan is based on the opinion that, over a space of time, "the minority is successful in dragging down the

Continued on Page Five.

20,000 ARE KILLED BY INDIAN QUAKES

Continued From Page One.

frontier, has lavish supplies of food available and is equipped with excellent hospital facilities. In normal circumstances Quetta could stand a siege of some months' duration and its water supplies are ample.

Sir Norman Cater, agent to the Governor General in Quetta, radioed that the second and third shocks were the severest, razing the railway headquarters, the civil government station and the native city. He said that the military station and staff college were not seriously harmed, however. According to other official messages from Quetta, the police force has been virtually wiped out.

It was revealed that Sir Norman saved his family and himself, when he first noticed the electric light pendants beginning to sway, by shouting to the members of the household, "Stand in the doorways!" Almost immediately the building crumbled, but the stout frames of the doorways held and all escaped with slight injuries.

The world famous fruit gardens surrounding the hill station, 5,500 feet above sea level, are in ruins, and the beautiful park has been turned into a casualty station, in which the sleepless doctors scarcely have time to separate the dying and the dead. Thousands of homeless refugees are being accommodated in tents on what was the race course and in the grounds of the wrecked Residency.

In the first list of the dead appear the names of Political Officer Meredith Jones, his bride of a fortnight and his mother-in-law, Mrs. Bradford. The children of several British officers whose bungalows were wrecked are missing.

A relief train has left Karachi with doctors, nurses, trained orderlies and plentiful supplies of ice and medicines, but it is not yet known how far it will be able to penetrate into the devastated area.

Relief airplanes were being mobilized at Lahore in readiness for the 500-mile flight to Quetta and expected word shortly that the landing ground there had been repaired. One large Victoria bomber was being reserved for forty military nursing sisters now being assembled from Kasauli, Umbala and Lahore hospitals.

Higher Toll Feared.

Copyright, 1935, by The Associated Press.

KARACHI, India, May 31.—Three tremendous rumbling earth shocks shattered the northwest frontier city of Quetta early today, killing an estimated 20,000 Europeans and natives. It was feared the death toll would go much higher with receipt of reports from outlying districts, especially that between Quetta and Kalat.

The town of Kandahar in Afghanistan also was reported in ruins, with an unknown number of casualties.

Tonight many of the dead still lay buried beneath débris, at which exhausted soldiers and volunteer relief workers were frantically tearing.

Scores of British and Indian troops dropped in the streets from sheer exhaustion after unbroken hours of digging, succoring the injured and organizing relief activities.

Few fresh details as to the extent of the catastrophe were forthcoming because of the destruction of the Quetta wireless station. Messages were being sent by way of Sibi, seventy miles from Quetta.

Meager advices said that fifty Europeans and 153 Indians injured in the quake had been extricated from the ruins by military rescue parties tonight and that hospital treatment had been given to them.

Populous Districts Razed.

Other reports declared that the Basu and Moti districts, the most

BRITON SAYS EARTH SEEMED TO GO MAD

Army Officer at Baluchistan Capital Asserts Tree Boughs Swept Ground in Quake.

CONGESTION ADDED TOLL

Houses in Native Quarter Fell on One Another, Imprisoning Whole Families.

Special Cable to THE NEW YORK TIMES.

LONDON, Saturday, June 1.— W. A. Myatt, in a dispatch to The Daily Mail from Quetta, capital of Baluchistan, says the most fearful toll in the earthquake there yesterday was taken in the native quarter and the bazaars, where people lived huddled together in almost suffocating congestion. He writes:

"So close are the houses together in this part that they fell one atop another, imprisoning whole families of shrieking, struggling people in the débris.

"Panic-stricken people who rushed into the narrow streets were overwhelmed as buildings crashed down, obliterating roadways and cutting

thickly populated parts of Quetta, had been completely razed. These sections were inhabited by Sindhis and various floating parts of the population.

Still other unconfirmed reports reaching Karachi said that the main bazaar on the Bruce Road to Quetta was afire. A severe storm followed the quake. The important frontier post of Chaman, sixty miles northwest of Quetta, was reported wiped out.

Two Royal Air Force planes were scheduled to take off here in the morning to assist in relief work.

Quetta's normal military and civil population of 60,000 had been swelled by thousands come from the lowland to escape the intense Summer heat. A wireless message from the town which gave the first complete estimate of the dead placed the figure at 20,000 or more, although earlier unofficial estimates were as high as 30,000. The message set the injured only "in the hundreds." The dead included at least three white children.

The main military barracks escaped the worst of the damage and soldiers were bearing the brunt of the relief work, for most of the town's policemen died.

An irrigation engineer named Francis and his wife were reported killed and the dead Royal Air Force aviators were said to include Flying Officer Charles Paylor.

Hundreds Killed in Streets.

Hundreds who fled for safety into the streets were caught and killed as buildings collapsed all about them.

The shocks laid waste the countryside around Quetta, tore up farm lands, shattered dwellings and disrupted communications. So violent were the quakes that birds were said to have been shaken out of their nests.

Hardest hit, apparently, was the Province of Baluchistan, which has 868,000 population. Meager reports said that one village, Mastung, with 4,000 inhabitants, lost 80 per cent of them. The villages of Larkana, Shikarpur and Ratodero also were known to have suffered. Terrified thousands all over the area were sleeping tonight in the open after praying to their Hindu gods for salvation.

An official report from Quetta said:

"Many casualties are feared to have occurred among the subordinate civil and police officers. The police force was almost wiped out. No railway officers were killed, but heavy casualties were feared among the subordinate personnel."

SCENES IN THE BALUCHISTAN EARTHQUAKE AREA.

Times Wide World Photo.

A birdseye view of the district around Quetta, where thousands are reported killed.

off all communication with the military station and railway. The narrow ways through the native quarter became shambles from which escape was almost impossible."

"Earth Seemed to Go Mad."

An army officer said:

"For a half minute the earth seemed to go mad. Boughs of trees, normally many feet from the ground swept the earth. The moon was dancing about crazily in the sky.

"Gradually the roar, which I can only liken to the sound of twenty express trains, reached its climax and died away. Then we heard the wailing of the dying and injured. Every street mongrel started howling."

Mr. Myatt adds:

"There is little left of the railway station and civil station. I have seen half-demented mothers, both white and native, wildly searching the ruins of buildings in the hope of discovering their children. It was as if some mighty wind had come rushing down Bolan Pass and blown the greater part of Quetta flat to the earth."

60,000 IN KANDAHAR AMID QUAKE PERILS

Capital of Afghan Province Is Important Trading Centre in Midst of Gardens.

Kandahar, which has suffered a severe earthquake, is the capital of a province of the same name in Southeastern Afghanistan. It has about 60,000 inhabitants.

It was the scene of a victory for British forces under General Frederick Roberts in 1880 during a war between Great Britain and Afghanistan. General Roberts later was elevated to the peerage in recognition of his victory and included the name of the city in his title.

Kandahar was supposed to have been founded by Alexander the Great, but did not take a place in history until the eighteenth century, when it was recognized as an important link in the trade routes to British India. After it had been conquered several times by Eastern nations the city was occupied by the British in 1839.

The city is at an altitude of nearly 3,500 feet. The straight, wide streets and impressive buildings are surrounded by a strong wall with bastions and a citadel. The city has 175 mosques and 1,600 marketplaces.

The chief exports are wool, cotton, asafoetida, fruit, silk and horses. The surrounding area contains many gardens yielding large quantities of semi-tropical fruits.

Times Wide World Photo.

A typical fruit stall in the Quetta market.

U. S. ENVOY NEAR EARTHQUAKE ZONE

Hornibrook Passed Through 6 Days Ago With Wife on Way to Afghanistan.

RED CROSS AWAITS CALL

Washington Experts Say There Is No Geological Connection With Recent Indian Quakes.

Special to THE NEW YORK TIMES.

WASHINGTON, May 31.—A report that no Americans were believed to be in the Quetta earthquake zone was received by the State Department today from Joseph G. Groeninger, United States Consul at Karachi, India.

William K. Hornibrook, United States Minister to Iran [Persia], who recently was appointed Minister to Afghanistan also, passed through the district six days ago en route to Afghanistan, where he presented his letters of credence. He was accompanied by Mrs. Hornibrook and their daughter.

Mr. Groeninger reported that thousands were killed in the earthquake and that the railway quarter and native city were razed. Only wireless communication was possible.

Red Cross Prepares to Aid.

Rear Admiral Cary T. Grayson, chairman of the American Red Cross, cabled sympathy today to the British Red Cross and asked the League of Red Cross Societies in Paris to keep him advised in regard to the need for relief.

On the seismograph at Georgetown University here the earthquake was recorded yesterday at 4:46:59 P. M. Eastern standard time as a very powerful shock. Georgetown scientists said the recording was complicated and that they had placed the earthquake centre nearer than India.

The shock was also recorded on the seismographs of the Coast and Geodetic Survey at Columbia, S. C.; Tucson, Ariz.; Bozeman, Mont.; Yukiah, Calif.; Sitka, Alaska; Honolulu, and San Juan, P. R. Reports from some of these stations are being collated.

"All the News That's Fit to Print."

The New York Times.

LATE CITY EDITION
WEATHER—Rain, slightly cooler today; tomorrow probably rain.
Temperatures Yesterday—Max., 71; Min., 56

Copyright, 1935, by The New York Times Company.

VOL. LXXXIV....No. 28,348. Entered as Second-Class Matter, Postoffice, New York, N. Y. NEW YORK, THURSDAY, SEPTEMBER 5, 1935. PP TWO CENTS In New York City. | THREE CENTS Within 200 Miles | FOUR CENTS Elsewhere Except in 7th and 8th Postal Zones.

ITALY IS DEFIANT AT GENEVA, RESERVING LIBERTY TO ACT; EDEN INVOKES LEAGUE PACT

ALOISI ATTACKS ETHIOPIA

Later Asserts Council Must Decide Which Stays in League.

SAYS ITALY IS IN DANGER

Jeze Denies Charges, Asking for Aid Against Threat of 'War of Extermination.'

EDEN PLEADS FOR PEACE

British Delegate Stresses Duty Is to Use the Machinery of Geneva to End Dispute.

By FREDERICK T. BIRCHALL.

Wireless to THE NEW YORK TIMES.

GENEVA, Sept. 4.—In a new and better atmosphere, cleared of suspicion by Secretary of State Hull's firm action on the Standard-Vacuum oil concession, the Council of the League of Nations began this evening its discussion of the Italo-Ethiopian problem.

It cannot yet be said that real progress toward a peaceful solution has been made. But on the whole these first results have not been wholly negative.

The Italians are staying here and continuing to discuss. That is a distinct gain. On the other hand their position, as stated in a lengthy declaration by Baron Pompeo Aloisi, can be described only as uncompromising.

Reserve Liberty of Action.

They deny the fitness of Ethiopia to take part on equal terms in the discussion now opening. They make "all reservations" as to their future course. But they have not actually demanded the expulsion of Ethiopia from the League, as it had been expected they would. However, Baron Aloisi's declaration, a bitter indictment of Ethiopia's action, closed with this paragraph:

"As we are concerned here with vital interests of primordial importance for Italian security and civilization, the Italian Government would be failing in its most elementary duties if it did not finally withdraw all its confidence with regard to Ethiopia and if it did not reserve to itself full liberty of action, with the view to adopting all measures that prove necessary for the security of her colonies and for safeguarding her own interests."

In press conferences in his hotel following the Council session Baron Aloisi was even more uncompromising.

Won't Reply to Ethiopia.

"You all heard my declaration on behalf of the Italian Government," he said. "It is irrevocable and unchangeable; it is our last position. In future discussions my part will be passive. I will not reply to Ethiopia, but, of course, I shall talk with other powers.

"We had a treaty of friendship with Ethiopia and we kept that treaty, but Ethiopia did not. My declaration today shows there is no more treaty, no more friendship with Ethiopia. I remain here merely as a courtesy to discuss the situation with the great powers."

"Then you regard Ethiopia as outlawed?" he was asked.

"Yes," he replied, "Ethiopia is outlawed as far as we are concerned."

"Do you then demand that she be expelled from the League?" was asked.

"You will have to decide finally whether Ethiopia or Italy is to be expelled," was the answer.

Explains "Free" Stand.

To an inquiry as to what he had intended to imply by saying that Italy reserved to herself "full liberty of action," he responded that he wished merely to register the fact that there was no agreement with the Council as to Italy's course.

"We retain our freedom of action," he repeated.

"What, then, is going to happen?" a journalist inquired.

"You had better ask a palmist," was Baron Aloisi's reply.

"But you intend, surely, to wait for the Council to decide whether a solution is possible?" was asked.

"That depends on the situation," was his reply. "We consider we are in great danger."

Some mirth was noticeable among

Continued on Page Fourteen.

When You Think of Writing Think of Whiting.—Advt.

The Complaint by Italy

By The Associated Press.

GENEVA, Sept. 4.—The text of important parts of the Italian memorandum against Ethiopia, placed before the Council of the League of Nations today, follows:

The Italian Government wishes to set forth, first of all, the particular political and juridical situation of Italy in regard to Ethiopia.

Immediately after the conclusion of a treaty, the Ethiopian Government began against Italy a series of hostile acts which, always more serious, led to armed conflict in 1895-96, which was concluded with a treaty of peace on Oct. 26, 1896.

Notwithstanding this past experience, the Italian Government resumed its policy of collaboration with Ethiopia, necessary for the Italian colonies in Eritrea and Somaliland, united to Ethiopian regions by a direct and close relationship.

The Italian Government concluded with Ethiopia a series of treaties and conventions, which sought to regulate all reciprocal relations. These accords stipulated the friendliest spirit and are the document of Italy's attitude of good-will toward Ethiopia, to whom Italy offered in peace every possibility of collaboration.

As a demonstration of the loyalty and benevolence with which the Italian Government treated Ethiopia there is this circumstance: That the largest quantity of arms and ammunition that was furnished Ethiopia before Italy, France and Britain concluded the treaty of 1930 came, in fact, from the Italian Government. The value of this amounted to 1,900,000 lire, of which amount the Ethiopian Emperor must still pay Italy 840,000 lire. With these very arms, furnished by Italy and not yet paid for, the Emperor is now preparing against Italy.

In recent years, as is known, Ethiopia anxiously sought warlike material. Her supplies of such material were appreciably augmented. It is clear that these arms have no other purpose except to be used against Italy.

The importance of the Ethiopian

Continued on Page Fourteen.

PRESIDENT SCORNS 'DOLLAR DIPLOMACY'

He Says Swift Cancellation of Ethiopian Oil Deal Proves End of Such Practices.

HOLDS AIR NOW CLEARED

State Department Shows Its Relief—Little Worried Over Chertok Concession.

Special to THE NEW YORK TIMES.

HYDE PARK, N. Y., Sept. 4.—The rapid negotiations that led to the cancellation by American Petroleum interests of the concession obtained from Ethiopia last week were hailed by President Roosevelt today as proof of the end of "dollar diplomacy."

"This is another proof," he said, "that since March 4, 1933, dollar diplomacy is no longer recognized by the American Government."

Speaks at Press Conference.

Mr. Roosevelt made this statement at a press conference this morning in response to a request for a statement of his reaction to the successful efforts made by Secretary Hull to have the American concessionaires relinquish their acquisition because of the embarrassing situation caused in diplomatic negotiations surrounding the Italo-Ethiopian question.

The President told newspaper men that by no stretch of the imagination had the President or the Secretary of State been concerned that the possession of oil leases would involve the United States in any way in the Ethiopian or Italian problems.

Nobody who knows the administration policy, he added, could think for a minute that there could be any such involvement. The only danger lay in the effect of the oil leases on negotiations between European powers and Ethiopia now going on at Geneva.

Withdrawal of the concession, Mr. Roosevelt said, was a fine thing because it cleared the air for those conferences.

Relief at State Department.

Special to THE NEW YORK TIMES.

WASHINGTON, Sept. 4.—An air of relief prevailed at the State Department today over the satisfactory solution of the troublesome Ethiopian oil concession, which Secretary Hull announced last night. Officials felt that the voluntary renunciation of the concession by the Standard-Vacuum Oil Company, owner of the African Exploration and Development Corporation, to which Emperor Haile Selassie granted exploitation rights to half of his kingdom, was the best possible outcome for an embarrassing situation.

The case of Leo Chertok, New York broker, who claims to have an option on a similar concession, is causing considerably less worry in high circles. One official described the deal Mr. Chertok says he put through with the Ethiopian Minister in London as "a freak and fantastic thing."

Mr. Hull indicated today that the

Continued on Page Fifteen.

GRAVITATION SEEN RE-FORMING EARTH

Prof. W. W. Watts Suggests Pull of Sun and Moon May Help in Making Land Masses.

ADMITS OTHER FORCES

He Offers Theory in Opening Meeting of British Group for Advancing Science.

By FERDINAND KUHN Jr.

Wireless to THE NEW YORK TIMES.

NORWICH, England, Sept. 4.—Scientists were told tonight by Professor William Whitehead Watts in his presidential address opening the meeting of the British Association for the Advancement of Science, that the tidal pull of the sun and moon might be one of the mysterious forces that help to cause the building of mountains and the formation of land masses on the surface of the earth.

For generations geologists here and abroad have tried in vain to account for these titanic stresses and strains. Was it simply a cooling of the earth's crust, they have asked, that had raised the gigantic rock masses of the Himalayas and made the ocean retreat from dry land? Or were other forces at work?

Theory of Earth Pulse.

A half century ago it was suggested that bursts of land-building energy had come at intervals of millions of years and that the earth, like its smallest organism, had a rhythmic pulse of its own. Present-day physicists and geologists think they have detected the driving power of such a pulse in radioactivity within the earth's crust.

Still others believe in the famous theory of continental drift—a hypothesis that is supported by the parallel outlines of the continents on both sides of the Atlantic, so that they would fit almost perfectly if pieced together on map.

But today Professor Watts, who is one of the foremost geologists, reviewed all these theories and admitted none of them was wholly proved. Unquestionably, he said, there is a "pulse within a pulse" helping to build the earth today, but its causes he found still obscure. Perhaps, he suggested, mountains have been pushed upward by the downward thrust of gravitation; perhaps there have been other forces still unknown.

"Isn't it possible, for instance," he suggested, "that tidal influence of the moon and sun, which is producing so much distortion of the solid earth that the ocean tides are less than they would be otherwise, and, dragging always in one direction is slowing down the earth's rotation, may exert permanent distortion influence on solid earth itself?

Sees Weakness Involved.

"May it not be that such a stress, if not sufficiently powerful to produce the greater displacements of continental drift and mountain building, may yet take advantage of structures of weakness produced

Continued on Page Twelve.

TIE-UP THREATENED IN GARMENT TRADE AS STRIKE SPREADS

15,000 Cloak and Dress Makers Said to Be Out Already in Sympathy With Clerks.

CONCILIATION MOVE FAILS

Union, Accused of Violating Contract, Asserts It Cannot Force Members to Work.

The strike of shipping clerks, push boys and allied employes in the garment district, which began last week, threatened yesterday to develop to proportions that may involve more than 100,000 garment workers of all classifications acting in sympathy with the strikers.

With 15,000 cloakmakers and dressmakers already idle after refusing to work in shops unwilling to meet the strikers' demands, David Dubinsky, president of the International Ladies Garment Workers Union, declared last night that his organization would not be responsible for the spread of the sympathetic strike movement "because our members do not work with strike breakers, no matter in what department, and we cannot urge them to do so."

Mr. Dubinsky's statement was made after an abortive conference called by him at the Hotel New Yorker with representatives of the employers' associations against whom the Ladies Apparel Shipping Clerks Union is striking. These are the same associations with which the International Ladies Garment Workers Union has collective agreements.

Employers Refuse to Yield.

The purpose of the conference was to prevail upon the employers to yield to the demands of the shipping clerks and enter into a collective agreement with their organization. The employers declined flatly to do so, saying that not more than 900 shipping clerks were on strike, and filed a protest both with Mr. Dubinsky and with the impartial chairman for the dress industry, Adolph Feldblum, charging violation of collective agreements by the International Ladies' Garment Workers' Union in permitting members of its affiliated organizations to walk out in sympathy strikes.

Mr. Dubinsky countered with a statement saying fully 12,000 shipping clerks and similar employes were on strike and refusing to assume responsibility.

Mr. Feldblum is on vacation in Bermuda and the date of his return is uncertain. Meanwhile the I. L. G. W. U. has objected to having the complaint of the employers heard before any of Mr. Feldblum's assistants.

Today, it is expected, 1,700 members of Truckmen's Union, Local 102, will carry out the union's original plan of calling a sympathetic strike and stopping all deliveries to establishments affected by the dispute. Mr. Dubinsky estimated the number of such establishments at nearly 3,000.

Clash in Dress Factory.

Yesterday's developments in the garment district were marked by a continuation of mass picketing, minor clashes between striking and non-striking workers and other acts of violence. A score of arrests were made. The situation bids fair to assume more aggravated form unless a settlement of the strike was reached.

Ten men were arrested, including the proprietor of a dress manufacturing shop, when the police arrived

Continued on Page Seventeen.

EMERGENCY PEAK IS DECLARED PAST BY THE PRESIDENT

He Orders Last Seven Recovery Agencies Under Control of Budget Director.

COVERS OPERATING COSTS

Action Follows Protests of Division Heads Who Had Curbs Cut From Acts.

By CHARLES W. HURD.

Special to THE NEW YORK TIMES.

HYDE PARK, N. Y., Sept. 4.—On the ground that the emergency peak had passed, President Roosevelt signed an Executive order today placing the administration expenses of the last seven recovery agencies under the Director of the Budget as of Oct. 15. The President later explained that economy was one of the objects sought.

Under today's order the seven agencies named, whose operations do not come under the Budget and Accounting Act of 1921, are the Agricultural Adjustment Administration, Commodity Credit Corporation, Federal Coordinator of Transportation, Federal Emergency Relief Administration of Public Works, Federal Emergency Administration, National Recovery Administration and Tennessee Valley Authority.

Today's order brings to a total of twenty the agencies placed under the budget and completes this work.

In discussing the various orders at his press conference today, where he announced the issuance of the final one, President Roosevelt said that he believed they would cut down overlapping of work by agencies and, in time, act to diminish the personnel.

His remark recalled a White House order issued on Saturday just before he left Washington in which the Work Relief Administration was directed to give special attention to the employment needs of workers dropped by the National Recovery Administration or who might be dismissed from other emergency agencies.

To Merge Credit Agencies.

He said today that the emergency agencies would have to cut their staffs soon, as the emergency phases of their work has for the most part been completed and they now are becoming principally administrative agencies.

As one example he cited the Home Owners Loan Corporation, which has completed receiving applications and hereafter will act more as a management corporation conserving the loans that have been made.

The National Recovery Administration, he added, has cut its staff from 4,900 to 3,300 persons and the personnel must be cut more deeply.

With the peak of the emergency passed, he went on, credit agencies also will probably be consolidated. As evidence of the passing of the credit emergency the President cited work by the government which, he said, has saved probably 1,000,000 homes for their owners, 1,000,000 farms on which mortgages otherwise would have been foreclosed and some 7,000 banks which otherwise would have been forced to close their doors.

Original Order Amended.

The Executive order issued today is an amendment of the original order issued Aug. 5, which referred to the Federal Home Loan Bank Board, Home Owners Loan Corporation, Federal Savings and Loan System, Federal Savings and Loan

Continued on Page Eight.

Schacht Bars Nazi Inquiry on Officials; Rebuffs Questions on Masonic Background

Wireless to THE NEW YORK TIMES.

BERLIN, Sept. 4.—Dr. Hjalmar Schacht, Minister of Economics and president of the Reichsbank, delivered another rebuff to the National Socialist party's attempt to project "coordination" into the past when he sent back questionnaires inquiring of all government officials whether they had ever belonged to the Freemasons, now dissolved, and to what lodge.

A batch of questionnaires intended for officials of the Reichsbank and Economics Ministry was returned by Dr. Schacht with the following curt remark:

"This question will not be answered by officials under my jurisdiction."

Dr. Schacht is a former Mason himself, and in his celebrated speech at the Koenigsberg Fair he denounced those contemporaries who "declared every former Mason to be a scoundrel."

By The Associated Press.

BERLIN, Sept. 4.—The Catholic question became vital again today after a pause broken by last Sunday's pastoral letter—which exhorted Catholics to "stand in the faith"—with a police order in Hamburg forbidding the wearing of uniforms by Catholic Youth groups.

Only organizations of a "purely religious nature" are exempt from the order, which forbids political and athletic activities among the young people's units and makes it illegal for them to wear insignia or to conduct meetings.

In Velten, a 62-year-old Jew accused of a racial crime was pushed through the streets wearing a placard worded "Race Violator." In Henningsdorf, workers for the Stuermer, Julius Streicher's Jew-baiting newspaper, photographed the patrons of Jewish merchants.

In his recent speech Dr. Schacht assailed individual actions against Jews as detrimental to German economy and subsequently had thousands of copies of the address run off by the Reichsbank printing presses after it had been censored in the newspapers. Last Saturday he announced the reinstatement of a Reichsbank official who had been denounced by Dr. Joseph Goebbels, Propaganda Minister, and sent to a concentration camp.

HURRICANE TOLL EXCEEDS 200; 164 TAKEN FROM THE DIXIE WHEN GALE HALTS RESCUES

SEAS ARE AGAIN RISING

Southwest Blow Stops Boats After Five Hours of Perilous Work.

11 SHIPS JOIN IN RESCUES

Crews Are Able to Work Only in Lulls Between Squalls—Will Resume Today.

FIRST OF RESCUED IN PORT

El Mundo and Cutter Reach Miami With 43 Passengers—4 Other Ships on Way.

Copyright, 1935, by The Associated Press.

MIAMI, Fla., Sept. 4.—Besieged for two days and two nights by a mad Atlantic storm in the Morgan liner Dixie, 164 passengers and members of the ship's crew were saved tonight from rocky French reef by gallant men of a rescue fleet.

Rising seas and rain cut short five hours of painstaking work by lifeboat, and six mercy ships hurried for port late tonight leaving an estimated 220 persons still aboard the stranded liner.

Late radio flashes from the Dixie's veteran skipper, Captain E. W. Sundstrom, said 165 persons, including 111 passengers and 54 members of the crew, had been saved.

A previous tabulation from the Dixie and owner's agents here gave a total of 164—110 passengers and 54 crew members—rescued, with 143 passengers and 77 members of the crew still aboard.

The Dixie carried 384 in all—253 passengers and 131 in the crew—when she was flung on the jagged reef during Monday's hurricane.

Hopes were high for completion of the transfer to an alert circle of ships, spread fanwise about the Dixie, by tomorrow. Owner's agents expected that another lull in the stubborn storm would allow waiting ships again to launch lifeboats by daylight.

Expects to End Transfers Today.

Captain Sundstrom himself reported:

"Expect transfer rest of passengers tomorrow and baggage."

The Dixie's skipper also radioed he had transferred "54 dismissed commissary crew at points where passengers could not be handled."

This explained, line officials said, why some of the crew went ahead of passengers in the lifeboats. They said the crew members, not needed on the boat, could help at debarkation points.

First of the rescue ships to complete the 60-mile trip to Miami was the El Mundo of the Morgan Line, with a score of rescued Dixie passengers aboard.

The Coast Guard cutter Carrabassett also entered the Miami slip and debarked twenty-three more passengers and the Dixie's purser, V. J. Slovin.

Two other ships—the Morgan liner El Occidente and the United Fruit liner San Benito—were bound for Miami.

Of the others, the United Fruit liner Atenas was ordered to Charleston, S. C., and the tanker Reaper to Wilmington, N. C.

Boats Fight Sea for Hours.

In the five hours that weary seamen from the rescue fleet bent over creaking oars in tossing lifeboats, terse radio flashes told a stirring story of their struggle with the sea.

Forced to row more than a mile and a half to reach the larger rescue craft, the boatmen fought stroke by stroke to reach the Dixie's rolling hull, manoeuvred with infinite care to her lee side and took passenger and sailor alike from the stricken ship.

There was not a single hint of loss of life in the story of the rescue that reached an anxious mainland tonight.

It was 7 P. M. (Eastern standard time), when a new blow cut short the work of rescue.

Then, the Dixie's wireless sent out word of the number saved and the ships that saved them.

Shortly before midnight tonight, the Radio Corporation of America reported that representatives of the Knight and Chapman Company of New York had boarded the Dixie

Continued on Page Two.

Liner Doric Sends S O S; In Crash With Freighter

By The Associated Press.

LONDON, Thursday, Sept. 5.—An S O S call was flashed from the Cunard White Star liner Doric today, saying the vessel had been in collision with the 2,160-ton French freighter Formigny.

The Doric is on a cruise, en route from Gibraltar to London.

The scene of the crash was off the Portuguese coast, about seventy miles off Oporto.

The distress call was picked up by the Land's End radio station, Lloyd's.

The British steamer Mooltan radioed the Lands End Wireless Station at 6:09 A. M. (1:09 A. M. Eastern daylight-saving time) that the British steamer Orion was standing by to take passengers from the Cunard-White Star liner Doric, which had sent out an SOS.

PASSENGERS TELL THRILLING STORIES

Some Among First Transferred From Dixie Say a Fire Was Quickly Put Out.

WATER OVER THEIR ANKLES

Priest Clung to One Place and Prayed for Five Hours, Giving Absolution.

Special to THE NEW YORK TIMES.

MIAMI, Fla., Sept. 4.—Nearly forty-eight hours after being trapped on the treacherous rocks of French Reef, sixty miles south of here, during a hurricane, passengers of the Morgan liner Dixie were en route once more for New York, this time aboard Coast Guard boats sent to their rescue. They will proceed to Miami, arriving about daybreak, here to be transferred to a special train for New York after a rest in a hotel.

Heavy seas had subsided sufficiently to permit the first transfer to the Coast Guard cutter Carrabassett shortly before 3 P. M. today, and little more than an hour later radio messages from a passing Pan American plane had told of four ships participating in the movement. The Dixie did not appear to be in serious danger at this time, although leaking and listing about five degrees to starboard.

Priest First Passenger.

Following V. J. Slovin, purser of the Dixie, who carried the ship's strong box and records, Father F. A. Wakeman, Catholic priest from San Diego, Calif., boarded the Carrabassett as the first of the passengers.

Father Wakeman said:

"I clung to one place in the ship and prayed for five hours. Several came to me for absolution. I firmly believe the vessel would have been lost had we not been driven on the reef."

Following him came I. M. Nobel of San Francisco and New York, manager of the boy violinist, Grisha Goluboff, according to Cecil R. Warren, Miami Daily News correspondent, in a copyrighted message from the Coast Guard cutter. Nobel is chairman of the passengers' committee planning a gift to the Dixie's crew. Nobel was cut on the foot by a piece of glass. It was his second experience in a shipwreck.

Get Order to Don Life Belts.

"We received orders to don life belts at 3 P. M. Monday," Nobel said. "Every one seemed resigned to his fate. There was no complaint from the passengers. It was quite dark by 4:30 P. M. When the lights were cut off we sang and played music to quiet any panic that might arise. Then the boats came last night and they were an inspiring sight to the passengers."

Additional radio messages from Warren aboard the Carrabassett described the night of terror spent by passengers aboard the Dixie. They huddled together in the ship's salon while four inches of water washed their feet, they reported, during the long hours passed Monday night in absolute darkness and without sign of relief.

Both officers and crew were praised by passengers for the exemplary courage shown as music was provided and fresh fruit was served to divert attention from the ship's struggle with high winds that

Continued on Page Two.

VETERANS LEAD FATALITIES

Only 11 of 192 Reported as Left Alive in One Florida Camp.

RELIEF ARMY RUSHING IN

Planes and Ships Speed to the Isolated Keys as Road Gangs Toil on Repairs.

STORM NOW DIMINISHING

Crossing Lower Georgia and Is Expected to Blow Out to Sea Over the Carolinas.

By The Associated Press.

MIAMI, Sept. 4.—Scenes of horror and desolation greeted the eyes of rescue workers tonight as they penetrated the storm-battered Florida keys to count the dead, estimated unofficially at upward of 200, while the hurricane apparently was blowing itself out in South Georgia.

Conservative estimates, which included tho made by the Red Cross, placed the number of dead at possibly less than 200, while other figures, received from various sources, ranged upward to between 400 and 500.

Leonard K. Thompson, Red Cross disaster relief chairman in the hurricane area, advised his Washington headquarters tonight he believed the death toll would be less than 200. This estimate, he said, was made after contact with all hitherto unheard from points in the area.

No estimate of the crop and property damage could yet be obtained and it was likely a factual total of the loss of life would not be available for days. The Red Cross figure was the first of a semi-official nature to be announced.

Rescue forces were being organized in all parts of the affected area, however, and it was hoped restoration of communication lines would quickly reveal the extent of the storm.

There were reports of high winds in Northwestern Florida tonight before the storm passed into Georgia, with some property damage, but no indication of loss of life. The Weather Bureau at Jacksonville said the disturbance, with decreased intensity but still attended by shifting gales, was expected to cross the lower tip of Georgia and pass out into the Atlantic through the Carolinas.

West Coast Property Damaged.

After lashing the keys early yesterday the hurricane had zigzagged across the southern tip of the mainland through sparsely settled sections and hurled part of its fury on Tampa, St. Petersburg, Fradenton, Sarasota and adjacent communities. No loss of life was reported from that section, although communication lines were paralyzed.

As for the widely varying estimates of the storm's toll, the Jacksonville Coast Guard station said that between 200 and 400 persons were dead at Matecumbe, where a number of World War veterans were engaged in a road-building project on the keys.

An estimate that the dead in the keys would not exceed 300 came from Dr. Joe Stewart, who late today completed an aerial survey of the storm-swept keys.

George Branch, station maste at Islamorado, toward the nort end of the island chain, reporte to the Florida East Coast Railroa that he counted nearly 150 bodie and estimated the storm ha claimed several hundred lives.

From Jack Combs, a Miami ur dertaker who led a rescue exped tion into the keys, came a repo that between 400 and 500 persor may have died.

Two Camps Isolated.

In his report to Washington, M Thompson said 100 known dea were from the neighborhood of Ve erans' Camp 1, on upper Mat cumbe Key. One out of every thre persons at that camp was said be dead.

Rescue workers for some tin had difficulty in reaching two oth veterans' camps, numbers 3 and located on lower Matecumbe, whic was isolated when winds and flo waters carried away the bridge

Continued on Page Six.

The Mt. Washington Hotel, Bretton Woo N. H. Broker's Office; Social Centre.—Ad

United Press International

An aerial view of lower Matecumbe Key, the site of F.E.R.A. camp Number Three, showing the widespread damage done by the flood waters following the hurricane.

HURRICANE TOLL NOW EXCEEDS 200

Continued From Page One.

highway and railroad tracks that linked that island in the key group.

It was in the Islamorado area, to the north, in the vicinity of Camp 1, that Station Master Branch reported he had counted nearly 150 bodies.

A radio message from a Coast Guard amphibian plane flying over the Keys said only seventy men remained alive in Camps 3 and 5 on lower Matecumbe. It added that three doctors were on hand and that survivors were being taken aboard three yachts and a Coast Guard cutter to be transferred to Miami.

Quarters for 683 Veterans.

FERA headquarters said it was not known exactly how many veterans were in the camps when the storm struck, as some were away on leave, but that there were housing accommodations for about 683.

The veterans were engaged in a FERA project of building an overseas highway linking Key West with the Florida mainland. Some of them were among the bonus seekers who marched on Washington. They came from all sections of the country.

Cooperating with Coast Guard, Red Cross and other relief agencies, the Pan American Airways turned over a number of its airplanes for relief work. A complete radio station was flown to one of the lower keys and set up to establish contact with the affected area. Four Miami doctors were flown into the stricken section to aid the injured.

Intercepted on his way to Kansas City for a speaking engagement, Dr. William de Kleine, medical director of the National Red Cross, entrained from St. Louis late today for the storm-swept area of Florida. He said the National Red Cross had eleven rescue and two hospital units in that area.

Sarasota Buildings Unroofed.

As the storm moved on north the Jacksonville division of the Coast Guard drew out its last available boat and plane to meet combined emergencies of distressed ships and devastating hurricane winds. Other divisions also rushed all available help to affected areas.

Uprooted trees, crippled communication lines and unroofed buildings were left in the path of the storm at Sarasota, on the west coast, and similar damage resulted at Bradenton, further north.

In Tampa the storm damaged some roofs, uprooted trees and broke windows, while at St. Petersburg, across Tampa Bay, "considerable" property damage and some injuries were reported in a dispatch from the Coast Guard cutter Nemesis.

High tides prevailed all along the coast, halting shipping, and torrential rain accompanied the swirling winds.

Several fish houses were blown down and small craft in the harbor shattered when the storm recurved and headed back inland near Cedar Key. No injuries were reported there, however.

Trees Reduce Intensity.

Presumably the storm passed into Georgia between Tallahassee and Madison. Once over land, where it encountered trees and other obstacles, the wind gradually diminished in intensity. The Weather Bureau said points further north might not get more than high winds. Crop damage was the principal consequences reported from Georgia.

Gainesville, Fla., where the State university is located, escaped with only minor damage to trees. A huge pine tree fell on the campus, however, and smashed windows in the engineering building.

Preparations were made tonight to start another rescue train from here to the Keys. An earlier one had been made up as men set to work repairing the tracks.

Representative J. Hardin Peterson said at Lakeland he had wired Harry L. Hopkins, Federal Relief Administrator, asking for an investigation of the deaths of veterans in the Keys. He wanted to find out, he said, why the islands were not evacuated when notice was given of the storm's approach.

"They had plenty of notice, and I want to fix the responsibility," Mr. Peterson asserted.

He said he was asked by Arthur R. Boring of Plant City, State commander of the American Legion, to take the action.

A boat owned by The Miami Daily News returned from the Keys tonight with fifty-two injured, fifty of them veterans. They were transferred to hospitals for treatment of injuries.

Relief Trucks Rushed Out.

Trucks loaded with medical supplies, food and clothing supplied by the Red Cross, National Guard and volunteer groups rumbled southward from here on errands of mercy to the injured and those left homeless by the storm's fury.

President Roosevelt personally ordered all available Federal forces to give aid and Coast Guard ships were dispatched to act as hospital bases in the isolated Keys.

Confronting the rescue workers was the task of removing to Miami the bodies of all those who perished on the Keys, some of which may be reached now only by boat, since highways and railroad beds were washed out.

Some rescuers reported that bodies could be seen pinned under the wreckage of their homes and others were strewn about in the open. Belief was expressed that some of the bodies may have been washed out to sea by the high tidal wave that struck the Keys.

Scenes of death, misery and destruction greeted the eyes of those who journeyed to the rugged Keys to lend a helping hand to the hurricane victims.

Houses and other buildings were crushed like match-wood and strewn about the countryside by the wind's fury. Highways were flooded and bridges and railroad tracks were washed away, completely isolating many of the Keys.

To some of the islands boats offered the only means of communication and the going was rough and hazardous.

Until rescue workers can reach the ragged Keys further south, belief was expressed by many that the heaviest loss of life probably was felt on the two Matecumbe Keys and fishing villages on Plantation Key and Key Largo.

"All the News That's Fit to Print."

The New York Times.

LATE CITY EDITION
Light rain and colder today. To-morrow generally fair with slowly rising temperatures.
Temperatures Yesterday—Max., 56; Min., 45

Copyright, 1936, by The New York Times Company.

VOL. LXXXV.....No. 28,544. Entered as Second-Class Matter, Postoffice, New York, N. Y. NEW YORK, THURSDAY, MARCH 19, 1936. PP TWO CENTS in New York City. | THREE CENTS Within 200 Miles | FOUR CENTS Elsewhere Except in 7th and 8th Postal Zones.

FLOODS SWEEP 12 STATES, MAROON THOUSANDS; PITTSBURGH IN DARKNESS, ALL TRAFFIC CUT OFF; NEW ENGLAND HARD HIT; JOHNSTOWN DESERTED

LOCARNO POWERS AGREE ON TERMS TO OFFER TO REICH

PLAN IS FRENCH VICTORY

Requires Submission of Franco-Soviet Pact to Hague Court.

DEMILITARIZED ZONE KEPT

It Would Be Internationally Policed Pending a Final Decision by Tribunal.

CABINETS WILL ACT TODAY

Condemnation of Germany Is Before League Council—Ribbentrop to Speak.

Texts of Eden and Grandi speeches to League on Page 10.

European Developments

LONDON—The Locarno powers provisionally agreed early this morning to a plan that includes submission of the Franco-Soviet pact to The Hague court for decision on whether it nullifies Locarno and meanwhile the creation anew of the demilitarized zone in Germany to be internationally policed. The plan is subject to Berlin's approval. Labor leaders of fifteen European nations gathered for a meeting today to frame a common policy toward the crisis. Also scheduled for today is a meeting of the League Committee of Thirteen to discuss peace in Africa.

BERLIN—Hope for "a square deal" in London was expressed in official quarters, which stressed the good-will behind Germany's peace proposals.

KOENIGSBERG—Continuing his campaign speaking tour, Chancellor Hitler avoided reference to the London situation, contenting himself with repetition of the German position. His tone was less truculent than previously.

Powers Draft a Plan

By AUGUR

Special Cable to THE NEW YORK TIMES.

LONDON, Thursday, March 19.—The conference of the Locarno treaty powers—Britain, France, Belgium and Italy—came to a dramatic end at 2:15 this morning after a laborious session. If the British Cabinet ratifies the agreement the French delegation has apparently carried its principal points:

First—A declaration for an obligatory appeal to The Hague Court for a decision on whether the Franco-Soviet pact invalidated the Locarno treaty.

Second—The demilitarized zone will be established anew on German territory.

Third—The zone will be occupied by a body of international troops with British participation.

[Establishment of the demilitarized zone would be temporary pending the outcome of the court hearings, according to The Associated Press.]

Fourth—Technical agreements, already drafted, must be signed immediately, providing measures for the immediate execution of the second and third decisions. This implies official permission to the British and French staffs to confer on establishing a joint plan of action.

British Approval Likely

The British Cabinet will meet today to examine the agreement. Approval is virtually certain because of the presence at the discussion of Anthony Eden, Foreign Secretary; Viscount Halifax, Lord Privy Seal, and Ramsay MacDonald, Lord President of the Council.

Pierre-Etienne Flandin, French Foreign Minister, will fly to Paris today in a special military plane to place the result of the conference before the Cabinet.

If Germany refuses to accept the plan further consultation of the Locarno powers will become necessary. Meanwhile the Council of the League of Nations is expected at today's meeting to express official condemnation of Germany for breaking treaties.

Thus the long, stormy Locarno session closes with a signal success for the French thesis. The British delegation long resisted any suggestion for pressure on Germany. Even at the last decisive meeting the British Ministers hesitated before acquiescing in the major part of the

Continued on Page Ten

When You Think of Writing Think of Whiting.—Advt.

Statesmen Drop Work To Attend Royal Levee

Wireless to THE NEW YORK TIMES.

LONDON, March 18.—The statesmen who have worked themselves to a frazzle over the international crisis for the last ten days had to don full dress and uniforms and spend several hours of precious time today attending the first levee of King Edward's reign.

Although many were busy into the early morning hours with the meeting of the Locarno powers and preparations for the session of the League of Nations Council this afternoon, their presence at Buckingham Palace was required because it was a diplomatic levee. The ceremony was held there for the first time in six years since St. James's Palace, where levees usually take place, is given over to the council.

Wearing the scarlet and gold uniform of the Colonel-in-Chief of the Brigade of Guards, King Edward, seated on a golden throne, received a thousand diplomats, Cabinet Ministers, officers of the fighting services and prominent professional men.

HEARST TELEGRAM GIVEN OUT IN HOUSE

McSwain Publicly Reads Message Which Publisher Sought by Suit to Suppress.

HE CHARGES SPITE, FALSITY

Senate Lobby Committee Cancels Subpoena and Prevents a Battle in the Courts.

Special to THE NEW YORK TIMES.

WASHINGTON, March 18.—Efforts of William Randolph Hearst, through injunction suits pending in the Supreme Court of the District of Columbia, to prevent the Senate lobby investigating committee from using as evidence or making public a telegram sent by Mr. Hearst to one of his editorial employes, were frustrated in the House today.

Representative John J. McSwain of South Carolina, chairman of the Committee on Military Affairs, on a question of personal privilege, read into the record the telegram in question. It proved to be a suggestion from Mr. Hearst to James T. Williams Jr., one of his editorial writers, that he write a series of editorials urging the impeachment of Mr. McSwain, who was described in the telegram by Mr. Hearst as "a Communist in spirit and a traitor in effect."

Later Elisha Hanson, counsel for Mr. Hearst, issued a statement in which he said that the telegram read by Mr. McSwain was "not a copy of a telegram sent by Mr. Hearst to one of his editors." Subsequently Mr. Hanson explained that it was a "garbled" copy. On the other hand, the Senate committee gave it to Mr. McSwain as a true copy.

Committee Drops Subpoena

Immediately following the reading by Mr. McSwain in the House, the Black committee withdrew its subpoena directing the Western Union to produce the message. Mr. Hanson said this was an effort by the committee to "evade a review of its action by the courts," and evidence that the committee was afraid "to meet the issue of its improper and illegal acts."

Practically every member of the House was in his seat when the Carolinian arose and asked recognition.

Time and again as Mr. McSwain denounced Mr. Hearst and Mr. Williams, the House cheered. When Mr. McSwain read the part of the telegram in which he was branded a "Communist" the House roared with laughter.

Following is the text of the telegram as read by Mr. McSwain:

"Los Angeles, Calif., April 5, 1935.
"James T. Williams Jr.,
"Washington, D. C.

"Confidential. Why not make several editorials calling for impeachment of Mr. McSwain? He is the enemy within the gates of Congress, the nation's citadel. He is a Communist in spirit and a traitor in effect. He would leave the United States naked to its foreign and domestic enemies.

"Please make these editorials for morning papers. Also make editorials extolling administration for

Continued on Page Two

ROOSEVELT SEEKS 1½ BILLION RELIEF; ASKS BUSINESS AID

Plea to Industry to Help in Jobs Marks Message on Fiscal Year's Needs.

FEDERAL 'TASK' STRESSED

Burden Cannot Be Shifted Yet to States and Communities, the President Declares.

The President's message on work relief is printed on Page 2.

By TURNER CATLEDGE

Special to THE NEW YORK TIMES.

WASHINGTON, March 18.—President Roosevelt asked Congress today for a new lump-sum appropriation of $1,500,000,000 with which to continue work relief for another year, beginning July 1, and at the same time urged private business to accept the responsibility for obviating such outlays in the future by another nation-wide drive for reemployment.

The President indicated that this amount was the least that would suffice. With it, he estimated that the government would have some $3,100,000,000 to meet the unemployment problem in the next fiscal year. This included $1,000,000,000 in unexpended balances of previous appropriations and $600,000,000 carried in the budget for the Civilian Conservation Corps and various public works.

He proposed to confine the Federal Government's assistance to 3,800,000 families and unattached persons classed as "employables." About 1,500,000 other cases would have to be carried on local and State relief rolls, which, he said, must henceforth assume full responsibility for "unemployables."

Address Intended for Country

The President's message was addressed to Congress, but was intended as well for the country. To Congress he simply made the request for the additional funds with which to continue his program of work relief. To the country, however, he made a plea for a more thorough solution of the unemployment problem, which, he said, was still "the most difficult one before the country."

The ultimate answer, he said, was with private industry.

"I present this problem and this opportunity definitely to the managers of private business," he said, adding the offer of aid and cooperation from all the appropriate Federal departments and agencies.

He intimated, however, that should private industry fail either to accept the responsibility or to find the solution, his administration intended to pursue his program of caring for the "employable" idle with expenditures from the Federal Treasury.

"Only if industry fails to reduce substantially the number of those now out of work will another appropriation and further plans and policies be necessary," was Mr. Roosevelt's way of putting it.

The message was accepted by the Democratic leadership in Congress as a matter of course. Plans were started immediately for attaching the new relief appropriation to the Second Deficiency Bill, now in process of formulation in the House Appropriations Committee. The prospects are that it will be reported to the floor for action within two weeks.

Republican critics reacted as they

Continued on Page Two

Power Sent by Chicago To Aid Flood Districts

Electric power is being transmitted from Chicago to aid communities in Pennsylvania and West Virginia affected by the floods.

Rising waters have forced the Springdale plant of the American Water Works and Electric system to cease operations, and replacement is coming from the Windsor plant, operated by this system jointly with the American Gas and Electric Company.

The area ordinarily supplied by Windsor is receiving power from the Chicago district.

ALL TRAFFIC LINES TO WEST PARALYZED

Railroads and Bus Companies Are Forced to Abandon Their Scheduled Runs.

PLANES UNABLE TO LAND

Failure of Power Plants Leaves Airports in Pittsburgh Area Without Lights.

Transportation facilities from New York to the flooded areas in Western Pennsylvania were tied up considerably yesterday

As the flood waters continued to rise during the day, railroad and bus companies, which had been maintaining a delayed service with difficulty, finally were forced to abandon their scheduled runs altogether, with the result that Pittsburgh, the center of the inundated area, was practically isolated.

With land transportation halted, the airlines, however, during the day responded to the emergency and, by pressing into service all available equipment, established a "shuttle" service to Pittsburgh. TWA, the Lindbergh line, rushed twelve planes to the area.

With the coming of night, however, even the planes were unable to land in Pittsburgh. The failure of power plants in that city left the airports without landing lights and all planes were forced to land at other points.

Planes Unable to Land

At 10 P. M. TWA announced that planes could not land and that those en route to the flooded city were being landed at Columbus, Ohio, some 200 miles away. All other flights scheduled for the night were postponed, and flying was not to be resumed until the morning.

Serious flood conditions were also reported in the vicinity of Binghamton, N. Y., but the railroad and bus lines asserted that traffic in that area was not halted, that their trains and buses were able to get through, although service was delayed

The floods in Pennsylvania affected the delivery of mail into that area, it was said by postal authorities late yesterday. At that time, it was stated, only first-class mail and special deliveries were being

Continued on Page Eighteen

Polo Pony Rescues Five in Deerfield Flood; Historic Old Village Is Nearly Isolated

Special to THE NEW YORK TIMES.

DEERFIELD, Mass., March 18.—The largest part of this historic old village is under water tonight, with several hundred of the population marooned in second-story rooms while the river bounding the village proper is rising at the rate of fourteen inches every hour. Rescue workers are hampered by fog and the collapse of the lighting system.

Rescue work began early this afternoon as the lower part of the village began to disappear beneath waters. At the Eaglebrook School, about 1,000 feet above the town on Mount Tocuntuck, Headmaster C. T. Chase Jr mobilized his forty students ranging between 7 and 16. They had a polo pony and two canoes.

"Pinto" the polo pony, became the hero of the town The cries of five persons on the second floor of a house on the bank of the river attracted the attention of the rescuers. The currents were treacherous and the canoes hard to handle.

Not so the polo pony, which swam out with a volunteer rider on his back to the marooned people. The volunteer, who would not give his name, put the five on the pony's back one at a time and made five successive trips to shore.

Throughout the night the boys were busy with their canoes, skirting carefully on the edges of the currents and retrieving whatever supplies, animals, valuables or other articles they could before the onrushing waters engulfed the houses.

The dormitories at the Deerfield Academy have been turned over to forty of the townspeople whose homes are gone, but the buildings themselves are in danger of following the homes of those they are housing if the flood continues to rise.

The railroad trestle over the Deerfield River, is the only remaining means of travel between the town and the world outside. An official of the road promised that a handcar would be sent to carry medical aid and supplies should they be needed. Supplies are low in the town and many are suffering in the cold and damp fog.

1,500 FLEE FROM TOWNS

Raging Connecticut River Engulfs Big Area in Massachusetts.

HUGE VERNON DAM IN PERIL

Power Officials Say Leaks Are Being Checked After Police Order Evacuations.

DAMAGE PUT AT MILLIONS

Bridges, Dams Go Out, Rail Traffic Crippled in Several States as Deaths Rise to 16.

By The Associated Press.

NORTHAMPTON, Mass., March 18.—The raging Connecticut River swept over the near-by towns of Hadley and Sunderland tonight, forcing the entire populace of the two towns to abandon their homes and flee to Amherst.

More than 1,500 flood refugees poured into the college city. Authorities at Massachusetts State College and Amherst College quartered them temporarily in their large gymnasiums.

To the north, 150 Hatfield residents were trapped in the Town Hall. Police Chief Arthur R. Breor at Hatfield informed State Police Headquarters at Northampton that the river waters, three feet deep, were swirling outside the building.

In this city the dike surrounding two sides of the city gave way, inundating another large residential section.

Huge Damage to Property

By The Associated Press.

BOSTON, March 18.—Flood-beleaguered residents of Western Massachusetts sent out frantic calls for help tonight as raging waters, whipped up by a steady southwest storm, ravaged New England for the second time in a week. The rain would continue until late tomorrow, Weather Bureau officials said.

The known dead in the week's period stood at sixteen, while property damage mounted into millions of dollars.

Two persons were missing.

Late tonight a message received at the office of Adjt. Gen. William I. Rose here announced that the huge dam at Vernon, Vt., had gone out.

State police and other officials immediately broadcast a warning to towns and cities in the Connecticut Valley below the dam.

Later, Superintendent Harry Ostron, at the Vernon Dam, said that it was still holding, though at both the Vernon and the New Hampshire sides the river was threatening to cut through.

Gangs of men worked steadily to stop the breach, throwing sandbags into the holes.

Frank D. Comerford, president of the New England Power Associates, said that he had talked with employes at the dam about midnight and that the engineer told him holes in the river bank at the sides of the dam had been plugged and the river had not risen in the last hour.

"The engineer said he thought the worst of the trouble was over," added Mr. Comerford.

Pittsfield Calls for Help

Meanwhile Pittsfield called for all possible assistance.

There the Pill electric dam was reported going out, and State police said that both the Plunkett dam at Pittsfield and the Eaton Crane and Pike dams both were going out. National Guardsmen were on duty at Pittsfield.

The Greenfield company of the National Guard was called out for service there, while three companies were on duty at Holyoke.

Governor James M. Curley, accompanied by a number of State officails, reached Springfield shortly before midnight to aid in directing relief work.

The rainstorm deluged the New England area during the day and night, and mountain snows, softened by continued unseasonably warm temperatures, poured thousands of tons of water into raging rivers, which, in turn, engulfed whole communities, submerged highways and railroad trackage, swept bridges before them and cut

Continued on Page Nineteen

The Floods at a Glance

By The Associated Press.

With at least fifty-seven persons dead, thousands of others homeless and the property damage increasing by millions hourly, devastating floods raged through twelve States last night, while tornadic winds, sleet and snow in other States increased the death list and losses.

To aid National Guardsmen, the Red Cross and authorities in the States, President Roosevelt mobilized the full forces of the Federal Government to give aid. WPA workers and army engineers were ordered to lend all aid in the zones of destruction and danger.

Pennsylvania

With the Monongahela and Allegheny Rivers at 45.9 feet, an all-time high, Pittsburgh was inundated, practically isolated and in darkness. The dead throughout the State were put at thirty-four. At Johnstown the waters were receding, but fear that weakened dams would give way kept the city tense. The dead there were put at six.

Southern States

In West Virginia, Wheeling and other cities were afloat. In Maryland, towns and cities, including Cumberland, Williamsport, Hancock and Harper's Ferry, were inundated. In Virginia, two were drowned in the Shenandoah Valley. In West Virginia, there were eleven deaths. In Georgia, two were killed in a windstorm.

New England

Towns in Massachusetts in the Connecticut Valley were being evacuated as part of the Vernon Dam in Vermont broke. Four lives were lost in Vermont. Boston faced a milk shortage, Worcester a power failure. Maine's Governor estimated the State's damage at $10,000,000. In Connecticut, three dams collapsed and a dozen building were swept away at New Hartford. In New Hampshire, the dam was swept away at Claremont.

New York State

In New York State there were 2,000 homeless, many communities were isolated, power lines down and highway traffic was paralyzed. Hundreds evacuated their homes in Binghamton and the militia there was mobilized.

7 TOWNS INUNDATED IN POTOMAC VALLEY

River Rises to 40 Feet at Williamsport, Md., and Sweeps Away Forty Houses.

DAMAGE PUT AT A MILLION

Hundreds of Families Homeless—Banks Closed and Troops on Guard at Cumberland.

By The Associated Press.

WILLIAMSPORT, Md., March 18—The worst flood in forty-seven years surged relentlessly down the Potomac River Valley tonight, inundating at least seven towns and making hundreds homeless.

Along a hundred-mile stretch from Cumberland to Point of Rocks the flood crest rolled. It swept houses, bridges and livestock before it and left desolation and destruction in its wake.

Only one death, and that indirect, was reported from the rampage of the usually placid river that flows in its upper reaches between Maryland and West Virginia, and lower down between Maryland and Virginia.

No estimate could be made of the property damage, but it easily amounted to more than $1,000,000. Uncounted hundreds were driven from their flooded homes along the river's banks.

Railway and vehicular transportation was stopped all through the stricken area because of washed out or shaky bridges and flooded roads. Communications were crippled only in isolated sections.

Water from five to ten feet deep swirled through the streets of the hapless towns that dotted the path of the flood.

Potomac 40 Feet Deep

At 2:15 P. M. the Potomac reached a height of forty feet here, two feet above its highest mark during the great Johnstown flood of 1889.

At Hancock, twenty miles above here, the river rose twenty feet during the day to pass its high-water mark of forty-seven years ago.

Families were driven from fifty homes in Hancock, where there was neither electric light nor drinking water. The town was inaccessible.

Several small buildings here were smashed to splinters by the rushing waters and a score or more of homes were abandoned. The Potomac Edison power plant was forced to shut down and the town was plunged into darkness.

Twenty miles below here Harpers Ferry, W. Va., at the juncture of the Potomac and the Shenandoah,

Continued on Page Sixteen

PANICKY RESIDENTS DESERT JOHNSTOWN

10,000 Flee to Hills on Rumor of Break in Huge Dam After the Flood Recedes.

MARTIAL LAW PROCLAIMED

Little Food Available and No Heat—Six Persons Dead—Looting Is Reported.

Special to THE NEW YORK TIMES.

JOHNSTOWN, Pa., March 18.—Homeless and without food, thousands of Johnstown's terror-stricken residents huddled in misery tonight upon the rain-soaked Conemaugh Hills above the city, battered by flood waters from the Conemaugh River and Stony Creek.

At least 10,000 fled the city this afternoon and took refuge in the hills as rumors flew that the huge Quemahoning Dam above Johnstown had broken, causing fears of a repetition of the great dam disaster which took more than 2,000 lives here in 1889. But the dam was found to be holding.

Flashlights of State and local police winked and bobbed in the otherwise dark streets while rain, causing fears of a new surge of flood waters, fell upon the receding waters of the overflowed streams.

Martial law was proclaimed late tonight as a regiment of National Guardsmen, mobilized from Indiana, Altoona, Greensburg and Somerset, started toward the city under command of Captain George Potts. It was expected here by dawn.

In the meantime Mayor Daniel J. Shields made public a series of thirty-day regulations which police were ordered to enforce until the arrival of the guardsmen. These provided for a 9 o'clock curfew, with no unaccredited persons permitted on the streets after that hour; no loitering in the restricted downtown area of about two square miles; no visitors or sightseers, and observance of the utmost precautions against fire.

The Dead Number Six

The known dead here numbered six. They were Frank W. Buchanan, a sportsman and authority on wild life, drowned as he left his place of business on Franklin Street; Hyman Torladsky, a furrier; Dan (Reds) Gallagher, a motorman; a Mrs. Hummel, who died of shock; a man named Geer and an unidentified woman.

The city counted its loss up to $10,000,000.

As the flood waters subsided some of the more venturesome residents went back to their homes and be-

Continued on Page Sixteen

PEAK PASSING PITTSBURGH

1,500 Guardsmen Patrol the Paralyzed City in Night of Terror.

THOUSANDS ARE TRAPPED

Isolated in Office Buildings or Waiting for Help on Tops of Surrounded Houses.

34 KNOWN DEAD IN STATE

With Rivers' Waters at All-Time High, Many Towns Face New Peril.

Pittsburgh Flood Receding

By The Associated Press.

PITTSBURGH, Thursday, March 19.—The flood waters in Pittsburgh receded a foot from an official peak of 45.9 feet early today and were dropping at the rate of six inches an hour.

Special to THE NEW YORK TIMES.

PITTSBURGH, March 18.—The worst flood in local history brought the terror of darkness to this city tonight as power plants were thrown out of use, and fifteen hundred National Guardsmen patrolled the streets while Mayor William McNair directed the mobilization of every agency against the danger of food and water shortages, pillaging and the spread of disease. Thousands were marooned in downtown office buildings.

There were five known dead here and 5,000 homeless; thirty-four were reported dead in the State.

Explosions and fires injured at least forty-nine persons here, destroying a half dozen industrial plants and other property as firemen met with almost insuperable difficulties in fighting the blazes.

The swirling waters, which came up almost without warning last night, submerged the "Golden Triangle," heart of the business district, under currents ten feet deep.

Five hundred men, women and children were reported trapped in the Blaine School in McKees Rock, a suburb. Frantic calls for aid said that the water had reached the second floor of the building, which might crumble any minute.

Rescue workers said they could not man skiffs in that section because of the swift current and the piles of débris.

Meanwhile cities and towns along the Ohio River Valley shuddered tonight as their hour of danger approached.

Scores of neighboring towns and cities were suffering. Among them were Altoona, Kittanning, Connellsville, Brownsville, DuBois, Kane, Hollidaysburg, Oil City, Point Marion, Towanda, Tyrone and Vandergrift. There were 3,000 reported homeless in Vandergrift alone and many places were isolated.

Several Serious Fires

Fires and explosions added terror to the situation here. A tank car in the yards of the Pittsburgh & Lake Erie Railroad was ignited when débris struck it and started a fire this evening which destroyed three business concerns, two houses and a municipal garage at a total damage estimated at $125,000.

The Etna Nut and Bolt Company, the Crucible Steel plant, the Waverly Oil Works and the Pittsburgh Steel Spring Company were also swept by disastrous blazes. Firemen stood hip-deep in water trying to extinguish them.

Thirty or more persons, including many women and children, were injured when an explosion shattered a home in the suburb of Lawrenceville in which they had taken refuge. They were showered with bricks and débris. Fire followed the explosion.

A small railroad bridge across the Monongahela River was reported on fire tonight, the latest in the long series of fires that had kept harassed firemen busy all day long.

All water and medical supplies were placed under the direction of the Red Cross by the City Council at an emergency meeting tonight, at which the Red Cross was also authorized to supervise and coordinate all relief, welfare and police

Continued on Page Fourteen

BANQUETS for 10 to 100—Phone The Parkside, 18 Gramercy Pk. GR. 5-6000.—Advt.

PITTSBURGH IS HIT BY WORST FLOOD

Continued From Page One

work. The council at the same time appropriated $1,000,000 for relief purposes.

Hundreds if not thousands of persons were still marooned late tonight on the rooftops of their homes in lowland sections of the city, and grave fears were felt for many of them. It was reported 500 were marooned in the McKees Rocks district alone.

In the Roosevelt Hotel on Penn Avenue, 575 guests and employes were marooned without water, food or heat while the flood raged seven feet deep in the lobby of the hostelry.

Police and National Guardsmen formed a cordon about the worst flooded areas and prevented any one except firemen and other uniformed relief workers from entering in boats as a safeguard against pillaging.

The city was in darkness through the failure of three major power plants of the Duquesne Power and Light Company. Two of the plants were put out of commission early in the day and the third went out of service in midafternoon.

Kerosene lamps, candles and pocket flashlights were at a premium in homes and for the use of the volunteers who manned rowboats, canoes and motor boats and ventured into the worst stricken regions on rescue missions.

Gas and steam lines throughout the city were wrecked by the waters, which in conjunction with the damage to the power plants threatened to leave at least parts of the city without heat, light, or cooking facilities for several days.

Street cars and buses throughout the city were halted, not only by the muddy streams which filled the flooded areas but by the failure of power.

Telephone and telegraph service was also badly crippled; at midday the telephone company requested that only emergency calls be placed.

With railroad and bus travel into the city halted, fears of a food shortage became acute. The Flood Menace Committee began a check-up of the stores available in the city and also began to make plans to prevent an outbreak of disease. Residents were urged to boil their drinking water.

Mayor McNair ordered police tonight to put an immediate halt to any attempt to profiteer, by the instant arrest of the proprietor of any restaurant or business concern that raised the price of food, clothing, or other necessities. The order prevailed throughout the city, including the non-flooded areas.

Dr. Richard Beban, president of the Alleghany County Medical Society, offered the services of its entire membership to the Red Cross, which had already established relief centers at vantage points. The Red Cross asked for all available cots and blankets, and for volunteers to aid the homeless.

Downtown the waters had risen almost to the second floor of business buildings, and brought about the closing of almost all theatres.

Steel mills and other manufacturing plants, most of which cluster along the banks of the swollen Alleghany River, were forced to close down, their fires extinguished by the rising waters. The usual veil of smoke over the city was missing.

The Stock Exchange and banks and business houses were forced to close.

Mayor McNair declared a legal holiday; he ordered that schools remain closed until Monday.

The Court House, the city-county buildings and other governmental centers were paralyzed by the failure of light and power.

Department stores and other retail establishments were badly hit by the surging floods, although this morning many merchants removed their most valuable portable stocks to safe regions on higher ground.

A gasoline shortage threatened the city tonight as the failure of the electric power supply put pumps out of commission, just when demands were extremely heavy as automobiles became almost the sole method of transportation in the non-flooded areas. In the absence of street and traffic lights, many mishaps were reported.

Officials of the city's water sup-

ply system said that about a day and a half's supply was on hand, although primary pump stations ceased operations this morning.

The entire South Hills residential district was without water, however, because of the exhaustion of the reserve supply of the South Pittsburgh Water Company, which serves about 3,000 families there.

WPA officials put their trucks and men at the disposal of the Red Cross and drew on the relief rolls for additional help to assist in distributing food and supplies.

Many industrial establishments offered cots and blankets, while citizens came forward with camping equipment for the homeless.

In response to an urgent appeal three truckloads of bedding and food supplies were rushed tonight to 500 refugees who had taken up temporary residences in the North Side police station, a Catholic school and a near-by library.

The high level of 48 feet reached by the flood waters at the juncture of the Alleghany and Monongahela compared with a previous record of 41.1 feet recorded twenty-nine years ago, in 1907. The disasterous flood of 1913 reached a high mark of 38 feet.

High watermarks left on many of the older buildings in the "Golden Triangle" by the disastrous flood of 1913 reached a history until that of today, were far surpassed by the swirling currents tonight.

Outbound traffic from the city was at a standstill except by air tonight, although the Pennsylvania and Baltimore & Ohio railroads maintained a shuttle service to some suburbs.

A shortage of boats handicapped the efforts of the recuers to reach the thousands of hungry men and women trapped on the upper floors of the business buildings downtown and in the thickly settled residential areas on the North Side, where many homes were flooded to the second floor.

The water had risen with unprecedented speed this morning. Thousands who went to work without difficulty were speedily trapped in their offices. Market Street was dry at 8 A. M. but hip deep at 10 A. M. The Sixteenth Street bridge, last link between the North Side and downtown, was closed at 10 A. M.

Municipal radio broadcasts at ten minute intervals over station KDKA kept up the spirits of many house holders until the failure of

electric power silenced most of the receiving sets.

Cots have been placed in garages, schools and churches throughout the metropolitan district tonight to give shelter to the homeless.

Business Section Is Closed

Copyright, 1936, by The Associated Press.

PITTSBURGH, March 8.—Beleaguered Pittsburgh closed its business section tonight to commerce. Thomas A. Dunn, Safety Director, told building owners in the "Golden Triangle"—where most of the nation's steel is bought and sold—not to open for business tomorrow. He suggested that office keys be surrendered to the men armed to guard them.

Military rowboats moved from building to building with food and blankets, but could not reach all those who needed them. Fires broke out and many burned unchecked because there were no telephone lines to carry alarms.

A tank car loaded with gasoline exploded in a railroad yard, starting a fire which destroyed six buildings. Flood waters prevented firemen from reaching it.

Gasoline stations exhausted their supplies. Sreet lights were dark. The South Pittsburgh Water Company lost one of its main plants and 250,000 customers feared that they would thirst after tomorrow noon, when an emergency supply at a substation will be drained.

Officials of light and power companies said they would need twenty-four hours to dry out electricity generating equipment after the flood subsides and an equal amount of time to restore steam and gas equipment. Three thousand homes in the South Hills residential district boiled water for drinking.

Residents of the populous north side were mostly badly trapped. Muddy water swirled through the district.

A score of explosions occurred as water struck hot boilers in homes and industrial plants. One of them injured thirty persons, another nineteen.

Air transportation avoided the unlighted Pittsburgh airport. Two Transcontinental and Western Air express ships stopped at Columbus, Ohio, for the night.

Guy's Mills Faces Lack of Food

MEADVILLE, Pa., March 18 (AP). —Snowbound residents of the near-

by farming community of Guy's Mills faced a food shortage tonight. A sudden storm clogged roads with eight to ten feet of snow, halting traffic and preventing movement of supplies to village stores.

Juniata River Dam Bursts

HARRISBURG, Pa., March 18 (AP).—The Highway Patrol reported tonight that part of the west wall of the Penn Central dam at Raystown, near Huntingdon, burst tonight.

Fairchild Aerial Surveys Photo.

An aerial view of the city of Pittsburgh showing the flooded business district between the Monongahela River in the foreground and the Allegheny River in the left background. It is in this section that the overflow reached a depth of eighteen feet in some places, surging through hotel lobbies, banks and stores, causing damage estimated at many millions of dollars. The houses in the foreground are in the Mount Washington section, which is above the flood level.

Associated Press Photo.

Flames raging in an oil plant where the flood hampered firemen

Flood Perils Told Over Radio; Rail Traffic Halts

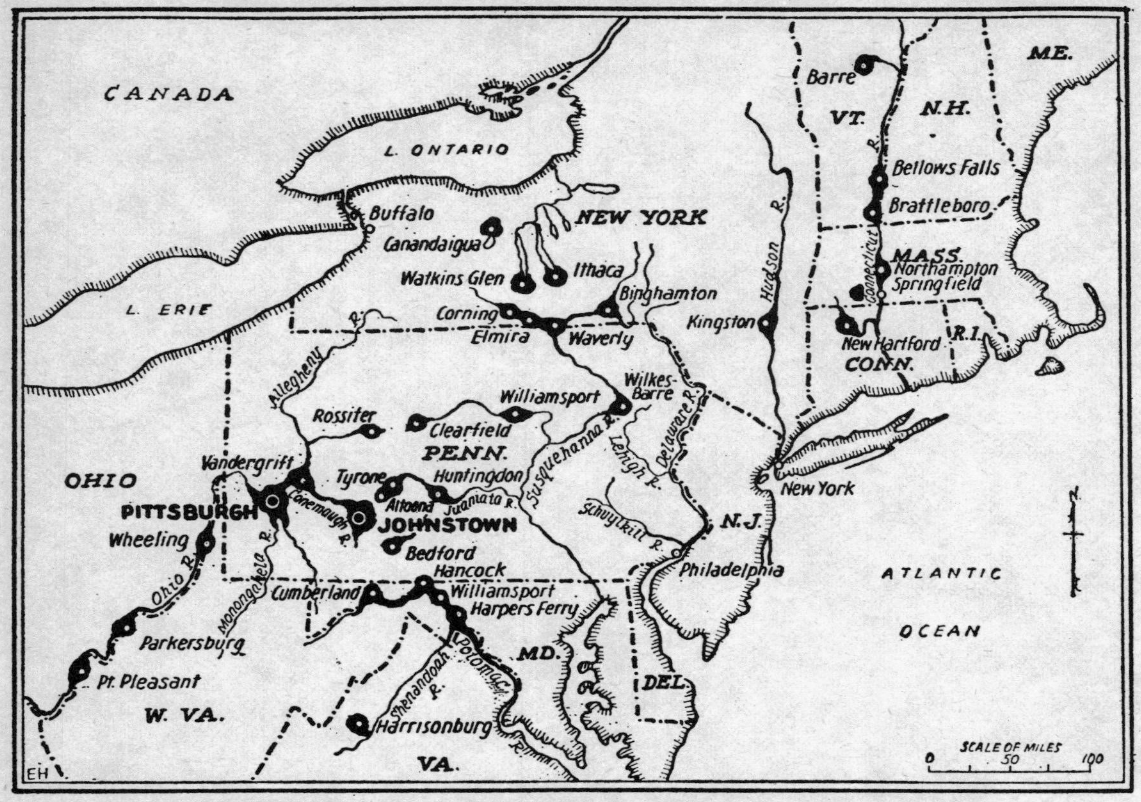

THE WIDE AREA IN THE EAST HIT BY FLOODS

The shaded cities and towns are those where overflowing rivers were reported causing heavy loss yesterday

ALL TRAFFIC LINES TO WEST PARALYZED

Continued From Page One

sent over the New York Central to Buffalo and Cleveland with the hope of getting the mail into the area from the north. Other mail was sent to Buffalo by other trains whenever convenient.

Late last night officials of the Pennsylvania Railroad announced that all service west of Lancaster, Pa., was discontinued. All trains of the line, bound for other western points, were being sent over the New York Central lines, through Albany and Buffalo to Cleveland, where they would again pick up their own line, it was said. All service has been "delayed," it was added.

Among the trains which were canceled yesterday by the flood conditions were the east and west bound Pennsylvania Limited from New York to Chicago; the Red Arrow, from New York to Detroit; the westbound American from New York to St. Louis, the westbound Broadway Limited and eastbound Golden Arrow from Chicago to New York.

At the offices of the Baltimore & Ohio Railroad it was asserted that all service on the line west of Washington had been halted at 4 P. M. According to an official of the company, the action was taken when "we were unable to get anything through from Washington to Pittsburgh."

Similar situations were also reported at the local offices of the Lehigh Valley and Lackawanna Railroads. The Lehigh Valley officials declared that they were able to get some trains through the flooded areas, but that in many cases their tracks were flooded and it was necessary to send the trains over some other companies' lines. The Lackawanna, which runs its trains through the Binghamton area, said that the floods in that vicinity were "serious," but that transportation was not being affected.

Later in the evening, however, the Lackawanna announced that all train schedules for Scranton and Binghamton had been canceled due to flooded tracks. The 9:55 train for Buffalo was canceled, while the Western Special from New York to Chicago, after being tied up at the Delaware Water Gap for several hours where water was four feet above the tracks, was forced to detour to the Lehigh Valley line at Philllipsburg, Pa.

Officials of the Greyhound, Safeway and Martz bus lines all reported that transportation in the area was halted. All three companies canceled bus service through the area at local depots.

Commissioner Alexander M. Damon, Eastern territorial commander of the Salvation Army, announced that the Army's relief force of thirty officers and 200 soldiers was in the flooded area. Using a fleet of twenty trucks, the force, according to Commissioner Damon, was distributing clothing, bedding and food supplies among the flood sufferers.

Flood conditions in New England disrupted service on several railroads in that area. At Springfield, Mass., trains of the Boston & Albany line rerouted over the New York, New Haven & Hartford Railroad and arrived in New York after some delay.

The New Haven reported that service on the line from Bridgeport, Conn., to Winston, Conn., was hampered by rising waters at Torrington, Conn., while officials of the Boston & Maine line north of Springfield declared that transportation was "pretty much disrupted."

Roundabout to Pittsburgh

With sixty passengers aboard, most of them home-going businessmen, the `ennsylvania Railroad's express train, Pittsburgher, ordinarily scheduled to leave from the Pennsylvania Station at 11:55 P. M. pulled out of Grand Central Terminal at 12:15 o'clock this morning.

The train, made up of fourteen cars, will travel to Pittsburgh over the New York Central lines to Cleveland and Columbus and enter its destination from the west. Officials of the railroad said that if all goes well it would reach Pittsburgh by 6 P. M., making the run in approximately 18 hours as compared with its regular run of about 9 hours.

TRAIN HERE 15 HOURS LATE

Special From Detroit Took Circuitous Route in Flood Area.

Delayed by floods and heavy snows, the Pennsylvania Railroad's Red Arrow Special arrived in the Grand Central Terminal at 12:30 o'clock this morning, about fifteen hours overdue.

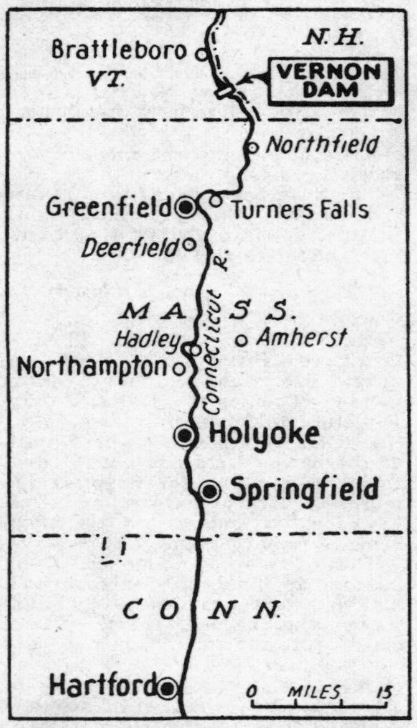

CONNECTICUT VALLEY

Towns suffering flood damage and facing much worse conditions should the Vernon dam, which is reported weakening, burst are shown.

The train started from Detroit at 4:30 P. M. Tuesday and was due in the Pennsylvania Station at 8:55 A. M. yesterday. Because some of the Pennsylvania's trackage was washed out by floods the train was forced to take a circuitous route by way of Girard, Ohio, thence to Erie, Pa., to Buffalo and from that point along the New York Central tracks to New York.

At no point along the run was the train marooned. The delay was caused by the precautionary measures taken. At various stops the train was held up, sometimes as long as two hours, until word was received that the road was open and safe.

Nothing but high praise came from the lips of the some ninety passengers that arrived. They received every consideration from the railroad officials, including free meals, they reported. When they arrived in New York, officials of the Pennsylvania Railroad were on hand to provide taxicabs for those who wanted to make connections with trains.

NEW ENGLAND HIT HARD BY FLOODS

Continued From Page One

lines of power, light and telephonic communication.

Worcester, Mass., battled tonight to retain its electric lights and power. Three fire companies were rushed to electric light stations with their pumpers.

The stations were flooded when the Leesville Dam went out. Worcester has a population of nearly 200,000 exceeded in the State only by Boston.

The deaths in New England today included:

Elizabeth, 7, and Donald Rattee, 5, drowned when they fell from a footbridge over a stream near Hancock, Vt.

Mrs. Hiram S. Drury of Williamstown, Vt., fell dead as she watched flood waters race down a hillside from a bursting dam near her home.

Harold L. Smith, 42, father of twelve children, drowned at Windham, Vt., while attempting to divert rising waters of a brook from flooding the basement of the lumber mill where he worked.

Harry R. Willard, railroad freight agent, swept to death at Leominster, Mass., when a bridge on which he was standing watching the flood water collapsed into the Nashua River.

At Springfield, Mass., the Connecticut River continued to rise at the rate of a foot an hour.

City Declares an Emergency

At Westfield, Mass., on the Westfield River, a Connecticut tributary, Mayor Raymond H. Cowing declared a state of public emergency and mobilized all available man-power to buttress menaced dikes and rescue marooned families.

Several hundred refugees crowded the American Legion Building and three churches; police commandeered every available boat, and fifty near-by CCC workers were pressed into service for relief duty.

The river, higher even than during the disastrous floods of 1927, which cost more than eighty lives in New England, isolated Westfield from all approaches but one.

In Northwestern Massachusetts the Hoosac River brought terror to two communities along its banks, Adams and North Adams. National Guardsmen were called out at both points. Small bridges were carried away at Adams and the municipal water supply was threatened. One of the principal gas mains was broken, hampering the light and fuel supply.

Seven truckloads of bedding and blankets were sent to North Adams upon orders of the National Guard.

All main line westward movement on the lines of both the Boston & Albany and the Boston & Maine Railroad was suspended.

Hundreds of passengers were temporarily stranded in Springfield's Union Station.

Late today State police reported that three bridges, including a New York, New Haven & Hartford Railroad span, had been swept away by the Connecticut at Montague, and that the débris had piled against a fourth bridge, that of the Boston & Maine Railroad, just below Montague at East Deerfield.

At Turners Falls on the Connecticut the river had reached a stage of 185,000 cubic feet a second, compared with 172,000 feet in 1927.

At Fitchburg, in North Central Massachusetts, the National Guard was called out as the Nashua River overflowed and conditions were described as the worst since 1850.

A break in the water main feeding the Fitchburg Hospital was restored by an emergency crew from the State Department of Public Health, but the hospital was using its own lighting system as power had failed in a large part of the city.

Cooperating with National Guardsmen, CCC workers, police and firemen toiled strenuously to salvage property in the path of the river and rescue marooned families. All factories near the river closed.

The Prince River, a tributary of the Ware River, swept away the Conners Pond bridge on the State highway between Barre and Petersham.

Three dams on the Prince River and one on the Ware River in that vicinity were threatened. A small power house on the Prince River was shifted about a foot by the flood.

Barre Plains was under water, with cellars of homes and stores flooded, largely from waters of Cleveland Brook, which became a raging torrent and piled up behind a blockade of sand and dirt that was washed against the county bridge. Residents appealed to county authorities to dynamite the bridge in the hope of opening up the brook channel.

At the Barre Wool Combing Company workmen dynamited floating ice that threatened a fifty-foot footbridge.

Railroad tracks were under water at Barre Plains.

At Brimfield, Mass., a dam on a pond gave way tonight and its waters flooded toward Fiskdale. Seventy-five residents in the path of the water fled from their homes.

Landslides covered railroad tracks in several spots between Greenfield and Fitchburg and train service was suspended early in the afternoon. Practically every highway between Fitchburg and North Adams was impassable.

Tonight the bursting of the retaining walls of the Plunkett Reservoir at Hinsdale, Mass., threw fresh torrents of water into the already flooded Housatonic, which eventually flows southward through Pittsfield.

At Williamstown, Mass., roads connecting Williams College with the town centre were washed out.

The Miller River in Central Massachusetts suddenly rose beyond the high levels of last week and, at Orange, flooded highways and threatened damage to the Reed textile plant, which suffered severe loss last week.

Water rose two feet above the highway between Orange and Athol, close to the Orange business center. Traffic was rerouted over back roads, but the rising water likewise menaced them. The water reached the Boston & Maine Railroad tracks in several places.

Serious flood conditions prevailed at Hinsdale, N. H., forcing rerouting of highway traffic from Kenne, N. H., to Greenfield, Mass., through Warwick, Mass. But in Warwick, Gale Brook increased to five times its normal size, washed sections out of the highway and overflowed three bridges.

Two Vermont communities, Johnson and Worcester, were cut off from telephone communication with the outside world.

The New England Telephone and Telegraph Company announced that it was unable to reach the central offices in either community and that they "apparently had been flooded out."

Johnson is an incorporated village of 659 population situated on a tributary of the Lamoille River. Worcester is a town of 470 population with a trading center on a tributary of the Winooski River.

Twenty-five families fled their homes at St. Johnsbury as a nine-mile ice jam swept down the Passumpsic River, burying highways and rail lines with ice and water. Telegraph poles were down and two feet of water ran in dwellings. Farmers in boats directed swimming cattle to safety.

To the south, at White River Junction, Vt., the Connecticut and White Rivers continued to rise. The fire station at White River was in a precarious condition. The grammar school was flooded.

The bridge over the Connecticut also was in danger, with the water only two feet away and rising rapidly. The railroad bridge was loaded with coal cars to hold it. At Hartford, Vt., the water was five feet over the falls.

Bellows Falls Is Isolated

Bellows Falls, Vt., was isolated by land. No mail came in during the day. Railroad transportation was at a standstill.

At Brattleboro, Vt., to the south, the situation was even worse, with loss placed unofficially at $250,000. The National Guard was on duty there tonight after a bridge across the Connecticut to Chesterfield, N. H., had been swept away. There had been no power or electric light since morning. Trains were tied up and many industrial plants were closed.

Destruction and Desolation in Maryland and South

PANICKY RESIDENTS DESERT JOHNSTOWN

PENNSYLVANIA AND MARYLAND CITIES INUNDATED BY RISING WATERS

Continued From Page One

gan shoveling silt and debris from their cellars.

Robert E. Bondy, Red Cross disaster relief director, set up a field hospital at the Westmont Upper Yoder High School, while CCC cots and blankets were rushed to Roxbury, another suburb, where temporary headquarters were established.

A measure of electrical and telephone service was restored as the night wore on.

But during most of the day and night there were no telephone connections, no city heat, no light, no power. Four of the city's five main bridges had collapsed into the torrents which last night and early today raced eighteen feet deep in places.

Highway, Rail Traffic Halted

All of the motor highways into the city were closed. The Pennsylvania Railroad, with two of its tracks washed into the Conemaugh and the other two of the four-track system unsafe, banned rail movement.

Only in the matter of the loss of human life did city authorities count the devastation appreciably less terrible than that of the "great flood" of May 31, 1889, when 2,235 men, women and children died.

Although the water was not more than a foot deep in the streets of Johnstown proper this evening and was rapidly draining off into slimy puddles, houses in near-by Ferndale stood in from six to eight feet of water.

While the official death list was set at six, unofficial reports held the loss of life to range from ten to forty. Governor Earle, who made a brief personal inspection of the city about midday, estimated that the toll eventually would be placed at somewhere between those limits.

With about 250 State police and State highway patrolmen already in the city, an additional 280 on the way from barracks and sub-stations as far east as Harrisburg, and 100 deputies supplementing the local force, the situation was kept well in hand pending the arrival of troops.

Furthermore, the emergency corps of the Red Cross was in the city, and these workers, with police, were tackling tonight the most difficult of the immediate questions— that of distribution of food supplies.

This was made difficult by the unreasoning panic which swept the city shortly before 3 o'clock this afternoon when the rumors spread of the breaking of the Quemahoning Dam, which is a gigantic reservoir of the Bethlehem Steel Corporation, sixteen miles from the city, on Stony Creek.

Men and women who were timidly picking their way back into the city from hillside refuges, since the flood waters were receding, heard the rumors and stampeded like frightened cattle.

"Run, run for your lives!" cries went up. "The dam's broken!"

Repeated assurances of State police that the dam, with its billions of gallons of potential destruction, was intact and in no danger of breaking might as well have been told to the wind.

With nerves at the breaking point due to last night's horror and sleepless, foodless and heatless hours, the evacuation of the city back to the hills began all over again.

Refugees Widely Scattered

Thus as food began to pour into the city from all over Cambria County, those for whom it was intended were scattered up and down the valley, in little groups, in unlighted houses and public structures, with no speedy means of transport to carry supplies to them.

Those who fled from Moxhan and Ferndale took refuge on the high ground at Prospect and Frankston. Orders were dispatched to all school buses in Cambria County to proceed as best they might to Johnstown, there to pick up and transport the homeless to the boroughs of Southmont, Westmont and Dale.

Four bridges spanning Stony

Associated Press Photo.

An aerial view of Johnstown, Pa., showing a section of the community where the residents were compelled to evacuate their homes yesterday because of the floods.

Creek — the Franklin, Ferndale, Maple Avenue and Riverside spans —were gone tonight. The sole remaining bridge connecting Johnstown with Conemaugh through the borough of Franklin was so severely damaged that it was expected to collapse momentarily.

The Conemaugh roundhouse of the Pennsylvania Railroad was washed out and four locomotives lay tonight half buried in the river.

With two of the four main tracks of the Pennsylvania washed out and their roadbeds seriously damaged, the other two are supposed to be unsafe, although there is no traffic in either direction to test them. Three trains which were reported to have left Harrisburg for Altoona were reported as not making any progress.

The William Penn Highway in the vicinity of Johnstown was again open, but secondary and rural roads were impassable. In low-lying areas, blocks of concrete had been ripped from the road, and wind-bound macadam and hard-surfaced roads were obliterated in some places.

10,000 Are Homeless

By The Associated Press.

JOHNSTOWN, March 18.—Red Cross agencies estimated that 10,000 were without homes in darkened Johnstown tonight, with 1,000 in great need.

Mayor Daniel Shields, who just three months ago became chief executive of the municipality, called upon all churches and other agencies to open their doors to the homeless. He also threw open all public buildings.

Larry B. Ashcom of The Johnstown Tribune quoted Mayor Shields as saying:

"Johnstown will have to be rebuilt."

Property damage, the Mayor was quoted as saying, would exceed by far that of the disastrous 1889 flood.

6 DIE IN WHEELING IN FLOOD AND BLAST

Island Home of 10,000 Persons in Ohio River Submerged and Water Keeps Rising.

THOUSANDS FLEE IN SOUTH

Harper's Ferry Under Water —Steel Mills and Mines Are Forced to Close.

By The Associated Press.

WHEELING, W. Va., Thursday, March 19.—The death toll from the floods sweeping through this city rose to six early today following an explosion in the southern part of Wheeling.

The Ohio River inundated Wheeling Island and crept into the business section and South Side of the city. The island is inhabited by 10,000 persons, one-sixth of the population of Wheeling.

The island was entirely submerged shortly before midnight and the water was near the second floors of homes. Most of the residents were believed safely transferred to the mainland but others remained in the top floors of their houses.

In downtown Wheeling, outside The Wheeling Intelligencer office, the water was four feet deep. Practically every road leading out of the city was under water. Telephone communication was uncertain.

The river's stage at midnight was 49.1 feet. Flood stage is 33 feet. Lockmaster J. R. Hill of Dam 12 at Warwood, north of here, said a crest of 54 feet was likely by 3 P. M. tomorrow.

Market Auditorium was thrown open for 4,000 refugees, and others sought shelter in schools and churches.

Among the dead were Buddy Harris, 2, drowned in the flooded basement of his home, and Mrs. Virginia Shahan of Wheeling Island, who died from exposure after being rescued from a sick bed by boat.

Two unidentified men were drowned after their skiff upset on Wheeling Island. Two unidentified persons were buried in the ruins of a two-family brick house which was wrecked by a gas explosion, injuring five others.

A driving rain was falling on the city. The river was rising at a rate of four-tenths to six-tenths of a foot an hour.

Two Lose Lives at Wellsburg, W. Va.

Copyright, 1936, by The Associated Press.

WELLSBURG, W. Va., March 18 —Two men were drowned in flood waters of the Ohio River tonight as one attempted to save the other from a flaming and partly submerged residence. Ten skiffs were used in an attempt to rescue 200 to 300 families which leaned out of windows and screamed for help.

Elmer Leonard, a glassworker, fell into the raging waters as he attempted to drag a young man identified only as "Deneen" from his blazing home into the skiff. Both were swept away before other boats could reach them.

As rescuers worked to evacuate the families from the second floors and roofs of their homes in the outer sections of the city, those further in shouted hysterically for help, but the workers ignored them, seeking first to remove those in the most dangerous positions.

Thousands Flee River Cities

Copyright, 1936, by The Associated Press.

CHARLESTON, W. Va., March 18.—Thousands of residents of Ohio River cities fled today before the menace of the greatest flood in history.

Flood stages of from fifty to fifty-eight feet at many communities were predicted for Thursday night or Friday morning by R. P. Powell, Federal meteorologist at Parkersburg.

The crest, he forecast, would send the waters rushing through streets at a height of eighteen feet in the little boat-building city of Point Pleasant; would cover half of Parkersburg and make 30,000 persons homeless in the industrial area of Wheeling.

Hurried preparations for rescue work were made by the State and communities.

Governor Kump's office announced late today that he had telegraphed to Secretary of War Dern asking permission to use all Federal equipment issued to the National Guard in flood areas. The office also said that the commandant of the Fifth Naval Area had authorized use of the Naval Reserve communications unit in Huntington to contact areas where communication had been cut off.

Carolinas Digging Out of Snow

CHARLOTTE, N. C., March 18 (P).— Western North Carolina sought today to dig from under the worst storm of the Winter which whipped up huge snowdrifts, paralyzed travel and marooned between 300 and 400 school children.

"All the News That's Fit to Print."

The New York Times.

LATE CITY EDITION
POSTSCRIPT
Fair and slightly warmer today.
Tomorrow showers.
Temperatures Yesterday—Max., 44; Min., 31

VOL. LXXXVI.....No. 28,909.

Entered as Second-Class Matter,
Postoffice, New York, N. Y.

NEW YORK, FRIDAY, MARCH 19, 1937.

TWO CENTS In New York City. | THREE CENTS Within 200 Miles. | FOUR CENTS Elsewhere Except in 7th and 8th Postal Zones.

Copyright, 1937, by The New York Times Company.

STRIKERS IN STORE EVICTED BY POLICE; 59 ARE ARRESTED

ALL-DAY SIEGE ENDS

Girls Scream, Weep as They Are Ousted From Woolworth Branch

POLICEMEN ARE BOOED

Union Officials Seized as Threats Are Made to Widen the Drive on Chain

C. I. O. CAMPAIGN ON TODAY

Seeks to Organize 1,250,000 in Textiles—Gains in Jersey as Company Signs Contract

Strike Developments

Sit-down strikers were cleared from a Woolworth store here by policemen and fifty-six strikers and three union officials were arrested. Page 1.

The C. I. O. will open its campaign today on a wide front to unionize 1,250,000 workers in the textile industry, it was announced here. Page 3.

In Woodbury, N. J., the Belber Bag and Trunk Company signed a closed-shop agreement with a C. I. O. union. Page 4.

In Detroit the police broke grip of sit-downers in department store as Governor Murphy's adjustment board to mediate strikes was formed in drive on labor upheaval. Page 5.

Chrysler counsel conferred with court and had hearing set for today to oust strikers. Page 1.

Remington-Rand, Inc., and union agreed on tentative terms for the settlement of a strike of 6,000 employees. Page 3.

Strikers Evicted Here

After a day of virtual siege warfare between sixty sit-down strikers and about thirty non-striking employes in the F. W. Woolworth 5 and 10 cent store at 33 West Fourteenth Street, the police cleared the store early last evening and arrested fifty-six strikers and three union officials who refused to leave.

Although the strikers, most of them girls who had been in the store since the strike was called at 11 A. M. Wednesday, screamed and wept and about 300 sympathizers gathered on the sidewalk booed and heckled the police, there was no attempt at resistance as twenty patrolmen from the Mercer Street station carried out the evictions.

Threats of broadening their drive against the Woolworth chain by calling strikes in anywhere from eight to twenty stores in the near future were voiced during the day by spokesmen for the union, Local 1,250 of the Department Store Employes Union, which is affiliated with the American Federation of Labor.

Brooklyn Store Kept Closed

They succeeded in keeping closed during the day the Woolworth store at 22 Sutter Avenue, Brooklyn, from which seventeen sit-down strikers had been removed by the police at 2 A. M. on charge of disorderly conduct. The strikers were arraigned during the day in the Pennsylvania Avenue Court but their case was not completed and will be continued today.

Two men and two women were arrested late in the afternoon at the F. & W. Grand Store at 1,645 Pitkin Avenue, Brooklyn, where thirty-five employes have been conducting a strike since Saturday. In a conference between representatives of the union and the H. L. Green Company, which operates five stores of the Grand chain which have been closed by strikes, was postponed until today because of the illness of one of the negotiators.

The arrests at the Fourteenth Street store were technically made by Thomas R. Lynn, a merchandising manager of the Woolworth company, assisted by the police, who were under the command of Inspectors Alexander C. Anderson and John W. Conway, and Captains Thomas Leahy and William Kent.

At 7 P. M. Mr. Lynn told the striking employes, who had verbally disputed possession of the store all day with twenty-seven non-striking clerks and a dozen uniformed private detective guards, that the store was closed and they

Continued on Page Two

San Juan Street Change Is the First in 200 Years

Special Cable to THE NEW YORK TIMES.

SAN JUAN, Puerto Rico, March 18.—The first extension to the original street plan of old San Juan proper in more than 200 years is now under way. It will add 200 feet to the south end of Cruz Street and permit the diversion of motor traffic from the congested retail and office section.

The street extension was made possible by the destruction of the building adjoining the Chase National Bank branch, which will give that bank frontage on three streets besides making traffic diversion possible.

City authorities say that the street extension, long contemplated, marks the first change from the earliest street plan of the city found in the archives. Long held up by litigation, the 200-foot addition to the street is now being made on the basis of a friendly agreement between the city and former property owners.

CHRYSLER MOVES TO OUST STRIKERS

Counsel, After Court Conference, Prepares for Hearing on Petition Today

MURPHY ASSAILS 'BANDITRY'

Governor Charges Strong-Arm Activity—Says Man He Sentenced Led Store 'Raid'

By RUSSELL B. PORTER
Special to THE NEW YORK TIMES.

DETROIT, March 18.—Attorneys for the Chrysler Corporation appeared before Circuit Judge Allan Campbell in chambers today, preparatory to asking for another court order looking toward the legal eviction of the 6,000 sit-down strikers who have held possession of eight of its plants here since a week ago Monday.

They announced later that they would appear before Judge Campbell in the Circuit Court at 9 o'clock tomorrow morning to press their application.

Governor Murphy tonight for the first time took direct charge of the Chrysler negotiations, when he called both sides into separate conferences in the Hotel Statler. K. T. Keller, president, and B. E. Hutchinson, executive vice president of the Chrysler corporation, conferred with him from 8 to 10 o'clock. Homer S. Martin, president, and Richard T. Frankensteen, Detroit organizational director for the United Automobile Workers, were with him from 10 o'clock till midnight. None would discuss the subject of the talks.

It was Judge Campbell who issued the injunction ordering John L. Lewis, chairman of the Committee for Industrial Organization; Homer S. Martin, president of the United Automobile Workers of America, and nearly 100 other officers and organizers of the two groups, as well as the actual sit-downers, to evacuate the plants by 9 o'clock yesterday morning under penalty of a ten-million-dollar fine to be levied against their property.

This order of the court was defied by the sit-downers and by a mob of 30,000 or more unionists and sympathizers who picketed the seized plants at the zero hour yesterday.

Several Moves Are Open

If the Chrysler Corporation follows the precedent set by the General Motors Corporation in the sit-down strikes at Flint, its application tomorrow morning will be for a writ of body attachment directing Sheriff Thomas C. Wilcox of Wayne County to arrest the sit-downers and bring them into court to answer charges of contempt.

Another procedure would be to ask an order to show cause, calling on attorneys for the union to argue why such a writ should not be issued.

In view of the fact that Mr. Lewis and other C. I. O. officers and organizers, who are out of the jurisdiction of the Michigan courts, were named as defendants in the Chrysler case, some other procedure may be contemplated.

Thomas R. Chawke, chief of the Chrysler counsel, who conferred with Judge Campbell, declined to say anything more about the company's plans than that he

Continued on Page Four

POPE BIDS NATIONS END RED 'RAVAGES'; URGES FAIR WAGES

In Anti-Communist Encyclical He Calls for Battle Against 'the Anti-God Campaign'

CITES CONDITIONS IN SPAIN

Asks Employers to Recognize Worker's 'Inalienable Right' to Sufficient Return

Official abstract of the Pope's encyclical is on Page 10.

Wireless to THE NEW YORK TIMES.

VATICAN CITY, March 18.—In another strong encyclical letter, running to 13,000 words, Pope Pius today called on all States "to prevent within their territory the ravages of the anti-God campaign," which shakes society in its very foundations.

He condemned communism as "a system full of errors and sophisms," deplored its effects in Mexico, Spain and Russia, and opposed to it the doctrine of the Catholic Church, which he said proclaims the equality and brotherhood of man and defends his liberty and his rights.

On the basis of these principles, he added, the Church recognizes and defends a hierarchy and the legitimate authority of society, because by proposing opportune social norms society should be a directing and coordinating force.

He even advocated the use of "legal means of constraint and repression when the activity of individuals or groups may tend to the detriment of the common good."

Opposes Party Exaggerations

However, lest a political interpretation might be given to his words, he pointed out in what was taken as a veiled reference to Nazism and fascism that the Church's doctrine "is equally removed from all extremes of error and all exaggerations of parties or systems which stem from error."

"It maintains the constant equilibrium of truth and justice, which it vindicates in theory and promotes and applies in practice, bringing into harmony the rights and duties of all parties," he declared.

At the same time the Pontiff suggested remedies against communism by urging on Catholics the world over the renewal of Christian life, detachment from worldly possessions, Christian charity, and above all justice, which "should induce employers and the wealthy to recognize the inalienable right of the working man to a wage sufficient for himself and his family."

He exhorted all priests to stand in the front line of this battle against communism with the cooperation of Catholic Action and auxiliary organizations and appealed to all Catholic workers and non-workers to put aside their differences and unite in this great struggle.

The Pope begged his "erring children" to "hear the voice of your loving father."

"We pray the Lord to enlighten

Continued on Page Ten

NEUTRALITY PLAN IS VOTED BY HOUSE; DISCRETION LIMITED

Measure Fixes a 2-Year Period for Presidential Right to Curb Shipments

BILL APPROVED 374 TO 12

Wadsworth, Opposing, Argues It Aids the Strong and Shuts Out the Weak

Special to THE NEW YORK TIMES.

WASHINGTON, March 18.—By an overwhelming vote of 374 to 12 the House passed today the McReynolds discretionary neutrality resolution, sending it to the Senate as a substitute for the Pittman mandatory legislation already adopted by that body.

The well-disciplined Democratic majority in the House beat down all amendments that were offered, except those which had the approval of Representative Sam D. McReynolds of Tennessee, chairman of the Foreign Affairs Committee.

Of these, the most important would provide a limitation of two years on Section 4 of the resolution, which would permit the President, in his discretion, to forbid American vessels to carry certain proclaimed categories of commodities, and which would permit him to put into effect a "cash and carry" policy for all commerce with belligerents.

Intended for Compromise

Offered by Representative James A. Shanley of Connecticut, with the endorsement of Mr. McReynolds, the amendment was intended to pave the way for an ultimate compromise with the Senate, where sentiment for mandatory legislation is as strong as the discretionary principle showed itself to be in the House. The Pittman resolution passed the Senate by a vote of 63 to 6.

The McReynolds resolution, as it finally passed the House, would set up machinery that the President of the United States could put into motion during time of international war at any time he found the peace and neutrality of this country threatened. He would not have to put it into effect automatically as soon as he found a state of war to exist, as he would have to do under the Pittman proposal.

In the main, the two measures would establish substantially the same machinery to prevent this country's involvement in foreign quarrels. They would both prohibit the export of arms, ammunition and implements of war and loans to all belligerents as soon as the President proclaimed that a state of war or civil strife existed anywhere in the world. They would both continue in effect existing means of controlling the munitions traffic sufficiently to carry out this purpose.

This much of the program is embodied in existing laws. The new departure that both resolutions would attempt to make is the regulation of the nation's foreign trade and the travel of its citizens in danger zones. In both measures provision would be made to avoid

Continued on Page Eight

500 PUPILS AND TEACHERS ARE KILLED IN EXPLOSION OF GAS IN TEXAS SCHOOL; 100 INJURED TAKEN FROM THE DEBRIS

RUINS ILLUMINATED

In Glare of Searchlights 3,000 Men Dig Wreckage With Gloved Hands

50 TRUCKS CLEARING SITE

School, Shattered by Series of Explosions, Reduced to Mounds of Brick, Steel

OVER IN A FEW SECONDS

Throng, Rushing Over Oil Fields, Snatched Children in Sight— Others Wedged by Concrete

By MEYER BERGER

NEW LONDON, Texas, Friday, March 19.—Three thousand men worked in the ruins of the $125,000 London Consolidated High School this morning under the glare of searchlights and gas flares, trying to find the bodies of school children and teachers still buried under the ruins of the building that collapsed yesterday afternoon after an explosion, with a loss estimated as at about 500 lives.

More than 400 bodies had been recovered before 2 A. M. They were taken to morgues in surrounding communities. Most of the bodies were unidentifiable.

Parents, kept from the ruins, went from one town to another in search of their children. The exact number of dead will not be known for at least three days, according to officials on the ground. Estimates of the total deaths varied from 500 to more than 700, but no one really knows.

The survivors and the dead taken from the ruins are scattered in communities all over Rusk County. They were carried away in trucks, ambulances and in private cars. Crim's Morgue in Henderson, ten miles from New London, had 160 bodies before 2 A. M. The searchers in the ruins still faced great mounds of debris that had not been touched.

Batteries of searchlights played on the ruins as the feverish workers, lifting brick by brick, continued their search for the bodies still remaining. It looked like a scene from the motion pictures. Over an area of three city blocks, oil field workers, farmers and white collar men from the surrounding New London dug at the debris with gloved hands.

Debris Is Carefully Searched

Fifty trucks were backed up to the ruins carrying the debris away to leave the field clear for further searching. They loaded the stuff into boxes, wash boilers, any type of container that came to hand.

Even the smallest bit of debris was searched carefully, for many of the bodies had been dismembered. Scattered here and there were text books, children's garments, odds and ends of school paraphernalia. As fast as a truck was loaded it rolled away, churning up the red clay, and headed off for the dumping ground. The workers still faced untouched mounds fourteen feet high. The largest mounds were in the center of the school grounds, where the auditorium had been.

The institution was called in these parts the richest rural school in America. All that remained of it was a small battered portion of the auditorium and a part of the right wing.

When the explosion occurred men at work in the near-by oil fields, supposed to be the richest oil community in America, said that the ground shook, and this whole forest of oil derricks trembled under the concussion. The explosion was heard over a distance of from twelve to fifteen miles.

Series of Explosions Described

What happened immediately after the explosion, they saw fire follow the flames. All agreed that there was no single explosion but rather a series of explosions in one building. The whole thing was a matter of a second, it was said.

They came tearing across the oil fields, men and women, and they said the front of the building was still standing and was just giving way when they got there. They had no idea that so many

Continued on Page Fourteen

Martial Law Is Declared

By The Associated Press.

AUSTIN, Texas, March 18.—Governor James V. Allred declared martial law tonight at the vicinity of the New London school disaster after ordering troops to proceed there.

He instructed officers to call out available troops at Tyler and Longview and take charge of the situation. About 200 National Guardsmen were available. The Governor issued the order after he was informed that thousands of sightseers were rushing to New London.

The Governor acted on statements that the State highway patrol and other officers might not be able to control the situation should the highways be thronged and relief work impeded.

The order was directed to Captain Arlie Goyne at Longview and Lieutenant Williams A. Johnson at Tyler.

"Proceed with all available men in your companies, taking charge of the entire situation," the order said.

Radio companies were requested by Mr. Allred to broadcast an appeal for people with no business there to stay away from New London.

Governor Allred characterized the disaster in the school house at New London, Texas, as "one of the worst in the history of our State," yesterday in a telephone conversation with a reporter for THE NEW YORK TIMES, from the Capitol at Austin.

"We have received only very meager information here, but we have received enough to know that this is one of the most tragic occurrences in many years," he said.

"Immediately upon receiving the report of the disaster, I issued orders for all State highway patrolmen and rangers to rush to New London by airplane and automobile to give the people of that stricken community every assistance possible."

Doctors and nurses and medical supplies were being rushed to New London and near-by communities from all over East Texas, Governor Allred said.

ROOSEVELT MOVES QUICKLY ON RELIEF

Red Cross and All Government Agencies Ordered to Lend Aid in School Disaster

DOCTORS FLY TO SCENE

Planes Also Take Nurses and Medical Supplies—Other Texas Cities Speed Help

Special to THE NEW YORK TIMES.

WARM SPRINGS, Ga., March 18.—President Roosevelt tonight called the Red Cross, of which he is honorary head, and all government agencies to help in the disastrous explosion in New London, Texas.

At the same time, the President issued a statement which read:

"I am appalled by the news of the disaster at New London, Texas, in which hundreds of school children lost their lives.

"A few hours ago I dedicated a school building here in Western Georgia with high hopes for the future service it could render. Tonight with the rest of the nation I am shocked and can only hope that further information will lessen the scope of this tragedy.

"I have asked the Red Cross and all of the government agencies to stand by and render every assistance in their power to the community to which this shocking tragedy has come."

Doctors Rush to the Scene

By The Associated Press.

NEW LONDON, Texas, March 18.—Thirty doctors and seventy-two nurses, twelve of them from the Red Cross, came here from Dallas to aid in the rescue work at the explosion-wrecked high school. Accompanying the doctors and nurses were twelve ambulances, twenty-five embalmers and five hearses.

Sobbing mothers pressed close to the rescue workers or moved from one group of the dead to another in what was most often a vain search for their children.

In many cases the clothes of the dead were tattered and their faces blackened by the blast and the fire that followed it.

Possibly eighty-five children were being treated at a Tyler hospital. Two were reported to have been taken alive from beneath the ruins.

Every school, church, club room and public building in the community has its quota of the dead or dying. The hospitals were jammed, but it seemed that those needing medical attention were getting it. Earlier in the day it was a different story, and many injured lay in their agony without care or a physician or nurse. There was no one to blame for that situation. There were not enough doctors and nurses.

As night fell workers set up spotlights and a half-dozen giant oil-field cranes were swung into position and set to clearing out the debris. They are working very carefully

Continued on Page Fifteen

CORONATION: Headquarters for hotel accommodations, Processions, seats, etc.
COOK'S, 587 Fifth Ave. VO. 5-1500.—Adv.

ROOF ROSE INTO AIR AS WALLS BUCKLED

Superintendent, Standing 50 Feet From School, Says There Was Not Much Noise

HEARD CHILDREN'S CRIES

He Had Just Stepped Outdoors —His Son, 17, Was in Class And Is Among the Missing

By Telephone to THE NEW YORK TIMES.

NEW LONDON, Texas, March 18.—W. C. Shaw, 61-year-old superintendent of the Consolidated School at New London, whose son, Sam, 17, was in the building when the explosion and fire leveled it, said tonight he was standing about fifty feet away from the structure at the time.

"It's unbelievable," he said. "There wasn't much noise. The roof just lifted up, then the walls fell out and the roof fell in.

"It was all over in a minute; no, less than that; half a minute. It's unbelievable."

Mr. Shaw, who has been superintendent of the school for six years, has his home on the grounds.

"I don't believe over a hundred children got out and a lot of them were so badly hurt they won't live," he said. "We haven't found our own boy, Sam. We're afraid he's gone, too."

Had Just Left the Building

There was no warning, the superintendent said. He had just come from the building. He had not detected no gas nor seen anything out of the way.

"The gas-steam system was operating, he said, with the gas turned on in a few of the radiators."

Accompanying the superintendent out of the building was E. W. Waggoner, a teacher. He was struck by flying debris, but his physical injuries were not of a major character.

"There can still hear some children in there," he kept repeating. "We can still hear some children in there."

The school grounds were roped off to keep back all except the workers, an army of whom tore desperately at the twisted steel and jumbled brick and concrete in their search for bodies, or the living.

From the oil well machine shops were brought acetylene torches to burn away the girders, while trucks hauled on heavy iron chains, pulling debris apart.

Flood lights on the football field immediately back of the main building, were turned on and other lights rigged on high poles in the oil fields.

It was a scene of ordered confusion. Workers had to make themselves heard above the groaning of the trucks and the roar of gasoline engines pumping up the pressure tanks for the torches.

"They are working very carefully," one of the workmen directing

Continued on Page Fourteen

RESCUERS TOIL ON

Night Crews Directed by Moans Coming From the Wreckage

740 IN BUILDING AT TIME

Bodies of 450 Already Found —Toll Is Third of School-Age Children of District

MOTHERS SEE DISASTER

Oil-Field Towns Aid and State Declares Martial Law—'Wet Gas' of Heaters Held Cause

By Telephone to THE NEW YORK TIMES.

NEW LONDON, Texas, Friday, March 19.—Nearly a third of the children of school age of this little town and the surrounding countryside in the heart of the rich East Texas oil fields were killed yesterday when a gas explosion brought their big, modern schoolhouse crashing down upon their heads.

Forty teachers and 700 children from 9 to 18 years of age were in the building at about 3:30 o'clock yesterday afternoon when this school of about 1,500 pupils drawn from the camps of oil field workers for miles around.

It was believed few more than 200 escaped with their lives. Many of those who did were so badly injured that it was feared they would die.

Police headquarters at Henderson, nine miles southeast of New London, reported that 448 bodies had been recovered at 12:30 o'clock this morning; that 300 had been identified, and that a new ambulance load of the dead was being brought into town every five minutes.

The bodies were being placed in garages, stores, undertakers' shops and police headquarters, according to the officer on duty. Outside all these buildings, he said, were groups of parents trying to identify their loved ones.

Final Count May Take Days

While it probably will be a day or two before a complete tabulation is made, the estimated death toll ranged between 500 and 530. Bodies of victims were sent to cities as far away as Shreveport, La., and undertakers within a 100-mile radius of the scene of the tragedy were summoned to assist in funeral preparations. An emergency call was sent out for coffins in which to bury the victims of the disaster.

The explosion which took such a terrific loss of life came late in the afternoon, scarcely ten minutes before the school's usual dismissal time. The parents of many of the children were near by and heard the blast and saw the puff of dust that wiped out the school house before their eyes as though it had been a mere mirage.

As the magnitude of the disaster became apparent, conditions in the little community verged on chaos, with nearly 10,000 residents of East Texas gathered near the school house, clogging the roads and blocking highways in and out of town.

Governor James V. Allred proclaimed martial law and sent 100 National Guardsmen and State highway patrolmen into the town under Colonel Clarence Parker of Tyler to preserve order and aid in the rescue work.

Parents First Attempt Rescues

At first frantic mothers and fathers tore with their bare hands at the twisted steel and broken brick and concrete which marked the spot where the big new $125,000 school house had stood.

Later, skilled workers arrived on the oil fields, which bear all of the first news of the disaster, cut away the crushing weight of concrete with their derricks and windlasses mounted upon trucks.

Men pressing close to the ruins heard the cries of children as the rescue work progressed with heart-breaking slowness.

In the corner of the schoolhouse it was discovered that the bent and twisted girders were keeping tons of concrete from falling; in upon a ground-floor room where twenty-seven children and their teacher were believed to have been when the blast shattered the walls of the school. It was here that rescuers

Continued on Page Fourteen

Garland and Twelve Associates Found Guilty On 43 Counts of Mail Fraud and Conspiracy

Wallace G. Garland, former honor student at Yale University, who became known as "The Wizard" because he developed patents on an "electric eye" system for traffic guidance, winning the approval and support of Professor Irving Fisher, economist; Arnold C. Mason, also a Yale graduate; eleven other persons and three corporations, were found guilty last night in Federal court on forty-three counts of mail fraud and conspiracy.

Federal Judge John C. Knox, before whom they had been on trial for more than a month, will impose sentences next Thursday. Each individual faces a possible 212 years in prison and fines totaling $230,000, although the court seldom imposes the maximum term.

The jury brought in a verdict of not guilty for the Automatic Signal Corporation, which Garland organized in 1927 to manufacture the "electric eye" devices for which he had patents. Professor Fisher, who invested heavily in that corporation, is now chairman of its board of directors.

The trial began last Feb. 9. The government, through William Power Maloney, Assistant United States Attorney, charged that Garland in his zeal to market the "electric eye" patents built up a succession of interlocking corporations, in which the value of the invention was greatly exaggerated.

The evidence showed that stock in the corporations sold to brokers for $5 a share was later sold to the public at $24 a share. So-called show contracts, it was testified, were prepared for the benefit of the Attorney General to give him the impression that brokers were paying $16 a share for the stock.

were the Public Service Holding Corporation of Delaware, stock of which Garland and his associates sold to the public; Elliott Myers & Co., Inc., and George Henriques & Co., brokerage firms.

The jury recommended leniency for the following defendants, who were found guilty on all counts: Walter M. Barr, 135 Brighton Road, Island City, L. I.; David Dubrin, 235 West Eighty-eighth Street; Harold Klein, 6,420 Gelenwood Road, Brooklyn; Harry Klein, 630 Avenue M, Brooklyn; Arthur Elliott Myers, 11 Van Corlear Place; Louis Fraino, 25 Central Park West; George Henriques, 600 West 116th Street; Russell Van Wyck Stuart, 105 West Fifty-fifth Street; William C. Toomey, 325 Seventy-fourth Street, Brooklyn; Joseph Winfield, 373 Ninety-second Street, Brooklyn; and David Weinstein, 25 Central Park West.

The corporations found guilty

Continued on Page Fourteen

500 DIE IN BLAST AT TEXAS SCHOOL

Continued From Page One

concentrated their efforts late in the night.

By 10 P. M. more than 100 ambulances from towns and cities as far away as Houston were on the scene with doctors and nurses.

Word was sent out from New London that no more doctors were needed but that there was urgent need for supplies of caffeine and glucose. A plane bearing these supplies got through from Houston late in the night after another one, chartered by the Humble Oil Company, had been forced back by fog.

Five of the dead and 100 injured victims of the disaster were rushed to Tyler, a near-by town, which only a few hours before receiving news of the catastrophe, had been celebrating the opening of its new hospital. The institution's equipment proved inadequate to meet the sudden emergency, and a call was broadcast for cots and blankets.

Undertakers' morgues for miles around were filled and telephone service in Eastern Texas was swamped under a deluge of calls from anguished parents seeking news of their little ones.

Most of the children and teachers were in the auditorium, which was situated in the center of the E-shaped building, 160 feet long and eighty feet deep, when the blast wrecked the school as though a bomb from an air-raider had found its mark.

Three hundred feet away in the gymnasium, a separate building, fifty or more mothers had gathered for a parent-teacher meeting when the rumble of the explosion sent them rushing to windows.

Where the school building had been they saw only a heap of twisted steel and a pile of brick and broken concrete with dry dust rising from it.

Mothers Struggle at Wreckage

Screaming hysterically, the mothers raced across the campus. With bare hands they clawed at the débris, trying desperately to reach children whose cries could be heard from beneath the crumbled structure.

As darkness fell on the ruins of the school, the community center for this region of scattered oil camps and small hamlets, the campus presented a macabre scene. Sightseers crowded elbow to elbow with grief-stricken parents, watching rescue crews at work with acetylene torches beneath floodlights from the football field and a string of electric bulbs hastily put in place above the wreckage.

Alongside the tragic pile, an ever-lengthening line of white told the magnitude of the disaster. The bodies of the little victims, before being taken to Henderson, were laid upon the grass and covered with sheets to await identification, which in many cases was difficult or impossible.

Hours after the explosion screams and moans of the injured could be heard beneath the wreckage.

Injured Taken to Near-By Towns

This little community, selected as the site for the consolidated school for its accessibility rather than for its size, had no hospital facilities, and doctors and nurses were scarce.

The injured, as they were extricated from the débris, were rushed to Henderson, Longview, Overton and Tyler. Private automobiles and delivery trucks were pressed into service as ambulances and a Baptist church at Overton served as an emergency hospital.

W. C. Shaw, the superintendent of the school, who saw it shattered before his eyes as he walked across the school yard, said at first he thought about 100 of the pupils and teachers in the building escaped death.

Many of the injured who were removed from beneath the tons of steel and concrete, he said, were so badly injured that they could not live. The superintendent's own 17-year-old son, Sam, was in the building and was believed to have died with his schoolmates.

Troy Duran, principal of the school, agreed with the estimate of the probable total of dead. He said that 300 bodies had been re-

moved by early evening, and that as many more lay buried beneath the wreckage.

Two teachers and twelve pupils, it was said, had been brought out alive and unscathed save for the shock they suffered. These fortunate ones, it was explained, had been saved from death by a huge bookcase which teetered over against a wall and created a sort of artificial cave, which held off the falling mortar from their heads.

Most of the younger children, in grades from the third to the sixth, had been dismissed before the disaster occurred and were out of harm's way.

Some were playing about the yard and saw the school building collapse upon their older schoolmates.

Goes Into School to Death

On one of the playgrounds, W. C. Waltrip, director of physical education, had directed a class in setting-up exercises, 100 yards from the school. One of the boys in the class was killed by a brick torn loose and sent hurtling through the air by the explosion.

Mr. Waltrip himself was killed in the explosion. A few minutes before the blast, he left his class and returned to the building to get some athletic equipment. He was caught under the deluge of brick and mortar and crushed to death.

J. R. Garner, who was teaching a class of sixteen children in history, escaped with all his pupils. They were in a wing of the building which stood up long enough to permit them to escape.

Eye-witnesses to the disaster said that the blast itself made little noise. All agreed that there was a muffled sound and a rumbling noise just before the building began to disintegrate.

First the walls seemed to bulge out, the horror-stricken witnesses said; then the roof lifted up and crashed in with a deafening roar, carrying most of the side walls with it. It was all over with such horrible quickness that there was no chance for escape and immediate rescue was impossible.

For a few minutes after the roof caved in, leaving jagged remnants

of wall still standing like the ruins of some medieval castle, flames shot out above the wreckage. The building, however, was of fireproof construction and the fire, having almost nothing to feed upon, soon died out.

From the lips of small children who lived through the horror and from the bereft parents of the dead, stricken almost dumb with tragedy, there came some graphic stories of the disaster.

Doris Derring, a 15-year-old student in the eighth grade, who found shelter under a desk when the roof fell in, said she saw her teacher buried alive. Before her eyes, she said, 100 of her schoolmates were blown from their desks into the schoolyard as the walls were ripped apart.

J. B. Jones, an employe of the Humble Oil Company, at work on a well three hundred yards from the school building, heard the first blast, saw the roof rise from the walls and then fall back with a crash that shook the earth beneath his feet.

Joe Davidson, another oil worker who lost three children in the disaster, declined to stop his rescue work to tell about it, saying that there was still a chance that some other children might be taken out alive. Another man, helping rescuers, came upon the body of his own little daughter, whom he had thought to be safe, amid the wreckage.

The wrecked school was part of a $1,000,000 educational plant erected by two school districts of Rusk County. It contained thirty classrooms and an auditorium big enough to accommodate half the pupils.

It was equipped to teach stenography, music, sewing and manual training, and it was the proud boast of the community that its school was as fine as could be found in any rural section of the country.

On one side stood the gymnasium and on the other was a grade school for children from kindergarten to the third grade, inclusive. All others attended classes in the building which was wrecked.

The home of the superintendent

stood on the school grounds, in the midst of the inevitable oil-well derricks, which, having provided the tax money from which the school was built, encroached even on its playgrounds.

First reports were that a boiler had exploded in the basement of the school directly beneath the auditorium in which the children were gathered for their regular daily assembly—half the school meeting in the morning and the other half just before dismissal time at 3:30 P. M.

School officials said, however, that there was no boiler or central heating plant in the building.

Instead, the school building was heated, when condition in the warm Texas atmosphere required, by separate steam radiators, heated by gas. With the abundant oil and natural gas fields near by, the fuel used was natural gas of the variety known as "wet gas," which is odorless.

The best guess regarding the disaster seemed to be that leaking gas had accumulated in the building unknown to pupils or teachers and had become ignited from the flame beneath one of the radiators, which, with the temperature down to 50 degrees, had been started in some of the classrooms and the auditorium.

The town of New London itself is a small community consisting of a dozen stores and a few scattered houses on the road between Henderson and Longview. All about it are the lank, grimy skeletons marking oil wells and the camps in which live the workers whose children were the victims of this afternoon's disaster. Among these camps word of what had happened spread rapidly and within less than an hour the roads into New London were choked with cars, making it difficult for the ambulance cars to make their way against traffic to emergency dressing stations.

Appeals Broadcast Over State

In the evening, appeals were broadcast over the State urging all but doctors and nurses to stay away from the scene of the worst tragedy in many years of Texas

history. Drug stores and hospitals all over East Texas were drained of their available supplies of bandages, germicides and unguents.

The biggest oil fields in the neighborhood are those of the Humble Oil Refining Company, Gulf Refining Company and the Tidewater Oil Company. All operations were suspended in these fields and the workers, numbering more than 1,000, were digging away the wreckage from the dead and injured.

They worked desperately, but with caution, with their torches, lest in cutting away the steel they loosen supports under masonry and let it down on some who still might be alive.

The explosion sent children hurtling through the air "like rag dolls with their clothes torn off," to quote one witness to the disaster.

As the dust settled, the broken bodies of many of the victims were seen lying on top of the débris. Some were decapitated. Others had legs and arms missing. A few were still alive. These were rushed to dressing stations at once in private cars.

Identification Is Difficult

Many parents, screaming hysterically or silently sobbing, ran from one body to another, seeking their loved ones. Occasionally a woman, slumping to the ground in a faint, indicated she had found what she had fearfully hoped she would not find. Mutilation of the bodies made the task of identification increasingly difficult. One couple hovered over the form of a little boy, his face and body so disfigured they could not be certain if he were their own.

"Oh, it's Jim, it must be Jim," sobbed the woman. Picking up one of the little victim's feet, she argued hysterically with her husband.

"See, it's his tennis shoes," she cried. "I remember he asked to wear them to school this morning."

"No, no," her husband replied almost happily. "Jim changed into his other shoes when he came home for lunch."

"Oh, merciful God, he may still be alive then," the mother cried as they got up and hurried away to scan other bodies.

Rescuers With Torches Battle Steel and Concrete to Bring Out Dying Children

Crowd gathers at ruins of the Consolidated School after the natural gas explosion which killed 500 children and teachers.

Wide World Photos

"All the News That's Fit to Print."

The New York Times.

LATE CITY EDITION
Fair today, temperature unchanged. Tomorrow fair, little change in temperature.
Temperatures Yesterday—Max., 71; Min., 54

Copyright, 1937, by The New York Times Company.

VOL. LXXXVI.....No. 28,958. Entered as Second-Class Matter, Postoffice, New York, N. Y. NEW YORK, FRIDAY, MAY 7, 1937. P TWO CENTS In New York City. | THREE CENTS Within 200 Miles. | FOUR CENTS Elsewhere Except in 7th and 8th Postal Zones.

HINDENBURG BURNS IN LAKEHURST CRASH; 21 KNOWN DEAD, 12 MISSING; 64 ESCAPE

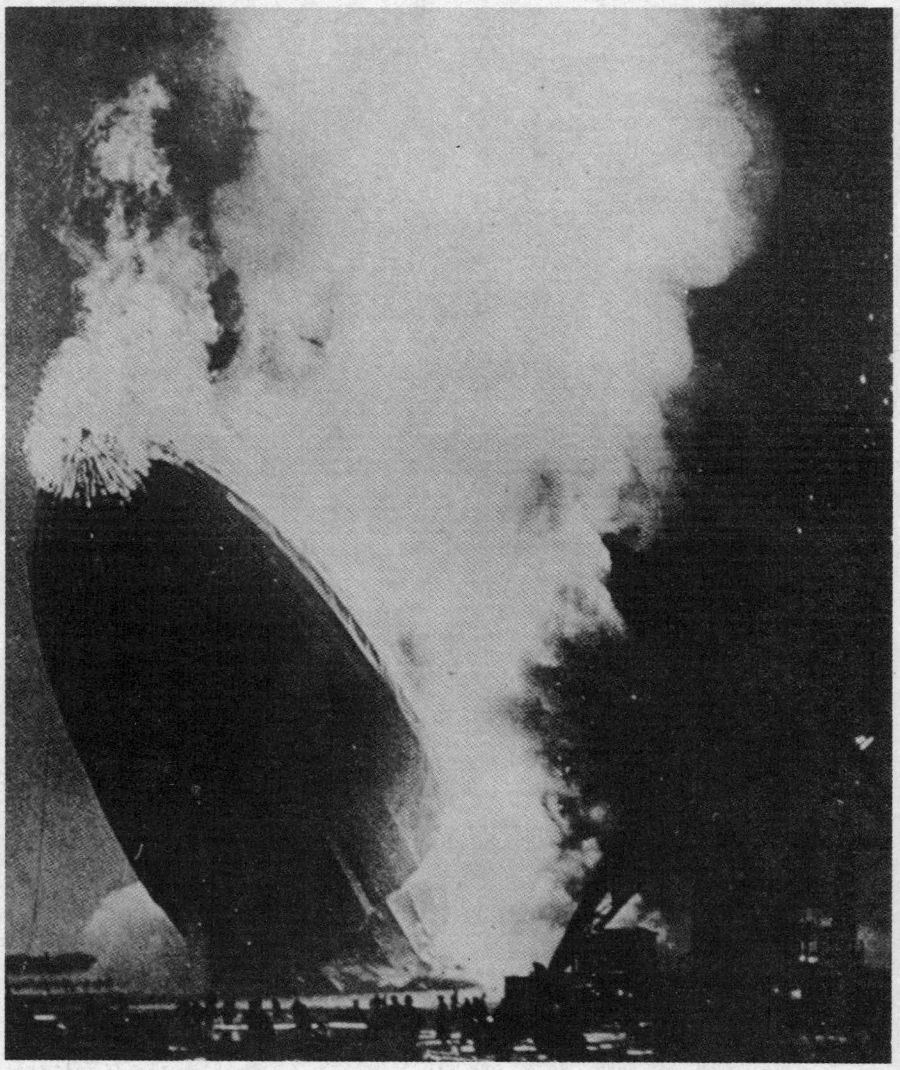

Associated Press Photo.

THE HINDENBURG IN FLAMES ON THE FIELD AT LAKEHURST

The giant airliner as she settled to the ground near her mooring mast at 7:23 o'clock last night

SHIP FALLS ABLAZE

Great Dirigible Bursts Into Flames as It Is About to Land

VICTIMS BURN TO DEATH

Some Passengers Are Thrown From the Blazing Wreckage, Others Crawl to Safety

GROUND CREW AIDS RESCUE

Sparks From Engines or Static Believed to Have Ignited Hydrogen Gas

A page of photographs of the disaster and survivors Page 20.

By RUSSELL B. PORTER
Special to THE NEW YORK TIMES.

NAVAL AIR STATION, LAKEHURST, N. J., May 6.—The zeppelin Hindenburg was destroyed by fire and explosions here at 7:23 o'clock tonight with a loss of thirty-three known dead and unaccounted for out of its ninety-seven passengers and crew.

Three hours after the disaster twenty-one bodies had been recovered, and twelve were still missing. The sixty-four known to be alive included twenty passengers and forty-four of the crew. Many of the survivors were burned or injured or both, and were taken to hospitals here and in near-by towns.

The accident happened just as the great German dirigible was about to tie up to its mooring mast four hours after flying over New York City on the last leg of its first transatlantic voyage of the year. Until today the Hindenburg had never lost a passenger throughout the ten round trips it made across the Atlantic with 1,002 passengers in 1936.

Two Theories of Cause

F. W. von Meister, vice president of the American Zeppelin Company, gave two possible theories to explain the crash. One was that a fire was caused by an electrical circuit "induced by static conditions" as the ship valved hydrogen gas preparatory to landing. Another was that sparks set off when the engines were throttled down while the gas was being valved caused a fire or explosion.

Captain Ernst Lehmann, who commanded the Hindenburg on most of its flights last year and was one of tonight's survivors, gasped, "I couldn't understand it," as he staggered out of the burning control car. Captain Max Pruss, commanding officer of the airship, and Captain Albert Stampf were also among the survivors.

Captain Lehmann was critically burned and injured; the other officers were also burned, but less seriously.

Experts in lighter-than-air operations who saw the accident said tonight that when the two landing lines were dropped by the dirigible at 7:20, they were immediately made fast to the mooring cars on the circular track about the mooring mast. The crew began to make the lines taut, but the ship had gathered too much momentum, according to these observers, and drifted several hundred yards past the mast. The starboard line pulled hard as the nose of the ship passed over the mooring mast at the top.

Order Not Heard

Captain Pruss, making his first trip in command of the dirigible, signaled and shouted, "Pay out!"

This order was heard by the operator on one mooring car, but not by the other, as the shout went against the wind and could not be heard. Consequently, one mooring car paid out and the other did not. The result was that the ship was thrown off its balance and lost the perfect equilibrium it had previously had.

Its nose dipped, forward ballast was dropped and the elevators were set to raise the ship. Instead the ship was held tight by one yaw line. The nose was pulled over and the elevators had an effect opposite to that which they were intended to have, according to this version. The tail dropped sharply and the bottom rudder hit the

Continued on Page Nineteen

Airship Like a Giant Torch On Darkening Jersey Field

Routine Landing Converted Into Hysterical Scene in Moment's Time—Witnesses Tell of 'Blinding Flash' From Zeppelin

By CRAIG THOMPSON
Special to THE NEW YORK TIMES.

LAKEHURST, N. J., May 6.—The Hindenburg, giant silver liner of the air, suddenly became a torch above the naval air station here tonight. What began as a routine landing of the transatlantic airship ended in a holocaust.

The ground crew, officials of the naval air base, spectators, reporters and press photographers were going about their customary business of aiding or watching the ship nose into the mooring mast.

Two ground lines had been dropped from the nose. These, attached to the cars running on a circular track around the mast, were holding the ship nose down at a thirty-degree angle, and helping it jockey into a position favorable with the wind for a mooring.

A thunderstorm had passed over the field a short time before and a drizzly rain was still falling. Twilight was beginning, although the visibility was still good.

So suddenly that it left spectators on the verge of hysteria for some time afterward, the ship burst into flame. Some one in the ground crew yelled "Run for your lives!" and the crew did. The stern of the ship settled and the photographers, squinting through the view finders of their cameras, ran toward the ship.

The occurrence sounded, witnesses said, like two explosions, one following the other about thirty seconds apart. Some said they saw one burst of flame, others two, but the noises they described as explosions gave way to the sounds of human screams.

In the "heavier-than-air" hangar, the pilot of an American Air Lines plane, waiting to ferry passengers from the airship into Newark, watched from a window.

"It seemed to happen so fast that I didn't think anybody could escape," he said afterward.

He was wrong, for about at that moment a man ran into the hangar.

"His face was black, but he seemed to be all right otherwise. He wanted to telephone his mother in Chicago."

The passenger was Herbert James O'Laughlin of Chicago.

On the field was an army detachment from Philadelphia, detailed there for just such an emergency. This detail promptly went to work, trucks scurrying over the field seeking the injured, while in the hangar telephone calls were being put through to all points in New Jersey and New York City calling for ambulances, doctors, nurses, medicine.

All this occurred while the flames spread toward the uptilted nose of the ship, while the stern sank to the ground to be followed shortly by the entire length, girder and strut, the bared ribs of the ship from which the skin had disappeared.

Robert Seelig, Murray Becker and Larry Kennedy, all newspaper camera men, related what they had seen.

"There was a noise that sounded like bullets coming out of the gondolas," Seelig said. "I saw nobody

Continued on Page Twenty-one

ANARCHISTS RENEW BARCELONA STRIFE; 5,000 LEAVE BILBAO

Revolters, Regaining Part of Catalan Capital, Demand Shock Troop Dissolution

SOCIALIST MINISTER SLAIN

Insurgents Reported Gaining Unresisted in Aragon as Foes Withdraw 12,000

EVACUATION IN NORTH SPED

British Warships Protect Craft Taking Women and Children From Bilbao to France

The Spanish Situation

PERPIGNAN—Anarchists were reported to have regained positions in Barcelona and to have demanded the dissolution of the government's shock troops. Withdrawal of 12,000 men from the Aragon front, to deal with the situation, was also reported, leading to an advance by the Rebel armies. Page 1.

ROME—A heavy concentration of Rebels, including Italians, to rescue the Italians cut off at Bermeo, was under way on the Bilbao front. Page 10.

BILBAO—Five thousand women and children were taken from the city, and vessels carrying them to France were guarded by British warships. More refugees were preparing to leave. (Follows the above.) Page 10.

LONDON—Foreign Secretary Eden revealed that the British Government had evidence that Guernica was destroyed by airplanes. He favored a neutral inquiry. Page 10.

Anarchists Give Ultimatum

Special Cable to THE NEW YORK TIMES.

PERPIGNAN, France, May 6.—The Anarchists are reported to have regained control in parts of Barcelona this afternoon after the Catalan Generalidad believed it had dominated the situation.

The Anarchists issued an ultimatum to the government demanding the dissolution of the shock troops patroling the city, the government's chief support, within twenty-four hours and declaring that otherwise they would take matters into their own hands and use every means in their power to suppress the shock troops.

The Anarchists also have obtained the upper hand at Junquera in addition to Figueras, according to news received here, and threaten, it is alleged, to use asphyxiating gas unless their ultimatum is obeyed.

Anarchist broadcasts have been picked up here stating that the casualties in the disorders in Barcelona since the Anarchist rebellion Tuesday amounted to 400 dead and 2,000 wounded. Declaring that "enough blood has flowed," the broadcasts continue to appeal for calm every ten minutes, and it is therefore believed that trouble still persists in Barcelona.

French Consulate Menaced

The French Consulate was threatened by Anarchists, who asserted that Rightist sympathizers had taken refuge there. The consul appealed to French warships in the harbor and 200 armed sailors reinforced the consulate guard.

Telephonic communication with Barcelona is still cut off tonight, and telegraphic and telephonic communication with the interior of Catalonia, which was re-established yesterday, was again interrupted this morning.

The Spanish Consul at Perpignan has recommended that Frenchmen and others should not go further than Figueras, and trains do not proceed beyond Gerona.

Francisco Ascasso, leader of the Anarchists in the Aragon Government, is reported to have been murdered.

Rebels Gain on Aragon Front

By The Associated Press.

PERPIGNAN, France, May 6.—Reports of an unresisted Insurgent advance along the whole Aragon front of Northeastern Spain and of the withdrawal of 12,000 government troops from it to keep the peace in troubled Barcelona, put a new and serious face on the Catalan Anarchist insurrection tonight. The reports emanated from Insurgent

Continued on Page Ten

Judge Sentences Himself By Signing Papers Unread

Wireless to THE NEW YORK TIMES.

MOSCOW, May 6.—A judge on one of the most important benches of the Moscow District Court who has the bad habit of signing unread any document placed before him has just sentenced himself to jail.

The court clerks, deciding he needed a lesson in "Bolshevik vigilance," presented to him a sheaf of papers including one reading: "To the chief of Butyrky prison: Under Magistrate Abramson is sent to you for further detention." Judge Abramson signed all the papers and picked up his newspaper again.

The clerks, of course, extracted the sentence and were passing it around laughingly when the judge found out about it. He destroyed it in a rage, declaring such jokes tended to undermine Soviet justice.

The government learned about it, however, and today Izvestia delivered to Judge Abramson a stinging rebuke for perfunctoriness, reminding him that he dealt not in inanimate goods but in human fate.

HUGHES SEES CHOICE IN LAW OR TYRANNY

Courts Must Be Maintained, He Tells Law Institute, or We Replace Reason by Force

TEST OF BAR TO ROOSEVELT

Stewardship Is Questioned by Laymen, He Writes in Warning of 'Critical Audience'

Text of Chief Justice Hughes's address is on Page 17.

Special to THE NEW YORK TIMES.

WASHINGTON, May 6.—Chief Justice Hughes made what his hearers construed as a reference to the Supreme Court when he told the American Law Institute today that if society is to choose the processes of reason as opposed to the tyranny of force, "it must maintain the institutions which embody those processes." It was the second time that the Chief Justice of the United States has broken his silence since the controversy over reorganization of the Supreme Court started three months ago.

Vigorous applause, lasting more than a minute, followed the Chief Justice's words, with which he concluded a speech in which he avoided any direct reference to the court issue.

President Roosevelt in a message to the institute likewise refrained from any positive statement about the Supreme Court, but remarked that "law interpreters," among other legal experts, are facing a sometimes critical audience.

President on Lawyers' Position

"I am happy to greet you members of the bench, the bar and the law school faculties who have assembled for the fifteenth annual meeting of the American Law Institute," the President stated.

"I have followed with interest your accomplishments within recent years in the restatement of the law and your proposals for improvement in the administration of criminal justice.

"Today our stewardship as lawyers is being questioned. The laymen of America are not, perhaps, quite so disposed to make a complete delegation of law matters to law men. At least the layman asserts his right to evaluate us.

"Law scholars, law practitioners, lawmakers, law administrators and law interpreters have the stage today. But more significant, they must play their rôles before an intense and sometimes critical audience.

"But this is well. The virtue of the common law was its adaptability to growth and improvement. In generations present and future the lawyer likewise will be measured by the same test.

"It is encouraging today that so many outstanding leaders of the profession assemble to give service in the important and worth-while task to which the American Law Institute is dedicated. I extend again my warm and cordial greetings to your membership and my best wishes for continued success."

Only at one other time since President Roosevelt made his recommendations to Congress on Feb. 5 has the Chief Justice made any

Continued on Page Seventeen

NOTABLES ABOARD

Merchants, Students and Professional Men on the Dirigible

LEHMANN IS A SURVIVOR

Veteran Zeppelin Commander, Acting as Adviser on Trip, Is Seriously Burned

CAPT. PRUSS IS ALSO SAFE

C. L. Osbun, Sales Manager, Who Survived a Plane Crash, Escapes Second Time

Notables from many walks of life were among the passengers on the ill-fated Hindenburg. They included merchants, students and business and professional men and women.

Many of the survivors owed their lives to the fact that they were apparently near windows in the dirigible when the accident happened and were able to leap through them to the ground in safety.

Among the survivors listed were Captain Ernst Lehmann, veteran Zeppelin commander; Captain Max Pruss, the new Hindenburg commander; Herbert O'Laughlin of Chicago, employed by the Consumers Company of Elgin, Ill.; Clifford L. Osbun, export sales manager of the Oliver Farm Equipment Company of Chicago, and Ferdinand Lammot Belin Jr. of Washington, D. C.

Lehmann's Condition Grave

Early this morning Dr. E. G. Herbener, staff surgeon at the Paul Kimball Hospital in Lakewood, said that Captain Lehmann was on the doubtful list. Captain Lehmann is suffering from shock and second and third degree burns of the face and body. Captain Pruss is suffering from second and third degree burns of the face, forehead and arms and will probably recover, Dr. Herbener said.

Among the passengers who were still unaccounted for were John Pannes, passenger traffic manager of the Hamburg-American Line and North German Lloyd at New York, and his wife; Ernst Rudolf Anders, partner of the firm of Seelig & Hille tea merchants of Dresden, Germany, and his son, R. Herbert Anders, and Hermann Doehner of Mexico, D. F.

Captain Lehmann and Captain Pruss were in the control gondola when the crash occurred. Both officers, together with several other members of the crew, leaped through the gondola windows to safety.

Lehmann an Adviser

Captain Lehmann, who was serving as adviser aboard the Hindenburg, had been commander of the ship until this year. He has had long experience with the lighter-than-air craft, and has been associated with Hugo Eckener, world-famous authority on Zeppelins, since 1931.

He was born March 12, 1886, at Ludwigshafen, on the Rhine, the son of a chemist. He became a naval cadet in 1905 and later entered the Polytechnic Institute at Charlottenburg, a borough of Berlin.

During the World War Captain Lehmann received the German Iron Cross award. After the war, as second in command to Eckener, he brought the dirigible Los Angeles to Lakehurst in 1924. When the Hindenburg was completed in 1936 Captain Lehmann was placed in command, a position he held until recently, when Captain Pruss was elevated as commander of the ship.

Mr. Osbun's escape from the disaster marked the second time that he had narrowly missed death as the result of a flying accident. Last year he was aboard a transport plane when it was forced down en route from Puerto Rico to Buenos Aires. Soon after he was transferred to a motorboat with other passengers and the motorboat blew up. Mr. Osbun escaped injury, but two other passengers were seriously burned.

Mr. Osbun declared that he was talking to fellow passengers in the dining salon, looking down through the observation window watching the ship being moored, when the disaster occurred. He was apparently blown through the window and thrown to the ground, suffering injuries. He was taken to the Paul Kimball Hospital in Lakewood, where his condition was said to be not serious.

Mr. Osbun is 37 years old, the fa-

Continued on Page Nineteen

DISASTER ASCRIBED TO GAS BY EXPERTS

Washington Sees Dangerous Combination of Hydrogen and Blue Gas as Cause

Special to THE NEW YORK TIMES.

WASHINGTON, May 6.—Washington airship experts and Congressional leaders received the news of the Hindenburg disaster with amazement and expressions of sorrow. But in every instance those who commented pointed out that the three disasters of the United States Navy were structural, while that of the German craft was due to the use of a combination of hydrogen and blue gas, the most dangerous of all gases for inflation of airships.

Dr. Hans Luther, the German Ambassador, said the disaster must not cause the world to lose faith in dirigibles and that it could not have been caused by technical defects.

"It is terrible," the Ambassador said. "I was horrified by the news, but it could not have been a technical matter. It must not cause us to lose faith in dirigibles because the Graf Zeppelin has operated safely and efficiently for eight years on the run from Europe to South America and elsewhere."

Secretary Hull sent the following message tonight to Konstantin von Neurath, the German Minister of Foreign Affairs:

"I extend to you and to the people of Germany my profound sympathy at the tragic accident to the dirigible Hindenburg and the resultant loss of life to passengers and crew."

"It is too terrible to believe," Admiral A. B. Cook, Chief of Naval Aeronautics, said. "From what I

Continued on Page Twenty-one

GERMANY SHOCKED BY THE TRAGEDY

At First Disbelieving, Line's Officials Tell of Receiving Message of Landing

Special Cable to THE NEW YORK TIMES.

BERLIN, Friday, May 7.—It was a few minutes after 1 o'clock this morning when the first news of the disaster to the Hindenburg reached Berlin by telephone from The New York Times Bureau in London. The bureau forwarded the brief bulletin to the effect that the airship had been destroyed while making its landing. No details were given.

At that hour the German newspapers were without news. Several first editions, in fact, had reported the Hindenburg's supposedly safe arrival on the strength of an erroneous telegram received by the company in Frankfort on the Main. It was almost two hours later before the news of the disaster with some few details reached the newspapers through the medium of the German official news agency.

Facts Difficult to Get

In the meantime such facts about the airship and its passengers proved difficult to obtain. The Frankfort and Berlin offices of the Zeppelin company were closed and no complete list of the passengers or crew was available. A list of twenty-one names comprising foreign passengers out of a total list of thirty-nine was obtained by telephone from Frankfort, where this correspondent had retained it since the sailing day.

Dr. Hugo Eckener, veteran chief of the Zeppelin service, was in Austria, where he had lectured last night in Vienna. The Vienna bureau of THE NEW YORK TIMES traced him to Graz and obtained his ad-

Continued on Page Nineteen

Great Crowds Here Watched Ship, With Many Notables Aboard, Sail to Her Doom

THOUSANDS IN CITY SAW LAST FLIGHT

Crowds in Times Square Gazed in Admiration, With No Thought of Disaster

AIRSHIP GLEAMED IN SUN

Dipped Low for Benefit of the Sightseers—Planes Gayly Flew Beside It

Thousands of persons craned their necks in Times Square yesterday afternoon as the Hindenburg, a familiar sight to this area, soared above the tall buildings in a brilliant sun.

From windows, rooftops, sidewalks, fire-escapes and other points of vantage they viewed the giant airliner, little realizing it was the last time they were to see the ship.

Traffic was impeded in some sections of the city as throngs choked thoroughfares and chauffeurs stopped their automobiles, left the steering wheels and gazed skyward as the ship, its motors roaring and swastikas gleaming, passed over the city.

Not only in the metropolitan area but in other sections the ship was greeted by the tooting of automobile horns. Crowds turned out to see the airship at Portland, Me.; Boston, New London and other places over which it flew at a comparatively low altitude.

After it had hove into sight near City Island on Long Island Sound, word was flashed to Manhattan by telephone to be on the watch for the airship.

As was customary in other flights of the Hindenburg, the commander, Captain Max Pruss, in charge of the westbound flight across the Atlantic for the first time, soared over the city for the sightseers' benefit.

At 3:12 P. M. the ship, which left Frankfort at 2:19 P. M. Monday, passed southward on the west side of Times Square.

Leaving Times Square, the dirigible, accompanied by several planes, including the big twin-motored Burnelli flown by Clyde Pangborn, which appeared like an ant moving beside an elephant, traveled to Brooklyn, where additional thousands dropped their work and looked up to see the Hindenburg for the last time.

At Ebbets Field, where the Brooklyn Dodgers were playing the Pittsburgh Pirates, the baseball fans temporarily took their minds off the game and stood up to gaze skyward.

Swinging the ship back toward the north, Captain Pruss headed for Manhattan, where throngs in the narrow downtown streets, attracted by the roar of the motors of the airship and the escorting planes, gathered on street corners and on the steps of the Treasury Building in Wall Street for a glimpse of the pride of the German air fleet.

Amateur photographers, perched at vantage points on the Empire State Building observation towers and atop Rockefeller Center, snapped pictures as the silvery ship swung by. Other pictures were snapped by newspaper photographers in airplanes.

Finally, after a return visit to midtown New York, the huge craft turned just south of the Empire State Building and began the flight that was to have ended with the landing at Lakehurst.

Passing over the Hudson River on the way to Staten Island, the passengers and crew of the Zeppelin were greeted for several minutes by a deafening roar of steamboat and other harbor vessel whistles.

BIRGER BRINK, EDITOR, OF SWEDEN, MISSING

Planned to Visit Governor Earle of Pennsylvania—Passenger Tells of His Escape

Special to THE NEW YORK TIMES.

LAKEHURST, N. J., May 6.—Birger Brink, one of the editors of the Stockholm Tidningen, whose body is believed to be among those buried in the twisted framework of the Hindenburg, was making a brief visit to this country to interview Governor George H. Earle of Pennsylvania and Dr. John H. Finley.

Having planned to return on the Hindenburg at midnight, Mr. Brink found the delayed arrival of the airship would interfere with his plans, so he sent a radiogram to Governor Earle requesting him to meet him in Philadelphia. The Governor agreed to do this, and to facilitate the interview sent a plane to meet the Hindenburg at Lakehurst in order that Mr. Brink would lose no time.

Dr. Amandus Johnson, director of the Swedish-American Historical Museum of Philadelphia, accompanied the pilot of the plane to Lakehurst. Einar Thulin, New York correspondent for the Tidningen, also was at Lakehurst to welcome the Swedish editor.

Mr. Thulin was about to enter his car, parked near the hangar, when the explosion occurred. It threw him to the ground. Then he ran toward the burning wreckage, hoping to find Mr. Brink among those stumbling from the twisted girders.

He was unable to find the editor, but Rolf von Heidenstam, whom he had known in Sweden, stumbled into his arms and collapsed. Mr. von Heidenstam had been watching the landing maneouvres from one of the dirigible's windows, he explained. According to Mr. Thulin, Mr. von Heidenstam was so dazed he could remember little of his experience.

Mr. von Heidenstam was badly burned about the head and was suffering from an injured back. Mr. Thulin was unable to learn to which hospital he had been taken.

By The Associated Press.

PHILADELPHIA, May 6.—Governor George H. Earle heard the news of the Hindenburg explosion as he waited here to confer with Dr. Birger Brink of Stockholm, a passenger on the ship.

Roosevelt Sends Hitler Message of Sympathy

Special to THE NEW YORK TIMES.

GALVESTON, Texas, May 6.—Shocked by the Hindenburg disaster at Lakehurst today, President Roosevelt tonight sent from his yacht The Potomac a message of sympathy to Adolf Hitler, the German Chancellor.

His message to Herr Hitler follows:

"His Excellency, Adolf Hitler, Reich Chancellor, Berlin.

"I have just learned of the disaster to the airship Hindenburg and offer you and the German people my deepest sympathy for the tragic loss of life which resulted from this unexpected and unhappy event."

At the same time, the President issued the following statement:

"I am distressed to hear of the tragedy of the Hindenburg, and extend my deep sympathy to the families of the passengers, officers and crew who lost their lives."

Both messages were sent to the temporary White House offices here for transmission, from the yacht on which the President is enjoying a fishing vacation.

NOTABLES ABOARD ILL-FATED LINER

Continued From Page One

ther of three daughters, Jean, 10 years old, Suzanne, 5, and Sally, 3, and lives at Parkridge, a suburb of Chicago. He was just concluding a three-month tour for his company which took him to South America, England and Germany.

A somewhat similar experience was had by Mr. O'Laughlin, who later told Dr. Jerome Kaufman of the Newark Hospital, who treated him on the scene for minor injuries, that he was in the main cabin of the ship with about fifteen other passengers when the ship "started to rock." He said he heard a "terrific noise" and that he jumped through a window to the ground. The ship at that time, he said, was only about fifteen feet from the ground.

Mr. O'Laughlin, who lives at 914 Bonnie Brae, River Forest, Chicago suburb, was returning to this country from a short European vacation which he started on April 11. His first act, when he was rescued, was to send a telegram to his mother in Chicago announcing that he was safe.

An early report listed Colonel Ira Nelson Morris, former United States Minister to Sweden from 1914 to 1923, as among the passengers. Colonel Morris called THE NEW YORK TIMES office last night and said that he was not aboard the ship, although his name headed the passenger list as given out by the Hamburg-American line.

Mr. Morris suggested that there might have been some confusion between his name and that of a nephew, Nelson Morris, who had been in Europe and had returned on the Hindenburg. The latter was among the survivors and was taken to a hospital for medical care.

Mr. Pannes, who had been employed by the Hamburg-American Line more than thirty years, was returning on the airliner with his wife. They had left here about one month ago on the Bremen for the purpose of returning on the Hindenburg.

Studied Air Service

Active in recent developments in the air traffic branch of this service since the first round-the-world flight of the Graf Zeppelin in August, 1929, Mr. Pannes made a special trip about one year ago on the Hindenburg to study the transit problems created by the entry of this airliner in transatlantic travel.

At that time he was engaged by the North German Lloyd Line in combining the regular shipping activity of the line with the duties of booking agent for the air line.

Mr. Belin Jr. is the son of a former American diplomat who has lived in Washington since his retirement from the foreign service. He was returning on a holiday visit to his home from Paris, where he had been a student at the Ecole des Sciences Politiques, in preparation for taking the examinations to enter the foreign service.

Mr. Doehner was general manager of the drug firm of Beick, Felix & Co., Mexico, D. F. His wife also was reported as missing, but their three children were listed as saved.

Business Man Missing

Another passenger on the ship who was unaccounted for last night was George Hirschfeld, a member of the Chamber for Industry and Trade of Bremen, Germany, and chairman of the committee for cotton. He was arriving to study the possibilities of developing business under the barter agreement recently made effective under which American cotton is shipped into Germany in exchange for German merchandise brought into this country.

Mr. Morris, member of the Chicago packing family, is the grandson and namesake of the founder of Morris & Co., which was merged several years ago with Armour & Co. He is 45 years old. His home in Homewood, a Chicago suburb, is regarded as one of the show places of that district.

Mr. Morris had been visiting in France with his wife, the former Blanche Bilboa, French actress, and was returning to Chicago on a business trip. He had intended to rejoin his wife in France. He was taken to the Paul Kimball Hospital in Lakewood following the disaster.

Other passengers who were still unaccounted for early this morning were the following:

Edward H. Douglas, who since 1930 has been living in Frankfort, Germany, where he was in charge of European agencies of the H. K. McCann Corporation, Ltd., an advertising firm. Mr. Douglas was born in Newark, N. J., in 1898 and served during the war as a petty officer in the United States Navy.

Moritz Feibusch, 57 years old, operator of the M. Feibusch Company, canned products and exporting firm of San Francisco. Mr. Feibusch had been on an extensive business trip to Europe. He lived at 2,201 Lincoln Way, San Francisco, which caused the passenger lists hastily compiled to give him a Lincoln, Neb., address on the first rep[illegible]s.

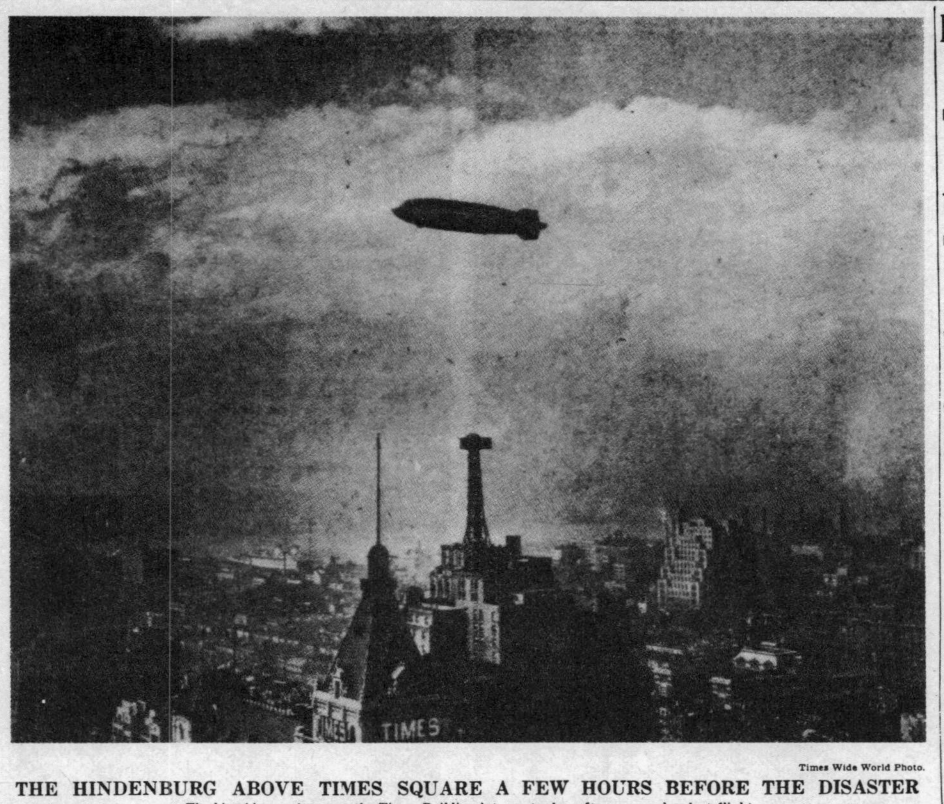

Times Wide World Photo.

THE HINDENBURG ABOVE TIMES SQUARE A FEW HOURS BEFORE THE DISASTER

The big ship passing over the Times Building late yesterday afternoon on her last flight

HINDENBURG FALLS IN FLAMES AT FIELD

Continued From Page One

earth. The ship bounded up again, then suddenly burst into flames and dropped to the ground.

It is understood that this version of the accident will be investigated by the naval board of inquiry convened for tomorrow and the Department of Commerce. The official investigation will also look into conflicting reports as to whether the fire was accompanied or preceded by explosions. Although most observers reported hearing a series of explosions, some insisted that there were no explosions until after the ship was almost destroyed by fire.

F. E. Fagg, head of the Bureau of Aeronautics of the Department of Commerce, flew in from Washington late tonight and conferred with Commander Charles E. Rosendahl, in charge of the air station. Mr. Fagg announced that Commander Rosendahl would preside over the board of inquiry to open tomorrow.

Commander Rosendahl, together with the 200 members of the ground crew, which had started to walk the dirigible to its mooring place, narrowly escaped injury when the Hindenburg fell in flames.

The catastrophe was witnessed by several hundred spectators, including several who had booked passage on the return trip of the Hindenburg to Germany, which had been scheduled to start at midnight tonight.

Delayed on Voyage

At the time of the crash, the Hindenburg was more than twelve hours late, having been due here at 6 o'clock this morning. Head winds delayed it coming across the Atlantic and down the coast from Labrador. On its last day it flew at reduced speed along the coast, waiting for dusk, as landing conditions are best at dawn and dusk.

After its scheduled landing tonight, it was to have been refueled quickly in preparation for the return voyage.

The airship was sighted here about 4:15 o'clock this afternoon. It flew over the landing field at a good altitude, but because of a strong wind, did not try to land. After circling the reservation, it pointed toward the coast again and disappeared. Shortly afterward thunderstorms blew up over the field and continued until about 7 o'clock.

A light rain was falling and the ground was well soaked when the Hindenburg reappeared, flying in from the coast at an altitude of about 500 feet.

Too high to land, the Hindenburg circled the field and came back at an altitude of about 150 feet. It flew over the mooring mast, doubled back and came in again heading slightly southwest, against the wind, with two lights in its bow against the gathering dusk.

During this turn over the field, the ship had begun to valve gas slightly and had dropped ballast twice to lighten its load for mooring. It was exactly 7:20 P. M. daylight saving time, according to official timing by company and naval authorities, when it dropped two lines to the ground crew.

Observers here said that the wind shifted just before the Hindenburg attempted to land, and that this made it difficult for the ground crew to manoeuvre her. A company representative said that normally the ship would have been expected to be perfectly safe the moment she dropped her lines.

Lined up on the field below the silvery cone-shaped airship, the ground crew grasped the lines and began to walk it the 100 yards to the mooring mast.

Muffled Boom Heard

At 7:23 o'clock those on the ground heard a low report or boom from the ship. Almost simultaneously there was a flash which lighted up the twilight, and sent a thrill of terror through the onlookers.

This was followed quickly by the bursting of flames from the rear gondola on the port side, where the engines had been throttled down in preparation for mooring. Then the flames spread forward, and in a moment the gigantic ship seemed to be enveloped in fire.

Horror gripped the spectators as the airship buckled aft of midships and began to settle slowly down to the ground in a mass of red flames and black smoke.

There was no sound from the ship except the crackling of flames as they crept forward and ate up the outer fabric so that her duralumin ribs could be seen before she struck the ground.

As the stern struck the earth there was another explosion. Then there was a series of explosions as the ship crumpled up and lay burning on the ground, with leaping forks of flame and billowing clouds of smoke rising into the air. There was something strange about the slow and gradual descent of the blazing ship. She came down so deliberately and settled upon the earth so quietly that spectators said afterward that they could not realize for a moment that a tragedy was taking place before their eyes.

This was but a momentary impression, for the shock of the sight, together with the scorching heat from the flames, drove the crowd running back several hundred feet. There were screams from women spectators, including Mrs. Rosendahl, who feared that her husband had been struck and killed by the falling airship.

Running around the ship until they could approach with the wind and not against the flames, rescuers dashed toward the burning dirigible. They included naval officers and sailors, company representatives and newspaper reporters and photographers.

Many of the survivors owe their lives to the heroic work of the volunteer rescue battalion. Others climbed out of the airship unaided, or were thrown clear when the ship grounded.

Some were hurled through the long isinglass strip on the side of the airship, through which passengers in the observation salon formerly looked out to see the country over which they were flying.

It was explained that the three ranking officers of the airship were saved because they were in the control car forward, whereas the original explosion or fire occurred aft, as did the buckling of the ship just before she dropped to the ground.

Because of this, the stern struck the ground first, and the flames, which enveloped the after part of the ship almost instantaneously, were comparatively slow in reaching the bow. This gave the officers in the bow, and more than half of the passengers, who were standing forward to watch the landfall, their chance to escape.

Had the slow fall of the ship taken much longer, however, nearly everybody aboard might have been burned to death, for a few moments after the bow struck the earth the whole ship was a mass of fire and soon nothing but a skeleton framework could be seen.

Can't Tell What Occurred

Passengers and crew members who were interviewed after the accident were unable to give much information as to the cause of the accident or the manner in which it occurred. Most of them said that it happened too quickly, and they were too stunned by the crash, to be able to tell exactly what had happened.

Commander Rosendahl took charge of the rescue work and summoned ambulances and fire engines from a wide area. Late tonight ambulances filled with doctors and nurses were still arriving here, from as far distant points as Jersey City.

While firemen fought the scorching flames rescuers dragged out injured persons and bodies of the dead. The burned and injured were carried from the wreck to a near-by road, where ambulances pulled up and took them aboard for hurried trips to the naval hospital here and hospitals in near-by cities. As the bodies were recovered they were taken to an improvised morgue on the naval reservation.

At midnight, although the flames had been put out, the embers were so hot that the rescuers were unable to complete their search of the wreckage. It was believed that additional bodies would be discovered tomorrow when the search is finished.

Coroner Raymond A. Taylor of Lakewood came here tonight and made plans for an inquest, which probably will be held tomorrow after all the bodies have been recovered. A hangar was being used as an impromptu morgue.

Commander Rosendahl ordered a cordon of sailors around the wreckage to keep sightseers away, and also set up guards outside the reservation to keep everybody out who did not have business inside. State troopers and marines were stationed at all cross-roads within a one-mile radius of the air station, closing the roads to all except police, officials, rescue workers and newspaper men.

Immediately after the disaster, special details of police cleared all highways to make way for doctors and nurses speeding to the scene from other points. Heavy fire engines and police emergency trucks clanging to the scene helped to keep the roads clear.

But while the rescue work was under way thousands of motorists converged toward the scene on all highways leading to Lakehurst. Before many of the injured had been taken from the first-aid stations on the field, lines of automobiles clogged the road for nearly ten miles on the main arteries to the north and south of the air station.

Harassed rescue workers and ambulance drivers complained that the press of the advancing crowd was so great that it was seriously hampering their work. As many policemen as could be spared were sent from the scene to patrol the surrounding roads and keep them clear.

A detail of National Guardsmen from Fort Monmouth took up stations on the main highways several miles from the air station and ordered motorists to turn back.

List of Saved and Missing

Following is an incomplete list of survivors, injured and missing in the Hindenburg disaster:

Survivors

At Fitkin Memorial Hospital, Neptune:

Eric Knocker.

Richard Kalmer, machinist in crew.

Ergin Brentele, machinist in crew.

Mrs. Eisa Ernst.

Philip Lentz, Frankfort on Main, Germany.

Herbert Dowe, wireless operator.

At the Royal Pines Hotel and Clinic, Pinewald:

Mrs. Mary Kleenmen, 51, Frankfort on Main, Germany.

Hans Fiund, 31, Frankfort on Main, Germany.

Alfred Grocinger, 20, Frankfort on Main, Germany.

George Grant, 63, London, England.

At Paul Kimball Hospital, Lakewood:

Captain Max Pruss, commander.

Captain Ernst Lehmann, former commander, condition critical.

Philip Mangone, 145 West Fifty-eighth Street, New York.

George Hirschfeld, Bremen and New York.

Colonel Nelson Morris, Chicago.

Otto C. Ernst, Hamburg, Germany.

And the following, unidentified as passengers or crew members: Albert Summit, William Stett, Theodore Ritter, Frank Herzog (condition critical), William Luthenberg, Hans Hugo, Adolph Fisher, Ray Fields Stahler, Joseph Lebrecht.

At Point Pleasant Hospital:

Mrs. Herman Doehner of Mexico, D. F., and her two sons, Walter and Werner; injuries reported not serious.

Survivors not at hospitals.

Mr. and Mrs. Leo Adelt, Berlin, Germany.

Pierre Belin, Washington, D. C.

Clifford Osburn, Chicago, Ill.

Joseph Spahs, Douglaston, L. I.

Herbert James O'Laughlin, Chicago, Ill.

Carl Otto Clemens, Bonn, Germany.

Irene Doehner.

Rolf von Heidenstamm.

Claus Rinkelbein.

Erich Knoscher.

Mrs. Margaret Mather.

Captain Albert Stampf.

Henry Bauer.

Walter Zeigler.

Radio Officer Speck.

Max Zabel.

Dr. Reudiger, ship's physician.

Staff Captain Wittemann.

Hans Hugo Witt.

Hinkel.

Emil Stoeckle.

Crew, Hospitals Unknown

Bulla.

Bahnolzer (critical).

Kurt Bauer.

Boetius.

Bernhardt.

Deeg.

Deutschler.

Iberfiein.

Franz.

Felber.

Freund.

Henneberg.

Schneuble.

Stach.

Schaedler.

Stoeffler.

Keppel.

Klein.

Kubis.

Lau.

Lens.

Zavier Maier.

Nunnenacher.

Nielsen.

Sauter.

Scweikard.

Scoenherr.

Listed as Missing

Among the passengers listed as missing are the following:

John Pannes, New York City.

Mrs. John Pannes, New York City.

Ernst Rudolf Anders, Dresden, Germany.

Herman Doehner, Mexico, D. F.

Edward Douglas, New York City.

H. Jackson, Dusseldorf.

Otto Reichhold, Vienna.

Hans Vinholt.

James Young.

Moritz Feibusch, San Francisco.

Birger Brink.

Burtis Dolan.

Fritz Erdman.

Identified Dead

Ludwig Feldber, crew.

HINDENBURG 129TH IN HONORED LINE

First Lighter-Than-Air Craft to Fly on Regular Schedule From Europe to the U. S.

TOOK TO AIR IN MARCH, '36

Landed at Lakehurst Year Ago After Flight of 61 Hours—18 Crossings Set This Year

Prior to establishing the first regular passenger service for lighter-than-air craft across the Atlantic, the Hindenburg, originally known as the LZ-129, first took to the air on March 4, 1936, for a trial flight over Lake Constance from her base at Friedrichshafen, Germany. She was manoeuvred about the sky for three hours and then was set down for final adjustments after meeting all technical requirements.

On March 26, 1936, about two weeks before the start of her maiden flight to the United States, the huge dirigible, which was twice as long as the Graf Zeppelin, had a minor accident as she was leaving the hangar. A sudden gust of wind grabbed her and set her down sharply, damaging one of the vertical stabilizers.

With the exception of this minor accident and the failure of one of her four sixteen-cylinder Daimler-Benz Diesel motors while crossing the Mediterranean during a South American trip, the Hindenburg had functioned well throughout her brief career. There have been several tense moments at her mooring masts when the big craft swayed dizzily under the velocity of high winds and when her ground crews found their task almost more than they could cope with, but she always came through safely.

Started First Flight Year Ago

Carrying fifty-one passengers and a crew of fifty-six the Hindenburg took off from Friedrichshafen at 4 P. M. on May 6, a year ago, for her first voyage to this country. With her gas volume of 7,300,000 cubic feet and a gross lifting capacity of 418,000 pounds she soared easily and pointed her nose westward for the 3,895 statute miles ahead.

Her four engines, which developed 4,400 horsepower, carried her swiftly over the Atlantic to Lakehurst, N. J., where she landed at 6:08 A. M. on May 9, after receiving a welcoming reception over this city that only New York knows how to give. When her nose was moored to the mast her log showed that the trip had been negotiated in 61 hours 35 minutes from her home base. This record was bettered several times on succeeding trips. As an indication of the comparative speed, the Los Angeles made her best crossing in 81 hours back in 1924.

The Hindenburg, the 129th in her line since Count Zeppelin, her namesake, soared over Lake Constance more than fifty years ago, had planned to make eighteen crossings this year. The schedule called for but a one-day stopover each time in Lakehurst. On her next proposed return flight from Germany, first planned for May 11 and later set for May 13 to arrange for coronation passengers, she had made arrangements to pick up photographs and news reels at London to be rushed to the United States.

Dr. Eckener Planned Service

Dr. Hugo Eckener, who was the Hindenburg's commander on most of her trips, first conceived the plan of transatlantic crossing in 1929 and hoped at that time for Germany and the United States to enter into a joint ownership of the line. This hope was shattered first by the depression and then by the crash of the Akron, the Macon and the British dirigible R-101, which fell in France. These things "created doubt" in some minds, Dr. Eckener afterward said.

During ten westward flights the Hindenburg averaged under sixty-four hours and on the eastward flights fifty-one hours. Some of her stop-overs were less than seven hours at Lakehurst.

The Hindenburg had a cruising range that would permit a flight from New York to China or a round trip between New York and Germany. On some of her stops here she was able to turn around and go back with scarcely any replenishing of her supplies outside of the fuel.

On her last successful crossing from Lakehurst to Frankfort on July 17, 1936, she carried fifty-seven passengers, which was a little better than average. Her smallest booking was twenty-one passengers for the westward flight on July 2, last year.

In five westward voyages last year she averaged better than forty-one passengers, 647 pounds of mail and 628 pounds of express. On the eastward trips the average number of passengers was more than fifty-two, with averages of 638 pounds of mail and 645 pounds of express. Her cargo has included such things as an airplane and a piano.

Despite the fact that the airship had been delayed by headwinds along the North Atlantic seaboard, preparations had been rushed at Lakehurst for refueling the airliner so that she could leave as scheduled. Standing at sidings were many railroad cars filled with more than 10,000 gallons of fuel waiting to be pumped aboard.

If the dirigible had left last night at 10 P. M., which was two hours after the original time set for the take-off on the return trip, it would have made the shortest stay in this country in its history.

Last year the Hindenburg made what were regarded as short stops when she left at midnight after arriving at dawn. In July of last year the Hindenburg made her fastest flight from this country to Germany, when she arrived over her German base forty-five hours and forty-three minutes after leaving Lakehurst.

On this trip the Hindenburg was carrying a ship's doctor for the first time. Also on board were two members of the United States Naval forces, Lieutenant Commander F. W. Reichelderfer and Lieutenant Richard W. Antrim.

Before her last eastward passage for the 1936 season the Hindenburg cruised for ten hours over six of the Eastern States as a farewell gesture, prior to her midnight sailing for home. The mammoth ship glistened in the sunlight for the edification of thousands on a roughly elliptical course from Boston to Philadelphia. Dr. Eckener said at the time it was done in appreciation of the welcome given the ship in this country. Guests on this trip included three admirals, the German Ambassador and representatives of the Department of State, the Department of Commerce and the press.

The Hindenburg carried passengers ranging in age from 6 months to 93 years. The child, the first so young to make the voyage, was the son of Melvin K. Whiteleather, a member of the Berlin staff of The Associated Press. The other extreme was a German professor who made the trip from Frankfort to Friedrichshafen, to hold the record as the oldest man to fly in lighter-than-air craft.

Ship Enlarged for Eighth Crossing

The ship was enlarged for passengers prior to her eighth crossing last year. On that voyage she carried her 1,000th passenger on the regular transatlantic service. In all there were 132 persons on board, including 72 passengers. Previously she could accommodate but 59 passengers and a crew of 55.

During the Winter months when the Lakehurst trip was not possible, the Hindenburg joined her sister ship the Graf Zeppelin in regular weekly trips to Rio de Janeiro. The weekly three-day service reached the market centers of Latin America.

The Hindenburg, always a matter of news when she was in flight, acquired special interest for readers the world over last September when she ferried three round-the-world reporters across the Atlantic on the first leg of their journey. Her performance on this trip was slightly disappointing owing to storms at sea but she negotiated the voyage without incident despite the fact that she arrived late, preventing the reporters from making planned connections on the Continent.

Performance Dispelled Doubt

The Hindenburg was built by the Luftschiffbau Zeppelin Company, which set up an operating company known as the Deutsche Zeppelin Reederei. Dr. Eckener, chairman of the board, and the American representative, F. W. von Meister, arranged for the docking facilities at Lakehurst, the western terminus.

Although there was considerable skepticism because of past performances of lighter-than-air craft, the Hindenburg schedule was carried out almost perfectly throughout the year. The courses were charted to suit the weather. Sometimes the ship would go as far north as Greenland and on other trips went south to the vicinity of the Azores but in the main adhered rather closely to the Great Circle.

Although the demand for travel this novel way increased with every trip, requiring the expansion of passenger accommodations, there was disappointment in the mail loads. The ship started off its regular flights by carrying 2,260 pounds of mail but this dropped gradually until it reached 167 pounds on one trip. The rates were forty cents for each half ounce. In the same way, freight cargoes varied from a peak of 2,500 pounds to sixty-three on the last successful westward journey.

The success of the Hindenburg and the frequent conferences based on this showing reached such proportions that it appeared America would again forget past disasters and once again engage in the lighter-than-air craft field.

GERMANY SHOCKED BY THE TRAGEDY

Continued From Page One

dress, whereupon this correspondent succeeded in awakening him and gave him the news by telephone. This was after the Zeppelin officials in Frankfort and Berlin, on the strength of their erroneous telegram reporting the ship's arrival, had been inclined to discredit any story of disaster.

Appeal to German People

Later brief details began to trickle in to newspapers and were used in the late editions, which devoted their entire front pages to the news.

All the newspapers feature an appeal to the German people, sent out by the official government service to "stand up under the blow." The government agency asserts that "the young and strong nations" can bear such disasters, and points out that a sister ship to the Hindenburg now is under construction in Friedrichshaven and soon will "take the place of the Hindenburg as ambassador from continent to continent, carrying the German flag over the ocean."

It is recalled that after preliminary trials the Hindenburg made its first long flight in company with the Graf Zeppelin in March of last year to propagandize for Hitler's plebiscite. It crossed the ocean ten times last Summer. It had made one flight to South America this year besides a number of trial flights in South Germany. This was the initial flight to New York for the season.

Film Plan for Airship

The loss of the Hindenburg occurred on the very day an interesting agreement was reached between the Zeppelin company and a group of American news photograph and film concerns. Under this agreement the airship was to have been instrumental in making a friendly German gesture toward Great Britain.

The next western trip was to have been delayed twenty-four hours to enable the airship to carry photographs and movie films of the British coronation ceremonies to New York.

The deal has been arranged by Berlin news bureaus of THE NEW YORK TIMES and The Associated Press.

Only Two Britons Aboard

Special Cable to THE NEW YORK TIMES.

LONDON, Friday, May 7.—The only two British passengers aboard the Hindenburg were said to be Captain Allen Charles Higgins, an army officer, and George Grant, steamship agent, both of London.

Officials of the Air Ministry and the German Embassy were appalled when THE NEW YORK TIMES telephoned to them the information of the disaster soon after 12:30 A. M. The Hindenburg was regarded here as the last word in safety and sound construction, and its series of successful transatlantic journeys with well-paying loads and keeping an accurate schedule had revived financial interest in the organization of a British airship service, which had been abandoned after the disaster to the R-101. It was revealed in a Berlin dispatch only last night that part of the duraluminum metal framework had been salvaged from the R-101, re-rolled and embodied in the Hindenburg. In the minds of experts consulted the most astonishing feature of the disaster was that the airship had burst into flames.

Doehner Prominent in Mexico

Special Cable to THE NEW YORK TIMES.

MEXICO, D. F., May 6.—Mr. and Mrs. Hermann Doehner of this city, who were aboard the Hindenberg with their three children, were prominent members of the German colony here.

This correspondent had a difficult task in breaking the news of the accident to the mother of Mr. Doehner by telephone. After thanking him for the news Mrs. Doehner burst into tears and hung up.

Going to the home later with further details of the accident, the correspondent talked briefly with Hermann Jr., a son. Near tears the youngster, about 15 years old, said he had been born in Mexico, his family having lived here for some time, but he was so broken up that he was unable to talk further.

Aviation Experts Give Their Opinions on the Probable Cause of the Disaster

DISASTER IS FIRST ON PASSENGER LINE

But Scores of Airships Built for War Use Have Crashed at Heavy Toll of Life

THREE LOST BY OUR NAVY

Shenandoah, Akron and Macon —Italia Blew Up in Arctic— Dixmude Fate Still Mystery

Since the experiments of Count Zeppelin, started in 1859, began, at the turn of the century, to hold out promise of serious pretentions for this type of aircraft, the career of lighter-than-air ships has been a checkered one. At one moment spectacular accomplishments have won the world's admiration; at the next equally spectacular destruction has cost many lives and shaken the faith of all but the most stanch adherents.

The Hindenburg, however, was the first commercial airship to meet a violent end. The rest have been military and naval ships.

The world production of rigid airships has been 151, of which, of course, by far the majority was made up by the war-type production of the Germans. Of the total only one major vessel, the veteran Graf Zeppelin, is now in commission to take in the air.

A sister ship of the Hindenburg, the LZ-130, nears completion at Friedrichshafen. The Los Angeles, of the United States Navy, is fit to fly but has been decommissioned and used as an experimental laboratory moored to the mast. Both the Akron and the Macon, pride of the navy while they lasted, have gone to destruction.

Most Airships Used Hydrogen

Of the rigid airships that have flown, 146 have used hydrogen as a lifting gas. Of these about one-half have burned. Of those using helium, a practical monopoly in the United States, none has burned but three. The Akron was smashed at sea by the blow-out of a storm center, the Macon was also wrecked at sea in turbulent air. The Los Angeles lived out a career full of accomplishment and is still serviceable and the navy's "tin balloon," the metal-clad ZMC2, is still in commission although seldom used.

When the World War was declared Germany had fourteen airships, of which eleven were in the military establishment. Building was feverish and the Zeppelins, of ever-increasing size and speed, proved of great usefulness as eyes of the fleet and as raiders which did so little material damage to the Allies and still greater damage to the morale of civil population. When the war closed only eight of the rigid airships remained to Germany out of a total of 124 in use during the period. These were surrendered to the Allies.

Great Britain got the L-64 in addition to the L-71; France the L-72, Z-113 and a commercial craft, the Nordstern; Italy the L-61 and the L-120 and the commercial Bodensee; Japan the L-37; Belgium the L-30 and the United States the L-126, which was to become the famous Los Angeles.

Long List of Successful Feats

Again at this point the balance of life and material lost the airship has a long list of successful feats to its credit. Enabled by inherent buoyancy to remain aloft under certain conditions that would spell disaster to the airplane, it has also proved able to fly in weather which grounded heavier-than-air transport. This was not illy exemplified by the Hindenburg. During her scheduled service last year she several times landed and departed under conditions of heavy rain and fog when low ceilings and visibility of only a few hundred yards kept all airplanes on the ground.

The airship has also proved able to make long distance flights with a load and at a speed with load which have been unattainable by other aircraft. It was in July, 1919, that the 2,000,000-cubic-foot British airship R-34, then the largest in commission, electrified the world by crossing the Atlantic under command of Major G. H. Scott to become the first lighter-than-air vessel to conquer the ocean and the first aircraft of any kind to make the westward crossing. Making her home port, she was also the first round-trip Atlantic voyager. Eleven years later another British airship, R-100, made the round trip crossing to Canada.

The Los Angeles was christened by Mrs. Calvin Coolidge, after the ship had been flown to this country in sixty-two hours by her German personnel, set an operating record which brought her world-wide praise.

Made Many Non-Stop Flights

In the course of it she flew to Bermuda, to Cuba, to the Pacific Coast, to Puerto Rico and to the Canal Zone, non-stop. The flight to Panama, the first non-stop journey to the Canal by aircraft of any sort, was made in 37 hours 30 minutes for a distance of 2,230 miles. The Los Angeles was used to develop many of the ground-handling, mooring and docking improvements worked out by such enthusiasts as Commander Charles E. Rosendahl and Admiral William A. Moffett, then Chief of the Bureau of Aeronautics, who was to lose his life on the Akron.

From the "L. A." the first glider took off from an airship, piloted by Lieutenant Ralph Barnaby; a forerunner of the routine hook-on and take-off of the nested planes of the Akron and Macon.

Abroad, the Italian airship Norge, under the oddly assorted leadership of Lincoln Ellsworth, Roald Amundsen and General Nobile, flew to the North Pole in 1926 and crossed the top of the world. Meantime the Germans had launched the Graf Zeppelin, destined to be among the most spectacular of airship performers. Previous peace time airship disasters have included the Shenandoah, the U. S. S. Akron, largest of this country's dirigibles, crashed off Barnegat lightship early on

Flood of Phone Inquiries Answered by The Times

Soon after the Hindenburg burst into flames yesterday phone calls poured into the telephone room of The New York Times. From 7:30 P. M. until 9:30 P. M. six telephone operators handled more than 5,000 calls.

The inquiries came from points as far distant as London, England. Many calls were received from various sections of Pennsylvania, Vermont and Massachusetts.

When informed that the airship had exploded the callers were unable to restrain expressions of sympathy and regret. One man, whose name could not be learned, but who said his wife was a passenger aboard the Hindenburg, apparently collapsed.

April 4, 1933, in a violent thunderstorm, bringing death to seventy-three.

Two years later, on Feb. 12, 1935, the Macon, sister ship of the Akron, plunged into the Pacific, but nearly all of her crew of eighty-three were saved. The Macon had cost the government about $4,000,000.

Shenandoah Disaster

The navy dirigible Shenandoah was caught in a seventy-mile-an-hour gale near Caldwell, Ohio, on Sept. 12, 1925, and was broken in two. The ship was dashed 7,000 feet to the ground, fourteen of the crew being killed and several others injured. Twenty-seven persons escaped.

Only five of the fifty-three persons aboard the British R-101 survived when it crashed into a hill in France early on the morning of Oct. 5, 1930. It was poking its way through a low-hanging fog when the accident happened.

On May 25, 1928, the Italian dirigible Italia, carrying General Umberto Nobile and his North Pole expedition, blew up in the Arctic. Most of the crew were killed, although some managed to keep alive for several months in the Arctic wastes until help came.

In a mystery disaster somewhere over the Mediterranean, the French dirigible Dixmude was destroyed in December, 1923. Fifty-two men lost their lives.

The Roma, Italian built, crashed near Hampton Roads, Va., in February, 1922, half an hour after leaving the ground. Thirty-four officers and men were killed.

The dirigible ZR-2, awarded to the British from Germany at the close of the World War, was destroyed in England in 1921. Forty-four persons died.

Another British ship, the R-34, was destroyed while moored at Howden, England, in January, 1921. Winds tore the envelope to shreds. In July, 1919, a blimp fell burning on the roof of the Illinois Trust and Savings Bank in Chicago, with the loss of ten lives.

On July 15, 1919, the British airship NS-11 fell into the North Sea after being struck by lightning, twelve lives were lost.

June 20, 1914, an airship and a plane collided over Vienna, killing nine persons.

Twenty-eight lives were lost in 1913, when the Zeppelin L-2 exploded over the Johannisthal Aerodrome. Fifteen were killed in the loss of the L-1 in 1913, and five died when the balloon Akron exploded in Atlantic City.

THE HINDENBURG AS SHE SAILED OVER MANHATTAN YESTERDAY

Rudy Arnold Aerial Photo.

The giant dirigible shown above the financial district on her way to Lakehurst in the late afternoon

Times Wide World Photo.

Captain Ernst Lehmann, veteran Zeppelin commander, who is in a hospital seriously injured.

Times Wide World Photo.

Captain Max Pruss, who was in command of the airship. He escaped death.

AIRSHIP CONVERTED QUICKLY INTO TORCH

Continued From Page One

jump. I heard everybody on the ground screaming. The heat made my face tighten up."

Becker said:

"I had my camera up to the eye level when the ship burst toward the tail end. It seemed to be in the center. The tail went first and the nose seemed to hang in the air. I saw no one jumping because I was so far back.

"I ran toward the ship and saw it enveloped in flames. In a fraction of a second there was nothing left but the skeleton. There wasn't much smoke. I saw a man walking toward me, assisted by two men. He had no clothes on. I saw a woman lying on a stretcher. There were screams from men and women on the field."

"I burst right over our heads." Kennedy said. "It flew apart as if made of paper. Pieces of the fabric fell on us. I saw one fellow jump out, or maybe he fell out. I think he was a passenger. He lay moaning on the ground."

The breathless, semi-hysterical and varying accounts given by the cameramen were typical of all the stories told by those who had seen the airship ignite. A member of the ground crew who was near the tail, where all apparently agreed that the fire was first seen, said:

"She dropped her lines at 7:20 daylight time. There was a burst of flame and a loud report which appeared to be just aft of the rear stern gondola. There was a loud shout, 'Run for your lives!' The second explosion came about thirty seconds later.

"With several of the others I ran as far out of the circle as I could. I saw the ship just sink down and the flames go through it. The fabric turned away in just a few seconds. I turned back with others to go as close to the ship as possible to pick up the survivors."

Mr. W. W. Walker of Toms River, N. J., who was about to enter the naval hospital overlooking the landing field, said the explosion was of sufficient force to shake the building. Half a dozen patients who were on the porch of the hospital said the flames spread so rapidly they believed there could be no survivors of the accident.

Alfred Snook, a dairyman who lives at the State hospital, on the Lakewood-Freehold Road, saw the accident as he alighted from his automobile to walk toward the airship, about 700 feet from his parking place.

"I saw a spurt of flames from the dirigible," he said. "It seemed to come from the rear of the ship. Then there was a terrific explosion and the entire airship suddenly became enveloped in flame. The nose of the airship was jerked upward and then the whole flaming hulk plummeted to the ground where the wreckage was instantly enveloped in thick black smoke.

"I saw a lot of people rushing from the hangar, which was about 1,000 feet from where the airship

American Plan to Build 2 Helium Ships Revealed

A plan by American interests to construct twin rigid airships of the Hindenburg class, but using non-inflammable helium, was revealed on April 27 at a hearing in Washington before the House Military Affairs Committee on a bill to produce helium at cost in government plants.

The Hindenburg was inflated with highly inflammable hydrogen, which led to its destruction. At the Washington hearing in April, T. E. Knowles, an engineer for the American Zeppelin Transport Corporation, which proposes to build the two new airships, said they might influence the Germans to discard hydrogen for helium in their airships.

Helium would provide an extra safety factor for the American airships, he testified. Their construction is impossible, however, he added, without a guarantee of a United States Government mail contract.

crashed. I did not see any life aboard the airship from the time it exploded until it struck the ground. A number of bodies jumped from the ship and I saw nothing fall. A light rain was falling at the time, but I saw no flash of lightning and I heard no thunder."

Go to Passengers' Aid

As rapidly as they recovered from their first shock, those on the field thought of the passengers. Walter Cullen, a ticket agent of the American Air Lines, and Herbert Holson, another employe of the line, were waiting on a truck to take the mail off the incoming ship.

"That blast was so terrific it blew both of us right off the truck," Cullen said. "The fire seemed to go right through the middle of the ship in an instant. Holson and I went to the ship as fast as we could run and the gondola was already on the ground when we got there. We climbed in and helped to pull several passengers out. But most of them took care of themselves."

Harry Thomas, a naval aviation, helped rescue a member of the crew.

Gill Robb Wilson, New Jersey aviation director, praised the conduct of the men on the ground.

"Those boys dived into the flames like dogs after rabbits," he said, "but the people in the body of the ship absolutely had no chance."

Marines on duty on the field also swarmed around the burning ship to aid in the rescues. With Commander Charles E. Rosendahl directing the work, temporary field hospitals were set up. Miss Dorothy Pyler, an American Air Lines stewardess and formerly a nurse, took an active hand in this.

At least forty persons were attended to at the temporary hospitals but some of them died shortly after that. Miss Pyler said.

The shortage of ambulances, doctors and nurses seriously impeded rescue work. Those on the field, however, did everything they could to make comfortable the injured while waiting for the response from hurried calls for medical supplies and equipment which went out to all parts of New Jersey and brought rapid response.

The entire field was a scene of mad confusion during this period out of which Commander Rosendahl worked mightily to make order as rapidly as possible. Help was supplied as fast as it could be. There were persons whose clothes were so badly burned that it was impossible to determine whether they were members of the crew or passengers.

Some were black from the flames and smoke, others had been stripped of their clothing by the blast and flames. Some were unable to speak, although they could walk or gesture. Others were unconscious.

The bodies of the dead were piled in the garage back of the naval hospital, which was closer to the ship than the lighter-than-air hangar. Last night efforts were made at identifying some of them, but for the most part identification will depend on examination of scraps of clothing or personal effects.

LEHMANN A VETERAN IN ZEPPELIN FIELD

Former Master of the Hindenburg in Command Year Ago When Ship Met Difficulties

Captain Ernst August Lehmann, former master of the Hindenburg, was injured seriously when disaster overtook the great ship yesterday. His recovery was reported "doubtful." Captain Lehmann is a veteran in the construction and flying of lighter-than-air craft. He is married.

Born fifty-one years ago on the shores of Lake Constance, he is the son of a chemist, Dr. Ludwig L. Lehmann. After finishing high school, he was trained for service in the German Imperial Navy. For six years he attended the Charlottenburg Technical College.

In 1913 he was assigned to command of the airship Sachsen for the German Airship Company at Frankfort, and, at the beginning of the World War, he continued in its command for the army.

For a time, during the war, he was in charge of development work on airships for the navy. Since the war he has been an official of the Luftschiffbau Zeppelin, and, from 1928 until a year ago, he was commander of the Graf Zeppelin, and associated with Dr. Hugo Eckener.

Last May he became executive captain of the Hindenburg, holding that post until the present trip. Recently he was assigned again to work on the construction of airships.

He has written numerous articles for European and American publications dealing with aeronautical subjects and collaborated on a book, "The Zeppelin." Among the decorations he has received is the Iron Cross, first and second class.

Captain Lehmann was in command of the Hindenburg, under Dr. Eckener, when the ship got into difficulties in April, 1936. Two of its four motors ceased to work off the African coast, near the southern border of Morocco. Permission was obtained from the French Government to take the shortest route back to Friedrichshafen, up the Rhone Valley and over Basle to Lake Constance. Captain Lehmann guided the ship safely to the home port on the power of half the ship's motors.

Captain Lehmann often expressed confidence that the air service could be established which would transport passengers across the Atlantic in three days or less. About two months ago he predicted that by 1940 there would be four Zeppelins operating regularly between Europe and North America, and that service would be established to the Far East.

American Plan to Build

(see above)

Atlantic Flown 170 Times by Capt. Pruss; His Career With Company Started in 1911

Captain Max Pruss, commander of the airship Hindenburg, who escaped in yesterday's crash, rose from the ranks, having joined the Zeppelin Company in a clerical capacity in 1911.

Although this trip marked the first time Captain Pruss was placed in charge of the dirigible on a trip to Lakehurst, he had been in command of the ship on previous trips.

Last year Captain Pruss commanded the ship when she flew from Lakehurst to Frankfort. He was also in charge of her crew during several of her flights to South America and back. In all, he flew the Atlantic Ocean about 170 times. Captain Pruss first visited the United States in 1924. At that time he was one of half a dozen German officers aboard the ZR-111, when that ship was brought to Lakehurst.

He spent five months here as an instructor at the United States Naval Station and then returned to Germany.

When the Hindenburg made her first flight to the United States Captain Pruss was one of four watch officers. With the promotion

of Captain Ernst A. Lehmann to succeed Dr. Hugo Eckener as commanding officer of the Hindenburg, Captain Pruss was elevated to the rank of first officer.

On Sept. 30, 1936, when the Hindenburg flew from Lakehurst to Frankfort, Captain Pruss was the commanding officer. On that occasion he flew directly out to sea, avoiding New York to pick up favorable westerly winds. He calculated correctly and completed his flight in three days.

Early this year Captain Lehmann was assigned to do construction and organization work in the expansion plant of Deutsche Reederei with Dr. Eckener. Captain Pruss was then placed in full command of the Hindenburg.

Captain Pruss was born in East Prussia on Sept. 29, 1891. He attended a local gymnasium and then spent a short time at a technical institute, where he studied aeronautics.

In 1911 Captain Pruss, then twenty years old, was employed by the Berlin office of the Zeppelin Company. Count Ferdinand von Zeppelin was alive at the time. Captain Pruss is married and has two sons.

SABOTAGE IS CONJECTURED

Kin of Inventor of Zeppelins, in Chicago, Gives Theory on Blast

CHICAGO, May 6 (P).—Count C. G. von Zeppelin, 30 years old, a nephew of the German inventor of the dirigible airship, who is in the United States on a business trip, expressed the opinion tonight that the explosion of the Hindenburg might be a case of sabotage.

He added that this was only a conjecture and gleaned from early reports of the disaster.

In his Loop hotel room he said he had read that the explosion had occurred in the stern of the ship and that the blast had surged forward. He said there was nothing to cause an explosion in the rear of the ship, as the gas cells were located in the middle third of the Zeppelins.

The Count said he was in the United States on a private business trip in connection with a netting manufacturing concern which he represents. He said his home was in Apeldoorn, Holland, and that a member of his family now was connected with the manufacture of the Zeppelins.

MOVIE CAMERA MAN SEES PASSENGER JUMP

Running to Film Landing When He Saw German Leap to Safety From Burning Airliner

By GEORGE WILLENS

Copyright, 1937, by NANA, Inc.

LAKEHURST, N. J., May 6. I was running like hell to get some movies of the landing and the big Zeppelin, was nosing down toward her mooring mast, ropes lowering. The front end of the Zep was exceptionally low, the tail high—a steeper landing than she took when I rode in her from Akron to Seville, Spain, in 1933.

Then I saw a stream of fire shoot backward over the top of the bag. From a distance of 300 feet, I saw a man hurl himself from a window of the ship, drop to the ground, get up limping and brush himself off. I was taking a movie of it. I never again saw a jump like that to hard ground.

I ran over to the spot and introduced myself to Joseph Shahs, a German acrobatic jumper.

"How on earth did you do it?" I asked.

"I don't know." he said, reeling himself to see if he really was all there. "Whew, am I lucky—not a scratch."

He said that he had heard a small explosion in the ship preceding the big one and that he had decided to jump for it despite the obvious risk. "I have never before and probably never will again see a jump like that to hard ground."

DIRIGIBLE TOUCHES GROUND IN LANDING

Tail Scrapes in Manoeuvring at Mooring Mast—Then Flames Envelop Big Ship

RESCUERS BRAVE THE HEAT

But Cannot Get Close to the Twisted Wreckage for Hours —Charred Bodies Found

By LEO V. KIERAN

Special to The New York Times.

LAKEHURST, N. J., May 6.—The German dirigible Hindenburg, largest lighter-than-air craft in the world, had been made fast to mooring cars and was being manoeuvered to the mooring mast of the Lakehurst Naval Air Station here when it caught fire in the stern and became enveloped in flames at 7:23 o'clock tonight.

The disaster occurred after the ship had returned to the field for the third time. A terrific downpour which had delayed the landing had just let up. There had been a shift in the wind from south-southwest to southeast, and Captain Max Pruss, in command, manoeuvered in to the mooring mast at the southwest corner of the field, a half-mile from the hangar, from the northwest.

Commander Charles E. Rosendahl, in command at the field, went to the mast, taking charge of ninety enlisted men attached to the air station and 110 civilian aides. Two landing lines were dropped. The ground crew dashed them fast to two mooring cars on the circular track about the mast. The crew began to make them taut.

Passengers Seen Laughing

With the ship only 200 feet aloft, passengers could be seen in the windows, laughing and waving to the men on the ground. But the ship had gathered too much momentum and had drifted several hundred yards past the mast. Captain Pruss signaled and yelled from the control cabin, "Pay out, pay out."

The crew could not pay out the lines far enough and let go. The ship lost the perfect balance that had been maintained up to that moment. Its tail touches, the ground. There was a roar as the stern burst into flames. The flames spouted out the nose, which rose in the air.

Within fifteen or twenty seconds before the metal framework could drop to the ground, the entire silver-painted envelope had been burned off the girders. When the ship crashed, it was nothing more than a skeleton, its interior blazing fiercely for more than forty minutes.

The members of the ground crew ran for their lives as the dirigible dropped, almost in their midst. None were believed to have been hurt. Five or six explosions were heard while the ship burned as the intense heat burst the fuel oil tanks. Sailors attached to the air station made repeated attempts to approach the wreckage while the flames burned, but they could not get near.

Several of the survivors told of leaping from the windows. Others were blown from the windows by the backdraft from the flames as they sprang from the stern to the bow of the ship. Others, away from windows, could not get out until the wrecked hulk had hit the ground.

Ground Crew Rushes In

The latter, their clothing burned, their bodies seared, scrambled and crawled to get away from the blaze and the all-pervading heat. Members of the ground crew ran in to help them, got them away to army trucks from an army emergency detail and to private cars in which they were rushed to the air station hospital and to near-by institutions.

Some who escaped were barely alive. Rescuers, whether breathing could be detected or not, sped them to institutions where emergency rooms were ready with equipment to effect resuscitation. Screams of the injured and dying spurred the rescue workers to supreme effort amid the confusion that filled the field.

It was several hours before the rescue workers could approach the twisted skeleton which was all that the fire had left of the ship. Even then the heat made it impossible for them to penetrate into the debris long. For it penetrated even the asbestos suits of emergency crews which had battled their way to the scene. They were able to bring out several bodies, however. All were charred beyond recognition.

The bodies were taken to the bachelor's quarters at the air station which were converted into a morgue. There they were laid out in rows while efforts at identification were made.

DISASTER ASCRIBED TO GAS BY EXPERTS

Continued From Page One

have been told it was entirely due to the use of hydrogen. It was not a structural problem, which has in the past figured in our own disasters. An explosion never occurred in any of our airships. There is no similarity between our disasters and that which occurred today.

Major General Oscar Westover, Chief of the Army Air Corps, and a pioneer lighter-than-air army expert, also pointed out that the United States has abandoned the use of hydrogen for helium, which is produced in greater quantities in the United States than in any other country.

Postmaster General James A. Farley made the following statement:

"I am inexpressibly shocked at the tragedy which has befallen the Hindenburg. To families of the ill-fated passengers and crew have my deepest sympathy."

"The explosion shocked every person who heard of it and will result in a great setback to airship development," Senator Walsh, chairman of the Naval Affairs Committee, said.

"A great distinction should be made between this loss and the three our own navy has experienced. The disasters of our navy have not been caused by explosions but by structural faults. We used helium gas, the Hindenburg used hydrogen.

"I believe that our navy has followed a wise course in suspending any further experiments with lighter-than-air ships. This catastrophe will generally discourage further experiments throughout the world in this apparently promising field of rapid travel.

"It has been our duty to conserve our supply of helium, just as we conserve our petroleum fields, and nothing can be said of that policy of protection."

Representative Lister Hill of Alabama, chairman of the House Military Affairs Committee said he was not surprised at "another" dirigible disaster.

"This terrible accident confirms the wisdom of our position not to build these dirigibles," he declared. "We have been wise and this proves it."

Representative Vinson of Georgia, chairman of the Naval Affairs Committee, declined to predict what effect the Hindenburg accident would have on the future development of lighter-than-air ships. It created a "terrible situation," he asserted.

Copeland Orders Inquiry

By The Associated Press.

WASHINGTON, May 6.—Chairman Copeland of the Senate committee investigating air safety said tonight he would order the committee investigator to begin an inquiry "at once" into the disaster to the German airliner Hindenburg.

Airship Men Give Views

While airship men both in and outside of the navy were unwilling last night to assign a definite cause for the destruction of the Hindenburg, there was one possible cause of which many of them were thinking. It was the valving of hydrogen into the outside air, especially during an electric storm.

The Germans believed they had taken all necessary precautions against fire in designing and operating their great airships. Every member of the crew and board wore rubber-soled shoes. Riggers working aloft rubbing against the huge and shifting gas cells wore asbestos lined suits in addition to rubber shoes and gloves.

They did not fear electric storms when they were high in the air when there was little need to valve gas. But German airship men did not know without this type of operation, have described a combination of circumstances that might well result in such a catastrophe.

Knowing the highly explosive mixture that results when leaking or escaping hydrogen mingles with the oxygen charged air, they were forever on the watch against such a condition.

However, the Germans always knew that on landing and last night they were landing in a rainstorm following close upon a sharp electric storm. Raindrops charged with electricity were falling on the big envelope. The ship itself, it was agreed by airship men, was at that the fire had left of the ship. Even then the heat made it impossible for them to penetrate into the debris long.

F. W. von Meister, vice president of the American Zeppelin Transport Corporation, agents in this country for the German company, who witnessed the explosion, said that either a spark from the static discharge igniting escaping hydrogen, or a spark from the engine exhaust might have been responsible.

There was a tendency, however, to discount this theory. It was pointed out that there were escape valves close to the part of the ship where eyewitnesses saw the first flame burst and that these valves released hydrogen at a point well above the hull of the ship, where it should have been dissipated before reaching the level of the ground.

Another theory advanced last night by officials attached to the German Embassy in Washington also was discussed at Lakehurst. As is customary during the landing process, the bridge officer made use of his engines, especially the rear motors, the possibility of a spark from the exhaust igniting hydrogen slipping along the hull of the ship was suggested.

Major George F. Hobson of Camp Dix in command of the army contingent in the ground crew said he saw a spark over the aft of the ship engines. An instant later, Major Hobson, a third of the Hindenburg was in flames.

Disaster Balks World Tour

OAKLAND, Calif., May 6 (P).—Destruction of the dirigible Hindenburg wrote finis today to Dr. Reginald Macgeorge's projected speed flight around the world by chodules in the Hindenburg. The Boston physician, who had depended on the Hindenburg to depart tomorrow for Hongkong on the Philippine Clipper. But he cancelled his reservation in view of the Zeppelin's explosion at Lakehurst, N. J.

The Hindenburg bursting into flames as it nosed toward the mooring post.

Wide World Photos

Photograph of the Hindenburg taken just before the second and third explosions sent it crashing to the ground.

N.Y. Daily News Photo

"All the News That's Fit to Print."

The New York Times.

LATE CITY EDITION
Cloudy and continued cool today. Tomorrow fair and slightly warmer.
Temperatures Yesterday—Max., 65; Min., 52

Copyright, 1938, by The New York Times Company.

VOL. LXXXVIII...No. 29,462. Entered as Second-Class Matter, Postoffice, New York, N. Y. NEW YORK, FRIDAY, SEPTEMBER 23, 1938. P THREE CENTS NEW YORK CITY and Vicinity | FOUR CENTS Elsewhere Except in 7th and 8th Postal Zones.

CHAMBERLAIN MEETS HITLER; TALKS TO CONTINUE TODAY; NEW GOVERNMENT IN PRAGUE

3-HOUR DISCUSSION

Many Questions Are Still Undecided Despite Basic Agreement

BRITON APPEALS FOR CALM

Fuehrer Wants Benes Ousted, Czech Army Reduced and Veto on Foreign Policy

Chancellor Hitler and Prime Minister Chamberlain conferred for three hours yesterday at Godesberg and will meet again today. They apparently had not found irreconcilable difficulties, but many questions were still undecided. Mr. Chamberlain issued an appeal to the populations of all countries concerned to remain calm, and asked that local conditions in Czechoslovakia remain orderly.

The official German news agency reported that Czech troops fired on celebrating Sudeten Germans in the Eger district and killed sixteen of them. This and other German reports of disorders in the Sudeten areas were not confirmed in Czechoslovakia, where it was said the border districts were calm. Czech troops continued to man the fortified line along the Reich frontier.

In Prague the Hodza Cabinet resigned and General Jan Syrovy, head of the army, took the Premiership and the War Ministry. He was believed to be distasteful to Germany because of his friendship for Soviet Russia. President Benes indicated broad negotiations might give a new aspect to the situation.

Britain suddenly redoubled air-raid precautions, and it was believed the dangerous features of the crisis were not over. It was said Mr. Chamberlain would be likely to choose resistance if Germany should use violence in Central Europe.

[All the above dispatches on Page 1.]

A German authority reported the Reich had as many warplanes as Britain, France and Czechoslovakia and it was understood at Godesberg this was a reason why France had wished to avoid war. [Page 6.]

A crisis in the French Cabinet was averted when three protesting Ministers were persuaded not to resign. [Page 5.]

Talk Lasts Three Hours

By FREDERICK T. BIRCHALL
Wireless to THE NEW YORK TIMES.

GODESBERG, Germany, Sept. 22.—For approximately three hours today Chancellor Adolf Hitler and Prime Minister Neville Chamberlain have been together, alone save for their joint interpreter, Paul Schmidt, in a frank and intimate conversation over the Czechoslovak situation.

They went into conference in the Fuehrer's suite at the Hotel Dreesen at 4:10 P. M. They emerged together smiling but serious and apparently in accord at 7:15, with nothing to say about what had passed between them except that their talk would be continued tomorrow morning.

The impression left on observers here is that upon the vital issues under review the two have not found their viewpoints utterly irreconcilable, but many questions are still undecided. The result, in fact, remains in the balance until tomorrow, when the discussion will proceed.

Chamberlain Issues Appeal

Returning to his hotel on the other side of the Rhine, Mr. Chamberlain immediately issued an appeal to the populations of all the countries concerned to remain calm and await the conclusion of the conversations now proceeding.

It is understood he would have liked Herr Hitler to join him in this appeal. Whether he made a direct request is not revealed, but the Fuehrer, it is understood, approved the statement's text before it was issued. It read:

The Prime Minister had a conversation with the Fuehrer which, beginning at 4 o'clock, continued until shortly after 7. The conversation will be continued tomorrow.

In the meantime, the first es-

Continued on Page Two

Germans Report 16 Slain by Czechs In Eger Area During Celebrations

Berlin News Agency Hears of Many Disorders in Sudeten Districts—Nazis There Seize Foes for Their 'Safety'

By The Associated Press.

BERLIN, Sept. 22.—Official German news agency dispatches tonight reported Czechoslovak troops had fired on celebrating Sudeten Germans of the Eger frontier district, killing sixteen men and women.

The dispatches from Eger asserted the outbreak occurred when troops, acting on orders from Prague, reoccupied areas previously evacuated after the government had agreed to cede them to Germany.

The official German news agency, DNB, said troops reappeared at 4 P. M. when village streets of the Eger district were crowded with joyously celebrating citizens, who had beflagged their towns after the police had withdrawn. Machine guns were said by DNB to have rattled from armored cars, instantly killing and wounding numerous bystanders.

DNB reports accused the Czechoslovak troops of firing on crowds in Koenigsberg, Graslitz, Falkenau, Joachinstal, Weipert and other places in the Eger district. German dispatches said the terrified Sudetens, hastily removing festive flags and garlands, closed their stores in Eger and Asch since they understood Czechoslovak troops were planning to take over these Sudeten towns during the night.

The dispatches asserted members of a "Red Guard," together with returned gendarmes, were patrolling Eger and Asch streets, where shooting, and scuffling were said to be continuing. Telephone communication with the two towns was disrupted.

The reports added to German apprehension that the Czechs might inflict severe damage on the Sudetenland before yielding it to Germany, a fear that deadened joy over Adolf Hitler's triumph.

Meanwhile, hurrying from camp to camp of fugitive Sudetens on this side of the border in Saxony, Konrad Henlein, leader of the Sudeten German (Nazi) party, admonished and encouraged his followers to hold out a short time longer.

At Annaberg, in the Erz Mountains, he addressed 10,000 cheering Germans and Sudetens from the balcony of the City Hall.

"We have come over to you," he said, "not because we were worried about our lives, but because we were determined to fight for the freedom of our homeland with the weapons in hand."

He referred to the armed Free Corps, which he organized after his

Continued on Page Ten

BRITAIN REDOUBLES AIR-RAID MEASURES

14 Gas Mask Stations to Open in London Today—Clamor Against Chamberlain Rises

By FERDINAND KUHN Jr.
Special Cable to THE NEW YORK TIMES.

LONDON, Sept. 22.—The British Government suddenly redoubled its air-raid precautions today as Prime Minister Neville Chamberlain and Chancellor Adolf Hitler began their meeting on the Rhine.

Millions of radio listeners throughout the country tonight heard a quiet announcement that new defense measures, coming closer to everyday households than ever before, would be applied immediately in London and many big cities of the provinces.

Between the radio announcements and the talks at Godesberg there was a direct connection, for it was the general impression here that the dangerous phase of the crisis was by no means over. Some in high places felt that the outcome of the Godesberg meeting would decide whether London's new air-raid precautions would have to be used in the near future.

Gas Mask Stations to Open

Tomorrow fourteen stations for fitting gas masks will be opened throughout the City of Westminster—the chief shopping, hotel and theatre district of London—and will be kept open for nine days until all the 130,000 residents of the district have had a chance to register. A statement by the Westminster City Council said that all men, women and children were expected to be measured for gas masks "except children under 5 years of age for whom other arrangements are being made."

In asking citizens to apply, the statement included the peremptory appeal, "the sooner the better." Distribution of gas masks will not be begun, but every one in Westminster will get a colored card according to the size and shape of mask needed. If an emergency comes air-raid wardens will go from house to house delivering masks according to the colors of the cards on the doors.

Simultaneously it was announced that thirty-four London hospitals had been made ready for "decanting" their movable patients at short notice so as to make room for air-raid casualties. The entire fleet of 300 powerful "Green Line" motor coaches, which run between London and the distant suburbs, will be used to take between 3,000 and 4,000 patients from the London hospitals to railroad stations. Ambulance trains will then take them to safer hospitals more than fifty miles from London.

The radio announcer assured listeners that all bus drivers already

Continued on Page Six

GEN. SYROVY FORMS NEW CZECH CABINET

250,000 Demonstrate in Prague Stressing Country's Unity in Crisis—Benes Asks Patience

By G. E. R. GEDYE
Wireless to THE NEW YORK TIMES.

PRAGUE, Czechoslovakia, Friday, Sept. 23.—Amid tremendous demonstrations of patriotic enthusiasm Premier Milan Hodza's "capitulation government" resigned yesterday morning. By last night a new government of "national concentration and defense" had been born under General Jan Syrovy, Inspector General of the Army. The new Cabinet contains two generals, the Ministry of Public Works being allotted to General Frantisek Nosal.

Foreign Minister Kamil Krofta and Finance Minister Joseph Kalfus were taken over from the Hodza government.

There are a few popular figures included as Ministers without Port-

Continued on Page Three

$12,000,000 GRANT IS MADE BY PWA FOR PARKWAY HERE

Moses Discloses Approval of Plan for $28,000,000 Artery in Brooklyn and Queens

TUNNEL PROJECT DROPPED

Time and Financing Held Bars to Allocation of Funds for Two-Borough Link

The Brooklyn-Manhattan vehicular tunnel, leading project on Mayor La Guardia's program of major improvements, has been rejected for PWA funds by Federal authorities, but a grant of $12,000,000, the amount sought for the tunnel, has been approved for the proposed $28,000,000 Circumferential Parkway in Brooklyn and Queens, Park Commissioner Robert Moses informed the Board of Estimate yesterday.

The parkway, an assessable improvement thirty-six miles long, with seventy bridges and six traffic lanes, will extend from Owl's Head Park, at the Narrows, around the entire outer border of Brooklyn and Queens to the Bronx-Whitestone Bridge under construction at Whitestone. The city's share of $16,000,000 will be borne by the city and the two boroughs. The Board of Estimate is expected to rush the project, as work must be completed by July 1, 1940, to comply with terms of the PWA grant.

On the urgent request of Commissioner Moses and Raymond V. Ingersoll, Borough President of Brooklyn, the board voted the preliminary steps to expedite the plan. The project was referred to the chief engineer of the board and the City Planning Commission for authorization and to the Director of the Budget for additional personnel to complete the plans. A public hearing on apportionment of costs and granting final authorization was set for Oct. 13.

Protest on Apportionment

With Stanley M. Isaacs, Manhattan Borough President, protesting the apportionment—80 per cent on the city and 10 per cent each on Brooklyn and Queens—as being unfair to Manhattan, which pays more than half the city's taxes, three alternative plans were accepted for consideration. Mr. Isaacs proposed 50 per cent on the city and 25 per cent on each of the two boroughs, while Borough President Harvey of Queens proposed 100 per cent on the city. The rules of the board call for 66 per cent on the city and 17 per cent on each of the two boroughs.

Mr. Moses said President Roosevelt had approved the $12,000,000 allotment for the parkway on Tuesday on recommendation of Secretary Ickes. Mr. Moses explained that the $77,000,000 tunnel project had been rejected chiefly because it would require four years to complete, or longer than the limit on PWA grants, and because of the necessity for the city to raise $20,000,000 by the sale of securities. The latest tunnel financing plan pressed by Mayor La Guardia also called for a $45,000,000 loan from the RFC.

The Park Commissioner said the

Continued on Page Twenty-eight

Second Hines Trial Will Begin on Nov. 14; Pecora to Sentence 3 Witnesses Dec. 5

The new trial of James J. Hines, Tammany district leader, and others on the indictment alleging conspiracy with Arthur (Dutch Schultz) Flegenheimer in the policy racket will start in General Sessions on Nov. 14, District Attorney Thomas E. Dewey announced yesterday. The date is that of the Monday following election day.

Motion papers for the trial were served on Hines's counsel of record, Joseph Shalleck. They are returnable tomorrow before Judge Owen W. Bohan in Part I of General Sessions. The papers contained a request for the selection of a blue-ribbon panel of 500 talesmen. This is an increase of 200 over the panel from which the jury was chosen before Supreme Court Justice Ferdinand Pecora in the first trial, which ended Sept. 12 as a mistrial.

Meanwhile Justice Pecora, with the consent of Mr. Dewey, discharged with the thanks of the court the extraordinary grand jury which handed up the indictment during seventeen months' service. During its tenure the grand jury had held 102 sessions and listened to 552 witnesses in a series of racket investigations by Mr. Dewey.

Justice Pecora, referring to the fact that J. Richard (Dixie) Davis, George Weinberg and George Schoenhaus, State witnesses against Hines, were awaiting sentence on their pleas of guilty before him, insisted on setting a tentative date for their sentencing.

"The Court has no desire or disposition to pronounce any judgment at any time that the District Attorney deems it would not be for the public interest to do so; the Court has no desire to do anything with regard to that matter that is not in the public interest," Justice Pecora said. He added he would be willing to postpone sentencing further if necessary.

Assistant District Attorney Charles P. Grimes replied: "Certainly I believe the imposition of any sentence should await further consideration, and possibly be held afterwards. As I understood it, Your Honor has stated to a representative of our office that Your Honor would be willing to abide by the combined recommendation of the District Attorney and the judge who finally hears the case to full completion and is, therefore, in a proper position to judge the value of the services rendered by those three defendants."

Justice Pecora denied this, saying that what he had said was that he would give "the utmost consideration" to any such recommendation. Mr. Grimes remarked, "It did not go as far as my understanding of what it was." Justice Pecora, declaring, "This Court or any other Court would be foolish, in my opinion, to say in advance what it will definitely do; I mean, I don't know," set Dec. 5 for sentencing.

Mr. Dewey indicated the trial would be held before Judge Charles C. Nott Jr. or Judge James Garrett Wallace.

STORM TOLL 462; THOUSANDS HOMELESS; 250 KILLED IN THE PROVIDENCE AREA; NEW ENGLAND STILL BATTLES FLOODS

RESORT IS WRECKED

Westhampton Beach Counts 15 Dead and Missing Exceed 30

ENTIRE ESTATES ARE GONE

Hunt for Bodies Pressed—Devastation Widespread on All Long Island

Special to THE NEW YORK TIMES.

WESTHAMPTON, L. I., Sept. 22.—Under smiling blue skies, fashionable Westhampton Beach — what was left of it—emerged today from the storm's ravages with a toll of fifteen dead and at least thirty-one persons still missing.

The damage to property was beyond any estimating. Whole Summer estates, with garages, cars and all the paraphernalia that goes with them, had been swept out to sea, leaving hardly a trace behind. Along the ocean front and in such debris as was left after the tidal swells subsided, more than 300 relief workers and policemen searched all day and far into the night for the other bodies which the sea and the ruins must inevitably yield.

From the nerve-racked survivors came stories of heroism and miraculous escapes that strained the imaginations of those relief workers who themselves were almost stupefied by the sights they saw. The eyewitness accounts given by the survivors were confused; such was the swiftness of the calamity that overtook that strand of sand dunes known as Ocean Beach and Dune Road.

Houses Swept Into Bay

But it appeared that at the very height of the storm yesterday the ocean suddenly rose in a series of gigantic tidal swells and swept in on the houses, all of them substantial structures, and then simply washed them over the beach into Moriches Bay. Those fortunate enough to cling to roofs, or cool enough to swim, were tossed up on the Westhampton Beach golf course or on the several sand hills and elevations in the vicinity.

The storm dealt out death indiscriminately. Among the victims were prominent members of the colony as well as Negro servants. Several of the bodies remained unidentified tonight.

The Westhampton Beach Club, a few weeks ago the scene of leisure and sociability, was an improvised morgue today, where hysterical persons sought frantically to identify their missing friends and relatives. The town itself was a shambles. Store windows were shattered, debris was piled high in the streets. The scenes of devastation were relieved here and there with grotesque incidents—a yacht deposited undamaged on a front lawn, behind a five-foot hedge.

Even the topography of the beach was materially changed during those furious hours when the sea tore sizable inlets through the island, in one instance an inlet that stretched nearly a mile into the heart of the town of Westhampton Beach.

The policing arrangements were perfected during the day through the cooperation of State troopers, the local authorities and volunteer groups, including Red Cross workers and members of the American Legion. Transportation was provided for the survivors, information clearing houses were set up, and all tourist traffic was kept far from the main scene.

16 Float on Roof 10 Hours

One of the most harrowing experiences involved nine adults and seven children, all members of the Summer colony, who went to the home of Mrs. Norvin R. Greene, wife of a New York investment broker, to attend a children's party, and ended up by floating on Moriches Bay for ten hours on the roof of Mrs. Greene's demolished home.

They were making merry at the Greene house on Dune Road when the storm came. The house was flooded, and the hostess and guests escaped to the roof after the men had smashed a hole through it. They clung there on the sloping, shingled roof, while part of the house floated three miles down to Quogue. There what little of the under-structure remained gave way entirely, and the roof was eventually beached at Quogue, where the party was rescued.

They were, besides Mrs. Greene, Mr. and Mrs. Harry McCarthy of Yonkers and their two children,

Continued on Page Twenty

Hurricane Victims Swept Into Sea As Tidal Wave Hit Rhode Island

Water 12 Feet Deep in Providence Streets Soon After Hurricane Broke—7 Children in One Section Found Drowned in School Bus

By JAMES P. McCAFFREY
Special to THE NEW YORK TIMES.

PROVIDENCE, R. I., Sept. 22.—Rhode Island tried hard tonight to shake off the effects of the hurricane that hit this city and surrounding territory late yesterday afternoon causing millions of dollars damage and resulting in the death of more than 250 persons with scores still missing.

The abnormal flood tide waters pushed up by the ninety-mile wind had receded and Rhode Island residents joined with public officials in checking up on the death toll and estimating the property damage. But Providence was still in darkness tonight and its communication lines, with the exception of the radio, had been cut off from the outside world.

Edward J. Kelly, superintendent of State police, in a report to Governor Robert E. Quinn said that more than 250 persons had been killed or drowned in the State. In a small community close to Westerly Mr. Kelly said that more than fifty bodies had been recovered. A police check-up indicated that 100 persons had been identified.

Not in the memory of any living person here, could a more fantastic story be recalled of the death and havoc that followed the tidal wave and the hurricane that hit this city shortly after 4 P. M. yesterday. With little or no warning, the waters of Narragansett Bay flooded downtown Providence to a height of twelve feet and department store shoppers headed for upper stories of the building to beat the flood.

Three hundred men, women and children were marooned in the City Hall, more than a quarter of a mile from the Providence River, which flows into Narragansett Bay, and they stayed at City Hall until morning.

Persons were killed by falling walls weakened by the flood waters. One man was drowned at Dorrance and Westminster Street, the Times Square of this community. Trees fell on moving automobiles and the drivers were killed or injured. Store fronts were damaged and looters grabbed for spoils before the waters receded.

While Providence, at the head of Narragansett Bay, felt much of the fury of the storm, the southern part of the State was caught squarely in the middle of the hurricane. Seven children were found drowned in a school bus at Jamestown on an island in Narragansett Bay.

Continued on Page Twenty-three

HARTFORD FIGHTS MENACE OF FLOOD

Sandbag Dikes Are Erected as Connecticut River Rises Far Above Safety Stage

By MILTON BRACKER
Special to THE NEW YORK TIMES.

HARTFORD, Conn., Friday, Sept. 23.—Auxiliary sandbag dikes were being erected here early this morning as the city sought to avoid possible repetition of the disastrous flood of 1936, when the business center was flooded and damage resulted estimated at $20,000,000.

The focal point of attack on the rain-swollen Connecticut River was the old Colt Embankment on the southwestern rim of the city, a thirty-two-and-a-half foot bulwark. At midnight the water stood two feet above that mark and was kept back only by the thousands of sandbags piled up by combined city and army engineers and WPA workers.

Thomas Foley, in charge of the emergency project, said the bags would be raised to thirty-eight feet, two feet higher than the river is expected to go. Since 2.30 P. M. yesterday its rise has never been more than four-tenths of a foot an hour, and the average increase led to the belief that it would reach its crest at about 6 A. M.

Park River Backs Up

Meanwhile there were other aspects of a flood in the city. But none quite as serious. The Park River backed up into Bushnell Park, in front of the State House. There lamp post bulbs glowed like floating Japanese lanterns. Several cellars in midtown were flooded and pumps were emptying them into Main Street. Some industrial areas on the East Side were partly submerged, but the city as a whole was not inconvenienced.

A few hundred home owners were evacuated to other parts of town, but in each case the step was precautionary and not due to advancing waters.

The record set in 1936 was about thirty-nine feet. Barring the possibility of further rain, there was no fear in official quarters that this would be matched.

Perfect Autumn weather throughout the rest of the State enabled volunteer workers to clear roads and rebuild homes damaged in Thursday's unprecedented storm.

National Guard Standing By

National Guardsmen and an emergency relief committee summoned by Mayor Thomas J. Spellacy stood by, however, in the event of more rain which did not seem likely tonight.

From the Saybrook Bridge, about six miles east, bridge workers looked down upon the vast spread of rough water and said it was little worse than at ordinary high

Continued on Page Twenty-two

SEAS 30 FEET HIGH HIT JERSEY COAST

Shore Resorts Buffeted by Tidal Waves—Boardwalks and Pavilions in Ruins

Special to THE NEW YORK TIMES.

MANASQUAN, N. J., Sept. 22.—The storm damage here as elsewhere along the shore was concentrated on the beach front, where the tidal waves which immediately followed the passage of the storm rolled to a height of more than thirty feet for an hour late yesterday afternoon.

The sea tore the entire fourteen blocks of the Manasquan boardwalk off its foundations and distributed it two blocks inland in driftwood. On the way the breaking sections crashed into casinos and pavilions fronting the ocean and into cottages on the side streets.

Porches were torn away and doors and windows smashed open to the wind, rain and sea, which left three feet of sand behind it. Ocean Avenue was buried in sand its entire length. The estimated damage was $250,000.

James Golden was swept more than a block inland in a whirl of water and splintered timber by the first of the tidal waves. When hauled to safety he was treated by the Manasquan first-aid squad for submersion and minor bruises and removed to his home here.

More than a dozen spectators and volunteer workers were treated for minor cuts and bruises received from flying pieces of the boardwalk. The most seriously hurt appeared to be Joseph Ehret, a Sea Girt contractor, who also was caught in the collapse of the Manasquan Boardwalk. He was pinned against a wall by the wreckage. He was admitted to the Fitkin Memorial Hospital, Neptune.

Delaware River Rising

Special to THE NEW YORK TIMES.

TRENTON, N. J., Sept. 22.—The flood following the fourth day of downpour yesterday remained today the chief menace inland in New Jersey, according to the United States Weather Bureau here. The Delaware River was expected to reach eleven feet above normal level before tomorrow.

At that level it would be over the seawall in back of the State capitol and would flood parts of Stacy Park.

Eight Jersey Towns Flooded

Special to THE NEW YORK TIMES.

MOUNT HOLLY, N. J., Sept. 22.—Rancocas Creek rose fourteen feet today and flooded eight towns in this vicinity, including Pemberton, Brownsville, Birmingham, Smithville, Hainesport and New Lisbon.

In Mount Holly the water was four feet deep over an area of twenty-

Continued on Page Twenty-three

RUIN WIDESPREAD

Deaths Are Reported in Seven States and in Canada

PRESIDENT DIRECTS AID

Fires and Shortage of Food in Many Areas — Railroad Service Hampered

As communications began to be re-established last night after the worst storm in the history of the northeastern section of the country, the list of dead from Wednesday's hurricane reached a total of 441, including at least 250 dead in Rhode Island alone. This figure for Rhode Island was the official estimate of the State Superintendent of Police late last night.

With many thousands homeless from the storm and fires and floods which had followed in its wake, grave fears were felt that disastrous floods, particularly in the valley of the Connecticut River, which was rising ominously, would add to the widespread suffering.

Seven States and one Canadian Province suffered losses of life from the storm which were placed at the following totals, as compiled from reports to The Associated Press, and other sources: Massachusetts, 108; Rhode Island, 250; Connecticut, 40; New York, 44, including 33 on Long Island; New Hampshire, 13; New Jersey, 3; Vermont, 2, and Quebec, 2.

Estimates Homeless at 10,000

Norman H. Davis, chairman of the American Red Cross, estimated in Washington that at least 10,000 families had been made homeless by the storm and the floods and fires that had followed in its wake. He expressed fear that this total would be greatly increased by floods in New England as reports came in that rivers there were rapidly rising.

Although he was confined to his bed by a cold, President Roosevelt kept in close touch with the situation and ordered the navy, the Coast Guard, the CCC, which has between 5,000 and 10,000 men in the stricken areas; the WPA and other government instrumentalities to give every possible help to rescue and relief work.

In Massachusetts Governor Charles F. Hurley declared a food and fuel emergency, while National Guardsmen patrolled twenty-three cities to direct the relief work and prevent looting. The situation was most acute in the vicinity of New Bedford, where there were reported to be thirty dead, and along the base of Cape Cod.

Boston and Providence were both completely shut off from railroad communication yesterday and for a long period the only contact that Providence had with the outside world was by radio. At Westerly, R. I., there were twenty-nine dead and more than fifty missing, according to fragmentary reports which came through by radio.

15 Dead in Westhampton

At Westhampton, the worst-stricken of the Long Island communities, the known dead totaled fifteen but at least thirty-one more persons were missing and it was expected that the toll would be considerably increased when 300 rescue workers completed their frantic search of the wreckage left there by a tidal wave washed up by the hurricane.

New York City, although spared the full violence of the 100-mile-an-hour storm, faced the possibility of a milk shortage by this afternoon as washouts of railroads and highways halted tank cars and greatly delayed milk trucks. Milk company officials said that there was a supply on hand sufficient for this morning. There was some danger of a shortage of highly perishable fruits and vegetables, but it was not expected to prove serious.

A shortage of electrical power here led Police Headquarters to broadcast a warning to the areas north of Fifty-ninth Street not to attempt the operation of automatic elevators, lest they halt between floors and fire start in the operating mechanism. The city subway system and the areas left in darkness for several hours Wednesday night were back to normal yesterday.

Communication with virtually all of New England and much of Westchester and Long Island was difficult yesterday as scores of trunk lines were broken and thousands of poles were down. Telephone company officials said that at the

Continued on Page Nineteen

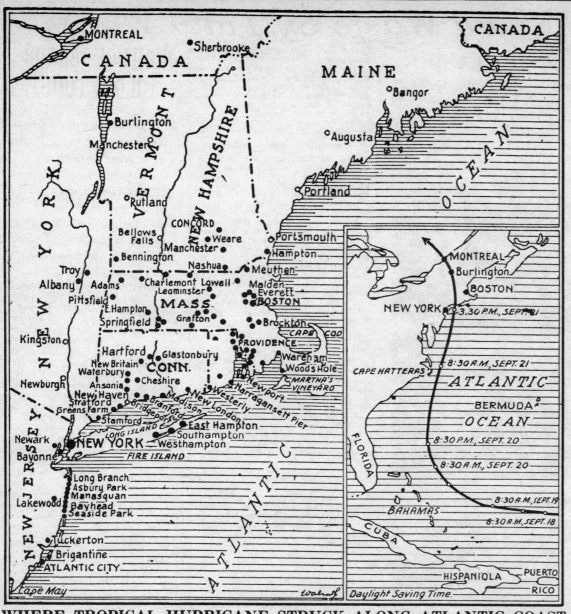

WHERE TROPICAL HURRICANE STRUCK ALONG ATLANTIC COAST

Map showing cities and towns which have reported damage from floods and wind. The inset shows the path of the hurricane. Cities not indicated by black dots are those which escaped the major brunt of the storm.

STORM TOLL IS 460; FLOODS THREATEN

Continued From Page One

height of the storm Wednesday evening only one cable line from New York to New England remained in service.

They placed the total of telephones still out of commission in the metropolitan area yesterday at 18,200, allocated as follows: Westchester, 3,200; Nassau and Suffolk, 8,661; Queens, 3,821, and Brooklyn, 2,391. They rushed 500 reserve operators and 600 repairmen into the worst damaged areas to try to restore service as rapidly as possible.

Railroads in New England were still almost completely paralyzed yesterday, while service to the south and west was somewhat delayed by storm damage. The New York, New Haven & Hartford Railroad reported its operations were at a standstill beyond New Haven. Its worst washouts were at East Lyme, New London, Mystic and Stonington, Conn.

The Long Island Railroad announced that service on the Rockaway and Montauk branches was still suffering from the storm, but that it had improvised bus service from Speonk to Montauk. The Edgemere section of the Rockaway line was still impassable. Other divisions of the Long Island were operating normally, according to officials of the road.

The New York Central's service on the Harlem division north of Golden's Bridge to Chatham and north of Briarcliff on the Putnam division to Yorktown Heights was still seriously impaired from falling trees and wires and other causes, it was said at the road's offices.

Insurance company officials in the city estimated yesterday that their losses in New York and its vicinity alone would reach $5,000,000 and pointed out that the total property damage would be far greater than this, for much of the damaged property was not insured. They pointed out that little flood or hurricane insurance is carried in this section of the country. No one was willing to hazard even the wildest guess at the total loss throughout the storm area.

The most threatening situation for the immediate future was along the valley of the Connecticut River, which at Hartford had already risen last night to 33.3 feet above low water level. The government meteorologist there expected it would reach the thirty-six-foot level today, only one foot below the all-time time record set in the $20,000,000 flood in 1936, and far above previous disastrous floods. At Springfield, Mass., 2,500 persons were evacuated from homes along the river there.

Fear that contaminated water supplies from broken mains and polluted reservoirs might start epidemics led public health authorities in several Connecticut and Massachusetts communities to warn the residents to boil all drinking water. New London, Conn., one of the hardest-hit cities in the whole storm region, sent a request for 400 packages of typhoid vaccine.

To meet the emergency caused by the almost complete disruption of railroad service in New England, the Interstate Commerce Commission temporarily suspended its regulations requiring railroads to route freight by the most direct route and permitted them to route it by any route that was open.

Airlines were swamped with demands from persons anxious to get to their homes and families in New England. American Airlines ran more than 100 flights between here and Boston, while Transcontinental and Western Air, which ordinarily does not fly to Boston, dispatched four twenty-one-passenger planes here as an emergency measure.

Ten deaths in the city were attributed to the storm—six in Queens, two in the Bronx and one each in Brooklyn and two on Staten Island. Five persons were injured and two were missing, while thousands of trees were destroyed and the damage to buildings was extensive.

Long Island, which reported thirty-three dead and thirty-one missing, was by far the worst hit of the areas about the city. The greatest center of suffering was at fashionable Westhampton, but the entire island felt the worst storm in its history. On Fire Island alone almost 600 houses was destroyed—95 at Fair Harbor, 200 at Saltaire and 300 at Ocean Beach.

Manhasset Bay was strewn with the wreckage of large and small yachts and pleasure boats, while it was estimated that between 500 and 700 small craft were destroyed off Fire Island. Several large launches were carried far inland by the tidal wave that struck the south shore of the island and were left there when it subsided.

Southampton, where the property damage was heavy, was isolated for hours Wednesday night and early yesterday. It was not until mid-afternoon that communication was restored. Meanwhile, J. P. Morgan & Co. had appealed to the coast guard for information as to the safety of. Mrs. S. Parker Gilbert, widow of the former agent general for reparations, who was eventually located at her home there, and Acting Mayor Newbold Morris had been greatly concerned about the safety of his two sons, who were found to be at the home of their grandmother, Mrs. J. C. Thaw. The roof of the Thaw home was partly blown off, but no one was injured.

Despite the damage done by the gale and the five-day downpour of rain, described as the worst in more than thirty years, Westchester County rallied quickly from the storm. With more than 1,500 extra men pressed into service, the authorities were able to reopen yesterday all the parkways and county roads, and to announce that telephone and lights had been restored through most of the county.

Tidal waves more than thirty feet high which rolled in on the New Jersey coast after the passage of the peak of the storm tore up many miles of boardwalk in the many resort cities there and distributed much of it as far as three blocks inland. Serious crop damage, especially to apples, was reported.

Among the dead in Connecticut were Henry L. Lewis of Stratford, owner of a factory in Bridgeport, whose wife, Mrs. Helen E. Lewis, was the Republican nominee for Secretary of State, first woman ever nominated for State office in Connecticut. Mrs. Lewis is among the missing. With their daughter, Cait, who was taken semi-conscious from the surf, they were swept into the sea when a tidal wave engulfed their Summer cottage ten miles east of New Haven.

Fear was felt for the safety of five or six members of the fishing boat Ocean View, which put out with a crew of twenty-three from Bridgeport Wednesday. The Ocean View sank in Long Island Sound, and her men took to two lifeboats, one of which turned over. Two bodies were recovered, and the fate of the other men in that boat, who were wearing life preservers, was not known.

Up-State New York was not as seriously punished by the storm as the coastal communities, but nevertheless dispatches brought word that three persons were dead and four were missing there. Fifty persons had to be removed from their homes at Mohawk, N. Y., because the Mohawk River was flowing four feet deep through the streets of the town.

At least 1,000 families were reported homeless and the property damage was placed at $4,000,000 at New London, Conn., which had five dead. In Stonington, Conn., there were four dead and five missing, and the entire population of the town, plus 275 persons from a stalled New York-to-Boston train, spent Wednesday night on two high spots in the flooded town. Four hundred school children remained in their school building all night there. Eight bodies were washed up on the beach at Old Saybrook.

Five hundred persons were reported homeless at Adams, Mass., while Worcester experienced a $100,000 fire during the storm. In the vicinity of Southbridge, Mass., the total damage was placed at $2,000,000. Seven persons were killed when a tugboat sank in Boston Harbor, out of which not a single vessel sailed yesterday.

Associated Press

DIRECTS RELIEF WORK
Robert E. Bondy, who flew to the storm area in New England.

Times Wide World

At Westhampton, looking toward the beach from the wreckage of the West Bay Bridge. Here before the hurricane stood a bath clubhouse and a row of large Summer homes.

Westhampton Beach Laid Waste by Tidal Waves

SCENES IN WESTHAMPTON AND FIRE ISLAND

Times Wide World

The remains of storm-wrecked houses which were blown onto Albee Road at Westhampton

Times Wide World

A view of Fire Island after the ocean broke through at Saltaire and poured across it into Great South Bay

DEVASTATION WIDE ON LONG ISLAND

Continued From Page One

Harry, 2½ years old, and Brenda, 10 months; Mrs. Greene's two children, Gair, 8, and Greta, 10; three unidentified children, and Joseph McFarland, Jean Arthur, John Gordon, Dorothy McAree and Mr. and Mrs. Leeman Chandler, all of Westhampton Beach.

Survivor Tells of Ordeal

Mrs. Anna King Hampton, daughter of John L. King, editor of The Westhampton Chronicle, and wife of Robert Hampton, was a survivor who suffered a harrowing experience. Her mother is one of the missing.

"Mother and my husband and I were in the house when the wave struck," she said. "It came so suddenly that I didn't realize what was happening. We were carried out of the house and started swimming.

I looked around and my mother was gone. My husband and I kept on swimming and finally got to shore."

J. W. Barnhart, business manager of The New York Daily News, and Mrs. Barnhart, who were also feared lost, floated in to shore during the night with two servants, having clung to a part of the roof of their home as it broke away. Mr. Barnhart was badly cut on the head and Mrs. Barnhart was suffering from shock.

George Burkhard, of 1 Gracie Square, New York City, and Mrs. Burkhard, swam from the island to the mainland and described to reporters the scenes of desolation in Moriches Bay as houses and people were toppled into the waters.

"The bay was like the ocean," Mrs. Burkhard said. "It was a wild, raging sea, filled with screaming people and all kinds of debris."

About forty houses were swept away from that stretch of beach which lies between Westhampton and Quogue bridges.

State Police in Charge

Inspector James Flynn of the State Police was in full charge of

the relief operations. He was assisted by fifty troopers, who took stringent measures against reported attempts to loot homes. Other relief agencies represented were the Salvation Army and volunteer firemen.

Daniel Schoonmaker, a 65-year-old resident of the Westhampton Beach colony, who suffers from paralysis, was unable to escape from the storm and lay on the beach all night until he was found in an exhausted condition by Coast Guardsmen early this morning.

The town was filled with homeless dogs who somehow found their own way out of the hurricane and who passed doleful hours today trying to find their homes, now swept away.

Other survivors were Arthur H. Brooks, 2 years old, of Montclair, who passed the night in a roofless house with his parent's two maids; and Harry McCarthy, his wife and their two children of Yonkers, who also suffered a night's exposure in a house with its roof blown off.

H. L. Carter, in command of the Coast Guard detachments at the scene, said that never in recorded history of Long Island were such

heavy seas seen as during the hurricane.

Mrs. George McKnight was alone in her house, her husband having gone to New York earlier in the day. She saw no hope for survival, so wrote him a farewell note and nailed it to a rafter.

Rescue workers found her this morning, and she tore up the note.

Couple Stranded on Island

Fred Schmidt and his wife of Mastic Beach, whose house was washed away, were cast away on Pattersquash Island in Moriches Bay. They were sighted by State Troopers in an airplane and were taken off by a rescue crew in boats.

It was David Potts of Westhampton Beach and Palm Beach whose yacht ended a day's cruising on the front lawn of a home. He had decided to ride out the storm in Moriches Bay in his 32-foot cabin cruiser Dorel. After fighting the storm for hours, he put an anchor down, and when the storm receded he found himself on the lawn, inside the five-foot hedge, over which he had floated.

Fire Island Sorely Hit

Special to THE NEW YORK TIMES.

FIRE ISLAND, L. I., Sept. 22.—Two persons were dead, most of the buildings were destroyed and three new channels were broken through from the ocean to Great South Bay, and the entire island was being evacuated today.

The dead were identified only as a Mrs. Bazinet and Mrs. Haas. A person listed as "Miss Davis, the school teacher at Kismet Park," was reported missing. The bodies of the two dead were recovered. Both had been drowned.

The Coast Guard ice breaker AB-25 evacuated seventy-five persons and the Saltaire Ferry brought forty more ashore, landing the passengers in both instances at Bay Shore. At least 125 cottages were swept away at Saltaire, and a channel eight feet deep was cut through the very center of the colony.

The other channel, of about the same depth, was cut through about two miles west of Saltaire at the naval radio station. The third was about four miles farther west, at the Coast Guard station. The foundation of the Fire Island lighthouse was cracked.

At Point o' Woods, only five cottages were washed away, but at Ocean Beach, a little to the west, about fifteen buildings of Camp Cheerful, a Rotary Club boys' camp, were washed to sea.

Fair Harbor, still farther west, reported six buildings alone remained standing, and that local residents found it difficult to tell where their vanished homes stood before the storm.

About thirty homes were washed away at Oak Beach, where fifteen persons were evacuated during the night. The bath house and pavilion at the Fire Island State Park were swept away.

25 Oak Beach Houses Gone

Special to THE NEW YORK TIMES.

OAK BEACH, L. I., Sept. 22.—Twenty-five houses were washed away here during the storm. Many of them were floating through the channel and the bay today. The beach itself was badly damaged by the storm and Lido Boulevard from Long Beach to Point Lookout was badly undermined. About twenty persons were rescued.

Martial Law in Southampton

Special to THE NEW YORK TIMES.

SOUTHAMPTON, L. I., Sept. 22.—A condition amounting to martial law was established in this devastated community today as firemen and members of the American Legion were assigned to police duty and the beach colony area was closed off to prevent looting. The total damage was estimated at $500,000 to $750,000.

In addition to the two deaths reported yesterday as a result of the storm, a third attributed indirectly to the storm was that of Arthur Kavanagh, 80 years old, retired vice president of the National City Bank of New York, who died of a stroke at his home at Water Mill, two miles from here, last night.

NIGHT OF TERROR TOLD BY COUNTESS

Wife of French Consul General Here Hails Ottman Butler as Westhampton Hero

FLED WITH BABY, NURSE

Three Local Youths Also Share Praise for Guiding Refugee Group to Shelter

WESTHAMPTON, L. I., Sept. 22 (AP).—A Countess who fled in overalls with her small baby clasped to her breast and a retinue of servants splashing at her heels gave thanks tonight that Providence had seen fit to spare her from last night's hurricane.

Still shaken from the ordeal, Countess Charles de Ferry de Fontnouvelle, wife of the French Consul General in New York, related her experience at the Summer home of Representative John J. O'Connor, the "purged" Democrat who will run for re-election as a Republican.

The refugee Countess, who waded out of her own Summer place just before it collapsed, found a haven in Mr. O'Connor's home after a terrifying night in the storm-battered residence of William Ottman Jr.

It was a disheveled, white-faced woman who came out of the storm, still clinging to her 23-month-old daughter, Ann Renée. She had discarded her overalls because they impeded her flight and was wearing only her underclothing when she reached the O'Connor home.

But, she said tonight, she was glad to be alive.

"I am convinced we were spared because of the baby," she added. "Providence looked down upon us through her eyes."

Thought Storm Was a Quake

The Countess said her first thought when the storm broke was of an earthquake.

"The whole house started to tremble," she went on. "We began to be afraid something was going to happen.

"Miss Agnes Zeigler [the baby's governess] said she would try to find help."

"I was never so frightened in my life," interjected Miss Zeigler. "The wind was howling and the water was up to the floor of the living room."

"She went out, but was unable to find any one," resumed the Countess. "So when she returned I bundled the baby in a blanket and we all started out together, Miss Zeigler, the baby, the cook and myself.

"Water swirled around our hips. Planks, branches and all sorts of things were flying through the air. It was only by the grace of God that we were not killed."

Butler Led Group to Shelter

They struggled to the Ottman home a half mile away, turning once in time to see their own big rambling frame house collapse with a roar. They found fifteen or twenty other refugees.

"The hero of everything was the Ottmans' butler," she recalled. "I wish I knew the name of that brave man. He quieted everybody when the storm was at its worst."

During a lull, the butler and Mlle. Zeigler went to the roof and began signaling with a flashlight. Off in the distance there came a flickering answer, but help never came.

Finally, just before midnight, the butler went out and returned with three husky boys, Stanley Wilson and Charles and Michael Goy. All together they linked arms and pushed through the storm to more sheltered places, the countess and her party stopping off at the O'Connor home.

"Thanks to God," she said, "my

Houses Swept Into Bay in Wake of Hurricane

two sons were in Washington and my husband in New York."

Butler's Identity Revealed

The unidentified butler lauded as a hero in the havoc of the hurricane and tidal wave at Westhampton Beach was revealed yesterday as Arni Benedictson.

Mr. Benedictson is a Norwegian and has been in the employ of Mr. and Mrs. William Ottman Jr. for about two years. He is credited with having saved at least twenty-five persons in the storm and with calming the fears and restoring the morale of the refugees who found a temporary haven in the Ottman beach home, which later was swept out to sea.

Mrs. Ottman, on her return to the city yesterday, told of efforts made by her husband to rescue the butler and three other members of their household staff, marooned in their home.

Miss Zeigler also paid high tribute to the butler's heroism in their ultimate rescue.

"About 4 o'clock yesterday our house began to tremble," she said. "The water began to come in, and when it reached the first floor, after flooding the basement, I waded through the water to a nearby house, where I found a chauffeur and a maid in the basement. I asked them to come and help us, but they wouldn't. So I went back to the house.

Pressed Through Wreckage

"The Countess wrapped the baby in a blanket, and the four of us started down the beach through the water. There were doors flying through the air, and all kinds of wreckage swirling past us on the crest of the sea. We made our way along the beach until we came to the Ottman home. There we found about twenty other refugees, with the butler calming their fears and trying to restore their morale.

"I heard the butler placidly remark that there might be some danger, and that it would be well to signal to the mainland that there was trouble on the beach. He then signaled, and afterward remarked that the situation as he observed it was disturbing. He then set out to the mainland to bring help."

He returned soon with three youths, Miss Zeigler continued, whom he had found at the bridge, which was in danger of collapsing. He advised that everybody follow him and make an effort to cross the bridge before it became too greatly weakened by the flood. Guided by the butler and three youths the group reached a zone of safety, she added.

According to Mrs. Ottman, the butler took out the Countess and her child and the others just a few minutes before their house collapsed. He was badly cut on the chin during the storm.

At her city home, 1,021 Park Avenue, Mrs. Ottman said:

"Our home was swept away, and we lost everything, including two cocker spaniels, an automobile and a station wagon.

"I was driving to Westhampton from New York when the storm broke. It was a strenuous ride, but I finally got through. I found my husband on the mainland with our 4-year-old son and his nurse. He had brought them over during the first part of the storm and had then returned to bring in the members of our household staff, the butler, two maids and a chauffeur.

"But he found it impossible to reach them. The wind blew with such force that his car was overturned and he came very near being drowned. Fortunately, as already told, our household staff got out of the house before it was swept away."

Atlantic Beach Damaged

Special to THE NEW YORK TIMES.

ATLANTIC BEACH, L. I., Sept. 22.—Damage to exclusive private beach clubs, including the Atlantic Beach Club, the Silver Point Beach Club, Nautilus Beach Club, Garden City Beach Club, Sea Glades Beach Club, Bath Club, Cabana Beach Club and others, is expected to exceed several hundred thousand dollars.

SOCIAL LEADER A VICTIM

Mrs. J. C. Norris a Resident of Philadelphia

Special to THE NEW YORK TIMES.

PHILADELPHIA, Sept. 22.—Mrs. John C. Norris, who perished in the storm at Narragansett Pier, was for many years a social leader in Philadelphia and at Narragansett. On hearing of her death and that of her son, John C. Norris Jr., 33 years old, several members of the family left by plane for Rhode Island.

Mrs. Norris, who was 66, was the former Maria S. Dobson, daughter of the late James Dobson, textile manufacturer here.

She went with her husband and son to Rhode Island, where they had spent the last thirty Summers, about July 1 and had not planned to return here before Thanksgiving Day. Soon after their arrival at the resort more than 150 guests, including many Philadelphians, attended Mr. Norris's seventy-ninth birthday celebration.

Mrs. Norris served many terms as president of the Narragansett Village Improvement Association. She was an expert in needlecraft, one of her chief hobbies. She also collected rare furniture, pictures and china.

Many Yachts Wrecked

Special to THE NEW YORK TIMES.

PORT WASHINGTON, L. I., Sept. 22.—Insurance men here estimated the damage done by the storm to about 400 boats tied up in the harbor at $1,500,000. Property damage was placed at $95,000.

About 1,000 boats, ranging in size from rowboats to sixty and seventy-foot yachts, were anchored in the harbor when the gale struck at 2 P. M. Most of the craft rode out the storm on their moorings, but about 400 were torn loose, and some of them were tossed on the shore or blown out to the Sound.

Freeport Loss Put at $200,000

Special to THE NEW YORK TIMES.

FREEPORT, L. I., Sept. 22.—Heavy losses to owners of boats tied up here, added to damage suffered by municipal services and private homes, brought the cost of Wednesday's storm to about $200,000 here, according to the estimate of Mayor Robert E. Patterson.

Losses at Center Moriches

Special to THE NEW YORK TIMES.

CENTER MORICHES, L. I., Sept. 22.—No fatilities occurred here, but the storm did much damage to property. A number of narrow escapes were reported. Frank G. Wild, a New York lawyer, escaped in a rowboat from his submerged home, and Frank N. Evanhoe, a retired New York police sergeant, made a similar escape.

The ballroom on the Masury estate, which was built over the water, collapsed into the sea. Hundreds of old shade trees were uprooted and destroyed. The damage to the big Summer estates of wealthy colonists was not immediately determined.

Electric Plant Disabled

Special to THE NEW YORK TIMES.

GLEN COVE, L. I., Sept. 22.—An estimated 90,000 homes in Long Island were without refrigeration today and will continue to be so for two or three days, officials feared, due to the suspension of service at the Long Island Lighting Company's No. 2 plant.

The plant, one of the most up-to-date anywhere, was built only seven years ago at Glenwood Landing, in Hempstead Harbor. At about 3:40 P. M. yesterday it was hit by a tidal wave that rose ten feet above the normal level of high tide and swept over the bulkhead.

In addition to the homes, which have also been without lights, radios, and, in some cases, telephones, delicatessen, grocery and other food stores are similarly affected.

HURRICANE BROUGHT DEATH AND DESTRUCTION

Times Wide World

Wrecked Westhampton homes in the vicinity where many buildings were washed out to sea

UP-STATE BEAVERS HOLD BACK FLOODS

Their Labors in Hurricane Are Credited With Preventing Interstate Park Damage

Special to THE NEW YORK TIMES.

STONY POINT, N. Y., Sept. 22.—Sixty beaver colonies manning dams in Palisades Interstate Park were credited today with having saved three arterial highways from serious flooding in yesterday's storm, preventing the certain destruction of at least one bridge and retarding the erosion of hundreds of acres of soil. The animals, known as "the earliest of all engineers," thus repaid a debt to mankind.

John J. Tamsen, superintendent of Bear Mountain Park, tramped through miles of soaking underbrush in the 47,000-acre preserve this morning accompanied by William H. Carr, director of the Trailside Museum, maintained by the American Museum of Natural History.

They agreed work accomplished by the busy creatures in controlling streams that drain into the Hudson and Ramapo Rivers was a "wonderful thing for the park." Evidence was found that beavers cut down trees the night of the hurricane, apparently intent on reinforcing their bulwarks of wood and mud.

Mr. Carr recalled that beavers were a familiar sight in this part of the State many years ago. Traces of century-old dams can be seen in the park today. But it was not until eighteen years ago that the National Park Service introduced the beaver here. Possibly a few of the oldest of them shared in the hectic task yesterday and last night.

Long Mountain Road (U. S. Highway 6) and the Johnstown Road would have been transformed into rivers for distances up to a quarter of a mile had not the beaver dams on higher land stemmed flood water, it was asserted. The same could be said of U. S. Highway 9W,

Associated Press

A Long Island train derailed by the gale near Westhampton

main road along the west shore of the Hudson, and Route 17, linking Tuxedo Park with Harriman to the north.

Rain of the past week, augmented by hillside torrents yesterday, soon caused park lakes and streams to overflow. They would have swept unchecked, carrying away the treasured topsoil, had it not been for the beaver dams "backing up perfectly terrific bodies of water, in some cases more than 200 yards across," Mr. Carr said.

Typical of the larger dams inspected was one 600 feet long and six feet high, with water spilling over the top. The naturalists estimated that at its base the dam must be fourteen feet thick.

Another was wedged between boulders thirty feet apart. It, too, stood firm despite the strain of the water. None of the dams showed signs of yielding, although most were completely submerged.

"All the News That's Fit to Print."

The New York Times.

LATE CITY EDITION
Fair today, rising temperatures in afternoon; snow tonight or tomorrow. Warmer tomorrow.
Temperatures Yesterday—Max., 31; Min., 9

Copyright, 1939, by The New York Times Company.

VOL. LXXXVIII...No. 29,587. Entered as Second-Class Matter, Postoffice, New York, N. Y. NEW YORK, THURSDAY, JANUARY 26, 1939. P THREE CENTS NEW YORK CITY and Vicinity | FOUR CENTS Elsewhere Except in 7th and 8th Postal Zones.

QUAKE RUINS 20 CHILE TOWNS; CONCEPCION CITY WIPED OUT; LOSS OF LIFE IN THOUSANDS

CHILLAN IS RAZED

Only Three Buildings Are Reported Standing in 144 Blocks There

INJURED STILL ENTOMBED

Relief Is Rushed Southward, but Railway Damage Delays Doctors and Officials

By CHARLES GRIFFIN
Special Cable to THE NEW YORK TIMES.

SANTIAGO, Chile, Jan. 25.—An earthquake last night virtually wiped out Concepcion, Chile's southern capital, and devastated twenty towns and cities in six rich agricultural provinces, with many thousands of dead and injured.

Two thousand were reported dead in Concepcion alone, with fires completing the devastation begun by the earth shock. Chillan, a city of 50,000, fifty miles inland from Concepcion, was reported as completely razed.

Only fragmentary reports, gathered by amateur operators at a hundred battery sets, last night linked the capital by short wave with the earthquake zone. Parties were organized at Talcahuano, the seaport of Concepcion, to reach that city, which during the day maintained an ominous silence.

The figure of 2,000 dead at Concepcion was reported here by the manager of the Chile Telephone Company at Tetuco and other nearby towns confirmed the estimate as probable, adding that 1,000 more were seriously injured.

Deaths Placed at 10,000

The newspaper Imparcial, usually well informed, confirms a report, not denied, it is said, in official circles, that no less than 10,000 met death last night in what is admittedly the worst earthquake in Chilean history.

The Governor of Concepcion sent a message to the Minister of the Interior estimating that the dead there reached many thousands, although it was not yet possible to form any clear idea. He asked the immediate dispatch of Red Cross aid, doctors, food and clothing.

Chillan, however, is now in the foreground, side by side with Concepcion, as the most stricken city. Aviators say that its destruction was almost complete.

[A Pan American-Grace Airlines pilot advised his headquarters at Lima, Peru, last night that 4,000 persons were dead at Chillan as a result of the earthquake and that the ruined city was in flames, according to The Associated Press.]

A theatre collapsed during a night show killing all in the audience, it is reported. The prison roof fell in, and all important buildings were destroyed. The streets are so filled with debris as to make rescue work utterly impossible. Light, power, water and drainage are gone.

Troops are doing their utmost to save the injured who are still entombed but as darkness sets in the task is most difficult. The dying, under the debris, are helplessly demanding aid.

Tents are being rapidly put up in surrounding fiel s. The lack of trains and other communications does not permit a sufficient supply of medical and sanitary requirements.

The wrecked streets are filled with the injured.

144 City Blocks Razed

A late report issued by a German Condor plane that flew over Chillan says that 144 blocks of dwellings and first class buildings were razed. Only three buildings are standing and can be inhabited.

The dead are being rapidly buried in open pits, presumably with the idea of avoiding an epidemic in the very hot weather and lack of water drainage. These pits are being dug in the streets adjoining the public plazas to bury the dead, it is reported, while the wounded are piled up in the old hospital awaiting medical attention, which is as yet scanty.

A government plane managed to land and bring back a few scribbled lines from many survivors and injured to distant relatives and to record brief pictures of tragedy and pathos.

Chillan is one of the most important cities of the South. A majority of its buildings were the old colonial type.

Private radio stations sending in reports said that the damage was not great in Valparaiso. There

Continued on Page Four

City Freezes in Northwest Gale; Today to Be Warmer, Snow Due

Mercury Drops 15 Degrees in Four Hours—Fierce Wind and Icy Highways Endanger Life and Property

Winter froze New York yesterday with unusually low temperatures and fierce northwest winds that blew virtually all day at gale force. The severe cold wave sent the temperature down to 9 degrees above zero at 10 o'clock last night. Although Weather Bureau officials had expected that the mercury would dip to 5 above zero, it began to climb shortly after 10 P. M. and at 11 o'clock, when the bureau closed for the night, it reached 12 degrees.

Fair weather and slightly rising temperatures were predicted for today, followed by light snow tonight or tomorrow and warmer weather tomorrow.

The bitter weather that caused discomfort in this city prevailed also in up-State New York, New Jersey, New England and the Great Lakes region.

The highest temperature recorded by the Weather Bureau here yesterday was 36 degrees at 3 A. M. By 6 A. M. the mercury had dropped to 32 degrees, the freezing point. From then on it remained below freezing. In the afternoon there was a sharp drop. From 28 degrees at 3 P. M., the temperature went down 15 degrees in the ensuing four hours, and it continued to fall during the evening.

The 9-degree reading at 9 and 10 P. M. was the lowest official one for the day and it equaled the previous low for this Winter, established on Monday. The official average for the day up to 11 P. M. was 22.5 degrees, seven and a half degrees below the normal average for Jan. 25.

The hourly temperatures were as follows:

1 A. M.	35	3 P. M.	28
2 A. M.	35	4 P. M.	24
3 A. M.	36	5 P. M.	20
4 A. M.	35	6 P. M.	16
5 A. M.	34	7 P. M.	13
6 A. M.	32	8 P. M.	11
7 A. M.	30	9 P. M.	9
8 A. M.	31	10 P. M.	9
9 A. M.	29	11 P. M.	12
10 A. M.	29	Midnight	*15
11 A. M.	28	1 A. M.	*14
Noon	26	2 A. M.	*12
1 P. M.	26	3 A M	*11
2 P. M.	26		

*Unofficial, at Times Square.

The lowest temperature for Jan. 25 was 4 degrees above zero in 1921 and the highest was 56 one year ago.

Most of the day the wind velocity measured from 40 to 52 miles an hour, thereby covering nearly the entire range given by the Weather Bureau for gale force—39 to 54 miles an hour. Only once did the northwester drop below the gale force minimum. That was at about 3 P. M.,

Continued on Page Fifteen

PLAN BOARD ZONES BIG EAST SIDE AREA

Restricts 170 Blocks for Home Development—First Step in City-Wide Program

An eight-year campaign by the East Side Chamber of Commerce for the comprehensive rezoning of 170 blocks in the Corlears Hook section of lower Manhattan was rewarded yesterday when the City Planning Commission voted a new zoning plan covering the district.

In its report to the Board of Estimate the commission said the district was formerly zoned almost entirely for business and unrestricted uses, though substantial residential developments exist there. The plan adopted yesterday seeks to bring the zoning into conformity with actual conditions and open the way for its development as a residential section.

"Under the proposed amendments," the commission reported, "about 42 per cent of the affected area would be zoned for residence uses, 33 per cent for retail purposes, 15 per cent for business and 10 per cent would be left as unrestricted districts."

"Most of the existing buildings are so old that they must soon be replaced by modern structures. There is no evidence of industrial expansion in this section, and most of the unrestricted uses consist of garages, warehouses and junk yards. Business uses are principally confined to retail stores on the ground floors of apartment houses. There are no longer any piers along the waterfront between Jackson Street and East Fourteenth Street, and those between Jackson Street and James Slip are largely used by various railroads for transferring freight."

Boundary Lines of District

The district involved is bounded by James Street, New Bowery, Chatham Square, Division Street, Straus Square, East Broadway, Jefferson Street, Pitt Street, Avenue C, East Eleventh Street, a line 100 feet west of the East River Drive, Mangin Street, Grand Street, Monroe Street, Corlears Street, Jackson Street, Cherry Street, South Street, Rutgers Slip, Water Street, Catharine Slip and Cherry Street.

In addition to rezoning, the commission also approved a "one-times-height district" for virtually the entire area. That restriction means that the height of buildings must not exceed the width of the street on which they front, and it would permit the erection of apartment buildings up to six stories in height.

"Since it may be assumed that future building in the retail districts will consist primarily of apartments," the commission said, "with such ground floors as the

Continued on Page Fourteen

WALSH ASKS LIMITS ON POWERS OF NLRB

Revision of Act Under A. F. L. Plan Put Before Senate, With New Rights for Employers

A digest of the amendments to the Wagner act, Page 10.

Special to THE NEW YORK TIMES.

WASHINGTON, Jan. 25.—Broad and detailed revision of the National Labor Relations Act was proposed today in a series of amendments introduced by Senator Walsh, carrying out recommendations prepared by the American Federation of Labor. The same amendments will be introduced soon in the House, it was learned.

The amendments were described by their sponsor as designed "to guarantee fair and equitable administration of the law by the National Labor Relations Board."

One of the amendments borrowed a provision from the New York State Labor Relations Act, which provides that the NLRB "may" investigate petitions for an employe election filed by an employer and order such an election. Under current practice, although this right was implied for employers, "the board arbitrarily refuses to entertain such petitions even though there is nothing in the NLRA which would close the door to such action," said Senator Walsh.

Objectives Are Described

The principal objectives of the amendments contained in the Walsh measure were described by Mr. Walsh and by the A. F. of L. in companion statements as follows:

"1. To make it obligatory on the board to respect the right of craft groups to decide for themselves by majority vote who their bargaining representative shall be.

"2. To curtail the assumed power of the board to invalidate legal contracts between employers and labor organizations.

"3. To correct the board's procedure so that all parties affected by any case will be given due notice, accorded a fair hearing, protected against abuses of discretion, and assured of adequate judicial review of wrongful decrees."

An important amendment to Section 9 of the NLRA, which was designed "to protect the integrity of craft unions," was written after the pattern of a similar provision in the Railway Labor Act.

Other amendments seeking to curtail the power of the NLRB to abrogate contracts were written in accordance with a recent decision by the Supreme Court of the United States in the Consolidated Edison case. These would prohibit board action unless "(1) the contract is with a company union, (2) the contract is for a closed shop and en-

Continued on Page Ten

BARKLEY FENDS OFF VOTE ON RELIEF CUT AS SENATE WAVERS

New Dealer Claims a Slight Majority for Restoring Fund to Roosevelt Estimate

MORE AT STAKE THAN WPA

Chamber Accepts Bill as Test of Line-Up Against Spending Policies of President

Special to THE NEW YORK TIMES.

WASHINGTON, Jan. 25.—Although claiming the votes to force a restoration by the Senate of $150,000,000 which was cut from the deficiency relief bill by the House, Senator Barkley, Democratic floor leader, again warded off a vote today to obtain time for a further canvass of the situation in the first real test in the new Congress of the Administration's strength in the Senate.

Mr. Barkley indicated after the session closed late in the day that a vote was unlikely tomorrow, but affirmed his confidence that he could out-vote the conservative coalition led by Senators Byrnes, Harrison and Adams.

The House voted a bill carrying $725,000,000 instead of $875,000,000 as requested by the President, to run the WPA from Feb. 1 to June 30, the end of the current fiscal year. The Senate Appropriations Committee approved the reduction by a vote of 17 to 7.

Meanwhile new controversies crept into debate which at many points represented little more than time-killing by advocates of the larger fund.

Senator Byrnes quoted from testimony by Colonel F. C. Harrington, before the House Appropriations Committee, which indicated that the WPA Administrator planned, in any event, to spend only about $750,000,000 of the requested $875,000,000 before June 30 and hold the rest for a carryover into the opening weeks of the next fiscal year.

"There has always been a carryover," Senator Byrnes said. "This testimony shows WPA really does not need much more than we propose to give them, despite tables produced here showing that drastic cuts would have to be made in the work-relief if we cut the requested appropriation by 17 per cent."

To Read Letter From Harrington

Senator Barkley said that tomorrow he plans to read a letter from Colonel Harrington to refute a charge made yesterday by Senator Adams that the WPA, whether intentionally or unintentionally, had concealed $56,000,000 which would be available after Feb. 1 in the form of a carry-over from current funds.

Senators Adams and Byrnes contended that this carry-over offset almost a third of the projected cut. Mr. Barkley said there was a simple explanation for the apparent discrepancy. The majority leader also said he would clarify other questions posed yesterday on a showing that the WPA and the Treasury Department disagreed to the extent of about $290,000,000 in favor of the WPA on the amount of "unobligated balances" remaining at the WPA's disposal as of last Dec. 31.

The debate was brief today because of an unexpected gift of time by Senator Barkley for a

Continued on Page Ten

MARTIN, ATTACKING LEWIS AS 'BETRAYER,' QUITS C. I. O. BOARD

Prepares Here for Legal Battle for Control of Auto Workers Union

MURRAY, HILLMAN RETORT

Motor Industry in Dilemma as Rival Factions Claim Jurisdiction Over Contracts

Text of Mr. Martin's letter will be found on Page 12.

Homer Martin, president of the United Automobile Workers of America, announced yesterday his resignation from the executive board of the Congress of Industrial Organizations and openly declared war on John L. Lewis as chairman of the C. I. O.

He declared that he and his faction in the automobile workers' organization would fight to the end to retain control of the union against what he termed Mr. Lewis's efforts to destroy its autonomy.

In a letter to Mr. Lewis informing him of his resignation, effective immediately, Mr. Martin accused the C. I. O. chieftain of betraying "the principles and policies of a democratic labor movement" and of aiming at a personal dictatorship over organized labor. He also charged Mr. Lewis with having formed an alliance with Stalinists in an alleged conspiracy to dominate the automobile workers' organization and warned him that "the intelligent union-conscious workers of America, loyally devoted to democratic principles and procedure, will never submit to such dictation."

Mr. Martin also maintained that Mr. Lewis's "lieutenants," Philip Murray, president of the Steel Workers Organizing Committee, and Sidney Hillman, president of the Amalgamated Clothing Workers, had held "secret conferences" with employers and members of the automobile workers' organization "for the purpose of transferring control of the organization to yourself."

Martin Names Counsel

Mr. Martin made public his letter to Mr. Lewis after he had conferred with Frank P. Walsh on the legal action arising from the setting up of two rival factions in the Automobile Workers Union. He announced retention of Mr. Walsh as counsel for his faction together with Frank Munholland of Toledo, attorney for the Railway Union Executives.

Mr. Walsh and Mr. Munholland will appear in court in Detroit Saturday to respond to the suit filed by officers of the rival group, which claims control of the union. This group, consisting of fifteen members of the executive board of the U. A. W. A. who have been suspended by Mr. Martin, has been recognized by the C. I. O.

Mr. Martin, declaring yesterday that this was an unconstitutional procedure, claimed the support of "the overwhelming majority of our union's membership." He asserted that the convention called by him in Detroit for March 4 would demonstrate that he and his followers had the backing of the membership.

Asked whether his resignation from the C. I. O. executive board meant that the United Automobile Workers were out of the C. I. O., Mr. Martin said that he acted in

Continued on Page Twelve

Rumania Lays a Plot to Fascists to Destroy Bucharest Buildings With Flame-Throwers

By The Associated Press.

BUCHAREST, Rumania, Jan. 25.—Rumanian police tonight uncovered a plot of terrorists to destroy many public buildings by a simultaneous attack with flame-throwers, and authorities said they believed remnants of the illegal Nazi-inclined Iron Guard were back of it.

Announcing the arrest of an officer of the chemical section of the Rumanian Army, who later was reported to have committed suicide, and the round-up of twenty-five other persons, the police said they had in their possession twenty-one of the unique flame-throwing devices that had been collected for the attack.

Buildings marked for destruction, authorities said, included the electric light plant, waterworks, post-office, radio building and the American-owned telephone building.

Among the prisoners being questioned were said to be a girl student, an army corporal, director of a petroleum works, engineer, doctor, lawyer and several chauffeurs and workmen.

Officials said that under Codreanu the Rumanian Nazi movement consisted almost entirely of students and youths.

"A different type of individual is concerned in the present conspiracy, but the motives and methods were those of the Iron Guard," an official said.

The inquiry that brought the flame-throwing plot to light started with a routine investigation into an explosion in a suburban house Jan. 8, in which a young public school instructor dabbling with explosives was killed.

An officer identified as Dimitrescu Nicholai is reported to have committed suicide in an ante-chamber of the military court building after a hearing. Authorities said he hanged himself with his belt after admitting details of the conspiracy.

Wireless to THE NEW YORK TIMES.

BUCHAREST, Rumania, Jan. 25.—Several leading Iron Guardsmen, including Corneliu Zelea Codreanu's successor, John Victor Vojen, have disappeared from Rumania, it was revealed today. There are unconfirmed rumors that several of them have gone to Carpatho-Ukraine, in Czecho-Slovakia. German activities in Carpatho-Ukraine for a Greater Ukrainian State are regarded as a threat to the Rumanian regime.

"When you think of writing think of Whiting."—Advt.

REBELS ISOLATE BARCELONA; DEFENDERS, CALLED TO YIELD, RETORT, 'INCH-BY-INCH FIGHT'

Insurgents Bomb Spanish Port While Americans Are Leaving

Missiles Drop Close to Boat Carrying Caldetas Refugees to Cruiser Omaha — French Warship Returns Fire

Wireless to THE NEW YORK TIMES.

ABOARD THE U. S. S. OMAHA, Near Barcelona, Jan. 25.—Twelve Spanish Insurgent bombers flew within plain view about 2,000 feet above this cruiser at 8:15 this morning. Each dropped two bombs over the villages of Arenys de Mar and Canet de Mar, about twenty miles up the coast from Barcelona. Most of the projectiles dropped into the sea about 200 yards off the villages.

In close proximity was the Omaha's motor whaleboat, carrying Rear Admiral Henry E. Lackey's flag lieutenant, Edward L. Woodyard, and Aviation Cadet Frank J. Peterson. They had gone ashore at Arenys to confer with the United States Naval Attaché, Captain Francis Cogswell, and the Military Attaché, Lieut. Col. Henry B. Cheadle.

The Omaha's boat left the ship at 9 A. M. to bring on board thirty American refugees.

Several bombs narrowly missed the British cruiser Devonshire, anchored 600 yards inshore from the Omaha.

Lieutenant James H. Flately Jr., an aviation officer on the Omaha, described the planes as fast modern bombers. He was under the impression that they were attempting to bomb a highway circling the two villages. One bomb made a direct hit on a truckload of ammunition in Arenys. The flames were distinctly visible from the Omaha's decks, and the deafening explosion sounded as if it had occurred alongside.

The Omaha's anti-aircraft guns were trained on the bombers, ready to fire at an instant's notice.

[Anti-aircraft shells were fired at the planes, according to The Associated Press, which all observers agreed must have come from a French warship, as the refugees insisted the Spanish Government had no anti-aircraft guns in the vicinity.]

Members of the United States Embassy staff were leaving on the Omaha for Marseille, France, tonight. They included Walter C. Thurston, the chargé d'affaires; Lieut. Col. Henry Cheadle, the military attaché, and W. M. Gibson, O. R. Paleu and William Kreiger, clerks. Also on the Omaha are Fred T. Caldwell, vice president of the International Telephone and Telegraph Corporation, and a Mr. Dennis, his assistant.

Wireless to THE NEW YORK TIMES.

PERPIGNAN, France, Jan. 25.—American citizens who wanted to

Continued on Page Two

ITALO-REICH ACTS ALARMING BRITAIN

London Especially Disturbed Over German Army Moves—Rome Warns France Anew

By FERDINAND KUHN Jr.
Special Cable to THE NEW YORK TIMES.

LONDON, Jan. 25.—The British Cabinet devoted most of a three-hour meeting today to a discussion of the European situation, which again looks thoroughly unpleasant to British eyes. The uneasiness of the past few days persisted in the best-informed quarters, and with it there came a renewal of nervous selling, with some forced liquidation on the Stock Exchange.

The calling up of 60,000 Italian reservists and the concentration of large bodies of troops at Genoa and Spezia did not make the outlook any brighter. But attention in government circles was directed less toward Italy than toward the reports of quiet military moves by Germany, which have followed the announcement of German Army changes last week-end.

Follow Last Summer's Pattern

In some ways the events in Germany are seen to be taking the same pattern as last Summer, when mobilization was begun as a prelude to the Czecho-Slovak crisis. Observers here are puzzled, for hey can see no possible justification for unusual military developments in Germany at the present time. There is no burning German "grievance," as in the case of Czecho-Slovakia, and no real or imaginary threat from outside.

The suspicion is that Germany may be preparing a show of force to back up probable Italian demands in the Mediterranean against France. It is hoped here that a clue will be provided by Chancellor Adolf Hitler's speech on Monday, for even the most unpleasant certainty is regarded as preferable to the haze of doubt that now surrounds German intentions.

Prime Minister Neville Chamberlain began work with his advisers today on the speech that he intends to deliver in his home city of Birmingham next Saturday. The speech is being carefully drafted as a prelude and perhaps a warning in advance of Herr Hitler's Reichstag utterance.

Simon Speech Recalled

One remembers Chancellor of the Exchequer Sir John Simon's speech at Lanark last Aug. 27, which was widely heralded in advance as a "warning," but which turned out to be ambiguous and entirely ineffective in preventing the crisis of the following month. The present belief at least is that Mr. Chamberlain's speech will be "strong" and will be framed in the light of the reports from Germany that have

Continued on Page Three

BARCELONA'S PLANS UPSET BY APATHY

People Found Unwilling to Work on Defenses—Remnant of an Army Carrying On

By HERBERT L. MATTHEWS
Wireless to THE NEW YORK TIMES.

PERPIGNAN, France, Jan. 25.—Doomed Barcelona was fighting hard at noon today. That is first-hand information, for I was only ten miles from the city at that time and checked with many drivers as well as with the military commanders of Granollers and Mataro. It would have been quite possible to go into the city and perhaps even pass the night, but there were no facilities for sending dispatches.

It is the ghost of an army that has thrown itself across the southern and western sides of the city—the once great Army of the Ebro, which has been broken by its gallant but hopeless struggle of the last thirty-three days and nights against enormous odds.

General Enrique Lister, who had twice called on his famous Fifth Corps for a truly superhuman effort—first at Borjas Blancas, then at Martorell—was making a last stand for Barcelona today. General Modesto, who commands the Army of the Ebro, was throwing in whatever fresh men he had who had come from Valencia.

Brigades of 120 Men

There are brigades in that army with 120 men left, companies that have twenty-five rifles, no machine guns and only fifteen to twenty cartridges daily per man. There are brigades with two machine guns and no artillery. There had been no reserves of men since the Fifth and Fifteenth Corps were thrown in during the second day of the offensive, until now, when some soldiers have been brought around from Valencia.

How can that army, which has fought more than a month against twice its number of always changing troops, hold now against an artillery concentration of one cannon every ten yards, against tanks and airplanes in far greater number than were used in any World War battle and against unlimited supplies of machine guns and submachine guns?

Rubi had fallen about midnight and Sabadell was threatened. The Rebels had established a bridgehead across the Llobregat south of Olesa de Montserrat. General Lister's bridgehead at Martorell, which had covered the retreat, was gone. All along the Llobregat down to the sea the Rebels were either in the line or there were no troops opposing them. The government's little bridgehead at Prat de Llobregat was pitifully weak.

That was the information that the few remaining foreign journalists

Continued on Page Three

ALL FLIGHT CUT OFF

Refugees Turn Back as Shells Make Road to North Impassable

2,000,000 CAUGHT IN CITY

Government Goes to Gerona—Labor Defies Demand of Franco for Surrender

Barcelona was virtually ringed and isolated by the Insurgents last night, but appeals to the populace to surrender were countered with a retort that the Rebels would face an "inch by inch" fight to take the city. [Page 1.]

Reports from correspondents who had left there, however, indicated that only a miracle could save the city; in recent days apathy on the part of the people was noted. [Page 1.] Moreover, the loss of Barcelona as an industrial center will impair further Loyalist resistance. [Page 3.]

Thirty Americans were menaced by Insurgent aerial bombs as they boarded American warships to sail for French ports. [Page 1.] The Insurgent planes ranged far yesterday; French anti-aircraft guns drove them away from the border at Portbou and a German bomber crashed on French territory. [Page 3.]

The trickle of refugees toward France continued. An arrangement was reported made under which a safety zone for them would be set aside on Spanish soil near the frontier. [Page 2.]

In Washington Senator Lewis opposed lifting the embargo on arms to Spain and a similar position was taken by Martin Conboy in a letter to THE NEW YORK TIMES. [Page 4.]

Capital Is Cut Off

By The Associated Press.

HENDAYE, France (at the Spanish frontier), Jan. 25.—Spanish Insurgents laid a ring of shellfire and steel about Barcelona tonight to meet a challenge that the city would be defended "inch by inch, street by street, house by house" as a demand was made for surrender of the 2,000,000 inhabitants.

[The Associated Press reported from London that the Spanish News Agency, in a dispatch dated from Barcelona this morning, said violent fighting was proceeding in several sectors around the former provisional capital.

["Republican forces with extremely high morale and fighting spirit counter-attacked heroically and in one counter-attack took fifty-four prisoners," the agency said.

[The communiqué listed sectors outside the city to the west and northwest as points where the battle was most savage.]

Ministries Move to Gerona

The government has moved to a new capital "somewhere" in Gerona Province."

[Minister of Communications Giner de los Rios, arriving at Perpignan, France, told a correspondent of THE NEW YORK TIMES that government Ministries were being established temporarily in the city of Gerona, about sixty miles north of Barcelona.]

The Barcelona radio station broadcast the challenge as the Spanish Press Agency in London reported that Socialist and Syndicalist trade union organizations had decided to hurl the joint declaration in the face of Generalissimo Francisco Franco's troops.

The escape of the 2,000,000 inhabitants, refugees and defenders was cut off by troops at the southern outskirts, by converging armies to the west and to the northwest and by a curtain of fire that covered the last coastal highway to the northeast.

"Determined Not to Yield"

The Barcelona broadcast declared:

"The taking of Barcelona will not be an easy matter.

"The population of Barcelona is ready, and the city will be defended inch by inch, street by street and house by house.

"Every man and woman is fiercely determined not to yield a step before foreign invaders."

Insurgent planes, which for days

Continued on Page Two

An old woman, badly injured, wanders aimlessly through the ruins at Chillan, Chile, while soldiers search the debris for bodies.

Wide World Photos

20 CHILEAN CITIES DAMAGED BY QUAKE

Continued From Page One

was no loss of life there, but the population was panic stricken and filled the streets and plazas, fearing a repetition of the 1906 earthquake which wiped out the city.

The earthquake was not felt farther north than the city of Iquique and the nitrate fields or farther south than Valdivia. There the streets were filled with panic-stricken crowds, but no loss of life was reported.

Damage was indicated at Curico and Talca. Talca has reported about twenty dead so far and hundreds injured. Churches were shaken and it is feared that many buildings will fall later.

Unconfirmed reports say that the city of Parral was seriously damaged. Many dead are reported there and many buildings shaken down.

Army and Navy in Charge

A decree was issued by the Minister of the Interior tonight placing all the administrative work in the six afflicted provinces under the control of the army and navy for an indefinite period. The military and naval chiefs are supposed to act in accordance with the civil governors, but will have full control.

All units of the Chilean fleet, headed by the dreadnought Almirante Latorre, have steam up and are ready to leave tonight for Talcahuano, conveying supplies, clothing and first aid. The military aviation is sending out more planes to cooperate.

The president of the Conservative party, Senator Maximiliano Errazuriz, head of the principal Opposition party facing the present Popular Front Government, offered the services of his organization to the government, in view of the serious

consequences of the quake and fires.

The extent of the damage to the industrial and agricultural districts around Concepcion is enormous.

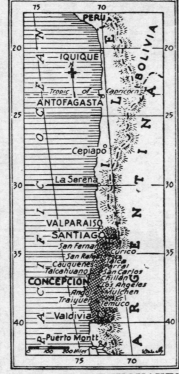

AREA OF EARTHQUAKES

The region of Chile most seriously affected is shown by shading, but shocks were felt Tuesday night as far north as Iquique and as far south as Valdivia.

Movements of trade and shipments from the near-by port of Talcahuano of the forthcoming harvests will suffer, but every measure will be taken as soon as possible by the authorities to begin the reconstruction.

Deeply impressed by reports from the various scenes of disaster, government officials face the tragic developments in silence. "We know very little yet," they say, "but whatever has happened we will confront the situation with confidence and the assurance of success."

In a descriptive statement broadcast this afternoon by the local Sociedad Nacional de Agricultura to New York an optimistic outlook was revealed, with the promise that reconstruction would begin immediately.

All News Censored

With communications still impossible the government is employing the naval radio station. To avoid unconfirmed rumors that might cause panic at distant points the government has ordered all broadcast stations and privately owned transmitters to cease transmitting or commenting in any way on the news of the disaster or on details from the stricken area.

The only information to be given out will be controlled by the Ministry of the Interior. Control measures have also been adopted on outgoing dispatches.

Turning over the government during his absence to the Minister of Foreign Relations, Abraham Ortega, President Pedro Aguirre Cerda with his wife, the Minister of the Interior and other officials, accompanied by numerous doctors, started south by train before daylight. He wished personally to inspect the situation.

His train and eleven other Red Cross convoys gradually advanced toward the scene of the disaster, crossing bridges with precautions. Linares was reached, and this was the last possible point of advance.

Moved by incoming reports, President Aguirre refused to make a

speech at Rancagua when his special train went through. He said that he wished personally to work in the south and not to talk.

When efforts to reach the afflicted proved vain, with trains definitely held up at San Rafael and Linares, President Aguirre stopped off at Talca with the idea of continuing south by car.

Doctors Enrolled

Trains with food and first aid followed the Presidential special.

Military units with motor trucks conveying food had left at sunrise for the South, heading for San Carlos, Chillan and other points. Hundreds of doctors, nurses, Red Cross ambulances and equipment departed from here while others were being rushed from different points.

Orders had been issued calling in all doctors, medical students and nurses and instructing them to be in readiness to travel southward to the stricken area.

The recently created Socialist militia throughout the provinces from Curico southward received orders from the emergency brigades to cooperate with the Carabineer forces to maintain order and help the injured.

Meantime Navy units headed by the destroyer Riquelme rushed to Talcahuano where the results of the quake were so serious that the population was without clothing and without food. Many buildings were destroyed, piers were damaged and the naval workshops were down.

The British cruisers Exeter and Ajax, on a courtesy visit to Valparaiso, have volunteered to go to this port to help, it is announced.

Army trucks with food and clothing made a long caravan along the dusty highways to the south. Hundreds of private cars, called on by the government, followed the same route with volunteers among the doctors and nurses, medical assistants, repair gangs and others.

Forgetting the political strife of the last two months, different groups issued orders for organized

aid for the afflicted section of the country. Communist organizations moved rapidly, ordering their supporters to reach Concepcion at the earliest moment. The Socialist militia received instructions to proceed immediately to the scene of the disaster.

The army took charge of the situation in the south with special troops of carabineer forces maintaining order.

Pan American-Grace Airways sent a plane to fly over the southern provinces to drop supplies. Planes endeavoring to reach Concepcion, however, were believed to have met difficulties and to have been unable to land because the runway was very short. In the mist and smoke the fliers could see wide fissures and sulphurous fumes.

Money for Relief

Arturo Natho, Socialist Secretary General of the government, authorized this evening public collections of funds for the victims of the disaster. It is expected to collect something like $25,000,000.

The Socialist parties here have decided to present a plan for the immediate enactment of a law by Congress establishing a forced loan of 500,000,000 pesos to help reconstruct. This project will go before Congress tomorrow morning.

An official statement says that the government has the situation well under control and that order is being maintained throughout the danger zone. It says that first reports were exaggerated, although the disaster is very serious.

This statement says that the destroyed cities will be reconstructed without loss of time while every help will be given to the stricken districts. It asks the population of the whole country to cooperate calmly, trusting in the government's well-directed efforts to face the situation.

The railroads are being repaired and bridges examined, but it will take time, it is reported, to establish regular service.

"All the News That's Fit to Print."

The New York Times.

LATE CITY EDITION
Fair, slightly warmer today. Tomorrow fair and warmer, showers in the afternoon or at night.
Temperatures Yesterday—Max., 75; Min., 61

Copyright, 1939, by The New York Times Company.

VOL. LXXXVIII...No. 29,715. Entered as Second-Class Matter, Postoffice, New York, N. Y. NEW YORK, SATURDAY, JUNE 3, 1939. P THREE CENTS NEW YORK CITY and Vicinity | FOUR CENTS Elsewhere Except in 7th and 8th Postal Zones.

MANTON TESTIFIES TO BIG CASH LOANS FROM LITIGANTS

BORROWED $664,000

Profited by $500,000 More From Various Financial Moves

WARNER LENT $250,000

I. R. T. Receiver Bought Stock in Manton Concern—Case May Reach Jury Today

Transcript of the testimony of Judge Manton, on Pages 8 and 9.

"Borrowings" of at least $664,000 from litigants and others, often on unsecured notes, for himself and for corporations he dominated, were described yesterday by Martin T. Manton, former senior judge of the Circuit Court of Appeals, in Federal court, where before Judge W. Calvin Chestnut and a jury, the trial of Manton on charges of selling justice moved swiftly toward its close.

Manton, the former tenth ranking justice of the United States judiciary, pictured himself under the questioning of United States Attorney John T. Cahill as a man who sat in his office, which co-incidentally was his Federal chambers, and arranged the "loans" and also executed financial manoeuvres by which he profited to the extent of at least $500,000 more.

These sums did not include what profits there might have been from a chicken farm his son operated on the Manton property on Long Island selling broilers to hotels operated by the Prudence Company for which he testified he had recommended the appointment of John M. McGrath as a trustee, or the profits from the sale of rugs to the same hotels—one order to the Essex House for $50,000 was specified—by the Modern Carpet Cleaning Company, in which Manton owned a half interest.

Many Records Used

Months of effort that began last Fall in the office of District Attorney Thomas E. Dewey and was continued in intensified form by the assistants headed by Mathias F. Correa of Mr. Cahill's staff, and by the agents of the Federal Bureau of Investigation, went into Mr. Cahill's cross-examination. Thousands of records of the most complex nature were distilled down to an inquiry that, lasting through the better part of one court day, spread out fanwise through many levels of the highly complicated corporate chaos that followed the depression.

These included admissions by Manton that:

He had approached Harry Warner of Warner Brothers Company and personally negotiated a loan of $50,000 between the time that a case in which the Warner Company was suing the Cinema Company, Inc., and the time the decision favorable to Warner was handed down by the court.

He had approached Louis Levy, of the law firm of Chadbourne, Stanchfield & Levy, and asked for a $25,000 loan while a suit brought by Richard Reid Rogers against the American Tobacco Company, charging that $10,000,000 in bonuses had illegally been paid to George W. Hill by the company was pending, in which Levy's firm was counsel for the company. A loan of $250,000, ten times the requested amount, was made to James J. Sullivan by Lord & Thomas, advertising agents for the American Tobacco Company, and all but $32,000, Manton testified, went into corporations he controlled.

$171,795 Loans Detailed

Cash borrowings from a procession of persons, including Nat Levy of the Kings Brewery, William W. Backmann of the Kips Bay Brewery, one Joe Gans, Barron Collier, the advertising man who had a contract for display cards in the I. R. T. subway; a lawyer named Weingarten connected with the London Character Shoe Company, a theatrical man named Robert Newman, and others which, in three years—1934, 1935 and 1936—came to $171,795.

In all of these borrowings the lenders marched into the judge's chambers, handed over the cash which he, he testified, put into his office safe for periods sometimes as long as two months, and took for their collateral promissory notes, otherwise unsecured. Most often by cashier's check this money flowed into Manton-controlled firms, or firms in which he had a substantial interest. With the sums testified to

Continued on Page Nine

Flying Boat Cavalier To Be Replaced in July

Special Cable to THE NEW YORK TIMES.

HAMILTON, Bermuda, June 2.—The council of the Bermuda Chamber of Commerce has been informed by its London representative that a new Imperial Airways flying boat to replace the Cavalier, which sank in the Gulf Stream with a loss of three lives Jan. 21, will leave England at the end of July to enter the service between here and the United States. The new ship will be similar to the Cavalier, which carried thirteen persons on its fatal trip.

The council also endorsed representations by its representative in London for a flying boat comparable to the forty-two-ton Boeing clippers of the Pan American Airways.

MARTIN DISPUTED BY GEOGHAN AIDE

Madden Denies He Agreed That Abortion Case Indictment Should Be Dismissed

Testifying yesterday as a prosecution witness at the bribery trial of his friend and former court room associate, Assistant District Attorney Francis A. Madden of Brooklyn contradicted Kings County Judge George W. Martin's version of a conversation they had concerning the jurist's decision to dismiss an indictment against Dr. Louis I. Duke, self-confessed abortionist.

Madden, who is awaiting trial under an indictment charging him with accepting $9,000 in bribes to protect Dr. Duke and another Brooklyn physician from criminal prosecution on abortion charges, said that he had argued at great length with Judge Martin against dismissing the Duke indictment and told the jurist "if that's not a case I don't know what a case is."

Judge Martin testified Thursday and also before the grand jury that Madden had agreed with him that "it wasn't much of a case" and that any action the jurist took would be "satisfactory."

Under defense counsel's questioning, Madden, the chief aide and so-called "brain trust" of District Attorney William F. X. Geoghan's office in recent years, indicated that he now regarded Judge Martin's action as justified and also depicted himself as a prosecutor who had never tried a criminal case before his appointment and who had been assigned to the Duke case, although he had never previously handled an abortion case.

Madden's testimony ended with counsel for both sides alternately firing questions at the witness in an effort to establish that their respective constructions of Judge Martin's reason for dismissing the Duke indictment were valid.

Accused by Three Witnesses

The prosecutor, Special Assistant Attorney General John Harlan Amen, presented three witnesses who testified that Judge Martin dismissed the abortion indictment after accepting a $1,000 bribe. Judge Martin testified that he dismissed the indictment on the law because it was his "honest judgment" that the evidence in the case was hearsay evidence based on "innuendoes and suspicions."

In support of its contention that Judge Martin's decision was prompted by a bribe the prosecution has put in evidence the grand jury minutes of the Duke case, a move which was objected to by Judge Martin on the ground that it would "wreck my entire case."

The defendant contended that if his action in dismissing the indictment was wrong it should have been appealed by the District Attorney's office, a step which was never taken. The indictment against Madden alleges that he received $5,000 from Dr. Duke and at the time it was handed up Samuel Isseks, legal assistant to Mr. Amen, said that the money was paid under an agreement not to appeal from Judge Martin's dismissal of the Duke indictment.

Earlier in the day the defense called to the witness stand Walter R. Hart, lawyer and former Alderman, who arranged for a dictograph recording of a conversation between Dr. Duke and one of Mr. Amen's assistants in which Dr. Duke asserted that he had never paid a bribe to any public official. Mr. Hart declared that while acting as attorney for Dr. Duke a few months ago he was told by the physician on several occasions that he

Continued on Page Seven

ROOSEVELT SHUNS BUSINESS APPEAL TO MEND LABOR ACT

White House Dinner Party Saw No Sign President Favored Change, Says Hopkins

HE RELIES ON LEISERSON

This Appointment to NLRB Will Remove Cause of Much Criticism, He Told Guests

By FELIX BELAIR JR.
Special to THE NEW YORK TIMES.

WASHINGTON, June 2.—Apparently unmoved by appeals of business and industrial leaders who told him at a White House conference last night that the National Labor Relations Act was retarding business recovery, President Roosevelt has no intention of sponsoring any revision of the statute in the immediate future, it was indicated today.

This impression, which was brought away from the after-dinner meeting with the Chief Executive by eight business leaders last night, was confirmed today by Secretary Hopkins, who told a special press conference that "there was no indication at the meeting that he (the President) was in favor of any amendment to the act—he did not so indicate."

Although many specific recommendations for amendment of the labor statute were suggested by the group last night, according to Mr. Hopkins, he said that it did not follow that either he or the President would necessarily pursue the recommendations of the Advisory Council. The success of the council did not require that "the government should meet business half way," he added.

Memorandum on Labor Act

The complete views of the Council on the Labor Relations Act which were given to the President informally were embodied today in a three-page memorandum left with Secretary Hopkins. Although it had been the intention of the group to present a formal draft of its views to Mr. Roosevelt it had not been completed when they left for the White House dinner party.

As one of their number reported today, it was because the group found the President indisposed and unable to attend the dinner party arranged for them that the business leaders did not present their views on the Wagner act more vigorously than they did. Some of them came away with the feeling that the meeting had been more on the social side than they would have had it, despite the frank discussion that took place.

President Roosevelt expressed the opinion, according to one of the conferees, that his appointment of Dr. William M. Leiserson as a member of the NLRB should remedy the cause of many of the criticisms against the board and make amendment of the act unnecessary, at least for the present. The business leaders were of a different opinion, holding that no one member on the board could remedy the conditions they complained of, but there was no meeting of minds on the subject.

The Secretary said in answer to a question that, of course, he had his own opinion on the need for revising the Wagner act or the lack of it, but that he did not care to discuss his views at this time.

"Obviously," he said, "the Ad-

Continued on Page Sixteen

Hitler Reported Ousting Generals Opposing Him

Special Cable to THE NEW YORK TIMES.

LONDON, June 2.—According to The Yorkshire Post, Chancellor Adolf Hitler has retired more than thirty officers who held leading appointments in the German forces owing to their opposition to a policy that might involve Germany in a war on two fronts.

This "purge," following that of February, 1938, prior to Herr Hitler's invasion of Austria, now involves, The Yorkshire Post says, Major Gen. Fritz Loeb, who is largely responsible for the military organization of industry under the Four Year Plan; General Edwin von Stuelpnagel, one of the highest officers in the German Air Force; General Quade, Commandant of the Air Force College; General Curt Liebmann, Commandant of the War Academy, and General Hermann Geyer, Commander in Chief of the Fifth Army Corps.

"If last year's precedent is any guide," The Yorkshire Post says, "there seems to have been a sharp tussle between political and military leaders of the Reich, ending once again in victory for the former."

CHAMBER SUBMITS TAX REVISION PLAN

Urges 15 P. C. Corporate Levy and Backs Morgenthau Views With Two Reservations

Special to THE NEW YORK TIMES.

WASHINGTON, June 2.—The Chamber of Commerce of the United States put before the Ways and Means Committee today its plan for immediate and long-range revision of the tax structure. It endorsed with two reservations the program submitted to the committee last week by Secretary Morgenthau.

Ellsworth C. Alvord, vice chairman of its committee on Federal finance, presented the chamber's recommendations, which call for a flat 15 per cent normal corporation tax with a specific credit of $2,000 on small incomes.

Mr. Alvord contended that with a business increase of 5 per cent, which, he said, could be expected from its enactment, the flat 15 per cent tax would have a yield equal to the $1,005,000,000 from the present 16½ per cent tax and the undistributed-profits tax.

Plans resulting from studies by both Treasury and Congressional tax experts project 22 and 18 per cent flat levies on corporations, it is understood, but modifications of other taxes bearing on corporations are a part of these plans.

The Ways and Means Committee decided tonight to restrict revision to corporate taxes and not attempt changes in individual income taxes.

The committee members of both parties joined in approving a motion to this effect, Chairman Doughton said.

Mr. Alvord submitted his program as the means for laying the groundwork for "maximum business activity." The phase of the program labeled "for immediate action" was:

"1. A flat rate normal corporation tax of 15 per cent, with a specific credit of $2,000 to reduce the applicable rate on small incomes.

"2. Outright repeal of the 2½ per cent undistributed profits tax.

"3. A carryover of net business losses for three years.

"4. Simplification of the individual capital gain provisions, eliminating the unnecessary distinction

Continued on Page Sixteen

House Group Votes $5 Rise in Old-Age Grant; Texas Adds 65,000 to Its Pensions Roll

Special to THE NEW YORK TIMES.

WASHINGTON, June 2.—The Ways and Means Committee voted tonight to recommend that the Federal contribution limit for old-age pensions be raised from $15 to $20 monthly, making possible pensions of $40 or more a month to those 65 years old or more.

The decision, on which only five of the twenty-five members of the committee were said to have dissented, was reached just before the committee completed action on amendments to the Social Security Act. These amendments, in the form of a bill, will be considered by the House next week under procedure decided upon by the leaders.

Committee members denied that the debate in the last two days that preceded defeat of the Townsend Plan in the House yesterday had demonstrated the political desirability of raising the pensions. They said that they saw no connection between the House's action yesterday and the committee's action today.

"It was entirely coincidental," said one member.

The committee voted to allow Puerto Rico to participate in the Federal grants for dependent children, maternal and child welfare under the act.

Special to THE NEW YORK TIMES.

AUSTIN, Texas, June 2.—Governor O'Daniel today signed the bill liberalizing the old-age pension law, adding 65,000 to 85,000 beneficiaries to the present roll of 118,000. The new law throws down the bars to all persons 65 years old or more.

It makes eligible for pension persons past the age limit who have not more than $1,500 of personal property, $1,000 life insurance, $350 cash and exempts a homestead, which under Texas law is 200 acres of land of any value so long as it is the permanent domicile of the pensioner. There are many instances where the declared homestead is valued at several hundred thousand dollars.

The ability of children to support their parents is also eliminated.

The monthly payment to each pensioner for June averaged $14.15. It came from borrowed money. The Legislature has been disputing since early in January over bills that sought to provide new revenue for meeting the pension roll which under the liberalized act would total $20,000,000 annually, it is estimated.

Adjournment is only a few days off, and it is indicated that no revenue measure for this purpose will be passed. It is reported that the Federal Government will not match the State expenditures.

STATESMEN ASSURE POPE THEY INTEND TO MAINTAIN PEACE

Pius Discloses Avowals From Governments—He Now Sees a Smoother Path to Accord

PONTIFF TO PUSH EFFORTS

Congratulated by Cardinals on Name Day—Greece Accuses Italy of Massing Troops

By HERBERT L. MATTHEWS
Wireless to THE NEW YORK TIMES.

VATICAN CITY, June 2.—Pope Pius XII said today that he had received "assurances of good-will and of a determination to maintain peace" from the governments he approached last month and that "other information" had given him greater hopes that influential statesmen could be induced to overcome obstacles to an understanding.

The Pontiff declared all this encouraged him to continue his efforts for peace.

This was the first public declaration that the Pope had made regarding his diplomatic efforts, and he incidentally made clear that the situation early last month, when he stepped in, had appeared singularly grave.

Today was the Pope's name day, and it was in responding to the congratulations that the dean of the Cardinals, Gennaro Granito Pignatelli di Belmonte, offered on behalf of the Sacred College that he made these references to peace.

The Vatican was beflagged and public officials had a holiday. Hundreds of telegrams came in from all over the world, while many members of the diplomatic corps went to the Vatican to sign a special register. The United States has no diplomatic representation at the Vatican and hence no United States official attended.

Cardinals Hope for Peace

It was 9:30 A. M. when the Pope received the Sacred College. Cardinal Pignatelli di Belmonte, in his statement, expressed the Cardinals' hope that the Pontiff would be spared "the many anxieties that afflict the church and its many beloved sons" and that he might see "that universal peace that he invoked from the first moment of his election."

The Pope began his response by thanking the dean and expressing his happiness at having such "intimate counselors and collaborators in the many sacred cares of the supreme pastoral office." He then went on to discuss the difficulties of the present hour, which is "charged in more than one quarter with ferments that are setting in motion or carrying through events about whose final results it is impossible for prudent discernment to say whether they will lead to construction or ruin."

The church has always taken action among men for the triumph of true peace, the Pontiff continued, and he said he was remaining faithful to this mission despite gravest difficulties "in a world of oppositions and divisions, of conflicts of feeling and interests, of exalted ideas and proud ambitions, of fear and daring; in the midst of a humanity that seems almost unable to make up its mind whether it should recognize and entrust the primacy of action and the decision of its own destiny to the sword or to the noble reign of law, to reason or to force."

Inspired by "Sacred Duties"

The Pope said he had not been able to refrain from taking action, because "it could not be reconciled with the sacred duties of our apostolic ministry if external obstacles or the fear of false interpretations or misunderstandings of our intentions and purposes—all of which are directed toward what is good—were to hold us back from the exercise of that salutary office of peace that is proper to the church."

It was at this point that the Pontiff recalled his recent diplomatic activities.

"Animated in the depths of our heart, as the common father was, by this spirit of peace and justice at a moment that appeared particularly grave in the lives of peoples, toward the beginning of last month," the Pope said, "we thought it timely, after mature deliberation, to make known to some statesmen of the great European nations the anxiety the situation was causing us at that moment and our fear lest international dissensions become aggravated to a point of degenerating into sanguinary conflict.

"This step met in general with the sympathy of the governments, we are glad to say, and after it had come to public attention, through no cooperation on our part, it met with the gratitude of the people. As a result of this step we received assurances of good-will and of a determination to maintain peace, which was so much desired by the people.

"Who could be more satisfied

Continued on Page Two

LOSS OF 86 IN SUBMARINE FEARED AS TIDE ENGULFS IT; 4 ESCAPE, SOME DIE IN EFFORT

TAPPING IS HEARD

British Divers Tell of Sounds as the Air in Vessel Fades

PLAN TO DRAG SHIP ASHORE

Vast Array of Rescue Craft Spurs Efforts, Though Hope for Men Is Small

By W. F. LEYSMITH
Special Cable to THE NEW YORK TIMES.

LONDON, Saturday, June 3.—With at least eighty-six air-starved men still entombed in the sunken British submarine Thetis, the stern of that vessel slipped from the grasp of rescuing ships in Liverpool Bay yesterday afternoon and from then on hope rapidly diminished of saving any more than the four men who yesterday morning floated to the surface from the submerged escape hatch of the ship.

At 2 A. M. divers, who in a strong tide were endeavoring to attach pontoon cables with which the Thetis might be floated and dragged to shallower water, reported they heard faint tappings within the submarine. The Admiralty adamantly refused to disclose any of the messages that passed between the imprisoned men and the outside world.

The depth at low water was approximately half the length of the submarine, and at most she was not tilted more than 45 degrees after her stern had slipped back, though it was understood the bow was deeply embedded in the mud.

Up to 2 A. M. the vessel had been submerged for 36 hours 20 minutes. [It was said yesterday that the Thetis's air supply was sufficient for 36 hours.]

Tells of Loss of Hope

Shortly after midnight an official of Cammell Laird, builders of the submarine, told relatives of the entombed men that there was no more hope for them. Mrs. G. H. Bolus, wife of the commander of the Thetis, had spent many hours encouraging wives and relatives of her husband's men—gathered at the Cammell Laird offices at Birkenhead.

The Admiralty notified Mrs. Caroline Hole last night that her husband, a stoker aboard the Thetis, was believed to have lost his life while trying to escape. This was the first intimation that any men, other than the four saved, had attempted to leave the Thetis.

Captain H. P. K. Oram, Commander of the Fifth Submarine Flotilla, who was the first man out of the Thetis, is said to have described a dramatic conference among the entombed men. It was decided, Captain Oram is reported to have said, that one civilian be paired with a naval man experienced in the use of the Davis escape apparatus until all civilians had been evacuated, for in the darkness of the escape chamber of the ship it was impossible for an untrained civilian to get out unaided.

The provisional theory is that one of the civilians, possibly the one who accompanied Mr. Hole, got jammed in the escape hatch and thus effectively closed the only avenue of escape to those remaining in the submarine.

Salvage Expert at Scene

Thomas MacKenzie, salvage expert who raised vessels of the sunken German fleet at Scapa Flow, arrived at the Thetis during the night, and, according to a lifeboat man who had been aboard one of the rescuing ships, an attempt was to be made during the night to drag the Thetis with the aid of pontoons into shallower water. The lifeboat man said it was believed all in the Thetis were dead.

Divers failed to connect air pipes, he said, owing to the rush of the tide, and the idea of cutting a hole in the stern was abandoned when it was found the imprisoned men were unable to reach that part of the submarine which was out of the water. Two attempts to raise the stern high enough to make cutting a hole worth while also failed.

For many hours between the tides yesterday eighteen feet of the stern of the submarine were above water—she was standing almost vertically on her nose in 130 feet of water—but frantic efforts of the officers and crews of more than twenty Admiralty vessels on the scene failed to get another man out.

Before a strong tide around 4 P. M. yesterday washed the subma-

Continued on Page Three

907 Refugees Quit Cuba on Liner; Ship Reported Hovering Off Coast

Rumor That United States Will Permit Entry Is Spread to Avert Suicides—Company Orders St. Louis Back to Hamburg

By R. HART PHILLIPS
Wireless to THE NEW YORK TIMES.

HAVANA, June 2.—The liner St. Louis, carrying 907 Jewish refugees from Germany whom the Cuban Government refused to permit to land, left Havana Harbor at 11:30 this morning in compliance with a decree signed by President Federico Laredo Bru.

The St. Louis cleared for Hamburg, Germany, according to the Cuban customs authorities. Her distraught passengers hope she will remain somewhere in the waters of the Western Hemisphere while friends, relatives and Jewish relief associations negotiate for their admittance to some other country.

Luis Clasing, agent here for the Hamburg-American Line, refused to discuss the possibilities of a later agreement with the Cuban immigration authorities. He said the ship had left for Hamburg.

"Of course, it might go elsewhere first," he added. "However, we have nothing definite on this."

Nestor Pou, Consul of the Dominican Republic, stated tonight that he had transmitted to Señor Clasing an offer by his government to receive the refugees before the St. Louis sailed. He said the only requirement was the deposit of a bond of $500 for each of the refugees.

Señor Pou said he had notified Lawrence Berenson of the National Coordinating Committee of New York, who is here attempting to solve the situation of the refugees, no reply from either.

So far, he said, he had received reply from either.

President Juan D. Arosamena of Panama has granted special authorization to Dr. and Mrs. Julius Lewith, passengers aboard the St. Louis, to enter his country, it was announced tonight by Dr. Ventura de Llunde, a Havana attorney.

Dr. Lewith, who was a prominent surgeon in Vienna, already has obtained quota numbers for himself and his wife for entry into the United States, according to Dr. de Llunde, and it is planned to transfer them at the first port the St. Louis enters.

The Lewiths have two sons residing in New York.

Dr. de Llunde also said an appeal had been made to the President of Panama to admit all the refugees on the St. Louis, since all have suf-

Continued on Page Four

CITY FOOD MENACED BY STORAGE STRIKE

Perishables in 22 Warehouses Tied Up by Walkout Over 40-Hour Week Demand

The city's supply of perishable foodstuffs was imperiled yesterday by a strike of employes in twenty-two cold-storage warehouses here and in Jersey City. Sixty million pounds of meat, butter, eggs, cheese, poultry and fresh and frozen fruits and vegetables pass through the warehouses each week.

Efforts by Nathan Frankel, Mayor La Guardia's labor-relations secretary, to settle the walkout, which began at noon, had no immediate effect. The dispute grew out of a demand by the Inland Warehousemen's Union, Local 818, of the International Brotherhood of Teamsters, an A. F. of L. affiliate, for a reduction in weekly hours from forty-four to forty with no change in the weekly pay of $35.

Both sides agreed that the strike was 100 per cent effective among checkers, laborers and other warehouse employes. The tie-up was made doubly menacing by the refusal of truck drivers, members of the same international union, to take anything in or out of the plants while the strike continued.

"Tremendous" Loss Feared

Officers of the Cold Storage Warehousemen's Association of the Port of New York, representing employers, described the situation as "most serious" and predicted that if the strike were not settled at once chaotic conditions, accompanied by "tremendous losses" in food and in money, would be inevitable.

When reports that a walkout was impending reached the 2,000 commission merchants and hotel and restaurant supply dealers for whom the cold-storage plants hold food under a loan system, they began to remove as much food as they could haul away. But Alexander Moir, chairman of the association's labor committee, said the perishables removed in this manner could not last longer than Monday, when conditions would become acute.

"There will be a critical food shortage by Monday," Mr. Moir declared. "Not one single piece of food has moved out of any of the warehouses since noon."

Edwin C. Maguire, counsel for the union, said he believed a crisis in the food supply would not set in for at least five or six days, but that after that the situation would be grave unless a settlement had been effected.

The strike was expected to make itself felt most immediately in the servicing of restaurants at the World's Fair, where little refrigeration space for the storage of food beyond a single day's supply is available, and in the provisioning of outbound ocean liners, which

Continued on Page Sixteen

NAVY STARTS WORK ON 24 WAR VESSELS

Two 45,000-Ton Battleships Lead in Contract Awards Totaling $350,000,000

Special to THE NEW YORK TIMES.

WASHINGTON, June 2.—Less than two weeks after a bill appropriating funds for an enlarged fleet was signed by President Roosevelt, the navy awarded contracts today for 159,800 tons of fighting ships, costing about $350,000,000.

Plans had been made and bids invited while the bill was pending, and construction can start immediately on the twenty-four ships, twelve by private companies and twelve in navy yards. Comprising two battleships, four light cruisers, eight destroyers, seven submarines, one aircraft carrier and two seaplane tenders, they will bring the total combatant tonnage of the navy, in commission and under construction, to 1,784,690.

In addition the navy awarded contracts aggregating $5,430,576 for propelling machinery for submarines.

The 45,000-ton battleships, the largest and most powerful ever designed, will cost $80,000,000 to $85,000,000 each and will be armed with 16-inch guns, according to Charles Edison, Acting Secretary.

In the main batteries these guns will number nine, three to a turret. Each battleship is expected to require 2,000 officers and men, and will have a top speed of more than twenty-eight knots, or better than five knots above that of the fifteen capital ships now in the line.

Submarines of Squalus Type

Six of the seven submarines in important respects will be like the Squalus, which sank last week off Portsmouth, N. H., indicating that the navy still has faith in this type.

Three submarines of 1,475 tons each were awarded to private shipyards, while three others of that size and one of 700 tons were allocated to navy yards.

Two 800-ton submarines of a new type, authorized in the 1939 Naval Bill, will be contracted for at a later date, probably within a month.

The four cruisers, assigned to private yards, are of a new type. Each will displace 6,000 tons and in speed will be among the fastest cruisers ever built.

The new battleships, now known as Nos. 61 and 62, will be built at the New York and Philadelphia Navy Yards, where materials are being assembled.

The first two of the authorized six 35,000-ton battleships, the North Carolina and the Washington, are on the ways at the New York and Philadelphia yards respectively, while three of the others went to private yards. In some quarters this was interpreted to mean that at least two 45,000-ton ships would be requested of Congress next year

Continued on Page Five

LOSS OF 86 LIVES IN THETIS FEARED

Continued From Page One

rine below the surface, an unsuccessful effort was made to cut a hole through the stern. The would-be rescuers had further failures when they attempted to lift the submarine bodily by pontoons or at least to keep the stern above water while a hole for escape was cut.

British naval reticence has prevented any authentic statement from reaching the public from the men saved, but it is believed the submarine, which was completing acceptance trials, either struck a submerged wreck during a prolonged dive, damaging and flooding forward compartments, or that there was some failure of the machinery in the forward torpedo tubes.

Newspaper men aboard the tug Troon reported that when nearing the scene of the disaster, off Great Orme's Head, their vessel "scraped over something," and Captain Alfred Lamey shouted to one of the Admiralty vessels: "We have struck a submerged object." It was suggested that that obstruction had disabled the Thetis.

The four men saved by the Davis escape "lung" are Captain Oram, Lieutenant F. G. Woods, and W. C. Arnold, stoker, both of the Thetis, and F. Shaw, a mechanic employed by Cammell Laird.

Mr. Shaw is said to have told one of his rescuers that two men tried to escape through one of the hatches and were drowned, while "another went mad and died."

"When I left," he is quoted, "the air was getting worse. The men were sprawled about in the compartments, but there was no panic. It was dark, and in a few more minutes I would have been too weak to escape.

"At first the men did not complain. I could hear them moving about and talking about sports. There is little hope of the others coming out alive."

Apparently one of the men to whom Mr. Shaw referred was the stoker, W. T. Hole, mentioned by the Admiralty in a message to his wife.

At 12:35 P. M. yesterday a flotilla of tribal class destroyers, equipped with latest anti-submarine devices, dashed up after an all-night forced-draft drive from Portland. Then it was decided to attempt to cut a hole in the stern.

Men with oxyacetylene cylinders and torches were put in rowboats and clambered upon the Thetis's stern. There flashed blue flame, and sparks cascaded into the brown water of the bay. Anxiously, thousands of men thronging the decks of the surrounding fleet watched these acetylene experts racing against time. They lost—beaten by the rushing tide.

One surging swell caught the Thetis in its grasp, and as the torch-wielders jumped to safety the wave rolled the submarine like a great fish beneath the surface.

The tide would not fall again until 6 P. M. There was still time to save the men, for it was calculated that even in the confined space there would be sufficient air to last them beyond last midnight. Cables were passed under the hull of the sunken craft and attached to huge pontoons, in the hope that the stern could be prevented from sinking deeper.

Divers at the Scene

But the air supply was the problem. There was no authentic information that divers—there were many on the scene—had been able to attach air pipes to emergency valves ringed with white circles on the hull.

The rescue squads seemed baffled at every turn. There were reports that cables attached to the pontoons snapped under the enormous strain. And then, as the tide receded at 6 P. M., the stern did not reappear as had been expected. The pontoons had failed to hold it, and the Admiralty sent out a grave message that hope of saving any more lives was diminishing.

However, more and heavier pontoons had arrived, and the warship crews worked desperately to get them to function.

Soon after dawn yesterday, when the tide was falling, the destroyer

Times Wide World Cablephoto

AT THE SCENE OF THE BRITISH SUBMARINE DISASTER EARLY YESTERDAY
Three boats from Admiralty warships gathered near the uptilted stern of the ill-fated Thetis before it disappeared under water later in day

Brazen, which with twenty-one other vessels had maintained a ceaseless all-night search, sighted an object protruding from the water about sixteen miles northwest of Great Orme's Head. Racing up, the officers saw that it was the stern of the submarine, jutting up almost vertically.

Her nose, perhaps shattered by some submerged wreck—there are many such relics of the submarine campaign of the World War in Liverpool Bay—was buried on the bottom. The water is about 130 feet deep there at high tide. As soon as the tide fell more and more of the submarine's hull became exposed, until eighteen feet of the tail was out of the water.

In a few moments boats manned by the Brazen's crew were alongside, and officers, tapping messages in Morse code on the submarine's side, were cheered when a reply from inside told that all the Thetis men were alive.

Immediately news was flashed to the Cammell Laird offices at Birkenhead, where, in a large waiting room, wives and relatives of many of the imprisoned men were keeping a strained vigil. Many, overcome, burst into tears at the report, which all too soon was taken to mean that safety was at hand.

Back over the waters of Liverpool Bay the Brazen was calling for assistance. Just as other vessels were closing around her, the heads of Captain Oram and Lieutenant Woods, encased in their Davis escape apparatus, bobbed above the surface. They had waited until they knew for certain that the Thetis had been located, and then, either by order or through drawing of lots, had made their way through the escape chamber amidships of the submarine to report the position, and assist in the direction of the rescue of their fellows. It was learned afterward that the forward escape chamber had been flooded.

A few minutes later, at 9:40 A. M. yesterday, Stoker Arnold, who had been in a similar accident off Malta, in the Mediterranean, when he was imprisoned in a submarine for thirty-six hours, and Mr. Shaw came to the surface.

The Brazen's crew then gazed anxiously into the water for others to appear.

All four of the rescued men were suffering badly even at that hour—

twenty hours after the diving of the submarine—from carbon dioxide poisoning, but they told how all the crew were still alive, though some of the older men were in dire straits.

There was a long wait. It was then 10 A. M. yesterday. Something must have gone wrong with the escape chamber.

Only those officers exchanging hammer signals with the entombed men knew what was really amiss.

It was announced that many more submarine experts were aboard the Thetis than was at first thought, among them Lieut. Comdr. R. N. Garnett, commanding the sister submarine Taku; Lieut. Comdr. T. C. C. Lloyd, commander of the sister submarine Trident, and Lieutenant P. E. J. Ryan and Lieutenant Engineer A. G. Jamison, also of the Trident.

In addition to the Thetis's commissioned crew of fifty-eight, there were twenty-six officials and workers from Cammell Laird, three armament experts from Vickers-Armstrongs, makers of gun equipment; two caterers and a Liverpool pilot.

Relatives Told of No Hope

BIRKENHEAD, England, Saturday, June 3 (P).—Sydney Woodward, secretary of Cammell Laird, builders of the submarine Thetis, brokenly told a crowd of the shipyards here early today:

"I am sorry, but there is no hope for the ninety men remaining in the submarine."

Women in the crowd of nearly 1,000 wept as he spoke. Many were wives or relatives, and some had been standing in the shipyards for nearly twenty-four of the thirty-four hours that had elapsed since the submarine became disabled in diving in Liverpool Bay, which is part of the Irish Sea.

The crowd was clustered around the gates of the Cammell Laird shipyard. Hundreds blocked the highway outside the gates of the plant.

Four of those who were in the vessel were saved through use of the Davis "lung" apparatus. Three others were said by a lifeboat crew to have perished in an attempt to follow the four to the surface.

The wife of Frank Shaw, one of the four who escaped from the submarine, said today her husband was

"dazed" and that after expressing deep concern for the safety of those left aboard he received a sleeping draught and was put to bed.

Mr. Shaw was suffering from shock and was under a doctor's care. He seemed "obviously shaken and somewhat unnerved," said a naval man who brought him ashore.

When he met his wife on the dock he embraced her warmly and talked briefly before being taken home. He praised Stoker W. C. Arnold for assisting him as they rose to the surface by the Davis lung apparatus, Mrs. Shaw said, but he did not give details.

Those on shore yesterday could guess fairly accurately why the rescue efforts were failing—they could see the tide and the deepening darkness. They were told that the British Navy had no such rescue chamber as had saved thirty-three from the sunken United States submarine Squalus off Portsmouth, N. H., last week.

But no one had any clear-cut idea of just what happened Thursday afternoon, when the shiny Thetis, a striking token of Britain's rearmament in a warlike world, became disabled in her diving test.

All that was permitted to seep from the official wall of secrecy was that the four rescued men had said their companions expected to follow them upward in the escape apparatus.

The shipyard was tense when Mr. Woodward, shortly after midnight, made his statement that hope had been given up. A crowd swarmed about him at the timekeeper's office when he appeared. It was there that many of the civilian workers and technicians who went down in the Thetis had often drawn their weekly pay.

"I must announce that the experiment of raising the Thetis's stern has not been successful," he began. Then he declared that there was no hope.

"The best thing you can do is to disperse and go home quietly," he concluded.

There was a minute or two of silence. Some one yelled:

"Where are your experts?"

But he was silenced by those around him.

Lifeboat Crew Tells of Its Helplessness During a Long Wait at Disaster Scene

By The Associated Press.

BIRKENHEAD, England, Saturday, June 3.—Members of a North Wales lifeboat crew that visited the chill, search-lighted scene of the submarine Thetis's sinking returned early today with the story that three occupants of the Thetis had perished in attempting to follow to the surface the only four survivors.

Their narrative suggested that others had died in desperately trying to save themselves with the Davis "lung" apparatus. The lifeboat men said that never before had they seen such a heart-rending drama.

"We have never felt so helpless," said one who often had participated in rescues in turbulent seas.

Early last evening they went to the scene, carrying doctors in their lifeboat—for hope had flamed in the afternoon, when a part of the Thetis's stern was visible.

"We were there for more than four and a half hours, and waited patiently, hoping some more would be able to get away from her," said Robin Williams, coxswain of the lifeboat. "She did not reappear at low tide. The strong tide had dislodged her from the mud bank in which she apparently stuck nose down, and the tide hitting against the stern pushed her down to the bed of the sea.

"There were rescue vessels of all kinds around. Divers and admirals. As time went on the chances of rescue became more and more slender. We could do nothing, of course, and when we came away no more had left the submarine."

"All the News That's Fit to Print."

The New York Times.

Copyright, 1939, by The New York Times Company.

LATE CITY EDITION
Cloudy today, little change in temperature. Tomorrow fair, temperature unchanged.
Temperatures Yesterday—Max., 20; Min., 12

VOL. LXXXIX...No. 29,923. Entered as Second-Class Matter, Postoffice, New York, N. Y. NEW YORK, THURSDAY, DECEMBER 28, 1939. P THREE CENTS NEW YORK CITY and Vicinity | FOUR CENTS Elsewhere Except in 7th and 8th Postal Zones.

FINNS AGAIN CROSS BORDER, IMPERIL RUSSIAN RAILROAD; SOVIET CALLS MORE TROOPS

6,000 DIE IN TURKEY AS QUAKES ARE FELT AROUND THE WORLD

Successive Shocks Take Heavy Toll in Life and Property in Anatolian Regions

LOS ANGELES AREA SHAKEN

Central America Is Affected—London Seismograph Broken by Severity of Tremors

Wireless to THE NEW YORK TIMES.

ANKARA, Turkey, Dec. 27—Fresh shocks added tonight to the terror and destruction in the regions of Eastern and Northern Anatolia, where seven earthquake shocks in quick succession today took a heavy toll of life and property.

Unofficial reports place the death total so far at more than 6,000, but disrupted communications prevented exact estimates. From a number of towns no news has reached the Turkish capital since the earthquakes.

[According to an Associated Press dispatch from Ankara more than 8,000 were killed in the earthquakes in Northern Anatolia.]

Latest reports from the earthquake district say that Erzingan, a city with a population of 25,000, has been completely destroyed. Three hundred are said to have perished there, but it is feared that the final figure will be bigger.

The shocks were particularly severe in the districts of Erzingan and Kemakh, where it is known that the death toll is 122, with more than 150 injured. Nearly every town and village in these districts is a pile of ruins.

Late tonight it was reported that fresh quakes, accompanied by subterranean rumblings, occurred.

Many terrified people fled from their shattered homes to the comparative safety of open fields. With nerves strained to the breaking point by each new tremor, their condition is desperate. They are facing intense cold and blizzards, with tents as their only protection. Relief parties with medical aid, food and other supplies have left for the scene, and the Turkish Minister of the Interior is personally directing operations.

Mosques' minarets, public buildings and houses alike toppled and crashed when the first shocks were felt at an early hour. Seven shocks came intermittently between 2 and 5 A. M. [7 and 10 P. M., New York time Tuesday].

Towns in several eastern departments were partly destroyed and whole villages were laid in ruins.

Army Patrols Search Ruins

ANKARA, Turkey, Thursday, Dec. 28 (AP)—Thousands of fearful Anatolians camped last night in open fields, numbed by icy winds, while Turkish Army patrols and fire brigades searched the smoking ruins of towns and villages for the bodies of hundreds believed to have perished in a catastrophic earthquake.

Most water mains, railway tracks and viaducts were put out of commission.

Although broken communications prevented a complete appraisal of the loss of life and damage, officials said such information as they had indicated a major catastrophe had taken place.

Heavy damage was reported at Samsun, a Black Sea port of 33,000 population; Sivas, an inland city of 34,000; Ordu, Tokat, Amasia, Yozgad and other places.

Apparently centering in Anatolia along the Black Sea coast, the severe shocks were felt between 2 A. M. and 5 A. M.

Aid was dispatched by the government and other agencies to the stricken zone, 100 to 250 miles east and northeast of this capital.

Although the force of the quake indicated serious damage had been done, observers pointed out that the loss of life might not prove comparatively great because of the light construction of dwellings and the rush of residents to flee to the open country.

Quake Felt in California

Special to THE NEW YORK TIMES.

LOS ANGELES, Dec. 27—Accompanied by an ominous deep-throated subterranean rumbling, a sustained earth shock of minor intensity jolted Los Angeles and near-by cities just before noon today.

No one was injured and property damage was almost negligible.

The earthquake, beginning in Los Angeles at 11:29 [2:29 P. M. New York time], swayed downtown buildings for from 10 to 45 seconds. Most observers described it as a sharp jolt, followed by a rotary movement, and terminated with two lighter shocks.

The epicenter was estimated by the Carnegie Seismological Laboratory in Pasadena as "about forty or fifty miles from Los Angeles" and

Continued on Page Six

When you Think of Writing Think of Whiting.—Advt.

Serious Crimes Increased In 316 Cities This Year

Special to THE NEW YORK TIMES.

WASHINGTON, Dec. 27—Increases in the first eleven months this year in the crimes of murder, rape, aggravated assault, burglary and larceny are shown in police reports received by the Department of Justice. Murders increased 4.6 per cent; rapes 5.9 per cent; aggravated assaults 1.8 per cent; burglary 3.3 per cent, and larceny by 6 per cent, according to reports from 316 cities of more than 25,000 population.

Decreases were shown in negligent manslaughter, 11.8 per cent; robberies, 3.8 per cent; and automobile thefts, 5.2 per cent.

November figures showed similar trends in a more pronounced form.

BANKHEAD OPPOSES REDUCING FARM AID

Senator Asks Roosevelt for Exception in Budget Cuts—O'Mahoney Pleads for West

By TURNER CATLEDGE
Special to THE NEW YORK TIMES.

WASHINGTON, Dec. 27—President Roosevelt received today a foretaste of Congressional resistance to drastic curtailment of some Federal expenditures as reports of budgetary reductions, which he is expected to send to the Capitol next week, increased on every hand.

In response to published rumors of slashes already made in budget estimates, Senator Bankhead of Alabama called upon the President to insist that he maintain parity payments to farmers. Senator O'Mahoney of Wyoming made just as urgent a plea opposing a reduction in expenditures for the reclamation service.

Reports were that the new budget would contain no specific estimate for parity payments and that the amount for reclamation, now aggregating close to $50,000,000 annually, would be cut nearly in half.

Neither Senator appeared to be encouraged so far as the budget for 1940-41 was concerned. Senator Bankhead tacitly confirmed the rumor that no recommendation would be included for parity payments which, although unbudgeted at the outset, were provided by Congress to the extent of $225,000,000 for 1939-40. The Senator insisted, however, that the President did not intend abandoning the principle of parity payments.

Says Parity Plan Will Stay

"As a result of our discussion I am in a position to say that there is no thought or intention of abandoning the principle of parity payments," Senator Bankhead said. "At this time it is not sufficiently known what money, if any, will be needed to carry out that principle because we don't know what the farm prices will be."

He recalled that when Congress appropriated $225,000,000 last Spring, disregarding the demand of President Roosevelt that new taxes be levied to cover it, it was after several months of the session had elapsed.

"It is the view of the Administration that because of war conditions it will not definitely be known what the prices of farm commodities will be and it may be that we won't need any new appropriation," he added.

He said that current prices of wheat were nearly three-fourths of parity and that cotton, selling at around 10 cents a pound, was within similar striking distance of the basic price. He noted like improvements in the prices of tobacco and rice.

Bankhead Is Silent on Issue

Replying to inquiries as to what he thought of the President's suggestion that Congress provide $550,000,000 in additional revenue to make up for the amounts which it voted for farm benefits in excess of budget estimates in the last two years, Mr. Bankhead said:

"I don't want to go into that because I am concerned primarily with the principle of parity payments which I sponsored in the Agricultural Adjustment Act of 1938.

"I would not, of course, want to take issue in a statement of fact with the President. I have always been in favor of passing taxes in the equivalent of any reasonable bill the Administration would recommend. However, I have not felt it was necessary because you don't need new taxes every time you increase the army and navy or other things."

In his budget message the President is expected to put before Congress three choices: First, to cut expenditures in unemployment relief, farm aid, rivers and harbors and flood control works and highways; second, to raise the necessary taxes; or, third, to raise the public debt limit, now fixed at $45,000,000,000, so that the Treasury could continue its deficit borrowing.

The debt will be pushing $45,000,000,000 early in the new fiscal year—it is now around $42,000,000,000—unless Congress takes one of the

Continued on Page Fifteen

COLD OF 11.9° HERE SETS WINTER LOW; NO CHANGE TODAY

Quarter of Inch of Snow Falls as a Biting Wind Adds to Discomfort in the City

4 FATALITIES IN JERSEY

Four Inches of Snow Reported in Parts of State—Storms Throughout the East

A biting northerly wind, driving gray, snow-laden clouds before it, brought to New York yesterday its coldest day of the Winter. Shortly before 10 A. M. the mercury dropped to 11.9 degrees above zero, and in the early afternoon snow flurries deposited about a quarter inch of dry, powdery snow throughout the metropolitan area.

The Northern States, east of the Rocky Mountains, felt a serious bite of Winter, according to The Associated Press. Several inches of snow fell in Pennsylvania, Ohio, New Jersey and other Eastern States, and snow and rains in the central and southern districts of the great plains area caused a "marked improvement" in drought conditions there, according to the Weather Bureau.

The mercury, which stood at 20 at midnight Tuesday in the city, began to fall during the early morning hours. By mid-morning it had reached its lowest point, 17 degrees below the normal for the date. Through the middle of the day it hovered in the low 'teens, but rose gradually toward nightfall, reaching 17 degrees at 6 P. M.

Drop Is Forecast

The lowest temperature recorded on any Dec. 27 in the city was 6 above in 1872, and the highest was 59 in 1936. The Weather Bureau expected temperatures possibly as low as 10 degrees above during the night, with little change in temperature during the day today, and cloudy weather.

The hourly temperature readings yesterday were:

Midnight	20	2 P. M.	12
1 A. M.	20	3 P. M.	14
2 A. M.	19	4 P. M.	15
3 A. M.	18	5 P. M.	17
4 A. M.	17	6 P. M.	17
5 A. M.	15	7 P. M.	17
6 A. M.	15	8 P. M.	17
7 A. M.	14	9 P. M.	17
8 A. M.	14	10 P. M.	17
9 A. M.	14	11 P. M.	*15
9:45 A. M.	11.9	Midnight	*15
10 A. M.	12	1 A. M.	*15
11 A. M.	13	2 A. M.	*14
Noon	14	3 A. M.	*14
1 P. M.	15		

*Unofficial, at Times Square.

For three-quarters of an hour from 2 P. M. snow flurries driven by a wind of four to eighteen miles an hour velocity swirled about the city. The Department of Sanitation found it necessary to put only forty machine sweepers on the bridges and the West Side Elevated Highway to clear away the snow before it turned to ice. The force was withdrawn about 6 o'clock, and only a stand-by crew was kept ready during the night, according to William J. Powell, Deputy Commissioner of Sanitation.

Rail transportation in and out of the city was not interrupted, and motor roads to up-State and New England points were clear. La Guardia Field was open to traffic all day, but flights to and from Washington, D. C., Pittsburgh and other Pennsylvania points were canceled owing to snow and poor visibility there. Planes from the West made emergency stops for

Continued on Page Twenty-three

'Red Tape' in Tax Reports Scored by Small Business

By The Associated Press.

BUFFALO, Dec. 27—One of "the biggest problems facing small business in the United States is the cost of preparing government tax reports," the Junior Chamber of Commerce stated today.

Roswell P. Rosengren, co-chairman of a committee which conducted a nation-wide survey on small business, said the report urged that the government eliminate red tape in reporting taxes. He went on:

"Whenever volume of business suddenly increases [holiday trade] there is no similar increase in net profits because the cost of preparing tax reports eats up excess profits."

NEGRO MAGISTRATE WILL BE PROMOTED

La Guardia to Name Paige to Special Sessions Jan. 1 to Succeed Voorhees

Mayor La Guardia announced yesterday that Myles A. Paige, New York's first Negro Magistrate, would be elevated to the Court of Special Sessions on Jan. 1, to become the first member of his race to sit in any part of Special Sessions in the city.

Magistrate Paige will succeed Justice A. V. B. Voorhees, who will retire when his term ends with the close of the year. The appointment will be for the regular term of ten years, and as Special Sessions justice Mr. Paige will receive an increase in salary of from $10,000 to $12,000 annually.

Mr. Paige, who starred at end for the Howard University eleven in 1920 and later worked as a Pullman porter while studying law at Columbia, has served as magistrate since his appointment by Mayor La Guardia in September, 1936. He is 41 years old, is married and has two children. He was admitted to the New York bar in 1925 and at one time was a deputy attorney general, in charge of the Workmen's Compensation Division.

Praised by Justice Bayes

Chief Justice William R. Bayes of the Court of Special Sessions, when asked to comment on the Mayor's announcement, indicated that he had had no previous knowledge that Magistrate Paige would receive the appointment. He made the following statement:

"Speaking for myself, Magistrate Myles A. Paige has sat here for brief assignments on several occasions, and I have a very high opinion of him. He has a very fine character and has fine ability. He will make an excellent judge. Should the Mayor appoint him, we will welcome him to this bench."

Although the first Negro justice, Mr. Paige will not be the first of his race to be active in the court, for Mrs. Eunice H. Carter, Negro lawyer, whom District Attorney Dewey appointed an Assistant District Attorney, is assigned to prosecutions in Special Sessions.

The Mayor made his announcement during an address of welcome to the Omega Psi Phi fraternity at the opening of its twenty-eighth annual conclave in the Harlem Branch of the Young Men's Christian Association, 180 West 135th Street. The opening of the four-day meeting was attended by 150 delegates from thirty-seven States. The organization has a membership of 7,500 Negro college men and 122 chapters.

Introduced by Richard E. Carey,

Continued on Page Fourteen

Drs. Buttrick and Adler Call on President; Two Peace Leaders See 'All in Agreement'

Special to THE NEW YORK TIMES.

WASHINGTON, Dec. 27—Means of restoring peace to the world were discussed today at the White House by President Roosevelt and leaders of the Protestant and Jewish faiths, who said afterward that "We are all in agreement."

Dr. George A. Buttrick, president of the Federal Council of the Churches of Christ in America, and Dr. Cyrus Adler, president of the Jewish Theological Seminary of America, called at the White House on the invitation of the President. The invitation was issued Saturday coincident with Mr. Roosevelt's announcement of a decision to send Myron C. Taylor to the Vatican as his personal representative "in order that our parallel endeavors for peace and the alleviation of suffering may be assisted."

"We discussed, in general, the issues obviously involved," Dr. Buttrick said as he and Dr. Adler left the White House after a long conference. "Beyond that we much prefer that the President issue any statement regarding the exact nature of our conference with him."

"We are all in agreement," Dr. Adler stated. "We are on call for further conferences."

In inviting the religious leaders to come to Washington, President Roosevelt expressed the wish that they would visit him "from time to time," and the clear indication which they gave after today's meeting that they would return was taken as further evidence that the Chief Executive does not plan a peace effort at this time.

Special to THE NEW YORK TIMES.

ATLANTA, Ga., Dec. 27—"American Baptists oppose any possible combine of the United States Government with the Vatican," Dr. W. O. Lewis, general secretary of the Baptist World Alliance, declared here today.

Dr. Lewis, who was in Atlanta for conferences with Baptist leaders, made the statement in commenting upon President Roosevelt's appointment of Myron C. Taylor as "a special peace emissary to the Vatican."

Dr. Louie D. Newton, an Atlanta Baptist pastor, yesterday sent a letter to President Roosevelt asking for more information concerning the appointment.

"I agree with Dr. Newton that a representative of this government to the Pope would be a dangerous

Continued on Page Three

MAYOR ACTS TO END CITY CHECK CASHING AT USURIOUS RATES

Denounces System Whereby Stores Get as Much as 25% of Election Workers' Pay

ISSUE UP TO PORTFOLIO

La Guardia Asks Him to Hold Up Assigned Vouchers to Curb 'Vicious Practice'

Denouncing the practice of discounting city employes' pay checks by as much as 25 per cent as an attempt to evade the usury laws of the State, Mayor La Guardia directed yesterday that payment by the city be refused on all checks that showed such assignments.

The Mayor based his action on a report from City Treasurer Almerindo Portfolio showing that assignments had been made by 1,199 election officials who earned $40 each in the last election. In a large number of cases, the workers could get their checks cashed only by assigning $4 of the $40 to the storekeepers who cashed the checks. In return the employes got orders for $4 in merchandise, but were required to spend an additional $6 in the discounters' stores before receiving the remainder of their checks in cash.

Mayor Writes to Portfolio

In a letter to Mr. Portfolio the Mayor said:

"It would appear from the statement of the attorney of one of the assignees that the assignee seeking payment can account for only 50 per cent of these $4 orders as actually having been exchanged for goods. It would appear that the system is so organized as to require each to spend at least $6 for goods in these stores. Therefore, some of the election officials actually spent $10 for which they received merchandise, while others spent $6 for merchandise and paid $4 for which they received no value.

"Then there is another set of assignments which you disclosed to me, where the $4 was deducted with no pretense that it was exchangeable for merchandise. This whole transaction savors of usury to me and surely is contrary to the banking laws of this State. I have long since adopted the policy of protecting city employes from loan sharks and usurers."

The Mayor pointed out that it was usually thirty days after the election before the officials received their compensation. To obtain the cash quickly, he said, the workers made their assignments immediately after the election.

Mayor Suggests a Test

"In order to test the validity of this action," the Mayor told Mr. Portfolio, "you are authorized to withhold delivery of these checks on any of the assignments. In the event that the assignee is willing to withdraw any of these assignments, you will then arrange for the payment in cash to the officials at any office of the City of New York nearest their homes. In this manner the validity of the assignments can easily be determined. The money is in the city treasury. No one stands any risk of losing a just payment. Perhaps we can put an end to this vicious practice."

After dispatching his letter to the City Treasurer, the Mayor said he would be most pleased if any of the assignees would sue the city for payment, adding that in such instances the city would enter the litigation on the side of its employe. The Mayor said the 1,199 election inspectors who had assigned part of their pay were among the 12,000 employed at the last election. With the $4 deduction alone, the Mayor said, the discount rate amounted to 120 per cent a year and 10 per cent for the thirty-day period. Employes who did not assign their earnings received their checks on Dec. 3.

Practice Is Not New

Mayor La Guardia said, sorrowfully, that the practice of discounting the pay checks of city employes was by no means new, and added that he thought the time had come to check it. He explained that his order forbidding payment on the assigned vouchers was in reality a means of inviting a suit against the city, in which he said the city would "interplead" with the hope of bringing all the facts into the open. Far from considering such transactions as being merely between the city employe and the assignee, the Mayor said he considered that a basic question of public policy was involved.

In a majority of cases, the Mayor said, the election officials took their pay vouchers to the storekeepers the day after election, made their assignments and fulfilled the conditions asked of them for the sake of getting some cash at once instead of waiting until Dec. 3 for their remuneration from the city. The law required the city to pay its election staff within thirty days after the date of the election.

Italian Press Says Soviet Forces Imperil Afghanistan, India, Iran

Newspapers Assert 700,000 Russian Troops Have Been Assembled—Britain Reported to Be Ready to Defend Khyber Pass

By The United Press.

ROME, Dec. 27—Italian newspapers reported today that Russia was massing 700,000 or more troops, Cossack cavalry and aviation along the frontier of Afghanistan, and that British, Afghan and Iranian forces also were being moved up to the border region.

Newspapers emphasized reports that Britons, Arabians and Iranians were rushing fortifications on the Persian Gulf and that Iran was sending reinforcements to the frontier with Russia.

The reported Russian-Afghanistan tension received prominence on the front pages of Italian newspapers, which told in detail of Afghan, Iranian and British Indian military preparations.

The newspaper Lavoro Fascista said that despite a formal denial by the Afghanistan Government that anything unusual was happening, soldiers had been sent to the Russian frontier while preparations were being made to organize all men capable of bearing arms.

"These measures are all the more opportune," Lavoro Fascista said, "in view of the news coming from the zones bordering Asiatic Russia, which is increasingly alarming.

"It is reliably reported that the Soviet has massed forty divisions of infantry on the Afghanistan border as well as strong units of Cossack cavalry and aviation. It is believed that motorized sections, which may form a part of this gigantic force, are being prepared and may be commanded, not by Russians, but by foreigners.

"It is believed that one can specify concerning this proposition that—to avoid the lack of success similar to that experienced by the Russians in Finland—these foreign of-

Continued on Page Three

The International Situation

East of Salla, where the Soviet border is nearest to the Russian railroad to Murmansk, the Finns were reported yesterday to have made their second crossing of the frontier. In the vicinity of Lieksa, where they had previously crossed, ski troops were said to be driving toward the railroad. While Russian aerial bombings continued, heavy fighting raged in Karelia. [Page 1.]

Britain's interest in Scandinavia, intensified by the Finnish hostilities, was evidenced by the signing of a war-trade treaty with Sweden. It is believed the British have made concessions to assure the Swedes' favor in whatever turn the war may take. [Page 1.] Moreover, the Allies are expected shortly to guarantee help to Sweden should Germany attack her because of open aid to the Finns. [Page 2.]

Italian newspapers implied Russia was planning a new adventure when they displayed reports that she was massing 700,000 troops on the border of Afghanistan. [Page 1.]

Patrol skirmishing continued on the Western Front, where the French were still busily reinforcing the Maginot Line. [Page 5.]

PIERCE SOVIET LINE

Second Wedge Driven Toward White Sea by Ski Raiders

FINNS REPULSED IN NORTH

Karelian Siege Continues, but Invaders Fail to Gain—Cities Are Bombed Again

By HAROLD DENNY
Wireless to THE NEW YORK TIMES.

HELSINKI, Finland, Dec. 27—Heavy fighting continued today on land, while in the air Soviet planes went on with their bombing offensive. According to Finnish official reports here tonight, the Red Army suffered further heavy losses of men and equipment, while their airplane attacks were ineffective in proportion to the efforts made.

The Russians are trying persistently to cross Lake Suvanto, and though in vain thus far are continuing the battle. The Finnish troops apparently are widening the salient they have driven into the Soviet lines north of Lake Ladoga, where on Christmas Day they crossed into Russian territory.

Tonight's communiqué reports that the Russians are falling back northeast of Lieksa toward their frontier in the direction of Rivivaara and the Finnish troops have advanced to Laklavaara, capturing seven tanks.

Cross Soviet Border Again

[Finnish troops crossed the border into Russia at a second point, it was reported from the region east of Salla, according to The Associated Press. At the first point, farther south in the vicinity of Lieksa, a picked ski battalion was reported to be driving toward the Murmansk Railway, a vital Soviet supply line. A Finnish general told The United Press that units had gone as far as Kandalaksha, fifty miles from the border.

[An eleven-word Moscow communiqué said "nothing important" had occurred on the fighting fronts. The Associated Press also reported that Russia had called more men to arms, presumably to provide large reinforcements in Finland.]

The Karelian Isthmus front, where recently some units of first-class Soviet troops have been found, in striking contrast with the nondescript cannon fodder the Finns had been mowing down heretofore, remains the scene of the most bitter conflict. The Russians continued to attack with great stubbornness and the Finns, conserving both men and ammunition and manoeuvring swiftly and surely through the rocky forests and frozen marshes that characterize that formidable front, have stopped one attack after another.

In one attack launched at noon yesterday north of Lake Hatjalahti, the Russians employed tanks and eight of these were destroyed, according to the Finnish communiqué tonight.

Tanks a Joke to Finns

Finnish officers and men, as I found on a visit to this front from which I have just returned, regard the Soviet tanks as a joke and take fierce delight in coming to grips with these monsters. Besides machine guns and anti-tank rifles, the Finns have a rough, home-made weapon that they find very effective. It is simply a mineral-water bottle half filled with gasoline, with a stick attached like a fuse.

The Finns hide in pits, over which the advancing tanks crawl. The moment the tanks pass, the Finns emerge, so close to the tanks that the latter's guns cannot open fire on them. The Finns then light the stick and hurl it at the tank. The bottle explodes and part of the blazing gasoline goes through openings in the tank, often igniting the monster's gasoline supply or exploding its munitions.

Soviet air activity today, though far less than had been expected after the punishment that Red Army planes inflicted on many cities and towns yesterday, was comprehensive enough, but again, so far as could be seen from fragmentary reports available here tonight, only civilian personnel and property were affected.

One civilian was killed and another wounded in another aerial bombardment of Tammerfors, chief

Continued on Page Two

Dear District Attorney Dewey: Those nightly laugh riots caused by "Morning's at Seven" at the Longacre Theatre call for an immediate investigation.—Advt.

ROME EAGER TO SEE POPE ON VISIT TODAY

Papal and Italian Flags Side by Side First Time Since 1870—King to Greet Pontiff

By CAMILLE M. CIANFARRA
By Telephone to THE NEW YORK TIMES.

ROME, Dec. 27—For the first time since 1870, when Italian troops captured Rome, thousands of Italian and Papal flags appeared in the streets today on the eve of Pope Pius's visit to King Victor Emmanuel. Wooden pillars decorated with the Italian and Papal colors were being erected with feverish haste late tonight along the itinerary from the Vatican to the Quirinal Palace.

In the Piazza Rusticucci, the small square marking the boundary between the Vatican and the Italian State, workmen were busy giving the finishing touches to the platform from which Prince Borghese, the Governor of Rome, will welcome the Pope on his arrival on Italian soil.

The meeting between the Pope and the King will take place at 10:30 A. M. It is clear from the details of the imposing ceremonial that nothing has been overlooked to give the greatest possible solemnity to what the press today calls "a historical event."

Identity of Views Stressed

Editorials stress how the church and Italy, though for different reasons, hold identical views in regard to certain problems and how they "deeply feel the present European moment."

In an editorial written by the Papal Secretariat of State, the Vatican City newspaper Osservatore Romano points out that tomorrow's event proves how complete is the reconciliation between the church and the Italian State. The lesson to be drawn from this, it explains, is that any question, no matter how difficult, as undoubtedly the Roman question was, can be solved, provided there is genuine good-will on all sides. The editorial implies the present European conflicts could be solved if the parties involved were truly desirous of attaining peace.

The Pope will leave the Vatican shortly after 10 A. M. He will be accompanied by Gennaro Cardinal Granito Pignatelli di Belmonte, dean of the Sacred College; Federico Cardinal Tedeschini, the

Continued on Page Six

TRADE PACT SIGNED BY BRITAIN, SWEDEN

Favorable Terms Are Believed Made by London to Win Help Against Germany

Special Cable to THE NEW YORK TIMES.

LONDON, Dec. 27—The British Government announced today that Sweden and the United Kingdom had signed a war-trade agreement designed to adapt the existing British-Swedish trade agreement to wartime conditions.

The new agreement is the result of weeks of negotiation. At the start of the war Swedish officials complained of the slowness of the British contraband control and pointed out that this severely hampered Swedish trade. The main object of the conversations was to overcome or to minimize the inconveniences caused to Swedish shipping by the British blockade and to find some way of helping Swedish traders to continue their trade with Britain despite the high wartime insurance rates and fluctuations of British currency.

It is believed Britain agreed to speed the examination of cargoes going to or coming from Sweden.

It is understood here that these negotiations were prolonged because Britain tried to stabilize the exchange of the currencies of the two countries. British officials asked the Swedes to enter a trade agreement for the duration of the war on the basis of the present rate of exchange between the pound and the Swedish krona. The Swedes refused on the ground that the pound might fluctuate with the trends of the war.

No details of the final agreement on this point were given, however, when the official announcement on the new pact was made.

Joint Committee to Be Created

Under the terms of the agreement a joint British-Swedish standing committee will be set up. It will meet periodically in London or Stockholm.

The decision of the British Government to seize all German exports, a decision against which

Continued on Page Two

Dispatches from Europe and the Far East are subject to censorship.

A view of a street in the town of Sivas. At left is the headquarters of the Governor of the province which was destroyed by the earthquake.

Wide World Photos

6,000 DIE IN TURKEY IN SERIES OF QUAKES

Continued From Page One

of so slight a nature as to preclude "much damage."

Householders in Maywood, Lynwood, Long Beach and Anaheim reported that dishes clattered from shelves, pictures shimmied on the walls and clocks were stopped.

Scant seconds after the earthquake began a high-tension power line collapsed on an oil refinery in the Santa Fe Springs field. Almost immediately oil started burning. Damage was estimated at approximately $1,000.

In Long Beach, scene of extensive damage during the March 10, 1933, earthquake, in which more than 100 persons lost their lives, damage was negligible.

Except for cracks in several streetlighting standards the city escaped damage.

On Terminal Island in Los Angeles Harbor several tiles fell from the roof of the California Institute of Technology weather observation station.

The Sheriff's substation at Malibu Beach was swamped with calls from residents who reported a "weirdly deep roaring, like a bass-voiced foghorn" from the ocean.

The sound was attributed to the earthquake, because the visibility was excellent and no ships were in sight at the time, deputies reported.

Seismograph Out of Action
Wireless to THE NEW YORK TIMES.

LONDON, Dec. 27—J. J. Shaw, seismologist, of West Bromwich, said today that on his return home after a short vacation he found that the indicator of the earthquake alarm bell had fallen. On investigation he found that the seismograph had been put out of action by the severest shock recorded in his observatory in a number of years.

Two essential couplers for the seismograph had been thrown from their sockets and had left the recording pointers lying helplessly upon the recording surface.

Italian Instruments Damaged

FAENZA, Italy, Dec. 27 (UP)—Professor Rafaele Bendandi, seismologist, said today that his instruments had recorded a four-hour earthquake, one of the most severe in thirty years, which he placed in Armenia and Asia Minor.

The quake began about 1 A. M. [7 P. M. Tuesday, New York time], he said.

"The violence of the vibrations damaged all my instruments," Professor Bendandi added. "The effect must have been disastrous."

"Terrific Earthquake" Recorded

GENEVA, Dec. 27 (UP)—Scientists of the Neuchatel Observatory announced today their seismograph recorded a "terrific earthquake" which probably centered near the border of European and Asiatic Russia.

They said it was registered at 1:02 A. M. [7:02 P. M. Tuesday, New York time] and was the most violent in twenty years.

The Zurich observatory placed the center of the quake in the Tiflis region of Russia, between the Black and Caspian Seas.

Zurich and Neuchatel scientists agreed that the quake must have caused widespread damage and many deaths if centered in a populous district.

Twelve hours previously, Tuesday at 7 A. M., an earthquake shook the Pacific Coast of Nicaragua, at the opposite side of the world from the location estimated for the shock recorded at Neuchatel.

San Salvador Feels Quake

SAN SALVADOR, El Salvador, Dec. 27 (UP)—A fairly heavy earthquake shook San Salvador at 5:55 A. M. today [6:55 A. M., New York time], frightening inhabitants but causing no damage locally.

Whether the shock caused damage in the provinces is not yet known. The quake was the second for El Salvador within a few hours. Several provinces were shaken late yesterday but no casualties or damage were reported.

EARTHQUAKES REPORTED WITHIN THIRTY-SIX HOURS

Shocks were felt, beginning Tuesday morning, successively in Nicaragua, Turkey, El Salvador and Los Angeles. The tremors indicated for Turkey were followed hours later by others, the times of which were not given. Dates and times shown on the map are in terms of New York.

In Turkey severe quakes early yesterday morning and last night jarred the towns shown by black squares. Deaths ran into the thousands and damage was extensive.

The New York Times.

"All the News That's Fit to Print."

LATE CITY EDITION
Warmer today.
Temperatures Yesterday—Max., 25; Min., 16

VOL. XCI. No. 30,698.

Entered as Second-Class Matter,
Postoffice, New York, N. Y.

NEW YORK, TUESDAY, FEBRUARY 10, 1942.

Copyright, 1942, by The New York Times Company.

THREE CENTS NEW YORK CITY and Vicinity

HOUSE CUTS 'FRILLS,' PASSES OCD BILL WITHOUT ROLL-CALL

$100,000,000 Measure, Shorn of Funds for Art and Dancers, Is Sent to the Senate

FULL INQUIRY IS PROMISED

Critics Assured of Hearing, While Mrs. Roosevelt Offers to Testify

By C. P. TRUSSELL
Special to The New York Times.

WASHINGTON, Feb. 9—Still revolting against dancers' arts and other so-called frills as parts of the national civilian defense program, the House of Representatives today stood formally and finally behind the restrictions it imposed tentatively last Friday upon the use of the $100,000,000 it was appropriating for the OCD.

So decisive was the voice vote that retained in the money measure an amendment prohibiting expenditures for instructions in physical fitness by dancers, fan dancers, street or theater shows that no member was forced to go on the record. The revolt, the oral edict disclosed, had spread deeply into Administration strongholds.

Although both majority and minority leaders had summoned all absentees back to town for a threatened roll-call showdown, the roll was not called on this highly controverted issue. The House seemed much relieved.

Donald Duck Voted Out

However, the House went on record to reach beyond the OCD and the quarrel which has involved Mrs. Eleanor Roosevelt, assistant director of OCD; Miss Mayris Chaney, her dancer protégée, and Melvya Douglas, movie star, and condemned the Treasury Department for what it viewed as a "frill" or a "turbelow."

By a roll-call vote of 259 to 112, the House refused to reimburse the Treasury for the $80,000 it already has paid out for a movie cartoon, now showing to the public, in which Donald Duck capers to boost the morale of the war-time taxpayer.

The House battle was as heated as that which was suspended on Friday, through abrupt adjournment, supposedly for a week-end cooling-off period. The interval, instead, appeared to have been only a period of preparation for further battle.

Through the afternoon the chamber echoed with charge and counter charge, most of them of a highly personal character, and with freshly coined war cries such as "Billions for defense, but not one cent for frivolities" and "Not a buck for Donald Duck."

First Lady Criticized

Mrs. Roosevelt figured largely in the debate, directly and by somewhat pointed indirection. Repeatedly, however, she received high praise for patriotism and perseverance as well as criticism for her activities in the OCD.

At one point of the debate, only the back stage intercession of House leaders prevented the voting of a suggestion from the floor, by a Democrat and member of the Appropriations Committee, that she resign her assistant directorate of OCD "and take her friends with her."

However, the House was told by leaders who fought the restrictive amendments, that the action regarding OCD physical fitness and theatrical activities was "entirely meaningless." Not a dime of the $100,000,000 being appropriated, said Representative Woodrum of Virginia, could be used, any way, to pay Miss Chaney or Mr. Douglas.

Foes of frills in civilian defense refused to concede that the result was meaningless.

"The intention of the amendment," said Representative Leland M. Ford, of California, its sponsor, "was to establish a principle here to show that we are not in favor of that type of boondoggling, to see that in the future these funds were not spent for any such purposes."

This principle, he said, had been set Friday and confirmed today.

But, Representative Cannon, of Missouri, chairman of the Appropriations Committee, protested that the fight on OCD activities had been waged by giving emphasis to the appointment to high posts in the OCD of only a few persons.

"Five per cent of all shells," he

Continued on Page Thirteen

Gen. Pershing's Son In Army as Private

Francis Warren Pershing, only son of General John J. Pershing, Commander in Chief of the A. E. F. during the World War, has enlisted in the Army as a private, it was disclosed here yesterday at the Army Building, 39 Whitehall Street.

Private Pershing, who was a broker with offices in 120 Broadway, enlisted on Feb. 4 and requested that recruiting authorities give out no publicity. He is married and has a son, 1 year old.

Private Pershing was inducted at Fort Dix, N. J., and then was sent to his present station in a Citizens Military Training Camp at Fort Snelling, Minn., in 1926, he was named the "best first-year soldier" of 2,000 men.

KERN SCOLDS MAYOR AT OUSTER HEARING

His and Sayra's Suspension Stands, Morton's Is Lifted— La Guardia in Gentle Mood

Paul J. Kern, president of the Civil Service Commission, and Wallace S. Sayre, commission member, remained under suspension in removal proceedings yesterday after a ninety-minute public hearing in City Hall at which Mayor La Guardia absolved Ferdinand Q. Morton, third member of the three-man agency, of all charges against him.

Mr. Morton, a Negro, told the Mayor he was ill at home when the Civil Service Commission issued a statement last Thursday which Mayor La Guardia construed as an attack on Corporation Counsel William C. Chanler. He added that he had had nothing to do with the commission's decision to file action against Mr. Chanler in an effort to compel him to represent the commission in litigation over the retention of four employes of the City Register's office.

On the basis of that explanation, the Mayor lifted Mr. Morton's suspension and ordered him back to work.

Adopting a mild paternal tone toward the six-foot-two, 33-year-old official who has been his protégé for twelve years, Mayor La Guardia addressed Mr. Kern as "Paul" throughout the hearing. The Mayor's attitude was like that of a father who believed punishment was in order, but disliked the idea of administering it.

Mr. Kern, in contrast, was stiff-backed and more than once reproached the Mayor for surrounding himself with "fawning sycophants" in preference to old friends

Continued on Page Fifteen

BRITISH FALL BACK

Japanese Dive-Bombers and Big Guns Pound Singapore Defenders

TANKS LAND, TOKYO SAYS

British Fighter Planes Battle Invaders, Who Claim Airport and Tell of Fires on Island

By The Associated Press.

SINGAPORE, Tuesday, Feb. 10—Under extreme pressure by Japanese invasion forces, British troops have executed a further withdrawal on Singapore Island, it was announced officially last night.

A communiqué from British headquarters said the withdrawal had been forced yesterday afternoon under the weight of Japanese dive-bombing and artillery bombardment and the menace of infiltrating ground forces.

Thus the first invaders ever to set foot upon this outpost of empire in the 123 years of its existence widened the foothold they established on a ten-mile stretch of the northwestern part of the island late Sunday night and yesterday morning. The struggle surged through thick mangrove swamps and rubber plantations.

[Tokyo broadcasts reported that Japanese tank units had been landed on Singapore Island and that the important Tenga airdrome, ten miles northwest of Singapore City, had been captured.]

The latest blow to the British fortunes came after it had seemed that the defenders had absorbed the first shock and were in a good position.

British headquarters issued the following communiqué at 10 o'clock last night:

"Strong enemy attacks which have developed from the landing on the west coast have been supplemented by dive-bombing and machine-gunning from the air throughout the day and by heavy enemy artillery bombardment. As a result of this pressure and enemy infiltration there has been some further

Continued on Page Two

The War Summarized

TUESDAY, FEBRUARY 10, 1942

British forces fought bitterly yesterday on a ten-mile front in west Singapore Island to destroy the Japanese bridgehead that threatens the Japanese bridgehead on one of the most strategically vital positions in the world, but last night a withdrawal was acknowledged. A Tokyo broadcast said the Japanese had captured Tenga airdrome, ten miles northwest of Singapore City. All over the island British positions were assaulted by dive bombers. [1:3; map, P. 2.]

In the Netherlands Indies Japanese planes machine-gunned two airports near Batavia and streets of that city, but were driven away from the harbor area. There was some damage to grounded aircraft, but no bombs were dropped. On Borneo Japanese patrols were reported pushing southward toward Banjermasin, a port only 300 miles across the water from Surabaya. [1:7; maps, P. 4.]

From the Philippines General Douglas MacArthur reported repeated Japanese assaults in the past two days had been repulsed everywhere and that fire from the forts at the entrance to Manila Bay had silenced some Japanese batteries. [3:1.]

In Burma troops were still being held in check along the Salween River front. The one hundred and first aerial combat victory for the American volunteer fliers was reported. Japanese plane losses in three months were estimated to total 220. [4:1.]

Moscow reported Soviet troops had broken through extensive German land mine fields in the Donets Basin, brought heavy losses to the Germans before Sevastopol, taken eighteen more villages on the central front and entered the outskirts of besieged Rzhev. The Germans claimed to have fought their way back to the outskirts of Mozhaisk, fifty-seven miles west of Moscow. [10:1.]

In Libya the Axis advance had apparently halted, and the British sent out patrols southwest of El Gazala and fought an engagement twelve miles west of there. Alexandria was bombed for the first time in five months, and the British bombed the German naval base at Salamis, Greece. [5:1.]

United States relations with Vichy were under great strain because of reports that the Pétain regime had turned over shipping to the Germans to aid their African campaign and was considering similar aid to the Japanese in Indo-China. [1:4.]

In London the Ministry of Information announced a Pacific Council would meet there today, with Australia, Great Britain, the Netherlands and New Zealand represented. [6:3.]

In the Netherlands Indies Japanese planes machine-gunned two airports near Batavia and streets of that city, but were driven away from the harbor area.

In Washington President Roosevelt sent a $26,740,000,000 Army and Maritime Commission appropriation request to Congress [3:6] and nominated Admiral William Standley, former chief of naval operations, as Ambassador to Russia. [6:4.]

FOR WANT AD RESULTS Use The New York Times. It's easy to order your ad. Just telephone Lackawanna 4-1000.—Advt.

U. S. WARNS VICHY OF POSSIBLE BREAK

Learns War Materials Were Sent to Rommel, While Indo-China Bargains With Japan

By JAMES B. RESTON
Special to The New York Times.

WASHINGTON, Feb. 9—A crisis is impending in the relations between the United States and Vichy France. Increasing evidence of collaboration between the Vichy Government and the Axis has led the State Department to review, though not yet to reverse, its policy of limited cooperation with the administration of Marshal Henri Philippe Pétain, it was learned tonight.

The immediate cause of this crisis is a report that Marshal Pétain has allowed the Germans to use French ships to supply the Axis forces in Libya and that his representatives in Indo-China are now negotiating with the Japanese to turn over the French ships there for action against the United Nations in Malaysia.

The negotiations with the Japanese are now being carried on by Admiral Jean Decoux, Vichy's Governor General of French Indo-China, whose public statements recently have been exceedingly favorable to the Axis. These negotiations are already in an advanced stage, and there is reason for stating that the United States will make it clear that the transfer of these ships to the Japanese will be interpreted as an unfriendly act that may result in a completely new United States policy toward Vichy France.

Embassy Denies Knowledge

The French Embassy in Washington disclaimed any knowledge tonight of the transfer of French ships either to the Germans or to the Japanese, but Viscount Halifax, the British Ambassador, took an entirely different story to the State Department this evening.

The precise amount of merchant tonnage in Indo-China is not known, but it is described in reliable quarters here as considerable. In addition, one French cruiser and a number of smaller warships are said to be under Admiral Decoux's control.

Lord Halifax placed before Sumner Welles, Under-Secretary of State, detailed evidence that French ships carried French war materials from French North Africa to Field Marshal Erwin Rommel for the

Continued on Page Five

Survivors Tell How Spark Caused Normandie Disaster

A clear account of the fire that damaged the liner Normandie at her pier yesterday came from the lips of sooty and blistered survivors as doctors and nurses worked over them in city hospitals. Pieced together these brief accounts cover the start of the fire,

tell its quick spread, and how more than 2,000 men tried in vain to stop it; how, eventually, all reached the pier alive, though many were injured and one died later.

Charles T. Collins, 18 years old, of 63 DeSales Place in Brooklyn, an ironworker, brought into Roosevelt Hospital to be treated for burns on the head and on the right hand, said he saw the fire start.

"I was working on a chain gang," Collins said. "We had chains around some pillars and eased them down when they were cut through. Two men were operating an acetylene torch. About thirty or forty men were working in the room, and there were bales and bales of mattresses.

"A spark hit one of the bales, and the fire began. We yelled for the fire watch and Leroy Rose, who was in our chain, and I tried to beat out the fire with our hands. Rose's clothes caught fire, and I carried him out. The smoke and heat were terrific."

Charles Florence, 22, a seaman in the Coast Guard, whose home is at 107 Fane Court, Brooklyn, told

Continued on Page Eight

ALBANY HITS MAYOR ON CITY GUARD PLAN

Gen. Brown Tells La Guardia State Law Forbids 'Little Private Armies'

By WARREN MOSCOW
Special to The New York Times.

ALBANY, Feb. 9—The State Administration today publicly rebuked Mayor La Guardia for his announced intention of establishing a regiment of volunteers in New York City to be known as the City Guard. The Mayor made known his intention to set up the guard in a radio address on Sunday. In the same broadcast he said he would quit his post this week as Federal Director of the Office of Civilian Defense.

Adjt. Gen. Ames T. Brown sent to the Mayor a telegram, the text of which was made public here, in which he told Mr. La Guardia that the military law of the State bars the setting up of "little private armies" by municipalities. Further, he told the Mayor also that he had the power to accomplish the same and by different means, including "the power to organize an auxiliary police force as recommended by the United States Director of Civilian Defense."

Lehman Approval Sensed

This telegram was sent by Brig. Gen. Brown, but it is almost certain that it was sent with the full knowledge of the Governor, since it has been known for weeks that the conduct of civilian defense in New York City has been a source of worry to Mr. Lehman as well as to the State's legislative leaders.

This development may serve to bring to a head a move which has now been hanging fire for at least ten days, namely, an appeal to the President of the United States for a group put the question up to the former District Attorney directly and got his pledge that under no circumstances would he change his mind.

"In addition, the occasion will mark Mr. Dewey's first important public appearance since he concluded a nationally applauded program of cleansing New York of countless bands of public, official, labor and political racketeers."

CAPITAL OF INDIES HAS ITS FIRST RAID

Japanese Attack Two Airports and Center of City—Harbor Defense Repels Enemy

By F. TILLMAN DURDIN
By Telephone to The New York Times.

BATAVIA, Netherlands Indies, Tuesday, Feb. 10—Batavia, the capital of the Netherlands Indies, was attacked by Japanese planes yesterday for the first time. The attack was carried out by eight fighter planes that swept in at a low altitude and machine-gunned two airdromes in the suburbs of the capital. Military planes were damaged, and at one field two passenger planes were splattered with bullets. One enemy plane was shot down and another probably was destroyed.

Coming just after noon, the raid upset the normal trend of life in Batavia to a considerable extent. Batavia's citizens, warned by sirens that probably saw the most blood-curdling yet brought into action, carried gas masks as they trooped to shelters. A new precaution against bomb blasts was in evidence. This is a chunk of rubber that is held between the teeth to keep the mouth open. Attached to

Continued on Page Four

12-HOUR FIGHT VAIN

Water-Logged Vessel Is Turned Over by Tide After Disastrous Fire

HAD BEEN ABANDONED

Ship Was Being Fitted Out as a Navy Auxiliary—Smoke Haze Covers Midtown

A blaze attributed to the sparks from a workman's oxy-acetylene torch led at 2:35 o'clock this morning to the keeling over at her West Forty-eighth Street pier of the former superliner Normandie, recently taken over by the United States Government and renamed the U. S. S. Lafayette.

The fire broke out shortly after 2:30 yesterday afternoon and was believed under control before 5. During the interval at least 128 men—sailors, Coast Guardsmen and civilians—had been injured, and one of the civilians died in Roosevelt Hospital at 6:50 P. M.

Yet, shortly before 3 o'clock this morning, with the stricken giant lying on her side in fifty to sixty feet of water and mud, the flames leaped again—primarily from a point beyond the rear funnel. One of the fireboats that had loitered near by eased in, a stream of water under high pressure arched through the darkness, and within an hour the new blaze seemed quenched.

Although the original fire was largely restricted to the three upper decks, and did damage considered as slight considering the size of the ship, fighting it involved pouring aboard an enormous quantity of water. This led to the list, which had reached a safe 16 degrees by 10 P. M., according to naval officials under Rear Admiral Adolphus R. Andrews, Third District commandant.

Loudspeaker Blares Warning

But, somehow, things got worse from then on. At 12:30 A. M., the loudspeaker in Pier 88, where the 83,423-ton former queen of the French Line had disembarked thousands of passengers, began to blare ominously:

"Admiral Andrews has ordered all hands to leave the ship . . . The Admiral has ordered all hands to leave the ship . . . The Admiral has ordered all hands to abandon the Normandie . . ."

At 1 A. M., the Third Naval District issued a brief statement somewhat qualifying the announcement. It said:

"The Admiral has ordered all hands off the ship as a safety precaution. It does not mean that the ship has been abandoned [in the usual sense] or hope given up but no one can be certain what the reaction of the ship will be to the flood tide."

Meanwhile observers at the darkened pier saw seamen from the United States Naval Receiving Station at Pier 92, a few blocks north, standing by with small ropes at the shipside. A spokesman said these were for last-minute rescues of any one who might be stranded aboard. Two small gangway crashed as the ship's tilt slowly increased toward an estimated 25 degrees.

Tugboats Are Withdrawn

Tugboats that had been nosing the ship toward the vertical were withdrawn as the list increased. Admiral Andrews, in his car parked at the stringpiece just opposite the oblique perpendicular of the ship's famous upsearing bow, commanded tersely on the broadcast order:

"The men have been ordered to evacuate the ship by reason of a dangerous list."

Asked directly if he thought she might topple, he shook his head non-committally.

Then, a little past 2 this morning, the increasing sag was reflected in clattering sounds from the upper decks, as articles began to topple toward the deep-dipping rail.

Tense watchers gasped, hoping the bottom mud would retain its precarious grasp on the keel. But at 2:35, quietly, with very little

Continued on Page Seven

Dewey Planning to Run Again For Governor, Leaders Declare

Special to The New York Times.

ALBANY, Feb. 9—Reports reaching Republicans here is that Thomas E. Dewey has definitely stated to party leaders his intention of running for Governor again this year. Mr. Dewey disclosed his plans to a small group of party leaders in response to a question from them, it was reported.

The question came up as a result of rumors, without foundation, that Mr. Dewey was thinking of not making the race. Since the leaders of the State organization were committed to his candidacy, and would have to get another candidate if the rumors were true, a group put the question up to the former District Attorney directly and got his pledge that under no circumstances would he change his mind.

The publicity, bearing the imprint of the National Republican Club, has been mailed out in envelopes of the Republican State Committee and contains complimentary references to Mr. Dewey. Speaking of the dinner, one of the releases said:

"The extraordinary interest in this year's affair stems from the fact that Thomas E. Dewey, New York's former District Attorney who set a precedent in metropolitan politics by arranging to turn over his office to a nonpartisan successor, is the principal speaker.

AS FLAMES SWEPT THE ONE-TIME PRIDE OF THE FRENCH MERCHANT MARINE

Smoke pouring from the Normandie as firemen attempt to bring the blaze under control   The New York Times. All photographs passed by U. S. Navy.

NORMANDIE UPSETS AT PIER AFTER FIRE

Continued From Page One

disturbance or noise, as searchlights played upon the great hulk erratically, the once-beautiful ship slipped over on her port side.

There was nothing of the convulsion in the river that onlookers had predicted. It was rather a subsiding, the ultimate completion of the giant's appointed course. The three great funnels lay clear of the icy murk— their lower rims barely three feet from the surface.

The pier was not affected by the turning over of the $56,000,000 vessel, for whose great bulk it had been especially constructed seven years ago. The question of possible salvage arose at once, but there was no way of getting official Navy comment at 3 A. M. From an emotional if not a practical standpoint there was the comment of one naval officer who has been intimately associated with the liner in her new status.

He stood grimly on the stringpiece as the mournful searchlight beams wavered over the looming gray form.

"That's my ship," he said. "We'll float her again."

At 8:20 P. M., when searchlights had played on the tilted gray strakes of the ship, Mayor La Guardia emerged from a temporary office in Pier 88, where the Nor-

mandie had landed thousands of passengers, and announced briskly:

"The chief's got his fire out and now the naval people will watch the ship. It's very tender—see how she listed—and now the job is to pump the wa————and that's what we're doing."

Officials, agreeing on the cause of the blaze, indicated nevertheless that several questions remained unanswered. They planned to locate and interrogate the wielder of the acetylene torch, and they were also interested in how much time—reputedly eleven minutes—elapsed between the outbreak of fire and the summoning of outside aid.

There were 1,500 men aboard the former French luxury liner when the fire started, 300 Navy, 400 Coast Guard and 800 civilians. All were declared to have escaped.

At the height of the blaze the smoke was blown over midtown aeras leaving a haze as far away as Times Square.

When the flames were declared "in hand" at 7 P. M., Fire Chief Patrick J. Walsh said officially that the three upper decks of the listing 83,423-ton sea queen had been "practically burned away."

Later, Chief Walsh amended, "the damage is slight considering the magnitude of the fire and the size of the ship."

Loss Matter of Time

In discussing the damage, Lieutenant Ernest Lee Jahncke Jr., aide to Rear Admiral Adolphus R. Andrews, Third Naval District Commandant, said "the thing now-

adays is not how many million dollars, it's how many days are lost." Later Admiral Andrews declined to estimate the number of days lost on account of the catastrophe.

The fire produced the greatest gathering of emergency apparatus since the United States entered the war.

In addition to the regular fire and police apparatus that normally responds to five alarms, the fire led to the assemblage near Pier 88 of units of all the various first-aid organizations that have sprung into being with the war.

The result was an unprecedented mingling of uniformed men and women in the vicinity of Twelfth Avenue and Forty-ninth Street. They ranged from Admiral Andrews to earnest young women of the American Women's Voluntary Services.

They included Mayor La Guardia, in corduroy-collared raincoat, sloshing grimly over tangled hoselines with Chief Walsh, and scores of mufti-clad auxiliary fire wardens, identifiable only by their armbands.

All afternoon, at varying intervals, stretcher-bearers emerged from the smoke-choked pier shed. Most of the victims seemed conscious, but in great distress. The one who died was Frank Trentacosta, 36 years old, of 2389 Nostrand Avenue, Brooklyn.

While the spectacle of the gray-painted hulk, tilting to port, lured thousands to the area, including at least a handful who had been passengers aboard the ship during its routine five-day crossings, rumors that more men were trapped

aboard persisted.

These rumors were finally quashed after dark when an engineman in a Twelfth Avenue shop, nearly exhausted and heavily blanketed, explained why the trapping had not occurred.

He said that although the automatic bulkhead system that had made the Normandie one of the safest ships afloat had started to grate into operation with the setting off of the alarm, the scaffolding rigged throughout the vessel for government purposes had prevented its effectively dividing the ship into water-tight compartments.

Admiral Andrews said merely that the automatic bulkhead system was not in operation. At any rate, all men aboard were thus enabled to get to safety. Many of them clambered down precariously directly from the uprearing tip of the Normandie's famous flaring bow—the rakish tip that enabled her to stretch 1,029 feet overall, although her waterline length is a modest 981.4 feet.

They executed this manoeuvre with the aid of an 85-foot firemen's extension ladder. Based on the West Side Express highway, from which traffic was diverted, this ladder thinly but safely bridged the gap between the overhead thoroughfare and the bow of the liner.

The ceaseless smoke, which started from a stack of kapok-stuffed life preservers off the main lounge where the metal-cutter had been using his torch, drifted over midtown, and cast an eerie pall

over the bright sun.

Fireboats, pushing against the port side of the burning ship, poured endless gallons of water aboard, and as the list increased to 10, 12, 15 degrees, much of it cascaded back into the Hudson. At night, when the worst was over, this rush of water from the ship's side was a cascade artificially illuminated by swerving beams of searchlights.

Two emergency lights on the ship's bridge played feebly on the forepart of the ship while from the pier stronger lights picked out patches of the hulk.

While the smoke thickened over what was once a carefree sports deck, the terrific clatter of the pumps on the fire-fighting vehicles filled the air.

There was endless noise, and always more smoke, and the strained faces of men. There were trucks and ambulances jolting over writhing hose lines. There was the deepening drone of low-flying planes, and the sad huddle of empty lifeboats clustered beneath the port bow.

But over all loomed the gray side of the almost legendary ship. It was she who barely seven years ago on her maiden voyage had brought the wife of France's President, here on an official visit. It was she in whose brilliant salons the society of both hemispheres had dined and danced. It was she toward whom the masters of all ships looked as the glamour ship of the Atlantic. And now it was she, deglamourized by the war, burning and listing at her slip.

The ship lists to port from the weight of the water poured in by fire fighters

Last night fireboats and tugs worked by floodlight

Oddly enough, the fire, which at times showed in bursts of crimson at openings in the bridge, did little damage to the outer surfaces of the ship. But the gray paint of the aft and dummy funnel did yield. And as it cracked and blistered away, it revealed the black and red of the pre-war Normandie—the only touch of the ship that was, in a setting for which she never had been built.

Sabotage Ruled Out

With all Federal and local officials ruling out the possibility of sabotage, there was unanimity as to the cause of the fire.

It began in a large public room on the promenade deck, where a group of workmen were engaged in clearing the space for government purposes. One of the best witnesses was former Alderman Edward J. Sullivan of Greenwich Village, who was a visitor aboard as a friend of a carpet company official engaged in a contract job.

Mr. Sullivan, who said he was standing only a few yards from the spot that first showed flame, put it this way:

"It happened in the grand salon on the promenade deck. One of the men had an acetylene torch. He was cutting down some decorative steel work. Another fellow was holding a shield for the sparks—it was about two by three feet. In the background were stacked some bales of what appeared to be excelsior. The sparks were flying but they'd hit the shield and bounce back."

He said the steel being cut was about eight feet high, generally triangular with an ornamental spiral construction. Six similar pieces, to which lamps apparently originally had been affixed, already had been cut down, he said. A deep horizontal gash already had been cut into the piece being worked on. Then, although the workman had turned off the torch, a few of the sparks from the last shower in some way got beneath, over or around the shield.

Ablaze in 3 Minutes

"In a flash, one of the men yelled 'fire.' The flames started up the bales and in a flash had run right up the stack to the ceiling. In three minutes it was all ablaze."

A Navy lieutenant identified by Mr. Sullivan as Henry Wood, took charge. Mr. Sullivan advised, "Get your local fire department right away." He said men began trying to fight the fire with available apparatus, but "I didn't see any hose." Like every one else aboard, he soon heard a hoarse voice repeating over the loud-speaker system:

"Get off the ship, get off the ship."

It was the same amplification system over which, for four years, visitors to sailings were good naturedly hurried to shore.

Some question remained last night as to just how long it took the first outside alarm to be sounded. Regardless, the first knowledge city firemen had of the outbreak was at 2:49 o'clock when a special building call was sounded that brought three engine companies, two hook and ladder companies and a battalion chief.

Eleven minutes later the first full alarm was sounded. This brought only one engine company and another chief of battalion, as the preliminary manual call is only that much short of the regular first daytime alarm. This was followed at one-minute intervals by the second and third alarms and at 3:12 the fourth alarm was turned in. The fifth alarm was ordered by Chief Walsh at 4:08 P. M.

43 Pieces of Apparatus Called

Despite the five alarms, there was only a total of forty-three pieces of fire apparatus at the scene, while about sixty-eight other companies were required to relocate so that other sections of Manhattan would be adequately protected. As darkness fell the searchlight truck was summoned along with an additional fuel wagon.

The apparatus at the fire included twenty-four engine companies, six hook and ladder trucks, three fireboats—The Firefighter, the James Duane and the John J. Harvey—one rescue company, one water tower, one gasoline and oil wagon, and one Fire Department ambulance. There was no need to summon any of the special new equipment, such as smoke ejector vehicles.

Seven police emergency squads also were sent to the scene to augment the normal complement of twenty-five mounted and foot men assigned to guard the vicinity of the pier. The usual detail from the sabotage squad, precinct detectives and a detail of FBI agents also were about when the fire started. As the alarms sounded additional policemen were ordered into the area and by nightfall there were about 200 police on duty, as well as a company of Negro soldiers to keep back the curious who managed to get through the fire lines established at Eleventh Avenue.

Admiral Gives Explanation

After several preliminary statements on the situation, which he observed during the day from the stringpiece and other vantages, Admiral Andrews at 10 P. M. rounded out the official version.

"The fire was started by sparks from a blowtorch of a worker in the grand salon," he said. "The sparks ignited the wrapping of a life preserver. The hoses were let out but the fire spread rapidly and within a very few minutes there was so much smoke that the men in the compartments had to get out."

Regarding the heavy smoke, he added:

"The life preservers were piled in bales, wrapped in tar paper with a burlap bag covering. It was the burlap that caught on fire. The fire then spread rapidly through the passageways into the bunks installed in the ship, the mattresses catching on fire. That is the cause of the fire spreading so rapidly. There was no powder or ammunition on the ship.

"Due to the list of the ship it was thought better at first to sink her, that is, to open the sluice valves and let the seawater in. She was not very far from the bottom and it was thought best to give her enough weight to put her on the bottom. It was later decided, on the advice of technical experts, not to sink her. Instead water was pumped into the starboard side amidships."

The admiral explained that a hole was cut in the side of the ship with acetylene torches, a hoseline was put through and water was pumped in.

Fire Marshal Brophy summed up the situation from his office's point of view. His version differed in no particular from the others, except in indicating that the material that actually ignited was the burlap covering of bales that contained the life preservers. He suggested that both the burlap and the kapok burned easily and hard.

Mayor La Guardia, arriving in mid-afternoon, accompanied Chief Walsh along the stringpiece and into the pier offices, cluttered with emergency workers. Too busy for interviewers, he merely turned his head and called, "The chief says we may soon have it under control," then disappeared into the smokey shed.

Most of the watchers were backed up to the other side of Twelfth Avenue with the arrival of the rifle-equipped troops.

Henri Morin de Linclays, general manager of the French Line in this country, reiterated last night that the Normandie originally had one of the finest equipped fire-fighting system ever installed on a ship.

Dock Men, Raid Wardens Direct Traffic at Fire

Four hundred dock workers and air raid wardens were pressed into service yesterday to assist sixty traffic policemen in re-routing automobiles around the Normandie fire zone. They performed their tasks so efficiently that Commissioner Valentine said that "traffic never was tangled seriously."

For more than three hours—until 6:15 P. M.—the West Side elevated highway was closed to northbound traffic at Twenty-third Street. Southbound service was halted at Seventy-second Street. Northbound traffic moved slowly because of curiosity seekers wanting a glimpse at the burning ship. Until night Eleventh and Twelfth Avenues were closed to vehicular traffic between Forty-third and Fifty-first Streets.

During the height of the fire the smoke was visible over a twenty-five-mile area and crowds lined the New Jersey shorefront, particularly at West New York and Weehawken. Many brought field glasses and cameras.

Fire Is Fourth to Sweep French Liners in Decade

Disastrous fires have swept three other large ships of the French Line in the last decade, it was recalled yesterday after the burning of the former Normandie.

L'Atlantique, $20,000,000 luxury liner that had been in service since September, 1931, between France and South America, burned off the Channel Islands on Jan. 4, 1933, under circumstances that caused French officials to voice suspicion of sabotage.

On May 5, 1938, the Lafayette was destroyed in dry dock at Havre, France, by a fire started by a blowtorch that was being used by a workman in the engine room.

The Paris, which before the building of the Ile de France and the Normandie had been the pride of the French fleet, was burned at Havre on April 19, 1939, by a fire that started in the ship's bakery.

SURVIVORS TELL HOW FIRE BEGAN

Continued From Page One

in the fire control room when the alarm came in over the telephone system.

"By the time our gang got to the scene there was too much smoke to see the fire," he said. "We never saw the flames, just smoke."

He was overcome by smoke after leaving the scene.

Louis Zarrelli, a seaman whose home is at Westport, Conn., was in bed amidships on A deck when smoke began pouring in through the ventilators. He had been off guard duty for a short time. He said he had no difficulty getting out, but later went back to make sure no one was trapped in the room. He collapsed on the pier from smoke poisoning after getting out a second time.

Joseph Centola, 32, a fitter, of

45 Atlantic Avenue, Brooklyn, told of the intense cold suffered by the fire fighters.

"I was in the condensing room on D deck with about a hundred other men when smoke began seeping down through the ventilators," he said. "We hollered for the fire watch but the smoke kept coming. Then our foreman told us to get off—evacuate.

"We were going down the gangway to the pier when I met firemen coming aboard. I am an auxiliary fireman with Engine 224 in Brooklyn and I went back with them. We went to A deck and we got water. It was swell working for a while, but we got drenched with water. It wasn't so bad while the water was on us but when it stopped I began to freeze. Coming down the ladder my pants froze into an L shape."

Centola was cut around the left hand breaking open a bulkhead to get at the flames and was also being treated for exposure at the Roosevelt Hospital.

Tells How Man Was Killed

George Deighan of 6914 Ridge Boulevard, Brooklyn, was working with Trentacoasta, or Trent, as he was known, when the latter was killed. Both were members of the fire watch.

"We were up forward on D deck about 2:30 when we were ordered to go to the top deck aft," he said. "It was all smoke. I was going down a ladder with Trent behind me when there was an explosion. There wasn't much noise or flame but a terrific concussion. I think it was a feeder tank for the torches. Trent was blasted right over my head and landed on the deck below. I went down and carried him off."

Deighan was able to leave Roosevelt Hospital around 7 o'clock after receiving treatment there for shock.

Most of the men who got close to the flames with hose came away as if they had been exposed to intense sun. The terrific heat, they explained, sent the hose spray back at them in the form of live steam and stung and reddened the skin. Those who were farthest from the fire's center, on the other hand, found their clothes froze almost instantly. Some, who tried to beat out the flames with blankets, had their shirtfronts seared.

Caught in Gun Magazine

William J. Kelly (Cannonball to his crew), 32, of 135 East Thirty-fifth Street, a master plumber, was caught in the ship's gun magazine with a work crew of about twenty-five helpers. At Bellevue Hospital, stalking up and down in hospital pajamas and blankets, he and his men coughed the smoke out of their lungs and talked of their experience.

"We were working three decks down," Kelly related, "when the fire started and came shooting down the four elevator shafts. Then smoke came pouring down the shafts too. We grabbed hose and played it on the flames as they shot out, but we were forced back and the smoke kept getting us.

"We saw a longshoreman working a winch over No. 1 hold. He hollered, 'All hands will have to leave. She's all afire,' but we kept working the hose until the smoke put us out." Kelly and his crew, incidentally, warmly praised the Coast Guardsmen and their heroic attempts to get at the heart of the flame through the dense smoke and the blistering heat.

Francis Dieck, 26, of 79-17 154th Street, in Flushing, Queens, a shipfitter's helper, was working on the main deck with six other men when, soon after the fire and smoke were discovered, the lights went out.

"We formed a human chain," Dieck said. "We felt our way through smoke that kept getting thicker by the minute. We groped our way up three decks to the air and then we took a hand with the hose until we were almost overcome."

Dieck told reporters three of his co-workers had put several bottles of acetylene gas on the promenade deck about twenty minutes before the fire started. He shared the opinion of others that the blaze had its origin in the salon. "No one could have held that blaze," he said. "It spread too quickly."

What worried Jack Panuzzo, 36, last night as he sat coughing in his home at 283 St. Marks Avenue, Brooklyn, was that he felt so bad he did not believe he would be able to get to work today.

Panuzzo is an iron worker who made four trips into the blazing salon on the promenade deck of the vessel at the height of the fire yesterday and brought out a man each time. Panuzzo finally collapsed himself and was carried to pier.

He refused to stay at the Polyclinic Hospital, despite the admonition from physicians that he had swallowed so much smoke that hospitalization was wise.

"I couldn't stay," he explained at his home. "I had to get back to my wife and baby. He smiled at his wife, Dorothy, and their child, Josephine, 2, who were near him in the living room of their fourroom apartment on the third floor of an old eight-family building.

Arnold Christofferson, 29, of 455 Forty-eighth Street, Brooklyn, a carpenter, sat in Bellevue Hospital emergency ward wrapped in a hospital blanket. He still wore his safety helmet strapped tight under his chin. His face and his hands were dark with soot and smudge. He gulped hot coffee, served by solicitous orderlies. All his clothes were in the hospital drier. They had frozen stiff.

"I was on B deck," Christofferson related. "We had a gang down there on paneling. I guess that's eight or nine decks down. A few of us whiffed this smoke. I looked out the port to see what was what. Two fellas are on the pier. They holler, 'The ship's burning,' and they point 'way over my head. I smiled. I though it was some kind of gag.

"Then one of the men on the pier crosses his heart. 'It's burning,' he hollers, and I see he means it. I stuck my head farther out and looked up and I see smoke pouring out of the windows high up the side of the ship. My eyes began to smart and I pulled in my head.

Smoke Got Thicker Below

"I told the other guys working with me, I said: 'I think the ship's burning. That's where the smoke's from. The smoke got thicker and the room got darker. I went aft on B deck to see could I help put this fire out, but I couldn't find the flames. Only smoke. I came to stairs and I went up two decks and the smoke kept getting worse.

"I reached a corridor. There the draft was behind me, and it blew the smoke past me, and forward. Thirty feet down that corridor it got so thick I couldn't breathe. I bent down. I went forward that way. I found there seemed to be better air near the floor. I wet a handkerchief and I covered my nose and mouth with it.

"I went as far as I could. I didn't know what I was getting into. I couldn't see my own hands. The corridor got warm and then real hot. I reached up to see was the ceiling hot. It didn't blister me or burn me, but it was awfully warm.

"I turned back. Some one away behind me in the corridor kept yelling 'Get out. Get out. Get below and get off on the gangplanks.' I figured if he was strong enough to yell like that the air must be better where he was. I stumbled along in the direction of his voice. When I got about where I thought the voice had been, it was gone. I didn't know what to do. I stood there a minute pressing the wet handkerchief against my lips and nose. It was hard to breathe.

"Then the whole corridor broke out in flame. I turned and backed away from it. How I got out, I don't know. I still had my tools in one hand—my hammer, my screwdriver and my ruler. Some

Ladders from the bow of the stricken vessel to the street

Lifeboats lie alongside

kind of naval officer, I guess he was Coast Guard, came through the corridor. He hollered, 'Come on. Come on. Get down to the pier.'

Voice Guided Men in Dark

"This officer posted different men where corridors crossed. That was a smart thing to do. If a guy came along and couldn't see, he would holler and one of the men at the cross point where two corridors met would hail him and send him on his way out. Water came flushing down the corridors. It got almost up to our ankles. I saw a sailor come through with hose. An officer called to him, but he wouldn't leave. He kept playing the hose."

Eventually Christofferson got out on deck. Men were pulling hose over the side. The carpenter carefully put his tools down and gave a hand with the hose. "We smashed windows," he recalled, "and we stuck the hose through and kept playing on the flames. I stayed until my pants and overalls got so stiff with ice I could hardly move my legs or my arms.

"A sailor came up with a load of blankets. He said 'You can't do any more. You've done all you could do.' He stripped me down and he wrapped a white blanket around me. I picked up my tools. Next thing I know I'm in the ambulance and here I am."

Carpenter Christofferson gulped more scalding coffee. He said when the smoke worked out of his throat in the hospital he called his fiancé in Court Street, Brooklyn, and told her he was all right.

"She had heard about the fire on the radio," he explained, "and she had seen it from the roof of the Court Street building where she works." The carpenter's red-rimmed eyes closed in a grin. He gathered the thick blanket around him. "My fiancé and me will get married the end of this month," he confided. He guarded his tools with his bare ankles.

Twice Overcome by Smoke

Fort Bartholomew, a Negro third-class seaman who had come from Norfolk only four days ago to be messman on the Normandie, was twice overcome by smoke as he fought the fire. At Roosevelt Hospital he told this story:

"I was in my room on B Deck when they gave the alarm to go off, and I went off with the rest of the fellows. When the firemen came and needed somebody to help with the hose, I went back on the ship with them. We were fighting the fire on the promenade deck when the smoke began to get me and I had to quit, but I wasn't out, so I went back. Then things got kind of warm there again, and they must have brought me over to the hospital."

Eddie Di Mayo, 25, a tester on the acetyline and air gas equipment, was alone on the sun deck when the fire began. He saw smoke rising from the promenade deck and looked for a rope with which to lower himself from the deck. By the time he had found a rope the smoke had become so thick that he could not see at all and the fire hose drenched his clothes and made his escape down the ship's side more perilous.

"All the News That's Fit to Print."

The New York Times.

LATE CITY EDITION
Rain, with moderate winds this morning.
Temperature Yesterday—Max., 49; Min., 32
Sunrise, 7:39 A. M.; Sunset, 5:30 P. M.

Copyright, 1942, by The New York Times Company.

VOL. XCII..No. 30,991. Entered as Second-Class Matter, Postoffice, New York, N. Y. NEW YORK, MONDAY, NOVEMBER 30, 1942. THREE CENTS IN NEW YORK CITY

BOSTON FIRE DEATH TOLL 440; NIGHT CLUB HOLOCAUST LAID TO BUS BOY'S LIGHTED MATCH

MANY MORE DYING

Dead May Pass 500 in Worst Disaster of Kind Since Iroquois Fire

BODIES HEAPED AT EXITS

Loss of Life Ascribed Almost Wholly to Panic—Means of Egress Plentiful

By FRANK S. ADAMS
Special to THE NEW YORK TIMES.

BOSTON, Nov. 29—This stunned and grieving city saw the list of known dead in the nation's worst fire disaster in almost four decades mount to 440 tonight while the critical condition of many of the 173 burned and injured persons in hospitals led to fears that the eventual death toll would pass the 500 mark.

Such was the condition of many of the bodies that officials voiced doubt of their identification. Only 289 of the dead had been identified tonight.

A lighted match, held by a 16-year-old bus boy in the city's best-known night club, the Cocoanut Grove, was responsible for the fire. He was perched precariously on a chair, trying to replace an electric light bulb that had been removed by a merry-making patron, when the match flame ignited an artificial palm tree. This was a little after 10 o'clock last night.

The fire spread with incredible swiftness along the walls of the darkened room in the basement of the rambling night club structure on Piedmont Street in the South End, at the edge of the theatre district. This room, known as the Melody Lounge, held about 130 patrons, while an additional 700 crowded the dine and dance floor above to its capacity.

Football Fans Swell Crowd

It was an exceptional night of patronage for the club, for one of the big football games of the year had taken place at Fenway Park in the afternoon. Holy Cross had defeated Boston College in a sensational upset and football fans adjourned to the club to celebrate the victory or temper the defeat.

Large delegations of Holy Cross followers had come from the Worcester area and there were alumni of both schools and just ordinary football fans from many sections. The attendance at the game was 41,000.

A girl's shrill cry of "fire!" precipitated a panic among the festive Saturday night patrons of the club. In semi-darkness, soon made dimmer by choking smoke, most of the 830 men and women in the club started a terrified rush for the exits.

Here and there calm heads tried to quiet the fear-maddened throng, but these efforts were futile. Women fell and were trampled under foot. Their shrieks only made others battle with greater frenzy to reach the doors.

Almost at the first rush the revolving door at the main entrance was blocked by the wild surge. When policemen and firemen untangled the terrible pile hours later

Continued on Page Twelve

Throng Seared by Flame In Spread of 15 Seconds

Terrorized by Waves of Fire, Night Club Patrons Trample Each Other in Scramble, Jamming Doors and Metal Windows

By MEYER BERGER
Special to THE NEW YORK TIMES.

BOSTON, Nov. 29—Fire broke out in the Cocoanut Grove night club here around 10:15 o'clock last night. Not one of the survivors can fix the exact time. One moment they were dancing, or enjoying their drinks at their tables or at the great cylindrical bar. Fifteen seconds later, seared by sudden tidal waves of flames, more than 800 persons were choking and gasping, scrambling for their lives.

About 700 of the guests were on the street floor. The rest were in the "Melody Lounge," which is connected with the main floor by concrete steps about ten feet wide, up a dozen concrete risers. The space nearest the walls, upstairs and down, was lined with imitation palm trees. Varicolored loops of silk hung from the ceiling. The lighting was dimmed.

The building rises only one story above the street level and the outer walls are of yellow dappled stucco. The front entrance was through a revolving door about six or seven feet wide. The large front windows were divided into small panes framed in strong monel metal. None but the thinnest of persons could have crawled through those windows.

The front of the night club faces on Piedmont Street. The rear gives upon Shawmut Avenue. All the rear windows were blind windows—that is, they were covered with boarding that let no light into the street. One small door at this end of the building gives on Shawmut Avenue. It had a lighted "exit" sign above it.

There was an extra exit from the Melody Lounge, but none of the patrons seemed to know about it. It led up a few steps into an office which, in turn, gave into Piedmont Street.

The impact of horror seemed to have swept from the minds of guests and employes all details of

Continued on Page Fourteen

VICTIMS DESCRIBE FIRE HORROR SCENE

Man Tells of Smashing Cellar Window in Heavy Smoke to Win Way to Safety

From a Staff Correspondent

BOSTON, Nov. 29—Vivid descriptions of the scenes attending the Cocoanut Grove fire were given today by survivors and spectators.

A graphic account was given by Charles W. Disbrow Jr., a Boston insurance executive, who was having dinner with his wife. They were sitting with a party of nine and were just completing their dinner when Mr. Disbrow observed what seemed to be a general disturbance at the bar.

"I saw a man jump up on the bar, which was raised above the main floor," he continued. "Two belches of flame seemed to be chasing him. I grabbed my wife and said, 'This is no place for us.' I knew there would be a panic and people had already started running away from the space near the bar. We made for the servants' door and went down a flight of steps into the basement."

Mr. Disbrow went on to describe how he and his wife were hemmed in by a swirling mob of patrons.

"There was no smoke in the cellar as we entered," he said. "There seemed to be a line of people down there, about two abreast, and they were going toward a dark corner. We went after them and then some one yelled:

"'We can't get out this way.'"

They attempted to fight their

Continued on Page Fourteen

ASK WOMEN SERVE ON FEDERAL JURIES

Judges Urge That All Social and Economic Groups Be Included in the Selections

Special to THE NEW YORK TIMES.

WASHINGTON, Nov. 29—Women should be made eligible for Federal jury duty in twenty States where they are still disqualified, according to recommendations for the improvement of the Federal grand and petit jury system filed here today by a committee of Federal judges.

The committee, reporting to the Judicial Conference of Senior Circuit Judges of the United States, further recommended that women not only be made eligible but also be required to serve, notably in fifteen States and the District of Columbia, where they are already eligible but may claim exemption if they wish.

In general, the committee recommended the repeal of the existing statutory requirement that Federal courts must observe the qualifications and exemptions prescribed for jurors in each State.

This would involve rejecting the color and property qualifications still operating in many States.

The committee emphasized the necessity of preventing discrimination in the choosing of juries, and stated that jurors in the Federal courts "should be drawn from every economic and social group in the community without regard to race, color or politics," but at the same time stated that the jurors should be "persons of as high a

Continued on Page Twenty-four

Pay-as-You-Go Tax Is Pushed in State

By The Associated Press

ALBANY, Nov. 29—Indications of pressure in the 1943 Legislature for application of the Ruml "pay-as-you-go" plan to ease the burden on payers of New York's personal income tax developed in two quarters today.

The Ruml plan, designed to prevent tax debt accumulation, would set the tax calendar one year ahead to bring collection in the same year in which income is earned. Under the State's present system taxes on 1942 income are collectible in 1943.

State Senator Thomas C. Desmond, Newburgh Republican, urged the State Tax Commission in a statement to report "promptly" on adaptability of the Ruml plan.

Bingo in Church Barred by Mayor As Just as Illegal as Elsewhere

Bingo and similar games of chance will be barred in churches as well as in motion picture houses and the rooms of fraternal organizations, if Police Commissioner Valentine follows a broad ruling laid down yesterday by Mayor La Guardia in his weekly radio "Talk to the People."

After announcing on Wednesday that after today bingo would not be permitted in motion picture houses and the quarters of fraternal groups, Mr. Valentine declared that it would be allowed on church premises if played under church auspices.

Mayor La Guardia, however, took the position that if bingo was unlawful it was unlawful regardless of where it was played, under whose auspices it was played and what was done with the proceeds. In his broadcast he did not refer to churches, but later, when asked whether his remarks applied to them, he reiterated his conviction that if the game was illegal to start with it could not be legalized by being played in a church under church auspices.

"I have received some inquiries regarding bingo," he said in his radio talk. "Well, I guess I'll have to answer them, and I think most of the inquiries could be answered by this statement:

"If a game is unlawful, the ultimate disposition of the funds, or the auspices under which the game is operated, or the place where the game is operated, does not make an unlawful game lawful. Do I make myself clear? If bingo is unlawful in one place, the same game

Continued on Page Eleven

FOR WANT AD RESULTS Use The New York Times. It's easy to order your ad. Just telephone LAckawanna 4-1000.—Advt.

FARM FOOD GOALS FIXED BY WICKARD TO SPUR WAR DRIVE

He Outlines 'the Most Crucial and Important Task' Ever Asked of the Growers

PRICE SUPPORT IS PLEDGED

Emphasis Put on Those Crops Most Essential for Needs of Military and Allies

Special to THE NEW YORK TIMES.

WASHINGTON, Nov. 29—United States food-production goals for 1943, "the most crucial and important task our farmers have ever been asked to perform," were announced today by Secretary Wickard.

At the same time Mr. Wickard disclosed a price-support program which pledges the department so far as possible to work out and maintain "a price policy during the year which will give maximum price assistance to the production program." Included in the program are specific price-support announcements for many major commodities.

The 1943 goals, designed to shape next year's production to the needs of the United Nations, are aimed in general at maintaining or exceeding the record level of production this year, but there are significant changes from this year's pattern which put emphasis on crops and livestock considered most essential to the war effort.

The goals and price-support programs are the result of consideration by the Food Requirements Committee, which regularly evaluates military and civilian and United Nations needs for our food and fiber products.

Goals Are Called Minimums

Mr. Wickard said the new goals "represent the minimum requirements for food produced in this country."

"These requirements, for our own military forces and for our Allies, now represent about one-fourth of estimated total food production in 1943," he added.

As the United Nations' offensive progresses, Mr. Wickard said, "we shall have the added responsibility of furnishing food for the peoples of countries freed from the Axis yoke. We shall need to use our food to rehabilitate the people in these countries so that they will be able to join us in the war against the aggressors."

Mr. Wickard said that the department would use every resource to ease the shortage of farm labor. This program, he said, would be directed to make labor available in these six ways:

1. The shifting of workers from

Continued on Page Ten

CHURCHILL TELLS ITALY TO OUST LEADERS OR FACE SHATTERING ALLIED AIR BLOWS; RUSSIANS BREAK NAZI DON DEFENSE LINE

SOVIET LISTS GAINS

100,000 Nazis Are Said to Have Been Killed in Last Ten Days

66,000 PRISONERS NETTED

Advances Are Continued on Stalingrad Front and in Area West of Moscow

By The Associated Press.

MOSCOW, Monday, Nov. 30—Russian armies have killed nearly 15,000 Germans in the new Soviet offensive west of Moscow and have crashed through a new German defense line on the east bank of the Don before Stalingrad in triumphant pursuit of the Nazis across the snows of Russia, it was announced early today.

A special communiqué said the grand offensive in the south alone had in the ten days between Nov. 19 and Nov. 29 netted the Soviet forces 66,000 German prisoners. The Nazi killed on all fronts, the Soviet newspaper Izvestia reported, totaled 100,000 in the past ten days.

The onrushing Red Army continued to sweep over populated places and towns before Stalingrad and west of Moscow, the communiqué said, and great masses of matériel were reported captured.

The regular Soviet communiqué, issued shortly after the special announcement, said the Russians were continuing their two offensives and regaining more occupied places.

"Immense Losses" Suffered

It added that the Germans were suffering "immense losses" southwest of Stalingrad, while all enemy attacks within the city, in the workers settlement of the northern part, were thrown back and "hundreds of enemy dead were left on the battlefield."

The special war report announced the capture of Obilnaya, which is seventy miles east of Kotelnikov, a city on the Stalingrad-Krasnodar railroad. This placed the lower fringe of the fighting well down on the Kalmuk steppe at the fringe of the Ergeni Hills in the upper Caucasus. In this area south of Stalingrad the Russians also reported the capture of the station of Nebikov.

Of the Stalingrad fighting, the

Continued on Page Eight

Allies Cut Road and Rail Line Linking Tunis and Bizerte

British First Army Ready to Launch Big Offensive From Key Town Only 10 Miles West of the Capital

By JAMES MacDONALD
Wireless to THE NEW YORK TIMES.

LONDON, Nov. 29—The Allied occupation of Djedeida, about ten miles west of Tunis, the capital of Tunisia, was officially announced today as the British First Army brought its guns within range of that important objective and awaited orders for a general attack, expected at any moment.

The seizure of Djedeida, northeast of Tebourba, was announced in an Allied Headquarters communiqué that said also that operations in the vicinity of Mateur were "proceeding satisfactorily."

Meanwhile aerial warfare continued at a sharp pace over the week-end, with Allied fliers attacking the airfield and docks at the strategic naval base of Bizerte and Axis planes attacking Bone, Algeria, a debarkation point for Allied supplies and reinforcements.

The Morocco radio reported tonight that the enemy forces had retired behind the semi-circular defenses in front of Tunis and Bizerte as the Allied troops continued lunging at them.

Axis troops in the northern sector kept up their work of blowing up bridges, railroad lines and highways to delay the Allied advance. In the southern sector, where the enemy retired more rapidly than in the north, communication lines are also being destroyed by the defenders.

The occupation of Djedeida gave the Allies a strategic advantage in preparation for their imminent drive to wrest Tunis from the enemy. It is an important railroad and highway junction, and now that it is in Allied hands, the railroad link between Tunis and Bizerte has been severed.

Following up this action, Allied parachute troops sought to pave the way for still another strategic step in the Mateur area. According to the Morocco radio, these

Continued on Page Two

PREMIER IS GRIM

Says African Clean-Up Will Give Springboard for Attacking Italy

SEES WAR END IN 2 STAGES

He Pledges Full Aid to U. S. in Pacific if Victory Is Won First in Europe

The text of Mr. Churchill's address is printed on Page 5.

Special Cable to THE NEW YORK TIMES.

LONDON, Nov. 29—Prime Minister Churchill, in a world broadcast on the eve of his sixty-eighth birthday, warned the Italian people tonight that the day of reckoning with them was drawing nigh, and implicit in his speech was an appeal to them to settle with their leaders who had misled them and to avoid now the holocaust that was awaiting them.

"It is for the Italian people, 40,000,000 of them, to say whether they want this terrible thing to happen to their country or not," he said.

Earlier in the day the British Broadcasting Corporation had broadcast an appeal to the Italian people to make a separate peace, and it was followed up by repeated broadcasts of Mr. Churchill's speech in their own language.

The Prime Minister warned his own people that the defeat of the Axis in Europe would not alone bring the blessings of peace. They must fight on, he said, beside the United States, China and the Pacific Dominions until Asia as well as Africa and Europe had been freed from the aggressors' domination.

Since the Prime Minister was broadcasting to the whole world, his words can be viewed not only as a warning to those at home not to dream of an early return to normal life but as a pledge of his government that when at last Reichsfuehrer Hitler and Premier Mussolini are vanquished in Europe Britain would not leave it to the United States to finish the job of fighting Japan single-handed.

Vows to Carry On in Pacific

Should the war come to a conclusion in two separate stages, west and east, so that the "Atlantic may be calm while in the Pacific the hurricane rises to its full pitch," Mr. Churchill vowed that Britain would of course bring all her forces to aid the United States and the people of Australia and New Zealand in their "valiant" struggles against the aggressions of Japan.

With such an ending to the turmoil in which the whole world is embroiled, Mr. Churchill found cause for optimism regarding the future, for he pointed out that the Allies would still be shaping the peace in Europe while still struggling against the common foe in the East. He continued:

"It seems to me that should the war end thus in two successive stages, there will be a far higher sense of comradeship around the council table than existed among the victors at Versailles. Then the danger had passed away, the common bond between the Allies had snapped. There was no sense of corporate responsibility such as

Continued on Page Five

2 Japanese Destroyers Hit, Believed Sunk Off Buna

By The United Press.

AT UNITED NATIONS HEADQUARTERS, Australia, Monday, Nov. 30—Allied airmen are believed to have sunk two more Japanese destroyers trying to reinforce the beleaguered New Guinea garrison around Buna, while to the west Allied naval forces intercepted a German auxiliary vessel of 8,000 tons and captured seventy-eight Nazis after they scuttled the ship, Allied headquarters announced today.

The German vessel, which was identified merely as an "auxiliary," was hit by Allied gunfire before the crew destroyed it, said the midday communiqué from General Douglas MacArthur's headquarters.

The communiqué said the ship was intercepted in the western sector—probably west of Australia in the Indian Ocean area which was a favorite hunting ground of German surface raiders in the first World War.

On the ground the battle for Buna raged through its sixteenth day yesterday with American and Australian troops, who have the enemy pinned with his back to the sea in a forty-square-mile area between Buna and Gona, maintaining pressure throughout the area.

Four Japanese destroyers tried to reinforce the besieged defenders, the communiqué said, but United States Flying Fortresses pounced on them and ran the Allied total to eleven Japanese ships sunk or damaged off the Buna-Gona area since Nov. 19.

Two of the destroyers were hit with 500-pound bombs which left them in flames. The communiqué said it was believed that they sank.

Continued on Page Six

TURIN HAMMERED WITH GIANT BOMBS

100,000 Incendiaries Also Are Dropped at Italian Industrial City—Many Fires Caused

By DAVID ANDERSON
Special Cable to THE NEW YORK TIMES.

LONDON, Nov. 29—A smashing blow was delivered at Turin last night by a large number of British aircraft, some carrying 8,000-pound bombs to Italy for the first time.

It was just one week and a day since the same city had been attacked in what was, up to then, the heaviest raid ever mounted against Italy. Last night's, in some respects, surpassed all previous records in severity, and at a cost of one Royal Air Force plane missing.

The punishment ladled out was described by the Air Ministry as heavy and concentrated—with good results. That understatement in high official quarters was matched by the testimony of Wing Commander G. P. Gibson, D. S. O., D. F. C. and Bar, who piloted a

Continued on Page Two

War News Summarized

MONDAY, NOVEMBER 30, 1942

Both a radio broadcast yesterday by Prime Minister Churchill and the developments in the Mediterranean zone indicated that a major effort to knock Italy out of the war was probably due in the not distant future.

Prime Minister Churchill warned the Italian people that their choice was to get rid of their leaders or be subjected to a prolonged air attack from Allied North African bases as well as from Britain. He warned his own people that the war would probably be long and costly. He greeted recent events in France as the end of the Vichy farce. The Prime Minister also intimated that the war in Europe might end with the defeat of Adolf Hitler before the end of the war in Asia. [1:8.]

British heavy bombers lent emphasis to Mr. Churchill's warning to the Italians with a second raid in eight days on the important Italian munitions center of Turin, in which four-ton bombs were used for the first time and 100,000 incendiaries. [1:6.]

Allied capture of Djedeida in Tunisia, twelve miles west of Tunis, was officially announced. The town lies across the road and an important railroad connection between Tunis and Bizerte. Progress was also reported from the Mateur area, twenty miles south of Tunis. [1:6-7; map, P. 2.]

German dissatisfaction over the outcome of the effort to seize the French Fleet at Toulon appeared to be threatening trouble for Pierre Laval. The German-controlled Paris radio said that Laval's "ambiguous" policy had fostered the wrong attitude among officers and men of the French Navy and Army. [3:1.]

Moscow reported the breaching of a new German line on the east bank of the Don near Stalingrad and the slaughter of nearly 15,000 Germans west of Moscow, where the central front offensive was reported making progress. [1:5; map, P. 8.]

From China came an announcement that United States fighter and bomber planes had destroyed twenty-three and possibly twenty-eight Japanese planes and had sunk two cargo ships in a raid Friday on Canton and had destroyed at least 100 barges in the Pearl River estuary. No United States planes were lost. [1:6-7.]

Two out of four Japanese destroyers attempting to reinforce besieged Buna, in New Guinea, were hit by bombs and believed sunk, United Nations Headquarters in Australia reported. To the northwest of Australia a German auxiliary vessel of 8,000 tons was trapped and scuttled by the crew. Seventy-eight Germans were captured. [1:6-7.]

The United States Navy announced the probable destruction by bombing of a small Japanese cargo vessel off Attu Island in the Aleutians, which is still occupied by the Japanese. [7:1.]

U. S. Fliers Down 23 Japanese In Our Biggest Attack on Canton

By The United Press.

WITH AMERICAN AIR FORCES IN CHINA, Nov. 29—American fliers, in their most successful operation of the war in China, shot down twenty-three, possibly twenty-eight, Japanese planes over Canton Friday and spread devastation among shipping and harbor facilities at the great Pearl River base.

Fighter planes of the Twenty-third United States Pursuit Group cleared the skies of enemy interceptor planes, and bombers dropped six tons of bombs on the Pearl River estuary, sinking two medium-sized freighters and about 100 barges. Huge fires were started among docks and warehouses.

No American planes were lost in the raid, the third against Canton in four days. It was the climax of a week of intensified air offensive against enemy centers in Burma, Indo-China, South China and Central China.

The greatest number of planes used in a single American operation in China took part in the raid. The first wave of bombers, commanded by Lieut. Col. Herbert Morgan of Freedom, Pa., scored three hits on the deck of an 8,000-ton freighter and sent about fifty barges surrounding the vessel to the bottom, possibly with a heavy loss of life.

"We consider that the freighter was definitely sunk," Colonel Morgan said. "Fighter pilots reported ten minutes later that the entire ship was ablaze and sinking fast.

A second flight of bombers, led by Major William Baste of Ind

Continued on Page Four

Savings insured up to $5,000 at Railroad Federal Savings & Loan Association, 441 Lexington Ave. (at 44th St.), N.Y.C.—Advt.

2-Month-Old Pledge Of Hitler Backfired

Exactly two months ago—on Sept. 30—Adolf Hitler in a broadcast to the German people spoke of Stalingrad as a city "which we shall take, you may depend on it," and at another point said, "The occupation of Stalingrad will be concluded."

Today the Russians have cleared the city's northern factory district of Germans, have swirled around the besieging armies from northwest and southwest, throwing them completely on the defensive, and Stalingrad still stands.

Local Stores Know the Answers in Buying Power Buffalo Courier-Express.—Advt.

DEATH TOLL AT 440 IN FIRE AT BOSTON

SCENE AT BOSTON NIGHT CLUB FIRE IN WHICH 300 ARE REPORTED DEAD

Continued From Page One

they found more than forty crushed and broken bodies jammed against this door.

Beside this revolving door was an auxiliary door, equipped with a panic lock of a type supposed to open readily to pressure from within. But for some reason still unexplained, this door had been bolted. In the wild excitement and terrific crush those forced up against it by the pressure behind were unable to find the bolt and open it.

The club had side and rear exits on Broadway and Shawmut Avenue. Some of the revelers escaped through these exits, but rushes by terror-stricken men and women quickly blocked them, leaving scores, frantic in the darkness, smoke and wild confusion, to mill about hopelessly.

In their mad rush for safety at least fifty men and women tried to escape through the kitchen, only to find themselves trapped. They were unable to find the only exit in the inky blackness that suddenly enveloped the club and virtually all of them died from smoke inhalation or injuries sustained as they battled aimlessly in whichever direction they thought safety might lie.

Police and fire officials agreed tonight, after a day-long investigation of the tragedy—the worst of its kind the United States has known since the Iroquois Theatre disaster took 603 lives in Chicago in 1903—that panic had claimed far more lives than the flames.

If only those within had waited patiently at their tables and filed out in orderly fashion, there would have been few if any deaths, the officials declared, since the fire itself was not a serious one. The firemen at the scene described it as a "flash fire" in the decorations of the night club and said they could have extinguished it quickly if they had been able to get at it.

Firemen Cannot Get In

But when they arrived at the club they found the same difficulty in trying to get into the smoke-filled club that those within were having in trying to get out. The first fire companies on the scene reported they had to clear away piles of bodies to force an entrance. Even with this terrible obstacle, the fire was put out within an hour after the first alarm was sounded at 10:15 P. M., according to the Fire Department, but it was not until 6 o'clock this morning that weary squads of firemen and police had finished the grim task of removing the dead and injured.

To understand the catastrophe, a description of the interior layout of the Cocoanut Grove is necessary. This establishment, which has had a checkered career since it first opened its doors fifteen years ago, has expanded recently under the pressure of wartime amusement seekers.

It originally occupied a brick building of one story and a half running between Piedmont Street and Shawmut Avenue. The Melody Lounge, down a few steps from the Piedmont Street level, was a darkened room with an oval bar, tables and booths.

Rolling Stage for Floor Show

On the upper level was the main dance floor, surrounded by tables. At one end of the room was a rolling stage for the floor show. Alongside it on the Piedmont Street side was another long oval bar, known as the Caricature Bar, while on the same floor level, but in another building fronting on Broadway, was a new cocktail lounge opened only two weeks ago. It had its own entrance on Broadway, but was connected with the older part of the club.

The Cocoanut Grove, which in its history has been played by Texas Guinan, Helen Morgan, Joe Frisco and other top-ranking night club stars, has been enjoying an almost unprecedented boom in recent months. Service men home for brief furloughs and war workers flush with overtime pay checks jammed it night after night.

Augmenting the customary Saturday night crowd last night were not only men and women who had attended the Holy Cross-Boston College football game but couples which included scores of service men winding up their Thanksgiving furloughs.

Mickey Alpert, leader of the orchestra, was just about to lift his baton to conduct "The Star-Spangled Banner" as a prelude to the floor show when the panic spread to the main floor. Every table in the dine and dance floor was filled and the crowd was standing three deep at the Caricature Bar.

Patron Removes Bulb

In the Melody Lounge downstairs, just before the fire started, five bartenders were busy filling the demands of the patrons. This room was ordinarily kept in semi-darkness, but apparently it was not dark enough to suit one of the patrons. He climbed up and unscrewed one of the few light bulbs, leaving one section of the room in almost total darkness.

John Bradley, one of the bartenders, summoned Stanley F. Tomaszewski, a 16-year-old bus boy, who lives at 17 Erie Street in the Dorchester section, and told him to replace the lamp. Tomaszewski got a fresh bulb and prepared to carry out orders.

"I got a chair and stood on it and lighted a match which I held in my left hand while I tried to screw the bulb back where it belonged," Tomaszewski told Police Captain John F. McCarthy, who took charge of the police investigation today.

"The match started an artificial palm tree burning. It was only about a foot from the socket where I was putting in the bulb. That's how the fire started."

Tomaszewski said that he tried to put the fire out and that Bradley came to his assistance but the flames spread with astonishing rapidity. Tomaszewski was burned on the right hand. He was questioned by the police until late tonight and then held as a material witness.

Fire-Resistant Was Applied

Fire Commissioner William A. Reilly said today that the leather-covered walls of the night club had been treated with a fire-resistant compound which kept them from bursting into open flame but caused them to give off dense clouds of thick smoke as the fire spread among ornaments that had been hung for the holidays.

The flames and smoke raced from the Melody Lounge into the larger rooms upstairs, throwing the throng there, most of its members in formal evening attire, into the most dreadful confusion.

Army and Navy officers, present in considerable numbers, tried vainly to stem the wild rush for the exits, but blind fear made most of the crowd oblivious to reason. Even those who wanted to stay out of the rush were swept along by the heedless flight of those behind them.

Some managed to make their way to windows, and jumped to the tops of parked cars in the street. But for some reason, which can be explained best by students of mob psychology, the great bulk of the crowd made for the main entrance, through which nearly all had come into the club.

Actually there were plenty of exits, enough to have provided egress for the crowd in short order, according to James H. Mooney, city building commissioner, and his assistant, Dennis Keohane, superintendent of construction. Mr. Keohane, who said he was familiar with the premises, said that there were in all four doors leading to Piedmont Street, four leading to Shawmut Avenue and one leading to Broadway. In addition, he asserted, the basement windows in the rear of the bar in the Melody Lounge could be used to reach the street without difficulty.

Mr. Mooney and Mr. Keohane reported that the building had been inspected by their department only recently and had been approved. Deputy Fire Chief John Kenney, in charge of Fire Department inspection, said that the club had passed an inspection by his men within the past year, but had been due for another inspection within the next few days.

Mr. Mooney, who helped direct the official activity at the scene, said that dead and injured were piled in heaps in some of the bottlenecks of the darkened passageways. He added that it was evident that "a terrific fight" had taken place in the darkness and tumult of the panic.

"Many of the bodies were actually torn apart," he declared.

While the terrible struggle went on within the club, there was confusion and wild excitement outside, also. The first fire alarm was quickly followed by three additional alarms, which brought a large quantity of apparatus to the scene.

The flames ate through the roof of the structure, and their reflection against the sky quickly brought a huge crowd, which added to the difficulties of the police and firemen.

Naval officers and enlisted men who were in the vicinity went to the assistance of the outnumbered police. Several officers told groups of enlisted men to lock arms and form a living chain, which helped press back the crowd from the immediate neighborhood of the burning building.

Service Men Give Help

Soldiers, Coast Guardsmen, sailors and a few civilians grabbed hose lines and helped the firemen stretch them. Priests hurried from near-by parishes to administer the last rites of the church to those being carried from the club.

Ambulances rushed to the scene from twenty-two hospitals in the city and suburbs but were unable to cope with the dreadful task of caring for the burned and injured. At least seventy-five taxicabs were pressed into emergency service as ambulances. Express trucks and newspaper trucks helped remove the dead.

Doctors and nurses by the scores hurried to the area as word of the disaster spread through Boston. An emergency dressing station was set up in a near-by garage and another in a drug store, while first aid was given on the sidewalks to many of the less seriously injured.

Many of those who escaped with slight injuries went to their homes before the overburdened police obtained any record of their names. But it was established today that there were about 830 persons in the club, which was supposed to accommodate only 800, when the fire started.

Inasmuch as the known dead and injured totaled 613, it can readily be seen that, with due allowance for those who went to their homes after receiving first aid, very few persons escaped from the flaming interior of the Cocoanut Grove unscathed.

Hospitals Are Burdened

As the injured began to descend in droves on the hospitals, their facilities threatened for a time to be overwhelmed. The situation was eased at the Boston City Hospital by the fact that more than 100 nurses and many internes and doctors were attending a dance in the nurses' home. They went on duty en masse.

The Boston chapter of the American Red Cross, which quickly mobilized 500 trained first aid volunteers under the direction of a dozen or more of its professional staff, received speedy assistance from New York. The New York Red Cross sent six skilled disaster relief workers here.

A shortage of some of the sulfa drugs threatened to develop as the burned and injured kept pouring into the hospitals, but the Red Cross put in a call to New York and in twelve minutes a large package of the drug was on its way. A special plane flew it to Boston in little more than an hour.

There was also a threatened shortage of blood plasma, but after a hurried conference of public officials permission was given to the hospitals to draw on the emergency blood banks that have been set up under the direction of civilian defense authorities as a safety measure against possible air raids. It was stipulated, however, that

Smoke pouring from the Cocoanut Grove last night as firemen battled the blaze

plasma drawn from these stocks must be replaced at the earliest possible moment.

Martial Law Proclaimed

As the news of the catastrophe spread through Boston and its neighboring towns and cities great crowds of men and women, some merely curious and other alarmed for the safety of friends and relatives, converged on the neighborhood of the club.

The crush grew so serious that at 1:58 A. M. martial law had to be proclaimed and a mixed force of policemen, soldiers, sailors and Coast Guardsmen established a picket line to prevent any one from approaching within 300 yards of the club.

Turned away from the neighborhood, hundreds of grief-stricken men and women besieged the hospitals and the city mortuaries in vain attempts to learn the fate of loved ones. The situation grew so acute that the authorities were forced to announce that bodies could not be viewed until they had been released by a medical examiner. Every medical examiner in the State was hurriedly summoned here to expedite the work.

Within the charred ruins the toiling rescue parties continued their task until almost daybreak. They found heartbreaking scenes as they proceeded. The body of a young girl was found in a telephone booth. Apparently in her terror she had tried to call some one she trusted to come to her assistance, only to be trapped by the flames.

Between 300 and 400 fur coats and evening wraps were found in the check room, most of them ruined by smoke and water. Army and Navy officers' caps to the number of about 200 also were found. Strewn through the wreckage were evening bags and vanity cases, high-heeled dancing slippers and torn fragments of evening gowns.

Air Raid Plan Gets a Test

The duty of listing the injured and identifying the dead was taken over by the Boston Committee of Public Safety, which had worked out an elaborate master disaster file system as part of the air raid precaution system here. In its first test this system functioned admirably.

Police prowl cars rushed volunteer workers and telephone operators to the headquarters of the committee at 9 Park Street to enable it to try to cope with the tremendous flood of inquiries from anxious relatives and friends. The system of using white cards for the missing, pink for the identified dead and green for the injured stood up well, officials said.

At the mortuaries, however, great difficulty was being encountered in identifying the women dead. Most of the male bodies had some identifying cards or papers in their billfolds, the attendants found, but the women, who were attired for a gay evening, had nothing to show their names.

Mayor Maurice J. Tobin, Fire Commissioner Reilly, Building Commissioner Mooney, Health Commissioner G. L. Gately, State Fire Marshal Stephen J. Garrity and Fire Chief Samuel Pope began a joint investigation of the disaster.

A hearing was opened today before Fire Commissioner Reilly, at which the six deputy Fire Chiefs who were at the fire testified to their observations. They agreed that the fire would not have been a difficult one to fight except for the terrified crowd and said that panic caused many more deaths than the flames.

List of Dead Is Read

Throughout the day and late into the night Boston's medical corps and facilities sought feverishly to save the lives of the critically burned. There were tragic scenes at both the North and South Mortuaries, where relatives and friends lined the sidewalks in an attempt to identify charred bodies.

A cold rain began to fall at about noon and scores of women who were waiting became hysterical. At about 5 P. M. Mayor Tobin and

Dr. James M. Manary, superintendent of City Hospital, arranged for their admittance into the amphitheatre of the morgue. The two officials alternately read lists of names of the dead. The reading was punctuated by grief-stricken cries. Other persons seeking the missing were told to supply all possible descriptive matter.

The North Mortuary listed 221 bodies and the South Mortuary 197. The Waterman Funeral Parlor opened its garage to receive about thirteen bodies.

In the line of waiting parents, relatives and friends was Edward J. McCormack, who was seeking his daughter, Mary, 20, the niece of Representative John W. McCormack. He was unable to receive any information.

William J. McDonald, a Coast Guardsman, with only an hour and a half of shore leave, arrived late in the afternoon and appealed to Police Captain Francis Tiernan to allow him inside the morgue to seek the body of his wife, Margaret. She was at the club and her automobile was discovered in front of the establishment.

As the rain increased in intensity the Red Cross and the Massachusetts Women's Defense Corps set up canteens and gave coffee to the persons waiting.

Four From Keene Are Victims
Special to THE NEW YORK TIMES.

KEENE, N. H., Nov. 29—Among four Keene casualties in the Cocoanut Grove fire was Mrs. Mabel (Rushaw) Clark, wife of Clyde C. Clark, formerly head dietitian of the New York City Hospital and former New York school teacher. Both Mr. and Mrs. Clark died and their 18-year-old daughter, Ann Marie Clark, was seriously burned. Fred P. Sharby Sr., proprietor of a chain of theatres in Maine, New Hampshire and Vermont, and his son, Fred Jr., also were burned to death. Mrs. Sharby was injured.

Another view of the rear entrance, made early yesterday morning, after the flames had been extinguished. Broken parts of chairs and tables and the personal effects of some of the patrons of the club litter the street.

The interior after it was swept by the flame

Associated Press Wirephoto

THRONG IS SEARED BY SWIFT BLAZE

Continued From Page One

what happened just before the fire broke out. Certainly it erased from their minds most of what followed. In each survivor's story there is

a definite hiatus. Somewhere between the first moment and the time when a woman or man found himself in the street or in a hospital there was at least one gap.

Swift Onrush of Flames

Some seemed to think the night club lights stayed on for several minutes after the flames rushed at them, and that the great rooms gradually filled with thick, rolling

smoke. Some seemed equally positive that the lights went out within one or two seconds after the first flame leaped across the ceiling and reached down for them.

Most of the guests and employes who were in the main room at street level recalled that the first sounds they heard were the crash of tables and the splintering of glass.

In that instant a wide tongue of flame shot up the stair well. It hardly touched the flimsy silk

A view outside the rear entrance of the Cocoanut Grove late Saturday night as city firemen and police, aided by service men, removed victims from the burning two-story building.

of younger persons, chiefly service men and their girls.

There was a disturbance, "a vague flurry," as he recalled it, which drew his attention toward the front door and the lobby. With it came the sound of a falling table or tables, the tinkling of many glasses breaking.

What confronted them when they turned in their chairs was something so different that the shock momentarily drained them of clear thought. They saw the great mass of flame belly up from the Melody Lounge.

Mr. Gill found himself saying: "Keep calm. It's fire. Keep calm. It's fire." But the panic and rush were on His words were drowned in women's screams and in men's hoarse outcries.

Mrs. Gill fell. So did other women at other tables. Persons sweeping past them with terror in their faces trampled them in the rush. Mr. Gill was swayed from side to side by men and women hurtling toward the doors.

As he fell, his body covered his wife's. Each time he tried to get her to her feet he was downed again, and she with him. They went over repeatedly, kicked and trodden by the hundreds foundering and milling in the dark, with occasional loops of flame reaching down and lighting the shambles.

Mr. Gill said he kept thinking, "They are going over us. They are heading toward a door. They are going over us to freedom."

His hair was singed, flame had licked and peeled his face and his hands were tender where fire had touched them over and over again. His clothes and his wife's were scorched. They beat wherever their garments seemed hottest and their palms were scorched.

BUCK JONES BADLY BURNED

BOSTON, Nov. 29 (P)—Charles (Buck) Jones, cowboy star of the motion pictures, was critically burned in the fire at the Cocoanut Grove night club.

Jones of Van Nuys, Calif., was under treatment at Massachusetts General Hospital today.

Visiting in Boston, the cowboy star had gone to the Cocoanut Grove last night with friends, among them Scott R. Dunlap, a movie producer of Van Nuys, who also was among the injured.

hangings. It just raced across them. Behind the chief path of flame great balloons of fire dropped on the tables, on the bar and on the bandstand.

Men and women said that they could recall no lapse of time between their first sight of flame and the time when they were beating at their hair, their clothing, their faces. One moment they were seated at their tables or at the bar or were slowly moving across the dance floor. The next second, almost, they were on the ground with the fire's hot breath reaching for them.

Screams and Shouts of Panic

John C. Gill of Arlington, head of the Catholic Youth of Boston College Alumni, was at a street-level table with his wife, Margaret. Around them were laughing men and women averaging around 35 to 40 years of age and a smattering

The upright support was all that remained of one of the revolving doors where many of the victims were crushed in an attempt to escape from the blazing structure.

Associated Press

The front entrance. This picture was made yesterday after the bodies had been removed.

"All the News That's Fit to Print."

The New York Times.

LATE CITY EDITION
Showers; warm in forenoon, cooler in afternoon; moderate winds.
Temperatures Yesterday—Max., 86; Min., 71
Sunrise, 6:37 A. M.; Sunset, 7:31 P. M.

Copyright, 1943, by The New York Times Company.

VOL. XCII. No. 31,272. Entered as Second-Class Matter, Postoffice, New York, N. Y. NEW YORK, TUESDAY, SEPTEMBER 7, 1943. THREE CENTS IN NEW YORK CITY

CHUTISTS RING FOE AT LAE; BRITISH PUSH AHEAD IN ITALY; RUSSIANS CAPTURE KONOTOP

M'ARTHUR IN PLANE

Chief Sees Americans and Australians Drop to Trap Foe

LAND FORCES ADVANCING

Up to 20,000 Japanese Circled the Lae-Salamaua Area by Surprise Coups

By FRANK L. KLUCKHOHN
By Wireless to THE NEW YORK TIMES.

SOMEWHERE IN AUSTRALIA, Tuesday, Sept. 7—Watched personally by Gen. Douglas MacArthur from an accompanying plane, a large force of United States and Australian paratroopers jumped on Sunday into the Markham Valley west of Lae, New Guinea, following up the surprise landings in the area by Australian troops the day before.

The Allied paratroop attack closed in the valley and, with the shore assault, encircled elements of four Japanese divisions estimated at 20,000 men.

The biggest aggregation of Allied planes ever assembled in the Southwest Pacific area carried over the objective the first paratroops employed as such in this theatre—a force officially said to be comparable in size to those forces used in North Africa and Sicily.

The Flying Fortress in which General MacArthur traveled led the "V" formations. On the return trip to his field headquarters one motor of General MacArthur's plane cut off and a crosswind developed over the air base, but the Fortress landed safely.

Australians Take Artillery

Carried by air in this huge operation, in which wave after wave of paratroopers plummeted to earth, was Australian artillery. Some of the men in the force had jumped only once before; for some it was the first leap.

General MacArthur, after getting back, explained:

"I did not want our paratroops to enter their first combat, fraught with such hazard, without such comfort as my presence might bring them."

Other ranking Allied officers in this theatre accompanied the dramatic expedition.

The paratroop attack was a complete surprise to the Japanese and, according to preliminary reports, more successful than any previous Allied operation of the sort.

Pride marked General MacArthur's face as he watched the attack of the formations that his careful planning and the work of his staff had developed, officers with him said.

General MacArthur sat next to the radio operator on the two-hour flight to the Markham Valley. Then shifting to a waist-gunner's window the Allied Commander in Chief viewed the laying of a smokescreen that contributed to the success of the mass landings and saw the hundreds of parachutes floating to earth.

Allied fighter planes weaved back and forth over the scene as protection against any Japanese planes. None of the foe appeared.

Foes Inland Escape Barred

ALLIED HEADQUARTERS IN THE SOUTHWEST PACIFIC, Tuesday, Sept. 7 (AP)—The Allied paratroops that floated down on the Markham Valley yesterday won fresh positions behind Lae to add to others that have been slowly forged eighteen miles to the southeast at Salamaua. Any hope the Japanese might have held of using the Markham Valley to flee out of Lae into the jungles was erased by the paratroopers who closed that inland route to the enemy.

The Australian forces above Lae, who since have pushed ahead until they met resistance at a plantation ten miles from Lae, suffered a few casualties from raiding Japanese planes but the paratroopers' surprise was even more complete. Striking on the fourth anniversary of Australian entry into the war, they encountered no air opposition. They were unmolested, therefore, in dropping to the valley and the

Continued on Page Seven

Allies Drive 10-Mile Salient Into Calabrian Mountains

Ten More Italian Towns and 1,000 New Prisoners Taken as Invaders Strengthen Bridgeheads—Naples Area Bombed

By MILTON BRACKER
By Wireless to THE NEW YORK TIMES.

ALLIED HEADQUARTERS IN NORTH AFRICA, Sept. 6—While Allied planes stepped up their attacks on airfields in the Naples area yesterday and last night, the ground troops in Calabria thrust a salient ten miles in depth to San Stefano d'Aspromonte, northeast of Reggio Calabria, in the difficult mountain country. They continued to advance on all sectors of the front.

Pushing ahead slowly in the face of exhaustive demolitions, the British and Canadian spearheads are now just east of Bagnara, in the north, and just east of Melito, in the south. At Bagnara they control the entrance to the southernmost trans-peninsular road, which winds to Bova Marina on the opposite coast.

Control of Strait Secured

The Navy has secured the control of the Strait of Messina and the flow of Allied reinforcements and supplies continues uninterruptedly. The thunder of the coastal guns trained on Sicily from the Italian mainland is only a memory. The invaders' bridgeheads are being strengthened and consolidated in every way necessary to support the lengthening lines of the forward troops.

[The front now runs from a point east of Bagnara back along the coast to Scilla, thence inland to San Stefano, back to the coast at Reggio Calabria and from there to Melito, The United Press said. Reports from Rome via Madrid said that the British Eighth Army had won almost complete control of the Aspromonte range, which extends forty miles northeastward from the "toe" of Italy, The United Press added. According to The Associated Press, the Allies have captured ten more towns.]

The capture of 1,000 more pris-

Continued on Page Four

FORTRESSES POUND STUTTGART IN REICH

Bag 70 Nazis in Attacks Also on Airfields—RAF Out Again After 1,500-Ton Rhine Raid

By The Associated Press.

LONDON, Tuesday, Sept. 7—Large formations of United States Flying Fortresses pounded Stuttgart yesterday to climax one of the greatest daylight bombing offensives of the war, and heavy Royal Air Force squadrons roared over the London area for more than two hours last night, outward bound to maintain the blows at Hitler's Europe.

Over Sunday night the RAF's big planes pounded Mannheim-Ludwigshafen in the South Rhineland with a 1,500-ton bombing attack.

A brief announcement early today said that the new RAF night raiders had again struck in Germany. Reports from Switzerland indicated the attack was once more in the Southern Reich.

More than seventy Nazi fighters were destroyed by the Flying Fortresses in fierce air battles that developed on the eight-hour, 900-mile flight to Stuttgart, center of southwest Germany's war industry and capital of Wuerttemberg Province.

A dozen more were shot down during joint RAF and United States Eighth Air Force attacks upon targets in France. Against this toll, thirty-five American and four British planes were missing in the day raids. The RAF lost thirty-four bombers over Sunday night.

"Flying Fortresses supported by Thunderbolts left fires burning in Stuttgart and bombed other targets, including airfields at Orleans

Continued on Page Ten

RED ARMY SEIZES 290 TOWNS IN DAY

Russians in Donbas Capture Makeyevka, Steel Center, 7½ Miles From Stalino

By The United Press.

LONDON, Tuesday, Sept. 7—The Russians took the great Donets Basin iron center of Makeyevka by storm yesterday, killing 3,000 Germans who tried desperately to hold them off, and captured Konotop, 127 miles northeast of Kiev, in a big Ukrainian break-through.

By capturing Makeyevka, a city of 240,000 people and site of the gigantic Kiroff iron works, the Red Army reached a point seven and one-half miles northeast of Stalino, Russia's twelfth city, of which Makeyevka is officially a suburb.

Slavyansk, Kramastorskaya and sixteen other key Donets cities also were taken in an advance of up to fifteen and one-half miles on a sixty-mile front.

In their Ukrainian break-through the Russians were advancing rapidly on Bakhmach, fifteen miles southwest of Konotop and 110 miles northeast of Kiev, to win control of the junction of railroads leading to Kiev, Gomel, Bryansk, Kursk and Odessa.

Konotop was one of the great German bases on what used to be the Kharkov front. The Russian communiqué, announcing the capture of Konotop, cited the Red Army's new gains as having been made in the Bakhmach direction in evident anticipation of a new triumph.

Moscow dispatches reported, incidentally, that the Red Army had now recaptured more than one-half of the immensely rich Donets Basin.

A Russian communiqué reported

Continued on Page Nine

Axis Prepares for New Invasions And Reports U. S. Army on Move

By The Associated Press.

LONDON, Sept. 6—The Germans were reported today to be rushing possible measures for the defense of the southern coast of France and other vulnerable spots along Europe's Mediterranean coast line.

German rumors of Allied intentions for the invasion of Europe flew so thick and fast that the British Broadcasting Corporation warned French listeners to "be careful of German provocations."

[The American Seventh Army embarked from North Africa on Sunday night for an unknown Mediterranean destination, The United Press reported from Madrid. It quoted a dispatch from Italy ascribing the report to usually reliable sources.]

The Germans were said to have cleared all French civilians from a fifty-mile strip of the southern coastal region, ten miles deep. Field Marshal Gen. Karl von Rundstedt, German Commander in Chief in western Europe, was also reported to be pushing additional fortifications in the Narbonne-Montpellier district of the Mediterranean coast to protect his headquarters at Montpellier.

Like the Marseille area, that district, which is flat and sandy and has several good ports, is particularly suitable for landing operations. Advices to the Allied Governments said that 5,000 to 10,000 engineers were also working frantically in the Marseille-Toulon area, throwing up fortifications.

For days the Germans have been trying to obtain some intimation

Continued on Page Five

CHURCHILL URGES POST-WAR ALLIANCE FOR WORLD PEACE

Honored at Harvard, He Says Anglo-American War Machinery Must Be Kept

IF WE DIVIDE, 'ALL FAILS'

Suggests Common Citizenship and Proposes 'Basic English' as a World Language

The text of Mr. Churchill's speech appears on Page 14.

By RUSSELL B. PORTER
Special to THE NEW YORK TIMES.

CAMBRIDGE, Mass., Sept. 6—The British and American peoples must not stop with winning the war, but must go on in cooperation for post-war organization and peace, declared Prime Minister Winston Churchill of Great Britain today after receiving the honorary degree of Doctor of Laws from Harvard University.

"You cannot stop," he warned. "It must be world anarchy or world order."

Saying that the British and American military leadership had attained a cooperation and unity that no allies had ever before enjoyed, he declared it would be "most foolish and improvident" to abandon this machinery as soon as the war were over. He urged that this machinery should be kept in operation, perhaps for a good many years, at least until some new form of world organization had been set up and proved successful in giving us an equal amount of security against being drawn into another world war.

He asserted that he did not know whether this would become a political issue in the United States, but was certain it could not become one in Great Britain.

Receives Ovation From Public

A nation-wide radio audience, as well as a distinguished academic gathering, heard the Prime Minister's address. He arrived this morning by special train from his conferences with President Roosevelt at Quebec and Washington. Receiving ovations wherever he appeared in public, he responded with frequent displays of the V for Victory sign with his fingers. He was heavily guarded by Secret Service men and State and local police. No advance word was published here about his visit, but word got around, and the vicinity of Harvard Square was crowded until he left town this afternoon for an undisclosed destination.

The Prime Minister was accompanied by a party which included his wife and his daughter, Subal-

Continued on Page Fourteen

MORE THAN 50 ARE KILLED IN WRECK OF SPEEDING CONGRESSIONAL LIMITED IN THE OUTSKIRTS OF PHILADELPHIA

SEARCHING THE WRECKAGE AFTER TRAIN DISASTER

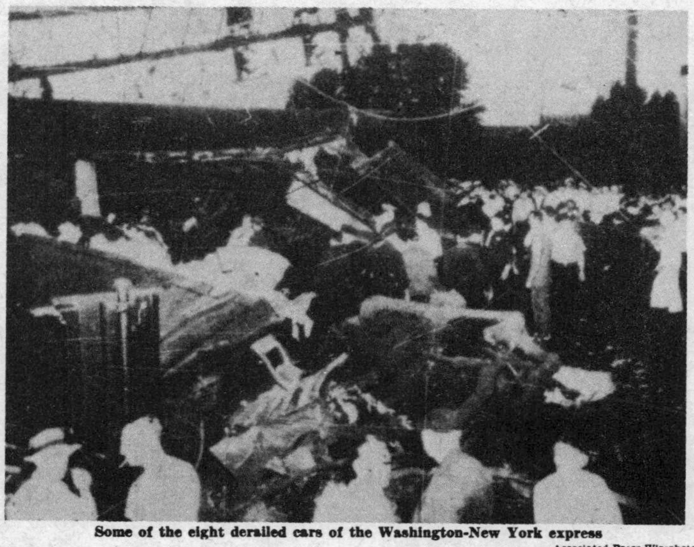

Some of the eight derailed cars of the Washington-New York express
Associated Press Wirephoto

8 CARS JUMP RAILS

Bodies of Victims Are Strewn Along Tracks at Frankford Junction

BIG TRAIN BROKEN IN TWO

Burned-Off Journal Box Is Blamed — Smashed Cars Block P. R. R. Main Line

By FRANK S. ADAMS
Special to THE NEW YORK TIMES.

PHILADELPHIA, Tuesday, Sept. 7—At least forty-three persons and probably more than fifty were killed when eight cars of the sixteen-car Congressional Limited, famous Washington-to-New York express of the Pennsylvania Railroad, were derailed at 6:08 last night at Frankford Junction, within the city limits, but four miles east of the North Philadelphia Station.

Announcing that forty-three bodies had been removed from the twisted steel wreckage, Pennsylvania railroad officials said at 2:30 A. M. that they believed the final total of dead would be somewhere between forty-eight and fifty-two. Local authorities believed the total would be considerably higher.

At midnight Dr. Saverio Brunetti, a police surgeon, had emerged from the car in which the heaviest loss of life occurred and said that thirty or forty bodies remained to be extricated.

A burned-out journal—the housing for the end of an axle—was the cause of the wreck, the nation's worst railroad disaster in many years, if not in the history of American railroading. The overheated axle at the forward end of the seventh car broke as the long train was rounding a curve at Glenwood and Frankford Avenues, almost at the point where the Pennsylvania's cutoff to New Jersey shore points leaves the main line.

FBI Starts Investigation

Twelve agents of the Federal Bureau of Investigation were sent to the scene from the Philadelphia office to investigate the circumstances of the wreck. It was reported that only a few hours before the Congressional Limited was due all switches along the route had been carefully inspected, by Government orders, and had been found to be working properly.

The train was moving at close to seventy miles an hour. The front end of the seventh car, a coach, was thrown almost vertically into the air by the sudden accident. As it came down it dragged with it from the tracks a second coach, two diners and four Pullman chair cars, but the last two cars of the train remained on the tracks. So did the first six cars, although the rear truck of the sixth car was derailed.

All eight of the derailed cars were sprawled like match sticks across the four tracks of the Pennsylvania's main line, completely blocking it to all traffic. The first day coach rolled over and over until it struck the base of a signal tower, which sheared through it like a giant can opener. It tore a gap through the middle of the car big enough for an automobile to pass through.

Torches Release Traps

Still coupled to this car, the second coach likewise rolled over and over, until it to came to rest against the shattered ruins of the other, whil ethe seven other cars were tossed by their impetus at crazy angles across the right of way. All of the loss of life occurred in the two day coaches.

When the first horror-stricken rescuers arrived they found that both ends of the two coaches had been sealed by the shattered steel of their vestibules. Police, firemen and railroad wrecking crews were forced to cut away tangled steel wreckage with acetylene torches before they could remove many of the occupants of these two cars.

Rescue workers searched the second of the two coaches for the body of a young Army lieutenant who had been traveling with an armed guard of four privates, ac-

Continued on Page Three

NON-PARTISAN PLEA MADE AT MACKINAC

Baldwin Heads Group Demanding World Stand by Republicans in Fight on 'Cabal'

By TURNER CATLEDGE
Special to THE NEW YORK TIMES.

MACKINAC ISLAND, Mich., Sept. 6—A demand by a group of Governors led by Raymond E. Baldwin of Connecticut that the Republican Post-War Advisory Council take at its meeting here a positive nonpartisan stand on post-war international problems threatened tonight to upset the plans of the "Washington cabal" to write a general, cover-all declaration and defer particulars to the future.

Supported by most of the New England Governors at the conference and either directly or in spirit by Gov. Edward J. Thye of Minnesota, who brought to the conference former Gov. Harold E. Stassen's plan for international collaboration, and by some State executives from the Far West, Governor Baldwin demanded that the council do more than promise

Continued on Page Eighteen

Survivors of Wreck Tell How Servicemen Helped

About 100 passengers who had escaped injury in the wreck of the Congressional Limited were brought to Pennsylvania Station at 10:15 o'clock last night in a special train made up of four cars which had gone through the disaster without damage.

Among the survivors were many who had been sickened by the sights of death and destruction at the scene. Some had had narrow escapes, having been within a few feet of persons killed outright.

The first of the injured to reach this city was a young woman, Miss Carolyn Brown of 1332 Fairmont Street, Washington, D. C., who is employed as an industrial analyst by the War Production Board. Miss Brown came into Pennsylvania Station just before midnight on a Lehigh & Reading Railroad train which was rerouted around the scene of the wreck.

She said she was seated in the sixth car when the wreck occurred.

"There were sudden jerks and then my car started rocking," she said. "Finally it turned over on its side. Most of the women in the car became hysterical. But the servicemen climbed around among the seats and quieted them.

"One woman was terribly hysterical. A sailor slapped her in the face, finally, saying, 'Close your damn mouth before everybody here becomes hysterical!' That quieted her down.

"I was lying there on the side of the car. Finally some of the sailors pulled me out, getting me outside through a back door, and I was taken to the Episcopal Hospital in North Philadelphia. An examination showed I had bad bruises of the left hand and left arm. After they treated me they let me continue on to New York."

Miss Brown, an attractive girl who is a native of Harrison, Ark., and a graduate of Park College in Missouri, hurried to New York because she had a date with Ensign Robert Kund of the Marine Air Corps at Floyd Bennett Field. She had come to New York to see him. She has been working in Washington for variour departments for

Continued on Page Three

'A' COUPONS TO LAST TO NOV. 22 IN EAST

OPA Dashes Hopes for Rise in Value of 'Gas' Ration at Any Early Date

Special to THE NEW YORK TIMES.

WASHINGTON, Sept. 6—Holders of "A" gasoline rations in the seventeen Eastern States and District of Columbia "must plan to make their A-6" coupons in their current books last through Nov. 22, the Office of Price Administration warned today. The agency's statement dashed the hopes of those who expected an early liberalization of the current gasoline allotment.

"The expiration date of Eastern motorists' present A books is undetermined," the OPA said. "It had been hoped that an improvement in the gasoline supply situation might make possible an increase in A rations for Easterners. This increase would have been accomplished by advancing the present expiration date of A-6 coupons from Nov. 21 to some time in October.

"At the present time, however, the supply situation in the East is not sufficiently improved to make an increase possible, and motorists must plan to make their A-6 coupons last through Nov. 22."

The revelation on A book rations was made in connection with an announcement by OPA giving instructions for mail renewal of the ration books in the shortage area.

The renewal procedure will be simple, OPA officials said. In some

Continued on Page Sixteen

War News Summarized

TUESDAY, SEPTEMBER 7, 1943

American parachute troops and heavy artillery dropped from the New Guinea skies behind the Japanese and completed the encirclement of 20,000 enemy troops in the Salamaua-Lae sector. The innovation took the enemy so completely by surprise that not a plane challenged the exploit. Simultaneously, the greatest armada of heavy and medium bombers in the history of the Pacific war roamed the battle area. Ninety-five tons of 1,000-pound bombs destroyed the main Japanese fortified bastion at Heath's Plantation defending Lae on the north. [1:1; map P. 7.]

United States planes for the first time flew 500 miles into southwest Germany yesterday to bomb Stuttgart. Other American aircraft hit airfields in France. Persistent fighter opposition was encountered and the Flying Fortresses shot down more than seventy of eighty-two enemy planes destroyed. Thirty-five bombers and four fighters failed to return. Sunday night the RAF dealt heavy blows to Mannheim-Ludwigshafen and other Rhineland targets. [1:2.]

Allied troops in southern Italy pushed a ten-mile salient to San Stefano, northeast of Reggio Calabria. Demolitions and mountainous terrain slowed the advance. The Strait of Messina was declared open to Allied navigation and aircraft again struck airfields and communications around Rome, Naples and southern Italy. [1:2-3; map P. 4.]

Germany and Italy were frankly worried over further invasions of the Continent. The continued absence of the American Seventh Army was a particular source of annoyance to the Axis, which expected a landing almost anywhere. [1:2-3; map P. 5.]

The pace of the Russian advance had not slackened yesterday. The Red Army captured nearly 300 more villages and was only a few miles from Stalino in the Donets Basin. Konotop was taken farther north. [1:3; maps P. 9.]

American and British planes, in a perfect example of cooperation with the Royal Navy, sank seven U-boats in the Bay of Biscay. The Germans were trying to run the Allied blockade in packs throwing up heavy anti-aircraft fire. [8:4-5.]

Anglo-American cooperation, characterized as unique among any allies by Prime Minister Churchill, must be carried on after the war, he said at Harvard, where the honorary degree of Doctor of Laws was conferred upon him. It would be "most foolish and improvident" to abandon this machinery, he said, urging a "stronger, more efficient and more rigorous" world organization than the League of Nations. American participation in world affairs and Anglo-American cooperation would never become political matters in England, he declared. [1:4.]

The French Committee of National Liberation added François de Menthon to its membership as Commissioner for Justice. M. de Menthon is co-director of Combat, a leading underground body in France. [11:1.]

Mosquito-Repelling Chemical Made For Army, Navy to Beat Malaria

By WILLIAM L. LAURENCE
Special to THE NEW YORK TIMES.

PITTSBURGH, Sept. 6—An impenetrable chemical wall against malaria-carrying mosquitos, which promises to answer the acute problem of quinine shortage for America's fighting forces in the jungle areas, was described here today at the opening sessions of the annual autumn meeting of the American Chemical Society.

The new chemical wall is an insect-repellent four to six times more lasting in its effect than any other similar substances hitherto known. Some details of its performance are still a military secret, but it is already safeguarding American soldiers and marines in areas infested with mosquitos, it was reported by Drs. Philip Granett, G. C. Furness and W. Rudolfs of the New Jersey Agricultural Experiment Station, Rutgers University, one of the group of chemists who synthesized the new chemical.

The chemical, known only as formula 612, promises to be the chemists' answer to Japan's cutting off the natural quinine supply in Java. Formula 612 promises to be much better than quinine, or similar anti-malarial drugs, for these chemicals do not cure malaria, whereas the new synthetic chemical acts as a preventive against that scourge of mankind.

The new compound is a colorless liquid. It has no unpleasant odor, according to Dr. Granett, and is

Continued on Page Twenty-one

MORE THAN 50 DIE IN DERAILED TRAIN

Continued From Page One

cording to other passengers. These passengers said that the lieutenant carried a small black leather case which they assumed contained important papers. The lieutenant and one of the privates were believed to have been killed and the other three privates injured.

Scores of injured persons had been thrown from windows of the other derailed cars or had crawled from the wreckage or been assisted by persons more fortunate than themselves. All available ambulances were summoned to the scene. They were busy for several hours removing the injured.

Railroad officials said at midnight that they had listed sixty-eight persons injured, but other observers at the scene believed that the total would reach at least 100. Many of the injured were so seriously hurt that there was little chance of their recovery, according to reports from the hospitals to which they were rushed.

Live wires dangling from the wrecked overhead power system of the railroad set fire momentarily to the wreckage of the first coach, but the blaze was extinguished almost at once by the first rescue workers to arrive. Some eye witnesses said that some of the injured were burned by the flames, but this was not confirmed by hospital reports.

Many Service Men Aboard

Many service men traveling to or from their homes on leave were among the passengers on the crack express. Aboard also were Government officials. Dr. Lin Yutang, the Chinese writer, and Roy W. Howard, president of the Scripps-Howard newspapers, were passengers on the train, but both escaped unscathed.

The train was the advance section of the celebrated Congressional Limited, long known as the Pennsylvania's fastest train. It left Washington at 4 P. M. and was due at the Pennsylvania Station in New York at 7:35 P. M. It had not stopped en route, but was scheduled to make one halt, at Newark.

It slackened speed a trifle below its normal seventy-five mile an hour to take a slight curve as it passed the Frankford Junction passenger station. Suddenly the seventh car was seen to lurch, and then shoot high into the air.

"The middle section of the train separated as the coupling broke," said Capt. H. Roberts of the Pennsylvania Railroad police, an eye witness. "The first car of this section jumped the tracks and telescoped the iron girder of the signal tower, almost directly over Castor Avenue. The girder opened up the steel railroad car just like a can opener would a can of sardines and split the entire car in two, from top to bottom and from front to back, making an opening big enough to drive a locomotive through.

Marine Describes Crash

"The car following was also derailed and smacked up against the car which had telescoped. Then the other cars went off the track."

Capt. S. G. Kitch of the Marines, a resident of Washington who was in one of the dining cars with two other Marine officers, said that "the first we knew of the trouble was the sound of a peculiar crunch.."

"Then the whole car lurched and swayed and everything, people, tables and food, were hurled into the aisles," he went on. "Suddenly, a tiny child went sliding by on the floor. We tried to grab it but missed. Later I learned it was unharmed."

Many of the estimated 250 passengers in the derailed cars were hurled through windows and some of them rolled down a steep embankment. Others remained lying along the right of way. The first rescue workers to arrive said that the whole area was filled with dazed and injured men, women and children.

Private automobiles and trucks from the streets nearest the scene of the crash were pressed into emergency service to rush as many of the injured as possible to hospitals and soon ambulances began to arrive to take over the task. At midnight ambulances were still lined up bumper to bumper beneath the Glenwood Avenue overpass.

Wreckage Pins Injured

Some of the injured were pinned within the twisted steel of the wrecked cars. Ambulance surgeons crawled in close to them to administer morphine to relieve their pain while the rescue workers toiled frantically to extricate them.

One woman, pinned from the waist down, was in such a position that she blocked the work until they could burn away the section of the car that was holding her. Eventually the rescuers burned off the top of the first smashed coach, thereby enabling other workers for the first time to get within the car.

Forty priests from near-by parishes arrived at the scene within a short time after the radio had carried the first word of the tragedy. They administered the last rites of the church to many of the dying and seriously injured.

Floodlights were strung overhead to permit the rescue work to go on unimpeded through the night while a strong guard of United States soldiers was stationed around the area to bar sightseers from impeding the task.

W. G. Higginbottam, general manager of the eastern division of the Pennsylvania, hurried to the scene and made a preliminary investigation of the cause of the accident. It was he who attributed it to a burned out journal box on the front truck of the seventh car of the train.

Other railroad officials, meanwhile, began a check on the number of persons who were aboard the express. They said early this morning that it carried a total of 541 passengers, of whom 410 were riding in coaches and 131 in Pullmans. They estimated that about 250 persons were in the eight derailed cars.

Within an hour after the disaster 300 civilian defense workers as well as crews of policemen, firemen and railroad employes were busy on the scene, while doctors and nurses from half a dozen hospitals had established temporary first aid headquarters.

A loud speaker system was set up to direct the rescue operations, with Police Inspector Thomas Burns in general command of the work. He directed concentrations of skilled crews at the points where they were most badly needed. The workers found it necessary to amputate legs of at least two of the victims who were caught beneath crumpled steel.

Judge Vincent A. Carroll took command of the civilian defense workers, while Superintendent of Police Howard Sutton and Inspector of Detectives George E. Richardson were in charge of the city's uniformed workers. Mayor Bernard Samuel and Director of Public Safety James H. Malone, both of whom had been passing the holiday at the shore, arrived in the evening.

Soldiers and Coast Guardsmen helped move the dead and injured. They also picked up large numbers of traveling bags and other personal possessions. One Coast Guardsman found a wallet containing $800, but having no identification papers.

Emergency wards of the city's hospitals, including Episcopal, Frankford, Methodist, Jefferson, Presbyterian, Jewish, Temple University and St. Joseph's Hospitals, were crowded with the injured. They reported that so many blood donors had appeared after news of the accident was broadcast over the radio that they had to turn away many of the volunteers. The Red Cross rushed blood plasma to the scene and to the hospitals.

All traffic along the main line of the Pennsylvania Railroad, one of the most important communication arteries for the war effort in the nation, was still blocked at 1 o'clock this morning. Railroad officials expressed hope that at least one track might be opened within a few hours, but it was expected noon today before normal service could be restored.

Meanwhile, some through trains were re-routed to New York over the tracks of the Reading Railroad, while the hourly service between New York and Philadelphia was operating only between Camden and New York. Passengers were being relayed to and from Camden by ferry from this city.

The derailment was the second major wreck on the Pennsylvania line within the last four months. Thirteen persons were killed on May 23 when five cars on an Atlantic City to New York passenger train were derailed near Delair, N. J., a few miles from the scene of tonight's wreck.

It also was the country's second major wreck within a week. At Wayland, N. Y., last Monday night, a Delaware, Lackawanna & Western Limited train was wrecked after sideswiping a locomotive, with twenty-seven persons killed and about seventy-five injured.

The Wreck of the Congressional Limited Near North Philadelphia That Cost Many Lives

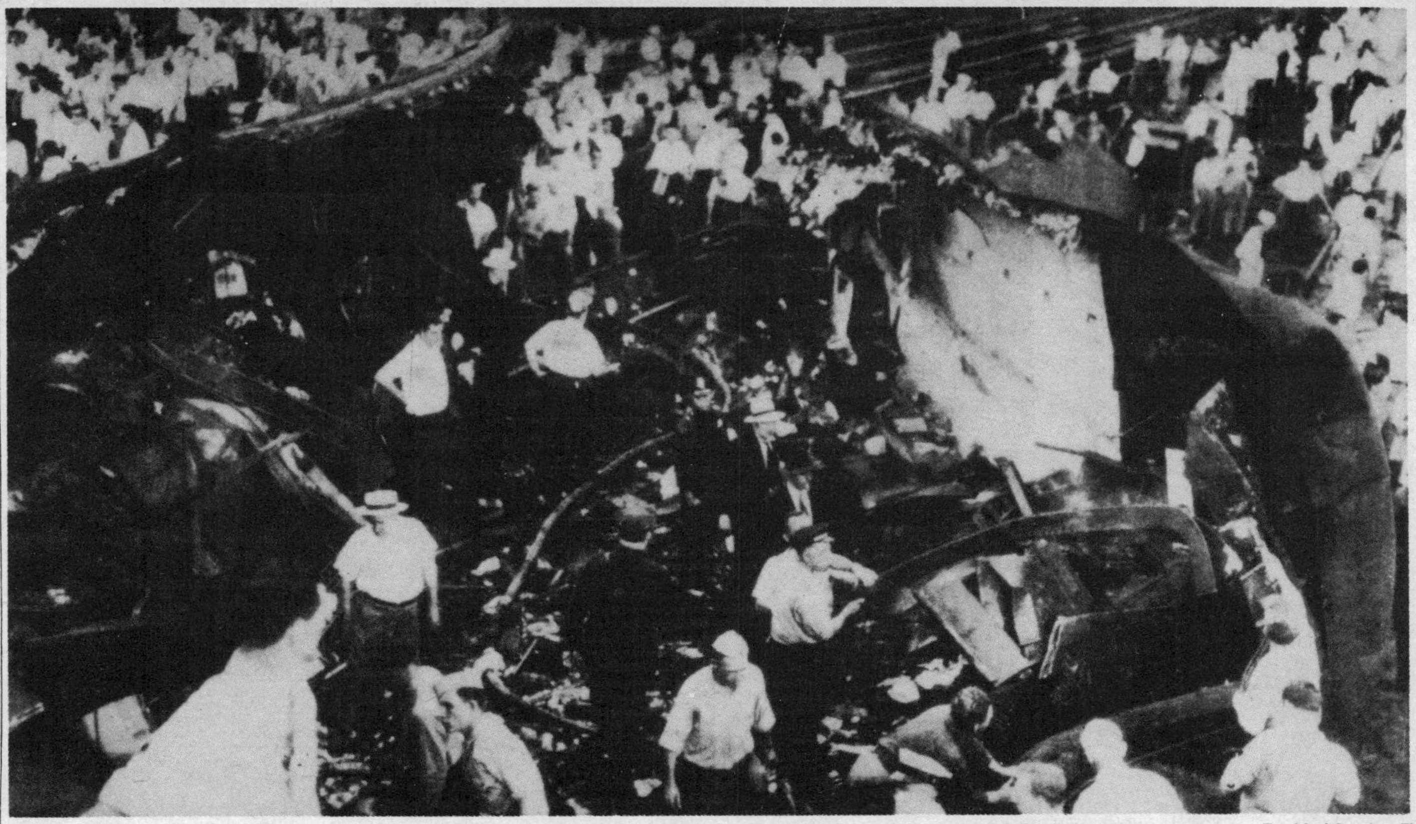

Rescuers, looking for the bodies of the dead and wounded, walk through the wreckage of a car that split in two in the disaster to the Pennsylvania Railroad's fastest passenger express at Frankford Junction. The wreckage on the left is believed to be the top of the car, while on the right are the floor and damaged seats.

Associated Press Wirephoto

Casualties in Philadelphia Rail Wreck

Special to THE NEW YORK TIMES.

PHILADELPHIA, Sept. 6 — A partial list of the dead and injured in the wreck of the Congressional Limited here tonight follows:

IDENTIFIED DEAD

BECKER, HAROLD, about 35, 2013 83d St., Brooklyn. Identified at the morgue through papers found in his wallet.
COLEMAN, Maj. ALFRED F., 60, 2400 16th St., N. W., Washington, D. C.
GODOFSKY, SAMUEL, 306 E. 171st St., New York.
HURLBURT, J. RUFUS, Washington.
OBERDORF, CALVIN, Washington.
SUGARMANN, ISADORE, 169 19th St., New York.
DISKIN, CLARENCE, 508th Parachute Infantry.
FABRIANT, SAMUEL, 235 Rochester Ave., Brooklyn.
FLANDERS, RAYMOND J., 400 Riverside Dr., New York.
KAHANEY, SAMUEL, 320 E. 176th St., New York.
KOLB, JOSEPH R., Marine Corps Reserve, 1810 2d Ave., New York.
KRAUSHWAR, LESTER A., 44 Curtis Pl., Maplewood, N. J.
KUSTER, HENRY, technician, 5th grade, Fifteenth Medical Depot, Camp Pickett, Va.
RYAN, Pvt. GEORGE, Rochester, N. Y.
WARD, GRACE, 525 Kingston St., Brooklyn.
WECHSLER, HARRY, 4574 Bedford Ave., Brooklyn.

INJURED

AT EPISCOPAL HOSPITAL

GUN, FRANK, 515 W. 157th St., New York City; broken back.
CAMPBELL, GEORGE, 20, Cambridge, Mass.; broken bones.
WARREN, HARRIET, 35 W. 90th St., New York, broken bones and contusions and lacerations.
MASON, VIVIAN, 44, of 155 Elm Ave., Mount Vernon, N. Y., possible broken back, lacerations of left leg.
MORRISON, EDITH, 235 W. 75th St., New York, lacerations.
STURMAN, MINNIE, 43, of 37-17 Riverdale Ave., New York, broken bones.
BUSHTA, GEORGE, 18, Jessup, Pa., shock.
RAFKY, MRS. BERTHA, 78, of 201 W. 89th St., New York, shock.
RAFKY, MISS HILDA, 28, daughter of Bertha, shock.
HAKEN, ROSE, 47, of 815 E. 14th St., Brooklyn, fractured spine.
REEVES, MARIE, 29, 414 7th Ave., New York; shock.
PETERSEN, BARBAR, 129 Derby St., Valley Stream, L. I.; leg injuries.
BROWN, CAROLYN, 21, Washington; contusions.
VAUGHAN, GERALD, 29, 19 W. 44th St., New York; contusions.
HOLM, ROSE, 23, Madison, N. J.; minor injuries.
JONES, GEORGIA ELIZABETH, 20, Lynchburg, Va.; minor bruises.
CLARK, MARY ELLA, 27, 91 Macon St., Brooklyn; minor injuries.
BREUSCH, BETTY, 21, of 139-12 34th Rd., Flushing, N. Y.; minor lacerations.
KNORR, HENRY P., 52, 1717 20th St., N. W., Washington; contusions.

ST. MARY'S HOSPITAL

FINER, Corp. DAVID N., 29, White Plains, on furlough from Fort Claiborne, La.; shoulder injury.
FINER, Mrs. JULIA, 26, wife of Corporal Finer; shock.
GREENBERG, EVELYN, 24, 109-11 8th St., Ozone Park, Queens, N. Y.; laceration of right hand.
MESISCAS, SARAH, 1044 Manor Ave., the Bronx, N. Y.; lacerations of hands and head.
SANPAGELLO ROSE, 50 MacDougal St., New York; broken bones.
LOWENTHAL, Mrs., 2188 Creston Ave., the Bronx, N. Y.; bruises of legs, thighs, hips, arms and burns of legs.
MINSKY, HARRIET, 2188 Creston Ave., the Bronx, N. Y.; bruises of head and shock.
QUIRK, DOROTHY, Washington; observation.

NORTHEASTERN HOSPITAL

VARTABEDIAN, VINCENT A., 46, Forest Hills, Queens, N. Y.
VARTABEDIAN, ARMAND, father of Vincent, Brooklyn.
GEORGINE, LOUIS, 35, Leonia, N. J.
HOWARD, MADELINE, 21, the Bronx, N. Y.; cook on the train.
GELD, IDA, 39, Brooklyn.
SMITH, RHODA, 19, the Bronx, N. Y.
PHALEN, LILLIAN, 25, New York.
BODNAR, JULIUS, Bronx, N. Y.
SANDBERG, RUTH, 19, the Bronx, N. Y.
WALSH, Tech. Sgt. JAMES P., 27, Richmond Hill, Queens, N. Y.
SCHUBERT, KATIE, the Bronx, N. Y.
NEARY, MARY, 22, the Bronx, N. Y.
LARKIN, Mrs. SARAH, the Bronx, N. Y.
ROBINSON, Mrs. ALBERT, 45, New York.
FALK, EVELYN, 23, Portchester, N. Y.
BENNES, CHARLES W., the Bronx, N. Y.
BROOM, CLARENCE O., 23, a marine, Fort Mill, S. C.
VOYNICK, JOSEPH, radio man 3d class, USN, Washington.
DAIL, HARRY W., 20, USN, Dumont, N. J.
MAY, JESSIE, 30, Baltimore.
McCAULEY, IAN, New York.
WINKLER, SHIRLEY, 23, the Bronx, N. Y.
WINKLER, SAMUEL, 26, the Bronx, N. Y.
BARBASH, IRVING, 63, New York.
HUN, Dr. BERNARD K., Richmond Hill, Queens, N. Y.
RISSETT, LILLIAN, 27, the Bronx, N. Y.
RISSETT, JULIA, 58; mother of Lillian, the Bronx, N. Y.
PARNES, Mrs. FLORENCE, 36, Jersey City.
DI ANGELLO, Mrs., Mount Vernon, N. Y.
DI ANGELLO, PATSY, Mount Vernon, N. Y.
MONROE, SAMUEL, New York.
MERCUR, AMMIE, New York.

AT FRANKFORD HOSPITAL

HOUSEMAN, Mr. and Mrs., Ossining, N. Y.
TADEN, JEAN, 373 Wilden Pl., South Orange, N. J.
TAYLOR, HERMAN, 1 Willow St., East Orange, N. J.
DUNSWORTH, EDNA, Washington.
GOLDMAN, IDA, 2386 Davison Ave., the Bronx, N. Y.
GORGAS, Mr. and Mrs. SAMUEL, 2219 Strauss St., Brooklyn.
CALVERT, ROBERT, Birmingham, Ala.
WARSAW, BLANCHE, Portchester, N. Y.
COHEN, BENNIE, 310 W. 3d St., New York.
RAVERI, RAY, no address.
COOPER, LUCILLE, 135 W. 225th St., New York.
TRYEE, LULA, 2555 Eighth Ave., New York.
TYREE, AHREND, same address.
TUTEN, THELMA, same address.
DAVIS, NATHANIEL, 929 E. 216th St., the Bronx, N. Y.
HENRY, MORRIS S., 1910 63d St., Brooklyn.
CARSON, W. P., 470 W. 150th St., New York.

AT NORTHEASTERN HOSPITAL

GHOLSTON, MARIE, Washington.
FRIEDMAN, ROSE, the Bronx, N. Y.
BIRNBAUM, SHIRLEY, Brooklyn.
SIMMONS, FLORENCE, Brooklyn.
SHUNKWEILER, Pfc. ALVIN L., Marine Barracks, Washington.
KAHANEY, GOLDIE, the Bronx, N. Y.
ROBINSON, ALONZO, merchant seaman, Sheepshead Bay, Brooklyn.
TEPHEN, JAMES, 478 Central Park West, New York.
RAMERI, Lieut. RAYMOND, of Washington.
GARRETT, L. W., 2010 7th Ave., New York.
PEFFIN, SAMUEL, no address.
BELL, VERNON, U. S. Army, Washington.
KING, EVELYN CURTIS, 271 W. 150th St., New York.
COWSICK, PETER, Quakertown, Pa.

TEMPLE UNIVERSITY HOSPITAL

BROOKS, JOHN, 18, Washington, shock and bruises.
ALLISON, PINKNEY, 56, 150 W. 140th St., New York, bruises of left leg.

NEWS BULLETINS
by The New York Times over Station WMCA—570 on the dial. Every hour on the hour 8 A.M. through 11 P.M.

SURVIVORS PRAISE SERVICEMEN'S AID

Continued From Page One

three years, she said. Her father is a statistician for the Missouri & Arkansas Railroad.

Cpl. Otis Tellis, returning from Langley Field, Richmond, Va., to his post in New Hampshire, said:

"I was in the fourth car from the engine. There was quite a bit of jerking and then the train came to a quick stop. We had just left Frankford Junction. When I got out I found the car directly behind mine—the fifth car from the engine—wrapped around a pole and completely cut in half.

"Several cars behind—maybe the seventh back from the engine—a car appeared to have had its roof torn off. There were no signs of panic, but there was quite a lot of crying. I had no idea how many people were killed and injured.

"I started to go to the aid of the injured, but I could not stand the sight of the blood all about, and I had to leave."

Brooklyn Man a Rescuer

Sol Rosen, a jewelry salesman, of 508 Williams Avenue, Brooklyn, had a narrow escape. He said:

"I don't know where I was riding; maybe it was in the seventh car from the engine. I think it was. All I can remember is that the roof was torn off the front half of the car. It was right over me. But all the people in front escaped injury and all the people in the back were hurt.

"I climbed out of the window. Looking around, I realized what had happened. I organized the men in my section of the car who weren't hurt—there were twenty-four, I think—into a team to help take out the injured through a window."

Seaman George Davis of the Navy, on his way from Washington to his home in Verona, N. Y., was in a car that was wrecked. He said:

"I don't know where my car was; it was the one just before the three that piled up. The train came to a sudden stop after there had been some severe jerking. There was a girl seated in the seat next to me and I threw her to the floor so she wouldn't be cut by the glass. I dont' know who she was.

"There was a lot of screaming. I managed to climb out of the window and I noticed that my car had cracked up against a trestle. After I had looked over the scene I climbed through the window back into the car and helped the girl out. She appeared to have escaped hurt. Then I pulled out several more passengers.

"Then I went in and saw a Negro soldier, apparently dead. He was badly mangled. I couldn't stand it any more and I had to quit."

Ensign Tells of Navy Aid

Ensign Doyle Seldenright of the Navy, who was on a trip with his wife, Ruth, from their home in Washington to New York, was just behind a group of cars which were badly wrecked. He said:

"We were in a parlor car in the rear, just in back of a dining car. Suddenly there was quite a bit of jolting and bouncing and the train stopped cold. I looked out of the window and I saw a signal bridge just ahead. All the cars in front seemed to be wrapped around the bridge and completely demolished.

"Just about that time a commander of the Navy came walking through my car and he asked all the service men to go out and aid the injured. I and some others went out, but we couldn't do much because we didn't have stretchers or medical supplies.

"Shortly afterward a Coast Guard detachment came up with ambulances, stretchers and supplies and we were able to get to work. The passengers who weren't hurt were remarkably calm.

"The most pitiful sight I saw was a 9-year-old Negro girl going around among the injured and the bodies looking for her mother. There was plenty of crying and wailing. I hope I never witness such a thing again.

One passenger saw very little of the disaster. He was George Christianson of 3409 Fulton Street, Washington, D. C., who is associated with the Norwegian Purchasing Commission. He was riding in the second car from the engine, on his way to New York.

"I felt a couple of jerks, looked out and saw that several cars had been derailed," Mr. Christianson said. "Everybody seemed to be quite calm; there was no panic whatever. Quite a few of the passengers were crying, however."

Two of the passengers arriving here had been in a car which crashed into a pole—the club car, which they said was the eighth. They were Ensign John Cassullo of San Diego, Calif., attached to the Maritime Service, and Sgt. Leo Selvitz of Los Angeles, a marine. They were traveling together.

As the train was leaving Philadelphia, Ensign Cassullo said, he went to the dining car to buy cigarettes. He had hardly returned to his seat when the car began to bounce and jerk. It crashed into a pole, he said, adding, "It was a terrible sight."

An Army major organized the servicemen in his vicinity to assist the injured and prevent panic among the uninjured, he said. He and Sergeant Selvitz had climbed out the window of their car, but then they climbed back and helped carry out the other passengers.

Gene Leibowitz of 32 Lenox Road, Brooklyn, said:

"I saw it all when the crash came. I was standing on the platform. The car I was on was not damaged, but we were tilted on an angle. I saw people hurt and dead."

A 12-year-old boy among the passengers told of having been thrown into a seat by the crash. He was Robert Paladino of 1734 Adams Street, the Bronx, who is in his last term at Public School 34. He was traveling with his mother, Mrs. Angie Paladino; her friend, Mrs. Ida Disperati of 1609 Melville Street, the Bronx, and the latter's daughter, Tina. The women had taken the children to see their fathers, who are in service and stationed in Washington.

"I was in the second car from the last, and walking forward from the water-cooler, when the crash happened," Robert said. "I wasn't hurt; I was thrown into a seat. We were helped out of the car."

As soon as the special train stopped, the passengers piled from the cars and hurried quickly to the platform. There many were greeted at the gates by anxious friends and relatives, some of whom had been waiting for hours. Others hurried to telephone booths and telegraph offices to inform their families that they were safe. Among them were a handful of children, with drawn, harried faces.

A. L. Stewart, Pennsylvania Railroad superintendent of passenger traffic, said last night that emergency arrangements had been made to use the facilities of the Lehigh Valley and Reading railroads for rerouting southbound Pennsylvania trains past the scene of the wreck and that westbound trains were rerouted over the "cut-off" from Trenton to Thorndale, Pa., which is normally used only for freight transportation.

Heavy Tolls Recorded In Other Train Wrecks

By The United Press.

Major train wrecks in the United States have included the following:

Dec. 29, 1876—Ashtabula, Ohio, 84 dead.
Aug. 10, 1887—Chatsworth, Ill., 81 dead.
Aug. 7, 1904—Eden, Col., 96 dead.
Dec. 30, 1906—Washington, D. C., 53 dead.
March 1, 1910 — Wellington, Wash., 96 dead.
July 4, 1912—Corning, N. Y., 40 dead.
Aug. 5, 1914—Tipton Ford, Mo., 40 dead.
June 22, 1918—Ivanhoe, Ind., 68 dead.
July 9, 1918—Nashville, Tenn., 115 dead.
June 17, 1925—Hackettstown, N. J., 50 dead.
June 19, 1938—Miles City, Mont., 46 dead.
April 19, 1940—Little Falls, N. Y., 30 dead.
July 31, 1940—Cuyahoga Falls, Ohio, 43 dead.
Aug. 30, 1943—Wayland, N. Y., 27 dead.

CALLS P. R. R. WRECK 'FATE'

Retired Engineer of Road Says That 'These Things Happen'

Special to THE NEW YORK TIMES.

JERSEY CITY, N. J., Sept. 6—To Edward V. Coar, 70 years old, of 2540 Hudson Boulevard, this city, who retired on Aug. 29 after twenty years as an engineer of the Congressional Limited, tonight's wreck of the crack flier was "fate—just fate."

Mr. Coar, who heard the news of the disaster while listening to the radio at his home, told newspaper men that although he had never been in a serious train accident, he had been "in tight spots several times."

"After all," he added, "these things happen now and then on other lines and to other trains and sometimes no one ever knows just why or how."

I. C. C. STARTS INQUIRY

Commission Sends Inspectors to Philadelphia Train Wreck

WASHINGTON, Sept. 6 (U.P.)—Shirley N. Mills, director of safety of the Interstate Commerce Commission, said tonight that field inspectors of the I. C. C. have been sent to Philadelphia to investigate the wreck of the Congressional Limited.

"It will be investigated in accordance with our usual practice," he said.

He said he expected no statement on the wreck before tomorrow morning.

SURVIVORS TELL SCENES OF HORROR

Brooklyn Man Says Coach Split and Part of Roof Fell and Car Lost Its Wheels

HEROIC WOMAN IS SAVED

Trapped Standing Up for Five Hours as Train Crew Works With Blow-Torch

Special to THE NEW YORK TIMES.

PHILADELPHIA, Sept. 6—Survivors of the Congressional Limited wreck told harrowing stories of hunting for friends and loved ones, of hearing the terrible sound of rending metal.

Joseph Haiken, 54 years old, of Brooklyn, N. Y., who was riding in the third coach behind the engine, said that just as the train passed the North Philadelphia station he had a feeling that something was dragging on the bottom of the train.

"The train slowed down and I looked at the coach behind. It seemed to split and a piece of the roof fell down into the aisle. The wheels were gone and the body of the car was resting on the tracks.

"I jumped down and ran along the tracks to the diner to find my wife. The diner was still on the tracks but was all smashed up inside. I found my wife. She was hysterical and screamed that two or three babies in the diner had been killed.

"The car in front of the diner was sideways across the track and by this time they were pulling out bodies of the dead."

The courage of Miss Christina Nix of Long Island City, Queens, was related by one of the first persons to reach the wreck.

Harry Hasher, who helped with the injured and dying, said he saw Miss Nix standing in the wreckage of the second coach to leave the tracks and wondered why she did not climb out.

"Then I saw," he continued, "her legs and feet were trapped in the mass of twisted steel. She was pinned in a standing position. Her cries of agony were pitiful but she remained conscious. I tried to comfort her in every way I could but there was no way for me to help her out.

"A smile formed on her pain-torn face. 'Thank God I'm Irish,' she whispered.

"Finally an emergency crew arrived and began to use acetylene torches to burn away the metal that pinned her legs. The pain must have been terrible but she wouldn't give up. Then some doctors saw her plight and periodically administered a sedative.

"At 11 o'clock they finally released her and took her to a hospital. Miss Nix had been pinned in the wreckage for almost five hours."

Matthew A. Roth, Chief Deputy Coroner, told of a woman who gave her name as Mrs. MacNeill of Washington, D. C. She was trapped in the dining car behind the coach.

"She gave me her watch," he said, "and then without a blink she told me she thought one of her legs was gone. Because of the position in which she was trapped I could not ascertain whether this was true."

He said that the woman lapsed into periods of unconsciousness and to keep her awake rescue workers talked to her continually. She was still trapped at 11 P. M., he said.

Miss Barbara Peterson, 20, of 129 Derby Street, Valley Stream, L. I., and a friend, Miss Florence McManus, 19, also of Valley Stream, were asleep in a coach in the center of the train. Miss Peterson escaped but did not know what happened to Miss McManus. The search for her was in vain.

"The car seemed to twist two or three ways at once," said Miss Peterson, who was taken to Episcopal Hospital. "I was thrown from my seat and my baggage and a lot of broken glass fell all around me."

She said that she kicked glass from a window and climbed out.

"The car was twisted sidewise and tilted so far over that I could step right out on the ground. Another car was almost on top of it."

She said that a sailor and his wife and little baby had been in the seat behind them.

"The sailor climbed out and gave me the baby to hold while he went back for his wife. They all got out safely."

Many passengers, who were thrown into the aisles as glass and baggage tumbled about them, said that the sides of the diners and coaches were covered with blood.

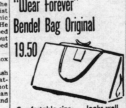

"Wear Forever"
Bendel Bag Original
19.50

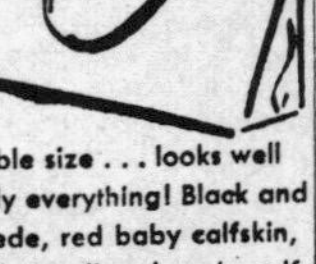

Comfortable size . . . looks well with nearly everything! Black and brown suede, red baby calfskin, green or beige lizard grain calf, black morocco, brown pearl- or pigskin-grain calf.

Bags, main floor

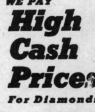

Henri Bendel
10 WEST 57
NEW YORK 19 NY

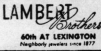

WE PAY
High Cash Prices
For Diamonds

Have you any old diamond jewelry? Have you any rings, pins, bracelets, brooches, heirloom pieces you no longer wear? Because of the war, diamonds are commanding high prices . . . We pay high prices for diamonds of every size and description. And our 67 year old reputation as neighborly jewelers is your assurance of fair dealing.

LAMBERT Brothers
60th AT LEXINGTON
Neighborly jewelers since 1877
OPEN THURSDAYS TILL 9 P M

"All the News That's Fit to Print."

The New York Times.

LATE CITY EDITION
Fair and cold today with moderate winds.
Temperatures Yesterday—Max., 34; Min., 21
Sunrise, 8:18 A. M.; Sunset, 5:34 P. M.

Copyright, 1944, by The New York Times Company.

VOL. XCIII..No. 31,404. Entered as Second-Class Matter, Postoffice, New York, N. Y. NEW YORK, MONDAY, JANUARY 17, 1944. THREE CENTS NEW YORK CITY

RUSSIA REJECTS POLISH PROPOSAL TO NEGOTIATE BOUNDARY DISPUTE; EISENHOWER ARRIVES IN BRITAIN

OUSTER OF KENNEDY AS TAMMANY HEAD SET FOR THIS WEEK

Foes of Leader Say They Now Have Necessary Votes in Executive Committee

ULTIMATUM IS DUE TODAY

If Resignation Is Refused Fay Will Get a Petition Forcing Meeting and Decisive Action

Claiming the signatures of a majority of the Tammany executive committee to a petition requesting Representative James H. Fay to call a meeting, members of the committee announced yesterday their intention of calling on Michael J. Kennedy today to ask him to resign as leader. Should Mr. Kennedy, as expected, refuse to resign, the petition will then be presented to Mr. Fay, the chairman, who under Tammany rules must call a meeting.

At the meeting, which is expected to be held before the end of this week, a motion will be made to oust Mr. Kennedy as leader. Edward V. Loughlin, secretary to Supreme Court Justice Ferdinand Pecora and leader of the Fourteenth Assembly District, who has taken the initiative in the circulation of the petition, is scheduled to be elected leader.

Although friends of Mr. Kennedy expressed doubt that a majority of the executive committee members had signed the petition, leaders in the movement to oust him declared that not only was there no doubt that a majority had signed but also that Mr. Loughlin had the necessary votes pledged to elect him leader. With the ex officio members there are twenty-seven and one-half votes in the executive committee and signers of the petition were said to represent sixteen and seven-twelfths votes.

Kennedy Refuses Comment

Mr. Kennedy had no comment on the attempt to depose him.

The movement to oust Mr. Kennedy grew out of his part in the nomination of Thomas A. Aurelio for Supreme Court Justice in an arrangement with Republican organization leaders. Mr. Kennedy and the Tammany executive committee sought, unsuccessfully, to rescind the nomination after disclosure by District Attorney Frank S. Hogan that Mr. Aurelio, who was later elected, owed his nomination in large part to Frank Costello, reputed racketeer.

Somewhat paradoxically members of the executive committee group that elected Mr. Kennedy leader and took an active part in bringing about the nomination of Justice Aurelio are now reported to be against Mr. Kennedy.

Assemblyman Patrick H. Sullivan, leader of the Eleventh Assembly District, who has been active with Mr. Loughlin in circulating the petition, said there was no doubt that a majority of the executive committee members had signed.

"We have the votes to oust Mr. Kennedy," he said.

Steady Decline in Influence

Should Mr. Kennedy resign or be ousted, he will be the third in recent years to be forced out of the leadership of Tammany. Since the death of Charles F. Murphy, the last really effective leader of Tammany, the local Democratic organization has decreased gradually in power and influence. George W. Olvany, who succeeded Mr. Murphy, resigned voluntarily. John F. Curry, who succeeded Mr Olvany, was ousted after defeat of Tammany in a city election. The late James J. Dooling, who possessed some qualifications for leadership, was in ill health when elected leader, and died while holding the leadership. Christopher D. Sullivan, who succeeded him, was ousted and died shortly after. Mr. Kennedy, elected to succeed Mr. Sullivan, won a primary fight easily and seemed to be on the way to a successful leadership until the Aurelio incident.

Kept out of control of the city administration by the election and two re-elections of Mayor La Guardia, Tammany's political influence has dwindled during the foregoing leaderships. Tammany Hall in East Seventeenth Street was sold to the International Ladies Garment Workers Union and the Tammany political organization was divorced from the 150-year-old Tammany Society. Technically the political Tammany is now the Democratic County Com-

Continued on Page Twenty

PURE WATER is vital to health. Drink Great Bear Ideal Spring Water.—Advt.

Bettors Face Arrest With the Bookmakers

Mayor La Guardia announced yesterday in his weekly radio broadcast from City Hall that he had written to Police Commissioner Lewis J. Valentine suggesting that in future bettors as well as bookmakers be arrested in gambling cases.

"District Attorney Charles P. Sullivan of Queens County suggests that when a bookmaker is arrested, we arrest those placing bets," the Mayor said. "We'll do that. We'll get their names and addresses, too. That is a very good suggestion and I have written to Commissioner Valentine about it and will confer with him during the week. I hope to put it into effect."

DREW ON CITY RADIO DENIES BIAS CHARGE

Mayor Also Introduces Heads of Three Police Groups to Tell of Religious Amity

Patrolman James LeRoy Drew, recently acquitted of departmental charges involving anti-Semitism, made a dramatic appearance yesterday on Mayor La Guardia's weekly radio broadcast from City Hall. Speaking at the Mayor's request, he reaffirmed his innocence of the charges, expressed regret that his case had disturbed the public and brought "sorrow" to the Mayor and Police Commissioner Lewis J. Valentine and declared that his record of seventeen years on the police force showed that he entertained no "evil antagonism" toward persons of the Jewish faith.

A board consisting of Frederick E. Crane and Edward R. Finch, former judges of the Court of Appeals, and former Police Commissioner George V. McLaughlin, recently reviewed the Drew case and found that Commissioner Valentine was justified, on the record, in dismissing the charges against the patrolman. The board was appointed by Mayor La Guardia.

Before Patrolman Drew spoke, Mayor La Guardia interviewed three members of the Police Department, representing Catholics, Jews and Protestants. They declared their belief that no racial or religious intolerance existed in the department.

"Recently there has been a great deal of discussion of a certain unfortunate case," the Mayor said. "In our country when one is acquitted that ends the case. Anything else would be persecution.

"I have asked Patrolman James Drew to come here today, and I am going to ask him to talk to you in his own words. Patrolman James Drew, the microphone is yours."

Patrolman Drew's Statement

Patrolman Drew took a chair opposite the Mayor and made his statement in a firm voice.

"My name is James LeRoy Drew," he said. "I have been a member of the Police Department for seventeen years. I am married and have five children. I am unhappy that I have been the cause of so much discussion and so much resentment because of a personal situation.

"I have been under charges. I have been tried and acquitted. I was not guilty of any of the charges preferred against me. My acquittal is, of course, a source of great personal satisfaction, not so much to me, but because of my family and my children. I know that my case was a source of great sorrow to my Commissioner and to you, Your Honor. I am greatly relieved that a board appointed by

Continued on Page Twenty-three

WAR BOND RALLIES WILL START TODAY AS CITY JUMPS GUN

Times Square Show With Array of Stars Among Many Events to Precede Formal Opening

NOON PARADE TOMORROW

Scores of Groups Will Begin Getting Pledges Tonight—Mayor Urges Purchases

The stage was set last night for the United States to start on its Fourth War Loan drive.

New York City—whose residents have a $698,500,000 quota in the four-week campaign for five and a half billion dollars in individual sales throughout the nation—was ready to get out the dollars for victory with an understanding of the seriousness of this home-front task, which was stressed by Mayor La Guardia in an official proclamation he made public yesterday afternoon.

Yet, in recognition of the gaiety that is part of the heritage of a free people, a huge outdoor show with entertainment stars is to be held at noon today in Times Square as a curtain raiser to the drive, which opens officially tomorrow with a military parade from the Battery to City Hall.

Mayor La Guardia, in his weekly radio talk from City Hall over WNYC, proclaimed the period from tomorrow to Feb. 15 as the Fourth War Loan drive and urged New Yorkers to put their money into war bonds as the soundest investment ever offered.

"It is better to loan your money to Uncle Sam and get interest than to have someone come over here and take it away," the Mayor said.

Many Stars on Program

New York's big show today will transform Times Square into an outdoor theatre. Jeanette MacDonald, Bill Robinson, Laraine Day and band leaders Tommy and Jimmy Dorsey—who will play in combination—are among the many entertainers enrolled by the motion picture industry's war activities committee, which has arranged the curtain raiser in cooperation with the Treasury Department.

Fifty war heroes, including wounded men from most of the fronts, who will ride in jeeps, will also take part in the Times Square rally.

Governor Dewey prepared a war loan proclamation, which is to be read at ceremonies in Albany this afternoon, calling upon all residents of the State to support the drive so that New York may take the lead in the fourth loan, as it did in the other three.

The drive's leg work, in this city, will be done largely by 20,000 Minute Men, recruited by the Treasury's war finance committee for New York, who will start a house-to-house canvass tomorrow morning to sell the bonds.

A whole series of preliminary events will take place today, followed by a stepping up of the tempo tomorrow after the drive becomes official. Mrs. George C. Marshall, wife of the Army Chief of Staff, and Mrs. Mark Clark, wife of the commanding general of the Allied Fifth Army, will attend a round of functions today. It had been announced incorrectly in yesterday's editions of THE NEW YORK TIMES that these functions were to take place yesterday.

The wives of the two generals

Continued on Page Eight

Argentine Quake Dead Reach 500; San Juan in Andes Is Devastated

By ARNALDO CORTESI
By Cable to THE NEW YORK TIMES.

BUENOS AIRES, Jan. 16—The city of San Juan, capital of the Andes Mountain Province of the same name, suffered catastrophic damage in an earthquake that struck most sharply for a period of fifty seconds at 8:48 o'clock last night.

Three more heavy tremors during the night and this morning—the third at 8:08 A. M.—hurled ruins down upon the stricken people of San Juan.

At 3 A. M. it had been officially announced that 200 persons were known to be dead and the injured numbered several times that figure. Estimates then were that in San Juan and the surrounding district 50 to 60 per cent of all buildings had been destroyed and heavy damage done to most others.

After the additional earth shocks this morning the Federal Commissioner or Interventor of the Province of San Juan, David Uriburu, calculated that 90 per cent of the buildings in the city were destroyed.

Unofficial reports placed the total dead at many times the figure first announced. Some estimates gave 2,000 killed and several thousand injured out of a population of about 36,000.

[Interior Minister Perlinger, who flew to San Juan, reported 500 bodies had been recovered in the city up to last night, said The Associated Press from Buenos Aires. Army control was established in the area.

[Provincial towns named in dispatches as suffering major casualties and damage included Trinidad and Concepcion, regard-

Continued on Page Eleven

French Fake Copies Of Lyon Newspaper

By Telephone to THE NEW YORK TIMES.

BERNE, Switzerland, Jan. 16—Copies of the Nouvelliste, a Lyon newspaper, bearing last Thursday's date, are passing from hand to hand throughout France and are being read avidly. The reason is that they are fakes—wherefore they contain real news.

On Wednesday night the Nouvelliste went to press as usual, filled with German communiqués and Vichy propaganda, but not a single copy reached the public. Instead, newsstands offered for sale an issue printed clandestinely that gave all the Allied bulletins and news items from British, American and Russian sources.

The substitution had been arranged very methodically. As the orthodox issues reached the streets from the presses, unknown men took charge of delivery trucks and drove off. Simultaneously other men supplied newsstands with the unorthodox issue. By the time the trick had been discovered and the police had gone to work, most of the newspapers had already been sold.

NEW BRITAIN DRIVE CAPTURES HILL 660

As U.S. Marines Score, Sio Falls to Australians—2 Warships, 7 Others Hit at Rabaul

By The United Press.

ADVANCED ALLIED HEADQUARTERS IN NEW GUINEA, Monday, Jan. 17—United States marines captured the vitally strategic Hill 660 on the Borgen Bay front of western New Britain Island Friday, overrunning strong Japanese defenses and advancing down the eastern slopes Saturday to break the anchor of the enemy's defense line, it was announced today.

As the marines crushed enemy resistance on the top of the important elevation, 660 feet in altitude, Allied bombers pounding the Japanese stronghold of Rabaul scored hits on one light cruiser, one destroyer and seven cargo ships in a damaging raid Friday.

Gen. Douglas MacArthur's Monday communiqué announcing these Allied triumphs in the bitter New

Continued on Page Six

GENERAL IS READY

Eisenhower Takes Over in Final Phase of Invasion Steps

TALKED WITH ROOSEVELT

Went to Washington and Also Conferred With Churchill Before Going to England

By DREW MIDDLETON
By Cable to THE NEW YORK TIMES.

LONDON, Jan. 16—Gen. Dwight D. Eisenhower has arrived in London to assume command of the invasion of northwestern Europe, the greatest military enterprise ever commanded by an American, and the final phase of the preparation for invasion has begun. Exuding confidence and enthusiasm, General Eisenhower arrived at the headquarters of this war's AEF—Allied Expeditionary Force—after conferences with President Roosevelt in the United States and with Prime Minister Churchill at Marrakesh, Morocco.

The supreme commander will immediately begin conferences with his chief lieutenants on details of the invasion. There is a likelihood that these will be followed by a quick inspection of the American and British Army units scheduled for combat duties and a tour of the vast supply depots scattered throughout Britain, on which these forces depend for ammunition, food and gasoline.

His arrival here completes the cast of invasion principals. Three Britons, Air Chief Marshal Sir Arthur Tedder, his deputy commander in chief; Air Chief Marshal Trafford L. Leigh-Mallory, who will direct all air forces involved, and Admiral Sir Bertram Ramsay, leader of the Allied navies, have already been named and are believed to be in the British Isles or in adjacent waters.

On the second level of command the name of the commander of the American invasion armies remains unannounced but not unknown. Gen. Sir Bernard L. Montgomery, his "opposite number" in command of the British armies that are destined to fight their way back into France, has already been named. His familiar figure, topped by a black beret, was seen in Plymouth yesterday.

Two other officers, who, although not directly connected with

Continued on Page Two

War News Summarized

MONDAY, JANUARY 17, 1944

Russia has turned down the proposal of the Polish Government in exile to negotiate their boundary differences. Moscow accused the Poles of having rejected the Soviet offer to use the Curzon Line as a border basis and of having attempted to mislead public opinion by suggesting the United States and Great Britain as mediators. The Russians also refused to consider resumption of diplomatic relations with the present Polish Government. [1:8.]

The Russian Army, again shifting the major weight of its attack, launched a drive between Nevel and Lake Ilmen. In three days of hard fighting in this northern sector Soviet forces gained up to five miles on a nine-mile front, capturing more than forty places and cutting the Novosokolniki - Dno - Leningrad railroad. Around Kalinkovichi the Russians crossed the Ippa River and widened the salient approaching Pinsk. Moscow said that 100,000 Germans had been killed on the First Ukraine Front from Dec. 24 to Jan. 13. [1:6-7.]

Americans of the Fifth Army in Italy stormed and captured Mount Trocchio controlling the Rapido Valley and the last high ground before Cassino and the Rome road. French forces seized Vallerotonda, two miles from Sant'Elia. Allied fliers heavily attacked the Florence area. [1:7; map P. 2.]

Nearly one-third of Leipzig's most densely built-up area was demolished in the surprise attack of Dec. 3, the RAF disclosed. [5:2.]

General Eisenhower arrived in England to prepare for the invasion of the Continent, the Supreme Headquarters of the Allied Expeditionary Force announced. It was revealed that he had conferred with Prime Minister Churchill in Africa and then with President Roosevelt and General Marshall in Washington en route to his new post. [1:5.]

Mr. Churchill, now fully recovered, had an "extremely cordial" talk of several hours with General de Gaulle at Marrakesh, Morocco, last Wednesday. Arming of the French underground, participation of French forces in the coming invasion and recognition of French authority over the liberated areas were among the subjects discussed. Leaders in Algiers were optimistic over the chances for improved relations. [3:1.]

Germany was reported to be rushing Gestapo agents and saboteurs to Spain in an effort to counteract the growing influence of the United Nations in that country. [1:6-7.]

American marines in New Britain captured Hill 660, overlooking Borgen Bay in the Cape Gloucester area, and Australians in New Guinea captured Sio and pushed on to Vincke Point. Forty Allied bombers attacked Rabaul and hit seven Japanese cargo ships, a cruiser and a destroyer. Sixty or seventy enemy aircraft rose to intercept the attack. Twenty-nine were shot down and sixteen more were probably destroyed. We lost two bombers and eight fighters. [1:4.]

RED ARMY STRIKES ON ANOTHER FRONT

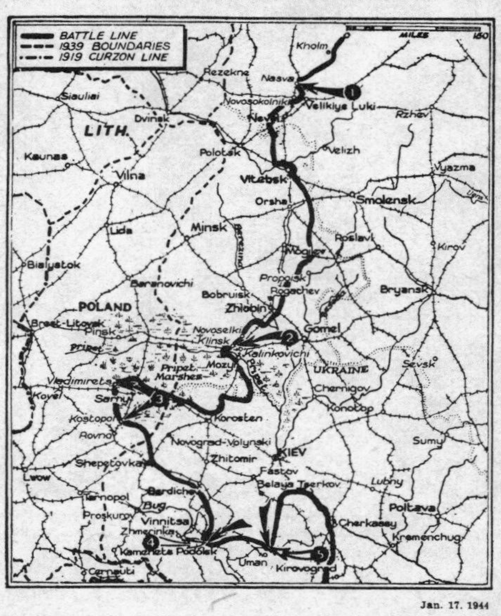

Jan. 17, 1944

In a smash in the direction of the Latvian border, Soviet troops cut the railroad running north from Novosokolniki around the station of Nasva (1). Progress in the Mozyr sector brought the capture of Novoselki and Klinsk village (2). The deepest westward penetration was registered at Vladimirets, and in this same area Kostopol was also seized (3). Strong German counterattacks continued east of Vinnitsa (4) and north of Uman (5).

Russians Open New Attack Above Nevel, Toward Baltic

By The United Press.

LONDON, Monday, Jan. 17—Gen. Ivan C. Bagramian's First Baltic Army veterans, renewing their offensive westward toward the Baltic States in the Nevel sector below Lake Ilmen, have hammered five miles into the German lines on a front nine miles long during a three-day offensive, Moscow announced last night. The new drive already has cut the railroad running north from Novosokolniki Junction to the Leningrad area, about seventy miles from the Latvian border.

Moscow announced that forty towns and settlements had been taken since that drive began Friday, and that at least one German infantry regiment of 3,000 to 4,000 men had been wiped out there yesterday.

A special communiqué revealed yesterday that Gen. Nikolai F. Vatutin's First Ukrainian Army had killed approximately 100,000 Germans and destroyed or captured 2,520 tanks in the first three weeks of an offensive that has carried the Russians fifty-nine miles into Poland on the northern end of a broadening front and within nineteen miles of the four-way rail junction of Rovno on the south.

Pripet Drive Forges Ahead

General Vatutin's southern forces, hurling back desperate German counter-attacks designed to keep the Russians from reaching vital railroads in the Vinnitsa and Uman sectors, wrecked 136 tanks and killed 2,000 Germans yesterday for a five-day total of 11,000 Germans killed and 431 tanks and self-propelled guns knocked out.

Gen. Konstantin K. Rokossovs-

Continued on Page Three

AMERICANS SEIZE PEAK NEAR CASSINO

Mount Trocchio Captured in Dual Assault—French Take 2 Towns and Heights

By Wireless to THE NEW YORK TIMES.

ALGIERS, Jan. 16—American infantrymen, charging up Mount Trocchio in a two-pronged assault powered by a shattering artillery barrage and met by sweeping rear fire from the Germans, seized the vital ridge overlooking Cassino yesterday.

Lieut. Gen. Mark W. Clark's Fifth Army attacked from the northeastern and southeastern corners of the spiny ridge, slightly more than two miles from Cassino, at 6:30 A. M. yesterday. By nightfall the 1,525-foot barrier had been conquered. For the first time the Allies have gained complete observation and dominance over the valley of the meandering Rapido River separating them from their objective.

Today the hard-won positions atop the ridge were being consolidated and the stage was set for

Continued on Page Two

Germans Pour Agents Into Spain In Last Stand Against Shift to Allies

The following article, received from Madrid by way of London, was not censored in Spain.

By HAROLD DENNY
By Cable to THE NEW YORK TIMES.

MADRID, Jan. 10 (Delayed)—Heavy new increments of German agents have been pouring into Spain in recent days in an obvious effort by Germany to save what she can of a situation that has gone badly against her here.

A thousand Gestapo agents and other German representatives have appeared in Madrid alone in the past fortnight. Significant additions to the German population have been noted in other parts of Spain. These reinforce the army of German spies, saboteurs and provocateurs already long active in chinks and crannies of the country's political and economic structure.

They are not easy to deal with, for Germany has extensive commercial interests in Spain and many of these agents are here in the plausible guise of executives, technicians and lesser employes of these interests, as well as cogs in Germany's vast diplomatic, consular and propaganda machinery. In Madrid, spies swarm in the big hotels in such numbers that even casual visitors cannot help noticing their presence.

It is such Germans who, in Allied quarters, are believed to have inspired the recent attacks on American and British consulates by young Spanish hoodlums, for which the Spanish Government has had to apologize. The same quarters fear that the new arrivals

Continued on Page Ten

DEADLOCK REACHED

Renewal of Diplomatic Ties With Regime in London Refused

EXILED CABINET SCORED

Accused of Trying to Mislead Public Opinion and Evading Issue of Curzon Line

By JAMES B. RESTON
By Cable to THE NEW YORK TIMES.

LONDON, Monday, Jan. 17—The Russian Government this morning rejected the Polish Government's offer to enter into negotiations on the Russian-Polish boundary dispute and refused to consider renewing diplomatic relations with Premier Stanislaw Mikolajczyk's Cabinet.

In a statement issued through its official news agency, Tass, in the middle of the night, the Russian Government charged that the Polish Government was trying to "mislead public opinion" by offering to discuss the boundary question with the aid of the United States and Britain. Moscow considers, the statement added, that the Polish Government's statement was a rejection of the Russian Government's proposal to make the Curzon Line the new Russian-Polish boundary. The Moscow statement deadlocks the most serious diplomatic crisis that the United Nations have had to face in recent months.

TEXT OF STATEMENT

The statement follows:

In reply to the declaration made by the Polish Government in London on Jan. 15, Tass is authorized to state:

"First, in the Polish declaration, the question of the recognition of the Curzon Line as the Soviet-Polish frontier is entirely evaded and ignored. This can be interpreted only as a rejection of the Curzon Line.

"Second, as regards the Polish Government's proposal for the opening of official negotiations between it and the Soviet Government, the Soviet Government is of the opinion that this proposal aims at misleading public opinion, for it is easy to understand that the Soviet Government is not in a position to enter into official negotiations with a government with which diplomatic relations have been broken.

"Soviet circles wish that it should be borne in mind that diplomatic relations with the Polish Government were broken off through the fault of that Government because of its active participation in the hostile anti-Soviet slanderous campaign of the German invaders in connection with the alleged murders in Katyn.

"Third, in the opinion of Soviet circles, the above-mentioned circumstances once again demonstrate that the present Polish Government does not desire to establish good neighborly relations with the Soviet Union."

[Soon after its broadcast of the statement, the Moscow radio announced appointment of a commission to investigate the alleged mass killing of Polish soldiers at Katyn, in the Smolensk area, The Associated Press said. A German report, vehemently denied by Russia, declared that 10,000 to 15,000 Poles had been executed there by the Red Army.]

Break Apparently Completed

This statement appeared to make complete the break between the Polish and the Russian Governments. Furthermore, it presented a great problem for the British Government, which was in constant contact with the Polish Government during the drafting of the latest Polish statement.

The controversy started on Jan. 5, when Premier Mikolajczyk's government issued a statement on the occasion of the Red Army's alleged crossing of the Russian-Polish frontier. This first statement drew attention to Poland's long fight against the Germans and contained a number of controversial statements that the Russian Government rejected in sharp language.

A Russian statement of Jan. 10 offered to discuss the establishment of the Russian-Polish boun-

Continued on Page Three

United Press International

Survivors of the earthquake that rocked western Argentina, virtually destroying San Juan and many adjacent towns, poke through the rubble of their former homes, hunting for the bodies of victims.

ARGENTINE QUAKE TAKES HUGE TOLL

Continued From Page One

ed along with San Juan as "totally destroyed," and Carpenteria, Cillakrause, Amgaco, Algaro Boverde and Media Agua.]

Many persons in the city of San Juan and in the dozen or more surrounding communities that were devastated were buried under fallen houses. Communications were broken, and an accurate count of the dead and injured will be possible only after wreckage has been cleared away.

The earthquake was regarded by seismologists as one of the most severe in Argentine history. It shook houses as far away as Montevideo, Uruguay, about 800 miles from San Juan. In Buenos Aires it caused the highest buildings to sway appreciably, but no damage was done here.

San Juan Struggles Through Night

San Juan City was described as a heap of ruins, the wreckage of what had been its buildings covering the streets and squares.

During the night women and children stayed in the open spaces while the men strove to organize aid and rescue persons trapped under fallen houses. Their task was rendered more difficult by the series of minor tremors that followed at brief intervals all night, with major shocks at 2:24 and 2:28 A. M.

The city had been plunged in darkness and all public services put out of commission by the first, heaviest shock. Appeals for help, especially for physicians, nurses, medical supplies and food, were sent out by portable Army radio.

Relief expeditions were organizer at once in all cities of western Argentina and in Chile—San Juan is about 100 miles from the border and 200 miles from Valparaiso—where the radio appeals were heard.

Mendoza, south of San Juan and ninety-seven miles away by rail, was the first outside center to get into action. A first train carrying doctors, nurses and the most necessary supplies left Mendoza soon after midnight, but it was unable to reach San Juan because the rail line had been destroyed about twenty miles from the stricken city.

By 2 A. M. more than 100 motor trucks and other vehicles had left Mendoza by road, but they also were unable to go directly to their destination because the highways were impassable from huge cracks and landslides.

Federal Chiefs Fly to Area

The Government in Buenos Aires, thirty hours away by rail, organized rescue efforts quickly. It ordered all troops within a wide radius to hurry to San Juan by whatever means were available.

The Vice President and War Minister, Gen. Edelmiro Farrel, and the Minister of the Interior, Gen. Luis C. Perlinger, left San Juan by air at dawn. Other Federal officials and ten physicians and ten surgeons accompanied them in the first group of planes.

Additional relief units were flown into the quake area soon afterward. A special train carrying sixty persons, mostly nurses and supplies, left Buenos Aires in the morning.

All available transport planes at the air base of Palomar, near Buenos Aires, were sent with medical supplies. All other military and civilian planes in the country were ordered held in readiness in case they should be needed.

Despite the difficulties of reaching San Juan, aid to the survivors proceeded apace. The first troops to get to the city dug into ruins to rescue the injured and set up first aid and relief stations.

Mendoza Provides First Help

From Mendoza 5,000 tents for survivors and 2,500 hospital beds for the injured were made available. All physicians, nurses and medical students were mobilized.

Mendoza itself suffered considerable damage in the quake and its wire communications were cut for several hours. No casualties were reported there.

ARGENTINE CITY ROCKED

Jan. 17, 1944

Four earth shocks wrecked San Juan (cross) and neighboring villages, rolling up a casualty list of thousands. Tremors were felt as far away as Montevideo, capital of Uruguay.

Trains got through to San Juan after the tracks had been repaired, and the first to return to Mendoza carried 300 injured.

The radio kept asking all day for volunteers for blood transfusions. Large stocks of food, medical supplies and blankets were made ready and started for San Juan.

The San Juan disaster deeply moved all Argentines, plunging the whole country into mourning. President Pedro Ramirez ordered the closing of all places of public amusement for the day and the suspending of all radio broadcasts except news and sacred music.

500 Bodies Recovered by Night

BUENOS AIRES, Jan. 16 (A)—Gen. Luis C. Perlinger, Minister of the Interior, reported from San Juan to President Ramirez tonight that 500 bodies had been recovered thus far. He said 900 persons were gravely injured and that 4,000 others were less seriously hurt.

David Uriburu, Federal Interventor of San Juan, who described the city as 90 per cent destroyed, said nearly all public buildings were gone. The only important edifice spared was the Rawson Hospital, which was evacuated because of its shaky condition.

The quakes last night were felt in a broad belt across the entire continent from Buenos Aires to Santiago, Chile.

Red Cross Here Ready to Act

WASHINGTON, Jan. 16 (U.P.)—The American Red Cross is prepared to rush medical supplies and assistance to the Argentine earthquake victims if needed, officials said today. Action will be withheld until full reports on conditions are available.

"All the News That's Fit to Print"

The New York Times.

LATE CITY EDITION
POSTSCRIPT
Sunny and hot today.
Temperatures Yesterday—Max., 90.1; Min., 72
Sunrise, 5:31 A. M.; Sunset, 8:30 P. M.

Copyright, 1944, by The New York Times Company.

VOL. XCIII..No. 31,576. Entered as Second-Class Matter, Postoffice, New York, N. Y. NEW YORK, FRIDAY, JULY 7, 1944. THREE CENTS IN NEW YORK CITY

LONDON IS FLYING BOMB TARGET, 2,752 KILLED, CHURCHILL REVEALS; AMERICANS GAIN AROUND LA HAYE

139 LIVES LOST IN CIRCUS FIRE AT HARTFORD

174 BADLY BURNED

Tiny Flame Wells Up Into Sheet of Fire, With Throngs in Big Tent

PANIC GRIPS THOUSANDS

Burning Folds of Canvas Fall on Struggling Mass—Many Children Are Victims

By MEYER BERGER
Special to THE NEW YORK TIMES.

HARTFORD, Conn., July 6—One hundred and thirty-nine dead and 174 badly burned persons were pulled from the charred ruins of the main Ringling Brothers and Barnum & Bailey circus tent in Hartford this afternoon after fire swept the enclosure end to end along its entire 520-foot length.

At least two-thirds of the dead and injured were children. Of the remainder all except five were women. Only five men, so far as could be figured tonight, died in the disaster, the worst in circus history.

The dead lay on Army cots in the State Armory all afternoon and all night, while a pitiful procession of parents and other relatives lifted Army blankets in attempts to identify their kin.

Sixty-four of the dead had been identified late tonight.

State's Attorney Hugh Alcorn Jr. figured that there were 6,789 paid admissions in the tent when the fire started. The tent has a seating capacity of twice that many.

Animals Are Controlled

More than 1,000 animals, including 40 lions, 30 tigers, 30 leopards, 20 bears, 40 elephants and lesser beasts, were in the corral just south of the big top when it flamed, but they were kept under control. None broke out.

Most of the persons under the big top escaped through tent sidewalls, five on either side, or through the front and rear exits. The others, as nearly as could be determined, were caught in the scramble to get out. The great top fell on them in huge flaming folds and set fire to their clothes and bodies.

The entire tent and all its poles and guy ropes were reduced to ashes within ten minutes after the first gust of flame was noticed near the main entrance at 2:40 P. M., just as the Wallendas, high-wire artists, were about to begin the third act.

No one seemed certain as to what started the fire. State's Attorney Alcorn and his detective staff remained on the grounds tonight, continuing their investigation. Officials, however, were ordered to remain on the four-acre circus lot.

Starts in Grandstand Section

Detective John F. Reardon, one of the county detectives, happened to be under the big top when the fire started. He said, as did most of the circus ushers, that the fire started in Section A of the grandstand.

This section was to the right, in the great tent, as one faced in through the main entrance. Between it and the main entrance was a row of what circus people call "blues" or bleacher seats. The sections ran around the tent in alphabetical order counter-clockwise. A cigarette dropped near the sidewall behind Section A might have been the cause. This seemed the common guess tonight in the absence of official proof.

Detective Reardon and the ushers had their eyes on the three rings as did all the children and women just before the cry of "fire" tore their eyes away.

Alfred Court's lions, tigers, jaguars, leopards and bears had just finished their act in the great steel-barred cages. The last ones had barely cleared the caged runs through which they re-enter their wagons when the fire swept up the tent walls.

High on their apparatus, the Flying Wallendas, third act of the show, were testing their wires. The spots had been trained on them and their figures were outlined

Continued on Page 11

"TEN LITTLE INDIANS," Broadway's newest hit. Broadhurst Theatre. Mats. Wed. & Sat. "Superlative mystery comedy"—W.-Tele.—Advt.

Mercury Up to 90.1°, Year's Hottest Day

The year's highest temperature was registered yesterday at 4:30 P. M. when the mercury touched 90.1 degrees. Today's forecast is for sunny and hot weather with moderate winds.

At 9 A. M. the thermometer registered 77 and continued to climb a degree or two an hour until 4 P. M. when it reached 90 degrees, a reading equal to the previous high mark for the year on June 27. To the man in the street, however, the day was not as uncomfortable as during the late June hot spell, as the humidity was below 50 per cent all afternoon.

A record week-day beach crowd of 612,000 was at the Rockaways, Queens, and the police and life-saving forces had a busy day. There were 326 first-aid cases reported; 144 rescues, and 126 children returned to their parents. Albert Johnson, 13 years old, of Elizabeth, N. J., was drowned in the Elizabeth River while swimming.

BOLT FROM DEWEY PRICE OF ALP AID

Connolly Admits Lamula Was Asked to Desert Governor to Get Endorsement

Eugene P. Connolly, secretary of the New York County committee of the American Labor party, conceded last night that the ALP had requested Assemblyman John P. Lamula, Republican, to sign a statement that he would not campaign directly or indirectly for the Dewey-Bricker ticket as a condition for giving him its endorsement for re-election in the Second Assembly District, Manhattan.

Asked if similar pledges were required of the Republican candidates for legislative and judicial offices who have received Labor endorsements, Mr. Connolly said, "No comment." Most of the Republicans receiving endorsements denied yesterday that they had made such pledges.

Mr. Connolly's concession was made in a formal statement issued from New York County headquarters of the Labor party last night in reply to a statement issued earlier in the day by Mr. Lamula in which he declared that he had refused an endorsement on such terms and had told those who made the proposal to "go to hell." Mr. Lamula also revealed that he had made arrangements for a series of radio talks assailing a fourth term for President Roosevelt, to which the Labor party is committed.

Mr. Connolly's statement on the incident said:

"Mr. John Lamula states that he was asked by the American Labor party to sign a statement to the effect that he would not campaign directly or indirectly for the election of Thomas E. Dewey.

"This is true.

"Mr. Lamula states that he told us to 'go to hell.' Mr. Lamula not only did not tell us to 'go to hell' but up to almost midnight of last night [Wednesday], the last night to file substitutions, he urged us to accept his verbal assurances he

Continued on Page 9

LAST-MINUTE PLEAS SPUR E BOND SALES; U. S. GOAL IN SIGHT

Willkie Joins Drive Leaders in Radio Appeal to People of City and State

TODAY PROCLAIMED 'E-DAY'

Total Purchases in Nation at $15,364,000,000 Are Within 4 Per Cent of Quota

With latest tabulations placing Fifth War Loan sales within 4 per cent of the $16,000,000,000 national goal, an eleventh hour appeal was made yesterday to increase the lagging sale of E bonds and other individual issues before the close of the formal drive tomorrow.

Attainment of the over-all quotas was assured by heavy corporate purchases aggregating $11,454,-000,000, or 115 per cent of quota for this category, increasing the total amount of bonds sold throughout the country to $15,364,-000,000.

Leaders of the War Finance Committee continued to stress the necessity for pushing E bond sales, however, and further rallies were scheduled for today and tomorrow. One of the principal rallies will be held at noon today before the giant cash register in Times Square.

Willkie Joins in Plea

In a radio address last night over station WJZ, Wendell L. Willkie joined with War Loan Drive leaders in urging the people of New York City and State to buy one more E bond in the remaining two days of the drive so that sales will come within reach of the quotas.

Mr. Willkie called attention to the robot bombings being inflicted on the British and the hardships endured by Russian civilians and the French underground, and asked that Americans "accept our small sacrifices in the way the civilians of our Allies have accepted their great ones."

Today has been proclaimed "E-Day" by Nevil Ford, State Chairman of the War Finance Committee, who has rallied volunteer workers for extra efforts in the last days of the drive.

Mr. Ford said that while the drive would end tomorrow, sales of the E bonds during the rest of the month would be recorded in the final totals. He asked, however, that the best possible showing be made by tomorrow.

"Many persons," Mr. Ford said, "are under the impression that the Fifth War Loan closes tomorrow night. While that is the case as far as the sale of open market issues is concerned, the campaign for E bonds and the other savings issues of F and G bonds and Series C tax savings notes will be pushed right through the end of July.

"This is in accordance with the practice in previous War Loans and does not mark an extension of the drive."

Day's Sales in City

Mr. Willkie and Mr. Ford both observed that the city and the State were lagging behind the national rate of E bond and individual issue sales, which, according to the latest report from the Treasury Department, stood at $3,910,-000,000, or 65 per cent of quota.

New York City registered single day sales of only $2,487,540 in E bonds, bringing the cumulative total to $90,511,691, or 39.8 of its quota.

In sales to all categories of investors the city fared much better. Single day's sales of $96,478,760 were registered, advancing the total to $3,887,594,333, or 93.3 per

Continued on Page 16

Police Headquarters Safe Robbed; Mayor Guffaws at Force's Chagrin

Some time between 6 o'clock Saturday night and early Monday morning a thief removed a small tin box, containing $402.75 in cash and $262.50 in war bonds, from the large safe in the Chief Inspector's Office at Manhattan Police Headquarters, and disappeared.

From Monday through Wednesday, policemen and laborers were questioned. Yesterday, when news of the theft leaked out, all lockers in the gray, somber five-story building at 240 Center Street, stretching from Broome to Grand Street, were searched.

Reporters called it a burglary. Police Commissioner Lewis J. Valentine, in response to a query, listed it as a "larceny."

"It is a larceny by a dishonest employe," he said, "and consists of a cash-box which was taken from an open safe in Room 108 between 3 P. M. of July 1 and 11:30 A. M. of July 3, containing $402.75 in cash and war bonds totaling $262.50, maturity value $350; the above amount of money having been collected from members of the department in connection with the Fifth War Loan. This matter is being thoroughly investigated by the Eighteenth Detective Division."

After Acting Deputy Chief Inspector William A. Turk, Deputy Inspector George P. Mitchell, in charge of the Sabotage Squad, members of the Safe and Loft Squad, fingerprint experts, had finished a taxing day, certain pertinent facts emerged:

The safe was left open. Twelve patrolmen and eight clerical men work in Room 108, which is on the

Continued on Page 16

KEY TOWN FLANKED

U. S. First Army Pushes Up Hill for Plateau Dominating Area

ADVANCE BELOW CARENTAN

Kluge Replaces Rundstedt as the Supreme Commander of Germans in West

5 A. M. Communique

By The Associated Press.

SUPREME HEADQUARTERS, Allied Expeditionary Force, Friday, July 7—American forces still are battling for La Haye du Puits, western anchor of the German line in Normandy, and other Yankee troops have advanced below Carentan, Supreme Headquarters announced this morning in communiqué No. 63.

The situation remained unchanged in the Caen sector on the eastern flank, the bulletin said.

In the drive down the Cherbourg Peninsula the American First Army pushed forward one to two miles in various sectors against heavy resistance and reached the Canal la Plessis, three miles south of St. Jores, and captured Le Mont, a mile and a half south of La Haye in an encircling move.

By DREW MIDDLETON
By Cable to THE NEW YORK TIMES.

SUPREME HEADQUARTERS, Allied Expeditionary Force, Friday, July 7—Doughboys of the American First Army are slowly and steadily hammering their way out of the iron ring that Field Marshal Gen. Erwin Rommel tried to draw around the Allies' beachhead in Normandy, while on the eastern sector Canadian tank and infantry forces are holding their lines in the protracted and bloody battle for the shell-pocked acres and shattered hangars of the Carpiquet airfield.

As the fighting went on yesterday Berlin announced that Adolf Hitler had removed Field Marshal

Continued on Page 3

THE PRESIDENT GREETS DE GAULLE

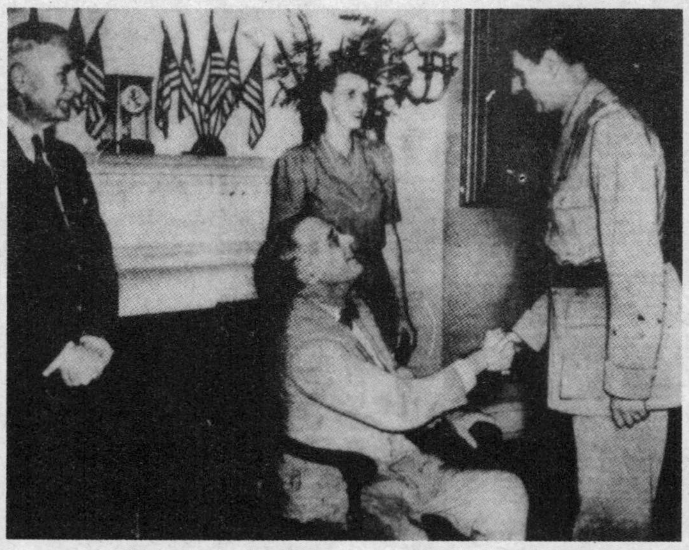

Mr. Roosevelt welcoming the French National Committee chief at the White House. The others are Secretary of State Cordell Hull and the Chief Executive's daughter, Mrs. Anna Boettiger.
Associated Press Wirephoto

DE GAULLE ARRIVES, MEETS ROOSEVELT

'My, I'm Glad to See You,' Says Host—Staff Chiefs on Hand —17 Guns Salute Visitor

By HAROLD CALLENDER
Special to THE NEW YORK TIMES.

WASHINGTON, July 6—Setting foot on American soil for the first time, Gen. Charles de Gaulle today stepped out of a big United States Army transport plane at the National Airport here in weather far hotter than that he had left in North Africa, made a little speech in English that he had carefully rehearsed in the plane and was received by President Roosevelt and his Cabinet at the White House.

At the airport General de Gaulle —though met by the three Chiefs of Staff, the military and naval

Continued on Page 3

War News Summarized

FRIDAY, JULY 7, 1944

London has been the main target of the German flying bombs since June 15, Prime Minister Churchill disclosed in the House of Commons yesterday. The enemy since then has sent over 2,754 missiles, a large proportion of which were destroyed before they could reach their mark. Those that did land, however, killed 2,752 persons—an average of a human being per bomb launched—and gravely injured 8,000 others.

Mr. Churchill saw little hope of an early end to the menace, saying even heavier rockets might strike Britain. He intimated that he had plans for future action but refused to discuss proposals for reprisals against Germany. The original launching sites had been wrecked by 50,000 tons of Allied bombs so that the robots were being projected from portable, pre-fabricated mountings. [All the foregoing 1:8; map, P. 4.]

Casualties, including some Americans, have been mainly civilian. Children were being evacuated from London and the city's deep shelters will soon be opened to the public. [4:1.]

More than 1,000 Eighth Air Force bombers and 750 fighters attacked flying-bomb sites in the Pas-de-Calais. Altogether more than 5,000 Allied planes from Britain, France and Italy raked enemy targets over a wide area including a triangle from Paris to the base of the Cotentin and Finisterre Peninsulas. [5:1.]

Americans, twice thrown out of La Haye du Puits by vicious counter-attacks, renewed the frontal assault on the town together with flanking drives, scoring gains on both sides. The advance from Carentan moved more rapidly. [1:4; map, P. 2.]

Hitler removed Field Marshal von Rundstedt as Supreme Commander in the west and in his place put Field Marshal Guenther von Kluge, several times beaten by the Russians. [3:5-6.]

Soviet armies captured Kovel, advanced to within twelve miles of Lithuania and thirty-two of Vilna, and were only nine miles from Baranovichi in a day that saw steady progress on all fronts. [1:7; map, P. 6.] In Italy the Allies ground out more gains along the entire line. [6:3.]

Assistant Secretary of War Patterson said the Allies were building up in Europe a firepower four times as great as that of the Germans. [3:1.]

It was revealed that fast carrier task forces operating over a vast area in the Pacific had sunk or damaged thirty-two Japanese ships in their recent attacks on the Bonin Islands. Pagan Island and Guam were also hit. [1:6-7.] Tiny Manim Island off Numfor was occupied by Allied forces, flanking the last enemy-held airfield on Numfor. [8:3.]

Chungking reported that the Japanese had begun a general retreat from their recent hard-won gains in Hunan and Honan Provinces. Adequate air support for the first time was credited with a major part in the turn of events in China. [1:6-7.] Chinese troops captured the mountain fortifications of Sungshan controlling the Burma Road crossing of the Salween River. [8:1.]

General de Gaulle was received by President Roosevelt shortly after his arrival for the first time in the United States. It is believed that Washington will accept the agreements drafted in London with the French Committee. [1:5.]

5 Japanese Ships Are Sunk In Bonins, 27 Are Damaged

By GEORGE F. HORNE
By Telephone to THE NEW YORK TIMES.

PEARL HARBOR, July 6—One of the fast carrier task groups that struck in the Bonin and Volcano Islands last Monday attacked the important enemy base on Chichi Island in the Bonins, sent five enemy craft to the bottom in the Chichi area, probably sank six and damaged ten others, Admiral Chester W. Nimitz revealed in a communiqué today. The craft ranged from luggers to a large cargo ship and included a number of naval vessels.

Additional information on the attack by the same carrier force on the same day on Haha Island in the Bonins added to the enemy's mounting ship and plane losses two small cargo vessels and nine luggers damaged, nine enemy aircraft shot down and three damaged on the ground and hits on buildings and defense installations. Thus thirty-two hitherto unreported vessels were added to the Japanese losses.

With increasing frequency the carrier groups are wearing away the enemy's defenses while our invaders of Saipan push his last troops farther and farther north toward the sea.

Pagan Island was attacked on Tuesday by carrier planes that hit the runway of the airfield and damaged buildings with bomb and strafing runs.

Large Fires Set on Guam

On the same day Guam was bombed through intense anti-aircraft fire and we started large fires on the island at the cost of only one plane.

For the first time it can be disclosed that Fleet Air Wing 2 has moved into position and is now operating against the enemy in support of advancing land troops. The Admiral said Group 1 of the Air Wing bombed gun positions at

Continued on Page 8

RUSSIANS ADVANCE SWIFTLY ON VILNA

32 Miles From Lithuanian City —Baranovichi Railroad Cut —Kovel Is Occupied

By The United Press.

LONDON, Friday, July 7—Russian troops, advancing westward twenty-four miles in twenty-four hours, smashed to within thirty-two miles of Vilna, capital of Lithuania, yesterday, while at the southern end of the Eastern Front Marshal Konstantin K. Rokossovsky's First White Russian Army occupied Kovel, great German base 175 miles southeast of Warsaw.

At the same time the Red Army began an encirclement movement against Baranovichi, drove to within nine miles of that vital rail junction and cut the Baranovichi-Luninets section of the Dvinsk-Luninets railroad, the intermediate German defense line before Poland and East Prussia.

Breaking through German reinforcements, including battalions of military police, Gen. Ivan D. Chernyakhovsky's Third White Russian Army advanced to within 132 miles of the pre-war border of East Prussia in its advance on Vilna.

More than 558 towns and settle-

Continued on Page 6

Japanese Begin Retreat in China; Our Air Blows Turn Battle Tide

By Reuter.

CHUNGKING, China, July 6—Japanese forces have begun a general retreat on the Hunan and Honan fronts of the China war theatre, it was declared here today.

Air reconnaissance reports today confirm that Japanese troops attacking Hengyang, key city in southern Hunan Province, are falling back northward toward Changsha, while there is practically no evidence of Japanese troops at Loyang, important city on the Lunghai Railway in Honan Province.

The Chinese Army has almost achieved the impossible.

While their garrison stubbornly held on to Hengyang, other Chinese columns launched a counter-attack along both sides of the Canton-Hankow railway.

The Japanese force that was besieging Hengyang for the past ten days has broken off the fight and begun to withdraw to the north.

There had been fears that Hengyang would certainly fall and that the Japanese would march on to Kweilin, capital of Kwangsi Province.

While the Chinese High Command carefully planned for the counter-offensive, they decided to adopt the cautious policy of not announcing its start until they were absolutely certain of victory.

The United States Fourteenth Air Force played a vital part in the reversal. Maj. Gen. Claire L. Chennault threw in everything he had. The American Air Force and the Chinese-American composite wing under his command bombed and machine-gunned Japanese concen-

Continued on Page 8

ROBOTS HURT 8,000

Premier Includes U. S. Losses—Holds Slight Hope for Future

PREVENTIVE AIDS SPEEDED

Intelligence Service Spotted Peril Year Ago—Children Sent to Country Havens

The text of the Prime Minister's speech, Page 4.

By RAYMOND DANIELL
By Cable to THE NEW YORK TIMES.

LONDON, July 6—Prime Minister Winston Churchill disclosed to the world today what has been a matter of bitter knowledge to Londoners for three long weeks—that this blitzed old capital of Great Britain has borne the brunt of the Nazi attack with flying bombs ever since it began in earnest on June 15.

In those three weeks, the Prime Minister reported, the Germans had launched 2,754 robot bombs, a large proportion of which were destroyed before reaching their target. Nevertheless, Mr. Churchill revealed that the flying bombs had killed 2,752 persons, or about one person for every projectile launched. In addition, he said, about 8,000 persons were seriously wounded.

For a weapon of "such proved inaccuracy," the nature, purpose and effect of which was "essentially indiscriminate," Mr. Churchill pointed out, this sprawling city, eighteen miles wide and twenty miles deep, made an ideal target. That the enemy has resorted to such a weapon, the Prime Minister said, "raises some grave questions upon which I do not propose to touch today."

Nor would Mr. Churchill allow himself to be drawn into any discussion of reprisals when Sir William Davison said he had scores of letters from constituents asking whether the Nazis should not be warned that, if the attacks continue, "we'll take whatever steps are necessary"?

Holds Out Slender Hope

Mr. Churchill replied:

"I have said deliberately that was a subject which raised grave considerations upon which I do not intend to embark. That is the best way to leave it."

The Prime Minister held out little hope for any early cure of the latest pestilence afflicting London, nor could he give any assurance that the huge explosive rockets that it was feared the Germans were preparing to use last year will not ultimately rain upon this embattled city. He could give no guarantee, he said, that the present or newer evils could be entirely prevented "before the time comes, as come it will, when the soil from which these attacks are launched has been finally liberated from the enemy's grip."

In the meantime, Mr. Churchill advised the House of Commons that, regardless of the cost of civilian life and property, the Government would not be diverted from the main battle in Normandy or from the strategic bombing of targets inside Germany. But earlier in his speech he said that preventive measures taken against the robot bombs had meant the

Continued on Page 4

U. S. 'Winged Bomb' Reported in Reich

By Reuter.

LONDON, July 6—The German radio reported today: "In their attacks on Cologne on May 28 and on Hamburg on June 18, the American bombers released some 'winged bombs' in the shape of small gliders."

The use of the "winged bomb" by the Americans was also mentioned in a second German broadcast today.

"This 'winged bomb,'" said the announcer, "is being released from a considerable distance, and the course it takes depends entirely on chance.

"Lacking even the semblance of accuracy, this missile is a terror weapon pure and simple."

The Worst Fire in Circus History Took Heavy Toll of Lives at Hartford

139 LIVES LOST IN CIRCUS FIRE

Continued From Page 1

against the hot sun glowing on the big top.

Suddenly the flame, at first just a little fire that might have been extinguished with a bucket of water, caught on the sidewall behind Section A. It leaped in one great, roaring column for the tent leaves, forty feet up.

Kenneth Grinnell, Mike Dare and Paul Runyon, three ushers, had started for the blaze with buckets, but the hot breath of flame scorched their clothes and drove them back. Before they could stop it, the fire spread at incredible speed.

It raced upwards, then along the sides and top of the great tent, quicker—according to some of the horrified witnesses—than the eye could follow it. Where it raced, great patches of canvas fell in hot gobs, blanketing the children and others on the seats.

There was little screaming or outcry, at first, because of the amazing speed with which the flame spread. Then men, women and children plunged or were pushed from the grandstands toward the center of the tent.

A breeze blowing through the tent's main entrance from the west —the length of he big top was stretched east and west—forced the fire toward the back, the direction taken by thousands who were not completely panicky.

The flame licked down at them with tremendous tongues. Canvas dropped and covered two to three hundred at a time, but in most instances the victims were able to tear the canvas away and get free. They made for the exits.

Elephants trumpeted outside in the great corral; lions, tigers and other great cats screamed, and the monkeys jabbered excitedly in their cages. Roustabouts and animal keepers moved about to restore quiet in the animal lines.

Run Under Burning Canvas

Witnesses seemed agreed that many deaths were caused by women and children running blindly under burning canvas that covered their heads. They ran into one another and great numbers crashed against the steel-ribbed runs through which Court's animals had just left the arena.

It was about three runs, or chutes, according to the police, that most of the dead were piled. In some places they lay two and three deep and the fire had eaten at their garments, their bodies and their faces.

Except for the "blues" sections immediately inside the main entrance, no part of the grandstand was spared by the flames. Every section, every steel rail, every great steel cage where the Court animals had performed, was blackened, bent, charred.

Even the bandstand, at the eastern, or far end from the main entrance, directly opposite the point where the fire started—a full 500 feet away—was burned to cinders. The electric organ, the kettledrums, the platform itself—these were charred inches deep.

The band, led by Pete Heaton, the organist, lived up to stage and circus tradition. The men kept blasting—that's the circus term for playing at top volume—until the last of the six great center poles toppled, and the last section of burning top with it.

Band's Uniforms Scorched

The band got away, faces blackened and uniforms scorched. So, apparently, did all the other circus performers and ushers. Even the Wallendas, high under the canvas, slid down the poles as the flames raced toward them and reached the ground—and exits.

Great clouds of dust rose over the grounds as survivors stampeded beyond the immediate heat zone.

"It was like you'd opened hell's doors," a big roustabout said later, "and you had all you could do to

Flame and smoke rise from the main tent as people flee just after the start of the catastrophe

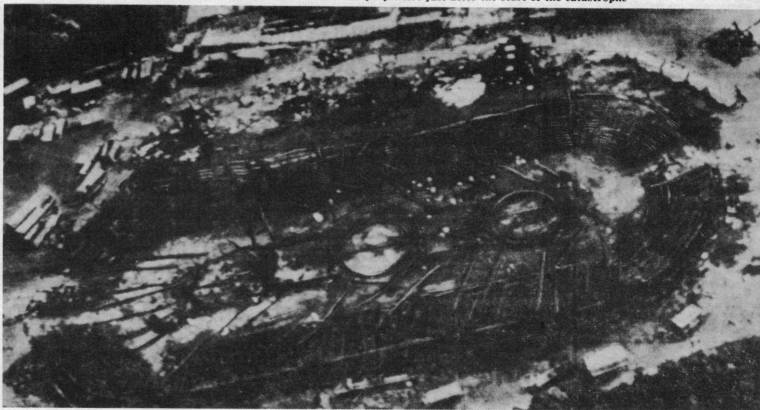

Three rings, charred poles and seats mark the site of the blaze as seen from the air   Associated Press Wirephotos

get your hands over your face and run t'other way."

Sergeant Copeland wrestled with one woman, her clothing charred, her face blackened, who tried to fight her way back toward the fire. The tent was entirely collapsed, then, flaming on the heaped dead. "My God," she kept screaming. "My God. My kid's in there."

Similar heart-breaking scenes were enacted in every corner of the lot. The roustabouts and the other circus workers had to fight with men and women to keep them from going back into certain death. Many collapsed on the grass after they were carried away.

Many Die on Way to Hospital

Ambulances, trucks, jeeps, private cars, raced from the circus toward the city's four largest hos——and started to take out the dead, the dying and the wounded.

They were ranged in rows on the ground between where the tent had stood and within the circle formed by circus supply wagons.

Priests rushed to the circus ground to administer absolution to the dying stretched in the sun. The Rev. Andrew J. Kelly, the Rev. Thomas McMahon and the Rev. Raymond La Fontaine administered to scores before they were borne from the lot.

Within a half hour, word of the disaster had spread over the town, by word of mouth and over the radio, and fathers, mothers and other kin who had children at the circus started toward the lot in Barbour Street on foot and in automobiles.

Storm Against Police Lines

Frantic women and tense fathers, perspiring in the hot sun and breathless from racing toward the lot, stormed against the hastily formed police lines. Mothers who had escaped ran around blindly crying for their young.

Policemen assigned to the disaster were tight lipped with worry about their own children.

Medical and police aid was astonishingly swift, but even if it had come on wings, according to those who saw the terrific drive of the flame it could not have saved those who died.

State police, auxiliary police, city police, defense units, soldiers from near-by Camp Bradley, and fire apparatus from Hartford, West Hartford, East Hartford and Bloomfield raced to the circus ground—all too late. All they could do was spray water on charred ruins.

The State Armory was thrown open to receive the unidentified dead, and militia and State police threw a cordon around it to hold back parents searching for missing children. Bodies were stretched on army cots.

Hartford had lost fewer lives on the beachheads in France than the circus fire had taken today.

"All the News That's Fit to Print"

The New York Times.

LATE CITY EDITION
Partly cloudy with moderate winds today.
Temperatures Yesterday—Max., 81; Min., 67
Sunrise, 5:40 A. M.; Sunset, 8:23 P. M.

Copyright, 1944, by The New York Times Company.

VOL. XCIII—No. 31,588. Entered as Second-Class Matter, Postoffice, New York, N. Y. NEW YORK, WEDNESDAY, JULY 19, 1944. THREE CENTS IN NEW YORK CITY

BRITISH RIP LINES EAST OF CAEN; AMERICANS WIN ST. LO JUNCTION; RUSSIANS NEAR LWOW IN NEW PUSH

DEMOCRATS FACE MANY-SIDED BATTLE ON VICE PRESIDENCY

Opponents of Wallace Fail to Agree on Single Man to Bear Brunt of the Contest

TRUMAN DRAWS SUPPORT

Senator Is Unwilling to Make Race—CIO Leaders Oppose the Boom for Byrnes

By TURNER CATLEDGE
Special to The New York Times.

CHICAGO, July 18—With Vice President Wallace rushing here from Washington to fight personally for his renomination and his opponents trying desperately but thus far unsuccessfully to center on a champion, the Democratic National Convention, scheduled to open at the Chicago Stadium at 11:30 A. M. tomorrow, appeared tonight to face the real possibility of an old-time Democratic battle royal over the selection of a running mate for President Roosevelt.

Seeking to forestall this possibility, an increasing number of anti-Wallace leaders were making a supreme effort to line their forces behind Senator Harry S. Truman of Missouri.

This was taking place at the end of a day which buzzed with rumors and counter-rumors concerning the opposition to James F. Byrnes by the Congress of Industrial Organizations and other groups, and additional reports that the President therefore would possibly ask his Director of War Mobilization not to permit his name to go before the convention.

Mr. Wallace's opponents considered themselves free to proceed following Mr. Roosevelt's mild endorsement of his 1940 running mate in a letter which reached the convention city last night and the added remark therein that the choice was up to the convention.

Byrnes "Stock" Seems to Slip

Mr. Byrnes was regarded until this morning as the focal point of forces intent on preventing the renomination of Mr. Wallace. His stock appeared to slip markedly, however, after word was put about that Philip Murray, president of the CIO, and Sidney Hillman, chairman of the CIO Political Action Committee, opposed him.

Mr. Murray and Mr. Hillman denied at an afternoon press conference that they were "against" Mr. Byrnes or anyone else. They said that they were simply "for" Mr. Wallace, for whom they have long been fighting, and would stand with him to the end.

Mr. Wallace's friends, meanwhile, experienced a considerable lift in spirits, following a few hours of virtual despair after the disclosure of the President's letter. One of the possibilities was that Mr. Roosevelt would be asked in the final stages to designate his choice, and that he would again demand Mr. Wallace, as he did in 1940, or turn to Associate Justice William O. Douglas.

Favorite Sons in Background

Senator Alben W. Barkley of Kentucky and at least a dozen other "hopefuls" stayed in the background as the Vice-Presidential contest was intensified. None of them seemed to be picking up strength, so far as word-of-mouth conversation around the Chicago hotels would indicate. Mr. Barkley was endorsed by the Kentucky delegation in a caucus; Gov. J. Melville Broughton of North Carolina was put forward by his delegation and several other delegations endorsed favorite sons.

Mr. Byrnes was not to be considered entirely out of the picture, although it was generally understood that he would not go to the post without the President's consent.

Reports that Senator Truman was to be the choice of the anti-Wallace forces were heard in the New York State delegation at a dinner and cocktail party. Earlier in the day, it was stated, Edward J. Flynn, New York national committeeman, in a conference with leaders, informed them that the decision of the Wallace opponents was to back Senator Truman, and that the New York delegation might be voting for him, at least after the first ballot. The group agreed to accede to this decision.

The word was passed along and it speedily became an open secret. The Truman boom found ripe territory in New York State, because of the fear of the New York City leaders that the alternative was

Continued on Page 12

THE GLOBE-SWEEPING, HEART-WARMING story of a man . . . a family . . . an era . . . a nation . . . a world: Darryl F. Zanuck's production of "WILSON" in Technicolor. A 20th Century Fox Picture. World Premiere. ROXY, AUG. 1. 9 P. M. Continuous thereafter.—Advt.

Convention Today

Special to The New York Times.

CHICAGO, July 18—The program of the Democratic National Convention for its first day is as follows:

Wednesday, July 19
FIRST SESSION
11:30 A. M., C. W. T.

Convention called to order by Robert E. Hannegan, national chairman.

Invocation—The Right Rev. John Zelezinski, Chicago.

National Anthem—Nona Vann, Chicago Civic Opera Company.

Call for convention, read by Mrs. Dorothy Vredenburgh of Alabama, secretary, Democratic National Committee.

Welcoming Speeches—Mayor Edward J. Kelly of Chicago and Senator Lucas of Illinois.

Presentation of distinguished visitors.

Remarks by Edwin W. Pauley, director of the convention.

Appointment of committees on credentials, permanent organization, rules and order of business, on resolutions and platform.

SECOND SESSION
8:15 P. M., C. W. T.

Called to order by Chairman Hannegan.

Invocation—The Rev. Harrison R. Anderson, Chicago.

Patriotic Song—Phil Regan.

Address—Mr. Hannegan, chairman of national committee.

Address—Mrs. Charles W. Tillett of North Carolina, assistant chairman, national committee.

Keynote address—Gov. Robert S. Kerr of Oklahoma.

DEWEY CHARGES WAR BALLOT PLOT

He Says 'Financial' Group Is 'Playing Politics' With Soldier Vote Rights

Special to The New York Times.

ALBANY, July 18—Governor Dewey declared today that a group with "unlimited financial resources' was "playing politics with the right of New York State's fighting men to vote."

He said that those advocating the use of the supplementary Federal ballot in New York ignored the fact that such ballots could not be counted under the State Constitution.

The Republican nominee did not identify the group he charged with a "campaign of deceit," in a prepared statement, but some elements of the CIO have been conducting a campaign to bring about use of the Federal ballot by New York service men and women. A delegation of 800 persons came to Albany last week to urge the Governor to authorize use of the Federal ballot.

The Governor asserted that the State soldier vote was drawn to fit precisely Title 2 of the Federal law and that it was a "model of simplicity."

TEXT OF STATEMENT

Following is the text of the formal statement:

"For some time now a group with unlimited financial resources has been playing partisan politics with the right of New York State's fighting men to vote. Instead of helping soldiers to vote, they have distributed millions of misleading circulars designed to confuse both the public mind and the mind of soldiers. It is time this campaign of deceit was labeled and exposed.

"Accordingly, I urge all families and friends of members of the armed services immediately to write to them, telling them the truth about their right to vote in the State of New York.

"The New York soldier vote law is a model of simplicity, drawn to fit precisely Title 2 of the Federal law. Every member of the armed forces all over the world will be

Continued on Page 11

AT LEAST 350 DEAD AS MUNITIONS SHIPS BLOW UP ON COAST

Two Vessels Being Loaded at Port Chicago Explode, Killing Virtually All at Spot

NAVY TOLL IS 200 TO 250

Enlisted Men Were Working as Stevedores—70 in Crews Die—Wide Land Damage

By LAWRENCE E. DAVIES
Special to The New York Times.

PORT CHICAGO, Calif., July 18—Three hundred and fifty or more persons were killed in the double explosion which shattered two munitions ships late last night, wrecked a Navy loading pier and left a "scorched earth" scene in this war boom town, forty miles northeast of San Francisco.

Material damage caused by the blast, one of the most disastrous in the country's history, was put at more than $5,000,000, excluding the value of the thousands of tons of munitions blown up. The munitions ships, both almost new, were valued at about $4,300,000. A Coast Guard crash boat and a fire barge also were destroyed and a tanker was damaged.

Hundreds of persons, possibly as many as a thousand, were injured. Every building in a radius of two or three miles was razed or damaged. Many stood at crazy angles, roofless or with walls caved in.

Summary of Death Toll

The death toll of Navy personnel, exclusive of members of the armed guard aboard the ships, was listed as "between 200 and 250," with some officials "guessing." Nine Navy officers supervising the loading of the ships by sailors lost their lives, as did fifteen Coast Guardsmen. Seventy Maritime Commission seamen were killed. Three civilian railroad workers riding on a locomotive and two cars near the explosion scene were never seen again and the pieces of the train were scattered over a wide area.

No civilian residents of the blast area are known to have been killed.

Six of the injured were at work in the Benicia Arsenal seven miles across the bay from Port Chicago. Col. Paul G. Rutten, commanding officer of the arsenal, estimated damages to arsenal buildings at about $150,000.

Capt. N. H. Goss, commanding officer of the naval ammunition depot at Mare Island, who has jurisdiction over the Port Chicago installation, voiced the belief that the cause of the explosion never would be known.

"We have no basis for giving any cause," he said, "as there are no close survivors to give evidence of what happened."

Navy Inquiry Expected

The Navy Department was expected to make a formal investigation.

The blast area, including Port Chicago and Martinez, was put under quasi-martial law as Sheriff James Long of Contra Costa County called for military aid in policing it.

Doubt was expressed that many of the bodies ever would be identified. It may be days before the death roster is complete. A Navy spokesman said that no death list would be made public until the next of kin had been notified.

Newspaper men, admitted to the area ten hours after the explosion, saw why some residents thought at first that there had been an enemy bombing. Acres of pier had been blown away, leaving the tops of piles sticking a few feet out of

Continued on Page 14

Race Issue Snarls the Platform; Southerners Halt Compromise

By CHARLES E. EGAN
Special to The New York Times.

CHICAGO, July 18—Sharp controversy over the racial issue stirred the Democratic resolutions committee today as it labored to complete an acceptable platform for presentation to the national convention on Thursday.

Insistence of leaders of the Congress of Industrial Organizations and Negro groups that a strong anti-discrimination plank be written into the platform was opposed by Southern delegates.

As the committee finished its work for the day, it was reported that statements by Philip Murray, CIO president, had so aroused delegates from the Southern States that efforts of Representative John W. McCormack of Massachusetts, the committee chairman, to effect a compromise were blocked.

A statement by Mr. Murray that labor demanded a courageous stand on the racial issue, and a telegram sent by Edgar C. Brown, director of the National Negro Council to President Roosevelt, urging him to take definite action to pledge his party to approve Negro demands and implement them by legislation, provoked resentment on the part of the Southern delegates, it was understood, and stiffened their resistance to even a mild anti-discrimination plank.

Mr. McCormack told reporters

Continued on Page 13

"TOMORROW AND TOMORROW AND TOMORROW . . ."—Wm. Shakespeare. And all New York is quoting him today—because tomorrow marks a truly important event in the world of entertainment—the World Premiere of M-G-M's stirring screen version of Pearl Buck's bestseller "Dragon Seed," starring Katharine Hepburn at Radio City Music Hall.—Advt.

AS 57,000 NAZI PRISONERS WERE PARADED IN MOSCOW

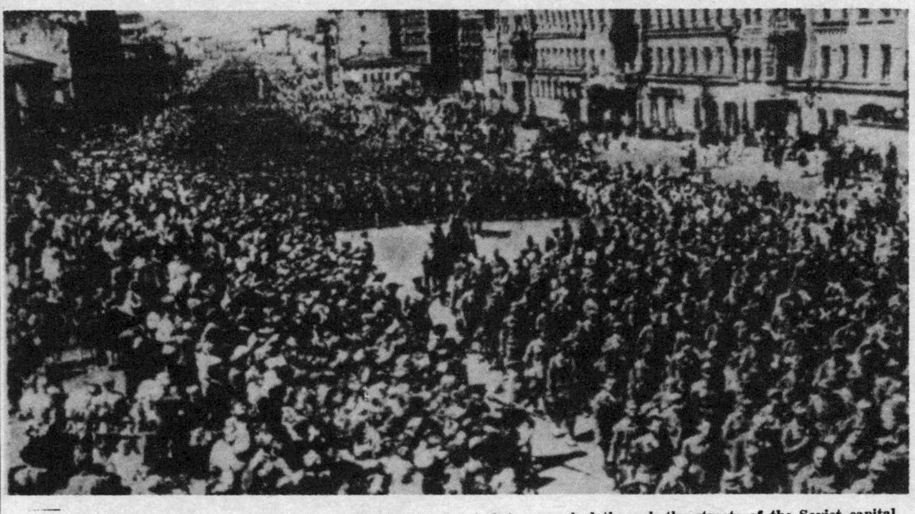

Some of Hitler's soldiers, captured on the White Russian front, being marched through the streets of the Soviet capital
The New York Times (Sovfoto Radiophoto)

JAPAN DROPS TOJO AS CHIEF OF STAFF

Umezu Heads Army in Shuffle Laid to Saipan as Premier Discloses National Crisis

After a five-month term as active head of the Japanese Army in the concurrent position of Chief of Staff, Premier General Hideki Tojo was "relieved" of that job yesterday in a drastic new High Command shake-up that was accompanied by the first Japanese acknowledgment of the loss of Saipan and a statement by Premier Tojo himself in which he told his people that "imperial Japan has come to face an unprecedentedly great national crisis."

After declaring that "Saipan Island has finally fallen into the enemy's hands," Premier Tojo was quoted by the Tokyo radio as telling the Japanese people:

"Now the day for the decisive battle is approaching."

Gen. Yoshijiro Umezu, Com-

Continued on Page 8

Soviet Troops Gain 31 Miles Through a 124-Mile Breach

By W. H. LAWRENCE
By Wireless to The New York Times.

MOSCOW, Wednesday, July 19—A great new offensive aimed at the very heart of Germany was announced late last night by Marshal Joseph Stalin, who said that forces of the First Ukraine Front in three days had driven thirty-one miles through a 124-mile-wide breach in the German lines, captured 600 inhabited points and crossed the Bug River almost at the 1941 Soviet-Polish frontier.

[The 1939 Polish partition line was reached at Skomorokhi, the Russian midnight communiqué said.]

The new drive, led by Marshal Ivan S. Koneff, who had replaced Marshal Gregory Zhukoff, was linked with the campaign on the First White Russian Front, commanded by Marshal Konstantin K. Rokossovsky.

Last night's High Command communiqué announced the capture of a total of 1,040 inhabited points as the Red Army drove forward on sectors west and northwest of Opochka, northwest and

Continued on Page 6

War News Summarized

WEDNESDAY, JULY 19, 1944

British and Canadian troops of the Second Army burst their bonds yesterday and shattered the German defenses about Caen. General Montgomery's finest divisions then started to roll across the plains east of the Orne and southeast of Caen, where a fierce battle of mobile forces raged all day.

The offensive was preceded by a gigantic aerial assault in which more than 2,000 Allied planes showered in excess of 7,000 tons of high-explosive and anti-personnel bombs on the Germans for four hours. Not a single enemy plane rose to challenge the armada from four Allied air commands.

At the other end of the Normandy line the Americans drove the Germans out of St. Lo, made Périers virtually untenable and improved their positions at other points. [All the foregoing 1:8; map P. 2.]

The bombing barrage at Caen carried the "bomb-line" forward ahead of the advancing troops and raised such clouds of smoke and dust that daylight was blacked out. [1:7.]

Allied air might is so great that at the same time more than 1,200 additional planes blasted Pennemuende and Zinnowitz on the Baltic coast, where the Nazis developed their flying bomb and rocket. Twenty-one of sixty German planes were shot down and at least forty-five more were destroyed or damaged in fights over rail and bridge targets in France. From Italy the Fifteenth Air Force attacked the Dornier works near Friedrichshafen. [3:8.]

The Russians opened another drive, this one aimed at Lwow. Moscow reported gains up to thirty-one miles on a 124-mile front. At one point the Red Army reached the Bug River and was twenty miles from Lwow. Elsewhere Soviet units pushed seven miles into Latvia, drove to within twenty-nine miles of Bialystok and to only five miles from Brest-Litovsk. [1:5-6; map P. 6.]

The Germans were also pushed back in Italy, where the Eighth Army menaced the Adriatic port of Ancona from the west and south and the Fifth Army reached the Arno River between Pisa and Florence. [1:6.]

Prime Minister Churchill was criticized in the House of Commons for insisting upon unconditional surrender by Germany. This, the critics contended, prolongs the war and discourages a workers' revolution. [5:1.]

Recently conquered Saipan in the Pacific was rapidly being converted into a strong American base. [9:1.] Allied forces in Burma were squeezing out further gains everywhere [8:4], and in China the Japanese were still being held from Hengyang. [8:7.] The Soviet journal War and the Working Class attacked Chungking's "reactionary policies" and refusal to unite with "patriotic and democratic forces" to crush Japan. [9:5.]

Tokyo shook up the Japanese High Command and "relieved" Premier Tojo as Chief of Staff of the Army. He was succeeded by Gen. Yoshijiro Umezu, military and diplomatic head in Manchuria. [1:4.] Secretary of State Hull interpreted the move as a sign of Japan's desperate military plight. [8:1.]

DONNIFORD MIXTURE. Companion tobacco for your finest pipe 30c.—Advt.

AMERICAN TROOPS REACH ARNO RIVER

Drive Between Florence and Pisa—Eighth Army Cracks Defenses of Ancona

By HERBERT L. MATTHEWS
By Wireless to The New York Times.

ROME, July 18—American troops of the Fifth Army, after having fought their way through difficult mountain terrain, reached the Arno River between Pisa and Florence today at the town of Pontedera.

Polish troops of the British Eighth Army, with Italians on their left flank, achieved a complete break-through in the German positions southwest of Ancona and the largest Italian port on the Adriatic seemed about to fall soon. The same fate is gradually overtaking Leghorn, on the Tyrrhenian, with this advance to Pontedera and the general tightening of the strangle-hold around the port.

The Eighth Army in the center is exploiting its surprise dash across the upper Arno and has taken Levane and Quarata. Thus three powerful thrusts, all initiated within the past four or five days, are driving the Germans back on what might be called the "Arno line," although it is really a series of natural positions that the enemy is expected to use to delay as long

Continued on Page 4

7,000 TONS OF BOMBS PACE BRITISH DRIVE

American, British and Dominion Planes in Thousands Blast Germans for 4 Hours

By JAMES MacDONALD
By Cable to The New York Times.

IN THE CAEN SECTOR, July 18—One of the mightiest air forces that ever took to the air—thousands of American, British and Dominions bombers and fighter-bombers—struck awesome blows early today at every enemy target northeast, east and southeast of Caen.

It was hell let loose. Seven thousand tons of bombs poured on the enemy in a few hours, and during that time the earth shook for miles around and the air throbbed with the roar of motors. Fires, explosions, the smell of cordite, occasional meteor-like streaks of flame as some of the Allies' planes hurtled to earth afire and the choking dust flung up by the bombs made the scene one that will not be forgotten by those who survived.

[Some 2,200 planes were employed and dropped 14,000 tons of bombs, The United Press reported.]

Attack Begins at Dawn

The curtain went up on this scene shortly before 5 A. M., just as day was breaking. From a vantage point of high ground well up in a forward area a group of war correspondents peered down on placid towns, villages and farmsteads. That placidity was a momentary thing in the stillness of early morning.

Suddenly through the stillness came the faint hum of airplane motors. The hum grew louder and louder and became an ear-splitting roar as a large formation of Royal Air Force heavy bombers circled

Continued on Page 3

German Staff Has Plans Now For Next War, Welles Warns

By JAMES B. RESTON
Special to The New York Times.

WASHINGTON, July 18—The German General Staff is aware of Germany's inevitable defeat and has already made "detailed plans for a later renewal of its attempt to dominate the world," Sumner Welles, former Under-Secretary of State, declares in a book to be published tomorrow.

Arguing for United States participation in an effective world peace organization and for the dismemberment of Germany, Mr. Welles says that, in "The Time for Decision," in order to carry out its plan for the third world war, agents of the German General Staff have already been naturalized, usually in two successive countries, "so that their future activities will be less suspect."

The majority of these men, Mr. Welles says, are being trained to appear as men of large commercial or financial interests, who will be able to dispose of considerable amounts of capital derived from the reserves which the German General Staff has already, during the past years, deposited under one guise or another in neutral countries.

"Our principal danger and the hope of the German General Staff," Mr. Welles says, "is that after the present war the people of the democracies, and particularly the people of the United States, will wish once more, as in 1920, to plunge themselves into the oblivion of 'normalcy.' "

"With this in mind," Mr. Welles

Continued on Page 5

IN COLUMBUS, Ohio, now a city of 400,000, there is a newspaper which is read daily in 97% of the city's homes—The Dispatch.—Advt.

MAJOR ASSAULT ON

British Armor Streams Into Open Country to Engage Germans

PACED BY RECORD BOMBING

Americans Cut Road to Lessay and Periers, Reported Abandoned by Foe

By DREW MIDDLETON
By Cable to The New York Times.

SUPREME HEADQUARTERS, Allied Expeditionary Force, Wednesday, July 19—The British Second Army has cracked the German defensive position around Caen in the successful opening of a major offensive.

British armored formations and mobile troops streamed onto the flat open country east of the Orne River and southeast of Caen last night to clash with élite German armored divisions in a crucial battle. The break-through, the most significant action on the Normandy front since the fall of Cherbourg, was preceded and supported by the heaviest air assault ever launched against an army in the field.

Lancasters and Halifaxes of the Royal Air Force's Bomber Command, Liberators of the United States Eighth Air Force and Marauders and Havocs of the Ninth Air Force blasted enemy strong points, field batteries, troop concentrations and fuel, ammunition and food dumps with more than 7,000 tons of bombs between 5:45 and 10 A. M. yesterday.

As the British army flooded through the breaches in the German lines on the eastern sector of the 100-mile front, the hard-hitting infantrymen of the American First Army fought their way into St. Lô, the hinge of the German positions on the western sector, and captured the German stronghold after a siege that had lasted eight days. This morning the Allies were rolling forward on both sectors after two brilliant initial successes.

Great Tank Battle Believed On

Massed British tanks supported by other mobile forces smashed into strong German forces in the flat country southeast of Caen, where one of the greatest tank battles of the war is believed to be raging. According to a German correspondent at the enemy's headquarters, the British Fifty-first Infantry Division—the famous Highland division that Gen. Sir Bernard L. Montgomery used in the Alamein break-through—is in the thick of the fighting with "several" British tank brigades. The Germans place the battlefield east of the Orne and about eight miles from the coast, or in the area of Banneville-la-Campagne and Emiéville.

"The advance has gone extremely well," a spokesman at Second Army headquarters declared yesterday afternoon as the British armor poured forward. According to reports from the front, the drive began toward Cuverville and Demouville, respectively four miles northeast and east of Caen, and toward the main Caen-Troarn road and the line of villages from Touffreville to Sannerville. A considerable number

Continued on Page 3

Nazi Sees Decision In Europe in 90 Days

By The Associated Press.

LONDON, July 18—Nazi radio broadcasts acknowledged tonight that Gen. Sir Bernard L. Montgomery had carried his attack east of the Orne and one commentator said the war would be decided in less than three months.

"The war is now in its decisive phase," said commentator Jean Paquis on the Nazi-controlled Paris radio. "In less than three months we shall know if the Allies have won or lost. On the east front it is now purely a question of life or death. On the west front the Allies have thrown into battle all the forces they can muster and the bitterest fighting must be expected."

2½ YEARS IN THE MAKING! 12,000 PLAYERS! 200 mighty scenes! 87 beloved melodies! Breathtaking spectacle: Darryl F. Zanuck's "WILSON" in Technicolor. A 20th Century Fox Picture! World Premiere, ROXY, AUG. 1, 9 P. M. Continuous thereafter.—Advt.

AT LEAST 350 DEAD IN BLAST ON COAST

Continued From Page 1

the water. Twisted stacks of lumber and rubbish were everywhere. A railroad track running out to the wrecked pier was dipping almost into the bay. Barracks at the loading station were demolished and other structures, including a carpenter shop, had disintegrated.

Observers had to take the word of Navy spokesmen that two ships had been tied up at the pier when the blasts went off at about 10:20 P. M. (1:20 A. M., New York time). The twisted bow of one ship lay on its side, protruding twenty feet or so out of the bay. A hundred feet away a propeller shaft was visible. Debris littered the water, but the ships, except for these parts, had sunk or been scattered. One sailor reported that a piece of sternpost landed in his barracks room a half mile away.

Port Chicago, with a peacetime population of about 1,500, lies a few miles west of the confluence of the Sacramento and San Joaquin Rivers, where they empty into Suisun Bay, an arm of San Francisco Bay.

In the development of the war loading port the Navy built acres of two-story barracks for pier workers. The barracks are a half-mile out of town. The population of the barracks, all of which were damaged, with many left uninhabitable, was put at around 1,400.

It was reported unofficially that most of the sailors working the loading shift at the time of the explosion were Negroes.

Tribute by Admiral Wright

Rear Admiral C. H. Wright, commandant of the Twelfth Naval

Automobiles parked near the dock area of Port Chicago, Calif., were blown apart. In the background are the ruins of one of the docks
Associated Press Wirephoto (U. S. Navy)

Two bits of wreckage sticking out of Suisun Bay were all that remained of the vessels
Associated Press Wirephoto

District, declared that all of those killed gave their lives "in the service of their country."

"Their sacrifice could not have been greater," he said, "had it occurred on a battleship or a beachhead on the war fronts. Their conduct was in keeping with the highest traditions of the United States naval service."

The destroyed vessels were the 10,000-ton Quinault Victory, a Victory ship delivered a week ago by the Oregon Shipbuilding Corporation at Portland, Ore., and the 7,500-ton E. A. Bryan, a Liberty ship delivered by Richmond Yard No. 2 March 8. Both yards are in the Henry J. Kaiser organization. The Quinault Victory was operated by the United States Steamship Lines and the Bryan by the Olivehumjl Olson Company. The damaged tanker was a Red Line ship.

One of the ships, according to Captain Goss, was loaded with "several thousand tons of explosives" and the other was "only slightly loaded" when the blasts occurred.

Capt. John Hendrickson and seven members of his crew of forty-one assigned to the Bryan were on authorized shore liberty last night and were presumed to be safe. Of fifty-two in the crew of the Quinault Victory sixteen had liberty passes and eight of these had reported in this afternoon.

Observers marveled that the damage had not been even greater. A munition train standing hardly more than a city block from the water's edge was undamaged.

Other freight cars dotted the reservation, but most of them were unscathed.

In the main barracks area, every wndow was blown out. Some of the war-built structures collapsed. The sides of others were blown out.

In Port Chicago the wall of a theatre was crushed, but with injury to only a few in the audience. At the Santa Fe depot broken glass strewed the floor. Store windows were smashed. A main street grocer, Pop Graham, found that 1,500 glasses of jellies and preserves had been broken.

The town was left without gas, electricity or running water. But late tonight the water supply was "reasonably well restored," relief workers announced, and progress was being made toward re-establishing electric and telephone service.

A man who was passed through the lines by State highway police and military sentries at about 5 A. M., said that he had waited for hours on the outskirts afraid to go to his home.

"I work in the steel mill over in Pittsburgh," he said, "I have a wife and five kids. I was afraid to come home. I was afraid they all were dead. My house is gone. But the family's safe."

The clock in the Port Chicago Hotel stopped at 10:19. This was the time the blast shook the bay area so hard that its force was registered on the seismograph of the University of California at Berkeley.

As pieced together by the authorities, the basic story is about as follows:

Gangs of Navy enlisted men, working as stevedores, were well along in the loading of the Quinault Victory with a cargo of high explosives of all types for use in the Allied offensive in the Pacific. The Bryan was tied up near by and the loading of her holds with munitions had just begun.

One ship blew up at 10:19, the others blew up about five seconds later. Flames shot toward the sky. A naval aviator flying over the installation at 8,000 feet had to climb to 10,000 feet to escape the fire and debris. A motorist described the rising mass of fiery debris as "a flaming doughnut."

As the force of the explosion was dissipated, air rushed in to fill the atmospheric vacuum. Its force was estimated at 150 miles an hour.

One 200-pound ship fragment sailed more than two miles.

Debris was hurled out into the bay for hundreds of yards. A warning was sent out for small craft to proceed through the adjacent waters with care.

Disaster relief units, military and civilian, formed early in the war to act in case of a Japanese attack, swung swiftly into motion. Doctors, nurses and hospital facilities throughout the bay area were "alerted." Ambulances were sent from points as far distant as Sacramento, sixty miles away. The number of civilian casualties was large, but few of the injuries were expected to be fatal.

For the first few hours relief workers labored in darkness or with flashlights. Before dawn brilliant floodlights illuminated the scene, but the full scope of the disaster was not revealed until daylight.

The walls of the Port Chicago theatre were blown in by the force of the blast
Associated Press Wirephoto

Concussion Coincides With Movie Bomb Scene

By The Associated Press.

PORT CHICAGO, Calif., July 18—As a result of the ammunition ship explosion, a mile and a half away, 195 movie theatre patrons in this town had a miraculous story to tell today.

They were watching a war film filled with bombing scenes last night. Then the wall blew in.

Joe Meyer, owner-manager of the theatre, said that he was operating the projector when the explosion occurred, just as a bombing scene with all its noise came on the screen.

He did not hear the ship blowing up, but one wall of the theatre caved in. Members of the audience, he said, got out safely with only minor scratches.

"All the News That's Fit to Print"

The New York Times.

LATE CITY EDITION
Showers, thunder showers; warm and humid today and tomorrow.
Temperature Yesterday—Max., 79; Min., 67
Sunrise today, 5:49 A. M.; Sunset, 8:19 P. M.

Section 1

NEWS INDEX, PAGE 41, THIS SECTION

Copyright, 1945, by The New York Times Company.

VOL. XCIV..No. 31,963. Entered as Second-Class Matter, Postoffice, New York, N. Y.

NEW YORK, SUNDAY, JULY 29, 1945.

Including Magazine and Book Review.

TEN CENTS New York City and Suburban Areas (15c Elsewhere)

SENATE RATIFIES CHARTER OF UNITED NATIONS 89 TO 2; TRUMAN HAILS AID TO PEACE

FOES ARE CRUSHED

With Hiram Johnson Ill, Only Shipstead and Langer Vote 'No'

WORLD OBLIGATION CITED

Leaders Say Today's Ratification Is 'Master Plan,' With Military Pacts Secondary

By JAMES B. RESTON

Special to THE NEW YORK TIMES.

WASHINGTON, July 28—The United States Senate paid a first installment on an old debt today. It ratified, 89 to 2, the United Nations Security Charter, successor to the League of Nations Covenant which it rejected twenty-six years ago, and thereby fulfilled Woodrow Wilson's prophecy that one day the upper chamber would reverse its decision.

The vote came 107 days after the death of Franklin D. Roosevelt, who helped guide the Charter past the pitfalls that defeated Wilson's Covenant, and at a moment when American statesmen were settling the fate of a defeated Germany and American warships were closing in on the heart of Japan.

The two Senators who voted against ratification were William Langer of North Dakota and Henrik Shipstead of Minnesota, both Republicans. Mr. Langer, who worked actively for Hiram Johnson and Robert M. La Follette when those two "irreconcilables" were candidates for President, said he was voting against the Charter because it would mean "perpetual war" and the "enslavement" of millions of poor people from Poland to India.

Hiram Johnson Sends Word

Senator Hiram Johnson, Republican, of California, sent word from the Naval Medical Center outside Washington that if he had been well enough to be present he would have joined Mr. Langer and Mr. Shipstead in opposition, but the four other members of the Senate who were with Mr. Johnson in the upper chamber during the League of Nations debate—Arthur Capper, Republican, of Kansas, and Peter G. Gerry of Rhode Island, Kenneth McKellar of Tennessee, and David I. Walsh of Massachusetts, Democrats, all voted for ratification.

As soon as the results were made known, President Truman and Cordell Hull, former Secretary of State, who started work on the Charter in the State Department in 1942, issued statements praising the Senate's action.

"It is deeply gratifying that the Senate has ratified the United Nations' Charter by a virtually unanimous vote," the President's message from Potsdam said. "The action of the Senate substantially advances the cause of world peace."

It was a grim-appearing Senate that rolled off the "ayes" on the final count this evening. Despite the long parliamentary debate in the chamber on the subject, and despite its overwhelming approval at the end, there was no sense of a job finished but merely of a difficult job just beginning.

Since a league to enforce peace had first been mentioned to members of this chamber by Woodrow Wilson in 1914, some 40,000,000 human beings, armed and unarmed, had been killed in two great wars. In the first German war total military casualties were estimated at 37,000,000 men; in the European phase of the second German war some 14,000,000 more had been killed, and our own casualties in this war, still unfinished, were over the million mark.

Chaplain Tells Senate's Hopes

Throughout the debate, the Senate seemed to realize this and to approach the problem more in hope than anything else.

"Under the old order of strife," the Senate's chaplain said in his prayer opening today's session, "we learned how to destroy ourselves. Under a new charter of mutual aid and tolerance of diversity, may we learn at last how to save ourselves."

Today's vote does not put the

Continued on Page 33, Column 4

EXECUTIVE, MFG. CORP. international in scope, sales volume of approximately 40 million dollars a year, in radio, electronics business, can use the services of a top ranking executive officer, preferably a man under 45 with mfg. and general executive experience. Fast growing organization, offering unparalleled opportunity to right man; salary commensurate with ability. Box W 362.—Advt.

Truman Deeply Gratified, He Says in Cable Message

President Promptly Recognizes Senate's Action as Advancing 'the Cause of World Peace'—Grew and Hull Applaud

Special to THE NEW YORK TIMES.

WASHINGTON, July 28—President Truman was swift to applaud the passage of the World Security Charter. In a message from Potsdam he said:

"It is deeply gratifying that the Senate has ratified the United Nations Charter by a virtually unanimous vote.

"The action of the Senate substantially advances the cause of world peace."

Joseph C. Grew, Acting Secretary of State, and Cordell Hull, former Secretary of State, also commended the Senate for its approval of the Charter.

Mr. Grew said:

"The passage of the United Nations Charter by the Senate today is a memorable event in the history of the United States and the world. By their action, the members of the Senate have taken a most important step toward establishing security and peace throughout the world.

"Millions of men, women and children have died because nations took to the naked sword instead of the conference table to settle their differences.

"The United Nations Charter, approved by such an overwhelming majority, represents the labor of citizens of fifty nations, united in their desire for a peaceful world. The Charter itself is the foundation and cornerstone on which the international organization to keep the peace will be built. This organization can survive only through the faith and labor of the citizens of all these nations.

"I congratulate the members of the Senate for their work today.

Continued on Page 33, Column 1

Poles, at Big 3 Meeting, Ask Stettin, Oder-Neisse Border

By RAYMOND DANIELL

By Wireless to THE NEW YORK TIMES.

BERLIN, July 28—A delegation of the Polish Government, including Vice Premier Stanislaw Mikolajczyk and, it is believed, Labor Minister Jan Stancczyk, has been here this last week to ask for a final delimitation of their country's western frontier to include Stettin and run from there southward along the east bank of the Oder-Neisse River line.

It was officially announced that Britain's new Prime Minister, Clement R. Attlee, and his Foreign Minister, Ernest Bevin, after formal calls on President Truman, Secretary of State James F. Byrnes, Premier Stalin and Foreign Commissar Vyacheslaff M. Molotoff, had participated today in a plenary session of the tripartite conference.

It is now believed, although there has been no inkling of their plans from official sources, that neither Winston Churchill nor former Foreign Secretary Anthony Eden will return. The new Prime Minister and his Foreign Secretary, who as Labor Minister in Mr. Churchill's coalition Government had access to all secrets of the War Cabinet, are the only new members of the British delegation. Inasmuch as Mr. Attlee sat in at all sessions of the Big Three before his election and saw all the official documents at the conference, it can hardly be said that he is a newcomer to the council table.

Parley Continuity Maintained

The downfall of the Churchill Government has caused little break in the continuity of the conference. Little more than forty-eight hours elapsed between Mr. Churchill's departure from Berlin and Mr. Attlee's return today.

In the absence of the head of the British delegation experts worked steadily to clear the decks

Continued on Page 5, Column 4

WOOLLEY DISMISSES ROSS IN OPA DISPUTE

Refuses to Grant the Public Hearing Demanded by Aide He Suspended June 22

Paul L. Ross, regional enforcement executive of the Office of Price Administration, who was suspended June 22 on charges of maladministration, was discharged yesterday by Daniel P. Woolley, regional OPA administrator, who refused to grant Mr. Ross the public hearing for which he had pleaded.

The discharge, effective at once, was contained in a registered letter mailed to Mr. Ross at noon, and followed by less than forty-eight hours the filing of Mr. Ross' reply to the administrator's charges.

In a brief statement, Mr. Woolley declared "utterly untrue and unfounded" serious counter-charges against him preferred by Mr. Ross in his answer. The enforcement officer had accused Mr. Woolley of hampering the enforcement of OPA regulations, interfering in behalf of certain alleged violators and obstructing the Federal enforcement policies.

Upon learning of his discharge,

Continued on Page 37, Column 5

Kweilin and Three Airfields Seized; Chinese Also Gain in Other Areas

By The Associated Press.

CHUNGKING, China, July 28—Chinese troops recaptured the airbase city of Kweilin yesterday and seized its three former American airfields from the Japanese, the Chinese High Command said tonight. The victory ended a six-week battle.

Kweilin, walled capital of Kwangsi Province, once was the biggest United States airbase in South-Central China. It had been occupied by the Japanese since last November. Its recapture was the most significant victory in the recent comeback of the Chinese armies.

Generalissimo Chiang Kai-shek's veterans smashed into the rubbled streets of Kweilin, 360 miles southeast of Chungking, at 4 P. M. yesterday after mowing down the defenders of the city's south and west gates. Most of the Japanese garrison had fled and enemy rearguard remnants swiftly were routed from machine-gun nests in cellars and on roofs, a communiqué said.

The Japanese, headquarters added, withdrew to the northwest to escape annihilation. Their escape route northeastward to Hengyang was severed several days ago. The Chinese said: "Our troops are in hot pursuit."

Kweilin, abandoned by the United States Fourteenth Air Force eight months ago, was the third former American airbase recovered in three days by the Chinese, whose current drive is rapidly strengthening American air power on the Asiatic mainland. It was

Continued on Page 3, Column 5

ENGINEERS—TRANSMITTING TUBES Expd in design & mfg. Technique of High Vacuum & Gas Filled Tube types. Good pay. Write Amperex, 25 Washington St., Bklyn.—Advt.

It's a wonder of laughs, "WONDER MAN" Starring DANNY KAYE, new Astor.—Advt.

When You Think of Writing Think of Whiting.—Advt.

NEW ZENITH HEARING AID, $40 to $50. LUGENE, INC., 604 Mad. Av. at 58 St.—Advt.

CRIPPLED WARSHIPS OF JAPANESE NAVY SMASHED BY FLIERS

2 Battleships and 3 Cruisers Set Afire in Saturday Strike by the Third Fleet

HYUGA IS FOUND SUNK

Returning U. S. Pilots Report Waters Off Kure Strewn With Burning Vessels

By Wireless to THE NEW YORK TIMES.

GUAM, Sunday, July 29—Two Japanese battleships, the Haruna and Ise, and three cruisers were set afire and a third battleship, the Hyuga, which was heavily damaged on Tuesday, was found to be resting on the bottom at her anchorage as United States Third Fleet carrier planes struck heavily Saturday at crippled remnants of the Japanese Navy in the Inland Sea.

An aircraft carrier also was further damaged.

Fleet Admiral Chester W. Nimitz today announced the results of the strike, which were incomplete. No reports had yet been received from British carrier pilots, who also participated.

Enemy Air Opposition Sporadic

The enemy's air opposition was sporadic, with American fighters shooting down one Japanese plane near Task Force 38, another eighteen near the target areas and destroying seventy-five on the ground. Fifty-six other parked enemy aircraft were damaged.

[Pilots returning from the Saturday strike reported waters off the Kure naval base littered with burning ships, and fleet dispatches said every major Japanese warship was believed to have been put out of action for the duration of the war, The United Press stated.]

The Third Fleet assault was directed at Japanese shipping between the once great ports of Kobe and Kure.

Pilots reported that the Hyuga, a modernized battleship with carrier type runway aft permitting it to handle aircraft, was on the bottom, water lapping over her main deck amidships.

It was disclosed also that Saturday's aerial assault, resulted in the sinking of three submarines, presumably in dry dock, and damage to four destroyers, two destroyer escorts, two medium-size freighter transports, three small cargo ships and an unidentified vessel.

Five Warships Left Burning

Whether these ships were among those damaged in the Tuesday attack, which battered twenty-three warships, was not revealed. However, it is definite that yesterday's attack further damaged six warships hit on Tuesday, the battleships Haruna and Ise, the cruisers Tone, Aoba and Oyodo and the escort carrier Kaiyo. All of these ships except the carrier were left burning in the latest assault.

Thus it seems that Admiral Halsey is well along toward his objective—the neutralization of Japan's remaining naval warships in order to provide a thoroughly clear field for future amphibious

Continued on Page 2, Column 2

BOMBER HITS EMPIRE STATE BUILDING, SETTING IT AFIRE AT THE 79TH FLOOR; 13 DEAD, 26 HURT; WIDE AREA ROCKED

WHERE BOMBER CRASHED INTO EMPIRE STATE BUILDING

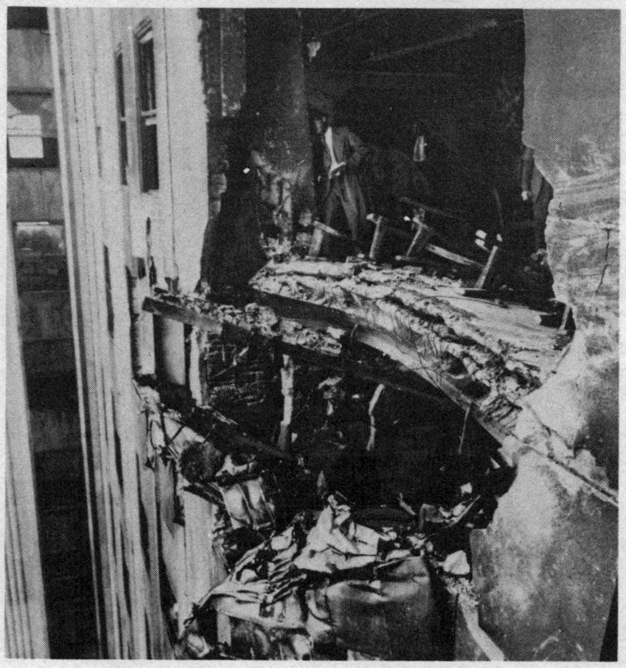

Hole torn between seventy-eighth and seventy-ninth floors   The New York Times (by Sisto)

B-25 CRASHES IN FOG

Hole 18 by 20 Feet Torn Through North Wall by Terrific Impact

BLAZING 'GAS' SCATTERED

Flames Put Out in 40-Minute Fight—2 Women Survive Fall in Elevator

By FRANK ADAMS

A twin-engined B-25 Army bomber, lost in a blinding fog, crashed into the Empire State Building at a point 915 feet above the street level at 9:49 A. M. yesterday. Thirteen persons, including the three occupants of the plane and ten persons at work within the building, were killed in the catastrophe, and twenty-six were injured.

Although the crash and the fire that followed wrecked most of the seventy-eighth and seventy-ninth floors of the structure, causing damage estimated at $500,000, Lieut. Gen. Hugh A. Drum, president of the Empire State, Inc., Corporation, said last night that an inspection by the city's building department and by other engineers and architects showed that the structural soundness of the building had not been impaired.

Landing Advice Disregarded

The plane, en route from Bedford, Mass., to Newark on a cross-country mission, had flown over La Guardia Field a few minutes before the crash, and its pilot, Lieut. Col. William F. Smith Jr., deputy commander of the 457th Bomber Group and recently decorated for his service overseas, was advised by the control tower to land. Instead he asked for the weather at Newark Airport and headed in that direction.

Horror-stricken occupants of the building, alarmed by the roar of engines, ran to the windows just in time to see the plane loom out of the gray mists that swathed the upper floors of the world's tallest office building. The plane was banked at an angle of about fifteen degrees as Colonel Smith swung it in a curve out of the northeast.

It crashed with a terrifying impact midway along the north or Thirty-fourth Street wall of the building. Its wings were sheared off by the impact, but the motors and fuselage ripped a hole eighteen feet wide and twenty feet high in the outer wall of the seventy-eighth and seventy-ninth floors of the structure.

Brilliant orange flames shot as high as the observatory on the eighty-sixth floor of the building, 1,050 feet above Fifth Avenue, as the gasoline tanks of the plane exploded. For a moment watchers in the street below saw the tower clearly illumined by the glare. Then it disappeared again in gray murk and the smoke of the burning plane.

Motor Hits Another Building

One of the plane's two motors hurtled clear across the seventy-eighth floor, tore a hole in the south wall of the building, and plummeted to the roof of the twelve-story office building at 10 West Thirty-third Street, where it started a fire that demolished the penthouse of Henry Hering, noted sculptor, with resulting damage estimated at $75,000.

A propeller was imbedded in the wall of the Empire State Building; the other motor and part of the landing gear crashed into an elevator shaft, where they fell to the sub-cellar 1,000 feet below, and other sections of the fuselage were blown as high as the eighty-sixth floor observatory. The steel girder at the seventy-ninth floor level was bent inward eighteen inches by the shock.

Cascading torrents of flaming gasoline poured through the seventy-eighth and seventy-ninth floors, setting fire to everything that was combustible. The burning fuel ran down stair wells into hallways as far as the seventy-fifth floor, while choking fumes

Continued on Page 25, Column 1

DRAFTSMEN-DESIGNERS: electrical, mechanical: experienced on electro-mechanical devices and instruments. Progressive national firm. Austin Co., 19 Rector, WH 4-6391.—Advt.

WOR—HEAR FATHER BROWN, famed Chesterton sleuth, at 5:00 P.M., Dial 710—WOR.—Advt.

B-29'S FIRE 6 CITIES IN PROMISED BLOWS

Oil Refinery Target on Honshu Added to List LeMay Gave Japanese in Advance

By Wireless to THE NEW YORK TIMES.

GUAM, Sunday, July 29—The Twentieth Air Force early today bombed six out of eleven Japanese cities that hardly twenty-four hours previously had been told that they were on a list of enemy communities marked for aerial destruction by Superfortresses.

Seven task forces of the B-29 bombers, totaling 550 to 600 planes, dropped more than 3,500 tons of incendiaries on the six industrial centers situated from Shikoku in the south to northern Honshu and demolition bombs on an oil refinery near Osaka.

[Gen. Douglas MacArthur reported Okinawa-based Army planes had sunk enemy shipping in Japan's Inland Sea area. He disclosed that our new B-32 super-bomber has been in action since May against the foe on Formosa and along the China coast.]

One of the B-29 task forces, sent

Continued on Page 4, Column 1

Catholic War Relief Office Is Chief Victim of Tragedy

By LARRY RESNER

An agency that has been in the vanguard of supplying aid and comfort to thousands of homeless and destitute persons in the war zones became yesterday, through one of those curious quirks of fate, the victim of the worst local tragedy of the war. The point of greatest impact of the low-flying bomber that crashed into the Empire State Building was at the seventy-ninth floor, where the principal tenant was the War Relief Services of the National Catholic Welfare Conference.

Throughout the war years, this agency has sent many field representatives into the lands laid waste by war to work with other relief and welfare agencies in helping war victims.

And only yesterday, as the bomber struck and destroyed their office, the reduced Saturday staff of workers was busily engaged in arranging the final details of a trip to Europe on Tuesday of two of their principal functionaries.

Only five of an estimated working staff of fifteen to twenty persons in the office, including men and women, were known to have escaped the flames that swept the skyscraper floor as the gasoline of the crashing plane exploded.

W. Paul Dearing, correspondent here for The Buffalo Courier-Express and publicity director of the War Relief Services for the last year, either jumped or was blown from his seventy-ninth-floor office to his death on a ledge on the sev-

Continued on Page 23, Column 3

SURVIVOR LIKENS CRASH TO A QUAKE

Building Moved Twice, Then Settled, Says Occupant Who Felt Shocks in China

By ALEXANDER FEINBERG

The towering Empire State Building that is a city of 102 stories, reaching 1,250 feet high, "moved" twice yesterday when struck by the bomber and then it "settled." That was a dread moment for one who had felt that double movement and the settling many times before.

Recently returned from China after twenty-seven years, the man who told of his sensations when the B-25 struck said the impact was precisely that of an earthquake, to which he is no stranger. Preferring not to give his name, he said he was in an office on the sixty-eighth floor of the building when he felt the double "move-

Continued on Page 28, Column 1

War News Summarized

SUNDAY, JULY 29, 1945

The United States Senate ratified, 89 to 2, the United Nations Security Charter. The two Senators who voted against ratification were William Langer of North Dakota and Henrik Shipstead of Minnesota, both Republicans. [1:1.]

Two battleships and three cruisers, all previously damaged, were hit again in the latest Third Fleet attack on the Inland Sea area, Admiral Nimitz disclosed, and it was found another battleship had been sunk. Returning pilots reported that the Japanese Navy probably was out of action for the rest of the war. [1:4.]

Between 550 and 600 Superfortresses set fire to six of the eleven Japanese cities warned previously of their coming destruction. [1:5; map P. 2.]

General Minami, chief of Tokyo's would-be totalitarian party, said Japan would be ready to discuss peace when East Asia was free from British-American "colonial exploitation." [9:1.]

Captain Zacharias, United States naval spokesman, broadcast to Japan a declaration that peace with Japan had now been made possible by the Potsdam proclamation. [4:5.]

Chinese forces took Kweilin and three former United States airfields. Other Chinese pressed toward Kukong, 120 miles north of Canton, gaining thirty miles in two days. [1:2-3; map P. 3.]

The British in Burma reported that the Japanese Twenty-eighth Army had been annihilated with more than 5,500 killed and the remnant fleeing toward Thailand. [3:1.]

Prime Minister Attlee and six new Ministers took the oath of office in London. [5-1.]

A Polish Government delegation was in Potsdam pleading for a western frontier running along the Oder and Niesse Rivers. Meanwhile, the conference was resumed with Mr. Attlee and Foreign Secretary Bevin in the places of Winston Churchill and Anthony Eden. [1:2-3; map P. 5.]

Michel Clemenceau accused Marshal Pétain at the latter's treason trial of having been indirectly responsible for handing over Georges Mandel, former Minister of Colonies, to the Germans who killed him. [12:1.]

Red Cross and Hospital Groups Speed to Aid of Victims, Rescuers

The last fireman barely had leaped from his truck to the raging four-alarm blaze caused by the bomber crash in the Empire State Building when hospital disaster units and two Red Cross Service canteen wagons were on the scene to aid the victims and rescuers of the catastrophe.

While fifteen Red Cross aides set up shop and dispensed hot coffee and doughnuts to the toiling fire fighters and others helping them, two disaster units from Bellevue Hospital, replete with the latest equipment, were making their way into the upper reaches of the building to assist in the rescue work.

Only twelve minutes elapsed between the sounding of the first alarm at 9:49 A. M. and the fourth alarm and from the moment the Telegraph Bureau at Police Headquarters received the first report the city's fire-fighting equipment, a small army of police and squads of Army and Navy units, mostly military police and shore patrols, moved with clock-like precision through the fog-shrouded streets.

The fire sirens screeched constantly as apparatus sped to the scene. The second alarm hit at 9:57 A. M., the third at 10 A. M. and the last at 10:01 A. M. After that there were other calls but only for specialized equipment.

The four alarms brought to the scene forty-one pieces of fire-fighting apparatus, including "walkie-talkie" radio units. All were under the immediate command of Fire Commissioner Patrick Walsh. Almost simultaneously the Police Department's ranking officers dispatched more than 400 policemen.

Continued on Page 32, Column 6

Tourneau CHRONOGRAPH, 45 min. recorder $71.50 TOURNEAU, 431 Madison Av., cor. 49 St.—Advt.

Food Dilemma? Read Margaret Pettigrew on the Woman's Page of The Brooklyn Eagle—Advt.

ENGINEERS - DRAFTSMEN, 150 all-time for N.Y.C. office. Makers of famous Thunderbolt needs permanent help for essential military and commercial projects for future development. Republic Aviation, 42 Broadway, WH 4-2864. W.M.C. rules.—Advt.

ARMY BOMBER HITS THE EMPIRE STATE

Continued From Page 1

and smoke rose upward to the observatory.

Betwe-n fifteen and twenty persons, most of them girl clerical workers, were at their desks in the offices of the War Relief Service of the National Catholic Welfare Conference, occupying the southwest section of the seventy-ninth floor, when the flaming flood burst in upon them.

Most of them ran in terror for the doors. At least four of them, it was established last night, safely reached the haven of the fireproof stair well, but several were overtaken by the flames as they ran and were burned to death. Three of them who had sought shelter in a separate office at the south side of the building were followed and killed there by the flames.

Paul Dearing, 37-year-old volunteer publicity man for the service, saw the flames approaching his desk near the west wall of the building, and jumped from a nearby window. He struck a ledge outside the seventy-second floor and was killed. He was identified by a police card showing he was formerly a reporter for The Buffalo Courier Express.

3 Occupants of Plane Perish

The bodies of the three occupants of the plane were hurled into the fiery inferno on the seventy-ninth floor, where, like those of the girl employes who were trapped there, they were burned beyond recognition. Two of the three were members of the crew of the plane, Colonel Smith and S/Sgt. Christopher S. Domitrovich, 31, of Granite City, Ill.

A Navy aviation machinist's mate, second class, who apparently had obtained a ride in the plane as a "hitch-hiker" when it left Bedford, was the third occupant. The Navy said last night that his identity apparently had been established, but in accordance with established procedure his name would not be announced until his next of kin was notified.

Fortunately, the seventy-eighth floor of the building was unoccupied, and was being used for the storage of various building supplies, which helped to keep the death toll down. However, one man, possibly a building employe, was trapped and burned to death there. He remained unidentified last night.

2 Women Fall 75 Stories

When the wreckage of the plane smashed into the north bank of elevators, it struck an I-girder between shafts numbers six and seven, weakening it and damaging some of the elevator cables. One car, which was empty, plunged immediately to the subcellar with a plane engine on top of it, but the other car figured in the most amazing of the many miraculous escapes of the day.

A girl elevator operator had opened the door of her car in another bank of elevators toward the south side of the building just as the explosion came. She was blown out of the car. Hysterical and burned by flaming gasoline, she was found by two young women employes of the Air Cargo Transport Corporation, with offices on the seventy-fifth floor.

These young women—Mrs. Barbara Brown of 222 East Sixty-first Street and Miss Penny Skepko of 104-42 126th Street, Richmond Hill, Queens—guided her back to their office, where first aid was administered. Then they took her to an elevator, that in shaft six. They were going to get in with her when Roy Penzell, president of Air Cargo Transport Corporation, advised them not to do so.

They turned her over to the care of the operator of car six and returned to their own office. Mr. Penzell, who remained in the hall, said that just as the elevator doors closed he heard the elevator cables snap with a crack like a rifle shot, and the car fell toward the subbasement.

Firemen had to cut a hole through a wall in the sub-basement to get into the car, fully expecting to find the occupants dead. Instead, a 17-year-old Coast Guard hospital apprentice, selected to be the first one through the hole because of his small stature, found the two women alive, although badly injured. Automatic devices evidently had slowed the falling car down enough to save their lives.

"Thank heaven, the Navy's here," said the burned girl as the Coast Guardsman, Donald Malony, administered first aid and then helped the two women out.

Because of the fog and bad visibility, there were only three persons in the upper observatory, at the 102d floor level, 1,250 feet above the street. One of them was Lieut. Allen Aiman, an aviation veteran of the South Pacific, who had with him his wife, Betty. Their home is in Columbus, Ohio.

"The visibility was zero," Lieutenant Aiman said later. "I was flabbergasted. I couldn't believe my own eyes when I saw the plane come out of the overcast. Then it struck the building with a force that sent a tremor through the whole structure."

The Aimans and Pat Hipwell, a guard on that level, whose home is at 32-10 Thirty-third Street, Astoria, found that the elevators had been put out of commission by the crash, but they made their way to safety down the stairs.

About fifty persons were in the glass enclosed observatory at the eighty-sixth floor level. Frank W. Powell, the tower manager, said that immediately after the crash flames shot up the elevator shafts, followed by a terrific cloud of dust and debris, while metal fragments of the plane landed on the open balcony outside.

Even at this terrifying juncture, however, the "canned" music that is wired into the observatory, continued to play and the soothing sounds of a waltz helped the spectators there to control themselves. There was no panic, but within a few minutes the heat and choking fumes from the fire below made the observatory uncomfortable.

The glass doors leading to the open balcony had been locked to keep people from going out into the fog and the slight rain that was falling. In the confusion, the keys could not be located, and so the three guards on the observatory level broke the doors open and let in the fresh air. After a few minutes, they also went down the stairs.

Many Offices Unoccupied

The staff of the National Broadcasting Company's television laboratory on the eighty-fifth floor had not yet arrived to begin the day's work, and the intervening floors between that point and the seventy-ninth were unoccupied, which undoubtedly helped to reduce the number of dead and injured.

Another factor in reducing casualties was the fact that the day was Saturday, when many offices are closed and others have reduced staffs. The War Relief Service of the NCWC, the largest sufferer from the disaster, would otherwise have had at least thirty persons in its offices instead of slightly more than half that number.

Joseph W. Bernstein of the publicity staff of the Empire State Building estimated that there were between 1,000 and 1,500 persons in it at the time of the accident. He said that if it had happened on a full business day there probably would have been 5,000 tenants, and 5,000 to 10,000 transients, in the building at that hour.

Most of those injured were on the upper floors of the building, but in a few cases persons walking along the sidewalks below suffered minor injuries from falling debris. It was considered astonishing, in view of the amount of broken glass and other debris that showered down, that these injuries were not more numerous and more serious.

Hundreds, if not thousands, of persons along Fifth Avenue and the near-by side streets saw the crash, and police headquarters was deluged almost immediately with calls from persons who wished to give the alarm. The first message was received at 9:49 A. M., which was listed as the official time for the disaster, although the Army in a statement placed it at 9:55.

Shock Felt Blocks Distant

The shock was felt for blocks around the busy intersection of Fifth Avenue and Thirty-fourth Street, and the explosion was heard more than a mile. Débris was thrown as far away as Madison Avenue, and one large chunk damaged the facade of a building at Fifth Avenue and Twenty-ninth Street.

By the time startled occupants of the lower floors of the building had made their way to the street, the first fire apparatus was arriving. Within eight minutes four alarms were sounded, bringing twenty-three fire companies and forty-one pieces of apparatus to the scene.

Thick smoke was pouring from the windows of the tower by that time, and a ruddy glow shone through the shattered openings, giving them a guide to the site of the fire. But the firemen had a difficult time getting up to fight it, because the building elevators could not operate above the sixtieth floor.

From that level the firemen toiled on foot to the seventy-eighth and seventy-ninth floors, where the fire was raging. Many of them carried hose and other types of portable apparatus. Much to their relief they found that the building's eight-inch stand pipes were undamaged by the blast and that there was ample water pressure to fight the flames.

Fire Commissioner Patrick Walsh, who arrived to take personal command of the fire-fighting, said that the blaze was the highest one in history, surpassing even the celebrated Sherry-Netherlands Tower fire of 1927, but that it was a comparatively easy one to extinguish. The flames were put out within forty minutes, he said.

Mayor Hurries to Scene

Mayor La Guardia was just getting out of his radio-equipped limousine at City Hall when the fourth alarm sounded. He recognized the number of the box as that at Fifth Avenue and Thirty-fourth Street and said to his driver: "That could be very bad. I'd better go up on that." So he sped to the scene.

Like every other early arrival, the Mayor had to walk up from the sixtieth floor, on the way getting soaked from the water that was cascading down from the fire hoses. When he reached the seventy-ninth floor he found that "a fiery furnace" was still raging there, but he remained until after the flames had been put out.

Thousands of spectators flocked to the vicinity of the building, but a force of 200 uniformed police, fifty detectives and twenty motorcycle and mounted men, under the command of Assistant Chief Inspector John W. Conway, formed lines and kept the area about the building clear. Even after the fire was out the adjoining streets were kept closed because glass kept falling from the hundreds of shattered windows in the lofty building.

Mayor La Guardia conferred at the building with John McKenzie, Commissioner of Marine and Aviation, who gave the first details about the appearance of the plane over La Guardia Field and Colonel Smith's decision not to land there. During the conversation the Mayor gestured violently with his fist and said audibly "I told them not to fly over the city."

Commissioner McKenzie later made a formal report, which was released by the Mayor from City Hall. It said that the plane called the La Guardia Field control tower, saying that it was fifteen miles to the south, and requesting the Newark weather. As that would place it close to Newark the chief operator, Victor Barden, suggested that it call Newark.

Within two minutes, however, the plane appeared directly southeast of La Guardia Field and Mr. Barden, thinking that it was about to land, gave it the necessary information about the runway to use and the wind velocity and direction. However, the pilot said that he wanted to go to Newark.

Col. H. E. Bogner, commanding officer of the Army Air Base at Sioux Falls, was at the Newark Airport waiting for the plane there, but when news of the accident arrived he left there and was not located later by newspaper men. He had spent last night at the Ambassador Hotel in this city, but checked out early yesterday morning and did not return there.

The plane, it was ascertained, arrived at the Bedford Army Air base, about twenty miles west of Boston, on Friday evening and left there at 8:55 A. M. yesterday. It was the belief there that a crew of four was on board the bomber, as well as at least one and possibly two Navy "hitch-hikers."

PHOTO-DIAGRAM OF THE PLANE CRASH

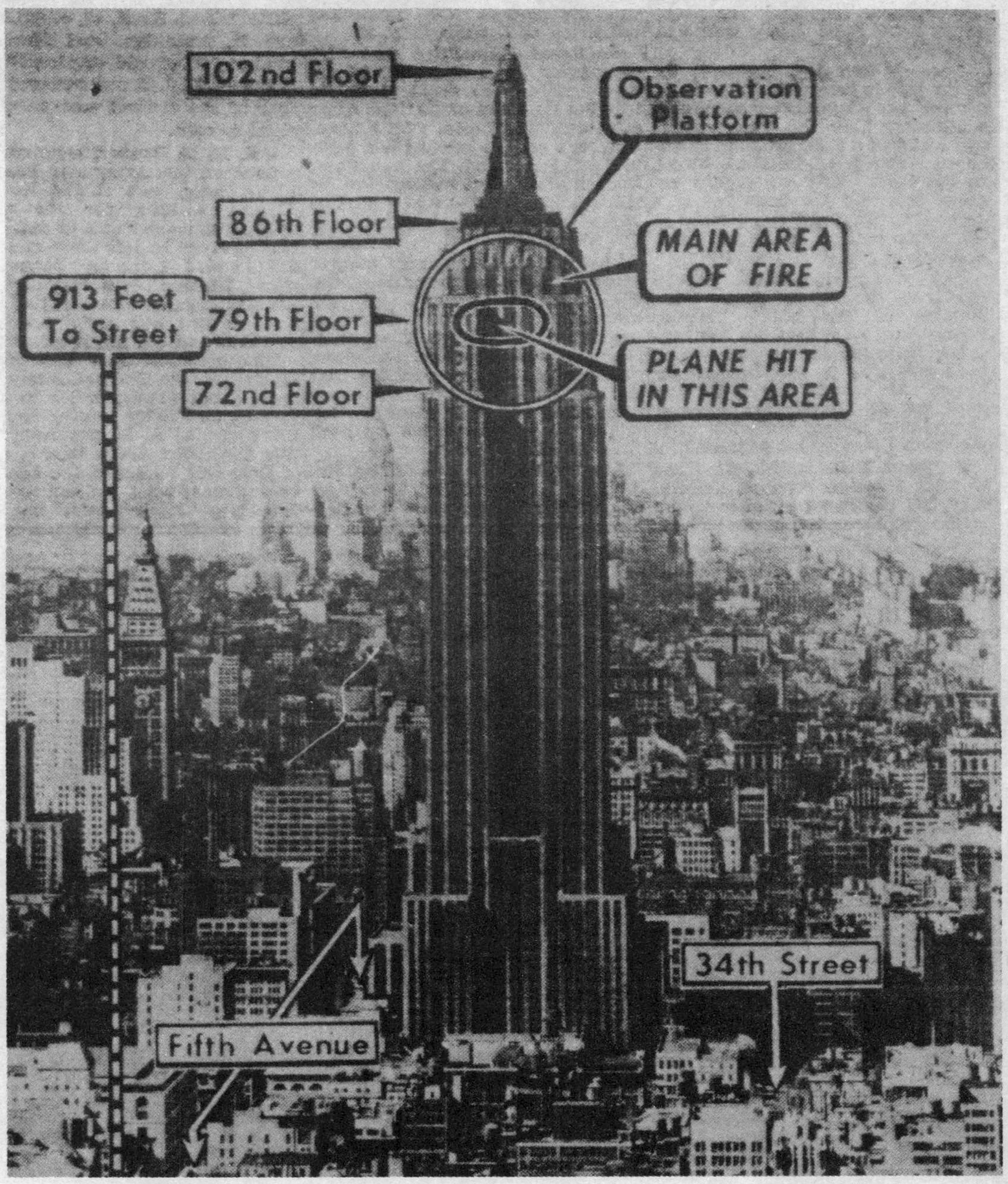

Key areas involved in the accident are located in this view looking south, with the north side of the Empire State Building shown.

Associated Press

"All the News That's Fit to Print"

The New York Times.

LATE CITY EDITION
Warmer, occasional showers today. Clearing tomorrow afternoon.
Temperatures Yesterday—Max., 44; Min., 36
Sunrise today, 5:40 A. M.; Sunset, 6:31 P. M.
Full U. S. Weather Bureau Report, Page 46

Copyright, 1946, by The New York Times Company.

VOL. XCV...No. 32,210. Entered as Second-Class Matter. Postoffice, New York, N. Y. NEW YORK, TUESDAY, APRIL 2, 1946. THREE CENTS IN NEW YORK CITY

CITY BUDGET SOARS TO $857,131,849; TAX RISE 5 POINTS

HIGHEST IN HISTORY

Program Submitted by Mayor Is $93,514,582 Above Current Total

5,899 NEW JOBS CREATED

Pay Increases of $15,099,442 Provided—Realty Taxes to Be $7,103,681 More

The text of O'Dwyer's budget message, Pages 17, 18 and 19.

By ROBERT W. POTTER

Mayor O'Dwyer submitted to the Board of Estimate yesterday an executive budget of $857,131,849 for 1946-47, representing an increase of $93,514,582 over the current budget of $763,617,266.

This increase, attributed by the Mayor to inevitably higher costs in the post-war reconversion period, will be met mostly by an indicated rise of five points in the basic tax rate, lifting it to 2.72, by an estimated yield of $67,000,000 from the new and additional taxes approved by the Legislature and by a $15,673,176 increase in State aid, chiefly for revised financing of relief. Real estate taxes are estimated to increase by $7,103,681.

While the budget, which can be cut or increased by the Board of Estimate and decreased by the City Council, is the largest in the city's history, including the amount to be raised by taxes, the indicated new tax rate will fall short of the record 2.89 rate of 1943-44 and be lower than any rate since the 2.64 of 1937, except this year's 2.67.

5,899 New Jobs Included

Heavy costs for materials and for repair and replacement of plant and equipment are indicated by an increase of $56,376,157 in other-than-personal costs, as compared with a $37,138,425 increase for personal costs, a total that is usually the larger. The total for other-than-personal service is $432,386,330, against $424,745,519 for personal service. The budget contains a total of 5,899 new jobs, including 3,028 police and 693 firemen. Straight pay increases totaling $1,738,851 are to go to 22,555 employes.

In his message Mayor O'Dwyer said the budget provided for $15,099,442 in 107,269 salary increases, increments and cost-of-living adjustments, to be paid to approximately the same number of employes, some of whom will benefit from more than one of the adjustments.

The salary increases, ranging from $120 to $240, go to low salaried employes for the most part, including library and museum employes and hospital workers. A lump sum appropriation of $5,000,000 is provided within which the Budget Director will work out increases and cost-of-living adjustments affecting a large number, including police and firemen, who in the maximum salaries will receive an $80 increase as a result of increasing the top pay from $3,000 to $3,150 and fixing their bonuses at $350 instead of the $420 bonus they now receive. Those receiving the maximum will thus get $3,500 instead of $3,420; all police will receive some increase.

Contrary to the hopes and demands of city employes, the cost-of-living bonus was not made a permanent wage increase. The Mayor said that while he thought many salary rates were inadequate for a fair standard of living, his efforts to make corrections were limited by the city's financial condition.

Hearings Start April 10

The Board of Estimate set hearings for April 10, 11 and 12. On April 10 civic organizations, taxpayers and departments will be heard at 10:30 A. M. The next day, at 2:30 P. M., civic organizations, taxpayers, the Board of Education, the Board of Higher Education and the libraries will be heard. On April 12, at 10:30 A. M. city employes from all departments will be heard. The board will take final action on the budget on April 26 at 2 P. M. The budget will then go to the City Council, which must act on it by May 21.

The Mayor said in his message

Continued on Page 19, Column 2

HOTEL GROSSMAN
In the Healthful Pine Belt
of Lakewood, New Jersey.—Advt.

Snow Brings April, Today to Be Balmy

April, arriving on the heels of a brisk Southeaster, put a chill end yesterday to the Florida-like weather in which the city had basked for much of the traditionally blustery month of March. Temperatures that hovered around 40 degrees, slight morning snow flurries and dull leaden skies ushered in the month.

Last month's average temperature, according to the Weather Bureau, was 49.7 degrees, three-tenths of a degree below the record high average for March, established last year. Last month also had 72 per cent of its highest potential sunshine, against an average of 61 per cent, a trace of snow as against an average of six inches, and only one day—March 11—when the temperature failed to go above normal.

The forecast says that with a shift of the wind to the south, the balmy zephyrs will be back today. Possible high, 60 degrees.

'DEATH SENTENCE' IS CONSTITUTIONAL

Supreme Court by 6-0 Backs Clause in Holding Company Act Ending Utility Empires

By LEWIS WOOD
Special to THE NEW YORK TIMES.

WASHINGTON, April 1—The legality of the long-discussed "death sentence" provision of the Public Utility Holding Company Act of 1935, compelling interstate gas and electric corporations to limit their activities to a single, integrated system, was sustained unanimously by the Supreme Court today.

The decision upheld a 1942 order of the Securities and Exchange Commission, forcing the $2,300,000,000 North American Company to divest itself of all its properties, except in the St. Louis area, merely one segment of its utility empire.

Only six justices, a legal quorum of the high court, participated in the ruling, which ended a determined four-year fight by North American against the constitutionality of the "death sentence" clause, carried in Section 11 (b) (1) of the act. Three other members of the court disqualified themselves.

Evils Are Charged

Justice Frank Murphy, who wrote the court's opinion, said that the SEC was perfectly right in treating North American "as possessing domination over its subsidiaries or the power to dominate them when and if necessary."

Mr. Murphy, in the opinion, said that Congress in enacting the "death sentence" clause, was concerned with "the economic evils resulting from uncoordinated and unintegrated public utility holding company systems." These evils, he went on, were "found to be polluting the channels of interstate commerce," and to take the form of transactions occurring in and concerning more States than one. Congress also found, he stated, that the national welfare "was thereby harmed, as well as the interests of investors and consumers."

"These evils, moreover," he con-

Continued on Page 21, Column 2

REPUBLICANS ELECT REECE AS CHAIRMAN; STASSEN IS CRITICAL

The Tennessee Representative Wins on Third Ballot Over Danaher and Hanes

NEGRO VOTE IS STRESSED

Minnesotan Says Selection Does Not 'Constitute a Decision' on Party's Policy

By JOHN D. MORRIS
Special to THE NEW YORK TIMES.

WASHINGTON, April 1—Representative B. Carroll Reece of Tennessee was elected Republican National Chairman today by National Committee delegates.

The former farm boy from Johnson City, a member of Congress for twenty-five years, won over his two principal contestants on the third ballot.

Nine delegates who had voted for former Senator John A. Danaher of Connecticut and one supporter of John W. Hanes of New York City, former Under Secretary of the Treasury, switched their ballots to Mr. Reece, along with two of the three delegates who originally voted for Senator Kenneth S. Wherry of Nebraska as a favorite son and possible dark horse candidate.

Only the names of Messrs. Reece, Danaher and Hanes were put in formal nomination, and the voting was restricted to them and Senator Wherry. Representative Clarence J. Brown of Ohio withdrew as a candidate to make the nominating speech for Mr. Reece.

Dewey Said to Back Danaher

Mr. Reece was regarded by some delegates as a candidate of supporters of Senator Robert A. Taft of Ohio, a 1948 Presidential possibility, while Mr. Danaher was said to have the backing of Governor Dewey, who is also a 1948 possibility.

That Mr. Reece's election was not looked on with favor by all Republican factions, especially by the liberal wing, was emphasized by Harold E. Stassen, former Minnesota Governor, and another aspirant for the 1948 Presidential nomination in his party, who issued a statement which said:

"It should be emphasized that the chairman's election by the national committee does not constitute a decision by the Republican party as to its policy or platform.

"That will be decided in the primary elections and convention of 1946 and 1948.

"It is, of course, well known that I do not approve of Chairman Reece's stand on many issues in the past. I will cooperate with him as the new chairman in the Republican Congressional election, and I will carry on the debate within the party on issues and principles."

Mr. Stassen did not attend the committee meeting.

Negro Vote Is Stressed

One aspect of Mr. Reece's election, emphasized privately and in speeches by delegates, was his influence with Negro voters.

Perry W. Howard, delegate from Mississippi, in seconding the nomination, recalled his "perfect" record of votes in the House on questions in which Negroes were interested. With Mr. Reece as chairman, he predicted "a general homecoming of the black Republicans in the fall of this year."

In the formal ballot which determined the successor of Herbert Brownell Jr., who resigned to devote his time to his New York law practice, Mr. Reece polled fifty-eight votes, compared with Mr. Danaher's twenty-two and Mr.

Continued on Page 48, Column 5

TRUMAN, BYRNES TALK ON U. N. CASE; SOVIET PUSHES IRAN

Russia Suggests to Teheran It Should Wish to Keep Red Army in Country

FOR SUCH AN AGREEMENT

But Premier Ghavam Shuns Idea—Moscow Wants Area Next to Turkish Frontier

By JAMES B. RESTON
Special to THE NEW YORK TIMES.

WASHINGTON, April 1—Secretary of State James F. Byrnes reported to President Truman today on his recent efforts to settle the Iranian case in the United Nations Security Council, but he had nothing to report on Premier Stalin's reaction to the Council's request for clarification of the Russo-Iranian negotiations.

In fact, there was not only no reply from either Moscow or Teheran to the Security Council's communication of Friday evening, but the official information reaching the State Department continues to indicate that the Russians have been keeping up their pressure on the Iranians for political and economic concessions in northern Iran.

One official dispatch reaching Washington, for example, indicates that the Soviet Union gave to Iranian Premier Ahmad Ghavam an aide memoire several days ago suggesting the possibility that the Iranian Government might wish to retain some of the Red Army troops in northern Iran. This aide memoire, it is understood, said that the Red Army troops would get out of Iran within five or six weeks, but it did not add—as the Russian official announcement added—that they would get out "if nothing unforeseen happens."

"Agreement" Enters

What it is reported to have said was that the Red Army evacuation would be completed in five or six weeks "provided no other agreement to the contrary is reached."

The importance of this distinction is that it is the first indication from Soviet documents that the Russians were actually negotiating or hoping to negotiate with the Iranians to keep their troops in northern Iran. The only public statement the Russians have made is that they were withdrawing in the next five or six weeks "if nothing unforeseen happens."

Now, the United States is apparently in possession of an official Soviet indication that the Russians were negotiating for the retention of their troops in Iran, and this is precisely why the Security Council asked Moscow and Teheran for the state of their present negotiations: the Council

Continued on Page 6, Column 5

TIDAL WAVES IN THE PACIFIC KILL 300, BATTER HAWAII, WEST COAST, ALASKA; UNDERSEA QUAKES CAUSE UPHEAVAL

SUBMARINE QUAKE RADIATES HAVOC IN EAST PACIFIC

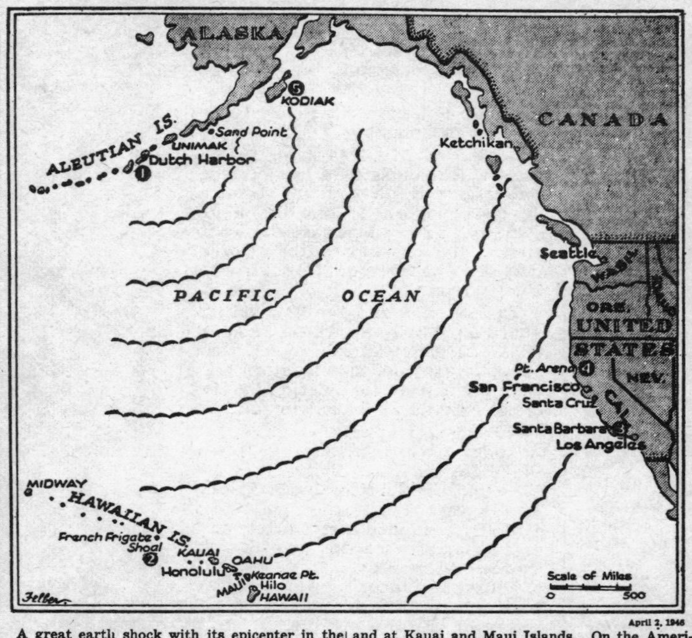

April 2, 1946

A great earth shock with its epicenter in the region of Dutch Harbor (1) started tidal waves that rolled across the ocean at an estimated rate of 300 miles an hour. The heaviest damage was reported from the Hawaiian Islands (2), particularly along the Honolulu waterfront, at Hilo and at Kauai and Maui Islands. On the American west coast the area hardest hit was between Santa Barbara (3) and Point Arena (4), although high waves also smashed ashore in Oregon and Washington. Last night the waves were reported to be rushing toward Kodiak (5).

DEVASTATION VAST

Water's Force Surges 300 Miles an Hour in 4,000-Mile Arc

5,000 HOMELESS IN HAWAII

Damage Is Put at Millions—Homes Crash, Boats Pulled to Sea as Waves Leap Barriers

A series of huge tidal waves, attributed by seismologists to underwater earthquakes centered near Dutch Harbor, Alaska, struck the Hawaiian Islands, the Aleutians and the West Coast of North America yesterday. A death toll of 300 was reported by Navy officers in the city of Hilo, Hawaii.

Reports from the Hawaiian Islands said property damage there was estimated in millions of dollars, with 5,000 persons made homeless on the island of Hawaii alone.

In California and the Pacific Northwest States the waves washed against the shores in freakish fashion, causing damage at some points and missing others a few miles away. In some places small buildings were swept from foundations and scores of boats broke from moorings.

The expanse affected was an arc of 4,000 miles. The wave impulse was said to race at a speed of 300 miles an hour.

Noise 'Like Big Wind'

By RICHARD MacMILLAN
By Wireless to THE NEW YORK TIMES.

HONOLULU, April 1—The latest total of known dead in the Hawaiian Islands in the wake of the tidal waves that struck today was seventy. Forty-eight bodies have been recovered on the Island of Hawaii.

Property damage was in millions of dollars. Five thousand persons were reported homeless on the island of Hawaii alone, whose principal city, Hilo, was heavily hit. Fifteen there were known to be dead. Shortly after noon the Army and Navy issued a joint warning that a new wave was possible and warned residents in low-lying areas to leave immediately. At 2 P. M. no new major wave had appeared, however.

At least three huge waves four to six feet high swept in from the sea about 7 A. M. Witnesses reported having heard a noise "like a big wind" and with waves hitting the islands at three-minute intervals.

A wall of water swept before it small boats moored in harbors, crushing flimsily built beach homes and drowning the victims. Honolulu, on the leeward side of the island of Oahu, escaped casualties, but property damage was heavy, especially along famed Waikiki Beach, where boats were washed up.

The wave swept up the Ala Wai Canal at Waikiki, beaching the sampan fleet moored there.

Hawaiian Guard on Alert

Gov. Ingram M. Stainback, who arrived from Washington yesterday, was keeping in close touch with the situation. The Army, Navy and Red Cross have volunteered aid. The Territorial Guard was alerted to duty.

On Hawaii, where apparently the biggest casualties were caused, a state of emergency was declared in Hilo. Twenty dead were brought to the Hilo Memorial Hospital. An unconfirmed report from the outlying district on the island was that thirty school children had lost their lives. A later communication, however, said that all the students were safe, but that four teachers had drowned. Eleven bodies were recovered on Maui, six on the windward side of Oahu and one on the island of Kauai. On a windward Oahu site beach homes of Honoluluans were heavily hit. Not one home was left undamaged in a beach settlement of Lanikai.

The immediate effect of the disaster was stunning. The waves hit Honolulu just as office workers were going to work. A Hawaiian Airlines pilot, Gilbert Teft, had just taken off in a DC-3 from Honolulu on a routine flight to Hilo when he saw a wave approaching

Continued on Page 3, Column 2

IRAN PREMIER ADDS WEIGHT TO U.N. PLEA

Gives Full Support to Ala in Message to Lie—U. S. and Britain Ready to Proceed

By W. H. LAWRENCE

A new pledge of unequivocal support from the Iranian Prime Minister, Ahmad Ghavam, for his United Nations' spokesman, Ambassador Hussein Ala, was coupled yesterday with renewed indications that the United States and Great Britain would insist upon overriding procedural objections to hear the substance of Iran's complaint

Continued on Page 8, Column 3

World Food Parley Called; Truman Orders Special Aid

By WALTER H. WAGGONER
Special to THE NEW YORK TIMES.

WASHINGTON, April 1—A conference of world and national food organizations and officials will start here May 20 to strengthen emergency famine relief and help individual governments map long-range food and farming programs as insurance against starvation conditions, the Food and Agriculture Organization of the United Nations announced today. The conference will last a week.

In a closely related move, President Truman called upon Secretary of Agriculture Anderson to take the lead in forming an inter-agency committee to work with the FAO on a world food program.

The committee, as outlined by the President, will consist of representatives of the Departments of Agriculture, State, Treasury, Commerce, Interior and Labor, the Federal Security Agency and the Bureau of the Budget. Secretary Anderson or a nominee of his selection will be chairman of the committee.

"This inter-agency committee shall have the responsibility for insuring that our Government aids to the fullest extent the proper functioning of the FAO," President Truman said.

He pointed out, however, that the State Department would continue to provide "policy guidance" on all international political questions and on general organizational and administrative matters as they affect the relationships of the FAO to the United Nations and other international organizations.

The President also asked Secre-

Continued on Page 4, Column 4

U. S. WILL GIVE UP CUBAN WAR BASES

Those Built During Hostilities to Be Relinquished May 20 —Guantanamo Unaffected

By The United Press.

WASHINGTON, April 1—Secretary of State James F. Byrnes notified Cuba tonight that the United States was giving up all the bases it built in Cuba during the war.

Cuban Ambassador Guillermo Belt, in issuing the news to correspondents, pointed out that negotiations over the bases had been proceeding since Sept. 24, 1945. This meant they were under study by the two Governments long before the Russian radio began discussing the matter at the height of the tension over the Iranian question at the United Nations meeting in New York.

Although the United States is entitled to keep the bases until six months after hostilities are for-

Continued on Page 6, Column 3

World News Summarized

TUESDAY, APRIL 2, 1946

Huge tidal waves towering to 100 feet brought death and destruction yesterday to a vast area of the Pacific reaching from the Aleutians to Hawaii and the West Coast. At Hilo, alone, the dead were estimated at 300. An under-water earthquake in the Dutch Harbor area was believed the cause. [1:8.]

Official information reaching the State Department indicated that Moscow was continuing its pressure on Teheran for political and economic concessions before withdrawing the Red Army from Iran, it was learned. Secretary Byrnes discussed the Security Council situation with President Truman. Neither Russia nor Iran had replied to the Council's questions seeking to clarify the state of affairs [1:4], but Ambassador Ala said he expected to receive replies today. [9:4.]

Premier Ghavam officially notified Secretary General Lie of the United Nations that Mr. Ala had his full support. The United States and Britain were reported determined to proceed with the Iranian question tomorrow should Russia fail to reply, recognizing that such action would constitute a serious challenge to the U. N. [1:5.] The Committee of Experts will recommend at least eighteen Council procedural rules on Thursday. [10:3.]

In Greece the royalist Populist party appeared to have won a clear majority in Sunday's elections, but not large enough to undertake to form other than a coalition government. [12:2.]

The United States will turn over to Cuba on May 20 all American-built bases, some of which have been evacuated. [1:7.] On May 1 the United States Army will disband the China theatre, leaving fewer than 4,000 soldiers there on miscellaneous assignment. The Marines, whose numbers are being reduced rapidly, will revert to Navy control. [2:5.]

General MacArthur informed the Far Eastern Commission that he was determined to hold Japanese national elections this month because reactionary forces there are now at their most disorganized state. [2:3-4.]

Moscow has rejected without explanation an invitation to join with eighteen other nations in the emergency conference on European cereal supplies opening tomorrow in London. [4:3.] The U. N. Food and Agriculture Organization has called an international meeting in Washington for May 20 in an effort to avert the recurrence of world famine conditions. [1:6-7.]

News on the labor front was discouraging. Transit workers brought transportation to a standstill in Detroit and Akron, Ohio. [1:6-7.] Negotiations in the eleven-week Westinghouse strike broke down again [16:6] and no progress was made toward an agreement in the soft-coal walkout. [1:2-3.]

Mayor O'Dwyer submitted an $857,131,849 budget, the largest in New York City's history. The increase of nearly $100,000,000 over the current budget arises mainly from cost of replacements and repairs, new jobs and pay increases. [1:1.]

Representative Carroll Reece of Tennessee was elected the new chairman of the Republican National Committee. [1:3.]

Coal Conferees Blame Each Other For No Progress as Strike Sets In

By LOUIS STARK
Special to THE NEW YORK TIMES.

WASHINGTON, April 1—Deadlocked in their efforts to agree upon a new contract to replace the one which expired last midnight, committees of the United Mine Workers of America and the Bituminous Operators negotiating committee blamed each other today for the impasse and adjourned until tomorrow morning.

The three-hour session, the first since the 400,000 soft coal workers began their strike, was marked by the presence of Paul Fuller, veteran conciliator of the Labor Department. He had no comment for publication, but he will report daily to Lewis B. Schwellenbach, Secretary of Labor, and Edgar L. Warren, the conciliation chief.

Mr. Fuller, assigned as a special mediator, worked in the coal mines as a youth but quit at the age of 18 when his right foot was crushed. Since then he has been a Methodist "circuit rider," superintendent in a steel mill, head of the CIO Flat Glass Workers' Union and, for the last four years, Federal conciliator in the rubber industry with headquarters in Akron.

The end of the meeting found John L. Lewis and his associates on the United Mine Workers committee still determined for a health and welfare fund to be paid by the operators.

The operators had again sought unsuccessfully to draw Mr. Lewis into a discussion of wages and hours, but he had countered with

Continued on Page 16, Column 3

Detroit Transit Strike May Grow; 1,800,000 Rides Thumbed in Day

Special to THE NEW YORK TIMES.

DETROIT, April 1—While 1,800,000 rides were thumbed by Detroiters to get to work and home again today in the worst public transportation tie-up this city has ever known, the American Federation of Labor Teamsters Union issued a threat that the strike might spread still further.

James Hoffa, business agent for the teamsters' union, said his group will "take a strong stand" if any attempt is made to break the strike of the street car and motor driver workers of the Department of Street Railways, the municipally owned transit system.

The strike started at 4 A. M. this morning when 5,200 members of Division 26 of the Amalgamated Association of Street Electric Railway and Motor Coach Employes of America ended their runs and refused to take out equipment.

The strike was voted at a mass meeting yesterday afternoon which was attended by about 2,000 members.

Efforts to reach a settlement today failed completely when officials of Division 26 and members of the Detroit Street Railway Commission met in Mayor Jeffries' office in the City Hall.

The union group asked that negotiations on the contract which expired at midnight, Sunday night, be reopened. Mayor Jeffries replied:

"There will be no negotiations, arbitration or wage concessions as long as you are on strike."

The Mayor and members of the

Continued on Page 15, Column 2

Drink GREAT BEAR Ideal Spring Water. It comes in Sterilized Bottles. GR 5-3810.—Advt.

TIDAL WAVES KILL 300 IN PACIFIC PATH

Continued From Page 1

Waikiki. He radioed to the airport and was diverted to the island of Maui, where he unloaded his passengers, picked up a portable radio transmitter and flew to Hilo to establish communications. An airline plane was standing by to take doctors, nurses and plasma to Hilo if needed.

Water Towers Fifty Feet

HONOLULU, April 1 (U.P.)—The great tidal waves, stemming from an earthquake on the ocean floor south of Alaska, swept over a 4,000-mile arc of the Pacific today.

It was reported unofficially that at least 330 persons had been killed, more than 300 in the Hawaiian chain.

The waves towered as high as fifty feet and traveled more than 300 miles an hour.

[A new 100-foot tidal wave was reported by the United States Navy to be rolling northeast along the Aleutian chain directly toward Kodiak Island, site of great American military installations.

[Naval headquarters at Anchorage, Alaska, reported Monday night a 100-foot surge of water was racing east and west from Unimak Island in the Aleutian chain and scout planes said it was heading for Kodiak at a thirty-knot clip. It was not known whether this wave originated from a new earth tremor similar to earlier ones.]

The Mayor of Hilo said in a broadcast intercepted by the Navy here that at least 300 persons were dead or missing.

10 Believed Killed in Lighthouse

KETCHIKAN, Alaska, April 1 (AP)—A tidal wave crashed today on the Aleutian island of Unimak, demolishing the Scotch Cap lighthouse, with an estimated loss of ten lives, but had apparently spent its force in the sea before it reached Dutch Harbor, 120 miles west.

The commander of the Alaska Sea Frontier said a minor wave had entered Dutch Harbor at 5:30 A. M., about an hour after it had struck Unimak. It carried away ferry barges that connected the base with the town of Unalaska and damaged small boat landings and pilings, the report said.

One body was reported recovered at Unimak but it was not identified. The Coast Guard cutter Cedar was sent from Kodiak and the cutter Clover from Adak to help the people of Unimak.

Two heavy earth tremors were reported early today at Sand Point in the Shumagin Islands, about 240 miles southwest of Kodiak, and it was thought locally the tidal wave may have started there.

A message from Unimak said the wave that struck the lighthouse was about 100 feet high.

The comamnder's message said earth shocks were continuing irregularly and he warned of a "possible recurrence" of the wave.

A Navy Privateer plane was dispatched from Kodiak to inspect the damage at Scotch Cap and lend assistance. In Kodiak the people prepared to evacuate to higher ground if the town siren sounded a danger signal.

Seven Waves Hit Coast

By LAWRENCE E. DAVIES

Special to THE NEW YORK TIMES.

SAN FRANCISCO, April 1—Tidal waves reaching a height of fifteen feet and traveling in a series of seven or eight struck the West Coast today, drowning at least one person, sweeping small buildings off their foundations and breaking scores of boats from moorings.

Some witnesses, including Coast Guard Seaman Richard Trainor of Pawtucket, R. I., who was in a rowboat in Bolinas Bay, twenty miles north of this city, when the first big wave struck, said it was "traveling darn fast."

However, James Healey, operator of a deep-sea fishing establishment in Princeton-by-the-Sea, fifteen miles south of here, described the waves as "slow and methodical, like molasses." Most of those who saw the water approaching agreed they had "never seen anything like it before."

The waves began hitting the West Coast about 10:30 A. M. and continued, in some places, more than an hour. The one death reported by nightfall occurred in Santa Cruz, fifty miles south of here. Cephus Smith was walking on Cowell's Beach with an unidentified companion when a big wave struck them. Mr. Smith grabbed for his companion, who was swept from his feet, but another wave tore him away and washed him to sea.

At Point Arena, more than 100 miles to the northwest, the waves reached a height of fifteen feet. The area affected extended south as far as Santa Barbara.

There was no evidence in San Francisco Bay that anything was amiss. The tide rose only two feet at Fort Point at the Golden Gate Bridge, but waves of unusual height struck along the beach at Sharps Park, at the southern border of San Francisco County.

Prof. Percy Byerly, University of California seismologist in Berkeley, said the earthquake was registered at 4:35:23 A. M. and continued for three hours.

Two major quakes were recorded at the California Institute of Technology in Pasadena and were estimated to be centered about 2,700 miles northwest of there. The first shock came at 4:30:06 A. M. and the second nearly six minutes later.

Origin Near Aleutian Deep

SAN FRANCISCO, April 1 (U.P.)—Seismologists said the underwater eruption occurred near the Aleutian Deep, a 15,000-foot chasm in the ocean floor south of the Shumagin Islands, just off the Alaskan peninsula.

The waves were set in motion by earth tremors that were believed to have their epicenter near Dutch Harbor, in the Aleutian chain west of Alaska.

The shores of Ala Wai, between Waikiki and Honolulu, are piled with fishing and pleasure craft that were washed upon the sands

Associated Press Wirephoto

HILO CITY ROLLED UP BY CRASH OF WATER

Hawaii Residents Cling to the Wreckage of Homes Swept to Sea by Tidal Wave

HILO, Hawaii, April 1 (AP)—This tragic city was a shambles today as rescue squads dug bodies of thirty-seven victims of the smashing tidal wave from the slimy wreckage and rubble.

No one knows how many dead there may be in this once-beautiful city. Navy officers here estimated that 300 had lost their lives when the terrific wall of water swept out of the Pacific and rolled to the beaches. Many were swept to sea and scores were reported clinging to wreckage of homes, trying to regain the shore.

On high ground stood weeping friends and relatives waiting to hear which names had been added to the death list. Troops patrolled the wrecked waterfront and permitted no one near the wreckage of buildings leveled by the rushing tons of water. Hilo's police chief, Anthony Paul, said thirty-seven bodies were recovered, but "there is no way to tell how many are dead."

Many are missing at Laupahoehoe, twenty-five miles northwest of Hilo, among them four mainland school teachers.

C. R. Ferdun, school principal, identified the four as Marsue McGinnis, Oxford, Ohio; Faye Johnson, Vinton, Va.; Dorothy Drake, Columbus, Ohio, and Helen Kingseed, Sidney, Ohio.

Cottages Driven Inland

Mr. Ferdun said the teachers lived in beach homes along the waterfront, which was inundated. Two of the cottages were swept out to sea. Three others near by were sent crashing inland.

"Eight school children are missing," the principal added. "There is little chance they are alive.

"After the first wave came in and then receded, the children ran down to the beach to see what happened, and the second wave engulfed them, according to witnesses."

A naval bomber dropped rescue equipment to four persons adrift on debris off Laupahoehoe and radioed the position of survivors to rescue craft.

There were no rescue craft at Laupahoehoe, but islanders put out to sea in a small outboard motor boat to try to reach men and women being carried farther to sea.

A correspondent flew to Hilo from Honolulu, and from the air looked upon a scene of devastation. Huge warehouses were flattened by the water. Buildings had been crushed like eggshells and swept from foundations.

The great million-dollar breakwater at Hilo's harbor is at least 50 per cent wrecked, officials said. Huge holes were pushed through thick concrete walls.

Railroad cars, automobiles, trucks, warehouses, molasses tanks, oil barges and boats were strewn about like toothpicks. One oil barge had been tossed through a warehouse.

City at a Standstill

All business life came to a standstill while soldiers and civilian crews dug for survivors. The homeless received food and shelter from those more fortunate.

A truck equipped with a loudspeaker cruised about town, asking residents to telephone names of missing relatives and friends to the Hilo police chief.

Martial law was not declared, but the Army is cooperating in maintaining order and protecting property.

Food was the urgent need. Much of the island's food supply had been in warehouses that were demolished.

Depth of Ocean Bed Set Tidal Waves' Speed; Father Lynch Puts Origin 10,000 Feet Down

The tidal waves that swept the Pacific yesterday may have been caused by a vertical drop in the ocean bed off Alaska or by a submarine landslide, Father Joseph Lynch, seismologist at Fordham University, said last night. Either of these phenomena may have been responsible, but it is not possible to determine which, he explained.

Judging by the speed at which the waves traveled, the original disturbance occurred in the ocean floor at a depth of about 10,000 feet, Father Lynch stated.

"In such waves we expect an average speed of about 100 miles an hour," he said, "but speed is dependent on the depth of the water in which the wave starts. From the speed with which these waves traveled—300 to 400 miles an hour—we surmise that the point of origin was about 10,000 feet deep."

The shock was recorded at 7:38 A. M. yesterday at the Fordham laboratory. The center of the quake was not far from Dutch Harbor, Alaska, Father Lynch said.

"The wave gathers as it goes along," Father Lynch said. "It takes some time to build up a rhythm and reach its peak—usually going more than 100 miles before it reaches a height of ten feet or more."

HARVARD, Mass., April 1 (U.P.)—The earth shock that set up the Pacific tidal waves was equal in magnitude to the catastrophic Tokyo quake of 1923 that killed 143,000 persons, Dr. L. Don Leet, director of the Harvard University Seismology Station here, said tonight.

"The only difference between them was that one occurred on land, where population was extremely heavy, and the other at sea," Dr. Leet said, adding in explanation of what happened:

"The earthquake causes the solid bottom of the ocean to break up and to slump to the deep bottom. Naturally, the water slumps too, causing a depression or dimple on the surface. Water from all sides rushes in to fill the depression, thus setting up a huge wave that goes out in all directions. The full effect of this moving mass of water is felt at the shoreline."

"All the News That's Fit to Print"

NEWS INDEX, PAGE 79, THIS SECTION

The New York Times.

LATE CITY EDITION
Fair and mild today and tomorrow.
Temperatures Yesterday—Max., 54; Min., 37
Sunrise today, 7:07 A. M.; Sunset, 4:29 P. M.
U. S. Weather Bureau Report, Page 7, Sect. 5

Section 1

Copyright, 1946, by The New York Times Company.

VOL. XCVI..No. 32,460. Entered as Second-Class Matter, Postoffice, New York, N. Y. NEW YORK, SUNDAY, DECEMBER 8, 1946. Including Magazine and Book Review. TEN CENTS New York City and Suburban Areas (15c Elsewhere)

LEWIS ENDS STRIKE, MINES OPEN TOMORROW; SURRENDERS AFTER LAWYERS SEE VINSON; RAIL EMBARGO, MAIL CURBS, DIMOUT HALT

127 KILLED BY FIRE IN ATLANTA HOTEL; MANY DIE IN LEAPS

Worst Such Disaster in U. S. Traps 280 in Their Rooms and Scores Are Injured

15-STORY BUILDING RUINED

Thousands of Spectators See Flames Engulf Victims—Bedsheets Aid Many Escapes

Special to The New York Times.

ATLANTA, Ga., Dec. 7—In one of the most tragic fire disasters in the country's history, the fifteen-story Winecoff Hotel on Peachtree Street in the heart of downtown Atlanta was destroyed early this morning with a toll estimated at 127 dead. Many scores were injured.

The deaths were fifty-six more than the previous record number of seventy-one hotel fire deaths in the burning of Newhall House in Milwaukee in 1883. Of the dead 114 had been identified.

At least twenty-five or thirty persons lost their lives by leaping from windows of the flaming building, Police Chief M. A. Hornsby said. Many other guests were carried to safety down firemen's ladders or jumped into fire nets.

Some of those who perished were burned beyond recognition, and it appeared that several days might be required before their identities were established.

About 280 guests were registered in the hotel's 194 rooms, it was said.

City Investigation Started

City authorities immediately began an investigation to determine the origin of the fire, which was believed to have started on the fourth or fifth floor of the structure and spread rapidly.

They expressed amazement when they learned that the hotel, regarded as one of the city's major establishments, had no fire escapes or other emergency means of safety.

The fire was first discovered by a Negro girl elevator operator at 3:15 A. M. Comer L. Rowan, the hotel's night manager, said he instructed the girl and a bellboy to awaken as many guests as they could and that he began phoning the rooms. The flames, however, apparently had made great headway before the alarm was given.

Persons on the upper floors could be seen at their windows pleading vainly for help. Several guests crawled out on ledges waiting for firemen to rescue them.

Some were observed lowering themselves from one floor to another on tied-up bed clothing. Several were seen to die when their grips gave way or the knotted sheets broke under their weight or were burned by flames.

Two Girls Jump Ten Floors

Two girls jumped from the tenth floor into a fireman's safety net and were saved.

One man was observed trying to reach a firemen's ladder. He swung down from a rope and hung between the building and the ladder. Two other persons jumped or fell from above and hit him and all three fell to their deaths.

Thousands of spectators jammed the area and occasional shrieks from the crowd in the streets could be heard amid scenes of heroism, tragedy and horror.

A woman yet unidentified was seen to jump from one of the upper floors and her body struck a steel cable and hung there over the street.

Another woman was said to have thrown two small children to their deaths in the street and then to have jumped to her own death. One man died when he missed a life net by inches, ripping the coat of one of the net holders in a last effort to save himself.

Three persons were seen in win-

Continued on Page 28, Column 1

New York Skyscraper Home Now Possible as U. N. Center

Mayor O'Dwyer Says City Offers New Bid for the World Capital—Rockefeller Site Considered a Likely Prototype

By GEORGE BARRETT
Special to The New York Times.

LAKE SUCCESS, N. Y., Dec. 7—The world capital of the United Nations may be established as a huge "international skyscraper" center in New York City, it was disclosed here today.

The construction in Manhattan of a separate international zone containing tall buildings and its own Assembly chambers was presented as a strong possibility tonight shortly after Mayor O'Dwyer had confirmed to reporters at City Hall that New York, in effect, was making another dramatic bid for the world capital.

The Mayor, questioned about reports that New York was going to increase its former offer of 350 acres of free land at Flushing Meadow to match the more pretentious offers made by Philadelphia, Boston and San Francisco, disclosed that he had only this morning attended "informal discussions with various members of the United Nations Site Committee and members of the United Nations." He added that he had "presented several possible sites inside the city, in addition to Flushing Meadow."

It had been reported here with increasing frequency during the last twenty-four hours that the United Nations was contemplating a permanent home within the limits of New York City if it would be possible to get enough land for the project. Mayor O'Dwyer elabo-

Continued on Page 11, Column 2

Byrnes Urges Troop Cuts As Big 4 Discuss Germany

By C. BROOKS PETERS

A drastic reduction of United States, British, Soviet and French forces of occupation in Germany, Austria, Poland and the Balkans was recommended to the Council of Foreign Ministers by Secretary of State Byrnes when the Council met yesterday morning to begin discussion of the peace treaty with Germany.

In an unanticipated move, Mr. Byrnes recommended two slashes in the number of occupying troops, both of which would affect most severely the Soviet armies deployed over Eastern Europe.

The United States proposal was contained in one of three memoranda submitted to the Council by Mr. Byrnes concerning the work the Council should do before completing its present session. Soviet Foreign Secretary Molotov also submitted a memorandum.

[The texts of the Byrnes and Molotov proposals appear on Page 20.]

Two Reductions Urged

The first cut would reduce to 620,000 men, including only 240,000 Russians, the forces of occupation in Germany, Poland, Austria, Hungary and Rumania on April 1, 1947.

The second reduction would reduce occupation forces proportionately in these countries another 25 to 33 1-3 per cent by April 1, 1948, "subject to such earlier withdrawal from Austria, Hungary and Rumania as may be required by the Austrian treaty."

The Ministers did not get round to discussing this issue yesterday. The basic question that confronted them in their two-hour meeting in the Waldorf-Astoria Hotel was what preparatory decisions they should make now to assure that the Council at its next session

Continued on Page 20, Column 1

U. S. WILL EXPEDITE GRAIN TO GERMANY

17 Ships to Sail From Albany This Month—Clay Says Food Is Vital to Occupation

Special to The New York Times.

WASHINGTON, Dec. 7—Asserting his determination to get enough food to Germany to prevent a collapse of our occupation program, Robert P. Patterson, the Secretary of War, estimated today that 300,000 tons of grains would be needed monthly.

To cope with the crisis afflicting the United States and British zones, Mr. Patterson added that a fleet of seventeen food-bearing ships would leave from Albany, N. Y., during December.

He said that food stocks in the United States zone were at "warehouse-bottom," and the British zone could survive only if United States food shipments reached it.

His summary of the situation was prompted by a warning from Lieut. Gen. Lucius D. Clay, Deputy Military Governor of the United States zone, that democracy would not win in Germany if the people were unable to obtain sufficient food.

"Food is the key to our entire

Continued on Page 23, Column 4

Atlanta Crowds View Hotel Ruin, Talk at Scene Is for More Safety

By BENJAMIN FINE
Special to The New York Times.

ATLANTA, Ga., Dec. 7—Pitiful sobbing women and tight-lipped men, with faces drawn and eyes reddened, swamped the hospitals and morgues of this proud city, seeking to identify relatives or friends who were trapped in the Winecoff Hotel fire early this morning.

Shocked and horrified, Atlanta residents by the thousand jammed the midtown section to view the gutted hotel structure. Until early afternoon the sheets and curtains that had been used by guests in their desperate efforts to get to safety still hung from the windows and fluttered in the breeze.

Unequalled heroism, together with miraculous escapes from death, marked the course of the country's most disastrous hotel fire. Praise was heard on all sides for a Negro girl elevator operator, identified only as Rosita, who was credited with being the first person to report the blaze. Comer L. Rowan, the hotel's night manager, said that the girl had reported the fire to him.

"I sent her to find the bellboy, who was making a routine floor check," he said, "and asked her to aid him in arousing the guests."

Wherever people were assembled today they talked about the fire.

"Something must be done to make hotels safer," a number said. Ironically enough, the Winecoff

Continued on Page 27, Column 1

RULES END QUICKLY

Federal Officials Rush to Restore the Normal Flow of Commerce

FREIGHT BANS OFF

Limits on Packages Are Removed, Restrictions on Coal Use Cease

By WALTER H. WAGGONER
Special to The New York Times.

WASHINGTON, Dec. 7—The Government moved swiftly this afternoon and evening to lift restrictive coal-conservation measures and to restore transportation, commerce and industry as quickly as possible to pre-strike normalcy.

John L. Lewis' sudden back-to-work order to his miners brought about prompt cancellation, or a promise of it in the immediate future, of the following emergency rulings:

The "brownout" of ornamental and non-essential lighting.

The Postoffice limitations on weight and size of parcel-post and mail shipments.

The general embargo on all rail freight and express transport imposed by the Interstate Commerce Commission.

The railroads' own ban on all freight shipments, except food and fuel, bound for export.

The 50 per cent cut in passenger service by coal-burning railroads, to have become effective Monday.

Most restrictions on use and movement of coal by commercial, industrial and utility users.

Officials Taken by Surprise

The suddenness of the Lewis announcement appeared to have caught Washington and the Federal Government completely off guard and unprepared. In view of the fact that Saturday is a normal Government holiday, many officials who otherwise would have

Continued on Page 5, Column 3

RUSH TO PITS DUE

Miners, Eager for Yule Cash, Expected Back on the Job Promptly

LAYOFFS WILL END

Eaton, Linked to Lewis Decision, Hails Him as 'Brilliant Leader'

By A. H. RASKIN
Special to The New York Times.

PITTSBURGH, Dec. 7—The first reaction of the nation's soft coal miners to John L. Lewis' back-to-work order was a mixture of puzzlement, disbelief and joy. Many, feeling the whole thing might be a hoax, said that they would wait for official instructions from the United Mine Workers before going back to their jobs.

Unworried over the prospect that there would be any resistance to ending the seventeen-day-old strike, jubilant operators and Government officials were making rush preparations tonight to reopen virtually all mines on Monday. Operators predicted that the full pre-strike production of 2,000,000 tons a day would be restored by Wednesday.

Union officials were equally confident that the 400,000 men would flock back to the mines as soon as official word was received.

"Boss Has Said It, That's All"

There was no rejoicing among the miners over the terms under which they were resuming work, but there was no disposition to question Mr. Lewis' authority to send them back as abruptly as he called them out.

"The boss has said it, and that's all," was the way William Blizzard, president of UMW District 17 in Charleston, W. Va., summed it up.

Most miners said that they were glad the strike was over, even though they could not understand

Continued on Page 4, Column 1

World News Summarized

SUNDAY, DECEMBER 8, 1946

John L. Lewis unexpectedly called off the soft coal strike yesterday afternoon. It was indicated that there would be no further interruption of production between now and April 1, 1947. [1:8.]

Miners were puzzled, incredulous and joyful, wondering what purpose had been served by their walkout, but it seemed likely that they would be back in the pits tomorrow. [1:5.]

The Government moved swiftly to cancel its various restrictions and conservation orders. [1:4.] In New York the dimout was lifted at 6 o'clock yesterday evening and the White Way blazed again as the city moved back toward normal. [1:6-7.]

In the broad struggle over labor's powers, the Ninth Circuit Court gave a decision that was held to place some statutory regulation on the interpretation of closed-shop contracts. [1:7.]

When the Council of Foreign Ministers met yesterday, Secretary Byrnes proposed a drastic reduction of United States, British, Russian and French occupation forces in Europe. Russia opposed some of the opening moves in discussing a treaty for Germany. [1:2-3.]

In the General Assembly White Russia was elected to one of the two remaining vacancies on the Social and Economic Council. [16:1.] The controversy between India and South Africa was sharply debated; the Assembly adjourned until today. [19:1.]

In the moot case of Spain, the United States announced that it would not be bound to any United Nations decision to break relationships. [13:1.] Madrid reacted in worried fashion to United Nations condemnation, the Cabinet denouncing "interference" in Spanish internal affairs. [14:1.]

In an exchange of letters with General Clay, Secretary of War Patterson asserted his determination to get enough food into Germany to prevent the collapse of the occupation program. [1:2.]

General Eisenhower, meanwhile, quoted the Secretary of War as having said that no atomic bombs and no fissionable material had been sent from the United States to any other country. [60:2.]

In United Nations circles there was further discussion of the problem of a site for the permanent headquarters. New York City suggested the possibility of erecting a "skyscraper city," within the metropolitan area itself. [1:2-3.]

There was temporary easement in the critical case of Iran when the Government refrained from issuing its expected order to troops to enter Azerbaijan to police elections. [21:1.]

The Palestinian situation was further vexed. An Arab spokesman said that Arab leaders would refuse to attend any more conferences on Palestine that considered partition. [41:2.]

The Indian stalemate continued. Pandit Nehru left London for New Delhi. The Congress party was cool to the British declaration that some accord was essential prerequisite to a Constitution. The Moslems, on the other hand, found some satisfaction in the British position. [46:2.]

City's Lights Go On Again; Thousands Recalled to Jobs

Mayor Quickly Proclaims Suspension of Brownout—Transport Agencies Act to Speed Return to Normal

By LAWRENCE RESNER

Few moments were wasted yesterday, after news of the calling off of the coal strike had been received from Washington, in starting New York City on the road back to normal business activity.

Mayor O'Dwyer issued a proclamation suspending the brown-out, thousands of furloughed railroad workers were recalled to work, and the business community generally heaved a deep sigh of relief.

Many of the theatres and amusements and business establishments on Broadway and in other parts of the city that had given almost perfect compliance to lighting restrictions were ablaze more than an hour in advance of the 6 o'clock deadline set by the Mayor in ending the brown-out.

The New York Central, the Pennsylvania Railroad, the Long Island Rail Road and the New York, New Haven & Hartford Railroad announced in swift succession that they had canceled the additional 25 per cent reduction of steam locomotive passenger service that was to have taken effect tonight. Other railroads were expected to follow the same program.

The New York Central, which was believed a typical case, said, however, that the first 25 per cent reduction in passenger service would remain unchanged until it started receiving new coal.

At the offices of the Railway Express, clerks who had been busy throughout the day notifying 6,500 of the agency's employes that they

Continued on Page 2, Column 2

Labor Law Revision Pushed To Prevent a Similar Crisis

Special to The New York Times.

TOLEDO, Ohio, Dec. 7—The end of the coal strike will not divert the Republican party's determination to prevent a recurrence of such a situation, Carroll Reece, Republican National Chairman, said today on his arrival in Toledo to address the executive committee of the Young Republican National Federation.

He reiterated his party's conviction that labor legislation was still the first and foremost problem facing the new Congress next month.

"Regardless of the Court action against John L. Lewis and the subsequent end of the coal strike, the basic problem involved in such a situation must be removed to prevent a recurrence," Mr. Reece said.

Congress Hails End of Strike

WASHINGTON, Dec. 7 (AP)—Members of Congress hailed the ending of the soft coal strike but some insisted that new labor legislation was still needed.

"Thank God, and I mean it with all due reverence," was the comment of Senator Edwin C. Johnson of Colorado.

Senator Scott W. Lucas of Illinois said: "As one United States Senator, I am happy that Mr. Lewis has seen fit to capitulate."

"I am glad the miners are going back," said Senator Bourke B. Hickenlooper of Iowa. "That meets the thing of immediate importance, the production of coal. But other vital issues must be met and settled, the threat of recurring situations hanging over the head of the American public. That issue and its solution must be one of the first problems of the new Congress.

Continued on Page 5, Column 1

CLOSED SHOP CURB IS UPHELD BY COURT

Worker Cannot Be Dropped for Preferring Another Union, It Is Held

Special to The New York Times.

WASHINGTON, Dec. 7—An important doctrine of the National Labor Relations Board, extending statutory limitations on the use of the closed shop, has been upheld in the courts for the first time.

The crux of the board's interpretation is that a union's right under its contract to expel a member and obtain his dismissal from employment cannot be invoked merely because the member exhibited a preference for another union at a collective bargaining election.

The decision enforcing the NLRB order was issued by the Ninth Circuit Court of Appeals. The principals were the Portland (Ore.) Lumber Mills, the Lumber and Sawmill Workers Union of the Brotherhood of Carpenters, AFL, the International Woodworkers Association, Congress of Industrial Organizations, and Ward Wilmarth, a member of the AFL union.

The AFL union had a closed shop contract with the company,

Continued on Page 3, Column 5

2 Held on Complaints by 32 GI's Of Swindle on Homes in Suffolk

Special to The New York Times.

LINDENHURST, L. I., Dec. 7—Acting on complaints of thirty-two ex-service men, the Suffolk County District Attorney's office caused the arrests last night and today of Benjamin Embinder, 45 years old, sales manager for "Lindenhurst Shores, Inc.," and Lawrence Calvert, a salesman, on charges of second-degree grand larceny.

According to the complaints the real estate concern sold lots to former GI's for $1,500 to $2,000 in the southern part of West Babylon. Complainants told the authorities that they got the impression that $10,000 homes would be built upon the lots within three to four months after the land had been bought. When the homes failed to materialize, the veterans scrutinized their contracts closely and found they had contracted only for the purchase of the lots.

Embinder, who gave his address as 656 West 204th Street, Manhattan, and Calvert, who lives at Lake Ronkonkoma, L. I., posted $500 bail each. They will have a hearing Wednesday in Lindenhurst Police Court before Justice William F. Wolters.

Investigation of the operations of Lindenhurst Shores, Inc., began several weeks ago when complaints began coming into various veterans' agencies. Former service men said they had bought lots in the development for prices ranging from $1,500 to $2,000, witn

Continued on Page 60, Column 4

CAPITAL SURPRISED

UMW Head Bows in Face of Court Action and Agrees to Negotiate

TRUMAN DROPS TALK

Mine Operation Ordered Till April 1—Contempt Case Still Pending

By JOSEPH A. LOFTUS
Special to The New York Times.

WASHINGTON, Dec. 7—John L. Lewis, president of the United Mine Workers of America, AFL, unexpectedly called off the country-wide soft coal strike today and directed all members to return to their jobs immediately.

He ordered the miners to continue working until April 1 at the wages and under the conditions existing before the stoppage.

With a bow to the United States Supreme Court and an acknowledgment of an economic crisis, the leader of nearly all the men who mine coal in the United States read to reporters at a suddenly called conference his letter of capitulation, directed to all UMW members and local unions in the bituminous districts.

He gave a virtual warranty of uninterrupted production at least until April 1, at the same time serving notice that the union would enforce the existing terms of employment at each mine.

Truman Cancels Address

The surprising announcement, on the fifth anniversary of the Pearl Harbor disaster and the seventeenth day of the strike, caught most of official Washington unprepared.

Within an hour President Truman canceled a radio address he was writing for tomorrow night. Revocation of the restrictions on transportation and coal consumption came later. Indeed, the Government at the time of Mr. Lewis' announcement was working on even more rigorous coal-conservation measures.

Mr. Lewis called his news conference for 2 P. M., a few hours after his lawyers and Government counsel conferred with Chief Justice Fred M. Vinson on the Government petition to the Supreme Court to take immediate jurisdiction of the contempt conviction and $3,510,000 fines levied against the union and its president.

It was learned that the United Mine Workers joined in the Government's petition to by-pass argument in the intermediate court of appeals. Lawyers left the Chief Justice with the impression that the court would accept the case immediately.

Court Argument May Be Delayed

The subsequent termination of the strike may alter that, however, perhaps to the extent of delaying argument for a few weeks. The national hardship factor has been eliminated by the strike termination, it was pointed out, even though the legal importance of the case remains.

Mr. Lewis' letter referred to the Administration's injunction as a "yellow dog" writ, which he said had "reached the Supreme Court." He called the Court "the protector of American liberties" and said the issues before it were "fateful for our republic."

"These weighty considerations," the letter continued, "and the fitting respect due the dignity of this high tribunal imperatively required that, during its period of deliberation, the Court be free from public pressure superinduced by the hysteria and frenzy of an economic crisis. In addition, public necessity requires the quantitative production of coal during such period."

Mr. Lewis said that in the meantime he would be willing to negotiate a new wage agreement

Continued on Page 3, Column 1

HYDE PARK WATCHES, "PRIDE OF TIME ACCURACY," for ladies and gentlemen. $37.50 to $1,000. At better jewelry stores. Emil Leichter Watch Co., Inc., 551 5th Ave., N. Y.—Advt.

HANOVIA ULTRAVIOLET ALPINE LAMPS. Most efficient source of ultraviolet. Help keep you physically fit.—Advt.

CASH FOR DIAMONDS AND JEWELRY Gimbels 5th Floor, Bway & 32 St.—Advt.

WOR—Hear Sister Kenny defend her work. 10:45 A. M. Dial 710—WOR.—Advt.

WHEN You Think of Writing Think of Whiting—Advt.

"TARAS FAMILY," unforgettable Russian Drama by Donskoy, director of "Rainbow." STANLEY 42 Street 7th Ave., Now.—Advt.

THE NEW YORK TIMES, SUNDAY, DECEMBER 8, 1946.

The Winecoff Hotel in Atlanta as It Burned Early Yesterday Morning

127 KILLED BY FIRE IN ATLANTA HOTEL

Continued From Page 1

dows on the thirteenth floor, shouting frantically for the attention of rescuers. One of them appeared to be praying. Suddenly the scene was obstructed by billowing flames which enveloped the trapped victims in certain death.

Doctors and Nurses Offer Aid

Hospitals in Atlanta and adjacent areas, including those at Fort McPherson and the Atlanta Naval Air Station, were called upon to supply ambulances, and several hundred nurses and doctors offered their services. The city's Grady Hospital was established as an official clearing center for bodies and for the injured. The American Red Cross set up emergency headquarters near the hotel, administering first aid.

The Atlanta Fire Marshal, Harry Phillips, said that the Winecoff had been inspected recently and had measured up to Fire Department safety requirements. Fire Chief C. C. Styron, called from his home, directed the firefighters attired in his pajamas under his fireman's coat.

Officials at Grady Hospital stated that many of those brought there were badly injured as the result of having jumped from windows.

Several guests made their way to safety down ladders put up by firemen from adjacent buildings. Among them were Maj. Gen. P. W. Baade of Washington, who commanded the Thirty-fifth Division during the war, and his wife.

Firemen fought the blaze for almost six hours before it was extinguished, aided by firefighters from three suburban towns, East Point, Hopeville and College Park.

At 9 A. M. the search began inside the hotel for the bodies of victims. Rescuers worked from room to room.

Newspaper reporters, accompanying stretcher-bearers into the building, witnessed the grim marks of the flames. Many bedrooms were a mass of charred furnishings.

Throughout most of the day ambulances were moving from the scene to the emergency morgue at Grady Hospital. One fireman in a rescue squad stated that many bodies were in the upper floors and that in one room on the top floor he found a woman's body and the bodies of five children.

Among the dead was W. F. Winecoff, 70 years of age, who built the hotel in 1913. Mr. Winecoff had lived there since his retirement in 1934. In that year Mr. Winecoff leased the hotel to Robert T. Myer of Birmingham, and in 1944 the property was purchased by W. H. Irwin of Atlanta, who then leased it to Arthur Geele Sr. and Robert O'Connell of Chicago.

Bedsheets Hang From Windows

ATLANTA, Dec. 7 (AP)—At daylight today the sides of the tall, chimney-like Winecoff Hotel were draped with torn bedsheets and blankets, marking where victims of the fire tried to escape. Eyewitnesses told how panic-stricken guests swung from tenth and twelfth-story windows on flimsy, make-shift ropes. A few were rescued, but most fell headlong as flames burned away their supports, or they lost their grip.

Others were seen briefly at flaming windows, shrieking and praying, then disappearing into the inferno.

At one time, a half-dozen bodies lay at the intersection of Atlanta's Peachtree Street and Carnegie Way, opposite the theatre where the world premier of "Gone With the Wind" was staged.

Some who kept their heads were saved. White-haired Mrs. Banks W eman, manager of the hotel cigar counter, pulled the wife and

children of her employer, Arthur Geele Jr., from the fourteenth floor to the top-floor apartment of Mrs. Arthur Geele Sr. There they huddled in a corner until the fire subsided.

The origin of the blaze apparently was buried in the charred wreckage or sealed with the dead. Fire Marshal Phillips could say only that the flames started in the corridors.

Marshal Phillips, accompanied by fire inspectors, said that in every instance the flames had burned into the rooms of the third, fourth and fifth floors, indicating

that the origin lay somewhere in the carpetted hallways.

The fire was out of control within a few minutes after it was discovered. The marshal said a bellhop testified that he had noticed no fumes or smoke when he delivered some soft drinks to a room on the fifth floor. But, when he turned to leave the room he found he was trapped by flames in the doorway.

The mystery of the fire's origin also gave rise to speculation as to how it could spread so rapidly through a fire-resistant building.

ARNALL TO ORDER INQUIRY

Assails 'Fraudulent' Advertising When Hotel Is Not Fireproof

PONTE VEDRA, Fla., Dec. 7 (U.P.)—Gov. Ellis Arnall said tonight that he would instruct the State Fire Marshal to make a full investigation of the Winecoff Hotel tragedy. He added that he would have the report submitted to the General Assembly for possible legislative action.

He declared, however, that he thought the enforcement of fire regulations in Atlanta was primarily a matter for the city to decide and that city officials ought to check the city's building code.

"This is a great tragedy," he said. "The public is being defrauded when a hotel is advertised as 'fireproof' but really isn't. Responsible agencies should prohibit the use of the word 'fireproof' when a hotel is not really fireproof as the Winecoff obviously was not."

Governor Arnall has been vacationing in Florida and expected to be back in Atlanta Tuesday.

A fireman searching one of the fire-charred rooms for victims

A woman leaps to her death

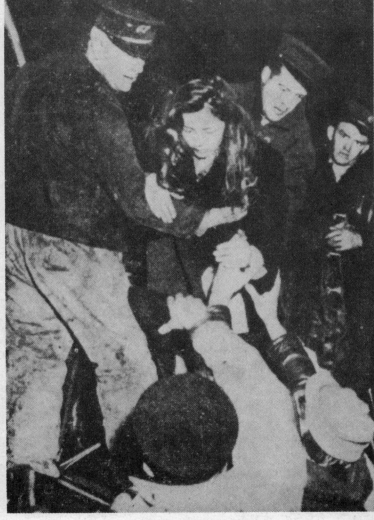
A guest is brought to safety

Associated Press Wirephotos

141

"All the News That's Fit to Print"

The New York Times.

LATE CITY EDITION
Clearing and cooler today. Fair and warmer tomorrow.
Temperatures Yesterday—Max., 55; Min., 44
Sunrise today, 5:16 A. M.; Sunset, 6:36 P. M.
Full U. S. Weather Bureau Report, Page 53

Copyright, 1947, by The New York Times Company.

VOL. XCVI..No. 32,590. Entered as Second-Class Matter. Postoffice, New York, N. Y. NEW YORK, THURSDAY, APRIL 17, 1947. THREE CENTS IN NEW YORK CITY

BLASTS AND FIRES WRECK TEXAS CITY OF 15,000; 300 TO 1,200 DEAD; THOUSANDS HURT, HOMELESS; WIDE COAST AREA ROCKED, DAMAGE IN MILLIONS

VISIT BY MARSHALL TO STALIN IS TERMED NO KEY TO IMPASSE

Basic Differences on German Settlement Are Expected to Continue in Big Four

COUNCIL TAKES UP AUSTRIA

Vienna Is Said to Plan Appeal to U. N. if Ministers Fail to Agree on Treaty

By DREW MIDDLETON
Special to THE NEW YORK TIMES.

MOSCOW, April 16—No break in the deadlock in the Council of Foreign Ministers on a German settlement is indicated, despite the conference last night between Secretary of State Marshall and Premier Stalin.

This is the opinion of reliable United States sources here. They do not, however, exclude the possibility of a conciliatory move by the Russians on minor points for propaganda purposes before the conference ends. But these sources do not expect that the Russians will take any other alternative to their present position on the major German question—reparations from current production.

Today the Council began consideration of the Austrian treaty. It agreed to listen tomorrow to a Yugoslav presentation of Marshal Tito's claim to part of Carinthia, and it accepted some of the Austrian treaty articles that already had been agreed upon by the Foreign Ministers' deputies.

Pessimism Regarding Pact

However, there was pessimism regarding the chances for obtaining an Austrian treaty at this session. And high Austrian sources disclosed that Vienna was planning to take the issue to the United Nations Security Council, or to ask one of the Allies to present it there.

The Austrians, it was said, take the view that if a treaty is not produced here in Moscow, and the occupation of Austria by foreign troops continues, the resulting situation will be a threat to world peace.

Regarding the general Soviet-United States deadlock in the Council, one American indicated today that it was not too late for the Russians to change their tactics, but the general advice was not to "expect too much" as a result of the conversation between Premier Stalin and Secretary Marshall.

If Soviet Foreign Minister Molotov, before the present Council session ends, makes a frank plea for reparations from current production based on the needs of the Soviet Union and the failure of the removal program in Germany to fulfill those needs, some accommodation might be worked out.

Position of U. S. Is Firm

But the United States will not give way on the question of reparations, any more than Secretary Marshall already has, so long as the Russians make reparations from current production the "absolute condition" of the economic unity of Germany.

Meanwhile, it is clear that the Russians hope that their present "grinding" tactics in the Council will in the end wear down the United States and British opposition to the Soviet policy for Germany. Following this theory, the Russians believe that some sort of adjustment can be made here or at the next meeting of the Foreign Ministers.

There is nothing to support the idea that any adjustments or concessions were made by either party during last night's meeting in the Kremlin, which lasted one and a half hours.

Secretary Marshall had taken the initiative in arranging the visit, since Premier Stalin is chief of the Soviet Government. The Secretary of State's delay in seeking the interview is explained by his reluctance to talk with the Premier until he felt that problems warranted it.

[Secretary Marshall asked for

Continued on Page 4, Column 5

SHEDD'S CORN MUFFIN MIX for quick party waffles.—Advt.

China Urges Big 4 To Act on Korea

Special to THE NEW YORK TIMES.

NANKING, April 16—Chinese Foreign Minister Wang Shih-chieh today dispatched a letter to Secretary Marshall urging the establishment of an independent government for a united Korea without further delay.

Dr. Wang said that if the occupying powers could not reach an agreement soon on Korean unity and independence, a "full consultation" should take place among the United States, Russia, Great Britain and China as parties to the Moscow Agreement of December, 1945.

The Minister's letter is in response to Secretary Marshall's note of April 8 to Foreign Minister Molotov. Dr. Wang sent copies of his letter to Mr. Molotov and to British Foreign Secretary Ernest Bevin.

Regret was expressed that no Korean Government had as yet been set up.

HOUSE GROUP VOTES MID-EAST AID BILL

Senate Action Due Tuesday—Vandenberg Warns Opponents We Must Defy Russia

By C. P. TRUSSELL
Special to THE NEW YORK TIMES.

WASHINGTON, April 16 — The $400,000,000 Greek-Turkish aid bill was approved formally by the House Foreign Affairs Committee today.

Twelve members voted "aye." Three members — Representatives Helen Gahagan Douglas of California and Mike Mansfield of Montana, Democrats, and Jacob K. Javits, Republican, of New York—voted "present." This maneuver, they explained, was not in complete disapproval of the program, but to reserve the right to criticize and seek to revise it.

The action came, after several weeks of committee hearings and deliberations, as the Senate in night session agreed to vote without further debate on its own Greek-Turkish aid measure at 4 P. M. next Tuesday.

Vote Accepted as Binding

Before coming to this decision, the Senators had plunged into their first sustained crossfire debate on the bill. Not all members, particularly those of the opposition, joined the bipartisan leadership push to let a prompt Senate vote be its "answer" to attacks on the Truman Doctrine by former Vice President Henry A. Wallace in Europe.

Not all members, particularly those of the opposition, joined the bipartisan leadership push to let a prompt Senate vote be its "answer" to attacks on the Truman Doctrine by former Vice President Henry A. Wallace in Europe.

Although ten members of the House Foreign Affairs group were absent when the test was made, the vote was accepted as final and binding. The reorganization act requires a vote of a committee majority. Thirteen of the twenty-five

Continued on Page 12, Column 3

BARUCH ASKS WORK FOR 44-HOUR WEEK TO STOP INFLATION

Proposes No Strikes, Layoffs Before 1949 to Maintain Production, Jobs and Buying

AIDING WORLD'S ECONOMY

At South Carolina Unveiling of His Portrait He Calls on America to Lead the Way

Text of Baruch's appeal for increased production, Page 21.

By The Associated Press.

COLUMBIA, S. C., April 16—Bernard M. Baruch said here today that the world "can get going only if men work" and that "if we accept the challenge to preserve civilization, it means greater effort than that exerted during the war."

Asserting that "we cannot achieve our purpose with the present hours and limitations on work," he urged a five-and-one-half-day week of forty-four hours, "with no strikes or layoff, to Jan. 1, 1949" to increase production.

"The result would be electrifying," he said.

Mr. Baruch spoke at the unveiling of his portrait in the hall of the State House of Representatives. The portrait, painted in 1928 by Oswald Birley, an English artist, was unveiled by Mr. Baruch's daughter, Belle. It was a gift from Mr. Baruch, made after $4,000 was authorized to be spent for a new painting.

New Outlook for Security

The native South Carolinian said that if his work proposal were adopted "production would flow smoothly, a sense of security would return to worker and employer; and the reaction upon the economy of the world would be deep and lasting."

"Until we have unity, until we straighten out and solve our own problems of production, and have internal stability, there is no basis on which the world can renew itself physically or spiritually," he added.

"Upon this change in our material outlook, there would follow a change in our sense of security. Make no mistake: our military lines are no stronger than the industry behind them.

"Unless we work, we shall see a vast inflation. Unless we work, we shall not be able to maintain our claim to power. That would be the greatest blow we could receive, for it would strip us of our strength to preserve our way of life."

He declared that such a program would meet the needs of other nations, asserting:

"There is no place left to which to turn for regeneration except to America. We must answer that call or we shall fail civilization in its most tragic moment, and thus ourselves.

"We cannot do it by loans, grants, subsidies, bonuses or pious

Continued on Page 21, Column 4

TEXAS CITY BURNING AFTER IT WAS ROCKED BY EXPLOSION

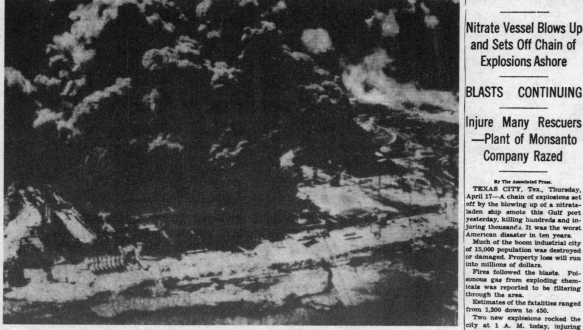

Air view of the industrial plants following the blast. In left center foreground is the sprawling Monsanto Chemical Company
Associated Press Wirephoto

SHIP STARTS HAVOC

Nitrate Vessel Blows Up and Sets Off Chain of Explosions Ashore

BLASTS CONTINUING

Injure Many Rescuers—Plant of Monsanto Company Razed

By The Associated Press.

TEXAS CITY, Tex., Thursday, April 17—A chain of explosions set off by the blowing up of a nitrate-laden ship smote this Gulf port yesterday, killing hundreds and injuring thousands. It was the worst American disaster in ten years.

Much of the boom industrial city of 15,000 population was destroyed or damaged. Property loss will run into millions of dollars.

Fires followed the blasts. Poisonous gas from exploding chemicals was reported to be filtering through the area.

Estimates of the fatalities ranged from 1,200 down to 450.

Two new explosions rocked the city at 1 A. M. today, injuring many persons who survived yesterday's disastrous blasts. There were no immediate reports of additional deaths.

John Coldron, reporter for The Beaumont Enterprise, said that another ship had blown up in the harbor. Earlier, the nitrate-loaded freighter, the High Flyer, was reported burning.

Warning of New Blast

W. H. Sandberg, manager of the Texas City Terminal Railways, had said there was an "even chance" that the High Flyer would explode.

Fire fighters from four cities poured streams of water on the vessel. A tug had attempted to pull it away from the dock and into the bay.

At near-by Lamarque, the State Highway Patrol said that one of the explosions was that of an oil tank on the Republic Oil Company's tank farm.

Mayor J. C. Trahan said he knew of 300 dead. G. B. Finley, State Highway Commission official, said at Austin that aides at the scene had indicated the toll would reach 1,200. Wiley Whatley, Houston police sergeant at the scene, estimated that the death total would be between 450 and 500.

Midwestern headquarters of the Red Cross at St. Louis reported that 500 bodies had been brought out of the explosion area late yesterday and that more bodies were being found constantly.

Gen. Jonathan M. Wainwright, hero of Bataan, visited the city and said:

"I have never seen a greater tragedy in all my experiences. I have come here to offer this stricken community every facility that the Army can place at its disposal."

He is now Commanding General of the Fourth Army.

Crew of Forty Killed

Mayor Trahan, who wears the Purple Heart for buzz bomb wounds received in Belgium, said that "no buzz bomb could ever compare with what happened here."

"It is such a terrific tragedy that the people have not been able to realize what happened," he added.

The chain of explosions was set off by the blowing up of the French freighter, Grandcamp, at 9:12 A. M. yesterday. The ship was obliterated and its crew of forty perished.

The Grandcamp explosion followed a fire that started at about 8:30 A. M. while it was being loaded with nitrate and, The Houston Post said, "possibly with small ammunition."

The Texas City Fire Department seemingly had the fire under control when the explosion came.

The huge war-built plant of the Monsanto Chemical Company was virtually destroyed by fire. It was

Continued on Page 18, Column 1

GREAT BEAR Ideal Spring Water is famous for its purity. Deliveries. GR. 5-3810—Advt.

PAY-AS-YOU-GO SET BY DEWEY AS POLICY

Reviewing Legislative Record, He Says Present Generation Should Not Mortgage Next

Dewey's radio review of the legislative session, Page 20.

By LEO EGAN
Special to THE NEW YORK TIMES.

ALBANY, April 16—Governor Dewey, in a review of this year's legislative record, emphasized tonight that his administration was committed to the pay-as-you-go policy with respect to public expenditures and believed that local

Continued on Page 20, Column 2

Doctors, Clergy Brave Fires And Fumes to Help Injured

By ROBERT E. BROWN
United Press Staff Correspondent.

TEXAS CITY, Tex., April 16—I flew over the Texas City disaster area today—over waves of black smoke which hid all but five huge clusters of licking flame. A rectangle roughly a mile long and a half mile wide along the waterfront was a mass of twisted steel structures and charred debris.

Clouds of smoke erased the sun. Fires were burning at the ruined plant of the Monsanto Chemical Company and in two oil refineries. Every few minutes another explosion spewed more flame and smoke into the sky.

Wading through the destruction area were doctors and nurses—grimy, sweaty and with blood on

Continued on Page 18, Column 8

PHONE UNION INSISTS ON PAY RISE OFFER

Beirne Says 'Pattern' Is Set—Arbitration Would Bring Wage 'Hodge-Podge,' He Holds

By LOUIS STARK
Special to THE NEW YORK TIMES.

WASHINGTON, April 16—The National Federation of Telephone Workers insists on a wage increase now because "millions of workers" have received such increases in recent months, according to Joseph A. Beirne, president of the federation. The "pattern" has been set in industry, he said.

In a broadcast tonight over the American Broadcasting Company network the union president defended his organization's rejection of the arbitration proposal made by Lewis B. Schwellenbach, Secretary of Labor.

The setback suffered by the Secretary of Labor when both the union and the American Telephone and Telegraph Company and asso-

Continued on Page 19, Column 2

RED CROSS SPEEDS AID TO TEXAS CITY

Allocates $250,000 and Flies Disaster Experts, Medical Supplies to Stricken Port

Special to THE NEW YORK TIMES.

WASHINGTON, April 16 — The American Red Cross made an initial appropriation of $250,000 today to aid victims of the Texas City explosion.

Basil O'Connor, chairman, indicated that the sum might be enlarged after a survey of the area.

Meanwhile, twenty trained disaster workers of the Red Cross are being rushed to the scene of the blast to assist and relieve volunteer workers from local chapters.

The organization has been forced to withdraw some of its trained disaster workers from duty at the scene of the recent Oklahoma-Texas Panhandle tornado, which also had a $250,000 allocation.

Three disaster specialists were flown from headquarters here to Texas City in a Navy plane. Another special plane left St. Louis with five Red Cross experts. Doctors and nurses are also on the way from a 100-mile radius of the scene.

Medical supplies, blood plasma and wholeblood, tetanus and gas gangrene antitoxin are being flown from the St. Louis office of the Red Cross

Galveston Red Cross is prepared to take in all refugees from Texas

Continued on Page 18, Column 7

World News Summarized

THURSDAY, APRIL 17, 1947

A nitrate-laden ship exploded in the Gulf port of Texas City, Tex., yesterday, killing 300 to 1,200 persons and injuring more than 1,000 others. The city of 15,000 was almost completely destroyed by a series of blasts that followed the ship explosion and fires. Poisonous gases hampered rescue work. Early this morning two new explosions rocked the city, injuring many rescue workers. First reports, however, gave no indication of any additional deaths. [1:8.]

The country's economic situation was widely discussed. Bernard M. Baruch said that to avoid inflation there must be a forty-four-hour week and no strikes through 1948. [1:3.] Congress was told that tax cuts and volume production had done more than price increases to raise profits last year [22:4], and a joint Congressional committee decided to seek civilian advice on price and related problems. [23:4.] General Motors Chairman Sloan said that business could not slash profits and simultaneously cut prices and increase wages. [22:2.]

General Motors offered its factory workers the same 15-cent hourly increase accepted by its electrical workers; the union demanded 23½ cents. [24:5.]

Striking telephone workers must receive a pay increase before they return to work, their leader said in Washington. [1:6.]

The House Foreign Affairs Committee, without a negative vote, favorably reported the Greek-Turkish aid bill with the Vandenberg amendment. [1:2.]

Former Premier Herriot denied that he had been asked to sign the "non-partisan" invitation to Henry A. Wallace to visit France although he was listed among the signers. Mr. Wallace delivered his final speech in Britain before an all-party meeting in the Commons. [9:1.]

General Marshall's talk with Generalissimo Stalin is not expected to close the gap between the American and Russian views on Germany. Austria was reported considering an appeal to the United Nations should the Foreign Ministers Council fail to agree on a treaty. [1:1.]

Armond D. Willis, former attaché to the United States Embassy in Moscow, is on his way home after having accused some members of the staff of being "anti-Soviet." Washington said he was being dismissed. [6:3.]

British forces in Palestine have been alerted for trouble following the execution of Dov Gruner and three other Zionist underground terrorists. An attempt was made to bomb a building of the Colonial Office in London. [1:2-3.]

Agreement was reached in China for a coalition government, with Gen. Chang Chun the Premier. [3:5.]

Russia has nominated Senator Georg Branting, Swedish Social Democrat, for Governor of the Free Territory of Trieste. [15:1.]

The Board of Estimate endorsed a contract leasing all city airports for fifty years to the Port of New York Authority, which will finance all improvements. [29:8.]

British Alert for Palestine Reprisal; Time Bomb Found in London Office

By CLIFTON DANIEL
Special to THE NEW YORK TIMES.

JERUSALEM, April 16—All of Great Britain's forces in this tumultuous country were alerted tonight against reprisals by the Jewish underground for the hanging of four convicted terrorists at Acre today. By a new decree, military justice was made supreme in the land.

Half the country's 700,000 Jews were confined indoors all day today as a precaution against popular demonstrations and terrorist retaliation.

The first furtive acts of defiance to the house curfew imposed on Jewish urban centers occurred in Tel Aviv, where dummy road mines were strewn and road blocks erected tonight. Near one of the

Continued on Page 13, Column 1

By CHARLES E. EGAN
Special to THE NEW YORK TIMES.

LONDON, April 16—A crudely made time bomb believed to be the work of Jewish terrorists was found in the Dover House offices of the Colonial Office shortly after 6 A. M. today. Dover House in Whitehall is within 200 yards of 10 Downing Street, official residence of Prime Minister Attlee.

Later in the day, an anonymous telephone call warned police that the War Office in Whitehall would be blown up at 4 P. M. Police cleared the building and searched it thoroughly without result.

Although they dismissed the telephone call as a hoax, Scotland Yard officials were working on the

Continued on Page 14, Column 3

When You Think of Writing Think of Whiting.—Advt.

U. S. Calls on Lewis and Operators To Meet for Talks on Bargaining

By JOSEPH A. LOFTUS
Special to THE NEW YORK TIMES.

WASHINGTON, April 16 — The Government moved today to bring together operators and miners in the soft coal industry in a resumption of collective bargaining.

Capt. N. H. Collisson, Federal Coal Mines Administrator, invited officials of the United Mine Workers and spokesmen for the forty-six coal operators' associations to meet here April 29. The suggested date is about two months before the end of Government possession of the mines.

"The purpose of the meeting," Capt. Collisson stated, "is to discuss the means by which a resumption of collective bargaining between the UMW and the coal operators may most effectively and expeditiously be accomplished."

The operators and the miners have not met face to face since early last fall, when attempts at negotiations failed to make progress.

The meeting was called as the National Labor Relations Board ruled that, despite Government operation, the mine employes still work for the private owners of the mines for purposes of the Wagner Act. The board said that the Supreme Court's decision in the contempt case against John L. Lewis and the UMW, of which he is president, did not alter that relationship.

The NLRB dismissed the peti-

Continued on Page 24, Column 3

MISS real cigar pleasure? Try PRINCE HAMLET all Havana Filler. 2-25c—Advt.

The Destruction That Followed in the Path of an Explosion in Texas City Yesterday

Smoke from burning oil refinerie- forms background for a wrecked home

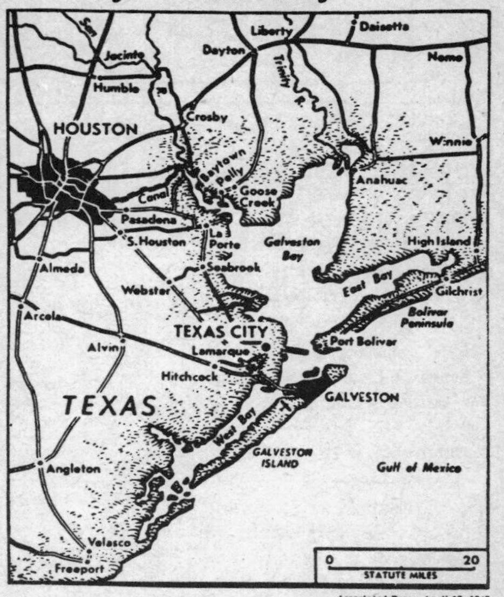

Associated Press, April 17, 1947

Where blasts touched off by an explosion in a nitrate-laden French ship brought destruction.

The area on fire after the French vessel exploded. At left is the Monsanto plant

Associated Press Wirephotos

1,200 FEARED DEAD IN TEXAS BLASTS

Continued From Page 1

at first reported that the fire was started by an explosion set off by the ship blast. An official of the company said in a wire from St. Louis last night, however, that "there was no explosion within the plant itself."

He was Dan J. Forrestal Jr., assistant director of industrial and public relations for the company, who flew to the scene yesterday afternoon for an investigation. A large proportion of the 500 persons employed by the plant were killed or injured, he said, and more than 100 were unaccounted for.

The blasts rocked the surrounding region for 150 miles.

Mr. Finley said: "Rescue parties bringing out casualties from the blast area estimated that about one out of every three persons had been killed, which would indicate around 1,200 dead."

He referred to the dock area, where the principal damage occurred and where there were about 3,500 persons when the explosions began.

A reporter flying over the scene likened it to bomb destruction of European cities in the recent war. The mushrooming cloud of smoke that arose was described as resembling the aftermath of the atom bombing of Hiroshima.

The first eye-witnesses to move into the area after the explosion saw workers stream from buildings with blood gushing from noses and ears, the result of concussion.

"Bodies were tossed about like playing cards," said a reporter for The Houston Chronicle.

Earlier, E. A. Boehler, a Houston policeman, had reported:

"Bodies can be picked up by the dozens in the fire area, but you cannot get in to them."

Relief and rescue workers swarmed into the city from all directions. National Red Cross headquarters in Washington set aside $250,000 for relief work and sent thirty disaster experts to the scene.

It was from records of the Metropolitan Life Insurance Company in Washington that the disaster was listed as the country's worst, in lives lost, in ten years. The next worst, the Atlantic coast hurricane of September, 1938, took 682 lives.

Tornado Area Sends Aid

It was the second major disaster in Texas within a week. A tornado swept the Panhandle and northwestern Oklahoma Wednesday, killing 132 persons in the two states. Relief workers still stationed in the tornado area rushed to the scene of the new calamity, hundreds of miles to the south.

The huge plant of the Monsanto Chemical Company was built in wartime at a cost of $19,000,000 to make styrene, an ingredient of synthetic rubber.

Fires still were raging in the Monsanto plant and fire fighters could hear the screams of some workers trapped inside. Rescue was impossible becaue of the heat and flames.

Fire fighters wore gas masks, fearing further explosions. Company officials said there were stocks of explosive chemicals in the buildings.

A reporter for the Houston Chronicle who flew over Texas City for an hour after the initial blast said there was a fire on the waterfront, another along the Santa Fe Railroad and a third in a gasoline refinery area. He said there were no fires in the city's business or residential areas.

The reporter gave this picture:

"Fire trucks were racing up from the south, presumably Galveston.

"The ship which is said to have started the fire could not be seen through the smoke.

"Flying toward the blaze, the smoke could be seen from Ellington Field, approximately thirty miles away. It reached 4,000 feet.

"One oil tank, about a thousand feet away from the blaze, was crumpled like a piece of tinfoil.

"Buildings along the Santa Fe Railroad tracks had had the ends blown out. The sides were intact. Pieces of metal could be seen from the air lying at the foot of the building.

"An industrial section close to the bay was afire with the biggest blaze. Smoke was pouring from tanks and buildings.

"A refinery west of the tracks also was burning. Several oil tanks were blazing brightly. A few tanks were crumpled by the force of the blast.

"A heavy cloud of smoke hung over the scene, shot with flashes of flame from the fires that still raged along the waterfront."

Officials of the Carbide and Carbon Chemicals Corporation in Texas City said that there were no injuries to employes at the plant, which was undamaged by the explosion.

At New York the Coast Guard said it had reports from its Texas units that as many as 1,000 persons might be dead and from 2,000 to 3,500 injured.

The National Guard was called out to help control the emergency.

The blases were so severe that windows were shattered at Galveston, eleven miles across the bay, and plaster was knocked from ceilings there. Many persons there fled from Galveston fearing an earthquake.

After the start of the chain of explosions flames raged unchecked because of damage to the water system.

Efforts to estimate the total of dead and injured were made difficult by the chaos and by disrupted communications. Although the telephone union ordered all strikers back on their jobs, lines were damaged and few were operating.

Residents were stunned and stumbled about the debris dazed. Many had burns or cuts from glass and steel and brick hurtled through the air.

The explosion was the worst in Texas history, exceeding even the New London school explosion in 1937 when 294 school children were killed. It was the second worst disaster in Texas history, being exceeded only by that of the Galveston hurricane in 1900, when 5,000 to 8,000 died.

Gov. Beauford H. Jester flew to the area to help direct relief. Rescue workers poured into Texas City from Galveston, Houston, Austin, San Antonio, and other cities.

Curious Among Dead

Relief was mobilized so quickly that Capt. Glenn Rose of the state highway patrol said at 2 P. M. that no additional doctors and nurses were needed.

The explosion on the Grandcamp followed a fire which had attracted several hundred curious to the docks to watch the fire fighters. Scores of these onlookers were killed.

W. H. Sanberg, vice president of the Texas City Terminal Railway Company, left the Grandcamp just five minutes before the explosion. He said that the concussion was "simply terrible."

"It blew out windows of every home in town," he declared. "It blew in ceilings in business buildings. It cracked new buildings from end to end. Doors were blown from their hinges."

He asserted that the Monsanto plant "doesn't exist any more."

Highways and causeways were blocked by frantic Texas City residents who work in Galveston as they rushed home to help.

Bill Nottingham, a Houston Post photographer who flew over the city, said that it looked as if a flight of B-29 superfortresses had bombed it. A war Air Force veteran, he said he had been on many raids "when we did less damage."

Wide Relief Mobilized

Port Arthur and Orange, 100 miles distant, said the blast was audible and that buildings rocked. At Pelly, 27 miles away, a man said the sound "hurt my eardrums."

Houston sent scores of doctors and nurses, and police and firemen. The state sent its highway patrolmen and disaster experts. The Eighth Naval District headquarters at New Orleans said that the commodore, three doctors and sixteen hospital corpsmen had been sent from the Orange Naval Station and others from the Naval Air Station at Hitchcock, Tex.

Without waiting for a call for help, the Fourth Army at San Antonio swung into action, sending a plane to St. Louis for blood plasma. Other planes were rushed to Fort Worth to get 10,000 blankets. A chemical officer was sent with 500 gas masks from the San Antonio General Depot. Nurses from Ellington Field and two Navy nurses were helping the injured in Galveston hospitals.

The Grandcamp, formerly the Benjamin R. Curtis, was built in Los Angeles for the Maritime Commission in 1942 and was sold to the French Line in July, 1946.

Texas City is heavily industrialized and a major Texas shipping center. The world's largest tin smelting plant is located here. Petroleum products form a major share of its industry. Cotton, cotton bagging, sulphur, grain, chemicals and other products pour through its ports. It was a major wartime war center.

Its outer harbor is shared by Galveston. The harbor is 800 feet wide and over five miles long, extending from the Gulf of Mexico between two protective breakwaters to Boliver Roads, the terminal of the Texas City, Galveston and Houston ship channels. It also is an intersection of the intracoastal canal.

The city is located on the mainland, across Galveston Bay from Galveston and eleven miles from the Gulf.

In commerce, it reached fourth place in Texas ports, with 3,907 vessels cleared and 13,441,248 net cargo tons moved last year.

Phone Strikers Ordered To Aid Stricken Area

By The Associated Press.

ST. LOUIS, April 16—All Southwestern Bell Telephone Company employes who are members of the Southwestern Telephone Workers Union, including operators, repairmen and any other necessary personnel, have been directed to return to their jobs in the area affected by the Texas City, Tex., ship explosion emergency.

Everett Cotter, general counsel for the union, said today the union members have been instructed not to resume their part in the nation-wide telephone strike until the emergency has been met.

Texas Mobilizes Relief for Blasted City; Army Flies in Big Loads of Blood Plasma

TEXAS CITY, Tex., April 16 (U.P.)—The state of Texas, assisted by the Red Cross, the armed services and veterans organizations, mobilized its resources tonight to handle the big job of relief in this blasted city.

The Fourth Army said at San Antonio that it was sending help. The Tenth Air Force was named coordinator of transportation, and immediately sent two airplanes to St. Louis to pick up 12,000 pounds of blood plasma.

Two Army planes at Bergstrom Field, Austin, Tex., were loaded with 8,750 pounds of plasma and sent here. All Army plasma in the San Antonio area was on its way, along with 500 Army gas masks.

Two C-47 cargo planes were sent to Forth Worth for 10,000 blankets. Braniff Airways said that doctors and nurses from all major cities on its routes were heading for this stricken city in its planes.

Gov. Beauford H. Jester alerted two battalions of Texas state guardsmen at Houston to add 400 men to the 150 state troopers who moved in from near-by Laporte.

Fire and Police Department men from Gulf Coast cities in an eighty-mile radius came in to help. The Texas Highway Department said that all the tractors and bulldozers in its system would be made available as needed to clear the wreckage.

The Coast Guard rushed a half dozen boats through Galveston Bay to Texas City and also set up a radio communications truck.

Dozens, possibly hundreds, of ambulances traveled between Texas City and Galveston, Houston and other towns in this area. As hospitals were filled, private homes were taken over.

An airplane carrying five doctors, five nurses, two Navy pharmacists mates and a load of supplies, including morphine and blood plasma, arrived from Corpus Christi, Tex. The Red Cross flew in a plane-load of gas masks from Lake Charles, La., and other masks arrived from Ellington Field, near Houston. The Navy put a 700-bed hospital at Houston and a 500-bed hospital at Fort Crockett, near Galveston, in the hands of the Red Cross.

Two Reported Killed In Plane Above Blast

By The Associated Press.

TEXAS CITY, Tex., April 16—An airplane flying over Texas City at the time of today's explosions was reported blown from the air and its two occupants killed.

A Houston Chronicle reporter said that the plane crashed near the plant of the Monsanto Chemical Corporation.

The occupants were said to have been identified as Fred Brumley and John Norris of Pelly, Tex.

Water Supply Condemned

By The United Press.

TEXAS CITY, Tex., April 16—Explosion after explosion ripped through this teeming oil city today, killing hundreds of persons and injuring hundreds more, and setting chemical plant, oil tank and ship fires that sent clouds of poisonous gas fumes across the devastated area.

Damage was estimated as high as $75,000,000.

The water supply was condemned and gas was shut off, adding to the difficulties of doctors trying to treat the injured. Jeeps and trucks rushed National Guard contingents here to guard the city and prevent looting. Refugees, many of them with their homes burned or blasted, streamed out of the city. One man who came in this afternoon saw several hundred sitting by the side of the road, apparently dazed and not sure what they ought to do.

Steel fragments were hurled for four and five miles in every direction, sending flaming splinters into the Monsanto plant, oil refineries and fifty oil tanks lining the waterfront, and slashing down people walking in the street and sitting in cars.

Two miles away a couple was found dead in a coupe. A piece of flying sheet metal had almost severed their heads.

The Monsanto plant caught fire and a shuddering series of blasts followed.

The fire spread to the near-by refineries and oil tanks. One by one they caught the blaze. Black smoke veiled the area. Beneath it seeped deadly fumes from the chemical plant and the explosive-laden freighters tied up there.

Two more ships exploded. A barge was lifted from the water, hurled 200 feet into the air and thrown across the broken hulks of the ships. A ten-car oil train was hurled against an embankment as though by a giant's hand.

Dr. W. H. Lane, a Monsanto official, was in the company's office 500 yards from the blasted ship.

"I saw scores of bodies as I left my office," he said.

Frank Taylor, a worker in one of the Monsanto warehouses, said that the blast caved in the building. Dazed and bleeding, he crawled through a hole in the wall and fell into Galveston Bay. Despite shock and injuries, he swam a half-mile up the bay to his home.

When he crawled upon shore he found his house a wreck. All members of his family were gone. He was searching for them tonight in the hope that they were among the survivors.

Ben Lapham, 29, of Mission, Tex., second mate of the freighter High Flyer, which was berthed two docks away from the French ship which blew up, said:

"The fire started in the No. 4 hold of the Frenchman about 8:30 this morning and everybody on our ship was standing around watching them fight the fire. The No. 4 hold had nitrate fertilizer in it and there were a lot of rumors that the No. 5 had ammunition.

"The fire burned about half an hour and about 9 o'clock or a little after there was the most terrible blast. The funny thing was that everything blacked out. I was knocked flat to the deck. It was like night for a minute or more. The blast blew our hatches open and killed several of our crew. Wreckage rained down for several minutes, but all I got was some bad scratches."

The big clock in Michael's jewelry store was stopped at 9:19 A.M., and Louis Alexander, the manager, who was standing about 20 feet from the door when it blew in on him, said that was "about" the time it happened.

Others thought it happened a few minutes earlier. Around 9:12 A. M. Jay Cohen, pressman for The Texas City Sun, was checking over his equipment. He said the force of the explosion lifted the linotype nearest him at least 3 inches off the floor.

T. W. Adams, a husky dockworker, said he was watching the fire aboard the ship. He saw a "little smoke" and then the explosion came. The blast knocked him about 20 feet. He scrambled to his feet and dashed into a parked car for protection. The top of the vehicle was crushed by the second blast and a big oil barge which had been tied at the dock landed near the car. Adams told his story and when he finished he fainted.

A policeman guarded the doorway to an automobile sales firm and garage which had been taken over as the main morgue. He said 250 bodies had been taken there by 4:30 P. M.

Food was being brought into Texas City tonight by truck. It consisted mainly of Army "C" rations.

The Volunteer Fire Department of Texas City was almost completely wiped out. F. H. Clement, one of the firemen, said he believed at least forty-five to fifty members of the department were among the dead. Almost all its equipment was destroyed.

Five hundred gas masks were rushed here from Ellington Field, near Houston, so rescue workers could penetrate to the waterfront blast area and reach the injured still trapped there.

The poisonous gas spreading in the city was nitrogen dioxide, which Dr. E. P. Schoch, Texas research chemist, said was "very dangerous at present" but probably would evaporate with the evening mists.

At Galveston, ten miles away, hospitals were overflowing with injured.

PRIEST VICTIM OF BLAST

He Is Fatally Hurt Attempting to Administer Last Rites

GALVESTON, Tex., April 16 (AP)—The Rev. William A. Roach, 38 years old, gave his life in the Texas City disaster today in attempting to reach the injured in the first blast and administer last rites.

Disregarding the warning of watchmen, the priest from St. Mary's Catholic church in Texas City approached the docks where the injured were lying and was hurt fatally in the second explosion. His parked car was found later about fifty feet from the water.

Father Roach was born in Philadelphia Aug. 5, 1908. With his twin brother, the Rev. John Roach, he came to Texas to study for the priesthood at La Porte Seminary.

Philadelphia Plasma on Way

PHILADELPHIA, April 16—(AP)—Sharpe and Dohme, pharmaceutical manufacturer, reported tonight it had put aboard a Transworld airliner twenty-five cartons of blood plasma consigned to Texas City.

Amateurs Get Clearance For Radio to Blast Area

Scores of new radio networks came temporarily into being throughout the country yesterday when, as a result of the disaster at Texas City, the Federal Communications Commission cleared an emergency wave-band for amateur operators. The purpose of the order was to permit amateurs to aid relatives and friends in the difficult task of communicating with persons in the devastated area.

How the plan worked was illustrated here by the experience of Joseph Gehegan, of 740 East 243d Street, the Bronx, operator of Station W2-ODO. Upon learning that the upper half of the regular amateur wave band had been ordered cleared for emergency use, he notified radio station WOR that he would transmit messages and WOR, in turn, made the fact public during its 6:30 P. M. broadcast.

An hour later, Mr. Gehegan said that he had established his "network" with the aid of stations W9-MLP, Chicago, and W5-MLK, near the scene of the explosion and fire. He had some twenty requests for information, he added. He was able to transmit them but authorities at Texas City, because of the strain even on amateur communications, ordered replies delayed until an unspecified later hour.

RED CROSS SPEEDS AID TO TEXAS CITY

Continued From Page 1

City if an order for evacuation is issued.

The Army has opened its hospital with 500 beds at Fort Crockett, and, together with the Navy, Coast Guard and Air Transport Command, has made available all its facilities for removing victims from the area.

Red Cross officials here were receiving reports on progress of their efforts from Roy Wingate, assistant manager of the Midwest area at St. Louis, who was in contact with the scene with two-way shortwave radio operated by the disaster chairman of the Freeport Chapter.

5 OFFICIALS MISSING, OIL COMPANY REPORTS

PITTSBURGH, April 16 (AP)—Five officials of the Texas City Tex., plant of the Republic Oil Refining Company, which has its main offices here, are missing in today's ship explosion, company officials said tonight.

"Some of our key personnel were at the docks when the ship exploded," said Walter S. Hallanan, president of the Plymouth Oil Company, of which Republic is a subsidiary.

Mr. Hallanan, who had just completed a telephone conversation with associates at Galveston, Tex., said eighteen to twenty members of the refinery's fire company, composed mainly of young engineers, were reported missing. He said they had been fighting the fire in the French cargo ship when the blast occurred.

Russell Holmsten, vice president and general manager of Republic, was listed as missing. He had been on the dock watching the fire.

Mr. Hallanan said that although the Republic plant is only about 3,000 feet from the point of the explosion, the only apparent damage was broken windows and the loss of a tank or two of crude oil.

"Our greatest loss, aside from the tragic death of our workers, was the destruction of our dock facilities," he said. "The explosion leaves us entirely cut off from water shipping, either for receipt of crude oil or shipment of the refined oil."

Salvation Army Starts Relief

Salvation Army National Headquarters reported last night that it had set up disaster relief headquarters in Texas City with twenty-five of its officers mobilized from Galveston, Orange, Lufkin, Houston and Beaumont and others on the way. The mobile canteen equipped with food, clothing, bedding and medicine has been sent into the zone.

VFW Chief Orders Aid for Area

WASHINGTON, April 16 (U.P.)—Louis E. Starr, national commander of the Veterans of Foreign Wars, telegraphed orders today to VFW members in Texas to "mobilize all resources" to aid victims of the Texas City explosion.

DOCTORS, CLERGY BRAVE FIRES, FUMES

Continued From Page 1

them. Priests were there and scores of volunteers.

Some donned gas masks rushed in from Fort Crockett at Galveston as they neared the docks where chemical fumes were heavy. Calls of the injured and dying could be heard faintly through the roar of the flames.

Twisted bodies lay everywhere. Rescuers stepped over the bodies as they hunted for the injured.

Along a street of small cafes and residences were scattered fragments of the ship which blew up to start this holocaust. There were also pieces of metal that were once part of the multi-million-dollar Monsanto chemical plant.

Roads leading into the center of the death area are closed. Some 1,500 law-enforcement officers and soldiers are here and only authorized persons can enter.

It is difficult to walk in Texas City. All the plate glass is gone, scattered in the streets. Bloody trails made by the injured are everywhere.

Chief Deputy Sheriff Jake Colca is in charge of identifying bodies. He said sixty-nine bodies were at the McGar garage and eight more at the Empken funeral home.

W. K. Otto of Lamar, who had been helping on a truck carrying out the dead, said he counted 200 bodies.

Mayor J. C. Traham of Texas City, an Army veteran, said the series of blasts sounded like an artillery barrage. He was in the city garage, two miles from the Monsanto plant, and he said the building "just disintegrated around me."

The dead at the McGar garage were covered with blankets. They lay on tar paper. A team of local men were trying to identify them. Some bodies were mutilated.

J. Crouch, State Highway patrolman, said when he first looked out of City Hall after the blast "you could see birds falling out of the air into the streets—killed by concussion."

Mrs. Adeline Flanikin, who was working in the Texas City Terminal office, said she went under a desk when she heard the explosion.

"I crawled back out to find the whole place down around me."

Policemen of Houston helped Texas City officers. Policemen were broadcasting from public-address systems mounted on automobiles, warning people of the danger of chlorine gas, which was released when tanks at the Monsanto chemical plant blew up. All persons were being warned to leave as quickly as possible.

The residents were leaving by the hundreds. At the outskirts of the town several hundred sat beside the highway. They appeared dazed.

In the downtown district, buildings remained upright. But most of them had all their window panes blown out. Roofs had been blown off many.

25 U. S. PLANES ALERTED

ATC Evacuation Fleet Ready to Aid Texas Victims

WASHINGTON, April 16 (U.P.)—The Army Air Transport Command's evacuation fleet of twenty-five airplanes was alerted today and placed at the disposal of authorities for aiding victims of the Texas City explosion.

Maj. Gen. Robert M. Webster disclosed that the entire fleet of C-47's and three C-54's, as well as flight nurses and medical attendants, have been authorized for use by the ATC Air Evacuation Officer in San Antonio.

Planes are standing by at Westover Field, Mass.; Warner-Robbins Air Base, Ga., and Lowry Field, Colo.

British Send Sympathy to Texas

LONDON, Thursday, April 17 (AP)—London's morning newspapers devoted major display today to stories and pictures of the disaster in Texas City, Tex. The editor of The Daily Express in a message cabled to Gov. Beauford H. Jester said that "Londoners who bore the strain of wartime blitz appreciate the immensity of suffering and associate themselves with me in offering the deepest sympathy to those bereaved."

Victims to Get U.S. Surplus Goods

WASHINGTON, April 16 (U.P.)—Robert M. Littlejohn, administrator, directed regional War Assets officers in the area today to make available at once any surplus supplies needed in the Texas City explosion.

"All the News That's Fit to Print"

The New York Times.

LATE CITY EDITION
Sunny and less humid today. Partly cloudy and warmer tomorrow.
Temperature Range Today-Max.,85; Min.,73
Temperatures Yesterday—Max.,86; Min.,73
Full U. S. Weather Bureau Report, Page 41

Copyright, 1948, by The New York Times Company.

VOL. XCVII..No. 33,059. Entered as Second-Class Matter. Postoffice, New York, N. Y. NEW YORK, THURSDAY, JULY 29, 1948. Times Square, New York 18, N. Y. Telephone Lackawanna 4-1000 THREE CENTS IN NEW YORK CITY

SENATE GOP AGREES TO CONSIDER BILLS ON PRICES, HOUSING

All Republicans in Chamber, Approving Leaders' Plans, Set Emergency Limits on Work

APPROPRIATIONS BARRED

No Nominations to Be Acted Upon—Tobey Asks Industry to Provide Inflation Curb

By C. P. TRUSSELL
Special to THE NEW YORK TIMES.

WASHINGTON, July 28—The general body of Republicans in the Senate agreed today that the extra session of the Eightieth Congress should consider only those recommendations made yesterday by President Truman which could "pass a test."

This test, established by the majority conference during a closed session lasting nearly three hours, set the qualifications for Congressional action as follows:

The proposed legislation must be emergency in character.

It must contain a problem of national importance.

It must be a program which can be processed properly within the time available to an emergency session.

This available time for processing would be no longer than a period of Congress which would not "interfere with the proper conduct" of the autumn campaigns.

The conference, composed of all Senate Republicans, approved a decision by the leaders to bring up in the upper chamber tomorrow the anti-poll tax bill, which is expected to run into a formidable filibuster by Southern Democrats.

Fund Bills, Nominations Out

The conference decided that there would be no appropriations bills, unless an unexpected emergency arose. Nor, it decided, would any consideration be given to the confirmation of nominations which might be sent to the Senate by the President.

In this way, the conference supported, without dissent, it was reported, the counterblast which the Congressional Republican high command directed last night at the President's message to the new session.

On policy matters, it was emphasized, the Republicans were in complete harmony.

It was conceded, however, that within the Senate Republican rank and file there was grumbling over the word statement in which the leaders flung most of the President's program back at him with direct or implied "noes."

Some Senators took exception to various phases of the leaders' statement. Others, it was said, found much fault with the issuing of such a statement before the declarations and recommendations had been submitted formally to conferences of all the Senate and House Republicans.

House GOP to Meet Today

The House Republican conference will meet tomorrow afternoon to go over the leaders' statement and discuss policies for the session.

As was indicated earlier, the Senate majority conference approved committee consideration of Presidential recommendations concerning housing and reductions in prices and living costs.

The price and housing situations fell into the jurisdiction of the Banking and Currency Committees. Both Senate and House groups will begin their hearings tomorrow. Paul A. Porter, former OPA chief, who was called in by the President to serve as liaison agent with the extra session will appear before the House group, speaking for the Administration's eight-point price control program. Marriner S. Eccles, of the Federal Reserve Board, will be the Senate committee's witness.

On the cost-of-living front the committees were expected to face such Administration recommendations as to present bank-lending systems, as these:

Governmental authority to call on the Federal Reserve Board to make a straight percentage increase in the amount of nonlendable reserves that banks are required to maintain with the Federal Reserve System.

Recommendation to ignore the Federal Reserve Board's pending request for authority to demand "special" reserves which banks could not put out as loans but could be used for investment in Government securities.

Authority for an increase in re-

Continued on Page 12, Column 3

IT'S NOT ENOUGH that SUNROC Water Coolers serve the world. We must also serve you. STillwell 8-2105.—Advt.

Southern Senators Pledged To Poll Tax Filibuster Today

Embattled 11 States Force 24-Hour Delay on Bill and Drive Wedge Into Republican and Northern Democrats' Opposition

By WILLIAM S. WHITE
Special to THE NEW YORK TIMES.

WASHINGTON, July 28—The Senate's embattled Southerners forced a twenty-four-hour delay today on the Anti-Poll Tax Bill and suddenly and materially improved their whole defensive position against this item in the civil rights program.

They then gathered their forces in a late afternoon caucus for the beginning tomorrow of a powerful filibuster against the measure in which twenty-one Senators from the eleven states of the South were pledged to take a hand.

In the meantime, they had driven slight but significant wedges into the hitherto overwhelming Republican-Northern Democratic phalanx drawn up along with President Truman against them.

Tonight, the highest Republican quarters were unwilling to claim an ultimate triumph and were not prepared to reject beyond recall a proposed Southern "compromise" which in fact would be a Southern victory.

This was a suggestion, which first arose outside the Southern camp from Senator Carl Hayden of Arizona, that the majority give up its insistence on passing a House bill directly abolishing the poll tax and substitute a constitutional amendment proposing abolition. This would leave the matter to the states where the Southerners wish it left.

Senator Richard Russell of Georgia, the leader of the Southern irreconcilables, made it plain that the Hayden plan would be acceptable on his side. He gave assurances that if it were adopted by the majority, more than half of the twenty-one Southerners would vote for it and that none of them would filibuster against it.

To this, however, he attached an

Continued on Page 14, Column 3

Pilots Believed Unconscious When DC-6 Crash Killed 43

By AUSTIN STEVENS

The huge DC-6 luxury airliner that crashed in eastern Pennsylvania on June 17, killing all forty-three persons aboard, may have been an uncontrolled plane manned by two nearly unconscious pilots. This possibility, it was learned yesterday, has become the chief line of inquiry of Government and aircraft investigators of the nation's third largest air disaster.

The plane, a West Coast to New York flight operated by United Air Lines, crashed into a mountain near Mount Carmel in circumstances that baffled aeronautic specialists.

Many well-known persons, including the theatrical producer Earl Carroll, perished when the 300-mile-an-hour airplane tore into a hillside.

Studies of the flight have produced the grim theory that the pilots of the plane, attempting to extinguish a fire—that possibly may not have existed—in a baggage compartment were overcome by carbon dioxide fumes seeping from the mechanical fire-fighting equipment of the plane.

Although the full story will never be known, exhaustive inquiry into what has become the most supportable reconstruction of the crash will be brought out in sworn testimony at a Civil Aeronautics Board safety bureau hearing to be held some time next month.

At that time the board will hear how in simulated flights of DC-6's, conducted since the crash, pilots who "pulled" fire extinguisher "bottles" found their cockpits filled with as high as a 12 per cent concentration of CO_2 fumes.

In these tests the pilot of the aircraft has worn an oxygen mask and his co-pilot has not. On some of these tests the man without an oxygen mask "conked out" from anoxia, or oxygen starvation.

Witnesses who observed the doomed airliner during its last minutes in the air—some of them pilots at a local airport near the crash scene—reported it flying at low altitude but with no apparent trouble with its engines or controls.

Eight minutes after radioing

Continued on Page 10, Column 4

MARSHALL STARTS U.N. 'SPY' INQUIRY

Names Committee of 3 Citizens to Study Question of Whether Agents Are Entering U. S.

By BERTRAM D. HULEN
Special to THE NEW YORK TIMES.

WASHINGTON, July 28—Secretary of State George C. Marshall appointed today a committee of three citizens to study the question of whether persons have entered the country in connection with the work of the United Nations or other international organizations whose presence is inconsistent with national security. The members of the committee are as follows:

Benjamin M. McKelway, editor of The Washington Evening Star.

James H. Rowe Jr., a former assistant attorney general, who is a member of the commission on organization of the executive branch of the Government.

Marcellus C. Shield, who was clerk of the House Appropriations Committee from 1916 to 1944, when he retired.

[At Lake Success, N. Y., delegates and members of the United Nations secretariat were shocked by the Marshall announcement. Arkady A. Sobolev, acting Secretary General of the U. N., said that "we have nothing to hide," but "we will not open our books to the committee."]

Creation of the committee resulted from hearings by a Senate judiciary subcommittee before which Robert C. Alexander, assistant chief of the State Department's visa division, testified that "perhaps several hundred" persons had come to the United States

Continued on Page 6, Column 2

Strike at Oppenheim Collins Voted by Union to Start Monday

By A. H. RASKIN

By a margin of 1,713 to 195, members of Local 1250 of the Retail, Wholesale and Department Store Union, CIO, voted last night in favor of a strike Monday at the Manhattan and Brooklyn stores of Oppenheim Collins & Co.

The local, which is made up of employes of Oppenheim Collins, Namm's, Loeser's, Hearn's and a number of other stores, also voted 1,665 to 233 to uphold the refusal of its officers to file non-Communist affidavits under the Taft-Hartley Law.

An American Federation of Labor union, Local 1601 of the Retail Clerks International Protective Association, has asked for a National Labor Relations Board election at Oppenheim Collins. Local 1250 cannot appear on the ballot unless it files the non-Communist affidavits.

In a speech made before the vote, Nicholas Carnes, president of the local, urged the members to approve the strike and to vote against filing the affidavits. Mr. Carnes also announced at the Manhattan Center meeting that he would seek election to Congress as candidate of the pro-Wallace American Labor party in the Twenty-sixth Bronx district.

The refusal of the local president to tell a House investigating committee whether he was a Communist or belonged to organizations listed as subversive by the Department of Justice was endorsed at the meeting by a vote of 1,676 to 214.

Mr. Carnes told the union members that Local 1250 would make "a final effort" to avert the Oppenheim Collins strike by proposing that its present contract, which expires Saturday night, be extended until Jan. 1. This proposal has

Continued on Page 15, Column 5

RED COACH GRILL, 7 East 58th St., will close Sundays during the Summer.—Advt.

EAST-WEST PARLEY TO SPUR JOINT TRADE PLANNED FOR FALL

Soviet Offers No Opposition to Satellites' Participation—Seen Resigned to ERP

YUGOSLAV CRISIS A FACTOR

Russian Asks U. N. to Seek Cooperation of Communist and Capitalist Worlds

By MICHAEL L. HOFFMAN
Special to THE NEW YORK TIMES.

GENEVA, July 28—A large-scale bargaining conference between the countries of Eastern and Western Europe aiming at a big increase in trade between the two regions is being prepared for some time this autumn, it was learned today.

Representatives of both Eastern and Western countries within the last few days have reached agreement that the time now is opportune to bring some or all of the countries participating in the European Recovery Program around a table with the Eastern countries to seek common agreement on how, when and where trade between the two groups can be increased.

The project still is in the groundwork stage and could be still-born as a result of any one of a number of political hazards that may arise. But it is learned on good authority that the top trade authorities of France, Poland, Czechoslovakia, the United Kingdom and the Organization for European Economic Cooperation in Paris are convinced of the necessity of some broader action in the field than heretofore has been possible.

An important, indeed vital, condition for the success of the plan is the absence of Soviet opposition to the participation of the Eastern countries.

A source very close to the Soviet delegation to the United Nations Economic and Social Council told this correspondent today that there was good reason to believe that the Soviet Union's attacks on the Marshall Plan in the current session marked the final appearance of this kind of effort to use that council and the United Nations Economic Commission for Europe, a subsidiary body, as a weapon to undermine the European Recovery Program.

That Soviet delegation is led by A. A. Arutiunian, who also is Russian representative on the Economic Commission for Europe.

This is not to say that the Russians will relent in their opposition

Continued on Page 9, Column 2

AFTER FARBEN EXPLOSION IN WHICH HUNDREDS DIED

Rescue workers searching ruins of chemical plant at Ludwigshafen, in French zone of Germany
Associated Press Radiophoto

250 DIE, 6,000 HURT AS BLASTS WRECK PLANT IN GERMANY

Full Toll at Farben Chemical Works in Ludwigshafen Is Not Known—Fires Rage

U. S. TROOPS AID IN RESCUE

600 at Scene as 1,000 Doctors and Nurses Treat Injured in French Zone City

By JACK RAYMOND
Special to THE NEW YORK TIMES.

LUDWIGSHAFEN, Germany, Thursday, July 29—At least 250 persons were killed and approximately 6,000 injured yesterday when explosions and fire wrecked the huge I. G. Farben chemical works in this French zone city.

Several hundred persons were trapped and some of them still were being dug out of the rubble early today. The rescuers could hear the cries of those caught between twisted beams and under piles of brick and wood.

United States and French troops and German laborers and policemen, working under searchlights in dense smoke, still were fighting the flames as explosions continued into the night. Amidst the confusion of speeding ambulances and grinding United States Army bulldozers and cranes, priests were administering last rites to the dying.

3,500 Outside Factory Hurt

The injured included more than 2,500 of the plant's employes and about 3,500 persons who suffered injuries while they were in their homes or in streets, some of them many blocks away from the chemical works.

The first explosion occurred yesterday afternoon in a room in a lacquer plant containing 4,000 cubic meters of chloroethyl (a cubic meter is 1.308 cubic yards). It came so suddenly and created such havoc that nerve-wracked officials at first estimated that several thousand persons had died. This was modified afterward, but there still was no accurate estimate of the toll in human lives. The disaster was comparable, it was said, with one in the same plant in 1921, when 600 were killed.

Twenty-two thousand persons were at work when the first blast ripped out the lacquer section. It threw workers in near-by buildings to the floor and smashed windows for several miles around. Fire spread into a methyl violet section and three more explosions came in rapid succession, knocking down the walls of unused, bombed-out buildings within the factory gates.

Hit by Beams and Pillars

Many persons were killed or injured later as falling steel beams and concrete pillars smashed them into the ground. In one instance a team of United States soldiers amputated a young man's leg to extricate him from a heavy machine, only to see him bludgeoned to death by a collapsing steel bar.

Two French petty officials were killed under the smashed ceiling of the administration building, at least 600 feet from the origin of the explosions. A German boy was hurled out a window of the same building to his death in a courtyard two stories below. One worker was reported drowned in a vat of tar in another building.

The factory, which was 80 per cent destroyed during the war, was known officially as the Badische Lime and Soda Factory. It was a unit of the former I. G. Farben cartel, at present under the control of a four-power committee. The factory was producing dyes, paints, lacquers, plastics, heavy chemicals, nitrogen, sulphuric acid and tanning agents.

Blast Felt in Heidelberg

Many Americans in United States Army Headquarters in Heidelberg, across the Rhine River about thirteen miles from Ludwigshafen, felt the first blast. Within half an hour the first detachments of United States soldiers, equipped with gas masks, and physicians and other rescue workers had joined the Germans and the French troops already on the scene.

Although the French and the Germans were nominally in charge, hundreds more Americans swarmed across the bridge connecting Mannheim and Ludwigshafen. A United States command post was established in a large courtyard of the factory. A map of the plant was spread out on a jeep and United States officers directed in wartime fashion the operations of

Continued on Page 3, Column 5

SALE MEN'S sport and summer shoes, reduced from \$8.95 to \$4.95 at new Regal store, 1 West 42nd Street. Wide choice of styles and sizes.—Advt.

SLAVS ASK U.N. CURB ON WEST IN TRIESTE

Belgrade Charges U. S., Britain Seek to Give Area to Italy in Violation of Pact

By A. M. ROSENTHAL
Special to THE NEW YORK TIMES.

LAKE SUCCESS, N. Y., July 28—Yugoslavia complained to the United Nations Security Council today that the United States and Britain were jeopardizing the peace by a steady campaign to give the free territory of Trieste to Italy.

In its first major international step since the break with the Cominform, Marshal Tito's Government asked for a verdict from the Council on long-standing Yugoslav-Soviet charges that the Western Allies were violating the Italian peace treaty.

United States delegation officials were waiting for word from Washington before making any comment but the British spokesman here said that Communist tactics of obstruction in Trieste made it doubtful whether the peace provisions for the Free Territory were workable now.

The five-page Yugoslav memorandum was immediately put under the diplomatic microscope here to

Continued on Page 6, Column 6

West to Urge Big Four Talks Include All European Issues

By HERBERT L. MATTHEWS
Special to THE NEW YORK TIMES.

LONDON, July 28—The United States, Britain and France are going to propose to the Soviet Union that talks be held not only on Germany but on Austria and Trieste as well, it was learned today.

Thus the Berlin issue has spread from that city to Germany as a whole and thence to much of Europe. Since Europe involves a whole complex of issues of all sorts between the Western democracies and the totalitarian East it has become symbolic of the world struggle.

That is why the next move on Berlin has been so long and carefully prepared. When the envoys of the United States, Britain and France see Foreign Minister Molotov, speak to him and present their aide-memoire, everything will depend on the Russian answer.

If once more it is a rejection, the Western Allies will most likely take the Berlin issue to the United Nations Security Council as endangering peace.

[In Berlin itself, the police force was split into Eastern and Western factions when the acting mayor refused to obey a Soviet order to reinstate the pro-Russian police chief, Paul Markgraf, who had been ousted by the Magistrate, and his deputy, Johannes Stumm, set up new headquarters in the United States sector.]

When today for the first time since the Berlin crisis started there were no three-power discussions here on the subject, the tendency was to look at the hopeful side of the situation.

Foreign Secretary Bevin's principal private secretary Frank Roberts, who has ministerial rank and who was in the British Embassy in Moscow for three years, left here to be Britain's envoy when the approach is made to Mr. Molotov.

Since he and Lieut. Gen. W. Bedell Smith will not arrive in Moscow before tomorrow afternoon the démarche is unlikely to take place before Friday.

However, nobody here can say precisely when it will take place for the obvious reason that it is up to Mr. Molotov to say when he

Continued on Page 3, Column 2

ISRAEL AND EGYPT BATTLING IN NEGEB

Attack on a Tel Aviv Convoy Is Held Cause of Outbreak—U. N. Truce Team Held Up

By GENE CURRIVAN
Special to THE NEW YORK TIMES.

TEL AVIV, Israel, July 28—It was announced here tonight that fighting between Egyptian and Israeli forces had broken out today in the Negeb region of Palestine.

The announcement added that as a result of the fighting a United Nations truce team had been prevented from reaching Gaza.

The truce team reached a point near Hatta but could not continue because of heavy firing by both sides.

According to a Government spokesman here the reason for the battle was an Egyptian attack on a supply convoy attempting to reach Negeb colonies in the Hatta-Karatiya area. The official statement said that Israeli forces were attacking Egyptian communications and vehicle concentrations at Faluja and Iraq el Manshiya to the southeast. It added that United Nations observers went to the scene this afternoon.

As the observers, led by Lieut. Col. Albert Perry, arrived there late in the afternoon during the height of the battle a truce attempt seemed impossible. Colonel Perry was there, not to negotiate a truce, but merely to deliver Col. Louis D. Cooper to the Gaza area where he was to be in charge of observers.

Today's development, although not considered important in the broad picture, does show, accord-

Continued on Page 8, Column 3

World News Summarized

THURSDAY, JULY 29, 1948

Hundreds of persons were killed and thousands injured in an explosion and fire that wrecked the I. G. Farben chemical works in Ludwigshafen, Germany, yesterday. Continuing blasts and fires hampered rescue work. The explosion came shortly before the 22,000 employes were to leave. [1:8; map P. 3.]

Another disaster took the lives of at least sixteen Americans when one of the three B-29's on an around-the-world flight crashed into the sea off Aden, Arabia. [1:6-7; map P. 10.]

It was reported in London that the Western Allies, in their note to Moscow, would propose that Austria and Trieste be included with Germany in four-power talks if Russia agreed to resume negotiations. [1:6-7.] Secretary Marshall, refusing to throw any light on the contents of the new Berlin note, called some news on it from abroad incorrect. [3:1.]

Frau Louise Schroeder, Berlin's Acting Mayor, rejected a Soviet demand to reinstate the ousted Communist chief of police. His successor, named by the City Council, moved to the American sector and the city had two police heads. [2:2.]

Plans were reported under way in Geneva to bring the countries of Eastern and Western Europe together in the fall in an effort to stimulate trade between the two regions. [1:4.]

The Yugoslav Communist party congress unanimously upheld Marshal Tito in his fight with the Cominform. [4:3.]

Trieste again was injected into the United Nations Security Council when Yugoslavia filed charges that the United States and Britain were endangering peace by striving to return the Free Territory to Italy. [1:5.] The Little Assembly voted unanimously to ask that its life be extended. [7:5.]

Three citizens were named by Secretary Marshall to study charges that aliens had used their credentials to the United Nations to carry on subversive activity in this country. [1:2.] United Nations officials were shocked and challenged the right of any nation to examine the body's records. [6:1.]

Fighting broke out between Egyptian and Israeli forces in the Negeb, preventing a United Nations truce team from reaching Gaza. [1:7.]

Senate Republicans, with some dissatisfaction on specific matters, approved the decision of their leaders to keep the special session of Congress short. It was agreed to act only on emergency or vital items. [1:1.]

Southern Democrats forced a twenty-four-hour delay on the anti-poll tax bill in the Senate and Republican leaders qualified their predictions of passage. Some support came to a Southern proposal to settle the issue by constitutional amendment rather than by legislation. [1:2-3.]

Liberal party endorsement in this state of President Truman's candidacy was believed indicated in the unanimous approval by a party group of the President's message to Congress. The party endorsed eleven Democratic and seven Republican candidates in New York County. [12:5.]

Should Congress pass a liberalized displaced persons bill, this state could employ 50,000, Industrial Commissioner Corsi said. [9:1.]

Peace was assured in the women's coat and suit industry by the signing of a three-year, no-strike agreement with an escalator wage clause. [15:1.]

An unresolved wage dispute between the management and the orchestra union brought doubt over opera at the Metropolitan this year. [23:1.]

16 on B-29 Lost in Sea Off Arabia; One of Crew of Global Plane Saved

By The Associated Press.

ADEN, July 28—One of three B-29 Superfortresses on an around-the-world flight crashed into the sea within sight of this port on the south coast of Arabia last night. At least sixteen American crewmen were believed lost.

One man was rescued but it was not learned immediately the exact number of men aboard the giant American bomber. Authorities here imposed restrictions on outgoing dispatches concerning the crash.

Five bodies were recovered from the sea during the day and were buried with full military honors in a funeral attended by the crews of the two remaining B-29's.

The crash occurred at 7 P. M. (11 A. M. Eastern standard time, Tuesday) shortly after the three planes took off for Ceylon.

The cause of the disaster still is unknown. Witnesses said the plane was airborne when the motors suddenly became silent. The other planes returned to Aden and are awaiting instructions.

United States Consul Charles Gidney and the consulate staff were present during rescue operations all through last night. Divers are working on the wreckage which is visible about a mile offshore at low tide.

The three planes carried a total of fifty-three men, according to an announcement when they left Tucson, Ariz., on the flight. The customary complement of a B-29 is nine men, but two of the globe-girdling planes carried double crews while the third carried seventeen men.

The lone survivor, identified only as Sergeant Gustafson, was picked up by local fishermen. He was reported resting comfortably in the RAF hospital.

[Capt. Percy H. Kramer, public

Continued on Page 10, Column 2

When You Think of Writing Think of Whiting—Advt.

German Red Cross workers removing bodies from the I. G. Farben chemical works after
the explosion and fire which killed 250 and injured 6000.

Wide World Photos

250 DIE, 6,000 HURT BY FARBEN BLASTS

Continued From Page 1

huge cranes, bulldozers and steam-shovels. A loudspeaker manned by a German ordered ambulances in nd out of the area as rescue workers hauled the dead and injured from the debris.

By midnight there were 600 Americans in the disaster area, in addition to about 500 French troops and German policemen. Emergency field hospitals, with Germans and Americans working side by side, were set up.

Medical Supplies Sent In

Under the order of Lieut. Gen. Clarence R. Huebner, Deputy United States Commander in Europe, that all possible aid be given, medical supplies poured in from United States Army hospitals. A field kitchen ready to feed 1,500 persons was established. Emergency gasoline stations, offering fuel to German ambulances and other rescue vehicles, in addition to Army equipment, were set up.

All available personnel from points as far away as Frankfort on the Main were drawn from German and occupation hospitals. About 1,000 physicians and nurses were reported in the area by 11 o'clock last night, when another explosion rocked the neighborhood. The factory grounds were immediately cleared of all persons except those engaged in disaster work. Many thousands of citizens whose homes had been shaken ringed the factory fence.

Water Pumped From Rhine

More than 40,000 feet of fire hose were used to pump water from the Rhine into the smoke and flames. Electric generators were hauled within the plant gates to supply floodlights as darkness fell. Smoky flame and lights from hand flashlights and lanterns produced an eerie scene.

The dead were taken immediately to the municipal cemetery. Because the bodies were charred beyond immediate recognition, friends and relatives were not permitted to attempt identification yet.

The streets for more than a mile around the factory were littered with glass and tumbled bomb ruins. Some streets were impassable by automobile, and special traffic routes were established to guide trucks and ambulances to and from the scene.

It was the third time, officials said, that the same factory had suffered such a disaster. In 1921 it was 98 per cent destroyed. In an explosion in 1943 the destruc-

tion was 52 per cent. As of Tuesday, the factory was back to approximately 89 per cent of its prewar production.

Workers at the factory said that yesterday's fire was worse than several fires set during the war in bombing raids.

Toll 300, Army Estimates

LUDWIGSHAFEN, Thursday, July 29 (AP)—More than 300 persons were killed in the blast that wrecked the Farben chemical works, according to a United States Army estimate.

American, French and German rescue workers braved minor blasts, flames and fumes early today as they continued bringing out survivors. The German police said that 1,000 persons were hospitalized in Ludwigshafen, 300 in Heidelberg and 300 in Mannheim. Other victims were taken to hospitals in Karlsruhe and Speyer.

The blast and resultant fire, which sent flames and smoke towering miles into the air, came just fifteen minutes before the factory's 22,000 workers would have gone home for the day.

Fire that followed the explosion yesterday spread like a gust of wind until an estimated eighteen buildings has been destroyed or damaged.

The factory had been producing

GERMAN CITY SHAKEN

The New York Times   July 29, 1948

Hundreds have been killed and thousands injured in an explosion at the I. G. Farben chemical works at Ludwigshafen (cross).

industrial chemicals, drugs and dyes. However, unconfirmed reports in recent months said the French also were using it to make high-explosive propulsion fluids for experiments with V-1 and V-2 rockets. Strong fumes from burning chemicals sent some survivors

reeling about the streets.

The terrific blast was comparable with the disaster in April of last year at Texas City, Tex., where an estimated 650 persons were killed and 3,000 injured when a French ship loaded with nitrates blew up in the harbor.

Helmeted French troops carrying rifles held back crowds of weeping relatives who tried to inch their way nearer the flaming wreckage and find a trace of the missing.

On the United States-occupied side of the Rhine other crowds lined the banks to watch the flames and a hovering column of smoke that had a base a half mile square. An automobile driver said he saw the smoke column when he was twenty miles from Ludwigshafen.

The origin of the blast and fire was not determined. Officials could not get close enough to the probable center of the blast to begin an investigation. They said they would make no statements until they had more information.

No American Deaths Reported

LUDWIGSHAFEN, Thursday, July 29 (UP)—No American casualties were reported in the blast that wrecked the Farben factory.

French Army authorities said they did not suspect sabotage. The cause of the blast may never be known because of the extent of damage.

"All the News That's Fit to Print"

The New York Times.

LATE CITY EDITION
Sunny and warm today; pleasant tonight. Fair and warm tomorrow.
Temperature Range Today—Max.,86; Min.,67
Temperature Yesterday—Max.,87; Min.,70
U. S. Weather Bureau Report, Page 7; Sect. 5

Section 1

NEWS INDEX, PAGE 63, THIS SECTION

Copyright, 1949, by The New York Times Company.

VOL. XCVIII..No. 33,433. Entered as Second-Class Matter. Postoffice, New York, N. Y. NEW YORK, SUNDAY, AUGUST 7, 1949. Including Magazine and Book Review. FIFTEEN CENTS New York City | Elsewhere 50 Mile Zone | Twenty Cents

U. S. REVIEW ON ORIENT GETS SPUR IN VISIT BY QUIRINO; VANDENBERG URGES CLARITY

Senator Says Policy Survey Must Aid Chinese People

Concession to Stalin, Insistence on Coalition Held Major U. S. Errors—Statement Indicates a Degree of Bipartisan Approach

Special to The New York Times.

WASHINGTON, Aug. 6—Senator Arthur H. Vandenberg of Michigan, ranking Republican member of the Foreign Relations Committee, stated today that the United States Government must make clear, in reviewing its Far Eastern policy, its support of the Chinese people and of freedom in the Far East. The State Department will undertake such a review starting on Monday.

The Senator depicted the China White Paper, released by the State Department yesterday, as a "post mortem" that would be of chief use in pointing out warnings for the future. He said that both China and the United States had made tragic errors in the past and called for a fresh look at our China policy "unhampered by past prejudices or emotions."

"Our chief mistakes," he commented, "were:

1. The price we paid at Teheran and at Yalta, at China's expense, for Russia's belated and unnecessary entry into the Japanese war.

2. Our well intentioned but impractical insistence upon a Nationalist-Communist coalition."

Mr. Vandenberg's brief statement today seemed to be in general agreement with the ideas Secretary of State Dean Acheson expressed in issuing the White Paper yesterday. The statement indicated a degree of bipartisan approach to Far Eastern policy that has been largely lacking recently.

Maj. Gen. Patrick J. Hurley, commenting on the White Paper, continued his feud with the career diplomats of the Foreign Service in a statement issued at his office here today.

He blamed them for what he

Continued on Page 2, Column 5

PACT PLAN IS ISSUE

President of Philippines to Push Anti-Red Bid on Pacific Defense

CHANGE IN EMPHASIS SEEN

Filipino Shifts Stress From Military Ties — Chiang and Rhee Meet in Korea

By HAROLD B. HINTON
Special to The New York Times.

WASHINGTON, Aug. 6 — The thorough review of United States policy toward the Far East, which the State Department is to undertake, starting next week, is expected to receive an initial impetus from the state visit of President Elpidio Quirino of the Philippine Republic, who will reach Washington on Monday.

President Quirino is the leading spirit in a movement to establish some kind of union of Southeastern Asian States to resist the aggressive tactics that the Chinese Communists are expected to employ as their forces move toward China's southern border. A month ago, he discussed this project with Generalissimo Chiang Kai-shek when the Chinese leader visited him in Baguio.

[Generalissimo Chiang arrived in Korea Saturday where he and President Syngman Rhee of Korea jointly confirmed that the main topic of their talks would be the formation of an anti-Communist Pacific defense pact.]

U. S. Not Consulted

The meeting of Generalissimo Chiang and President Quirino was arranged without consultation of the State Department by either of them and only mild interest was displayed here. At that time, it appeared that President Quirino had in mind a Pacific pact to follow the lines of the recently signed North Atlantic pact.

He already had urged a parallel course for the nations bordering on the Pacific some months previously. He declared for a pact among the free countries of Southeast Asia, with the active support of the United States.

Pending the formulation of a new Far Eastern policy—one presumably to be based on the assumption that the National Government is doomed in China and that the Chinese people themselves must decide whether they will live under the rule of the Communists, the only official indication of what the United States might do in the event of aggression, overt or covert, against the countries to the south of China was given by Secretary of State Dean Acheson yesterday in transmitting the China White Paper to President Truman.

He indicated that if the Chinese Communists attempted to engage in aggression against China's neighbors, the United States would bring the matter before the United Nations as a situation threatening international peace and security.

Change of Emphasis Seen

President Quirino's ideas, however, envisage some sort of regional organization within the United Nations that will be able to take preventive action. He has just recalled to Manila Brig. Gen. Carlos Romulo, the Philippines representative to the United Nations, to undertake an active campaign of sounding out the interested governments of Southeastern Asia. It is assumed that he himself will do the sounding out in Washington.

In his instructions to General Romulo, President Quirino stated that he envisaged the projected union "to be essentially an act of common faith on the economic, political and cultural level in tune with work of the Economic Cooperation Administration in the Far East and the program of the United Nations Educational, Scientific and Cultural Organization," and that it would involve no military commitments.

This statement of objective is interpreted here as a change from the reasoning that motivated his talks with Generalissimo Chiang, during which, it is believed, the matter of reciprocal military commitments was perhaps uppermost. The Romulo instructions contain a

Continued on Page 5, Column 6

8-CENT BUS FARE BEGINS TOMORROW ON 3D AVE. LINES

Nearly 1,800,000 Riders Will Pay Rise From 7 Cents Under Court Ruling

ARKWRIGHT SIGNS ORDER

Company Promises Improved Service—25 New Vehicles Expected This Week

By KENNETH CAMPBELL

Nearly 1,800,000 persons using Third Avenue Transit Corporation buses will pay a fare of 8 cents instead of 7 beginning tomorrow at 12:01 A. M., it was announced yesterday.

The announcement of the fare increase, granted by the Public Service Commission in spite of objections by Mayor O'Dwyer and the Board of Estimate, was accompanied by assurances from the company that the service would be improved.

James Hodes, president of the Third Avenue Transit Corporation, said after the announcement of the increases that his company hoped to have twenty-five new buses operating in the Bronx by the end of the week.

"The eight-cent fare will permit us to give constantly improving service," Mr. Hodes said. The company operates seventy-six bus lines in Manhattan, the Bronx and Westchester. Vehicles of the Third Avenue system operating in Westchester will not be affected by the fare rise. When the company applied for the increase it said that it had lost $2,048,500 between Jan. 1 and June 1.

The Third Avenue Transit Corporation is in receivership and the Transport Workers Union is seeking $1,100,000 due Third Avenue employes in retroactive pay and is demanding a new contract.

Court Authorized Increase

On Tuesday Federal Judge Samuel H. Kaufman authorized trustees of the bankrupt bus company to file with the Public Service Commission an eight-cent fare schedule to become operative at the Commission's discretion. At the same time Judge Kaufman denied the trustees' application to lift an injunction restraining the city from bringing action in the State courts to decide the validity of the franchise clause that the city contends gives it the right to void the franchise if fare increases are granted without Board of Estimate approval.

A City Hall spokesman for Mayor O'Dwyer, who reached the Mayor at his executive residence, quoted him as saying:

"I have nothing further to add to what has already been said on the subject."

The order granting the increase was signed by Public Service Commissioner George A. Arkwright yesterday after it seemed that Third Avenue bus riders would get

Continued on Page 52, Column 3

Major Sports News

BASEBALL

Successive ninth-inning homers by Tommy Henrich and Joe DiMaggio enabled the Yankees to beat the Browns, 9 to 8, at the Stadium yesterday. DiMaggio's smash, his second of the afternoon, broke an 8-8 tie. The Dodger winning streak was stopped at six when the Brooks lost at Cincinnati, 5 to 2. However, the Dodgers stayed a half-game out of first place as the pacemaking Cards were beaten by the Giants in a night contest, 3—1.

HORSE RACING

Round View, from the Sanford Stud Farms, won the $20,000 added Whitney Stakes at Saratoga, with Donor second and the favored My Request third over the mile-and-a-quarter route. The winner paid $14. More Sun, paying $7.90, carried the Brookmeade Stable silks to victory in the United States Hotel Stakes at six furlongs, the secondary Spa attraction. At Monmouth Park, Count-A-Bit took the Choice Stakes.

GOLF

The Montclair team of William Dear Jr. and Kenneth Gordon reached the final of the Anderson Memorial tourney at the Winged Foot course with William Schappa and E. B. Vaughan of the home club. Dear and Gordon downed Bob and Bill Kuntz of Bonnie Briar, 1 up, and Schappa and Vaughan defeated Ted Bishop and Ed Wyner of Boston, 2 and 1.

(Full details in Section 5.)

Gulf Stream Shifts Closer to Jersey

Special to The New York Times.

SPRING LAKE, N. J., Aug. 6—The Gulf Stream, normally about eighty miles off the North Jersey coast at this season, was reported today to be only twenty-two miles off shore, resulting in the discovery of many rare tropical fish in the nets of fishermen.

Capt. Vincent Droughton, veteran navigator in Northern and Southern waters, measured the distance of the stream from Manasquan Inlet. Old-time fishermen have also declared the stream to be closer to shore than ever before.

By The Associated Press.

ATLANTIC CITY, N. J. Aug. 6—Tropical fish were reported running off the New Jersey coast today. Flying fish, which normally never get farther north than Florida, were seen near here, according to fishermen returning tonight, who also told of unusually high catches of other summer fish.

FORD CALLS ON MEN TO REJECT STRIKE

Company Takes Full Pages and Radio Time on Vote Eve —Reuther Assails Plea

Special to The New York Times.

DETROIT, Aug. 6—The Ford Motor Company began an intensified campaign today to persuade its 87,000 hourly paid workers in Michigan to vote against a strike in an election beginning Monday.

The company took full-page advertisements in the three Detroit Sunday newspapers — The Free Press, The News and The Times. It bought time on four Detroit stations for spot announcements urging employes to vote "no" on the strike ballot. The appeal was directed as much to the wives of the workers as to the men themselves.

Mr. Ford told the workers that "it is the apparent hope of union leadership that you will vote yourself into another long strike." He reiterated the company's previously announced purpose, "to keep the greatest possible number of people at work at present high rates" rather than "a much smaller number at higher rates."

In Lansing today the State Supreme Court denied a motion by Ford to block the strike vote on charges that the State Labor Mediation Board had been "unfair" in refusing to conduct the strike vote on company property, and, instead, ordering it held in the immediate vicinity of union offices. The company's application was ordered held in abeyance indefinitely.

Walter P. Reuther, president of the United Automobile Workers, CIO, in a thirty-minute radio talk last night, accused the company of falsely attempting "to sell the workers a bill of goods" in regard to putting their job security first.

He assailed the company's demand for revision of seniority rights, which, he said, was an indirect contradiction of the company's announced objective of keeping the maximum number of employes at work.

"Ford wants to return to its pre-union practice of working the life out of an employe and then tossing him out of the gate," Mr. Reuther declared.

He called his program for pensions and job security a means of taking care of workers when "they are too old to work but too young to die."

The company's appeal to the

Continued on Page 51, Column 1

EMERGENCY DECREE ISSUED IN HAWAII; DOCKS SEIZURE SET

Governor Quickly Uses Crisis Powers Voted by Special Session of Legislature

DEMANDS END OF STRIKE

Refusal to Mean Territorial Operation of Stevedoring—Tie-Up Reaches 98 Days

By The Associated Press.

HONOLULU, Aug. 6—Gov. Ingram M. Stainback proclaimed tonight a state of emergency in Hawaii's dock strike and called upon the stevedoring industry and the strikers to resume operations. He acted under a law he signed this afternoon which empowers him to take "possession of any or all stevedoring companies."

The proclamation was issued after a three-hour meeting of the Territorial Attorney General's staff, officials of two Honolulu stevedoring companies and the president of Hawaii Stevedores, Ltd., a non-union firm formed after the strike began.

There was no discussion with the CIO International Longshoremen's and Warehousemen's Union.

Legislature Clears Bill

Special to The New York Times.

HONOLULU, Aug. 6—Governor Stainback signed into law today a bill giving him temporary powers to act in the dock strike which began ninety-eight days ago.

The bill, which cleared both houses in a special session of the Territorial Legislature early today, was designed specifically to deal with the present walkout. It gives the Governor power to operate Hawaiian docks, using such manpower and equipment as is available, including striking members of the International Longshoremen's and Warehousemen's Union, CIO, and personnel and equipment of struck concerns. The act will be in effect for 180 days.

Union Members Act Quickly

But even as the legislators were passing the measure they hope will bring an end to the current strike, members of the union were voting to refuse to return to work under the terms of the bill. In this they were backed up by their president, Harry Bridges, who flew here yesterday from San Francisco. Mr. Bridges announced that his union would also attack the constitutionality of the new measure.

The principal clauses of the bill are these:

1. The Governor is authorized to take over and operate the stevedoring industry and related facilities.

2. So far as is possible the Governor will employ the personnel of struck companies, including strikers at the prevailing wage rates prior to the strike.

3. The companies shall have ten days in which to take the option of accepting a fair rental on their equipment or the profits under governmental operation. This clause is modeled after the Massachusetts Utility Act.

4. If the companies elect to share in the profits of the operation the Territory will deduct an operating fee of one-fourth of 1 per cent. At about $1,500 a month based on operations here before the strike. A $250,000 revolving fund is set up to cover operations.

5. It will be unlawful to strike dur-

Continued on Page 51, Column 1

Bulgars Reshuffle Ministers in Cabinet

By The Associated Press.

SOFIA, Bulgaria, Aug. 6—Bulgaria got a new Foreign Minister and Minister of the Interior tonight.

Vassil Kolarov, who was named Premier July 20 to succeed the late Georgi Dimitrov, resigned his old post as Foreign Minister. The new Foreign Minister is Vladimir Poptomov, a member of the Bulgarian Politburo.

The Ministry of the Interior went to Russi Hristozov. He succeeds Anton Yugov, who remains a Deputy Premier.

Vulko Chervenkov was succeeded as President of the Culture, Science and Arts Commission by Karlo Lukanov. He remains a Vice Premier.

Cyril Lazarov who was named president of the State Planning Commission to succeed Dobri Tarpichev, who remains a Vice Premier.

Prof. Petko Kunin was named Finance Minister. He succeeds Ivan Stefanov. Vulko Gochov was named Minister of Industry, replacing Professor Kunin.

ARMS AID FATE TIED TO MILITARY HEADS

Tydings Says if They Justify Plan in Terms of Guns, Tanks, Congress Is Likely to Agree

By CHARLES HURD
Special to The New York Times.

WASHINGTON, Aug. 6—The fate of the $1,450,000,000 foreign military assistance program will rest on the justification this country's military leaders give for it, Senator Millard E. Tydings of Maryland, chairman of the Senate Armed Services Committee, predicted today.

"It's up to the Chiefs of Staff," he said, "to explain in terms of guns, tanks and planes the need for the full $1,450,000,000. I think the Congress will give them what they say is necessary to carry out the defense plan."

Not all members have shown agreement with Senator Tydings by any means, but his statement pointed up the interest with which the Senate is awaiting a first-hand report from the military leaders, who are in Europe. They are Gen. Omar N. Bradley, Army Chief of Staff; Admiral Louis Denfeld, Chief of Naval Operations, and Gen. Hoyt S. Vandenberg, Chief of Staff of the Air Force.

They are expected to return in time to testify on Wednesday before a joint session of the Senate Committees on Foreign Relations and the Armed Services.

A similar joint committee session

Continued on Page 2, Column 2

4 DEFENSE PLANS WEIGHED BY CHIEFS; MAIN TALKS ENDED

An Atlantic Defense Committee Would Direct Pact Signers Under Each Alternative

REGIONAL GROUPS FAVORED

U. S. Leaders Said to Support Idea Emphasizing 'Self-Help' —Head for Vienna Today

By BENJAMIN WELLES
Special to The New York Times.

LONDON, Aug. 6—The United States Joint Chiefs of Staff, currently in Europe discussing the future North Atlantic pact military organization with their European colleagues, are considering four alternative types of organization, it is authoritatively learned here.

Any one of these, if adopted by the twelve pact signatories, would be directed by an Atlantic Defense Committee based in Europe, on which all twelve powers would have their military representative. This committee would in turn be led by a small, tight knit Executive Committee of United States, Britain, probably Canadian and possibly French delegates. The question of French participation at this level is one of the principal problems facing the United States Chiefs in their talks in Europe.

Over the entire military setup, it is understood, would be an Atlantic Political Council, consisting of one political representative from each of the twelve powers and operating under the authority of Article 9 of the Atlantic pact.

Four Alternate Organizations

The four alternative defense organizations that the United States Chiefs are now considering are:

1. An expansion of the Western Union military organization, which at present consists of Britain, France, Belgium, the Netherlands and Luxembourg. The new organization would include the seven other Atlantic pact powers but it would necessitate altering the fifty-year Brussels Treaty, which is now the keystone of the Western Union.

2. A new military organism consisting of all twelve pact powers, who would create a common headquarters and draw up their defense plans there together.

3. An organization in which each of the twelve powers would draw up its own defense plans separately, sending them to the Atlantic Defense Committee for modification as needed and for

Continued on Page 2, Column 5

Communists Raise Land Tax A Hundredfold in Shanghai

By HENRY R. LIEBERMAN
Special to The New York Times.

SHANGHAI, Aug. 6—Both Chinese and foreign owners of property in Shanghai, accustomed to paying their taxes in depreciated currency under the Kuomintang, are rubbing their eyes at whopping bills now being rendered for land tax by the Communist Government here.

The land tax has been set at 100 times the standard values originally fixed for 1949 last November while the Kuomintang still controlled Shanghai. In addition to presenting bills on this basis for the next six months, the Communists have in a number of cases claimed arrears from institutions whose property formerly was exempt from taxation.

Foreign-owned mission property is subject to taxation. Still unsettled is the question of property owned by foreign consulates whose legal status is not recognized by the Communists in the absence of formal diplomatic relations. The United States consulate, it is reported, has received bills for a "house tax," but the bills have not yet been paid.

American School to Close

The Shanghai American School, heretofore exempt as an educational institution, was reported preparing to close today after having received a bill amounting to ¥76,000 (U. S.) to cover a land tax for the next six months plus alleged tax arrears.

British owners of the unused Shanghai race course, which did not reopen after VJ-Day, are wondering what to do about their own tax bill amounting to about $180,000. The race course is located inside the city. The Nationalists, who frowned upon horseracing from the standpoint of austerity, exempted

Continued on Page 7, Column 5

SYRIAN SYNAGOGUE BOMBED, 6 KILLED

Act in Damascus Held the Work of Terrorists Demonstrating Against Palestine Talks

By ALBION ROSS
Special to The New York Times.

BEIRUT, Lebanon, Aug. 6—Six or seven persons were killed and twenty-seven injured in the bombing last night of a synagogue in Damascus, Syria, by terrorists believed to have been demonstrating against the Palestine peace negotiations conducted by the United Nations Conciliation Commission in Lausanne, Switzerland.

The bomb, apparently handmade, was thrown into the entrance of the synagogue just as preparations were being made for the Sabbath Eve service. The building was damaged considerably and windows of other buildings in the vicinity were shattered.

The best guess seems to be that the fanatical son of a very wealthy family was responsible for the crime. He is understood to have set fire to a Jewish establishment in Damascus last year, but nothing serious came of it and the matter was ignored by the previous Gov-

Continued on Page 22, Column 1

World News Summarized

SUNDAY, AUGUST 7, 1949

The arrival in Washington tomorrow of President Quirino of the Philippines is expected to have a marked effect on the State Department's review of Far Eastern policy. President Quirino has long been a champion of a defense alliance in Southeast Asia to meet the threat of Communist aggression. The only official indication of what the United States may do in the event of such aggression was the emphasis placed in the China White Paper on containment of communism within China's boundaries. [1:8.]

Generalissimo Chiang Kai-shek flew to Korea with five top-ranking advisers to discuss with President Syngman Rhee the prospects for setting up such a Pacific pact against Communist aggression. [7:1.]

A fresh approach to United States policy in the Far East was urged by Senator Vandenberg as the State Department prepared to begin its review tomorrow. The Republican leader called the China White Paper a "post-mortem," valuable principally in avoiding past errors. [1:6-7.]

While the Chinese Nationalists declined to make official comment on the White Paper, considerable resentment over the document was expressed informally by subordinate officials. The Acheson report was attacked by Canton leaders as "a move to whitewash the State Department." [4:1.]

In Shanghai, foreign property owners found the Communist regime increasing land taxes as much as one hundred times the 1949 rates established by the Nationalist Government. [1:6-7.]

In Damascus, terrorists believed to be protesting the Palestine peace negotiations in Lausanne bombed a synagogue, killing a half-dozen persons and injuring twenty-seven. [1:7.]

Four alternate types of military organization to implement the Atlantic pact were reported to be under consideration by the United States Joint Chiefs of Staff. Any one of these would be under an Atlantic Defense Committee of all twelve pact signatories, which in turn would be led by an Executive Committee of the United States, Great Britain, probably Canada, and possibly France, it was reported. The inclusion of France in this group was held to be one of the major questions facing the United States officers during their European tour. [1:5.]

Passage of the Administration's $1,450,000,000 military aid program will depend directly on the evidence collected by the Joint Chiefs of Staff during their European tour, a Senate spokesman said. The three officers are expected to present their report to the Senate committees on Wednesday. [1:4.]

The Ford company launched an intensive campaign among 87,000 employes, seeking to persuade them to vote against a strike in tomorrow's election. The company utilized extensive radio and newspaper advertisements directed at labor. [1:2.]

The Governor of Hawaii has issued a proclamation of emergency in the ninety-eight-day-old dock strike, acting under a bill which he signed into law yesterday afternoon. The law empowers him to take possession of any or all stevedoring on the islands. [1-3.]

In this city the Third Avenue Transit Corporation received permission from the Public Service Commission to raise its bus fares from 7 to 8 cents, effective at 12:01 A. M. tomorrow. [1:1.]

5,000,000 More Fake 3c Stamps Found in Burlap Bags in Bronx Lot

Another cache of counterfeit three-cent stamps, this one totaling at least 5,000,000, was found yesterday in the Bronx, less than two blocks from where 2,000,000 had been discovered the day before.

The second batch was uncovered at 11 A. M. in a vacant lot along the East River near Whittier Street by Eddie De Fabrizio, 20 years old, a junkman, who was looking for saleable refuse.

He found four large burlap bags, similar to those used for potatoes, in a clump of weeds about fifteen feet in from the curb. Ten feet away he found three other burlap bags.

He called the police, who found in each bag two large bundles wrapped in heavy brown paper—the same sort of covering as on the stamps found the previous day. Inside the bundles were sheets of 100 three-cent stamps. The sheets were gummed, but not perforated. The stamps were copies of the usual purple three-cent stamp bearing a portrait of George Washington. They were identical with the stamps found on Friday.

A postal expert said he could not tell the counterfeit stamps from real ones when he examined them side by side, the police said.

Detectives John Mulcahy and Frank Morgal of the Simpson Street station estimated that yesterday's find totaled between 50,000 and 60,000 sheets of stamps. This number of bonafide three-cent stamps would be valued at $150,000 to $180,000.

The false stamps were taken at 9:10 P. M. by Secret Service agents to their headquarters at 90 Church Street.

Earlier in the day the Secret Service widened its investigation of counterfeit stamps and money

Continued on Page 37, Column 3

1,400 Dead in Ecuador Earthquake; New Shocks Cause Panic in Ambato

By The Associated Press.

Mounting reports from Ecuador's earthquake-ravaged area said late last night that more than 1,400 persons had been killed and thousands injured.

In one small town alone—Patate —more than 1,000 lost their lives.

The full extent of Friday's tragedy unfolded as additional disaster reports filtered through to the outside world over crippled communication lines.

Ecuadorean President Galo Plaza Lasso said in broadcast heard in Lima, Peru, that more than 1,000 were killed at Patate. He spoke from Ambato, where more than 400 were dead and 1,000 injured.

The Ecuadorean Embassy in Washington raised the Ambato figure, saying 500 were known dead there, and more than 2,000 injured.

New shocks were felt at Ambato at 8:10 A. M. and 10:33 A. M. (Eastern standard time) yesterday, the Shell Petroleum Company radio said in a report heard at Guayaquil, Ecuador. These shocks felled the walls of buildings already wrecked by the previous quakes and created considerable panic.

Latest reports from Quito, Ecuador, said at least twenty persons died in the town of Pillaro, which was leveled by the quake.

At Latacunga there were eleven known dead and thirty injured. Two churches, the government house and about fifty dwellings were destroyed.

Various sources reported the destruction of Salcedo. Damage also was believed heavy at Pujili, Banos, Pansaleo, Mocha, Guano, Cujibies, Squisili, Cevallos, Riobamba, Guaranda, San Andres, Cochimabama, Guamote and Santa Rosa.

The Governor of Chimborazo

Continued on Page 24, Column 2

DELEVISION—What to demand of the set you buy. For new sound advice, see the DuMont advertisement on Page 17 of today's New York Times Magazine.—Advt.

WHEN You Think of Writing Think of Whiting.—Advt.

United Press International

Blocks of stone strewn over what was a principal thoroughfare in Ambato, Ecuador.
The auto at left and truck at right were crushed to junk by the weight and force of stones
falling from surrounding buildings.

QUAKE TOLL RISES; NEW SHOCKS FELT

Continued from Page 1

Province reported many dead and injured in his capital city, Riobamba.

President Plaza and Interior Minister Salazar Gomez were in Ambato directing rescue work. All other Cabinet members were in Quito on twenty-four-hour duty coordinating relief operations

Thousands Are Homeless

QUITO, Ecuador, Aug. 6 (UP)— A rich farming and industrial area in central Ecuador dug out from its ruins today after a devastating earthquake that left 30,000 homeless in its wake.

An intensity of 8 degrees in the Sieberg scale, only 2 degrees below the maximum intensity, was recorded in the earth shocks.

A local radio station estimated that the death toll might reach 2,000, and said the stricken area now was menaced by floods of the Ambato River, dammed by landslides.

Ambato, garden spot of Ecuador, is 8,382 feet above sea level, in an Andean valley, surrounded by large fruit and vegetable orchards. It also was fast becoming one of the country's chief industrial centers.

Disaster struck also in the heart of a densely populated farming area. The towns of Banos, Guano, Mocha and Pelileo were hit almost as hard as Ambato.

Everywhere roads were clogged with fleeing human columns. They moved without knowing where they were going. Many fell by the roadside exhausted. Plazas and parks were jammed.

Because of the fear of epidemics bodies were buried as fast as possible in huge trenches. Others were cremated.

In Ambato 30 per cent of all public and private buildings were estimated to have been destroyed completely; 60 per cent were made unusable and the remainder were cracked but still inhabitable.

Five Ambato textile mills were destroyed; the roof and walls collapsed over the works; damage was estimated at $2,000,000.

The Quito-Guayaquil railway, chief communication artery in the country, was severed at many places. Luis Cordovez, president of the line, said there were twenty-seven landslides in a stretch of ten miles south of Ambato. It would take at least two weeks to clear them up, he estimated.

Scores of automobiles and trucks parked along the curbs, especially in the downtown section of Ambato, were crushed by the falling buildings.

Special civil guard platoons kept looters from the ruins, with orders to shoot on sight.

Ambato was without electricity, and all rescue work, including emergency surgical operations, was carried out by lantern light.

New York-born President Galo Plaza Lasso assumed personal command of relief operations. He set his headquarters in an army tent in the main Ambato plaza, with a staff of 200 doctors and scores of nurses and aides.

He also asked every able-bodied person to donate blood to the local blood bank.

Offers of cooperation came immediately from the governments of unscathed towns; local newspapers organized public subscriptions for the survivors; foreign diplomats from neighboring countries offered to rush doctors, plasma, medicines and other necessities by plane.

Private airlines placed their planes at the Government's disposal.

Seven Army transport planes were used as ambulances to bring the most seriously injured to Quito hospitals. More than 100 of them were moved during the day.

Luis Mena, director of the Quito Observatory, said the quake was of tectonic nature, its epicenter located some 100 miles south of Quito.

Señor Mena said he believed the quake was caused by the displacement of huge masses of rock in the high Andes.

34 Rescuers Die in Crash

QUITO, Ecuador, Aug. 6 (UP)— Thirty-four persons were killed today when a Shell Oil Company plane, flying rescue workers from Mera Nueve to the earthquake-stricken city of Ambato, crashed in the mountains twenty miles from Ambato. Most of the victims were employes of the Shell Oil Company. The wildness of the terrain at the scene of the crash forced rescue workers to postpone efforts to recover the bodies until tomorrow.

U. S. Red Cross Offers Aid

WASHINGTON, Aug. 6 (AP)— Basil O'Connor, president of the American National Red Cross, cabled the Red Cross Society of Ecuador that medical supplies and food would be sent to the stricken area if needed. He asked for a report on the damage done.

"All the News That's Fit to Print"

The New York Times.

LATE CITY EDITION
Mostly sunny today, warm tonight.
Occasional showers tomorrow.
Temperature Range Today-Max., 79; Min., 64
Temperatures Yesterday—Max., 76; Min., 66
U. S. Weather Bureau Report, Sect. 3; Page 10

Section 1

NEWS INDEX, PAGE 95, THIS SECTION

Copyright, 1949, by The New York Times Company.

VOL. XCIX..No. 33,475. Entered as Second-Class Matter. Postoffice, New York, N. Y. NEW YORK, SUNDAY, SEPTEMBER 18, 1949. Including Magazine and Book Review. FIFTEEN CENTS New York City / 50 Mile Zone { Elsewhere Twenty Cents

207 LOST AS A CRUISE SHIP BURNS IN NIGHT FIRE AT TORONTO PIER; SCORES LEAP OFF; 110 IN HOSPITALS

12 NATIONS CREATE A DEFENSE SYSTEM FOR ATLANTIC PACT

U. S. to Participate 'Actively' in the Military Plans for Safeguarding Europe

DECISIONS TAKEN SWIFTLY

Council Is Formally Set Up—Regional Groupings Are Backbone of Program

Text of the communique on the North Atlantic Council, Page 3.

By WALTER H. WAGGONER
Special to THE NEW YORK TIMES.

WASHINGTON, Sept. 17—The twelve nations bound by the North Atlantic pact created the framework of a Western military organization today in which the United States would participate "actively" in the defense planning of Europe.

The foreign ministers of the signatory nations of the treaty, forming a North Atlantic Council, voted in a brief routine meeting also to establish a Defense Committee comprising the defense ministers of all the member nations and a Military Committee on which all the chiefs of staff or their equivalent would be represented.

The only task of selection was in the naming of a central or "Standing Group" in the Military Committee consisting of the United States, Britain and France. This would in effect be the unit seeing to it that the work of the all-member Military Committee was accomplished.

The Military Committee's particular tasks would be general policy guidance for the whole organization and recommendations to the Defense Committee for "military measures for the unified defense of the North Atlantic area."

U. S. in the Key Role

The United States will occupy a singularly key role for a non-European nation in the military defense of Europe not only by its membership on the three-member "Standing Group" of the Military Committee but also by virtue of a special request to "participate actively" in the security planning of the five Brussels Pact countries that otherwise comprise the Western European regional defense planning group.

Canada also was included in the request, which, according to a communiqué issued at the conclusion of the meeting, said that the two North American members "have been requested and have agreed to participate actively in the defense planning as appropriate."

A group of United States officers, however, has been attending the Western Nations military planning sessions, which are under the command of Field Marshal Viscount Montgomery at Fontainebleau, but their positions have been those of observers only.

Except for the planning and coordinating assigned to the "Standing Group," the basic work of the North Atlantic defense organization will be handled by five planning groups embracing the geo-

Continued on Page 4, Column 3

Major Sports News

BASEBALL

The Yanks protected their two-and-a-half-game American League pennant lead yesterday by defeating the Tigers, 5 to 4. The second-place Red Sox downed the Browns, 3—2. In the National League, the Dodgers lost to the Pirates, 7—2, but remained two and a half games behind the leading Cards, who were beaten by the Braves, 4 to 2.

GOLF

United States pros took six of eight singles matches from the British to retain the Ryder Cup by a final score of 7 to 5. Lloyd Mangrum of Chicago beat Fred Daly, British match play champion, 4 and 3, in the closing match. Mrs. Dorothy Germain Porter won the women's national title by defeating Miss Dorothy Kielty, 3 and 2.

HORSE RACING

Miss Request, paying $14.40, won the Beldame Handicap at Aqueduct. Harmonica finished second, but was disqualified and placed out of the money. Plunder was advanced to second and Mother to third. Donor took the Narragansett Special by a head over Vulcan's Forge, with Ponder, 1-to-2 favorite, third. Donor paid $17.60.

[Full details in Section 5.]

A High Czech Cleric Held to Aid Regime

Special to THE NEW YORK TIMES.

PRAGUE, Czechoslovakia, Sept. 17 — Dr. Frantisek Onderik, Apostolic Administrator at Cesky Tesin (Teschen), has issued a statement approving the Government's proposed new church law despite the fact that it has been condemned as unacceptable by the rest of the Catholic hierarchy, the official Czechoslovak news agency announced tonight.

If this is confirmed, it would represent the first major breach in the solid front of the Roman Catholic Church hierarchy opposing the Government's efforts to bring the church under its control.

Although he does not have the title of Bishop, Dr. Onderik is a member of the Council of Bishops and has signed all recent pastoral letter circulars to the clergy, including the memorandum to the Government drawn up by the Bishops at Trnava on Aug. 14. His name appears last on the list of signers, as "Apostolic Administrator of the Czech Part of Vreclau Archdiocese (Tesin)." The rest of the Archdiocese is in Poland.

AID TO CHIANG VAIN, U. S., BRITAIN AGREE

French Join in Pessimism—Loss of Formosa to the Reds Is Expected Now

Special to THE NEW YORK TIMES.

WASHINGTON, Sept. 17 — The foreign policy spokesmen of the United States and Britain presented individual but almost uniformly gloomy appraisals of the Chinese situation today in a discussion of Far Eastern affairs with France.

Secretary of State Dean Acheson and British Foreign Secretary Ernest Bevin met with French Foreign Minister Robert Schuman this afternoon in a second meeting in Mr. Acheson's office for the purpose of consolidating their views, if possible, on the major foreign policy issues of the world that will face the General Assembly of the United Nations opening Tuesday.

A brief communiqué issued jointly by the three principals after their talk said only that they had exchanged views "on matters of concern to the three governments in the Far East."

"As a result of this exchange," the statement continued, "the Ministers found that their views on

Continued on Page 12, Column 3

World News Summarized

SUNDAY, SEPTEMBER 18, 1949

Fire roared through the Great Lakes cruise steamship Noronic at her Toronto pier early yesterday morning when nearly all of the 511 passengers and most of the crew aboard were asleep, and exacted a fearful toll. Late in the day 207 persons had been listed as dead or missing. [1:8.] Survivors agreed that fire warnings had been too tardy to get most of the sleeping passengers out of their rooms safely. [1:5-6.] Mourning relatives and friends of the victims, many of whom were holidaymakers from Detroit and Cleveland, converged upon the scene of the tragedy, traveling by planes, trains and buses to get to Toronto as quickly as possible. [1:7.]

The twelve nations allied under the North Atlantic treaty met in Washington and agreed to form a Defense Committee of all the defense ministers of the member nations and a Military Committee that would include all the Chiefs of Staff or their equivalent. The committees have the task of planning the defense of Western Europe. The United States will participate "actively" in the program. This nation was named with Britain and France to a three-member Standing Group in the Military Committee that has the task in effect of supervising the work of the Military Committee. [1:1.]

Secretary of State Acheson, British Foreign Secretary Bevin and French Foreign Minister Schuman held a private conference on the Far East. Mr. Acheson and Mr. Bevin agreed, it was reported, that at the present time there were no Nationalist groupings left in China worth supporting. [1:2.]

In the Budapest treason trial one of the defendants, Lazar Brankov, the former counselor of the Yugoslav Legation in Moscow, testified that Winston Churchill was one of the leaders among British, Americans and Yugoslavs who had plotted to seize the Balkans. He maintained that Americans and Britons had promised military support to Marshal Tito if the Yugoslav leader would take up arms against the Soviet Union as part of the alleged plot to take over Eastern Europe. [9:1.]

The Senate Foreign Relations and Armed Services Committees estimated that the Soviet Union had more than 5,000,000 men under arms, in a formal joint report on the $1,414,010,000 foreign military aid bill. [1:6-7.]

The 480,000 members of the United Mine Workers appeared headed for a new strike under the slogan of "no welfare, no work," although John L. Lewis had issued no official strike call. District officials of the union reported that the miners were "boiling mad" because of the suspension of pension and medical payments and predicted that all coal mines would be shut by Wednesday. [1:3.]

The prospects of achieving a peaceful solution for the other strike threat overhanging the nation, that in the steel industry, took a gloomier turn as President Philip Murray of the United Steelworkers of America, CIO, charged the steel companies were reluctant to grant modest pensions to their workers while extending generous retirement benefits ranging up to $100,000 a year to their top executives. [1:4.]

In this city, President Michael J. Quill of the Transport Workers Union, CIO, expressed deep dissatisfaction with the attitude of the Board of Transportation toward union demands for more pay and shorter hours of work and warned that there might be a slowdown in the city's subway operations within two or three weeks. [1:5.]

COAL STRIKE LOOMS ON ISSUE OF ENDING PENSION PAYMENTS

Owners See 'Familiar Pattern' in Early Walkouts That May Be Complete by Wednesday

'NO WELFARE, NO WORK'

New Slogan Rouses Workers, With Anthracite Miners Also Reported Ready to Quit

By A. H. RASKIN
Special to THE NEW YORK TIMES.

PITTSBURGH, Sept. 17—"No welfare, no work" became the slogan of the nation's coal miners today as indications poured in from all parts of the country that a new strike by the 480,000 members of John L. Lewis' United Mine Workers was on.

There was still no official strike call from Mr. Lewis's headquarters in Washington, but district officials in many areas reported that the miners were "boiling mad" over the suspension of pension and medical payments by the United Mine Workers Welfare Fund. The district leaders predicted that few miners would be in the pits Monday and that virtually all the mines would be shut by Wednesday.

Operators called it the start of "a familiar pattern," with the union ordering a general strike under the guise of a spontaneous walkout by the miners. They accused Mr. Lewis of "steaming up" the men by making it appear that the shortage of welfare funds stemmed from the refusal of some large southern operators to continue their royalty payments of 20 cents a ton.

Northern mine owners, who have had little sympathy for the course followed by the southern group in its negotiations with Mr. Lewis, maintained that the union's efforts to shift the onus to the operators was "a smoke screen."

The owners said the fault lay with Mr. Lewis, both because he had cut the fund's income through his own imposition of a three-day work-week and because he had brushed aside employer warnings that he was establishing pensions and other benefits on a basis too generous for the industry to bear.

The northern operators are scheduled to make their monthly remittance of about $3,000,000 to the welfare fund on Tuesday. Some owners favor withholding the money if the miners quit work,

Continued on Page 64, Column 3

FATAL FLAMES LIGHT CRUISE VESSEL AT CANADIAN BERTH

The Canadian Steamship Lines steamer Noronic burning at her Lake Ontario pier in Toronto
Associated Press Wirephoto

'DOUBLE STANDARD' CHARGED TO STEEL

Murray Says Companies Pay for Executives' Pensions but Bar Funds to CIO

Special to THE NEW YORK TIMES.

PITTSBURGH, Sept. 17—The hopes of Federal mediators for averting a national steel strike received another jolt tonight when Philip Murray, president of the United Steelworkers of America, CIO, accused the industry of applying a double standard in pensions for workers and pensions for executives.

In a statement buttressed with figures credited to the files of the Securities and Exchange Commission, Mr. Murray asserted that steel companies had set up pension systems under which their top executives would receive retirement benefits ranging up to $100,000 a year without any contribution by the executives themselves.

Deriding the industry's contention that it was "socialistic" for President Truman's Steel Fact-Finding Board to recommend that employers pay the full cost of pensions and social insurance, Mr. Murray said:

"A study of the steel companies' own official statements filed with SEC is truly an exposé of the inconsistent position of the steel industry. It resolves itself to this: For an official of a company to receive a pension paid for solely by the company is a good thing. For the worker to receive the same benefits is a 'loss of his freedom.'"

Capital Parley Tomorrow

The Murray statement was issued as company and union officials were preparing to leave this steel center to attend a Government-sponsored peace conference in Washington Monday. Most company offices were closed when the latest union attack was released, so there was no immediate comment from industry leaders.

Virtually all the large steel companies have informed the union that they believed workers should share in the cost of their own pensions and social insurance. United States Steel Corporation characterized the Truman board's proposal that employers bear the whole cost as a "revolutionary doctrine." Similar expressions have been made by the other companies.

The companies contend that noncontributory welfare funds are wrong in principle because they strip the individual of any responsibility for his own future security. The companies also feel that there will be no ceiling to union demands for liberalization of

Continued on Page 61, Column 1

ARCO—"Rules the World"—Rulers, Sandwiches for School—Office—Home.—ADV.

Survivors Say That Alarm, If Sounded, Came Too Late

By AUSTIN STEVENS
Special to THE NEW YORK TIMES.

TORONTO, Sept. 17—Most of those who perished when flames enveloped the pleasure steamer Noronic early this morning never left their tiny staterooms. At 1 o'clock a dance had ended, the bar had closed down and late merrymakers had retired. Hundreds of others had gone to their rooms hours before and were sound asleep when the cries of "Fire!" were heard.

Conflicting on details, survivors were in agreement on one thing—whatever alarm had been sounded came late.

If an alarm bell was sounded, few heard it. Those who reached the pier safely recounted that in most cases they had been awakened by screams or by the few passengers who were awake and who did what they could do to rouse others, before scrambling oversides on ramps or rope ladders.

As the flames roared down the narrow passageways in a ship that had been designed with the greatest space devoted to its public rooms, passengers said, they found no one of the crew to direct them to exits. Passengers who boarded the steamer at Cleveland said there had been no fire drill.

A former assistant purser, however, said emphatically there was

Continued on Page 39, Column 1

SLOWDOWN THREAT RENEWED BY QUILL

Unless 'Package' Demands Are Met, He Tells TWU Rally, Subway Trains Will Crawl

By STANLEY LEVEY

Michael J. Quill, president of the Transport Workers Union, CIO, threatened yesterday a slowdown on the city's subway lines in "two or three weeks."

He told 1,500 union members packed in front of the offices of the Board of Transportation at 250 Hudson Street that unless the board acts affirmatively on the TWU's 1949 "package" demands the situation "will get out of hand."

The rally, which had been expected to bring out 10,000 persons, was called to force approval of the union program first presented to the board more than three months ago.

A report made public yesterday by the Board of Transportation for the first year of operation under the 10-cent fare cast doubt on the possibility of a pay rise in 1949 for city transit employes. Revenues exceeded operating expenses by $13,353,085, but after applying $11,067,500 to outstanding budget notes issued in 1947 and 1948 to cover old deficits of the city system, the remaining surplus revenue totaled only $2,285,585.

Contents of the "Package"

The "package," whose total cost has been estimated at $72,000,000, includes the following points:

Reduction in the hourly work-week from forty-eight to forty with no loss in pay; an additional wage increase of 21 cents an hour; three weeks' vacation instead of two, eleven holidays instead of seven and other concessions.

These are substantially the same demands made of private bus companies. In the case of the private lines, the union's program is now in arbitration. Sidney Sugerman, former chairman of the National Wage Stabilization Board for New York and New Jersey, is the arbitrator. Dr. Emanuel Stein is hearing the case involving the union and the Third Avenue Transit System.

John J. Woods, deputy commissioner of transportation, is reportedly preparing an analysis of the

Continued on Page 60, Column 5

VICTIMS' KIN TAX TRAVEL FACILITIES

Extra Planes and Trains Rush Relatives, Many From Detroit and Cleveland, to Scene

Cleveland and Detroit echoed the tragedy of the Toronto ship fire yesterday as relatives and friends sought to get transportation to the scene. Many of the victims came from those two cities.

Trans-Canada Airlines used every available plane on a shuttle service between Windsor, Ont., and Toronto, on a one-hour schedule. The Canadian Pacific and Canadian National Railways added extra coaches to their trains for the 200-mile journey. In Detroit, Charles E. Wilson, president of General Motors, sent his private transport plane to Toronto with doctors, nurses, and medical equipment.

In Cleveland, the American Red Cross used casualty lists as a basis for plane priorities. Relatives of the dead and seriously injured left the city by plane, while relatives of the less seriously injured were routed to trains and buses.

Private cars in steady streams choked the Detroit-Windsor Tunnel and the Ambassador Bridge

Continued on Page 43, Column 1

Russia Has 5 Million in Military, Senate Is Told in Arms Aid Report

By JOHN D. MORRIS
Special to THE NEW YORK TIMES.

WASHINGTON, Sept. 17—Russia has more than 5,000,000 men under arms and is constantly increasing her military strength, the Senate Foreign Relations and Armed Services committees reported today.

That appraisal of the Soviet Union's war potential was given by the committees in their formal joint report on the $1,414,010,000 foreign military assistance bill, which the Senate is scheduled to take up Monday. The strength of United States armed forces is 1,616,600.

In the face of the Soviet armed power, the committees stated, the military assistance program "cannot possibly provide the strength required to undertake aggression."

Thus, despite contentions that it marks the beginning of United States participation in a global armament race, "the program is wholly defensive in nature."

"The United States," the report added, "remains committed to the purposes and principles of the United Nations and is fully ready to cooperate in any program of armament regulation worked out by the United Nations, as again stated in the present bill, if such program will provide adequate safeguards to assure the observance by all parties of any resolution or convention restricting armaments.

"It has been Soviet intransigence, not a reluctance on the part of the United States, which has so far prevented the accomplishment of such a program."

There is no intention under the arms bill to build up military forces comparable to Russia's, the report emphasized.

"That nation," it said, "has consistently maintained the largest military force in the post-war world, with over 5,000,000 men under arms.

"It has increased its military budget for 1949 by 19 per cent over that of 1948; there has been progress in the training of troops—the ground forces are estimated to be in better condition than at any time since the war; it has increased the security measures along its borders and the borders of its satellites.

"The Soviet force in Germany

Continued on Page 12, Column 1

WHEN You Think of Writing Think of Whiting.—Advt.

373 ESCAPE BLAZE

Passengers Are Roused by Flames Starting Near Vessel's Bar

FIGHT THEIR WAY TO DECK

Noronic, Largest Pleasure Ship on Lakes, Was Making Season's Last Trip

By ALEXANDER FEINBERG
Special to THE NEW YORK TIMES.

TORONTO, Sept. 17—The Noronic, largest passenger ship on the Great Lakes, burned at her pier early today in one of the worst disasters of North American maritime history. It was feared that 207 persons had perished in the blaze that swept the 6,905-ton vessel from stem to stern in fifteen minutes after a fire was discovered on C deck aft, near the ship's bar, at 2:38 A. M.

The known toll of lives was 112, with ninety-five more persons missing and believed dead. Of those aboard the ship, including 511 passengers, 110 persons were hospitalized at first and 373 escaped, many of these suffering injuries regarded as slight.

With the ship's hull completely burned out, the shell of what had been the pride of the lake fleet lay in thirty feet of water at Queen's Quay. Drawing twenty-five feet she sank to a depth of five feet by the stern.

Pumping Effort Fails

A day's effort of pumping had failed to lift two of her five decks out of the water. An exhausted army of rescuers had given up by 1:30 P. M. the grim labor of extricating all the bodies they could reach. Of those listed as missing most were believed to have drowned.

Canada Steamship Lines issued a passenger list late this afternoon which showed that 324 persons had boarded the cruise ship at Cleveland and 187 persons at Detroit. The vessel, making her last cruise of the summer, had docked here at 6 P. M. yesterday.

First, passengers were picked up at Detroit. Then she made her way across Lake Erie to Cleveland where the majority of the holiday voyagers embarked, proceeding down the Welland Canal and across Lake Ontario to Toronto.

The cruise was to have continued to Prescott, Ont., and the Thousand Islands. The steamer had been scheduled to leave her berth here at 7 o'clock tonight.

Passengers Were Asleep

Terror-stricken passengers, many of them roused from their sleep and clad in night garments, fought their way to what they believed was the sanctuary of the decks. They found the decks ablaze.

Some teetered on the edge of the railings, then leaped overboard. Others stood rooted in fear. Still others slid down ropes and hawsers.

Through the flaming circles of the portholes, helpless observers saw panicky faces appear, disappear and reappear.

The splash of passengers jumping into the water provided a strange accompaniment to the ship's whistle which kept blowing incessantly.

The frenzied holiday-makers rushed to the starboard side and this weight caused the vessel to list so that her superstructure crashed into the pier.

So quickly did the blaze spread that there was no time to get the lifeboats off their davits. They still hung there tonight, charred, with the exception of one boat that lay half-submerged.

The first firemen on the scene, responding, from all accounts, to an alarm sounded on shore, were from the Adelaide Street fire station. Survivors insisted that the ship's alarm had not been sounded until some time after the vessel was ablaze.

Fifty pieces of apparatus, marshalled by the City of Toronto, battled the flames. Firemen threw aerial ladders to the ship making a bridge to safety for many of the

Continued on Page 41, Column 3

"LEARN THE FACTS OF LUGGAGE" Read the Amelia Earhart Luggage advertisement—Page 23, this section.—Advt.

Rescue workers removing bodies from *Noronic*.

Wide World Photos

207 LOST AS SHIP ON CRUISE BURNS

Continued from Page 1

trapped passengers. One ladder snapped in two and half a dozen persons were plunged into the water.

A raft was standing by and those who had fallen from the broken ladder and some of those who had leaped to escape the flames made for it. Then the firemen turned another of their ladders downward to the raft and the survivors climbed up to the dock.

At least five separate explosions were heard as the flames continued to sweep the ship. Until 3:25 A. M., the fire appeared to be largely confined to the deck level but a short time after that, flames were seen reddening the portholes.

Other Ships Moved

The steamships Cayuga and Kingston, tied on the east side of Pier 9, were moved to safety out into Toronto Bay. They had been on the opposite side of the Noronic's berth, at the same pier. Flames burned the pier planking and scorched the roof and a sign over the pier offices.

Many of the victims were trapped in their cabins while asleep. Others were in the cocktail bar where the first blaze was reported. Survivors said that late parties had been in progress, both at the bar and in some staterooms.

Anxious relatives clustered on the dockside questioning crew members about the fate of their kin. Inquiries flooded newspaper offices here. In the absence of an official passenger list, the newspapers compiled their own from the inquiries, checking these names against the names of those reported dead, injured or escaped.

The dead were brought to the Horticultural Building of the Canadian National Exhibition, where an emergency morgue was set up.

Injured passengers were taken to Western, St. Michael's, Wellesley and General Hospitals. Other survivors were brought to the King Edward, Royal York and other Toronto hotels.

Capt. William Taylor of Sarnia, Ont., home port of the ill-fated ship, got off safely after rousing as many passengers as he could reach. His crew also debarked safely. Best available reports, however, were that only a skeleton crew had been aboard.

Three Investigations Set

Three investigations were launched into the fire that destroyed the $5,000,000 liner. The Dominion Department of Transport appointed Capt. W. N. Morrison of Toronto to conduct a preliminary inquiry. Capt. Sam Hill of the Toronto Fire Marshal's Department, opened a second inquiry and Chief Coroner Smirle Lawson was holding an inquest on the deaths.

A sister ship of the Noronic, the Hamonic, burned near Sarnia in 1945. One person was killed and 325 were rescued. The Noronic was built in 1913 at Port Arthur, Ont., and with this trip would have completed her thirty-sixth year of lake cruises.

The Canadian Red Cross, the Salvation Army, the Toronto Corps, and other welfare organizations rushed their forces to the scene of the disaster. They were joined by clergymen of all denominations who comforted the bereaved. The St. John Ambulance Corps, an organization of volunteers, set up a first-aid station. Fifty nursing sis-

ROUTE OF ILL-FATED CRUISE SHIP

The New York Times   Sept. 18, 1949.

The Noronic burned and sank, with a heavy loss of life, while berthed at Toronto (cross) on her way from Detroit and Cleveland. She was on a voyage to the Thousand Islands.

ters and fifty men of the corps established an emergency 100-cot hospital within three hours.

Red Cross to Aid Victims

From Washington, the American Red Cross dispatched Colin Herrle, its national disaster director, to Toronto. It was announced that the Red Cross would make funds available to aid the families of victims.

St. Michael's Hospital, to which many of the injured were removed, was like a battle station. Its emergency ward was filled. Friends and relatives added to the crowding.

The survivors told tales of horror, confusion and heroism. Several of the injured told of a crew member who had helped passengers down the ropes while he stood on the top deck with flames all around him. A doctor's assistant was cited by others, who said she had gone from cabin to cabin breaking windows to help the people get out.

Neither officials nor survivors could account for the quick spread of the flames. Some crew members said there had been a "bad slip-up" in the fire alarm system, and fire officials indicated that a delay in sounding a shore alarm had been occasioned by the ship's officers trying themselves to fight the fire.

Those who knew the Noronic declared, however, that the ship had seemed almost "fireproof." They said that the fire-fighting equipment had been constantly inspected, that hose lines had been ample and that fire extinguishers and other fire-fighting equipment had been liberally placed through the corridors.

The United States consul here, H. Earle Russell, said he had notified Washington authorities of the disaster because most of the passengers were United States nationals.

Mr. Russell declared he did not intend to make a separate investigation into the fire, saying, "I believe the investigation is in very capable hands right now."

"All the News That's Fit to Print"

The New York Times.

LATE CITY EDITION
Foggy, some drizzle early today, showers later, ending tomorrow.
Temperature Range Today—Max., 71; Min., 59
Temperatures Yesterday—Max., 73; Min., 57
Full U. S. Weather Bureau Report, Page 47

Copyright, 1950, by The New York Times Company.

VOL. XCIX No. 33,725. Entered as Second-Class Matter, Post Office, New York, N. Y. NEW YORK, FRIDAY, MAY 26, 1950. Times Square, New York 18, N. Y. Telephone Lackawanna 4-1000 FIVE CENTS

BROOKLYN TUNNEL COSTING $80,000,000 OPENED BY MAYOR

Woman Pays First Toll After 72-Mile-an-Hour Ride With Husband on Motorcycle

10,563 CROSS IN 5½ HOURS

Cerémonies Honor Moses, Who Still Insists Bridge Would Have Been Better Deal

By JOSEPH C. INGRAHAM

The Brooklyn-Battery Tunnel was opened to traffic yesterday ten years after President Franklin D. Roosevelt broke ground for the $80,000,000 project.

Thousands of persons in the skyscrapers rimming the Manhattan plaza of the longest, deepest and most costly vehicular crossing in the United States, dropped torn paper and ticker tape as Mayor O'Dwyer cut the gold-colored ribbon stretched across the west tube of the facility at 11:37 A. M. to open the of [illegible] fast new [illegible] under the mouth of the East River.

Then the Mayor, Cardinal Spellman, Robert Moses, chairman of the Triborough Bridge and Tunnel Authority, which completed the city's most ambitious post-war project, and Mrs. Moses, led a motorcade of 338 cars through the 9,117-foot long tube.

At 12:25 P. M. wooden barriers across the Manhattan entrance on West Street were removed. One minute later the procedure was repeated at the Brooklyn side. The time difference was a sporting gesture on the part of George E. Spargo, general manager of the authority, to make more even the race for the honor of paying the first toll, as the eleven collection booths are at the Brooklyn end.

Woman Pays First Toll

The distinction of starting the mammoth tunnel on its way to realizing its heavy cost went to Fortunate Conti. She nervously leaned from the motorcycle her husband, Charles Conti, was piloting and at 12:28 P. M. dropped a begrimed quarter into the hand of Herman Liebowitz, the collector.

Mrs. Conti's nervousness was understandable. It was her first trip on her husband's month-old motorcycle and she made it solely on his promise of trying to be the first to traverse the bore from Manhattan to Brooklyn, she said.

At about the same time the driver of a Brooklyn bakery panel truck out-maneuvered eight other vehicles to shoot through the east tube to Manhattan. Without taking his foot off the "gas" the bakery driver whizzed past the toll booth, slapped 35 cents into the dazed collector's hand and was on his way without bothering to identify himself.

The Contis were more cooperative. Flagged down by a tunnel officer, they obligingly paused on their way to their home at 64 Bay Eighth Street, Brooklyn, and explained how they had out-distanced others vying for the honor. It was simple, said Mr. Conti, a 32-year old printer. "I went through the tunnel at 72 miles an hour." The legal speed limit is forty miles.

Brewery Truck Also a "First"

The first "pay-load" through the tunnel was hauled by the driver of a brewery truck who started from Newark Wednesday. He waited patiently through the night until the tube was opened to keep his promise to a customer to be the first to bring him his beverage by way of the short, fast link between the tip of Manhattan and Red Hook.

The truckman, James Carovillano of Rutherford, N. J., was the first of an estimated 150,000 commercial users that will travel the underwater crossing during the next twelve months. The tunnel will cut the running time between the waterfront areas of Brooklyn and Manhattan by thirty-five minutes, saving truckers $1,000,000 annually. Truck tolls range from 35 cents to $1.25, depending on weight and size.

In addition, an estimated 9,000,000 passenger-car operators, who will pay more than $3,000,000 into the authority coffers this year, at the rate of 35 cents a trip, now can move free of traffic lights from the West Side Highway through the Belt Parkway.

The first mad dash for fleeting glory over, vehicles flowed through the twin tubes at a steady, fast-moving pace. At 6 P. M. the automatic counters showed that the four-lane facility had attracted 10,563 cars, vans and motorcycles. The traffic, Mr. Spargo said, about equaled that through the 10-year-

Continued on Page 3, Column 1

WRECKED CHICAGO TROLLEY IN WHICH MANY DIED

Firemen looking for victims in street car following collision with gasoline truck (on right)
Associated Press Wirephoto

33 Burn to Death in Chicago As Street Car Hits 'Gas' Truck

Special to THE NEW YORK TIMES.

CHICAGO, May 25—At least thirty-three persons died and twenty-four were injured, four critically, tonight in the flaming crash of a crowded street car and a double trailer gasoline truck near Sixty-third and State Streets on Chicago's South Side.

Thousands of gallons of gasoline poured out of the torn sides of the trailers, engulfing the street car in flames and setting fire to several automobiles and eight buildings.

Officials feared that other bodies would be found in the ruins of five buildings that were destroyed on the east side of State Street. Many persons were dining when the disaster occurred at 6:30 P. M., and it was believed some might have been trapped in their apartments. Three other buildings were damaged.

Thirty-two persons died in the street car, which was one of the new streamlined type. They died in a mass near the exits as they tried to escape.

Only one tentative identification was made among the victims on the street car. A charred bill found in the pockets of a man identified him as John E. Storey. Another victim was believed to have been Paul Manning, 42 years old, motorman of the car. William Lidell, 29, the conductor, escaped with some other passengers by climbing through a rear window.

Police were told that the truck, loaded with 7,000 to 8,000 gallons of gasoline, was driven by Mel Wilson, an employe of the Sprout & Davis Company of Whiting, Ind., which owned the truck. He died in the cab of the truck that jack-knifed in the northbound traffic lane, about 200 feet north of Sixty-third Street. The street car came to rest diagonally across the street.

The victims' bodies were put temporarily on the sidewalk when firemen were able to enter the charred street car after playing streams of water on it for almost an hour.

Later the bodies were removed to the Cook County Morgue, where the difficult task of identification was begun. Because of the charred condition of the bodies and destruction of wallets and identifying papers, it was feared weeks might be needed before identification was completed.

The crash occurred as the street car, moving south on State Street,

Continued on Page 24, Column 2

NO PAY RISE IN '50, TEACHERS ARE TOLD

Mayor Says He Won't Confer With Them Until They End Their 'Horsewhip' Strike

Declaring that he could do nothing this year to raise teachers' salaries because there was no money available, Mayor O'Dwyer said yesterday that he would not discuss the matter with the teachers until they ended their extra-curricular work stoppage.

Speaking at the Public Education Association's fifty-fifth annual meeting in the Cosmopolitan Club, 122 East Sixty-sixth Street, the Mayor accused the teachers of using their walkout, in effect since April 17, as a "horsewhip to get money that isn't there."

He charged that the Board of Education, because of its failure to halt the walkout, was poorly administered. Among the 100 persons who heard his remarks were Maximilian Moss, president of the board, and Dr. William Jansen, Superintendent of Schools, who have been at odds over the handling of the situation.

Mr. O'Dwyer spoke extemporaneously for twenty-five minutes. Before his arrival, Mr. Moss read a speech prepared for Mr. O'Dwyer in which the Mayor reiterated his contention that the board should be fiscally independent and that its members should be elected by the people. At present board members are appointed by the Mayor for seven-year terms.

After telling his listeners that his mother and father had been teachers and that five members of his family were still teaching, Mr. O'Dwyer said that although his sympathies were with the teachers he considered their stoppage of after-school services to children

Continued on Page 21, Column 7

TRUCKERS APPROVE A NO-STRIKE PACT

4-Year Contract to Be Signed With Union Here Expected to End Tie-Ups, Restore Trade

By A. H. RASKIN

The last obstacle to a four-year no-strike pact in the city's strife-ridden general trucking industry was removed yesterday. Approval by a committee representing 1,800 trucking employers cleared the way for formal signing of the contract early next week.

City officials joined representatives of union and management in voicing the hope that the peace plan would eliminate tie-ups in what has been one of the most turbulent sections of New York's economic life and thus stem the diversion of export and import trade to other ports.

Strikes in 1946 and 1948 halted the movement of food, medical supplies, newsprint and merchandise of all kinds. These strikes caused losses estimated at several hundred million dollars and left a permanent heritage of unemployment for many truck drivers.

Local 807 of the International Brotherhood of Teamsters, A. F. L., the city's biggest trucking local, endorsed the stabilization pact in a referendum completed last month. Its ratification by the employers at a meeting at the Statler Hotel

Continued on Page 16, Column 5

TRUMAN ANNOUNCES 3-POWER ARMS PLAN FOR ARABS, ISRAELIS

Agreement to Regulate Sale on Basis of Parity—President Sees Stability Bolstered

MUNITIONS RACE IS SCORED

Move Against Soviet Is Held by Officials to Be Secondary Aspect of the Accord

Texts of three-power and Truman statements, Page 6.

By ANTHONY LEVIERO
Special to THE NEW YORK TIMES.

WASHINGTON, May 25—President Truman announced today an agreement with Great Britain and France to regulate the sale of arms to Middle Eastern countries on a basis of parity between the Arab states and Israel.

An achievement of the London meetings of the foreign ministers of the three countries, the treaty would contribute to the stability and security of the Middle East, Mr. Truman said.

This country's participation in the consultations resulting in today's simultaneous declaration by the three countries, said the President, "emphasizes this country's desire to promote the maintenance of peace in the Near East."

In the joint declaration the three countries reaffirmed their opposition to "an arms race between the Arab states and Israel."

Hope for Reduction in Arms

Informed officials said that the agreement should not be interpreted as a stimulus to arms shipments to the countries that were engaged in bloody strife before the establishment of Israel as an independent nation. They added rather that the agreement should bring about a reduction of arms to the troubled area by the contribution it would make toward a stable political situation there. They stressed their hope that this would be the ultimate result.

The declaration based the new arms policy on three points, as follows:

1. The three Governments recognized that the Arab states and Israel had to maintain defensive systems to provide for their "legitimate self-defense and to permit them to play their part in the defense of the area as a whole."
2. The three Governments have

Continued on Page 6, Column 6

World News Summarized

FRIDAY, MAY 26, 1950

The Senate, after defeating determined Republican assaults on the Point Four program, passed and sent to the White House yesterday the bill authorizing aid to foreign nations. The vote was 47 to 27. Congress must still vote funds for the six programs, including the third Marshall Plan year. [1:8.]

Unless economic equilibrium is restored to the world before the end of the Marshall Plan, Europe's efforts toward freer trade and less governmental control will fail, the United Nations Economic Commission for Europe reported. [4:1.] West Germany's upper house voted, 27 to 16, to join the Council of Europe. [10:4.]

The Western occupying powers completed plans for the military protection of the Western sectors of Berlin during the week-end demonstration of Communist youths. Steps were taken to minimize the chance of "incidents." [1:6.] Young Communists massing in the Soviet sector were forbidden by the People's Police to enter Western areas. [10:2.]

An agreement to regulate arms sales to the Middle East and equalize supplies to the Arab states and Israel as a contribution to stability in that area was announced by the United States, Britain and France. The three promised to see that frontier or armistice lines were not violated. [1:5.] The decision to include Israel in the arms plan was welcomed by Tel Aviv. [6:3.]

Moscow was said to be engaged in integrating North China into the Soviet economic structure as a move toward eventual domination of all northern Asia. [8:2.]

The State Department is sending John Foster Dulles to Japan next month to discuss a possible Japanese peace treaty with General MacArthur. [1:6-7.]

Marshal Tito scolded the major powers for starting an arms race and "wasting time" on atomic debate instead of attacking "potential causes of war." He said the "unequal" relations between large and small states were a major cause of friction. [5:5.] Trygve Lie, returning from his European mission to end the "cold war," said the "ordinary" people of both East and West Europe wanted peace. [5:1.]

In Washington, the compromise bill extending Federal rent controls beyond June 30 was cleared for House action after June 12. [46:1.] A start on the $2,476,468,850 Federal low-cost housing program is expected early next month. [25:5.]

An outside panel recommended that the Atomic Energy Commission name an assistant general manager to head all phases of atomic security. [14:1.] A wildcat laborers' strike halted construction work at the Oak Ridge, Tenn., plant. [1:6-7.]

Truck owners in this city approved a four-year, no-strike contract already accepted by the union. [1:4.]

A Federal official advised the city to institute a broad program of land management in the watershed to increase the storage yield of rain. [25:3.]

Mayor O'Dwyer formally opened the Brooklyn-Battery twin-tube tunnel to traffic. [1:1.]

The City Council voted to replace the Traffic Commission with a Traffic Department. [25:1.]

At least thirty-three persons were burned to death in a collision between a Chicago street-car and a gasoline truck. Five buildings near by were destroyed and two others were damaged. [1:2-3.]

Index to other news appears on Page 24.

Roosevelts Renounce Trustee Suit To Find if President Died a Soldier

By The Associated Press.

POUGHKEEPSIE, N. Y., May 25—The family of the late President Roosevelt today renounced any claims of tax benefits his trust estate might receive if it were established that he died as a soldier and not as a civilian.

The members of the family disassociated themselves from an action of the majority of trustees of the Roosevelt trust estate brought before Dutchess County Surrogate Frederick S. Quinterro. The trustees asked an intermediate account of their actions.

The trustees of the trust estate of $1,232,558.03—not the entire amount left by the late President—are Basil O'Connor, chairman of the National Foundation for Infantile Paralysis; Henry T. Hackett, a Poughkeepsie lawyer, and James Roosevelt.

But James Roosevelt joined with his mother, three brothers and sister in protesting the action.

In effect, the trustees want the court to determine whether they would be held responsible for failure to press for application of tax provisions that would work to the advantage of the trust estate.

They asked the court if the trust estate had any legal rights to a refund of Federal income and estate taxes. Both refer to tax benefits to individuals who died in the active service of the armed forces in World War II.

Existing law provides for a refund of income taxes paid during the war years by anyone who died in active service and a refund of the bulk of estate taxes paid between Dec. 7, 1941, and Jan. 9, 1947.

The question before the court, therefore, is whether the late President, as Commander in Chief, died as a member of the armed forces or as a civilian.

Last month an Internal Revenue agent ruled that claims of the trustees for refund of $164,485.76 in income taxes under provisions of the law were invalid.

The surrogate pointed out in a

Continued on Page 17, Column 3

Wildcat Strike Halts Building Of Atom Plants at Oak Ridge

Walkout by 3,000 A. F. L. Workers Ties Up Big Construction Project—Davis of Labor Panel and Union Order Men Back

By The Associated Press.

OAK RIDGE, Tenn., May 25—A wildcat strike by 3,000 American Federation of Labor workers halted construction today on a gigantic $227,000,000 atomic energy project.

The sudden and officially unexplained walkout began yesterday afternoon when about 700 laborers and hodcarriers left their jobs. It increased overnight to include all A. F. L. craftsmen working on the construction project.

Union leaders themselves immediately denounced the strike, calling it "unauthorized" and ordering the strikers to return to their jobs at once. But there was no indication the strikers would heed the order.

The project involves construction of two plants, known as K-29 and K-31, to increase the nation's output of fissionable uranium-235, the atomic bomb ingredient. Work on the project was begun last year, but the Atomic Energy Commission has not given a progress report on it.

Failure of an arbitration board to hand down an immediate decision in a wage dispute involving Local 818 of the laborers and hodcarriers apparently touched off the walkout.

The three-member arbitration board, named by Chairman William H. Davis of the Atomic Energy Labor Relations Panel, completed a hearing on the laborers' dispute Tuesday and took the findings under advisement.

Some of the strikers told newsmen that they had been promised an immediate decision in the dispute. They said they expected the decision Tuesday, immediately following the hearing. They did not say who made the "promise."

Both the union and the Maxon Construction Company, contractor for the project, had agreed in advance to abide by the arbitration board's decision.

The laborers struck for a week last month to back up their de-

Continued on Page 16, Column 3

U. S. CHIEF IN BERLIN ACTS TO BAR CLASH

Taylor Limits Use of Highway by Americans—Confident West Will Guard Rights

By DREW MIDDLETON
Special to THE NEW YORK TIMES.

BERLIN, May 25—The Germans and Western Allies in Western Berlin are ready to withstand the shock of the mass Communist youth demonstrations and any consequent incidents in the free half of the city this week-end, Maj. Gen. Maxwell D. Taylor, United States Commandant in the city, declared tonight.

All preparations have been made on the military side to protect "this island in the sea of Red hostility" and the Western powers are aware of their trusteeship for the lives of more than 2,000,000 persons in their sectors, General Taylor declared.

The United States authorities, eager not to afford the Communists the occasion for manufactured incidents, forbade United States personnel to use the Berlin-Helmstedt Autobahn between 5 P. M. and 7 A. M. until further notice.

Their action followed a letter from Col. Alexei I. Yelisarov, Deputy Soviet Commander, denying that there would be any limitation of movement on the roads of the Soviet zone in connection with the youth rally.

Colonel Yelisarov stated that the highway between the city and the Western zones would be open "as usual" with the exception of one stretch that would be closed, necessitating a detour of ten to fifteen kilometers (six to nine miles) until June 1.

The United States command acknowledged the detour in a statement that said all traffic between the two points mentioned in Colonel Yelisarov's letter (Kleistow and Alt Langewisch) would be diverted

Continued on Page 11, Column 1

U. S. ECONOMIC HELP TO INDO-CHINA SPED

Special Mission to Viet Nam, Laos and Cambodia Named—Washington Asks Stability

By The Associated Press.

SAIGON, Indo-China, May 25—A program of United States economic aid to French-sponsored Indo-China was announced today by the United States Legation. What it amounts to was not disclosed.

The announcement, made by Edmund Gullion, United States chargé d'affaires, warned that France and the Indo-Chinese states must bear the main responsibility for restoring security and stability to Indo-China.

[In Washington, The Associated Press said, the Economic Cooperation Administration had set up a special mission to Southeast Asia to develop the program. It will be headed by Robert Blum, formerly with the E. C. A.'s mission to France.

[E. C. A. Administrator Paul G. Hoffman said that plans called for "industrial rehabilitation projects and other economic help" in the states of Cambodia, Laos and Viet Nam. He said the amount and type of aid were still under discussion but aid in the fields of health and agriculture was considered of "primary importance."]

It is expected here that the program will be inaugurated with an allocation of $23,500,000. This amount was reported to have been recommended by the United States mission to Southeast Asia under R. Allen Griffin.

The announcement said the aid was designed to reinforce joint efforts of France, Viet Nam, Cambodia and Laos and that the help was complementary "without any intention of substitution."

The aid will be granted under separate bilateral agreements to be

Continued on Page 9, Column 5

Dulles Will Visit Japan for Talks With MacArthur on Peace Treaty

Special to THE NEW YORK TIMES.

WASHINGTON, May 25—John Foster Dulles, Republican adviser to Secretary of State Dean Acheson, will go to Japan early next month for talks with General Douglas MacArthur about the possibility of writing a Japanese peace treaty.

Plans for Mr. Dulles' trip have not yet been prepared in detail, but a tentative schedule will take him to Tokyo at about the time of the visit planned by Secretary of Defense Louis Johnson and Gen. Omar N. Bradley, chairman of the Joint Chiefs of Staff.

In a recent shift of State Department assignments, Mr. Dulles was named specifically to handle the Japanese peace treaty problems.

When the forthcoming trip to the Far East of Secretary Johnson and General Bradley was announced, no mention was made of talks with General MacArthur about the Japanese treaty. It was learned on good authority, however, that such talks were one of Mr. Johnson's intentions.

The State Department, meanwhile, had apparently begun to consider such a mission for Mr. Dulles about the time or shortly after Mr. Johnson's trip was announced.

One of the reasons for the decision to send Mr. Dulles, according to well informed authorities, is that the State Department desires its own report of conditions in Japan bearing on the treaty situation.

Among the difficulties that face the Government in seeking to reach a national policy on the treaty is a difference of opinion between the State and Defense Departments. Secretary of State Acheson has stated a number of times that a treaty with Japan is of great urgency, and it is the State Department's position that this should be done swiftly, even without the participation of the Soviet Union and Communist China.

The Defense Department, largely on the basis of recommendations

Continued on Page 9, Column 3

FOREIGN AID VOTED BY SENATE, 47-27; POINT 4 INCLUDED

$3,200,000,000 Authorization for Year Beginning July 1 Goes to the President

MANY SHIFT ON FINAL POLL

Hoffman Predicts the Marshall Plan Costs Will Be $3,000,000,000 Below Estimate

By C. P. TRUSSELL
Special to THE NEW YORK TIMES.

WASHINGTON, May 25—After three days of bitter contest, the Senate approved and sent to the White House late today an authorization for $3,200,000,000 of economic assistance to foreign countries through the fiscal year starting July 1. The vote was 47 to 27. Provision of the actual money involved rests with appropriations committees in later actions.

With this authorizing budget, covering six foreign-aid programs including the third year of the Marshall Plan, Congress gave its first approval of President Truman's Point Four program which he requested in his inaugural address as "a new and bold" venture looking to world peace. Its stated objective is to help economically undeveloped areas of the world, through technical assistance and exchange of know-how, rise to greater productivity and commerce, higher living standards and improved democratic morale.

Other programs covered by the authorization called for $100,000,000 for economic assistance to the Republic of Korea, $94,000,000 for aid in China and its general area, $27,450,000 for the help of Palestine refugees and $15,000,000 for international welfare work for children.

Republicans, led by Senator Robert A. Taft of Ohio, minority policy leader, fought the version of the Point Four plan that was before the Senate until the last moment. They contended that in the adjustment of Senate and House of Representatives differences an entirely new program was presented for final Senate action.

Investment Guarantees Assailed

In the place of the program for purely technical assistance which the Senate approved by a bare lead of 37 to 36 on May 5, was the House version, Mr. Taft and his allies asserted. This, they held, expanded the program to one of promotion of American capital investment at any underdeveloped point in the world with implied governmen guarantees against financial loss.

Here, it was contended by those who sought to return the measure to conference for a rewriting of the Point Four phase to conform to original Senate decision, was a plan for a permanent economic aid program to spread throughout the world when the Marshall Plan ended in 1952.

Proponents of Point Four, as contained in the measure due for final Congressional action, debated that Mr. Taft and his colleagues of the opposition were envisaging back-breaking financial and other commitments in declarations of policy designed to emphasize American good-will and desire to help those underdeveloped areas that sought to cling to democratic living.

They conceded that the language of the House version policy declarations were "flowery." But this, interjected Senator Walter F. George, Democrat of Georgia, was a sort of habit Congress had fallen into. He added that he did not like it.

Senator Taft and Senator Eugene D. Millikin, Republican of Colorado, insisted, in effect, that although the intention might have been merely to plant verbal flowers, the implications of the declarations of policy promised American guarantees.

Connally Defines Commitment

Senator Tom Connally, Democrat of Texas and chairman of the Foreign Relations Committee, denied this repeatedly. The American commitment under Point Four, he said, involved $35,000,000 out of a total foreign aid program of $3,200,000,000, of which some $10,000,000 would be used in this hemisphere. So, he argued, Point Four assistance could not go beyond the giving of technical aid with $25,000,000.

At this point attention was shifted to the Marshall Plan. Paul G. Hoffman, head of the Economic Cooperation Administration, was telling the Senate Appropriations Committee in closed session that present estimates indicated that

Continued on Page 4, Column 4

Charred bodies of some of the victims of the collision lie in the rear end of the street car.

Wide World Photos

33 BURN TO DEATH IN CHICAGO CRASH

Continued From Page 1

swung suddenly to the left to enter a switch-back siding in a vacant lot on the east side of State Street. A flooded underpass a block south had made it necessary to reroute the car.

Witnesses said that the car struck the side of the northbound truck. Chicago Transit Authority officials were told that the trolley car was moving rapidly when it entered the switch. A flagman asserted that he waved his flag frantically at the motorman to warn him that the switch was "open" for a turn at that point. The car continued on, he said.

The first police and firemen to reach the scene put into effect an emergency plan that brought all available police and fire ambulances and rescue squads to the scene.

Fire Marshal Anthony J. Mullaney estimated the property damage in excess of $150,000. He said that the heat from the flames was so intense that it cracked bricks and concrete in the street pavement.

Hours after the fire in the street car was extinguished, firemen still were battling the flames in the buildings. Walls collapsed in several of them.

Witnesses Describe Scene

A crash, a few sparks and then a deep roar of black smoke and billowing flame that surged up the street like rolling flood waters was the description of eye witnesses to the collision.

Passengers on the street car who were able to flee from the inferno inside the blazing street car were too dazed as they received treatment in half a dozen hospitals to give many details of the sudden disaster.

Peter Simadis, owner of a State Street tavern, said he heard a loud crash and looked out to see a wall of flame rolling up the street.

"The fire was traveling like a series of explosions, spreading so fast that no one could have escaped its path," Mr. Simadis said. "I ran to the telephone, but before I could complete a call to the fire department the front window of the tavern cracked under the intense heat and then fell inside the tavern.

Mr. Simadis said there were six persons in the tavern at the time and all rushed out the back door, feeling the heat even that far from the fire.

Walter Skonicki, a repairman for the Board of Education, was sitting by his front window and looked out as the southbound State Street streamliner-type car turned left on a switch and struck the truck.

"There was a sudden 'boom' and then heavy flames rolled up instantly," he said. "I saw a number of persons jump off the back end of the street car, some of them with their clothing afire, some with legs and arms cut by glass."

Windows Melted by Heat

Mr. Skonicki said he dashed out to rescue his daughter's auto, parked in front of his home, but was forced back inside by the heat and fled with his family out the back door as windows at the front of the house melted.

The Rev. Robert J. Sidney, assistant pastor of the South Shore Baptist Church, said he was getting gasoline in a station a short distance up the street. He looked and saw a street car

"When I looked again," he said, "something like air blew over the street car and then it was enveloped in flames. In a second the entire car was hidden by fire. The flames went in all he open windows.

"One woman thrust her head out but couldn't get her body through the opening. She raised her clenched fists over her head and just shuddered and then slumped to the floor. I saw people with their hair on fire. It was miserable."

Mrs. Ella Flowers, 76 years old, was sitting at the front window of her second-floor apartment when she heard a crash. She said she ooked out and saw a mass of flame that hid the streetcar. Then the fire billowed up past her window. She called to others and rushed out the back door as the building caught fire.

Passenger Tells of Escape

Edward W. White Jr. was sitting near the rear of the car on the right side.

"The car was packed with people standing in the aisle," Mr. White said. "At Sixty-third Street the car hit an open switch, turned left and hit the truck head on. The whole car was in flames within a second.

"I kicked the glass out of the back door and jumped out. The flames were right behind me. It was so hot I just rolled over to the curb. A woman put her coat around me."

Mr. White's leg was severely cut when he kicked out the door glass. A bystander applied a tourniquet to stop the flow of blood and he was put in a police squad car for a quick trip to Provident Hospital.

Mrs. Ora Mae Bryant said she fell to the floor when the car and truck crashed.

"Everyone was screaming and yelling," she related. "We couldn't get the door open. Finally someone broke a window and we crawled out."

"I heard someone shout 'Look out!' and then there was a crash," said Mrs. Mary Poorney, who was taken to Englewood Hospital.

"The car tilted a litle and then righted itself," she added. "People were thrown to the floor. Suddenly there were black smoke and flames all around. People tried to get off, but the doors were locked. Someone finally forced the back door. I followed other and leaped off the car and ran as fast as I could."

"All the News That's Fit to Print"

The New York Times.

LATE CITY EDITION
Mostly cloudy, continued cold today. Cloudy, showers tomorrow.
Temperature Range Today—Max.,47; Min.,32
Temperature Yesterday—Max.,43; Min.,31
Full U. S. Weather Bureau Report, Page 71

Copyright, 1950, by The New York Times Company.

VOL. C..No. 33,906. Entered as second-Class Matter. Post Office, New York, N. Y. NEW YORK, THURSDAY, NOVEMBER 23, 1950. K Times Square, New York 18, N. Y. Telephone Lackawanna 4-1000 FIVE CENTS

75 KNOWN DEAD IN L. I. WRECK IN RICHMOND HILL; TOLL MOUNTING IN CRASH OF EASTBOUND EXPRESS INTO STANDING TRAIN; CAUSE IS UNDETERMINED

ALLIES PUSH AHEAD IN MOVE TO CLEAR NORTHEAST KOREA

Meanwhile the Two Sides Spar Cautiously in West Below Main Red Defense Line

PATROLS NEAR CHONGJIN

Advance Units of South Korea Capital Division Eight Miles From Industrial Center

By LINDESAY PARROTT
Special to The New York Times.

TOKYO, Thursday, Nov. 23—United States and South Korean forces drove ahead yesterday in new advances to clear the Korean northeast. Meanwhile the main forces on both the Communist and United Nations sides continued cautious sparring in the west some miles below what is now believed to be the main Communist defense position, about fifty miles south of the Manchurian frontier on the Yalu River.

The longest advance was again scored by the South Korean Capital Division on the east coast. Supported by naval gunfire of United Nations warships north of the Forty-first Parallel, advanced elements of the Capital Division marched ten miles to the vicinity of Yonhyang. It was a twenty-mile advance in two days, according to official accounts.

The South Koreans met only light resistance, with no indication thus far of the enemy reinforcements previously reported moving down into the area from the north.

Reports from Korea said that the Capital Division's patrols were within eight miles of the city of Chongjin, last important settlement below the Soviet border, north of the Forty-second Parallel.

Chongjin Again Heavily Bombed

Chongjin, an industrial town and large port and railway junction, has been heavily pounded by United States bombers. B-29 Superforts yesterday again returned to the city, to plaster the docks, industrial areas and railroad yards, boring through low clouds and dropping their explosives by radar techniques.

Superforts also put seventy-ton demolition bombs on "military targets" at Musan, on the Yalu River—this time in a visual attack as radar bombing along the Manchurian border is prohibited in the fear of international complications resulting from poor aim. Musan is one of the areas where Chinese troops have been reported concentrating for a possible attempt to break out of the trap forged around them in the northeast, when the United States Seventh Division reached the river and cut them off in the northeastern corner of Korea.

Fighters and light bombers attacked the enemy airfield at Kanggye, in the central sector—another reputed concentration point of reinforcements and supplies from China. F-80 Shooting Stars returned to strike at the Korean side of the international bridge across the Yalu at Sinuiju, one of the main links in the communications

Continued on Page 3, Column 5

China Reds Free 27; Shun War, They Say

By Reuters.

YONGBYON, Korea, Thursday, Nov. 23—Twenty-seven wounded American prisoners were released yesterday by Chinese Communists three miles from American lines. The Americans brought back the oral message: "Chinese do not want to fight Americans."

The Americans were released yesterday morning north of Yongbyon, in the central sector.

The twenty-seven, all wounded, included three sergeants and four corporals but no officers. The men reported that they had been well fed and well treated. They said a Chinese woman interpreter talked to them daily.

When You Think of Writing Think of Whiting.—Advt.

Russia Dominates U. S. Reds, McGrath Formally Charges

Government Demands Financial Accounting and List of Members of Party Which 'Regularly Reports' to Moscow Regime

By LEWIS WOOD
Special to The New York Times.

WASHINGTON, Nov. 22—The Communist party of the United States is dominated and controlled by Soviet Russia, Attorney General J. Howard McGrath charged tonight.

He made the accusation in a long petition filed with the Subversive Activities Control Board, in which he asked an order to force the Communists to register under the new Internal Security Act of 1950. They have so far refused to register.

The McGrath petition, a 4,800-word history of the Communist party machinations and attitude toward the United States, is the first such step taken under the new law.

Released here, copies of the petition were simultaneously served by air mail on Communist headquarters at 35 East Twelfth Street, New York City. The document was marked for the notice of William Z. Foster, party chairman, and Gus Hall, secretary, whom the Justice Department portrayed as a "high functionary."

Attorney General McGrath demanded that the party reveal its financial details and furnish a list of all its members in the United States.

Strong opposition is expected from the Communist organization. Under the law it was supposed to register voluntarily with the Attorney General on or before Oct. 23. It has not done so; its officials have flatly announced their refusal. From all indications the party will start an action in the courts to have the new law declared unconstitutional, with the

Continued on Page 41, Column 3

Text of Attorney General's petition is on Page 40

Chemist, Woman Aide Guilty, Espionage Jury Here Finds

After deliberating for three hours and fifty minutes, a Federal Court jury of seven men and five women found Abraham Brothman, chemical engineer, and his business partner, Miriam Moskowitz, guilty yesterday of conspiring to mislead a 1947 Federal grand jury investigating espionage.

It also found Brothman guilty on a second count of influencing Harry Gold, admitted atomic spy, to tell the grand jury a fabricated story of their relationship with each other and with other figures in a Soviet spy ring.

Setting next Tuesday at 10:30 A. M. as the time for sentencing, Judge Irving R. Kaufman remanded the defendants to the Federal House of Detention, 427 West Street, without bail. He told the jury it had reached the only possible verdict in the light of the evidence and paid tribute to United States Attorney Irving H. Saypol and his staff for their painstaking preparation of the case.

On the conspiracy count, both defendants face a possible maximum penalty of five years imprisonment and $10,000 fines. On the second count, the maximum punishment for Brothman could be five years in jail and a fine of $5,000.

Brothman, 36-year-old father of two children, lives at 41-08 Forty-second Street, Sunnyside, Queens. Miss Moskowitz, 34 and single, lives at 151 Eighth Avenue. When the verdict was announced, both maintained the same impassive attitude they had shown during most of the trial.

The Government had charged that for a period of years begin-

Continued on Page 43, Column 3

2 MORE SEIZED HERE IN PLOT ON TRUMAN

Chief and Ex-Head of Local Puerto Rican Nationalists Held in $50,000 Bail Each

By EDWARD RANZAL

The president of the Nationalist party of Puerto Rico in New York and his predecessor were held in $50,000 bail each yesterday by United States Commissioner Edward W. McDonald on a charge of being co-conspirators in the attempt to assassinate President Truman on Nov. 1.

They were arrested by Secret Service agents in City Hall Park after they had left the United States Court House, following their appearance before the Federal grand jury. Twelve other persons also testified before the panel investigating the assassination plot.

The defendants are Julio Pinto Gandia, 42-year-old president of the party, of the Hotel Ledonia, 42 East Twenty-eighth Street, and Juan Bernardo Lebron, 28, a cook, of 800 East 108th Street, who was president of the party last year. The party, which has its local headquarters at 1241 Southern

Continued on Page 19, Column 1

U. S. Steel, Set to Grant Pay Rise, Sounds the Government on Prices

By JOSEPH A. LOFTUS
Special to The New York Times.

WASHINGTON, Nov. 22—The United States Steel Corporation and the United Steel Workers, C. I. O., are on the verge of an agreement raising wages 15 to 30 cents an hour, but there is a hitch in the bargain—prices.

The company is taking informal soundings in government to assure itself that a price increase will not be disturbed.

The company, it was reported, has conditionally decided to grant "fifth-round" wage rises of 15 cents in the lowest bracket, with step-ups of one-half cent an hour all along the line. There are thirty-two wage classifications in the current contract, so that employes in the top bracket, very few in number, would get a rise of about 30 cents.

Company and union negotiators, it was learned, had held high hopes that the agreement could be closed this week. The Government's authority to fix prices, however, has made this a three-cornered bargain, in effect.

If the necessary assurances could have been obtained in time the agreement would have been signed in Chicago, where the steel workers' president, Philip Murray, is presiding over the C. I. O. convention.

John D. Stephens, United States Steel's vice president in charge of industrial relations, had been reported ready to fly to Chicago for the signing. Instead, he left New York tonight for his home in Pittsburgh. A delay in the final agreement until next week was indicated.

The Government's price and wage control machinery is not fully geared up yet. No ceilings have been set. Later on, however, prices and wages could be rolled

Continued on Page 32, Column 5

TAMMANY RIVALS FACE GRAND JURY ON GANGSTER TIES

Hogan Opens Inquiry Into the Charges Made by Factions of DeSapio and Sampson

RAO AND STACCI NAMED

Pressure Against Mancuso Is Laid to Them—Appeal on Hall for Meeting Is Argued

District Attorney Frank S. Hogan announced last night that he had started a grand jury investigation of underworld influence in Tammany Hall.

The inquiry is a direct outgrowth of the struggle now in progress—with charges and counter-charges of ties with gangsters—between Carmine DeSapio, present leader of Tammany, and Frank Sampson, a former leader, for control of the organization.

In the recent election, Mr. DeSapio was the nominal sponsor and one of the chief supporters of former Supreme Court Justice Ferdinand Pecora, the Democratic-Liberal candidate for Mayor. Mr. Sampson backed Mayor Impellitteri and is due for appointment as an executive assistant to the Mayor upon Mr. Impellitteri's return from a Southern vacation.

One of the charges he is sifting, Mr. Hogan said, relates to efforts being made to unseat former General Sessions Judge Francis X. Mancuso as a Tammany leader in the Sixth Assembly district. Mr. Mancuso supported Mr. Pecora in the election but afterward joined with Mr. Sampson in a struggle to depose Mr. DeSapio.

"As If They Had Leveled a Gun"

It has been charged that Joey Rao and Joseph (Joe Stretch) Stacci, notorious underworld characters, attended a meeting of election district captains of the Sixteenth District and officials of the Pocasset Democratic Club last Sunday evening at the home of Fred Cincotti, a building contractor, at 333 East 116th Street.

Mr. Hogan said:

"It is charged that Rao and Stacci made known their opposition to the continuance of Francis X. Mancuso as the Democratic leader of the district. Following the meeting, opponents of Mr. Man-

Continued on Page 47, Column 1

AT THE SCENE OF LONG ISLAND TRAIN WRECK

Emergency squads from police and fire departments and volunteer workers alongside one of the cars in fatal collision in Queens. The New York Times (by Edward Hausner)

2 RETIRED OFFICERS TO FACE BET JURY

Former Heads of Brooklyn Police to Be Questioned in $50,000 Realty Deal

By MILTON HONIG

Two recently retired high-ranking police officers have agreed to appear on Monday before the Brooklyn grand jury investigating gambling to explain a $50,000 real estate deal in Florida, District Attorney Miles F. McDonald announced yesterday.

The two are former Assistant Chief Inspector Edward C. Moran, who was in command of Brooklyn and Richmond, and his partner, former Acting Lieut. Paul W. Twiley, who was supervisor of Brooklyn plainclothes men.

Mr. McDonald said that their appearance would be voluntary and that they would not sign waivers of immunity. This would be Mr. Moran's second call. On Oct. 2

Continued on Page 52, Column 5

Floodlights Etch Tragedy And Heroism in Wreckage

Floodlights from emergency police and fire equipment focused on the locale of last night's train wreck in Richmond Hill illuminated a scene of major disaster. The cries of the injured mingled with the impatient shouts of rescue workers as a subdued crowd of more than 5,000 stood by, shocked by the immensity of the tragedy.

Priests administered the last rites to the dying. White-coated doctors and ambulance attendants hurried from victim to victim administering morphine injections to those in pain and soothing the frightened with words of comfort.

As the night wore on and the cold became more penetrating, the doctors and nurses draped blankets over their hospital attire.

The rescue work was carried out under considerable difficulty, for the railroad tracks at the scene are on embankments fifteen feet above street level. Wooden planks were thrown across the slippery banks to enable the stretcher bearers to carry the injured to the ambulances below.

The crowd began to dwindle by 11 P. M., but the rescue workers continued to help the injured. Climbing into the telescoped cars, they reached the victims pinned under the wreckage. So strenuous was the relief work that several of the workers required first-aid themselves.

Friends and relatives of the passengers had rushed to the scene as news of the wreck spread. Many wept as they waited for identification of the victims. Residents of the area, who had witnessed the early rescue work, tried to reassure them that immediate meas-

Continued on Page 23, Column 1

TRAIN PASSENGERS DESCRIBE HORRORS

Employes of Road Knocked to Floor and Cut—Limp Hands Sag at Windows

As rescue workers toiled to free imprisoned victims of the crash on the Long Island Rail Road last night, survivors and neighborhood residents described the accident and the agonies of the trapped passengers.

Some of those able to walk away from the scene told of brakes slamming on suddenly, a flash of light and the impact of one train tearing into another. Others related the efforts of passengers to pick themselves up from the aisle floors and stagger among broken glass to the ground outside.

Home owners in the neighborhood recounted their efforts to carry bleeding and moaning persons to private houses turned into first aid centers.

Survivors told of carrier equipment twisted by the crash and encasing smashed bodies. They spoke of blood-spattered hands hanging

Continued on Page 21, Column 1

World News Summarized

THURSDAY, NOVEMBER 23, 1950

At least seventy-five persons were killed and ninety-nine hurt when one Long Island Rail Road train crashed into the one ahead in Richmond Hill last evening. Both trains were crowded with suburbanites and Thanksgiving Day visitors. [1:8.]

Rescue work was carried on under floodlights as near-by residents helped passengers and officials aid the injured. [1:6-7.] The first train had made an emergency stop. [1:7.]

Twenty-one persons on a missionary plane were believed lost when their craft crashed into a Wyoming mountain. [49:1.]

The Communist party in this country is "substantially dominated and controlled by the Government and Communist party of the Soviet Union," Attorney General McGrath charged in a petition to compel the party to disclose financial details and file a list of members. [1:2-3.] A Federal jury convicted Abraham Brothman and Miriam Moskowitz of conspiring to mislead a Federal grand jury investigating Communist espionage. [1:2-3.] The President and former president of the Puerto Rican Nationalist party in this city were arrested and held in $50,000 bail each on charges of being co-conspirators in the attempt to kill President Truman. [1:2.]

Secretary Acheson said the State Department would continue its foreign policy talks with Republican Congress leaders, including Senator Taft. [27:1.]

Americans and South Koreans pushed ahead in clearing northeast Korea as other United Nations forces advanced cautiously toward the Communists' defense line. [1:1, map P. 2.]

France has decided to strengthen her forces in Indo-China and hasten virtual independence for the three states. [3:1.]

North Atlantic military leaders have devised a new formula on use of German troops in defense of Europe. [12:1.] Bonn's inability to decide on its own contribution was said to delay reinforcement of United States troops in Germany. [11:1.]

Britain suspended shipment of tanks to Egypt until the dispute over troops in the Suez Canal zone had been adjusted. [14:1.]

The Communist-dominated peace congress in Warsaw ended after naming a peace council to act as a watchdog over the United Nations. [4:3.]

A grand jury investigation into alleged underworld connections of the DeSapio and Sampson factions in Tammany Hall was disclosed. [1:4.]

Two former police officials agreed to tell the Brooklyn gambling grand jury how they got $50,000 to buy a Florida orange grove. [1:5.]

NEWS BULLETINS FROM THE TIMES
Every hour on the hour
7 A.M. through Midnight
WQXR AM 1560
WQXR FM 96.3

Index to other news appears on Page 36.

Thoughts of War Overshadowing Thanksgiving Festivities Today

Thoughts of peace and prayers for the fighting forces in Korea appeared to overshadow all else as America prepared to celebrate the Thanksgiving holiday today.

All faiths planned special services and many non-religious groups tempered their feasts and festivities with sober thoughts of world problems and of the men battling in bitter cold mountains far from home.

A last-minute rush of air travel was believed indicative of the desire of many to be with relatives and friends this year. One of the unusual features of this Thanksgiving air travel was the number of family groups with children who sought plane space. Usually the largest number of holiday air passengers are business men rushing to reach their homes.

The rush on air travel broke all previous records for Thanksgiving. By late afternoon officials at both Eastern and American Airlines were using such adjectives as "amazing," "unprecedented" and "totally unexpected." An official at American Airlines, who predicted that the "whole holiday week-end will prove a record," said that twenty-nine extra sections, three more than planned, "suddenly had to be thrown into the breach" both into and out of the New York area at La Guardia and Newark airports.

With 3,022 air travelers reported last Thanksgiving out of New York, he placed this year's estimate at 3,500, an increase of nearly 500.

At Eastern Airlines, where a 10 per cent gain from advance bookings was indicated, an official said that "suddenly the lid blew off and we wished that we had two fleets instead of one."

"Demands for seats—and we couldn't find a remaining seat to any place—became so heavy that

Continued on Page 61, Column 5

CARS TELESCOPED

Hempstead Train Halts in the Path of One Going to Babylon

50 ARE IN HOSPITALS

Red Cross Rushes Aid—Holiday Travelers Among Victims

A partial list of the dead and injured is printed on Page 20.

The Long Island Rail Road had the grimmest disaster of its ill-starred career last night when at least seventy-five persons were killed and ninety-nine suburban-bound Thanksgiving eve travelers, were injured, some probably fatally, in the collision of two eastbound trains in the Richmond Hill section of Queens.

The collision occurred at 6:26 P. M., when the front of a twelve-car train telescoped the rear of another twelve-car load of passengers at an elevated point in the express tracks on 125th Street near Eighty-third Avenue, between Lefferts Boulevard and Hillside Avenue.

Both trains were heading for Jamaica as the first stop. The first, No. 780, bound for Hempstead, L. I., with more than 1,000 passengers, had left the Long Island station in Manhattan at 6:09 P. M. The second, No. 174, en route to Babylon, L. I., with 1,200 passengers, many of them having to stand, followed at 6:13 P. M.

First Train Stopped

Official reports were that the Hempstead bound train stopped. The second train was headed for the same Babylon destination as the one wrecked on Feb. 17 at Rockville Centre, when thirty-two persons were killed and more than 100 injured.

The second train was operated by B. J. Pokorny, whose home address was not learned and telescoped the one ahead, which was being run by Motorman William W. Murphy. The latter escaped unharmed but at an early hour this morning police and fire crews had not found the body of Mr. Pokorny in the twisted mass of wreckage. Mr. Murphy was taken to the 103d Police Precinct in Queens for questioning.

A spokesman for the railroad said he expected that the tracks would be cleared some time this morning, but was unable to say at what time. He pointed out, however, that because of the Thanksgiving holiday, no morning "rush hour" was anticipated.

Early this morning trains leaving the Pennsylvania Station were being delayed for about an hour, he said. At the Pennsylvania Station prospective Long Island passengers were being told merely that all trains on that road were "subject to delay."

Mistake on Signal Seen

As far as the police could determine, Mr. Murphy's train got the "go ahead" signal and was beginning to roll ahead at fifteen miles an hour, then faltered and stopped as the brakes "grabbed" and the driver of the second train, seeing the signal to proceed, kept on at high speed and rammed the last car of Murphy's train.

The terrific impact was such that passengers were mangled in the last car of the first train and

Continued on Page 20, Column 2

2 Internes Credited With Saving Scores

Physicians said last night that two-thirds of the surviving injured of the Long Island train wreck owed their lives to the heroism of two young hospital internes.

The internes, Dr. Paul E. Soffer and Dr. Arnold R. Sanders, squeezed their way between telescoped cars. There they worked for four and a half hours, ministering to trapped passengers.

Then the two young physicians crawled out and collapsed.

Scene at Fatal Long Island Rail Road Train Crash in Richmond Hill

Firemen trying to reach some of the victims

DEATH TOLL RISING IN L. I. TRAIN WRECK

Continued From Page 1

the first car of the following one.

Some bodies were decapitated. Others were so badly mangled that identification seemed impossible. Pieces of human limbs were found later at the scene.

The roar of the collision startled thousands of persons in the vicinity and 5,000 civilians hurried to the scene to watch the police and fire crews rip the wrecked trains apart with acetylene torches as floodlights illuminated the wreckage. Many civilians offered blood for transfusions on the spot, as doctors and internes, summoned from many Queens hospitals, worked over the victims.

As news of the wreck reached them, the city's ranking officials drove to the scene from their homes. Among those who went there to supervise the rescue work were Acting Mayor Joseph T. Sharkey, Police Commissioner Thomas F. Murphy and other department heads.

At 12:15 o'clock this morning the police reported that ninety-six persons had been treated for injuries at four hospitals. Of these, forty-four remained there for further treatment.

Acting Mayor Sharkey issued the following statement at the scene at 1 A. M.:

"Something must be done to stop this carnage. If public ownership is the answer, that's it."

He called for a unified investigation by all agencies "to get to the bottom of this and learn why these things must happen on this particular line."

"It's about time that we should find out the cause of these wrecks on the Long Island Rail Road," he declared. "Something must be done quickly in the interests of public safety. I'm not interested in the financial operations of the road but in the safety of the people."

At 12:15 o'clock this morning it was reported that ninety-nine persons had been treated for injuries at four hospitals. Of these, fifty remained in the hospitals for further treatment.

Hospitals throughout Queens were filled almost to overflowing as ambulances brought the injured and dying to the Queens General, Mary Immaculate, Kew Gardens and Jamaica Hospitals and the Red Cross rushed extra supplies of blood plasma to them.

Of thirty-three victims taken to Queens General Hospital, twenty-four stayed for further help. Mary Immaculate Hospital treated sixteen persons, five remaining. Of the twenty-nine treated at Jamaica Hospital, eight remained. Thirteen of the twenty-one taken to Kew Gardens Hospital stayed.

There was no accurate estimate available of the number of persons treated at the scene and in private homes.

Dr. Randy Wyman, a director of the Municipal Hospital System, alerted all hospitals in Queens to be prepared to receive at least fifty bodies.

Meanwhile, onlookers heard shrieks and moans of other victims still trapped in the wreckage as doctors fought to reach them and give first aid. Priests from various churches gave last rites to those believed to be dying.

Shortly after the collision, which occurred on an embankment about eight feet above street level, wrecking cranes, equipped with powerful cranes, arrived on the local tracks and began the work of helping to separate the two interlocked trains. It was reported that the tie-up would not be cleared until sometime this forenoon at the earliest and possibly not until this afternoon.

One of the survivors was an official of the railroad, David George of Cherry Valley Apartments, Garden City, L. I., who handles public relations for the line. He said that the "rending crash" threw passengers off their seats in the rear car of the first train amid shattered glass.

Reporters at the scene said they saw in the wreckage some bodies that had been hurled to the ceiling of the last car of the front train.

A list of the dead and injured was posted on the bulletin board at the Richmond Hill police station. Friends and relatives continued to come there all night.

An undetermined number of passengers were driven to their homes, where they received treatment from their private physicians. Meanwhile, women living in the area set up first-aid stations for the less badly injured, providing hot coffee, tea and soup.

Andrew Papps, a State Public Service Commission Supervisor of Railroad Equipment, and Thomas Cullen, Assistant Queens District Attorney, issued a joint statement saying:

"If we find any evidence of criminal negligence on the part of any person, there will be prosecution."

Mr. Murphy, motorman of the first train, has forty-five years of railroad experience, according to the police, who said he was 61 years old.

As far as could be learned, Mr. Pokorny was 55 years old. It was presumed that he died at his post in the lead car of the second train. It was believed that his body had been jammed back twenty feet or more into the twisted mass of steel. A policeman said he thought he had seen Mr. Pokorny's body near the fifth window of the front car.

"At least," the policeman said, "the man I saw was wearing motorman's gloves."

Mr. Pokorny, a native of Chicago, joined the Long Island Railroad in 1919.

A physician who treated some of the victims at the scene and who had been inside one of the wrecked cars described it as "a bloody, bloody mess," than which war "couldn't be any worse."

The estimate of seventy-five killed, with possibly more deaths to ensue, would make the disaster the worst in the United States since 1943, when seventy-nine persons were killed in a railroad wreck at Frankfort Junction, Philadelphia.

Law suits are still pending as a result of the Long Island Rail Road wreck in Rockville Centre last February, when two trains crashed head on on a stretch of temporary track. Jacob Kiefer, motorman of one train, was tried for manslaughter. He was found innocent after he said he "blacked out" and did not remember the signal light.

Last Aug. 5 a young brakeman opened the wrong switch on the Long Island near Huntington on the North Shore, with the result that a passenger train rammed a freight. More than fifty persons were injured but no one was killed.

At 2:15 o'clock this morning District Attorney Charles P. Sullivan of Queens issued a statement at the Richmond Hill police station, which, he said, was Motorman Murphy's account of the behavior of his train brakes.

"Mr. Murphy said that when he left the Pennsylvania Station his brakes were in working order," Mr. Sullivan reported. "He said he had even tested the brakes in the tunnel en route to Queens and that they responded satisfactorily.

"He also reported that he had given the brakes a final test at Winfield, which is located between Long Island City and Woodside. He said that when he reached Kew Gardens he was proceeding at the rate of thirty-five miles an hour and that he slowed the train to fifteen miles an hour when the train reached the westerly approach to the Jamaica station.

"At that particular time, Mr. Murphy said, he was ninety seconds behind time. He said that when he attempted to pick up speed his brakes 'refused to respond' to release. He added that he then tried to use his electrical apparatus and finally his air pressure and that his train came to a standstill. It was at this point, he said, that the crash occurred."

Mr. Sullivan, who was conducting his investigation at the station house, said that the engineer had said he had been working as a motorman for the railroad for thirty-one years. He gave his age as 61.

100TH ANNIVERSARY
"All the News That's Fit to Print"
1851 1951

The New York Times.

LATE CITY EDITION
Rain, windy and mild today. Clearing and much colder tomorrow.
Temperature Range Today—Max., 50; Min., 35
Temperatures Yesterday—Max., 45; Min., 31
Full U. S. Weather Bureau Report, Page 59

Copyright, 1951, by The New York Times Company.

VOL. C..No. 33,982. Entered as Second-Class Matter, Post Office, New York, N. Y. NEW YORK, WEDNESDAY, FEBRUARY 7, 1951. Times Square, New York 18, N. Y. Telephone LAckawanna 4-1000 FIVE CENTS

74 KILLED, 330 HURT IN JERSEY TRAIN WRECK; CROWDED COMMUTER CARS PLUNGE OFF RAILS AT TEMPORARY ROAD OVERPASS IN WOODBRIDGE

RAIL STRIKERS BACK IN EAST, BUT TIE-UP WIDENS IN MIDWEST

Lines Here to Give Commuters and Through Passengers Full Service Today

FREIGHT IS STILL SNARLED

Embargoes Relaxed—Chicago Reports Break in Walkout—Plant Lay-Offs Continue

By STANLEY LEVEY

Striking railroad switchmen went back to their jobs in the East yesterday, permitting partial resumption of passenger and commuter service, but many other points in the nation were still locked in the grip of the walkout.

The Pennsylvania, New York Central, New York, New Haven & Hartford, Erie, Lehigh Valley and Jersey Central, operating in the metropolitan area, planned virtually full service on through passenger and commuter lines today.

But the major part of cross-country traffic was still snarled at such key transfer points as Chicago, Cleveland, St. Louis and St. Paul-Minneapolis.

A break in the strike was reported in Chicago last night. Many switchmen were reported to have telephoned that they intended to report for work on shifts late last night or early today.

At Los Angeles Southern Pacific switchmen voted 207 to 119 late last night to end their "sickness" strike and return to work at once. In the Pacific area also the Santa Fe and the Union Pacific reported normal service in major centers.

"Show" Is Not Yet Over

In general outside of the East and West Coast the back-to-work movement by members of the Brotherhood of Railroad Trainmen was scattered at best.

A spokesman for the railroads described the situation thus:

"Any idea that the show is over is completely erroneous. Wherever one group goes back there's another bunch that goes out."

The freight blockade was broken somewhat, but thousands of cars still were not rolling. The Pennsylvania here lifted its embargo on the reception of freight at New York, Philadelphia, Trenton and Buffalo. But the embargo remained in force at Chicago, St. Louis, Cincinnati and Toledo.

While the Railway Express Agency removed its embargo on shipments between New York and New England and New York and New Jersey points, it kept in force its ban on the movement of freight between fourteen Northeastern states and the rest of the country and within the fourteen-state area.

The New York Central continued its embargo on the delivery of all freight west of Buffalo.

More Lay-Offs in Sight

An official of the Association of American Railroads here said that while it would be possible to clean up the accumulation of freight cars in sixty yards in the New York harbor area in a "few days," such improvement would depend on improvements at other points.

At its peak the strike had probably caused idleness for 250,000 persons. Only a small fraction of that number went back to work yesterday. In Detroit, the automobile industry, worst sufferer from the strike, was still beset by shortages of parts and materials and 100,000 workers were without jobs.

Major manufacturers said that even if all the rail strikers went back, the effects of the tie-up would continue to hamper their operations. Detroit's freight service was almost normal, but supply lines from Chicago and Toledo were still clogged. More lay-offs were in sight today.

Industry and labor in the Chicago area continued to experience heavy losses. The United States Steel Company said the strike had caused the loss of 20,000 tons of steel production at the company's big mills in south Chicago.

Cutbacks at the company's Gary (Ind.) mills had cost 6,100 tons of

Continued on Page 17, Column 2

New 'Seabury' Investigation For City Is Slated by Albany

Costello Especially Mentioned as Manhattan Republicans Introduce Resolution With Reported Backing of Governor

By LEO EGAN
Special to THE NEW YORK TIMES.

ALBANY, Feb. 6—A Seabury-type investigation into underworld influence in New York City politics and the general administration of municipal government in New York was proposed today by two Republican legislators from Manhattan, with the reported backing of Governor Dewey.

Indications were strong that the proposal would be approved by the Republican majorities in both branches of the Legislature before the current session adjourns about the middle of next month.

One purpose of such an inquiry would be to provide a Republican backfire to anticipated disclosures before the Crime Investigating Committee of the United States Senate that gambling has flourished in New York State areas under Republican control.

Sol Gelb, former chief Assistant District Attorney of New York County and a member of Governor Dewey's staff during the time he was District Attorney, is being mentioned in Capitol corridors as a probable choice for chief counsel to the State Investigating Committee.

Mr. Gelb's recent court appearances as counsel for Frank Erickson, the gambler now serving a penitentiary sentence for bookmaking, and as counsel for Gerard Purcell, secretary-treasurer of the Uniformed Firemen's Association, who is under indictment for misappropriation of association funds, are not regarded here as any bar to his selection.

Others being mentioned for the committee's staff are Murray R. Gurfein and Jacob Grumet, both of whom served on Mr. Dewey's staff when he was District Attorney. Mr. Grumet received an interim ap-

Continued on Page 32, Column 3

NIGHT SCENE GRIM

Rescue Work Is Pushed Long After Dark by Fire and Railroad Crews

FLOODLIGHTS GLARE

Ambulances, Aided by Trucks, Carry Off the Dead and Injured

Special to THE NEW YORK TIMES.

WOODBRIDGE, N. J., Feb. 6—The floodlights of the Woodbridge Volunteer Fire Department and other fire units lit up a tragic scene of death and confusion here tonight. At 11 P. M. rescue workers had not yet completed the task of bringing the dead and injured from the twisted passenger cars of The Broker, Pennsylvania Railroad commuter train that crashed down a twenty-six-foot temporary red gravel embankment after leaving the rails on a sharp curve.

A worker's acetylene torch showed the faces of the dead at close range in a weird bluish glare as he struggled desperately to burn away the twisted steel that held the victims prisoner. Trucks, pressed into service by the police, carried away both dead and injured as fast as possible.

Train Partly Over Bridge

The train had passed partly over a temporary wooden bridge on the embankment erected recently to carry the tracks over the new route of State Highway 4. Beyond the bridge, which was opened only today, the tracks curve more sharply than the old right-of-way, which runs on lower ground fifty feet away.

As the crashing of glass and screams of the passengers mingled with the hiss of escaping steam, residents in the vicinity left their homes and rushed to the scene.

The bridge, as one witness described it afterward, was still standing but appeared to have sunk into the gravel under the weight.

One of the derailed cars was twisted almost into the shape of

Continued on Page 25, Column 6

AT SCENE OF RAIL DISASTER IN NEW JERSEY

Police, firemen and emergency workers aiding victims in cars of the Pennsylvania commuter train The Broker, which was derailed in Woodbridge last night. The New York Times (by Edward Hausner)

SPAN JUST OPENED

11-Coach P.R.R. Carrier Jumbled as 6th Car Breaks Trestle

TROOPS CALLED OUT

Engineer Says He Was Going 25 M. P. H., Not Speeding, as Charged

Special to THE NEW YORK TIMES.

WOODBRIDGE, N. J., Wednesday, Feb. 7—Seventy-four persons were killed and 330 injured here yesterday when a Pennsylvania Railroad train jammed with rush-hour commuters jumped from a temporary track section, strewing the wreckage of eight cars along the side of a steep embankment.

The accident—the third major railroad tragedy in the New York area within twelve months—occurred at 5:43 P. M. as the eleven-car southbound train, known as The Broker, bound from Jersey City to Bay Head Junction, swung into a sharp turn and mounted a temporary overpass opened only three hours earlier to carry trains over construction work on the New Jersey Freeway here.

The exact cause of the disaster was undetermined, but it appeared to observers that a temporary wooden trestle had collapsed after the engine and the first five cars had cleared it.

Might Top L. I. R. R. Toll

Early this morning, as rescue workers still labored with acetylene torches under the glare of floodlights to free the last victims from the wreckage, it appeared the death toll might exceed the total of seventy-nine who died in the Nov. 22 crash of two Long Island Rail Road trains at Richmond Hill, Queens. Thirty-two died in another Long Island crash at Rockville Centre last Feb. 17.

Shortly after 1 A. M. Alexander Eber, assistant prosecutor of Middlesex County, who assumed charge of the investigation, announced that seventy-one bodies had been counted in a temporary morgue here, in the Middlesex County Morgue, Perth Amboy, and elsewhere. Fifteen of these, and two other bodies visible in the wreckage, were still unidentified.

Many among the injured were on the critical list at hospitals in Perth Amboy, South Amboy and Rahway. Scores of others were admitted for treatment of minor injuries and discharged.

Army and Guard Summoned

Police and fire equipment from a score of surrounding communities responded to a general emergency call sent out by the first rescuers to reach the scene. Army troops from near-by Camp Kilmer and New Jersey National Guardsmen were called to clear away a dense throng of onlookers that impeded rescue workers in the narrow street paralleling the tracks at the scene of the wreck.

Woodbridge, a town of 28,000 inhabitants, is about twenty miles south of the Jersey City terminal. The wreck occurred a quarter of a mile south of the Woodbridge station, a block from the main business center.

Although a Pennsylvania Railroad detective said the train was traveling at top speed when it cracked up, the injured engineer said he entered the trestle at no more than 25 miles an hour.

"I entered the trestle at about 25 miles an hour and the speed of the train certainly couldn't be blamed for the crash," said Joseph H. Fitzsimmons, 57 years old, of Point Pleasant, N. J., the engineer, from a bed in the Perth Amboy General Hospital.

He suggested that the "over-crowded coaches and the temporary trestle caused the accident."

"The moment my engine passed over the trestle and lurched sharply I felt the rest of the cars would never make it," he added. "When I started to sway I applied the brakes but apparently it was too late."

Mr. Fitzsimmons suffered head cuts and fractured ribs when he

Continued on Page 25, Column 2

RAIL DISPUTE TALKS FAIL TO FIND ACCORD

Union Negotiators Confer With Mediators, Then Seek to End Differences on Demands

By JOSEPH A. LOFTUS
Special to THE NEW YORK TIMES.

WASHINGTON, Feb. 6—The railroads and four operating unions were still locked in dispute tonight, and management estimated that the traffic jam resulting from the "sick" strike of switchmen showed little improvement, considering the country as a whole.

Union negotiators, after conferences among themselves, went into session with the National Mediation Board late this afternoon. After a meeting of more than two hours, a dinner recess was taken.

A night meeting also was recessed and the union leaders went into a further study of differences in their respective demands. The board asked both unions and the carriers to remain "on call."

Hints that a settlement was imminent cropped out on Capitol Hill, but a spokesman for the railroads said he did not have "the slightest idea" of the basis for such a rumor.

The railroads also said that new walkouts by switchmen, members of the Brotherhood of Railroad Trainmen, practically offset the return of switchmen in some places.

"The magic word hasn't gone out yet," a railroad spokesman said.

The union group was reported to have spent most of the day put-

Continued on Page 17, Column 5

M'GRATH TO HANDLE COURT PRICE TESTS

Feud With Justice Agency Cut Off by Johnston, Aide Says—DiSalle Sought Full Role

By CHARLES E. EGAN
Special to THE NEW YORK TIMES.

WASHINGTON, Feb. 6—The Department of Justice today won its fight to handle civil as well as criminal cases arising out of violations of the nation's price ceilings, according to a spokesman for Eric Johnston, economic stabilization administrator.

After an hour's talk with Peyton Ford, deputy attorney general, the Johnston spokesman said his superior had reached an agreement with the Department's representative giving full authority to the Justice Department in the field of price-administration prosecutions.

Earlier, F. Joseph Donohue, in charge of enforcement for the Office of Price Stabilization, which is under Mr. Johnston's jurisdiction, was reported ready to resign if the claim of the Department of Justice that it exercise control over civil prosecutions of price ceiling violations prevailed.

Reached after the Johnston-Ford compromise, Mr. Donohue said that he would remain in his post at least "until this enforcement branch of O. P. S. is properly staffed."

Michael V. DiSalle, director of price stabilization, was in Toledo and not available for comment when Mr. Johnston reached his agreement with Mr. Ford. Mr. DiSalle, however, was scheduled to

Continued on Page 20, Column 3

CITY COUNCIL VOIDS POLICE BILL CHANGE

3-Vote Switch Kills Softening Rider to Measure Requiring 30-Day Wait for Pensions

A switch of three votes enabled the City Council yesterday to rescind its adoption on Jan. 26 of an amendment that would have softened materially Council legislation requiring members of the Police Department to wait thirty days before their retirement applications could be effective.

Parliamentary obstacles, however, blocked any immediate police pension reform. Action on the bill was put over until the Council's next scheduled meeting, Friday, Feb. 16.

To avoid any possible question of legality as to the Council's ac-

Continued on Page 32, Column 6

Reds Draw Back 5½ Miles To New Seoul Defense Line

By LINDESAY PARROTT
Special to THE NEW YORK TIMES.

TOKYO, Wednesday, Feb. 7—Chinese Communist troops on the western Korean front pulled back five and one-half miles to new defense positions in the hills six miles below the Han River and the old Korean Republican capital of Seoul as United Nations armored task forces for the second day yesterday probed deeply into enemy advance positions below the city's southern outskirts.

With allied forces moving forward in strong tank and infantry teams, the Chinese Communists moved back from their previous line of resistance along the coastal road from the ruined temple city of Suwon. An Eighth Army headquarters spokesman said today that the United Nations capture of Hill 431, twelve miles southwest of Seoul, after a battle, had rendered the enemy line untenable.

The Chinese Communist withdrawal began thirty-six hours ago while enemy rearguards fought stubborn delaying actions covering the retreat. The spokesman said that enemy positions along the Han had been heavily reinforced and that the Communists meant to make a determined fight south of the river.

The United Nations advance yesterday came along the main north-south highway through Anyang. Probing forces pressed within about four miles of Seoul in the deepest penetration.

In the central sector, a tank and infantry team, which jumped off Monday from Hoengsong, had pushed a total of six miles through the mountains.

Eighth Army Headquarters es-

Continued on Page 3, Column 2

MOSCOW STRESSES GERMANY IN NOTE

Reply on Four-Power Parley Does Not Bar Other Issues —French Disappointed

Text of one of the Soviet notes to Western powers, Page 12.

By HAROLD CALLENDER
Special to THE NEW YORK TIMES.

PARIS, Wednesday, Feb. 7—While not declining to discuss other questions, the Soviet Union in its note on the four-power conference, as it was published in Paris today, once more placed the emphasis entirely upon Germany, as though its demilitarization was the principal issue.

The note again attacks the policy of the Western powers for reviving the German industry of war and raising the question of the resurrection of the German armies, and this despite the fact that the Western powers have in fact slowed down their measures for the rearmament of Western Germany.

The Soviet note goes on to com-

Continued on Page 12, Column 3

World News Summarized

WEDNESDAY, FEBRUARY 7, 1951

Seventy-four persons were killed and at least 330 others injured in the derailment of a southbound Pennsylvania commuter train at Woodbridge, N. J., at 5:43 P. M. yesterday. [1:8.]

The East recovered somewhat from the crippling effects of the railroad strike as workers returned to their posts. Virtually normal train service by today was forecast. The rest of the country, however, saw little of the back-to-work movement, and in the Far West there were reports of a further spread of the walkout. As a result most cross-country traffic was at a standstill. [1:1.]

Representatives of the carriers and the unions were still deadlocked and a spokesman for the railroads said there was no basis for a report that a settlement of the dispute was imminent. [1:2.]

Strong opposition in Congress to the proposal to draft youths of 18 has caused Administration leaders to believe that Congress eventually will approve a compromise measure calling for the induction of youths at 18½ years and forbidding their dispatch to combat areas before they reach 19. [15:1.]

Full authority was given the Department of Justice to prosecute civil as well as criminal cases of violations of price ceilings. [1:3.]

The Atomic Energy Commission set off its fifth and most powerful atomic blast in eleven days, concluding its current series of test explosions near Las Vegas, Nev. The commission said the tests had saved "invaluable time" in the atomic development program. [16:2.]

In Korea Chinese troops below Seoul fell back five and a half miles to new defense positions only six miles below the Han River, which skirts the former South Korean capital. [1:6-7; map P. 2.]

A Soviet note to the Western powers emphasized that German militarization should have the top consideration at the proposed meeting of the Council of Foreign Ministers, but did not bar discussion of other issues. [1:7.]

Washington was said to be unenthusiastic about new diplomatic discussions with Moscow at this time. If such negotiations do take place Washington will insist that an Austrian treaty, the rearmament of Soviet satellites in Eastern Europe and other issues affecting the security of Yugoslavia also be put on the agenda. [5:3.]

The recent reprieve of twenty-one Germans convicted of war crimes was dictated by political expediency, according to the views of the German public as revealed by a survey. [14:1.]

Dr. Vladimir Clementis, former Foreign Minister of Czechoslovakia, may be in Western Germany, according to a United States High Commission official, who said "we had nothing to do with bringing him here." [13:1.]

The participation of Spain as a full-fledged member of the North Atlantic Treaty Organization was held a long-range policy of this country. [1:6-7.]

NEWS BULLETINS FROM THE TIMES
Every hour on the hour
7 A.M. through Midnight
WQXR AM 1560
WQXR FM 96.3

Index to other news appears on last page of this section.

Tests of Atomic Artillery Indicated; Greatest Nevada Blast Lights West

By WILLIAM L. LAURENCE

While the five atomic explosions at the gunnery range near Las Vegas are of necessity shrouded in official mystery, certain facts, known to scientists but unfamiliar to the public, make it possible to arrive at reasonable conclusions about them.

A tremendous blast—likened to a bursting sun—that was felt in Los Angeles and sighted more than 500 miles away wound up the present series of Nevada experiments yesterday at 5:46 A. M., Pacific standard time. It was the most powerful in the series.

To understand the nature of the tests, one must first understand the nature of the atomic bomb and its constituents. The active material in a bomb consists of rather small quantities of either one of two fissionable materials—uranium 235 (U-235) or plutonium.

The fissionable material is limited by what is known as the critical mass, the exact amount of which is a top secret. It is known, however, that the weight of the critical mass is in terms of pounds.

For purposes of illustration, let us assume that the critical mass is ten kilograms (twenty-two pounds). On the basis of this figure, no amount of fissionable material less than ten kilograms could be made to explode. On the other hand, any mass of fissionable material more than ten kilograms would explode automatically in a manner analogous to spontaneous combustion in a chemical reaction.

While the actual explosive material is thus weighed in terms of pounds, the auxiliary apparatus required to produce an efficient atomic explosion, including the shell, must be thought of in terms of tons. It is known that the atomic bomb used over Japan and at Bikini substantially filled the bomb bay of a B-29.

The principal problem in designing and constructing an efficient

Continued on Page 16, Column 3

Pitfalls Lie in the Path of Spain To a Defense Alliance With West

This is the first of five articles on Spain by the Chief Foreign Correspondent of THE NEW YORK TIMES.

By C. L. SULZBERGER
Special to THE NEW YORK TIMES.

MADRID, Jan. 27—It is clear that United States policy toward Spain is founded upon the hope that some day Spanish manpower and the nation's raw materials, industrial ability and geographic position may be incorporated into the North Atlantic Treaty Organization.

This is a relatively long-range aspiration on the part of Washington. It apparently was formulated before the revision of the United Nations' attitude on full diplomatic representation in Madrid. Evidently, that change in relations was the first step toward accomplishing the objectives fixed by Washington.

Before any other truly significant advances in the direction of the desired goal can be registered two other achievements are regarded as necessary: first, France must be visibly strengthened as a military power with *élan vital* (along the lines now being followed but by no means yet achieved); second, the question of West Germany's participation in the North Atlantic Treaty Organization mechanism must be at least formally settled.

The basic issue concerning Spanish cooperation with the Atlantic Alliance is deeply intricate. It involves far more than United States good-will, or even than the type of coordinating occidental defensive measures against a common threat, regardless of individual national, political, or economic divergences.

Essentially it is a political question to which may be appended a profoundly important economic corollary.

Diplomatic and Ideological

Continued on Page 6, Column 3

SCENES OF FATAL TRAIN WRECK WHICH TOOK HEAVY TOLL

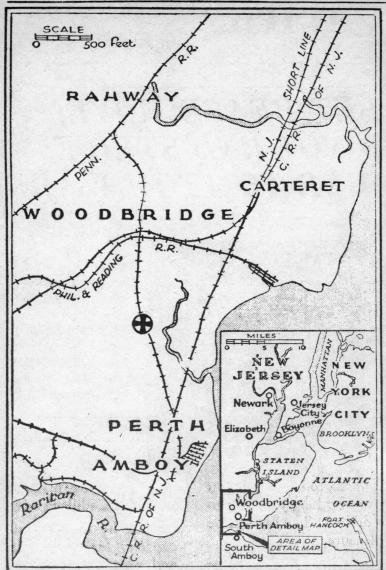

The New York Times   Feb. 7, 1951

Cross shows where commuter train crashed over embankment in Woodbridge, between Rahway and Perth Amboy.

Rescuers use ladders to remove injured from the twisted coaches of the Pennsylvania commuter train

A New Jersey state trooper looking at the overturned engine of the derailed commuter train   Associated Press

The New York Times (by George Alexanderson)

A view of one of the wrecked cars showing the caved-in trestle

JERSEY COMMUTERS DIE IN RAIL WRECK

Continued From Page 1

was thrown from the engine cab. A. M. Dunn, also of Point Pleasant, the fireman, died of injuries in the Perth Amboy Hospital at 7:20 last night.

A Pennsylvania spokesman issued a statement at 11:45 P. M. saying that the accident was under investigation but asserting that it was not caused by failure of the trestle. The temporary trackage was opened at 1:01 P. M. and the first train passed over it at 1:50 P. M., followed by five others before the wreck occurred, the spokesman said.

In Haddonfield, The United Press ported, Gov. Alfred E. Driscoll said all state officials had been ordered to "take every necessary step to determine the cause" of the wreck.

Mr. Eber said Attorney General Theodore Parsons had assigned two of his assistants to aid in the inquiry on the scene.

A commuter on a train that preceded the wrecked one by fifteen minutes noted that the train seemed to wabble slightly in passing over the temporary trackage on the embankment.

From the position of the cars after the wreck, observers reconstructed the accident as follows:

The locomotive, tender and first five cars of the eleven-car train passed safely over the trestle, one car length across and supported by eighteen wooden piles. Wheels of the sixth car apparently broke through the wooden bridge, causing a whip-lash action to convulse the train.

The steam locomotive toppled over on its side but remained on top of the embankment. The tender fell to the west down the twenty-five-foot embankment, landing in Fulton Street, which parallels the tracks on the west.

The first and second cars slewed part way down the embankment, perilously tilted but not overturned. The third and fourth cars plunged farther down the embankment and were the worst damaged. They contained most of the dead and critically injured.

The fifth car rested on its side in the mud of the embankment just south of the bridge, while the sixth, under which the trestle appeared to have collapsed, spanned the trestle, resting on the concrete abutments at either end. One of its wheel trucks had dropped through the bridge and rested in Legion Place below.

The seventh and eighth cars appeared to have sheared past the sixth car, ripping open their sides and plowing down the embankment near the third and fourth coaches. The last three cars remained to the north of the bridge, upright on the tracks.

Arnold Szeles, who was in his home at 275 Fulton Street, immediately opposite the scene when the wreck occurred, told of a "tremendous crash" followed by a dense cloud of smoke that obscured the scene. When it lifted, he and other residents ran to the overturned cars and began assisting the injured.

Soon they were joined by the first emergency vehicles from Woodbridge and calls for help from farther afield were issued.

At Rahway General Hospital, a man who suffered only face lacerations told hospital attendants he saw dead and injured piled up together inside the splintered cars. He was one of twenty-five casualties, most of them in critical condition, taken to the hospital in the first hour.

The first of the victims at the South Amboy General Hospital were five men, all walking cases, who suffered only minor cuts and bruises. The hospitals' ambulances had returned to the wreck to bring other loads.

Perth Amboy General Hospital, closest to the scene, had received ten injured persons within half an hour after the accident and attend-

ants said "many more" were on the way.

A Pennsylvania spokesman emphasized that the recent "sickness" strike of the railroad switchmen had nothing to do with the accident. He said the train was manned by its regular crew.

The train left Jersey City at 5:10 P. M. after picking up passengers from a connecting train through the Hudson Tubes that left Hudson Terminal, Manhattan, at 5:02 P. M.

After making a first stop at Newark, The Broker picked up speed heading for Perth Amboy, its next stop.

The rear cars remained upright on the tracks and passengers in them received, for the most part, only minor injuries, from being thrown against obstacles by the force of the crash. The last car, according to a railroad spokesman, was a club lounge privately rented by a group known as the Jersey Shore Commuters Club, executives who commute daily to Newark and New York.

An immense crowd of bystanders collected rapidly at the scene in this Middlesex County town of 28,000 inhabitants. Police and fire emergency squads and ambulances from a score of other near-by communities and State Police vehicles were hampered initially by private vehicles clogging the scene. The wreck area was cordoned off by police to give rescue crews unhampered access to the scene.

The line is double-tracked at the point of the wreck and railroad officials said other trains were being routed around the wreck.

100TH ANNIVERSARY
"All the News That's Fit to Print"
1851 1951

The New York Times.

Copyright, 1951, by The New York Times Company.

LATE CITY EDITION
Fair today and tomorrow, except partly cloudy both afternoons.
Temperature Range Today—Max., 70; Min., 53
Temperatures Yesterday—Max., 66; Min., 54
Full U. S. Weather Bureau Report, Page 63

VOL. C..No. 34,072. Entered as Second-Class Matter, Post Office, New York, N. Y. NEW YORK, TUESDAY, MAY 8, 1951. Times Square, New York 18, N. Y. Telephone LAckawanna 4-1000 RAG PAPER EDITION SEVENTY-FIVE CENTS

MARSHALL SAYS M'ARTHUR UPSET PEACE MOVE; HOLDS GENERAL'S PLAN COULD NOT END STRIFE; TRUMAN DEFENDS POLICY AS BAR TO ATOM WAR

REGENTS PROPOSE STATE TV NETWORK TO AID EDUCATION

Board Will Seek $3,500,000 From Legislature to Build Stations in Ten Areas

CHANNELS ASKED OF F.C.C.

Head of Special Unit Studying Plan Says Airways Are as Valuable as Schoolhouses

By JACK GOULD

A plan for a state network of eleven educational television stations, under which the resources of colleges, schools, museums, art galleries and libraries would be used to provide special video programs for both school children and adults, was announced yesterday by the Board of Regents.

The board revealed that it would ask the Legislature for $3,500,000 with which to construct two transmitters in this city and one each in Buffalo, Rochester, the Albany-Schenectady-Troy area, Binghamton, Ithaca, Syracuse, the Utica-Rome area, Poughkeepsie and Malone.

Disclosure of the plan, by far the most comprehensive yet suggested for educational use of the television medium, was made in a document filed in Washington with the Federal Communications Commission, which was asked by the board to set aside the non-commercial channels necessary for the projects success.

Freeze on Construction Noted

Actual operation of the network could not begin for a year or two, it was noted, because of the governmental "freeze" on the construction of new stations.

John P. Myers, chancellor of the Board of Regents, and Dr. Lewis A. Wilson, State Commissioner of Education and president of the University of the State of New York, agreed that the proposed network would provide "unlimited opportunities" to extend the state's educational program.

The board's approval of the plan was based on recommendations made by a special committee of Regents appointed to study television, including Jacob L. Holtzmann, chairman; Vice Chancellor Edward R. Eastman and Roger W. Straus.

Mr. Holtzmann said that he viewed with "extreme criticism some of the bad things made available to children on television" and that he personally disapproved of children being told about the pleasures of beer drinking while they watched the Brooklyn Dodgers.

"Whether a laxative works or not or perspiration disappears under your arm, that is a matter of taste," he continued. "We wouldn't say don't do that. What we want to do is to provide an alternative."

Will Fight for Channels

Mr. Holtzmann acknowledged that the Regents might run into conflict with commercial interests that also sought the limited number of television channels available, but made it clear that the Regents were prepared for any contest that might develop.

"It is as important for the educational system to have television channels as schoolhouses, and I don't know in the future which will be more important," he said. "The television channels are the most valuable natural resource the people possess today.

"We, the Regents, maintain we have a first mortgage on those channels and we're going to fight for them."

The Regents, who have supervisory authority over more than 8,000 public and private educational cultural institutions in the state, filed its plan with the F. C. C. only a matter of hours before the deadline for comment on the commission's proposed allocations of new channels for video outlets.

For the most part the Regents endorsed the commission's proposals for educational outlets in New York State, but in the case of several cities proposed further

Continued on Page 44, Column 2

Salvador Quake Kills 1,000 In One City; Other Towns Hit

Many Hundreds Are Hurt in Two Stricken Areas—Tremor Large-Scale

By The Associated Press.

SAN SALVADOR, May 7—A major disaster struck this country yesterday when an earthquake in southeastern El Salvador took approximately 1,000 lives in the city of Jucuapa alone. The figure was made public by the Government.

Hundreds more were injured. The President of the republic, Lieut. Col. Oscar Osorio, accompanied by high military and civil officials, and rescue teams from all over the country rushed to the stricken area. The Government decreed three days of national mourning.

New earthquakes were reported in southeastern El Salvador today, in the wake of yesterday's tremors. The new shocks were reported in the cities of Santiago de María and in Be[illegible]n, both in Usulutan Department. No casualties have been reported thus far in today's quake.

The greatest damage was reported in Jucuapa, a city of about 12,000, about ninety miles east of

GUAT.
HONDURAS
0 20 40 Mi.
Santa Ana
Lempa
Jucuapa
Chinameca
San Salvador
San Miguel
Usulutan
EL SALVADOR
NIC.
0 200 Mi.
FLA.
Miami
Gulf of Mexico
CUBA
MEXICO
Caribbean Sea
BR.HOND.
HONDURAS
GUAT.
EL SALVADOR
NICARAGUA
PANAMA
AREA OF DETAIL MAP
COSTA RICA
Pacific Ocean

The New York Times May 8, 1951
Cross indicates stricken area

San Salvador, and at Chinemeca, about 17,000 population, two miles farther east. The near by towns of Nueva Guadalupe, Santiago de

Continued on Page 12, Column 6

Richter Is Pulitzer Novelist; No Prize Given for Drama

By CHARLES GRUTZNER

The fields of drama and reporting of national affairs went without awards in the announcement yesterday by the trustees of Columbia University of the thirty-fourth annual selections of Pulitzer Prizes in journalism, letters and music.

Conrad Richter's "The Town"—final book in a trilogy on an American pioneer family—won the award as the best novel by an American, and Carl Sandburg's "Complete Poems" was named the year's best book of American poetry. This was the second Pulitzer prize won by Mr. Sandburg.

The absence of an award for national reporting was explained by Dr. Grayson Kirk, vice president and acting head of Columbia University, as due to the finding by the advisory board, which makes the award recommendations, that the outstanding achievement in that field had been the exclusive interview with President Truman obtained by Arthur Krock, the Washington correspondent of THE NEW YORK TIMES. Mr. Krock, who had won Pulitzer prizes for national reporting in 1935 and 1938, is now a member of the advisory board, whose policy it is not to make any award to a member.

There was not, however, any explanation for the absence of a drama award. Questions about the omission drew "no comment" replies from Columbia officials. Four times previously Pulitzer awards have been withheld from the theatre—in 1919, 1942, 1944 and 1946.

The war in Korea made a heavy impact on the field of prize jour-

Continued on Page 29, Column 1

65 POLICEMEN FACE INDICTMENT TODAY

Leibowitz Set to Arraign Men Named in 8-Month Inquiry on 'Protected' Gambling

By MILTON HONIG

A sealed indictment accusing sixty-five to seventy present and former members of the Police Department of conspiracy to obstruct justice will be handed up today by the Brooklyn rackets grand jury.

The true bill, bringing to a climax an eight-month investigation into the police-protected bookmaking activities of Harry Gross, head of a $20,000,000-a-year syndicate, will cite about twenty-five as defendants, while the others will be listed as co-conspirators.

The indictment is scheduled to be opened tomorrow before County Judge Samuel S. Leibowitz. At that time, the defendants, who range in rank up to inspector, will appear for arraignment.

Meanwhile, District Attorney Miles F. McDonald announced that

Continued on Page 35, Column 3

Thieves' Car Kills Man on Walk; 3 Others Hurt in 18th St. Getaway

One pedestrian was killed and three others seriously injured at 5:40 P. M. yesterday on Eighteenth Street between Broadway and Fourth Avenue when two suspects fleeing from postal inspectors drove wildly through the crowded thoroughfare in a jeep station wagon.

The suspects abandoned the wagon when it got jammed between two Railway Express Agency trucks and escaped on foot.

The action started at Fifth Avenue and Twentieth Street. Postal Inspectors Peter Maichiello and Walter Crowe, in plain clothes, were on an investigation unconnected with the incident when they saw two men loitering near the curb. As the inspectors approached the men ran south and jumped into the station wagon, parked at the west curb between Eighteenth and Nineteenth Streets.

The inspectors had no car in which to follow but the suspects, thought by the police to have been package thieves, did not know this and put on speed, rounding the corner of the avenue and Eighteenth Street, headed east. The fleeing car went safely until it reached the southeast corner of Broadway, where it jumped the curb and struck Paul Metzler, 30 years old, of 3100 Brighton Seventh Street, Brooklyn, as he was buying a paper from the corner newsdealer.

The car veered sharply left and mounted the north curb opposite 35 East Eighteenth Street, striking and killing Raymon Vazquey, 24, of 450 West Nineteenth Street, knocking over a sidewalk ventilator and smashing a window of the Leonardo Furniture Company at 35.

The driver, apparently terrified, and seeing home-going crowds emerging from the buildings around, then wrenched the wheel again and the car zigzagged across to the south curb. It ran along the sidewalk for fifty feet at fifty miles an hour, knocking down

Continued on Page 34, Column 5

KOREA ALLIES DRIVE

Push Back Communist Invaders in an Attack Northwest of Seoul

FOE QUITS CHUNCHON

Abandons the Road Hub Eight Miles South of the 38th Parallel

By LINDESAY PARROTT
Special to THE NEW YORK TIMES.

TOKYO, Tuesday, May 8—South Korean forces jumped off in an attack northwest of Seoul yesterday and pushed back the Communist invaders one to three miles in stubborn fighting.

Front-line dispatches said that United Nations forces had reached positions ten to thirteen miles above the capital, regaining about half the ground lost to the Communists' spring offensive before it withered in Seoul's outskirts under heavy United Nations artillery barrages. The South Koreans, spearheading the allied advance, fought an estimated two regiments, which withdrew slowly northward.

The Communists abandoned the important road hub city of Chunchon, in central Korea, and yielded ground before United Nations assaults at the eastern end of the line, near Inje.

Lieut. Gen. Matthew B. Ridgway's headquarters said this morning that tank-infantry teams scored "limited advances" both in the east and west. They met "moderate" resistance northwest of Seoul, but only scattered opposition inland from the Sea of Japan, in the eastern sector.

[According to The United Press, advancing United Nations forces on the east coast placed units at Kangson, ten miles above the Thirty-eighth Parallel.]

A United Nations armored patrol rolled into Chunchon at 2:30 o'clock yesterday afternoon, Eighth Army headquarters reported. It found no enemy in the city, which

Continued on Page 3, Column 5

PRESIDENT WARNS

Asserts Single Nuclear Blast Could Cause Toll Above Korea's

NOTES RED SETBACKS

Reports Drive in Asia Checked, 'Conspiracy' Hard Hit Elsewhere

The text of President Truman's address is on Page 20.

By W. H. LAWRENCE
Special to THE NEW YORK TIMES.

WASHINGTON, May 7—President Truman warned the nation tonight that the possibility of many atomic bombs' falling upon American cities was a stake in the debate over General of the Army Douglas MacArthur's removal because of the war policies he advocated in the Far East.

"Remember this. If we do have another world war, it will be an atomic war," the President said in a late addition to his speech. "We could expect many atomic bombs to be dropped on American cities and a single one of them could cause many more casualties than we have suffered in all the fighting in Korea."

Mr. Truman said that we must assume both that the Soviet Union had atomic bombs and the capacity to deliver them upon our cities no matter how effective our air defenses might be made.

This fact, he continued, was one of several reasons why he felt he could not accept the risks of a third world war inherent in the policy of limited warfare against Communist China advocated by the ousted general.

The President asserted that the progress of Communist imperialism throughout Asia had been checked by the firm stand of the United Nations in Korea and that the battle against aggression there had "dealt a heavy blow to the

Continued on Page 19, Column 3

World News Summarized

TUESDAY, MAY 8, 1951

Defense Secretary Marshall and President Truman yesterday defined the differences with General MacArthur as springing from the dismissed commander's demand for extending the war against Communist China at the risk of starting a new world war and wrecking the coalition of Western Allies.

Secretary Marshall told the Senate inquiry that not even the MacArthur plan could bring an early end to the Korean fighting. A "fundamental divergence" between General MacArthur's judgment and that of those setting United States policy, he said, reached a crisis when General MacArthur offered the enemy an armistice in the field at the moment that President Truman had about finished clearing his plan for a truce with the other allies.

It was because General MacArthur, who had always followed military directives, had ignored those against public statements on policy that he was removed, Secretary Marshall said. The Secretary disputed General MacArthur at all points and said the Joint Chiefs' statement that the former commander had relied on contained sixteen points, not only the four that had been quoted. [All the foregoing, 1:8.]

"Our foreign policy," President Truman told national civilian defense leaders, "is to try to prevent atomic war," in which many bombs would fall on this country, and to "stand and work with the other free peoples of the world." Warning against "impatience or defeatism," he said the Kremlin could score no greater victory than by disrupting the Allies. "We cannot go it alone in Asia and go it in company in Europe," he declared, and if we engaged in an "all-out struggle in Asia" we would expose Europe "to the Soviet armies." [1:5.] Only 500,000 have volunteered for civilian defense, although 15,000,000 are needed. [29:1.]

General MacArthur announced he was returning his plane to the Government. [10:3.]

British and French opposition to United States proposals that the United Nations impose an arms embargo on Communist China appeared to be disappearing. [3:1.] Britain denied the shipment of strategic materials to Red China. [5:3.]

In Korea, South Koreans drove north of Seoul as the allies pushed deeper into areas recently lost. [1:4; map P. 2.]

Moscow renewed its demand that the United States, Britain, Communist China and the Soviet Union meet to draw a Japanese peace treaty. [1:6.] The British saw the note as a move to split the Western allies. [8:3.]

Lieut. Gen. Wedemeyer, whose 1947 report on Korea was made public last week, has applied for retirement. [1:7.]

A United States armed services contingent landed in Iceland to help defend that country. [13:3, with map.]

An earthquake in El Salvador killed more than 1,000. [1:2-3.]

Conrad Richter's "The Town" won the Pulitzer Prize for the best American novel. No awards were made in drama or national reporting. [1:2-3.]

NEWS BULLETINS FROM THE TIMES
Every hour on the hour
7 A.M. through Midnight
WQXR AM 1560
WQXR FM 96.3

Index to other news appears on last page of this section.

TESTIFIES FOR THE ADMINISTRATION

Secretary of Defense George C. Marshall in witness chair
The New York Times (by Bruce Hoertel)

SOVIET ASKS PARLEY ON JAPANESE PACT

Assailing U. S. Draft, Moscow Calls for Meeting of States Involved in Peace Treaty

By HARRISON E. SALISBURY
Special to THE NEW YORK TIMES.

MOSCOW, May 7—The Soviet Union in a memorandum handed to United States Ambassador Alan G. Kirk today proposed calling the Council of Foreign Ministers of the United States, the Soviet Union, Britain and Communist China in June or July to draft, in consultation with all the other states that participated in the Far Eastern war, a peace treaty for Japan.

The Soviet proposal sharply attacked not only the draft proposals for a peace treaty with Japan prepared by the United States but the manner of preparation, which, it charged, was designed to impose an American "diktat" upon Japan and to exclude the Soviet Union, China and other countries from full participation in the treaty preparations.

The Soviet statement declared it was "perfectly obvious" that without participation of Communist China in the peace treaty "a real peaceful settlement in the Far East is impossible."

The Soviet memorandum was handed to Admiral Kirk by Acting Foreign Minister Alexander Bogomolov at the Foreign Office at noon today. Mr. Bogomolov is act-

Continued on Page 7, Column 1

WEDEMEYER SEEKS ARMY RETIREMENT

Aide Says 'Coincidence' With the MacArthur Developments Makes Action 'Spectacular'

By LAWRENCE E. DAVIES
Special to THE NEW YORK TIMES.

SAN FRANCISCO, May 7—Lieut. Gen. Albert C. Wedemeyer, 53-year-old commander of the Sixth Army, with headquarters at San Francisco's Presidio, acknowledged today that he had applied for retirement.

The news, six days after his long-secret recommendations on Korea had been made public in their essentials by the combined Senate Armed Services and Foreign Relations Committees, caused wide speculation, on all phases of which the general himself remained silent. The committees are now holding hearings in Washington on the dismissal of General of the Army Douglas MacArthur from his Far East commands.

[The United Press reported that General Wedemeyer would not confirm or deny reports circulated last week that he would accept the chancellorship of the University of California at Los Angeles.]

General Wedemeyer refused to reply to such questions as whether his action was influenced by the situation involving General MacArthur. One Presidio source, voicing doubt that President Truman's dismissal of General MacArthur

Continued on Page 9, Column 2

McGee Dies in Mississippi Chair; Final Plea to Justice Vinson Vain

By JOHN N. POPHAM
Special to THE NEW YORK TIMES.

LAUREL, Miss., Tuesday, May 8—At 12:05 A. M. today, 2:05 New York time, Willie McGee, 37-year-old Negro convicted of raping a white woman, died in a portable electric chair set up in front of the jury box in the same county court room where he had stood trial.

McGee's case had attracted world-wide attention and Mississippi officials were deluged with several thousand letters and telegrams, including some from Moscow and Red China. It had also resulted in a series of public protest demonstrations by leftists in cities throughout the country, as well as inviting the attention of the State Department.

As death came to McGee, a crowd of 500 men, women and children, who had milled about the courthouse lawn for three hours, gave vent to a few cheers, then broke up quietly and left the square.

Several men and boys had climbed to the upper branches of trees shading the courthouse walls and viewed the execution through an open window on the second floor.

Some fifty witnesses observed the execution, including the husband of the woman who was raped. He sat in the fourth row of seats. Flanking him were several members of his immediate family.

McGee's execution followed a turbulent day in which his attorneys moved on three legal fronts to obtain a stay of a death sentence that had previously been set aside five different times in almost six years.

While McGee was being transferred from one county jail to another in preparation for the execution, lawyers appealed to Federal jurists in Jackson, New Orleans and Washington for elev-

Continued on Page 32, Column 2

GENERAL IS BLAMED

Secretary Says Truce Steps in Korea Spoiled Work of President

HITS M'ARTHUR CASE

Denies Chiefs Approved Ideas—Reveals Truman Wanted Wider Air War

The text of Secretary Marshall's testimony, Pages 16 through 18.

By WILLIAM S. WHITE
Special to THE NEW YORK TIMES

WASHINGTON May 7—Secretary of Defense George C. Marshall accused General of the Army Douglas MacArthur today of having destroyed, in violation of orders, the only chance to date of negotiating an end to the Korean war.

He asserted as well that General MacArthur's rejected policy for more aggressive military action in Korea not only might have mortally involved the United States with the Soviet Union but would not, in any case, have decisively defeated the Communists in Korea.

In this, Secretary Marshall said, he was speaking with the concurrence of the highest military authorities, the Joint Chiefs of Staff. No plan—not the MacArthur plan, not the existing plan for limited commitment in Korea—was going to make an early end to the fighting, the Secretary said, unless the Chinese Communists found their losses insupportable.

Recalls MacArthur Offer

Testifying before the joint Senate Armed Services and Foreign Relations Committees in closed session, Secretary Marshall, himself a General of the Army, supported in every detail President Truman's decision to remove General MacArthur from high command in the Far East.

General Marshall will return to the witness stand at 10 A. M. tomorrow. His questioning by the committees was far from done.

General MacArthur, the Secretary declared, had never ignored strictly military directives "but in relation to public statements [involving policy] he has."

The most damaging of these utterances, Secretary Marshall added, was General MacArthur's offer of March 24 to meet the enemy commander in the field to seek a way to armistice.

That statement had been made by General MacArthur, General Marshall went on, in the face of warnings against such declarations and in the face of specific prior information that the President was working on the subject of peace negotiations.

At the time General MacArthur spoke, Secretary Marshall said, the President had about finished clearing his plan with the thirteen other Allied nations having troops in Korea.

Says Chiefs Listed 16 Points

"In view of the serious impact of General MacArthur's statement on the negotiations with these nations," the Secretary continued, "it became necessary to abandon the effort, thus losing whatever chance there may have been at that time to negotiate a settlement of the Korean conflict."

General Marshall said all Washington officials—himself, the Joint Chiefs of Staff and the President—had approved General MacArthur's request for authorization to give enemy planes "hot pursuit." This is a term applied to the chasing of enemy aircraft beyond the Korean boundary, without taking the initiative in fighting over the line. However, General Marshall testified, the thirteen other nations with troops in Korea opposed this approval, and the matter was dropped.

He hit at nearly every view and contention General MacArthur had offered in his own defense before the committees—hit, by "very distressing necessity," he said, at a "brother officer."

He accused General MacArthur

Continued on Page 15, Column 1

QUAKE KILLS 1,000 IN SALVADOR CITY

Continued From Page 1

Maria, Usulutan and Caserios also suffered considerable damage.

The Government bureau of information gave no death toll for Chinemeca but said that 200 injured had been removed from that city to a hospital in near-by San Miguel. The Government announcement described the destruction at Chinemeca as "50 per cent less" than the damage at Jucuapa.

Although El Salvador is in a volcanic region, the country has never before experienced so destructive a quake. The entire country is subject to periodic heavy earth shocks.

The National Meteorological Observatory said today that the disaster might be attributable to a volcanic peak called El Limbo, about three miles south of Chinameca. Meteorologists said, however, that neither the old volcano nor the near-by volcano of San Miguel had given any recent signs of activity.

The observatory placed the epicenter of the quake about sixty miles southeast of the capital. The Government is requiring safe-conduct passes for all persons seeking to enter the devastated region. This step was taken to facilitate rescue work and make it easier to maintain public order and security.

Dr. Frank Press, director of the Columbia University Seismograph Station at Palisades, N. Y., said yesterday that the Salvadorean quake was of magnitude 6, which indicates a quake of major proportions. The greatest earthquake of recent years was the Assam earthquake of last Aug. 15, which was of a magnitude 8½. The historic San Francisco quake of 1906 was tabulated at 8¼.

Last year's Assam quake was considered the biggest since volcanic Krakatoa Island, Indonesia, exploded in 1883. The number of homes razed in the Assam shocks was given as 100,000. Because of the remoteness of the area, no accurate report of the number killed was available, but it was estimated that 5,000,000 people were affected.

Stunned victims of the earthquakes, their faces still reflecting the shock, wait helplessly for relief.

United Press International

Rescue workers search through the rubble for survivors. In the background is one of the few buildings left standing in Jucuapa.

United Press International

The New York Times.

Copyright, 1951, by The New York Times Company.
NEW YORK, TUESDAY, JULY 17, 1951.
VOL. C..No. 34,142.
FIVE CENTS
LATE CITY EDITION
Scattered showers today; cooler, less humid tonight and tomorrow.
Temperature Range Today—Max., 83; Min., 72
Temperature Yesterday—Max., 87; Min., 71
Full U. S. Weather Bureau Report, Page 40

FLOODS ROLL SOUTH; 'STAGGERING' LOSS IN FOOD REPORTED

Oklahoma Town Inundated—850,000 Acres of Farm Land in 3 States Under Water

'OPERATION PORKCHOP' ON

Stored Meat in Kansas City Moved, Much Feared Ruined—Truman to Visit Zone

By WILLIAM M BLAIR

Bail of 14 Reds Voided Again; New Bonds Required Today

Ryan Disqualifies Civil Rights Congress—Gives Defendants Until Noon to Raise $165,000 Elsewhere or Be Jailed

By RUSSELL PORTER

Kem Rider Substitute Backed To Curb Trade With Russia

By WILLIAM S. WHITE

O. P. S. SETS SURVEY OF GROCERY PRICES

Agency Will Try to Establish Uniform Ceilings on Items in Each Community

By CHARLES GRUTZNER

De Gasperi and His Cabinet Resign In Split Within the Premier's Party

By ARNALDO CORTESI

Dr. Alcide de Gasperi

LONDON, PARIS SEND BITTER OBJECTIONS TO U. S.-SPAIN PACT

2 European Allies in Western Defense Renew Opposition—Britain Will Not Resist

SHERMAN, FRANCO CONFER

Washington Is Noncommittal About Meeting—A Second Interview Is Possible

IRAN ARRESTS REDS; HARRIMAN CONFERS

Sunday Riot Inciters Rounded Up—U. S. Adviser Is Silent on 2 Talks With Premier

By SYDNEY GRUSON

World News Summarized

TUESDAY, JULY 17, 1951

TRUCE SESSIONS MAKE 'SOME PROGRESS'; BOTH SIDES STRESS OWN AGENDA AIMS; NEGOTIATORS BACK AFTER 5TH MEETING

THE COMMUNIST NEGOTIATORS AT KAESONG TALKS

Left to right: Gen. Hsieh Feng, Gen. Tung Hua, the Chinese delegates; Gen. Nam Il, chief spokesman; Maj. Gen. Lee Song Cho and Maj. Gen. Chang Pyong San, North Koreans, at the conference house Monday.

New Soviet Moves for Amity With West Noted in Moscow

By HARRISON E. SALISBURY

SATELLITE UNREST REPORTED GROWING

Slowdowns, Sabotage, Lower Quality of Production Mark Dissatisfaction With Reds

By DREW MIDDLETON

Leopold III of Belgium Abdicates In Favor of His Son, Baudouin, 20

REDS CITE ISSUES

Peiping Radio Says Aim at Talks Is Return of Korea Status Quo

PARLEY LENGTH IN DOUBT

Allied Briefing Officer Asserts Conferees Must Agree First on Subjects to Discuss

By LINDESAY PARROTT

Flood Waters Recede in Kansas and Missouri; Oklahoma Town Inundated

Sandbagging along the Missouri River.

The New York Times

FLOODS ROLL SOUTH; FOOD LOSSES HIGH

Continued From Page 1

estimated the loss to Topeka at $100,000,000.

Manhattan, Salina and other Kansas cities reported the high water was receding but that it would be at least three weeks before services were normal.

Throughout the flooded area telephone service was on an emergency basis. Some 32,000 telephones were out in Kansas City at one time. Fifty operators were reported flying in from New York tonight for the emergency.

The Red Cross regional headquarters at St. Louis estimated tonight that there were 165,300 "disrupted" persons in the flood area. This meant homeless, out of work and displaced.

Stored Food Losses Feared

In addition to farm damage, which may run to $100,000,000 in Kansas alone according to some land experts, the two Kansas Citys faced the loss of great amounts of meat, eggs and frozen food stocks stored in warehouses caught in the flood.

A packing house official estimated that at least 25,000,000 pounds of meat were in the plants here of the "Big Four" packing companies—Armour, Swift, Wilson and Cudahy. All are in the flooded industrial areas.

"Operation Porkchop," as it is called by weary Army engineers, started this afternoon to remove the meat. Boats maneuvered into the flooded plant area to carry the meat to big refrigerated trucks that would rush it to cold storage. Some of the meat had been kept in condition by dry ice carried in by boat at the height of the flood after the water knocked out refrigeration machinery.

Boats were working at the Armour and Swift plants as Government inspectors stood by to pass on the meat and condemn spoiled beef, pork and other products. Cudahy officials also asked for boat help and Wilson was expected to try to get its stocks moved shortly.

A Swift spokesman said most of the beef at that plant had spoiled and that stocks being taken out included frozen pork loins and shoulders and sweet pickled (cold cuts) meat. He declined an estimate of the damage to the packing industry but said it would be four to six weeks before the major plants resumed operations.

One of two major cold storage warehouses, with water up to the third floor, began the removal by boat of some 5,000 cases of eggs. The warehouses also contain frozen vegetables, meats, fruits and fruit juices and a variety of other foods.

The warehouses were attempting to get elevators in working order to bring down food stocks from as high as ten floors. But, barring repairs, they planned to construct slides to get the food cases down to boats.

Some 10,500 head of livestock trapped in the Kansas City stockyards were being trucked out as water receded. Giant road graders and dirt hauling trucks were towing big diesel vans through two and three feet of water to the concrete hog pens to take out the cattle, hogs, sheep, horses and mules. The vans then were towed back to a roadway and dispatched, with police escorts, to outlying feeder lots, pasture and other yards, including the stockyards at St. Joseph, Mo., sixty miles north of here.

The livestock were moved to the safety of the upper decks of the hog pens early Friday and had been fed since by supplies carried by boat.

Yard officials said the livestock included approximately 3,500 head of cattle, 6,000 hogs and 1,500 sheep. Trading has been suspended indefinitely at the yards, which may require extensive rehabilitation because of the mud and debris deposited by the swirling flood tide.

Joseph M. Nolan, city councilman and livestock commission buyer, emphasized that it was necessary for the industry to turn its attention to rehabilitation of the yards in order to "prepare to handle the 300,000 cattle expected from the grass country in the next few months."

A warehouse spokesman said that if the total estimated damage

Oil (black streak, left), from tanks that burst, flowing down flood-covered street in the central industrial area of Kansas City, Mo. At right is burned out section, scene of huge fire Friday.

The Associated Press

The flood, moving down the Neosho River, had crossed into Oklahoma, inundating part of the town of Miami (A). The mingled waters of the Kansas and Missouri Rivers poured toward St. Louis as the tide rapidly ebbed in Kansas City area.

to the sprawling industrial districts was near $750,000,000. then "at least half of it was in food."

There remained the possibility, however, that the dry icing and other emergency measures had saved much of it.

Industrialists and business men were inclined to believe that the $750,000,000 damage figure that Maj. Gen. Lewis A. Pick, Chief of Army Engineers, reported to President Truman today was "too low." They expected the damage to be more in the neighborhood of $1,-000,000,000 and sources close to General Pick said he was being conservative. No accurate estimate can come until much later when salvage operations are well under way.

Meanwhile, in Topeka, Kan., H. L. Collins, Federal-state crop expert for the Kansas area, said that crops in the lower Kansas River Basin had been destroyed or so badly damaged as to be worthless.

"The loss," he said, "greatly exceeds 1903, the last big major flood damage." Wheat and corn bore the brunt of the damage and the next crop report likely will show a further drop in wheat and corn. The July 1 crop report showed that wet weather and floods had cut the wheat crop down to 147,854,000 bushels, a decrease of 13,000,000 bushels from June in the country's top wheat state. There were no estimates how much more the crop would be cut."

Wheat harvesting has been under way in Southern Kansas coun-

ties but in the big central belt, crews have been kept from the fields by rain, high water and floods. The wheat growth has been heavy, but it is lodging, or falling down, and shattering, making it useless. Harvesting has not begun in northern counties and unless there is a continued dry spell there may be some loss there as the wheat is ripening rapidly.

An aerial survey of the lower Kansas River Valley shows stacks of hay sticking out of the high water. Some of the inundated hay will be rotted. The same situation exists along the Missouri and tributaries and farmers reported that much hay was caught in windrows on the ground.

One of the major losses is expected to be in farm building, machinery and equipment. According to agriculture sources, little machinery and equipment was moved out of the flooded areas because the rivers rose so rapidly under the heavy rains over a three-day period last week.

The one bright spot was the condition of pasture land. Mr. Collins reported that it was lush from the rains and provided excellent summer forage for livestock.

Heartened by Truman Visit

Kansas Cityans were heartened by the news that President Truman would visit here tomorrow.

Officials were looking to him to push flood control plans in Congress to prevent a recurrence of the disaster. It was learned today that groups that had consistently

opposed plans of the Army Engineers and other Federal agencies in the vast Missouri River Basin had asked Army Engineers to go over the plans with them again.

Brig. Gen. Don G. Shingler, Missouri River Division chief of the Army Engineers, flew to Topeka this afternoon to confer with one powerful opposition group in that hard-hit community. He took with him Col. L. J. Lincoln, district Army engineer here, and others to show what was planned in the way of dams, reservoirs and local protection works to harness the Kansas and its turbulent tributaries.

Meanwhile, the two Kansas Citys moved ahead on the arduous task of cleaning up the mud, restoring crippled water facilities and rehabilitating industral plants, businesses and several thousands of homes.

Contractors and union labor organizations joined with Kansas City, Mo. in setting up a nonprofit organzation to clean out flooded public areas and cooperate with similar operations by private plant owners and other private organizations.

Will Speed Rehabilitation

The contractors and the American Federation of Labor and Congress of Industrial Organizations leaders carried the plan to the city. Methods of financing were brushed aside temporarily as more pressing rehabilitation work was discussed.

Union men will be thrown into the big task at reduced wage rates and contractors will slice rental fees on needed equipment. A single man will head the organization, directing the work from City Hall.

"This is a community effort and all we want to do is get the job done," said Perrin D. McElroy of the A. F. L. "Plasterers and bricklayers, and others, skilled and semi-skilled, they'll all be handling shovels. It must be and shall be a nonprofit organizaton."

Some 4,000 residents evacuated as a precautionary measure from North Kansas City, across the Missouri River from Kansas City, Mo., started to move back to their homes today. The city, where dikes held after a hard fight by volunteers, came alive as residents converged on homes by auto, truck, bus and on foot.

Kansas City (Mo.) officials were confident that the Turkey Creek Pumping Station would be in operation by the end of the week to relieve the drastic water situation. That northeast pumping station, which was inundated, was being dried out as water dropped below the floor level. Kansas City, Kan., won its three-day fight to save the light and water plant with an emergency dike.

The most common sights in the area today were glass jars, wooden casks and other containers filled with boiled water or with water purified with halazone tablets. There were wry faces over the tablets, which imparted a dank taste to the water, but health officials continued to urge boiling and use of the tablets, which have been distributed free. Almost every business house, including hotels and restaurants, had emergency water rations.

Stores Open Four Hours

Thousands of persons continued to get typhoid inoculations, especially those working in the flooded areas or residents preparing to return to inundated homes. This was true all through the Kansas River Valley, at Salina, Manhattan, Oakland and elsewhere.

Department stores and other commercial houses opened for four hours today, 11:30 A. M. to 3:30 P. M., but crowds were small.

Taverns and bars also were closed and the traditional Monday washday was out. Only institutional laundry, such as hospital work, was permitted.

At least one railroad hoped to restore its service directly into Kansas City, Mo., by tomorrow.

The Rock Island line said its Golden State Limited and Imperial would leave Chicago and Los Angeles tomorrow, heading here. One of the big difficulties with railroad service has been a technical one. Trains must make a turn-around here in a big track loop before moving east or west. The loop tracks have been flooded.

Many passengers bound east, west and south have been stranded here. The Rock Island said it still had some Los Angeles passengers to move. All lines dispatched passengers by bus and other means to points of service. In some cases passengers were taken as far as Oklahoma City to resume their journeys.

The Rock Island will not be able to resume its southbound service to Oklahoma and Texas for some time.

A spokesman for the Santa Fe said it would be two weeks before they could get under way here. Westbound Santa Fe trains have been moving from Chicago to Galesburg, Ill., on the line's own tracks, thence to Omaha and Lincoln, Neb., and on to Denver over Burlington tracks, where they pick up Santa Fe rails again.

In the case of the Union Pacific, passengers boarding at St. Louis are carried to Omaha on Wabash lines and then onto the main Union Pacific tracks.

Other lines affected by the high waters are the Frisco, Katy (Missouri-Kansas-Texas), Wabash, Milwaukee and Kansas City Southern. The Missouri Pacific's St. Louis-Colorado run has been detoured over Burlington and Milwaukee tracks to St. Joseph, Mo., and thence west.

Steel Union Sends Flood Aid

PITTSBURGH, July 16 (AP) — Philip Murray, president of the United Steelworkers and the Congress of Industrial Organizations, said today the steel union had sent a $10,000 check to the C. I. O. Emergency Flood Relief Committee at Kansas City, Mo. Mr. Murray added the C. I. O. would send a similar amount. He urged all C. I. O. unions to aid the flood-stricken community.

A flooded district of Miami, Okla., where 400 homes were inundated Sunday. At left is one of the city's main east-west streets, turned into a stream by the overflowing Neosho River.

Associated Press Wirephotos

Truman to Fly Over Flood Area; Congress, Agencies Rush Relief

Wilson to Go Along With President Today to Note Disaster Steel Needs—House Increases Fund to $25,000,000

By HAROLD B. HINTON
Special to The New York Times.

WASHINGTON, July 16—President Truman will fly to Missouri tomorrow for a personal inspection of the flood-damaged area around Kansas City, where he spent most of his early life. He will be accompanied by Mrs. Truman and their daughter, Margaret, who has just returned from Europe.

Another passenger in the Presidential airplane, the Independence, will be Charles E. Wilson, Director of Defense Mobilization, who will try to evaluate the damage to military production plants in the flooded region. In this way he will seek to estimate the amount of structural steel that will have to be allocated for plant rehabilitation and for the restoration of bridges, railroads and similar structures that have been damaged. The amount of steel required may be of sufficient volume, some officials believe, to transmit its impact to the arms production program.

House Votes $25,000,000 Aid

At the Capitol, the House passed an appropriation of $25,000,000 for disaster relief in the area, without a dissenting vote. The Senate was not in session today, but is expected to ratify the action tomorrow.

Representative Ben F. Jensen, Republican of Iowa, proposed an amendment under which $2,000,000 of the immediate $25,000,000 fund be earmarked for flood control construction from Sioux City, Iowa, to Kansas City. This, however, was put aside for concentration on disaster aid.

The Senate Appropriations Committee met while the House was debating its own aid resolution and voted promptly for appropriating $15,000,000. When it learned that the House had increased the sum, the group decided to meet again tomorrow morning, consider the increase, and make its recommendations as the Senate convened.

The original sum proposed to the House was $15,000,000, based on earlier estimates. On motion of Representative John W. McCormack of Massachusetts, the Majority Leader, however, the increase was made without opposition.

House leaders had expected the relief measure to be speeded through to adoption with little or no debate. The House, however, talked at length, not in controversy over the assistance, but to demonstrate two issues uppermost in the minds of many members as they received the steady reports of devastation in Kansas and Missouri. These members told of having similar flood danger areas in their home districts, some on large rivers, some on small ones.

Digest of Relief Measures

Reports include the following:

R. F. C.—Concentrating its total disaster fund of $35,000,000 on the flood area * * * set up emergency field examiners who will aid in restoring the homes to pre-disaster status.

PUBLIC HEALTH — Flying in ten to twelve portable water purifying units from various parts of the country * * * will undertake noculation program to fight disease.

FOOD AND DRUG ADMINISTRATION — Working with chain stores and other food interests to determine what foodstuffs are edible.

RED CROSS — Has raised allocated disaster funds to $750,000.

AIR FORCE—Has forty planes in the flood region, running in supplies and evacuating victims. To date, the Air Force has air-lifted 160 tons of supplies.

ARMY CORPS OF ENGINEERS—Reports 1,000 persons are working in area.

MAYOR TUCKER — Fears that every day 170,000 people are out of work means a daily payroll loss of $1,300,000.

LABOR DEPARTMENT—Three of its seven offices in the flood areas are under water but the records have been saved. Unemployment insurance, as a result, can be paid out to those who have been made idle and who are covered.

AGRICULTURE DEPARTMENT — Supplies such as powdered milk, eggs, and cheese are being dispatched to critical points.

A break in dike (right, center) at Kansas City, Kan., caused floods in many plants, including Phillips Petroleum (top).

"All the News That's Fit to Print"

The New York Times.

LATE CITY EDITION
Cloudy and cold today; clearing, colder tonight. Fair tomorrow.
Temperature Range Today-Max., 35; Min., 28
Temperatures Yesterday—Max., 39; Min., 31
Full U. S. Weather Bureau Report, Page 39

Copyright, 1952, by The New York Times Company.

VOL. CI..No. 34,374. Entered as Second-Class Matter, Post Office, New York, N. Y. NEW YORK, WEDNESDAY, MARCH 5, 1952. Times Square, New York 36, N. Y. Telephone LAckawanna 4-1000 RAG PAPER EDITION SEVENTY-FIVE CENTS

MORAN SENTENCED TO 15½-28 YEARS IN FIRE SHAKEDOWN

Judge Mullen Says 'Genius' of Racket Cached or Passed On $300,000 for Future

WAY FOR 'TALK' LEFT OPEN

Commitment Papers Unsigned —$1,000 Pay-Off to Cover a Deputy Chief Is Bared

By ALFRED E. CLARK

A prison sentence of fifteen and one-half to twenty-eight years was imposed yesterday in General Sessions on James J. Moran, former First Deputy Fire Commissioner, convicted as "guiding genius" of a $500,000-a-year fuel oil shakedown racket.

The 50-year-old ousted official must first serve the state prison sentence before he begins a five-year Federal term that was imposed in addition to a $2,000 fine for perjury committed last spring before the Senate Crime Investigating Committee.

Moran, a political protégé and close friend of former Mayor William O'Dwyer, was characterized by Judge John A. Mullen as "a shining example of everything a public official should not be."

The sentence, which well might mean that Moran will end his days behind bars, confirmed reports that the convicted man had refused to cooperate with District Attorney Frank S. Hogan and to divulge the identity of the "person or persons" who had divided the "lion's share" of the lucrative profits with him.

Four "Bagmen" Aided State

Since Moran's conviction last Feb. 5, when he was remanded to City Prison, it had been hoped by Assistant District Attorney Alfred J. Scotti that the prisoner would cooperate. It was the fulfillment of a similar hope in the case of four fire inspectors, convicted as Moran's "bagmen," that brought the official to his present plight. The inspectors received stiff jail terms and then turned state's evidence to gain clemency.

Judge Mullen loosed a scathing denunciation on Moran before imposing sentence. He rejected the prisoner's contention, made to probation authorities, that he was the victim of the conspiracy rather than its head.

"The jury rejected that idea and so do I," said Judge Mullen, who went on to picture Moran as the "creator and director of a gigantic conspiracy throughout New York City to shake down fuel oil equipment installers."

Pointing out that the accused had lived "well within" his $10,000-a-year salary as deputy fire commissioner, Judge Mullen charged he had either cached the $300,000 or "else you have passed the money on to some other person or persons whom you can call on some time in the future."

Ousted by Impellitteri

Moran, married and the father of four children, 13 to 20 years old, was appointed to the Fire Department in February, 1946. Shortly before Mr. O'Dwyer resigned as Mayor in the summer of 1950 to become Ambassador to Mexico, he appointed Moran to the Board of Water Supply, a lifetime post paying $15,000 annually. He resigned on orders of Mayor Impellitteri after being indicted by a Federal grand jury on perjury charges.

Judge Mullen refused to postpone Moran's commitment for thirty days and the prisoner was hustled back to his cell in the City Prison. However, it was learned that the judge had left court without signing commitment papers that would authorize Moran's removal to Sing Sing Prison.

As a result, speculation arose late yesterday as to whether Moran might still avail himself of an opportunity to "talk," even though he had shown no disposition to do so. One observer put it tersely: "All last month he didn't even say 'Hello.' Now he's got time to mull it over."

In an unusual move, Judge Mullen released the eleven-page probation report that had been submitted to him in connection with the Moran case. The most significant parts of the report were disclosures of two other alleged shakedown attempts by the defendant.

One occurred in 1917 when the International Fire Chiefs Association held a convention here at the Pennsylvania Hotel (now the Statler). The report said that Moran

Continued on Page 16, Column 4

SWISS INDUSTRIES FAIR—AT BASLE: ... textiles, fashions. APRIL 19-29, 1952. Advt.

Shift in Income Distribution Is Reducing Poverty in U. S.

Rise in National Output Benefits 'Forgotten Man'—Vast 'Leveling Up' Held Proof of Our Vitality—No Similar Soviet Record

By WILL LISSNER

The United States has undergone a social revolution in the last four decades, and particularly since the late Thirties.

The marginal worker, the first to lose his job in times of depression, and once regarded as the "forgotten man" of American capitalism, has been the greatest beneficiary of recent gains in national output. The American dream of rising in the income pyramid to comfortable levels of living has been realized by millions of families.

The gains substantially outweighed pre-Korea price rises.

As a result of little-appreciated changes in the distribution of a rapidly growing national income, the United States has gone about half the way toward eliminating inequities in incomes. But it has done this, not by leveling down, but by leveling up. These are some of the changes:

¶The very poor have become fewer by two-thirds of their 1939 number.

¶The poor have become better off. Where three out of four families had incomes of less than $2,000 a year in 1939, only one out of three fell into that class ten years later.

¶The well-to-do and the rich have become more numerous. In the late Thirties, one family in about fifty was in the $5,000 and over income class, and one out of 100 was in the $10,000 and over class. In the late Forties, one family out of six was in the $5,000 and over class, and one out of twenty in the $10,000 and over class.

¶Over the years, the very rich have become poorer because the rise in labor incomes has been ac-

Continued on Page 24, Column 2

Aluminum Buying in Canada On Big Scale Studied by U. S.

By THOMAS E. MULLANEY

Proposals for augmenting the nation's aluminum supply through a seven-year purchase contract with Canada for 3,500,000,000 pounds of that country's metal in ingot form and through additional domestic expansion of productive facilities have been drafted by Samuel W. Anderson, deputy administrator for aluminum of the Defense Production Administration.

This two-point program is expected to be placed before top officials of the United States aluminum industry at a meeting in Washington today and before a large group of key Government and industrial representatives there tomorrow at a panel on aluminum policy presided over by Defense Mobilizer Charles E. Wilson.

The objectives of these proposals, which cover the years 1953 through 1959, are these: to assure all military requirements for this pivotal metal; to provide for all civilian needs, and to create a huge surplus for the nation's emergency stockpile of critical materials.

With respect to a further enlargement of domestic facilities, Mr. Anderson suggests the building of a plant or plants capable of turning out 280,000,000 to 300,000,000 pounds of raw aluminum annually, or a 10 per cent increase of the industry's size, when it completes next year the defense expansion program started in 1950 and 1951.

The long-range procurement contract with Canada would see the bulk of the metal coming here in the period 1955 through 1959. Informed sources say that about 3,000,000,000 of the 3,500,000,000

Continued on Page 15, Column 3

NO INQUIRY ASKED ON TREASURY AIDE

After Foley Testifies Briefly, Hoey Says Investigation Was Not Ordered

By CLAYTON KNOWLES

Special to THE NEW YORK TIMES.

WASHINGTON, March 4—A Senate subcommittee questioned Edward H. Foley Jr., Under Secretary of the Treasury, for twenty minutes today about the interest he took in pending tax cases and, after the closed session, announced that "no investigation was ordered and none asked."

Senator Clyde R. Hoey, Democrat of North Carolina who heads the permanent investigating subcommittee of the Senate Expenditures Committee, made this statement after Mr. Foley had given his answers under oath to questions raised by Senator Joseph R. McCarthy, Republican of Wisconsin.

Mr. McCarthy originally had asked that the Under Secretary be questioned before the full committee but this group, now engaged in considering President Truman's plan for reorganizing the Bureau of Internal Revenue, turned the

Continued on Page 20, Column 4

DEMOCRATS WARY OF AUTHORITY PLAN FOR CITY TRANSIT

Implied Fare Rise Threatens Them Politically, They Feel as They Study State Program

STEINGUT TO SEE MAYOR

Moore Bringing Proposals for Solving Local Fiscal Problem for Impellitteri's Perusal

By LEO EGAN

Special to THE NEW YORK TIMES.

ALBANY, March 4—Democratic legislators became alarmed today over the possibility that they would be asked to vote in favor of transferring New York's publicly owned transit lines to an independent authority that would be required to operate them without any tax subsidy.

Any such vote, they feared, would be equivalent to voting for a fare increase with all its attendant political dangers, including the possibilities of primary opposition for renomination and defeat for reelection.

As a result, Irwin Steingut of Brooklyn, Democratic leader of the Assembly, made hasty arrangements this afternoon for a series of conferences with Mayor Impellitteri and the Democratic leaders of the five New York City counties before the city administration agreed to such a transfer as part of a solution of its financial problems.

Moore to Present Program

Mr. Steingut's conferences will take place after Lieut. Gov. Frank C. Moore has acquainted the Mayor and other city officials with the details of the program that has been devised by the state administration and Republican legislative majorities to enable the city to obtain the money it needs to balance its budget for the fiscal year that starts July 1.

The state program, of which Mr. Moore is the chief architect, was formulated as an answer to city requests for $63,800,000 in new state grants plus the right to raise $280,000,000 through new local taxation to bring the city budget for next year into balance.

The city's program contemplated continued operation of the transit system by the Board of Transportation with the city making good a $54,000,000 operating deficit and a $13,500,000 pension deficit from tax collections. It further contemplated reduction of the sales tax from 3 to 2 per cent.

Although details of the state program have not been made public as yet, its keystone is understood to be the transfer of the transit lines either to the Triborough Bridge and Tunnel Authority, headed by Robert Moses, city construction coordinator, or to a new authority. In either event, the authority would be required to

Continued on Page 22, Column 2

102 Perish in Brazilian Train Disaster

Associated Press Radiophoto

Wrecked coaches on a bridge over Pavuna River near Rio de Janeiro

Special to THE NEW YORK TIMES.

RIO DE JANEIRO, March 4—One of the worst train disasters in Brazil's history occurred near the capital this morning, killing at least 102 persons and injuring 200, of whom fifty were on the danger list. Accurate figures still were impossible to get this evening because of the scale of the catastrophe and the consequent confusion, but the death toll was expected to mount above the present total.

The wreck took place when two old wooden cars of a badly overloaded train bound for Rio de Janeiro skidded off the tracks on a bridge over the Pavuna River, about twenty miles from here, near Anchieta, and were rammed by a fast electric train traveling in the opposite direction.

It was believed that poor condition of the rails had caused the wreck. According to capital newspapers, a freight train was derailed at the same place a few days ago, but without casualties.

The shattered wooden cars

Continued on Page 11, Column 1

PRESIDENT INSPECTING THE VOICE OF AMERICA SHIP

The New York Times (by Bruce Hoertel)

Mr. Truman talking with Capt. Oscar C. V. Wev, skipper of the Courier, after dedicating the vessel in Washington yesterday.

TRUMAN REASSURES EAST BLOC PEOPLES

He Says 'We Are Your Friends' in World-Wide Broadcast Dedicating 'Voice' Ship

Text of the President's address appears on Page 4.

By ANTHONY LEVIERO

Special to THE NEW YORK TIMES.

WASHINGTON, March 4—President Truman became the Voice of America today and sent a message of hope and peace around the world.

Speaking particularly to people behind the Iron Curtain who have been confused by the Communist "storm of falsehood," the President dedicated the Coast Guard Cutter Courier to the cause of truth in the struggle for men's minds.

The ship from the mothball fleet will course the Atlantic to pierce holes through the electronic shield maintained by the Soviet Union to keep news of the free world out of its uneasy empire. Today the 1,250 Russian jamming stations were busy as usual, trying to blot out the President's voice with their deliberate cacophony.

Relays Combat the Jamming

Powerful relay stations lifted the President's voice, however, and poured his message of peace into the Soviet Union, and the satellite countries, as well as to free men everywhere.

"We have no quarrel with the people of the Soviet Union or with the people of any other country," President Truman said. He recalled the two centuries of friendship that had marked the relationships of people of this country and the peoples of Russia and China. He also recalled how the United States had gone to the assistance of those two countries in World War II and added:

"I want to say to these people today, as we said then: We are your friends. There are no differences between us that cannot be settled if your rulers will turn from their senseless policy of hate and terror and follow the principles of peace."

In dedicating the ship, Mr. Truman joined with Cabinet officials and civil leaders in memorializing the first ten years of the Voice of America.

"There is a terrific struggle going on today to win the minds of people throughout the world," said Mr. Truman.

He declared truth was America's best weapon and pointed out that it would do no good if people never heard it.

Acheson Stresses Truth Drive

Secretary of State Dean Acheson speaking briefly ahead of the President, reiterated that the "campaign of truth is the central part of our foreign policy today."

The former Navy cargo vessel wore a coat of fresh gray for the ceremony on Washington's Potomac waterfront.

Mr. Truman spoke under a canopy on the "flight deck" from which the Courier will send up a special aerial with helium balloons to a height of 900 feet, or about twice as high as the Washington Monument.

For its new mission of carrying a "cargo of truth," as Mr. Truman expressed it, the Courier received a new United States flag from Donald McQuade, National Commander of the Catholic War Veterans.

Mrs. Hiram Cole Houghton,

Continued on Page 4, Column 3

Truce Parley Is Stalemated On 3 Main Points in Dispute

By LINDESAY PARROTT

Special to THE NEW YORK TIMES.

TOKYO, Wednesday, March 5—The Korean truce negotiations reached a complete deadlock yesterday on all disputed points when Communist and United Nations negotiators failed to find an answer to the impasse over the voluntary repatriation of prisoners, inclusion of the Soviet Union as one of the "neutral" armistice controllers and designation of ports of entry at which impartial inspectors should be stationed after a cease-fire.

Rear Admiral Ruthven E. Libby told correspondents after a two-hour session at Panmunjom that the talks on the prisoner exchange were "right back where they were Dec. 18," when the military committee began consideration of the issue. The North Korean representative, Maj. Gen. Lee Sang Cho, in a formal statement three times repeated that the Communists would "never" agree that prisoners should have the right to decide whether to return to their former allegiance, the Admiral said.

[The Associated Press reported that Allied Sabre jets had shot down five MIG craft and probably destroyed another when they surprised a formation of seventy enemy planes crossing the Yalu River from Manchuria into North Korea.]

Exchange of Information

Much of the debate centered on the exchange of information regarding captives not included in the rosters exchanged last year between the two commands. The Communists demanded data on approximately 44,000 originally reported by the United Nations as war prisoners, later found to be South Koreans and reclassified as interned civilians.

Such information would be handed over, Admiral Libby informed the enemy negotiators, only when parallel data was forthcoming regarding the approximately 50,000 South Koreans listed as missing and believed to have been impressed in the Communist armies.

General Lee argued that the Allied Command was obliged to return reclassified men since these previously had been called pris-

Continued on Page 2, Column 5

ATTLEE WINS TEST ON BEVAN REBELS

Ex-Prime Minister Gets 3-to-1 Backing of Labor M. P.'s in Showdown on Defense

By RAYMOND DANIELL

Special to THE NEW YORK TIMES.

LONDON, March 4—Former Prime Minister Clement Attlee and his moderate leadership of the Labor party won a striking victory over Aneurin Bevan, left-wing leader, whose political fortunes have been rising lately, at a private meeting today of the Labor members of Parliament.

Mr. Attlee and his colleagues in the recent Labor Government defeated by a margin of three to one Mr. Bevan's contention that expenditure on defense should be cut rather than that social services should be curtailed. For the first time the Bevanites challenged the party leadership on their favorite issue. The result of the meeting indicated that one in every four Laborites supported Mr. Bevan on this subject.

There are 294 Labor seats in Parliament, but many members were absent from the meeting. The vote was reported to have been 41 for Mr. Bevan and about 120 for the official party line. It has been estimated that the basic strength of the rebels in the House of Commons is between 80 and 100. The lower figure would roughly preserve the ratio of today's vote.

However, despite the victory for the moderates, the Labor party decided to offer an amendment to the Government's motion, on which tomorrow's defense debate, in which Prime Minister Churchill will take part, is to be held. The Govern-

Continued on Page 9, Column 3

U. S. Says Czechs Held Queens G. I. For Year, Then Sent Him to Poland

Special to THE NEW YORK TIMES.

WASHINGTON, March 4—The United States accused Communist Czechoslovakia today of having seized and jailed a United States Army corporal more than a year ago, held him incommunicado and then turned him over to Poland last month.

Cpl. Alexander S. Czarnecki, son of Mrs. Sophie Czarnecki, 87-11 Ninety-seventh Avenue, Ozone Park, Queens, had been listed as absent without official leave from United States forces in Germany since Dec. 15, 1950. United States authorities have known since early last June, however, when they received a brief note from him, that the corporal was in a Prague jail. Embassy officials have been trying since then both to see the corporal and to get him released. Both efforts have been in vain.

With the case of the missing corporal mentioned in today's Rude Pravo, Communist party newspaper in Prague, the State Department released the details of the corporal's disappearance for the first time.

Czechoslovak claims that the corporal had deserted from the army and sought "asylum" in Poland—he is of Polish descent—because he disagreed with "aggressive" United States policies were denounced by the State Department as the handiwork of Communist propagandists.

A note from Czechoslovakia last Friday was the first official acknowledgment by Prague authorities that Corporal Czarnecki had been in the satellite country. It stated that he had been "taken over by Polish authorities on Feb. 22 after he had requested asylum in Poland."

The note also alleged, according to Michael J. McDermott, State Department press officer, that the corporal had deserted from the Army "because he disagreed with"

Continued on Page 5, Column 1

U. M. T. IS SHELVED IN HOUSE, 236-162, AS COALITION WINS

Bill Sent Back to Committee, Where Vinson Declares He Will Not Ask Any Action

RAYBURN PLEADS FOR PLAN

Says 'Those Who Stand With Us,' Meaning the NATO Allies, Will Lose Heart

By HAROLD B. HINTON

Special to THE NEW YORK TIMES.

WASHINGTON, March 4—The House of Representatives refused today to authorize the Administration to start a program of Universal Military Training for men at 18 years of age, followed by seven and a half years of Reserve obligation.

The action was the result of a confused parliamentary situation in which the merits of the proposal never were frankly at issue, but it appeared to be a final shelving of the bill for this session of Congress.

The House, after reversing itself on an important amendment, voted by 236 to 162 to refer the Administration bill back to the Armed Services Committee, ostensibly for further study. Representative Carl Vinson, Democrat of Georgia, chairman of the committee, said after the session that he would not ask the committee to consider the question again at this session.

A Parliamentary Maneuver

However, Representative Paul J. Kilday, Democrat of Texas, a member of the committee who has favored the program, said the chairman might reconsider his position if the Senate passed a bill and sent it to the House for concurrence. Such a proposal is on the Senate calendar, having been unanimously recommended by its Armed Services Committee.

After spending last week on general debate, the members of the House were ready for action when the bill reached the stage of reading for amendment today. Sitting as the Committee of the Whole for this purpose, the House had hardly been called to order by Representative Jere Cooper, Democrat of Tennessee, as chairman, when the maneuvering began.

Representative William H. Bates, Republican of Massachusetts, who resigned from the Navy after more than nine years of service when elected to the House in 1950 to succeed his father, Representative George J. Bates, offered a motion to strike out the bill's enacting clause.

Had this prevailed, it would have automatically shelved the measure, but Administration leaders rallied enough votes to defeat it by 196 to 167. It looked, at that point, as if Mr. Vinson would be able to pilot the bill to a successful haven later in the week.

The Amendments Grow

Speaker Sam Rayburn made one of his rare speeches, urging that the motion be defeated on the ground that shelving the bill in such a manner would cause "those who stand with us," meaning the other members of the North Atlantic Treaty Organization, to lose heart.

Mr. Vinson then offered an amendment that would have limited the Universal Training system to the period between enactment and July 1, 1958, and would have forbidden its application at any time Selective Service was being used to draft men for actual military service.

This was adopted, 126 to 19, but it was to be the last success the Democrats were to enjoy. Thereafter, a well-organized coalition of nearly all the Republicans and several conservative Democrats took charge and maneuvered the bill to its ultimate downfall.

The first step was the adoption

Continued on Page 10, Column 4

News Summary and Index

For greater convenience of the reader the summary of the news has been combined with the index and placed on the last page of this part of The Times. The "News Summary and Index" provides a compact yet comprehensive view of the day's developments classified by subjects. It appears each day on the

Last Page of This Part of The Times

Rescuers search for bodies of victims amidst the mangled wreckage of these coaches, after two trains collided and burned at a crossing.

United Press International

102 DEAD IN WRECK OF BRAZILIAN TRAIN

Continued From Page 1

jack-knifed upward, and mangled bodies were caught in the wreckage. This evening firemen and policemen still were working to extricate the victims, who were mostly persons bound for their jobs in the capital.

The train was reported traveling slowly, but at 8:40 A. M., as it crossed the bridge, the engineer applied the brakes. Suddenly, the two cars swerved off the rails and came to rest on a parallel track just as the more modern electric suburban train arrived. Before the latter could be stopped, it plowed into the packed wooden cars.

Investigation of the disaster was hampered because the engineer of the wooden train had fled in the steam locomotive and then had abandoned it to hide. Because of a peculiarity in Brazilian law, an engineer, if arrested at the scene of an accident, can be held indefinitely without bail, but if he succeeds in escaping arrest for forty-eight hours, he can remain free unless his responsibility is formally established by the court.

Suburban trains of the Central Railroad of Brazil, on which the crash occurred, habitually are overloaded. Frequently, clusters of passengers cling outside the cars and ride on the bumpers between them. Fatal accidents are daily occurrences, but the shortage of equipment has prevented any improvement of conditions.

Projects for overhauling suburban train service are under study by the joint Brazilian-United States Commission for Economic Development. However, by a decision of the Brazilians themselves, improvement of long-distance distribution of food and raw materials has received priority over suburban passenger traffic.

Economic Factor Important

This traffic also is a matter of general economic importance, however, since thousands of man-hours are lost daily while workers wait for trains, on which they often cannot find room. It was one of these heavily overloaded trains, with extra passengers hanging on the outside of the old wooden cars, that was wrecked today.

One witness described the spectacle of outside riders flung in all directions as the crash occurred.

As many ambulances as possible were sent from Rio de Janeiro, together with rescue squads from four fire stations, to help extricate the victims. Local buses, and even trucks, were pressed into service. All off-duty personnel of three big hospitals were summoned to help with first-aid work.

A special train was sent to bring the bodies to the capital. Special police details were put around the Dom Pedro Segundo Station here for fear that families of the victims might stage violent demonstrations.

Reached Bridge Together

RIO DE JANEIRO, March 4 (AP) —A spokesman for the Central Railroad gave this account of the disaster today:

A wooden coach train left the Brazilian capital at 8:30 A. M., bound for Juiz de Fora, in the state of Minas Geras, 100 miles north of here. Seventeen minutes later, a crowded steel commuter train left Nova Iguacu, thirty-six miles from the capital.

The two trains thundered onto the Pavuna River bridge at the same time. As they neared each other, some cars of the coach train jumped the tracks and swung across the span. The commuter train then ploughed through the sides of the wooden cars.

"All the News That's Fit to Print"

The New York Times.

LATE CITY EDITION
Rain today; rain ending tonight. Clearing and warmer tomorrow.
Temperature Range Today-Max., 59; Min., 51
Temperatures Yesterday—Max., 55; Min., 50
Full U. S. Weather Bureau Report, Page 37

Copyright, 1952, by The New York Times Company.

VOL. CI..No. 34,428. Entered as Second-Class Matter, Post Office, New York, N. Y. NEW YORK, MONDAY, APRIL 28, 1952. Times Square, New York 36, N. Y. Telephone LAckawanna 4-1000 FIVE CENTS

176 MISSING AS U. S. DESTROYER SINKS IN NIGHT CRASH WITH CARRIER WASP; 61 MEN ARE RESCUED IN MID-ATLANTIC

COLLIDE DURING MANEUVERS AT SEA

Associated Press

The destroyer-minesweeper Hobson, which went to the bottom

The New York Times

Aircraft carrier Wasp, whose bow was damaged

BIG SHIP DAMAGED

75-Foot Gash Cut in Side as Flat-Top Wheels in Dark During Games

HEADS HERE FOR REPAIRS

Bringing Survivors Back to U. S. —Skipper of Smaller Craft Believed Among the Lost

By JAY WALZ
Special to The New York Times.

WASHINGTON, April 27—The destroyer-minesweeper Hobson sank after colliding with the aircraft carrier Wasp last night, and the Navy announced late today that 176 men were missing.

The Atlantic Fleet operating base at Norfolk, Va., said sixty-one survivors had been picked up by the Wasp and another destroyer-minesweeper, the Rodman. They are being returned to the United States.

At Charleston, S. C., the Hobson's home port, Rear Admiral William V. O'Regan, Navy Mine Force commander, said fourteen officers and 223 enlisted men had been aboard the ship that went down.

The Navy sent notices to the next of kin of the 176 men—seven officers and 169 enlisted men—reporting them as "missing." Of the survivors fifty-four are enlisted men and seven are officers.

No News on Rescue Efforts

Twenty-four hours after the accident, a Navy Department spokesman here said that, in the absence of reports to the contrary, the situation appeared to be that none, beyond the sixty-one listed survivors, had been saved. He said he had no information that rescue operations were continuing. He would not make a flat statement that all the rest were lost, however.

Since his name did not appear on the list of those rescued, the Navy presumption was that the commander of the Hobson, Lieut. Comdr. W. J. Tierney, was among the lost.

The huge Wasp was slashed along her starboard water line for a distance of about seventy-five feet from the bow. The Navy said no casualties aboard the carrier had been reported and it was presumed there had been none.

Tonight the Wasp was proceeding under her own power at 10 knots toward New York for repairs. Accompanied by the Rodman, she is expected to arrive at the New York Naval Shipyard, Brooklyn, Friday or Saturday.

Part of a Task Group

Navy offices here reported the collision took place at 1:38 A. M. today, Greenwich time, or 8:38 P. M., Eastern standard time, yesterday. The location was given at Lat. 42 degrees 21 minutes N., Long. 44 degrees, 13 minutes W. This point on a map of the Atlantic showed the collision to have occurred about 1,775 miles northeast of Norfolk and about 725

Continued on Page 11, Column 1

TRUMAN CONCEDES CONSTITUTION PUTS LIMITS ON POWERS

STEEL STEP A 'DUTY'

President Argues Basic Law Requires He Act for Nation's Safety

REPLIES TO QUESTIONER

Denies 'Pro-Labor' Wage Board —Insists Steel Profits Are High After Tax Payments

Exchange of letters and excerpts from steel case briefs, Page 13

By JOSEPH A. LOFTUS
Special to The New York Times.

WASHINGTON, April 27—President Truman said today the powers of the President were derived from, and limited by, the Constitution, but he felt the Constitution did not require him to "endanger our national safety by letting all the steel mills shut down in this critical time."

Mr. Truman's statement ostensibly was a reply to a man who asked him five questions about his seizure address to the nation on April 8. Actually, it amounted to public disavowal of controversial statements made by Government counsel in United States District Court here last week in opposing an injunction that would undo seizure of the steel mills.

When Judge David A. Pine asked whether the Department of Justice was contending that the Constitution limited Congress and the courts but not the President, Holmes Baldridge, assistant attorney general, replied in the affirmative. This and other statements in court have aroused widespread criticism. Judge Pine has the issue under consideration now, and promised counsel on Friday a decision within a week.

'Realized' Action Was Drastic

The pertinent sentences in the President's letter to C. S. (Casey) Jones, the noted aviator of Washington Crossing, Pa., said:

"I realized that the action I was taking in this case was very drastic, and I did it only as a matter of necessity to meet an extreme emergency. In so doing, I believe that I was acting within the powers of the President under the Constitution—and, indeed, that it was the duty of the President under the Constitution to act to preserve the safety of the nation.

"The powers of the President are derived from the Constitution, and they are limited, of course, by the provisions of the Constitution, particularly those that protect the rights of individuals.

"The legal problems that arise from these facts are now being examined in the courts, as is proper, but I feel sure that the Constitution does not require me to endanger our national safety by letting all the steel mills shut down in this critical time."

Mr. Truman then said he twice had sent messages to Congress asking it to prescribe a course in the steel case if it disagreed with his action.

Justice Department Stand Noted

The written position of the Department of Justice in the steel seizure case is not at variance with the President's statement today with respect to the Constitution. The statements of Mr. Baldridge that made headlines and provoked criticism were made orally and in most, if not all, cases were not volunteered but were replies to testing questions asked by the court.

Some lawyers sympathetic with the Government's position felt that Mr. Baldridge was led into making, or acquiescing in, unnecessarily broad statements.

The department's brief in the case says at one point:

"It should be noted that we do not contend that the President has a residuum of powers outside of the Constitution inherent in his position as Chief of State, as plaintiffs [the steel companies] would have this court believe our position to be. We contend only that he has such powers under the Constitution and concede that his actions are subject to constitutional limitations. In the instant case, the applicable limitation is

Continued on Page 12, Column 2

WHAT HAPPENED? See the "11th Hour News" presented by National City Bank of New York, WPIX, Chan. 11, 11:00 p.m.—Advt.

WROTE TO TRUMAN

Associated Press

C. S. (Casey) Jones

RUSSELL DISAVOWS CIVIL RIGHTS PLANK

Would Not Be Bound by Such a Proposal if Nominated, He Says, Citing Smith in '28

By JOHN N. POPHAM
Special to The New York Times.

TAMPA, Fla., April 27—Senator Richard B. Russell of Georgia said today that if he received the Democratic Presidential nomination and the national party platform recommended compulsory fair employment practices legislation, then he would "declare flatly that I am not bound by any such proposal."

"When Alfred E. Smith was the Democratic nominee in 1928, there was a prohibition plank in the party platform which he refused to be bound by, and that's exactly what I would do on the fair employment issue," Senator Russell declared.

The Georgian's remarks were made in a press conference at which he was asked to comment on the civil rights stand taken by Senator Estes Kefauver of Tennessee, who is opposing Senator Russell in Florida's Presidential preferential primary election on May 6.

Senator Kefauver, while stumping this state last week in his first bid for Southern support at the polls, declared that, although he favored voluntary and persuasive fair employment practices legislation, as the party's nominee he would feel "morally bound" to accept its platform even if it included compulsory measures in the civil rights field.

Meanwhile, it appeared evident

Continued on Page 16, Column 7

CONTROLLER WANTS LARGER CITY STAFF TO SPUR TAX YIELD

Joseph Sees $775,000 Added Cost More Than Offset by Increased Collections

TO HIRE 100 ACCOUNTANTS

Also Seeks Pay Rises for 253 He Has and 40% Increase in His Clerical Force

By PAUL CROWELL

Controller Lazarus Joseph announced yesterday that he would ask the Board of Estimate soon for a supplementary appropriation of $775,000 to enable his office to increase and expedite the collection of special city taxes.

The additional funds, which would have to be provided by issuing budget notes, would be used, according to Mr. Joseph, to make possible the employment of 100 extra accountants, increase the salaries of the 253 accountants now working in the Bureau of Excise Taxes and raise by 40 per cent the manpower of the clerical staff.

Mr. Joseph offered no estimate of the additional tax revenue the bureau hoped to collect as a result of the increased appropriation, but a spokesman for his office said it would be "substantial." State fiscal authorities have conservatively estimated that, even with the present staff, increased efficiency and streamlined procedure in collecting special city taxes would increase their annual yield by at least $1,000,000.

Problem Under Study for Year

Mr. Joseph's staff of fiscal experts has been planning methods of stepping up the collection of special city taxes, with special attention to the sales tax, ever since it became apparent last year that financing of the 1952-53 budget would force the fullest exploitation of all sources of city revenue.

Specifically, Mr. Joseph recommended the employment of 100 additional accountants in the Bureau of Excise Taxes to augment its present staff of 253. He suggested that the new men be employed at a starting salary of at least $4,300 a year at an annual cost of $430,000. This is the amount now paid by the Federal Government for such employes and is more than Mr. Joseph's accountants now receive.

In addition, Mr. Joseph said, the salaries of the present staff of 253 accountants should be increased to at least $4,300, involving an additional cost of $175,000, and the bureau's clerical staff should be increased by 40 per cent at an estimated annual cost of $170,000.

Approval of the three recommended steps, Mr. Joseph said, would increase excise tax revenues far beyond the total extra cost of $775,000.

Admitting that many of the bureau's accountants are doing outside work for private clients in order to supplement their city pay, Mr. Joseph declared that the Court

Continued on Page 27, Column 2

HUGE RED BUILD-UP DURING TRUCE TALK LISTED BY RIDGWAY

Army of 750,000 Is Massed Behind a 'Siegfried Line' in Korea, General Says

NEW CONFERENCE BEGINS

Chief Allied Delegate Refuses to Divulge Proceedings at the Full Armistice Session

By LINDESAY PARROTT
Special to The New York Times.

TOKYO, Monday, April 28—The Communist Command in Korea used the period of the armistice negotiations to make a substantial increase in its armies, building up a ground force of more than three quarters of a million men, well armed and behind powerful fortifications, and an air strength of more than 1,500 aircraft based in Manchuria, Gen. Matthew B. Ridgway's headquarters said yesterday.

The United Nations commander, in an information bulletin, asserted that, although the enemy forces—now mostly made up of Chinese—indicated no immediate offensive intentions, all factors showed that the Chinese "intend to maintain a strong position in Korea."

Headquarters noted a steady increase in enemy artillery and armor, and the presence of some new weapons, such as Soviet-designed rocket launchers, and compared the belt of fortifications built across the peninsula since the truce talks began last July to Germany's Siegfried Line of World War II.

General Ridgway's estimate came as the armistice negotiators at Panmunjom resumed the meetings of the full delegations this morning in an attempt to solve the virtual deadlock on all issues of the truce.

Deliberations Secret

The full delegations met on schedule at 11 A. M. [10 P. M. Sunday, Eastern daylight time]. Under some arrangement with the Communists that has as yet not been announced, it appeared that these sessions, like previous futile meetings of staff officers, were to be secret.

Vice Admiral Charles Turner Joy, senior United Nations negotiator, made no announcement from where his instructions had come, but said: "I regret I am not at liberty to make any statements regarding the nature or substance of this or any future conferences."

When he was asked why this had happened, his answer was: "Please don't ask me any questions," dispatches from Korea said. There was no indication this afternoon that any progress had been made in the new round of conversations.

The session had been set for yesterday morning, but was called off suddenly by the United Nations side without a reason for the postponement.

Staff officers debating Item 3 of the proposed agreement—terms for enforcement of the cease-fire—met for thirty minutes yesterday to hear North Korean Col. Chang Chun San, the principal enemy representative, again denounce the United Nations' "unreasonable demands" for a limitation on the construction of military airfields north of the Thirty-eighth Parallel during the truce.

"It was very obvious they were not trying to make any progress," Col. Don O. Darrow, senior United Nations staff officer, told correspondents.

Truce Would Bar Build-Up

General Ridgway's information bulletin said the enemy generally had been able to make excellent use of the long period of the truce negotiations, during which armed pressure has been at a minimum. The inference was left to be drawn that at least up to now the Communists might have had little reason to seek a formal armistice, since six months of virtual inactivity along the front have given them the opportunity for such a build-up of strength. On the other hand, a truce such as the United Nations seeks would prohibit a further increase of the forces of either side on the peninsula.

During the long-drawn-out negotiations, headquarters said, "the strength of the Chinese and North Korean forces has materially increased, rather than decreased." The release went on to itemize the advantages that had accrued to the enemy.

"Personnel and equipment losses largely have been replaced, training continued and some additional equipment has arrived," the bulletin said. Despite continued United Nations air superiority "over the

Continued on Page 2, Column 3

Sheen in Rome Says Red Agents Tried to Infiltrate the Priesthood

By The Associated Press

ROME, April 27—American Communists were under secret orders in 1936 to infiltrate the Roman Catholic priesthood, Bishop Fulton J. Sheen said today.

The 57-year-old Auxiliary Bishop of New York, speaking before an overflow congregation in the American Catholic Church of Santa Susanna, said:

"In 1936 the [Communist] wolves went into the forces which control public opinion * * *. There was hardly a prominent newspaper commentator who did not have a Communist secretary, although he or she did not necessarily know it.

"This was the beginning of the planting of forces of evil communism within the religious communities to destroy them from within. * * * A call for volunteers to enter religious orders and make the great sacrifices of the life of a seminarian was made at a secret Red meeting in a large [American] city."

Bishop Sheen, in Rome for his annual report as United States director of the Pontifical Society for the Propagation of the Faith, said the Communists even attempted to infiltrate his own office.

"A man from Moscow tried to install himself in my office," the Bishop related. "He had written a book on communism and came with introductions from sixty-three American editors. He told me he wanted to fight communism with me.

"As he went out the door, I called the F. B. I. [Federal Bureau of Investigation] and told them I had a Communist agent. The F. B. I. called back within half an hour to say they had traced this man through China and Mongolia but did not know he was in the U. S. A."

Although he did not mention him by name, Bishop Sheen strongly indicated in his sermon that the case of Alighiero Tondi, 44, Italian Jesuit priest who has just "embraced the Communist idea," paralleled American Communist infiltration. Communist propagandists have been stressing the defection of Tondi strongly.

Bishop Sheen also warned, in a clear reference to the approaching May 25 municipal elections in Italy, that Rome was coming to a crisis and that Romans were "face to face with tyrannical danger." The Communists are making an earnest fight to win in Rome.

Sheen Leaves for Paris

ROME, April 27 (UP)—Following an audience with the Pope, Bishop

Continued on Page 7, Column 6

Japan Wins Freedom Today; Treaty With Chiang Is Settled

Yoshida Warns the Country of Communist Designs to Conquer World

Special to The New York Times.

TOKYO, Monday, April 28—Premier Shigeru Yoshida, in a message on the eve of Japanese independence today, warned the newly sovereign nation against Communist designs to "conquer the world through insidious propaganda and infiltration, and by force." He called for a systematic increase in the country's defensive power.

Mr. Yoshida, leader of the Japanese conservatives and recently a daily target of a Communist propaganda broadcast to Japan, made the statement in a press release twelve hours in advance of the nation's resumption of independent rule at 10:30 tonight [9:30 A. M. Eastern daylight time], when deposit of the instruments of ratification of the San Francisco peace treaty will officially launch a new historic era for Japan.

The statement was one of the strongest anti-Communist pronouncements by the Premier, who made it clear that, as head of a sovereign government, he would follow the same guiding principle he frequently has announced as administrator under the Allied occupation.

"At long last we are free," Mr. Yoshida told the Japanese. "We are independent. Japan now joins the family of nations as a sovereign equal."

But he added that Japan, "grate-

Continued on Page 3, Column 5

Tokyo Renounces Claims to Formosa and Pescadores in Separate Accord

By The Associated Press.

TAIPEI, Formosa, April 27—A separate treaty of peace between Japan and Nationalist China was completed tonight. It will be signed at a ceremony here tomorrow afternoon.

The treaty will be signed at the Nationalist Government guest house, formerly the official residence of Japanese governors of Formosa.

Nationalist Foreign Minister George Yeh said the treaty was written in the spirit of the general Japanese peace treaty, signed in San Francisco on Sept. 8, and which becomes effective tomorrow. Nationalist China did not participate in that peace conference.

The Chinese-Japanese treaty's main points are:

¶Japan renounces title to Formosa and the Pescadores Islands, between Formosa and the Chinese mainland.

¶Japanese property and claims in Formosa will be disposed of by special arrangement between the two parties.

¶Japan recognizes as nationals of the Republic of China the residents of Formosa and the Pescadores who are of Chinese nationality.

¶Japan renounces her former assets in China.

¶The Republic of China and Japan agree to apply the principles

Continued on Page 3, Column 3

U.S. Jet Dives Into English Village; Pilot and British Couple Are Killed

Special to The New York Times.

LONDON, April 27—A blazing United States F-84 Thunderjet hurtled from the sky over the placid village of St. Peter's in Southeast England today and crashed on a little bank building in the main street.

The pilot, Capt. Clifford V. Fogerty Jr., of New York, and an elderly couple, William and Evelyn Read, were killed and several other villagers injured.

A United States officer said tonight that the pilot was told by radio to keep his damaged plane away from Broadstairs, a populous shore resort a little more than a mile away. The sea is two miles from the spot where the plane crashed.

Despite the horror that struck the village like a bursting bomb, the main topic tonight was what might have been.

At 12:16 P. M., when the crash took place, the narrow street was virtually deserted. A few minutes later it would have been filled with worshipers going home from morning service at the Twelfth Century church just 150 yards from where the plane crashed.

"Had I finished my sermon promptly, it is unquestionable that 30 per cent of my congregation of between 300 and 400 people would have been walking along the high street when the Thunderjet crashed," said the vicar, the Rev. Laurens Sargent. "Between twenty and thirty would have been waiting at the bus stop almost at the scene of the crash."

The plane came from the near-by United States Air Force station at Manston, Kent. It was one of a formation of four that whistled over the village less than a minute after taking off.

An eyewitness, Charles Scho-

Continued on Page 3, Column 4

VAST SAVING TO U. S. SEEN IN MUTUAL AID

Committee on Present Danger Puts 2-Year Gain at 12 Billion —Asks Greater Efficiency

By FELIX BELAIR Jr.
Special to The New York Times.

WASHINGTON, April 27—The Committee on the Present Danger told Congress today that an effective Mutual Security Program would save the nation $12,000,000,000 in defense expenditures in two years but that administrative changes were needed to get the most from this country's aid dollars.

In a report to the Senate Foreign Relations and House Foreign Affairs Committees, which are considering the Administration's $7,900,000,000 security program, the nonpartisan citizens group said that helping Western Europe to build its defenses now was "militarily the best—and perhaps the only—way to create a sound defense of the United States."

Report Follows Inquiry

Only by joining in this joint rearmament effort now can the United States hope to cut back its own huge defense budget in the near future, it added, and avoid the drafting of more thousands of young men into the armed forces.

The Committee on the Present Danger was formed two years ago with fifty members prominent in the fields of education, business, industry, labor, agriculture, publishing and the professions. Its purpose is to create a greater public awareness of the threat of Communist aggression and to urge timely action to meet it.

The report filed with the Congressional committees was the result of an investigation of the Mutual Security Program here and abroad and the conditions it is designed to meet.

Critical of Scattered Set-Up

The committee was critical of the present scattered administration of the program among the Defense and State Departments and the Mutual Security Agency.

Despite a provision for the coordination of all operations through a Director for Mutual Security, the report said, "so far the set-up has not functioned to utilize effectively the European economies to produce what they could for their own defense."

"So-called offshore procurement is still held up by legal questions, by procurement regulations which were designed for contracting in this country for the supply of our own forces and by administrative complications," it declared.

The report did not mention the amount of military orders thus far placed in Western Europe but other sources have indicated that

Continued on Page 4, Column 3

2d Elizabeth Crash Mystifies Air Board

By AUSTIN STEVENS
Special to The New York Times.

WASHINGTON, April 27—The second of the three recent air disasters that brought death and fear to the residents of Elizabeth, N. J., was listed officially today as a mystery that had defied three months of intensive investigation.

The Civil Aeronautics Board, reporting on the circumstances of the Jan. 22 crash in which twenty-three persons aboard an American Airlines Convair inbound to Newark airport were killed and seven persons on the ground were fatally injured, said there was insufficient evidence on which to base a conclusion.

Former Secretary of War Robert P. Patterson was among the passengers who died in the plunge of the twin-engined transport.

Baffled on almost all counts, the board's accident specialists offered as the only possibility they had seriously considered the chance

Continued on Page 27, Column 3

Aircraft carrier Wasp with damaged bow.

The New York Times

DESTROYER SINKS IN CRASH; 61 SAVED

Continued From Page 1

miles northwest of the western-most Azores.

At Norfolk this afternoon, Admiral Lynde D. McCormick, Commander in Chief of the Atlantic Fleet, said the two ships involved in the accident were part of a task group en route to the Mediterranean to join the Sixth Fleet.

The Wasp, commanded by Capt. Burnham C. McCaffree, was engaged in night flight operations with destroyer-minesweepers Hobson and Rodman at plane guard stations near-by. Usually, such stations are taken from a half mile to a mile off and the ships stand by for action in the event a plane crashes or falls in the water.

The collision occurred as the Wasp was turning into the wind to recover her aircraft returning from a simulated night air strike against other ships in another area. Both the Hobson and the Rodman had been somewhat aft of the carrier.

The Hobson was struck on the starboard side amidship. The Navy said it did not know how long the destroyer remained afloat afterward.

Headed for Gibraltar

Other ships in the task group headed for Gibraltar to relieve units of the Sixth Fleet were the carrier Palau, the cruisers Worcester and Baltimore, and fifteen destroyers. Rear Admiral H. B. Harrett, who commands Cruiser Division Four, was aboard the Worcester and was in command of this task group. Rear Admiral C. C. Wood was in command of the fifteen destroyers.

The fleet oiler Pawcatuck and

two submarines also were in the group.

The Hobson was a 1,630-ton Bristol class destroyer, converted to a destroyer-minesweeper in December, 1944. Her home port was Charleston, S. C. She normally carried thirteen officers and 212 enlisted men, but the Navy reported tonight that she had aboard a few more than this complement when she embarked on the present assignment.

The Wasp, an Essex class carrier, has a normal complement of 2,500 officers and men, including the carrier air group. The eighth naval vessel and the second aircraft carrier to bear that name, she was recommissioned at the New York Naval Shipyard last fall.

This was the second accident to have befallen the Navy within a week. Last Monday, thirty seamen were killed in a blast in the forward gun turret of the heavy cruiser St. Paul, off the Korean coast.

The St. Paul was engaged at the time in firing on Communist targets, but the Navy stressed that the explosion was accidental; that it did not result from enemy action.

Hampered by Weather

WASHINGTON, April 27 (Æ) — The rescue operations following the sinking of the Hobson were hampered by the dark, and by foul weather.

A Navy dispatch timed at 3 A. M., Eastern daylight time, reported "15 knots southwest wind, sea rough and confused." That was nearly five hours after the crash.

First word from naval headquarters on the collision merely reported the sinking and the fact that it occurred in night maneuvers, and added:

"Rescue operations are continuing. It is not known at present how many personnel lost their

U. S. Navy

Capt. Burnham C. McCaffreey, skipper of the Wasp.

lives. That information will be released as reports are received.

"Damage to the carrier Wasp was limited to the first seventy-five feet of her bow. There was no report of casualties aboard the carrier and the presumption is that there were no casualties. The Wasp is returning to the United States for repairs."

The accident was one of the greatest non-combat disasters the Navy suffered in recent times. On Feb. 18, 1942, the destroyer Truxton and the cargo ship Pollux were lost in a storm off Newfoundland

U. S. WARSHIP IS SUNK IN ATLANTIC ACCIDENT

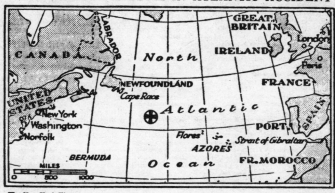

The New York Times   April 28, 1952

The destroyer-minesweeper Hobson went down in mid-Atlantic (cross) after she had collided with the carrier Wasp.

with 204 dead. On April 19, 1942, 218 lives were lost when the destroyer Ingraham was involved in an Atlantic collision.

Ships' Distinguished Records

WASHINGTON, April 27 (UP)— The two Navy ships that collided in the Atlantic last night both had distinguished records in World War II and had survived some of the bitterest sea fighting in history.

The Wasp is the second carrier to bear that name. Her predecessor was sunk by a Japanese torpedo in the early days of the war.

The destroyer-minesweeper Hobson took part in the Allied landings in Normandy and southern France. Commissioned at the Charleston, S. C., Navy Yard in January, 1942, she also participated in anti-submarine patrols in the Atlantic, in the landings in North Africa and in a carrier strike at Bodo, Norway.

While operating as a destroyer,

the Hobson won the Presidential unit citation for sinking a German submarine and for other outstanding actions in the Atlantic.

After being converted to a fast destroyer-minesweeper at Charleston in late 1944, the Hobson moved to the Pacific where she participated in the American landings on Okinawa. Four of her crew were killed and five wounded in an attack by a Japanese Kamikaze suicide plane.

The present Wasp was commissioned in November, 1943, after being built by the Bethlehem Ship Building Company at Quincy, Mass. She first saw action in the war in a raid on the Japanese-held Marcus and Wake Islands, in May, 1944. Later engagements took her to Saipan, Tinian, Guam, Iwo Jima, the Philippines, Formosa, Okinawa and the Japanese islands themselves.

During one week in March of 1945, the Wasp and her planes were credited with destroying twenty Japanese planes.

"All the News That's Fit to Print"

The New York Times.

LATE CITY EDITION
Fair and cold today. Not quite so cold, snow likely tomorrow.
Temperature Range Today—Max., 26; Min., 11
Temperature Yesterday—Max., 51; Min., 17
Full U.S. Weather Bureau Report, Page 41

Copyright, 1953, by The New York Times Company.

VOL. CII..No. 34,708. Entered as Second-Class Matter, Post Office, New York, N. Y. NEW YORK, MONDAY, FEBRUARY 2, 1953. Times Square, New York 36, N. Y. Telephone Lackawanna 4-1000 FIVE CENTS

EISENHOWER TO GIVE DOMESTIC POLICIES IN MESSAGE TODAY

Details on Foreign Program Also Due to Be Divulged at Joint Session of Congress

VIEWS ON TAXES AWAITED

Move for Controls Extension Believed Unlikely—Nominee for Air Post to Testify

By CLAYTON KNOWLES

Special to THE NEW YORK TIMES.

WASHINGTON, Feb. 1—President Eisenhower will appear before a joint session of Congress tomorrow to spell out the course he proposes to follow at home and abroad in the year ahead.

The general expectation is that the President's Message on the State of the Union, which will be broadcast nationally by all major radio and television networks, will give the first clear insight into the domestic policies of the new Administration.

The Administration's outlook on world affairs was sketched in broad strokes in the President's Inaugural Address, but his address tomorrow is likely to deal with specific points.

It is widely known that the President proposes to use the occasion to announce that the Seventh Fleet will be relieved of its assignment of "neutralizing" Chinese Nationalist forces on Formosa.

Important as such an announcement will be, millions of Americans will find greater interest in details of the Administration's program on the home front, which were discussed only in general terms in the recent political campaign.

Virtually every citizen will be affected in one way or another by the course the President charts on the budget, taxes, controls and defense, and large segments of the population will follow with interest what is said on the labor law, farm price supports, civil rights, natural resources and other subjects.

Division on Tax Policy

Most observers, for example, do not expect the President to recommend that price and wage controls be continued beyond April 30, when present regulations expire. But great interest will attach also to whether the President will keep rent control or urge that stand-by controls be voted to replace discontinued direct controls. General Eisenhower's own party is split on both points.

Similarly, President Eisenhower will have the opportunity to state whether the budget must be balanced before taxes are cut. Here, too, there is a divergence of viewpoint among Republicans.

Any pronouncement by the President on fair employment practice legislation, segregation and other aspects of the civil rights controversy also will be widely followed.

President Eisenhower's appearance before the two houses of the Congress tomorrow will not be his first. In the late spring of 1945, when he had returned to the United States as the victorious commander of Allied forces in Europe, he was invited to address a similar gathering.

Many look to the President's appearance tomorrow as an opportunity to throw into the shadow some of the unpleasantness of the last two weeks that resulted when some key appointees encountered trouble in getting confirmed. Also, through mixed signals from the White House, certain reorganization authority that was sought recently was voted out of committee on a restricted basis.

Talbott to Be Questioned

Neither situation will have been completely resolved when the President goes to Capitol Hill tomorrow. Before his arrival, Harold E. Talbott, Secretary-designate of the Air Force, will have been recalled before the Senate Armed Services Committee for further questioning, even though that committee voted 14 to 1 last Thursday to recommend his confirmation.

Mr. Talbott is being brought back before the committee at the request of Senator Estes Kefauver, Democrat of Tennessee, who wants to question him about two Congressional reports in which his name figured.

One of these reports, made in 1951 by a House subcommittee, charged the Government had been forced to pay $305,000,000 extra for automobile parts over a two-year period because of questionable price and trade agreements in the automobile industry.

The second report, prepared by

Continued on Page 15, Column 4

REGISTER TODAY. OVER 1,000 Credit Courses! Adult... Columbia University, School of ... Studies. UN 5-4000.—Advt.

More Indictments Mapped On Evidence in Pier Inquiry

Hogan and McDonald Are Using Record Provided by Commission as Basis for Further Prosecutions

By CHARLES GRUTZNER

Additional indictments of waterfront racketeers were foreseen yesterday as a result of the study by local prosecutors on both sides of the East and Hudson Rivers of testimony given at the State Crime Commission's hearings.

District Attorneys Frank S. Hogan in Manhattan and Miles F. McDonald in Brooklyn, who have developed independently several pier crime cases, expect to increase the number of indictments on the basis of leads obtained from the record of the private and public hearings of the Crime Commission.

In Brooklyn, Assistant District Attorney Julius Helfand, head of the special investigation unit, is presenting to a grand jury new cases resulting from the cooperation between him and the Crime Commission. Similar situations exist in Staten Island, where William B. Herlands, special prosecutor, is working up cases based on his independent investigation and also on information obtained from the commission and from the New Jersey Counties of Bergen, Essex and Hudson.

Former Supreme Court Justice Joseph M. Proskauer, chairman of the Crime Commission, made it clear yesterday that his agency was leaving the development of cases against individuals to the local prosecutors. He said the commission would concentrate now on preparing its report on the nature and extent of waterfront evils, with recommendations for remedial legislation.

The prosecution of malefactors is regarded by the Crime Commission as outside its main purpose. For that reason it will make all the information it has gathered available to the prosecutors.

The lurid record of unsolved West Side murders, of extortion, assault, "loan-sharking," gambling and other crimes which the commission accumulated at the series

Continued on Page 16, Column 3

DOCK UNION PURGE BY A.F.L. EXPECTED

Time to End 'Hands Off' Rule, Chiefs at Miami Parley Feel —Coup by Reds Feared

By A. H. RASKIN

Special to THE NEW YORK TIMES.

MIAMI BEACH, Feb. 1—Strong indications that the American Federation of Labor would take direct action to force a clean-up in its racket-ridden affiliate on the New York waterfront, the International Longshoremen's Association, developed tonight as the federation's fifteen-member Executive Council gathered here for the opening of its midwinter meeting tomorrow.

Angered by disclosures that gangsters were using the pier union as an instrument for systematic shakedowns and victimization of the union rank and file, high A. F. L. officials said they felt it was time to abandon the federation's traditional "hands off" attitude toward the internal affairs of its autonomous international unions.

The big question tonight was what the A. F. L. actually could do to help drive racketeers out of positions of control in the longshore union. Federation leaders said that recent testimony before the New York State Crime Commission had made it clear that the union's high command was "so shot through with corruption" that it was doubtful there was any element in the leadership around which to reorganize.

If the parent organization revoked the longshoremen's charter, dock workers on the Atlantic and Gulf coasts would be stripped of their sole links to honest unionism and left entirely at the mercy of the gangs, one federation leader asserted.

Another warned that any cancellation of the charter might open the way for a successful Communist campaign to take over the

Continued on Page 16, Column 2

BOY, 15, IS ACCUSED AS YOUTH'S SLAYER

Patient Investigation by Police Uncovers Suspect in Bronx Rock-Bashing Mystery

Diligent day-by-day investigation by detectives who questioned more than 200 youths produced yesterday what the police called the solution to the murder of a 15-year-old Bronx boy found beaten to death last Dec. 26 in a junk-filled lot at 175th Street and Carter Avenue in the Tremont section.

The development came shortly after midnight when a youth questioned about the crime for the third time mentioned the name of a boy who had not previously been associated with the case.

The suspect was identified as Thomas Morgan, 15, of 2059 Webster Avenue, the Bronx.

The victim, Paul Peltz of 2134 Aqueduct Avenue, was found dead three days after he had left his home. He had informed his parents, Mr. and Mrs. Emanuel Peltz, that he was going out to make a "gun trade" and that he would return in about a half-hour.

A tragic tale of youthful intrigue and trickery was unfolded by Deputy Chief Inspector Edward W. Byrnes, in command of Bronx detectives, who had guided the hunt for the killer since the body was found, and other authorities as they recounted the events that led up to the crime.

According to the story, the Peltz boy had a "mania for guns." An acquaintance, Milton Thordsen, 14, of 406 East 175th Street, the Bronx, told Paul some days before the crime that he knew of another boy who had two .22 caliber automatics that he would like to "swap" for Paul's air rifle and .22 caliber rifle. Actually, there were no automatics to be traded and, according to Chief Byrnes, it was a fake deal from the outset.

Only a few days earlier young

Continued on Page 22, Column 4

Eisenhowers Join Capital Church In Simple Presbyterian Ceremony

Special to THE NEW YORK TIMES.

WASHINGTON, Feb. 1—President and Mrs. Eisenhower were received into membership of the National Presbyterian Church today in a private ceremony described by the pastor as "simple and modest."

The Eisenhowers were among fifty new members taking part in a short, private session that preceded a regular communion service at 9 A. M. Dr. Edward L. R. Elson, pastor of the church, said that in keeping with the wishes of the President to keep his religious life out of the public eye, he could report few details of the service.

"The President and Mrs. Eisenhower were received according to the standards of the Presbyterian Church," Dr. Elson told a reporter.

Persons who state a desire to join the church are received at such a session by the pastor and elders of the church, Dr. Elson explained. Those seeking membership are examined and their Christian faith is confirmed.

The pastor said President and Mrs. Eisenhower were so examined and confirmation of their Christian faith was made.

After this private ceremony, which took place off the main church auditorium, the Eisenhowers, joined by the other new communicants, became full members of the church when they received Holy Communion at the 9 o'clock service.

Accompanying the Eisenhowers at this service, which lasted an hour without a formal sermon, was the President's brother, Dr. Milton S. Eisenhower.

The church was filled as the President and his wife took their places in Pew No. 41, which is near the front on the left hand side of the church.

Leaving the church, the Eisenhowers passed through a small throng gathered outside to greet them as, escorted by Dr. Elson, they stepped to the limousine for the ride back to the White House.

Dr. Elson said President Eisenhower's action today was the "climax of long consideration by the President and instruction by the pastor."

"He (the President) is a man of simple faith, who takes his religious doctrine very sincerely," the pastor commented.

Dr. Elson noted, also, that Presi-

Continued on Page 13, Column 3

CITY ACTS TO AVERT SHORTAGE OF FUEL IN TUGBOAT STRIKE

Mayor, Ordering Conservation Plans, Sees No Immediate Danger of Scarcities

SUPPLIES HERE CHECKED

Philadelphia and Norfolk Also Tied Up—No Settlement in Sight in Pay Deadlock

By EMANUEL PERLMUTTER

The Port of New York girded last night for possible shortages in coal and fuel oil as the strike of 3,500 towboat workers on 450 harbor craft moved into its second day with no indications of a settlement.

The ports of Philadelphia and Norfolk also were affected by the work stoppage, which resulted from the breakdown of contract negotiations between three locals of the United Marine Division of the International Longshoremen's Association, A. F. L., and the shipowners.

City officials, directed by Mayor Impellitteri, began checking the municipality's fuel supplies and formulating plans for conservation. Mr. Impellitteri reported there was no immediate danger of shortages that might curtail public utility services or public school operations.

Foods that normally come in from New Jersey by barge can be brought over by truck. However, edibles transported by ocean-going vessels would be affected.

No Peace in Sight

No settlement of the strike appeared in sight. A similar stoppage in 1946 caused a "brownout" of the city's lighting and conservation of heating in homes, industrial plants and municipal buildings.

Negotiations on wage increases, welfare benefits and other contract improvements for workers up to captain collapsed Saturday night despite the intervention of Federal and city mediators. The union sought wage raises of between 30 to 50 per cent. Company negotiators offered 5 per cent.

Promise of strike support by Joseph P. Ryan, international president of the union, has posed the possibility of sympathy walkouts by longshoremen.

Meanwhile, Police Commissioner George P. Monaghan conferred several times with the Mayor and then with his own aides later at Police Headquarters, mapping plans for the emergency. He said that members of the force would have to work longer days if the strike caused much disruption.

A spokesman for the Consolidated Edison Company said the utility had a week's supply of fuel at its stations, as well as a large stockpile in Astoria, Queens. It would be difficult to move the supplies from Astoria, however, because barges towed by tugs usually are employed.

Negotiation Efforts Go On

Although the effects of the strike were felt only slightly yesterday because of the normal Sunday lull in traffic, efforts to end the stoppage continued.

James McFadden, representing Daniel Kornblum, director of the city labor relations division, reported that the union and the Marine Towing and Transportation Employers Association still adhered to their positions of Saturday night, but that he was still trying to meet with them today.

The principals in the dispute will hold their own meetings today. The operators will meet at 11 A. M. in the New York Towboat Exchange, 17 Battery Place, to discuss future plans. James McAllister, head of the owners negotiating committee, said representatives of ninety-five companies would attend.

Union negotiators will hold sessions all day at their headquarters, 107 Washington Street.

Capt. William V. Bradley, president of Local 333, which is on strike, said yesterday that the union was willing to continue negotiations. He asserted that the tie-up of coal and oil deliveries by water was 100 per cent effective.

Several vessels managed to depart from local docks and berth here on their own power. The American Manufacturer, of the United States Lines, sailed early yesterday morning at slack tide from Pier 61, North River. The United Fruit ship Comayaga berthed at Weehawken at 11:25 A. M., also at low tide.

The Cunard liner Media entered the harbor at 11:15 A. M. Although she was scheduled to dock in Hoboken at 2 o'clock in the afternoon, she anchored overnight in

Continued on Page 16, Column 4

FREE TO PUBLIC: Children's Dental Health Exposition, ... Fifth Ave., cor. 89th. Opens Mon., Feb. 2d. ...—Advt.

Associated Press Radiophoto

HAVOC WROUGHT BY FLOODS: Air view showing long line of trailers piled up after they were washed against a stone wall at Skegness, Lincolnshire, England.

CITY TERCENTENARY MARKED AT SERVICE

Prince Bernhard of Netherlands Leading Figure as the Formal Observance Opens in Church

New York's 300th anniversary as an incorporated city was marked yesterday by special services in the Protestant Episcopal Church of St. Mark's-in-the-Bouwerie, Second Avenue and Tenth Street. Prince Bernhard of the Netherlands took part.

The ceremony, which actually celebrated the incorporation of the city as New Amsterdam, was arranged by the Saint Nicholas Society. Lee Thompson Smith, president of the society, wore the fringed, three-cornered hat that Washington Irving had worn in 1835.

James J. O'Brien, the city's official Father Knickerbocker, was at the church, too, but not in uniform. Mayor Impellitteri and Park Commissioner Robert Moses—who has done more to lift the face of the city than any one person, certainly in the last two decades—occupied a front pew.

In the morning, there were references to the anniversary in several other pulpits. But in view of the very nature of the occasion, it was only proper that a group whose present officers include men

Continued on Page 27, Column 5

Dulles in Paris to Discuss Obstacles to Defense Unity

By HAROLD CALLENDER

Special to THE NEW YORK TIMES.

PARIS, Feb. 1—John Foster Dulles, United States Secretary of State, and Harold E. Stassen, head of the Mutual Security Agency, arrived today and spent the afternoon and evening listening to more than a score of United States officials—political, economic and military—in a rapid briefing on the outlook for European defense and unity.

Secretary Dulles will face tomorrow French Premier René Mayer and at least four other ministers, who will be on the defensive in view of their desire to reconsider the European army treaty, which President Eisenhower and Secretary Dulles apparently are impatient to get ratified.

As if to soften the shock caused here by his speech Tuesday suggesting United States policy might change if Europe did not unite, Mr. Dulles began his Paris visit at the airport by praising the "creative thinking" shown by the French in devising plans for the European Coal and Steel Community and the European army that had "caught the imagination" of the American people.

The French plea to Mr. Dulles will be in effect that this "creative thinking" should be permitted to go on unhampered by undue advice or pressure from the sidelines until it creates an army treaty that can pass the French Parliament

Continued on Page 5, Column 4

B-29 BOMBERS RAID REDS' BATTLE POSTS

Big Korean Front-Line Strike Made Before Dawn—Sabres Add to Tally of MIG's

Special to THE NEW YORK TIMES.

TOKYO, Monday, Feb. 2—Ten United States Superfort bombers from bases in Japan and Okinawa dropped 100 tons of high explosives on Communist front line positions early today in what the Air Force called the largest B-29 attack against the enemy's battle posts in more than a year.

The B-29 attack was carried out shortly before dawn. Air crewmen reported only moderate flak opposition. The effects of the raid and the location were not reported immediately.

Just before last midnight other Superforts dropped 500-pound bombs on a Communist supply center at Paeksong village, near the west coast south of Chinnampo. The B-29 target area contained 145 barrack-type buildings, and aerial reconnaissance had spotted heavy vehicular traffic moving into the sector recently.

Pilots back from the strike on Paeksong reported sighting two enemy night fighters, and one of them made a non-firing pass at the Superforts. After the bombing, crewmen said they saw fires in the area from as far away as sixty miles.

Yesterday, United States Sabre jet pilots rounded out fourteen straight days of aerial battles with Russian-made MIG's over northwest Korea, with two fights in which they damaged one enemy jet.

Credit for the crippling of the MIG went to First Lieut. Raymond A. Kinsey of Texas, who downed a Soviet-designed TU-2 bomber off the Korean west coast Friday.

The two engagements yesterday in "MIG Alley," the sky between the Yalu River and the Sinanju area, pitted eighteen F-86 Sabres against seventeen enemy jet fighters.

In other air activities, Allied

Continued on Page 2, Column 3

'Service' Stations Return in Britain; Rival Brands of Gasoline Are Back

By THOMAS F. BRADY

Special to THE NEW YORK TIMES.

LONDON, Feb. 1—All the gasolines that make a motor purr, give it that smoo-oo-ooth zip, keep microbes out of cylinders, contain anti-knock specifics or provide that extra getaway came back to Britain today.

With the brand names, and the privilege of using the appellation super and of charging 3 to 5 cents a gallon more for high grade petrol, the competitive spirit has reappeared—at least among the major oil companies. And they are trying to reinstitute it among their service station employes.

In the years since the beginning of the war, when gasoline brand names were merged to form Government-controlled low-grade "pool petrol," filling station "service" in the American sense disappeared. Many gasoline vendors established a charge for checking tires. Drivers learned to get out and clean their own windshields—called windscreens here—while they waited for a grudging attendant to detach himself from a cup of tea in the back room to pour a few gallons of pool petrol into their tanks at a price roughly equivalent to 48 cents an American gallon.

When a driver with an American accent committed the solecism of asking for a cloth for his windshield, he was politely rebuked with a cool stare and the comment: "I'm afraid we don't have anything of that sort, sir." Only by combining patience with firm pleading could a driver persuade attendants to check the oil and water.

Today that all began to change in the service stations cornered by the major companies in a war for outlets that has been going on for

Continued on Page 10, Column 5

FLOODS DEVASTATE NORTH SEA COASTS; HUNDREDS KILLED

200 Die and Thousands Lose Homes in Britain When Tide Sweeps Far Inland

SOME U. S. TROOPS LOST

Water Brings Disaster to Low Areas of Netherlands, With Known Toll There 230

Special to THE NEW YORK TIMES.

LONDON, Monday, Feb. 2—A storm and floods that devastated the east coast of Britain yesterday and Saturday night took at least 200 lives. Thousands of persons were homeless and communications were still so badly disrupted this morning that it was impossible to establish the number of dead or the extent of damage.

Some reports put the loss of life as high as 350. To these tragic figures can be added the 132 persons who drowned in the Irish Sea, in the sinking of the ferry Princess Victoria Saturday.

[The North Sea also inundated large areas of the Netherlands and Belgium, as well as northern France, and penetrated to Duesseldorf in Germany. In the Netherlands 230 persons were reported dead and hundreds missing as the waters broke dikes and surged inland as much as forty miles in some places. Dutch officials said the "position is getting worse." At Le Havre, France, a number of ships were torn loose from their moorings, but the damage was not serious.]

Some United States service men and their families were feared drowned at Hunstanton, Heacham and Snettisham, on The Wash in Norfolk. Reports from near-by King's Lynn said that more than 100 beach bungalows had been swept away, and at Hunstanton twelve persons were known to have drowned early last night.

Toll in Town May Exceed 40

It was feared that the death toll at Hunstanton might exceed forty—among them American service men who lived in bungalows. Other Americans from an air base at Sculthorpe helped to evacuate stranded families in the area.

The sea invaded the land at low-lying points all along the coast, from the Orkneys to Dover. Hardest hit were the lowland counties of Lincoln and Norfolk.

An abnormally high tide was built up and driven inland by a gale from the north until it approached the proportions of a tidal wave.

Throughout yesterday, people were evacuated by boats and trucks from flooded regions. Thirteen thousand residents of Canvey Island in the Thames Estuary were brought to the mainland after a heavy loss of life—probably more than 100.

Five thousand persons were evacuated from an eighteen-mile stretch of the Lincolnshire coast near Mablethorpe. Another thousand were moved out of King's Lynn. A rescue attempt will be made later this morning on Foulness Island, also in the Thames Estuary, where 300 were stranded and believed in danger.

Although the wind moderated late yesterday afternoon, the police in eastern England were still advising householders to abandon their homes and move inland.

The flood was the worst natural disaster in recorded British history since the plague of 1665. Reliable estimates put the number stranded and homeless at 50,000.

A drydock at Sheerness on the

Continued on Page 3, Column 3

To Suburban Readers

The strike of newspaper deliverymen against suburban wholesalers has curtailed distribution of The New York Times outside New York City within a 50-mile radius. The Times may be obtained, however, at all newsstands within the New York City line. Suburbanites in New York during the evening are advised to get their copies before going home. Temporary mail subscriptions may be ordered for the duration of the emergency at no increase over the regular newsstand price by telephoning The Times. Information on how and where to get The Times is given at the end of The New York Times News Bulletins, which are broadcast every hour on the hour over WQXR, 1560 on the AM dial, and WQXR-FM, 96.3 on the FM dial.

FLOODS DEVASTATE NORTH SEA COASTS

Continued From Page 1

Violent Storms Lash Britain's East Coast, Causing Large Loss of Life and Property

southern shore of the Thames Estuary was flooded, and the submarine Dirdar and the naval frigate Berkeley Castle, which were being refitted, sank in the dock.

The Cunard Liner Queen Mary, delayed twenty-four hours, sailed for Cherbourg and New York at noon yesterday. Eight tugs were used to get her to sea.

Sea walls all along the Lincolnshire coast from the Humber to The Wash were breached by the huge waves. The flood in some places went more than three miles inland. At Sutton-on-Sea, a Lincolnshire town, rescue work was nearly impossible because the sea had penetrated two miles behind the town.

The ultimate scope of the tragedy will not be known for several days. The only communications in some areas were police car radios. The danger will continue for another forty-eight hours because abnormally high tides will continue and defenses against the sea have been breached.

The risk of an epidemic also exists, and people in stricken areas were warned to drink only boiled water.

The disaster on Canvey Island, which has an area less than ten square miles, was most concentrated. The lashing tide struck the island early yesterday morning, and a protecting wall broke in more than a dozen places. Half an hour later, the town was flooded to a depth of nine feet and 13,000 inhabitants were imperiled.

Reports this morning indicated that up to 200 had drowned or were missing before the evacuation was completed yesterday afternoon. The rescue work was carried out by a fleet of small boats reminiscent of the Dunkirk evacuation of British troops in World War II. Highways in the area were closed so trucks and buses could bring the evacuees to London hospitals and reception centers—hastily converted military installations.

Second Tide Hits Island

A second high tide, worse than the first, swept over the island at 2:30 P. M., before the evacuation was finished. By 7 P. M., 136 casualties, six dead on arrival, had been admitted to local hospitals. Houses on the island were pounded to pieces, and furniture swirled in the streets. It will be months before the island is fully habitable again.

The Thames River was swollen as far up as London, and there were minor overflows in lower London itself.

Farther north, the Ouse and Humber Rivers also flooded, with more deadly results. Parts of the ports of Hull and Grimsby were closed off after the inundation.

Evacuees from coastal Lincolnshire were received at military centers inland, and hospitals were crowded with casualties.

The inundation was caused by north to northwesterly winds reinforcing spring tides, which followed a full moon. The wind lashed masses of water before it and to its right, down into the southern part of the North Sea, battering Continental lowlands as well as England. Although Scotland was hard hit Saturday night, it actually escaped the worst of the disaster yesterday.

ELIZABETH VIEWS RESCUE

Duke of Edinburgh Helps Save Cattle on Norfolk Farm

LONDON, Feb. 1 (P)—Queen Elizabeth II and her husband, the Duke of Edinburgh, drove today through the embattled Norfolk districts, where their neighbors were fighting disastrous floodwaters.

The Royal Family has been staying at Sandringham, their Norfolk estate. Sandringham for the most part is on high ground, but the Duke went out last night to help rescue seventy steers on the royal farm.

This air view illustrates the extent of floodwaters covering the countryside at Sutton-on-the-Sea, Lincolnshire. Evacuation of the entire area has been started.

Associated Press Radiophoto

6 Americans Dead and 7 Missing As Floods Sweep English Resort

HUNSTANTON, England, Feb. 1 (P)—Forty persons, many of them Americans, were believed to have drowned today in North Sea flood waters that overwhelmed this Norfolk coastal resort.

Only the heroic efforts of United States airmen and British civilians prevented the death toll from going higher as waters crushed and swept away houses. The American airmen were attached to the nearby Sculthorpe air base.

A United States Air Force spokesman said at least six Americans were known to be dead when rescue operations halted tonight. He said the dead included one service man and five dependents. Seven other Americans were missing, he said—two service men and five dependents. An undetermined number of Americans were injured.

Twelve bodies were recovered.

The houses that took the force of the storm were occupied by British families and American service men and their families.

While the storm raged 500 United States airmen, armed only with inadequate equipment, left their base for rescue operations. The Sixty-seventh Air Rescue Squadron was the nucleus of this force. Its commanding officer, Capt. Gerald A. Wethermon of Electra, Tex., fought the wind and waves in a fragile rubber dinghy until he collapsed from exposure and was taken to a hospital.

Airman Third Class Reis L. Leming, 22, of Toppenish, Wash., rescued American service men and British civilians until he was himself dragged unconscious from the icy waters. He was credited with saving eighteen lives.

"We went from wrecked bungalow to wrecked bungalow, put the marooned people onto life rafts or rubber dinghies and held them afloat as we walked through the water beside them," he said later at a hospital.

Late tonight the high wind was still blowing, but all inhabitants of Hunstanton had been lodged safely in the higher part of the town. The American airmen—some of whom had had no sleep for forty-eight hours—remained in the town for any further help that might be needed.

Hunstanton was without fresh water as a result of flood damage. Royal Air Force water trucks distributed water for essential needs.

Among the Americans injured was Lieut. Charles Smith, public information officer at Sculthorpe air base, who was trapped in his bungalow at Hunstanton and narrowly escaped drowning. He is now in a hospital.

The New York Times   Feb. 2, 1953

The raging waters brought havoc to the Lincoln-Norfolk region (1), the Thames estuary (2), areas deep in the Netherlands and Belgium (3), Le Havre (4) and Duesseldorf (5). The bodies of sixty-three persons of the 132 who died in the sinking of a ferry between Ireland and Scotland (6) on Saturday were recovered.

FERRY TOLL IS 132; 44 SURVIVE SINKING

Ships Searching for Bodies Off North Ireland Find 63—All Women and Children Die

DONAGHADEE, Northern Ireland, Feb. 1 (UP)—Ships' nets were dragging from the sea today the bodies of victims of the ferry Princess Victoria, which sank in a storm with a loss of 132 lives yesterday in the North Channel off this port.

Sixty-three bodies were recovered. The British destroyer Contest radioed that she had picked up forty-five today. Twelve were pulled from the sea by a lifeboat, and six were found earlier.

Among the bodies recovered were those of Maj. J. M. Sinclair, 56, Northern Ireland Deputy Premier and Finance Minister; Sir Walter Smiles, 69, Ulster Unionist Member of Parliament, and Capt. James Ferguson, skipper of the ferry, who went down with his ship.

Officials finally agreed that forty-four persons survived this greatest British shipping disaster since World War II. Of the fifty-four-member crew, ten were saved.

All women and children passengers perished in the raging seas. All those saved were men.

Malcolm McKennon, 31, a crewman who launched a lifeboat, said he saw another boat crowded with passengers, many of them women, "lifted up by the waves and broken in half like a radish on the ship's screws."

"Their bodies flew through the air into the sea," he added.

Another crewman, Angus Nelson, told of seeing Capt. James Ferguson salute while standing on the deck as the ship slid under the waves.

"During all those terrible hours Captain Ferguson was grand," he said. "All the men helped stewardesses wrap the women and children in blankets. I cannot explain why none were saved."

The weather was cold and clear today. A fifty-mile gale piled whitecaps up in twenty-foot waves as two destroyers, two lifeboats, six merchantmen and four trawlers criss-crossed the area searching for the bodies of the victims.

Investigation Ordered

Special to THE NEW YORK TIMES.

BELFAST, Northern Ireland, Feb. 1—A. T. Lennox-Boyd, British Minister of Transport, ordered today an investigation of the capsizing of the 2,694-ton ferry Princess Victoria yesterday on a trip from Stranraer, Scotland, to Larne, Northern Ireland.

Officials of the state-owned British Railways, which operated the ships, are also conducting an investigation. J. L. Harrington, chief marine officer of the British Railways, said he was satisfied that everything possible had been done to save the vessel and her passengers and crew.

The death of John Maynard Sinclair, Northern Ireland's Minister of Finance and Deputy Prime Minister, in the sinking of the Princess Victoria leaves a serious gap in the Government. He had been regarded as the most probable successor to Lord Brookeborough as Prime Minister.

Mr. Sinclair served in France and Palestine as an infantry captain in World War I. An authority on finance, he was appointed financial secretary to the Ministry of Finance in 1941 and became Minister of Finance and Deputy Prime Minister in 1943.

Lieut. Col. Sir Walter Doring Smiles, who was also drowned, had sat in the House of Commons as a Conservative member since 1931.

Eddy to Fly to Netherlands

FRANKFURT, Germany, Feb. 1 (P)—Lieut. Gen. Manton S. Eddy, commander of the United States Army in Europe, will fly to the flood-stricken Netherlands tomorrow to make an on-the-spot investigation as to what aid can be rendered by the United States Army, a spokesman announced tonight.

"All the News That's Fit to Print"

The New York Times.

LATE CITY EDITION
Fair and warmer today. Partly cloudy, warmer tomorrow.
Temperature Range Today—Max., 80; Min., 62
Temperatures Yesterday—Max., 77; Min., 60
Full U. S. Weather Bureau Report, Page 46

Copyright, 1953, by The New York Times Company.

VOL. CII..No. 34,845. Entered as Second-Class Matter. Post Office, New York, N. Y. NEW YORK, FRIDAY, JUNE 19, 1953. Times Square, New York 36, N. Y. Telephone Lackawanna 4-1000 FIVE CENTS

U. S. INSISTS RHEE RETAKE P. O. W.'S; REDS ACCUSE US, SEE TEST OF FAITH; WEST CONDEMNS SOVIET ON BERLIN

COURT HEARS SPY DEBATE; RULES TODAY

CASE SEEN IN PERIL

Rosenbergs May Fight Indictment if Death Sentence Is Upset

By LUTHER A. HUSTON
Special to The New York Times.

WASHINGTON, June 18—The Supreme Court is expected to announce at noon tomorrow its decision as to whether it will set aside the stay of execution granted to Julius and Ethel Rosenberg the atom spies, by Justice William O. Douglas.

Until that decision is made known the stay remains in effect. In consequence, the Rosenbergs escaped death in Sing Sing prison tonight for conspiracy to betray the secrets of the atomic bomb to Soviet Russia. The execution of their death sentences had been set for 11 P. M.

The high court heard three hours of arguments today on the question of whether the Atomic Energy Act of 1946 was applicable to the Rosenberg case. Then it considered the matter for three hours in its conference room.

At 6:29 P. M., Associate Justice Harold H. Burton ascended the bench alone and said:

"The court will stand in recess until tomorrow at 12 noon."

Special Term Convened

The court met at noon in a special term convened by Chief Justice Fred M. Vinson on application of Attorney General Herbert Brownell Jr., who had asked the court to invalidate the stay granted by Justice Douglas.

Although it had been expected that some of the justices would not be able to be present, inasmuch as they had left Washington when the court recessed on Monday for the summer, all nine were on the bench. Justice Douglas, who had started for the West by motor car, turned back at Uniontown, Pa.

The question the court was convened to decide was whether the provisions of the Atomic Energy Act applied to the Rosenbergs' case, rather than the General Espionage Act under which they had been convicted and sentenced. Justice Douglas found a legal doubt that the sentences had been imposed under the proper statute and ordered a stay of execution until the point was decided by the courts.

If the Atomic Energy Act applied, the death sentences imposed by Federal Judge Irving R. Kaufman would be illegal. Under that act the death sentence, or life imprisonment, may not be imposed in espionage cases except on recommendation of the jury. The jury that convicted the Rosenbergs made no such recommendation.

Whole Case in Doubt

Soon after the arguments began the question was raised as to the effect a decision holding the atomic act applicable would have upon the Government's case.

While Robert L. Stern, acting Solicitor General, was arguing that the act did not apply, Justice Robert H. Jackson remarked:

"The probabilities are that if the Atomic Energy Act covers this case, the whole case is out."

The apparent point was that if the sentences passed under the

Continued on Page 8, Column 4

Legislature Takes Up Pier Crime Thursday

By WARREN WEAVER Jr.
Special to The New York Times.

ALBANY, June 18—Governor Dewey announced tonight that he was calling the members of the Legislature back to the capital for a special session beginning at noon Thursday, June 25, to deal with corruption uncovered by the investigations of the State Crime Commission.

The Governor indicated in a statement that the chief reason for having reconvened the Legislature before the regular session next January was his desire to improve "the scandalous conditions which have prevailed on docks" in the Port of New York.

Mr. Dewey declared, however, that he would also place before the lawmakers legislation involving the administration of criminal justice in general, based on the Crime Commission's inquiries into gambling, official

Continued on Page 15, Column 5

HOPE FOR FAST END OF SHIP TIE-UP DIMS

Union Raises Wage Demands It Had Made of the Tanker and Dry-Cargo Operators

By JOSEPH J. RYAN

Hope for a quick end of the three-day seamen's strike, which is slowly clamping a vise on one-half of the nation's privately operated merchant fleet, faded late yesterday when the National Maritime Union, C. I. O., suddenly increased the monetary formula it had demanded earlier of 100 tanker and dry-cargo ship operators.

A tanker negotiating committee, which was prepared to concede a 2 to 6 per cent wage and overtime increase, met at the Commodore Hotel yesterday with a union group headed by Joseph Curran, N. M. U. president. The committee represents the owners of 239 deep-sea vessels.

This formula had been pressed by the union at meetings with the operators on Tuesday and Wednesday. Both the dry-cargo passenger ship operators and the tanker representatives had steadfastly refused the demand and offered a 3 per cent across-the-board increase.

In an interview yesterday at union headquarters, 346 West Seventeenth Street, Mr. Curran said the union would insist on the 2 to 6 per cent formula or an agreement by the operators to submit the wage demands to arbitration. Later the union's stand was backed up by the unanimous vote of its national council to strike formally for the demands.

Offer Is Reconsidered

Carl F. Vander Clute, Gulf Oil Company official, and spokesman for the tanker committee, said yesterday that the oil companies had reconsidered the wage offer and asked the union group to a meeting at the Commodore Hotel.

In a telephone conversation prior to the meeting, Mr. Vander Clute said he first had asked Mr. Curran to "shave the demand to 2 to 4 per cent," but finally indicated that the companies would pay the higher formula. He added that Mr. Curran had raised the demand to 5 per cent during the conversation, but agreed that "we might do business at the lower figure."

Mr. Vander Clute said that Mr. Curran and his group then insisted on the 5 per cent rise at the meeting and, when the operators objected, walked out of the session with his committee. "It was the most dastardly action I ever heard of in labor relations," he said.

Asked to comment on Mr. Vander Clute's statement, Mr. Curran permitted himself to be quoted by an associate to the following effect:

"A man who identified himself as Vander Clute, who sounded like Vander Clute and convinced me he was Vander Clute made an offer of 5 per cent across the board. When the union officers called at the Commodore to discuss it I was astounded to find they had withdrawn the 5 per cent. I'm not too surprised, as the tankermen's tactics have been deceptive since the start."

The union spokesman added that the N. M. U. had insisted on the

Continued on Page 45, Column 2

Marie Is Rejected As French Premier

By LANSING WARREN
Special to The New York Times.

PARIS, Friday, June 19—France's longest political crisis since World War II continued into its fifth week today with the rejection by the National Assembly of André Marie, the Radical party's wartime resistance hero, by a vote of 272 in M. Marie's favor to 209, with more than 100 abstentions. He required 314 votes.

M. Marie obtained the support of the Independents, a large section of the former Gaullists and a scattering of other groups outside his party but he failed to win over the Roman Catholic Popular Republican party whose most noted leaders are the former Foreign Ministers Robert Schuman and Georges Bidault.

Pierre-Henri Teitgen, Popular Republican spokesman, attributed his group's abstention to M. Marie's intimation of wavering over ratification of the European defense

Continued on Page 6, Column 6

129 SERVICEMEN DIE IN JAPAN AIR CRASH, WORST IN HISTORY

All Aboard Korea-Bound C-124, U. S. Crew and Troops, Perish in Fiery Spin Near Tokyo

By The Associated Press.

TOKYO, Friday, June 19—The world's worst air disaster killed every one of 129 United States servicemen aboard a giant Globemaster transport plane in a fiery crash near Tokyo yesterday.

The great, two-decked C-124, its engines failing after a take-off for Korea, was trying desperately to get back to Tachikawa Air Base, twenty-five miles west of Tokyo. It never made it.

The Globemaster went into a flat spin, staggered and plummeted nose down into a muddy farm.

Japanese farmers said there was a terrific flash and a roar as the 3,000 gallons of gasoline aboard burst into flame. Then the dead and dying were incinerated in a towering funeral pyre.

Through the night, by searchlight, and up to noon today, United States Air Force crews worked to recover the charred bodies. One victim was found still clasping a rosary, as he had been praying when his fate overtook him.

The Air Force said it would hold an immediate investigation to try to discover the cause of the crash. The long list of victims will not be released until next of kin are notified.

Of the total aboard, seven were crew members and the rest were airmen and Army engineers attached to air bases returning to Korea from rest leave in Japan.

All Far East C-124's, four-engined giants capable of carrying 222 passengers, had just gone back into service after being grounded over the week-end with generator trouble. [Later Friday, all C-124's were again grounded by order of Far East Air Forces.]

Weather Called 'Safe'

The Air Force said, however, there was nothing to indicate coming trouble on the fatal flight. The weather, while rainy and murky, was well within safe flying limits.

"I heard a tremendous sound of engines," said Hiroji Kato, 35, a Japanese farmer who was burned by hot metal thrown from the wreck.

"I looked up. The huge plane was falling on me. I almost fainted. Then it crashed and exploded."

Other Japanese witnesses said the plane came down so steeply it almost somersaulted, and that bodies were thrown around the wreckage.

Japanese firemen dragged out seven dying men before flames drove them back.

The previous record was the crash of another C-124 last Dec. 20 at Moses Lake, Wash., when eighty-seven persons died. There were some survivors at Moses Lake.

Far East Air Forces said the giant Korea-bound craft rolled down the two-mile runway at Tachikawa and was airborne at 4:31 P. M.

There was a 1,000-foot ceiling with broken clouds, a mile visibility, and light rain and some fog. Safety limits for Air Force flight are a 250-foot ceiling and a half-mile visibility.

As soon as the plane was in the

Continued on Page 5, Column 2

Egypt Now Republic; Naguib Her President

By ROBERT C. DOTY
Special to The New York Times.

CAIRO, June 18—The Kingdom of Egypt was proclaimed a republic shortly after 10 o'clock tonight with Maj. Gen. Mohammed Naguib, leader of the military group that seized power last July, as its first President and Premier.

As the army swept away the last vestiges of monarchy and moved to tighten its control of the Government, three of eleven other members of the military Revolution Council abandoned their positions as controllers behind the scenes to assume direct charge of key ministries from civilian incumbents. A fourth assumed the post of Commander in Chief of the armed forces, surrendered by General Naguib as he assumed the Presidency and continued as Premier.

The decisions announced tonight merely make formal a

Continued on Page 10, Column 4

RED PLOT ALLEGED TO SLAY M'CARTHY

F.B.I. Ex-Agent Tells Senators of Hearing 'Goon Squad' Head Boast of Getting Assignment

By C. P. TRUSSELL
Special to The New York Times.

WASHINGTON, June 18—A former Federal Bureau of Investigation undercover agent swore to the Senate Investigating subcommittee today that he attended a secret meeting last December when a "goon squad" organizer announced that the Communist party had selected him to "liquidate" Senator Joseph R. McCarthy, Republican of Wisconsin. Mr. McCarthy is chairman of the Senate group.

As Joseph D. Mazzei of Millvale, Pa., testified, Lou Bortz, the man he accused, was among the spectators. Senator Karl E. Mundt, Republican of South Dakota, the acting chairman, called him to the witness stand.

Senator McCarthy had turned the gavel over to Mr. Mundt, since the testimony was to concern him. The Wisconsin Senator arranged, however, for Mr. Mazzei and Mr. Bortz to sit elbow to elbow as questioning continued. Mr. Mazzei, who said that he had posed as a Communist for twelve years until last March 26, directly identified Mr. Bortz as the man he was accusing. But Mr. Bortz refused, under constitutional protection, to say whether he knew his accuser.

When asked whether he had been assigned to kill Senator McCarthy and had so told the meeting in Pittsburgh on Dec. 4, Mr. Bortz replied that any answer he gave "might be self-incriminating."

He also refused to answer other

Continued on Page 9, Column 2

GERMAN EXECUTED

Allies Demand Russians Lift Military Barriers Splitting Berlin

By WALTER SULLIVAN
Special to The New York Times.

BERLIN, June 18—The three Western powers demanded tonight that the Soviet Union lift its military barrier virtually cutting Berlin in two and denounced as a "travesty of justice" the Soviet execution of a West Berliner as an alleged instigator of yesterday's riots.

A note sent to their Soviet counterpart by the British, French and United States commandants in Berlin condemned the Russians' "irresponsible recourse to military force" in quelling the disorders in the Soviet sector.

The note declared that a "considerable number" of West Berliners had lost their lives or had been wounded by resulting gunfire. The Allied note also was sent in the names of the three Western High Commissioners in Bonn.

Under the martial law proclaimed by Maj. Gen. P. T. Dibrova, Soviet commandant in East Berlin, a Russian firing squad executed a man charged with having helped to start the riots "on the orders of a foreign intelligence agency." The Western note denied the executed man had any such connection with the rioting.

It described the execution as an "act of brutality which will shock the conscience of the world." The wife of the executed man said he must have been caught in the disorders while passing through the Soviet sector to collect unemployment benefits.

Soviet Guns Calm Sector

Under the guns of Soviet troops and tanks East Berlin appeared to be calm, but large numbers of workers still had not returned to work.

The Soviet sector of Berlin was virtually sealed off from Western eyes. Only doctors, nurses and residents of East Berlin were allowed to cross the line from West Berlin.

One or two Soviet tanks were stationed at the most important street crossings in the downtown area. Their guns were trained on West Berlin as though to underline the Communists' contention that the primary source of their trouble lay with West Berlin "rowdies" and agents of foreign powers, who were alleged to have led the rioting.

The West Berlin police raised their total of known casualties in yesterday's fighting to five dead and 119 wounded. Of the dead, all but one were West Berliners, most of whom were reported to have been hit by Soviet gunfire at Potsdamerplatz, where the British, Soviet and United States sectors converge.

Some of the wounded were East Berliners though all were in West Berlin hospitals, West Berlin police officials added. They believed

Continued on Page 12, Column 5

Rhee Rebuffs Eisenhower; Prisoner Escapes Continue

South Korean Leader Says Truce Cannot Be Bought by Pledges of Aid or Security —Armistice Meeting Is Postponed

By LINDESAY PARROTT
Special to The New York Times.

TOKYO, Friday, June 19—The Government-controlled Peiping radio charged today that Americans had "deliberately connived" with Dr. Syngman Rhee, President of South Korea, in staging the mass outbreak of anti-Communist prisoners of war. The broadcast said the world was now waiting to see how the United States Government would deal with Dr. Rhee's rebellion.

Meanwhile, mass escapes continued. Nearly 1,500 prisoners stormed through barbed wire stockades and barrages of tear gas last night at camps at Yongchon and Inchon. They were in addition to almost 25,000 North Koreans who had escaped earlier.

A third new outbreak took place this morning, when ninety-seven prisoners escaped from a hospital at Pusan.

Dr. Rhee tartly informed President Eisenhower that Korean support for an armistice on the peninsula could not be bought by promises of economic aid or military security for the young republic.

The Communists abruptly called off the only meeting that had been scheduled at Panmunjom today to complete the draft of an agreement for an armistice—now possibly severely threatened by Dr. Rhee's action in liberating the prisoners.

[News agencies said that Soviet newspapers had described the release of the prisoners as "a provocative action of the Syngman Rhee clique."]

The Peiping radio broke its silence this morning on the outbreak of the prisoners. The official broadcast gave no hint as to whether the Communist command would now break off the truce negotiations at Panmunjom.

The mass outbreaks, involving

Continued on Page 4, Column 4

RHEE IS ASSAILED BY HAMMARSKJOLD

U. N. Secretary Calls Freeing of Captives Contrary to Stand of the World Organization

By A. M. ROSENTHAL
Special to The New York Times.

UNITED NATIONS, N. Y., June 18—Secretary General Dag Hammarskjold stepped publicly into the Korean situation for the first time today with a denunciation of the Republic of Korea for releasing North Korean prisoners of war.

The Swedish chief of the United Nations staff issued a statement branding the Republic's action as unilateral and contrary to the position of the world organization. He said it had hurt the chances for the peaceful unification of the country.

"From the United Nations point of view it is regrettable that the Republic of Korea, by the unilateral act of releasing prisoners of war and other recent actions, has increased the difficulty of establishing a state of affairs in which the United Nations may successfully engage in the rehabilitation of that country and in a peaceful and constructive approach regarding the unification of Korea," said Mr. Hammarskjold.

"Yesterday's grave developments are not only in clear contradiction of the United Nations position, but come strangely from the Government of a country—the Republic of Korea—which has for years been the beneficiary of so much effort and sacrifice by members of the United Nations."

Keeps Close Touch on Korea

Mr. Hammarskjold's advisers said that the Secretary General had been keeping in close touch with the Korean situation. Any information on Korea is relayed to the Secretary General through the United States delegation. The chief of the delegation, Henry Cabot Lodge Jr., flew to Washington today and will take his usual seat at the Friday meeting of the President's Cabinet.

Western and Asian delegates generally had only harsh words to say about President Syngman Rhee's action. They called it "irresponsible" and a threat to everything the United Nations had done in Korea.

As far as the United Nations as a political organization is concerned, delegates said, there is nothing that can be done until it becomes clear whether or not there is to be a truce. Some delegates said that they believed the truce would be agreed to anyway. But they had no answer to the question as to what the United Nations would do if Dr. Rhee ordered his forces to keep on fighting.

Several Western delegates declared that the commitment of the United Nations in Korea was only

Continued on Page 3, Column 3

CAPTIVES INQUIRY ASKED BY SENATOR

Hendrickson Would Seek to Learn U. S. 'Culpability' in Release by South Korea

By WILLIAM S. WHITE
Special to The New York Times.

WASHINGTON, June 18—A Senate investigation to "determine the extent of American culpability" in South Korea's release of anti-Communist North Korean war prisoners in defiance of the United Nations was proposed today by Senator Robert C. Hendrickson, Republican of New Jersey.

Congress generally sought more information on the whole affair, which President Eisenhower was said by Congressional callers to have regarded as a serious one.

One of these callers, Senator Styles Bridges, Republican of New Hampshire, told reporters that the President had not commented on whether an armistice would be jeopardized but had "discussed the seriousness of the thing as another angle complicating the situation."

Senator H. Alexander Smith, Republican of New Jersey, called for tomorrow morning, an urgent meeting of the Far Eastern subcommittee of the Senate Foreign Relations Committee. As chairman of the subcommittee, he asked John Foster Dulles, the Secretary of State, to attend.

Mr. Dulles, it was made clear, would be asked many questions, including what the United States proposed to do now and in the future about Dr. Syngman Rhee, the South Korean President.

Senator Leverett Saltonstall, Re-

Continued on Page 2, Column 3

WASHINGTON ANGRY

Dulles Bluntly Says Seoul Broke Pledge to U. N.—Premier Flies Home

By W. H. LAWRENCE
Special to The New York Times.

WASHINGTON, June 18—President Eisenhower today dispatched to President Syngman Rhee of the Korean Republic a secret but sharply worded message demanding the immediate recapture of thousands of anti-Communist North Korean prisoners of war set free by South Korean guards in violation of United Nations agreements.

The text of the Presidential message to Dr. Rhee was not made public, but Secretary of State John Foster Dulles, speaking to newspaper men at the White House, bluntly charged the South Korean Government with "unilateral action" flouting "the authority of the United Nations Command to which the Republic of Korea had agreed."

Paik Too Chin, South Korean Premier, abruptly cut short a scheduled three-day visit to Washington and left here by plane late this afternoon for Korea so he could give to Dr. Rhee and other officials a first-hand report of the angry Washington reaction.

Paik Indicates Urgency

Mr. Paik told reporters at National Airport here that "I must go back." He repeated this twice. "I was merely paying a courtesy call on General Eisenhower," he added.

Dr. You Chan Yang, South Korean Ambassador, who accompanied Mr. Paik to the airport, said the Premier wants "to get out as fast as he can on account of the crisis." Dr. Yang said he knew of no special message Mr. Paik might have for Dr. Rhee but added that the Premier would relay President Eisenhower's views, expressed at the White House yesterday.

At mid-afternoon, there still was no official or unofficial comment from the Communist Chinese and North Korean leaders with whom the United Nations had been expected to sign a cease-fire agreement within the next few days.

Officials quite frankly feared that Dr. Rhee's defiant act might wreck the truce talks and any early hope of ending the bloodshed. The South Koreans, of course, had openly proclaimed their opposition to an armistice that would leave Korea divided, but officials had believed that, in the final showdown, Dr. Rhee's Government would go along with the settlement and take no overt action to keep the war going.

Dulles' Remarks Sharp

Official Washington's anger with Dr. Rhee and the South Korean Government was stated bluntly by Secretary Dulles after a lengthy meeting of the National Security Council with President Eisenhower. Mr. Dulles' comment, dictated to White House reporters, was an unusually strong denunciation of one ally by another in the middle of a shooting war.

"I have been in conference with the President regarding the unilateral action taken by the Republic of Korea to release prematurely

Continued on Page 2, Column 5

Yugoslavia Will Let Soviet Flotilla Pass Down Danube From Vienna

Special to The New York Times.

BELGRADE, Yugoslavia, June 18—Yugoslavia, which agreed to exchange Ambassadors with the Soviet Union last week at Moscow's request, has granted permission for twenty-six Soviet war vessels, now docked in Vienna, to pass through the Yugoslav section of the Danube River on their way to the Black Sea area for repairs.

The ships, the first Soviet war vessels to be sent through Yugoslavia since Belgrade's break with the Cominform in 1948, will sail in five groups, starting Monday and finishing by July 13. They will go to Izmail, a large river port in the Soviet Ukraine on a branch of the Danube delta at the Rumanian border.

The Soviet request was made in a note three days ago and was granted by the Yugoslav State Secretariat for Foreign Affairs, it was announced today. Experts on the Soviet Union here suggested that the move might be a Soviet step to pave the way for a settlement on a treaty for Austria.

[Moscow named a civilian High Commissioner for its occupation zone of Austria last week, relegating the military to a secondary role, and reduced restrictions on Austrian citizens' travel across the zone's boundary. Later the United States, Britain and France criticized the Soviet Union for obstructing a state treaty with Austria, on which negotiations have been under way sporadically since 1946, and called on Moscow to provide the "exact text" of a treaty it would be willing to sign to end the Austrian occupation.]

The Yugoslav announcement said permission for passage had been granted in accordance with the Danube Convention but that,

Continued on Page 6, Column 4

Associated Press Radiophoto

DAVID AND GOLIATH: Two demonstrators in Wednesday's anti-Communist riot in East Berlin, having no other weapons on hand, tossed stones at these two Soviet tanks on Leipzigerplatz. Soviet occupation authorities extended martial law yesterday to areas adjoining East Berlin.

Firemen pour foamite on the still smoldering wreckage of the giant C-124 Globemaster which crashed near Tachikawa Airbase outside of Tokyo.

Wide World Photos

129 Servicemen Die in Air Crash; Korea-Bound C-124 Falls in Japan

Continued From Page 1

air the pilot reported engine trouble by radio. His message said: "One engine out—returning to field for GCA landing."

At 4:34 he crashed.

A "GCA" is a ground-controlled approach, or instrument, landing. Tachikawa lies about twenty-five miles due west of Tokyo and is one of the largest air bases in the world. The crash was at the town of Kodaira, four miles north-northeast of the field.

The crash scene was amid small farms and woodlots that are intermingled amid small towns on the western fringes of Tokyo. The countryside is flat, brilliantly green and, from above, picturesque with its tidy villages, turned-up tile and thatch roofs and clusters of bamboo groves.

The flight was a special called to carry the airmen and soldiers back from "R-and-R"—five days' rest and recreation leave in Japan. The Far East Command cancelled all "R-and-R" leaves in Japan today because of the tense prisoner-of-war situation in Korea. The leaves were extended again tonight, however, and none of the men aboard the C-124 was among those specially recalled. The C-124's also have been flying regular courier service to and from Korea,

carrying other military personnel, army civilians, war correspondents and others.

First positive word of the crash came from an Air Force helicopter pilot who circled the scene moments after the impact and sent a message by radio: "No survivors," to the Tachikawa control tower.

"This is a great tragedy," said Gen. O. P. Weyland, commander of the Far East Air Forces. "I grieve for these men's families."

The Air Force issued the following statement:

"A United States Air Force C-124 Globemaster, returning for a landing, crashed shortly after take-off from Tachikawa air installation west of Tokyo at 4:34 this afternoon, with approximately 120 passengers and a crew of seven on board.

"The four-engined transport crashed and burned in a clearing near the village of Kodaira, four miles east-northeast of the air installation twenty-five miles west of Tokyo.

"First reports said there was one Japanese injured by the crash.

"Emergency medical teams and crash crews from near-by Air Force installations rushed to the scene immediately. An Air Force helicopter circled the crash area immediately and reported there were no survivors."

C-124's Again Grounded

TOKYO, Friday, June 19 (UP)—Far East air forces again ordered all C-124 Globemaster transports grounded. An announcement today with the order said an investigation of yesterday's crash at Kodaira showed no connection between that crash and the generator trouble that had caused the previous gorunding order June 13.

"In yesterday's crash," the Air Force said, "one engine failed shortly after take-off, but a check of the generator of the troubled engine, whose prop was feathered, showed it to be in good condition."

The Air Force said the commander of the plane was "exceptionally well qualified on the C-124" with 62,00 flying hours, 489 hours logged in the C-124. The pilot and co-pilot also had more than 6,000 hours each.

Air Crew Found Strapped In

KODAIRA, Japan, June 18 (AP)—Searchers found the pilot and crewmen still strapped to their seats in the demolished Air Force Globemaster.

Cutting their way with axes into the nose of the huge double-decked plane, the searchers found part of the craft untouched by fire. Farther back, the passenger compartment was partly burning. The first passenger bodies to be recovered from the worst air disaster in history had been strapped in their bucket seats on the upper deck.

Investigators Fly to Japan

WASHINGTON, June 18 (AP) — An Air Force investigation team is flying to Japan to determine the cause of the crash of the C-124

The New York Times   June 19, 1953

SCENE OF CRASH: A United States C-124 fell near Kodaira (cross), killing 129 American service men.

The Air Force crash crew, which arrived at this muddy Japanese rice farm twenty-five minutes after the crash, said the force of the impact had torn watches off the wrists of some of the passengers.

The rain turned the scene into a swamp. Lines of ambulances threaded their way down a long, narrow lane and then across the soggy field. They picked up the bodies and then filed slowly out, bouncing over the furrowed rice paddy.

Globemaster transport that took 129 lives. Gen. Hoyt S. Vandenberg, Air Force Chief of Staff, said that the team was led by Maj. Gen. Victor E. Bertrañdias, deputy inspector general of the Air Force, and included two representatives of the Douglas Aircraft Corporation, builders of the plane.

Highest Previous Air Toll Was 87, Dec. 20, 1952

The highest death toll from an air crash before yesterday's disaster near Tokyo was the eighty-seven persons killed when a C-124 Globemaster crashed at Moses Lake, Wash., Dec. 20, 1952.

Other major air disasters, as listed by The United Press, include—

March 12, 1950—Crash of Avro Tudor airliner near Cardiff, Wales, eighty killed.

June 24, 1950—Crash of Northwest Airlines DC-4 in Lake Michigan, fifty-eight killed.

Dec. 16, 1951—Crash of nonscheduled C-46 passenger liner at Elizabeth, N. J., fifty-six killed. (This was the worst of three crashes at or near Elizabeth within a four-month period with a total of 119 deaths.)

Nov. 1, 1949—Collision of a P-38 fighter plane with an Eastern Airlines DC-4 at Washington, D. C., fifty-five killed.

Aug. 31, 1950—Crash of a Trans-World Airlines Constellation in the Egyptian desert, fifty-five killed.

"All the News That's Fit to Print"

The New York Times.

LATE CITY EDITION
Cloudy, cooler today; showers likely tonight. Rain tomorrow.
Temperature Range Today—Max., 64; Min., 54
Temperatures Yesterday—Max., 74; Min., 57
Full U. S. Weather Bureau Report, Page 56

Copyright, 1954, by The New York Times Company.

VOL. CIII..No. 35,187. Entered as Second-Class Matter, Post Office, New York, N. Y. NEW YORK, THURSDAY, MAY 27, 1954. Times Square, New York 36, N. Y. Telephone LAckawanna 4-1000 FIVE CENTS

BLASTS ON CARRIER KILL 91, INJURE 200; HELICOPTERS FLY VICTIMS TO SHORE FROM THE BENNINGTON IN ATLANTIC

Associated Press Wirephoto

HELICOPTERS EVACUATE CASUALTIES: Four helicopters wait on deck of the aircraft carrier Bennington to fly injured seamen back to shore, a rescue technique perfected in Korean war. One elevator is below deck, apparently preparing to bring injured to helicopters. The plane with folded wings on left rear of deck is part of carrier's complement.

CHEOPS TREASURE, SHIP OF THE DEAD, FOUND AT PYRAMID

RELIC OF 2900 B. C.

Perfumed Funeral Craft in Deep Passage Is 55 Yards Long

By KENNETT DOVE
Special to The New York Times.

CAIRO, May 26—A perfumed ship built by a Pharaoh nearly 5,000 years ago to carry his soul to heaven was discovered today in a subterranean corridor beside a pyramid.

The ship, constructed and furnished by Cheops, was found in a limestone passageway next to his vast pyramid at Giza, south of Cairo.

Oars and a rudder sweep were placed in the gunwales as if ready for instant embarkation on a celestial voyage. Linen ropes were coiled on the deck of sacred sycamore and cedar wood. The hull of the ship, which is believed to be one of a pair, is fifty-five yards long.

The corridor in which it was found is hollowed out in the bedrock of a hill at the desert's edge overlooking the green Nile Valley. The ship has at least six decks and is estimated to be nine yards deep.

The discovery was described as explosive by Dr. Mustafa Amer, head of the Egyptian Department of Antiquities. The find, expected by authorities here to prove one of the most important in Egyptian archaeological history, was made by Kamal el-Malakh, 34-year-old Egyptologist and architect, who is director of archaeological work for Giza and Lower Egypt.

Mr. el-Malakh said there was no doubt that the ship had been built by Cheops, second king of the Fourth Dynasty, which lasted from 2900 to 2750 B. C.

Furniture and Artifacts

The importance of the find lies in the fact that it contains the first furniture and artifacts of Cheops' reign to be found. Except for the tomb of his mother, Hetep-Heres, discovered at the bottom of a shaft a short distance away in 1925, no other funeral chamber had been overlooked by robbers. All other pyramids have been plundered repeatedly since the world's first revolution of record overthrew the sixth Egyptian dynasty 2,500 years before Christ.

The funeral ship, which began evolving in prehistoric times, has been unearthed in many forms. The most magnificent ones were built around Cheops' time, but until today their contents could only be surmised.

Mr. el-Malakh penetrated into the corridor yesterday after his workmen had chiseled through one of the fifteen-ton limestone blocks that had sealed it from the weather and treasure-seeking ghouls through five milleniums. He had suspected that the blocks, uncovered three weeks ago in the construction of a tourist road circling the Great Pyramid, were the ceiling of a corridor leading to the southern tomb of Cheops. The tomb was mentioned in hieroglyphics found on a stone scarab two years ago.

The hole was enlarged enough this morning to permit the young

Continued on Page 4, Column 3

Anti-U.S. Plot Is Laid To 17 Puerto Ricans

By EDWARD RANZAL

Seventeen leaders of the terrorist Nationalist party of Puerto Rico were indicted here yesterday on charges of seditious conspiracy.

The indictment returned by a Federal grand jury stemmed from the shooting in Washington last March 1 of five Representatives in the chamber of the House. It also followed twenty-two years of violence by party members, who seek total independence for Puerto Rico.

In early morning raids Federal Bureau of Investigation agents arrested eleven of the defendants—four here, six in Chicago and one in Ponce, P. R. The remaining six are in prison, four in Washington in connection with the March 1 shooting, and two in Danbury, Conn., for contempt.

On the recommendation of United States Attorney J. Ed-

Continued on Page 14, Column 4

U. S. DETAINS SHIP FOR ARMS SEARCH

French Freighter at Panama Held on Report of Unlisted Weapons in Cargo

By WALTER H. WAGGONER
Special to The New York Times.

WASHINGTON, May 26—United States customs officials are inspecting a French merchant ship at the Panama Canal on suspicion that her cargo may include unlisted weapons.

The State Department, which announced this tonight, did not specify what the inspection of the vessel was expected to uncover.

Other United States officials made it clear, however, that recent reports of new arms shipments bound for Guatemala had prompted the Government to take new precautionary measures against Communist threats to the Western Hemisphere.

[Dispatches from Panama said the freighter was being detained on suspicion that she was carrying arms. A spokesman in New York for the French Line said he had been given to understand the ship carried "a few cases of hunting guns consigned from Belgium to a sporting goods outlet in a Central American country."]

Action Is Explained

After a careful study this evening of reports that the French Line merchant ship might hold a cargo of arms not listed on her manifest, the State Department issued the following statement:

"Before entering the canal the French Line merchant vessel S. S. Wyoming, which is now at Cristobal, is undergoing inspection by United States Customs inspectors to determine whether there has been a violation of customs regulations. The ship's manifest reflects a miscellaneous cargo comprised principally of machinery. Included are five boxes of sporting arms, but it is understood that no question is being raised about these.

"The inspection is being conducted with the knowledge and approval of the French Government and the French Line."

United States authorities said the inspection was to make certain that the machinery listed on the manifest was really machinery. They said it was not yet known what the destination or origin of the ship was. These questions are now being studied.

Officials pointedly separated the detention of the Wyoming from recent reports that two additional shipments of arms for Communist-dominated Guatemala were on their way from undisclosed Baltic ports. But they added that it was clear that certain information had reached the United States indicating that the cargo of the French vessel might contain more weapons than the five boxes of sporting arms.

The Government's alarm over the possibility of secret arms shipments to Guatemala developed suddenly about ten days ago when it was discovered that a

Continued on Page 6, Column 3

DRIVE New Convertible—Sedans. Kent Auto [illegible] 320 E. 48 St. MU [illegible]—Advt.

Nixon Urges Dewey To Seek Re-Election

By JAMES A. HAGERTY

Vice President Richard H. Nixon made an appeal last night to Governor Dewey to run for re-election in November.

Speaking at the $100-a-plate dinner of the Republican State Committee at the Waldorf-Astoria Hotel, Mr. Nixon said of Mr. Dewey:

"I don't know what his future plans are, but I would just like to say that I am among the great numbers of people in other states in America, interested in the cause of good government, who hope that he might continue to give the nation's most populous state the incomparable leadership he has given to it for the last twelve years."

Prolonged applause and cheers followed the Vice President's statement.

Mr. Nixon, whose speaking

Continued on Page 39, Column 6

McCARTHY INQUIRY DISMISSES CASES OF HENSEL, CARR

Republicans Carry 4-3 Vote and Democrats Denounce It as 'a Slick Whitewash'

Excerpts from transcript of the hearing are on Page 20.

By W. H. LAWRENCE
Special to The New York Times.

WASHINGTON, May 26—Four Republican Senators outvoted three Democrats today to dismiss misconduct charges against H. Struve Hensel, Assistant Secretary of Defense, and Francis P. Carr, staff director for the McCarthy investigating subcommittee.

Joseph N. Welch, special counsel for the Army in its dispute with Senator Joseph R. McCarthy, called the decision "a stab in the heart."

Democrats denounced it as "a slick whitewash."

The action came at the close of the Army's presentation of its side of the case on the twenty-first day of public televised hearings before the Senate Permanent Subcommittee on Investigations.

Roy M. Cohn, counsel for the committee under Senator McCarthy, Republican of Wisconsin, was then sworn and will take the stand at 10 A. M. tomorrow to lead off the McCarthy side of the wrangle.

Senator Stuart Symington, Democrat of Missouri, threatened to appeal the committee's decision on the Hensel and Carr cases to the floor of the Senate. He said he would raise the matter also in the Senate Armed Services Committee, of which he is a member.

Motives Are Questioned

While the Republicans asserted their motion had been motivated by the lack of any evidence against Mr. Carr and Mr. Hensel, the Democrats charged that the real purpose of the move had been to relieve Mr. Carr of a requirement that he testify under oath as requested by Army representatives.

A Democratic motion to call Mr. Carr as the first witness on the McCarthy side was voted down, four to three, on straight party lines.

Mr. Carr had been accused by the Army of having participated with Senator McCarthy and Mr. Cohn in attempting by improper means to obtain preferential treatment for Pvt. G. David Schine.

Private Schine, a wealthy New Yorker, was an unpaid staff consultant to the McCarthy subcommittee before he was drafted last November.

Senator McCarthy had charged that Mr. Hensel "masterminded" the Army charges against the McCarthy staff to stop the subcommittee from investigating him. The Senator alleged that Mr. Hensel had acted improperly in organizing a private firm supplying shipping companies while he was a wartime Navy Department official.

Senator McCarthy specifically refused to withdraw his charges

Continued on Page 21, Column 1

PIER UNIONS' VOTE FAILS TO DECIDE CONTROL OF PORT

I.L.A. Takes Lead of 319 but Labor Board Must Rule on 1,797 Challenged Ballots

By A. H. RASKIN

For the second time in five months a fiercely contested National Labor Relations Board election failed last night to settle the interunion fight for control of the Port of New York.

The old International Longshoremen's Association, battling for its life against the combined assault of the American Federation of Labor, Governor Dewey and the Waterfront Commission, emerged from the balloting with a margin of 319 votes over its A. F. L. rival.

But the victor will not be known until the Labor Board disposes of 1,797 challenged ballots, a process that may take a month or more.

Twenty thousand dock workers participated in the balloting, which was conducted in an atmosphere of churchlike calm in contrast to the turbulence and bloodshed that forced invalidation of a similar poll last December.

The official result, as announced at 11 P. M. by Charles T. Douds, regional director of the Labor Board, gave the I. L. A. 9,110 votes to 8,791 for the A. F. L., with 1,797 ballots in dispute, 49 void and 51 against both unions.

Vote Is Increased

The new pier union, set up by the federation last September to bring honest unionism to the crime-steeped waterfront, bettered the record it made in the first election. At that time it ran 1,492 votes behind the I. L. A., with 4,396 ballots challenged.

Most observers expected, however, that a count of the disputed votes in yesterday's poll would guarantee victory for the I. L. A. Patrick J. Connolly, executive vice president of the old union, estimated that 1,500 of the challenges had been filed by the A. F. L. against I. L. A. stalwarts.

He demanded that the election results be certified without delay so the I. L. A. could negotiate a new wage agreement with the New York Shipping Association. He hinted at a new strike if the Labor Board engaged in protracted hearings before giving his union the green light to bargain with the employers.

No concession of defeat came from the A. F. L. John Dwyer, its port chairman, said he felt "very confident" the new union would get a majority of the challenged ballots and win the right to speak for all of the port's 26,000 dock workers. He made it plain that the A. F. L. had no intention of abandoning its drive to clean up the harbor, even if it did wind up on the short end of the final count.

Mr. Douds, who praised the vote as the "most orderly" he had ever seen, declared that it might take six weeks to two months to complete an investigation of the challenged ballots and decide which should be counted. Each union has five days in which to file objections to the conduct of

Continued on Page 55, Column 3

French Lean to Divided Indochina; Troops Quit Two Posts in Delta

Cabinet Gives Bidault Right to Seek to Compromise Red and Paris Plans

By LANSING WARREN
Special to The New York Times.

PARIS, May 26—The French seemed today to be moving toward acceptance of a partition of territory in Indochina.

The extent of the territory to be yielded to the Vietminh and the new line of defense depends on an international guarantee of the partition, in which the United States and other nations at the Geneva conference would join.

Georges Bidault, French Foreign Minister, returned tonight to Geneva, where the Far Eastern conference is being held. He was armed with the Cabinet's vote of confidence enabling him to seek a compromise between the new Vietminh proposal and the latest French plan for a cease-fire on the Indochina front.

The chances of obtaining this were said to depend on Allied solidarity to convince the Soviet bloc the Allies were united and that there would be no way of

Continued on Page 6, Column 2

Positions on Southern Rim Are Blown Up—Vietminh Pincer Drive Develops

By The Associated Press.

HANOI, Vietnam, May 26—French Union defenders of the Red River delta, menaced by an apparent Vietminh pincers advance, today blew up two of their posts on the southern rim of the delta.

As tanks, armored cars and planes furnished protective cover, the French evacuated and dynamited the posts at Thannhe and Doaithon, about sixty miles southeast of Hanoi. The posts, six miles southeast of Thaibinh, a market center, had been subjected to constant encircling maneuvers and harassing night attacks.

The pincers threat developed last night as Vietminh units, moving southeasterly along Route 41 from smashed Dienbienphu, suddenly struck off northeastward.

French Army headquarters here said bombers, from land and carrier bases, and fighter planes bombed and strafed the advancing column.

Military sources here believe

Continued on Page 3, Column 3

T. W. U. TO BATTLE FOR STRIKE RIGHT

Plans Suit on Condon-Wadlin Law—700 on Joint Board Unanimous for Walkout

By LEONARD INGALLS

Union preparations for a legal battle over the right of Transit Authority employes to strike were being made yesterday.

Michael J. Quill, president of the Transport Workers Union, C. I. O., defied the transit agency in its threat to seek an injunction against a walkout and to invoke the Condon-Wadlin Law, which makes dismissal mandatory for public employes who strike.

Rejection by the authority of fact-finding proposals that would have strengthened the T. W. U. as the representative of 34,000 of the agency's 44,000 employes led to the threat of a strike.

A strike at 12:01 A. M. June 14 was voted unanimously last night by 700 members of the union's local joint executive board at the Capitol Hotel. An open vote on the strike date during the next ten days by the rank and file was authorized. Plans for picketing at twenty-six places on the transit system during a walkout were made.

Earlier in the day, after a meeting of union lawyers, Mr. Quill announced that "there is considerable legal opinion that the Condon-Wadlin law has no application to the pending walkout by the T. W. U. in the New York City transit system."

The legal aspects of the situation were explored by Arthur J. Goldberg, general counsel of the Congress of Industrial Organizations, and John F. O'Donnell, general counsel of the T. W. U.

Another meeting was scheduled for June 4 and a union announcement said that the general counsels of all C. I. O. international unions would gather here then for "a council of war on New York State's anti-labor Condon-Wadlin Law."

The law was voted by the Legislature and approved by Governor Dewey in 1947. It has never been subjected to a major court test.

A spokesman for the Governor said yesterday that Mr. Dewey

Continued on Page 28, Column 3

Survivors Fight the Flames To Organize Instant Rescue

By WILLIAM M. FARRELL
Special to The New York Times.

QUONSET POINT, R. I., May 26—Rescue work aboard the aircraft carrier Bennington got under way almost simultaneously with the blasts and fire this morning. Sailors and marines were wrenched from sleep or routine tasks and plunged into the work of saving shipmates who lay burned.

The damage and injury were mostly in sleeping, dining and recreation areas, or in passages connecting such areas.

To reach the casualties, some of the survivors had to fight their way out of the blast-torn areas. Those who could get hold of mask-type breathing devices put them on, and worked for hours searching out and moving the injured. Others kept at the task as long as they could stand the suffocating atmosphere.

One of those who narrowly missed injury and helped to organize the rescue work was Marine Lieut. Carl Gage of Lynnfield, Mass. He and Capt. David Twomey, commander of the ship's detachment of marines, were asleep in their stateroom when the fire started.

They had barely awakened

Continued on Page 16, Column 6

Soviet Party Rising To a Par With State

Special to The New York Times.

MOSCOW, May 26—Parity or duality of the Communist party and the state in the Soviet Union has been growing.

Observers in the foreign diplomatic corps note, for example, that at the recent session of the Supreme Soviet, two important addresses of equal importance were delivered.

The first was that of Premier Georgi M. Malenkov to the Council of Nationalities. The second was that of Nikita S. Khrushchev, first secretary of the Communist party, to the Council of Union.

Although the meeting of the Supreme Soviet is what might be called a "Government" occasion, none the less the party secretary, Mr. Khrushchev, spoke on a basis of full parity with Premier Malenkov.

This parallel role of party and

Continued on Page 2, Column 4

CENTRAL VOTE IN; MEETING RECESSED

2,200 Stockholders Attend Noisy Session on Control—Count Starts Today

By ROBERT E. BEDINGFIELD
Special to The New York Times.

ALBANY, May 26—The noisy battle of the last eighteen weeks for control of the giant New York Central Railroad quieted today to a shuffling of a stack of 40,979 papers—representing votes.

That quiet, however, did not descend until 4:48 P. M., when the Central stockholders' meeting in the Tenth Regiment Armory here was recessed until Tuesday.

For the preceding four hours and forty-eight minutes some 2,200 Central shareholders had participated in a session more like a rousing political convention than an annual meeting of a century-old railroad.

It will be days, maybe weeks, before those shareholders and the ones who participated by proxy know whether they re-elected fifteen men to manage their $2,600,000,000 investment for the next year or elected an insurgent slate of fourteen men and a woman.

The count of proxies by the inspectors of election, three professors of law, will begin tomorrow at 9 A. M. in the Ten Eyck Hotel here. A tedious process, it will continue to 8 P. M. daily until completion. The professors are Robert W. Miller of Syracuse University, John Hanna of Columbia University and Covington Hardee of Harvard Law School.

The present board is headed by William White, 57-year-old

Continued on Page 41, Column 2

For a pleasant Memorial Day Week-End be sure to stock up on WHITE ROCK Q-9 Quinine Water.—Advt.

SHIP REACHES PORT

Explosions Cause Fire 75 Miles at Sea—Origin Unknown

By MURRAY SCHUMACH
Special to The New York Times.

QUONSET POINT, R. I., May 26—Explosions and fire aboard the aircraft carrier Bennington killed at least ninety-one men and injured more than 200 today.

It was one of the worst peacetime disasters in modern United States naval history.

The blasts originated on the deck below the hangar deck, the first one occurring at about 6:20 this morning. The hangar deck is just below the flight, or top, deck of the ship.

The 41,000-ton vessel was in the Atlantic about seventy-five miles south of Newport, R. I., when she was rocked by the explosions.

The carrier, escorted by the destroyer Ingraham, was on her way north to this naval air station from Norfolk, Va.

The Secretary of the Navy, Charles S. Thomas, who flew here from Washington to inspect the ship and talk to eyewitnesses, said the cause of the explosion was not known.

A court of inquiry will begin here tomorrow. According to Rear Admiral John M. Hoskins, commander of air activities here, the inquiry will "try to determine the cause of the accident; to learn if anyone was at fault and try to make sure that it never happens again."

Ambulances Stand By

From the first of three explosions, until the last man left the ship, the scenes often were reminiscent of wartime. Heroism was mingled with death as rescuers fought through smoke and bent steel to find comrades. The fire raged for about four hours after the explosions.

Helicopters made as many as a dozen trips out to sea to bring the critically injured to hospitals. Ten of the victims were on the critical list and some personnel were missing.

Long lines of ambulances were on the pier here before the carrier arrived, and later in the day many hearses occupied the same area.

While ranking Navy officers held conferences, hundreds of wives and parents sat tensely in a theatre here, waiting to learn if their men were alive.

Several theories advanced to explain the disaster were discredited during the day. Capt. William F. Raborn of Oklahoma City, skipper of the ship, suggested at first that a fuse magazine might have exploded. Later, however, he said a check had shown this to be unlikely.

The possibility of sabotage was discounted by Admiral Hoskins, but he added he could not dismiss this entirely until the investigation was concluded.

Other officers, including Captain Raborn, said they did not think the trouble began in the catapult room, which contains mechanism for launching planes.

At the time of the accident Captain Raborn was on the navigation bridge and the ship was

Continued on Page 16, Column 2

Student Body to Pay I.R.T. Melee Damage

Dismayed by last Thursday's disorder on the subway, the student body of the High School of Commerce has offered to pay for the damage.

The melee, which occurred on the I. R. T. subway trains and stations between the Van Cortlandt Park terminal and Ninety-sixth Street, involved hundreds of high school boys and girls. It occurred after a rain squall had forced cancellation of the school's field day in the park.

The day after the disorder representatives of the student government of the school, at 155 West Sixty-fifth Street, met with the principal, Vincent McGarrett, to discuss a plan of restitution. The proposal was then submitted to school's 2,000 students and overwhelmingly approved.

A spokesman for the Transit Authority said the principal damage was the smashing of electric

Continued on Page 28, Column 5

The Vigil at the Pier: Ambulances Await the Injured as Families Seek Word of Their Kin

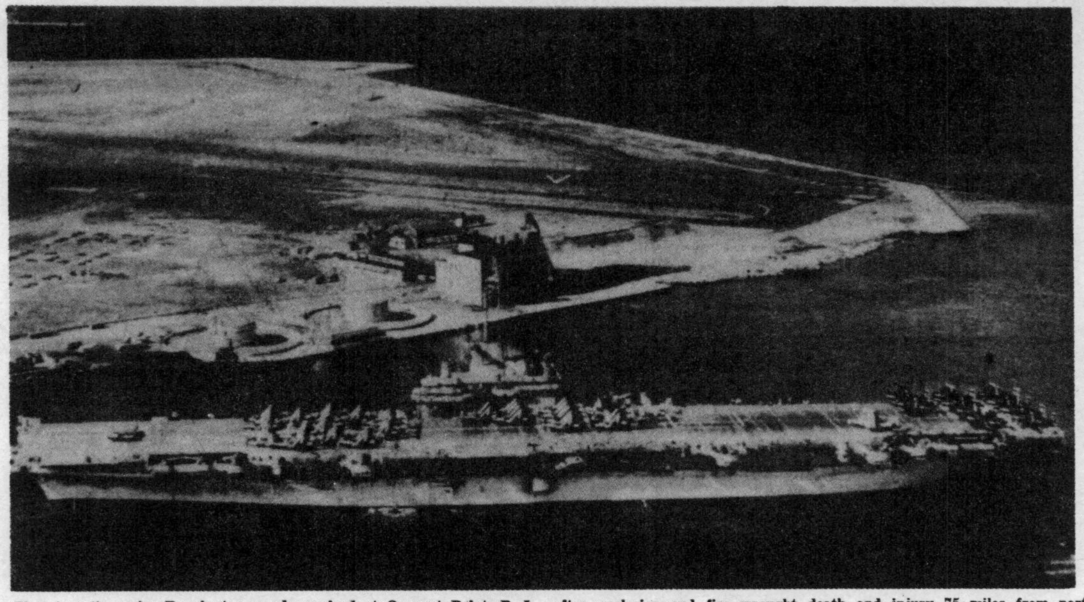
The aircraft carrier Bennington as she arrived at Quonset Point, R. I., after explosion and fire wrought death and injury 75 miles from port

On the pier, ambulances wait to take injured sailors to hospital. Some were removed by air.

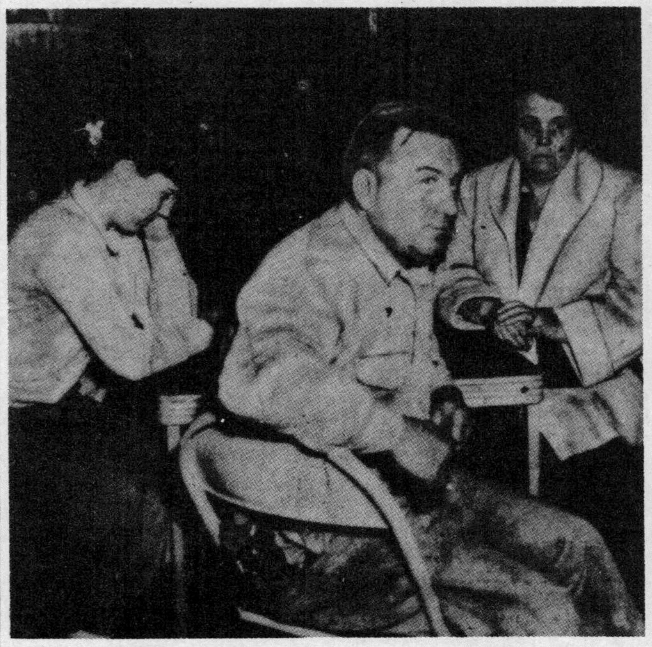
Anxious eyes tell of parents' grief. Wife of sailor silently shares the pangs of doubt.

The New York Times (by Meyer Liebowitz)
Some crew members of the carrier lean against a fighter plane to write telegrams assuring families of their safety

WITNESSES LAUD CREW'S BEHAVIOR

Wounded Never Whimpered—Men 'Acted Like Seamen,' Helped in Rescues

By IRVING SPIEGEL
Special to The New York Times.

QUONSET POINT, R. I., May 26—Eyewitness accounts of the Bennington disaster were told today by weary survivors who were flown into this Naval Air Base by helicopters and by those who were on the carrier when she docked here.

His face still blackened by smoke, Robert Pierro of Corona, Queens, in New York City, an electronics technician, said he had been on duty in an enclosure on the hangar deck when the first explosion occurred.

Knocked Down by Blast

"Almost immediately," he said, "the ship's gong sounded general quarters over the loudspeaker.

"That first explosion knocked me down. I noticed smoke and fire from the deck below. I rushed down, men were lying on the deck, bleeding and crying for help, bodies were floating in the water. The deck was a mess with twisted steel tables and chairs."

Harold Gibbs of Pittsfield, Mass., a medical corpsman, one of the first of the Quonset Naval Air Station to board the Bennington, paid high tribute to the efficiency of the medical treatment to the injured.

Gibbs, who gave first-aid treatment to the wounded for superficial burns, said that scores of the wounded were lined up on the deck awaiting removal to the hospital.

"Not a whimper from these guys," he said. "Once in a while, one of the fellows would turn around and say 'Hey, fellow, give me a hand with this bandage.'"

Robert Cheyne, of Attleboro, Mass., an electrician's mate, said he was asleep in his bunk when he heard the first explosion which hurled "me clear out of the rack."

"I saw smoke," he added, "I hit the deck fast and as I started to go forward, I heard another explosion. I hit the deck."

Helped With Wounded

Cheyne said he made his way to another part of the ship, where he took a hand in aiding the wounded.

Jerry Tye, of Barbourville, Ky., electrician's mate, said he was in the mess room with several hundred other seamen.

"We heard the explosion, and most of the guys sitting near me felt that it might have been a small thing," he said. "We saw the smoke and flames and heard more explosions. The fellows behaved like seamen, we exited quickly but orderly to the decks, and then scattered."

George Robinson of Charles City, Va., a seaman, related how he had been sleeping on the "third deck portside when I heard a helluva noise."

Hurled 15 Feet

"Something dumped me out of the rack," he said. "I made my way to the second deck. I tried opening the hatch. It was locked. There was another bang, and I was hurled fifteen feet against a bulkhead. The next thing I knew I was on the hangar deck covered with blankets. The guy next to me was dead."

Robinson was treated for minor bruises and shock.

Similarly, James Wynne of Elmhurst, Queens, in New York, an electrician's mate, said he had been on the sixth deck when he had heard the first explosion.

Wynne said he had made his way also to the second deck but the "hatches were secure."

"I made my way down, but I guess the fumes got me," he said. "I passed out. When I came to I was on the hangar deck." He was treated for smoke poisoning.

Chief Warrant Officer Greely Goodwin of Mount Pleasant, S. C., was in the engine room with a crew when dense smoke began filtering into the room from the ventilator system.

"I beat it up to the hatch and cried out for help," he said.

"I heard the explosion. I didn't know what to expect, but I figured we needed more men for the engine room. I still don't know how we kept those engines going through all that smoke. The guys were coughing and choking but they stood fast at those engines."

91 DEAD, 200 HURT IN CARRIER BLASTS

Continued From Page 1

doing twenty knots. Rear Admiral Edgar Cruise, commander of Carrier Division 6, was aboard. He had made the Bennington his flagship.

Captain Raborn said that his first knowledge that something was wrong came about 6:20 A. M. when he saw a puff of white smoke from below the flight deck. Shortly thereafter he felt a "minor" explosion, followed by two stronger blasts.

General quarters was sounded and the captain organized and directed rescue parties. He said his men performed many acts of heroism, saving comrades trapped in smoke-filled compartments in which the water used to fight the fire was often more than a foot deep.

While directing operations below deck, the captain ordered planes still aboard to take off. Twenty aircraft, including jets, left the carrier before the accident. In the next few minutes another twenty took off. The captain said none of the planes was damaged—they landed at the Quonset Naval Air Station.

Not all the planes on the carrier were flown off. Some that were on the hangar deck at the time of the explosion were moved up to the flight deck as the ship made for port.

During midafternoon, after inspecting the carrier, the captain said there were no bodies remaining aboard the vessel and that all the injured had been removed.

In announcing the organization of a court of inquiry, Admiral Hoskins said it would include, in addition to himself, Admiral Cruise, Capt. James E. Leeper, commander of Fleet Air Wing 3, here, and Capt. R. J. Zanzot, matériel officer of the staff of the commander of destroyers in the Atlantic.

Admiral Hosknis said that, except when classified information was discussed, the court of inquiry would be open to the press. An inspection of the ship by the court will take place tomorrow, he declared.

Admiral Hoskins said he did not yet know the exact location of the first explosion. He described the tragedy as "the worst I can recall offhand in peacetime."

He asserted, "I don't believe there is any possibility of sabotage. However, I can't be certain about that until the inquiry is completed."

The admiral praised Captain Raborn for his work in controlling the fire and limiting the damage to a "comparatively small area of the ship."

Secretary Thomas, who came aboard the Bennington about an hour after she arrived here at 12:25 P. M., said he knew there was "nothing I could do, but I wanted these men and their families to know the deep, personal interest I had in these men."

The Secretary, whose son is serving aboard another carrier, vowed the injured would get the best possible medical care. He praised not only the rescue workers, but also civilian doctors and nurses who volunteered their services.

Mr. Thomas said he was particularly proud of the work done by the helicopter pilots. Their efficiency, he said, would undoubtedly mean the difference between life and death to some of the injured.

The Secretary said he assumed he would make a report but indicated that this matter obviously could not be discussed in detail pending completion of the court of inquiry.

The Bennington left Norfolk on Monday. She was conducting air operations at sea and was not due here until Friday. The carrier had last been at this naval air station over the week-end of May 15 and 16.

Telephone facilities here and in surrounding areas were so badly snarled that calls were generally held up for about three hours. The Navy had priority for official business and relatives swamped the switchboards in their anxiety to learn the fate of men aboard the carrier. Reporters at the scene were hampered in relaying stories to their offices in consequence.

House Group Votes Rise In Pensions to Veterans

WASHINGTON, May 26—(UP)—The Veterans Committee of the House of Representatives today unanimously approved an increase of nearly 10 per cent in Federal pension and compensation payments to ex-service men and their dependents.

The proposed increase, which faces an uncertain fate in Congress, would go to all but a handful of the 3,676,872 veterans and dependents currently carried on Veterans Administration rolls.

Detailed figures were not available. But it was estimated the proposal would cost the Treasury about $230,000,000 a year in additions of the $2,500,000,000 already spent on such programs.

The benefit increases, designed to offset increases in living costs, were approved by the committee Tuesday for most disabled veterans and their dependents.

Heavy Loss Aboard Bennington Not the Navy's Worst Disaster

175 Perished in 1952 When Hobson Was Rammed—Typhoons in Pacific Swept More Than 400 Seamen to Death

By IRA HENRY FREEMAN

The appalling loss of life by explosion and fire aboard the aircraft carrier Bennington yesterday ranked among the worst disasters to befall United States naval vessels by accident.

Aside from many greater losses occurring in combat, one of the greatest disasters in recent years occurred on April 26, 1952, when the minesweeper Hobson was cut in two by the aircraft carrier Wasp 700 miles west of the Azores and sank in four minutes.

One hundred seventy-five of her crew perished and only sixty-one were rescued by the Wasp and other ships in the task force heading for the Mediterranean.

During World War II many American sailors died aboard their ships by accident, not by enemy action. The destroyer Ingraham sank in twenty-five seconds after a collision in a fog off Canada in August, 1942, with a loss of 218 men. The destroyer Turner exploded in the Lower New York Bay on Jan 3, 1944, and 138 of her crew died.

Nature also has been destructive. A typhoon in the Pacific sank the destroyers Hull, Monaghan and Spence in January, 1945, drowning more than 400 of their complement. An Atlantic hurricane overwhelmed the destroyer Warrington, two Coast Guard patrol ships, a lightship and a minesweeper in September, 1944, with a total loss of 344 men.

A freezing gale in February, 1942, blew the destroyer Truxton and the transport Pollux on the beach in Newfoundland in February, 1942, and 189 crewmen died.

There were fifteen noncombat submarine disasters from 1915 to 1943, with an aggregate loss of 247 sailors.

The largest loss among these submarines was forty, the entire crew of the S-4, which rammed the Coast Guard destroyer Paulding off Provincetown, Mass., and sank Dec. 16, 1927.

Other notable submarine losses included the R-12, which sank off the east coast of this country in June, 1943, with a loss of twenty-eight men; the S-26, which went down off Panama after a collision with another naval vessel on Jan. 24, 1942, with only three of her crew of thirty-five rescued, and the Squalus, which sank off Portsmouth, N. H., on May 23, 1949. In the last accident, thirty-three of the crew were raised by diving bell, but twenty-six were lost.

Other important accidents involving large loss of life aboard naval vessels in recent years include:

Oct. 16, 1953—Carrier Leyte, exploded and burned in Boston drydock, thirty-seven dead, forty injured.

Aug. 25, 1950—Hospital ship Benevolence collided with freighter Mary Luckenbach in fog off San Francisco, twenty-three dead.

May 31, 1948—liberty launches off the carrier Kearsage sank in Norfolk, Va., harbor, thirty sailors drowned.

Jan., 1946—minesweeper Minivet hit mine off Japan, thirty-one lost, five injured.

April 23, 1945—patrol boat PE56 exploded and sank off Cape Elizabeth, Me., forty-nine drowned.

In addition, two Navy munitions ships blew up in San Francisco Bay in July, 1944, causing 322 deaths and more than 1,500 injuries, these, however, included Army men and civilian workers as well as Navy personnel.

During World War I, 431 men, mostly American soldiers, died when the Otranto, a British transport, sank in a collision off Scotland. Just after the Civil War, 1,450 Union war prisoners lost their lives in explosion of the steamer Sultana, which was evacuating them from Memphis on April 27, 1865.

The New York Times May 27, 1954
SITE OF DISASTER: Explosions rocked the Bennington at sea (cross), some 75 miles south of Newport, R. I.

SURVIVORS FIGHT FIRE FOR RESCUE

Continued From Page 1

when a blast caved in two temporary metal bulkheads and flames burst from the ventilator.

Slightly burned, the two men found themselves trapped in their room. Using a rifle as a crowbar, they managed to get a door opened, only to find a fire blazing in the passage outside.

"We put out that fire, and started up a ladder to the hangar deck," Lieutenant Gage said. "The top of the ladder was blocked by two bodies, and we had to move them to get by."

The two men found others groping into the area, and organized them into rescue parties. Time after time, their work was blocked by debris, or by the bodies of injured shipmates.

Groups led by Lieutenant Gage, Ensign William Schultz and other officers made their way through passages choked with twisted steel plates, among bulkheads coated with oil. Fuel lines had burst, either causing or adding to the emergency.

"I think the last blast blew out the fire," Lieutenant Gage said. "The chief obstacles to the rescue work were the deadly fumes and the blocked passages.

"We couldn't use stretchers down there—it was hard enough just to walk," the lieutenant said. "We carried the men by hand till we could get them into clear spaces, then they were put on stretchers and moved to one of the bays on an upper deck.

"Most of them had had their clothes burned off, and many were bleeding from the mouth. I believe their lungs had been singed. Some died while we were trying to get them out.

"We were able to get to all of the men, though, and it was wonderful the way everyone helped. After we had taken out all we could find, we checked staterooms and other places to see that nobody had been overlooked."

Fire Forward of Island

The areas wrecked by the fire and blasts were on the first and second decks below the hangar deck, generally forward of the ship's "island," or superstructure. This part of the body of the vessel is thickly armored, so that externally there was virtually no sign of the damage.

Inside, however, the officers' wardroom and the warrant officers' wardroom, as well as the crew's mess, were badly damaged. The crew's quarters were more heavily in use, and casualties there were severe. Officers' staterooms also suffered sharply.

Many entries to the area were blocked, and compartment doors were closed to confine the damage. A passage on the lower of the two decks affected, and two hatches, provided the routes over which the burned and injured men were carried.

On the hangar deck, from which the ship's "island" rises alongside the flight deck, hospital corpsmen and others set up aid stations for the administration of blood plasma and sedatives. Some of the injured had been cut or hurt by water pitchers, crockery and anything else that was not secured when the blasts knocked everything about.

While the personnel of the Bennington concentrated on controlling the disaster, she followed her escort, the destroyer Ingraham, up Narragansett Bay.

76 at Naval Hospital

Special to The New York Times.

NEWPORT, R. I., May 26—The seventy-six most seriously injured aboard the Bennington were brought to the Naval Hospital here today by helicopter and boat.

Hardly had the Bennington arrived off Brenton Point shortly before 11 A. M. when five Navy and Coast Guard helicopters went into action to maintain a continuous shuttle service between the ship and the land near the hospital. They brought sixty-two of the most serious cases to the hospital immediately.

Capt. John L. Enyart, commandant of the Naval Hospital, commandeered a vacant lot a few hundred yards east of the hospital grounds for the larger helicopters to land. A dozen ambulances kept on a continuous move between the fields and the hospital door. The small Coast Guard helicopter landed at the hospital baseball field within the base limits. A landing pier on the ocean side also was used.

During the afternoon thirteen more stretcher cases were brought by crash boat from the Quonset Air Station, twelve miles up Narragansett Bay, and landed at the naval station dock. Here ambulances stood by to rush the men to the hospital.

Newport Hospital Aids

Every available Navy nurse and hospital corpsman in the area was summoned to duty. The Newport Hospital, a private institution, sent twelve doctors from its staff, as well as supplies.

The Newport Hospital also set up a blood bank where 500 volunteer donors reported during the day. As a result 120 pints of blood plasma were collected and sent to the Naval Hospital.

All Navy chaplains in the area reported to the Naval Hospital to assist in the wards and all Roman Catholic victims received the last rites of the church.

During the afternoon Charles S. Thomas, Secretary of the Navy, who had flown to Quonset, came to Newport and visited the victims in the hospital wards.

The helicopter service attracted thousands of sight-seers to the vicinity, creating a serious traffic congestion at noon. As a result, William A. Gildea, Newport City Manager, called in every off-duty policeman and sealed off the area.

The Newport Red Cross stood by to furnish assistance, but its work will come later in looking out for families of the injured and in relaying information on the hospital patients to their families over the country. Charles Estil, regional Red Cross representative, came to Newport to take charge of the relief work.

'COPTERS TO AID HUNT FOR INJURED CLIMBER

FAIRBANKS, Alaska, May 26 (AP)—One young mountain climber was killed and another lay seriously injured at the 14,000-foot level on Mount McKinley after a "terrible spill" that ended a student expedition.

Two battered survivors of the accident brought the story here last night. A rescue mission was organized today to try to rescue the injured man.

The four-man expedition of University of Alaska students or former students went up the 20,300-foot mountain April 17. They had been listed as overdue ten days. A search had started yesterday. The survivors were found by chance by an unidentified forest ranger who was working on an outlying road job in Mount McKinley Park.

The rescue party will try to go by helicopter to the 8,000 or 9,000 foot level and then climb to the gravely injured man, George Argus.

Fragmentary reports said the five-day food supply left him in an improvised tent shelter would run out today.

The man killed in the fall was Elton Thayer, a well-known Alaska climber.

Word of the disaster and desperate rescue plans was relayed here today by the Civil Air Patrol and the Seventy-fourth Air Rescue Squadron. The report said the four were tied together when they hurtled down the precipice.

Yonkers Licenses Bus Line

Special to The New York Times.

YONKERS, May 26—The Common Council last night licensed one bus line to operate to the new Cross County Center but withheld a permit from a second. Westchester Surface Ways, Inc., got its permit to run buses from Mount Vernon to the center, but the Yonkers Railroad Company's petition was referred to the Transit Committee because its proposed bus route along Central Park Avenue would coincide in part with that of the Club Transportation Corporation.

The New York Times.

"All the News That's Fit to Print"

LATE CITY EDITION
Fair and mild today. Partly cloudy and mild tomorrow.
Temperature Range Today—Max., 77; Min., 58
Temperature Yesterday—Max., 73; Min., 61
Full U. S. Weather Bureau Report, Page 41

VOL. CIV..No. 35,310.

Entered as Second-Class Matter, Post Office, New York, N. Y.

NEW YORK, MONDAY, SEPTEMBER 27, 1954.

Copyright, 1954, by The New York Times Company.

Times Square, New York 36, N. Y.
Telephone LAckawanna 4-1000

FIVE CENTS

M'CARTHY REPORT IN CENSURE STUDY TO BE MADE TODAY

Sources Close to 6 Senators on Special Panel Say They Will Criticize Wisconsinite

RUMORS FILL WASHINGTON

One Forecast Asserts Rebuke Will Be Recommended on at Least 3 Counts

Special to The New York Times.

WASHINGTON, Sept. 26—The Senate Select Committee that investigated the censure charges against Senator Joseph R. McCarthy will make public its report tomorrow at 9 A. M.

Unofficial predictions were circulated today on the contents of the 65,000-word document that will put before a reconvened Senate on Nov. 8 the question of whether to censure or absolve the Wisconsin Republican.

There was no official comment on what the committee would say. However, sources close to the six-member group said again privately that the report would criticize the Senator but that was as far as it would go.

The three Republicans and three Democrats that make up the group maintained their silence, but one, Senator Francis Case, Republican of South Dakota, did say that not even the White House had any advance information.

One forecast among the many today, however, was that the committee in its unanimous report would recommend the censure of Senator McCarthy on three counts.

Abuse of Zwicker Cited

They were said to be as follows:

1. That he was contemptuous of the Senate Privileges and Elections subcommittee that had investigated his activities in 1951 and 1952.

2. That he used vulgar language in referring to Senator Robert C. Hendrickson, Republican of New Jersey.

3. That he used abusive tactics in his questioning last Feb. 18 of Brig. Gen. Ralph W. Zwicker.

These counts represent three of the five general categories of charges against the Senator that the committee considered in nine days of public hearings that ended Sept. 13.

Originally forty-six charges were leveled against the Senator and referred to the committee. But the group selected thirteen for study and put them into the five categories.

The two other categories are incidents of encouragement of United States employe to violate the law and their oaths of office or Executive orders and incidents involving receipt or use of confidential or classified information from Executive files.

It was asserted but not confirmed here today that the committee would dismiss as irrelevant to its inquiry the specific charge that the Senator misused fully received a 2½-page abstract of a paper sent by the Federal Bureau of Investigation to the Army on alleged security risks.

It was said the committee would criticize the Senator for possessing the document but would not rule on censure on this point.

The contents of the document,

Continued on Page 8, Column 3

Almost 1,000 on Ferry Die As Typhoon Sweeps Japan

About 50 Americans Lost on Craft Upset in Strait —Damage Widespread

By LINDESAY PARROTT
Special to The New York Times.

TOKYO, Monday, Sept. 27—A train ferry capsized last night, drowning almost 1,000 persons, including more than fifty Americans—troops and Army dependents and other civilians.

The blunt-bowed, open-ended vessel turned over in typhoon winds that swept Tsugaru Strait, between Honshu and Hokkaido. The typhoon did widespread damage over the main islands of Japan. Gusts were estimated at seventy miles an hour and the storm was recorded as the most violent here since 1938.

The 4,337-ton ferry Doya Maru left Hakodate at 6:30 P. M. bound for Aomori, terminal of the main rail line on northern Honshu.

The Doya Maru capsized at an emergency anchorage off Nanaihama, west of Hakodate, after a four-hour battle with winds and storm-lashed waves.

The vessel carried soldiers of the United States First Cavalry Division transferring from Hokkaido to new posts on Honshu and their dependents.

More than twelve hours after the ship had turned over and sunk, 101 persons were known to have been rescued and taken to hospitals, out of more than 1,100 who had sailed aboard the craft. According to an unofficial count, 450 bodies had been washed ashore or recovered from the wreck.

Besides those drowned many were apparently killed when rail-

Continued on Page 12, Column 6

[Map caption:]
The New York Times Sept. 27, 1954
Scene of capsizing (cross)

Failings of Weather Bureau Laid to Federal Parsimony

By ROBERT ALDEN

The United States Weather Bureau, charged with a grave responsibility in terms of life, property and commercial interest, is severely handicapped by a lack of funds to carry out a complex operation. As a case in point, meteorologists say that if the trend toward eliminating weather observation stations continues there is a very real danger that the bureau's forecasts will become less accurate.

In 1947 there were 443 such weather stations. Next year there will be 321. In 1949 the Weather Bureau had 4,517 full-time employes. Next year there will be 3,728.

The plight of the Weather Bureau was brought into focus by Hurricane Carol, which roared into an unprepared New England at the end of August, killing sixty persons and causing damage estimated at $500,000,000.

As a result of that storm this newspaper interviewed about forty persons in the field of weather study and prediction, most of them privately employed and thus holding no special brief for the Weather Bureau.

To a man they agreed that the bureau had been treated penuriously by Congress and by the Bureau of the Budget and that, consequently, its product was not up to what it could be.

One description characterized the Weather Bureau as a neglected "horse-and-buggy outfit struggling to get along on just a pittance—a fraction of the money it should have."

The more generously inclined commented that in spite of severe budgetary handicaps the Weather Bureau through constant struggle was "almost" managing to keep abreast of the times in a branch

Continued on Page 12, Column 1

JAVITS WON'T CURB HIS LIBERAL VIEWS

Says He Is Running on Own Record, Not Dewey's, and Is Ives' 'Personal Choice'

By DOUGLAS DALES

Representative Jacob K. Javits, Republican candidate for Attorney General, served notice yesterday that he was not toning down his liberal views to suit conservative elements in the Republican party.

"I will be what I was in my office I serve in," he declared at an interview in his law office, 630 Fifth Avenue. He added:

"I believe all the things I worked for. I'll stand and fight for all the same beliefs that I stood for in the Congress."

Mr. Javits, describing himself as "liberal by philosophy," said his nomination "represented something of a success for modernism in the Republican party, and that is all to the good."

The candidate conceded that he had been critical in the past on several points in the record of Governor Dewey, but on the whole, he said, he believed it had been a good record.

"But I'm not running on Dewey's record," he asserted. "I'm running on my own record."

Has Disagreed With Dewey

Mr. Javits did not see eye-to-eye with the State Administration on the 15 per cent across-the-board rent increase authorized in 1951, and he differed in details on the handling of the transit situation.

Presumably referring to opposition within the Republican party in his bid last year for the Republican nomination for Mayor, Mr. Javits said he was the "personal choice" for Attorney General of Senator Irving M. Ives, the candidate for Governor.

"Suffice it to say," he observed, "if there had been no Ives, there would have been no Javits."

Asserting that Tammany Hall, the New York County Democratic organization, was in control of the Democratic party in the state, Mr. Javits said a Democratic victory would mean that "Tammany would control both city and state, with no check and no balance."

With a Republican administration in Albany, he added, "the people of New York have had the check and the balance of an effective state government since 1945 upon what Tammany might do with the town."

"Tammany Hall's record in New York City, in the way it has run the city, has a background of waste and corruption that is not ancient history because the Crime Commission has backed up these findings within the very recent past."

Mr. Javits said it was not his business to say what went on in

Continued on Page 13, Column 4

Mitchell Says Nixon 'Lies' on Red Ousters

By CLAYTON KNOWLES
Special to The New York Times.

WASHINGTON, Sept. 26—Stephen A. Mitchell, Democratic National Chairman, charged today that Vice President Richard M. Nixon had told an "outright lie" about the number of Communists removed from Government jobs by the Eisenhower Administration.

He based his charge, he said, on an Associated Press dispatch quoting Mr. Nixon as having said Sept. 18 at Huron, S. D., that the Administration had "kicked the Communists out of Government not by the hundreds but by the thousands."

Appearing on the National Broadcasting Company television program "Youth Wants to Know," Mr. Mitchell, renewing a charge he had made in New Hampshire last night, said:

"Now he [Mr. Nixon] knows

Continued on Page 15, Column 6

A.F.L. MOVES TO AID FEDERAL CLEAN-UP OF WELFARE FUNDS

At Final Session Today, It Also Will Ask Inquiries of Brokerage Fees

By A. H. RASKIN
Special to The New York Times.

LOS ANGELES, Sept. 26—Stirred by disclosures of union welfare rackets, the American Federation of Labor prepared today to pledge its aid in Government moves to root out abuses in administration of the funds.

This break with the Federation's historic policy of fighting Government interference in internal union affairs is scheduled for formal approval at tomorrow's closing session of the A. F. L. convention here.

The Federation will set forth its readiness to cooperate in any objective survey of the problems involved in keeping welfare funds honest. It will urge that such surveys by Congressional and state investigators put the spotlight on the sins of insurance companies, brokers and employers, as well as of corrupt union officials.

However, the A. F. L. will emphasize that its call for a balanced inquiry is not intended to shift attention away from union crooks or to shield them from punishment. The A. F. L. will demand that all its 113 affiliated unions exercise maximum vigilance in cleaning their own houses and bringing wrongdoers to justice.

Primary A. F. L. Problem

George Meany, A. F. L. president, has made it plain in conferences with other union chiefs that he believes a clean-up of welfare funds is the primary internal problem confronting the organization. He has set forth his conviction that legislative remedies will be necessary to supplement the self-policing activities of A. F. L. unions.

Much of the Federation's fire will be directed against state laws requiring the payment of brokerage fees and commissions on welfare fund accounts. Millions of dollars each year go to insurance agents for writing welfare contracts.

Investigation in New York and other states have shown that these fees often become the basis for "kickbacks" to union officials or members of their families.

In some instances, the broker performs no service in return for his commission. Experts on the union's own staff advertise for competitive bids from insurance companies and select the one that offers the desired protection at the lowest premium cost to the welfare fund.

The union then learns that it cannot legally apply the commission that would normally be paid to an agent in a way that would allow a saving to the fund. Either an agent must be brought in to collect the commission or the money is kept by the insurance company. As a result of this situation, many union officials have arranged to have relatives obtain agent's licenses and pocket thou-

Continued on Page 29, Column 7

[Photograph]

Associated Press Radiophoto
DULLES IN LONDON: The Secretary of State, right, is greeted by Winthrop W. Aldrich, U. S. Ambassador to Britain, as Mr. Dulles left plane yesterday at London Airport.

MEXICAN STRIKERS BLOCKADE 3 CITIES

Halt U. S. Tourists in Fight on Gasoline Price Rise —Troops Held Ready

By SYDNEY GRUSON
Special to The New York Times.

MEXICO CITY, Sept. 26—Federal troops were held ready in barracks today to break a spreading transport strike that has paralyzed three cities. They are Tampico and Madero, on the Gulf of Mexico, and Victoria, about 200 miles south of Brownsville, Tex.

The spread of the strike to Victoria caused considerable hardship to United States tourists motoring to Mexico City. As in Tampico and Madero, taxi and truck drivers, incensed over a rise in gasoline prices, blockaded Victoria's streets and highways, preventing vehicles from entering or leaving.

According to reports in the Mexico City press, a number of tourists were forced to spend the night in their automobiles outside Victoria.

The strike was touched off Friday when Pemex, the Government's oil and gas monopoly, raised gasoline prices on an average of 30 per cent throughout northern Mexico in an effort to make up for revenue losses resulting from last April's devaluation of the peso. Leadership of the strike came from the taxi drivers, who complained bitterly that the Government had promised to maintain the pre-devaluation cost of living for the poorer classes.

Tampico Situation Gravest

The situation was considered gravest in Tampico, one of Mexico's most important ports and a major center of the oil industry. On an average, gasoline had sold in the Tampico-Madero area for the equivalent of 13 cents a gallon. The new price posted Friday was 17 cents, a rise that taxi drivers said threatened their livelihood.

Organized business and agriculture of the region seemed solidly united behind the strikers, though the blockade was costing Tampico's commerce and industry losses of possibly $100,000 a day. The Tampico Chamber of Commerce threatened to initiate a general strike in support of the strike.

So far the blockade has been almost 100 per cent effective, according to Tampico officials. The strikers allowed only food supplies to enter or circulate in the city, which has a population of 150,000, and there were fears that electricity would soon have to be shut off for lack of fuel.

Farmers of the Tampico-Madero area have lent the strikers tractors and trucks to block roads, and launch owners are reported to have allowed their boats to be used to shut down traffic on the three rivers flowing into the Gulf of Mexico at Tampico and Madero.

The Associated Press reported Sunday that the Com-

Continued on Page 7, Column 2

Mendes-France Says Nation Cannot Rely on Outside Aid

By LANSING WARREN
Special to The New York Times.

PARIS, Sept. 26—France must rebuild her economy without more foreign aid, Premier Pierre Mendès-France said today. In a speech at the town hall in Annécy, he said that outside help henceforth must come only in the form of military aid.

"Beginning in 1955, France must balance her foreign trade and balance her accounts without external aid," he said. "A country that fails to do this in the end gets into an impossible situation, both for itself and for the countries that are helping it."

The Premier added that "no doubt it would be normal" for France, with military obligations beyond her strength, to receive a powerful supplement of support from her allies in organizing a common defense.

"But we cannot count on any exceptional resources to fill in the balance of our accounts," he added.

Before leaving for London to attend the nine-power conference on arming West Germany, which opens Tuesday, M. Mendès-France went to Annécy to open an industrial and agricultural fair and to address France on his economic projects.

He feels that his essential task, after he gets pressing foreign problems off his hands, lies in achieving internal reconversion and recovery. He said he was certain this could be done.

"It has been said that France is on the decline," he remarked. "On the contrary, the possibilities that are offered by the resources of our country and North Africa allow us every hope. We can place our bets on France. We are at the dawn of a new era."

Because in his three months in office he has been almost wholly engaged with problems of Indo-china, Tunisia, the European Defense Community Treaty and Germany, the Premier has encountered delays in starting his economic program.

The first of the decrees by which the National Assembly authorized him to operate his re-

Continued on Page 3, Column 2

DULLES WILL MEET FRANCE'S PREMIER TODAY IN PRIVATE

Diplomats to Weigh Means of Improving Relationship Between Their Countries

PARLEY ON TOMORROW

Britain Will Press German Sovereignty—Plans to Offer Europe Stronger Ties

By DREW MIDDLETON
Special to The New York Times.

LONDON, Sept. 26—John Foster Dulles, United States Secretary of State, will meet privately tomorrow with Pierre Mendès-France, French Premier and Foreign Minister, in an effort to improve United States-French relations.

The aim will be to facilitate progress toward European unity in the nine-power conference opening here Tuesday.

Conscious of what he termed the "imperative" need for good results from the conference, Mr. Dulles took the initiative and arranged the meeting soon after his arrival from Washington today.

As he landed at the London airport, Mr. Dulles sighted René Massigli, French Ambassador to Britain, who was waiting for M. Mendès-France. Mr. Dulles asked the envoy to arrange a meeting for him with the French Premier tomorrow.

Tonight Mr. Dulles and Anthony Eden, British Foreign Secretary, conferred for three hours at the home of Winthrop W. Aldrich, United States Ambassador to Britain. There will be other meetings of leaders of various delegations tomorrow in preparation for the start of the conference.

Represented at the conference will be Britain, the United States, France, Canada, West Germany, Italy, Belgium, the Netherlands and Luxembourg.

Sovereignty to Be Pushed

Contrary to expectation, the first day of the meeting is likely to produce solid progress toward one of the two main purposes of the conference: the granting of sovereignty to West Germany.

The British delegation will propose Tuesday morning that a working party of the United States, French, German and British diplomats start immediately to draft a declaration liquidating the Allies' occupation of West Germany.

Another augury for progress at the conference is a report from authoritative British sources that Britain will be willing to negotiate some agreement with European powers fixing the duration of the British military commitments on the Continent.

The British Cabinet is understood to be willing to discuss with France and other interested powers a guarantee that at least two British divisions will remain in any European defense force for a fixed term of years.

Support for a deeper and more extensive British commitment in any continental organization to take form this week came from The Times of London.

Stronger Commitment Urged

This newspaper, long a voice of governing Britain, calls in an editorial in tomorrow's edition for a declaration by Mr. Eden that Britain is ready "to play her full part in a European Defense Community, not contrived as a hashed-up makeshift because nothing better is possible, but born in a new determination that the century-old hammering out of European unity shall be given a new impetus."

These words are the high point of an editorial two columns long. Diplomatic observers in London regard it as the strongest lead the most influential British newspaper has given to the Government in recent years.

The atmosphere has noticeably brightened as a result of the day's events. The scheduled meeting between M. Mendès-France and Mr. Dulles, Britain's willingness to promise more in support of a European alliance than had been expected and the goading by The Times have raised hopes that

Continued on Page 3, Column 3

LABORITES CHEER BID TO MALENKOV

Pre-Convention Meeting Also Hails Invitation to Chou to Pay Visit to Britain

By THOMAS P. RONAN
Special to The New York Times.

SCARBOROUGH, England, Sept. 26—British Labor party delegates cheered their approval tonight of an invitation by Dr. Edith Summerskill, party vice chairman, to Georgi M. Malenkov and Chou En-lai to visit Britain.

The more than 1,200 Labor representatives, gathered here for the annual party conference that will open tomorrow, heard Dr. Summerskill's account of the invitation at a pre-convention rally.

She yelled their approval when she said neither Premier had declined to come. She extended the invitations during her visit to the Soviet Union and Red China last month with a Labor party group. Mr. Malenkov, she said, had asked jovially if she could promise him a visa.

"I asked the Ambassador if he would issue a visa to Mr. Malenkov and he solemnly assured me he would," Dr. Summerskill recounted.

Clement R. Attlee, head of the party and former Prime Minister, who led the Labor group that visited the Soviet Union and China, told the delegates tonight that "there is no alternative to coexistence except perhaps codeath."

Mr. Attlee, with characteristic caution, underlined both sides of

Continued on Page 3, Column 7

Senate Inquiry Opens Here Today On $14 Million Housing Windfalls

By CHARLES GRUTZNER

How eighteen operators got windfalls totaling more than $14,000,000 from forty-four housing developments will be put into the record of the Senate Banking Committee, beginning today.

The windfalls resulted when the Federal Housing Administration issued guarantees for mortgages that far exceeded the costs of construction of the projects. The differences were pocketed by the builders.

Senator Homer E. Capehart, committee chairman, said last night that the cases involved metropolitan area housing projects that had not figured in the committee's previous disclosures. Most of the new cases are of apartment developments in Brooklyn and Queens. There are some in other parts of this city and some in New Jersey and other suburban communities.

The new series of public hearings will be held in the Hotel Astor, starting at 10 A. M. The Senate committee will recess for two days after today's session, and will meet again Thursday and Friday.

"Mortgaging-out [windfall] has been far worse in Greater New York than in any other part of the United States," Mr. Capehart said. "The best this committee can do is scratch the surface."

The committee has conducted investigations and held public hearings in Los Angeles, New Orleans, Chicago, Indianapolis and Detroit since its hearings here a month ago. At that time it disclosed huge profits by builders and what Senator Capehart called corrupt practices in the F. H. A.

"In every city where we have investigated we've had at least one F. H. A. employe admitting corruption," Senator Capehart said. He explained, when questioned about this, that the employe had admitted to acts that he and his colleagues had called corrupt, although some of the employes had contended their actions had not been corrupt.

In addition to the witnesses in the new cases, the committee has subpoenaed Abraham Traub, of the Farragut Gardens developers in Brooklyn, to bring the books and other records of that enterprise, which netted a $4,000,000 windfall, to

Continued on Page 12, Column 5

One of the eighteen new cases got a windfall of $1,750,000 on an original cash investment of $5,000, Senator Capehart, an Indiana Republican, said.

Czechoslovakia Is Facing Ouster From Monetary Fund by Year End

Special to The New York Times.

WASHINGTON, Sept. 26—Czechoslovakia, last Communist member of the International Monetary Fund, will be expelled from this organization at the end of this year unless she supplies information about her foreign trade and internal economy, authoritative sources said tonight.

The Board of Governors of the Fund and the International Bank, now holding its ninth annual meeting here, can be expected to make this decision in the next few days, the sources said. It will act on recommendations made by the board's committee on finance and organization.

The Associated Press reported Sunday that the Committee of Governors on Organization of the International Monetary Fund had voted "overwhelmingly" to suspend Czechoslovakia from the Fund for refusal to supply full fiscal and economic data as required for membership. The Fund's governors are expected to endorse the committee on Wednesday.]

The Czechoslovakian Communists have declined on grounds of national security to supply the Fund with information required from all members to show whether they are cooperating with the organization's objectives.

The Monetary Fund's sister organization, the International Bank, had previously suspended Czechoslovakia from it on Dec. 31, 1953, because the Czechs had refused to pay the required portion of their capital.

If Czechoslovakia has not paid by the end of this year she will be expelled from the Bank.

Including Czechoslovakia, the

Continued on Page 15, Column 6

Russia Re-Viewed

Today's installment of the series by Harrison E. Salisbury, a correspondent of The New York Times who has just returned to this country after five years in the Soviet Union, will be found on Page 23.

ALMOST 1,000 DEAD IN CAPSIZED FERRY

Life boats and a life raft from the ferry *Toya Maru* lie on the debris-strewn beach after the typhoon had subsided.

Wide World Photos

Continued From Page 1

road cars on the ferry broke loose and crushed passengers.

Listed as missing are Thomas M. West, 60, an agent for the Max Factor cosmetics company, and Dean Leeper of Ohio, a Y. M. C. A. secretary.

The ferry, one of those that link the Hokkaido and Honshu railroad systems in a seventy-mile trip across the strait, loaded last night with passengers and cars of the express train bound for Ueno Station in Tokyo.

As far as could be learned to date, the Doya Maru immediately met heavy seas. Spray and solid water, pouring over the bow and through the cutaway after deck and open stern, quickly soaked and incapacitated one of the twin engines.

Losing power, the Doya Maru was carried off her course and swept toward the shore southwest of Hakodate. The crew of the ferry dropped anchor off the Nanaihama breakwater, hoping to ride out the storm. As the disaster was reconstructed by local authorities of Japan's Maritime Safety Board in the absence of survivors' accounts, the anchor chains apparently snapped.

The Doya Maru, rolling and careening in the offshore surf, staggered toward the beach without sufficent power left in the engines to claw out to the open water. The vessel overturned when it hit a reef running out from the Hokkaido shore.

The violent typhoon, which swept northward over Japan, also sank four small coastwise ships at sea, the Maritime Safety Board said.

A United States LST (landing ship tank) carrying troops was reported safely beached near Hakodate in the same area where the Doya Maru was grounded.

Fire whipped by high winds destroyed 80 per cent of the town of Iwanai on Hokkaido where the storm was apparently at its worst. Iwanai has a population of 25,000, but no report of casualties was immediately available.

The Tokyo newspaper Asahi Shimbun said this afternoon a preliminary inquiry indicated the Doya Maru had been "overloaded and undermanned." [The largest Staten Island ferry, of 2,500 tons, carries up to 3,000 persons, but no railroad trains.]

Toll Great in the Area

TOKYO, Monday, Sept. 27 (Æ) —The United States Army commander on the scene at Hakodate reported today the typhoon death toll in that area was believed to be 1,490.

The newspaper Asahi, reported here that four other big ferries besides the Doya Maru were sunk and badly damaged. It said four were busy in rescue work. Only two out of fourteen were in service.

Japanese police reported seventy-seven persons killed in other typhoon destruction and that forty others were buried by landslides or were missing.

"All the News That's Fit to Print"

The New York Times.

LATE CITY EDITION
Mostly sunny and hot today. Fair, hot and more humid tomorrow.
Temperature Range Today—Max., 96; Min., 74
Temperature Yesterday—Max., 84; Min., 66
Full U. S. Weather Bureau Report, Page 34

Copyright, 1955, by The New York Times Company.

VOL. CIV....No. 35,637. Entered as Second-Class Matter. Post Office, New York, N. Y. NEW YORK, SATURDAY, AUGUST 20, 1955. Times Square, New York 36, N. Y. Telephone LAckawanna 4-1000 FIVE CENTS

FLOODS BATTER THE NORTHEAST; 67 KILLED, DAMAGE IN BILLIONS; 4 STATES DECLARE EMERGENCIES

The New York Times (by Carl T. Gossett Jr.)

FLOOD SCENE IN WATERBURY: Swirling water damages buildings and rail facilities in Connecticut city

MOSCOW ACCEPTS ADENAUER'S PLAN TO DISCUSS UNITY

Also Approves Sept. 9 as Date for Start of Conference With German Chancellor

AVOIDS PRISONER ISSUE

Says, However, Any Question of Interest to Both Parties Is Open to Discussion

By CLIFTON DANIEL
Special to The New York Times.

MOSCOW, Aug. 19.—Without a quibble, the Soviet Government agreed today to discuss the German reunification question with Chancellor Konrad Adenauer when he comes here next month.

It also readily agreed to the date—Sept. 9—proposed by the Bonn Government for the beginning of the Chancellor's visit to the Soviet capital.

It required a diplomatic note of only three sentences for the Kremlin to express its consent to Bonn's proposals. The note was handed to Baron Vollrath von Maltzan, West German Ambassador in Paris, today by Sergei A. Vinogradov, Soviet Ambassador.

"Of course the Soviet Government does not see any obstacle to an exchange of opinions on this [the reunification] question, as well as other international questions that may interest both parties," the Soviet note said.

The tone was that of the Russian word "pozhaluista," which in four syllables wraps up all the meanings of "please, by all means of course and why not?"

Prisoner Issue Omitted

The note, however, did not mention the second question raised by Bonn, the "release of those Germans who are still detained within the territory or sphere of influence of the Soviet Union or are otherwise prevented from leaving this area."

At the same time Moscow agreed that other questions connected with the negotiations could be discussed. That left the way open for Dr. Adenauer to raise the question of prisoners, which he undoubtedly will do.

The agenda that has now been agreed upon as a result of the exchange of notes between the two Governments include the following:

The establishment of diplomatic relations, the conclusion of a commercial treaty and a cultural treaty, questions relating to those points, and the reunification of Germany.

The negotiations will be conducted on the German side by a Government delegation led by Dr. Adenauer.

On the Soviet side there may be Nikita S. Khrushchev, First Secretary of the Soviet Communist party, Premier Nikolai A. Bulganin and Vyacheslav M. Molotov, Foreign Minister. Those three leaders are now on vacation but presumably they will return to Moscow before Dr. Adenauer arrives. They might be joined in the negotiations by Anastas I. Mikoyan when trade relations are being discussed.

The Soviet Government's decision to invite Dr. Adenauer to come to Moscow to discuss the establishment of diplomatic relations was communicated to the

Continued on Page 3, Column 2

O'Malley Is Fearful Of a One-Team City

By SYDNEY GRUSON

The possibility was raised yesterday that two of New York's baseball teams—the Dodgers and the Giants—might have to leave the city.

Walter F. O'Malley, president of the Dodgers, suggested the prospect of this calamity. For more than an hour, he pleaded the Dodgers' case for a new city-aided ball park to Mayor Wagner. Then he concluded:

"This problem is bigger than the Dodgers alone. It's unlikely that one club or the other would move. You'll find that the two will move. If one team goes, the other will go.

"It is serious, Mr. Mayor, very serious."

Mr. O'Malley recited figures to support his belief that, without the draw of the fierce interborough rivalry, the Giants

Continued on Page 19, Column 3

GALLAGHER GETS A LIFE SENTENCE

Sergeant Is Found Guilty of Murder of Fellow P.O.W.'s and of Assisting Reds

By ARTHUR J. OLSEN

Sgt. James C. Gallagher was found guilty yesterday of the murder of two fellow prisoners of war and flagrant collaboration with the enemy in the Korean prison camps.

A military court of eight officers sentenced him to dishonorable discharge, forfeiture of all pay and allowances and life imprisonment at hard labor.

The verdict was read in a small, crowded courtroom at Fort Jay, Governors Island, on the fourteenth day of a general court-martial. The 23-year-old youth, a trim military figure in starched khakis, accepted the judgment stoically. He said later he had received a fair trial.

Ten specific offenses were alleged against Gallagher, who joined the Army in 1948 to escape "bad company" in his native Brooklyn and who fell into much worse company when captured near Kunu-ri, Korea, on Nov. 2, 1950.

The sergeant was found guilty on seven charges—two unpremeditated murders, collaboration, three instances of maltreatment of fellow prisoners and one of informing on his comrades.

The court acquitted him on a second informing specification and a third murder count. Midway in the trial it directed a verdict of not guilty on a charge that he signed a "go home" appeal to United Nations troops. Ironically, the accused later acknowledged this act, his only admission of any misdeed during three days of testimony.

In finding Gallagher guilty of collaboration, the court ac-

Continued on Page 2, Column 4

PRESIDENT RAISES BICYCLE DUTY 50%; PRICES WILL GO UP

Eisenhower Invokes Escape Clause—His Rate Is Under F.T.C. Recommendation

Text of the President's letter is printed on Page 6.

By CHARLES E. EGAN
Special to The New York Times.

WASHINGTON, Aug. 19—President Eisenhower increased duties on all imported bicycles by 50 per cent today.

Under terms of the Presidential order, the new rates became effective immediately. The higher duties were imposed under the "escape clause" of the Reciprocal Trade Agreements Act. The clause is intended to protect domestic manufacturers from intensive foreign competition that threatens serious injury to their industry.

[New York retailers said the price of imported bicycles would rise about 10 per cent. British lightweight bicycles have sold here for from $29.98 to $79.98. The new prices will be from about $33 to $86.]

The order today was based on recommendations to the President by the Federal Tariff Commission. It fell short, however, of granting the full tariff protection the Federal agency had recommended.

The Tariff Commission had suggested a flat tariff rate of 22½ per cent of the foreign wholesale value be applied to all imported bicycles. Instead the President raised the present duty of 7½ per cent to 11¼ per cent on the lightweight models. On all other types of bicycles, dutiable at 15 per cent, the order raised the duty to 22½ per cent in accordance with the commission's recommendations.

Triple Rise Recommended

To raise the tariff on lightweight cycles as the Tariff Commission recommended, the President said, would have imposed a duty triple the previous rate.

The President wrote identical letters to Senator Harry F. Byrd, Democrat of Virginia, as chairman of the Senate Finance Committee, and Representative Jere Cooper, Democrat of Tennessee and chairman of the House Ways and Means Committee. In them he explained why he had declined to advance the duty on lightweight bicycles as much as the commission had suggested.

The President said the "ingenuity and resourceful efforts of foreign producers and American importers" had been responsible "almost entirely" for the development of the large American market for the lightweight type of bicycles.

"As for the other varieties of imports—the balloon tire, middleweight and junior sized types, for example," the President

Continued on Page 6, Column 6

RAINS SET RECORD

Worst in Pennsylvania, Jersey, Connecticut, Massachusetts

By EDWIN L. DALE Jr.

Severe floods struck large areas of the northeastern United States yesterday.

Great river systems in eastern Pennsylvania, New York, New Jersey, Massachusetts and Connecticut were unable to contain a record downpour of rain. The result was at least sixty-seven deaths, more than a dozen persons missing and damage estimated in billions.

Hurricane Diane, her winds reduced to a comparative whisper, had retained an unadvertised kick far worse than anything her winds could do. She sucked in vast quantities of moisture-laden air from over the Atlantic and then dumped the water by the ton in advance of her leisurely path.

It was water, water everywhere—and in some places not a drop to drink.

As the skies finally dried over Boston in the evening and earlier to the southward, the Weather Bureau had the day's one comforting note: it predicted no more rain for at least three days.

Disaster Areas Proclaimed

This was the situation in summary:

¶Connecticut was declared a disaster area, with Gov. Abraham Ribicoff wiring President Eisenhower for Federal help. The Governor estimated the damage "in the billions" in the western part of the state, where three big rivers and many smaller ones were on the loose.

¶In northeastern Pennsylvania one large city—Scranton—was without water supply, as were several smaller towns. The Delaware River was breaking flood crest records. Thousands were homeless and were being cared for by the Red Cross. Gov. George M. Leader declared a state of emergency.

¶The Delaware burst its banks in the corner of New York, New Jersey and Pennsylvania in the Port Jervis-Sussex County area. Most of northwestern New Jersey was declared a disaster area, as smaller streams flooded districts missed by the Delaware. Resort communities below the Catskills in New York were isolated.

¶Gov. Christian Herter of Massachusetts also declared an emergency. Several towns in the western part of the state were in trouble and cut off. Worcester, to the east, was swamped by rainfall alone.

¶Hundreds of main highways and smaller side roads in the five-state area were impassable, cutting off scores of hard-hit communities. All trains heading west out of Boston were canceled, and five railroads had to suspend service on one or more routes. Rail and highway bridges crumbled or were dangerously

Continued on Page 8, Column 6

MINERS MAY GAIN PAY RISE IN NORTH

Lewis Is Said to Have Won First Increase in 3 Years for Soft Coal Pits

The United Press

WASHINGTON, Aug. 19—John L. Lewis, president of the United Mine Workers, and northern producers have negotiated the first wage increase for soft coal miners in three years, an informed source said today.

The agreement was said to provide for a wage increase of $1.20 a day, effective Sept. 1, and an 80-cent increase, effective April 1, 1956, bringing the total rise to $2 a day.

This would raise the basic daily wage to $20.25, ranking it with auto and steel industry wages.

The source said the agreement was negotiated secretly by Mr. Lewis and representatives of the Bituminous Coal Operators Association, which represents northern commercial producers and the so-called "captive"

Continued on Page 21, Column 6

Upstate Resorts Isolated; Helicopters Save Scores

Large sections of southeastern New York State, including heavily populated resort areas, lay under swirling flood waters yesterday. The Red Cross declared the city of Port Jervis and its environs a disaster area. Heavy rains and rapidly rising rivers caused property damage estimated in the millions. Thousands of homes and summer cottages had to be abandoned, bridges, highways and railroad tracks were washed out or flooded and more than 100 marooned persons had to be rescued by Army helicopters. At least two persons, one a New York City resident, died as a result of the storm.

Mayor Eugene Glusker of Ellenville, an Ulster County town of 4,000 in the heart of the Catskill resort area, reported a "chaotic condition" with hundreds homeless. In a telegram to Governor Harriman, Mayor Glusker said 200 homes had been destroyed, water mains damaged, and several streams were flowing into the village.

Throngs of children were removed from summer camps in the area and National Guard amphibious ducks made many rescues. A troop of thirty-six Boy Scouts was among those evacuated by helicopter.

In Sullivan County an emergency was declared as farmlands and villages along the Delaware and other streams were flooded.

Parts of Port Jervis, a city of 10,000 at the confluence of the Delaware and Neversink Rivers in Orange County, were cut off for much of the day. More than 1,200 persons were evacuated to high ground by Army helicopters and ducks. Streets in the business district

Continued on Page 10, Column 6

DELAWARE RISES, MENACES TRENTON

Thousands Flee Low-Lying Areas—Sussex, Passaic and Bergen Hard Hit

The rain-swollen Delaware River and countless other streams sent thousands of New Jersey residents and campers fleeing yesterday. Helicopters, scows, boats and amphibious vehicles were used to rescue men, women and children from flooded or threatened low-lying areas.

The greatest damage occurred along the Delaware, western boundary of the state. All bridges north of Trenton were closed, and many were damaged. A crest nine feet above normal flood level was expected by 5 o'clock this morning.

Conditions were acute at Phillipsburg, across the river from Easton. Two bridges were under water, and 1,000 Pennsylvanians were stranded on the Jersey shore. Gov. Robert B. Meyner ordered the state police to take the stranded persons to Hackettstown and other points at a safer distance from the swollen river.

Small Boats Sought

Civil Defense disaster control officials in conjunction with the police in cities along the river called for persons with small boats to stand by to help where evacuation was needed.

In Trenton a partial emergency was declared when the river invaded the residential area along its banks. Two thousand persons were taken to higher ground. Blankets and cots were sought for the refugees. To protect the city's threatened filtration plant, an appeal for an additional 500 sandbags went to the Mercer County Civil Defense coordinator.

At 12:30 o'clock this morning Governor Meyner proclaimed a state of emergency in Trenton. Earlier he had proclaimed emergencies in the three northwestern counties of Sussex, Warren and Hunterdon. Parts of Mercer County had also declared a state of emergency on a local basis.

The Governor is remaining in Trenton during the critical period.

Bergen and Passaic Counties in the northeast part of the state were also hard hit.

There was a possibility, Governor Meyner said, that [illegible]

Continued on Page 11, Column 2

CONNECTICUT RAIN AT DISASTER STAGE

Floods Are Called Worst in State's History, With New Blows Facing Hartford

By MERRILL FOLSOM
Special to The New York Times.

HARTFORD, Conn., Aug. 19—Storms sweeping northward from the Atlantic swamped Connecticut today, creating the worst floods in the state's history.

Highways were washed out, bridges wrecked, dams smashed, factories flooded, railroad tracks undermined, homes washed away and thousands of acres of corn, tobacco and other crops destroyed.

Mayor Raymond E. Snyder of Waterbury said late last night that fifteen was "a fairly accurate estimate" of the number of dead in his city. Earlier, the State Office of Civil Defense reported that ten persons were dead in Naugatuck and three in Washington.

Mayor Snyder was quoted by The Associated Press as saying the destruction caused in Waterbury by the rampaging Naugatuck River was "the worst in history" and "just unbelievable." Power lines and bridges were reported swept away by the swollen river, which was reported racing along at fifty miles an hour.

The Merritt Parkway and many other main roads escaped serious damage. Scores of towns were not seriously affected, particularly near Long Island Sound.

Revising an earlier estimate of one billion dollars damage,

Continued on Page 8, Column 2

The Young One Steals Eisenhower Show in the West

Associated Press Wirephoto

The President supervises grandson, David, in practice with a 9-iron at Colorado camp

By RUSSELL BAKER
Special to The New York Times.

FRASER, Colo., Aug. 19—This is a story about a President and a 7-year-old scene stealer. Its moral, if you insist on one, is that Dwight D. Eisenhower can be pushed out of the limelight if the competition is a bright-eyed youngster wearing a cowboy hat and named Eisenhower. This morning, some forty newsmen were admitted to the President's ranch hideaway for the conventional vacation pictures. This is an annual set piece

Continued on Page 7, Column 1

4 British Officers Confess 'Irish' Raid

Special to The New York Times.

LONDON, Aug. 19—Four junior British Army officers have confessed that they had staged a raid on a camp in North Wales Monday as a "practical joke."

The War Office announced today that the officers, whose names were not disclosed, had volunteered information on their roles in the mock raid. The announcement said they had expressed "deep regret" to the public and to the police for the trouble and alarm they had caused.

Lieut. Gen. Sir Lashmer Whistler, commanding the Army's Western Command, has also apologized to the police in the Army's behalf and is investigating the full circumstances, the announcement said.

The pre-dawn prank at Camp Kinmel, near Rhyl, in which an enlisted guard was trussed up and two others threatened at

Continued on Page 3, Column 4

U.S. Vaccine Report Due to Clear Cutter

Special to The New York Times.

WASHINGTON, Aug. 19—The impending Public Health Service report on polio cases that followed inoculation by Cutter vaccine is expected to criticize inadequate Federal safety standards, rather than the Cutter Laboratories in Berkeley, Calif.

While this report will not be issued until next week, its contents have become known to the vaccine manufacturing industry and were divulged today by an industry spokesman.

The Department of Health, Education and Welfare, of which the Public Health Service is a part, refused to discuss the report and issued the following brief statement:

"When released the report will speak for itself. Until it is released the department of course cannot comment on its contents. It is hoped that the report will be made public

Continued on Page 11, Column 6

Paths of Devastation Are Traced In a Flight Over Flooded Regions

By CLARENCE DEAN

From the air yesterday, the flooded areas presented a nightmare in full daylight.

Grotesque pathways of boiling, muddied water twisted through the lush Naugatuck Valley in Connecticut, the resort counties of Sullivan and Ulster in New York, up to the foothills of the Catskills and south along the Delaware River into Pennsylvania.

The chocolate-colored torrents carried debris, sometimes large parts of buildings. Factories, business places, even communities stood out as islands in low places where the rivers had swept into lakes.

South of the Waterbury, Conn., railroad station, the mainline tracks were torn away. Railroad cars were tumbled into the water like toy trains.

All through the Naugatuck Valley cities, helicopters buzzed like giant insects, landing on factory roofs, hovering over flooded houses, rescuing persons who had been trapped by the suddenly rising water.

In Connecticut, where, from the air, the damage seemed worst, the muddy water of the Naugatuck River swept out from Stratford, discoloring Long Island Sound for miles.

At Seymour, the river had torn away a dam, and the water had spread over a wide area of Derby just below. Lumber from storage piles in yards floated like match sticks. At Seymour, a railroad bridge was torn in half.

Above, in Naugatuck, the yellow helicopters of the United States Air Force Air-Sea Rescue Service and the blue helicopters of the Navy were shuttling back and forth between flood-isolated buildings and a point on higher ground. At the high point a string of buses waited to transfer the evacuees.

In Waterbury, the next large

Continued on Page 9, Column 7

New England Rail Service Disrupted; Marooned Lackawanna Passengers Rescued

WASHOUTS HALT MANY RAILROADS

324 Stranded on 2 Trains Evacuated to Scranton by Buses and Army 'Copters

NEW HAVEN ALSO TIED UP

Service on Central and Erie Is Cut Off—Flooding Forces Closing of Some Highways

Railroad service linking New York with Boston, the Berkshire Hill towns of Connecticut and Massachusetts and the Pocono resorts of Pennsylvania was halted yesterday by washouts and earthslides on the tracks.

Many highways were closed by floods and bridges were under water at hundreds of points in New York, New Jersey, Connecticut, Massachusetts and Pennsylvania. Scores of communities were isolated and could be reached only by boat, amphibious vehicle or helicopter.

The railroad hit hardest in this area was the Delaware, Lackawanna and Western, which serves the area between Hoboken, N. J. and Buffalo. All service on the main line between Hoboken and Scranton, Pa., was suspended about 8 A. M. A spokesman said it was the worst tie-up on the railroad in forty years and that full service would not be restored for "three or four days."

324 Passengers Marooned

On the Lackawanna, 324 passengers on two trains were marooned all Thursday night in the Pocono Mountains. They were evacuated yesterday by a fleet of buses and ten Army helicopters to Scranton, which nearly was cut off by flooded roads itself.

Two hundred and thirty-five persons were aboard a train bound from Hoboken to Buffalo that was stopped by washed out trackage at Cresco, Pa., at 8 P. M. on Thursday. Eighty-nine passengers were on a train bound from Binghamton, N. Y., to Hoboken when it was halted at Tobyhanna, Pa., at 7:30 P. M.

By mid-morning yesterday, the railroad got some buses through to take the passengers from Tobyhanna to Scranton. Second Army Headquarters sent ten helicopters from Fort Meade, Md., to air lift passengers from Cresco between 9:30 A. M. and 3 P. M. Each helicopter could carry six to twelve passengers.

Under Brig. Gen. William Verveck, chief of the Pennsylvania Military District, the "whirlybirds" began ferrying passengers the twenty-two miles to Scranton. At 1 P. M., however, five big buses arrived from the Tobyhanna Signal Corps Storage Depot and took all remaining passengers to Scranton by a less thrilling surface route.

New Haven Road Hit

On the New York, New Haven and Hartford Railroad, the line between Norwalk, Conn., and Pittsfield, Mass., was washed out before dawn, as was the main line between New Haven and Springfield, Mass. The rail connection between Providence, R. I., and Boston was flooded at three points, so the important express line from New York to Boston ended at Providence.

The Boston and Albany Division of the New York Central was unable to run between those two cities, since the line passes through Pittsfield and Worcester, Mass.

The New York Central also had no service on its Harlem Division north of Pawling, N. Y.

At Holyoke, Mass., floods stopped the Montrealer, on its way from Washington to Montreal, and the Washingtonian, making the same run south.

The New Haven Railroad cancelled its Bar Harbor Express from Philadelphia to that famous Maine resort.

In the New York commuting area, twenty-five trains on three Westchester divisions of the New York Central were delayed up to thirty minutes by a landslide and floods near Brewster, N. Y.

The most important highways flooded, according to the Automobile Club of New York and official state agencies, were as follows:

NEW YORK STATE

Taconic Parkway—A four-mile stretch near Route 55 in the Poughkeepsie area and twenty-four miles between Poughkeepsie and Red Hook.
U. S. 9—Between N. Y. 301 and N. Y. 52.
N. Y. 17—Near Wurtsboro.
N. Y. 97—From Calicoon to Narrowsburg and twenty-nine miles between Narrowsburg and Barryville.
U. S. 209 and N. Y. 55—Near Kerhonkson.
N. Y. 208—Near Washingtonville.
Routes 42, 52, 207, 17B—Various points in Sullivan and Ulster Counties.

NEW JERSEY

U. S. 22—For fifteen miles east of Phillipsburg.
N. J. 23—Northwest of Butler.
U. S. 206—At Frankford and Somerville, in Somerset County.
N. J. 29—Between Trenton and the bridge to Yardley, Pa.
U. S. 46—Near Belvidere, Warren County.
N. J. 12—At Frenchtown, Hunterdon County.
In addition, nearly all secondary roads in Bergen County, many roads in the Pompton Lakes area of Passaic County and numerous roads in Sussex County, where fifty highway bridges were damaged or destroyed. All vehicular bridges across the Delaware River north of Trenton were closed to traffic in mid-afternoon.

CONNECTICUT

U. S. 6, 7 and 8—Near New Milford and Torrington.
A highway bridge over the Naugatuck River at Waterbury and another at Naugatuck collapsed. All roads into Torrington were impassable except by "ducks." Many secondary roads in northwestern Connecticut were closed by the State Police.

Associated Press Wirephoto

WATERBURY: A factory worker rescued by breeches buoy from produce warehouse

Associated Press Wirephoto

AGAWAM, MASS.: Overturned car in ditch where highway collapsed after heavy rain

The New York Times

TORRINGTON, CONN.: Swollen creek spills into streets and washes away sections of several buildings in its path

CONNECTICUT RAIN AT DISASTER STAGE

Continued From Page 1

Gov. Abraham A. Ribicoff reported by telegram tonight to President Eisenhower that the damage would "run to billions" and that the President should declare Connecticut a "major disaster area for Federal aid." The Governor called the day "one of the darkest in Connecticut's history."

The Army sent word to Governor Ribicoff tonight that $500,000 had been allocated to Army engineers for emergency work in Massachusetts and Connecticut. This work is expected to concern highway repairs, restoration of drinking water supplies and other such necessary projects. The Governor said this allocation would barely scratch the surface of the relief work needed.

Of the swollen rivers, the Housatonic, the Naugatuck, the Farmington, the Connecticut, the Hockanum, the Willimantic and the Quinebaugh sent cascades of water rushing across the state. Rain slackened this afternoon, and the sun even shone briefly, but the floods may reach high levels toward Long Island Sound tomorrow.

River 19 Feet Over Average

The Connecticut in Hartford, swamped with 13.77 inches of rain in a day, rose 19.5 feet above average this afternoon. This amounted to three feet above flood level but tomorrow it is expected to be more than six to eight feet higher as torrents from the north reach here.

Thirteen inches of rain fell in the Torrington area in less than twenty-four hours. Power and telephone lines by the thousands were torn down. Gas lines were flooded and extra hazards were created by the extinguishing of pilot lights by flood waters. Some water lines were undermined and washed away, leaving neighborhoods without drinking water.

Severely hit was the Farmington River Valley in northwestern Connecticut. For a time it seemed that the 1888 Otis Dam, just across the boundary in Massachusetts, would be washed away. Evacuations of towns and farms in a twenty-mile strip of Connecticut Valley below the dam was begun by the Office of Civil Defense and the National Guard. But floodgates and flashboards were opened at the dam. This reduced the hazard.

Thirty important highway bridges were shattered or dangerously undermined. Among those wrecked were the memorial bridges in Naugatuck and Waterbury, the Marbledale Bridge near Northville, one in Unionville, one in Collinsville, two in Putnam, three in Somers, one in West Willington and one in Suffield.

Washed away or badly undermined and sunken were the railroad bridges in Seymour, Unionville and Farmington, also two sections of the Eagleville Dam in Coventry and part of the Baltic Dam in Sprague.

The Army arranged tonight to ship six portable, temporary bridges from Ohio factories. They are scheduled to arrive Sunday.

Governor Ribicoff was awakened in the executive mansion at 1 A. M. by a telephone call from Mayor William Carroll of Torrington.

"We've got trouble," the mayor shouted. "Things are pretty bad, rivers are running through the main streets, stores and homes are flooded, and it's getting worse."

The Governor notified Civil Defense and National Guard heads, jumped into some clothes and rubber boots and left the mansion by car. The Governor's official driver, Arthur Horan, was at the wheel and state policemen later joined the party.

Heading for Torrington, the Governor ran into trouble. Every road he tried had a washed-out bridge, six-foot gullies across the pavement, ten feet of water or pavement turned on end.

"When other conditions were all right, we could hear boulders crashing down the hillsides onto the road," the Governor later recalled.

Using two-way radio communication, the Governor heard from the state police that Winsted was under water and the Otis Dam might burst any minute.

4,000 Guardsmen Out

Reaching Maj Gen. Frederick G. Reincke, State Adjutant General, John C. Kelly, State Police Commissioner, and Leo J. Mulcahy, State Director of Civil Defense, Governor Ribicoff declared a state of emergency.

Then came the Governor's job of trying to return to Hartford. Roads had washed out behind him and at Burlington he became isolated on an island of mud and shattered concrete. Abandoning his limousine, he waded waist deep across a stream and hailed a milk truck that was functioning all right at the moment.

The driver, Ernest Griswold, was somewhat astonished but he eagerly took on the task of chauffeuring the Governor. After eight miles the water became too deep for the milk truck, though. The Governor transferred to a high-wheeled emergency road truck and then to a state police car. He got to Hartford at 6:30 A. M. Forsaking the capital for the day, he went to the near-by armory and in shirtsleeves directed the rescue operations.

His conclusions were summed up in his telegram to President Eisenhower, which followed an informal conversation with aides of the President in the White House.

"The State of Connecticut," the Governor wired, "is in a very critical position because of torrential rains, floods, washouts and impaired communications. We are faced with a major disaster. Widespread hazardous conditions exist on our roads and highways. A state of emergency has been declared. Damage estimates run to billions of dollars with loss of life, damage to food and medical supplies and suffering of the homeless. I firmly believe Federal assistance is required.

"The National Guard, local and state Civil Defense organizations, local and state police, the American Red Cross and other community charitable institutions are operating in maximum effort. All available state, town and city funds and other resources will be committed to alleviate suffering and to restore essential public facilities.

"I am hereby requesting that to meet this emergency you declare the State of Connecticut a major disaster area and that you allocate Federal funds and other assistance as outlined under Public Law 875."

General Reincke and Governor Ribicoff agreed that the flood was considerably worse than those of 1936 and 1938. The general said the disaster was the worst of any kind that had ever hit the state.

Col. Edward Wozenski, commander of the 169th Infantry Regiment of the Connecticut National Guard, flew by helicopter this afternoon over the Torrington and Winsted areas. He reported "devastation everywhere." He rescued twenty persons from rooftops. At Litchfield he saw a new house washed into the Bantam River and carried piecemeal downstream.

Town of 8,000 Evacuated

The State Guard was also mobilized tonight by the Governor.

Seymour, a community of 8,000 on the Naugatuck River south of Waterbury, was evacuated tonight by Guardsmen. Two hundred persons were taken in ducks and trucks to the armory in nearby Ansonia.

The American Red Cross reported to the Governor tonight that it had obtained adequate allocations of drugs and medical supplies for delivery by helicopter and military trucks.

Thirty persons were known to be marooned tonight on rooftops at Granby. Helicopters were not able to reach them because of interference from the trees.

Thirty-seven helicopters and twenty-two mechanical ducks were used by state police, National Guardsmen and Civil Defense volunteers to rescue home owners from rooftops. Some of the rescue apparatus was borrowed from the New York National Guard, the Army and helicopter manufacturers.

More helicopters were being flown here by the Navy and the Marines. Bradley Field, near Hartford, is the base of operations. Small reconnaissance planes are being used to spot people on rooftops, boats and rafts, and then the helicopters are flown in. Nightfall caused suspension of the work until tomorrow.

Winsted, a community of 9,000 in the northern part of the state, was cited tonight by the Governor and his aides as a typical place in distress. Lieut. Col. Robert Schwolsky of the National Guard said after a helicopter flight over Winsted:

"In all my life I never saw anything like it. Automobiles on every street seem to have just been thrown at each other, landing on their sides and their roofs."

The colonel and others reported that 85 per cent of the factories in Winsted were flooded or destroyed, and that the community had no gas, electricity or water, and no food except that in homes.

Power failures became increasingly numerous in the larger cities tonight. In Hartford, power in the newspaper plant of The Courant failed, and the printing of the paper was transferred to the plant of its rival, The Times.

In Putnam, fires and explosions added to the flood crisis. Mayor John Dempsey was quoted by The Associated Press as saying that fire had broken out in a magnesium plant and explosions had set fire to "a couple of homes." The plant was completely surrounded by water, preventing firemen from reaching the scene.

A large unwieldy barge broke loose on the Housatonic River at Devon, and it was feared that it would smash a bridge of the New York, New Haven and Hartford Railroad at Devon. Four small Coast Guard boats, the only craft available, undertook to intercept the barge.

Thomas Scadden, Civil Defense Director at Waterbury, reported that the damage in that city alone amounted to $150,000,000.

In Naugatuck 1,500 persons were evacuated, chiefly to the Beacon Valley Range School on high ground on the edge of the community. Red Cross workers and neighbors fed and bedded the evacuees.

A dam at Bolton on the Hop River northeast of Hartford broke at 9:45 o'clock tonight and flooded low areas.

Floods Pummel the Northeast; 4 States Declare Emergencies

Continued From Page 1

cutting off scores of hard-hit communities. All trains heading west out of Boston were canceled, and five railroads had to suspend service on one or more routes. Rail and highway bridges crumbled or were dangerously undermined—the total, already more than fifty, was rising.

The Red Cross was caring last night for several thousand homeless people in three states.

The eroded, hilly country of northeastern Pennsylvania was perhaps the worst hit, as the Delaware, Susquehanna, Schuylkill and Lehigh Rivers and their tributaries could not begin to cope with the rush of water from the hills. Western Massachusetts and Connecticut, along the South-flowing Housatonic and Naugatuck Rivers, were swamped. The corner of New York, New Jersey and Pennsylvania in the Port Jervis-Sussex County area caught the flood crest of the Delaware as it swept south toward Trenton.

A measure of the rivers' burden came in a single statistic: the city of Holyoke, Mass., took 14.67 inches of rain in forty-eight hours. This sort of drubbing from the elements occurred across much of Diane's path.

It was a sudden drubbing that came only a week after the heavy rains that accompanied Hurricane Connie. The damage and misery that followed would probably add up to less than the great floods of 1936, but for many areas it was the worst in recent history. The Delaware, biggest of the area's rivers, broke several records for flood crests along her winding valley.

More Trouble Due

For some communities—particularly in New England—the worst was probably not over. The peak crest of the Connecticut River was due to hit Hartford this morning. The Delaware packed some potential trouble for Philadelphia and points south.

For the New York metropolitan area, the rains merely added to an August precipitation that already had broken all records. The damage was confined to flooding in the city streets in much less proportion than during the downpours brought by Connie.

In the South, streams in northern Virginia swelled the Potomac to flood proportions, but damage was relatively minor. The floods in Virginia had begun to abate by early yesterday afternoon, unlike the situation in many places farther north.

Yesterday's floods picked their spots. Western Connecticut was hit harder than ever before, but the eastern part of the state and the shore communities got no more than a bad soaking from the rain. Next-door New York State went almost scot-free, except in the Port Jervis area.

Yesterday's floods were unusual, however, in that some communities nowhere near a big river took a severe beating simply from the effects of heavy rains on small streams. It appeared to be completely a matter of nature's whim: Newark reported it got only two and one-fourth inches of rain in the twenty-four hours ended at 8:30 yesterday morning, while upstate the totals ran to six inches or more.

Reports of the human toll were conflicting. The Associated Press added up at least seventy-three deaths, with an unknown number missing. United Press casualty figures had at least seventy-seven persons listed as dead, with twenty-nine others missing.

Typical of the impossibility of obtaining an accurate count was Stroudsburg, Pa. All through the afternoon it was cut off from communications. By late afternoon the town was reporting nine persons "definitely dead" and "possibly twenty others" missing. The over-all totals were sure to rise.

Besides Scranton and Stroudsburg, the communities that took the worst beating included Waterbury, Winsted, Torrington, Naugatuck, Seymour and Danbury in Connecticut; Tamaqua and Easton in Pennsylvania; Branchville and many small towns in the entire northwestern corner of New Jersey, and a set of villages in the Farmington River valley of Massachusetts.

Waterbury seemed to have the unenviable record of the highest death toll. Mayor Richard C. Lee of New Haven quoted the Waterbury Mayor, Raymond E. Snyder, as counting "at least fifteen persons" dead.

It was a long, hard—and successful—day for the rescuers. A fleet of Army and National Guard helicopters removed 235 passengers from a Delaware, Lackawanna and Western Railroad train marooned overnight in the Pocono Mountains at Cresco, Pa. The Red Cross rushed bottled water to the six hospitals in Scranton.

A relay team of nineteen helicopters removed 110 boy and girls campers from an island in the Delaware River forty-five miles north of Philadelphia. More than 100 persons in Connecticut were taken from housetops and hillocks by helicopters of the Sikorsky Aircraft Division of the United Aircraft Corporation.

Near Philadelphia an intrepid naval officer swung down into a tree from his hovering helicopter and lifted three persons into the craft. The Coast Guard and various local civil defense organizations rushed amphibious military ducks to stricken communities cut off from access by road.

An extra danger in the Schuylkill area came when the river swept 10,000 electric blasting caps from the Atlas Powder Company shipping warehouse. The police alerted homes and businesses in towns along the river against the danger of explosions and distributed 50,000 placards in Philadelphia warning against touching the loose caps.

Property damage was heaviest in industrial plants along the river banks. In Danbury the Barden Corporation, maker of precision ball bearings, reported at least $1,000,000 worth of damage. A pond—not river—overflowed its normally quiet banks in the village of Easthampton, Mass., and so undermined the United Elastic Corporation plant that a section of the building collapsed into the pond.

In Winsted, swamped by thirty feet of water, four of every five factories were reported flooded or destroyed. Reports from Pennsylvania concentrated on the problems of people, not industrial plants, but damage was heavy in industrial towns along the upper Schuylkill and through parts of the Delaware valley.

The effects of the flood were due to be felt for several days by thousands of people who escaped immediate harm. The Lackawanna railroad reported the worst damage in forty years to its roadbed from water and landslides and found two of its bridges washed away. Services, the railroad said, will not be normal for at least three or four days.

Even animals suffered from nature's soaking forty-eight hours. Reports from Milford, Pa., near the Delaware Water Gap—after the town's communications were restored at 7 A. M. yesterday following ten hours of isolation—were that there had been serious destruction of wild game that could not escape the waters.

The Red Cross here reported hundreds of calls from parents worried about children in summer camps. It gave assurance that all campers were safe, as far as was known. A number of children were evacuated from isolated spots in the Port Jervis area, but not a camper had been hurt or injured at latest reports. The Red Cross warned parents against trying to travel to the area, because roads were still impassable.

Nassau Gets Off Lightly

Special to The New York Times.

MINEOLA, L. I., Aug. 19—Heavy rain that fell last night and early today caused only minor damage in Nassau County. The Long Island Lighting Company reported power failures put the lights out in only 1,000 homes. At the same time about 2,000 telephones were knocked out of service, according to the New York Telephone Company.

NEW RAIN RECORD IN MASSACHUSETTS

Peaks Listed for 48 Hours and Month—11 Deaths in State Are Laid to Storm

Special to The New York Times.

BOSTON, Aug. 19—A record rainstorm pounded Massachusetts today, causing at least eleven deaths and damage running into the millions.

Gov. Christian A. Herter declared a state of emergency in central and western Massachusetts, the sections most affected.

The action was taken as a precautionary measure. It will enable the state to ask for use of Federal troops until the Massachusetts National Guard returns tomorrow from training at Camp Drum, N. Y. Authorities at Fort Devens, Mass., told the Governor that troops were alerted and would move into any area where they were needed.

The Small Business Administration in Washington designated Berkshire, Franklin, Worcester, Hampshire and Hampden Counties as disaster areas. Residents of these zones will be eligible for emergency loans to repair flood damage.

Governor Herter said that the Federal Government had made $500,000 available to the Army Engineers for emergency purposes in the flooded areas if no other funds were available.

Floods caused by two days of virtually unremitting rain were responsible for most of the devastation. In some areas damage was greater than that caused by last year's two-punch hurricanes.

Weather Bureau Records

The Boston Weather Bureau recorded more than fifteen inches of rain in thirty-six hours, seven inches more than the previous record for forty-eight hours. Almost nine inches of the downpour came in twenty-four hours. The rain stopped here at 8:46 P. M. The previous August rainfall record was 13.38 inches.

Transportation facilities were the most conspicuous victims as washouts cut every line in the area. The flood waters also virtually halted the movement of mail in and out of Boston. Some preferential first-class mail was flown to New York.

The New Haven Railroad experienced its worst emergency since the 1938 hurricane. Only one short commuter line, with an improvised schedule, ran out of South Station this afternoon.

"We've used every bus we could beg, borrow or steal in New England," said a railroad spokesman.

The Federal Express, which left Washington at 11 o'clock last night and was due in Boston at 8:10 o'clock this morning, was stranded in Holbrook, Mass., this afternoon. More than 100 passengers were brought to Boston, twenty miles away, by bus or taxicab. A forty-foot washout had halted the train on the last lap of its improvised route.

Rail Service Canceled

The Boston and Albany and New York Central Railroads canceled all service today.

The Boston and Maine halted service from North Station until tonight, when the Montrealer and the "Gull" to the Maritime Provinces left.

The Metropolitan Transit System in Boston was forced to curtail service on some lines for several hours. Water forced closing of the Tremont Street subway station downtown for four hours.

By tonight, however, all lines except two short suburban stretches were reported operating again.

Highways in eastern Massachusetts were under water at many points but most bus lines managed to run. Most main roads in the Worcester area and western Massachusetts were impassable.

Power failed at the Haynes Memorial Hospital in Boston and nurses, doctors and attendants operated respirators by hand until emergency generators went on. The hospital handles a large share of the city's polio cases.

Emergency in Worcester

Worcester in central Massachusetts was particularly hard hit, recording almost eleven inches of rain in thirty hours. Residents were asked to keep off the streets. City Manager Francis J. McGrath declared a state of emergency, as did town officials in the near-by communities of Shrewsbury, Marlboro and Milford.

'ISLANDS' IN BAY STATE

Northampton and Other Towns Isolated by Washouts

Special to The New York Times.

NORTHAMPTON, Mass., Aug. 19—Northampton was one of a series of municipal islands in rain-swept western Massachusetts today.

The communities were cut off from one another by highway washouts caused by two days of steady downpour. The state university's weather station at Amherst, nine miles east, reported that 8.62 inches of rain had fallen in forty-eight hours.

Washouts were reported also to have isolated Holyoke, Southampton, Easthampton, Sandisfield and Russell.

Shortly before noon a Coast Guard duck, an amphibious craft, rolled into Northampton from New London, Conn. It was followed by a busload of Air Force personnel from Westover Air Force Base at Chicopee, Mass. The detail was sent to Easthampton, from which an emergency call for assistance had been sent this morning to Gov. Christian A. Herter by William A. Herrman, chairman of the Board of Selectmen.

Swollen waters of Nashawanuck Pond so undermined the United Elastic Corporation plant at Easthampton that a section of the building collapsed and toppled into the pond.

Floods in Eastern Pennsylvania Take 37 Lives and Cause Damage in the Millions

GOVERNOR SEEKS DISASTER RELIEF

National Guardsmen Help in Evacuation of Hundreds—21 Persons Drowned

TWO MEN ELECTROCUTED

Wide Area Is Inundated—Communities Cut Off as Bridges Collapse

Special to The New York Times.

PHILADELPHIA, Saturday, Aug. 20—Eastern Pennsylvania counted at least thirty-seven dead and millions of dollars in damage this morning as the result of this area's most violent and destructive flood in generations.

Missing persons were being sought by anguished relatives. Others were searching for washed-away homes, furniture, automobiles and other belongings. Government officials, working around the clock, mobilized Federal, state and local agencies to stem the tides and to rescue persons trapped by the swirling waters.

Gov. George M. Leader made a quick inspection tour of the ravaged areas last night and then asked President Eisenhower by telegram to declare the region a disaster area, a declaration that would make communities eligible for Federal aid.

Severe rain storms that lashed eastern Pennsylvania Thursday night inundated many cities and towns from Philadelphia northward. Thousands of homes, business establishments and industrial plants were flooded and many bridges were washed away. Road damage was estimated by the Highway Department at $10,000,000.

The roaring Delaware River was expected to crest at Trenton, N. J., and at Easton, Pa., later this morning and in Philadelphia a short time thereafter. The crest probably will reach 38.1 feet at Easton, just short of the record of 38.6 feet set in 1902.

32 Drowned, 2 Electrocuted

Of the known dead, thirty-two were drowned, two were electrocuted and three perished in traffic accidents.

Numerous spectacular rescues were accomplished. Navy helicopters evacuated 400 Boy Scouts from Treasure Island, a camp in the Delaware River near Point Pleasant. Helicopters also rescued 108 boys and girls from Camp Pennington, on another island fifteen miles farther north, when it was threatened by flood waters.

Scranton, Pennsylvania's fourth largest city, with a population of 120,000, was without water supply and a state of emergency was declared. Water mains and several bridges, including a large cement structure, collapsed.

In Easton, power and water supplies were cut off yesterday and residents were warned to use water sparingly. Water from the Delaware backed up into the Lehigh River, causing that waterway to overflow also. The two rivers converge in Easton.

Flood waters from the Lehigh swirled into a distributing plant of the metropolitan Edison Power and Light Company, forcing that plant to shut down. The Easton Express was forced to print its Friday editions at The Bethlehem Globe-Times plant and radio station WEST had to rely on a gas generator for power.

Two bridges joining Easton with Phillipsburg, N. J., across the Delaware, were washed out.

Poconos Roads Closed

The Monroe County water supply for drinking purposes also was cut off. Nearly all roads into the Pocono Mountains resort were flooded.

Along the Delaware River, from Stroudsburg to Easton, observers reported at least twenty bridges washed out. Thousands of persons who live on one side of the river and work on the opposite bank were stranded at their places of employment.

At least thirty small bridges in Monroe County also were said to be damaged or washed away. Toll bridges at Allentown and Bethlehem were opened for free travel until the emergency ends.

The southern section of Stroudsburg as well as adjoining East Stroudsburg and Canadensis were inundated by up to seven feet of water for a time. East Stroudsburg was placed under martial law last night. National Guardsmen patroled several other areas, also, and helped in the evacuation of residents.

In suburban Philadelphia thousands of homes and industrial plants were flooded. Four hundred persons were evacuated in Norristown.

At Tamaqua an estimated 10,000 electric blasting caps floated out of the Atlas Powder Company into the Schuylkill River. State police warned that, though wet, the caps were dangerous and wired to explode on impact.

The Pennsylvania Railroad said this morning all service affected by the flooding had been restored to normal. The Reading Railroad said it hoped to have its operations back to normal later today. Trains of two other lines, the Erie and the Baltimore and Ohio, used the Pennsylvania's tracks yesterday for detours in areas where they could not operate.

Associated Press Wirephoto

STROUDSBURG, PA.: Waters of Pocono Creek flow across collapsed highway bridge on U. S. Route 209. The bridge in west end of town links Stroudsburg to roads in central part of state. It collapsed during the night.

Associated Press Wirephoto

SCRANTON, PA.: Air Force helicopter about to swing a man to safety from roof of house. Another man in window awaits rescue. Helicopter saved many flood victims.

ARMY FLIES HELP TO SCRANTON AREA

City Without Drinking Water—Governor Visits Flood Zone—Many Evacuated

Special to The New York Times.

SCRANTON, Pa., Aug. 19—Flash floods following a steady, twenty-four hour rainfall took four lives, caused damage estimated at millions of dollars and left thousands of persons homeless today in Scranton and northeastern Pennsylvania.

At 10 A. M. Mayor James T. Hanlon declared a state of emergency when this city of 124,000 was left without drinking water in the wake of the rampaging flood of the Lackawanna River. The Mayor appealed to Gov. George M. Leader and to the White House to send Federal and state aid of any type available.

A fleet of Army and National Guard helicopters removed 235 passengers from a Lackawanna Railroad train marooned overnight in the Pocono Mountains at Cresco. The 109th Infantry Regiment of the Twenty-Eighth Division sent two helicopters to the Hoboken-Scranton train and at least five others were sent from other Army units in the East. The passengers were evacuated to Scranton-Wilkes-Barre airport at near-by Avoca.

Train to Hoboken Cut Off

A second Lackawanna Railroad train en route from Scranton to Hoboken, N. J., was cut off by flood waters at Tobyhanna, twenty-eight miles southeast of here. Its eighty-nine passengers were removed by bus to this city.

Scranton's water supply failed this morning. Citing the health hazards, Mayor Hanlon called upon all factories, business houses and stores to close immediately. The Mayor also closed theatres and other amusement places. The Red Cross was hauling water to the city's six hospitals.

One of the city's main bridges, on Cedar Avenue, collapsed before the pounding waters of the swollen Roaring Brook, a large stream that flows through the east and south end of the city.

Smaller communities south and north of here suffered heavy flood damage and almost all were also without water.

Today was bright and sunny and the flood waters receded rapidly.

The New York Times (by Carl T. Gossett Jr.)

MILFORD, PA.: Farmland flooded by the swollen Delaware River. This is a view looking toward Port Jervis, N. Y.

FACTORIES FLOODED IN LITCHFIELD AREA

Special to The New York Times.

LAKEVILLE, Conn., Aug. 19—Heavy rains and floods created disaster in areas in three sections of Litchfield County today and isolated many small towns.

Most affected were Torrington, where the overflowing Naugatuck River flooded the factory and downtown areas; Winsted, where the Mad River flooded Main Street and the mill section; and Norfolk, where sections of the plant of the General Electric Company were floated away. In all three cities hundreds were made homeless and were evacuated by units of the Connecticut State Guard. The homeless were being cared for by the American Red Cross.

Power and telephone lines were knocked out in all three cities early in the day.

Elsewhere in the county Canaan was isolated, as were other towns along the Housatonic River such as Falls Village and West Cornwall. The Pittsfield line of the New Haven Railroad was washed out at Cornwall Bridge. Route 7, the main traffic artery in the western part of the county, was impassable.

Swollen streams rising suddenly into pasture lands brought heavy losses to dairy farmers when cows were swept into the water. Milk was piling up for delivery to New York and Fairfield County.

FAMILIES EVACUATED

River at Norwalk Overflows—Power at Silvermine Fails

Special to The New York Times.

NORWALK, Conn., Aug. 19—Thirty-five Rowayton families left their homes today when the Five Mile River overflowed its banks. Seven Darien families living along the Noroton River were evacuated.

Also swollen far beyond their usual high levels were the Norwalk and Silvermine Rivers and the Saugatuck, in Westport, where the ground floors of several buildings were flooded.

Although tides were higher than usual, no extensive damage was reported by shore residents.

About 1,000 homes in the Silvermine area were without power for about two hours through cable failure in a substation of the Connecticut Light and Power Company in the north end of the city. The station was flooded. W. Irving Hubbell, district manager, reported that the water had come to within two inches of a high water mark set by a previous storm.

EMERGENCY IN DANBURY

$3,000,000 Damage Caused by 6-Foot Rise in River

Special to The New York Times.

DANBURY, Conn., Aug. 19—A state of emergency was declared here today as swollen waters of the Still River ramNo paged through residential, factory and business districts. Early estimates put the loss at more than $3,000,000.

The river, usually not more than a foot deep, rose more than six feet during a rainfall of more than five inches in twenty-four hours.

Twenty-five families in a residential area bordering the river were evacuated in police emergency boats. Water flooded a number of factories. The Barden Corporation, maker of precision ball bearings, reported at least $1,000,000 in damage when the first floor was inundated.

Water up to three feet deep covered the White Street business area.

'36 Floods Killed 168, Routed 429,000; Damage in 13 States Was $500,000,000

The last time the northeastern states felt anything like yesterday's floods was in March, 1936. For two weeks rampaging rivers from Virginia to Maine wrought more than $500,000,000 damage in thirteen states, caused the deaths of 168 persons and left 429,000 others homeless.

Swollen by two extraordinarily heavy rainstorms, the Connecticut River that year spilled over in three states, the Merrimack overran its shores in New Hampshire and Massachusetts, as did the Susquehanna, Juaniata, Conemaugh and Monongahela Rivers in Pennsylvania, the Shenandoah and the Potomac in Virginia, the Ohio River and the Finger Lakes in upstate New York.

Most sections of the country have suffered major flood disasters since the most famous of all took 2,100 lives at Johnstown, Pa., on May 31, 1889. That small community eighty miles east of Pittsburgh was swallowed by the rushing Conemaugh River when a dam eighteen miles upstream broke.

More than 450 persons perished by floods in Ohio and Indiana in March, 1913, while the total damage exceeded $100,000,000. The Miami River was the most serious offender, leaving Dayton a mass of mud and debris.

The mighty Mississippi rose to the highest levels in its history in April, 1927. It roared across more than 18,000,000 acres of land, drove more than 300,000 persons from their homes and took the lives of 391. Most of the poor farmers along the 1,090-mile river bed south of Cairo, Ill., lost nearly all their possessions. The flood inspired a memorable, nation-wide rescue and relief movement.

In January, 1937, the Ohio River set in motion a series of floods in eleven Midwestern states, killing more than 900 persons and causing $400,000,000 damage.

The Midwest also has suffered the severest floods since World War II. In July, 1951, the Missouri River took forty-one lives and caused $1,000,000,000 damage. More than two million acres were flooded and 100,000 persons were left homeless in Missouri, Mississippi and Red River floods in April, 1952.

BEACHES ARE CLOSED

Westchester Official Acts on L. I. Sound Shores After Rain

Special to The New York Times.

WHITE PLAINS, Aug. 19—Long Island Sound beaches today were ordered closed for at least twenty-four hours by Westchester County Health Commissioner William A. Holla as many residents cleaned out flooded cellars. The rain registered from three inches in the southern half of the county to five and one-half inches in the northern sector.

The closing of the beaches was necessitated, Dr. Holla said, by the overloading of the sewage disposal systems because of the heavy rain. Sewage-laden water that normally drains through the sewage disposal plant was bypassing through storm drains and emptying directly into the Sound.

Associated Press Wirephoto

FARMINGTON, CONN.: Mrs. Leon Berchard clutches her 1-year-old daughter, Lorna Mae, crying: "Don't take my baby from me." She is aided by rescue worker after having seen her older child, Patricia Ann, 3, drown. Rescue boat taking them to safety from flooded home had capsized.

Union Jumps Strike Deadline

MEMPHIS, Tenn., Aug. 19 (AP)—C. I. O. United Automobile Workers have struck the International Harvester plant here four days ahead of the date set by a national strike vote. Negotiations to write a new contract are under way in Chicago.

DAMAGE IS WEIRD AS SEEN FROM AIR

Continued From Page 1

community to the north, some of the big brass and copper plants were encircled by water. The area near the railroad looked devastated. Not only were the tracks torn away, but long sections of roadways disappeared under the flood. Automobiles were almost completely covered. Five helicopters were plying back and forth in one small area.

In near-by Terryville, bridges were washed away. Streets were under water.

At Torrington, by yesterday afternoon the Mad River—always prone to flooding—had begun to recede. It had left what looked from the air like huge mud flats and stagnant lakes surrounding crushed, teetering buildings.

At Winsted, farther north on the Mad, water was still coursing down the main streets, carrying debris that piled up against bridges. Sections were shorn from buildings.

Everywhere through the valley there were startling scenes—houses pitched or turned awry, gaping open through a wall torn away; outdoor motion picture theatres discernible only by the tips of their big white screens; home owners trying to rescue their belongings by rowboat and canoe.

The railroad yards were partly under water. The airport was almost completely covered.

The Delaware River, whipped to even greater force by a northwest wind, swirled perilously close to the floorboards of a bridge in the center of town. Houses near by were surrounded by water. Streets were impassable.

Roads Dip Under Water

To the north, in the lower reaches of the Catskills, the roads that led to resorts repeatedly dipped beneath floods.

At one point, cars were managing to creep through. Then one driver, attempting a different technique, entered the water with a flying start. He cast up a spray higher than the car before coming to a dead stop after about fifty feet. A wrecker, apparently stationed on the dry part of the road for such contingencies, moved slowly in to pull the car out.

South of Port Jervis, just over the border of Pennsylvania, the Delaware seemed to have wreaked a special violence on the little town of Milford. One section of a main roadway bridge had been ripped asunder. Twisted from its foundations, it dangled into the surging river.

Highways were cut away as though by a giant bulldozer. Roofs of buildings were coursing downstream.

From the air, flooding appeared sporadically in upper New Jersey. At Sussex, a big trailer truck stood helplessly midway in a stretch of flooded road.

The weird pot-pourri of destruction seemed the more unreal because it lay among a setting of neat fields and sweeping hills, greener because of the rains. The sun had come out, and big white clouds scurried across the sky, throwing patches of shadow on the secure uplands. But in the valleys ran the serpentine paths of muddy rain.

Japanese Floods Kill Nine

SAPPORO, Japan, Aug. 19 (AP)—More torrential rains fell throughout central Hokkaido today and the toll from flash floods mounted to nine killed and three missing. Thousands of houses have been flooded, destroyed, or washed away and thousands of acres inundated on Hokkaido, Japan's northernmost island.

Flood Closes a Playhouse

The Bucks County Playhouse at New Hope, Pa., canceled its performance last night when the flood waters reached the porch of the theatre. The current attraction at the playhouse is "A Palm Tree in a Rose Garden," a new play by Meade Roberts.

New Heat Wave Today; Held Back by Hurricane

New Yorkers who desire to be properly outfitted for the weather are advised to take off their rubbers and get out their fans. A new heat wave of at least two days' duration is to start today, according to the 11 o'clock weather forecast last night.

There will be nothing puny about the heat wave. The predicted high for today is 96 degrees. The prospect for the week-end is the middle and upper 90s and mostly sunny.

The cause of the expected heat is warm air that had been hovering over the West and Northwest but now is pushing into the North Atlantic States.

The only good word for Hurricane Diane came from the Weather Bureau. It said the heat would have struck New York a day earlier had not Diane unleashed the torrents that wrought such havoc in various states.

ARMY DUCK MIRED ON RESCUE MISSION

Special to The New York Times.

NEWBURGH, N. Y., Aug. 19—An amphibious Army duck got stuck in the mud trying to rescue stranded campers along a rain-swollen creek near here today.

The vehicle, sent from West Point to evacuate 100 vacationing children at Moodna Camp, was mired for thirty minutes until it was pulled loose by a construction company tractor. There were twenty-five children aboard. The campers got caught in rising waters at 6 A. M.

Two major highways in the Newburgh area were closed by flood waters this morning. Routes 17K and 52 were blocked for hours by water that surged six feet over the pavement. A golf course along Route 17K was inundated. There was five feet of water in the clubhouse shower room.

Several streets in the city were flooded but no serious damage was reported. A creek's raging waters cracked a concrete reinforced steel bridge over Wisner Avenue.

In the adjoining town of Newburgh three roads were closed and Town Highway Superintendent Edward Wolfrum had to stand in twelve inches of water in his office to use the telephone. Utility companies reported only minor damage.

WATER MAIN BREAKS

65 Families Evacuated From 2 Apartments in Brooklyn

Sixty-five families in two Williamsburg apartment houses in Brooklyn were evacuated yesterday when a sixty-six-inch water main on South Fifth Street burst at midnight.

The main, one of the principal lines carrying water from the Catskill watershed to the Williamsburg section, was still spouting water hours after it had broken.

The break occurred in front of two six-story houses at 353 and 357 South Fifth Street. Basements of both buildings were quickly flooded. A 10-by-12-foot section of sidewalk collapsed, creating a hole two feet deep. The water spread to adjoining properties and into the yards of South Fourth Street houses. Basement and ground floors at 344 South Fourth Street were evacuated.

The police roped off South Fifth Street and crews from the Department of Water Supply, Gas and Electricity struggled to reach the break and shut off the flow of water.

Federal Aid in Diane's Wake

FRASER, Colo., Aug. 19 (AP)—President Eisenhower today qualified North Carolina for Federal aid to repair damage from Hurricane Diane. Last Monday the President declared regions of the state hit by Hurricane Connie as a major disaster area and allocated $1,000,000 in Federal money for relief.

Railroad Tracks Are Washed Out, Roads and Bridges Closed by Swirling Waters

TAMAQUA, PA.: Raging flood waters of the Little Schuylkill River wash out one lane of highway running through the town. Telephone repairmen in rowboat use pneumatic drills to free the downed lines from the broken slabs of concrete.

Associated Press Wirephotos

MOUNT POCONO, PA.: Swirling Delaware River southeast of the town tears through plant on river edge, undercutting the bank and tilting water tower. At top is a washout on line of Delaware, Lackawanna and Western Railroad.

SPARE TIRE USED IN 'COPTER RESCUE

Pilot With Korean Service Fashions Makeshift Winch to Reach Difficult Spots

A helicopter pilot with a war-proved knack for unorthodox rescues displayed his talent again in yesterday's flood crisis.

Frank Yirrell, a 31-year-old Sikorsky test pilot, was assigned to one of the company's H-34 Army helicopters to fly rescue missions in the hardest-hit Connecticut areas.

The plane, basically a troop transport, can carry fourteen passengers and two pilots. But it has a serious disadvantage when it comes to rescue operations. It lacks the electrically driven winch mechanism, standard on the Navy version, which can lower a cable to a person in trouble and haul him up into the plane.

Mr. Yirrell's test craft did not even have on board the customary Army cargo net that can be hung below the plane. But he did not have time to worry about the state of his equipment when the emergency call went out for the ten available Sikorsky company helicopters to save Connecticut residents stranded by the floods.

The pilot had worked under handicaps before. In Korea, as a Navy pilot, he had performed the first night rescue behind enemy lines. Coincidentally, the co-pilot who held the flashlight over his shoulder in a makeshift effort to light the way on that Korean mission is a Sikorsky engineer who flew co-pilot for him again yesterday. His name is Richard S. Stephanski.

24 Rescued in Derby

The two pilots and a crewman, Tony Orphanis, flew first to the town of Derby. They landed on a factory roof and, in two shuttle flights to a near-by highway, they rescued twenty-four persons.

Next the helicopter flew to Seymour and took off about seven or eight persons from the tops of houses or factories. The lack of a winch was no handicap as yet. The craft could hover alongside the small rooftops while passengers stepped aboard.

While flying to Beacon Falls, where he made a single rescue, Mr. Yirrell noticed many homes with arched roofs or surrounding trees. It would be impossible to land on such roofs. The trees would make it equally impossible to get down low enough to hover alongside the windows.

For future use, he borrowed a length of tough rope from a fireman. Then he flew on to Naugatuck, which was in desperate shape because of the collapse of a bridge. He saw a number of people stranded in homes with arched roofs or surrounding trees.

At this point, he landed on a highway near a gas station and appropriated a spare tire. The tire was attached to the rope and made a good substitute for the conventional rescue device.

Device Works Well

The tire arrangement was lowered first to a woman standing at a top-floor window. She climbed into the tire. But when she was unable to squeeze through the window, she got cold feet and decided to wait for a boat.

The helicopter sidled over to another house. The tire was lowered to a woman on a rooftop, and she climbed into it, sitting like a child on a tire swing in the back yard. Instead of reeling her in, Mr. Yirrell left her suspended down below, flew a half mile to a highway, and set her down gently.

That broke the ice. It ended any skepticism about the tire device. The tire was used to rescue two women and seven men in Naugatuck before the gas ran low and Mr. Yirrell had to head back to Bridgeport.

All in all, ten helicopters from the Sikorsky plant, most of them equipped with winches or floats, took part in the rescue operations. They were flown by fourteen pilots; nine Sikorsky employes, two Air Force men stationed at the plant, and two from the Navy and one from the Marines. The last three have been in training on the company's planes.

By nightfall, the company fleet reported it had made 451 rescues. But a number of pilots, including Mr. Yirrell, were still out on follow-up missions.

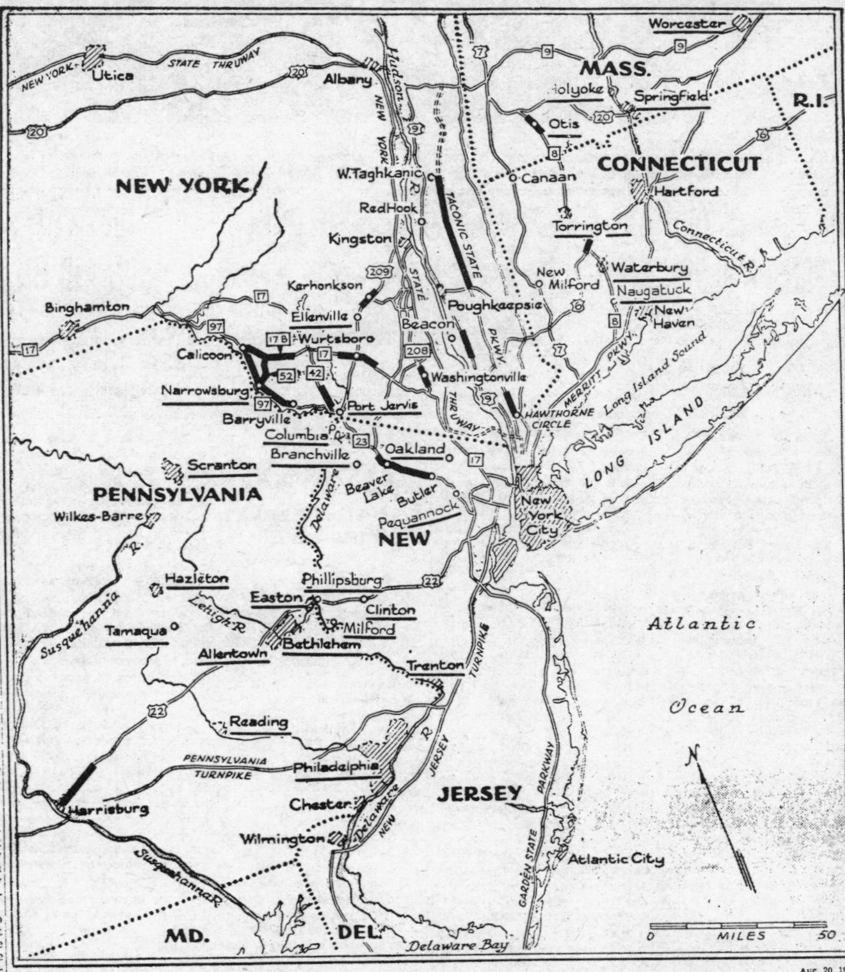

The New York Times — Aug. 20, 1955

FLOOD DAMAGE: Underlined cities were among those hit. Heavy lines show sections of highways affected by water.

DAM BREAKS, SOAKS RHODE ISLAND AREA

WOONSOCKET, R. I., Aug. 19 (AP)—A massive section of Horseshoe Dam burst under pressure tonight, spilling tons of water over a four-square-mile area of congested tenements and small stores.

Five hundred families in the district had been evacuated several hours before, as the Blackstone and Mill Rivers, which join at Woonsocket, reached the flood danger point. The crest of the flood was not expected on the Blackstone River until tomorrow.

Farther downstream, Pawtucket and Central Falls were alerted. Volunteers piled sandbags along the rising Blackstone. Residents of low areas of Central Falls were evacuated.

Those evacuated in Woonsocket were housed in the State Armory, the Naval Reserve Armory, the high school gym and a public housing recreation hall. The Red Cross arranged to feed them.

The collapse of the right side of Horseshoe Dam came several hours after an upstream barrier in Hopedale, Mass., had crumbled, sending raging flood waters downriver.

Task Force Will Clear Storm Debris in City

The Sanitation Department will employ a special task force tomorrow to remove tons of debris left over from recent storms.

Commissioner Andrew W. Mulrain said the extra force would concentrate in Brooklyn and Queens. Normal sanitation crews, aided by personnel and equipment from the borough presidents' offices, will be sufficient in the Bronx and Richmond.

The special force will be augmented by equipment from Manhattan sanitation centers because Manhattan suffered the least storm damage. Five hundred men and ninety trucks will be used in Brooklyn and Queens.

Since last week-end the department has been hard pressed to maintain regular waste collection schedules in the face of the burden added by the storms, Mr. Mulrain said. He asked the public to be patient.

Japan Said to Buy British Jet

TOKYO, Saturday, Aug. 20 (AP)—The newspaper Yomiuri said today Japan had signed a contract Monday with the De Havilland Aircraft Company of Britain for the purchase of a Vampire jet. The British training plane, costing £70,000, will be delivered Nov. 15, the newspaper said.

PENNSYLVANIA TOWN ISOLATED TEN HOURS

Special to The New York Times.

MILFORD, Pa., Aug. 19—This borough of 1,135 persons was an isolated island from 9 o'clock last night until 7 A. M. today. The Delaware River and its tributaries, not yet recovered from the saturation of Hurricane Connie last week, spilled over without restraint as Diane poured nearly thirteen hours of new rains upon this area. The downpour lasted from 4 P. M. yesterday until 4:45 o'clock this morning.

Latest reports, skimpy and irregular because of broken communications, showed no deaths in this area below the Delaware Water Gap.

However, several persons were injured, one was reported missing and there were numerous rescues. Seven bridges and two approaches to bridges were swept away. This region, known for its hunting, also suffered serious destruction of wild game.

The Delaware River is now seventeen feet above normal here and is a deep, dark, muddy stream carrying the debris of trees and homes. Sawkill Creek, Dingman's Creek, Raymondskill Creek and others, which usually have little or no water at this time of the year, are now as much as twenty feet deep and 200 feet wide.

Shortly before last midnight, a woman and two children were rescued from their home in Dingman's Ferry, just before the structure was torn loose by rushing waters. In this community, two men tied together by ropes carried a woman to safety from her apartment above a garage. More than a dozen families have been evacuated here to higher ground.

A Mr. Rowe, described as a Highway Department employe, has been unreported for twenty hours. A bridge collapsed as Robert Blood was driving across it and he and the car were dropped fifteen feet into Sawkill Creek. He swam ashore. Richard Hummell drove into a hole where a bridge once had crossed the Raymondskill Creek. He was saved by passers-by.

FLOODS CUT OFF UPSTATE RESORTS

Continued From Page 1

were under more than a foot of water, causing damage estimated at $1,000,000. Thirty National Guardsmen helped police to protect 500 abandoned homes. By 7 P. M. some roads out of the city were open and the Erie Railroad's line to New York was reported running.

Mayor James E. Cole declared an emergency at 2:35 A. M. Since Wednesday night, seven and a half inches of rain have fallen in Port Jervis.

Thousands of New Yorkers headed for week-ends in the resort area came to Port Jervis by train or road and could go no further last night. They strained all available accommodations to capacity.

Governor Harriman said last night that every department of the State Government had been instructed to give as much help as possible.

"It is a bad situation," he said. "The immediate problem is health and safety, of course. Then we must get roads open and communications that are down restored. We will deal with future needs in a constructive and sympathetic way."

At Goshen, water covered the one-mile track on which the famed Hambletonian harness race is run. Below Middletown, some homes were flooded by the surging Wallkill River.

In Kingston police and firemen, aided by residents of the Rosendale area, removed 100 men, women and children from their flooded homes along Rondout Creek early Thursday night. Many of them spent the night in local churches.

The streets of Rosendale were under three feet of water yesterday morning. Only the roofs of some homes in the lower areas of the village were visible. The water began receding at 3 P. M. yesterday.

Ramapo River High

Along the New York Thruway, water cascaded down the mountainside between Suffern and Harriman, running off into the Ramapo River, already dangerously swollen.

Last night the State Civil Defense Commission reported that the flood situation was "generally improved and under control" in five counties.

In Port Jervis, it was said, conditions were not entirely cleared up, but "the worst is over." Rockland County officials said everything was under control and no assistance was needed. Ulster County's report was similar.

Sullivan County communications were disrupted in the western areas. The county has thousands of vacationers and many of their cottages were destroyed.

In Dutchess County, the hardest-hit section was in Pleasant Valley. However, floods were receding, and all main roads, except those through Pleasant Valley, were open.

At Hillburn, seven inches of rain turned the Ramapo River into a turbulent stream that swept one house from its foundations and poured three feet of water into the buildings of the International Fermont Company, which manufactures generators.

Many resorts, including children's summer camps, sustained heavy damage and vacationers often were imperiled by the raging waters.

At a resort called Eddy's Farm near Port Jervis, 300 guests were removed by Army ducks and helicopters. At the Bianca Hotel, near Ellenville, rescue workers erected a cable and pulley conveyance and brought fifty-three guests and five dogs to safety across the Ramapo.

It was in this vicinity that a New York City resident was killed. The victim was Jacob Perlmutter, a 42-year-old hosiery distributor, who lived at 815 West 181st Street. He and seven friends were walking across a bridge over Beerkill Creek when they were swept into the waters. Mr. Perlmutter's companions were saved.

In Putnam County a creek running through Camp Madison, a children's resort, overflowed. Sixty girls and nineteen women counselors were stranded on one side without supplies. Army ducks from the armory at Peekskill hauled a two-day supply of food to them.

Three other camps in Putnam County were isolated. According to the Red Cross, however, they are on high ground and the children were reported safe. These camps were Greenhill and Talcott operated by the Young Men's Christian Association, and Camp Cejwin, operated for boys and girls by the Central Jewish Institute.

In near-by Godeffroy thirty-three boys and girls were rescued from flood-surrounded Camp Jubilee by helicopters from the Stewart Air Force Base at Newburgh.

In Columbia County, the Bash Bish Creek jumped its banks in the early dawn and sent four feet of water cascading into the village of Copake. The flood washed out a bridge on Route 22, a main artery into the New York City area, and another on a road leading into the Taconic State Park. A section of Route 22 near the Columbia-Dutchess County line also was washed out.

Automobiles Washed Away

Twelve persons occupying a two-family camp in the park fled to safety just before their living quarters were swept away. Two automobiles disappeared in the tumbling flood.

Forty-five persons were evacuated from the park and sixty children were taken from a private camp over a temporary road.

A forty-mile stretch of Taconic State Parkway was closed for several hours because of high water, but was reopened in mid-afternoon.

In the Monticello area, 8.06 inches of rain fell in the twenty-four hours ending yesterday at 8 P. M. This made a total of twenty-one inches since Aug. 7. It was the greatest rainfall in the twenty-four-hour period there since a twelve-inch downpour one day in 1928.

Jersey, Amid Its Flood, Scans Water Shortage

Special to The New York Times.

TRENTON, Aug. 19—While flood waters lapped at the back of the State House today, a legislative hearing inside grappled with another problem: the water shortage.

In the Assembly Chamber, State Senator John Summerill, Republican of Salem County, was presiding at a hearing of a joint legislative committee. The subject was New Jersey's need of additional water resources, illustrated in the recent drought.

William Baumer of the State Chamber of Commerce proposed immediate acquisition of reservoir sites at Round Valley, Chimney Rock and the rest of the Wharton tract in Burlington County. The New York engineering concern of Tippetts, Abbett, McCarthy and Stratton, in a special report for the Legislature, recommended only the development of Chimney Rock. This report was criticized as "incomplete" by several persons. The hearing will continue at 10 A. M. Monday in the Assembly chamber.

Back of the building, where the grounds slope down to the Delaware River, state workers were piling up sandbags to keep the flooding stream out of the boiler room.

RAIL WRECK IN SOUTH KILLS 5, INJURES 50

MARKED TREE, Ark., Aug. 19 (UP)—Four cars of the Frisco Railroad's Kansas City to Florida special jumped the track here today. Five persons were killed, including a mother and her 18-month-old son when a car was demolished. At least fifty persons were injured.

O. P. Rainey, Frisco traffic manager, attributed the wreck to a rod or pin in the switch, which apparently had broken from vibration, permitting the switch rail to open.

The fourth-from-last of the eight-coach train jumped the track and slammed into two side-tracked boxcars, demolishing all three. The three coaches on the rear also were hurled from the track but did not overturn, although the rear club car was left leaning at a 45-degree angle. The wreck happened at about 9:30 A. M.

The wreck occurred about two blocks from Marked Tree's main street.

Frank Woods of Springfield, Mo., conductor of the train, estimated the speed of the train at the time of the wreck at forty miles an hour. He said the train was on time on its run from Kansas City to Memphis.

C. A. P. AND ARMY HELP

Former Lights Hospital and Latter Orders Bailey Bridges

WASHINGTON, Aug. 19 (AP)—The Civil Air Patrol asked its organizations in four states—Connecticut, Massachusetts, Pennsylvania and New York—today to get ready to help rescue or bring relief to flood victims.

Headquarters here said light-plane pilots already were in the air in areas where the weather would permit flying and had reported one dam and two bridges destroyed in Connecticut.

The organization said one of its mobile power supply units was providing emergency power for a hospital at Derby, Conn. Another unit is hauling barrels of water from Allentown to Stroudsburg, Pa., because of flood pollution.

The Army said that troops and facilities in the First and Second Army areas have been ordered to provide direct aid in the floor-stricken sections in the Northeast. First Army headquarters is in New York and Second Army headquarters is at Fort Meade, Md.

Associated Press

OGDENSBURG, N. J.: Cows have difficult time of it after the heavy rain inundated farm

"All the News That's Fit to Print"

The New York Times.

LATE CITY EDITION
Condensation of U. S. Weather Bureau forecast: Chance of showers, warmer today. Partly cloudy tomorrow.
Temperature range today: 79—60.
Temperature range yesterday: 64.8—56.2.
Full U. S. Weather Bureau Report, Page 62.

© 1956, by The New York Times Company.

VOL. CV..No. 35,943. Entered as Second-Class Matter, Post Office, New York, N. Y. NEW YORK, THURSDAY, JUNE 21, 1956. Times Square, New York 36, N. Y. Telephone LAckawanna 4-1000 FIVE CENTS

PINEAU URGES U.S. HEED SOVIET BIDS TO EASE TENSION

Tells National Press Club He Thinks West Could Gain by Such an Experiment

TALKS WITH PRESIDENT

Dulles Is Cool to Proposals That Allies Coordinate Contacts With Kremlin

Texts of Pineau's speech and communiqué on Page 8.

By DANA ADAMS SCHMIDT
Special to The New York Times.

WASHINGTON, June 20—Christian Pineau, French Foreign Minister, urged Americans today to try the "experiment" of friendlier relations with the Soviet Union.

He devoted his entire speech before the National Press Club to explaining why he thought the Soviet Union was undergoing certain "irreversible" changes, and why he thought it to the advantage of the West to accept Soviet offers of increased cultural and economic exchanges.

He spoke just after he had had a ten-minute conversation about Algeria with President Eisenhower at Walter Reed Hospital.

M. Pineau, who was accompanied by Secretary of State Dulles, found the President propped up on pillows in bed. Mrs. Eisenhower was present.

The President explained, by way of apology, that he was in bed because he already had done his daily walking exercise and had spent a prescribed period sitting in a chair.

According to M. Pineau's account when he came out of the hospital suite, the President asked about "the situation of the French people in Algeria."

President's Interest Cited

"He was very interested by my answer," M. Pineau said, "and I am sure expects, like me, a prompt solution of this problem. I gave him the best wishes not only from the French Government but from all the French people. We expect his prompt re-establishment, and his illness will be finished."

The question of the United States attitude toward France's painful problem in Algeria was one to which the Foreign Minister attached particular importance throughout his visit. This is the most difficult question facing his Government.

Many political observers in Washington believe that sooner or later France is doomed to lose Algeria, at least to the extent she has lost in Morocco and Tunisia, and that the Socialist party of France is destined to bear the onus for this loss.

The joint communiqué issued by Mr. Dulles and M. Pineau took a brighter view. It noted that Mr. Dulles had "expressed the hope of the United States Government" for a "liberal and just solution which should enable the European and Moslem populations to live and work together in peace and harmony."

Unlike the speech delivered by C. Douglas Dillon, United States Ambassador to France, in Paris last March, however, the communiqué did not say the United States "supports" France.

Continued on Page 9, Column 1

Red Weapons Mark Huge Cairo Display

By OSGOOD CARUTHERS
Special to The New York Times.

CAIRO, June 20—Premier Gamal Abdel Nasser showed his new Communist weapons today in one of the largest displays of Arab armed strength ever seen in the Middle East.

The massive parade featured the third day of celebrations marking the withdrawal of the last British troops from Egyptian soil after seventy-four years of occupation of the Suez Canal base.

New Stalin tanks, MIG jet fighters and Ilyushin twin-jet bombers were the highlights of a four-hour parade in which token forces from every Arab country except Iraq joined thousands of Egyptian troops in a review before Premier Nasser.

Another unit that drew a rousing cheer from the thou-

Continued on Page 5, Column 4

ZHUKOV SEES TITO AS AN ALLY IN WAR

Predicts Joint Stand as Two Nations Sign Government and Party Agreements

Texts of the Soviet-Yugoslav declarations on Page 10.

By JACK RAYMOND
Special to The New York Times.

MOSCOW, June 20—Marshal Georgi K. Zhukov said today that if war were imposed on Soviet and Yugoslav military forces they would fight shoulder to shoulder for the benefit of mankind.

This statement by the Soviet Defense Minister highlighted a three-part ceremony in the Kremlin that sealed the renewal of relations between Yugoslavia and the Soviet Union, their Communist parties as well as Governments.

Speaking slowly, seriously and extemporaneously, Marshal Zhukov said:

"Soviet and Yugoslav military forces fought shoulder to shoulder against German fascism. Soviet and Yugoslav military forces are struggling to maintain peace, but should war be imposed upon us we will struggle shoulder to shoulder for the benefit of mankind."

President Tito of Yugoslavia, who was standing near by, nodded and gripped Marshal Zhukov's hand firmly.

[In Washington United States officials saw no evidence that Yugoslavia had returned to the Soviet-dominated camp.]

At a news conference this afternoon Koca Popovic, Yugoslav Secretary of State for Foreign Affairs, avoided endorsing the idea that Soviet-Yugoslav relations had reached the point where military collaboration of the nature envisioned by Marshal Zhukov could be commented upon.

"We hope there will be no

Continued on Page 11, Column 1

RADFORD PLEADS FOR AID AS VITAL TO WEST'S SAFETY

Wilson Also Tells Senators Military Fund Cut Would Offer 'Serious Risks'

By WILLIAM S. WHITE
Special to The New York Times.

WASHINGTON, June 20—Admiral Arthur W. Radford appealed to the Senate in strong terms today not to make material reductions in the mutual security program.

The Chairman of the Joint Chiefs of Staff told the Senate Appropriations Committee that even if the pending $4,457,575,000 foreign aid bill survived intact in the Senate "our struggle for military security will be hampered."

Further, to cut its military provisions, he said in effect, would be to go below the irreducible minimum that was necessary for the comparative safety of the West.

Charles E. Wilson, the Secretary of Defense, testified before the same committee. He warned:

"To cut military assistance materially at this time would present serious risks to the defense of the United States and the free world and would require a complete revaluation of our international position and of our own military budgets."

One of the results, he added, would be to force a heavy increase in the United States armed forces "at a very much greater cost in manpower and money."

Admiral Radford and Secretary Wilson, in their testimony, were fighting against an additional Senate reduction in the aid bill as it had come from the Foreign Relations Committee.

A Two-Phase Struggle

That measure, though short by more than $300,000,000 of the $4,900,000,000 originally requested by President Eisenhower, nevertheless was some $700,000,000 more than the House of Representatives had voted.

The Administration's struggle is in two phases. First, there is the problem of bringing unharmed through the Senate the authorizing measure brought out by the Foreign Relations Committee.

Next, there is the task of influencing generous treatment in the separate appropriations measures.

The Appropriations Committee represents one of the second hurdles.

The Foreign Relations Committee, meanwhile, issued a report admonishing the Senate that it would be "an enormous national folly to abandon or drastically to curtail" the aid program.

The committee nevertheless defended its refusal to give the Administration the $4,900,000,000 that it had sought while at the same time resisting efforts to cut down the $4,457,575,000 bill.

The report noted that the foreign aid outlay for the current

Continued on Page 3, Column 3

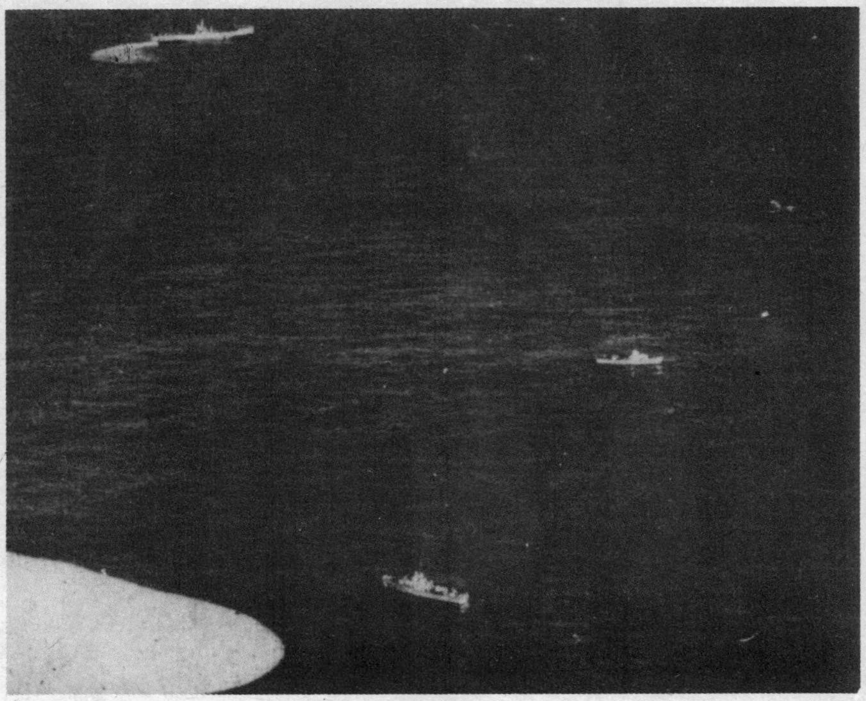

Associated Press

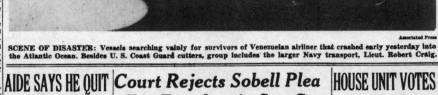

SCENE OF DISASTER: Vessels searching vainly for survivors of Venezuelan airliner that crashed early yesterday into the Atlantic Ocean. Besides U. S. Coast Guard cutters, group includes the larger Navy transport, Lieut. Robert Craig.

74 DEAD IN CRASH OF PLANE AT SEA; SEARCH IS IN VAIN

Coast Guard Brings Bodies of 6 to City From Scene of Disaster Off Jersey

24 STUDENTS ON BOARD

Venezuelan Investigators on Way Here — Eisenhower Expresses 'Deep Regret'

By PETER KIHSS

Searchers yesterday failed to find a single survivor of the seventy-four persons aboard a Venezuelan airliner that crashed into the Atlantic Ocean at 1:32 A. M. It was the worst disaster on a scheduled airliner in history.

The accident, which occurred thirty-two miles east of Asbury Park, N. J., took the lives of twenty-four Venezuelan children returning home for vacations after studying in the United States.

It destroyed the budding careers of a brother-and-sister team of pianists—boy 12 and 14 years old—on their way from North Hollywood, Calif., to play concerts in South America. It left a 10-year-old boy, who had stayed with grandparents in Brooklyn, bereaved of his father, mother, sister and brother.

Besides a crew of ten, the airliner carried sixty-four passengers. Eighteen passengers and two stewardesses were United States citizens. Most of the others were Venezuelans.

Coast Guard vessels brought back six bodies last night.

The search closed at nightfall, with an electrically lighted marker buoy left in the shark-infested waters. Seamen had worked there all day.

To Resume Search Today

At sunrise today, the Coast Guard proposes to resume the search with a cutter and planes in an effort to glean bits that might somehow explain why the tragedy occurred.

The four-engined airliner had radioed an emergency call at 12:46 A. M., reporting its left inboard engine had failed. A Coast Guard twin-engine amphibian plane had flown out to escort the Venezuelan Super Constellation back to New York International Airport, Idlewild, Queens, from which it had taken off at 11:16 o'clock Tuesday night.

Lieut. Comdr. Frederick J. Hancox, pilot of the Coast Guard plane, reported the airliner began dumping gasoline at 1:29 A. M. A minute later he saw a "flicker of fire" from the right wing. Two minutes later, the ship, entirely aflame, plunged into the moonlit water 8,000 feet below.

The jettisoning of fuel is a normal procedure to reduce the hazard of fire in a plane with engine trouble. In this case, it would have been necessary to bring the aircraft's weight down for landing, inasmuch as it probably was still carrying more than 5,000 of the 6,550 gallons with which it had left Idlewild.

In Caracas, Venezuelan authorities said they would "investigate to the last detail." They reported the plane had been thoroughly overhauled just before it left New York, so that they believed the engine trouble

Continued on Page 22, Column 7

AIDE SAYS HE QUIT AT BENSON BEHEST

But McLeaish Denies Heavy Drinking—'Disgruntled' Ex-Employes Scored

By ALLEN DRURY
Special to The New York Times.

WASHINGTON, June 20—Robert B. McLeaish, who resigned yesterday as head of the Farmers Home Administration, told Senate investigators today that Ezra Taft Benson, Secretary of Agriculture, had "strongly suggested" he quit.

Mr. McLeaish's sudden resignation followed earlier hearings by the Senate Post Office and Civil Service Committee at which witnesses testified that he and several other high officials of the agency drank excessively.

The committee's investigation is part of a study of the agency's operations in which Democrats, on the committee have sought to show both irregularities of conduct and undue political pressure from Washington to have Republicans appointed to the agency's state and county committees.

The agency, a part of the Agriculture Department, makes loans and participates in such programs as emergency drought relief.

So far, the investigation has concentrated principally on the charges that Mr. McLeaish and others drank excessively. Today Mr. McLeaish denied this.

"When I get through work,

Continued on Page 25, Column 1

Court Rejects Sobell Plea For Freedom in Spy Case

By EDWARD RANZAL

Morton Sobell's bid for freedom or a new trial was turned down yesterday by Federal Judge Irving R. Kaufman.

Sobell, serving thirty years in Alcatraz prison, was convicted in 1951 of conspiracy to commit wartime espionage. He was a co-defendant with Julius and Ethel Rosenberg, who were executed for their part in the conspiracy to transmit atomic secrets to the Soviet Union.

With apparent reference to the recent statements of Sobell's "innocence" by Bertrand Russell,

Excerpts from judge's opinion will be found on Page 14.

British philosopher, and Jean-Paul Sartre, French writer, Judge Kaufman wrote in a forty-seven-page opinion:

"This petition is so entirely devoid of merit that perhaps it has been unduly dignified by the minute consideration and analysis it has received in this opinion.

"However, an effort has been made to lay to rest with finality baseless contentions and accusations which have been repeated not primarily to aid Sobell but rather to embarrass and injure our courts and country."

Judge Kaufman found that the issues now raised by Sobell were not new and in most instances had been reviewed by the United States Court of Appeals.

In his motion Sobell contended that he had been kidnapped in Mexico by the Federal Bureau of Investigation and forcibly brought back to this country. He said that as a result the court

Continued on Page 14, Column 5

CONFEREES AGREE ON ROAD PROGRAM

Act on 33.4 Billion Network Covering 41,000 Miles—Financing Parley Next

Special to The New York Times.

WASHINGTON, June 20—A Joint Congressional Conference Committee reached agreement today on a record $33,400,000,000 road-building program.

Construction features of bills passed earlier by the House of Representatives and the Senate had been referred to the Senate-House committee for adjustment of differences.

The agreement cleared the way for a separate conference committee to settle relatively minor differences in provisions for financing the program by higher taxes on motor fuel, tires, trucks and buses.

The House bill called for an $18,814,000,000 increase in these levies over a sixteen-year period. The Senate reduced this to $14,518,000,000 by modifying a proposed special impost on heavy trucks and buses.

Under today's conference agreement, the final bill would authorize Federal outlays of $25,000,000,000 for completion of a 41,000-mile interstate highways network in the next thirteen years. The Federal Government

Continued on Page 19, Column 2

HOUSE UNIT VOTES SCHOOL AID BILL

Southerners Fight Measure—Bid for U. S. to Pay Cost of Integration Is Killed

By JOSEPH A. LOFTUS
Special to The New York Times.

WASHINGTON, June 20—The Rules Committee of the House of Representatives cleared the Kelley School Aid Bill today for floor action, possibly next week.

The measure would provide $1,600,000,000 in grants to states, on a matching basis, over four years for new school facilities. It is sponsored by Representative Augustine B. Kelley, Democrat of Pennsylvania.

The House Education and Labor Committee, meanwhile, killed another school bill. This measure, sponsored by Representative Stewart L. Udall, Democrat of Arizona, would have had the Government pay the cost of integrating public schools. Southern Democrats and Republicans formed the majority in a 14-10 vote. Opponents of the bill contended that nobody knew how much the Government would have to pay.

Strong opposition to the Kelley bill has developed among Southern Congressmen. They fear that states that do not integrate their schools will not get any of the school construction funds.

Representative Adam Clayton Powell Jr., Democrat of Manhattan, planned to offer a floor amendment that would require the Administration to withhold funds from school districts that had not made a start on integration.

Cleared by 8-3 Vote

The Kelley bill was cleared by an 8 to 3 vote. The "no" votes were cast by the chairman, Representative Howard W. Smith of Virginia, and William M. Colmer, Democrat of Mississippi, and Leo E. Allen, Republican of Illinois.

The "aye" votes were cast by: Ray J. Madden of Indiana, James J. Delaney of Queens, James W. Trimble of Arkansas, Richard Bolling of Missouri, Thomas P. O'Neill Jr. of Massachusetts, all Democrats; Clarence J. Brown of Ohio, Harris Ellsworth of Oregon, and Henry J. Latham of Queens, Republicans.

The committee voted an open rule—permitting amendments on the floor—and six hours of debate.

Chairman Smith carried the fight against the bill to the floor even before the bill got there. Permitted to speak "out of order," he told the House that "the aggregate amount involved is $8,350,000,000," not $1,600,000,000.

This bill, Mr. Smith told the House, "sets up a situation where the Federal Government is

Continued on Page 28, Column 3

DON'T miss VICTOR RIESEL'S answer to his attackers—a fighting series 'MY WAR WITH THE MOB.' The Mirror's crusading labor columnist cracks down on labor mobsters. Buy the SUNDAY MIRROR.—Advt.

Oxford Honors Truman, Hails His Courage

Ex-President Called 'Truest of Allies' as He Gets Degree

By DREW MIDDLETON
Special to The New York Times.

OXFORD, England, June 20—Harry S. Truman was hailed as the personification of simple courage when he received an honorary degree of Doctor of Civil Law from Oxford University today.

The former President's admission to the ancient fellowship of Oxford took place in the Sheldonian Theatre, designed by Sir Christopher Wren. The Earl of Halifax, former Foreign Secretary and British Ambassador to Washington and now Chancellor of the University, conferred the degree.

The man from Missouri, serious but unabashed by the weight of dignified knowledge around him, stood in the center of the theatre while the Public Orator, T. F. Higham, read the citation of "Harricum Truman" in Latin.

Then Lord Halifax, also speaking in Latin, conferred the degree with words that, translated, said:

"Truest of allies, direct in your speech and in your writings and ever a pattern of simple

Continued on Page 13, Column 3

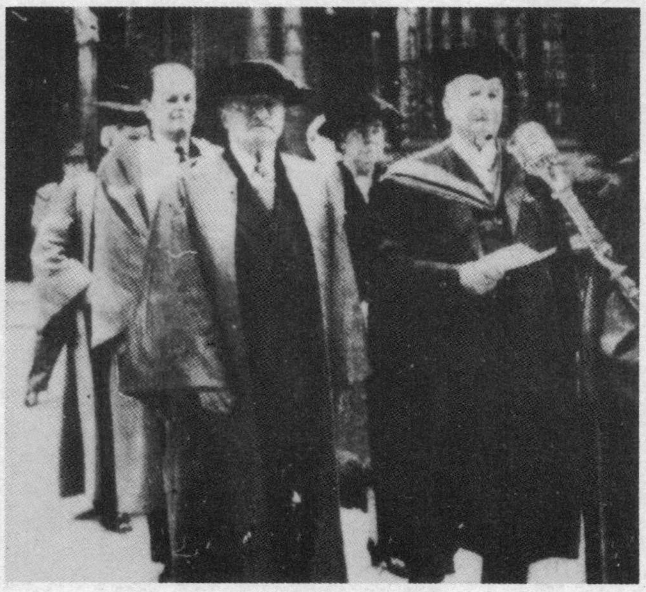

Associated Press Radiophoto

Former President Truman walks in the procession at Oxford University with T. F. Higham, right, the university's Public Orator. Mr. Truman received a Doctor of Civil Law degree.

Duplessis Triumphs In Quebec Election

By RAYMOND DANIELL
Special to The New York Times.

QUEBEC, June 20—Despite the power and prestige of the Federal Liberal Government, Premier Maurice Duplessis and his National Union Government were swept back into power in today's elections in Quebec Province.

In a victory speech from his home town, Trois Rivières, Mr. Duplessis promised to be generous to his defeated foes. The rights of minorities, he said, would always be protected in Quebec.

The victory gave Premier Duplessis, according to a count before midnight, seventy-two seats in the ninety-three seat Legislature, a gain of seven seats. The Liberals led by Georges Lapalme and allied with the Social Credit party and backed by the Federal Government, won twenty seats, a

Continued on Page 2, Column 3

Agents Hunt a 'Bug' In Lehman's Office

Special to The New York Times.

WASHINGTON, June 20—Two men with badges walked into Senator Herbert H. Lehman's office today and scrutinized his refrigerator closet.

Security being what it is, no one can be certain what they were looking for, but circumstantial evidence suggests they suspected a "bug," an electrical or electronic device used for long-range eavesdropping.

The Senator's closet is adjacent to a Senate hearing room where hyper-secret Defense Department information is being submitted to an Armed Services subcommittee investigating the nation's aerial preparedness for war.

The subcommittee revealed yesterday that security police were guarding the air around the room against potential devices for eavesdropping.

The agents' job, according to the subcommittee, is to in-

Continued on Page 16, Column 4

Witness Says Plane Was a 'Ball of Fire'

Special to The New York Times.

SAN JUAN, P. R., June 20—Charles Edward Fisher, an Eastern Airlines captain, said the Venezuelan airliner looked like a "ball of fire" as it crashed into the sea today.

Captain Fisher had just taken off from New York International Airport, Idlewild, Queens, on a flight to Puerto Rico when the airport tower told him that the incoming Venezuelan plane was in trouble.

Shortly thereafter, he intercepted radio messages between a Coast Guard plane and the Venezuelan airliner. Minutes later, he had both planes in sight.

This is the way he described the crash:

"The Venezuelan advised the Coast Guard he was going to dump his gas. The Venezuelan asked if it was okay to dump in that area and New York ad-

Continued on Page 32, Column 3

74 DEAD IN CRASH OF PLANE AT SEA

Continued From Page 1

came from some "unforeseeable defect."

Because the disaster occurred on the high seas past the twelve-mile limit, it was technically not within United States jurisdiction.

However, the Civil Aeronautics Board in Washington offered complete assistance in the inquiry through the Venezuelan Embassy. Investigators here collected transcripts of the plane's final communications. A Coast Guard patrol boat brought back the engineer's log book, found in the floating debris.

In Washington, President Eisenhower announced a personal message through diplomatic channels to President Marco Perez Jiminez of Venezuela, expressing "deep regret over the tragic accident."

Reporting the tragedy, José R. Roncajolo, general manager of the Venezuelan airline, Linea Aeropostal Venezolana, in New York, said:

"L. A. V. regrets to announce the loss of one of its Super Constellation aircraft. According to present reports from the Coast Guard, there are no survivors.

"L. A. V. has been operating since 1946 to New York City, and has completed more than 5,000 flights without any accident and has transported safely more than 140,000 passengers between New York and Caracas."

"L. A. V. never had an accident on any international flight which operates to Havana, Miami, Lisbon, Madrid, Rome and Lima, as well as New York.

"Capt. Luis Plata, pilot of the lost aircraft, has been flying since 1940, and had logged approximately 12,000 hours.

"He was president of the Venezuelan Pilots Association and his loss will be greatly felt by L. A. V., as well as the loss of the other members of his crew.

"L. A. V. extends its sincerest sympathy to all relatives and friends of the passengers and crew of the lost aircraft."

The Venezuelan airliner was one of two Super Constellations that had been delivered to L. A. V. by the Lockheed Aircraft Corporation on Oct. 23, 1954. The flight was to have been piloted by Capt. Gonzalo Parraga, 36 years old. It turned out that he was scheduled for a so-called refresher flight here yesterday, so Captain Plata substituted for him.

Baggage loading delayed the take-off about eighteen minutes Tuesday night. But the Civil Aeronautics Administration said its Idlewild control tower had reported the take-off at 11:16 P. M. "was normal in all respects."

Engine Failed at 12:24

The first intimation of trouble came at 12:24 A. M. The plane reported to the C. A. A. overseas radio station at Sayville, L. I., that its No. 2 engine was out and it was returning to Idlewild. It was then about 250 miles east of Norfolk, Va.

At 12:46 A. M. it radioed a declaration of emergency. The C. A. A. notified the Coast Guard Search and Rescue Office at Floyd Bennett Field in Brooklyn.

Commander Hancox, a 35-year-old career officer who lives in Wantagh, L. I., was summoned from bed at the base to set out with a four-man crew in a twin-engined Grumman Albatross to escort the limping plane.

They took off at 1:02 A. M. Nine minutes later they established radio contact. At 1:25 A. M. they saw the Venezuelan and moved toward escort position, a thousand feet above and slightly aft.

At almost the same time, an Eastern Airlines plane bound for San Juan, P. R., from Idlewild, saw both aircraft. Capt. Charles E. Fisher of Asheville, N. C., its pilot, said later he heard the Venezuelan plane tell the Coast Guard it was going to dump its gas. Captain Fisher said he heard the Venezuelan radio ask if it was "okay to dump in the area and New York advised if it was over open water it was okay."

'No Anxiety' in Radio Voice

"The person making radio contact from the Venezuelan plane had no note of anxiety in his voice, but was very cool and calm," Captain Fisher said. "He spoke good English with a Latin-American accent."

A Lockheed spokesman in New York explained that a Super Constellation carries four main gasoline tanks. Each has a separate ejection chute, which is operated from the cockpit and which extends vertically two feet below the trailing edge of the wing.

The Venezuelan airliner, with its capacity load, had presumably been close to its maximum take-off weight of 135,400 pounds. Its maximum allowed landing weight was 110,000 pounds.

At a consumption of 300 to 400 gallons of gasoline an hour —six pounds to the gallon—it could not have used up enough fuel to get down to the landing limit without jettisoning, the manufacturer's spokesman said.

In dumping gasoline, the recommended speed is between 140 and 185 miles an hour, the spokesman added. The Coast Guard reported Commander Hancox observed no adverse conditions, as the Venezuelan went down to perhaps 150 miles an hour to start unloading his fuel at about 8,000 feet of altitude.

The airliner was less than half an hour's flying time from Idlewild when it radioed: "Roger, we're cleared to drop gas." Then it added: "Roger, we have New York in sight."

Apparently it had thereupon cut off radio circuits in a normal course of starting to jettison gasoline. For when Commander Hancox saw the spurt of fire and yelled a warning over his radio he got no answer.

The "flicker of flame" on the shining aluminum right wing burst into a "ball of fire," Commander Hancox reported later at Floyd Bennett Field. The airliner nosed over into a steep dive and screamed a spiral course into the ocean.

"It burned bright about ten minutes," Commander Hancox, weary and sickened, related.

Then darkness closed in. The Coast Guardsman dropped flares and a marker.

He swooped low, and saw an oil slick and debris. "There was no chance at all of survivors," he said.

The first vessel to reach the scene was the Navy transport Lieut. Robert Craig, at 3:43 A. M. It had left here Tuesday midnight bound for Bremerhaven, Germany.

Four Coast Guard cutters— the Tamaroa and Firebush from St. George, S. I.; the Gentian from Cape May, N. J., and the Yeaton from New London, Conn. —followed, along with seven patrol boats from East River Pier 9, Rockaway, Short Be ch and Fire Island, L. I., and Sandy Hook and Manasquan, N. J. The Coast Guard sent a seaplane and a land plane as well as the Albatross amphibian for air search.

No Sign of Life Found

At 4:50 A. M., the Lieutenant Craig recovered one body and sighted others, but warned that it believed no survivors would be found. The warning was confirmed, as other rescuers found only parts of bodies, despite considerable quantities of clothing, documents and fragments of the airliner.

The Coast Guard used both grappling equipment and sonar in the effort to locate the plane, which had disintegrated so thoroughly in 120 feet of water that the search covered four square miles.

The Lieutenant Craig eventually transferred its pitiful findings to the Coast Guard vessels. Patrol boats had brought only six bodies here before the Coast Guard at 7:30 P. M. announced the search was ended for the night. The Firebush left a marker buoy, reporting this was now "five miles further out than originally estimated."

AT THE SCENE: The Gentian, a Coast Guard ship, searching area of the crash in the Atlantic Ocean thirty-two miles east of Asbury Park, N. J. Coast Guard plane hovers above.

BALL OF FIRE SEEN BY CRASH WITNESS

Continued From Page 1

vised if it was over open water it was okay. At this time my plane was coming abreast of him. He was still to my left and slightly below me. The ceiling and visibility were unlimited and the moon was above me to my right, which gave me a good view of him.

"A few seconds after his last radio contact I observed a large white puff behind him. Then, a very brief space and then, a steady trail of mist behind him. I noticed at this time his running lights were still blinking. We were just passing abreast, with him still below me, and in just a very few seconds dumping had begun.

'Ball of Fire'

"Then all I could see was a large ball of fire. He appeared to proceed on course for a few seconds then he made an abrupt turn to the right of approximately ninety degrees. Then he began what appeared to me a long shallow dive. Just after making the turn, a small ball of fire — when compared to the mass—fell from the plane.

"He continued this dive for a short while then seemed to be making a shallow, slightly climbing turn to the left. This continued for a very few seconds, when three more small balls of fire dropped from the mass.

"The mass appeared to continue upward for a few moments and then appeared to arc over and drop straight down. Its appearance on the way down was that of a falling star, and apparently there was no explosion until it hit the water.

"There was a large explosion and fire on impact. The fire lasted as one large mass for perhaps thirty seconds and subsided some and then divided into one good-sized one with four or five smaller ones.

"We, of course, were circling in shallow turns. The Coast Guard plane had descended and was out of the ultra-high frequency radio range with New York.

"However, New York had us both on radar and gave me a position, which I relayed to the Coast Guard plane.

Calmness Reported

"The person making radio contact from the Venezuelan plane had no note of anxiety in his voice, but was very cool and calm.

"I would place the time of the crash at approximately 12:31 A. M., Eastern standard time [1:31 A. M., Eastern daylight time]. It was obvious that I could be of no further assistance, so I proceeded on course."

Captain Fisher, who has been with Eastern for seventeen years, was asked for his personal feeling.

It was "one of helplessness— what can you do?" he said.

Mary Blair of Upper Sandusky, Ohio, a stewardess on Captain Fisher's plane, said, "we saw a bright light in the water, and we informed the passengers of what we knew because we were circling as is the custom.

"There were the lights of New York visible on one side and the plane in the water—so close to have something like that happen."

Another witness was Miss Elizabeth Brown of Mount Vernon, Ohio, who was going to San Juan on vacation. She said that when she first saw the "light in the water she thought it was a ship burning. Then we were told what it was—such a pity."

BELONGINGS of plane's sixty-four passengers and ten crew members are sorted from debris by Coast Guardsmen.

"All the News That's Fit to Print"

The New York Times.

LATE CITY EDITION
Condensation of U. S. Weather Bureau forecast:
Warm and humid with thunder showers late today and tomorrow.
Temperature range today: 89-67
Temperature range yesterday: 81-62.2
Full U. S. Weather Bureau Report, Page 59

NEWS SUMMARY AND INDEX, PAGE 59

© 1956, by The New York Times Company.

SECTION ONE

VOL. CV—No. 35,953. Entered as Second-Class Matter, Post Office, New York, N. Y. NEW YORK, SUNDAY, JULY 1, 1956. Including Magazine and Book Review. TWENTY-FIVE CENTS

TWO AIRLINERS CARRYING 128 VANISH IN WEST; WRECKAGE OF ONE SIGHTED IN GRAND CANYON

Steel Strike Under Way; Prolonged Shutdown Is Feared

650,000 ARE OUT

Mills Are Closed as Tenure of Contract Snags Parley

Company and union statements will be found on Page 34.

By A. H. RASKIN

A national strike of 650,000 steel workers began last midnight.

Peace talks collapsed six hours before the strike deadline, and no arrangements for new conferences were made by either side.

Union and industry leaders expressed fear that the stoppage would last at least a month, with a strong possibility that it might outrun the crippling eight-week tie-up in 1952.

The mills that normally turn out nine-tenth of the country's most basic metal were stilled long before the first pickets arrived. They stopped pouring steel hours before the official shutdown.

The strike will halt a daily flow of 250,000 tons of steel and cut off upward of $10,000,000 a day in wages. A long stoppage would extend the pall of joblessness and economic loss over scores of other industries.

A foretaste of such hardship already is being felt in the Birmingham area, where 25,000 members of the United Steelworkers of America have been away from their jobs nine weeks because of a strike of 264 railroad unionists.

Exchange Recriminations

The advent of the national steel strike was marked by a fresh exchange of recriminations between the union and the twelve principal steel producers. Each group insisted it had done everything possible to reach an agreement, and blamed the other for the breakdown of negotiations.

The companies said that their offer of a five-year no-strike contract embodied "the largest increase in actual purchasing power" the union had attained in any five-year period.

"The only proposals that the union has made have been so excessive that they afforded no realistic basis for bargaining," a formal industry statement declared.

David J. McDonald, president of the union, said that the industry was "making more money than ever before, and it is more adamant than ever before."

"The steel industry is intent on shutting down the mills," the 53-year-old union chief declared. "The steel union will follow its traditional policy of 'no contract, no work' at midnight."

He made his announcement in a grim mood as he left the negotiating room in the Roosevelt Hotel after the final meeting with the management committee. He summoned the union's 170-member wage policy committee to a meeting this morning. After that the union high

Continued on Page 34, Column 4

Major Sports News

BASEBALL

Junior Gilliam had four hits and Gil Hodges walloped a homer yesterday as the Dodgers beat the Phillies, 10 to 7. The Senators, behind the pitching of Chuck Stobbs, halted the Yankees, 5—1. The Giants downed the Pirates, 6—4.

TRACK AND FIELD

Lou Jones set a world record of 45.2 seconds in winning the 400-meter run as the final Olympic trials were completed at Los Angeles.

HORSE RACING

Red Hannigan, $29.80, captured the $58,500 Carter Handicap at Belmont. Favored Nashua finished in seventh place, out of the money for the second time in a row. Flower Bowl was first in the $156,500 Delaware Handicap.

TENNIS

Vic Seixas, Ham Richardson and four American women reached the quarter-finals at Wimbledon.

Details in Section 5.

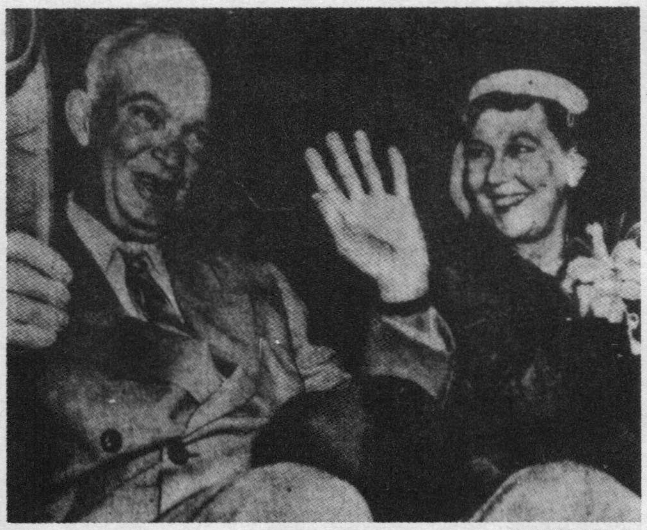

Associated Press Wirephoto

PRESIDENT LEAVES HOSPITAL: President and Mrs. Eisenhower bid good-by to Walter Reed Army Hospital. They went yesterday morning, in auto, to farm in Gettysburg.

President Quits Hospital, Goes to His Farm for Rest

By JOSEPH A. LOFTUS
Special to The New York Times.

GETTYSBURG, Pa., June 30—President Eisenhower was discharged from Walter Reed Army Hospital today. He checked in at his Gettysburg farm two hours later for a convalescence of at least two weeks.

The seventy-five-mile auto trip tired the President a little, but not more than was expected. He went to bed immediately on arrival.

James C. Hagerty, White House press secretary, said:

"The doctors tell me that the trip was very satisfactory as far as they were concerned, medically speaking, and that there was no strain on the President other than the fact that he did feel a little tired, which they said was perfectly natural."

The trip took about twenty minutes longer than usual, but Mr. Hagerty said there was no deliberate slowdown.

The final medical bulletin issued at the hospital said:

"The President slept almost continuously last night for seven and one-half hours. He awoke feeling refreshed. His temperature, pulse, blood pressure and respiration are normal. He is being discharged from the hospital this morning. His spirits and his morale are high. The physicians in attendance wish to thank you ladies and gentlemen for your courtesy and kindness, and for your fair and accurate reporting during the President's stay at Walter Reed Hospital."

The bulletin was signed by Maj. Gen. Leonard D. Heaton, who operated on General Eisenhower for ileitis on June 9; Dr. Isador Ravdin, who assisted at the operation, and Maj. Gen.

Continued on Page 38, Column 4

GOLF CASH PRIZES HALTED IN JERSEY

Essex Prosecutor Acts Under Court Ban on Games of 'Skill' as Gambling

Special to The New York Times.

BELLEVILLE, N. J., June 30—The State Supreme Court's ruling on gambling threw New Jersey's sports world today into a state of consternation.

The Essex County Prosecutor acted under the ruling to block prize payments at the state Professional Golfers Association championship, after a complaint was filed by an irate Jersey shore concessionaire.

The concessionaire was one of those shut down by the court's ruling that all games in which players wagered money were prohibited by the state's anti-gambling law.

In professional tournaments in golf—and many other sports as well—the participants pay entry fees that go into the pool from which prize money is paid.

About $2,000 in prize money was involved in today's tournament at Hendricks Field, the first P. G. A. tournament in the state to be held at a public course.

It was won by Stan Mosel of Essex Fells, who staged a comeback to defeat Al Mengert of Echo Lake. They did not learn of the withdrawal of the prizes until the thirty-first hole.

There Jim Warga, P. G. A. tournament chairman, told them the committee had been required to assure Prosecutor Charles Webb that no prizes would be awarded.

Mosel would have won between $600 and $800, while Mengert would have won about $300 to $400.

While the prosecutor acted, there were strong indications in Trenton that Gov. Robert B. Meyner would veto a bill designed to counter the effect of the court's ruling. The bill was rushed through the Legislature Thursday night.

Some of the Governor's closest advisers expressed serious doubts as to the constitutionality of the bill. The State Constitution forbids any extension of

Continued on Page 48, Column 3

Best kiss in town—Barton's Almond Kisses. Buy a pound, get a half pound free. Barton's Bonbonniere.—Advt.

WHEN you think of writing—Think of Whiting. WHITING PAPER COMPANY.—Advt.

Highways Jammed As Holiday Nears

Good weather, the ending of the school year and the start of the vacation season joined yesterday to lure thousands of New Yorkers to what they wistfully hoped would be the open road.

Automobile traffic on virtually all main highways leading out of the city was reported to be heavy. There were numerous delays at various key points because of the congestion.

For some of the more fortunate, the day provided an early start to next Wednesday's celebration of the Fourth of July. Most, however, will have to turn homeward by tonight to face the usual driving hazards, irritations and jangled nerves for a fresh work week.

Delays were reported on the Bronx-Whitestone and Henry Hudson Bridges, the Marine Parkway to the Rockaways

Continued on Page 32, Column 3

STEVENSON JOINS POLITICAL PICNIC

At Fete in Westchester He Asks Grass-Roots Support in Harriman's State

By RICHARD AMPER
Special to The New York Times.

BEDFORD VILLAGE, N. Y., June 30—Adlai E. Stevenson made his first challenge for grass-roots support in Governor Harriman's home state today.

The leading candidate for the Democratic Presidential nomination perspired through a fifty-minute appearance at a political picnic in suburban Westchester County, where he pursued these campaign tactics:

He kissed and was kissed by a baby, and was bussed by several women admirers. He ate spun sugar candy under protest, rode a miniature fire engine loaded with children, hit a softball four times, shook innumerable hands, signed autographs, but drew the line at mounting a pony.

He also got in a tacit dig at Mr. Harriman. It was during a brief speech he made standing on a grassy, sun-drenched slope on the seventy-acre estate of Cass Canfield, executive of the publishing concern of Harper & Brothers, who was picnic host.

Mr. Stevenson said he had been told that a postcard poll conducted by the Democratic

Continued on Page 36, Column 1

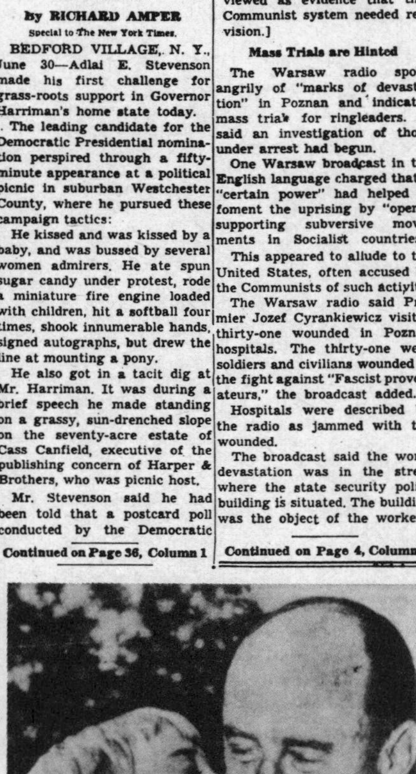

The New York Times (by Joseph Schiffano)

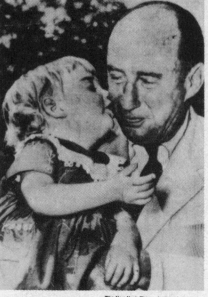

BABY KISSES CANDIDATE: Adlai E. Stevenson receives a kiss from 2-year-old Margaret Waller of Katonah, at picnic given for him at Bedford Village by campaign backers.

POLISH ARTILLERY REPORTED ENDING REVOLT IN 3D DAY

Westerners Returning From Poznan Fair Tell of Gunfire Dying Out in Afternoon

By The Associated Press.

BERLIN, June 30—Polish heavy artillery and tanks tonight appeared to be crushing the last holdouts of a workers' bread-and-freedom revolt in Poznan.

Westerners returning from the Poznan industrial fair reported that tanks and artillery had thrown a ring of steel around the city. A Frenchman told of artillery firing directed at the center of Poznan.

Gunfire echoed through the streets in the morning but was dying down in the afternoon, Westerners said.

Two Portuguese business men said they had been told that 400 to 600 Poles had been killed in three days of street fighting. The Warsaw radio increased its estimate of the number of dead from thirty-eight to forty-eight.

[East Germans, meanwhile, received a warning based on the Polish rioting. Their top Communist paper said "the workers' and peasants' state can be of steel-hard vigor." In Italy, however, the left-wing press sided with the demonstrators. The rioting was viewed as evidence that the Communist system needed revision.]

Mass Trials are Hinted

The Warsaw radio spoke angrily of "marks of devastation" in Poznan and indicated mass trials for ringleaders. It said an investigation of those under arrest had begun.

One Warsaw broadcast in the English language charged that a "certain power" had helped to foment the uprising by "openly supporting subversive movements in Socialist countries."

This appeared to allude to the United States, often accused by the Communists of such activity.

The Warsaw radio said Premier Jozef Cyrankiewicz visited thirty-one wounded in Poznan hospitals. The thirty-one were soldiers and civilians wounded in the fight against "Fascist provocateurs," the broadcast added.

Hospitals were described by the radio as jammed with the wounded.

The broadcast said the worst devastation was in the street where the state security police building is situated. The building was the object of the workers'

Continued on Page 4, Column 1

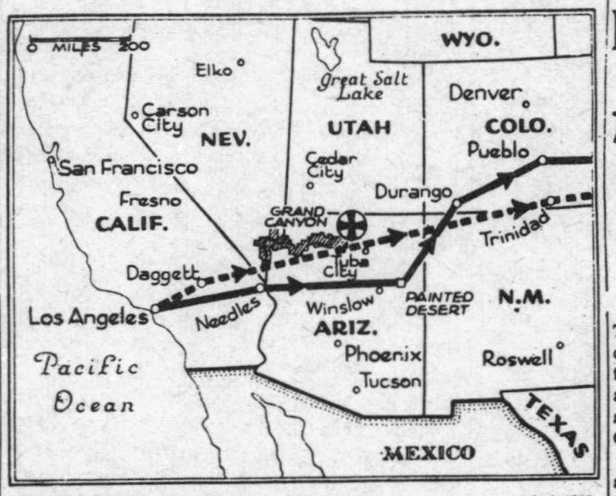

The New York Times July 1, 1956

ROUTES OF TWO PLANES: Wreckage of T. W. A. Super Constellation (broken line) seen in Grand Canyon (cross). The United Air Lines DC-7 (solid line) is still missing.

U.S. Offers to Send Food To Ease Distress in Poland

Special to The New York Times.

WASHINGTON, June 30—The United States offered today to send free food to the people of riot-torn Poznan and other areas in Poland. Acting Secretary of State Herbert Hoover Jr. made the offer in a letter to Harold Starr, general counsel of the American Red Cross.

Mr. Hoover asked that the American organization find out "immediately" through the International League of Red Cross Societies whether the food would be accepted to relieve the "reported hunger and distress of the Polish people."

The offer was transmitted at once to League headquarters in Geneva, where it will be sent to the Polish Red Cross.

In his letter, Mr. Hoover said the riots in Poznan seemed to be marked by demands of the populace for bread. Moreover, he said, there seem to be "serious food shortages" through the Communist-ruled country.

"The people of the United States, many of whom are of Polish descent, have a sympathetic concern for the welfare of the Polish people," Mr. Hoover continued.

Accordingly, he said, the United States Government is ready to make available through the Red Cross "appropriate" quantities of wheat, flour and other foods.

The food, which would come from surplus farm commodities, would be turned over to the Red Cross societies without cost at an "appropriate port of entry in Poland." The only other stipulation would be that the food be "labeled for distribution as a gift from the American people."

Lincoln White, State Department press officer, said he did not know how much food the United States was prepared to send, but added it should be enough.

The food would be shipped under legislation that permits surplus foods to be shipped in emergencies to friendly peoples

Continued on Page 5, Column 1

Dulles Hails Victory Of Aid Bill in Senate

By CHARLES E. EGAN
Special to The New York Times.

WASHINGTON, June 30—John Foster Dulles lauded the Senate today for its action last night in authorizing $4,500,000,000 for foreign aid.

The Secretary of State said that if the Senate's action was concurred in by the House of Representatives and backed by the necessary appropriations, the Mutual Security Program "can be carried forward for the benefit of the free world."

Mr. Dulles, who is vacationing in Canada, made the comments in a statement issued here.

Mr. Dulles emphasized that the foreign aid measure was not a "give-away" but one designed to promote the peace and safety of the country.

Senator Walter F. George, Democrat of Georgia, who is chairman of the Foreign Rela-

Continued on Page 6, Column 2

SOVIET PUBLISHES LENIN TESTAMENT

It Ends 33 Years' Silence—U. S. Prints Documents on Stalin and Party

Texts of Soviet documents as released by U. S., Pages 2-3.

By JACK RAYMOND
Special to The New York Times.

MOSCOW, June 30—The text of Lenin's "testament" was published here today after its suppression in the Soviet Union for thirty-three years. In the testament Lenin proposed the removal of Stalin as general secretary of the Communist party.

It was accompanied in Kommunist, the party's theoretical journal, by the heaviest public indictment yet of the late dictator's conduct of his office, including his foreign policy.

"Stalin committed serious errors in leadership over agriculture, military affairs and in the field of foreign policy," it was emphasized in the preface to the text.

[The State Department made public Saturday eighteen documents it said were distributed at the Soviet Communist party congress in February to supplement the anti-Stalin speech by Nikita S. Khrushchev, First Secretary of the party. The department said the documents had been obtained "through a confidential source."]

The article in Kommunist reinforced the belief that the text of Nikita S. Khrushchev's secret speech describing Stalin's regime of terror could shortly be published.

The speech, which was referred to this week in Pravda, the Soviet Communist party newspaper, was delivered at the closing session of the Soviet Communist party's twentieth congress last February.

Kommunist explained that the Lenin documents published today were made available to the delegates of the twentieth congress and were being published in accordance with a decision of the Central Committee.

They included memoranda dictated by the founder of the Soviet Union in December, 1922, and January, 1923, for the party congress that took place in May, 1924, after Lenin's death in January of that year.

A paraphrase of part of the testament was published here May 18 without identification. It was contained in a story in the youth newspaper Komsomolskaya Pravda in an effort to explain the downgrading of Stalin.

As late as 1927 references to the testament were published in the Soviet Union, once by Stalin himself, in which he defended

Continued on Page 4, Column 3

NO SIGN OF LIFE

70 on Crashed T. W. A. Plane—United Craft Is Still Missing

By The Associated Press.

WINSLOW, Ariz., June 30—Two airliners disappeared over desolate northern Arizona in a thunderstorm today. The wreckage of one, carrying seventy persons, was spotted tonight in the Grand Canyon.

The wreckage was identified as that of a Trans World Airline Super Constellation on its way from Los Angeles to Kansas City.

No sign of survivors was reported.

Still missing and presumed to have crashed was a United Air Lines DC-7 with fifty-eight aboard. It was bound for Chicago and Newark, N. J.

Capt. Byrd Hyland, head of a search and rescue team from March Air Force Base in California, said "there is a possibility" that the planes had collided in flight.

Captain Hyland said later the wreckage might also include that of the United Air Lines DC-7. The Air Force captain said there was no way of ascertaining before daylight whether the wreckage was that of one or two planes.

The two planes took off from Los Angeles' International Airport within minutes of each other and were flying virtually the same easterly route.

Lynn Coffin, chief ranger at Grand Canyon National Park, said wreckage of the Super Constellation was sighted from the air about twenty-five miles northeast of Grand Canyon Village, which is on the south rim of the canyon.

Brothers Spot Wreckage

Mr. Coffin said the find was made by Palen and Henry Hudgin, brothers who operate the Grand Canyon Airlines.

The brothers said the wreckage was on the side of a butte about 1,000 feet above the Colorado River, in rugged terrain difficult to enter.

The wreckage was scattered over the hillside, they said, and two fires were burning in the area.

Mr. Coffin said Nellis Air Force Base, in Nevada, had been notified that the wreckage had been found and was making arrangements to fly to the area in the morning.

Air Force officials at Winslow said rescue teams might be sent into the area by parachute tomorrow morning.

The Hudgin brothers said they had clearly seen the Super Constellation's tail.

The two planes had been missing for more than ten hours when the wreckage of the T. W. A. plane was sighted.

The search for the United Air Lines DC-7 by military, civil and airline authorities, working on

Continued on Page 42, Column 4

Mollet Says Nasser Has 'Megalomania'

By The United Press.

LILLE, France, June 30—French Premier Guy Mollet accused Egyptian President Gamal Abdel Nasser today of suffering from "megalomania"—delusions of grandeur.

In some of the strongest language yet aimed by a high French official against Egypt, which many French feel is aiding the Algerian rebels, M. Mollet said:

"I denounce the megalomania of Colonel Nasser. He hopes to line up behind himself not only the Arab world but the entire Moslem world. One would think oneself back in the Middle Ages. Today, Pan-Islamism is a threat to peace."

M. Mollet spoke at a rally of his Socialist party, which has been split over his get-tough policies against the rebel

Continued on Page 6, Column 3

This is an aerial view of the vast gorge where two airliners fell into the Grand Canyon.
These buttes are a two-day hike over dangerous terrain from the nearest road.

Wide World Photos

2 AIRLINERS LOST WITH 128 ABOARD

Continued From Page 1

Continued From Page 1

the ground and in the air, was halted by darkness until daylight.

The area over which the planes disappeared is a broad expanse of wasteland covering thousands of square miles of high, jagged mountains, deep canyons and parched desert.

Heavy thunderclouds hung over the area during the day, but no one in authority would speculate as to what might have happened to the planes.

The total number of persons aboard the craft raises the possibility of the worst commercial air disaster in history in event they may have collided or otherwise been involved in a single mishap.

The worst commercial crash in history was that of a Venezuelan airliner off New Jersey's coast June 20 in which seventy-four persons died. The worst air disaster was the crash of a military C-124 at Tokyo in 1953 in which 129 persons died.

United Airlines and T. W. A. said each plane had enough fuel for eight-and-a-half hours when it began its flight. That means both would have run out of fuel about 6:30 P. M., Mountain standard time, 9:30 P. M. Eastern daylight time.

The T. W. A. Constellation carried sixty-four passengers, mostly T. W. A. employes or relatives of employes, and six crew members. United's craft had fifty-three passengers and a crew of five aboard.

The first word that the planes were in trouble came from Winslow, in northern Arizona. The Civil Aeronautics Authority reported it had started a search for the planes at 11:46 A. M., M. S. T., after trying unsuccessfully for an hour to establish radio contact.

As the Air Force, civil aviation authorities and law enforcement agencies throughout northern Arizona organized for a search, there was a flurry of reports that wreckage of one or both planes had been spotted.

The T. W. A. plane left Los Angeles bound for Kansas City by a route taking it over Daggett, Calif., Trinidad, Colo., and Dodge City Kan. It was last reported at 10:55 A. M., M. S. T., over Lake Mohave, a desert lake near the California border.

The United craft's route to Newark was by way of Needles, Calif., Painted Desert, Ariz., Durango and Pueblo, Colo., Hutchinson, Kan., St. Joseph, Mo., Joliet, Ill., Chicago, Detroit and Philadelphia. The last report from it was at Needles at 10:58 A. M., M. S. T.

The most persistent of the wreckage reports had one or both planes down in the Marble Canyon-Tuba City area at the western end of the vast Navajo Indian Reservation.

The planes entered the desolate area within fifty miles of each other where the Colorado River divides Arizona and California. The terrain ahead ranged from the Grand Canyon —the world's deepest gorge—to the 12,000-foot San Francisco peaks—Arizona's highest mountains.

The terrain features sparsely populated ranchlands, Indian reservations and forestlands with few communities, few roads and virtually no communications.

RECORD TOLL SEEN FOR AIR DISASTER

Total of 128 Deaths in Two Missing Planes Will Exceed 1950 Wales Crash by 48

The disappearance of two airliners in the West yesterday may result in the blackest day in the history of commercial aviation.

If all the passengers and crew members aboard the Trans World Airline Super Constellation and the United Air Lines DC-7 were killed, the death toll would stand at 128, the highest in a single day of commercial flying.

Up until yesterday, the worst commercial air disaster claimed the lives of eighty persons. It occurred on March 12, 1950, when a chartered Avro Tudor transport plane went down near Cardiff, Wales.

The greatest catastrophe to a scheduled commercial airplane in history was written in the sky only last week. On June 20, a Venezuelan Super Constellation with seventy-four persons aboard caught fire and plunged into the sea off the Jersey coast, killing everyone aboard.

Four days later, a British Overseas Airways Corporation Argonaut crashed in North Nigeria, killing twenty-six of the forty-five persons aboard. One person was listed as missing.

The greatest number of persons killed in any aviation disaster occurred June 18, 1953, when a military plane, an Air Force C-124 Globemaster, crashed near Tokyo, killing 129 persons. The plane was carrying United States service men back to Korea from leave.

In another military airplane crash, eighty-seven service men lost their lives when a Globemaster fell at Moses Lake, Wash., on Dec. 20, 1952.

Following are other civilian and military air crashes in which fifty or more persons were killed, with the number of fatalities in each case:

66—United Air Lines DC-4 at Laramie, Wyo., Oct. 7, 1955.
66—Navy DC-6 at Honolulu, March 21, 1955.
66—Collision and crash of two Air Force Flying Boxcars in Germany, Aug. 11, 1955.
58—Northwest Airlines DC-4 into Lake Michigan, June 24, 1950.
57—Israeli El Al Airlines Constellation shot down by Bulgarian Communist anti-aircraft batteries near Petrich, Bulgaria, July 27, 1955.
56—Nonscheduled C-45 passenger transport at Elizabeth, N. J., Dec. 16, 1951.
55—Collision of P-38 fighter plane with Eastern Airlines DC-4 at National Airport, Washington, Nov. 1, 1949.
55—Trans World Airlines Constellation on the Egyptian desert, Aug. 31, 1950.
54—Air Force B-24 near Freckleton, England, Feb. 15, 1947.
53 — Avianca Airlines DC-4 on mountain in Colombia, Feb. 15, 1947.
53—Eastern Airlines DC-4 near Port Deposit, Md., May 30, 1947.
53—Chartered transport near San Juan, Puerto Rico, June, 1947.
53—United Air Lines DC-6 at Bryce Canyon, Utah, Oct. 24, 1947.
52—French transport plane at sea 400 miles off Cape Verde Islands, Aug. 1, 1948.
52—Pan American Airways DC-4 off San Juan, Puerto Rico, April 11, 1952.
52—C-124 Globemaster on mountain in Alaska, Nov. 23, 1952.
50—Capital Airlines DC-4 at Lookout Rock, Va., June 13, 1947.
50—United Air Lines DC-6 into Rocky Mountain National Park, Colo., June 30. 1951.
50—Pan American World Airways plane in Brazilian jungle, April 30. 1952.
50—United Air Lines DC-6B near Decoto, Calif., Aug. 24, 1951.

BROKERAGE OFFICIAL WAS ON T.W.A. PLANE

One of those listed as a passenger on the TWA Super Constellation was Richard C. Noel, a partner in the investment and brokerage concern of Van Alstyne, Noel & Co., Inc., of 52 Wall Street.

His home is at 5 Carstensen Road, Scarsdale.

Mr. Noel is a governor of the American Stock Exchange and a vice-president and director of Hercules Steel Products Corporation. He also is a director of the Circle Wire and Cable Corporation, Consolidated Diesel Electric Corporation, Diana Stores Corporation, Kin-Ark Oil Company and New Idria Mining and Chemical Company.

He was born in Silver City, N. M., on June 9, 1891. Mr. Noel was graduated from the Institute of Law at St. Louis University.

He and the former Marietta Thompson were married in New York on Sept. 24, 1919.

They have two children, Richard Curtis Jr. and Mrs. Martha Baskowitz.

Mr. Noel formed the investment concern, with eight other partners, in 1943. One of the limited partners is his wife.

T. W. A. HOSTESS 2 YEARS

Upstate Woman Was Aboard Craft Missing in West

RICHFIELD SPRINGS, N. Y., June 30 (AP)—Beth Ellis Davis, hostess on the Trans World Airline plane missing over northern Arizona, had been employed by the airline for about two years.

Her parents, Mr. and Mrs. Milburn Davis of Richfield Springs, were notified by T. W. A. tonight that the plane was overdue and "presumed lost."

"All the News That's Fit to Print"

The New York Times.

LATE CITY EDITION
Condensation of U. S. Weather Bureau forecast:
Fair and warm today. Hot, humid, afternoon thunderstorms tomorrow.
Temperature range today: 86—71.
Temperature range yesterday: 86.7—79.5.
Full U. S. Weather Bureau Report, Page 40.

© 1956, by The New York Times Company.

VOL. CV..No. 35,979. Entered as Second-Class Matter, Post Office, New York, N. Y. NEW YORK, FRIDAY, JULY 27, 1956. Times Square, New York 36, N. Y. Telephone LAckawanna 4-1000 FIVE CENTS

1,117 ANDREA DORIA SURVIVORS ARRIVE HERE; 7 DEAD, 52 MISSING, 1,652 SAVED IN COLLISION; ITALIAN LINER SINKS; STOCKHOLM DUE TODAY

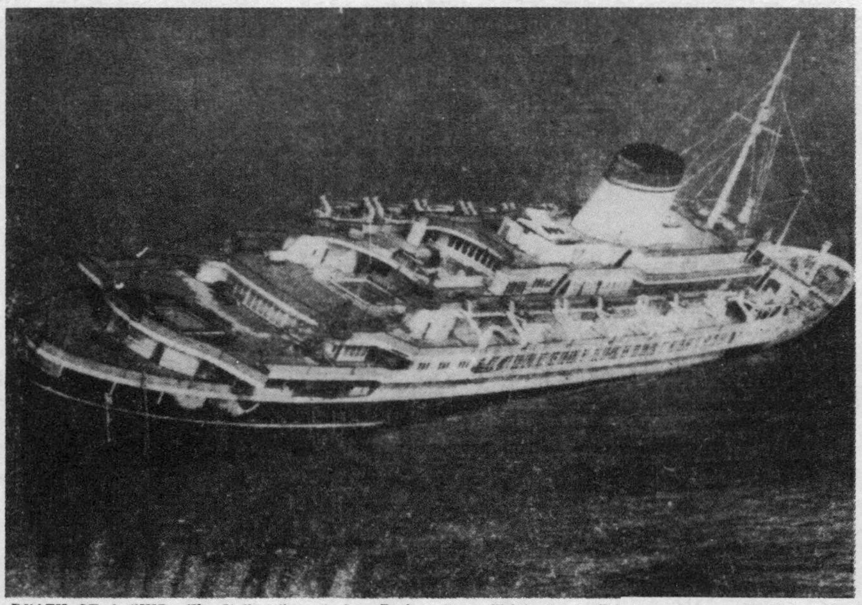

DEATH OF A SHIP: The Italian liner Andrea Doria, after collision at sea, lists toward damaged side and . . .

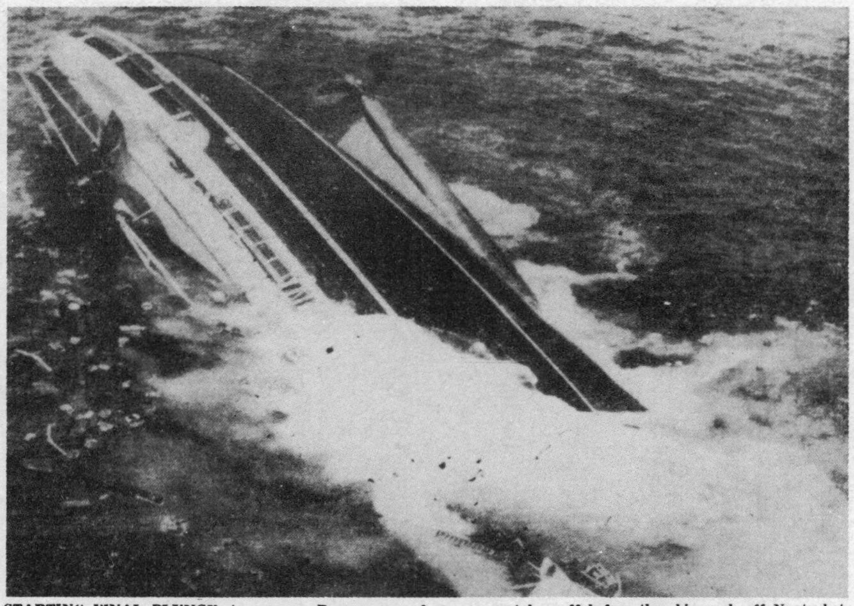

STARTING FINAL PLUNGE, turns over. Passengers and crew were taken off before the ship sank off Nantucket.

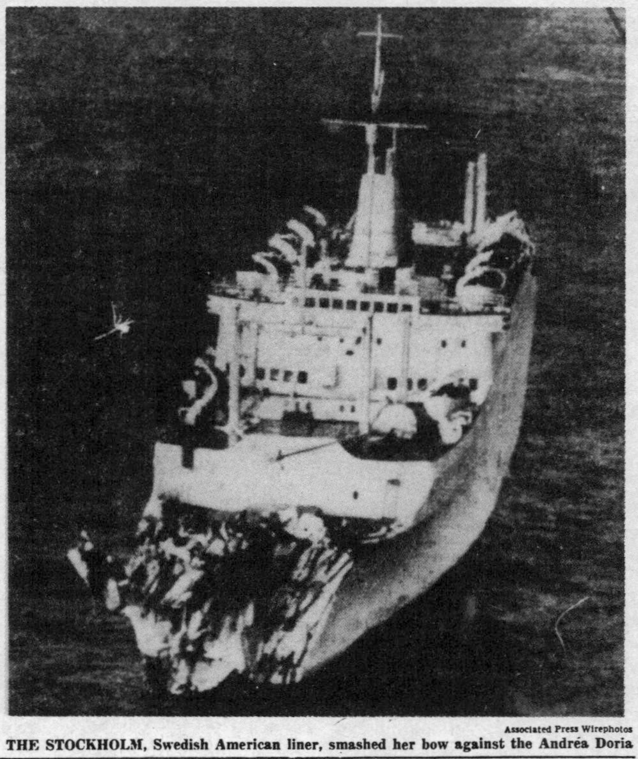

Associated Press Wirephotos

THE STOCKHOLM, Swedish American liner, smashed her bow against the Andrea Doria

Egypt Nationalizes Suez Canal Company; Will Use Revenues to Build Aswan Dam

Nasser Retaliates Against West's Denial of Aid—London Stunned

Special to The New York Times.

CAIRO, July 26—President Gamal Abdel Nasser's revolutionary regime seized full control of the Suez Canal today. The Egyptian leader announced that profits of the internationally controlled waterway would be used to build the High Dam at Aswan.

President Nasser proclaimed emotionally the nationalization of the Suez Canal Company, which for eighty-seven years since the canal was opened, has been run by foreign interests, largely French and British.

It was Egypt's drastic retaliation against the Western withdrawal of offers to help finance the giant project to harness the Nile River. It was apparent by this action that the Egyptian leader also had given up any plan or hope of getting a counter-offer of aid from the Soviet Union.

[Prime Minister Eden conferred with Cabinet officials and with United States and French diplomats immediately after he had heard the news about the seizure of the canal. British officials were stunned by the Egyptian move.]

The instant President Nasser made his announcement Egyptian officials of the Suez Canal Company marched to the company's headquarters in Cairo with a squad of police and took over the premises.

The police cordoned off the canal company's headquarters which is just across the street from the United States Embassy compound.

At Port Said the Egyptian Governor of the Suez Canal,

Continued on Page 2, Column 4

Eisenhower's Four Years

Analysis of 'Partnership' on Resources And Democrats' 'Give-Away' Charges

This is the sixth of a series of articles analyzing the record of the Eisenhower Administration at the start of the Presidential election campaign.

By ALLEN DRURY

Special to The New York Times.

WASHINGTON, July 26—Dwight D. Eisenhower was elected President of a nation endowed much more than most with natural resources. In his first State of the Union Message he summarized a philosophy for their management that was to lay the groundwork for one of the hottest political issues of his Administration.

"The best natural resources program for America," he said, "will not result from exclusive dependence on Federal bureaucracy. It will involve a partnership of the states and local communities, private citizens and the Federal Government, all working together. This combined effort will advance the development of the great river valleys of our nation and the power they can generate. Likewise, such a partnership can be effective in the expansion throughout the nation of upstream storage, with sound use of public lands, the wise conservation of minerals, and the sustained yield of our forests."

Around these words, so sincere in sound and earnest in intent, so insistent upon the good old American themes of "partnership" and "working together," there was soon to develop a raging controversy, full of implications and consequences neither Democrats nor Republicans can yet fully foresee.

Politically, the controversy boils down to two conflicting catch-words: the "partnership" of the President, the "give-away!" snapped out by Harry Truman and chorused by fellow Democrats. But beyond these

Continued on Page 4, Column 3

TIMES MAN KILLED

Cianfarra of Madrid and Two Daughters Among the Dead

At least seven persons were killed in the collision Wednesday night between the Andrea Doria and the Stockholm.

Among the dead were Camille M. Cianfarra, Madrid correspondent of The New York Times, his stepdaughter, Linda Morgan, and his daughter, Joan Cianfarra.

Mr. Cianfarra's wife, Jane, was injured in the collision and rescued by the Ile de France.

She was taken from the rescue ship by ambulance to St. Clare's Hospital with fractures of the arm and leg. Her condition was said to be "not serious."

Mrs. Martha Peterson, wife of Dr. Thure C. Peterson of Upper Montclair, N. J., also was killed. Other victims were Mrs. Walter J. Carlin, whose husband is prominent in Democratic politics in Brooklyn; Alf Johannsen of the crew of the Stockholm, and one unidentified man.

The Cianfarras were returning to the United States aboard the Andrea Doria for home leave. They had embarked at Gibraltar last Saturday.

Mr. Cianfarra was 49 years old. His stepdaughter, Linda, 14, was the daughter of Mrs. Cianfarra and her former husband, Edward P. Morgan, a commentator on the American Broadcasting Company radio network. Mr. and Mrs. Cianfarra's daughter, Joan, was 8.

In a twist of fate, Mr. Cianfarra had tried to book passage on the Cristoforo Colombo, sister ship of the Andrea Doria. Told in Morocco that accommodations on the former vessel were unavailable, the correspondent then was successful in

Continued on Page 9, Column 6

4 RESCUE SHIPS IN

Ile de France Brings 753 From Disaster—Other Craft Due

By MEYER BERGER

Four rescue ships stood in from the sea yesterday with 1,117 survivors of the collision between the Italian Line steamship Andrea Doria and the Swedish Line's Stockholm off the New England coast before midnight Wednesday.

The Ile de France brought 753 into this port, the freighter Cape Ann 129, the Military Sea Transportation Service transport Pvt. William H. Thomas 158 and the Navy destroyer escort Edward H. Allen 77. Two other survivors arrived separately. The Stockholm, with the last of the survivors, is due today. Scores of the rescued were bruised, shocked or hurt in other ways.

The Andrea Doria and the Stockholm crashed in deep fog off Nantucket Light at 11:22 P. M. Wednesday, apparently because of "radar blindness." The Andrea Doria sank within a mile or two of where she was wounded. She went down at 10:09 A. M. yesterday, a little less than eleven hours after the collision.

Seven persons were feared dead; fifty-two were unaccounted for. Of the 1,709 persons aboard the Andrea Doria—crew and passengers — 1,652 were known saved. This would include those brought in yesterday and due today.

Five of the seven reported dead were Andrea Doria passengers; two were seamen off the Stockholm, killed in a rescue effort.

The wounded Stockholm with a forty-foot hole in her bow, has 533 survivors aboard. She is steaming back to port very slowly, under Coast Guard escort. She was expected to

Continued on Page 6, Column 6

ISRAEL AND ARABS GET NEW U. N. BID

Hammarskjold Sends 'Strong Appeal' on Keeping Truce

By MICHAEL L. HOFFMAN

Special to The New York Times.

GENEVA, July 26—Dag Hammarskjold has sent a new "strong appeal" to Israel and neighboring Arab countries to take measures for enforcing their cease-fire agreements.

Mr. Hammarskjold, Secretary General of the United Nations, announced this today just before departing for New York. [He is scheduled to arrive at New York International Airport, Idlewild, Queens, at 7 P. M. Friday.]

The Secretary General had planned to take a brief holiday in Sweden, his native country, before returning to his headquarters. But the wounding of three United Nations observers on the Israeli-Jordanian frontier within the last three days was assumed here to have altered his plans.

"I am grieved by the injuries suffered," Mr. Hammarskjold said, "and I extend my warm sympathy to the United Nations observers who have been seriously injured while on duty in the cause of peace."

Sources in a position to know

Continued on Page 2, Column 7

HOUSE APPROVES 3.7 BILLION IN AID

Compromise Bill Is Assured of Passage by Senate

By WILLIAM S. WHITE

Special to The New York Times.

WASHINGTON, July 26—A compromise foreign aid appropriation of $3,766,570,000 was approved today by the House of Representatives as the Democratic Eighty-fourth Congress moved toward adjournment.

Senate concurrence in the foreign aid bill was assured. It cleared the House by voice vote with only murmurs of dissent. It would provide, with $240,000,000 of reappropriated funds, a total of $4,006,570,000 to carry the mutual security program forward in fiscal year that opened July 1.

The President originally had asked $4,900,000,000, though the appropriation for the fiscal year that just ended was only $2,700,000,000.

Final action on this last great foreign policy issue of the session was accomplished in an atmosphere of exertion over a dozen other questions as Congress pressed on toward the end.

These were some of the day's important actions:

The Administration's meas-

Continued on Page 41, Column 3

Warren Will Make India Goodwill Tour

By RUSSELL BAKER

Special to The New York Times.

WASHINGTON, July 26—Chief Justice Earl Warren will make a goodwill tour of India next month.

With White House approval, he has accepted an Indian invitation to make the trip in his official capacity as Chief Justice of the United States.

Officially, he will be responding to an invitation to visit India to observe the country's judicial system in action. In fact, however, the trip is bound to have diplomatic significance far overshadowing Mr. Warren's education in Indian law.

It comes in the wake of two

Continued on Page 4, Column 3

Stassen Holds Fire Pending a New Poll

By JAMES RESTON

Special to The New York Times.

WASHINGTON, July 26—Harold E. Stassen declared a temporary cease-fire in his one-man war against Vice President Richard M. Nixon today pending completion of another private poll on the comparative strengths of all potential Republican Vice-Presidential nominees.

Mr. Stassen is backing Gov. Christian A. Herter of Massachusetts for the Republican Vice Presidential nomination.

The President's special assistant on disarmament had breakfast this morning with the man whom he accused

Continued on Page 5, Column 2

CAPTAIN ARRIVES, SILENT ON CAUSES

Lauds Crew and Rescuers—Gives No Clue to Crash

Capt. Piero Calamai of the sunken Andrea Doria arrived in New York last night, haggard and weary, yet fully composed. But he offered no clue to the cause of his ship's collision with the Stockholm late Wednesday night.

The luxury liner's master arrived aboard the Navy destroyer escort Edward H. Allen. Seventy-six of his crew preceded him onto a Brooklyn Army Base pier. They were stooped and disconsolate. Many were dressed in makeshift clothing, some of it stained with blood. They responded only occasionally to the efforts United States Navy men made to ease their loss.

Captain Calamai, although his arrival was marked by none of the triumph that greeted the Andrea Doria's maiden voyage here in January, 1953, appeared tough and in full control of himself.

He paid tribute to the discipline and calmness of the passengers, and to the sense of duty of his men.

The Edward H. Allen docked

Continued on Page 9, Column 3

Safety Men Puzzled By Failure of Radar To Prevent Collision

By GEORGE HORNE

The loss of the Andrea Doria posed today two critical puzzles for American maritime safety experts.

In New York and Washington these questions were raised: How could two well-equipped ships collide with their radar working? And why did the Andrea Doria's vaunted stability fail?

Still another question was raised in New York. A group of survivors accused the Andrea Doria's crew members of having failed in their seafaring responsibilities. Other passengers, however, said they thought the picture of crew insufficiency was exaggerated and the natural result of excitement in the hours of travail. Some passengers praised the work of the Italian seamen under stress.

There appeared to be a fair chance that the enigmas would not be fully explored, at least in this country, because the United States Coast Guard lacks jurisdiction in Wednesday night's crash off Nantucket Lightship. The Coast Guard is the national arbiter on safety

Continued on Page 7, Column 6

PASSENGERS TELL OF FEAR IN NIGHT

But Survivors Also Recount Heroism on Board Liner

By HARRISON E. SALISBURY

Tales of bravery and sudden tragedy in the night were told yesterday by many of the 760 survivors of the Andrea Doria who arrived on the Ile de France.

The accent in the stories of the passengers was upon heroism. Apparently there was a minimum of panic and confusion aboard ship.

Because it was the ship's last night out, many passengers had not retired when the Stockholm struck. Many of them cited this as a reason for the comparatively low death toll. Some returned to their cabins to find the walls crushed by the sudden impact of the collision.

One of the most tragic stories was that reported about Col. Walter G. Carlin, a prominent Brooklyn Democratic political figure, and his wife.

The Carlins occupied Cabin 46 on the upper deck. It was here that the main brunt of the Stockholm's blow was felt.

Shipboard friends of the Carlins, Mr. and Mrs. Alfred Green

Continued on Page 6, Column 2

Huge Geysers Seen As Ship Goes Down

The following account was written by a news pool reporter, Edward McCarthy of The United Press. He flew over the scene of the collision at sea in a Coast Guard plane from Floyd Bennett Field, Brooklyn.

We hugged the shoreline of Long Island until we arrived at Nantucket. The ships in distress were located without any trouble, and at 9:50 A. M. we circled over the scene. We noted that the Andrea Dorea was listing 45 degrees on her starboard side with her bow partly submerged, the water-line up to the main deck.

The photographers took their pictures and we made a three-

Continued on Page 4, Column 3

Federal and City Officials Relax Regulations to Help Collision Survivors Enter U. S.

PASSPORT RULES ARE LAID ASIDE

Foreigners to Be Excused From Usual Procedures on Immigration

ITALIAN CONSUL AIDING

Public Health Service and Custom House Will Waive Ordinary Formalities

By JACQUES NEVARD

Federal, city and Italian Government officials joined forces yesterday to ease the entry into the United States of survivors of the collision between the Italian luxury ship Andrea Doria and the Swedish liner Stockholm.

The State Department waived its passport requirements for United States citizens who had lost their belongings aboard either vessel.

The Immigration and Naturalization Service anounced that foreign survivors of the Andrea Doria would be excused from formal immigration inspection for the time being and would have to furnish only their names and United States addresses at present.

The United States Public Health Service said it would limit its inspection of incoming survivors to a check for communicable diseases.

Italian Charge d'Affairs Egidio Ortona flew here from Washington to join officials of the Italian Consulate General in New York in offering assistance to Italian nationals who had been aboard the Andrea Doria.

Blank Declarations Planned

Robert W. Dill, Collector of Customs at the Port of New York, said that survivors of the Andrea Doria would be given blank Customs Declarations to sign if they had saved less than $500 of their possessions. He said he doubted that anyone had managed to carry that much into the lifeboats.

The officials announced these steps to the press after a meeting yesterday afternoon in Mr. Dill's office in the Custom House at the foot of Broadway.

Edward J. Shaughnessy, District Director of the Immigration and Naturalization Service, spoke for both the Passport Office and his own agency.

The meeting was attended by officials of the Italian Line and the Swedish American Line, operators of the two ships involved in the collision.

Capt. Piero Ferrari, Italian Line Port Captain, expressed his "deepest appreciation of the Government authorities and other steamship companies that went so gallantly to the rescue of the passengers and crewmen of the vessels."

He said his company would "do all we can to simplify the plight of these poor people."

Captain Ferrari added that the Italian Line would put up in hotels those survivors who had no other place to stay in the city.

Praise for Coast Guard

Mr. Dill had particular praise for the Coast Guard sea and air units that participated in the rescue.

New York City's Department of Marine and Aviation offered to put at the disposal of the rescuing vessels any open pier in the harbor.

The offer was made at a time when it was believed that Andrea Doria survivors aboard the French liner Ile de France would be taken off the ship at Quarantine by means of lighters. The idea was abandoned later in the day when it was learned that the Ile de France would proceed to her regular berth at West Forty-eighth Street and the Hudson River to discharge those whom she had rescued.

Mr. Shaughnessy said that brief instructions, in both English and Italian would be given to all alien survivors of the crash, informing them that immigration inspection was being dispensed with at this time.

The instruction sheet continued:

"We are merely asking for your name and address and any documents which you may have readily available.

"At a future date you will hear from an officer of the [Immigration and Naturalization] service closest to the address given and you will be instructed concerning the procedures which you should follow at that time.

"We make one request—that you notify the New York office of any change of address from the one given to us today."

Man Who Once Crossed Sea in Sloop Is Survivor

A Swedish yachtsman crossed the Atlantic early this month in his thirty-three-foot sloop and concluded that the most bothersome aspect of the voyage was "the feeling of loneliness."

Yngve Cassel, a 47-year-old machine parts manufacturer, moored his trim craft, the Casella, at City Island, the Bronx, eighty-three days and 6,478 miles from Falmouth, England. In an interview on July 5 he said that sailing was for unhappy people, that the trip was more "lonely" than hazardous.

Mr. Cassel's only shipmate, Klas Lindberg, a 23-year-old marine engineer, went job-hunting. Mr. Cassell planned to sell his sloop and waited for his wife Doris to join him by plane. The Cassels were aboard the liner Stockholm en route back to Europe Wednesday night when she collided with the Andrea Doria.

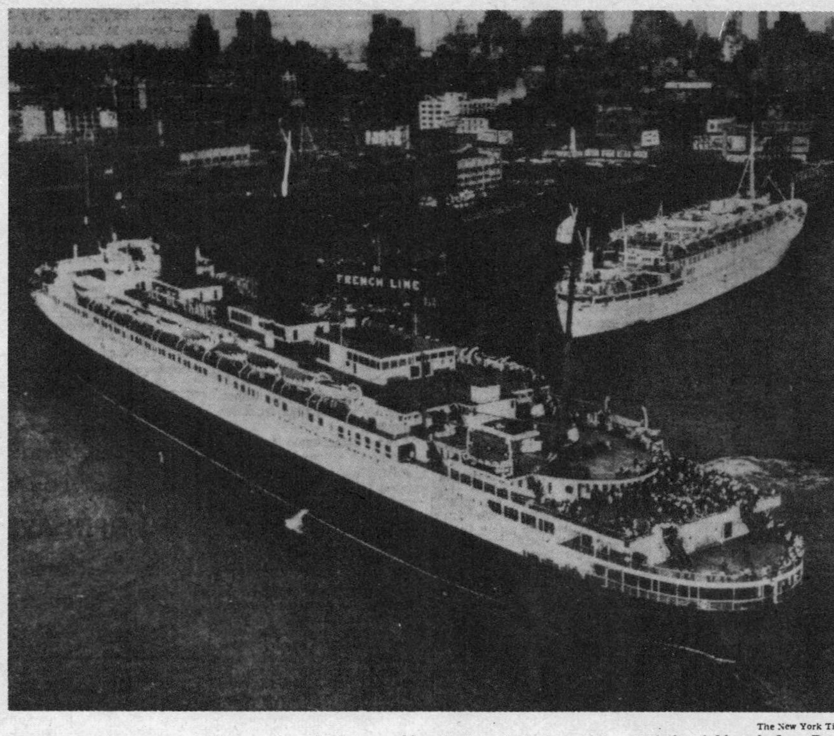

The New York Times

RESCUE SHIP: The Ile de France, largest of many ships that went to the assistance of the sinking Andrea Doria, moves up to Hudson River pier at Forty-eighth Street. She returned to put ashore throngs of survivors of the disaster.

PASSENGERS TELL OF FEAR IN NIGHT

Continued From Page 1

of New Rochelle, had invited them to join them in the lounge for a drink. But the Carlins were tired and declined. Mrs. Carlin had retired and was reading in her bed. Mr. Carlin was brushing his teeth toward the end of a fairly long corridor leading from the cabin.

At that moment the collision occurred. Mr. Carlin was knocked from his feet. When he picked himself up, dazed, and made his way toward the cabin, the Greens reported, he saw nothing but a gaping hole. The side of the ship had been sheered off and Mrs. Carlin had vanished, apparently a victim of the tragedy.

Narrow escapes were common. Istvan Rabovsky and his wife, Nora Kovach, ballet dancers who fled from their native Hungary in a spectacular crossing of the Iron Curtain, again came close to tragedy. They occupied a cabin not far from that of the Carlins and had retired before the shock came.

Both rushed to the promenade deck in their underclothes. They reported—as did many passengers—that there was considerable smoke in the area where the ship was hit.

Ruth Roman, the motion-picture actress, was returning from Italy with her 3½-year-old son, Dickie. She was dancing in the Belvedere Room when "we heard a big explosion like a firecracker." She said she saw smoke coming from the general area of her cabins, 82 and 84, but when she reached there her son was fast asleep.

'Going on a Picnic'

Miss Roman and a companion, Mrs. Grace Ells, awoke the boy and told him: "We are going on a picnic."

There was a considerable wait for lifeboats. Finally, Miss Roman handed the boy over to seamen who lowered him to a boat. She started to climb down a rope ladder to join the boy, but when she was half way down the lifeboat pulled away. She shouted but it continued away from the Andrea Doria.

She was put on the next lifeboat and had received no further word of her youngster as he apparently was put aboard another rescue boat.

Miss Roman was convinced her son was safe. She said she thought he probably would get a thrill out of the excitement without realizing the danger in which he had been.

There were several Roman Catholic sisters aboard the Andrea Doria. Among them were Sister Marie Raymond, Grand Rapids, Mich., and Sister Mary Callistus, London, Ont., returning after a year of music studies in Florence.

The sisters traveling together in cabin class, said that a moment after the impact "we heard screaming."

"We had no idea what had happened," one said. "We put on our clothes and our life preservers and got on the deck. We had had boat drill and we went to our muster stations. The people were marvellous. There was a steward there and he made everyone feel very secure. They took off the women and children first. The children were taken by the seamen who tied them together for safety."

Crash Knocked Down Tables

Among the passengers also was a group of executives of the Standard Oil Company (New Jersey). They included Dr. Stewart Coleman of 365 Barrett Road, Cedarhurst, L. I., and his family, Marion W. Boyer of Greenwich, Conn., and his wife, both directors of the concern, and H. G. Burks Jr., of Elizabeth, N. J., and his wife.

"We were playing bridge on the boat deck when the crash occurred," Mr. Burks said. "It was a substantial jar and it knocked down tables and drinks. We headed for our cabins, which were away from the collision area."

Mr. Burks said his party picked up coats and life preservers and went to the deck. The vessel was listing sharply to starboard.

"We took a place where we thought we would be clear if the ship sank," Mr. Burks said. "After a time the rescue boats arrived and they began to take the ladies and children off."

Mr. Burks said the Andrea Doria crew behaved well. However, he criticized the failure of the ship's management to make any announcement in English of what had happened.

"It was bad to be left in the dark so far as any official word of what was going on was concerned," he said. "However, both crew and passengers were very orderly."

The bridge party in which the Burks were participating at the moment of the accident included Dr. Coleman and Dr. and Mrs. R. B. Boggs, Manhasset, N. Y.

Moris Novik, president of radio station WOV, New York, and his wife were in the Belvedere room at the time of the accident.

The orchestra, Mr. Novik recalled, was playing "Arrivaderci, Roma" (Farewell, Roma).

"They had been playing that tune all night," Mr. Novik said. "They had just started again when the crash came. At first it didn't seem too bad. Of course the tables went over and drinks were spilled."

The fog was very heavy at the time of the crash, Mr. Novik said. By the time the Ile de France arrived the fog had lifted a bit and the moon had come out.

Mr. Novik said that the Andrea Doria had listed so badly that it was extremely difficult to get people down to the boats.

"We formed chains of hands on the deck," he said, "and passed the women down the chain until a member of the crew picked them up and helped them over the side and down the ladder."

Mayor Richardson Dilworth of Philadelphia and his wife occupied cabin No. 80 on the upper deck. The Stockholm plowed into the Andrea Doria about sixty to seventy feet ahead of the Dilworth's cabin.

"We were in our cabin asleep," the Mayor said. "The crash not only awoke us—it threw us face to face. Thank God the lights stayed on. We threw on some clothes. There was a lot of smoke in the hall. We had to crawl down the passageway and up the gangways because the boat had tilted so badly. It must have taken us twenty minutes to climb up to the boat deck."

Mayor Dilworth said it was extremely difficult to get the life boats off because of the extreme list.

"The decks were like skating rinks," he said. "Half the passengers were over 45. It was quite wonderful to see how they reacted without panic and without pushing around. Quite a few people got broken arms on the slippery decks. Mrs. Dilworth was badly bruised."

Mrs. Ellen Dean of Baltimore said she was in the ballroom dancing.

"I happened to look out the window," Mrs. Dean said, "and there was another ship. It was right on top of us. A moment later it struck us. I could see its lights and everything. The rails almost touched ours. It was the Stockholm."

Betsy Drake, actress wife of Cary Grant, emerged from the disaster in her stocking feet.

"I was getting ready for bed," she said, "when there was a big bang. Everything flew across the room. My cabin was on the boat deck. I got dressed and found the decks very difficult and slippery. Finally one of the sailors told me to get into a boat and I slid down the deck to the ladder."

Ile de France Sails for Le Havre Again; Schedule Disrupted by Her Rescue Job

When the Ile de France sailed again at 8:20 last night for Europe she was thirty-six hours behind her schedule in what is still the peak of the season.

Franch Line officials here were not certain how the delay would affect future sailings, but they hoped that the lost time would be made up by the end of her next voyage.

The 23-knot liner originally was due to arrive at Le Havre next Wednesday and sail from there for the return trip next Friday. She will now probably arrive on Friday. It was possible that she might make an immediate turn-around, or at latest sail again on Saturday, Aug. 4.

The 44,500-ton, 793-foot ship was launched at the Penhoet shipyards in St. Nazaire, France in June 1926 and made her maiden voyage just one year later. At the time she was the largest ship launched since World War I. She quickly built up a reputation as one of the most pleasant to travel on in spite of larger ships which later sailed in competition.

In six years of World War II duty she carried 626,000 troops to every corner of the globe, and she was a tired and battered craft at the end of hostilities. The Penhoet yards then rebuilt her "from the portholes in" installing new machinery and modern passenger accomodations. Minus one of her three original smokestacks, but with the same old distinguished lines of her hull, she made her first post-war crossing as a full-fledged luxury liner in July 1949.

FOREIGN AID STUDY SET

Senate Unit Will Serve While Congress Is Not in Session

WASHINGTON, July 26 (UP)—Senator Walter F. George, Democrat of Georgia, named today six members of a special Senate committee to study foreign aid to serve as an executive committee while Congress is not in session.

Senator Theodore Francis Green, Democrat of Rhode Island, who is in line to succeed Mr. George as chairman of the Foreign Relations Committee, was named chairman of the executive committee.

Other members are Senators Richard B. Russell of Georgia and J. William Fulbright of Arkansas, Democrats, and Styles Bridges of New Hampshire, H. Alexander Smith of New Jersey and William F. Knowland of California, Republicans.

The special committee is composed of all members of the Foreign Relations group, plus the ranking Democratic and Republican members of the Appropriations and Armed Services Committees.

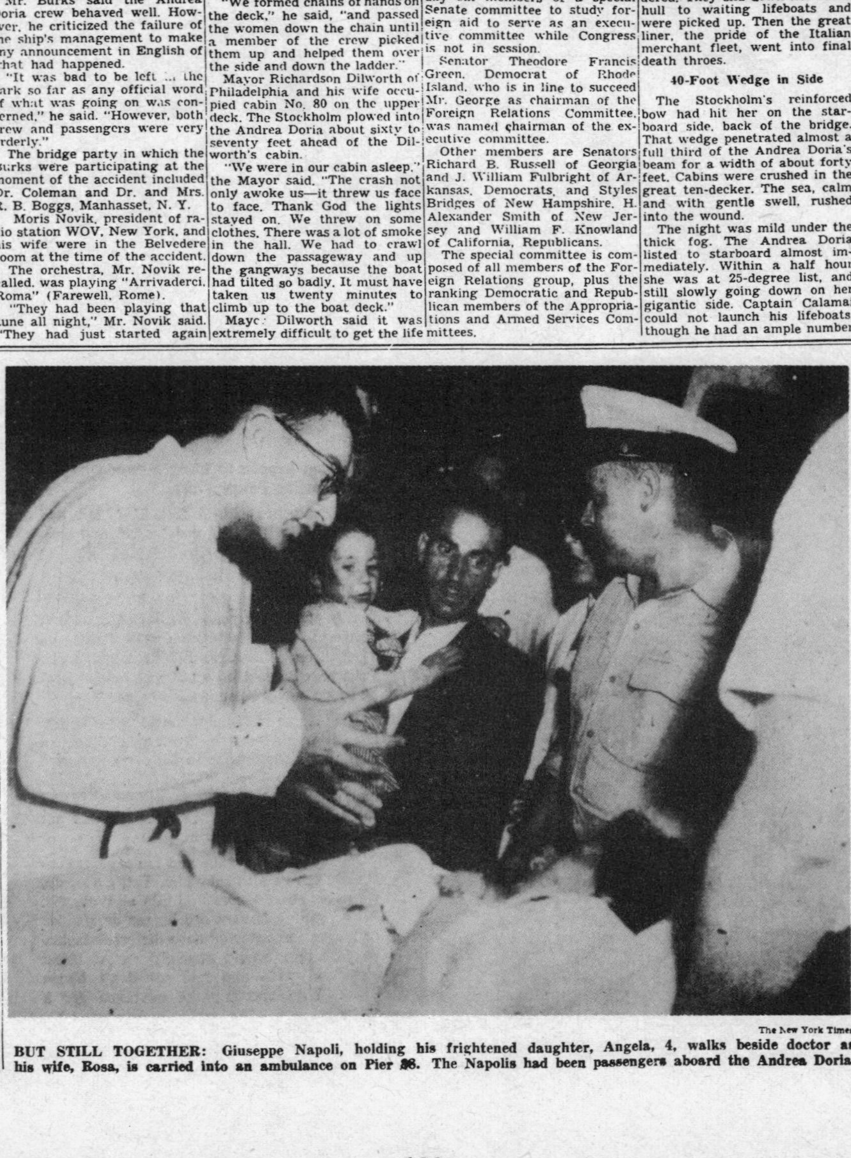

The New York Times

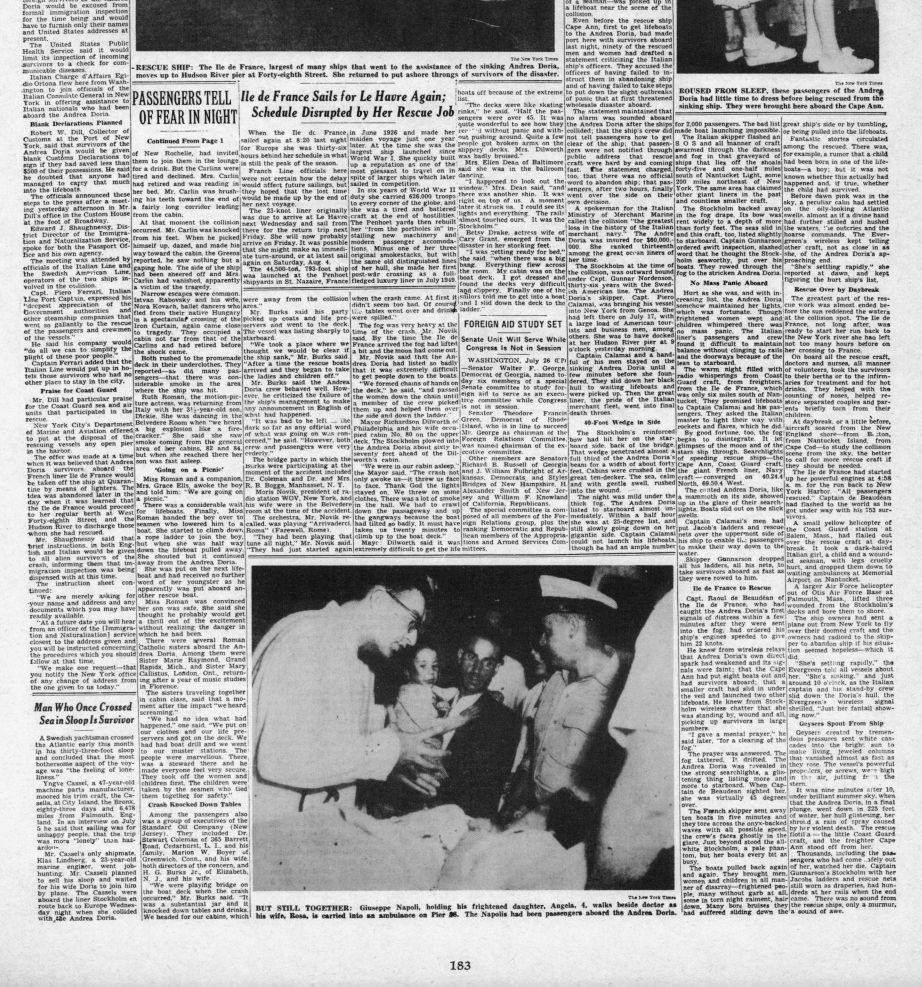

BUT STILL TOGETHER: Giuseppe Napoli, holding his frightened daughter, Angela, 4, walks beside doctor as his wife, Rosa, is carried into an ambulance on Pier 88. The Napolis had been passengers aboard the Andrea Doria.

4 SHIPS ARRIVE WITH SURVIVORS

Continued From Page 1

make her pier in the Hudson River around noon today if the seas held calm and smooth, as they were off Nantucket at the moment of collision.

The Coast Guard was still checking the total number of survivors last night by radio recount with incoming rescue craft, with hospitals on Nantucket Island and with Boston.

On the list of the dead were included Camille Cianfarra, New York Times correspondent, and his two children, Linda, 14 years old, Joan, 8. Mr. Cianfarra was returning from his Madrid post for a vacation in New York. (Mrs. Cianfarra, pinned by a timber in her cabin, was rescued but has leg injuries. She was brought in on the Ile de France.)

Others feared to have died were: Mrs. Martha Peterson, wife of Dr. Thure S. Peterson of the Chiropractic Institute of New York, whose home is in Upper Montclair in New Jersey; Mrs. Walter Carlin, wife of Col. Walter J Carlin, a prominent figure in Democratic politics in Brooklyn Alf Johannsan of the crew of the Stockholm was flown to Nantucket Island with other persons. He died soon afterward.

Another body—apparently that of a seaman—was picked up in a lifeboat near the scene of the collision.

Even before the rescue ship Cape Ann, first to get lifeboats to the Andrea Doria, had made port here with survivors aboard last night, ninety of the rescued men and women had drafted a statement criticizing the Italian ship's officers. They accused the officers of having failed to instruct them in abandoning ship and of having failed to take steps to put down the slight outbreaks of panic that at first threatened wholesale disaster aboard.

The statement maintained that no alarm was sounded aboard the Andrea Doria after the ships collided; that the ship's crew did not tell passengers how to get clear of the ship; that passengers were not notified through public address that rescue craft were hard by and coming fast. The statement charged, too, that there was no official word to abandon ship; that passengers, after two hours, finally went over the side on their own decision.

A spokesman for the Italian Ministry of Merchant Marine called the collision "the greatest loss in the history of the Italian merchant navy." The Andre Doria was insured for $60,000,000. She ranked thirteenth among the great ocean liners of her time.

The Stockholm at the time of the collision, was outward bound under Capt. Gunnar Nordenson, thirty-six years with the Swedish American line. The Andrea Doria's skipper, Capt. Piero Calamai, was bringing his vessel into New York from Genoa. She had left there on July 17, with a large load of American tourists and business men, among others. She was to have docked at her Hudson River pier at 9 o'clock yesterday morning.

Captain Calamai and a handful of his men stayed on the sinking Andrea Doria until a few minutes before she foundered. They slid down her black hull to waiting lifeboats and were picked up. Then the great liner, the pride of the Italian merchant fleet, went into final death throes.

40-Foot Wedge in Side

The Stockholm's reinforced bow had hit her on the starboard side, back of the bridge. That wedge penetrated almost a full third of the Andrea Doria's beam for a width of about forty feet. Cabins were crushed in the great ten-decker. The sea, calm and with gentle swell, rushed into the wound.

The night was mild under the thick fog. The Andrea Doria listed to starboard almost immediately. Within a half hour she was at 25-degree list, and still slowly going down on her gigantic side. Captain Calamai could not launch his lifeboats, though he had an ample number for 2,000 passengers. The bad list made boat launching impossible.

The Italian skipper flashed an S O S and all manner of craft swarmed through the darkness and fog in that graveyard of ships that lies off the shoals forty-five and one-half miles south of Nantucket Light, some 200 miles northeast of New York. The same area has claimed other giant liners in the past and countless smaller craft.

The Stockholm backed away in the fog drape. Its bow was rent widely to a depth of more than forty feet. The seas slid in and this craft, too, listed slightly to starboard. Captain Gunnarson ordered swift inspection, slashed word that he thought the Stockholm seaworthy, put over his boats. They rowed through the fog to the stricken Andrea Doria.

No Mass Panic Aboard

Hurt as she was, and with increasing list, the Andrea Doria somehow maintained her lights, which was fortunate. Though frightened women wept and children whimpered there was no mass panic. The Italian liner's passengers and crew found it difficult to maintain balance without clinging to rails and the doorways because of the lean to starboard.

The warm night filled with radio whisperings from Coast Guard craft, from freighters, from the Ile de France, which was only six miles south of Nantucket. They promised lifeboats to Captain Calamai and his passengers. They asked the Italian master to light their way with rockets and flares, which he did.

By good fortune, too, the fog began to disintegrate. It let glimpses of the moon and of the stars slip through. Searchlights of speeding rescue ships—the Cape Ann, Coast Guard craft, the giant French liner, Navy craft — converged on 40.24.4 North, 69.50.4 West.

The canted Andrea Doria, like a mammoth on its side, showed up in the glare of their searchlights. Boats slid out on the slick swells.

Captain Calamai's men had put Jacob's ladders and rescue nets over the uppermost side of his ship to enable the passengers to make their way down to the water.

Skipper Gunnarson dropped all his ladders, all his nets, to take survivors aboard as fast as they were rowed to him.

Ile de France to Rescue

Capt. Raoul de Beaudéan of the Ile de France, who had caught the Andrea Doria's first signals of distress within a few minutes after they were sent into the fog, had ordered his ship's engines speeded to give him 22 knots.

He knew from wireless relays that Andrea Doria's own direct spark had weakened and its signals were faint; that the Cape Ann had put eight boats out and had survivors aboard; that a smaller craft had slid in under the veil and launched two other lifeboats. He knew from Stockholm wireless chatter that she was standing by, wound and all, picking up survivors in large numbers.

"I gave a mental prayer," he said later, "for a clearing of the fog."

The prayer was answered. The fog tattered. It drifted. The Andrea Doria was revealed in the strong searchlights, a glistening thing listing more and more to starboard. When Captain de Beaudean sighted her, she was virtually 45 degrees over.

The French skipper sent away ten boats in five minutes and they tore across the onyx-backed waves with all possible speed, the crew's faces ghostly in the glare. Just beyond stood the all-white Stockholm, a pale phantom, but her boats every bit as busy.

The boats pulled back again and again. They brought men, women and children in all manner of disarray—frightened people, many without garb at all, some in torn night raiment, hair down. Many bore bruises they had suffered sliding down the great ship's side or by tumbling, or being pulled into the lifeboats.

Fantastic stories circulated among the rescued. There was, for example, a rumor that a child had been born in one of the lifeboats—a boy; but it was not known whether this actually had happened and, if true, whether the child had survived.

Before dawn pink was in the sky, a peculiar calm had settled on the oily-looking Atlantic swells, almost as if a divine hand had further stilled and hushed the waters, the outcries and the hoarse commands. The Evergreen's wireless kept telling other craft, not as close in as she, of the Andrea Doria's approaching end.

"She's settling rapidly," she reported at dawn, and kept figuring the hurt ship's list.

Rescue Over by Daybreak

The greatest part of the rescue work was almost ended before the sun reddened the waters at the collision spot. The Ile de France, not long after, was ready to start her run back to the New York river she had left not too many hours before on her crossing to France.

On board all the rescue craft, doctors and nurses, all manner of volunteers, took the survivors to their berths or to the infirmaries for treatment and for hot drinks. They helped with the counting of noses, helped restore separated couples and parents briefly torn from their children.

At daybreak, or a little before, aircraft soared from the New England shore—from Boston, from Nantucket Island, from Cape Cod—to study the collision scene from the sky, the better to call for more rescue craft if they should be needed.

The Ile de France had started up her powerful engines at 4:58 a. m. for the run back to New York Harbor. "All passengers rescued." Captain de Beaudéan had flashed to the world as he got under way with his 753 survivors.

A small yellow helicopter of the Coast Guard station at Salem, Mass., had flailed out over the rescue craft at daybreak. It took a dark-haired Italian girl, a child and a wounded seaman, with legs cruelly hurt, and dropped them down to waiting ambulances at Memorial Airport on Nantucket.

A larger Air Force helicopter out of Otis Air Force Base at Falmouth, Mass., lifted three wounded from the Stockholm's decks and bore them to shore.

The ship owners had sent a plane out from New York to fly over their doomed craft and the owners had radioed to the skipper to abandon ship if his situation seemed hopeless—which it did.

"She's settling rapidly," the Evergreen told all vessels about her. "She's sinking," and just around 10 o'clock, as the Italian captain and his stand-by crew slid down the Doria's hull, the Evergreen's wireless signal shrilled, "Just her fantail showing now."

Geysers Spout From Ship

Geysers created by tremendous pressures sent white cascades into the bright sun to make living, jeweled columns that vanished almost as fast as they rose. The vessel's powerful propellers, or screws, were high in the air, jutting from the stern.

It was nine minutes after 10, under brilliant summer sky, when that the Andrea Doria, in a final plunge, went down in 225 feet of water, her hull glistening, her shroud a rain of spray caused by her violent death. The rescue flotilla — the little Coast Guard craft, and the freighter Cape Ann stood off from her.

Thousands, including the passengers who had come safely out of her, watched her die. Captain Gunnarson's Stockholm with her Jacobs ladders and rescue nets still worn as draperies, had hundreds at her rails when the end came. There was no sound from the rescue ships, only a murmur, a sound of awe.

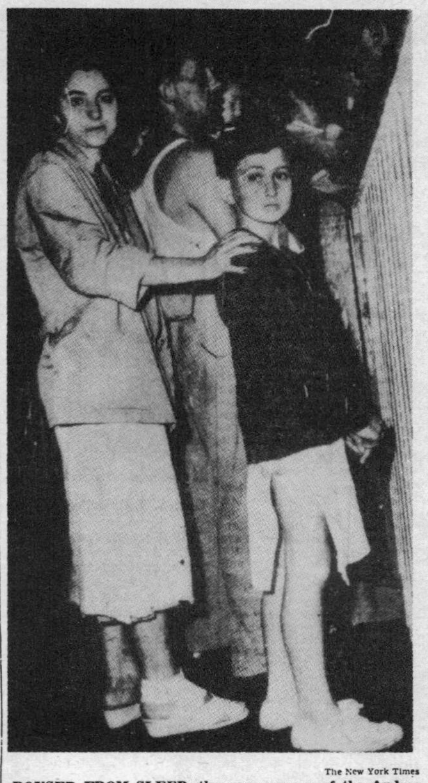

The New York Times

ROUSED FROM SLEEP, these passengers of the Andrea Doria had little time to dress before being rescued from the sinking ship. They were brought here aboard the Cape Ann.

Liner Stockholm Is Expected to Arrive at Pier 97 This Noon With 533 Survivors

SHIP IN NO DANGER; MOVES AT 7 KNOTS

Coast Guard Cutter Escorts Damaged Vessel on Her Return to Dock Here

PASSENGERS TO BE AIDED

Line Is Making Plans for New Passage on Other Craft for Those Brought Back

The stricken Swedish liner Stockholm is moving toward New York under her own power at an estimated speed of seven knots and was expected early today to reach here this noon.

The ship, being escorted by the Coast Guard Cutters Owasco and Tamaroa was said to be proceeding "satisfactorily" and appeared to be in no danger. She is bringing 533 survivors of the Andrea Doria—320 passengers and 213 crew—in addition to her own 535 passengers and 215 crewmen.

Communication with the vessel, at least in so far as the Swedish American Line was concerned, was virtually impossible throughout yesterday. Only two or three terse wireless messages were received from the Stockholm's master, Capt. Gunnar Nordenson, and those related to the condition of the liner, the number of survivors aboard and the estimated arrival time here.

A spokesman for the line said executives at the office had been unable to contact the ship by radiotelephone, as her facilities had been under "emergency" use. He said a list of the survivors aboard should be available early this morning.

The Swedish American Line has decided to bring the damaged vessel to her own dock, Pier 97, Hudson River, at West Fifty-seventh Street. However, it was emphasized that no visitors would be permitted to enter the pier. Arrangements have been made to disembark the Stockholm's passengers via a forward gangplank, while the survivors of the Andrea Doria will use an aft gangway.

Survivors to Go to Pier 84

The passengers and crew of the Italian liner will be whisked off Pier 97 as soon as they debark and taken in buses to Pier 84 at West Forty-fourth Street. Pier 84 was the usual berth for the Andrea Doria.

Meanwhile, the Swedish American Line will attempt to make as many rerouting arrangements as possible while the Stockholm's passengers are still on the pier. An official of the line said arrangements had been made to transfer 200 persons to the Norwegian America Line's Bergensfjord, which will depart for Scandinavian ports next Wednesday morning. About forty more will sail on the Kungsholm, another Swedish American Line vessel, when she leaves next Friday morning.

The official said offers of space had been received from virtually all airlines flying the Atlantic, along with proffers of berths aboard ships headed for Europe.

Every effort will be made, he said, to complete as many arrangements for Stockholm passengers as possible on the dock, but representatives of the line will be in contact with passengers at the hotels they are placed in. The company's offices will remain open throughout the week-end to facilitate the rerouting, it was explained.

A three-man "inspection" group is flying from Sweden to survey the damaged Stockholm, the company announced yesterday afternoon. Capt. John Petterson, a director of the line; Hilding Bergenheim, from its technical department, and a representative of the underwriters are expected to reach here this morning.

Arrangements have been made for repairs to the Stockholm to be made here by the Todd Shipyards Corporation. Officials of the Swedish American Line declined to estimate the extent of the ship's damage or the length of time she will be out of service.

Islamic Groups Meet Today

The fifth annual convention of the Federation of Islamic Associations in the United States and Canada will open today at the New Yorker Hotel. Yesterday the Islamic Council of New York announced through its president, Ibrahim Chowdry, that it would not participate. Mr. Chowdry said the Islamic Council did not "approve of the acts or the spirit of the host organization, which represents a handful of people in this area."

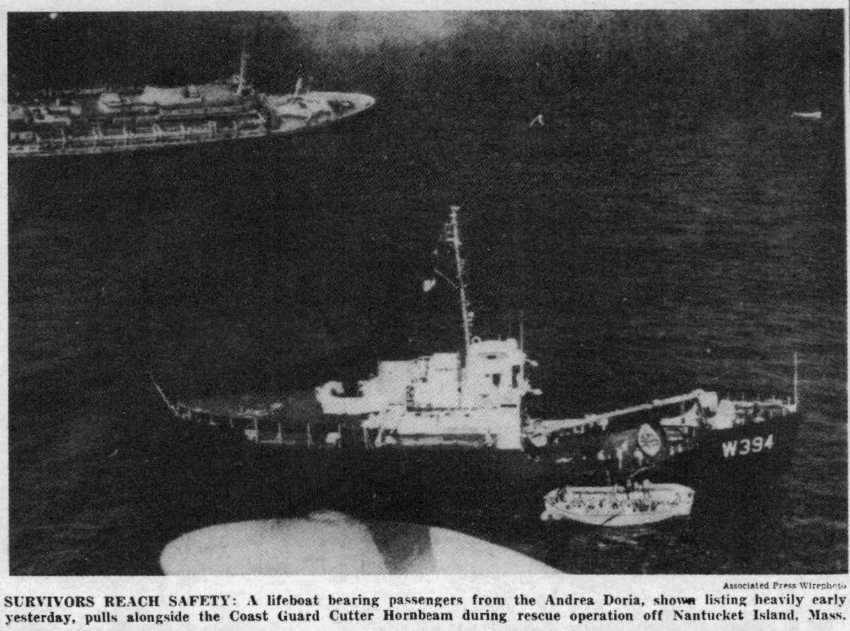
W394

Associated Press Wirephoto

SURVIVORS REACH SAFETY: A lifeboat bearing passengers from the Andrea Doria, shown listing heavily early yesterday, pulls alongside the Coast Guard Cutter Hornbeam during rescue operation off Nantucket Island, Mass.

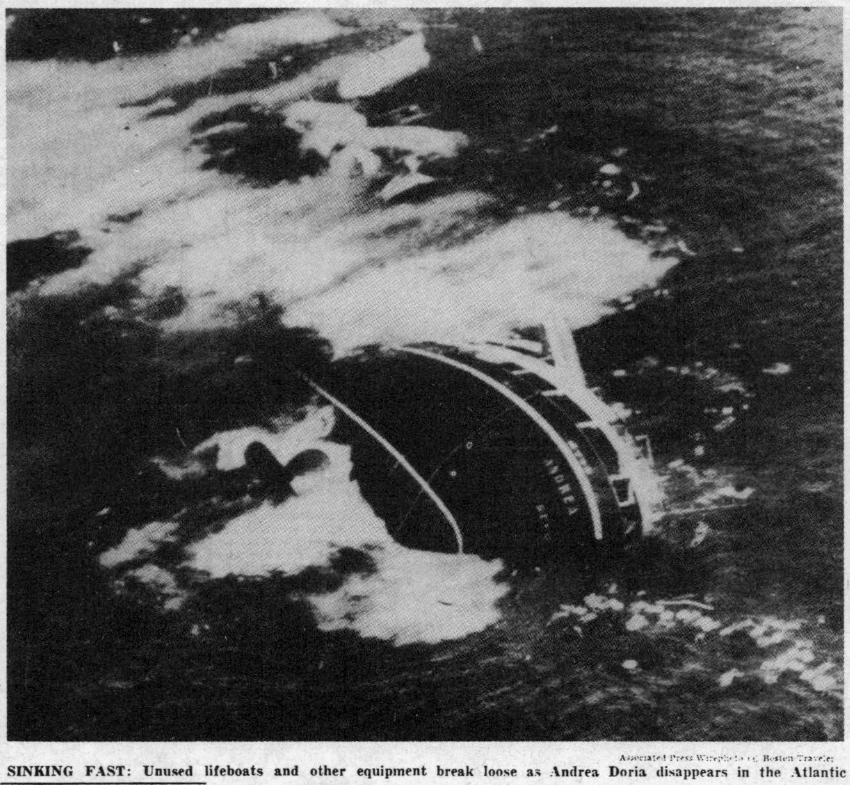

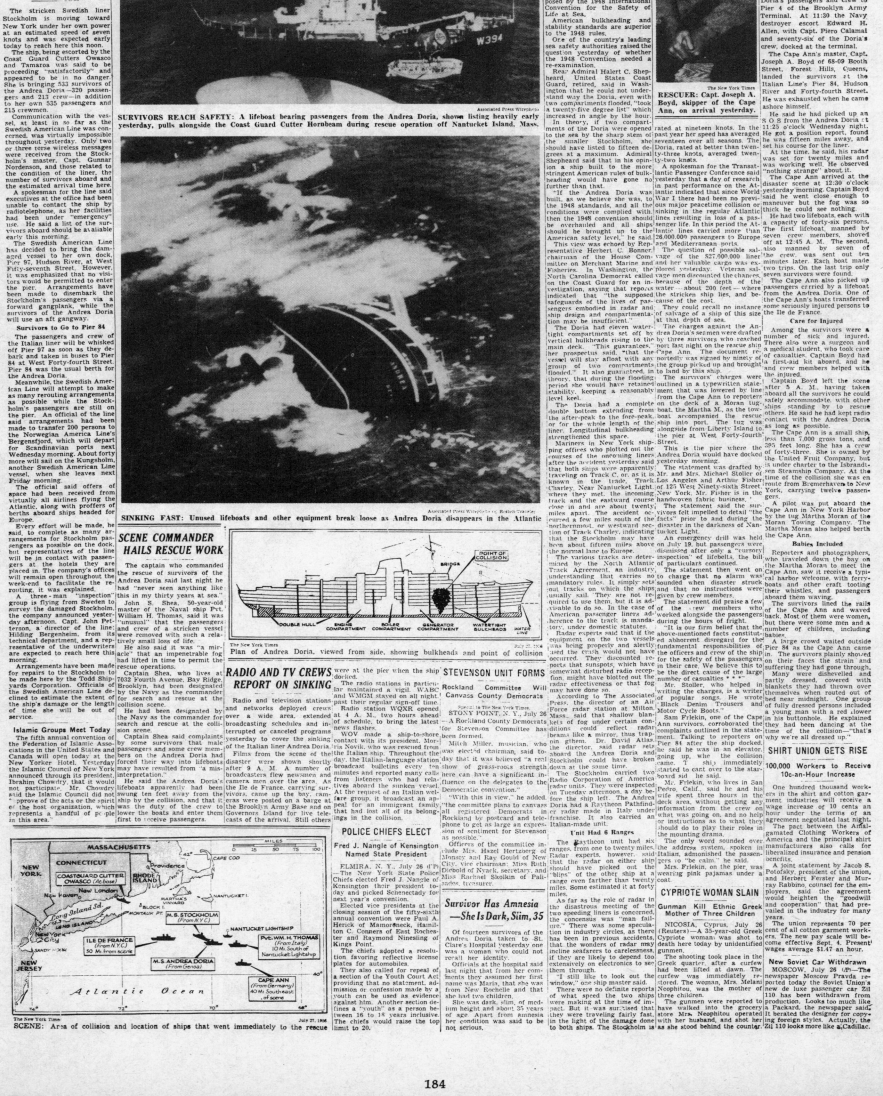

Associated Press Wirephoto via Boston Traveler

SINKING FAST: Unused lifeboats and other equipment break loose as Andrea Doria disappears in the Atlantic

SCENE COMMANDER HAILS RESCUE WORK

The captain who commanded the rescue of survivors of the Andrea Doria said last night he had "never seen anything like this in my thirty years at sea."

John S. Shea, 50-year-old master of the Naval ship Pvt. William H. Thomas, said it was "unusual" that the passengers and crew of a stricken vessel were removed with such a relatively small loss of life.

He also said it was "a miracle" that an impenetrable fog had lifted in time to permit the rescue operations.

Captain Shea, who lives at 7032 Fourth Avenue, Bay Ridge, Brooklyn, had been designated by the Navy as the commander for search and rescue at the collision scene.

He had been designated by the Navy as the commander for search and rescue at the collision scene.

Captain Shea said complaints by some survivors that male passengers and some crew members on the Andrea Doria had forced their way into lifeboats may have resulted from "a misinterpretation."

He said the Andrea Doria's lifeboats apparently had been swung ten feet away from the ship by the collision, and that it was the duty of the crew to lower the boats and enter them first to receive passengers.

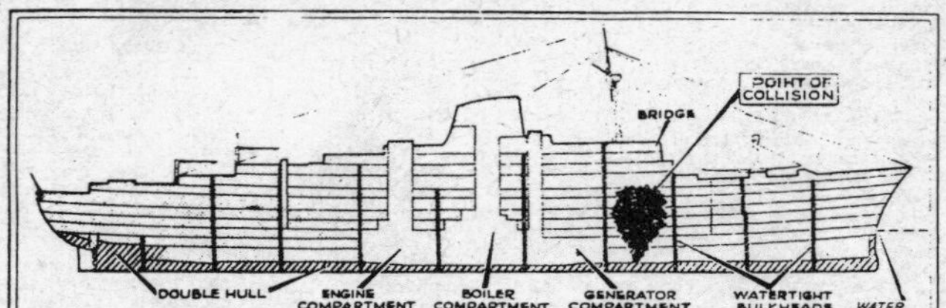
POINT OF COLLISION
BRIDGE
DOUBLE HULL
ENGINE COMPARTMENT
BOILER COMPARTMENT
GENERATOR COMPARTMENT
WATERTIGHT BULKHEADS
WATER LINE

The New York Times July 27, 1956

Plan of Andrea Doria, viewed from side, showing bulkheads and point of collision

RADIO AND TV CREWS REPORT ON SINKING

Radio and television stations and networks deployed crews over a wide area, extended broadcasting schedules and interrupted or canceled programs yesterday to cover the sinking of the Italian liner Andrea Doria.

Films from the scene of the disaster were shown shortly after 9 A. M. A number of broadcasters flew newsmen and camera men over the area. As the Ile de France, carrying survivors, came up the bay, cameras were posted on a barge at the Brooklyn Army Base and on Governors Island for live telecasts of the arrival. Still others were at the pier when the ship docked.

The radio stations in particular maintained a vigil. WABC and WMGM stayed on all night, past their regular sign-off time.

Radio station WQXR opened at 4 A. M., two hours ahead of schedule, to bring the latest news flashes.

WOV made a ship-to-shore contact with its president, Morris Novik, who was rescued from the Italian ship. Throughout the day, the Italian-language station broadcast bulletins every ten minutes and reported many calls from listeners who had relatives aboard the sunken vessel. At the request of an Italian welfare group, it broadcast an appeal for an immigrant family that had lost all of its belongings in the collision.

POLICE CHIEFS ELECT

Fred J. Nangle of Kensington Named State President

ELMIRA, N. Y., July 26 (UP)—The New York State Police Chiefs elected Fred J. Nangle of Kensington their president today and picked Schenectady for next year's convention.

Elected vice presidents at the closing session of the fifty-sixth annual convention were Paul A. Herick of Mamaroneck, Hamilton C. Conners of East Rochester and Raymond Ninesling of Kings Point.

The chiefs adopted a resolution favoring reflective license plates for automobiles.

They also called for repeal of a section of the Youth Court Act providing that no statement, admission or confession made by a youth can be used as evidence against him. Another section defines a "youth" as a person between 16 to 18 years inclusive. The chiefs would raise the top limit to 20.

STEVENSON UNIT FORMS

Rockland Committee Will Canvass County Democrats

Special to The New York Times.

STONY POINT, N. Y., July 26—A Rockland County Democrats for Stevenson Committee has been formed.

Mitch Miller, musician, who was elected chairman, said today that it was believed "a real show of grass-roots strength here can have a significant influence on the delegates to the Democratic convention."

"With this in view," he added, "the committee plans to canvass all registered Democrats in Rockland by postcard and telephone to get as large an expression of sentiment for Stevenson as possible."

Officers of the committee include Mrs. Hazel Hertzberg of Monsey and Ray Gould of New City, vice chairman; Miss Ruth Diebold of Nyack, secretary, and Miss Rachael Skolkin of Palisades, treasurer.

Survivor Has Amnesia —She Is Dark, Slim, 35

Of fourteen survivors of the Andrea Doria taken to St. Clare's Hospital yesterday one was a woman who could not recall her identity.

Officials at the hospital said last night that from her comments they assumed her first name was Maria, that she was from New Rochelle and that she had two children.

She was dark, slim, of medium height and about 35 years of age. Apart from amnesia her condition was said to be not serious.

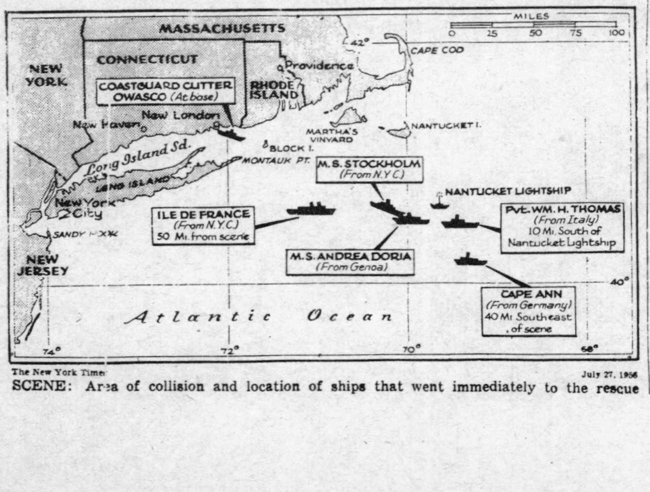
MILES
0 25 50 75 100
MASSACHUSETTS
CONNECTICUT
NEW YORK
COASTGUARD CUTTER OWASCO (At base)
RHODE ISLAND
Providence
CAPE COD
42°
New London
New Haven
MARTHA'S VINYARD
NANTUCKET I.
BLOCK I.
MONTAUK PT.
Long Island Sd.
LONG ISLAND
New York City
M.S. STOCKHOLM (From N.Y.C.)
NANTUCKET LIGHTSHIP
ILE DE FRANCE (From N.Y.C.) 50 Mi. from scene
Pvt. WM. H. THOMAS (From Italy) 10 Mi. South of Nantucket Lightship
M.S. ANDREA DORIA (From Genoa)
NEW JERSEY
40°
CAPE ANN (From Germany) 40 Mi. Southeast of scene
Atlantic Ocean
74°
72°
70°
68°

The New York Times July 27, 1956

SCENE: Area of collision and location of ships that went immediately to the rescue

SURVIVORS ASSAIL THE DORIA'S CREW

Continued From Page 1

matters. In the case of American ships involved in sea disasters and of ships of any flag involved in trouble in American waters, it conducts a formal and exhaustive inquiry.

The inquiries usually result in an assignment of blame.

Both ships were under foreign flag and the crash occurred beyond local waters, so the Coast Guard will not hold an inquiry unless requested to do so by Sweden or Italy. Litigation in admiralty through damage cases may bring out the details, however.

The Andrea Doria was built stritctly to the standards imposed by the 1948 International Convention for the Safety of Life at Sea.

American bulkheading and stability standards are superior to the 1948 rules.

One of the country's leading sea safety authorities raised the question yesterday of whether the 1948 Convention needed a re-examination.

Rear Admiral Halert C. Shepheard, United States Coast Guard, retired, said in Washington that he could not understand why the Doria, even with two compartments flooded, "took a twenty-five degree list" which increased in angle by the hour.

In theory, if two compartments of the Doria were opened to the sea by the sharp stem of the smaller Stockholm, she should have listed to fifteen degrees at a maximum. Admiral Shepheard said that in his opinion a ship built to the more stringent American rules of bulkheading would have gone no further than that.

"If the Andrea Doria was built, as we believe she was, to the 1948 standards, and all the conditions were complied with, then the 1948 convention should be overhauled and all ships should be brought up to the American safety level," he said.

This view was echoed by Representative Herbert C. Bonner, chairman of the House Committee on Merchant Marine and Fisheries. In Washington, the North Carolina Democrat called on the Coast Guard for an investigation, saying that reports indicated that "the supposed safeguards of the lives of passengers embodied in radar and ship design and compartmentation may be insufficient."

The Doria had eleven watertight compartments set off by vertical bulkheads rising to the main deck. "This guarantees," her prospectus said, "that the vessel will stay afloat with any group of two compartments flooded." It also guaranteed, in theory, that during the flooding period she would have retained stability, keeping a reasonably level keel.

The Doria had a complete double bottom extending from the after-peak to the fore-peak, or for the whole length of the liner. Longitudinal bulkheading strengthened this space.

Mariners in New York shipping offices who plotted out the courses of the oncoming liners after the accident yesterday said that both ships were apparently traveling on Track C, or, as it is known in the trade, Track Charley, Near Nantucket Light, where they met, the incoming track and the eastward course close in and are about twenty miles apart. The accident occurred a few miles south of the northernmost, or westward section of Track Charley, indicating that the Stockholm may have been about fifteen miles above the normal lane to Europe.

The various tracks are determined by the North Atlantic Track Agreement, an industry understanding that carries no mandatory rules. It simply sets out tracks on which the ships usually sail. They are not required to use them, but it is advisable to do so. In the case of American passenger liners adherence to the track is mandatory, under domestic statutes.

Radar experts said that if the equipment on the two vessels was being properly and alertly used the crash would not have occurred. They discounted reports that sunspots, which have somewhat disturbed radio reception, might have blotted out the radar effectiveness or that fog may have done so.

According to The Associated Press, the director of an Air Force radar station at Milton, Mass., said that shallow blankets of fog under certain conditions could reflect radar beams like a mirror, thus trappin gthem. Dr. David Atlas, the director, said radar sets aboard the Andrea Doria and Stockholm could have broken down at the same time.

The Stockholm carried two Radio Corporation of America radar units. They were inspected on Tuesday afternoon, a day before the ship left. The Andrea Doria had a Raytheon Pathfinder radar made in Italy under franchise. It also carried an Italian-made unit.

Unit Had 6 Ranges

The Raytheon unit had six ranges, from one to twenty miles. Radar experts, however, said that the radar on either ship should have picked out the "blips" of the other ship at a range even farther than twenty miles. Some estimated it at forty miles.

As far as the role of radar in the disastrous meeting of the two speeding liners is concerned, the concensus was "man failure." There was some speculation in industry circles, as there has been in previous accidents, that the wonders of radar may incline seafarers to carelessness, if they are likely to depend too extensively on electronics to see them through.

"I still like to look out the window," one ship master said.

There were no definite reports of what speed the two ships were making at the time of impact. But it was surmised that they were traveling fairly fast, in the light of the damage done to both ships. The Stockholm is

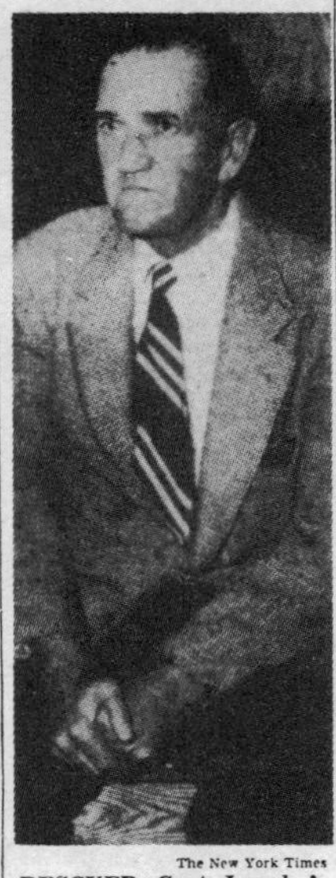

The New York Times

RESCUER: Capt. Joseph A. Boyd, skipper of the Cape Ann, on arrival yesterday.

rated at nineteen knots. In the past year her speed has averaged seventeen over all seasons. The Doria, rated at better than twenty-three knots, averaged twenty-two knots.

A spokesman for the Transatlantic Passenger Conference said yesterday that a day of research in past performance on the Atlantic indicated that since World War I there had been no previous major peacetime collision or sinking in the regular Atlantic lines resulting in loss of a passenger life. In this period the Atlantic lines carried more than 26,000,000 passengers to Europe and Mediterranean ports.

The question of possible salvage of the $27,000,000 liner and her valuable cargo was explored yesterday. Veteran salvage men discounted the chances, because of the depth of the water — about 200 feet — where the stricken ship lies, and because of the cost.

They could recall no instance of salvage of a ship of this size at that depth of sea.

The charges against the Andrea Doria's seamen were drafted by three survivors who reached port last night on the rescue ship Cape Ann. The document reportedly was signed by ninety of the group picked up and brought to land by this ship.

The survivors' charges were outlined in a typewritten statement that was lowered by line from the Cape Ann to reporters on the deck of a Moran tugboat, the Martha M., as the towboat accompanied the rescue ship into port. The tug was alongside from Liberty Island to the pier at West Forty-fourth Street.

This is the pier where the Andrea Doria would have docked yesterday morning.

The statement was drafted by Mr. and Mrs. Michael Stoller of Los Angeles and Arthur Fisher of 125 West Ninety-sixth Street, New York. Mr. Fisher is in the handwoven fabric business.

The statement said the survivors felt impelled to detail "the facts" prior to and during the disaster in the darkness of Nantucket Light.

An emergency drill was held on July 19, but passengers were dismissed after only a "cursory inspection" of lifebelts, the bill of particulars continued.

The statement then went on to charge that no alarm was sounded when disaster struck and that no instructions were given by crew members.

The statement did praise a few of the crew members who worked alongside the passengers during the hours of fright.

"It is our firm belief that the above-mentioned facts constituted abhorrent disregard for the fundamental responsibilities of the officers and crew of the ship for the safety of the passengers in their care. We believe this to be the direct cause of the large number of casualties * * *"

Mr. Stoller, who helped in writing the charges, is a writer of popular songs. He wrote "Black Denim Trousers and Motor Cycle Boots."

Sam Frlekin, one of the Cape Ann survivors, corroborated the complaints outlined in the statement. Talking to reporters on Pier 84 after the ship docked, he said he was in an elevator, going up, when the collision came. The ship immediately started to cant over to the starboard side he said.

Mr. Frlekin, who lives in San Pedro, Calif., said he and his wife spent three hours in the deck area, without getting any information from the crew on what was going on, and no help or instructions as to what they should do to play their roles in the mounting drama.

The only word sounded over the address system, spoken in Italian, admonished the passengers to "be calm," he said.

Mrs. Frlekin, on the pier, was wearing pink pajamas under a coat.

CYPRIOTE WOMAN SLAIN

Gunman Kill Ethnic Greek Mother of Three Children

NICOSIA, Cyprus, July 26 (Reuters)—A 35-year-old Greek Cypriote woman was shot to death here today by unidentified gunmen.

The shooting took place in the Greek quarter, after a curfew had been lifted at dawn. The curfew was immediately restored. The woman, Mrs. Melani Neophitou, was the mother of three children.

The gunmen were reported to have walked into the grocery store Mrs. Neophitou operated with her husband, and shot her as she stood behind the counter.

3 SHIPS BRING IN 364 FROM DORIA

Freighter and 2 Navy Craft Dock Here With Crewmen and Passengers of Liner

By RUSSELL PORTER

Three rescue ships last night brought a total of 364 survivors of the Andrea Doria to New York.

The freighter Cape Ann landed 129 men and women at 8 P. M. at the Italian Line's Pier 84, Hudson River and Forty-fourth Street. At 9:45 P. M. the Naval ship Pvt. William H. Thomas brought in 158 of the Doria's passengers and crew to Pier 4 of the Brooklyn Army Terminal. At 11:30 the Navy destroyer escort Edward H. Allen, with Capt. Piero Calamai and seventy-six of the Doria's crew, docked at the terminal.

The Cape Ann's master, Capt. Joseph A. Boyd of 68-09 Booth Street, Forest Hills, Queens, landed the survivors at the Italian Line's Pier 84, Hudson River and Forty-fourth Street. He was exhausted when he came ashore himself.

He said he had picked up an S O S from the Andrea Doria at 11:25 o'clock Wednesday night. He got a position report, found he was fifteen miles away, and set his course for the liner.

At the time, he said, his radar was set for twenty miles and was working well. He observed "nothing strange" about it.

The Cape Ann arrived at the disaster scene at 12:30 o'clock yesterday morning. Captain Boyd said he went close enough to maneuver but the fog was so thick he could see nothing.

He had two lifeboats, each with a capacity of forty-six persons. The first lifeboat, manned by seven crew members, shoved off at 12:45 A. M. The second, also manned by seven of the crew, was sent out ten minutes later. Each boat made two trips. On the last trip only seven survivors were found.

The Cape Ann also picked up passengers carried by a lifeboat from the Andrea Doria. One of the Cape Ann's boats transferred some seriously injured persons to the Ile de France.

Care for Injured

Among the survivors were a number of sick and injured. There also were a surgeon and a medical student, who took care of casualties. Captain Boyd had a first-aid kit aboard, and he and crew members helped with the injured.

Captain Boyd left the scene after 5 A. M., having taken aboard all the survivors he could safely accommodate, with other ships standing by to rescue others. He said he had kept radio contact with the Andrea Doria as long as possible.

The Cape Ann is a small ship, less than 7,000 gross tons, and 395 feet long. She has a crew of forty-three. She is owned by the United Fruit Company, but is under charter to the Isbrandtsen Steamship Company. At the time of the collision she was en route from Bremerhaven to New York, carrying twelve passengers.

A pilot was put aboard the Cape Ann in New York Harbor by the tug Martha Moran of the Moran Towing Company. The Martha Moran also helped berth the Cape Ann.

Babies Included

Reporters and photographers, who traveled down the bay on the Martha Moran to meet the Cape Ann, saw it receive a typical harbor welcome, with ferryboats and other craft tooting their whistles, and passengers aboard them waving.

The survivors lined the rails of the Cape Ann and waved back. Most of them were women, but there were some men and a number of children, including babies.

A large crowd waited outside Pier 84 as the Cape Ann came in. The survivors plainly showed on their faces the strain and suffering they had gone through.

Many were dishevelled and partly dressed, covered with blankets they had thrown over themselves when routed out of bed near midnight. One group of fully dressed persons included a young man with a red flower in his buttonhole. He explained they had been dancing at the time of the collision—"that's why we're all dressed up."

SHIRT UNION GETS RISE

100,000 Workers to Receive 10c-an-Hour Increase

One hundred thousand workers in the shirt and cotton garment industries will receive a wage increase of 10 cents an hour under the terms of an agreement negotiated last night.

The pact between the Amalgamated Clothing Workers of America and the principal shirt manufacturers also calls for liberalized insurance and pension benefits.

A joint statement by Jacob S. Potofsky, president of the union, and Herbert Ferster and Murray Rabbino, counsel for the employers, said the agreement would heighten the "goodwill and cooperation" that had prevailed in the industry for many years.

The union represents 70 per cent of all cotton garment workers. The new pay scale will become effective Sept. 4. Present wages average $1.47 an hour.

New Soviet Car Withdrawn

MOSCOW, July 26 (AP)—The newspaper Moscow Pravda reported today the Soviet Union's new de luxe passenger car Zil 110 has been withdrawn from production. Looks too much like a Packard, the newspaper said. It berated the designer for copying foreign styles. Actually, the Zil 110 looks more like a Cadillac.

Italy Receives News of Loss of Pride of Her Merchant Navy as National Calamity

TRAGEDY SHOCKS ROME AND GENOA

Newspapers Publish Extras—Bulletin Broadcast by Government Radio

PREMIER SEGNI NOTIFIED

Cause of Collision Creates Speculation—Mrs. Luce Expresses Sympathy

By ARNALDO CORTESI

Special to The New York Times.

ROME, July 26—The news that the Andrea Doria, pride of the Italian Merchant Navy, had been gravely damaged in a collision with the Stockholm and subsequently had sunk was received in Italy as a national calamity.

There was a run on newspapers throughout the country as edition after edition came off the presses with the latest details of the tragedy that was being enacted off Nantucket Island.

Shock and anxiety were particularly intense in Genoa, a city of seafarers, where the Italian Line has its central offices and where a majority of the crew was recruited. The Andrea Doria was launched in near-by Sestri Ponente in 1951. Large crowds stood in stunned silence all day in the Piazza de Ferrari outside the biulding where the board of directors of the Italian Line sat continuously from the moment when the first news of the collision was received to long after the Doria had settled to the bottom of the ocean

In Rome Gennaro Cassiani, Minister of the Merchant Navy, was also in his office all day in constant touch with the developments on the American side of the ocean. It was he who issued the dramatic order to Capt. Pietro Calamai to abandon his ship when it was clear that the Doria could not be saved. Signor Cassiani was in constant touch also with Premier Antonio Segni who asked for a minute-to-minute account of how the Doria was faring.

First News at 6:15 A. M.

The first news of the collision was given by the semi-official Ansa news agency at 6:15 A. M., Rome time [1:15 A. M. New York time]. Ansa said merely that the Doria and the Stockholm had been in a collision, that there had been no loss of life but that the Doria was being evacuated and that rescue ships were on the way. The first full report of what had happened was given by Ansa at 9:32 o'clock, Rome time. At 11:06 o'clock Ansa announced that all on board had been saved.

Shortly before noon the Government-controlled radio network interrupted a musical program for a special news bulletin saying that the Doria had been rammed. Shortly afterward, the noon papers were in the streets with a full story up to that time. Giornale D'Italia was out first with a special giving a well-rounded story of the collision and subsequent events. Many newspapers underlined the immediacy with which aid was rushed from all sides to the stricken Italian ship.

Crash Is a Mystery

Most Italians feel that there is some kind of mystery about the way their ship was sunk. The Doria was fitted with the most modern radar equipment and presumably the Stockholm was also. People here find it difficult to understand how two ships could collide under such circumstances even if the visibility was reduced to zero by fog. Moreover, the Doria was represented as virtually unsinkable owing to her many watertight compartments.

A possible explanation of the collision was furnished by Prof. Marino Algeri, president of the Superior Italian Council of Telecommunications. He said that shipboard radar equipment used excessively short wave lengths because longer wave lengths increased the bulk of the equipment. He said that shorter wave lengths are more easily absorbed by fog with the result that their effective radius was not great.

Among the messages received by the Italian Government was one from United States Ambassador Clare Boothe Luce. It was addressed to the Minister of the Merchant Navy through the American Embassy in Rome. After expressing her sympathies for the loss of the ship, she rejoiced at the 'magnificent discipline of the crew and officers" which, according to the information available when she wirelessed from her yacht in the western Mediterranean, had enabled all persons aboard to be saved.

The Italian line as yet has made no announcement as to how it proposes to deal with 1,200 passengers who were booked on the Doria's return trip to Europe.

Aug. 14 Sailing Scheduled

ROME, July 26 (AP)—The collision left hundreds of Americans in Italy wondering today how and when they could get home.

The Italian liner was scheduled to leave Genoa on its next sailing for New York on Aug. 14.

"It's the very height of the westbound tourist season," said an official of a large tourist agency. "Everything from Italy is booked up solid. But one way or another, it will have to be worked out."

Pope Voices Sorrow

CASTEL GANDOLFO, Italy, July 26 (AP)—Pope Pius XII was informed of the Andrea Doria tragedy at his summer home here today and expressed his sorrow.

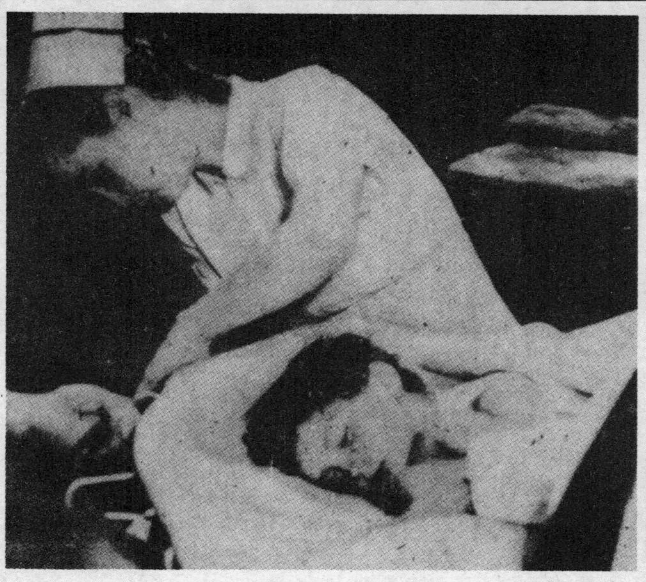

Associated Press Wirephoto

HURT IN CRASH, this 7-year-old passenger of the Andrea Doria was taken aboard the Stockholm and removed by helicopter to Boston. Here a nurse attends her at hospital.

GEYSERS SIGHTED AS LINER GIVES UP

Continued From Page 1

mile circle of the area. The second time we went over the Andrea Doria, about five minutes later the list had increased to about sixty-five degrees. The Stockholm was about three miles away and around the Stockholm was about a mile-square area of oil slick.

The entire area of three miles was littered with debris. Three lifeboats drifted empty and aimlessly. In the area we could make out two destroyer escorts, four Coast Guard cutters and one merchant ship. They were some distance from the Andrea Doria.

We circled the ship a third time. It was about 10 A. M. She was now on her side, apparently just sinking. We could see six lifeboats ripped loose and floating freely. We saw huge geysers coming from the sides of the ship; apparently the air pressure had blown out the portholes.

Capsized With Stern High

Debris was blown high in the air. She keeled over and we could see both screws free of the water. In our fourth pass over the ship at 10:10 A. M., the ship had turned turtle. Her nose was forward in the water with her stern completely out of the water. She hung on for three or four minutes and then disappeared.

The force of the suction caused a tremendous whirlpool and, with it, debris poured out and to the surface from the whirlpool. For about fifteen minutes, this suction continued, changing the water into varied colors—a million different colors.

We watched and then made our way to the Stockholm, which had begun to move. We could see numbers of passengers on the deck and we could see her bow. It appeared to have been struck by a bomb.

As we flew the lowest we had—we came down to an altitude of about 200 feet—we could see parts of the bow dangling and falling off. The ship appeared to have a slight starboard list and, as she started off toward New York, she left about a two-mile trail of debris.

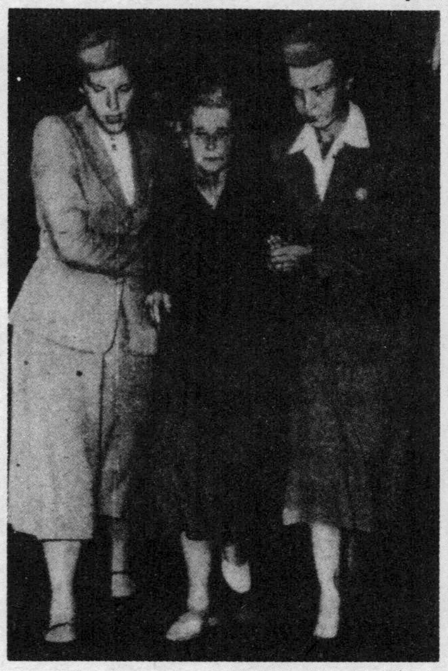

The New York Times

VOLUNTEER WORKERS assist a woman brought here aboard Ile de France after her rescue from Andria Doria.

Ship's Death Throes Viewed

By MILTON BRACKER

Special to The New York Times.

NANTUCKET, Mass., July 26—The 30,000-ton liner Andrea Doria sank in blue water, under clear skies today, not quite eleven hours after her collision with the Stockholm.

Through the early hours of a perfect morning, the stricken ship turned increasingly on her starboard side. Meanwhile, near by, helicopters buzzed over the stern of the Swedish ship, removing seriously injured survivors.

The drama of the doomed Andrea Doria was played out in inexorable stages. Until the very last, many who flew over—admiring the intact portside, with a line of lights gleaming brightly along the promenade deck—were hopeful, even confident that she would stay afloat.

In fact, despite the tilt of her decks, the sleek black liner looked more of a ship as she lay on her side in the water than did the battered Stockholm. The Swedish vessel's bow had been crumpled back between thirty and fifty feet; she stood as if foreshortened by a dull and clumsy ax, wielded by a giant. The Andrea Doria looked tired but serene.

Ships a Mile Apart at 8:30

At 8:30, when this writer flew over, the water was lapping at the starboard rail of the Andrea Doria and the port propeller was jutting starkly from the placid sea. Water foamed from a vent in the elevated portside and cascaded into the sea, making it milky.

About a mile away the creamy-white Stockholm looked curiously like a ghost riding out of faint mist. But the blue circle of the Swedish American Line, with its enclosed crowns, showed clearly on the erect funnel. On the fantail, people were clustered beneath the hovering helicopters.

But while the Andrea Doria was hiding her wound, the bow of the Stockholm was crushed back nakedly. Actually, the impact had been felt a little more deeply to port, so that the jagged line of wreckage did not cut quite squarely across the beam. On the starboard side there was a twisted bulge of metal as if the strakes had been rolled back upon themselves.

Circling back to the Andrea Doria, one saw the gilt letters of its name proud on its side. The mast still stood perpendicular to the slanting decks. The three swimming pools showed their pale turquoise bottoms to the sun. In one, some water remained along the down-tilted edge.

Lifeboats Tell Own Story

Most indicative of what happened was the state of the lifeboats. On the low starboard side, there were only empty davits, showing that the small craft had gotten away. On the grotesquely raised port side, eight boats hung stiffly, symbol of their own futility.

At 10 A. M., Bob Caddigan, pilot of the Nantucket Flying Service, made another trip to the scene. He reported that the ship had turned further. The decks were awash, but she still appeared to be riding reasonably securely.

Then, nine minutes later two business men in a private plane saw the end. They were William E. Barbour, chairman of the board of Tracerlab, Inc., Boston electronics manufacturer, and a friend, Samuel Carr of Milton, Mass.

Both men described how, as the decks gradually became perpendicular to the surface, the Andrea Doria's bow gradually tipped. The ship began to subside along her whole length, but with a slight thrust at the bow.

Mr. Barbour said he actually saw the last of the water spill from the swimming pool. The port propeller broke water along its entire shaft, and the great bulk went under. There was a bright spread of foam, then a strong upsurge of bubbles. Gradually the water turned from blue to green. In it, two spinning lifeboats appeared—they had broken loose from the davits at the last.

At 10:15, another plane flew over the bubbles. It bore Capt. Carlo Fava, New England representative of the Italian line, who was piloted from Boston by Ralph Hynes.

When Captain Fava reached Nantucket, his eyes showed how he felt.

"When we got over there, she was gone" he said.

Andrea Doria's Haggard Captain Arrives, But Gives No Clue to Cause of Collision

Continued From Page 1

at 11:30, but it was an hour before the Italian line's master stepped off. A corps of seventy-five newsmen had beseiged the vessel with pleas for a statement from him. At first he declined.

Then, in the company of Navy officers and Italian consular officials he appeared with a statement written out in pen. He read it hurriedly amid the furor at dockside and retreated to the ship. Few had caught more than a phrase or two.

Captain Calamai finally acceded to demands that he reread the statement in a pier lounge. In a high voice, in good English, he declared:

"As you know, the Andrea Doria last night was hit by the Swedish ship Stockholm. The damage was so great that it was necessary to disembark all passengers and crew. We have been helped brilliantly by the U. S. Army, Navy and Coast Guard. The successful rescue was made possible by the discipline and calmness of the passengers and the sense of duty of my officers and crew."

The stocky veteran of forty years of sea duty wore a blue beret, white shirt, blue tie and the regular blue uniform in which he commanded the Andrea Doria's bridge on fifty previous successful Atlantic crossings.

Firmly he refused to answer questions about the tragedy and the complaints of some passengers about the debarkation.

Besides Italian diplomatic officials, Captain Calamai was met by his brother, Mario, and a nephew, Dr. Bruno Galasso. They and police Inspector Edward G. McGlone hurried him off to an unknown place.

Monitors of Disaster Hear of Tropical Storm

Within a few hours of the ship disaster off Nantucket, the season's first tropical storm, Anna, started brewing over the southwest Gulf of Mexico.

Ironically, one of the men at the Coast Guard Search and Rescue Center, 80 Lafayette Street, "called" the event. As the Guardsmen worked at top speed to facilitate rescue operations, Lieut. Donald D. Davidson said, "All we need now is a hurricane."

Fifteen minutes later, at 4 P. M., word came that Anna was causing heavy seas and squalls as she moved inland toward Tampico, Mexico. The storm was blowing itself out last night, the Weather Bureau said.

LINER SYMBOLIZED REBIRTH OF ITALY

Andrea Doria Called 'Floating Art Gallery'—A Nation Helped Decorate Her

By SANKA KNOX

The Andrea Doria was looked upon as the symbol of a renascence in Italy's maritime history.

At the bottom of the sea with the broken Italian flagship lie other symbols of Italy's rebirth since World War II—the fruits of her artists and artisans.

In the tragedy perished original works of art and decorations created by scores of artists. And in the cargo, in other evidence of burgeoning crafts and industry, were silks, woolens, cottons, furniture, wines, and olive oil, valued at about $2,000,000.

Exquisitely decorated, the vessel was called "a floating art gallery." Many of Italy's leading painters, sculptors, ceramists and designers shared in creating beauty for their first post-war ship of the northern run.

Modern from the exotic blond wood panelling to the occasionally surrealist style of its murals, the decorations had one among them that came from a distant past.

This was a crest in silver, the coat of arms of Andrea Doria, valiant sixteenth century Genoese admiral for whom the ship was named. It was on a bulkhead of the main deck, close to a larger-than-life bronze statue of the admiral.

The crest, presented by a Doge of Genoa in recognition of victories at sea, was affixed to the portico of the admiral's mansion. When the Andrea Doria left Italy on her maiden voyage on Jan. 14, 1953, the crest had become part of the ship, the gift of a direct descendant of the admiral, the Marquis Gianbattista Doria.

Marine Scene in Mirrors

One of her treasures was a "Carnival of the Sirens," a nocturnal marine scene done all in inlaid mirrors. The technically complex and delightful work, in the first class dining room was by Felicita Frai, a well-known painter of Milan.

The walls of the cabin class dining room were partly covered with decorations gilded in relief and in color on crystals. The artist was Prof. Angelo Bragalini of Bologna.

In the Winter Garden of the Promenade Deck were ceramic creations by Guido Gambone, one of Italy's most distinguished artists and craftsmen. In a first class lounge hung a fantastic tapestry woven with a scene of North and South American Indians.

A loom was built especially for the tapestry, which took a year to weave.

Originality in art was carried throughout the ship. In tourist class, an original technique of graphite painting was employed by Prof. Ugo Rossi in dining room panels of animals and still life.

$100,000 CAR IS LOST

Chrysler's New 'Idea' Vehicle Was on the Andrea Doria

DETROIT, July 26 (UP)—A $100,000 "idea" car that took more than two years to design and built went down with the Andrea Doria.

The Chrysler Corporation announced the loss of the car, which was designed by Chrysler's engineering division and built by Ghia of Turin, Italy's world-noted sports car designers and builders.

The car, named the "Norseman," was on Chrysler drawing boards for a year. It took another fifteen months to hand-built it in Italy.

Chrysler said the car was covered by insurance.

The car had no door posts. Cantilever arches on each side held the top from the rear with the same strength of present cars with front posts. Rear body panels were made of aluminum to reduce weight, and the body was streamlined along aerodynamic principles.

COLLISION INQUIRY ASKED

House Unit Seeks Report, but U. S. Has No Jurisdiction

Special to The New York Times.

WASHINGTON, July 26—Representative Herbert C. Bonner, chairman of the House Merchant Marine Committee, today asked the Coast Guard for a full report on the collision of the Andrea Doria and Stockholm.

The North Carolina Democrat said his group would look into the incident to determine whether the two vessels had lived up to international agreements on maritime safety. He asked that the Coast Guard investigation include testimony from the captains of the ships.

It was noted here that while the committee could investigate the disaster, it had no real jurisdiction because the accident happened to foreign ships outside of United States waters.

Young Chenault Bails From Jet

WENDOVER, Utah, July 26—(UP)—Capt. Claire P. Chenault, son of Gen. Claire Lee Chenault who commended the Flying Tigers of World War II fame, escaped injury today when he was forced to bail out of a jet fighter high over the Bonneville salt flats. He was returning from an exercise when the engine of his F84F Thunderstreak fighter-bomber flamed out. A helicopter picked him up within minutes.

Yemen Expects Soviet Aid

BEIRUT, Lebanon, July 26 (Reuters) — Yemen's Foreign Minister, Crown Prince Seif el Islam el Badr, said here today that the Soviet Union would finance some economic projects in his Arab kingdom. The prince is on his way home from a visit to Moscow.

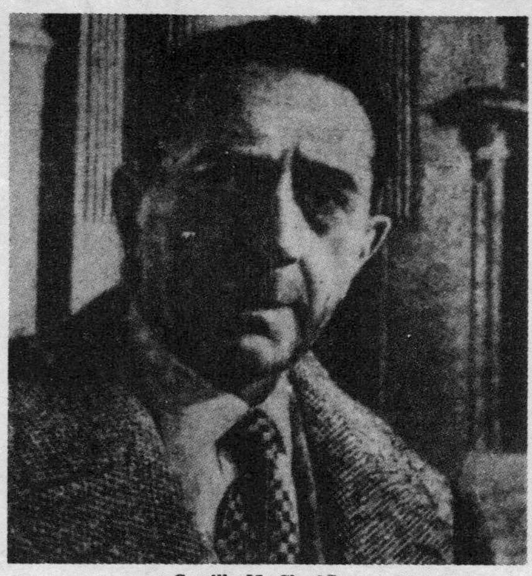

Camille M. Cianfarra

TIMES MAN KILLED IN SHIP DISASTER

Continued From Page 1

booking passage for himself and his family on the Doria.

Late yesterday the Ile de France brought 753 survivors of the sunken Andrea Doria into New York. They had many stories to tell of nightmare aboard a luxury liner.

The grimmest story among the hundreds told by the disaster's survivors was that of Dr. Peterson, 57 years old, a quiet-spoken chiropractor.

Dr. Peterson, with the aid of a helpful crew member, Rovelli Giovanni, rescued Mrs. Cianfarra from almost certain death in the sinking luxury liner.

Dr. Peterson's own wife, Martha, died as he and Signor Giovanni worked frantically to free her from the smashed structure of the ship. Mr. Cianfarra, Dr. Peterson reported, was killed instantly, as were the two Cianfarra children.

The Petersons occupied Cabin 56 on the upper deck on the starboard side of the Andrea Doria. The Cianfarras occupied the adjoining cabins, 54 and 52. The Cianfarras children were in No. 52.

The Cianfarras and the Petersons had retired shortly after 10:30 P. M.

Thrown Into Next Cabin

At 11:22 P. M. Dr. Peterson was thrown from his bed by the shock of the collision. So violently was he hurled that he found himself in an adjoining cabin, No. 58. He had been knocked unconscious. When he regained consciousness he found himself partly trapped by wreckage.

Dr. Peterson called out. He heard screaming. With great difficulty he made his way back to his own cabin. He found his wife pinned fast between a bulkhead and the outside of an elevator shaft. He heard Mrs. Cianfarra calling for help from her cabin.

Dr. Peterson found Signor Giovanni and took him back to the Peterson cabin. The chiropractor examined his wife. She had two broken legs and a broken back. Dr. Peterson gave her morphine, but the two men were unable to free her to administer further aid.

Dr. Peterson and Signor Giovanni then went to the Cianfarra cabin. Mrs. Cianfarra was jammed between a bulkhead and the spring of her bed. Mr. Cianfarra was dead.

The rescue team managed to find a pair of wirecutters to cut the bedsprings and free Mrs. Cianfarra.

Pushing his way back to his own cabin, Dr. Peterson again tried to free his wife. Failing again, he managed to locate a jack. Dr. Peterson and Signor Giovanni began prying beams off Mrs. Peterson's body. While they were doing this, she died.

Mrs. Peterson was 55 years old. She was a native of Stockholm, Sweden. She is survived by Dr. Peterson and two married daughters.

It was reported that the bodies of Mr. Cianfarra and his daughters went down with the Andrea Doria.

Heads Chiropractic Group

Dr. Peterson is president of the Chiropractic Institute of New York. He had been lecturing in Europe, then had taken a holiday in Switzerland with Mrs. Peterson. On the voyage the Petersons had become casually acquainted with the Cianfarras.

Another passenger was Betsy Drake, wife of Cary Grant, the actor. She had met the Cianfarras in Spain in connection with a magazine article Mrs. Cianfarra was writing on Mr. Grant.

Mr. Morgan, the father of Linda Morgan, Mr. Cianfarra's stepdaughter, spoke last night at 7 o'clock on his regularly scheduled news program.

He never mentioned to his audience that his daughter had been killed.

Mr. Cianfarra had been The Times correspondent in Spain since November, 1951. Before that he had been a member of the newspaper's Rome bureau, where, over the years, he won wide recognition as an expert on Vatican affairs.

For a four-year period, between August, 1942, and May, 1946, he had served as The Times correspondent in Mexico.

Mr. Cianfarra took to his coverage of Vatican City the advantages of an Italian background and a fluency in the Italian language combined with his viewpoint as a native American.

An outgoing, easygoing person, he made many friends and important contacts in Italian political and social circles. He enjoyed a high reputation in Papal diplomatic circles.

Mr. Cianfarra was a close friend of Pope Pius XII. He wrote the the stories of the death of Pope Pius XI and the election and coronation of Eugenio Cardinal Pacelli as Pope Pius XII.

Several years ago Mr. Cianfarra—known to his myriad friends and acquaintances as "Cian"—scored a world scoop for The Times. He reported that Vatican archaeologists had uncovered the tomb of St. Peter. Mr. Cianfarra had spent two months gathering the story.

Mr. Cianfarra was ribbed occasionally by his friends as a man who spoke Italian with an American accent and English with an Italian accent.

He was born on March 29, 1907, in Long Island City, Queens, to Camille and Giulia Rollini Cianfarra, both of whom had been born in Italy.

At the age of 6, the younger Cianfarra was taken to Rome. His father had been appointed Rome correspondent of The New York American. The elder Cianfarra later became manager of the United Press Bureau in Rome, at which post he remained until his death in 1925.

In Rome, the younger Cianfarra studied at a Roman Catholic School run by Irish priests. There he received his elementary and high school education.

In 1928 Mr. Cianfarra returned to the United States and, for a time, attended City College. He worked for various Italian-language newspapers in New York, including The Bollettino Della Sera and The Corriere d'America.

In 1933 he joined the staff of The United Press in New York. A year later he was shifted to London as a correspondent for The United Press there. In August, 1935, he joined the Rome bureau of The New York Times.

Shortly after the start of World War II, Mr. Cianfarra, along with other American correspondents, was interned at Siena by the Italian Government. After five months, he was released and returned to the United States.

In August, 1942, he was sent to Mexico City as correspondent there. After nearly four years in Mexico he was reassigned to Rome. In November, 1951, Mr. Cianfarra became Madrid correspondent.

Mr. Cianfarra frequently was sent on detached service to cover such events as the United Nations General Assembly in Paris in 1948 and various North Atlantic Treaty Organization conferences in Lisbon and Paris.

In 1945 Mr. Cianfarra married Jane Stolle Morgan of Boise, Idaho, who was then Mexico correspondent of The New York Post. She is the daughter of Mrs. Charles E. Daches of Seattle, Wash. Mr. Cianfarra had previously been married to the former Edda de Mistura. She died in Mexico City in 1944. They had no children.

Mr. Cianfarra was the author of two books, "The Vatican and the War," and "The Vatican and the Kremlin."

In addition to his widow, he is survived by his mother and a sister, both of Rome.

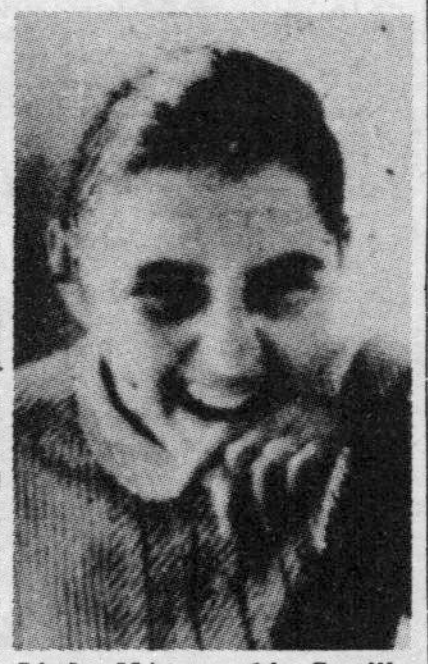

Linda Morgan, 14, Camille M. Cianfarra's stepdaughter.

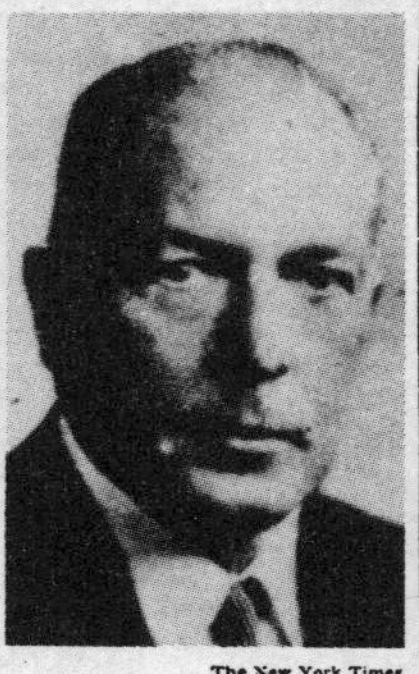

The New York Times

Dr. Thure C. Peterson, whose wife died on the Andrea Doria. With the aid of a crew member he rescued Mrs. Camille C. Cianfarra.

108 SAVED IN 1950 BY THE STOCKHOLM

Radar Picked Up Foundering Craft Off Denmark as Other Ships Failed

Radar, which failed to prevent the collision of the liners Andrea Doria and Stockholm, once made it possible for the Swedish ship to rescue 108 persons.

They were aboard the Danish mail boat Kronprins Olav, which was foundering in a heavy fog off Denmark in 1950. Numerous vessels tried to reach her without success. The rescue was effected only when the Swedish American Line vessel was able to pick up the distressed craft on the large twelve-inch view scope of her radar set.

The 11,000-ton Stockholm, less than half the size of the Andrea Doria, is the largest passenger vessel ever built in Swedish yards and is the third ship to carry that name.

The first, a 547-foot vessel of 12,835 tons built in Germany in 1900, was sold to interests that converted her into a whaling factory vessel and renamed her the Solglimt.

The second Stockholm, a handsome 28,000-ton motorship, was built in Italy. She was destroyed by fire of unknown origin in December, 1938, just before she was to be commissioned. The vessel was being rebuilt when the Italian Government took her over and converted her into a troopship. She sank in Trieste in May, 1945.

Has Racy Appearance

The current Stockholm, sleek and white, looks like a cross between a super-yacht and a man o' war. She was launched at Gothenburg, Sweden, in 1946, and has a sharp, rakish bow that gives her a fast, racy appearance.

She completed her maiden run to New York March 1, 1948, and won unusual praise from William S. Ireland, Sandy Hook pilot, who said she was "really a pearl from a sailor's point of view.

"She can turn around on a dime and give you 8 cents change," he said. "She is the finest ship I have ever been aboard."

She arrived, bedecked from stem to stern with multi-colored signal flags, and was welcomed by the whistles of steamers in the harbor and by fireboats shooting streams of water into the air.

In February, 1954, she arrived here after having her interior altered. Her accommodations were increased to provide for 586 passengers, instead of 395, and the tourist class lounge was more than doubled in size. En route, while backing out of her berth in a fog at Halifax, N. S., she brushed a British freighter, the Starcrest, but was undamaged.

She made the news columns several other times. An Israeli group considered purchasing her in 1952 but negotiations were not consumated. A ponderous, black, armored car once owned by Adolf Hitler was brought to this country in her in 1948 and longshoremen hissed and booed as the vehicle was unloaded.

The $29,000,000 Andrea Doria, a 30,000-ton luxury ship, was launched in Genoa on June 16, 1951. She signalized the rebirth of Italy's merchant marine, which had been 90 per cent destroyed in World War II.

The vessel, which emphasized gracious living and air-conditioning even in the automobile storage section, was named for a sixteenth-century statesman and naval hero in Genoa who was very active in European affairs.

The vessel, painted black and noted for her handsome lines, was the thirteenth in gross tonnage among the ocean liners.

Nearly 20,000 persons swarmed to Pier 84 at West Forty-fourth Street, on Jan. 25, 1953, to welcome the luxury liner when she arrived on her maiden voyage. Some sight-seers stood in line as long as three and a half hours to get aboard. The crowd was so great that the police had to establish barricades and turn away thousands who wanted to get aboard.

The 697-foot craft, whose top trial speed was reported to be 25.30 knots, cruised at twenty-three knots. She had three permanent outdoor swimming pools. The ship was called the queen of the Italian fleet until a slightly larger successor, the Cristoforo Colombo, was commissioned in 1954.

BRAZIL LOANS NEAR

Export-Import Bank Expected to Aid in Development

Special to The New York Times.

WASHINGTON, July 26—Diplomatic sources reported today that the Export-Import Bank was nearly ready to announce the granting of development loans to Brazil.

It had been anticipated that the agreement would be announced about the time President Eisenhower left at the end of last week for the Panama meetings of American chiefs of state. However, it is now understood that the details will be made public early next week.

The total amount is understood to be about $148,000,000.

House Votes A.E.C. Fund Rise

WASHINGTON, July 26 (UP)—The House authorized the Atomic Energy Commission today to spend an additional $24,000,000 for laboratories and other facilities needed in atomic research. It passed unanimously and sent to the Senate a bill raising the commission's authorization for the purchase of expansion of research facilities from $295,000,000 to $319,000,000.

"All the News That's Fit to Print"

The New York Times.

LATE CITY EDITION
Condensation of U. S. Weather Bureau forecast:
Mostly fair today; chance of showers tonight and tomorrow.
Temperature range today: 85—68.
Temperature range yesterday: 87.4—67.8.
Full U. S. Weather Bureau Report, Page 48.

VOL. CV..No. 35,992.

Entered as Second-Class Matter,
Post Office, New York, N. Y.

NEW YORK, THURSDAY, AUGUST 9, 1956.

© 1956, by The New York Times Company.

Times Square, New York 36, N. Y.
Telephone LAckawanna 4-1000

FIVE CENTS

PRESIDENT PLANS A FULL CHECK-UP BEFORE ELECTION

Gives Pledge to Tell Nation If He Ever Has Reason to 'Believe I Am Not Fit'

LIMITS TALK OF HEALTH

Also Refuses New Comment on Stassen Fight on Nixon —Thinks Views Are Clear

Transcript and summary of news conference, Page 10.

Special to The New York Times.

WASHINGTON, Aug. 8—President Eisenhower told the American people today that he would have another thorough physical examination before the election on Nov. 6.

While revealing that at his news conference, he renewed his promise to let the public know whether at any time he thought himself physically "unfit" to serve a second term.

General Eisenhower told about his plans for a check-up after having rebuffed a reporter's question about the "Stassen-Nixon-Herter affair."

The reporter had asked whether the President would elaborate on previous remarks about the efforts of Harold E. Stassen to displace Vice President Richard M. Nixon from the ticket this fall. Mr. Stassen, the President's disarmament aide, is urging Gov. Christian A. Herter of Massachusetts for the Vice-Presidential nomination.

To this question the President answered:

"If I didn't make myself clear on the subject you mentioned, and on my health, I am never going to be able to do it, and those subjects I don't intend to discuss again.

"I dealt—with respect to the second one, a question here I have raised myself, I believe I did promise this: That at an appropriate time in the—sometime later this year, but certainly before the election, I will have another complete examination, and to determine that there has been no change in my situation, and I said, believe I will put it this way: If at any time I have any reason to believe that I am not fit, as I believe myself to be now, I will come before the American public and tell them."

Further Discussion Shut Off

With that remark, the President shut off further discussion of his health or of the "Stassen-Nixon-Herter affair."

Should his next physical examination suggest to him that he should not run for a second term, party machinery could take care of the emergency. The Republican National Committee could call a new convention if there were time. Otherwise the committee itself could make the new nomination.

Meanwhile, it was announced that the President's only vacation plans at this time called for three or four days at Cypress Point Club, near San Francisco. This vacation would start after his appearance at the Republican National Convention on the final day in that city. That is expected to be Thursday, Aug. 23 or Friday, Aug. 24.

At his conference, the President had said only that he

Continued on Page 10, Column 3

Wife Says Doctors Cleared Roosevelt

By CLAYTON KNOWLES

Mrs. Franklin D. Roosevelt said yesterday that her husband's doctors had told him less than three months before his campaign for a fourth term that he "could quite easily go on with the activities of the Presidency."

She emphasized her husband had never had a heart attack, despite recurrent rumors to the contrary. He died of a cerebral hemorrhage about three months after his inauguration in 1945.

Mrs. Roosevelt recalled that the President had undergone a series of physical examinations in May, 1944. She said that the only advice given by the doctors, who found him "well and active," was that he should "rest each day" to ease a heart weakened by the strain of the war years in the White House.

The statement by Mrs. Roosevelt, elicited during an interview, took on significance in

Continued on Page 10, Column 7

33 Hurt as Excursion Boat Strikes Bridge on Harlem

Circle Line boat tied up yesterday at 138th Street, the Bronx, after it had hit bridge

The New York Times (by William C. Eckenberg)
These young swimmers took mooring lines ashore for the boat's captain after the accident. From the left they are James Seidel, Robert Hughes, Dennis Sullivan and William Weber.

By EDITH EVANS ASBURY

A sight-seeing boat carrying 195 passengers around Manhattan Island struck a bridge yesterday afternoon and thirty-three persons were injured. Ten of them were hospitalized, but nine were re-

leased soon afterward. The Circle Line's ninety-nine-ton Sightseer IX veered out of control in the Harlem River as it approached the Madison Avenue Bridge, which joins Manhattan and the Bronx at East 138th Street. The guide's

running description of the sights ashore was suddenly interrupted by the voice of Capt. John Milcetich, 70-year-old skipper of the excursion boat, directing everyone to lie

Continued on Page 29, Column 3

Stevenson Stand on Rights Perils First-Ballot Victory

By W. H. LAWRENCE

Special to The New York Times.

CHICAGO, Aug. 8—Backers of Adlai E. Stevenson conceded privately tonight that the controversy over civil rights might cost him a first-ballot nomination as the Democratic Presidential candidate. They made new efforts to repair the damage to their cause.

The setback resulted from Mr. Stevenson's suggestions for a strong civil rights platform plank "unequivocally" endorsing the Supreme Court's decision against racial segregation in public schools.

Southern spokesmen said that big blocs of votes previously counted as favorable to Mr. Stevenson must now be classified as doubtful. They said the doubt probably would continue until the shape of the platform was finally determined.

While Mr. Stevenson's managers remained confident of victory on an early ballot, they no longer talked with certainty of sufficient votes to put their candidate over on the first count of delegates. A total of 686½ votes, a majority, is required to nominate a candidate in the convention, which opens here Monday.

For the record, James A. Finnegan, Mr. Stevenson's campaign manager, claimed this afternoon "over 600" first-ballot votes for his candidate. Reminded that he had claimed 630 votes yesterday, he amended his figure upward. He said "a few" delegate votes might have been lost, but, in general, the 1952 nominee had maintained his

Continued on Page 12, Column 2

G.O.P. DENOUNCED OVER RESOURCES

Chapman Offers Democrats a Draft Plank Charging 'Betrayal of Heritage'

By WALLACE CARROLL

Special to The New York Times.

CHICAGO, Aug. 8—The Democrats warmed up today to one of the major issues of the coming election campaign—the natural resources policies of the Eisenhower Administration.

Oscar L. Chapman, who was Secretary of the Interior in the Truman Administration, offered the Committee on Platform and Resolutions of the Democratic National Convention a "give-em-hell" draft plank on the resources issue. It accused the Eisenhower Administration of "a betrayal of our heritage."

Tomorrow, former President Harry S. Truman will appear before the platform makers and offer his advice on the issues of the coming Presidential and Congressional campaigns.

Mr. Chapman went before the platform group as chairman of the party's natural resources advisory committee. On behalf of his group he urged the platform writers to press the natural resources issue against the Republicans "uncompromisingly and on the broadest basis."

The receptive attitude of the platform committee made it clear that this advice would be taken. Questions by far western delegates in particular indicated that an aggressive attitude might swing a good number of Senate and House seats in that section besides winning voters in the Presidential contest.

The draft plank that Mr. Chapman presented described the Eisenhower stewardship over the nation's land, water and energy resources as "a faithless performance" and "a sordid page in history."

It charged that the Republicans had encouraged "raiding and grabbing" of water power resources, of timber in the national forest and of oil in the tidelands.

In outlining an alternative Democratic policy, Mr. Chapman's draft proposed the addition of two new points to what

Continued on Page 12, Column 5

Agreement Reached In Aluminum Strike

By STANLEY LEVEY

The Aluminum Company of America and the United Steelworkers of America reached an agreement yesterday on terms for a contract that will end the eight-day strike.

A formal announcement of the settlement is expected today. It will be followed by an early call to 18,000 strikers to return to their jobs. The walkout, plus a simultaneous strike by 10,000 employes of the Reynolds Metals Company, has cut the nation's aluminum production in half.

The basis of the agreement was the wage-benefit package that ended the recent national steel strike. The cost of the package will be 45.6 cents an hour for the duration of a three-year contract. This was expected to set the pattern for settling the union's strike against Reynolds.

The Aluminum Workers In-

Continued on Page 26, Column 4

TEAMSTERS SIGN 4-YEAR PACT HERE IN FIGHT ON HOFFA

3½-Cent Package Covering 10,000 in Local 807 Also Aimed at Racketeers

Agents for 10,000 union truck drivers and 1,250 employers in the metropolitan area signed a new wage agreement yesterday that promised peace between them until 1960.

The four-year pact provides a package increase of 18½ cents an hour for members of Local 807, International Brotherhood of Teamsters. It is expected to increase local trucking costs by 7½ to 12 per cent.

Significantly for both parties, the agreement marked the high point of a joint effort to keep the local free from domination by James R. Hoffa, the Midwest teamster leader, and from the influence of trucking industry racketeers.

The contract was signed by Joseph M. Seiler, chairman of the Local Cartage Conference of the Empire State Highway Transportation Association, Inc., and John E. Strong, president of Local 807, at the office of Hugh E. Sheridan, impartial chairman of the local trucking industry.

For the first time in many years Local 807 had refused to join in area-wide bargaining with nine other teamsters' locals, principally on the ground that these negotiations were being led by union men from the Hoffa camp.

Break by Other Locals Seen

Mr. Sheridan predicted that other locals would break away from the area-wide talks, now under way. Mr. Strong said "there may be a change" toward independent bargaining by Local 816, headed by Martin T. Lacey, who also has opposed the Hoffa group.

Local teamsters complain that Mr. Hoffa operates mainly in the interest of over-the-road truckers. Mr. Lacey has charged that Mr. Hoffa is the prime mover in an asserted conspiracy to gain control of the Teamsters Joint Council here.

Against this background, a Federal grand jury has been searching for racketeers in the trucking industry here and District Attorney Frank S. Hogan has charged that underworld elements are trying to gain control of the Joint Council.

Joseph M. Adelizzi, managing director of the Empire State Highway Transportation Association, appeared to be voicing the sentiments of both parties yesterday when he said the Local 807 agreement was a blow "for honest unionism in this area and its right to represent the men."

However, Thomas L. Hickey, secretary-treasurer of Local 807, indicated that the local eventually might return to area-wide negotiations. "These area-wide committees will come more and more into play in the future," he said.

The four-year term of the contract, effective Sept. 1, was seen as a device to prevent the Hoffa interests from taking over bar-

Continued on Page 49, Column 5

DORIA'S HANDLING DEFENDED BY LINE

Vessel Followed Rules, but Stockholm Was 20 Miles Off Route, Dr. Ali Holds

By GEORGE HORNE

The Italian Line defended the seamanship of its lost liner Andrea Doria yesterday.

For the first time the company gave its official version of the fateful meeting of the Doria and the Swedish American liner Stockholm off Nantucket Light on the night of July 25.

A statement from the company, backed by an interview given by Dr. Giuseppe Ali, head of the line here, contradicted charges made the previous day by owners of the Swedish ship.

The Italian ship, which went down with a presumed loss of forty-seven of the 1,709 passengers and crew aboard, followed international rules of the road exactly and the Stockholm broke the rules, causing the crash, Dr. Ali charged.

Damage and loss suits resulting from the disaster are mounting. In Federal Court yesterday Judge Lawrence E. Walsh moved to consolidate the cases against Swedish American Line at the

Continued on Page 26, Column 6

India to Attend Suez Talks; Likely to Speak for Egypt

Nehru, Indicating Cairo Will Reject Bid, Criticizes Big Three Western Powers— Conditional Soviet Acceptance Seen

By A. M. ROSENTHAL

Special to The New York Times.

NEW DELHI, India, Aug. 8—India today took the carefully considered political decision that hoped would allow her to serve as a bridge between Britain and Egypt in the critical Suez situation.

After almost a week of consultations with London and

Text of the Nehru statement will be found on Page 4.

Cairo, Prime Minister Jawaharlal Nehru told Parliament that India would attend the international conference on the Suez Canal called by Britain, France and the United States.

The Prime Minister made it plain he had information Egypt would not attend. He said India realized Egypt "could not and would not" participate in a conference about which she had not been consulted in advance.

Mr. Nehru made it plain, too,

that India backed Egypt's right to nationalize the Suez Canal Company, resented British and French mobilization and blamed the United States' withdrawal of support for the proposed Aswan High Dam for the current trouble.

In a sense, these comments will make Mr. Nehru Cairo's principal spokesman at the conference, scheduled to open in London Aug. 16.

[Further reports that Egypt would refuse to attend the conference were attributed to high political sources in Cairo. Meanwhile, the Soviet Union was said to have indicated that it would participate, although with some reservations.]

Prime Minister Nehru's speech was delivered in deliberately dispassionate tones, and the lan-

Continued on Page 4, Column 3

State Ruling Backs Teachers' Refusal To Inform on Reds

Text of the Allen decision in teachers' case, Page 8.

By LEONARD BUDER

The State Education Commissioner ruled yesterday that a teacher could not be discharged for refusing to name other teachers who are or were Communist party members.

Commissioner James E. Allen Jr. reversed the suspension of four New York City public school teachers and one principal and the dismissal of a municipal college faculty member for refusing to name others. He declared that compelling teachers to become informers "would do more harm than good and that this type of inquisition has no place in the school system."

A school spokesman, however, asserted that the five school employes still had other charges confronting them that were not annulled by the Commissioner's action and that they would probably be kept on suspension.

Meanwhile, Peter Campbell Brown, the city Corporation Counsel, said that he would challenge the Commissioner's ruling in the courts.

The ruling," Mr. Brown declared, "radically affects the conduct of the entire anti-subversive program of the Board of Education and Board of Higher Education, and involves interpretation of the fundamental rights and obligations of teachers. This is a problem of such importance that I feel compelled, in the public interest, to obtain a definitive declaration from the courts."

Dr. Allen handed down his decision in connection with a series of appeals made by eight New York City educators. Two

Continued on Page 8, Column 6

EISENHOWER SEES NO WAR OVER SUEZ

Expects 'Good Sense' to Bar Hostilities, but Does Not Rule Out Use of Force

By DANA ADAMS SCHMIDT

Special to The New York Times.

WASHINGTON, Aug. 8—President Eisenhower expressed his conviction today that there would be no war over the Suez Canal.

But he went on to indicate that he was not letting down the British and the French and that there were circumstances under which force might be used.

The President said at his news conference that he thought there was "good reason to hope that good sense" would prevail. He added that he thought "a little sober thinking" was going to prevail.

[Secretary General Dag Hammarskjold of the United Nations is to confer with Secretary of State Dulles in Washington Friday on the Suez problem.]

The Suez Canal dispute is "one of those things that just has to be settled," the President declared, adding that "damage and destruction is no settlement."

On the basis of these remarks a British correspondent asked whether the President meant that he was "opposed to the use of military force under any circumstances."

The President stiffened and flushed.

"I didn't say that," he asserted. "I was very careful not to say that," he added, and went on to explain that all he meant was that questions interesting more than one nation should be settled by negotiation.

"We have tried to substitute

Continued on Page 2, Column 4

EDEN SAYS NASSER IS THE SOLE ENEMY IN CRISIS ON SUEZ

Asserts Britain's 'Quarrel Is Not With Egypt, Still Less With the Arab World'

ASKS NATIONS' SUPPORT

Prime Minister, in Broadcast, Also Reaffirms Aim to Use Force as Last Resort

Text of the Eden broadcast on Suez appears on Page 2.

By KENNETT LOVE

Special to The New York Times.

LONDON, Aug. 8—Prime Minister Eden told a vast radio and television audience tonight that President Gamal Abdel Nasser of Egypt was Britain's sole and personal enemy in the dispute over the Suez Canal.

"Our quarrel is not with Egypt," the Prime Minister said, "still less with the Arab world. It is with Colonel Nasser."

Sir Anthony appealed for world support in the quarrel. His fifteen-minute talk was the first program ever carried simultaneously by Britain's two television networks, both the Government-sponsored and the commercial. It was also carried by British and United States broadcasting hook-ups.

President Nasser was portrayed by Sir Anthony as a Fascist plunderer whose appetite grew with feeding and whose word was worthless.

He said President Nasser's seizure of the Suez Canal was a matter of life and death for Britain and Europe because it placed countries dependent on Middle Eastern oil supplies at the mercy of one man. He reaffirmed Britain's intention to use force as a last resort to make sure that the great trading nations of the world could not be "strangled at any moment."

Reinforcements Continue

The reinforcement of British Middle East forces continued by air and sea. Four troopships are scheduled to sail in the next six days with units of artillery, anti-aircraft, air dispatch and maintenance and infantry troops. Air charter company officials were called to the Air Ministry for consultations.

Sir Anthony spoke in careful, measured phrases. He reminded his British viewers that many of them had served in Egypt and had helped to defend the Suez Canal in the two world wars.

At one point he gestured with both hands to emphasize the "preposterous amount" of oil revenues President Nasser wanted to meet with canal revenues.

Sir Anthony outlined Britain's intentions regarding the possible use of force to restore international control over the canal at the end of an eloquent statement covering all important aspects of the situation. He said:

"Meanwhile, we have too much at risk not to take precautions. We have done so. That is the meaning of the movements by land, sea and air of which you have heard in the last few days.

"My friends, we do not seek a solution by force, but the broadest possible international agreement. That is why we have

Continued on Page 2, Column 3

276 Miners Trapped In Belgian Pit Fire

Special to The New York Times.

BRUSSELS, Belgium, Aug. 8—Two hundred and seventy-six coal miners were trapped by fire 2,200 to 3,500 feet below ground level today in Marcinelle. They still were there late tonight.

Seven men reached the surface safely in a mine shaft elevator when the fire broke out. After having been beaten back once by fumes, rescuers equipped with oxygen apparatus went down this elevator and rescued the seven men at a level of 2,500 feet. The miners were taken to a hospital but late tonight it was doubted that any would survive.

The elevator, in another shaft elevator, was put out of action when the cables melted from the heat of the fire. [The Associated Press reported twenty-five men had escaped before the elevator jammed.]

Salvage teams descending a

Continued on Page 6, Column 4

Death Toll in Blast in Colombian City Is Estimated as High as 1,200

Associated Press Wirephoto
This is downtown Cali, where seven truckloads of dynamite exploded Tuesday, tearing the center of the Colombian city

By The Associated Press.

CALI, Colombia, Aug. 8—The death toll in yesterday's dynamite blast in the heart of this city was estimated today to be as high as 1,200. Relief poured in, and the task of burying the dead went on.

Authorities said tonight 357 victims had been buried so far in a common grave. Ninety other bodies are still awaiting identification by relatives, it was added. Up to 2,000 buildings may have been destroyed by the explosion, some sources

said. Damage to business and industry was estimated as high as $40,000,000. The blast left a crater eighty-five feet deep and about 200 feet wide. No North Americans were reported killed or injured in the disaster, in which seven trucks

loaded with dynamite exploded. The trucks had been parked for the night Monday in a densely populated area of slums, warehouses, small hotels, stores and fac-

Continued on Page 6, Column 6

276 Trapped in Belgian Mine
When Flames Cut Off Escape

Continued From Page 1

third shaft, newly drilled and not yet in operation, recovered three bodies after having groped through a labyrinth of passages and removed a hatch from a six-foot-thick concrete wall that separated the new shaft from the old mine.

The fire broke out at 8:15 A. M. in two disused galleries situated above those in which the men are trapped. It was caused when a derailed coal truck fell against an electric cable, cutting it and causing a short circuit.

Relatives of the trapped miners, many of whom had migrated from Italy, rushed sobbing to the pithead as news of the disaster spread through Marcinelle, a mining community of 23,000 near Charleroi.

Fears were growing tonight that this might become the third largest mine disaster in history. The Honkeiko, Manchuria, mine disaster in 1942 caused 1,549 deaths and in a disaster in Coullière, France, 1,027 coal miners lost their lives in 1906.

Rescue operations are hampered by the heat and intense smoke but there still are hopes that at least a few more men can be rescued. Air is being pumped into the galleries where the men are trapped.

King Baudouin visited the scene of the disaster tonight, as did Premier Achille van Acker and several of his Cabinet Ministers.

The New York Times   Aug. 9, 1956

Belgian miners were trapped by fire at Marcinelle (cross).

Italians Irked at Disaster

ROME, Aug. 8 (UP)—The Italian Government dispatched its Labor Minister and Foreign Affairs Under Secretary to Belgium tonight amid an outcry over the latest Belgian mine disaster involving Italian workers.

The Government, which suspended the migration of Italian miners to Belgium six months ago as a result of previous mine disasters, prepared to appeal to the European Coal and Steel community to prevent a repetition of today's disaster in Marcinelle.

Italian union leaders charged that safety measures in Belgian mines were inadequate.

Hundreds of anxious relatives and friends wait outside the gates of the Amercoeur Works at the Du Bois De Cazier coal mine for news of the miners trapped by flames and smoke a half mile or more beneath the surface of the earth.   *United Press International*

Rescue workers search in the wreckage of the Cali railroad station after a tremendous dynamite blast razed eight city blocks in the downtown area of the city.   *United Press International*

COLOMBIA BLAST SAID TO KILL 1,200

Continued From Page 1

tories. President Gustavo Rojas Pinilla charged that the blast, which destroyed the center of this city, was an act of political sabotage.

Some officials said there never might be an accurate count of the dead. Many bodies disintegrated in the blast. Most of the dead died in their sleep.

The newspaper Diario de Colombia of Bogotá estimated the dead at 1,200.

The explosion came about 1:20 A. M. yesterday. The day was the anniversary of the 1819 Battle of Boyaca, a national holiday celebrating a decisive battle in the War for Independence from Spain.

The seven trucks in the explosion were part of a convoy of ten carrying explosives from the port of Buenaventura to the Public Works Ministry in Bogotá. The drivers decided to spend the night sleeping in the trucks.

Fourteen hours after the explosion, a fireman digging in ruins where several adults had perished found a 2-month-old boy lying unharmed in the wreckage.

Bulldozers pushed debris aside in an effort to uncover more bodies. Dust and smoke still hung over the disaster area under a hot sun.

Most of the population of this city of 285,000 was helping to give aid in one form or another. Doctors, nurses, medical supplies and food were flown in from Bogota and other cities.

The American Red Cross in Panama sent two tons of medical supplies. Thousands of blood donors lined up in Bogotá in response to an appeal.

General Rojas, in his sabotage accusation, hinted that the explosion came as the result of a joint statement by former Presidents Alberto Lleras Camargo and Laureano Gomez, appealing to their rival Opposition parties to unite and overthrow the Government.

The President, who was heavily guarded, declared in a radio statement that, "before God and man, the armed forces will not rest until the authors of this treacherous and criminal attempt receive exemplary punishment."

Comment by Ex-President

MIAMI, Fla., Aug. 8 (P)—Former President Lleras Camargo of Colombia said in a statement reaching here today that he and former President Gomez had been linked to the Cali explosion because they were political opponents of General Rojas.

"I have heard with the deepest surprise that the President of the Republic explained the tragedy by naming in his communiqué as responsible those who are working for harmony among political parties and of Colombia itself," Dr. Camargo said.

"All the News That's Fit to Print"

The New York Times.

LATE CITY EDITION

U. S. Weather Bureau Report (Page 36) forecasts: Rain early, clearing later today. Fair tonight and tomorrow. Temp. range: 81—67. Yesterday: 80.7—71.6.

VOL. CVI..No. 36,316. © 1957, by The New York Times Company. NEW YORK, SATURDAY, JUNE 29, 1957. Times Square, New York 36, N.Y. Telephone LAckawanna 4-1000 FIVE CENTS

DEATH TOLL 120 IN GULF HURRICANE; HUNDREDS INJURED AS TIDAL WAVES RAVAGE LOUISIANA COASTAL TOWNS

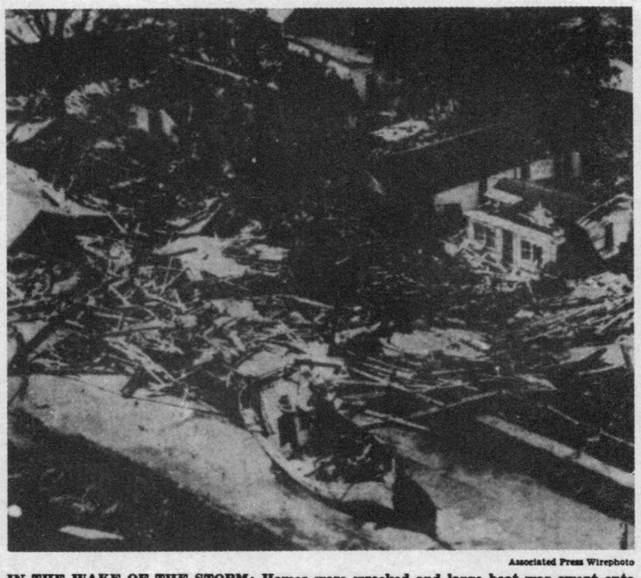

Associated Press Wirephoto

IN THE WAKE OF THE STORM: Homes were wrecked and large boat was swept onto a highway as hurricane swept through Cameron, in southwestern Louisiana near the Gulf.

ARMY SENDS HELP

Helicopters and Boats Hunt for Survivors in Cameron Area

By The Associated Press.

LAKE CHARLES, La., June 28—Smashing tidal waves swamped the Louisiana coast today in the wake of Hurricane Audrey, leaving an estimated 120 dead and hundreds injured.

The waves slipped slowly back to sea tonight, unveiling wild wreckage.

Maj. Gen. Raymond Hufft, state Civil Defense Director, said the expected loss of life in Cameron parish was about 100 persons. This was a downward revision from the 150 he previously had expected in the marshy area south of Lake Charles.

General Hufft said the dead in the area now totaled fifty-two, with 150 missing. He expects about one-third of the missing to be dead. Other fatalities occurred in scattered areas over the state.

An armada of helicopters and fleets of boats roamed through the flooded area in the southwest corner of Louisiana, concentrating on the twenty-mile, below-sea level strip across the bottom of the state.

Fewer Believed Dead

Sheriff O. B. Carter of Cameron Parish said he had fifty-two dead. He gave his total in an amateur radio broadcast from the flood-beleaguered town of Cameron, south of Lake Charles. His earlier estimate had been 200 dead or presumed dead.

Most estimates of the dead made it clear that there was room for error and the total could be higher or lower. Communications prevented comparisons of estimates by various sources.

Civil defense officials said Army units had come in to assist civil defense leaders in cleaning up. They furnished equipment, water purification units and other needed material.

Rescue teams brought hundreds out of the towns of Cameron, Grand Chenier and Black Bayou and other communities. However, the receding water later permitted some to remain at Cameron.

Many were rescued from high spots, rooftops and trees, where they had been for long hours without food or water.

Rescued From Tree

R. A. Whatley, 40 years old of Grand Chenier, told how he had clung to a tree for eighteen hours with his injured wife, Dorothy, 35.

"We were at a friend's house," he said. "We went to the attic. Then we jumped into the water and grabbed a tree. Three of the people died."

Ken Dixon, managing editor of The Lake Charles American Press, said that the bodies of two-thirds of the victims would be swept into the Gulf of Mexico by the receding tidewaters.

The first hint of the scope of the disaster came early this morning when Deputy Sheriff D. P. Vincent, rescued by boat

Continued on Page 18, Column 1

President Speeds Aid in Storm; Peterson Sent to Direct Relief

Special to The New York Times.

WASHINGTON, June 28—President Eisenhower directed the mobilization of Federal resources today for relief in the hurricane-stricken area of southern Louisiana.

As reports of casualties and damage flowed into the White House, he dispatched a personal representative to the scene of the disaster.

The President telephoned the orders from his farm at Gettysburg, Pa., where he had motored for a long week-end with Mrs. Eisenhower.

The President named Val Peterson as his "personal representative" and directed him to fly to Louisiana tonight. Mr. Peterson, who recently resigned as Federal Civil Defense Administrator, will be accompanied by Lewis E. Berry Jr., acting Civil Defense Administrator; Maj. Gen. Albert M. Gruenther, president of the American National Red Cross, and Maj. Gen. Emerson Itschner, Chief of the Army Engineers.

Mr. Peterson was instructed to see that all Federal facilities were utilized, including those available at military installations in the stricken area. He also was directed to make available medicines, food, shelters, road equipment and other Federal resources.

An initial report to the President from General Gruenther at Red Cross headquarters here said that the national organization had sent forty-five persons from Washington to join Louisiana chapters in relief work.

General Gruenther said that the Red Cross already had sheltered and fed some 40,000 persons in eighty relief stations.

James C. Hagerty, White

Continued on Page 18, Column 2

BILL TO PROTECT F.B.I. FILE VOTED BY SENATE GROUP

Subcommittee Backs Move to Provide Only 'Relevant' Data to Defendants

BROWNELL MAKES PLEA

Says Supreme Court Ruling Stirs 'Grave Emergency in Law Enforcement'

By JAY WALZ

Special to The New York Times.

WASHINGTON, June 28—An Administration move to limit the use of files of the Federal Bureau of Investigation by defendants in criminal cases won quick approval today from a Senate Judiciary subcommittee.

The subcommittee, voting unanimously, reported out a bill within a few minutes after Attorney General Herbert Brownell Jr. testified that a Supreme Court decision of June 3 had brought a "grave emergency in law enforcement."

The bill would open the secret F. B. I. files only for information found "relevant" by the judge in the case. A number of Senators, including Joseph C. O'Mahoney, subcommittee chairman, sponsored the measure, which was drafted in the Department of Justice.

A similar bill, introduced by Representative Kenneth B. Keating, Republican of upstate New York, was bypassed yesterday by a House Judiciary subcommittee in favor of a "stronger" measure sponsored by Representative Francis E. Walter, Democrat of Pennsylvania.

Conviction Voided

The Supreme Court decision causing concern upset the conviction of Clinton E. Jencks, a New Mexico labor leader, who had been found guilty of filing a false non-Communist affidavit. A majority of five justices ruled that Mr. Jencks should have been permitted to see reports that Government witnesses made about him to the Federal Bureau of Investigation.

The bureau, with Executive backing, has long has held that its files must remain secret because exposure of its informants would dry up sources of information.

Mr. Brownell assured the Senate subcommittee that "we accept the principle" of the Supreme Court decision. However, he urged that access to the secret information be limited to avoid "serious miscarriage of justice in Federal criminal cases."

The high court majority said that if Government prosecutors felt they could not disclose files when they were requested, they should drop the cases.

Broadly Interpreted

The Attorney General said that one Rhode Island court had interpreted the Jencks decision so broadly that it could result in the "freeing of a convicted tax evader and four convicted kidnappers."

Last night, Mr. Brownell related, the Justice Department received notice that four defendants who were convicted of kidnapping on May 29 in Rhode Island had demanded all reports of the F. B. I. relating to the alleged kidnapping as well as any statements, oral or written, made to the F. B. I. agents by parents of the victim.

In a recent criminal income

Continued on Page 7, Column 2

Budget Aide Chosen As a T.V.A. Director

By WILLIAM M. BLAIR

Special to The New York Times.

WASHINGTON, June 28—Arnold R. Jones of Kansas, Deputy Director of the Bureau of the Budget, was selected by President Eisenhower today to be a director of the Tennessee Valley Authority.

The nomination, for a nine-year term, is to be sent to the Senate next week. It is expected to touch off another round in the public-vs.-private-power fight that the Democrats, taking the public power side, are seeking to build into a major issue for the 1958 and 1960 elections.

Mr. Jones is a Republican. He is a certified public accountant. He is on leave from Kansas State College, which he joined in 1945 as controller at the request of the President's brother, Dr. Milton S. Eisenhower, then

Continued on Page 8, Column 2

House Panel Acts to Deny Long-Term Aid Authority

Committee Cuts 400 Million From Total Approved by Senate—3-Year Fund for Foreign Loans Is Refused

By WILLIAM S. WHITE

Special to The New York Times.

WASHINGTON, June 28—The House Foreign Affairs Committee recommended tonight the elimination of a long-term authority for the foreign aid program that the Senate had granted.

The committee, by undisclosed vote in closed session, accompanied this thrust at the Eisenhower Administration with yet another. It proposed a $400,000,000 cut below the $3,637,000,000 authorization that the Senate had granted.

The Administration originally had sought $4,400,000,000. But the President subsequently reduced this by $500,000,000.

The House committee expects to complete final action on the bill by Monday.

Neither this nor the authorization, approved by vote of 57 to 25 in the Senate on June 14, has any aspect of finality as to what money is actually to be allowed.

Both involve grants of authority to continue the program with only suggested monetary ceilings. The actual allocation will be determined later by separate appropriations bills.

Thus the decision of the House committee to resist a grant to the Administration of the long-term commitment power was of greater significance than its recommendation for a $400,000,000 reduction.

Specifically, the committee struck out a proviso by which the Administration would be guaranteed at least a three-year loan fund for economic assistance—the heart of its "new approach" of this year to mutual security.

Left in the bill was only an item of $500,000,000 for this purpose for the fiscal year opening Monday. Stricken were general-

Continued on Page 7, Column 3

EISENHOWER CUTS DEFENSE BUILDING

Trims 456 Million From New Outlay—Senators Vote 34 Billion for Arms

By JOHN D. MORRIS

Special to The New York Times.

WASHINGTON, June 28—President Eisenhower trimmed nearly half a billion dollars today from projected new outlays for military construction.

He sent Congress a request for appropriations of $1,665,500,000 to finance improvements of existing installations here and abroad and to build new ones. This was $456,500,000 less than he had proposed in his Budget Message last January.

The President meanwhile won another skirmish in his battle for what he regards as adequate funds for other military programs.

The Senate Appropriations Committee unanimously approved a bill appropriating $34,534,229,000 to build up the country's armed strength in the 1958 fiscal year, which starts Monday.

The panel sustained without change a subcommittee's decision to restore $971,504,000 that the House of Representatives had cut from President Eisenhower's requests. The President and his military advisers had sought the restoration of $1,274,-

Continued on Page 8, Column 3

President and Wife Doff Shoes at Rites Dedicating Mosque

By W. H. LAWRENCE

Special to The New York Times.

WASHINGTON, June 28—President and Mrs. Eisenhower removed their shoes today to join Moslems from sixteen countries in opening formally a new Islamic Center on Massachusetts Avenue.

While hundreds watched beneath a broiling sun, the President declared that the mosque was an example of America's prized religious freedom and tolerance and a symbol of the long friendship of this country and the nations of Islam.

The crowd was a distinguished one, including many other leaders of the United States Government and the Ambassadors of Saudi Arabia, Afghanistan, Egypt, Indonesia, Iran, Iraq, Jordan, Libya, Morocco, Pakistan, Sudan, Syria, Tunisia, Turkey and Yemen.

For many, the high point came when the President, in the traditional gesture of respect, removed his shoes before a brief inspection tour of the prayer room. The room faces toward Mecca, the center of the Moslem faith.

Arab League Ambassadors had said in advance that the President, as a Protestant, was not required to remove his shoes, but could slip them into cloth coverings before stepping in the deep pile of Persian rugs that

Continued on Page 9, Column 6

DULLES RULES OUT U.S. RECOGNITION OF CHINESE REDS

Asserts Any Ties Would Only Prolong 'Passing Phase' of Communist Control

The text of Dulles' address is printed on Page 6.

By GLADWIN HILL

Special to The New York Times.

SAN FRANCISCO, June 28—Secretary of State Dulles emphatically reiterated today the United States determination to give no comfort to Communist China diplomatically, commercially or culturally.

He said international communism's grip on the 600,000,000 people of mainland China was regarded as "a passing and not a perpetual phase" that would only be prolonged by any kind of recognition.

Mr. Dulles' declaration, made to a convention of Lions International, was the Administration's first comprehensive delineation of its China policy in three years. Billed by the State Department as a "major" pronouncement, it shaped up as an inferential rejection of international undercurrents of accommodation to the regime of Mao Tse-tung.

Peiping U. N. Role Urged

Recently both Britain and Japan have expressed willingness to carry on degrees of trade with Red China, and the Communists have been building up pressure for Communist China's representation in the United Nations.

Mr. Dulles said the United States' China policy, "like all our policies," was under "periodic review," but that there appeared to be no reason at this time for altering it.

About 5,000 delegates in San Francisco's Civic Auditorium applauded and cheered a half dozen times during the Secretary's twenty-minute speech, which was televised nationally. The Lions are a federation of local service clubs, dedicated to fellowship and community good works.

'Negative' Policy Denied

Secretary Dulles did not mention the current controversy about the State Department's ban on visits by United States reporters to Red China. He said however:

"We doubt the value of cultural exchanges which the Chinese Communists are eager to develop. They want this relationship with the United States primarily because, once that example were given, it would be difficult for China's close neighbors not to follow it. These free nations, already exposed to intense Communist subversive activities, could not have the cultural exchanges that the

Continued on Page 6, Column 5

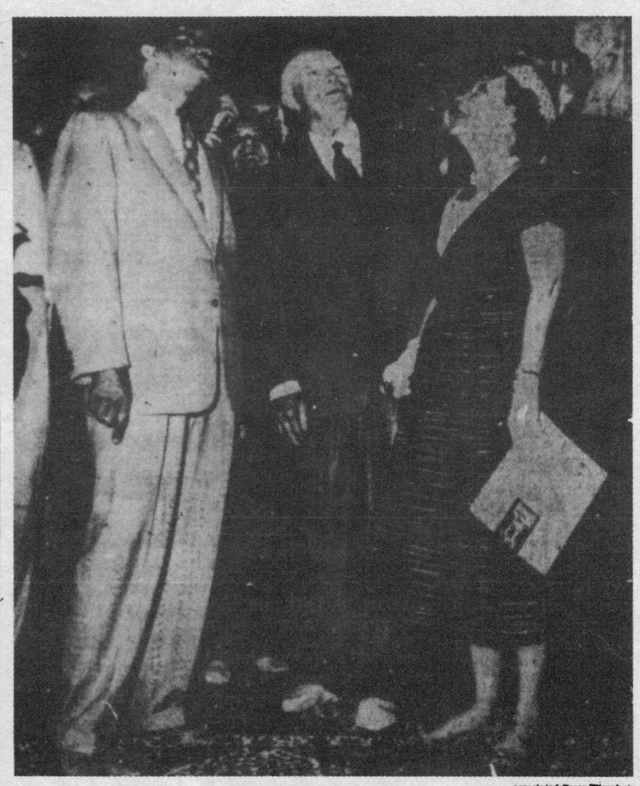

Associated Press Wirephoto

ISLAMIC CENTER DEDICATED IN WASHINGTON: Sheikh Abdullah al-Khayyal, left, showing President and Mrs. Eisenhower around the mosque at the center on Massachusetts Avenue yesterday. In accordance with Moslem custom, they had removed shoes.

NATO TO DISCUSS ARMS PLAN TODAY

U. N. Delegations in London Go to Paris—Stassen Asks for Airport Inspection

By LEONARD INGALLS

Special to The New York Times.

LONDON, June 28—Western delegates to disarmament talks here flew to Paris tonight to consult with their Atlantic pact allies.

The representatives of the United Nations Disarmament Subcommittee will meet tomorrow with the Permanent Council of the North Atlantic Treaty Organization.

The delegates left soon after the presentation of strong Western points on an arms reduction control system to the subcommittee. After the Paris discussions the United States is scheduled to submit to the five-power United Nations group next week major proposals on limitations of nuclear weapons.

With the support of Britain, France and Canada, Harold E. Stassen, chief United States representative, today told Valerian A. Zorin, head of the Soviet delegation, that any initial disarmament treaty must include safeguards against a surprise attack, including the inspection of airports.

In proposals made to the subcommittee April 30, the Soviet Union omitted surveillance of airports in its suggestion for a first-step disarmament agreement.

A few hours after the subcommittee meeting, Mr. Stassen, Jules Moch of France, Ivor Pink of Britain and Capt. M. H. Ellis of Canada, flew to Paris for the Atlantic pact council discussions.

Disarmament Subcommittee

Continued on Page 3, Column 2

City Approves Sale Of Manhattantown; Work to Begin Soon

By CHARLES GRUTZNER

The Board of Estimate yesterday approved William Zeckendorf's plan to put up the money and know-how to get the stalled Manhattantown redevelopment under construction.

The Webb & Knapp realty interests, headed by Mr. Zeckendorf, will advance $1,088,000 at once to purchase controlling stock interest in Manhattantown, Inc., and pay up that corporation's debts. They will also furnish a $900,000 bond to guarantee completion of the first three buildings in two years.

Manhattantown is to consist of nine sixteen-story apartment buildings and a shopping center in the six-block area between Central Park West and Amsterdam Avenue, from Ninety-seventh to 100th Street. Webb & Knapp will furnish additional bonds later to guarantee completion of the entire redevelopment by 1962.

Early Start Is Planned

The realty concern is to begin excavation within two weeks after taking over control of Manhattantown, Inc. The changeover is to be effected not later than July 15, and requires two preliminary actions. These are formal discontinuance of the city's foreclosure action and approval of the transfer by the Housing and Home Finance Agency.

William R. Peer, executive secretary to Mayor Wagner, said the city would file a discontinuance of the foreclosure next week in State Supreme Court. Federal approval of the transaction is believed certain. The Government agency had extended the expiration date of its mortgage insurance for the first three buildings to permit the change in control to be negotiated.

Division of the Outlay

Of the $1,088,000 outlay, $170,000 represents the purchase of 138 of the 200 shares of Manhattantown stock by the Webb & Knapp Construction Corporation from Jack Ferman and Seymour Millstein and members of the Ferman and Millstein families. The purchaser is a wholly owned subsidiary of Webb & Knapp, Inc. William Zeckendorf is president and William Zeckendorf Jr. is vice president of both concerns.

The remainder of the immediate outlay, for which Webb & Knapp will receive notes on Manhattantown, Inc., will pay off the following debts:

¶$620,000 to the city for back taxes and interest.

¶$200,500 for notes, with interest, held by the Fermans and Millsteins.

¶$60,000 on a note held by the Chemical Corn Exchange Bank on Manhattantown, Inc., and personally guaranteed by the Fermans and Millsteins.

¶$37,500 to Daniel J. Riesner for legal services rendered to

Continued on Page 17, Column 3

LANZA ATTORNEY UPHELD BY COURT

Appellate Division Supports Cosentino's Silence About Tape-Recorded Parley

The Appellate Division yesterday upheld Sylvester Cosentino's refusal to answer official questions based on his talks with Joseph (Socks) Lanza. The ruling was unanimous.

A lawyer, Mr. Cosentino contended that the questions asked of him by Arthur L. Reuter, acting State Investigation Commissioner, would violate his lawyer-client relationship with Lanza.

In a formal opinion, Associate Justice Francis Bergan declared that Commissioner Reuter's questions were based on a surreptitiously recorded conversation between Mr. Cosentino and Lanza at the Westchester County Jail.

Although the state's highest court has ruled that the Joint Legislative Committee on Government Operations is free to make this recording public, Mr. Cosentino cannot be questioned about it, the opinion held.

Referring to the use of electronic devices to intercept and record the conversation, Justice Bergan continued:

"The law does not lie helpless because there may arise ingenious facilities to circumvent its safeguards; if the constitutional guaranty of the aid of counsel is to be of value, the court must afford to every man the right to talk with his lawyer with assurance that the lawyer will not be required or permitted to disclose what is said.

"To the extent that information thus wrongfully obtained

Continued on Page 33, Column 2

U.S. Bars Arab Plea To End Aid to Paris

By E. W. KENWORTHY

Special to The New York Times.

WASHINGTON, June 28—The State Department rejected today a request by eleven Arab nations that the United States suspend military aid to France.

In parallel notes to the Arab diplomatic missions here, the United States also reaffirmed its policy that Israeli shipping has the right to pass freely through the Gulf of Aqaba and the Suez Canal.

On May 24, representatives of the Arab states called on Secretary of State Dulles and read a 5,000-word statement asking the United States to stop military aid to France on the ground that the French were using it to suppress Algerian nationalism.

The Arabs' note accused the French of "outrageous acts of terror and atrocities" in Algeria.

The State Department's reply

Continued on Page 3, Column 4

Sections of Texas and Louisiana Along the Gulf of Mexico Are Hard Hit by the Year's First Hurricane

The six men clinging to these two liferafts were washed ashore safely yesterday after being in the storm-tossed Gulf of Mexico since Thursday. An oil-drilling platform on which they were working had capsized eighteen miles south of Sabine Pass, Tex. This photograph was taken Thursday afternoon by John D. Vaughn, helicopter pilot for Magnolia Petroleum.

A refuge from the high winds and floods marking Hurricane Audrey in Cameron, La., was courthouse at right. It is on comparatively high ground, and sheltered numerous refugees. Cars parked in lot apparently were lifted and crashed together at height of blow. National Guard and Army units, Red Cross and Coast Guard and private groups aided rescue.

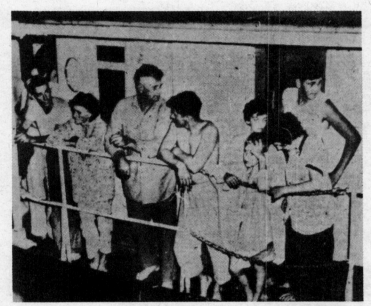

These are some of the persons whose homes in Cameron, La., were destroyed by the hurricane. Refugees were taken from Gulf village to Lake Charles aboard Coast Guard cutter.

Associated Press Wirephotos

The New York Times

June 29, 1957

Hurricane and tidal waves that hit the coast of the Gulf of Mexico practically destroyed Cameron, La. (cross), and wrought heavy damage in the underlined cities and towns.

GULF HURRICANE TAKES 120 LIVES

Continued From Page 1

from Cameron, said he felt "3,000 or 4,000 drowned" there.

Stanley Meisler, Associated Press reporter, reporting by mobile amateur radio from isolated Cameron, told of the grim hunt by survivors for relatives.

Charles LeBoeuf of Cameron, looking for his mother, said:

"I may find her body, but not her. She slipped away from my brother because she was too heavy to hold."

Mr. Meisler described the battered areas, hit by waves twenty feet high, as "shocking and almost unbelievable." He said water remained as much as six feet deep in places, although it was falling tonight.

He said best estimates indicated several thousand persons had remained in Cameron Parish yesterday because many of them thought the hurricane would not reach land until night. It struck in the middle of the morning.

National Guardsmen patrolled sections of Lake Charles and Cameron Parish to prevent looting.

Dr. Cecil Clark of Cameron worked around the clock, although his wife, three children, parents and sister were swept away by the waves.

Bill Mertena, an American Press reporter, toured the Cameron area by plane and helicopter.

He said Cameron was about 90 per cent destroyed, with "at least 50 per cent of the buildings demolished completely and many others so badly damaged they were a total loss."

Mr. Mertena covered almost eighty miles of coastline in his flights and reported only one home out of every twenty-five still standing.

"Only projecting foundations and chimneys told where there had been houses," he said. "The resort community of Holly Beach no longer exists. It was completely wiped off the map."

Bodies of dead cattle, horses and wild animals littered stretches of the marshlands.

Cars Spotted On Road

Mr. Mertena said he had counted more than seventy-five cars scattered along roads where people had made vain efforts to flee. The fate of the occupants was unknown.

General Hufft, after his tour of the area, said bodies of the dead animals constituted a major health problem.

About 350 survivors of the hurricane evacuated Pecan Island after medical and parish authorities warned of a possible outbreak of disease. Isolation of the island, loss of electric power and contamination of drinking water caused a disease threat, an official stated.

Pecan Island, actually a ridge about eight feet high at its high-

est point, is set in flat marshlands that extend six miles southward to the Gulf of Mexico. It is about fifty miles southeast of Lake Charles.

Elsewhere, 400 persons were rescued by one boat alone, the majority picked off rafts, trees and remnants of rooftops. Some were swimming or floating when spotted by rescuers.

John Washington, 32 years old, of Cameron, said, "I was living in a rooming house and it just tore down."

Mrs. Wade C. Haley, 26 years old, said she and her husband and four children were in their trailer home when the hurricane hit.

"I don't know where the trailer is now," she said. "It was already floating before we got out of it. A boat picked us up at a two-story house later and took us to the courthouse."

Many refugees gathered at the courthouse before being brought into Lake Charles.

The steel and concrete courthouse was the only Cameron building still intact. Water was knee deep on the first floor.

Refugees were sent to an arena at McNeese State College in Lake Charles. Most had only the stained, mud-spattered clothes they wore.

Relatives and friends took some into their homes. Hundreds remained in the arena tonight on cots, eating in shifts in the college cafeteria.

No over-all damage estimates were available.

Mr. Dixon said it would run into the millions in Lake Charles alone. The city suffered plate glass and roof damage, broken power lines, and water damage.

Oil Rigs Destroyed

Oil companies, whose offshore rigs were destroyed by the 105-mile-an-hour winds, said their loss would run at least $15,000,000.

A herd of 30,000 Brahman cattle in the Pecan Island area was wiped out. Sheriff Jack Moss at Abbeville said the herd was "easily worth millions."

Four of the dead were in the Pecan Island section, a big area of Vermilion Parish that adjoins Cameron Parish and also lies below sea level.

At Cameron, boats 75 and 100 feet long were lying hundreds of yards inland. Some had been carried miles. A huge drilling barge was left blocking the highway from Lake Charles to Cameron.

National Guards units moved thousands of cots and blankets into the area and 400 Red Cross officials helped bring some order at refugee camps.

PRESIDENT SPEEDS AID TO STORM BELT

Continued From Page 1

House press secretary, said reports from civil defense officials on the scene were being relayed to the President in Gettysburg.

Teams from the Civil Defense Administration moved in rapidly to investigate and evaluate reports from the troubled area. This was a legal preliminary essential to a declaration by the President that places hardest hit by Hurricane Audrey in "a major disaster area."

Mr. Hagerty said that Governor Peterson had been called in because of his long experience as Civil Defense Administrator in meeting other disasters, such as the New England flood of 1955.

Ready for Envoy's Post

Mr. Peterson, who had been scheduled to be sworn in Monday as the new ambassador to Denmark, said that "we'll throw the book at the disaster, utilizing every resource of Government to bring every bit of relief possible."

The Peterson group was scheduled to fly directly to New Orleans. They will be met by Acting Gov. Lether Frazier and civil defense officials.

Mr. Peterson will stay in Louisiana as long as necessary, making plans to meet the emergency

and keeping the President informed of the steps he thinks the Federal Government must take.

Maj. Gen. Raymond E. Hufft, Louisiana Adjutant General and Civil Defense Administrator, flew over the Cameron-Chenier area today and reported to the White House that the destruction was heavy.

He also reported that helicopters offered the only means of reaching Cameron, although the Army already had road clearing equipment in the area.

The Coast Guard moved into rescue operations ahead of the President's general order to other service units, including the Army, Navy and Air Force, to lend their manpower and equipment to help the stricken area.

From Fourth Army headquarters nine helicopters were dispatched to work under Coast Guard direction.

White House aides followed reports from the Louisiana coastal area. Civil Defense officials from the regional offices at Denton, Tex., and Alexandria, La., were directed to move into the area at once and to confer with state officials on assistance needed from the Federal Government.

The Small Business Administration designated eight parishes in Louisiana and two counties in Texas as disaster areas tonight.

This will enable owners of homes and businesses damaged or destroyed in the hurricane to apply for reconstruction loans from the Federal agency. The long-term loans are available at 3 per cent interest.

"All the News That's Fit to Print"

The New York Times.

LATE CITY EDITION

U. S. Weather Bureau Report (Page 45) Includes...
Chance of showers today; clearing tonight. Mostly fair tomorrow.
Temp. range: 87—73. Yesterday: 84.7—73.2

VOL. CVII..No. 36,728. | © 1958, by The New York Times Company. Times Square, New York 36, N. Y. | NEW YORK, FRIDAY, AUGUST 15, 1958. | Not beyond 200-mile zone from New York City. Higher in air delivery cities. | FIVE CENTS

U. S. CONSIDERING BID TO U. N. CHIEF TO GO TO JORDAN

AMMAN ASKS AID

Opposes a U. N. Force but Seeks Arms for Self-Defense

Lloyd's speech and excerpts from others, Page 4.

By THOMAS J. HAMILTON
Special to The New York Times.

UNITED NATIONS, N. Y., Aug. 14—The United States disclosed tonight that it might ask the General Assembly to request Secretary General Dag Hammarskjold to go to Jordan to discuss strengthening the United Nations position there.

Henry Cabot Lodge of the United States told Latin American delegates that such action might be necessary as a result of a statement today to the Assembly by Abdul Monem Rifai, the Jordanian representative.

Mr. Rifai, brother of the Jordanian Premier, Samir el-Rifai, said that his Government would not permit United Nations forces or observers to be stationed on Jordanian territory. But he added that Jordan needed money and arms for self-defense.

Vetoed Plan Is Basis

Mr. Lodge told the Latin American delegates that the United States wanted the Assembly to adopt a resolution on Lebanon and Jordan reproducing the essential points of a Japanese proposal vetoed by the Soviet Union during the Security Council debate last month.

The new resolution, which is to be introduced by Norway and possibly other Western countries, will call on Mr. Hammarskjold to take additional measures to insure the territorial integrity and political independence of Lebanon and Jordan, Mr. Lodge said.

The same basic line is being taken by Selwyn Lloyd, British Foreign Secretary. He told the Assembly this morning that it should ask Mr. Hammarskjold to take the necessary steps, in consultation with the two governments, to insure these objectives for Lebanon and Jordan.

Key Section Cited

The impending Norwegian resolution will be based on the operative part of the Japanese resolution. It will read:

"The Assembly

"Requests the Secretary General to make arrangements forthwith for such measures, in addition to those envisaged by the resolution of 11 June, 1958, as he may consider necessary in the light of the present circumstances, with a view to enabling the United Nations to fulfill the general purposes established in that resolution, and which will, in accordance with the Charter, serve to ensure the territorial integrity and political independence of Lebanon, so as to make possible the withdrawal of United States forces from Lebanon."

In addition, it is understood,

Continued on Page 5, Column 1

The New York Times

SPEAKS FOR JORDAN: Abdul Monem Rifai at the U. N. General Assembly.

TUNISIA WILL GET U. S., BRITISH ARMS

Move to Strengthen Nation Against Algerian Rebels Approved by French

By MICHAEL JAMES
Special to The New York Times.

TUNIS, Aug. 14—The United States and Britain will supply arms to Tunisia.

The step is apparently designed to permit this small pro-Western nation to protect herself against Algerian rebels, who are leaning increasingly toward the United Arab Republic.

The news that this decision had been taken was unofficial, but it came from the most reliable sources.

[United States officials denied that the arms shipments were motivated by fear of a coup by Algerian rebels. A British spokesman refused to comment on this point. French officials said France had approved the arms deal.]

Bourguiba Requested Arms

It is not possible here to determine just what quantities and types of weapons will be made available. President Habib Bourguiba has publicly asked for sufficient infantry matériel to arm his little army of 6,000 men.

Algerian rebels operating on the western edge of Tunisia are armed only with infantry weapons. Their big weakness, should there be trouble with Tunisia, is a lack of transport. The Tunisians have that.

It was also impossible here to determine the day of delivery but it is understood that the British at least would start shipping weapons in the very near future.

Previously Britain and the

Continued on Page 10, Column 4

RATE OF DISCOUNT RAISED ON COAST TO BAR INFLATION

San Francisco Bank Moves to 2% as Reserve Board Shifts to Tighter Policy

By EDWIN L. DALE Jr.
Special to The New York Times.

WASHINGTON, Aug. 14—The Federal Reserve Board, in a major switch in policy, authorized an increase today in the discount rate at the Federal Reserve Bank of San Francisco. It was changed from 1¾ to 2 per cent.

According to experience, the other eleven Reserve banks, including New York, will soon follow San Francisco in going to the higher rate. However, it may take a little longer than usual for the whole system to reach the new level.

The switch was a direct signal that the Federal Reserve considered recovery from the recession to be solidly under way and that renewed inflationary pressure was now the threat. Never before has the system moved toward higher interest rates so early in the recovery period, particularly with 5,000,000 people still unemployed.

Bank Borrowings Low

The discount rate is the interest rate charged member banks who borrow from the Federal Reserve. These borrowings have been extremely low in recent months. Thus the main effect of the move may be psychological. But that does not lessen its importance as a signal of Government policy.

Ironically, today's move coincided with a reduction in Britain of the discount rate, which is called the bank rate there. A mild recession is just getting under way across the Atlantic, and the authorities in Britain are interested in spurring activity.

The British rate was reduced from 5 to 4½ per cent.

Reserve Board officials, as usual, discussed their move cautiously. They took note of the recent improvement in the business statistics and a surge of inflationary sentiment that has struck the financial markets. This sentiment has produced a sharp rise in the stock market and a sharp fall in the market for Government bonds.

Follows the Market

They also pointed out that money conditions had already tightened somewhat, producing a rise in sensitive short-term interest rates, such as the rate on ninety-one-day Treasury bills. To that extent, today's move followed rather than led the market.

Behind the move today was one other major factor. Top authorities in the Federal Reserve are convinced, and have said so publicly, that the system acted too slowly to check the recovery from the 1953-54 recession. They feel that the subsequent inflation might have been less if monetary restraint had been applied sooner.

It has long been evident that they had no intention of letting the same thing happen again if they could prevent it. Hence the quick restraining move, even though the degree of restraint is very mild.

The increase, effective tomorrow, was requested by the San Francisco Bank.

Significance Discounted

The fact that the first increase came on the West Coast was not regarded here as of major significance. The recession has always been less severe there than elsewhere, and the San Francisco Bank was behind the others when the discount rate was moving down. It was considered a natural innovator in a move toward higher rates.

But the main point was that the board here in Washington approved any increase in the rate.

The discount rate reached its post-war peak last August just as the boom was about to turn into a recession. At that time it was fixed at 3½ per cent.

Then in mid-November, in a major signal that the Federal Reserve felt that recession had begun, the rate was reduced from 3½ to 3 per cent. It fell in stages between November and April down to the level of 1¾ per cent that had prevailed until today.

The Federal Reserve affects day-to-day conditions in the money market by its buying

Continued on Page 45, Column 2

Woman Confirmed In High U.S. Office

By BESS FURMAN
Special to The New York Times

WASHINGTON, Aug. 14—The Senate confirmed today the appointment of Miss Bertha S. Adkins as Under Secretary of the Department of Health, Education and Welfare.

A few minutes before confirmation she held her final news conference as assistant chairman of the Republican National Committee, a job she held for eight years.

Miss Adkins said that an air-conditioned bus from her home town of Salisbury, Md. would bring friends to the department auditorium, where she will be sworn in Tuesday at 11:30 A. M. Such ceremonies there are usually held in a smaller conference room.

She said that for the last week, along with recently appointed Secretary Arthur S.

Continued on Page 12, Column 3

2 TRANSIT UNIONS FAIL IN UNITY TALK

M.B.A., Blaming T.W.U. for Impasse, Makes Appeal to Meany for Charter

By STANLEY LEVEY

Merger negotiations between the Motormen's Benevolent Association and the Transport Workers Union have failed, the motormen reported yesterday.

The motormen's group placed all the blame for the impasse on the T. W. U. It accused that union of bargaining in bad faith and of repudiating a merger plan agreed to by its own counsel. The T. W. U. did not answer the charges, reserving comment until after a meeting of its executive board in a few weeks.

Apparently abandoning hope of peace with the T. W. U., the motormen speedily applied to the American Federation of Labor and Congress of Industrial Organizations for a federal charter giving them jurisdiction in this area.

Loos Writes To Meany

The request was contained in a letter from Theodore Loos, M.B.A. head, to George Meany, president of the merged labor group.

Mr. Loos will head a four-man delegation to the meeting of the A. F. L.-C. I. O. executive council at Forest Park, Pa., next week. Labor observers regarded the union's chances of receiving a direct charter as slight.

A report on the transit negotiations was made at a meeting of the motormen last night by Louis Waldman, the group's general counsel. The members approved a recommendation by their board of directors that a federal charter be sought. The session was held at Roosevelt Auditorium, Fourth Avenue at Seventeenth Street.

The merger talks were start-

Continued on Page 14, Column 3

HOUSE APPROVES FARM PROP CUTS; UPHOLDS BENSON

Measure Affects Corn, Rice and Cotton—Concurrence By Senate Is Expected

Special to The New York Times.

WASHINGTON, Aug. 14—The House of Representatives approved overwhelmingly today a farm bill supported by Ezra Taft Benson, Secretary of Agriculture.

The vote assured passage of farm legislation before Congress adjourns. The Senate has already passed a similar bill.

The action today was regarded as a great victory for Mr. Benson—in particular for his drive toward lower price supports on key crops. The "leverage" he used was a provision in existing law that forced a drastic reduction in rice and cotton acreage in the absence of new legislation.

Last week Mr. Benson gambled to get a better bill by mustering enough Republican votes to block passage of a bill approved by the House Agriculture Committee.

Rayburn Had Balked

For a while it appeared the gamble had lost, because House Speaker Sam Rayburn, Democrat of Texas, said he would not permit any further attempts at farm legislation.

But the pressure from rice and cotton states in the South proved too strong for the Speaker. The Agriculture Committee last night approved two key amendments further lowering price supports. Mr. Benson approved the bill, the Republicans rallied round, and the bill went through the House today on a voice vote.

The only opposition came from die-hard members of the dwindling farm bloc from both parties. They could not even muster enough support to demand a roll-call vote. Mr. Rayburn declared the bill passed by the necessary two-thirds majority on the basis of the voice vote.

Major Provisions of Bill

The bill's main provisions are as follows:

¶It ends all acreage controls on corn and drops price supports immediately to 65 per cent of parity, or about $1.14 a bushel. Under the House bill, farmers would have to approve this change by referendum. The original bill in the House contained a floor of $1.18 a bushel.

¶It gives individual cotton farmers, for the next two years, a choice between 80 per cent of parity with low acreage or 65 per cent of parity with higher acreage. By 1963 there will be a floor of 65 per cent for all cotton, or about 27 cents a pound under the present parity formula. The original bill had a floor of 30 cents, and this was the heart of Mr. Benson's objection.

¶It gradually reduces rice supports to 65 per cent with

Continued on Page 12, Column 4

99 ON DUTCH AIRLINER LOST OFF IRELAND ON TRIP HERE; 51 OF VICTIMS AMERICANS

Associated Press Radiophoto from London

SMOKE MARKER in Atlantic shows way to KLM crash site for the approaching French trawler General Leclerc.

LIFE RAFTS FOUND

8 Bodies Recovered but Rescuers See No Survivors

By The Associated Press.

SHANNON, Ireland, Friday, Aug. 15 — A New York-bound Dutch Super-Constellation carrying ninety-nine persons plunged into the Atlantic yesterday. Fifty-one of the passengers were Americans returning home.

If all were killed, as appeared likely, it is the worst disaster ever involving a single commercial plane.

The KLM-Royal Dutch airliner fell into the squall-whipped sea on a flight from Amsterdam shortly after taking off from Shannon airport. It fell about 130 miles west of Ireland.

Searchers recovered eight bodies, all afloat, plus some partly inflated life rafts.

A KLM spokesman said the plane evidently was in one piece when it hit.

No Sign of Life Seen

At Aldergrove, Northern Ireland, crewmen of the first Royal Air Force Shackleton plane to sight the wreckage said they saw six bodies, but no sign of life during an eight-hour patrol.

Lieut. Comdr. James Whyte, harbor master, said there were several tiny, uninhabited islands about fifty miles from where the plane went down. He said "there is a remote possibility some might have reached them."

"I don't think there are any survivors, but there is a slim chance," he said.

Liam Meeling, KLM station manager at Shannon Airport, said the plane evidently crashed almost immediately after making its first check call back to Shannon.

Under normal conditions a plane could radio if it was in trouble. Even if two of the four engines were disabled, most of today's trans-Atlantic airliners, including the Super-Constellations, would be able to go on or turn back to the nearest airport.

Storm in the Area

The plane had headed into an area where other aircraft ran into a storm. Fliers here did not rule out the chance that lightning had hit the plane.

The Cunard liner Caronia, an Irish pleasure cruiser, an Irish naval corvette and the Canadian destroyer Crusader headed for the scene. They were not expected to reach it before daybreak.

In addition to ninety-one passengers, the plane carried a Dutch crew of eight. The pilot was Capt. A. E. Roelofs. According to an airline spokesman, forty-one women, six children and forty-four men passengers were aboard.

Among the passengers were six Egyptian fencers bound for a tournament at Philadelphia.

Twenty of the victims, mostly

Continued on Page 11, Column 5

Harriman Backs Finletter; Murray Is Second Choice

By WARREN WEAVER Jr.
Special to The New York Times.

ALBANY, Aug. 14—Governor Harriman is supporting Thomas K. Finletter for the Democratic nomination for United States Senator, but he is prepared to settle for Thomas E. Murray. The Governor has told friends and close political associates that he feels that Mr. Finletter, a former Secretary of the Air Force, is the best qualified candidate and would make the strongest running mate with him on the party ballot this fall.

He has taken this position despite Mr. Finletter's enthusiastic campaign for Adlai E. Stevenson for the Democratic Presidential nomination two years ago. Mr. Harriman sought that nomination himself and most of New York's Democratic leaders supported him.

Pressure From Liberals

The Governor has been under considerable pressure from the Liberal party to persuade other Democratic leaders, notably Carmine G. De Sapio, that Mr. Finletter should be the unanimous choice of the party's nominating convention.

Thus far Mr. Harriman has not been successful in this move, and he has told advisers that the political situation may force him to shift his support to another of the five Senate candidates if the Finletter cause bogs down hopelessly. He does not feel that that time has arrived.

Should Mr. Finletter's nomination prove to be politically impossible, the Governor is prepared to swing his support to Mr. Murray, a former member of the Atomic Energy Commission. Mr. Murray has the private endorsement of Michael H. Prendergast, the Democratic state chairman.

The factor that may force the Governor to shift to Mr. Murray is the campaign for the nomination being waged by James A. Farley, former Postmaster General and Democratic National Chairman.

Farley Influence Cited

Mr. Farley has seriously damaged his chance for the nomination by his direct personal attacks on the Governor. But his following among conservative Democrats is considered strong enough to influence the selection of a Senate candidate other than himself.

The rationale now under consideration by Mr. Harriman runs like this: If the "Farley wing" of the party is to be mollified when its candidate is passed by, the Senate nominee must be a man who will appeal specifically to that group.

Mr. Harriman believes that Mr. Murray would meet this test. He is of Irish descent, a prominent Roman Catholic layman and a successful business man of considerable means who has seen Government service in Washington. All these are attributes he shares with Mr. Farley.

The Governor has told friends he does not believe Tammany Hall is committed to seeking the Senate nomination for District Attorney Frank S. Hogan of New York. It is Mr. Harri-

Continued on Page 14, Column 7

GEROSA BIDS CITY CURTAIL SPENDING

Public Works Are Creating $2 of Debt for Every $1 of Redemption, He Warns

By PAUL CROWELL

Controller Lawrence E. Gerosa warned the Wagner Administration yesterday that its public works construction program must be curtailed. He said this was necessary to keep the city's debt and basic real estate tax rate within reasonable limits.

It was the fourth time in the last twelve months that Mr. Gerosa had flashed the stop sign against what he considered excessive borrowing to finance capital programs.

In a statutory report to the Board of Estimate, Mr. Gerosa indicated that the city was incurring $2 of new debt for every $1 of debt redemption.

The report went also to the City Planning Commission and Budget Director Abraham D. Beame. The planning agency is now preparing its proposed capital budget for 1959 and a capital program for the next five years.

The Gerosa report disclosed that the city's gross bonded debt stood at $4,033,320,000 on July 1, an increase of $263,548,000 over the $3,769,772,000 outstanding on July 1, 1957.

The report said the increase resulted from incurring new debt of $508,354,000 while only $244,806,000 of old debt was being retired.

"This amplifies my repeated

Continued on Page 19, Column 2

Report of U.S. Surrender Study Arouses Angry Debate in Senate

By ALLEN DRURY
Special to The New York Times.

WASHINGTON, Aug. 14—The Senate engaged in angry debate today and tonight on whether to deny funds for any Government study of possible plans for surrender by the United States in a future war.

After a tumultuous session, the Senate recessed until noon tomorrow without taking a vote on the proposal.

Debate began early in the afternoon, lapsed for a while and then resumed early in the evening to run until almost 11 P. M.

It stemmed from an amendment to a pending appropriations bill that would withhold funds for such a study. The amendment was offered by Senator Richard B. Russell, Democrat of Georgia.

Senator Russell's amendment was based on a newspaper report that such a study had been conducted for the Defense Department. Republican Senators declared that President Eisenhower had no knowledge of the study and had ordered an immediate investigation when he was informed of it on Tuesday morning.

The recess until tomorrow was moved by the Senate's Democratic leader, Lyndon B. Johnson of Texas, after members on both sides of the aisle had tried without success to persuade Senator Russell to withdraw his amendment.

Senator Johnson said it was his own opinion that "it would be the better part of wisdom if we stand up like men and face up to the amendment, which means just what it says and vote upon it now."

"It's my opinion," he said, "that the longer we play with it the worse it gets."

He said, however, that "many of my friends on both sides of the aisle want to think on it and chew on it and study it over night," and so he would ask for the delay.

The decision to recess was first requested by the Senate Republican leader, William F. Knowland of California, in an obvious move to allow time for Senator Russell to be persuaded to withdraw his amendment or to modify it.

Senator Russell at adjournment time showed no intention of doing either, although there was a possibility that he might change his mind by tomorrow.

Prior to the recess the Senate had engaged in perhaps its most

Continued on Page 3, Column 3

Eisenhower Regrets Jamming Of U. N. Broadcasts by Soviet

By FELIX BELAIR Jr.
Special to The New York Times.

WASHINGTON, Aug. 14—President Eisenhower expressed astonishment and regret today over Soviet jamming of broadcasts of the proceedings of the United Nations General Assembly meeting on the Middle East.

George V. Allen, head of the United States Information Agency, had reported the jamming to the President. All sixteen frequencies being used by the Voice of America for Russian-language broadcasts are being jammed, Mr. Allen said.

The powerful Soviet jamming signals not only drowned out President Eisenhower's statement of his six-point program for the Middle East but the speech by Andrei A. Gromyko, Soviet Foreign Minister.

Since the beginning of the United Nations meeting all Russian-language broadcasts by the Voice of America, and several in English, have sounded like a buzz saw going through a wet plank.

"The President had hoped that the peoples of the world would be able to listen to the full proceedings of the General Assembly," James C. Hagerty, White House press secretary, said. "It was with astonishment and regret that he learned that the Russians were jamming the broadcasts."

In his report to the President, Mr. Allen said the Voice of America was broadcasting the United Nations proceedings around the clock in the five official languages of the United Nations. They are English, French, Spanish, Russian and Chinese.

All eighty-five transmitters and relay bases of the Voice of America are engaged in the

Continued on Page 6, Column 1

Morhouse Implies Rockefeller Is Sure of G. O. P. Nomination

By LEO EGAN

L. Judson Morhouse yesterday implied that Nelson A. Rockefeller was assured of the Republican nomination for Governor.

The implication was contained in a call Mr. Morhouse issued as Republican state chairman for a meeting of the Republican state committee to elect a new chairman. The meeting was set for Aug. 24, the eve of the state convention.

Traditionally meetings of the state committee to elect a chairman are held immediately after the convention. This practice gives the candidate for Governor an opportunity to make his choice known.

Mr. Morhouse's re-election as chairman is regarded as certain if Mr. Rockefeller is the candidate for Governor. But it is viewed as doubtful if either State Senator Walter J. Mahoney of Buffalo or Leonard W. Hall of Oyster Bay should be the choice.

The call provides for a meeting of the state executive committee in Rochester on Sunday, to be followed the same day by a meeting of the full state committee. The convention opens in Rochester on Monday, Aug. 25, and continues through Aug. 26.

Mr. Hall told a luncheon meeting of the New York Young Republican Club at Schwartz' restaurant, 15 Broad Street, yesterday that he regarded the convention as "wide open." The choice of a candidate for Governor, he continued, would be decided by delegations that have taken no position as yet.

Mr. Hall predicted that Governor Harriman's failure to make New York State more

Continued on Page 14, Column 3

The New York Times   Aug. 15. 1958

Site—Cross marks spot

99 BELIEVED DEAD IN AIRLINER CRASH

Continued From Page 1, Col. 8

persons of college age, were returning from a Church of the Brethren tour of Europe in connection with an anniversary celebration of the church.

The plane was in radio contact with Shannon Airport for about half an hour after taking off from here. Then radio silence caused a large air search to be started from both sides of the Atlantic.

Hours later, a British rescue plane, guided by a radar trace from a British commercial airliner, spotted wreckage, bodies and half-inflated life rafts tossing on the water.

The airliner was believed to have run into the stormy zone as it climbed after leaving Shannon.

Pilot Reports Squall

A Trans World Airlines pilot, Capt. Everett Wolf, after a crossing from New York to Shannon, reported that he had hit a "very bad squall and if that KLM plane had engine trouble he might really have been in a bad way."

The plane was equipped to crash-land in the ocean, KLM officials said. It carried inflatable life preservers for passengers and crew and four inflatable lifeboats, each able to hold twenty-five persons.

A little more than twelve hours after the airliner crashed, a French trawler reported that it had sighted survivors on life rafts. But later the trawler, the General Le Clerc, ran among the rafts and dinghies and reported it could see no survivors.

Two Royal Air Force planes, equipped to drop rescue equipment, circled the wreckage and reported sighting rafts and dinghies with signs of life. However, KLM airline officials at Amsterdam said there was little hope that anyone survived.

"We must to our regret assume that hope for survivors is slight." KLM said.

From the pilot of a British Shackleton came a terse radio message to Shannon late tonight:

"There are no survivors."

The pilot did not say whether he intended that report to cover the whole area or the segment assigned him to patrol.

Time of Departure

The plane, named Hugo de Groot after a seventeenth century Dutch law expert, had left Shannon Airport at 3:05 A. M. (9:05 P. M. Eastern standard time Wednesday).

The aircraft made its routine callback to the Shannon ocean control office at 3:40 A. M. There was silence when its next callback was due at 4:50 A. M.

A watch found on the body of one of the men pulled from the sea had stopped at 4:48. There was no clue to wether it was running on Greenwich Mean Time or an hour ahead on European Time, or perhaps British Summer Time.

The crash mars a record that had led regular scheduled airlines to call the North Atlantic the world's safest air route. More than 5,000,000 persons had flown the route aboard regularly scheduled airlines since World War II without a loss.

However, there have been aviation accidents in those waters. A flying boat ditched off the British Isles in 1948. A chartered British plane with thirty-nine aboard — mostly troops—went down off Ireland in 1953.

At least nine nationalities were represented aboard the plane.

KLM described the plane, a Lockheed Super-Constellation. Model 1049-H, as the latest of Lockheed's planes designed to carry either cargo or passengers. It said this type of aircraft had only been in operation on KLM runs for three or four months.

KLM said the plane's load was not out of the ordinary. Ships on its economy flights have ninety-five seats for passengers. Other trans-Atlantic lines have similar flights. Economy flights take a third-class rate, below those for first and tourist classes.

First Economy Flight Crash

SHANNON, Aug. 14 (UPI)— The crash was the first crack-up of an economy-class airliner in the four-month-old cut-rate trans-Atlantic economy service. Passengers aboard the ill-fated airliner, which was an extra flight because of heavy traffic, paid $408.60 for a New York-to-Shannon round trip.

13 Victims From One County

Special to The New York Times.

LANCASTER, Pa., Aug. 14— Thirteen persons from this area were among the Americans feared lost when a KLM-Royal Dutch Airline plane plunged into the Atlantic Ocean early today. They included two sisters, a man and wife, and a young couple who planned to be married soon.

Should the present search for survivors be unfruitful, the casualty list would be the largest in one accident in Lancaster County history.

All those from Lancaster County were members of the Church of the Brethren, who were on a tour to Europe to mark the 250th anniversary of the founding of the denomination.

Eleven other Lancaster County residents who had been a part of the tour returned home earlier this week on another KLM airliner. One of the eleven experienced by that craft early Tuesday over Labrador.

Tension at Idlewild and the Plane That Never Came

The New York Times

Waiting for word—This was the scene yesterday at KLM offices at New York International Airport in Queens after airliner from Amsterdam had crashed at sea. On the fourth line at left side of sign in rear the arrival time of Flight 607E had been removed.

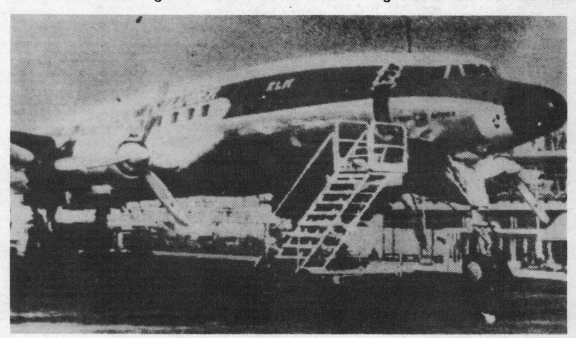

Associated Press Radiophoto

Ill-fated airliner—This is the Royal Dutch Airlines plane Hugo de Groot, which went down in the Atlantic Ocean carrying ninety-nine persons. Plane was en route to New York via Shannon. The airliner is shown recently at Schiphol Airport, the Netherlands.

GIRL AVOIDS CRASH BY REVISING PLANS

Dutch Traveler, Scheduled for Ill-Fated Plane, Shifts to an Earlier Flight

By JAMES FERON

One bright ray pierced the gloom that settled yesterday over the KLM passenger lounge at New York International Airport, Idlewild, Queens.

It came because an 18-year-old Dutch girl's reservation aboard the ill-fated Flight 607E had been changed to an earlier flight a few hours before take-off Wednesday night.

Marijke Pennock had been scheduled to leave Amsterdam on the 9 P. M. flight to meet her parents, arriving in New York from Michigan, and the representative of a New Jersey sanatorium. There she would be treated for tuberculosis contracted in the former Dutch East Indies.

Early Wednesday evening the KLM-Royal Dutch Airlines office in Amsterdam said it had one seat left on Flight 635, leaving at 7:30 P. M. Marijke grabbed her luggage and boarded it.

Father Voices Gratitude

In New York, John and Maria Pennock were terrified when they learned of the apparent fate of their daughter. Marijke, who arrived at 9:10 A. M., was detained filling out a detailed health and immigration form.

Later in the morning the Pennocks finally met. "It's an act of Providence," Mr. Pennock said. "I still don't know why we should be singled out, but I'm happy we were."

Others arriving in the KLM lounge through the morning and early afternoon felt other emotions. A few collapsed in tears, most wandered around in a daze.

Associated Press

Pilot—Capt. A. E. Roelofs

The New York Times.

LATE CITY EDITION
U. S. Weather Bureau Report (Page 74) forecasts:
Mostly fair today and tonight.
Some cloudiness tomorrow.
Temp. range: 36—26. Yesterday: 34.4—23.8.

VOL. CVIII..No. 36,837.   © 1958, by The New York Times Company. Times Square, New York 36, N. Y.   NEW YORK, TUESDAY, DECEMBER 2, 1958.   10c beyond 100-mile zone from New York City. Higher in air delivery cities.   FIVE CENTS

STATE G.O.P. EYES TAX RISE ON 'GAS AND CIGARETTES

Leaders, at Meeting With Rockefeller, Are Said to Reverse Former View

GOVERNOR-ELECT SILENT

But He Reports Agreement on Economic Study and Continued School Aid

By DOUGLAS DALES

In their search for more revenue to meet an expected deficit of $200,000,000 in the state budget next year, Republican leaders are considering increases of 2 cents in the gasoline tax and 1 cent in the cigarette tax.

This was learned yesterday as Governor-elect Nelson A. Rockefeller met with Republican legislative leaders for the first time since his return from a post-election vacation in Venezuela.

At a news conference after the meeting, Mr. Rockefeller said agreement had been reached among the leaders to support two of his campaign pledges.

One involves setting up a fifteen-member commission to study the state's economy with a view to increasing business and job opportunities. The second approves the continuation of $53,000,000 in extra school aid voted by the Legislature at its last session.

Weekly Meetings Planned

Mr. Rockefeller announced that he planned to meet with the legislative leaders at 2 P. M. every Monday until he assumed the Governorship at midnight Dec. 31. The meetings will be held at his temporary headquarters 20 West Fifty-fifth Street.

Attending the meeting yesterday were Senator Walter J. Mahoney of Buffalo, the majority leader; Assembly speaker Oswald D. Heck of Schenectady; Assemblyman Joseph F. Carlino of Long Beach, the majority leader in the lower house; Senator Austin Erwin of Geneseo, Senate finance chairman; Lieut. Gov.-elect Malcolm Wilson, of

Continued on Page 26, Column 1

LEHIGH MAY DROP PASSENGER TRAINS

Railway Cites Huge Losses From Little-Used Service

By ROBERT E. BEDINGFIELD

The Lehigh Valley Railroad plans to quit the passenger traffic business and to operate solely as a freight carrier.

Cedric A. Major, president, said yesterday that "with the greatest regret" the railroad would file within ten days with the Interstate Commerce Commission and other regulatory agencies for authority to drop its passenger train services. He estimated the "legal gymnastics" required before the last passenger train pulled out would take at least four months.

"As a railroad man for forty-two years, I hate to see this," Mr. Major told forty municipal officials and newspaper men at a luncheon at the Links Club here. "However, we are going broke unless we can get this authority."

He also said that the carrier was losing $4,000,000 to $5,000,000 a year on the operation of its passenger trains.

The Lehigh Valley operates 1,130 miles of railroad in New Jersey, Pennsylvania and the upstate counties of New York, adjoining Lake Ontario and Lake Erie. Its main line runs from Jersey City and Perth Amboy through Newark and Phillipsburg, N. J., Bethlehem, Allentown, Wilkes-Barre, Pa. and Geneva, N. Y., to Buffalo. Branch lines serve Rochester, Ithaca, Canastota, Cortland and Elmira, N. Y., in the Pennsylvania anthracite region.

The road, which reaches Pennsylvania Station in Manhattan under a trackage rights agreement with the Pennsyl-

Continued on Page 55, Column 2

Million Student-Days Lost In Closings, Flemming Says

Secretary Calls Shutdown in Integration Fight 'Indefensible'—Fears Great Harm to Pupils and Teachers

By BESS FURMAN
Special to The New York Times.

WASHINGTON, Dec. 1—Arthur S. Flemming reported today that more than a million student-days already had been lost by the closings of public schools to avoid integration. The Secretary of Health, Education and Welfare repeatedly referred to this loss and other losses of school time as "indefensible."

In a statement at a news conference he tallied these losses by localities—for four schools in Little Rock, Ark., six in Norfolk, Va., two in Charlottesville, Va., and one in Warren County, Va. He also evaluated the total educational loss in terms of the effect on teachers, the effect on young people, and the effect on American ideals.

Secretary Flemming's statement followed the morning ses-

Text of Flemming's statement is printed on Page 40.

sion of his all-day conference with the heads of voluntary organizations concerned with elementary and secondary education. Many conferees, particularly representatives of labor groups, asserted that the questions of human rights raised by the closing of the schools would result in dire national and international consequences. A spokesman for the American Friends Service committee asked Mr. Flemming to make an "objective study" of the closed schools.

The Secretary replied that the statement he had prepared for today constituted "at least a beginning of the process of evaluating the impact."

In his statement, Secretary Flemming noted that this week the closed schools "are passing the deadline when it is impossible for them to complete the

Continued on Page 40, Column 3

Examiner Advises F.C.C. To Void Miami TV Award

By ANTHONY LEWIS
Special to The New York Times.

WASHINGTON, Dec. 1—A special hearing examiner recommended today that the Federal Communications Commission revoke its grant of television Channel 10 in Miami because of attempts at improper influence.

But the examiner, Horace Stern, retired Chief Judge of the Pennsylvania Supreme Court, did not accept the Justice Department's view that such activity should automatically disqualify an applicant. The F. C. C.'s general counsel had joined in this suggestion.

Judge Stern recommended instead that the commission simply weigh any impropriety as a factor when it considered competing applications for the channel. He said an applicant might be able to overcome the "serious burden" of such "derelictions" and show that a grant to it was still in the "public interest."

Two Leading Contenders

The two leading Channel 10 applicants are Public Service Television, Inc., a National Airlines subsidiary, which won the F. C. C. grant originally, and WKAT, Inc.

Judge Stern found both guilty of "persistent" and "grossly improper" off-the-record approaches to Richard A. Mack, then one of the seven members of the Federal Communications Commission. Mr. Mack has since been indicted in the case and is awaiting trial.

As to WKAT, Judge Stern found that its principal figure, A. Frank Katzentine, had made numerous approaches to Mr. Mack himself and through "emissaries." Among these he

Continued on Page 33, Column 5

72 VESSELS TIED UP BY BOYCOTT IN U. S.

But World Action Against 4 'Flags of Convenience' Is Only Partly a Success

By EDWARD A. MORROW

American transport workers yesterday tied up seventy-two "flag of convenience" ships in a boycott scheduled to last until Thursday.

Longshoremen and teamsters respected picket lines set up by unlicensed seamen in ports throughout the United States.

Six of the target ships were in the New York Harbor area yesterday. On two of these, unloading operations were completely halted. On three others, members of an independent oil workers' union disregarded the picket lines and unloaded the ships. A sixth vessel, a tanker, spent six hours searching for a berth late last night and finally began unloading operations.

There was a question last night whether three tankers included in the New York group would be able to sail today because of the boycott.

Picket Boats Appear

Picket boats cruised the harbor to advertise the seamen's action against American-owned ships flying the flags of Panama, Liberia, Honduras and Costa Rica.

The boycott in this country, led jointly by the National Maritime Union and the Seafarers International Union, was the backbone of a world-wide demonstration called by the International Transport Workers Federation.

The federation had called upon its affiliates in sixty-two countries to boycott ships flying the flags of the four "convenience" countries.

The boycott was aimed primarily at ships not covered by wage agreements with one of the federation's affiliates.

The ensigns of the four countries are known as "flags of convenience" because owners registering their vessels under them enjoy tax benefits and labor regulations below the standards of traditional maritime nations.

Dispatches from ports over the world indicated that on a global basis the boycott was only a limited success. Omer Becu, general secretary of the federation, summed up the reports he had received as "neither favorable nor unfavorable," according to an Associated Press dispatch from London.

A majority of the target ships in Great Britain were made idle.

But the boycott was considerably weakened in the Netherlands.

Continued on Page 27, Column 1

Sir Hubert Wilkins Dead at 70; Explored Polar Regions by Plane

First Flier of America-Europe Arctic Route Tried Submarine Trip Under Ice Cap in '31

FRAMINGHAM, Mass., Dec. 1—Sir Hubert Wilkins, the noted polar explorer, was found dead of a coronary occlusion today in his hotel room here. He was 70 years old.

The bearded veteran of many polar explorations had been working as a geographer and consultant at the Army Quartermaster Corps Research and Development Center in neighboring Natick.

A chambermaid found the body in the explorer's room at the Park Central Hotel. The body was fully clothed, including an overcoat. Police Chief Edward T. McCarthy of Framingham said Sir Hubert apparently had been stricken when he returned to his room yesterday afternoon.

Sir Hubert's wife, Lady Suzan Wilkins, who lives in their New York apartment, was notified. She is the former Suzan Bennett, an artist, singer and actress.

Associated Press
Sir Hubert Wilkins

eral of the Army, in a statement in Washington, said that Sir Hubert's contributions were reflected in the "countless im-

Continued on Page 57, Column 2

ADENAUER MEETS OPPOSITION CHIEFS ON BERLIN CRISIS

Chancellor Seeks to Mold National Policy on Soviet Free-City Proposal

By SYDNEY GRUSON
Special to The New York Times.

BONN, Germany, Dec. 1—Chancellor Konrad Adenauer took the unusual step today of conferring with the leaders of West German political parties other than his own in an effort to mold a national policy on the Berlin crisis.

Meeting with the 82-year-old head of the ruling Christian Democratic Union were representatives of the Social Democrats, the country's major Opposition group; the Free Democrats and the German party, which is allied with the Chancellor's party.

Not since West Germany's crucial nuclear armament debate last spring has the Chancellor, who likes to keep a tight personal hold on policy-making, sought the advice or the opinions of other party leaders. Dr. Heinrich von Brentano, the Foreign Minister, also attended the meeting.

More Meetings Planned

A brief communiqué said only that more meetings were contemplated. Erich Ollenhauer, party chairman, and Herbert Wehner, his principal deputy, represented the Social Democrats.

National unity already has been achieved in the agreement of all politicians and parties that the Soviet proposal to transform West Berlin into a demilitarized free city is unacceptable. It is on what should be done next that the Chancellor and his Socialist opponents are most likely to disagree.

The new crisis has led to some discussion among rank and file party members on the possibility of a national government to meet what they believe to be a national danger.

Coalition Is Doubted

The consensus of Western observers is that no coalition embracing Dr. Adenauer and the Social Democrats is possible at this time. For one thing, Dr. Adenauer is against such a move, and he has a way of prevailing if he wants or does not want something strongly enough.

The Social Democrats' ideas on West German foreign policy also would seem to rule out an acceptable basis for a coalition.

Most political observers here agree that the Soviet proposal on West Berlin is bound to force the West Germans into a reappraisal of the various plans to set up a neutral zone between the Western and Soviet forces in Central Europe.

There is nothing to indicate that either the Chancellor or the Social Democrats have changed their basic views on these plans. The Chancellor rejects the ideas as leading to a situation in which West

Continued on Page 2, Column 4

WEST MAY RESIST GERMAN RED ROLE

Possibility of Letting Eastern Regime Control Traffic to Berlin Believed Ended

By ARTHUR J. OLSEN
Special to The New York Times.

BERLIN, Dec. 1—The Soviet Union's insistence on turning over its occupation responsibilities to East Germany has voided any chance that the Western Allies might accept East German control of access to Berlin, according to responsible diplomatic sources.

Secretary of State Dulles said last week that the Western powers "might" allow the East Germans to check their traffic between Berlin and the West. Informants here said this possibility rested upon the Soviet designation of the East Germans as their agents. In view of the Soviet note that announced Moscow's intention to give East Germany sovereign control over East Berlin, the basis for an "agent" solution has been eliminated, the Western sources said.

The United States view is understood to be that the essential measure to preserve the freedom of West Berlin is to maintain the presence of the United States garrison in the city.

Interference Ruled Out

Any attempt to undermine that position—and this would include East German attempts to impede the communications of the garrison—would be regarded as an act of war, diplomatic sources here said.

The estimate of the situation prevalent in responsible Western quarters here is that a "limited war" in the three air corridors linking Berlin with the West would be a distinct possibility.

The United States would be expected to enforce rights it regards as absolute to fly along the prescribed routes into the city. It would be up to the other side to make the first move toward a general war, informants said.

In the United States view, a showdown as to whether the Western Allies could maintain the status quo in Berlin probably would take place in the air.

A clear-cut decision on rights of access might be difficult to bring about on the roads and waterways that link West Berlin with West Germany, according to expert appraisals.

Four-power agreements setting forth the rights of the Western Allies to water and surface communications are less

Continued on Page 2, Column 3

90 PERISH IN CHICAGO SCHOOL FIRE; 3 NUNS ARE VICTIMS; SCORES HURT; PUPILS LEAP OUT WINDOWS IN PANIC

Associated Press Wirephoto
FIRE IN PAROCHIAL SCHOOL: Firemen attempting to bring the blaze under control yesterday at Our Lady of the Angels Roman Catholic school in Chicago's West Side.

Panic Grips Classrooms; Confusion Increases Toll

Special to The New York Times.

CHICAGO, Dec. 1—Panic aided the flames at Our Lady of the Angels School today. While some children recalled the disciplines of fire drills to make their way to safety, others perished in their confusion.

Some pupils jumped from windows; others were pushed. Still others were trampled as they groped for exits. The smaller ones huddled in confusion in corridors. Efforts to get some to move were of little avail.

In a few classrooms teachers were able to maintain control.

Mrs. Eda Shanahan, one of the nine lay teachers, talked soothingly to her pupils, urging them to wait for firemen and ladders at the open windows of her second floor room.

Pupils Descend by Ladder

Meanwhile the Rev. Charles Hunt, assistant pastor of Our Lady of the Angels Church, and James Raymond, a janitor at the school, managed to get a fire ladder in place on the building outside Mrs. Shanahan's room. Her charges reached the ground safely.

Another teacher told how she had persuaded pupils to form a human chain by clutching each other's clothing and leading them to safety.

A nun who made three trips into the burning building to rescue children said:

"I felt untold strength."

One teacher, who was not identified, told of leading her charges to the head of a stairway and rolling them down to safety.

Continued on Page 28, Column 4

DE GAULLE IS SURE TO BE PRESIDENT

Coty Decides Not to Seek Re-election, Leaving the General Unopposed

By HENRY GINIGER

PARIS, Dec. 1—The last obstacle to Premier Charles de Gaulle's assumption of the French Presidency was removed today by President René Coty.

M. Coty informed the Premier at a meeting in the Elysée Palace that he would not seek re-election. The news was announced by the Premier's office and its implication was that Premier de Gaulle himself would seek election as the Fifth Republic's first President.

The election, to be held Dec. 21, will be the third major act of political renovation in France.

The first was the strong approval in a popular referendum Sept. 28 of a new Constitution providing for a strengthened Presidency and a weakened National Assembly and commonly considered as tailor-made for General de Gaulle.

Newcomers Win Office

The second act was performed in the elections yesterday and the preceding Sunday, in which the country chose a National Assembly that it found difficult to recognize today. It returned only 166 out of 440 representatives of continental France in the old Assembly and produced a huge crop of 188 Gaullists, most of them political newcomers.

A new round of elections will take place next Sunday. Municipal and departmental general councils will then gather to select most of the 75,000 electors, who in turn will choose a President two weeks later. Barring his own last-minute withdrawal, Premier de Gaulle is expected to run unopposed and in this new-Gaullist country to be elected with virtual unanimity.

President Coty, who is 76 years old, will be an ex officio member of the important Constitutional Council and may become the honorary President of General de Gaulle. Premier de Gaulle paid tribute today to

Continued on Page 5, Column 2

L. I. Boy Kills Sister, Mother and Himself

Special to The New York Times.

GREAT NECK, L. I., Dec. 2—A 14-year-old boy shot his mother and sister and then turned his .22-caliber repeating rifle on himself in the family's nine-room split level home in Saddle Rock Village near Great Neck tonight, the Nassau County police said.

The police said that the mother, Mrs. Dorothy Wiener, 47 years old, and her daughter, Laurie, 21, had both been shot in the head by James Wiener with his rifle. James then shot himself.

Mrs. Wiener's husband, Max Wiener, the proprietor of the Wiener Advertising Art Studio at 12 East Thirty-seventh Street, Manhattan, was not home at the time of the shooting. The police said that he was

Continued on Page 2, Column 8

1,500 ARE RESCUED

24 in One Class Die at Desks—Closing Bell 18 Minutes Away

By RICHARD J. H. JOHNSTON
Special to The New York Times.

CHICAGO, Dec. 1—A fast-spreading fire today killed at least eighty-seven Chicago school children and three nuns.

The disaster occurred at Our Lady of the Angels Roman Catholic School at 3808 West Iowa Street, eighteen minutes before the bell that would have closed the school day. About 1,515 grade-school and 120 kindergarten children were attending classes.

At least 100 other children were taken to seven hospitals where the condition of many was listed as critical. It was feared the death toll would continue to mount.

Many children had leaped from windows in panic.

Priests of the parish dashed from the church and joined teachers in rescue efforts.

Two Buildings Occupied

It was believed that nuns, lay teachers, priests, janitors and passers-by had rescued more than 1,000 of the children.

The children occupied two buildings, which made up the school facilities of Our Lady of Angels parish.

The fire occurred at 2:42 P. M. in the older two-story brick building.

Firemen who fought their way into a classroom found twenty-four children sitting dead at their desks. Books and homework assignments for tomorrow were stacked neatly before the children.

Fire Commissioner Robert Quinn said the boiler room of the building appeared to be intact. An earlier report said that an explosion had occurred there.

Blaze in Stairwell

Heavy black smudges were found on the stairwell leading from the room, Mr. Quinn said. He reported that the fire might have started from an oily type of blaze in the stairwell. He said he was mystified as to how the fire had spread so rapidly.

City officials, at the direction of Mayor Richard J. Daley, immediately ordered what was promised to be "one of the greatest fire investigations in the city's history."

Mr. Quinn said the tragedy might have been caused by a "touch-off." Touch-off is the firemen's word for arson.

Chicago schools have been targets of anonymous phone

Continued on Page 28, Column 1

MEXICO INSTALLS A NEW PRESIDENT

Lopez Begins 6-Year Term —Cites Educational Need

By PAUL P. KENNEDY
Special to The New York Times.

MEXICO CITY, Dec. 1—Adolfo Lopez Mateos, 48-year-old lawyer and former Minister of Labor, was inaugurated today for a six-year term as President of Mexico.

He named a Cabinet consisting mainly of middle-of-the-road men experienced in administrative or diplomatic duties under the outgoing President Adolfo Ruiz Cortines.

In his forty-five-minute inaugural address, Señor Lopez Mateos spoke at length of Mexico's need for increased educational facilities and for economic development. He sounded an apparent warning to groups that have incited demonstrations in recent months. He also pledged that Mexico would play a constructive international role.

Anti-United States demonstrations that were predicted for today did not materialize. A few leaflets were scattered in the streets calling on Secretary

Continued on Page 20, Column 4

Children and Nuns Victims in Chicago as Flames Race Through Grammar School

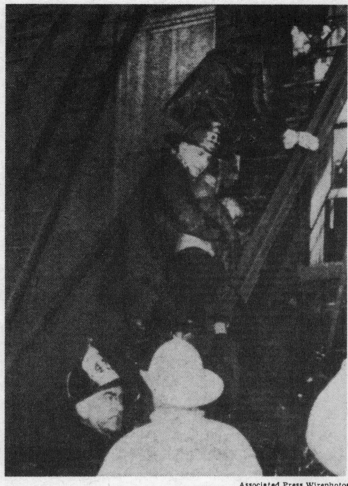

RESCUER brings an injured child out of the building

Associated Press Wirephotos

AERIAL VIEW of burning Our Lady of the Angels Roman Catholic School in Chicago

GRIEF is reflected in faces of parents and others as they watch firemen battle blaze

CHILDREN PANIC, LEAP TO GROUND

100 Are Taken to Hospitals, Many Critically Injured— 24 Found at Desks

Continued From Page 1, Col. 8

callers who reported that bombs had been planted in buildings. Schools have been evacuated for hours and classes have been canceled while firemen searched the premises.

Drew Brown, head of the Police Arson Squad, said that the fire appeared to have started in a corridor below the first floor in a corner of the building.

He said that rubbish might have been left there and could have been the source of the flames. At 8:30 P. M. he said that no evidence of arson had been found.

The city's Building Commissioner, George L. Ramsey, said after a preliminary inspection of the building that he had found six exits from the second floor of the building. He said that they and the width of the corridors were adequate for escape.

Mrs. Barbara Glowacki, owner of a grocery store less than a block north of the school, added to the mystery of the fire's origin. She told investigators that twenty minutes before she heard the fire engines a strange man entered her store and asked if she had a public telephone.

Police Hunt Man

She said she did not. She quoted him as saying, calmly, "I was going to report that the school's on fire."

He then walked out, Mrs. Glowacki said. The police are searching for the man.

The police said they found a thirty-gallon metal can, sealed at both ends, at the foot of the basement stairway where the fire was believed to have started. It was taken to the Police Crime Laboratory for examination.

Pupils of the school, including two boys detailed to empty waste baskets in the larger building's boiler room, told of hearing strange sounds from the building's radiators just before the flames raced through the building.

A janitor of the school ran through the halls seconds later, shouting, "Call the Fire Department."

Jump in Panic

Flames spread so rapidly that scores of children had been killed, many at their desks, or had leaped from windows before firemen arrived. Others were trampled or crushed by their companions in a panic dash for safety.

Panic raged through the school and in the streets adjacent. Scores of parents rushed to the scene, where they saw billowing smoke and towering sheets of flames swirling from the building in which their children were trapped or too frightened to escape.

So rapid was the spread of the flames that carefully rehearsed fire-drill procedures were forgotten by many of the children.

Within minutes, hundreds of parents pressed frantically against the police and fire lines in an attempt to enter the school to find their children.

Mothers Plead to Enter

Hysterical mothers raced futilely up and down the safety lines pleading to be permitted to enter the building.

The neighborhood of the school is a quiet residential section made up chiefly of single family frame houses and two-family buildings. Most of the residents are second and third-generation Chicagoans of Italian, Irish and German extraction. The neighborhood is heavily populated by Roman Catholics.

It was a typical, calm, early winter day with the sun shining and the temperatures in the upper twenties.

Some f the mothers of the younger pupils had already donned ats to go to the school yard to meet their children.

Persons living in the vicinity of the school became aware of the mishap when the sounds of school letting out were strangely different. Instead of happy shouts and laughter they heard young voices screaming in terror.

Smoke in Classrooms

Within minutes smoke swirled through the classrooms and flames licked through stairways.

Without heeding their teachers children began to open and leap through windows on the first, second and third floors. Those on the lower floors managed to flee.

The children dropping from the upper floors lay still where they fell or crawled in pain away from the burning building.

Others huddled in panic in their rooms or jammed the corridors, unheeding the efforts of their teachers to organize them for an orderly evacuation.

Later when firemen were able to enter the building they found children's bodies, some burned so badly that identification was difficult or impossible.

They lay in groups or sprawled singly down the corridors and on the stairways.

Among the earliest to arrive at the scene was Chicago's recently appointed Archbishop Albert Meyer. The Archbishop of the largest Roman Catholic diocese in the nation stood with tears coursing his cheeks. Mayor Daley stood beside him.

Firemen arrived at the scene in time to help hundreds of children down the ladders. Others had found their way to the school fire escapes and had assisted classmates to safety.

"All the News That's Fit to Print"

NEWS SUMMARY AND INDEX, PAGE 95

The New York Times

LATE CITY EDITION

U. S. Weather Bureau Report (Page 95) forecasts: Mostly fair today; chance of showers tonight and tomorrow.

Temp. range: 75—60; yesterday: 71.0—62.9.

SECTION ONE

VOL. CIX..No. 37,136.

© 1959, by The New York Times Company. Times Square, New York 36, N. Y.

NEW YORK, SUNDAY, SEPTEMBER 27, 1959.

35c outside New York City, its suburban area and Long Island. Higher in air delivery cities.

TWENTY-FIVE CENTS

EISENHOWER, KHRUSHCHEV TALK PRIVATELY ALL DAY; GERMAN ISSUES DOMINATE

MOOD HELD 'GOOD'

Today's Meetings May Decide if Progress Can Be Made

By HARRISON E. SALISBURY

Special to The New York Times.

GETTYSBURG, Pa., Sept. 26 — President Eisenhower and Premier Khrushchev talked almost all day today privately about Berlin and the German question. But whether they had made progress toward a solution was not yet certain.

General Eisenhower and the Soviet leader spent many hours at the President's Catoctin Mountain lodge retreat and at the President's near-by Gettysburg home discussing world problems.

Most of the time they talked alone and most of the time they talked about Berlin and Germany. James C. Hagerty, White House press secretary, said in a 9 P. M. briefing for newsmen that the Berlin situation had not yet been changed by the talk.

Mr. Hagerty said further talks would have to be held tomorrow morning "so that it may be determined if progress has been or can be made" on the issue.

Herter Talks With Gromyko

While President Eisenhower and Premier Khrushchev talked between themselves with the aid of interpreters, their principal foreign policy advisers, Secretary of State Christian A. Herter and Foreign Minister Andrei A. Gromyko, worked on other problems.

The atmosphere of the talks, Mr. Hagerty said, "is good." He added that the subjects of discussion were serious and revolved around the questions of Berlin and Germany.

Mr. Hagerty emphasized that, until it could be determined what if any progress was being made on Berlin and Germany it was impossible to determine what the outcome of the discussions would be.

Disarmament Discussed

The principal topics discussed by the principal advisers of the two leaders were disarmament, exchange agreements and nuclear test suspension.

Thus far, Mr. Hagerty's words made it clear that no tangible steps have been taken toward the kind of progress to justify a summit meeting. What tomorrow will bring is another matter. But for tonight those Americans with some access to direct knowledge of the course of the day's talks at Camp David appeared to have their fingers crossed. They were neither optimistic nor pessimis-

Continued on Page 40, Column 1

ARRIVE FOR TALKS: Vice President Richard M. Nixon and John A. McCone, chairman of Atomic Energy Commission, arrive by car yesterday at gates of Camp David, Md.

Associated Press Wirephoto

MITCHELL WARNS OF NEW LAY-OFFS IN STEEL STRIKE

Finds Economy Strong Now, but Fears October Dip—Confers With Finnegan

FACTORY JOBS DECLINING

Secretary Reports 600,000 Idle in Tie-Up—Loss of Pay Put at 700 Million

By C. P. TRUSSELL

Special to The New York Times.

WASHINGTON, Sept. 26—The Secretary of Labor and the chief of the Federal Mediation and Conciliation Service conferred in closed session today on the discouraging developments of the steel strike.

Negotiations between the steel companies and the union spokesmen broke down last night. It appeared in some quarters that the next move was up to the Government.

According to a Labor Department report issued today, more than 600,000 are idle because of the steel strike. The loss of pay to those involved directly or indirectly had reached some $700,000,000. This was the situation as of Sept. 15. It was predicted that later reports would show a worse situation, despite industry's ability thus far to ward off serious damage.

Decisions Not Revealed

What might have been decided today by James P. Mitchell, the Secretary of Labor, and Joseph F. Finnegan, the chief Federal mediator, was not disclosed.

They would not comment on their discussions, but let it be known that they would confer further over the week-end.

In the wake of their silence, however, there were predictions that the Government, which has kept hands off so far, would invoke the Taft-Hartley Law to force an eighty-day "cooling-off" period if the picture became darker. Such a "cooling-off" injunction would put strikers back to work for eighty days.

The Labor Department report indicated that the situation would become darker by Oct. 15.

Today's report was the fourth issued by the Labor Department since the steel strike started on July 15. It covered surveys in thirty-one steel producing and consuming areas.

Consumers Little Hurt

While the steel consumers are more or less holding their own thus far, the report said, the strike is making increasing inroads on employment.

At this point, Secretary Mitchell reported, the over-all economic situation remains strong. He said, however, that the impact of the strike was being felt on factory employment, in which steel products constitute the backbone.

In Detroit, for instance, Secretary Mitchell pointed out, there was a threat to the drive of automobile manufacturers to

Continued on Page 63, Column 3

SUPPORTERS: Governor Rockefeller being greeted by a group of about 200 enthusiastic welcomers as he arrived just after midnight yesterday at airport in Manchester, N. H. The Governor was in New Hampshire to attend a reunion of his Dartmouth class.

Associated Press Wirephoto

524 DIE, 2,296 HURT IN JAPAN TYPHOON, WORST SINCE 1945

More Than 700 Are Missing—Storm Sweeps to North After Battering Honshu

By The Associated Press.

TOKYO, Sunday, Sept. 27 — Typhoon Vera raged northward today leaving a trail of death and destruction. The heaviest toll was in Central Honshu, west of Tokyo.

Weather officials called it the worst storm here since World War II ended in 1945.

National Police headquarters here reported about noon that there were 524 dead, 741 missing and 2,296 injured.

The National Police, in giving these figures on the known casualties, said the toll of the storm may go even higher when full reports are received.

Americans Apparently Escape

No casualties were reported among American military personnel stationed in Japan.

The National Police gave this report of damage: 5,655 houses totally destroyed, 10,546 partially destroyed and 230,012 flooded.

The storm was screaming up the Sea of Japan toward Hokkaido, Japan's northernmost main island. Winds on the edge whipped Tokyo and caused some casualties here.

The typhoon, which first slammed into south-central Honshu, the middle main island, late yesterday, was reported by United States Air Force weathermen to be centered this morning near Misawa, North Honshu, and moving northeast at forty-six miles an hour. Maximum winds in the storm were fixed at 92 miles an hour.

The weather observers said the storm was expected to be 200 miles northeast of Chitose on Hokkaido Island by mid-afternoon.

Nagoya Is Hardest Hit

According to incomplete reports from Nagoya, that industrial city had so far suffered the heaviest casualties, including forty-five dead, 116 missing and 248 injured. Nagoya officials estimated 5,800 homes had been destroyed.

One report said an apartment house in Nagoya collapsed during the height of the storm, pining eighty-four persons under debris. Rescue work was reported hampered by torrential rains that flooded the area.

Fringe winds from Typhoon Vera toppled a concrete chimney in Tokyo during the night, crushing one person to death and seriously injuring two others, the police reported.

The Japanese maritime safety agency reported a 7,412-ton British ship had run aground and sprung a leak off Nagoya, 180 miles southwest of Tokyo, while Typhoon Vera was sweeping across Central Hon-

Continued on Page 3, Column 4

Rockefeller's Visit Spurs New Hampshire Backers

By WARREN WEAVER Jr.

Special to The New York Times.

HANOVER, N. H., Sept. 26—The drive to put Governor Rockefeller in the nation's first Republican Presidential primary gained momentum today. As the Governor made his first visit to New Hampshire since the "draft Rockefeller" movement was begun here, the Rockefeller supporters revealed plans to expand their numbers and their influence.

In a few days the committee of forty prominent New Hampshire Republicans that has urged Mr. Rockefeller to enter the primary will be expanded to 150 in an effort to put more pressure on the Governor and to promote his popularity locally.

Among the most significant of the new Rockefeller recruits, according to a local leader, will be Dr. John Sloan Dickey, president of Dartmouth College, the Governor's alma mater. Dr. Dickey was host to Governor and Mrs. Rockefeller tonight.

Backers Confident

As the Governor toured Concord and the Dartmouth campus here on visits political and otherwise, his chief New Hampshire supporters expressed confidence that he would permit his name to be entered and that he could defeat Vice President Richard M. Nixon in their first contest. Nixon supporters have already announced plans to enter his name in the primary.

At a morning news conference, the Governor repeated his statement that he was "not in a position now to respond either positively or negatively" to the invitation to enter the Presidential lists here next March.

One of the most influential Republican leaders and outspoken Nixon supporters in the state hinted to Mr. Rockefeller privately at a breakfast gathering that his position was not entirely inflexible.

Senator Styles Bridges re-

Continued on Page 46, Column 3

U. S. DOLLAR GAINS STRENGTH ABROAD

Monetary Fund Chief Credits Recovery to Restraint on Credit and Spending

By EDWIN L. DALE Jr.

Special to The New York Times.

WASHINGTON, Sept. 26 — The managing director of the International Monetary Fund said today that there was more foreign confidence in the dollar now than was the case six months or a year ago.

According to the Monetary Fund chief, Per Jacobsson, the main reason is the financial policy of the United States Government—a balanced budget and credit restraint by the Federal Reserve System.

Mr. Jacobsson told a news conference that the recent deterioration of the United States balance of payments, with its resulting outflow of gold, was in considerable part due to the financial measures taken to fight last year's recession: a big budget deficit and a huge expansion of credit.

"The general credit principles apply to the United States like everyone else," he said. "Thus the United States must do — and is doing — what the European countries have done to strengthen their balance of payments."

Besides a balanced budget and credit restraint, Mr. Jacobs-

Continued on Page 55, Column 3

CEYLON APPOINTS ANTI-RED PREMIER

Education Chief Succeeds Bandaranaike—Nation Is Calm After Murder

By PAUL GRIMES

Special to The New York Times.

COLOMBO, Ceylon, Sept. 26—A stanch anti-Communist was sworn in today as Prime Minister of Ceylon to succeed S. W. R. D. Bandaranaike, who died of wounds inflicted by an assassin yesterday.

The new Prime Minister is Wijayananda Dahanayake, formerly Education Minister in Mr. Bandaranaike's Cabinet.

The Governor General, Sir Oliver Goonetilleke, administered the oath of office shortly before noon at Queen's House, his official residence. Meanwhile, Colombo calmly mourned the death five hours earlier of Mr. Bandaranaike, who was shot four times yesterday morning by a yellow-robed Buddhist monk.

Mr. Dahanayake declared in an interview tonight that "nothing has taken place to make us think of any alteration of the policy that was pursued by Mr. Bandaranaike."

"We should set our minds and hearts to work, more work and

Continued on Page 3, Column 3

President Takes Premier To His Gettysburg Farm

By WILLIAM J. JORDEN

Special to The New York Times.

GETTYSBURG, Pa., Sept. 26—President Eisenhower and Premier Khrushchev interrupted their discussion of world problems this afternoon to visit the President's farm and country house near here.

The twenty-mile trip from Camp David to the farm was made by helicopter. The President showed Mr. Khrushchev his herd of prize Black Angus cattle, introduced him to his daughter-in-law and grandchildren and conversed with the Soviet visitor on the back porch.

It was the second time the two leaders interrupted their meetings at Camp David, in the Catoctin Mountains of Maryland, to go off together for private conversations. This morning they visited a bowling alley in a recreation hall while strolling inside the Camp David area.

President Eisenhower and the Soviet leader boarded a helicopter at Camp David at 4:33 P. M. With them were the President's son, Maj. John Eisenhower; the President's naval aide, Capt. E. P. Aurand, and the Premier's interpreter, Oleg A. Troyanovsky. They were followed by Secret Service men and Soviet security agents in another helicopter.

The flight lasted twelve min-

Continued on Page 40, Column 3

U.S. AND SOVIET SET TO WAR ON DISEASE

Accord Reached for Joint Studies in Cancer, Polio and Heart Ailments

By BESS FURMAN

Special to The New York Times.

WASHINGTON, Sept. 26—The United States and the Soviet Union have agreed to engage in joint health research projects, it was announced today.

The agreement followed talks at the National Institutes of Health, Bethesda, Md., between leading United States and Soviet health officials.

The joint projects reported today as part of "wide areas of agreement" constitute a major step beyond the growing number of exchanges that already have taken place and are planned for the future.

The projects will cover studies in cancer, heart disease and poliomyelitis. They are the first major joint effort in peaceful scientific pursuits announced since Premier Khrushchev's visit to the United States, although other bilateral programs in atomic energy and commercial air transportation have been indicated.

Dr. H. van Zile Hyde, Assistant Surgeon General for International Affairs, disclosed the areas of agreement with the Soviet medical leaders follow-

Continued on Page 41, Column 2

Mme. Khrushchev Visits Official's Home and Family

Mme. Khrushchev greeting long line of neighborhood youngsters yesterday outside home of John Armitage, State Department employe, at 3706 Taylor Street in Chevy Chase, Md.

Associated Press Wirephoto

By EDITH EVANS ASBURY

Special to The New York Times.

WASHINGTON, Sept. 26—Mme. Nina Petrovna Khrushchev seized a sudden opportunity today to visit an American home in a more modest price range than the stately apartments and ambassadorial quarters she has been seeing in the United States. A State Department employe, John Armitage, invited her to stop at his Chevy Chase home on the way back to Washington from a visit to the National Institute of Dry Cleaning. She promptly accepted. Mr. Armitage, a native Tennessean, telephoned

Continued on Page 41, Column 8

A Free East Europe Among G.O.P. Goals

By RUSSELL BAKER

Special to The New York Times.

WASHINGTON, Sept. 26—The Republican party has tentatively decided to proclaim a policy of peaceful "emancipation" from Soviet rule for the Communist states of Eastern Europe.

This is made clear in a working paper of the Republican Committee on Program and Progress, charged with drafting a long-range statement of G. O. P. policy and objectives.

The committee, whose formation was announced from the White House in February, is headed by Charles H. Percy, an industrialist of Kenilworth, Ill. Although a finished draft of its policy guide for the G. O. P. is not expected until next month, the committee's tentative conclusions were obtained today in a lengthy working paper deal-

Continued on Page 41, Column 7

Police Pressing Gangland Leads In Killing of Pisano and Woman

The police were following several leads yesterday in the murder of Little Augie Pisano and a woman in Queens late Friday night. They indicated the shootings were an underworld job.

"There is no dearth of suspects in this case," said Deputy Chief Inspector Walter F. Henning, who is in charge of Queens detectives.

Pisano, whose real name was Anthony Carfano, lived in Atlantic Beach, L. I. In the Twenties he had been a lieutenant in Brooklyn for Al Capone.

The woman slain with him was identified as Mrs. Janice Drake of 63-60 102d Street, Forest Hills, Queens. She was at Pisano's side when they were killed by several shots fired from the back seat of a car he was driving.

Police officials yesterday afternoon indicated that Mrs. Drake might have been with Pisano because of a chance meeting early Friday evening at the Copacabana night club, 10 East Sixtieth Street.

She was the wife of Allan Drake, a television comedian, and the mother of a 13-year-old boy, Michael. Chief of Detectives James B. Leggett said there was no evidence that the dead couple had been romantically involved.

It was recalled that Mrs. Drake had been questioned seven years ago in the murder of Nat Nelson, a garment district playboy.

Nelson was shot to death at his bachelor apartment, 360 West Fifty-fifth Street, on Feb 9, 1952. Detectives learned that he had been on a tour of Greenwich Village night spots with Mrs. Drake the night before.

The Nelson case was never

Continued on Page 45, Column 3

Sports News

BASEBALL

The Braves defeated the Phillies, 3—2, at Milwaukee yesterday and tied the Dodgers, who lost to the Cubs, 12—2, for the National League lead. Each team has one game to play. The Giants downed the Cardinals, 4—0, in a game halted in the eighth because of rain. Sam Jones hurled a seven-inning no-hitter for the Giants, who will end their regular season play in a double-header at St. Louis today.

HORSE RACING

Sword Dancer won the $109,800 Woodward Stakes at Aqueduct, beating Hillsdale in the final yards. Round Table was third in the mile-and-a-quarter race and Inside Tract last in the field of four.

FOOTBALL

Army routed Boston College and Columbia defeated Brown. Scores of leading games:

Army	44	Boston Coll	8
Columbia	28	Brown	6
Cornell	20	Colgate	15
Harvard	36	Massachus'ts	22
Holy Cross	31	Dartmouth	8
Louisiana St.	10	Texas C. U.	0
Navy	29	Wm. & Mary	2
Northwest'n	15	Oklahoma	13
Notre Dame	28	N. Carolina	8
Pennsylvania	26	Lafayette	0
Rutgers	8	Princeton	6
Syracuse	35	Kansas	21
Yale	20	Connecticut	0

Details in Section 5.

Today's Sections

Index to Subjects

Flood waters rage through the streets of Nagoya, Japan. More than 1,000 bodies were found in this city, one of the hardest hit by the typhoon.

The New York Times

Typhoon Takes Toll in Japan In Sweep North to Hokkaido

Continued From Page 1, Col. 5

shu from the Pacific to the Sea of Japan.

The ship, identified as the Changsha, owned by the China Navigation Company, Ltd., was reported to have been carrying 222 persons besides her crew.

The National Railways reported that twenty-two trains were stranded and rail traffic disrupted in eighty places. The railway canceled twenty runs, including seven fast expresses connecting Tokyo and Osaka. All domestic plane flights were suspended.

There was at least one power failure, for fifteen minutes, in Downtown Tokyo.

Earlier this year three typhoons and the fringe of a fourth had swept Japan, leaving 215 dead, 995 injured and 321 missing:

July—Fringe rains brought on by Typhoon Billie, which caused widespread death and destruction in Taiwan, left 45 dead, 75 injured and 16 missing in Japan.

Aug. 10—Ellen: 11 killed, 11 injured, 5 missing.

Aug. 15—Georgia: 137 dead, 712 injured, 108 missing.

Sept. 17-18—Sarah: 22 dead, 197 injured, 192 missing.

Bodies Recovered From River

TOKYO, Sunday, Sept. 27 (UPI)—Reports of the typhoon's effect in Central Japan said that the bodies of eighty-five victims were recovered today from the Nagara River. The storm broke the levee on which they had taken refuge.

Two hundred persons were killed and 300 missing at Handa, near Nagoya, when typhoon-

The New York Times   Sept. 27, 1959

Nagoya (1) was hit. Then the typhoon swept toward Misawa (2) and northward on the east of Chitose (3).

driven waves broke up a sea-wall, weakened when a 1,000-ton shop was dashed against it.

Korean Fishing Fleet Missing

SEOUL, Korea, Sept. 26 (UPI)—A Seoul newspaper reported today that 1,200 Korean fishermen had failed to return from a commercial fishing expedition. They were feared lost in typhoon Sarah, which struck southern Korea last week.

The newspaper Hankuk Daily News said the fishermen left Oerarodo Island off the port of Pusan Aug. 28 aboard a fleet of forty-six ships. None of the ships has returned.

Typhoon Sarah left 3,750 casualties, including 669 dead, elsewhere in South Korea. The United States Army is distributing 3,000,000 pounds of relief supplies.

The New York Times

Survivors of typhoon Vera stand on a hillside overlooking their flooded homes.

"All the News That's Fit to Print"

The New York Times

LATE CITY EDITION
U. S. Weather Bureau Report (Page 74) forecasts: Fair and cold today. Cloudy, cold, chance of snow tomorrow.
Temp. range: 36—19; yesterday: 31.7—22.

VOL. CIX..No. 37,293. © 1960, by The New York Times Company. Times Square, New York 36, N. Y. NEW YORK, WEDNESDAY, MARCH 2, 1960. 10 cents beyond 50-mile zone from New York City except on Long Island. Higher in air delivery cities. FIVE CENTS

RUSSELL HARDENS FILIBUSTER STAND ON VOTING RIGHTS

Discounts Talk of an Accord as Deadlock in Senate Heads for Third Day

MAJORITY IS CONFIDENT

Forces Roll-Call on Motion and Beats It, 55 to 6—Catches Foes Napping

By RUSSELL BAKER
Special to The New York Times.

WASHINGTON, Wednesday, March 2—The Senate was still locked in a stand-off contest of will and stamina today as the non-stop session to force a civil rights vote continued toward its third day.

At 3 A. M. Senator Sam J. Ervin, Democrat of North Carolina, was winding up a speech about the sins of the Supreme Court. He had taken the floor at 11 P. M.

Southern members, sworn to talk until doomsday if necessary to block a vote, had held the floor for thirty-nine hours and were still breathing easily.

A large bipartisan bloc of civil rights advocates, equally determined to force a vote, stayed massed in makeshift sleeping quarters near the Senate chamber ready to prevent the Southerners from getting any undue relaxation.

No Progress Made

Shortly after sun-up yesterday the majority was even cocky enough to force a roll-call vote on a motion to adjourn—a motion they handily defeated, 55 to 6, while most Southerners were caught sleeping in far-off hideaways.

On the floor there was no sign of progress toward writing a bill, although the consensus is that the Southerners will ultimately be forced to yield.

Senator Richard B. Russell, chief strategist for the Southerners, contributed the only substantive declaration about the chances of getting a bill, and it was discouraging.

The Georgia Democrat, who Monday had rated voting-rights provisions far down on his list of "obnoxious" proposals before the Senate, said yesterday that he did not mean the South would consider a compromise bill dealing with voting rights.

Solution Is Sought

"Some persons apparently got the idea that I was wrapping the olive branch around a white flag and that I was looking for some way to compromise this issue," he said. "Such a thought was the furtherest on earth from my mind."

Nevertheless, in the private offices beyond the Senate arena powerful support was gathering for a solution that would center on new voting rights measures and strike out some of the proposals dealing with school desegregation.

Among the most offensive of all these proposals to the Southerners is a section that would put Congress on record as endorsing the Supreme Court desegregation decision of 1954 as "the supreme law of the land."

This section and a companion provision affording Federal "technical assistance" for school districts planning desegregation appear to have little chance of

Continued on Page 23, Column 3

U. S. Delays Firing 9,000-Mile Missile

By RICHARD WITKIN
Special to The New York Times.

WASHINGTON, March 1—An Air Force attempt to fire an Atlas missile 9,000 miles into the South Indian Ocean was canceled today. It will not be rescheduled until after President Eisenhower returns Sunday from his South American tour.

Informed sources said today that the attempt was to have been made before the President's return, but officials in Washington were reported to have become worried about the political aspects of the project.

It was understood here that an effort had been made to put the issue before the President on his tour of South America. It was not clear what reply, if any, had come back, but it did not include a

Continued on Page 5, Column 2

DILLON STRESSES U. S. AID TO LATINS

Tells Caribbean Assembly of Rising Private Investment —Cites Available Fund

By SAM POPE BREWER
Special to The New York Times.

DORADO BEACH, Puerto Rico, March 1—The United States asserted tonight that its private investors were creating wealth for Latin America by pouring in capital at the rate of $600,000,000 a year.

At an inter-American meeting, Douglas Dillon, Under Secretary of State, made a vigorous rebuttal of charges often heard in Latin America that the United States had not offered adequate economic help to countries there.

He told the Caribbean Assembly that direct bilateral loans from the United States to Latin-American countries in the last ten years had totaled more than $3,500,000,000. He said $1,000,000,000 was available now through the Inter-American Development Bank for the use of all Latin-American countries except Cuba, which is not a member of the bank.

Answering charges sometimes made by Latin Americans that foreign investors are draining wealth from their countries, Mr. Dillon said:

¶Latin-American governments get 15 per cent of all their revenues from United States companies.

¶Tax payments by United States companies to Latin-American Governments are double the profits the companies send home.

¶United States companies

Continued on Page 14, Column 3

PRESIDENT DENIES CHARGE THAT U. S. BACKS DICTATORS

Replies to Latin Criticisms in Speeches in Chile—Visit to Uruguay Due Today

Eisenhower talks and letter will be found on Page 16.

By TAD SZULC
Special to The New York Times.

SANTIAGO, Chile, March 1—President Eisenhower said today that allegations that the United States supported dictatorships were ridiculous.

On the second day of his visit to Chile the President gave special attention to what he called "serious misunderstandings" among the American republics. These "impede the resolution of many problems that beset us," he said.

Chile is the third nation the President has visited in his South American tour. He will leave Santiago tomorrow morning by plane for Montevideo, Uruguay, the last Latin capital on his itinerary.

Americans Hear Speech

In a speech at a midtown movie house in Santiago this morning before an audience of United States Embassy employes and other members of the American community here and their friends, the President mentioned misunderstandings of United States policies he had encountered during his tour.

"And then I have heard it said that the United States supports dictators," he said. "This is ridiculous. Surely no nation loves liberty more, or more sincerely prays that its benefits and deep human satisfactions may come to all peoples than does the United States."

"We repudiate dictatorship in any form, Right or Left," the President said. "Our role in the United Nations, in the Organization of American States, in two world wars and in Korea stands as a beacon to all who love freedom," he asserted.

Communiqué Issued

In a joint communiqué published tonight after two days of private talks, President Eisenhower and President Jorge Alessandri Rodriguez urged a concerted effort to solve the economic problems of the hemisphere and to reach a general limitation on arms purchases throughout Latin America.

The statement was issued after a dinner given by General Eisenhower for the Chilean President at the United States Embassy residence. It also reaffirmed the Pan-American policy of nonintervention in the internal affairs of other states.

The declaration contained no

Continued on Page 16, Column 7

RUBBLE OF A CITY: Pedestrians walk through a debris-filled street of Agadir, Morocco. Two earthquakes and tidal wave that hit city yesterday reportedly killed more than a thousand persons and left most of inhabitants homeless. Associated Press Radiophoto

KHRUSHCHEV VIEW OF CHINA CRITICAL

Indonesians Say He Finds Peiping Is Industrializing 'at Too Great a Cost'

By BERNARD KALB
Special to The New York Times.

JAKARTA, Indonesia, March 1—Premier Khrushchev told President Sukarno that Communist China's industrial achievements were being made "at too great a cost," authoritative Indonesian sources said today.

While the Soviet Premier did not elaborate, his remark was interpreted by his Indonesian listeners to mean "human cost."

Mr. Khrushchev was said to have added he had great respect for Peiping's strides in turning China into an industrialized modern state.

This was one of many exchanges between the Soviet Premier and the Indonesian President during Mr. Khrushchev's thirteen-day visit to this neutralist country. He departed this morning for Afghanistan via Calcutta on the last leg of his Asian tour.

[In Calcutta, the Soviet Premier had a forty-five-minute talk with Prime Minister Jawaharlal Nehru.]

In a farewell statement, prior

Continued on Page 3, Column 1

Governor Insists Assembly Pass His Road Safety Plan

By WARREN WEAVER Jr.
Special to The New York Times.

ALBANY, March 1—Governor Rockefeller today challenged recalcitrant Republican Assemblymen to accept his program for the promotion of highway safety.

The Governor declared that it would be "unthinkable" if the Legislature did not approve four key bills in the highway field. The Assembly majority has indicated it will not accept any of them in their present form.

The Rockefeller statement was sufficiently strong to leave very little room for compromise between the Governor and the Republican lawmakers in their first major clash of the 1960 session.

By serving notice that he would attempt to force his bills through, Mr. Rockefeller set up an intractable political situation in which either he or the Assemblymen must give ground. There were no signs that the Assembly views had changed.

Poor Issue Seen

Some observers felt that the Governor had chosen a poor issue on which to bring to a head his differences with his own party members, largely because it appeared unlikely that he could soften Republican opposition to the highway safety program.

The measures on which the Governor staked his political prestige would result in these changes:

¶Eliminate the requirement that a policeman pursue a speeder for at least a quarter of a mile before arresting him. This would authorize convictions on radar evidence alone.

¶Penalize New York drivers —when the offense called for license suspension and revocation—for motor-vehicle convictions in neighboring states.

¶Provide new penalties for those who drive after drinking but are not legally intoxicated.

¶Enact a new definition of speeding to replace one declared unconstitutional by the courts as too vague.

In a closed conference last week, Republican Assemblymen rejected the first two proposals outright and indicated that the third would be acceptable only

Continued on Page 30, Column 4

'61 STATE BUDGET VOTED BY SENATE

Assembly Debate Continues as G.O.P. Seeks Tax Cut and School Aid Rise

By DOUGLAS DALES
Special to The New York Times.

ALBANY, March 1—The Senate approved and sent to the Assembly today a budget that neither the Republicans nor the Democrats were too happy about.

After a five-hour debate the lower House adjourned shortly after 8 P. M., postponing a final vote until tomorrow.

The main budget bill provides for a spending program of $2,035,000,000 for the fiscal year starting April 1. This would be $32,000,000 more than last year.

Democrats made attempts to amend Governor Rockefeller's proposals in twelve respects in the Senate and in fifteen areas in the Assembly. As usual, the amendments were defeated by strictly party votes.

Other Proposals Studied

As the budget came to a vote, Republicans were still studying proposals to increase school aid beyond the $25,000,000 in additional aid that is provided for in the budget. They also wrestled with the question of an income tax cut.

The spending program approved today is the largest in the state's history. And it is expected to be somewhat higher when further appropriations are made in the supplemental budget.

The budget has been hailed by Governor Rockefeller as a pay-as-you-go formula, which means that it will be balanced by current revenues without the use of any bond moneys for capital construction.

In addition to meeting expenditures, revenues next year are expected to provide a surplus of $32,000,000, according to Mr. Rockefeller's estimate.

The surplus estimate has been disputed by both parties. Republicans are having their own forecast prepared with a view toward justifying additional school aid and possibly a tax cut.

At a conference of Assembly

Continued on Page 31, Column 5

TRAIN HITS TRUCK; 17 DIE IN WRECK

55 Hurt on Coast as Flyer Crashes Into Oil Vehicle —Cars Are Derailed

Special to The New York Times.

BAKERSFIELD, Calif., March 1—A speeding Santa Fe passenger train collided in a fiery explosion this afternoon with an oil tank truck. A spokesman for the railroad said that seventeen persons had been killed and fifty-five injured.

The accident occurred about five miles northwest of here at the Snow Road and Allen Lane crossing about 5:15 P. M. Pacific Coast time (8:15 P. M. New York time).

Within minutes emergency calls were issued by the Kern County Emergency Sheriff's Office and the California Highway Patrol for all ambulances and medical services in this city of 100,000 population, which is 110 miles north of Los Angeles.

The train was the eastbound San Francisco Chief. It left Richmond, Calif., across the bay from San Francisco, at 12:59 P. M., on the regular run to Chicago.

Engineer Is Killed

Among the nine known dead were the train's engineer and a fireman and the truck driver. Seventy-two passengers were reported to have been on the train. A brakeman told reporters the train had been going about seventy-five miles an hour in a "high-speed area" when the crash occurred.

At three hospitals here spokesmen said that at least fifty-one persons had been brought from the scene. Among those critically injured was John Horst, the train brakeman.

Nine of the eleven passenger cars plummeted in flames into a ditch.

The three Diesel units caught fire. The first coach telescoped on top of them, and the second and third coaches wound up in zig-zag position.

The crash attracted thousands

Continued on Page 75, Column 3

1,000 FEARED DEAD AS QUAKES WRECK MOROCCAN RESORT

Agadir Is Heap of Rubble—Tidal Wave and Fire Hit Port City on Atlantic

THOUSANDS ARE INJURED

Americans Among Missing —Power and Water Failure Hinder Rescue Work

By MARVINE HOWE
Special to The New York Times.

AGADIR, Morocco, March 1—Two earthquakes, a tidal wave and fire left this resort a vast heap of rubble and cracked shells of houses. The toll of the dead was estimated tonight at more than 1,000 and of the injured additional thousands. Most of the city's 45,000 inhabitants were homeless.

The first quake struck this important Atlantic port and resort shortly before last midnight. The second came about an hour later.

As the sun set on the razed city this evening, Moroccan Army troops, police and surviving townspeople were digging frantically in the ruins for persons buried by the quake. The Moroccan radio said the Government had ordered a total evacuation of the city.

Town Lies in Darkness

Agadir lay in total darkness tonight, except for occasional candles. Electricity and water are cut off, and telephone lines are down, greatly hampering rescue operations.

Estimates of the number of casualties ranged as high as 5,000. It was impossible to give the exact toll since rescue teams must still dig out a number of four and five-story apartment buildings where hundreds were known to be trapped.

All day a stream of survivors, fearing another quake, fled from Agadir by cars, trucks, bicycles and on foot. About 80 per cent of the city lies in ruins. Tonight it was largely deserted except for rescue teams and those that were trapped.

A French naval air base, four miles south of Agadir, has been transformed into a giant refugee camp. The base, untouched by the quake, is the center of the evacuation operation.

More than 500 injured have been evacuated by French planes put at the disposal of the Moroccan Government. Hundreds of homeless French civilians have set up cots and makeshift tents on the grounds of the base.

The United States Air Force

Continued on Page 18, Column 3

SEWER DATA GONE, CONTRACTOR SAYS

Records of West Side Job Are Reported Stolen

By PETER KIHSS

A contractor has told a state investigation that extensive records, some of them bearing on perhaps 94 per cent of a $2,000,000 West Side sewer job, were stolen last year from a trailer parked at the project.

The disappearance was disclosed yesterday in State Supreme Court as the sewer contractor and a private carting company sought to quash subpoenas for records issued by the State Commission on Governmental Operations of the City of New York.

In defending the subpoenas, Whitney North Seymour Jr., the commission's chief counsel, told Justice Thomas A. Aurelio that his agency was studying the effectiveness of city supervision over contract costs.

The commission, he added, also is investigating the Union Carting Company, which collects refuse from commercial establishments, in part to check whether the city itself should take over all such work.

Purchasing Chief Queried

In another development, the commission questioned Joseph V. Spagna, the city's Purchase Commissioner, for five hours in a private hearing at its office, 386 Park Avenue South, on his department's procedures and buying.

Mr. Spagna later told reporters the questions had been

Continued on Page 31, Column 3

Filibuster Diary: First 24 Hours

Southern Forces Dig In and the Majority Protects Its Flanks

By E. W. KENWORTHY
Special to The New York Times.

WASHINGTON, March 1—Leather lungs, oak legs, a cast-iron stomach, an expert knowledge of Jefferson's Manual, a panoramic view of United States history, a fund of anecdote and a store of righteous indignation—these are the qualifications for a varsity filibusterer.

By contrast, the attacking majority needs only the knowledge of the manual and the ability to rouse from a sound sleep in the middle of the night to answer the quorum bell.

There were, undoubtedly, giants in the Senate in the old days. But yesterday's opener in the round-the-clock showdown on the civil rights bill was worthy of the past.

Here is what happens in a filibuster—at least what happened in the first twenty-four hours of this one:

Noon, Monday, Feb. 29—Most of the Senators are on the floor. The public galleries are only partly filled. Vice President Nixon is on hand. The Senate chaplain, the Rev. Frederick Brown Harris, offers a prayer—"Fix our wills upon a world of human wretchedness with wrongs to be set right."

12:02 P. M.—The majority leader, Senator Lyndon B. Johnson of Texas, asks, as usual, for unanimous consent to dispense with reading of The Journal—a lengthy summary of the previous day's proceedings. Senator Richard B. Russell, Democrat of Georgia, leader of the eighteen Southern stalwarts, objects. "I do not propose to waive any potential [time-consuming] advantage, however minute."

12:08 P. M.—Senator Everett McKinley Dirksen of Illinois, the minority leader, asks that business be suspended each day for the customary noon prayer. Senator Russell agrees: "If there is anybody on earth that needs prayer at the present time, it is the Senate of the United States."

12:12 P. M.—Senator Allen J. Ellender, Democrat of Louisi-

Continued on Page 29, Column 1

Senator Vance Hartke, Indiana Democrat, eats a quick breakfast in his office as his wife brings clean shirt. Associated Press Wirephoto

1,000 Negroes Join March in Alabama

By CLAUDE SITTON
Special to The New York Times.

MONTGOMERY, Ala., March 1—A thousand Negro students prayed and sang the National Anthem today on the steps of the first capital of the Old Confederacy in a peaceful protest against segregation.

Neither the police nor white hoodlums, one of whom attacked a Negro woman with a miniature baseball bat last week-end, attempted to interfere.

High state officials watched from the entrance to the building, which now serves as Alabama's capitol, with an occasional muttered comment.

The likelihood remained that at least some of the demonstrators would be punished. Gov. John Patterson has strongly implied that their leaders should

Continued on Page 29, Column 5

Avail soon Exec Asst 36 Hvy Mod Sis Promo, Mgmt, Edit'rl. 27716 Times. Advt.

Soviet Is Adamant On Berlin Air Lanes

Special to The New York Times.

BERLIN, March 1—A Soviet spokesman said today that the Western Allies must negotiate with East Germany and the Soviet Union if they wanted to fly above the Soviet-imposed 10,000-foot ceiling in the air corridors linking West Berlin with the West.

Sources in Washington disclosed Monday that the United States had decided to resume supply flights into the city above that ceiling, in agreement with Britain and France.

Yuri Beburov, First Secretary at the Soviet Embassy in East Berlin, said Allied flights to and from Berlin above an altitude of 10,000 feet would be considered "unilateral violations of East Germany's air sovereignty" unless an agreement was reached previously.

The West accepts no limita-

Continued on Page 3, Column 5

NEWS INDEX

4 Radio Licenses Held Up by F.C.C.

Special to The New York Times.

WASHINGTON, March 1—The Government called upon four Massachusetts radio stations today to justify renewal of their Federal licenses in the light of payola that they or their employes may have received.

The Federal Communications Commission notified the stations that public hearings on their applications for license renewals might be necessary because of testimony on payola before Congressional investigators.

The stations are WMEX, WILD and WORL in Boston and WHIL in Medford. The commission indicated, in letters to the stations, that they had failed to comply fully with an F. C. C. questionnaire calling for full disclosure of payola, undercover payments to disk

Continued on Page 75, Column 2

1,000 Feared Dead as Quakes Hit Moroccan Port

AGADIR IS TURNED INTO RUBBLE HEAP

Tidal Wave and Fire Wreak Havoc in Beach Resort— Americans Are Missing

Continued From Page 1, Col. 8

will operate an airlift for the injured throughout the night from Agadir to the Benguérir and Nouaseur air bases. The United States Ambassador, Charles W. Yost, flew to the scene of the disaster and made available $10,000 to the Moroccan Government for food and medical supplies.

On a stretcher in the hangar of the French air base a United States Air Force first lieutenant, Gerald Martin, waited desperately for news of his wife, buried among the ruins of a hotel. The lieutenant and his family were on a vacation at Agadir.

He and his 1-year-old daughter Diane were rescued this afternoon from the debris of the hotel where they had been buried since the quake struck. Lieutenant Martin, who comes from St. Albans, W. Va., suffered leg injuries. The child was unhurt.

Moroccan authorities have made urgent appeals for help. The immediate need was for medical personnel and work crews to dig the city out of its grave. Six United States Air Force and Navy physicians and several nurses flew with the first American relief plane to Agadir today.

The panic-stricken population began its exodus at daybreak, heading for inland villages at Taroudant, Inezgan and Ait Melloul, which were untouched by the quake.

Some Remain to Search

The few families who remained in the city to continue the search for friends and relatives huddled together in small groups on the beach or in gardens, out of danger of falling walls.

The old Moroccan quarter known as Tal Borj lies destroyed. Little remained of the casbah, an ancient fortress and favorite tourist site overlooking the sea. In the modern European city, the four-story luxury hotel Es Saada is a heap of stone and glass.

Hotels, restaurants, fashionable shops and the central market were badly damaged. Most of the villas and apartment houses of more than one story crumbled under the violence of the quake.

Americans Among Missing

Special to The New York Times.

RABAT, Morocco, March 1— In one of the gravest catastrophies in Moroccan history, nothing is known of the fate of the seven American families reported to be living there.

Agadir, 400 miles south of Casablanca on the Atlantic coast, has a population of 45,-000. Many foreign tourists were in the city when disaster struck. Approximately 95 per cent of the old city is reported destroyed and 70 per cent of the new city, and a third of the industrial area.

Immediate aid to the stricken was made all but impossible by the light failure caused by the twelve-second shock.

At the Es Saada Hotel, the most luxurious building in Agadir, very few of its tourist guests survived. Some of the town's inhabitants who escaped by car arrived in Mogador, north of Agadir in pajamas. King Mohamed V arrived in Agadir this morning.

The downtown hospital is unusable, making the French air base hospital the main center for care of the injured.

The United States has sent teams from all its bases in Morocco. One American couple fell from their third-floor room in the Es Saada Hotel to the basement, from which they were extricated six hours later with only bruises.

To ward off epidemics, United States and French medical teams are inoculating survivors against typhoid and typhus.

Tidal Wave Follows Quake

CASABLANCA, Morocco, March 1 (AP)—The tidal wave that followed the first tremor swept some 300 yards into the stricken city. Fires broke out while rescue work was in progress.

Lieut. (j. g.) Norman Lefton of the United States Navy, on his honeymoon in Agadir, suffered broken legs. His wife, the former Margaret Banks, was flown out of Agadir to an unknown destination.

The disaster was the second major earthquake to hit North Africa in less than two weeks. More than forty persons were killed in a quake Feb. 21 at Melousa, Algeria.

Town to Be Rebuilt

RABAT, March 1 (Reuters) —King Mohamed returned to Rabat tonight and presided at a Cabinet meeting. The Cabinet decided to rebuild Agadir as soon as possible.

It appointed Crown Prince Moulay Hassan as head of a special "National Commission for the Reconstruction of Agadir." The Crown Prince is in charge of rescue operations.

First Quake Strongest

STRASBOURG, France, March 1 (UPI)—The Geophysical Institute here said the first temblor did most of the damage but that lesser temblors continued for forty-five minutes.

Maugham's Nephew Hurt

LONDON, March 1 (Reuters) —Lord Maugham, a nephew of Somerset Maugham, the novelist, was identified tonight as having been injured in the quake. His injuries are said to be not serious.

Lord Maugham, 43 years old, writes under the name of Robin Maugham. He is in a hospital in Casablanca.

Agadir a Scene of Destruction; Residents Flee Shattered City

AGADIR, Morocco, March 1 (UPI)—Americans, British and German tourists as well as the permanent inhabitants of Agadir wandered in confusion through the rubble of this ruined city tonight.

Many tourists wintering on the sunny Atlantic shore were believed to be among the hundreds killed or injured in the earthquake that struck Agadir shortly before last midnight.

The confusion was so great that no reliable estimate of casualties had emerged tonight.

For the tourists it could have been worse. Most of the big new hotels in the main tourist section withstood the quake fairly well.

But the Saada Hotel, on the fringe of the new European quarter of the city, lay in ruins. At least fifty tourists were believed to be trapped under the crumbled wreckage.

"It collapsed so slowly that you might have thought the buildings were groaning in pain," a witness said.

Three Americans were among those known to have escaped from the rubble of the Saada. Their names were lost in the confusion.

Wife Saved as Husband Waits

A tall German in pajamas was hovering by a pile of rubble into which rescuers were digging in the sunshine of the early afternoon. After hours of waiting, he wept with relief when they dug out his wife, injured but alive, and rushed her to a hospital.

From a plane flying over the bay of Agadir toward the undamaged airfield, the scene looked almost peaceful. Only a spreading patch of yellow sand in the blue of the water indicated the upheaval that took place in the night.

Then as the plane swooped low for a landing it was possible to see the destruction in the European "new city" and the Moslem quarter. It looked as if a giant foot had stepped on the city and squashed it flat.

Along the road from the airport to the city, hundreds of Europeans and Moslems walked in a daze, some with bundles of belongings and with children clutching their hands.

The city itself was a scene of destruction. Big houses had burst outward. Furniture, mattresses, sheets and broken dishes were spilled from the broken walls.

Some of the wreckage was bloodstained. Everywhere the bright sun glittered on broken glass.

Many Workers Escape

Hundreds of Arab workers living on farms and ramshackle buildings on the outskirts of the city escaped death by fleeing after the first mild tremor yesterday noon. They collected their families and slept outdoors. In the morning most of their homes were in ruins.

But for the majority in the city who did not want to forsake their homes, it was a night of terror.

This is an account given by Mme. Yvette Dehri, who lives in the "new city":

"At first the shock seemed to tip us sideways. We were thrown out of our beds. The whole house rocked in the midst of a terrifying, roaring noise.

"We scrambled out of the house, grabbed our two oldest children and started up the road. But then we saw that in the panic we had left our third child behind.

"How we got back down the street I shall never know. But we collected the boy and headed for open ground.

Associated Press Radiophoto

HIT BY EARTHQUAKES AND TIDAL WAVE: An aerial view of damaged buildings in Moroccan port of Agadir

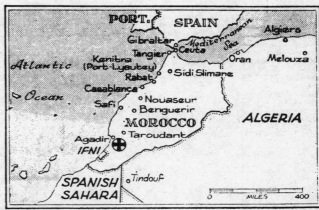

The New York Times   March 2, 1960

Two earthquakes and a tidal wave struck Agadir (cross)

"All the News That's Fit to Print"

The New York Times.

LATE CITY EDITION
U. S. Weather Bureau Report (Page 78) forecasts: Mostly fair and warm today, tonight and tomorrow.
Temp. range: 72—54; yesterday: 68.6—54.7.

VOL. CIX..No. 37,377. © 1960, by The New York Times Company. Times Square New York 36, N. Y. NEW YORK, WEDNESDAY, MAY 25, 1960. 10 cents beyond 50-mile zone from New York City except on Long Island. Higher in air delivery cities. FIVE CENTS

SATELLITE TO SPOT MISSILE FIRINGS PUT INTO ORBIT IN AIR FORCE TEST; ALLIES DEFEND U.S. IN U.N. DEBATE

STATE LAYS FRAUD TO CONTRACTORS AT YONKERS TRACK

Charges Profiteering Sent Costs of Clubhouse From 7.5 Million to 18 Million

HEARING IS BEGUN HERE

Lane Cites Profits to Thugs as Investigation Group Gets First Data in Case

By EMANUEL PERLMUTTER

The State Investigation Commission charged yesterday that contractors who built the $18,000,000 clubhouse at Yonkers Raceway in 1958 had defrauded the taxpayers by inflating the construction costs.

Under a statute enacted in 1956 and repealed last year, the state is committed to reimburse harness tracks for capital improvements made while the law was in effect. The money is to be paid out of the state's tax income from pari-mutuel betting.

Among those who shared in the excessive construction fees, according to Myles J. Lane, the commission chairman, were the late Anthony Carfano and Vincent Rao, two underworld figures.

3-Day Hearing Started

Carfano, alias Little Augie Pisano, was a former henchman of Al Capone, the late Chicago gangster. Little Augie was murdered with a woman companion in a car last September in Queens. Rao was one of the men who attended the 1957 gangland meeting at Apalachin, N. Y. His brother Charles also shared in the construction profit.

The charges of contract profiteering were made by Mr. Lane as the investigation commission opened three days of public hearing on the Yonkers Raceway project in its offices at 270 Broadway.

He explained that the new clubhouse was originally projected at $7,525,000, but that with extra items and work and general contractors' and architects' fees the cost was exceeded by about $11,000,000.

Mr. Lane intimated that the facts brought out by the commission might result in the state's recapturing part of the $20,000,000 it had already paid or earmarked for payment to the raceway for capital improvements.

Lane Promises Details

"The information which we have now obtained in this investigation will illustrate a more complete picture of the grossly excessive cost of the construction of Yonkers Raceway," he declared. "The evidence will concern the techniques employed in the granting of contracts to favored firms, and the loose procedures and supervision which permitted these overcharges to be made for alleged extra work performed by way of so-called change-orders.

"More specifically, the evidence presented may serve as a basis for future action by appropriate state agencies to entirely re-evaluate and review the certified costs of the Yonkers Raceway construction program, and to disallow and recover by all legal means the excessive costs previously paid

Continued on Page 30, Column 3

Florida Runoff Won By States' Rightist

By United Press International.

MIAMI, May 24—Farris Bryant, a lawyer, pledged to maintain segregation and to champion states' rights, won Florida's Democratic run-off primary for Governor tonight.

The 45-year-old Ocala legislator defeated Doyle E. Carlton Jr., 37, of Wauchula. Mr. Carlton, son of a former Governor, was making his first bid for the state's highest post. It was Mr. Bryant's second try for the governorship.

With 1,910 of 1,971 precincts reported, the vote was Mr. Bryant 488,416 and Mr. Carlton 406,090.

Victory in the primary is the equivalent of election in the heavily Democratic state.

Mr. Bryant will oppose George Petersen of Fort Lauderdale, the Republican nominee, in November.

Mr. Bryant not only beat a strong rival, but he also over-

Continued on Page 27, Column 3

Collins and Church Named To Democratic Convention

Florida Governor Will Be the Permanent Chairman and Idahoan Keynoter—Butler Calls G.O.P. 'Soft' on Reds

By LEO EGAN

Gov. LeRoy Collins of Florida, a Southern moderate on racial issues, was selected yesterday as the permanent chairman of this year's Democratic national convention.

Senator Frank Church of Idaho, a civil rights advocate and one-time winner of the American Legion's national oratorical contest for high school students, was picked at the same time for temporary chairman, or keynote speaker.

Paul M. Butler, the Democratic national chairman, announced both selections at a news conference that followed a three-hour meeting of the fourteen-member committee on arrangements for the convention.

The choices are subject to ratification by the convention delegates when they meet in Los Angeles on July 11.

In answer to questions, Mr. Butler charged that the Eisenhower Administration was "too soft on communism." He also predicted that the Democrats would carry all fifty states in this year's Presidential election.

In Washington, Senator Church said he was "deeply moved" by his selection as keynoter. He said he would deliver a "fighting speech directed at the appalling failures of the Republican Administration," but that he would not hit "below the belt."

Also in Washington, James C. Hagerty, President Eisenhower's press secretary, commenting on

Continued on Page 22, Column 3

SENATE UPHOLDS JOBLESS-AID VETO

Bill's Backers Lack 11 Votes to Override—Democrats See Campaign Issue

By JOHN D. MORRIS

Special to The New York Times.

WASHINGTON, May 24—The Senate sustained today President Eisenhower's veto of the depressed-area bill.

The vote of 45 to 39 for overriding was eleven short of the two-thirds majority required to pass a measure over a veto.

Democratic managers of the bill served notice that they would carry the issue "to the people" in the Presidential and Congressional campaigns this fall. They discounted the prospect of action on any compromise measure.

The bill called for $251,000,000 in Federal loans and grants to bring new industry and employment to chronically depressed areas of the country. President Eisenhower had proposed a $53,000,000 program.

A new Administration bill, introduced since the veto May 13, would set up a $180,000,000 program. Some Republicans justi-

Continued on Page 25, Column 1

Rockefeller to Get Party's Plea Today To Go to Convention

By WARREN WEAVER Jr.

Special to The New York Times.

ALBANY, May 24—Republican leaders will urge Governor Rockefeller tomorrow to reconsider his decision not to attend the Republican national convention in Chicago in July.

The move will be made at a meeting of the party's county chairmen with the Governor. It will be preceded by a gathering of the Republican state executive committee, which Mr. Rockefeller is not expected to attend.

The Governor announced earlier this month that he would not attend the national convention. His aim was to avoid lending any possible encouragement to efforts to draft him for the party's nomination for Vice President.

This decision, however, has raised serious party problems. The principal one involves the selection of a successor to Governor Rockefeller as chairman of the New York Republican delegation.

Both United States Senators—Jacob K. Javits and Kenneth B. Keating—have made informal bids to head the delegation if Mr. Rockefeller should re-

Continued on Page 24, Column 4

CHILE VOLCANOES ADDING TO HAVOC; DEATH TOLL 1,000

2,000,000 Are Homeless—180 Perished in Waves in Japan and Okinawa

By The Associated Press.

SANTIAGO, Chile, May 24—Volcanic eruptions added to the massive devastation by earthquakes, tidal waves and landslides in southern Chile today.

The Government said more than 1,000 had died in the four-day disaster and that perhaps 2,000,000 were homeless.

[Japan and Okinawa counted 180 dead and missing in the wake of tidal waves fanning out from the quake area and racing across the Pacific. The swells battered coastlines on an arc from Alaska to New Zealand.]

At least five volcanoes were in eruption, and a new one was reported born in the midst of the horror and panic.

Four volcanoes — Osorno, Caulle, Carral and Casablanca—were active in Osorno Province, about 500 miles south of Santiago, authorities said.

Cities Are Evacuated

The near-by cities of Lanquihue and Osorno, with a combined population of about 26,000, were ordered evacuated.

A pilot reported 7,350-foot Puyehue volcano near Osorno also was spewing smoke and fire. Farther north, in Cautin Province, a new volcano started emitting a column of flame and smoke.

A new earthquake this afternoon shook Quinchao in Chiloe Province, the Government reported. It had no details because of chaotic communications.

Tidal waves also carried more than 100 to death at Aleta today.

Another crushing wall of water eighteen feet high engulfed the small seaside resort of Mehuin early today. Mehuin is near Queulen and is about 560 miles south of Santiago.

New earthquakes also rocked the mountainous southern provinces, precipitating landslides into the Pacific at Maullin, a town of 1,500 about 600 miles south of Santiago.

Whole villages have been swept away by tidal waves as high as twenty-four feet.

Other villages with which no contact has been made may have been destroyed by tidal waves or landslides, Interior

Continued on Page 2, Column 3

Damage Left by Tidal Waves in Japan and Hawaii

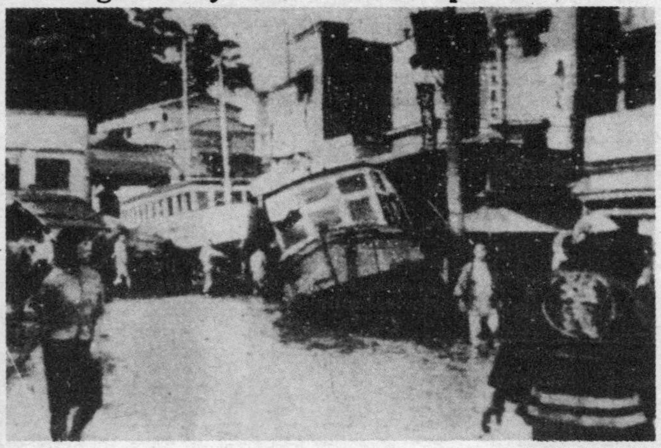

Associated Press Radiophoto

Sight-seeing boat rests against store front on flooded main street of Shiogama, Japan

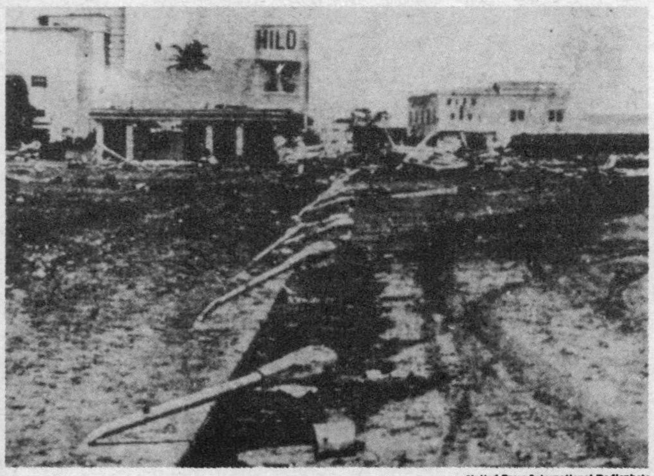

United Press International Radiophoto

Bent parking meters attest to the force of huge waves that swept into Hilo, Hawaii

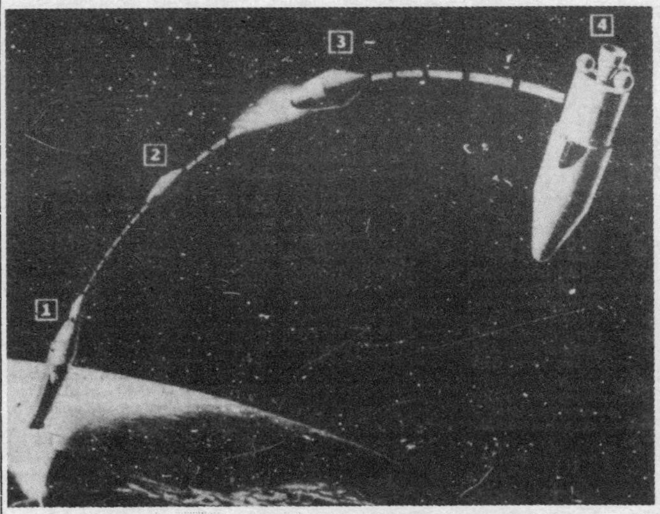

Missiles and Space Division, Lockheed Aircraft Corporation

EYE IN THE SKY: Drawing depicts launching of Midas II satellite. Midas is carried aloft (1) by a modified Atlas missile. It coasts after separation (2), then integral engine ignites (3) to place it into orbit, during which it points toward earth (4).

ATLAS IS BOOSTER

Path of Midas Near the Equator Avoids Most Red Lands

By JACK RAYMOND

Special to The New York Times.

WASHINGTON, May 24 — The Air Force placed a 5,000-pound experimental satellite in orbit today in its program to devise space sentries that would give a speedy warning of surprise missile attacks.

The satellite, named Midas for Missile Defense Alarm System, was launched from Cape Canaveral, Fla., this afternoon with a modified Atlas intercontinental ballistic missile as booster.

When orbital success was verified, the heavily instrumented space vehicle, twenty-two feet long and five feet in diameter, was reported to be circling the earth once every 94.34 minutes.

The satellite is scheduled to pass over territory 28 degrees north and south of the Equator. This path avoids the Soviet Union, but it does carry the vehicle over three Communist or Communist-dominated countries—China, North Vietnam and Tibet.

Low to the Equator

At 6:16 P. M., Midas' apogee, or highest point above the earth's surface, was calculated at 316 miles; its perigee, or lowest point, was 300 miles.

This was said to be the lowest orbit in relation to the Equator that it is possible to achieve from Cape Canaveral. Officials would not comment whether they had tried to avoid sending the satellite over the Soviet Union, but they said that the orbit itself, together with reports of well-functioning instruments within it, showed good space marksmanship.

More than that, however, the test underscored the United States' intensive effort to develop means of protection against possible surprise nuclear attack by long-range ballistic missiles.

The Midas functions by detecting, with its infrared sensors, the heat given off by a missile engine's exhausts. The Midas will track a rising rocket for as long as its missile engine burns, or about five minutes.

Coincides With U. N. Talks

This information, relayed to ground stations, would give the missile's approximate course. Radar screens would then refine the information for a quick and accurate fix on the rocket's course.

The Air Force is planning tests for the infrared devices in the next few days.

Today's test originally had been scheduled to take place before the summit meeting as a demonstration of United States space prowess.

Instead, it coincided with the United Nations debate over the U-2 spy plane incident, which United States officials have emphasized stemmed from this

Continued on Page 4, Column 1

REPUBLICANS BACK INQUIRY ON SUMMIT

Fulbright Gains Bipartisan Support in Senate Unit for Hearing on Paris Failure

By RUSSELL BAKER

Special to The New York Times.

WASHINGTON, May 24—Republicans assured bipartisan support today for a Senate inquiry into the failure of the summit conference.

Senator J. W. Fulbright, chairman of the Foreign Relations Committee, which will conduct the inquiry, said in the midst of rising political uproar over the collapse of the Paris meeting that he was "consciously striving" to prevent the hearing from "becoming partisan."

The Arkansas Democrat said the first witness when the inquiry opened Friday would be Secretary of State Christian A. Herter. He added that later witnesses would include Thomas S. Gates Jr., Secretary of Defense; Allen W. Dulles, director of the Central Intelligence Agency, and officials of the National Aeronautics and Space Administration.

Meanwhile, the White House challenged Moscow to let the Soviet people hear President Eisenhower's report tomorrow night on the collapse of the summit conference. The Voice of America will beam the speech to the Soviet Union in eight languages.

[Senator John F. Kennedy, Democratic candidate for the Presidential nomination, called in Newark Tuesday for an early summit meeting between the next President and Premier Khrushchev.]

Replying to questions, Mr. Fulbright said the committee

Continued on Page 12, Column 1

Britain and France Deny Aggression in U-2 Flight

By THOMAS J. HAMILTON

Special to The New York Times.

UNITED NATIONS, N. Y., May 24—Britain and France defended the United States today against the Soviet charge that flights of American reconnaissance planes over Soviet territory constituted "aggressive acts."

Sir Pierson Dixon of Britain told the Security Council that if a Western disarmament pro-

Excerpts from U. N. debate will be found on Page 8.

posal had been in effect, the U-2 plane incident would not have occurred.

The British representative alluded to a disarmament plan submitted in Geneva last March by Western members of the ten-power disarmament group. It contained a provision for international air inspection as an assurance against surprise attack.

'Menace' Seen by France

Armand Bérard of France said the direct cause of the present situation was "the menace revived from time to time by those who claim that they have the means of annihilating the rest of the world."

M. Bérard said that this menace would be averted only when a system of disarmament accompanied by appropriate controls had been established. He declared that earth satellites also constituted a menace.

Earlier today Henry Cabot Lodge of the United States submitted to Secretary General Dag Hammarskjold a memorandum detailing the activities of eleven Soviet spies apprehended in the United States since the death of Stalin. The memorandum was distributed to members of the Security Council.

Argentina, Nationalist China and Italy also told the Security

Continued on Page 8, Column 3

SOVIET TO RELEASE 9 WITH U.S. PLANE

Craft Forced Down in East Germany Is Expected to Fly Back to West Today

By ARTHUR J. OLSEN

Special to The New York Times.

WIESBADEN, Germany, May 24—The Soviet Army agreed today to release at once nine Americans and the C-47 Air Force transport forced down Friday by Soviet fighter planes in East Germany.

The two-engine aircraft, which was not damaged in the incident, is expected to take off tomorrow morning from a small airfield near the Baltic coast to fly to West Germany.

United States officials were surprised by the prompt acquiescence of Col. Gen. Ivan I. Yakubovsky, commander of Soviet forces in East Germany, to a request for the "immediate return" of the Americans. The officials had been prepared for a long wrangle over the terms of release.

'Violation' Protested

In a letter to Gen. Clyde D. Eddleman, commander of the United States Army in Europe, General Yakubovsky coupled his offer to release the aircraft, its five crew members and the four passengers with a protest against a "violation" of the frontiers of East Germany.

A United States Air Force officer set out immediately for Schwerin, in the northwest corner of East Germany, to make arrangements to bring the downed transport and the interned Americans to West Germany.

At 9:30 P. M. the United States Army in Berlin announced that the plane would take off early tomorrow from a small airfield near the Baltic coastal village of Kluetz. The plane was said to be in good flying condition, but bad weather prevented a take-off tonight.

United States Air Force headquarters here said that Lieut. Col. Clarke T. Baldwin was under orders to fly the C-47.

Continued on Page 18, Column 4

Secret Agents Seized Killer Nazi Abroad and Took Him to Israel

By LAWRENCE FELLOWS

Special to The New York Times.

JERUSALEM (Israeli Sector), May 24—Adolf Eichmann, captured S. S. colonel who headed the section for Jewish affairs in Hitler's Secret State Police, was spirited from his home in an undisclosed country by Israeli security agents.

Israel charges Eichmann with having played a leading role in planning and carrying out the killing of 6,000,000 Jews.

Premier David Ben-Gurion announced yesterday that Eichmann had been captured and would stand trial for his life.

This afternoon the head of Israel's Security Service called a news conference to state that Eichmann had been traced and captured through the efforts of his agents alone. He added that no foreign officials had been bribed into cooperating with the Israeli agents nor would any money be passed to them in the future.

However, it is suspected here that one or more foreign countries were deeply involved in the case, if only in permitting Israeli agents to work freely in their search for people they consider their enemies.

Speculation in the Israeli press is narrowing to South America.

Eichmann is accused of having committed his crimes against Jews in his dual capacity as an important official in the Gestapo (Geheime Staatspolizei) or secret police and the S. S. (Schutzstaffel), the black-uniformed military and political élite of the Nazi movement, led by Heinrich Himmler.

Evidence is being assembled in preparation for the trial of Eichmann. One highly placed legal authority suggested today that the trial might not come

Continued on Page 20, Column 4

NEWS INDEX

Cairo Newspapers Seized by Nasser

By JAY WALZ

Special to The New York Times.

CAIRO, May 24—Almost all the Egyptian press was in effect nationalized today.

A Government decree removed four major Cairo newspaper and magazine publishing houses from private direction and "reorganized" them under control of the National Union. This is the political organization President Gamal Abdel Nasser has established to give the United Arab Republic a one-party Government.

Under the official order, the publishers who are put out of business will be compensated for their properties. Editors and writers will not lose their jobs in journalism. In the future, any Egyptian wishing to work as a journalist must have authorization from the National Union, the decree specified. An official explanation published with the decree said that the publications

Continued on Page 21, Column 3

Residents of Valdivia, in southern Chile, look over buildings wrecked by series of earthquakes.

Wide World Photos

QUAKES CONTINUE TO BATTER CHILE

Continued From Page 1, Col. 4

Minister Jaime Silva told a news conference.

Two Chilean freighters, Santiago and El Canelo, sank in raging seas off Puerto Corral. No survivors were reported.

In addition to the more than 1,000 dead, at least 500 are missing, and reports to the Government indicate that nearly 2,000,000 persons, or 65 per cent of the population in eleven southern provinces, may be homeless.

Wide areas of the mountain and lake country were reported in seizures of panic and destruction.

Nine persons yesterday were reported killed by a landslide down the slope of another live volcano, Osorbo, fifty-five miles east of Puyuhue.

New quakes continued spasmodically today and high waves continued to smash at coastal villages.

The Interior Ministry said a new volcano had been created in Cautin Province, farther north, and that it was emitting fire and smoke. No further details were given.

San Carlos de Bariloche, Argentine Andean resort visited by President Eisenhower last February, was reported darkened by volcanic ash. It is about fifty miles east of Puyehue.

Two small mountains disappeared as a result of quakes that continued spasmodically in an area extending for 600 miles down the narrow Chilean spine.

Seven persons were killed at Maullin and two others were missing as a result of today's quakes.

The four-day sequence added up to Chile's worst disaster since 1939, when an earthquake killed 20,000.

The University of Chile's Seismological Institute said the first quakes last Saturday and Sunday were of maximum intensity and were capable of greatly changing the configuration of the surface. Rock faults underlying the southern region are responsible for the tremors that shake the area periodically, the institute said.

Called Stronger Than 1939's

Experts believed the tremors Saturday and Sunday were even stronger than those of 1939.

But Señor Silva said the more modern buildings withstood the shaking better than the houses and offices did twenty-one years ago.

The minister said the Government has not even begun reckoning the damage, but it will run into many hundreds of millions of dollars.

Reconstruction will take years, he said, pointing out that hydroelectric plants, port works, foundries, roads and bridges as well as buildings had been destroyed and damaged.

President Jorge Alessandri was in the stricken zone directing relief operations into which the Government has put every available resource.

Fleets of military and civilian planes took doctors, nurses and emergency supplies southward. Planes and helicopters from the United States, Argentina, Chile and Peru joined in the operation. Two United States Air Force Globemasters flew medical supplies and clothing from the Panama Canal Zone.

Pope John XXIII sent condolences to the Government and directed that a personal contribution of funds be distributed by Archbishop Opilio Rossi, Apostolic Nuncio in Santiago.

WAVE TOLL IS 180 IN JAPAN, OKINAWA

Swells From Chile Quakes Hit Coasts From New Zealand to Alaska

TOKYO, Wednesday, May 25 (AP)—The people of this island nation, no strangers to natural disaster, today began the task of clearing debris left by giant tidal waves that battered the western Pacific basin from Japan to New Zealand.

The devastating waves, generated by earthquakes in Chile, left at least 180 persons dead or missing in Japan and Okinawa with another 850 reported injured. Property damage was estimated in the millions of dollars.

The casualty figure is expected to rise as communications are restored.

The New York Times   May 25, 1960
MORE MISERY: Underlined cities in Chile are hit by new devastation.

The semi-official Japan Broadcasting Corporation reported 150,000 persons homeless, 4,600 homes washed away or damaged, 43,000 homes flooded and 1,900 boats cast adrift or damaged.

Waves Struck at Dawn

Northern Honshu and the northernmost island of Hokkaido were battered hardest. Huge waves began pounding the Japanese coast at dawn yesterday almost without warning.

Wave after towering wave, ranging as high as twenty feet, unleashed fury on twenty-five communities. At least ten were inundated.

The waves left havoc and chaos along the rugged coast, stretching like a bow for 500 miles from Kushiro, Hokkaido, to Shiogama on Japan's main island of Honshu.

A survivor at Onagawa, one of the hard hit towns in northern Honshu, said:

"As dawn began breaking across the horizon we saw the tide recede. It kept receding. We realized it was a tidal wave so we dashed for the hills. Two hours later we returned. Our homes were a mass of debris but we saved our lives."

An eight-foot tidal wave lashed the United States-administered island of Okinawa in the Ryukyus, south of Japan. It left three dead, 1,000 homes flooded and hundreds of acres of rice fields blanketed with salt water.

Damaged Formosa

Both Formosa and the Philippines, where giant waves struck the Pacific coastline, reported some damage. The extent of casualities, if any, was not known.

Hong Kong reported surging tides but their strength was spent and no damage was reported.

The French islands in the South Pacific, New Zealand and Australia all reported waves but only minor damage.

In Japan the waves crushed houses, mauled property, banged boats about and hurled many ashore. People were swept out to sea. Others, terrified, escaped to higher ground.

In Shizukawa 800 fishing craft were cast adrift or sunk and twenty persons killed. One survivor there said: "In about one hour two waves devoured 300 houses and wrecked 500 more."

Eight waves almost wiped out Kiritappu, a small village in Hokkaido. Ten people clinging to wrecked houses were swept out to sea.

United States armed forces stationed here offered to help. Japanese troops also were called in.

Controversy arose on why Japan had not received better warning. Japan's Central Meteorological Agency said reports had been received from the Pacific Tidal Wave Center in Hawaii Monday morning and night.

"But both referred to tidal waves in the South Pacific," said the director, Kiyoo Wadachi. "We could not issue a warning here on the basis of these reports, but we could have if we at least had reports of damage in Hawaii."

Hawaii a Disaster Area

WASHINGTON, May 24 (AP) —The Island of Hawaii was declared a disaster area today by the Small Business Administration. It also has been given that designation by the Department of Agriculture.

61 Dead and Missing at Hilo

HONOLULU, May 24 (AP)— Hilo mourned its thirty-eight dead today and fearfully waited word on twenty-three persons still missing. Some were believed carried out to sea yesterday by the series of four

"All the News That's Fit to Print"

The New York Times.

LATE CITY EDITION
U. S. Weather Bureau Report (Page 80) forecasts: Fair today; variable cloudiness, milder tonight and tomorrow. Temp. range: 65—49; yesterday: 63.4—48.6.

VOL. CX...No. 37,510. © 1960 by The New York Times Company. Times Square, New York 36, N. Y. NEW YORK, WEDNESDAY, OCTOBER 5, 1960. 10 cents beyond 50-mile zone from New York City except on Long Island. Higher in air delivery cities. FIVE CENTS

RELAY SATELLITE FOR GLOBAL RADIO IS ORBITED BY U.S.

Eisenhower Utilizes Courier Sphere to Send Message to Herter at the U.N.

LAUNCHING 26TH BY U.S.

Third Anniversary of Space Age Also Sees a Test of Scout Research Rocket

By JOHN W. FINNEY
Special to The New York Times.

WASHINGTON, Oct. 4—The United States celebrated the third anniversary of the space age by sending a message from President Eisenhower to the United Nations by way of a new communications satellite launched today.

The 500-pound Courier satellite, a forerunner of a space communications system that will permit instantaneous global transmission of radio and television programs, was launched from Cape Canaveral, Fla. at 1:50 P. M. Eastern Daylight Time.

On its first orbit around the earth, the satellite transmitted a message from President Eisenhower to Secretary of State Christian A. Herter at the United Nations in New York. Mr. Herter then delivered the message to Frederick H. Boland, President of the General Assembly.

On Third Anniversary

The Presidential message arrived at the United Nations almost three years to the hour after the United States received the jolting news that the Soviet Union had placed the first satellite in space.

With Courier, the United States has now launched twenty-six civilian and military earth satellites and two deep-space probes. The Soviet Union has launched six earth satellites, one deep-space probe and impacted one payload on the moon.

Another development indicating the accelerating pace of the United States space program was the first successful test flight today of the Scout rocket, which is designed to serve as a relatively inexpensive "work horse" for the launching of small scientific satellites.

The seventy-two-foot tall, 36,600-pound rocket was fired from the National Aeronautics and Space Administration's station at Wallops Island, Va. into an arching seventy-nine-minute flight that carried it some 3,500

Continued on Page 3, Column 4

Macmillan and Khrushchev Meet Again; Briton Urges Big Four Talks Early in '61

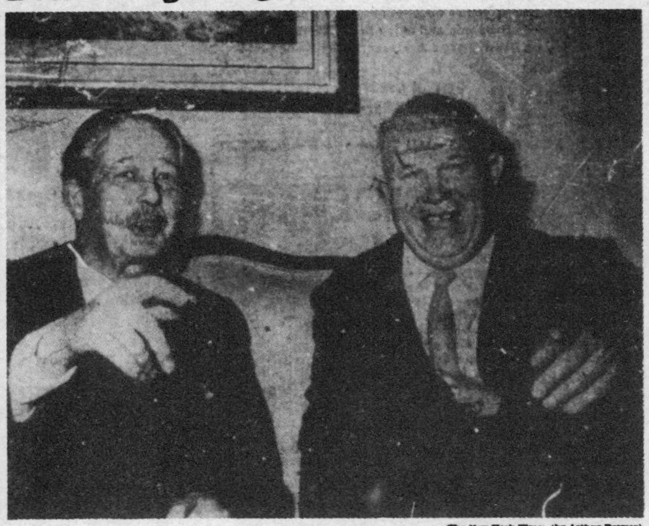

The New York Times (by Arthur Brower)

A meeting of minds—As photographers shouted for "just one more," Prime Minister Macmillan and Premier Khrushchev gave this response. Among the many subjects discussed at Briton's Waldorf suite, they agreed on at least one: this was the last picture.

INDIA-SOVIET PACT ON AID HELD NEAR

Deal Covers Military Help for Regions Threatened by Chinese Reds

By PAUL GRIMES
Special to The New York Times.

NEW DELHI, India, Oct. 4—India was reported today to be near an agreement for large-scale Soviet aid to develop her northern communications.

The agreement was described as "strictly one of trade and commerce." It could have the effect, however, of placing India in a position of accepting foreign military aid for the first time—and aid from one Communist country to guard her against another.

The potential deal was described in The Times of India in a signed article by Prem Bhatia, the paper's chief editorial executive in Delhi. Defense Ministry sources said they could give no information on the subject.

Road Equipment Involved

Mr. Bhatia said teams of Indian officials would go to Moscow shortly to conclude the deal. He said it would involve Soviet transport aircraft, helicopters and engineering equipment for a 150,000,000 rupee ($31,500,000) program of India's Border Roads Development Board.

Prime Minister Jawaharlal Nehru is chairman of the board and Defense Minister V. K. Krishna Menon is deputy chairman. Both are attending the United Nations General Assembly session in New York.

Defense Ministry sources reported last month that India was likely to place a sizable order for Soviet helicopters. The sources said they were needed to carry reinforcements and supplies to military units in remote mountain outposts near the Chinese frontier.

Mr. Bhatia's article indicated considerably more was involved. He said heavy transport aircraft were essential to carry

Continued on Page 2, Column 3

Prime Minister Suggests 'Let Dust Settle' Before New Parley on Berlin

By THOMAS J. HAMILTON

Prime Minister Macmillan told Premier Khrushchev yesterday that he hoped that the Big Four could resume negotiations on Berlin in January or February at the level of either the heads of government or the foreign ministers.

In their talk at the Waldorf Towers, the British Prime Minister said, according to a reliable source, that it would be "better to let the dust settle" from the current session of the General Assembly before negotiations were resumed.

Mr. Khrushchev's reply was not disclosed. However, the Soviet Premier said after the hour-and-a-quarter-talk that it had been "very productive."

Berlin Blockade Ruled Out

At a Soviet reception last night, Premier Khrushchev discussed the Berlin question and gave "full assurances" that the city would not be blockaded.

However, he again warned that the Soviet Union would sign a peace treaty with East Germany, ending the state of war and the occupation status of Berlin.

Mr. Khrushchev paid a courtesy call on Mr. Macmillan after learning that the British leader would leave for home this afternoon. The two men also conferred for two hours last Friday evening.

Mr. Macmillan was understood to doubt that the Soviet Union would take any such drastic action on the Berlin question as concluding a peace treaty with East Germany in the next few months, particularly without first consulting the Western powers.

In his speech in the opening week of the Assembly, Mr. Khrushchev suggested another summit meeting "within a few months," and he indicated that he would delay any action regarding Germany and Berlin pending the convening of such a meeting.

John Russell, a spokesman for Mr. Macmillan, said that the question of an eventual summit meeting had again been dis-

Continued on Page 18, Column 1

4 NEUTRALS WOO ASIA-AFRICA BLOC

Nkrumah, Sukarno, Nasser and Nehru Seek Backing for U. S.-Soviet Talks

Special to The New York Times.

UNITED NATIONS, N. Y., Oct. 4—Four of the five heads of neutral states who have urged a meeting between President Eisenhower and Premier Khrushchev appealed today for unanimous Asian-African support of their move in the General Assembly.

Debate on the item was scheduled to open tomorrow.

The four leaders, Prime Minister Jawaharlal Nehru of India, President Sukarno of Indonesia, President Gamal Abdel Nasser of the United Arab Republic and President Kwame Nkrumah of Ghana, came to a meeting here at the bidding of U Thant of Burma, head of the Asian-African group.

He explained later that the purpose was to hear the reasoning of these leaders while they were available here. There was no discussion of the resolution from the floor nor questions asked.

President Tito of Yugoslavia, who had joined the four others in pressing for an Eisenhower-Khrushchev meeting, left for home today and did not attend the session.

When Mr. Nehru was leaving, someone wanted to know whether the resolution was still alive in view of its speedy re-

Continued on Page 18, Column 5

KENNEDY AGREES WITH PRESIDENT ON KHRUSHCHEV

Says Eisenhower Showed 'Judgment' in Declining to Meet Russian

By LEO EGAN
Special to The New York Times.

INDIANAPOLIS, Oct. 4—Senator John F. Kennedy endorsed tonight President Eisenhower's refusal to seek a meeting with Soviet Premier Khrushchev.

In a televised interview here, the Democratic candidate for President said he thought Mr. Eisenhower had shown "good judgment" in rejecting a suggestion from five neutral nations that he meet with the Russian leader.

"There is no sense having a meeting unless there is an atmosphere before the meeting that leads you to hope there will be success," Senator Kennedy commented.

The five nations were India, Indonesia, the United Arab Republic, Yugoslavia and Ghana.

Calls G. O. P. Wasteful

The Senator recorded the interview for later showing over Indiana television stations just before he accused the Republican National Administration of wasting billions of tax dollars through inefficiency and mismanagement in an address to a Democratic rally and fund-raising dinner here tonight.

The manager of the Indianapolis Coliseum, where the rally was held, estimated attendance at 10,500. Of these, he said, 1,700 had paid $100 for a dinner before the rally.

The crowds that greeted Senator Kennedy this afternoon on his arrival here by plane from Chicago for tonight's rally were small and undemonstrative compared with those that have greeted him in other places.

His caravan followed a circuitous route from the airport into downtown Indianapolis to pass through most of the Democratic sections of the city.

Even so, there were only a few blocks that turned out more than a hundred persons to watch him pass.

Appears Curious

The Senator's welcoming crowds in Utica, N. Y., which has only one-quarter of Indianapolis' population, were twice as big and five times more demonstrative. Today's welcome appeared motivated more by curiosity than by hero worship.

In contrast, Vice President Nixon is reported to have drawn a crowd of 30,000 when he opened his campaign here on Sept. 12.

Besides his endorsement of President Eisenhower's ban on a meeting with Mr. Khrushchev, Senator Kennedy made the fol-

Continued on Page 33, Column 3

NIXON SAYS FOOD WILL GO UP 25% IF KENNEDY WINS

Tells Consumers on Tour of Jersey That Farm Plank Perils Their Pocketbooks

By WARREN WEAVER Jr.
Special to The New York Times.

WEST ORANGE, N. J., Oct. 4—Vice President Nixon charged tonight that the Kennedy farm program would raise family food costs 25 per cent, reduce beef and pork supplies to war-time rationed levels and put 2,000,000 Americans out of work.

In a speech at a party rally at the armory here, the Republican Presidential candidate made one of his most outspoken attacks on a program sponsored by his opponent, Senator John F. Kennedy.

On the basis of the Kennedy farm plan alone, Mr. Nixon declared, "the people should reject his candidacy for the Presidency of the United States."

Besides raising consumer costs and Government expenses and driving farmers off the land, Mr. Nixon said, the Democratic farm proposals would encourage Soviet agricultural supremacy.

Soviet Boast Recalled

"Mr. Khrushchev publicly boasts of his intention to catch up with the United States in the production of such farm products as milk and meat," the Vice President declared. "If Senator Kennedy's plan is put into effect, Mr. Khrushchev can realize his ambition for a number of farm products. This specifically includes milk."

Mr. Nixon's attack on the Kennedy farm program was the highlight of a lengthy day of campaigning by motorcade through northern New Jersey, with speeches in Paterson, Hackensack, Elizabeth, Plainfield, Newark and here.

By day's end he had spoken before 50,000 persons. Thousands more had seen his motorcade pass.

Turnout in Paterson

The Vice President made two of his stops in the same communities that Mr. Kennedy had visited on a Jersey tour two weeks ago. In City Hall Plaza in Democratic Paterson, the police estimate of the Nixon crowd was 5,000 to 7,500, but the actual number appeared much nearer 10,000.

According to reporters who covered Mr. Kennedy in the same place, the Democrat had drawn as much as twice as many, but again the estimates varied.

In Elizabeth, in front of the Winfield Scott Hotel, Mr. Nixon spoke to a crowd the police put at 3,000. In a different location—a park in front of City Hall—Mr. Kennedy's audience had ranged from 4,000 to 7,500.

The Kennedy farm program calls for high, rigid price sup-

Continued on Page 27, Column 1

61 DIE, 11 SURVIVE AS AIRLINER FALLS IN BOSTON HARBOR

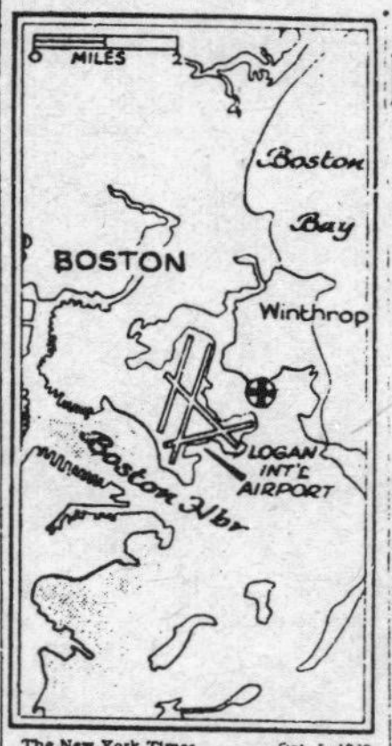

The New York Times Oct. 5, 1960

PLANE DISASTER: Cross marks site of Boston crash.

PLANE SINKS FAST

Hits After Taking Off on Eastern Air Lines Southbound Flight

By JOHN H. FENTON
Special to The New York Times.

BOSTON, Oct. 4—An Eastern Air Lines Electra airliner crashed and exploded after its takeoff from Logan International Airport today. Sixty-one persons were believed killed.

There were eleven survivors among the sixty-seven passengers and five crewmen aboard. But several were in critical condition. Sixteen bodies were believed trapped in the after-part of the broken fuselage.

The turboprop airliner took off at 5:40 P. M. Two minutes later it veered and plunged into Pleasant Park Channel, a shallow area in Boston Harbor about 200 yards off the suburban town of Winthrop. It broke in two. Within moments, volunteer rescuers were wading through mud at low tide to pull bodies ashore.

Many Trapped in Seats

Many on board were trapped in their seats, still fastened. Rescuers found them with heads down in the muddy water.

Among the passengers were fifteen Marine recruits who had been inducted earlier in the day. They were bound for training camp. Some of their relatives saw the crash from an observation deck at the main terminal building at the airport.

The crash was the second involving an Electra in less than three weeks. In three previous Electra crashes, a total of 162 persons died. In one at La Guardia Airport Sept. 14, all on board escaped without serious injury.

Today's craft was Flight 375, bound for Philadelphia, Charlotte, N. C., Greenville, S. C. and Atlanta.

There were conflicting reports as to whether the craft had exploded before or after it hit the water. Winthrop residents said they were so accustomed to hearing planes break the sound barrier that they had not paid

Continued on Page 21, Column 6

SURPLUS CUT 75% IN BUDGET STUDY

But Revision to 1.1 Billion From 4.2 Billion Assumes Business Will Pick Up

By RICHARD E. MOONEY
Special to The New York Times.

WASHINGTON, Oct. 4—The Government estimated today that its budget for the current fiscal year would show a surplus of $1,100,000,000, assuming a strong pick-up in economic activity in the next few months.

A surplus of $4,200,000,000 was estimated by President Eisenhower when he presented the budget to Congress in January. The major reason for the reduced figure was the failure of corporate profits to live up to the January estimates.

The new estimate assumes that this year's profits, and the tax revenues they yield, will be no greater than those of last year.

The new estimate was in the midyear review that the Budget Bureau presents after Congress has finished its work. The fiscal year 1961 ends June 30.

Optimism Is Voiced

In comment on the review Maurice H. Stans, Director of the Budget, declared at a news conference that the outlook was "strengthening and improving" business conditions. He added that "we see no need for concern about a possible recession in the first half of next year."

Still discussing calendar periods, he said that a seasonal upturn was in prospect for the remainder of the year and that, for that reason, the Government saw no need for measures to reduce unemployment.

Detailed new budget estimates, as offered today, compared with actual results for the last two fiscal years, were as follows, in billions of dollars:

	1959	1960	1961
Receipts	$68.3	$78.4	$81.5
Spending	80.7	77.2	80.4
Deficit	12.4	...	...
Surplus	...	1.2	1.1

The President estimated in

Continued on Page 12, Column 3

ANTI-TITO PICKETS REPORT REPRISALS

Ask U. S. to Study Belgrade Acts Against Relatives

By PETER KIHSS

Demonstrators against President Tito charged here yesterday that his Government had taken reprisals against their relatives in Yugoslavia. They asked the State Department to investigate.

The complaint was made as Marshal Tito sailed for home yesterday afternoon. Before he left he said the "cold war had intensified" and that he was leaving "in a less optimistic mood than when I arrived."

George Vaughn, spokesman for the American Serb Committee, said at least nine New Yorkers had received word from Belgrade of reprisals.

Letters Tell of Reprisals

Mr. Vaughn said the reports had come in letters, telegrams, and, in two cases, telephone calls from relatives in Yugoslavia. He said the messages blamed the demonstrations here for the reprisals in Yugoslavia.

Mrs. Judith Solujich, a committee representative, translated letters that reported three incidents.

One letter told of the arrest of a demonstrator's brother. A second reported that Yugoslav authorities had seized a passport to the United States from a demonstrator's mother. A third said a demonstrator's daughter had been threatened with the loss of her job.

A spokesman for the Yugoslav mission to the United Nations said that "allegations by those groups are not worthy of comment."

He said the pickets had

Continued on Page 19, Column 4

Algeria Rebels Say They Helped 5,000 Desert the Foreign Legion

Special to The New York Times.

RABAT, Morocco, Oct. 4—Eleven deserters from the French Foreign Legion in Algeria were presented here today as conscientious objectors to colonial wars.

The Provisional Government of Algeria announced at the same time that its services had helped more than 5,000 deserters from the Foreign Legion to cross the Algerian borders.

Ahmed Alaoui, the Moroccan Minister of Information, presented the eleven deserters at a news conference. He described their desertion as a "political act of the utmost importance" and the beginning of an "international protest" against the war in Algeria.

"Morocco will do everything in its power to encourage the development of desertions in the French colonial army in Algeria," Mr. Alaoui said. "It is just to revolt against an unjust war."

The Moroccan Government spokesman praised a recent movement of French intellectuals in support of military insubordination. He described as "true patriots" all those in France who declared they favored a refusal of military service or desertion.

A representative of the Algerian nationalist Government also praised the "courage" of the French intellectuals who have signed a manifesto asserting the right of Frenchmen to refuse military service in Algeria. The Algerian rebel spokesman called this "an efficient contribution toward peace in Algeria."

The eleven deserters were unanimous in asserting that

Continued on Page 20, Column 3

Johnson Pays Homage to Babies and Food in Queens

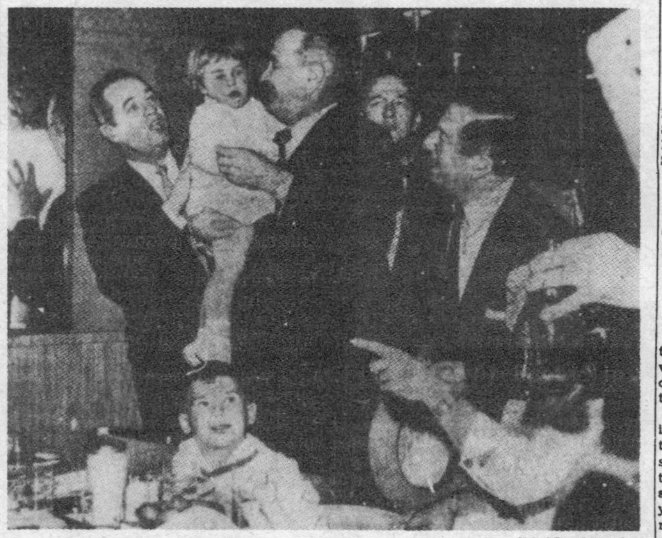

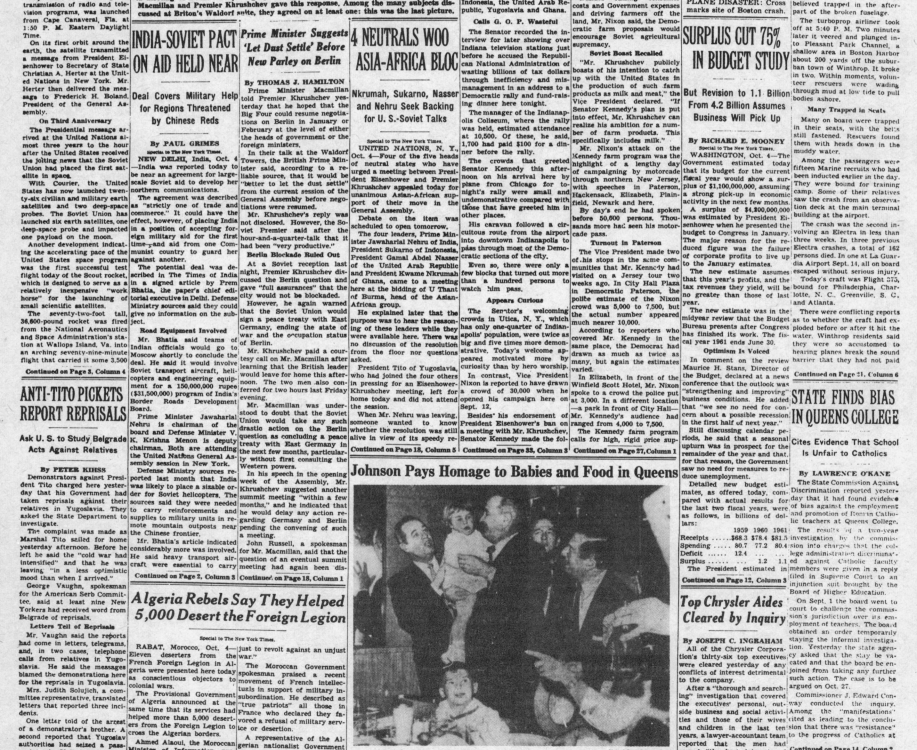

United Press International

Senator Lyndon B. Johnson holds 2-year-old Andrea Pollak of Plainview, Nassau County, during campaign stop at Turnpike Restaurant in Queens. Her 4-year-old brother, Stuart, is in foreground. (A little food for thought: Mr. Pollak is a Republican committeeman.)

By ANTHONY LEWIS

Lyndon B. Johnson followed the gastronomic route into New York politics yesterday by sampling pickles at a Queens delicatessen. "So what happened here?" Irving Steinberg, the delicatessen owner, cried as a caravan of politicians and their attendants marched into the Turnpike Restaurant on Queens Boulevard in Forest Hills. "An invasion, oh my God!" The Democratic nominee for Vice President wandered around the tables shaking hands, giving hugs and passing out admission cards for the last session of the Senate. "Hey, Senator," John T. Clancy, Queens Borough President

Continued on Page 31, Column 1

Top Chrysler Aides Cleared by Inquiry

By JOSEPH C. INGRAHAM

All of the Chrysler Corporation's thirty-six top executives were cleared yesterday of any conflicts of interest detrimental to the company.

After a "thorough and searching" investigation that covered the executives' personal, outside business and social activities and those of their wives and children in the last ten years, a lawyer-accountant team reported that the men had served "the best interests of Chrysler * * * and had faithfully performed their duties."

The findings were supported by special counsel employed by nonmanagement directors to make sure that the company-hired investigators had adequately pursued every facet that might show wrongdoing by top management officials.

The special counsel, Dewey,

Continued on Page 35, Column 2

STATE FINDS BIAS IN QUEENS COLLEGE

Cites Evidence That School Is Unfair to Catholics

By LAWRENCE O'KANE

The State Commission Against Discrimination reported yesterday that it had found evidence of bias against the employment and promotion of Roman Catholic teachers at Queens College.

The results of a two-year investigation by the commission into charges that the college administration discriminated against Catholic faculty members were given in a reply filed in Supreme Court to an injunction suit brought by the Board of Higher Education.

On Sept. 1 the board went to court to challenge the commission's jurisdiction over its employment of teachers. The board obtained an order temporarily staying the informal investigation. Yesterday the state agency asked that the stay be vacated and that the board be enjoined from taking any further such action. The case is to be argued on Oct. 27.

Commissioner J. Edward Conway conducted the inquiry. Among the "manifestations" cited as leading to the conclusion that there was "resistance" to the progress of Catholics at

Continued on Page 14, Column 2

NEWS INDEX

Associated Press Wirephoto

GRIM TASK: Firemen and rescue workers search tail section of four-engine Electra that fell into Boston Harbor yesterday shortly after take-off. Most of the turbo-prop plane, which carried sixty-seven passengers, sank quickly.

AIRLINER CRASHES IN BOSTON HARBOR

Continued From Page 1, Col. 8

too much attention at first to the crash.

Hours after the crash, agents of the Federal Bureau of Investigation and armed service investigators were examining bits of wreckage for what was described as "an important article."

Thomas L. Hackett of the Office of Special Investigation, Air Force branch, said the article was "not top secret." The F. B. I. refused comment.

Even scraps of paper fished out of the water were being taken to a compound at the airport for examination.

One of the first to reach the scene was Navy Comdr. Donald Regan, who lives at Winthrop. He paddled out in a kayak, a single-passenger canvas boat.

"When I got there, part of the plane was still afloat," he said. "A good many of the passengers were strapped to their seats and couldn't get out. The seats were floating. I noticed that their weight was pulling them over so that their heads were in the water."

A Marine who survived the crash said the plane started to circle after having left the runway. The next thing he knew, he said, he was going through a porthole. He identified himself as Albert Nordin, 21 years old, of East Bridgewater, Mass. He had just enlisted and was on his way to training camp at Parris Island, S. C.

Commander Regan said he and others in small boats had pulled out five or six persons alive, as well as some dead.

"We tried to get everyone who was apparently alive first," he said. "It was very difficult. With the kayak I could get right alongside the bodies and work them over to the larger boats. Then I'd get out of the kayak and work with the rowboats."

Rescuers converged on the scene in small boats, by helicopter and in Navy and Coast Guard rescue craft. Among the first were members of the Cottage Park Yacht Club at Winthrop. Several were teen-agers.

J. T. O'Brien, a club member, said a dozen dinghys had rushed to the scene. Police boats came up the harbor from Boston proper.

Among the survivors were Pat Davis of Jacksonville, Fla., and Joan Berry of Memphis, Tenn., the stewardesses.

A call for skin divers brought more than 200 from many parts of Massachusetts.

Survivors taken ashore on the Winthrop side were removed to the Winthrop Community Hospital. There were fifteen, but five were dead on arrival. One died later and three were in serious condition.

Two survivors brought ashore at the airport were taken to Massachusetts General Hospital.

Most of the victims were covered with oil when pulled out of the water. Some survivors had swallowed oil and were sick. Most suffered cuts on faces and legs.

It was still twilight when the rescue operation began, and before long searchlights were playing on a tangled scene of stretchers, watersoaked luggage, shoes, torn clothing and personal belongings of the victims.

Military policemen from Fort Banks, at Winthrop, joined Boston, state and Winthrop policemen to control the thousands crowding along the shore on either side of the yacht club.

Many bodies were taken to the Winthrop fire headquarters and others to police headquarters. Still others were assembled in a temporary morgue set up at the edge of the airport.

Physicians worked in corridors to treat survivors brought to the small Winthrop Hospital. Many were given blood plasma.

It was the worst tragedy in New England aviation history. Attaches of the airport said it

ACCIDENT IS FIFTH FOR THE ELECTRA

162 Died in Earlier Crashes of Lockheed Aircraft— Speed Was Reduced

By RICHARD WITKIN

The crash of a Lockheed Electra last night in Boston harbor was the fifth major accident involving this type of airliner. The turbine-propeller Electras have been in use less than two years.

Since March this year, all the more than 130 Electras operating in this country have been compelled to fly at sharply curtailed speeds.

The restriction was imposed by the Federal Aviation Agency after the second of two crashes in which wings were ripped off in flight.

The manufacturer has announced a $25,000,000 program to strengthen the plane's structure and permit a return to normal operations.

was the first time anyone had been killed in a commercial crash at Logan.

An east wind was blowing about twenty-five miles an hour when the crash happened. There was a slight chop to the water in the channel, but not enough to interfere seriously with the operations there.

The area of the crash scene was once a pleasure boating bay off Winthrop. When the airport was built about thirty years ago, two islands offshore were leveled and runways were created with the fill. Since then, pleasure craft from Winthrop have used a narrow ship channel to skirt the airport in reaching deep water.

There was no immediate indication what had led to last night's crash.

162 Died in Accidents

The two other previous crashes occurred in approaches to La Guardia Airport. In neither case was the accident due to any structural defect.

A total of 162 persons was killed in three of the four previous accidents. In the fourth, which occurred Sept. 14 at La Guardia, all seventy-six persons on board escaped with their lives even though the plane flipped on its back and burned.

The Electra is a graceful-looking four-engine plane. Its turbo-prop engines burn fuel like a pure jet, but the exhaust is harnessed to drive conventional propellers. Pure jets obtain their push from a reaction to the rearward thrust of the exploding gases.

First Crash at New York

The first Electra crash occurred Feb. 3, 1959, shortly after the planes first began to haul regular passengers.

The craft belonged to American Airlines. It was coming in to land at La Guardia Airport but put down in Flushing Bay about a mile short of the runway. Sixty-five of the seventy-three persons on board were killed.

The second crash occurred Sept. 29, 1959 near Buffalo, Tex. A Braniff International Airways plane with thirty-four persons on board was flying from Houston to Dallas when the left wing snapped off and the plane spun to the earth. All on board were killed.

There was no widespread suspicion that anything basic was wrong with the plane until the third crash occurred March 17, 1960, at Tell City, Ind. This involved a Northwest Airlines Electra bound from Chicago to Miami.

The pattern of disaster was much like that in the Buffalo, Tex., crash, except that it was the right wing that snapped

instead of the left. All sixty-three persons on board were killed.

It was shortly thereafter that the F. A. A. ordered the sharp cut in the plane's speed.

Normal cruising speed is about 400 miles an hour. The speed was cut in two increments to a maximum of 329 statute miles an hour.

The airspeed meter maximum is much less. Altitude and temperature account for the difference between meter reading and the actual speed over the ground.

At the time of the speed cut, the Civil Aeronautics Board, which investigates crashes, recommended that the F. A. A. ground all Electras that had not as yet been subjected to minute inspection. The recommendation was not followed. This brought some criticism of Elwood R. Quesada, head of the F. A. A.

Mr. Quesada had repeatedly assured the public that the speed restriction gave the Electra "a structural margin as great, if not greater than, any aircraft" in the transport field.

F.A.A. Has No Plan To Ground Electras

Special to The New York Times

WASHINGTON, Oct. 4 — Elwood R. Quesada, head of the Federal Aviation Agency, said tonight that no connection had been established so far between the Boston plane crash and the crashes of other Electras because of structural failures.

The agency has no plans to ground the Electras, he said.

He said that he would join other F. A. A. officials and investigators at the crash scene tomorrow morning.

"There doesn't seem to be any relation between this crash and any structural problems with the airplane," he said. "From information on hand now, tonight's crash did not establish any fault with the plane.

"We do not know what caused the crash."

The New York Times.

LATE CITY EDITION
U.S. Weather Bureau Report [...] Forecast:
Cold, chance of snow flurries today;
fair and cold tonight and tomorrow.
Temp. range: 35-22 yesterday: 40-1-30.

VOL. CX..No. 37,583.   © 1960 by The New York Times Company. Times Square New York 36, N.Y.   NEW YORK, SATURDAY, DECEMBER 17, 1960.   10 cents beyond 50-mile zone from New York City except on Long Island (higher in air delivery cities)   FIVE CENTS

127 DIE AS 2 AIRLINERS COLLIDE OVER CITY; JET SETS BROOKLYN FIRE, KILLING 5 OTHERS; SECOND PLANE CRASHES ON STATEN ISLAND

STATEN ISLAND: Wreckage of Trans World Airlines Super Constellation in New Dorp   BROOKLYN: Rescue workers gather near ruins of United Air Lines DC-8 jet in Seventh Avenue at Sterling Place, in the Park Slope section

The New York Times

ETHIOPIAN REVOLT SAID TO COLLAPSE; SELASSIE HAILED

Envoys in U. S. and Britain Report Rebels Seized —Emperor in Asmara

Special to The New York Times.

WASHINGTON, Dec. 16 — The Ethiopian Embassy here reported today that the attempt by the Imperial Guard to overthrow Emperor Haile Selassie I had "ended in complete failure early this morning."

Ambassador Mikael Imru issued a statement saying that the army and air force, which had remained loyal to the Emperor, had captured Addis Ababa, the capital, and "overpowered and seized" the "disgruntled officers" of the Imperial Guard. The rebels had seized the city Wednesday.

[The Emperor arrived in Asmara, Ethiopia, Friday and received a tumultuous welcome from his loyal subjects there. He was told that the palace rebel ion had failed.]

Prince Not Mentioned

The rebel group was reported at first to have been led by the Emperor's son, Crown Prince Asfa-Wossen. Later reports suggested that the Crown Prince might have acted "under duress."

The Ambassador's statement this noon made no mention of the part played by the Crown Prince and threw no light on his fate or his whereabouts.

Nor did the Ambassador say anything about his father, Ras Imru, the 68-year-old cousin of the Emperor, who was reported to have been appointed Premier of the government formed by the rebels.

The Ambassador stated that the loyal forces had been led by Maj. Gen. Merod Mengsha, Chief of Staff; Maj. Gen. Kebede Guebre, army commander.

Continued on Page 2, Column 4

New Pact to Expand Cuban-Soviet Trade

By MAX FRANKEL
Special to The New York Times.

HAVANA, Dec. 16 — Cuba and the Soviet Union plan to exchange goods valued at $168,000,000 next year, the Ministry of Commerce disclosed here tonight.

The expanded trade dealings will be in addition to exchanges of sugar and other products for Soviet oil that had been agreed upon last February.

Although no details about the new arrangements were disclosed, it appeared almost certain that the Soviet Union would purchase considerably more Cuban sugar than it originally had planned.

Whatever the terms of the new trade agreement, it will

Continued on Page 6, Column 3

Dillon Appointed Secretary of Treasury; Kennedy's Brother Is Attorney General

Second Republican Gets Post in New Cabinet— President Approves

By W. H. LAWRENCE
Special to The New York Times

WASHINGTON, Dec. 16—President-elect John F. Kennedy designated a Republican, Douglas Dillon, as his Secretary of the Treasury today and named his brother, Robert F. Kennedy, as Attorney General. Mr. Dillon, now serving the Eisenhower Administration as Under Secretary of State, dis-

The texts of Kennedy's news conferences are on Page 14.

closed that he had sought the assent of President Eisenhower this morning and of Vice-President Nixon earlier.

"Neither of them had any objection if I felt that this was something that would be in the national security interest of the country, and if we were to work toward a sound fiscal policy as is the case," Mr. Dillon said.

Both appointments long had been forecast. But the choice of Robert Kennedy, 35 years old, is expected to provoke a political storm. Senator Kennedy set a precedent by naming his brother to the Cabinet.

Senator Kennedy said he would complete his Cabinet tomorrow by naming his Postmaster General from the family home at Palm Beach, Fla., where he is planning a prolonged holiday through Christmas and New Year's Day.

At the same time, he said Byron R. White, Denver attorney and former All-America football star at the University of Colorado, would be Deputy Attorney General. Harry J. Anslinger, Commissioner of Narcotics in the Treasury Department, has agreed to stay in that position, Senator Kennedy said.

Appointments Forecast

Highly placed Democrats forecast the following other major appointments by Senator Kennedy shortly:

¶Mrs. Elizabeth Smith, California's Democratic national committeewoman, as Treasurer of the United States, replacing Mrs. Ivy Baker Priest.

¶Fred Dutton of California as secretary of the Kennedy Cabinet. He is a former executive secretary to Gov. Edmund G. Brown of California.

Mr. Dillon, 51 years old, becomes the Cabinet's second Republican. He will serve with

Continued on Page 14, Column 6

PRO-WEST FORCES TAKE VIENTIANE

New Premier Enters Laos Capital as Fighting Ends

Because of communications difficulties, the following dispatch was filed jointly by correspondents in Vientiane.

VIENTIANE, Laos, Dec. 16—Prince Boun Oum, the new Premier of Laos, and the rightist pro-Western general, Phoumi Nosavan, drove into Vientiane at dusk today and announced the liberation of this shattered administrative capital.

At the same time, Capt. Peng, a cheerful Laotian tank officer, was busy cleaning from hold-out positions at the Vientiane airport the stubborn remnants of Capt. Kong Le's pro-Communist paratroops and guerrillas of the Communist-led Pathet Lao movement.

The seventy-six-hour battle for Vientiane ended at 5 P. M. local time [5 A. M. Friday, Eastern Standard Time].

Rightist Troops Hold City

By JACQUES NEVARD
Special to The New York Times.

VIENTIANE, Dec. 16—The troops of Gen. Phoumi Nosavan held the center of Vientiane this morning eighteen hours after they had captured it for a second time in a seesaw battle with tenacious pro-Communist defenders.

Mortar, machine-gun and small-arms fire could still be heard as tanks and armored cars cruised through the streets.

After a night lull the battle turned hot and fierce again. The heart of this usually somnolent

Continued on Page 4, Column 3

U.S. Offers NATO A Nuclear Arsenal And 5 Submarines

By DREW MIDDLETON
Special to The New York Times.

PARIS, Dec. 16—The United States offered Western Europe a mighty new nuclear armory today for defense against the Communist bloc.

Secretary of State Christian A. Herter announced what he termed a new concept for operation of medium-range ballistic missiles to the Ministerial Council of the North Atlantic Treaty Organization late this afternoon.

The offer was conditional upon agreement by the European allies on political control of the weapons, which were described by Mr. Herter as offering the best means for providing a common defense in the field of medium-range ballistic missiles.

The offer calls for commitment to the Atlantic alliance before the end of 1963 of five ballistic missile submarines armed with eighty Polaris missiles, the Secretary of State said. The step would enlarge the alliance's military capabilities and reaffirm the United States' commitment to Europe's defense, he said.

The United States would then expect other members of the

Continued on Page 13, Column 4

WIDE U. N. POWER IN CONGO IS URGED

100-Day Blanket Authority Sought for Hammarskjold

By LINDESAY PARROTT
Special to The New York Times.

UNITED NATIONS, N. Y., Dec. 16—An urgent meeting of the General Assembly heard a proposal tonight to grant blanket emergency powers to Secretary General Dag Hammarskjold for 100 days to meet the growing crisis in the Congo.

Francisco Milla Bermudez of Honduras read the text of a proposed resolution that would give effect to the plan.

The purpose of the series of recurring emergencies in the new African state, he said, was full interim powers for the Secretary General might be the best way to bring peace and order to the country under the terms of the Charter.

The Assembly adjourned at 10:35 P. M. to meet again at 10:30 A. M. tomorrow, with the United States delegate scheduled as the first speaker.

Latin-American sources said that some other Latin-American nations had been consulted on the Honduran proposal, though none joined in sponsoring the plan. Señor Milla Bermudez announced that he was prepared to consider changes in his text and would introduce it formally if others agreed.

The proposal would permit the Assembly to revoke the Secretary General's special authority if necessary or extend it beyond the 100-day period if Mr. Hammarskjold seemed to be succeeding.

The Honduran proposal was

Continued on Page 3, Column 6

A PILOT OFF ROUTE, U.S. OFFICIALS HINT

C.A.B. and F.A.A. Open Wide Inquiries—Tape Records of Flights to Be Studied

By RUSSELL PORTER

A preliminary investigation of the air disaster here yesterday suggested that the two planes collided because one was off its course.

An extensive inquiry was opened by the two Federal agencies concerned with civilian aviation, the Civil Aeronautics Board and the Federal Aviation Agency.

E. R. Quesada, Administrator of the Federal Aviation Agency, which is responsible for the operation of the airways, said last night that it was "very probable" that there had been a collision.

Alan S. Boyd, a member of the C. A. B., which investigates air accidents, was present when Mr. Quesada made his statement at New York International Airport. The two officials held a joint news conference.

They said that the investigation was just starting and little had been learned, but that the Trans World Airlines plane had fallen in three parts in Staten Island in a way indicating that it could not have been broken up by hitting the ground.

They said this made it appear likely there had been a collision, but there was as yet no positive evidence of a collision.

"All we know is that two planes crashed eleven miles apart," they said.

Shortly before the disaster, they said, the T. W. A. plane flew over the Linden, N. J., area

Continued on Page 10, Column 1

10 Brooklyn Houses Burn After Plane Hits a Church

By JOHN F. MURPHY

Ten four-story tenement buildings and an empty church were set afire when the United Air Lines DC-8 jet crashed and exploded in the populous Park Slope district of Brooklyn yesterday. More than 250 firemen and about fifty pieces of apparatus rushed to the seven-alarm blaze, which took more than two hours to bring under control.

There were several hundred persons in the buildings when the airliner plummeted through one tenement on Sterling Place and rammed into the Pillar of Fire Church across the street.

A rapid-fire series of small explosions followed, igniting roofs and spraying wreckage over a wide area.

Tenants Race From Homes

As soon as the plane crashed, women, children and elderly persons came pouring out of the buildings into the street, dressed in houseclothes, sweaters and pajamas. They ran panic-stricken from the smoldering wreckage.

Men, women and children saw the flaming wreckage of a Trans World Airlines Super-Constellation plunge toward them—and fall short. And although all forty-four persons on board were killed, no one on the ground was even scratched by the fall of the shattered airliner.

The one victim identified was Charles J. Cooper, 34 years old, a sanitation worker, who had been shoveling snow. Those missing were Wallace E. Lewis, 90, the caretaker of the church at 123 Sterling Place; Joseph Colacano, 29, and John Oppersano, 35. Mr. Colacano Mr. Oppersano had been selling Christmas trees on the sidewalk.

The first fire alarm was sounded at 10:36 A. M. When

Continued on Page 9, Column 1

DISASTER IN FOG

DC-8 Plunges Into Park Slope Street, Missing School

By HOMER BIGART

Two airliners collided over New York harbor yesterday in fog and sleet, killing 127 passengers and crewmen. One plane crashed in Brooklyn, killing five more persons on the ground, and the other fell on Staten Island.

A United Air Lines DC-8 plunged into the crowded Park Slope section of Brooklyn shortly after 10:30 A. M. All but one of its seventy-seven passengers and the crew of seven were killed. The survivor was an 11-year-old boy.

The plane demolished a church and killed a Department of Sanitation worker who was shoveling snow. Burning debris caused a seven-alarm fire, destroying ten brownstone apartment buildings, several shops and a funeral home. Nine persons were injured on the ground.

Three Unaccounted For

Three persons were unaccounted for, including the 90-year-old custodian of the Pillar of Fire Church, 123 Sterling Place, a Gothic structure that was leveled by flames.

At almost the same instant as the Brooklyn disaster, a Trans World Airlines Lockheed Super-Constellation crashed near Miller Army Air Field, New Dorp, S. I., eleven miles to the southwest.

This plane, out of Dayton and Columbus, Ohio, apparently exploded in the air just before the crash. All thirty-nine passengers and the crew of five were killed or fatally injured. Parts of the plane fell in the Lower Bay and parts on the northwest corner of Miller Field.

Three victims were taken by Coast Guard helicopter to the Public Health Service Hospital

Continued on Page 8, Column 1

S. I. HOMES SPARED BY FALLING DEBRIS

Parts of Airliner Land in Backyards—No One on Ground Is Injured

By THOMAS BUCKLEY

Distances that can be paced off quickly—50 feet, 150 feet, 200 yards—were the measure of life and death on quiet streets on Staten Island yesterday.

Aside from those on the plane who were killed, five persons on the ground died. These five presumably included three men who were missing, but the police said even more bodies might be found beneath the fuselage.

The flaming forward section of the craft, from which twenty-nine bodies were taken, smashed to earth on the northwest corner of Miller Army Air Field, less than 150 feet from the eighth-room frame home of Edward Brody, at 324 Boundary Lane, Midland Beach. Dozens of other homes on tree-lined streets stood near by.

"I saw it coming right at us," Mrs. Brody said. "I ran upstairs to get my daughters.

Continued on Page 11, Column 1

Boy, 11, Only Survivor of Crash

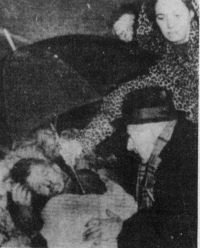

© New York Journal American
Steven Baltz is comforted by passers-by at scene of crash

Condition Is Critical —Parents and Sister at His Bedside

By ROBERT CONLEY

An 11-year-old boy, flying here to meet his mother and sister, was the only survivor of yesterday's airliner collision.

He was thrown from the tail section of a United Air Lines jet and found in a Brooklyn snowbank, his clothes aflame.

The youngster, Steven Baltz of Wilmette, Ill., regained consciousness last night but was still in critical condition early today with burns and broken bones.

His mother and sister were at his bedside when he awoke at Methodist Hospital in Brooklyn. They had flown here from Chicago ahead of him. His father, William S. Baltz, flew in late in the day and reached the bedside just after dark.

"He's coming along quite well, very well," the father said after

Continued on Page 11, Column 6

4 Cardinals Named; One Is an American

By ARNALDO CORTESI
Special to The New York Times

ROME, Dec. 16—The Most Rev. Joseph Elmer Ritter, Archbishop of St. Louis, and three other prelates were named today by Pope John XXIII to become Cardinals Jan. 16.

The elevation of Archbishop Ritter will return the number of American Cardinals to six, as it was up to the death of John F. Cardinal O'Hara, Archbishop of Philadelphia, less than four months ago.

The present American Cardinals are Archbishops Francis Spellman of New York, James F. McIntyre of Los Angeles, Richard Cushing of Boston, Albert G. Meyer of Chicago and Aloysius J. Muench of Milwau-

Continued on Page 2, Column 1

Airliners Collide Over City and Crash in Brooklyn Street and Field in Staten Island

DISASTER WORST IN U.S. AIR ANNALS

Jet From Chicago Plunges in Park Slope as 2d Plane Falls in New Dorp

Continued From Page 1, Col. 8

on Staten Island. Two were dead on arrival and the other died shortly after.

Several eyewitnesses said they had seen the plane disintegrate. The tower operator at Miller Field, a Sergeant Logsdon, said two or three large pieces of burning wreckage had come hurtling down through the clouds. The plane was in its death spin, and one of its wings separated just before the crash.

Federal agencies were investigating the crashes. The United jet was due at New York International Airport at 10:45 A. M. The T. W. A. plane was due at LaGuardia at 10:40 A. M.

Approaching the city, the United jet was ordered by traffic controllers to fly a holding, or stacking, pattern 5,000 feet over Preston, N. J., until cleared to proceed to Idlewild. The TWA plane was directed to fly a holding pattern 6,000 feet over Linden, N. J., until cleared for La Guardia. Their courses from the holding pattern to the airports would have been several miles apart.

Toll Exceeds One of '56

It was the worst air disaster in United States history. The death toll exceeded that of the worst previous crash, over Grand Canyon in 1956, when 128 died. That collision also involved United Air Lines and T. W. A. planes.

Last night, under floodlights, policemen and firemen were still engaged in the grim task of searching for bodies in the debris at Seventh Avenue and Sterling Place, Brooklyn. Eighty-seven bodies had been taken to the Kings County Hospital morgue. The three missing persons were presumed to be among them.

The search centered on the ruins of the Pillar of Fire Church. The stone facade of the church, which had towered over the four-story brownstones of Sterling Place, had collapsed, and it was feared that several bodies of passengers lay under tons of debris.

Wallace Edward Lewis, the 90-year-old caretaker who lived on the third floor of the church, was missing and believed dead.

Also missing were two Christmas-tree salesmen who had been setting up their trees in a dirty snowbank outside a vacant Sterling Place store when the plane came hurtling down. They were Joseph Colacano, 29, of 14 East Second Street, Brooklyn, and his uncle, John Opperisano, 34, of Massapequa, L. I.

At midnight, firemen digging in the rubble surrounding the fuselage on the church site uncovered another body, bringing the total of those presumed to have been killed on the ground to five. The police said there was a possibility that other bodies would be found under the fuselage.

Jet Misses School

As the jet neared the end of its plunge it narrowly missed the St. Augustine parochial school and high school at Sixth Avenue and Sterling Place, where more than 1,000 children were in classes. Then it sheared off the steeply gabled roof of the Pillar of Fire Church and burst into flames.

The rear of the fuselage plunged into the intersection of Seventh Avenue and Sterling Place, setting fire to two blocks of brownstones on the west side of Seventh Avenue.

Flying debris struck and killed a street cleaner who was shoveling snow near the intersection. He was Charles J. Cooper, 34, of 2348 Sixty-first Street, Brooklyn.

The only surviving passenger, Steven Baltz, 11, of Wilmette, Ill., who was flying here to meet his mother, was thrown clear of the blazing wreckage and landed in a snowbank.

Later, in Methodist Hospital, the boy was able to describe the last desperate minute of the flight.

He told a physician of looking out the plane window at the snow falling on the city, just before the crash.

"It looked like a picture out of a fairy book," he said. "It was a beautiful sight."

Priests from St. Augustine's ran to the scene with holy oils. They found the intersection ablaze with jet fuel. Flaming rivulets raced down the slope of Sterling Place and enveloped parked automobiles, setting off a chain of popping explosions as the fire reached the gasoline tanks.

Flames Three Stories High

"The heat was terrific and the flames were shooting three stories high," said the Rev. Raymond Morgan, assistant pastor of St. Augustine's. "We couldn't get near the plane, so we helped people out of threatened houses. We heard no screams from the wreckage."

For fifteen minutes after the disaster police and firemen did not know they were dealing with the wreckage of a giant jet airliner. They thought at first that a propeller plane had crashed and that no more than a dozen persons were aboard. Not until the arrival of aviation accident investigators was it indicated that scores of persons lay dead in the wreckage.

After the extent of the disaster was apparent, all auxiliary policemen in Brooklyn alarm blaze brought out 250 were ordered out. The seven-firemen and fifty pieces of apparatus.

Mayor Wagner, Police Commissioner Stephen P. Kennedy, Fire Commissioner Edward F. Cavanagh Jr. and Robert E. Condon, Civil Defense director, went to the scene.

The Mayor, who observed with shock that "most of the bodies are horribly mutilated," also went to the auditorium of St. Augustine's, where scores of women and children, driven from their homes by the fire, had taken refuge.

Within seconds after the jet smashed into the Pillar of Fire Church, the rear of the three-story building occupied by the McCaddin Funeral Home, on the corner of Seventh Avenue and Sterling Place, burst into flame.

The undertaker, Henry McCaddin, and his wife were having a mid-morning cup of coffee in their third-floor quarters. Their year-old daughter, Donna Marie, played under the kitchen table.

Suddenly the house shook. Mrs. Caddin started to reach for Donna Marie, but a neighbor, who had seen flames pouring from the building, rushed in, snatched up the baby and led the McCaddins to an escape over the roof.

Across Sterling Place a Chinese laundry and a delicatessen were sideswiped by burning fuselage and caught fire. For a while it was feared that the laundry owner, 70-year-old James Moy, known in the neighborhood as "Jimmy the Laundryman," had been burned to death. But he turned up later.

He said he had been in the front of his shop, ironing a shirt, when the plane crashed. He was able to reach the street only slightly singed.

Bishop Arthur K. White, head of the Pillar of Fire Society, is the father of a United Air Lines pilot. When he heard of the disaster he made an urgent telephone call from his headquarters at Zarephath, N. J. to Newport Beach, Calif., where his son lives. His son, Horace Merrill White, answered the phone.

The ceiling over Park Slope was only about 600 feet when the disaster struck. Sleet came spitting down out of the dirty gray clouds and gutters were brimming with slush.

The once quiet and sedate neighborhood is running down, but the area is still thickly dotted with churches and funeral homes.

Flatbush Avenue Extension, a major artery, only a few blocks away, was closed to traffic during most of the afternoon.

Commissioner Kennedy broadcast an appeal asking the curious to stay away from the scene. But thousands were drawn to it and police lines had to be formed on all sides.

Fire Commissioner Cavanagh said the final death toll might not be known for hours. He said:

"It seems reasonable that when we get down farther into the wreckage of these buildings we may find bodies of occupants who were caught there when the crash came."

The Federal Bureau of Investigation sent from Washington a team of specialists to aid in identifying the dead.

A temporary morgue was set up in a garage next to the Pillar of Fire Church.

In Washington, Senator Norris Cotton, Republican of New Hempshire, said, "This catastrophe is of the magnitude that would demand special attention. As a member of the Aviation subcommittee, I am requesting a special investigation. There should be no delay."

The New York Times

FROM THE SKY: Wreckage of the United Air Lines jet is strewn across the intersection of Sterling Place and Seventh Avenue, Brooklyn

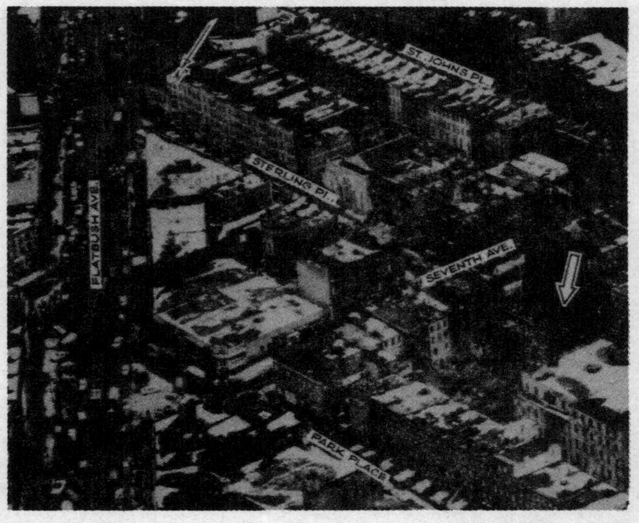

Speed Hanzlik for The New York Times

AREA IN BROOKLYN: Arrow indicates the crash site of the United Air Lines jet at the intersection of Sterling Place and Seventh Avenue. The view is to the south.

Grief and Sobbing Fill Lounge At Idlewild After the Disaster

Friends and Relatives Told of Crash an Hour Later—Some Give Up Hope and Try to Identify Bodies at Morgue

By NAN ROBERTSON

Agonizing suspense and then grief filled a United Air Lines waiting room at New York International Airport yesterday as relatives and friends of passengers aboard United's Flight 826 from Chicago learned the plane had crashed in Brooklyn.

The first clue that something was wrong came shortly before 11 A.M. when the flight listing was removed from an illuminated board. The DC-8 jetliner had gone down after apparently colliding with a Trans World Airline Super Constellation moments before, but the knowledge of the disaster was withheld for at least an hour from those who waited.

When airlines officials revealed there had been an "accident" and when it became increasingly clear there were many dead among the seventy-six passengers and seven crew members aboard, men and women in the lounge milled around dazedly or began to sob quietly.

Mrs. Ruth Skolsky of 157-29 Twelfth Avenue, Beechhurst, Queens, was waiting for her husband Alvin, 34, to whom she had been married less than a month ago.

"What am I going to do, what am I going to do?" she asked as tears streamed down her cheeks.

When others tried to assure her that her husband, a sales executive for a television program, was still alive, Mrs. Skolsky sobbed: "No, no, there's only one survivor." She had just learned this from news reports.

Christmas Reunions Planned

Some of those looking forward to Christmas reunions waited at Idlewild for as much as six hours until all hope was gone that some passengers had missed the plane or changed their minds.

They then faced the ordeal of searching among the bodies at the Kings County Hospital morgue to identify their dead.

The victims aboard the other airplane, Trans World Air Line Flight 266, which crashed on Staten Island, were taken to the Bellevue Hospital morgue in Manhattan.

A T. W. A. spokesman at LaGuardia Airport, where this plane was preparing to land, said only a few persons had awaited its arrival and they had left the airport immediately after learning of thee crash.

Most of the passengers were "commuters" on the "business man's flight" from Columbus and Dayton, Ohio. At 3 P. M. yesterday, the flight arrival board at LaGuardia still carried Flight 266 as scheduled to arrive at 10:36 A. M.

Early yesterday at Idlewild, Mrs. Florence Crapanzano of Upper Montclair, N. J., said: "I am better off than all these other poor people." She said she was awaiting her 18-year-old daughter Adele, a student at the University of Chicago.

"I am not really certain that she was aboard that plane," Mrs. Crapanzano said. "At least, I can hope."

Except for muted sobbing, the United lounge at Idlewild was almost completely silent. From the main floor of the building, the sound of tinkling music being played over a public address system could be heard. Those waiting for news had been gradually shepherded to a second-floor "V. I. P." lounge.

An auburn-haired woman, an airlines passenger agent, stood at the door, tears in her eyes. "We told them what has happened and they know the plane has crashed," she said.

Huddled inside were Charles Dileo, his wife, Margery, and three of their children, Raymond, Ronnie and Mrs. Margery Ostermeier.

They were waiting for a third son, Frank, a 21-year-old senior majoring in physical education at the University of Utah.

Mr. Dileo tried to maintain his composure, but broke down frequently as he spoke. "Frank was coming home for Christmas," he said. "He hasn't been home since Christmas two years ago."

Sent Him Money

The father, an accountant, who lives at 75 Cedar Place, Floral Park, Queens, said he had bought Frank's ticket a month ago. "But last night we were advised through the airline at Salt Lake City that he didn't have enough money, so we sent it to him."

Mr. Dileo was not sure if his son had made the connection at Chicago. "We are still hoping and we're going to stay here," he said.

Another father who had separated from his daughter yesterday morning at Chicago because they could not find seats on the same plane also fought to remain calm.

The father, George LaRiviere, of Greenwich, Conn., said he had been with his daughter, Peggy, a freshman at Barat College in Lake Forest, Ill., at Chicago's O'Hare Airport just several hours earlier. She had planned to take an American Airlines plane with her father for New York at 10:10 A. M., but was forced to switch to the doomed United Flight 826.

A woman awaiting news of her daughter hoped not only that she was alive, but that her husband would not fly to New York from Buffalo to join her.

Mrs. Charles T. Post of Pleasantville, N. Y. said she believed her 18-year-old daughter Catherine was aboard the United jet liner. Mr. Post was in Buffalo on business yesterday and advised his wife that he was trying to get to New York by private plane.

"I hope he doesn't get one," she said. "I don't want him to fly." Her husband is business manager for Iron Age, a trade publication. The Posts have another daughter, Penelope, 21, and a son, Charles Jr.

George Loughran, of 40-07 248th Street, Little Neck, Queens, wrung his hands as he worried about his 24-year-old son Thomas, also listed as a passenger.

The son is a Chicago representative of Standard & Poor's. "I'm so upset I can't remember his Chicago address," Mr. Loughran said.

Last night, officials at the Kings County and Bellevue morgues turned away relatives and friends who went to identify the victims. Many of the bodies were so badly burned or mangled as to make physical identification impossible.

Those who came were asked to wait until at least tomorrow before returning. Policemen from the Missing Persons Bureau took down descriptions, hoping to spare relatives by making preliminary identifications, wherever possible, through physical characteristics, papers or clothing.

Brooklyn Scene: A Quiet Byway Is Invaded by Death and Chaos

Sterling Place, an Area of Run-Down Houses, Ripped Asunder by Crashing Plane—Residents Tell of Escape

By CLARENCE DEAN

A quiet Brooklyn neighborhood of brownstones and turn-of-the-century apartment houses became an inferno in a few quick seconds yesterday morning.

At 10:30 A. M., about the only sound on Sterling Place from Sixth to Seventh Avenues was the slushing passage of an occasional car. A wet snow was falling, and the clouds were low-hung.

Moments later, the narrow thoroughfare was filled with death and bedlam. The wreckage of a fallen DC-8 jet airliner lay scattered upon the neighborhood, partly embedded in buildings. Flames flared in the street and swirled from under roofs.

Only the outlines of Sterling Place were visible through the yellow-tinged smoke. The sound of sirens was everywhere. On the outskirts of the disaster, stunned and incredulous residents huddled in doorways and gathered in stores.

The neighborhood is two blocks south of busy Flatbush Avenue and about half a mile northwesterly down the hill from Prospect Park, on the fringes of the once-fashionable Park Slope area.

Area in Transition

It is a neighborhood of the type known as "in transition." Lower-income families have been moving in, some of the brownstones have become rooming houses and the once-spacious apartments have been cut into smaller units.

Many of the older residents have hung on, however, and Sterling Place has remained a respectable street. It is a place where neighbors gather on front stoops of a summer evening to chat and drink beer, and where everyone knows everyone.

Christmas wreaths had begun to appear in windows along Sterling Place yesterday. Trash barrels were waiting at the curb for the sanitation men delayed by the storm that began last Sunday. People had gone to work, children were at school and, because the weather was bad, few shoppers had ventured out.

In the third-floor living quarters above the McCaddin Funeral Parlor at 24 Seventh Avenue, on the northwest corner of Sterling Place, Mr. and Mrs. Henry McCaddin were having a mid-morning cup of coffee. Donna Marie, 1 year old, was playing under the kitchen table.

Across the street, at 122 Sterling Place, Mrs. Henrietta Enright was sleeping late in her top-floor apartment.

At the intersection of Sterling Place and Seventh Avenue, Salvatore Manza, a Department of Sanitation worker who lives at 270 First Street, Brooklyn, was shoveling snow. Mr. Manza, white-faced, told later of his experiences.

"I heard this whistling sound, and I looked up," he said. "I saw this plane, not even fifty feet up. It was coming from there toward there." He pointed from southwest to northeast.

"All of a sudden," Mr. Manza went on, "the right wing dipped. It hooked into the corner of that apartment house roof, and the rest of the plane slammed into the church and the apartment house across the street. All at once everything was on fire, and the fire from the plane in the street was as high as the houses."

The apartment where Mrs. Enright was sleeping was the building where the plane first touched. "I can't tell you anything," she said. "I don't know what happened. I was sleeping, and then suddenly I was looking up through the roof at the sky, and they were carrying me out."

Mrs. McCaddin described what had happened.

"We were having our coffee, and I said to Henry, 'My goodness, that plane sounds awfully low!' And just then the whole house shook like it had been hit by a bomb, and the room was all flames.

"I started to grab the baby, and I saw Mr. Carter run in, and he grabbed the baby, and somehow we all got out."

Mr. Carter—Robert Carter, 29 years old—who runs a hairdressing establishment at 5 Seventh Avenue, said:

"I saw the flames coming out of McCaddin's, and I ran over. Afterward I tried to get near the wreckage of the plane, but the fire was so bad, it singed my eyebrows."

The scene was an orderly kind of pandemonium. The air was filled with sirens, the throbbing of the fire pumpers and commands issuing from loudspeakers.

The procession of apparatus, ambulances, Civil Defense vehicles and emergency workers of many kinds kept coming.

The New York Times Dec. 17, 1960

BROOKLYN: Airliner fell into street (cross), setting fires in a row of houses.

Policemen ringing the wooden barricades kept opening and closing them. Hoses tangled the slushy streets for blocks.

Outside the barricades, several hundred feet from the disaster point, newspaper men complained bitterly as their entrance was barred by the police, who readily opened the barriers to television camera men and a seemingly endless stream of fire buffs equipped with honorary badges.

The gray stucco church into which the plane rammed was a three-story, gabled structure known as the Pillar of Fire Church. Its congregation is part of the Holiness denomination, a Fundamentalist group.

The impact of the crash and the fire that followed demolished all except the facade of the building. Wallace E. Lewis, 90 years old, the caretaker of the building, was missing and presumed dead in the wreckage.

At the height of the fire ten residential buildings and the church were burning. Walls had collapsed and there was burning, smoking debris everywhere.

Fire Commissioner Edward F. Cavanaugh Jr. said: "It may be weeks before we can comb through that rubble."

Body Found in Street

Aside from the bodies removed from the plane's wreckage, five others were recovered. One was identified as that of Charles J. Cooper, 34, of 2348 Sixty-first Street, Brooklyn, a Sanitation Department worker, who had been clearing snow.

Two persons, who were selling Christmas trees, were missing and presumed dead. They were Joseph Colacano, 29, of 14 East Second Street, Brooklyn, and his uncle, John Opperisano, 31, of Massapequa, L. I.

The scene suggested a wartime bombing.

The granite cornice of a four-story apartment house on the south side of Sterling Place had been torn away. Part of the roof was shorn.

Across the street, next to the burning church, there was only a cavity where a similar four-story house had stood. Next door, at the corner of Seventh Avenue, flames poured steadily from the roof of the red-brick funeral home.

Part of a wing lay hooked in the torn roof of the apartment house. The forward section of the fuselage was imbedded in the debris across the street.

A thirty-foot section of the tail lay grotesquely askew in the intersection of Sterling Place and Seventh Avenue. In color and shape it resembled a huge elephant on its side. The tip of the tail rested atop the cab of a red truck.

On Sterling Place, firemen wading through ankle-deep water carried body after body to temporary morgues in two garages. The procession of the olive drab stretchers continued while other firemen removed charred mail and documents from the wreckage.

As dusk approached, the Fire Department put its emergency searchlight units into action, bathing the scene in an eerie white light. In the glare, hundreds of firemen continued to search the rubble and wreckage turning up bits of evidence to help identify the victims.

The wet streets began to freeze, adding to the difficulty of the work.

Hundreds of motorists, sightseers and homeward-bound commuters, added to an already chaotic situation. For a mile around the scene, side streets were clogged with autos.

Southbound traffic on Flatbush Avenue was being diverted to St. Marks Avenue, three blocks from the scene. Flatbush Avenue, from Bergen Street to Prospect Park, was closed to all but emergency equipment.

Red Cross and Salvation Army units were giving hot coffee, soup and doughnuts to disaster workers. Welfare Department workers were on hand to assist those evacuated from the stricken buildings. Many of the homeless were congregated in the lobbies of near-by theatres and churches.

Children Evacuated From Private School

The Berkeley Institute evacuated its 400 pupils yesterday to an adjoining gymnasium within minutes of the airliner crash in Brooklyn.

The private school building at 181 Lincoln Place, two blocks from the crash site, was shaken.

Immediately, teachers went from class to class instructing the children to go downstairs to put on their boots and coats. Classes filed down in the fire-drill procedure and were sent to the gym.

The school had been scheduled to end its day at noon for the Christmas holiday. Those children who live near the school were sent home when their parents called. Others waited for the school buses.

Girls of the senior class guided the younger children to the buses. A few teachers took some of the pupils home by subway.

2 Schools in Crash Area Inspected by Theobald

Superintendent of Schools John J. Theobald hurried from a meeting at City Hall yesterday morning to visit two Brooklyn schools near the scene of the airliner crash.

No damage was reported at either school, although debris from the crash landed within two blocks of the Public School 9 Annex at 279 Sterling Place. Dr. Theobald also visited P. S. 614 at 227 Sterling Place, about a block from the accident.

The meeting between school officials and the Mayor's special committee of labor leaders appointed to work out differences between teachers and the Board of Education was "practically postponed," according to David Dubinsky, a vice president of the American Federation of Labor and Congress of Industrial Organizations.

No date was set for another meeting.

10 Brooklyn Houses and a Church Are Set Ablaze by the Flaming Wreckage

OCCUPANTS PANIC, FLEE TO SIDEWALK

Church Caretaker Is Among Missing — Hunt Pressed for Victims of Crash

Continued From Page 1, Col. 6

Engine Company 269 arrived a few minutes later, the firemen immediately sounded another alarm, bringing more equipment to the crash site.

Plane Fuselage Broken

Six more alarms were sounded within the next thirty-six minutes, bringing firemen from Queens and Manhattan as well as Brooklyn.

The first job of the firemen, according to the Chief of Department, George David, was to put out the fire in the plane itself.

The tail assembly landed ablaze in the intersection of Seventh Avenue and Sterling Place. The fuselage of the plane was broken into several pieces that were scattered along Sterling Place, and the nose and engines of the jet were buried in the wreckage of the church.

Luckily, Sterling Place slopes down from the scene of the disaster, and as firemen sprayed water on the fires the plane's tanks floated away toward Sixth Avenue.

Foam Rushed to Fire

A special fire unit brought chemical foam to the scene for use on the jet fuel fires, but it was not needed.

A flaming section of the left wing had landed atop a four-story building at 124 Sterling Place, setting fire to the roof. The fire spread to similar structures at 122, 120 and 118, on the south side of the street.

In its descent, the jet also ignited six buildings on Seventh Avenue, Nos. 18, 20, 22, 24, 26 and 28.

While fighting the fires, Fire Chief Joseph Henry and Fireman Robert Burns were injured and taken to Methodist Hospital for treatment. Both were reported in good condition last night.

Chief David said there had been no problem in evacuating the buildings because the occupants had fled and most of them were on the streets by the time the first firemen arrived.

He said all supplies of gas and electricity in an eight-block area had been shut off to prevent further fires.

Rescue crews with stretchers moved in as soon as the fire in the plane was out to remove bodies from the wreckage. These were taken to near-by stores and garages and later transferred to hospitals.

After the plane fire was put out, the firemen went to work on the tenements. They hoisted ladders to play hoses on upper stories where pieces of wreckage had smashed through walls and burned holes in the floors below.

By 12:42 P. M. the fire was declared under control and the long job of cleaning up and removing the dead began.

Top Officials at Scene

Commissioner Cavanagh, who was being interviewed on a radio program when he heard of the crash, arrived at the scene after the second alarm and remained there until late last night directing operations.

Police Commissioner Stephen P. Kennedy and Mayor Wagner also were at the scene.

Mr. Cavanagh said the recovery of any casualties from the burned buildings would be a "long, slow process."

He explained that the four-square-block area between Sixth and Seventh Avenues and St. John's Place and Park Place would remain roped off until firemen had made a complete search of the damaged buildings.

Many of the persons who fled the burning buildings were in a state of shock and were given sedatives and treatment at the scene by doctors.

By nightfall all of them had gone to stay with relatives or had been assigned to one of the emergency shelters established near the crash.

Commissioner Cavanagh called it "an act of God" that the major impact of the crash had been on the vacant church rather than on any of the surrounding buildings.

TEACHERS STAY ON JOB

Care for Children in School Near Scene of Crash

Officials at Public School 4 at 35 Berkeley Place, Brooklyn, stayed on the job yesterday because of the emergency situation.

The school serves the area in which a United Air Lines plane crashed.

By 4 P. M. about 500 pupils had been called for by parents and guardians. The remaining 200 children were escorted to their homes by teachers and attendance personnel. The children whose parents were not at home to receive them were taken to a temporary shelter set up at St. Augustine's Roman Catholic parochial school at Park Place and Sixth Avenue.

School officials reported that all of the children had been picked up by 6:10 P. M.

Spellman Begins Yule Tour

Cardinal Spellman left here last night for Elmendorf Air Force Base, Anchorage, Alaska, to begin his annual Christmas trip to Armed Forces stationed overseas.

The New York Times

SEARCH: Police and firemen carry a victim from the wreckage of the Pillar of Fire Church on Sterling Place, rammed by United Air Lines jet plane

Army of Rescuers at 2 Crashes, But Few Rescues Are Possible

Police, Fire, Defense and Medical Units Led by Mayor and High Aides— City-Wide Disaster Signaled

By IRA HENRY FREEMAN

Great numbers of policemen, firemen, civil defense teams, Coast Guardsmen, doctors and nurses, Red Cross and Salvation Army personnel, Boy Scouts and volunteers flocked to the two sites of the airplane crashes in Brooklyn and Staten Island yesterday.

However, the actual rescues made by this small army of disaster units were tragically few.

The sole person alive in the Brooklyn crash, 11-year-old Steven Baltz of Wilmette, Ill. was saved by passers-by and off-duty patrolmen.

Two men and a woman were pulled from the wreckage of the plane at Miller Army Air Field on Staten Island by soldiers on duty there.

A Coast Guard helicopter flew the men to the United States Public Health Service at New Dorp, S. I., while the woman was driven there in a private automobile. The woman and one man were dead on arrival at the hospital. The other man died at 1:03 P. M.

The mobilization of civil defense was quickly put into action, not the usual mock drill.

City officials concerned with civil defense were quickly on the scene. Mayor Wagner, Police Commissioner Stephen P. Kennedy, Fire Commissioner Edward F. Cavanagh Jr. and Robert E. Condon, civil defense director, rushed to Brooklyn. Dr. Morris A. Jacobs, Hospital Commissioner, went first to the Staten Island crash scene and then to Brooklyn.

Shortly after the first alarm was flashed into Police Headquarters, thirty-nine patrol cars, four emergency rescue trucks and 265 men were at the Brooklyn crash.

Five fire alarms were rung in Brooklyn firehouses and two in Manhattan for the Brooklyn crash. Fifty-six pieces of apparatus—pumpers, ladder trucks, rescue trucks, searchlight trucks and a radio truck—went to the Sterling Place blazes set off by the crash.

Fire Commissioner Cavanagh expressed gratification that nearly 200 off-duty firemen had voluntarily come to the scene to help their comrades, about equal in number, who were on duty there.

Disaster Signal Given

Mr. Condon turned in a city-wide disaster signal, as though a bomb had struck. This brought 500 men and women civilians—trained as auxiliary policemen, firemen, first-aid men, drivers, messengers, nurses —to the scenes of the two crashes.

Two mobile communications trucks were set up at the Brooklyn site by civilian defense workers. The police had a similar truck there and the New York Telephone Company quickly strung special telephone lines.

Kings County Hospital sent four ambulances, twenty doctors, eight nurses and eight attendants to the Brooklyn scene. Bellevue Hospital's similar disaster unit went first to Staten Island and then to Brooklyn. A score of city and voluntary hospitals in Brooklyn also sent ambulances, doctors and nurses to Sterling Place, but there was little for them to do.

About 100 refugees from burned-out tenements were sheltered and fed by civil defense units at Public School 9, Sterling Place and Vanderbilt Avenue, and at St. Augustine's Roman Catholic School, Sterling Place and Sixth Avenue.

Red Cross workers set up a shelter and canteen within half an hour in the Carlton movie theatre at Flatbush Avenue and Seventh Avenue.

The Red Cross also brought in 400 pints of blood, with 200 more close by.

Within fifteen minutes after the crash, the Salvation Army doughnut and coffee truck was off, ready to feed rescue workers in Brooklyn. Food carts of the Red Cross and the Three Alarm Association arrived only a little later.

Boy Scouts of Troop 22, attached to St. Francis Xavier Roman Catholic Church in Brooklyn, served as runners for civil defense workers in Brooklyn.

The first rescuers at the Staten Island crash were artillery men and aircraft maintenance men stationed at Miller Field. Lieut. Victor Boner, post marshal, came from Fort Wadsworth, S. I., to take charge. The Coast Guard helicopter was flown in from Floyd Bennett Field in Brooklyn by Lieut. Comdr. Moses Walker with Lieut. James Esposito and Coast Guardsman Martin Tierney.

Since the crash was on an open, little-used airfield and the fire less serious than in Brooklyn, there was a much smaller mobilization of disaster teams on Staten Island.

The police forces included eighteen patrol cars, three emergency trucks, and 136 men. There were also three police helicopters from Floyd Bennett hovering over the scene. Communications were taken care of by two police radio trucks and a telephone switchboard trailer, lent by the New Jersey Bell Telephone Company. The trailer was hooked up to temporary telephone lines to the spot.

3 Ambulances Sent

Seaview Hospital sent its disaster team of three ambulances. Fifty doctors responded, but only the three fatally injured persons were in need of medical aid and they were taken to the hospital.

Because debris littered the Lower Bay off New Dorp, it was feared some plane victims might be in the water. Twenty-five Coast Guard boats, from forty-foot picket launches to 180-footers, with a total of 200 men aboard them searched the water in vain from 11 A. M. until darkness fell. Four police launches, with fifteen men aboard, joined the futile search.

Small gasoline fires on the crash were easily handled by six engine companies and three trucks.

To help identify the dead, the Federal Bureau of Investigation sent men to New York. There were twenty-four bodies in the Richmond County Morgue at Seaview, and a much larger number in the Kings County Morgue.

Many helpful passers-by did their best to rescue victims at he Brooklyn scene. Among these were Anthony Troiano, 27, years old, and his brother, Neil, 0, both plumbers, who were working near the scene. They aided the Baltz boy, helped firemen lift a girder off a man pinned in the wreckage and led some tenants safely out of the burning houses.

Many physicians from "doctors' row," Brooklyn's Eighth Avenue, rushed to the scene but found little to do.

GEAR FORCES JET BACK

Emergency Chicago Landing Made by American Airliner

CHICAGO, Dec. 16 (AP)—An American Airlines Boeing 707 jet airliner with ninety-four passengers aboard made an uneventful emergency landing today at O'Hare Airport after the pilot reported that its landing gear would not retract.

The plane departed for New York's International Airport at 9:49 A. M., Central Time. It abandoned course when the mechanical failure was discovered and returned. After circling the area to reduce fuel load and allow time for deployment of airport emergency equipment, the plane landed forty-nine minutes after take-off.

Crash Witnesses Describe Destruction on the Ground

By CHARLES GRUTZNER

A photoengraver, walking to his job on Brooklyn's Park Slope, has his gaze drawn skyward about 10:40 A. M. yesterday by what seemed to be "a large bolt of lightning." He saw the fuselage of an airliner smash into a row of Seventh Avenue brownstones. They burst into flame.

Near by, a grocer rushed into the street when a blast broke his window. He found the tail section of a plane spanning the roadway in front of his door. He stared in horror as a boy from the plane, his clothing afire, collapsed in the snow.

At about the same time in New Dorp, S. I., ten miles away, a service station owner heard "a big thump," ran outside and saw a thirty-foot midsection of a plane gushing flames and "twirling like a bright toy" descending into a field.

A real estate broker, driving along Staten Island's Hylan Boulevard, heard a "terrible grinding noise" that made him think something had gone wrong with the car engine. He shut off his motor, stepped out and found that the noise was coming from a plane about 300 feet overhead. As he watched, the burning plane broke into several parts and showered debris over a wide area.

Early Confusion

In these ways did some of the eyewitnesses first become aware of the air disaster. Other witnesses gave varying accounts, amid the early confusion at the ground scenes, of how things happened.

But through every personal account there ran the same thread of surprise and horror.

The scene in Brooklyn, where one plane fell in a densely populated district, reminded one witness of the bombed and burning villages of the Korean war.

In Staten Island, where the wreckage narrowly missed a community of wooden homes and a public school, witnesses said the blood-drenched snow and the bodies made them think of a battlefield.

Most of the Staten Island observers of the falling Trans World Airline plane mentioned the sickening horror of the slow earthward spiraling of the fuselage that carried so many to their death.

"I prayed that it would be over soon," said Tom Griffo, operator of a service station at New Dorp Lane and Hylan Boulevard.

Here is the scene as pieced together by witnesses in the vicinity of Seventh Avenue and Sterling Place, Brooklyn:

Saw Plane Come Apart

Michael Egan, on his way to his job at the Kennedy Photo Engraving Company, said he looked upward and "saw a large plane falling."

"It came apart," he said. "The tail snapped off and fell across Seventh Avenue. The fuselage plowed into a row of brownstone rooming houses. People came rushing out of the lower floors. Parts of the wreckage were falling all around.

"The people were dazed and didn't seem to know what to do. Then they started running away from the scene, but by this time the sight-seers were rushing up from every side street and clogging up everything. Human nature is a funny thing."

Mr. Egan said the crowds impeded rescue efforts until the police ordered them away and roped off an area of sixteen city blocks. The wildest rumors spread when rescuers began carrying bodies from the burning buildings. It was not known then whether the bodies were those of plane passengers or of residents of the row of buildings.

Joseph Turner was stacking milk containers in the rear of his grocery at 26 Seventh Avenue when a blast shattered a window. Running outside, he saw wreckage and burning buildings. But what shocked him most, he said, was this:

"I saw a young boy crawl out from under the plane. He was on fire. He fell in the snow. A woman came and put a blanket over him."

John Fitzgerald, owner of a bar and grill at Flatbush Avenue and Prospect Place, two blocks away, heard a loud noise that made him think of the explosion that wrecked the Luckenbach pier in South Brooklyn four years ago.

Mr. Fitzgerald went outside to see.

"The rescuers hadn't got into the buildings yet," he said. "They were blazing furiously. It seemed as if gasoline from the plane had sprayed them."

Mr. Fitzgerald said he saw two bodies taken out of a car that had been crushed by the plane's tail section.

Mrs. Constance Ciazzo, watching from the window of her flower shop at 312 Flatbush Avenue, said she had seen a boy about 18 running from the scene with blood streaming down his face.

Sees Distraught Boy

"He was screaming 'Oh, those people are burning to death'," recounted Mrs. Ciazzo. "His eyes were bulging. My husband grabbed him and shook him but he kept running. I think he was out of his mind."

Peter Brook, a salesman, said he heard a "whistling" noise and looked up to see part of the plane hit the Pillar of Fire Church and fall almost at his feet.

"I dove behind a four-foot picket fence and hit the snow," said Mr. Brook. "Just as I landed flat there was a tremendous explosion. I was dazed and lay about five minutes until two policemen picked me up. I was lucky. The cops showed me a piece of metal that had hit the fence."

James O'Berg, driver of a Seventh Avenue bus, was in the block of the crash—between Park Place and Sterling Place—when there was "a terrific explosion and a couple of smaller ones."

"It was a complete inferno," said Mr. O'Berg. "People were running all over. I saw a woman with her clothes on fire and I tried to help her but somebody—I don't know who—restrained me and said 'Don't go near her!' She fell in the snow, I think. I don't know what happened to her."

Thought It Was Air Raid

Mr. O'Berg said he thought there had been an air raid. He told his passengers to lie flat and cover their heads, but they ran from the bus. One left behind a bag of groceries.

Anthony Fontana, a former Air Force man, was on his way to work for a printing company when he saw the plane heading towards him.

"It was a big one, and it was coming in out of control," he said. "It was coming in too low and the left wing was dipped. Someone said, 'It's going to hit!' and the next second it hit with a terrible roar.

"It bounced off these houses and then it plowed into the church and just demolished it. The name of the church was the Pillar of Fire—ain't that something!"

Huddled in a corner drugstore with three neighbors, Mrs. Josephine Paterson, 84, of 10 Seventh Avenue, declared: "It fell in flame and smoke, and a black object fell in front of my home. It was an engine. Then a large generator fell near by.

"It looked as though the plane was going to fall on the housing development, but it missed. The Police and Fire Departments arrived almost immediately."

Mr. Griffo, operator of the service station, said that while the fuselage was falling in flames, "hundreds of other parts of the plane were dropping over an area of eight or ten blocks.

"Then I saw an engine on the right side blow up," he said. "The second engine on the right side blew after that, and when it did, it blew the tail section to pieces. I saw a couple of people falling out of the plane."

Mrs. John S. Bailey, a New Dorp housewife, said she was reminded of a spinning toy as the plane "kept turning around and went down in spirals."

Arthur Huss, who has a furniture store on Hylan Boulevard, said he saw "millions of pieces go by." Two of his men, Charles Kneuer and Fred Schramel, who were outside loading a truck, ran into the store for shelter when the pieces started flying like shrapnel.

Thought Burner Blew Up

Richard Petosa, a petroleum inspector, was in his home in New Dorp. He said that when he heard the explosion his first fear was that his own oil burner had blown up. He ran to near-by Miller Field.

"I've seen worse in Korea as a marine," said Mr. Petosa. "But you were never prepared for it there. This is more of a shock."

The Rev. Raymond Morgan, the pastor, and three assistant priests from St. Augustine's Roman Catholic Church, gave last rites to six dead persons lying near the Brooklyn wreck without knowing whether the victims were Catholics.

Among the first at the Staten Island crash were another pair of brothers, Peter and Gerard Paul of Castleton, S. I., were Christmas shopping near by. They left their packages, scaled an airfield fence and helped drag bodies out of the burning wreckage until soldiers under Lieut. Edward Monroe arrived.

7 Missile and Air Aides Die on T.W.A. Plane

Among the passengers who died on the T. W. A. plane that crashed on Staten Island were at least seven specialists in missile and aircraft development who had hoped at Dayton, home of Wright-Patterson Air Force Base.

E. R. Quesada, director of the Federal Aviation Agency, was in Dayton when the crash occurred. He had gone there to lay wreaths on the graves of the Wright brothers on the fifty-seventh anniversary of their first flight.

Mr. Quesada, a retired Air Force lieutenant general, flew immediately to New York to supervise the investigation.

Heard 'Terrible Noise'

Mrs. George Weber of New Dorp said:

"My niece and I were in the kitchen making cookies when we heard this terrible noise. She said: 'Listen to the thunder.' We went to the window and there was this terrible ball of fire. It was huge and it must have been a mile off.

"I watched, and it was terrible. We could see now it was a plane. It seemed to fall a few feet and there was another huge burst of flame. And then the plane went down. It went down in a terrible way, one wing gone, and it turned over and over very slowly. You could watch it all the way and it was always red from the flames."

George Dorfman, a State Islander who was driving toward his Manhattan real estate office when he stopped his car because of the "terrible grinding" noise, said the plane had crashed only 300 yards from him.

"I was scared of the debris that was showering all around and I got back in my car," he said.

Frank Maybury, Staten Island dispatcher for Transit Authority buses, was in his radio car at the time of the crash.

"I heard a noise from his doorstep he saw "a sight no one can ever forget." The entire intersection of Seventh Avenue and Sterling Place was enveloped in "a huge, orange ball of flame," he said.

He started to help a young man who was running with his clothes afire, but other neighbors pulled the young man into the snow to smother the flames.

The pastor returned to his church and opened it to those evacuated from the burning buildings and to tired rescue workers.

A Sanitation Department worker, Salvatore Manza, was removing snow when the plane hit. He said:

"Then the whole thing splashed into the street. There was an explosion and a ball of fire. Another sanitation worker and I ran and recovered the body of one of our men, Charles Cooper."

Vincent Pacilio, who had parked his car at the intersection while he went to work in the neighborhood, said:

"I heard the crash and ran down there to get my car out. Flames and smoke were all around. There were screams from inside the wreckage. It was the worst sound I ever heard!"

Others said also they had heard screams from inside the buildings and from cars that had been crushed or set afire.

Police Race Airliner

On Staten Island, where open space permitted better observance of the path of the second doomed airliner, police cars and their rescue equipment raced the falling plane to the crash.

The Rev. Milton Perry was sitting in his third floor apartment in the Charlesbury Homes development, where about 1,500 persons live, when he "felt the earth shake."

"I thought it was a bombing," Mr. Perry said. "I saw the plane

United Press International

ALL THAT REMAINS: Fireman turns hose on the ruins of a brownstone house demolished by the crash of the jet

Federal Agencies Say Evidence Suggests One Airliner Was Off Course Near City

A BROAD INQUIRY INTO CRASH BEGUN

Tapes of Pilots' Talks With Towers and Logs of Jet Focus of the Studies

Continued From Page 1, Col. 5

at 6,000 feet, and received permission by radio from traffic controllers to descend to 5,000 feet on its approach for a landing at LaGuardia Airport.

The last known position of the other craft, a United Air Lines jet, was 5,000 feet over Preston, N. J., south of Linden, where it had been ordered to fly in a holding pattern—that is, circling until it was notified a runway was clear and it could approach for a landing at Idlewild.

While both planes were in holding patterns over New Jersey, the officials said, a buffer zone of five miles should have separated them, according to Federal rules.

The officials said the T. W. A. plane was being cleared to leave its holding pattern and make its landing approach when its last message was heard. Its flight pattern then called for it to go across New Jersey, pass a check-point off Coney Island and then fly across Brooklyn to LaGuardia. It was to have gone over the Ebbets Field-Prospect Park section of Brooklyn.

The jet, when it got permission to make its landing approach, was to pass a check-point off the Rockaways and fly over Rockaway Beach and Jamaica Bay to Idlewild.

'Human Error' Possible

Asked how they could have collided under these circumstances, he replied:

"It could have been human error, to which we are all subject, but this is sheer speculation and the evidence so far has been only superficially examined."

He declined to say specifically that either pilot was off course.

He said he did not know whether the United plane had been tracked by the Idlewild radar station but thought it had not. At the time of the disaster, he said, the United plane was under the control of the Idlewild air-traffic center.

"As far as we know at this time he was not lost," Mr. Quesada said, referring to the pilot of the jet.

The planes carried radar equipment for weather purposes but not for tracking other planes.

Mr. Quesada said an automatic flight recorder carried by the jet had been recovered intact. This is a fireproof and crashproof device that records flight data, including altitude, speed, position and time.

The flight recorder and tape recordings of talks between traffic controllers on the ground and the two airliners' pilots were expected to provide vital clues to the cause of the accident. Investigators were analyzing the taped conversations and the data in the flight recorder.

No Evidence of Failures

Mr. Quesada said there was no evidence of structural or navigational failures on the planes or of failure on the part of the traffic controllers.

The C. A. B. said the inquiry would be the most extensive it has held. Two C. A. B. members and twenty-nine investigators took part, including a number who flew here yesterday from Washington.

F. A. A. officials questioned traffic controllers at the air-traffic center at International and at LaGuardia Airport.

Incoming planes are controlled by the air-traffic center until they reach an a a near their destination, when they are transferred to control of the local towers. Officials were trying to find out, among other things, whether the air-traffic center or the control towers had charge at the time of the disaster.

Edward E. Slattery Jr., public-information officer for the C. A. B., said traffic-control

DISASTER: Two airliners in holding patterns west of the city that were to follow dotted lines to airports here collided. United Air Lines jet crashed on Brooklyn street (1) while a Trans World Airlines Constellation came down on Staten Island (2).
The New York Times — Dec. 19, 1960

Flaw in Ground Control

Crash of Two Planes Under Guidance Shows Chance of Error Still Remains

By RICHARD WITKIN
Special to The New York Times.

DALLAS, Tex., Dec. 16—There was one thing about today's air disaster in New York that, from a cold technical point of view, appeared to overshadow all else. It was the first time, as far as experts could recall, that planes involved in a midair collision had both been under firm control of "traffic cops" in control stations on the ground.

In all other cases, at least one of the planes had been operating outside the jurisdiction of ground stations.

What this absence of two-plane control meant, essentially, was that controllers could not be counted on to keep the two planes from colliding. They could not be counted on because they did n.t know exactly where one, or both, planes were. In such situations, the main reliance for avoiding collisions lies in pilot eyesight. But with the increase in the speed of airplanes the reliability of pilot eyesight for such duty has decreased sharply. In addition, this "see and be seen" system is obviously usable only when planes operate outside cloud formations.

Directions From Ground

But yesterday both planes were supposed to have been strictly following traffic directions radioed from the ground. Their respective altitudes would have been dictated by controllers, as would their flight paths from town to ' . .t and from check point to check point. Their precise times over successive check points also would have been dictated.

Finally, and most important of all, their progress would have been carefully followed by radar operators so that, if they deviated from orders, the pilots could be warned and a new volume and speed system would have been worked out to avert potential collision avoided.

Something went wrong. To what extent the error was human, to what extent mechanical, can hardly be guessed at right now, and may never be precisely known.

Many possibilities suggest themselves. One pilot may have misunderstood his orders, because of radio static or a mental slip. A controller may have given incorrect orders. Navigation equipment on one of the planes may have given a false reading.

But what about radar? When one or both of the planes deviated from 'its assigned course, should not a controller have seen the radar blips converge and have radioed emergency corrections?

Theoretically, yes. But radar, like any other piece of machinery, is not infallible. The blips could have been blurred by rain or snow or signal reflection from buildings or other ground objects.

In addition, radar currently in use has one immense shortcoming. It shows only a plane's geographical position over the ground, not its altitude. So, the converging of blips does not necessarily mean an impending collision, since the planes could be thousands of feet above and below each other.

Still, a controller normally works on the most pessimistic assumption. He will take action if blips at unknown altitudes head for one another.

There is some speculation that one significant factor in yesterday's tragedy may have been the fact that the two planes were nearing different, though neighboring, airports.

A building disaster on Aug. 22, 1891, sixty-four persons died when the upper floor of a building on Park Place collapsed.

Almost a century ago, in 1883, a series of fires, set by rioters protesting the Civil War draft act, killed 1,200 persons and destroyed forty-three buildings.

Ground controllers directing traffic headed for a single airport might be expected to be less attuned to the possibility that a plane they are handling might conflict with one handled by a controller who is miles away and has not yet seen the collision course.

News Analysis

Investigators learned that at about the time of the accident the ceiling at Idlewild was 700 feet, with broken clouds. The sky was overcast at 1,500 feet and visibility was one mile. There was light rain and fog and a wind from the northwest at eleven knots.

In a few minutes the ceiling dropped to 600 feet, the wind increased to twelve knots and light snow was added to the light rain and fog.

Appeal Made to Public

Investigators appealed to anyone finding pieces of the wrecked planes to leave them where they are and notify the police immediately. The investigators said wreckage might contain important clues to the cause of the disaster.

Investigation headquarters were set up at the Seaway Idlewild Hotel, near the Federal Building at Idlewild, where the C. A. B. and F. A. A. have their regional offices.

Officials of the C. A. B. who came from Washington included the board members, G. Joseph Minetti and Alan S. Boyd, and Melvin N. Gough, director of the Bureau of Safety, who heads the investigating team.

Joseph Fluet, chief of the operations division of the Bureau of Safety and former supervisor of the bureau in the New York region, also flew here for the investigation.

In Washington Representative John Bell Williams, Democrat of Mississippi, said the House aeronautics subcommittee, of which he is chairman, would postpone its investigation until the C. A. B. developed more facts.

Senator Norris Cotton, Republican of New Hampshire, a member of the Senate aviation subcommittee, demanded a special board of inquiry without delay.

Francis McDermott, executive director of the Air Traffic Control Association, said the disaster showed the need for more effective control systems.

1,021 Lost in 1904 Slocum Fire Was Biggest Toll in City History

The disaster in the city's history, most costly of life was a fire aboard the vessel General Slocum on June 15, 1904 that killed 1,021 passengers. Included were many children on a Sunday school outing.

The blaze started as the excursion ship was making its way along the East River off Hell Gate.

Another fire took place on March 25, 1911, in the Triangle shirtwaist factory on Washington Place near Greene Street. Hundreds of workers were trapped at cutting tables at one of them tossed a match in to a bundle of fluffy fabric. The fleeing women found that the exits had been locked. The fire took 145 lives.

On Dec. 5, 1876, 295 persons were killed in a fire in the old Brooklyn Theatre on Fulton Street, in what is now the Borough Hall section of Brooklyn.

In a subway disaster, ninety-seven persons were killed and 100 were injured on Nov. 2, 1918, in the wreck of a BMT

Brighton line train in the Malbone Street tunnel in Brooklyn, not far from the area where the DC-8 fell yesterday.

An explosion aboard the ferryboat Westfield in New York harbor on July 30, 1871, killed 100 passengers.

The most recent major air disaster in New York, in which sixty-five persons were killed, was the crash of an American Airlines turbo-prop airliner on Feb. 3, 1959.

Continued From Page 1, Col. 5

centers and control towers automatically recorded all radio conversations between pilots and traffic controllers.

Under board policy, he went on, the records will not be made public until they are introduced in evidence at the public hearing that will close the investigation. Witnesses and all persons concerned with the aircraft will testify. Thereafter, the board will make a detailed report, which will be made public in Washington.

The whole process may take many months, judging by investigations of previous disasters. Under weather conditions like those prevailing yesterday, there are about 1,200 instrument flights a day in and out of Idlewild and LaGuardia, according to Martin L. Sonnett, F.A.A. air traffic specialist. Both the United and T. W. A. planes were flying on instruments.

TUNNEL LANE KEPT CLEAR IN EMERGENCY: The approach to the Brooklyn-Battery Tunnel, with one lane kept ready to serve ambulances or other vehicles on the way to the area in Brooklyn where plane wreckage fell.
The New York Times

2d Airliner Collision of Its Kind Raises '60 Death Toll to Record

1956 Crash Over Grand Canyon Killed 128—Elizabeth Disasters and Bomber That Hit Empire State Also Recalled

By RALPH KATZ

The airline collision here yesterday was the second such disaster in the nation's aviation history involving commercial airliners in which fatalities occurred.

The only parallel accident was the collision on June 30, 1956, of two planes over Arizona's Grand Canyon with a loss of 128 lives By coincidence, the planes were operated by the same companies as those in yesterday's accident—Trans World Airline and United Air Lines.

The planes had left Los Angeles minutes apart and flown east, the T. W. A. plane was a Super Constellation; the United, a DC-7. Their flight patterns came together over the Painted Desert, near Tuba City in north-central Arizona.

The unusualness of what appeared yesterday to be a repetition of the 1956 collision was pointed up by Jerome Lederer, director of the Cornell-Guggenheim Aviation Safety Center and the Flight Safety Foundation.

He said that in the twelve years covering 1948-59 there had been seven collisions involving scheduled airliners in the nation in which there had been fatalities. In only the Grand Canyon disaster had two commercial airliners met, he said.

Two Convairs Collided

There had been, he added, a collision between two commercial craft on Aug. 26, 1955, over Michigan City, Mich., in which there were no fatalities. The collision involved two Convair planes, one operated by United, the other by American Airlines.

Mr. Lederer said that there had been 25,000,000 airline flights in the twelve years. Collision fatalities involving commercial planes occurred in one of 3,500,000 flights, he said.

The death toll this year in scheduled commercial airline accidents, including yesterday's crash, came to 336 passengers and forty-two crew members, compared with 257 passengers and thirty-seven crew members in 1959. The disaster yesterday broke the record for fatalities that was s^t in 1959.

Added to the similarities of the New York and Grand Canyon disasters was the almost exact number of deaths. In the accident here 127 persons aboard the planes lost their lives; in the 1956 collision, 128.

Altogether, in the twelve years, there have been twenty collisions in the air. Those involving airliners and other craft killed forty-three persons, while collisions of private planes and collisions of military planes.

That yesterday's accident occurred over populated areas recalled the series of three airline crashes at Elizabeth, N. J., between Dec. 16, 1951, and Feb. 11, 1952. It also recalled the crash of an Army Air Forces B-25 bomber into the Empire State Building in 1945.

Among the other coincidences in yesterday's crash was that it

Cabinet Aide Died

came on the ninth anniversary of the first Elizabeth crash.

On Nov. 24, 1959, a four-engine T. W. A. Constellation cargo plane crashed in the pre-dawn dark, near Midway Airport, Chicago. The three-member crew was killed, together with eight residents of the area.

Another crash over a populated area occurred on April 5, 1952. A twin-engined C-46 Commando cargo plane went down in a rainstorm in Jamaica, Queens.

The two crew members were killed, together with two men in their homes and a police inspector in his car. In the crash and resultant fire, five homes were destroyed and twenty-two automobiles damaged, ten of them demolished.

The New Jersey crashes involved three passenger planes taking off or approaching Newark Airport for landings. The total death toll came to 116 persons, including ten persons killed in their homes by the planes.

The first Elizabeth crash killed all fifty-six passengers and crew members of a Curtis C-46 Commando taking off for Florida. The twin-engined, nonscheduled airliner, operated by Miami Air Line, Inc., went down in the city's midtown area.

In the second crash, among the twenty-nine passengers and crew members who died were Robert P. Patterson, former Secretary of War. Also among the dead were six persons in three houses hit by the American Airlines Convair descending in thick fog and rain.

In the third crash, which led to the temporary closing of Newark Airport, twenty-seven passengers and crew members of a National Airlines plane were killed, together with four tenants of a three-story apartment struck by the craft. Forty-three persons, mostly passengers, were injured.

The Army burned the fog-swathed Empire State Building on July 28, 1945. Its three-member crew was killed, together with two men and eight women.

The plane hit the 102-story building at the seventy-ninth floor, where the civilians who were killed had been working for the War Relief Services of the National Catholic Welfare Conference.

The year 1960 got off to a grim start. On Jan. 6, a National Airlines DC-6B disintegrated in flight over Bolivia, N. C., with a death toll of thirty-four, including five crew members. On Jan. 18, a Capital Airlines Viscount crashed and burned in a swampy ravine at Holdcroft, Va., with a loss of fifty lives.

Exploded in Flight

Other major air accidents this year included the deaths of sixty-three persons on March 17 when a Northwest Orient Airlines Lockheed Electra turbo-prop plane exploded in flight over Tell City, Ind., and the deaths of sixty-two passengers on Oct. 4 when an Eastern Airlines Electra crashed into Boston Harbor soon after take-off.

On Oct. 25, a Northeast Airlines DC-6 crashed in flames near Frenchtown, Mont., with a loss of twelve passengers and crew members. Seventeen Americans were among thirty-seven passengers and crew members killed when an Aviance Colombian National Airline's Super Constellation crashed into Montego Bay, Jamaica, on Jan. 21.

On Oct. 29, sixteen members of the California Polytechnic College football team were among twenty-two fatalities when a chartered C-46 plane crashed at Toledo, Ohio. Twenty-five other passengers and crew members survived.

Sixty-five persons died last year when an American Airlines Lockheed Electra crashed into the East River on an approach to a landing at La Guardia Airport on Feb. 3.

On June 26, 1959, thirty-four Americans were among the sixty-eight persons killing when a T. W. A. Constellation crashed in a thunderstorm near Milan, Italy. The plane had just taken off for Chicago by way of Rome on a flight from Athens, Greece.

Viscount Crashed

On May 12, a Capital Airlines Viscount crashed near Baltimore, killing twenty-seven passengers and four crewmen. The plane was believed to have been struck by lightning.

On Sept. 29, 1959, twenty-seven passengers and six crew members were killed when a Braniff Airways Lockheed Electra turbo-prop plane exploded in midair over Buffalo, Texas.

One of the worst crashes last year occurred on Nov. 16 when a National Airlines DC-7B disintegrated over the Gulf of Mexico, killing fifty-nine passengers and five crewmen. Senator A.S. (Mike) Monroney, Democrat of Oklahoma, who headed an investigation committee, declared that a bomb had been exploded in the craft. Robert V. Spears, a 45-year-old Dallas "naturopath," or nonmedical healer, whose name listed on the passenger manifest, had induced a crony and former prison-mate to take his place on the plane. Regarded as a "mystery man" in the explosion, was sentenced to two five-year prison terms for auto theft and performing an abortion.

Phone Lines Jammed For Hour After Crash

Telephone lines to Staten Island and the Brooklyn crash area were jammed for almost an hour following the air disaster yesterday. Calls were delayed several minutes during the period.

The New York Telephone Company said there was a wide effect on telephone service in the city. Callers unable to get connections or dial tones dialed "operator." The operators, in turn, became so busy trying to help that their own lines became overloaded.

Long-distance lines to Columbus. O., and Chicago, from which the planes came, also were overloaded.

Service was restored to normal before noon.

PILOTS LAUD ORDER FOR COCKPIT TAPES

WASHINGTON, Dec. 16 (UPI)—The nation's airline pilots today applauded a new Government order requiring voice recorders in the cockpits of all airliners to catch the last conversations on planes that crash. They called for recorders in the passenger compartments also.

C. N. Sayen, president of the Airline Pilots Association, urged that indestructible recorders should be "strategically located" in the passenger cabins to pick up "valuable information" for determining the cause of airline disasters.

Mr. Sayen made the proposal in a statement issued an the House aeronautics subcommittee.

F. A. A. Chief E. R. Quesada disclosed at a subcommittee hearing Wednesday that his agency had ordered airliners to install indestructible voice recorders in their cockpits.

These devices would be designed to retain only the last few moments of conversations, to avoid any charge of infringement on any pilots' privacy. Mr. Quesada said the recorders would help the F. A. A. determine the cause of airline crashes.

But those are the facts, and they should keep the public crashes. Mr. Sayen urged the importance of fear that such tragedies are likely to be repeated.

dimensional radar that will show altitude as well as position over the ground. Work is also under way on cockpit devices that will automatically alert pilots to impending collisions. But there is much less optimism about perfecting such devices than about most of the other desired equipment.

It is meager comfort to say that yesterday's disaster was the first of its kind and that the control system—despite excessive burdens on controllers and a still too-high danger of collision—appears to be essentially a good one and promises to become an excellent one.

But what about radar? The radar controller in the tower at New York International directs only planes destined to land there. The same goes for the controller in the LaGuardia tower.

Of course, each radar should show them the blips not only of the planes for which they are responsible, but also those headed for the neighboring airport. But what if the radar acted up at a critical moment?

Ultimately, once the plane is squared away for a straight-in approach to the landing strip, control is turned over by the tower radar room to another tower man who watches the plane come into actual view.

No system devised by man can be perfect. No one would have claimed, even before yesterday, that the traffic-control system was the best man could devise.

But it is far ahead of what it was two or three years ago. And an energetic modernization program is beginning to gain impressive momentum.

The big trouble is that modernization started late—very late. As postwar traffic soared, as aircraft speeds also soared, planning to take care of the new volume and speed was woefully inadequate.

Emergency Study Made

It was not until late 1954 or early 1955 that the nation began to face up to the immensity of the collision hazard—as it already existed, and as it promised to grow with the rapid maturing of the jet age.

A Presidential committee made an emergency assessment of the situation. Its alarmed report reflected a study of the airline industry that contended there were four near-collisions involving airliners every day.

The proposed budget for traffic control submitted early in 1956 showed a jump from about $5,000,000 the previous year to about $40,000,000. After the Grand Canyon collision, Congress jumped the outlay to $75,000,000 for the fiscal year ended June 30, 1957.

A new Presidential commitment was out to devise a thorough short-range and long-range plan for modernizing the entire traffic-control system. This report led to the creation of the Federal Aviation Agency and to the prompt initiation of the ambitious modernization program now well under way.

The old system, in use since the days of the DC-3, worked on the most pessimistic assumption. He will take action if blips at unknown altitudes made in flight plans and positions.

More and more planes—eventually all airliners—will be handled by the control system, in good weather and bad. Engineers have developed the computers and other automation devices that will start being installed in significant numbers in two of three years. These will relieve controllers of clerical work and let them concentrate on the main job of making decisions.

Work is under way on three-

Specifications on the Two Planes in Crash Are Listed

A United Air Lines DC-8 Jet Mainliner of the kind that crashed yesterday in Brooklyn

A Trans World Airlines Super Constellation like the one that fell in Staten Island
Associated Press

The aircraft in yesterday's crash represent two of the nation's biggest propeller and jet planes.

The United Air Lines DC-8 Jet Mainliner is a product of the Douglas Aircraft Company. It can carry 113 passengers—sixty first-class and fifty-three coach. The plane, which costs about $5,000,000, is 150 feet, 6 inches long and slightly over 42 feet high. It has a wingspan of 142 feet, 5 inches and can carry 12,000 pounds of cargo.

The plane is powered by four Pratt & Whitney J-57 or J-75 engines. According to United, these models have accumulated about 3,000,000 hours of flying time. Each J-57 delivers a maximum thrust of 13,000 pounds and the J-75 delivers 15,000 pounds for the J-75.

The DC-8's maximum take-

off weight with J-57 is 270,000 pounds; with J-75 it is 281,000 pounds. The cruising air speed is 516 to 591 miles an hour. The plane's fuel capacity is 17,600 gallons and its range is 2,340 to 3,710 miles.

Douglas Aircraft announced plans to build the DC-8 in June, 1955. Four months later, according to a spokesman for United, that airline became the first in this country to make a firm commitment to buy the jet aircraft. The company ordered thirty DC-8's at first and increased the order to forty in November, 1957.

The first DC-8 came off the production line on April 9, 1958, and made its first flight on May 30, 1958. The first of United's forty DC-8's left the factory in August, 1958, and entered an intensive test program. The DC-8 received a

type certificate from the Federal Aviation Agency Aug. 31, 1959.

Trans World Airline's Super Constellation is a Lockheed model 1049A and has been in operation by T. W. A. since September, 1952. Its length is 113 feet, 7 inches and its wingspread is 123 feet. Its gross take-off weight is sixty-tons and it can carry a payload of 23,750 pounds.

The Super Constellation seats sixty-four persons during daytime flights. At night it accommodates forty-eight in seats plus eight upper and lower berths. A luxury lounge in the rear seats seven.

Powered by four Curtiss-Wright C1A-2 engines, each having 2,700 horsepower, it has a cruising speed of 318 miles an hour. It can cruise at 20,000 feet with a full payload for 3,250 miles, nonstop.

"All the News That's Fit to Print"

The New York Times.

LATE CITY EDITION
U. S. Weather Bureau Report (Page 6) forecasts Mostly fair today and tonight. Chance of rain tomorrow.
Temp. range: 41—30; yesterday: 44—36.

VOL. CX....No. 37,644. © 1961 by The New York Times Company. Times Square, New York 36, N. Y. NEW YORK, THURSDAY, FEBRUARY 16, 1961. 10 cents beyond 50-mile zone from New York City except on Long Island. Higher in air delivery cities. FIVE CENTS

KENNEDY WARNS OF RISKS OF WAR IN A UNILATERAL ACTION IN CONGO; HAMMARSKJOLD FIRM; RIOT IN U.N.

VIOLENCE AT U. N.: United Nations guards battle with demonstrators in gallery of Security Council chamber

Associated Press

18 U.S. SKATERS AMONG 73 DEAD IN A JET CRASH

BELGIAN DISASTER

All Lost When Plane Falls at Brussels—49 Americans

By HARRY GILROY
Special to The New York Times.

BRUSSELS, Belgium, Feb. 15—A Sabena Airlines Boeing 707 jet crashed near the Brussels Airport early today, killing seventy-three persons, including the eighteen members of the United States figure-skating team.

The plane, en route from New York, plunged to earth after it had twice circled the airport. The dead included the sixty-one passengers, the crew of eleven, and a farmer in the field where the plane fell.

The passengers included forty-nine Americans, a Swiss, a Frenchman, a German, a Canadian, a Nicaraguan and seven Belgians.

The American figure-skating team was on its way to a world championship meet in Prague. Its members included Mrs. Maribel Vinson Owen, 49 years old, of Winchester, Mass., and her two daughters, both of them champions. Mrs. Owen was the United States figure-skating champion nine times. On the current trip she was the coach for her daughters.

Worst Sabena Crash

The crash was the worst ever suffered by Sabena. It also marked the first time any passengers had been killed in a Boeing 707 accident. The last serious Sabena crash occurred May 18, 1958, when a DC-7C crashed at Casablanca, killing fifty-six passengers and nine crew members.

The four-engine jet came in sight of the control tower shortly before 10 A. M. in a cloudless sky. The plane, which had left New York at 7:30 P. M. yesterday, would have landed at once except that another plane was moving along the runway to take off, an airport official said.

Persons in the little farming hamlet of Berg, northeast of Brussels, saw the airliner circling overhead at an altitude of about 600 feet. Officials at the control tower were also watching the plane with field glasses.

Suddenly the plane fell. An airport official placed the time at 10:05 A. M.

Plane Strikes Farmer

The plane came down at a 70 degree angle onto a small farm field. It plunged into a grove of trees, narrowly missing three houses. It struck Theo de Laet, a young farmer noted as an amateur cyclist, killing him. A piece of debris tore a leg off another farmer, Marcel Lauwers.

Parts of the plane were thrown 200 yards but the bulk of the airliner burst into flames, preventing anyone from approaching until firemen arrived from the airport.

William de Swarte, director general of Sabena, said tonight that "something must have gone wrong with the controls of the plane." He said the plane

Continued on Page 18, Column 1

U. S. Backs 3d Loan For New Haven Line

By ROBERT E. BEDINGFIELD

The New York, New Haven and Hartford Railroad will be able to meet its $1,560,000 payroll tomorrow, thanks to another lifeline tossed to it by the Federal Government.

The Interstate Commerce Commission agreed yesterday to guarantee a $3,500,000 unsecured bank loan that the carrier said it needed to meet immediate obligations and avert bankruptcy. The railroad had asked for a guarantee of a $5,000,000 loan, but the commission scaled down the amount.

The New Haven is obtaining the loan from a group of banks headed by the Chase Manhattan. The loan carries a 5 per cent interest rate and matures Nov. 3. The Interstate Commerce Commission has guaranteed payment of both interest and principal to the lenders under the

Continued on Page 34, Column 2

Meany Denounces Foes of Wage Rise

By A. H. RASKIN
Special to The New York Times.

BAL HARBOUR, Fla., Feb. 15—George Meany called today for higher wages as the key to national prosperity and economic growth.

The president of the American Federation of Labor and Congress of Industrial Organizations derided arguments that wage increases had been responsible for pricing United States goods out of world markets.

His talk at a luncheon of the federation's Maritime Trades Department in the Americana Hotel was an indirect reply to moves by some White House advisers to put the brakes on wage increases as a means of spurring recovery and combating competition.

Mr. Meany took specific exception to a suggestion by Sen-

Continued on Page 21, Column 2

GEROSA PREDICTS NO NEW TAXATION

Says General Fund Will Be 872 Million—Criticizes Mayor on Estimating

By CHARLES G. BENNETT

Controller Lawrence E. Gerosa estimated yesterday that the city's general fund would reach a record total of $872,636,000 for the fiscal year beginning next July 1. This, he said, "indicates there will be no need for new taxes of any kind."

At the same time, Mr. Gerosa criticized a proposal by Mayor Wagner that the Mayor's office take over the estimation of general fund receipts. A "spending Mayor," the Controller said, "could have one of his subordinates tailor-make the estimate to fit his spending needs."

The general fund consists of miscellaneous revenues—largely the proceeds from licenses, permits, water charges and excise taxes—including the 3 per cent retail sales tax. Other sources of revenue are the real estate tax and money received from the state and Federal Governments.

Mr. Gerosa also reported that business in New York City in 1960 "appeared to run against the nation-wide tide of economic contraction." He made a guarded prediction that the city's prosperity would continue.

The Controller's prediction on the general fund forecaw a cash carry-over of $67,560,000 from 1960-61, plus funds withdrawn from the stabilization reserve. Mr. Gerosa forecast that

Continued on Page 25, Column 1

PRESIDENT CALLS SPEED ESSENTIAL TO COMBAT SLUMP

Renews Plea to Congress—Says 'Recession' Is Right Word for Business Lag

By RICHARD E. MOONEY
Special to The New York Times.

WASHINGTON, Feb. 15—President Kennedy said tonight that anyone who considered all the available evidence would agree that "it is necessary to take action" to combat the recession.

He spoke, at his news conference, in reply to a Republican charge that he had overstated the nation's economic problems for political reasons. [Question 12, Page 16.]

He defended the use of the word "recession" to describe the present situation, and called once again for quick Congressional action on his economic proposals—unemployment compensation, aid to depressed areas and other measures.

He also announced two lesser stimulating actions that will be taken under existing authority—a speed-up in post office construction and a liberalization of the criteria for awarding defense contracts to small businesses.

Cites '58 Recession

The President said he saw "no necessity or desirability of minimizing our problems." There has been a recession for "some months," and the difficulty is compounded by the fact that the country never fully recovered from the 1958 recession, he said.

He called for the cooperation of the leaders of both parties in Congress. And he took exception to the view of the Senate Republican leader, Everett McKinley Dirksen of Illinois, that the State of the Union message had had no more impact than "a snowflake falling on the bosom of the Potomac."

In his opening statement at the news conference, Mr. Kennedy reviewed all the economic actions taken by his Administration, and all the proposals it had made.

Wants Action 'This Winter'

"This country is most concerned about the very serious problem of unemployment which we have faced this winter," he stated. He said he was hopeful "that we can move forward this winter so that some relief can be given to our fellow Americans."

Mr. Kennedy cited five statistics to underscore his belief that "it is necessary to take action"—inventories of 1,000,000 unsold new automobiles, more than 5,500,000 unemployed workers, 600,000 of this jobless group who have exhausted their unemployment-benefit rights, slack operations in the steel industry and a decline in over-all business activity since the middle of last year.

"I hope we can get action as soon as possible," he said. "We want to see the American economy get back on its feet."

The President also said tonight that his Administration

Continued on Page 17, Column 2

Khrushchev Urges 'Strict' Arms Curbs In Wire to Kennedy

By SEYMOUR TOPPING
Special to The New York Times.

MOSCOW, Feb. 15—Premier Khrushchev told President Kennedy today that any disarmament agreement should include "strict international control."

The Soviet leader urged a speedy solution of the disarmament problem in a telegram acknowledging the congratulations extended by the President on the launching of the Soviet Venus rocket.

Noting that Mr. Kennedy, in his inaugural address, had proposed a pooling of efforts in the struggle against disease, the conquest of space and the development of culture and trade, Mr. Khrushchev said:

"We consider that the solution of the disarmament problem would provide conditions favoring the earliest realization of these noble tasks before mankind. And we would like every country to exert every effort for the solution of this problem with the establishment of such strict international controls that no one could arm in secret and commit aggression."

Mr. Khrushchev also said:

"All are in agreement that the solution of the disarmament problem depends to a great extent on the agreement

Continued on Page 6, Column 1

RIOT IN GALLERY HALTS U.N. DEBATE

American Negroes Ejected After Invading Session—Midtown March Balked

More than two dozen persons were injured yesterday when a group made up mostly of American Negroes set off the most violent demonstration inside United Nations headquarters in the world organization's history.

About sixty men and women burst into the Security Council chamber, interrupting the session, and fought with guards in a protest against United Nations policies in the Congo and the slaying of Patrice Lumumba, former Congo Premier.

Last night, 200 demonstrators virtually took over the north side of Forty-second Street in a march from First Avenue westward across Manhattan, chanting "Congo, yes! Yankee, no!"

When they refused to abandon an advance toward Times Square, mounted policemen charged the demonstrators at Sixth Avenue and Forty-third Street and dispersed them.

Groups Anti-Colonialist

The demonstrators inside the Security Council chamber included members of the United African Nationalist Movement, the Liberation Committee for Africa and On Guard, groups apparently of nationalist and anti-colonialist hue.

The public was excluded for the rest of the day and will be barred again today.

Later, picketing outside the United Nations on First Avenue at Forty-third Street appeared

Continued on Page 10, Column 2

Reds Virtually Lift Berlin Entry Curbs

Special to The New York Times.

BERLIN, Feb. 15—East Germany announced today a virtual lifting of restrictions on the entry of West Germans into East Berlin.

The announcement, from Communist police headquarters, said that effective at midnight tonight it would "simplify and ease" the regulations under which West Germans have been required since last fall to obtain special permits to enter East Berlin.

High-ranking sources in West Berlin said the Communists in effect had agreed to lift their ban under the impact of West German threats to take sharp measures of reprisal. These sources said the East German announcement was phrased so as to allow the Communists to "save face."

Dr. Kurt Leopold, West Ger-

Continued on Page 2, Column 7

ON FATAL FLIGHT: Members of U. S. figure-skating team at Idlewild Tuesday before departure for Brussels. Front row, from left: Deane McMinn, coach; Laurence Owen, Stephanie Westerfield and Rhode Michelson. Others, bottom to top, from left: Douglas Ramsey, Gregory Kelley, Bradley Lord, Maribel Owen, Dudley S. Richards, William H. Hickox, Ray Hadley, Laurice Hickox, Dallas Pierce, Ila Hadley, Roger Campbell, Diane Sherbloom, Donna Lee Carrier, Robert Dineen and Patricia Dineen. Plane was Sabena jet.

Associated Press

U. N. Chief Tells Russians He Won't Be Forced Out

By LINDESAY PARROTT
Special to The New York Times.

UNITED NATIONS, N. Y., Feb. 15—Secretary General Dag Hammarskjold told the Soviet Union today that he would not be driven out of his post. His resignation and the substitution of a three-man committee for the office of Secretary General, which have been demanded by the Russians, would destroy the world organization at its most critical moment, he said.

Statements at U. N. on Congo are on Pages 12 and 13.

The Swedish diplomat told the Security Council that he meant to stay on as long as the organization needed him.

The Council's debate on the Congo crisis was interrupted by what officials here called the worst outbreak it ever has witnessed. Shortly before noon, as the new United States representative, Adlai E. Stevenson, was making his first major address to a United Nations body, thirty or more demonstrators started a minor riot in the spectators' gallery.

Lumumba Death Protested

The demonstrators, many of them Negroes, were protesting the murder of Patrice Lumumba, the deposed Congolese Premier.

The day's debate in the Council seemed to indicate that, despite friendly gestures by the new United States Administration and by the Kremlin, the American and Soviet delegations were as far apart as ever on the crucial questions of the Congo and of the "cold war."

The discussion of the Congo situation was adjourned just before 7 tonight and will be resumed at 11 A. M. tomorrow.

Mr. Stevenson said that a statement issued last night in Moscow and a draft resolution laid before the Council today by Valerian A. Zorin, the chief Soviet delegate, constituted a "declaration of war" on the United Nations. The resolution would call for an end of United Nations operations in the Congo within a month. The Soviet Union, in its Moscow statement, also declared its non-recognition of Mr. Hammarskjold as Secretary General.

Mr. Hammarskjold, defending his record in carrying on United Nations operations in the Congo, said he had done his

Continued on Page 10, Column 1

NEWS INDEX

	Page		Page
Books	29-29	Music	24-26
Bridge	28	Obituaries	31
Business	42-43	Real Estate	51-52
Buyers	42	Screen	24-26
Crossword	29	Ships and Air	61
Editorial	30	Society	36
Events Today	29	Sports	38-41
Fashions	35-36	TV and Radio	62-63
Financial	43-51	Theatres	24-26
Food	35-36	U. N. Proceedings	11
Letters	30	Wash. Proceedings	19
Man in the News	5	Weather	61

News Summary and Index, Page 33

POLISH MOB SACKS BELGIAN EMBASSY

Rioters Assault Diplomats in Protest on Lumumba—Files Are Burned

By ARTHUR J. OLSEN
Special to The New York Times.

WARSAW, Feb. 15—A mob of young Poles, protesting the death of Patrice Lumumba, sacked the Belgian Embassy today and assaulted diplomats who tried to defend it.

The demonstrators fed a bonfire on the street outside the four-story building with papers and files thrown from the embassy windows.

Bricks and cobblestones shattered virtually every window in the building, which also houses the Netherlands Embassy. Furniture was broken and marred with crimson dye.

At the end of the twenty-minute foray, the four Belgian diplomats and local employes of the embassy were crimson stained with dye and shaken but uninjured.

Second Attack on Building

The mid-afternoon assault was the second "spontaneous" demonstration against Belgium in eighteen hours. Last night a mob of nearly 1,000, mostly youngsters from Warsaw Polytechnic Institute, hurled stones at the embassy building and shouted and orated against the "murderers" of Mr. Lumumba.

The Polish Government was actively encouraging today the spirit of indignation over the death of the Congolese politician. Premier Jozef Cyrankiewicz sent a telegram of condolence to Antoine Gizenga, whom he addressed as Vice Premier of the Congolese Government.

The President of the Sejm (Parliament) denounced the slaying. Polish members of the Interparliamentary Union issued a statement of protest. The official press excoriated "colonialists" and "imperialists" in vengeful terms.

About fifty riot policemen were on duty at the Belgian Embassy in a residential section of Warsaw when the crowd began forming at 1:30 P. M. Witnesses said that most of the protestors arrived in buses. A

Continued on Page 11, Column 3

New! Whipped butter in bars. Hotel Bar WHIPSTIX. Smoothest, tastiest.—Advt.

ALLIES IN ACCORD

Strong Stand Backed as West Appraises Soviet Position

Transcript of news conference and summary, Page 16.

By W. H. LAWRENCE
Special to The New York Times.

WASHINGTON, Feb. 15—President Kennedy pledged tonight that the United States would defend the Charter of the United Nations by opposing any attempt by any Government to intervene unilaterally in the Congo.

The President declared at a nationally televised news conference that massive, unilateral intervention by any country would bring with it "risks of war."

He did not mention the Soviet Union, but it was obvious his statement was directed to the Soviet leadership in the light of its newest attack on the United Nations operation in the Congo and on Secretary General Dag Hammarskjold.

President Kennedy spoke in cautious diplomatic language, but a solemn and careful appraisal of the situation was made here with the principal Western allies before he spoke.

Decision Is Reached

This produced agreement that a strong position was necessary and strategically possible since the Western allies are closer to the Congo than the Soviet Union. Accordingly a decision was reached to speak out at once in the hope of deterring the Soviet Union from intervening unilaterally.

The President declared he was "seriously concerned at what appears to be a threat of unilateral intervention in the internal affairs of the Republic of the Congo."

"I find it difficult to believe," he added, "that any Government is really planning to take so dangerous and irresponsible a step."

Then he made clear his intention to defend the United Nations authority in the Congo and his belief that the only legitimate government for that country was that of President Joseph Kasavubu.

Nehru's Stand Endorsed

President Kennedy declared his strong agreement with India's Prime Minister Jawaharlal Nehru, that it would be "a disaster" if the United Nations left the Congo.

The overriding concern of the half-hour news conference, held in the auditorium of the new State Department building, was the deepening crisis in the Congo and the threat posed to the United Nations by yesterday's declaration by the Soviet Union that it no longer would recognize Mr. Hammarskjold or the Kasavubu Government with which the United Nations has been dealing.

President Kennedy discussed the Congo with a carefully drafted statement he read be-

Continued on Page 10, Column 8

Nehru Offering U.N. Congo Combat Force

Special to The New York Times.

NEW DELHI, India, Feb. 15—India has offered to send "combat" troops to assist the United Nations command in the Congo.

Prime Minister Jawaharlal Nehru told Parliament today that the offer had been made in response to a request from the world body some weeks ago. He said a reply had been sent saying that India believed the United Nations should continue to function in the Congo, but that it should be made more effective.

If that could be done, Mr. Nehru said, "we would get over our reluctance and help the United Nations even by sending some combat troops." India now has some troops in the Congo. She has described these as noncombatant personnel.

Mr. Nehru said the reply had

Continued on Page 11, Column 6

Crash in Belgium Kills 73, 18 on Figure-Skating Team

ALL ON PLANE DIE; 49 ARE AMERICANS

Craft Falls Near Brussels After Atlantic Flight— Hits Man on Ground

Continued From Page 1, Col. 1

had recently been through a complete test.

He said that an international convention reached at Chicago provided that in cases of accidents on international airlines the country in which the crash occured could not proceed alone with the inquiry.

M. de Swarte said the plane had been in radio contact with the Brussels Airport from the time it crossed the Belgian coast, a few minutes before its scheduled arrival time of 9:50 A. M.

The pilot, Capt. Louis Lambrechts, indicated by radio that everything was operating perfectly. There was nothing to indicate that anything was wrong as the plane began to circle the airfield, although the pilot no longer spoke to the tower.

A farmer named Verhoeven said he had watched the plane "try to land twice and then go up again." He thought it possible that photographs were being taken from the plane because it was such a beautiful day.

Premier Gaston Eyskens and other members of the Cabinet visited the disaster scene this morning. M. Eyskens said the Government was "deeply disturbed by this new tragedy in Belgium and extends its sympathy to all who are bereft."

The lower house of Parliament observed a minute of silence for the victims at the start of its daily session.

King Visits Crash Scene

King Baudouin and Queen Fabiola visited the crash scene this afternoon. The King talked with salvage workers as they dug into the wreckage and uncovered bodies. He and the Queen visited the family of the dead farmer and went to the hospital where the injured man is in serious condition.

A woman who saw the crash told King Baudouin that she was convinced that the pilot had deliberately come down at a steep angle to avoid crashing into a row of houses in the center of Berg.

Observers at the airport said it seemed probable that controls on one side of the plane had failed to function.

The fact that a Boeing was involved in the crash added to the distress felt in this country because these planes won the personal regard of the Belgians during the airlift of Belgian refugees from the Congo last summer. During the period from July 9 through July 28 the five Sabena Boeings, including the one that crashed today, made sixty-two round-trip flights between Belgium and Africa.

Sabena recently announced that the five Boeing planes had transported in one year 139,900 passengers, 2,500 tons of freight and mail and had covered more than 6,000,000 miles.

KENNEDY IN TRIBUTE TO VICTIMS OF CRASH

President and Mrs. Kennedy led the nation in mourning the deaths of the eighteen members of a United States figure-skating team in an airplane crash at Brussels, Belgium.

Extending sympathy to the families and friends of the athletes yesterday, the nation's

Associated Press Radiophoto

NO SURVIVORS: Wreckage of the Sabena jet airliner is scattered over a field near Brussels airport after plane crashed in attempt to land. The 73 passengers, including the 18-member U. S. figure-skating team, were killed.

U. S. GROUP URGES TITLE MEET GO ON

Skating Official Estimates Plane Disaster Set Back Sport Here 2 to 4 Years

Despite the sudden and tragic loss of the entire United States team in the crash of a Sabena airliner, the United States Figure Skating Association asked yesterday that the world championships, at Prague, Czechoslovakia, be held on schedule.

There were conflicting reports about the question of cancellation. When reports of the crash reached F. Ritter Shumway of Rochester, vice president of the skating organization, he immediately cabled a request to Dr. Jacob Koch, president of the International Skating Union, that he "carry on." Earlier, a dispatch from Europe had said that the championships would be canceled.

"We appreciated the tribute to our skaters," explained Mr. Ritter, the top ranking United States skating official since the recent death of Hobart Herbert, former president of the United States Association. "But we thought the competition should continue as the skaters, I know, would want it that way. Accordingly I cabled Dr. Koch."

Cancellation Is Urged

In Geneva, Dr. Koch called for a cancellation of the championships. However, the Czechslovak association was in favoring of carrying on and the question was put to a vote of the executive committee.

A United Press International dispatch from Davos, Switzerland, quoted George Haelser, secretary general of the International Skating Union as having said that the championships "will be canceled." However, a Reuters report from Prague stated "the championships will go ahead as scheduled."

Mr. Ritter asserted the "personal tragedy" of the crash had "overwhelmed him."

He said he believed that the United States would require "two to four years" to recover its international competitive strength in this sport.

Three of the first five finishers in the United States men's championships two weeks ago in Colorado Springs were on the plane. They were Bradley Lord of Boston, who finished first, Greg Kelley of Colorado Springs, second, and Doug Ramsey of Detroit, fourth.

The third-place finisher, Tim Brown of Berkeley, Calif., and 16-year-old Bruce Heiss of Ozone Park, Queens, who finished fifth, were not named to the team for the Prague event.

Laurence Owen, Stephanie Westerfield and Rohe Michelson, who placed one, two, three, respectively, the United States

The New York Times   Feb. 16, 1961.

TRAGEDY IN BELGIUM: The airliner crashed near Brussels' airport (cross).

women's singles, also were aboard the plane. Miss Owen won the women's title in the North American championships Sunday in Philadelphia.

A 6 to 10 Year Task

"Skating has received an incalculable setback", asserted Pierre Brunet, coach of the Olympic champion, Mrs. Carol Heiss Jenkins, who is now a professional. Mr. Brunet planned to leave on Friday for Prague as the tutor of Donald Jackson, the Canadian who won the North American championship.

In Mr. Brunet's view the future of figure skating in the United States depends on the development of 14 and 15 year olds.

Mr. Brown is studying medicine and Bruce Heiss will be starting college in the fall. That means they will be unable to devote as much time to skating.

"To become an expert skater," Mr. Brunet said, "takes from six to ten years, depending on the individual. You have to practice three hours daily, summer or winter, if you want to climb to the top."

One of the requisites is the ability to trace on ice what are

known as "school figures." They have a value of approximately 60 per cent when tabulations are made in deciding a championship.

The other phase of the test consists of "free skating," which is skated to music. This can have spectacular and artistic overtones, depending upon the competitor.

"There are ninety-six school figures that have to be skated by the time you reach senior competition," explained Mr. Brunet. "They are skated on both the right and left foot and are done forward and then backward."

Mr. Brunet said that it was possible that Nancy Heiss, Mrs. Jenkins' sister, might return to competition. Miss Heiss, who is 18 years old, is a sophomore at Michigan State. She has been out of major competition for two seasons since breaking a bone in her foot.

Top Prospect Retired

Two weeks ago, Miss Heiss gave an exhibition of free skating at the Dartmouth winter carnival in Hanover, N. H. Nancy Heiss finished second to her sister in the 1959 United States championship.

Mrs. Barbara Ann Pursley, the former Barbara Ann Roles of Los Angeles, who finished third in the 1960 Olympics, has retired from skating competitions. She could be a leading prospect in the women's ranks, according to Mrs. Howard Meredith, official and skating judge for more than twenty years. However, Mrs. Meredith thinks the real hope for the sport depends on how quickly the youngsters can mature.

Loraine Hanlon, a 15-year-old Boston girl, and recent winner of the national junior title; Carol Noir, 14, of West Orange, N. J., holder of the Eastern senior title; Tina Noyes, 12, of Boston, national novice champion, and Joya Utermohlin, 14, of New York, Eastern junior champion, were listed as likely prospects by Mrs. Meredith.

Chief Executive said in a message issued from the White House:

"I was distressed and saddened to learn of the airline crash in Brussels this morning.

"This disaster has brought tragedy to many American families and is a painful loss to the international community of sports as well.

"Our country," the President's message continue, "has sustained a great loss of talent and grace which had brought pleasure to people all over the world.

"Mrs. Kennedy and I extend our deepest sympathy to the families and friends of all the passengers and crew who died in this crash."

J. Lyman Bingham, executive director of the United States Olympic Committee, said of the athletes who perished:

"The U. S. Olympic Committee is greatly shocked by this tragedy. They were many fine people who were on the threshold of brilliant careers, not only in their chosen sport, but as useful and representative American citizens."

Associated Press

KILLED IN SABENA CRASH: Mrs. Maribel Vinson Owen, the former figure-skating champion, practicing with her daughters last week in Boston before North American championships at Philadelphia. At left is Laurence, 16. At right is Maribel, 20. Both were national champions. The girls and their mother were en route to the world championship in Prague when they and the rest of U. S. team were killed in jet crash near Brussels.

Toll of Athletes High in Planes; 16 Collegians Died in '60 Crash

Members of California Polytechnic Football Team Killed en Route Home—Soccer Hard Hit

The crash of the Belgian jet that killed the eighteen members of the United States figure-skating team yesterday was the second air tragedy in four months to affect American athletes.

On Oct. 29 a chartered plane crashed and burned in an attempted take-off from the Toledo airport. Members of the California State Polytechnic College football team were aboard and sixteen of them were among the twenty-two passengers killed. They were on the way home to San Luis Obispo from a game with Bowling Green College of Ohio.

European soccer has suffered by far the worst losses in air travel. The latest tragedy occurred last July 16, when a chartered plane crashed at Copenhagen, killing eight of Denmark's leading players.

The first crash to strike at sports on a massive scale took place May 4, 1949, in the Italian Alps. The fourteen-man Italian national soccer squad, hailed as the greatest in Italy's history, was wiped out and twenty-eight persons in all were killed.

English Team Decimated

England's greatest soccer team, Manchester United, was decimated Feb. 6, 1958, when a British plane crashed after a take-off from Munich en route home. Seven players were among the twenty-one persons killed and other athletes were so badly injured they were unable to play again.

In 1950 thirteen Brazilian athletes died in a plane crash in their native land. In Czechoslovakia in 1956, six members of the Banik ice hockey team failed to survive an air tragedy.

The sports world felt the impact of an aviation disaster for the first time March 31, 1931, when Coach Knute Rockne of the Notre Dame University football team perished with seven others in Southeast Kansas. Rockne was considered one of the greatest of coaches.

Since the Manchester United crash there has been a movement among professional sports leagues in the United States to set up "disaster plans."

One Plan in Effect

One of these plans, designed to restock a club in the event of an air, train or bus disaster, has been put into effect already, but for a different reason. By utilizing this plan, the American League stocked two new baseball clubs this winter in expanding from eight teams to ten.

All the disaster plans are similar. A certain number of star players on a team are "protected" and the others are made available to a team that must be stocked or restocked.

Although major-league baseball has been first to make use of its plan—and probably will do so again next winter in stocking two new National League teams—the National Basketball Association was also among the earliest to adopt a disaster plan. It did so shortly after the Manchester United crash.

The National and American Football Leagues and the National Hockey League have made provisions to aid disaster-stricken members.

Related to accidents involving sports figures was the crash of a British plane March 12, 1950, at Cardiff, Wales. The tragedy took the lives of eighty soccer fans returning from a championship match in Dublin.

Mrs. Owens' Mother Is Sole Survivor of Skating Family

WINCHESTER, Mass., Feb. 15 (AP)—Mrs. Gertrude C. Vinson, 80-year-old sole survivor of the famous Vinson-Owen skating family, was near collapse today upon learning that her daughter and two granddaughters were among the seventy-three persons killed in a Belgian plane crash.

Killed were Laurence Owen, 16, North America's new figure-skating champion; her sister, Maribel, 20, also a skating champion, and their mother, Mrs. Maribel Vinson Owen, nine-time United States women's figure-skating champion.

The only member left of the family is Mrs. Owen's mother, Mrs. Vinson.

losing her balance on a double axel jump. She just excelled Wendy Griner, the Canadian champion, for the title.

They Skated as One

After the competition, Mrs. Owen, whose cheers for her daughter were audible, was asked if she felt as if she were in the rink with Laurence. "You bet," she said. "I skated every stroke with her."

Laurence, a senior at Winchester (Mass.) High School, had recently been accepted for study at Radcliffe College next year.

While her sister, Maribel, was not quite as polished a skater as Laurence, she teamed with Dudley Richards last month at Colorado Springs to win the national senior pairs championship. Maribel was a senior at Boston University.

Mrs. Owen married Guy R. Owen, a Canadian, in 1938. They were divorced in 1949. Mr. Owen died in 1952. They had skated as a pair for many years and later formed their own ice show. Mrs. Vinson is survived by her mother, Mrs. Gertrude C. Vinson.

CRASH IS LINE'S 2D FOR ATLANTIC RUN

Sabena's First, in 1946 in Newfoundland, Killed 27

The crash of a Sabena airliner in Brussels yesterday was the second fatal crash on the trans-Atlantic run for that airline in its fourteen years of service on the Atlantic route.

The first was on Sept. 18, 1946, when a DC-4 en route from Brussels crashed near Gander, Nfld., killing twenty-seven of the forty-four persons on board.

The crash yesterday was the sixth involving a United States-built jetliner and the second of these to take the lives of passengers. The other jet crash fatal to passengers was the collision of a United Air Lines DC-8 jet and a Trans World Airlines piston-engine Super Constellation last Dec. 16 over Staten Island.

That collision—the worst air accident in history—killed 134 persons, including six on the ground.

Sabena began jet service across the Atlantic a little more than a year ago, on Jan. 24, 1960. It abandoned piston-powered aircraft on the route last April. The airline has four remaining Boeing 707 Intercontinental jets.

Its schedules include daily service out of New York for Brussels and three flights a week from Montreal, of which two originate in Mexico City.

According to Sabena spokesmen here, the airline is the eighth largest international line, with routes into 109 cities in forty countries. It first began operations in 1919 and through 1960 had carried 8,684,373 passengers a total of 8,302,260,488 passenger miles.

3 Owens, All Star Skaters, Die

Mrs. Maribel Vinson Owen, who was killed with her two daughters in the crash of a Sabena airliner yesterday, was a tireless athlete whose exuberance won her a host of friends at ice rinks in many parts of the world, but her pride and joy were her daughters Laurence and Maribel.

Mrs. Owen's life was a full one, from the time she attained skating prominence with a third place in Olympic competition in 1932 behind Sonja Henie to her last coaching victory, when Laurence won the North American championship in Philadelphia last Sunday.

Figure skating was a labor of love for Mrs. Owen. A bold and daring skater, she was a master of school figures. When she began taking lessons there were some who doubted that she would ever be a top-flight skater. Since the day she made her skating debut on double runners in Cambridge, Mass., when she was 3 years old, she had accounted for numerous laurels here and abroad.

Junior Champion at 12

She won the national junior title when she was 12 and remained unbeaten in senior competition after winning the na-

Mother, Nine Times Champion, Rejoiced in Girls' Feats

tional crown—the first of nine—in New Haven at the age of 16. Her string of triumphs was interrupted in 1934, when she skated in Europe and did not defend her national title.

As a member of the United States Olympic team in 1928 she placed fourth in the international tests. That season she finished second to Miss Henie in the world championships. Mrs. Owen placed third in the 1932 Olympic Games and fifth in 1936. She was a close friend of Miss Henie.

She also scored in pairs, winning six national championships, two with the late Thornton Coolidge as a partner and four with George E. B. Hill of Boston. She also won the North American crown with Hill in 1935.

Mrs. Owen's father, the late Thomas M. Vinson, was a standout in the old American school of figure skating.

Slender, comely and graceful, Mrs. Owen once said that "nothing short of a decade can make a champion skater." She

was an all-around athlete. Aside from skating, she was an expert swimmer, tennis player and sculler.

She achieved fame as a coach and her protege, Tenley Albright, won the 1956 Olympic title at Cortina d'Ampezzo, Italy.

Daughter Her Succesor

Her greatest hope was centered on Laurence. It was under her mother's guidance that Laurence won the United States and North American championships. Laurence was the only American winner in the recent North American competition.

Mrs. Owen's job was coaching others in the exacting sport and devoting her free time to her daughters. Laurence placed sixth in the 1960 Winter Olympics at Squaw Valley, Calif.

Sports Illustrated said of Laurence recently: "Her free skating has an air, a style, an individuality which sets it apart from all the work done in recent years."

Many persons prominent in figure skating termed Laurence a carbon copy of her mother. Pretty and graceful, she had her mother's drive and ability. She appeared to be America's only hope for a medal winner in the 1964 Olympics.

In the North American championships, Laurence managed to win the free skating despite

Captain and Members of the Crew Who Perished in Jet Airliner Crash in Belgium

Louis Lambrechts, captain

Jean Eugene Roy, co-pilot

Jean Marie Kint, navigator

Jacqueline Trullemans

Associated Press

Jacqueline Rombaut

Plane Circled Brussels Airport, Then 'Fell in a Series of Spins'

Control Tower Official Says Sabena Jet 'Disintegrated'—Wreckage Is Hurled Over Wide Area by Tremendous Blast

BRUSSELS, Belgium, Feb. 15 (AP)—A nightmare occurred today in warm, bright sunshine —the blazing destruction of a Sabena Boeing 707 jet and seventy-three persons.

Villagers of Berg, four miles north of Brussels, thought something might be wrong as the huge airliner coming from the coast approached the Brussels Airport. The roar of its engines sounded odd and the flight pattern looked erratic.

The plane circled the field a time or two, lowered its undercarriage, retracted it, turned again and fell spinning to the ground.

The airliner was visible from the airport control tower.

"Suddenly the plane fell in a series of spins," an airport official said. "It literally disintegrated."

There was a tremendous explosion as the stricken airliner hit near a woods. Flaming, twisted wreckage spewed over a wide area. Seventy-two persons on the plane were killed. So was a farmer who had been tilling his cabbage patch.

Fire Trucks Alerted Early

A motorcycle policeman patrolling a near-by road sped to the scene.

Dozens of fire trucks and ambulances, their sirens screaming, converged on the wreckage. State police quickly threw a cordon around the area.

Even before the plane crashed, fire trucks had been alerted.

"We saw the crash coming," an airport officer said. "It looked as if the plane's controls had been lost completely."

"The fire trucks were actually on their way before the crash, he added. "They couldn't have been faster, but there was nothing they could do."

A physician found one passenger victim under a wing. Beside him were the dead farmer and a badly injured dog that had to be shot.

Near by was a farm laborer with one leg severed. The physician said the laborer's life had been saved by a rescuer who applied a tourniquet.

A state policeman said: "The heat was so intense I saw pieces of aluminum melting like butter."

A fire officer reported that before the flames could be controlled there was a series of explosions as the fuel tanks blew up.

Authorities set up an emergency morgue at the airport to house the bodies.

Amid the mud and mire lay plane fragments, luggage and bodies.

The control tower commander said the plane had been in contact by radio after crossing the coast, but shortly before the crash "we lost contact."

"The plane circled two or three times normally as a Caravelle jet was just taking off," he said. "All seemed all right then suddenly we realized something was going wrong. There were no more contacts."

Crash Seen From Train

Passengers aboard the Liege-Brussels train, passing close by, were among the witnesses of the disaster. One said that the plane did not appear to have its wheels down as it came in for a landing.

Airport personnel, however, said they saw the plane let down its landing gear, then withdraw it unexpectedly and climb up again. They described a series of "strange turns" such as are made during a test flight.

Another passenger on the train said:

"The plane appeared to be making a normal approach to land when it suddenly reared up, pointing almost vertically nose up into the sky. Then it fell back like a great stone and we heard an explosion."

François de Kleermaeker, a coal merchant, said he saw the plane drop from the sky "just like in wartime when a plane fell after being hit."

Canadian Skaters Weep

PRAGUE, Czechoslovakia, Feb. 15 (Reuters) — Members of the Canadian team here to participate in a skating meet wept today when they heard of the deaths of the members of the American team in a plane crash in Belgium. The announcement over the loudspeaker at the Prague airport was the first the Canadian team had heard of the disaster.

Believes Pilot Avoided Homes

BRUSSELS, Feb. 15 (UPI)—Mrs. Heloise Vereyken of Steenokerseel, near the site of the Sabena crash, ran outdoors to see what was happening after she heard a plane make several turns overhead.

"I saw the plane coming," she said, "and I believe the pilot did not want to crash on the houses but was desperately looking for a clear spot."

U.S. VICTIMS GOING TO SKATING MEET

Ex-Champions and Officials as Well as Competitors Die in Air Disaster

Following are sketches of passengers who were killed in yesterday's plane crash in Brussels:

HOWARD R. LILLIE

A well-known scientist, Howard R. Lillie, 59 years old, was president of the International Commission on Glass. He was en route to a Brussels meeting of the commission's executive committee.

Manager of the research and development division of Corning Glass Works, Mr. Lillie had been with the company since 1927. He held major patents and was the author of many technical articles. He was a past president and fellow of the American Ceramics Society.

His daughter, Alice, is a student at the University of Pisa, Italy. He had planned to visit her.

WALTER S. POWELL

A retired executive and director of the Brown Shoe Company of St. Louis, Walter S. Powell, 81, was a former president of the United States Figure Skating Association. A figure-skating enthusiast, Mr. Powell was active in promoting United States competition in Olympic figure skating. He was a native of Philadelphia.

MARTIN S. SORIA

Martin S. Soria, 49, an associate professor at Michigan State University, was an international authority on Spanish arts, especially the work of Velasquez. He was en route to Madrid, at the invitation of the Spanish Government, to read a paper at the fourth annual conference for intellectual cooperation in the Institute for Hispanic Culture.

A native of Berlin, Professor Soria held degrees from Madrid, Zurich and Harvard Universities. He taught at City College here and Princeton before joining the East Lansing, Mich., faculty in 1948. Professor Soria was the author of four books and collaborated on three others with Prof. George Kubler of Yale. He is survived by a wife and three children.

JULIAN BAGINSKI

A restaurateur, Julian Baginski, 33, of Englewood Cliffs, N. J., was a partner in the Italian Pavilion, a restaurant at 24 West Fifty-fifth Street.

Mr. Baginski was on his way to Warsaw to visit his mother, who is dying of cancer. He leaves a widow, a son, Julian 3d, and a daughter, Antonia, 9 months old. The family moved to New Jersey from Elmhurst, Queens, a year ago.

PIERRE BALTEAU

A Belgian manufacturer, Pierre Balteau was president of the Balteau Electric Company of Liège, which produces industrial X-ray machines. M. Balteau was returning from a visit to his company's plant in Stamford, Conn.

MAX SILBERSTEIN

A diamond importer, Max Silberstein, 50, of 18 Manitou Road, Westport, Conn., maintained Manhattan offices at 576 Fifth Avenue. He was on a business trip.

He was born in Belgium. He is survived by his wife, the former Ruth Rosenstein; a daughter, Margo, 13; a son, Alex, 10; his father, Morris Silberstein of New York; two sisters, Mrs. Julius Manes of Bennington, Vt., and Mrs. Benjamin Davis of New York, and two brothers, William of Scarsdale and Jesse of Larchmont.

H. HERBERT MYERS

President of the Charles Beseler Company of East Orange, N. J., manufacturers of Photography equipment, for the last seventeen years, H. Herbert Myers, 63, of 67 South Munn Avenue, East Orange, was on a business trip.

Mr. Myers was a istee and former vice presider of Temple Sharey Tefilo. He survived by his wife, the former Lee Vasa; a son, Martin, and a daughter, Mrs. Ruth Berman.

HAROLD G. KELLETT

Harold G. Kellett of 270 Bronxville Road, Yonkers, was a vice president of Scott and Williams, New York manufacturers of hosiery machinery. He was about 50. He was on a business trip to Brussels. He leaves a widow, Margaret.

MRS. MARGARET POZZUOLO

Mrs. Margaret Pozzuolo, 20, of Philadelphia, was en route to join her husband, who is in the Army in Munich, Germany. She was expecting a child.

BRADLEY LORD

Bradley Lord, 21, of Swampscott, Mass., was this country's top-ranking amateur skater. He won the senior men's title in the national figure-skating championships in Colorado Springs Jan. 28.

Mr. Lord placed fourth in the nationals last year when David Jenkins completed a four-year sweep. This time he picked up three first-place ballots from the five judges, narrowly beating Greg Kelley, 16, who was also on the ill-fated plane.

ROBERT, PATRICE DINEEN

Robert and Patrice Dineen, a well-known figure skating pair, lived at 433 West Thirty-fourth Street. They were married two years ago and have a son, Robert, Jr., 9 months.

DALLAS PIERCE

Dallas (Larry) Pierce, 24, of Indianapolis, Ind., was national dance-skating champion with Diane Sherbloom, also of Indianapolis.

Mr. Pierce was the winner of thirteen national and Midwestern skating awards since 1957. He started figure skating at 17, attended Indiana University for several years, then went to work with his father, Dallas H. Pierce, a plumbing and heating dealer.

DOUGLAS RAMSAY

Douglas Ramsay, 16, of Detroit, was the youngest of the competitors in the American senior men's skating competition at Colorado Springs. Only the first three winners were to compete in the world's championships at Prague. Tom Brown of Los Angeles beat Ramsay for third place.

Mr. Brown was unable to go to Prague and the United States Figure Skating Association gave his place to young Douglas. He got special permission to take time off from high school where he was a junior.

Douglas had been a skater for nine years. He won the National Junior Championships last year at Seattle and the Midwest senior men's title in Minneapolis.

C. WILLIAM SWALLENDER

C. William Swallender, 52 years old, of Southfield, Mich., was a coach who had trained many outstanding skaters. He was Douglas Ramsay's coach and he had coached Ginny Baxter, who placed fifth and third in the world championships in 1952.

Mr. Swallender leaves his wife, Genevieve, and two sons.

DONNA LEE CARRIER

Donna Lee Carrier, 20, of North Hollywood, Calif., was the daughter of the Rev. and Mrs. Floyd Carrier. They formerly lived in Albany and Troy. Miss Carrier was a graduate of Troy High School and a member of a figure-skating club called the RPI Club because it uses the Rensselaer Polytechnic Institute field house.

THE KELLEYS

Gregory Kelley, 16, was runner-up for the United States senior men's skating championship. He had placed third in the North American men's singles in Philadelphia.

Gregory and his sister, Nathalie, who was accompanying him, were the children of Dr. and Mrs. Vincent J. Kelley of 1032 Center Street, Newton Center, Mass.

THE HADLEYS

Ila Ray Hadley, 18, and Ray Hadley Jr., 17, were a figure-skating pair. They were trained by their parents, Ray Hadley Sr. and Alvah Hadley, (who had been a professional skater under the name of Linda Hart). Their parents operate an ice studio in Seattle.

"All the News That's Fit to Print"

The New York Times.

LATE CITY EDITION
U. S. Weather Bureau Report (Page 36) forecasts: Hot, humid with early showers today. Chance of rain tonight and tomorrow.
Temp. range: 94—75; yesterday: 94—71.
Temp.-Hum. Index: near 80; yesterday: 81.

VOL. CX....No. 37,842. © 1961 by The New York Times Company. Times Square, New York 36, N. Y. NEW YORK, SATURDAY, SEPTEMBER 2, 1961. 10 cents beyond 50-mile zone from New York City except on Long Island. Higher in air delivery cities. FIVE CENTS

ALL 78 ON PLANE KILLED IN CRASH OUTSIDE CHICAGO

FAMILIES PERISH

Piston Craft Plunges Into Field Minutes After Take-Off

By AUSTIN C. WEHRWEIN
Special to The New York Times.

CHICAGO, Sept. 1—A Trans World Airlines Constellation plunged into a cornfield twenty miles west of here early today, killing all seventy-eight persons aboard.

The crash was the fourth worst in United States air history. It was also the worst single-plane disaster in United States commercial aviation.

The four-engined piston plane crashed four minutes after taking off from Midway Airport here for Las Vegas, Los Angeles and San Francisco.

Family groups—one of seven, another of six, another of five—were among the victims. Many of those aboard were on Labor Day holidays.

More than a third of the seventy-three passengers had boarded the plane at New York International Airport, where it arrived from Boston at 9 o'clock last night.

The others had boarded either at Boston, where the flight began, at Pittsburgh or at Midway Airport here.

Slight Rain Falling

The plane, eight minutes behind schedule when it took off here at 2:03 A. M. Central Daylight Time, crashed in a gentle rain.

Federal aviation officials said this afternoon that there was nothing so far to indicate an explosion in the air. However, they said the plane had swooped to earth fast, and at a steep angle.

The plane came down near Hinsdale, on the still-rural edge of Clarendon Hills, a well-to-do suburb.

No houses were hit, but flaming debris fell on the barn of Jerry Broz, a 55-year-old farmer, who was jolted out of bed by the crash.

He climbed to the roof of the barn and stamped out the flames, and then came down to find one of the big landing

Continued on Page 37, Column 4

President to Press Care of Aged in '62

By RUSSELL BAKER
Special to The New York Times.

WASHINGTON, Sept. 1—President Kennedy pledged today that he would assign the "highest priority" in next year's Congressional session to a program of medical care for the aged under Social Security.

The President's assurance was given in a letter to Senator Pat McNamara, Democrat of Michigan and chairman of a Senate subcommittee on problems of the aged.

The President's letter was made public in response to an earlier letter from Mr. McNamara seeking White House assurance that the bill would be pressed next year "with all possible vigor."

Although Mr. Kennedy listed the medical-care bill early this year as priority legislation, the House Democratic

Continued on Page 7, Column 2

KENNEDY APPEALS FOR SAFE HOLIDAY

President Urges 'Patience and a Clear Head' on Road —Heat Stalls Many Cars

By RICHARD J. H. JOHNSTON

President Kennedy made an appeal yesterday for care and consideration on the nation's highways as the last long weekend holiday of the summer got under way.

As the President called on motorists to drive "with patience and a clear head," the National Safety Council predicted that at least 420 persons would die in traffic accidents before Tuesday morning.

Supporting the President's appeal, major bus and truck lines instructed their drivers to operate with headlights burning throughout the daylight hours of the holiday period to remind all drivers to "take it easy."

The plan called for nationwide participation in a campaign of "Truck Lights On For Safety." In Iowa, Missouri, Texas and Illinois, all drivers of pleasure cars were asked to keep their headlights on for the same purpose.

The scramble by car, bus, rail and plane for resorts and country and shore places got under way in midafternoon yesterday as the temperature soared to 94 degrees.

Traffic was moderate to heavy on all major roads lead-

Continued on Page 36, Column 3

LEVITT DEMANDS BIGOTRY INQUIRY

5 Campaign Exhibits Sent to Attorney General

By DOUGLAS DALES

State Controller Arthur Levitt urged Attorney General Louis J. Lefkowitz yesterday to investigate "the practice of political bigotry and to bring to stern account those who are responsible for these outrageous tactics."

The request by the Democratic organization candidate for Mayor was accompanied by five exhibits in support of his charges that Mayor Wagner's campaign workers were appealing for votes on the basis of racial and religious bigotry.

Mr. Lefkowitz, who is the Republican candidate for Mayor, said he would have no comment on Mr. Levitt's request until he had had a chance to examine the exhibits.

Lehman Assails Charge

In a statement Thursday, Mr. Levitt said 600 city sanitation workers in Queens were using the argument that "a victory for Levitt will leave a Jew to run against a Jew."

As a result of the charges, there were these other developments yesterday:

¶Former Senator Herbert H. Lehman, who had been called upon by Mr. Levitt to repudiate the alleged tactics, denounced Mr. Levitt's charges as "a transparent, despicable foul blow * * * the most malicious tactic of any campaign I recall."

¶Mayor Wagner, attributing the Levitt charges to "Boss" Carmine G. De Sapio's "bag of campaign tricks," said he had been told that "De Sapio now

Continued on Page 5, Column 2

GOULART RETURNS TO BRAZIL TO PUSH PRESIDENCY CLAIM

100,000 Hail Leftist Leader Opposed by Military as a Successor to Quadros

By JUAN de ONIS
Special to The New York Times.

PORTO ALEGRE, Brazil, Sept. 1—Vice President João Goulart flew into Brazil by a secret route in a blacked-out jet airliner tonight to lay claim to the Presidency.

He received the biggest, most enthusiastic public welcome in the history of this embattled state capital.

Senhor Goulart was received at Salgado Filho Airport by Gov. Leonel Brizzola and Gen. José Machado Lopes, commander of the Third Army, which is based here and which has declared its loyalty to Senhor Goulart.

Senhor Goulart embraced Governor Brizzola, who is his brother-in-law, and then the general in an emotional meeting as he stepped off the plane.

Senhor Goulart's claim to the Presidency, which was vacated last Friday by Dr. Janio Quadros, has met with stiff opposition of the nation's military leaders, who have charged Senhor Goulart with a vulnerability to Communist infiltration.

Escorted by Troops

Throughout the day radio stations controlled from the Governor's Palace here had broadcast reports that Senhor Goulart was coming overland by car from Montevideo.

His trip here in a Varig Airlines Caravelle jet was kept secret until he landed after a one hour and ten minute flight from the Uruguayan capital.

A crowd of more than 100,000 persons had gathered in front of the Governor's Palace to await Senhor Goulart.

He drove from the airport with an escort of combat cars filled with about fifty soldiers in battle dress and carrying sub-machine guns and entered the palace by a private entrance.

Flight Kept Secret

After a three-day stopover in Paris and a six-hour visit between flights in New York, Senhor Goulart flew into Montevideo yesterday.

There he received reports from Brazilian political leaders on the situation in his own country after careful plans were made for his return to this southernmost state capital. Senhor Goulart raced to Montevideo's Carrasco Airport and boarded the jet airliner.

As the Caravelle approached the Brazilian frontier, all lights were turned off and curtains were drawn. The big plane raced in darkness at over 450 miles an hour on a flight plan that was kept secret until the plane landed.

It was learned that Senhor Goulart had told visitors in Montevideo that he was willing

Continued on Page 6, Column 6

HOUSE UNIT BACKS FOREIGN AID CUT OF 896 MILLIONS

Administration Sees Danger to Its Program in 23% Reduction in Funds

By E. W. KENWORTHY
Special to The New York Times.

WASHINGTON, Sept. 1—The House Appropriations Committee approved reductions in foreign aid funds today that left Administration officials stunned and angry.

The committee upheld cuts initiated by a subcommittee headed by Representative Otto E. Passman, Democrat of Louisiana. Two days ago the subcommittee ignored a plea by President Kennedy and slashed $896,000,000 from the appropriations bill.

Today the full committee, headed by Clarence Cannon, Democrat of Missouri, brushed aside a last-minute appeal by Secretary of State Dean Rusk and Secretary of Defense Robert S. McNamara. They asked the committee to appropriate the full amount authorized yesterday by the House and Senate—$4,253,500,000.

Secretaries Join in Plea

Having learned that the committee was about to approve the cut, the two Secretaries joined in a letter to Mr. Cannon. They said:

"We urge your committee to review with the utmost care the proposed reduction and to reinstate in full the amounts involved. This nation finds itself in an atmosphere of mounting crisis in which the forces of international communism stand poised to seize upon every opportunity to exploit any sign of weakness in the free world. Your action is being watched by peoples everywhere."

At Gettysburg, Pa. former President Dwight D. Eisenhower issued a statement saying that "these slashes are incomprehensible to me, especially in light of present world tensions."

Taxpayer Savings Seen

"I am sure," he went on, "that the large majority of thinking American citizens, Democrats and Republicans alike, would join me in urging vigorous support of efforts to remedy the damage that would result from these reported committee recommendations."

But Mr. Passman said at the end of the two-hour committee hearing:

"This is a great day for the taxpayers."

The subcommittee's recommendation of an appropriation of $3,357,500,000 represents a 23 per cent cut from the maximum amount permitted—the amount set in the authorization bill. This is the deepest cut in years at this stage of the appropriation process.

The reduction of $896,000,000 came on top of a cut of $509,000,000 that Congress made in authorizing the program. The President originally requested $4,762,500,000. The total cut now

Continued on Page 7, Column 3

SOVIET EXPLODES ATOMIC WEAPON OF INTERMEDIATE FORCE OVER ASIA; NASSER ASSAILS TEST RESUMPTION

BELGRADE TALKS START: President Gamal Abdel Nasser of United Arab Republic greets fellow delegates at meeting. At right is President Habib Bourguiba of Tunisia.

Associated Press Radiophotos

BERLIN IS DISCUSSED: President Sukarno of Indonesia speaks. At right is Prime Minister Nehru of India. Behind Mr. Nehru is V. K. Krishna Menon, Indian Foreign Minister.

ATMOSPHERE TEST

Long-Range Devices of U.S. Detect and Identify Blast

By TOM WICKER
Special to The New York Times.

WASHINGTON, Sept. 1 — The White House announced today that the Soviet Union resumed the testing of nuclear weapons early this morning by exploding a device over Soviet Central Asia.

The announcement said the explosion took place "in the atmosphere" at Semipalatinsk, about 350 miles south of Novosibirsk.

Andrew Hatcher, the assistant White House press secretary, said the explosion was detected "early this morning, Western time" by what he described as "long-range detecting equipment." It was apparently the first nuclear test by the Soviet Union since its announcement Wednesday that it would resume testing.

Event Was Anticipated

Mr. Hatcher said that after the detection of the explosion was confirmed as a nuclear device, the news was given to President Kennedy at the White House at 3:15 P. M. He explained that the lag between detection and the report to the President was caused by the time required to check the information obtained by United States detection equipment.

"This has been anticipated," he said. "It didn't come as a surprise."

There was no precise estimate of the size of the nuclear device. The announcement said only that it had had "a substantial yield in the intermediate range." Mr. Hatcher said this yield meant that the Soviet device was larger than the "average atomic bomb" and larger than the bomb exploded over Hiroshima in 1945.

First Test Since Agreement

He further explained that the device was not in the range of a megaton, the equivalent explosive force of 1,000,000 tons of TNT. Rather, he described it as being in the kiloton range. This would mean an explosive force of hundreds of thousands of tons of TNT, perhaps between 100,000 and 500,000 tons. The Hiroshima bomb was twenty kilotons, or the equivalent of 20,000 tons of TNT.

The Soviet explosion was the first known nuclear test by one of the three nuclear powers—Britain, the Soviet Union and the United States—that agreed in the fall of 1958 to refrain from testing while trying to negotiate a test ban. France, however, has set off four nuclear devices since then, one of them this year.

Despite the moratorium on testing, the United States maintained its secret global system that has detected atomic explosions in the Soviet Union over the years.

Semipalatinsk is an industrial and transportation center

Continued on Page 3, Column 1

U. S. BUTTRESSES BERLIN AIR CASE

Cites 1947 Soviet Document to Prove Commitment on Civilian Planes' Access

Text of 1947 Soviet document is printed on Page 5.

By MAX FRANKEL
Special to The New York Times.

WASHINGTON, Sept. 1—The United States presented more evidence today supporting the Western powers' right to fly civilian planes through Communist East Germany to West Berlin.

The State Department published a fourteen-year-old hitherto-secret translation of a Soviet document to buttress its contention that Moscow is committed to give Allied planes—civilian and military—unrestricted access to Berlin.

In an admittedly thin legal dossier on the subject, the document is considered by the department to be the best available, even though it deals only obliquely with the point at issue.

Allied access to Berlin derives from an oral agreement between Marshal Georgi K. Zhukov of the Soviet Union, then Soviet military governor, and Gen. Lucius D. Clay, then United States military governor.

The air corridors, as well as rules for access by land and water, were later defined by the military commanders of the occupation authorities in Germany. But there was never a written agreement explicitly

Continued on Page 5, Column 4

Khrushchev Asserts His Aim Is to Shock Allies Into a Parley

By SEYMOUR TOPPING
Special to The New York Times.

MOSCOW, Sept. 1—Premier Khrushchev was quoted today to the effect that he had decided to resume the testing of nuclear weapons to shock the Western powers into negotiations on Germany and disarmament.

The Soviet leader gave this explanation to Sir Leslie Plummer and Konni Zilliacus, two Left-wing members of the British Labor party, in a three-hour interview yesterday at his summer home near Yalta, on the Black Sea.

There was no announcement here up to midnight of the Soviet nuclear test in the atmosphere over Central Asia, as disclosed in a White House statement.

However, the Ministry of Defense announced that the Soviet northern fleet would hold joint maneuvers with rocket troops and the air force in the Barents and Kara Seas this month and next.

"In accordance with the plan of military preparations, military exercises with the actual use of various types of modern weapons will be held," the communiqué said.

Allies Rejected Proposal

The announcement implied that rocket weapons, possibly with nuclear warheads that would contaminate the area, would be employed.

The region of the maneuvers was declared dangerous for navigation for Soviet and foreign ships and to flights of aircraft between Sept. 10 and Nov. 15.

On the decision to resume tests, Sir Leslie, who was reached at Yalta by telephone, quoted Mr. Khrushchev as having said that if he felt it was only by such threats that the Western powers would be compelled to enter East-West talks.

By taking a tough line, Premier Khrushchev said, he hoped to make the Atlantic alliance agree to merging the discussions at Geneva on a nuclear test ban treaty with negotiations for general and complete disarmament.

The United States and Britain rejected this proposal at Geneva on the ground that it would delay an agreement on a test ban treaty.

Sir Leslie and Mr. Zilliacus

Continued on Page 3, Column 4

NASSER PROPOSES TALKS AT SUMMIT

Tells Neutrals at Belgrade That Nuclear Tests Make Parley Vital to Peace

Excerpts from conference talks will be found on Page 2.

By M. S. HANDLER
Special to The New York Times.

BELGRADE, Yugoslavia, Sept. 1.—The conference of the nonaligned countries opened today and heard President Gamal Abdel Nasser of the United Arab Republic denounce the Soviet decision to resume nuclear testing. He urged an immediate summit conference to save the peace.

President Nasser said that the world was moving closer to the brink of disaster and that no effort must be spared to facilitate negotiations. The only alternate course to negotiations, he said, is military conflict.

The twenty-four governmental leaders assembled at 10 A. M. around an oval mahogany table in the main hall of the Yugoslav Parliament building.

A cautiously worded speech by President Tito of Yugoslavia paved the way for Mr. Nasser's criticism of the Soviet Union's announcement on the resuming of nuclear testing.

President Tito's speech, which opened the conference, appeared designed to set out failures of the bloc systems without offending the members of the two competing systems. He emphasized that the nonaligned nations planned no bloc.

The speeches were by no

Continued on Page 2, Column 7

U. N. in Congo Cuts Ties With Katanga

By Reuters.

ELISABETHVILLE, the Congo, Sept. 1—The United Nations mission here severed relations today with secessionist Katanga Province.

It repeated its charges that Godefroid Munongo, the province's Interior Minister, had organized "a murderous conspiracy" against United Nations troops and officials. It said that relations would remain severed until Mr. Munongo was dismissed from his post.

The United Nations also reiterated its charge that Mr. Munongo was responsible for atrocities committed by Katanga forces against tribesmen in the Kasai Province.

Mr. Munongo said at a news conference yesterday that the United Nations was trying to oust him because officials considered him the main obstacle

Continued on Page 6, Column 3

NEWS INDEX

Bomb Defense Widely Doubted; Rockefeller Calls Shelter Parley

Feeling of Futility Voiced

By NAN ROBERTSON

If a sampling of New Yorkers and residents of near-by counties is typical, Americans feel that protection against a superbomb at this time is almost hopeless.

Interviews yesterday with more than 100 persons showed that almost all knew that the Soviet Union was resuming nuclear tests. They knew, too, that the Russians had announced they could make a 100-megaton bomb of terrifying power and had the rockets to send it anywhere on earth.

Most of the New Yorkers were apartment dwellers and none had built bomb shelters, although a few home owners with the space had considered doing so.

Almost all believed that the

Continued on Page 4, Column 5

Governors Are Summoned

By The Associated Press.

ALBANY, Sept. 1—Governor Rockefeller called a meeting of the Civil Defense Committee of the Governors' Conference today. He said the Governors needed to discuss fall-out shelters and other defense problems "in view of international developments."

The meeting will be held Sept. 17 in Washington.

Mr. Rockefeller apparently referred to the decision of the Soviet Union to resume the testing of nuclear weapons.

The Governor is chairman of the committee. He said the meeting would be designed to enable the members of the Governors' Conference to develop a civil defense program to put to their respective legislatures.

The Republican Governor said

Continued on Page 4, Column 6

President Is Host to 18 Children at Candy Store

Associated Press Wirephoto

The President, at golf cart's wheel, waits for children to get set for trip from store

By The Associated Press.

HYANNIS PORT, Mass., Sept. 1—President Kennedy loaded eighteen youngsters aboard his big white golf cart tonight for a twilight visit to the neighborhood candy store.

He wound up the trip with a weeping youngster in his lap.

As Mr. Kennedy started the cart for the block and a half trip back to his summer home, three youngsters toppled off the rear. One sat down hard. The boy started crying, and a policeman picked him up and carried him to the President. Mr. Kennedy soothed the little boy, and drove home with the youngster in his lap. The boy was one of the seven children of Attorney General Robert F. Kennedy, the President's brother. Mr. Kennedy pulled the cart around the corner and the children made a beeline for the shop with the President's daughter, Caroline, among the front-runners. The children got candy bars, and the bill was about $1.50. The President will spend the week-end here.

Stretcher bearers carry bodies from cornfield near Hinsdale, Ill., after TWA plane crashed shortly after takeoff. Twisted metal from burned plane is at right.

Wide World Photos

ALL 78 ON PLANE KILLED IN CRASH

Continued From Page 1, Col. 1

wheels had slammed through the barn door.

Within minutes, the first of more than thirty suburban fire departments and fifty suburban, state and county police detachments were on the way to the scene.

One witness said the plane "fell like a comet."

A deputy sheriff put in a call to a carnival for a truck with an arc light, and for a time it was the only illumination at the misty scene.

"My farmyard is a cemetery without crosses," Mr. Broz said later as dawn came on the hot, humid day.

Bed sheets and newspapers covered the burned and shattered bodies that were later moved by a caravan of ambulances to the Cook County Morgue in Chicago.

Twisted metal, snapped-off cornstalks and heaps of acrid-smoking ashes marked the site of the crash.

Halaby at Crash Site

Federal officials and investigators arrived later, led by Najeeb E. Halaby, Federal Aviation Administrator. He was accompanied by Whitney Gillilland, a member of the Civil Aeronautics Board, and Melvin N. Gough, director of the C. A. B.'s Bureau of Safety.

At a news conference in a basement room of the Air Line Pilots Association building adjacent to Midway Field, they played a tape recording of the final conversation between the control tower and the aircraft captain, James H. Sanders, 40

years old, of Manhattan Beach, Calif. They described it as routine, and without clues to what happened.

Although Mr. Halaby emphasized that the cause of the crash was yet to be determined, he said the "navigation facilities were in order and the control tower functioned in accordance with regulations."

The transcript of the tape-recorded conversation showed, he said, only a routine request for a routine take-off. The visibility was three miles, the cloud ceiling 15,000 feet and the wind from the south at eight miles an hour.

Under Radar Control

Mr. Halaby said the plane has been under radar control until four minutes after its departure, when it disappeared off the radar scope—indicating the moment of the crash.

The visibility from the Midway tower at that moment was good enough for a glow of bright light on the western horizon to be seen.

The tower then asked a Northwest Airlines pilot in the area if he had seen an "explosion or something." The pilot replied that he had, that "it's spread over a quite wide area" and that it "looks like a brush fire."

Mr. Gough, the Safety Bureau director, also said there was nothing thus far to indicate that the aircraft had exploded in air.

He was asked whether there was any indication of sabotage. "I don't think we can afford to rule out anything," he replied.

He did say that the plane had come down at "a steep angle and very hard," and estimated the angle at 20 degrees.

"I never tried to land one in this position or attitude," Mr. Gough replied, referring to the angle of descent.

Aviation experts later said

that a normal approach would be three degrees.

Tail Found Far Away

It appeared, according to some aviation experts, that a third of the plane's tail section had fallen away before the crash.

The tail section was found almost a quarter of a mile from the first impact point. It seemed to be less damaged than other parts of the wreckage, and to have drifted slightly east of the descending line, which was unaccountably to the north.

Asked about this, Mr. Gough replied that it was "very significant and would surely be a point of interest in the investigation."

Replying to another question, Mr. Gough said it was not "reasonable" for the tail section to land as it did.

Mr. Halaby discounted a report that the T. W. A. plane had had mechanical difficulties en route to Chicago. He said the co-pilot on the incoming leg, who stayed behind in Chicago, had reported "no discrepancies," meaning no mechanical trouble.

This morning's crash was the fifth major one at or near Midway Airport and it took the greatest toll of life.

On July 17, 1955, a Braniff Airways plane, approaching Midway, clipped a filling station sign outside the airport fence and overturned on landing. Twenty-two persons died.

Twelve were killed when a Delta Air Lines plane crashed after taking off from Midway on March 10, 1948, and eight died when a United Air Lines transport struck a house at Sixty-third Street and Keating Avenue on Dec. 4, 1940.

A B-24 Liberator bomber coming in for a landing at Midway struck a gas storage tank on West Seventy-third Street

on May 21, 1943, killing the twelve Air Force men aboard.

The Air Line Pilots Association sent an accident investigation team to the scene of today's crash. The team will aid Federal authorities and also conduct its own independent investigation, the union said. It is headed by T. G. Linnert, head of the association's engineering and air safety department.

Reports Questioned

Many persons living within a radius of half a mile to a mile of the crash reported that an explosion and fire occurred before the plane struck the ground.

Careful screening of all statements, however, caused the investigators to disregard the reports.

Weather at the crash scene varied from misty and foggy to showery during the hours between midnight and dawn. The weather was not considered a factor in the accident, but possibilities of turbulence were still a question.

The Constellation was flown from the East Coast to Chicago by a crew listed by T.W.A. as A. Van de Velde, captain; P. J. van Reeth, first officer or co-pilot; F. O. Dak, flight engineer, and D. Duffy and C. Thompson, stewardesses, all of Chicago.

The crew members who died, besides Captain Sanders, were Dale Tarrant, first officer; James C. Newlin, flight engineer, and Nanette Fidger and Barbara Pearson, stewardesses, all of the Los Angeles area.

Instructions Heard

Because the flight was heavy with fuel the climb rate was leisurely. The crew acknowledged the departure instructions by radio steadily for the next three minutes, never indicating

The New York Times Sept. 2, 1961

Plane with 78 aboard left Chicago's Midway Airport (1) and crashed near Hinsdale suburb (2) west of city.

that there were difficulties of any sort.

"About four minutes out they simply stopped acknowledging or talking," said a tower man. "We were just about to turn the flight over to Chicago air traffic control radar in a normal hand-off when we became aware that they were down."

Charles C. George Jr, 26, who was spending the night at his parents' home in Clarendon Hills, said:

"I was awakened by a sudden roar of aircraft engines. I opened my eyes and looked out the window and saw a big airplane—a great big one—silhouetted against the sky. And it was very low, skimming just above the trees and wires along Sixty-first Street. It wasn't over fifty feet up.

"I saw it pass over the trees and then touch down in the cornfield and instantly there was an explosion like an earthquake that shook our house. And the plane disappeared in a fountain of flame. I was stunned."

The New York Times.

LATE CITY EDITION
U. S. Weather Bureau Report (Page 18) forecasts:
Early fog, rain today, turning
Cloudy, showers, colder tomorrow.
Temp. range: 42—32; yesterday: 35—30.

VOL. CXI....No. 37,949. © 1961 by The New York Times Company. Times Square, New York 36, N. Y. NEW YORK, MONDAY, DECEMBER 18, 1961. 10 cents beyond 50-mile zone from New York City except on Long Island. Higher in air delivery cities. FIVE CENTS

500,000 IN BOGOTA GREET PRESIDENT ON ALLIANCE TOUR

Aide Calls Crowd Biggest to Welcome Kennedy on Any of His Trips

AID PLEDGE IS RENEWED

Speech Assails Communism as Tour of Venezuela and Colombia Is Completed

Caracas statement and excerpts from Bogotá talk, Page 14.

By TAD SZULC
Special to The New York Times.

BOGOTA, Colombia, Monday, Dec. 18—A crowd of 500,000, nearly half the population of Bogotá, turned out yesterday to give a rousing welcome to President and Mrs. Kennedy.

Dressed in their Sunday best, the crowd filled Bogotá's streets, sometimes twenty deep, in a warm outpouring of friendship for the United States and its President.

[The President took off for Puerto Rico on his way home just after 1 A. M., news agencies reported.]

As he completed his two-day visit to Venezuela and Colombia, President Kennedy said that his trip demonstrated "the determination of the people of the United States to eliminate poverty and hunger from the Americas."

Pierre Salinger, White House press secretary, said last night that the Bogotá turnout was larger than any reception for the President anywhere, including his visits to Paris, Vienna and London and campaign appearances in the United States.

Welcome Pleases Kennedy

Mr. Salinger said that his own estimate of the number in the crowd here was 1,000,000 people. Colombian estimates were more conservative.

Mr. Salinger said that President Kennedy had thanked Colombia's President, Dr. Alberto Lleras Camargo, for the enthusiastic welcome.

In a speech last night at a dinner given by Dr. Lleras Camargo, President Kennedy said that democracy had an "unparalleled power" to reshape societies. Democracy can meet "new needs without violence, without repression, without a discipline which destroys liberty," he added.

Following Saturday's visit to Caracas, Venezuela, where despite fears of hostile demonstrations by extreme Left-wing elements President Kennedy found an unexpected favorable reception, the Bogotá welcome clearly made the President's weekend in Latin America a major success.

The message President Kennedy brought was that Latin America could look forward to economic development and a

Continued on Page 14, Column 5

SIBERIANS EAGER FOR KENNEDY TEXT

Copies of Izvestia Interview Pass From Hand to Hand

By HARRISON E. SALISBURY
Special to The New York Times.

MOSCOW, Dec. 17—President Kennedy's interview with Izvestia's editor is still fresh news in the remote areas of the Communist world nearly three weeks after it was published.

In Outer Mongolia and eastern Siberia, torn and hand-soiled copies of Izvestia's Nov. 29 issue containing the interview by Aleksei I. Adzhubei, the paper's editor, who is a son-in-law of Premier Khrushchev, are still in active circulation.

The reaction of the typical reader in out-of-the-way sections was that the interview showed that the United States President was so eager for peace as the Soviet people.

In a two-week trip through these areas, this correspondent was asked a number of times about the interview by persons who had heard of it but had been unable to lay hands on a copy of the newspaper.

In a physics laboratory of Ulan Bator University, half a dozen students and instructors were avidly poring over a copy of the interview instead of carrying on with their studies. On

Continued on Page 12, Column 3

WELCOME TO BOGOTA: President Kennedy at airport yesterday.

Balaguer Forms Council To Take Over Government

By R. HART PHILLIPS
Special to The New York Times.

SANTO DOMINGO, Dominican Republic, Dec. 17—President Joaquín Balaguer announced today the appointment of a Council of State to govern the Dominican Republic. Dr. Balaguer will preside over the new council.

The President coupled the announcement with a pledge to resign as soon as the Organization of American States lifted the diplomatic and economic sanctions imposed on the country more than a year ago.

Dr. Balaguer, who said he hoped the sanctions would be lifted immediately so that he could leave office by Feb. 27, made the announcement in a broadcast to the Dominican people from the Presidential Palace.

His talk was followed by a message from Maj. Gen. Pedro Rafael Rodríguez Echavarría, Secretary of State for Armed Forces, who declared his full support of Dr. Balaguer's plan.

Assembly to Lose Power

The former air force officer, who led military elements in preventing a coup d'état by members of the Trujillo family and forced them into exile last month, said the country could not live in "a permanent state of agitation."

Dr. Balaguer, who said he would preside over the Council of State until his resignation, added that the body would assume the authority of the National Assembly, which is formed by the Senate and the Chamber of Deputies.

The council, Dr. Balaguer added, will call elections by Aug. 16 for a constituent assembly to modify the Dominican Constitution and will set general election by Dec. 20 of next year.

Dr. Balaguer said the current National Assembly would declare itself in recess until the Constituent Assembly could be called.

The President's plan for this transition follows closely the demands of opposition political groups during the long negotiations that were broken off Dec. 10, when the armed forces refused to accept demands for Dr. Balaguer's resignation.

At that time Gen. Rodríguez

Continued on Page 15, Column 1

EISENHOWER BACKS EASING OF TARIFFS

Sees Solid Economic Gains in Gradual Liberalization Proposed by Kennedy

Special to The New York Times.

WASHINGTON, Dec. 17 — Former President Dwight D. Eisenhower has given strong advance support to President Kennedy's program for foreign trade liberalization.

General Eisenhower made his statement after a long talk with Christian A. Herter, Secretary of State in his Administration. The former President said:

"It is clearly necessary that our trade policies and procedures should have sufficient flexibility to meet the new conditions created by the establishment of the Common Market in Europe.

"While there are difficulties, of course, I am convinced that a steady, gradual liberalization of trade restrictions, with adequate consideration for possible injury, can yield solid benefits for the American economy."

Tariff Cuts Proposed

A little-noted statement on the issue was released in Gettysburg, Pa., Friday afternoon. It contained a number of General Eisenhower's views on international matters. News accounts had emphasized other points dealing with nuclear testing and the Congo situation.

Mr. Herter and William L. Clayton, Under Secretary of State for Economic Affairs under President Harry S. Truman, have been leading advocates for granting the President new and broadened power to cut tariffs on a reciprocal basis so that the United States will be able to compete successfully in the European market.

In fact Mr. Herter and Mr. Clayton have gone further in their recommendations than the Administration intends to go at the outset, in a report Nov. 1 to a joint Congressional subcommittee on foreign economic policy they proposed that the United States form a "trade partnership" with the European Economic Community, or Common Market.

Television Interview

In another development today, Alfred M. Landon, Republican candidate for President in 1936, intimated that he might break with his party if the Republican leadership in Congress opposed the President's trade liberalization program.

In a televised interview on "Washington Conversation," a program of the Columbia Broadcasting System, Mr. Landon was reminded that in a recent speech at the National Press Club he said the question of his remaining a Republican in 1964 would depend on what happened

Continued on Page 6, Column 4

Negro Groups Split On Georgia Protest

By CLAUDE SITTON
Special to The New York Times.

ALBANY, Ga., Dec. 17—A leadership conflict developed today between the two regional organizations in the Negro protest movement here.

An open break occurred between the Southern Christian Leadership Conference and the Student Nonviolent Coordinating Committee.

It involved the Rev. Dr. Martin Luther King Jr., head of the conference, who was asked to wait until yesterday, and several of his former supporters in the student organization.

The development was regarded as having important implications for the future of the civil rights movement throughout the South. It reflects the growing competition for financial support and power

Continued on Page 31, Column 1

U.N. FORCES ENTER HEART OF CAPITAL IN KATANGA FIGHT

Troops Reported Moving on Presidential Palace — Limited Truce Sought

By The Associated Press.

ELISABETHVILLE, the Congo, Dec. 17 — United Nations forces battled their way into the heart of this secessionist capital tonight. They were reported trying to capture the official residence of Moise Tshombe, President of Katanga Province.

Some reports said that Mr. Tshombe was inside. Others said he was in an area south of Elisabethville.

United Nations officials earlier listed the Presidential palace and the Katanga radio station as the two remaining objectives for United Nations troops. Seizure of both would give the United Nations virtual control of the city.

Fighting erupted in the center of the city after a concentrated mortar barrage. Five thousand United Nations troops moved on Elisabethville in a pincer attack.

Tshombe Returns

A Katangese spokesman said Mr. Tshombe had returned to the capital earlier in the day after an overnight trip to Kipushi on Katanga's frontier with Northern Rhodesia.

United Nations jets firing rockets attacked the headquarters of the Union Minière in Haut-Katanga, the Belgian-controlled mining company, and several homes. The buildings were left in flames. United Nations authorities said the homes and offices had been used as sniper bases against United Nations troops.

[In New York, the United Nations command ordered its military command in Katanga to urgently consider a temporary cease-fire in the area near the Union Minière installation to permit the evacuation of civilians.]

Belgian Aide Killed

Officials at the Belgian Consulate reported that during the fighting last night, Guillaume Derriks, a top Union Minière adviser, and his 87-year-old mother were killed.

[In Brussels, Union Minière officials charged that United Nations troops had murdered the Derriks and their servants.]

During the day the prongs of the United Nations pincer advance moved slowly against stiff Katangese resistance from the northern and western suburbs.

The fighting in Katanga began early this month after Katangese officials denounced a Nov. 24 Security Council resolution authorizing the United Nations command here to use force, if necessary, to expel mercenaries and foreigners in

Continued on Page 3, Column 1

KENNEDY PRESSING CONGO TRUCE TALK

Asks U. S. Envoy to Escort Tshombe to a Meeting With Premier Adoula

Special to The New York Times.

WASHINGTON, Dec. 17 — President Kennedy received word today that the Congo's Premier, Cyrille Adoula, was willing to confer with Moise Tshombe, President of secessionist Katanga Province. The President acted immediately to speed such a meeting.

The State Department made public a note to Mr. Tshombe noting that the United States Ambassador to the Congo, Edmund Gullion, had been asked to fly to Elisabethville from Leopoldville in an American plane to "escort" Mr. Tshombe to the proposed meeting and return him safely.

Ambassador Gullion Sent

The message, which was forwarded by Mr. Gullion to Mr. Tshombe in Elisabethville, the embattled capital of Katanga, said President Kennedy was glad that Mr. Tshombe was "prepared to enter immediate talks" with Premier Adoula "with a view to finding a solution to the differences" now dividing them.

"The President hopes that you can proceed to Kitona for this purpose within a matter of hours," the message said. Kitona is in the Congo, not far from the Katanga border.

President Tshombe had asked President Kennedy to try to end the fighting in the Congo and had expressed willingness to meet Premier Adoula. There

Continued on Page 2, Column 3

Circus Tent Fire Kills 285, Injures 600, in Rio Suburb

Scores of Children Die in Flames and Panic — Arson Suspected

Special to The New York Times.

RIO DE JANEIRO, Dec. 17 — At least 285 persons, most of them children, were killed and 600 injured today in a fire that swept a circus tent at suburban Niterói this afternoon.

The police of Rio de Janeiro state, who reported the figures for the casualties, said that many in hospitals might die of injuries.

Many of those killed were trampled to death in the panic of the circus audience to escape the flames.

About 2,500 were watching the show when the fire broke out about 2 P. M. The police said the flames consumed the canvas tent in a few minutes. The police said about 1,400 children had been in the circus audience.

Parents went from hospital to hospital and to the Niterói morgue searching for missing children who had been at the parties. Children in the streets cried for their missing mothers.

The disaster was one of the worst recorded in circus history. At Hartford, Conn., on July 6, 1944, fire killed 168 persons and injured 487 in the circus tent of Ringling Brothers Barnum and Bailey.

All the performers and animals escaped in the Niterói fire. The flames were confined to the big tent.

The police said they had not determined the cause of the fire. They were investigating reports of arson.

Niterói hospitals called Rio de Janeiro by radio for plasma, narcotics and ice. Ambulances and other aid from Rio de Janeiro had to cross Guanabara Bay by ferryboats, which took half an hour for the trip, to

Continued on Page 17, Column 3

Scene of the fire (cross)

INDIA INVADES 3 ENCLAVES OF PORTUGUESE ON COAST; U.S. MAY URGE U. N. TO ACT

RUSK MEETS AIDES

They Weigh Going to Security Council if Lisbon Does Not

By E. W. KENWORTHY
Special to The New York Times.

WASHINGTON, Dec. 17—The United States was weighing tonight whether to go to the United Nations Security Council on the Goa crisis if Portugal did not immediately move to do so.

The news that Prime Minister Jawaharlal Nehru had decided to take over the three Portuguese enclaves of Goa, Damão and Diu by force aroused dismay and consternation in the Administration.

Only a few days ago President Kennedy had sent a letter to Mr. Nehru beseeching him not to use arms to take over the colonies, which Indians regard as part of their national territory.

The President also sent a letter to Portugal's Premier Antonio de Oliveira Salazar, urging a peaceful settlement.

[U Thant, Acting Secretary General of the United Nations, also sent notes to Mr. Nehru and Dr. Salazar appealing for a preservation of peace. Mr. Nehru rejected this appeal. His and Dr. Salazar's replies blaming each other were disclosed at the United Nations.]

Activity Is Intense

The Indian Government's announcement of the attack set off intense diplomatic activity here. Secretary of State Dean Rusk, who returned only last night from the ministerial meeting of the North Atlantic Treaty Organization, immediately summoned a meeting in his office.

Under Secretary George W. Ball; Phillips Talbot, Assistant Secretary for South Asian Affairs; and Harlan Cleveland, Assistant Secretary for International Organization (United Nations) Affairs, attended.

The United States' only official statement was an expression of regret. A State Department spokesman said that the United States had been urging India not to use force.

U. S. Action Expected

The feeling was strong here that if Portugal did not take the initiative, the United States, probably in concert with other Western powers, would do so. There was no question whatever, judging from remarks made privately, that the United States would support a resolution condemning India's action.

"I would only anticipate that the United States would take the same position that we took against Britain and France in the case of Suez," one official said, referring to 1956, when the United States opposed Britain and France in their battle in Egypt.

Several officials emphasized

Continued on Page 11, Column 1

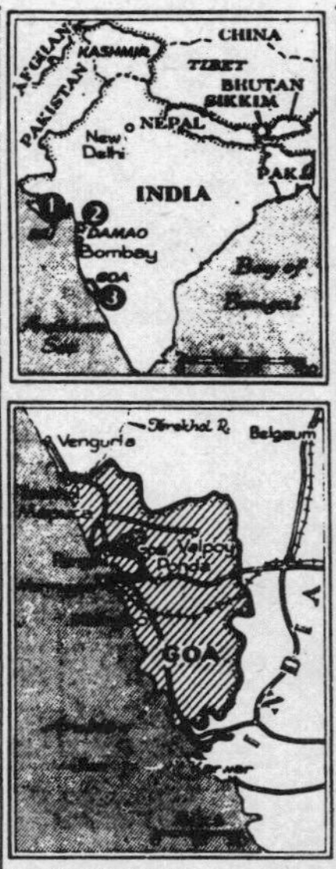

State to Be Asked To Add 38 Judges

By PETER KIHSS

The State Judicial Conference prepared yesterday to recommend that the Legislature create thirty-one new Supreme Court and seven new County Court judgeships to shorten delays in personal injury and criminal cases.

The proposal would provide eleven additional Supreme Court justices for Nassau and Suffolk Counties, which will become the new Tenth Judicial District Sept. 1. It now takes sixty-seven months for accident cases to reach jury trials in Nassau and fifty-five months in Suffolk.

Queens, which will become the Eleventh Judicial District, would get seven new Supreme Court justices; Kings and Richmond Counties, making up the Second District, would get

Continued on Page 5, Column 4

GOA RESISTS MOVE

Krishna Menon Cites Provocative Acts— Peace Bids Fail

By The Associated Press.

BELGAUM, India, Monday, Dec. 18—Indian troops invaded Goa and Portugal's two other enclaves on India's west coast early today.

The invasion was announced by the Indian Government. It was intended to end four-and-one-half centuries of Portuguese rule over parts of the Indian subcontinent.

The sound of fighting reaching this command post a few miles from the Goa border indicated that the Portuguese were carrying out their pledge to fight to the bitter end to defend Goa, the largest enclave, about 225 miles south of Bombay.

India's Defense Minister, V. K. Krishna Menon, said in New Delhi that India's Seventeenth Infantry Division was invading Goa from three directions with instructions to use the minimum force necessary.

Surrender Expected

Later reports said Indian troops successfully bridged Portuguese defenses at a number of points and were spreading out inside Goa. Portuguese artillery and mortar fire answered the Indian pre-attack barrage. However, the Indian army command here said the invasion was going as planned and confidently predicted that Goa would fall within two or three days.

[Communications between Lisbon and Goa were cut after an Indian air attack early Monday, according to a report by Reuters.]

Official reports reaching here said there was only nominal resistance in Damão and Diu, the two smaller enclaves north of Bombay, which, together, comprise about fifty square miles and have a total population of about 50,000.

Breakdown Charged

Mr. Krishna Menon said India ordered troops into Goa because of what he called a complete breakdown in civilian administration and provocations against Indian borders.

Portugal has ruled Goa, which has 1,537 square miles and a population of 650,000, since 1510. Mr. Krishna Menon said the Portuguese were there illegally.

The invasion announcement came within eight hours of fresh accusations by Indian officials of a Portuguese crossing along the 180-mile Goa border, and of firing upon an Indian patrol. It marked the end of efforts by the United States, Britain and the United Nations to prevent the crisis from erupting into fighting.

The invasion of Goa was announced at 12:30 A. M. today. A half hour later the invasion of Diu and Damão was announced.

The action was under the command of Lieut. Gen. Joyanto Chaudhuri. He commanded

Continued on Page 10, Column 4

LISBON SAYS INDIA 'DISREGARDS' U. N.

Accuses Nehru of 'Contempt' for World Law—Indians Are Ordered Interned

By BENJAMIN WELLES
Special to The New York Times.

MADRID, Dec. 17 — Alberto Franco Nogueira, Portuguese Foreign Minister, described the Indian invasion of Goa tonight as an example of "international immorality."

He called the invasion "disregard for the law, defiance of the United Nations Charter, contempt for the International Court of Justice and utter contempt for world public opinion." He placed responsibility for such conditions on Prime Minister Jawaharlal Nehru of India.

[The Portuguese Government at once ordered the internment of all Indian subjects residing in Portuguese overseas territories, according to Reuters.]

Opinion Seen Flouted

In a telephone interview, the Portuguese Foreign Minister said that the Indian Government had flouted "public opinion in many parts of the world, even among peoples who were not primarily sympathetic to Portugal."

"This is the first step by India to achieve the political unity of the Indian subcontinent," he declared. "It can have very serious consequences for other countries near by whose turn may come next."

Portuguese officials have been warning in recent days that India's long-awaited attack on Goa would be a prelude to a series of aggressive measures against India's other small neighbors: Pakistan, Nepal, Bhutan, Sikkim and Ceylon.

Portuguese authorities also stated in Lisbon that India's assault on the 650,000 Portuguese nationals had highlighted the ineffectiveness of United States policy toward the African-Asian bloc.

"America has been currying the favor of the Africans and Asians since the Kennedy Administration took office," one source noted today. "This is the first obvious result of Ambassador Adlai Stevenson's tactics in the United Nations," he said.

Other Portuguese indicated

Continued on Page 6, Column 3

Algerians Training Angolan Guerrillas

By LLOYD GARRISON

UNITED NATIONS, N. Y., Dec. 17 — A contingent of African rebels from Portuguese Angola is being trained in guerrilla warfare by Algerian nationalists at camps in Tunisia.

The Algerian National Liberation Front began training forty Angolans three months ago. Twenty-five of the Angolans are reported on their way back to Angola, accompanied by six Algerian advisers.

According to an Algerian source at the United Nations, the six advisers will help the rebels to organize militarily and politically. The source said the advisers would particularly stress the importance of political indoctrination along the lines of the Algerian rebels' slogan. "The leaflet precedes the

Continued on Page 8, Column 3

Emergency crews sift through debris following the tragic fire which destroyed the main tent of the Circo Americano.

United Press International

CIRCUS FIRE DEAD AT 285 IN BRAZIL

Continued From Page 1, Col. 5

Rio de Janeiro, the Brazilian Air Force Hospital began to receive Niteroi victims late in the day. The military services provided physicians and rounded up nurses.

Niteroi is the capital of the State of Rio de Janeiro.

Lopo Coelho, acting Governor of the state of Guanabara, which adjoins the Federal District of Rio de Janeiro, went across the bay and rallied help personally as well as by formal appeal.

Señhor Coelho said more than 2,000 men and women had lined up in front of the Niteroi morgue seeking missing relatives and friends.

The Federal and state authorities both declared the fire a public calamity. Federal troops were called up to help transport bodies to the morgue

and the injured to hospitals. They used military trucks in the shortage of ambulances.

Survivors of the fire generally were at first almost incoherent as they tried to describe the brief terror in the flaming tent. They said the exits seemed to have been blocked almost at once with bodies.

One man got out with all his five children by ducking under the stands instead of trying to escape through the desperate crush.

President Joao Goulart's wife, Senhora Teresa Goulart, who is chairman of the Brazilian As-

sistance legion ordered her organization mobilized to help the fire victims. The organization supplements Red Cross activities.

The State Governor, Celso Pecanha, who had been away, returned to Niteroi and took over direction of the relief work. He convened the State Legislature to vote emergency funds.

As the Niteroi morgue became crowded, some bodies were laid out in the city's Sports Stadium for relatives' identification.

The circus had the name of Great North American. It was set up in front of this railroad station in Niteroi. It had run in this city for some time before crossing the bay to the suburb.

The circus manager estimated the owners' loss at 50,000,000 cruzeiros (about $125,000). He said the circus company, despite its name, had no connection with United States or other North American interests.

The circus was operated by the Estavanovich brothers of Brazil and employed performers from many countries.

"All the News That's Fit to Print"

The New York Times.

LATE CITY EDITION

U. S. Weather Bureau Report (Page 69) forecasts: Mostly fair, not so cold today and tonight. Some cloudiness tomorrow. Temp. range: 35—18; yesterday: 31—15.

VOL. CXI. No. 37,974.
© 1962 by The New York Times Company. Times Square, New York 36, N. Y.
NEW YORK, FRIDAY, JANUARY 12, 1962.

10 cents beyond 50-mile zone from New York City except on Long Island. Higher in air delivery cities.

FIVE CENTS

KENNEDY ASKS NEW TARIFF POWER AND RIGHT TO CUT TAXES IN SLUMP; STATE OF UNION TALK IS CONFIDENT

United Press International Telephoto

STATE OF THE UNION MESSAGE: President Kennedy addressing joint session of Congress. At rear are Vice President Johnson and House Speaker John W. McCormack.

34 REQUESTS MADE

Economic and Welfare Plans to Strengthen U. S. Are Stressed

Text of the message appears on Pages 12 and 13.

By JAMES RESTON
Special to The New York Times.

WASHINGTON, Jan. 11—President Kennedy asked the Eighty-seventh Congress today to give him new authority to reduce tariffs, cut personal income taxes in an economic emergency and strengthen the welfare programs of the nation.

In a confident State of the Union message that gave unusual emphasis to economic and welfare issues rather than military measures, the President called for a low-tariff trade partnership with the free world and a domestic program designed to improve the nation's economy, social well-being and education.

The President, looking fit at the end of his first year in the White House, was well received by the Democratic majority in Congress. The Republicans, however, showed little enthusiasm for what they obviously regarded as a liberal election-year shopping list that would be sharply modified and by the end of the session.

5-Year Tariff Plan

Altogether, the President made thirty-four legislative requests. Among them was a proposal for a new five-year Trade Expansion Act. The President suggested that the new law permit the gradual elimination of all tariffs in the United States and the European Common Market countries on all items in which the United States and the Common Market countries together supply 80 per cent of the world's trade. The plan would allow the gradual reduction of duties up to 50 per cent on other goods.

These requests, however, were surrounded by verbal commitments to assure that the "benefits far outweigh any risks" and to assist employers to adjust to import competition. Accordingly, the President's outline was criticized by Congressional protectionists, who thought it too liberal, and by representatives of some Common Market countries, who thought it too protectionist.

Other Proposals

The President's other foreign-policy proposals included the following:

¶A $3,000,000,000 long-term Latin-American Alliance for Progress program.

¶Legislation to underwrite a $200,000,000 bond issue for the United Nations, which the President warmly supported.

¶Funds for an international communications satellite system, the details of which will be set forth in a later message.

In addition to these legislative requests in the foreign field, the President spoke confidently of the nation's relations with its

Continued on Page 13, Column 1

WEST TO BROADEN TALKS IN MOSCOW ON BERLIN ISSUES

Thompson Gets Wider Power to Probe Soviet Intentions on Full Negotiations

MAY SEE GROMYKO SOON

Allied View on Rights in City and Outlook for Agreement Expected to Be Topics

By SYDNEY GRUSON
Special to The New York Times.

BERLIN, Jan. 11—The United States Ambassador in Moscow, Llewellyn E. Thompson Jr., has received new instructions for his next round of talks with the Soviet Union on the Berlin problem.

Mr. Thompson is expected to see Foreign Minister Andrei A. Gromyko soon, possibly this week. He is acting on behalf of the Western Big Four—the United States, Britain, France and West Germany—to see whether a basis can be found for formal negotiations on Berlin.

The new instructions are believed here to allow Mr. Thompson to go somewhat further than in his discussion with Mr. Gromyko on Jan. 2, when the renewed probing of Soviet intentions got under way.

French Restriction Stands

Allied officials emphasized, however, that Mr. Thompson was not empowered to negotiate on behalf of the Allies and that the French restriction on going beyond trying to find out what the Russians are willing to settle for still held good.

Nevertheless, it is understood that Mr. Thompson will now be able to discuss the Allies' view of their rights in Berlin, which are based on the occupation of the city after World War II, and, if Mr. Gromyko shows himself amenable, the possibility of rewriting West Berlin's links with West Germany into an agreement on the city's future.

The question of these links is a sensitive issue here. But the Allies' view, it is understood, is that West Germany and West Berlin cannot continue to insist at the same time on a constitutional relationship between the two and the retention of the city's occupation status and the presence of Allied troops. The former is considered more important not only for the Allies, including West Germany,

Continued on Page 4, Column 3

Peru Landslide Kills 450; 3,000 Reported Missing

Mountain Town Buried by Avalanche—Rise in Toll Expected

Special to The New York Times.

LIMA, Peru, Jan. 11—An avalanche entombed the Andean village of Ranrahirca last night, killing all but fifty of its 500 people. The tiny community was buried under forty feet of ice, boulders and mud.

Many more people are believed to have been buried by the massive avalanche as it dropped suddenly from Huascarán, a 22,205-foot extinct volcano that is the highest in Peru, and crashed through other settlements in the valley.

The missing were reported to total 3,000 to 4,000, but this figure is still guesswork because the region is marked by deep ravines and sharp slopes that would take days to survey. The final death toll may have to be established by checking census figures computed last July.

The New York Times — Jan. 12, 1962

Area hit by slide (cross)

One of the survivors was Mayor Alfonso Caballero of Ranrahirca, who reported that only about fifty of the 500 inhabitants of his village had survived the disaster.

The Mayor could give an accounting of only his own village, which is 200 miles north-

Continued on Page 3, Column 6

RIGHT TO QUESTION ACCUSERS IS GIVEN IN PASSPORT CASES

State Department to Forbid Communists to Make Any Trips Outside U. S.

By ANTHONY LEWIS
Special to The New York Times.

WASHINGTON, Jan. 11—The State Department will announce tomorrow new regulations that bar passports to Communist party members but allow anyone accused of party membership to confront and cross-examine his accusers.

This is believed to be the first time that the Government has provided such an absolute right to confrontation in any internal security program. The use of confidential information has been a characteristic of many security proceedings.

Under the new regulations, the Federal Bureau of Investigation or other security agencies will still be able to insist on anonymity for a confidential informant. But in such a case, the State Department will have to issue a passport to the person accused by the informant.

Attorney General Approves

The confrontation provision was worked out in extensive discussions among State and Justice Department lawyers. It has the approval of Attorney General Robert F. Kennedy.

Communist party members have been free to obtain passports since 1958. The Supreme Court then held that State Department regulations barring passports to persons affiliated with communism had not been authorized by Congress.

The new move against party members results from the Supreme Court's upholding last June of the Internal Security Act of 1950.

The court said that the Communist party must register under the law as a "Communist-action" group. The party has refused to do so and is being prosecuted.

Warning to Be Printed

The law of 1950 provides that no member of a group directed to register, whether actually registered or not, may apply for or use a passport. The maximum penalty for violation is a fine of $10,000, five years in jail or both.

To implement the Internal Security Act, the State Department will print a warning about the passport provision at the top of every passport application. It is also distributing signs to passport offices around the country warning that it is a crime for Communists to apply.

Under the act, only present party membership is a reason for withholding a passport. If any passport official has reason to believe an applicant is a member, he will tentatively deny the application.

The applicant is then entitled

Continued on Page 17, Column 1

U. S. and Britain Confer On Actions Taken by U. N.

By E. W. KENWORTHY
Special to The New York Times.

WASHINGTON, Jan. 11—A group of United States and British officials began today a review of the problems facing their countries in the United Nations. In both Britain and the United States, there has been increasing debate—inside the Government as well as in the press—over some of the activities of the United Nations, particularly in the Congo.

There has also been concern over what the Earl of Home, British Foreign Secretary, has called "the demonstration of power without responsibility" by many of the new nations.

Even as the British and American diplomats began two and a half days of talks, President Kennedy gave renewed expression of United States support for the United Nations in his State of the Union message.

Basic to Our Strength

"Our strength and our hope" in keeping the peace, the President declared, "is the United Nations."

The President said he could see "little merit in the impatience of those who would abandon this imperfect world instrument because they dislike our imperfect world."

"The troubles of the United Nations," he continued, "merely reflect the troubles of the world. A weakening of the organization could only increase those troubles."

The President urged Congress to support his request to purchase up to half the $200,000,000 bond issue of the United Nations. The proceeds of the bonds will be used largely to finance the peace-keeping oper-

Continued on Page 14, Column 6

ALGERIAN CITIES ASK MORE TROOPS

French Aides Urge Army to Bolster Algiers and Oran as New Violence Looms

By PAUL HOFMANN
Special to The New York Times.

ALGIERS, Jan. 11—Top French officials here asked the army today to move additional troops into the seething cities of Algeria.

Further military reinforcements for Algiers and Oran were demanded as European extremists and Moslem urban guerrillas were reported to be preparing for showdown battles.

Jean Morin, French Delegate General and highest French Government representative in Algeria, presided at today's emergency meeting at the French administrative center in Rocher-Noir, thirty-three miles east of here. The session was attended by prefects heading the thirteen departments of administrative districts of northern Algeria and high police officials.

A Government source said the prefects voiced "some apprehension" about the present tense situation but were on the whole "confident" that large-scale clashes could be avoided if the army was strengthened in the big coastal cities.

Strong French forces had already moved into Algiers and Oran last week-end. It is thought that the army will not send in further reinforcements unless it expects a cease-fire with the rebels that would produce a quieter situation in Algeria's huge hinterland. Army forces are understood to be spread very thin in vast areas.

Tension in Algiers mounted

Continued on Page 2, Column 4

ELECTRIC STRIKE HAS MILD IMPACT

Other Crafts Keep Working as Power Is Maintained

By STANLEY LEVEY

New York's first major strike in the electrical industry in forty years began yesterday, but the initial impact was slight.

Nine thousand members of Local 3 of the International Brotherhood of Electrical Workers did not report for their jobs with 600 electrical contractors at 8 A. M.

In their place at building construction sites were several hundred men sent in by the union to maintain power and light so that other work could go on.

Local 3 posted no pickets and made no effort to keep other building craftsmen from their jobs. Nor did the union turn off the power, as the contractors had feared. As a result, construction activity in the $1,250,000,000-a-year industry was slowed but not stopped.

However, industry spokesmen warned that the effects of the strike would be cumulative. In three or four days, they said, the pace of construction will begin to lag as work reaches the point where the electricians normally would take over. After that, they predicted, the tie-up will accelerate until it involves all workers in the construction field.

The electricians on strike include all those on construction jobs and some who do maintenance and installation work.

The strike was made certain early yesterday morning when, despite the eleventh-hour intervention of Mayor Wagner, ne-

Continued on Page 22, Column 1

City Is Drawing Up Rent Control Law

By PAUL CROWELL

Mayor Wagner said yesterday that the city was drafting a local law setting up its own rent-control machinery.

It was indicated at City Hall that the measure would create a local rent control board with power to promulgate administrative regulations.

The Mayor's declaration was in reply to a statement made by Governor Rockefeller at a press conference on Wednesday, accusing him of trying to avoid the responsibility of handling rent control locally.

The Mayor said: "However ready he is with the words, he is certainly careless with the facts."

Mr. Wagner added that Mr. Rockefeller should have known that city and state representatives had already conferred on the transfer of rent control re-

Continued on Page 16, Column 1

B-52 Flies Halfway Around World

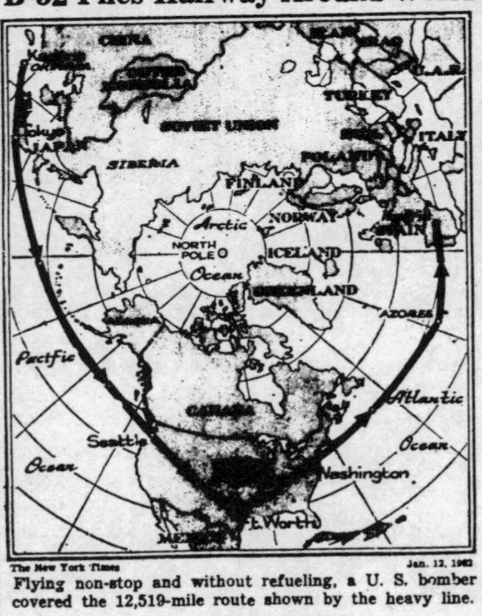

The New York Times — Jan. 12, 1962

Flying non-stop and without refueling, a U. S. bomber covered the 12,519-mile route shown by the heavy line.

By The Associated Press.

MADRID, Jan. 11—A United States Air Force B-52H superbomber equipped for launching missiles broke a world record today by flying 12,519 miles non-stop from Okinawa to Madrid without refueling. The jet plane, which is powered by eight turbofan engines, exceeded by 1,283.4 miles the old distance record without refueling, set in 1946 by a United States Navy patrol plane named the Truculent Turtle. The jet, in its flight halfway around the world, claimed ten other speed and course marks. It took off yesterday with a gross weight of nearly 500,000 pounds from

Continued on Page 6, Column 4

ARMY'S RESERVES FACING OVERHAUL

Pentagon Bars Major Cuts in Drill-Pay Units—Kennedy to Seek More Missiles

By JACK RAYMOND
Special to The New York Times.

WASHINGTON, Jan. 11—Plans for a thorough overhaul of the Army Reserve forces, but without major reductions in their total strength, will be made known to Congress next week.

These plans, to be announced by Secretary of Defense Robert S. McNamara, will call for fairly small reductions in the total of 700,000 men on drill-pay status. They will eliminate some low priority Reserve and National Guard units and shift others.

The plans also will ease earlier readiness programs that counted on bringing 89,000 Reservists, including two Guard divisions, to active duty on three weeks' notice. At the same time, increases in Congressional appropriations will be sought for the Reserves to accelerate over-all readiness.

President Kennedy called attention to the pending revisions in a brief review of military affairs in his State of the Union message today.

He cited spending increases over the last twelve months to strengthen the armed forces—"not in the expectation of war

Continued on Page 13, Column 7

Congress Sees New Goals As Long-Range Program

By JOHN D. MORRIS
Special to The New York Times.

WASHINGTON, Jan. 11—Members of Congress viewed much of President Kennedy's enlarged legislative program today as a glittering prospectus of goals that were unlikely to be achieved this year, if ever.

The feeling was that several major proposals in the State of the Union message had been put forward "for the record" as long-range objectives rather than in the hope or expectation of action in the 1962 session.

Members listed high in that category recommendations for stand-by authority to reduce taxes and increase public works in a recession.

Doubts On School Aid

They also included the President's renewed requests for aid to public schools and an overhaul of the unemployment compensation system.

Mr. Kennedy's promise to support some proposals for civil rights legislation now pending in Congress was similarly classified by legislators.

So was his advocacy of a broad public welfare program for the relief and rehabilitation of the indigent, at least to the extent that the scope, yet to be disclosed, was likely to exceed realistic expectations.

Regardless whether Mr. Kennedy was outlining such proposals for action this session, the prospect was that with the possible exception of public welfare proposals they would be

Continued on Page 14, Column 1

PRESIDENT SEEKS RECESSION CURBS

Request for Tax Authority Renews Economic Issue—Stiff Opposition Seen

By RICHARD E. MOONEY
Special to The New York Times.

WASHINGTON, Jan. 11—President Kennedy asked Congress today for authority to combat recessions with quick, temporary cuts in personal income taxes.

His plan, which economists have discussed for years, would be a sharp change in the taxing power bestowed on Congress by the Constitution.

The Administration does not expect the plan to be enacted on this first try. It believes, however, that the idea offers such an important anti-recession weapon that Congress and the public should start thinking about it.

Seeks Change on Jobless

The tax-cutting proposal was the first of three anti-recession measures that the President proposed on the argument that "the time to repair the roof is when the sun is shining."

The second was a proposal that he had announced before, to give the President stand-by authority to speed up spending for Federal construction and on state and local construction that receives Federal aid, if unemployment should rise by an amount to be specified in the law.

The third was a repeat request for approval of last year's proposals to strengthen the unemployment insurance system.

The message also pressed three proposals "to expand our growth and job opportunities"

Continued on Page 13, Column 7

Minow Asks More TV Outlets; Educational Program Pressed

All-Channel Sets Urged

Special to The New York Times.

WASHINGTON, Jan. 11—Newton N. Minow said today that the country urgently needed more television stations to give the public a greater choice of programs.

As the most effective step in that direction he urged Congress to pass an all-channel receiver bill. This would require manufacturers to make television sets capable of receiving all channels. Mr. Minow is chairman of the Federal Communications Commission.

Most of the 55,000,000 television sets now in use in the United States can receive only twelve very-high-frequency channels—numbers 2 through 13. They cannot get the seventy ultra-high-frequency channels

Continued on Page 70, Column 2

National Policy Sought

Special to The New York Times.

WASHINGTON, Jan. 11—A special study group called today for a national policy for development of educational television.

The suggestion was made by the Educational Media Study Panel after more than a year of study. A report was released by Dr. Sterling M. McMurrin, Commissioner of the Office of Education.

Dr. McMurrin said his office was prepared to carry out immediately the panel's suggestion for establishment of national and regional exchange centers for educational television teaching materials.

He said this would be done under the educational media provisions of the National Defense Education Act.

In calling for a national pol-

Continued on Page 70, Column 6

Automation Buffer Is Favored by Panel

By PETER BRAESTRUP
Special to The New York Times.

WASHINGTON, Jan. 11—The President's Committee on Labor-Management Policy submitted its first recommendations today. It called for compensation, education and retraining for workers to cushion the unemployment arising from automation.

The nineteen-member committee is headed by Secretary of Labor Arthur J. Goldberg and includes seven top corporation executives, seven union leaders and five public members. It was set up by President Kennedy last March to recommend private and public policies in labor-related areas.

The panel agreed unanimously on the following statement: "Achievement of technological progress without sacrifice of human values requires a com-

Continued on Page 14, Column 5

NEWS INDEX

The path of the avalanche, roaring down Mt. Huascarah in the Peruvian Andes.

Wide World Photos

Landslide in Peru Kills 450; 3,000 Are Reported Missing

Continued From Page 1, Col. 3

west of Lima and thirty miles north of the hot springs resort city of Huarás. But more than 7,000 persons live in surrounding ranching and mining communities and other areas near by.

Witnesses of the disaster. who were on high ground that was bypassed by the slide, said that the mass of rock, mud and ice was about three quarters of a mile wide when it plunged into the valley.

Mayor Caballero said that it took only eight minutes for Ranrahirca to be "wiped off the map." The avalanche was started when an ice mass, loosened by Peru's summer sun. broke off the mountain top and carried snow, water, rock and mud along with it.

The avalanche started about 7 P. M. when the mountain communities had settled in for the night, dropped with a roar and a cloud of dust and snow, sweeping quickly over the church, the village hall, the school and other buildings. It swept on to the edge of the Santa River.

Relief Planes Sent

It was hours before officials at Lima were able to get reports of the disaster because telephone and other communication lines were engulfed in the slide.

Planes of the Peruvian Air Force left for the area early this morning with relief supplies and high Government officials. Additional relief supplies were being sent overland. and tractors and bulldozers were being rushed to Huaras to supplement emergency equipment.

Avalanches, called "huaycos" by Peruvian Indians, are the most terrifying phenomena in the Andes during the rainy season. They strike with tremendous force in unpredictable places.

A similar disaster occurred Dec. 13, 1941, partly destroying Huarás, the largest town in the valley. The loss of life then was estimated at a total of more than 3,000 persons.

The area of yesterday's disaster, Callejon de Huaylas, is often called the Switzerland of South America because of its glacier-capped peaks and scenic beauty.

Villages Wiped Out

HUARAS, Peru, Jan. 11 (UPI) — The Peruvian villages of Saccha, Huaraschuco, Uchucoto and others between Yungay and Carhuaz in the rich agricultural Huarás Valley were wiped out by the avalanche, according to reports reaching here.

The Huarás Valley, between the massive ranges of the Andes, is rich agricultural country.

Red Cross Aid Offered

Special to The New York Times.

GENEVA, Jan. 11 — The League of Red Cross Societies sent an offer today of international help for the Peruvian Red Cross.

The league. which has eighty-seven national affiliates, said it would immediately call on its members for emergency action if assistance was required.

"All the News That's Fit to Print"

The New York Times.

LATE CITY EDITION
U. S. Weather Bureau Report (Page 56) forecasts
Mostly sunny today. Fair tonight.
Some cloudiness tomorrow.
Temp. range: 84—56; yesterday: 84—55.
Temp.-Hum. Index: low 70's; yesterday 73.

VOL. CXI...No. 38,117.   © 1962 by The New York Times Company.
Times Square, New York 36, N. Y.   NEW YORK, MONDAY, JUNE 4, 1962.   10 cents beyond 50-mile zone from New York City
except on Long Island. Higher in air delivery cities.   FIVE CENTS

MACMILLAN VISIT REASSURES PARIS ON TRADE BLOC TIE

Parley With de Gaulle Clears Atmosphere for Further Talks, French Aides Say

COMMON GOALS CITED

Two Leaders Pledge to Push Ahead in Negotiations— Briton Returns Home

By ROBERT C. DOTY
Special to The New York Times.

PARIS, June 3—President de Gaulle and Prime Minister Macmillan ended today a week-end of conversations that French sources said had dissipated mutual suspicions arising from negotiations for British entry into the European Common Market.

The two leaders issued a communiqué affirming their agreement on the existence of a "community of interests" between France and Britain on major issues and their determination to pursue negotiations with those common interests in mind.

The Prime Minister and his wife, Lady Dorothy Macmillan, flew back to London late this afternoon after their twenty-four-hour visit with the French President and his wife at the Château de Champs, east of Paris.

Talks Viewed as Success

The two leaders conferred last night and this morning with only an interpreter present. They were joined later by Premier Georges Pompidou, Foreign Minister Maurice Couve de Murville and the French and British Ambassadors to London and Paris, respectively.

Informed French circles described the result of the conversations as one likely to improve the atmosphere of the current negotiations in Brussels on Britain's application to join the six-nation European Economic Community.

The French have suspected that Britain sought to obtain for herself the best of two worlds—entry into the Common Market and maintenance of her special trade links with the Commonwealth.

Ties to U. S. a Problem

It has also been feared that Britain could not be brought to a whole-hearted acceptance of a European orientation inevitably involving some sacrifice of her special relationship with the United States.

French sources said Mr. Macmillan gave the impression here that he was determined to bring Britain into the Community without reservations and extra-European attachments that

Continued on Page 3, Column 3

ADENAUER SCORNS RETIREMENT TALK

Asserts His Era Is Not Over —Affirms Support of U. S.

By GERD WILCKE
Special to The New York Times.

DORTMUND, Germany, June 3—Chancellor Adenauer told his party today that "the Adenauer era has not ended yet."

He indicated in a speech opening the annual congress of the Christian Democratic Union that he would not step down next year, as has been widely assumed in West Germany.

He repeated that he would give up his office before the next Federal elections in 1965, but he insisted that in agreeing last year not to serve another full term "I did not state the day or year when this will be done."

The opposition Social Democrats have demanded Chancellor Adenauer's retirement. The Free Democrats, junior partners in his Government, have indicated that they have received his pledge to resign next year.

The 86-year-old Chancellor, who also is party chairman, came to this bustling coal and steel city apparently determined to straighten the record on his future role and also on his views about Western unity.

He said his critics "must have slept for twelve years if they think I have basically different views" from those of other Western leaders on how to

Continued on Page 4, Column 4

Terrorists in Algeria Split On Talks With Nationalists

Pirate Broadcasts From Two Cities Conflict on Status of Parley

By THOMAS F. BRADY
Special to The New York Times.

ALGIERS, June 3—The unity of the Right-wing terrorist Secret Army Organization appeared tonight to have been destroyed.

A pirate broadcast on the television sound channel at Oran declared that the command of the Secret Army of European terrorists was in the Oran region, in western Algeria, and not at Algiers. The broadcast denounced as without authority the "negotiations" that have been reported to be taking place here.

At the same time, a pirate broadcast in Algiers said the "contacts" that were in progress had thus far been the "maneuvers of politicians."

The Algiers broadcast said that if a "satisfactory response" was not received by Tuesday at midnight, the truce that has prevailed here for nearly four

Continued on Page 8, Column 3

Pope Asks Racial Accord in North Africa and End Of Extremist Killings

By PAUL HOFMANN
Special to The New York Times.

ROME, June 3—Pope John XXIII called today for an end to bloodshed in Algeria and appealed for racial peace in North Africa.

The Pope's plea at a general audience in St. Peter's this morning was understood to have been directed above all to European extremists in Algeria.

"May all inhabitants of the Mediterranean coast from Tunis to Morocco shake hands," the Pontiff declared. "May the rights of all be respected in the bloodstained lands of Africa."

French observers here read into the Pope's words an appeal also to Moslem nationalists in Algeria, Tunisia and Morocco to show understanding for the legitimate interests of the European minorities.

It was widely believed that Pope John had timed his mes-

Continued on Page 9, Column 3

U. S. Urged to Widen Aid To World on Atom Power

By JOHN W. FINNEY
Special to The New York Times.

WASHINGTON, June 3—A State Department advisory committee recommended today that the United States give greater support to the International Atomic Energy Agency in promoting and safeguarding the global development of nuclear power.

The committee found that after a difficult and somewhat discouraging start, the agency could now begin to fulfill its originally intended function of helping to develop and build atomic power plants.

[In Moscow, the Soviet Union warned that the international situation would be aggravated if the United States set off a series of high-altitude nuclear test explosions.]

The brightening prospect for the agency, the committee said, springs from the newly encouraging outlook for the development of economically competitive electricity from nuclear power.

"Indeed nuclear power "will be commercially attractive in a number of countries in the near future."

The committee said that with this improved outlook for atomic power had come a need for the United States to support the agency with "increasing vigor" if this country were to further its "Atoms for Peace" program and prevent fissionable materials from being diverted to military purposes.

The eight-man advisory committee is headed by Dr. Henry D. Smyth of Princeton University, the United States representative to the international agency. The committee was

Continued on Page 2, Column 3

VENEZUELA ARMY CRUSHING REBELS

120 Loyal Troops Believed Killed in Fight to Drive Insurgents From City

By United Press International.

PUERTO CABELLO, Venezuela, June 3—Loyal Government troops appeared tonight to have broken the back of a Leftist revolt after bloody block-by-block fighting in the heart of this city.

Snipers' bullets whined through the streets, but some of the rebel marine units here were reported trying to escape to mountains in the south.

Rebel units entrenched in the downtown area earlier had repulsed a dawn attack by Government troops and had forced them to retreat.

By nightfall, however, loyal forces were encountering only sporadic resistance in the city, mostly from snipers.

Loyalist casualties alone were estimated to have totaled at least 120 dead.

Snipers in City

Several hundred rebel snipers remained scattered throughout the city, but a Government military spokesman predicted that mopping-up operations would crush remaining resistance within twenty-four hours.

[Cuba apparently sought to assist the rebels, according to a Reuters dispatch from Caracas. The dispatch said the Havana radio, heard in Venezuela, had asked the rebels to get in touch with Cuba by radio and called on the Venezuelan people to support the rebels.]

Hard fighting forced the insurgents out of the big naval base last night after they had staged the country's third military revolt in a year against the regime of President Romulo Betancourt.

Rebel Chief Defiant

Navy Comdr. Pedro Medina Silva, one of the revolt leaders captured in the fierce battle, was reported to be still defiant. "There has been Carúpano and Puerto Cabello and there will be more to come," sources quoted him as having said. Carúpano is an important naval base that was the scene of a revolt earlier this year.

Troops, heavy tanks and mobile artillery patrolled the city streets as the Government ordered a curfew for civilian residents of this city.

A Government chaplain, the Rev. Natalio D. Rivera, estimated that loyalist casualties alone were "no less than" 120 dead and between 300 and 400 wounded. There was no immediate indication of rebel losses.

Military commanders said the fighting here probably was

Continued on Page 18, Column 1

Wyszynski Defies Polish Regime With Letter Attacking Atheism

Cardinal Bids Catholics Pray for Return of Country's 'Godless' to the Faith

By ARTHUR J. OLSEN
Special to The New York Times.

WARSAW, June 3—An episcopal letter of the Roman Catholic Church, published over official objections, called upon Poland's Christians today to fast and to pray that atheists return to the faith.

The episcopal letter, signed May 15 by Stefan Cardinal Wyszynski and all sixty-four Polish Bishops, had been scheduled for publication last Sunday. The document became known to Government authorities, however, and Cardinal Wyszynski was pressed to withhold it.

Cardinal Wyszynski, who has been increasingly disturbed by Government-supported efforts to educate young Poles against "superstition" and "medieval practices," refused to withhold the letter, although he hesitated for a week.

Retaliation appears to have started as soon as the regime learned of the letter. Sources close to the church said that a number of young seminarians

Associated Press
Stefan Cardinal Wyszynski

studying for the priesthood in the Rzeszow and Kielce areas received military draft notices last week. Two years ago the Government suspended the exemption of the student clergy from military service, but only a few seminarians had been called up before last week.

The letter, read in every church in Poland during masses, proclaimed the Octave of

Continued on Page 7, Column 3

CONGRESS FACING HEAVY WORK LOAD ON RETURN TODAY

Senate Is Expected to Send 4.6 Billion Aid Bill to House by Week-End

By RUSSELL BAKER
Special to The New York Times.

WASHINGTON, June 3—Congress will return from a long Memorial Day vacation this week to attack a heavy backlog of work.

On Tuesday the Senate will start action on the Administration's $4,662,000,000 foreign aid authorization bill, which is somewhat less freighted with political controversy this year than usual. It is expected to pass without substantial cuts and go to the House by the week-end.

The House Foreign Affairs Committee has reported a bill carrying about the same amount of money but apportioning it differently. The House will wait for the Senate to act.

Although the foreign aid authorization does not face its usual perils this year, largely because its most controversial features were decided last year, authorization is only the first and easier of two steps for the aid program.

Battle Coming Up

It must be followed by a separate bill that makes the authorized funds available for spending. And here the Administration faces the usual hard fight late in the session to avoid deep cuts.

The House, which has been unusually quiet for the last month, still has no major floor fights on its immediate schedule, but trouble lies just over the horizon.

The Senate Ways and Means Committee is expected to report to the House the trade bill, the top-priority measure on President Kennedy's legislative agenda for this year. The leadership has tentatively planned to start floor action on June 18.

No Senate activity has begun yet on the trade bill and none is scheduled until mid-July when the Finance Committee will start hearings.

Farm Bill Awaits Action

Another major controversy will move toward resolution this week when the House Rules Committee is asked to clear the Administration's drastic new farm bill for floor action.

The farm bill, as passed by the Senate, is one of the most stringent production controls in history on wheat and livestock feed grains such as corn, barley and grain sorghums. The House Agriculture Committee has retained the most controversial control provisions of the bill, and its rate on the House floor is in doubt.

In the Senate, the issue was settled in the Administration's favor through a series of virtually solid party-line votes, with the Southern Democrats providing the critical margin of

Continued on Page 20, Column 1

121 IN ATLANTA ART GROUP KILLED AS JET AIRLINER CRASHES AT PARIS; 9 OTHERS DEAD, 2 IN CREW SURVIVE

United Press International Telephoto
FRENCH AIR DISASTER: Firemen and police sift wreckage near tail section of the Air France jet airliner that crashed and burned at Villeneuve-le-Roi, outside Paris.

A NEW COMMUNITY PROPOSED BY CITY

Project in Brooklyn Would Offer Low-Rent Housing, Schools and Stores

By PAUL CROWELL

The city's Housing and Redevelopment Board has completed preliminary plans for the establishment of a $63,800,000 residential community on a 150-acre site fronting on Jamaica Bay in the Paerdegat Basin section of Brooklyn.

Milton Mollen, chairman of the board, said yesterday that the proposed community, to be constructed on largely vacant land, would supply middle and low rent housing. The site also would have park areas, new public schools, cultural and shopping centers, hospital facilities and a marina.

Mr. Mollen said that the housing units would be of varying heights. It is planned, he said, to have a new elementary school and a new junior high school on the site.

The general boundaries of the proposed community are Paerdegat Avenue, Ralph Avenue, East Sixty-sixth Street, Island Avenue and Avenue T.

Approval to be Sought

The Housing and Redevelopment Board, Mr. Mollen said, will soon submit the project for consideration by the City Planning Commission and the Board of Estimate, whose approval is required if the project is to advance.

Mr. Mollen gave no details of the proposal, but a recent report of the Housing and Redevelopment Board estimated the cost of the project at $63,-800,000, the number of dwelling units at 2,341 and the amount of commercial space at 253,000 square feet.

The report estimated that the city would derive $1,200,000 a year in real estate taxes from the area after completion of the project, as compared with a present annual yield of $30,000.

It was indicated that these estimates may have changed, but not materially, since the report was issued a few weeks ago.

Both public and private hous-

Continued on Page 25, Column 1

Atlanta Is Stunned by Loss Of Many Cultural Leaders

By CLAUDE SITTON
Special to The New York Times.

ATLANTA, June 3—Shocked disbelief followed by mourning swept Atlanta today with the news that many of its cultural leaders had died in the crash of an Air France jetliner in Paris. Not since 119 died here in the Winecoff Hotel fire of 1946 has this city suffered a comparable disaster.

Members of more than one hundred families, many of them prominent in civic, social, business and political affairs, died in the crash. Expressions of sorrow for their loss were coupled with concern over the city's cultural future.

The last air accident in which numbers of persons from the same area were killed was the crash last Nov. 8 of a chartered airliner near Richmond, Va., that took the lives of seventy-seven persons. Most of them were Army recruits on their way to basic training, including thirty-one who had been picked up in Wilkes-Barre, Pa., and seventeen in Baltimore. Twenty-six of the recruits were from North Jersey communities.

Most of the victims of the Paris crash were either officials or members of the Atlanta Art Association, which operates museums and galleries containing several valuable collections of paintings and sculpture. The association's president, Del R. Paige, and his wife were among the dead.

Mr. Paige also headed a committee of civic leaders that was laying plans for an Atlanta center for the performing arts. He and others on the jetliner were active in the fields of music, ballet, opera and the theater. "Atlanta has suffered an

Continued on Page 23, Column 1

WRECKAGE BURNS

Flames Bar Rescue in Worst Single-Plane Disaster in History

By ROBERT ALDEN
Special to The New York Times.

PARIS, June 3—One hundred thirty persons were killed today when an Air France Boeing 707 jet crashed and burned while taking off from Orly Airport for New York.

The only survivors were two stewardesses. A steward was found alive in the wreckage, but he died ten hours later.

It was the worst disaster involving a single airplane in the history of aviation.

All of the victims except seven crew members and one passenger were Americans, and most of these were from Atlanta. A group of 121 had come to Europe on an art-appreciation tour sponsored by the Atlanta Art Association and had chartered the plane for the return flight to New York and Atlanta.

The crash wiped out six members of one family from Atlanta. They were Frederick W. Bull; his wife, Elizabeth; two daughters, Ellen, 10 years old, and Betsy, 16; Mr. Bull's mother, Mrs. Mary Bull, and his uncle, Robert S. Newcomb.

Sky Was Sunny

The accident took place in bright sunlight and with barely a cloud in the sky. The jetliner, heavily weighted with fuel for the long trans-Atlantic flight and with a capacity passenger load, began to roll down the long Orly runway twenty-five minutes after noon.

According to eyewitnesses, the plane gathered runway speed quickly. As it reached the speed at which it apparently should have become airborne, it rose about six feet and then faltered. It appeared that the plane's air speed was not sufficient to sustain flight.

The jet settled to the runway, and there is evidence in marks on the runway that the pilot tried to brake the 140-ton craft. His efforts were in vain.

The plane careened crazily as it ate up the remaining yardage to the end of the runway. It smashed some lights on one side of the runway, the right wing grazed the ground, and parts of the plane began breaking away.

2 Explosions Follow

The jetliner then crashed through a low wooden fence and raced into a flat open field that borders the little French town of Villeneuve-le-Roi at the edge of the airfield. As the landing gear broke away and the jet engines scraped the earth, flames burst out at the front.

Two muffled explosions were reported as the jet caught fire—20,000 gallons of it—took fire. The flames roared high as the plane disintegrated against the side of a low, lightly wooded hill.

Parts of the wreckage plowed into and destroyed an uninhabited house, and other parts struck low garden walls in the town. No one in the town was killed, although fierce fires began burning everywhere in the fields just fifty yards from Villeneuve-le-Roi.

No Chance for Passengers

Townspeople, most of whom were at lunch, rushed from their houses, but there was no chance of saving the passengers trapped inside the burning plane.

Firefighters who raced to the scene from the Orly hangars found the two stewardesses. Francoise Authie and Jacqueline Gillet, who had been thrown clear of the jet.

Mlle. Gillet was lying about fifty yards from the wreckage, moaning and sobbing. Her legs were slightly burned, but she did not seem badly hurt.

Mlle. Authie was found wandering in the midst of the burning wreckage. She appeared unhurt.

More than an hour after the crash, firefighters found

Continued on Page 22, Column 2

PAY INCREASE DUE AT CITY COLLEGES

Rosenberg Expects 3 Million —Cites Mayor's Promise of Parity With Schools

By NAN ROBERTSON

Teachers in the City University of New York will receive $3,000,000 in salary increases for the coming school year, Gustave G. Rosenberg, chairman of the Board of Higher Education, said yesterday.

Mr. Rosenberg disclosed in a television program that Mayor Wagner had assured him of the raise, based traditionally on 10 per cent of each salary increase for the entire city school system.

The $3,000,000 raise would affect, Mr. Rosenberg said later, about 3,000 full-time faculty members, plus other part-time teachers in seven colleges in the municipal system.

The system includes City College, Hunter, Brooklyn and Queens Colleges, and the Bronx, Queensborough and Staten Island community colleges. The faculty of the City University is equal to about 10 per cent of the teaching staff

Continued on Page 21, Column 1

Internes' Salaries to Be Doubled At Montefiore Hospital by 1964

By EMANUEL PERLMUTTER

The salaries of internes at Montefiore Hospital will be doubled, the hospital announced yesterday. The Bronx institution listed increases almost as great for resident doctors.

The new salary scale will go into effect in July and will be completed by 1964. It will raise internes to $4,000 a year and residents to a high of $6,250, making the salary scale the highest of its type in the city.

Internes are usually newly graduated doctors who are spending a year in a hospital working with patients. Residents have completed internship and are usually training for two to four years in their specialized fields of medicine, including surgery.

The new schedule will increase the salary of internes from $1,920 to $3,000 in July; to $3,500 in 1963, and to $4,000 in 1964.

Residents will have their base

Continued on Page 14, Column 5

In announcing the new salary scale for Montefiore, Victor S. Riesenfeld, president of the hospital, said it was designed to "help eliminate the added burden of very low wages to the already rigorous demands of post-graduate medical training."

"This change is being made because we believe it is time for a break with tradition," he added. "In the interest of fairness to young doctors and the society they will serve, house staff salaries must be made commensurate with their skills, training and high purpose."

The city's municipal hospitals pay their chief residents $4,800 a year, a spokesman for the

130 Killed as Jetliner Crashes Attempting to Take Off

ALL BUT 9 VICTIMS IN ATLANTA GROUP

2 of Crew Survive as Craft Roars Through Fence and Explodes in Open Field

Continued From Page 1, Col. 8

steward, Marcel Lugon. He was lying among several bodies in the wreckage, unconscious and with severe burns. He was taken to the hospital in critical condition.

A gendarme who was on his way home for lunch saw the crash and ran toward it. But the wreckage was burning so fiercely that he was unable to get close to it. He finally retreated, his legs singed.

Policemen and ambulances from surrounding towns were on the scene in minutes. But there was nothing they could do to save further lives. Within an hour and a half firemen extinguished the last of the flames.

The rescue force sifted through the wreckage to recover the bodies, many of them burned beyond recognition.

The bodies were placed side by side in a scorched apple orchard. Later they were taken in convoys of ambulances to an improvised morgue at Orly's old air terminal.

Since it was a Sunday and a pleasant one, thousands of French motorists were on the road in the vicinity of Orly Airport. They heard the news of the crash on their car radios, and the roads about the airport soon became clogged.

The long line of ambulances moving out of Villeneuve-le-Roi rolled past the stalled motorists.

Investigations Open

Air France and the French Government immediately began investigations into the disaster. But in today's early stages of the inquiry no one at the scene would even guess as to the cause.

[The Civil Aeronautics Board in Washington sent a representative to Paris to act as an observer in the investigation of the crash, United Press International reported.

[A C. A. B. spokesman said the representative, George W. Haldeman, departed for Paris within hours after the disaster.

[The spokesman explained that while the investigation would be under French jurisdiction, the C. A. B. liked to "keep on top" of any accidents involving planes of American manufacture.

[According to another Government aviation official, early reports of the disaster indicated "some similarity" to the crash of an American Airlines 707 in New York last March 1 in which ninety-five persons were killed.

[The official noted that the Air France plane was reported to have listed sharply to starboard just before the crash. The American Airlines plane also listed to starboard after taking off and rising several hundred feet.]

Roger Dusseaulx, French Minister of Transport and Public Works, will be in over-all charge of the investigation. He arrived at Orly this afternoon, and the control tower told him that after the captain of the Air France flight had received permission to take off and had acknowledged it, there was no further communication from the jet.

Dream Ends in Tragedy

Today's disaster brought a tragic end to what had been a dream come true—a first visit to Europe—for a large group of Georgians.

They had arrived in France on May 10 to see Europe in general and its museums in particular.

After their arrival, most went their separate ways. But forty-five went on a special tour arranged by American Express for the Atlanta Art Association. The group visited Britain, Germany, Switzerland, the Netherlands and Italy.

All of the Georgians—those who went their private ways and those who went on the special tour—were at Orly this morning to return to the United States. The only non-American passenger among them was Paul S. Doassans, Atlanta district manager for Air France.

The scheduled take-off, 12:25 P.M., was punctual.

The residents of Villeneuve-le-Roi are used to the sound of jet engines, roaring at full throttle down the runway at neighboring Orly and then up over the town. Today's roar, they said, was different. It seemed as if the whole town would be consumed by its ferociousness.

Firemen at Annual Dinner Rush to Scene of Jet Crash

VILLENEUVE - LE - ROI, France, June 3 (Reuters)—The firemen of this city of 16,715 persons were preparing to sit down to their annual dinner today when the Air France Boeing 707 jetliner crashed and burned among neat gardens and red-tiled villas near Paris' Orly Airport.

The firemen leaped up from the table and rushed to the disaster scene in their dress uniforms.

Villeneuve also was celebrating the anniversary of the release of its prisoners-of-war from German camps after World War II. But the blare of the city's band soon gave way to the sirens of ambulances as rescue teams rushed through the main street to the blazing wreck of the plane.

TOLL SETS RECORD FOR SINGLE PLANE

The toll of 130 lives in the jet crash in Paris yesterday was the highest ever incurred in a single-plane disaster, and it was the sixth airplane accident in history to cause more than 100 deaths.

The crash yesterday killed more persons actually aboard the aircraft than any other accident in the annals of aviation.

The worst of all accidents occurred here on Dec. 16, 1960, when a United Air Lines DC-8 jet and a Trans World Airlines Super-Constellation collided over Staten Island. A total of 134 persons was killed.

However, six of the persons killed were on the ground and 128 were aboard the planes — eighty-four on the jet and forty-four on the propeller-driven plane.

In the Tokyo disaster in 1953, a United States Air Force C-124 Globemaster crashed, killing 129 servicemen. This was the worst military accident on record and, until yesterday, the worst accident involving only one plane.

A total of 128 persons was killed June 30, 1956, when a United DC-7 and a T. W. A. Super-Constellation collided over Grand Canyon in Arizona.

Two other crashes earlier this year each took more than 100 lives. On March 15 a Constellation chartered by the Flying Tiger Line from the Military Air Transport Service disappeared over the Pacific Ocean with 107 persons aboard. On March 4 a chartered Caledonian Airlines DC-7C crashed at Douala in the West African Republic of Cameroon, killing 111.

Associated Press Radiophoto

FIRES FOLLOW CRASH: Flames that spread from ruins of the Air France jetliner that crashed on take-off yesterday being fought in fields in the vicinity of Orly Airport.

The New York Times   June 4, 1962
CRASH SITE: Plane fell near Orly Airport (cross).

Columnist on Airliner Had Described Atlanta Group's Travels

ATLANTA, June 3 (UPI) — "Spring is late everywhere..."

Those were the words of Margaret Turner, club editor of The Atlanta Journal, who died with 129 others today in the crash of an Air France Jet near Paris.

"So far our summer clothes have remained packed in our suitcases," she wrote in an Atlanta Journal column sent from Rome Friday, two days before she died.

"We have not been out of our winter coats a single day since leaving Atlanta May 9," she said in detailing the activities of members of the touring Atlanta Art Association.

"Spring is late everywhere we've been, which accounts for the gorgeous display of all kinds of blooms and flowering shrubs."

The fateful trip to Europe was a volunteer assignment for Mrs. Turner, said Jack Spalding, editor of The Journal.

Mrs. Turner's husband died several months ago and "we all thought that the trip to Europe would be a wonderful opportunity to cheer her up," he said.

Mrs. Turner's apparently final writing effort for The Journal was printed in the paper's society section last Friday. The column was reprinted today in a special edition.

Mrs. Turner wrote that some members of the art group had become ill with a virus infection while in Venice, shortly before departing for Paris. She said that patients were on the mend but that laryngitis "still plagues most of us . . . which doesn't help matters when it comes to the language barrier."

"Some say the virus was caused by exposure," she wrote. "But we can't decide if we had been exposed to too many paintings and nude sculpture, too many dark and dank castles, too many steps, too much rain or too much of each other."

There were those who mistrusted Italian drinking water, she wrote.

"Mrs. R. K. Stow of Atlanta [one of the victims] drops a purifying pill in each glass before drinking, while some have found that a dash of scotch or bourbon makes the best water purifier in the world."

". . . today in Rome, sick or well, nobody intends to miss the sights in this ancient city. It's stupendous . . . we run into Atlanta people everywhere we go. . . ."

MOURNERS FLOCK TO ATLANTA MUSEUM

ATLANTA, June 3 (AP) — Tragedy opened the Atlanta Art Museum today. The museum usually is closed on Sundays.

Scores of persons came to the museum when they heard that more than 121 persons in an Atlanta art group had been killed in a plane crash in Paris. Of the victims, eight were Georgia artists.

Those who showed up at the museum said "we just wanted to help in some way." ———

United Press International Radiophoto

WRECKAGE OF JETLINER litters yard outside house near Villeneuve-le-Roi after the fatal accident yesterday.

"All the News That's Fit to Print"

The New York Times.

LATE CITY EDITION
U. S. Weather Bureau Report (Page 30) forecasts: Fair and pleasant today, tonight and tomorrow.
Temp. Range: 78—59; yesterday: 76—63. Temp-Hum. index: low 70's; yesterday: 75.

VOL. CXI . No. 38,208. © 1962 by The New York Times Company. Times Square, New York 36, N. Y. NEW YORK, MONDAY, SEPTEMBER 3, 1962. 10 cents beyond 50-mile zone from New York City except on Long Island. Higher in air delivery cities. FIVE CENTS

PRESIDENT LEADS SALUTE TO LABOR; RAIN CUTS TRAFFIC

Kennedy Hails High Output Rate of Union Workers—Mayor Joins in Tribute

ROAD DEATHS MOUNTING

Safety Council Fears Toll May Reach 500 by Close of 3-Day Period Tonight

Text of Kennedy's statement will be found on Page 31.

By EMANUEL PERLMUTTER

Rain, gray skies and cool weather marred the second day of the Labor Day week-end for most New Yorkers yesterday.

Highway traffic in the area fell below the holiday norm and beaches and other outdoor recreational facilities were patronized sparingly. For many families, an afternoon near the television set replaced a drive in the country.

A Labor Day statement by President Kennedy praised the high production of American workers and recounted their general achievements. Other public figures, including Mayor Wagner, also saluted the working men and women of the nation as well as the record of the labor movement.

Raincoats and topcoats were in evidence yesterday as the temperature dropped from 76 degrees at 3 A. M., to 63 at 10:50 A. M. It remained in the sixties through most of the day. The record high for the date here was 102 in 1953, and the low, 51 degrees in 1886.

Weather Outlook Bright

The weather outlook for Labor Day is brighter. The Weather Bureau forecast a mostly sunny day in New York, with a high temperature near 80 degrees.

It was generally clear and warm throughout the country yesterday, except for areas in the East. This good weather contributed in part to the continued high death rate in auto accidents. The National Safety Council said that automobile highway fatalities were mounting and might reach 500 before midnight tonight, the end of the three-day holiday week-end.

The Associated Press reported early today that 334 persons had lost their lives in automobile accidents since 6 P. M. Friday, the start of the holiday week-end.

President Kennedy, noting that about 70,000,000 were now employed, said:

"We are a blessed land. More

Continued on Page 31, Column 3

Morgenthau to Quit Post And Seek Governorship

U. S. Attorney Will Take Step Before Primary—O'Connor Vows Fight

By CLAYTON KNOWLES

Robert M. Morgenthau will resign early this week as a United States Attorney to run for Governor. His resignation as Federal prosecutor for the Southern District of New York will be submitted to Attorney General Robert F. Kennedy before the Thursday primary election.

This timing will enable the 43-year-old Bronx resident, a son of former Secretary of the Treasury Henry Morgenthau Jr., to take over the direction of the campaign, started by his friends, for the Democratic nomination for Governor.

The resignation will serve several purposes.

It will apprise all those seeking delegate seats at the Demo-

Continued on Page 12, Column 2

Rockefeller Begins Tour of 9 Counties Today in Pre-Convention Drive

By LAYHMOND ROBINSON

Governor Rockefeller will embark today on a tour that will take him into at least nine counties in advance of the Republican state nominating convention in Buffalo Sept. 18 and 19.

Mr. Rockefeller, who has called for the greatest campaign effort in his party's history in the fall elections, will meet thousands of prospective voters from some of the state's major voting blocs.

He will speak before labor, business and civil rights groups. He will also attend nonpartisan county fairs, picnics and outings as well as the usual partisan dinners sponsored by Republican organizations.

The Governor will spend most of today at the Columbia Coun-

Continued on Page 12, Column 5

BEN BELLA FOES AND LOYAL TROOPS CLASH IN CASBAH

35 Reported Dead and 70 Hurt in Exchange of Fire—March on Algiers Halts

By THOMAS F. BRADY
Special to The New York Times.

ALGIERS, Sept. 2—Heavy rifle and machine-gun fire erupted in the Casbah, the ancient Moslem quarter of Algiers, shortly before dusk tonight. It continued for more than an hour.

The number of casualties was not known, but one unconfirmed report said that thirty-five persons had been killed and at least seventy wounded.

Troops of the command of Willaya 4 cordoned off the Casbah when the shooting started.

The clash was apparently between followers of Col. Yacef Saadi, a Casbah leader loyal to the Political Bureau and Vice Premier Ahmed Ben Bella, and the forces of Willaya 4, the military region that controls Algiers and opposes the Bureau. The Bureau is Algeria's de facto Government.

Second Clash in a Week

It was the second clash in the Casbah in less than a week. On Wednesday, five Willaya 4 soldiers were killed in a fight with Colonel Saadi's men. One civilian was also reported to have been killed.

[In Boghari, in central Algeria, Algerian Army troops commanded by officers supporting the Political Bureau were stymied in an attempt to march on Algiers in response to a call from the Bureau. Blocked by hostile troops of Willaya 4, leaders of the march negotiated with Willaya 4 officers.]

The Willaya 4 command issued an ultimatum Friday demanding that Colonel Saadi and his men, described as the "underworld" of the Casbah, surrender their arms within forty-eight hours. Colonel Saadi responded by declaring that his men would never give up their arms. The ultimatum expired at noon today.

French Deny Charge

Some officers of the Willaya 4 command charged tonight that French Army units had joined in the firing in the Casbah. The French Army still has more than 200,000 men in Algeria. These charges were vague, however, and the French Embassy here immediately issued a denial.

Benyoussef Ben Khedda, Premier of the now powerless Provisional Government, issued a call by radio tonight for a fifteen-day truce among all elements in the Algerian struggle while political leaders sought a negotiated solution.

The truce would apply not only to the Casbah but also to the conflict in the Southwest between the forces of Willaya 4 and troops who support Mr. Ben Bella and the Political Bureau.

Belkacem Krim, a Deputy Vice Premier who is opposed to the Bureau, declared tonight that if no agreement could be

Continued on Page 5, Column 1

3,000 Are Killed in Iran's Worst Quake; Thousands Hurt and 200 Towns Leveled

Associated Press Radiophoto
Survivors huddle before rubble at Moradtapeh, one of villages devastated by earthquake

Special to The New York Times.

TEHERAN, Iran, Sept. 2—More than 3,000 people in western Iran were reported dead today in perhaps the most severe and disastrous earthquake in the country's modern history.

The earthquake last night lasted only one minute, but it destroyed more than 200 towns and villages, left thousands homeless and seriously injured at least 4,000.

Although the Government radio announced that more than 3,000 were killed, some reports placed the death toll as high as 8,000.

No Americans were reported anywhere near the earthquake area. Nor did any reports reach this capital of European casualties.

About 3,000 people are reported to have perished in one village alone—Daresfahan near Kazvin in the center of the disaster area.

Another report said 1,500 had died in the village of Avaj, between Kazvin and Hamadan.

Convoys of injured arrived in Teheran during the day from the devastated areas and were sent to ten hospitals in the city.

The earthquake affected an 8,500-square-mile area about

Continued on Page 6, Column 1

MOSCOW AGREES TO ARM AND TRAIN MILITARY IN CUBA

Soviet Also Will Provide Economic and Industrial Aid Under New Pact

GUEVARA WINS ACCORD

Action Is Termed Response to Threats by 'Imperialists' Against Castro Regime

Text of communiqué on Soviet aid to Cuba, Page 2.

By SEYMOUR TOPPING
Special to The New York Times.

MOSCOW, Sept. 2—The Soviet Union announced tonight that it had agreed to supply arms to Cuba and to provide technical specialists to train Cuban forces.

Moscow said the agreement with the Cuban Government was made in response to Havana's request for aid to meet the "threats" of "aggressive imperialist quarters." This policy will be continued as long as the threat stands, the announcement said.

The United States was not cited by name, but the announcement made it clear that the Soviet Government was using the quarrel between Washington and Havana as justification for strengthening the Castro regime.

The Soviet statement was contained in a communiqué issued here on the talks conducted by Maj. Ernesto Guevara, Cuban Minister of Industry, with Premier Khrushchev and other Soviet leaders.

New Mill to Be Built

The communiqué did not disclose the quantity or type of armaments to be supplied to Cuba, nor did it say how many military instructors would be sent.

On other matters, the communiqué said that Moscow had agreed to help Cuba build an iron and steel mill, and to expand the capacity of three existing plants from 110,000 to 350,000 tons of steel annually.

Additional specialists in agriculture are to be sent to Cuba to help with irrigation projects, land reclamation and hydraulic engineering problems.

The statement was the most emphatic declaration of Soviet military involvement in the Caribbean since Premier Khrushchev on July 9, 1960, implied that Soviet rockets would defend Cuba against any armed invasion.

Remark Qualified

Mr. Khrushchev later qualified this remark as symbolic after there were signs in Moscow of public uneasiness at the extent of the commitment.

After the rebel landings in Cuba in April, 1961, Mr. Khrushchev warned President Kennedy that the Soviet Union would give Cuba all necessary assistance to beat back any armed attack.

The forces of Premier Fidel Castro crushed the rebels quickly, using military equipment from Soviet-bloc countries.

The Soviet public has not been told of the military aid already provided to Cuba. Several Cuban military missions have visited Moscow without announcement of the results of their negotiations.

This was the case with the

Continued on Page 2, Column 4

U.S. BANKRUPTCIES FOUND INCREASING

Rise Is 400% in Decade—Most Filed by Individuals—Several Causes Given

By JOSEPH A. LOFTUS
Special to The New York Times.

WASHINGTON, Sept. 2—Americans are going bankrupt in record numbers. Ninety per cent of the bankruptcies involve individuals. Only 10 per cent are business bankruptcies.

The individuals, for the most part, voluntarily go to court to declare their insolvency. A few of them—about one out of eight—offer to work out some kind of settlement with their creditors.

The others just throw up their hands and say they can't pay. In these cases the creditors seldom recover any assets of consequence. Generally, unless fraud is proved, the bankrupt gets a legal discharge from his debts — and the department store, the loan company and the automobile agency write them off as bad debts.

Free to Make New Debts

When the bankrupt gets a discharge he is free from harassment on these old debts. He can run up new debts, creditors being willing.

Bankruptcy filings have increased by 400 per cent in the last ten years, according to reports of the Administrative Office of the United States Courts. The report for the year ended last June 30, not yet published, will show new bankruptcy cases totaling 147,780.

Record-breaking though this is, the figure has one encouraging side: it was not as high as expected. It went up only 1,137 from the preceding year.

This is baffling the experts just as much as the rise of 36,609 the year before.

Every year since World War II, bankruptcy cases have increased. However, there has

Continued on Page 23, Column 4

Kerr Sees Pledge To Control Imports As Trade Bill Aid

By The Associated Press.

WASHINGTON, Sept. 2—Senator Robert S. Kerr, Democrat of Oklahoma, said today he expected the Kennedy Administration to pledge action to block excessive imports of specific items before its trade bill came to a Senate vote.

The Oklahoman, a key member of the Finance Committee now considering the bill, said he expected these assurances to be given on textiles, perhaps shoes, and on some other products.

The Administration already has negotiated a multi-nation agreement to limit textile imports but has been under strong pressure from the industry for more action.

Some Congressional critics have complained the Administration is pushing a broad trade bill and at the same time agreeing to all sorts of unilateral restrictions on various products.

Appears With Keating

Senator Kerr's views were given in a radio-television interview with Senator Kenneth B. Keating, Republican of New York, recorded for New York stations.

The Oklahoman said he expected the Finance Committee to make some language changes in the trade bill as it came from the House, but that "I do not think it will make substantial changes in the principle."

This principle, he said, is that broad new authority must be granted the President to deal with the rapidly developing European Common Market.

He said he hoped the bill would "put our nation in a position to compete with the Common Market, the European Economic Community, both for the domestic market within their boundary and in the channels of trade and commerce in the world, at the same time letting us be friends as well as competitors."

Senator Kerr said he thought language changes would be introduced to make more specific

Continued on Page 6, Column 7

40 NATIONS ASKED TO SKILLS PARLEY

President Sets Up Meeting In October for Improving Uses of Manpower

By E. W. KENWORTHY
Special to The New York Times.

NEWPORT, R. I., Sept. 2—President Kennedy announced today the convening of an international conference on the role of skilled manpower. Its aim is to accelerate the economic progress of underdeveloped countries.

The conference will be held in San Juan, P. R., from Oct. 10 to 12 under the sponsorship of the Peace Corps with the cooperation of the Department of State and Labor.

The United States Government has invited more than forty nations to attend the conference. Thirty-six already have accepted the invitation. Most of the nations will be represented by important Government officials.

Johnson to Head U. S. Group

The United States delegation will be headed by Vice President Johnson and will include the new Secretary of Labor, W. Willard Wirtz, and Anthony J. Celebrezze, the Secretary of Health, Education and Welfare.

In announcing the conference President Kennedy said:

"Many recent studies, including surveys of the development of the United States, have indicated that human skills and technology are an even greater factor than capital investment in effecting a rapid transition to a developed country."

The time has come, the President stated, when past experience should be combined with new technology in teaching skills so as to speed economic

Continued on Page 3, Column 5

Allies Tell Soviet To Change Route Into West Berlin

Special to The New York Times.

BERLIN, Sept. 2—The Western powers told Soviet military officials today to stop bringing relief guards for the Soviet war memorial in West Berlin through the East-West crossing on the Friedrichstrasse.

In a set of instructions issued by the three Allied commandants here, the Russians were told to use one of two other crossings much closer to the monument in the British sector's Tiergarten.

The action, agreed on by Washington, London and Paris, was viewed as a move to decrease the Soviet presence in West Berlin. The Russians began using armored vehicles to transport their guards to the monument twelve days ago after West Berliners stoned buses that were used to carry the guards.

Soviet Colonel Listens

A United States official read the Allied instructions this afternoon to a Soviet colonel in charge of the guards at Checkpoint Charlie, the United States military post at the crossing, after the Russian convoy had returned from the memorial.

Informed sources said the chiefs of the three Western liaison missions at Potsdam would deliver notes with the text of the Allied order at Soviet army headquarters tomorrow. Only after Gen. Ivan I. Yakubovsky, Soviet commander in East Germany, has received the official Allied notification can it be considered in effect.

There was agreement that the Western step could result in an East-West confrontation if the Russians refused to comply.

Allied officials declined to give details of the order.

Continued on Page 3, Column 2

MODERNIZED ARMY CALLED CUBA'S AIM

But U. S. Says Soviet's New Move 'Merely Confirms' Recent Arms Aid

By TAD SZULC
Special to The New York Times.

WASHINGTON, Sept. 2—Experts here believe that a Soviet announcement today of additional military and arms aid for Cuba presages a campaign to streamline Cuba's armed forces.

A communiqué made public in Moscow called for additional Soviet military training mission and weapons to be sent to Cuba.

It was believed here that the announcement was intended to cover recent Soviet deliveries of weapons. The communiqué was signed by Cuba's Minister of Industries, Maj. Ernesto Guevara, and the head of the Cuban militia, Capt. Emilio Aragones Navarro. It came at the end of a six-day visit to the Soviet by the two officials.

A spokesman for the State Department said the announcement in Moscow "merely confirms what has been going on in recent months."

U. S. Sees Nothing New

The spokesman said: "The announcement does not seem to represent anything new. We have been saying right along that the Soviet Union has been sending military equipment and technicians to Cuba."

However, the fact that the Soviet Union chose at this time to openly proclaim the scope of its military assistance to Cuba was seen here as highly significant.

The Moscow announcement appeared to constitute a firm Soviet commitment to the defense of Cuba, although it was not regarded as a direct threat against the United States. Such threats characterized past pronouncements on alleged United States plans for an invasion of Cuba.

For the first time, Moscow conceded that military advisers were accompanying the new arms shipments. This suggested to some officials in Washington that the Russians might be ready to risk a major increase in tension with the United States on the Cuban issue.

Both the Soviet Union and the Kennedy Administration have referred to the Soviet military personnel in Cuba as "tech-

Continued on Page 2, Column 5

SCHOOL PROBLEMS VEXING SUBURBS

Integration Newest Issue—Classes Begin This Week

By LEONARD BUDER

Several old problems and one relatively new problem dominate the suburban school scene as the new term gets under way this week.

The old problems stem from the continuing increase in suburban school enrollment, reflecting the post-war population shift from the big cities and the rise in the birth rate. These problems include serious shortages of qualified teachers and satisfactory school facilities in many communities.

The relatively new problem involves school integration. In many communities, controversies have developed over allegedly discriminatory school policies.

Several school systems, including those in Newark, Montclair and Jersey City, are taking new steps this fall to promote greater integration.

Large concentrations of Negro pupils in some schools have brought, or threaten to bring, disputes in other communities. These include Malverne, Glen Cove, Hempstead, Manhasset, Roosevelt, Freeport, Westbury and New Rochelle in New York and Englewood, Orange and Plainfield in New Jersey.

Despite the many problems, the suburban school picture is by no means bleak. In many areas, school officials report

Continued on Page 7, Column 1

All Civilian Planes Grounded 5½ Hours by Raid Test

Associated Press
Command-post staff at Stewart Air Force Base, Newburgh, N. Y., during Operation Sky Shield. Base is headquarters for Boston Air Defense Sector of the continental command.

For five and a half hours yesterday the skies over the United States and Canada were the exclusive domain of 1,600 bombers and fighter aircraft. The planes were taking part in the third annual staging of the operation called Sky Shield, a vast exercise by the North American Defense Command (NORAD) to test continental defenses. About 1,000 B-52 and B-47 bombers of the Strategic Air Command pretended to be enemy attackers making runs on cities from New York to Los Angeles. More than 600 interceptor aircraft streaked

Continued on Page 6, Column 6

Mob in London Pummels Mosley And Routs His Backers at Rally

By JAMES FERON
Special to The New York Times.

LONDON, Sept. 2—Sir Oswald Mosley, leader of the Union Movement, was kicked and punched today as a turbulent crowd of 3,000 in London's East End broke up a meeting of his followers. Forty-four persons were arrested.

Police reinforcements, standing three to eight deep, attempted to protect Sir Oswald, the British Fascist leader before World War II. He was struck as he left his car for the platform to make a speech. His first dozen words were drowned out by the crowd's screams. After two minutes he left at the suggestion of the police.

Sir Oswald had gone to Bethnal Green to speak in favor of a united Europe, his aides said, and had selected the East End because he had supporters there. Opponents said he had gone there to antagonize the large Jewish population. The incident was almost a duplicate of one last month in another section of the East End. On that occasion Sir Oswald was knocked down.

Tonight's was the latest in a series of outdoor meetings sponsored by three British Fascist or neo-Fascist organizations. Their anti-Negro, anti-Jewish speakers have attracted larger and larger crowds and greater violence.

The Government barred the use of Trafalgar Square to the ultra-right-wing groups last month. Last week it imposed a ban on all political processions for this week-end.

Elsewhere in the East End, today, the newly formed Yellow

Continued on Page 3, Column 3

NEWS INDEX

Embassy of India Raided in Jakarta

By The Associated Press.

JAKARTA, Indonesia, Monday, Sept. 3—Indonesian demonstrators broke into the Indian Embassy today in a violent climax to the stormy Asian Games. The raiders left part of the building's interior a litter of broken glass and damaged art objects.

Security forces prevented an attempted by about fifty raiders to tear down the Indian flag.

Then an estimated 4,000 persons, many dressed in green military-style uniforms, marched a mile down a six-lane highway as police cleared their path to the fourteen-story luxury hotel housing the Indian and other delegations to the games. There was no violence reported at the hotel, although groups

Continued on Page 20 Column 6

TONIGHT at 8:05 P.M.: "Carnival." Complete Score. Radio Station WVNJ, 620 AM-100.3 FM.—Advt.

One of the thousands of orphans of the earthquake that hit a vast area of Iran sitting alone amid the ruins of Bouein.

Wide World Photos

Iran's Worst Quake Kills 3,000; Thousands Hurt in 200 Towns

Continued From Page 1, Col. 7

100 miles from Teheran in a triangle formed by the towns of Kazvin, Saveh and Hamadan.

It took place at 10:20 P. M. (2:20 P. M. New York time). [Other reports said it occurred at 10:52 P. M. Teheran time.]

Severe shocks were registered by the Teheran seismograph until early this morning. Tremors also were felt along the route of the Trans-Iranian Railway, and telegraph service was halted. Train service was suspended pending a check on rail damage.

In Teheran the severe shocks terrorized residents, with hundreds rushing out of their homes in night clothes.

Shah Mohammed Reza Pahlevi, vacationing at a Caspian resort, ordered Premier Assadollah Alam to use all possible means to provide immediate relief.

Army units, gendarmerie and police forces were alerted.

Truckloads of tents, blankets, medicine, food and other supplies and medical teams were rushed to the devastated areas. Planes stood by to airlift victims and drop supplies.

Troops and relief teams were digging out dead in the disaster areas. Relief centers and mobile hospitals have been set up for the injured and for the feeding of children and other victims.

Authorities feared many more were still buried beneath the rubble and that the death toll would rise. Many villages in remote mountainous areas had not yet been reached by relief teams. Supplies were being air-dropped to them.

Teheran seismograph experts said last night's earthquake was an extension of tremors that occurred in Turkey, Greece and Italy.

Shah's Sister Directs Relief

The Shah's sister, Princess Shams, who is honorary head of Red Lion and Sun, the Iranian equivalent of the Red Cross, is conducting relief operations and the International Red Cross has been informed of the extent of damage and fatalities.

Premier Alam appealed to the public over the Teheran radio today to make all efforts to help disaster victims.

Relief teams on horseback were on their way to remote villages in mountainous areas and fresh supplies of food, bread and cheese were sent from Teheran tonight for victims whose homes were destroyed.

Tank trucks were rushing water to areas where the supply was cut off or contaminated.

Special measures were taken to prevent the spread of disease. Recovered bodies were being buried immediately.

Premier To Visit Area

TEHERAN, Sept. 2 (UPI)—Premier Alam announced tonight that he would go to the stricken areas before dawn but that he would remain in his office until then to direct operations to save any victims who might have been buried alive. The Shah broke off his vacation to rush here.

Earlier in the day Dr. Hussein Khatibi, director of the Red Lion and Sun Society, estimated that 1,000 persons had been killed and many more thousands injured. He added: "I expect to have very sad and sorrowful reports later today."

Dr. Khatibi, who personally inspected the ruined areas around Karaj, ordered additional rescue units into the village.

In a report to the Premier, he said "everything is incredibly bad."

Witnesses described the disaster scenes as "desolate, gloomy, desperate," with parents of dead children near hysteria. The reports said families of victims clustered together and prayed.

Premier Alam ordered troops to guard villages against possible attacks by starving wolf-packs.

A Government communiqué broadcast tonight by the Teheran radio said:

"The victims are living under more pitable conditions than it was thought at first. The number of dead and injured is more than was believed at first. Some of the villages are in such a condition that most of their inhabitants are believed to have died.

"Other villages could not be reached due to the lack of proper roads for the motor vehicles. News from these areas is extremely tragic."

In Sweden, the Uppsala Seismological Institute said the

The New York Times Sept. 3, 1962

The area most severely affected in the disaster is shown by diagonal shading.

shock from the earthquake was 100 times more severe than the one recorded in the quake that killed 12,000 persons in Agadir, Morocco, March 1, 1960. The temblors were recorded as of disaster scale as far north as Moscow.

The newspaper Ettelaat, which had a correspondent at the scene in northwestern Iran, estimated the death toll at 4,000 with "several times" that number injured. The newspaper said the area looked as if it had been leveled by a nuclear explosion.

Lighter Shocks Follow

The earthquakes first struck Iran last night with a one-minute temblor followed by a series of lighter shocks over a six-hour period.

Officials said the mud brick huts in which most of the victims lived collapsed and buried the inhabitants while they slept. One Iranian newspaper, El Kayhan, said the toll might go as high as 8,000.

An Ettelaat reporter who toured the section around Ipak, a village of about 1,000 inhabitants eighty miles west of here, said he found it a pile of rubble.

Officials said the epicenter of the earthquake was recorded somewhere between Hamadan and Kazvin, about 140 miles west of here.

"All the News That's Fit to Print"

The New York Times.

LATE CITY EDITION

U. S. Weather Bureau Report (Page 66) forecasts: Mostly sunny, breezy and cool today; fair and cold tonight. Fair tomorrow.

Temp. range: 52—35; yesterday: 48—38.

VOL. CXII .No. 38,428. © 1963 by The New York Times Company. Times Square, New York 36, N. Y. NEW YORK, THURSDAY, APRIL 11, 1963. TEN CENTS

ATOM SUBMARINE WITH 129 LOST IN DEPTHS 220 MILES OFF BOSTON; OIL SLICK SEEN NEAR SITE OF DIVE

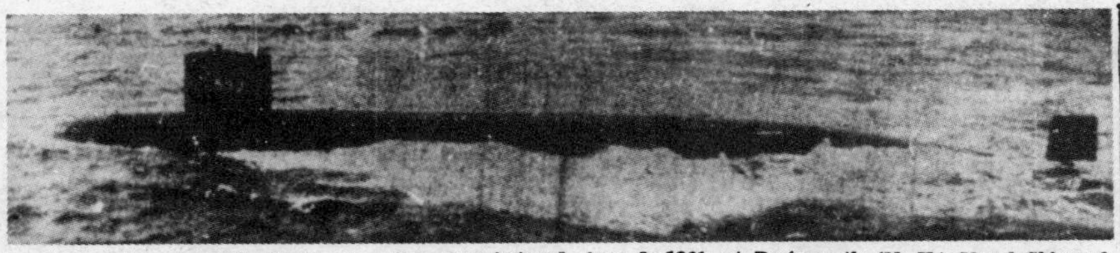

Thresher, nuclear-powered attack submarine, commissioned Aug. 3, 1961, at Portsmouth (N. H.) Naval Shipyard

THRESHER HUNTED

Rescue Craft Search Area of Last Test in 8,400-Foot Water

By ROBERT F. WHITNEY

Special to The New York Times

WASHINGTON, April 10—The Navy said tonight that its atomic submarine Thresher and 129 men aboard "appeared to be lost" in the Atlantic.

An oil slick was reported to have been sighted in the area where the vessel took a deep test dive at about 9 o'clock this morning in water 8,400 feet deep, 220 miles east of Boston.

"At that depth," said Adm. George W. Anderson, Chief of Naval Operations, "rescue would be absolutely out of the question."

Loss of the Thresher and 129 men would be the Navy's worst peacetime submarine disaster.

However, the Navy still clung to the possibility that there had been a communications failure and the $45,000,000 submarine was unable to report by radio or otherwise.

This appeared to be a dim hope after the ship, named for the thresher shark, had not been heard from since early morning.

Radiation Peril Denied

Admiral Anderson announced that the accident would be investigated by a court of inquiry headed by Vice Adm. Bernard Austin, president of the Naval War College.

Admiral Anderson, who was at the Pentagon answering reporters' questions about the disaster, assured them that there was "no chance of nuclear explosion in the submarine" or of "radioactive contamination" dangers to shipping.

The Navy chief said quietly: "To those of us who have been brought up in the traditions of the sea it is a sad occasion when a ship is reported lost."

The Navy's first announcement that the Thresher was missing came after reports flooded Newport, R. I., that a submarine was "on the bottom and unable to rise."

Rescue Vessels Sent

With the Thresher missing, the Navy sent destroyers from Newport and aircraft from the Quonset, R. I., Air Station. They are probing for possible radio signals and a fix on the submarine's position.

The 129 men aboard include 96 enlisted men, 16 officers and 17 civilian technicians from the Portsmouth, N. H., Navy Yard.

The Thresher had recently been at Portsmouth for overhaul and had gone out for deep diving tests. With her was the submarine rescue ship Skylark, which lost contact after the Thresher's dive.

The depth at which the Navy thinks the Thresher may be lying would doom the vessel and her crew. Pressures at such a depth would crush the hull, it was said.

Presumably this was the reason why Admiral Anderson said

Continued on Page 14, Column 1

United Press International

Lieut. Comdr. John Wesley Harvey, skipper of craft.

The New York Times April 11, 1963

Thresher reported down in the Atlantic at cross.

NATO TO PROCEED ON ATOMIC FORCE INCLUDING FRENCH

Paris Expected to Contribute Two Squadrons to Carry U. S. Nuclear Weapons

NASSAU PLAN APPROVED

Progress Reported in Effort to Heal Rift Over British Tie to Common Market

By DREW MIDDLETON

Special to The New York Times

PARIS, April 10—The North Atlantic alliance is to establish an allied nuclear force, including French squadrons, informed sources said tonight.

The United States will contribute three Polaris submarines and Britain her V-bomber force while France, West Germany and other European powers will make available planes and missiles capable of delivering nuclear weapons provided by the United States.

The assumption that France will contribute to this force rests on the American conviction that President de Gaulle will agree to the inclusion of two French fighter-bomber squadrons for purposes of strategic coordination, including the assignment of targets.

French Go Part Way

The establishment of the force, which is to be completed at a NATO meeting in Ottawa next month, can thus be represented as the acceptance of the United States-British project for an interallied nuclear force as laid down in last year's Nassau agreement.

The French, qualified sources said, are unlikely to go that far. But they have made known to Secretary of State Dean Rusk and others their willingness to play a role in any cooperative allied nuclear effort.

President de Gaulle rejected the Nassau proposal for an interallied force last December. The present American view apparently is that he will cooperate as long as the nuclear force is not called by that specific term.

The disclosure of French willingness to contribute to the force was made known after a meeting this afternoon of the North Atlantic Council attended by Mr. Rusk and the Foreign Ministers of Britain, France, West Germany and Italy.

Strengthening of Alliance

The North Atlantic alliance, rattled in recent months by France's pursuit of an independent national policy, appears on the surface to be considerably strengthened by the events of the last three days.

Mr. Rusk talked with President de Gaulle and received the French leader's assurances on his belief in the importance of the Atlantic alliance. The Earl of Home, Britain's Foreign Secretary, met Maurice Couve de Murville, the French Foreign Minister, and some degree of cordiality on defense issues was reintroduced into the British-French relationship.

The American and British ministers remained firm in contending that Britain should be a member of the European Economic Community. The initiative for an improvement in

Continued on Page 3, Column 5

SEATO Reaffirms Support for Laos

By HENRY GINIGER

Special to The New York Times

PARIS, April 10—The eight nations of the Southeast Asia Treaty Organization reaffirmed their support today for a neutral and independent Laos in the face of a renewed Communist menace.

In a communiqué capping a three-day meeting, the Council of Ministers of the organization expressed concern over "continued and increased threats weighting on the security" of the area.

There was no question of the intervention of the organization in Laos. As a neutral nation Laos has asked to be no longer a beneficiary of the treaty group's help.

It was strongly hinted, however, that some of SEATO's members would be prepared to take a military stand such as taken in May, 1962, when

Continued on Page 6, Column 3

SOVIET'S CONCERN ON BERLIN GROWS

Moscow Says That NATO's Atomic Program Causes a Special Urgency

By SEYMOUR TOPPING

Special to The New York Times

MOSCOW, April 10—A Soviet diplomatic source said today that the talks between the United States and the Soviet Union on Berlin had acquired a new urgency because of Western plans to establish a nuclear force in the North Atlantic Treaty Organization.

The source asserted that the dangers stemming from West German access to nuclear weapons through such a NATO force would be raised by Anatoly F. Dobrynin, the Soviet Ambassador in Washington, at his next meeting with Secretary of State Dean Rusk.

Mr. Dobrynin and Mr. Rusk are scheduled to meet Friday for their second conversation on Berlin and Germany in the current exploratory talks.

Interruptions Over Cuba

The private talks were resumed on March 26 after having been interrupted by the Cuban crisis last October.

Soviet officials here suddenly are evincing a new interest in the Berlin talks after a period of a month in which they appeared content to accept the status quo. They now say that a renewed effort must be made to achieve an understanding on Germany before any Western arrangement is made that would give West Germany access to nuclear weapons.

The Soviet position on the possible creation of a nuclear force for the Western military alliance was stated in notes to the Western powers published yesterday. The notes dismissed the United States argument that the proposed nuclear

Continued on Page 2, Column 4

POPE JOHN URGES A WORLD NATION TO GUARD PEACE

His Encyclical on Problems of Atomic Age Proposes Broadening of U.N.

Text of encyclical appears on Pages 17, 18 and 19.

By ARNALDO CORTESI

Special to The New York Times

ROME, April 10—Pope John XXIII proposed in an encyclical today the establishment of a world political community or public authority, a kind of supernation to which all countries should belong. Its aim would be to insure peace.

"The moral order itself," he said, demands that a public authority be established on a worldwide basis.

He made it clear that this new world organization should not be in contrast to or competition with the United Nations, of whose existence the 81-year-old Pontiff took note with satisfaction. He expressed hope that "the day may come when every human being will find therein an effective safeguard for the rights which derive directly from his dignity as a person."

Pope's Eighth Encyclical

The Pope's proposal was contained in an encyclical, or circular letter, dealing with present-day problems of peace. He signed it at the Vatican yesterday. It bears tomorrow's date, Holy Thursday.

The encyclical, the eighth of John XXIII's four-and-a-half-year Pontificate, is known by the first significant words of the Latin text, "Pacem in Terris" ("Peace on Earth"). In a departure from precedent, it was addressed not only to the Roman Catholic episcopacy, clergy and faithful but also to "all men of goodwill."

The Pontiff warned that nuclear warfare could destroy mankind. He noted the "enormous stocks of armaments that have been and still are being made in more economically developed countries" and said that they "should be reduced equally and simultaneously."

Other Principal Points

Other principal points made in the encyclical were these:

¶Governments and men must avoid the frequently committed error of supposing that relationships between men and states are controlled by the same laws as the physical universe.

¶Gains made by the working classes, the participation of women in public life and wider recognition of the equality and dignity of men bespeak progress toward a more just society.

¶Civil authorities must promote as well as protect the rights of individuals.

¶Governments must protect all racial minorities.

The essential part of the en-

Continued on Page 16, Column 1

House Votes Works Plan; Backs President, 228-184

By JOHN D. MORRIS

Special to The New York Times

WASHINGTON, April 10—Administration forces won the first major skirmish today in what promises to be a session-long battle over Federal spending. The House of Representatives overrode Republican opposition and approved an appropriation of $450,000,000 for a public works program designed to create jobs in communities with high rates of unemployment.

The roll-call vote was 228 to 184. This affirmed an earlier count of 202 to 172, taken by tellers.

The majority on the roll-call, which reversed an action taken by the House Appropriations Committee last week, included 208 Democrats and 20 Republicans. Voting against the fund were 151 Republicans and 33 Democrats.

Republican Foes Assailed

The White House issued a statement hailing the action as a victory "in the fight against unemployment." The statement also accused Republicans who voted against the appropriation of "blind opposition."

Republican leaders, who have resolved to cut total requests for new spending authority by at least $10,000,000,000, said they were not disheartened by the outcome.

They noted that they were handicapped today by the fact that the program at issue promised Federal funds for local projects in the districts of many Representatives. It was politically hazardous for members to vote against the appropriation in the face of strong pressure from home.

The pressure rose to a high point before the voting as many telegrams and telephone calls from Governors, Mayors and other public officials were received by House members.

The funds were added to an omnibus bill providing supplementary appropriations for various agencies in the remaining months of the fiscal year 1963, which ends June 30.

The bill, as passed by voice

Continued on Page 34, Column 4

CLAY ADVOCATES FURTHER AID CUT

Declares Additional Savings Won't Be 'Tremendous'—Opposes 'Stroke of Ax'

By FELIX BELAIR Jr.

Special to The New York Times

WASHINGTON, April 10—Gen. Lucius D. Clay called today for a bigger cut in foreign aid spending than the $400,000,000 President Kennedy has pruned from his January budget estimate of $4,900,000,000.

General Clay, head of a Presidential advisory commission on foreign aid, indicated that any additional savings "would not be tremendous," but he declined to estimate the further potential economies.

At a public hearing before the House Foreign Affairs Committee, he said that such an estimate would entail a country - by - country analysis that he would give only behind closed doors.

"But I am sure that a careful analysis would show the possibility of some further savings," General Clay said. "We on the committee were very gratified that the President did cut his original request. The new request contains programs that we have not reviewed, but I would say that his proposals for continuing programs are very closely in agreement with our report."

In its report, the Clay committee proposed tighter administrative criteria and a gradual termination of economic aid programs in some countries. It proposed that military aid be

Continued on Page 6, Column 5

Revival of Saloons, Outlawed Since '34, Is Studied by State

By CHARLES GRUTZNER

The corner saloon may stage a legal comeback in New York State with safeguards against its antisocial features.

The saloon was outlawed by name in the state alcoholic beverage control law adopted in 1934, right after the repeal of Prohibition.

It could be restored to respectability and legality through the elimination of some current restrictions on licensed drinking places. These restrictions will be examined by the Moreland Act Commission, which was appointed by Governor Rockefeller to review and recommend changes in liquor and beer controls.

Rule on Meals a Factor

The main restriction—which is being widely circumvented—is the requirement that any drinking place be operated as part of a bona fide eating place, at which regular meals are available. The law says specifically that sandwiches and salads alone do not fill the bill.

The commission chairman, former Federal Judge Lawrence E. Walsh, said yesterday that the major areas of the inquiry, which will take a year or more, would include the requirements for full-meal facilities and a full view from the street, and the prohibition against swinging doors on drinking places.

Mr. Walsh said the whole subject of liquor control would be reviewed by the commission in the light of social changes since 1934. He said there was a question whether some of the "minute" regulations were making it too difficult for conscientious persons to comply with all the rules.

One field of inquiry will involve whether the state's fixing of liquor prices should be abolished.

Continued on Page 36, Column 4

KENNEDY WEIGHS STEEL PRICE MOVE

Puts Off Trip and Confers With His Advisers After Wheeling Concern Acts

By RICHARD E. MOONEY

Special to The New York Times

WASHINGTON, April 10—President Kennedy maintained a conspicuous silence today on the Wheeling Steel Corporation's price increase.

He postponed overnight his planned departure for a long Easter weekend in Florida. Pierre Salinger, his news secretary, said that this was because "the President has a number of matters here at the White House that he feels he should attend to this afternoon." But it was widely interpreted as a psychological move to make the steel industry apprehensive.

[Most of the nation's major steel producers declined Wednesday to discuss the Wheeling company's announcement.]

Meeting Is Held

The President met in the late morning with a half-dozen members of his Cabinet and top-ranking aides, essentially the same group that drafted the Administration's counterattack on the United States Steel Corporation's price increase a year ago today. There was also one outsider present—Clark M. Clifford, the Washington lawyer who was the President's private agent in dealing with United States Steel last year.

There were two later meetings of the group. One, with Walter W. Heller, chairman of the President's Council of Economic Advisers, followed the morning meeting with the President. Then in the late afternoon the group met with the President again.

There had been no announcement of any meetings, though the word had spread fast. It was evident that at the first meeting the conferees had decided that the Administration should sit tight for the moment and gather facts.

Mr. Salinger said "no comment" to all questions about steel all day, and other officials were told to do the same. At a late hour it was still not known whether the President would make a statement and the White House lobby was jammed with reporters in anticipation.

The Administration was disturbed, though not completely surprised, by Wheeling's move

Continued on Page 54, Column 1

Mississippi Faculty Backs Artist Arrested for Painting Integration Riots

The New York Times (by Claude Sitton)

G. Ray Kerciu, assistant professor of art at University of Mississippi, with his painting "America the Beautiful"

By CLAUDE SITTON

Special to The New York Times

OXFORD, Miss., April 10—Faculty members urged the University of Mississippi today to support an artist under attack for a painting portraying the desegregation riots here last September. In a unanimous resolution, the local chapter of the American Association of University Professors called on the school's administrators to take the following steps: First, to issue a vigorous public statement upholding the right of G. Ray Kerciu, assistant professor of art, to express his convictions through the painting "America the Beautiful." Then, to direct the university attorney to represent Mr. Kerciu in his trial on charges of obscenity and desecration of the Confederate flag. "If this is not done, it is the belief of this body that the individual members of this faculty can only con-

Continued on Page 21, Column 4

Rockefeller Scores U.S. Cuban Policy

By WARREN WEAVER Jr.

Special to The New York Times

WASHINGTON, April 10—Governor Rockefeller sharply criticized today United States policy on Cuba.

At a news conference the New York Governor said that he found it "very hard to understand" why the Administration was supporting "freedom fighters" in South Vietnam and "holding them back and preventing them from operating in Cuba."

"I hope it is not as a means or an endeavor to placate or to appease the Soviet," he said.

Mr. Rockefeller was asked if he had any evidence that appeasement of the Russians was involved in the attempt to prevent refugee raids on Cuba.

"It is hard to see what other reason there would be, in view

Continued on Page 10, Column 4

Ex-Lefkowitz Aide Is Silent at Inquiry

By JACK ROTH

A former law associate of State Attorney General Louis J. Lefkowitz refused yesterday to sign a waiver of immunity and testify before the grand jury investigating the State Liquor Authority.

The former associate, Hyman D. Siegel, who said he had worked for Mr. Lefkowitz from 1930 until 1957, entered and left the grand jury room in less than five minutes. Outside the room he met with reporters, but let his lawyer, Matthew H. Brandenburg, respond to most of the questions.

Mr. Lefkowitz was asked later to comment on Mr. Siegel's refusal to testify. A spokesman would not go beyond a statement that Mr. Lefkowitz had not practiced law since assuming his state post and that Mr.

Continued on Page 36, Column 1

Belmont Park Shut; Track Held Unsafe

By JOE NICHOLS

Belmont Park, accepted as the finest race course in the world since its founding in 1905, will be closed "for reasons of public safety" for at least two years. This was announced by James Cox Brady, chairman of the board of the New York Racing Association, after a meeting of the board of trustees yesterday.

A state of "progressive deterioration" of the physical properties of the plant, discovered in a spring engineering inspection, prompted the N.Y.R.A. to ask the New York State Racing Commission for permission to keep the park closed. Ashley Trimble Cole, the commission chairman, attended the meet-

Continued on Page 39, Column 1

NEWS INDEX

Tonight at 8:45 PM! "Stop The World I Want To Get Off". Complete Score Radio Station WVNJ; 620 AM—100.3 FM.—Adv.

Atom Submarine With 129 Is Missing in the Depths 220 Miles From Boston

OIL SLICK IS SEEN NEAR SITE OF DIVE

Hope Is Dim for Craft, Not Heard From for 12 Hours —Navy Plans Inquiry

Continued From Page 1, Col. 8

that the depth "precludes any possibility of salvage if the submarine is indeed missing." But he added to reporters:

"We are always hopeful that perhaps this is a case of communications failure and that the submarine might conceivably be proceeding to port.

The Thresher was launched in 1960 and commissioned in August, 1961. She is a nuclear attack craft, the newest of her class, which are the fastest and deepest operating submarines in the fleet.

Her length is 278 feet and beam 21 feet and she displaces 3,700 tons.

The commanding officer is Lieut. Commander J. W. Harvey, of Waterford, Conn.

Next of Kin Being Told

The next of kin of all aboard are being notified that the Thresher is overdue.

The Navy said that the approximate position where the Thresher was last heard from was Lat. 41 degrees and 44 minutes N., Long. 64 degrees and 57 minutes W.

Winds in the area ranged from 25 to 40 knots and seas were high.

Merchant ships in the area have been notified to help in the search.

Should it prove that the Thresher is indeed down but not at a depth that would doom her, her crew would have oxygen for an indefinite time if her equipment was working.

This oxygen would come from storage flasks and in addition from apparatus for extracting it from sea water. The vessel of course has equipment for extracting carbon dioxide and other contaminants from her atmosphere.

The possible crushing of the Thresher's hull immediately raised a question as to whether her nuclear reactor would be torn apart and the area of sea contaminated with radio-activity.

Admiral Anderson said he had checked this with Vice Adm. Hyman G. Rickover, the Navy's nuclear propulsion expert, and received assurances that this was a "negligible possibility."

The Thresher was the first of her class of nuclear attack submarines. Two others, the Permit and the Plunger, are in operation and 22 more are under construction.

An attack submarine like the Thresher is said to be able to operate as deep as 1,000 feet below the surface. It is believed that ships of this class have an underwater speed in excess of 30 knots.

The actual maximum depths at which United States submarines can operate are secret, but presumably they would not be much beyond 1,400 feet.

However, the so-called bathyscape can go much lower than this and the Government is planning some scientific vessels, among them the "Aluminaut," a vessel of aluminum that presumably might operate down to 5,000 feet.

Submarine Rescue Vessels

The submarines of the Thresher's class have the so-called albacore hull—resembling the shape of the fish—are sonar geared, and carry torpedoes and other weapons. They were designed for attacking shipping and finding and destroying other submarines.

In addition to the destroyers and planes, three submarine rescue vessels are involved in the search for the Thresher.

The submarine's skipper Commander Harvey, is a graduate of the class of 1950 of the Naval Academy at Annapolis, Md. He has had nine years in nuclear submarines and has been in command of the Thresher for six months.

Commander Harvey had served on the first nuclear submarine Nautilus and was with it on a North Pole cruise. He was executive officer of the submarine Sea Dragon when she made her rendezvous with the Skate under the North Pole last summer. Both of these vessels are nuclear-propelled.

Commander Harvey was born Sept. 4, 1927, in the Bronx, New York City.

The officer is married and is the father of two children. His wife is the former Irene Nagorski of Philadelphia. His father and mother live at 680 Rennard Street, Philadelphia.

The officer in charge of the search and possible rescue operation is Rear Adm. Lawson P. Ramage, deputy commander of the submarine force of the Atlantic Fleet.

Other Contacts Denied

The last report received from the Thresher, according to a submarine officer at the Pentagon, was soon after 9 A.M. today, when she was aproaching her test depth in her dive. There has been no further word, although about an hour later the Skylark began calling her on underwater communications equipment.

Navy officials were asked if there had been any reports of unidentified or suspicious submarines in the test area. There were no other contacts they said.

The text of the Navy's statement announcing that the vessel was missing follows:

"The next-of-kin of the crew of the nuclear submarine U.S.S. Thresher (SSN-593) are being notified that the ship is overdue and presumed missing.

"The Thresher has been conducting routine tests some 220 miles east of Boston. The submarine rescue vessel U.S.S. Skylark was accompanying the Thresher. This procedure is normal for submarine tests and trials following an overhaul.

"Skylark reported that Thresher has not communicated as scheduled since submerging shortly after 9 A.M., E.S.T. this morning."

Ships Speed to Area

NORFOLK, Va., April 10 (UPI)—Adm. Robert L. Dennison of the Atlantic Fleet headquarters said tonight the submarine rescue ship Skylark and the salvage vessel Recovery already were on the scene of the Thresher's disappearance tonight and that other ships were steaming to the area.

Admiral Ramage was expected to arrive on the scene at 9:30 A.M. tomorrow aboard the destroyer Blandy. Five additional destroyers—Yarnell, Wallace Lind, Warrington, The Sullivans and S. B. Roberts—as well as the destroyer leader Norfolk, the submarines Sea Owl and Seawolf and an additional submarine rescue vessel, the Sunbird, were speeding to the area.

Four Neptune aircraft from Brunswick, Me., were on the scene and additional aircraft were expected soon.

A statement from Admiral Dennison's headquarters said:

"Thresher departed the U. S. Naval Shipyard in Portsmouth, N. H., at 8 A.M. E.S.T. April 9 in company with Skylark. She dove at 12:22 P.M. E.S.T. yesterday about 30 miles southeast of Portsmouth, N. H., and was in communication with Skylark until 9:17 A.M., E.S.T., this morning, when communications were lost.

"Tests being conducted involved a dive to depth in excess of 400 feet and was due to last six hours. At the end of the six-hour time period, Thresher was to ascend to a depth nearer the surface and return submerged to Portsmouth."

Sabotage Question Raised

WASHINGTON, April 10 (UPI) — Admiral Anderson said tonight that sabotage to the Thresher was "probably a remote possibility" that would be looked into.

The Admiral said the Navy was considering bringing the deep-diving experimental vessel Trieste from the West Coast to try to locate the Thresher.

But he pointed out that if the submarine was down in 8,400 feet of water, it would be impossible to bring her to the surface.

Associated Press

LAUNCHING OF THRESHER: This was the scene as Thresher was launched, July 9, 1960, at Portsmouth (N.H.) Naval Shipyard. Vessel is one of the latest nuclear craft.

Associated Press Wirephoto

MAKING STATEMENT: Adm. George W. Anderson, Chief of Naval Operations, speaking at the Pentagon on loss of the Thresher.

Names of Men on Missing Submarine

WASHINGTON, April 10 (UPI)—Following is a list of those missing aboard the submarine Thresher as made public by the Navy tonight:

OFFICERS

ALLEN, Lieut. Cmdr. Philip H., North Hampton, N.H.
BABCOCK, Lieut. j.g. Ronald C., Portsmouth, N.H.
BIEDERMAN, Lieut. Robert D., Hampton, N.H.
BILLINGS, Lieut. Cmdr. John H., South Berwick, Me.
DI NOLA, Lieut. Cmdr. Michael J., Rye, N.H.
GARNER, Lieut. Cmdr. Pat M., Mystic, Conn.
GRAFTON, Lieut. j.g. John G., Dewitt, N.Y.
HARVEY, Lieut. Cmdr. John W., New London, Conn.
HENRY, Lieut. j.g. James J. Jr., son of James J. Henry, 4591 Kings Highway, Brooklyn, N.Y.
KRAG, Lieut. Cmdr. Robert L., New London, Conn.
LYMAN, Lieut. Cmdr. John S. Jr., Kittery, Me.
MALINSKI, Lieut. j. g. Frank J., Phoenix, Ariz.
PARSONS, Lieut. j. g. Guy C., Jr., husband of Marjorie Parsons, 90 Greenridge Avenue, White Plains, N.Y.
SMARZ, Lieut. John, Portsmouth, N.H.
WILEY, Lieut. j. g. John J., Kittery, Me.
COLLIER, Lieut. Merrill F., Gales Ferry, Conn.

ENLISTED MEN

ARSENAULT, Tilmon J., husband of Hilda Mary Arsenault, Portsmouth, N.H.
BAIN, Ronald E., Mount Vernon, Ill.
BELL, John E., Mystic, Conn.
BOBBITT, Edgar S., Midland, Tex.
BOSTER, Gerald C., St. Louis, Mo.
BRACEY, George, Groton, Conn.
BRANN, Richard P., Somersworth, N.H.
CARKOSKI, Richard J., Grand Island, Neb.
CARMODY, Patrick Wayne, Toledo, Ohio.
CAYEY, Steven G., Norwich, Conn.
CHRISTIANSEN, Edward, son of Oliver Christiansen, 3900 Greystone Avenue, Bronx, N. Y.
CLAUSSEN, Larry W., Topeka, Kan.
CLEMMENTS, Thomas E., husband of Elaine R. Clemmments, 740 First Street, Westfield, N. J.
CUMMINGS, Francis M., Wellesley Hill, Mass.
DABRUZZI, Samuel J., Kittery, Me.
DAY, Donald C., Newburyport, Mass.
DENNY, Roy O., Kittery, Me.
DIBELLA, Peter Joseph, Portsmouth, N.H.
DUNDAS, Don R., Russell, Kan.
DYER, Troy E., Groton, Conn.
DAVISON, Clyde E. Hobbs, N.M.
FORNI, Elwood H., Mystic, Conn.
FOTI, Raymond B., Hampton, N.H.
FREEMAN, Larry W., Kittery, Me.
FUSCO, Gregory J., Kittery, Me.
GALLANT, Andrew Joseph Jr., McKinley, Me.
GARCIA, Napoleo T., Washington, D.C.
GARNER, John E., Vallejo, Calif.
GAYNOR, Robert W., Groton, Conn.
GOSNELL, Robert H., Raleigh, N.C.
GRAHAM, William E., North Stonington, Conn.
GUNTER, Aaron J., Portsmouth, N.H.
HALL, Richard C., Arlington, Va.
HAYES, Norman T., Temple City, Calif.
HEISER, Laird Glenn, Topen, Pa.
HELSIUS, Marvin Theodore, Trout Cheek, Mich.
HEWITT, Leonard H., Kittery, Me.
HODGE, Joseph H., Hampton, N.H.
HODGE, James P., Tarrant City, Ala.
HUDSON, John F., Groton, Conn.
INGLIS, John P., Spokane, Wash.
JOHNSON, Brawner G., Groton, Conn.
JOHNSON, Edward A., North Bay, Me.
JOHNSON, Richard L., Hendricks, Minn.
JOHNSON, Robert E., Kittery, Me.
JOHNSON, Thomas B., Montoursville, Pa.
JONES, Richard W., Milford, N.H.
KALUZA, Edmund J. Jr., Willimanset, Mass.
KANTZ, Thomas C., Ann Arbor, Mich.
KEARNEY, Robert D., Denville, N. J.
KEILER, Ronald D., Green Bay, Wis.
KIESECKER, George J., Exeter, N. H.
KLIER, Billy M., Groton, Conn.
KRONER, George Ronald, Cleveland, Ohio.
LANOUETTE, Norman G., next of kin, Florence B. Lanouette, 2050 Montgomery Street, Rahway, N. J.
LAVOIE, Wayne W., Gonic, N. H.
MABRY, Templeman N. Jr., Albuquerque, N. M.
MANN, Richard H. Jr., North Hampton, N. H.
M'CLELLAND, Douglas R., Portsmouth, N.H.
M'CORD, Donald J., Exeter, N.H.
M'DONOUGH, Karl P., Titusville, N.J.
MIDDLETON, Sidney L., Groton, Conn.
MARULLO, Julius F., Jr., Groton, Conn.
MUISE, Ronald A., Los Angeles, Calif.
MUSSELWHITE, James A., Kittery, Me.
NAULT, Donald E., Groton, Conn.
NOONIS, Walter Jack, Portsmouth, N.H.
NORRIS, John D., Groton, Conn.
OETTING, Chesley C., Mankato, Minn.
PENNINGTON, Roscoe C., Groton, Conn.
PETERS, James G., Kittery, Me.
PHILLIPPI, James F., Yucaipa, Calif.
PHILPUT, Dan A., Dover, N.H.
PODWELL, Richard, Exeter, N.H.
REGAN, John S., Groton, Conn.
RITCHIE, James P., Burlington, Vt.
ROBISON, Pervis, son of Pervis Robison, 8 Passaic Avenue, Nutley, N. J.
ROUNTREE, Glenn A., Portsmouth, N. H.
RUSHZTSKI, Anthony W., Allentown, Pa.
SCHIEWE, James M., Bristol, Conn.
SHAFER, Benjamin N., Gales Ferry, Conn.
SHAFER, John D., Groton, Conn.
SHIMKO, Joseph T., Newmarket, Ala.
SHOTWELL, Burnett M., next of kin Burnett E. Shotwell, 25 Cooper Blvd., Red Bank, N.J.
SINNETT, Alan D., Groton, Conn.
SMITH, William H. Jr., next of kin Agnes Smith, 542 Faitout Avenue, Roselle Park, N.J.
SNIDER, James L., Uncasville, Conn.
SOLOMON, Ronald H., Exeter, N.H.
STEINEL, Robert E., Salisbury Beach, Mass.
VAN PELT, Roger E., Kittery, Me.
WASEL, David A., New Britain, Conn.
WALSKI, Joseph A., Hampton, N.H.
WIGGINS, Charles L., Exeter, N.H.
WISE, Donald E., Arlington, Mass.
WOLFE, Ronald E., Jewett City, Conn.
ZWEIFEL, Jay H., LaCrosse, Wis.

CIVILIANS

ABRAMS, Fred P., Kittery, Me.
BEAL, Daniel W., Jr., Somersworth, N.H.
CHARRON, Robert E., Newburyport, Mass.
CORCORAN, K. R., Charlottesville, Va.
CRITCHLEY, Kenneth J., Biddeford, Me.
CURRIER, Paul C., Exeter, N.H.
DES JARDINS, Richard R., Kittery, Me.
DINEEN, George J., Bideford, Me.
FISHER, Richard K., Durham, N.H.
GUERETTE, Paul A., Portsmouth, N.H.
JAQUAY, Maurice F., Middletown, R.I.
KEUSTER, D., West Hyattsville, Md.
MOREAU, Henry, Portsmouth, N.H.
PALMER, Franklin J., Durham, N.H.
PRESCOTT, Robert D., Sanford, Me.
STADTMULLER, D., Roslyn, N.Y.
WHITTEN, Laurence E., Northwood, N.H.

OBJECTS 'FLOAT' BELOW SURFACE

Compressibility of Water Is Factor in Phenomenon

By WALTER SULLIVAN

If the Thresher, which disappeared off Massachusetts yesterday, had been almost buoyant when she dove, she could float well above the 8,400-foot ocean bottom in the region where she went down—if her hull were strong enough.

The reason is that certain metal objects are less compressible than water. They sink until the water around them has been squeezed to a density greater than that of the object, and then they remain suspended.

It is this that has led imaginative artists to depict ships of ancient vintage hanging at mid-depths in the deep ocean.

This, however, would only happen to a submarine if her tanks were partly blown, making her almost buoyant to begin with. Furthermore, the hull would have to be strong enough to withstand the pressure at the depth where she became buoyant. This appears unlikely.

At the bottom depth where the submarine is believed to have gone down—some 8,400 feet—the pressure is more than 3,630 pounds to the square inch. The exact pressure is dependent on such variables as water temperature and salinity.

It seems unlikely that a submarine hull could withstand that pressure. On Jan. 23, 1960, a United States Navy bathyscaph descended 35,800 feet into a trench in the floor of the western Pacific.

A bathyscaph consists of a spherical hull of extremely thick steel suspended from a blimp-like container of gasoline.

Because gasoline is lighter than water, the bathyscaph rises to the surface when ballast is dropped. The passengers ride in the sphere.

A submarine could be designed to withstand pressures comparable to those encountered by a bathyscaph, but this would severely limit her military usefulness.

While many students of elementary physics are led to believe that water cannot be compressed, this is untrue.

It is, in fact, more compressable than certain metal bodies. This made it possible, a few years ago, for John C. Swallow, the British oceanographer, to invent the so-called neutral buoyancy float.

This is a long, pipe-like arrangement that is marginally buoyant. It can be set to hover at pre-determined depth, emitting high frequency sounds that enable surface ships to follow its drift.

It was with such buoys that a deep countercurrent was found flowing in the opposite direction beneath the Gulf Stream.

Submarine Veterans Honor 1,900 Lost in World War II

PHILADELPHIA, April 10 (UPI)—Submarine veterans held memorial services tonight for 1,500 comrades who lost their lives in World War II. They did not know that 129 men were missing and presumed dead aboard the Thresher.

The ceremonies were held at the naval base here aboard the submarine Hake.

A wreath was tossed into the Delaware River by the next of kin of a submariner who died in that war.

Canadian and British Ships Stand By to Aid in Search

HALIFAX, N. S., April 10 (Canadian Press) — The Navy said tonight that ships of the Atlantic Command were standing by should the United States Navy ask for Canadian assistance in the search for the missing nuclear submarine Thresher.

Also ready to sail was the British submarine Auriga, based here.

Navy Has Many Contact Devices

Buoys, Sonar Sounds and Flares Part of Ship's Equipment

Special to The New York Times

WASHINGTON, April 10 — Slicks of oil, wreckage, puffs of smoke escaping through the heavy seas — these were the signs the Navy looked for in its search for the missing nuclear submarine Thresher.

The Navy can make contact with submerged submarines in many ways, which are classified. But officials said they had failed to reach the Thresher.

There was no indication whether contact was being sought by testing for the location of the nuclear reactor. Officials said there was no radiation danger from the disablement of the submarine.

As time wore on, it was feared tonight that the Navy had suffered its worst peacetime submarine disaster.

Little hope was held that any of the 129 men aboard the 3,700-ton Thresher might still be alive if the big submarine were lying helplessly on the bottom.

The estimated depth of the water where the Thresher was believed to have sunk is 8,400 feet. That is too deep for the boat's hull to sustain the terrific pressure, a Navy expert said.

Although the Thresher was the first of her class and was said to be capable of diving deeper and cruising faster than any other submarine, her 278-foot hull, 21 feet at the beam, would be crushed if she were at the bottom.

Indications were the Thresher had met with an accident that had prevented her officers from signaling for help. Various types of signals had been available to her.

All submarines have huge sonar domes in the rounded nose, which can be used to send out high-pitched "pings."

Surface vessels can also send out sonar sounds, hoping for an echo from the target, or can receive the sound of a stricken submarine. But such contact with the Thresher had not been reported.

The Thresher, like other submarines, has large, cylindrical metal buoys, eight feet long and three feet in diameter. These are intended to be released as surface markers to draw attention in emergencies.

At a late hour tonight, no buoys had been spotted.

Normally a submarine should be able to emit smoke signals and flares. These can be puffed from her tubes into the water and bubbled up to the surface.

The rescue ship Skylark, which had accompanied the Thresher, was also helpless because of the depth at which the submarine had been operating.

The Skylark, a surface vessel of about 1,200 tons, can conduct salvage operations down to 800 feet. She is equipped with a large diving bell and has expert divers aboard.

In another major submarine disaster, the Squalus sank in 240 feet in 1939. She was immediately located. Surface ships succeeded in placing slings under the hull, lifting her enough to permit pumping operations to free her of water. Thirty-three crewmen were saved and 26 drowned.

Had the Thresher been in only a few hundred feet, the crew could have attempted to escape individually.

The technique calls for donning life jackets, inflating them and slipping out from the forward escape trunk.

This method has been adopted in recent years in place of the Monson lung. The Monson is an air bladder worn on the chest with a mouthpiece, into which a man can breathe. He uses it as an auxiliary lung as he leaves through escape hatches.

2d Submarine Involved In Accident This Week

Special to The New York Times

NEW BEDFORD, Mass., April 10—Another submarine was involved in a sea accident in New England waters late Monday, but damage was minor.

The fishing vessel Sunapee, of New Bedford, reported that a submarine had gone through its nets, causing a loss of about $3,000.

Navy investigation determined that the submarine was the Alexander Hamilton, a nuclear-powered Polaris missile craft. There was no indication of any damage to the submarine.

Associated Press

SALVAGE OF SQUALUS: The bow of the submarine Squalus emerging from the waters off New Hampshire coast where she went down during a practice dive on May 23, 1939.

Disaster Recalls Loss of Squalus

New Devices Saved 33 in 1939—Toll on O-9 Was 33

By GEORGE BARRETT

Tragedies—and rare victories—have marked a long series of accidents to the men and the submarines that have penetrated the depths of the oceans.

The last major disaster involving a United States Navy submarine in peacetime occurred, however, almost 22 years ago, when the training submarine O-9 failed to return from a test dive off the Maine coast.

The craft, with two officers and thirty-one men, submerged on June 16, 1941, in a test dive 24 miles east of Portsmouth Navy Yard. According to all indications she was "crushed like an eggshell" when she sank to a depth of more than 400 feet.

Six days later, following intensive salvage and rescue operations, the Navy abandoned all hope of rescuing the trapped crew and a naval burial service was held above the spot aboard another submarine.

The tragedy to the O-9 followed a dramatic episode involving the submarine Squalus in the same area a little more than two years earlier.

In the case of the Squalus the Navy brought into practical application for the first time a newly devised rescue apparatus. With the device—a steel shell shaped like an inverted pear—the rescue teams brought up 33 of the 59 men trapped on the bottom.

The Squalus went down a few miles off the New Hampshire coast for a one-hour practice dive at 8:40 A.M. on May 23, 1939. The 299-foot craft was one of the newest products of the Portsmouth Navy Yard.

When the Squalus failed to reappear, a sister ship, the Sculpin, steamed past the Isle of Shoals in search of her.

A smoke bomb released from the sunken vessel revealed her position, and near it the Sculpin found a yellow buoy with a brass plate bearing the legend:

"Submarine Squalus sank here. Telephone inside."

The telephone, connected by wire with the Squalus, brought word of the accident and rescue ships converged. The rescue chamber that was used so successfully had been developed by research spurred by the disaster in 1927 to the submarine S-4, whose forty men were lost when she was rammed and sunk off Provincetown, Mass.

Four Trips Made

It took four trips to the "diving bell" to rescue the thirty-three crew members still living. Twenty-six of the crew were dead, trapped in the flooded after compartment. The Squalus was brought up later, by means of pontoons, and was recommissioned and renamed the Sailfish. With some members of her original crew aboard, she made her first trials safely and later joined the fleet.

The accident occurred to the S-4 on Dec. 17, 1927, when the Coast Guard destroyer Paulding — an old four-stacker — drove at eighteen knots through rough seas into the harbor of Provincetown, Mass., and crashed into a "stick in the water" that her officer of the deck thought was a fisherman's marker. It was the conning tower of the S-4, which sank immediately. She had been on her trial runs.

The world waited tensely while rescue operations were started. A chief torpedoman found the sunken craft, walked slowly around her and kept hammering her hull hoping to get a response. At the bow there came from inside the metal hull the dot-and-dash signal that the diver had been hoping to hear.

There were six men in that section of the submarine, trapped in space that was no more than 30 feet in length and seven feet wide and quickly using up the compartment's air.

As rescue operations began, Provincetown — in winter — became almost a resort town again as crowds poured into the area and boats took spectators out to the scene of the disaster at $15 to $35 a passenger.

But Christmas came — and went — and hope was abandoned for the six men. The final raps from inside the metal hull were "faint, confused tappings." The first bodies were brought out through opened hatches on Jan. 5, but it was March before the S-4 was raised. She was refitted and put to use on experimental salvage work. To test new rescue gear she was sunk and raised a dozen times.

One of the greatest tolls taken in a United States submarine sinking occurred during World War II when sometime in January, 1943, the Argonaut was sunk by the Japanese near New Britain Island, taking with her 102 crew members.

On Sept. 25, 1925, the submarine S-51 collided with the steamer City of Rome off Block Island. Thirty-four lives were lost.

Another dramatic undersea rescue occurred on Dec. 1, 1920, when the S-5 sank during a dive off Delaware Capes. Heroic efforts of the crew in pumping out water brought the stern to the surface and the steamship General Goethals rescued the entire crew after they had been under water for thirty-seven hours.

Two submarines rammed into each other on Dec. 17, 1917, off San Diego, Calif. The collision, between the F-1 and F-3, took 19 lives.

Two years earlier, on March 24, 1915, the submarine F-4 sank in 300 feet of water off Honolulu. She was brought to the surface once by rescuing ships, but the cables slipped and the craft went back to the bottom of the sea. The crew of 22 perished.

One of the most tragic accidents involving foreign submarines took 99 lives when the British submarine Thetis sank in the Irish Sea on June, 1939.

And a French submarine, the Ondine, sank after colliding with a Greek steamship off Portugal on Oct. 3, 1928, with a loss of 43 lives.

Thresher Damaged in June

GROTON, Conn., April 10 (AP)—The nuclear submarine Thresher, apparently lost in the Atlantic, suffered minor damage in Florida last June. She was berthing at Port Canaveral when she was rammed by a tug. A three-foot gash was ripped in her hull over the ballast tanks. Damage was so slight that the Thresher was able to make it all the way to a shipyard here for repairs.

Mother Hopes the Lord Will Care for Skipper

PHILADELPHIA, April 10 (UPI) — Mrs. Manning J. Harvey, mother of the skipper of the missing nuclear submarine The Thresher, said tonight she was "hoping the Lord will take care of him."

Mrs. Harvey said she felt that "something has gone wrong with the communications system" in the submarine. She said she had "great faith in God" and in her son, Lieut. Comdr. John W. Harvey.

Mrs. Harvey said her son had taken command of the Thresher at Portsmouth in January. She said he had had previous experience on the Sea Dragon and the Nautilus.

Craft's 'Silent Quality' Could Hamper Rescue

PORTSMOUTH, N. H., April 10 (UPI) — The missing nuclear-powered submarine USS Thresher was described as having a "built-in silent quality" at her launching July 9, 1960, at the Portsmouth Naval Shipyard.

The 278-foot craft was hailed by the Navy as the "lead ship of the world's most advanced class of nuclear attack subs." She incorporates features allowing her to operate deeper and more noiselessly than any of her predecessors.

These very abilities, which led the Navy to label her "one of the most effective antisubmarine warfare weapons in the Navy arsenal," could serve tonight to hinder rescue efforts.

The Thresher was the first submarine in Naval history to be launched bow-first and the first Navy ship to be so launched in 40 years.

Thoroughbred thrills this Saturday. $25,000 Excelsior at the Big A. Excitement you can find nowhere else. Make a day of it. An excellent lunch. Then 9 fabulous races. First race, 1:30 PM. Come any day, Mon. thru Sat. By car along the L.I. parkways toward Idlewild to the Aqueduct turnoff. By IND subway from 42nd St. & 8th Ave. or Hoyt Schermerhorn. Or come by bus. Grandstand admission, just $2.00

BIG A

"All the News That's Fit to Print"

The New York Times.

LATE CITY EDITION
U. S. Weather Bureau Report (Page 44) forecasts: Sunny, very hot and humid today. Clear tonight. Fair, hot tomorrow.
Temp. range: 97—74; yesterday: 96—72. Temp.-Hum. Index: low 80's; yesterday: 83.

VOL. CXII..No. 38,535.
© 1963 by The New York Times Company. Times Square, New York 36, N. Y.
NEW YORK, SATURDAY, JULY 27, 1963. TEN CENTS

KENNEDY AND KHRUSHCHEV CALL PACT A STEP TO PEACE BUT NOT A WAR PREVENTIVE

RUSSIAN CAUTIOUS

Says a Nonaggression Accord Is Necessary to Assure Peace

By SEYMOUR TOPPING
Special to The New York Times

MOSCOW, July 26—Premier Khrushchev declared today that the conclusion of a treaty for a partial nuclear test ban had created favorable opportunities for a further advance toward ending the cold war.

The Soviet leader described the initialing here yesterday of a treaty to forbid nuclear testing in the atmosphere, in space and under water as "an event of great international importance."

But Mr. Khrushchev cautioned that the treaty "does not mean an end of the arms race and hence by itself cannot avert the danger of war." He asserted that an East-West nonaggression pact was required to assure world peace.

The Premier made his comments in replies to written questions submitted by Pravda, the Soviet Communist party organ, and Izvestia, the Government newspaper.

Copies Distributed

Correspondents were summoned to the Ministry of Foreign Affairs at 4 P.M. to receive advance copies of the interview. It appeared that Mr. Khrushchev wished his remarks about the treaty to be published along with President Kennedy's speech tonight.

An hour earlier W. Averell Harriman, the United States delegate to the three-power talks, which concluded the treaty, was warmly received by Mr. Khrushchev in his Kremlin office.

The Premier beamed as Mr. Harriman entered the room accompanied by two of his advisers at the talks: Foy D. Kohler, United States Ambassador here, and Carl Kaysen, a member of President Kennedy's staff.

Khrushchev Seems Pleased

With outstretched arms Mr. Khrushchev strode across the room, grasped Mr. Harriman's hand and then, reaching up to take hold of the shoulders of the tall American diplomat, he cried: "Molodets!" This is a Russian expression that means "bravo" or "fine fellow."

Mr. Khrushchev appeared delighted that the accord had been reached. He urged Mr. Harriman to return to Moscow next month with Secretary of State Dean Rusk for the ceremonial signing of the treaty.

Mr. Harriman, Under Secretary of State for Political Affairs, is scheduled to leave Moscow tomorrow at 10 A.M. aboard a United States Air

Continued on Page 3, Column 1

Red China Expects Atom Arms Soon

Special to The New York Times

HONG KONG, July 26—A Chinese Communist official expressed confidence today that China would have nuclear weapons "in the not too distant future."

The statement was made by Kuo Mo-jo, a deputy chairman of the Standing Committee of the National People's Congress, at a rally in Peking to mark the 10th anniversary of the Korean armistice.

He declared: "The present attempt of a small number of countries to control the destiny of the people of the world by means of monopolizing nuclear weapons will certainly be smashed in the not too distant future."

His statements followed the announcement from Moscow that the United States,

Continued on Page 3, Column 2

PRESIDENT ON TV

Tells Nation Treaty Is 'Victory for Mankind' but Not Millennium

Text of Kennedy's address is printed on Page 2.

By TOM WICKER
Special to The New York Times

WASHINGTON, July 26 — President Kennedy, speaking to the nation tonight in a "spirit of hope," described the treaty for a limited nuclear test ban as a "victory for mankind" in its pursuit of peace.

The treaty, initialed in Moscow yesterday by representatives of the United States, the Soviet Union and Britain, would ban nuclear tests in the atmosphere, in space and under water.

Describing the agreement as a "shaft of light cut into the darkness" of cold-war discords and tensions, Mr. Kennedy nonetheless warned that it was "not the millennium."

"It will not resolve all conflicts, or cause the Communists to forego their ambitions, or eliminate the dangers of war," he said. "It will not reduce the need for arms or allies or programs of assistance to others.

'A Step Away From War'

"But it is an important first step—a step toward peace—a step toward reason — a step away from war."

If "this short and simple treaty" could now be made a symbol of "the end of one era and the beginning of another," the President said, it could lead on to further reductions of tensions and broader areas of agreement.

Among them, he suggested, might be "controls on preparations for a surprise attack, or on numbers and types of armaments."

"There could be further limitations on the spread of nuclear weapons," he added.

The important point, Mr. Kennedy said, is that "the effort to seek new agreements will go forward."

The President appeared on all three national television networks and his words also were heard on four radio networks. He spoke from his office in the West Executive Wing of the White House.

Immediately after the speech, he departed for a weekend at Hyannis Port, Mass. There he

Continued on Page 2, Column 6

NEW RAIL TALKS OPENED BY WIRTZ; I.C.C. BILL DELAYED

Secretary Summons Carrier and Union Men to Parley at Pastore Suggestion

SENATOR HALTS HEARING

Inquiry Into Kennedy's Plan Recessed a Day to Let Negotiators Try Again

Special to The New York Times

WASHINGTON, July 26—Secretary of Labor W. Willard Wirtz plunged into a new effort tonight to mediate a settlement in the bitter and tangled railroad work-rules dispute.

The Secretary met with officials of the railroads and the five train-operating unions at his office.

In this evening's meeting, the Secretary asked both sides to define precisely in writing their positions on the issues. No agreement was reached, but the meetings were scheduled to continue tomorrow.

The Secretary said he was engaged in "an effort to do everything possible to see if this dispute can be settled by collective bargaining."

The new round of mediation developed at a hearing this afternoon by the Senate Commerce Committee on the Administration's proposal to refer the dispute to the Interstate Commerce Commission for a ruling that would be binding on both sides for two years unless they negotiated their own settlement.

Wirtz Acts Immediately

Senator John O. Pastore, Democrat of Rhode Island, acting committee chairman, suggested that the committee could call a temporary halt to its consideration of the President's proposal to allow a final effort to settle the dispute through bargaining.

Mr. Wirtz called this "an eminently sound suggestion" and announced to the crowded hearing room that he would call the two sides together again.

The Secretary added that the President's plan contemplated that the dispute should eventually be resolved by bargaining.

Senator Pastore recessed the hearing until 9 A.M. tomorrow.

Some of the immediate urgency went out of the situation yesterday when the railroads agreed to postpone their work-rules changes, which would trigger a strike, to Aug. 29. They had planned to make them Tuesday.

The changes would permit them to abolish thousands of jobs they contend are unnecessary and that they say cost

Continued on Page 21, Column 1

Quake Devastates Skoplje, Yugoslavia; At Least 500 Dead; Toll May Top 2,000

Associated Press

Rescue workers dig through ruins of building destroyed by earthquake in Yugoslav city of Skoplje. Photograph was made available by Tanyug, official Yugoslav news agency.

By DAVID BINDER
Special to The New York Times

SKOPLJE, Yugoslavia, Saturday, July 27—A massive earthquake devastated the city of Skoplje at dawn yesterday while most citizens slept, leaving more than 500 dead and 3,000 injured.

Officials said the death toll was expected to rise well above 2,000. Rescue crews were still removing survivors and bodies from the rubble.

More than half the population of 170,000 in Skoplje were left homeless. Authorities estimated that 85 per cent of the living quarters of the Macedonian Republic city, the fourth largest in Yugoslavia, were no longer habitable.

Thousands set up tents and spent the night in the open park around the city.

The quake struck at 5:15 A.M. with an intensity of eight or nine on the international scale.

A ninth-grade quake indicates a disaster strong enough to cause almost total ruin of buildings and numerous human casualties. A second weaker quake followed later.

"I thought it was a hydrogen bomb," a Skoplje man said. "There was a terrible roar. I woke up, looked out the window, and saw the Hotel Macedonia swaying from side to side."

Continued on Page 4, Column 5

ATLANTA'S MAYOR BACKS RIGHTS BILL AS HELP TO CITIES

Calls Public Facility Clause Key to Averting Strife—Senator Praises Views

Excerpts from Mayor Allen's testimony are on Page 7.

By E. W. KENWORTHY
Special to The New York Times

WASHINGTON, July 26—The Mayor of Atlanta appealed to Congress today to pass legislation to eliminate segregation, which he called "slavery's stepchild."

"We cannot dodge the issue," Mayor Ivan Allen Jr. told the Senate Commerce Committee. "We cannot look back over our shoulders or turn the clock back to the eighteen-sixties. We must take action now to assure a greater future for our citizens and our country."

In the last several years Atlanta has desegregated city parks and golf courses, public schools, lunch counters, principal restaurants and its leading hotels for the holding of conventions.

Mr. Allen, who was elected Mayor in 1961, took pride in the progress. He said, "It has been a long, exhausting and often discouraging process and the end is far from being in sight."

Asks Passage of Bill

What Atlanta has accomplished, Mr. Allen said, has been done partly by voluntary action and partly as a result of court orders. But the task of dealing with discrimination in public accommodations would have been easier if there had been a national law to guide local officials and businessmen, he said.

He does not believe, he said, that any American wants the Federal Government to restrict unnecessarily the rights of private business.

However, he added, "I am firmly convinced that the Supreme Court insists that the same fundamental rights must be held by every American citizen."

Therefore, any failure by Congress to pass the bill "would amount to an endorsement of private business setting up an entirely new status of discrimination throughout the nation," he declared.

Fears Return to Turmoil

"Cities like Atlanta might slip backwards," he warned. "Hotels and restaurants that have already taken this issue upon themselves and opened their doors might find it convenient to go back to the old status."

The result might well be "the old turmoil of riots, strife, demonstrations and picketing," Mr. Allen asserted, continuing: "Gentlemen, if I had your problem, armed with the local experience I have had, I would pass a public accommodations bill."

He asked the Senators whether it was all right for the Negro to go down Main Street depositing his earnings at the bank and purchasing food at the supermarket just like any other customer, and then be

Continued on Page 7, Column 5

United Press International Telephoto

BACKS CIVIL RIGHTS PROVISION: Mayor Ivan Allen Jr. of Atlanta, testifying before Senate Commerce Committee yesterday, urges passage of section barring segregation in privately owned public accommodations.

JUNE PRICE INDEX AT RECORD LEVEL

Sugar, Tobacco and Taxes Main Factors in Rise of 0.4 Per Cent Over May

By EILEEN SHANAHAN
Special to The New York Times

WASHINGTON, July 26—A huge jump in sugar prices and the first general price rise for cigarettes in more than five years helped push the consumer price index to a record level in June.

The Labor Department reported today that the index had increased four-tenths of 1 per cent in June to 106.6. That meant that the purchases of a typical city family, which cost $10 in the 1957-59 period, cost $10.66 last month.

Increases in sales taxes in New York City and Pennsylvania and in real estate taxes in several other areas also contributed to the rise in the index.

Sugar prices increased by 32 per cent in June and were 44 per cent above those of a year earlier, the department said.

The increase of 7 cents a carton on most brands of nonfilter cigarettes raised the cost of tobacco products generally by more than 3 per cent.

Other foods whose prices increased during the month included pork, apples, grapefruit and frozen and canned orange juice.

The prices of fresh oranges declined slightly as did those of beef, eggs, milk and many fresh vegetables.

On balance, food prices in-

Continued on Page 14, Column 6

New U.S. Directives Bar Discrimination In Apprentice Plan

By JOHN D. POMFRET
Special to The New York Times

WASHINGTON, July 26—Strict new regulations were issued today to prevent racial discrimination in union-management apprenticeship programs sponsored by the Government.

The regulations, issued by the Labor Department's Bureau of Apprenticeship and Training, will apply to about 9,000 joint programs with 150,000 apprentices.

Programs that do not adhere to the new standards will lose their Federal support.

The action provoked a storm among labor and management leaders in the construction industry. They asked Labor Secretary W. Willard Wirtz to suspend the plan until they could confer with him.

They said the regulation threatened the existence of the apprenticeship system.

Loss of Federal registration

Continued on Page 8, Column 4

PENTAGON FIGHTS BIAS NEAR BASES

Lets Military Commanders List Areas as Off Limits if Discrimination Persists

By JACK RAYMOND
Special to The New York Times

WASHINGTON, July 26—The Pentagon authorized military commanders today to designate as off limits to servicemen any areas in the vicinity of military bases that practice "relentless discrimination" against Negroes.

A directive issued by Secretary of Defense Robert S. McNamara said that commanders were responsible for opposing discriminatory practices affecting their men not only on bases but "also in nearby communities where they may live or gather in off-duty hours."

In a memorandum on the subject to President Kennedy, Mr. McNamara said that "military effectiveness is unquestionably reduced as a result of civilian racial discrimination against men in uniform."

The Secretary also declared in the memorandum:

"Certainly the damage to military effectiveness from off-base discrimination is not less than that caused by off-base vice, as to which the off-limits sanction is quite customary."

The directive and memorandum were in response to a request June 21 by President Kennedy to Mr. McNamara to report within a month his action on complaints of discrimination cited by a special committee.

The committee, known as the

Continued on Page 8 Column 2

GERMANS CAUTION ON PACT'S SEQUEL

Bonn Holds Nonaggression Treaty Must Be Linked to Solution of Its Problems

By ARTHUR J. OLSEN
Special to The New York Times

BONN, July 26 — West Germany raised a warning voice today against the political consequences in Europe that could flow from the new Soviet-Western nuclear test treaty.

West Germany's concern focuses on a nonaggression arrangement between the North Atlantic Treaty Organization and Warsaw Pact alliances that Premier Khrushchev advocates as the next step in a progressive easing of international tensions. The Warsaw Pact is the Communist counterpart of NATO.

But informed officials declared that the test ban treaty itself might pose an awkward problem for the West German Republic.

Consultation Is Urged

A Government spokesman said that a nonaggression arrangement could make sense "only if it can be linked with the first steps toward the solution of problems that are responsible for tension in Europe."

In Bonn's view the partition of Germany and Communist pressure against West Berlin are the main sources of tension.

The governing Christian Democratic party said today that it was now necessary for the Western allies to consult on the Soviet proposals to determine "the true Soviet intentions."

"The agreement must not lead to a freezing of the unsatisfactory political situation in the world, particularly in Europe," said Dr. Heinrich von Brentano, former Foreign Min-

Continued on Page 2, Column 2

DE GAULLE URGED TO GIVE UP TESTS

Pleven and Le Monde Warn Against Defying Opinion

By DREW MIDDLETON
Special to The New York Times

PARIS, July 26 — Former Premier René Pleven warned President de Gaulle today against defying public opinion by ignoring the United States-Soviet-British nuclear test ban treaty and continuing French tests.

A warning in similar terms appeared in the influential afternoon newspaper Le Monde, which suggested that the Government learn from the United States the price of adherence to the treaty. The thought, shared by some politicians, is that France might get nuclear information in return for adherence and save a lot of money.

The sharpness of the reaction in a country where political conformity has become fashionable reflected the belief that the initialing of the treaty presented General de Gaulle with a com-

Continued on Page 3, Column 5

NORTHEAST LOSES FLORIDA AIR RUNS

C.A.B. Also Votes, 3-2, to Restore Airline's Subsidy

Special to The New York Times

WASHINGTON, July 26 — The Civil Aeronautics Board stripped Northeast Airlines of the valued New York-Florida route today. The vote was 3 to 2.

At the same time, the board announced it intended to restore the 29-year-old airline to subsidy status to prevent bankruptcy and preserve its New England air service.

The board majority held that there was no present need for a third carrier on the New York-Florida run. The decision leaves National Airlines and Eastern Air Lines in the market.

In a sharp dissent, Robert T. Murphy, C.A.B. vice chairman, and G. Joseph Minetti asserted that "there is a substantial continuing need for a third carrier in the flourishing, heavily traveled New York-Florida market."

They also said in a statement that the New York-Florida route, plus a subsidy to which Northeast was "entitled for local service" in New York, erased any "serious doubt as to its fitness and ability to continue as a sound, viable carrier."

"Solicitude for the well-being of Eastern has undoubtedly influenced the majority decision to eliminate Northeast in the

Continued on Page 21, Column 3

Broadcast Satellite Hangs Over Atlantic

By The Associated Press

CAPE CANAVERAL, Fla., July 26 — Syncom II, a new breed of space communications station, rocketed into orbit today. It cleared two big hurdles toward its goal as the world's first synchronous satellite—one that hangs over one area of the globe.

The glittering space package was shot into a great egg-shaped orbit. As it raced upward it received and transmitted back to earth the music of "The Star-Spangled Banner."

Five hours and 33 minutes after launching, a small motor aboard the satellite fired over Africa to arrest the vehicle near a 22,543-mile altitude.

At this point the satellite was in near-synchronous orbit and drifting slowly westward.

On its present course, Syncom II would follow an equa-

Continued on Page 45, Column 2

U.S. WILL OPPOSE BLOW AT LISBON

Allies Are Against Embargo Proposed by Africans

By THOMAS J. HAMILTON
Special to The New York Times

UNITED NATIONS, July 26—The United States, Britain and France told the Security Council today that they would not vote for an African-Asian resolution that would order all members of the United Nations to apply a partial embargo against arms shipments to Portugal.

The resolution, introduced by Ghana, Morocco and the Philippines, would forbid shipments of arms and military equipment or any assistance that would enable Portugal "to continue its repression of the peoples of the territories under its administration."

The resolution would also ask the Secretary General, U Thant, to insure compliance with the resolution, and to report the results to the Council by Sept. 30.

Adlai E. Stevenson, head of the United States delegation, said most members of the Council were in agreement on objectives, and urged them not to "surrender to the emotion and frustration that this issue has created."

He appealed to the authors of the proposal to change the provision regarding arms shipments so that, instead of issuing

Continued on Page 6, Column 4

Swiss Defy Cubans, Hold U.S. Embassy

By HEDRICK SMITH
Special to The New York Times

WASHINGTON, July 26 — Switzerland has informed Cuban authorities that she will not abandon the United States Embassy in Havana unless physically forced by Cuba to do so.

Informed sources here said the decision to "stand fast" was made by the Swiss themselves, not at the United States' request.

[In a speech in Havana, Premier Fidel Castro called for Cuban-style revolutions in other countries of Latin America and pledged Soviet support for them, The Associated Press reported.]

The Castro Government said Wednesday that the $1,219,000 United States Embassy on the Havana waterfront must be "nationalized and adjudicated."

Continued on Page 6 Column 7

Vietnamese Give Up Base in Reds' Area

By DAVID HALBERSTAM
Special to The New York Times

SAIGON, Vietnam, July 26—South Vietnamese forces have withdrawn from a highly publicized and supposedly permanent base in the heart of Zone D, a long-time holding of Communist guerrillas. Americans protested the pull-out.

The Americans are angry because the troops left behind approximately 800 antipersonnel mines, buried throughout the area. Information here is that the Communists now know there are mines in the area. They are said to have lost a few men trying to dig them out.

The next move, logically, would be to bring in trained ordnance technicians to take them out. Then they would be available for use against Government troops and Americans.

Another setback for the Gov-

Continued on Page 6 Column 3

NEWS INDEX

Macedonian City's Buildings Razed

Half of Skoplje's Population Homeless After Quake

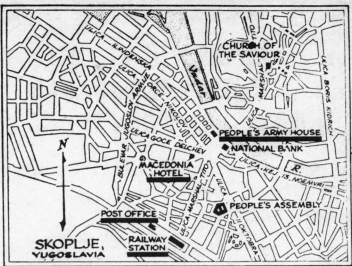

The New York Times   July 27, 1963

Underlined names designate some of the major structures damaged in earthquake (the street plan is based on material supplied by C. S. Hammond & Co.).

Associated Press

Aerial view of Skoplje, on Vardar River in Yugoslavia, before earthquake devastated it

YUGOSLAV QUAKE TAKES HIGH TOLL

Continued From Page 1, Col. 4

The Hotel Macedonia had 180 beds and it was full of tourists. Only a few guests were rescued. It was estimated that many, including foreigners, lay buried in the rubble. By noon only an Italian child could be identified.

A second hotel, the Skoplje, was also completely smashed. Only the wall of the main post office remained standing and the center of the railroad terminal fell in on hundreds of travelers waiting to catch the early morning trade for Belgrade.

A modern five-story building known as Karpus suddenly became only a three-story building as the earth swallowed up the first floors.

An ancient mosque on the left bank of the Vardar River was completely shattered.

From the air Skoplje looked as if it had been struck by a heavy bombing raid. There were gaping holes where roofs had been. A haze of brick and mortar dust hung over the city.

From the ground the scene was more appalling. Many streets were impassable because buildings had fallen across them. Homeless men, women and children toiled tirelessly in the rubble, carrying the few belongings they could save.

Thousands of rescue crews worked feverishly as the sun set.

Rescuers Seek Girl

On the top of a huge ruin rescuers were looking for a 17-year-old girl. At the small opening in the heap of rubble there had been a four-story house. They cried: "Mira, Mira, Mira," but no answer came.

The identity of many of the dead could not be determined immediately and officials declined to release names.

Bora Causey, the Macedonian Minister of Home Affairs, said that at least one member of the Macedonian Executive Council had been killed.

Many of the city's leading citizens lost their lives, another official said. They pointed out that three apartment buildings and physicians lived and crashed in ruins, leaving none alive.

He said that there was an initial moment of panic with people running headlong in the streets and out of the city, but that calm soon prevailed. This correspondent, who arrived eight hours after the quake, found the citizens silent and disciplined. Only the sound of ambulances and the roar of truck motors broke the quiet.

Hundreds of shop windows were broken and goods were

The New York Times   July 27, 1963

The cross marks Skoplje

for the taking. However, there was no sign of looting.

Officials said the main danger was the possibility of an epidemic. They warned the citizens not to use water from the city system. Water was brought in by a tank truck, which was virtually mobbed by the thirsty citizens. The temperature on the cloudless day had been above 90 since morning.

Mr. Causev said he started the official rescue and evacuation operation 20 minutes after the earthquake hit. He set up field headquarters in the park opposite the republic's Parliament and soon got in touch with Belgrade authorities by means of a portable radio.

More than 10,000 were called in to help, most of them from the National People's Army and the militia. Three field hospitals were established.

Petar Stambolic, President of the Yugoslav Executive Council, flew to Skoplje about five hours after the quake with a group of Government officials. He promised immediate federal emergency aid. President Tito was due in Skoplje this morning.

Planes, trucks, jeeps, bulldozers and buses soon began arriving from all over Yugoslavia with medical teams, rescue specialists and supplies of plasma and whole blood. United States Ambassador George F Kennan, on the last day of his service in Yugoslavia, donated a pint of blood.

Mr. Causev said that no martial law was in force but that a sort of emergency mobilization status had been declared. A curfew was called at 7 P.M. last night, forbidding movement on the streets.

Electric power and regular communications were also cut off.

Mr. Causev said one reason rescue operations started so quickly was that Skoplje authorities had had the experience of coping with a major flood that struck the city Nov. 24.

The high water mark of the flood, which did more than $4,000,000 in damage, was at the same point as the center of the quake on the main city square. Two building on that square,

Tanyug via Associated Press

Army club was one of the hundreds of buildings in city left in ruins by the earthquake

SKOPLJE'S LEGEND 2,500 YEARS LONG

Byzantine Emperor Helped City After One Quake

By M. S. HANDLER

Skoplje, which was devastated by an earthquake yesterday, has been a focus of power the People's Bank and the House of the Army, were devastated by the quake.

Among the other buildings lost were high schools, the Technical Institute of Skoplje University, which burned, and the Kursumlin Han, an ancient Turkish caravansary that served as the city archeological museum.

At 11 o'clock last the Skoplje radio began broadcasting the names of victims.

in the Balkans since the ancient times. Under President Tito it has been a center from which Yugoslav power has radiated throughout Macedonia.

Its population is 170,000. About two-thirds of these have been added to the city since World War II.

The city has had a continuous history of at least 2,500 years. It was an important center under the primitive Illyrians, the Romans, the Byzantines, the Serbs, the Turks, and finally the Serbs again.

Situated astride the Vardar River, about 70 miles from the northern frontier of Greece, Skoplje, the capital of Yugoslav Macedonia, has been built up as a strong point directed toward Bulgaria and Albania.

Marshal Tito's regime invested more money per capita in the modernization of Macedonia, one of the most neglected regions of Europe, than in any of the other republics of the Yugoslav Federation.

The natural resources of the region had to be rediscovered by geologists and developed by engineers. Macedonia was on the way to an industrial might and commercial prominence it had never known before when the earthquake struck.

What the original Illyrians called their settlement no one knows. The conquering Romans called the province Dardania and the capital Scupi, from which Skoplje is derived.

When the Srbi crossed the Danube and occupied the area, Justinian accepted the fact. He helped them rebuild the city, as Justinana Prima, in 518 after an earthquake.

Stephen Dushan, the Serbian hero, was crowned at Skoplje in 1346. The barrier he erected against the oncoming Turks fell in 1392.

The Turks ruled all Macedonia — today divided among Yugoslavia, Greece and Bulgaria — from the ancient city, which they called Uskub.

"All the News That's Fit to Print"

The New York Times.

LATE CITY EDITION
U. S. Weather Bureau Report (Page 82) forecasts: Sunny today; clear tonight. Mostly sunny and warmer tomorrow.
Temp. range: 71—48; yesterday: 65—50.

VOL. CXIII..No. 38,610. © 1963 by The New York Times Company. Times Square, New York 36, N. Y. NEW YORK, THURSDAY, OCTOBER 10, 1963. TEN CENTS

GIANT DAM FALLS IN ITALY; HUNDREDS REPORTED DEAD AS WATER ENGULFS TOWNS

ALPINE VALLEY HIT

Rains and Landslides Cause Collapse in Piave River Area

By The Associated Press

BELLUNO, Italy, Thursday, Oct. 10—The 873-foot-high Vaiont Dam collapsed under the weight of torrential rains and mountain landslides last night. Rescue officials said they believed hundreds and possibly thousands were killed as a wall of water crashed into the Piave River valley.

The collapse of the dam, one of the world's highest, sent millions of tons of stored-up water into sleeping communities in the valley in northeast Italy.

[In Venice, a fireman returning from the disaster scene said: "You can't count the dead. There are hundreds and hundreds of them." One village and half a town were reported wiped out, according to United Press International.]

The dam is 10 miles north of Belluno, which is on the Piave River 50 miles north of Venice.

Longarone, a community of 2,000 people close to the dam, was reported to be completely submerged. At least half a dozen other communities were hit.

Many Reported Hurt

Hospitals in communities surrounding the stricken area reported receiving a growing stream of injured persons.

In Rome, the Interior Minister, Mariano Rumor, ordered all public security forces in the stricken area—Italy's northeast Alps between Venice and the Austrian border—to rush aid to the victims.

Calls went out to United States military bases at Verona and Vicenza, both south of the danger zone, for helicopters to aid the rescue operations.

The Vaiont Dam, finished in 1961, was the third highest concrete dam in the world. It was a tapered structure narrowing at its base The dam was not on the Piave River itself. It held back water in a side reservoir.

The Piave River valley, scene of the Italian Army's stand against the Austrians after the Caporetto defeat of World War I, was familiar to millions as the setting of Ernest Hemingway's novel "Farewell To Arms."

Rains Loosen Rocks

Civil authorities in Belluno and in Venice reported that in the last few days thousands of tons of earth and rock on Mount Toc above the dam had been loosened by torrential rains.

Hours after the disaster there was still no precise description of what had happened.

The Vaiont Reservoir was planned to hold about 1.5 million tons of water. It was part of an extensive hydroelectric complex in this Alpine area.

The volume of water released by the collapse was so great that here in Belluno the level of the Piave River suddenly rose 16 feet. The river flooded fields and roads in this area.

In the immediate hours after first word of the disaster, there was uncertainty over whether the dam had given way or whether a massive mountain landslide had dropped into the reservoir and sent a huge flood plunging over the dam into the valley below.

Town Is Sea of Mud

The Longarone area was reported to be a sea of mud from the deluge.

At the community of Pontenell' Alpi, halfway between Belluno and Longarone, a policeman found a phone line and reported that the community was under three feet of water. But he said that as far as he knew there were no serious injuries there.

He said there was no contact with communities farther north, and added:

"The flood waters hit this place with such speed I'm afraid something terrible must

Continued on Page 3, Column 4

Associated Press

VAIONT DAM, near Belluno, Italy, which collapsed because of torrential rains and mountain landslides.

FRENCH AIR UNIT WITH ATOM BOMBS NOW OPERATIONAL

Group Is Said to Comprise 6 Mirage Bombers With 40-Kiloton Weapons

By DREW MIDDLETON
Special to The New York Times

PARIS, Oct. 9—France joined the United States, the Soviet Union and Britain today as a military atomic power.

The first elements of the French nuclear striking force, a symbol of France's independence in the Western alliance, are now operational.

What was described as "the concrete beginning" of French nuclear power consists of an undisclosed number of Mirage-IV supersonic bombers armed with 40-kiloton plutonium atomic bombs.

Double the Hiroshima Bomb

The allied military consensus is that France now has six Mirage-IV bombers in service. Each of the 40-kiloton bombs is twice as powerful as the atomic bomb dropped on Hiroshima by the United States in 1945. A kiloton of explosive force is the equivalent of 1,000 tons of TNT.

[Canada has now agreed to the United States supplying Canadian and United States air defense forces in Canada with nuclear air-to-air missiles, Ottawa reported.]

France's move into nuclear independence was first made known, in a roundabout way, as diplomats were concluding that high-level talks in Washington had done little to bridge the gap between United States and French foreign policies.

The French striking force is President de Gaulle's cherished symbol of military independence of the United States and a prestige factor to advance his aim of political leadership in Europe.

U. S. Attitude Remarked

It may only have been coincidence, but the existence of the force's first element was disclosed after the French Government had learned that the United States Administration remained hostile to French claims to independence within the alliance. These had been put forward by Foreign Minister Maurice Couve de Murville in talks with President Kennedy and Secretary of State Dean Rusk.

The existence of the first element of the striking force was reported in a communiqué issued after a Cabinet meeting this morning.

The key paragraph said:

"The Minister of Defense [Pierre Messmer] reported on the imminent end of the evacuation of Bizerte, begun in July, 1962, conforming to the decisions of the Government. Thus, as has been foreseen and announced, the creation of new means that the armed forces are beginning to have at their disposal permits the termina-

Continued on Page 2, Column 4

KENNEDY AUTHORIZES WHEAT SALE TO RUSSIANS TOTALING $250,000,000; SENATE TO CONSIDER WIDER TRADE

POLICY STUDY SET

Panel Is Dissatisfied Over Current Curbs on U.S. Exports

By FELIX BELAIR Jr.
Special to The New York Times

WASHINGTON, Oct. 9—The Senate Foreign Relations Committee agreed today to review United States trade policy with a view to expansion of exports to the Soviet Union and its satellite countries.

Senator J. W. Fulbright, the committee chairman, said that "considerable dissatisfaction" over current restrictions had been voiced by members while questioning Secretary of State Dean Rusk in secret session about the pending sale of American wheat to the Soviet Union.

The dissatisfaction was with the results of certain legislative restrictions that penalize United States exporters while benefiting some of the nation's allies and other recipients of its aid programs, according to Mr. Fulbright.

Cites Johnson Act

He referred specifically to the Johnson Act of 1934. This prohibits loans or commercial credits to countries in default on debts to the United States.

On many occasions, Mr. Fulbright explained, Canada and other friendly nations have financed their exports to Communist countries through New York banks, an expedient denied United States exporters.

Mr. Rusk was before the committee with David E. Bell, International Development Administrator, primarily to discuss the Administration's $4.5 billion foreign aid authorization request.

Questions U. S. Trade

"As it turned out, the discussion devoted to foreign aid consumed very little time," Mr. Fulbright said. "Most of the questions concerned trade policy and the fact that we've been financing the trade of our friends with the Communist bloc for years."

"I detected from the expressions of the members that there is considerable dissatisfaction with our present policies," he said. "They apparently felt that we should be dealing directly with the Communist bloc ourselves. We intend to pursue the subject and to review it with the State Department."

Mr. Fulbright described the upshot of the committee session as "the beginning of a movement in a somewhat dif-

Continued on Page 21, Column 3

U.S. Protests to Canada Over Fixed Wheat Prices

Aides Assert 'Secret Deals' With Japan and Soviet Union Imperil Trade Ties and Undermine the Free Market

Special to The New York Times

WASHINGTON, Oct. 9—The United States has lodged a strong official protest with Canada over the sale of wheat at fixed prices.

Spokesmen for the Department of Agriculture, disclosing the protest today, asserted that recent Canadian actions in the sale of wheat had jeopardized traditional Canadian-United States consultations and undermined historic world commercial market practices based on supply and demand.

The protest was touched off by the sale of 30,000,000 bushels of wheat to Japan for delivery over eight months at a fixed price. The sale came at a time when prices were rising and the United States, which holds the bulk of the world supply of wheat, stood to benefit from higher prices.

[In Ottawa, Trade Minister Mitchell Sharp denied that Canada's pricing of wheat in the sale to Japan was a reversal of policy. The Wheat Board followed its usual marketing practice, selling at current prices for future delivery, he said.]

A further United States-Canadian disagreement has arisen in Ottawa's announced intention of establishing a trusteeship over two Great Lakes maritime unions involved in a jurisdictional dispute that at times has held up ships in lake ports. The United States is reported to fear such a move would intensify the dispute.

The spokesmen for the Agriculture Department said that the Canadians were offering a fixed-price contract with the United Kingdom for 40,000,000 bushels. Britain is a traditional

Continued on Page 21, Column 6

AID TO PEACE SEEN

President Also Calls Deal Beneficial to U.S. Economy

Transcript of news conference and summary, Page 13.

By WILLIAM M. BLAIR
Special to The New York Times

WASHINGTON, Oct. 9 — President Kennedy approved today the sale of $250 million worth of wheat to the Soviet Union.

The wheat—150 million bushels—will be sold through private commercial channels at the world price for cash or short-term credit. It will be for use only in the Soviet Union and Eastern Europe. This ruled out wheat to Cuba and Communist China.

The President's action opened the way for sales to other Soviet-bloc countries. Czechoslovakia, Bulgaria and Hungary have asked for wheat. Their request covers about $60 million. This would make the total sale $310 million.

[Wheat futures advanced smartly Wednesday on the expectation that the President would approve the sale of the grain to the Soviet Union. Prices rose 2 to 3 cents a bushel on the Chicago Board of Trade.]

Seeking Other Products

At the same time, the President told his news conference that the Soviet Union and satellite countries were interested in American surplus livestock feed grains and other farm products. [Opening statement, Page 18.]

In what amounted to a summation of his views on the wheat deal, Mr. Kennedy said:

"This particular decision with respect to sales to the Soviet Union, which is not inconsistent with many smaller transactions over a long period of time, does not represent a new Soviet-American trade policy. That must await the settlement of many matters.

"But it does represent one more hopeful sign that a more peaceful world is both possible and beneficial to us all."

The President said the Soviet was being treated "like any other customer in the world market." The proposed sale, he said, demonstrates the "willingness" of this country to help countries with short supplies of foodstuffs and to relieve world tensions.

Sees Payments Deficit Cut

The wheat sale will benefit other sectors of the United States economy besides farmers, he said. These include shippers and the whole agricultural complex of traders and food processors. It also would reduce the United States balance-of-payments deficit.

The balance of payments represents the money coming into and going out of the country. The payments for the grain would increase the money coming into the country and thus cut the United States deficit by the amount of the payments.

The world price that the Russians will pay is expected to be about $1.79 a bushel. The domestic price includes also a Federal subsidy of about 55 cents a bushel, which would make it $2.34.

Part of the subsidy is used to pay the farmer the difference between the world price and the support price guaranteed him by the Government, now $2 a bushel. The rest of the subsidy goes toward handling, transportation and related costs in getting the wheat to the ships. This latter part of the subsidy benefits the farmer also, because it pays for charges that

Continued on Page 20, Column 1

TORIES NOW HUNT FOR NEW LEADER

Party Meeting Opens With Behind-Scenes Issue on Macmillan Successor

By SYDNEY GRUSON
Special to The New York Times

BLACKPOOL, England, Oct. 9 — The Conservative party's annual conference opened today. Routine floor proceedings were overwhelmed by a sharpening behind-the-scenes struggle for the party leadership brought on by Prime Minister Macmillan's illness.

Mr. Macmillan was resting comfortably in a hospital and was said to be in good condition for an operation he will undergo tomorrow morning to relieve obstruction of the prostate.

The conference took on all the flavor of a deadlocked party convention in the United States, for regardless of what was being said publicly, the consensus of the politicians was that a new leader must be chosen soon.

Macmillan Comfortable

A bulletin from King Edward VII Hospital in London said:

"The Prime Minister has had a comfortable day. The results of the investigations are satisfactory and the operation of prostatectomy will be performed tomorrow."

A medical dictionary defines prostatectomy as "removal of a part or all of the prostate," a gland a little smaller than half

Continued on Page 2, Column 2

KENNEDY DEFENDS C.I.A. SAIGON ROLE

Denies Agency Is Following Course of Its Own—Says Work Is Eyed Closely

Special to The New York Times

WASHINGTON, Oct. 9—The Central Intelligence Agency operation in South Vietnam was vigorously defended today by President Kennedy.

It is "wholly untrue," the President said at his news conference, that the agency has been following a course of action contrary to that of other Government agencies. [Question 2, Page 18.]

News reports from Saigon and comments by officials here have indicated that there was a policy dispute between Henry Cabot Lodge, the United States Ambassador in Saigon, and John H. Richardson, the C.I.A. chief there.

He Cites the Record

Mr. Kennedy said that he had reviewed the record carefully over the last nine months and found nothing to indicate the C.I.A. had done anything but support policy.

"I can just assure you flatly," he said, "that the C.I.A. has not carried out independent activities but has operated under close control of the Director of Central Intelligence," who he said was operating under the "National Security Council and under my instructions."

"I think they've done a good

Continued on Page 5, Column 1

Use of Vernacular For Part of Mass Is Voted in Council

By MILTON BRACKER
Special to The New York Times

ROME, Oct. 9 — The Ecumenical Council placed strong emphasis today on the role of the parish priest. It also approved, as expected, the reform that will eventually authorize him to say parts of the mass in the vernacular—for example, English in the United States.

The Council voted another amendment. It will require the preaching of a homily, or sermon, at masses on Sundays or holy days when a congregation is present.

In the United States, an American Archbishop explained, sermons are not widely neglected, but they tend to diminish during the summer and are sometimes replaced by letters from the bishop.

Session's Eighth Meeting

The amendment also declared that a homily should properly deal with the "mysteries of the faith and the norms of Christian life," rather than be a topical address on morality not directly associated with the scriptural content of the mass.

In its eighth meeting since the resumed session was opened by Pope Paul VI Sept. 29, the Council, officially designated Vatican II, touched more on the regular churchgoing habits of Roman Catholics than it had at any previous meeting.

The Council was again doing two things at once. It was continuing the debate on the structure of the church—the second chapter of the schema "De Ec-

Continued on Page 3, Column 1

PRESIDENT NUDGES GOLDWATER'S HAT

Says He Thinks Senator Can Be G.O.P. Nominee—Stops Short of a Prediction

Special to The New York Times

WASHINGTON, Oct. 9 — Senator Barry Goldwater of Arizona might well be the Republican Presidential nominee in 1964, if he can survive "a trying seven or eight months which will test his endurance, his perseverance—and his agility," President Kennedy said today.

But the President, replying to questions at his news conference, stopped short of predicting that Senator Goldwater would win the nomination — and just short of saying that John F. Kennedy would be his Democratic opponent. [Questions 11 and 13, Page 18.]

The President left little doubt on the latter point, however, when asked if he was ready to announce his own candidacy.

Decision Put Off

"No, I think I will wait," he said, smiling. "Next year, I can wait longer."

More seriously, he closed his news conference with the prediction that the 1964 campaign would be a "hard, close race."

He also outlined what he apparently believed would be the major issues of the Presidential election, but he refused to predict whether they would benefit or damage him. [Question 22.].

In 1964, Mr. Kennedy said, "we will have to decide whether

Continued on Page 19, Column 1

Mrs. Nhu Advises Kennedy on Reds

The New York Times

Mrs. Ngo Dinh Nhu speaking before Overseas Press Club

By ROBERT C. DOTY

Mrs. Ngo Dinh Nhu, controversial Vietnamese political figure, said yesterday that if she were President Kennedy, she would "inform the people" of the Communist danger "instead of being inclined to lull them into a false sense of security." She expressed this view in response to a question at the first public appearance of her 21-day tour of the United States—a luncheon of the Overseas Press Club at the Waldorf-Astoria Hotel. A tiny figure in turquoise silk brocade, Mrs. Ngo Dinh Nhu peered over a lectern in the grand ballroom, made a short speech in hesitant but adequate English, and fielded questions from

Continued on Page 4, Column 3

Moses Rejects Council Parley On 25c Fee for Pupils at Fair

By CHARLES G. BENNETT

Robert Moses notified the City Council yesterday that he would not attend a Council committee meeting next Tuesday to discuss a reduction of admission charges for schoolchildren at the World's Fair.

The president of the fair corporation also, in effect, rejected the Council's proposed resolution demanding that reduced admission fees be set for children attending the fair in classes.

"In large part," Mr. Moses said, "the resolution makes statements which are contrary to fact." He gave his answer to the Council in a letter to Eric J. Treulich, the Council's vice chairman and majority leader.

Mr. Moses had first rejected outright a proposal by education officials that a 25-cent admission charge be established for schoolchildren. Later he suggested it might be possible to admit children for 25 cents on Mondays during July and August.

Meanwhile, as Mayor Wagner pressed at City Hall for a 25-cent admission for schoolchildren at all times, it became known that the World's Fair 18-member executive committee might meet earlier than Oct. 28, as previously announced, to take up the controversial proposal.

Deputy Mayor Edward F. Cavanagh Jr. and City Council President Paul R. Screvane, both members of the committee, are under instruction from Mayor Wagner to move for the children's reduced rate whenever the committee meeting is held.

"I think the fair should work

Continued on Page 33, Column 1

Peking Bars a Moscow Break; Dispute Ideological, Chou Says

By United Press International

TOKYO, Oct. 9 — Premier Chou En-lai of Communist China said today that there was no possibility of a diplomatic break between Peking and Moscow.

The Chinese Communists have faith that the Soviet Union would come to their aid in event of war, Mr. Chou said. He declared that the Soviet-Chinese treaty of alliance and amity was "still very much alive."

He asserted that the dispute between the big Communist powers would not get any worse, that their differences were ideological and not political.

Mr. Chou assessed Chinese-Soviet relations in an interview with the former Japanese Premier, Tanzan Ishibashi, now head of a Japanese industrial exhibition in Peking.

The interview was reported by Japanese newsmen and radio broadcasters now covering the industrial show. The Mainichi newspaper carried the report in its Thursday morning edition and NHK, the Japanese Government's radio outlet, broadcast it.

The Mainichi Daily News, an English-language paper, reported that Mr. Ishibashi asked Mr. Chou: "Why are you engaged in such a foolish thing as the Chinese-Soviet ideological dispute?"

Mr. Chou replied that Peking's position was "based on China's basic (Communist) principle."

"China does not want to bring it up as a political dispute between China and the Soviet Union, but the Soviet Union has brought it up as an international problem," he went on.

"The Soviet Union has recalled its technical experts from China, but China has not asked her technicians in the Soviet

Continued on Page 6, Column 1

NEWS INDEX

News Summary and Index, Page 43

NON NON BECOMES OUI OUI When Ricard the French drink. 90 pf. Imp'td by Mons.Henri Wines Ltd. N.Y.-Advt.

"GRETCHEN GRANT IS WONDERFULLY WILD!" SEE PAGE 53—ADVT.

Rescue workers probe for victims in wreckage of village of Pilago. Arrow points to approximate location of Vaiont Dam.

Wide World Photos

HIGH DAM FALLS IN ITALIAN ALPS

Continued From Page 1, Col. 1

have happened to the places north of here, especially Langarone."

The policeman reported that most of Pontenell' Alpi's 6,000 inhabitants were asleep when the Piave River suddenly smashed over its banks.

"But somebody must have seen the flood coming," he said, "because there were screams and shouts of alarm just before the water hit and many people were out of bed when it came."

"Everybody else is still blocked inside houses, afraid to come out in the water," he said.

The first bodies reported recovered were found buried in deep mud on a road three miles outside Langarone.

Rescue workers pushing into the stricken area saw a nightmare scene of muddy wastelands filled with debris and giant trees ripped up from their roots like fragile weeds.

The Italian Red Cross ordered a field hospital into the area.

Reports filtering back from survivors from communities outside Langarone told of a horrifying roar that preceded the crash of the waters.

The roar came minutes before the flood and many residents managed to flee to higher ground before the wall of water fell on their homes.

The first workers back from the area said it was utter chaos. They reported it was abso-

lutely impossible to make any firm estimates of dead at this stage, but agreed that hundreds of people must be buried under the rubble of Langarone itself.

"It's just about completely wiped away," one man said.

The Vaiont Dam was designed as part of a hydroelectric complex of five reservoirs and four power stations. The complex is not complete, but the Vaiont Dam has been providing power since last year.

It was built of reinforced concrete across a deep gorge just east of Langarone across the Piave River. Langarone is on the west side of the river.

Dam Was 72 Feet Thick

BELLUNO, Thursday, Oct. 10 (UPI)—The Vaiont Dam was said to be the world's highest arch dam. It was 72 feet thick and it crumbled without warning.

Part of the village of Fae was washed away.

The main road from Belluno to the Dolomites and the Austrian border was cut by the flood.

The dam, a mass of 50,000 tons of concrete across a mountain gorge, caved in shortly after 11 P.M. (6 P.M. Eastern daylight time.)

The flood area, 1,550 feet up in the Alps, is just south of the Dolomite range. The Piave River flows through the area from north to south in a narrow valley flanked by mountains 8,500 to 9,000 feet high.

How full the dam was when it burst was not known, but it was believed to be close to capacity.

It was built several years ago by the Adriatic Electric Society.

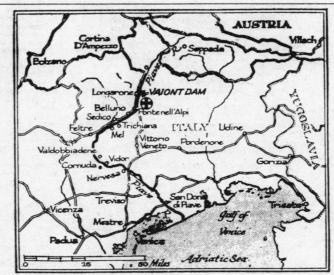

The New York Times   Oct. 10, 1963

ALPINE DISASTER: Heavy casualties were caused by the collapse of the Vaiont Dam (cross) in northern Italy.

Rail Line Carried Away

ROME, Thursday, Oct. 10 (Reuters) — Motorists reaching Belluno from the disaster area said part of the local rail line had been carried away.

The village of Longarone and the smaller villages of Fae, Codissago and Castellavazzo all had been hit by the onrush of water, they said.

The parish church of Longarone was reported destroyed.

Motorists said there were scenes of panic in the villages as the waters engulfed them.

The injured in Belluno Hospital were in too great a state of shock to give a coherent account of what happened, they added.

Rescuers from the Belluno area took little-used mountain paths to reach the disaster area. All the normal road and rail routes were blocked.

Belluno officials said they had asked for 600 policemen from surrounding prefectures, for medical teams and for helicopters from the United States Air Force base at Vicenza.

It will not be possible to form a full picture of what happened till after sunrise, they said.

All roads in the area were

reported to be covered by masses of mud, slime, tree trunks and branches.

According to an engineer in Belluno, about 75 per cent of the dam collapsed.

As dawn broke, rescuers reported hearing cries for help from marooned victims.

Four battalions of the Italian Army were ordered to the area to join rescuers.

The prefect of Belluno, trying to make his way through to the disaster area, reported that outlying houses in Longarone had been inundated.

Hundreds Reported Dead

Special to The New York Times

VENICE, Thursday, Oct. 10— A fireman returning from the disaster scene said: "You can't count the dead. There are hundreds and hundreds of them."

The rush of water caught villagers as they were asleep or preparing to go to sleep late last night.

The town of San Dona di Piave on the Piave River, about 12 miles from where the river empties into the Northern Adriatic, has been ordered evacuated, Venice firemen said.

San Dona di Piave has a population of more than 25,000.

United States troops at North Atlantic Treaty Organization bases in Verona and Vicenza were preparing to go to the aid of the stricken villagers later today.

The Piave River is the fifth largest in Italy. It rises in the Carnic Alps and flows 137 miles to the Adriatic Sea about 20 miles northeast of Venice. The river drains a basin of 1,550 square miles.

"All the News That's Fit to Print"

The New York Times.

LATE CITY EDITION
U. S. Weather Bureau Report (Page 46) Forecast: Cloudy with showers today; clearing tonight. Fair and cooler tomorrow. Temp. range: 58—45; yesterday: 63—41.

VOL. CXIII. No. 38,632. © 1963 by The New York Times Company. Times Square, New York 36, N. Y. NEW YORK, FRIDAY, NOVEMBER 1, 1963. TEN CENTS

KENNEDY DOUBTS SOVIET HAS ENDED RACE TO THE MOON

Does Not Regard Statement by Khrushchev as Giving Up on Lunar Program

WOULD PRESS U.S. BID

Tells News Conference He Would Not Make Any Bets on Russians' Intentions

Transcript of news conference and summary, Page 14.

By JOHN W. FINNEY
Special to The New York Times

WASHINGTON, Oct. 31 — President Kennedy expressed doubt today that Premier Khrushchev had taken the Soviet Union out of any race to the moon.

The President suggested that the United States proceed on the assumption that it was still racing the Soviet Union to land men on the moon and should continue with a space program he described as "essential" to the national security.

As he put it at his news conference:

"I would not make any bets at all on Soviet intentions." [Question 21, Page 14.]

The effect of the President's statements was to recast the Apollo lunar expedition more firmly in terms of a race than the Administration has been accustomed to do in recent months.

Justified as Race

When the United States lunar expedition was first proposed in May, 1961, it was justified by the President largely in terms of a race with the Soviet Union for national prestige.

But in recent months the Administration has been arguing that its objective was not necessarily to beat the Soviet Union to the moon but rather to achieve "pre-eminence" in space.

At a time when the space program was in budgetary trouble on Capitol Hill, Premier Khrushchev caused consternation in the Administration ranks by making comments that were widely interpreted as indicating the Soviet Union was not racing to the moon.

In an interview with correspondents last week, the Russian leader said "We are not at present planning flights by cosmonauts to the moon."

The reaction of many Admin-

Continued on Page 14, Column 6

SENATE LEADERS PROPOSE AID CUTS

Urge 385 Million Slash in Move to Balk Opponents

By FELIX BELAIR Jr.
Special to The New York Times

WASHINGTON, Oct. 31 — Senate leaders of both parties joined today in proposing a reduction of $385 million in the $4.2 billion foreign aid authorization bill. They acted in an effort to head off a possibly deeper slash and further delay.

The offer from Senator Mike Mansfield, the majority leader, to cut combined economic and military aid to $3,815,000,000 in the current fiscal year was immediately rejected by Senator Wayne Morse. The Oregon Democrat is trying to have the measure sent back to the Foreign Relations Committee for trimming as well as new policy directives.

The proposal had the further immediate effect of winning new recruits to the "liberal revolt" engineered by Senator Morse for returning the bill to the committee. Several Senators on that committee expressed resentment at not having been consulted on the leadership move and said they would now support the Morse motion to recommit.

Although the leadership agreement is expected to prevail in the end, one of its purposes — to end the extended debate mounted by Senator Morse and a few other Democrats — appeared doomed. The Oregon Senator said he would "speak at length" against the bipartisan amendment tomor-

Continued on Page 12, Column 1

Johnson Promised Place On a '64 Kennedy Ticket

President Discounts Talk of 'Dumping' Vice President—He Twits Goldwater on 'Busy Week Selling T.V.A.'

By JOSEPH A. LOFTUS
Special to The New York Times

WASHINGTON, Oct. 31 — Vice President Johnson's place on the Democratic ticket in next year's election was assured today by President Kennedy. The basic assumption, of course, is that Mr. Kennedy himself will run again.

A questioner at today's news conference, noting reports that Mr. Johnson would be "dumped" or "purged," asked Mr. Kennedy whether he would be retained.

"Yes, he will, no question he will," the President replied. [Question 25, Page 14.]

The speculation on Mr. Johnson's future derives from doubts as to his usefulness as a campaigner in the South.

His strong public position on civil rights since the election in 1960 has hurt his popularity in those states he helped hold for the Democratic ticket three years ago.

There are a number of reasons, other than party loyalty, for retaining the Vice President for another campaign. The principal one seems to be that nobody has suggested a more practical substitute.

Another is that even if Mr. Kennedy should write off most of the South, he is not writing off Texas's 25 votes. Dropping Mr. Johnson would probably be tantamount to giving away these votes.

President Kennedy dealt lightly with an accusation by Senator Barry Goldwater today that the Administration had been guilty of "blackouts, distortions, fabrications and falsi-

Continued on Page 22, Column 6

PRESIDENT GIVES BONN ASSURANCE ON COMBAT FORCE

Says 6 Divisions and Other Units Will Stay in Germany as Long as Need Exists

By MAX FRANKEL
Special to The New York Times

WASHINGTON, Oct. 31 — President Kennedy assured West Germany today that he planned no reduction in the number of United States combat forces on German soil.

In fact, the President said, he intends to keep there not only the six divisions pledged to the North Atlantic Treaty Organization but also three artillery battalions, two armored battalions and one armored cavalry regiment that were sent to Germany as temporary reinforcements during the 1961 Berlin crisis.

The purpose, he added, would be to offset unfulfilled pledges by the other members of the Atlantic alliance.

The President said, however, that noncombat personnel would be reduced.

Move to Ease Tensions

Mr. Kennedy's statement, most of which was read from a text, was made in answer to the first question at his news conference. It dealt with logistics but was intended to remove tensions between the United States and West German Governments and within the Administration. [Questions 1 to 4, Page 14.]

Over the last two weeks, as often before, the West German Government has been upset by suggestions that the United States could or should bring home some of the forces kept in Europe since the end of World War II.

Many Germans have feared such a move as the "beginning of the end" of Washington's commitment to defend them and, more recently, as a sign that President de Gaulle's lack of confidence in future United States Administrations might be justified.

Kennedy's Visit Recalled

Washington has repeatedly denied these intentions. President Kennedy did so on his visit to West Germany last June and Secretary of State Dean Rusk did so in Frankfurt last Sunday.

Mr. Kennedy's voice was needed because doubts both here and in Europe were damaging the Administration's determined effort to woo the new West German Government of Chancellor Ludwig Erhard away from the influence of President de Gaulle.

The doubts would not die because of discord within the Administration over the policies that have kept 1,000,000 Americans, including about 250,000 in Germany, stationed permanently overseas. Many in the Defense Department, strongly sup-

Continued on Page 5, Column 3

Court of Appeals Upholds City Betting Referendum

Special to The New York Times

ALBANY, Oct. 31—The Court of Appeals today gave New York City approval to conduct a referendum on off-track betting next Tuesday. The state's highest court unanimously upheld the Appellate Division, which had rejected two suits designed to prevent the referendum.

The Court of Appeals heard arguments late yesterday and handed down its ruling without an opinion.

It said only that "the Appellate Division had acted within its power in dismissing the case because of delay in bringing it."

The suits were filed this month by John H. Young 3d, an unsuccessful candidate for the Democratic nomination for councilman at large in Manhattan, and by Councilman Theodore R. Kupferman, Manhattan Republican.

Dismissal Explained

And, although the suits were rejected by the Appellate Division, that court said it had done so only because the actions had been started too close to the election. The five-man lower court asserted that the betting question clearly should not be on the ballot.

Although the City Council passed a local law on Aug. 20 authorizing the referendum, the first suit was not started until Oct. 7. Both suits were dismissed on Oct. 23 by Supreme Court Justice Samuel M. Gold.

The question before the voters in Tuesday's election will be whether a committee should be created and financed to formulate a plan for off-track betting in the city. Mayor Wagner has

Continued on Page 22, Column 5

UNEMPLOYED RATE REMAINS AT 5½%

Jobless Total at 3.4 Million in October—Employment Shows Slight Increase

By JOHN D. POMFRET
Special to The New York Times

WASHINGTON, Oct. 31— The national unemployment rate failed to change significantly in October.

The Labor Department put it today at 5.5 per cent, one-tenth of a point below the September figure after adjustment to eliminate seasonal factors.

Experts attributed the change principally to a rounding off of figures. The October rate was two-tenths of a point above that of a year before.

Unemployment, at 3.4 million, was not significantly changed from the previous month's 3.5 million.

Long-Term Total Remains

Employment was at 69.8 million. That also was no significant change from September's total of 69.5 million.

The gain, in line with seasonal expectations, occurred in nonfarm jobs, which rose from 64.2 million to 64.5 million.

Unemployment has been above 5 per cent, a level generally agreed to be too high—since late 1957.

President Kennedy was asked at his news conference today about the impact of automation on jobs.

"Machines can make life easier for men if men do not let the machines dominate them," he replied. [Question 9, Page 14.]

Most of the conforts people now enjoy are the result of

Continued on Page 15, Column 6

Harvard's Students Cautioned on Sex

Special to The New York Times

CAMBRIDGE, Mass., Oct. 31 —Harvard students have been told that permission to have women visit their rooms has become for some students "a license . . . for wild parties and sexual intercourse."

Dean John U. Munro made the statement in a letter to The Crimson, the university's daily newspaper.

He said that it was believed that a majority of students were not implicated, but he added:

"We have been badly shaken up recently by some severe violations of our rules of decent behavior."

"We are worried about the behavior of a few, and the general laxness in administration may bring the whole sys-

Continued on Page 67, Column 1

Development Company Planned To Fight Appalachian Poverty

Roosevelt Jr. Tells Senate of Economic Blight in Mountains of 10 States

Special to The New York Times

WASHINGTON, Oct. 31—A Presidential commission plans to recommend the creation of a development corporation to overcome poverty and backwardness in 10 Appalachian states.

Under Secretary of Commerce Franklin D. Roosevelt Jr. described the plan today in testimony before the Senate Labor subcommittee on employment and manpower.

Mr. Roosevelt heads the Appalachian Regional Commission, which is working out a plan to revive the economy of the region. It was named by President Kennedy in April, and consists of representatives of 14 Federal departments or agencies, the Conference of Appalachian Governors and the states.

The region in question lies along both sides of the mountain chain and runs southwest from Pennsylvania to Alabama. It includes the highlands of the 10 states.

Mr. Roosevelt drew a grim picture of the area's problems. Appalachia, he said, is an almost uninterrupted community winding along valleys and up hollows, enclosed by steep, empty hills.

"This ribbon town has no water system, either for supply or waste removal, no firehouse, no hospital, no doctor, no library, no police station," he said. "And it has none of these because it is not a town. Yet it goes on for miles and miles, and thousands of people live in it."

The average educational level of its residents is two years

Continued on Page 15, Column 5

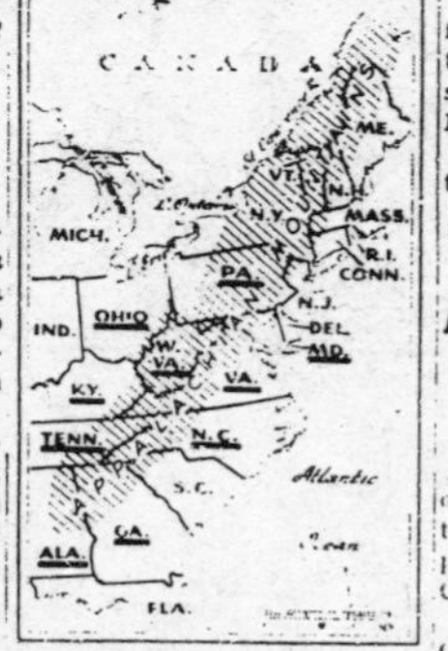

The New York Times Nov. 1, 1963

Aid plan covers parts of 10 states (underlined) in Appalachian chain (shading).

62 Dead and Hundreds Hurt In Blast at Indiana Ice Show

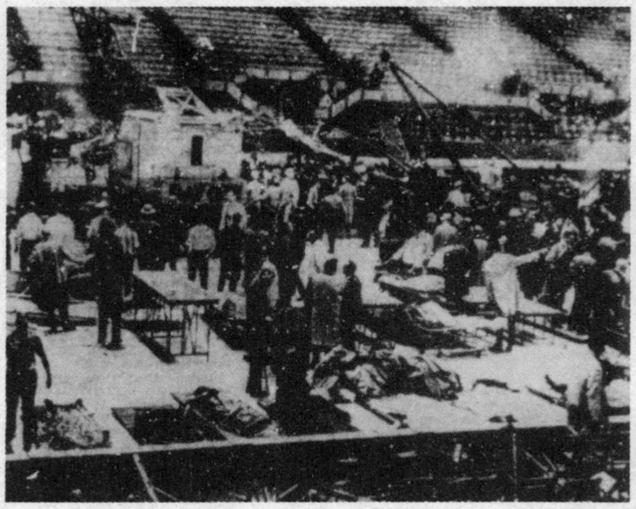

Associated Press Wirephoto

Rescue workers search for survivors in explosion at Indiana State Fairgrounds Coliseum

By The Associated Press

INDIANAPOLIS, Oct. 31—At least 62 persons were killed and hundreds were injured tonight in an explosion during the opening performance of the Holiday on Ice revue at the Indiana State Fairgrounds Coliseum. Heavy equipment was being moved in to search for more bodies under the debris. Fire Chief William Lynch said he had counted 62 bodies removed from the shattered remains of bleachers and structural concrete. The state police said there were unconfirmed reports of five more dead. Many of the victims were children.

The injured were being taken to several Indianapolis hospitals in taxis, ambulances, cars and buses. Deputy Sheriff Bernard Gohmann said there were indications that a gas explosion had occurred under a refreshment stand beneath the seats. After the blast, rows of bodies were lined up under blankets on the ice. Other rows were started outside the building in a drizzling rain. "They went up in the air like flies," said a woman

Continued on Page 21, Column 1

HOUSE UNIT FINDS AIR DEFENSE HURT

Calls Pentagon 'Misleading' in Reports on Closings of Radar and Warning Posts

By JOHN D. MORRIS
Special to The New York Times

WASHINGTON, Oct. 31 — A Congressional investigating subcommittee reported today that United States air defenses had been weakened by the shutdown of four SAGE direction centers and 17 long-range radar facilities.

The five-man subcommittee, of the House Armed Services Committee, said that the shutdowns had been ordered by the Defense Department over the opposition of the Air Force.

It accused the Pentagon of issuing a "misleading and inaccurate" announcement of the decision. And it said that Secretary of Defense Robert S. McNamara had "incorrectly informed the President as to the manner in which the proposed changes would be carried out."

Data Coordinated

SAGE stands for semi-automatic ground environment. The system consists of centers to receive and coordinate information on approaching aircraft and direct interception operations. Computers and radar are employed.

The investigating subcommittee's report was classified as "top secret," but some of the findings were outlined in a letter by the chairman, Representative Porter Hardy Jr., Democrat of Virginia.

The letter was addressed to the chairman of the full com-

Continued on Page 13, Column 2

U. N. Group, 97-1, Asks More Effort For Full Test Ban

By SAM POPE BREWER
Special to The New York Times

UNITED NATIONS, N. Y., Oct. 31—A resolution calling for intensified work toward a total ban on nuclear tests was adopted today by the General Assembly's Political Committee.

The vote was 97 to 1. Albania voted against the resolution. The Central African Republic, Cuba and France abstained. Cambodia was present, but not participating, and other members were absent.

The action completed the 111-member committee's work on the question of "the urgent need for suspension of nuclear and thermonuclear tests."

The resolution calls on all states to adhere to the treaty for a partial ban on testing "and to abide by its spirit and provisions." The treaty was signed Aug. 5 in Moscow.

Geneva Action Sought

The new measure asks the 18-nation Disarmament Committee to continue its Geneva negotiations toward a complete ban on tests. Specifically, the resolution "requests" the committee to work for the objectives named in the Moscow treaty: "To achieve the discontinuance of all test explosions of nuclear weapons for all time."

The present treaty does not cover underground tests.

The resolution asks the 18-nation group to report on its progress to the General Assembly as soon as possible, and in any case not later than next year's session.

France's abstention today was in accordance with her general refusal to take part in the

Continued on Page 5, Column 6

CASTRO SAYS C.I.A. USES RAIDER SHIP

He Asserts Cuba Captured Small Boats From Vessel—Miami Owner Denies It

By The Associated Press

WEST PALM BEACH, Fla., Oct. 31—Premier Fidel Castro charged last night that the Central Intelligence Agency was operating a raider ship called the Rex, and that she had been used in a sabotage mission against Cuba. He said two small boats from the Rex and several C.I.A. agents had been captured.

Premier Castro described the Rex as a 150-foot diesel vessel flying the Nicaraguan flag. He said she was based in West Palm Beach.

A vessel called the Rex, 174 feet long, returned to Palm Beach Monday and was tied up today in the Port of Palm Beach. She flies the Nicaraguan flag and carries large searchlights, radar and a crane on the stern. Two motor launches were missing from their davits.

The port director, Joel Wilcox, said, "The dockage is paid by the Sea Key Shipping Company from a post office box. I know nothing of the Rex's activities."

Oil Man Claims Ship

J. A. Belcher, a Miami oil company executive, told The Miami Herald that the Rex belonged to him, but denied that it had participated in raids against Cuba.

He said he bought the vessel from the Paragon Company, identified by The Herald as a Nicaraguan firm formerly owned by the family of Luis Somoza, an ex-President of Nicaragua.

Mr. Belcher told The Herald that for most of the year he had leased the Rex for electronic and oceanographic research to the international division of the Collins Radio Company of Dallas. He said the ship's captain, identified as Alexander Brooks, had told him the Rex had never been in Cuba's waters.

Premier Castro, in a radio

Continued on Page 15, Column 2

Restaurants Urged Not to Serve Water Unless Diners Request It

The diner who wants a glass of water with his meal will have to ask for it now, if eating places heed a new appeal from City Hall.

At the close of the driest October on record, the water level of the city reservoirs has dropped below 30 per cent of capacity, Armand D'Angelo, Commissioner of Water Supply, reported yesterday.

He asked restaurants not to serve water unless patrons called for it; barbers not to leave the hot water tap running, and truck and taxicab owners not to wash their vehicles more than twice a week.

The appeal to business users of water to curb consumption followed a series of comparable suggestions to householders by Mayor Wagner last week. Mr. D'Angelo said he was "grateful" at the residents' response, which has already produced good results. He said he hoped to have figures on the extent of the saving in a day or two.

The new measures, he said, are not "panic" proposals but part of a step-by-step schedule he drew up some time ago in preparation for any extended drought.

Water storage has dropped to 29.6 per cent of capacity. Mr. D'Angelo reported, with 141.2 billion gallons left in the city's six reservoirs. Full, they hold 476.5 billion gallons.

Even before October ended at midnight, the Weather Bureau said it would prove drier than October, 1924, which held the previous record of 0.24 of an inch of rain. In spite of light showers last evening, the new record stood at 0.14 of an inch. Normal precipitation for October is 3.14 inches.

The month also produced the

Continued on Page 25, Column 1

MOROCCO BREAKS TIES WITH CUBANS OVER ALGERIA AID

Also Recalls Ambassadors From Syria and U.A.R.—Cites 'Extreme Hostility'

TROOP HELP IS CHARGED

Rabat Says Castro Vessels Carried Volunteers to Join in Border Fight

By PETER GROSE
Special to The New York Times

RABAT, Morocco, Oct. 31— The Moroccan Government broke diplomatic relations today with Cuba and recalled its ambassadors from Syria and the United Arab Republic. It said that the three countries had shown "extreme hostility" toward Morocco during the country's border conflict with Algeria.

Morocco also ordered nearly 350 teachers from the United Arab Republic working in Morocco on a cultural mission to cease their activity pending expatriation.

Two United Arab Republic cultural centers were closed earlier by the Moroccans.

Ahmed Balafrej, the Moroccan Foreign Minister, accused Cuba of having sent shiploads of weapons, ammunition and volunteers to Algeria to take part in combat against Morocco.

Formal Break Possible

Mr. Balafrej said Cuba's "hostile action" justified the breaking of relations. He accused Syria and the United Arab Republic of "hostile attitudes" and said the recall of the ambassadors might lead to a formal break in relations.

These diplomatic repercussions of the Algerian-Moroccan border crisis came a day after the two countries agreed on a cease-fire. Signed in Bamako, the capital of Mali, the cease-fire is to take effect at midnight tomorrow.

Mr. Balafrej did not specify Morocco's complaint against Syria, but he accused the United Arab Republic of sending troops to bolster the ill-trained Algerian Army.

The Foreign Minister's reference to volunteers from Cuba was the first report that soldiers as well as matériel had arrived from Havana. Three Cuban airloads of tanks, artillery and jet fighters were reported to have arrived at the Algerian port of Oran last week.

Most of the matériel was So-

Continued on Page 2, Column 4

MISSION IN YEMEN EXTENDED BY U.N.

Thant Says Saudi Offer to Pay Permits Retention

Special to The New York Times

UNITED NATIONS, N. Y., Oct. 31 — The United Nations observation mission in Yemen was extended tonight until Jan. 4.

The Secretary General, U Thant, announced that Saudi Arabia had agreed to pay half the costs for the extension. He said that since the United Arab Republic and Yemen had already expressed a wish to continue the mission, he had canceled orders for its withdrawal.

The mission is observing compliance with a disengagement agreement between the United Arab Republic and Saudi Arabia, which have supported opposite sides in Yemen's civil war.

In a report to the Security Council published yesterday, Mr. Thant had announced that the mission would be withdrawn Monday for lack of financial support.

He had also said he did not believe "that the solution of the problem or even the fundamental steps which must be taken to resolve it can ever be within the potential of the United Nations observation mission alone, and most certainly not under its existing limited mandate."

The mission was authorized by a Security Council resolution of June 11, with the understanding that it was to be supported financially by Saudi Arabia and the United Arab Republic. They guaranteed it for two months from the be-

Continued on Page 3, Column 2

NEWS INDEX

Dwight D. Eisenhower's 'The White House Years' appears on Page 35

Aftermath of the Explosion at Indianapolis Fairgrounds Ice Show

Wide World Photos

Large cranes work in the background to free those buried under the rubble of concrete following an explosion at the Indiana State Fairgrounds coliseum. Dead and injured lie in the foreground.

62 IN INDIANA DIE IN ICE SHOW BLAST

Continued From Page 1, Col. 7

who survived the explosion. Methodist Hospital, near the scene, was quickly jammed with at least 40 injured. Stretchers packed the hospital halls.

The Marion County Coroner called for a large truck to gather personal belongings — mink stoles, billfolds, purses and clothing — scattered across the bloody ice and debris.

Leon Eaton of Osgood, Ind., a spectator sitting on the opposite side of the rink, said flames shot 30 feet into the air. He went on:

"One whole section was ripped out, bleachers and everything. There were people lying there halfway across the ice in pools of blood. There was a big boom, just like a charge of dynamite."

The blast ripped out a 50-foot section of high-priced box seats at the east end of the south side of the arena. Giant chunks of concrete from the basic structure of the arena were hurled into the air and came down on the spectators.

The audience was estimated at 6,000 persons. The coliseum seats about twice that number.

Harvey Ambrose of Columbus, Ohio, who sells novelties with the show, said, "There was a tremendous explosion. The whole area rose up like a fountain. I was hit by falling bricks but not injured seriously."

Donna Walters of Indianapolis said her grandfather, Ray Walters, and a woman friend were killed. She said she and others of their party were thrown out of their seats and were injured only slightly.

The exterior of the building remained intact.

A temporary morgue was set up at the coliseum, which is situated about five miles from the downtown area.

The seats in the immediate area of the blast held 368 persons. Of that number, 128 were in box seats above the explosion. Some 240 were in temporary seats beneath the tumbling concrete blocks and seats. The blast hurled the entire box section into the air and down again onto the bleachers.

Members of the chorus of the ice revue were skating around the rink to Dixieland music when the explosion occurred. The girls screamed and fled. A spokesman for the show said none of the troupers was known to be injured.

Live Wires Delay Search

As one giant crane lifted a chunk of blasted concrete weighing tons, flames broke out again briefly in the wreckage. Hoses were turned on the area.

Associated Press Wirephoto

Woman, trapped by fallen section of the bleachers, receives assistance from another survivor of the explosion.

Then rescuers were delayed by sparking live wires buried in the debris. Electricians cut the wires at the source and the search continued.

Many of the dead were believed to be prominent citizens. At least a dozen of the dead women were expensively dressed, many in mink.

Mrs. Helen Fritz of Indianapolis, who was in a chair near the front of the rink, but away from the main blast area, said:

"We were hit by the people flying through the air, then seats, bricks and concrete slabs. Then the fire broke out almost immediately. We were trying to crawl to the other side to safety. We were buried. Those people in the bleachers, they had no idea what happened."

She escaped with a bruised face.

The band continued playing as the screaming crowd sought refuge. Officials credited their coolness with averting worse casualties through a mass panic.

Toured the World

The "Holiday on Ice" show is an internationally known revue produced by Morris Challen of Minneapolis. Its four companies, featuring such stars as Dick Button, have toured all over the world, including the Soviet Union.

Each company travels with a big ice-making machine, which pumps brine through five miles of pipe to freeze the flooded floor of an arena.

The New York Times.

LATE CITY EDITION
U.S. Weather Bureau Report (Page 9) forecast:
Sunny and mild today; cloudy tonight. Fair, mild tomorrow.
Temp. range: 63—45; yesterday: 59—51

SECTION ONE

VOL. CXIII—No. 38,641. © 1963 by The New York Times Company. Times Square, New York 36, N.Y. — NEW YORK, SUNDAY, NOVEMBER 10, 1963. — THIRTY CENTS

WAGNER REVISES HOUSING POLICY TO LIMIT RENTS

Relieves Mid-Income Project Sponsors of Relocation and Demolition Tasks

PLAN SUGGESTED BY U.S.

City to Manage Condemned Buildings—Mayor Also Moves to Cut Graft

By LAWRENCE O'KANE

Mayor Wagner announced a major change in the city's urban renewal policy yesterday that he said would mean a reduction of at least $2.50 a month in the rental of new middle-income apartments.

Costs for owners of cooperative apartments would also be cut, but no estimate of the amount was given.

Until now, private sponsors of urban renewal developments have paid for demolishing buildings and relocating tenants on urban renewal sites. This cost was reflected in the rents charged for new apartments.

Under the new policy, the city will take over demolition and relocation, paying the costs out of urban renewal funds, two-thirds of which come from the Federal Government and one-sixth each from the city and state governments. This cost will not be reflected in the rents paid by tenants.

The city will also take over the interim management of condemned properties on urban renewal sites.

Acts to Cut Graft

The Mayor also acted yesterday to simplify building regulations affecting all construction in the city. He ordered that all new rules on construction be cleared through his deputy, Charles H. Tenney, to eliminate overlapping and confusing regulations. The move was designed to speed construction and to reduce the possibilities for graft.

The change in urban renewal policy had been urged by the Mayor's top housing policy advisers and by the Federal and state governments. It brings New York's policy closer to that followed by other cities.

Other cities sell vacant land to urban renewal developers. New York sells land and buildings and offered a discount in the sales price in return for the developer's assuming the responsibility of interim management, relocation and demolition.

With sites acquired at a fraction of their market value, the temptation for developers to delay construction while collecting rents from the properties was strong.

In the days of the city's Committee on Slum Clearance, headed by Robert Moses, the sponsors of three projects sold out.

Continued on Page 43, Column 4

Sports News

FOOTBALL

Harvard upset Princeton yesterday before 25,000 fans.

Air Force..48	U. C. L. A...21
Army 7	U'tah 7
Boston Coll.15	Buffalo 3
Bucknell ..11	Colgate 5
Clemson ...11	N. Carolina. 7
Conn. 22	Boston U....15
Cornell 28	Brown 0
Dartmouth .47	Columbia ...6
Duke 39	Wake For....7
Ga. Tech...15	Florida 3
Harvard ...21	Princeton ...7
Holy Cross..14	V. M. I......7
Indiana 20	Oregon St...15
Iowa 27	Minnesota ..13
Memphis St..9	S. Carolina...0
Michigan ...14	Illinois 8
Mich. St....27	Purdue 7
Mississippi .41	Tampa 0
Miss. St....57	Auburn 0
Navy 35	Maryland 7
Nebraska ...23	Kansas 9
N. C. State. 15	Va. Tech.....7
Oklahoma ..24	Iowa St......9
Oregon 31	Wash. St.....7
Penn St....10	Ohio. St......7
Pitt. 27	N. Dame 7
Rutgers 49	Lafayette 6
Syracuse ...15	West Va......11
So. Calif...21	Stanford 11
Texas 7	Baylor 0
Washington .36	California ...39
Wisconsin ..17	N'western ..14
Yale 21	Penn 8

HORSE RACING

Hurry to Market survived a foul claim and won the $317,290 Garden State Stakes.

Details in Section 5.

Roosevelt Raceway Begins Cleaning Up After Rioters

This was the scene late Friday night at the trackside entrances to the grandstands.
United Press International

Yesterday teams of glaziers worked to replace the glass knocked from the rows of doors.
The New York Times (by Robert Walker)

Leaders of Raceway Riot Sought in Study of Films

Special to The New York Times

MINEOLA, L. I., Nov. 9—The Nassau County police today impounded movies taken during the rioting last night at Roosevelt Raceway in a move to identify the leaders of the violence. Fifteen men were arrested after the riot, which broke out when the track management declared the sixth race official even though only two of the eight horses finished.

During the outbreak, about 500 fans smashed the tote board, battled the police, set fires and caused other damage estimated at $30,000.

Tonight's racing was conducted without incident. Plainclothes policemen circulated among the 31,398 patrons, but they found no disorder. The crowd was about average for a Saturday night. [Details on racing in Section 5.]

Twin Double Threatened

The twin double may be in jeopardy, because of the riot. This is a form of wagering in which bettors try to pick the winners of the last four races. The sixth race is the first one of the four.

Disgruntled holders of twin-double tickets were believed to have started the riot.

There were 85,574 tickets sold on the twin double last night. Because of a spill that knocked six horses out of contention, only 3,563 tickets were "alive" for a chance at the big prize. This meant that the holders of the 82,011 remaining tickets were disqualified in mid-night.

Continued on Page 83, Column 1

CITY VOTE URGED ON FLUORIDATION

Councilman Sees Dangers—Referendum Would Prevent Action Now

By CHARLES G. BENNETT

A move for a referendum on the fluoridation of New York City's water supply developed in the City Council yesterday.

If upheld by the Council, it would block for some time to come the plans of the Wagner administration to put fluoridation into effect in the next few months.

Councilman Edward V. Curry, Democrat of Richmond, said yesterday that he would introduce a resolution calling for a referendum at Tuesday's meeting of the Council.

The proposal now pending at City Hall for immediate consideration of fluoridation would be shelved until after the referendum.

A public hearing on immediate fluoridation is scheduled at City Hall at 10 A.M. on Monday, Nov. 18, before the Board of Estimate and the Finance Committee of the City Council.

Warns of Danger

Acting in response to the pleas of medical, dental and other organizations, Mayor Wagner and City Council President Paul R. Screvane have announced their strong support of the fluoridation proposal. A majority of the Board of Estimate, it has been indicated, supports the plan.

The Curry resolution warns that "a mechanical failure in the equipment disseminating" fluorides into our water supply system could be extremely dangerous to millions of our residents," and adds:

"If the proposal to fluoridate our water is approved, 8 million people of the City of New York will have no choice in the matter, and will be forced to use fluoridated water."

The resolution declares that "more time is needed for a program of research and education, so that answers may be provided to the many questions

Continued on Page 43, Column 6

Jewel Bandits Left 85% of Loot; Fingerprints in Vehicles Studied

The robbers who took jewelry said to be worth at least a million dollars from a messenger service here Friday left about 85 per cent of the loot behind, the police said last night.

The station wagon, which was seized with its six guards on East 41st Street about 1 o'clock Friday afternoon, contained 2,000 envelopes with necklaces, rings and brooches. Some of the envelopes were in six different bags and the rest in fiber boxes resembling small suitcases. There were also some gold bars weighing 15 to 20 pounds each.

At the West 30th Street station house, the police questioned 20 men with criminal records for possible clues, and also several persons who may have witnessed the robbery. No possible witnesses scanned the rogues

Continued on Page 83, Column 5

OTEPKA ACCUSERS PLACED ON LEAVE

State Department Studies Case of Two Who Altered Testimony on Phone Tap

By MAX FRANKEL

WASHINGTON, Nov. 9—The Otepka security case took a dramatic turn today that jeopardized the Government careers of the accusers as well as the accused. The development also raised important new questions about executive-branch procedures and relations with Congress.

Beside the central controversy over the right of a State Department security officer to pass secret documents to a Senate committee, there suddenly flared an argument over the department's right to tamper with the telephones of an employee and over Senate charges of deception and possible perjury about one such eavesdropping attempt.

Two of three State Department officials who this week "amplified" their earlier denials of electronic eavesdropping on a colleague were placed on administrative leave" today. The indications were that Secretary of State Dean Rusk would reluctantly ask both, and perhaps all three, to resign.

The central figure in the case is Otto F. Otepka, who was dismissed last Tuesday as chief security evaluations officer in

Continued on Page 47, Column 1

BAKER PROMOTED TAX CHANGE IN '62 TO AID HIS MOTEL

Attempted to Ease Financial Plight—Congress Acted Quickly on Amendment

By EILEEN SHANAHAN

WASHINGTON, Nov. 9—Robert G. Baker used his influence to get tax legislation through Congress that he hoped would help him out of financial difficulties over a luxury motel he had built.

The legislation, added to the Administration's tax bill last year as an amendment, would have made it easier for the former secretary to the Senate Democratic majority to sell units in the motel and set it up as a cooperative or condominium.

Mr. Baker and his associates conceived this tax plan in the summer of 1962 when they found themselves in difficulties as a result of large loans they had made to finance the motel in Ocean City, Md.

The amendment, put into the tax bill on the Senate floor with almost no debate and without a formal vote, was sponsored by Senator John J. Sparkman, Democrat of Alabama.

No Objection Offered

It was accepted in the House-Senate conference committee's draft of the final bill. There was no House debate on it.

Treasury officials said today they had offered no objection because they believed it was a justifiable change that would eliminate an inconsistency in tax laws.

They also said they had known Mr. Baker's interest in the amendment, but only after it had passed the Senate. The officials said they had heard the legislation characterized as "the Bobby Baker amendment" after its passage.

That characterization was based on comments by Senators and Senate staff members.

How Mr. Baker had succeeded in pushing through the amendment was still a secret. Knowledgeable officials said only that he had been behind the amendment, and refused to go into details.

Sparkman Vague

Senator Sparkman said today he was not certain whether he had been aware of Mr. Baker's interest in the legislation when he proposed it.

He said he thought the legislation had been "suggested" to him by members of the home-building or savings and loan industry, but his memory was vague on the matter.

Other Senators, by their remarks in the brief debate on the amendment, indicated they were familiar with it.

They were: Jacob K. Javits, Republican of New York, who noted that he owned a cooperative apartment; George A. Smathers, Democrat of Florida,

Continued on Page 44, Column 1

Mine Blast and Rail Crash Kill at Least 491 in Japan

327 Dead, 348 Injured in Shaft—Toll Is 164 in 3-Train Pile-Up

Special to The New York Times

TOKYO, Sunday, Nov. 10—A coal-mine explosion and a rail wreck killed at least 491 persons in Japan yesterday. Hundreds of persons were injured and several hundred miners were trapped with little hope of escape.

[Rescuers said it appeared that a giant fireball touched off by the explosion, cave-ins and carbon monoxide had killed miners who tried to reach safety in isolated underground chambers, The Associated Press reported.]

The mine disaster at Omuta took at least 327 lives. Omuta is in Fukuoka Prefecture in Kyushu. A total of 348 miners were said to have been seriously injured.

The rail accident, in which 164 persons died, including an American student from Colorado, happened just outside Yokohama on Japan's main north-south Tokaido trunk line. More

Coal-mine blast occurred at Omuta (1). Two trains hit a third near Yokohama (2).
The New York Times   Nov. 10, 1963

Continued on Page 3, Column 5

House Headwaiter Went to NATO Talk With Congressmen

By NAN ROBERTSON

WASHINGTON, Nov. 9—The headwaiter in the House dining room was disclosed today to have accompanied a group of Representatives attending the NATO parliamentarians' conference in Paris.

Ernest Petinaud, the headwaiter, made the trip as a guest of Representative Wayne L. Hays, Democrat of Ohio. The Washington Daily News reported Mr. Hays is a member of the House Administration Committee, which serves as a watchdog over Congressional junkets.

There was no immediate confirmation here or in Paris that the headwaiter had been the guest of Mr. Hays. It was reported from Paris that both Mr. Hays and Mr. Petinaud checked out of their hotel there today.

Their destination was reported to be Bonn, West Germany, but no one could be found in that city who was expecting them.

[The supervisor of the House restaurant said Mr. Petinaud told him earlier this year that Mr. Hays had invited him to go to Europe, The Associated Press reported. Mr. Petinaud had accumulated three weeks of vacation time, he added.]

The delegation, which flew to Paris Nov. 1, included nine Representatives, the wives of seven of them, and two women employees in Mr. Hays's office.

The meeting of members of the parliaments of the member nations of the North Atlantic Treaty Organization began on Monday and ended last

Continued on Page 44, Column 4

Senators to Renew TFX Study With Testimony From Gilpatric

By JACK RAYMOND

WASHINGTON, Nov. 9—A Senate subcommittee plans to resume the TFX hearings Nov. 18, with testimony from Deputy Defense Secretary Roswell L. Gilpatric.

He will be asked, among other things, to explain in detail his links with the General Dynamics Corporation as a lawyer before he took office in January, 1961.

Mr. Gilpatric was a partner in the firm of Cravath, Swaine & Moore of New York city. The General Dynamics Corporation, winner of the controversial $6.5 million contract to produce the TFX airplane, was a client of the firm at the time Mr. Gilpatric was one of the partners.

The panel, the Senate Permanent Investigating Subcommittee, is under the chairmanship of Senator John L. McClellan, Democrat of Arkansas. It also plans to recall former Secretary of the Navy Fred Korth.

Mr. Korth will be asked about possible conflict of interest in the selection of the company to manufacture the new jet fighter, experimental as tactical fighter, or TFX. The military chiefs of the Navy and Air Force recommended Boeing.

The hearings, which have been stormy on occasion, were

Merits of a contract proposal

by General Dynamics, which planned to produce the plane in Fort Worth, Tex., where he was a prominent banker.

The losing bidder, the Boeing Company of Seattle, planned to produce the plane in Wichita, Kan.

"If you find or this committee finds that I am not in a man of integrity I certainly you should so recommend to the President and I will promptly hand in my resignation," Mr. Korth said under questioning July 22.

Mr. Korth resigned as Secretary Oct. 14 to return to private business. He acknowledged that he had used his official stationery in contacts with business associates.

The subcommittee has been investigating the TFX contract intermittently since Feb. 25. It is searching, for possible evidence of favoritism in the selection of General Dynamics in the manufacture of the new jet fighter

Continued on Page 42, Column 1

U.S. WILL RESUME KEY AID PROGRAM IN SOUTH VIETNAM

Commercial-Imports Plan, Suspended Under Diem, Involves 95 Million

MOVE BOLSTERS BUDGET

Supply of Consumer Goods and Funds for Military Won't Be Interrupted

Special to The New York Times

WASHINGTON, Nov. 9—The United States has decided to resume a key program of economic aid to South Vietnam. The program was suspended in August in an effort to get Ngo Dinh Diem, then President, to introduce political reforms.

[Two hundred armed opponents of the ousted South Vietnamese Government who are Social Democrats have rallied to the support of the new Government, The Associated Press reported from Saigon. On the fighting front, a sergeant from Kansas was killed by Communist fire.]

Officials in Washington said today that action was being taken in Saigon to end the suspension of the commodity-import program. The program, which had been running to about $95 million a year, was used to finance much of South Vietnam's commercial importing and, indirectly, to support the Government's budget.

Bulk of Aid Continued

The bulk of these aid programs continued throughout the Buddhist crisis and the coup d'état that overthrew the Ngo family.

President Ngo Dinh Diem and his brother Ngo Dinh Nhu were killed during the revolt by military leaders last Friday and Saturday.

The commodity-import program was the only economic-aid program suspended during the final months of Ngo Dinh Diem's Government. But the United States did support military support to South Vietnam's Special Forces, which were being used largely for political and security purposes by the Saigon Government.

At the time, Washington stipulated that these forces were returned to their original function of fighting the Communists, such aid would be resumed. Instead, however, President Ngo Dinh Diem decided to keep some Special Forces personnel in Saigon for his personal protection.

Presumably the military support, which amounts to about $3 million a year, will be resumed as the new Government puts the Special Forces

Continued on Page 5, Column 1

DE GAULLE SEEKS POWER UNTIL 1970

Aides Say He Wants to Be at Helm to Help Change Atlantic Alliance Policy

By DREW MIDDLETON

Special to The New York Times

PARIS, Nov. 9—President de Gaulle believes he must retain office until 1970, a year after the military agreements of the North Atlantic alliance come up for revision, according to a qualified source.

The President, the source said, has made his intention known in conversations in the last two weeks. He is not concerned with the way he prolongs his stay in power, although this will be "constitutional," but simply in being at the helm to defend France's interests.

General de Gaulle is said to hope that "the Anglo-Saxons," meaning the United States and Britain, will understand that he intends to uphold his policy of national military and political independence when the Atlantic alliance treaty is revised.

He Seeks 'Continuity'

He is also said to be interested in maintaining "continuity" of his policy toward Eastern Europe, which is based on his opposition to the Yalta agreements by the United States, Britain and the Soviet Union gave the Russians a free hand in Eastern Europe.

The French leader's present position appears to be an extension of one he took Sept. 25. He said then that he believed he should be able to continue to lead France and maintain her independence of Washington's and Moscow's "double hegemony."

He obviously now believes his leadership must be extended until the end of the present decade to insure retashioning of the Atlantic alliance. His term, which is for seven years, expires in 1965.

[President de Gaulle is 73 years old. His last meeting

Continued on Page 12, Column 1

Texas Voters Balk Repeal of Poll Tax

By JOSEPH A. LOFTUS
Special to The New York Times

DALLAS, Nov. 9—Texas voted today to keep their 61-year-old poll tax, a decision that might bear significantly on next year's Presidential race in this state.

Both advocates and opponents of the repeal proposal were certain that it would have "added thousands of liberal voters to the registration rolls, thus reinforcing a Kennedy-Johnson ticket in 1964.

President Kennedy carried Texas in 1960 by only 46,000 votes. The state has 25 votes in the Electoral College.

Little more than one-fourth of the qualified electorate cast ballots on the proposed amendment to the state constitution.

With returns nearly complete,

Continued on Page 77, Column 4

BLAST AND CRASH KILL 491 IN JAPAN

Continued From Page 1, Col. 7

mine's tunnels. The mine explosion occurred at 3:15 P.M. (1:15 Saturday morning, Eastern standard time.)

The train wreck happened just before 10 P.M. when a freight train hit a truck on a grade crossing. The first three cars of the freight train were derailed and they overturned. The wreckage was hit almost instantly by two passenger trains coming from opposite directions on adjacent tracks. The forward coaches of both trains were derailed and wrecked.

About 480 of the 1,221 workers who were in the mine at the time of the blast were brought to the surface. Most were led or carried to safety in small groups by rescuers working from three main entrances.

Blast Heard for Miles

The blast was heard for many miles. Rescued miners described the scene as one of confusion and horror.

The mine, operated by the Mitsui Mining Company, is one of the largest in Japan. Its tunnels extend far under the waters of Ariakeno Bay. Kyodo, Japan's national news agency, reported that rescue efforts were being hampered by poison gas in the mine and the loss of all electric power below the surface.

The American who died in the train crash was identified as William Scott of Colorado Springs, Colo. He was a student at International Christian University in Tokyo.

Rescue workers toiled through the night to remove the dead and injured from the twisted wreckage.

The police sent vehicles and ambulances to take the injured to 13 hospitals in the Yokohama area. Train service on the Tokaido line, which links the Tokyo-Yokohama area with the Kyoto-Osaka-Kobe region 350 miles south, was disrupted.

Train Bound for Tokyo

One of the passenger trains involved was bound for Tokyo. The other was filled with commuters returning to the suburban area south of Yokohama. Its destination was Zushi on the shore of Sagami Bay.

The rail accident was the second major disaster on Japan's extensive Government-operated rail system in 19 months. A wreck in the Arakawa district of Tokyo in May, 1962, killed 160 persons and injured 296. The accident subjected the Japan National Railways to severe criticism.

The Mikawa coal mine, site of yesterday's explosion, is situated in one of Japan's biggest coal-producing centers. The Mikawa mine and two others near by turn out about 5 million tons of coal a year.

The area has been beset by bitter labor strife in recent years following efforts by the Mitsui Mining Company in 1960 to reduce its work force by 2,000 men because of the inroads being made into coal consumption by increasing imports of petroleum.

Japan Jolted by Tragedies

TOKYO, Sunday, Nov. 10 (AP)—The tragedies jolted Japan in the midst of a crisp, pleasant autumn weekend.

Until last night, Japanese had been following the news of the state visit of West Germany's President, Dr. Heinrich Lübke, who was host to the Emperor and the Empress at a gala performance of the Berlin Opera.

Early-morning broadcasts and newspapers changed all this with accounts of the mine accident. These were succeeded six hours later by stories of the train crash. Lists of the dead were transmitted over nationwide television networks throughout the night.

Japan Shaken by Train Wreck and Mine Disaster

Aerial view of the wreckage of the trains that collided and overturned near Yokohama

JAPAN FAMILIAR WITH CALAMITY

Population Density Makes for High Casualties

The disasters in Japan yesterday struck a nation that has already had more than its share of natural and man-made catastrophes.

Three of the 11 worst railroad wrecks and several of the worst mine disasters in history have occured in Japan and her empire.

On Sept. 1, 1923, the fourth most lethal earthquake in a record of more than 1,000 years, killed 143,000 Japanese.

Part of the explanation appears to lie in Japan's population density of 650 persons to the square mile — one of the greatest in the world and about 13 times that of the United States.

A record for casualties in a mine disaster was set in April, 1942, in the Honkeiko Colliery, in Manchuria, then under Japanese operation, when 1,549 miners were killed.

1,060 Died in France

At Corrières, France, on March 10, 1906, an explosion killed 1,060 miners—the second-highest toll. On Jan. 21, 1960, at Coalbrook, South Africa, 417 miners were killed. The worst mine disaster in the United States, with 25 that have claimed more than 100 victims, was on Dec. 6, 1907 at Monongah, W. Va., with 361 dead. In February, 1962, 298 West German miners died in a gas explosion in a coal mine at Saarbrücken.

The death toll in Saturday's train crash was the third-highest in Japanese history, the 11th in world railroad history.

The greatest disaster in rail history occured at Modane, France, on Dec. 12, 1917 when a French troop train was derailed, killing 543 persons. Another wartime accident—the derailing of an Italian train in a tunnel near Salerno on March 2, 1944—claimed 426 lives. Many died of asphyxiation from fumes confined in the tunnel.

At Gretna Green, Scotland, a three-train crash took 227 lives on May 22, 1915—again in wartime.

Worst Japanese Crash in '40

Japan's own worst rail crash, one of three that took 200 lives and ranks fourth in casualties, occurred on Jan. 29, 1940 near

Rescue workers carry out bodies of victims after explosion ripped through mine at Omuta

Osaka. Identical death tolls resulted from accidents at Cuartla, Mexico, in 1881, and at Nowy Dwor, Poland, in 1949.

Other high-casualty crashes were those at Sakvice, Poland, in 1953—186 dead; Kendal, Jamaica, B.W.I., 1957—175 dead; Wellington-Auckland, New Zealand, 1953—150 dead; Tokyo, 1962—147 dead, and between Bandjar and Bandung, Indonesia, 1959—110 dead.

The worst United States railroad crash occured at Nashville, Tenn., on July 9, 1918,

when 101 passengers and crewmen were killed.

In recent years, the 84 commuters killed in the derailment of a commuter train at Woodbridge, N. J., on Feb. 6, 1951, and the 79 killed less than three months earlier at Richmond Hill, N. Y., were the highest fatality lists in American railroading.

Between September, 1954, and January, 1955, four Japanese ferryboats were lost with a death toll of 1,611. The sinking

229

"All the News That's Fit to Print"

The New York Times.

LATE CITY EDITION
U. S. Weather Bureau Report (Page 52) forecast: Chance of showers or snow today; clear tonight. Fair, cold tomorrow.
Temp. Range: 56—36; yesterday: 60—47.

VOL. CXIII... No. 38,661. NEW YORK, SATURDAY, NOVEMBER 30, 1963. TEN CENTS
© 1963 by The New York Times Company. Times Square, New York 36, N. Y.

JOHNSON NAMES A 7-MAN PANEL TO INVESTIGATE ASSASSINATION; CHIEF JUSTICE WARREN HEADS IT

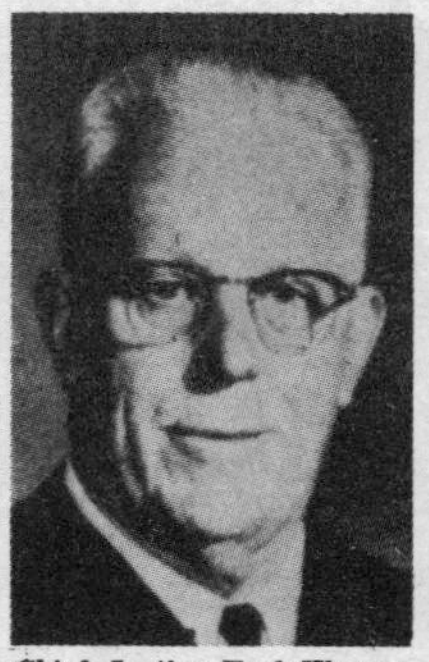
Chief Justice Earl Warren

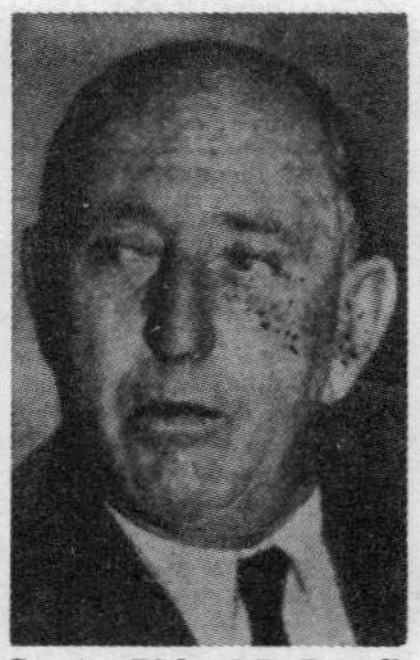
Senator Richard B. Russell

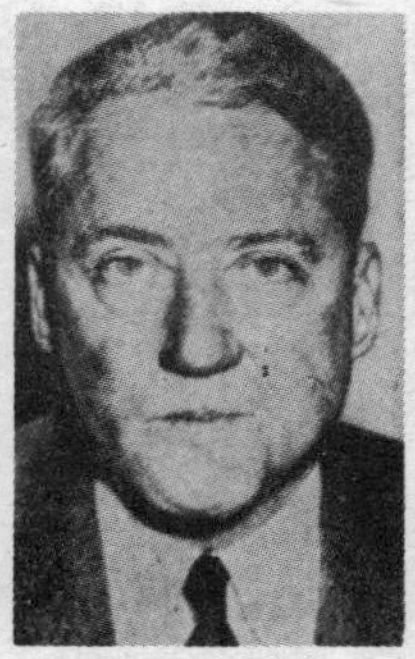
Senator John S. Cooper

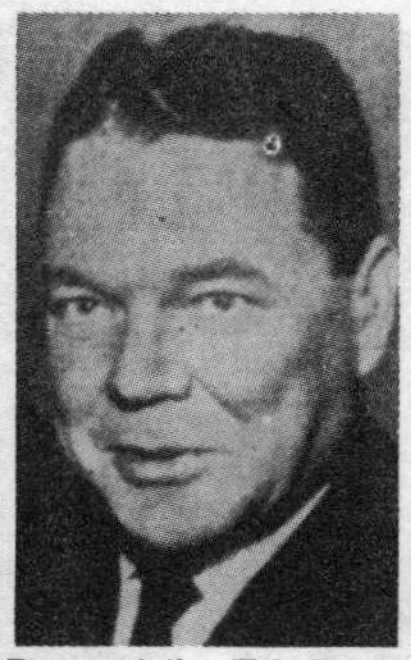
Representative Hale Boggs

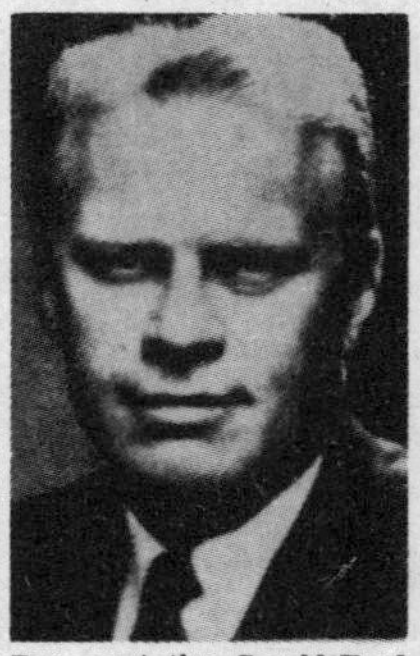
Representative Gerald Ford

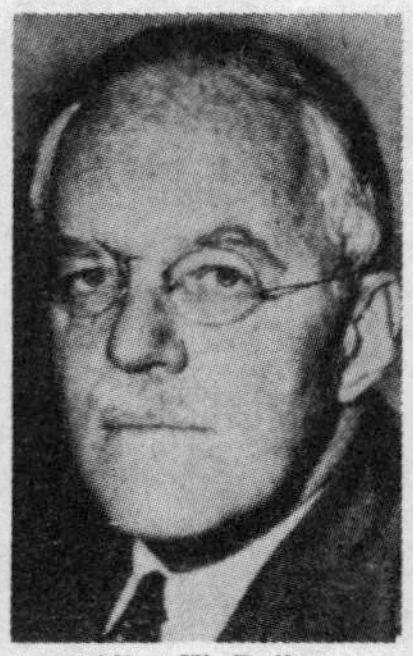
Allen W. Dulles

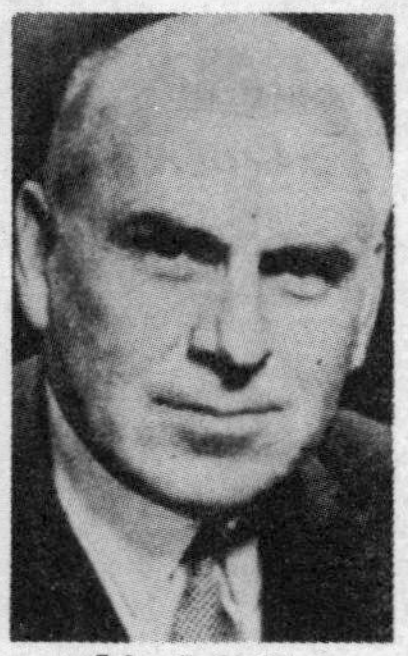
John J. McCloy

TEXAS OFFERS AID

President Asks Board for a Public Report After Full Inquiry

By JOHN D. MORRIS
Special to The New York Times

WASHINGTON, Nov. 29—President Johnson created a special commission tonight to investigate the assassination of President Kennedy. He appointed Chief Justice Earl Warren to head the panel.

The White House, in announcing the action, said the Chief Justice would serve as chairman of a seven-member commission that also includes two Senators, two Representatives and two former Administration officials.

It added:

"The President is instructing the special commission to satisfy itself that the truth is known as far as it can be discovered, and to report its findings and conclusions to him, to the American people and to the world."

Will Evaluate Data

Others appointed to the commission were: Senator Richard B. Russell, Democrat of Georgia; Senator John Sherman Cooper, Republican of Kentucky; Representative Hale Boggs, Democrat of Louisiana; Representative Gerald R. Ford, Republican of Michigan; Allen W. Dulles, former director of the Central Intelligence Agency, and John J. McCloy, former disarmament adviser to President Kennedy.

The commission, according to the White House statement, will be instructed "to evaluate all available information concerning the subject of the inquiry."

It said that this would include evidence obtained by the Federal Bureau of Investigation in a special inquiry previously ordered by Mr. Johnson. The F.B.I. report on that investigation is expected to be ready next week.

Texas to Cooperate

The Attorney General of Texas, Waggoner Carr, has "offered his cooperation," the White House said. This means, officials explained, that evidence obtained by a state court of inquiry created by the Attorney General will be available to the Presidential commission.

Officials also said that the timing of the inquiry and the procedures — whether public hearings would be held, for example—would be determined by the Chief Justice.

They reported that "all necessary powers, including subpoena powers," would be provided.

Congress's Aid Expected

Within the general authority of his office, the President can appoint such commissions to make inquiries as he wishes. An act of Congress, however, will be required to provide the power to subpoena witnesses and documents.

It was taken for granted that Congress would promptly pass a bill providing such power.

The commission will investigate the killing of Lee H. Oswald, President Kennedy's accused slayer, as well as "all facts and circumstances relating to the assassination of the late President," according to the White House announcement.

Besides naming the members of the commission, the announcement said:

"The President today announced that he is appointing a special commission to study and report upon all facts and circumstances relating to the assassination of the late President, John F. Kennedy, and the subsequent violent death of the

Continued on Page 12, Column 3

118 ON JET DIE AS IT CRASHES AT MONTREAL

DISASTER IN RAIN

Toronto Shuttle Falls in a Field 4 Minutes After Taking Off

Special to The New York Times

MONTREAL, Nov. 29—All 118 persons on a Trans-Canada Air Lines jet were killed tonight when the plane crashed and burned in a driving rainstorm.

The crash, about 20 miles north of Montreal, was the worst in Canada's history.

The jet, a four-engine DC-8F, plunged into a soggy field near the town of Ste. Thérèse de Blainville, a few hundred feet from the main highway leading to the Laurentian Mountains.

One witness said she had seen what looked like "a long red streak in the sky" just before the crash.

The plane was going from Montreal to Toronto on a regular Friday night shuttle. It took off from Montreal International Airport four minutes before the crash.

A Trans-Canada spokesman said the passengers were believed to have been mostly Canadians. The first casualties to be identified were the plane's officers. They were:

Capt. J. D. Snider, 47 years old, the pilot, of Toronto; First Officer H. J. Dyck, 35, of Leamington, Ont., and Second Officer E. D. Baxter, 29, of Toronto.

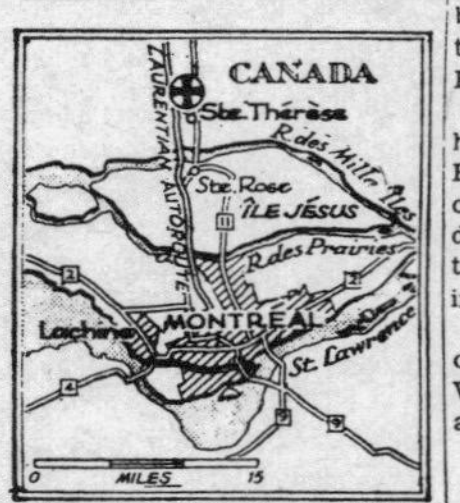

The New York Times Nov. 30, 1963
Scene of the crash (cross)

The red-trimmed, silver jet dug a huge crater in the ground that soon began to fill with rainwater.

Rescue parties were hampered by deep mud around the wreckage. Although parts of the plane were scattered over a wide area, the craft broke into two main sections when it struck the ground.

The Quebec provincial police issued an emergency call for all available ambulances when word of the disaster was received. Two hours later the ambulance call was canceled.

The plane, Flight 831, took off in the rain from the airport runway used in bad weather. It first headed northeast and had started to circle to get back on course for Toronto, about 400 miles to the southwest.

It crashed at Ste. Thérèse at 6:32. An unconfirmed report said the airport tower had had no communication with the plane after it was airborne.

The site of the crash was a flat field away from houses in the town of 12,000 people. The main sections of the wreckage lay about halfway between Highway 11 and the Laurentian Autoroute. Despite the heavy

Continued on Page 53, Column 2

Home Vows Effort To Ease Tensions

Special to The New York Times

LONDON, Nov. 29—Prime Minister Sir Alec Douglas-Home pledged tonight "all the ingenuity and penetration" of British diplomacy to reduce tensions between East and West.

Lest anyone see in this the promise of an independent initiative, he emphasized that British efforts would be made only as a loyal ally of the West, and of the United States in particular.

Some voices have been raised here to suggest that President Kennedy's death provided Britain with an opportunity to assume his role in international affairs until

Continued on Page 2, Column 7

VENEZUELA SEEKS DRIVE ON CASTRO

Betancourt Urges Action by Hemisphere to Erase Communist Foothold

By RICHARD EDER
Special to The New York Times

CARACAS, Venezuela, Nov. 29—President Romulo Betancourt called today for an effort by Western Hemisphere nations to overturn the Government of Premier Fidel Castro.

In the toughest statement he has made on Cuba, President Betancourt said that it had become "necessary to have joint definite action to finish with this bridgehead of Communism in America."

Mr. Betancourt's speech coincides with the close of the Venezuelan election campaign, amid new threats by terrorists.

[In Washington the Administration pledged every effort to isolate Cuba and prevent the export of Communist subversion to the rest of Latin America.]

At noon today the Armed Forces of National Liberation sent a statement to news agencies saying that Col. James K. Chenault, an American kidnapped Wednesday, would be freed in exchange for the release of 70 women said to be held prisoner by the Government.

[The Associated Press reported an exchange offer, but said Colonel Chenault was to be traded for six persons who hijacked a plane Thursday and made the pilot fly it to Port of Spain, Trinidad. The six were returned to Caracas.]

The clandestine National Liberation force also announced

Continued on Page 2, Column 2

SOVIET GRAIN SALE IS SNAGGED AGAIN ON SHIPPING RATES

Negotiations Are 'Dormant'—Broken Glass Is Found in Wheat From Canada

By EDWIN L. DALE Jr.
Special to The New York Times

WASHINGTON, Nov. 29—The on-again, off-again negotiations with the Soviet Union for the sale of American wheat are off again.

The two chief Russian negotiators have left the country and the talks are described by officials here as "dormant." No one will say whether the talks are off for good, but the Soviet postion is that the next move must come from the United States.

Sergei A. Borisov, First Deputy Trade Minister, who arrived here Oct. 23, is understood to have flown back to Moscow with Anastas I. Mikoyan, a First Deputy Premier, who came here for President Kennedy's funeral.

Freight Rates the Issue

Leonid Matveyev, head of the Soviet grain trading agency, has gone to Ottawa, where he previously concluded a massive wheat purchase from Canada. He has established a temporary residence there.

Lesser officials in the Soviet negotiating delegation are also understood to have left the United States.

The talks on the sale, expected to amount to about $250 million, have snagged over the issue of shipping. The United States insists that at least 50 per cent of the wheat be shipped in American-flag vessels, whose rates are higher than those available on foreign-flag ships. The Russians consider this "discriminatory" and refuse to pay the extra freight charges.

[In Montreal it was confirmed that broken glass had been found in shipments of Canadian wheat to the Soviet Union. It was believed that the contamination was the result of carelessness rather than sabotage.]

U. S. Position Is Modified

The United States has considerably modified its original position on the shipping question, with the result of somewhat reducing the extra charge to the Russians. But this is still not satisfactory to the Russians.

The present Soviet position is that if the United States has a better offer, it can be communicated to Moscow or the Soviet Embassy here. The Russians have given no sign of wishing to resume negotiations until there is such a move.

The question may be put up to President Johnson. Only he could decide whether to relax still further the requirement of shipping in United States vessels. This has already been relaxed from a requirement of shipping in American bottoms "where available" to a requirement that 50 per cent of the

Continued on Page 2, Column 2

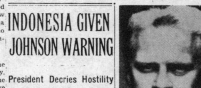

INDONESIA GIVEN JOHNSON WARNING

President Decries Hostility to Malaysia in Conference With Defense Minister

Special to The New York Times

WASHINGTON, Nov. 29—President Johnson has conveyed to Gen. Abdul Haris Nasution, Indonesia's Defense Minister, the deep disquiet felt by the United States over Indonesia's threatening attitude toward Malaysia.

In an earlier talk with Zulfikar Ali Bhutto, the Foreign Minister of Pakistan, Mr. Johnson also expressed concern at Pakistan's apparent drift toward Communist China.

Officials said briefing papers had been prepared for the guidance of the President for both these talks.

Talk 'Very Friendly'

General Nasution has been considered better disposed toward the United States than President Sukarno of Indonesia. When the general emerged from his meeting with Mr. Johnson today, he said that the talk had been "very friendly," and that assurances had been given on both sides that the friendly relationship would continue.

General Nasution said that he had explained to President Johnson the Indonesian view of the Malaysian situation and that Mr. Johnson had expressed hope for "an Asian solution."

The general said he had told the President that "we will not start a clash from our side," but that Indonesia would defend herself "if attacked."

Relations between the United States and Indonesia in the last few months have not been marked by friendliness. On Sept. 25 President Sukarno said Indonesia was threatened by the

Continued on Page 3, Column 2

Joint Chiefs See President; Hear Demand for Economy

By E. W. KENWORTHY
Special to The New York Times

WASHINGTON, Nov. 29—President Johnson had his first White House conference with the Joint Chiefs of Staff today. He emphasized to them that he expected their cooperation in redeeming his pledge to get a dollar's value for each military dollar spent.

In turn, the Joint Chiefs familiarized the President with their operating procedures. Andrew T. Hatcher, acting White House press secretary, said afterward that the President contemplated no change in these procedures.

Mr. Johnson put in a long, arduous and crowded day, dividing his attention among foreign, domestic and legislative problems.

Despite the best efforts of Bill D. Moyers, an old friend who has been shifted from second in command at the Peace Corps to become the President's man-of-all-work, Mr. Johnson was far behind his schedule by noontime.

Johnson Sees Wilkins

The President finally left the White House for his residence at 10:27 P.M. after a series of conferences with members of his staff.

He had a 45-minute session with Roy Wilkins, executive secretary of the National Association for the Advancement of Colored People. Afterward Mr. Wilkins told reporters, "We have very great faith in the new President's attitude on civil rights."

The members of the Joint Chiefs of Staff, who met with Mr. Johnson, are Gen. Maxwell D. Taylor, chairman; Gen. David M. Shoup of the Marine Corps; Gen. Curtis E. LeMay of the Air Force; Adm. David L. McDonald of the Navy and Gen. Earle G. Wheeler of the Army.

The President also held a conference with Robert S. McNamara, Secretary of Defense; John A. McCone, director of the Central Intelligence Agency, and McGeorge Bundy, the Presidential assistant for national security affairs.

Later, Secretary of State Dean Rusk briefed Mr. Johnson on foreign policy problems. After a session with Lawrence F. O'Brien and Myer Feldman on pending legislation, the President met with Dr. Glenn T. Seaborg, chairman of the Atomic Energy Commission.

Sees Pakistani Minister

He also kept in touch by phone with the Senate Democratic leader, Mike Mansfield of Oklahoma, and the speaker of the House, John W. McCormack of Massachusetts. In midafternoon, he saw Charles A. Horsky, his adviser on District of Columbia affairs.

At the end of the day, he met with Zulfikar Ali Bhutto, the Foreign Minister of Pakistan, and Gen. Abdul Nasution, the Indonesian Defense Minister.

He also issued an Executive order formally renaming the Cape Canaveral space installation in Florida the John F. Kennedy Space Center.

Most members of President Kennedy's White House staff

Continued on Page 8, Column 1

OSWALD PLANNED A BOOK ON RUSSIA

Stenographer in Fort Worth Tells of Typing His Notes Criticizing Soviet Life

By JOHN HERBERS
Special to The New York Times

FORT WORTH, Tex., Nov. 29—A public stenographer disclosed today that she had typed notes for Lee H. Oswald that were to be the basis of a book on the hardships of life in Russia.

Pauline V. Bates said the man accused of assassinating President Kennedy walked into her office on June 18, 1962, with a manila envelope full of notes. He wore a zipup jacket, a white T-shirt and dark slacks.

"I saw your name in the telephone book," he said. "Can you do some typing for me?"

Miss Bates said she worked at brief intervals for the next few days typing the notes that had been made on various kinds and shapes of paper. Mostly, she said, they described the harshness of life in Russia.

The 24-year-old Oswald lived in Russia for three years after finding life in his own country unbearable.

He returned to this country June 13, arriving at New York by ship. He left New York June 14 for Fort Worth. His ticket was paid for by his

Continued on Page 9, Column 1

Thousands of Students in Paris Battle With Police

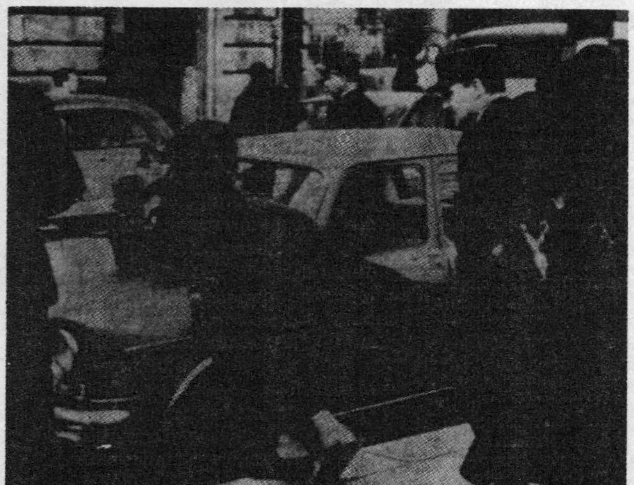
Associated Press Cablephoto
Paris policeman uses a weighted cape to subdue student taking part in riot on Left Bank

By HENRY GINIGER
Special to The New York Times

PARIS, Nov. 29—A sharp debate on French education erupted into violence today as thousands of university students clashed with the police in many areas of the Left Bank. The police used rolled-up capes weighted with pieces of lead, riot sticks and high-pressure fire hoses to break up the ranks of students determined to demonstrate, despite a ban, their discontent with insufficient school facilities. About 300 demonstrators were arrested and 30 policemen were reported injured, one by a paving stone. The number of injured students was unknown. Most of

Continued on Page 4, Column 3

Hasty Independence Is Deplored in U.N.

By DAVID ANDERSON
Special to The New York Times

UNITED NATIONS, N. Y., Nov. 29—Chile warned in the General Assembly today that the smaller colonial territories throughout the world must not be granted independence hastily or indiscriminately.

Ceylon endorsed the Chilean view that states unprepared for independence risked "falling under the pernicious and selfish influences of larger states."

This was the first time that anti-colonialist spokesmen had raised such warnings in General Assembly debate.

Oscar Pinochet of Chile said he felt entitled to speak out "clearly and frankly" on so delicate a subject "since our anti-

Continued on Page 3, Column 5

Mrs. Johnson to Put TV Stock in a Trust

By United Press International

WASHINGTON, Nov. 29—Mrs. Lyndon B. Johnson moved today to transfer her controlling interest in a Texas radio and television station to trustees.

A lawyer for Mrs. Johnson filed an application with the Federal Communications Commission requesting permission to transfer her control of KTBC-AM-FM-TV in Austin to A. W. Moursand and J. W. Bullion of Johnson City, Tex., as trustees.

They already control 184 shares, or 30.9 per cent, of the stock in the LBJ Company, which owns the stations. The application filed today said this stock was being held in trust for the Johnsons' daughters—

Continued on Page 8, Column 3

Kennedy Chose Site at Harvard For Presidential Library Oct. 19

By BEN A. FRANKLIN
Special to The New York Timer

WASHINGTON, Nov. 29—President Kennedy had picked a site at Harvard University for the library and museum that will house the personal and official papers of his Administration.

It was learned today that, on a weekend visit to the Boston area Oct. 19, Mr. Kennedy inspected several locations that Harvard had offered for the building. He was accompanied by John Carl Warnecke, the California architect who is now designing Mr. Kennedy's tomb at Arlington National Cemetery.

The site Mr. Kennedy chose is next to the graduate school of business administration. It faces the Charles River and Winthrop House, the dormitory in which Mr. Kennedy spent his upperclass days at Harvard. He was graduated in the class of 1940.

President Kennedy often urged his Cabinet, the principal members of his White House staff and other ranking officials of his Administration to preserve their personal and official papers.

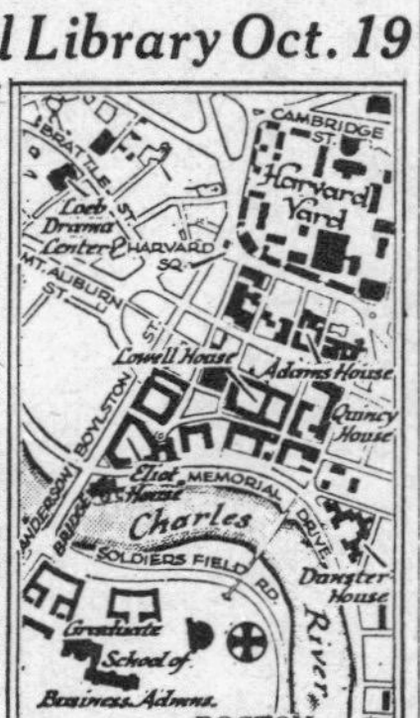

The New York Times Nov. 30, 1963
Site of the library (cross)

The building, therefore, which will be called the Kennedy Presidential Library and Museum, will be "a complete record of

Continued on Page 14, Column 4

NEWS INDEX

Helicopter view of the scattered remains of the Trans-Canada DC-8F jet which crashed near Montreal.

Wide World Photos

118 on Jetliner Killed in Crash At Montreal During Rainstorm

Continued From Page 1, Col. 1

rain, the plane burned for about two hours. The police and Canadian soldiers quickly cordoned off the area to keep spectators away.

Although the plane was headed for Toronto. it was believed that many of the passengers were planning to go on to Vancouver, B. C., to attend the Grey Cup professional football game tomorrow between the Vancouver Lions and the Hamilton Tiger Cats. The game is the championship playoff between Eastern and Western teams.

The plane was due to arrive at Toronto at 7:15 P.M.

'Terrible Explosion'

One witness living near the crash site said she was in her kitchen when "I heard a terrible explosion and saw a huge red ball of fire in the air. The plane crashed just about right away after that, and my husband called the police."

A temporary morgue was set up at a nearby Canadian Army ordnance depot.

Within an hour of the crash, traffic along Highway 11 and the expressway was completely stalled as motorists tried to drive to the scene.

The Canadian Minister of Transport. George McIlraith. said Government investigators were going to the site. The airline is Government-owned.

The airline marked its 25th anniversary in the spring of 1962. At that time it was reported that the line had carried more than 28 million passengers and had flown 1.5 billion revenue miles.

Line Founded in 1937

The airline was founded in 1937 by an act of Parliament. It first flew a 122-mile route between Vancouver and Seattle. It now serves 40 Canadian communities, six cities in the United States and points in Europe and the Caribbean.

One of the line's planes crashed seven years ago on a flight from Montreal to Vancouver. All 62 persons aboard were killed.

Aviation's worst disaster involving a single plane occurred in Paris in June, 1962, when an Air France jetliner crashed, killing 130 persons, 121 of them Americans.

The highest death toll in the history of aviation occurred in December, 1960, when 134 persons were killed when two planes collided over New York City. Six of the dead were on the ground.

In 1953, a United States Air Force C-124 crashed and burned near Tokyo, taking the lives of 129 persons. It was the worst single military air disaster.

United Press International
Capt. J. D. Snider, who was the pilot on the fatal flight.

"All the News That's Fit to Print"

The New York Times.

LATE CITY EDITION

U. S. Weather Bureau Report (Page 63) forecasts: Fair, breezy and cold today; cloudy tonight. Fair and cold tomorrow.
Temp. Range: 46—35; yesterday: 49—37.

SECTION ONE

NEWS SUMMARY AND INDEX, PAGE 63

VOL. CXIII. No. 38,781.

© 1964 by The New York Times Company. Times Square, New York, N. Y. 10036

NEW YORK, SUNDAY, MARCH 29, 1964.

40¢ beyond 50-mile zone from New York City, except on Long Island. 50¢ beyond 200-mile zone from New York City, higher in air delivery cities.

THIRTY CENTS

SCORES PERISH IN ALASKA QUAKE AND TIDAL WAVES ON WEST COAST; ANCHORAGE SUFFERS WORST LOSS

DELAYS REPORTED IN FRANCE'S DRIVE FOR ATOMIC FORCE

Severe Engine Difficulties Said to Stall Production of Mirage-4 Bombers

SUBMARINES ALSO LAG

Plan for Nuclear-Powered Craft With Missiles May Not Be Met Before '72

By DREW MIDDLETON
Special to The New York Times

PARIS, March 28—France's nuclear force, the military foundation for President de Gaulle's claim to European primacy, has encountered acute technical difficulties, according to highly qualified sources.

On the basis of their observations, these sources have concluded that there has as yet been no important French breakthrough in nuclear weaponry.

The first phase of France's advance into the nuclear age is the construction of a bomber fleet capable of carrying atom bombs of the type dropped on Hiroshima in 1945. It had been thought that the French Air Force had at least a squadron of these Mirage-4 bombers in operation.

The sources said, however, that France had no more than three prototype Mirage-4 bombers operational and, at most, three other bombers of this type from regular production.

Flight Needs Lacking

Both the prototypes and the production models are reported to be plagued with engine troubles and not yet capable of the flights envisaged.

Consequently, there is no production line for these aircraft, as far as the sources know. There have even been hints that the French Air Force would be interested in American-built engines if this could be reconciled with General de Gaulle's conviction that the nuclear force must be entirely French in construction.

A few atomic bombs are ready for the Mirage-4 bombers, the sources said.

The second phase of France's nuclear effort will take the form of three nuclear-powered submarines armed with Polaris-type missiles. This program also is lagging, the sources report.

The French estimate, they said, is that the submarines will be ready by 1968 or 1970. The sources believe that two or three

Continued on Page 3, Column 2

CITY SAID TO LOSE MILLIONS ON DRUG

Pills Bought in U.S. Cost 5 Times More Than Imports

By RONALD SULLIVAN

The city is losing millions of dollars by paying five times more than the Federal Government pays for tetracycline, the most widely used antibiotic.

A Federal spokesman reported yesterday that tetracycline was purchased in Italy for 1.6 cents a tablet. Deputy Commissioner of Purchase Gabriel A. Wechsler said the city had to buy it from American companies for 8.7 cents a tablet.

Sold under various trade names in drugstores, tetracycline's prescription price is from 30 to 40 cents a tablet.

"The city is a captive of high American drug prices," Mr. Wechsler said. "But we are trying desperately to get loose."

Mr. Wechsler's comments followed a charge by William F. Haddad, a reform Democratic candidate for Congress, who declared yesterday:

"In the purchase of tetracycline the city is being cheated, threatened and intimidated by American drug companies."

Mr. Haddad, who is opposing Representative Leonard Farbstein in the Democratic primary in the 19th Congressional District, said that otherwise "the city has an excellent record of purchasing drugs at low prices."

Tetracycline is purchased by the Government and the city for use in hospitals. The Department of Purchases estimates that it spends $1 million a year for tetracycline under trade

Continued on Page 25, Column 1

Buying a home? See The Dime FIRST. A mortgage takes fast action. The Dime Savings Bank of Brooklyn. TR 5-3000 —Advt.

U.N. Troops Take Over in Kyrenia

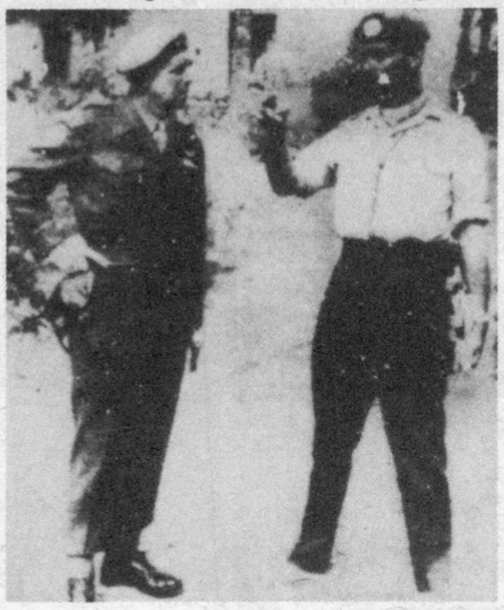

Associated Press Cablephoto

Maj. Pat Tremblay, right, of the Canadian peace-keeping force on Cyprus, with Maj. John Pegg of the British Army.

By LAWRENCE FELLOWS
Special to The New York Times

KYRENIA, Cyprus, March 28—A company of United Nations soldiers, French-Canadians of the Royal 22d Canadian Regiment, arrived here today to take over the task of keeping the peace between Greek and Turkish Cypriotes.

Although Kyrenia itself has been spared from the intercommunal fighting that covered much of Cyprus, trouble broke out all around the perimeter of this harbor

Continued on Page 7, Column 1

Saud Stripped of Power; Faisal Takes Full Control

By DANA ADAMS SCHMIDT
Special to The New York Times

BEIRUT, Lebanon, March 28—King Saud, after three days of pressure, submitted today to decisions of a council of the royal family and of religious leaders reducing him permanently to the role of figurehead. He was expected to leave Saudi Arabia, possibly forever, "for reasons of health."

The King signed a decree stripping him of his armed protection, of most of his revenue and half his income. But at his request the decree will not be published.

The sons of the King who led a campaign defending him, particularly Prince Mohammed, are expected to leave Saudi Arabia by air within a few days.

Crisis Began Monday

Crown Prince Faisal, Saud's half-brother, is now in full control of the kingdom, although the King was left his title.

The crisis began last Monday with a meeting of all leading members of the royal family except Saud, along with 34 religious patriarchs, known as ulema, and tribal leaders. The tribal chiefs had been summoned by Faisal to answer a demand by the King that his powers be restored in full.

The gathering upheld Faisal and proposed to remove Saud from the throne and proclaim the Prince as ruler. But Faisal insisted that Saud retain the title. All that mattered, he said, was that the King should leave power in Faisal's hands and not

Continued on Page 18, Column 1

JOHNSON TO TOUR POVERTY SECTORS

At News Parley, He Says He Disagrees With Fulbright on Panama and Cuba

By TOM WICKER
Special to The New York Times

AUSTIN, Tex., March 28—President Johnson said tonight that he would soon make a personal inspection trip "to view conditions first hand" in poverty-stricken areas of the nation.

He said he had no plans, however, to fly to Alaska to inspect Anchorage and other cities hit by an earthquake Friday night.

In an unscheduled news conference around the massive desk in his paneled office at the LBJ Ranch near here, Mr. Johnson also said that he had "given very strong instructions and followed through very vigorously" that Air Force planes were to observe the limits of air corridors through East Germany to West Berlin.

By doing so, he said, he hoped there would be no repetition of the incident in which three United States fliers were shot down in East Germany after their RB-66 strayed out of the central corridor.

The United States, he said, will continue to "do all we can to ease the tensions that exist." He said he was "very happy" at the release of the three fliers. He insisted that they had not been "on any clandestine or spy mission."

The President reiterated his disagreement with Senator J. W. Fulbright, Democrat of Arkansas, who is chairman of the

Continued on Page 31, Column 1

A.E.C. Post Given To Radcliffe Head

Special to The New York Times

AUSTIN, Tex., March 28 — President Johnson today named Mrs. Mary Ingraham Bunting, president of Radcliffe College, to the Atomic Energy Commission.

The 53-year-old Dr. Bunting, a microbiologist and biochemist, will be the first woman to serve on the five-member commission.

The salary for the post is $22,500 a year.

In appointing a woman, President Johnson resolved a deadlock between labor and business groups that had been fighting to place a representative on the commission ever since the seat became vacant Feb. 1. Then Dr. Robert E. Wilson, a former oil

Continued on Page 30, Column 1

INDONESIA FACING A CRISIS ON FOOD; MILLIONS HUNGRY

Rations on Java Reported Insufficient for Health—Rice Harvest Delayed

By SETH S. KING
Special to The New York Times

SEMARANG, Indonesia, March 26 — During the next six weeks, President Sukarno will have to pass through one of the most dangerous periods he has faced since he became leader of Indonesia 14 years ago.

Until the country's rice crop is harvested in early May, food supplies in this normally bountiful land will remain dangerously low.

Estimates are that more than two million Indonesians, most of them on this island of Java, now do not have enough to eat to remain healthy.

In several areas of Java and in a few scattered pockets in Bali there are people today who are lying down in the streets and dying of starvation. Hundreds have been hospitalized from the effects of lack of food.

Relief Effort Ineffective

The Sukarno Government has not been able to mount effective relief operations to prevent the widespread hunger. In these scattered areas people are dying while there is more than enough food in adjoining valleys barely 20 miles distant.

Families of impoverished villagers, hungry and in rags, have been making their way into the cities of Jakarta, Semarang, Jogjakarta and Surabaja to beg on the streets and sleep on the sidewalks.

Yet a traveler touring Bali and crossing the lush rice-producing areas along the 475 miles of roadway between Surabaja and Jakarta could see no evidence this week that Indonesia faced a major food shortage.

A long dry season and hordes of rats reduced last year's rice crop in Indonesia by at least 10 per cent.

The Rains Late Again

The rains have been late again this year. As a result the 1964 crop in the major rice-growing areas will be at least two months late and again at least 10 per cent below normal.

About two million children have been added in the year, presenting two million more mouths to feed and bringing the country's estimated population to 103 million.

President Sukarno's campaign to crush the new Federation of Malaysia has cut off most of the shipping that normally brought rice imports from Burma and Thailand through Singapore. Indonesia's credits abroad both for chartered shipping and for rice have been virtually exhausted. So have the country's foreign currency reserves with which to buy for cash abroad.

The Sukarno Government has already purchased 40,000 tons

Continued on Page 9, Column 1

Jews and Christians Worship As Feast Days Occur Together

Easter to Be Sunny

By PAUL L. MONTGOMERY

Many of the world's Christians will rejoice today in the commemoration of the Resurrection.

In the city, Easter services are planned beginning at dawn and running through much of the day. Among the earliest are the sunrise ceremonies at 5:45 A.M. in Carl Schurz Park, at 86th Street and the East River and at Kennedy International Airport.

Many churches will have double or triple services to accommodate overflow crowds.

The Weather Bureau expects mostly a bright setting for the day's festivities, which include the annual Easter parade on Fifth Avenue. The day is expected to be sunny, with the afternoon temperatures in the high 40's.

In Christian churches, the event commemorated by Easter is the basis of all services during the year. The Resurrection means to Christians that the influence of Jesus and His teachings did not end with His Crucifixion around 28 A.D. but was continued when His followers found His tomb empty on the third day afterward. In

Continued on Page 26, Column 3

ROBERTS Fine Furniture, Greenwich, Conn. Famous Baker Royal Bedding.—Advt.

Passover Celebrated

By IRVING SPIEGEL

Worshipers gathered in temples and synagogues yesterday morning for special services in observance of the first day of Passover, the Jewish festival celebrating the liberation of the Israelites from Egyptian bondage.

In sermons, rabbis called attention to the festival's emphasis on religious freedom and deplored the continuing suppression of the spiritual and cultural activities of Jews within the Soviet Union.

Last night, the second seder, the meal-worship service, was held in Jewish homes. The story of Moses delivering the Jews from the tyranny of Pharaoh, as recorded in Exodus, was retold.

Both Easter and Passover are observed during the advent of spring although not necessarily on the same date.

However, this year through a coincidence of the calendar Easter occurs during the Passover week. Passover is celebrated according to the lunar calendar. Its celebration begins on the 14th day of the Hebrew month of Nisan. This fell at sundown on Friday, which was Good Friday for Christians.

Easter is determined by the

Continued on Page 26, Column 7

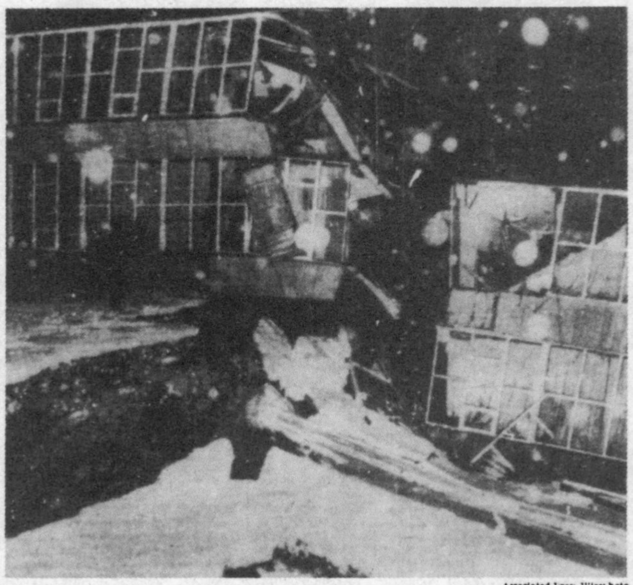

Associated Press Wirephoto

Ruins of Government Hill School, Anchorage, which was torn apart by earth fissure, left

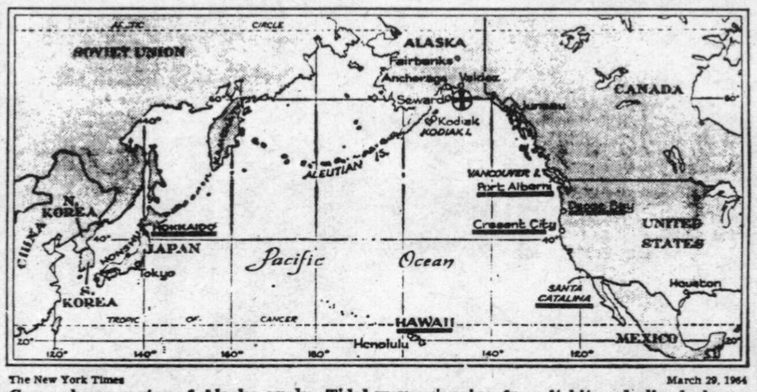

The New York Times — March 29, 1964

Cross shows center of Alaska quake. Tidal waves fanning from it hit underlined places.

WHITE HOUSE ACTS

Emergency Is Declared—Alaskans Starting to Clear Rubble

By The Associated Press

ANCHORAGE, Alaska, March 28—One of history's mightiest earthquakes spread devastation in Alaska, but the still-quivering, snowy ruins tonight yielded a surprisingly low toll of known dead.

The Governor's office in unharmed Juneau, far to the south of the quake center, reported total deaths in America's largest state might not exceed 50.

"Casualties are less than we ever dreamed they could be," Secretary of State Hugh Wade said.

Authoritative figures were unlikely for several days.

Anchorage, Seward, Valdez and a score of smaller communities on the Gulf of Alaska dug through frigid rubble and reeled apprehensively from at least 42 aftershocks of the temblor that occurred at 5:36 P.M. Good Friday evening (10:36 P.M. Eastern standard time).

President Johnson declared the state a major disaster area and pledged all Federal resources in providing aid.

Damage Is Estimated

Gov. William A. Egan estimated the damage through the state at a minimum of $250 million.

Anchorage, Alaska's largest city, with a metropolitan area of 100,000 persons, suffered spectacular damage from the shock. Official death tallies 24 hours later ranged from seven to 16.

Hard-hit Valdez, 150 miles south on Prince William Sound, counted six dead and 24 missing. Seward, 60 miles southeast of Anchorage across the Kenai Peninsula, had three dead and 20 missing.

Giant seismatic sea waves generated by the quake smashed a half-dozen smaller towns rimming the Gulf of Alaska to the south and on Kodiak Island to the southwest. Tidal waves set off by the quake were reported across the Pacific.

At least 12 died and 15 were reported missing at Crescent City, Calif., more than 2,000 miles south of the quake's epicenter. One child drowned and three were missing when the waves caught a sleeping family on a beach near Depoe Bay, Ore.

The waves slashed at the Hawaiian Islands without major damage and finally spent them-

Continued on Page 48, Column 1

ITALIAN AIRLINER HITS MT. VESUVIUS

All 45 Aboard, Including 7 Americans, Are Killed in Crash During Rain

By Reuters

NAPLES, Italy, Sunday, March 29—All 45 persons aboard an Alitalia Viscount turboprop airliner were killed last night when the plane crashed in flames on the slopes of Mount Vesuvius.

[The Associated Press in Naples reported that seven Americans were among the 45 dead.

[They were listed as Major Lawrence Mancini of Brooklyn, his wife, Fay, and two children, Jill and Steven; Lieut. Robert I. Adkison and J. H. McFadden, both of New York, and Thomas Vendur of Norfolk, Va.]

Naples firemen who reached the wreckage shortly after 3 A.M. local time reported that the aircraft had struck the mountain slope and then slid downward.

Left Rome at 10:10 P.M.

The Viscount was on a normal Turin-Rome-Naples flight and left Rome at 10:10 P.M. local time.

It was due to land at Naples 45 minutes later.

The airport at Naples reported it was in radio contact with the aircraft when it was maneuvering for a landing. Contact was broken off at 10:37 P.M., the airport said.

Rescue parties reached the Vesuvius volcano observatory in cars, but then had to make their way on foot over the lava bed from a 1944 eruption.

Once across, they forced their way slowly through thick bush and mud and slush caused by incessant rain that fell in the area during the day. Fog hampered the rescue teams.

The plane crashed in the region of the "Cresto Cardo" (thistle crest) on the rim of the crater out of which the volcano

Continued on Page 50, Column 2

PORT CHESTER SHADE & AWNING CO. Awnings of Every Description 914—WE 9-0441—Advt.

Missile Defenses Keep Functioning During the Quake

Text of Pentagon briefing appears on Page 49.

By MAX FRANKEL
Special to The New York Times

WASHINGTON, March 28—The Defense Department moved swiftly this morning to make sure that missile and air defense systems had survived the Alaska earthquake and to organize disaster relief missions.

Military installations in Alaska suffered some damage, but the early warning systems that guard North America against attacks from the Soviet Union functioned throughout the disaster. Some communications were disrupted, but there was no break in contact with the area.

Thus by 7 A.M., eight hours after the first tremors struck, Lieut. Gen. Raymond J. Reeves, Commander in Chief for Alaska, was able to inform Washington:

"The Alaskan Command still maintains its full capability to carry out its assigned mission — defense of Alaska — despite some damage to buildings and equipment."

Aid by Military Units

Military units in Alaska were by that time moving to assist the stricken civilian communities, though bad flying weather and torn-up roads disrupted the effort.

Another major concern here through the night was the effect of tidal waves on the northwestern United States and Hawaii. It was not until 4 A.M. that officials found this danger to have passed with relatively little damage in most places.

The capital then turned to organizing itself for disaster relief, a job that required coordination among a half-dozen Government agencies. It was supervised by the White House Office of Emergency Planning and the Defense Department.

Officials of both agencies assembled at the Pentagon at 7 A. M. to obtain a full report on the situation. Among those at the meeting were Cyrus R. Vance, Deputy Secretary of De-

Continued on Page 49, Column 1

WEST COAST HIT BY TIDAL WAVES

Flooding Set Off by Quake Leaves at Least 12 Dead at Crescent City, Calif.

By WILLIAM M. BLAIR
Special to The New York Times

CRESCENT CITY, Calif., March 28 — Tidal waves 12 to 15 feet high, set off by the Alaskan earthquake, swept out of the Pacific early today and wrecked the business district of this town, causing at least 12 deaths.

The death toll was expected to rise as Federal and state relief units moved in to aid the stricken community in northwestern California near the Oregon border.

Sheriff O. E. Hovgaard, who was coordinating the aid work, estimated that as many as 25 persons might have perished in the water that rolled in about 1:40 A.M., Pacific standard time (4:40 A.M., Eastern standard time).

[The waves left death and destruction from British Columbia to Southern California, United Press International reported. The highest wave, one of 17 feet, hit Vancouver Island. Four children in a family sleeping on a beach near Depoe Bay, Ore., were swept away by the sea.]

Elderly Couple Drowned

The bodies of 10 of the 12 known dead here have been recovered.

The number of homeless was placed at from 75 to 100 persons. Their homes were knocked off their foundations in the 29-block business area hit by the rolling waves. Several persons were in the hospital.

Some bodies were seen floating out on the receding tide from the low-lying areas.

A visitor at a motel near the waterfront reported seeing an elderly couple drowned as they were swept away from another motel nearby.

The 12 known dead were 10 adults and two preschool chil-

Continued on Page 48, Column 7

Need $3,000, $5,000, $10,000? It's easy to refinance your mortgage at The Dime Savings Bank of Brooklyn. TR 5-3000.—Advt.

Today's Sections

Index to Subjects

Scores Die in Alaska Quake and West Coast Tidal Waves; Anchorage Hardest Hit

PRESIDENT SPURS EMERGENCY HELP

Buildings Collapse, Utility Lines Snap and Cracks Appear in the Earth

Continued From Page 1, Col. 8

selves lapping Japan and Siberia.

President Johnson's disaster relief chief arrived here by plane tonight. He met immediately with state, local and military leaders to organize the recovery efforts.

Edward A. McDermott, director of the Office of Emergency Planning, left the Presidential plane after a 3,700-mile flight from Washington, and went at once to the meetings at Elmendorf Air Force Base.

Today the series of aftershocks created fear at the quake scene but raised no new sea waves. The strongest tremor registered 6.2 on the Richter scale. This would rate as a dangerous quake in itself, but it was a minor annoyance compared with the terrific initial shock of last evening.

That tremor, rated from 8.2 to 8.7 on the Ritcher scale, jostled seismographs around the world.

If the reading were finally put at 8.7, this would be the strongest earthquake scientifically recorded. The San Francisco disaster of April 18, 1906, rated 8.25, and more recent, less destructive quakes in isolated areas have reached 8.5 and 8.6.

In Anchorage, the largest devasted area, Mayor George Sharrock told newsmen there were only four known dead and three presumed dead, plus undetermined injured and missing.

Another estimate came from John Alcantra, assistant to Governor Egan, who placed the Anchorage toll at 16. Mr. Alcantra listed seven in the Turnagain residential area of swank homes, four in the new J. C. Penney building, four in a coin arcade and one at the Anchorage International Airport, where the tower collapsed.

Troops patrolled a 30-block area of downtown Anchorage through the day and night. No one was permitted to enter or leave the district after dark.

Seek to Restore Service

Some large buildings in this section were swallowed up by deep fissures that opened in the earth. Others were tilted so dangerously that dynamiting was planned to avoid further danger.

However, G. E. Evans, a New York engineer, estimated to newsmen that only 5 per cent of the city's buildings were a total loss and 35 per cent escaped with little damage.

City workers strove all day to restore electric, gas and water services, cut off when the quake shattered lines.

Most Anchorage and other residents of the stricken areas still huddled by candlelight around emergency fires tonight, however, and drank melted snow.

Valdez, a town of 1,200 persons, was completely evacuated during the day. Most residents drove their cars to a camp at Gulkana, 117 highway miles to the northeast. Fire destroyed the Valdez business district.

Seward, where a great smoky fire from ruptured oil tanks burned all day, reported the fire was confined to the dock area.

One late report from Seward said, "Doing O.K., all things considered."

As the initial nerv us reaction wore off, fears disease and worries over food supplies became uppermost.

Markets opened briefly during the day, some selling groceries that the shock had left heaped in aisles.

Typhoid Shots Planned

The public was urged not to use sewer facilities for fear of water contamination. Metal receptacles were distributed in Anchorage.

Typhoid fever inoculations were planned to begin tomorrow.

There was a foot or two of snow on the ground throughout most of the area. Downtown Anchorage had 4 inches.

Temperatures ranged from 22 to 27 degrees—mild for Alaska at this early season but bitter in heatless quarters.

Meanwhile, reports continued to trickle in from outlying towns.

The village of Kaguyak on the southern tip of Kodiak Island reported two residents were missing and 60 had been evacuated by boat.

A sketchy report from the village of Chenega, south of Whittier on Prince William Sound, said half the population was missing, but failed to give any number or further details.

From the town of Kodiak, Adm. R. E. Riera, commander of the Alaska Sea Frontier, reported there had been no casualties, contrary to first unconfirmed reports of 50 dead.

Smoke Covers Peninsula

By LAWRENCE E. DAVIES

Special to The New York Times

ANCHORAGE, Alaska, March 28—Early reports that deaths here might reach 300 or more were tremendously exaggerated. By this evening, after hundreds of rescue workers had searched dwellings and downtown business structures, the deaths in Anchorage itself were estimated at seven.

Fires continued to burn at Whittier and Seward, on the Kenai Peninsula south of this city. Great pillars of smoke swirled up from the Seward fire all day. Flames glowed this evening from six fuel tanks afire at Whittier, a port used by the Army in World War II.

Smoke covered the whole peninsula, site of oil and gas drilling operations by the Standard Oil Company of California, the Richfield Oil Corporation, the Shell Oil Company, the Union Oil Company and other operators.

Mayor George Sharrock of Anchorage met late in the day with Gov. William A. Egan, who had flown from the capital at Juneau on an inspection tour taking in Anchorage, Kodiak and Valdez, his home town.

Soldiers Patrol Streets

"It is possible," Mr. Sharrock said, "there may be additional deaths, but the remarkable thing is that the list is not higher. Moreover, there was no panic whatever despite the severity of the quake. And there has been very, very little looting of property. The police got on the job right away and we called for help from the National Guard and Army."

The Mayor said that martial law had not been declared. But uniformed soldiers were on every downtown street intersection to keep civilians out of the area.

"We are looking into water and sewage disposal problems," the Mayor said. "We have limited water supplies and have arranged scheduled deliveries with tankers and tank trucks in part of the city."

"The food situation we are inventorying now to determine the extent of the supplies and how much of them are usable," he said.

The Mayor said very few homes had heat and power.

"We have two gas turbines that we hope to get in use soon and get the gas line reopened," he went on. "Sixty per cent of our power capacity is out of operation but it is slowly coming back."

No businesses were permitted to operate during the day in the downtown section. The no-business edict will be continued at least through tomorrow, Mayor Sharrock said.

Among the residential areas, the attractive Turnagain section, a mile long and several blocks wide, was hardest hit.

At the meeting of Governor Egan and Mayor Sharrock, the question of early reopening of the banks in quake-affected areas was discussed with Elmer Rasmuson, president of the National Bank of Alaska.

Mr. Rasmuson told the Governor, "We need passes to get into our buildings to see what damage has been done."

Mayor Sharrock promised that passes would be made available to all businessmen of the downtown area intent on such missions.

Governor Egan, joined the Mayor in urging Mr. Rasmuson and his fellow bankers to try to get their institutions open "as soon as possible."

Mayor Sharrock, normally a quiet, placid executive, showed fire when he was asked whether Anchorage planned to rebuild.

"You bet we'll rebuild," he retorted. "There's no question of that."

The downtown damage was especially heavy along Fourth Avenue, the city's main business thoroughfare, and on Fifth Avenue.

The two highest apartment buildings in Anchorage, the McKinley Apartments and the L Street Apartments, each 14 stories high, remained standing. The L Street building appeared cracked but was regarded safe for occupancy.

Military Presses Cleanup

WASHINGTON, March 28 (AP)—The armed forces in Alaska reported tonight they had mounted a full-scale rescue and cleanup operation on the earthquake-battered peninsula.

A late report by telephone was received at the Pentagon from Lieut. Gen. Raymond J. Reeves of the Air Force, the Alaskan commander.

All boats under the command of the Alaska Sea Frontier were being used to evacuate survivors from outlying districts.

General Reeves reported the aerial medical evacuation of 40 military men and their dependents from the Elmendorf Air Force Base and said, "Medical facilities north of the Alaskan Range report capability to receive 125 patients."

The general said there were two 36-bed hospitals now on the way to Alaska and that additional field hospitals had been alerted for movement into the stricken zone.

These were hospitals at Fort Sam Houston, Tex., and Fort Lewis, Wash.

Meanwhile, the general reported 150 Army troops had been air-lifted by helicopter into Seward.

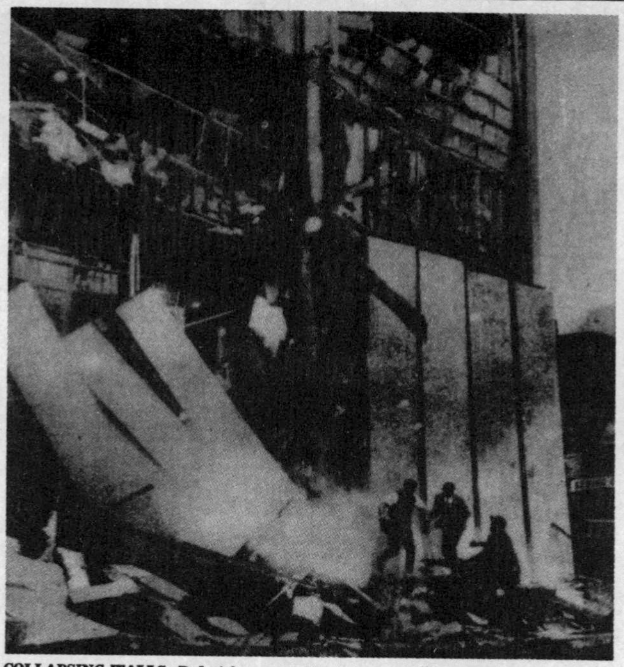

COLLAPSING WALLS: Pedestrians scramble to escape as five-story J. C. Penney store in Anchorage is destroyed by the earthquake that wrecked the city's downtown area.

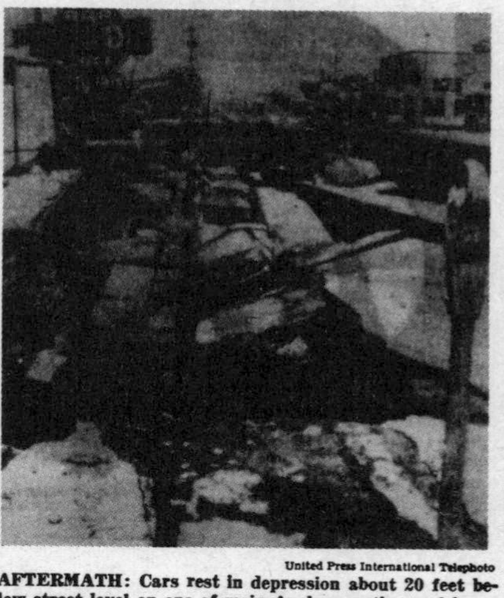

United Press International Telephoto

AFTERMATH: Cars rest in depression about 20 feet below street level on one of main Anchorage thoroughfares.

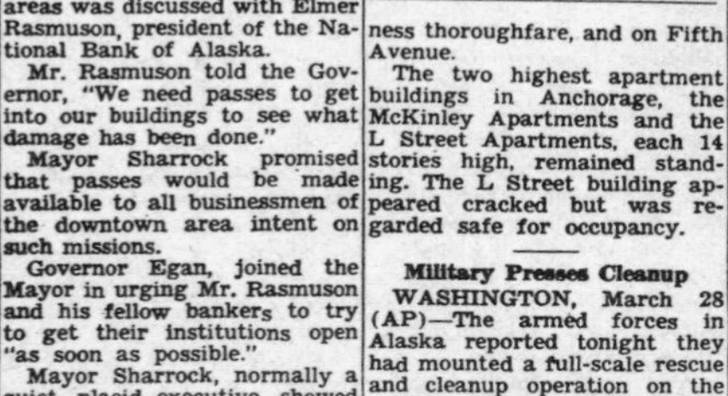

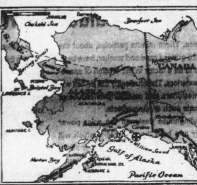

The New York Times March 29, 1964

QUAKE CENTER has been placed near the coast (cross)

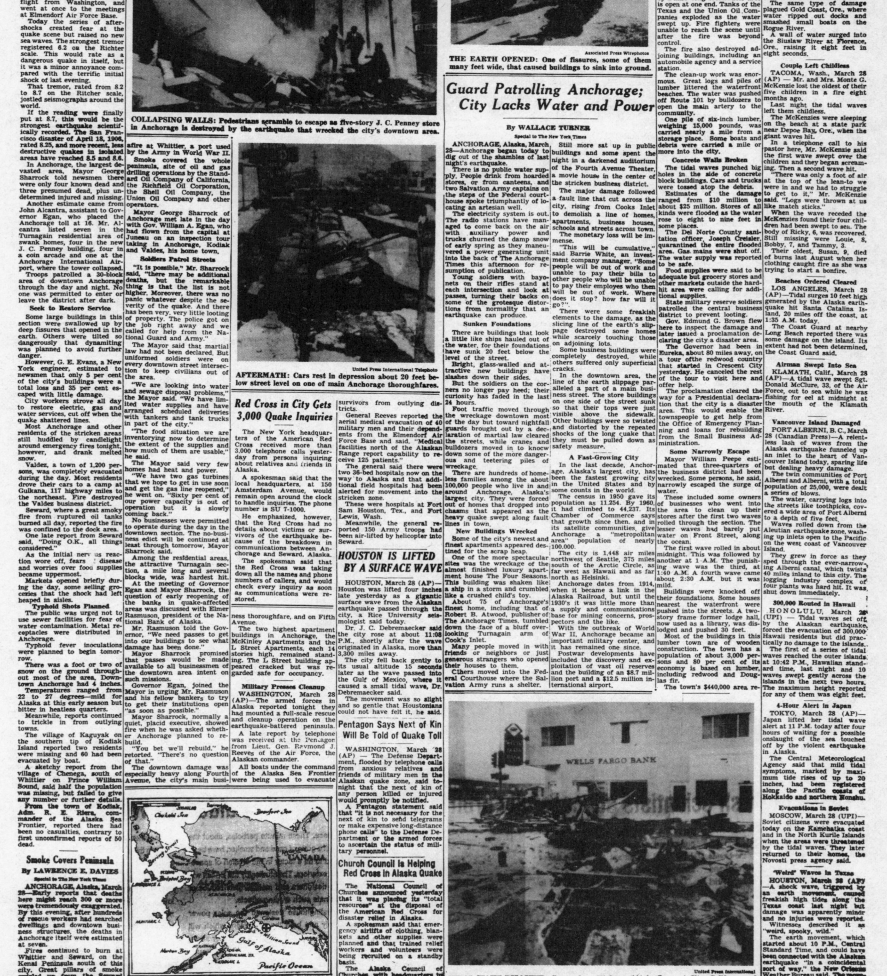

Red Cross in City Gets 3,000 Quake Inquiries

The New York headquarters of the American Red Cross received more than 3,000 telephone calls yesterday from persons inquiring about relatives and friends in Alaska.

A spokesman said that the local headquarters, at 150 Amsterdam Avenue, would remain open around the clock to handle inquiries. The phone number is SU 7-1000.

He emphasized, however, that the Red Cross had no details about victims or survivors of the earthquake because of the breakdown in communications between Anchorage and Seward, Alaska.

The spokesman said that the Red Cross was taking down all the names and phone numbers of callers, and would check every inquiry as soon as communications were restored.

HOUSTON IS LIFTED BY A SURFACE WAVE

HOUSTON, March 28 (AP)—Houston was lifted four inches late yesterday as a gigantic surface wave from the Alaskan earthquake passed through the city, a Rice University seismologist said today.

Dr. J. C. Debremaecker said the city rose at about 11:08 P.M., shortly after the wave originated in Alaska, more than 3,300 miles away.

The city fell back gently to its usual altitude 15 seconds later as the wave passed into the Gulf of Mexico, where it caused a small tidal wave, Dr. Debremaecker said.

The movement was so slight and so gentle that Houstonians could not have felt it, he said.

Pentagon Says Next of Kin Will Be Told of Quake Toll

WASHINGTON, March 28 (AP) — The Defense Department, flooded by telephone calls from anxious relatives and friends of military men in the Alaskan quake zone, said tonight that the next of kin of any person killed or injured would promptly be notified.

A Pentagon statement said that "it is not necessary for the next of kin to send telegrams or make expensive long-distance phone calls" to the Defense Department or the armed forces to ascertain the status of military personnel.

Church Council Is Helping Red Cross in Alaska Quake

The National Council of Churches announced yesterday that it was placing its "total resources" at the disposal of the American Red Cross for disaster relief in Alaska.

A spokesman said that emergency airlifts of clothing, blankets and other supplies were planned and that trained relief workers and volunteers were being recruited on a standby basis.

The Alaska Council of Churches, with headquarters in Anchorage, is cooperating in the program.

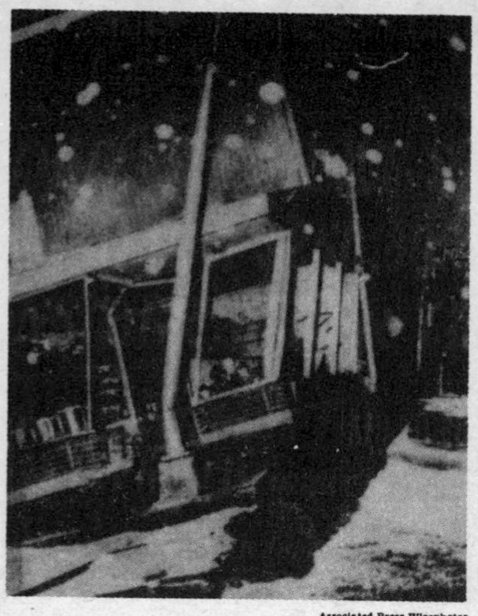

Associated Press Wirephotos

THE EARTH OPENED: One of fissures, some of them many feet wide, that caused buildings to sink into ground.

Guard Patrolling Anchorage; City Lacks Water and Power

By WALLACE TURNER

Special to The New York Times

ANCHORAGE, Alaska, March 28—Anchorage began today to dig out of the shambles of last night's earthquake.

There is no public water supply. People drink from hoarded stores, or from canteens, and two Salvation Army captains on the steps of the Federal courthouse spoke triumphantly of locating an artesian well.

The electricity system is out. The radio stations have managed to come back on the air with auxiliary power and trucks churned the damp snow of early spring as they maneuvered a power generating unit into the back of The Anchorage Times this afternoon for resumption of publication.

Young soldiers with bayonets on their rifles stand at each intersection and look at passes, turning their backs on some of the grotesque distortions from normality that an earthquake can produce.

Sunken Foundations

There are buildings that look a little like ships hauled out of the water, for their foundations have sunk 20 feet below the level of the street.

Bright, glass-walled and attractive new buildings have slashes down their sides.

But the soldiers on the corners no longer pay heed; their curiosity has faded in the last 24 hours.

Foot traffic moved through the wreckage downtown most of the day but toward nightfall guards brought out by a declaration of martial law cleared the streets, while cranes and bulldozers moved in to knocw down some of the more dangerous and teetering piles of wreckage.

There are hundreds of homeless families among the about 100,000 people who live in and around Anchorage, Alaska's largest city. They were forced out of homes that dropped into chasms that appeared as the heavy quake swept along fault lines in town.

New Buildings Wrecked

Some of the city's newest and finest apartments appeared destined for the scrap heap.

One of the more spectacular sites was the wreckage of the almost finished luxury apartment house The Four Seasons. This building was shaken like a ship in a storm and crumbled like a crushed child's toy.

About 75 of Anchorage's finest home, including that of Robert B. Atwood, publisher of The Anchorage Times, tumbled down the face of a bluff overlooking Turnagain arm of Cook's Inlet.

Many people moved in with friends or neighbors or just generous strangers who opened their houses to them.

Cthers moved into the Federal Courthouse where the Salvation Army runs a shelter.

Still more sat up in public buildings and some spent the night in a darkened auditorium of the Fourth Avenue Theater, a movie house in the center of the stricken business district.

The major damage followed a fault line that cut across the city, rising from Cooks Inlet to demolish a line of homes, apartments, business houses, schools and streets across town.

The monetary loss will be immense.

"This will be cumulative," said Barrie White, an investment company manager. "Some people will be out of work and unable to pay their bills to other people who will be unable to pay their employes who then will be out of work. Where does it stop? how far will it go?".

There were some freakish elements to the damage, as the slicing line of the earth's slippage destroyed some homes while scarcely touching those on adjoining lots.

Some business buildings were completely destroyed, while others suffered only superficial cracks.

In the downtown area, the line of the earth slippage paralleled a part of a main business street. The store buildings on one side of the street sunk so that their tops were just visible above the sidewalk. Other buildings were so twisted and distorted by the repeated shocks of the long quake that they must be pulled down as safety measure.

A Fast-Growing City

In the last decade, Anchorage, Alaska's largest city, has been the fastest growing city in the United States and by some counts in the world.

The census in 1950 gave its population as 11,254. By 1960, it had climbed to 44,237. Its Chamber of Commerce says that growth since then, and in its satellite communities, give Anchorage a "metropolitan area" population of nearly 100,000.

The city is 1,448 air miles northwest of Seattle, 375 miles south of the Arctic Circle, as far west as Hawaii and as far north as Helsinki.

Anchorage dates from 1914, when it became a link in the Alaska Railroad, but until the 1930's it was little more than a supply and communications base for mining concerns, prospectors and the like.

With the outbreak of World War II, Anchorage became an important military center, and it has remained one since.

Postwar developments have included the discovery and exploitation of vast oil reserves and the building of an $8.7 million port and a $12.5 million international airport.

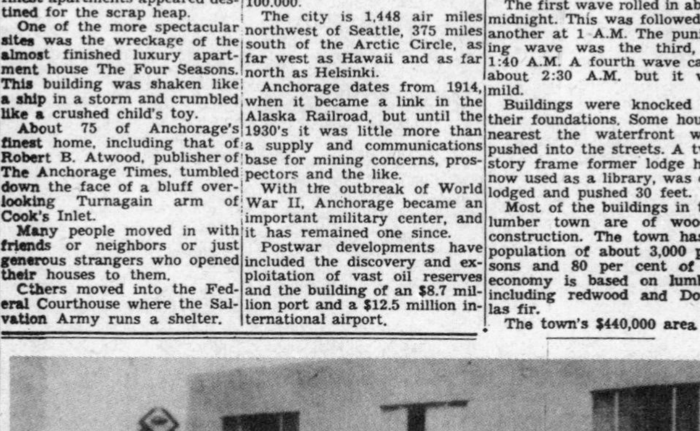

United Press International

TIDAL WAVE DISASTER: Scene along Highway 101 in Crescent City, Calif., one of the areas hardest hit by the tidal waves that accompanied the earthquake in Alaska.

West Coast Hit by Tidal Waves; 12 Dead in Crescent City, Calif.

Continued From Page 1, Col. 7

dren. The youngsters had been staying with grandparents near the waterfront.

Debris, including giant redwood logs in this lumber community, were tossed onto the roads and streets and into stores. Streets in the city and in adjacent areas near the ocean were covered with mud.

There were reports of extensive damage to boats and beaches. Gold Beach, a wild beach area near the Prairie Creek Redwoods State Park, was torn up and water channels cut in it.

A fire still burned today in a bulk oil and gasoline plant on the harbor, which is enclosed by a mile- long breakwater that is open at one end. Tanks of the Texas and the Union Oil Companies exploded as the water swept up. Fire fighters were unable to reach the scene until after the fire was beyond control.

The fire also destroyed adjoining buildings, including an automobile agency and a service station.

The clean-up work was enormous. Great logs and piles of lumber littered the waterfront beaches. The water was pushed off Route 101 by bulldozers to open the main artery to the community.

One pile of six-inch lumber, weighing 15,000 pounds, was carried nearly a mile from a storage place. Some boats and debris were carried a mile or more into the city.

Concrete Walls Broken

The tidal waves punched big holes in the side of concrete block buildings. Cars and trucks were tossed atop the debris.

Estimates of the damage ranged from $10 million to about $25 million. Stores of all kinds were flooded as the water rose to eight to nine feet in some places.

The Del Norte County sanitation officer, Joseph Creisler, quarantined the entire flooded area. Gas mains were shut off. The water supply was reported to be safe.

Food supplies were said to be adequate but grocery stores and other markets outside the hard-hit area were calling for additional supplies.

State military reserve soldiers patrolled the central business district to prevent looting.

Gov. Edmund G. Brown flew here to inspect the damage and later issued a proclamation declaring the city a disaster area.

The Governor had been in Eureka, about 80 miles away, on a tour ofthe redwood country that started in Crescent City yesterday. He canceled the rest of the tour to visit here and offer help.

The proclamation cleared the way for a Presidential declaration that the city is a disaster area. This would enable the townspeople to get help from the Office of Emergency Planning and loans for rebuilding from the Small Business Administration.

Some Narrowly Escape

Mayor William Peepe estimated that three-quarters of the business district had been wrecked. Some persons, he said, narrowly escaped the surge of water.

These included some owners of businesses who went into the area to clean up their stores after the first two waves rolled through the section. The lesser waves had barely put water on Front Street, along the ocean.

The first wave rolled in about midnight. This was followed by another at 1 A.M. The punishing wave was the third, at 1:40 A.M. A fourth wave came about 2:30 A.M. but it was mild.

Buildings were knocked off their foundations. Some houses nearest the waterfront were pushed into the streets. A two-story frame former lodge hall, now used as a library, was dislodged and pushed 30 feet.

Most of the buildings in this lumber town are of wooden construction. The town has a population of about 3,000 persons and 80 per cent of its economy is based on lumber, including redwood and Douglas fir.

The town's $440,000 area redevelopment project, along the waterfront, on which a start was recently made, was torn up.

Damage Along Coast

SAN FRANCISCO, March 28 (UPI)—Walter Marion, University of California seismographic engineer, estimated the speed of the tidal wave at 500 miles an hour and possibly faster.

All along the coast fishing boats and yachts were torn from their moorings.

In San Francisco Bay, a wall of water surged through the Golden Gate, setting adrift a beached ferry boat.

At Seaside, Ore., tidal waters pushed back the Necanicum River, flooding a trailer park.

Power and telephone service were cut off at Cannon Beach and the wave toppled several houses off their foundations.

The same type of damage plagued Gold Coast, Ore., where water ripped out docks and smashed small boats on the Rogue River.

A wall of water surged into the Siuslaw River at Florence, Ore., raising it eight feet in eight seconds.

Couple Left Childless

TACOMA, Wash., March 28 (AP) — Mr. and Mrs. Monte G. McKenzie lost the oldest of their five children in a fire eight months ago.

Last night the tidal waves left them childless.

The McKenzies were sleeping on the beach at a state park near Depoe Bay, Ore., when the giant waves hit.

In a telephone call to his pastor here, Mr. McKenzie said the first wave swept over the children and they began screaming. Then a second wave hit.

"There was only a foot of air at the top of the lean-to we were in and we had to struggle to get to it," Mr. McKenzie said. "Logs were thrown at us like match sticks."

When the wave receded the McKenzies found their four children had been swept to sea. The body of Ricky, 6, was recovered. Still missing were Louie, 8, Bobby, 7, and Tammy, 3.

Their oldest, Susan, 9, died of burns last August when her clothing caught fire as she was trying to start a bonfire.

Beaches Ordered Cleared

LOS ANGELES, March 28 (AP)—Tidal surges 10 feet high generated by the Alaska earthquake hit Santa Catalina Island, 20 miles off the coast, at 1:35 A.M. today.

The Coast Guard at nearby Long Beach reported there was some damage on the island. Its extent had not been determined, the Coast Guard said.

Airman Swept Into Sea

KLAMATH, Calif., March 28 (AP)—A tidal wave swept Sgt. Donald McClure, 33, of the Air Force, out to sea while he was fishing for eel at midnight at the mouth of the Klamath River.

Vancouver Island Damaged

PORT ALBERNI, B. C., March 28 (Canadian Press)—A relentless lash of waves from the Alaska earthquake funneled up an inlet to the heart of Vancouver Island today, sparing life but dealing heavy damage.

The twin communities of Port Alberni and Alberni, with a total population of 25,000, were dealt a series of blows.

The water, carrying logs into the streets like toothpicks, covered a wide area of Port Alberni to a depth of five feet.

Waves rolled down from the Aleutian earthquake zone, washing up inlets open to the Pacific on the west coast of Vancouver Island.

They grew in force as they sped through the ever-narrowing Alberni canal, which twists 40 miles inland to this city. The logging industry complex of four plants was hard hit. It was shut down immediately.

300,000 Routed in Hawaii

HONOLULU, March 28 (UPI) — Tidal waves set off by the Alaskan earthquake, forced the evacuation of 300,000 Hawaii residents but did practically no damage to the islands.

The first of a series of tidal waves reached the outer islands at 10:42 P.M., Hawaiian standard time, last night and 10 waves swept gently across the islands in the next two hours. The maximum height reported for any of them was eight feet.

4-Hour Alert in Japan

TOKYO, March 28 (AP)—Japan lifted her tidal wave alert at 11 P.M. today after four hours of waiting for a possible onslaught of the sea touched off by the violent earthquake in Alaska.

The Central Meteorological Agency said that mild tidal symptoms, marked by maximum tide rises of up to 20 inches, had been registered along the Pacific coasts of Hokkaido and northern Honshu.

Evacuations in Soviet

MOSCOW, March 28 (UPI)—Soviet citizens were evacuated today on the Kamchatka coast and in the North Kurile Islands when the areas were threatened by the tidal waves. They later returned to their homes, the Novosti press agency said.

'Weird' Waves in Texas

HOUSTON, March 28 (AP)—A shock wave, triggered by an earth movement, caused freakish high tides along the Texas coast last night but damage was apparently minor and no injuries were reported.

Witnesses described it as "weird, spooky, wild."

The earth movement, which started about 10 P.M., Central Standard Time, and could have been connected with the Alaskan earthquake "in a coincidental sort of way," the New Orleans Weather Bureau said. The movement churned waves up to six feet in some areas.

"All the News That's Fit to Print"

The New York Times.

LATE CITY EDITION
U.S. Weather Bureau Report (Page 74) forecast:
Partly cloudy today; rain developing tonight. Rain tomorrow.
Temp. range: 46—36; yesterday: 61—48.

VOL. CXIV..No. 39,098.
© 1965 by The New York Times Company. Times Square, New York, N. Y. 10036
NEW YORK, TUESDAY, FEBRUARY 9, 1965.
TEN CENTS

84 LOST AS DC-7 CRASHES IN SEA OFF JONES BEACH MINUTES AFTER TAKE-OFF

DEBRIS IS FOUND

Ships Search Area—Eastern Plane Was on Way South

By HOMER BIGART

An Eastern Air Lines plane with 84 persons aboard plunged into the Atlantic Ocean off Jones Beach early last night. There were no signs of survivors.

The plane, a DC-7B that had taken off from Kennedy Airport, apparently never pulled out of a steep bank to the south, according to the Federal Aviation Agency. It crashed 8 miles south of Jones Inlet.

The plane exploded as it hit the sea, not in mid-air as some early reports indicated, according to the Federal agency.

A massive search by surface craft and helicopters yielded not even one piece of debris for more than two hours. Then Coast Guard cutters began finding small pieces—headrests, bits of metal, a torn maroon blazer—and finally bodies.

"In my judgment there will be no survivors," an F.A.A. spokesman said.

79 Passengers Aboard

The plane, Eastern's Flight 663, was carrying 79 passengers and five crew members when it went down about 6:30, a few minutes after taking off. It was bound for Richmond, Charlotte, N. C.; Greenville, S. C., and Atlanta in a flight that had originated in Boston.

One minute the plane was a normal blip on the airport's radar screens. Then it vanished as completely and suddenly as a plunging star.

The weather was clear, the visibility good. No word of any trouble aboard the plane preceded the crash.

Despite the swift arrival of rescue craft and the relative calmness of the sea, nothing was found until shortly before 9 P.M., when an oil slick was spotted five miles south of Long Beach, L. I. Then Coast Guard cutters began finding pieces of debris.

Water 75 Feet Deep

The depth of the sea in the crash area was reported to be 75 feet.

The plane took off at 6:20 from Kennedy's Runway 31 Left. It made the normal take-off and noise-abatement maneuvers, and radio contact with the control tower was maintained until 6:25.

At about that time the plane was "handed over" to the New York Air Traffic Center at MacArthur Field, near Ronkonkoma, L. I. However, the center never received the hand-over, an official source said.

After his last contact with the plane, the radarman at Kennedy took another look at his screen. The plane was not there.

At just about that time the New York Air Traffic Center began asking about Eastern's Flight 663, and the search was started.

When the DC-7B left the runway, the pilot, Capt. Frederick R. Carson, probably made a left turn from the runway and headed for the ocean. It was

Continued on Page 28, Column 1

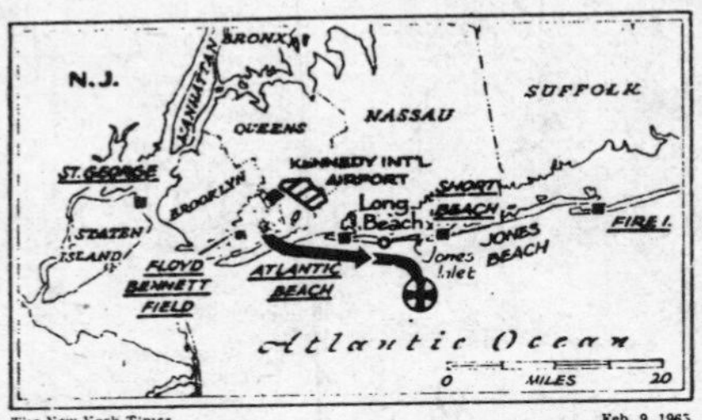

The New York Times Feb. 9, 1965

CRASH SCENE: Heavy line denotes course believed taken by plane before it fell at area marked by cross. Underlined are Coast Guard stations joining in search for survivors.

2 Witnesses See Flash

By MARTIN GANSBERG

The first word that Eastern Air Lines Flight 663 was down in the Atlantic Ocean came from Mrs. Thelma Gutman of 47 Allevard Street, Lido Beach, L. I., who called the Coast Guard about 6:30 P.M. to say that she had seen "a ball of fire fall into the sea."

Mrs. Gutman and her husband, Alfred, received no further word from the Coast Guard, but they said they realized what they had reported after they heard about the crash on the radio.

About the same time, Seaman Dale Bishop, 19 years old, on duty atop the 75-foot observation tower at the nearby Short Beach station, made a similar report.

"I heard a thud, or something that sounded like a small firecracker," Seaman Bishop said. "I looked in a south-by-southwest direction and saw this red ball of fire about 10 feet high above the water."

He notified the officer on duty, who alerted five stations in the New York area. Two minutes later—at 6:34—Lieut. Bobby Wilkes took off

Continued on Page 29, Column 1

REVOLT DIES OUT IN LEGISLATURE

Zaretzki and Travia Reward Backers, but Some Key Posts Go to Opponents

By R. W. APPLE Jr.
Special to The New York Times

ALBANY, Feb. 8—Senator Joseph Zaretzki of Manhattan and Assemblyman Anthony J. Travia of Brooklyn took the reins of the Legislature firmly into their hands tonight. Democratic opposition to the two new leaders evaporated.

Mr. Zaretzki was named Temporary President of the Senate last Friday and Mr. Travia was elected Speaker of the Assembly the next day. But because they won with the help of Republican votes, some Democratic legislators had threatened to challenge their authority.

No such challenge developed tonight as the two houses went through brief organizational sessions that were as stylized as an 18th-century minuet.

Mr. Zaretzki and Mr. Travia allotted most of the key patronage positions to men who had supported them during the furious 30-day struggle over legislative leadership, but they gave key committee chairmanships to some of their opponents.

In both the Assembly and the Senate, last year's rules were readopted without a dissenting vote.

Assemblyman Moses Weinstein of Queens, who delivered his borough's 12 votes to Mr. Travia on each of the 28 leadership ballots, was named majority leader in the lower house. He is the chairman of the Democratic organization in Queens.

Although the appointment was

Continued on Page 30, Column 6

U.S. SEEKS CURBS ON FOUNDATIONS

Treasury Would Ban Private Gain by Funds and Limit Influence in Business

By EILEEN SHANAHAN
Special to The New York Times

WASHINGTON, Feb. 8—Broad new restrictions on the activities of tax-exempt charitable foundations were proposed today by the Treasury Department.

The restrictions would primarily seek to prevent the use of foundation funds for private gain and to reduce the broad economic power that some foundations now exercise through their ownership and control of private commercial businesses.

The proposals, the outgrowth of more than a year of study by the Treasury Department, would all require legislation.

Initial Congressional comment came from two long-time critics of foundations who asserted that the Treasury's recommendations did not go far enough.

The critics, both Democrats, were Representative Wright Patman of Texas, chairman of the House Banking Committee, and Senator Albert Gore of Tennessee. It seemed certain, however, that some other members of Congress would feel that the proposals went too far.

Large Foundations Absolved

The Treasury said its lengthy study had showed that "the preponderant number of private foundations perform their functions without tax abuse."

It said, however, that the study "has also produced evidence of serious faults among a minority of such organizations."

Although the Treasury did not name the foundations that it said had abused their tax-exempt status, officials indicated that all or nearly all of the large and widely known foundations had been absolved. The large foundations, for example, generally do not make loans to their officers or contributors, a practice the Treasury wants to forbid.

Some of the most famous foundations, however, including the Ford Foundation, by far the largest of all, would be affected by other Treasury recommendations designed to reduce a foundation's control and influence over commercial enterprises.

The Treasury made two basic recommendations designed to reduce the economic power of foundations and the families of those who establish them. It proposed that no foundation be

Continued on Page 18, Column 3

PRESIDENT ASKS FEDERAL POWER TO END POLLUTION

Outlines Plan to Bar Fouling of Air and Water at Source—Omits Hudson Proposal

Excerpts from President's message are on Page 27.

By WILLIAM M. BLAIR
Special to The New York Times

WASHINGTON, Feb. 8—President Johnson took several steps today toward new Federal enforcement powers to clean up the nation's water supplies, air and countryside.

His Special Message to Congress on Natural Beauty proposed permitting the Federal Government to set standards to halt water pollution at its source and to prevent air pollution.

Administration officials viewed these steps as the beginning of a new enforcement program that would first summon a national effort to combat "ugly America" and then would back it up with broadened Federal power at a later stage if necessary.

For Preserving Hudson

The President's message ranged over a wide variety of beautification projects for cities and rural areas, including more recreation areas and parks and the cleaning up of junkyards along highways.

He singled out the Hudson River for mention as an urban river that could best be preserved by the same sort of cooperative state and local program planned for the Potomac River. Thus, Mr. Johnson appeared to have doomed for the immediate future proposals now before Congress to create a national scenic riverway along the lower Hudson, a plan also opposed by Governor Rockefeller of New York as a Federal intrusion.

The Administration does not, however, favor construction of the $162 million Hudson River power plant near Cornwall sought by the Consolidated Edison Company.

'New Conservation' Emphasized

Other suggestions in the President's message included more Federal grants to states and local communities, mustering university aid on planning, enlarged research in all areas of the cleanup program and possible tax incentives to industry to encourage conservation.

Mr. Johnson emphasized "a new conservation," which he described as concerned "not with nature alone, but with the total relationship between man and the world around him."

"Its object is not just man's welfare but the dignity of man's spirit," he declared.

He said that a White House conference on natural beauty would be held in mid-May under the chairmanship of Laurance S. Rockefeller, chairman of the New York State Council of Parks. Mr. Rockefeller, a businessman and well-known conservationist, headed the Federal Outdoor Recreation Resources Review Commission, which pinpointed the need for recreation

Continued on Page 27, Column 1

SOUTH VIETNAM PLANES HIT NORTH; U.S. THEN CALLS A HALT TO STRIKES; SOVIET PLEDGES RED DEFENSE AID

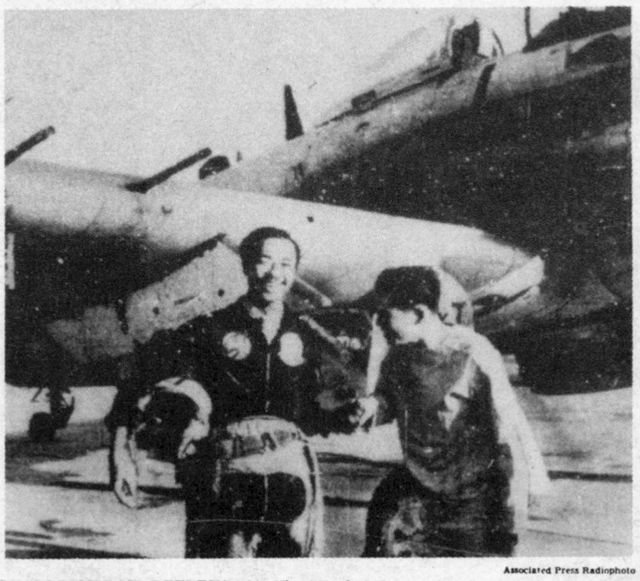

Associated Press Radiophoto

LEADER OF RAID RETURNS: Air Vice Marshal Nguyen Cao Ky, standing before his plane after leading raid against North Vietnam. With him at Danang is another pilot, in hospital garments, who had parachuted from a damaged plane over South Vietnam.

U.S. SENDS ESCORT

Jets Provide Cover as Communications Center Is Bombed

By SEYMOUR TOPPING
Special to The New York Times

SAIGON, South Vietnam, Feb. 8—South Vietnamese air force planes, accompanied by United States jet fighters, bombed and strafed a military communications center today in the Vinhlinh area of Communist North Vietnam in a follow-up of yesterday's attack across the border by American aircraft.

Lieut. Gen. Nguyen Khanh, commander in chief of the armed forces, said at a news conference that 24 South Vietnamese planes had struck at Vinhlinh at 3:30 P.M. He said 70 per cent of the targets had been destroyed, according to preliminary estimates.

[Informed sources in Washington said a number of United States Air Force F-100 Supersaber jet fighters escorted the Vietnamese planes, providing protective cover and suppressing enemy ground fire, United Press International reported. Reconnaissance also was said to have been carried out by Air Force RF-101 Voodoo jets.]

Marshal Leads Attack

General Khanh reported that the planes had encountered heavy antiaircraft fire. The strike was led by Air Vice Marshal Nguyen Cao Ky, 31-year-old commander of the air force, who returned to the base at Danang with a bullet-punctured cockpit.

One plane, hit by ground fire, developed engine trouble as it headed for its home base. The pilot bailed out and was rescued.

The Hanoi radio, monitored here, asserted that antiaircraft guns shot down six United States planes. Yesterday, North Vietnam said four planes had been shot down and others damaged. Washington said only one plane was lost yesterday.

The Vinhlinh area is just north of the demilitarized zone, which includes the 17th Parallel. Under the 1954 Geneva agreement, the 17th Parallel divides North and South Vietnam. There are important highway and rail connections in the area, as well as North Vietnamese military installations.

Holds News Conference

General Khanh announced the air strike at a news conference in the officers' club of the joint chiefs of staff headquarters shortly after a communiqué was issued by the United States Embassy.

The communiqué said: "In furtherance of the action announced yesterday by the Acting Prime Minister [Nguyen Xuan Oanh] and the U. S. Ambassador [Maxwell D. Taylor] it was made known that military action was taken today by Vietnamese and United States aircraft against other military installations in North Vietnam."

Ambassador Taylor conferred with Mr. Oanh before the communiqué was issued.

The communiqué emphasized, as did that published yesterday, the joint nature of the operation. Bad weather prevented South Vietnamese planes from

Continued on Page 12, Column 1

JOHNSON UPHELD ON U.A.R. AID PLEA

House, in Reversal, Rejects G.O.P. Bid for Insistence on Ban—Vote Is 241-165

By FELIX BELAIR Jr.
Special to The New York Times

WASHINGTON, Feb. 8—House Democrats gave President Johnson an overwhelming vote of confidence today and a free hand to permit or prevent continued surplus-food shipments to the United Arab Republic in the national interest.

The party-line vote of 241 to 165 rejected a Republican move to instruct House negotiators to stand firm on an earlier ban on such shipments in conference with the Senate. The effect of the vote was to enable House managers to accept a milder Senate amendment, which would leave the matter for the President to decide.

Both legislative branches will have another opportunity to vote on the question when the conference negotiators report back to their respective bodies with their recommendations on Wednesday. But the margin of the President's victory today and the appeals for party loyalty on which it was based left no uncertainty about the final outcome.

In today's vote, 37 Democrats defected to the 128 Republicans

Continued on Page 10, Column 5

Moscow and Peking Warn They Will Not Fail Hanoi

By THEODORE SHABAD
Special to The New York Times

MOSCOW, Tuesday, Feb. 9—The Soviet Government warned early today that it would be "forced, together with its allies and friends, to take further measures" to aid North Vietnam's defense against United States air attacks. A Government statement said:

"No one should doubt that the Soviet Union will do this,

Texts of Soviet and Chinese statements, Page 12.

that the Soviet people will fulfill its international duty to the fraternal Socialist country."

[Communist China called the United States action an "undisguised war provocation" and said its people would "definitely not stand idly by." The North Vietnamese Government termed Sunday's air attack a "new and utterly grave act of war" but said nothing could save the United States "from failure in South Vietnam." Page 12.]

The Soviet statement, made public shortly after midnight by Tass, the official press agency, was the first formal Government reaction to two days of United States and South Vietnamese air raids against North Vietnam. The raids followed an attack by South Vietnamese guerrillas against a United States base early Sunday.

In a speech yesterday at a Soviet Embassy reception in Hanoi, the North Vietnamese capital, Premier Aleksei N. Kosygin said that the situation created by the United States attacks was "fraught with serious complications."

The Soviet Government said in its statement that United States planes over North Vietnam had "bombed and strafed many houses and even a hospital."

"There is loss of human life," it added.

Referring to the American "military actions" against North Vietnam and to the build-up of "armed forces and weapons in South Vietnam," the Moscow statement said:

"In the face of the abovementioned actions of the United States, the Soviet Union will be forced, together with its allies and friends, to take further measures to safeguard the security and strengthen the defense capability of the Democratic Republic of Vietnam."

There was no indication what

Continued on Page 12, Column 5

U. S. STOPS RAIDS TO ASSESS EFFECT

Johnson Promises to Try to Keep Peace, but Won't Bar Future Strikes

By MAX FRANKEL
Special to The New York Times

WASHINGTON, Feb. 8—The United States called a halt to air strikes against North Vietnam today to assess the military and diplomatic reactions of several Communist nations, especially the Soviet Union.

President Johnson and his advisers refused, however, to rule out further retaliatory raids or to define the circumstances under which they would be resumed.

In a brief public comment Mr. Johnson expressed hope that no one would misjudge the character, strength and fortitude of the United States.

"We love peace," the President said. "We shall do all that we can in honor to preserve it—for ourselves and for all mankind. But we love liberty the more and we shall take up any challenge, we shall answer any threat, we shall pay any price to make certain that freedom shall not perish from this earth."

After reporting to the National Security Council, McGeorge Bundy, the President's special assistant for security affairs, voiced optimism on South Viet-

Continued on Page 13, Column 1

L.I. Bank Plans to Lend Fair $3.5 Million Needed to Open

Head of Franklin National Says He Will Do All He Can To Help Second Season

By ROBERT ALDEN

The World's Fair apparently has succeeded in raising the $3.5 million it needs to insure its opening for the 1965 season.

Arthur T. Roth, president of the Franklin National Bank of Mineola, said last night that "while we will have to look at the fair's financial statements, there is not the slightest doubt in my mind" that the loan on short term notes would be made. He said he expected that his and, possibly, other banks would provide the money.

"We certainly are interested in helping the fair continue for a second season and we'll do everything we can in that direction," Mr. Roth said.

The Franklin National has assets of $1.5 billion and the $3.5 million that the fair has said it needs to insure its opening on April 21 is well within the loan limits of the bank, as established by Franklin National's by-laws.

Mr. Roth said that Mr. Moses telephoned him yesterday morning and asked him if he were willing to get together

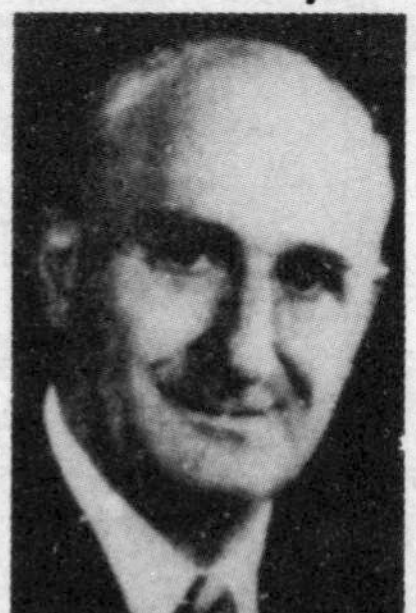

Arthur T. Roth

with other banks—"not any of those banks that walked out on us"—to lend the money that was needed.

By "those banks that walked out on us" Mr. Moses is believed to have referred to five of nine bankers on the fair's finance committee who resigned on Jan. 18 because they said they had not received adequate audited information on the fair's financial situation.

The five bankers who re-

Continued on Page 15, Column 4

Nonprofit Group Proposed Here To Keep Business and Spur Jobs

The Commerce and Industry Association of New York called yesterday for the creation of a private, nonprofit corporation to reverse the flow of business out of the city and provide new jobs.

H. C. Turner Jr., the president of the association, said the corporation would seek the support and advice of Federal, state, city and private agencies in creating programs that would improve the city's business climate.

He noted that the city had lost 76,000 manufacturing jobs in five years.

The Commerce and Industry Association, founded in 1897 as the Merchants Association of New York, has more than 4,000 member concerns, including large and small businesses and corporations with headquarters here.

The association also announced yesterday that it was inviting top business leaders and others interested in the city's business status to a meeting early next month "to develop programs aimed at creating more job opportunities and to carry out the first important steps toward improving the business climate in the city."

The association's board of directors received a report from a committee that suggested that the new corporation "set

Continued on Page 26, Column 1

British Will Ban Cigarette Ads On TV for Reasons of Health

By JAMES FERON
Special to The New York Times

LONDON, Feb. 8—The Government said today it would ban cigarette advertising on television "as soon as practicable" because of the danger of smoking to health.

The decision, announced in the House of Commons, came nearly three years after Britain's Royal College of Physicians reported that "cigarette smoking is a cause of lung cancer."

Last year, after a similar study, the United States Public Health Service said that the use of cigarettes contributed substantially to the American death rate that "appropriate remedial action" was needed.

Kenneth Robinson, the Minister of Health, told the House that deaths from lung cancer continued to increase in Britain despite an intensive Government health education program.

"The Government has decided that the time has come to end the advertising of cigarettes on television," he said. The Minister added that measures against "other forms of cigarette advertising" were being considered.

The ban, which is expected to take effect in about two months, will cause considerable disruption in the 17 stations of the

Continued on Page 2, Column 3

NEWS INDEX

OLD MOTHER HUBBARD'S CUPBOARD wouldn't have been bare if she had followed shopping and cooking suggestions on The New York Times women's page.—Advt.

KIND OF SHAKES YOU UP! Read: "The Shuddering Earth," February FORTUNE.—Adv.

INTRIGUE IN THE DEN. With Schaber & Righter's Tangle. It's just as much fun as their Scrabble, and Parcheesi games.—Adv.

84 Lost as DC-7 Crashes Into Atlantic Near Jones Beach

DEBRIS IS FOUND BY SEARCH SHIPS

But No Survivors Are Seen —Eastern Airliner Had Left Here for South

Continued From Page 1, Col. 1

estimated that the plane was about 13 miles from the airport when its blip disappeared from the radar screen.

The Coast Guard said that at 6:31 it received a phone call from a woman who said she had seen "a big explosion" about two miles off Lido Beach, which is east of Long Beach and west of Jones Inlet.

A minute later, the Coast Guard said, Floyd Bennett Field was alerted by the tower at Kennedy Airport that Flight 663 was believed to have gone down.

Then at 6:33 came the announcement from the Federal Aviation Agency that the plane had crashed into the Atlantic.

There were conflicting reports on an explosion and fire aboard the plane.

Federal Aviation Agency officials questioned a Pan American World Airways pilot whose jet was near the area at the time of the crash.

Capt. Stephen Marshall said he was at 3,500 feet inbound from San Juan, P. R., flying Pan American Flight 212.

Report Clarified

Captain Marshall was first reported to have said that the Eastern plane had exploded, and his initial radio message pointed to the possibility of sabotage.

He later denied this first report.

"I did not see the plane crash," he told newsmen. "I saw it before it went down."

He refused to say anything more, explaining that he was still being questioned by F.A.A. officials and that they would release his report.

A Coast Guard lookout on Jones Beach, Seaman Dale Bishop of Easton, Pa., provided a report that an explosion had occurred on the plane. He said the plane was at an altitude of about 3,500 feet when it exploded and plunged flaming into the sea.

This report stirred suspicions of sabotage. But further investigation indicated that the plane exploded on impact with the sea after failing to pull out of a steep bank.

Events Reconstructed

Late last night, an F.A.A. spokesman gave this reconstruction of the events surrounding the crash:

"Eastern Flight 663 departed Runway 31L at 6:20 P.M., Eastern standard time.

"At 6:25:05 E.S.T. the pilot reported he was at 2,700 feet.

"At 6:25:40 E.S.T. he reported he was turning to the left for a heading of 170 degrees. That was his last transmission.

"At 6:27 E.S.T. an Air Canada Viscount, Flight 627, which left right behind the Eastern flight, reported spotting an explosion in the ocean.

"Around the same time Pan American Airways Clipper Flight 212 reported sighting an aircraft in an exceptionally steep turn and then an explosion on the ocean.

"At 9:25 P.M. the Coast Guard reported finding debris 14 to 17 miles southeast of Kennedy Airport and 7½ miles due south of Jones Inlet. The debris consisted of seat cushions, Eastern Air Lines brochures, a headset and some honeycomb metal."

The Federal Aviation Agency

Surface craft and helicopters search site of Eastern Air Lines DC-7B crash site off Long Island.

The New York Times

2 Witnesses See Ball of Fire, Alerting Coast Guard

Continued From Page 1, Col. 3

in a Coast Guard helicopter from Floyd Bennett Field, Brooklyn. In a matter of minutes he and five other Coast Guard pilots, in helicopters and seaplanes, were over the crash scene.

Comdr. Fred Merritt, chief of operations at Floyd Bennett, had all 135 men and 25 officers ready to assist the operation. By 6:45 P.M. he received the first report from his pilots.

Meanwhile, Louis Ferrari of 120 Cedarhurst Avenue, Oceanside, L. I., heard the explosion as he was resting in his home. He rushed out to the beach and saw four helicopters, like a flock of birds, following one after another. He said they dropped flares to illuminate the sea, but it was too hazy for him to make out much.

While the copters hovered overhead, more than 15 surface craft sped to the scene. There was some cloudiness, but the temperature was in the 50's and the sea was relatively calm.

Coast Guard officials held little hope at 10 o'clock that anyone could have survived in the sea. An officer said that the survival period for anyone in the water at the time of the crash would have been a maximum of an hour.

"With this cold wind blowing up now," he said, "the survival time would have been cut down considerably."

During the early hours of the search, the men in the air or at sea were pessimistic as they reported back to their bases. Lieut. Comdr. Leo Donohue, who returned to Floyd Bennett at 9 o'clock after an hour and a half in the air, said:

"It looks bad. We may have to wait for morning before any wreckage turns up."

About half an hour later, however, a 40-foot picketboat reported by radio that it was recovering parts of the airliner. It said it had found a seat intact and a three-foot headset identified as belonging to Eastern Air Lines. Other ships began reporting wreckage, too.

Reports of bodies having been recovered began funneling to Coast Guard stations soon after 11 P.M. A fishing boat picked up the body of an unidentified woman and transferred it to a Coast Guard cutter.

Another vessel said that it had found the body of a child about eight miles south of Jones Beach.

The Jess Lu IV, a 55-boat fishing boat that operates out of Freeport, returned to South Beach with debris it had picked up at sea. The captain, Jay Porter, said that his crew had recovered part of the plane's cabin.

"When we got the cabin, the body of one of the pilots was in it," he said. "But it flicked into the water while we were lifting the cabin aboard."

The sea in the area where the plane was first seen to have gone down was lighted by a host of ships and planes, so that it was not too difficult to make out any items picked up.

Ships played lights on the water as helicopters and seaplanes continued to drop flares. Each ship reported some discovery — smashed foam-rubber seats, plastic bags or other items that might have been aboard a plane in flight.

Radio Reports Received

A little after 11 P. M. a fishing boat, Miss Peconic II, captained by Buddy Dorman and operating out of Freeport, L. I., returned to the Short Beach station. The crew had debris that had been salvaged from the sea. It included a woman's mohair coat, a brown handbag, a soft pillow, a foam rubber cushion and a white pillow clearly labeled "Property of Eastern Air Lines."

On shore meanwhile hundreds of curious stood along the edge of the beaches and watched out over the sea. Motorists, hearing of the crash on their radios, created a traffic jam on the Jones Beach Parkway.

The military police barred all but authorized personnel from the Short Beach Coast Guard base. High-level officers and police officials from nearby communities listened to radio reports at the base.

At Kennedy International Airport some relatives and friends had returned to the Eastern Air Lines terminal after hearing of the crash. They were taken to special quarters, where public relations officers for the airline tried to keep them informed. Three nurses were on hand to care for them.

Two priests, faculty members at Archbishop Molloy High School in Queens, arrived at the airport to console relatives of victims. They said they had heard the news over the radio.

By 9:50, with about 10 persons still waiting at the terminal, Eastern officials announced that there would be no further word and suggested that those waiting return to their homes. The officials said they were being deluged for information by telephone.

Passengers on another Eastern flight—No. 806 from Tampa, Fla.—arrived as the confusion of the crash took hold in the terminal. Two of them, Robert Vautrain, 17, and his sister, Sandra, 13, of South Hadley, Mass., described the search at sea.

They said they were sitting at window seats and saw "flares from under our plane and boats in the ocean." Their mother, Mrs. Robert Vautrain, said it looked like a "Fourth of July spectacle" below them.

spokesman, Chris Walk, chief of the flight standards division, Eastern region, said weather conditions were good at the time of crash. There was a 12,000-foot ceiling and eight miles' forward visibility.

Nor was overloading a factor. Flight 663 had an estimated gross weight at take-off of 104,-700 pounds, well within its permissable limit of 126,000 pounds.

According to Mr. Walk, "the take-off was absolutely normal."

Was there sabotage? he was asked.

"We have no information to indicate any sabotage," he said.

Was there still any hope for survivors?

"I do not believe there were any survivors," he said, and a moment later, added, "In my judgment there will not be any survivors."

He also said that "preliminary information we have now does not indicate any explosion prior to impact."

Later Captain Marshall told newsmen that he first noticed the Eastern plane passing to the right of the nose of his Pan American jet.

"The aircraft started a right turn which became progressively steeper as it passed on our right," he said. "About 30 seconds later we saw a bright glow from behind and below us."

Captain Marshall said he put his jet into a left turn to prepare for a landing at Kennedy when he noticed flames on the water.

Used Longest Runway

The plane left from Kennedy's Runway 31, which parallels Jamaica Bay and runs east and west on the south edge of the airport. It is the world's longest runway—11,600 feet.

"All the News That's Fit to Print"

The New York Times.

LATE CITY EDITION
U. S. Weather Bureau Report (Page 58) forecasts: Partly cloudy today; cooler tonight. Fair tomorrow.
Temp. Range: 85—72; yesterday: 83—72.
Temp.-Hum. Index: upper 70's; yesterday: 79.

VOL. CXIV . No. 39,280. © 1965 by The New York Times Company. Times Square, New York, N. Y. 10036 NEW YORK, TUESDAY, AUGUST 10, 1965. TEN CENTS

PRESIDENT SIGNS $280 MILLION BILL FOR HEALTH STUDY

Will Name Panel to Define Goals—'Staggering Era' Foreseen for Medicine

DR. TERRY LEAVING POST

Surgeon General to Join University of Pennsylvania —Successor Is Sought

By NAN ROBERTSON
Special to The New York Times

WASHINGTON, Aug. 9 — President Johnson signed today a $280 million health research bill and announced that he would soon form a White House study group to define United States goals in health, education and "happiness."

He indicated that Marion B. Folsom, Secretary of Health, Education and Welfare under President Eisenhower, would be on the panel, which will be under Presidential direction. Mr. Johnson said that the group, made up of leaders in Government and private life, would be chosen within a few days.

In a surprise move, the President also announced the resignation of Dr. Luther L. Terry as Surgeon General of the Public Health Service. He told his audience of 1,000 persons at the National Institutes of Health that Dr. Terry would leave Sept. 30 to become vice president of the University of Pennsylvania.

Looks for Successor

Mr. Johnson pledged that he would look for "the most adventurous and most imaginative doctor in the country" to take Dr. Terry's place.

"I don't know where he is, but we're going to start looking for him," he declared.

Dr. Terry, who is 53 years old, is a native of Alabama. He took his medical degree from Tulane University. He has been Surgeon General since Jan. 15, 1961, after serving as assistant director of the National Institutes of Health.

Dr. David E. Price, the assistant Surgeon General, has also resigned. He plans to leave about Sept. 9 for New Delhi, where he will be on the staff of the Ford Foundation working on family planning.

The President was in an evangelistic mood as he ticked off the recent advances against such killers as polio and asserted that "a staggering era for medicine has begun."

"Our nation today leads a

Continued on Page 12, Column 4

Fire Traps 48 in a Titan Silo; 19 Killed, Rest Feared Dead

2 Workmen Escape in Arkansas—Crew Was Altering Missile Site

By ROY REED
Special to The New York Times

SEARCY, Ark., Aug. 9 — Fire trapped 48 civilian workmen in a Titan II missile silo 10 miles northwest of here this afternoon. Nineteen of the men were found dead tonight, and little hope was held for the 29 others.

Two men working near the top of the cylinder holding the intercontinental missile escaped from the underground complex with minor injuries.

The silo is more than 150 feet deep, and workers were engaged in a modification project all up and down it beside the 103-foot-tall missile.

An Air Force spokesman said the missile's atomic warhead had been removed earlier and there was no chance of a nuclear explosion.

The missile was still filled with fuel, and that added to the hazard of the rescue operation. The rescue squad, more than 100 Air Force personnel, also was slowed by dense smoke and heat and by cramped quarters.

The Air Force spokesman said the cause of the fire was not known. It apparently broke out suddenly on Level 2 of the eight-level silo, about 40 feet beneath the mouth of the hole.

The dead men were not immediately identified. The Air Force said none of the workmen would be identified until all were accounted for.

The two men who escaped were Hubert A. Saunders, 59

Continued on Page 10, Column 3

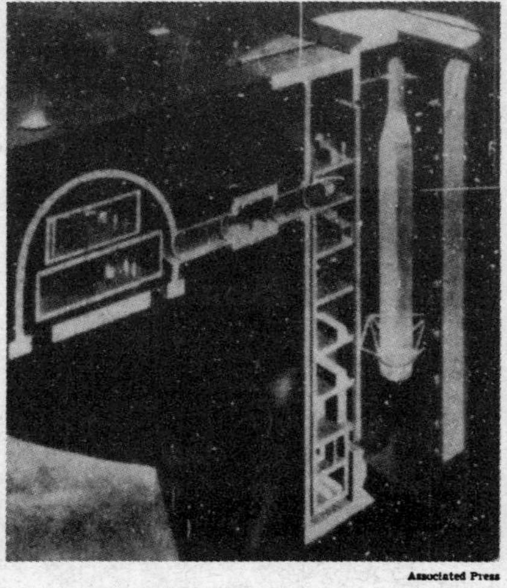

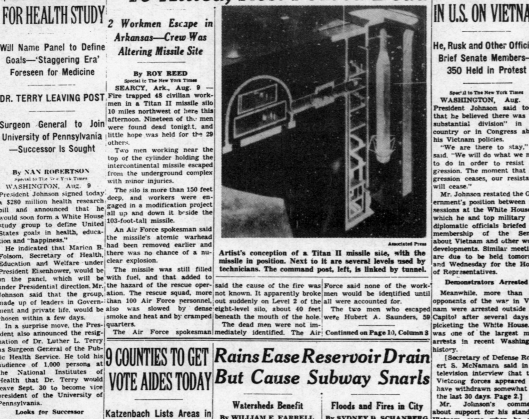

Associated Press

Artist's conception of a Titan II missile site, with the missile in position. Next to it are several levels used by technicians. The command post, left, is linked by tunnel.

9 COUNTIES TO GET VOTE AIDES TODAY

Katzenbach Lists Areas in South Considered as the Most Discriminatory

By JOHN HERBERS
Special to The New York Times

WASHINGTON, Aug. 9—Attorney General Nicholas deB. Katzenbach today designated nine counties in Alabama, Mississippi and Louisiana to which Federal examiners will be sent tomorrow to begin registering eligible Negroes under the Voting Rights Act of 1965.

These are considered to be the worst counties in the South in terms of discrimination against Negro voters. Other counties that had been tentatively designated for examiners were taken off the list because of recent registration of Negroes or promises by local or state officials to do so.

Counties Designated

The nine counties designated are:

Alabama — Dallas, Hale, Lowndes and Marengo, all in the Black Belt, where the Rev. Dr. Martin Luther King Jr. led demonstrations last winter and spring.

Louisiana — East Carroll, East Feliciana and Plaquemines Parishes.

Mississippi — Leflore and Madison.

Immediately after designating these for examiners, John W. Macy Jr., chairman of the Civil Service Commission, dispatched two examiners to each county. They are expected to arrive and open offices tomorrow morning.

Under the act, which was signed Friday by President Johnson, the Attorney General is instructed to consider in calling for examiners whether the ratio of nonwhite to white persons registered to vote suggests violation of the 15th Amendment and whether efforts are being

Continued on Page 14, Column 5

Rains Ease Reservoir Drain But Cause Subway Snarls

Watersheds Benefit

By WILLIAM E. FARRELL

The city's gloomy water picture brightened a bit yesterday.

Even before the day's cloudbursts, the Department of Water Supply, Gas and Electricity announced that the city's upstate watersheds had received an average of an inch of rain over the weekend.

Last night the Weather Bureau said that one-quarter of an inch to an inch of rain fell in the watershed area yesterday. "We can't indicate at this time what the runoff into the reservoirs will be," a bureau official said.

In addition, the bureau reported that numerous places in the state had received heavy rains. More than two inches fell in Newburgh in six hours, and nearby Poughkeepsie reported nine-tenths of an inch.

Consumption Reduced

Because of the weekend rain the level of the reservoirs dropped only 500 million gallons during the 24 hours ending at 8 A.M. yesterday. The daily average drop has been just under a billion gallons.

The latest figures released by the department showed a total of 208 billion gallons in storage, or 43.7 per cent of capacity. Yesterday's water consumption was held to 899 million gallons. At the same time last year the reservoirs contained 341.1 billion gallons, or 71.6 per cent of capacity.

Commissioner Armand D'Angelo said the weekend rainfall in the Delaware River basin

Continued on Page 15, Column 3

Floods and Fires in City

By SYDNEY H. SCHANBERG

Sudden thundershowers pelted the city yesterday afternoon, bringing a temporary respite from the heat and the dry spell, but snarling subways and streets for thousands of persons on their way home from work.

The drenching rains, which lasted only a few hours, flooded subway tracks in Lower Manhattan, knocking out evening rush-hour service on the Broadway-Seventh Avenue line from Times Square to the Borough Hall station in Brooklyn.

Another massive snarl developed—this one on the East Side and involving street traffic—when a fire broke out in Consolidated Edison's underground electric lines at Madison Avenue and 48th Street.

Two Streets Closed

The blaze came at the height of the downpour, shortly after 3 P.M. It blew off four manhole covers. No one was injured, but the police were forced to close off the avenue from 47th to 49th Street.

A Con Edison spokesman said water flooding the lines might have been the cause.

Except for these major disruptions, it was like any other torrential shower in the city. Cellars in downtown Manhattan got flooded, parts of the East River Drive temporarily resembled a bayou and a section of a street in the Bronx caved in.

Mayor Wagner, waxing humorous, issued a brief state-

Continued on Page 15, Column 2

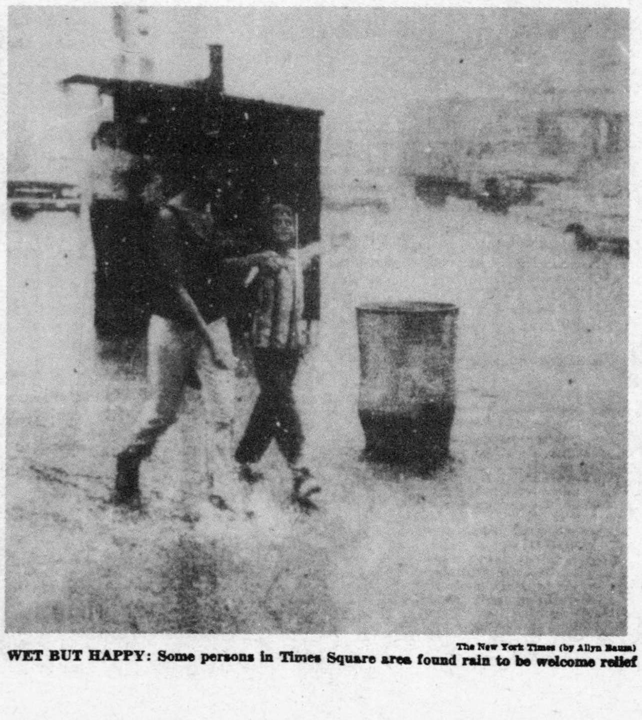

The New York Times (by Allyn Baum)

WET BUT HAPPY: Some persons in Times Square area found rain to be welcome relief

COPTERS TO LINK TETERBORO TO L.I.

Service From New Jersey to Kennedy Due Next Year

By EDWARD HUDSON
Special to The New York Times

TETERBORO, N. J., Aug. 9 —Plans to develop Teterboro Airport as a base for passenger helicopter service to Kennedy International Airport were announced here today.

Under the program announced for the light-plane field, air travelers from New Jersey and vicinity will be able to check their baggage at Teterboro Airport and board a helicopter for Kennedy, there to continue their journey. The service is expected to start next spring.

The plans call for Pan American World Airways to take over the operation of Teterboro Airport, 12 miles from Times Square, about Jan. 1 from the Port of New York Authority.

Pan American will continue to run Teterboro as a base for general aviation—business and private flying. It will also make it the base for its sales of Fan Jet Falcons, eight-passenger jets designed for corporate use.

It was disclosed last February that Pan American was negotiating with the Port Authority to take over Teterboro, which the latter contends has been losing money. But the date of the takeover, the terms and such details as the new helicopter service were made public for the first time at a news conference here today. The agreement is for a term of 30 years.

At the conference, Gov. Richard J. Hughes of New Jersey

Continued on Page 30, Column 1

Figure Art Studio, Camera Hobbyists Welcome. 66 W. 39. WI 7-4961. Advt.

Safety of Public Put First by Bar's Chief

By FRED P. GRAHAM
Special to The New York Times

MIAMI BEACH, Aug. 9—The president of the American Bar Association today placed the right of citizens to be free from criminal attack ahead of the constitutional rights of persons accused of crimes.

The statement by Lewis F. Powell of Richmond, Va., brought thunderous applause from the 3,000 lawyers at the initial session of the association's convention.

The delegates also applauded —an unusual informality at A.B.A. assemblies—when Mr. Powell criticized what he called the role of sit-in demonstrations in creating disrespect for law.

Mr. Powell also told the assembly that the association was planning to tighten its rules

Continued on Page 12, Column 3

PRESIDENT DENIES SUBSTANTIAL SPLIT IN U.S. ON VIETNAM

He, Rusk and Other Officials Brief Senate Members— 350 Held in Protest

Special to The New York Times

WASHINGTON, Aug. 9— President Johnson said today that he believed there was "no substantial division" in the country or in Congress about his Vietnam policies.

"We are there to stay," he said. "We will do what we need to do in order to resist aggression. The moment that aggression ceases, our resistance will cease."

Mr. Johnson restated the Government's position between two sessions at the White House in which he and top military and diplomatic officials briefed the membership of the Senate about Vietnam and other world developments. Similar meetings are due to be held tomorrow and Wednesday for the House of Representatives.

Demonstrators Arrested

Meanwhile, more than 350 opponents of the war in Vietnam were arrested outside the Capitol after several days of picketing the White House. It was one of the largest mass arrests in recent Washington history.

[Secretary of Defense Robert S. McNamara said in a television interview that the Vietcong forces appeared to have withdrawn somewhat in the last 30 days. Page 2.]

Mr. Johnson's comments about support for his stand in Vietnam came when he was asked if it was true that some members of Congress were "disagreeing privately" with his course of action.

He replied: "I find that members of my party, and the other party, and people throughout the country frequently disagree with me on a good many things. I don't think it's private, though."

Asserts He Has Mandate

The President added that he did not seek uniformity and "we don't ever reach unanimity in situations as difficult as Vietnam."

Mr. Johnson recalled that last August, Congress at his request overwhelmingly approved a resolution that he said "goes just as far as we know how to go" in vesting authority in the President to conduct the war in Vietnam.

"I have authority and I am exercising it," he said.

"I would warn any would-be hopeful enemy of the United States that they must not make the miscalculation that other people have done in the past, to believe this country is divided, and that the course of action that has been established by three Presidents is going to be affected by dissent here or there."

The President repeated that United States policies in Vietnam had been established through the administrations of three Presidents. He then said: "There is no substantial division

Continued on Page 2, Column 3

Figures in the Malaysian Crisis

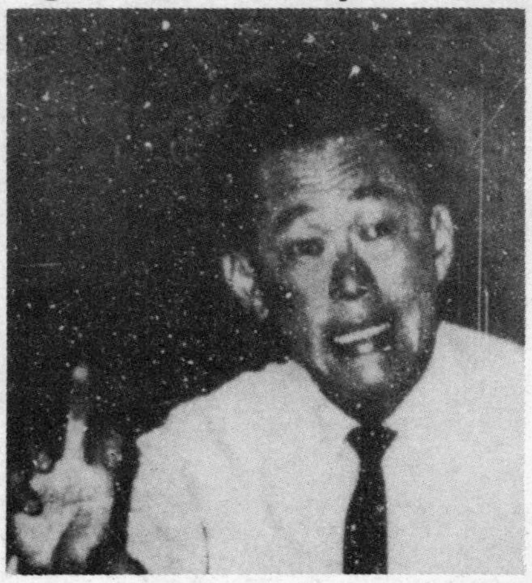

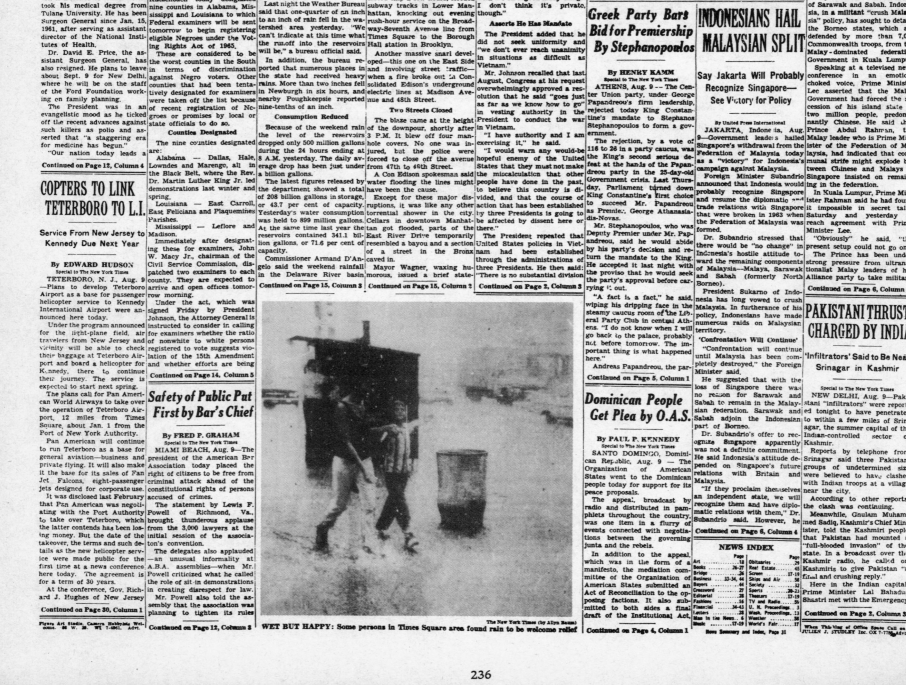

Associated Press Wirephoto

Prime Minister Lee Kuan Yew at Singapore press conference. He said he wanted trade ties with Communists.

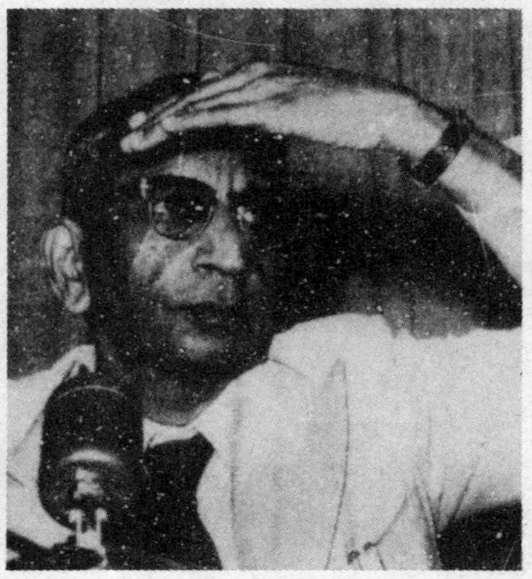

United Press International

Radhakrishna Ramani, Malaysian Ambassador to United Nations, at news conference yesterday at which he announced Singapore would apply for separate seat in U.N.

Greek Party Bars Bid for Premiership By Stephanopoulos

By HENRY KAMM
Special to The New York Times

ATHENS, Aug. 9 — The Center Union party, under George Papandreou's firm leadership, rejected today King Constantine's mandate to Stephanos Stephanopoulos to form a government.

The rejection, by a vote of 116 to 26 in a party caucus, was the King's second serious defeat at the hands of the Papandreou party in the 25-day-old Government crisis. Last Thursday, Parliament turned down King Constantine's first choice to succeed Mr. Papandreou as Premier, George Athanasiadis-Novas.

Mr. Stephanopoulos, who was Deputy Premier under Mr. Papandreou, said he would abide by his party's decision and return the mandate to the King. He accepted it last night with the proviso that he would seek the party's approval before carrying it out.

"A fact is a fact," he said, wiping his dripping face in the steamy caucus room of the Liberal Party Club in central Athens. "I do not know when I will go back to the palace, probably not before tomorrow. The important thing is what happened here."

Andreas Papandreou, the par-

Continued on Page 5, Column 1

Dominican People Get Plea by O.A.S.

By PAUL P. KENNEDY
Special to The New York Times

SANTO DOMINGO, Dominican Republic, Aug. 9 — The Organization of American States went to the Dominican people today for support for its peace proposals.

The appeal, broadcast by radio and distributed in pamphlets throughout the country, was one item in a flurry of events connected with negotiations between the governing junta and the rebels.

In addition to the appeal, which was in the form of a manifesto, the mediation committee of the Organization of American States submitted an Act of Reconciliation to the opposing factions. It also submitted to both sides a final draft of the Institutional Act,

Continued on Page 4, Column 1

INDONESIANS HAIL MALAYSIAN SPLIT

Say Jakarta Will Probably Recognize Singapore— See Victory for Policy

By United Press International

JAKARTA, Indonesia, Aug. 9—Government leaders hailed Singapore's withdrawal from the Federation of Malaysia today as a "victory" for Indonesia's campaign against Malaysia.

Foreign Minister Subandrio announced that Indonesia would probably recognize Singapore and resume the diplomatic and trade relations with Singapore that were broken in 1963 when the Federation of Malaysia was formed.

Dr. Subandrio stressed that there would be "no change" in Indonesia's hostile attitude toward the remaining components of Malaysia—Malaya, Sarawak and Sabah (formerly North Borneo).

President Sukarno of Indonesia has long vowed to crush Malaysia. In furtherance of his policy, Indonesians have made numerous raids on Malaysian territory.

'Confrontation Will Continue'

"Confrontation will continue until Malaysia has been completely destroyed," the Foreign Minister said.

He suggested that with the loss of Singapore there was no reason for Sarawak and Sabah to remain in the Malaysian federation. Sarawak and Sabah adjoin the Indonesian part of Borneo.

Dr. Subandrio's offer to recognize Singapore apparently was not a definite commitment. He said Indonesia's attitude depended on Singapore's future relations with Britain and Malaysia.

"If they proclaim themselves an independent state, we will recognize them and have diplomatic relations with them," Dr. Subandrio said. However, he

Continued on Page 6, Column 4

NEWS INDEX

News Summary and Index, Page 31

SINGAPORE PLANS TO SEEK ACCORDS WITH COMMUNISTS

But New Independent State Will Continue Cooperation With Britain in Defense

INDONESIAN TIE WEIGHED

Lee Says Malaysia Forced Secession—Rahman Cites Failure of Secret Talks

By SEYMOUR TOPPING
Special to The New York Times

SINGAPORE, Aug. 9—Prime Minister Lee Kuan Yew declared today that newly independent Singapore would cooperate with Britain in defense matters, but would seek new understandings with Communist countries and with Indonesia.

The Prime Minister said Singapore wanted trade ties with all Communist countries, would accept a trade mission from the Soviet Union and was ready to re-establish consular relations with Indonesia. He made these arrangements conditional on respect for Singapore's sovereignty.

The 43-year-old Prime Minister, who is of Chinese parentage, made his policy statement during a tearful explanation of the weekend events that resulted in the surprise withdrawal of Singapore from the Federation of Malaysia at 12:01 A.M. today and its establishment as an independent nation.

Relations Strained

The secession has put a severe strain on relations between the three remaining members of the federation, which was founded Sept. 16, 1963, under the aegis of the British Commonwealth.

The remaining members are Malaya and the Borneo states of Sarawak and Sabah. Indonesia, in a militant "crush Malaysia" policy, has sought to detach the Borneo states, which are defended by more than 7,000 Commonwealth troops, from the Malay-dominated federation Government in Kuala Lumpur.

Speaking at a televised news conference in an emotion-choked voice, Prime Minister Lee asserted that the Malay Government had forced the secession of his island state of two million people, predominantly Chinese. He said that Prince Abdul Rahman, the Malay leader who is Prime Minister of the Federation of Malaysia, had indicated that communal strife might explode between Chinese and Malays if Singapore insisted on remaining in the federation.

In Kuala Lumpur, Prime Minister Rahman said he had found it impossible in secret talks Saturday and yesterday to reach agreement with Prime Minister Lee.

"Obviously" he said, "the present setup could not go on."

The Prince has been under strong pressure from ultranationalist Malay leaders of his Alliance party to take militant

Continued on Page 6, Column 4

PAKISTANI THRUST CHARGED BY INDIA

'Infiltrators' Said to Be Near Srinagar in Kashmir

Special to The New York Times

NEW DELHI, Aug. 9—Pakistani "infiltrators" were reported tonight to have penetrated to within a few miles of Srinagar, the summer capital of the Indian-controlled sector of Kashmir.

Reports by telephone from Srinagar said three Pakistani groups of undetermined size were believed to have clashed with Indian troops at a village near the city.

According to other reports, the clash was continuing.

Meanwhile, Ghulam Muhammed Sadiq, Kashmir's Chief Minister, told the Kashmiri people that Pakistan had mounted a "full-blooded invasion" of the state. In a broadcast over the Kashmir radio, he called on Kashmiris to give Pakistan "a final and crushing reply."

Here in the Indian capital, Prime Minister Lal Bahadur Shastri met with the Emergency

Continued on Page 2, Column 3

When Thinking of Office Space Call on JULIEN J. STUDLEY Inc. OX 7-7780. Advt.

Rescue workers rest for a few minutes after removing the 46th body from the Titan II missile site.

United Press International

Continued From Page 1, Col. 4

years old, of Conway, Ark., and Gary Wayne Lay, 18, of Clinton, Ark. The Air Force said that most of the workmen were from Arkansas.

They are employes of the Peter Kiewit & Sons Co. of Omaha. The company has a contract to modify and improve the physical facilities of several of the 18 Titan missile sites north of Little Rock.

The fire began about 1:30 P.M. Rescue workers reported that by 8:30 tonight the heat was subsiding, indicating that the fire perhaps had gone out.

Until then, the rescuers had not been able to stay in the pit more than 30 minutes at a time because of the intense heat and dense smoke.

Newsmen who interviewed Mr. Saunders and Mr. Lay before they were put under sedation at a Searcy hospital quoted the two as saying they had been working on Level 1 and Level 2 of the silo. Suddenly they were engulfed in fire and smoke, and they began running for the opening.

The first four bodies were found on Level 2. The other workmen apparently were trapped below Level 2.

The silo is entered from an access portal several feet away from the silo. The top of the silo is covered by a 75-ton steel lid that is not used for normal entry. The access portal tunnels down, then across and into the side of the silo.

Military Men Unhurt

Mr. Saunders and Mr. Lay escaped through the access portal.

Four military personnel were in another section of the complex, the launching control center. This is about 100 feet away and connected to the silo by a cableway, or tunnel. The men in the control center reportedly were not hurt.

Rescue operations were being conducted through the access portal.

The workmen were said to include painters, electricians, plumbers and carpenters.

The maintenance work has been going on about six weeks.

An early report was that the fire had broken out in a diesel generator. Capt. Douglas Wood,

director of information at Little Rock Air Force Base, where the missile operation maintains headquarters, said that this had not been confirmed.

Air Force rescuers were flown from Little Rock Air Force Base in helicopters. They went into the silo wearing asbestos suits.

Air was pumped in through the access portal in an attempt to push out the heavy smoke and provide oxygen for any workmen who might have survived.

Gov. Orval E. Faubus sent state police troopers and state civil defense workers to direct traffic and aid in the rescue effort.

Escape Cut Off

SEARCY, Ark., Aug 9 (UPI) —The airmen on the control center of the missile site, seeing that they could not get into the silo and help the trapped workmen, sealed off the control center as they fled, it was disclosed tonight. They were afraid that if the rocket fuel got much hotter it would explode.

Sealing the hatch smothered the fire but also cut off all possible escape for the trapped men.

"There was no other decision to be made," Capt. Douglas Wood, information director of Little Rock Air Force Base, said.

'Heard Men Screaming'

SEARCY, Ark., Aug 9 (AP) —"I heard men screaming and crying," said 18-year-old Gary Wayne Lay. "I heard a man shouting 'Help me, help me.'"

Mr. Lay, a laborer on the Titan II missile silo near here, spoke from a bed in a hospital after escaping from the silo's launching tube after fire broke out in it.

"It was horrible," he said. "I couldn't see. I just felt my way out. If it hadn't been for God, I don't guess I'd ever gotten out."

Mr. Lay said he would not guess the fate of other men unaccounted for in the missile silo.

"When the fire flashed, I tried to go down a ladder, but it was jammed up with men,"

he said. "So I went up the top, through the fire"

He suffered burns on the hands, face, neck and legs, doctors said.

Another workman, Hubert A. Saunders, 59, also escaped by climbing up a ladder out of the silo.

He said most of the workmen went down the ladder to a hatch because the smoke was drifting upward.

"I heard a man crying 'Help me! Help me!' but I couldn't see him," Mr. Saunders said. "I was in the tube. The missile was in there I moved, I got out of there.

"The fire and smoke billowed into the tube, and I ran up that ladder," he said.

Johnson Orders Aid

WASHINGTON, Aug. 9 (AP) — President Johnson ordered that every effort be made to save the men trapped in a Titan missile silo near Searcy, Ark., the White House announced tonight.

The President directed also that an immediate investigation be made to determine the cause of the fire.

"All the News That's Fit to Print"

The New York Times.

LATE CITY EDITION
U.S. Weather Bureau Report (Page 82) forecasts: Fair, cold today; becoming cloudy tonight. Cloudy tomorrow.
Temp. Range: 35—20; yesterday: 38—26.

VOL. CXV..No. 39,448. NEW YORK, TUESDAY, JANUARY 25, 1966. TEN CENTS

© 1966 by The New York Times Company. Times Square, New York, N. Y. 10036

KEY SENATORS ASK THAT U.S. CONTINUE PAUSE IN BOMBING

Fulbright and Aiken Request Foreign Relations Unit Be Consulted on Resumption

RUSK BARS ASSURANCES

Decision to Renew Attacks on North Vietnam Near, Informed Sources Say

By TOM WICKER
Special to The New York Times

WASHINGTON, Jan. 24 — Strong opposition to a resumption of the bombing of North Vietnam was registered by leading Senators today as President Johnson continued to weigh in silence his next moves in the Southeast Asian war.

With the Lunar New Year lull ended and with fighting in South Vietnam resumed, United States bombers were absent from the skies over North Vietnam for the 31st day.

Secretary of State Dean Rusk and Secretary of Defense Robert S. McNamara indicated in separate Congressional hearings that the President had made no decision yet to end the bombing "pause."

This was confirmed privately by well-informed sources. But they expressed the belief that "the fuse is getting shorter." They said that a resumption of the bombing now appeared virtually inevitable, although no timetable could be stated.

A Sharply Differing Stand

Meanwhile, Senator J. W. Fulbright of Arkansas, chairman of the Foreign Relations Committee, and Senator Mike Mansfield of Montana, the majority leader, urged the Administration to continue the pause. Senator Fulbright asked that it be continued "for a longer time," and Senator Mansfield, "indefinitely."

Mr. Fulbright moved sharply away from the Administration position by advocating that the Vietcong be invited to participate in peace negotiations. He said he believed the absence of such an invitation might be the main obstacle to negotiations.

The Administration has taken the position that the Vietcong could have their views represented at any peace conference, but it has refused to accept

Continued on Page 2, Column 5

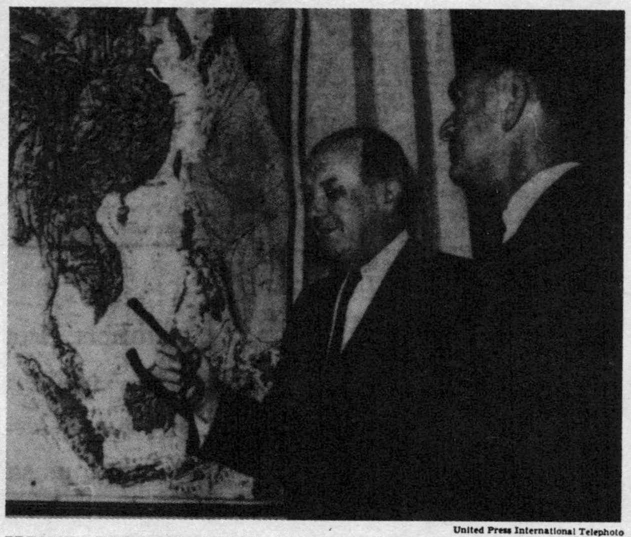

PRESENTS VIEWS ON VIETNAM: Secretary of State Rusk with Senator J. W. Fulbright, chairman of Foreign Relations Committee, before Mr. Rusk testified on fighting. (United Press International Telephoto)

47 AMERICANS DIE IN VIETNAM CRASH

Transport Aircraft Carried 43 G.I.'s and 4 Crewmen

By United Press International

SAIGON, Tuesday, Jan. 25—A United States Air Force C-123 transport plane carrying 47 American servicemen crashed and burned in the Central Highlands of South Vietnam today, killing all aboard.

The plane crashed about five miles east of Ankhe, headquarters and base camp of the United States Army's First Cavalry Division (Airmobile).

A United States military spokesman reported that 43 men from the Seventh Cavalry Regiment and four crewmen were aboard the plane. He said there were no survivors.

The cause of the crash was not known. The plane, attached to the 315th Air Commando Squadron, was carrying the troops to a staging area.

Vietcong Attack Base

By NEIL SHEEHAN
Special to The New York Times

SAIGON, Tuesday, Jan. 25—The Vietcong staged a mortar attack on the big United States and South Vietnamese air base at Danang early today, killing two Americans and two Vietnamese Government soldiers.

[Three Americans were killed, according to an Associated Press dispatch.]

Informed sources said 11 Americans and 11 Vietnamese were wounded in the attack on the base, which is 380 miles north of Saigon.

No planes were hit, an American military spokesman said, but two gasoline tanker trucks, an asphalt spreader and a mobile crane were damaged.

Four Vietnamese civilian dependents of military personnel were wounded when several shells fell near the Vietnamese

Continued on Page 3, Column 1

Mayor Ties Cash Saving To Increased Productivity

By CLAYTON KNOWLES

Mayor Lindsay said yesterday that his campaign pledge to cut $300-million to $400-million from the city's operating costs could not be construed in terms of dollar savings alone. He said a substantial part of the savings would be "in terms of increased productivity without any reduction in essential city services."

The Mayor insisted at a City Hall news conference that he was not giving a new interpretation of his campaign promise.

"I have always said that," he maintained. "Eliminate waste and duplication where it exists and get proper program planning and there is a real chance for increasing productivity . . .

"When I'd talk about it during the campaign, however, the headline that always came out on this was: 'Lindsay Promises Millions in Cuts.'"

Campaign Paper Quoted

In a campaign white paper of Oct. 26 titled "From Fiscal Decay to Recovery," Mr. Lindsay said:

"By keeping the expense level steady, by increasing productivity by several hundred million dollars annually, increased services can occur in the future without accompanying staggering increases in the annual budgets.

"We will institute—in contrast to the present primitive substitutes — immediate short and long range program planning which will project the city's expenses and revenues. This planning will be backed up by a strict performance-control system with teeth in it. We will thereby save the city $300-million to $400-million annually by eliminating untold waste and duplication."

A week ago, in his first fireside chat, the Mayor declared that it was now his objective "to achieve selected savings of at least $150-million during the next 18 months."

That will be done, he said, by having all departments try for 10 per cent reductions in operating cost. He said he proposed to "save" $50-million to $75-million more over the next 18 months through his "job freeze" order barring the filling of vacancies.

The job-freeze order caused a furor among civil service employes and unions representing

Continued on Page 36, Column 8

PRICE AND POLICE SETTLE DISPUTE

Deputy Mayor Admits Using Patrol Cars 3 Times but Not to Bring Coffee

By ERIC PACE

Deputy Mayor Robert Price met yesterday with officials of the Patrolmen's Benevolent Association in an effort to resolve complaints that he had made undue demands on the police force.

He conferred for an hour with John J. Cassese, the association's president, and Norman Frank, an aide. The meeting was set up after the organization said last week that Mr. Price's office had been "naive to the point of unbelievability" in asking the Police Department to hold open six high-ranking detective jobs.

The P.B.A. also reported complaints by policemen that Mr. Price had ordered a police radio car to bring coffee and sandwiches to City Hall, that he had used a police car for his personal transportation and that he had ordered the ticketing of some cars for traffic violations.

Mr. Cassese emerged smiling from the confrontation at City Hall and said: "I'm convinced there was nothing politically motivated [in Mr. Price's behavior toward the police], nor would I construe it as interference in the Police Department."

Appears With Price

He appeared with Mr. Price at a news conference in the Mayor's Blue Room and said: "I believe we have an understanding now, and what has transpired in the past will not happen later on."

At the news conference, Mr. Price defended himself against the complaints. Mr. Cassése, whose organization includes more than 90 per cent of the police force, did not take issue with Mr. Price's rebuttals.

On the complaint that Mr. Price had ordered a police car to bring coffee and sandwiches to City Hall, Mr. Price said he did not doubt that a call had been made in his name, but he said, "I had no knowledge of it." Mr. Cassese called the charge "imaginary."

Mr. Price said that he had indeed asked policemen to ticket illegally parked cars. "All citizens try to work with the police to build a safer city," he observed. Mr. Cassese agreed that Mr. Price's actions had been proper.

The Deputy Mayor repeated

Continued on Page 36, Column 8

NEWS INDEX

LOTTERY IS LIKELY TO PASS IN ALBANY

Brydges Opposes Plan, but Will Apply 'No Pressure' to G.O.P. Colleagues

By SYDNEY H. SCHANBERG
Special to The New York Times

ALBANY, Jan. 24 — The Democratic proposal to authorize a state lottery was assured of approval by the Legislature today.

The only possible obstacle — opposition by the Republican majority in the Senate — was removed when the majority leader, Earl W. Brydges, said that while he was going to vote against the plan, he would apply "no pressure" on his colleagues to follow suit.

Mr. Brydges, in fact, predicted that the lottery — whose proceeds would go exclusively for state aid to schools—would be approved, as it was last year, "with considerable Republican support."

Opposed by Governor

Approval of a public lottery requires an amendment to the State Constitution. This means the measure has to be passed by two separately elected Legislatures and then by the voters in a referendum. If the present Legislature approves the amendment it will be put on the ballot in the November election. The amendment could not take effect before next Jan. 1.

Governor Rockefeller has said he opposes lotteries in principle, but his approval is not required on constitutional amendments.

The indications today were that the lottery measure might come up for a vote as early as next week, at least in the Assembly.

Last year it swept through the Assembly by a vote of 116 to 18, and the Senate by a 35 to 18 tally.

Assembly Speaker Anthony

Continued on Page 36, Column 2

A Gaullist Deputy Linked to Abduction

By HENRY TANNER
Special to The New York Times

PARIS, Jan. 24—A Gaullist Deputy and close friend of Interior Minister Roger Frey was accused today by the weekly magazine L'Express of having been personally involved in the abduction here of Mehdi Ben Barka, an exiled Moroccan Opposition leader.

Mr. Ben Barka was kidnapped in daylight Oct. 29 on the busy Boulevard Saint - Germain-des-Prés, apparently with the help of French police officers and gangsters. He is believed to be dead now.

The French Government has charged that Gen. Mohammed Oufkir, the Moroccan Interior Minister, and two Moroccan security officers were involved.

L'Express, a respected news magazine, said that Pierre Lemarchand, the Gaullist Dep-

Continued on Page 10, Column 3

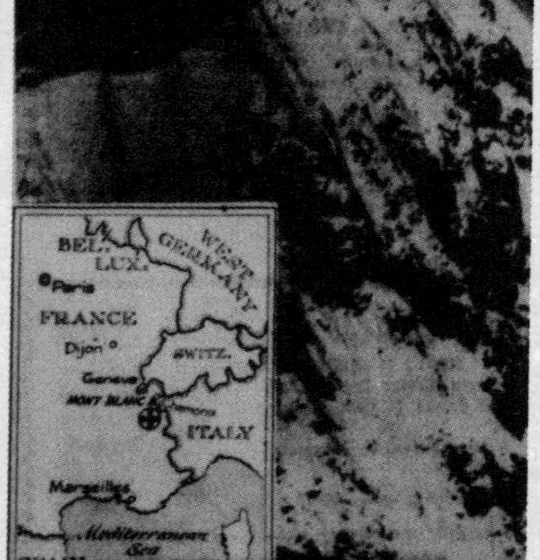

The New York Times Jan. 25, 1966 (Associated Press Cablephoto)

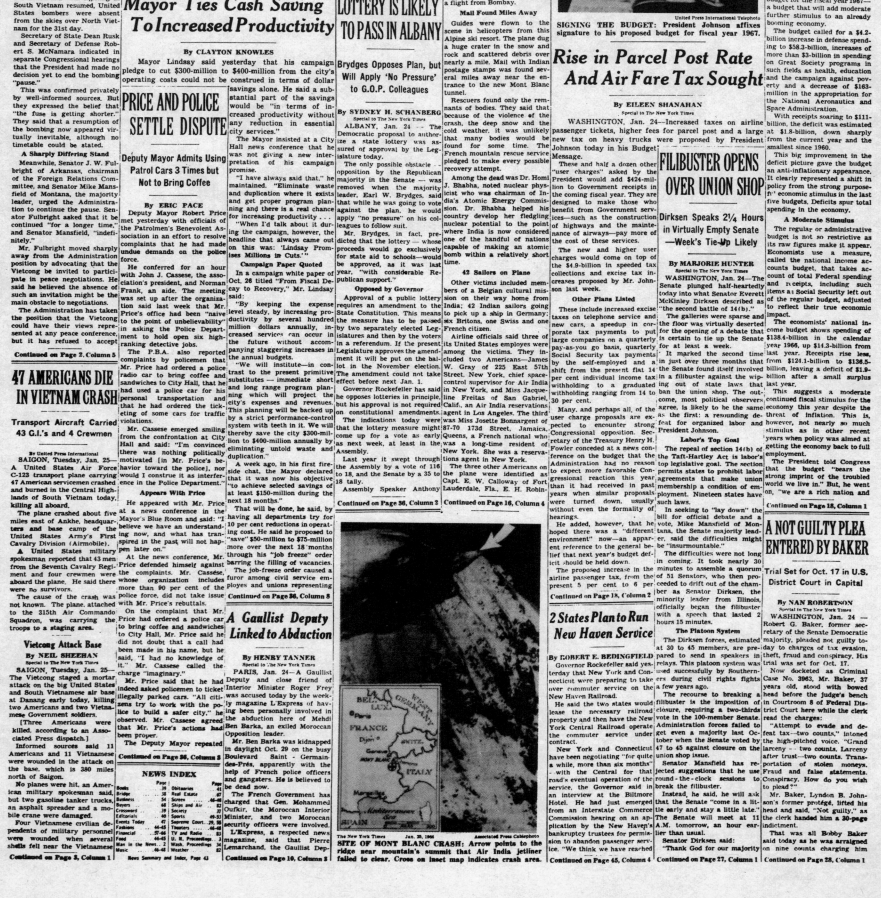

SITE OF MONT BLANC CRASH: Arrow points to the ridge near mountain's summit that Air India jetliner failed to clear. Cross on inset map indicates crash area.

117 ON INDIAN JET DIE AS IT CRASHES INTO MONT BLANC

5 Americans on Boeing 707 That Was Coming Here—Atom Scientist a Victim

By United Press International

CHAMONIX, France, Jan. 24—An Air India Boeing 707 jetliner crashed into a ridge today near the three-mile-high summit of Mont Blanc, killing all 117 persons aboard. With 45 feet more of altitude the plane would have cleared the ridge.

The captain of the New York-bound airliner served as co-pilot of the Indian plane that carried Pope Paul VI on his flight to India in December, 1964. India's top atomic scientist was among the passengers.

Five Americans were reported among those killed as the plane crashed in fog and 22-below-zero temperature minutes before it was due at Geneva on a flight from Bombay.

Mail Found Miles Away

Guides were flown to the scene in helicopters from this Alpine ski resort. The plane dug a huge crater in the snow and rock and scattered debris over nearly a mile. Mail with Indian postage stamps was found several miles away near the entrance to the new Mont Blanc tunnel.

Rescuers found only the remnants of bodies. They said that because of the violence of the crash, the deep snow and the cold weather, it was unlikely that many bodies would be found for some time. The French mountain rescue service pledged to make every possible recovery attempt.

Among the dead was Dr. Homi J. Bhabha, noted nuclear physicist who was chairman of India's Atomic Energy Commission. Dr. Bhabha helped his country develop her fledgling nuclear potential to the point where India is now considered one of the handful of nations capable of making an atomic bomb within a relatively short time.

42 Sailors on Plane

Other victims included members of a Belgian cultural mission on their way home from India; 42 Indian sailors going to pick up a ship in Germany; six Britons, one Swiss and one French citizen.

Airline officials said three of its United States employes were among the victims. They included two Americans—James W. Gray of 225 East 57th Street, New York, chief space-control supervisor for Air India in New York, and Miss Jacqueline Freitas of San Gabriel, Calif., an Air India reservations agent in Los Angeles. The third was Miss Josette Bonnargent of 87-70 173d Street, Jamaica, Queens, a French national who was a long-time resident of New York. She was a reservations agent in New York.

The three other Americans on the plane were identified as Capt. E. W. Calloway of Fort Lauderdale, Fla., E. H. Robin-

Continued on Page 16, Column 4

$112.8-BILLION BUDGET ADDS TO SPENDING FOR DEFENSE AND 'GREAT SOCIETY' GOALS

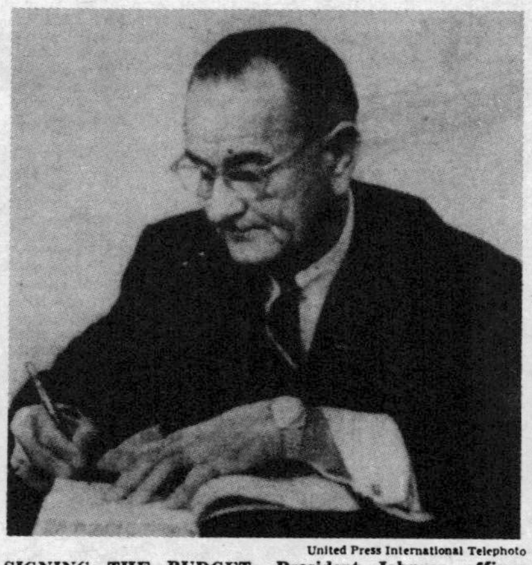

SIGNING THE BUDGET: President Johnson affixes signature to his proposed budget for fiscal year 1967. (United Press International Telephoto)

DEFICIT REDUCED

$1.8-Billion Expected by Johnson—Aid to Economy Likely

The Budget Message: A Slip-Out Section, Pages 19-26.

By EDWIN L. DALE Jr.
Special to The New York Times

WASHINGTON, Jan. 24 — President Johnson sent to Congress today his $112.8-billion budget for the fiscal year 1967—a budget that will add moderate further stimulus to an already booming economy.

The budget called for a $4.2-billion increase in defense spending to $58.3-billion, increases of more than $3-billion in spending on Great Society programs in such fields as health, education and the campaign against poverty and a decrease of $163-million in the appropriation for the National Aeronautics and Space Administration.

With receipts soaring to $111-billion, the deficit was estimated at $1.8-billion, down sharply from the current year and the smallest since 1960.

This big improvement in the deficit picture gave the budget an anti-inflationary appearance. It clearly represented a shift in policy from the strong purposeful economic stimulus in the last five budgets. Deficits spur total spending in the economy.

A Moderate Stimulus

The regular or administrative budget is not so restrictive as its raw figures make it appear. Economists use a measure, called the national income accounts budget, that takes account of total Federal spending and receipts, including such items as Social Security left out of the regular budget, adjusted to reflect their true economic impact.

The economists' national income budget shows spending of $138.4-billion in the calendar year 1966, up $14.3-billion from last year. Receipts rise less, from $124.1-billion to $136.5-billion, leaving a deficit of $1.9-billion after a small surplus last year.

This suggests a moderate continued fiscal stimulus for the economy this year despite the threat of inflation. This is, however, not nearly so much stimulus as in other recent years when policy was aimed at getting the economy back to full employment.

The President told Congress that the budget "bears the strong imprint of the troubled world we live in." But, he went on, "we are a rich nation and

Continued on Page 18, Column 1

Rise in Parcel Post Rate And Air Fare Tax Sought

By EILEEN SHANAHAN
Special to The New York Times

WASHINGTON, Jan. 24—Increased taxes on airline passenger tickets, higher fees for parcel post and a large new tax on heavy trucks were proposed by President Johnson today in his Budget Message.

These and half a dozen other "user charges" asked by the President would add $424-million to Government receipts in the coming fiscal year. They are designed to make those who benefit from Government services—such as the construction of highways and the maintenance of airways—pay more of the cost of these services.

The new and higher user charges would come on top of the $4.9-billion in speeded tax collections and excise tax increases proposed by Mr. Johnson last week.

Other Plans Listed

These include increased excise taxes on telephone service and new cars, a speedup in corporate tax payments to put large companies on a quarterly pay-as-you go basis, quarterly Social Security tax payments by the self-employed and a shift from the present flat 14 per cent individual income tax withholding to a graduated withholding ranging from 14 to 30 per cent.

Many, and perhaps all, of the user charge proposals are expected to encounter strong Congressional opposition. Secretary of the Treasury Henry H. Fowler conceded at a news conference on the budget that the Administration had no reason to expect more favorable Congressional reaction this year than it had received in past years when similar proposals were turned down, usually without even the formality of hearings.

He added, however, that he hoped there was a "different environment" now—an apparent reference to the general belief that next year's budget deficit should be held down.

The proposed increase in the airline passenger tax, from the present 5 per cent to 6 per

Continued on Page 18, Column 2

FILIBUSTER OPENS OVER UNION SHOP

Dirksen Speaks 2¼ Hours in Virtually Empty Senate —Week's Tie-Up Likely

By MARJORIE HUNTER
Special to The New York Times

WASHINGTON, Jan. 24—The Senate plunged half-heartedly today into what Senator Everett McKinley Dirksen described as "the second battle of 14(b)."

The galleries were sparse and the floor was virtually deserted for the opening of a debate that is certain to tie up the Senate for at least a week.

It marked the second time in just over three months that the Senate found itself involved in a filibuster against the wiping out of state laws that ban the union shop. The outcome, most political observers agree, is likely to be the same as the first: a resounding defeat for organized labor and President Johnson.

Labor's Top Goal

The repeal of section 14(b) of the Taft-Hartley Act is labor's top legislative goal. The section permits states to prohibit labor agreements that make union membership a condition of employment. Nineteen states have such laws.

In seeking to "lay down" the bill for official debate and a vote, Mike Mansfield of Montana, the Senate majority leader, said the difficulties might be "insurmountable."

The difficulties were not long in coming. It took nearly 30 minutes to assemble a quorum of 51 Senators, who then proceeded to drift out of the chamber as Senator Dirksen, the minority leader from Illinois, officially began the filibuster with a speech that lasted 2 hours 15 minutes.

The Platoon System

The Dirksen forces, estimated at 30 to 45 members, are prepared to send in speakers in relays. This platoon system was used successfully by Southerners during civil rights fights a few years ago.

The recourse to breaking a filibuster is the imposition of closure, requiring a two-thirds vote in the 100-member Senate. Administration forces failed to get even a majority last October when the Senate voted by 47 to 45 against closure on the union shop issue.

Senator Mansfield has rejected suggestions that he use round-the-clock sessions to break the filibuster.

Instead, he said, he will ask that the Senate "come in a little early and stay a little late." The Senate will meet at 11 A.M. tomorrow, an hour earlier than usual.

Senator Dirksen said:

"Thank God for our majority

Continued on Page 27, Column 1

2 States Plan to Run New Haven Service

By ROBERT E. BEDINGFIELD

Governor Rockefeller said yesterday that New York and Connecticut were preparing to take over commuter service on the New Haven Railroad.

He said the two states would lease the necessary railroad property and then have the New York Central Railroad operate the commuter service under contract.

New York and Connecticut have been negotiating "for quite a while, more than six months" — with the Central for that road's eventual operation of the service, the Governor said in an interview at the Biltmore Hotel. He had just emerged from an Interstate Commerce Commission hearing on an application by the New Haven's bankruptcy trustees for permission to abandon passenger service. "We think we have reached

Continued on Page 45, Column 4

A NOT GUILTY PLEA ENTERED BY BAKER

Trial Set for Oct. 17 in U.S. District Court in Capital

By NAN ROBERTSON
Special to The New York Times

WASHINGTON, Jan. 24 — Robert G. Baker, former secretary of the Senate Democratic majority, pleaded not guilty today to charges of tax evasion, theft, fraud and conspiracy. His trial was set for Oct. 17.

Now docketed as Criminal Case No. 3963, Mr. Baker, 37 years old, stood with bowed head before the judge's bench in Courtroom 8 of Federal District Court here while the clerk read the charges:

"Attempt to evade and defeat tax—two counts," intoned the high-pitched voice. "Grand larceny — two counts. Larceny after trust—two counts. Transportation of stolen moneys. Fraud and false statements. Conspiracy. How do you wish to plead?"

Mr. Baker, Lyndon B. Johnson's former protégé, lifted his head and said, "Not guilty," as the clerk handed him a 30-page indictment.

That was all Bobby Baker said today as he was arraigned on nine counts charging him

Continued on Page 28, Column 1

117 ON INDIAN JET DIE AS IT CRASHES

Continued From Page 1, Col. 5

son, an employe of the Union Carbide Company and R. J. Homan. The addresses of the latter two were not given.

The passengers also included Patrick C. Coates, the Burmah Oil Company's chief representative in India, and Baroness Degley, a Belgian.

The airline identified the pilot as Capt. J. T. D'Souza, a veteran of 18 years' service and one of the line's most experienced pilots. He had flown the run over the Alps hundreds of times.

The flight was named Kanchenjunga, after the Himalyan peak. The plane crashed along the French-Swiss border close to where an Air India Constellation crashed Nov. 3, 1950, killing all 48 aboard.

News of the disaster reached New Delhi shortly after Mrs. Indira Gandhi was sworn as India's first woman Prime Minister. It cast a pall over the inauguration festivities.

The crash occurred around 8:25 A.M. (2:25 A.M. E.S.T.) when the jetliner was still going at its full speed of about 600 miles an hour, but was about to start slowing down for landing at Geneva, local sources said.

The plane hit a ridge of the 15,771-foot peak about 700 feet from the summit. The crash occurred at a point where the Boeing left the Italian radar beam and was to be picked up by Geneva's radar.

Officials said the pilot probably would have cleared the obstacle had not a violent snowstorm broken out over the Mont Blanc range at just that time.

Gerard Devouassoux, a Chamonix mountain guide, said the plane skirted the peak and crashed just below the ridgetop.

Mountain guides brought the remains of some of the victims to Chamonix tonight. They also found the bodies of 15 monkeys that were being transported.

Some of the wreckage could be seen with binoculars from Chamonix this afternoon after the storm cleared. Jagged pieces of metal jutted from the snow and glittered in the sun.

"The wreckage was strewn over a wide area," said a rescue official. "There were no survivors. In fact, only pieces of arms and legs can be found."

Workmen at Chamonix, France, unload bodies from rescue helicopter after jetliner crashed on nearby Mont Blanc.

Wide World Photos

Plane Crash Victim Led India's Nuclear Effort

Dr. Bhabha Was His Country's Foremost Atomic Scientist

Dr. Homi Jehangir Bhabha, who was killed yesterday in a plane crash on Mont Blanc, was India's foremost atomic scientist and the dominant figure in that country's plans to harness the atom. He was 56 years old.

A brilliant physicist, he held the two top posts in India's nuclear energy program for more than a decade. He was chairman of the country's Atomic Energy Commission and directed the Indian Atomic Energy Department, which operates directly under the Prime Minister.

Under his direction India moved rapidly toward the exploitation of nuclear energy to supply the country's critical needs for electric power. India expects next year to begin the harvest of this work, when the first of a series of nuclear power stations is due to go into service.

Last November Dr. Bhabha denied reports that India was secretly preparing to explode a nuclear device. He said in an interview then that India was 18 months from such an event and that "we are doing nothing to reduce that period." He said India's nuclear program was devoted to production of power and other peaceful purposes.

Last-Minute Change

The scientist was on his way to Vienna yesterday for a conference of the International Atomic Energy Commission. He was originally scheduled to travel on an Air India flight Saturday to Geneva, but changed his plans at the last moment.

India's new Prime Minister, Mrs. Indira Gandhi, described his death as "a personal loss."

"To lose Dr. Bhabha at this crucial moment in the development of our atomic energy program is a terrible blow for our nation," she added.

Dr. J. Robert Oppenheimer, director of the Institute for Advanced Study at Princeton, N. J., said Dr. Bhabha "will be sorely missed as a scientist who in his work and example did so much to promote physics in his country and elsewhere."

A stocky, handsome man, Dr. Bhabha wielded an influence among Indian scientists and in Government councils that was said to have been compounded of many things: scientific emi-

Associated Press

Dr. Homi Jehangir Bhabha

nence, wealth, family ties, his friendship with the late Indian Prime Minister, Jawaharlal Nehru, a quick intelligence and a flair for the arts.

Dr. Bhabha was fond of plants and filled the porch next to his penthouse apartment in Bombay with many exotic varieties, some of which he introduced to India.

He played the violin and was an accomplished painter. At the new Tata Institute building he once proudly showed a visitor a lobby full of paintings by young Indian artists.

His apartment was decorated with his own abstract works, done in the nineteen-thirties when he was in England.

A descendant of a prominent Indian family, Dr. Bhabha became widely known in the West as chairman of the first United Nations Conference on the Peaceful Uses of Atomic Energy, held in Geneva in August, 1955.

At that conference he predicted that by 1975 man would

Denied Secret Preparations to Set Off an Explosion

find a way to control the fusion of atoms to provide limitless industrial power. Fusion, the process used in the hydrogen bomb, combines atoms to provide energy, in contrast with fission, which splits atoms.

That goal is still not in sight and many scientists have taken a less optimistic view on its chances of achievement.

Dr. Bhabha's prediction marked the first public discussion of the possibility of controlled fusion and led to revelations by the United States and Britain of work they had been conducting in that field.

Dr. Bhabha, a bachelor, was a native of Bombay. He was born Oct. 30, 1909, to wealthy Parsee parents. He started his education in Bombay and continued his college studies in England, where his brilliance earned him a number of scholarships.

He received his bachelor's degree at Cambridge University in 1930 and his Ph.D. four years later.

Headed Tata Institute

Returning to India in 1940, he began to do research in theoretical physics and cosmic rays. In 1945 he was named director and professor of theoretical physics of the Tata Institute of Fundamental Research in Bombay, which he built into India's largest research laboratory.

He was appointed the first chairman of the Indian Atomic Energy Commission in 1948. In 1954 he was named secretary of the Atomic Energy Department headed by Prime Minister Nehru.

Dr. Bhabha was a fellow of science academies in many countries, including the American Academy of Arts and Science, and a foreign associate of the United States National Academy of Sciences. He was named a fellow of the Royal Society in London in 1941.

He was a prolific author of papers on quantum theory and cosmic radiation, and his articles were published in United States, British and Indian publications.

"All the News That's Fit to Print"

The New York Times.

LATE CITY EDITION

U. S. Weather Bureau Report (Page 57) forecasts: Snow flurries ending this afternoon; fair tonight and tomorrow. Temp. Range: 30—23; yesterday: 35—28.

VOL. CXV..No. 39,459. © 1966 by The New York Times Company. Times Square, New York, N. Y. 10036 NEW YORK, SATURDAY, FEBRUARY 5, 1966. TEN CENTS

Picture From Moon: Crust Seems Firm

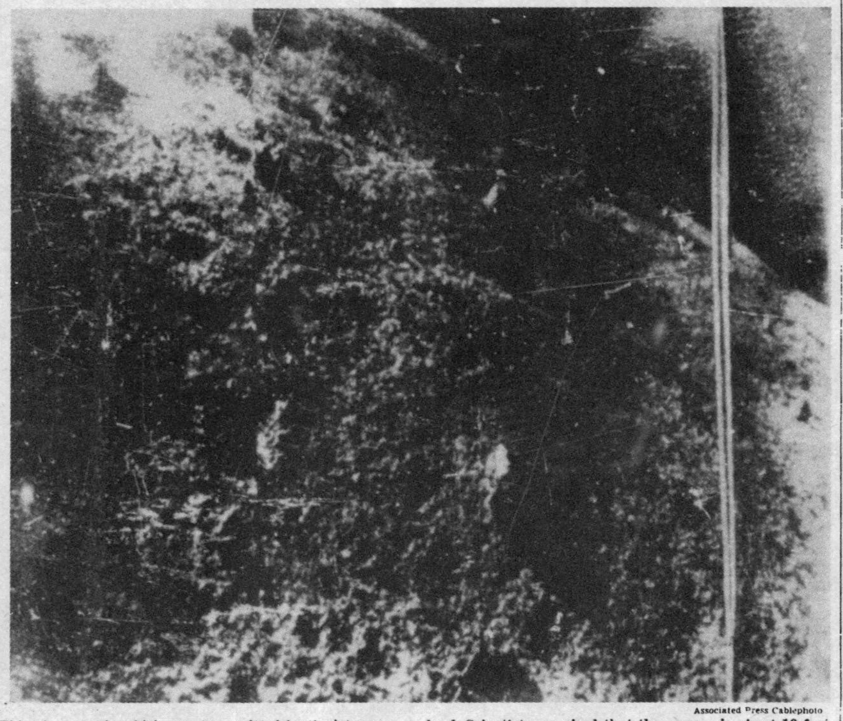

Associated Press Cablephoto

This photograph, which was transmitted by Soviet spacecraft Luna 9 after it landed on moon, faces south. It was intercepted at radio observatory at Jodrell Bank, England. Scientists surmised that the camera is about 10 feet above floor of a shallow crater, with horizon, upper right, not far away. Transmission flaw caused lines at right.

Porous Surface Is Dotted By Oddly Shaped Rocks

By WALTER SULLIVAN

The Soviet Union's Luna 9, from its location on the moon, has sent to earth pictures showing a moonscape covered with peculiar porous material and scattered with oddly shaped rocks.

The presence of the rocks suggests that the underlying surface is strong enough to support a man or a large spacecraft.

The pictures were not made public by Moscow but by the radio astronomy observatory at Jodrell Bank, near Manchester, England.

The British, with their huge radio antenna, 250 feet in diameter, were able to extract at least two photographs from radio transmissions intercepted from the Soviet spacecraft. The transmissions were received immediately after the vehicle landed on Thursday night and yesterday afternoon. The pictures were produced by running the radio signals through a newspaper's wirephoto equipment.

One problem in assessing the photographs is the fact that, until the Russians interpret the pictures, the scale of features showing in them will be uncertain.

Thus Dr. Gerard P. Kuiper, director of the Lunar and Planetary Laboratory at the University of Arizona, believes Luna 9 is sitting inside a shallow crater. He notes that in the south-facing photograph there is little foreshortening of the most distant rocks and other features.

He therefore takes the horizon to be the near rim of the crater. The rocks, he believes, are only a foot high.

A similar view was expressed by Dr. Eugene M. Shoemaker of the Astrogeology Branch of the United States Geological Survey.

Reached by telephone last night, Dr. Shoemaker said that, from the shadows, it appeared that the two pictures were taken in opposite directions. The view with the longer horizon, he said, was looking south. The other, with two elongated objects, faced north. He believes those objects are a fiction of faulty transmission.

The vehicle seems from these two pictures to be near the center of a crater with its horizon formed by a rim only a few hundred feet away, Dr. Shoemaker said. The north-facing picture, he added, shows a peculiar patch of rubble in its lower part. He pointed out that Amer-

Continued on Page 10, Column 1

U.S. SUES UNIONS TO HALT JOB BIAS

5 Building Trades Groups in St. Louis Are Accused of a Discrimination 'Pattern'

By JOHN HERBERS

Special to The New York Times

WASHINGTON, Feb. 4—The Department of Justice announced tonight it had filed the first "pattern of practice" lawsuit under the Fair Employment Practices Section of the Civil Rights Act of 1964.

The suit was filed in United States District Court in St. Louis earlier in the day against construction trades unions accused of discriminating against Negroes.

The unions are affiliated with the American Federation of Labor and the Congress of Industrial Organizations.

In Effect since July 2

Attorney General Nicholas deB. Katzenbach said in announcing the suit that it also was the first action seeking to enforce the nondiscrimination clause that appears in all Federal contracts.

The section of the Civil Rights Act which bans discrimination in employment, Title VII, has been in effect since last July 2. For several years the Government has tried by executive order to eliminate employment discrimination in work done under Government contract.

In the past, however, the Government has tried to achieve compliance by negotiation. Filing of a lawsuit is permitted under the Civil Rights Act where there is an indication of a widespread practice of discrimination.

Defendants in today's lawsuit are the Building and Construc-

Continued on Page 13, Column 4

Distribution Center Planned in Midtown

Plans for a 15-story distribution center to provide storage facilities for manufacturers west of the General Post Office in midtown Manhattan were submitted yesterday to the City Planning Commission for its approval.

The plans were filed by Lazard Frères & Co., the investment banking firm, which presented them as the first phase of a development that would total $44.2-million.

The banking concern would like ultimately to build at least 1,600 apartments on the eastern portion of the site, which would be between 31st and 33d Streets from Ninth to Tenth Avenues.

William Zeckendorf bought the site for the Webb & Knapp real estate company from the Pennsylvania Railroad eight

Continued on Page 34, Column 1

Bishop Pike's Son Is Believed A Suicide in Broadway Hotel

A 22-year-old man believed to be the elder son of the Rev. James A. Pike, the Episcopal Bishop of California, shot and killed himself in a hotel room here yesterday.

Bishop Pike was addressing 600 delegates in San Francisco at the opening of the 115th convention of the Episcopal Diocese of California at the time the tentative identification was made. San Francisco policemen waited for him to finish speaking and then told him of the suicide.

"I just don't understand it," the Bishop said. "He seemed reasonably happy." Shaken, he repeated the words several times.

The Bishop left the convention to tell his wife about the death.

Chaplain Richard Bayfield of the San Francisco church said yesterday that Bishop Pike would not come to New York. He said positive identification of the body would be made sometime today by staff members of the Cathedral Church of St. John the Divine, where the Bishop served for six years before going to California in 1958.

The body, tentatively identified by the New York police as that of James Albert Pike, was found on the bed of his sixth-floor room at the Hadson Hotel at 31st Street and Broadway.

A .30-30 rifle lay beside the body, and the police reported they had found a note.

A detective described its message as "rambling." He said it mentioned the names of many persons and ended with "Good-by. Good-by."

Last September young Pike had accompanied his father to Cambridge, England, where the Bishop was studying while on a sabbatical leave. The son, too, registered at Cambridge, but decided to come back with his father last Wednesday.

They did not come back on the same plane, however, the son being delayed because his passport was lost and he had to get a new one. The police found a United States passport issued by the American Embassy in London in the dead man's effects.

On Wednesday, the police said, young Pike checked into the hotel at 8:20 in the evening. He asked for a room for two days and paid $10.50 in advance.

Just before 2 o'clock yesterday afternoon, a bellboy, Louis Wells, entered the room and found the body clad in a red shirt, blue trousers and white socks.

Detectives of the West 30th Street precinct said that the man had fired two shots from the rifle, the first of which had

Continued on Page 58, Column 1

NEW BILL ATTACKS CITY AIR POLLUTION

Measure Would Curb Use of Soft Coal and Restrict Incinerator Design

By CHARLES G. BENNETT

Legislation designed to mount a broad attack on New York's air pollution was filed with the City Council yesterday.

The bill would forbid the use of bituminous coal two years after passage of the law. It would also clamp rigid controls on the use of coal and fuel oil for other purposes, including the generation of power.

Flue-fed incinerators would be barred in all new apartment buildings, and other restrictions would be imposed to help rid the city of its air contamination.

Time Limits Set

Fines up to $1,000 would be imposed; the top fine now is $500.

Within one year after passage of the law, existing incinerators in all buildings other than apartment houses of six stories or less would have to be modernized. The exempted apartment houses would have to modernize their incinerators within two years.

Councilman Robert A. Low, Manhattan Democrat-Liberal, who is one of the bill's sponsors, declared it was designed "to keep the city from choking itself to death."

He said Mayor Lindsay's panel on air pollution would be invited to make recommendations for inclusion in the bill, if it desired.

The Consolidated Edison Company would be affected particularly by a requirement

Continued on Page 15, Column 3

Patrolman Is Held In 3 Store Holdups

By JACK ROTH

A policeman who was twice honored for capturing holdup men was arrested yesterday on charges of robbing a food store in his own Manhattan precinct three times.

The District Attorney's office said he was part of a ring that had committed a number of robberies in other boroughs. Three other men were arrested as part of the ring and charged with other robberies.

The 35-year-old patrolman, Frederick Eisenbach, a heavy six-footer who lives at 87 North Henry Street, Brooklyn, was seized in his home yesterday morning and was ordered booked after being questioned for several hours in the prosecutor's office.

Eisenbach, who was attached

Continued on Page 60, Column 4

U.S. TO INCREASE GRAIN SHIPMENTS FOR INDIA FAMINE

Johnson Orders Movement of 3 Million Tons, Nearly Doubling Year's Relief

By FELIX BELAIR Jr.

Special to The New York Times

WASHINGTON, Feb. 4—President Johnson authorized today the shipment of three million more tons of grain to India for famine relief.

In announcing the action at an impromptu news conference, he said the grain would be shipped "as quickly as possible." [India Statement, Page 8.]

The President also let it be known that he was considering a request to Congress for emergency legislation authorizing him to step up American food shipments substantially and to take the lead in marshaling contributions from all other countries to relieve the famine in India. [Question 1.]

Mr. Johnson said that the newly authorized shipment would include two million tons of wheat, worth about $160-million, and a million tons of "maize," valued at from $45-million to $50-million. Food officials said the maize was a grain sorghum called milo.

Will See Mrs. Gandhi

He said he was planning to see Prime Minister Indira Gandhi here in Washington in "the reasonably near future" and at her convenience. He said they would discuss mutual problems and measures that might be taken by the governments and people of India and the United States to help each other.

The precise time of Mrs. Gandhi's visit to Washington is a matter for her to announce, the President said. [Question 3.]

In response to a question, he said that he would not foreclose or preclude the resumption of conventional economic foreign aid to India pending the Prime Minister's visit. Aid to both India and Pakistan was cut off with the outbreak of border fighting last year.

Plan Still Being Formed

At the moment, he said, he is passing only on the most urgent matter of emergency food allocations. These, he said, would bring total grain shipments to India to 6.5 million tons in the current fiscal year, ending June 30. [Question 4.]

The President emphasized that the emergency food legislation under consideration was still in the idea stage, that its form remained to be determined and that it might not be submitted at all. He did not indicate whether the legislation was one of the matters he planned to discuss with the Prime Minister.

However, the President said that the plan he had in mind would be entirely apart from the message to Congress next

Continued on Page 8, Column 6

JOHNSON TO FLY TO HAWAII TO MEET SAIGON LEADERS FOR 3-DAY REVIEW OF WAR

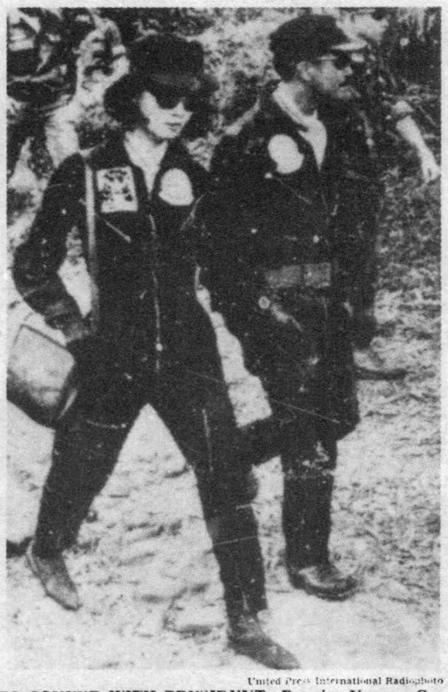

United Press International Radiophoto

TO CONFER WITH PRESIDENT: Premier Nguyen Cao Ky of South Vietnam, shown with his wife on visit to Bongson battlefield, is to meet with Mr. Johnson in Hawaii.

HE LEAVES TODAY

Lodge, Westmoreland and 4 From Cabinet Will Attend Talks

Transcript of news conference is printed on Page 8.

By JOHN W. FINNEY

Special to The New York Times

WASHINGTON, Feb. 4—President Johnson announced today that he would fly to Hawaii tomorrow to confer with South Vietnamese leaders and American military and diplomatic representatives stationed in Vietnam.

The President said he planned a three-day review of political and military developments in South Vietnam, with emphasis upon the rural "pacification" program recently instituted by the Saigon Government.

Mr. Johnson announced the surprise conference, which will be his first meeting with South Vietnamese leaders, at an unscheduled news conference in his White House office.

He said that no specific military or political developments in South Vietnam had prompted the conference. The meeting is not expected to result in any change in American policies in Vietnam, he added. [Vietnam statement, and Question 15, Page 8.]

Senate Hearing Is On

It appeared, however, that domestic political considerations, both in Washington and in Saigon, played an important part in Mr. Johnson's decision to meet the South Vietnamese.

The Presidential announcement came in midafternoon as the Senate Foreign Relations Committee was beginning the second session of its televised hearings on the Vietnamese war.

An obvious effect of the announcement was to divert at least some attention from the hearings, which have been marked by Senatorial concern over the course of the Administration's policies in Vietnam.

For the South Vietnamese leaders, the Presidential trip—Mr. Johnson's first overseas since his assumption of office—will represent an important vote of confidence in the eight-month-old Saigon Government, which is viewed by the Administration as still fragile but holding promise for political stability and economic progress.

Lodge to Arrive Sunday

The two principal leaders of the Saigon Government — the chief of state, Maj. Gen. Nguyen Van Thieu, and the Premier, Air Vice Marshal Nguyen Cao Ky — are to participate in the conference. Accompanied by Henry Cabot Lodge, the United States Ambassador, they will arrive in Honolulu on Sunday.

President Johnson will leave tomorrow afternoon on a 10½-hour nonstop flight to Honolulu. He said he planned to return to Washington Tuesday evening.

The President will be accompanied by his leading military and diplomatic advisers — Secretary of State Dean Rusk, Secretary of Defense Robert S. McNamara, Gen. Earle G. Wheeler, Chairman of the Joint Chiefs of Staff, and McGeorge Bundy, special Presidential assistant for national security.

In addition, because of the emphasis expected to be placed in the talks on rural-development programs in South Vietnam, Secretary of Agriculture Orville L. Freeman and John W. Gardner, Secretary of Health, Education and Welfare, will be in the Presidential party.

The talks will also involve

Continued on Page 8, Column 8

Division-Size Unit Widens G.I. Drive On Vietnam Coast

By R. W. APPLE Jr.

Special to The New York Times

BONGSON, South Vietnam, Saturday, Feb. 5—The United States threw more troops into the battle for Binhdinh Province today, making it the first division-size American operation of the Vietnamese war.

Maj. Gen. Harry W. O. Kinnard, commander of the First Cavalry Division (Airmobile), took personal charge of the huge offensive, which has been redesignated Operation White Wing. He moved his mobile command post into the combat area.

Despite the increased commitment, the Americans failed for the fourth day in a row to track down the mixed enemy force of North Vietnamese regulars and Vietcong guerrillas with whom they fought a series of battles late last week.

Three battalions, organized into the division's Third Brigade, will operate in the immediate vicinity of Bongson, 275 miles northeast of Saigon, and three others will be responsible for a sector between Bongson

Continued on Page 5, Column 3

M'NAMARA BALKS AT PUBLIC INQUIRY

Morse Angry as Secretary Says Testimony on War Might Harm Security

By E. W. KENWORTHY

Special to The New York Times

WASHINGTON, Feb. 4—Secretary of Defense Robert S. McNamara objected today to testifying at public hearings on United States policies in Vietnam.

But Mr. McNamara told Senator J. W. Fulbright, chairman of the Senate Foreign Relations Committee, that he would be willing to appear in closed sessions.

Senator Fulbright made known Mr. McNamara's opposition to public testimony at the end of a four-hour morning hearing held by the committee.

At the hearing, David E. Bell, administrator of foreign aid, was subjected to intensive, and at times sharp, questioning on the direction of United States policy in Vietnam as well as the direction of the aid program.

Mr. Fulbright said that he had asked Secretary McNamara and Gen. Earle G. Wheeler, chairman of the Joint Chiefs of Staff, to testify publicly next week.

Secretary McNamara, Mr. Fulbright explained, said at first that he and General Wheeler were scheduled to appear before the House Appropriations Committee next Monday and Tuesday, the days suggested by the chairman.

The Arkansas Democrat said that when he asked Mr. McNamara whether they could appear later in the week, the Sec-

Continued on Page 7, Column 3

133 Japanese on Airliner Die As It Crashes Into Tokyo Bay

Boeing 727 Was Approaching Airport—Accident Worst Involving One Plane

By The Associated Press

TOKYO, Saturday, Feb. 5—A Boeing 727 jet airliner carrying 133 Japanese plunged into Tokyo Bay last night sending up a pillar of fire. No survivors were found, making the crash the worst disaster involving a single plane.

Flying in perfect weather, the All-Nippon Airway plane was minutes away from Tokyo Airport when its pilot radioed he would land visually without instruments. Then the airliner vanished from radar screens.

Villagers along the shore and the pilot of another plane said they saw flames stab the darkness of the bay at about 7 P.M., the moment the plane was due to land.

Then fishermen and Japanese Defense Force boats began picking up bodies from the murky waters of the bay. They had picked up about a score when an airline spokesman announced the fuselage had been found with scores of bodies inside. This led to the belief that all aboard were dead.

Grappling hooks from a Coast Guard boat brought up the wreckage.

The plane carried 126 passengers and a crew of seven. Most passengers were returning from the annual winter carnival at Chitose, 600 miles north of Tokyo and point of origin for the flight.

The worst previous single-plane air crash involved a Boeing 707. An Air France liner crashed June 3, 1962, in Paris killing 130. Before that the worst had been another Tokyo crash in 1953 of an Air Force C 124 Globemaster that killed 129 United States servicemen.

The worst disaster involving more than one plane was the death of 134 persons in the

Continued on Page 57, Column 3

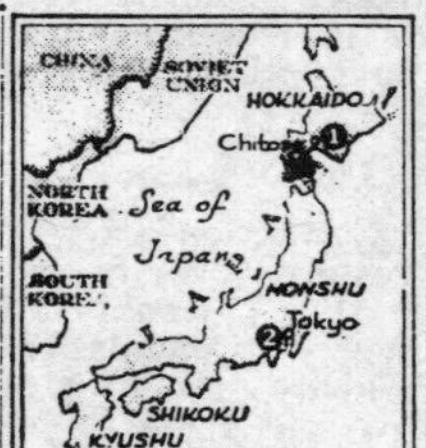

The New York Times Feb. 5, 1966

Jet plane from Chitose (1) crashed in Tokyo Bay (2).

Strike Threat Ousts Cabinet in Belgium

By United Press International

BRUSSELS, Feb. 4—The Government of Premier Pierre Harmel, which had just achieved the settlement of a crisis in the coal-mining area of eastern Belgium, resigned tonight under the threat of a nationwide strike by doctors.

Mr. Harmel submitted the resignation of his six-month-old Social Christian-Socialist Cabinet to King Baudouin. The action followed a day-long session with doctors and health insurance officials in a vain attempt to resolve the crisis.

A palace spokesman later announced that the King had reserved his decision on whether to accept the resignation.

Henry Fayat, Secretary of State for European Affairs, said a problem had arisen at the Cabinet session during discussions

Continued on Page 2, Column 4

NEWS INDEX

Newsmen and relatives of victims look on as a Japanese Coast Guard boat carries in a section of fuselage of the 727 jet airliner which crashed in Tokyo Bay.

United Press International

TOKYO AIR CRASH TAKES 133 LIVES

Continued From Page 1, Col. 6

collision of two airliners over New York City on Dec. 16, 1960.

The disaster was the fourth involving a Boeing 727 in the last six months. The other three, all in the United States, took a total of 127 lives.

Kaheita Okazaki, president of All-Nippon, said the line's five other Boeing 727s would continue to fly unless the Japanese Civil Aviation Board grounds them.

In the early morning hours, he met with reporters and said; "I'm still praying that there will be at least one or even two survivors. Then all will not have been lost."

C.A.B. Offers Help

The Japanese authorities ordered an inquiry, and the Transport Ministry scheduled an initial hearing later today. The plane was reported missing for more than five hours yesterday. Then an airline spokesman announced that bodies and debris had been spotted about eight miles southeast of Tokyo Airport which sits on the edge of the bay.

The bodies were carried back to a Tokyo pier, where relatives awaited to identify the victims. Many of the relatives had been at the airport waiting for the plane. Others rushed there as word that the plane was missing spread over the Japanese television and radio stations.

They waited hopefully until the first bodies were reported found. Then many began to wail. Some fainted.

Twenty of the victims had flown to Chitose only yesterday, sent there by their employer on a one-day holiday to attend the winter carnival, noted for its giant snow statues.

Fourth Boeing 727 Crash

The crash of the Boeing 727 in Tokyo Bay was the fourth fatal accident involving the three-engined jetliner since last Aug. 16 when a United Air Lines plane with 30 aboard crashed in Lake Michigan while preparing to land in Chicago.

On Nov. 8, an American Airlines Boeing 727 with 58 aboard plowed into a hillside while preparing to land at Cincinnati. Four persons survived. Only three days later on Nov. 11, another United Boeing 727 crashed on landing at Salt Lake City and burst into flame. Of the 91 persons aboard, 43 died.

Following the crashes, each taking place during some phase of the landing operation, the United States Civil Aeronautics Board investigated the accidents and reconsidered the airworthiness of the plane. So far, the plane has not been faulted.

Although 81 per cent of the wreckage of the August crash has been recovered from the bottom of Lake Michigan, the cause of the accident remains a mystery. The board is still investigating the other two crashes. But it has noted that circumstances in each differed substantially and that "there is no single causal pattern which would lead us to suspect that the 727 is unairworthy. Because of the rapid burning of the 727 in Salt Lake City, however, the Federal Aviation Agency has recommended certain corrective measures dealing with fire prevention.

Had Perfect Record

Before the four crashes, the Boeing 727, warmly praised by pilots, had a perfect safety record since its introduction on Feb. 1, 1964.

The 133 persons aboard the All-Nippon plane were slightly more than are permitted in the United States.

The maximum number of passengers and crew varies with different airlines. It is figured on the basis of how fast the airline can evaluate the plane. The highest number in the United States is 122 passengers and six crewmen for Pacific Southwest Airlines. United Air Lines carries a maximum of 119 passengers and six crew.

In Washington, the Civil Aeronautics Board, through the State Department, offered aid to the Japanese Government in investigating the crash. The aid would consist of one or two safety experts or accident investigators and use of the board's flight recorder readout machine. The Japanese Government accepted the offer last night.

"All the News That's Fit to Print"

The New York Times.

LATE CITY EDITION
U. S. Weather Bureau Report (Page 95) forecasts: Variably cloudy today; fair and colder tonight and tomorrow. Temp. Range: 45—36; yesterday: 45—39.

NEWS SUMMARY AND INDEX, PAGE 95

SECTION ONE

VOL. CXV..No. 39,488. | NEW YORK, SUNDAY, MARCH 6, 1966. | 50c beyond 50-mile zone from New York City, except on Long Island, higher in air delivery cities | THIRTY CENTS

© 1966 by The New York Times Company, Times Square, New York, N. Y. 10036

LINDSAY CONCEDES HIS TAX PROGRAM PROVIDES SURPLUS

If It Is All Approved, City Will Have $130-Million to Spare, He Reports

15-CENT FARE IN DOUBT

He Links It to Fiscal Plan —Legislature May Balk at Full Program Now

By THOMAS P. RONAN

Mayor Lindsay conceded yesterday that if his entire tax program was adopted and the Legislature authorized an increase in the real estate tax, as he has requested, the city would have a "surplusage" of about $130-million.

He said this could be used to improve city services, to help correct "the dangerous condition" of the financial reserves, or to make "a very small reduction" in the massive debt burden.

He also declared during a television interview that there was doubt as to whether the 15-cent subway and bus fare could be maintained, but he said that how serious that doubt was "remains to be seen." He said studies were under way into all aspects of the situation, including the use of fare zones.

May Affect Legislators

The Mayor's concession that there might be a surplus could make it more difficult for him to persuade the Legislature to enact his full program, as he has repeatedly urged.

When Mr. Lindsay formally made public his tax program on Thursday, some Democratic leaders of the Legislature questioned whether he really needed all that he asked.

Joseph Zaretzki, who as the Democratic leader in the Senate is expected to play a key role in the Legislature's discussions, suggested the Republican Mayor was trying to amass a money cushion so that he would not have to raise taxes again.

'Build-Up' Seen

"I have a sneaking suspicion," Senator Zaretzki said, "that he's trying to build up a tremendous surplus which will carry him through the next four years in contour-seat comfort."

Mr. Lindsay made his comments on the tax program and fare during an interview being taped for use on the WNBC-TV "Searchlight" program at 11 o'clock this morning.

This program is usually presented live, but it was taped at Mr. Lindsay's request because he is trying to keep his Sundays clear of engagements so that he can spend them with his family.

On Wednesday Mr. Lindsay estimated that the budget for the fiscal year beginning July 1 would show a deficit of almost $600-million. The real estate tax increase to which he

Continued on Page 42, Column 1

AND NOW LINDSAY, SONG-DANCE MAN

His Rebuttal Routine Brings Down Inner Circle House

Mayor Lindsay, with straw hat, white gloves and cane, did a five-minute song-and-dance routine last night with a Broadway star and brought down the house at the annual Inner Circle evening of New York political writers.

Breaking a tradition that is many years old, the Mayor took the stage after the three-act lampooning of his administration given by the writers, saying:

"Maybe I can save this show yet!"

In years past, New York's Mayor has been given time for a "rebuttal" of the satire directed at him. But this always has been done in the form of a speech and while members of the journalistic cast were still on stage.

But last night Mr. Lindsay—who acted in his college days and in an off-Broadway show—asked for an empty stage for his rebuttal.

In a style reminiscent of the

Continued on Page 56, Column 1

WORLD'S LEADING PRODUCER of Folk Music on Records. Write for free catalog. Dept. T. Folkways, 165 W. 46 St. NYC—Advt.

Wagner Urges City To Provide Details On Police Shake-Up

By MURRAY SCHUMACH

Former Mayor Robert F. Wagner called on the Lindsay administration yesterday to give full answers to questions about political intervention in the selection of top officers of the Police Department.

"I sincerely hope," he said, "that these questions can be answered satisfactorily and in some detail rather than just a flat denial."

Mr. Wagner said that while he hoped that statements made so far by Mayor Lindsay and Police Commissioner Howard R. Leary were truthful, complete clarification was imperative to restore public confidence in the police.

Mayor Lindsay, who was not aware of Mr. Wagner's comments, contended yesterday that the morale of the vast bulk of the Police Department had not been affected by charges that City Hall interfered unnecessarily in the operations of the department.

Mr. Lindsay predicted that the morale of the police would rise steadily under his administration and that the department would give better pro-

Continued on Page 42, Column 1

HUMPHREY HEADS YOUTH JOBS PANEL

Cabinet Unit, Appointed by Johnson, Will Seek Ways to Reduce Summer Unrest

By JOHN D. POMFRET
Special to The New York Times

SAN ANTONIO, Tex., March 5 — President Johnson created today a study group of Cabinet rank to develop a major Federal program to alleviate teen-age unemployment and other problems of social unrest this summer.

The group will be headed by Vice President Humphrey, who headed a similar panel last summer. But Mr. Humphrey's new mandate is much broader and the group is getting an earlier start this year.

The President has asked for a report by April 1 on what can be done. Last year, he did not set up the group until May 21, and it devoted its energy almost exclusively to trying to persuade private industry and organizations to give summer jobs to youths.

Tension Found in Slums

It is obvious that Mr. Johnson wants to avoid a repetition of such social explosions as the riot in the Watts section of Los Angeles. The riot, which began last Aug. 11 and continued for five days, took 34 lives, injured 1,032 persons and caused millions of dollars in property damage, with total destruction of 200 buildings and damage to 600 more.

The Administration has had reports from some people who are studying racial tensions in the slums that the situation remains potentially explosive in many small cities as well as in the larger ones that have traditionally been the focus of concern.

Mr. Johnson's memorandum to the Vice President creating the study group was released by the White House press office here.

Mr. Johnson is spending the weekend at his ranch 70 miles northwest of San Antonio. It is his first visit to the ranch since

Continued on Page 45, Column 3

ALL 124 ON PLANE ARE DEAD IN CRASH INTO JAPAN'S FUJI

89 Victims From U.S. Include 75 on Tour—Disaster Is Tokyo's 2d in 24 Hours

By ROBERT TRUMBULL
Special to The New York Times

TOKYO, Sunday, March 6—All 124 persons aboard a British jetliner were killed when the Boeing 707 plane caught fire above Mount Fuji yesterday afternoon and crashed on the sacred mountain's eastern slopes.

Among those killed, at least 89 were listed as Americans. These included 75 members of a tour party of sales agents for the Thermo King Company, a Minneapolis concern manufacturing refrigerators, and members of their families.

Scores of persons on the ground watched as the British Overseas Airways Corporation plane began to smoke soon after taking off from here on a flight to Hong Kong. Some said that an explosion tore off the plane's tail fins and that they could see people spilling from the fuselage as the plane fell from an altitude of 3,000 feet.

Wind Suspected

Despite these reports of a fire and explosion aviation experts said that adverse wind conditions around the volcanic cone about 40 miles south of Tokyo may have caused the crash. The vicinity of the 12,388-foot peak is notorious for tricky air currents.

[Technicians in New York said that a condition could exist where turbulent air could have caused the aircraft to undergo a drastic maneuver that might lead to a crash. Such violent forces, they said, might have caused an engine to disintegrate, possibly setting fire to the wing or fuselage.]

The crash on Mount Fuji, which airline pilots frequently fly over to give passengers a close-up look, was the second major air disaster in the Tokyo area within 24 hours and the third in a month. Friday night, a Canadian Pacific Airlines DC-8 jet crashed on the runway while landing at the Tokyo International Airport, killing 64 of the 72 persons aboard.

133 Killed on Feb. 4

Four weeks earlier, on Feb. 4, the worst single plane crash in aviation history occurred near the same airport when 133 persons died as a Boeing 727 jet belonging to All-Nippon Airways, a Japanese domestic line, plunged into Tokyo Bay while preparing to land.

Two more deaths were added to the month's toll this morning when a Japanese military helicopter, searching for bodies still unrecovered from the Boeing 727 crash, made a forced landing in Tokyo Bay and killed two members of the crew.

In all, 323 persons died in the four accidents.

The dense fog that had contributed to the loss of the Canadian jet Friday night was also a factor in the B.O.A.C. tragedy. Instead of landing at Tokyo on schedule Friday, the British plane had been diverted to the United States Air Force base at Itazuke, about 600 miles south, because of the fog.

The plane, with a crew of 11, came to Tokyo yesterday morning and picked up 103 of its 113 passengers for Hong Kong and points west. Normally, the plane would have stayed overnight in Tokyo Friday night

Continued on Page 54, Column 4

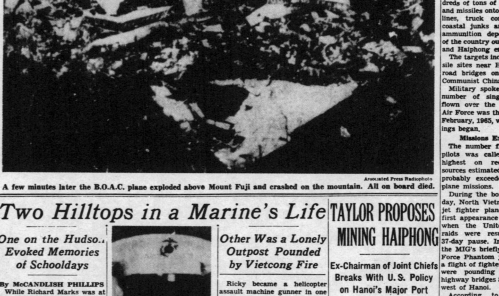

Jetliner Crashes on Mount Fuji After Take-Off From Tokyo Airport

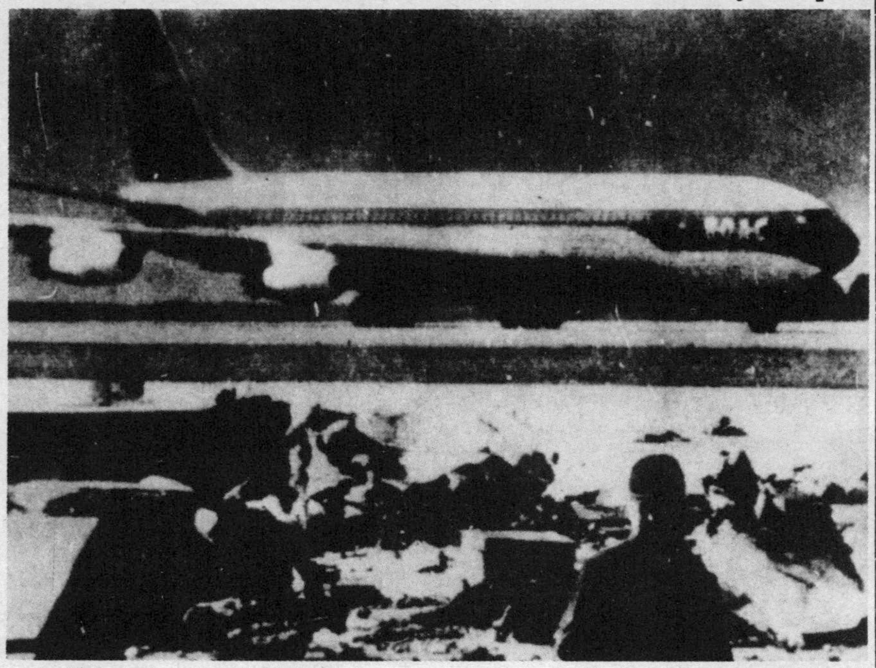

NHK-TV, Tokyo, via Associated Press Radiophoto

Preparing to take off yesterday, B.O.A.C. jet passed wreckage of plane that crashed on Friday at the same airport

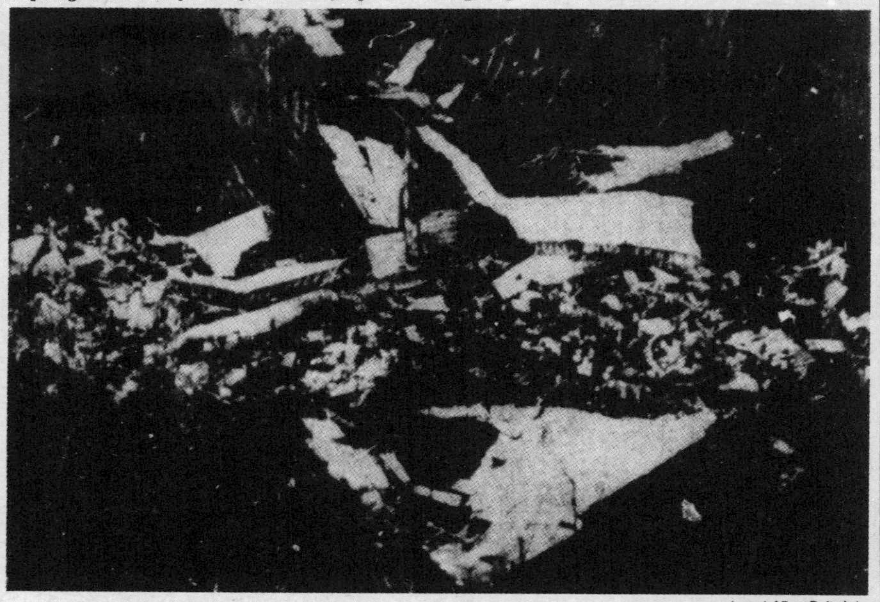

Associated Press Radiophoto

A few minutes later the B.O.A.C. plane exploded above Mount Fuji and crashed on the mountain. All on board died.

Two Hilltops in a Marine's Life

One on the Hudson Evoked Memories of Schooldays

By McCANDLISH PHILLIPS

While Richard Marks was at the Hackley School in Tarrytown he was a quietly agreeable, serious boy. Sometimes he would roam the school's wide hilltop clearing and gaze down at the silvery Hudson or climb to the highest outlook to trace the shimmering outlines of the vast city to the south.

Two hilltops became important in Ricky's life. He loved the high hill at Tarrytown, with its tall shade trees and spell-inducing vistas and the ivy that rustled against the weathered gray stones of the central building. He was one of 380 boys at the preparatory school in 1961 to 1963.

The other hill is just called Hill 69, a combat outpost in Vietnam from which, in the words of one of his letters, "they will probably try to push us off in the next few nights."

Letters Trace Growth

"It is now dusk and we are observing artillery fire in the area around us—it is truly beautiful in a morbid sort of way," he wrote to Peter Whiting, a mathematics instructor at Hackley.

This letter, and dozens of others received from combat zones by his mother and Mr. Whiting, tell a story of troopship impressions, excitement at travel, loneliness, yearnings, fright in battle and cherished plans for civilian tomorrows—a story known to thousands of American youths now serving in Vietnam.

The letters of Pfc. Richard E. Marks of the United States Marines—written in small-figured longhand and often running to five pages—trace the expanding consciousness of a

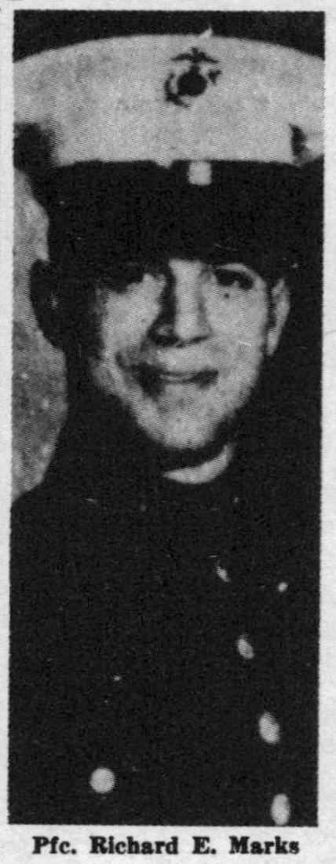

Pfc. Richard E. Marks

young man placed under prolonged and terrible stress.

For Ricky Marks, the transitions from boyhood, to raw Marine recruit, to assault trooper "trained to kill," to the intensity of battle were very swift.

He was born in New York City and reared in Eastchester and California. His father, Robert B. Marks, vice president of a music publishing firm here, died in 1963.

He entered Hackley as a freshman in 1961, but quit school after his sophomore year. After working briefly, he joined the Marines.

Snapshots sent home show Ricky as a trim, muscular young man 5 feet 10 and 150 pounds, before a low-grade fever began to gnaw him down.

Other Was a Lonely Outpost Pounded by Vietcong Fire

Ricky became a helicopter assault machine gunner in one day (they told him he'd have to learn "the hard way.") At the age of 18 he found what it was to be "scared to death" and to feel his bones "aching all the time."

The monsoons and combat patrols of Vietnam stripped him of 30 pounds.

Last July his sergeant told him he had nine more months in Vietnam. "I'll go crazy," he wrote in a letter to his mother, Mrs. Stephen Kramer. "So far we have already had six Marines in the battalion go crazy, and one Sea Bee. This place is too much for an extended period of time."

Mission Is Vetoed

As he saw men die, whole companies almost wiped out Ricky, however, came deeply to believe in the military job of "restoring peace to this troubled land."

From a combat perspective in Vietnam, the letters show, the matters that began perplexing Ricky early were the student demonstrations here in support of Vietcong ambitions and—in his view—political interference with pursuit of the enemy in Vietnam.

"The only complaint I have about our work here is that we cannot do a complete job," his letter last July 30 to Mr. Whiting said. He cited "red tape" that prevented seizing strategic advantages.

"I have seen on more than one occasion when artillery targets (a large number of V.C. troops) were left unfired upon because the permission to fire had to be okayed by so many

Continued on Page 2, Column 3

Pope Pius's Appeals on Jews Published to Counter Accusers

Special to The New York Times

ROME, March 5 — The late Pope Pius XII, during World War II, exhorted the bishops of Germany to help the "oppressed and persecuted" not only of the Roman Catholic faith but everyone "in the name of basic human dignity," according to letters made public today by the Vatican.

There are few direct references to Jews in the Pope's letters, written between 1939 and 1944 and published as the second volume in a series, "Acts and Documents of the Holy See concerning the Second World War."

But the printing of the letters, many of them hitherto unpublished, was regarded by observers as part of the Vatican defense of the Pope against accusations that he did not speak out often enough or vigorously enough against the Nazis' persecution of the Jews.

The volume, consisting of 124 letters, of which 103 are written in German and the rest in Latin, follows the publication last December of the first volume, dealing with the prewar situation.

In one letter, written on April 30, 1945, to Msgr. Konrad von Preysing, then Bishop of Berlin, Pope Pius praised Msgr. Bernhard Lichtenberg, provost of Berlin's St. Hedwig Cathedral, who died in a Nazi prison after his arrest for praying in

Continued on Page 13, Column 1

TAYLOR PROPOSES MINING HAIPHONG

Ex-Chairman of Joint Chiefs Breaks With U.S. Policy on Hanoi's Major Port

By MAX FRANKEL
Special to The New York Times

WASHINGTON, March 5 — Gen. Maxwell D. Taylor, in a conscious dissent from Administration tactics, has publicly called for the mining of Haiphong harbor, North Vietnam's major port.

In his first significant break with official policy, the former Chairman of the Joint Chiefs of Staff opposed the known views of Secretary of State Dean Rusk and other officials who have thus far persuaded President Johnson to avoid direct action against Soviet and other shipping to North Vietnam.

The Administration contends that the mining of Haiphong or a blockade around it would plunge the United States into a direct and serious confrontation with the Soviet Union. This, it is said, would create a crisis over the movement of supplies that have had only a marginal effect on the war in South Vietnam.

A challenge to Soviet ships near Vietnam, officials maintain, would probably evoke a much harsher reaction from Moscow than the partial blockade of Cuba during the missile crisis in 1962.

Other nations, too, it is said, would vigorously object and thus retreat in their support of the United States in Vietnam.

General Taylor, who has been a part-time consultant to President Johnson since he retired

Continued on Page 3, Column 6

CORRECT Metropolitan Opera advertisement appears on Page 30 of this section. (Advt.)

U.S. MARINES FIGHT BIG NORTHERN UNIT ON VIETNAM COAST

They and Southern Troops Oppose 2,000 Regulars—Enemy Death Toll High

AIR RAIDS SET A RECORD

Jets Bomb 2 Missile Sites Near Hanoi—Reds' MIG's Attack American Pilots

By NEIL SHEEHAN
Special to The New York Times

SAIGON, March 5 — United States marines and South Vietnamese paratroops fought a ferocious battle with 2,000 North Vietnamese regulars yesterday and today in the coastal province of Quangngai.

The action, along with two smaller battles in the country, was said to have cost the enemy 759 men dead and 100 weapons lost.

In the Quangngai clash, American and South Vietnamese losses were officially described as light in relation to the total forces involved. But reliable military sources said that some Marine and paratroop units had suffered heavy casualties, including a large number of wounded.

The number of marines and South Vietnamese troops in the battle was estimated at 7,000.

Bombers Range Widely

The action came as American bombing attacks against North Vietnam reached record intensity.

Air Force and Navy pilots made 61 raids against North Vietnam yesterday, raining hundreds of tons of bombs, rockets and missiles onto transportation lines, truck convoys, barges, coastal junks and supply and ammunition depots over most of the country outside the Hanoi and Haiphong enclaves.

The targets included two missile sites near Hanoi and railroad bridges on the route to Communist China.

Military spokesmen said the number of single-plane raids flown over the North by the Air Force was the highest since February, 1965, when the bombings began.

Missions Exceed 250

The number flown by Navy pilots was called one of the highest on record. Military sources estimated that the total probably exceeded 250 single-plane missions.

During the bombings yesterday, North Vietnamese MIG-17 jet fighter planes made their first appearance since Jan. 31, when the United States air raids were resumed after a 37-day pause. In one instance the MIG's briefly attacked Air Force Phantom jets protecting a flight of fighter-bombers that were pounding railroad and highway bridges 80 miles northwest of Hanoi.

According to a military spokesman, three MIG's suddenly dived at the Phantoms. Each MIG made a single fir-

Continued on Page 3, Column 4

Today's Sections

*Included in all copies in the New York metropolitan area and adjacent territory.

Index to Subjects

All 124 on Jet Are Killed in Crash on Mount Fuji

89 FROM U.S. DIE; CAUSE DISPUTED

Witnesses Tell of Fire and Midair Explosion—Others Blame Wind Currents

Continued From Page 1, Col. 3

and left for Hong Kong about two hours earlier yesterday.

Numerous members of a Japanese military unit training on the slopes of Mount Fuji witnessed the explosion of the plane at about 2:17 P. M. (12:17 A. M. New York Time). One of the witnesses, who watched the crash through binoculars, told Japanese reporters that the plane "began to emit a white smoke from its tail" while flying above the mountain, 40 miles south of Tokyo.

"An explosion blew off the plane's tail fins and it started to fall in corkscrew fashion," he said. "As the falling plane reached a point about 3,000 feet above the ground, we could see clothes dropping out of the burning fuselage like feathers from a bird, and human beings falling from the plane with their arms spread wide as if they were practicing sky-diving."

The main part of the plane plunged into the dense brush on the mountainside below the snow line, at about 4,500 feet above sea level. Bits of the wreckage were spread over a wide area near the town of Gotemba, a popular ski resort.

Rescue parties reaching the crash site reported that all 124 bodies were recovered within hours. Authorities discounted early reports of a collision in the air between the jetliner and a smaller aircraft.

By nightfall, the police reported, more than 60 bodies had been carried down the mountain to the Daijoji and Zenryuji Buddhist temples in Gotemba, where they were placed in wooden coffins. Buddhist temples are the traditional collecting stations for victims of mass tragedies in this disaster-prone country, which is hit frequently by earthquakes, fires, floods and typhoons.

Mountains are revered in Japan and Mount Fuji is the most sacred of all. The graceful volcanic peak is venerated by Buddhists and Shintoists alike.

Police Chief Saw Smoke

TOKYO, Sunday, March 6 (UPI)—Zenzo Kawano, Police Chief of the suburban town of Gotemba near the crash site, said that smoke attracted his attention to the falling plane.

"The tail appeared to be coming apart and several pieces dropped to the ground," he said. "Then the plane went into a spiral and slammed into the side of the mountain."

Mr. Kawano said he did not hear any explosion while the plane was in air and did not remember seeing any flames until the main fuselage hit the ground.

"Then there was a huge puff of smoke," he said. "I suppose some of the fuel exploded."

United States Marines on a nearby firing range were among the first to reach the scene. Some of the passengers still were strapped in their seats, they said.

Lieut. Thomas Quinn of Modesto, Calif., said when he arrived on the scene he "found wreckage scattered all over the side of the mountain."

"I don't know what happened, but the plane must have blown up in the air," he added.

There was other evidence to substantiate this view. The rear stabilizer and rudder — both pieces of the tail assembly — were found lying near a road

The New York Times   March 6, 1966
BRITISH jet crashed on Mt. Fuji (1) a day after Canadian plane crashed at airport (2) while landing. Japanese aircraft plunged into Tokyo Bay (3) Feb. 4.

about five miles from the crash scene. Both were covered with scorch and smoke marks.

Investigators on Way

TOKYO, Sunday March 6 (Reuters) — B.O.A.C.'s board chairman, Sir Giles Guthrie, was to arrive in Tokyo today with a six-man team to investigate yesterday's crash.

Japanese Premier Eisaku Sato today cabled his "deepest sympathy" over the crash to British Prime Minister Harold Wilson.

CRASH CUT SHORT A 'FABULOUS' TRIP

75 Aboard on Orient Tour Offered by Company

"Seventeen fabulous days in the Orient" was the enticing promise offered 75 Thermo King Corporation dealers and their wives. It was their reward for hard work.

They had had just seven of those days, seeing the palaces and wonders of Japan, when the jetliner that was taking them to Hong Kong crashed against the side of Mount Fuji yesterday, killing all aboard.

The tragedy was felt in a score of states, among them Colorado, Michigan, California, New York, Iowa, Wisconsin, Minnesota, Pennsylvania, Ohio, Missouri, Massachusetts, Arkansas, Utah and Minnesota, home state of the corporation, which has its headquarters in Minneapolis.

Detroit was the home of Mr. and Mrs. Charles Heemstra, who had been married just two weeks ago and for whom the trip was to be a honeymoon. They had just bought a new home and were to move in when they returned. Mrs. Heemstra leaves two children from a previous marriage.

From Philadelphia came Mr. and Mrs. David Weiss and Mr. and Mrs. Jack Weiss. The men were brothers and partners in a local dealership for Thermo King, manufacturers of refrigerating equipment. The David Weisses leave two sons and three grandchildren. The Jack Weisses had no children.

From upstate New York were Mr. and Mrs. Joseph H. Richings Sr. of Derby; John T. Dooley Sr. of Buffalo; Louis J. DeCarolis of Rochester, and Charles Galbo of Cheektowaga.

The Richings leave five children under 18 years of age.

Mr. Galbo had a premonition that he might not return from the trip. He told that to a friend. The friend said: "We had a standing joke that if anything happened to him he'd will me his gas tank and outboard motor. Only yesterday I got a

card from him saying he was going to give them to me."

Several of the dealers who won the trip for outstanding sales records last year decided not to go. Bobby Brown of Little Rock, Ark., sold his tickets because it was inconvenient for him to leave his business.

Leonard Herlinger of Cincinnati was prepared to take the trip but then "decided in the last few days not to go," he said.

Michael Ligeros of Detroit gave his tickets to Mr. and Mrs. Leland Long of Pueblo, Colo. "They were really excited," Mr. Ligeros said. "It was the first time the Longs had left Colorado."

Mr. Ligeros's brother and sister-in-law, Mr. and Mrs. William G. Ligeros of Salt Lake City were aboard the plane.

"It's almost impossible to believe," said an official of the travel agency that made arrangements for the Japanese part of the tour. "They had such a pleasant stay in Japan and were looking forward to seeing Hong Kong." The group was also to visit Hawaii.

The three teen-age children of Mr. and Mrs. Ralph Kerwin of Minneapolis received a heartening telegram early yesterday morning. It said: "We're OK. Love, Dad."

Only later did the children learn that telegram had been sent because their father thought they might be worried about a plane that had crashed

in Tokyo the day before.

Mr. Kerwin was controller of the Thermo King company.

In Minneapolis, a spokesman for Thermo King said, "this has got to be the most disastrous thing a company could experience." He said almost everyone of the firm's top dealers was on the plane.

OTHER DISASTERS IN AIR RECALLED

Fuji Crash Was 4th Worst Involving One Plane

Yesterday's air crash near Tokyo, in which 124 persons were killed, was the fourth worst air disaster involving a single plane. Two of the others also took place near the Japanese capital.

The worst was last Feb. 4, when an All-Nippon Airlines Boeing 727 plunged into Tokyo Bay, killing all 133 persons aboard.

On June 18, 1953, 129 United States servicemen lost their lives when a C-124 Air Force Globemaster crashed near Tokyo.

The death toll yesterday was also exceeded on June 3, 1962, when 130 persons were killed in the crash of a Boeing 707 jet at Orly Airport in Paris.

On Promotion Tour

Seventy-five of the victims in yesterday's crash into Mount Fuji were members of the sales force of a Minneapolis refrigerator manufacturing company and their relatives, who had been touring the Far East in an annual promotional event.

In the Orly crash 121 of the victims were members of the Atlanta Art Association.

A two-plane collision over Staten Island on Dec. 16, 1960, killed 134 persons—127 in the planes and seven on the ground.

Earlier aviation accidents in which groups of Americans died included a crash of a Belgian Airlines Boeing 707 while it was approaching Brussels from New York on Feb. 15, 1961. Among the 73 victims were 18 members of the United States figure-skating team who had been on their way to the world figure-skating championships in Prague.

Many members of the California State Polytechnical football team were among the 22 persons killed when a chartered aircraft crashed on take-off at Toledo's airport on Oct. 29, 1960.

Associated Press Radiophoto
ON A TRAGIC COURSE: B.O.A.C. jetliner, trailing smoke, plunges toward crash on Mount Fuji and death for 124 persons aboard. Photo was taken by Hiroaki Ikegami, an amateur photographer vacationing near mountain. His 35-mm. camera had 200-mm. lens.

"All the News That's Fit to Print"

The New York Times

LATE CITY EDITION

U.S. Weather Bureau Report (Page 95) forecasts: Light rain then variably cloudy today; fair tonight and tomorrow. Temp. Range: 53—44; yesterday: 54—36.

NEWS SUMMARY AND INDEX, PAGE 95

SECTION ONE

VOL. CXVI..No. 39,733. © 1966 by The New York Times Company. Times Square, New York, N. Y. 10036 NEW YORK, SUNDAY, NOVEMBER 6, 1966. 50c beyond 50-mile zone from New York City, except on Long Island. Higher in air delivery cities. 35 CENTS

REPUBLICAN GAINS IN HOUSE LIKELY TO BE MODERATE

Major Rise Found Blocked by Strength of 28 of 48 Democratic Freshmen

NO SENATE SHIFT SEEN

Nationwide Report Shows G.O.P. Will Pick Up Net of Five Governorships

By WARREN WEAVER Jr.

Special to The New York Times

WASHINGTON, Nov. 5 — Three of every five of the Democratic Congressmen who carried Republican districts in their party's landslide in 1964 appear likely to win re-election next Tuesday.

This relatively strong showing by four dozen Democratic freshmen looks like a major factor in an election that will probably produce Republican gains of about average off-year size in the House and a little less in the Senate.

The Republicans might ordinarily have expected to reclaim all or most of these 48 House seats this fall, on the reasonable assumption that they would revert to past political preferences in the absence of a Presidential contest.

Had the Republicans done so, this recapture, plus the 10 traditionally Democratic seats they expect to win next week, could have built something like the 50-to-60-seat victory some of their leaders have optimistically forecast.

Figure Could Rise

An end-of-the-campaign survey by The New York Times indicates, however, that about 28 of the 48 Democratic freshmen will be returned to Congress. This figure could rise to 34 on a heavy Democratic tide or fall to 23 under Republican pressure.

The Times survey, the last of three checks of political trends in all 50 states during the campaign, produced the following conclusions:

¶Republicans are favored to gain a net of five Governors, win 20 of the 35 state elections and oust Democrats in Arizona, California, Minnesota and Nebraska, among other states.

¶The Senate election appears to be a stalemate, with Republicans winning 15 of 35 seats, the same number they now hold. At best, the Repub-

Continued on Page 68, Column 1

PRINCETON HALTS HARVARD BY 18-14

Upset Causes Four-Way Tie in Ivy League Title Race

Harvard and the University of California, Los Angeles, lost their first college football games of the season, while Notre Dame and Michigan State remained undefeated yesterday.

Princeton downed Harvard, 18-14, to cause a four-way tie for the Ivy League lead. Washington beat U.C.L.A., ranked No. 3, 16-3; Notre Dame, No. 1, routed Pittsburgh, 40-0, and Michigan State, No. 2, whipped Iowa, 56-7.

Scores of other leading games:

Alabama	21	L. S. U.	0
Arkansas	31	Rice	20
Army	20	Geo. Wash.	7
Colgate	20	Bucknell	0
Cornell	23	Brown	14
Dartmouth	56	Columbia	14
Duke	9	Navy	7
Georgia	27	Florida	10
Ga. Tech	14	Virginia	13
N. Car. St.	24	Maryland	21
Nebraska	21	Kansas	13
Ohio State	7	Indiana	0
Purdue	23	Wisconsin	0
S. M. U.	21	Tex. A&M.	14
Syracuse	12	Penn State	10
Texas	26	Baylor	14
So. Calif.	35	California	9
Yale	17	Penn	14
Miami (Fla.)	10	Tulane	10

BASKETBALL

The New York Knickerbockers won their sixth game in 10 starts by defeating the Detroit Pistons, 115-104, before 12,620 fans at Madison Square Garden. Willis Reed led the New York scoring attack with 32 points.

HORSE RACING

Destro defeated Straight Deal by a nose to win the $56,500 Ladies Handicap at Aqueduct.

Details in Section 5.

O'Connor Attacks Slums; Governor Acts on Addicts

Democrat Urges State Insurance Protection for Homeowners

By MAURICE CARROLL

"Slums have gotten infinitely worse" during the eight years of the Rockefeller administration, Frank D. O'Connor said yesterday as he proposed his own state housing program.

The Democratic candidate for Governor suggested a plan that would include state-sponsored insurance to help families save their homes if the chief wage-earner died or was disabled, and a state subsidy of interest payments on mortgages held by local housing authorities.

Mr. O'Connor was the only one of the four major candidates to do any active campaigning yesterday, the final Saturday before the state election.

At Stake on Tuesday

Close to 6 million New Yorkers, voting from 6 A.M. to 9 P.M. on Tuesday, will choose a Governor, Lieutenant Governor, Attorney General and Controller, the entire Legislature, all of the state's delegation in the House of Representatives and members of next year's constitutional convention, and will vote on a dozen state questions.

In a midday news conference at the Hotel Commodore, Mr. O'Connor said yesterday that his housing program would cost "not in excess of $12 to $13-million" a year. He headed in

Continued on Page 88, Column 3

2,000 Narcotics Users to Be Committed Here in City-State Plan

Governor Rockefeller, apparently convinced that crime in the streets is a pivotal election issue, announced yesterday a major city-state plan for getting New York City's narcotics addicts off the streets and treating them.

Although the announcement was described as a joint one with the city, it was made by the Governor's office alone only three days before the state elections.

Mr. Rockefeller, hoarse from his long campaign, also hit hard at the narcotics-breeds-crime issue at a morning news conference in the New York Hilton hotel, his campaign headquarters.

'Cautiously Optimistic'

It was his only public activity on a day devoted largely to preparing for two television debates today and for a round-the-state barnstorming trip by air on Monday.

The Governor described himself as "cautiously optimistic" about the outcome.

Under the new city-state plan, which will be part of the Governor's controversial program of compulsory commitment, 2,000 addicts convicted of narcotics misdemeanors will be committed for a three-to-six-month induction process at the Rikers Island Penitentiary. Then

Continued on Page 88, Column 5

BROWN PRESSING TO CATCH REAGAN

Trailing in Polls, He Pins Hope on Last-Minute Aid From the Undecided

By GLADWIN HILL

Special to The New York Times

LOS ANGELES, Nov. 5—At noon on Thursday, as Ronald Reagan was being showered with confetti and cheered by thousands in a downtown San Francisco parade, Gov. Edmund G. Brown was airborne on the way to San Diego from Los Angeles.

At San Diego, the Governor addressed a small roomful of people at a state museum, called on the Mayor and spoke at a shopping center rally where juveniles outnumbered prospective voters.

The contrasting vignettes reflected, albeit in exaggerated proportion, the differing impetus of the two rivals' campaigns as California's gubernatorial race approached the finish line next week.

The 55-year-old Republican actor's drive had the glow of victory within reach. The Democratic Governor's bid for a third four-year term was taut with hope.

On the basis of the latest opinion surveys, Mr. Reagan appeared to have a commanding lead. But the standings

Continued on Page 70, Column 4

Minutemen Accused Of Having Informer Among State Police

By WILL LISSNER

Queens authorities said yesterday that for two years a state policeman had stolen heavy weapons for the right-wing Minutemen and had tipped them off on state and Federal investigations.

District Attorney Nat H. Hentel of Queens said that the informer was one of three state troopers who had formed a Minuteman drill team upstate. He declined to name the man because the investigation of his activities was continuing.

The prosecutor said that according to the state trooper's own statements, he did the following for the organization, which fears that a Communist uprising is imminent:

Found During Raids

¶Stole or otherwise obtained antitank cannons, grenades, a mortar, a recoilless rifle and other weapons.

¶Passed on at least one state police investigation report, communications data about upstate police and other governmental agencies and a library of military training manuals, including some covering demolition devices and explosive charges.

¶Acted as an organizer for them and recruited two National Guardsmen as possible organizers of Minutemen groups.

The information about the trooper's activities was found in material seized on Oct. 30

Continued on Page 27, Column 1

GIANT BLACKOUTS STILL POSSIBLE, U.S. STUDY FINDS

But Report to Johnson Cites Steps Taken to Prevent Another 1965 Failure

By EILEEN SHANAHAN

Special to The New York Times

WASHINGTON, Nov. 5 — Electric companies in the Northeastern United States and Canada have not done enough during the last year to insure against widespread power failures, the Federal Power Commission said today.

In a report on the long-term consequences of the 80,000-square-mile blackout in the Northeast that took place a year ago next Wednesday, the commission said many steps had been taken to make the recurrence of such failures "less likely."

But the commission expressed its "greatest concern" over the continuing unreadiness of individual utilities "to take positive and timely actions" to make sure their power systems would continue operating in the face of a major disruption in service elsewhere in the Northeast.

Improvements Noted

"All of the utilities [in the Northeast] have improved their readiness for such an eventuality," the commission said, "but only a few have adopted a program of automatic actions."

The Northeastern power systems still need stronger interconnections to serve as emergency sources of power, the commission said.

Until these interconnections are strengthened, it said, the over-all system could again split apart, leaving isolated utility systems unable to cope with their power needs, "if a severe, though unlikely, incident should occur."

"In such a case, prevention of another cascading failure could depend upon prompt action in shedding part of the load of the systems affected," it added.

Coordinated arrangements for automatic load shedding—that is, cutting off service to low-priority customers in order to continue to serve the rest—have not been made, the commission said.

Action Here Cited

There are also other aspects of coordinated emergency planning on which the 21 principal utilities in the Northeastern United States and Canada have not reached "a full and satisfactory consensus," according to the report.

The commission said progress had been "more conclusive and encouraging" in planning for restoration of power after a failure.

In New York City, where the power was off as long as 13 hours in last year's blackout, the commission noted that new equipment was being installed to permit faster restoration of service and to minimize the danger of equipment damage, which prolonged the blackout there.

The commission found that the chances of another power failure triggered by exactly the same cause as last year's

Continued on Page 44, Column 3

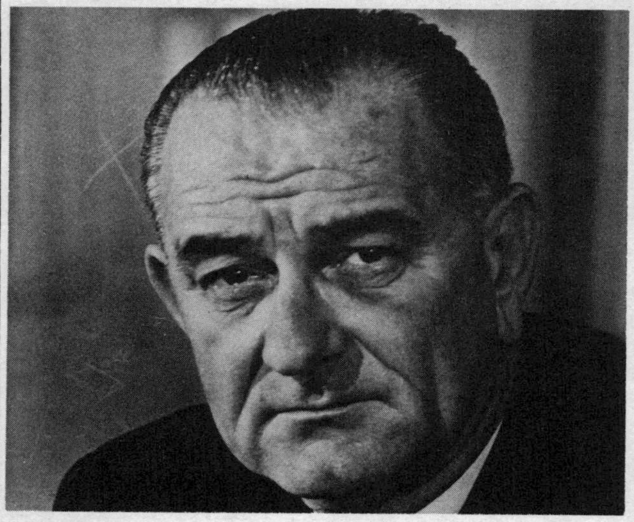

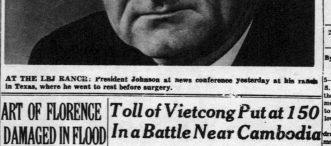

AT THE LBJ RANCH: President Johnson at news conference yesterday at his ranch in Texas, where he went to rest before surgery.

ART OF FLORENCE DAMAGED IN FLOOD

Some Places Under 10 Feet of Water—Death Toll in 3 Nations Put at 87

By ROBERT C. DOTY

Special to The New York Times

ROME, Nov. 5—Irreparable damage to some of the world's great art treasures in Florence was part of the cost of the gales and floods that swept Italy yesterday and today.

[At least 87 persons were known dead in floods and landslides caused by storms in Italy, Austria and Switzerland, according to Reuters. Page 3.]

Torrential rains and winds up to 90 miles an hour battered the country for several hours beginning early Friday, centering on Tuscany and its capital, Florence. Venice, Grosseto and Trento were also hard hit.

The Arno River burst through its banks, flooding much of Florence to depths of up to 10 feet, cutting rail, road and wire communications and, farther downstream, inundating parts of Pisa.

"Damage is incalculable," said Mayor Piero Bargellini of Florence, who is a writer and renaissance art expert. "The war, all of the last war, probably did not do as much damage to Florence as the Arno did yesterday."

Door of Paradise Damaged

The greatest single loss yet identified was the damage to the sculptured bronze door of the Baptistry facing the city's Cathedral, Il Duomo.

Five of the ten panels of the East Door, or Door of Paradise, executed by the 15th-century Florentine sculptor Lorenzo Ghiberti, depicting biblical scenes, were swept off by flood waters. [They were later recovered from the mud, badly scratched and marked, United Press International reported from Florence.]

Paintings and pieces of sculpture in the Uffizi Gallery, near the Piazza della Signoria, were spared, except for some works undergoing restoration in ground-floor studios, but the entire collection of more than 130,000 photo negatives of art works stored in the basement was destroyed.

Causes of Deaths Varied

The death toll included victims of drowning, collapse of houses, highway accidents caused by wind and rain, asphyxiation from broken gas mains and exhaustion of rescue workers.

Property damage was certain to be many billions of lire, perhaps as much as a billion dollars.

The streets of Florence, Venice, Grosseto and smaller towns were a shambles of floodwater, mud, hundreds of automobiles piled helter-skelter on top of one another, household goods and contents of stores floating on the muddy current. Water, gas and power lines were out of service in Florence. Drinking water was being distributed from trucks.

In the Florence area and in other parts of Italy, air force and police helicopters were being used to rescue scores of people still marooned on housetops 24 hours after the storm began. An Italian reporter, accompanying a rescue flight, described women with babies in

Continued on Page 3, Column 2

Toll of Vietcong Put at 150 In a Battle Near Cambodia

Special to The New York Times

SAIGON, South Vietnam, Nov. 5—More than 150 Vietcong guerrillas have been killed in fighting in the thick jungles northwest of Saigon near the Cambodian border, it was reported tonight. Two companies of 80 to 90 South Vietnamese militiamen have suffered crippling losses in separate actions, but so far American losses have been slight.

[United States Air Force pilots shot down two MIG-21 jets northwest of Hanoi late Saturday in an air clash that lasted under three minutes, The Associated Press reported. Page 36.]

Reinforcements Called In

The fighting northwest of Saigon, which began last Thursday, has been largely between units of a company or less in strength. Each time the Americans have found the enemy, however, they have called in company after company of reinforcements.

A United States military spokesman said tonight that the campaign had grown to multibrigade strength, and some observers estimated that 7,000 to 8,000 American troops were moving through the jungles within a radius of 20 miles of Tayninh, the capital of Tayninh Province, 50 miles northwest of Saigon.

According to intelligence sources, the enemy troops be-

Continued on Page 36, Column 1

F.B.I. Seizes Two And Charges Plot On Zambia Copper

By ARNOLD H. LUBASCH

Federal agents arrested two American citizens yesterday, charging a bizarre conspiracy to blow up a vital railroad bridge in the African nation of Zambia.

The two were accused of planning to make a substantial profit in copper speculation by causing a serious international shortage of the metal. Zambia is the world's second largest copper producer.

The bridge is a key link in the only railroad used to transport Zambian copper to East African ports for shipment to world markets, the Federal agents said here. They said destruction of the bridge could seriously interrupt the supply of copper and substantially raise its price.

'Like a Dime Novel'

The agent who released the announced of the arrests observed of the alleged plot: "When I first heard it, I thought it was fantastic. It's almost like a dime novel. Fantastic. But it happened."

Agents of the Federal Bureau of Investigation made the arrests, which were announced by Acting Attorney General Ramsey Clark.

F.B.I. Director J. Edgar Hoover identified the two alleged conspirators as Rolf Duenbier, vice president and New York manager of a German metals concern, and Jay Aubrey Elliott, a professional diver and yacht captain.

Mr. Hoover said the 36-year-old Duenbier was born in Aachen, Germany, came to the United States several years

Continued on Page 18, Column 4

GHANA RELEASES GUINEAN ENVOYS

Haile Selassie and Nasser Persuade Ankrah to Act—African Parley Saved

By THOMAS F. BRADY

Special to The New York Times

ADDIS ABABA, Ethiopia, Nov. 5—Emperor Haile Selassie of Ethiopia announced tonight that Guinean diplomats held in Ghana for a week had been released.

An agreement for the release was reached in a 3½-hour session by the Emperor, Lieut. Gen. Joseph A. Ankrah, Ghana's Chief of State, and President Gamal Abdel Nasser of the United Arab Republic.

The grim-faced General Ankrah, who had yielded to the others' pressure, emerged from the bargaining session with the Emperor and President Nasser, who were wreathed in smiles, to tell the newsmen the three had succeeded in saving the current top-level conference of the Organization of African Unity from threatened disintegration over the Ghana-Guinea dispute.

President William V. S. Tubman of Liberia, who had also participated in the bargaining, had left an hour and a half earlier.

Emperor Reads Statement

Standing on the steps of Africa Hall, the headquarters of the Organization of African Unity, Haile Selassie read the statement saying that the conferees had reached agreement and that the Guinean diplomats, headed by their Foreign Minister, had already been released and were en route here to participate in the conference.

The statement said also that the chiefs of state had telegraphed President Sékou Touré of Guinea to join them here tomorrow.

In return, the statement continued, Haile Selassie, Mr. Nasser and Mr. Tubman had made themselves responsible for obtaining the release of Ghanaians "who may be detained against their will in Guinea."

The statement referred only to the diplomats held by Ghana. The group of Guineans arrested Oct. 29 included four members of the delegation en route to Addis Ababa and 15 Guinean students who were flying on the same plane.

The scene that meant that the facade of African unity at least would survive was lighted by the neon tubes that illuminate the big new Africa Hall.

General Ankrah was dressed in the splendor of a Ghanian tribal chief, wearing a red, green and gold cloth draped over one shoulder like a toga. Haile Selassie and Mr. Nasser wore dark business suits, sharply contrasting with the primitive costume for which General Ankrah had abandoned the general's uniform that is his usual garb.

The solution that ended the week of suspense here was at

Continued on Page 14, Column 3

M'NAMARA PLANS REDUCED BUILD-UP IN VIETNAM IN '67

Draft Calls to Be Cut Back for the Next 4 Months if Present Trends Continue

HE TALKS WITH JOHNSON

Secretary Says the Enemy's Morale Has Deteriorated as Attacks Increase

Transcript of news conference is printed on Page 43.

By ROBERT B. SEMPLE Jr.

Special to The New York Times

JOHNSON CITY, Tex., Nov. 5—Secretary of Defense Robert S. McNamara said today that the American troop commitment in Vietnam would continue to grow, but at a substantially lower rate than in 1966.

This means, he said, that the draft calls for the next four months "will be significantly smaller."

Mr. McNamara flew to the LBJ ranch this morning and conferred with President Johnson on the defense budget for next year and the military situation in Southeast Asia.

This afternoon he met with reporters in the front yard of the Johnson home. He read from a prepared statement and then answered a few questions.

The President, who sat next to Mr. McNamara and occasionally offered comments, arrived here yesterday to rest before minor surgery sometime in the next three weeks.

Mr. McNamara was the first of what is expected to be a stream of official visitors.

Laboratory Tests Due

Mr. Johnson will undergo laboratory tests in San Antonio Monday and will vote Tuesday in an election in which Republicans have sought to make his conduct of the war in Vietnam an issue.

In general, Mr. McNamara's tone was optimistic. He declared, as he has before, that the North Vietnamese "can no longer achieve a military victory."

He also said that a new study based on the interrogation of enemy prisioners showed that allied efforts on the ground and in the air had impaired North Vietnamese morale, exposed jungle sanctuaries, reduced the enemy's food supplies, and brought the level of enemy deaths in combat to 1,000 a week.

Mr. McNamara cautioned that his predictions were subject to "unforeseen contingencies."

He said there was a strong possibility of further cuts in the "planned rate" of production of air ordnance—bombs, rockets and ammunition.

No "sharp increases" are planned in the number of air attacks in Vietnam, now averaging about 25,000 individual sorties a month, he said.

The secretary said that the total number of men inducted into the armed services in Au-

Continued on Page 43, Column 1

Aircraft in Disaster Test Land on City Piers and Lots

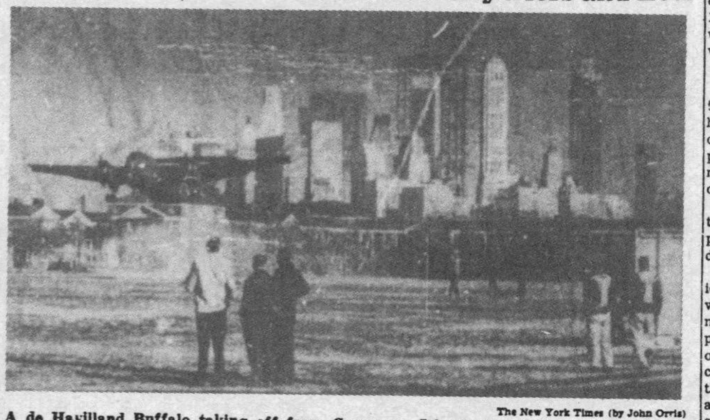

The New York Times (by John Orris)

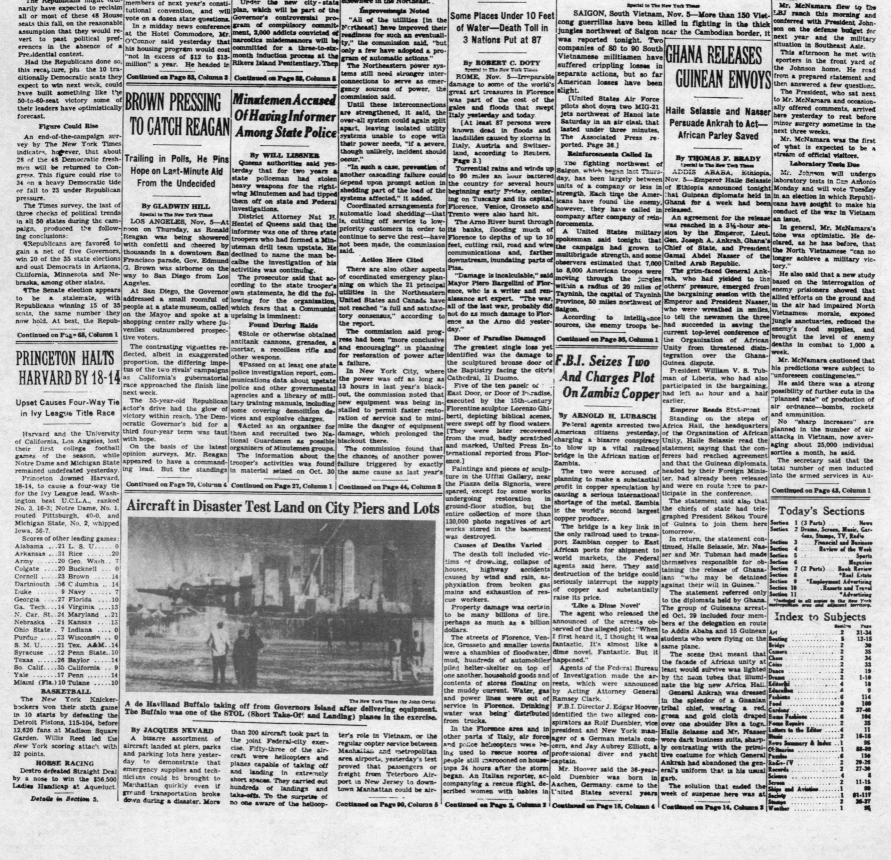

A de Havilland Buffalo taking off from Governors Island after delivering equipment. The Buffalo was one of the STOL (Short Take-Off and Landing) planes in the exercise.

By JACQUES NEVARD

A bizarre assortment of aircraft landed at piers, parks and parking lots here yesterday to demonstrate that emergency supplies and technicians could be brought to Manhattan quickly even if ground transportation broke down during a disaster. More than 200 aircraft took part in the joint Federal-city exercise. Fifty-three of the aircraft were helicopters and planes capable of taking off and landing in extremely short spaces. They carried out hundreds of landings and take-offs. To the surprise of no one aware of the helicopter's role in Vietnam, or the regular copter service between Manhattan and metropolitan area airports, yesterday's test proved that passengers or freight from Teterboro Airport in New Jersey to downtown Manhattan could be air-

Continued on Page 90, Column 5

Today's Sections

Index to Subjects

ART OF FLORENCE DAMAGED IN FLOOD

Continued From Page 1, Col. 5

their arms who were waving from perches inaccessible to the helicopter because of adjoining obstacles and were forced to await rescue by boat.

The 11th-century Ponte Vecchio, the only one of the Florence bridges left standing by retreating German forces in 1944, again survived, but was badly damaged.

Seventy prisoners in the Florence jail escaped during the flood and one was found dead in his cell.

The Adige River broke its banks at Trento, causing at least nine deaths in the city and forcing thousands to flee.

At Least 87 Are Dead

ROME, Nov. 5 (Reuters)—At least 87 persons were counted dead today in floods and landslides caused by storms in Italy, Austria and Switzerland.

More than 50 of the dead were pelled from the mud and water that covered much of Italy, 20 persons were known dead in Austria, and an avalanche in Switzerland killed five.

The Italian Cabinet met under Premier Aldo Moro and allocated 10-billion lira ($16-million) for emergency relief.

Damaged art in Florence included, in the old abbey of San Salvi, the "Last Supper," a 16th-century fresco by Andrea del Sarto, which was still under water.

In the Bargello Museum, a collection of arms was under a mound of mud. The ground floor of the Museum of Natural History of Science was damaged and its collection of wax models destroyed.

Floodwater filled the Strozzi Palace 10 feet deep, drowning its 400-year-old archives and a collection of furniture.

Refugees Huddle in Church

FLORENCE, Italy, Nov. 5 (AP)—Inside the basilica of Santa Croce, hundreds of Florentine homeless huddled among the stone tombs of Michelangelo, Galileo, Machiavelli and other giants of the Renaissance.

Other Museums Listed

FLORENCE, Nov. 5 (UPI)— Ugo Procacci, Superintendent of Galleries, gave this damage report on other places housing art works:

Academy and San Marco Museums: all art works salvaged; Horne and Santa Croce Museums: still flooded, situation considered "very grave;" Bardini Museum: still unreachable, collections of ancient musical instruments "certainly" under water; Bueonarroto House: still isolated, but art works possibly salvaged by director; Medici Chapel: damaged, but extent not known; State Archives: six feet of water destroyed or damaged all documents on the lower shelves.

Mr. Procacci had no report on the National Library, Italy's second largest, where tens of thousands of books were reported to be under water in the basement.

The Arno River Recedes After Flooding Historic Areas in Italian City

United Press International Cablephoto

A boat was left stranded in Florence's Piazza della Signoria, once the Forum of the Republic, after flood ebbed. At right, in the Loggia dei Lanzi, a meeting place, stands Cellini's Perseus holding the head of Medusa. To the left is a copy of Michelangelo's David, and beyond is Bandinelli's Hercules and Cacus. Palazzo Vecchi is at left.

The famed Ponte Vecchio (Old Bridge) across the Arno River in the center of Florence, heavily damaged by the flood.

Wide World Photos

The New York Times.

VOL. CXVI..No. 39,816.   © 1967 by The New York Times Company.   NEW YORK, SATURDAY, JANUARY 28, 1967.   10 CENTS

500,000 IN THE CITY GO WITHOUT HEAT IN HOUSING STRIKE

Elderly Are the Hardest Hit in Public Developments Affected by Dispute

6,000 EMPLOYES ARE OUT

'Real Progress' Is Reported by Union as Negotiations With Officials Resume

By DAMON STETSON

Nearly all of the 500,000 residents in public housing developments here were left without heat or hot water yesterday by a strike of 6,000 employes of the City Housing Authority.

Chicago Is Crippled By a 23-Inch Snow; Police Kill Looter

By DONALD JANSON
Special to The New York Times

CHICAGO, Jan. 27—A city accustomed to snowstorms succumbed to one today.

NATION'S BANKS SET 5¾% RATE; REBUKING CHASE

Prime Borrowing Cost Falls From 6% but Not to Level of 5½%, Kept by Leader

By H. ERICH HEINEMANN

LINDSAY ORDERS O'DWYER OUSTED

But Procaccino Says Board Counsel Will Stay On in Transit Subsidy Suit

By SETH S. KING

3 APOLLO ASTRONAUTS DIE IN FIRE; GRISSOM, WHITE, CHAFFEE CAUGHT IN CAPSULE DURING A TEST ON PAD

BEFORE AN EARLIER TEST: Lieut. Col. Virgil I. Grissom, left, Air Force Lieut. Col. Edward H. White 2d, center, and Navy Lieut. Comdr. Roger B. Chaffee in front of the launching pad. Photograph was released Tuesday.

HOURS BEFORE THE TRAGEDY: Colonel Grissom walking to the Apollo spacecraft ahead of Commander Chaffee, yesterday, some 5½ hours before the fire broke out. The capsule was atop a Saturn 1-B rocket, 218 feet above pad.

TRAGEDY AT CAPE

Rescuers Are Blocked by Dense Smoke— Cause Is Studied

By The Associated Press

CAPE KENNEDY, Fla., Jan. 27—The three-man crew of astronauts for the Apollo 1 mission were killed tonight in a flash fire aboard the huge spacecraft designed to take man to the moon.

APOLLO PROGRAM DEALT HARD BLOW

The Slim Margin for Failure Believed Jeopardizing a Moon Landing by '70

By EVERT CLARK

ARMY OPPOSITION TO MAO REPORTED

Troops in 2 Regions Said to Resist Orders to Help in Ousting Party Officials

By CHARLES MOHR

TOWAWAY POLICY IS EASED FOR U.N.

City to Extend Parking Area for Diplomats and Chase Other Motorists Out

62 Nations Sign Treaty To Curb Arms in Space

By MAX FRANKEL

Fire on Spacecraft Captured on Film

By MARTIN WALDRON

Einstein Relativity Theory Challenged

By WALTER SULLIVAN

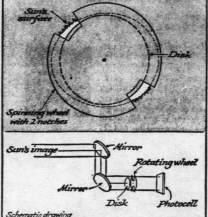

Schematic drawing

Three Apollo Astronauts Killed by Fire in Capsule During Test on Pad at Cape

GRISSOM, WHITE AND CHAFFEE DIE

Deaths Are Instantaneous as Spacemen Are Trapped Behind Closed Hatches

Continued From Page 1, Col. 8

flight, with Colonel Grissom occupying the command pilot's seat on the left, Colonel White in the middle, and Commander Chaffee on the right.

In Washington President Johnson mourned the death of the astronauts. He said the three men had given their lives in the nation's service.

Representative Joseph E. Karth, Democrat of Minnesota, said a dinner meeting of space program executives was underway in Washington when the announcement was made that there had been "a flash fire resulting from the use of pure oxygen . . ." He said no further explanation had been given at the dinner.

The fire was reported during a "plugs out" test of the booster and Apollo 1 craft. Mr. Haney said the test meant that the booster and spacecraft had been operating on their own power systems and not power from the ground.

NASA officials later said the Apollo's escape system could not have been used. The system required an astronaut to trigger a rocket attached to the top of the Apollo. The rocket would jerk the spacecraft away from its booster.

A spokesman said a gantry had been wrapped around the entire rocket during today's test, enclosing the escape rocket. He said the only way the astronauts could have escaped would have been to open the hatches and scramble out.

Mr. Haney said the rehearsal had reached the minus 10-minute mark, meaning it was 10 minutes away from a simulated liftoff. The hatches were sealed.

A NASA official said minor difficulties had cropped up during the countdown with two systems, a communications system and the environmental control system.

Cause of Fire Unknown

Officials said they did not know whether the fire stemmed from the two troublesome systems. All data were held pending an investigation.

Space officials said the three victims possibly had no knowledge there was a serious problem aboard. The spacecraft and rocket were not fueled and explosive devices aboard the spacecraft had been inactivated and could not have caused the disaster, they said.

The Air Force and NASA jointly impounded all data. The space agency said reporters would not be permitted to the scene until tomorrow morning at the earliest and any pictures of the incident that might reveal details were also being withheld.

The backup astronauts for the scheduled 14-day flight—postponed indefinitely — now become the prime pilots for Apollo 1.

'There Was a Flash'

CAPE KENNEDY, Fla., Jan. 27 (UPI)—The spacecraft was on Launching Pad 34 atop a two-stage Saturn 1 rocket. A closed circuit television camera aboard the craft was relaying pictures of the astronauts, who were five hours into a crucial test of the ship, when suddenly "there was a flash and that was it."

A spokesman watching the screen in the Saturn blockhouse a few hundred yards away said, "There were no communications with the crewmen at that time." They were never heard from again.

It took 10 to 15 minutes for the first ground crewman to rush up a high speed elevator and try to rescue the astronauts.

"Emergency crews encountered dense smoke in removing the hatches" on the spaceship, said a spokesman for the National Aeronautics and Space Administration.

"We will go ahead with the space flight program," said NASA's Administrator, James E. Webb, in Washington.

Dr. Edward C. Welsh, executive secretary of the agency, said the Soviet Union may have lost some of its astronauts in similar disasters "but we don't know if they have."

"Although everyone realized that someday space pilots would die, who could have thought the first tragedy would be on the ground?" Mr. Webb said.

Normal procedure in case of fire in the cabin would be for the astronauts to throw open the three hatches, run along an access arm to the red tower flanking the rocket, and take a high-speed elevator to the ground.

The fire struck so swiftly, and with such intensity that the astronauts "apparently died instantly," an official said.

Tass Reports Apollo Deaths

LONDON, Saturday, Jan. 28 (AP)—Tass, the Soviet press agency, briefly reported the Apollo disaster in its Russian-language service for overseas today. It quoted Associated Press reports that the three American astronauts, Virgil I. Grissom, Edward H. White 2d and Roger B. Chaffee, had died as a result of a fire on ground tests of an Apollo spaceship.

NASA

THE SPACE WALK: Lieut. Col. Edward H. White 2d outside the Gemini 4 on June 3, 1965. He was first American to walk in space, and first human to maneuver by jet power.

Associated Press

SPACE VEHICLE: Saturn 1-B rocket of type that would have carried the craft. Apollo capsule rests atop it.

APOLLO PROGRAM SUFFERS SETBACK

Continued From Page 1, Col. 7

which Mr. Johnson made his remarks, James E. Webb, the NASA administrator, said he believed an American could be put on the moon late in 1969. But he warned that there were not enough rockets for the usual amount of testing or for substitution if one failed.

Then the technical setbacks that usually occur in a research and development program—chiefly losses of rocket stages in ground tests—began to add up. Only last November, NASA reshuffled the Apollo flight plans, canceling one set for 1966 and delaying by several months the first launching of an Apollo spacecraft aboard the huge Saturn 5 rocket that will eventually boost an Apollo to the moon.

Less than a week later, the President sounded a note of caution. He said the Apollo program was "much more complicated" than the Gemini program that had just ended successfully.

Apollo, he said, "has more elements of as yet unproven capability. The months ahead will not be easy as we reach toward the moon. We must broaden and extend our know-how based on the increased power of these mighty new boosters. But with Gemini as the forerunner, I am confident that we will overcome the difficulties and achieve another success."

White House officials said at the time that the President was not trying to warn that the 1970 goal might be missed. Rather, they said, he was cautioning that Apollo might not go so smoothly as Gemini had because of its inherently greater difficulties.

Despite these assurances, senior space agency officials said at that time that the 1970 goals were "a reasonable possibility" but "no longer a sure thing."

There have been other technical setbacks since, including the explosion of a Saturn rocket stage last week at Sacramento, Calif., in which the rocket was destroyed and the test stand damaged.

Nevertheless, the budget sent to Congress this week by the President said:

"The achievement of the manned lunar landing by 1970 will demonstrate clearly our position as a space-faring nation."

In his own message accompanying the budget, the President also spoke of the 1961 resolve to "send a manned expedition to the moon in this decade."

"Much hard work remains and many obstacles must still be overcome before that goal is met," he said.

Then the President went on to describe an ambitious post-Apollo program that would "set our course for the more distant future."

"Indeed, we have no alternative unless we wish to abandon the manned space capability we have created," the President said.

Mr. Webb said tonight, "We'll go ahead with the space flight program."

Astronaut Toll of U.S. Is Now 6, But None Has Been Lost in Space

Special to The New York Times

WASHINGTON, Jan. 27—The irony of the deaths of three Apollo astronauts tonight is that 36 men have flown in space for the United States and the Soviet Union and returned safely to earth.

Yet this country has now lost six astronauts in aircraft or ground accidents.

Since the space age began nine years ago, there have been rumors that Soviet astronauts have died in space or in launching-pad accidents.

But American officials have always denied knowing of any such accidents.

In the 10 manned Gemini flights, the United States accumulated almost 1,900 man-hours of space flight with no deaths or injuries and only one close call.

American officials have cautiously pointed out, since before a Russian pilot, Col. Yuri A. Gagarin, became the first man to fly in space on April 12, 1961, that space flight would almost certainly cost a life someday.

An Air Force captain, Theodore C. Freeman, 34 years old, was the first American astronaut to die. A goose struck the windshield of his T-38 jet trainer as he attempted to land at Ellington Air Force Base near Houston on Oct. 31, 1964. He had not flown in space.

The two men who were to fly the Gemini 9—Elliot M. See Jr. and Maj. Charles A. Bassett 2d of the Air Force—died last Feb. 28, when their T-38 jet struck the McDonnell Aircraft Corporation building in St. Louis, where the Gemini capsules were made.

Scholarships Available To Astronauts' Children

LAFAYETTE, Ind., Jan. 27 (AP)—The children of astronauts Virgil I. Grissom and Roger B. Chaffee will be able to follow their fathers at Purdue University on full scholarships, Purdue's president, Frederick L. Hovde, said tonight.

Both astronauts, who died with Edward H. White 2d in an Apollo spacecraft fire at Cape Kennedy, were Purdue graduates. Colonel Grissom was graduated in 1950 and Commander Chaffee in 1957.

Colonel Grissom has two sons, Scott, 16 years old, and Mark, 13, and Commander Chaffee's children are Sheryl, 8, and Stephen, 5.

SENATE UNIT ASSAYS SOVIET SPACE GOALS

WASHINGTON, Jan. 27 (AP) — Although the Soviet Union has not put any of its astronauts into space recently, it still plans to beat the United States in landing a man on the moon, a Senate committee said today.

This and many other details of the Soviet space program and goals were included in a 920-page report released by the Aeronautical and Space Sciences Committee.

There is no evidence of "either Soviet disenchantment with the program or a desire to cut it back," the report said.

The report was released by Senator Clinton P. Anderson, Democrat of New Mexico, the committee chairman. It was prepared by the Legislative Reference Service of the Library of Congress.

The survey, covering 1962-65, includes unclassified material and documents related to the Soviet efforts, goals and purposes.

Over all, the Soviet program was rated as "well planned, orderly and vigorously pursued with concentration on specific, limited objectives, each achieving a marked advance beyond the one preceding."

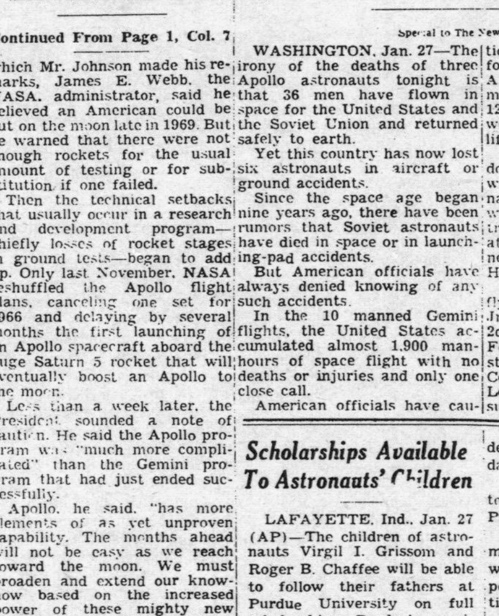

The New York Times Jan. 28, 1967

SITE OF TRAGEDY: Cross indicates Complex 34, area of Cape Kennedy where accident killed three astronauts.

Johnson Voices Sorrow at Loss Of 'Three Valiant Young Men'

WASHINGTON, Jan. 27 (AP) —President Johnson, in a statement here tonight, expressed sorrow at the loss of three Apollo astronauts in an accident tonight at Cape Kennedy.

"Three valiant young men have given their lives in the nation's service," the President said. "We mourn this great loss and our hearts go out to their families."

Vice President Humphrey and James E. Webb, administrator of the National Aeronautics and Space Administration, joined the President in expressing sorrow for the loss of the three astronauts.

Some members of Senate and House Committees that deal with space, while expressing shock at the deaths, commented that they did not believe the accident would slow the United States space effort.

Mr. Humphrey, who is chairman of the National Aeronautics and Space Council, said, "The United States will push ever forward in space and the memory of these men will be an inspiration to all future spacefarers."

Cites Astronauts' Bravery

The Vice President, who often visits the Cape Kennedy space center to observe its operations, said:

"The deaths of these three brilliant young men, true pioneers and wonderfully brave, is a profound and personal loss to me.

"I have had such close relationships with them that my sorrow is very deep. My heart goes out to their families and loved ones."

Mr. Webb said, "We in NASA know that their greatest desire was that this nation press forward with manned space flight exploration, despite the outcome of any one flight. With renewed dedication and purpose, we intend to do just that."

Mr. Webb went on:

"I have extended my sympathy and that of all employees of NASA to the families of Astronauts Grissom, White and Chaffee.

"The nation tonight feels a great sense of loss. That feeling is even greater among those of us who worked with those competitive young men who were so completely devoted to enlarging man's capability in space flight."

Secretary of Defense Robert S. McNamara sent the following message to the families of the three astronauts, who were also members of the armed forces:

"Our brave men in uniform, whether in Vietnam or seeking the frontiers of the future, mourn with all of us the tragic loss of three gallant and dedicated American airmen. To the families of Lieut. Col. Grissom, Lieut. Col. White and Lieut. Comdr. Chaffee we send our deepest condolence."

In addition to his formal statement, President Johnson sent personal messages to the families of the three astronauts.

'Tragic Loss to Nation'

PALM DESERT, Calif., Jan. 27 (UPI) — Former President Dwight D. Eisenhower, in whose administration the American space program began, said tonight in a statement issued from his vacation home here:

"The accident that took the lives of three of our highly trained, skilled and courageous American astronauts is a tragic loss to our entire nation. Mrs. Eisenhower and I extend to their families our deepest sympathy. Our thoughts and prayers are with them."

Message From Thant

Special to The New York Times

UNITED NATIONS, N. Y., Jan. 27 — Secretary General Thant sent a message of condolences to President Johnson tonight on the death of the three American astronauts.

The message was sent only a few hours after Mr. Thant sent a greeting to the United States hailing the signing of the treaty on the peaceful explorations of outer space.

The message from Mr. Thant said: "It is with shock and sadness that I hear of the tragic accident that has today taken the lives of the three gallant American astronauts in the course of their preparation for another historic venture into space."

"I know that the international community which the U.N. represents mourns their deaths and appreciates the sacrifices which these three men have made," he said.

SPACECRAFT FIRE CAPTURED ON FILM

Continued From Page 1, Col. 8

and Washington flew to Cape Kennedy tonight to begin a study of the available data.

In a late-night press conference, the first held by any space official after the accident, Mr. Haney said that the astronauts at the time of the fire were in pressurized suits and were being fed pure oxygen, an indication that the fire burned inside the spacesuits as well as outside.

Mr. Haney said that the spacecraft was "heavily damaged," both inside and outside.

The fire lasted only four minutes before crews inside the gantry around the spacecraft and its rocket could open the hatch atop the spacecraft. Mr. Haney said 26 workmen had inhaled smoke while trying to open the hatch. Two of the men were hospitalized.

The Apollo spacecraft is not equipped with ejection seats, as were the Gemini spacecraft, which was flown in training missions during 1965 and 1966.

Even if there were no fire inside the spacecraft, it would take a minimum of 90 seconds for the three astronauts to open the Apollo hatch and emerge, a NASA technician said.

The astronauts were reported to have been fatally burned almost instantly by the sweeping fire.

Mr. Haney said space officials were conferring late tonight in the blockhouse headquarters near the site of the accident, poring over the sequence of events leading to the fire.

NASA said it did not have a copy of the time sequence of the tests that were being made by the three astronauts.

Officials who were studying the situation included Dr. Kurt Debus, director of the Kennedy Space Center; Robert R. Gilruth, director of the Manned Spacecraft Center at Houston; Rocco Petrone, assistant director of the Kennedy Space Center; Maj. Gen. Sam Phillips, director of the Apollo program; Dr. Joseph Shea, director of the Apollo spacecraft program, and Dr. Max Faget, director of engineering and development at the Manned Spacecraft Center.

Mr. Haney said the bodies of the astronauts were still in the spacecraft four hours after the fire. Photographs were being made, he said.

"I am sure that the accident will have a major effect on the Apollo program," he said. However, he would not speculate on the length of time the program might be delayed.

The first Apollo flight was scheduled for Feb. 21, and there had been an indication that the first flight to the moon might come as early as late in 1968.

NASA officials would not speculate on the cause of the fire.

Mr. Haney said that the inside of the spacecraft apparently was a mass of flames.

"I think it is a fair assumption that death was instantaneous," he said. "Everything was burning, everything."

Bulletins on Astronauts Interrupt TV Schedule

The program schedules of the national television networks were interrupted last night for bulletins and then special reports on the deaths of the three astronauts in a flash fire at Cape Kennedy.

Between 8:12 and 8:17 P.M., the National Broadcasting Company, the American Broadcasting Company and the Columbia Broadcasting System carried the first word of the deaths of Lieut. Col. Virgil I. Grissom, Lieut. Col. Edward H. White 2d and Lieut. Comdr. Roger B. Chaffee.

N.B.C. pre-empted a half-hour at 9:30 P.M., while C.B.S. subsequently inserted a report in its Friday night movie, and A.B.C. delayed the start of regular shows at 9:30 and 10 P.M.

Additional special programs were scheduled for later in the evening and for today.

News Session Excerpts

Special to The New York Times

HOUSTON, Jan. 27—Following are excerpts from a transcript of a news conference held at the Manned Spacecraft Center here by Paul P. Haney, public affairs director of the center:

Q. Concerning the program, can you say right now what—was the spacecraft a total loss? What about the service module, and so forth?

A. I really don't know anything about the service module. The spacecraft was severely damaged, according to all the visual reports.

Q. Did you confirm, Paul, if the outside of the spacecraft was actually charred? A. There was some fire damage externally as well.

Q. Paul, could you tell us what a "plugs out" test is? And I gather this is what was going on today. And presumably this test is a similar kind of a test that you run through in Gemini. And was this particular event today a part of the routine prior to launching a spacecraft into space with men in it?

A. It was a full-scale pressure test.

Internal Power

Q. Can you tell us a little bit about this test and what it entailed?

A. Plugs out literally means you're running on internal power. You do every function that you would do in a normal countdown. I think this particular test called for a countdown to zero, then a simulated boosted flight phase with an early termination immediately after that.

Q. In other words, Houston Mission Control was up— A. Houston was up and monitoring, all the data coming back and forth, yes. And they were establishing their time lines, the dressing procedure. As you know, on this flight we planned to dress over in the manned spacecraft operations building and ride over to the pad fully suited, instead of as we did in Gemini, where we dressed at Pad—at the area there, at Pad 16, right beside this pad.

Q. So the spacecraft was on internal power, oxygen was coming from the ECS system [environmental control system]. Right?

A. Yes.

Q. Now this is not the first time this spacecraft's been like this. Right? In other words, you've run a manned test for six days in a vacuum chamber over here and, of course, this didn't even involve altitude conditions. Right?

A. This particular spacecraft would have been through at least two chamber runs, which is virtually the same configuration—even more so, in that it was the inner vacuum.

Both Manned

Q. And were both manned? A. Uh-huh.

Q. Chamber runs. This particular spacecraft? A. Yes. At least two.

Q. How many hours are we talking about, roughly? A. Oh, a chamber run takes 12-13 hours.

Q. Were you in the control center at the time, Paul?

A. No I was not. I had just left the office.

Q. Were they getting television from the Cape? A. At the Cape I believe they had some television monitors.

Q. Well, were they getting voice communication from the astronauts? A. Yes there was communications with the blockhouse and members of the crew and here.

Q. Do you know what was the last thing that was said to them? Or said from them? A. When I'm at liberty to discuss those—all the data, including the voice data, has been impounded, pending the outcome of this investigation.

Critical Substances

Q. Paul, other than the environmental control system and matter of oxygen, were there any other critical substances on board during this kind of test? A. Critical substances?

Q. Such as, like in— down in the service system, you've got your hydrogen. A. The booster was not fueled, nor was the service module.

Q. How much heat is the Apollo spacesuit capable of withstanding? A. The heat shield itself?

Q. The suit. A. That'd be a good question for a spacesuit engineer. I would have no way of knowing.

Q. Did I understand you to say that they were conducting this plugs out test when this flash fire occurred. A. That's right.

Q. Paul, is there anything —do you know anything to indicate what will be done with Mission 204 [Apollo 1]? What spacecraft will fly now? And maybe, how long? A. No, honest, I don't.

Q. Did you ever speculate on what caused the fire? A. No. I'm not speculating.

Q. Do you know? A. No.

Blaze Confined

Q. Paul, the flash fire, as it is quoted in your statement, was all confined to the spacecraft area? A. Yes.

Q. Is there anything combustible in the command module other than oxygen? A. No. But that in itself, of course, saturates all the insulation, and all the other surfaces that it sees in the spacecraft.

Q. Does oxygen burn explosively? Or does it burn relatively slowly? A. In this particular case it would be very explosive—flash.

Q. Were the suits pressurized? A. Yes.

Q. They were pressurized. Was the hatch also pressurized? A. No. The spacecraft itself was not pressurized. It was sealed.

Q. It was sealed and there was— A. I would say the suits were at least partially pressurized.

Q. But there was oxygen both within the suit and within th espacecraft cabin? A. Yes.

Q. Well, Paul, the fire itself—did it just naturally die itself out? Or did they use chemicals to put the fire out, or what?

A. Well, I think the release indicates the hatch was opened four minutes after the fire report came in and there was still dense smoke. The Cape has come up with 26 names of people who suffered smoke inhalation. Two of them are being held overnight.

Q. Paul, these people that were injured at the Cape, where they injured during an effort to open the craft? A. Uh-huh.

Possibility of Accident Didn't Upset Astronauts

Two of the astronauts killed yesterday were matter-of-fact recently when asked about the possibility of an Apollo mishap.

In an interview filmed by the Columbia Broadcasting System last month which was not televised until last night, Lieut. Col. Virgil I. Grissom was asked by Nelson Benton, a reporter, whether the law of averages "so far as the possibility of a catastrophic failure" bothered him.

"There's always a possibility that you can have a catastrophic failure, of course," Colonel Grissom answered. "This can happen on any flight. It can happen on the last one as well as the first one. So you just plan as best as you can to take care of all these eventualities."

Lieut. Comdr. Roger B. Chaffee, asked if there was "anything scary" about a first space flight, replied that there were a lot of "unknowns" and "problems." "This is our business," he said, "to find out if this thing will work for us. I don't see how you could help but be a little bit excited. I don't like to use the word scary."

Hondurans Going to Vietnam

WASHINGTON, Jan. 27 (AP)—Honduras will send a group of military observers to Vietnam, it was announced here today. It will be the first Latin-American military representation in the Vietnam conflict, although it wil not be a combat unit. Ricardo Midence, the Honduran Ambassador here, said the Honduran military observers "will stay one week in Vietnam inspectign civic action programs and military operations."

Congo Sentences Ex-Minister

KINSHASA, the Congo, Jan. 26 (Reuters)—Bertin Mwamba, the former Congolese Minister of Post, Telephones and Telegraph, was sentenced tonight to seven years and eight months in prison by a military court here. He was charged with embezzling more than $560,000 and had pleaded innocent.

Like 'em racy looking?

(Cars, that is)

•

You'll find a big selection advertised in The New York Times Automobile Exchange today in the Sports Pages

"All the News That's Fit to Print"

The New York Times

LATE CITY EDITION

Weather: Partly cloudy today, tonight and tomorrow. Temperature range: today 83-69. Wednesday 82-69. Temp.-Hum. Index 76; Wed. 76. Complete U.S. report on Page 74.

VOL. CXVI..No. 39,989 © 1967 The New York Times Company. NEW YORK, THURSDAY, JULY 20, 1967 10 CENTS

NEW NAVY CHIEF AMONG 82 KILLED IN AIR COLLISION

John T. McNaughton Dies With Wife and a Son in North Carolina Crash

79 VICTIMS ON AIRLINER

3 Dead on Smaller Plane, Which Tower Official Says Was 12 Miles off Course

By The Associated Press

HENDERSONVILLE, N. C., July 19—A Boeing 727 airliner and an off-course private plane collided over the Blue Ridge foothills of western North Carolina today, killing 82 persons, including the Secretary of the Navy-designate, John T. McNaughton, 45 years old.

There were no survivors among the 74 passengers and five crewmen aboard the Piedmont Airlines plane, or in the smaller craft, which carried two Missouri businessmen and their pilot.

The airline first said the jet carried 73 passengers, and issued a casualty list. Hours later a Piedmont spokesman said there were 74 passengers.

Harold Roberts, chief of the Federal Aviation Administration tower at the Asheville airport, said, "The small plane was about 12 miles south of where it should have been."

Wreckage Near Camp

Wreckage showered down 50 yards from a summer camp occupied by 145 teen-agers and their counselors. Camp directors held a songfest to keep their charges away from the crash scene.

Also killed were Mr. McNaughton's wife, Sarah, 46, and their younger son, Theodore, 11.

The McNaughtons boarded the airliner at nearby Asheville, minutes before the collision. They had been in the area to pick up their son, who had been in a summer youth camp.

The airliner, in service about four months, was Flight 22 from Atlanta to Washington. It had left the Asheville airport at 11:58 A.M. The time of the crash was put at 12:01.

A witness said the smaller aircraft, a twin-engine Cessna 310, struck the airliner "nose

Continued on Page 22, Column 3

Rusk Asserts Foe Is 'Hurting Badly'

Special to The New York Times

WASHINGTON, July 19—Secretary of State Dean Rusk reported today that the enemy was "hurting very badly" in Vietnam but cautioned that there was "still a long, tough job ahead" before Hanoi would be willing to talk seriously about peace.

At his first news conference in nearly four months, Mr. Rusk presented a generally encouraging picture on the course of the war in Vietnam and political developments in Saigon. He dismissed the suggestion that a stalemate was developing in the war, argued against any change in the current United

Continued on Page 6, Column 4

U.S. ARMS MAY GO TO MIDEAST AGAIN

Rusk Hints at Renewed Aid for Israel, Jordan, Saudi Arabia to Counter Soviet

By JOHN W. FINNEY

Special to The New York Times

WASHINGTON, July 19—Secretary of State Dean Rusk indicated today that the Administration was moving toward a revival of its policy of providing sufficient arms to maintain a military equilibrium in the Middle East between the nations dependent upon Soviet military aid and those dependent on Western aid.

In a State Department news conference he noted that the introduction of new Soviet weapons into the region was raising security problems for Israel and certain pro-Western Arab nations.

The Secretary said that the Administration was giving special attention to the question of resuming military as well as economic aid to Jordan. A resumption of aid to Jordan as well as certain other states in the area is "a matter of great preoccupation at the present time," he said.

State Department officials said that a review of arms shipments was focusing on Jordan, Israel and Saudi Arabia. Before the Arab-Israeli war last month, the United States was committed to provide Israel with two squadrons of A-4 at-

Continued on Page 2, Column 4

ISRAEL SAYS PRICE FOR WITHDRAWAL IS PEACEFUL TIES

Rafael Asserts Gromyko's Demand Would Lead to New Assault by Arabs

By DREW MIDDLETON

Special to The New York Times

UNITED NATIONS, N. Y., July 19—Israel declared today that normal relations with the Arab states was the price of the withdrawal and disengagement of her occupation forces.

"In the view of the Government of Israel," Gideon Rafael, the Israeli delegate, said in a letter to the President of the Security Council, "an integral and inseparable link exists between the withdrawal and disengagement of forces, and the establishment of normal, peaceful and good neighborly relations between the states of the region."

The withdrawal of Israeli forces without "simultaneous and parallel action" by the Arabs to establish peace would lead, in Israel's view, "to a renewed Arab assault on Israel at a date and in circumstances more favorable to the Arab aim of destroying Israel's independence," Mr. Rafael said.

A Reply to Gromyko

The Israeli letter to Endalkachew Makonnen of Ethiopia, this month's President of the Council, replied to a demand yesterday by the Soviet Foreign Minister, Andrei A. Gromyko, for withdrawal of Israeli forces. This demand was incorporated in a letter to Mr. Makonnen and to the General Assembly as well.

Mr. Rafael's letter will also be circulated in the General Assembly, Israeli sources said.

The letter was described as a major policy statement by Israeli diplomats because it spelled out in formal language the connection the Israeli Government draws between withdrawal and disengagement and recognition by Arab states.

These actions, Mr. Rafael made clear, are to be followed by peace negotiations. Now that a cease-fire has been established and its observance overseen by United Nations observers, he said, "conditions are ripe for the Middle Eastern states to reach agreements for the establishment of peaceful conditions free from external

Continued on Page 4, Column 4

United Press International

SEARCH FOR STOLEN WEAPONS: Guardsmen and policemen leaving house in the Negro section of Plainfield, N. J.

Israelis Assembling Tanks and Big Guns On Suez East Bank

By TERENCE SMITH

Special to The New York Times

QANTARA, United Arab Republic, July 19—Israel has assembled a formidable collection of heavy artillery and tanks on the east bank of the Suez Canal to reinforce her position in occupied Sinai.

The build-up began during heavy Israeli-Egyptian fighting last weekend and continued on Monday, when the Egyptians announced that they would fire on any boat the Israelis attempted to put in the canal.

Since then the Israelis have not put any craft in the canal, but they have gathered the equipment necessary to enforce their stipulation that either both countries will use the waterway or neither will.

They are also ready to launch a small fleet of patrol boats at a moment's notice. One such boat, with heavy machine guns fore and aft, was resting on a trailer in a street in Qantara, which is on the canal.

No one here doubts that a comparable build-up has taken place on the Egyptian side, though all that can be seen

Continued on Page 2, Column 6

NIXON PINS HOPE ON THE PRIMARIES

Says That if He Decides to Run He Must Display His Strength in Early Votes

By WARREN WEAVER Jr.

Former Vice President Richard M. Nixon said yesterday that he would withdraw from Presidential competition next spring if he failed to demonstrate in the early primaries that he was the strongest candidate the Republican party could field.

"I'm not going to the convention as a second or third string candidate to sit on a clump of delegates and try my hand at brokering," he said in an interview. "By that time, assuming I decide to run, I'll either be in or out."

Mr. Nixon prefaced any political discussion with the disclaimer that he had not yet decided whether to seek the Republican nomination. He will formally announce his plans next December or early in January. No one expects him not to run.

Rejects Goldwater Strategy

He rejected any updated version of the 1964 Goldwater strategy, which involved quietly locking up delegates in the states with no primary competition. If he won the nomination that way, he said, he would lose the election.

As things now stand, the Nixon demonstration of strength would be made in a half-dozen primaries, beginning with New Hampshire in March. In addition to the major contests in Wisconsin, Nebraska and Oregon, Mr. Nixon is considering Indiana and South Dakota.

He discussed his political future in his Broad Street law office, 24 floors above the financial district, his chair tilted back and his feet on a large walnut desk.

"Basically, I'm fatalistic about the Presidency," he said. "As far as I'm concerned, I'm

Continued on Page 25, Column 5

Riot Bill Voted by House; Fate in Senate Is in Doubt

By JOHN HERBERS

Special to The New York Times

WASHINGTON, July 19—After five hours of emotional speeches, the House passed tonight a bill that would make it a Federal crime to use interstate facilities or to cross state lines to incite a riot.

The vote was 347 to 70. The measure now goes to the Senate, where its fate is uncertain.

Sponsors of the legislation said that they were giving President Johnson and the Justice Department a new weapon with which to fight crime and violence and particularly to put down urban rioting that has afflicted many areas of the country.

But it was a weapon that the Administration had not requested. Also, the Administration was reported to feel that the bill would be ineffective against the civil disturbances that have erupted in Negro ghettos.

'A Futile Gesture'

It was passed over the objections of Representative Emanuel Celler, Democrat of Brooklyn, chairman of the House Judiciary Committee.

"I consider this bill to be a futile gesture, neither preventive nor curative," he told a hushed House. "The basic disorder is the discontent of the Negro, his disenchantment as to promises made but not fulfilled, the dreary, slow pace by which he achieves equality."

"This bill will not allay his anger and frustrations," he said with deep emotion. "Instead, it will arouse his anger and frustration more deeply. His leaders ask for better housing for their fellows. You offer them jails.

"His leaders ask for better facilities for education. You read them a riot act. They ask for decent living. You feed them a drastic statute. They ask for more employment. You give jobs in prison garb.

Constructive Action Stressed

"You cannot fight fire with fire. You can only fight fire with water. You can only fight the distress of the Negro with the lotion of human kindness, with constructive, not negative, action."

But before the vote came, Mr. Celler's words were followed by speech after speech declaring that riots were incited in city after city by outsiders who had crossed state lines in order to set a match to tinder boxes in the inner city.

The main body of the bill, written by Representative William C. Cramer, Republican of Florida, says:

"Whoever travels in interstate or foreign commerce or uses any facility in interstate or foreign commerce, including the mail, with intent to (A) in-

Continued on Page 26, Column 4

PANEL IN JERSEY TO STUDY RIOTING

Hughes Appoints a Biracial Group to Find Causes and Recommend Solutions

By WALTER H. WAGGONER

Special to The New York Times

TRENTON, July 19—Gov. Richard J. Hughes named a "blue ribbon" committee today to investigate the causes of the recent riots and racial disorders in the state and to recommend solutions to the problems that underlie such disturbances.

The committee is biracial and includes two former Governors.

Mr. Hughes said the committee would also look into complaints that the state troopers and National Guard members engaged in excessive and indiscriminate shooting in combating the riots and sniping that swept Newark for nearly six days beginning last Wednesday night.

Study to Be Broad

Back in his State House office after working round the clock in Newark during the worst of the violence, the Governor said that the formation of the "very blue-ribbon" committee was one of the steps being taken to prevent further upheavals.

The Governor named Robert Lilley, president of the New Jersey Bell Telephone Company, chairman of the new committee.

Its members are Robert B. Meyner, a Democrat, and Alfred E. Driscoll, a Republican, both former Governors; Bishop John J. Dougherty, president of Seton Hall University; Bishop

Continued on Page 28, Column 5

TROOPERS SEARCH PLAINFIELD HOMES FOR STOLEN GUNS

But House-to-House Hunt Is Ended After Negroes Complain of Damage

SOME WEAPONS FOUND

Heavily Armed Troopers Act Without Warrants Under Proclamation by Hughes

Text of Hughes proclamation is printed on Page 28.

By THOMAS A. JOHNSON

Special to The New York Times

PLAINFIELD, N. J., July 19—Heavily armed National Guard men and state troopers swarmed into the Negro community here today in a house-to-house search for stolen weapons, then halted their mission when angry residents complained that their homes were being damaged.

Despite the resentment, the city had a relatively quiet day. At midnight, there had been no reports of renewed racial trouble. "Everything is quiet," one Negro leader said. "If a wave is made, Whitey will make it."

The search by 300 troopers and guardsmen in a mile-square area of the cordoned-off West End was carried on without warrants under the authority of a declaration of emergency proclaimed by Gov. Richard J. Hughes.

The proclamation, prepared two days ago, was read from the steps of the Plainfield police station shortly after noon by Col. David B. Kelly, superintendent of the state police.

'State of Disaster'

The city was declared in "a state of disaster and emergency," giving the Governor the right to invoke extraordinary powers "until such time as it is declared by me that a state of emergency no longer exists in the City of Plainfield."

Less than two hours later, a task force spearheaded by four armored personnel carriers bristling with .50-caliber machine guns stood poised at Central Avenue and West Fourth Street.

As the personnel carriers, loaded with guardsmen armed with M-1 rifles, bayonets, carbines, .45-caliber submachine guns and pistols, began to inch forward, Paul N. Ylvisaker, Commissioner of Community Affairs, sprinted into the intersection waving his arms in protest. He yelled "Stop! Stop!"

Mr. Ylvisaker disclosed there had been a misunderstanding—the heavy equipment was not supposed to be there.

"This is a peaceful community," he said. "This will be an orderly search."

Mr. Ylvisaker said he had conferred with Colonel Kelly, who agreed that the carriers should not precede the 20 patrol jeeps convoying 12 truckloads of searchers into the area.

The carriers turned back.

The objective of the search was 46 semiautomatic weapons

Continued on Page 28, Column 7

New Navy Secretary's Family Reunion Is Followed by Tragedy in Air

Secretary of the Navy-designate and Mrs. John T. McNaughton with their son Theodore, 11, at breakfast yesterday in Asheville, N. C. They were among the victims of mid-air collision between a jetliner and a smaller plane.

Associated Press Wirephoto

Firemen and rescue workers searching smoking wreckage of the Boeing 727 near Hendersonville, N. C., yesterday

Mexico Arrests 13; Links China to Plot

By The Associated Press

MEXICO CITY, July 19—The Government reported in an official statement tonight that it had foiled a plot financed from Communist China that had sought to establish a "popular Socialist" regime in Mexico.

The Attorney General's office said that a Venezuelan and a Salvadorean were among 13 persons arrested in the case.

According to the statement, the group was preparing subversive actions both in Mexico City and the provinces and had already dynamited an army truck in a rural road in the state of Guerrero seeking to procure arms.

The statement said the Mexican branch of Hsinhua, the Chi-

Continued on Page 14, Column 3

The Strategy of Riot-Control: Newark Assesses Use of Guns

By PETER KIHSS

Did city and state police and the New Jersey National Guard invoke excessive gunfire in quelling Newark's riots? Was there indiscriminate—even backlash — shooting by law enforcement officers? What strategy did they employ?

In the wake of the six days of disorder that led to 26 deaths, 1,200 injuries, 1,300 arrests and damage exceeding $15-million, community groups were marshaling complaints yesterday. Governor Hughes promised a "blue-ribbon" independent inquiry beyond the investigations undertaken by the three law-enforcement agencies themselves.

Mayor Hugh J. Addonizio supported his Newark policemen. He said they had started on a policy of "restraint and containment — better broken windows than broken heads." He said the guardsmen and state police had acted well in re-establishing control; there were indications elsewhere that at midpoint the Mayor had sought to soften the massive use of state force.

Col. David B. Kelly, superintendent of the state police, laid down the strategy that cordoned off and sectored first one-third and then one-half the city with clockwise and counterclockwise motor patrols. Maj. Gen. James F. Cantwell said his National Guard acted under the state police orders by providing the muscle

Continued on Page 29, Column 1

NEWS INDEX

GIVE CLOSED-IN CHILDREN country vacation. Give to The Fresh Air Fund, New York 10036. The New York Times Appeal for The Fresh Air Fund—Advt.

82 ON 2 AIRCRAFT DIE IN COLLISION

Continued From Page 1, Col. 1

to nose." The small plane exploded and went down immediately.

The airliner flew on momentarily as the pilot apparently tried to recover from the impact. Then it, too, blew up. Debris showered down over the area two miles northeast of Hendersonville, a mountain summer resort city of 10,000.

Bodies were strewn over a wide area.

One witness said the airliner apparently tried to head for nearby Interstate 26, a four-lane artery 150 yards from where the main wreckage fell. The explosion rattled windows in downtown Hendersonville.

Among the airliner passengers were 25 persons headed for a meeting of the Stokely Van Camp food products company at White Sulphur Springs, W. Va. They were to have left the plane at Roanoke, Va.

One of the victims was Ennis Parker of Griffin, Ga., a vice president of Stokely Van Camp. He and the other delegates to the company's meeting boarded the plane at Atlanta.

3rd Crash in Line's History

Piedmont serves 10 states and the District of Columbia on its 7,000 miles of routes. This was the third fatal crash in its 18-year history.

The Boeing 727 had gone into service for Piedmont only about two months ago. It was being leased by Piedmont from Boeing at $1,000 a day.

Mr. McNaughton had been appointed by President Johnson to succeed Paul H. Nitze as Navy Secretary. He had been confirmed by the Senate but had not been formally sworn.

The Cessna, owned by Lansair, Inc., of Springfield, Mo., a commercial insurance and trucking concern, was occupied by Dave Addison, about 40, the pilot, of Lebanon, Mo.; and passengers Robert E. Anderson, about 42, a consultant for Community Development Consultants, Inc., and Ralph Reynolds, about 40, a vice president of Lansair, both of Springfield.

An Eyewitness Report

Clarence Huder, a sign painter who lives nearby, said he saw the big jet circling near the Asheville airport shortly after take-off.

He said he saw the small plane hit the airliner. "It looked like the small one hit the bottom of the big plane," he said. "In about a second, there was an explosion."

Mr. Huder said it appeared the pilot of the airliner tried to straighten the craft, but then there was another explosion.

"A thousand pieces fell from the plane," Mr. Huder said. "Some of them, including bodies, fell on lawns and rooftops."

Mr. Huder said he heard two other explosions as he drove toward the scene.

Another witness, Thomas A. Conner, 39, said his 12-year-old son Alden yelled: "Look, daddy, that little plane is going to hit the big one."

Mr. Conner said the smaller craft appeared to rise directly up from underneath the airliner and hit it "nose to nose." The airliner then made a sharp turn, Mr. Conner said, as if trying to reach Interstate 26.

'About Leveled Off'

"He was about leveled off," Mr. Conner said, "when he exploded."

Counselors at the nearby summer youth camp acted immediately to get their charges out of the crash area. The program director, Marvin Nockow, 50, of Miami, and other staffers moved the children to the opposite side of the camp area before holding the songfest.

The National Transportation Safety Board in Washington sent investigators to the scene.

The flight and voice recorders of the Piedmont jet were found, according to the head of the board, former Gov. John H. Reed of Maine.

Mr. Reed told a news conference that the two instruments "appear to be in relatively good condition." He said they were sent to Washington for study.

A spokesman for the board said the airliner left Asheville on an instrument flight plan, and two minutes later reported leaving the 5,000-foot altitude to climb to a flight altitude of 21,000 feet.

The Cessna, also on an instrument flight plan, had been cleared to the Asheville radio beacon at 6,000 feet, and had reported over the navigation station at 11:58 A.M.

Weather observers said the area had broken clouds at 2,500 feet, with a visibility of four miles in a haze.

Safety Setup Planned

Early this month the domestic airline industry reached agreement with several prospective manufacturers on a technical description of an airborne collision avoidance system. Prototypes of the system are expected to be available for airline evaluation by early 1969.

But the system is considered too costly (estimated at $30,000 to $50,000 a plane), too heavy and too much of a drain on aircraft electrical power for small planes. And unless both planes in potential danger are equipped with it, it will not help.

Studies are under way on modified versions for light aircraft, but as yet none have been acknowledged as the solution.

United Press International Telephoto

WHERE JET CRASHED: Smoke rising from the spot where the Piedmont Airlines Jetliner fell near Interstate 26 at Hendersonville, N. C., yesterday, as seen from the air.

"All the News That's Fit to Print"

The New York Times

LATE CITY EDITION

Weather: Mostly sunny today. Fair tonight and tomorrow. Temp. range: today 86-68; Sat. 83-67. Temperature-Humidity Index 77. Sat. 77. Complete U.S. report on Page 67.

SECTION ONE

VOL. CXVI. No. 39,999

© 1967 The New York Times Company.

NEW YORK, SUNDAY, JULY 30, 1967

60c beyond 50-mile zone from New York City, except Long Island. Higher in air delivery cities. 40 CENTS

PRESIDENT CALLS FOR FREE INQUIRY ON NATION'S RIOTS

Orders Commission to Find Answers Without Regard to 'Conventional Wisdom'

DETROIT GETS U.S. AID

Johnson Acts to Give City's Small-Business Men Help —Soldier Kills Negro

By ROY REED

Special to The New York Times

WASHINGTON, July 29 — President Johnson put his new commission on civil disorders to work today on a long list of questions, charging it to find the answers without regard to "conventional wisdom."

As he posed them, the questions about the recent racial riots boiled down to three that were basic:

"What happened?"

"Why did it happen?"

"What can be done to prevent it from happening again and again?"

Meanwhile, Mr. Johnson ordered the Small Business Administration to make available long-term, low-interest loans to home owners and small-business men whose property was damaged in the Detroit violence. [Page 52.]

[An Army paratrooper shot and killed a fleeing Negro in Detroit Saturday night. It was the first shooting by a Regular Army man since paratroopers entered the city. Page 52.]

Cites Need for Advice

The President, calling the commission to its first meeting at the White House, told the 11 members that he wanted advice on short-term measures to prevent riots and on better ways to contain them if they began.

Moreover, he said he wanted to know of long-term measures "that will make them only a sordid page in our history."

The commission is to make an interim report by March 1, 1968, and a final report not later than a year from today.

It met for 3½ hours and then adjourned until next week, when it will begin conferring with Federal officials and others familiar with racial unrest. The commission expects to begin by asking Congress for the power to subpoena witnesses.

"Let your search be free," Mr. Johnson urged in a statement laying down guidelines for the investigation.

"Let it be untrammeled by what has been called the 'conventional wisdom.'"

He said he had appointed the commission not to approve his ideas, but to guide the Administration "through a thicket of tension, conflicting evidence and extreme opinions."

He told the bipartisan, interracial commission:

"One thing should be absolutely clear: This matter is far,

Continued on Page 53, Column 1

Army's Entry Into Detroit: How Decision Was Made

White House Views Action as Swift and Prudent—Michigan Finds Tension Raised by Dispute Over Wording

The riots in Detroit last week were brought under control through the uneasy collaboration of two political leaders who are potential rivals for the Presidency next year. Whether political considerations influenced their actions is an issue of speculation and comment. Here is how Washington and Detroit look back on the events.

By MAX FRANKEL

Special to The New York Times

WASHINGTON, July 29—In the view of the White House, the Army moved into Detroit last Monday as swiftly as possible but also as prudently as necessary, with only a few minor flaws in the public presentation of the operation.

Stung by charges that they let politics interfere with public policy and safety, President Johnson and his advisers have carefully recorded their moves and motives, and they cite that record not only in self-defense, but also with pride.

Their record includes several major ingredients: the President's reluctance to send Federal troops against rioters for the first time in 24 years; what they view as Gov. George Romney's vacillation for nearly 20 hours about the need for the troops; the relatively poor training and use of National Guard forces, and the highly efficient and disciplined performance of the Army.

Despite their pride, White House officials here worry that a precedent has been set and shudder at the thought of many Governors turning riot control

Continued on Page 50, Column 1

By GENE ROBERTS

Special to The New York Times

DETROIT, July 29—A dispute over the use of two words—"request" and "insurrection"—delayed the use of Federal troops in Detroit and increased tensions between Gov. George Romney and the Johnson Administration.

This is the view of public officials who were present as Governor Romney communicated by telephone and telegram with the Administration while Detroit was ripped apart by fire-bombers and looters.

Governor Romney was reluctant to use the word "insurrection" in applying and writing for Federal troops because he felt this might invoke escape clauses in insurance policies and prevent hundreds of property owners from being reimbursed for their losses.

He also thought the Administration was "quibbling" when it said he should use the word "request" in wiring for Federal aid. Governor Romney preferred to say that he "recommended" Federal troops.

The Johnson Administration, on the other hand, referred Governor Romney to a Federal

Continued on Page 50, Column 2

U. S. Navy via Associated Press Radiophoto

AFTER DISASTER STRUCK: Crewmen fighting the blaze on flight deck of the Forrestal. Fire destroyed 25 planes.

AT LEAST 70 DEAD IN FORRESTAL FIRE; 89 OTHERS MISSING

78 Injured Aboard Carrier in Blaze and Explosions Off North Vietnam

CRAFT IS OUT OF ACTION

She Will Go to Philippines After Delivering Victims to Hospital Ship Repose

By R. W. APPLE Jr.

Special to The New York Times

SAIGON, South Vietnam, Sunday, July 30—At least 46 United States Navy men were killed yesterday as flames surged through the aircraft carrier Forrestal.

Eighty more men were listed as missing, and it was feared that many had drowned after throwing themselves into the sea to escape the flames. Fifty-six were injured, many seriously, after a fuel tank accidently dropped from a jet plane, setting off the explosion and blaze.

[In a later dispatch, The Associated Press put the toll at 70 dead, 89 missing and 78 injured.]

The Navy, issuing its casualty report today, said that 25 aircraft had been destroyed or had rolled overboard in the blaze, rather than 29 as first reported, but it added that 31 other planes had suffered damage ranging from light to serious. The carrier's full complement of planes is 80 to 85, the Navy said.

Flames Raged 10 Hours

Not until 8:30 last night, nearly 10 hours after it broke out, was the fire brought under control, the Navy reported. The last flames were not extinguished until 12:20 A.M. today.

By then the Forrestal was steaming toward a rendezvous with the hospital ship Repose in the Gulf of Tonkin. Later today, after transferring her injured crewmen, she is to head for the United States naval base at Subic Bay, in the Philippines.

The 75,900-ton carrier, nearly 12 years old, was said to have suffered extensive damage. Four holes were blown in her flight deck by exploding 750-pound bombs, a Navy spokesman said.

Four more holes had to be cut in the deck to fight the stubborn flames, which swept through the maze of cables and piping between the flight deck and the hangar deck below.

Naval experts said it seemed certain that the Forrestal, which joined the assault against North Vietnam less than a week ago after long service in the Mediterranean and the Atlantic, would have to return to the United States for re-

Continued on Page 3, Column 1

Mayor Hears Angry Pleas In Brooklyn Ghetto Walk

Negroes Shout Demands

Angry Negroes met Mayor Lindsay with demands for immediate economic relief yesterday as he toured streets in Bedford-Stuyvesant, Brooklyn, where bands of young Negroes had gone on a rampage before dawn yesterday.

Half of the Mayor's hour-long visit was spent in a Congress of Racial Equality office on Fulton Street between Nostrand and Bedford Avenues, where a CORE representative, Sonny Carson—often waving a finger within inches of the Mayor's face—led a condemnation of the city for asserted failures.

Shortly before midnight last night, in the same area, a crowd of Negroes threw rocks at firemen who had come to put out a small rubbish fire. Some windows were broken and some stores were looted, the police said. Eleven persons were arrested.

The earlier rampage was explained to Mayor Lindsay by Mr. Carson.

"The main reason for the small insurrection this morning is because certain things have not been done," Mr. Carson

Continued on Page 55, Column 1

Spellman in East Harlem

By EMANUEL PERLMUTTER

Cardinal Spellman went to East Harlem last night to lead its Puerto Rican residents in special prayers of thanks for the return of "peace and brotherhood" to the ghetto.

The religious service in St. Paul's Roman Catholic Church, at 117th Street between Park and Lexington Avenues, was preceded by a candlelight procession of [illegible] 700 men, women and children through the area, known as El Barrio. The district had been racked by several nights of rioting earlier in the week.

The Cardinal, wearing an orange robe and an orange skull cap, stood at the head of the stairs in the church lobby and greeted the marchers when they returned at 9 P.M.

Then he concluded the hour-long mass with a brief blessing for those who had taken part in religious processions earlier in the week to help restore quiet to the community.

Standing at the lectern, his voice barely audible, he said in Spanish: "I greet you in this mass of thanksgiving.

"I have always looked upon

Continued on Page 55, Column 4

Mt. Vernon Mayor Offers Job Program Paying $100 a Week

By RALPH BLUMENTHAL

Special to The New York Times

MOUNT VERNON, N. Y., July 29—Mayor Joseph P. Vaccarella told ghetto residents here tonight that the city would support a new job-recruitment campaign in the ghetto and would guarantee wages of not less than $100 a week.

The oral assurance followed a confrontation between the Mayor and Negro residents. But no one was very clear on the details. A United States Labor Department official who was present described the agreement as "hairy" with problems.

The Negroes were jubilant.

"You just saw history being made," said Lloyd King, president of the local chapter of the National Association for the Advancement of Colored People. "You saw a reasonable confrontation with black power."

Mayor Vaccarella said the Board of Estimate, of which he is one of three members, would appropriate $250,000 Tuesday to subsidize salaries below $100 a week for men hired under the new employment program. It would affect jobs in private industry as well as the government.

Negroes at the meeting said that about 200 jobs were needed in the recruitment campaign.

The Mayor repeated his program later in the evening at

Continued on Page 52, Column 5

NEWBURGH RALLY ENDS IN VIOLENCE

30 Negroes Are Arrested in Rampage After Argument at a Neo-Nazi Meeting

Special to The New York Times

NEWBURGH, N. Y., Sunday, July 30—Negro youths in their teens and 20's went on a rampage for several hours in the Negro section last night, smashing store windows and stoning police, after the holding of a long-postponed meeting in the Orange County Courthouse by the neo-Nazi National Renaissance Party. More than 30 Negroes were arrested.

Three policemen were injured after having been struck by bricks and unopened beer cans, and at least two stores were reported broken into.

The disturbance, the first racial violence in this Hudson River city of 27,000, began after Negroes first jeered and taunted, and then walked out of the Renaissance party meeting.

There was one shooting incident, Police Chief John E. Tierney said. He said someone had fired from a speeding car at two policemen in an unmarked car at the intersection of Broadway and Lander Street. Neither policeman was hurt.

Firemen put out a blaze that had been started in a small clothing plant at 45 Clark Street at about 1 A.M.

The City Manager, Paul L. McCauley, who earlier in the evening had appealed to residents to stay indoors, said after midnight, "We're not playing any more."

Continued on Page 43, Column 1

U.S. Jets From Thailand Hit Barracks Near Hanoi

By United Press International

SAIGON, South Vietnam, July 29—American warplanes swept over North Vietnam yesterday to batter a previously untouched army training school near Hanoi and warehouses within eight miles of Haiphong, United States officials said today.

Jet fighter-bombers flew 157 missions through cloudless skies and left a trail of destruction that ranged from the rich Red River delta through the southern panhandle into the demilitarized zone between the two Vietnams.

The United States spokesman said Air Force F-4C Phantoms and F-105 Thunderchiefs from Thailand apparently took by surprise the Sontay army barracks 23 miles west of Hanoi. The first attack on the school destroyed about 30 of the 50 or 60 buildings in the occupied complex.

A band of Navy A-4 Skyhawks from the carrier Bon Homme Richard strafed the Loi-dong warehouse area eight miles north of Haiphong and hit it with 250-pound and 500-pound bombs.

The raid was the closest to Haiphong this week.

Other Skyhawks from the carrier Oriskany and F-4 Phantoms, launched from the carrier Forrestal before it caught fire, bombed the Hatou naval support area and nearby Hongai explosives dump 30 miles northeast of Haiphong and ship repair facilities eight miles north-

Continued on Page 2, Column 4

Navy to Let All U.S. Ships Use Secret Navigation by Satellite

By JOHN NOBLE WILFORD

Special to The New York Times

BRUNSWICK, Me., July 29—Vice President Humphrey announced here today that the United States would permit commercial ships and ocean researchers to use the previously restricted Navy navigation satellites.

The move means that any American ship at sea could be equipped to tune in the coded radio signals from the three Navy satellites that are a key to guiding the nation's Polaris-missile submarine fleet.

Ships of other nations may eventually be allowed to use the system, too. However, Mr. Humphrey sidestepped this issue today, deleting from his original text a remark that consideration was being given to selling the necessary equipment to "our close allies."

Mr. Humphrey made the announcement in a speech at a conference of Maine and New Hampshire marine scientists being held here at Bowdoin College. The Vice President, who also serves as chairman of the National Council on Marine Resources and Engineering Development, is on a five-day tour of oceanographic centers in New England.

In his speech, the Vice Presi-

Continued on Page 28, Column 1

The New York Times (by Barton Silverman)

GREETS MARCHERS: Cardinal Spellman at the entrance to St. Paul's Roman Catholic Church in East Harlem. Auxiliary Bishop Terence J. Cooke is next to the Cardinal.

Sports News

PAN-AMERICAN GAMES

The United States swept the first three men's track and field events yesterday at Winnipeg, Man. Van Nelson of Minneapolis broke the games record in winning the 10,000-meter run in 29 minutes 17.4 seconds. Randy Matson of Pampa, Tex., and Frank Covelli of Long Beach, Calif., also won gold medals in the shot-put and javelin throw, respectively.

BASEBALL

The Mets and Yankees both lost. Al Ferrara's two-out home run in the bottom of the ninth inning brought the Los Angeles Dodgers a 2-1 victory over the Mets. The Yankees bowed, 6-2, to the Kansas City Athletics. The Chicago White Sox edged the Detroit Tigers, 4-3, and acquired Rocky Colavito from Cleveland.

THOROUGHBRED RACING

Ethel D. Jacobs's Straight Deal, ridden by Bob Ussery, rallied to win the $118,275 Delaware Handicap at Delaware Park. At Monmouth Park, Queen of the Stage, piloted by Braulio Baeza, took first place in the $103,650 Sorority Stakes. Fort Marcy, with Ron Turcotte up, captured the $58,400 Tidal Handicap at Aqueduct.

Details in Section 5

Huge U.S. Park Urged in Adirondacks

By MURRAY SCHUMACH

The creation of a huge national park within the sprawling boundaries of what is now the Adirondack Mountains State Park was urged yesterday in a report from Laurance S. Rockefeller, chairman of the State Council of Parks.

The proposed Federal park would contain some 1,720,000 acres and would be exceeded in size only by the Yellowstone and Mt. McKinley national preserves, which have 2,221,772 acres and 1,939,398 acres, respectively.

The report urged the additional acquisition of nearly 600,000 privately owned acres in this area to make the park the largest in the United States.

Mr. Rockefeller conceived the idea for the National Park about two years ago and later put a panel headed by Conrad L. Wirth, former director of the National Park Service, to work on studying its feasibility. The group recommended that the state turn over its land in the area to the Federal Govern-

Continued on Page 27, Column 3

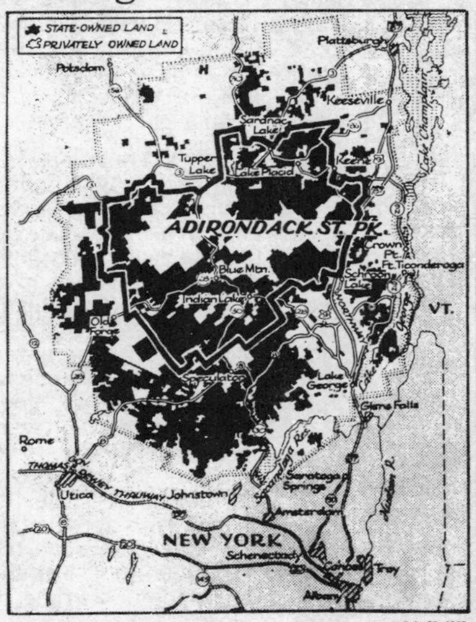

The New York Times July 30, 1967

National Park (dark line) would be within state preserve

Today's Sections

Index to Subjects

THE FRESH AIR FUND STILL GIVES
Give to The Fresh Air Fund, New York 10036. The New York Times Appeal for The Fresh Air Fund.—Advt.

70 Crewmen Dead in Fire Aboard Carrier Forrestal Off North Vietnam

Flight deck of the carrier. It took crewmen more than an hour to extinguish flames on the deck; fires burned longer in the hangar deck and below.

Continued From Page 1, Col. 8

pairs that would take many months.

The fire began as the carrier was swinging into the wind to start launching her aircraft for the day's attack against North Vietnam.

An auxiliary gas tank of a Douglas A-4 Skyraider fighter-bomber was said to have dropped to the deck from its position under the wing as the plane was warming up for launching. The 250-gallons of volatile fuel splashed across the flight deck, and in a moment it was ignited by the superheated steam of the carrier's four-catapult launching system.

The flames quickly engulfed the Forrestal's four-acre flight deck—a vast steel platform almost as big as a square block in New York City. Bombs, rockets and fuel tanks on waiting planes caught fire.

Turned to the Starboard

The Forrestal turned to starboard immediately to cut the 40-mile-an-hour winds over her decks, which were fanning the flames. When the fire was put out, she headed south to meet the Repose, which was steaming from Danang Harbor.

According to the official account, the fire broke out at 10:53 A.M., seven minutes before the ship was to have begun launching aircraft. The Forrestal was on Yankee Station, 175 miles north of Danang, with two other carriers, the Oriskany and Bon Homme Richard.

The Oriskany returned to the waters off North Vietnam on July 15, having been refitted after a fire on Oct. 26, 1966, in which 43 crewmen were killed, three men injured seriously and 35 suffered minor injuries.

That fire was caused by the ignition of magnesium flares in a locker below deck.

Minutes after the general quarters alarm resounded on the Forrestal, other ships sped to her aid. The Repose hoisted anchor at Danang, the heavy cruiser St. Paul, which had been bombarding targets in North Vietnam, turned to sea and ships near the Forrestal pulled alongside.

The Rupertus and the Henry W. Tucker—the destroyers in the Forrestal's screen—poured water onto the carrier's flaming decks. The Oriskany and the

The New York Times   July 30, 1967

Forrestal was on station in Gulf of Tonkin (cross) when fire began on flight deck.

U. S. Navy via Associated Press Radiophoto

A helicopter and a destroyer rush to aid the stricken Forrestal. Copter was from one of two other carriers in area.

Bon Homme Richard sent doctors by helicopter and took off casualties.

Firemen of the Forrestal, clad in heat-resistant aluminum suits, sprinted to the flight deck and to the vast hangars below, to which the flames quickly spread. They covered the burning planes with foam.

Capt. John K. Beling, the ship's commanding officer, was uninjured and stayed on the bridge. The propulsion system of the carrier, a 1,039-foot long craft, continued to function through the crisis.

Plane-handling trucks pushed burning aircraft over the side, and firefighters hurled pieces of other planes into the sea. Big bombs and rockets were thrown overboard.

Rear Adm. Harvey P. Lanham, commander of Carrier Division 2, who flies his flag from the Forrestal, said that in the first hour of the disaster, "I saw more heroic incidents that I could count."

Lieut. Comdr. Larry Forderhase, the ship's catapult officer, told of seeing crash crews calmly unloading bombs from the

wings of blazing aircraft and unscrewing their fuses.

"People were carrying these bombs," he was quoted as having said. "Carrying 250-pound bombs and throwing them over the side."

Commander Forderhase said he had seen a sailor, wearing a shiny aluminum fire-resistant suit, pushing a fork-lift truck against a burning plane despite exploding rockets and cannon ammunition until he got it off the deck and into the sea.

In the brief time that the inferno raged on deck, it destroyed more planes than the gunners in North Vietnam have brought down in the average month since the air war began in February, 1965. About 625 United States planes have been lost in the north since the bombing began—an average of 21 a month.

The Forrestal carries about 4,300 men and six squadrons of aircraft.

The Forrestal will probably be replaced on Yankee Station by the Constellation, the flagship of the Seventh Fleet's carrier strike force, which was on

her way to the Philippines for crew liberty.

Included in the new gear, which brought the Forrestal up to date with such carriers as the Enterprise, the Independence and the Kitty Hawk, were the latest radar and computer systems.

On Thursday, two small fires broke out — one below decks and one in a plane—but were quickly extinguished.

When the fire broke out yesterday, the flight deck was ready for the launchings with several dozen aircraft lined up on and behind the catapults.

Deck crews, clad in bright green, red and blue jerseys and wearing special caps to block out the roar of the jets, were swarming around the planes, fully exposed to the flaming fuel.

It appeared that the planes ready for launching were the ones that burned. These were believed to be the Phantoms and Skyhawks, which would suggest that the loss in equipment ran to more than $50-million.

"All the News That's Fit to Print"

The New York Times

LATE CITY EDITION

Weather: Partly cloudy, windy and cold today, tonight and tomorrow. Temp. range: today 37-27; Friday 39-31. Full U.S. report on Page 81.

VOL. CXVII—No. 40,138 © 1967 The New York Times Company. NEW YORK, SATURDAY, DECEMBER 16, 1967 10 CENTS

ALGERIA REPORTS CRUSHING REVOLT BY ARMY FACTION

Dissidents Led by Ex-Staff Chief 'Put Out of Action' as They Head for Capital

BOUMEDIENE IS VICTOR

President Takes Command of Forces When Former Ally Attempts a Coup

Special to The New York Times

ALGIERS, Dec. 15 — Troops loyal to President Houari Boumediene have foiled an attempted coup against his regime by dissident army units led by the former Army Chief of Staff, Col. Tahar Zbiri, the Algerian official news agency said tonight.

The agency added that the rebel elements were "blocked, encircled and put out of action" last night in the El-Affroun-Mouzalaville district, which is about 40 miles southwest of Algiers, by troops loyal to Mr. Boumediene.

The agency indicated that clashes had occurred between the opposing forces. It said the action of the rebels had caused several deaths among the population of the troubled area.

The agency declared that Colonel Zbiri, supported by some members of his family who are all army commanders, led the units under their command "in an adventure without issue."

Algiers Reported Target

Informed sources said that the rebel units, which included a tank battalion, had headed toward Algiers from Orléansville, about 130 miles southwest of Algiers. These sources declared the rebel units had been stopped outside Blida, which is the headquarters of the strong Third Military Region.

The agency linked last night's events to what it called the combined efforts by imperialism against revolutionary regimes. It indicated that the rebellion had been financed by a foreign intelligence service that it did not identify.

The agency said that many regional commanders were sending telegrams of support to President Boumediene.

Soldiers Get an Appeal

The rebellion was revealed by the President in a nine-minute nationwide broadcast earlier today in which he appealed to all officers and soldiers to put it down.

"Your duty commands you to fight rebellion under all its forms until your last breath and to destroy at the roots all germs of adventurism," he said.

Mr. Boumediene added that he was sure his loyal troops would "assume their responsibilities with courage" and would "strike at the counter-revolutionaries with firmness."

Although appealing to his loyal troops to stifle the rebellion, the President indicated in his speech that the rebellion had been crushed.

Life in Algiers was calm and business went on as usual throughout the day. Many peo-

Continued on Page 2, Column 4

U.S. Pursues Study Of Vietcong Plan

By HEDRICK SMITH
Special to The New York Times

WASHINGTON, Dec. 15—The United States, at first inclined to view the distribution of the Vietcong political program at the United Nations yesterday as a propaganda move, is trying through diplomatic channels to learn whether the Viet-

Excerpts from U.S. statement and captured notes, Page 12.

cong intended it as an opening toward negotiations.

Administration officials almost totally discounted any intention by the Vietcong to move toward political compromise.

The Government, in a prepared statement, affirmed its opinion that the program "reflects no significant change" in the position of North Vietnam or the National Liberation Front, political arm of the Vietcong.

The State Department asserted that there was no evi-

Continued on Page 12, Column 4

GOLD PURCHASES ARE HEAVY AGAIN

Anxiety in Europe Mounts as Changes Are Rumored in Monetary Measures

By ANTHONY LEWIS
Special to The New York Times

LONDON, Dec. 15—There was heavy buying of gold today in Europe's major financial centers as a feverish week in the gold markets ended. Today's surge made it the biggest gold-buying week since Britain devalued the pound on Nov. 18.

In London, dealers felt early action by the United States and other members of the gold pool was essential to stop the rush.

Much of the immediate pressure came from uncertainty about reports that the gold pool members might soon clamp restrictions on gold dealings. The announcement of rumored measures could well come this weekend.

But underlying the whole gold rush more deeply is a genuine concern among European financial men that American fiscal and balance-of-payment excesses may undermine the stability of the dollar.

Tomorrow's Financial Times says: "Opinion is hardening on

Continued on Page 71, Column 6

WESTERN POWERS REBUFF GREEK BID FOR RECOGNITION

A Junta Leader Invites King to Return at Will, Subject to 'Certain Procedures'

By SYDNEY GRUSON
Special to The New York Times

ATHENS, Dec. 15 — The major Western powers have rebuffed the new Greek Government's first approach for recognition.

The Ambassadors of the United States, Britain, Italy, France and West Germany ignored an invitation yesterday to meet Col. George Papadopoulos, who crushed King Constantine's attempted coup Wednesday and made himself Premier and Minister of Defense.

No other nation has extended recognition to the colonel's Government. The result has been to create a sense of isolation that diplomats here believe is having an effect on the Government's actions.

Stopped Off in Rome

There were many rumors tonight that the Government was seeking a reconciliation with the King, and that this was the mission of Foreign Minister Panayotis Pipinelis in Rome today.

The Foreign Minister, reputed to be a strong monarchist, stopped in Rome to see the King on his way to Athens from Brussels.

[A leading member of the junta, Brig. Stylianos Patakos, said King Constantine could return any time, The Associated Press reported. "We didn't send him away, and his throne is here," Brigadier Patakos added. But he said "certain procedures" would have to be followed. The Primate of Greece, Ieronymos, flew to see the King in Rome.]

Publishers Jailed Earlier

A good deal of what the junta is up to remains shrouded in secrecy. But it became known today that a wave of arrests had followed the King's attempted coup. The names of at least 15 people taken into custody were known.

There seemed to be no set pattern for the arrests. They were mostly of politicians, but three members of the King's staff and two newspapermen were also seized. The newspapermen were L. V. Karapanayotis and Stelios Moussis,

Continued on Page 16, Column 2

ALL THAT WAS LEFT: Smashed automobiles and trucks lie amid a tangled mass of steel and concrete on a stretch of land under the Ohio end of the collapsed bridge. It had linked Point Pleasant, W. Va. and Kanauga, Ohio.

Associated Press Wirephoto

Johnson Welcomes Upton Sinclair, 89, At Meat Bill Signing

By MAX FRANKEL
Special to The New York Times

WASHINGTON, Dec. 15 — President Johnson embraced muckrakers, housewives and even journalists today at another White House ceremony designed to demonstrate his thesis that this year's legislative record has been good, if not great.

Mr. Johnson invited Upton Sinclair to witness the signing of the Wholesome Meat Act, which will gradually plug loopholes left by the first Federal meat inspection law.

Mr. Sinclair, 89 years old, helped enact that law as a politician, as a Government employe and, above all, through his exposure of unsanitary conditions in the meat industry in a book "The Jungle" in 1906.

In a wheelchair, attended by a nurse, daughter and son-in-law, Mr. Sinclair applauded

Continued on Page 53, Column 4

U.S. TO SPEED AID TO THE NEW HAVEN

Johnson Moves to Provide $28.4-Million for 144 Cars and Modernized Stations

By RICHARD L. MADDEN
Special to The New York Times

WASHINGTON, Dec. 15—President Johnson, declaring that the New Haven Railroad "is close to financial disaster," announced today a three-part program to help the line buy new passenger cars and improve service.

Until a permanent solution to the New Haven's problems is found, the President said, he has authorized the following "immediate actions":

¶Approval by the Department of Housing and Urban Development of a $28.4-million capital grant for new equipment and other improvements to provide better commuter service between New York City and its northern suburbs over the next few years.

¶A speed-up by the Department of Transportation of a $500,000 payment to improve the New Haven's right-of-way as part of the department's demonstration program for high-speed ground transportation.

¶Agreement by the Federal Government of a debt deferral plan to free $1.7-million in immediate cash, which the line had set aside for debt payments.

Federal officials said that the $28.4-million urban mass transit capital grant would go to buy 144 new multiple-unit, self-propelled cars, to modernize

Continued on Page 45, Column 3

New Setup Urged For City Hospitals

By MARTIN TOLCHIN

A special commission appointed by Mayor Lindsay recommended yesterday that the city's hospitals and health services be operated by a public corporation appointed by the Mayor.

This would allow improvements, the commission said, by freeing the agencies from "the constraining regulations and procedures" of governmental machinery.

"The commission concludes that conditions in the city hospitals are not only deplorable but, under existing arrangements, irremediable," the report said. It was based on a 12-month study headed by Gerard Piel, publisher of Scientific American magazine.

The report said that plan-

Continued on Page 26, Column 3

Ohio River Span Crashes; Heavy Death Toll Feared

By The Associated Press

POINT PLEASANT, W. Va., Dec. 15—A towering suspension bridge collapsed during rush-hour and Christmas shopping traffic today, sending an estimated 75 cars and trucks 80 feet down into the Ohio River. Five bodies were recovered and estimates were that the death toll might go higher when daylight permitted searching the river.

"The whole bridge is in the river," a policeman said at Gallipolis, near the Ohio end of the 1,750-foot-long bridge. "There isn't any bridge any more."

[United Press International quoted Sheriff Denver Walker of Gallia County in Ohio as saying: "This is just a drop in the bucket. I'm afraid there are about 60 dead." At least 18 persons were reported hospitalized.]

The bridge carries traffic on U.S. 35 between Kanauga, Ohio, and Point Pleasant, which is 57 miles northwest of Charleston, W. Va.

Heavy Traffic Flow

A considerable stretch of the 40-year old bridge at the Ohio end was over land. An estimated 35 to 40 automobiles and trucks lay amid the tangle of concrete and steel where this part of the span fell. Wrecker trucks and cranes worked at retrieving the smashed vehicles.

Where the bridge wreckage lay in the water a skin diver searched for bodies in the strong current until the search was called off for the night at 10 P.M. Other divers had been summoned. The channel is 70 feet deep at this point.

In Washington, Lowell K. Bridwell, Federal Highway Administrator, announced that he was sending a team of bridge experts here to try to determine the cause of the collapse.

An accurate count of the number of vehicles that had been streaming across the bridge was impossible. Aside from the usual heavy flow of commuter traffic from both Ohio and West Virginia, there were many Christmas shoppers and weekend travelers.

Millard Halstead, Chief Deputy Sheriff of Mason County, W. Va., said, "It will be days before we know how many people were on the bridge. It may be days before some tour-

Continued on Page 34, Column 3

NEWS INDEX

EXP'D College Bartenders for your parties. Call Cocktails Unlimited, 864-0304—Adv't.

DIRKSEN AND FORD REBUT PRESIDENT

On TV, They Decry Attack on G.O.P. and Denounce Johnson on Inflation

Excerpts from the G.O.P. rebuttal are on Page 28.

By WARREN WEAVER Jr.
Special to The New York Times

WASHINGTON, Dec. 15—The Republican leaders of Congress went on television tonight to defend their colleagues against political charges leveled by President Johnson earlier in the week.

Senator Everett McKinley Dirksen of Illinois voiced dolorous resentment over the President's characterization of Republican House members as "wooden soldiers of the status quo."

"Generally speaking," the Senator said, "the wooden soldiers have not only been sustaining the Commander in Chief, but we have been sustaining the live soldiers in Vietnam, which is infinitely more important."

Representative Gerald R. Ford, the House Republican leader, displayed a dollar bill and reported that its value had gone down 13 per cent since

Continued on Page 28, Column 8

Postal Annex Swept By Fire, 1,800 Flee

A spectacular fire, spouting flame and smoke through shattered windows into the subfreezing night, raged through one of the city's major postal stations last night, destroying tons of Christmas mail.

Some 1,800 to 2,000 postal employes were safely evacuated from the Morgan station in Manhattan after the fierce, fast-moving blaze broke out on a basement conveyer belt at around 9:30 P.M.

At 3 A.M. the flames were reported still out of control, but were contained within the station, occupying the block between 29th and 30th Streets and Ninth and 10th Avenues. Morgan station is primarily devoted to handling foreign mail.

About 350 firemen and 50 pieces of equipment, including the Fire Department's super-

Continued on Page 82, Column 3

CONGRESS CLEARS FOUR MAJOR BILLS AND ENDS SESSION

Votes Social Security Rise, Poverty and Foreign Aid Funds and School Help

WILL RETURN ON JAN. 15

Mansfield Plans to Take Up a Civil Rights Bill Then, Assuring a Filibuster

By JOHN HERBERS
Special to The New York Times

WASHINGTON, Dec. 15—The first session of the 90th Congress, which opened last Jan. 10, adjourned tonight after approving four major bills that created controversy and dissension until the end.

The bills, sent to the White House for President Johnson's signature, provide the following:

¶Scaled-down foreign aid and antipoverty appropriations.

¶Increases in Social Security benefits along with new restrictions on welfare payments.

¶Authorization of Federal aid to elementary and secondary education for two more years.

The House adjourned sine die at 6:36 P.M. and the Senate at 6:50. In the House, about 20 members who were left on the floor whooped for joy when the adjournment motion passed.

In the Senate, the end came with a discussion of Cambodia and with Mike Mansfield of Montana, the Democratic majority leader, expressing hope that "peace will come next year."

Tax Bill Study

The 1967 session, which lasted 340 days, was the fifth-longest since World War II. The longest was 365 days in 1950.

Despite the session's length, however, a large portion of President Johnson's legislative program received no action and was put over until next year.

Both houses voted to begin the next session on Jan. 15, when work will resume on uncompleted legislation.

Wilbur D. Mills, Democrat of Arkansas, chairman of the House Ways and Means Committee, announced today that the committee would resume consideration of the main Administration bill carried over—

Continued on Page 20, Column 1

TAX RISE FACING NEW HOUSE STUDY

But Mills Bars Commitment in Sessions Next Month

By EILEEN SHANAHAN
Special to The New York Times

WASHINGTON, Dec. 15 — The House Ways and Means Committee will take another look in late January at the Administration's proposed 10 per cent tax surcharge, Representative Wilbur D. Mills, chairman of the panel, said today.

Mr. Mills made no commitment, however, that the committee would approve the tax increase even then.

In a short statement issued by his office, the Arkansas Democrat indicated that he would not abandon his drive to force the Administration to hold down Government spending as the price of favorable action on the tax bill.

In addition, the statement implied that the renewal of speculation in gold against the value of the dollar had been Mr. Mills's chief reason for announcing his intention to reconvene the committee.

Mr. Mills issued his statement shortly after a meeting in his office with Secretary of the Treasury Henry H. Fowler.

It had been known for some time that the Treasury was pressing Mr. Mills to issue a statement before Congress adjourned indicating that the tax bill was still alive for consideration next year.

Such a statement, it has been hoped, will reassure financial circles, in this country

Continued on Page 19, Column 1

CRUSADING AUTHOR HONORED: Upton Sinclair, in wheelchair, was the President's guest yesterday at signing of a bill to improve protection against abuses in meat packing. Yuki, Presidential pet, extended friendly paws to the writer, who is 89 years old.

Associated Press Wirephoto

Pontiff Sets Jan. 1 As a 'Day of Peace'

By ROBERT C. DOTY
Special to The New York Times

ROME, Dec. 15—Pope Paul VI asked all "men of goodwill" today to celebrate a worldwide "Day of Peace" on Jan. 1, 1968, and every future New Year's Day.

The Pontiff made public a message, already transmitted to all governments and churches of the world, asking "all true friends of peace"—Christian and non-Christian alike—to exercise "their own initiative to be expressed in a free manner" for peace. He particularly counseled the honoring and strengthening of international organizations with their "great mission" of peace.

He reviewed the hopes of redeeming humanity from "its sad and fatal bellicose con-

Continued on Page 18, Column 1

Ohio River Span Falls; Heavy Death Toll Feared

ists are reported missing."

Deputy Halstead said witnesses to the collapse told him they had heard victims screaming for help in the water, but they could not be seen in the darkness.

One trailer truck floated several hundred yards downstream after it plunged into the water, he said.

The disaster blocked all traffic on the Ohio River. The Corps of Engineers at Huntington said no boats were moving in the area of the bridge collapse.

The superstructure of the two-lane concrete and steel bridge tumbled on top of the cars as they hit the frigid, swirling waters.

"Traffic was bumper to bumper," said 25-year-old Todd Mayes, a teacher at the Kyger Creek High School in Ohio.

"I don't know how many cars were on it but traffic stretched all the way across the bridge.

"I looked up and it was gone," said Mr. Mayes, who had turned onto the Ohio-side bridge ramp on the way to his Point Pleasant home seconds after the span collapsed. Normally, he was on the bridge daily at 5 P.M., but he had stopped to buy a can of paint near the bridge approach.

Among those reported missing were the 18-year-old wife of Howard Boggs and his 17-month-old daughter.

"They just went down and they didn't come up with me," sobbed the 24-year-old Mr. Boggs. "I don't know how I'm going to live without them.

"That old bridge was bouncing up and down like it always does. Then all of a sudden

The New York Times   Dec. 16, 1967
Scene of collapse (cross)

everything was falling down. My feet touched the damned bottom of the river."

"I don't know how I came up. I must have blacked out again because the next thing I knew, I was hanging onto this barrel. I thought I was going to freeze to death before that tugboat picked me up.

"I just hope to God Marjorie and the kid got out okay."

Ambulances from cities and towns on both sides of the river, along with police and fire department rescue units, sped to the scene. Point Pleasant is a light industry town of 6,000.

Civil Defense officials dispatched amphibious trucks and other rescue equipment from Columbus and Marysville, Ohio. The authorities here issued a call asking the aid of owners of searchlight-equipped boats in the night rescue effort on the river. The temperature was near freezing.

Gov. Hulett C. Smith of West Virginia and Burl A. Sawyer, West Virginia Road Commissioner, left Charleston by car for Point Pleasant. Gov. James A. Rhodes of Ohio and P. E. Masheter, Ohio Highway Director, left Columbus by plane for the scene.

The bridge belongs to West Virginia. A spokesman for the West Virginia Road Commission said the state bought it from the Ohio-West Virginia Bridge Company in 1941. The bridge was dedicated in 1928 and was last inspected in April, 1965.

Aerial view shows what is left of the Pt. Pleasant-Kanauga bridge. A railroad bridge is pictured to the right of the broken span.

Wide World Photos

Associated Press

The bridge at rear in photo made some time ago is the one that collapsed completely yesterday, except for its piers. The West Virginia side is at left, the Ohio side at right.

"All the News That's Fit to Print"

The New York Times

LATE CITY EDITION

Weather: Thundershowers likely today; cloudy, cool tonight, tomorrow. Temp. range: today 64-55. Frid. 75-53. Full U. S. report on Page 78.

VOL. CXVII... No. 40,278 © 1968 The New York Times Company. NEW YORK, SATURDAY, MAY 4, 1968 10 CENTS

PEACE TALKS SET FOR PARIS; U.S. ACCEPTS HANOI'S PLAN TO BEGIN IN ABOUT A WEEK

JOHNSON DEMANDS INCREASE IN TAXES DESPITE ELECTION

Calls on Congress Members to 'Stand Up Like Men' and Help Their Country

REPUBLICANS ARE ANGRY

Rep. Byrnes Says Chances of Passing Bill Have Been 'Killed' by President

News conference transcript will be found on Page 16.

By EDWIN L. DALE Jr.
Special to The New York Times

WASHINGTON, May 3—President Johnson, using unusually strong language about Congress, demanded at a news conference today that the members "stand up like men" and pass a tax increase "even in an election year."

The time has come, the President said with emotion, for the members of Congress to "bite the bullet" and "do what ought to be done for their country." [Question 9, Page 16.]

"Don't hold up a tax bill until you can blackmail someone into getting your own personal viewpoint over on [expenditure] reductions," he cried, gesticulating fervently.

"We are courting danger by this continued procrastination," Mr. Johnson warned.

The nationally televised session was held in the East Room of the White House.

Death Blow Is Seen

Republican reaction in Congress was prompt and unfavorable. Representative John W. Byrnes of Wisconsin, the senior minority member on the Ways and Means Committee, said from his office in Green Bay, Wis.:

"The President at his press conference killed the chances for a tax bill."

Republicans have been demanding deeper spending reductions than the President is willing to accept as a price for their support of a tax increase.

The President said today he agreed this week upon a $4-billion expenditure reduction "reluctantly" even though "we do not think it's the wisest course for the nation."

"In my judgment," he continued "if Congress is left alone, it probably will not reduce appropriations the 10 billion planned and will not rescind the 8 billion. And will

Continued on Page 16, Column 1

CHALLENGES CONGRESS: President Johnson calls for tax rise at his news conference. His wife sits at left.

Associated Press

PRESIDENT VOICES CONCERN ON MARCH

'Many Inherent Dangers' in Poor People's Campaign in Capital Discerned

By BEN A. FRANKLIN
Special to The New York Times

WASHINGTON, May 3—President Johnson said today that the Government was concerned about the "many inherent dangers" in the planned camp-in here in the Poor People's Campaign.

At his news conference, he expressed the hope that the period of demonstrations would be brief, so as to avoid "possibilities of serious consequences." [Question 7, Page 16]

Mr. Johnson also said that the Government had made "extensive preparations" for trouble if it came. He did not say so, but it is known that the preparations include plans for a large deployment of troops in and around the capital when the big demonstrations begin the week of May 26.

The President voiced in a straightforward manner his second expression of concern in recent weeks about the prolonged, large-scale demonstrations that leaders of the Southern Christian Leadership Conference have planned.

He said that he expected Congress to give "due consideration" to the demands of the Poor People's Campaign, which includes jobs, housing and nutrition for the impoverished and hungry for all races. But he declared that "then we expect to get on with running the Government as it should be run."

This was obviously a reference to the pledge of the Rev.

Continued on Page 17, Column 1

Columbia and Student Unit Modify Stands in Dispute

By MURRAY SCHUMACH

A newly formed organization at Columbia University that says it represents 4,000 striking students refused yesterday to call for the resignation of the university's president and vice president in submitting its first list of demands for settling the dispute.

Other student groups have demanded the resignation of President Grayson Kirk and Vice President David B. Truman since the Columbia crisis began on April 23 when students began seizing buildings on the campus.

The demand became even more insistent after violence broke out last Tuesday as the police cleared students from the five occupied buildings.

Beyond Personalities

"We dropped the demand for the resignations for the time being," said Mark Rudd, president of the school's radical Students for a Democratic Society, which is part of the new broad-based Columbia Strike Coordinating Committee.

"We don't want to suggest that only personalities are responsible for the problems of the university," he said, after making public the coordinating group's program.

The development was one of a number during the day that indicated a drift, perhaps only temporary, toward greater moderation among faculty as well as student factions and a stronger hope for resumption of a more normal school life next week.

Other indications were these:

¶Announcement by Prof. Lionel Trilling, in behalf of the 12-man executive committee of the faculty, that his group had begun meetings with diverse groups among students and faculty "to restore the shattered frame of confidence."

¶Return to class by hundreds of students at the Law School, despite the pleas of a few dozens pickets to remain away.

¶Support for the 12-man faculty group by the Committees on Instruction of Columbia University on Morningside Heights, a group of some 90 members representing 13 faculties. This was the first time in Columbia history that this group has met as a body.

¶Indications that top officials at the university were considering the possibility of dropping criminal charges against students arrested early Tuesday morning.

¶Growing evidence that the university's board of trustees was prepared to share some of its authority with other groups at Columbia.

Concession by Truman

¶A concession by Dr. Truman, during a three-hour appearance on WNDT, Channel 13, that "clearly there were some breakdowns in the police action."

¶Some 600 signatures by students on petitions calling for resumption of all classes on Monday "so that the destructive processes of anarchy not be given the opportunity to make the rebuilding process more difficult." The petition was addressed to "moderates."

The backdrop for these activities was a generally cheerful campus yesterday that had classes on the lawn, animated discussions, embracing couples and music by a rock 'n' roll group.

There were signs of tension in the occasionally heated arguments among knots of students

Continued on Page 28, Column 1

SORBONNE CLOSED AS STUDENTS RIOT

500 Are Arrested in Paris as Police Evict Leftists —Scores Are Injured

By LLOYD GARRISON
Special to The New York Times

PARIS, May 3—More than 500 students were arrested and scores injured today when armed riot policemen charged the quadrangle of the Sorbonne and evicted left-wing demonstrators.

While battles between students and the police continued to erupt tonight along the Boulevard St.-Michel, Jean Roche, the rector of the Sorbonne, announced that France's oldest and most prestigious university would close tomorrow for the first time in recorded history. The Sorbonne was founded in 1253.

By nightfall, clashes between students and the police had spread throughout much of the Latin Quarter, with many streets clouded with tear-gas fumes.

Students Strike Back

Boulevard St.-Michel resembled a battleground. Many students, incensed by earlier police violence in clearing the university, struck back with bricks, paving blocks and tin cans filled with gasoline and ignited by home-made fuses.

By 10 P.M., 21 steel-helmeted policemen had been injured, one seriously. The police had no count of the number of students injured. At least a dozen were carried away from the scene in ambulances. Among those requiring medical treatment were two news photographers, one of whom had been badly beaten during a police charge.

One teen-age girl, clubbed half-conscious and crying "Mama, Mama," lay for more than 40 minutes on the pavement of Boulevard St.-Michel before an ambulance arrived.

Tactical Victory for Students

The Sorbonne's closing was a major tactical victory for the New Left student-power movement, which earlier this week forced the closing of the University of Nanterre in suburban Paris.

The New Left in France is composed of many fractious groups—Communists, Socialists, anarchists and Marxist devotees of the slain Latin-American revolutionary, Ernesto Che Guevara.

They are united in two general goals—more student control of university administration, and in the political field, the violent overthrow of the "capitalist establishment" in general.

Although they constitute a small minority among French students—many of whom are apolitical—leaders of the New Left have been able to exert increasing pressure on university administrations. At Nan-

Continued on Page 30, Column 5

ALLIES MAUL FOE

Kill 856 Near Dongha and Repel Division —Jets Strike North

By United Press International

SAIGON, South Vietnam, Saturday, May 4 — United States marines and South Vietnamese troops have hurled back a North Vietnamese division near Dongha, killing 856 of the enemy, military spokesmen said today.

American casualties in the four-day battle were 68 men killed and 323 injured seriously enough to be evacuated, the spokesmen said. South Vietnamese casualties were described as light.

The spokesmen said that the assault on the Marine base at Dongha, in South Vietnam's northernmost province, was the first time in the war that the enemy had massed a full division of troops for a single strike.

The spokesmen said that the battle for the base was opened Tuesday by some 8,000 North Vietnamese troops who swept southward from the demilitarized zone.

The allies, with a total force of about 5,000 men, broke the back of the attack yesterday when the enemy withdrew after making a counterattack about five miles north of Dongha.

United States jets struck repeatedly at the retreating North Vietnamese.

Action Heavy Near Saigon

By JOSEPH B. TREASTER
Special to The New York Times

SAIGON, May 4—South Vietnamese troops and American helicopter crews killed 194 Vietcong soldiers yesterday in a daylong battle 28 miles southwest of Saigon.

Military spokesmen said the South Vietnamese had suffered light losses. The Americans reported no casualties.

In an air strike in North Vietnam, United States Air Force pilots reported having destroyed more than 800 drums of petroleum, oil and lubricants in a storage area 24 miles north of the Mugia Pass, a major funnel for infiltration into South Vietnam. Each drum contained 100 gallons.

A United States military spokesman said that bombs from the Air Force planes had set off 12 explosions on the ground and that black smoke swirled 7,000 feet into the air as the fuel burned.

The fighting southwest of Saigon, in the rice paddies of the Mekong Delta, began when a South Vietnamese battalion spotted elements of the 263d

Continued on Page 10, Column 1

A Role for de Gaulle Forecast by French

Special to The New York Times

PARIS, May 3—The choice of Paris as the site for preliminary peace talks led informed French observers to predict today that President de Gaulle would eventually play a major active role in the search for a settlement in Vietnam.

The French Government had no official comment on the agreement by the United States and North Vietnam to meet here, but representatives of practically all parties expressed joy and gratification.

An especially jubilant statement came from Robert Poujade, the spokesman of the Gaullist movement. He made it clear that the regime regarded the event as a triumph of its policy of independence and neutrality.

Mr. Poujade said the fact

Continued on Page 14, Column 6

JOHNSON CAUTIOUS

But Voices a Hope for 'Serious Movement' for a Settlement

Text of Hanoi broadcast is printed on Page 14.

By MAX FRANKEL
Special to The New York Times

WASHINGTON, May 3—The United States and North Vietnam agreed today to begin formal talks in Paris next Friday or soon thereafter.

The break in the deadlock over a place to meet was apparently unexpected here. It came during the night in a message delivered to the United States Embassy in Laos. President Johnson accepted the arrangements in a return message this morning and then announced the agreement at a news conference that had been previously scheduled. [Opening statement, Page 16.]

Mr. Johnson said he hoped the agreement "can represent a mutual and a serious movement by all parties toward peace in Southeast Asia," but he cautioned that he foresaw "many, many hazards and difficulties ahead."

As Hanoi's statement was interpreted at the White House, one of the immediate difficulties will be the agenda for the first round of talks.

Hanoi Holds to Its Views

North Vietnam held to the view that the purpose of the talks was to enable the United States "to decide" on an unconditional halt in the bombing of all of North Vietnam "and all other acts of war" against it. Other matters, it said, could be talked about later.

Mr. Johnson chose not to argue this point in public, saying only that "I assume that each side will present its viewpoint in these contacts."

But he and his senior advisers have made it clear that they still will insist on the San Antonio formula, outlined by the President in a speech there, which stipulates that a complete halt to the bombing of North Vietnam will come only if the United States is given reason to assume that Hanoi will not take military advantage of the cessation.

Feels Vindicated

After 34 days of diplomatic dickering with Hanoi about a suitable place to meet, Mr. Johnson seemed to feel vindicated in his tactics. He had resisted formal talks in Cambodia or Poland, places that he felt to be disadvantageous to the United States and to its allies, particularly South Vietnam.

After previous rhetorical offers to meet any place, any time, the President was heavily criticized as procrastinating over the last month, both by North Vietnam and by many Americans, including two of his party's candidates for the Presidential nomination — Senators Eugene J. McCarthy and Robert F. Kennedy.

The President suggested today that it had been worthwhile to wait. Paris, he pointed out, was a place in which all parties to the war "should expect" fair and impartial treatment and where they all maintained diplomatic representation.

Mr. Johnson again appealed to the candidates not to mislead the enemy about who speaks for the United States,

Continued on Page 14, Column 1

PARTY IS ASSAILED AT PRAGUE RALLY

Student Meeting Displays Anti-Communist Tone — Dubcek Flies to Moscow

By DAVID BINDER
Special to The New York Times

PRAGUE, May 3 — A student rally today in Prague's Old Town Square supporting the democratization of Czechoslovakia swiftly assumed a markedly anti-Communist character.

It took place amid growing evidence of political tension on both domestic and external fronts.

It was disclosed tonight that Alexander Dubcek, the new Communist party chief, had flown to Moscow for meetings with the Soviet Government.

A brief announcement by the Czechoslovak press agency said he was accompanied by Oldrich Cernik, the Premier; Josef Smrkovsky, head of Parliament, and Vasil Bilak, head of the Slovak wing of the party.

According to reliable sources, these topics were on the agenda of his Moscow talks: Economic relations between Czechoslovakia and the Soviet Union, as well as economic cooperation with other Communist countries, and negotiation of a gold-ruble credit from the Soviet Union for modernizing the Czechoslovak consumer-goods industry.

It is understood that, from the Czechoslovak side, questions will be raised as to how much the Dubcek leadership

Continued on Page 12, Column 4

HOUSE UNIT VOTES RISE IN URBAN AID

$13.8-Billion Bill Lists Half a Billion for Model Cities

By MARJORIE HUNTER
Special to The New York Times

WASHINGTON, May 3 — Despite pressure to trim domestic spending, the House Appropriations Committee voted today to increase the flow of Federal funds into city programs.

The action by the normally economy-minded committee reflected Congressional concern over recent riots and other forms of urban unrest.

Among the city programs funded under the $13.8-billion money bill approved by the committee to finance 21 Government agencies were the following:

¶Model cities, the Administration's program designed to rehabilitate city slums, $500-million. This is $150-million less than requested by President Johnson but $188-million more than appropriated for the fiscal year 1968 that ends June 30.

¶Federal subsidies for low-rent housing, $350-million. This is $8-million less than the President proposed but $75-million above the current fiscal year appropriation.

¶Rent supplements, under which the Government subsidizes a portion of the rent payments for poor families, $25-

Continued on Page 17, Column 7

84 Killed in Crash of Braniff Electra in Texas

4-Engine Turboprop Airplane Falls in an Electric Storm

By United Press International

CORSICANA, Tex., May 3—A Braniff International Electra flying through blinding rain and lightning crashed in a ball of flame tonight in a pasture in central Texas. All 84 persons aboard were killed.

A witness said the four-engine turboprop Electra, a later version of the trouble-plagued Lockheed aircraft that was grounded for a while in the early nineteen-sixties, had blown up before it hit the ground, and pieces "fishtailed" down through sheets of rain.

The Federal Bureau of Investigation said in Washington that there was no reason to suspect foul play.

It was the first major United States airline crash in 1968 and the first serious one since Nov. 20, 1967, when a Trans World Airlines Convair jetliner bound from Los Angeles to Boston

The New York Times May 4, 1968

fell short of the runway at Greater Cincinnati Airport and killed 69 persons.

Braniff said the plane left Houston at 5:11 P.M., Eastern daylight time, on a flight to Dallas. It was scheduled to go on to Tulsa, Okla., and Memphis. Braniff officials said the plane had sent a routine message after leaving Houston. The crash occurred some time between 5:30 and 5:41.

Eyewitness Reports That It Exploded While in Air

Cloyce Floyd, postmaster of the little town of Dawson, about a mile away from the crash scene, said he was driving along in a driving rain and saw a "red flash."

"I looked over to the left and I could see this red ball of fire hanging back there about the size of the sun," he said. "From the glare of the fire I could see the fuselage sort of fishtailing down. Then it hit and exploded."

Rex Owen, a fireman from Mexia, Tex., was among nearly 100 volunteer rescue workers who went to the scene.

"It [the wreckage] was scattered all over the place," he said.

Rescue vehicles clogged the muddy roads carrying bodies back to morgues. The Mayor of Dawson, Charles Renfro, told

Continued on Page 24, Column 3

City May Cut Realty Tax Rise Because Investments Earn More

By CHARLES G. BENNETT

City property owners were told yesterday by Controller Mario A. Procaccino that their 1968-69 real estate tax rate would probably be lower than had been predicted.

He said an improved interest yield from the Federal and municipal securities in which the city invests its sinking fund money had reduced by $8.5-million the allocation for debt retirement.

This reduction, he said, will pare the predicted 1968-69 tax rate by 2.6 cents on each $100 of property valuation.

In February, Michael Freyberg, president of the Tax Commission, forecast for the fiscal year beginning July 1 a basic realty tax rate 5 to 8 cents more than the current figures of $5.07.

Contrasted with Mr. Freyberg's February forecast of a probable tax rate of $5.12 to $5.15, the Controller's figures would make this range $5.09 to $5.12, with allowances for added fractional amounts.

Taking a median estimated basic tax rate within Mr. Procaccino's range of $5.11, the owner of a house assessed at $20,000 would pay a basic tax of $1,022, and the owner of a commercial building assessed at $1-million would pay a basic tax of $51,100.

Mr. Freyberg's prediction of a tax rate was made as he announced a tentative assessed valuation of the city's taxable real estate for 1968-69 of $33,849,357,210.

The tax rate on city real estate must be set for the coming fiscal year by the City Council not later than June 25. To the basic citywide rate the Council will add borough rates to reduce the debt for local improvements.

In a letter to Mayor Lindsay,

Continued on Page 23, Column 3

NEWS INDEX

84 Dead in Crash of Braniff Airliner

United Press International

Workmen search the wreckage of the Braniff airliner that crashed in farm country while approaching Dallas Love Field on a flight from Houston.

Continued From Page 1, Col. 4

curiosity seekers to stay away. He said they were making "a general nuisance" of themselves.

Braniff identified the crew of five as:

Phillips, J. R., the captain.

Foster, Jack, first officer.

Crossland, D. W., second officer.

Brand, Jo Carol, stewardess.

Renz, Suzanne, stewardess.

Mr. Phillips and Mr. Foster were from Dallas and Mr. Crossland lived in Irving, a suburb of Dallas. Miss Brand was from Taylor, N. D., and Miss Renz from South Orange, N. J., but both stewardesses were stationed at Dallas.

Two other Braniff employes were on the plane. They were identified as Molly Ann Deware, a secretary from Jefferson, Tex.; and John Allen Roberts, a construction engineer from Dallas.

The crash site, near a farmhouse about 24 miles south of Corsicana and about half a mile south of Texas Farm Road 709, was lit with emergency power as workers toiled through the night in a wet drizzle trying to remove all the bodies.

The plane was one of the few that Braniff had not painted in its new rainbow color motif.

It still bore the red, blue and silver colors the line used in years past.

The wreckage was still smoldering hours later. The fuselage was a jumble of torn and tangled metal. The scorched trees around it were hung with metal and fabric.

A tornado watch was out for the whole area and violent thunderstorms and lightning were reported in central Texas when the plane went down.

A Braniff public relations official at Dallas said the cause of the crash was not known.

"It appears that this plane exploded prior to hitting the ground inasmuch as it scattered over a large area," he said. "We were unable initially to find anything to identify the plane. This thing is scattered all over the country, and the mud is ankle deep."

In Washington, the F.B.I. said its "disaster squad" would be sent to the scene at Braniff's request to assist in identifying victims. But, the bureau said, there was no reason to suspect foul play.

The crash site was in rolling hill country where farmers grow mostly cotton and sorghum. Dawson is the only town in the area.

The Texas Department of Public Safety rushed fingerprint and chemical technicians to the

scene to help with the identification.

Striking members of the Communications Workers of America lifted their picket lines in Corsicana to allow telephone operators to go back to work to handle emergency calls.

Tragedy struck the Electra when it first began flying nearly a decade ago.

The airliner began flying in January, 1959. By 1960 it was the center of controversy.

It had suffered two fatal accidents which claimed 97 lives. An Electra operated by Braniff crashed near Buffalo, Tex., Sept. 29, 1959. On March 17, 1960, a Northwest Airlines Electra crashed near Tell City, Ind.

In both cases, a wing of the plane ripped away. A Civil Aeronautics Board investigation traced the weakness to a vibration known as "whirl mode:" mounts holding the engine in place became loose.

This, in turn, set up a vibration that was transmitted to the wing. Investigators found that at certain speeds the wing would break loose.

Lockheed recalled all of the airplanes after the 1960 crash.

The defect was corrected at a cost of $25-million.

The last fatal Electra crash occurred Sept. 17, 1961.

Associated Press

Rescue workers carry a body from wreckage of airliner

"All the News That's Fit to Print"

The New York Times

LATE CITY EDITION
Weather: Rain, windy, cool today. Cloudy, chance of rain tomorrow. Temp. range: today 56-50; Monday 59-48. Full U.S. report on Page 93.

VOL. CXVII . No. 40,302 | NEW YORK, TUESDAY, MAY 28, 1968 | 10 CENTS
© 1968 The New York Times Company.

$6-BILLION BUDGET ASKED BY LINDSAY, 16% OVER '67-'68

Most of $840-Million Rise Would Go for Education and Welfare Expenses

HE CALLS IT 'AUSTERE'

Only Major New Program Is Expansion of Police—Revenue Need Cited

The text of Mayor's budget is printed on Page 34.

By RICHARD REEVES

Mayor Lindsay submitted a $6,082,455,491 expense budget to the City Council and Board of Estimate yesterday to cover the day-to-day costs of running the city during the year that begins July 1.

Described by Mr. Lindsay as an "austerity" budget, the 1968-69 financial plan lists expenditures $840-million—or 16 per cent—higher than last year's. Most of the increase will be used to meet rising welfare and education costs.

The new $6.1-billion budget is the largest in the city's 300-year history and the second largest in the nation—topped only by the $186.1-billion Federal budget. The city's budget is $400-million higher than the State of California's proposed 1968-69 budget, $700-million higher than New York State's, and higher than any Federal budget before President Franklin D. Roosevelt's first term.

Difficulties Stressed

In submitting the budget for Council and Board approval, Mr. Lindsay emphasized that revenue shortages and legal requirements for a balanced budget made it impossible to plan major city programs in the coming year.

"My basic objective," he wrote on the first of 2,075 pages in three books distributed at City Hall yesterday afternoon, "is the continuation of essential public services without disastrous reductions."

The only significant new program listed in the summary is a $25-million allocation to increase the size of the police force by 3,000 men, to 31,938 men.

Balance Is Tipped

But there are 46 items listed under the heading "Economies, Program Reductions." Those reductions range from a $5.9-million cut in the education appropriation because of the elimination of after-school recreational and study programs in nonpoverty areas to a $155,000 cut effected by eliminating 47 of 129 paid chaplains who serve city departments.

The budget was delicately balanced last Saturday afternoon by a combination of economies, additional state aid and a 10-point package of new taxes and fees, including a small real-estate tax increase and a $10 automobile use tax.

But the balance was tipped later the same day when the State Legislature rejected one

Continued on Page 35, Column 1

Justices Tell South To Spur Integration Of All Its Schools

Special to The New York Times

WASHINGTON, May 27—The Supreme Court ruled unanimously today that "freedom of choice" desegregation plans are inadequate if they do not undo Southern school segregation as rapidly as other available methods would.

In its first detailed review of the adequacy of the means being used to implement the landmark school desegregation decision of 1954, the Court declared that "delays are no longer tolerable." It stopped short, however, of granting the full relief that civil rights lawyers had requested.

The Court did not declare freedom of choice plans inherently unconstitutional. This would have required many Southern communities to begin taking affirmative steps to mix more Negroes with whites in the schools. About 9 out of 10 Southern communities now employ the freedom of choice plan, which

Continued on Page 33, Column 4

HIGH COURT BACKS BAN ON BURNING OF DRAFT CARDS

Rules Out 'Symbolic Speech' Appeal in Upholding '65 Curb on War Protesters

Excerpts from Court decision will be found on Page 32.

By FRED P. GRAHAM
Special to The New York Times

WASHINGTON, May 27—The Supreme Court upheld today a law of 1965 that makes it a crime to burn or otherwise destroy or mutilate a draft card.

In a 7-to-1 opinion by Chief Justice Earl Warren, the Court gave a strong and sweeping endorsement to the power of Congress to strengthen the Selective Service laws.

It also discounted the assertion of the lone dissenter, Justice William O. Douglas, that the Supreme Court should consider whether the Selective Service laws could constitutionally be used to draft young men to fight in an undeclared war.

The law, an amendment to the Selective Service laws, was enacted by Congress in response to a series of antiwar protests that involved public destruction of draft cards. It was declared unconstitutional by the United States Court of Appeals for the First Circuit as an infringement on free speech.

Lower Court Reversed

But in the opinion today, Chief Justice Warren rejected the lower court's contention that draft card burning is "symbolic speech" and that Congress is forbidden by the First Amendment's free-speech guarantees to outlaw it.

"We cannot accept the view that an apparently limitless variety of conduct can be labeled 'speech' whenever the person engaging in the conduct intends thereby to express an idea," the Chief Justice said.

He also rejected a contention that the circumstances of the law's enactment proved that it had been intended to quash antiwar dissent.

It is a "hazardous matter" to try to determine the subjective motive of the members of Congress in passing the law, he said, and since there are legitimate reasons why Congress might want to prevent the destruction of draft cards, the Court would not assume that Congress had acted for unconstitutional reasons.

The opinion listed a number of reasons why it thought the draft system would function more smoothly if registrants were forbidden to destroy or multilate their draft cards. It concluded that the law against

Continued on Page 32, Column 6

U.S. Nuclear Submarine With 99 Overdue

Search for Scorpion Is Begun by Craft of Atlantic Fleet

By WILLIAM BEECHER
Special to The New York Times

WASHINGTON, May 27—The nuclear-powered attack submarine Scorpion, with 99 men aboard, was reported overdue tonight.

A widespread search by planes, ships and submarines of the Atlantic Fleet was quickly ordered. It stretched from the Virginia Capes to the Azores, west of Portugal.

By 10 P.M. some 18 ships were involved, two of them dispatched from a base in Spain, the remainder from American ports.

Adm. Thomas L. Moorer, Chief of Naval Operations, said the Scorpion had been scheduled to return to Norfolk, Va., at 1 P.M. today after completion of a three-month training exercise with ships of the Sixth Fleet in the Mediterranean.

She was last heard from last Tuesday night, he said, and gave her position—about 50 miles south of the

United Press International
The crew of the Scorpion lining the pier for her commissioning in 1960 at Groton, Conn.

Azores—together with her easterly course, her 18-knot speed and her estimated time of arrival in Norfolk.

The Navy is making no presumption that the Scorpion is lost, Admiral Moorer insisted. There have been numerous occasions over the last several years, he said, in which nuclear submarines have been late and unheard from for a matter of hours, only to turn up safe.

In the case of the Scorpion, he said, the skipper, Comdr. Francis A. Slattery, may have decided to delay his approach over the shallow waters on the continental shelf because of storms and rough seas. Waves of 15 to 20 feet were churning the area, he said.

Such stormy weather may also have prevented the skipper from communicating with

Continued on Page 3, Column 2

FRENCH STRIKERS TURN DOWN PACT, CONTINUE SIT-INS

Voting With Raised Hands, Workers Defy Leaders—Walkout Still Spreads

35,000 RALLY IN PARIS

Students and Unionists Urge End of Gaullist Regime—Referendum June 16

By HENRY TANNER
Special to The New York Times

PARIS, May 27 — An overwhelming majority of French workers decided today to go on with their strike and to reject the far-reaching concessions that Premier Georges Pompidou made to their union leaders early today.

The strikers continued to occupy the thousands of factories throughout the country that they have held for a week to 10 days. Red flags still flew over the plants. Public transportation was still halted. Economic analysts, looking at the rejected pact, predicted that France faced a bout of inflation.

As if to demonstrate the hardening of the workers' position, strikers at the nationalized gas and electricity company of Paris cut off current in most of the capital for half an hour after lunch.

Demonstration Is Held

Also students, workers and opposition political leaders, a crowd of 35,000, marched to a Paris stadium, where they held a demonstration calling for an end of the Gaullist regime.

The referendum, on which President de Gaulle has staked his presidency, was set for June 16. The date was officially announced today. The text that will confront the voters will be published Wednesday.

Because of the overwhelming rejection of the wage package, the back-to-work movement, expected by many, did not materialize. This was a blow to the Government, which had hoped that a 35 per cent rise in minimum wages and other proposed benefits would end the strikes, which began 10 days ago.

Leaders Watch Vote

The strike movement, in fact, expanded in some regions. Barge traffic stopped on the Seine, the Oise and the Moselle Rivers. The workers at the Government's nuclear center in St.-Paul-lès-Durance, in southern France, walked out, following their colleagues in the nation's other nuclear installations.

The strikers in the nation's key industrial plants gave the signal for the defiance. They met in factory assemblies and voted, almost unanimously, by raising arms over their heads.

The first results came from the auto plants of Renault and Citroën in the Paris region; Berliet, the big truck builder, in Lyons; the Michelin tire factory in Clermont-Ferrand, in central France, and Rhodiaceta, the biggest plastic-fiber manu-

Continued on Page 16, Column 1

SUBWAY DELAYS EXPECTED TODAY

IRT Between Manhattan and Brooklyn Disrupted by Transformer Fire

A power failure disrupted large portions of the subway system yesterday and, despite emergency repairs, was expected to prevent any continuous service on the IRT between Brooklyn and Manhattan this morning.

The Transit Authority reported that it would run special trains between the New Lots and Flatbush terminals in Brooklyn and Atlantic Avenue, where passengers may transfer without cost to the BMT for the rest of the trip into Manhattan.

Because of the power failure, which was caused by a transformer fire, the IRT trains will operate at only half their normal speed.

In announcing that the emergency would extend at least through the morning rush hour, the Transit Authority urged those who normally used the IRT in Brooklyn to switch to alternative routes whenever possible. The IND and BMT will be running normally, the authority spokesman said.

The failure on the IRT cut out all service to four IRT stations in Brooklyn—Nevins, Hoyt, Clark and Borough Hall. In Manhattan, Wall Street and

Continued on Page 59, Column 3

M'CARTHY FORCES FORESEE VICTORY

Kennedy Holds Slight Lead in Latest Polls on Eve of Primary in Oregon

By WARREN WEAVER Jr.
Special to The New York Times

PORTLAND, Ore., May 27—The critically important Oregon Democratic primary campaign closed today with the exuberant forces of Senator Eugene J. McCarthy claiming that victory over Senator Robert F. Kennedy was within their grasp.

Senator Kennedy still enjoyed a very narrow lead in the latest public opinion polls, but his margin was so small that any big movement of undecided voters toward the Minnesota Senator could wipe it out.

A victory in Oregon is considered almost essential for the New York Senator's prospect of winning the nomination. Senator Kennedy himself has said he must win here to remain "a viable candidate."

Import for California

A loss could endanger the advantage a strong campaign has built for him in California, where the primary will be held June 4.

[In Harrisburg, Pa., a majority of Pennsylvania's delegates to the Democratic National Convention voted to support Vice President Humphrey for the nomination for President.]

The most recent poll, taken by Oliver Quayle for the National Broadcasting Company and made public tonight, gave Senator Kennedy 34 per cent, Senator McCarthy 32, Vice President Humphrey (who is not on the ballot) 10, President Johnson (who is) 9, others 4 and undecided 11.

In their previous primary contests in Indiana and Nebraska, Mr. McCarthy has picked up roughly two-thirds

Continued on Page 8, Column 1

5,000 Farmers Stage Protest in Brussels

By CLYDE H. FARNSWORTH
Special to The New York Times

BRUSSELS, May 27—Five thousand farmers swarmed into central Brussels today to protest against any lowering of dairy price supports by the European Common Market.

The farmers listened to speeches, disrupted traffic, waved posters, let air out of automobile tires and bombarded policemen with eggs and cheese.

The police retaliated by shooting water at the demonstrators from water cannons kept in reserve around the Palais des Congrès.

This low, sprawling complex of buildings on a hill in the downtown area is where farm ministers from the six member states—France, Italy, West Germany, the Netherlands, Belgium and Luxembourg—are meeting to try to work out common dairy policies.

The purpose of the demonstration was to get the farmers' point of view across to the ministers.

The market has been wrestling with the problem for months. Farmers thought the question was settled two years ago when common prices for dairy products were originally agreed upon.

The establishment of these relatively high prices led to the building up of huge butter surpluses. West Germany and Italy have been complaining that the cost of financing this surplus production is too great.

Now a plan has been put forward to lower the support price for butter, to put a tax on margarine and to defer until next year the knotty problem of how to finance the surpluses.

The farm ministers are trying to reach agreement in three days. They are negotiating under pressure of a July 1 deadline, when the member states are scheduled to eliminate all industrial duties in trade with each other.

France has said that if common prices for dairy products are not worked out

Continued on Page 16, Column 6

ECONOMISTS URGE ASSURED INCOME

1,000 in Universities Urge Payment Based on Need, With Work Incentives

Special to The New York Times

WASHINGTON, May 27 — More than 1,000 academic economists endorsed today "a national system of income guarantees and supplements."

The brief statement was sponsored by five well-known economists and was issued here and in Cambridge, Mass. It supported, by implication, the demand of the Poor People's Campaign here for a "guaranteed annual income."

The statement said the cost of an income guarantee or supplement plan would be "substantial but well within the nation's economic and fiscal capacity." It also said such a plan was "feasible and compatible with our economic system."

The five sponsors were Profs. Paul A. Samuelson of the Massachusetts Institute of Technology, John Kenneth Galbraith of Harvard, James Tobin of Yale and Harold Watts and Robert Lampman of the University of Wisconsin.

The signers were from 125 colleges and universities, with 10 universities having 15 or more signers.

The statement did not endorse any of the specific proposals for guaranteed income, such as a "negative income tax." But it said:

"A workable and equitable plan of income guarantees and

Continued on Page 22, Column 3

Hanoi Is Believed Shifting On Denial It Uses Troops

By ANTHONY LEWIS
Special to The New York Times

PARIS, May 27—Amid harsh words today at the fifth session of the preliminary talks on Vietnam, Hanoi's delegation took an apparent step toward acknowledging that North Vietnamese troops are in the South.

The American spokesman, William J. Jorden, said later that the chief North Vietnamese delegate, Xuan Thuy, had come "about as close as he has to date to admitting" the presence of North Vietnamese regulars in the South. Others saw potential significance in the language used by Mr. Thuy, who said:

"Vietnam is one country, the Vietnamese people are one... When the United States commits aggression against Vietnam, any Vietnamese has the right to fight them, and that on any portion of his dear country's territory. This is a sacred and inalienable right."

Somewhat similar comments have been made in the past, but experts regarded today's formulation as more emphatic and forthright. It was given added import by the fact that the Government in Hanoi made a statement to the same effect today, using some of the same phrases.

W. Averell Harriman, the chief United States negotiator, has attached much weight to the need for an acknowledgement by the North Vietnamese here that their troops are in the South.

He said nine days ago that such an admission would provide a basis for considering Hanoi's demand for cessation of American bombing — and later to consider "the withdrawal or regroupment" of all non-South Vietnamese forces from South Vietnam.

Hanoi has never formally admitted that regular North Vietnamese units are in the South, and it seems unlikely that it will. The question is whether today's language, with its im-

Continued on Page 14, Column 1

Republicans Revolt in Jersey; Lean to Hughes on Urban Aid

By RONALD SULLIVAN
Special to The New York Times

TRENTON, May 27—A major Republican revolt in the Legislature and a "rich people's march" on the state capital combined here today to project new hope for Gov. Richard J. Hughes's urban-aid and capital-construction programs.

The revolt saw Republican legislators from Bergen and Essex Counties reject their party's announced fiscal program in favor of higher measures that come closer to the programs advocated by the Democratic Governor.

Meanwhile, about 2,000 people, most of them well-dressed women from well-to-do suburbs, attended a bipartisan Majority Response for Urban Aid Rally on the steps of the War Memorial Building near the Statehouse. The rally was held to generate support for the Governor's $126-million urban-aid program.

Former Governors Alfred E. Driscoll, a Republican, and Robert B. Meyner, a Democrat, were co-chairmen of the sponsoring committee.

In the Legislature, the Bergen and Essex defections were considered significant because the two counties command the biggest delegations in both houses, which the Republicans control

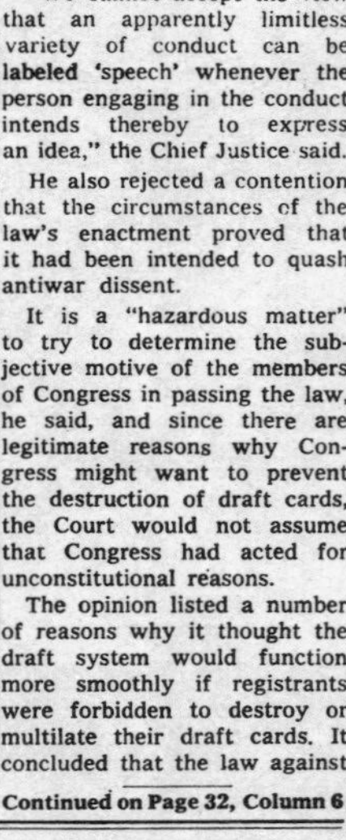

United Press International
Alfred E. Driscoll, former Governor, is a leader in the move to increase urban aid.

by 3-to-1 majorities. The margins would normally be enough to override a gubernatorial veto and enact a fiscal program independent of Mr. Hughes.

Along with his urban-aid program, the Governor has proposed a $1.75-billion bond issue for capital construction.

However, the Republican legislative leadership announced last week that it had agreed upon an $890-million bond issue and a $58.4-million local-aid program that would in many cases give more aid

Continued on Page 24, Column 4

Guilty Verdict Given In Crimmins Trial

By EDITH EVANS ASBURY

After more than nine hours of deliberation, an all-male jury early this morning found Mrs. Alice Crimmins guilty of manslaughter in the first degree in the death of her 4-year-old daughter almost three years ago.

Mrs. Crimmins sat shaken but without tears as the jury filed into the courtroom preceded by a racing crowd of spectators. Her husband, Edmond, and her brother, John Burke, a teacher, both sobbed audibly as the foreman declared the jury's findings.

Harold Harrison, the lawyer for the 29-year-old defendant, asked that the jury be polled and each man stood in turn and told Supreme Court Justice Peter Farrell that he had in-

Continued on Page 94, Column 2

Montreal, San Diego In National League

The National League voted last night in Chicago to expand to 12 teams next year, awarding baseball franchises to Montreal and San Diego. Each of the new teams will pay $10-million for its franchise.

The 10 owners of the present clubs in the league agreed on the two cities after almost 10 hours of deliberation.

Warren Giles, league president, said that Montreal will play in Expo Stadium, which will be enlarged to seat 45,000. The city will have completed a domed stadium seating 55,000 by 1971. San Diego will play in its new $28-million stadium, which seats 45,000.

The choice of Montreal marks the major leagues' first expansion out of the United States.

Details on Page 55

Allies to Yield Last Occupation Powers to Bonn

Step Is Linked to Expected Passage of Emergency Laws by German Parliament

By PHILIP SHABECOFF
Special to The New York Times

BONN, May 27—The United States, Britain and France agreed today to surrender vestigial occupation rights in West Germany as soon as Bonn's new emergency laws go into effect. The laws would entitle the Government to suspend constitutional rights in time of national emergency.

The allied agreement means that West Germany will achieve legal sovereignty for the first time since the fall of the Third Reich at the end of World War II in 1945.

Meanwhile, a fresh outbreak of strikes and demonstrations against the emergency laws erupted at schools and universities.

Henry Cabot Lodge, the new United States Ambassador, along with the French ambassador and the British chargé d'affaires, met today with Willy Brandt, the West German Foreign Minister, to declare their willingness to give up the reserve powers they hold under the convention of 1954 ending the occupation status of West Germany.

Earlier, Mr. Lodge presented his credentials to President Heinrich Lübke.

The most important powers that will be yielded by the Western allies are the right to tap telephones and inspect letters in West Germany. These rights were retained after 1954 to enable the allies to protect the security of their military forces on West German soil.

The West German Government will take over the telephone and postal surveillance after the controversial emergency laws pass their third and final reading.

The laws and the agreement today will not affect the status of Berlin. The three Western allies will continue to function as occupation powers in West Berlin. The Soviet Union, formally the occupying power in East Berlin, ceded its rights to the East German Government in 1955, an action the three Western powers do not recognize.

For some years the Western allies have stated their readiness to give up their reserve rights in West Germany as soon as Bonn produced legislation enabling it to preserve public order and maintain a viable government in time of national emergency.

Such legislation first was drafted more than a decade ago.

Continued on Page 2, Column 6

NEWS INDEX

"THE SPIRIT OF '76"—HAPPY BIRTHDAY JENNIE GROSSINGER JUNE 16, 1968—Advt.

U.S. Nuclear Submarine With 99 Aboard Is Overdue at Norfolk

Continued From Page 1, Col. 7

shore, the admiral said. But he noted that not even fragmentary messages had been picked up.

Five years ago, the nuclear attack submarine Thresher was similarly reported overdue and later was found to have sunk in 8,400 feet of water 220 miles east of Cape Cod with 129 men aboard.

A court of inquiry attributed the Thresher loss to a piping system failure in the engine room, believed to have caused flooding that pulled the submarine down to the ocean floor.

A Navy spokesman said the Scorpion went through her last normal overhaul during most of last year. At that time all the ship's piping systems were thoroughly tested as was her watertight condition. The Scorpion was launched three years before the Thresher.

Normally, Admiral Moorer said, a nuclear submarine returning to the United States would stay submerged and off the air until just before she approached port. There had been no report of mechanical trouble from the vessel at any time during her three months away, he said.

As submarines approach the shallow waters of the continental shelf, extending about 55 miles offshore from Norfolk, they often come up to the surface, Admiral Moorer said. Because of the high seas today, he continued, this might have been a dangerous maneuver and the skipper could well have decided to delay his approach.

"It would be safer to wait," the admiral said.

"Naturally I'm concerned," the admiral said. "But I've been through this many times."

He then added that perhaps when the seas grew calm the Scorpion, with her 12 officers and 87 enlisted men, would proceed into port without further incident.

If, however, the Scorpion did sink while crossing the shallows above the continental shelf, he said, there are ways to rescue the crew. The men could swim out one at a time, or a diving bell could be lowered to lift several out at a time.

If the vessel sank in deeper water, Navy rescue vessels are equipped to operate several hundred feet down, he said.

The Scorpion is one of six Skipjack class submarines designed primarily for antisubmarine warfare. Such vessels carry homing torpedoes and long-range antisubmarine missiles that can carry both high explosives and nuclear warheads.

These submarines have the mission of protecting American Polaris submarines as well as surface ships against enemy surface and submarine threats.

There are 28 other nuclear attack submarines commissioned and 31 more in various stages of construction, for a total of 65.

In addition there are 41 Polaris submarines, each carrying 16 strategic missiles.

The Navy said that Rear Adm. Douglas Plate, aboard the destroyer William Wood, was in charge of search operations in the area around the Virginia Capes.

Vice Adm. Arnold Schade, commander of the Atlantic submarine force to which Scorpion belonged, happened to be at sea aboard the submarine Pargo and joined the search as soon as heard of the Scorpion's being overdue.

FIVE SUBMARINES LOST SINCE 1950

Sinkings Cost Lives of 330 —Thresher Had 129 Aboard

The Thresher, the Squalus, the Thetis. Each was the name of a submarine involved in a major naval disaster. Those few persons—close relatives and members of the submarine service—who know the special anxiety that attends the long silence of a submarine were hoping last night that the missing Scorpion would not be added to them.

A total of 330 lives have been lost in five submarine disasters since 1950—the year the British submarine Truculent was rammed by the Swedish tanker Divina and lost in the Thames Estuary at a cost of 65 men.

It was on April 9, 1963, that the nuclear submarine Thresher began her brief and tragic career. She was the proud first of her class of long-range attack craft made to run silent, run deep and run fast.

She had gone through nine months of tuning up and renovations in the Portsmouth (N. H.) Naval shipyard. With 129 men aboard, she went out for a series of check dives on the morning of April 10.

Deepest Diver for U.S.

The sea was calm with a slight swell. An escort vessel hovered nearby. The Thresher was the deepest diving combat submarine in the world.

About 7:45 A.M. she sent out a routine diving message and then slid silently into the sea some 220 miles east of Cape Cod, never to be seen again.

Soon a series of hasty, garbled messages began reaching the escort ship, reporting increasing difficulties. Sounds received in the listening post on the surface suggested the breaking up of a sinking ship. The Thresher, with all hands, was lost. After a fruitless, 25-hour search by planes, surface ships and other submarines, the Navy abandoned hope. The loss of the Thresher was the worst submarine disaster in the Navy's history.

The Thresher had exceeded her collapse depth. Apparently she was totally flooded. More than three dozen ships subsequently engaged in extensive searches of the ocean floor for her remains.

A five-month-long search for the hull was called off in September. All that had been found was some scattered debris, including a 30-foot section of pipe that was identified as part of the Thresher, some twisted metal and sections of her steel plating, salvaged from a depth of 8,450 feet.

Inquiry Conducted

A Naval Court of Inquiry heard that the crew was still testing the Thresher's diving planes and rudder mechanisms the night before her fatal voyage.

Later, Congressional testimony disclosed that the submarine had been permitted to go on the test cruise despite indications of poor workmanship and defective piping aboard.

One inspection showed that several hundred joints in the ship's critical salt-water piping system could have been defective. To meet its deadline for the Thresher, the shipyard had permitted her to go on the shakedown cruise without inspecting all the joints, according to the testimony.

On May 23, 1939 in somewhat similar circumsetnces the submarine Squalus went down a few miles off the New Hampshire coast. She was one of the newest products of the Portsmouth Navy Yard.

The Squalus lay in mud 240 feet below the surface. An air induction valve had failed to close and water had flooded the after compartments. The Squalus could not rise, but she sent a smoke bomb to the surface to mark her position.

In long hours of suspenseful operations, 33 members of the 59-man crew were brought

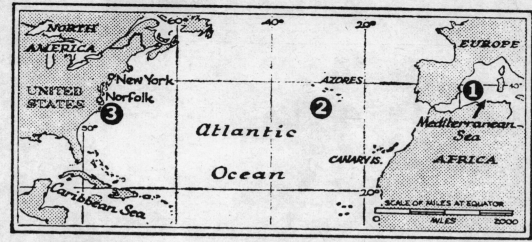

The New York Times   May 28, 1968

The Scorpion, after training exercise in Mediterranean (1), last reported from about 50 miles south of the Azores (2). She is overdue at home port of Norfolk, Va. (3).

Wives of Scorpion's Crewmen 'Hopeful' as They Await Return

Special to The New York Times

NORFOLK, Va., May 27— Mrs. Francis A. Slattery, wife of the commander of the missing nuclear submarine Scorpion, waited in her suburban home tonight for news of the Navy's air-sea search.

Naval personnel refused to allow reporters into the Slattery home in Virginia Beach, a suburb of Norfolk. They would say only that Mrs. Slattery and "five or six" other wives of Scorpion crewmen were waiting together.

"They are hopeful," said an unidentified man who answered the door of the Slattery home.

Commander Slattery assumed command of the Scorpion last fall.

The 36-year-old officer is married to the former Dorothy L. Record. Their three children are Steven, 12, Joline, 11, and Judy, 10. The family lives in Virginia Beach, Va.

Commander Slattery was graduated from the United States Naval Academy in 1954 and from the Naval War College in 1967. Before taking command of the Scorpion, he served on two other submarines, the Nautilus and the Tunny.

His parents, William A. and Doris M. Slattery, live in West Paris, Me., the commander's home town. He was graduated from West Paris High School in 1950.

Associated Press

Comdr. Francis A. Slattery, the captain of the Scorpion.

safely to the surface. Twenty-six men had drowned inside the craft.

The submarine was salvaged, recommissioned at a cost of $1.4-million and renamed the Sailfish.

A few days after the Squalus disaster, on June 1, 1939, the British submarine Thetis was lost at a cost of 99 lives in the Irish Sea. That made it the worst submarine disaster in naval history to that time.

When found, at dawn the next day 14 miles from Great Ormes Head, a Welsh promontory, 18 feet of the tail section of the submarine was showing above the water. The sunken craft was tilted in a deep dive position, her nose stuck at the bottom.

Late tonight there were 10 vessels involved in the search from Norfolk, three from Charleston, S. C., three from New London, Conn., and two from Rota, Spain.

Storm Peril Doubted

WASHINGTON, May 28 (UPI) —Veteran submariners said the Atlantic storm itself posed little if any threat to the submarine because most of the storm's impact would be absorbed by the first few feet of water.

A submarine running just below even the roughest sea would be in relatively calm waters, they said.

They also noted that the Scorpion could not use her regular radio communications unless she could get her 45-foot whip antenna above the surface.

Thus, the Scopion, unless she resorted to other, more complicated ways of communication, could not, for example, tell rescuers she was lying disabled on the bottom, unable to surface.

When the atomic-powered Scorpion was launched in December, 1959, she was listed among the world's two fastest and most maneuverable undersea craft, rivaled only by a sister ship, the Skipjack. Her cost was put at $40-million.

The submarine, with her stout, whale-shaped hull, was christened at Groton, Conn.,

by Mrs. Elizabeth S. Morrison of Arlington, Va., the daughter of the late Comdr. Maxmilian G. Schmidt. Commander Schmidt, the last commanding officer of the Scorpion of World War II, went down with his ship on a Pacific Ocean mission.

The Scorpion is 252 feet long. It was said that in some respects the Scorpion and Skipjack seemed "more like airplanes than submarines." An airplane-type joystick, rather than a ship's wheel, controlled the submarine's maneuvers.

A previous silence-in-the-deep of the Scorpion caused a false alarm in September, 1960, when the ship was engaging in North Atlantic Treaty Organization maneuvers 300 miles west of

Ireland. The British Admiralty reported that there had been no radio contact with the Scorpion for more than 24 hours.

An alert went out to ships, planes and shore stations to lend their sonar ears to a search for the submarine's radio signals. After some hours of anxiety, the Navy in Washington announced that the Scorpion had been instructed not to receive or send any messages for the first five days of the maneuvers.

The Scorpion had sent a message saying she was diving and would remain out of contact until the predetermined hour.

"All the News That's Fit to Print"

The New York Times

LATE CITY EDITION

Weather: Rain today; clearing and cool tonight. Fair, mild tomorrow. Temp. range: today 74-66; Sunday 75-63. Temp.-Hum. Index: yesterday 70. Complete U.S. report Page 56.

VOL. CXVII . No. 40,399 · © 1968 The New York Times Company. · NEW YORK, MONDAY, SEPTEMBER 2, 1968 · 10 CENTS

MUSKIE REGARDS POLICE IN CHICAGO AS OVERREACTING

Appears to Take a Softer View of Demonstrations Than Humphrey Does

ALSO SCORES 'ANARCHY'

Vice President Is Firm—He Arrives Here by Plane for Labor Day Parade

By WALTER RUGABER
Special to The New York Times

PORTLAND Me., Sept. 1—Senator Edmund S. Muskie of Maine, in reacting to the street disorders that shook the Democratic National Convention last week, displayed today an attitude that was somewhat softer than Vice President Humphrey's.

The party's Vice-Presidential nominee, in his first major appearance since becoming Mr. Humphrey's running mate, said that he had an "impression" that the police "overreacted" in their suppression of youthful protesters last Wednesday.

The Vice President, in remarks yesterday, said, "We ought to quit pretending that Mayor Daley did something that was wrong" in taking a hard line toward demonstrations outside the Conrad Hilton Hotel.

Again today Mr. Humphrey, in a talk in his home town of Waverly, Minn., denounced "militant, strident, violent" people who take to the streets to settle their problems.

[Mr. Humphrey, preparing to open his Presidential campaign with an appearance today in New York City's Labor Day Parade, arrived by chartered plane at 10:10 P.M. Sunday at La Guardia Airport, where about 50 persons picketed him.]

Not 'Clear Endorsement'

Senator Muskie, questioned on the National Broadcasting Company's "Meet the Press" program, said that he did not consider Mr. Humphrey's statement yesterday a "clear endorsement" of the police performance in Chicago.

He also declared that there had been "troublemakers" bent on disrupting the city, and that Mayor Daley had had no choice but "to organize to take care of the situation."

"I doubt that Mayor Daley would deliberately provoke trouble," he said of the Chicago Mayor.

Later in the program, he said that officials should be "firm" with protesters, and that no city could "tolerate anarchy."

But he also noted that "a lot of innocent people were hurt" when the Chicago police had waded into crowds outside the convention headquarters at the Conrad Hilton, swinging riot sticks and spraying Chemical Mace.

The police sometimes overreacted, Mr. Muskie said, because they are "human beings, moved by events," but they "should not assume that every-

Continued on Page 20, Column 5

Associated Press

COUNTRY GENTLEMAN: Vice President Humphrey vaults a fence after inspecting sheep at his Triple H homestead in Waverly, Minn. He took newsmen with him on his tour.

Sutton Seeks a Coalition For Democratic Reforms

By WILL LISSNER

Borough President Percy E. Sutton of Manhattan said yesterday that he and some other Democratic leaders were going to try to form "a new coalition" to restructure the party in New York State.

Mr. Sutton, who was a protégé of the late Senator Robert F. Kennedy and a supporter of Senator Eugene J. McCarthy, said the "coalition" would seek to embrace people in the McCarthy and Kennedy camps, backers of Senator George S. McGovern, and "progressive supporters of Hubert H. Humphrey."

Mr. Sutton termed the move entirely separate from the current election campaign. He said he would go "all-out" in the campaign to elect Paul O'Dwyer to the Senate seat held by Jacob K. Javits, a Republican, but would defer his decision on whether to support Mr. Humphrey for President.

His support of Mr. Humphrey will depend, he said, on whether the Vice President yields to public pressure and reformulates his position on Vietnam.

O'Dwyer Discusses Position

Mr. O'Dwyer, who has said he would not support the Vice President, said yesterday that he would do nothing to injure Mr. Humphrey's chances and denied that he had said he would not vote for him.

Mr. Sutton disclosed his plans for the coalition in an appearance on the WNBC-TV program "Man in Office" and in an interview later.

The coalition, he said, would be designed to bring about a "restructuring" of the party to make it an outstanding example of "participatory democracy."

Mr. Sutton was a delegate to the convention, but he gave up his seat in a protest that won greater representation for Negroes and Puerto Ricans. He participated from "outside the hall," he explained.

"One of the things I saw at this convention was a number of people that I want to be identified with in the future," he went on. "They were a new

Continued on Page 20, Column 2

TEACHERS WARN OF SCHOOL STRIKE

May Balk Monday Opening Over Brooklyn Dispute and Decentralization

By PETER KIHSS

The head of New York City's 55,000 unionized teachers said yesterday that the chances were "a little better than 50-50" that the city's public schools would not reopen on schedule next Monday.

Albert Shanker, president of the United Federation of Teachers, warned of a citywide shutdown in case of two circumstances:

One would be if the Board of Education failed to reinstate 10 teachers whom the Ocean Hill-Brownsville demonstration district tried to force out last May 9. The other would be if the board failed to modify its pending decentralization plan for all schools, so as to assure protection for teachers.

The administrator of the eight-school Ocean Hill-Brownsville district, Rhody A. McCoy, told newsmen yesterday: "I don't think anything will make those 10 acceptable."

But Mr. McCoy suggested

Continued on Page 17, Column 5

Cleveland Searches for Reasons For 4-Day Race Battles in July

This report on the violence in Cleveland was prepared by Anthony Ripley, Thomas A. Johnson and C. Gerald Fraser. The article was written by Mr. Ripley.

Special to The New York Times

CLEVELAND — "There is something wrong with our society," said Mayor Carl B. Stokes. "Many of us have known this for a long while and have searched for the answers. But the answers have obviously not been found."

Something went wrong in Cleveland on the night of July 23 and for four days afterward, and the search for answers is still continuing.

Eleven men were shot to death—three white policemen and eight black civilians — in about 80 hours. The police believe at least two other Negroes were shot and killed, but no trace of them has been found and no one has been reported missing.

The Cleveland [illegible] been called [illegible] police and an armed uprising by Negroes. However, the weight of evidence indicates that it was closer to spontaneous combustion.

Armed black civilians met armed white policemen and shots were fired, tumbling Cleveland into civil disorder.

Weeks later the police were still trying to piece fragments together at their headquarters in the grimy old central police station. Some of their reports were in obvious error, and most were unavailable to the press.

What had happened in Cleveland?

It began with a 65-minute gun battle between the police and black nationalists starting at 8:25 P.M. on a Tuesday

Continued on Page 12, Column 1

Labor Day

Today is Labor Day. Following is a list of services that are affected:

Parking—Sunday regulations in effect.

Post Offices—Closed except for special delivery.

Stores—Most department and other retail stores closed.

Banks and Stock Exchanges—Closed.

Sanitation—No regular refuse collection.

Central Park Drives—Closed to automobiles, 6 A.M. to 9 P.M.

Invasion of Czechoslovakia: The First Week

Entry by the Armies of 4 Nations Stirred Wide Resistance

The following reconstruction of events in the first seven days of the occupation of Czechoslovakia was prepared by Tad Szulc and Clyde H. Farnsworth, New York Times correspondents in Prague.

Special to The New York Times

PRAGUE, Sept. 1—A Soviet MIG-21 jet fighter screeched over the roofs of sleeping Prague a few minutes after 1 o'clock on the morning of Wednesday, Aug. 21. As it landed at Ruzyne International Airport, its wing companion flew on a direct approach to the airport.

There was silence for a few minutes, and then the first Antonov-12 four-engine turbo-prop transport pierced the clear night sky over this city, its green and red running lights blinking against the darkness on its descent to Ruzyne.

Within a minute another heavy AN-12 followed from the east. Then the roar over the capital was unabating as, at 50-second intervals, transport planes touched down at Prague Airport, disgorging crimson-bereted Soviet airborne troopers.

Two hours earlier, a column of Soviet T-55 tanks had crossed the Czechoslovak frontier from East Germany at Cinovec, a quiet village 60 miles northwest of Prague, and now its forward elements were nearing the residential suburb of Kobylisy. Young Soviet tankmen in black leather headgear peered out of their turrets, their hands on their 50-caliber machine guns.

Gamma-Pix

Soviet armor near headquarters of the Czechoslovak news agency C.T.K. recently. A bomb was set off in the street there early yesterday, shattering some of the building's windows.

The invasion of Czechoslovakia had begun.

At 1:50 A.M., Prague was told in a radio broadcast, delivered in quiet tones:

"Last night, Aug. 20, about 11 P.M., the armies of the Soviet Union, the Polish People's Republic, the German Democratic Republic, the Hungarian People's Republic and the Bulgarian People's Republic crossed the national frontiers of Czechoslovakia without the knowledge of the President of the Republic, the National Assembly, the Government, the First Secretary of the Communist party or any of their bodies."

Then the radio station went off the air.

The airlift was the biggest ever carried out by the Soviet Union outside its frontiers. Within the first seven hours, 250 aircraft put down here a full airborne division complete with small armored vehicles, fuel and supplies.

Along with the Soviet, East German, Polish, Hungarian and Bulgarian columns entering Czechoslovakia through 18 crossing points from the north, northwest, south and east, this airlift formed the

Continued on Page 6, Column 1

Foe Shells Danang With Big Rockets, Killing at Least 10

By DOUGLAS ROBINSON
Special to The New York Times

SAIGON, South Vietnam, Monday, Sept. 2—The city of Danang came under a heavy enemy rocket attack this morning.

At least 10 civilians were killed and 43 injured when the large 122-mm. rockets crashed into several heavily populated areas along the Danang waterfront.

The South Vietnamese command here said that 25 rockets had been fired into the city during the shelling, which began shortly before 2 A.M.

The American military headquarters in Danang said six rounds or more hit in a naval storage area, causing light damage. There were no American casualties.

Most of the heavy rockets smashed into private homes near the waterfront and in the crowded downtown section of the city.

In the last several weeks, the Danang area has been the target of rocket attacks on at least four occasions. Last week, a small-scale ground attack fol-

Continued on Page 2, Column 5

IRAN'S QUAKE TOLL PUT IN THOUSANDS

8,000 Bodies Are Reported Found—Area Struck by Severe New Tremor

By ERIC PACE
Special to The New York Times

TEHERAN, Iran, Monday, Sept. 2—Iranian relief officials reported last night that more than 8,000 people were known to have been killed in earthquakes that struck the northeastern province of Khurasan over the weekend.

A second severe tremor in the area was reported by Teheran's Geophysics Institute yesterday morning, 21 hours after the first quake. This was confirmed by a provincial telegraph operator, who tapped out the words "earthquake, earthquake" before his wire went dead. The extent of the second earthquake was not immediately known.

All told, Iranian officials said, there were at least 2,500 people injured as of yesterday evening, and several thousand others were missing.

One hundred villages were

Continued on Page 3, Column 2

Associated Press

DESOLATION: In the town of Kakhk in eastern Iran, a young boy sits amid the rubble from homes destroyed by the earthquakes that struck the region this weekend. Kakhk, with a population of more than 14,000 was at the center of first quake, on Saturday.

U.S. Now Doubts Invasion Of Rumania Is Imminent

Intelligence Assessed

Special to The New York Times

WASHINGTON, Sept. 1 — United States intelligence officials said tonight that the latest intelligence information received from Eastern Europe had satisfied the Johnson Administration that a Soviet invasion of Rumania was not imminent.

But the officials repeatedly declined to discuss the content of the intelligence, other than to say that it did not involve an assurance from Moscow that an occupation would not take place.

On Aug. 20 Soviet, East German, Polish, Hungarian and Bulgarian troops and armor invaded Czechoslovakia to prevent that country's further drift toward liberal policies.

Last Friday, unconfirmed intelligence received in Washington raised the possibility that more Soviet military action in Eastern Europe might be in the offing. Over a period of time Rumania also has taken steps to escape complete Soviet domination. On the basis of the Rumanian reports, President Johnson-

Continued on Page 3, Column 4

Bucharest Reiterates View

By JOHN M. LEE
Special to The New York Times

BUCHAREST, Sept. 1—Faced with rumors of an impending invasion, Rumania's Communist leaders fought back today with more arguments for national independence and against armed intervention.

The invasion fears were based on reports of unusually heavy concentrations of Soviet forces along Rumania's 830-mile frontier with the Soviet Union, and by President Johnson's weekend reference to the rumors.

But there has been no evidence of unusual military activity in Rumanian border areas. Nor has there been any comment on the matter from official Rumanian sources.

The war of words continued, however.

Ceausescu's View

President Nicolae Ceausescu, head of state and of the Rumanian Communist party, in a speech published this morning in Scinteia, the party paper, declared:

"We have never thought that force could ever be used among Communists, among socialist countries, to impose a certain point of view."

Mr. Ceausescu recalled the statement commonly attributed to Louis XIV: "L'état, c'est moi"—"I am the state."

"There are some theoreticians," Mr. Ceausescu said, "who take upon themselves the right of giving definitive judgments, on the principle, 'Le marxisme c'est moi.'

"No, nobody can affirm that 'I am Marxism.' Marxism-Leninism is nobody's property, it is a scientific principle."

Premier Ion Gheorghe Maurer was also quoted in Scinteia. He said in a speech:

"We are building socialism in such a way that it could never be said that we have de-

Continued on Page 3, Column 6

NEWS INDEX

CZECH PARTY ADDS LIBERAL LEADERS IN SURPRISE MOVE

Only 2 Backers of Moscow Kept in New 21-Member Pro-Dubcek Presidium

SOME REFORMERS STAY

Ruling Body Also Includes 7 From Clandestine Group Held Illegal by Soviet

By TAD SZULC
Special to The New York Times

PRAGUE, Sept. 1—The Moscow-backed Central Committee of the Czechoslovak Communist party elected today an enlarged and, under the circumstances, startlingly liberal ruling Presidium.

Of the 21 full members of the new Presidium, only two could be regarded as unconditional supporters of the Soviet Union, whose armies have led a five-nation occupation of Czechoslovakia since Aug. 20.

The two conservatives are Vasil Bilak, removed last week from his post as First Secretary of the Slovak Communist party, and Jan Piller, who sought to persuade President Ludvik Svoboda after the invasion to head a pro-Moscow government.

Both Mr. Bilak and Mr. Piller were among the 11 regular members of the pre-invasion Presidium, chosen last April, but other conservative figures on the old body were dropped.

Congress Met Secretly

Instead, seven of the 16 new members came from a clandestine liberal Presidium elected on Aug. 23 by an extraordinary party congress. It met secretly at a Prague industrial plant after the Russians had interned Alexander Dubcek, the First Secretary; Premier Oldrich Cernik, Josef Smrkovsky, President of the National Assembly, and Frantisek Kriegel, President of the Communist-led National Front, the popular-front group.

The Russians have declared the clandestine party congress illegal and have refused to recognize its 160-member Central Committee and its 27-member Presidium. Since his release from Soviet custody, Mr. Dubcek has sought to reconcile the conflicting memberships of the clandestine and pre-invasion party bodies to Moscow's satisfaction.

Dubcek Keeps Top Post

Mr. Dubcek, who continues as the party's First Secretary, Premier Cernik and Mr. Smrkovsky were re-elected to the Presidium. However, Mr. Kriegel was dropped from both the Presidium and the Central Committee, apparently because he was unacceptable to the Soviet Union.

Political observers were baffled after the Prague radio, in its 7 P.M. broadcast, announced the composition of the new Presidium and other changes in the party leadership.

When the Central Committee opened its two-day meeting yesterday at Hradcany Castle, the seat of the presidency, the expectation was that the new Presidium would be evenly balanced between the Dubcek liberals and the pro-Moscow conservatives, presumably in an attempt to placate the Russians.

Bigger Central Committee

The 87 new members proposed today for the Central Committee, which is to be enlarged from about 100 to about 190 when the party congress approves them at a session later this year, are also predominantly liberal.

It was unclear whether this surprising dominance of liberals was intended as defiance of the Soviet Union, which appeared to be doubtful, or had Moscow's tacit approval.

Along the lines of the second theory, the renewed censorship, instituted late last week as one of the conditions for the eventual withdrawal of occupation troops under the Moscow agreement signed with the Prague leadership last Monday, has proved thus far to be extremely mild.

In a speech [illegible]

Continued on Page 4, Column 4

Toll in Iran Earthquake May Run Into Thousands

Continued From Page 1, Col. 5

said to have been damaged by the first sudden sharp jolt Saturday afternoon, which shook hundreds of square miles of arid farming country about 800 miles east of here. Centered around Kakhk, a mud-brick village, the afflicted area extends toward the borders of the Soviet Union and Afghanistan.

The Iranian relief organization, the Red Lion and Sun Society, reported 800 people were killed in Kakhk and two neighboring villages and 80 per cent of the houses destroyed.

Though the area is relatively sparsely inhabited, casualties ran high because the mud-brick cottages of the peasants were easily wrecked by the tremor, which was about as strong as the one six years ago that killed 12,000 people.

Relief workers, soldiers and rural policemen fanned out to help victims in the battered countryside. It was feared that large numbers of people remained trapped.

Shah Mohammed Riza Pahlevi remained in seclusion at his summer palace overlooking Teheran today, hearing reports and directing rescue operations. The young Empress, who was with him, was reported to have wept as the casualty figures came in.

As far as could be learned, no disaster aid from foreign countries was requested or received. Red Lion and Sun officials said that relief workers had found 8,222 bodies.

No Reports of Epidemics

There were no reports of fire or epidemic or of looting or other disorders. Eyewitnesses said ruined villages were filled with weeping women, some scrabbling at the rubble of their homes with their bare hands.

Iranian journalists at the quake scene estimated that the number of dead might reach 14,500, but this figure was not corroborated by officials.

Estimates of the number of people made homeless ranged up to a hundred thousand and beyond.

People in the stricken area subsist largely from wheat and cotton farming and are known as skilled carpet makers and lovers of poetry. One of the battered towns, Ferdows, was named for a famous poet.

Private cars moving through Khurasan were being stopped and asked to ferry casualties to aid centers.

Premier Amir Abbas Hoveida and four ministers were at the site today and the Shah was expected to visit the area soon.

Iranian authorities airlifted two field hospitals to the Kakhk area alone, each with facilities for 300 casualties. These included a four-year-old girl who was rescued from the rubble today after being traced by her screams. Elsewhere, schools and mosques were being used as field clinics.

Since earthquakes damaged many canals, some areas were also faced with water shortages. Many villagers, afraid of further quakes, were camping out in the countryside.

In the Kakhk area, one village telegraph operator tapped out a halting message calling for "blood . . . medicine, supplies." A Kakhk villager who reached the town of Meshed said he had heard a "terrifying rumble . . . I looked back at the village and there was only rubble, the smell of blood and wailing. We had not even picks and shovels to dig out bodies that were buried in rubble."

More Tremors Reported

TEHERAN, Sept. 1 (Reuters) — More severe earthquake shocks hit two cities today in the devastated area of northeast Iran. Heavy damage was reported in Birjand and Turbat-i-Haidari.

Rescue workers search through the rubble of a home destroyed by the earthquake which hit northeastern Iran.

United Press International

The New York Times   Sept. 2, 1968

Iranian towns (underlined) struck by strong earthquake

Associated Press

This Iranian family in the town of Kakhk survived Saturday's earthquake, but officials of the Red Lion and Sun, Iran's equivalent of the Red Cross, estimated that hundreds of people had been killed or injured in the Kakhk area. The town itself was devastated.

"All the News That's Fit to Print"

The New York Times

LATE CITY EDITION

Weather: Sunny and seasonable today. Fair tonight and tomorrow. Temp. range: today 49-33. Sunday 50-33. Full U.S. report on Page 76.

VOL. CXVIII... No. 40,595 NEW YORK, MONDAY, MARCH 17, 1969 10 CENTS

© 1969 The New York Times Company.

U.S. ARMOR FIGHTS ENEMY IN THE DMZ FOR THREE HOURS

Amphibious Vehicles Enter Sector for the First Time Since Last November

SUPPORT FOR MARINES

Rocket Position Is Hunted—Allies Lose 11 Men as Patrol Is Ambushed

Special to The New York Times

SAIGON, South Vietnam, March 16—United States marines entered the demilitarized zone with armored vehicles yesterday for the first time since last November, a United States military report said.

Just south of the zone, an allied force fought a sharp and costly engagement after having been ambushed by North Vietnamese troops, according to reports from the field.

A United States Army spokesman said that the fighting inside the demilitarized zone broke out after a Marine force on patrol in the zone observed several heavy rockets being fired into South Vietnam from the demilitarized zone, which was established by the Geneva accords of 1954.

Mile Inside Zone

Seeking the rocket position, the marines engaged a North Vietnamese Army force about three miles northeast of Gio-linh and a mile inside the southern edge of the six-mile-deep zone. As the fighting intensified, the marines were reinforced by several tanklike amphibious vehicles, which operated against the enemy for about three hours. The enemy then withdrew and the marines returned to their base outside the zone.

After the fight, the bodies of 10 North Vietnamese regulars were found in the area, the United States spokesman said. No United States casualties were reported.

United States forces regularly patrol the southern half of the zone, below the border between the two Vietnams, which bisects the zone.

A U. S. Condition

When the United States halted the bombing of North Vietnam last Nov. 1, one condition—never publicly acknowledged by North Vietnam—that Washington said it had insisted on was that the buffer zone not be "abused" by the enemy. The regular American patrols and constant aerial surveillance of the zone have found the enemy generally more restrained in its use of the zone since the bombing halt.

In the fighting farther south of the zone, initial reports from the field said that a combined American and South Vietnamese force had been ambushed by North Vietnamese regulars.

These reports said that the allied force was on patrol in an area 6 miles south of Giolinh and 10 miles north of Quangtri. The North Vietnamese were

Continued on Page 11, Column 1

At Least 150 Die and 100 Are Injured As Jet Falls Into a Venezuelan Suburb

Associated Press

Rescue workers search wreckage left after DC-9 crashed in Maracaibo residential area

By United Press International

MARACAIBO, Venezuela, March 16—A Venezuela DC-9 airliner crashed into a populous suburb of Maracaibo on takeoff today, killing at least 150 persons aboard the plane and on the ground. It was the worst airline disaster in history.

Forty-seven persons from North America were reported to have been aboard.

The VIASA airlines twin-engine jet, carrying 83 persons including the crew, lost altitude and fell in the suburb of La Coruba two minutes after it took off for Miami at 11:45 A.M. Five square blocks of the area were damaged heavily in the crash.

Spokesmen for the Anatomical Hospital of the University of Zulia in Maracaibo, which was being used as a central morgue, said at 11 P.M. that the hospital had received 150 bodies. Other hospitals reported that they had been attending more than 100 persons suffering severe burns, broken bones and shock.

The worst previous airline disaster occurred on Dec. 16, 1960, when a Trans World Airlines Superconstellation and a United Air Lines DC-8 collided over New York City. The death toll included 6 on the ground and 128 passengers.

On Feb. 14, 1966, a Japanese plane crashed into Tokyo Bay, killing all 133 persons aboard. Last April 20, a South African Airways plane crashed and burned at Windhoek, South-West Africa, killing 122.

83 Aboard the Plane

Officials of the Venezuelan line said all 83 persons aboard the flight, which originated in Caracas, were presumed to have been killed.

United States Consulate officials in Maracaibo were checking the line's list of 47 passengers from North America to determine how many were United States citizens. Immigration officials in Caracas said that a minimum of 15, many of whom had been attending a convention of the Clark Equipment Company of Battle Creek, Mich., were from the United States.

Officials of the airline said tonight that the plane had inexplicably lost altitude two minutes after leaving Grano de Oro Airport, then smashed into the suburb, splintering telephone poles and trees, crushing homes, buses, cars and trucks and spreading burning fuel over the five-block area.

At least seven houses burned. A family of five, identified only as Rodriguez, were crushed to death at the dinner table when the plane smashed into their home.

City officials proclaimed Maracaibo a disaster area and the police blocked off the area where the damage was most severe. Only firemen, ambulance crews and policemen were allowed into the area, which was obscured by a thick pall of black smoke.

Witnesses reported initially that the plane had appeared to explode in flight just before it crashed.

Airline officials at first announced that fire had broken

Continued on Page 14, Column 1

SOVIET SAYS CHINA USED A REGIMENT IN USSURI ATTACK

Accuses Foe of an Invasion Aimed at Seizing Territory —Peking Claims Victory

By HENRY KAMM

Special to The New York Times

MOSCOW, March 16—The Soviet Union charged today that Communist China used forces on the scale of an infantry regiment in yesterday's border clash over a disputed island on the frozen Ussuri River. For the first time, the Russians accused the Chinese of an invasion aimed at seizure of Soviet territory.

A description of the fighting made public today by Tass, the official press agency, said the regimental-sized Chinese force and its support units had covering fire from artillery and mortar batteries.

[United States Government specialists in Washington said that an average Chinese Army regiment consisted of about 3,000 men, including headquarters and support units. They put the strength of an average infantry company—the unit said to have been involved in previous clashes—at about 150 men. But they stressed that individual unit strengths might vary greatly.

[The Peking radio reported Sunday that the Chinese had held a victory celebration on Chenpao Island after Saturday's clash. The Chinese reports indicated, however, that the battle may have been mainly a duel of artillery fire and maneuver.]

Blunt Accusation Made

The Tass account of the latest fighting, in contrast with the Soviet reporting of the incident of March 2, involving the same Far Eastern island, bluntly accused China of seeking to capture the disputed territory.

The uninhabited island on the border river is known to the Russians as Damansky Island.

The Soviet description of yesterday's clash, according to observers, constituted a significant stepping-up of Moscow's grievance against Peking. It marked the first time that China had been directly accused of invading the Soviet

Continued on Page 5, Column 4

Associated Press

DR. KING'S WIDOW IN LONDON: Mrs. Martin Luther King Jr. speaking yesterday from the pulpit of St. Paul's Cathedral—the first woman to do so at a regular service in the Anglican edifice. An account of her visit is on Page 22.

CITY HIGH SCHOOLS ORDERED TO NAME SECURITY OFFICERS

Junior Highs Are Included in Action by Donovan Aimed at Student Disruptions

PRINCIPALS AGAINST IT

Association Calls the Plan Inadequate—Lindsay Adds His Own Assurances

By M. A. FARBER

Superintendent of Schools Bernard E. Donovan ordered every high school and junior high school in the city yesterday to name a security official as part of a plan to stem increasing student disruptions and violence.

The officials would be responsible for overseeing order in the schools, confirming that school entrances were being watched to prevent access by people without legitimate business, maintaining regular contact with the police and working with parent's associations.

Dr. Donovan also said that trained security aides would be placed in 20 of the most troubled high schools and junior high schools, but it was not clear whether the aides would be uniformed or whether they would be armed. This program, to be started after Easter, may be expanded to other schools later.

The Superintendent's plan, which was immediately denounced by the High School Principals Association as inadequate and misconceived, was presented by him at a closed meeting of 120 high school principals and district superintendents.

Some Schools Closed

Mayor Lindsay, who attended the one-hour session at Board of Education headquarters in Brooklyn, assured the principals that they were not being "abandoned" at a time when increasing disruptions have resulted in the temporary closing of some schools.

The Superintendent said he would issue a fuller statement this week on the new security measures.

A spokesman for the Board of Education, Assistant Superintendent Jerome G. Kovalcik, said that the security officials to be named in all city high schools and junior high schools would be present members of the schools' administrative staffs and would perform their new roles in addition to their other duties.

However, a leader of the principals' association said he understood that the officials would be extra personnel and would operate on a full-time basis.

Mr. Lindsay said at a news conference after the meeting that the city would not tolerate "unlawful activity" or disturbance in the schools. He said the Police Department would give "highest priority" to help-

Continued on Page 31, Column 3

Mayor Tells Aides: I'll Run; Kheel Announces He Won't

Lindsay to Make Plans Public This Week

By RICHARD REEVES

Mayor Lindsay informed his closest political associates yesterday that he would announce his candidacy for re-election this week, probably tomorrow.

The Mayor, who will seek the Republican and Liberal nominations as he did in 1965, invited a small group of advisers to Gracie Mansion last night to discuss the timing of his announcement, the wording of his statement and the selection of running mates for City Council President and Controller.

Although preparations for the Lindsay campaign have been under way since last November, the Mayor apparently did not assure anyone of his intention to run again until the weekend. At that time he spoke to members of his family and a group of advisers including his campaign manager, Richard R. Aurelio, and two old friends, former United States Attorney General Herbert Brownell and Bethuel Webster.

Mrs. Lindsay Opposed

The decision to seek a second term was not easy, Mr. Lindsay said, and was opposed by his wife, Mary, and many old friends.

One of the reasons for the opposition of friends was their recognition that private polls showed that the Mayor would be entering the race as a de-

Continued on Page 19, Column 1

Mediator Rules Himself Out Irrevocably

By CLAYTON KNOWLES

Theodore W. Kheel, the labor mediator, said yesterday that he was irrevocably out of consideration for the race for Mayor.

"I am not a candidate, I won't be a candidate, and there is no set of circumstances that could lead me to accept a nomination," he said in ruling out a contest that many leading city Democrats had urged him to make.

These Democrats had said that the 54-year-old Riverdale lawyer's ability to reconcile group differences, revealed in many national, state and city mediation cases, would make him the strongest party candidate against Mayor Lindsay.

Pledge of Cooperation

Mr. Kheel, in barring a race, pledged the fullest cooperation to the Mayor who takes office Jan. 1 in resolving "conflicts in intergroup relations that are not illegal but are overlapping and hence extremely difficult."

"I came to realize as I examined my position that I could claim no special competence in administration or in politics," he said in an interview. "But I do feel a competence in mediating group conflicts that I believe will enable me to make my greatest contribution to the city in that role."

Mr. Kheel, who has handled

Continued on Page 18, Column 1

A Moderate Living Costs $9,977 a Year Here

By PETER MILLONES

It costs more to maintain a moderate or good standard of living in New York City than in any other city in the continental United States, but it is cheaper to maintain a low standard here than in 14 other cities.

These findings, published yesterday by the United States Bureau of Labor Statistics, show that a family of four in the New York area had to spend $6,021 a year to maintain a low standard of living, $9,977 for a moderate standard and $14,868 for a good standard.

The surprise in the figures—the comparatively low cost of a low standard of living here—is a result of cheaper public transportation and rent-controlled housing, which largely benefit those in lower-income brackets.

But for those families of four attempting to live at moderate or higher levels, New York costs are about 10 per cent more than the urban average for food and about 22 per cent more for housing. These figures exclude Honolulu, which is in a high-priced world of its own.

A four-person family that spends $14,868 a year here, including taxes, for what would generally be considered a good living standard, would have to spend $13,325 in Chicago, and $13,645 in Los Angeles for a comparable standard of living.

The budget figures for the three living standards in New York compare with a national urban average of $5,915, $9,076 and $13,050.

These figures are actually conservative, because they were compiled in the spring of 1967 and since then there have been sizable increases in consumer prices. It is not clear why the Bureau of Labor Statistics in Washington took two years to analyze its figures before releasing them, although this is the first time it has prepared such a survey.

The bureau made a re-examination of some budget costs as of last fall. That study indicates that the national figures may have risen by now by about $300 for the low standard and by about $600 for the high standard. The increases may be even greater in New York because, in general, prices here have risen more than in other cities.

Continued on Page 32, Column 3

Biafra, in 6 Months, Has Moved Away From the Edge of Defeat

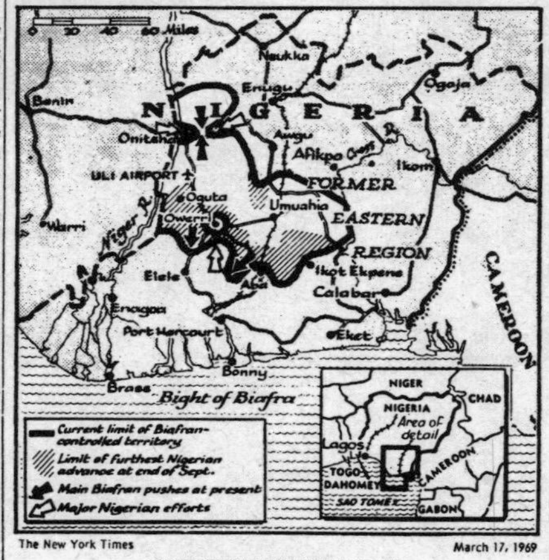
50 Miles
NIGERIA
Benin
Onitsha
ULI AIRPORT
Owerri
Umuahia
FORMER EASTERN REGION
Warri
Ikot Ekpene
Calabar
Port Harcourt
Bonny
Brass
Bight of Biafra
CAMEROON
Ogoja
Ikom
Current limit of Biafran-controlled territory
Limit of furthest Nigerian advance at end of Sept.
Main Biafran pushes at present
Major Nigerian efforts
NIGER
CHAD
NIGERIA
Lagos
Area of detail
TOGO
DAHOMEY
CAMEROON
GABON

The New York Times March 17, 1969

By LLOYD GARRISON

Special to The New York Times

UMUAHIA, Biafra (Nigeria), March 5—Six months ago, Biafra appeared on the verge of total military and internal breakdown after more than a year of the civil war that followed its secession from Nigeria.

The Nigerian "final push" was in full swing and federal troops were within artillery range of Uli airport, Biafra's last outlet to the rest of the world. Civilians, most of them children, were starving, with some relief agencies estimating the death toll at 6,000 persons a day.

Refugees clogged the roads and Biafra's leader, Lieut. Col. Odumegwu Ojukwu, openly discussed plans to split the army into guerrilla units if Biafra's towns and main roads were finally overrun.

That was in September. Since then there has been a reversal in Biafra's fortunes.

Gone is the air of panic in the heartland of the Ibos, the largest tribe in Nigeria's former Eastern Region.

There are now no refugees on the roads except in the most forward areas where there is actual fighting. Most of the more than one million uprooted people of Biafra have been housed in schools, churches and even lean-tos. The amount of

Continued on Page 6, Column 3

Maddox at Work: A Study in Paradox

By ANTHONY RIPLEY

Special to The New York Times

ATLANTA — When Lester G. Maddox ran for Governor three years ago, the right-wing, Bible-quoting, pistol-waving segregationist told everybody he was against big government, big spending, welfare and Federal control.

Since he has been in office, Georgia's welfare services have expanded, its bureaucracy has fattened, higher taxes are in prospect, and a statewide War on Hunger has been declared, the last with a call for direct Federal intervention.

The bald, puckish Governor has headed off into these unexpected areas like a bicycle rider seated backward but peddling forward, a stunt that he likes to show off, in real life, on the driveway of the Executive Mansion.

The contrast between the vast sweep of his right-wing rhetoric and the slow but steady expansion of social programs during his administration has puzzled both backers and opponents.

Some people may laugh at the Governor's troubles. He was the central character of a recent Broadway musical satire, "Red, White and Maddox," in which he blithely reduced the nation to nuclear ashes.

But in Georgia he is the subject of much serious debate. Some say that concern for social problems has tempered his political opinions.

Others feel that in his role as "the little people's man" he has struggled to keep clear of political and bureaucratic intrigue.

Still others contend that inexperience as an administrator has left him unable to control his subordinates, who have moved ahead with social programs despite his political opinions.

"The understanding I have is that the man just doesn't administrate," Paul Anthony, director of the Southern Regional Council, said recently. "Look at his background. He's a restaurant owner and the champion of a cause."

As a rule in Georgia, Mr. Anthony said, Governors work closely with the Legislature on such controversial subjects as taxes, carefully balancing forces and working to achieve a joint effort.

But this year, he said, Governor Maddox's tax program was sprung upon the legislators with almost no consultation and with what many

Continued on Page 24, Column 3

Industry Seeks Executives in Military

By LEONARD SLOANE

Spurred partially by the growing unrest at campus recruiting centers and partially by the need to hire more young professional and technical employes, corporations are increasingly turning to the military as a source of new executives.

As a result, junior officers with college degrees are being wooed with almost frenetic intensity. Agencies have been created to bring together companies and men being separated from the service.

Among major concerns using this method of recruitment are the Chase Manhattan Bank, Armco Steel Corporation, Continental Can Company, Johnson & Johnson and International Business Machines Corporation.

"We've reduced our campus recruiting activity 25 per cent this year to get at the large number of junior officers getting out of the service," says Albert H. Barlow, a second vice president of the Chase bank. "And these junior officers are going to have a terrific impact on the labor market in the future."

"We find this an excellent source of employes," adds Joseph K. Harrison, coordinator of management and technical recruiting at Armco. "They're more mature individuals, they're more serious about their careers and our attrition rate with these men is extremely low."

One recruiter, remaining anonymous, observes, "It's a great delight to talk to applicants who have haircuts."

Recruiting of new engineers, accountants and other professionals at colleges has long been an important part of corporate employment programs. But, within the last few years, disturbances on some campuses have developed when these recruiters appear. Such disturbances began with protests against the Dow Chemical Company for its manufacture of napalm. They have spread more recently to many big companies for a variety of reasons.

At the same time, the needs of industrial and finan-

Continued on Page 53, Column 4

NEWS INDEX

QUAGGA. Look THAT up in your Funk & Wagnalls Standard College Dictionary. (Advt.)

WINE TASTERS WANTED. Many openings. Take Japan Air Lines, 8 pm flight to Paris. Advt.

QUAGGA. Look THAT Up in your Funk & Wagnalls Standard College Dictionary.—Advt.

INSTANT MAIL. Accountants use it to send tax forms and financial statements coast-to-coast in 2 hours or less. Shouldn't you? Call Insta Fax (212) 866-6000.—Advt.

$1000 HAIRPIECE CLUB. Membership includes two custom pieces, fully guaranteed and serviced without charge for two years. Unexcelled. The Penthouse. PL 2-6140. (Advt.)

Wide World Photos

Residents of the La Trinidad and Ziruma districts of Maracaibo run towards their burning homes minutes after a VIASA DC-9 jet aircraft plunged into the Venezuelan city and exploded.

PLANE CRASH KILLS 150 IN VENEZUELA

Continued From Page 1, Col. 4

out in the port engine after the take-off. A later airline announcement said, however, that the plane had crashed while making a low pass and it did not clarify whether there was in-flight fire.

The area is relatively close to downtown Maracaibo, a city of 800,000, which is the oil capital of Venezuela.

Airline officials said that two Latin-American baseball players on their way to join American professional teams and two other prominent local baseball officials were among the passengers.

They were identified as Hec-

tor "Latigo" Chaz, who was reporting to the Phoenix, Ariz., branch of the San Francisco Giants; Carlos Santeliz, reporting to the Shreveport, La., team of the Atlanta Braves system; Antonio Herrera, owner of the Barquisimeto Cardinals, and his son, José; and the Barquisimetto club administrator, Ali Hernandez.

List of Those on Plane

Special to The New York Times

MIAMI, March 16—Following is the list, furnished by VIASA, the Venezuelan airline, of the passengers and crew aboard the DC-9 that crashed today in Venezuela:

BOARDED AT CARACAS

ASHMORE, R., United States.
ASHMORE.
BENJAMIN, H., United States.
BENJAMIN, R., United States.
BROWN, R., United States.
BROWN, United States.
BUCKSON, Andrew.
BUCKSON, Leila, United States.
CARTER, P., United States.
CHEW, D.
DAVISON, A., United States.

The New York Times   March 17, 1969

THE PLANE'S ROUTE: Flight started in Caracas (1), then picked up more passengers in Maracaibo (2), and crashed on take-off, heading for Miami (3).

DAVISON, G., United States.
DEELSNYDER, Basil, United States.
DEELSNYDER, Jane, United States.
DE MADERO, Gloria, United States.
DE MALASUNA, Gertrude.
DE TORREALBA, Ana, Venezuela.
DOGWEL, B., United States.
DOGWEL, L., United States.
D. ANNA L., United States.
GRAZNA, D., United States.
HACKER, John J.
HENEY, Adelina, United States.
HENEY, John, United States.
HUNT, R., Venezuela.
JAEN, Juan, Venezuela.
KEESE, Florence, United States.
KOOBER, Magrita, United States.
LIBORIAN, G.
LUCES, Kevin, Venezuela.
MEJIA, Aura B., Venezuela.
NELSON, N., United States.
NELSON, United States.
OATES, A., United States.
OATES, P., United States.
RIC..., Joe, United States.
RODRIGUEZ, Henriquez, Venezuela.
VENEZIA, United States.
VENEZIA, J., United States.
WHITMAN, Charles, United States.

In addition, three persons boarded at Caracas at the last minute and their names did not appear on the list.

BOARDED AT MARACAIBO

AMERIGO, Tavoleri.
BAGLEY, Linda.
BAGLEY, Tony.

BARCLAY, Susan.
BOCARROSA, Michael.
DEE, Clarice.
GRANERO, Adolfo.
GRANERO, Elvira.
HAYWOOD, James.
HASSENICH, Hans.
HERNANDEZ, Alis.
HERRARA, Jose A.
HERRARA, Antonio.
ITALO, Romero.
JARRIN, Carlota.
JOHNSON, Willis.
MARBUENJUR, Max.
MAY NINA, Gene.
OSORIO, Raul.
OSROUS, Amis.
RIPPA, Frank.
ROGERS, Mary Elizabeth.
ROMANS, Harmon.
ROMERO, Carmen.
SANTELI, Carlos.
SOTO, Isabella.
SUSAN, Barclay.
URDANETA de ROMERO, Alicia.

CREW

SABELLI MALDONALDO, Emiliano, Captain.
RODRIGUEZ SILVA, José, Captain.
PARKAS, Jorge, Co-pilot.
RADA, Miguel, First officer.
FIRRICIA, Ernesto, Purser.
HEREDIA, Ernesto, Steward.
GOSSELAIN, Claude, Steward.
FUENTAS, Alba, Stewardess.
FRANCO, Abigail, Stewardess.
SAINSBURY, L., Flight Dispatcher.

"All the News That's Fit to Print"

The New York Times

LATE CITY EDITION

Weather: Chance showers, cooler today. Fair tonight and tomorrow. Temp. range: today 78-66; Monday 82-67. Full U.S. report on Page 93.

VOL. CXVIII..No. 40,673 © 1969 The New York Times Company. NEW YORK, TUESDAY, JUNE 3, 1969 10 CENTS

PRESIDENT SEEKS 2-YEAR EXTENSION OF POVERTY DRIVE

Had Planned One-Year Bill —He Delays Request for Legislative Changes

PROGRAM TO BE STUDIED

Director Tells House Panel He Needs Time Before Asking Major Shifts

By MARJORIE HUNTER

Special to The New York Times

WASHINGTON, June 2—President Nixon asked Congress today to extend the Government's multibillion-dollar antipoverty program for two years. Earlier, he had said he would seek a one-year extension.

The decision was announced both at the White House, in a statement issued by the President, and on Capitol Hill, in testimony by Donald Rumsfeld, the new director of the antipoverty agency, the Office of Economic Opportunity.

The President has recommended $2,048,000,000 to finance the program in the fiscal year starting July 1. This is $100-million more than the agency's appropriations for the fiscal year just ending.

Mr. Rumsfeld told the House Education and Labor Committee that the Administration would not propose legislative changes in the antipoverty program at this time.

Effective Next Month

Noting that he had been on the job just seven days, Mr. Rumsfeld said he wanted to review the antipoverty efforts before proposing any major changes.

While not seeking changes in the basic law, the Administration plans to go ahead with previously announced decisions to delegate operation of several antipoverty programs—including the Head Start preschool program and the Job Corps — to other departments.

The President has assigned Head Start to the Department of Health, Education and Welfare, and the Job Corps to the Department of Labor, effective July 1.

These planned shifts have been denounced by some members of Congress, including the chairman of the House Edu-

Continued on Page 28, Column 5

Australian Ship Slices U.S. Destroyer; 56 American Sailors Listed as Missing

United Press International

American destroyer Frank E. Evans, whose bow sank after collision with aircraft carrier

By The Associated Press

PEARL HARBOR, Hawaii, June 2—An Australian aircraft carrier sliced in two the United States destroyer Frank E. Evans during maneuvers in the South China Sea today, and the destroyer's bow sank, the Navy reported.

One American sailor is known dead, 56 are missing and 216 were rescued, the Navy said. There were no casualties listed aboard the Australian carrier, the Melbourne, which had a four-foot hole in her bow about 12 feet above the water line. Her flight deck was also damaged.

The bow of the destroyer sank within minutes. The remainder of the ship was lashed to the carrier and remained afloat.

The collision occurred about 650 nautical miles southwest of Manila at 4:12 A.M. Tuesday, Philippines time, which is 10:12 A.M. Monday Hawaiian time.

The 2,200-ton Evans and the Melbourne were participating in the Southeast Asia Treaty Organization exercise known as Sea Spirit.

The skipper of the Evans, Comdr. Albert S. McLemore, and his executive officer were among those saved, the Navy said.

Several ships involved in the exercise went to the aid of the Evans's survivors. Among them were the American ships James E. Kyes and Everett E. Larson, the British ship Cleopatra and the new Zealand ship Blackpool.

In addition, it was reported that other ships were in the area and that the United States carrier Kearsarge was standing by.

Informed of the disaster as he was campaigning in a by-election in Melbourne, Prime Minister John G. Gorton of Australia said: "I am most distressed

Continued on Page 17, Column 1

HIGH COURT BACKS NEGROES' RIGHTS IN THREE RULINGS

Decides Voting, Recreation and School Cases as End of Warren Term Nears

By FRED P. GRAHAM

Special to The New York Times

WASHINGTON, June 2—The Supreme Court acted with near-unanimity today in issuing three decisions upholding Negroes' rights to equality in education, recreational opportunity and voting.

Although the Court is deeply split over some issues as Chief Justice Earl Warren's final term nears an end, it was demonstrated today that civil rights—one of the areas of the "Warren Court's" most notable activity—was not one of them.

Disposing of all of the year's civil rights cases in one sitting, the Court did the following:

¶Ruled unanimously that a recalcitrant Southern school board could be required to move toward the elimination of recognizable "Negro" schools by assigning its teachers according to racial ratios set by the Federal judiciary.

¶Held, 7 to 1, that even a lake recreation area in an out-of-the-way Arkansas location was covered by the public accommodations provision of the Civil Rights Act of 1964 and must admit Negroes.

¶Upheld a lower court decision, by a 7-to-1 margin, that a North Carolina county had used a literacy test to discriminate against Negroes — and thus could not be excused from coverage under the Voting Rights Act of 1965—because it had once segregated them in inferior schools that left many illiterate.

First Approval of Ratios

The school decision, written by Justice Hugo L. Black of Alabama, marked the first time that the Supreme Court had given its approval to the use of racial ratios in achieving school desegregation.

Justice Black stressed that the racial ratio approved today was not a universal constitutional requirement. Rather, he said, it is an expedient that was found to be necessary to break up the pattern of segregation in the Montgomery, Ala., schools that existed before the Supreme Court declared school segregation unconstitutional in 1954.

Federal District Judge Frank M. Johnson Jr. had tried to make up for years of foot-dragging by Montgomery school officials by ordering them to begin immediately to move toward a goal of a ratio of three white to two Negro teachers in each school. This is the ratio of white to Negro teachers in the school district as a whole.

School officials complained

Continued on Page 18, Column 1

U.S. SAID TO PLAN AN OKINAWA DEAL BARRING A-BOMBS

Nixon Decision Reported—Timing Hinges on Terms for Isle's Return to Japan

By HEDRICK SMITH

Special to The New York Times

WASHINGTON, June 2—President Nixon has decided to remove American nuclear weapons from Okinawa once an over-all plan for turning the island back to Japanese rule has been agreed upon, well-placed informants disclosed today.

The actual timing of the removal of the weapons to other sites in the Pacific area will depend on the terms of the reversion agreement, the sources indicated. Japan wants the weapons removed and the island returned, with the rest of the Ryukyu chain, by 1972.

Mr. Nixon's decision, reportedly made after a National Security Council meeting in late April on the Okinawan question and related issues, is an important one. It is understood to reflect the judgment of the President's civilian advisers that maintenance of sound, long-term relations with Japan is more important than the military advantage of retaining complete freedom of operation on Okinawa.

Negotiations to Continue

Informed sources said Mr. Nixon's decision had not yet been communicated formally to the Japanese Government. But presumably it will be made known in the course of negotiations with Tokyo on the Okinawa issue this summer and fall.

The Japanese Foreign Minister, Kiichi Aichi, met with President Nixon for 40 minutes this morning at the White House to present his Government's request that the Ryukyu Islands, held by the United States since 1945, be returned to Japanese rule by 1972.

Mr. Aichi's call on the President marked the formal beginning of negotiations on the Okinawa issue, though there have been months of preliminary discussions at lower levels. The negotiations are expected to culminate in November with a visit to Washington by Japan's Premier, Eisaku Sato.

Now Under Military Rule

Mr. Aichi told the President today that Japan would like American bases in Okinawa to function after reversion on the same basis as United States installations in Japan's four home islands.

Under present conditions, with the Ryukyus governed by a United States administration headed by a military High Com-

Continued on Page 14, Column 1

Dirksen Denounces Kennedy Criticism Of Tactics in War

By JOHN W. FINNEY

Special to The New York Times

WASHINGTON, June 2—The Senate Republican leader, Everett McKinley Dirksen, rebuked Senator Edward M. Kennedy today for his criticism of military tactics in Vietnam, suggesting that the Senate Democratic whip was undercutting field commanders and impairing troop morale.

The Senate Democratic leader, Mike Mansfield, promptly came to the defense of his absent assistant. He said that the Massachusetts Senator had "a right to speak as he sees fit."

Only a handful of Senators were on the floor for the Dirksen-Mansfield exchange, which was pointed but lacking personal animus. Senator Kennedy was in Arizona delivering a commencement speech before the Rough Rock Indian school.

In the politics of the Vietnam war, the exchange may mark an important turning

Continued on Page 16, Column 3

O.A.S. CHIEF CITES RANCOR OVER U.S.

Confers With Rockefeller—White House Supports Mission's Continuation

By JUAN DE ONIS

Special to The New York Times

PORT OF SPAIN, Trinidad, June 2—Galo Plaza, Secretary General of the Organization of American States, said today that student violence against Governor Rockefeller's fact-finding mission reflected an increasing disillusionment and frustration in Latin America toward the United States.

Mr Plaza, who had breakfast here with Mr. Rockefeller and his advisers, told them not to fool themselves into thinking that student protests in Latin America were just the work of an extremist minority.

Mr. Rockefeller later flew to New York, two days ahead of schedule, because of the cancellation of his planned visit to Venezuela. Before his departure, he declared that he had no intention of canceling any of the 11 visits remaining on his itinerary in two future Latin-American trips.

[In Washington, the White House said that it supported the Governor's decision and that the two remaining trips would not be canceled.]

Mr. Plaza, a former President of Ecuador, who was educated in the United States and is an old friend of Governor Rocke-

Continued on Page 2, Column 4

POMPIDOU VICTORY APPEARS ASSURED; REDS TO ABSTAIN

Communist Call to Backers Not to Vote in Presidential Runoff Is Blow to Poher

'REACTIONARIES' SCORED

Interim Leader Is Urged by Gaullists to Withdraw, but He Insists He Will Run

By HENRY TANNER

Special to The New York Times

PARIS, June 2—The French Communist party tonight told its supporters to abstain from voting in the runoff presidential election on June 15 between Georges Pompidou and Alain Poher.

A statement issued by the party's Central Committee said that both candidates were reactionaries and stooges of capitalism, and that members of the working class therefore could not vote for either.

In the view of most observers and politicians, the party's decision was tantamount to assuring the election of Mr. Pompidou, the Gaullist candidate.

Mr. Pompidou won yesterday's first-round election by getting more than 44 per cent of the valid ballots. He needs only an additional 6 per cent to attain the required majority.

Poher Needs Leftist Votes

Mr. Poher, France's Interim President since the resignation of President de Gaulle, ran a poor second with slightly more than 23 per cent. He could win the runoff only if he obtained most or all of the votes that went to the Communist candidate, Jacques Duclos, and to other leftist candidates.

At least four out of every five Communist voters are not members of the party, which claims a membership of about half a million. The members undoubtedly will heed the party directive. Of the others some may go along with the party line and others are likely to split their vote between Mr. Pompidou and Mr. Poher—with Mr. Poher nevertheless the victim.

Mr. Pompidou also is the benefactor from another point of view, political observers noted. The Communist action will have the effect of reducing the total number of valid ballots, and thus the number of votes required to get a majority.

No More Would Be Needed

Thus, if the nearly five million people—21 per cent of the total—who voted for Mr. Duclos were to follow the party line and not vote in the runoff, Mr. Pompidou would not have to win any new votes. The total he obtained yesterday would give him a majority.

Despite the Communist action, Mr. Poher reiterated his determination to remain in the race. Last night Gaullist officials began a campaign to persuade him to withdraw, hoping to face Mr. Duclos in the runoff. They believe that against the Communist candidate Mr.

Continued on Page 3, Column 4

PANEL URGES SHIFT IN M.I.T. RESEARCH

Retention of Defense-Allied Laboratories Backed, With Stress on Civilian Role

By ROBERT REINHOLD

Special to The New York Times

CAMBRIDGE, Mass., June 2—A special committee at the Massachusetts Institute of Technology recommended today that the institute retain its two controversial defense-connected laboratories but attempt to shift their emphasis toward socially oriented civilian projects.

The panel stopped short of recommending that weapons research be ended, as some students and professors have urged. The members made clear their belief, however, that the laboratories were too heavily engaged in military research and should "energetically explore new projects to provide a more balanced research program."

Appointed last month by M.I.T.'s president, Howard W. Johnson, the committee consisted of 22 professors, students, alumni, staff and trustees of the prestigious institution. At the time Mr. Johnson ordered that new classified research be declined while the panel was deliberating.

Mr. Johnson issued a statement today endorsing the committee's recommendations and lifting the ban on new classified projects. The recommenda-

Continued on Page 33, Column 1

Violent Rainstorm Floods City Roads And Halts Subway

By DAVID K. SHIPLER

New Yorkers were awakened by the crack and roll of thunder in the hours before dawn yesterday as a quick, violent storm materialized over the city and dumped 2.35 inches of rain in two and a half hours.

Water flowed across major highways and poured into subway tunnels, snarling rush-hour traffic, knocking out some electric power and infuriating millions who had begun to regard the weather as an ally during the sunny, pleasant Memorial Day weekend.

All but one of Brooklyn's subway lines were halted for several hours, and the only trains that ran in Queens were those on elevated tracks. The Long Island Rail Road diverted its Brooklyn-bound trains into Manhattan's Penn Station, adding 20,000 passengers to the influx there.

Flooding closed sections of the Franklin D. Roosevelt Drive, the Grand Central Parkway, the Belt Parkway, Queens Boulevard and other major arteries. But the chain reaction of delays and detours, both above and below ground, reached far beyond the stricken areas.

The New York and American Stock Exchanges opened 45 minutes late—at 10:45 A.M.—and the American Exchange suspended trading for a short time when wet cables knocked

Continued on Page 38, Column 2

JUSTICES RESTRICT MILITARY TRIALS

Give Civil Courts Authority Over Off-Base Offenses in U.S. in Peacetime

Special to The New York Times

WASHINGTON, June 2—The Supreme Court ruled today that servicemen could not be court-martialed in peacetime for crimes committed off military bases within the United States.

The ruling is expected to fall heavily on the court systems of small communities near military bases, where military courts have customarily punished many off-base infractions by servicemen.

Before today's ruling, military officials and local prosecutors in such communities usually conferred informally to decide which authority would prosecute military personnel. The Court was told that the services had prosecuted about 15 per cent of all off-duty offenses.

The Supreme Court ruled today, 5 to 3, that those courts-martial were unconstitutional because they did not grant the accused servicemen their rights to trial by jury and to indictment by grand jury, which are guaranteed by the Fifth Amendment.

"Courts-martial as an institution are singularly inept in dealing with the nice subtleties of constitutional law," Justice

Continued on Page 22, Column 4

400 FROM SLUMS URGED FOR C.C.N.Y.

Faculty Senate Backs Plan for More Black Students

By SYLVAN FOX

The City College faculty senate last night approved a plan to admit 400 additional students from minority groups in the 1969-70 academic year and 400 more from minority groups the following year.

In adopting the plan, the 87-member faculty senate cast aside a controversial dual admissions proposal, which called for 50 per cent of the 1970 freshman class to come from poverty areas without regard to academic performance, an action that would have substantially increased the number of black and Puerto Rican students.

The senate's action must now go to the Board of Higher Education, which has ultimate authority over any admissions changes at City College. The faculty senate recommended that the admissions pattern it adopted be made applicable to the entire City University.

Under the senate plan, 300 students from selected high

Continued on Page 34, Column 1

The Changing City: Crime on the Rise

This is the third report in a series on the problems of New York City.

By DAVID BURNHAM

The Police Department has modernized its equipment, increased its manpower and reorganized patrolling operations in the last three years, but reported crime in the city has continued to rise.

This anomaly has left residents of almost every neighborhood in the city fearful of the mugger, the burglar and the vandal. It also has led more and more policemen, criminologists and government officials to challenge widespread views of how to combat crime.

One key problem is that very little is known about crime and how to fight it. Shortly after Howard R. Leary assumed command of the New York Police Department in 1966, for example, he doubled the size of the Narcotics Bureau to 300 men.

Asked recently whether this move had reduced the traffic in illegal drugs or the crimes committed by the city's estimated total of 50,000 addicts, Commissioner Leary replied:

"I can't answer that question. I could pop my mouth off, but there really isn't any hard information."

Despite the lack of concrete evidence, many criminologists and law enforcement officials are convinced that attempts to suppress crime must go far beyond the police to the broader realm of the city's attempts to solve the economic, social and racial problems that have divided and scarred its citizens.

"To a considerable degree law enforcement cannot deal with criminal behavior," James Vorenberg, former director of the National Crime Commission, says in explaining this position. "The most important way in which any mayor could be held responsible for crime is the extent to which he failed to fight for job-training programs, better schools and decent housing."

New Yorkers live with an enormous amount of crime. In 1968, 904 murders, 1,840 rapes, 54,405 robberies, 28,515 felonious assaults, 173,559 burglaries, 146,319 larcenies of $50 or more and 74,440 car thefts were reported to the police.

In addition, projections based on studies by the Na-

Continued on Page 35, Column 1

The New York Times

MEET IN WASHINGTON: President Nixon with Kiichi Aichi, Foreign Minister of Japan, at White House yesterday. Mr. Aichi presented request for return of Pacific islands.

Mayor Asks Ruling On $6,000 in Gifts

By MARTIN TOLCHIN

Mayor Lindsay will return $6,000 in campaign funds raised by the President of the City Tax Commission, if the Board of Ethics finds that his fund-raising was improper, the Mayor's press spokesman said yesterday.

The funds were obtained by Benjamin G. Browdy from 18 contributors, some of whom may be lawyers who practice before the commission, according to Mr. Browdy.

The tax agency official, who said that he saw nothing unethical in this fund-raising, formally requested a ruling yesterday from the Board of Ethics.

The Mayor's spokesman said: "We will be guided by the

Continued on Page 37, Column 5

NEWS INDEX

	Page		Page
Books	44-45	Music	40-43
Bridge	44	Obituaries	47
Business	61, 73-74	Society	39
Buyers	74	Sports	52-58
Crossword	45	Supreme Court	18, 72
Editorials	46	Theaters	40-43
Fashions	50	Transportation	93
Financial	55-74	TV and Radio	94-95
Food	50	U. N. Proceedings	14
Man in the News	3	Wash. Proceedings	22
Movies	40-43	Weather	93

News Summary and Index, Page 49

DISCOVER WHO DISCOVERED EUROPE Today. On the book page.—Advt.

KENNETH GARTNER Plays Beethoven THIS SUNDAY AT TOWN HALL —Advt.

Australian Carrier Slices U.S. Destroyer; 56 Americans Missing

Wide World Photos

Damage is shown on the bow section of the Australian aircraft carrier *Melbourne* after its collision with the U.S. Navy destroyer *USS Frank E. Evans.* The two ships collided in the South China Sea while engaged in the six-nation SEATO operation "Sea Spirit."

Continued From Page 1, Col. 4

and upset about it." He expressed his sympathy to the relatives of the American victims.

The Melbourne had only recently returned to service after a $7.8-million refitting necessitated by a collision in 1964. In that collision, the carrier sliced through the Australian destroyer Voyager.

The Melbourne carries American-built Skyhawk fighters and Grumman antisubmarine tracking aircraft.

Inquiry Is Up to U.S.

Special to The New York Times

CANBERRA, Australia, Tuesday, June 3—The Navy Minister, Charles R. Kelly, said today that an official inquiry into the collision would be the responsibility of the United States,

since the Melbourne was under the command of an American admiral at the time of the collision.

"This admiral was controlling the whole exercise," he said, referring to the SEATO maneuver. "The Australian Navy will of course be represented at the inquiry."

Mr. Kelly said that the Australian carrier and the American destroyer had been steaming together, with the destroyer acting as an escort while the carrier took on planes that had been in the air for the maneuver.

"Normally the ships would be between 200 and 300 yards apart," he said.

Mr. Kelly said that after the collision had sliced the American destroyer in two, the after portion of the stricken vessel had "drifted past" the Melbourne. The Australian ship grappled the after portion of

the destroyer and took the survivors aboard. The Melbourne then disengaged and the after section sank.

Evans Launched in 1944

The 2,200-ton destroyer, the Frank E. Evans, was launched on Oct. 3, 1944, in Staten Island. The ship, named after the late Brig. Gen. Frank E. Evans of the Marine Corps, was designed specifically to outmatch and outmaneuver the cruiser-destroyers built by Japan before World War II.

On May 11, 1945, the Evans teamed with the destroyer Hugh W. Hadley in a 45-minute battle off Okinawa in which 38 Japanese planes were demolished. In all, 88 Japanese planes were knocked out of the sky in what was described as an epic battle.

The other Japanese craft were brought down by marine

Corsair pilots. Four of the planes crashed on the Evans's decks, and the hull took hits that flooded one engine room.

Exercise Sea Spirit began in Manila on May 30. It is a convoy exercise from the Philippines to the Gulf of Thailand, with some SEATO navies exercising antisubmarine warfare capabilities. It is estimated by Pentagon sources that there have been about 30 SEATO exercises in the past involving both this kind of maneuver and amphibious exercises.

A Pentagon official said he believed that the countries other than the United States and Australia participating in Exercise Sea Spirit were Thailand, the Philippines, Britain and New Zealand.

Commander McLemore has been in the Navy since 1949. He participated in the first amphibious landing of the Ko-

The New York Times   June 3, 1969

Ships collided southwest of the Philippines (cross.)

rean war. The Evans is his first command. He has been captain of the destroyer since February 1968. He is married and has five sons.

"All the News That's Fit to Print"

The New York Times

LATE CITY EDITION

Weather: Chance of showers today, tonight. Partly cloudy tomorrow. Temp. range: today 88-75; Monday 88-73. Temp.-Hum. Index yesterday 80. Complete U.S. report on Page 85.

VOL. CXVIII . No. 40,750
© 1969 The New York Times Company.
NEW YORK, TUESDAY, AUGUST 19, 1969

10 CENTS

C. F. HAYNSWORTH NAMED BY NIXON FOR HIGH COURT

U.S. Appellate Judge Chosen for Vacancy Created by Resignation of Fortas

SENATE APPROVAL SEEN

South Carolinian Is Favored by Conservative Leaders of Judiciary Committee

By NEIL SHEEHAN

Special to The New York Times

SAN CLEMENTE, Calif., Aug. 18—President Nixon announced today the nomination of Judge Clement F. Haynsworth Jr. of South Carolina to be an Associate Justice of the Supreme Court.

The nominee, a 56-year-old native of Greenville, is chief judge of the United States Court of Appeals for the Fourth Circuit, which has headquarters in Richmond.

Judge Haynsworth, a fifth-generation lawyer, has a conservative record on civil rights and a mixed conservative and liberal record on criminal cases.

He is to fill the seat vacated last May by Abe Fortas, a liberal who resigned in the controversy over his acceptance of a fee from the family foundation of Louis Wolfson, a convicted stock manipulator.

Easy Approval Foreseen

The nomination is not expected to encounter any serious opposition from the Senate Judiciary Committee, which is dominated by conservatives.

The committee chairman, James O. Eastland, Democrat of Mississippi, and Senator Everett McKinley Dirksen, of Illinois, the ranking Republican, have both strongly endorsed Judge Haynsworth.

Judge Haynsworth is also expected to win confirmation on the Senate floor, although the opposition there may be more serious because of what appears to be a coalescing protest from civil rights and labor groups.

Ronald L. Ziegler, the Presidential press secretary, said that in his choice of Judge Haynsworth, the President believed "he has selected a man who has a proven record as a jurist, both as associate judge and chief judge on one of the country's busiest courts of appeals."

"Judge Haynsworth meets the qualifications which the President believes are essential for an Associate Justice for the Supreme Court," Mr. Ziegler said. "The President feels that during Judge Haynsworth's years on the bench, he has demonstrated judicial temperament,

Continued on Page 27, Column 1

Chosen for U.S. Supreme Court

United Press International

Clement F. Haynsworth Jr., chief judge of U.S. Court of Appeals for the Fourth Circuit, in his office yesterday.

Right of Relief Recipients To Bar Home Visits Upheld

By EMANUEL PERLMUTTER

In a decision that could radically affect welfare procedures, a three-man Federal Court ruled here yesterday that recipients may not be denied public assistance solely for refusing to allow caseworkers into their homes without a warrant.

The court said that the granting of Federal assistance could not require recipients to waive their protection against search and seizure under the Fourth Amendment.

[In Washington, lawyers concerned with legal aspects of welfare reform welcomed the decision as one of the most significant in an increasing number of court-mandated safeguards of the poor.]

Appeal Decision Delayed

Barbara James, a Bronx mother, was granted a permanent injunction preventing the Department of Social Services from carrying out its decision to terminate welfare payments to her and her pre-school son, Maurice, because she had refused to permit visits to her home by an investigator. Her address and marital status were not divulged.

John L. Costa, Deputy Social Services Administrator, said that his department would have to study the decision before deciding whether to file an appeal.

Because a special constitutional court heard the case, an appeal would have to be made directly to the United States Supreme Court.

At present, state and city

Continued on Page 49, Column 2

STATE FUND PLANS 4 SCHOOLS IN CITY

1,440 Apartments Are Part of $50-Million Renewal Project in Yorkville

By EDWARD C. BURKS

A $50-million plan to provide Yorkville with four new public schools and to develop air rights above them for 1,440 apartments was announced yesterday.

The New York City Educational Construction Fund, a state authority that will handle the development at no cost to the city, reported that three old schools would be torn down and four new ones put up.

The first site to be developed, and the largest, according to Daniel Z. Nelson, executive director of the fund, is an abandoned city asphalt plant covering four acres at 90th Street and Franklin D. Roosevelt Drive.

A school complex for 830 pupils and 1,000 middle-income apartments is scheduled to be constructed on the site, just one block north of Gracie Mansion, the Mayor's residence.

The other combined school-

Continued on Page 30, Column 1

ULSTER TO FORM CIVIC COMMITTEE TO SEEK A TRUCE

Catholic Priest at Meeting of 20 Community Leaders—More Soldiers Due

By ALVIN SHUSTER

Special to The New York Times

BELFAST, Northern Ireland, Aug. 18—Prime Minister James Chichester-Clark called community leaders together tonight to discuss way of restoring peace and understanding in this strife-torn territory.

The 20 leaders agreed after a three-hour meeting to form a reconciliation committee of representatives from the churches, industry, universities and the legal professions in an effort to restore "peace and confidence." The chances of success appeared doubtful in the present atmosphere.

"The first solution is to get fear out of the minds of people," said Harold Sloan, who represented the Methodist Church. "The people of both sides are crazy with fear."

William Cardinal Conway, Roman Catholic Primate of Ireland, declined the invitation to attend the meeting. Catholic civil-rights leaders later called the talks a "sham" and "an attempt at window-dressing."

The conference, attended by a Catholic clergyman, was held on the eve of Major Chichester-Clark's meeting in London with Prime Minister Wilson on the sectarian violence, which has claimed eight lives here since Thursday.

March Near Barricades

Catholics and Protestants buried their dead today with solemn marches near the rubble and barricades of still-tense neighborhoods. Protestants buried one man. Catholics buried five persons, including two boys, aged 9 and 15.

The British Army disclosed that by Thursday 2,000 more soldiers would arrive in Northern Ireland, bringing the total to 6,000. The commanding officer of the forces warned that his soldiers "may come under attack from both sides" if the two Prime Ministers fail to end the violence, which has followed a civil-rights campaign that the Catholic minority began last fall.

Lieut. Gen. Sir Ian Freeland, who commands British troops in Northern Ireland, said that unless "something more constructive and helpful" emerged from the talks in London, "the honeymoon period could end in a few hours."

Slow Return to Normal

Belfast still struggled today to return to normal after the shootings and arson of the last week. A few stores in the hard-hit areas reopened this morning, and milk and bread trucks drove past armed troops to resume deliveries. Because 54 buses were stolen last week for use in makeshift barricades, local transportation was spotty. At rush hour some lines of workers stretched for a block.

There were only a few incidents of violence late tonight. A gasoline bomb was thrown through the window of a community center and a few win-

Continued on Page 3, Column 1

Hurricane Leaves Wake of Destruction in Mississippi

A house was blown from its foundation and onto a railroad track near Gulfport, Miss.

Associated Press

Ships in Gulfport area were washed ashore by winds estimated to be 190 miles per hour

HURRICANE DEAD REPORTED AT 101; TOLL MAY GROW

Thousands Left Homeless in 3 States Along Gulf Coast —Fires Out of Control

NIXON AIDS MISSISSIPPI

Declares It a Disaster Area —Storm Heads Northward While Its Winds Slacken

By The Associated Press

GULFPORT, Miss., Aug. 18—The death toll from Hurricane Camille reached 101 tonight as rescue workers probed the shattered areas of the Louisiana and Mississippi coasts.

Civil defense officials in Mississippi reported 100 dead from all along the coast and expected the toll to increase to between 150 and 200. In Louisiana, one man was killed when the storm struck low-lying areas below New Orleans.

In San Clemente, Calif., President Nixon declared Mississippi a major disaster area and allocated the state $1-million in relief funds

Fires burned out of control because firefighting units could not reach them. Buildings burned in Bay St. Louis, Miss., 15 miles west of Gulfport near the Louisiana border. Communications were disrupted.

Storm Moves Inland

The hurricane moved inland today, hitting Hattiesburg and other cities along the way with high winds, up to 100 miles an hour in Hattiesburg.

The storm moved northward into the Mississippi Delta country north of Jackson this afternoon.

As Camille moved inland, its winds dropped to less than 50 miles an hour, taking it out of the hurricane classification.

Later today, the Weather Bureau called Camille a "dying storm" as it passed through Greenwood, Miss. The bureau said the storm would disintegrate into rain squalls as it moved farther north.

Thousands of persons in Mississippi, Louisiana and Alabama were left homeless in the hurricane's wake. High winds and flood waters pounded the coasts of all three states and the storm buffeted New Orleans on its way inland across Mississippi. The winds were reported as high as 190 miles an hour.

Coast Guard Planes Used

In Miami, the National Hurricane Center said Camille was the second strongest hurricane ever to hit the United States. An unnamed hurricane that struck the Florida Keys in 1935 was measured as being stronger.

The Coast Guard put 16 helicopters and two planes in the air to scour the 30-mile stretch of Mississippi's coast between Waveland and Biloxi for further damage. This was the point of Camille's impact when the hurricane left the waters of the Gulf of Mexico.

Most of the Gulf Coast was without electricity, gas or drinking water.

The eye of the big storm moved across the coast last night. The Red Cross report-

Continued on Page 24, Column 1

19-HOUR CONCERT ENDS BETHEL FAIR

Producer Says Town Has Asked Festival to Return

By WILLIAM E. FARRELL

Special to The New York Times

BETHEL, N. Y., Aug. 18 — Undaunted by rain, mud, wet clothes and chilly mountain breezes, thousands and thousands of youths sat on a rural hillside here for a marathon 19-hour session of folk-rock music that ended at 10:30 A.M. today and brought the Woodstock Music and Art Fair to a close.

Within minutes after Jimi Hendrix, an electric guitar player, and his group played what was called a searing, "mind blowing" rendition of the national anthem, the hillside was cleared for the first time in nearly four days of the hordes of youths — estimated at one time to total 300,000 —who came here for three days of music, companionship and, in many cases, drugs.

The death of one youngster during the music fair was attributed by authorities to drug overdoses, and another youth died when he was run over by a tractor. Lesser injuries,

Continued on Page 34, Column 1

80,000 SQ FT modern, air cond office space (4 flrs); 5 Ave & 34 St area; rent all or part. Data processing facilities & other extras. (212) 986-1111. —Advt.

Mies van der Rohe Dies at 83; Leader of Modern Architecture

Special to The New York Times

CHICAGO, Aug. 18 — Mies van der Rohe, one of the great figures of 20th-century architecture, died in Wesley Memorial Hospital here late last night. He was 83 years old.

Mr. van der Rohe had entered the hospital two weeks ago.

He is survived by two daughters, Mrs. Georgia van der Rohe and Mrs. Marianne Lohan; five grandchildren and six great-grandchildren.

Expressed Industrial Spirit

By ALDEN WHITMAN

Ludwig Mies van der Rohe, a man without any academic architectural training, was one of the great artist-architect-philosophers of his age, acclaimed as a genius for his uncompromisingly spare design, his fastidiousness and his innovations.

Along with Frank Lloyd Wright and Le Corbusier, the German-born master builder who was universally known as Mies (pronounced mees) fashioned scores of imposing structures expressing the spirit of the industrial 20th century.

"Architecture is the will of an epoch translated into space," he remarked in a talkative moment. Pressed to ex-

Associated Press, 1958

Mies van der Rohe

plain his own role as a model for others—a matter on which he was shy, as he was on most others—he said:

"I have tried to make an architecture for a technological society. I have wanted to keep everything reasonable and clear — to have an architecture that anybody can do."

A building, he was convinced, should be "a clear and true statement of its times"—cathedrals for an age of pathos,

Continued on Page 28, Column 3

City Aide Would Cut Bill if a Phone Fails

By DAVID BIRD

A city official testified yesterday that if the telephone company failed to deliver adequate service "the customer is freed of his obligation to pay the company's rates."

Mrs. Bess Myerson Grant, the city's Commissioner of Consumer Affairs, said, "No one has an obligation to pay for service which is not in fact received—even to a colossus like the telephone company."

Mrs. Grant testified at a hearing called by the State Public Service Commission as part of its investigation into the growing difficulties plaguing telephone service in the metropolitan area.

The hearing, highly emotional at times as subscribers de-

Continued on Page 40, Column 4

DETAINED BERETS OUT OF STOCKADE

Men in Vietnam Case Given Rooms in Normal Quarters

By JAMES P. STERBA

Special to The New York Times

SAIGON, South Vietnam, Aug. 18 — The Special Forces officers and men held in a stockade in connection with the reported slaying of a Vietnamese intelligence agent were transferred today to ordinary Army quarters.

The move was made less than two weeks after the Army disclosed that the eight soldiers of the Special Forces, or Green Berets, were being held pending an investigation that could result in court-martial charges of murder and conspiracy to commit murder. The case, surrounded by mystery, has resulted in charges and denials of involvement by the United States Central Intelligence Agency.

Sources familiar with the investigation have disclosed that the Vietnamese whose death is at issue was a double agent who had betrayed an allied intelligence network monitoring infiltration on the Cambodian border. It has been asserted that he was killed on instructions from the C.I.A., an assertion

Continued on Page 13, Column 1

What the Hurricane Did

By ROY REED

Special to The New York Times

GULFPORT, Miss., Aug. 18 —Just what will a hurricane wind of 190 miles an hour do?

It will snatch three large oceangoing ships from their moorings and set them down on the beach, nosed together like three rowboats tied to a single chain.

It will make a concrete-block service station disappear, leaving only the gasoline pumps to identify what once was there.

It will enter a broken window of a beach front house and stir the heavy pieces of furniture so playfully that the living room couch ends up in the dining room, and the heavy china closet holding a woman's antique cutglass comes to rest at a 45-degree angle, propped against the wall like a drunkard.

"These antiques are from Kentucky," said Mrs. Edward M. Sternberg as she surveyed the cutglass, the stately chairs and tables and the water-soaked carpet.

She did not explain the significance of their being from Kentucky, and there was a suggestion of mist in her eye that did not invite questions.

The Sternbergs were back to look over the remains of their home after Hurricane Camille. They were grateful to be alive.

"Every house on the beach is like this," said a neighbor, Allen Kerr. "It's a good thing we left, or we'd all have been killed."

Gulfport and Biloxi, a few miles to the east, were the pride of Mississippi, the favorite playground of rich and poor for miles around, until the hurricane struck last night. Now the playground is a wreck.

The wreckage extends all along the Mississippi coast and beyond. Mobile on the east and New Orleans on the west were also in the hurricane's path, although neither was damaged as heavily as the little Mississippi towns in between.

Most of the residents of the little towns were too

Continued on Page 24, Column 3

NEWS INDEX

Heart Experts Urge Caution on Implants

By SANDRA BLAKESLEE

Total heart transplant operations are here to stay but should be continued only on a controlled experimental basis, several leading heart experts said yesterday.

The surgeons and immunologists interviewed expressed their opinions in light of the death Sunday of Dr. Philip Blaiberg, who was the world's longest-surviving heart transplant recipient.

Dr. Blaiberg, a South African dentist, lived for 563 days with a transplanted heart, until chronic rejection of his second heart killed him. He was 60 years old.

Several of the doctors expressed the hope that what

Continued on Page 25, Column 1

BOWNE (noun: rhymes with downtown) Bowne of New York City, Inc., the foremost corporate and financial printer.—ADVT.

BAY ST. LOUIS: An elderly woman is helped to helicopter for treatment in New Orleans

BILOXI: Half of church in the Mississippi city was torn away and half left standing by freakish winds of hurricane

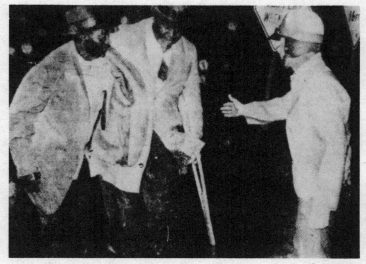

NEW ORLEANS: Policeman extending hand to residents fleeing waters of leaking levee

Hurricane's Toll Heavy;
Winds Off Gulf Abate

Continued From Page 1, Col. 8

ed its shelters housed more than 70,000 persons in Louisiana, Alabama and Mississippi during the night.

Gov. John Bell Williams of Mississippi spent much of the day in Gulfport, conferring with disaster rescue officials.

Comment by Williams

Following a ride over stretches of broken pavement between Gulfport and Biloxi, the Governor declared:

"I just couldn't believe it could be this bad until I actually saw it."

Governor Williams said he thought damage would be "in the hundreds of millions of dollars."

Fear about unreported damage grew in Louisiana. Gov. John J. McKeithen flew over the area after daybreak. Telephone communications — even ham radio operations — were nonexistent.

High water prevented searchers from entering the area. High water was a major problem below New Orleans. The city escaped with high winds and some damage along the Lake Pontchartrain seawall. Most damage was below New Orleans in the marshlands.

The Alabama coastline around Mobile suffered wind and water damage. The Florida panhandle also felt some of the storm's winds.

Radio Station Destroyed

The storm lifted a house near Gulfport from its foundations and dropped it on a railroad track. Three big cargo ships were blown from their moorings against piers and onto the beach.

The Buena Vista Hotel on the coast of Biloxi had water eight feet deep on its ground floor, destroying all the facilities of radio station WLOX.

The Gulfport Daily Herald

building was battered and water crept into the building.

Downtown Gulfport was a battleground for man against nature. Shattered glass littered the streets and buildings were damaged to the point of near collapse.

It's gone — not destroyed — it's gone," said Luke Petrovich, the Plaquemines (La.) Parish Public Safety Commissioner of a 10-mile strip between Buras and Fort Jackson.

'There Is No More Buras'

NEW ORLEANS, Aug. 18 (UPI)—Hurricane Camille practically wiped the river town of Buras off the map and left Bogalusa without electrical power or water.

"There is no more Buras," said one survivor driven out of the disaster area today. "It's all gone, flattened, nothing, just nothing."

Civil defense officials said waters from the Mississippi River broke through levees on the West Bank and inundated Buras in minutes.

One hundred National Guardsmen were ordered into Bogalusa after the Mississippi border city lost all electrical power and water services. Twenty more state troopers were also sent in to help handle the Bogalusa emergency.

No Alabama Fatalities

MOBILE, Ala., Aug. 18 (AP) —The hurricane left widespread destruction along coastal Alabama but apparently spared human life.

Unofficial estimates indicated that damage from Camille—the first hurricane to hit Alabama since 1926—would amount to several millions of dollars.

Bay St. Louis Damage

BAY ST. LOUIS, Miss., Aug. 18 (UPI)—This scenic coastal town was struck by the storm's

most devastating winds.

The business district of Bay St. Louis, a lumber milling and seafood packing center, had been concentrated on one street. Half of it is gone. Stores on the east side of the street caved into the Bay of St. Louis.

Three Killed in Cuba

HAVANA, Aug. 18 (Reuters) —The hurricane ravaged the western part of Cuba over the weekend, killing three persons and forcing 25,000 to be evacuated, the Communist party newspaper Granma said today.

There was no information about whether the hurricane, which flooded large areas of the west, damaged the vital sugar and tobacco harvests.

Eligible for U.S. Loans

WASHINGTON, Aug. 18 (AP) — Gulf Coast regions damaged by the hurricane were declared disaster areas today by the

Small Business Administration. The areas were made eligible for 3 per cent reconstruction and repair loans.

Hilary J. Sanodval Jr. ,administrator of the Federal agency, said the organization was prepared to act swiftly to provide aid to hurricane victims in Florida, Mississippi, Alabama and Louisiana.

Meanwhile, three teams from the Agriculture Department have been sent into Mississippi and Louisiana to help with food relief.

One team was reported to be in the Hattiesburg area; a second was working north from Jackson, and a third was headed into New Orleans, the department said.

Under Secretary of Agriculture J. Phil Campbell said 90,000 pounds of Government food was on its way from a Shreveport warehouse to Gulfport and Biloxi.

Damage Compared

Hurricane Betsy probably caused more damage in 1965 than Hurricane Camille did over the weekend, a Federal official said yesterday.

Betsy resulted in $1.4-billion in damage to private, state and Federal facilities, covering a greater area of Louisiana and Mississippi than the latest hurricane.

For those in the direct line of the hurricane, however, Camille has been as severe as Betsy, according to George A. Lincoln, director of the Office of Emergency Preparedness.

A 1964 hurricane named Hilda caused 23 deaths along the Louisiana coast as tornadoes on the outer edges of the hurricane smashed whole city blocks to pieces.

BAY ST. LOUIS: Toll bridge on route 90 near Mississippi town stands out amid litter of debris piled up by storm winds

"All the News That's Fit to Print"

The New York Times

LATE CITY EDITION

Weather: Cloudy today and tonight. Fair and continued cold tomorrow. Temp. range: today 40-31; Tuesday 48-35. Full U.S. report on Page 94.

VOL. CXIX.. No. 40,926

© 1970 The New York Times Company.

NEW YORK, WEDNESDAY, FEBRUARY 11, 1970

10 CENTS

PAKISTANI TROOPS REPORTED SERVING WITH JORDANIANS

Infantry Regiment of 2,000 to 3,000 Is Said to Join Two Training Missions

A VICTORY FOR HUSSEIN

Amman Officials Reinstitute Curbs on the Guerrillas—Palestinians Angered

By DANA ADAMS SCHMIDT
Special to The New York Times

BEIRUT, Lebanon, Feb. 10—Pakistan has quietly moved an infantry regiment into Jordan, high officials close to King Hussein's palace in Amman said today.

The sources said that the troops were in addition to two Pakistani military-training missions—one for the Jordanian Air Force and one for armored units—that have been in Jordan for three or four months. The regiment was said to number 2,000 to 3,000 men, while the training missions were said to total 200 to 300 men.

In another development in Amman, the Government issued an order reasserting earlier measures for controlling Palestinian guerrillas, particularly the prohibition against carrying arms in towns. The new order requires the guerrillas to turn in their arms and ammunitions to the authorities.

Palestinians Angered

A committee representing the Palestinian groups answered angrily that the measures "were meant to push the countries to the verge of civil war" and that the Jordanian authorities alone would be responsible for "any bloodshed that may ensue."

The Jordanian Army of about 55,000 men is already reinforced by the presence of about 12,000 Iraqis and 5,000 Syrian troops, as well as several battalions of Saudi Arabians, totaling about 1,500 men. [Western intelligence sources have confirmed that a Pakistani antiaircraft-training unit is known to have been active in Jordan for the last month.]

Pakistan is the first non-Arab Moslem country to give an Arab country military support against Israel, although the Pan-Islamic conference at Rabat, Morocco, last September voted in principle to support the Palestinian cause.

Result of King's Efforts

The arrival of the Pakistani regiment was the fruit of King Hussein's efforts over many years to foster close relations with Pakistan. He visited that country two months ago and is reported about to go there again after a state visit to the Persian Gulf sheikdom of Abu Dhabi later this week.

In August, 1968, Crown Prince Hassan of Jordan married Sarvath Ikramullah, the daughter of a Pakistani carcer diplomat.

The commander of the Pakistani Air Force, Air Marshal Rahim Khan, spent five days in Jordan and was decorated with Jordan's highest military order last week, just before King Hussein went to the meet-

Continued on Page 4, Column 3

Youth Hostel Takes Main Force of Fatal Avalanche in the French Alps

People at Val d'Isère gathering around the 8-year-old hostel after snow roared through its ground floor yesterday

Associated Press

Rescuers using rods to probe for victims after the avalanche stopped. Belgian and French youths occupied the hostel.

Grenades Miss Dayan Son In Arab Attack in Munich

By DAVID BINDER
Special to The New York Times

BONN, Feb. 10—Three Arabs armed with grenades, in an apparent attempt on the life of the son of Defense Minister Moshe Dayan of Israel, killed an Israeli airline passenger and wounded 23 persons in attacks yesterday on a bus and a lounge at the Munich airport.

Assaf Dayan, who was unhurt, was among the Israeli passengers aboard El Al flight 435, which stopped at Riem Airport in Munich on its way from Tel Aviv to London. Mr. Dayan, 24 years old, is an actor.

A grenade was thrown onto an airport bus that 19 of the plane's passengers had just boarded for the ride back from the terminal to the plane, the police said.

The explosion killed Ari Katzenstein, a 32-year-old engineer from Haifa, and wounded several, including an Israeli actress, Hanna Maron, and the pilot and co-pilot. Young Mr. Dayan was already aboard the plane.

Another of the Arabs threw a grenade into the lounge, which was crowded with 100 persons. One suspect was seized just as he had pulled the pin on his grenade, which exploded in his hand, wounding him. After a brief gun battle with the police, the two others were captured and disarmed.

After interrogating the three suspects, the Munich police chief, Manfred Schreiber, said there was reason to believe that Mr. Dayan had been the target of the attacks.

The police said that their

Continued on Page 4, Column 3

United Press International

Assaf Dayan at the airport in Munich after the attack.

39 DIE IN FRANCE UNDER SNOWSLIDE

Skiers at Val d'Isere Resort Engulfed at Breakfast—37 Youths Injured

By CLYDE H. FARNSWORTH
Special to The New York Times

BOURG - ST. - MAURICE, France, Feb. 10—An avalanche of snow thundered down on the fashionable Alpine resort of Val d'Isère today, killing at least 39 young skiers.

The avalanche, believed to be the worst in French history, injured 37 youths as it smashed into the bottom floors of a student chalet at breakfast time.

Information tonight indicated that Belgian and French youths were staying in the chalet. There were no reports of any Americans among the victims or survivors.

More than 100,000 cubic yards of snow crashed down from a treeless, 7,000-foot crest known as le Dôme, rushed 700 yards across the Alpine source of Isère River, engulfed a section of National Route 202, and smashed into the chalet.

The three-story structure, owned by a youth club known as the Union of Fresh Air Centers, housed about 200 persons, mostly in their early twenties.

The avalanche struck at 8:05 A.M., roaring through the ground floors and windows of the eight-year-old concrete building. Survivors said the only warning they had was "a terrible noise" just before the mountain of snow hit the dining room.

The building remained intact. Rescue workers immediately came to the scene and began digging out bodies and survivors.

It was the first time in 50 years that an avalanche had struck the village about 20

Continued on Page 14, Column 3

Lindsay Says Lack Of Funds Hinders Fight on Narcotics

By MARTIN TOLCHIN

Mayor Lindsay said yesterday that despite the rapidly growing narcotics problem and mounting pressures for government action on all levels, the city could not substantially expand its programs against drug abuse because of lack of funds.

"The most serious problem we have is insufficient funding from all sources," Mr. Lindsay told a City Hall news conerence.

The Mayor, who variously referred to the narcotics problem as a "crisis," "dilemma," "one of our most desperate problems," and "a direct threat to the future of the city," said that the city lacked funds to expand substantially beyond the current $13-million-a-year drug abuse program that affects 2,000 of the city's 100,000 addicts. Of the $13-million, $5.4-million comes from the Federal Office of Economic Opportunity, the Mayor said.

The 2,000 narcotics addicts in the city's drug program include 1,100 inpatients, of whom 200 are teen-agers. An additional 693 youths 18 or under are outpatients.

In a related development,

Continued on Page 50, Column 5

SENATE IN ALBANY VOTES STATE SHIFT ON PAROCHIAL AID

Passes, 41-15, Bill Repealing the Blaine Amendment—Debate Lasts 3 Hours

By WILLIAM E. FARRELL
Special to The New York Times

ALBANY, Feb. 10 — The Senate, by an overwhelming majority, took a first step today toward repealing the strict language of the State Constitution that prohibits direct or indirect state financial aid to schools with religious affiliations.

After nearly three hours of debate, the Senate voted, 41 to 15, to replace the language of Article XI, section 3 of the Constitution, known as the Blaine amendment, with the less restrictive language of the First Amendment of the United States Constitution.

The controversial bill now goes to the Assembly, where it is expected to be taken up and passed after more debate tomorrow. If the bill is approved, Governor Rockefeller is expected to sign it. The Governor called for repeal of the Blaine amendment last month in his annual program message to the Legislature.

1972 Effective Date

To alter the Constitution, legislation must pass two separately elected Legislatures and then be submitted to the voters in a statewide referendum. Assuming approval of the repeal measure during these subsequent steps, it could not take effect before 1972.

The repeal bill, sponsored by Senate Majority Leader Earl W. Brydges, Republican of Niagara Falls, sparked the lengthiest debate of the session and touched on a variety of sensitive issues, such as the separation of church and state, whether the Senate was espousing a dual system of public education and the possible effects of state aid to private and parochial schools on the hard-pressed public school system.

"All through my tenure in this body we have been confronted with a restrictive measure," Mr. Brydges said, alluding to the Blaine amendment, "more restrictive than the First Amendment, and we had to seek ways to get around this restrictive language."

Aid Program Held in Peril

But, Mr. Brydges said, despite the fact that programs such as textbook aid to parochial school children had not been thrown out by the courts, they were "just in a wee bit of jeopardy."

The status of such programs, he argued, would be more secure, if the 76-year-old Blaine amendment was deleted and replaced by the Federal Constitution's less restrictive wording—that, in this case, the Legislature "shall make no law respecting an establishment of religion."

While representatives of 25 civic, religious and educational organizations voiced their opposition to repeal of the Blaine amendment in a news conference, the debate moved along in the ornate Senate Chamber.

Continued on Page 50, Column 2

De Sapio Sentenced To 2 Years in Prison For Kickback Plot

Associated Press

Carmine G. De Sapio after he was given his sentence.

By CRAIG R. WHITNEY

Carmine G. De Sapio, once a powerful figure in state and national Democratic politics, was sentenced yesterday to two years in prison and fined $4,500 for his part in a conspiracy to bribe former Water Commissioner James L. Marcus and obtain kickbacks on Consolidated Edison Company contracts.

De Sapio protested his innocence and said he would appeal.

He was nervous and choked with emotion as he stood before Federal Judge

Continued on Page 30, Column 6

GARELIK OPPOSES MORGENTHAU JOB

City Council Blocks Lindsay Request to Set Up a Third Deputy Mayor's Office

By MAURICE CARROLL

Mayor Lindsay's plans to set up a third Deputy Mayor's office that would cost more than $500,000 a year were blocked yesterday in the City Council and criticized afterward by Sanford D. Garelik, the Council President.

Mr. Garelik, who won election as the Mayor's running mate, said that he had "serious questions" to ask when the proposal comes up in an executive session of the Board of Estimate today.

He conceded that he had helped block approval in the board last week.

To Take Office Sunday

Yesterday's developments made it probable that Robert M. Morgenthau would take office as the third Deputy Mayor on Sunday without authorization for his salary, his office or his staff.

"It's hard to imagine that the necessary legislation won't be passed soon," said a spokesman for Mr. Lindsay, and there were indications that interim financial arrangements would be made to put Mr. Morgenthau, a Democrat who used to be United States Attorney here, to work without complication.

Mr. Garelik, who sat at his City Hall desk looking over a six-page single-spaced report from Deputy Mayor Richard R. Aurelio justifying the proposed

Continued on Page 34, Column 8

PRESIDENT OFFERS PLAN FOR CLEANUP OF AIR AND WATER

Message to Congress Asks Expanded Action in Four Environmental Areas

SOME SURPRISES LISTED

Curbs on Industry Urged—U.S. Researchers to Seek a Pollution-Free Car

Text of the Nixon message is printed on Pages 32, 33.

By ROBERT B. SEMPLE Jr.
Special to The New York Times

WASHINGTON, Feb. 10—President Nixon asked Congress today for a variety of tools—some old, some new and some experimental—to help clean the air and purify the nation's polluted waters.

Having stressed environmental problems in his State of the Union Message nearly three weeks ago, Mr. Nixon chose the same issue as the subject for his first legislative message to Congress of the new year.

"Like those in the last century who tilled a plot of land to exhaustion and then moved on to another," he said, "we in this century have too casually and too long abused our natural environment. The time has come when we can wait no longer to repair the damage already done."

Four Areas for Action

To undertake these repairs, the President called for "expanded Government action" in four major areas: water pollution control, air pollution control, solid waste disposal and the orderly increase of park lands and open space.

Some of the major elements of the plan had already been forecast by the President in his State of the Union and Budget Messages. Most notable of these were a $10-billion program to build municipal waste treatment plants, to which the Government would contribute $4-billion, and a new financing device that would, in effect, guarantee a market for the $6-billion in municipal bonds that localities must sell to meet their share of the program.

However, the message contained a sizable list of surprises, including, most prominently, the following:

¶Nationwide air quality

Continued on Page 33, Column 1

CITY SAYS 13 TOOK POLLUTION BRIBES

Inspectors Are Suspended—6 Businessmen Seized

By EDWARD RANZAL

Thirteen city air-pollution inspectors—about 15 per cent of the 83-man inspection force—were suspended yesterday and six businessmen were arrested on charges of having bribed inspectors to overlook violations. Warrants were issued for the arrest of two more businessmen.

Commissioner of Investigation Robert K. Ruskin said that bribes ranging from $5 to $40 had been systematically collected over the last 11 years, with some businessmen paying off at least twice a month.

"I wish to make it clear," he said, "that if this kind of happy partnership continues it will only be at the jeopardy of both the businessman who pays and the inspector who receives."

His department's inquiry, he said, "is still active and continuing."

Merril Eisenbud, Administrator of the Environmental Protection Administration, said:

"This sort of thing has greatly diluted the effectiveness of our enforcement program."

So flagrant was the alleged corruption that two policemen attached to Mr. Ruskin's office said they had collected bribes by merely identifying themselves as air pollution inspectors.

In both instances, the policemen said, they were immedi-

Continued on Page 30, Column 8

Top Court in India Bars Nationalization of Banks

But 10-1 Vote Striking Down Plan Is Held Likely to Push Mrs. Gandhi Farther Left

By SYDNEY H. SCHANBERG
Special to The New York Times

NEW DELHI, Feb. 10 — The Indian Supreme Court struck down Prime Minister Indira Gandhi's Bank Nationalization Act today, ruling that the take-over of the 14 biggest private banks last July was "hostile discrimination" since other Indian banks and foreign banks were excluded.

The ruling, by a vote of 10 to 1, is thought likely to push Mrs. Gandhi, for reasons of political prestige, to go farther to the left and introduce legislation nationalizing all banks.

Turning back would be difficult for the 52-year-old Prime Minister, who had staked her political reputation and her new socialist course on the bank move. It won strong backing among leftists in and out of the governing Congress party.

Actually the nationalization, implemented first by ordinance and then by parliamentary statute, never really went into effect since representatives of the private banks immediately challenged the move in the courts. For the last seven months the Government has been able to do little but prepare the machinery for the day when it hoped nationalization would be upheld judicially.

The Supreme Court decision was not only of major political and economic significance but also made legal history. It upset a long-standing precedent under which the social objective of a Government measure was held to have priority over individual rights or property rights.

The lone dissenting justice, A. N. Ray, contended that Parliament was "the best judge of what should subserve public interest" and held that it was logical and reasonable to select the biggest banks for nationalization because of their resources. He also said that the Constitution's requirements had been met in awarding compensation.

In part the bank take-over precipitated Mrs. Gandhi's split with the conservative old guard of the governing Congress party and left her dependent for her majority in Parliament on Communists, other leftists and independents.

She has made it clear that she would prefer not to tamper with the foreign banks, which could deter or scare off the foreign investment India badly

Continued on Page 13, Column 1

NEWS INDEX

Colorado Atom Plant Is Called Radiation Hazard

By ANTHONY RIPLEY
Special to The New York Times

WASHINGTON, Feb. 10—A group of Colorado scientists contends, on the basis of its investigations in the Denver area, that one of the nation's key atomic bomb manufacturing plants has been releasing dangerously radioactive plutonium into the air, water and soil.

Officials of the Atomic Energy Commission acknowledged that over the years small amounts of plutonium had been released by its Rocky Flats plant, 16 miles northwest of downtown Denver, but emphasized that the amount was too "minuscule" to pose a public health hazard.

A different conclusion was reached by the private scientific group in Colorado, which found that enough plutonium had been released to pose "a serious threat to the health and safety of the people of Denver."

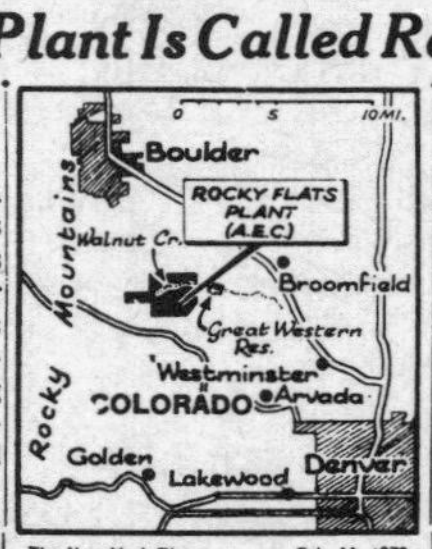
0 5 10 MI.
Boulder
ROCKY FLATS PLANT (A.E.C.)
Walnut Cr.
Broomfield
Great Western Res.
Rocky Mountains
Westminster
COLORADO
Arvada
Golden
Lakewood
Denver

The New York Times Feb. 11, 1970

The group recommended that the plant be phased out of production and rebuilt elsewhere with much more stringent safety precautions.

The plant, operated for the Atomic Energy Commission by the Dow Chemical Company, makes plutonium triggers for atomic devices. Last May 11 it was struck by a $45-million fire when plutonium, which ignites spontaneously, caught fire in a work room. It was one of the largest of a long series of fires over the 18 years that the plant has been in operation.

The investigation of that fire led the Atomic Energy Commission to conclude that there was no danger involved and that the radiation was entirely contained within the plant itself and the immediate vicinity.

But the scientists, a group of five working independently of the commission, reported finding plutonium deposits not only from the fire but also from years of leakage from the plant.

Their findings were contained in a report sent Jan. 13 to Dr. Glenn T. Seaborg, chairman of the commission, by Dr.

Continued on Page 33, Column 5

United Press International

Rescuers search the debris for survivors of an avalanche which engulfed a youth hostel in Val D'Isere, France.

Continued From Page 1, Col. 4

miles from here, in a blustery mountain corridor at an altitude of about 5,000 feet between Chambéry and Turin, Italy.

President Pompidou, declaring the avalanche a national tragedy, sent Interior Minister Raymond Marcellin and Joseph Comiti, Secretary of State for Youth Sports, to oversee the rescue efforts.

But the weather was so bad at Val d'Isère that neither man was able to get to the village tonight. They remained here at Bourg-St.-Maurice, where those injured by the avalanche were being brought all day today by ambulance down a treacherous mountain road.

By this evening only 23 of the dead had been identified. Rescue workers said that the reported number of dead was not definite.

Thirty-two injured youths were brought down from the mountain to a hospital at Bourg-St.-Maurice. Five others, with lesser injuries, were treated by local doctors.

Mr. Marcellin told reporters that the identified dead were mostly French. Some Belgian youths were also among the dead, he said.

One survivor, Mike Benoit, 21-year-old, from Brussels, told reporters from his hospital bed that he had been headed up the stairs toward his bedroom from the dining room when the avalanche struck.

He said that the snow crashed through the staircase window, and carried him down a corridor and out through another window. Luckier than most, he suffered a badly cut arm. Vivianne Euzanat, also 21, from Paris, was dragged unconscious from an air hole in the snow, near the staircase in the dining room. Many of the youths found safety under the staircase. One survivor had been buried up to his neck in snow.

Tonight Bourg-St.-Maurice was a scene of tearful encounters of parents with rescue workers and those compiling lists of casualties.

Communications with Val d'Isère were extremely difficult and many parents could not find out whether their children were among the dead, injured or unhurt.

A father, wandering the corridors of the hospital, told of his frustration in trying to learn of his son, who was staying in the chalet. "They really don't know anything," he said.

Freakishly warm weather and high winds were held responsible for the avalanche. Heavy snows have fallen in the region in recent days. The high winds and above-freezing temperatures loosened the snow.

The mayor of Val d'Isère, Noel Machet, reported tonight by telephone to interior Minister Marcellin that winds were higher than 100 miles an hour.

Mr. Machet said there were at least eight points on the road between Bourg-St. Maurice and Val d'Isère where avalanches could strike.

All road and air links with Val d'Isère were severed tonight.

Others Urged to Move

VAL D'ISERE, France, Feb. 10 (AP)—The blizzard continued tonight, and the police advised occupants of chalets and hotels outside the center of town to stay in emergency dormitories set up in a theater and public buildings, or to sleep in the highest floors of their houses.

Many of the guests at the chalet were French postal and railway workers. There were about 20 Belgians and six West Germans staying at the camp's

The New York Times   Feb. 11, 1970

hostel, according to reports.

Some bodies, including those of ski-trail workers going to their jobs, were hurled high in the air. The slide's 100 yard-front caught autos and carried them 100 yards.

"There was a gay, happy atmosphere at the dining tables," said Jean Charles Loos, 25, who suffered head and hip injuries.

"We were talking about where we would go skiing.

"Suddenly, there was this rumbling sound. As the noise became deafening, I realized it was an avalanche. I just had time to dive against the wall for protection. Then a great wall of snow burst through the door and hit me. I was submerged and I remember no more until I woke up in a neighboring house."

Chantal Demur, 22, said she had been buried for about two hours in a pocket of air under the snow before she was dug out.

"I tried to get people out," said Jacques Sifferlen, a student trapped in the slide, "but a lot of them were stuck like in concrete. You couldn't pull them out and had to cut people free with steel blades."

Val d'Isère is the home of French ski champions Jean Claude Killy and Marielle and Christine Goitschel.

It was the greatest loss of life in an avalanche in Europe since 1900, according to the Swiss Avalanche Research Center near Davos. Snowslides in Austria in January, 1954, killed more than 100 persons, but the deaths were in several communities.

Responsibility for measures against avalanches and for evacuation when one threatens normally lies with local authorities in France, a procedure called haphazard and amateurish in a statement by Melchior Schild of the Swiss service.

"All the News That's Fit to Print"

The New York Times

LATE CITY EDITION

Weather: Partly sunny, humid today. Chance of rain tonight, tomorrow. Temp. range: today 85-65; Monday 87-65. Temp.-Hum. Index yesterday 78. Full U.S. report on Page 78.

VOL. CXIX.. No. 41,037
© 1970 The New York Times Company.
NEW YORK, TUESDAY, JUNE 2, 1970

15 CENTS

HOUSE COMMITTEE CUTS $555-MILLION FROM FOREIGN AID

Expected Approval Would Make Appropriation Bill Lowest in Postwar Era

BUDGETARY PINCH CITED

Reduced Total Is $1.6-Billion — Economic Assistance Is Trimmed Hardest

By JOHN W. FINNEY

Special to The New York Times

WASHINGTON, June 1—The House Appropriations Committee, citing domestic budgetary problems, voted today for a $555-million cut in the Administration's foreign aid program.

The committee approved a bill providing $1,644,950,000 for foreign aid in the fiscal year that begins July 1. If the committee's recommendation is upheld—and there is every indication that it will be—the foreign aid program will be reduced to the lowest level in the postwar period.

The bill is scheduled to be called up on the House floor later this week, with the expectation that the House will accept the bill presented by its influential Appropriations Committee.

Senate in Similar Mood

In contrast with the past, the Administration cannot safely look to the Senate to restore cuts. In the Senate, the mood also has shifted against the foreign aid program to the point that Senator Mike Mansfield, the Majority Leader, has declared he will vote against any foreign aid appropriations on the ground that they lead only to foreign military involvements.

Foreign aid appropriations, which reached their high point of $6-billion to $7-billion in the early years of the Eisenhower Administration, have gradually been declining as first the executive branch and then Congress reduced the program.

The Administration this year submitted the smallest request since the program began. It asked for $2.2-billion, which was $509-million below last year's request and $388-million more than Congress appropriated last year.

Subcommittee Acted

The House foreign aid appropriations subcommittee, headed by Representative Otto E. Passman, Democrat of Louisiana, made a 25 per cent cut, which was endorsed today by the full committee.

The committee pointed to the financial situation confronting the nation. "The committee feels that Federal expenditures must be curtailed wherever reasonably possible, in order to combat the destructive effect of inflation," an accompanying report said.

The reductions were greater in the area of economic assistance for 77 countries. The bill would provide $1,276,200,000 for economic assistance, $537-million less than requested by the Administration.

Left untouched was the $350-

Continued on Page 9, Column 1

Mrs. Smith Warns of Repression

She Assails Militant Students and Their Critics in Capital

Special to The New York Times

WASHINGTON, June 1 — Senator Margaret Chase Smith spoke today of a "national sickness" pervading the land, and she denounced protesting student militants. She also attacked their critics in the Administration.

It was the 20th anniversary of a speech in which the Maine Republican, speaking from the same Senate desk, attacked the late Senator Joseph R. McCarthy of Wisconsin for irresponsible political tactics, and she recalled some of that speech today.

"I spoke as I did 20 years ago because of what I considered to be the great threat from the radical right—the threat of a government of repression," Senator Smith declared.

"I speak today," she said, "because of what I consider to be the great threat from the radical left that advocates and practices violence and defiance of the law—again, the threat of the ultimate result of a reaction of repression."

Recalling her floor speech of June 1, 1950, Senator Smith

Associated Press

Margaret Chase Smith talks to newsmen after speech

said: "We had a national sickness then from which we recovered. We have a national sickness now from which I pray we will recover."

While she was sharply critical of student demonstrators who commit crimes, the 72-year-old Senator indicated her belief that overreaction by Administration officials — she declined to name names—con

Continued on Page 16, Column 3

THAILAND TO SEND VOLUNTEER FORCE TO AID CAMBODIA

Premier Says That Troops Will Free Pnompenh Units for Combat Service

By Reuters

BANGKOK, Thailand, June 1—Premier Thanom Kittikachorn said today that Thailand would send volunteer soldiers to defend Pnompenh from attack and to enable Cambodian troops to go into action against Communist forces.

The Premier's announcement follows the resumption of diplomatic relations between Cambodia and Thailand on May 13 and a Cambodian request for military aid.

Speaking to newsmen, Premier Thanom said the Thai volunteers would be trained in battalion-size groups over a period of eight weeks. Unlike the 12,000 Thai troops serving in South Vietnam, who are financed by Bangkok, the volunteers are to be equipped, armed and paid by the Cambodian Government.

[The Cambodian Government put martial-law regulations into effect Monday and staged a one-hour general alert drill in Pnompenh, the capital.]

Reservists to Be Chosen

Premier Thanom did not say how many men, to be chosen from among army reservists and Thai citizens of Cambodian origin, would be sent to Cambodia.

Thailand has already announced that she would send 20 gunboats to take part in anti-Communist patrols along the Mekong River, would provide uniforms and other equipment for 50,000 Cambodians and would conduct joint air reconnaissance along the border with Cambodia.

These moves were announced Thursday by the Interior Minister and army chief, Gen. Praphas Charusathien, when he returned to Bangkok at the head of a Thai delegation that had visited Pnompenh.

Gunboats to Go Soon

Informed sources said today that the gunboats, manned by Thai sailors, would move to Cambodia early this month. Air reconnaissance along the land and coastal borders is expected to start in a few days.

Mr. Thanom said that Thailand also had agreed to train noncommissioned officers for the Cambodian armed forces.

The Premier conceded that there was some opposition to sending troops into Cambodia, but said that the majority of Thais favored the move.

Cambodian leaders were reported last week to have asked

Continued on Page 3, Column 4

PERU ESTIMATES 30,000 DIED IN QUAKE THAT WIPED OUT SCORES OF TOWNS IN NORTH

Associated Press

Destruction from the earthquake on a street in Huarmey, a Peruvian city in the Andes

AID IS REQUESTED

Pilots Surveying Area Report Landslides and Burst Dams

By H. J. MAIDENBERG

Special to The New York Times

LIMA, Peru, June 1 — The Peruvian Government believes that more than 30,000 people were killed in the earthquake that devastated large areas of northern Peru yesterday.

The figure, which the military Government stressed was based on aerial surveys, was given to foreign embassies late this afternoon as sketchy reports from the affected regions filtered through broken communications lines to Lima.

Although the Government's estimate of the number of deaths was higher than earlier, nonofficial estimates, members of the foreign diplomatic community indicated that they were inclined to place credence in the Government figure.

Peruvian Air Force pilots surveying the valleys flooded by burst dams and buried under landslides radioed headquarters here that scores of communities "are no longer on the map." Whole valleys have become raging rivers and roads have been hidden by tons of rocks, they added.

In response to foreign ambassadors who asked for estimates of damage and offered relief services, the Peruvian President, Gen. Juan Velasco Alvarado, said: "We believe that at least 30,000 are gone, just based on estimates of the population in the areas surveyed by air today. We need help."

Amateur and mining company radio operators in the Andean areas today reported hundreds of deaths and devastating de-

Continued on Page 8, Column 4

Justices Rule U.S. Courts Can Enforce Strike Bans

Special to The New York Times

WASHINGTON, June 1—The Supreme Court ruled 5 to 2 today that Federal judges may bar workers from striking in violation of no-strike clauses of collective bargaining contracts.

Reversing a contrary ruling issued in 1962, the Court held that the Norris-LaGuardia Act of 1932 does not prohibit injunctions against strikes when unions have agreed to settle their grievances by arbitration, instead. The act forbade Federal judges to issue injunctions "in any case growing out of any labor disputes."

The Court ruled that subsequent acts of Congress had declared a strong policy in favor of "the peaceful resolution of labor disputes" through arbitration. It concluded that this policy would be enhanced if Federal judges were permitted to order workers to live up to no-strike agreements, which are commonplace in collective bargaining contracts.

The result is a substantial modification of the longstanding hands-off policy declared by the Norris-LaGuardia Act, which was enacted following complaints by labor union interests that Federal judges had been too quick to enjoin strikes as "illegal."

Under the ruling handed down today, Federal judges can order unions to submit their disputes to arbitration and to refrain from striking, if their contracts include the typical clauses that require disputes to be settled in this way.

Today's decision was sharply criticized by Justice Hugo L. Black, who wrote the Court's opinion in 1962. He said that

Continued on Page 28, Column 8

COURT POSTPONES DEATH ROW RULING

Freeze on Executions in U.S. Is Continued—Two Cases on the Issue Accepted

By FRED P. GRAHAM

Special to The New York Times

WASHINGTON, June 1—The Supreme Court postponed today an important decision on capital punishment until the Court term that begins in October, leaving intact a judicial freeze that has stopped all executions in the United States for the last three years.

Today's action sent back to the trial court the case of William L. Maxwell, a Hot Springs, Ark., Negro. He had taken to the Supreme Court a broad challenge to the procedures followed when he was sentenced to death in 1962 for raping a white woman.

Maxwell's appeal, which was supported by the N.A.A.C.P. Legal Defense and Educational Fund, Inc., had widely been expected to produce a landmark capital punishment ruling.

However, the Court disposed of the appeal today on narrow grounds, apparently avoiding the important capital punishment issues for two reasons. The Justices, for one thing, are narrowly divided. In addition,

Continued on Page 29, Column 1

8 More Newsmen Vanish in Cambodia; Total Missing at 24

By SYDNEY H. SCHANBERG

Special to The New York Times

PNOMPENH, Cambodia, June 1—Eight more newsmen were reported missing in Cambodia today and were believed captured by North Vietnamese and Vietcong troops.

The eight were members of television teams from the National Broadcasting Company and the Columbia Broadcasting System. There were two correspondents among them — Welles Hangen of N.B.C. and George Syvertsen of C.B.S.

Their disappearance brings to 24 the number of non-Cambodian newsmen missing in the recent fighting in Cambodia.

The television newsmen's three vehicles, including a jeep, burned, were found today 32 miles south of Pnompenh on Route 3, a few miles from the town of Angtassom.

Besides Mr. Hangen and Mr. Syvertsen, the newsmen reported missing today were Yoshihko Waku, Japanese, a soundman; Roger Colne, French, a cameraman, both from N.B.C.; and from C.B.S.: Jerry Miller, a producer; Ramnik Lekhi, Indian, a cameraman; Kojiro Sakai, Japanese, a soundman; and Tomaharu Ishii, Japanese, a cameraman. Mr. Syvertsen and Mr. Miller were traveling in the jeep.

In addition to the eight, three

Continued on Page 5, Column 4

SOVIET PUTS 2 MEN IN ORBIT AT NIGHT

Soyuz-9 Flight Is Termed 'Solitary,' Indicating No Link-Up With Others

By BERNARD GWERTZMAN

Special to The New York Times

MOSCOW, Tuesday, June 2—The Soviet Union launched a two-man spacecraft into earth orbit last night with one of the pioneers of the space age in command of the Soyuz-9 vehicle.

The official announcement by the press agency Tass, which was released about a half hour after blast-off, said that Soyuz-9, piloted by Col. Andrian G. Nikolayev, would carry out an extensive program of scientific and technical research and experiments "in the conditions of a solitary orbital flight."

The reference to a solitary flight seemed to rule out other crafts' joining Soyuz-9. Recent flights in the Soyuz series have been marked by "group missions," which have been described as preliminary to eventual creation of a permanent manned orbital space station around the earth.

As usual with Soviet space shots, this one was kept secret until the announcement was made at 10:30 P.M. Moscow time (4:30 P.M., Eastern Daylight Time), when a special program interrupted regular Soviet radio and television transmissions.

A taped fragment of the launching, which was said by Tass to have taken place at 10 P.M. (1 A.M. Tuesday at the launching site), was shown on the screen. It was an eerie sight because of the floodlights that illuminated the launching pad, which was presumed to be situ-

Continued on Page 26, Column 3

Jersey High Court Backs Police Files on Activists

By RONALD SULLIVAN

Special to The New York Times

TRENTON, June 1—The New Jersey Supreme Court today upheld the compiling by the police of secret intelligence dossiers on civil rights activists and other protesters that had been ordered destroyed last year by a lower court in Hudson County.

In a unanimous decision here by the court, the state's highest, Chief Justice Joseph Weintraub maintained that state and local law enforcement agencies had the right to collect and maintain intelligence files on persons suspected of taking part in civil demonstrations despite charges that such information violated guarantees of freedom of speech and assembly under the First Amendment.

"Lawlessness has a tyranny of its own," the state court ruled, "and it would be folly to deprive the government of its power to deal with that tyranny merely because of a figment of a fear that government itself may run amok."

The files, which remained intact under an injunction that superseded the order to destroy them, were challenged by the Jersey City branch of the National Association for the Advancement of Colored People and members of the Students for a Democratic Society.

The case was handled by the

Continued on Page 26, Column 2

Suspect in 20 Bank Robberies Seized

By ROBERT D. McFADDEN

An alleged bank robber, dubbed Dashing Dan by the Federal Bureau of Investigation for his mannerly method of dealing with tellers, was arrested outside his Queens home yesterday, less than an hour after he reportedly held up another bank—his 20th job in three months.

F.B.I. agents and Queens detectives were waiting for the suspect, 44-year-old Raphael Pavia, when he stepped out of a taxi at 2:05 P.M. near his apartment building in the Rochdale Village Houses, at 163-35 130th Avenue, Jamaica.

The police said they found $1,910 in the suspect's possession—the exact amount taken in a holdup at the Bankers Trust Company branch at 345 Park Avenue at 1:20 P.M. Mr. Pavia was unarmed and offered no resistance, the police said.

The authorities had known for some time what the suspect looked like. Pictures taken of the robber by hidden cameras during nearly all of the 20 bank holdups in the metropolitan area had made him one of the most photographed suspects in history.

Pictures showing Dashing Dan from a variety of angles and articles describing his neatly tailored appearance and orderly, polite approach to bank robbery had appeared in

Man believed to be Raphael Pavia leaving Bankers Trust Company branch at 345 Park Avenue yesterday with handful of money. Photograph was taken by a hidden camera.

newspapers here in recent days.

The F.B.I., in announcing the arrest, said it had been brought about "as a direct result" of Federal and city police cooperation and "the assistance of news articles, which have appeared recently publicizing his activities."

Mr. Pavia, described as an immigrant from Tunisia who has been working here as a

Continued on Page 22, Column 1

Teamsters Break Custom and Back Rockefeller

By EMANUEL PERLMUTTER

Governor Rockefeller yesterday picked up the support of a big segment of organized labor when New York Teamsters Joint Council 16 endorsed him for re-election.

Nicholas Kisburg, legislative representative of the 169,000-member council, said it was the first time that New York City teamsters had endorsed a Republican candidate for Governor. In 1966 they backed Frank D. O'Connor, the Democratic nominee, and in previous years they had either supported the Democrat or remained neutral.

In announcing the teamster endorsement, Mr. Kisburg asserted that Governor Rockefeller's "unprecedented and magnificent performance in the area of labor legislation warrants and compels this departure from traditions."

He said also that Mr. Rockefeller's re-election "is a must if we are to have justice and order." And he accused Arthur J. Goldberg and Howard J. Samuels, who are contending for the Democratic nomination, of being "divisive and advocates of racial and generational conflict."

The endorsement gave Mr. Rockefeller the support of his second big labor bloc. He has already won the backing of the 200,000-member Greater New York Building and Construction Trades Council.

In addition, the Governor's candidacy has been endorsed by the State Council of the United Brotherhood of Carpenters and Joiners; the State Council of the International Brotherhood of Operating Engineers, and New York City Musicians Local Union 802. These three and the construction workers also backed him four years ago.

The Governor gave a reception yesterday for labor leaders at the Americana. He stood in a reception line and greeted the beaming representatives of blue-collar, public-employe and white-collar workers.

Edward V. Regan, the Republican candidate for Controller, and Attorney General Louis J. Lefkowitz and United States Senator Charles E. Goodell, the Governor's running mates for re-election, were at his side.

A small orchestra played soft music as the guests consumed

Continued on Page 30, Column 1

NEWS INDEX

Protests by Scientists in Soviet On Biologist's Arrest Reported

By JAMES F. CLARITY

Special to The New York Times

MOSCOW, June 1—Reliable sources said today that the recent arrest of Zhores A. Medvedev, a biologist, had brought protests by four of the Soviet Union's most prominent scientists, including nuclear physicists.

The sources said the protest represented rising discontent with increasing repression of liberal intellectuals in various fields.

Mr. Medvedev, who has written a book published in the West attacking genetic theories imposed under Stalin, was detained Friday in Obninsk, an atomic research center 60 miles southwest of Moscow. He was reported taken by the police and a psychiatrist to a mental institution at nearby Kaluga.

The sources said that a group of psychiatrists from Moscow examined Mr. Medvedev yesterday in Kaluga and declared him normal, but said he would remain in the hospital for a week for observation.

According to the sources, the examination was a result of personal telegrams sent to the Kaluga authorities by the four scientists. They were identified as Andrei D. Sakharov and Pyotr L. Kapitsa, nuclear physicists; Vladimir A. Engelhardt, a biochemist, and Boris L. Astaurov, a geneticist. All four are members of the prestigious Academy of Sciences.

A prominent literary figure, Aleksandr T. Tvardovsky, former editor of the monthly Novy

Continued on Page 7, Column 1

Smooth things over with a Norelco Speedshaver. Korvette's. Advt.

Youngsters in the port city of Chimbote look over the ruins of homes left by the massive earthquake which struck Peru.

Wide World Photos

Peru Estimates 30,000 Died in the Quake

Continued From Page 1, Col. 8

struction. Among the hardest hit centers was Chimbote, a fishing and mining community where 200 were known dead and almost three-fourths of the flimsy houses destroyed. The epicenter of the earthquake was placed at 12 miles off Chimbote in the Pacific Ocean.

Peruvian military aircraft reported that the neighboring resort area of Huarás had been leveled. Mining company stations said that at least 160 people were dead.

5 Dead in Lima

Here, in the capital, there were five known dead, four from heart attacks, and little damage. Some sections of the city were without lights as utility lines snapped. Communications by telephone and cable were broken. Roads north of Lima were blocked by landslides that affected many spots along the narrow coastal region to the Ecuadorian border.

The Government announced that the earthquake registered 7.75 on the Richter scale, the worst recorded here since May 24, 1940, when 200 were killed. Foreign Ministry spokesmen

said that they were appealing to the United Nations and international relief organizations for medical and other supplies. [In Washington, the State Deer death tolls were reported in Trujillo and the valley of Callejon de Huaylas.

When the earthquake struck, many Peruvians were indoors listening to the World Soccer Cup match between Mexico

partment said the United States was ready to give aid if asked, The Associated Press reported.]

Chile sent several planeloads of medicine and food and reported that medical teams were being assembled to fly here.

Other Andean cities severely affected were Huarmey, where 30 were known dead, and Caraz, where a dam broke and washed out several hundred homes. Efforts to reach the mountain community were hampered by landslides. Small-and the Soviet Union in Mexico City. Peru is in the finals and interest in the games is intense here. The earthquake came 40 minutes before the Sunday matinees at movie houses, many of which were reported destroyed.

According to the Peruvian Geophysical Institute, Peru is subject to as many as 1,500 earth tremors each year. In fact, Lima experienced four lessor tremors between 3:24 P.M. yesterday, when the big quake struck, and midnight.

The quakes, to which the entire west coast of South America is subject, are attributed to the geological immaturity of the Andes, a relatively young mountain chain. The growing pains of the Andes are emphasized by the numerous active volcanoes that push upward in the region.

Deep faults in the seabed off the coast receive the displaced earth pushed down by the rising mountains. The side to side movements of the earth—the quakes—are the result.

Despite the frequency of earth movements here, few are important enough to warrant

fright among Peru's population of 12.7 million. The last major quake occurred on Oct. 16, 1966, when 110 died.

Thant Offers U.N. Aid

UNITED NATIONS, New York, June 1 (Reuters) — Secretary-General Thant today sent a message of condolence to the Government of Peru over yesterday's severe earthquake and he offered all possible United Nations assistance to alleviate suffering caused by the disaster.

"I am requesting the resident representatives of the United Nations Development Program in your country to get in touch with the officials in your excellency's Government to determine the best manner in which we could offer necessary assistance," he said.

4 From U.S. Reported Killed

LIMA, June 1 (AP) — Two Roman Catholic nuns from the United States were killed in Chimbote yesterday when an earthquake struck Peru, and two Peace Corps volunteers were reported missing and "presumed dead" in Huaras.

The nuns were identified as Sister Gabriel Joseph Gussin, 52 years old of St. Louis, and a Sister Edith Mary, whose last name was unavailable and who was believed to be from Pittsburgh.

The Peace Corps workers were identified as Miss Marie Clutterbuck 20, of Cambellesport, Wis., and Miss Gail Gross 23, of Freemansburg, Pa. The Peace Corps director, Ed Barker, said the girls were seen in a building that was swept away, and "are presumed dead."

Cities Damaged From Coast to Amazon

By LAWRENCE VAN GELDER

From Peru's ocean port of Chimbote, through the Callejon de Huaylas winding between two Andean ranges, to the jungle-girded city of Iquitos and in countless other communities, Sunday's earthquake traced a path of ruin and death.

Chimbote embodied many of Peru's hopes for the future. The city, a rare, naturally protected port, has served as the foundation for heavy investment designed to foster a steel industry begun in 1958.

In a relatively short time—amid the unfolding of plans to bring electrical energy, iron ore and coal into Chimbote—the city's population swelled 50-fold to about 200,000. Chimbote also exports large quantities of fish meal to Europe and the United States.

Valley Hit Hard

The Callejon de Huaylas offers a striking contrast to Chimbote. Filled with picturesque villages and small towns with narrow, cobblestoned streets, the Callejon de Huaylas is a valley that runs for 80 miles between the Andean coastal range known as the Cordillera Negra and the main Andean range, known in the area as the Cordillera Blanca.

The heavily populated valley was struck hard by the earthquake. Peruvian military aircraft reported the leveling of of Harás, the chief town in the area, which resembles Switzerland.

Huarás, about 10,000 feet high and about 200 miles north of Lima, has a population of slightly more than 50,000. Silver, coal and cinnabar are mined in the area, and the local archeological museum contains

monoliths carved by valley stonecutters in the era before Christ.

On a road outside Huarás, the capital of the department of Ancash, large numbers of boulders can be seen scattered to either side, remnants of a 1941 avalanche that caused 6,000 deaths.

While the earthquake struck such cities on or near the coast as Nazca, Lima, Trujillo, Chimbote and Chiclayo, it also struck deep inland at the remote eastern jungle city of Iquitos, capital of the Loreto Department. Iquitos, with a population of about 100,000, is in the heart of an area that produces gold, oil, iron, rubber, quinine and palm oil.

More than 50 years ago, Iquitos was a boom town, and the rubber barons who flocked to the jungle built fine homes adorned with tiles from Portugal and Italy and ironwork from England.

Today vultures are seen in the streets, and the waterfront slum teems with huts built on rafts. The town market has been slipping down a river embankment for years. Statues of forgotten men stand in town squares.

While students at the University of Loreto study engineering and agriculture, visitors may travel a short distance by river from Iquitos to watch the Indians demonstrating their skill with blowpipes and poisoned arrows.

Iquitos, on the west bank of the Amazon, lies 2,300 miles from the river's mouth and is known as the world's furthest inland port.

Trujillo, also hit by the earthquake, is 343 miles north of Lima on the Pacific coast.

"All the News That's Fit to Print"

The New York Times

LATE CITY EDITION

Weather: Cloudy with occasional rain or drizzle through tomorrow. Temp. range: today 59-50; Sunday 65-49. Full U.S. report on Page 93.

VOL. CXX..No. 41,190 © 1970 The New York Times Company. NEW YORK, MONDAY, NOVEMBER 2, 1970 15 CENTS

142 Are Killed by Fire in Locked Dance Hall in France

After the fire, residents of Saint-Laurent-du-Pont gather outside the smoldering building where victims were trapped

United Press International

Relatives check descriptions of bodies and personal effects of young people on coffins that fill town gymnasium.

$100-MILLION RISE IN REQUIRED COSTS IS FACED BY CITY

Total Deficit for Year Could Go as High as $300-Million, Budget Director Warns

By PETER KIHSS

The city's Budget Director said yesterday that mandatory increases in costs alone could result in an increase of $100-million in spending out of city tax funds above the original estimates for the current budget.

When that is added to shortfalls in predicted revenue, a deficit of $200-million to $300-million could result, the Budget Director, Edward K. Hamilton, said.

Mr. Hamilton added that the city faced this large deficit even before counting the costs of its current negotiations with unions. He said that pending demands by policemen and firemen could more than double their departments' present budgets to $1-billion and $750-million respectively.

The prospective deficit, Mr. Hamilton said, will have to be met by cutting planned expenditures, such as through the job freeze ordered by Mayor Lindsay, and by seeking more state and Federal aid. Mr. Hamilton estimated that the average city employe costs $15,000 to $20,000 a year in wages and benefits.

Opposes Use of Reserves

Any use of the city's rainy-day reserve—now about $50-million, after a $35-million drawing to balance the 1969-70 budget—or short-term borrowing would only push taxpayers' problems into the next budget year, he added.

Mr. Hamilton discussed an increasingly gloomy picture of the city's $7.7-billion operating budget that went into effect last July 1 during an interview and on a WNBC-TV "Man in Office" broadcast.

A prospective decline of $100-million to $150-million in estimated yields from stock transfer, personal income and business taxes had already been reported to Mayor Lindsay in September. The decline was ascribed to the national economic slowdown.

Mr. Hamilton said the spending side of the budget had since begun reflecting similar trouble. He cited the major prospective added costs facing taxpayers as including:

¶$20-million more for welfare costs, as the city's share of a $60-million increase if the rise in relief rolls continues to

Continued on Page 34, Column 4

G.O.P. Expected to Fail In Bid for Senate Control

Party Regarded as Likely to Gain One to Three Seats, With Seven Needed to Reverse Democratic Majority

By R. W. APPLE Jr.

Special to The New York Times

WASHINGTON, Nov. 1—President Nixon's primary political goal of 1970, Republican control of the Senate, appears to lie beyond his reach.

Despite Mr. Nixon's and Vice President Agnew's unprecedented midterm campaigning, which has carried them into 35 states; despite the fact that Republican committees have outspent the Democrats by 5 to 1; despite Republican efforts to capitalize on the national perturbation over crime and violence—despite all this, it seems almost certain that the Democrats will have a majority in the Senate next year.

Late polls and reports indicate a probable Republican gain of one to three seats in the voting on Tuesday, with a gain of seven needed for control.

A Democratic gain of one seat is an outside possibility. It is also possible that there will be no change in the present 57-43 alignment.

The Democrats have a good chance of gaining at least five and possibly as many as eight governorships, the polls and reports show, including several in major industrial states. Democrats now control 18 of the 50 Governors' mansions.

The Democrats appear likely to gain no more than a half-dozen seats in the House, if that.

In an ordinary year, the Democrats' projected showing in the balloting would be considered poor. In off-year elections from 1950 to 1966, the party holding the Presidency lost an average of 29 seats in the House and three in the Senate.

Republican leaders, including Mr. Agnew, have already begun to interpret this year's campaign along classic lines.

But 1970 has been no ordinary year. For one thing, Mr. Nixon was the first newly elected President in over a century with both houses of Congress arrayed against him, which makes historical precedent a questionable political test.

Moreover, he and his party

Continued on Page 57, Column 6

GOVERNOR, RIVALS ARGUE ON CHANGE IN ABORTION LAW

Sharp Dispute on the Need for Revision Marks Last Confrontation of Race

TWO DEBATES ARE HELD

Rise in Commuter Tax and the Nixon-Agnew Tactics Also Are at Issue

By FRANK LYNN

Governor Rockefeller and Arthur J. Goldberg, debating for the last times in the gubernatorial campaign, sharply disagreed yesterday on the need for changes in the state's abortion law, a possible commuter tax increase and the campaign tactics of President Nixon and Vice President Agnew.

However, both agreed on the effect of the election of the other. "A disaster," said Mr. Rockefeller of a Goldberg election. "A major disaster," said Mr. Goldberg of a Rockefeller re-election for a fourth term.

While many voters spent a sunny and mild Sunday outdoors or watching televised professional football, the two gubernatorial candidates and their Conservative opponent, Paul L. Adams, spent a good part of the afternoon in television studios for their hour-long debates on WNBC-TV and WCBS-TV.

On the abortion issue Mr. Goldberg warned against changing the law while Mr. Rockefeller said some amendments would be needed and Dr. Adams called for repeal of the liberalized law.

Six Million to Vote

The eight-month-long campaign will end tomorrow when more than six million New Yorkers are expected to vote between 6 A.M. and 9 P.M. to choose a Governor, Lieutenant Governor, Attorney General, State Controller, Representatives, State Senators, Assemblymen and local officials and judges.

Despite occasional flashes of anger during the two debates, the gubernatorial candidates, in their last scheduled meeting of the campaign, were friendly toward each other at the end.

However, the final debate was spiced by the surprise appearance of Democratic State Chairman John J. Burns in the studio immediately after the televised encounter.

Confronting the Governor, Mr. Burns said that Mr. Rockefeller had "maligned" him by asserting that Mr. Burns was one of those who had offered the chairmanship of the Metropolitan Transportation Author-

Continued on Page 56, Column 3

Last Senate Race Debate Marked by Harsh Charges

By C. GERALD FRASER

New York's three Senatorial candidates attacked one another with such phrases as "misrepresentation and fraud," "despicable" and "if you can read English" yesterday in their fourth and final television debate of the campaign.

Senator Charles E. Goodell, the Republican-Liberal candidate, displayed a full page newspaper advertisement, in support of Richard L. Ottinger, his Democratic opponent, that he said was "a misrepresentation and a fraud."

Mr. Ottinger, a Westchester Representative, accused James L. Buckley, the Conservative candidate, of "despicable" actions in charging that Mr. Ottinger was associated with "bomb-throwing groups."

Mr. Buckley replied: "The fact is, if you read English, I made no such charges."

The three men were seen on a special hour-long "Direct Line" program on WNBC-TV, yesterday morning. Vic Roby, the program's regular moderator and Mrs. Lionel Robbins, New York State first vice president of the League of Women Voters, put a total of eight questions to the candidates that opened the way for the attacks.

As the program opened, and Mr. Ottinger got his first opportunity to speak, he accused Mr. Buckley of "going up to the Western regions of this state to associate me with every violent, terrorist group in this entire country." And this, Ottinger said, is nothing less than "despicable."

Mr. Ottinger said: "I challenge you . . . to let me appear on that half hour [television program] that you bought on tomorrow and we'll have it out with respect to these irresponsible charges that I'm associated with Panthers and Lords and all other kinds of bomb-throwing groups."

Challenged by Mr. Ottinger to explain his campaign slogan—"Isn't it about time WE had a Senator," Mr. Buckley said the "we" meant "all of us people who have been disenfranchised, whether black, white, rich or poor, Protestant or Jewish or Catholic."

Discussing his support, Mr. Buckley said: "As an indication of the breadth of my support, and the moderation of my support, I point to Mr. John Marchi [1969 Republican mayoral candidate] and Mr. [Mario] Procaccino [1969 Democratic mayoral candidate] . . . they have

Continued on Page 58, Column 7

Giants Defeat Jets, 22-10

The Giants defeated the Jets yesterday, 22-10, before a record crowd of 63,903 at Shea Stadium. (See Page 71).

U.S.-SOVIET TALKS TO RESUME TODAY

Moscow Aides, in Helsinki for Arms Parley, Stress Opposition to Polemics

By BERNARD GWERTZMAN

Special to The New York Times

HELSINKI, Finland, Nov. 1—The Soviet delegation arrived by train from Moscow today for the resumption tomorrow of negotiations with the United States on the limitation of strategic arms.

Vladimir S. Semyonov, a Deputy Foreign Minister and the leader of the Soviet delegation, said on his arrival here that his side was "awaiting with interest" its third round of talks with the Americans, whose chief delegate is Gerard C. Smith, director of the Arms Control and Disarmament Agency. The United States delegation arrived on a special Air Force flight from Washington on Friday night.

Mr. Semyonov's brief, noncommittal statement heightened curiosity among American delegates about whether the talks would continue on the rather businesslike course they have followed so far or would become a source of Soviet-American polemics.

At a reception tonight given by the Finnish Foreign Ministry's press department, Soviet sources were stressing the need for an absence of polemics. This was in accord with a

Continued on Page 22, Column 1

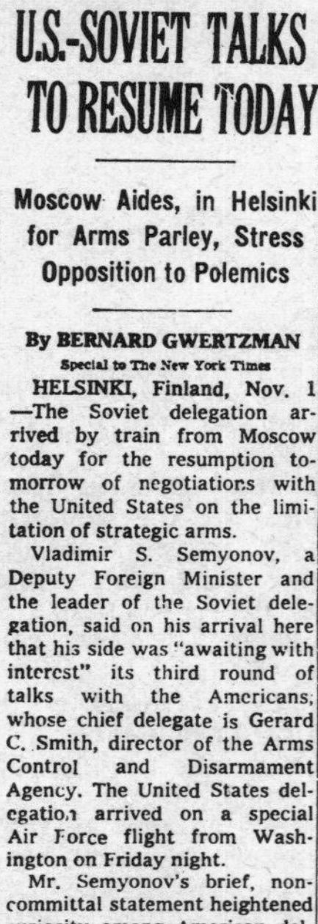

United Press International

Vladimir S. Semyonov arriving in Helsinki yesterday.

20 Survive Flames Outside a Village Near Grenoble

By The Associated Press

SAINT-LAURENT-DU-PONT, France, Nov. 1 — A fire in a dance hall in this village killed 142 persons early today, trapping them behind emergency exits that firemen and survivors said had been padlocked and then nailed shut with planks to keep out anyone without a ticket.

Investigating magistrates heard charges of negligence as well as the contention of a kitchen worker that the doors could have been opened from inside, but that the crowd had panicked.

The fire broke out at 1:45 A.M. while about 165 dancers were in the building just outside Saint-Laurent-du-Pont, a town 14 miles northwest of Grenoble in southeastern France. The victims, all 17 to 25 years old, had come to hear a new rock group.

Breaking into the Club Cinq Sept, rescue workers found bodies piled near the exits. Eight persons, three in critical condition, were hospitalized. About 10 other survivors did not require treatment.

"If the safety doors hadn't been blocked, almost everybody could have been saved," said Dominique Guette, 17 years old, who had been at the dance.

Police and fire officials were

Continued on Page 31, Column 1

'BIG MINH' IMPLIES HE'LL FIGHT THIEU

General Says People Have Lost Faith in Leaders—Urges Reconciliation

By ALVIN SHUSTER

Special to The New York Times

SAIGON, South Vietnam, Monday, Nov. 2—Maj. Gen. Duong Van Minh, one of the most popular figures in South Vietnam, broke a year-long political silence yesterday with a broad hint that he would challenge Nguyen Van Thieu for the presidency next year.

The 53-year-old general, the most serious potential rival to President Thieu, declared in a National Day statement that South Vietnam was becoming more destitute, its society more heart-rending and the life of its people more miserable. He charged that the nation's sovereignty was increasingly impaired and that the people were losing faith in their leaders.

As South Vietnamese ended their National Day celebration, terrorists fired four rounds of rockets into Saigon early this morning. Officials said that at least six civilians had been killed and 15 injured. [Page 3.]

The general, known throughout the country as Big Minh, called for "national reconcilia-

Continued on Page 8, Column 1

Key Polish Official Is Killed by Truck At Karachi Airport

Special to The New York Times

KARACHI, Pakistan, Nov. 1—A Polish Deputy Foreign Minister, Zygfryd Wolniak, and three Pakistanis were killed today at Karachi International Airport when an airline van ran into a reception line formed to welcome the Polish President, Marshal Marian Spychalski, here.

Also injured in the incident were the Polish Ambassador to Pakistan, Alojzy Bartoszek, and the Polish Consul General in Karachi, W. Duda.

There were unconfirmed reports that the driver of the truck shouted slogans when he was arrested. Some witnesses were reported to have heard the driver, identified as Mohammed Feroze, say that he had completed his mission. However, there is no confirmation of the reports.

The mishap occurred shortly after Marshal Spychalski's arrival here from Islamabad, Pakistan's new capital, 1,000 miles to the northeast, for the final stop in a five-day state visit to Pakistan.

As President Spychalski was being introduced to members of the welcoming party, consisting of leading citizens of Karachi

Continued on Page 11, Column 1

The Case History of a Housing Failure

By JOHN HERBERS

Special to The New York Times

ST. LOUIS, Oct. 29 — In the midst of an acute housing shortage, St. Louis is boarding up 26 eleven-story apartment buildings, part of a $36-million housing project built 15 years ago and not yet paid for.

The 17 remaining buildings in the Pruitt-Igoe public housing complex continue in use, at least for the time being.

But there are officials here who hope for the day when all 43 structures, which rise like great granite cubes on 57 acres of central-city land, will be torn down, the mountains of concrete, steel and brick carted away and the name of Pruitt-Igoe erased forever from the St. Louis map.

For years the housing project has been plagued with rampant crime, vandalism, physical deterioration, accidental deaths and serious injuries.

"It was like building a battleship that would not float," said Thomas P. Costello, acting director of the St. Louis Housing Authority. "The damn thing sank."

Probably no other public housing failure in the nation is as monumental as that of Pruitt-Igoe. Nevertheless, it is indicative, not only of housing problems but also of the web of urban distress that, in varying degrees, grips large cities across the country.

Here the distress is stark and visible and the cause is easily traced.

Pruitt-Igoe was built in 1955 and 1956 on a site that had been cleared of slums. It was proclaimed in architectural magazines as an innovation in high-rise living for the poor, with clean walls of brick and glass providing a sharp contrast to the decayed tenements and row houses a few blocks away.

Yet, almost from the beginning, it was a disaster—socially, architecturally and financially. Various efforts over the years to make it work have failed. It is now a scene of vast devastation. The poorest of the poor would rather live in a dilapidated hut than endure Pruitt-Igoe's concentrated misery. And a destitute housing au-

Continued on Page 36, Column 1

For Congress, Mrs. Ray Rice recommends responsible, reasonable, resourceful, remarkable Republican Ray Rice. She knows. Citizens for Rice, J. Wells, Dir., 1398 N. Blvd., Manhasset, N.Y. advt.

NEWS INDEX

The six (6) Rice girls ask you to vote for their daddy, Ray Rice, for Congress. They know. Citizens for Rice, J. Wells, Dir., 1398 N. Blvd., Manhasset, N.Y. advt.

Campaign Aides Go All Out in a Last-Minute Effort to Sway Votes

The New York Times (by William E. Sauro and Ernest Sisto)

Firemen search the burnt out dance hall "Le Cinq Sept" at Saint-Laurent-Du-Pont, France.

Wide World Photos

Fire in French Hall Kills Many Trapped Behind Locked Doors

Continued From Page 1, Col. 2

working on the theory that a prank—a cigarette tossed at a youth's coat — might have caused the blaze.

Two young men ran nearly a mile to give the alarm in town. In five minutes, 30 volunteer firemen were fighting the blaze, but it had spread quickly, fed by the dance hall's paper and plastic decorations.

The firemen thought at first that most of the dancers had escaped, so quiet was the building when they arrived. One

fireman, Henri Fattalini, said: "There wasn't a murmur or a cry. Imagine our horror when the first group succeeded in getting the door open and then felt bodies falling on them."

Another fireman, Georges Rostan, said he had to break down two locked doors.

Officials felt that the dancers had rushed toward the doors in panic. The only door that all witnesses agreed had been in working order was partly blocked by a turnstile.

The most detailed accounts of the fire came from a group of four friends who were

drinking at the club's bar when the fire broke out. Mr. Guette said: "I had this intuition when I smelled smoke. Then I saw the first flames over the bar. I screamed and then I rushed toward the door and a little wall. There was a woman who was blocking my way. I pushed her over the top of the wall, and I jumped. She's alive."

"After that we tried to help out buddies," he continued. "We heard a woman screaming behind one of the emergency exits. They had nailed planks to the doors, as if the padlocks weren't enough. Then we took a beam and were able to knock in the door and pull out a young woman. When the door gave way, there were people piled up behind, reaching out

with their arms. Five minutes later they were all dead."

Another friend, Jean-Luc Bastard, 17, continued the account:

"We did everything to save as many people as possible. We pulled on their arms and legs and we soaked our jackets in the stream near the dance hall and we smothered the flames on clothes of the people we could pull out."

"People in cars stopped on the side of the road and looked at us," he said. "Some of them were kidding around and laughing at what we were doing and refused to help. There were only three or four who helped."

The building was left a charred shell. The ceiling had burst in the heat.

One of those who escaped was a director of the dance hall. His two partners were killed.

"All the News That's Fit to Print"

The New York Times

LATE CITY EDITION

Weather: Rain today and tonight. Mostly cloudy, cooler tomorrow. Temp. range: today 51-47; Saturday 56-48. Full U.S. report on Page 91.

SECTION ONE

VOL. CXX . No. 41,203 © 1970 The New York Times Company. NEW YORK, SUNDAY, NOVEMBER 15, 1970 — 75¢ beyond 50-mile zone from New York City except Long Island. Higher in air delivery cities. — 50 CENTS

CITY AIDES TO ASK $50-MILLION RISE IN TAXICAB FARES

Cost of Average Ride Would Increase From $1.35 to $1.90 on the Meter

HOPE TO AVERT STRIKE

Surcharge of 25 Cents for Additional Passengers Would Be Imposed

By EMANUEL PERLMUTTER

City officials seeking to avert a threatened taxi driver strike were reported ready yesterday to recommend a $50-million a year fare increase that would include raising the present $1.35 average ride to $1.90 on the meter.

Also in the package would be an extra charge of 25 cents for every passenger in addition to the person who engaged the cab.

The rise in the cost of the average ride would be accomplished through new rates of 50 cents for the first fifth of a mile; 10 cents for each additional fifth, and 10 cents for each one and a half minutes of waiting time. These rates are now charged in Boston, Cleveland, Detroit and Philadelphia.

Present New York taxi rates are 45 cents for the first sixth of a mile; 10 cents for each additional third of a mile, and 10 cents for each two minutes of waiting time. The average ride is 2.4 miles.

Last Increase in 1968

A City Hall source said that Mayor Lindsay would present these suggestions to the City Council, which alone has the power to set taxi fare rates. A fare increase was enacted by the Council in 1968 after it had been proposed by the Mayor.

There were indications that any plan to tax additional passengers might run into trouble in the Council. A source close to the Council leadership said last night, "Some Council members would be likely to oppose the 25 cent head tax as inequitable."

He explained that a businessman using a taxi paid for on his company's expense account would probably not complain

Continued on Page 40, Column 1

WRECKAGE OF CHARTERED PLANE: Charred remains of Southern Airways DC-9 jet after it crashed on approach to airport at Huntington, W. Va. Seventy-five persons, including the Marshall University football team, were on board. (Associated Press)

City to Press State For Wide Changes In Health-Care Law

By JOHN SIBLEY

The Lindsay administration will press for major changes in health care, both public and private, in the next session of the Legislature.

A package of bills that is now being drafted by lawyers for the city's Health Services Administration includes the following proposals:

¶Institution of financial incentives to hospitals to provide comprehensive care for families and to do away with the impersonal assembly-line procedures that characterize many outpatient departments.

¶Creation of a new class of health professionals — physicians' assistants — to relieve doctors of routine chores.

¶Establishment of a comprehensive program of treatment of alcoholism.

¶Elimination of conflicts between the state and city mental health programs and guaranteeing that the state would pay localities 50 per cent of the cost of public health programs.

Statewide Laws Sought

Tentative versions have been written for eight pieces of legislation, all of which would be effective statewide. Gordon Chase, the city's Health Services Administrator, has already begun a series of meetings to rally support from medical societies, government agencies, citizens groups and legislative leaders.

Explaining the proposal on family care by hospitals, Mr. Chase said that it would create a state fund for use by public and private hospitals that submit acceptable plans for ambulatory care units.

Families would be seen regularly by the same doctors—groups of specialists working as teams—and not be repeatedly greeted by different physi-

Continued on Page 54, Column 4

DEMOCRATS FIGHT MONEY PROBLEMS

Party Has $9.3-Million Debt but Election Results Are Viewed as Fund Spur

By R.W. APPLE Jr.

Special to The New York Times

WASHINGTON, Nov. 14—The Democratic party is like a halfback who played out the season with a bad knee and showed surprising zip in the big game, but must still undergo surgery in the off-season if he is to be right for next year.

For the Democrats, the problem is money, and the surgery will begin in a few weeks.

The Democratic National Committee is still $9.3-million in debt. In the last 10 months, the figure has not been reduced, partly because national fund-raisers were afraid of detracting from the campaigns of Democratic candidates for the Senate, the House of Representatives and governorships.

Keeps Party Afloat

Robert Strauss, the Texas lawyer who was elected national treasurer in March, has kept the party afloat through 1970 by developing a list of 50,000 small donors and by persuading 700 larger contributors to provide $100-a-month for nine months. These contributions have met the national committee's $135,000-a-month expenses.

Mr. Strauss hopes to raise enough money in the next eight months to slice at least $2-million to $3-million off the debt.

"It will be easier now than it was before Election Day," Mr. Strauss said in an interview Thursday. "A lot of potential contributors were waiting to see whether we came out of last Tuesday with any reasonable shot at the White

Continued on Page 39, Column 1

75 on Football Team Plane Die in West Virginia Crash

By United Press International

HUNTINGTON, W. Va., Nov. 14 — A chartered airliner, carrying the Marshall University football team and coaching staff and state civic leaders and legislators, crashed and burned in light fog and rain tonight near the Tri-State Airport in the Appalachian Mountains.

The authorities said all 75 persons aboard were killed.

The plane, a twin-jet DC-9 owned by Southern Airways in Atlanta, was in communication with the airport until just before the crash at about 7:40 P.M., after a 40-minute flight from North Carolina, where the Marshall team played an afternoon game.

Control tower officials said that "everything was perfectly normal and there was no indication of trouble."

The death toll was the highest this year in an airplane accident in the United States. All of the fatal airliner crashes this year were on charter or nonscheduled flights; none occurred in commercial scheduled flights.

It was the nation's third airliner accident—the second this year—involving a college football team. Thirty-one persons, including 14 Wichita State University players, were killed last Oct. 2 when their plane crashed in the Colorado Rockies. In 1960, a plane crash in Toledo, Ohio, killed 22 persons, including 16 members of the California State Polytechnic College team.

The DC-9, which has twin jets on either side of the tail assembly, can carry 95 passengers.

The civic leaders and legislators aboard the plane were members of a boosters' club composed of prominent citizens who helped the football team financially. A spokesman for the university said members of the club who were on the plane included six prominent physicians.

The Federal Aviation Administration said the plane carried 70 passengers, a crew of four and a baggage handler.

The pilot was making an ap-

Continued on Page 48, Column 1

Thousands of Pakistanis Are Killed by Tidal Wave

Cyclone in Bay of Bengal Hits Coastal Region—Communications Cut

Special to The New York Times

DACCA, Pakistan, Nov. 14—A cyclone-driven tidal wave that swept in from the Bay of Bengal Thursday night drowned tens of thousands of people in the offshore islands and coastal districts of East Pakistan.

The Pakistan radio originally reported from Karachi that nearly 50,000 people were believed dead in the 120-mile-an-hour cyclone and the 20-foot tidal wave. The radio said later today that 11,000 deaths had been confirmed and that the final toll might be at least twice that number.

The areas most affected were the islands of Hatia, Sandwip, Kutubdia and Dubla and the districts of Noakhali, Barisal and Chittagong.

Under Water 8 Hours

Hatia, in the Ganges Delta, reported 5,000 dead. An earlier report on the number of deaths on the island, which has a population of 120,000, was based on a message from a magistrate that said "half the islanders may have drowned." The message said that half the island's 242 square miles had been under 20 feet of water for eight hours.

On Dubla, an island in the Bay of Bengal south of the port of Mungla, nearly 15,000 Hindu pilgrims attending a religious festival were originally believed to have drowned, but official reports said there were no known casualties on the island.

Islands Out of Contact

The exact extent of the devastation was not known because communications have been disrupted and 100 small islands remained out of contact with the mainland.

The disaster was described as "the worst in this century" by a newspaper in Chittagong, the largest port and the second largest city of East Pakistan.

East Pakistan's worst cyclones and tidal waves in the recent past struck on Oct. 10 and 31, 1960, killing 10,000 persons. A cyclone in 1965 killed 12,000 people. There have been eight cyclones in the last ten years here.

A pilot who flew over the

Continued on Page 7, Column 1

The New York Times — Nov. 15, 1970

Island of Hatia was hard hit by massive tidal wave.

MILITARY APPEARS TO CONTROL SYRIA

It Takes Over From Rivals in Baath Party — Tanks Watch Guerrilla Camps

By ERIC PACE

Special to The New York Times

DAMASCUS, Syria, Nov. 14—Syrian Army tanks and armored cars were deployed around Arab commando camps near Damascus today after the military faction of the ruling Baath party apparently seized power yesterday.

Informants close to the left-wing Baath party said that the military leadership, headed by the Defense Minister, Lieut. Gen. Hafez al-Assad, had dismissed leaders of As Saiqa from their posts in the Syrian-backed guerrilla group. General Assad was said to have replaced the Saiqa leaders with regular army officers to neutralize any opposition from the commandos' ranks.

A drive through Syria and a tour of Damascus today showed the nation to be calm, although somewhat subdued. The so-called political faction of the Baath party, whose leaders have been arrested by the military, gave no sign of trying to regain power through force. There has been no known bloodshed so far.

An old conflict between the two factions of the party

Continued on Page 23, Column 1

SOVIET'S REMOVAL OF VESSEL IN CUBA IS AWAITED BY U.S.

Submarine-Support Ship Is Expected to Go as Result of an Understanding

NUCLEAR ARMS AT ISSUE

American Officials Hopeful Secret Talks Resolved Dispute Over Base

By BENJAMIN WELLES

Special to The New York Times

WASHINGTON, Nov. 14—For seven weeks, the United States has been engaged in secret diplomacy to prevent the Soviet Union from basing nuclear-missile submarines or installing nuclear weapons in the Western Hemisphere. Now American officials believe that an understanding has been reached.

The officials said they would regard the departure of a Soviet submarine tender from the Cuban port of Cienfuegos in the coming days as proof that the Russians accept the understanding. The vessel normally carries spare nuclear weapons and such facilities as high-powered cranes for handling submarine nuclear arms.

Early Departure Likely

The officials disputed a report from another highly credible source that the tender would leave within the next two or three days.

Current discussions between Washington and Moscow over this issue are in such a delicate state, the officials warned, that the national interest might be impaired by anything that Moscow might misinterpret as an ultimatum, even through press reports.

They did confirm that he United States had warned the Soviet Union that anything resembling a permanent nuclear facility in Cuban or other Hemisphere waters would seriously jeopardize American-Soviet relations.

Heart of Understanding

Reliable American sources indicate that the heart of the understanding is an unwritten pledge by the Soviet Union not to base missile-carrying nuclear submarines, store nuclear weapons or install repair and servicing facilities anywhere in the Western Hemisphere.

In return, the American sources indicate, the United States will closely watch but not obstruct periodic visits by the Soviet fleet to Cuban or other Hemisphere ports for shore leave for crewmen and for routine ship maintenance.

Other sources, including some in the intelligence community, know enough of the facts to express considerable

Continued on Page 22, Column 3

JOINT EFFORT DUE ON CITY'S WASTE

U.S., the State and Industry to Help Solve Problems

By DAVID BIRD

A combination of new efforts by Federal and state governments and private industry may soon be helping to solve the city's solid-waste problem, a problem that until recently was considered to be solely a municipal responsibility.

The entrance of Federal and state authorities into the problem is a realization by them, they say, that the situation, which they generally agree has reached a critical stage, can no longer be solved by municipalities alone.

Business has turned to the problem, knowing that it is a major producer of the waste that needs cleaning up. Its concern is spurred by fear that stiff new regulations will be laid down by government if business does not do the job itself.

As William F. May, chairman and president of the American Can Company, told an industry group here last week:

"We have failed in the past in carrying out our business, to consider society's environmental needs."

Mr. May's company is a large manufacturer of containers that end up being a major littering and solid-waste problem for the nation's cities.

Mr. May warned his business audience at a meeting of the Packaging Education Foundation that they would have to expect some deductions in the

Continued on Page 78, Column 3

VERMONT'S famous Crowley Cheese—See Magazine Page 131—ADVT.

Rising Protests and Lawsuits Shake Routine in State Prisons

By MICHAEL T. KAUFMAN

Within the last few months tremors of discontent and protest and a heavy file of lawsuits have shaken the bureaucracy, the routine and the discipline of the state prison system.

At prisons in Attica, Napanoch and Auburn inmates have demonstrated, refusing to report to their work details. At the same time the courts have been flooded with writs seeking to extend prisoner rights and curb the traditional prerogatives of prison administrations.

"There is no doubt that the prisons are under attack," said Paul D. McGinnis, the Commissioner of Correction, who announced last week that he would retire next Jan. 1 after 46 years of state service.

Russell G Oswald, who is rumored as the man who will take over the new state superagency governing prisons, parole and the state police when it becomes operative on Jan. 1, concurs. Mr. Oswald, who is now chairman of the Parole Board, feels that the prison turmoil is part of a larger social upheaval.

"What's happening in the prisons," he said, "is a reflection of what has happened outside. Most of the country's institutions have come under attack—the colleges, the schools, the courts — now, it's the prisons."

But unlike these other institutions, prisons are sealed off from public view and are usually in remote regions. Still, disquiet has been seeping

Continued on Page 79, Column 1

A Devoted Few Strive to Save Wild Horses

Hope Ryden—"America's Last Wild Horses"

A lone stallion races through plains of Nevada. Wild horses, once in huge bands, are vanishing from the West.

By ANTHONY RIPLEY

Special to The New York Times

DENVER, Nov. 14 — Hounded by human enemies, America's once huge bands of wild horses are disappearing from the Western plains and mountains

In remote gullies, mesas and deserts where only the hardiest survive are the remaining descendants of the tough, small Spanish mustangs brought to the horseless New World by the conquistadores 400 years ago.

At the turn of the century, there were an estimated two million wild horses ranging through the immense grasslands that run west of the Mississippi River to the Rocky Mountains, past the Continental Divide and through the deserts beyond to the Pacific Coast.

Today, the Bureau of Land Management of the Department of the Interior estimates that only 16,000 are alive, scattered in 11 Western states. The wild horse is hunted down for sport or slaughtered for pet food or killed because it competes for grass with antelope, deer, cattle and sheep.

The plight of the horses has touched off a growing movement among conservationists to protect the last of the vanishing breed. But the efforts so far have brought only slight advances. Mustang hunters in airplanes still stampede the wild horses till they drop from exhaustion, capture them and sell them as horsemeat for 6 cents a pound.

The story of the horses, and the efforts to save them, is told in a just-published book, "America's Last Wild Horses," by Hope Ryden of New York, a documentary film producer for A.B.C. News.

Miss Ryden said, "They need protection from cruelty and extinction. Many livestock people want to remove all predators and competitors.

Continued on Page 60, Column 4

Today's Sections

Index to Subjects

JOBS IN THE MEDICAL FIELD. Openings for professional and non-professional workers appear today in The New York Times. See Section 4 and 9. Section 9 is distributed in New York and vicinity.—Advt.

The New York Times

Villagers wait on line in front of a doctor's tent. In background, the remains of a schoolhouse smashed by the cyclone.

Victims of the cyclone awaiting relief.

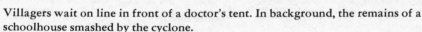

TOLL IN PAKISTAN PUT AT THOUSANDS

Continued From Page 1, Col. 6

town of Bhola said: "Nothing remains in Bhola. All is gone." He said that at least 1,000 persons had fled there. A major part of Bhola was under water, it was reported.

In Noakhali district, about 340 bodies were counted on the small island of Dudharam.

Several ocean-going vessels at Chittagong and Mungla were reported damaged by the storm. The airports at Chittagong and at Cox's Bazar were said to be under three feet of water for several hours Friday morning, and the control tower at Chittagong Airport was badly damaged.

Thousands of dead cattle were reported floating in the country by more than a thousand miles of Indian territory. Damage to houses, crops and other property was described by officials as "colossal." ficials as "colossal."

Doctors Flown In

In Hatia, a medical team and emergency supplies were brought in by helicopter today. Three gunboats of the Pakistani navy and a hospital ship with three doctors and 14 other medical personnel left Chittagong for Hatia, Sandwip and Kutubdia, carrying relief supplies and medicines.

Communication links between the offshore islands and Chittagong are still cut. A central control room has been set up in Chittagong to collect data on the cyclone disaster. A cyclone is the Indian Ocean equivalent of a hurricane in the Atlantic and a typhoon in the Pacific.

President Agha Mohammad Yahya Khan returned to Dacca, the East Pakistani capital, from Peking after a five-day state visit to China. He directed the Governor of East Pakistan, Vice Adm. S. M. Ashan, to direct relief work.

General Yahya said at the airport that the disaster followed by only a few weeks a milder cyclone and large-scale floods that caused considerable damage.

No Aid Request Yet

WASHINGTON, Nov. 14 (UPI) —The State Department said today that the United States had received no request so far from Pakistan for relief assistance.

Department officials said that reporting from United States diplomats in Pakistan had been sketchy but there had been no reports of American casualties.

75 on Plane Carrying Football Team Killed in West Virginia Crash

Continued From Page 1, Col. 5

proach to the airport's Runway 11 when the crash occurred about 7:40 P.M., after a 40-minute flight from Kinston, N. C. The Marshall team had played East Carolina College at Greenville, N. C., and lost, 17-14.

There was a 300-foot ceiling and visibility was five miles, the aviation agency said.

The plane came down about a mile and a half from the airport, near a point where Interstate 64 crosses the Big Sandy River into Kentucky. The Appalachians rise to a height of about 1,000 feet in the area.

Mrs. Don Bailey, a resident of the area, said: "I heard the plane overhead. Then it made a funny sound. I went to the back porch and saw a streak of fire and then an explosion. My house shook. Then it seemed like there was nothing but fire

The New York Times   Nov. 15, 1970

in the sky."

Mrs. Bailey's husband added, "I don't see how anybody could have gotten out of that plane."

Steve Stanley, an air traffic control specialist at the airport, said he was on the field "taking a breather" when the crash occurred.

"I saw a large ball of fire, an explosion, about two miles from Runway 11," Mr. Stanley said.

Other eyewitnesses reported that the plane struck the top of a hill, skidded down into a valley and exploded.

State Trooper W. F. Donohoe, one of nine state policemen at the crash scene, said the wreckage still burned two hours after the crash.

A spokesman for Marshall University, which has an enrollment of 9,100, said the plane carried 37 football players, members of the coaching staff, a West Virginia State Assemblyman, a Huntington television station sportscaster and members of the Big Green Boosters Club. The Marshall team's nicknames are Thundering Herd and Big Green.

John Ontague, East Carolina's athletic director, said that Marshall's athletic director, Charles Kautz, and the university's head football coach, Rick Tolley, were aboard the plane, which left Kinston at 6:38 P.M.

The Marshall team, depleted because of a recent recruiting scandal and Mid-American Conference suspension, opened the season with a 40-man squad. Only about a half-dozen players were from West Virginia. Others were from Florida, Texas, Massachusetts, Ohio and New Jersey.

Marshall was placed on probation by the National Collegiate Athletic Association because of recruiting methods and alleged payments to players. The players mentioned in the alleged irregularities dropped out of school or transferred to other schools. The team had three victories and six losses this year.

Marshall University, which is located in Huntington in the tri-state region where West Virginia, Ohio and Kentucky meet, is more familiar to sports fans for its basketball teams than its football teams.

The school was founded in 1837, two years after the death of Chief Justice John Marshall of the United States.

Some From Jersey

HUNTINGTON, W. Va., Nov. 14 (AP)—The traveling roster of players and coaches for Marshall University's football team included: Ted Shoebridge, Lyndhurst, N. J.; Kevin Gilmore, Harrison, N. J.; Art Harris, Passaic, N. J.; Marcelo Lajterman, Lyndhurst, N. J., and Dennis Foley, Carteret, N. J.

"All the News That's Fit to Print"

The New York Times

LATE CITY EDITION

Weather: Partly sunny, cold today; fair and cold tonight, tomorrow. Temp. range: today 32-19; Tuesday 36-29. Full U.S. report on Page 85.

VOL. CXX . No. 41,290 — NEW YORK, WEDNESDAY, FEBRUARY 10, 1971 — 15 CENTS

© 1971 The New York Times Company

APOLLO ASTRONAUTS LAND WITHIN A MILE OF TARGET AFTER A 'TERRIFIC FLIGHT'

New York Times/C.B.S. News

Capt. Alan B. Shepard Jr., center, and Comdr. Edgar D. Mitchell, right, Navy, with Maj. Stuart A. Roosa of Air Force in quarantine aboard U.S.S. New Orleans after recovery.

NIXON HAILS CREW

Men, Quarantined on Pacific Carrier, Tell of 'Super' Voyage

By JOHN NOBLE WILFORD

Special to The New York Times

HOUSTON, Feb. 9 — The Apollo 14 astronauts rode their spaceship to a safe, successful and precise splashdown in the Pacific Ocean at 4:05 P.M. today, Eastern standard time.

It marked the end of the nation's 24th manned space flight, the sixth mission to the moon and the third to have landed men who explored that desolate world some 238,000 miles from the earth.

Less than an hour after splashdown, Capt. Alan B. Shepard Jr. and Comdr. Edgar D. Mitchell of the Navy and Maj. Stuart A. Roosa of the Air Force stepped aboard the U.S.S. New Orleans, a helicopter carrier.

They had hit the water four miles from the ship and less than a mile from their aiming point about 900 miles south of American Samoa.

Shepard Elated

"We have had a terrific flight," Captain Shepard, the 47-year-old Apollo commander, said after a prayer by the ship's chaplain and words of welcome. "It's been just completely super all the way around."

Captain Shepard spoke from inside the crew's quarantine quarters. The astronauts were immediately placed in quarantine as a precaution against the spread of lunar organisms—in the unlikely event there were any disease for the astronauts to contract on the moon.

Shortly after the astronauts arrived aboard, President Nixon telephoned to offer his congratulations. Mr. Nixon watched the splashdown on the television in an aide's office. A White House statement by the President said:

"To each and every one of the many people who contributed to the success of Apollo 14, a grateful nation says 'Well done' and to the astronauts themselves—to Captain Shepard, Commander Mitchell and Major Roosa—we all will add an equally hearty welcome home."

On their nine-day mission, Captain Shepard and Commander Mitchell spent 33½ hours on the lunar surface in the Fra Mauro highlands.

They set up a nuclear-powered science station that continues to transmit data and returned with 96 pounds of

Continued on Page 24, Column 2

Stock Volume at Peak

Volume on the New York Stock Exchange soared to 28,250,000 shares yesterday, setting a record for the second straight day. Two blocks of two million shares each in Greyhound Corporation stock helped to swell the volume. Details, Page 59.

21 Policemen Face Knapp Investigation In a Theft of Meat

By DOUGLAS ROBINSON

The Knapp Commission, which has been investigating reports of police corruption, has subpoenaed 21 policemen for questioning about the burglary of a Greenwich village meat-packing plant last month.

Michael F. Armstrong, the chief counsel to the commission, confirmed that the subpoenas had been issued, but declined to discuss details of the case.

The police said the investigation started when an anonymous informant told of seeing uniformed policemen loading meat into radio patrol cars.

The subpoenas, which are returnable today at the commission's office at 51 Chambers Street, call for the appearance of a lieutenant, three sergeants and 17 patrolmen.

All but one of the patrolmen are attached to the Charles Street station in Greenwich Village. The other man is assigned to the Manhattan South Patrol Borough.

The burglarized meat concern, the Great Plains Packing Company, Inc., at 449 West 13th Street, is owned by James E. Reardon, a former plainclothesman who was an associate of Harry Gross in the $20-million-a-year bookmaking scandal in the nineteen-fifties.

Reardon resigned from the police force in 1947 and became an associate of Gross, who paid the police $1-million a year for protection.

In 1952, the former police-

Continued on Page 32, Column 3

COMMON MARKET WILL UNIFY MONEY

Agreement Reached to Make Bloc Into Single Currency Area Over Next Decade

By CLYDE H. FARNSWORTH

Special to The New York Times

BRUSSELS, FEB. 9 — After months of argument, the six members of the European Economic Community agreed today on a concrete plan to make their trade bloc into a single currency area over the next decade.

The historically important accord means that Europe is developing a distinct monetary personality and loosening itself from the influence of the dollar. The agreement, which will be put into effect retroactively to Jan. 1, 1971, could provide a new thrust of uniting Europe politically.

The accord, reached by Ministers from the six Common Market countries— Belgium, France, Italy, Luxembourg, the Netherlands and West Germany—at a council meeting in the Palais des Congrès, was strung together by a series of compromises, chiefly over the federal institutions that might be established as monetary integration deepened.

France and West Germany, the main antagonists, buried their differences, in effect, by postponing decisions over federalizing the customs union while agreeing to move ahead in a trial of intensified eco-

Continued on Page 61, Column 1

Business Group Planning Improvements in Midtown

Civic Group Is Formed

By RICHARD REEVES

More than 100 of the city's most prominent business leaders have formed an association to deal with municipal problems, beginning with a privately financed program to clean midtown streets.

The Association for a Better New York—organized by a core group of the city's largest real-estate men — will operate on a $2.5-million, three-year budget in much the same way that chambers of commerce work in smaller communities.

"We're all tired of groups and committees, but we had to do something, and this is really a desperation move," said Preston Robert Tisch, president of Loew's Corporation. He is one of the men who began putting the association together last fall when the General Telephone and Electronics Corporation announced it was moving its headquarters from the city to Connecticut.

The association's primary goal is to establish a positive image for New York, the im-

Continued on Page 86, Column 1

A Plan to 'Save' 5th Ave.

By MICHAEL STERN

Mayor Lindsay announced yesterday a zoning proposal designed to preserve the prestige retail character of Fifth Avenue, now threatened by competing uses, rising rents and soaring land values.

If adopted by the City Planning Commission and the Board of Estimate, the proposal would return housing to the midtown section of the avenue and initiate the building of as many as 25 tall, triple-purpose towers flanked by sidestreet arcades and combining stores, offices and apartments.

Under the proposal, the section of the avenue from 38th to 59th Street would be designated a special retail district, and at least the two lower floors of all new buildings erected in the district would have to be rented to retail tenants.

Builders who elected to pro vide more than the minimum retail space would be given a bonus in the form of permission to erect a larger structure, with the extra floors to be

Continued on Page 86, Column 5

U.S. AIDES BELIEVE THRUST MAY COST FOE YEAR OR MORE

Aims of Laos Drive Defined —Rogers and Laird Give Report to Legislators

By WILLIAM BEECHER

Special to The New York Times

WASHINGTON, Feb. 9—Administration planners asserted privately today that the allied military incursion into Laos could buy a year or possibly two during which it would be extremely hard for North Vietnam to mount an effective offensive of any size in either South Vietnam or Cambodia.

That result could be achieved, they said, not only through the temporary destruction and disruption of enemy military supplies but also by establishing a precedent for South Vietnamese operations in southern Laos.

Senior Pentagon and State Department officials cited those aims as the specific objectives of the Laotian campaign.

Goals Are Explained

Its purpose was described in more general terms by the Secretary of State, William P. Rogers, and the Secretary of Defense, Melvin R. Laird, in Congressional appearances today. They said the goals were to improve South Vietnam's security and facilitate continued withdrawals of American troops.

[On the fighting front in Laos, bad weather virtually cut off United States air support, including helicopter supply runs. The South Vietnamese advance forces were said to be about six miles from the border, with advance units as far as 12 miles in. Page 14.]

Mr. Laird, who had appeared before the Senate and House Armed Services Committees insisted to reporters on Capitol Hill that the Laos operation, rather than widening the war, as critics have asserted, had shortened it.

Senator George D. Aiken, Republican of Vermont, emerged from a briefing by Mr. Rogers for the Senate Foreign Relations Committee to report that the drive should permit the United States to withdraw men more safely and probably at an earlier date than would have been possible otherwise. [Page 15.]

Administration's Analysis

The Administration's analysis is based on the contention that the North Vietnamese cannot mount major, sustained offensives unless they are able to move thousands of tons of war material along the 1,500 miles of dirt roads and tracks that make up the Ho Chi Minh Trail.

Heavy American bombing throughout the war, the officials say, achieved the destruction of considerable supplies, but until the closing of Cambodian ports to North Vietnam last year the enemy was able to get enough rockets, grenades, mortars and other basic requirements to support extensive attacks. Now the enemy is dependent on overland routes.

Ground assaults have always been regarded as more effective on weapons caches than bombing truck convoys, which

Continued on Page 14, Column 1

Newton Denounces 2 Missing Panthers

By EDITH EVANS ASBURY

Huey P. Newton, national leader of the Black Panther party, denounced two New York Panther leaders yesterday as "enemies of the people" who had put party leaders and members in jeopardy by "disappearing" while on trial here.

The two New Yorkers, Richard Moore and Michael Tabor, are among 13 Black Panthers who have been on trial here since Sept. 8 for an alleged bomb conspiracy. They failed to appear for trial Monday and again yesterday, forfeiting bail totaling $150,000 and being declared fugitives, with warrants issued for their arrest.

Assistant District Attorney Joseph A. Phillips said, "In my opinion, they may have at-

Continued on Page 36, Column 1

HEAVY QUAKE IN LOS ANGELES AREA KILLS AT LEAST 35; HUNDREDS HURT; HOUSES, HOSPITALS, FREEWAYS HIT

The New York Times/Robert Smith

Attendants at San Fernando Veterans Hospital working on one of first patients pulled from the leveled building

ISRAEL IS WILLING TO DISCUSS CANAL

But Mrs. Meir, in a Reply to Sadat Speech, Still Bars Withdrawal of Troops

By PETER GROSE

Special to The New York Times

JERUSALEM, Feb. 9—Premier Golda Meir declared today that Israel was ready to support the reopening of the Suez Canal, and to discuss with the United Arab Republic a "mutual de-escalation of the military confrontation."

She declared that, if reopened, the canal should be available to shipping of all nations, including Israel.

In a policy address to the Knesset, or parliament, Mrs. Meir replied to the speech of the Egyptian President, Anwar el-Sadat, last Thursday, in which he suggested that the Suez Canal, which has been closed since 1967, could be reopened after a "partial withdrawal" of Israeli troops from the eastern bank.

Mrs. Meir reiterated Israel's long-standing refusal to withdraw troops until a peace agreement had been reached, but she used unexpectedly mild language in referring to the

Continued on Page 10, Column 1

At a California Hospital, 'Everything Came Down'

By ROBERT A. WRIGHT

Special to The New York Times

SYLMAR, Calif., Feb. 9—It was a bright 82-degree afternoon, and the men tearing at the rubble of the San Fernando Veterans Hospital were sweating in the warm sun as they went on digging through the ruins of the hospital, where the force of the earthquake hit hardest, still searching for bodies.

The sloping lawns of the hospital were overrun by 500 policemen and rescue workers and their heavy equipment, but spectators stood in the pleasant shade of trees to watch the rescue efforts.

"We're not even counting the injured," said one of the doctors who had been brought to the hospital by car and helicopter to treat the injured as they were brought out from the wreckage. "We're just trying to put them in beds in any hospital we can find."

At least 19 persons were killed, 25 were rescued and by this evening about 30 were believed to be still trapped beneath the rubble.

Palm trees and telegraph poles angled out from under the wreckage of the stucco walls that had collapsed when the earthquake wrenched the area early this morning.

Some of the doctors clambered down into the rubble to give morphine shots to the trapped survivors. "Some of them were lying in there with rocks as big as this," said Dr. Donald Yadusky, holding his hands an arm's length apart. Dr. Yadusky, an internist who lives on the hospital grounds, said he had helped to rescue three men buried under the walls of Ward 5.

"Some of them were moaning at first, but later there was just a silence around here."

Another doctor examined a patient just carried out from the wreckage and shook his head: "No way," he said. "No how. No way," and ordered the patient evacuated.

Maxine Price, a nurse at the Olive View Sanitarium, also in Sylmar, where two persons died, said: "Everything came down around us —the lights, the walls."

The $23-million sanitarium

Continued on Page 30, Column 6

A MAJOR DISASTER

Loss Is Put at Billion —A Dam Cracks, Thousands Flee

By STEVEN V. ROBERTS

Special to The New York Times

LOS ANGELES, Feb. 9 — A major earthquake rumbled through southern California early today, killing at least 35 persons, injuring hundreds and causing more than a billion dollars in damage to homes, businesses and roadways in Los Angeles and the surrounding areas.

Centered near Newhall, 40 miles north of Los Angeles, the quake was felt in Fresno, 200 miles to the north; at the Mexican border, 130 miles to the south, and in Las Vegas, 225 miles to the northeast.

Thousands of residents threw clothing and food into their cars and tried to leave, but gargantuan traffic jams slowed their progress.

The death count was expected to rise beyond 50 as rescue workers dug through tons of rubble from dozens of collapsed buildings.

Hospital Buildings Collapse

President Nixon declared a major disaster in the area and dispatched representatives of the Office of Emergency Preparedness and other agencies to the scene. Vice President Agnew is expected to arrive tomorrow to meet with Gov. Ronald Reagan and other local officials to discuss relief efforts.

The worst disaster was at a Veterans Administration hospital in Sylmar, a community about 25 miles from downtown Los Angeles and 10 miles from Newhall. About 80 persons were trapped when two hospital buildings collapsed. Twenty-five were rescued, 19 were known dead and about 30 were missing.

A mile from the hospital, two persons were found dead at Olive View Sanitarium, where walls were collapsed by the shock. The institution is a new $23-million complex.

Tonight, John A. LaBie, the Los Angeles County Engineer, estimated that 1,000 private buildings in Los Angeles County had suffered damage totaling $1.3-billion. County buildings

Continued on Page 30, Column 1

United Press International

DANGER POINT: Water pushing against earthfill retaining wall after a concrete wall of the lower Van Norman Dam in San Fernando Valley collapsed during the earthquake.

NEWS INDEX

Many Dead in Heavy Quake in Los Angeles Area

OVERPASS COLLAPSES: Bridge lies on Golden State Freeway (I-5) in northern San Fernando Valley

The New York Times/Doug Andrews

United Press International

TOPPLED VETERANS HOSPITAL: Rescue workers search for survivors in San Fernando

Quake Damage Is Put at Over $1-Billion

Continued From Page 1, Col. 8

suffered $125-million in damage.

The sheriff's office put the injured figure at 850.

The tremor struck only seconds after 6 A.M. and lasted for close to a minute. It registered 6.5 on the Richter scale, making it the strongest quake to hit Los Angeles since 1933. The famous San Francisco quake of 1906 would have registered about 8.5 if the scale had been in use at that time.

The shock waves were so powerful that they knocked out the seismographic instruments at the California Institute of Technology in Pasadena, the home of Dr. Charles F. Richter, who devised the Richter Scale.

Many lives were undoubtedly saved because of the time that the quake occurred. Most people were in bed and out of the way of falling debris. An hour or two later the freeways and business district would have been jammed with potential victims.

A sense of danger continued to hover over the city throughout the day. The Van Norman Lakes, a series of reservoirs in the hills about the San Fernando Valley, the area's main bedroom community, were badly shaken by the tremor. The cement facing of one dam fell away and a large crack appeared in the remaining earthen barrier.

Gov. Ronald Reagan reported that thousands of people were being evacuated from a 12-square-mile area as workmen frantically tried to pump out the lake's 7 billion gallons of water. They were pumping the water into the Los Angeles River, which flows into the Pacific.

By midday, the threat of collapse ended, but large waves on the lake continued to eat away at the dam.

Officials estimated that 90,000 persons lived in the evacuated area, which is made up mainly of middle-class homes, with few businesses or industries. Most of the people went to the homes of friends or to several evacuation centers set up in local schools and other public buildings.

As working people tried to return home tonight, they were kept out of the threatened area, and police set up an emergency number where members of separated families could leave messages for one another.

Plants that feed chlorine into the city's water supply were knocked out, and residents of the San Fernando Valley were advised to boil water before drinking it.

An 800,000-volt intertie that brings electricity to southern California from the Northwest was also damaged, but adequate power was available from other sources. In Houston, Mission Control reported that four tracking stations for Apollo 14 were temporarily affected but that backup systems kept communications with the astronauts going.

Just about everything that could be damaged was damaged. The huge Lockheed plant in Burbank was forced to close. A 40-foot church steeple in Eagle Rock tumbled. A runway at the Burbank Airport buckled. Employes at the studios of the National Broadcasting Company found plaster ankle-deep in some stairwells.

The oldest building in Los Angeles, the Villa Adobe on Olivera Street, suffered severe damage in five rooms. It was the first time in 153 years that the structure had been harmed by a quake. Nearby, a winery was shaken so badly that hundreds of bottles crashed and broke, sending an alcoholic aroma to the street, which is where the city of Los Angeles was founded.

The Division of Highways tallied at least $5-million in damage to major routes, saying the Golden State Freeway near Newhall buckled, with slabs tilted as much as five feet above the roadbed. Major damage was reported to seven freeway structures.

Five major highways were closed: the Golden State Freeway (Interstate 5); the San Diego Freeway (Interstate 405) near San Fernando due to a bridge collapse; Interstate 210 near Newhall; California 14 near Newhall, and California 2 near La Canada.

In thousands of homes throughout the city, dishes and glasses shattered. Said one secretary: "Everything is broken everywhere."

Most of the damage in downtown Los Angeles appeared to be in the old Skid Row district, a hodge-podge of secondhand shops, cheap bars and liquor stores, rundown restaurants and missions.

At the Midnight Mission, an aging two-story building of standstone-colored brick at Los Angeles and Fourth Street, a quarter of the roof collapsed, killing at least one man and spewing bricks onto the sidewalk in front and down a flight of inside stairs.

Henry Richmond, director of the mission, which has operated at its present site since 1929, remained in his office, although the building had been officially closed as hazardous. He was trying to arrange sleeping accommodations for some of his staff and the regulars whose only home was in the narrow cots that jammed the barracks-like second story.

Following the quake, many areas of the city were left without power and telephone service, but the situation gradually improved as crews tackled the tremendous repair job.

Several major freeways were blocked as overpasses collapsed and roadways buckled. For a while, the town of Newhall was completely blocked off and a bulldozer gouged a pathway in the rubble to get fire equipment through.

Skyscrapers Little Hurt

Until recent years, Los Angeles imposed a height limit on buildings, partly out of fear of an earthquake. But damage was greatest to the older, lower buildings. Several cracks appeared in the walls of the Hall of Justice, site of the Sharon Tate murder trial. At the county library, most of the shelves collapsed, carpeting the floors with three feet of books.

But in most of the new skyscrapers, which reach up to 42 stories, damage was slight. Within hours after the tremor, workmen were back on the steel skeletons of half-finished towers, apparently untroubled by the rumbles of the earth many floors below.

At the Sylmar Juvenile Detention Center, about 100 delinquent teen-agers escaped in the confusion after the center had suffered heavy damage.

By far the most serious damage occurred at the Veterans Administration Hospital, where the roof collapsed on a wing holding tuberculosis and emphysema patients. Workmen "operated like surgeons", according to one observer, carefully removing chunks of rubble to get at the victims. Doctors and nurses scrambled about, administering morphine to victims.

Late in the afternoon, searchers estimated that 50 to 75 bodies might eventually be found.

Bob Dutton, a patient on the third floor of the V.A. hospital, said that he was in a wheelchair suffering from a back injury when the quake struck.

"I learned to walk, he said. "I jumped for the door and when I reached the hall and turned around to look back, there was nothing there—just wide-open space. It looked like someone had sliced the building."

In Newhall, a farming community that was closest to the quake's center, one observer said that the main street looked as if it had been "hit by a bomb." Most buildings in the town were reported damaged, and dozens of small fires were ignited when gas mains ruptured.

Southern California has a long history of earthquakes, and most residents here are used to general tremors that rattle the windows occasionally. But today was different. The early hour added to the eeriness.

"I awakened to a nightmare," said Michael Snitkowsky, a student at San Fernando Valley State College. "I found myself on the floor, and my bed seemed to stand on end."

He ran into the hallway to find a scene that was repeated all over the city. People in pajamas and bathrobes held portable radios to their ears and talked in nervous, frightened tones. One had been cut by flying glass; another was hurt when a bookcase fell on him.

"Everyone was scared," he said, "they didn't know what to do."

Many people likened the quake to a rough sea. "I was actually seasick in bed," said one young girl.

"I was knocked to my knees," added a public relations man, "and while I was there, I prayed a little."

And a woman who was 12 days overdue with her first child suddenly went into labor when the quake hit. "Let's go to the hospital," she said to her husband. "It only took an earthquake, but I'm finally going to have it."

Most scientists felt that the quake had a more practical origin. Late today, they were still trying to determine which of the many faults that crisscross the state caused the latest tremor.

Dr. William Kaufmann, director of the Griffith Park Observatory, speculated that the quake might have been caused by an unusual alignment of the sun, the moon and the earth, which produced a lunar eclipse.

Associated Press

RESCUE OPERATION: A patient of the Olive View Sanitarium in Sylmar, Calif., being carried from recreation wing that toppled

Nurse: 'Everything Came Down'

Continued From Page 1, Col. 7

had been described as "earth-quake-proof;" it was completely destroyed by the quake. County Supervisor Warren Dorn said there was a "20-foot hole in the ground" where a 50-bed mental health unit was simply swallowed up. The building, Mr. Dorn said he had been told, was located near a "dead [inactive] fault."

A teen-age girl standing near a mound of rubble at the hospital stared and said: "It's my mom. She's in there. The firemen heard her yell. She's in there."

Dr. John D. Arberberry, who had been in the sanitarium's emergency room giving oxygen to an asthma patient when the earthquake occurred, said: "The building shook like it was being wrung by the neck. We were all knocked to our knees."

Scouts Help Police

Boy scouts augmented the strained police forces directing traffic at intersections where there were no working traffic lights and signaling drivers along roads furrowed by huge buckles in the concrete.

Nearby, suburban streets were flooded because of broken water mains and damage to the many swimming pools in the area.

There was a strong odor of gas hanging in the air, and, besides the water from cracked swimming pools and split water mains that sloshed in the gutters, 5,000 gallons of water were spilling down the hills from a huge tank that was smashed not far from the veterans hospital.

And there was fire. Seven buildings blazed at a San Fernando shopping center, where an aircraft manufacturing firm also burned.

A few food stores managed to open. They did not allow their customers inside their stores, which were strewn with shards of glass and scattered merchandise, but sold milk and other necessities to long lines of people at the front doors.

From an airplane that toured the area in the early morning hours, two massive concrete overpasses at the intersection of the San Diego and Golden State Freeways—main commuter arteries for Los Angeles—lay splintered across the roadways as if they were toys knocked over by an angry child.

At the apex of a triangle formed by the northernmost end of the San Fernando Valley, giant cracks were etched on the water side of the dam in the water system that supplies the Van Norman Reservoir, Los Angeles's largest. Massive chunks of concrete, some as large as

buses, had been dislodged from the dam by the quake.

And to the north, near a smaller lake that is part of the system, the earth was distorted by giant fissures. At least one was large enough for a man to fall into; from the air, others seemed no more than a foot wide.

Thousands of persons in the 12-square-mile area just below the reservoir were evacuated from their homes in the early morning. They spent the day waiting to learn if their homes would be lost under seven billion gallons of water.

But they showed little panic. The police toured the area in loudspeaker cars, telling the people to get out, and they drove to evacuation centers — such as the Granada Hills High School —with few of their household goods.

It was not that way all over. "People were running up and down the street, the middle of the street, in every direction—north, south, east and west—and screaming," said a liquor store dealer in a Skid Row section of Los Angeles.

And, as the plane came in for a landing at Van Nuys Airport after the tour, several foursomes could be seen playing golf on an adjacent course.

Nixon Declares Major Disaster And Begins Wide Relief Effort

WASHINGTON, Feb. 9 — President Nixon declared the southern California earthquake zone a major disaster area today and asked Vice President Agnew to leave tomorrow for Los Angeles to meet with Gov. Ronald Reagan and Mayor Samuel W. Yorty.

The relief effort is to be coordinated by the Office of Emergency Preparedness. John Coleman, a spokesman for the agency, said representatives from the regional office in Santa Rosa, Calif., were already on the scene.

Several Federal agencies are taking part in the aid effort, including the Army Corps of Engineers and the Small Business Administration, which is offering low-interest loans to help rebuild businesses and homes damaged by the quake.

The President is authorized to provide aid under the Disaster Relief Act of 1970 upon application from state officials. Governor Reagan telephoned George A. Lincoln, the director of the Office of Emergency Preparedness, this afternoon to report that California's disaster aid fund was seriously depleted and to request Federal aid. California has had serious recent forest fires and floods.

Mr. Lincoln and Donald Johnson, the administrator of the Veterans Administration, will accompany Mr. Agnew

tomorrow morning.

A spokesman for the disaster aid agency said that the relief efforts would focus on providing loans, removing debris and providing food and water.

All agencies of the Federal Government have been alerted to the situation and may offer emergency aid, such as the early mailing of Social Security checks, according to the spokesman.

The American Red Cross has opened at least four shelters in the San Fernando Valley area to assist the homeless and injured.

President Nixon also declared the State of Washington a disaster area today because of floods last month in the southwestern portion.

Quake Insurance Is Carried by Few;

LOS ANGELES, Feb. 9,(UPI) —Most of the damage in today's earthquake probably was not covered by insurance.

Although several insurance companies offer earthquake coverage, its cost and a substantial deductible provision make it unattractive to buy, according to Kenneth H. Klee, president of the Insurance Brokers Association of California.

An Earthquake Theory Predicted 1971 Would Be a Bad Year

Big Tremors Tied to Abrupt Changes in Earth's Spin Axis

By WALTER SULLIVAN

The Commerce Department made public last Thursday a report noting that one theory of earthquake indicated that 1971 would be a peak year for them.

On Saturday an earthquake devastated the town of Tuscania in Italy, killing 14 and injuring more than 100. Yesterday another struck the north edge of Los Angeles, producing even greater casualties. In the last two days there have also been quakes in the Aleutians and south of South America.

They do not prove the theory, but they will be seized upon by the growing number of scientists who consider it plausible. The hypothesis links major earthquakes to slight but abrupt changes in the earth's spin axis.

Yesterday's earthquake occurred on or near the San Andreas Fault. However, it was not considered intense enough to constitute the long-predicted release of strain along the San Andreas.

Aftershocks Detected

Scientists at the California Institute of Technology in nearby Pasadena said a preliminary look at data from eight of the institute's field stations showed aftershocks originating along a line roughly at right angles to the San Andreas Fault. It appeared that the original rupture occurred some five miles below the surface, which is typical of quakes in that area.

The spin axis of the earth changes the earth's orientation with respect to the stars, in several ways. One is the so-called precession of the equinoxes in which the spin axis drifts slowly under the gravitational influence of the sun, moon and planets.

This precession comes full circle every 26,000 years. It means that 12,000 years from now the star Vega, now prominent in the summer sky, will be near the north pole of the heavens (now occupied by the star Polaris).

There is also, however, a much less radical wobble in a 14-year cycle. Known as the Chandler Wobble, it causes the position of the North Pole of the earth to vary by as much as 72 feet. At its maximum, this motion of the pole reaches six inches in a single day.

It is because several major earthquakes have been correlated with this period of maximum motion, and because 1971 should be such a period, that a peak in earthquake activity has been predicted for this year.

One of the mysteries about the Chandler Wobble is what keeps it going. Students of the earth's spin believe the wobble should fade away. This led two scientists at the University of Western Ontario — Lalantendu Mansimha and Douglas Smylie — to propose in 1967 that it is earthquakes that periodically jolt the earth enough to stimulate the wobble.

The debate has become a chicken-and-egg proposition. Some believe the wobbles cause the earthquakes and some think it is the other way around.

Charles A. Whitten, chief geodesist of the National Ocean Survey in the Commerce Department's National Oceanic and Atmospheric Administration, believes that both schools may be correct: that the wobble, at its maximum, triggers quakes, which then feed new energy into the wobble.

It was his analysis of the relationship between global earthquake activity and the rate of spin change over the last 70 years that led to the prediction for 1971 made public last week. The relationship is clearest, he said, during the last 20 years, when worldwide records were relatively complete.

The extent of the wobble is determined by high-precision astronomical observations made at a number of observatories around the world. Whether a jump in the axis occurred just before or after yesterday's quake will not be known until the most recent observations are analyzed.

If the wobble does, in fact, stimulate quakes, it does so, as a rule, in areas where accumulated strain in the earth's crust has set the stage for such an energy release. The Pacific is surrounded by a "ring of fire" in terms of volcanic activity and frequent earthquakes.

This is thought to be related to the movement of crustal rock beneath the ocean floor from mid-ocean ridges. It is in these ridges that molten rock rises from the depths and moves toward the coastlines. This rock movement seems responsible for earthquakes along the west coast of South America, like that in Peru which killed some 30,000 people last May.

There is clear evidence that the ocean floor is pushing under the continent there. However this does not appear to be the pattern in California. The chief observed movement there is that along the San Andreas Fault in which the motion on the far side of the fault is always to the right.

Yesterday scientists from Caltech were flying over the stricken area by helicopter, looking for signs of rupture in the earth's surface and for evidence indicating whether or not this was the pattern of slippage.

Richter Scale Invented By California Scientist

The Richter Scale used to measure earthquakes was developed in 1931 by Charles Francis Richter, a California Institute of Technology seismologist, who is now retired.

The scale measures the magnitude of earthquakes, and anything above a magnitude of 4.5 is considered potentially dangerous.

The San Francisco earthquake of 1906, which took 700 lives, has been estimated at 8.5 on the Richter Scale. Yesterday's quake in Los Angeles measured between 6 and 6.5.

The Richter Scale differs from other earthquake measurement devices in that readings do not have to be taken at the scene of the earthquake. It is widely accepted as the most common standard.

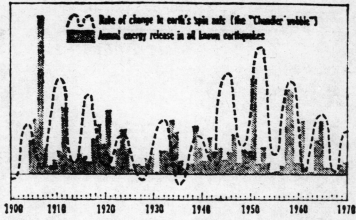

This graph, prepared by Charles A. Whitten of the National Ocean Survey, relates energy released by known earthquakes, from 1900 to 1970, with the daily shift in the spin axis of the earth because of the so-called Chandler Wobble. Particularly in recent years, when records were most complete, there seems a correlation, indicating that 1971 should be a year of many quakes.

FREEWAY DAMAGE: Chunks of roadway of Golden State Freeway were thrust up by yesterday morning's earthquake. In rear is overpass that collapsed during tremor.

Millions Have Died in Past Earthquakes

By United Press International

Earthquakes throughout history have taken millions of lives and caused damage in the hundreds of billions of dollars.

Following are some of the worst earthquake disasters of modern times:

Nov. 1, 1775—More than 80,000 people were killed in a quake centered in Portugal and felt over an area of one million square miles. Thousands were swallowed up by the ocean.

Feb. 5-March 27, 1783—A series of quakes on the tip of the Italian boot destroyed 181 towns and villages and caused 30,000 casualties.

Feb. 4, 1797—Forty-one thousand lives were lost as a series of quakes rocked Quito, Ecuador, and surrounding area.

Dec. 16, 1811—One of the three most destructive earthquakes on the North American continent occurred in southeastern Missouri. The shocks changed the course of the Mississippi River, ruined for years some 50,000 square miles of farmland and were felt in Arkansas, Kentucky and Tennessee.

Nov. 19, 1822—At Valparaiso, Chile, an upheaval of land caused the ocean to recede, and thousands died. Thirteen years later, Concep-cion, Chile, was destroyed by a quake.

Oct. 28, 1891—In Mino and Owari Provinces, Japan, some 7,200 were killed and at least 200,000 buildings leveled. Five years later, at Sanriku, Japan, a submarine quake caused the deaths of 28,000 persons.

April 18, 1906—An earth tremor, the most disastrous in United States history, struck San Francisco, causing a fire in which 452 persons were killed and 28,188 buildings destroyed.

Dec. 28, 1908—Messina and Baratti, Italy, were flattened in a quake that took 80,000 lives.

Jan. 13, 1915—Thirty thousand died in a quake in central Italy.

Sept. 1, 1923—Tokyo and Yokohama were struck. The death toll was 99,331, and 576,262 homes were destroyed. Fire damage was set at $4-billion to $6-billion.

Sept. 1, 1962—More than 10,000 were killed in a quake in northern Iran.

May 31, 1970—The northern part of Peru was devastated by a quake that reduced several towns to rubble, leaving at least 30,000 and perhaps as many as 50,000 persons dead.

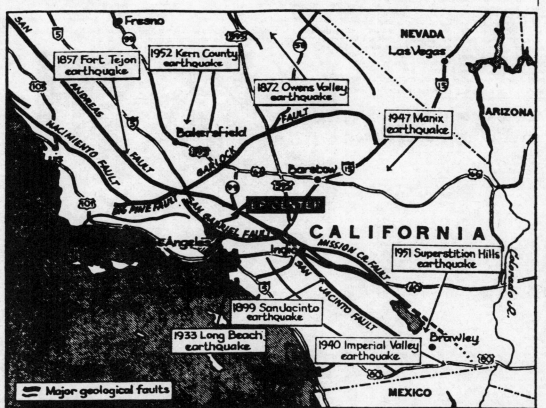

The New York Times   Feb. 10, 1971

Yesterday's earthquake is believed by scientists at the California Institute of Technology to have occurred near the San Andreas Fault but may have been unrelated to it. Shown above are major California faults and locations of some recent earthquakes.

"All the News That's Fit to Print"

The New York Times

LATE CITY EDITION

Weather: Cloudy, seasonable today and tonight. Fair, mild tomorrow. Temp. range: today 40-56; Monday 37-54. Full U.S. report on Page 81.

VOL. CXXI . . No. 41,716
© 1972 The New York Times Company
NEW YORK, TUESDAY, APRIL 11, 1972

15 CENTS

I.T.T. Aide Says He Feared Further Leaks

Representative Bob Wilson, California Republican, before Judiciary Committee.

By FRED P. GRAHAM
Special to The New York Times

WASHINGTON, April 10 — The head of the International Telephone and Telegraph Corporation's Washington office testified today that he had ordered the shredding of office files after Jack Anderson obtained a controversial memorandum because "there might be a lot of others in there like that."

The executive, William R. Merriam, a vice president of the company, told the Senate Judiciary Committee that he had decided that it was "time to clean house" after Mr. Anderson, the columnist, obtained a memorandum purportedly written by Mrs. Dita D. Beard, a lobbyist.

Mr. Merriam and Representative Bob Wilson, Republican of California, gave testimony today that contradicted each others' statements and testimony by other witnesses.

"Somebody's not telling the truth; take your pick," concluded Senator Quentin N. Burdick, Democrat of North Dakota,

Continued on Page 32, Column 1

Associated Press

William R. Merriam, head of the Washington office of I.T.T., after he testified.

QUAKE HITS IRAN; TOLL ESTIMATED AT 2,000 TO 4,000

Wide Area of South Struck, Radio Communication Out —Shah Speeding Relief

By Reuters

TEHERAN, Iran, April 10—An earthquake struck southern Iran today and thousands were feared dead. A provincial governor told of villages leveled and of heartbreaking scenes as survivors dug in the rubble for relatives.

Unofficial reports from the ancient town of Shiraz put the death toll at 2,000 to 4,000, but no official estimate has been given. A Government spokesman said that radio communication with rescue teams had broken down and that no reliable figures on casualties would be known until tomorrow.

Tremors were felt over a radius of 250 miles from where the quake struck in an area about 600 miles south of Teheran and 100 miles southeast of Shiraz. The destruction ranged over 20 to 30 villages and townships in an area 40 miles long and 12 miles wide.

Trapped as Houses Fall

Nearly all the houses in the farming villages of Ghir and Karzin, at the center of the quake, collapsed on their sleeping occupants. Men who had gone to the fields or to morning prayers escaped. Many of the casualties are believed to be women and children.

Four further quakes followed in the afternoon around Ghir, Karzin and the town of Jahrum, a Government spokesman here said.

In the province of Jahrum, already ravaged by the original quake, the later shocks brought down the remains of shattered buildings in ruined villages.

Mohammed Riza Pahlevi, the Shah of Iran, ordered relief and rescue operations sped as the extent of the disaster became apparent, and sent his younger brother, Prince Mahmoud, to supervise work on the spot. A relief coordinating center was established in Teheran.

Chief Tours Stricken Area

The first quake struck in Fars Province, whose ancient Persian capital was Shiraz. The provincial Governor-General, Manouchehr Pirouz, reported by telephone that he had flown over the stricken area and had landed at the villages hardest hit.

Ghir and Karzin had been leveled, he said; not a wall was standing in Ghir. He said he had seen old men and women weeping as they searched the rubble of their homes for missing children and small children crying for parents they could not find.

The Governor General could

Continued on Page 7, Column 1

NORTH VIETNAM'S LOSSES IN A DAY IN QUANGTRI AREA PUT AT 1,000 MEN, 30 TANKS

Nixon Indirectly Criticizes Soviet Arms Aid to Hanoi

By BERNARD GWERTZMAN
Special to The New York Times

WASHINGTON, April 10 — In a clear allusion to the Soviet Union's military aid to North Vietnam's forces, President Nixon said today that the big powers had a special responsibility to discourage others from mounting attacks on neighbors.

Although no nation was named, Mr. Nixon's remarks were seen as part of the Administration's effort to focus attention on the Soviet Union's aid program, which has provided Hanoi with tanks, artillery and missiles. In Washington's view this aid has made possible the offensive against South Vietnam.

Every "great power," the President said, must follow the principle that it should not encourage, "directly or indirectly, other nations to use force or armed aggression against its neighbors."

In a news conference Friday, Secretary of Defense Melvin R. Laird criticized the Russians for placing "no restraints" on Hanoi's use of Soviet equipment outside North Vietnam. The State Department had said earlier that the attack could not have been made without Soviet equipment.

Mr. Nixon, who had not previously spoken, even indirectly, about the offensive, couched his comments today in diplomatic language unlikely to offend the Russians publicly or jeopardize plans for his Moscow trip next month.

He spoke at ceremonies at the State Department marking the signing of a United Nations convention that bars the

Continued on Page 17, Column 1

BOMBING HEAVIER

B-52's Fly Deeper Into the North—Ground Action Subsides

By FOX BUTTERFIELD
Special to The New York Times

SAIGON, South Vietnam, Tuesday, April 11—Allied military commanders said yesterday that the North Vietnamese appeared to have suffered a serious setback in their drive into Quangtri Province in the northern part of South Vietnam.

A count on the battlefield revealed, according to reports from the scene by American officers and newsmen, that the Communists lost more than 1,000 soldiers and 30 tanks in their attacks Sunday west of the city of Quangtri.

In the wake of these assaults, the only battles reported in the area yesterday were three smaller clashes around Quangtri, with South Vietnamese marines and rangers reporting they had killed 243 more enemy troops.

Saigon's Losses Heavy

Accurate estimates of Government casualties for Sunday's battles are not available, but they also are said to have been heavy.

Meanwhile, the American retaliatory bombing campaign against North Vietnam intensified.

[B-52's, flying deeper into North Vietnam than ever before, struck at the Vinh area, 145 miles north of the demilitarized zone, The Associated Press reported. Official sources said all planes returned safely. But the Hanoi radio said two United States Navy fighter-bombers and one jet fighter had been downed in the area.]

Little fighting was reported during the day yesterday in the southern part of South Vietnam on the front north of Saigon.

An enormous Government relief column of tanks, howitzers and troops drawn from the Mekong Delta crept cautiously northward trying to relieve the South Vietnamese Fifth Division, which has been surrounded by the enemy at Anloc, 60 miles north of Saigon.

With little action reported for

Continued on Page 16, Column 1

Argentine Leftists Kill a Top General And Fiat's Director

By JUAN de ONIS
Special to The New York Times

BUENOS AIRES, April 10—Political extremists assassinated a powerful Argentine general today and a few hours later killed Oberdán Sallustro, the Italian industrialist who was kidnapped 19 days ago.

The two slayings, particularly that of Gen. Juan Carlos Sánchez in an ambush in Rosario, 170 miles northwest of here, infuriated the military Government of President Alejandro A. Lanusse and shocked most Argentines.

After a meeting of the National Security Council, presided over by General Lanusse, it was announced that all terrorist crimes will be judged by military courts with the power to impose the death sentence for kidnapping or for assault on members of the armed forces and the police.

General Lanusse then met at Government House here with political and labor leaders. A spokesman said General Lanusse had said that "nothing and nobody, and much less the

Continued on Page 8, Column 1

70 STATES REJECT BIOLOGICAL ARMS

U.S., Soviet Among Those Signing Accord That Also Calls for Destruction

By HEDRICK SMITH
Special to The New York Times

MOSCOW, April 10—More than 70 nations, including the United States, the Soviet Union and Britain, signed a convention today that outlaws biological weapons and, for the first time under a modern arms-control measure, requires states to destroy their stocks of such weapons.

The signing ceremonies took place in Moscow, Washington and London. The treaty will go into force as soon as 22 nations, including the three major nuclear powers, have deposited instruments of ratification. France and China, the other nuclear powers, were not among the signatories.

President Nixon, in Washington, and the Soviet President, Nikolai V. Podgorny, here in Moscow, took the occasion to emphasize their hopes of

Continued on Page 4, Column 2

Associated Press

CAPTURED TANK SHOWN IN QUANGTRI: One of many tanks lost by North Vietnamese over the weekend is viewed by South Vietnamese civilians. It is a Soviet-made T-54.

LINDSAY DESPAIRS OF MORE STATE AID

Rejects New Taxes Beyond Unused Nuisance Package, but May Turn to Notes

By MARTIN TOLCHIN

Mayor Lindsay said yesterday he despaired of any substantial increase in state aid to meet the $795-million gap he anticipates in his proposed $10-billion expense budget, and instead saw "less desirable but more feasible short-term solutions" that might include short-term budget notes.

Mr. Lindsay said that he sought no new city taxes, beyond the $141-million in nuisance taxes authorized last year by the Legislature but not yet enacted by the City Council. He rejected proposals by the City Council leadership for increases in the income tax and the stock-transfer tax.

"Temporary solutions are never wholly satisfactory," Mr. Lindsay said in a mimeographed statement released at City Hall. "It has become clear, however, that until this city digs in its heels and says 'no' to further tax increases, the taxpaying New Yorker will be asked to shoulder much more than his share of the burden. This is the year when we say 'no.'"

'More and More Unlikely'

Deputy Mayor Edward K. Hamilton said at an impromptu news conference in his office, which adjoins the Mayor's, that enactment of the Big Six Mayors' Program for state assumption of the costs of welfare and education "looks more and more unlikely in Albany."

Mr. Hamilton said that he thought the city had "a good shot" at state restoration of $15-million, which would save the jobs of 1,067 city workers involved in state financed programs. These workers are scheduled to be laid off May 1.

"Beyond that, we've been given nothing but pessimism

Continued on Page 31, Column 5

C.A.B. Chief Urges Study Of U.S. Air Security Role

Crimes Stir Concern

By RICHARD WITKIN

The chairman of the Civil Aeronautics Board, Secor D. Browne, suggested yesterday that President Nixon name a high-level commission to explore the possibility of giving a Federal agency the job of providing airline and airport security.

Mr. Browne, in an interview, made the suggestion because, he said, the system for preventing airline hijacking is inadequate and impractical.

In the international area, the C.A.B. chief urged that the President seek to hasten ratification of treaties calling for extradition or local punishment of air pirates and that consideration be given to even stronger measures.

Expressing deep concern following four aircraft crimes over the weekend, Mr. Browne said:

"We've grabbed the problem

Continued on Page 19, Column 1

F.B.I. Recovers $499,970

By ANTHONY RIPLEY
Special to The New York Times

SALT LAKE CITY, April 10 — The Federal Bureau of Investigation announced today it had recovered $499,970 from the home of Richard Floyd McCoy Jr., who was arrested yesterday and charged with air piracy in the armed take-over of a United Air Lines 727 jetliner.

The amount was only $30 short of the $500,000 paid to an airline hijacker. The man, wearing a false mustache, wig and mirror sunglasses, bailed out of the plane Friday night over the Provo, Utah, airport after commandeering the jet on a flight from Denver to Los Angeles and diverting it to San Francisco. There he picked up the money and four parachutes, allowed the passengers to disembark and took off with five crew members aboard.

Mr. McCoy, who is held with-

Continued on Page 18, Column 3

LABORITE LEADERS QUIT OVER MARKET

Deputy Chief and 2 Others Protest the Party's Stand Against British Entry

By ALVIN SHUSTER
Special to The New York Times

LONDON, April 10—The Labor party's leadership split openly today over British entry into the Common Market with the resignation of Roy Jenkins as the party's deputy leader.

Two other party leaders also resigned their posts in what amounted to a sharp rebuke for Harold Wilson, the party leader.

When Mr. Wilson was Prime Minister he favored British entry into the Common Market but changed his mind after losing the elections in 1970 to Edward Heath. Since then Mr. Jenkins has led the Labor party wing that has insisted that Britain should join.

Negotiator Resigns

The two other leaders to resign were Harold Lever, the party's spokesman on power, and George Thomson, the spokesman on defense. Mr. Thomson was Britain's Common Market negotiator in the last Labor government.

A fourth leader, Mrs. Shirley Williams, Labor's spokesman on home affairs, threatened to resign if the party refused to adopt a "more constructive" approach to joining the Market.

Although Mr. Wilson argues that he is not against the principle of entry but the terms, Mr. Jenkins and his colleagues argued differently today. They said the party was now moving

Continued on Page 9, Column 1

3 More Gangland Killings Bring Total to 6 in 5 Days

By ERIC PACE

Two more men were slain in gangland style here yesterday a few hours before a cortege of black Cadillacs escorted the body of Joseph Gallo, the murdered Mafia chieftain, to his grave in Brooklyn.

Early this morning, the police announced that yet another man had been found slain in gangland style. This victim, whose body was discovered at 10:30 last night in an automobile in the Sheepshead Bay section of Brooklyn, was still not identified at 3 o'clock this morning.

The two victims who were identified were Gennaro Ciprio, who was killed outside his restaurant in the Bath Beach section of Brooklyn, and Frank Ferriano, a New Jersey laundryman, whose 340-pound body was found in a lower West Side parking lot.

Both men had arrest records, both had been shot in the head, and both were found with large sums of money in their pockets. The police said this showed the motive for their murders was revenge, not robbery.

"Perhaps we're getting a rash of Mafia killings, like you get a rash of hijackings or bombings," said Deputy Police Commissioner Robert Daley, "but there's no indication yet that these guys are related to the Gallo killing."

The unidentified man found last night was in a parking lot in front of 2800 Coyle Street with a number of bullet wounds

Continued on Page 82, Column 1

'Face-to-Face' Review Set In All City Relief Cases

By PETER KIHSS

The city will conduct "face-to-face recertification" of its entire relief caseload, interviewing clients in all 503,291 cases, totaling 1,255,721 persons, by latest count. The review will take at least a year to carry out.

Plans for the complete check-up were announced yesterday by the Human Resources Administrator, Jule M. Sugarman, who asserted that the city's latest samplings made for the state and Federal Governments showed that an average of only 3.8 per cent of the cases were "totally ineligible" for aid.

He also said, however, that 3 per cent could not be located at the time of sampling, 1 per cent refused to cooperate and 3.1 per cent had been classified into wrong categories, raising problems about Federal and state reimbursement. This would raise the total of questionable cases to 10.9 per cent, although many of these could have been at least initially eligible.

Mr. Sugarman added that errors in overpayments and underpayments affected an additional 28.7 per cent of the caseload. He attributed much of the problem to understaffing of the city Department of Social Service and a changeover from caseworkers to clerks for income maintenance. Experience, he added, has shown a need to modify the simple declaration-of-need system.

The net cost of mispayments and ineligibility was estimated by Mr. Sugarman at $63-million annually. The current city budget for actual cash grants to welfare recipients totals nearly $1.2-billion, of which the Federal Government pays almost half, with the city and state sharing the rest.

For the state Department of

Continued on Page 30, Column 2

NEWS INDEX

TOM Stoppard has arrived for previews of Real Inspector Hound—Theatre Four.—Advt.

Morning Telegraph Ceases Publication

By EMANUEL PERLMUTTER

The Morning Telegraph—the dedicated horse-player's daily guide and encyclopedia—ceased publication yesterday after 139 years as a newspaper specializing in news of thoroughbred and harness racing.

I'm taking Epitaph
he wins it by a half
According to this here
in the Telegraph.

"Fugue for Tinhorns." Copyright 1950 Frank Music Company. Words and music by Frank Loesser. Reprinted by permission.

The paper, which was shut last Monday by a strike of union printers, had a staff of 260 and a daily circulation of about 50,000. It was on sale at race tracks throughout the country and at many newsstands. Besides carrying race entries, selections and results, it ran movie and theater reviews and feature articles about the racing world.

Readers of the paper, which frequently ran to 32 pages, were not limited to the Runyonesque "tinhorns" of "Guys and Dolls." It was pored over by shabby men in subway cars, by well-dressed customers waiting their next in barber shops and, occasionally, by a housewife with a love of horseflesh and a hope of augmenting the household allowance.

The decision to cease publication was announced by Stewart Hooker, publisher of both The Morning Telegraph and The Daily Racing Form, a companion daily racing paper that has been in operation since 1874. Each paper carried a $1 newsstand price.

Both papers have been pub-

Continued on Page 81, Column 6

OTB Aqueduct Off-Track Betting

• Official OTB Code Letters, Entries, Comment.
• Past Performances and Expert Selections

Aqueduct
Pimlico
Hialeah Park
Suffolk Downs
Narragansett Park
Past Performances

The MORNING TELEGRAPH

Founded in 1833

PRICE $1.00

★★★★★

An Iranian carries his possessions on his back through a street in the devastated village of Ghir, Southern Iran.

Wide World Photos

QUAKE HITS IRAN, HEAVY TOLL SEEN

Continued From Page 1, Col. 5

give no casualty figures, but he said the Mayor of Ghir and his family had died, as had several policemen who had been in their station when it collapsed.

The normal population of Ghir and Karzin is about 18,000. The people are farming families who live in mud huts and whose land produces rice, dates, cotton and citrus fruit.

U.S. Offering Aid

WASHINGTON, April 10 (AP) —The United States Government has made a "preliminary contribution" of $25,000 to the Red Lion and Sun Society, the Iranian relief organization, to help victims of the earthquake that struck the country today, the State Department said.

"We stand ready to give additional help if requested," said the State Departmente spokesman, Robert J. McCloskey. He said there were no reports of any American casualties in the quake.

"All the News That's Fit to Print"

The New York Times

LATE CITY EDITION
Weather: Mostly sunny, cool today; fair and cool tonight and tomorrow.
Temp. range: today 48-63; Saturday 57-72. Full U.S. report on Page 107.

News of special interest to readers in New Jersey will be found on pages 75 to 106.

VOL. CXXI....No. 41,777   © 1972 The New York Times Company   NEW YORK, SUNDAY, JUNE 11, 1972   75¢ beyond 50-mile zone from New York City, except Long Island. Higher in air delivery cities.   NJ   50 CENTS

9.4-BILLION BUDGET ADOPTED FOR CITY; LAYOFFS FORESEEN

Lindsay Requests No Added Taxes, but Warns of Cuts Through Full Attrition

BORROWING PREDICTED

$65-Million From Current Contract Funds Employed to Obviate New Levies

By MARTIN TOLCHIN

Mayor Lindsay yesterday adopted a $9.407-billion city operating budget, abandoning his request for new taxes, but warning of impending layoffs of an undisclosed number of city employes and the continued loss in Police, Fire and Sanitation Department strength.

Mr. Lindsay, caught in a tax revolt by both the Board of Estimate and City Council, which spurned his requests for new property taxes, for final action on a budget that represents one of the smallest percentage increases in the city's recent history — 9.3-per cent over the present $8.6-billion budget. The new budget will be $600-million below the $10-billion "skin-tight," "hold-the-line" budget originally submitted by the Mayor.

'Tightest Restrictions'

In addition to layoffs, the new budget will require continued attrition—the nonreplacement of city employes who leave jobs through death, Hall meeting with his top aides.

"This budget imposes the tightest restrictions on expenditures, so that for the second consecutive year we will have full attrition in the police, fire and sanitation services. Mr. Lindsay said. Yesterday was the deadline for his action on the budget, which he announced after a two-and-a-half-hour City Hall meeting with his top aides.

"This will result in a decrease of 3,500 uniformed personnel from these three essential services" — a condition which will be felt in every neighbor-

Continued on Page 62, Column 4

U.S. Agrees to Aid 2d Avenue Subway

Special to The New York Times

WASHINGTON, June 10—The Federal Government has agreed to help finance New York City's Second Avenue subway, according to officials here.

The decision on the East-Side line, which has been a goal of transit planners since the 1930's, is expected to insure completion of the system within a decade. The system will cost nearly $1-billion.

The Urban Mass Transportation Administration will announce by the end of this month a grant of $25-million for construction of the subway, the officials have revealed.

No formal commitment will be made publicly on the rest of

Continued on Page 45, Column 1

General Bombed in North Before President's Order

Lavelle Relieved of Air Force Command After He Reported Strikes in Early 1972 as 'Protective Reaction'

By SEYMOUR M. HERSH
Special to The New York Times

WASHINGTON, June 10—Gen. John D. Lavelle was relieved as commander of United States Air Force units in Southeast Asia in March and demoted after ordering repeated and unauthorized bombing attacks of military targets in North Vietnam.

He reported the raids to higher headquarters as officially sanctioned "protective-reaction" strikes, military and Congressional sources said in a series of interviews.

Raids Approved in April

The current bombing attacks on the North were approved by President Nixon in April, the month after General Lavelle was relieved as commander by Gen. John D. Ryan, the Air Force Chief of Staff. An official Air Force announcement a month later said that the general had retired "for personal and health reasons."

Last month, more than eight weeks after he was ordered to return to the United States and retire, the White House nominated General Lavelle for retirement at the three-star rank of Lieutenant General. It is believed to be the first time in modern military history that a four-star general or admiral has been nominated to retire at a lower rank.

During the first three months of this year, Administration spokesmen repeatedly insisted

General Lavelle, who as head of the Seventh Air Force was responsible for all Air Force combat flights in Southeast Asia, was said by these sources to have ordered the bombing raids over a three-month period that began in early January.

During those months, these sources said, the targets included airfields, radar sites, missile sites and antiaircraft batteries throughout the southernmost panhandle region of North Vietnam.

Continued on Page 14, Column 1

Gen. John D. Lavelle

Extra Physicians on Duty To Examine Sick Firemen

The Fire Department yesterday made extra doctors available to cope with the recent sharp upturn in the number of firemen reporting sick after fires.

A spokesman for the Fire Department said that in addition to the two doctors always on call who respond to major fires and examine firemen on the scene, an extra two doctors on each shift would be kept on stand-by.

The spokesman, Paul M. O'Brien, said, however, that the sick calls had "tapered off" slightly in the 24-hour period that ended at 8 A.M. yesterday.

A total of 102 fire fighters reported injuries in the 24-hour period, compared with 124 in the preceding 24-hour period, he said.

From 8 A.M. yesterday to midnight, at least another 70 firemen reported themselves sick or injured after fighting fires.

The total included 14 of those called to a two-alarm blaze at 157 Prospect Place in the Park Slope area of Brooklyn and 15

at a two-alarm blaze in a vacant, six-story building at 285 East Third Street on the Lower East Side, according to Mr. O'Brien.

The two department doctors normally on duty examined the 29 firemen on the scene—as they usually do when there are two or more alarms—and granted them "recuperative time on duty in their firehouses," he said. Reports on their ailments have not been filed yet, Mr. O'Brien added.

The upturn in sick calls came as the 2,700-member Uniformed Fire Officers Association complained about the city's refusal to include in the proposed contract specific language on pay differentials with other unions.

Frank LeMuscio, a spokesman for the fire officers, said was unperturbed by the policy of sending doctors to the scene. He asserted that each man should automatically report to a medical officer after a fire.

"We've been trying to get men to do that all the time."

Continued on Page 54, Column 1

WRECKAGE IN RAPID CITY: Autos left in jumbled pile after Rapid Creek flood that struck city in South Dakota

United Press International

BURNS URGES BOND FOR A TAX REFUND

Seeks to Avoid Inflationary Effect Next Spring From Money Overwithheld

By EDWIN L. DALE Jr.
Special to The New York Times

WASHINGTON, June 10—Arthur F. Burns, chairman of the Federal Reserve Board, has suggested to Congress that taxpayers now experiencing significant overwithholding of their Federal income tax, voluntarily or otherwise, be offered next spring a special Treasury bond with a high interest rate that they could choose instead of a tax refund.

Mr. Burns is known to be greatly worried that the massive refunds now in store for next spring, as a result of overwithholding, could contribute to a burst of consumer spending at just the wrong time—when Mr. Burns believes the economy will be in a state of near-boom.

The idea of an economy nearing stage of a dangerous boom—with a revival of strong "classic" inflationary pressure—as early as next year may seem strange after two and one-half years of subpar performance and high unemployment. But some economists, Mr. Burns among them, noting the already distinct pickup so far this year, believe this is a real possibility.

The Federal Reserve chairman made his suggestion this week in a closed session of the House Ways and Means Committee, which was considering legislation on the national debt

Continued on Page 29, Column 1

14-Week Nixon Drive Gets $10-Million

By BEN A. FRANKLIN
Special to The New York Times

WASHINGTON, June 10—The main Republican campaign treasury for the re-election of President Nixon has received more than $10-million in early 1972 gifts from contributors whose identity apparently will never be known, the President's first full Federal election finance statement disclosed today.

At the same time, financial reports by the Democrats showed their accounts depleted by heavy spending in the primaries this spring.

The financial statement of the four principal Nixon fundraising committees, directed by former Secretary of Commerce Maurice H. Stans—the Finance Committee to Re-elect the President, the Media Committee to

Re-elect the President, the Television Committee to Re-elect the President and the Radio Committee to Re-elect the President—were among the last ones filed here today.

They came by messenger at 4:38 P.M., hard on the deadline for all candidates for Federal office to submit campaign spending reports under the new Federal Election Campaign Act and slightly over an hour before the filing clerk was scheduled to close his office.

In signing the reform measure last Feb. 7, President Nixon praised the act as a mechanism for restoring "public confidence in the integrity of the electoral process."

The effective date of the law was April 7. Thus, the names of those who contributed to the party war chests before that

date do not have to be disclosed in the financial statements required by it.

The source of contributions made to Presidential candidates under the pre-April 7 law, the widely discredited Federal Corrupt Practices Act of 1925, could legally be obscured.

Today's Nixon financial statements reported $10.1-million in receipts during the 14 weeks between Jan. 1 and April 7—the period of legal nondisclosure—and only $1.2-million in the eight weeks between April 7 and May 31, the cut-off day for the reports due today.

In February and March Mr. Stans was touring the country and urging Republican contributors to whom anonymity was an important consideration to give early, before the

Continued on Page 59, Column 1

McGovern's Route to the Top

By CHRISTOPHER LYDON
Special to The New York Times

WASHINGTON, June 10—"I honestly don't think there has been a major surprise in the last two years," said Gary Hart, the 34-year-old manager of Senator George McGovern's Presidential campaign, speaking calmly of a revolution in Democratic party politics that caught almost everyone else unawares.

He suffered one dark moment last January, Mr. Hart confessed. Watching the virtual parade of Democratic leaders to endorse Senator Edmund S. Muskie, he had looked ahead to the first primary and pictured himself and Joe Grandmaison, his New Hampshire coordinator, standing alone on a street corner passing out leaflets as

the candidate drove his own car around to the state's college campuses.

But depression passed quickly, and only three days after Mr. McGovern's remarkably strong second-place showing in the March 7 New Hampshire primary, Mr. Hart finished reconnaissance of Florida and declared unemotionally: "It's all over. Ed Muskie has got to get off the ground here and he isn't doing it. John Lindsay has got to get off the ground and he isn't doing it either. That means the race through the

rest of the primaries is going to be us against Hubert Humphrey, and that means we're going to win."

George McGovern's candidacy was still being widely discounted three months ago when the feeling of anticlimax settled on Mr. Hart. Even now the blossoming of George McGovern—a baldish, former minister and rural radical who campaigned for a full year without exceeding 5 per cent in the Democratic preference polls and is now on the verge of winning the nomination—is generally considered mysterious. How did he do it?

Some of the critical elements in the emergence of this onetime 500-to-1 long shot were beyond his control, including the acceleration of the war in Vietnam at the culmination of his all-important drive in Wisconsin; the heavy damage that Gov. George C. Wallace of Alabama inflicted on the Demo-

Continued on Page 56, Column 3

Riva Ridge Wins

Riva Ridge won the $155,900 Belmont Stakes yesterday at Belmont Park by seven lengths. Ruritania ran second and Cloudy Dawn third as 54,635 spectators watched the 104th running of the race for 3-year-old thoroughbreds. Riva Ridge paid $5.20, $4.80 and $3.80 for $2 across the board. Details in Section 5.

FLOOD KILLS 155 IN SOUTH DAKOTA; 5,000 HOMELESS

Rapid City Area Smashed as Creeks Swollen by Rains Roar Out of Black Hills

A LAKE DAM GIVES WAY

Injured Fill Two Hospitals —500 Feared Missing in National Disaster Zone

By ANTHONY RIPLEY
Special to The New York Times

RAPID CITY, S. D., June 10—More than 155 persons were reported dead today and 5,000 were homeless in a flash flood that swept through this city and several smaller towns on the eastern edge of the Black Hills last night.

More than 500 residents were believed missing and property damage was estimated at between $80-million and $120-million.

There was no word on the fate of 4,000 tourists believed to be camping in the Black Hills this weekend.

The number of dead was expected to climb as reports from isolated hill communities came in.

Looting Reported

A 9 P.M. curfew was declared after reports of looting and gunfire in the city.

Mayor Donald V. Barnett said that at least 10 per cent of the buildings in this city of 43,000 had been totally destroyed and "well over" 50 per cent damaged.

City and civil defense officials had no count of the injured, who filled both of the city's two hospitals. Many lay on mattresses in the halls.

The flood, triggered by exceptionally heavy rains that varied from more than two to seven inches in a thunderstorm that struck the Black Hills last night, came in two waves, the Mayor said. The first came between 9:30 and 10 P.M. and the second at midnight, when Canyon Lake dam in a city park gave way.

Explosions and Fires

Ruptured gas mains and felled power lines touched off explosions and fires across the city. For a time, all electric and gas service was shut off after water mains for fear that the water was contaminated.

President Nixon, after conferring with his disaster relief aide in Washington, declared the area a national disaster area, making it eligible for emergency Federal aid.

Also, Gov. Richard F. Kneip, in the state capital at Pierre, declared the city a disaster area and ordered 1,000 Air National Guard members at a training center just outside of the city to help in the rescue. Regular Army troops were

Continued on Page 64, Column 5

Slaughter in Burundi: How Ethnic Conflict Erupted

By MARVINE HOWE
Special to The New York Times

BUJUMBURA, Burundi, June 9—This nation is just beginning to realize the extent of the slaughter that has taken place here over the last six weeks in struggles between the country's two major ethnic groups.

The complete story of an attempted coup at the end of April, and the counteroffensive that followed, cannot be told since only official sources can be quoted and they are clearly biased. Other sources, as well as foreigners, are still generally terrorized and reluctant to jeopardize lives of friends or risk expulsion. However, a six-day visit to Burundi has produced a plausible account of the catastrophe out of a web of rumors, lies and contradictions.

Clear statistics on the extent of the massacres are hard to come by. Information is limited because movement has been severely curtailed by official barricades and curfews. Foreigners must have travel permits and these are very difficult to obtain. Above all, most people are terrorized and re-

Continued on Page 3, Column 1

Hutus in Kiganda listen as a Government official announces that rebellion has ended

The New York Times/Marvine Howe

Community Plans Bring New Hope for Retarded

By B. DRUMMOND AYRES Jr.
Special to The New York Times

OMAHA, June 10—Two years ago, Mike S. was just another severely retarded 6-year-old staring vacantly at the drab walls in one of the jam-packed wards at the state home in Beatrice, a farm town about 100 miles southwest of here.

He had been in the 1,400-bed institution since shortly after birth. He was still in diapers and could not dress himself, speak sentences or walk without wobbling. There was very little money or manpower for treating him, Beatrice being a typical state home. And everyone expected him to remain there until death.

Today, however, Mike is out of Beatrice, living in a comfortable "hostel" in Omaha with half a dozen

other retarded children. He is toilet-trained, can talk and sing, dresses himself, moves about without difficulty and goes to special classes in reading and writing.

What happened?

The answer lies in a quiet metamorphosis that is slowly changing the whole approach to treating mental retardation, an illness that affects more than six million Americans—or three of every hundred—and annually costs the country some $5.5-billion in lost productivity and abnormal hospital expenses.

It is not any breakthrough in medicine, for there is still no cure-all for retardation

Continued on Page 44, Column 4

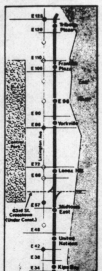

The New York Times/June 11, 1972

DO YOU KNOW ANY IMPORTANT MAN IN BUSINESS WHO DOES NOT READ FORBES MAGAZINE?—ADVT.

LANN—BIRTH & and JOSEPH. Happy 50th Wedding Anniversary son, L.—ADVT.

Flood Ravages Rapid City, S.D.; Death Toll High

Continued From Page 1, Col. 8

Fort Carson, Colo., were also dispatched, and Air Force personnel at Ellsworth Air Force Base, a Strategic Air Command post near Rapid City were bringing in tanks of drinking water.

Witnesses to the two floods said that water swirled into the city from two canyons to the west, tumbling cars end over end.

Homes were moved off their foundations, some totally collapsed and others were thrown across highways. The main path of destruction was in a belt about a block wide on either side of Rapid Creek, which winds through this resort town.

Senator George McGovern of South Dakota was briefed in Washington on the disaster throughout the day and announced that he would fly to his home state at 6:45 A.M. tomorrow.

Also in Washington, President Nixon ordered his chief aide for disaster relief to expediate all appropriate assistance.

"The President has been following closely reports from Rapid City and is deeply disturbed at the loss of life and widespread destruction that has occurred," Mr. Nixon's press secretary, Ronald L. Ziegler, said.

Like Flaming Barges

At the West Side Trailer Court just off Main Street here, the water wiped out more than a score of mobile homes. Other mobile homes, their propane gas tanks set afire by fallen power lines, floated off into the flood waters like flaming barges.

The tide of water was the result of freak weather conditions, according to Elroy Balke, regional hydrologist at the Weather Service's Kansas City Office. At one small town outside Rapid City, he said, seven inches of rain fell in six hours.

Associated Press

WHERE A HOME ONCE STOOD: Water-filled foundation of house in Rapid City, struck by flood yesterday. House, ripped off base, lies ruined in background. Broken gas mains and power lines caused explosions and fires in area.

The New York Times/June 11, 1972

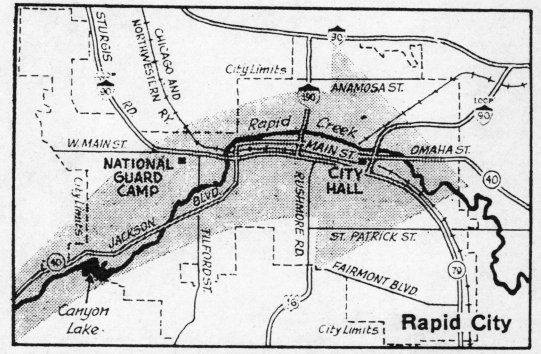

Floodwaters surged through city by way of Rapid Creek

"The probability of that much rainfall and those particular weather conditions can be expected once in a hundred years," he said.

The first of the two big waves came from water running off drainage areas in the low mountains to the west and then rushing into Lime and Rapid Creeks. The two creeks join in Rapid City and Sioux Park, just below Canyon Lake dam.

Canyon Lake dam was holding back more water from other streams.

But at midnight the dam broke, releasing a wall of water into the town. It was this second, larger wave that did the most damage, according to residents.

Below the dam, the creek follows an "S"-shaped bed through Sioux Park and the city. The flood waters ignored the creek banks, however, and raced directly across the park, a shopping center and the city.

In its wake it left a jumble of cars, machinery, house trailers, homes and trees.

The flood, however, did not take the townspeople completely by surprise.

According to Mayor Barnett, he received a call from an unidentified man shortly before the first wave struck. The man told the Mayor that he was 18 miles west of Rapid City and said, "Mr. Mayor, it looks to me like you've got 20 minutes."

The Mayor said that he immediately went on the local radio station and sent out the police with orders to warn people along the creek to leave their homes.

Local radio stations broadcast repeated emergency messages through the day: "If you find a body, do not touch it. Call." "Stay in your homes and do not impede emergency vehicle traffic." "Don't drink the water." "Boats are needed immediately.

"Now we're worried about water contamination," said Donald Kosmicki," a spokesman for St. John McNamara Hospital. He said the city had shut off the water supply to check for contamination, and that hospitals had been notified to conserve water.

The western section of the city was hit hardest, with floodwaters reaching depths of 10 feet at some points. Homes in the Cleighborn and Canyon Lake areas were either washed away or severly damaged.

Jerry Mashek, an editor of The Rapid City Journal, who toured the city today, described scenes of devastation across Rapid City. The first wall of water, he said, "sounded like a freight train in the night."

"All the News That's Fit to Print"

The New York Times

LATE CITY EDITION

Weather: Occasional rain today; chance of rain tonight, tomorrow. Temp. range: today 62-71; Sunday 64-68. Temp.-Hum. Index yesterday 65. Full U.S. report on Page 66.

VOL. CXXI . . No. 41,785 NEW YORK, MONDAY, JUNE 19, 1972 15 CENTS

© 1972 The New York Times Company

SOVIET PRESIDENT SAYS PEACE TALKS WILL RESUME SOON

Podgorny Asserts Moscow Will Do All Possible to Help Resolve Vietnam Issue

ENDS 3-DAY HANOI VISIT

Kremlin Leader Is Confident During Calcutta Stop—U.S. Officials Voice Interest

By The Associated Press

CALCUTTA, India, June 18—President Nikolai V. Podgorny of the Soviet Union, stopping off here on his way home from a three-day visit to Hanoi, predicted today that the Paris peace talks would resume soon and indicated that the Soviet Union would work to insure their success.

Asked at a news conference during a 30-minute stopover here if the Paris talks would be resumed, Mr. Podgorny said: "Yes, soon."

"The Soviet Union will do everything possible for a de-escalation of the Vietnam war," he said.

Talks Suspended by U.S.

His remarks came four days after the United States rejected another Communist request to resume the peace talks. The Paris meetings have been suspended since May 4 when the United States delegation charged the Communists with failing to negotiate seriously.

[In Washington, officials expressed interest in the forecast by the Soviet President of an early resumption of the Paris talks but advised against undue optimism. Page 8.]

It is thought that President Podgorny may have succeeded in getting Hanoi to agree to United States terms for reopening the peace talks. Reports from Paris last week said that one possible United States condition would be a return to Paris of the chief North Vietnamese delegate, Xuan Thuy, from Hanoi.

The Soviet leader made his stopover here as Mr. Thuy's special adviser, Le Duc Tho, flew back to Hanoi after conferring with the Chinese Premier, Chou En-lai, in Peking. Mr. Tho left Peking on the eve of the arrival there of President Nixon's national security adviser, Henry A. Kissinger, for a four-day visit.

"Consultations" Planned

The announced purpose of Mr. Kissinger's trip is to have "concrete consultations with Chinese leaders to further the normalization of relations between the People's Republic of China and the United States and continue the exchange of views on issues of common interest." But it is considered likely that the war in Vietnam will be discussed.

Holding a rare news conference, the 69-year-old President Podgorny appeared ebullient

Continued on Page 9, Column 1

United Press International

SCENE OF AIR DISASTER: Tail section of British European Airways jet that crashed after take-off lies on a field near Heathrow Airport, London. Man on ladder searches for box with flight recorder. Plane apparently broke up when it crashed into field.

All 118 Killed in Worst British Air Crash

By ALVIN SHUSTER
Special to The New York Times

LONDON, June 18—A British European Airways jet plunged into a field minutes after taking off from Heathrow airport today, killing all 118 aboard. It was Britain's worst air disaster.

The Trident-1 aircraft, heading for Brussels, fell near Staines, just four miles from Heathrow. One survivor, pulled from the wreckage, died later in the hospital.

The plane, its wheels up, apparently broke up when it crashed into the field. Eyewitnesses said the tail section snapped off and the rest of the fuselage plowed another 50 yards up to a line of trees.

"The pilot got his undercarriage up," said a spokesman for the British Airline Pilots Association. "This indicates he made a good take-off. But he landed with no undercarriage and it's a complete mystery what could have gone wrong."

Of the 118 killed, 109 were passengers, including an infant, and nine crew members.

LONDON
Heathrow Airport
Wraysbury Res.
King George VI Res.
Staines Res.
Staines
Thames River
Queen Mary Res.
Chertsy
Sunbury
0 2 MI.

The New York Times/June 19, 1972

The full passenger list was withheld tonight, but the airline said that among those aboard 29 were Americans, 29 Belgians, 28 Britons and 12 Irish.

Among the victims were several prominent Irish businessmen who were going to Brussels on Common Market matters. The pilot, Capt. Stanley Key, 51 years old, was one of the line's most experienced captains.

It was an unusually full plane for a Sunday Brussels flight. Officials said some passengers might have been trying to beat the worldwide pilots strike scheduled for tomorrow morning in protest against assertedly lax international measures against air

Continued on Page 6, Column 4

McGovern Gains Backing; State Will Vote Tomorrow

6 States and Puerto Rico Choose Delegates

By R. W. APPLE Jr.

Senator George McGovern of South Dakota picked up sizable blocs of delegates at Democratic conventions in four mountain states and in Connecticut, North Dakota and Puerto Rico this weekend.

Experienced Democratic professionals at the conventions and in Washington, though still perturbed by Mr. McGovern's economic proposals, which some of them consider radical and ill-conceived, were prepared to concede him the party's Presidential nomination.

Some aides to Senators Edmund S. Muskie of Maine and Hubert H. Humphrey of Minnesota, while maintaining publicly that they still expected the South Dakotan to fall short, said privately that the two were remaining in the race mainly in the hope of persuading Mr. McGovern to moderate some of his positions and thus foster party unity.

Mr. McGovern moved his delegate-vote total to 1,091.55 at the seven weekend meetings. The mountain states where he scored successes were Colorado, Montana, Utah and Idaho.

More Votes Coming

In tomorrow's New York primary, Mr. McGovern is expected to gain at least 200 of the 248 delegates to be elected.

Next weekend, he is expected to gain 24 more votes among the 30 to be allotted by the New York State Democratic Committee, two more when Nebraska chooses its national committee members and eight at the Delaware convention.

Some new commitments from formerly uncommitted delegates and from supporters of Mr. Muskie are expected after the New York balloting. But even without those, Mr. McGovern

Continued on Page 22, Column 3

Major Democratic Races Enliven Primary Here

By FRANK LYNN

Eight major contests for Congressional nominations, the first primary for the State Court of Appeals and scores of legislative contests highlight the statewide Democratic primary tomorrow.

The primary also has national significance, with Senator George McGovern favored to win against scattered opposition at least 200 of the state's 278 delegates to the Democratic National Convention. A total of 248 of those delegates will be elected in Congressional districts tomorrow and the remaining 30 will be appointed by the Democratic State Committee next Saturday.

The Republican primary will be considerably quieter, with a score of contests for Congressional and legislative nominations, but few of them of any major significance.

The polls will be open from 3 P.M. to 10 P.M. in the city and from noon to 9 P.M. in the rest of the state.

Confusion Seen Here

Polls are opened in primaries only in districts where there is a contest, but because of the contest for the Democratic nominations for the Court of Appeals judgeships, which are statewide posts, every polling place in the state will be open.

There could be some confusion over polling places in the city, however. The Board of Elections, in an economy move, has consolidated many polling places, so voters may have to go to different polling places than in the past and in many cases they are farther from their homes than the old ones. Each of the 2 million affected voters is supposed to have

Continued on Page 24, Column 1

Associated Press

CALLS FOR SHUTDOWN: Capt. J. J. O'Donnell, U.S. pilots' association leader. He asked in TV interview for members to stay home.

GLOBAL STOPPAGE SNARLS AIRLINES; U.S. PILOTS CURBED

Burger Upholds Order by Appeals Bench Forbidding Americans to Join Strike

UNION CHIEF IS DEFIANT

Says Members Will Stay Off Jobs Today Despite Any Step by Supreme Court

By RICHARD WITKIN

A 24-hour global work stoppage called for today by pilots and maintenance men to press for more stringent measures against hijacking has disrupted major portions of airline operations.

How extensive the shutdown of international and domestic flights would be on this country's airlines remained uncertain even as the 2 A.M. deadline for the beginning of the strike passed this morning. But many foreign airlines had already canceled flights, including those out of New York.

At 5:45 P.M., Chief Justice Warren E. Burger upheld a temporary order by the United States Court of Appeals for the District of Columbia prohibiting members of the Air Line Pilots Association from joining the stoppage.

However, the American union's president, Capt. J. J. O'Donnell, who earlier called on his members to stay home today whatever the Supreme Court decided, said, "There is no way under our control that we can roll back the suspension of service."

Some Refuse to Strike

Pilots of two of the nation's largest carriers, United Air Lines and American Airlines, were on record as refusing to participate in the shutdown, but there appeared to be sizable rebellious elements in the United group.

In the rest of the world, there were no significant court actions, and the picture was much clearer.

"The stoppage is very much on," said a spokesman for the International Federation of Air Line Pilots Associations, which called for the one-day demonstration. The spokesman, Terry Middleton, said that the shutdown, scheduled for 2 A.M. today, New York time, was being supported by 40 to 45 of the federation's 64 units in 62 countries.

The outlook for air travelers in the United States, as of last night, was mixed.

Early this morning, officers

Continued on Page 26, Column 3

DEMOCRATIC RAID TIED TO REALTOR

Alleged Leader Said to Have G.O.P. Links and to Have Aided C.I.A. on Cuba

By TAD SZULC
Special to The New York Times

WASHINGTON, June 18—The apparent leader of five men arrested yesterday for breaking into the headquarters of the Democratic National Committee here was identified today as an affluent Miami real estate man with important Republican party links in Florida.

He was also said to have been one of the top planners of the Central Intelligence Agency's abortive invasion of Cuba in 1961.

Five men were arrested at gunpoint in the raid. The police said that they possessed sophisticated eavesdropping devices and photographic equipment.

The five alleged raiders are being held at the District of Columbia jail. Private and official sources who know the five suspects and their background said that the leader was Cuban-born Bernard L. Barker, who, under the code name of "Macho," acted for the C.I.A. in planning the Bay of Pigs operation.

One of the other men arrested is James W. McCord, a former employe of the C.I.A. who is currently employed as a security agent by both the Re-

Continued on Page 20, Column 1

South Vietnamese Troops Raid 2 Enemy-Held Areas

By CHARLES MOHR
Special to The New York Times

SAIGON, South Vietnam, Monday, June 19—South Vietnamese troops have raided two areas occupied by North Vietnamese forces, according to military spokesmen.

A large force of South Vietnamese marines crossed the Mychanh River line into Quangtri Province and reported killing 36 North Vietnamese by early yesterday afternoon. The South Vietnamese put their own losses at one man killed and four wounded.

[American fighter-bombers resumed attacks Monday above the 20th Parallel in North Vietnam after a four-day suspension during the visit to Hanoi of President Nikolai V. Podgorny of the Soviet Union, United States military sources disclosed, The Associated Press reported.]

The South Vietnamese advance was described by a military spokesman as a "raid," indicating that the marines would not try to hold the five-mile-deep salient they had opened northeast of Hailang.

Quangtri, the northernmost province in South Vietnam, has been occupied by the North Vietnamese since May 1. Marines have previously raided the province twice and then pulled back. The size of the present force was not announced but was understood to be about 3,000 men.

In another move Saturday, about 100 men of the South Vietnamese 23d Division were flown by helicopter into the Central Highlands town of Tancanh, north of Kontum, which the North Vietnamese had overrun earlier.

The raiding force fought its way through the town, freeing nine South Vietnamese prisoners of war and picking up 58

Continued on Page 10, Column 1

HONG KONG RAINS TAKE MANY LIVES

100 Feared Dead, Thousands Homeless After Landslides

Special to The New York Times

HONG KONG, Monday, June 19—More than 100 people were feared dead and thousands were homeless in Hong Kong today following three days of torrential rain that sent hundreds of tons of earth and rock sliding down the steep hillsides on which much of this British colony is built.

Most of the dead lost their lives in two major landslides yesterday—a chain-reaction incident that affected four buildings, and the collapse of a huge section of a hillside onto 78 huts providing temporary housing for about 400 people.

In the last three days more than 25 inches of rain have fallen on Hong Kong. Early today, as more rain was forecast, hundreds of workers, in-

Continued on Page 3, Column 1

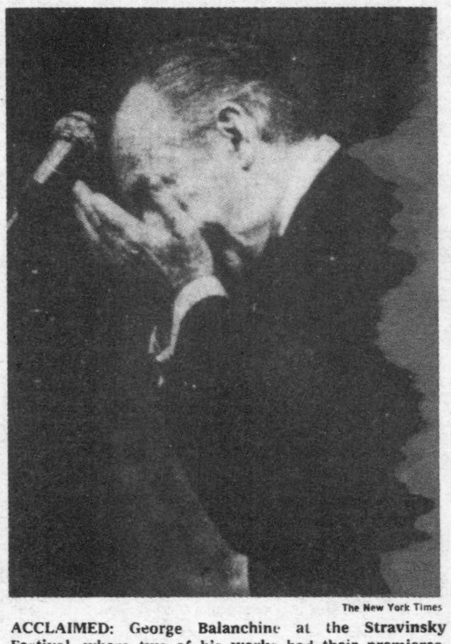

The New York Times

ACCLAIMED: George Balanchine at the Stravinsky Festival, where two of his works had their premieres.

Children's-Book Writer Is Slain In Landmark House in 'Village'

Irma Simonton Black, a writer and editor of children's books, was found stabbed to death yesterday in the Greenwich Village landmark house she had lived in for more than 30 years.

Mrs. Black, who was 66 years old, was to retire in August as chairman of publications and communications for the Bank Street College of Education. She had been on the faculty of the college for 40 years and had created the Bank Street readers, a series of school books in which the traditional Dick and Jane prototypes were replaced by urban children in city settings.

Mrs. Black's husband, James Hammond Black, a partner in the Wall Street law firm of Sowers, Herrick & Black, was away over the weekend attending the wedding of a niece in Savannah, Ga. He returned home two hours after the murder was discovered at 2 P.M.

At that time two neighbors, whose suspicions had been aroused by a broken basement window, went through the house at 26 Jones Street off Bleecker Street.

The neighbors, Mrs. Hope Dibbell and Tony Buttita, told the police that they had found the door to Mrs. Black's third-floor apartment open and that the writer's body, clad in pajamas, lay in the living room.

The police surmised that the killer was a burglar. They said the murder weapon was a fork from a carving set. They said Mrs. Black, who was stabbed in the left shoulder, had apparently resisted the intruder.

They also reported that closets and desks in two other apartments in the building had been opened and ransacked. On the second-floor landing, the police said, neighbors found a pair of men's boots that may have belonged to the intruder.

The police theorized that the murderer had fled through the skylight in the Black apartment, which was found unlatched.

Detectives had not yet established the time of Mrs. Black's death, but they said she was murdered some time after 8 P.M. Friday, when she

Continued on Page 37, Column 4

Associated Press

SOMETHING NEW: Sporting a mustache, President Nikolai V. Podgorny of the Soviet Union makes stopover in Calcutta, India. He returned to Moscow after Hanoi visit.

City Ballet Triumphs in Stravinsky Fete

By CLIVE BARNES

So it has started! Last night at the New York State Theater, the New York City Ballet, in front of a quite extraordinarily glamorous audience (tout New York, as they might say in Paris), opened its week-long Stravinsky Festival. It opened it with an appreciation of times past and a recognition of times future.

During these performances there will be some 20 world premieres, to say nothing of revivals. The message—bright and clarion clear—is simply that Stravinsky lives.

For the entire history of New York City Ballet the company has enjoyed a special relationship with Stravinsky. Now in celebration of his 90th birthday, which would have been on Saturday, George Balanchine, Jerome Robbins, John Taras and the dancers and choreographers of the company are making one creative effort to achieve a living monument to a man who has indirectly meant so much to American dance. Here and now is a danced library of Stravinsky scores.

In an opening speech, the company's general director, Lincoln Kirstein, said: "The last six days have been a miniature Normandy landing." He then paid tribute to some of the company's founding fathers, the strange but potent consortium of Serge Diaghilev, Newbold Morris, Morton Baum and Nelson Rockefeller.

Mr. Balanchine had more than a speech for us. He had an unannounced treat.

In 1902, two years before Mr. Balanchine was born (but, as George said, "he wrote it for me without knowing it") Stravinsky composed a now-lost sonata.

Efforts were made to get a score from the Soviet Union but to no avail. Then Mrs. André Malraux, who had seen and remembered a facsimile of the score, offered to play the second movement, a scherzo, from memory.

It was this two-and-a-half minute 70-year-old fragment that got the festival under way, with Mrs. Malraux playing and Sara Leland and John Clifford dancing. It was a small, sweet taste of the evening to come, an unexpected hors d'oeuvre to a banquet.

This is already a remarkable season. On this first night, apart from the trimmings and the speeches, the company offered one minor-major work by Mr. Robbins, two major-major works by Mr. Balanchine and a refurbished, and much improved revival of the Balanchine/

Continued on Page 40, Column 1

Nicklaus Wins Open

Jack Nicklaus won the United States Open golf championship for the third time yesterday with a final-round 74 for 290, beating Bruce Crampton of Australia by three strokes. It was Nicklaus's 13th major title, tying the record of Bobby Jones. Details on Page 43.

NEWS INDEX

	Page		Page
Bills in Wash.	36	Movies	38-41
Books	30-31	Music	38-41
Bridge	30	Obituaries	36
Business	49, 51	Op-Ed	33
Crossword	31	Society	29
Editorials	32	Sports	43-48
Family/Style	28	Theaters	38-41
Financial	49-54	Transportation	66
Going Out Guide	38	TV and Radio	67
Letters	32	U. N. Proceedings	2
Man in the News	26	Weather	66

News Summary and Index, Page 35

Only 1 day to go before the birth of the new WORLD: a magazine addressed to the life of the mind. ADVT.

All 118 Aboard Killed Near London in Britain's Worst Air Crash

Wide World Photos

Part of the fuselage of the British European Airways Trident airliner after the plane crashed shortly after taking off from London's Heathrow Airport on a flight to Brussels.

Continued From Page 1, Col. 4

piracy. The crash, the first by a passenger-carrying Trident in its eight years of service, was the third major air tragedy in five days. A Japan Air Lines plane crashed in flames on Wednesday on its approach to New Delhi, killing 87. And, the next day, a Cathay Pacific plane with 80 aboard plunged into the Central Highlands of South Vietnam.

The three-engine Trident took off from Heathrow in dull and rainy weather shortly after 5 P.M. and crashed just a few hundred yards from the main shopping street of Staines. The site was about four miles from the end of the runway.

"Nothing was heard from the captain which would indicate anything was wrong with the aircraft," said Henry Marking, chairman of the airline.

Rescue workers and investigators worked through the wreckage tonight in a light rain. Bodies of the victims were carried on stretchers to the surrounding grass and then moved to a temporary mortuary at Heathrow Airport.

Sightseers contributed to the chaos by trying to get to the crash scene. Roads were blocked for miles around Staines and those who reached the area were asked through police loudspeakers to leave.

Most Died on Impact

Rescue workers and clergymen who rushed to the area said most passengers apparently died on impact. A policeman said that he pulled a young girl from the plane alive but she died before an ambulance could arrive. A passenger identified as a businessman from Dublin was rushed to a nearby hospital, but died there of head injuries.

"I heard a plane circling overhead and then there was a sound as though the engines were cutting out," said one local resident. "There was a thud like a clap of thunder and the windows in the house shook."

Airline officials said tonight that the so-called "black box" flight recorder had been recovered and turned over to Government investigators. They said that the tapes would be replayed quickly to see if the cause could be determined.

Until today the worst air disaster in Britain had been that of March, 1950, when an Avro Tudor V, carrying passengers from a Rugby game in Belfast, crashed in Glamorgan, Wales, killing 80. Last October a British European Airways Vanguard plunged into a field in Belgium, killing all 63 aboard.

"All the News That's Fit to Print"

The New York Times

LATE CITY EDITION

Weather: Partly cloudy today; fair tonight. Mostly sunny tomorrow. Temp. range: today 67-79; Monday 70-86. Temp.-Hum. Index yesterday 71. Full U.S. report on Page 69.

VOL. CXXI . . . No. 41,842 NEW YORK, TUESDAY, AUGUST 15, 1972 15 CENTS

© 1972 The New York Times Company

The New York Times/Barton Silverman

New York District Attorneys meeting with Michael Whiteman, counsel to Governor Rockefeller. From left: Thomas J. Mackell, Queens; Frank S. Hogan, Manhattan; Eugene Gold, Brooklyn; Mr. Whiteman; John M. Braisted Jr., Staten Island, and Burton B. Roberts, the Bronx.

Nixon Prods Auto Makers To Cancel '73 Price Rise

Rumsfeld Holds Meeting at White House to Ask Withdrawal of Plans

By EDWARD COWAN
Special to The New York Times

WASHINGTON, Aug. 14—The White House has intervened directly with the automobile industry in an attempt to get the four manufacturers to withdraw their proposed price increases on 1973 model cars.

Donald Rumsfeld, director of the Cost of Living Council, met today at the White House with representatives of American Motors, Chrysler and General Motors. He is scheduled to talk with a Ford executive tomorrow.

Associated Press
Donald Rumsfeld

The White House let it be known that Mr. Rumsfeld had arranged the meetings at the direction of President Nixon. A White House spokesman stopped short of saying that Mr. Rumsfeld had asked the companies not to raise prices, but other authoritative sources said that the purpose of the meetings was "to talk them out of price increases, if possible."

Increases Proposed

The Chrysler Corporation, the Ford Motor Company and the General Motors Corporation have applied to the Price Commission for increases averaging $85 to $91 a car to cover costs incurred in meeting Federal emission-control and safety standards, particularly the requirement for stronger bumpers.

The American Motors Corporation has asked for $78 to cover such costs, plus $68 for what it said were other cost increases.

The meetings marked one of the few instances of Administration "jawboning" since the Phase Two program of wage-price controls began last November. In the spring, food-chain executives were summoned to Washington twice to discuss prices of meat and other food.

The fact that the White House resorted to this sort of pressure against auto prices was regarded by some observers as suggesting that the Price Commission could find no ground to disapprove the proposed increases.

A public commitment by the industry to hold the price line and absorb any cost increases out of profits, which are up sharply this year, would be an important victory for the Administration's campaign to dis-

Continued on Page 69, Column 7

KISSINGER HOLDS ANOTHER SESSION WITH HANOI AIDES

Meets With Thuy and Tho Third Time in Paris, Then Flies to Switzerland

DETAILS ARE WITHHELD

Talk Comes at a Time of Greater Polemics Between Hanoi and Washington

By BERNARD GWERTZMAN
Special to The New York Times

WASHINGTON, Aug. 14—Henry A. Kissinger, President Nixon's adviser on national security, held another private meeting with North Vietnam's negotiators in Paris today, the White House announced.

He then flew to Switzerland to help celebrate his parents' 50th wedding anniversary. The White House said he would leave Switzerland tomorrow, but declined to say where he would go from there.

The latest private Paris meeting—the third in a month—came at a time of increased public polemics between Hanoi and Washington and an intensification of political debate in this country over the Nixon Administration's handling of the Vietnam negotiations.

Details Withheld

The White House gave no further details on the session, other than that Mr. Kissinger met with Le Duc Tho, the Hanoi Politburo member charged with Vietnam negotiations, and Xuan Thuy, the regular North Vietnamese delegate to the semipublic sessions between North Vietnam and the Vietcong on one side and the United States and South Vietnam on the other. The 155th such session is scheduled for Thursday, with no apparent sign of a breakthrough.

Ronald L. Ziegler, the White House press secretary, told newsmen of the Paris meeting today while it was going on and said that Mr. Kissinger would then go to Laax-Flims near Zurich. His parents, Mr. and Mrs. Louis Kissinger of New York, were vacationing there.

Newsmen told Mr. Ziegler that his silence on Mr. Kissinger's ultimate destination would lead to speculation that he might go back to Paris for another session. But Mr. Ziegler refused to elaborate on the travel plans.

The session today was Mr. Kissinger's 16th in a series that dates from 1969. The first 12 were completely secret and

Continued on Page 4, Column 3

BURGER ASKS END OF 3-JUDGE COURTS

Also Appeals to Congress for 'Impact Statements' Before Passing Laws

By FRED P. GRAHAM
Special to The New York Times

SAN FRANCISCO, Aug. 14—Chief Justice Warren E. Burger called upon Congress today to abolish three-judge Federal District courts. Congress created them 62 years ago as a states' right measure but the result has been that the Federal courts have been loaded with additional work.

He also urged Congress to avoid adding to the Federal courts' work burden, by refusing to pass any laws creating new Federal crimes or civil actions without first preparing a "court impact statement" showing how many more judgeships should be created to handle the new cases.

This would be patterned after the environmental impact statements that Federal agencies must prepare before they may approve roads, dams or other projects that could affect the environment.

The Chief Justice's remarks, delivered at the San Francisco Hilton Hotel in his third annual "State of the Judiciary" speech to the American Bar Association, which is holding its annual convention here, were the most direct proposals he has made to Congress since he became the nation's chief judicial officer in 1969.

Chief Justice Burger began his addresses amid some speculation that Congress would invite him to make an annual address before a joint session, patterned after the President's State-of-the-Union speech.

His two prior speeches, delivered before the unofficial bar association forum, were mostly couched in general terms, steering away from direct advice to Congress.

But no invitation for a Con-

Continued on Page 55, Column 1

Police Say a Hired Killer Slew 2 in Error

By EMANUEL PERLMUTTER

Two businessmen shot to death Friday night in an upper East Side restaurant were apparently gunned down by a hired killer who mistook them for members of the Mafia family of Joseph A. Colombo Sr., Police Commissioner Patrick V. Murphy said yesterday.

Mr. Murphy said at a news conference at the West 82d Street police station that the two slain men and two business associates wounded in the shooting were standing at a place at the bar that had been vacated a few minutes earlier by the four Mafia members.

He said the four mobsters had retired to a table in the rear of the restaurant, the Neopolitan Noodle, 320 East 79th Street, and were sitting there when the businessmen were shot.

The shootings, he said, were undoubtedly a continuation of the gang warfare between the Mafia families of Joseph Colombo Sr. and the late Joseph (Crazy Joe) Gallo, who was slain earlier this year in a Little Italy restaurant in Manhattan. The Gallo slaying is believed to have been in retaliation for the critical wounding of Colombo last year in Columbus Circle.

Innocent People Victims

"This was a terrible crime, a frightening crime," Commissioner Murphy said. "It is a materialization of what I have been fearing, that as a result of organized crime violence innocent persons could be killed."

One of the gunman's targets, Mr. Murphy said, was Alphonse (Little Allie) Persico, the elder brother of Carmine (The Snake) Persico, a leader of the Colombo crime family who is now serving a 14-year sentence in Illinois for interstate theft.

Carmine Persico's son, also named Alphonse Persico, was also seated at the table, Mr. Murphy said, as was Jerry Langella, a bodyguard to Little Allie. A fourth man at the table was not identified by the Commissioner.

Mr. Murphy pointed out that there had been more than a score of gangland killings in the last two years and said they were part of a power struggle in the underworld. Thomas Eboli, one of the top Mafia leaders in the metropolitan area, was slain on a Brooklyn street last month in an as yet unsolved murder.

The commissioner said that, in an effort to get the "higher-ups" in organized crime, he

Continued on Page 22, Column 3

MURPHY SUPPORTS KNAPP'S PROPOSAL

Asserts a State Prosecutor of Corruption in the City 'Would Be Great Help'

By JAMES M. MARKHAM

Police Commissioner Patrick V. Murphy yesterday endorsed the Knapp Commission's recommendation that Governor Rockefeller appoint a special deputy attorney general to prosecute official corruption, while the city's five District Attorneys met with the Governor's counsel to oppose it.

The five District Attorneys met for an hour and 40 minutes with Michael Whiteman, counsel to the Governor, and marshaled their arguments against the suggestion that a citywide prosecutor was needed to investigate corruption among the police, prosecutors and judges.

Ronald Maiorana, the Governor's press secretary, said Mr. Whiteman, having conferred last week with Whitman Knapp, the lawyer who led the initial inquiry into police corruption, would report the views of "both sides" to the Governor. Mr. Whiteman asked the District Attorneys to submit records of indictments, convictions and current investigations in the area of official corruption.

But Mr. Maiorana gave no indication of the thinking of the Governor on the matter. Mr. Rockefeller returned early

Continued on Page 40, Column 3

Clark Says North Vietnam May Free a Few P.O.W.'s

By WALLACE TURNER
Special to The New York Times

SAN FRANCISCO, Aug. 14—Ramsey Clark, a former United States Attorney General, said here today that he thought that a few American prisoners of war would be released soon by North Vietnam.

Mr. Clark's statement was made at a news conference following a two-week visit to North Vietnam that ended Saturday.

"I urged them to release some prisoners, and I say frankly I think they will—a few, I don't know when," he said. "But what they tell you—and you know I have a little difficulty arguing with it—is 'we can't release pilots when pilots are bombing our children.'"

Mr. Clark chose his words carefully when asked whether American military commanders had attempted deliberately to destroy the system of dikes in North Vietnam.

"I saw damage to dikes, sluices and canals of a substantial nature at least six places," he said in the news conference at the St. Francis Hotel here. "At a couple of places, it was evident that it was a massive assault. At the time I saw it, there were no military targets there."

He said also that he recognized that such targets, perhaps antiaircraft batteries, could have been moved away before he saw the dike damage.

In a 40-minute statement and in the 20 minutes of questioning that followed, Mr. Clark repeatedly attacked the bombing on moral grounds. He said he had seen a hospital that was destroyed by bombs between last December, when, he said, it was

Continued on Page 2, Column 4

156 Are Killed in Air Crash In a Suburb of East Berlin

By Reuters

BERLIN, Aug. 14—An East German airliner crashed in a suburb of East Berlin today and all 156 people aboard were killed, the East German press agency reported.

EAST GERMANY
TEGEL AIRPORT
West Berlin
East Berlin
TEMPELHOF AIRPORT
Potsdam
SCHÖNEFELD AIRPORT
Königs Wusterhausen
0 Miles 10

The New York Times/Aug. 15, 1972

It was the second largest death toll in the history of civil air disasters. In Japan, in July, 1971, an All-Nippon Airways Boeing 727 collided with an F-86 Saber jet fighter, and 162 were killed.

The German plane, a four-engine, Soviet-built Ilyushin 62, crashed minutes after it had taken off from East Berlin's Schönefeld Airport on a vacation charter flight for Burgas, a Bulgarian resort city on the Black Sea. The Ilyushin, which belonged to Interflug, the East German state airline, carried 148 passengers and a crew of eight.

An airline spokesman said that all the passengers were East German tourists. [West German television accounts of the disaster said that some West Berliners were among the passengers, The Associated Press reported. Travelers from West Berlin have regular access to flights at Schönefeld, it said.]

The jet crashed at Königs Wusterhausen, six miles from the airport, in an area of lakes and forests. The East German agency, A.D.N., said that the cause was not known.

There were no survivors, the agency reported, despite immediate action by fire brigades and medical teams. Soon after

Continued on Page 10, Column 4

TWO TOP OFFICERS RESIGN FROM H.I.P.

They Leave in Dispute Over Financing as Health Group Accepts 15% Rate Rise

By NANCY HICKS

The two top executive officers of the Health Insurance Plan of Greater New York resigned yesterday in the latest phase of a running dispute over the future structure and financing of H.I.P., the second-largest prepaid health insurance group in the country.

The resignations of James Brindle, the president, and Martin Cohen, executive vice president, were accepted at a meeting of the board of directors held at H.I.P.'s headquarters, 625 Madison Avenue. At the same meeting the board reached a compromise agreement on a rate increase with the City of New York, whose employes make up about half of H.I.P.'s 740,000 subscribers.

5-Man Panel in Control

The 15 per cent increase, agreed to by both parties, was half the amount approved by the state and hoped for by H.I.P. officers to carry out a reorganization plan. That plan is aimed at making all participating physicians full-time H.I.P. employes and at consolidating the 28 groups into larger, hospital-based prepaid group plans.

The organization's general counsel, Allan Kornfeld, will become acting administrator for H.I.P., which will be temporarily run by a five-man committee headed by William

Continued on Page 17, Column 1

City to Build a Terminal for Trailerships

By EDWARD RANZAL

The city took another step yesterday in its bid to recapture waterfront business that it has lost as Mayor Lindsay announced plans for a $16-million trailership terminal on Staten Island.

It was the fifth major move for revival of the city's waterfront in the last three months.

In June the American President Lines returned to the city after 45 years, the Northeast Container Terminal opened in Brooklyn and the Dovar Shipping Company became a major tenant of Northeast. Last month the city announced plans to redevelop the Chelsea piers in Manhattan into the nation's first air-cargo terminal.

The Port of New York, which includes terminals in New Jersey as well as New York City, is still the No. 1 port in the nation for general cargo, according to the city's Commissioner of Ports and Terminals, Edgar C. Faber. But the city at one time handled two-thirds of all cargo in the Port of New York and now handles only one-third, he continued.

The Mayor, Mr. Faber added, wants to recapture the one-third of shipping business that the city has lost to other ports, largely Newark, Elizabeth and Philadelphia.

The Staten Island terminal, which will be operated by Trans American Trailer Transport, will be built partly on landfill on a 42-acre site in Stapleton, just south of the St. George ferry terminal.

When completed in 1975, the facility will support 500 jobs, about 250 more workers than presently employed by Trans American, now operating from nearby piers.

Three abandoned piers will

Continued on Page 69, Column 5

BAY ST.
PIER 7
PIER 8
NEW LAND
New York Bay
PIER 11
PIER 12
PIER 13
Area of planned marine terminal
St. George
Stapleton
BROOKLYN
NARROWS
STATEN ISLAND
VERRAZANO-NARROWS BRIDGE

The New York Times/Aug. 15, 1972

DO YOU KNOW ANY IMPORTANT MAN IN BUSINESS WHO DOES NOT READ FORBES MAGAZINE?—ADVT.

NEWS INDEX

LEARN CHESS WITH YOUR CHILDREN ILLUS. BOOK "THE ROYAL GAME" SHOWS HOW. AT BOOKSTORES.-ADVT. Vanguard Press, 424 Madison Ave., N.Y.C.

The Nobility of Chess: Every Grandmaster Is a King

By HAROLD C. SCHONBERG
Special to The New York Times

REYKJAVIK, Iceland, Aug. 14 — The grandmasters of chess, those suzerains of the 64 squares, have been here in force, watching Boris Spassky and Bobby Fischer slug it out for the world championship title.

Miguel Najdorf came from Argentina a few weeks ago. Bent Larsen came from Denmark. They have since left. Svetozar Gligoric and Dragoljub Janosevic of Yugoslavia are still around. So is Fridric Olafsson of Iceland. So are Efim Geller and Nikolai Krogius of the Soviet Union. So is Lothar Schmid of West Germany. So are Robert Byrne, Larry Evans and Lubomir Kavalek of the United States. Counting Spassky and Fischer, about one-seventh of the world's 80-plus grandmasters have come to Reykjavik.

Chess fans watch them from a distance, goggle-eyed, much as a squire in King Arthur's court might watch Sir Lancelot, Sir Gareth or Sir Tristram.

One gets to be a grandmaster by beating other grandmasters. (It is a little more complicated than that, but that is the basic idea.)

These grandmasters are the nobility of chess, the ultimate authorities to whom all defer. In their heads are more variations than a Mahler symphony has notes. In their psyches vibrates the

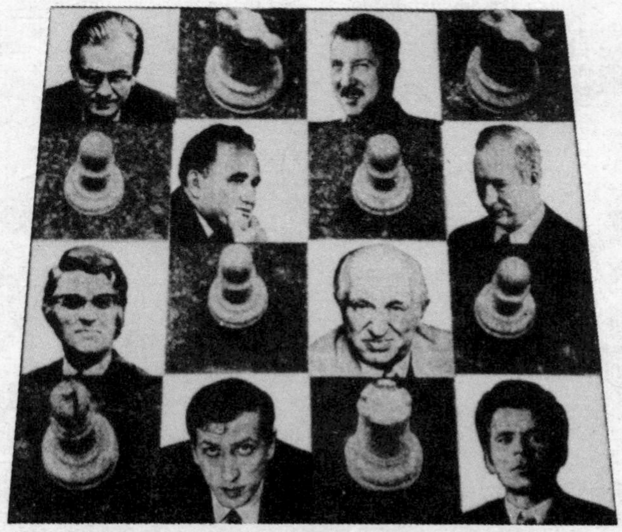

Chess grandmasters, from the left in each row, beginning at the bottom: Bobby Fischer and Boris Spassky; Lothar Schmid and Miguel Najdorf; Efim Geller and Robert Byrne, and, at the top, Bent Larsen and Svetozar Gligoric.

confidence of a Ty Cobb coming to bat. In their secret hearts is the opinion that they, not Fischer or Spassky, should be on the stage of Exhibition Hall playing for the title.

They stand in small knots talking to each other, these grandmasters do. Normally grandmasters talk only to other grandmasters. Nobody else can understand them or follow their split-second, machine-gun analyses.

"Spassky just moved rook d8," says one to another. "I don't understand it. Why not pawn g6, forcing king to h8 followed by pawn f5, knight f4, rook a3 and bring it over."

"But if pawn g6," says the other, "perhaps Spassky can then play pawn h7 instead of king h8. This position is like in the game Braunschweig-Garcia at Baden-Baden, 1925,

Continued on Page 32, Column 4

What appears to be a wing lies among still-smoldering bits and pieces of the crashed East German Interflug jet.

Wide World Photos

EAST GERMAN JET CRASHES, 156 DIE

Continued From Page 1, Col. 3

the crash, a Government commission, headed by Otto Arndt, the Transport Minister, was sent to the scene to investigate.

The Ilyushin 62 is a long-haul airliner with a maximum seating capacity of 150 and a cruising speed of about 520 miles an hour. Interflug began using the planes in July, 1970.

A men who saw the crash said that the plane had caught fire immediately after it swept over the roof of his house at what appeared to be less than 100 feet of altitude.

The witness said the pilot then appeared to try to raise the nose, but that the plane exploded a few yards above the ground and crashed into a field.

He said that the wreckage was scattered over a wide area.

Another eyewitness said that she had not seen flames in the air but had heard several loud blasts. "The plane exploded and parts fell on our field," she said. "We first saw the flames after the plane had already crashed. The rescue teams got there very quickly."

Königs Wusterhausen, an old city, has for 50 years served as a railroad junction and a radio transmission center.

The transmission equipment and radio masts serve East Germany's long-wave radio station.

"All the News That's Fit to Print"

The New York Times

LATE CITY EDITION
Weather: Unseasonably mild today; cool tonight. Rain likely tomorrow. Temp. range: today 37-48; Saturday 39-41. Full U.S. report on Page 47.

SECTION ONE

VOL. CXXII . No. 41,973
© 1972 The New York Times Company
NEW YORK, SUNDAY, DECEMBER 24, 1972

75¢ beyond 50-mile zone from New York City, except Long Island. Higher in air delivery cities.

50 CENTS

HEAVY RAIDS GO ON FOR SEVENTH DAY IN NORTH VIETNAM

SECRECY IS TIGHT

U.S Withholds Any Reports on Foe's Defense Action

By JOSEPH B. TREASTER
Special to The New York Times

SAIGON, South Vietnam, Sunday, Dec. 24—Heavy American bombing of North Vietnam continued for a seventh day today while the United States military command drew even tighter its curtain of secrecy over the operation.

[American military sources in Saigon said the United States plans a short halt in the bombing of North Vietnam for Christmas, The Associated Press reported.]

For the first time, the command refused yesterday to disclose any information about North Vietnamese air defenses, withholding reports on how many surface-to-air missiles were believed to have been fired, how intense the conventional antiaircraft fire had been and whether any MIG's had been seen in the skies.

Disclosures at Minimum

The command had been releasing that information daily since the full-scale bombing of the North was resumed on Monday. Asked to explain why it was withheld yesterday, a command spokesman, Maj. Gilbert L. Whiteman, said only that "I have no comment on any operations over the North at all."

Throughout this latest period of bombing, the command's policy has been minimal disclosure. After searches and rescue efforts have been completed, it has made public hard-

Continued on Page 5, Column 1

HOSPITAL DEATHS

Hanoi Aide Says 25 Staff Members Are Killed by Bombs

By Agence France-Presse

HANOI, North Vietnam, Dec. 23—The North Vietnamese Vice Minister of Health said tonight that 25 doctors, pharmacists and male and female nurses had been killed at Bach Mai Hospital during American bombing raids on Hanoi in the last few days.

The minister, Dr. Nguyen Van Tin, spoke as he showed foreign newsmen the destroyed building, one of the seven largest hospitals in the capital. It was bombed on Tuesday and again last night, he said.

[In Saigon, South Vietnamese intelligence officials were circulating a report that Gen. Vo Nguyen Giap, the North Vietnamese Defense Minister, was killed when a delayed-action bomb went off in Hanoi Friday. But American intelligence officials said that they could not confirm the report, and in Paris, it was dismissed by the North Vietnamese delegation to the four-party peace talks as an attempt at "psychological warfare."]

The Bach Mai Hospital had reportedly been damaged during bombing last June. Today, practically nothing remained. The operating rooms were razed and pharmaceutical stocks destroyed.

The Health Minister said that about $3-million damage had been done by fighter-bombers and B-52's, which, he said, dropped about 30 bombs on the

Continued on Page 3, Column 3

Dr. Harrison H. Schmitt/NASA

THE EARTH, seen from the Apollo 17 spacecraft. The South Pole is visible at bottom, Africa left of center, the Arabian peninsula at top. According to NASA, this is the first Apollo photo in which no part of the earth is in shadow.

THOUSANDS DEAD AS QUAKES STRIKE NICARAGUAN CITY

CAPITAL BATTERED

Fires Follow Temblors in Managua—U.S. Is Sending Aid

The New York Times/Dec. 24, 1972

By United Press International

MEXICO CITY, Dec. 23—A series of powerful earthquakes destroyed a large part of the Nicaraguan capital of Managua early today, crumpling buildings and sparking fires that killed or injured tens of thousands of persons.

Reports from neighboring Costa Rica said the Nicaraguan Health Ministry said at least 18,000 persons had been killed, either by collapsing buildings or fires that followed. An additional 40,000 persons were injured and 200,000 left homeless, the health ministry said. The city has a population of 325,000.

[In Tegucigalpa, Honduras, Carlos Gomez Andino, chief of the Honduran Red Cross, said after a visit to Managua that the death toll was more than 10,000 and the number of injured was "incalculable," Reuters reported.]

Fires Out of Control

Pilots who flew over Managua said as much as 70 per cent of the city was in ruins. Fires started by the earthquake burned out of control. The water supply was cut off and there was no water for fire-fighting or for drinking. Electricity also was knocked out.

Communications from Managua were virtually cut off. Only amateur radio operators provided links with the outside world.

The two-and-a-half hour series of quakes touched off explosions and fires, and a large portion of the city was engulfed by flames almost 24 hours after the quakes struck around midnight.

Former President Anastasio Somoza-Debayle, who turned over the leadership of the country to a triumvirate last May but remains its military strongman, sent a cable to President Nixon saying that the capital had been devastated. Mr. Nixon ordered immediate relief help for the stricken nation.

Roads Are Jammed

An international relief operation began almost immediately. The governments of Honduras, El Salvador and Guatemala sent in relief supplies.

In Managua, survivors fled in panic, jamming all roads around the city, which is on a lake east of the Pacific coast.

"Hundreds of mutilated bodies were strewn along the streets, some still wrapped in bedsheets, some missing heads, hands or feet," said one witness fleeing the city.

Juan Castenera, manager of the Communications Satellite Corporation's station on the outskirts of Managua, described the scene as "like the end of the world."

Mr. Castenera, reporting by radiotelephone to Washington, said he had not been able to get into the city because of the thousands of refugees stream-

Continued on Page 18, Column 4

SERVICES BELIEVE DISCIPLINE HOLDS

Forces, Especially the Navy, Have Problems but Most Leaders Are Hopeful

By DREW MIDDLETON

Discipline in the United States armed forces remains effective despite the impact of hundreds of thousands of volunteers from what military men regard as a permissive society and widespread reforms in military life, officers and noncommissioned officers assert.

A wide-ranging series of interviews with these men, who are responsible for maintaining military discipline, disclosed that all three services do have disciplinary problems and that the Navy is suffering most at present.

But the prediction of most officers and noncommissioned officers of the Army, Navy and Air Force is that a more liberal approach to a higher type of recruit will result in forces marked by individual enter-

Continued on Page 30, Column 3

Youths Rejecting Heroin, But Turn to Other Drugs

By JAMES M. MARKHAM

A combination of law-enforcement pressures, therapeutic efforts, differing rates of availability of certain drugs and subtle changes in community moods and youthful fads appears to have slowed the spread of heroin addiction in New York.

But, according to a variety of people close to the city's multifaceted drug scene, the apparent slowing of the heroin epidemic has been accompanied by a rise in the abuse of other substances, notably methadone, barbiturates, cocaine and alcohol.

Blacks 'Turning Off'

According to some people, the current situation is such that tinkering with several variables might produce significantly different results. Thus, for example, an easing of a half-year heroin shortage and a simultaneous shrinking of a currently plentiful street-methadone supply could conceivably fuel a rise in heroin use.

One trend, however, does appear to be relatively firm: heroin is no longer "cool" among many young people in heavily addicted slum communities.

"No question about it," said Dr. Beny J. Primm, executive director of the Addiction Research and Training Corporation in Bedford-Stuyvesant. "I see a turning off, particularly among the black and Puerto Rican community. They are intolerant to the new abuser."

But, highlighting the faddish nature of much drug abuse, Dr. Primm expressed concern over a recent upsurge in cocaine use among young blacks, which he contended was aggravated by "Super Fly," a popular film about a black cocaine pusher.

"If you want to hang out, you've got to move with the fad," observed Carlos Suarez, a South Bronx youth who has been a heroin-dabbler, a gang president and a Marine and who is now involved in teaching karate and organizing tenants in Hunts Point.

Mr. Suarez maintained that radical political ferment had stigmatized the junkie as a

Continued on Page 34, Column 3

DEVICES EXPLODE IN 5TH AVE. STORES

Minor Damage Reported as Thousands of Shoppers Prepare for Holiday

By MICHAEL KNIGHT

Stores were jammed with last-minute Christmas shoppers yesterday, but the festive spirit was slightly disrupted by the detonation of two incendiary devices at Bonwit Teller and the igniting of a third device at Bergdorf Goodman.

There were no injuries in either incident and damage was reported to have been minor.

Bomb squad detectives said the devices had been placed in the stores by radical demonstrators but would not reveal the name of any particular group they held responsible.

The police said the devices appeared to consist of battery-operated timers attached to explosive material in cigarette cases, similar to fire bombs that have been detonated sporadically in department stores over the last

Continued on Page 38, Column 2

Europe Reacts to Bombing With Increasing Protests

By ALVIN SHUSTER
Special to The New York Times

LONDON, Dec. 23—Western Europe is reacting to the American bombing of North Vietnam with growing protests and a mixture of sadness, disgust and anger.

Correspondents in major capitals report that almost all shades of opinion have joined in denouncing the resumption of the heavy American raids. There was talk among some left-wing groups and unions of organizing boycotts of American goods and ships.

Street demonstrations have been held in London, Rome, Copenhagen, Zurich and Amsterdam. In Rome 25,000 people heeded the call of the Italy-Vietnam Committee, a left-wing group, and turned out in a parade and rally last night. About 7,000 joined in a protest in Copenhagen today.

At official levels in the capitals, there were expressions of regret over the continued warfare and of concern that the raids might jeopardize the new relationship developed between the Soviet Union and the United States after President Nixon's visit in May. Other officials in Bonn, London and elsewhere took the view that the bombing would serve further to tarnish the image of the United States.

[At the United Nations, Secretary General Waldheim said he was greatly concerned at the continuing bombing and called for a resumption of the cease-fire negotiations.]

Despite the scattered street demonstrations, the depth of feeling among Europeans toward the bombing is difficult to gauge. The mining of Haiphong and bombing earlier this year failed to stir widespread protests. And some officials believe that, like many Americans, Europeans have grown rather numb to the events in Indochina after all the years of warfare.

The harshest official attack

Continued on Page 4, Column 1

Today's Sections

Index to Subjects

BARCO BUSINESS EQUIPMENT STORES WISH YOU A VERY HAPPY HOLIDAY SEASON AND A HAPPY NEW YEAR. Advt.

Truman's Condition

Former President Harry S. Truman was described as "slightly improved" but still in critical condition last night after he had become "completely unresponsive" earlier in the day at a Kansas City hospital. Page 32.

Racial Ideas Change in South Africa's Ruling Group

By CHARLES MOHR
Special to The New York Times

PRETORIA, South Africa, Dec. 18 — Perhaps because their story was a poignant one, no people have been more intoxicated with their history than the Afrikaners, the whites, mostly of Dutch descent, who rule South Africa.

It seemed not only strange but significant, therefore, that the Afrikaners' most sacred folk festival, known as the Day of the Covenant, was not so much celebrated as it was ignored this year.

A forlorn crowd of 2,000 gathered in the amphitheater at the Voortrekker Monument Saturday, leaving 12,000 seats empty. Crowds elsewhere in the Republic of South Africa also were small.

To some observers the small crowds reflected a slow, gradual change in the traditional thinking and racial beliefs of Afrikaners.

These crowds heard a recitation of how the Afrikaner nation was slowly born of a blend of Dutch, German and fiercely Calvinist French Huguenot settlers who began coming to the Cape of Good Hope in the 17th century.

These "Boers," or farmers, spread into a hostile interior, where they gradually developed their own language, Afrikaans, which is something like Flemish but with elements of simplified Dutch. The settlers gradually came to think of themselves not as European expatriates but as an African people.

The holiday crowds also heard again the story of how their Boer ancestors, the Voortrekkers, wandered like Biblical Israelites in the South

Continued on Page 2, Column 1

The New York Times/Michael Irwin

Afrikaners, some dressed in traditional costume, attend festival at Pretoria amphitheater. Attendance was sparse.

Hog Prices Reach Record, Portending Consumer Rise

By SETH S. KING
Special to The New York Times

CHICAGO, Dec. 23 — In the long history of this nation, no common hog ever brought a price as high as was paid Thursday at the stockyards in Peoria.

At $34 a hundred pounds, No. 1 grade hogs shattered all previous records, pushing Christmas season income for hog raisers even higher than in the banner year 1948 and portending still higher supermarket prices for consumers.

This surge in hog prices ended, with a resounding bang, an agricultural year in which most Midwestern farmers not only had record crop yields to sell, but also had one of the best markets in memory.

Cattle Prices Rising

The average prices paid to farmers for all agricultural products were more than 13 per cent higher than those in 1971, the Agriculture Department noted.

This helped explain why food costs for consumers rose more than 4 per cent over the year and why in the next six months these consumer prices will probably remain as high or go even higher.

Farm prices for fattened beef cattle, which declined in November to their lowest level in six months, were on the rise again this week, moving up to about $37 a hundred weight for choice grade steers. This was about $2.50 more than a year ago.

Even though there is now an increase of 10 per cent in the number of beef cattle being fattened for market, agricultural economists expected consumption of beef to continue climbing and prices paid to farmers to reach the $40 level in the next few months.

There are no Federal price controls on raw farm products.

Continued on Page 23, Column 1

Tupolev Dead at 84

Andrei N. Tupolev, the aircraft designer whose name became synonymous with the Soviet aviation industry, died yesterday at 84. His new supersonic airliner, the TU-144, rivaled only by the British-French Concorde, is expected to go into service in 1975. Details on Page 41.

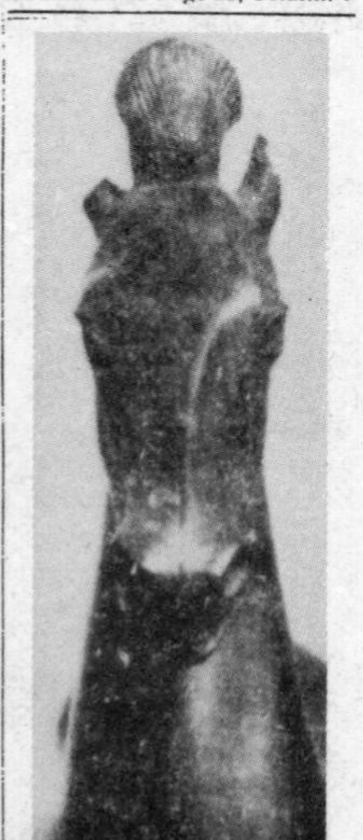

NOW TERMED GENUINE: Bronze horse called "fraud" in 1967 is now described as a genuine, ancient masterpiece by Metropolitan Museum experts. See Page 33.

Thousands Killed as Earthquake Smashes Nicaragua's Capital

Wide World Photos

Children sit in front of their destroyed home in Managua, Nicaragua, after the earthquake rocked the capital city.

Continued From Page 1, Col. 8

ing out of it. He estimated that a great portion of the city had been leveled by the quakes and that about a third was engulfed by flames hours later.

The earthquake was the second that has devastated the city this century and the third major one in its history. Managua was destroyed March 31, 1931, by an earthquake and fire that killed 2,000 persons, and it was leveled by an earlier quake in 1885.

The first of the series of quakes came at about 11:10 P.M. (12:10 A.M. New York time) and another followed 10 minutes later, producing some panic among the populace. The strongest in the series were at 1:30 A.M., and registered 6.25 on the Richter scale at observatories throughout the hemisphere. An aftershock that followed the main quake registered 5.50, and lesser aftershocks continued for some time afterward.

By comparison, the major Alaskan earthquake on March 27, 1964, registered 8.4 on the scale and the San Francisco quake of 1906 that destroyed most of the city registered 8.3.

In the United States the National Earthquake Information Center in Boulder, Colo., said the epicenter of the quake was in or near Managua itself.

In Managua, one radio amateur reporting from his mobile station in his car, the only source for his electric power, said: "The most immediate problem now is drinking water."

Managua lies on the shore of Lake Managua, 25 miles east of the Pacific, but the lake is so polluted that its water is undrinkable.

Had Series of Disasters

Managua, a former Indian village on whose site Spanish conquistadores founded a city in the 16th century, has been repeatedly stricken by disaster. In addition to the earthquakes of 1885 and 1931, the latter recording 6 on the Richter scale, the city was ruined by floodwaters from Lake Managua in 1876, was heavily damaged when an arsenal exploded in 1902, and was devastated by civil war in 1912.

Howard Hughes, the industrialist and recluse, was among the 3,000 Americans in Managua when the earthquakes struck. His associates in Los Angeles said they had received

word that Mr. Hughes and his staff were safe.

Commercial airline pilots arriving in Mexico City after flying over the devastated city said some lakeside areas appeared to have sunk lower than the lake and were being flooded. There were no reports of flooding, however, when telephone links were established late this afternoon between Managua and Tegucigalpa, capital of neighboring Honduras, 150 miles to the north.

The Las Mercedes airport outside Managua continued functioning on an emergency basis after the earthquake, and various types of planes began an airlift to transfer injured to Tegucigalpa and to the Costa Rican capital of San José, 200 miles southeast of Managua.

All of Managua's hospitals were destroyed, according to the Nicaraguan National guard. The Honduran ministry of defense said the Nicaraguan National Guard advised them to be prepared for more than 20,000 injured.

Nicaraguan troops were guarding the entire downtown section of stores and offices and particularly the banks.

Among the buildings demolished by the quakes were the Presidential Palace; the Cathedral; the newspaper offices of La Prensa and Novedades; the United States Embassy; two of the city's three major hotels, the Balmoral and the Gran Hotels; and all the public utilities offices. Most of the other buildings and homes were either destroyed or heavily damaged.

The secretary to the American ambassador, Rose Marie Orlich, 36, of Philadelphia was killed, the State Department said in Washington. In Tegucigalpa, Honduras, American officials said a friend of Miss Orlich, identified only as Valeri Slugy, also was reported killed.

Water mains were ruptured, and there was no water available either for drinking or to fight the rapidly spreading fires.

Relief flights into the stricken capital began today. The United States Southern Command, based in the Panama Canal Zone, and the United States Readiness Command in Tampa, Fla., coordinated American rescue efforts. At least two mobile hospitals were to be flown to Managua tomorrow. The State Department said rescue planes

would begin evacuating all Americans—estimated to number about 3,000—tomorrow.

'Managua Has Disappeared'

GUATEMALA City, Dec. 23 (Reuters) — Danilo Arias, a Costa Rican believed to be the first foreign newsman to reach Managua, reported by radio today that hundreds of bodies were lying in the streets.

In his report, monitored here, Mr. Arias said: "Those of us who knew Managua will never see it again.

"Managua has disappeared. All is desolation, death and tragedy."

Pope Expresses Sorrow

ROME, Dec. 23 (UPI)—Pope Paul VI expressed his sorrow to the victims of the Nicaraguan earthquake today in a cable to the Archbishop of Managua.

The cable said the Pope "prays for eternal peace for the dead and hopes for the prompt recovery of the injured while he is close to the most beloved Nicaraguan brothers with the comforting and fatherly papal blessing."

"All the News That's Fit to Print"

The New York Times

LATE CITY EDITION

Weather: Partly sunny, mild today; fair tonight. Sunny, mild tomorrow. Temp. range: today 45-59; Monday 35-54. Full U.S. report on Page 76.

VOL. CXXII . No. 42,003 NEW YORK, TUESDAY, JANUARY 23, 1973 15 CENTS

© 1973 The New York Times Company

LYNDON JOHNSON, 36TH PRESIDENT, IS DEAD; WAS ARCHITECT OF 'GREAT SOCIETY' PROGRAM

High Court Rules Abortions Legal the First 3 Months

State Bans Ruled Out Until Last 10 Weeks

National Guidelines Set by 7-to-2 Vote

By WARREN WEAVER Jr.

Special to The New York Times

WASHINGTON, Jan. 22 — The Supreme Court overruled today all state laws that prohibit or restrict a woman's right to obtain an abortion during her first three months of pregnancy. The vote was 7 to 2.

In a historic resolution of a fiercely controversial issue, the Court drafted a new set of

Excerpts from opinion and dissent are on Page 20.

national guidelines that will result in broadly liberalized anti-abortion laws in 46 states but will not abolish restrictions altogether.

Establishing an unusually detailed timetable for the relative legal rights of pregnant women and the states that would control their acts, the majority specified the following:

¶For the first three months of pregnancy the decision to have an abortion lies with the woman and her doctor, and the state's interest in her welfare is not "compelling" enough to warrant any interference.

¶For the next six months of pregnancy a state may "regulate the abortion procedure in ways that are reasonably related to maternal health," such as licensing and regulating the persons and facilities involved.

¶For the last 10 weeks of pregnancy, the period during which the fetus is judged to be capable of surviving if born, any state may prohibit

Continued on Page 20, Column 5

Cardinals Shocked —Reaction Mixed

By LAWRENCE VAN GELDER

Reaction to the Supreme Court decision on abortion fragmented yesterday along predictable lines, as leaders of the Roman Catholic Church assailed the ruling while birth control and women's rights activists praised it.

In the forefront of Catholic reaction were Cardinal Cooke of New York and Cardinal Krol of Philadelphia, who is also

Statements by Cooke and Krol appear on Page 20.

the president of the National Conference of Catholic Bishops.

Cardinal Cooke issued a statement calling the Court's action yesterday "shocking" and "horrifying." Cardinal Krol called the decision "an unspeakable tragedy for this nation."

But William Baird, a crusader for birth control and abortion, called the decision "a triumph" that culminated a long struggle.

"I'm delighted to see that our position—that women have the right to control their own bodies—has been vindicated," he said.

Dr. Alan F. Guttmacher, president of the Planned Parenthood Federation of America, called the decision "a wise and courageous stroke for the right to privacy, and for the protection of a woman's physical and emotional health."

"By this act," he said, "hundreds of thousands of American women every year will be

Continued on Page 20, Column 1

Ruling Seems to Forestall Abortion Debate in Albany

By WILLIAM E. FARRELL

Special to The New York Times

ALBANY, Jan. 22—The United States Supreme Court's abortion decision today appeared to quash the hopes of Right to Life and other anti-abortion groups for a full-scale debate in the Legislature again this year on repealing the state's liberalized abortion law.

"No way," replied Assemblyman Constance E. Cook, a Republican of Ithaca and a sponsor of the liberalized abortion law, when asked if the issue of restoring the old state statute would be seriously discussed again.

The liberalized state law permits a woman to have an abortion or demand until the 24th week of pregnancy. The old law permitted abortions only when a woman's life was in jeopardy.

Rendered 'Useless'

The Supreme Court's 7-to-2 ruling, Mrs. Cook said, rendered efforts by antiabortion lobbyists to force it to the floors of the Senate and Assembly "a useless show of strength."

Similarly, Assembly Speaker Perry B. Duryea, Republican of Montauk, said he felt it would be "futile" to bring repeal legislation up for debate again.

Well-organized opponents of the liberalized abortion law succeeded in having it repealed in both houses last year despite a pledge by Governor Rockefeller that he would veto a repeal measure. The Governor kept his promise.

Mr. Rockefeller, who did not comment on the court decision today pending a review of it by his legal staff, reaffirmed that he would again veto a repeal measure this year, but the antiabortion groups were undaunted.

Today, the comments of abortion opponents contained some of the emotional comments that the issue has always elicited here.

From his newly opened lobbying office near the Capitol, Edward J. Golden, chairman of the New York State Right to Life Committee, said, "virtually all protection under law has

Continued on Page 22, Column 1

3.7 MILLION CARS RECALLED BY G.M. TO CORRECT FLAW

Shields Will Be Installed to Prevent Entry of Gravel Into Steering System

By JERRY M. FLINT

Special to The New York Times

DETROIT, Jan. 22 — The General Motors Corporation recalled today 3.7 million 1971 and 1972 cars, its full-size Chevrolet, Pontiac, Buick and Oldsmobile models.

G.M. said it would install a shield at the bottom of the car to keep gravel from bouncing into the steering mechanism, which could jam the steering.

The automaker insisted that the trouble was rare, and rejected the idea of a recall on this problem last year. But at the same time the company said it had received reports of 96 incidents allegedly tied to the trouble, with 23 turned into accidents in which 12 injuries were reported.

Criticism by Nader

The recall is one of the largest but does not match the recall for correction of safety defects of 6.7 million G.M. cars in 1971 or 4.4 million Fords last June.

Ralph Nader, the auto industry's major critic, has criticized G.M. for its failure to recall cars to correct this problem, and last August the Government's safety agency issued a consumer warning bulletin on the problem.

At that time, General Motors said that it did not believe the safety hazard was serious but offered to repair the cars without charge. Reports of the trouble kept appearing and the company has changed its position.

Steering May Jam

The condition, General Motors said, can become a problem only if a car "is driven over loose gravel, on extremely rutted roads at speeds which caused the car to pitch excessively." If the front frame cross-member, a cross bar similar to a step on a ladder, dips so low to the ground that it scoops up loose stones or gravel "it then is possible that stones of a certain size and shape may lodge between the steering coupling and the frame." The stones fall out of the car if turned to the right, G.M. said, but the steering may

Continued on Page 78, Column 2

KISSINGER IN PARIS; CEREMONIAL SITE CHOSEN FOR TALKS

Use of Conference Center Indicates Both Sides View Truce Round as Vital

By FLORA LEWIS

Special to The New York Times

PARIS, Jan. 22 — Henry A. Kissinger arrived here tonight, and it was announced that his talks tomorrow with Le Duc Tho of North Vietnam would be moved to the ceremonial setting of the International Conference Center.

Hanoi and Washington announced jointly last week that this next round of negotiations would complete a cease-fire agreement for Vietnam. Today there was still no official word on how long that task would take, but the choice of location — after months of meetings in secluded private quarters — suggested that the two sides considered tomorrow's session important.

The announcement that the talks would be moved to the center was made by the North Vietnamese here tonight, then confirmed by the American delegation.

The conference center is the old Hotel Majestic, on the Avenue Kléber, site of the formal four-sided Paris peace conference for over four years.

At the airport Mr. Kissinger said nothing more than "I am glad to be here." He went directly to the residence of the South Vietnamese Forign Minister, Tran Van Lam, though it was nearly midnight and he had left Washington early in the morning.

That was apparently a proto-

Continued on Page 6, Column 4

NATION IS SHOCKED

Citizens Join Leaders in Voicing Sorrow and Paying Tribute

By ROBERT D. McFADDEN

Shock, sorrow and the sense of a historic leader lost were the mourning themes of public officials and private citizens across the nation last night as word spread that Lyndon Baines Johnson was dead.

From the White House and the halls of Congress where he had served, and in cities and towns across the land where he had campaigned and made his policies felt, there was an outpouring of tribute to the former President, Senator and Representative from Texas.

Statement by Nixon

Many recalled Mr. Johnson's efforts to promote racial equality, to fight poverty and to improve education; others said that his deep commitment to the war in Indochina had prevented him from achieving all his domestic goals.

President Nixon, in a statement, declared: "To President Johnson, the 'American Dream' was not a catch phrase—it was a reality of his own life. He believed in America, in what America could mean to all its citizens and what America could mean to the world. In the service of that faith, he gave himself completely."

Mr. Nixon noted that in more than three decades of public life, Mr. Johnson "knew times of triumph and times of despair—he knew controversy and adulation. Yet, no matter what the mood of the moment, at the center of his public life—and at the center of his spirit—was an unshakeable convic-

Continued on Page 25, Column 1

The New York Times/George Tames

LYNDON BAINES JOHNSON, 1908—1973

STRICKEN AT HOME

Apparent Heart Attack Comes as Country Mourns Truman

Special to The New York Times

SAN ANTONIO, Tex., Jan. 22 —Lyndon Baines Johnson, 36th President of the United States, died today of an apparent heart attack suffered at his ranch in Johnson City, Tex.

The 64-year-old Mr. Johnson, whose history of heart illness began in 1955, was pronounced dead on arrival at 4:33 P.M. central time at San Antonio International Airport, where he

An obituary article appears on Pages 26 through 29; an appraisal, Page 25.

had been flown in a family plane on the way to Brooke Army Medical Center here.

A spokesman at Austin said that Mr. Johnson's funeral would probably be held Thursday at the National City Christian Church in Washington. He said the body would lie in state at the Johnson Library in Austin from noon tomorrow until 8 A.M. Wednesday, with an honor guard, and then would be taken to Washington, where it will lie in state at the Capitol rotunda until the funeral. Mr. Johnson will be buried at the L.B.J. Ranch.

Death came to the nation's only surviving former President as the nation observed a period of mourning proclaimed less than a month ago for former President Harry S. Truman.

A Legacy of Progress

Although his vision of a Great Society dissolved in the morass of war in Vietnam, Mr. Johnson left to the nation a legacy of progress and innovation in civil rights, Social Security, education, housing and other programs attesting to his fundamental affection for his fellow Americans.

At Fort Sam Houston, where Brooke Army Medical Center is situated, flags were hoisted to full staff and then immediately lowered again in respect for the Texan who was thrust into the Presidency on Nov. 22, 1963, when an assassin's bullet took the life of President Kennedy in Dallas.

Ironically, Mr. Johnson died in what appeared to be the waning days of the Vietnam war. The man who won election in 1964 to a full term as President with the greatest voting majority ever accorded a candidate was transformed by that war into the leader of a divided nation.

Amid rising personal unpopularity, in the face of the lingering war and racial strife at home, Mr. Johnson surprised the nation on March 31, 1968, with a television speech in which he announced, "I shall not seek and I will not accept the nomination of my party as your President."

Stage Set for Defeat

He thus renounced an opportunity to cap with a second full term a career in public life that began in 1937 with his election to Congress as an ardent New Dealer and led to the majority leadership of the Senate and to the Vice-Presidency and the Presidency. His renunciation set the stage for Democratic defeat at the polls in 1968.

Two days before Mr. Johnson's death, Richard M. Nixon, the Republican who was elected in 1968, took the oath of office for his second term as President. Mr. Nixon telephoned Mrs. Johnson today at the hospital here to express his sympathy.

At a news briefing tonight in Austin at KTBC, the Johnson family's television and ra-

Continued on Page 25, Column 5

Foreman Stops Frazier In 2d Round, Wins Title

By RED SMITH

Special to The New York Times

KINGSTON, Jamaica, Jan. 22 —Under Caribbean skies that had never witnessed anything remotely like it, big George Foreman smashed Joe Frazier to the floor six times tonight and won the heavyweight championship of the world in 4 minutes 35 seconds.

Arthur Mercante, the referee from New York, stopped the uneven match with Frazier on his feet but hardly in the contest.

A crowd of 36,000 paying $412,000, substantially more than had been expected, saw one of the most startling upsets in two and a half centuries of heavyweight title matches. Frazier, in his 10th defense of the title New York State conferred on him in 1968 and his third since he whipped the former champion, Muhammad Ali, in 1971, had been favored at 1 to 3 in the betting shops here.

Foreman, unbeaten in 37 fights and author of 34 knockouts since he won the Olympic heavyweight title in 1968, had been recognized as Joe's most formidable opponent since Ali, but most boxing men doubted that he could stand up under the ceaseless pressure of a characteristic Frazier attack.

They'll never know now whether they were right or wrong, for Joe never got a chance to apply pressure. Looking rather thick in the middle at 214 pounds, the champion tried to "come out smoking" but Foreman used his greater size and longer reach to smother the fire. At 6 feet 3 inches, the challenger had three and a half inches in height and a five-inch advantage in reach.

Reaching out with both hands, he fended off Frazier's early rushes, turning the challenge aside. Then he sank a hook deep into Joe's body, and the crowd had the first hint of what was in store. In a moment Foreman was moving forward, using both hands with authority. Even so, there was an instant of shocked silence when an uppercut sent Joe sprawling.

The champion got to his feet immediately and resumed his jigging style, both hands high,

Continued on Page 33, Column 6

Black Muslims Accused By Rival Sect in 7 Killings

Leader of Hanafis Calls for Muhammad Ouster

By PAUL DELANEY

Special to The New York Times

WASHINGTON, Jan. 22 — The leader of the Hanafi community of Moslems here today blamed the Black Muslims for the slaying last Thursday of seven of his followers, including three of his children, and he, in effect, declared war on the Black Muslims.

The leader, Hamaas Abdul Khaalis, called on other Moslem groups in this country and abroad to assist in deposing the Black Muslims and their leader, Elijah Muhammad.

The slayings and Mr. Hamaas's statement at a news conference evoked apprehension among law enforcement authorities and Islamic experts that more bloodshed would come.

Meanwhile, a team of Washington detectives went to New York today to investigate the possibility of a connection between the Moslem feud and the attempted robbery of a Brooklyn gun store that resulted in a 47-hour siege over the weekend. The belief is that the aborted robbery, which came one day after the mass killings here, was an attempt to obtain arms for the pending battle.

The slayings occurred at the headquarters of the Hanafi, a three-story stone mansion in the interracial "Gold Coast" section, where many of the city's black middle-class citizens reside. The seven victims included five children, four of whom were drowned, ranging in age from 9 days to 10 years old.

Mr. Hamaas revealed some

Continued on Page 77, Column 2

Four Held for Murder in Brooklyn Siege

By PETER KIHSS

The four men seized in the 47-hour weekend siege and shootout at a Brooklyn sporting goods store were held without bail yesterday on charges of murdering a policeman—which could lead to a death penalty—and of kidnapping 10 hostages.

Three were arraigned in Kings County Criminal Court with the proceedings virtually walled off by a tight guard of a dozen uniformed court officers ranged in front of the court railing.

The fourth was arraigned in Kings County Hospital, where he had undergone surgery for a bullet wound in the stomach.

District Attorney Eugene Gold told Judge Robert M. Haft that two of the defendants each had a previous arrest — one in 1964 and one in 1966. Both apparently were then about 16 years old, and Gerald Lefcourt, a defense lawyer, said the men told him the charges had been dismissed.

Outside of court, Robert M. McKiernan, president of the Patrolmen's Benevolent Association, demanded prosecution that could lead to electrocution for the fatal shooting of Patrolman

Continued on Page 77, Column 3

Pilgrims' Jet Crashes in Nigeria; 180 Are Feared Dead, a Record

By THOMAS A. JOHNSON

Special to The New York Times

LAGOS, Nigeria, Jan. 22 — A chartered jetliner carrying Nigerian Moslems home from a pilgrimage to Mecca crashed and burned today while landing in fog in northern Nigeria, and it was feared that 180 people had been killed.

Twenty-two of the 202 aboard survived, among them the pilot and several other crew members, according to reports from the airport at Kano, 525 miles north of here.

A death toll of 180 would make the crash the worst air disaster in history. Previously, the crash of a Soviet airliner near Moscow on Oct. 13, in which 176 people died, had been listed as the worst. The chartered jet, a Boeing 707 that belonged to Royal Jordanian Airways, was one of many planes involved in transporting Nigerian Moslems, as about

Continued on Page 10, Column 4

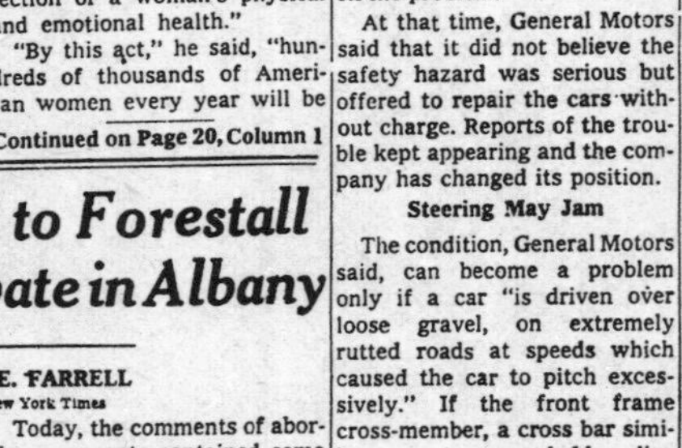

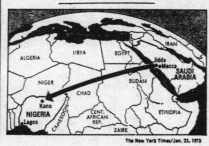

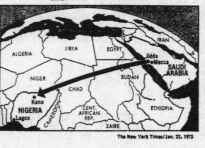

The New York Times/Jan. 23, 1973

Iceland Evacuates 7,000 on Isle After an Ancient Volcano Erupts

By The Associated Press

REYKJAVIK, Iceland, Tuesday, Jan. 23—Seven thousand people were being evacuated from an offshore Icelandic island early today as a volcano that had been quiet for more than a thousand years erupted.

Police authorities on the tiny island of Heimaey, one of a group off the south coast of Iceland, said boats and planes were being used to get the inhabitants of the town of Vestmannaeyjar to safety on the mainland.

But, they said, a hail of ash from the belching volcano of Helgafell was making operations from the island's airstrip difficult. They said a stream of molten lava also threatened to seal off the harbor, trapping boats.

Telephoned reports to Reykjavik—70 miles northwest of Heimaey—said a fissure 2,000 to 3,000 yards long opened and was spewing out lava and ash.

Fiery explosions were hurtling molten debris more than 1,500 feet into the air.

One side of Vestmannaeyjar

The New York Times/Jan. 23, 1973

is only 150 yards from Helgafell.

The police said the lava was flowing away from the town and into the Atlantic, but they said this could change at any time.

Women and children were being evacuated by air along with patients from the town's hospitals.

Others were boarding boats in the harbor. Iceland's big fishing fleet, Coast Guard vessels and other merchant ships were ordered to the island, the police said.

The United States Air Force base at Keflavik promised to

Continued on Page 10, Column 3

NEWS INDEX

	Page		Page
Art	44	Movies	44-47
Books	37	Music	44-47
Bridge	36	Obituaries	41
Business	48-62	Op-Ed	39
Chess	36	Society	42
Crossword	37	Sports	32-36
Editorials	38	Theaters	44-47
Family/Style	30	Transportation	76
Financial	48-62	TV and Radio	77-79
Going Out Guide	44	U. N. Proceedings	9
		Weather	76

News Summary and Index, Page 41

America! mañana. EL COCA-COLA GRANDE troupe leaves London for Nuevo York!—Advt.

A nuclear-like cloud of smoke and ashes rises from the Helgafell volcano on Iceland's Heimaey Island.

Wide World Photos

7,000 EVACUATED ON ICELANDIC ISLE

Continued From Page 1, Col. 7

send helicopters. A small earthquake last night heralded the eruption, the police said. The volcano had not erupted since the Vikings discovered Iceland in 864 A.D.

Nation Declares Emergency

REYKJAVIK, Iceland, Tuesday, Jan. 23, (Reuters)—A general emergency was declared in Iceland today and the authorities ordered that three primary schools in the capital be used to house refugees from Vestmannaeyjar.

Ships were heading for Vestmanneyjar from Reykjavik and the southwest fishing towns of Thorlakshoefn and Grindavik. Refugees were to be taken by sea to Thorlakshoefn and from there by bus to Reykjavik.

Eyewitnesses reported from Vestmannaeyjar that terrified inhabitants crowded the streets after the eruption at 2:30 P.M.

A harbor management source said the island's fishing boats had been sailing away carrying 30 to 100 refugees each.

The Mayor of Vestmannaeyjar, Magnus Magnusson, urged people to be calm and made repeated calls for everyone to gather at the harbor.

Cars were lying all over the harbor area, abandoned by owners anxious to be evacuated.

Many people had only the clothes they were wearing. Others had stuffed small suitcases with whatever they could lay their hands on quickly.

The town was blacked out when the eruption began. Some small earth tremors were reported but they caused no damage.

Many Active Vents in Area

Iceland is considered by many geologists to be one of the greatest lava fields of modern times. Between 20 and 30 active vents have been said to mark the area, with uncertainty as to the exact number stemming from the fact that some are probably hidden beneath ice sheets.

In November, 1963, a volcanic eruption led to the creation of a mile-long, 600-foot-high island 20 miles off Iceland's southern coast. Named Surtsey—the Island of the Black One, the god of fire and destruction—it is composed of pumice and volcanic ash.

180 Are Feared Dead in Nigerian Crash

Continued From Page 1, Col. 3

30,000 made the trip to Mecca this year.

The crash was witnessed by a crowd attracted to the scene by word that 80 pilgrims, none identified by name, had died during the pilgrimage to the Saudi Arabian city that Moslems regard as the most sacred.

The plane crashed after a flight of about 2,100 miles from Jidda, near Mecca.

[In Amman, a spokesman for the Jordanian airline identified the pilot as an American, Capt. John Waterman, and said the company had been informed that he and seven other crewmen were among the survivors, The Associated Press reported.]

Communication with Kano was difficult, and early reports on the crash thus were sketchy. Those reports said that the jet burst into flames as it was making its approach to the Kano airport. It was not clear whether the wheels had touched down at the time.

Witnesses reported that many persons leaped from the emergency exits of the plane and were then trapped in flames roaring all around them.

Hundreds of soldiers, policemen and volunteer workers, on hand to control the large crowds of returning pilgrims and their waiting relatives and friends, rushed to the wreckage of the plane after it crashed.

"It was a pathetic, ghastly sight," one airport worker said afterward.

The Nigerian Government announced an investigation of the crash, which occurred in mid-morning, and a team of experts left Lagos for Kano. Aviation sources here said that the experts were considering a number of theories, including poor visibility at the airport.

Runway Said to Collapse

AMMAN, Jordan, Jan. 22 (AP)—A statement on the air crash in northern Nigeria issued today by the Jordanian Government said the crash occurred because the runway collapsed as the plane landed.

It said that the undercarriage of the jet then fell apart and the fuselage spun 180 degrees and burst into flames after a series of explosions.

A spokesman for Royal Jordanian Airways said the aircraft had been chartered by Nigeria Airways. He said the plane's pilot, Capt. John Waterman, was an American whose wife and children live in Beirut, Lebanon.

Pilot's Wife Gives Report

BEIRUT, Lebanon, Jan. 22 (AP)—Mrs. John Waterman, the pilot's wife, said she had heard from aviation sources that the runway had collapsed at the point where the plane touched down.

She said that her husband had been flying for 20 years in the Middle East and had logged 20,000 hours of air time.

He was born in Fresno, Calif., but has not maintained a home in the United States for many years, she added.

"All the News That's Fit to Print"

The New York Times

LATE CITY EDITION

Weather: Partly cloudy today; cold tonight. Chance of rain tomorrow. Temp. range: today 36-51; Wed. 36-48. Full U.S. report on Page 90.

VOL. CXXII ... No. 42,082 © 1973 The New York Times Company NEW YORK, THURSDAY, APRIL 12, 1973 15 CENTS

Auto Makers Win a Delay Of Year on Exhaust Curbs

Ruckelshaus Postpones Standards Set for 1975 but Lists Interim Rules—California Gets Stricter Controls

By E. W. KENWORTHY
Special to The New York Times

WASHINGTON, April 11 — William D. Ruckelshaus, administrator of the Environmental Protection Agency, gave automobile makers today an additional year to produce new cars meeting the 1975 standards for reducing emissions of hydrocarbons and carbon monoxide, the two major exhaust pollutants.

At the same time, as the law requires, Mr. Ruckelshaus set interim exhaust standards for new cars sold in 1975 in all states except California. These interim national standards will go "half the distance" toward those that were to have been met by 1975, he said.

For California, Mr. Ruckelshaus set interim standards that go two-thirds of the way toward the original 1975 Federal standards. The Clean Air Act of 1970, which requires the agency to set pollution standards, permits a difference for California provided such standards are stricter than the national ones. Last May Mr. Ruckelshaus rejected the manufacturers' plea to delay the 1975 standards, contending that the industry had not proved that the technology required to meet the standards was unavailable.

Today, acting under a court order to reconsider his decision, he explained he had decided that a suspension was in the public interest because manufacturers might not be able to produce enough properly equipped vehicles to meet the national demand. The delay's effect on the campaign against air pollution will be "minimal," he said.

Mr. Ruckelshaus said his decision would mean that meeting the interim national standards would increase the cost of a 1975 car about $100 over that of a 1973 model. In California, where a car would have to be equipped with a "catalytic

Continued on Page 22, Column 1

HAIG WILL CONFER WITH NIXON TODAY ON THE CEASE-FIRE

General to Report on Talks in Southeast Asia—National Security Council to Meet

By WILLIAM BEECHER
Special to The New York Times

WASHINGTON, April 11 — The White House announced today that Gen. Alexander M. Haig Jr., President Nixon's special envoy to Indochina, would meet with the President tomorrow morning immediately upon returning from a four-day assessment of the military situation in Southeast Asia.

Administration officials said the report given to the President would serve as a focus for a major decision on what to do about what they describe as a deterioration of the cease-fire.

A session of the National Security Council was scheduled for 10 A.M., following the general's report to the President.

No Announcement Due

However, Ronald L. Ziegler, the White House press secretary, told newsmen not to expect any major announcement after the President's discussions with General Haig and the subsequent Security Council meeting.

The announcements today came as two legal scholars and a former Attorney General appeared before the Senate Foreign Relations Committee to support legislation that would restrict the President's war powers and to argue that Mr. Nixon had no constitutional authority to continue bombing in Cambodia. [Page 5.]

In Cambodia, meanwhile, a senior Government official discounted somewhat reports of a crisis in Phnom Penh. He denied that the capital was under Communist siege and implied that the United States airlift of fuel to the city was an American, not a Cambodian, idea.

Concern Voiced in Capital

Here in Washington, sources in various Government departments described the White House as deeply disturbed by continuing reports of a weapons build-up by North Vietnam and of military activities by its forces, particularly in South Vietnam and Cambodia, since the Vietnam cease-fire officially went into effect on Jan. 28.

On a number of occasions recently, the President has

Continued on Page 7, Column 1

Javits, Not Rose, Initiated the Fusion Drive

By MURRAY SCHUMACH

Senator Jacob K. Javits

Governor Rockefeller

The quest for a fusion candidate for Mayor was initiated by Senator Jacob K. Javits, not, as has been believed, by Alex Rose, the Liberal party leader, or by Governor Rockefeller.

The Republican - Liberal Senator touched off the intricate political negotiations, and he was also the secret middleman, along with Attorney General Louis J. Lefkowitz, who brought Mr. Rose and Governor Rockefeller together for their first meeting since 1967.

And Senator Javits, not former Mayor Robert F. Wagner, was the first choice of the Governor and Mr. Rose to run for Mayor, under the joint endorsement of the Republican and Liberal parties. Only after the Senator refused was the pressure applied to Mr. Wagner to run for the job he gave up eight years ago after three terms.

"Jack is the one who started the whole thing with a telephone call last November," Mr. Rose recalled the other day, during one of a few interviews in which he traced the sequences of the cliffhanger that now enters a new phase with the refusal of Mr. Wagner to run for Mayor on any ticket.

One of the strangest episodes in the story was that Mr. Rose, though he conferred with Governor Rockefeller, Senator Javits, Mayor Lindsay, other eminent New Yorkers and several aspirants for Mayor, rarely met with Mr. Wagner, who became his strongest choice.

"I didn't want to talk to Bob too much," said Mr. Rose, with a smile. "I knew that if I pressed him he would turn me down. I never said to him: 'Bob, will you run or not,' because I figured that if I did he would say no."

Mr. Rose said that as early as last December he was certain that Mayor Lindsay would not run for re-election and that this was one of the reasons he felt free to seek some other nominee.

Mr. Rose retraced the political labyrinth of the past few months in a modest office on the 25th floor at 245 Fifth Avenue, at 25th Street, headquarters of the United Hatters, Cap and Millinery Workers International Union, of which he is president. On the walls were pictures of Mr. Rose with Presidents, Governors, Mayors. In the room, where President Kennedy had sat on three occasions, was a bust of the slain

Continued on Page 50, Column 3

Robert F. Wagner

Alex Rose

WAGNER DECLINES TO RUN FOR MAYOR 'ON ANY TICKET'

Says He Lacks the Desire Needed for Job Despite Concern About City

A DIFFICULT DECISION

Son's Council Race Is Cited as Factor—Liberals Must Select New Candidate

By FRANK LYNN

Robert F. Wagner declined yesterday to run for Mayor, declaring that he did not have the "overriding desire" needed for the post and expressing concern that he might hurt the election prospects of his son, Robert Jr., who is a candidate for councilman at large in Manhattan.

"I do not plan to be a candidate for Mayor in this election, on any ticket," the former Mayor declared in a brief statement ruling out not only a Liberal party candidacy but also an independent run for Mayor.

The statement meant that it was very unlikely that the 63-year-old Democrat, who has been a major figure in the city's politics for more than two decades, would ever again seek elective office.

Abortive Attempt

It was also the final chapter in one of the most bizarre political arrangements in recent municipal history — the agreement between Governor Rockefeller and Alex Rose, the Liberal party leader, to attempt to bring back to City Hall the Democratic Mr. Wagner eight years after they had joined to support Mayor Lindsay, then a Republican, to end 12 years of Wagner rule.

The Rockefeller-Rose alliance began wavering when Republican county leaders publicly balked over the choice of their longtime political nemesis, Mr. Wagner, and collapsed completely when Mr. Wagner faced challengers in both the Republican and Liberal primaries.

State Senator John J. Marchi of Staten Island has announced his candidacy for Mayor on the Republican line while J. Stanley Shaw, Queens Liberal chairman and foe of Mr. Rose, is seeking the Liberal mayoral nomination.

But Mr. Wagner did not allude to these challenges in his statement.

The former Mayor, who was not available to newsmen to elaborate on his statement, said that the decision not to run had been difficult because of his "concern about the condition of the city."

"I have thought it over from

Continued on Page 50, Column 3

Counselor to Nixon Terms Watergate a Blow to Party

By JOHN HERBERS
Special to The New York Times

The New York Times
Anne Armstrong

WASHINGTON, April 11 — Anne Armstrong, Counselor to President Nixon, said today that the Watergate affair was hurting the Republican party across the nation.

Mrs. Armstrong, who acts as liaison between the White House and the Republican National Committee, said that she agreed with an unusually strong statement by Senator Barry Goldwater, Republican of Arizona, that the Watergate controversy was harming party fund-raising efforts and could damage Republican candidates next year unless the matter was cleared up.

Meanwhile, the grand jury investigating the Watergate break-in heard testimony today from Dwight L. Chapin, a former appointments secretary to President Nixon; Gordon C. Strachan, former assistant to H. R. Haldeman, the White House chief of staff, and Donald H. Segretti, who was paid between $30,000 and $40,000 in Republican campaign funds.

"Senator Goldwater keeps on top of Republican matters, and I must assume he is correct," Mrs. Armstrong said at a breakfast meeting with reporters. "I think he is absolutely right at the present. We are being hurt now, but I am convinced the Administration is determined to clear up this to the satisfaction of the American public."

This was the first acknowledgement from the White House that the case of political espionage last year by members of the Committee for the Re-election of the President was causing major trouble in the President's party.

Because Mrs. Armstrong is one of the President's chief aides and came to the meeting prepared to speak out on the Watergate matter, her remarks were taken as an indication of increasing concern in the White House about recent developments in the case.

Mrs. Armstrong was appointed to the Presidential staff last Dec. 18. She was co-chairman

Continued on Page 40, Column 3

184-Truck Convoy, First in 3 Weeks, Gets to Phnom Penh

Special to The New York Times

PHNOM PENH, Cambodia April 11 — A large convoy of supply trucks arrived here this afternoon, the first to make its way from the sea past Communist positions in three weeks, but a senior figure in the Government took issue with reports that Phnom Penh had been under siege.

He described the American airlift of fuel that began yesterday as "helpful but not vital" and said people here "don't get alarmed so quickly" as Europeans and Americans, implying that the airlift was an American idea.

"We are used to living simply," he declared.

The main utility of the airlift, according to Cambodian officials, is to reduce the speculative hoarding and blackmarket sales of gasoline that had created what the officials said was an artificial shortage.

The convoy that arrived today consisted of 184 trucks, carrying supplies such as food, salt, lumber and cement, but no fuel. However, fuel is expected to be arriving by road soon from Kampong Saom, the country's only seaport, now that Route 4 from the sea has been reopened.

A convoy of 120 tank trucks escorted by armored vehicles

Continued on Page 8, Column 1

Nixon Acts on Pensions

President Nixon asked Congress yesterday to establish Federal standards for improving private pension systems for 35 million workers. Details are on Page 34.

ELLSBERG TELLS OF SHIFT IN VIEWS

Describes to Jury Sights in Vietnam That Turned Him Against U.S. Role There

By MARTIN ARNOLD
Special to The New York Times

LOS ANGELES, April 11—Dr. Daniel Ellsberg testified today at the Pentagon papers trial that his feelings about the Vietnam war had been changed by such experiences as standing amid burning huts or watching schools built with American supplies turn to dust and "blow away" on the wind.

He said that at first he had been a hawk. In 1964, while working for the Defense Department, he said, he helped to plan "covert actions" against North Vietnam, such as the shelling of that country and a program to arrest and interrogate North Vietnamese fishermen.

Dr. Ellsberg said that he had participated in the planning of the bombing of the North and that he had helped gather the official signatures necessary to put the bombing operation into effect.

Became a Dove

But after he got to Vietnam, he said, he began to change to a dove, and he told the jurors of incidents that led to this change.

In his second day on the witness stand, he said:

"I saw school after school in which if you poked your heel down in the floor of the school your heel went through what was called cement. If you took a coin you could scrape away the wall."

"In a high wind it would blow away because they were mostly sand, the cement supplied by American aid," he said. "We were building schools not

Continued on Page 13, Column 1

Jurors in Mackell Inquiry Return Sealed Indictment

By DAVID BURNHAM

A special state grand jury investigating corruption in the criminal justice system of New York City handed up an unknown number of sealed indictments yesterday in State Supreme Court in Queens.

The jury, which has been taking evidence presented by the special deputy state attorney general, Maurice H. Nadjari, has been investigating the way in which the office of Queens District Attorney Thomas J. Mackell handled a criminal case against a man with whom a number of his staff members had invested money.

The indictments were presented to Supreme Court Justice John M. Murtagh by the grand jury foreman at 4:55 P.M. They were sealed at the request of Stephen Sawyer, an assistant deputy attorney general in charge of Mr. Nadjari's investigations in Queens.

Mackell's Sons Questioned

Earlier in the day, the grand jury questioned two sons of Mr. Mackell, a step the Queens District Attorney called "the worst type of Gestapo tactic."

Mr. Mackell said last night through a spokesman that he did not know what was in the indictments and therefore could not comment on them.

Similarly, Mr. Nadjari's office, through its spokesman, said it had no comment on the sealed indictments.

Mr. Sawyer refused to make any substantive comment about yesterday's indictments, declining to say how many persons were involved or when they would be arrested. He said the indictments would be made public "when the person or persons named are in custody."

The comments of witnesses who have been called to testify indicate the jury has investigated the following:

¶The handling by Mr.

Continued on Page 36, Column 3

JUDGE HALTS MOVE TO DISBAND O.E.O.

Rules Administration Lacks Authority for Cutbacks in Current Fiscal Year

By BILL KOVACH
Special to The New York Times

WASHINGTON, April 11—A Federal judge branded the Nixon Administration's efforts to dismantle the Office of Economic Opportunity as "illegal" today and ordered a halt to curtailment of the program in the current fiscal year.

In a strongly worded 41-page opinion, Judge William B. Jones of the United States District Court for the District of Columbia ordered Howard Phillips, Acting Director of the O.E.O., to halt his termination of agency programs immediately because such action was "unauthorized by law, illegal and in excess of statutory authority."

Attorneys involved in the suit, brought on behalf of four Community Action agencies threatened with termination and several labor unions representing O.E.O. employes, described Judge Jones's action as "sweeping" and "historic." One lawyer said it should offer members of Congress new support in their struggle with the Administration over the impoundment of funds appropriated by Congress.

Harold Himmelman, attorney for the Lawyers Committee for

Continued on Page 19, Column 1

A Mothers' Holiday, Then Grief in British Villages

By RICHARD EDER
Special to The New York Times

AXBRIDGE, England, April 11—Six small boys were swinging on the iron schoolyard fence in this bereaved Somerset village.

"I'll tell you a secret," said Neil Hopkins, who is 10 years old and thin and wore a heavy red wool sweater. He smiled persistently but looked very white. "My mum was on the plane."

Vance Harding broke in. "My sister was lucky," he said. "She sat in the part of the plane that didn't get all smashed to flinders."

Neil's mother, Brenda Hopkins, had organized the one-day shopping and sightseeing trip to Basel for the Axbridge Ladies' Guild. Seventy members went, and only 27 are definitely listed as survivors of yesterday's plane crash in which more than 100 died.

Mrs. Hopkins's name is not on the initial list of survivors. What remains of her family's hopes, and those of dozens of families in the village, rest in the fact that by tonight three injured survivors had still not been identified.

Last night, Mr. Hopkins, a builder, recalled the start of what was to have been a one-day holiday escape for doz-

Continued on Page 10, Column 1

Associated Press

Villagers in Axbridge, England, going to church yesterday to pray for victims and survivors of plane crash in Switzerland. Most passengers were women from Somerset.

Arabs and Israelis Battle in Europe, Too

By PAUL HOFMANN
Special to The New York Times

ROME, April 11—The recent spectacular actions by Arab and Israeli commandos have been accompanied by a chain of deadly but obscure duels among secret networks all over Europe and elsewhere, intelligence specialists here say.

Between the attack on Israeli athletes by Black September guerrillas at the Olympic Games in Munich last September and the Israeli attack on Arab guerrillas in Lebanon yesterday, at least four Arabs be believed to have played undercover roles were killed in Rome, Paris, and Nicosia, Cyprus, and an Israeli security agent was shot to death in Madrid.

Security experts here say they are convinced that Arab and Israeli clandestine organizations have contributed to the rash of letter bombs since last September that has killed an Israeli diplomat in London and caused injuries to other people in various places.

The assassination of an Iraqi in Paris last Friday is believed here to have been yet another episode in Arab-Israeli underground warfare. The victim was Basil el-Kubaisi, 40, who was identified as a teacher at the American University in Beirut, but the university denied that he was on the faculty. The Popular Front for the Liberation of Palestine, a leftist guerrilla organization, said in Beirut that the slain man was a member on a mission in Paris.

Mr. Kubaisi had been traveling extensively in Europe, and security sources here say that he was probably trailed by Israeli agents for some time. He was walking in the Madeleine district of Paris late at night when, according to a witness, he was shot by two young men who escaped.

Several similar attacks have been reported in West Germany in recent months. Since the beginning of 1972 at least seven Palestinians, all believed to have been connected with secret organizations, are said to have been killed or to have disappeared in West Germany.

In Rome, gunmen who remain unidentified killed a pre-

Continued on Page 16, Column 1

NEWS INDEX

F.P.C. PLAN POINTS TO GAS PRICE RISE

National Ceiling Sought to Replace Regional Control

By EDWARD COWAN
Special to The New York Times

WASHINGTON, April 11 — The Federal Power Commission, in a step apparently designed to raise natural gas prices, began today a streamlined proceeding to establish a uniform national ceiling price for gas from new wells in all parts of the United States.

The higher prices presumably would be passed on to most industrial and residential consumers and might also tend to nudge up the prices of competing fuels, notably oil. Gas accounted for one-third of all energy supplies last year and more than 55 per cent of the nation's homes were heated by gas.

The three present commission members — two seats are vacant — are known to believe that gas prices must go higher to encourage more exploration and discovery of additional gas supplies.

The new rate would apply to wells begun after Jan. 1, 1973. It would replace the seven so-called area rates, or regional ceilings on producer prices, now in effect. Produc-

Continued on Page 72, Column 4

A Mothers' Holiday, Then Grief in British Villages

Continued From Page 1, Col. 1

of families in the village, rest in the fact that by tonight three injured survivors had still not been identified.

Last night, Mr. Hopkins, a builder, recalled the start of what was to have been a one-day holiday escape for dozens of mothers in this lovely, quiet, strawberry-growing part of the Somerset countryside.

"I never like saying good-by to my wife," he said, "but this morning she came upstairs and said, 'See you tonight, love,' and I replied, 'I hope so. I hope so.'"

The crash of the four-engine Vanguard airliner owned by Invicta, a tour-flight operator, has crushed the flow of life in half a dozen villages around here. In Cheddar, three miles west of here, the vicar, the Rev. Donald Denman, said:

"It has been worse than Aberfan. Here it is the mothers of whole families who died." At the Welsh mining village of Aberfan in 1966, a hill of coal waste collapsed, killing 116 children and 28 adults.

3 Survivors Out of 23

Cheddar, whose "Mums'-Night-Out Club" had joined the **Axbridge** Ladies' Guild in booking seats for the flight, has only three survivors of some 23 who took the trip.

With figures still unclear, it is estimated that 40 to 60 small children from Axbridge, Cheddar and the nearby villages of Yatton, Wrington

The New York Times/April 12, 1973

A women's group from Axbridge was aboard plane that crashed near Basel.

and Congresbury have been left motherless.

Nowhere is the sense of shock and grief more tangible than here in Axbridge, a tiny town whose main square is surmounted by a 12th-century Norman church and whose men work in the strawberry fields or in 'the local stores.

"All their lives, all their grandfathers' lives have been spent here," said the Rev. Richard Impey, who had come from Wells to assist Axbridge's overburdened vicar, the Rev. Anthony Martin.

Last night Mr. Martin led a night service at the church. Today the church was empty and the vicar, a thin, slight man, was tracing and retracing his steps, through the village streets, head bent low, to visit the bereaved.

At the post office, which doubles as a small general store, Mrs. Mary Cox was talking with the postmistress, Mrs. Jill Helps, and her husband, Brian.

"I've never been on a plane. I always wanted to." said Mrs. Cox wonderingly.

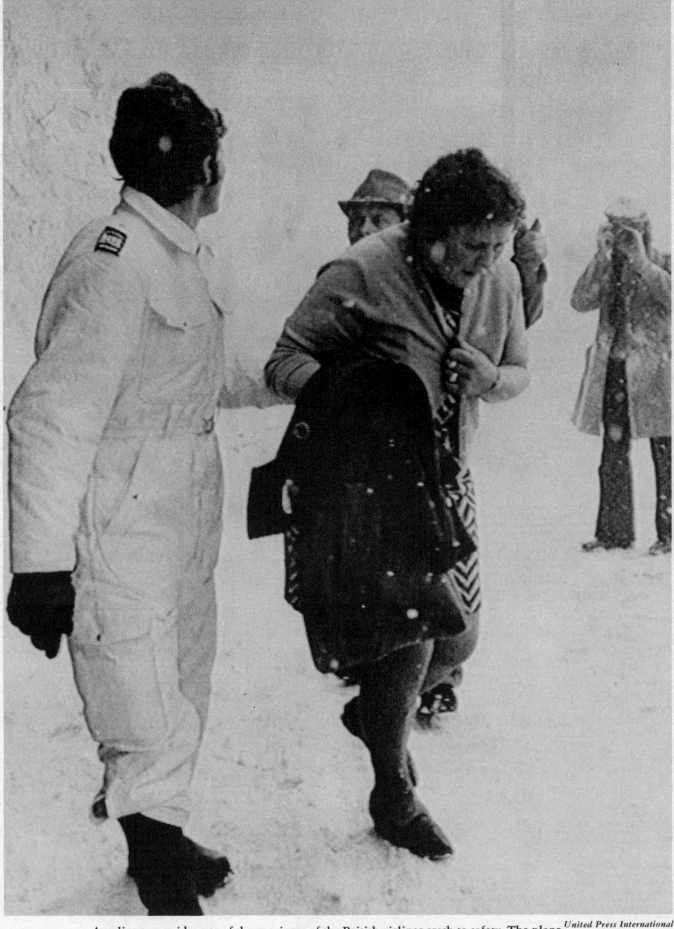

A policeman guides one of the survivors of the British airliner crash to safety. The plane was making a second instrument landing attempt in fog and blinding snow when it crashed and exploded.

United Press International

"We shan't be flying again, Mrs. Cox," said Mr. Helps. "People are heartbroken here," said Mrs. Helps. "So many lovely girls, super mums—just one day they went off and this was it." She added:

"They weren't in the habit of holidays." It was this point—that the disaster had claimed women for whom this was to have been a first sampling of foreign travel—that the villagers stressed over and over.

"Take Mrs. Sandford, the butcher's wife," said Kenneth Limp, who manages a local bank. "I don't think she'd had more than a day off in

her life—maybe one or two Sundays at Weston-super-Mare."

The High Street, a row of low stone houses and stores, was utterly quiet except for an occasional passing car, its windshield magnifying the stiff, swollen faces within. Every few shops bore a notice, "Closed today," and at one, an announcement for a cheese and wine party carried the word "Canceled" in thick red crayon.

Everyone in the village was drawn, on any excuse, or none, to the square. At one end, in the Oak House Hotel—three of its waitresses

died—volunteers from local organizations were taking telephone calls, comforting relatives, and trying to make up a list of who had died and who had survived.

Inside, the volunteers pressed past each other in the narrow hall, carrying coffee, or lists. One woman rubbed the feet of an old man who had collapsed on a sofa and lay weeping, his face shielded by a wrist encased in a starched cuff.

The villagers waited outside, wandering through the square or standing in knots, edging toward each other and away from two dozen cameramen who circulated

among them. At 4 in the afternoon two buses pulled up and were quickly loaded with relatives who were to go to Bristol to catch special flights for Basel.

Most of those who sat waiting for the buses to pull out did not know whether they would be identifying the dead or greeting one of the three unidentified injured.

The buses left and a young man with curly hair, who had just seen his sister off, moved away. Two old women went up and hugged him.

"If there's anything we can do, don't hesitate to let us know, will you, Raymond, my love," the older one said.

"All the News That's Fit to Print"

The New York Times

LATE CITY EDITION

Weather: Partly cloudy today; fog tonight. Chance of rain tomorrow. Temp. range: today 68-79; Tuesday 68-86. Temp.-Hum. Index yesterday 78. Full U.S. report on Page 78.

VOL. CXXII... No. 42,193 © 1973 The New York Times Company NEW YORK, WEDNESDAY, AUGUST 1, 1973 — 15 CENTS

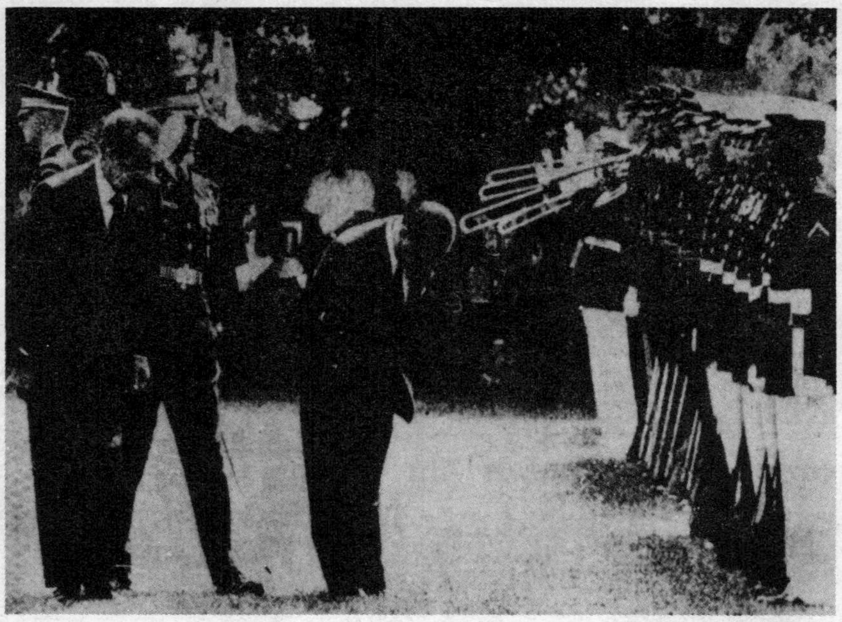

Premier Kakuei Tanaka of Japan bowing to honor guard before reviewing it with President Nixon — United Press International

HALDEMAN CHALLENGED BY PANEL ON VERSION OF CONTENTS OF TAPES; NIXON ALONE TO DECIDE ON ACCESS

PRESIDENT'S GOAL

Aide Says Nixon Will Judge Who Can Help Him Learn Facts

By R. W. APPLE Jr.

Special to The New York Times

WASHINGTON, July 31—The White House said today that President Nixon, acting alone, would decide who should be given access to the tape recordings of his conversations about the Watergate case.

Mr. Nixon made his decisions, said the deputy Presidential press secretary, Gerald L. Warren, "based on the President's judgment of who could best assist him in determining the facts of the Watergate matter without jeopardizing the confidentiality of the tapes."

The matter was raised by reporters as a result of testimony yesterday by H. R. Haldeman, Mr. Nixon's former chief of staff, who told the Senate Watergate committee that he had listened to two crucial tapes—one of them at his home several weeks after he left the Government's employ.

Dozens of Questions

Of all the present and former White House aides accused of involvement in the Watergate affair, Mr. Haldeman is the only one known to have heard any tapes.

Mr. Warren was asked dozens of questions, few of which he was willing to answer. Most of them dealt with two central problems: the confidentiality of the recordings and the fairness or unfairness of giving some persons access while denying it to others.

Mr. Nixon has refused to honor subpoenas from the committee for certain tapes and from his special prosecutor, Archibald Cox, on the ground that they are private Presidential papers protected from subpoena by executive privilege and the separation of powers.

Difficulty Is Cited

But his lawyer, Prof. Charles Alan Wright of the University of Texas, said at a news briefing last Thursday:

"It is very difficult to make any claim of privilege for material that is no longer confidential. I don't rule out the possibility that there will be some cases in which it could happen, but I can't offhand think of an example of a nonconfidential document as to which you have a constitutional privilege."

One of the documents that Mr. Nixon agreed to turn over to Mr. Cox, while rejecting his subpoena demanding others, was a memorandum that had lost its confidentiality when

Continued on Page 20, Column 7

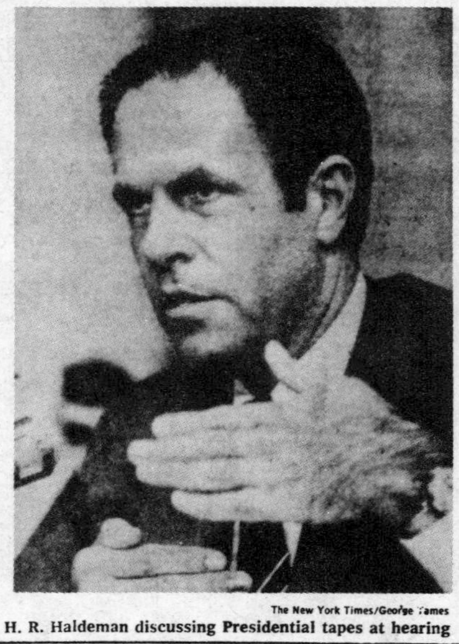

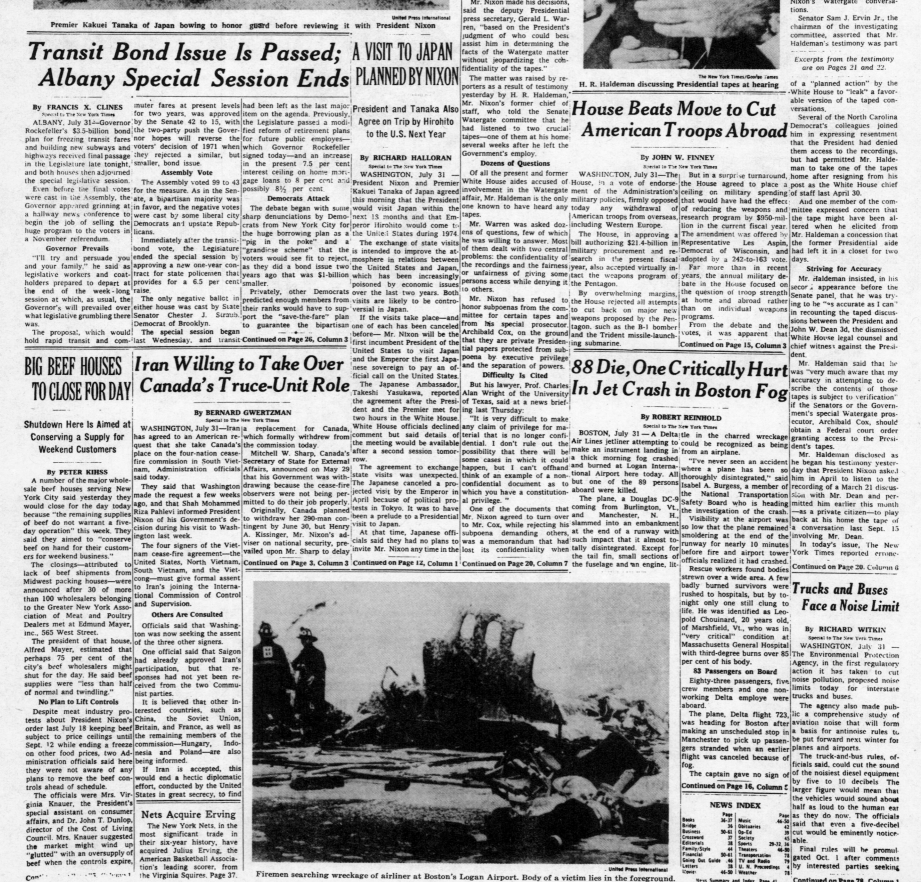

The New York Times/George Tames

H. R. Haldeman discussing Presidential tapes at hearing

SENATORS IRATE

Ervin Sees a 'Planned Action' to Leak a Version of Talks

By JAMES M. NAUGHTON

Special to The New York Times

WASHINGTON, July 31—The Senate Watergate committee challenged, in terms of alarm and indignation, the testimony today of H. R. Haldeman about the contents of secret White House recordings of President Nixon's Watergate conversations.

Senator Sam J. Ervin Jr., the chairman of the investigating committee, asserted that Mr. Haldeman's testimony was part

Excerpts from the testimony are on Pages 21 and 22.

of a "planned action" by the White House to "leak" a favorable version of the taped conversations.

Several of the North Carolina Democrat's colleagues joined him in expressing resentment that the President had denied them access to the recordings, but had permitted Mr. Haldeman to take one of the tapes home after resigning from his post as the White House chief of staff last April 30.

And one member of the committee expressed concern that the tape might have been altered when he elicited from Mr. Haldeman a concession that the former Presidential aide had left it in a closet for two days.

Striving for Accuracy

Mr. Haldeman insisted, in his second appearance before the Senate panel, that he was trying to be "as accurate as I can" in recounting the taped discussions between the President and John W. Dean 3d, the dismissed White House legal counsel and chief witness against the President.

Mr. Haldeman said that he was "very much aware that my accuracy in attempting to describe the contents of those tapes is subject to verification" if the Senators or the Government's special Watergate prosecutor, Archibald Cox, should obtain a Federal court order granting access to the President's tapes.

Mr. Haldeman disclosed as he began his testimony yesterday that President Nixon asked him in April to listen to the recording of a March 21 discussion with Mr. Dean and permitted him earlier this month—as a private citizen—to play back at his home the tape of a conversation last Sept. 15 involving Mr. Dean.

In today's issue, The New York Times reported errone-

Continued on Page 20, Column 6

Transit Bond Issue Is Passed; Albany Special Session Ends

By FRANCIS X. CLINES

Special to The New York Times

ALBANY, July 31—Governor Rockefeller's $3.5-billion bond plan for freezing transit fares and building new subways and highways received final passage in the Legislature late tonight, and both houses then adjourned the special legislative session.

Even before the final votes were cast in the Assembly, the Governor appeared grinning at a hallway news conference to begin the job of selling the huge program to the voters in a November referendum.

Governor Prevails

"I'll try and persuade you and your family," he said as legislative workers and coat-holders prepared to depart at the end of the week-long session at which, as usual, the Governor's will prevailed over what legislative grumbling there was.

The proposal, which would hold rapid transit and commuter fares at present levels for two years, was approved by the Senate 42 to 15, with the two-party push the Governor hopes will reverse the voters' decision of 1971 when they rejected a similar, but smaller, bond issue.

Assembly Vote

The Assembly voted 99 to 43 for the measure. As in the Senate, a bipartisan majority was in favor, and the negative votes were cast by some liberal city Democrats and upstate Republicans.

Immediately after the transit-bond vote, the Legislature ended the special session by approving a new one-year contract for state policemen that provides for a 6.5 per cent raise.

The only negative ballot in either house was cast by State Senator Chester J. Straub, Democrat of Brooklyn.

The special session began last Wednesday, and transit had been left as the last major item on the agenda. Previously, the Legislature passed a modified reform of retirement plans for future public employees—which Governor Rockefeller signed today—and an increase in the present 7.5 per cent interest ceiling on home mortgage loans to 8 per cent and possibly 8½ per cent.

Democrats Attack

The debate began with some sharp denunciations by Democrats from New York City for the huge borrowing plan as a "pig in the poke" and a "grandiose scheme" that the voters would see fit to reject, as they did a bond issue two years ago that was $1-billion smaller.

Privately, other Democrats predicted enough members from their ranks would have to support the "save-the-fare" plan to guarantee the bipartisan

Continued on Page 26, Column 3

A VISIT TO JAPAN PLANNED BY NIXON

President and Tanaka Also Agree on Trip by Hirohito to the U.S. Next Year

By RICHARD HALLORAN

Special to The New York Times

WASHINGTON, July 31 — President Nixon and Premier Kakuei Tanaka of Japan agreed this morning that the President would visit Japan within the next 18 months and that Emperor Hirohito would come to the United States during 1974.

The exchange of state visits is intended to improve the atmosphere in relations between the United States and Japan, which has been increasingly poisoned by economic issues over the last two years. Both visits are likely to be controversial in Japan.

If the visits take place—and one of each has been canceled before— Mr. Nixon will be the first incumbent President of the United States to visit Japan and the Emperor the first Japanese sovereign to pay an official call on the United States.

The Japanese Ambassador, Takeshi Yasukawa, reported the agreement after the President and the Premier met for two hours in the White House. White House officials declined comment but said details of the meeting would be available after a second session tomorrow.

The agreement to exchange state visits was unexpected. The Japanese canceled a projected visit by the Emperor in April because of political protests in Tokyo. It was to have been a prelude to a Presidential visit to Japan.

At that time, Japanese officials said they had no plans to invite Mr. Nixon any time in the

Continued on Page 12, Column 1

House Beats Move to Cut American Troops Abroad

By JOHN W. FINNEY

Special to The New York Times

WASHINGTON, July 31—The House, in a vote of endorsement of the Administration's military policies, firmly opposed today any withdrawal of American troops from overseas, including Western Europe.

The House, in approving a bill authorizing $21.4-billion in military procurement and research in the present fiscal year, also accepted virtually intact the weapons program of the Pentagon.

By overwhelming margins, the House rejected all attempts to cut back on major new weapons proposed by the Pentagon, such as the B-1 bomber and the Trident missile-launching submarine.

But in a surprise turnaround, the House agreed to place a ceiling on military spending that would have had the effect of reducing the weapons and research program by $950-million in the current fiscal year. The amendment was offered by Representative Les Aspin, Democrat of Wisconsin, and adopted by a 242-to-163 vote.

Far more than in recent years, the annual military debate in the House focused on the question of troop strength at home and abroad rather than on individual weapons programs.

From the debate and the votes, it was apparent that

Continued on Page 15, Column 3

BIG BEEF HOUSES TO CLOSE FOR DAY

Shutdown Here Is Aimed at Conserving a Supply for Weekend Customers

By PETER KIHSS

A number of the major wholesale beef houses serving New York City said yesterday they would close for the day today because "the remaining supplies of beef do not warrant a five-day operation" this week. They said they aimed to "conserve beef on hand for their customers for weekend business."

The closings—attributed to lack of beef shipments from Midwest packing houses—were announced after 30 of more than 100 wholesalers belonging to the Greater New York Association of Meat and Poultry Dealers met at Edmund Mayer, Inc., 565 West Street.

The president of that house, Alfred Mayer, estimated that perhaps 75 per cent of the city's beef wholesalers might shut for the day. He said beef supplies were "less than half of normal and twindling."

No Plan to Lift Controls

Despite meat industry protests about President Nixon's order last July 18 keeping beef subject to price ceilings until Sept. 12 while ending a freeze on other food prices, two Administration officials said here they were not aware of any plans to remove the beef controls ahead of schedule.

The officials were Mrs. Virginia Knauer, the President's special assistant on consumer affairs, and Dr. John T. Dunlop, director of the Cost of Living Council. Mrs. Knauer suggested the market might wind up "glutted" with an oversupply of beef when the controls expire,

Con[illegible]3, Column 1

Iran Willing to Take Over Canada's Truce-Unit Role

By BERNARD GWERTZMAN

Special to The New York Times

WASHINGTON, July 31—Iran has agreed to an American request that she take Canada's place on the four-nation cease-fire commission in South Vietnam, Administration officials said today.

They said that Washington made the request a few weeks ago, and that Shah Mohammed Riza Pahlevi informed President Nixon of his Government's decision during his visit to Washington last week.

The four signers of the Vietnam cease-fire agreement—the United States, North Vietnam, South Vietnam, and the Vietcong—must give formal assent to Iran's joining the International Commission of Control and Supervision.

Others Are Consulted

Officials said that Washington was now seeking the assent of the three other signers.

One official said that Saigon had already approved Iran's participation, but that responses had not yet been received from the two Communist parties.

It is believed that other interested countries, such as China, the Soviet Union, Britain, and France, as well as the remaining members of the commission—Hungary, Indonesia and Poland—are also being informed.

If Iran is accepted, this would end a hectic diplomatic effort, conducted by the United States in great secrecy, to find a replacement for Canada, which formally withdrew from the commission today.

Mitchell W. Sharp, Canada's Secretary of State for External Affairs, announced on May 29 that his Government was withdrawing because the cease-fire observers were not being permitted to do their job properly.

Originally, Canada planned to withdraw her 290-man contingent by June 30, but Henry A. Kissinger, Mr. Nixon's adviser on national security, prevailed upon Mr. Sharp to delay

Continued on Page 3, Column 3

Nets Acquire Erving

The New York Nets, in the most significant trade in their six-year history, have acquired Julius Erving, the American Basketball Association's leading scorer, from the Virginia Squires. Page 37.

88 Die, One Critically Hurt In Jet Crash in Boston Fog

By ROBERT REINHOLD

Special to The New York Times

BOSTON, July 31 — A Delta Air Lines jetliner attempting to make an instrument landing in a thick morning fog crashed and burned at Logan International Airport here today. All but one of the 89 persons aboard were killed.

The plane, a Douglas DC-9 coming from Burlington, Vt., and Manchester, N. H., slammed into an embankment at the end of a runway with such impact that it almost totally disintegrated. Except for the tail fin, small sections of the fuselage and an engine, little in the charred wreckage could be recognized as being from an airplane.

"I've never seen an accident where a plane has been so thoroughly disintegrated," said Isabel A. Burgess, a member of the National Transportation Safety Board who is heading the investigation of the crash.

Visibility at the airport was so low that the plane remained smoldering at the end of the runway for nearly 10 minutes before fire and airport tower officials realized it had crashed.

Rescue workers found bodies strewn over a wide area. A few badly burned survivors were rushed to hospitals, but by tonight only one still clung to life. He was identified as Leopold Chouinard, 20 years old, of Marshfield, Vt., who was in "very critical" condition at Massachusetts General Hospital with third-degree burns over 85 per cent of his body.

83 Passengers on Board

Eighty-three passengers, five crew members and one non-working Delta employe were aboard.

The plane, Delta flight 723, was heading for Boston after making an unscheduled stop in Manchester to pick up passengers stranded when an earlier flight was canceled because of fog.

The captain gave no sign of

Continued on Page 16, Column 5

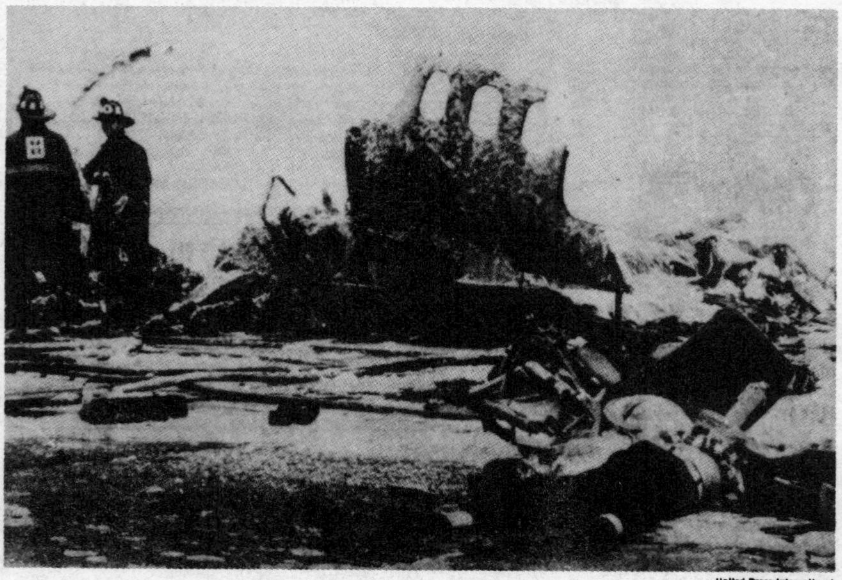

United Press International

Firemen searching wreckage of airliner at Boston's Logan Airport. Body of a victim lies in the foreground.

Trucks and Buses Face a Noise Limit

By RICHARD WITKIN

Special to The New York Times

WASHINGTON, July 31 — The Environmental Protection Agency, in the first regulatory action it has taken to cut noise pollution, proposed noise limits today for interstate trucks and buses.

The agency also made public a comprehensive study of aviation noise that will form a basis for antinoise rules to be put forward next winter for planes and airports.

The truck-and-bus rules, officials said, could cut the sound of the noisiest diesel equipment by five to 10 decibels. The larger figure would mean that the vehicles would sound about half as loud to the human ear as they do now. The officials said that even a five-decibel cut would be eminently noticeable.

Final rules will be promulgated Oct. 1 after comments by interested parties seeking

Continued on Page 78, Column 1

NEWS INDEX

One of the victims of the Delta DC-9 that crashed and burned as it attempted to land in heavy fog at Logan International Airport lies in the foam as firemen search through the scattered wreckage for other victims.

United Press International

88 Die and One Is Hurt in Jet Crash in Boston Fog

Continued From Page 1, Col. 7

difficulty as the craft swooped down over Boston Harbor toward runway 4 Right, which juts out into the water. An official of the Federal Aviation Administration said the pilot maintained normal voice contact with the control tower until impact.

The fog was so thick that the crash at the end of the 10,000-foot runway could not be seen by the tower. It was not until 11:18, nine minutes after it occurred, that the airport fire station learned of the accident from some construction workers who were working near the site.

Men aboard fire trucks and rescue vehicles dispatched by the Massachusetts Port Authority, which operates the airport, found a scene of incredible horror.

Firemen sprayed the burning parts of the wreckage with fire-extinguishing foam as scores of ambulances and rescue vehicles surrounded the fuselage of the plane.

Everything seemed to have been torn apart. Blue and red seats, many with passengers still strapped in, littered the runway. Two pairs of landing gear lay askew about 200 feet from the main wreckage. A section of the tail assembly lay against the concrete abutment.

There was almost no sign of life. The bodies, wrapped in white sheets, were carried out on stretchers and taken by truck to the fire station a mile away, where they were placed on the floor. By mid-afternoon, 20 or so bodies had not yet been retrieved.

The crash was the first major accident at Logan since Oct. 4, 1960, when an Eastern Airlines Electra crashed, resulting in 62 deaths.

The underlying cause of the accident was not immediately known, but it appeared that the craft touched the ground about 3,500 feet short of where it should have, according to Richard E. Mooney, aviation director of the Port Authority.

Ferris J. Howland, regional director of the F.A.A., said the plane appeared to have struck the seawall several hundred feet beyond the lower end of the runway.

Despite the dense fog, airport officials insisted the weather conditions were satisfactory.

"We were open and operating normally — we had no problems," said Ron Brinn, a spokesman for the Port Authority.

Mr. Howland concurred, saying, "Without a doubt the weather was within operating conditions." The final decision on whether to land under such conditions is made by the pilot, and Mr. Howland reported that two other pilots veered off before landing just after the Delta crashed. This was before the accident was discovered, after which the airport was shut down for about two hours.

Michael Cicarelli, an F.A.A. spokesman, said that the minimum conditions for landing depended on the type of equip-

ment aboard the plane and the qualifications of the pilot. At the time of the crash, he said, the ceiling was 400 feet and the visibility was a half-mile to a mile.

The F.A.A. said that all airport and tower instruments were in working order. The officials expect to reconstruct the Delta jet's path from the flight recorder, which has been retrieved intact and sent to Washington for analysis.

Even though he was making an instrument landing, officials said, the pilot required visual contact with the runway for the touchdown. Since he signaled no distress before impact, it was possible that he mistook the earthen embankment between the water and the pavement for the runway.

Because of the fog, there were few eyewitnesses. One was Geoffrey Keating, a construction worker on the field. "I looked up and saw a sheet of flame—it was like a field of fire," he said, "and then I heard a loud thud."

The New York Times/Aug. 1, 1973

First in 20 Years

ATLANTA, July 31 (UPI)— The crash of a Delta Air Lines DC-9 at Boston today was the first fatal accident for one of the airline's scheduled passenger flights in more than 20 years. Delta said the last such accident occurred May 17, 1953, when a DC-3 crashed at Marshall, Tex., killing 16 passengers and three crew members.

"All the News That's Fit to Print"

The New York Times

LATE CITY EDITION

Weather: Extremely hot today; very warm tonight. Hot tomorrow. Temp. range: today 79-98; Tuesday 77-98. Temp.-Hum. Index yesterday 85. Full U.S. report on Page 74.

VOL. CXXII . No. 42,221 © 1973 The New York Times Company   NEW YORK, WEDNESDAY, AUGUST 29, 1973   15 CENTS

1,000 Trapped in an IRT Tunnel Accident

Man Dies of Heart Attack in 115° Heat —18 Need Stretchers as Ceiling Falls

By PAUL L. MONTGOMERY

One man died and 1,000 passengers were trapped in 115-degree heat and heavy smoke yesterday after an archway in the ancient Flushing line tunnel under the East River collapsed on the first car of a Queens-bound IRT train.

At least 18 passengers were carried from the tunnel on stretchers by sweating policemen and firemen, and scores of others had to be assisted to the street for treatment before they were sent home. The dead man apparently suffered a heart attack in the heat, smoke and confusion.

Normal service on the Flushing line was restored at 8:46 P.M. after the track at the site of the collapse, near First Avenue and 42d Street, had been cleared.

A chunk of concrete 20 feet long apparently worked loose from iron retaining rings at an archway of the two-track tunnel and crashed into the side of the first car of an 11-car train that had left Grand Cen-

The 1 hour 20 minutes that the passengers were trapped in the intense heat and smoke was a time of terror and quiet **Continued on Page 44, Column 3**

heroism, of chaos and people finding a moment to be kind to one another. Many remarked about the minimum of hysteria.

"There was no panic, compliments to the people," said a fireman, Edward Boljonis, of Ladder Company No. 2.

The accident, the first in the subways since 1971 involving a passenger fatality, occurred at the Manhattan end of the old Steinway tunnel between Long Island City, Queens, and Grand Central Terminal, two blocks east of the Grand Central stop. The tunnel, the oldest in the system, was built at the turn of the century for trolley cars.

The New York Times/Larry Morris
Mother accompanies fireman carrying child from subway

The New York Times/Michael Evans
Passengers at Grand Central Station after leaving train, which was pulled back from tunnel after mishap

98° Heat Record for Year; City Power Usage at Peak

By FRANK J. PRIAL

New York sweltered through its hottest day of the year yesterday, and the city consumed more electricity than ever before although Consolidated Edison was forced to cut the voltage by 5 per cent.

The temperature in the city hit 98 degrees at 3:30 P.M., a record for the year and only 2 degrees under the record for the date, 100 degrees in 1948. Con Edison said its customers were using 8,161 megawatts of electricity, a record at 2:30 P.M. The previous high demand was 8,136 megawatts recorded on Aug. 10.

The tropical temperatures

Official Temperatures

were expected to hold, probably until Friday, as were record high pollen counts, which caused distress for hay-fever sufferers.

The illegal opening of fire hydrants, particularly in poor neighborhoods, caused the Department of Water Resources to post its first water alert, setting off a series of internal procedures devised to cope with falling water pressure. The alert was in effect from 2 P.M. to 6 P.M., Water Resources Commissioner Martin Lang reported.

Mr. Lang said the opening of fire hydrants coincided with especially heavy water consumption attributable to the heat. He estimated that water was being used yesterday at a rate of 1.9 million gallons a day, compared with a usual 1.3 million gallons.

Most New Yorkers coped **Continued on Page 44, Column 7**

AN AGNEW FRIEND SAID TO AID INQUIRY

Financier in Baltimore Is Believed Ready to Talk in Exchange for Immunity

By BEN A. FRANKLIN
Special to The New York Times

BALTIMORE, Aug. 28—Another key witness in the Federal investigation of the possible role of a number of officials, including Vice President Agnew, in kickbacks from Maryland contractors was reported today to be cooperating with the United States Attorney's office here in return for preferential treatment.

Informed sources said that I. H. Hammerman 2d, one of Mr. Agnew's closest friends in this city, was negotiating with George Beall, the United States Attorney for Maryland. In return for limited immunity from prosecution, sources familiar with the investigation here said, Mr. Hammerman is prepared to provide the prosecutor with information.

It could not be learned whether his testimony, if it ever reached the grand jury, would concern directly the allegation of bribery, extortion and Federal tax fraud that Mr. Beall has told Mr. Agnew by letter were the focus of an investigation surrounding the Vice President. Mr. Agnew also has extensive friendships and connections with others under investigation here.

Mr. Agnew and Mr. Hammerman were sixth-graders together here, and Mr. Hammerman has recently been a leader in **Continued on Page 22, Column 1**

Solzhenitsyn Tells Of Threats to Life

By The Associated Press

MOSCOW, Aug. 28—Aleksandr I. Solzhenitsyn, in a rare and bluntly outspoken interview with two Western newsmen, has declared that his life has been threatened. The Nobel Prize novelist, whose writings are banned in his homeland, added that if he was imprisoned or killed, "the main part of my works will be published."

Mr. Solzhenitsyn, winner of the Nobel Prize for Literature in 1970, said he and his family — he and his second wife have two children — had received warnings. "If I am declared killed or suddenly mysteriously dead," he added, the **Continued on Page 8, Column 1**

WIDE PRICE SURGE INCREASING COSTS PAID BY FACTORIES

Purchasing Agents Report Rises That Certainly Will Be Passed to Consumers

By MICHAEL C. JENSEN

The nation's manufacturers in the last two weeks have experienced the strongest surge of price increases for the materials they buy since the Nixon Administration's original Phase 1 price freeze ended in 1971, according to a survey of 250 companies.

The new price increases represent the bulge that the Administration said would appear at the end of its second freeze on Aug. 13. The higher costs are certain to be passed along to customers in the form of more expensive consumer goods.

The survey which was tabulated yesterday by the National Association of Purchasing Management, is scheduled for release in about two weeks.

More Next Month

Next month is expected to bring even sharper increases because many large companies, which must give the Government 30 days notice before raising most prices, will be allowed to increase prices under Phase 4 rules.

Although price increases in industrial commodities are not as visible to consumers as rises in the cost of groceries and other retail goods, they play a pivotal role in checking or fueling inflation.

When a company has to pay higher prices for raw materials (like chemicals and copper), or finished products (like office supplies and cardboard cartons), those costs are quickly reflected in higher retail prices for the company's own products.

Officers Comment

Telephone interviews with corporate officers across the country reinforced the survey's conclusion that prices had risen rapidly and broadly following relaxation of the Administration's price freeze.

"We've been hit left and right," said Arlo E. Carney, director of purchases for the Belden Corporation, a Chicago wire manufacturer that uses a variety of fabricated metal products.

Like other corporate executives who were queried, Mr. Carney said he had been bombarded with increases since the **Continued on Page 45, Column 1**

MORE THAN 500 DIE IN MEXICAN QUAKE AND TOLL IS RISING

The Injured Exceed 1,000 as Temblor Devastates Towns and Villages

By The Associated Press

MEXICO CITY, Aug. 28—A predawn earthquake ripped through the center of Mexico today, devastating towns and villages in the country's worst disaster in modern history. More than 500 persons were reported dead and more than 1,000 injured.

[A Government communiqué said Wednesday that 575 deaths had been confirmed, Reuters reported.]

Most of the 80 persons reported dead in Orizaba, in Veracruz state, were in a five-story building badly damaged by the quake.

Cracks 100 yards wide surrounded a string of devastated small towns in much of the stricken area across the states of Puebla, Veracruz and Oaxaca. The three states form a belt across central Mexico south of the capital.

Blood Donors Sought

President Luis Echeverria Alvarez ordered immediate full-scale aid for the area. Public appeals were issued for blood donors.

"It was before dawn when the earthquake began and then I thought it was going to be the end of the world," said Santiago Martínez, 67 years old, of Tehuacán, about 160 miles east of Mexico City. He said his son had been killed in the quake.

The earthquake, the strongest in Mexico in decades, measured variously 5.5 and 6.5 on the open-ended Richter scale.

The quake added thousands to the list of homeless in central and eastern Mexico. The area was just recovering from the effects of a hurricane and a month of torrential rains that **Continued on Page 12, Column 3**

INDIA TO RELEASE 90,000 PAKISTANIS IN PEACE ACCORD

Hard-Sought Settlement of the 1971 Conflict Is Reached—War Crimes Issues Appear to Be Resolved

Special to The New York Times

NEW DELHI, Aug. 28—India and Pakistan signed an agreement here today clearing the way for the release of most of the 90,000 Pakistani prisoners held in India and for settlement of other problems arising from their war in December, 1971.

The accord, reached after 19 days of difficult negotiations spread over two months in Islamabad and New Delhi, also provides a procedure for Pakistani recognition of Bangladesh. Bangladesh, the Bengali region that until December, 1971, was the eastern wing of Pakistan, did not participate in the negotiations since her independence had not yet been recognized by the Pakistanis.

However Sheik Mujibur Rahman, Prime Minister of Bangladesh, had been consulted by India during the negotiations, and his Foreign Minister, Kamal Hossain, said today in Dacca: "We are fully satisfied with the agreement. It has our full concurrence."

A Tacit Agreement

Other key provisions call for the release of Bangladesh and Pakistani nationals stranded in the two countries.

The most crucial point was said to be tacit agreement by Bangladesh, in exchange for the recognition by Pakistan, to drop her threat to hold war-crimes trials. In return Pakistan appears to have dropped her plan to hold 203 Bengalis for trial as a reprisal for any war-crimes action in Bangladesh.

Bangladesh had named 195 of the 90,000 Pakistani prisoners of war as persons to be tried **Continued on Page 4, Column 5**

on charges of war crimes. But the issue, according to the agreement, is to be the subject of talks between Bangladesh and Pakistan. The release is expected to start within two weeks.

Details of the agreement, signed by the two chief negotiators, Parmeshwar Narain Haksar of India and Aziz Ahmed of Pakistan, are to be made public officially tomorrow. Informed sources, who reported the broad outlines of the accord, expressed confidence that it would lead to a durable peace.

Other Provisions Listed

India and Pakistan have gone to war three times since they became independent nations in 1947. Besides the 17-day war of December, 1971, which ended with the defeat of Pakistan and the emergence of Bangladesh, they fought twice over Kashmir, in 1948 and 1965.

According to the informants, the accord signed today includes the following:

¶Pakistan agrees to a firm time table for recognizing Bangladesh and discussing the prisoner issue on the understanding that she will not oppose Bangladesh's admission to the United Nations.

¶Pakistan is to release all stranded Bengalis, their number to be ascertained by "neutral agencies."

¶Pakistan is to admit from Bangladesh an unspecified number of Biharis. Many of these non-Bengali Moslems collaborated with the Pakistanis in at-**Continued on Page 4, Column 5**

West Point Simplifies Cadet Regulations

By JAMES FERON
Special to The New York Times

WEST POINT, Aug. 28—The United States Military Academy has rewritten its book of regulations, replacing decades of accumulated restrictions with a simplified code emphasizing self-discipline.

The revised version, which took four months to complete and went into effect yesterday, is part of a new philosophy that the Academy is introducing to adapt to a changing society as well as to respond to its critics.

Broad Outlines Offered

The revised code, described by officers here as the most comprehensive regulation change in the academy's 171-year history, simplifies many rules and offers broad outlines on others.

The commandant of cadets, Brig. Gen. Phillip R. Feir, said some prohibitions in the old code were self-evident. "For example, one regulation stipulated that 'No shoes will be worn into the shower room' and 'Showers will be fully turned off after use.'"

"We've been manning the bastions here, hanging tight to

our standards in a society that was saying there were no standards," General Knowlton said. "Now we feel the pressure is off, and the first step was to redo the 'blue book.'"

The words remain out of bounds, although regulations no longer contain pages of cross-hatched areas marking each potential trysting place. "For me to say cadets will stay out of the woods will not keep them out," General Feir said.

'Area Tours' Retained

The new rules also will eliminate some traditional disciplinary measures—including the hated confinement—while leaving others unchanged, such as "area tours" (marching back and forth in full uniform with a rifle, sometimes hours).

Confinement meant that cadets could be restricted to their rooms during free-time periods for up to six months. "This was stifling and counter-productive," General Feir said.

The superintendent said he had asked General Feir to come **Continued on Page 18, Column 4**

Robert Dowling Dies

Robert W. Dowling, former president and chairman of the City Investing Company, died yesterday at his home in the Pierre Hotel. He was 77 years old. He served on many civic, cultural, educational and professional organizations. Details on Page 40.

'Culture' Bus Route To Run Weekends

By EDWARD C. BURKS

The Transit Authority is starting an experimental "culture loop" bus route this Saturday to run 17 miles through midtown and upper Manhattan with all-day, multiride tickets costing $1.

The project will allow passengers to get off as many times as they want at cultural institutions along the way and reboard later buses without paying any additional fares.

The route of 22 stops includes museums, churches, Lincoln Center, Rockefeller Center, the Central Park Zoo and the United Nations.

Operating on Saturdays, Sundays and holidays, the specially designated air-conditioned buses will run every 15 minutes from Pennsylvania Station.

The first bus each day will **Continued on Page 23, Column 6**

Civil Rights Unity Gone In Redirected Movement

This is the fourth in a series of articles examining conditions and attitudes 10 years after the march on Washington.

By PAUL DELANEY

Ten years ago, Hannah D. Atkins, a State Representative in Oklahoma, and J. L. Chestnut, a Selma, Ala., lawyer, frequently entertained whites in their homes.

Today, neither bothers, unless it is absolutely necessary.

Ten years ago, there was a spirit of togetherness among blacks and whites and it was the guiding principle of the civil rights movement.

Today, blacks snicker at the refrain, "black and white together," from the theme song of the movement, "We Shall Overcome." If anybody still

sings the theme, it is possibly a nostalgic white citizen.

Neither Mrs. Atkins nor Mr. Chestnut is regarded as a wild-eyed radical or as antiwhite.

But because both may fairly be regarded as solid black bourgeois, their attitudes raise one of the central questions worth asking 10 years after the Rev. Dr. Martin Luther King Jr.'s dramatic speech during the march on Washington on Aug. 28, 1963: What has become of the civil rights movement of the sixties?

On the face of it, the answer is clear: the "movement"—at least to those who knew it as mass protest, spirited rhe-**Continued on Page 16, Column 1**

NEWS INDEX

United Press International
SIEGE IN SWEDISH BANK ENDS, HOSTAGES SAFE: Jan-Erik Olsson, one of two gunmen who surrendered last night in Stockholm when police piped tear gas into vault, is led out in handcuffs. Four hostages, who had been held since the attempt to rob the bank began last Thursday, emerged unhurt. Details are on Page.

Quake in Mexico Kills Nearly 500

Continued From Page 1, Col. 6

killed 70 persons and left hundreds without shelter.

The authorities said about 400 persons were feared dead in Puebla state, where huge cracks could be seen from the air and 90 more in Veracruz state.

Communications with many areas were cut off and the death toll was expected to rise as new reports filtered into the larger cities.

Clusters of people could be seen standing around wrecked homes in Serdán, a town of 22,000 about 120 miles east of Mexico City that was reported virtually destroyed.

From the air church steeples could be seen toppled in piles of debris in communities across Puebla state, which is noted for its many colonial churches.

No damage was reported in Mexico City, although buildings swayed briefly when the quake hit. Hundreds of tourists in their nightclothes ran into the streets when their hotel rooms began to tremble.

Many survivors in Puebla state told newsmen the first indication of the quake was a huge cloud of dust seen hovering a mile high to the southeast before dawn.

"I ran out of my house with my wife and both of us knelt and started praying," said a man in Tehuacán. "But my son . . . I couldn't wake him. When I looked back our house had collapsed. Later a friend and I pulled out his body."

The New York Times/Aug. 29, 1973

Towns with names underlined are in area hard hit by earthquake.

The National Seismology Institute in Mexico City measured the quake at 5.5 on the Richter scale. Any reading of 4.5 or above is considered potentially dangerous.

In Richter measurements, an earthquake whose intensity is 7 is 10 times more severe than one of 6, which in turn is 10 times greater than one of 5.

The weather station at Veracruz on the Gulf Coast, which measured the quake at 6.5, said its center appeared to be near the cities of Orizaba and Córdoba, about 170 miles east of Mexico City.

Shocked townspeople wander through the ruins of Cuidad Serdan in southeastern Mexico after an earthquake badly damaged the city.

Wide World Photos

"All the News That's Fit to Print"

The New York Times

LATE CITY EDITION

Weather: Mostly sunny, cool today; cold tonight. Fair, mild tomorrow. Temp. range: today 35-46; Thursday 43-53. Additional details on Page 73.

VOL. CXXIII...No. 42,314 © 1973 The New York Times Company NEW YORK, FRIDAY, NOVEMBER 30, 1973 15 CENTS

CHAPIN IS INDICTED ON CHARGE HE LIED ON SEGRETTI LINKS

4 Perjury Counts a Result of Testimony Defendant Gave to Watergate Grand Jury

JAWORSKI IS ACCUSER

Ex-White House Aide Faces Up to 5 Years and $10,000 Fine on Each Allegation

By ANTHONY RIPLEY

Special to The New York Times

WASHINGTON, Nov. 29—President Nixon's former appointments secretary, Dwight L. Chapin, was indicted today on four counts of perjury in the Watergate scandals.

The special Watergate prosecutor, Leon Jaworski, charged that Mr. Chapin on four occasions last April made statements before the Watergate grand jury that Mr. Chapin knew to be false.

All four alleged instances of perjury were connected with Mr. Chapin's dealings with Donald H. Segretti, who has admitted he infiltrated, sabotaged and spied upon Democratic Presidential campaigns in 1972.

Each of the four counts, which are under the perjury section of the United States Code, is punishable by a maximum penalty of five years in prison and a $10,000 fine.

'False Declaration'

Technically the charge is "making false declaration before a grand jury" and carries a heavier fine than the old five years and $5,000 fine for perjury. It was added to the criminal code in 1970.

With Mr. Chapin's indictment today, a total of 26 individuals and seven corporations have been involved in court action arising from the Watergate scandals and related matters.

Reached by United Press International at his home in Winnetka, Ill., Mr. Chapin was quoted as saying that he was "just not sure" about his next move and would wait to hear from his lawyer before deciding what to do. His lawyer, Jacob A. Stein of Washington, could not be reached for comment.

Ronald L. Ziegler, President Nixon's press secretary, commented on the indictment today, saying it "in no way undercuts a presumption of innocence."

Mr. Chapin left the White House late last January amid reports he was being forced

Continued on Page 22, Column 3

Shortage of Drugs Is Termed Critical; Industry Seeks Oil

By RICHARD SEVERO

Because of the oil situation, the United States faces a critical shortage of penicillin, cortisone and other vital drugs, an industry spokesman said yesterday.

He added that the shortage would get worse unless the Federal Government acted soon to divert more crude oil to the petrochemical industry.

This assessment came from a spokesman for key elements in the pharmaceutical industry in New Jersey, where large makers of ethical drugs have facilities. The situation is so grave that a group of industry executives is going to Washington next Monday to meet with John A. Love, President Nixon's chief energy adviser.

Ralph Schmidt, manager of plant operations for the Beecham-Massengill Pharmaceuticals Division of Beecham, Inc., Piscataway, N. J., explained that

Continued on Page 42, Column 2

NEWS INDFX

NON-FICTION WRITERS' WORKSHOP, NYU LOEB Center, Sat., Dec. 8. $30. (212) 598-3791—ADVT.

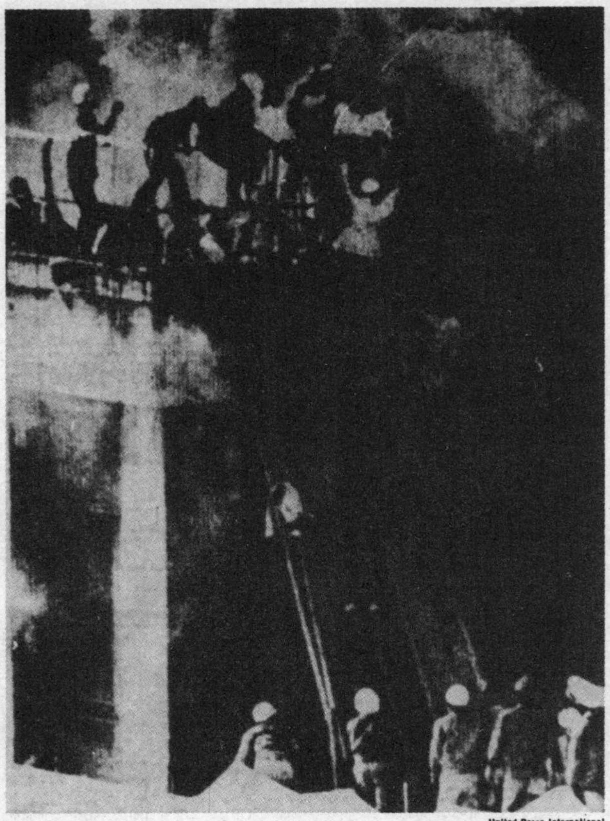

United Press International

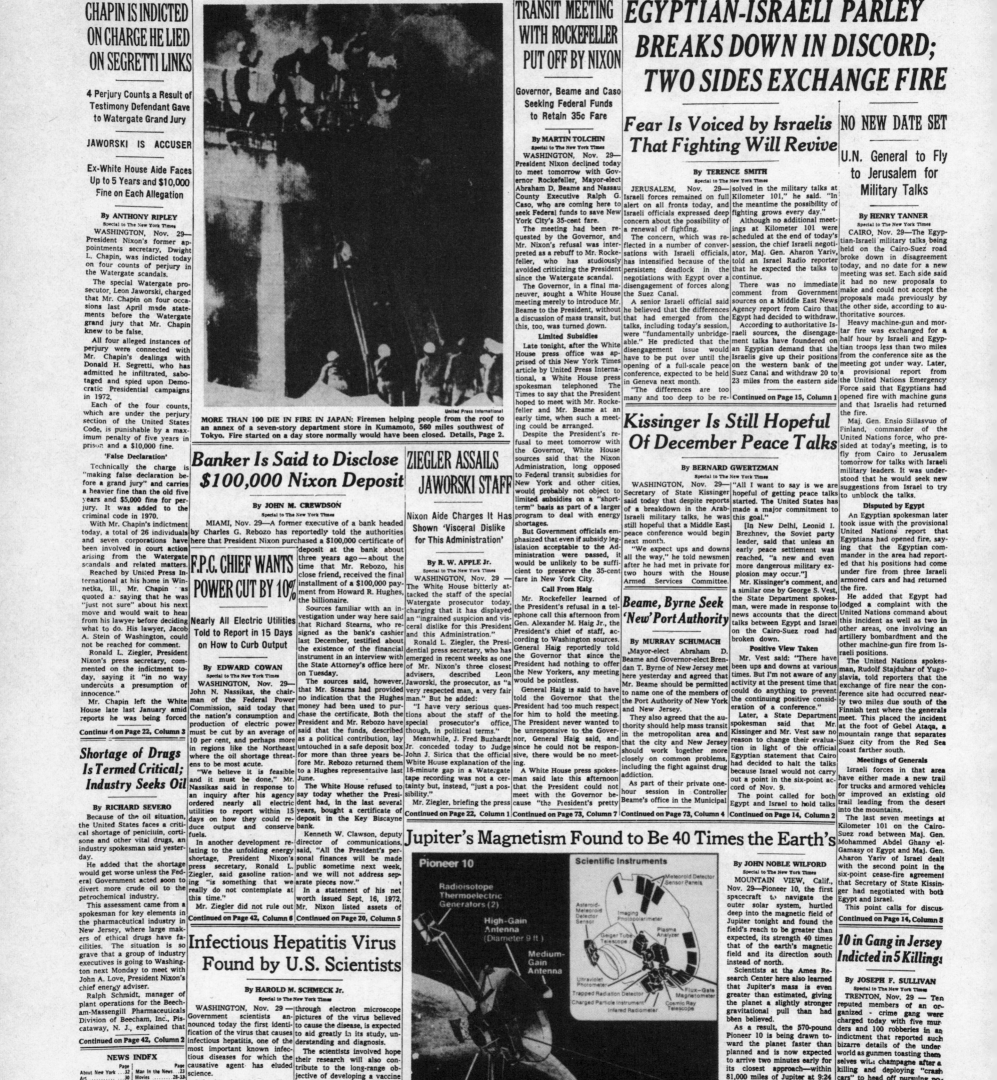

MORE THAN 100 DIE IN FIRE IN JAPAN: Firemen helping people from the roof to an annex of a seven-story department store in Kumamoto, 560 miles southwest of Tokyo. Fire started on a day store normally would have been closed. Details, Page 2.

Banker Is Said to Disclose $100,000 Nixon Deposit

By JOHN M. CREWDSON

Special to The New York Times

MIAMI, Nov. 29—A former executive of a bank headed by Charles G. Rebozo has reportedly told the authorities here that President Nixon purchased a $100,000 certificate of deposit at the bank about three years ago—about the time that Mr. Rebozo, his close friend, received the final installment of a $100,000 payment from Howard R. Hughes, the billionaire.

Sources familiar with an investigation under way here said that Richard Stearns, who resigned as the bank's cashier last December, testified about the existence of the financial instrument in an interview with the State Attorney's office here on Tuesday.

The sources said, however, that Mr. Stearns had provided no indication that the Hughes money had been used to purchase the certificate. Both the President and Mr. Rebozo have said that the funds, described as a political contribution, lay untouched in a safe deposit box for more than three years before Mr. Rebozo returned them to a Hughes representative last June.

The White House refused to say today whether the President had, in the last several years, bought a certificate of deposit in the Key Biscayne bank.

Kenneth W. Clawson, deputy director of communications, said, "All the President's personal finances will be made public sometime next week, and we will not address separate pieces now."

In a statement of his net worth issued Sept. 16, 1972, Mr. Nixon listed assets of

Continued on Page 20, Column 5

F.P.C. CHIEF WANTS POWER CUT BY 10%

Nearly All Electric Utilities Told to Report in 15 Days on How to Curb Output

By EDWARD COWAN

Special to The New York Times

WASHINGTON, Nov. 29—John N. Nassikas, the chairman of the Federal Power Commission, said today that the nation's consumption and production of electric power must be cut by an average of 10 per cent, and perhaps more in regions like the Northeast where the oil shortage threatens to be most acute.

"We believe it is feasible and it must be done," Mr. Nassikas said in response to an inquiry after his agency ordered nearly all electric utilities to report within 15 days on how they could reduce output and conserve fuels.

In another development relating to the unfolding energy shortage, President Nixon's press secretary, Ronald L. Ziegler, said gasoline rationing "is something that we really do not contemplate at this time."

Mr. Ziegler did not rule out

Continued on Page 42, Column 6

ZIEGLER ASSAILS JAWORSKI STAFF

Nixon Aide Charges It Has Shown 'Visceral Dislike for This Administration'

By R. W. APPLE Jr.

Special to The New York Times

WASHINGTON, Nov. 29—The White House bitterly attacked the staff of the special Watergate prosecutor today, charging that it has displayed an "ingrained suspicion and visceral dislike for this President and this Administration."

Ronald L. Ziegler, the Presidential press secretary, who has emerged in recent weeks as one of Mr. Nixon's three closest advisers, described Leon Jaworski, the prosecutor, as "a very respected man, a very fair man." But he added:

"I have very serious questions about the staff of the special prosecutor's office, though, in political terms."

Meanwhile, J. Fred Buzhardt Jr. conceded today to Judge John J. Sirica that the official White House explanation of the 18-minute gap in a Watergate tape recording was not a certainty but, instead, "just a possibility."

Mr. Ziegler, briefing the press

Continued on Page 22, Column 1

Infectious Hepatitis Virus Found by U.S. Scientists

By HAROLD M. SCHMECK Jr.

Special to The New York Times

WASHINGTON, Nov. 29—Government scientists announced today the first identification of the virus that causes infectious hepatitis, one of the most important known infectious diseases for which the causative agent has eluded science.

Infectious hepatitis is a liver disease. It afflicts at least 50,000 Americans a year; perhaps many more. While not commonly fatal, it can involve many weeks of debilitating illness.

The successful identification, through electron microscope pictures of the virus believed to cause the disease, is expected to aid greatly in its study, understanding and diagnosis.

The scientists involved hope their research will also contribute to the long-range objective of developing a vaccine or some other preventive measure against the illness.

A more certain prospect is that it will enlarge scientists' understanding of the true scope of infectious hepatitis

Continued on Page 48, Column 1

WILLCOX & GIBBS' Nine Months Revenues were up 32% (WG-ASE)—Advt.

ED SULLIVAN SAYS: "I LOVE 'MOLLY' And Kay Ballard Is Sensational."—Advt.

TRANSIT MEETING WITH ROCKEFELLER PUT OFF BY NIXON

Governor, Beame and Caso Seeking Federal Funds to Retain 35c Fare

By MARTIN TOLCHIN

Special to The New York Times

WASHINGTON, Nov. 29—President Nixon declined today to meet tomorrow with Governor Rockefeller, Mayor-elect Abraham D. Beame and Nassau County Executive Ralph G. Caso, who are coming here to seek Federal funds to save New York City's 35-cent fare.

The meeting had been requested by the Governor, and Mr. Nixon's refusal was interpreted as a rebuff to Mr. Rockefeller, who has studiously avoided criticizing the President since the Watergate scandal.

The Governor, in a final maneuver, sought a White House meeting merely to introduce Mr. Beame to the President, without a discussion of mass transit, but this, too, was turned down.

Limited Subsidies

Late tonight, after the White House press office was apprised of this New York Times article by United Press International, a White House press spokesman telephoned The Times to say that the President hoped to meet with Mr. Rockefeller and Mr. Beame at an early time, when such a meeting could be arranged.

Despite the President's refusal to meet tomorrow with the Governor, White House sources said that the Nixon Administration, long opposed to Federal transit subsidies for New York and other cities, would probably not object to limited subsidies on a "short-term" basis as part of a larger program to deal with energy shortages.

But Government officials emphasized that even if subsidy legislation acceptable to the Administration were passed, it would be unlikely to be sufficient to preserve the 35-cent fare in New York City.

Call From Haig

Mr. Rockefeller learned of the President's refusal in a telephone call this afternoon from Gen. Alexander M. Haig Jr., the President's chief of staff, according to Washington sources. General Haig reportedly told the Governor that since the President had nothing to offer the New Yorkers, any meeting would be pointless.

General Haig is said to have told the Governor that the President had too much respect for him to hold the meeting. The President never wanted to be unresponsive to the Governor, General Haig said, and since he could not be responsive, there would be no meeting.

A White House press spokesman said late this afternoon that the President could not meet with the Governor because "the President's pretty

Continued on Page 73, Column 7

EGYPTIAN-ISRAELI PARLEY BREAKS DOWN IN DISCORD; TWO SIDES EXCHANGE FIRE

Fear Is Voiced by Israelis That Fighting Will Revive

By TERENCE SMITH

Special to The New York Times

JERUSALEM, Nov. 29—Israeli forces remained on full alert on all fronts today, and Israeli officials expressed deep concern about the possibility of a renewal of fighting.

The concern, which was reflected in a number of conversations with Israeli officials, has intensified because of the persistent deadlock in the negotiations with Egypt over a disengagement of forces along the Suez Canal.

A senior Israeli official said he believed that the differences that had emerged from the talks, including today's session, were "fundamentally unbridgeable." He predicted that the disengagement issue would have to be put over until the opening of a full-scale peace conference, expected to be held in Geneva next month.

"The differences are too many and too deep to be resolved in the military talks at Kilometer 101," he said. "In the meantime the possibility of fighting grows every day."

Although no additional meetings at Kilometer 101 were scheduled at the end of today's session, the chief Israeli negotiator, Maj. Gen. Aharon Yariv, told an Israel Radio reporter that he expected the talks to continue.

There was no immediate comment from Government sources on a Middle East News Agency report from Cairo that Egypt had decided to withdraw.

According to authoritative Israeli sources, the disengagement talks have foundered on an Egyptian demand that the Israelis give up their positions on the western bank of the Suez Canal and withdraw 20 to 23 miles from the eastern side

Continued on Page 15, Column 1

NO NEW DATE SET

U.N. General to Fly to Jerusalem for Military Talks

By HENRY TANNER

Special to The New York Times

CAIRO, Nov. 29—The Egyptian-Israeli military talks being held on the Cairo-Suez road broke down in disagreement today, and no date for a new meeting was set. Each side said it had no new proposals to make and could not accept the proposals made previously by the other side, according to authoritative sources.

Heavy machine-gun and mortar fire was exchanged for a half hour by Israeli and Egyptian troops less than two miles from the conference site as the meeting got under way. Later, a provisional report from the United Nations Emergency Force said that Egyptians had opened fire with machine guns and that Israelis had returned the fire.

Maj. Gen. Ensio Siilasvuo of Finland, commander of the United Nations force, who presided at today's meeting, is to fly from Cairo to Jerusalem tomorrow for talks with Israeli military leaders. It was understood that he would seek new suggestions from Israel to try to unblock the talks.

Disputed by Egypt

An Egyptian spokesman later took issue with the provisional United Nations report that Egyptians had opened fire, saying that the Egyptian commander in the area had reported that his positions had come under fire from three Israeli armored cars and had returned the fire.

He added that Egypt had lodged a complaint with the United Nations command about this incident as well as two in other areas, one involving an artillery bombardment and the other machine-gun fire from Israeli positions.

The United Nations spokesman, Rudolf Stajduhar of Yugoslavia, told reporters that the exchange of fire near the conference site had occurred nearly two miles due south of the Finnish tent where the generals meet. This placed the incident at the foot of Gebel Ataqa, a mountain range that separates Suez city from the Red Sea coast farther south.

Meetings of Generals

Israeli forces in that area have either made a new trail for trucks and armored vehicles or improved an existing old trail leading from the desert into the mountains.

The last seven meetings at Kilometer 101 on the Cairo-Suez road between Maj. Gen. Mohammed Abdel Ghany el-Gamasy of Egypt and Maj. Gen. Aharon Yariv of Israel dealt with the second point in the six-point cease-fire agreement that Secretary of State Kissinger had negotiated with both Egypt and Israel.

This point calls for discus-

Continued on Page 14, Column 5

Kissinger Is Still Hopeful Of December Peace Talks

By BERNARD GWERTZMAN

Special to The New York Times

WASHINGTON, Nov. 29—Secretary of State Kissinger said today that despite reports of a breakdown in the Arab-Israeli military talks, he was still hopeful that a Middle East peace conference would begin next month.

"We expect ups and downs all the way," he told newsmen after he had met in private for two hours with the House Armed Services Committee. "All I want to say is we are hopeful of getting peace talks started. The United States has made a major commitment to this goal."

[In New Delhi, Leonid I. Brezhnev, the Soviet party leader, said that unless an early peace settlement was reached, "a new and even more dangerous military explosion may occur."]

Mr. Kissinger's comment, and a similar one by George S. Vest, the State Department spokesman, were made in response to news accounts that the direct talks between Egypt and Israel on the Cairo-Suez road had broken down.

Positive View Taken

Mr. Vest said: "There have been ups and downs at various times. But I'm not aware of any activity at the present time that could do anything to prevent the continuing positive consideration of a conference."

Later, a State Department spokesman said that Mr. Kissinger and Mr. Vest saw no reason to change their evaluation in light of the official Egyptian statement that Cairo had decided to halt the talks because Israel would not carry out a point in the six-point accord of Nov. 9.

The point called for both Egypt and Israel to hold talks

Continued on Page 14, Column 2

Beame, Byrne Seek 'New' Port Authority

By MURRAY SCHUMACH

Mayor-elect Abraham D. Beame and Governor-elect Brendan T. Byrne of New Jersey met here yesterday and agreed that Mr. Beame should be permitted to name one of the members of the Port Authority of New York and New Jersey.

They also agreed that the authority should help mass transit in the metropolitan area and that the city and New Jersey should work together more closely on common problems, including the fight against drug addiction.

As part of their private one-hour session in Controller Beame's office in the Municipal

Continued on Page 73, Column 4

Jupiter's Magnetism Found to Be 40 Times the Earth's

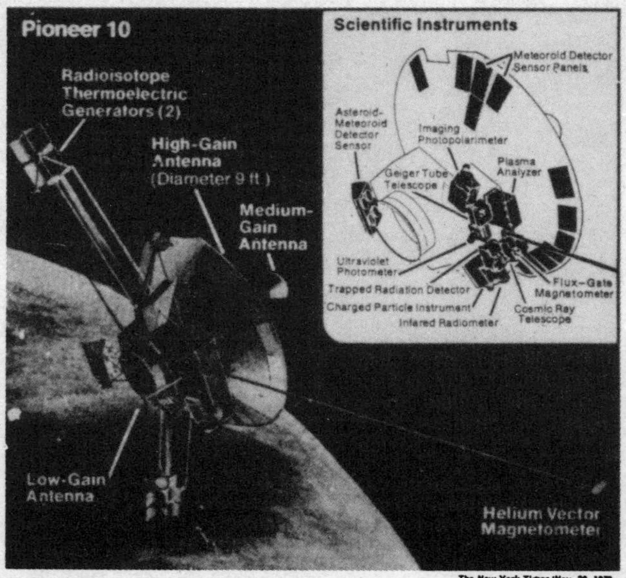
Pioneer 10
Radioisotope Thermoelectric Generators (2)
High-Gain Antenna (Diameter 9 ft.)
Medium-Gain Antenna
Low-Gain Antenna
Helium Vector Magnetometer
Scientific Instruments
Meteoroid Detector Sensor Panels
Asteroid-Meteoroid Detector Sensor
Imaging Photopolarimeter
Plasma Analyzer
Geiger Tube Telescope
Ultraviolet Photometer
Trapped Radiation Detector
Charged Particle Instrument
Infared Radiometer
Flux-Gate Magnetometer
Cosmic Ray Telescope

The New York Times/Nov. 30, 1973

Instrument-laden Pioneer 10, facing possible radiation hazards near Jupiter, is powered by nuclear generators rather than solar panels because of long distance from sun. Radio signals from Jupiter, traveling at speed of light, take 45 minutes to reach earth.

By JOHN NOBLE WILFORD

Special to The New York Times

MOUNTAIN VIEW, Calif., Nov. 29—Pioneer 10, the first spacecraft to navigate the outer solar system, hurtled deep into the magnetic field of Jupiter tonight and found the field's reach to be greater than expected, its strength 40 times that of the earth's magnetic field and its direction south instead of north.

Scientists at the Ames Research Center here also learned that Jupiter's mass is even greater than estimated, giving the planet a slightly stronger gravitational pull than had been believed.

As a result, the 570-pound Pioneer 10 is being drawn toward the planet faster than planned and is now expected to arrive two minutes early for its closest approach—within 81,000 miles of Jupiter at 9:24 P.M. Eastern standard time Monday. The spacecraft will send back to earth the first close-up images of the largest planet in the solar system.

The first scientific discoveries to be gleaned from the spacecraft's radioed data were reported by scientists at a news

Continued on Page 25, Column 1

10 in Gang in Jersey Indicted in 5 Killings

By JOSEPH F. SULLIVAN

Special to The New York Times

TRENTON, Nov. 29 — Ten reputed members of an organized-crime gang were charged today with five murders and 100 robberies in an indictment that reported such bizarre details of the underworld as gunmen toasting themselves with champagne after a killing and deploying "crash cars" to head off pursuing policemen.

The six-count state indictment was hailed by law-enforcement officials here as the "most complete picture" ever presented of underworld activities because, for the first time the violence was shown to support a gambling and narcotic

Continued on Page 41, Column 1

Department Store Fire in Japan Kills 100

KUMAMOTO, Japan, Nov. 29 (AP)—Fire and smoke stampeded thousands of panicky shoppers in a department store here today and the police said more than 100 were killed and 100 injured in the worst such blaze in Japan's history. Casualties were expected to mount.

There were conflicting reports but the police said that 107 persons, 67 of them women, were killed. Many were burned beyond recognition.

The fire raged for eight hours through the seven-story building in the center of this southern provincial city of 480,000 on the island of Kyushu, about 560 miles southwest of Tokyo.

The fire occurred on a day when the store normally would have been closed and when sprinklers were not working because they were under repair for fire prevention week, officials said.

Smoke and fumes continued to hamper rescue work as building materials used in remodeling the 20-year-old Taiyo Department store still smoldered.

'It Was Like an Inferno'

"It was like an inferno, full of cries of fleeing mothers and children," said Junko Nagai, a waitress who survived the fire. "I am lucky to be alive."

Masatoshi Tsuruya, a 22-year-old university student, said: "I was almost overwhelmed by smoke before I reached a window from which I escaped by a ladder." He said he saw people tumbling down a stairway like an avalanche.

Kinuko Miyagawa, a waitress, recalled she was pouring tea for a customer when black smoke suddenly poured into the restaurant.

"I tried to escape but was soon overcome by smoke," she said. "I latched onto someone and managed to reach the roof. There were about 30 persons in the restaurant at the time but I don't know what happened to them."

The store was open for the beginning of the pre-Christmas and year-end sales season and was filled with about 10,000 shoppers. Witnesses said the shoppers stampeded when someone shouted "Fire!" at the sight of smoke.

Only about 1 per cent of Japanese are Christians, but since World War II Christmas has been celebrated with major gift giving in addition to the traditional New Year's holiday.

The fire broke out in the bedding sales department on the third floor around 1:20 P.M. and raced up the stairs of the building.

100 Stranded on Roof

The shoppers and store employes headed for the windows, then ran for the stairs and escalators, adding to the confusion. Hundreds ran out of the store, witnesses said.

About 100 persons managed to reach the roof, where they screamed for help.

Fire-fighting equipment was rushed to the store. Ladders were raised to rescue those on the roof. But the police said there were not enough fire trucks with ladders to handle the job. Helicopters were brought into service.

Witnesses said some people on the lower floors of the building tried to escape by climbing down dangling ropes, others tried to leap to a nearby shop awning.

Firemen, soldiers and policemen wearing oxygen masks had difficulty forcing their way into the building because of fumes caused by the building materials used to line the walls and floors of the store, the police said.

Witnesses said many customers were choking and kept covering their faces with handkerchiefs and towels.

Wide World Photos

An aerial view of the burning Taiyo department store engulfed in billowing dense smoke.

"All the News That's Fit to Print"

The New York Times

LATE CITY EDITION

Weather: Cloudy and cold with rain likely today, tonight and tomorrow. Temp. range: today 27-38; Friday 31-37. Additional details on Page 58.

VOL. CXXIII ... No. 42,378 — NEW YORK, SATURDAY, FEBRUARY 2, 1974 — 15 CENTS

© 1974 The New York Times Company

NIXON PREDICTS SHARP INFLATION WITH LITTLE GROWTH IN ECONOMY; SEES BETTER TIMES LATER IN YEAR

ANNUAL MESSAGE

Largest Jobless Rise in 4 Years Reported by Labor Department

By EDWIN L. DALE Jr.
Special to The New York Times

WASHINGTON, Feb. 1—President Nixon and his Council of Economic Advisers predicted today severe inflation in the months immediately ahead, with little or no economic growth, but foresaw better times in the second half of the year.

The President's annual Economic Message to Congress coincided with a report by the Labor Department that unemployment increased significantly last month. The unemployment rate rose to 5.2 per cent of the labor force from 4.8 per cent in December, the largest increase for a single month in four years, with the energy shortage playing an important role.

Text of Economic Report appears on Page 10.

In his economic report, Mr. Nixon said that if his forecast of a period of stagnation of the economy, with improvement in the second half, proved too optimistic, "We will be prepared to support economic activity and employment by additional budgetary measures, if necessary."

Unpredictable Factor

Both the President in his message and the Council of Economic Advisers in the much longer companion report emphasized that the outlook was "highly uncertain" this year, largely because of the unpredictable nature of the energy shortage.

Although the message forecast a continued high rate of inflation, particularly in the first half of the year, the President said, "We will continue our policy of progressive removal of price and wage controls in order to restore the flexibility needed for efficiency and expansion in a time of economic strain."

A long analysis of controls by the council concluded that they probably did not do much good in curbing inflation last year and had reached the point of threatening needed business investment.

As if to confirm the President's announcement, the Cost of Living Council ended price controls today in the retail sector of the economy, except for food, fuels and automobiles.

Estimate of G.N.P.

The council's report predicted a gross national product—total output of goods and services—of $1,390-billion in 1974, a rise of 8 per cent. But of this, only 1 per cent would be "real" growth and the rest inflation. This forecast is close to that of the majority of private economic forecasters.

Herbert Stein, chairman of the council, said inflation in the second half of the year should drop below a rate of 5 per cent on the assumption that the big rise of food and fuel prices would be "behind us" by then.

Although the council's report did not make a specific prediction, Mr. Stein said that the council's estimate was that consumer prices would rise about 6 per cent from the end of 1973 to the end of 1974, compared with 8.2 per cent last year.

As for unemployment, the Economic Report said unemployment for the year would "average a little above 5.5 per

Continued on Page 10, Column 5

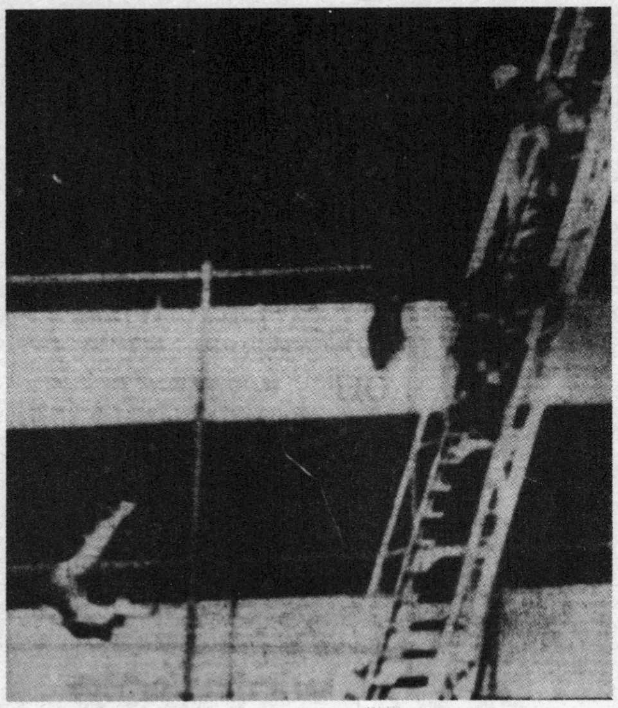

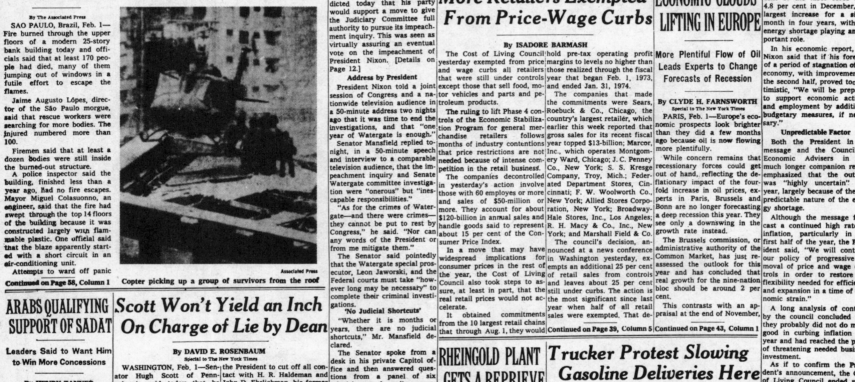

Firemen watch helplessly as occupant of burning building in São Paulo plunges to death

170 Dead in Brazilian Office Fire

By The Associated Press

SAO PAULO, Brazil, Feb. 1—Fire burned through the upper floors of a modern 25-story bank building today and officials said that at least 170 people had died, many of them jumping out of windows in a futile effort to escape the flames.

Jaime Augusto Lópes, director of the São Paulo morgue, said that rescue workers were searching for more bodies. The injured numbered more than 100.

Firemen said that at least a dozen bodies were still inside the burned-out structure.

A police inspector said the building, finished less than a year ago, had no fire escapes. Mayor Miguel Colasuonno, an engineer, said that the fire had swept through the top 14 floors of the building because it was constructed largely with flammable plastic. One official said that the blaze apparently started with a short circuit in an air-conditioning unit.

Attempts to ward off panic

Continued on Page 58, Column 1

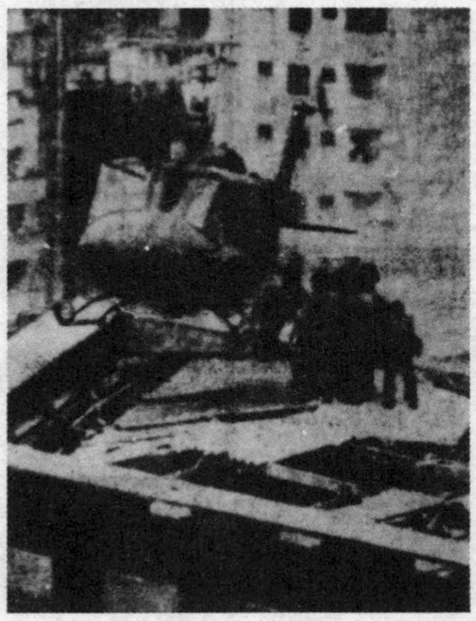

Associated Press

Copter picking up a group of survivors from the roof

MANSFIELD BARS WATERGATE'S END IN REPLY TO NIXON

Bids Congress and Courts Pursue Inquiry to Cleanse U.S. Political Processes

By JAMES M. NAUGHTON
Special to The New York Times

WASHINGTON, Feb. 1—The Senate Democratic leader, Mike Mansfield, declared tonight that Congress and the courts must pursue their Watergate investigations "in order to cleanse the political processes of the nation."

The Senator from Montana, responding on behalf of the Democratic majority in Congress to President Nixon's State of the Union Address on Wednesday, pledged that his party would put "the regular business of the nation" ahead of Watergate.

Excerpts from the Mansfield speech are on Page 11.

But Mr. Mansfield said that Congress would deal "fully" with the inquiry into the possible impeachment of the President, and he specifically rejected Mr. Nixon's plea for an end to the Watergate investigations.

Meanwhile, John J. Rhodes, the ranking Republican in the House of Representatives, predicted today that his party would support a move to give the Judiciary Committee full authority to pursue its impeachment inquiry. This was seen as virtually assuring an eventual vote on the impeachment of President Nixon. [Details on Page 12.]

Address by President

President Nixon told a joint session of Congress and a nationwide television audience in a 50-minute address two nights ago that it was time to end the investigations, and that "one year of Watergate is enough."

Senator Mansfield replied tonight, in a 50-minute speech and interview to a comparable television audience, that the impeachment inquiry and Senate Watergate committee investigation were "onerous" but "inescapable responsibilities."

"As for the crimes of Watergate—and there were crimes—they cannot be put to rest by Congress," he said. "Nor can any words of the President or from me mitigate them."

The Senator said pointedly that the Watergate special prosecutor, Leon Jaworski, and the Federal courts must take "however long may be necessary" to complete their criminal investigations.

'No Judicial Shortcuts'

"Whether it is months or years, there are no judicial shortcuts," Mr. Mansfield declared.

The Senator spoke from a desk in his private Capitol office and then answered questions from a panel of six television and radio correspondents.

Senator Mansfield told the panel that he would favor live television coverage of impeachment proceedings should they come to a vote of the House floor and during any Senate trial of charges against the President.

He spoke deliberately and almost professorially as he read

Continued on Page 11, Column 1

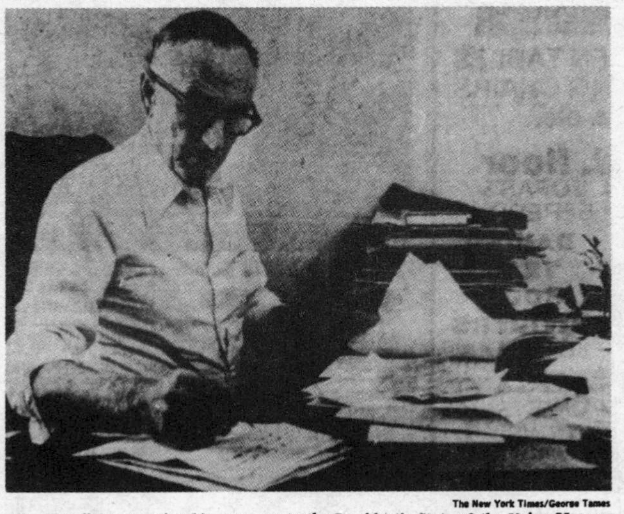

The New York Times/George Tames

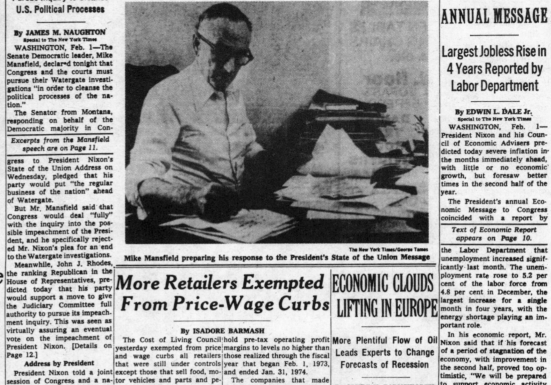

Mike Mansfield preparing his response to the President's State of the Union Message

More Retailers Exempted From Price-Wage Curbs

By ISADORE BARMASH

The Cost of Living Council yesterday exempted from price and wage curbs all retailers that were still under controls except those that sell food, motor vehicles and parts and petroleum products.

The ruling to lift Phase 4 controls of the Economic Stabilization Program for general merchandise retailers follows months of industry contentions that price restrictions are not needed because of intense competition in the retail business.

The companies decontrolled in yesterday's action involve those with 60 employes or more and sales of $50-million or more. They account for about $120-billion in annual sales and handle goods said to represent about 15 per cent of the Consumer Price Index.

In a move that may have widespread implications for consumer prices in the rest of the year, the Cost of Living Council also took steps to assure, at least in part, that the real retail prices would not accelerate.

It obtained commitments from the 10 largest retail chains that through Aug. 1, they would hold pre-tax operating profit margins to levels no higher than those realized through the fiscal year that began Feb. 1, 1973, and ended Jan. 31, 1974.

The companies that made the commitments were Sears, Roebuck & Co., Chicago, the country's largest retailer, which earlier this week reported that gross sales for its recent fiscal year topped $13-billion; Marcor, Inc., which operates Montgomery Ward, Chicago; J. C. Penney Co., New York; S. S. Kresge Company, Troy, Mich.; Federated Department Stores, Cincinnati; F. W. Woolworth Co., New York; Allied Stores Corporation, New York; Broadway-Hale Stores, Inc., Los Angeles; R. H. Macy & Co., Inc., New York; and Marshall Field & Co.

The council's decision, announced at a news conference in Washington yesterday, exempts an additional 25 per cent of retail sales from controls and leaves about 25 per cent still under curbs. The action is the most significant since last year when half of all retail sales were exempted. That de-

Continued on Page 39, Column 5

ECONOMIC CLOUDS LIFTING IN EUROPE

More Plentiful Flow of Oil Leads Experts to Change Forecasts of Recession

By CLYDE H. FARNSWORTH
Special to The New York Times

PARIS, Feb. 1—Europe's economic prospects look brighter than they did a few months ago because oil is now flowing more plentifully.

While concern remains that recessionary forces could get out of hand, reflecting the deflationary impact of the fourfold increase in oil prices, experts in Paris, Brussels and Bonn are no longer forecasting a deep recession this year. They see only a downswing in the growth rate instead.

The Brussels commission, or administrative authority of the Common Market, has just reassessed the outlook for this year and has concluded that real growth for the nine-nation bloc should be around 2 per cent.

This contrasts with an appraisal at the end of November,

Continued on Page 43, Column 1

ARABS QUALIFYING SUPPORT OF SADAT

Leaders Said to Want Him to Win More Concessions

By HENRY TANNER
Special to The New York Times

CAIRO, Feb. 1—President Anwar el-Sadat won support for his disengagement agreement with Israel from most of the other Arab leaders during his recent tour of their capitals, according to informed sources here, but there is a time limit on their commitment.

Mr. Sadat, the sources say, must achieve further Israeli withdrawals beyond the new truce line, and other Israeli concessions, to assure continued Arab support.

The qualified nature of the Arab backing is believed to be the reason that Mr. Sadat has gone out of his way to stress the limitations of the Israeli-Egyptian agreement.

At a meeting here last night,

Continued on Page 3, Column 4

Scott Won't Yield an Inch On Charge of Lie by Dean

By DAVID E. ROSENBAUM
Special to The New York Times

WASHINGTON, Feb. 1—Senator Hugh Scott of Pennsylvania said today that he was not "backtracking one single inch" on his charge that John W. Dean 3d had lied about President Nixon's role in the Watergate cover-up.

Mr. Scott, the Senate Republican leader, made the statement to reporters after meeting with Mr. Nixon to discuss the budget for the next fiscal year.

An assistant special prosecutor, Richard J. Davis, said in court yesterday that the prosecutor's office had no reason to believe that Mr. Dean had not told the truth.

Meanwhile, there were the following related developments:

¶A former White House speech writer said that Secretary of State Kissinger and Gen. Alexander M. Haig Jr., the White House chief of staff, had urged the President to cut off all contact with H. R. Haldeman and John D. Ehrlichman, his former top aides, but that Mr. Nixon had refused to do so.

¶Ronald L. Ziegler, Mr. Nixon's press secretary, said that from now on he would cut short reporters' questions about Watergate issues.

¶The attorney for Rose Mary Woods, the President's personal secretary, asserted that the court-appointed technical experts who found that the tape of an important Watergate conversation had been manually erased were "not experts [but] six professors who don't know what they're doing."

Senator Scott hinted that his charge that Mr. Dean had committed perjury might have been based on evidence that the special prosecutor had not seen. He told reporters that he hoped

Continued on Page 12, Column 6

Pension Plan Improved

The United Steelworkers of America and the three major aluminum companies reached agreements yesterday that reduce the normal retirement age from 65 to 62 and provide cost-of-living supplements for workers who retire. Page 34.

RHEINGOLD PLANT GETS A REPRIEVE

Judge Gives Two Unions at Brewery Until Monday to Appeal Earlier Ruling

By FRED FERRETTI

A Federal judge last night temporarily extended the life of the famous Rheingold brewery in Brooklyn, where workers were sitting in to protest the planned permanent closing of the plant.

The stay, issued by Federal District Court Judge John R. Bartels, prohibited the company from closing the 119-year-old landmark before midnight Monday, to give attorneys for two brewery workers unions time to appeal Judge Bartels's earlier ruling that had refused to halt the closing.

The closing is being sought by Rheingold's parent company, Pepsico, Inc.

Eugene F. Kelly, a Rheingold vice president, said last night that his company would "certainly abide by any court decision" to remain open. Pending receipt of the judge's order and discussion with Rheingold's lawyer, however, he said he did not know what provisions would be made to reopen the brewery on Monday.

The plant was closed officially as of 4 P.M. yesterday—before Judge Bartels's reprieve—and the majority of its 1,500

Continued on Page 60, Column 2

Trucker Protest Slowing Gasoline Deliveries Here

Picketing at Terminals Curtails the Output

By FRANK J. PRIAL

Thousands of motorists in the metropolitan area, their fuel-gauge needles quivering dangerously close to "E," were denied their first tankful of February's gasoline allotments yesterday by picketing independent truck drivers who were protesting the fuel squeeze on their industry.

Those motorists who were lucky enough to find service stations selling gasoline—in some parts of the region fewer than 50 per cent of the stations had fuel—endured interminable lines and paid up to 6 cents a gallon more than they had last month when they finally reached a working pump.

The impact of the protest was particularly acute in New Jersey. The Shell Oil Company's terminal in the Sewaren section of Woodbridge was closed down for most of the day after pickets threatened company drivers. Around 3:30 P.M. several tank trucks filled with gasoline left the terminal driven by Shell supervisors.

A Shell spokesman said the regular drivers had been given a choice between "driving out or punching out" for the day. All of them chose to go home for the day, the spokesman said.

Normally, the Shell trucks

Continued on Page 16, Column 2

Shipments of Fruits and Steel Are Disrupted

By AGIS SALPUKAS
Special to The New York Times

DETROIT, Feb. 1—The spreading fuel protest by independent truckers was seriously disrupting the shipment of fruit, produce, meat and steel today, forcing some distributors and plants to close and threatening others with shutdowns next week.

One spokesman for the truckers said that the protest was now "extremely effective" in 28 states.

In Pennsylvania, Gov. Milton J. Shapp activated elements of two National Guard battalions to insure the free movement of trucks after stones and other heavy objects were thrown from overpasses at trucks whose drivers were not joining the stoppage.

Gov. John J. Gilligan authorized the Ohio National Guard to use helicopters to search for snipers and stone throwers, and Gov. Reubin Askew of Florida offered Guard trucks to deliver fuel to police, fire and ambulance units on the fuel-starved southwest coast.

George Rynn, president of the Council of Independent Truckers, one of the major groups organizing the protest, made the estimate that the protest was "extremely effective" in 28 states, but he said it was

Continued on Page 16, Column 5

500 Germans, Own Colleges Full, Will Study in U.S.

By IVER PETERSON
Special to The New York Times

WASHINGTON, Feb. 1—About 500 German students, perhaps the first of thousands, will enroll next year in American colleges, where there is ample room, to relieve overcrowding in German universities.

Under the new program, announced today at Georgetown University here and in Bonn, 500 precollege students from the German state of Rhineland-Palatinate will enroll, at their state's expense, in the American colleges as the first step in the experiment.

If, after five years, the program is successful, as many as 30,000 college-prepared German students who are annually denied admission to their own country's universities because of overcrowding could cross the Atlantic for their bachelar's and masters' degrees.

The new program was worked out by Dr. Christian Schwartz-Schilling, executive secretary of the Christian Democratic Union party in the state of Hesse, and the Rev. Edmund G. Ryan, executive vice president of Georgetown University. Father Ryan made the announcement here.

The overcrowding of German universities, with the consequent exclusion of thousands of otherwise qualified students, has become a minor political issue in Germany. Dr. Schwartz-Schilling approached Father Ryan last year when he heard that American campuses, by contrast, were reporting about half a million unfilled spaces as enrollments slipped and student tastes changed.

The first 500 students will be enrolled as sophomores in the fall of 1975 in a number of American public, private and sectarian colleges grouped in five states across the country. The colleges have not yet been decided on, Father Ryan said, but they will be in Missouri, Michigan, Washington State, Texas and Washington, D.C. Georgetown will enroll 20 of the students.

The costs of sending the students to American colleges will

Continued on Page 27, Column 4

NEWS INDEX

The upper floors of a Sao Paolo, Brazil, office building burn while people on the balconies wait to be rescued.

Wide World Photos

A man jumps to his death as fire rages in the 25-story building.

Many Are Dead in Fire in Brazilian Bank Building

Continued From Page 1, Col. 1

were generally failures. Several sheets, painted with the injunctions "Calm," "Danger is past" and "Wait," were held on the street for people in the building to see.

But ladders reached only to the 11th floor of the building. "People became desperate and jumped from the building when they saw that our ladders could not reach them," said the military police commander in São Paulo.

Some people on the upper floors tried to lower themselves by sheets and ropes. Bodies lay among the debris and broken glass from the building.

"The bottom of their feet were burned," said First Sgt. Alicio Zanca of the São Paulo police. "That made them desperate." Crowds in the streets watched many victims jump or fall as huge flames and black smoke enfulfed most of the building.

One witness, Lineu Bernardes dos Santos, said that he saw about 30 persons falling from windows and balconies. Officials estimated that 10 to 15 fell.

Among the comparatively few bodies identified by late tonight was that of William Franz Williams, an American employed by the Brazilian bank who previously had worked in Brazil for National City Bank of New York. His hometown in the United States was not available.

Roque Abado, an official of Banco Cresiful de Investimento, said the savings and investment bank rented the new building's top 14 floors, which are offices. The bottom 11 floors, which did not burn are a parking garage.

Mr. Abado said that the fire apparently started with a short circuit in an air-conditioner on the 12th floor. The building's air-conditioners are in the windows, which can be opened.

The bank began moving into the building in April, 1973, while construction was being finished.

At the height of today's fire, which was brought under control in about two hours, at least 25 persons on the roof waved frantically at helicopters that circled the building without landing because of the heat and smoke.

At times, those on the roof disappeared in clouds of smoke, and flames leaped toward them from below.

After the flames had been extinguished helicopters began landing on the roof and carrying survivors to safety.

Ladders were unable to reach beyond the 13th and 14th floors of the building, and many on upper floors tried to lower themselves to the ladders using sheets.

Others panicked in the heat and jumped. One policeman said that he saw about 15 persons jump.

Neasa de Souza, a municipal nurse with alomst 20 years' experience, cried convulsively while watching victims waiting for help on the pavement. "The people are dying and we can't do anything!" she said.

Urban Disasters Familiar

In February, 1972, another São Paulo skyscraper—that one a 29-story department store and office building—was ravaged by a fire in which nine people died.

In December, 1970, 15 died and 200 were injured when fire swept through a large section of the sprawling Volkswagen do Brasil factory 12 miles east of São Paulo. The plant is Brazil's largest auto factory, employing more than 23,000 people.

São Paulo, which enjoys year-round pleasant climate at a site 2,500 feet above sea level, has been confronted with such disasters and with the urban problems produced by a rapidly increasing population.

Pushed by a dynamic work ethic, São Paulo has been described by boosters as the fastest growing major city in the world. Greater São Paulo has a population of nine million, and the city itself is approaching six million, making it the largest city in South America.

São Paulo employs 650,000 industrial workers in more than 25,000 industries, one of the largest being the manufacture of automobiles.

As it has moved up economically, the city has also become known for excellence in the arts.

São Paulo is celebrating its 420th anniversary.

"All the News That's Fit to Print"

The New York Times

LATE CITY EDITION

Weather: Drizzle, then partly sunny today. Cloudy tonight, tomorrow. Temp. range: today 41-60. Sunday 38-41. Additional details on Page 68.

VOL. CXXIII ... No. 42,408 © 1974 The New York Times Company NEW YORK, MONDAY, MARCH 4, 1974 20¢ beyond 50-mile radius of New York City, except Long Island. Higher in air delivery cities. 15 CENTS

345 KILLED AS JUMBO JET DIVES INTO FRENCH FOREST IN HISTORY'S WORST CRASH

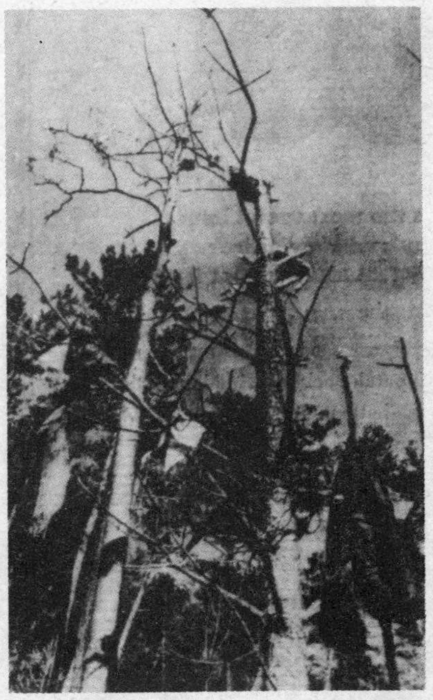

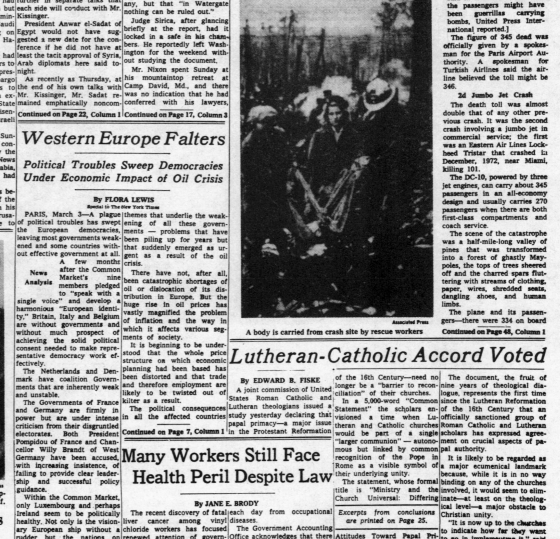

Bits of clothing litter the trees in the forest of Ermenonville, northeast of Paris, where Turkish DC-10 crashed.

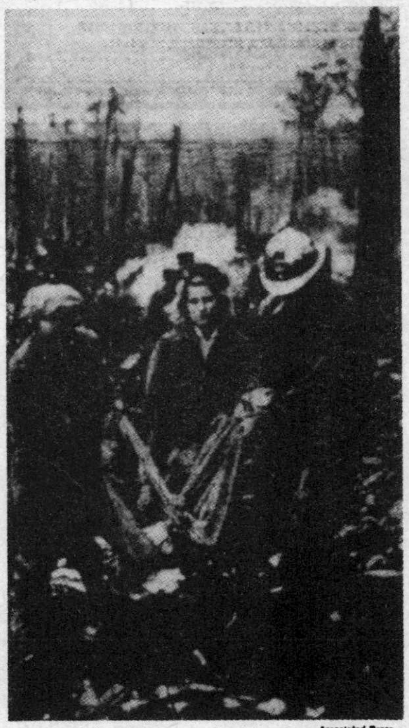

Associated Press

A body is carried from crash site by rescue workers

EXPLOSION HEARD

Turkish Airliner Falls Soon After Leaving Paris for London

By NAN ROBERTSON

Special to The New York Times

PARIS, March 3 — A Turkish jumbo jet plunged into a forest 26 miles northeast of here today, killing all 345 persons aboard. It was the worst air disaster in history.

A witness reported hearing an explosion and seeing the tail fall off the Turkish Airlines DC-10 shortly after it took off for London from Orly Airport. Six bodies were found nine miles from the crash site in the forest of Ermenonville, near Mortefontaine.

The cause of the crash has not been determined, and the Turkish Minister of Communications, Ferda Guley, said in Ankara that sabotage could not be ruled out. Aymar Achille-Fould, the French Secretary of State for Transportation, said that the fact that bodies had been found so far from the place where the plane fell "tends to prove that the explosion occurred in flight."

[Turkish airline sources said in Istanbul that five of the passengers might have been guerrillas carrying bombs, United Press International reported.]

The figure of 345 dead was officially given by a spokesman for the Paris Airport Authority. A spokesman for Turkish Airlines said the airline believed the toll might be 346.

2d Jumbo Jet Crash

The death toll was almost double that of any other previous crash. It was the second crash involving a jumbo jet in commercial service; the first was an Eastern Air Lines Lockheed Tristar that crashed in December, 1972, near Miami, killing 101.

The DC-10, powered by three jet engines, can carry about 345 passengers in an all-economy design and usually carries 270 passengers when there are both first-class compartments and coach service.

The scene of the catastrophe was a half-mile-long valley of pines that was transformed into a forest of ghastly Maypoles, the tops of trees sheered off and the charred spars fluttering with streams of clothing, paper, wires, shredded seats, dangling shoes, and human limbs.

The plane and its passengers—there were 334 on board

Continued on Page 48, Column 1

MRS. MEIR STATES SHE WILL NOT HEAD NEXT GOVERNMENT

Announces Surprise Move at Labor Party Meeting After Severe Criticism

ISRAELI CHIEFS STUNNED

Attempts to Sway Premier Are Unavailing So Far—New Election Possible

By TERENCE SMITH

Special to The New York Times

JERUSALEM, March 3—Premier Golda Meir stunned her party and the country tonight by announcing that she was giving up her five-week effort to form a new coalition government.

She stated her decision in a moment of apparent pique at a closed-door meeting of her Labor party after members of Parliament from the right and the left had criticized her leadership and her attempts to form a minority government.

Mrs. Meir's decision—if she sticks to it—means that she will decline to continue as Prime Minister in the next government and that new elections may well be required to overcome Israel's deepening political crisis.

Attempts at Dissuasion

Efforts were already under way tonight, however, to get the 75-year-old Premier to change her mind. A delegation representing the different factions within her splintered party spent three hours talking with Mrs. Meir at her Jerusalem residence. A large crowd of Israeli and foreign newsmen waited in the tree-lined street for developments.

Emerging from the meeting, the Labor party leaders said that Mrs. Meir had not changed her position. But they added that they hoped some solution could be found tomorrow morning that would encourage her to head the government.

Despite this domestic political deadlock, Israel was expected to go ahead with plans to participate in negotiations with Syria over a disengagement of forces. Israel and Syria agreed over the weekend to send delegations to Washington later this month to begin talks under American auspices. The present Government, which wil continue in office on a caretaker basis, is anxious to begin those negotiations as soon as possible.

Mrs. Meir's decision to give up her efforts to form a government came as a complete surprise.

"She's fed up," one Labor party official explained later. "She realized that while the different factions of the party would give her new cabinet lip-service support they would not back her up when it came to

Continued on Page 4, Column 3

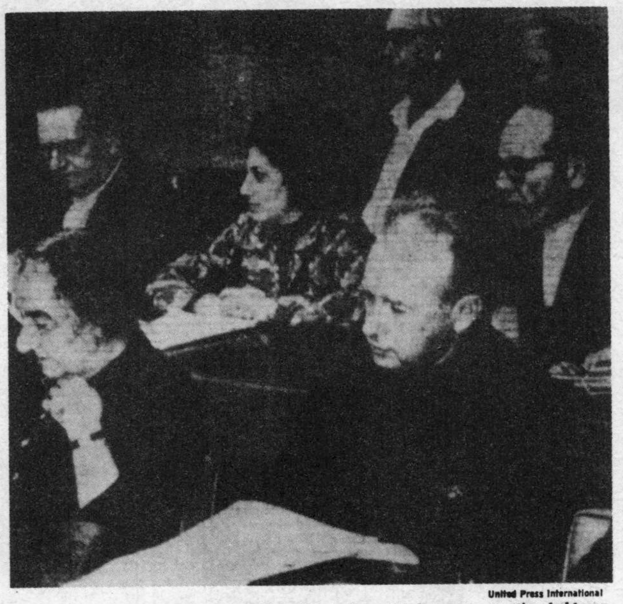

United Press International

Premier Golda Meir and Yitzhak Rabin, next to her, at Labor party meeting held yesterday in Jerusalem. In the second row, from left, are Avraham Silberberg, Nuzhat Katzav and Moshe Shahal; in the third row, David Koren and Moshe Dayan.

SIRICA'S DECISION ON JURY'S REPORT COULD COME TODAY

Findings of Nixon's Alleged Tie to Watergate May Be Given to House Panel

By R. W. APPLE Jr.

Special to The New York Times

WASHINGTON, March 3 — Chief Judge John J. Sirica of the United States District Court is expected to decide this week, possibly tomorrow, what to do with a sealed report handed down to him on Friday by one of the Watergate grand juries, well-placed sources said today.

The 50-page report is said to outline the grand jury's conclusion that President Nixon was involved in a conspiracy to cover up the Watergate bugging. It was accompanied by a recommendation that the jury's findings, and the evidence supporting them, be turned over to the House Judiciary Committee, which is considering Presidential impeachment.

Courses for Judge

A source close to the prosecution reported that Leon Jaworski, the special prosecutor, expected a ruling from Judge Sirica tomorrow. The judge can order the report resealed or can send all or part of it to the committee; he can also decide whether to order that the report be released publicly.

D. Todd Christofferson, the judge's law clerk, said that no official proceedings had been scheduled for tomorrow. He added that he did not expect any, but that "in Watergate nothing can be ruled out."

Judge Sirica, after glancing briefly at the report, had it locked in a safe in his chambers. He reportedly left Washington for the weekend without studying the document.

Mr. Nixon spent Sunday at his mountaintop retreat at Camp David, Md., and there was no indication that he had conferred with his lawyers,

Continued on Page 17, Column 3

ARABS HIJACK JET, FREE 102, BURN IT

Amsterdam Police Capture Gunmen in Runway Chase —Passengers All Safe

By United Press International

AMSTERDAM, the Netherlands, March 3—Two gunmen who identified themselves as members of an Arab youth organization hijacked a British Airways jetliner with 102 persons aboard today, forced it to land outside Amsterdam and then set it afire after allowing all the passengers and crew members to flee.

The police captured the hijackers, who had guns and hand grenades, in a runway chase at Schiphol Airport. No shots were fired.

The passengers and crew members slid down the emergency chutes of the VC-10 aircraft moments before smoke and flames began pouring out. The police said two persons had injured their ankles hitting the ground.

A British Airways spokesman said there were 92 passengers and 10 crew members aboard the four-engined jetliner that was making a regular flight to

Continued on Page 48, Column 1

Egypt Urges Arab Talks On Easing Oil Embargo

By HENRY TANNER

Special to The New York Times

CAIRO, March 3—Egypt has proposed that the oil ministers of Arab oil-producing countries meet in Tripoli, Libya, next Sunday to consider, among other things, the easing of their oil embargo against the United States.

A similar conference had been scheduled for Feb. 14 but was canceled at the last minute at the request of Saudi Arabia and Egypt, acting on behalf of Syria's President, Hafez al-Assad.

The Syrian President had asked the other Arab leaders to continue to maintain the pressure of the total embargo against the United States to strengthen Syria's hand in exchanges with Secretary of State Kissinger about military disengagement on the Syrian-Israeli front.

Egypt's proposal of next Sunday as a new date for the conference was announced by the official Middle East News Agency. It said Saudi Arabia, Kuwait and Abu Dhabi had agreed to the date.

The Egyptian action was believed to be a reflection of the fact that Mr. Kissinger, in his visits to Damascus and Jerusalem last week, was able to nudge the two hostile countries a step closer toward consultation on disengagement.

As a result of the Secretary's efforts in the two capitals, Syrian and Israeli representatives will go to Washington to explore each other's positions further in separate talks that each side will conduct with Mr. Kissinger.

President Anwar el-Sadat of Egypt would not have suggested a new date for the conference if he did not have at least the tacit approval of Syria, Arab diplomats here said tonight.

As recently as Thursday, at the end of his own talks with Mr. Kissinger, Mr. Sadat remained emphatically noncom-

Continued on Page 22, Column 1

Western Europe Falters

Political Troubles Sweep Democracies Under Economic Impact of Oil Crisis

By FLORA LEWIS

Special to The New York Times

PARIS, March 3—A plague of political troubles has swept the European democracies, leaving most governments weakened and some countries without effective government at all.

News Analysis

A few months after the Common Market's nine members pledged to "speak with a single voice" and develop a harmonious "European identity," Britain, Italy and Belgium are without governments and without much prospect of achieving the solid political consent needed to make representative democracy work effectively.

The Netherlands and Denmark have coalition Governments that are inherently weak and unstable.

The Governments of France and Germany are firmly in power but are under intense criticism from their disgruntled electorates. Both President Pompidou of France and Chancellor Willy Brandt of West Germany have been accused, with increasing insistence, of failing to provide clear leadership and successful policy guidance.

Within the Common Market, only Luxembourg and perhaps Ireland seem to be politically healthy. Not only is the visionary European ship without a rudder but the nations on which it was to be built seem unable to set themselves a definite course. By and large, the same is true of most other Western democracies.

The specific political problems that have undermined the authority and cohesion of government vary widely in Europe. Scandal, corruption, inflexibility, personal and partisan feuds, and the deterioration of aging political concepts appear to be among the causes of ailing government from capital to capital.

But there are common themes that underlie the weakening of all these governments — problems that have been piling up for years but that suddenly emerged as urgent as a result of the oil crisis.

There have not, after all, been catastrophic shortages of oil or dislocation of its distribution in Europe. But the huge rise in oil prices has vastly magnified the problem of inflation and the way in which it affects various segments of society.

It is beginning to be understood that the whole price structure on which economic planning had been based has been distorted and that trade and therefore employment are likely to be twisted out of kilter as a result.

The political consequences in all the affected countries

Continued on Page 7, Column 1

BRANDT SET BACK IN HAMBURG VOTE

The Social Democrats Lose Seats in State Legislature

By CRAIG R. WHITNEY

Special to The New York Times

BONN, March 3—Chancellor Willy Brandt's Social Democratic party suffered a severe setback today in elections for the Hamburg state legislature, losing the absolute majority it has held since 1957.

The party had expected some losses in Hamburg, a city as well as a state, and can continue governing in coalition with the Free Democrats, who increased their share of the 120 seats in the legislature.

But nearly complete returns tonight gave the Social Democrats only about 45 per cent of the vote—down from the 55.3 per cent the party won in the last state elections in 1970.

One of Mr. Brandt's advisers said today that local issues did not seem to be the reason for the party's decline in popularity but rather a general malaise that extended to the rest of the country.

"The party appears to the

Continued on Page 6, Column 1

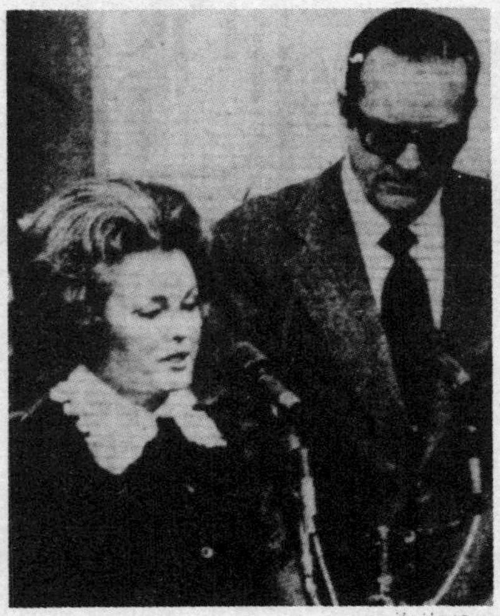

Associated Press

Mr. and Mrs. Randolph A. Hearst broadcasting their appeal yesterday from their home in Hillsborough, Calif.

Hearst Pleads With Kidnappers

By EARL CALDWELL

Special to The New York Times

HILLSBOROUGH, Calif., March 3 — A month after the abduction of his daughter and 10 days since the last message from the kidnappers, Randolph A. Hearst made a new appeal today for some word from 20-year-old Patricia Hearst.

"You might ask the people who are holding you if you could be allowed to send us a letter or get in touch with us by tape," the newspaper executive said.

Mr. Hearst, with his wife at his side, made his appeal during a televised news conference in the driveway of his mansion here. Their daughter was taken from her Berkeley apartment Feb. 4 by a group calling itself the Symbionese Liberation Army.

Although $2-million has already been turned over to feed California's poor and $4-million more has been promised if Miss Hearst is released, there was still no

Continued on Page 25, Column 1

Lutheran-Catholic Accord Voted

By EDWARD B. FISKE

A joint commission of United States Roman Catholic and Lutheran theologians issued a study yesterday declaring that papal primacy—a major issue in the Protestant Reformation of the 16th Century—need no longer be a "barrier to reconciliation" of their churches.

In a 5,000-word "Common Statement" the scholars envisioned a time when Lutheran and Catholic churches would be part of a single "larger communion" — autonomous but linked by common recognition of the Pope in Rome as a visible symbol of their underlying unity.

The statement, whose formal title is "Ministry and the Church Universal: Differing Attitudes Toward Papal Primacy," was adopted by the 26-member Lutheran-Roman Catholic Consultation in the United States.

Excerpts from conclusions are printed on Page 25.

The commission, which comprises 13 Roman Catholics and 13 Lutherans, was appointed in 1965 by the National Committee of the Lutheran World Federation and the Committee for Ecumenical and Interreligious Affairs of the National Conference of Catholic Bishops. The Lutheran delegation includes representatives of all major branches of Lutheranism in this country.

The document, the fruit of nine years of theological dialogue, represents the first time since the Lutheran Reformation of the 16th Century that an officially sanctioned group of Roman Catholic and Lutheran scholars has expressed agreement on crucial aspects of papal authority.

It is likely to be regarded as a major ecumenical landmark because, while it is in no way binding on any of the churches involved, it would seem to eliminate—at least on the theological level—a major obstacle to Christian unity.

"It is now up to the churches to indicate how far they want to go in implementing it," said the Rev. George A. Lindbeck,

Continued on Page 25, Column 3

Many Workers Still Face Health Peril Despite Law

By JANE E. BRODY

The recent discovery of fatal liver cancer among vinyl chloride workers has focused renewed attention of government, labor, industry and medicine on the thousands of known, suspected and as yet unsuspected health hazards that face 60 million working Americans.

Despite the passage three years ago of the Occupational Safety and Health Act, granting every American the right to work without job-induced threats to life and health, the overwhelming majority of workers are not yet protected by the law's provisions. For lack of this protection, hundreds of workers are dying each day from occupational diseases.

The Government Accounting Office acknowledges that there has not been nearly enough money and staff allocated to make a dent in the vast problem of occupational health. In addition, fundamental scientific knowledge is lacking upon which to base remedial actions, and without more funds the necessary research is not forthcoming.

Historically, occupational health has been a low-priority item for both government and medicine.

Yet, each year one of every

Continued on Page 20, Column 1

NEWS INDEX

"Ziggy" [illegible] WILLCOX & GIBBS (WG-AMEX) — Advt.

Rescuers carry the body of one of the 345 victims of the Turkish DC-10 jetliner which crashed in the Ermenonville forest, north of Paris.

Wide World Photos

345 on a Jumbo Jet Killed Near Paris

Continued From Page 1, Col. 8

at take-off plus 11 crew members—were ripped apart.

The valley floor was smothered with a chaos of debris and shards of metal. Sleet showers alternated with sun, turning the ground into a bog.

A shell of part of the red-striped white fuselage lay canted crazily between two trees, the largest chunk of the plane that remained.

Rescue workers in blue-and-white uniforms spoke in low voices as they poked and stirred the ruins with splintered branches, looking for bodies, passports and clothing that could be used for identification. Occasionally a small plane buzzed and circled overhead.

Searchers packed the remains into blankets and bags or placed them on stretchers. As night gathered, portable floodlights were brought to illuminate the valley and allow them to continue their labors.

The silence at the crash site contrasted with the chaos on the roads that led to the forest, a favorite place on a sunny Sunday for picnics and strolling.

Ambulances, police cars and fire engines brayed their warnings as they tore through tangles of civilian automobiles. The curious also came on foot by the thousands with children in their arms or tugging at dogs.

Thousands of policemen and troops blocked their way, but a few left the muddy forest trails and slipped through the

The New York Times/March 4, 1974

tangled and slimy underbrush to approach the scene.

An official said it would take a week to gather the wreckage. At nightfall, a tight police cordon was set up around the scene. A temporary morgue was established in the gothic vaulted hall of an old church at Senlis.

Turkish Airlines said that 216 passengers boarded the DC-10 at Orly. Many were British, joining another large contingent of Britons flying from Istanbul.

A sudden strike of Engineers at London's Heathrow Airport had forced the cancellation of many British Airways flights and passengers in Paris had switched to the Turkish jet. About 40 Japanese passengers were reported on board.

The pilot of the plane today gave no sign of trouble in the brief moments before the crash. The French state-owned television network reported tonight that the plane's landing gear

had been lowered as if the pilot were trying to make an emergency landing at the new Charles de Gaulle Airport at nearby Roissy-en-France.

Then the wheels were apparently retracted again as the jumbo jet lunged toward the forest.

Late this afternoon, part of the flight recorder, which might give some clue to the cause of the crash, was recovered.

One of the witnesses of the plane's last seconds was Maurice Lhote, who works in the control tower at Le Bourget Airport.

He was walking with his family in the forest of Ermenonville when he saw the jet flying at about 2,400 feet. "I noticed that its angle of flight was not normal," he said. "I thought the pilot was trying to land at Le Bourget, but he wasn't in the proper approach path. Seconds later the plane vanished."

The National Transportation Safety Board in Washington said the United States was sending a three-man team to observe the investigation of the crash.

"Though the accident occurred on French soil, it was a U. S. - manufactured aircraft," said Edward F. Slattery, a spokesman. "We want to be on hand to know as rapidly as possible what happened. I would say more than 100 DC-10s are used by the American fleet. If there were a malfunction or a fault in the design, we want to be able to take corrective

measures as fast as possible."

The DC-10, manufactured by the Douglas Aircraft Division of the McDonnell Douglas Corporation, was introduced in 1971 and costs about $20-million.

Guerrilla Action Suggested

ISTANBUL, Turkey, March 3 (UPI)—Turkish airline sources said tonight that five passengers on the Turkish Airlines plane that crashed north of Paris might have been guerrillas carrying bombs that exploded in flight.

The sources said the airline had information indicating that three Japanese and two Arabs who were said to have boarded the plane at Paris for the flight to London were guerrillas.

They said the guerrillas had planned to sabotage a British Airways flight from Paris to London but that the flight had been canceled and they were transferred to the Turkish plane. Their bombs exploded after take-off, causing the crash, they said.

The sources said all the airline's information had been given to the Turkish Ministry of Communications.

345 Toll Worst by Far; Earlier Record Was 176

By United Press International

The crash of a Turkish airliner carrying 345 persons near Paris yesterday was by far the worst air disaster in history.

Previous air disasters include these:

On Jan. 23, 1973, a Jor-

danian Boeing 707 crashed at Kano airport in Nigeria killing 176 persons.

On Oct. 13, 1972, a Soviet Aeroflot jetliner carrying 176 persons crashed near Moscow, killing all aboard.

On July 30, 1971, a Japanese jet fighter and an All Nippon Airways 727 jet collided near Morioka in northern Japan, killing 162.

On Aug. 14, 1972, an East German Soviet-built Ilyushin jetliner crashed and exploded in a suburb of East Berlin, killing 156.

On Dec. 3, 1972, a Convair 990 owned by a Madrid charter company crashed at Santa Cruz De Tenerife, Canary Islands, killing 155 persons.

On March 16, 1969, a Viasa DC-9 crashed in Maracaibo, Venezuela, killing 155 persons.

London Strike Diverted Britons to Turkish Jet

LONDON, March 3 (Reuters) —A strike of ground staff at London's Heathrow Airport diverted many British passengers to the Turkish Airlines DC-10 that crashed near Paris today, a spokesman for British Airways said.

British Airways said many of its own passengers were booked on the Turkish plane at Paris after a strike of engineers at Heathrow grounded all of its European flights. About 200 of the passengers on the Turkish plane were rebooked in Paris from British airlines.

"All the News That's Fit to Print"

The New York Times

LATE CITY EDITION

Weather: Showers likely today; cloudy and mild tonight, tomorrow. Temp. range: today 60-70; Thursday 53-75. Additional details on Page 74.

VOL. CXXIII..No. 42,440 | © 1974 The New York Times Company | NEW YORK, FRIDAY, APRIL 5, 1974 | 20¢ beyond 50-mile radius of New York City, except Long Island. Higher in air delivery cities. | 15 CENTS

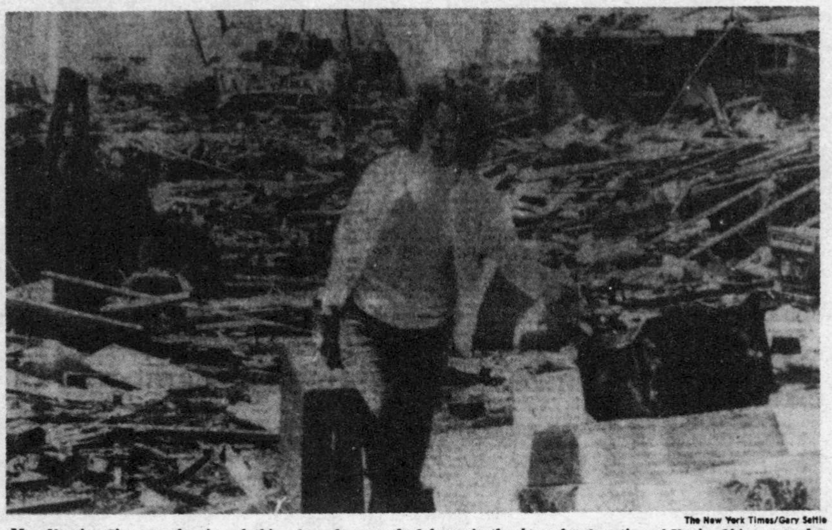

The New York Times/Gary Settle

Mrs. Vernice Simons salvaging clothing from her wrecked home in the Arrowhead section of Xenia, Ohio, yesterday

City in Ohio Stays Calm Amid Twister's Debris

By DOUGLAS E. KNEELAND

Special to The New York Times

XENIA, Ohio, April 4—It was too soon—or too late—for tears in Xenia today.

Yesterday this old Miami Valley city of 25,000 people, about 10 miles east of Dayton in southwestern Ohio, was one of the worst hit of any of the communities caught in what the United States Weather Service has called the most severe rampage of tornadoes in the nation since 1925.

When Xenia's own particular twister roared through late in the afternoon, it left as many as 30 persons dead, hundreds injured and thousands homeless in a wake three or four miles long and several hundred yards wide.

Slashing through town from the southwest, it ripped apart new housing developments, downtown businesses, shopping centers, schools, churches and old neighborhoods alike.

And today, under a warm April sun that compensated for the brisk wind that played dangerously with loose wires, dangling signs and traffic lights, and broken branches, Xenia was trying to put it all back together again.

As in most disasters too overwhelming to contemplate, there was a strange calm about the place, as if the people of Xenia got up every morning of their lives and sifted through the splinters that were once their homes, scraped unrecognizable debris from their streets, sawed up the fallen trees that once shaded their yards.

Hundreds of Ohio National Guardsmen were on the streets, out-of-town policemen were everywhere, bulldozers and fork lifts growled

Continued on Page 16, Column 4

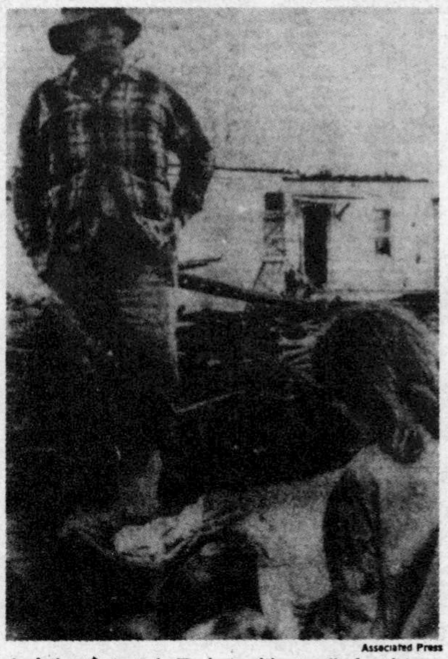

Associated Press

A victim of storm in Xenia awaiting medical assistance

TORNADOES' TOLL IS PLACED AT 310, 1-BILLION DAMAGE

Five States Are Designated Disaster Areas by Nixon —Kentucky Worst Hit

By JUDITH CUMMINGS

Cones of vicious winds that slashed across 11 states of the South and Middle West pushed the death toll to more than 300 persons yesterday and evoked tornado watches for six additional states, in the worst tornado disaster in 49 years.

The twisters, nearly 100 of them striking within eight hours in an area from Georgia to Michigan, had left 310 known dead last night, including eight persons who were killed in the Canadian border-city of Windsor, Ont. Early estimates of property damage exceeded $1-billion.

Although most of the storms occurred late Wednesday, a few sporadic tornado formations were reported yesterday, including one that caused the death of a Virginia teen-ager when his mobile home was snatched up, hurled 100 yards and dropped on its roof.

Nixon Heeds Pleas

Responding to pleas from state officials, President Nixon declared Alabama, Kentucky, Ohio, Indiana and Tennessee disaster areas. A White House spokesman said Mr. Nixon was awaiting further information on the situation in Georgia, Illinois, Michigan and North Carolina before taking action in those states.

Designation as a disaster area makes the states eligible for massive Federal aid and clears the way for low-interest loans to homeowners and businessmen.

While searches for survivors continued across a center swath of the country, Kentucky appeared to be the worst hit. As the death count reached 71, Gov. Wendell Ford called it the most tragic day in the state's history.

Water Supply Critical

Five persons were killed and more than 200 injured in Louisville, where the roaring funnels ripped out large sections of neighborhoods. The water supply was termed critical after a tornado hit the city's main source at the Crescent Hill Plant.

Fifty miles to the southwest, the Ohio River town of Brandenburg all but disappeared, leaving 40 dead, and the winds cut through more than a dozen other Kentucky towns and cities, including Frankfort. Power lines were reported down and telephone service

Continued on Page 16, Column 1

Aides Say Nixon's Tax Bill Will Force Him to Borrow

He Will Pay Major Part of the $432,787 in Cash—Spokesman Says Payment Will Severely Cut His Wealth

By JOHN HERBERS

Special to The New York Times

WASHINGTON, April 4—White House officials said today that President Nixon's personal wealth would be severely reduced when he pays his tax bill of $432,787 plus interest.

"A payment such as this is a major impact on his financial position," said Gerald L. Warren, deputy White House press secretary.

A White House official who asked not to be identified said, "The President is going to have to borrow a substantial amount in order to meet this obligation."

Both Mr. Warren and this official said that the President had enough cash on hand to pay a major portion of the tax bill, which Mr. Nixon said yesterday he would pay in full even though he contends he does not owe it. But the remainder, something less than half, will be paid with borrowed money.

President Nixon's net worth was set at about $1-million last December, when the President made his most recent financial disclosure. But because he subsequently promised to give his San Clemente estate to the public and because of his decision to pay back taxes and interest, Mr. Nixon's personal holdings, in effect, would be wiped out, according to his assistants. It has not been determined when the transfer of the estate is to be made.

Mr. Nixon still will not be a poor man. He receives a salary and expense allowance of $250,000 a year. The Government maintains the White House and pays many of the necessities for him and his family. Apparently he will be able to continue the mortgage payments on his villas in Key Biscayne, Fla., and San Clemente.

His aides, however, sought

Continued on Page 18, Column 5

House Unit Bids President Yield on Tapes by Tuesday

By JAMES M. NAUGHTON

Special to The New York Times

WASHINGTON, April 4—The House Judiciary Committee demanded today that President Nixon decide by Tuesday whether he will turn over to it tape recordings of some 42 Watergate-related conversations it seeks for its impeachment inquiry.

"We will subpoena them if we must," the committee chairman, Representative Peter W. Rodino Jr., Democrat of New Jersey, warned. He said that "the patience of this committee is wearing thin" after waiting 38 days for a White House reply to the panel's request of Feb. 25.

Congressional officials close to the inquiry said later that they expected the committee to vote next week, perhaps as early as Wednesday, to subpoena the tapes if they are not volunteered by the President.

Two of the President's lawyers, James R. Prochnow and Larry G. Gutterridge, were among the spectators, taking notes, at a meeting of the Judiciary Committee when Mr. Rodino declared.

"We have gone forward assuming good faith and cooperation. As regards the President himself, we have been respectfully patient. The courts were patient. The House has been patient. The people have been patient for a long, long time."

At the White House, a Presidential spokesman declined comment on the committee's deadline, reiterating that the tapes issue was the subject of

Continued on Page 21, Column 5

Wholesale Prices Up 1.3% in March

Special to The New York Times

WASHINGTON, April 4—The strong surge of wholesale prices continued in March despite an unaccustomed drop in farm and food prices, the Department of Labor reported today.

The rise in the wholesale price index was 1.3 per cent after adjustment for normal seasonal changes in some prices, about the same as in February but less than in the three preceding months.

The index was marked last month by a near-record jump of 2.9 per cent in prices of industrial commodities, a category covering thousands of items at all stages of process-

Continued on Page 51, Column 6

NIXON TAX INQUIRY IS CLOSED BY I.R.S. AND CONGRESS UNIT

But Several Democrats Are Said to Feel Report Hints Constitutional Violation

PRESIDENT COMMENDED

Joint Committee Lauds His 'Prompt Decision' to Pay $432,787 in Back Levies

By EILEEN SHANAHAN

Special to The New York Times

WASHINGTON, April 4—The Internal Revenue Service and the Congressional Joint Committee on Internal Revenue Taxation formally closed today their inquiries into President Nixon's tax payments for his first four years in the White House.

The committee, by a 9-to-1 vote, officially noted its agreement with the substance of most of the recommendations of its staff, which had concluded that Mr. Nixon underpaid his taxes by $444,022 in the years 1969-72. The sole dissenter from the endorsement of the staff's work was Senator Carl T. Curtis, Republican of Nebraska.

Meanwhile, it was learned that Mr. Nixon's pre-Presidential papers would apparently remain in the National Archives. [Page 19.]

Constitutional Violation

In another development, sources close to the House Judiciary Committee, said that several Democrats on that panel were convinced that yesterday's report on President Nixon's taxes pointed to a violation of a constitutional provision prohibiting a President from receiving extra compensation or emoluments. [Page 19.]

The Joint Committee commended Mr. Nixon "for his prompt decision" to pay the taxes. He will pay the somewhat smaller amount of $432,787 that Internal Revenue found he owed for the four years.

The White House announced last night that Mr. Nixon would pay the figure assessed by Internal Revenue, plus interest. But he has apparently decided not to pay the interest on his 1969 delinquency, which is by far the largest amount for any year. He can legally avoid the payment of interest for that year, which would amount to $40,000, because the three-year statute of limitations has run out on his 1969 return.

In fact, he could also legally avoid payment of the entire

Continued on Page 18, Column 6

Aaron Ties Babe Ruth With 714th Homer

First-Inning Drive in Season Opener Equals Record

By DAVE ANDERSON

Special to The New York Times

CINCINNATI, April 4—With the unobtrusive grace that has symbolized his career, Henry Aaron tied Babe Ruth's record today with his 714th home run—a 400-foot, three-run line drive over the fence in left-center field at Riverfront Stadium on his first swing of the major league baseball season.

The historic home run, in the first inning off Jack Billingham of the Cincinnati Reds, momentarily silenced the sellout crowd of 52,154, including Vice President Ford, as the 40-year-old slugger of the Atlanta Braves trotted around the bases in his casual, unemotional manner.

By the time Aaron approached home plate all his teammates had run out of their dugout and were waiting to congratulate him. Johnny Bench, the Reds' catcher, also shook his hand.

"I thought that tying the record would mean a lot to me," Aaron said later, "but it was just another home run. It's a load off my back, but losing the ball game took

Continued on Page 43, Column 3

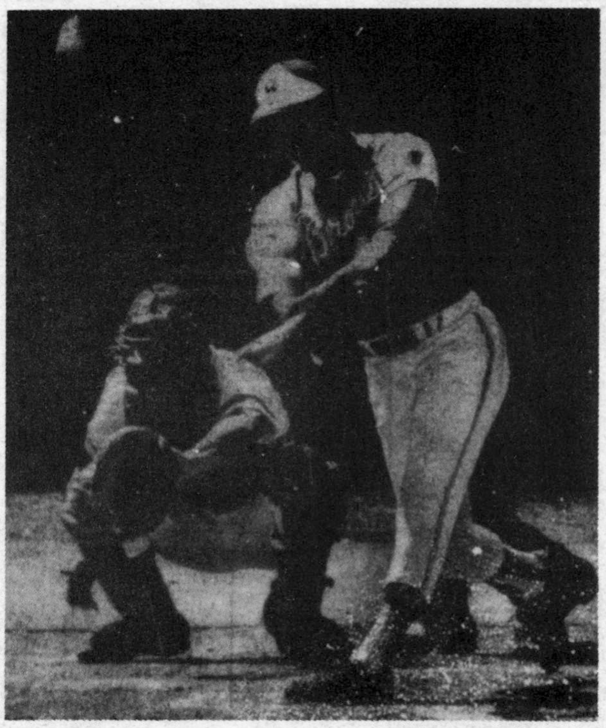

United Press International

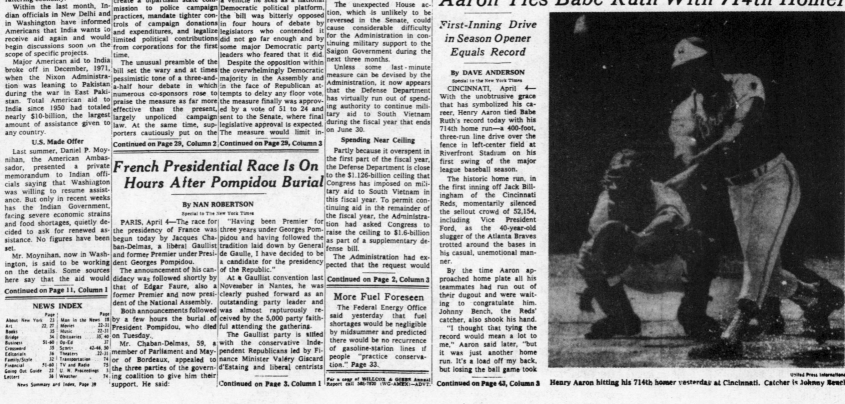

Henry Aaron hitting his 714th homer yesterday at Cincinnati. Catcher is Johnny Bench.

INDIANS ASK U.S. TO RESTORE AID

Request Emphasizes Anxiety Over Economic Travails—U.S. Was Major Donor

By BERNARD WEINRAUB

Special to The New York Times

NEW DELHI, April 4—India has quietly asked the United States to resume aid, a move that underlines the anxiety here about food shortages and the faltering economy.

Within the last month, Indian officials in New Delhi and in Washington have informed Americans that India wants to receive aid again and would begin discussions soon on the scope of specific projects.

Major American aid to India broke off in December, 1971, when the Nixon Administration was leaning to Pakistan during the war in East Pakistan. Total American aid to India since 1950 had totaled nearly $10-billion, the largest amount of assistance given to any country.

U.S. Made Offer

Last summer, Daniel P. Moynihan, the American Ambassador, presented a private memorandum to Indian officials saying that Washington was willing to resume assistance. But only in recent weeks has the Indian Government, facing severe economic strains and food shortages, quietly decided to ask for renewed assistance. No figures have been set.

Mr. Moynihan, now in Washington, is said to be working on the details. Some sources here say that the aid would

Continued on Page 11, Column 1

NEWS INDEX

	Page		Page
About New York	23	Man in the News	18
Art	22, 27	Movies	22-31
Books	35	Music	22-31
Bridge	34	Obituaries	35, 40
Business	51-60	Op-Ed	37
Crossword	35	Sports	42-46, 50
Editorials	36	Theaters	22-31
Family/Style	32	Transportation	74
Financial	51-60	TV and Radio	75
Going Out Guide	22	U. N. Proceedings	3
Letters	36	Weather	74

News Summary and Index, Page 39

2 State Legislatures Press For Election Reform Laws

Albany Assembly Acts

By FRANCIS X. CLINES

Special to The New York Times

ALBANY, April 4—The State Assembly today voted overwhelming approval of broad new controls of campaign practices in a bill whose language conceded "the prevailing lack of confidence and participation of the citizens of this state in the election process."

The measure, which passed by a vote of 133 to 6, would create a bipartisan state commission to police campaign practices, mandate tighter controls of campaign donations and expenditures, and legalize limited political contributions from corporations for the first time.

The unusual preamble of the bill set the wary and at times pessimistic tone of a three-and-a-half hour debate in which numerous co-sponsors rose to praise the measure as far more effective than the present, largely unpoliced campaign law. At the same time, supporters cautiously put on the

Continued on Page 29, Column 2

Bill Backed in Jersey

By RONALD SULLIVAN

Special to The New York Times

TRENTON, April 4—A highly controversial measure mandating the public financing of gubernatorial elections in New Jersey received initial legislative approval this evening in the Assembly.

An attempt to make it apply also to primaries was defeated.

A cornerstone of Governor Byrne's legislative program and a vehicle he sees as a national Democratic political platform, the bill was bitterly opposed in four hours of debate by legislators who contended it did not go far enough and by some major Democratic party leaders who feared that it did.

Despite the opposition within the overwhelmingly Democratic majority in the Assembly and in the face of Republican attempts to delay any floor vote, the measure finally was approved by a vote of 51 to 24 and sent to the Senate, where final legislative approval is expected. The measure would limit in-

Continued on Page 29, Column 3

HOUSE BARS RISE IN VIETNAM AID

Rejects Administration Call for $474-Million More in Military Assistance

By JOHN W. FINNEY

Special to The New York Times

WASHINGTON, April 4—The House, by a vote of 177 to 154, tonight rejected the Administration's request for a $474-million increase in military aid to South Vietnam.

The unexpected House action, which is unlikely to be reversed in the Senate, could cause considerable difficulty for the Administration in continuing military support to the Saigon Government during the next three months.

Unless some last-minute measure can be devised by the Administration, it now appears that the Defense Department has virtually run out of spending authority to continue military aid to South Vietnam during the fiscal year that ends on June 30.

Spending Near Ceiling

Partly because it overspent in the first part of the fiscal year, the Defense Department is close to the $1.126-billion ceiling that Congress has imposed on military aid to South Vietnam in this fiscal year. To permit continuing aid in the remainder of the fiscal year, the Administration had asked Congress to raise the ceiling to $1.6-billion as part of a supplementary defense bill.

The Administration had expected that the request would

Continued on Page 2, Column 3

French Presidential Race Is On Hours After Pompidou Burial

By NAN ROBERTSON

Special to The New York Times

PARIS, April 4—The race for the presidency of France was begun today by Jacques Chaban-Delmas, a liberal Gaullist and former Premier under President Georges Pompidou.

The announcement of his candidacy was followed shortly by that of Edgar Faure, also a former Premier and now president of the National Assembly.

Both announcements followed by a few hours the burial of President Pompidou, who died on Tuesday.

Mr. Chaban-Delmas, 59, a member of Parliament and Mayor of Bordeaux, appealed to the three parties of the governing coalition to give him their support. He said:

"Having been Premier for three years under Georges Pompidou and having followed the tradition laid down by General de Gaulle, I have decided to be a candidate for the presidency of the Republic."

At a Gaullist convention last November in Nantes, he was clearly pushed forward as an outstanding party leader and was almost rapturously received by the 5,000 party faithful attending the gathering.

The Gaullist party is allied with the conservative Independent Republicans led by Finance Minister Valéry Giscard d'Estaing and liberal centrists

Continued on Page 3, Column 1

More Fuel Foreseen

The Federal Energy Office said yesterday that fuel shortages would be negligible by midsummer and predicted there would be no recurrence of gasoline-station lines if people "practice conservation." Page 33.

For a copy of WILLCOX & GIBBS Annual Report call 361-7820 (WG-AMEX)—ADVT.

Ohio City Stays Calm Amid Debris

Continued From Page 1, Col. 2

where shoppers usually stroll, sirens whined persistently. But the people went about their strange tasks with certain hands and serene faces.

At one end of East Main Street, a graying man and a slender boy of about 12 years worked together in front of a used car lot, unidentifiable because its sign had been shredded by the storm and its shiny merchandise had been crushed and battered.

While the boy used a snow shovel to scoop the rubble from the street, the man methodically picked up stray wires and twisted sheets of metal. Like hundreds of Xenians today, they were just volunteers.

As he dragged the tangled sheet of tin to the heap he was slowly building, the man smiled and said:

"If everybody pitches in, it won't take long."

Down the street a bit, Chester Freelan stood in a doorway of one of the old buildings that line Main and Detroit Streets, the heart of downtown Xenia. Behind him were the wooden stairs to his apartment above his "pool room and beer joint," whose sign had been ripped off and windows shattered.

Flee to Basement

"It sure tore up that apartment upstairs," said Mr. Freelan, unshaven after a night of little sleep. Then, nodding to either side, "I think they'll have to tear these three buildings down."

What "it" was he did not have to say, nor did any of the other thousands who had their own stories to tell in Xenia today.

"I come to the door," he went on, grinning and pointing, "and right there, about that fifth traffic light, I seen it. I told those guys they'd better hit for the basement. Everybody that was in there, they run for the basement. There wasn't nobody hurt."

Down on Detroit Street, not far from the old stone Greene County Courthouse, where off-duty Guardsmen lounged on the lawn below the smashed clock tower, the local Army recruiting officers had placed a sign on their door in an aging gray brick building.

"Sorry, we're closed," the sign said. So was almost everything in town, but the Army had as good an excuse as anybody. The roof had been torn from the building.

In a parking lot across the street, Harry Anthony, in a gray business suit and the yellow hard hat that most people working around town were wearing today, was carefully lettering his own sign on the side of a streamlined motor home. "Gallagher Insurance Agency, Motorists Mutual Company, Emergency Claims Office," it said.

Clock Marks Time

Mr. Anthony and his associates were open for business —more business than usual. But where was the regular office?

"Across the street," Mr. Anthony said ruefully, nodding at the gray building with the missing roof.

On the other side of De-troit Street, William Hitchcock, in a plaid cap and gray jacket, carrying a raincoat despite the sunshine, stood in the entrance to his locked jewelry store, a casual-appearing sentry.

"It hit at 4:40," he said, looking up at the clock in his twisted sign. The hands were frozen at 4:40 P.M.

"We close on Wednesday afternoon," he said, "so I was away from the store at the time, but it passed just a little south of our home. It sounded like a fast passenger train. It was really just filling the air with stuff, really violent."

The windows of his store were shattered and barren.

"Everything I had in the windows was gone," he said, "and I got down here about an hour after it happened. I don't know whether the storm sucked the stuff out or what."

So he stood his ground in the doorway, looking reluctant to leave.

Almost Proved Fatal

Out in the Arrowhead subdivision, a new home development that was one of the most devastated sections, a handful of National Guardsmen drove up to help Vernice Simons, who was picking through the remains of her house.

Looking around, one of the Guardsmen sighted a soft-water tank that seemed to have survived amid the carnage. "Do you want that?" he asked.

"I never want to see that damn thing again," she said. "It almost killed me."

She and her family had hidden in a closet when they heard the tornado coming, she explained, and the tank had blown on top of them. Everyone but her husband escaped unscathed. He was in a hospital with broken ribs.

In much of Xenia today, the gas had been shut off for fear of leaks and explosions, the electricity and telephones were out, people were forced to boil water because of possible contamination and traffic was so snarled it could take an hour or more to get in or out of town. But nobody seemed to be complaining.

And helping hands kept appearing in unusual places. In one afternoon traffic jam, several youngsters on a creeping National Guard truck heading into town even handed out popsicles to motorists who were leaving the city.

One man, reaching for a tossed popsicle, missed and then looked back in chagrin as the truck rolled on. The boys shrugged and laughed.

It was that kind of a day in Xenia—too soon—or too late—for tears.

Mr. and Mrs. William McAdams carrying away belongings in wheelbarrows yesterday in Xenia, Ohio, after tornado leveled buildings there

The New York Times

Associated Press

A resident of Brandenburg, Ky., stares silently at wreckage left in the path of tornado

Tornadoes' Damage $1-Billion

Continued From Page 1, Col. 5

knocked out through the central portion of the state.

Five more dead were reported in Xenia, Ohio, yesterday, bringing the total to 30 in that community of 25,000 in the southwestern part of the state. Another 1,000 were injured by a tornado that leveled half the town and there were unconfirmed reports of more than 40 missing.

Gov. John J. Gilligan ordered 1,500 National Guard troops into Xenia to help relief workers and to prevent looting. The Governors of Indiana, Kentucky and Tennessee also ordered guardsmen to duty in stricken communities in their states.

Vice President Ford, who was flown on an inspection tour of damaged areas of Ohio, called the destruction "unbelievable . . . you can see where the houses were reduced to matches." Thirty-five were dead in the state.

In Washington, Senator Birch Bayh, of Indiana requested an additional $100-million in disaster relief funds to supplement the $63-million that he said remained available for use until the end of June, out of an original $400-million fund. Roll call votes in the Senate were canceled for Friday and most of Monday so that Senators from affected states could go home.

Indiana had 52 dead and at least 1,000 were injured, with the heaviest damage at Hanover, in the south.

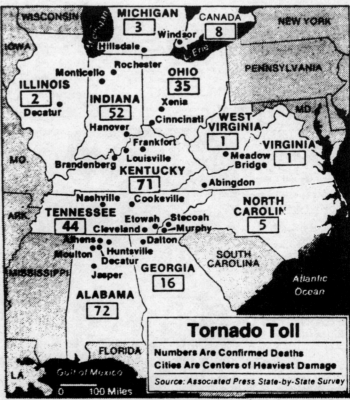

Tornado Toll

Numbers Are Confirmed Deaths
Cities Are Centers of Heaviest Damage

Source: Associated Press State-by-State Survey

The New York Times/Louis Craca/April 5, 1974

"All the News That's Fit to Print"

The New York Times

LATE CITY EDITION

Weather: Partly sunny, mild today; cloudy tonight. Fair tomorrow. Temperature range: today 60-72; Saturday 70-80. Details on Page 67.

SECTION ONE

VOL. CXXIV..No. 42,610 | © 1974 The New York Times Company | NEW YORK, SUNDAY, SEPTEMBER 22, 1974 | $1.00 beyond 50-mile zone from New York City, except Long Island. Higher in air delivery cities. | 60 CENTS

Ford Foundation Weighs Reducing Grants by 50%

Falling Security Market and Inflation Are Cited —Dissolution Possible

Allen Green

McGeorge Bundy

By M. A. FARBER

The Ford Foundation, squeezed like most private philanthropies by falling stock and bond markets and mounting inflation, is considering a reduction of as much as 50 per cent in its annual grants.

McGeorge Bundy, the president of the foundation, which is the wealthiest in the country, said that a cut of 50 per cent in Ford's $220-million-a-year program budget was one of several alternatives that he had presented to the trustees of the foundation for review at their quarterly meeting last week.

'Hard Look' Needed

Mr. Bundy said in an interview that the other options included smaller reductions or dissolving the foundation by distributing its assets, which have fallen from $3-billion to $2-billion in market value in the last year.

Ford's trustees rejected the idea of dissolution in 1967, when the foundation began reducing its grants from a level of more than $300-million annually. Mr. Bundy declined to comment on the likelihood of the trustees' voting the foundation out of business, but few trustees are believed to favor dissolution.

"We need to take a hard look at our situation," the Ford executive said. "The question is how much action to take now. If we continue to spend at our

Continued on Page 47, Column 1

ASSEMBLY OF U.N. SETS FULL DEBATE ON PALESTINIANS

Israel Objects to Separate Discussion of Issue as Agenda Is Adopted

By PAUL HOFMANN

Special to The New York Times

UNITED NATIONS, N. Y., Sept. 21—The General Assembly of the United Nations, in an unusual Saturday meeting, decided today to hold a full-fledged debate on the "Palestinian question" despite an impassioned protest by Israel.

No formal vote was taken as the full Assembly adopted the agenda for its 13-week meeting, as proposed by its General Committee.

The Palestinian discussion will be item 108 on the Assembly's agenda of 110 items. An earlier draft agenda contained 113 items, but some of them were combined.

Kissinger to Speak

The session's general debate, in which spokesmen for the member nations outline their Governments' policies, is item 9 on the agenda and will open on Monday. Secretary of State Kissinger will be one of the first speakers.

Mr. Kissinger is expected to discuss the world's economic problems, especially the interdependence of the energy and food crises, and to devote a part of his address to the situation in the Middle East.

The status of the Palestinians was regularly discussed as part of other Middle East problems in previous General Assembly sessions.

Last week, all 20 Arab nations represented in the world organization and many African and Communist nations requested that the Palestinian question be debated at the current session as a separate item.

No U.S. Opposition

Israel immediately served notice that she was opposed to the move on the ground that it would increase tension in the Middle East.

The United States has not opposed the move for a separate Palestinian debate. The American delegation here appears prepared to consult with other members when a draft resolution on the matter is circulated.

Today, the Israeli delegate,

Continued on Page 4, Column 1

United Press International

FORD AND GROMYKO CONFER: The President and Andrei A. Gromyko, Soviet Foreign Minister, chat outside the White House following their meeting. At center is Viktor M. Sukhodrev, interpreter; at left, Ambassador Anatoly F. Dobrynin. Behind Mr. Gromyko are Secretary of State Kissinger and Maj. Gen. Brent Scowcroft. Page 10.

TOLL IN HONDURAS FROM HURRICANE NOW PUT AT 3,800

5,000 Are Reported Missing and 60,000 Homeless—Crops Are Flattened

AIRLIFT BRINGS RELIEF

U.S. Sends Planes—Many Towns Still Cut Off With No Casualty Estimates

By ALAN RIDING

Special to The New York Times

TEGUCIGALPA, Honduras, Sept. 21 — The Government announced tonight that at least 3,800 bodies had been found and 5,000 people were missing as a result of a hurricane that struck Thursday.

The authorities said that vast areas of the Caribbean coastal region were flooded and many towns and villages were still cut off from this capital.

Col. Eduardo Andino, chief coordinator of the nation's National Emergency Committee, said that the disaster zone stretched across the entire northern lowlands, where most of the country's agricultural products are grown.

"The banana plantations have been flattened," he said after flying over the area this afternoon. "People are sitting on rooftops, holding tiny children in their arms and waving for help."

A report by Colonel Andino to the National Emergency Committee said that 3,800 bodies had been found so far and over 60,000 people were homeless. But in many towns that were badly hit by the hurricane and subsequent flash floods, there were still no estimates of casualties.

Path of Destruction

The United States, Nicaragua and Guatemala began to send emergency supplies. So far, the United States Army has sent six helicopters, two U-21 light aircraft and two C-130 cargo carriers in response to the disaster.

The hurricane, propelled by 130-mile-an-hour winds and lashing rains, cut a path of destruction across Nicaragua, Honduras, El Salvador, Guatemala, and Belize, the former British Honduras, before it died down over southeastern Mexico last night.

The Mexican Weather Bureau said that what was left of the hurricane was centered at midday yesterday about 100 miles southeast of Acapulco and moving west with winds of 60 miles an hour. Officials estimated that 2,000 to 8,000 Mexicans were homeless.

The small Honduran town of Choloma, 18 miles north of the

Continued on Page 12, Column 3

Sindona Resigns His Post As Franklin Bank Director

By JOHN H. ALLAN

Michele Sindona, the largest shareholder in the parent company that owns the beleaguered Franklin National Bank, yesterday announced his resignation as a director. His announcement signaled the fact that the Italian financier, whose own banking holdings have been crumbling in recent weeks, would not fulfill his earlier promise to supply up to $50-million to the Franklin.

The resignation removed one roadblock to acceptance by Federal regulatory authorities of the bank's plan to remain independent as a Long Island-based institution.

Two Alternatives

Mr. Sindona has been a controversial figure to Federal authorities because of his tangled international financial activities. He is also under investigation by the Internal Revenue Service for allegedly having offered to contribute $1-million to the Committee to Re-elect the President (former President Richard M. Nixon). The revenue service is seeking to learn whether the contribution was ever made and where he planned to obtain the funds.

In a letter sent last Thursday to the 20,000 shareholders of Franklin, Joseph W. Barr, chairman of the bank, said his proposals, which were submitted to the Federal Deposit Insurance Corporation last Sept. 16, were the only hope for re-

Continued on Page 29, Column 1

Bellevue Project Is Limited as State Holds to '65 Costs

By MURRAY SCHUMACH

The state has told the city that if it wants the psychiatric facilities planned more than a decade ago for the new $150-million Bellevue Hospital, it must abide by a construction budget set in pre-inflationary 1965.

City mental-health experts retort that this is impossible and that the four top floors at the hospital that were supposed to have opened this month as a desperately needed psychiatric center here would remain empty indefinitely.

"This is completely irrational," said Dr. Alexander Thomas, director of the antiquated psychiatric center in the old Bellevue building. "To say, on the one hand, that the program is approved, and, on the other hand, to say that it has to operate within a figure that is unrealistic, puts the whole program in a straitjacket beforehand. It sounds to me like a runaround. And it certainly is."

A Beame Appeal

The latest development in the bitter Bellevue situation was revealed in an exchange of letters between leading state and city mental-health officials. The letters have been obtained by The New York Times in its continuing investigation of deficiencies of the state's mental-health program.

The clash between the state

Continued on Page 32, Column 1

WATERGATE HURTS POLITICAL FUNDING

Area Legislators Say Money Is Harder to Get—Need for Integrity Stressed

By MARTIN TOLCHIN

Special to The New York Times

WASHINGTON, Sept. 21—In the aftermath of Watergate, members of Congress from New York, New Jersey and Connecticut say they are having trouble raising campaign funds, have become more cautious about handling money and are more conscious of the need for integrity.

Many of the members say that the Watergate scandal is a major reason that the New York delegation is losing one-fifth of its House members—8 of 39.

"They lost heart in the entire political system," said Representative Benjamin S. Rosenthal, Queens Democrat.

Despite the criticism of politicians engendered by Watergate, however, most members of the tristate Congressional delegation said that they had not changed their day-to-day operations, nor their dealings with lobbyists, contributors and constituents. But some nevertheless conveyed a sense of change.

"I'm sure that Watergate has changed each of us," said Representative Howard W. Robi-

Continued on Page 36, Column 4

Teacher Groups Increase Election Campaign Outlay

By DAVID E. ROSENBAUM

Special to The New York Times

WASHINGTON, Sept. 21—The nation's teachers' organizations have vastly increased the amount of money they are giving to political candidates this year and have become one of the best financed special interest groups in the nation.

Reports of contributions filed under Federal law and interviews with officials of various organizations indicate that teachers may spend more than $2-million before the November election.

Most of the money will be donated to candidates for state and local office, but it seems likely that from $600,000 to $750,000 will be given to candidates for Congress.

In 1972, the teachers gave about $100,000 to Congressional candidates.

An idea of the magnitude of the teachers' contributions and of the potential lobbying strength it gives them in Congress can be seen by comparing their spending with that of the American Medical Association.

The A.M.A. and its state affiliates, which have long been considered one of the richest and one of the most powerful lobbies in Washington, gave $475,000 to Congressional candidates in 1972.

At the forefront of the teachers' move into big-time political financing is the National Education Association.

Stanley J. McFarland, who is the director of the association's Political Action Committee and the director of its Government Relations Office, ex-

Continued on Page 56, Column 3

POWER REACTORS FACE SAFETY TEST

21 of 50 to Be Checked for Cracks in Cooling Pipes—A.E.C. Aide Quits Post

By DAVID BURNHAM

Special to The New York Times

WASHINGTON, Sept. 21—The Atomic Energy Commission has ordered 21 of the 50 nuclear reactors producing commercial electric power in the United States to close down within the next 60 days to determine whether cracks are developing in the pipes of their cooling systems.

Meanwhile, a leading nuclear safety expert announced he was quitting his job with the commission "in order to be free to tell the American people about the potentially dangerous conditions in the nation's nuclear power plants."

Suggests Complete Halt

Carl J. Hocevar, author of one of the commission's basic methods of analyzing nuclear power plant safety, said in his letter of resignation to the commission chairman, Dixy Lee Ray, "In spite of the soothing reassurances that the A.E.C. gives to the uninformed, misled public, unresolved questions about nuclear power safety are so grave that the United States should consider a complete halt to nuclear power plant construction while we see if these serious questions can, somehow, be resolved."

Mr. Hocevar, one of several safety research experts who have recently resigned from the commission's Idaho Safety Research Center, said in a statement that he planned to work with critics of nuclear reactors, such as the Union of Concerned Scientists in Massachusetts and Ralph Nader, the consumer advocate, to inform

Continued on Page 44, Column 1

Yanks Win, Lead by 1

The Yankees rallied to beat the Cleveland Indians yesterday, 14-7, and take a one-game lead over the Baltimore Orioles with nine games left in the hot Eastern Division race. The Orioles lost to the Boston Red Sox, in 10 innings. Details in Section 5.

After Robust Decade, South's Growth Lags

By B. DRUMMOND AYRES Jr.

Special to The New York Times

ATLANTA, Sept. 21—The Southern economy is beginning to falter and stumble after a decade of robust growth.

Both prices and unemployment are now rising more rapidly south of the Mason-Dixon line than in the country as a whole.

Economists blame many of the same factors that have hurt business in other parts of the United States. But they say that some special factors have exacerbated the situation in Dixie.

For one thing, prices are spiraling faster in the South because the region's unusually rapid growth over the years has inevitably diminished a once-plentiful supply of cheap labor.

In Tidewater, Va., for example, black women who once were lucky if they could get a maid's job at $50 a week now make more than $100 a week in food processing plants. The plants are advertising for still more workers.

New minimum wage coverage and more and more unionization have also pushed up labor costs. Only a few weeks ago cotton mill workers unionized the J. P. Stevens & Co., Inc., plant in Roanoke Rapids, N. C., a step that will almost certainly have far-reaching impact on Dixie's huge, antiunion textile industry.

Like the diminution of the cheap labor pool, such a devel-

Continued on Page 52, Column 4

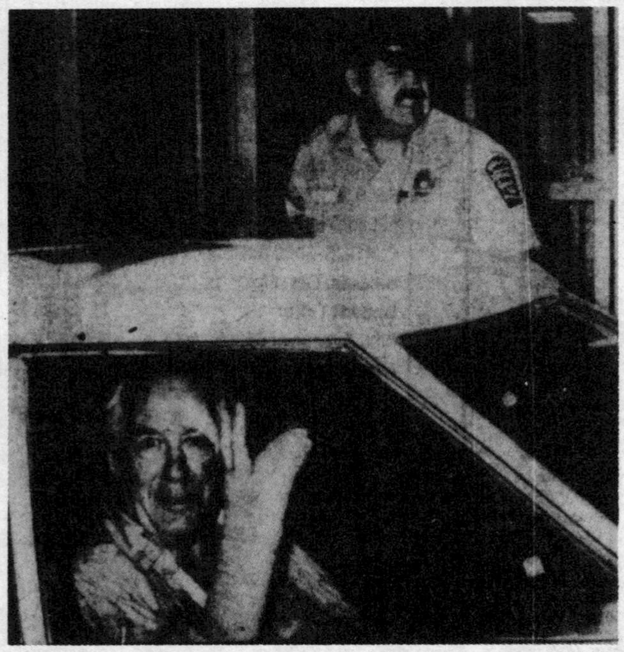

Associated Press

CHIEF JUSTICE HURT TRYING OUT BICYCLE: Warren E. Burger leaving Arlington (Va.) Hospital after suffering a fractured rib, a dislocated finger and a cut over the eye Friday night near his home. The police said that, while pedaling on a major road, he swerved to avoid a car. The bicycle was a gift for his 67th birthday Tuesday. A Supreme Court spokesman said Mr. Burger was later readmitted for a few days of "tests."

Wall Street Tries Hard to Forget Nixon

By VARTANIG G. VARTAN

Wall Street once gave its heart, its hurrahs and its campaign money to Richard M. Nixon. But lately the nation's nerve center of finance has been doing its best to forget about the President who resigned amid scandal on Aug. 9.

"From the Street's point of view, Nixon doesn't exist any more," declared Clarke D. Young, a vice president of Rauscher Pierce Securities Corporation. "A lot of people stuck by Nixon until the last tape disclosure just before his resignation," noted Mr. Young, an Easterner who displays individuality by wearing a wide-brim Western hat.

"But when it became apparent he had lied—that he really was Tricky Dick—there was disillusionment down here."

In Wall Street, a bastion of Republican strength, the sense of relief over Mr. Nixon's departure and the urgency to forget about him—"like last year's bad stock," as one broker put it—was underscored repeatedly in other interviews.

Dollar Signs Tell All

Overlying the Street's attitude toward Mr. Nixon, and towards virtually everything else, is the appalling state of the stock market and the crisis of profits confronting the securities industry. While the rest of the country is edging into recession and while housewives fret over high food prices, Wall Street has been mired in a deepening depression of its own for more than a year.

It is a business in which a brokerage-house salesman suddenly pulls up stakes without even saying good-by to his friends. The dollar signs tell everything, and a week ago Wednesday a seat on the Big Board was sold for $66,000, compared with a high of $515,000 only six years ago.

But for all its silence on Mr. Nixon, the Street finds that scar tissue can be penetrated in the most unexpected ways. The first trading day after President Ford announced his unconditional pardon of Mr. Nixon, the stock market responded with a jarring 15-point drop in the Dow Jones industrials.

On the trading floor of the stock exchange, where water-pistol fights and talcum-powder dousings of members ranked among the headier pranks of balmier times, the mood was grim.

When asked about the floor's

Continued on Page 51, Column 2

A Lawyer Hunted In Prison Killings Is Active in Hiding

By HENRY WEINSTEIN

Stephen M. Bingham, the radical lawyer who disappeared three years ago amid charges that he had helped plot an attempted prison escape by the black revolutionary author George Jackson, is alive, is continuing his political work underground, and has no intention of turning himself in.

In an interview last month in a Canadian city, the 32-year-old Mr. Bingham appeared calm, healthy and in good spirits, even though he was resigned to the life of a hunted man for whom a new identity and constant security precautions had become second nature.

To avoid giving any hint of his whereabouts, he would not discuss where he lived—neither the geographic region nor whether it was an urban or rural area—and he would not say whether he had a job, whether he lived alone or whether he was in contact with other leftists underground, including the Weatherpeople.

Nor would he confirm or deny

Continued on Page 41, Column 1

SAVINGS ON BOOKS UP TO 90%! Nearly 600 titles! For catalog write: Dept. FP, Columbia University Press, P.O. Box 196, Irvington, N.Y. 10533.—Advt.

Today's Sections

Index to Subjects

Wide World Photos

A wall of water, earth and rocks swept away much of the town of Choloma in northwest Honduras or left the buildings in a sea of mud.

Honduras Hurricane Toll Now at 3,800

Continued From Page 1, Col. 8

city of San Pedro Sula, appears to have been hit worst. Already 2,760 bodies have been found there and many more people were missing.

Engulfed by River

The town, which has a population of 6,000, was engulfed by a wall of water on Thursday night when a swollen river burst through a dike.

The valley of Aguan, in the northeast of the country, has also been designated a major disaster area even though no rescue teams have so far reached the farm settlements where some 10,000 people live.

"The mud is eight feet deep in places," Colonel Andino said. "We just have no idea of how many people may be trapped. It may be weeks before we dig through the mud and find the bodies."

The hurricane, known as Fifi, first struck Honduras Tuesday, but its full fury was only felt Thursday when winds of up to 110 miles an hour and torrential rains swept across the northern lowlands and brought heavy rain to the entire country.

In this mountain capital, damage was light and only a few houses were tumbled by flash floods.

On the Caribbean coastline, the Government has announced that at least 1,000 people were dead and 5,000 homeless in La Ceiba, but in Puerto Trujillo, Tocoa, Iriona, Puerto Cortes and other towns battered by the storm, theer was still no word on the number of dead.

The United States, which has already sent disaster survey teams from the United States Army Southern Command in the Panama Canal Zone, was expected to provide a water purification plant and water-cleansing tablets in the coming days. Mexico is expected to send 29 planeloads of food and medicine as well as doctors and nurses.

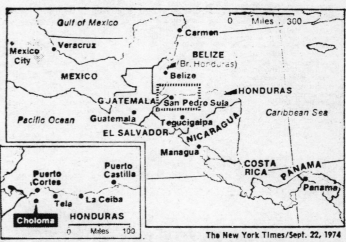

The New York Times/Sept. 22, 1974

Hurricane wiped out whole communities in Honduras, with toll apparently heaviest in Choloma.

"All the News That's Fit to Print"

The New York Times

LATE CITY EDITION

Weather: Clear, seasonable today, tonight. Turning cloudy tomorrow. Temperature range: today 27-40; Wednesday 35-40. Details, Page 74.

VOL. CXXIV . . No. 42,705 | © 1974 The New York Times Company | NEW YORK, THURSDAY, DECEMBER 26, 1974 | Price higher in air delivery cities. | 20 CENTS

Intruder in Car Smashes White House Gate

U.S. Aide's Son Gives Up; Held Off Police for 4 Hours

By PHILIP SHABECOFF
Special to The New York Times

WASHINGTON, Dec. 25—A young man, dressed like an Arab and seemingly laden with explosives, interrupted the Christmas calm of the capital today when he crashed his car through a White House gate at 7:07 A.M. and then stood for four hours a few feet from the executive mansion.

With President Ford and his family out of town, the building was empty except for staff. There were Secret Service agents and security guards on the grounds.

The incident ended when the man, identified as Marshall H. Fields, 25 years old, the son of a deceased American official, surrendered to the White House security police at 11 A.M. After questioning, he was taken to St. Elizabeth's Hospital for psychiatric examination.

Wired to the man's body were emergency warning flares, which are considered relatively harmless.

A Secret Service spokesman said Mr. Fields's only demand was to speak to the ambassador of Pakistan. He surrendered after the Howard University radio station met his demand to broadcast an appeal for a meeting with the ambassador.

The ambassador, Sahabzada Yaqub Kahn, had no intention of meeting with Mr. Fields, according to a spokesman for the embassy.

The Secret Service already had a file on Mr. Fields, a college dropout and former taxi driver, as a person who had made a threat against Government officials, a spokesman for the service said. The threat was reportedly not against the President.

State Department security

Continued on Page 24, Column 1

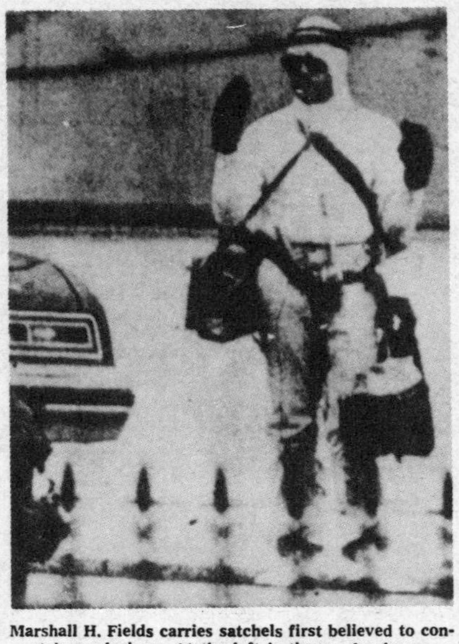

Marshall H. Fields carries satchels first believed to contain explosives. At the left is the car he drove.

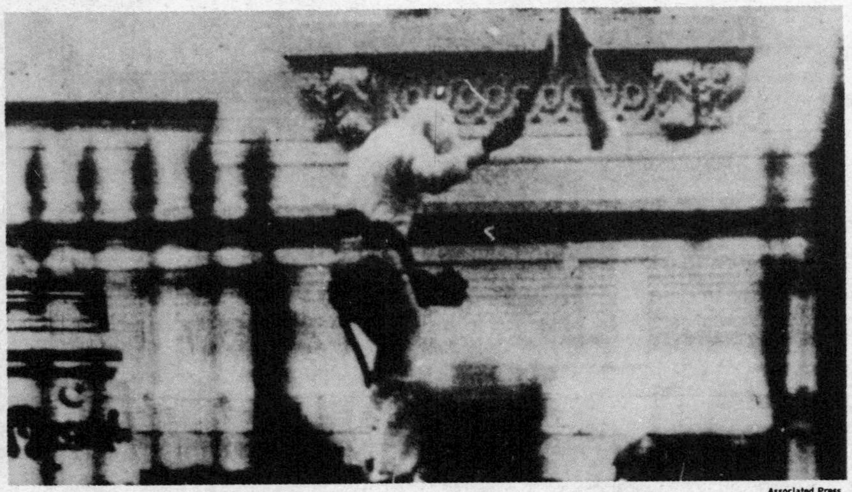

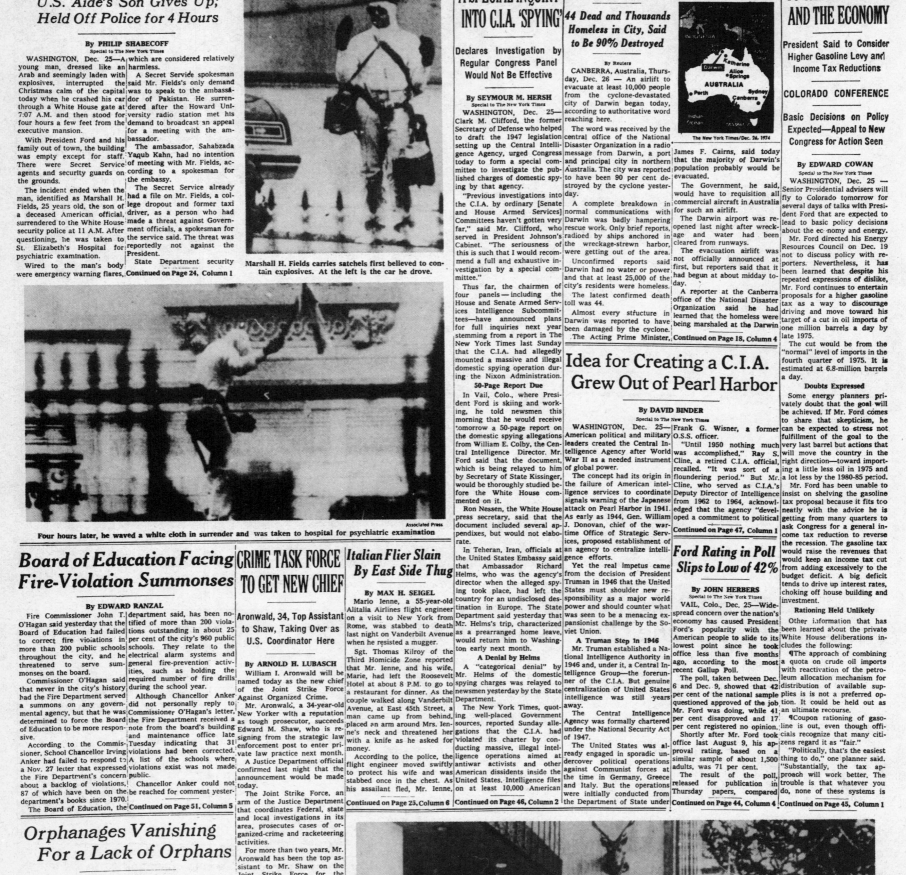

Associated Press

Four hours later, he waved a white cloth in surrender and was taken to hospital for psychiatric examination

CLIFFORD FAVORS A SPECIAL INQUIRY INTO C.I.A. 'SPYING'

Declares Investigation by Regular Congress Panel Would Not Be Effective

By SEYMOUR M. HERSH
Special to The New York Times

WASHINGTON, Dec. 25—Clark M. Clifford, the former Secretary of Defense who helped to draft the 1947 legislation setting up the Central Intelligence Agency, urged Congress today to form a special committee to investigate the published charges of domestic spying by that agency.

"Previous investigations into the C.I.A. by ordinary [Senate and House Armed Services] Committees haven't gotten very far," said Mr. Clifford, who served in President Johnson's Cabinet. "The seriousness of this is such that I would recommend a full and exhaustive investigation by a special committee."

Thus far, the chairmen of four panels—including the House and Senate Armed Services Intelligence Subcommittees—have announced plans for full inquiries next year stemming from a report in The New York Times last Sunday that the C.I.A. had allegedly mounted a massive and illegal domestic spying operation during the Nixon Administration.

50-Page Report Due

In Vail, Colo., where President Ford is skiing and working, he told newsmen this morning that he would receive tomorrow a 50-page report on the domestic spying allegations from William E. Colby, the Central Intelligence Director. Mr. Ford said that the document, which is being relayed to him by Secretary of State Kissinger, would be thoroughly studied before the White House commented on it.

Ron Nessen, the White House press secretary, said that the document included several appendixes, but would not elaborate.

In Teheran, Iran, officials at the United States Embassy said that Ambassador Richard Helms, who was the agency's director when the alleged spying took place, had left the country for an undisclosed destination in Europe. The State Department said yesterday that Mr. Helms's trip, characterized as a prearranged home leave, would return him to Washington early next month.

A Denial by Helms

A "categorical denial" by Mr. Helms of the domestic spying charges was relayed to newsmen yesterday by the State Department.

The New York Times, quoting well-placed Government sources, reported Sunday allegations that the C.I.A. had violated its charter by conducting massive, illegal intelligence operations aimed at antiwar activists and other American dissidents inside the United States. Intelligence files on at least 10,000 American

Continued on Page 46, Column 2

Australia to Airlift 10,000 Out of Cyclone-Hit Darwin

44 Dead and Thousands Homeless in City, Said to Be 90% Destroyed

By Reuters

CANBERRA, Australia, Thursday, Dec. 26 — An airlift to evacuate at least 10,000 people from the cyclone-devastated city of Darwin began today, according to authoritative word reaching here.

The word was received by the central office of the National Disaster Organization in a radio message from Darwin, a port and principal city in northern Australia. The city was reported to have been 90 per cent destroyed by the cyclone yesterday.

A complete breakdown in normal communications with Darwin was badly hampering rescue work. Only brief reports, radioed by ships anchored in the wreckage-strewn harbor, were getting out of the area.

Unconfirmed reports said Darwin had no water or power and that at least 25,000 of the city's residents were homeless.

The latest confirmed death toll was 44.

Almost every structure in Darwin was reported to have been damaged by the cyclone.

The Acting Prime Minister, James F. Cairns, said today that the majority of Darwin's population probably would be evacuated.

The Government, he said, would have to requisition all commercial aircraft in Australia for such an airlift.

The Darwin airport was reopened last night after wreckage and water had been cleared from runways.

The evacuation airlift was not officially announced at first, but reporters said that it had begun at about midday today.

A reporter at the Canberra office of the National Disaster Organization said he had learned that the homeless were being marshaled at the Darwin

Continued on Page 18, Column 4

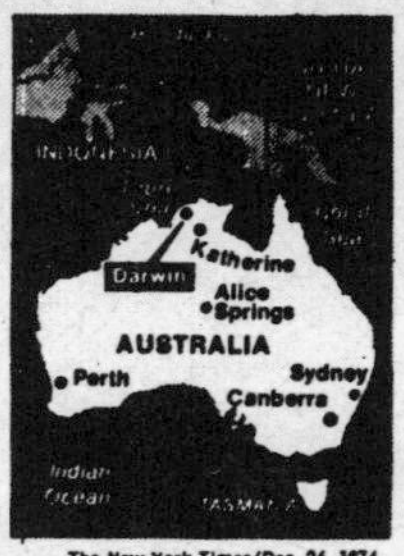

The New York Times/Dec. 26, 1974

Idea for Creating a C.I.A. Grew Out of Pearl Harbor

By DAVID BINDER
Special to The New York Times

WASHINGTON, Dec. 25—American political and military leaders created the Central Intelligence Agency after World War II as a needed instrument of global power.

The concept had its origin in the failure of American intelligence services to coordinate signals warning of the Japanese attack on Pearl Harbor in 1941. As early as 1944, Gen. William J. Donovan, chief of the wartime Office of Strategic Services, proposed establishment of an agency to centralize intelligence efforts.

Yet the real impetus came from the decision of President Truman in 1946 that the United States must shoulder new responsibility as a major world power and should counter what was seen to be a menacing expansionist challenge by the Soviet Union.

A Truman Step In 1946

Mr. Truman established a National Intelligence Authority in 1946 and, under it, a Central Intelligence Group—the forerunner of the C.I.A. But genuine centralization of United States intelligence was still years away.

The Central Intelligence Agency was formally chartered under the National Security Act of 1947.

The United States was already engaged in sporadic undercover political operations against Communist forces at the time in Germany, Greece and Italy. But the operations were initially conducted from the Department of State under Frank G. Wisner, a former O.S.S. officer.

"Until 1950 nothing much was accomplished," Ray S. Cline, a retired C.I.A. official, recalled. "It was sort of a floundering period." But Mr. Cline, who served as C.I.A.'s Deputy Director of Intelligence from 1962 to 1964, acknowledged that the agency "developed a commitment to political

Continued on Page 47, Column 1

Ford Rating in Poll Slips to Low of 42%

By JOHN HERBERS
Special to The New York Times

VAIL, Colo., Dec. 25—Widespread concern over the nation's economy has caused President Ford's popularity with the American people to slide to its lowest point since he took office less than five months ago, according to the most recent Gallup Poll.

The poll, taken between Dec. 6 and Dec. 9, showed that 42 per cent of the national sample questioned approved of the job Mr. Ford was doing, while 41 per cent disapproved and 17 per cent registered no opinion.

Shortly after Mr. Ford took office last August 9, his approval rating, based on a similar sample of about 1,500 adults, was 71 per cent.

The result of the poll, released for publication in Thursday papers, compared

Continued on Page 44, Column 4

FORD CALLS AIDES TO WEIGH ENERGY AND THE ECONOMY

President Said to Consider Higher Gasoline Levy and Income Tax Reductions

COLORADO CONFERENCE

Basic Decisions on Policy Expected—Appeal to New Congress for Action Seen

By EDWARD COWAN
Special to The New York Times

WASHINGTON, Dec. 25 — Senior Presidential advisers will fly to Colorado tomorrow for several days of talks with President Ford that are expected to lead to basic policy decisions about the economy and energy.

Mr. Ford directed his Energy Resources Council on Dec. 19 not to discuss policy with reporters. Nevertheless, it has been learned that despite his repeated expressions of dislike, Mr. Ford continues to entertain proposals for a higher gasoline tax as a way to discourage driving and move toward his target of a cut in oil imports of one million barrels a day by late 1975.

The cut would be from the "normal" level of imports in the fourth quarter of 1975. It is estimated at 6.8-million barrels a day.

Doubts Expressed

Some energy planners privately doubt that the goal will be achieved. If Mr. Ford comes to share that skepticism, he can be expected to stress not fulfillment of the goal to the very last barrel but actions that will move the country in the right direction—toward importing a little less oil in 1975 and a lot less by the 1980-85 period.

Mr. Ford has been unable to insist on shelving the gasoline tax proposal because it fits too neatly with the advice he is getting from many quarters to ask Congress for a general income tax reduction to reverse the recession. The gasoline tax would raise the revenues that would keep an income tax cut from adding excessively to the budget deficit. A big deficit tends to drive up interest rates, choking off house building and investment.

Rationing Held Unlikely

Other information that has been learned about the private White House deliberations includes the following:

¶The approach of combining a quota on crude oil imports with reactivation of the petroleum allocation mechanism for distribution of available supplies is is not a preferred option. It could be held out as an ultimate recourse.

¶Coupon rationing of gasoline is out, even though officials recognize that many citizens regard it as "fair."

"Politically, that's the easiest thing to do," one planner said. "Substantially, the tax approach will work better. The trouble is that whatever you do, none of these systems is

Continued on Page 45, Column 1

Board of Education Facing Fire-Violation Summonses

By EDWARD RANZAL

Fire Commissioner John T. O'Hagan said yesterday that the Board of Education had failed to correct fire violations in more than 200 public schools throughout the city, and he threatened to serve summonses on the board.

Commissioner O'Hagan said that never in the city's history had the Fire Department served a summons on any governmental agency, but that he was determined to force the Board of Education to be more responsive.

According to the Commissioner, School Chancellor Irving Anker had failed to respond to a Nov. 27 letter that expressed the Fire Department's concern about a backlog of violations, 87 of which have been on the department's books since 1970.

The Board of Education, the department said, has been notified of more than 200 violations outstanding in about 25 per cent of the city's 960 public schools. They relate to the electrical alarm systems and general fire-prevention activities, such as holding the required number of fire drills during the school year.

Although Chancellor Anker did not personally reply to Commissioner O'Hagan's letter, the Fire Department received a note from the board's building and maintenance office late Tuesday indicating that 31 violations had been corrected. A list of the schools where violations exist was not made public.

Chancellor Anker could not be reached for comment yester-

Continued on Page 51, Column 5

CRIME TASK FORCE TO GET NEW CHIEF

Aronwald, 34, Top Assistant to Shaw, Taking Over as U.S. Coordinator Here

By ARNOLD H. LUBASCH

William I. Aronwald will be named today as the new chief of the Joint Strike Force Against Organized Crime.

Mr. Aronwald, a 34-year-old New Yorker with a reputation as tough prosecutor, succeeds Edward M. Shaw, who is resigning from the strategic law enforcement post to enter private law practice next month.

A Justice Department official confirmed last night that the announcement would be made today.

The Joint Strike Force, an arm of the Justice Department that coordinates Federal, state and local investigations in its area, prosecutes cases of organized-crime and racketeering activities.

For more than two years, Mr. Aronwald has been the top assistant to Mr. Shaw on the Joint Strike Force for the Southern District of New York, covering Manhattan, the Bronx and nine more counties extending north to the border of Albany County.

Mr. Shaw, who was an assistant United States attorney for several years until he became head of the Joint Strike Force in July, 1972, successfully prosecuted Representative Frank J. Brasco of Brooklyn this year on a charge of conspiracy to accept bribes to help a Mafia-controlled truck company.

In early 1972, while still an assistant United States attor-

Continued on Page 50, Column 6

Italian Flier Slain By East Side Thug

By MAX H. SEIGEL

Mario Ienne, a 55-year-old Alitalia Airlines flight engineer on a visit to New York from Rome, was stabbed to death last night on Vanderbilt Avenue when he resisted a mugger.

Sgt. Thomas Kilroy of the Third Homicide Zone reported that Mr. Ienne, and his wife, Marie, had left the Roosevelt Hotel at about 8 P.M. to go to a restaurant for dinner. As the couple walked along Vanderbilt Avenue, at East 45th Street, a man came up from behind, placed an arm around Mrs. Ienne's neck and threatened her with a knife as he asked for money.

According to the police, the flight engineer moved swiftly to protect his wife and was stabbed once in the chest. As his assailant fled, Mr. Ienne,

Continued on Page 25, Column 6

Orphanages Vanishing For a Lack of Orphans

By LINDA AMSTER

"Christmas was the day you got chicken, you got an orange. Just a day off from school, and better eating."

That is what John E. Harding remembers most vividly about the holidays he spent at the Mission of the Immaculate Virgin, on Staten Island, where he lived from 1905 to 1909. There were some 1,200 children then at Mount Loretto, as it is known, and the 79-year-old New York City executive recalled that most of them had lost both parents or, like himself, were left with only one, who could not afford to keep them.

But Christmases and times have changed at Mount Loretto and other institutions like it. The child they once sheltered is so rare today that orphanages have virtually disappeared in the United States. Like the daguerreotype that once recorded them, orphanages have faded into the memorabilia of another time.

As Robert Schlesselman, director of Lutherbrook, a child care facility in Addison, Ill., said:

"There used to be eight, 10, 12 children in one family. There was a lot of illness and disease. People died and these children were left. Who was going to take them in? There was nothing like Aid to Dependent Children, insurance or workmen's compensation.

"Now there are no orphans. Not many parents are dying. And when death does occur, relatives take the children in. I've been all over the country. I don't know of any orphanages. There aren't any."

But medical advances and social legislation are not the only reasons orphanages

Continued on Page 67, Column 5

NEWS INDEX

	Page		Page
Books	35	Movies	53-59
Bridge	34	Music	53-59
Business	65-67	Obituaries	40
Chess	34	Op-Ed	37
Crossword	35	Sports	60-64
Editorials	36	Theaters	53-59
Family/Style	52	Transportation	74
Financial	65-67	TV and Radio	75
Going Out Guide	56	Weather	74

News Summary and Index, Page 39

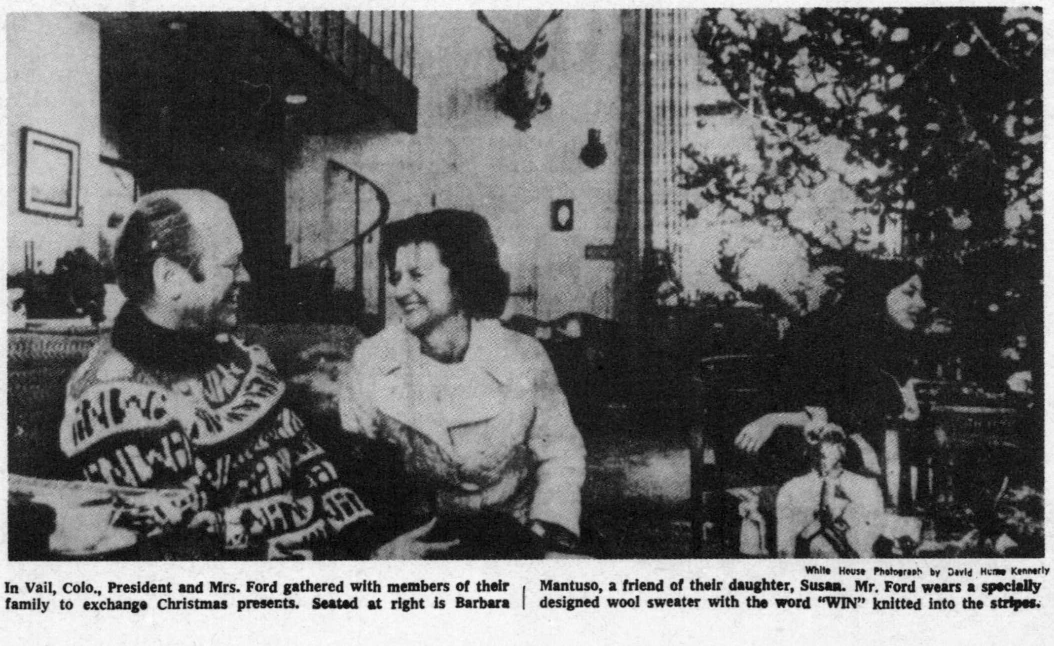

White House Photograph by David Hume Kennerly

In Vail, Colo., President and Mrs. Ford gathered with members of their family to exchange Christmas presents. Seated at right is Barbara Mantuso, a friend of their daughter, Susan. Mr. Ford wears a specially designed wool sweater with the word "WIN" knitted into the stripes.

Australia Airlifting 10,000 Out of Cyclone-Devastated Darwin

Wrecked homes and leaning utility poles in Darwin, Australia, which was hit by a cyclone Wednesday. Search for victims continued yesterday.

Continued From Page 1, Col. 7

airport and that two planeloads had taken off. In addition, he said, military aircraft were taking out the injuries.

The weather bureau said that the cyclone had also struck the town of Katherine, 190 miles southeast of Darwin.

All telephone lines to the Katherine area were out of service. In one of the last telephone conversations with Darwin, a police sergeant there told a staff member of a newspaper in Sydney, The Australian:

"It has fairly demolished the place. It went right over the top of us. There were fierce winds right over the top of the town. It shifted cars all around in the street. It blew trees down. The damage will be fantastic."

The sergeant was reported to have said that Darwin had a three-day warning of the cyclone but that this had been of little help. "You can't hold your roof on," he was quoted as having said.

Hundreds of people were injured in Darwin, a port on the northern coast, when the winds of up to 125 miles an hour roared into the city from across the Timor Sea.

Roofs were torn from the main hospital and from many homes. Windows were shattered, cars overturned and power lines brought down. The city was left without electricity and drinking water.

Many of the dead were caught in their cars driving home from Christmas Eve parties.

Hundreds of homes were leveled and others hurled from their wooden pillars, which are used in housing construction in the tropical region of Darwin to permit air to circulate under

United Press International

Refugee of cyclone, wrapped in cloth, at rescue center

the houses.

A pilot who flew over Darwin said that the area near the airport had been most severely damaged. He described the city as a scene of devastation.

The harbor area was also battered. Many vessels were sunk or driven aground.

Shipping losses in the Darwin harbor included two navy patrol boats—one ran aground

and the other was reported by the state radio to have sunk after its magazine blew up when it collided with a wharf. Two freighters were also reported aground.

Mr. Cairns, the Acting Prime Minister, said simply: "It's a national disaster."

The weather Bureau in Sydney said that the new cyclone posed a serious threat to nomadic aboriginal tribes living in

remote areas east-southeast of Darwin.

A Weather Bureau spokesman said that the storm was moving eastward over remote desert country and that there was still the danger that it could regain its full intensity if it returned to the sea over the gulf of Carpentaria, about 320 miles east of Darwin.

At last report the cyclone was within 150 miles of the coast.

United Press International

Jackie Yu, 9 months old, one of the victims flown out of Darwin, is carried to an ambulance in Sydney.

Survivors Leaving Darwin

SYDNEY, Australia, Thursday, Dec. 26 (AP)—The first survivors to leave Darwin reached Alice Springs, 900 miles away, last night and related how their homes had disintegrated in the cyclone.

Planes began to arrive in the city early today, but officials said rescue operations were being hampered by rain and wind.

"All the News That's Fit to Print"

The New York Times

LATE CITY EDITION

Weather: Sunny, cooler today; cold tonight. Chance of rain tomorrow. Temperature range: today 33-46; Monday 41-49. Details on Page 42.

VOL. CXXIV ... No. 42,710

© 1974 The New York Times Company

NEW YORK, TUESDAY, DECEMBER 31, 1974

Price higher in air delivery cities.

20 CENTS

KREMLIN CANCELS BREZHNEV'S VISIT TO MIDDLE EAST

Trip to Egypt, Syria and Iraq Is Put Off Indefinitely—No Explanation Given

CAIRO AIDES END TALKS

Ministers in Moscow Affirm Interest in Geneva Parley With Palestinian Seat

By CHRISTOPHER S. WREN

Special to The New York Times

MOSCOW, Dec. 30—Leonid I. Brezhnev, the Soviet leader, has indefinitely postponed his visits to Egypt, Syria and Iraq next month, it was announced today.

No immediate explanation was available for the indefinite postponement, which amounts to a cancellation in diplomatic terms, although several theories were advanced.

It appeared that the Kremlin had accepted a setback in its new efforts to enhance Soviet visibility in the Middle East. Western diplomats speculated that the postponement signaled difficulties in Moscow's relations with Cairo.

However, this was challenged by a Soviet-Egyptian statement issued tonight to wind up a hasty three-day visit to Moscow by high Egyptian officials.

Geneva Forum Favored

The statement stressed the "firm friendship" between the two countries and asserted their joint pledge to work for a resumption of the Geneva conference on the Middle East "at an early date," with the participation of the Palestine Liberation Organization.

[In Washington, the postponement of Mr. Brezhnev's trip came as a welcome surprise to Administration officials, who had feared that the visit might lead to a resurgence of Soviet influence in Egypt. Page 2.]

The Soviet Government's press agency, Tass, in announcing the postponement of Mr. Brezhnev's trip, gave no reason for the action.

The announcement came two days after Egypt's Foreign Minister, Ismail Fahmy, and the newly appointed Minister of War, Gen. Mohammed Abdel Ghany el-Gamasy, appeared here for talks.

Their arrival was thought by Western diplomats to be con-

Continued on Page 2, Column 6

Pakistan Estimates Quake Killed 4,700 in 9 Towns

Ground Contact With Disaster Area, in Mountains of the North, Is Cut Off—Toll in One Village Put Over 500

By The Associated Press

PATTAN, Pakistan, Dec. 30—The earthquake that struck northern Pakistan over the weekend killed 4,700 persons and injured 15,000 in nine towns, according to official estimates.

The toll is expected to rise as runners make contact with regions farther north that have been cut off since the quake came Saturday night and continued intermittently for 24 hours.

The only way into the disaster area at present is by helicopter over the peaks of the Karakoram Mountains. An army operation, based in Pattan, is carrying out rescue work and helicopter-lifts of drugs, food, and clothing.

The army says that 500 people died here in Pattan, that 2,000 were injured and about 400 houses destroyed or badly damaged. [In Karachi, other sources put the Pattan death toll at 700.]

Stone, mortar and wooden houses here lie collapsed in heaps of rubble. By day, women and children pick their way through the ruins, searching for loved ones and looking for possessions; at night, most of the village's population of about 10,000 sleep in the open, in temperatures near zero.

"When the quake started at dusk I was saying my prayers with five other policemen in the police station mosque," said Constable Miana Zar, who suffered leg and chest injuries. "Suddenly the whole building started shaking. The roof over the mosque collapsed. Three of my colleagues were killed. Myself and two others survived to be rescued."

Musha Koov, a farmer, said the quake came just after he and two brothers went to cut wood in his yard. "Almost before I had time to turn around, the whole house collapsed," he said. He and his brothers

Continued on Page 2, Column 1

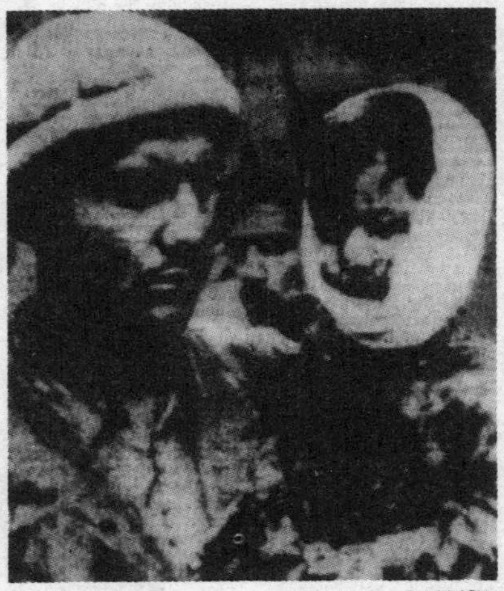

Associated Press

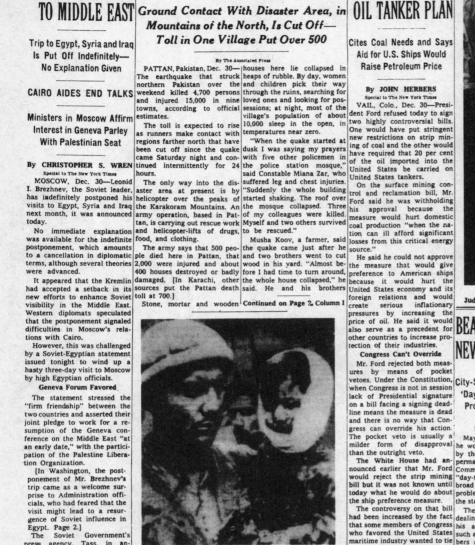

A man in Pattan, northern Pakistan, holding an injured young survivor of Saturday's earthquake.

PRESIDENT VETOES STRIP MINING BILL, OIL TANKER PLAN

Cites Coal Needs and Says Aid for U.S. Ships Would Raise Petroleum Price

By JOHN HERBERS

Special to The New York Times

VAIL, Colo., Dec. 30—President Ford refused today to sign two highly controversial bills. One would have put stringent new restrictions on strip mining of coal and the other would have required that 20 per cent of the oil imported into the United States be carried on United States tankers.

On the surface mining control and reclamation bill, Mr. Ford said he was withholding his approval because the measure would hurt domestic coal production "when the nation can ill afford significant losses from this critical energy source."

He said he could not approve the measure that would give preference to American ships because it would hurt the United States economy and its foreign relations and would create serious inflationary pressures by increasing the price of oil. He said it would also serve as a precedent for other countries to increase protection of their industries.

Congress Can't Override

Mr. Ford rejected both measures by means of pocket vetoes. Under the Constitution, when Congress is not in session lack of Presidential signature on a bill facing a signing deadline means the measure is dead and there is no way that Congress can override his action. The pocket veto is usually a milder form of disapproval than the outright veto.

The White House had announced earlier that Mr. Ford would reject the strip mining bill but it was not known until today what he would do about the ship preference measure.

The controversy on that bill had been increased by the fact that some members of Congress who favored the United States maritime industry wanted to tie it to the foreign trade bill, which contains a provision sponsored by Senator Henry M. Jackson, Democrat of Washington, intended to ease the emigration of Soviet Jews.

Mr. Ford has strongly favored the trade bill, which is now on his desk for his signature. A deal was made, Administration officials confirmed, in which the President would not oppose the ship preference bill in Congress in order to get the trade bill.

No Deal on Veto

However, no compromise was made, both Congressional and Administration officials said, that the President would not veto the bill. It was promoted at the urging of the United States maritime industry, which already operates under heavy Federal subsidies and protection.

In a memorandum of disapproval issued by the White House, Mr. Ford said the meas-

Continued on Page 9, Column 3

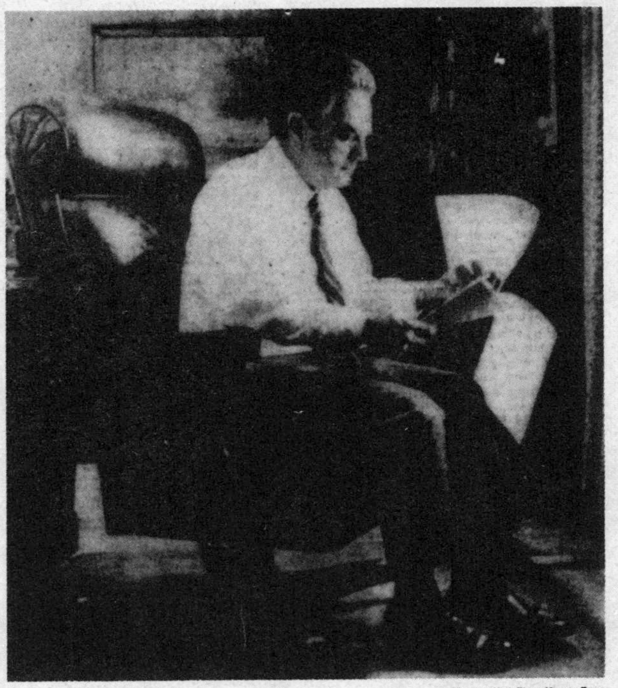

The New York Times/George Tames

Judge John J. Sirica in his chambers yesterday after he charged the Watergate jury

WATERGATE JURY RECEIVES CHARGE; WEIGHS FATE OF 5

Panel Deliberates 4 Hours in Cover-Up Case Before Recessing Until Today

NO QUICK VERDICT SEEN

Sirica Rejects Request of the Jurors to See Large Sections of Testimony

By LESLEY OELSNER

Special to The New York Times

WASHINGTON, Dec. 30—A jury of nine women and three men began to deliberate today the case against the five former White House and Nixon campaign aides charged in the Watergate cover-up.

The jurors deliberated for nearly four hours this after-

Excerpts from judge's charge to jury are on Page 6.

noon before recessing until tomorrow, without a verdict and amid signs that the deliberations would be long.

The jurors began their discussions at 1:55 P.M. after receiving instructions on the law this morning from Judge John J. Sirica.

About 5:30 this afternoon, the jurors sent a note to Judge Sirica, asking for three sets of testimony: the trial testimony of former Attorney General John N. Mitchell, one of the defendants; Mr. Mitchell's testimony before the grand jury in April, 1973, and the trial testimony of the Government's three main witnesses, John W. Dean 3d, Frederick C. LaRue and Jeb Stuart Magruder.

Judge Calls Conference

Judge Sirica held a conference in his chambers with the lawyers.

Then, a few minutes before 6 o'clock, he summoned everyone in the case to the courtroom. He called in the jurors, and read aloud their note — sent by the jury's foreman, James A. Hoffar, a 57-year-old retired park policeman who was elected by the jurors at the start of their deliberations.

He told them that he could not grant their request.

First of all, he said, the transcript of the trial contained much that they were not to see — legal arguments and bench conferences, for instance. Thus, a court reporter would have to read the testimony aloud.

"It would take three weeks," he said. "It would be impossible. We'd be trying this case all over again."

Judge Sirica told the jurors that if they had a more limited request—if they wanted only a few pages of testimony—it could be granted. He told them, too, that they could have any exhibit they wanted. Then, he recessed court until tomorrow, sending the jurors to the hotel where they are sequestered.

The other defendants in the case are John D. Ehrlichman,

Continued on Page 6, Column 1

BEAME TO PROPOSE NEW FISCAL PANEL

City-State Body Would Deal 'Day-to-Day' With Broad Problems and Solutions

By FRED FERRETTI

Mayor Beame said yesterday he would propose the creation by the State Legislature of a permanent City-State Fiscal Commission to discuss on a "day-to-day ongoing basis" the broad spectrum of the fiscal problems facing the city and the state's role in their solution.

The Mayor, in an interview dealing with the first year of his administration, said that such a commission—with members appointed by the Governor, the legislative leadership and himself, and "staffed with fiscal experts"—would "enable us to come up with the city-state financial policies we need rather than the continual reliance of the city on its annual pleas for money from the state."

Recently Mr. Beame said that eliminating the city's current deficit of $135.4-million and promoting financial solvency in the 1975-76 fiscal year and beyond lay with the state and its responses to the city's pleas.

A deficit of more than $1-billion has been projected for the city by some financial observers, including Controller Harrison J. Goldin, and the Mayor has said that the city will start the new fiscal year, beginning July 1, with a built-in $300-million deficit because of state-ordered programs that the state financed for this year only and for which financing will not be repeated.

To reduce the deficit in the

Continued on Page 42, Column 1

Hunt Tells of Early Work For a C.I.A. Domestic Unit

By SEYMOUR M. HERSH

Special to The New York Times

WASHINGTON, Dec. 30 — E. Howard Hunt Jr., a Watergate burglar who pleaded guilty, told the Senate Watergate committee last year in still unpublished testimony that he served as the first chief of covert action for the Central Intelligence Agency's Domestic Operations Division.

Mr. Hunt, testifying before the Senate investigators in closed session on Dec. 18, 1973, revealed that his domestic activities included the secret financing of a Washington news agency as well as the underwriting of the popular Fodor's travel guides.

A copy of Mr. Hunt's testimony before the Watergate committee, marked "confidential," was made available today to The New York Times.

[In a report to President Ford, William E. Colby, Director of Central Intelligence, has confirmed allegations that the C.I.A. spied on thousands of United States citizens under previous Administrations, according to The Los Angeles Times.]

In a telephone interview today, Mr. Hunt said that he spent about four years working for the Domestic Operation Division, beginning shortly after the unit was set up by the C.I.A. in 1962.

Mr. Hunt, who is now free and living in Miami pending the appeal of his Watergate conviction, denied any involvement or knowledge of domestic spy-

Continued on Page 4, Column 2

3 Killed and 9 Wounded By an Upstate Sniper, 18

By ROBERT D. McFADDEN

A teen-aged sniper described as an honor student killed three persons and wounded nine others with rifle and shotgun fire in and around the Olean (N.Y.) High School yesterday before surrendering to state troopers and city policemen who stormed the school under a barrage of tear gas and gunfire.

National Guard tanks, police armored vehicles and fire trucks rumbled into a cordon around the school during a two-and-a-half-hour siege that stunned the city of 18,200 about 55 miles south of Buffalo, just above the Pennsylvania border.

At least 10 persons were trapped on the first floor of the four-story red-brick school in central Olean as the suspect, 18-year-old Anthony Barbaro, a senior at the school and the best shot on its 10-man rifle team, ranged over the third and fourth floors, spraying the streets and surrounding neighborhood with rifle fire.

The police said he had shot and killed a janitor on the building's third floor, a man walking in the street outside and a young woman driving a

Continued on Page 42, Column 5

$170,000 in Illegal Gifts Admitted by Ashland Oil

By ANTHONY RIPLEY

Special to The New York Times

WASHINGTON, Dec. 30—In a second round of answering charges of making illegal corporate contributions to political campaigns, Ashland Oil, Inc., acknowledged today that it gave an additional $170,000 in company funds to prominent politicians of both major parties from 1970 to 1972.

The Kentucky-based oil company pleaded guilty more than a year ago to giving illegally $100,000 to Richard M. Nixon's 1972 Presidential re-election campaign.

Today, lawyers for Ashland appeared in Federal District Court here to plead guilty to five new charges brought by the Watergate special prosecution against the corporation. Chief Judge George L. Hart Jr. fined Ashland the maximum of $25,000.

The illegal contributions listed in the new charges included the following:

¶$50,000 in cash delivered from June, 1970, to February, 1972, to Robert S. Straus, then treasurer and now chairman of the Democratic National Committee, for the committee's use.

¶$100,000 in cash delivered from September, 1971, to February, 1972, to Carl F. Arnold, a Washington oil and gas lobbyist, "for redelivery by said Carl Arnold to candidates for election" to the Senate and House of Representatives and to political committeemen. Mr. Arnold was then a fund-raiser for the Presidential bid of Representative Wilbur D. Mills, Democrat of Arkansas.

¶$6,864.65 spent by the corporation from July, 1970, to September, 1972, to reimburse

Continued on Page 6, Column 6

Connecticut to Build Solar-Heating Plant In Housing for Aged

By LAWRENCE FELLOWS

Special to The New York Times

HARTFORD, Dec. 30—Connecticut has been granted Federal funds to build a $1-million, 40-unit housing project for the elderly in which half the project will draw heat from the sun, Gov. Thomas J. Meskill said today.

Because there is no other project like it in the country, the state has been awarded a Federal grant of $130,700 to cover the cost of designing the solar-energy installation, the Governor said, adding: "Never before have we had solar heating in a multifamily housing project . . . or in public housing."

Construction on the experimental housing project is to begin next July in Hamden, north of New Haven. It should take a year to complete.

All 40 units will be supplied with heat drawn from a conventional source, probably gas-fired or oil-fired furnaces.

But for the 20 units in the solar experiment, the conven-

Continued on Page 24. Column 1

Mills Reveals Alcoholism; Plans to Stay in Congress

By MARJORIE HUNTER

Special to The New York Times

WASHINGTON, Dec. 30—Representative Wilbur D. Mills, attributing his recent erratic behavior to alcoholism, pledged total abstinence today as he announced that he would retain his seat in Congress.

Publicly contrite over his well-publicized escapades with

Text of the Mills statement appears on Page 5.

an Argentine strip-tease dancer, the once powerful chairman of the House Ways and Means Committee said he now knew that he had been a "sick man."

His statement, issued through his Congressional office, was prepared from his bed at Bethesda Naval Hospital, where he had been a patient since Dec. 3.

Close friends say that Mr. Mills had considered resigning from Congress, but that he decided yesterday to keep his seat after discussing the matter with his family and associates.

"Perhaps the easier path would have been to resign my seat and disappear from public life and public scrutiny," the 65-year-old Arkansas Democrat said in his prepared statement.

"I have never been one to quit in the face of adversity and I will not be a quitter now," he continued. "I know what it

Continued on Page 5, Column 1

NEWS INDEX

By appointment only—the utmost in exclusive travel, strictly deluxe—write Air France Dept. NYC-P.J. Box 747, N.Y. 10011—Advt.

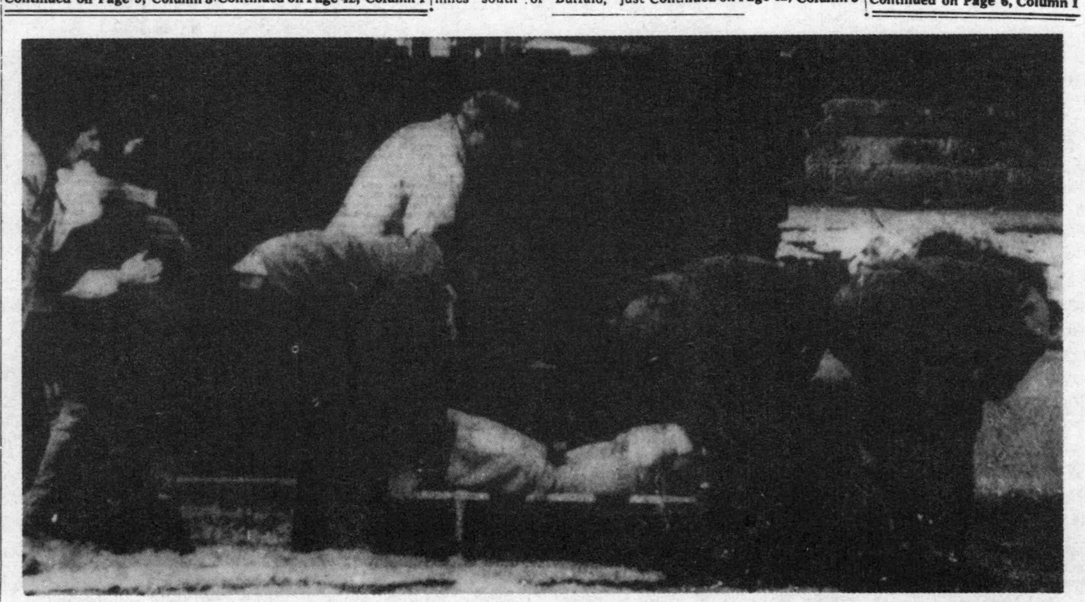

United Press International

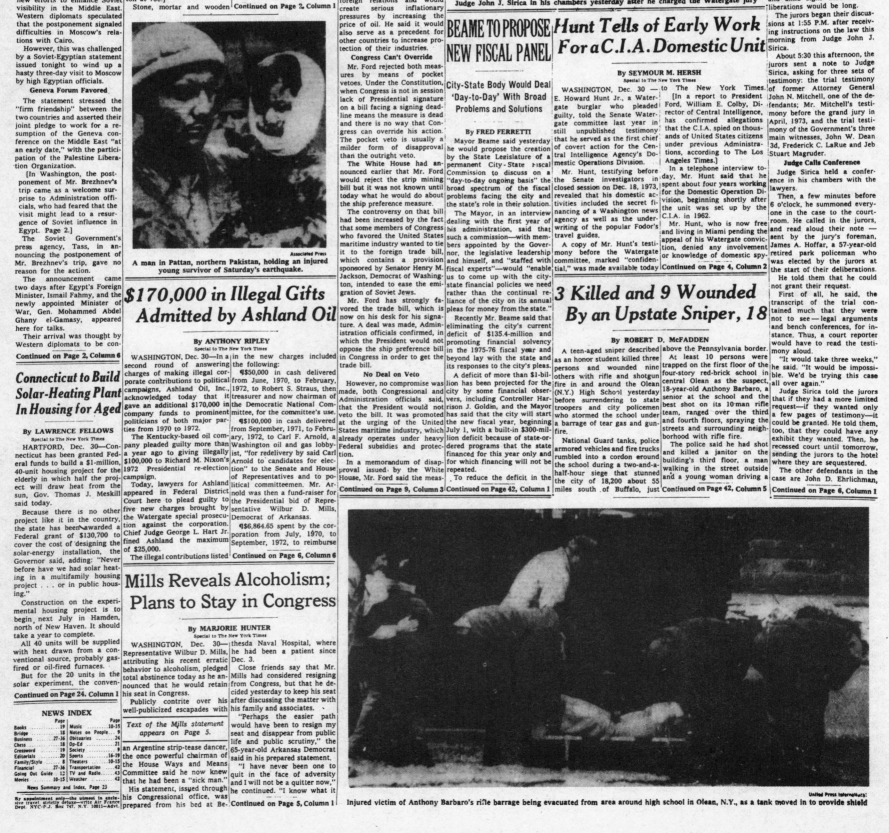

Injured victim of Anthony Barbaro's rifle barrage being evacuated from area around high school in Olean, N.Y., as a tank moved in to provide shield

Pakistan Estimates Death Toll of Earthquake at 4,700 in 9 Towns

Continued From Page 1, Col. 3

clawed at the wreckage but they were unable to save his mother and three nephews who were buried. He said eight cousins of his were killed in another part of the village.

Jamil Khan, a laborer, said that 10 of his relatives were killed and 10 injured, and that the dead included his 3-year-old daughter and infant son.

The New York Times/Dec. 31, 1974

Pattan (top map) is base for rescue work. Places with names underlined were among those hardest hit by the earthquake.

Some houses that escaped destruction in the initial shock were crushed by boulders that the tremor sent down from the surrounding mountains.

A team of seven army and civilian doctors has set up a field hospital here.

Efforts to bring in blankets and tents have been hampered because the Karakoram Highway, which runs through the disaster region, has been either severed or demolished along a 70-mile stretch.

The highway, which runs down from the Chinese border, is the main route through which vital commodities are brought into the deprived northern areas of Pakistan. It was completed with Chinese assistance and is known as the silk route.

Partial Breakdown Given

Special to The New York Times

KARACHI, Pakistan, Dec. 30 —The Pakistani news agency, Associated Press of Pakistan, quoting official sources, made public a partial breakdown of deaths in the earthquake Saturday.

It said that Shorgarah had apparently suffered 500 dead; the villages of Dubair and Alai, 1,000; Pattan, 700; Kayal, 300, and the villages of Kiru and Zaidkhar, 1,000.

Worst in 2 Years

LONDON, Dec. 30 (Reuters) —The earthquake Saturday in Pakistan has killed the highest number of people since the Christmas, 1972, quake in Managua, Nicaragua, in which 8,000 to 10,000 died.

Pakistan's last large-scale earthquake, in 1935, took 30,-000 lives.

Wide World Photos

A youth wearing the clothes of the North Pakistan mountain people stands amid the debris after the earthquake devastated the village of Pattan.

"All the News That's Fit to Print"

The New York Times

LATE CITY EDITION

Weather: Clear and cold today and tonight. Fair and warmer tomorrow. Temperature range: today 28-42; Friday 30-37. Details on Page 58.

VOL. CXXIV . No. 42,805 — © 1975 The New York Times Company — NEW YORK, SATURDAY, APRIL 5, 1975 — Price higher in air delivery cities. — 20 CENTS

OVER 100 VIETNAM ORPHANS KILLED WITH 25 ADULTS IN SAIGON CRASH; HANOI SAID TO SEND MORE TROOPS

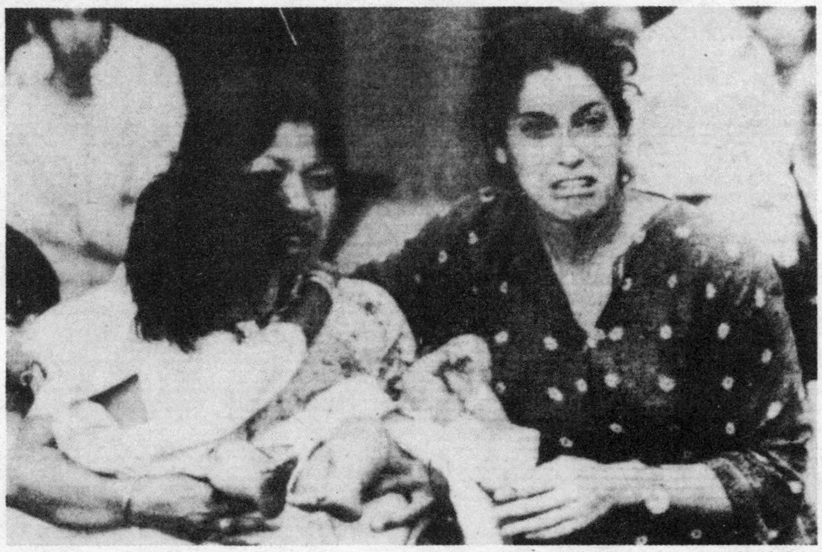

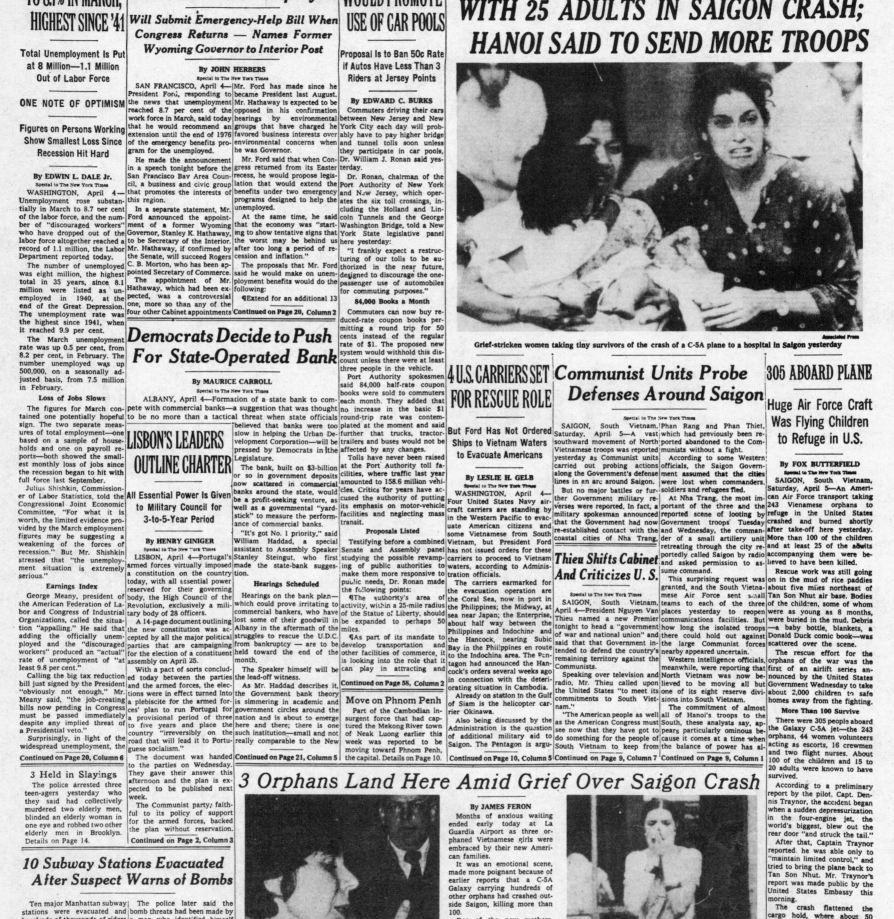

Associated Press

Grief-stricken women taking tiny survivors of the crash of a C-5A plane to a hospital in Saigon yesterday

305 ABOARD PLANE

Huge Air Force Craft Was Flying Children to Refuge in U.S.

By FOX BUTTERFIELD

Special to The New York Times

SAIGON, South Vietnam, Saturday, April 5—An American Air Force transport taking 243 Vietnamese orphans to refuge in the United States crashed and burned shortly after take-off here yesterday. More than 100 of the children and at least 25 of the adults accompanying them were believed to have been killed.

Rescue work was still going on in the mud of rice paddies about five miles northeast of Tan Son Nhut air base. Bodies of the children, some of whom were as young as 8 months, were buried in the mud. Debris—a baby bottle, blankets, a Donald Duck comic book—was scattered over the scene.

The rescue effort for the orphans of the war was the first of an airlift series announced by the United States Government Wednesday to take about 2,000 children to safe homes away from the fighting.

More Than 100 Survive

There were 305 people aboard the Galaxy C-5A jet—the 243 orphans, 44 women volunteers acting as escorts, 16 crewmen and two flight nurses. About 100 of the children and 15 to 20 adults were known to have survived.

According to a preliminary report by the pilot, Capt. Dennis Traynor, the accident began when a sudden depressurization in the four-engine jet, the world's biggest, blew out the rear door "and struck the tail."

After that, Captain Traynor reported he was able only to "maintain limited control," and tried to bring the plane back to Tan Son Nhut. Mr. Traynor's report was made public by the United States Embassy this morning.

The crash flattened the cargo hold, where about 50 children had been strapped in. "Some of us got through a chute from the top of the plane, but the children at the bottom of the plane didn't have a chance," one survivor said.

The orphans were to be taken to Travis Air Force Base in California. They were to be adopted by American families

Continued on Page 8, Column 1

Communist Units Probe Defenses Around Saigon

Special to The New York Times

SAIGON, South Vietnam, Saturday, April 5—A vast southward movement of North Vietnamese troops was reported yesterday as Communist units carried out probing actions along the Government's defense lines in an arc around Saigon.

But no major battles or further Government military reverses were reported. In fact, a military spokesman announced that the Government had now re-established contact with the coastal cities of Nha Trang, Phan Rang and Phan Thiet, which had previously been reported abandoned to the Communists without a fight.

According to some Western officials, the Saigon Government assumed that the cities were lost when commanders, soldiers and refugees fled.

At Nha Trang, the most important of the three and the reported scene of looting by Government troops Tuesday and Wednesday, the commander of a small artillery unit retreating through the city reportedly called Saigon by radio and asked permission to assume command.

This surprising request was granted, and the South Vietnamese Air Force sent small teams to each of the three places yesterday to reopen communications facilities. But how long the isolated troops there could hold out against the large Communist forces nearby appeared uncertain.

Western intelligence officials, meanwhile, were reporting that North Vietnam was now believed to be moving all but one of its eight reserve divisions into South Vietnam.

The commitment of almost all of Hanoi's troops to the South, these analysts say, appears particularly ominous because it comes at a time when the balance of power has al-

Continued on Page 9, Column 1

Thieu Shifts Cabinet And Criticizes U. S.

Special to The New York Times

SAIGON, South Vietnam, April 4—President Nguyen Van Thieu named a new Premier tonight to head a "government of war and national union" and said that that Government intended to defend the country's remaining territory against the Communists.

Speaking over television and radio, Mr. Thieu called upon the United States "to meet its commitments to South Vietnam."

"The American people as well as the American Congress must see now that they have got to do something for the people of South Vietnam to keep from

Continued on Page 9, Column 7

4 U.S. CARRIERS SET FOR RESCUE ROLE

But Ford Has Not Ordered Ships to Vietnam Waters to Evacuate Americans

By LESLIE H. GELB

Special to The New York Times

WASHINGTON, April 4—Four United States Navy aircraft carriers are standing by in the Western Pacific to evacuate American citizens and some Vietnamese from South Vietnam, but President Ford has not issued orders for these carriers to proceed to Vietnam waters, according to Administration officials.

The carriers earmarked for the evacuation operation are the Coral Sea, now in port in the Philippines; the Midway, at sea near Japan; the Enterprise, about half way between the Philippines and Indochina and the Hancock, nearing Subic Bay in the Philippines en route to the Indochina area. The Pentagon had announced the Hancock's orders several weeks ago in connection with the deteriorating situation in Cambodia.

Already on station in the Gulf of Siam is the helicopter carrier Okinawa.

Also being discussed by the Administration is the question of additional military aid to Saigon. The Pentagon is argu-

Continued on Page 10, Column 5

JOBLESS RATE UP TO 8.7% IN MARCH, HIGHEST SINCE '41

Total Unemployment Is Put at 8 Million—1.1 Million Out of Labor Force

ONE NOTE OF OPTIMISM

Figures on Persons Working Show Smallest Loss Since Recession Hit Hard

By EDWIN L. DALE Jr.

Special to The New York Times

WASHINGTON, April 4—Unemployment rose substantially in March to 8.7 per cent of the labor force, and the number of "discouraged workers" who have dropped out of the labor force altogether reached a record of 1.1 million, the Labor Department reported today.

The number of unemployed was eight million, the highest total in 35 years, since 8.1 million were listed as unemployed in 1940, at the end of the Great Depression. The unemployment rate was the highest since 1941, when it reached 9.9 per cent.

The March unemployment rate was up 0.5 per cent, from 8.2 per cent, in February. The number unemployed was up 500,000, on a seasonally adjusted basis, from 7.5 million in February.

Loss of Jobs Slows

The figures for March contained one potentially hopeful sign. The two separate measures of total employment—one based on a sample of households and one on payroll reports—both showed the smallest monthly loss of jobs since the recession began to hit with full force last September.

Julius Shishkin, Commissioner of Labor Statistics, told the Congressional Joint Economic Committee, "For what it is worth, the limited evidence provided by the March employment figures may be suggesting a weakening of the forces of recession." But Mr. Shishkin stressed that "the unemployment situation is extremely serious."

Earnings Index

George Meany, president of the American Federation of Labor and Congress of Industrial Organizations, called the situation "appalling." He said that adding the officially unemployed and the "discouraged workers" produced an "actual" rate of unemployment of "at least 9.8 per cent."

Calling the big tax reduction bill just signed by the President "obviously not enough," Mr. Meany said, "the job-creating bills now pending in Congress must be passed immediately despite any implied threat of a Presidential veto."

Surprisingly, in light of the widespread unemployment, the

Continued on Page 20, Column 6

Ford Acts to Extend to '77 Aid Plan for Unemployed

Will Submit Emergency-Help Bill When Congress Returns — Names Former Wyoming Governor to Interior Post

By JOHN HERBERS

Special to The New York Times

SAN FRANCISCO, April 4—President Ford, responding to the news that unemployment reached 8.7 per cent of the work force in March, said today that he would recommend an extension until the end of 1976 of the emergency benefits program for the unemployed.

He made the announcement in a speech tonight before the San Francisco Bay Area Council, a business and civic group that promotes the interests of this region.

In a separate statement, Mr. Ford announced the appointment of a former Wyoming Governor, Stanley K. Hathaway, to be Secretary of the Interior. Mr. Hathaway, if confirmed by the Senate, will succeed Rogers C. B. Morton, who has been appointed Secretary of Commerce.

The appointment of Mr. Hathaway, which had been expected, was a controversial one, more so than any of the four other Cabinet appointments Mr. Ford has made since he became President last August. Mr. Hathaway is expected to be opposed in his confirmation hearings by environmental groups that have charged he favored business interests over environmental concerns when he was Governor.

Mr. Ford said that when Congress returned from its Easter recess, he would propose legislation that would extend the benefits under two emergency programs designed to help the unemployed.

At the same time, he said that the economy was "starting to show tentative signs that the worst may be behind us after too long a period of recession and inflation."

The proposals that Mr. Ford said he would make on unemployment benefits would do the following:

¶Extend for an additional 13

Continued on Page 20, Column 2

RONAN TOLL PLAN WOULD PROMOTE USE OF CAR POOLS

Proposal Is to Ban 50c Rate if Autos Have Less Than 3 Riders at Jersey Points

By EDWARD C. BURKS

Commuters driving their cars between New Jersey and New York City each day will probably have to pay higher bridge and tunnel tolls soon unless they participate in car pools, Dr. William J. Ronan said yesterday.

Dr. Ronan, chairman of the Port Authority of New York and New Jersey, which operates the six toll crossings, including the Holland and Lincoln Tunnels and the George Washington Bridge, told a New York State legislative panel here yesterday:

"I frankly expect a restructuring of our tolls to be authorized in the near future, designed to discourage the one-passenger use of automobiles for commuting purposes."

84,000 Books a Month

Commuters can now buy reduced-rate coupon books permitting a round trip for 50 cents instead of the regular rate of $1. The proposed new system would withhold this discount unless there were at least three people in the vehicle.

Port Authority spokesmen said 84,000 half-rate coupon books were sold to commuters each month. They added that no increase in the basic $1 round-trip rate was contemplated at the moment and said further that trucks, tractor-trailers and buses would not be affected by any changes.

Tolls have never been raised at the Port Authority toll facilities, where traffic last year amounted to 158.6 million vehicles. Critics for years have accused the authority of putting its emphasis on motor-vehicle facilities and neglecting mass transit.

Proposals Listed

Testifying before a combined Senate and Assembly panel studying the possible revamping of public authorities to make them more responsive to public needs, Dr. Ronan made the following points:

¶The authority's area of activity, within a 25-mile radius of the Statue of Liberty, should be expanded to perhaps 50 miles.

¶As part of its mandate to develop transportation and other facilities of commerce, it is looking into the role that it can play in attracting and

Continued on Page 58, Column 2

Move on Phnom Penh

Part of the Cambodian insurgent force that had captured the Mekong River town of Neak Luong earlier this week was reported to be moving toward Phnom Penh, the capital. Details on Page 10.

Democrats Decide to Push For State-Operated Bank

By MAURICE CARROLL

Special to The New York Times

ALBANY, April 4—Formation of a state bank to compete with commercial banks—a suggestion that was thought to be no more than a tactical threat when state officials believed that banks were too slow in helping the Urban Development Corporation—will be pressed by Democrats in the Legislature.

The bank, built on $3-billion or so in government deposits now scattered in commercial banks around the state, would be a profit-seeking venture, as well as a governmental "yardstick" to measure the performance of commercial banks.

"It's got No. 1 priority," said William Haddad, a special assistant to Assembly Speaker Stanley Steingut, who first made the state-bank suggestion.

Hearings Scheduled

Hearings on the bank plan—which could prove irritating to commercial bankers, who have lost some of their goodwill in Albany in the aftermath of the struggles to rescue the U.D.C. from bankruptcy — are to be held toward the end of the month.

The Speaker himself will be the lead-off witness.

As Mr. Haddad describes it, the Government bank theory is simmering in academic and government circles around the nation and is about to emerge here and there; there is one such institution—small and not really comparable to the New

Continued on Page 21, Column 5

LISBON'S LEADERS OUTLINE CHARTER

All Essential Power Is Given to Military Council for 3-to-5-Year Period

By HENRY GINIGER

Special to The New York Times

LISBON, April 4—Portugal's armed forces virtually imposed a constitution on the country today, with all essential power reserved for their governing body, the High Council of the Revolution, exclusively a military body of 28 officers.

A 14-page document outlining the new constitution was accepted by all the major political parties that are campaigning for the election of a constituent assembly on April 25.

With a pact of sorts concluded today between the parties and the armed forces, the elections were in effect turned into a plebiscite for the armed forces' plan to run Portugal for a provisional period of three to five years and place the country "irreversibly on the road that will lead it to Portuguese socialism."

The document was handed to the parties on Wednesday. They gave their answer this afternoon and the plan is expected to be published next week.

The Communist party, faithful to its policy of support for the armed forces, backed the plan without reservation.

Continued on Page 2, Column 3

3 Held in Slayings

The police arrested three teen-agers yesterday who they said had collectively murdered two elderly men, blinded an elderly woman in one eye and robbed two other elderly men in Brooklyn. Details on Page 14.

10 Subway Stations Evacuated After Suspect Warns of Bombs

Ten major Manhattan subway stations were evacuated and hundreds of thousands of riders were delayed for an hour in the homebound rush last night by the bomb threats of an alleged bank-extortionist who had set off a device earlier as authorities seized him on a crowded corner at Herald Square.

City and Transit Authority policemen began herding crowds out of the stations in midtown and lower Manhattan at 5:40 P.M., and police bomb experts searched platforms, tracks, lockers and lavatories for time bombs that the suspect had said were set to go off at 6 P.M.

About 45 minutes after that deadline, the alert was called off and straphangers poured back into the stations, which had been bypassed by trains during the bogus emergency.

The police later said the bomb threats had been made by a man who identified himself as Edward Williams, 26 years old, of 317 Jones Drive, Paterson, N. J. He was taken into custody outside Macy's at 34th Street and Broadway shortly after 1 P.M. by Federal and city law-enforcement officers posing as bankers with a payoff.

As he was seized, the suspect hurled a suitcase that contained gunpowder packed in a mayonnaise jar. It exploded, inflicting second-degree and third-degree burns on the face of Bruce Brotman, a Federal Bureau of Investigation agent, and slightly injuring several other law-enforcement officers.

Authorities said the suspect earlier had walked into two branches of the Bankers Trust

Continued on Page 58, Column 7

3 Orphans Land Here Amid Grief Over Saigon Crash

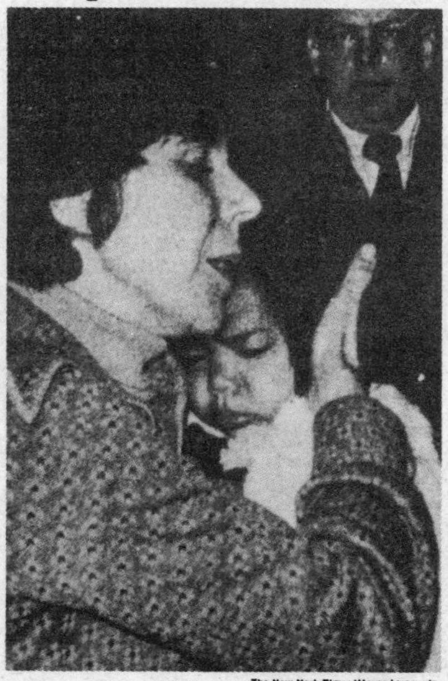

The New York Times/Meyer Liebowitz

At La Guardia Airport, Adell Kolinsky of Spring Valley, N.Y., greeted child she and her husband are adopting.

By JAMES FERON

Months of anxious waiting ended early today at La Guardia Airport as three orphaned Vietnamese girls were embraced by their new American families.

It was an emotional scene, made more poignant because of earlier reports that a C-5A Galaxy carrying hundreds of other orphans had crashed outside Saigon, killing more than 100.

One of the new mothers, Adell Kolinsky, wept when she heard the news. For Ronnie Starr, who had waited two years for her child, anxiety briefly turned to sorrow "for those children and those people waiting for them."

A few hours later, as Mrs. Kolinsky embraced Nguyen Thi My Huong, whom she renamed Robyn Lan, she murmured: "We love her so. It's so good to save one."

The children blinked and gazed from face to face as they were carried from the plane, an Eastern Airlines flight from Los Angeles. The youngsters seemed confused and weary after a series of flights that began in Qui Nhon and Diem Phuc and ended in Spring Valley and

Continued on Page 8, Column 6

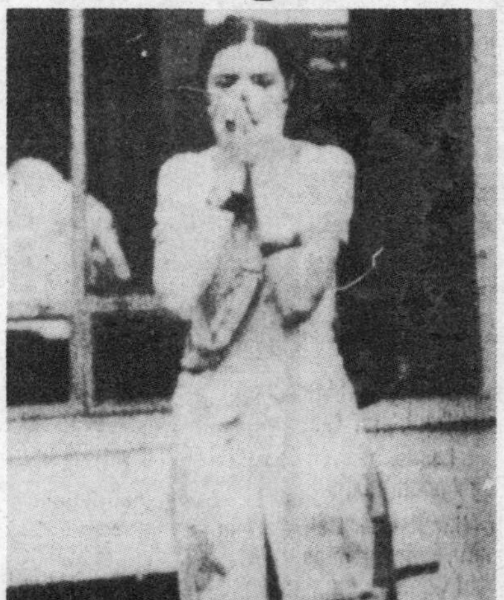

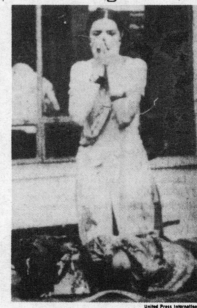

United Press International

In Saigon, a survivor of the crash in which orphans were killed grieved as she saw a victim taken to a hospital.

NEWS INDEX

More Than 100 Vietnamese Orphans and 25 Adults Are Killed in Saigon Crash

305 WERE ABOARD U.S.-BOUND PLANE

Huge Jet Plunges Shortly After Take-Off—Search for Survivors Still On

Continued From Page 1, Col. 8

in what President Ford described as a "humanitarian effort."

"This is the least we can do, and we will do much, much more," the President said of the airlift Thursday in San Diego. The $2-million it will cost to transport the 2,000 came from a special foreign aid fund for children.

The women escorts aboard the plane were said be volunteers, mostly secretaries working in the United States embassy or wives of members of the American defense attaché office.

Other American secretaries and wives of officials stood around the hospital tonight weeping and supporting each other as each new ambulance-load of bodies arrived.

Rosemary Taylor, who was head of the Friends of All Children orphanage, which provided most of the children on the flight, stood alone and silent against a hospital wall. An Australian nurse, she was well known in Saigon's foreign community for her aggressive support of orphan causes.

Crowds of Vietnamese also stood around watching the arrival of the victims, but most of the people helping with the bodies were Americans.

Victor Urbach, a Pan American World Airways pilot who was flying above and behind the Air Force plane, said the C-5A pilots "had done one heck of a job," to avoid a worse disaster. Mr. Urbach, from San Francisco, said the trouble had occurred over the South China Sea near Vung Tau, 40 miles east of Saigon.

The pilots managed to maintain partial control of the plane, Mr. Urbach related, but according to their radio messages they realized they would not be able to make it safely back to Tan Son Nhut before hitting the ground. Instead of crashing into a heavily populated area near the airfield, they tried to land in the rice field, and the craft exploded.

Copters Get Survivors

The survivors, many covered with mud, were picked up from the wreck by Air America helicopters and brought to the Seventh Day Adventist hospital next to Tan Son Nhut.

Until the Paris peace agreement of 1973, the Seventh Day Adventist hospital was the U.S. Army Third Field Hospital, a major center for treating wounded American soldiers.

An American doctor, who declined to be identified, said many of the children were "in amazingly good condition."

According to hospital sources, eight members of the Air Force crew perished in the crash. The others escaped practically unscathed. They sat quietly in the hospital this evening, drinking coffee offered them by nurses. When asked about the accident, a sergeant said, "we were ordered to say nothing."

Captain Traynor, the pilot of the C-5A, said in his report that after the rear door blew out and struck the tail, the elevator was frozen and the hydraulic line ruptured.

He then declared an emergency and began returning to Tan Son Nhut. He lowered his landing gear and attempted to get on an approach to the airfield, he continued.

"But at about 2,000 feet," he saw that his rate of descent was "too fast and applied full power." The plane then crashed into the field.

Air Force investigators are on their way from the United States to check into the cause of the accident, an Embassy spokesman said today.

The C-5A, made by the Locheed Corporation, has long been a controversial and trouble-plagued plane because of enormous overruns in its cost and faults in its design.

Ford Sends Condolences

Special to The New York Times

SAN FRANCISCO, April 4—President Ford, here to make a series of speeches and appearances, issued the following statement today on the crash of a military plane carrying Vietnamese orphans to the United States:

"I am deeply saddened at the loss of so many lives in the crash of the United States C-5A mercy flight today near Saigon.

"I wish to convey my heartfelt condolences to the families and friends of the victims, many of whom were coming to new homes in the United States, and to the volunteers who were caring for them on the flight.

"Our mission of mercy will continue. The survivors will be flown here when they are physically able. Other waiting orphans will make the journey.

Housing Policeman Indicted

A Housing Authority policeman, Stanley Metz, 30 years old, was indicted yesterday on a charge of offering a bribe to another policeman on behalf of a man who had been arrested on a drug charge, according to Maurice H. Nadjari, the special state anticorruption prosecutor. The arrested man was identified as Robert Torres, 35, of 35 Jackson Street.

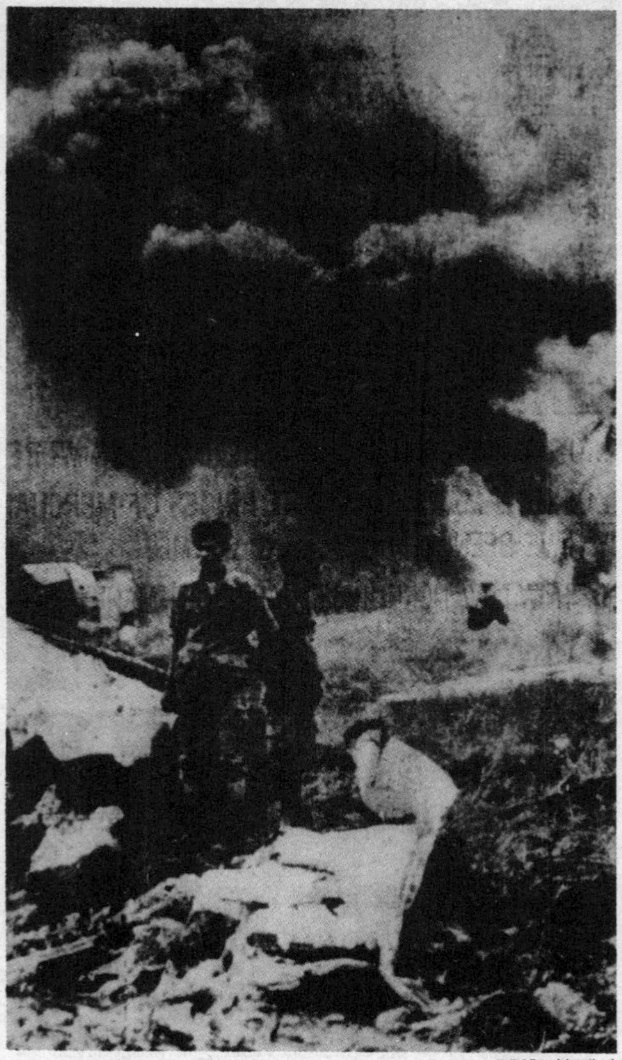

United Press International

Rescue workers among the smoldering wreckage of the plane that crash-landed in rice fields a few miles northeast of Tan Son Nhut air base soon after taking off with 305 persons, mostly orphaned children.

Crash of Galaxy Is Puzzling to Experts

By RICHARD WITKIN

Military and civilian aviation experts were deeply puzzled yesterday over reasons for the crash of a United States Air Force cargo plane near Saigon with 243 Vietnamese orphans aboard.

Among the questions that arose were the following:

Was the huge cargo-loading entryway under the rear of the plane improperly closed when the 350-ton craft, the largest plane in the world, took off?

Was there any warning on a cockpit indicator that the coverings over the entryway were in an unsafe condition? Could the plane possibly have been sabotaged?

Once the entryway came open, how was it possible for parts of the loading ramp, or other equipment swept out by the decompression, to produce the critical damage to the tail section?

The plane, a C-5A, or Galaxy, has had an unhappy history, despite unquestioned successes in ferrying to Vietnam and other war zones, equipment far greater in tonnage and dimensions than any other aircraft could accommodate.

Technical and Cost Problems

Its record has been marred by severe technical problems, huge cost overruns and political disputes—all of which helped bring the manufacturer, the Lockheed Aircraft Corporation, to the verge of bankruptcy.

Earlier troubles centered on the fact that the wings had considerably less strength and life expectancy than called for by the design. The C-5A also came in for repeated criticism for alleged poor workmanship and use of untested materials in the production work at the Marietta, Ga., plant.

There was no indication of any connection between those troubles and what happened yesterday on what was to have been the first leg of a flight to bring 243 war orphans to the United States. Previously, there had not been a single death in more than 190,000 hours of flights by the 81 C-5A's that have been produced.

There was one previous crash landing, and two Galaxies were destroyed on the ground by fire. A mechanic servicing one of the planes was killed.

The crash in Vietnam, according to the account of the pilot as relayed by Air Force spokesmen in Washington, began with the sudden opening of the entryway under the rear fuselage.

The opening is actually sealed, to withstand pressurization inside, by a ramp that can unfold through the opening. A grouping of three unpressurized doors close over the ramp. Two open horizontally in clam-shell fashion, and the third is hinged to move upward.

The Air Force plane was climbing through 23,000 feet when the trouble began. At that altitude, the air outside was extremely rarefied, and the interior of the double-decked craft was powerfully pressurized to provide the passengers with a near-normal atmospheric environment.

The sudden opening of the entryway, whether because of the inside pressure or some other cause, produced a violent outward rush of the plane's air—known as explosive decompression.

The pilot, Capt. Dennis Traynor, who was reported to have escaped unhurt, believed that the pressure-sealing loading ramp had blown out and torn open the clam-shell doors behind it, the Air Force said.

About the same time, he lost all control of the elevator and rudder controls on the tail, as well as of some of the plane's flap system and of the No. 1 and No. 2 hydraulic systems. These two systems apparently run through the vertical tail surface.

The abrupt door-opening recalled the loss of a rear cargo door that led to the crash of a Turkish Airlines DC-10 near Paris a year ago, killing all 346 on board. In that case, the depressurization of the cargo compartment caused the floor of the still-pressurized passenger cabin above to collapse, severely damaging the control lines.

But in yesterday's crash, there was evidently little danger of a floor collapse because of large grilled openings between the upper and lower decks that equalized pressure above and below.

Normally, the lower deck is used only for cargo, but yesterday it carried many of the orphans and other passengers. The upper deck is ordinarily available for about 80 servicemen, crewmen for trucks, tanks or other vehicles carried below.

There was considerable dispute yesterday about how the C-5A's controls might have been damaged. The most prevalent theory was that pieces of the loading ramp or other loose items rammed violently into the vertical tail.

Others thought this next to impossible. They did not see how, with the plane moving at perhaps 350 miles an hour, any emerging debris could have made its way from under the very rear of the fuselage to the tail surface on top of the fuselage. They conceded that the air currents would have been powerful and perhaps unpredictable. But they still doubted this theory.

If they were right, there was still the possibility of sabotage or of some other malfunction no one has thought about.

The pilot turned back toward Saigon, using the ailerons on his wings and differential power settings on his four engine throttles, the Air Force said.

Seven miles from the field, at 5,000 feet he lowered the 28-wheel landing gear and started a final 90-degree turn to the final approach. It was at this point that the plane began to settle rapidly.

The pilot, deciding he could not make the runway, put down in a fairly normal attitude in the paddy five miles short. The giant plane broke into three sections and burned.

Tatters of Tragedy in a Paddy Field

SAIGON, South Vietnam, April 4 (AP)—The huge transport plane lay broken into four main sections, its debris strewn over an area the size of two football fields.

Toys, cushions, a baby bottle, flight manuals, a Donald Duck comic book and the bodies of orphans were scattered in the soggy paddy field.

Helicopters ferried small bodies wrapped in ponchos to Saigon morgues.

The immense United States Air Force C-5A Galaxy that crashed Friday afternoon a half hour after leaving Saigon's Tan Son Nhut airport was carrying 243 Vietnamese orphans to new homes and safety in America.

More than a hundred of them died.

Some South Vietnamese militiamen at a post one and a half miles from the airport had been preparing their evening meal at the time. "We looked straight up in front of us and we saw debris flying all over the paddy field. It was a horrible thing to see."

The pilot, Capt. Dennis Traynor, said a cargo door blew out and the sudden decompression crippled his controls. He was flying back to Saigon when he crashed.

Air Force Sgt. Jim Hadley, a medical technician from Sacramento, Calif., recalled what happened after the cargo door blew. He was on the second level of the plane's three levels, all packed with orphans.

"You could see the hole in the back of the plane. You could see the sunlight streaming in.

"Things started flying around. Eyeglasses. Pens. Pieces of insulation tore off the ceiling. The pillows exploded—they were plastic lined."

Sergeant Hadley said that oxygen masks dropped down automatically, but the children were sitting two to a seat and there weren't enough masks to go around.

"We had to keep moving them from kid to kid," Sergeant Hadley said.

A flight nurse said: "There were about 120 kids in the second level with us, almost all of them infants. After we crashed, someone opened the emergency exit. I think I was the first one out. I looked around and everything looked stable and we started getting the children out. The crew members were all handing kids up the aisles."

The nurse, who was injured, didn't want her name used because her parents didn't know she was on the flight.

"I felt like I was waiting to die," she said, describing the moments during which the plane tried to reach the runway for an emergency landing. "I knew the cargo door had blown out. We could see it. We're all so thankful to be out alive and that we got so many kids out."

"The children were beautiful," she said. "They were noisy when we took off. They were scared, and they didn't like the straps holding them down. Once the decompression condition hit, the kids didn't say a word. They quieted down right away. I think the kids were quiet because they were getting dopey from an absence of oxygen."

For Childless Couple, Three Instant Sons

By GRACE LICHTENSTEIN

Special to The New York Times

DENVER, April 4—Larry and Linda Moritz got the son they long wanted. Dave and Bobbie Johnson became instant parents of three boys after six years of childless marriage. Tony and Denise Ingram found a new playmate for their two previously adopted Vietnamese girls.

In a touching, quietly joyous scene, the three American couples were finally united here today with the Vietnamese orphans they had been awaiting for weeks.

More than 100 persons—parents, friends, relatives, volunteer case workers and translators—showed up at 1 A.M. in the otherwise deserted Denver Airport to meet 17 orphans, part of the group flown to the United States from beseiged Saigon.

Twelve of the children, many of them carrying balloons, toy telephones and stuffed animals, were met by local families who put them up temporarily before sending them along to their new parents elsewhere.

But for Tom Moritz, 4 years old, Camille Ingrams, and for three young brothers, Jeremy, Peter and Matthew Johnson, the 10,000-mile journey ended when their new parents embraced them as they stepped off the commercial Western Airlines flight from San Francisco.

Greeting by Children

The moment was particularly moving because of the backgrounds of the three adoptive families and because Denver is the home of Friends of Children of Vietnam, the organization largely responsible for bringing these orphans to this country.

Dozens of toddlers brought by their parents played with the new arrivals on the airport floor and gave them presents. Two previously adopted Vietnamese boys, identically dressed in mini-football jerseys, plunked themselves down in the group.

Linda Moritz of Loveland, Colo., fought back tears as she stroked the hair of the wide-eyed, silent Vietnamese boy she and her husband have named Tom.

"I was afraid I wouldn't recognize him because all we had seen were pictures with his head shaved," she said. "But isn't he beautiful? Oh, sweetheart," she crooned, "Mama loves you. Mama won't hurt you."

The Moritzes' two daughters, aged 4 and 7 reached up to clutch the boy's hand and to offer him a brown and white teddy bear. A young Air Force veteran whispered in Vietnamese, "You're safe, don't cry."

Tom immediately buried his head in his new mother's shoulder and wept.

"Here," Mrs. Moritz said, handing the boy gently to her husband, who manages a service station in Fort Collins, "Here's your son."

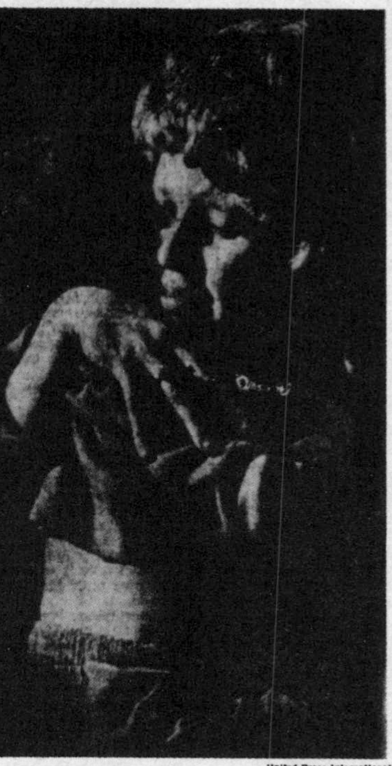

United Press International

Linda Moritz embracing the Vietnamese boy she and her husband are calling Tom. He was one of 17 children who arrived in Denver yesterday and are being adopted.

Like Mr. and Mrs. Moritz, Mr. and Mrs. Johnson of Berthoud, Colo., had arranged their adoption after finding it impossible to adopt an American child. Also like the Moritzes' they became excited about the prospect of adopting a Vietnamese child when they visited some of the families in the Loveland-Berthoud area who over the years have taken in 11 of the homeless young war victims.

But for the Johnsons the arrival of the three Vietnamese brothers, aged 5, 6 and 7, whom they have adopted, meant the start of a "total change in life-style," as Mrs. Johnson put it. The Johnsons have been unable to have their own natural children.

Sign Language at Start

"We've gone through a lot of soul-searching," Mrs. Johnson, a teacher, explained. "But we're probably better mentally prepared than most parents who go through a nine-month pregnancy. It's going to take a lot of patience and a lot of love. We're going to use a lot of sign language. And we've learned a few words of Vietnamese—like the word for potty."

Mr. and Mrs. Ingram made the four-hour drive from their home in Casper, Wyo just in time to meet Camille, a part-black orphan who will be the third Vietnamese girl in their family. They also have two young sons of their own.

The Ingrams know better than most what problems they'll encounter with their new daughter. It took five weeks before their first adopted Vietnamese would let her new father touch her. Their second cried "for two weeks solid at night," Mr. Ingram said. "But now they fit right in."

Mr. Ingram, the superintendent of a trailer home company, added that he had been concerned when his wife first "hit me with the idea" of a racially mixed child. "But it makes no difference," he said, hugging Camille. "What you're doing is saving a life."

Few Vietnam Orphans Eligible to Come to U.S.

Special to The New York Times

SAIGON, South Vietnam, April 4—There are 25,000 orphans in institutions in South Vietnam at the moment. Untold thousands more are cared for by Vietnamese families. Only about 1,500 are eligible to emigrate to the United States.

To qualify an orphan must be under 9 years of age and in the care of one of seven American-licensed institutions here—Holt Children's Services, International Social Services, Friends for All Children, Friends of the Children of Vietnam, Catholic Relief Services, the Pearl Buck Foundation and World Vision.

Virtually all of the 1,500 have been spoken for by families in the United States, which will claim them as soon as they are delivered. The orphans will be issued immediate residence visas and will eventually hold citizenship.

Other Vietnamese, apart from those with husbands or close relatives in the United States, do not have such privileges.

Orphans Land Amid Grief Over Crash

Continued From Page 1, Col. 5

Mahopac Falls, N.Y.

For some the arrival of the children represented a surprise.

The Kolinsky's, who have three sons—Jeffrey, 16; Steven, 14, and Gary, 10—had expected a 5-year-old girl, but Robyn is 2 or 3.

A few hours later, at the Kolinsky's Spring Valley home, Robyn was sitting on a bed decorated in pink, surrounded by her brothers, laughing and clapping "like she's been here forever," Mrs. Kolinsky said.

During the day, Gary was seen racing across the lawn to the house next door.

"I've got to borrow some Pampers," he shouted over his shoulder. "She's still in diapers. And we don't have a crib, either." The Kolinskys' neighbor, Mary Ellen Kerpoff, adopted a 21-month-old Korean child six weeks ago.

The two other orphans on the flight were Nguyen Thi Thu Cuc, 3, renamed Kathleen Marie by the Robert Flanigan family of Edison, N. J., and Tham Thi Thu Huong, who will be 3 in October, renamed Shalli Naté by Ronnie Starr of Mahopac Falls.

Airline officials emptied the plane of regular passengers and then, one by one, stewardesses carrying the children read the name tags, linking them finally to their adoptive families.

The first was handed to Miss Starr, who lives with her mother and is a dog groomer. "Life is beautiful," she said as she was handed her new daughter.

Later, she spoke of herself and her motivation in adopting a Vietnamese child.

"I can remember wanting to do this since I was 10," she said. "I came from a home with a mother who worked hard to raise my brother and sister and myself. She was a mother who cared and I felt everyone should have someone who cares."

Miss Starr, who is 28, said she had completed arrangements for the adoption of another child last year, "but she died before we could get her here."

She praised the Denver-based Friends of Children in Vietnam, which handled the adoption, "especially because single-parent adoption can be so difficult."

The same agency helped the Flanigans, whose girl was the second to be carried from the plane. Mr. Flanigan, a grocer, was accompanied by his wife, Josepha, and three adopted children, Caroline, 9, Robert, 7, and James, 5, all of whom came to the Flanigans through the Catholic Welfare Bureau in Trenton.

"We wanted more children," Mr. Flanigan said, "but there seems so few available in this country now, what with the pill and abortion. We tried more than 100 agencies, and even when a child was available, we had a low priority because we already had three."

Mrs. Flanigan wept as she was handed Kathleen Marie, who also cried a few minutes later, but more from fright than joy. Caroline kept offering her new sister a doll, but the lights and confusion were overwhelming.

Mrs. Kolinsky, who is 37, could scarcely contain herself when she was handed Robyn, the last off the plane.

"I love the world and I love Robyn," she said. "She's precious and she's mine. Look at her. She's not just a picture any more. She's a person. Do it—adopt a child. It's beautiful."

Benjamin Kolinsky is a pharmacist and his wife a supervising nurse who specializes in pediatrics at Letchworth Village in Rockland County.

Mr. Kolinsky, who also praised the Friends of Children in Vietnam, said his efforts began last year when the family's contributions to a Vietnamese orphanage developed into discussion of adoption.

"We wanted a girl," Mr. Kolinsky said, "and after all, the surest way to get one is to adopt her."

They began the long process of filling out forms and writing letters.

Events moved slowly, however, until the military situation in Vietnam worsened. On Tuesday, Mr. Kolinsky said, the State Department loosened restrictions and the departures began in earnest.

As the families separated at the airport this morning, each child seemed destined for vastly different experiences. Kathleen Marie, for example, will share a Roman Catholic environment, and Robyn Lan will enter a Jewish home.

"Until recently Ben could never get Friday night off," Mrs. Kolinsky said. "So we didn't do the ritual Sabbath ceremony. Now he's got Fridays off and we are starting to observe it, with the wine and the challah and everything. As soon as I can, I will begin teaching Robyn how to light the candles and what it is to be a Jewish mother. I think it's time we had a girl in this family."

Later, as they waited for a friend to get the car, Mrs. Kolinsky said to her husband: "You know, I think she looks like you." They laughed, and Robyn grinned. "Now we are six," Mrs. Kolinsky said.

Veteran Is 'Just Hoping' New Son Wasn't Aboard

By LEE DEMBART

A Vietnam veteran and his wife, who have been renovating their upstate home to make room for a Vietnamese orphan, waited apprehensively by their telephone yesterday for word on whether their child was aboard the plane that crashed near Saigon.

"We're just hoping," the veteran, David Shakow, a 32-year-old father of two, said by telephone from Mechanicville, N.Y., north of Albany. His voice breaking, Mr. Shakow added: "We have no way of knowing. We can't piece it together. We're hoping he wasn't on the plane."

"We wanted to do this right along for many years," Mr. Shakow went on. "I was in Vietnam in the sixties, and that convinced us to go with a Vietnamese child.

"We started back in December, '73. It's time-consuming. Six to seven months that the agency studies the home. Then immigration. The paperwork is unreal. To get it all down to one day at the end, I can't believe it."

Last month, the Shakows received a photograph of 13-month-old Minh Khiet Luu, who was in a Saigon orphanage.

"He looked to be a healthy little boy," Mr. Shakow said. "I've got a little boy of 3, and we've got all the clothes ready. We didn't have to buy anything special.

"We've been renovating the house to get the extra bedrooms. We may be crowded for a while, but it's O.K. If things break on the happy side, we won't give a damn."

Mr. Shakow, who works for an insurance company, said he had heard about the crash on the radio yesterday morning and had tried to call the adoption agency, Friends of All Children, in Boulder, Colo.

At first there was no answer, then the agency said it did not have a passenger manifest. Mr. Shakow took the day off from work to stay by the phone with his wife, Nancy.

"We were hoping that we could get him here sooner, and then things started to fall apart there," Mr. Shakow said. "We sent the air fare, and a few days before it was broadcast that a chartered 747 would take the children out. Why they switched over to military we don't know."

The doomed craft, which crashed shortly after take-off from Saigon, was a United States Air Force transport plane taking children from a Saigon orphanage.

"Friends for All Children has four orphanages there," Mr. Shakow said. "We are just hoping that ours didn't come from that orphanage. If he was, ours could sit up; so be probably wasn't in the cargo. From what we've heard, the kids who were strapped down in the upper part were the only ones who made it."

The Shakows did not tell their son or 4-year-old daughter about the crash, but "they know there's something wrong," Mr. Shakow said. "We're not like our usual selves."

"We head one rumor that we should hear something tomorrow," he said, his voice choking up again. "If you hear anything please let us know."

Cambodia Expels Newsman

Special to The New York Times

PHNOM PENH, Cambodia, April 4—The Government ordered today that the Phnom Penh bureau chief for Agence France-Presse, Charles de Nerciat, be expelled. The bureau will remain open. The action was officially described as due to "tendentious reporting."

"All the News That's Fit to Print"

The New York Times

LATE CITY EDITION

Weather: Mostly sunny today; mild tonight. Fair, pleasant tomorrow. Temperature range: today 68-85; Tuesday 73-93. Details on Page 86.

VOL. CXXIV ... No. 42,886 © 1975 The New York Times Company NEW YORK, WEDNESDAY, JUNE 25, 1975 — Price higher in air delivery cities. — 20 CENTS

109 FEARED DEAD AS JET FALLS NEAR KENNEDY DURING A STORM; FIRST BIG CRASH HERE SINCE '65

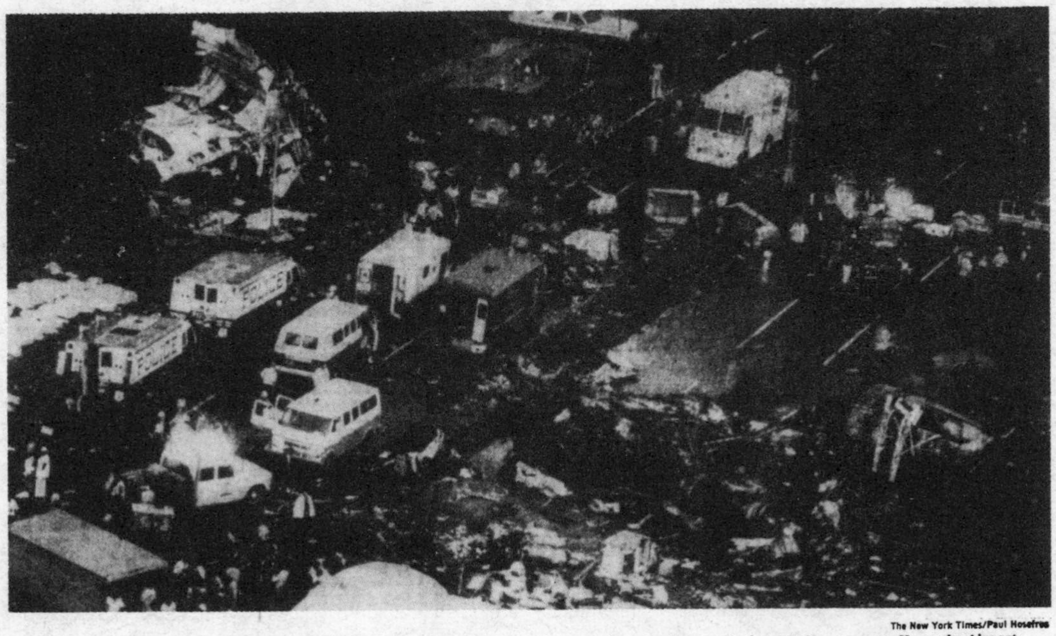

The New York Times/Paul Hosefros

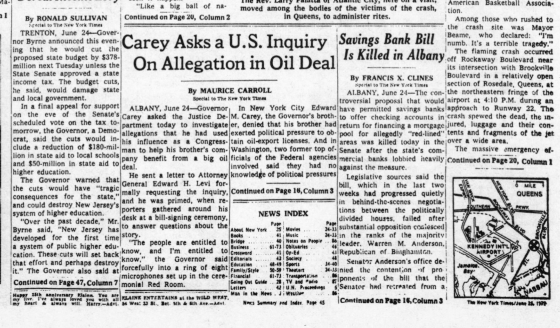

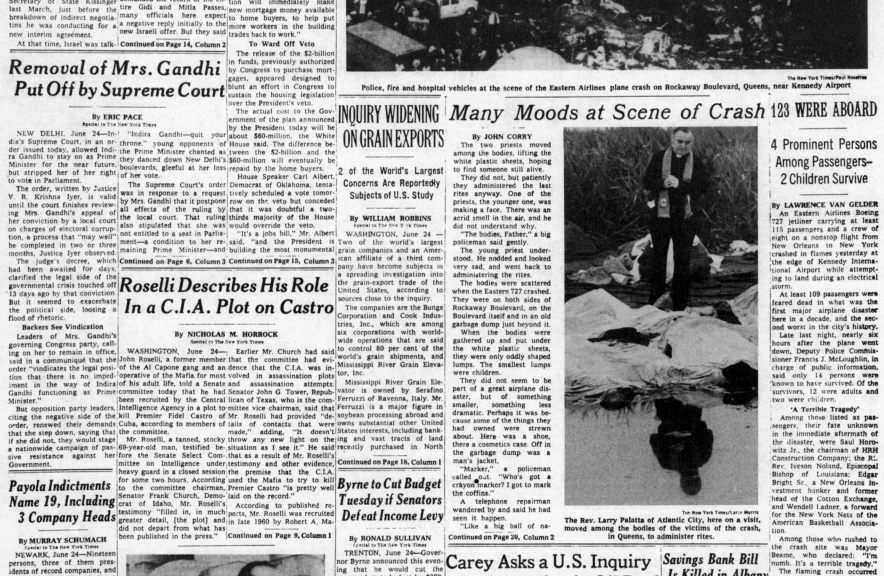

Police, fire and hospital vehicles at the scene of the Eastern Airlines plane crash on Rockaway Boulevard, Queens, near Kennedy Airport

123 WERE ABOARD

4 Prominent Persons Among Passengers—2 Children Survive

By LAWRENCE VAN GELDER

An Eastern Airlines Boeing 727 jetliner carrying at least 115 passengers and a crew of eight on a nonstop flight from New Orleans to New York crashed in flames yesterday at the edge of Kennedy International Airport while attempting to land during an electrical storm.

At least 109 passengers were feared dead in what was the first major airplane disaster here in a decade, and the second worst in the city's history.

Late last night, nearly six hours after the plane went down, Deputy Police Commissioner Francis J. McLoughlin, in charge of public information, said only 14 persons were known to have survived. Of the survivors, 12 were adults and two were children.

'A Terrible Tragedy'

Among those listed as passengers, their fate unknown in the immediate aftermath of the disaster, were Saul Horowitz Jr., the chairman of HRH Construction Company; the Rt. Rev. Iveson Noland, Episcopal Bishop of Louisiana; Edgar Bright Sr., a New Orleans investment banker and former head of the Cotton Exchange, and Wendell Ladner, a forward for the New York Nets of the American Basketball Association.

Among those who rushed to the crash site was Mayor Beame, who declared: "I'm numb. It's a terrible tragedy."

The flaming crash occurred off Rockaway Boulevard near its intersection with Brookville Boulevard in a relatively open section of Rosedale, Queens, at the northeastern fringe of the airport at 4:10 P.M. during an approach to Runway 22. The crash spewed the dead, the injured, luggage and their contents and fragments of the jet over a wide area.

The massive emergency ef-

Continued on Page 20, Column 1

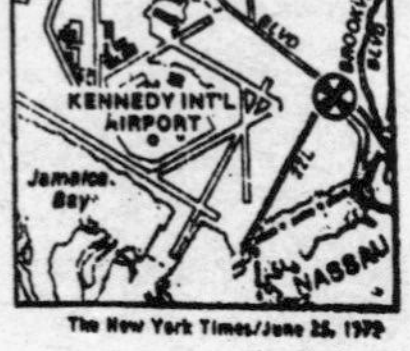

The New York Times/June 25, 1975

Many Moods at Scene of Crash

By JOHN CORRY

The two priests moved among the bodies, lifting the white plastic sheets, hoping to find someone still alive.

They did not, but patiently they administered the last rites anyway. One of the priests, the younger one, was making a face. There was an acrid smell in the air, and he did not understand why.

"The bodies, Father," a big policeman said gently.

The young priest understood. He nodded and looked very sad, and went back to administering the rites.

The bodies were scattered when the Eastern 727 crashed. They were on both sides of Rockaway Boulevard, on the Boulevard itself and in an old garbage dump just beyond it.

When the bodies were gathered up and put under the white plastic sheets, they were only oddly shaped lumps. The smallest lumps were children.

They did not seem to be part of a great airplane disaster, but of something smaller, something less dramatic. Perhaps it was because some of the things they had owned were strewn about. Here was a shoe, there a cosmetics case. Off in the garbage dump was a man's jacket.

"Marker," a policeman called out. "Who's got a crayon marker? I got to mark the coffins."

A telephone repairman wandered by and said he had seen it happen.

"Like a big ball of na-

Continued on Page 20, Column 2

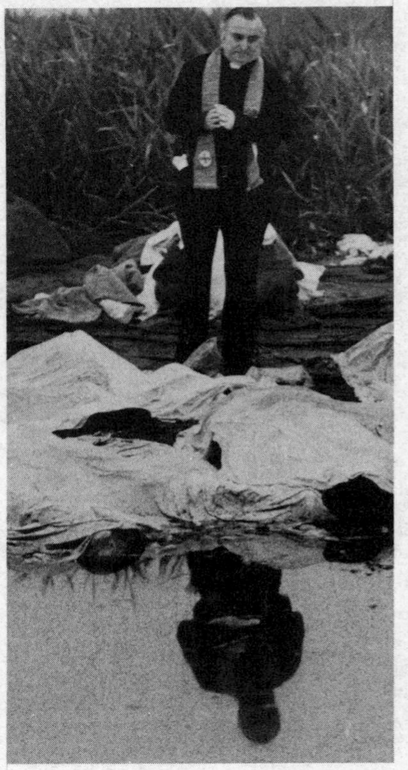

The New York Times/Larry Morris

The Rev. Larry Palatta of Atlantic City, here on a visit, moved among the bodies of the victims of the crash, in Queens, to administer rites.

Israel Offers Compromise To Egypt on Sinai Accord

Cuts Duration of a Pact to 3 or 4 Years and Proposes Corridor to Oilfield—Sadat and Aides Respond Quickly

By TERENCE SMITH
Special to The New York Times

JERUSALEM, June 24—Israel proposed a new disengagement agreement with Egypt that would last three to four years and would include a land corridor to an oilfield at Abu Rudeis in what is now occupied Sinai.

Israeli Government officials, in reporting this, said Israel had also offered to withdraw from the western parts of the Gidi and Mitla Passes in Sinai. But, they added, Israel wants to retain control of the eastern ends of the passes and access to electronic surveillance stations she maintains in the Gidi Pass.

The proposal, which was outlined to President Anwar el-Sadat of Egypt yesterday by the American Ambassador to Cairo, represents a modification of an Israeli position discussed by Secretary of State Kissinger last March, just before the breakdown of indirect negotiations he was conducting for a new interim agreement.

At that time, Israel was talking of evacuating only an enclave around the Abu Rudeis area itself and allowing land access through her lines along a road with United Nations checkpoints. Now, Israeli officials said, she offers a land corridor along the coast between the town of Suez and the oilfield and asks that Israeli vehicles be permitted to patrol it under United Nations supervision.

In March, Israel was pressing for an accord that would last five to seven years. Now she wants one that would last a minimum of three years, preferably four.

In exchange for the withdrawals, Israel wants an Egyptian commitment not to use force for the duration of the interim agreement.

Since Egypt has repeatedly demanded the return of the entire Gidi and Mitla Passes, many officials here expect a negative reply initially to the new Israeli offer. But they said

Continued on Page 14, Column 2

PRESIDENT VETOES $1.2-BILLION BILL FOR AID TO HOUSING

Asserts Economy Would Be Damaged but Frees Funds for Buying Mortgages

By JAMES M. NAUGHTON
Special to The New York Times

WASHINGTON, June 24—President Ford vetoed today a $1.2-billion emergency housing measure that he contended would "damage the housing industry and damage the economy."

But the President ordered the immediate release of $2-billion for Government purchase of home mortgages at subsidized rates, and he asked Congress to authorize $7.75-billion more for the existing mortgage assistance program.

"The steps I have announced today are the best way to meet the problems of housing in this country at the present time," Mr. Ford said in a brief statement before television cameras in the White House. "This action will immediately make new mortgage money available to home buyers, to help put more workers in the building trades back to work."

To Ward Off Veto

The release of the $2-billion in funds, previously authorized by Congress to purchase mortgages, appeared designed to blunt an effort in Congress to sustain the housing legislation over the President's veto.

The actual cost to the Government of the plan announced by the President today will be about $60-million, the White House said. The difference between the $2-billion and the $60-million will eventually be repaid by the home buyers.

House Speaker Carl Albert, Democrat of Oklahoma, tentatively scheduled a vote tomorrow on the veto but conceded that it was doubtful a two-thirds majority of the House would override the veto.

"It's a jobs bill," Mr. Albert said, "and the President is building the most monumental

Continued on Page 15, Column 3

Removal of Mrs. Gandhi Put Off by Supreme Court

By ERIC PACE
Special to The New York Times

NEW DELHI, June 24—India's Supreme Court, in an order issued today, allowed Indira Gandhi to stay on as Prime Minister for the near future, but stripped her of her right to vote in Parliament.

The order, written by Justice V. R. Krishna Iyer, is valid until the court finishes reviewing Mrs. Gandhi's appeal of her conviction by a local court on charges of electoral corruption, a process that "may well" be completed in two or three months, Justice Iyer observed.

The judge's decree, which had been awaited for days, clarified the legal side of the governmental crisis touched off 13 days ago by that conviction. But it seemed to exacerbate the political side, loosing a flood of rhetoric.

Backers See Vindication

Leaders of Mrs. Gandhi's governing Congress party, calling on her to remain in office, said in a communiqué that the order "vindicates the legal position that there is no impediment in the way of Indira Gandhi functioning as Prime Minister."

But opposition party leaders, citing the negative side of the order, renewed their demands that she step down, saying that if she did not, they would stage a nationwide campaign of passive resistance against her Government.

"Indira Gandhi—quit your throne," young opponents of the Prime Minister chanted as they danced down New Delhi's boulevards, gleeful at her loss of her vote.

The Supreme Court's order was in response to a request by Mrs. Gandhi that it postpone all effects of the ruling by the local court. That ruling also stipulated that she was not entitled to a seat in Parliament—a condition to her remaining Prime Minister—and

Continued on Page 6, Column 3

INQUIRY WIDENING ON GRAIN EXPORTS

2 of the World's Largest Concerns Are Reportedly Subjects of U.S. Study

By WILLIAM ROBBINS
Special to The New York Times

WASHINGTON, June 24—Two of the world's largest grain companies and an American affiliate of a third company have become subjects in a spreading investigation into the grain-export trade of the United States, according to sources close to the inquiry.

The companies are the Bunge Corporation and Cook Industries, Inc., which are among six corporations with worldwide operations that are said to control 80 per cent of the world's grain shipments, and Mississippi River Grain Elevator, Inc.

Mississippi River Grain Elevator is owned by Serafino Ferruzzi of Ravenna, Italy. Mr. Ferruzzi is a major figure in soybean processing abroad and owns substantial other United States interests, including banking and vast tracts of land recently purchased in North

Continued on Page 18, Column 1

Roselli Describes His Role In a C.I.A. Plot on Castro

By NICHOLAS M. HORROCK
Special to The New York Times

WASHINGTON, June 24—John Roselli, a former member of the Al Capone gang and an officer of the Mafia for most of his adult life, told a Senate committee today that he had been recruited by the Central Intelligence Agency in a plot to kill Premier Fidel Castro of Cuba, according to members of the committee.

Mr. Roselli, a tanned, stocky 69-year-old man, testified before the Senate Select Committee on Intelligence under heavy guard in a closed session for some two hours. According to the committee chairman, Senator Frank Church, Democrat of Idaho, Mr. Roselli's testimony "filled in, in much greater detail, [the plot] and did not depart from what has been published in the press."

Earlier Mr. Church had said that the committee had evidence that the C.I.A. was involved in assassination plots and assassination attempts. Senator John G. Tower, Republican of Texas, who is the committee vice chairman, said that Mr. Roselli had provided "details of contacts that were made," adding, "It doesn't throw any new light on the situation as I see it." He also said that as a result of Mr. Roselli's testimony and other evidence, the premise that the C.I.A. used the Mafia to try to kill Premier Castro "is pretty well laid on the record."

According to published reports, Mr. Roselli was recruited in late 1960 by Robert A. Ma-

Continued on Page 9, Column 1

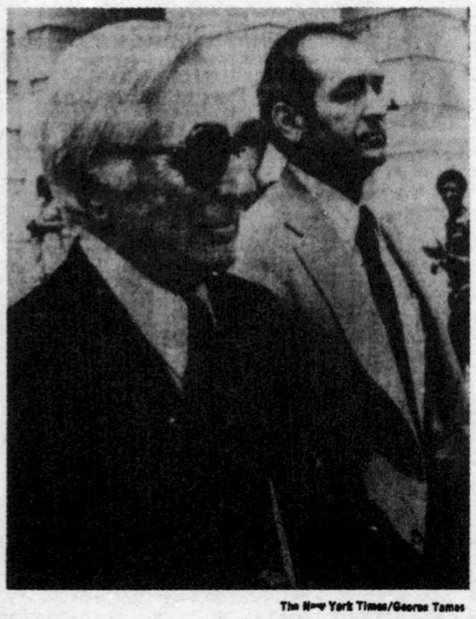

The New York Times/George Tames

A man identified as John Roselli leaving the Capitol

Byrne to Cut Budget Tuesday if Senators Defeat Income Levy

By RONALD SULLIVAN
Special to The New York Times

TRENTON, June 24—Governor Byrne announced this evening that he would cut the proposed state budget by $378-million next Tuesday unless the State Senate approved a state income tax. The budget cuts, he said, would damage state and local government.

In a final appeal for support on the eve of the Senate's scheduled vote on the tax tomorrow, the Governor, a Democrat, said the cuts would include a reduction of $180-million in state aid to local schools and $50-million in state aid to higher education.

The Governor warned that the cuts would have "tragic consequences for the state," and could destroy New Jersey's system of higher education.

"Over the past decade," Mr. Byrne said, "New Jersey has developed for the first time a system of public higher education. These cuts will set back that effort and perhaps destroy it." The Governor also said at

Continued on Page 47, Column 7

Payola Indictments Name 19, Including 3 Company Heads

By MURRAY SCHUMACH
Special to The New York Times

NEWARK, June 24—Nineteen persons, three of them presidents of record companies, and six corporations were indicted yesterday as "the first step" in a nationwide payola investigation by the United States attorneys of Newark, New York, Philadelphia and Los Angeles.

Charges in the seven indictments included, in addition to illegal payments to radio station personnel by record companies, income-tax evasion, mail fraud and interstate transportation of stolen property.

Jonathan L. Goldstein, United States Attorney here, stressed repeatedly, at a news conference, that after two years of investigation this was only "the beginning" of the inquiry into payola in the billion-dollar pop-record industry.

Mr. Goldstein, who has been coordinating the investigation, in explaining why no disk jockeys had been indicted, said they had been very cooperative

Continued on Page 40, Column 5

Carey Asks a U.S. Inquiry On Allegation in Oil Deal

By MAURICE CARROLL

ALBANY, June 24—Governor Carey asked the Justice Department today to investigate allegations that he had used his influence as a Congressman to help his brother's company benefit from a big oil deal.

He sent a letter to Attorney General Edward H. Levi formally requesting the inquiry, and as he was primed, when reporters gathered around his desk at a bill-signing ceremony, to answer questions about the story.

"The people are entitled to know, and I'm entitled to know," the Governor said forcefully into a ring of eight microphones set up in the ceremonial Red Room.

In New York City Edward M. Carey, the Governor's brother, denied that his brother had exerted political pressure to obtain oil-export licenses. And in Washington, two former top officials of the Federal agencies involved said they had no knowledge of political pressures

Continued on Page 16, Column 3

Savings Bank Bill Is Killed in Albany

By FRANCIS X. CLINES
Special to The New York Times

ALBANY, June 24—The controversial proposal that would have permitted savings banks to offer checking accounts in return for financing a mortgage pool for allegedly "red-lined" areas was killed today in the Senate after the state's commercial banks lobbied heavily against the measure.

Legislative sources said the bill, which in the last two weeks had progressed quietly in behind-the-scenes negotiations between the politically divided houses, failed after substantial opposition coalesced in the ranks of the majority leader, Warren M. Anderson, Republican of Binghamton.

Senator Anderson's office denied the contention of proponents of the bill that the Senator had retreated from a

Continued on Page 16, Column 3

NEWS INDEX

HAPPY BIRTHDAY HENRY—My husband, lover & best friend.—Priscilla.—ADVT

Happy 25th anniversary Elaine. You are my live. I've always loved you with all my heart & always will. Harry.—Advt.

ELAINE ENTERTAINS at the WILD WEST, 54 West 33 St., Bet. 5th & 6th Ave.—Advt.

109 Feared Dead as Jet Falls Near Kennedy in Storm

Removing the bodies of victims.

The New York Times

First Big Crash Here Since '65

Bishop From Louisiana Listed as a Passenger

Continued From Page 1, Col. 8

fort touched off by the crash sent policemen, firemen, ambulances, helicopters, detectives, rescue crews and civil officials racing to the scene while hospitals mobilized to receive the injured and dead.

Crowds gathered at the scene to gape at the twisted metal and foam-covered debris of the burned wreckage of what had once been Eastern's Flight 66. Eyewitnesses came away shaken.

"I was about three blocks away," Neal Rairden, a 23-year-old mechanic at the Rosedale Shell station at 249-15 Rockaway Boulevard, told newsmen.

"I saw the plane coming in. It was raining very hard at the time, about 4:10. All of a sudden there was lightning. I looked up and all I saw was smoke and flames and no plane.

"I said, 'Holy God!' I knew that plane had gotten hit by lightning."

Cause Not Determined

There was no immediate confirmation of the speculation

that the plane had been struck by lightning; nor was it immediately known if any cars had been struck when the plane crashed short of the runway.

"He came in too low, hit a landing light on one of the towers, apparently rose up and missed the next three of them and then slammed right into the ground," said Lieut. Alfred Mantenfel of Engine Company 301 from Hollis, Queens.

Frank Pugliese, a public affairs spokesman for the Federal Aviation Administration said: "There was a pretty severe storm at the time. There was some thunder. It was a typical summer electrical storm that varied in intensity. Just when you thought it was over, it started up again."

F.A.A. investigators were immediately sent to the scene to begin the effort to determine the cause of the crash of the three-engine jet plane.

The airport was closed at 4:11 P.M., a peak period. Flights were diverted elsewhere until the airport was reopened to traffic at 4.53 P.M.

At the time of the crash, the F.A.A. said, the general conditions consisted of a six-knot

wind, a 3,000-foot ceiling and five-mile visibility—conditions not particularly adverse for an experienced airline crew.

Beame at Scene

Mayor Beame and Police Commissioner Codd were among those who hurried to the crash scene. The Mayor, upon learning that the flight had originated in New Orleans, telephoned Mayor Moon Landrieu to assure him that "everything possible will be done to ease the suffering of the survivors."

United Press International reported that in New Orleans, Nils Haugen, the Norwegian Vice Consul General, said that 19 Norwegian sailors were aboard the flight, "going home on vacation." The sailors, he said, were from two Norwegian ships docked in Louisiana ports. At least one of the Norwegians was reported in a hospital, badly burned.

Flight 66 was running behind schedule when it crashed. It had been scheduled to touch down at Kennedy Airport at 3:45 P.M.

The plane, with its blue and white markings, was heading for Runway 22 at Mrs. Victor Gomez, accompanied by her 6-year-old daughter, Michele, was walking to her home at 148-81 Brookville Boulevard, just across a swampy field from the airport.

"I looked up, and saw it was

coming in too low," she said. "In bad weather we hear planes come in too low all the time, and I often say to myself, 'Uh-oh, that one's not going to make it to the runway,' so I didn't pay much attention this time."

She heard a thud. Later her husband, an airline employe, called from Manhattan to see if his family was still there. It was then she learned of the crash and through her living room window she saw smoke rising over the wreckage.

At the Cedarhurst Tennis Club, just down Brookville Boulevard from Mrs. Gomez's home, Doris Boehmann, the 24-year-old club manager, was drawn to the window for reasons she could not explain.

"It was thundering and lightning," she said. "I heard the planes coming in low and I was looking out to watch them land." Then, about 500 yards in front of her, moving across the tennis courts, she saw a plane—far too low.

"It was just about 40 or 50 feet off the ground, and then there was fire," she said before trying to describe how the plane "just began to break up in the air and fall" out of her line of sight.

A pillar of smoke rose from where the plane had disappeared.

"Lightning hit the plane," said another eyewitness, Paul Moran, a Nassau County police officer.

"The plane veered to the right," he said. "The right wing went down. The left wing went

up. Then about 35 yards later, the plane hit the ground. All I could see was a ball of flame about a hundred yards long and about 50 feet high."

As the plane descended it struck at least five of the 35-foot light towers marking the approach to the runway.

"I saw this big flash of fire like the atomic bomb goes off," Moe Friedman, an airport employe reported. "The flames went up in the air about 500 or 600 feet. She went right across the highway. The rain was coming down pretty heavy."

At Jamaica Hospital's emergency room, one of the Norwegian survivors, Egon Luftaas, although badly burned, told reporters what he remembered:

"Going in for a landing, the pilot went too much to the left. You know, with one wing down, not two. There was an explosion. Everyone was flinging around. After that I only remember the fire."

Above the site, police aviation crews were reporting, "Debris scattered over a large area."

Soon, policemen and firemen hauling stretchers made of red metal were picking their way through the wreckage. The dead, under white shrouds, lay at the side of the road.

The living were rushed to Jamaica and South Shore Hospitals in Queens and Jacobi Hospital in the Bronx.

Among the survivors were two flight attendants, Mary

Firemen inspecting the plane's burned remains.

The New York Times

Mooney, 28 years old, of Tulsa, Okla. and Robert Hoefler, 29, of the Bronx, who were taken to the South Shore Division of Long Island Jewish-Hillside Medical Center at 327 Beach 19th Street in Far Rockaway, Queens. According to Dr. Ilene Raisfeld, director of the department of internal medicine, who treated them, both were in serious but stable condition.

Under Observation

Miss Mooney. Dr. Raisfeld said, suffered injuries to the bones in her back, but was expected to make a full recovery. Mr. Hoeffler suffered broken ribs and was under observation for possible neurological injuries.

The doctor said the crew members had said they were sitting in the tail section of the plane when they felt a shudder. The next they knew, they were outside and running. A passing policeman picked them up and drove them to the hospital, where they were admitted at about 4:15 P.M. in a state of shock.

Nick Rasch, a 44-year-old engineer for the F.A.A. from Turnersville, N. J., who witnessed the crash from his office about a half mile away, told of reaching the site and seeing survivors after notifying the control tower.

"We got to the plane just as the first fire trucks were pull-

ing in" Mr. Rasch said. "Part of the fuselage and tail were on fire. We saw three survivors, two of them lying down and one walking up the road.

"You couldn't tell if it was a man or a woman. The person was all bloody. Somebody told the person to sit down and the first ambulance that came took the three away. What I was surprised about, the other two didn't bleed."

Speaks With Restraint

Frank Borman, the former astronaut who is the president and chief operating officer of Eastern Airlines, met with newsmen at Kennedy Airport after flying down from Boston and inspecting the crash site. Looking grim and speaking with evident restraint, he said it had been a "very bad crash," which had been accompanied by "a severe fire."

Mr. Borman declined to speculate about the cause of the crash. One of the worst problems about crashes, he asserted, was speculating before the facts were in. "I'm not going to do that," he said.

The National Transportation Safety Board, which is empowered to investigate all air crashes, sent 18 men to the scene — eight from its Eastern Region office at Kennedy Airport and 10 from Washington. George A. Van Epps, the regional director, who was in im-

mediate charge of the investigation, said the jetliner's flight recorder and voice recorder had been recovered and flown to Washington for analysis. The flight recorder would trace for investigators the plane's final maneuvers, and the voice recorder would contain the crew's cockpit conversations as the craft approached the field.

An official police spokesman raised the possibility that the death toll would rise above 109. He said he had been told by an Eastern Airlines spokesman of the possibility that infants, uncounted in the passenger total, had been aboard the plane. A small pine box was seen being unloaded at the morgue.

A police spokesman said two people were arrested at the crash site for impersonating police officers and emergency workers. "They were either curiosity seekers or thieves." he said. "We don't know which. One guy had a doctor's bag and white coat and another took a coat, hat and boots off a fire truck."

The last disaster at a New York area airport also involved an Eastern plane near Kennedy. It occurred on Feb. 8, 1965, when 84 persons were killed in the crash of a DC 7-B shortly

2 Priests Administer Rites at Mournful Scene of Crash

Continued From Page 1, Col. 5

palm," he said.

"I heard it." Bruce Hardwick, another telephone man, said. It had sounded like thunder, he said.

The crash had come at 4:10 P.M., and immediately people began to gather at the scene. Cars filled Rockaway Boulevard in minutes and soon a little hill overlooking the garbage dump was crowded. The people on the hill had come to see a disaster. They were, however, very quiet.

Along the boulevard, winding through South Jamaica, civilians stood at intersections, waving emergency vehicles through, and even sending some of the sightseers away. The civilians

after take-off.

The worst aviation disaster here was the collision of a DC-8 with a Super Constellation in a fog over Staten Island on Dec. 16, 1960. A total of 134 persons died in that crash—all those aboard the two planes and six who were killed when wreckage from the planes fell to the ground.

seemed to take their work very seriously.

Teen-agers by the thousands were streaming in by bicycle and on foot. They weren't sure what they would find because the first reports were sketchy. They said only that there had been a disaster.

Nonetheless, some of the teen-agers who came got bored quickly. When the first ambulances left carrying some of the bodies away, they went with them, hanging on the rears of the vehicles. Angrily, policemen shouted at them. Sometimes, the teen-agers got off.

Within minutes after the crash the police had set up a big yellow plastic tent and hung a sign on it.

"Missing Persons Section," it said. Rescue workers wandered in and out of the tent, but it hardly mattered. The passengers inside were all dead.

Then it began to rain again, and the field with the bodies and wreckage was beaten into a sodden mulch. Mosquitoes came out. The policemen and rescue work-

Police and rescue workers search for victims.

The New York Times

ers began to swear. Everyone seemed to be getting in everyone else's way.

A plump motherly woman from the Salvation Army appeared, carrying a plastic bag full of sandwiches.

"They're very fresh," she said shyly, and gravely a big police sergeant took one.

"Thank you, ma'am," he said politely.

Meanwhile, another policeman was shouting over a public-address system. "All vehicles clear the roadway," he said. "We must have an access path."

By 9 P.M., the last bodies were being taken away from the garbage dump. Policemen loaded them on stretchers, took them across Rockaway Boulevard and moved them into the big yellow tent.

It was no longer called the "Missing Persons Section." Now it was called the morgue.

As the floodlights came on, a rescue worker collapsed. He lay on the ground, his mouth opening and closing and then, along with some of the bodies, he had just been ministering to, he was taken away in an ambulance.

From out of the darkness, Police Commissioner Michael Codd appeared. His back was to the hill where the teenagers had been standing before. "Grisly work," he said. "Very hard work."

On Rockaway Boulevard the ambulances were carrying the last bodies away.

19 Norwegian Sailors Listed as Passengers

Among the survivors of yesterday's Eastern Airlines crash at Kennedy International Airport was a Norwegian tourist, Egon Luftaas, who said he was traveling with a group of 14 Norwegians. Mr. Luftaas was taken to Jamaica Hospital in serious condition with burns over most of his body.

According to the Norwegian Consulate General here, the plane's passengers included 19 Norwegian sailors going home on vacation from the vessels Fernwave and Nopal Tellus.

Crash Underscores Axiom: The Landing Is Critical

By RICHARD WITKIN

Yesterday's Eastern Airlines crash reinforced a fact of airline life that has been pointed up ... repeated accident surveys. The most dangerous part of a flight is the final approach and landing. A 1972 study by the National Transportation Safety Board showed that, in the 1964-to-1969 period, one in every three fatal crashs of United States airliners occurred in this phase of the flight.

News Analysis

And subsequent experience has further demonstrated the vulnerability of flights on the final descent to the runway, though complete updated statistics were not readily available.

Among the approach and landing accidents in recent years in this country were the jumbojet crash in the Florida Everglades, the crash of a twinjet DC-9 at Boston's Logan International Airport and the crash of a Boeing 727 on a mountainside last winter as it was descending toward Dulles International Airport.

There was no immediate indication yesterday as to what had caused the Eastern 727 to plummet to the ground about a half mile short of the runway at Kennedy International Airport.

Suspicions—and that is all they were—centered on the foul weather in the area.

A spokesman for the Federal Aviation Administration said an intense thunderstorm had erupted shortly before the crash, producing heavy rain and tricky winds.

There was also a report from a policeman that a ball of lightning had struck the craft's tail just before it veered to the right and plunged eartward. But safety experts thought it unlikely that lightning had precipitated the crash since planes are fitted with reliable devices to cope with the lightning danger.

Soon after the accident, the National Transportation Safety Board dispatched investigators from Washington to Kennedy to take over the official inquiry into the causes of the tragedy. Following procedures developed in decades of crash inquiries, the N.T.S.B. officials will form teams of specialists to review every conceivable aspect of the fatal flight: the condition of the fuselage, the engines, the weather, the history of the particular craft, and the record of air-to-ground conversations between New Orleans and New York.

Participating on the teams, in addition to N.T.S.B., F.A.A. and other government officials, will be representatives from the aircraft and engine manufacturers, from the airline, and from pilot groups and other groups.

The high incidence of landing accidents (compared with takeoff crashes and en route crashes caused by fires, collisions, storms and sabotage) has brought a series of major governmental steps in the last few years designed to lessen the risk.

A heavy proportion of F.A.A. funds continues to go into installation of electronic Instrument Landing Systems (I.L.S.'s) to guide aircraft through bad weather to the runway threshold. Many experts, spearheaded by the Air Line Pilots Association, have continued to complain that the installations are not being made fast enough.

Air-traffic controllers have been instructed to warn crews if altitude data—added to radar gear only in recent years—show planes descending dangerously below assigned altitudes either on a landing approach or en route between cities.

While yesterday's crash fell into the largest statistical category, it was actually not the most likely type of landing accident. Night-time operations have tended more often to lead to fatal crashes than daytime flights. Furthermore, there have been relatively few fatal accidents in which the crew had available a standard I.L.S., as did the Eastern crew yesterday.

Many disasters, both here and abroad, have occurred when pilots were trying to reach runways that lacked a standard I.L.S. and had to guide themselves by less precise radio aids.

How I.L.S. Works

An I.L.S. is an invisible electronic pathway that brings a plane down to the runway as though the craft were rolling down a moderately inclined slide. The pilot keeps the plane on the proper pathway by centering two needles on a cockpit instrument. Or it can be done "hands off" through use of an automatic pilot.

Except in rare cases on a handful of specially equipped runways, the human pilot takes over from the automatic pilot shortly before touchdown.

A question raised by some knowledgeable observers yesterday was whether, in view of the storm in the area, the F.A.A. controllers should not have temporarily halted landings, at least on the runway the Eastern jet was aiming for.

There were reports, widespread though not officially verified, that the pilot of a jet of another airline had found conditions so inclement just before the Eastern crash that he changed plans to land at Kennedy and diverted to Boston.

There were other, similar, reports that a jet landing shortly before the crash had experienced severe downdraft that caused the plane to drop precipitously for about 1,500 feet before finally making it safely onto the runway.

This would have been consistent with information that there was a sharp shift in the direction of the wind just about the time of the accident.

One other question raised by some experts was whether the controllers had been bringing in traffic over the most prudent route and onto the most desirable runway.

Was the storm heaviest to the northeast, as some weather reports were said to have indicated? In that case, could the plane have been steered around the worst of the weather and come in safely on a longer runway headed in a different direction? The winds at ground level, despite the storm, were said to have been moving at relatively low speeds.

The issue of weather was one of the prime matters the N.T.S.B. inquiry was bound to concern itself with.